THE COMPLETE 100-BOOK APOCRYPHA

Ultimate Collection

Including 1–3 Enoch, Giants, Jasher, Jubilees, Lost Gospels, Sibylline Oracles, Key Early Church Writings and more

Featuring Deuterocanon, Ethiopian Canon, Pseudepigrapha, Apocalypses, Testaments, Apostolic Fathers, Infancy Gospels, Gnostic Gospels, Passion Gospels, Epistles, Acts & Other Apocryphas

SYBILLINE ORACLES — BONUS
ACTS OF JOHN — BONUS
ACTS OF PETER — BONUS
ACTS OF THOMAS — BONUS

ASHER WILSON

Copyright Notice:

2024 ASHER WILSON. All rights reserved. This publication arranges and presents selections of texts in the public domain. No part of this publication may be reproduced or transmitted in any form or by any means, electronic or mechanical, including photocopying, recording, or any information storage and retrieval system, without permission in writing from the publisher, except for the inclusion of brief quotations in a book review.

Disclaimer:
This book is a curated collection of several texts in the public domain, intended to provide an accessible format for study and reflection. The introductions and conclusions are the contributions of the author and are intended for contextualization and commentary purposes only.

Limitation of Liability:
The author and publisher disclaim all legal liability for any losses or damages that may result from the use of the information in this book. This book is provided "as is" without warranty of any kind, either express or implied. Efforts have been made to ensure the content is presented in a thoughtful and respectful manner, reflecting the spiritual and historical significance of the texts.

TABLE OF CONTENTS

- Introduction 4
- Old Testament Apocrypha 5
  - Deuterocanon 5
    - The Prayer of Manasses 5
    - The First Book of Esdras, or Ezra Kali 5
    - The Second Book of Esdras, or Ezra Sutu'el ... 12
    - The Book of Tobit 24
    - The Book of Judith 28
    - The First Book of the Maccabees 34
    - The Second Book of the Maccabees 46
    - The Third Book of the Maccabees 56
    - Additions to Esther 60
    - Psalm 151 64
    - The Wisdom of Solomon 65
    - The Wisdom of Jesus the Son of Sirach 71
    - The Book of Baruch 85
    - The Letter of Jeremiah 87
    - The Song of the Three Holy Children 90
    - The History of Susanna 95
    - Bel and the Dragon 96
  - Ethiopian Canon 97
    - The Book of Jubilees, or The Little Genesis .. 97
    - The Book of Enoch 123
    - The Fourth Book of the Maccabees 144
    - The Book of Meqabyan I 150
    - The Book of Meqabyan II 164
    - The Book of Meqabyan III 172
    - 4 Baruch, or Paralipomena of Jeremiah ... 176
  - Pseudepigrapha 178
    - The First Book of Adam and Eve 178
    - The Second Book of Adam and Eve 194
    - Life of Adam and Eve, or Vita Adae et Evae ... 201
    - Slavonic Life of Adam and Eve 204
    - Five Psalms of David 205
    - The Psalms of Solomon 206
    - The Martydom of Isaiah 210
    - The Ascension of Isaiah 212
    - Fragments of a Zadokite Work 215
    - The Letter of Aristeas 220
    - The Story of Ahikar 231
    - The Biblical Antiquities of Philo 237
    - The Book of Jasher 261
    - Bonus Guide 332
  - Apocalypses 333
    - The Second Book of Enoch 333
    - The Third Book of Enoch 339
    - The Revelation of Esdras 351
    - The Apocalypse of Sedrach 353
    - 2 Baruch, or Syriac Apocalypse of Baruch .. 355
    - 3 Baruch, or Greek Apocalypse of Baruch .. 365
    - The Apocalypse of Abraham 368
    - The Apocalyse of Daniel 370
    - The Apocalypse of Moses, or Revelation of Moses ... 372
  - Testaments 374
    - The Testaments of the Twelve Patriarchs .. 374
    - The Testament of Abraham 388
    - The Testament of Job 390
    - The Testament of Solomon 394
    - The Testament of Moses 400
- New Testament Apocrypha 402
  - Apostolic Fathers 402
    - The Didache, or Teaching of the Twelve Apostles ... 402
    - The General Epistle of Barnabas 404
    - The First Epistle of Clement to the Corinthians ... 410
    - The Second Epistle of Clement to the Corinthians ... 417
    - The Shepherd of Hermas 419
    - The Epistle of Ignatius to the Ephesians ... 439
    - The Epistle of Ignatius to the Magnesians .. 440
    - The Epistle of Ignatius to the Trallians 441
    - The Epistle of Ignatius to the Romans 442
    - The Epistle of Ignatius to the Philadelphians .. 443
    - The Epistle of Ignatius to the Smyrnæans .. 444
    - The Epistle of Ignatius to Polycarp 445
    - The Epistle of Ignatius to the Philippians .. 446
    - The Martyrdom of Ignatius 448
    - The Epistle of Polycarp to the Philippians .. 450
    - The Martyrdom of Polycarp 451
    - The Epistle of Mathetes to Diognetus 454
    - The Fragments of Papias 456
  - Infancy Gospels 458
    - The Gospel of the Birth of Mary 458
    - The Protoevangelium of James, or The Gospel of James ... 460
    - The Arabic Infancy Gospel, or Syriac Infancy Gospel . 463
    - Thomas's Gospel of the Infancy of Jesus Christ ... 468
    - The History of Joseph the Carpenter 469
  - Gnostics 472
    - The Gospel of Thomas 472
    - Apocryphon of James, or The Secret Book of James ... 475
    - The Gospel of Mary 477
    - The Book of Marcion, or The Gospel of the Lord ... 478
    - The Gospel of Philip 481
    - The Secret Gospel of Mark 486
    - Apocalypse of Adam 487
    - The Odes of Solomon 489
  - Passion Gospels 494
    - The Gospel of Peter 494
    - The Gospel of Bartholomew 495
    - The Gospel of Nicodemus, or Acts of Pontius Pilate ... 498
    - Letters of Herod and Pilate 506
    - The Avenging of the Saviour 509
    - The Narrative of Joseph of Arimathaea 511
    - The Book of John the Evangelist 513
  - Epistles 514
    - The Epistles of Jesus Christ and Abgarus King of Edessa ... 514
    - The Epistle of Paul to the Laodiceans 515
    - The Epistles of Paul to Seneca, with Seneca's to Paul .. 515
    - The Epistula Apostolorum, or Epistle of the Apostles .. 517
  - Acts And Other Apocryphas 522
    - The Acts of Andrew 522
    - The Apostles' Creed 528
    - The Acts of Paul and Thecla 529
    - Tertullian On Specticals 532
    - Tertullian On Prayer 538
    - Tertullian On Patience 543
    - Tertullian On Martyrs 547

INTRODUCTION

The term "apocrypha" comes from the Greek word "apokryphos," meaning "hidden" or "secret." These texts encompass a diverse collection of ancient writings not included in the canonical Bible. They span centuries, cultures, and religious traditions, offering a rich tapestry of stories, teachings, and insights into early Judaism and Christianity.

OLD TESTAMENT APOCRYPHA

DEUTEROCANON: The Deuterocanonical books, part of the Catholic and Eastern Orthodox Bibles, include prayers, wisdom literature, and historical accounts. Notable texts are *The Prayer of Manasses*, *The Books of Esdras*, and *The Books of Maccabees*, which recount Jewish resistance against Hellenistic oppression. *The Wisdom of Solomon* and *Ecclesiasticus* (Sirach) offer philosophical reflections, while additions to *Esther* and *Daniel* provide further narrative depth.

ETHIOPIAN CANON: The Ethiopian Orthodox Church includes unique texts like *The Book of Jubilees*, which retells Genesis with added angelology. *The Book of Enoch* (1 Enoch) influenced early Christian thought with its visions of heaven and judgment. The *Books of Meqabyan* recount stories of martyrdom, while *4 Baruch* offers unique Jewish and Christian traditions.

PSEUDEPIGRAPHA: The Pseudepigrapha, meaning "falsely attributed writings," includes texts attributed to biblical figures, covering a range of genres. *The Books of Adam and Eve* expand on Genesis with detailed stories. The *Psalms of Solomon* and *The Martyrdom and Ascension of Isaiah* reflect Jewish piety. The *Damascus Document* and the *Letter of Aristeas* provide insights into Jewish sectarian movements. *The Story of Ahikar* and *Pseudo-Philo* weave folklore and biblical history, while *The Book of Jasher* offers additional historical narratives.

APOCALYPSES: Apocalyptic literature features visions of the end times and heavenly revelations. *The Books of Enoch* (2 and 3 Enoch) describe heavenly secrets. The *Revelation of Esdras*, *Apocalypse of Sedrach*, and *Apocalypses of Baruch* explore divine judgment themes. *The Apocalypse of Abraham* and *The Apocalypse of Moses* (often synonymous with *The Life of Adam and Eve*) add further enigmatic visions.

TESTAMENTS: The Testaments present final speeches and teachings of biblical patriarchs. *The Testaments of the Twelve Patriarchs* encapsulate Jacob's sons' moral exhortations. The *Testaments of Abraham*, *Job*, *Solomon*, and *Moses* (or *Assumption of Moses*) blend moral instruction with apocalyptic elements, offering rich early Jewish and Christian theology.

NEW TESTAMENT APOCRYPHA

APOSTOLIC FATHERS: The Apostolic Fathers' writings bridge the New Testament and later Christian theology. *The Didache* is an early Christian ethics manual. *The Epistles of Barnabas* and *Clement* offer theological guidance. The *Shepherd of Hermas* presents visions on repentance. Epistles of *Ignatius* and *Polycarp* highlight early Christian struggles, while the *Epistle of Mathetes to Diognetus* and *Fragments of Papias* provide further insight into early Christian thought.

INFANCY GOSPELS: The Infancy Gospels expand on Jesus' early life. The *Gospel of the Birth of Mary* and *Protoevangelium of James* detail Mary's life. The *Arabic Infancy Gospel* and *Thomas's Gospel of the Infancy* include miraculous tales of Jesus' childhood. *The History of Joseph the Carpenter* focuses on Joseph's life.

GNOSTICS: Gnostic literature contrasts with orthodox Christianity, offering alternative narratives. The *Gospel of Thomas* and the *Gospel of Mary* provide mystical teachings. The *Book of Marcion* and *The Gospel of Philip* present divergent theological reflections. The *Secret Gospel of Mark* and *Apocalypse of Adam* reveal diverse early Christian thought, while the *Odes of Solomon* add a lyrical dimension.

PASSION GOSPELS: The Passion Gospels recount Jesus' crucifixion and resurrection with unique details. The *Gospel of Peter* and *Gospel of Bartholomew* offer alternative accounts. The *Gospel of Nicodemus* and *Letters of Herod and Pilate* explore the political aspects of Jesus' crucifixion. *The Narrative of Joseph of Arimathaea* and *The Book of John the Evangelist* provide additional perspectives. *The Avenging of the Saviour* reflects early Christian legend.

EPISTLES: The apocryphal epistles include correspondence attributed to Jesus and Paul. The *Epistles of Jesus Christ and Abgarus King of Edessa* and the *Epistle of Paul to the Laodiceans* are notable examples. The *Epistles of Paul to Seneca* and the *Epistula Apostolorum* assert apostolic authority and doctrinal orthodoxy.

ACTS AND OTHER APOCRYPHAS: The Acts literature recounts the apostles' adventures and teachings. The *Acts of Andrew* and *Acts of Paul and Thecla* highlight the spread of Christianity. Other writings include doctrinal treatises like the *Apostles' Creed* and Tertullian's works (*On Spectacles*, *On Prayer*, *On Patience*, *On Martyrs*), illustrating early Christian doctrine development.

Unlock a World of Timeless Wisdom!

Immerse yourself in the rich heritage of ancient scripture with our exclusive offer… **download the FREE digital version** of these four incredible books:

- **The Sibylline Oracles:** A fascinating collection of prophetic writings attributed to ancient sibyls… blending pagan mythology with Jewish and Christian themes to deliver profound esoteric knowledge.
- **The Acts of John:** An intriguing account of the Apostle John's missionary journeys and miracles… showcasing his unwavering faith and the transformative power of the Christian message.
- **The Acts of Peter:** A compelling narrative detailing the Apostle Peter's travels and acts… illustrating his pivotal role in spreading Christianity and his profound spiritual insights.
- **The Acts of Thomas:** A remarkable story of the Apostle Thomas's missionary efforts in India… highlighting his encounters, teachings, and the establishment of early Christian communities.

Don't miss this opportunity to explore these revered books that have stood the test of time. Get your free copy today and experience the wisdom they have to offer.

Go to the Bonus chapter on page 332 and discover how to get your bonuses now!

OLD TESTAMENT APOCRYPHA

DEUTEROCANON

The Prayer of Manasses

The Prayer of Manasses is recognized as Deuterocanonical Scripture by the Greek Orthodox and Russian Orthodox Churches. It is included in an appendix to the Latin Vulgate Bible.

King of Judah, When He Was Held Captive in Babylon

1

¹ O LORD Almighty in heaven, God of our fathers Abraham, Isaac, and Jacob, and of their righteous offspring, ² you who have made heaven and earth, with all their order, ³ who have bound the sea by the word of your commandment, who have shut up the deep, and sealed it by your terrible and glorious name, ⁴ whom all things fear, yes, tremble before your power, ⁵ for the majesty of your glory can't be borne, and the anger of your threatening toward sinners is unbearable. ⁶ Your merciful promise is unmeasurable and unsearchable, ⁷ for you are the Lord Most High, of great compassion, patient and abundant in mercy, and relent at human suffering. ⁸ ᵃYou, O Lord, according to your great goodness have promised repentance and forgiveness to those who have sinned against you. Of your infinite mercies, you have appointed repentance to sinners, that they may be saved. You therefore, O Lord, who are the God of the just, have not appointed repentance to the just, to Abraham, Isaac, and Jacob, which have not sinned against you, but you have appointed repentance to me, a sinner. ⁹ For I have sinned more than the number of the sands of the sea. My transgressions are multiplied,ᵇ O Lord, my transgressions are multiplied, and I am not worthy to behold and see the height of heaven for the multitude of my iniquities. ¹⁰ I am bowed down with many iron bands, so that I can't lift up my head by reason of my sins,ᶜ neither have I any relief; for I have provoked your wrath, and done that which is evil before you:ᵈ I didn't do your will, neither did I keep your commandments. I have set up abominations, and have multiplied detestable things. ¹¹ Now therefore I bow the knee of my heart, asking you for grace. ¹² I have sinned, O Lord, I have sinned, and I acknowledge my iniquities; ¹³ but, I humbly ask you, forgive me, O Lord, forgive me, and please don't destroy me with my iniquities. Don't be angry with me forever, by reserving evil for me. Don't condemn me into the lower parts of the earth. For you, O Lord, are the God of those who repent. ¹⁴ In me you will show all your goodness, for you will save me, even though I am unworthy, according to your great mercy. ¹⁵ Then I will praise you forever all the days of my life; for all the army of heaven sings your praise, and yours is the glory forever and ever. Amen.

The First Book of Esdras, or Ezra Kali

The First Book of Esdras is recognized as Deuterocanonical Scripture by the Greek Orthodox and Russian Orthodox Churches. It is not recognized by the Roman Catholic Church, but 1 Esdras is placed as an appendix to the Latin Vulgate Bible.

1

¹ *Josias held the Passover in Jerusalem to his Lord, and offered the Passover the fourteenth day of the first month, ² having set the priests according to their daily courses, being arrayed in their vestments, in the Lord's temple. ³ He spoke to the Levites, *the temple servants of Israel, that they should make themselves holy to the Lord, to set the holy ark of the Lord in the house that King Solomon the son of David had built. ⁴ He said, "You no longer need to carry it on your shoulders. Now therefore serve the Lord your God, and minister to his people Israel, and prepare yourselves by your fathers' houses and kindred, ⁵ according to the writing of King David of Israel, and according to the magnificence of Solomon his son. Stand in the holy place according to the divisions of your Levite families who minister in the presence of your kindred the descendants of Israel. ⁶ Offer the Passover in order, prepare the sacrifices for your kindred, and keep the Passover according to the Lord's commandment, which was given to Moses. ⁷ To the people which were present, Josias gave thirty thousand lambs and kids, and three thousand calves. These things were given from the king's possessions, as he promised, to the people and to the priests and Levites. ⁸ Helkias, Zacharias, and ᵉEsyelus, the rulers of the temple, gave to the priests for the Passover two thousand six hundred sheep, and three hundred calves. ⁹ Jeconias, Samaias, Nathanael his brother, Sabias, Ochielus, and Joram, captains over thousands, gave to the Levites for the Passover five thousand sheep and seven hundred calves. ¹⁰ When these things were done, the priests and Levites, having the unleavened bread, stood in proper order according to the kindred, ¹¹ and according to the several divisions by fathers' houses, before the people, to offer to the Lord as it is written in the book of Moses. They did this in the morning. ¹² They roasted the Passover lamb with fire, as required. They boiled the sacrifices in the brazen vessels and caldrons with a pleasing smell, ¹³ and set them before all the people. Afterward they prepared for themselves and for their kindred the priests, the sons of Aaron. ¹⁴ For the priests offered the fat until night. The Levites prepared for themselves and for their kindred the priests, the sons of Aaron. ¹⁵ The holy singers also, the sons of Asaph, were in their order, according to the appointment of David: Asaph, Zacharias, and Eddinus, who represented the king. ¹⁶ Moreover the gatekeepers were at every gate. No one needed to depart from his daily duties, for their kindred the Levites prepared for them. ¹⁷ So the things that belonged to the Lord's sacrifices were accomplished in that day, in holding the Passover, ¹⁸ and offering sacrifices on the altar of the Lord, according to the commandment of King Josias. ¹⁹ So the children of Israel which were present at that time held the Passover and the feast of unleavened bread seven days. ²⁰ Such a Passover had not been held in Israel since the time of the prophet Samuel. ²¹ Indeed, none of the kings of Israel held such a Passover as Josias with the priests, the Levites, and the Jews, held with all Israel that were present in their dwelling place at Jerusalem. ²² This Passover was held in the eighteenth year of the reign of Josias. ²³ The works of Josias were upright before his Lord with a heart full of godliness. ²⁴ Moreover the things that came to pass in his days have been written in times past, concerning those who sinned and did wickedly against the Lord more than any other people or kingdom, and how they grieved him ᶠexceedingly, so that the Lord's words were confirmed against Israel. ²⁵ *Now after all these acts of Josias, it came to pass that Pharaoh the king of Egypt came to make war at Carchemish on the Euphrates; and Josias went out against him. ²⁶ But the king of Egypt sent to him, saying, "What do I have to do with you, O king of Judea? ²⁷ I wasn't sent out from the Lord God against you, for my war is against the Euphrates. Now the Lord is with me, yes, the Lord is with me hastening me forward. Depart from me, and don't be against the Lord." ²⁸ However, Josias didn't turn back to his chariot, but tried to fight with him, not regarding the words of the prophet Jeremy from the Lord's mouth, ²⁹ but joined battle with him in the plain of Megiddo, and the commanders came down against King Josias. ³⁰ Then the king said to his servants, "Carry me away out of the battle, for I am very weak!" Immediately his servants carried him away out of the army. ³¹ Then he got into his second chariot. After he was brought back to Jerusalem he died, and was buried in the tomb of his ancestors. ³² All Judea mourned for Josias. Jeremy the prophet

---

ᵃ *1:8* The Alex. MS. omits You... saved.
ᵇ *1:9* The Alex. MS. omits O Lord... multiplied.
ᶜ *1:10* Some authorities omit by reason of my sins.
ᵈ *1:10* The Alex. MS. omits I did... commandments.

* **1:1** 2 Kings **23:21**; 2 Chronicles **35:1**
* **1:3** Numbers **3:9**
ᵉ *1:8* Jehiel, 2 Chronicles **35:8**.
ᶠ *1:24* Or, sensibly Judges **16:17**.
* **1:25** 2 Chronicles **35:20**

lamented for Josias, and the chief men with the women made lamentation for him to this day. This was given out for an ordinance to be done continually in all the nation of Israel. ³³ These things are written in the book of the histories of the kings of Judea, and every one of the acts that Josias did, and his glory, and his understanding in the law of the Lord, and the things that he had done before, and the things now told, are reported in the book of the kings of Israel and Judah. ³⁴ * The people took ᵃJoachaz the son of Josias, and made him king instead of Josias his father, when he was twenty-three years old. ³⁵ He reigned in Judah and Jerusalem for three months. Then the king of Egypt deposed him from reigning in Jerusalem. ³⁶ He set a tax upon the people of one hundred talents of silver and one talent of gold. ³⁷ The king of Egypt also made King Joakim his brother king of Judea and Jerusalem. ³⁸ And Joakim imprisoned the nobles and apprehended his brother Zarakes, and brought him up out of Egypt. ³⁹ *Joakim was twenty-five years old when he began to reign in Judea and Jerusalem. He did that which was evil in the sight of the Lord. ⁴⁰ King Nabuchodonosor of Babylon came up against him, bound him with a chain of brass, and carried him to Babylon. ⁴¹ Nabuchodonosor also took some of the Lord's holy vessels, carried them away, and stored them in his own temple at Babylon. ⁴² But those things that are reported of him, and of his uncleanness and impiety, are written in the chronicles of the kings. ⁴³ Then Joakim his son reigned in his place. When he was made king, he was eighteen years old. ⁴⁴ He reigned three months and ten days in Jerusalem. He did that which was evil before the Lord. ⁴⁵ So after a year Nabuchodonosor sent and caused him to be brought to Babylon with the holy vessels of the Lord, ⁴⁶ and made Sedekias king of Judea and Jerusalem when he was twenty-one years old. He reigned eleven years. ⁴⁷ He also did that which was evil in the sight of the Lord, and didn't heed the words that were spoken by Jeremy the prophet from the Lord's mouth. ⁴⁸ After King Nabuchodonosor had made him to swear by the name of the Lord, he broke his oath and rebelled. Hardening his neck and his heart, he transgressed the laws of the Lord, the God of Israel. ⁴⁹ Moreover the governors of the people and of the priests did many things wickedly, exceeding all the defilements of all nations, and defiled the temple of the Lord, which was sanctified in Jerusalem. ⁵⁰ The God of their ancestors sent by his messenger to call them back, because he had compassion on them and on his dwelling place. ⁵¹ But they mocked his messengers. In the day when the Lord spoke, they scoffed at his prophets ⁵² until he, being angry with his people for their great ungodliness, commanded to bring up the kings of the Chaldeans against them. ⁵³ They killed their young men with the sword around their holy temple, and spared neither young man or young woman, old man or child; but he delivered all of them into their hands. ⁵⁴ They took all the holy vessels of the Lord, both great and small, with the treasure chests of the Lord's ark and the king's treasures, and carried them away to Babylon. ⁵⁵ They burned the Lord's house, broke down Jerusalem's walls, and burned its towers with fire. ⁵⁶ As for her glorious things, they didn't stop until they had brought them all to nothing. He carried the people who weren't slain with the sword to Babylon. ⁵⁷ They were servants to him and to his children until the Persians reigned, to fulfill the word of the Lord by the mouth of Jeremy: ⁵⁸"Until the land has enjoyed its Sabbaths, the whole time of her desolation shall she keep Sabbath, to fulfill seventy years.

2

¹ In the *first year of King Cyrus of the Persians, that the word of the Lord by the mouth of Jeremy might be accomplished, ² the Lord stirred up the spirit of King Cyrus of the Persians, and he made a proclamation throughout all his kingdom, and also by writing, ³ saying, "Cyrus king of the Persians says: The Lord of Israel, the Most High Lord, has made me king of the whole world, ⁴ and commanded me to build him a house at Jerusalem that is in Judea. ⁵ If therefore there are any of you that are of his people, let the Lord, even his Lord, be with him, and let him go up to Jerusalem that is in Judea, and build the house of the Lord of Israel. He is the Lord who dwells in Jerusalem. ⁶ Therefore, of those who dwell in various places, let those who are in his own place help each one with gold, with silver, ⁷ with gifts, with horses, and cattle, beside the other things which have been added by vow for the temple of the Lord which is in Jerusalem. ⁸ Then the chief of the families of Judah and of the tribe of Benjamin stood up, with the priests, the Levites, and all whose spirit the Lord had stirred to go up, to build the house for the Lord which is in Jerusalem. ⁹ Those who lived around them helped them in all things with silver and gold, with horses and cattle, and with very many gifts that were vowed by a great number whose minds were so moved. ¹⁰ King Cyrus also brought out the holy vessels of the Lord, which Nabuchodonosor had carried away from Jerusalem and had stored in his temple of idols. ¹¹ Now when King Cyrus of the Persians had brought them out, he delivered them to Mithradates his treasurer, ¹² and by him they were delivered to ᵇSanabassar the governor of Judea. ¹³ This was the number of them: one thousand gold cups, one thousand silver cups, twenty-nine silver censers, thirty gold bowls, two thousand four hundred ten silver bowls, and one thousand other vessels. ¹⁴ So all the vessels of gold and of silver were brought up, even five thousand four hundred seventy-nine, ¹⁵ and were carried back by Sanabassar, together with the returning exiles, from Babylon to Jerusalem. ¹⁶ *In the time of King Artaxerxes of the Persians, Belemus, Mithradates, Tabellius, ᶜRathumus, Beeltethmus, and ᵈSamellius the scribe, with their other associates, dwelling in Samaria and other places, wrote to him against those who lived in Judea and Jerusalem the following letter: ¹⁷"To King Artaxerxes our Lord, from your servants, Rathumus the recorder, Samellius the scribe, and the rest of their council, and the judges who are in Coelesyria and Phoenicia: ¹⁸ Let it now be known to our lord the king, that the Jews that have come up from you to us, having come to Jerusalem, are building that rebellious and wicked city, and are repairing its marketplaces and walls, and are laying the foundation of a temple. ¹⁹ Now if this city is built and its walls are finished, they will not only refuse to give tribute, but will even stand up against kings. ²⁰ Since the things pertaining to the temple are now in hand, we think it appropriate not to neglect such a matter, ²¹ but to speak to our lord the king, to the intent that, if it is your pleasure, search may be made in the books of your ancestors. ²² You will find in the chronicles what is written concerning these things, and will understand that that city was rebellious, troubling both kings and cities, ²³ and that the Jews were rebellious, and kept starting wars there in the past. For this cause, this city was laid waste. ²⁴ Therefore now we do declare to you, O lord the king, that if this city is built again, and its walls set up again, you will from then on have no passage into Coelesyria and Phoenicia." ²⁵ Then the king wrote back again to Rathumus the recorder, Beeltethmus, Samellius the scribe, and to the rest that of their associates who lived in Samaria, Syria, and Phoenicia, as follows: ²⁶"I have read the letter which you have sent to me. Therefore I commanded to make search, and it has been found that that city of old time has fought against kings, ²⁷ and the men were given to rebellion and war in it, and that mighty and fierce kings were in Jerusalem, who reigned and exacted tribute in Coelesyria and Phoenicia. ²⁸ Now therefore I have commanded to prevent those men from building the city, and heed to be taken that there be nothing done contrary to this order, ²⁹ and that those wicked doings proceed no further to the annoyance of kings." ³⁰ Then King Artaxerxes, his letters being read, Rathumus, and Samellius the scribe, and the rest of their associates, went in haste to Jerusalem with cavalry and a multitude of people in battle array, and began to hinder the builders. So the building of the temple in Jerusalem ceased until the second year of the reign of King Darius of the Persians.

3

¹ Now King Darius made a great feast for all his subjects, for all who were born in his house, for all the princes of Media and of Persia, ² and for all the local governors and captains and governors who were under him, from India to Ethiopia, in the one hundred twenty seven provinces. ³ They ate and drank, and when they were satisfied went home. Then King Darius went into his bedchamber slept, but awakened out of his sleep. ⁴ Then the three young men of the bodyguard, who guarded the king, spoke one to another: ⁵"Let every one of us state what one thing is strongest. King Darius will give he whose statement seems wiser than the others great gifts and great honors in token of victory. ⁶ He shall be clothed in purple, drink from gold cups, sleep on a gold bed, and have a chariot with bridles of gold, a fine linen turban, and a chain around his neck. ⁷ He shall sit next to Darius because of his wisdom, and shall be called cousin of Darius." ⁸ Then they each wrote his sentence, sealed them, and laid them under King Darius' pillow, ⁹ and said, "When the king wakes up, someone will give him the writing. Whoever the king and the three princes of Persia judge that his sentence is the wisest, to him shall the victory be given, as it is written." ¹⁰ The first wrote, "Wine is the strongest." ¹¹ The second wrote, "The king is strongest." ¹² The third wrote, "Women are strongest, but above all things Truth is the victor." ¹³ Now when the king woke up, they took the writing and gave it to him, so he read it. ¹⁴ Sending out, he called all the princes of Persia and of Media, the local governors, the captains, the governors, and the chief officers ¹⁵ and sat himself down in the royal seat of judgment; and the writing was read before them. ¹⁶ He said, "Call the young men, and they

---

* **1:34** 2 Kings 23:30; 2 Chronicles **36:1**
ᵃ *1:34* Another reading is, Jeconias.
* **1:39** 2 Chronicles 36:4- 5
* **2:1** 2 Chronicles 36:22, 23; Ezra 1:1
ᵇ *2:12* Another reading is, Simanassar.
* **2:16** Ezra 4:7
ᶜ *2:16* Rehum,
ᵈ *2:16* Shimshai.

shall explain their own sentences. So they were called and came in. ¹⁷ They said to them, "Explain what you have written." Then the first, who had spoken of the strength of wine, began ¹⁸ and said this: "O sirs, how exceedingly strong wine is! It causes all men who drink it to go astray. ¹⁹ It makes the mind of the king and of the fatherless child to be the same, likewise of the bondman and of the freeman, of the poor man and of the rich. ²⁰ It also turns every thought into cheer and mirth, so that a man remembers neither sorrow nor debt. ²¹ It makes every heart rich, so that a man remembers neither king nor local governor. It makes people say things in large amounts. ²² When they are in their cups, they forget their love both to friends and kindred, and before long draw their swords. ²³ But when they awake from their wine, they don't remember what they have done. ²⁴ O sirs, isn't wine the strongest, seeing that it forces people to do this?" And when he had said this, he stopped speaking.

4

¹ Then the second, who had spoken of the strength of the king, began to say, ² "O sirs, don't men excel in strength who rule over the sea and land, and all things in them? ³ But yet the king is stronger. He is their lord and has dominion over them. In whatever he commands them, they obey him. ⁴ If he tells them to make war the one against the other, they do it. If he sends them out against the enemies, they go, and conquer mountains, walls, and towers. ⁵ They kill and are killed, and don't disobey the king's commandment. If they win the victory, they bring everything to the king– all the plunder and everything else. ⁶ Likewise for those who are not soldiers, and don't have anything to do with wars, but farm, when they have reaped again that which they had sown, they bring some to the king and compel one another to pay tribute to the king. ⁷ He is just one man! If he commands people to kill, they kill. If he commands them to spare, they spare. ⁸ If he commands them to strike, they strike. If he commands them to make desolate, they make desolate. If he commands to build, they build. ⁹ If he commands them to cut down, they cut down. If he commands them to plant, they plant. ¹⁰ So all his people and his armies obey him. Furthermore, he lies down, he eats and drinks, and takes his rest; ¹¹ and these keep watch around him. None of them may depart and do his own business. They don't disobey him in anything. ¹² O sirs, how could the king not be the strongest, seeing that he is obeyed like this?" Then he stopped talking. ¹³ Then the third, who had spoken of women, and of truth, (this was Zorobabel) began to speak: ¹⁴ "O sirs, isn't the king great, and men are many, and isn't wine strong? Who is it then who rules them, or has the lordship over them? Aren't they women? ¹⁵ Women have given birth to the king and all the people who rule over sea and land. ¹⁶ They came from women. Women nourished up those who planted the vineyards, from where the wine comes. ¹⁷ Women also make garments for men. These bring glory to men. Without women, men can't exist. ¹⁸ Yes, and if men have gathered together gold and silver and any other beautiful thing, and see a woman who is lovely in appearance and beauty, ¹⁹ they let all those things go and gape at her, and with open mouth stare at her. They all have more desire for her than for gold, or silver, or any other beautiful thing. ²⁰ A man leaves his own father who brought him up, leaves his own country, and joins with his wife. ²¹ With his wife he ends his days, with no thought for his father, mother, or country. ²² By this also you must know that women have dominion over you. Don't you labor and toil, and bring it all to give to women? ²³ Yes, a man takes his sword and goes out to travel, to rob, to steal, and to sail on the sea and on rivers. ²⁴ He sees a lion and walks in the darkness. When he has stolen, plundered, and robbed, he brings it to the woman he loves. ²⁵ Therefore a man loves his wife better than father or mother. ²⁶ Yes, there are many who have lost their minds for women, and become slaves for their sakes. ²⁷ Many also have perished, have stumbled, and sinned, for women. ²⁸ Now don't you believe me? Isn't the king great in his power? Don't all regions fear to touch him? ²⁹ Yet I saw him and Apame the king's concubine, the daughter of the illustrious Barticus, sitting at the right hand of the king, ³⁰ and taking the crown from the king's head, and setting it upon her own head. Yes, she struck the king with her left hand. ³¹ At this, the king gaped and gazed at her with open mouth. If she smiles at him, he laughs. But if she takes any displeasure at him, he flatters her, that she might be reconciled to him again. ³² O sirs, how can it not be that women are strong, seeing they do this?" ³³ Then the king and the nobles looked at one another. So he began to speak concerning truth. ³⁴ "O sirs, aren't women strong? The earth is great. The sky is high. The sun is swift in its course, for it circles around the sky, and returns on its course again in one day. ³⁵ Isn't he who makes these things great? Therefore the truth is great, and stronger than all things. ³⁶ All the earth calls upon truth, and the sky blesses truth. All works shake and tremble, but with truth there is no unrighteous thing. ³⁷ Wine is unrighteous. The king is unrighteous. Women are unrighteous. All the children of men are unrighteous, and all their works are unrighteous. There is no truth in them. They shall also perish in their unrighteousness. ³⁸ But truth remains, and is strong forever. Truth lives and conquers forevermore. ³⁹ With truth there is no partiality toward persons or rewards, but truth does the things that are just, instead of any unrighteous or wicked things. All men approve truth's works. ⁴⁰ In truth's judgment is not any unrighteousness. Truth is the strength, the kingdom, the power, and the majesty of all ages. Blessed be the God of truth!" ⁴¹ With that, he stopped speaking. Then all the people shouted and said, "Great is truth, and strong above all things!" ⁴² Then the king said to him, "Ask what you wish, even more than is appointed in writing, and we will give it to you, because you are found wisest. You shall sit next me, and shall be called my cousin." ⁴³ Then he said to the king, "Remember your vow, which you vowed to build Jerusalem, in the day when you came to your kingdom, ⁴⁴ and to send back all the vessels that were taken out of Jerusalem, which Cyrus set apart when he vowed to destroy Babylon, and vowed to send them back there. ⁴⁵ You also vowed to build the temple which the Edomites burned when Judea was made desolate by the Chaldeans. ⁴⁶ Now, O lord the king, this is what I request, and what I desire of you, and this is the princely generosity that may proceed from you: I ask therefore that you make good the vow, the performance of which you have vowed to the King of Heaven with your own mouth." ⁴⁷ Then King Darius stood up, kissed him, and wrote letters for him to all the treasurers and governors and captains and local governors, that they should safely bring on their way both him, and all those who would go up with him to build Jerusalem. ⁴⁸ He wrote letters also to all the governors who were in Coelesyria and Phoenicia, and to them in Libanus, that they should bring cedar wood from Libanus to Jerusalem, and that they should help him build the city. ⁴⁹ Moreover he wrote for all the Jews who would go out of his realm up into Judea concerning their freedom, that no officer, no governor, no local governor, nor treasurer, should forcibly enter into their doors, ⁵⁰ and that all the country which they occupied should be free to them without tribute, and that the Edomites should give up the villages of the Jews which they held at that time, ⁵¹ and that there should be given twenty talents yearly toward the building of the temple, until the time that it was built, ⁵² and another ten talents yearly for burnt offerings to be presented upon the altar every day, as they had a commandment to make seventeen offerings, ⁵³ and that all those who would come from Babylonia to build the city should have their freedom–they and their descendants, and all the priests that came. ⁵⁴ He wrote also to give them their support and the priests' vestments in which they minister. ⁵⁵ For the Levites he wrote that their support should be given them until the day that the house was finished and Jerusalem built up. ⁵⁶ He commanded that land and wages should be given to all who guarded the city. ⁵⁷ He also sent away all the vessels from Babylon that Cyrus had set apart, and all that Cyrus had given in commandment, he commanded also to be done and to be sent to Jerusalem. ⁵⁸ Now when this young man had gone out, he lifted up his face to heaven toward Jerusalem, and praised the King of heaven, ⁵⁹ and said, "From you comes victory. From you comes wisdom. Yours is the glory, and I am your servant. ⁶⁰ Blessed are you, who have given me wisdom. I give thanks to you, O Lord of our fathers. ⁶¹ So he took the letters, went out, came to Babylon, and told it all his kindred. ⁶² They praised the God of their ancestors, because he had given them freedom and liberty ⁶³ to go up and to build Jerusalem and the temple which is called by his name. They feasted with instruments of music and gladness seven days.

5

¹ After this, the chiefs of fathers' houses were chosen to go up according to their tribes, with their wives, sons, and daughters, with their menservants and maidservants, and their livestock. ² Darius sent with them one thousand cavalry to bring them back to Jerusalem with peace, with musical instruments, drums, and flutes. ³ All their kindred were making merry, and he made them go up together with them. ⁴ These are the names of the men who went up, according to their families among their tribes, after their several divisions. ⁵ The priests, the sons of Phinees, the sons of Aaron: Jesus the son of Josedek, the son of Saraias, and Joakim the son of Zorobabel, the son of Salathiel, of the house of David, of the lineage of Phares, of the tribe of Judah, ⁶ who spoke wise words before Darius the king of Persia in the second year of his reign, in the month Nisan, which is the first month. ⁷ *These are the of Judeans who came up from the captivity, where they lived as foreigners, whom Nabuchodonosor the king of Babylon had carried away to Babylon. ⁸ They returned to Jerusalem and to the other parts of Judea, every man to his own city, who came with Zorobabel, with Jesus, Nehemias, ᵃ Zaraias, Resaias,ᵇ Eneneus, Mardocheus, Beelsarus,ᶜ

---

* 5:7 Ezra 2:1　|　ᵃ 5:8 Seralah.　|　ᵇ 5:8 Or, Enenis.　|　ᶜ 5:8 Mispar.

Aspharsus,[a] Reelias, Roimus, and Baana, their leaders. [9] The number of them of the nation and their leaders: the sons of Phoros, two thousand one hundred seventy two; the sons of[b] Saphat, four hundred seventy two; [10] the sons of[c] Ares, seven hundred fifty six; [11] the sons of[d] Phaath Moab, of the sons of Jesus and Joab, two thousand eight hundred twelve; [12] the sons of Elam, one thousand two hundred fifty four; the sons of[e] Zathui, nine hundred forty five; the sons of[f] Chorbe, seven hundred five; the sons of Bani, six hundred forty eight; [13] the sons of Bebai, six hundred twenty three; the sons of[g] Astad,[h] one thousand three hundred twenty two; [14] the sons of Adonikam, six hundred sixty seven; the sons of[i] Bagoi, two thousand sixty six; the sons of[j] Adinu, four hundred fifty four; [15] the sons of[k] Ater, of Ezekias, ninety two; the sons of Kilan and Azetas, sixty seven; the sons of[l] Azaru, four hundred thirty two; [16] the sons of[m] Annis, one hundred one; the sons of Arom, the sons of[n] Bassai, three hundred twenty three; the sons of Arsiphurith, one hundred twelve; [17] the sons of Baiterus, three thousand five; the sons of[o] Bethlomon, one hundred twenty three; [18] those from Netophas, fifty five; those from Anathoth, one hundred fifty eight; those from[p] Bethasmoth, forty two; [19] those from [q] Kariathiarius, twenty five: those from Caphira and Beroth, seven hundred forty three; [20] the Chadiasai and Ammidioi, four hundred twenty two; those from [r]Kirama and [s]Gabbe, six hundred twenty one; [21] those from [t]Macalon, one hundred twenty two; those from [u]Betolion, fifty two; the sons of [v]Niphis, one hundred fifty six; [22] the sons of [w]Calamolalus and [x]Onus, seven hundred twenty five; the sons of [y] Jerechu, [z]three hundred forty five; [23] and the sons of [aa]Sanaas, three thousand three hundred thirty. [24] The priests: the sons of [bb]Jeddu, the son of Jesus, among the sons of Sanasib, nine hundred seventy two; the sons of [cc] Emmeruth, one thousand fifty two; [25] the sons of [dd]Phassurus, one thousand two hundred forty seven; and the sons of [ee]Charme, one thousand seventeen. [26] The Levites: the sons of Jesus, Kadmiel, Bannas, and Sudias, seventy four. [27] The holy singers: the sons of Asaph, one hundred twenty eight. [28] The gatekeepers: the sons of[ff] Salum, the sons of[gg] Atar, the sons of Tolman, the sons of[hh] Dacubi, the sons of[ii] Ateta, the sons of[jj] Sabi, in all one hundred thirty nine. [29] The temple servants: the sons of[kk] Esau, the sons of[ll] Asipha, the sons of Tabaoth, the sons of[mm] Keras, the sons of[nn] Sua, the sons of[oo] Phaleas, the sons of Labana, the sons of[pp] Aggaba. [30] The sons of[qq] Acud, the sons of Uta, the sons of Ketab, the sons of[rr] Accaba, the sons of[ss] Subai, the sons of[tt] Anan, the sons of[uu] Cathua, the sons of[vv] Geddur, [31] the sons of[ww] Jairus, the sons of[xx] Daisan, the sons of[yy] Noeba, the sons of Chaseba, the sons of[zz] Gazera, the sons of[aaa] Ozias, the sons of[bbb] Phinoe, the sons of Asara, the sons of[ccc] Basthai, the sons of[ddd] Asana, the sons of[eee] Maani, the sons of[fff] Naphisi, the sons of[ggg] Acub, the sons of[hhh] Achipha, the sons of[iii] Asur, the sons of Pharakim, the sons of[jjj] Basaloth, [32] the sons of[kkk] Meedda, the sons of Cutha, the sons of[lll] Charea, the sons of[mmm] Barchus, the sons of[nnn] Serar, the sons of[ooo] Thomei, the sons of[ppp] Nasi, the sons of Atipha. [33] The sons of the servants of Solomon: the sons of[qqq] Assaphioth, the sons of[rrr] Pharida, the sons of[sss] Jeeli, the sons of[ttt] Lozon, the sons of[uuu] Isdael, the sons of[vvv] Saphuthi, [34] the sons of[www] Agia, the sons of[xxx] Phacareth, the sons of Sabie, the sons of Sarothie, the sons of[yyy] Masias, the sons of Gas, the sons of Addus, the sons of Subas, the sons of Apherra, the sons of Barodis, the sons of Saphat, the sons of Allon. [35] All the temple-servants and the sons of the servants of Solomon were three hundred seventy two. [36] These came up from[zzz] Thermeleth, and[aaaa] Thelersas,[bbbb] Charaathalan leading them, and Allar; [37] and they could not show their families, nor their stock, how they were of Israel: the sons of[cccc] Dalan the son of[dddd] Ban, the sons of[eeee] Nekodan, six hundred fifty two. [38] Of the priests, those who usurped the office of the priesthood and were not found: the sons of[ffff] Obdia, the sons of[gggg] Akkos, the sons of Jaddus, who married Augia one of the daughters of[hhhh] Zorzelleus, and was called after his name. [39] When the description of the kindred of these men was sought in the register and was not found, they were removed from executing the office of the priesthood; [40] for Nehemias and Attharias told them that they should not be partakers of the holy things until a high priest wearing[iiii] Urim and Thummim should arise. [41] So all those of Israel, from twelve years old and upward, beside menservants and women servants, were in number forty two thousand three hundred sixty. [42] Their menservants and handmaids were seven thousand three hundred thirty and seven; the minstrels and singers, two hundred forty five; [43] four hundred thirty and five camels, seven thousand thirty six horses, two hundred forty five mules, and five thousand five hundred twenty five beasts of burden. [44] And some of the chief men of their families, when they came to the temple of God that is in Jerusalem, vowed to set up the house again in its own place according to their ability, [45] and to give into the holy treasury of the works one thousand minas[jjjj] of gold, five thousand minas of silver, and one hundred priestly vestments. [46] The priests and the Levites and some of the people lived in Jerusalem and the country. The holy singers also and the gatekeepers and all Israel lived in their villages. [47] But when the seventh month was at hand, and when the children of Israel were each in their own place, they all came together with one purpose into the broad place before the first porch which is toward the east. [48] Then Jesus the son of Josedek, his kindred the priests, Zorobabel the son of Salathiel, and his kindred stood up and made the altar of the God of Israel ready [49] to offer burned sacrifices upon it, in accordance with the express commands in the book of Moses the man of God. [50] Some people joined them out of the other nations of the land, and they erected the altar upon its own place, because all the nations of the land were hostile to them and oppressed them; and they offered sacrifices at the proper times and burnt offerings to the Lord both morning and evening. [51] They also held the feast of tabernacles, as it is commanded in the law, and offered sacrifices daily, as appropriate. [52] After that, they offered the continual oblations and the sacrifices of the Sabbaths, of the new moons, and of all the consecrated feasts. [53] All those who had made any vow to God began to offer sacrifices to God from the new moon of the seventh month, although the temple of God was not yet built. [54] They gave money, food, and drink to the masons and carpenters. [55] They also gave carts to the people of Sidon and Tyre, that they should bring cedar trees from Libanus, and convey them in rafts to the harbor of Joppa, according to the commandment which was written for them by Cyrus king of the Persians. [56] In the second year after his coming to the temple of God at Jerusalem, in the second month, Zorobabel the son of Salathiel, Jesus the son of Josedek, their kindred, the Levitical priests, and all those who had come to Jerusalem out of the captivity began work. [57] They laid the foundation of God's temple on the

---

[a] *5:8* Reclaiah
[b] *5:9* Shephatiah.
[c] *5:10* Arah.
[d] *5:11* Pahath-moab.
[e] *5:12* Zattu.
[f] *5:12* Zaccai.
[g] *5:13* Asgad.
[h] *5:13* According to other readings, **3622**, or **3222**.
[i] *5:14* Bigvai.
[j] *5:14* Adin.
[k] *5:15* Ater of Hezekiah.
[l] *5:15* Another reading is, Azuru.
[m] *5:16* Another reading is, Annias.
[n] *5:16* Bezai.
[o] *5:17* Bethlehem.
[p] *5:18* Azmaveth.
[q] *5:19* Kiriath-arim or Kiriath-jearim.
[r] *5:20* Rumah.
[s] *5:20* Geba.
[t] *5:21* Michmas.
[u] *5:21* Bethel.
[v] *5:21* Magbish
[w] *5:22* Lod, Hadid.
[x] *5:22* Ono.
[y] *5:22* Jericho.
[z] *5:22* Another reading is, two
[aa] *5:23* Senaah.
[bb] *5:24* Jedaiah.
[cc] *5:24* Immer.
[dd] *5:25* Pashhur.
[ee] *5:25* Harim.
[ff] *5:28* Shallum.
[gg] *5:28* Ater.
[hh] *5:28* Akkub.
[ii] *5:28* Hatita.
[jj] *5:28* Shobai.
[kk] *5:29* Ziha.
[ll] *5:29* Hasupha.
[mm] *5:29* Keros.
[nn] *5:29* Siaha.
[oo] *5:29* Padon.
[pp] *5:29* Hagaba.
[qq] *5:30* Akkub.
[rr] *5:30* Hagab.
[ss] *5:30* Shamlai.
[tt] *5:30* Hanan.
[uu] *5:30* Giddel.
[vv] *5:30* Gahar
[ww] *5:31* Reaiah.
[xx] *5:31* Rezin.
[yy] *5:31* Nekoda.
[zz] *5:31* Gazzam.
[aaa] *5:31* Uzza.
[bbb] *5:31* Paseah.
[ccc] *5:31* Besai.
[ddd] *5:31* Asnah.
[eee] *5:31* Meunim.
[fff] *5:31* Nephisim.
[ggg] *5:31* Bakbuk. According to other readings, Acum, or Acuph.
[hhh] *5:31* Hakupha.
[iii] *5:31* Harhur.
[jjj] *5:31* Bazluth.
[kkk] *5:32* Mehida.
[lll] *5:32* Harsha.
[mmm] *5:32* Barkos.
[nnn] *5:32* Sisera.
[ooo] *5:32* Temah.
[ppp] *5:32* Neziah. Another reading is, Nasith.
[qqq] *5:33* Hussophereth.
[rrr] *5:33* Peruda.
[sss] *5:33* Jaalah.
[ttt] *5:33* Darkon.
[uuu] *5:33* Giddel.
[vvv] *5:33* Shephatia.
[www] *5:34* Hattil.
[xxx] *5:34* Pochereth-haz-zebaim, Ezra **2:57**.
[yyy] *5:34* Another reading is, Misaias.
[zzz] *5:36* Telmelah.
[aaaa] *5:36* Telharsha.
[bbbb] *5:36* Cherub. Addan.
[cccc] *5:37* Delaiah. Another reading is, Asan.
[dddd] *5:37* Tobiah Another reading is, Baenan.
[eeee] *5:37* Nekoda.
[ffff] *5:38* Habaiah, or Hobaiah.
[gggg] *5:38* Hakkoz.
[hhhh] *5:38* Barzillai. Another reading is, Phaezeldaeus.
[iiii] *5:40* Gr. the manifestation and truth.
[jjjj] *5:45* A mina is about **570** grams or **1.25** pounds.

new moon of the second month, in the second year after they had come to Judea and Jerusalem. ⁵⁸ *They appointed the Levites who were at least twenty years old over the Lord's works. Then Jesus, with his sons and kindred, Kadmiel his brother, the sons of Jesus, Emadabun, and the sons of Joda the son of Iliadun, and their sons and kindred, all the Levites, with one accord stood up and started the business, laboring to advance the works in the house of God. So the builders built the Lord's temple. ⁵⁹ The priests stood arrayed in their vestments with musical instruments and trumpets, and the Levites the sons of Asaph with their cymbals, ⁶⁰ singing songs of thanksgiving and praising the Lord, according to the directions of King David of Israel. ⁶¹ They sang aloud, praising the Lord in songs of thanksgiving, because his goodness and his glory are forever in all Israel. ⁶² All the people sounded trumpets and shouted with a loud voice, singing songs of thanksgiving to the Lord for the raising up of the Lord's house. ⁶³ *Some of the Levitical priests and of the heads of their families, the elderly who had seen the former house came to the building of this one with lamentation and great weeping. ⁶⁴ But many with trumpets and joy shouted with a loud voice, ⁶⁵ so that the people couldn't hear the trumpets for the weeping of the people, for the multitude sounded loudly, so that it was heard far away. ⁶⁶ * Therefore when the enemies of the tribe of Judah and Benjamin heard it, they came to know what that noise of trumpets meant. ⁶⁷ They learned that those who returned from captivity built the temple for the Lord, the God of Israel. ⁶⁸ So they went to Zorobabel and Jesus, and to the chief men of the families, and said to them, "We will build together with you. ⁶⁹ For we, just like you, obey your Lord, and sacrifice to him from the days of King ᵃ Asbasareth of the Assyrians, who brought us here." ⁷⁰ Then Zorobabel, Jesus and the chief men of the families of Israel said to them, "It is not for you to build the house for the Lord our God. ⁷¹ We ourselves alone will build for the Lord of Israel, as King Cyrus of the Persians has commanded us." ⁷² But the heathen of the land pressed hard upon the inhabitants of Judea, cut off their supplies, and hindered their building. ⁷³ By their secret plots, and popular persuasions and commotions, they hindered the finishing of the building all the time that King Cyrus lived. So they were hindered from building for two years, until the reign of Darius.

6

¹ Now *in the second year of the reign of Darius, Aggaeus and Zacharius the son ofᵇ Addo, the prophets, prophesied to the Jews in Judea and Jerusalem in the name of the Lord, the God of Israel. ² Then Zorobabel the son of Salathiel and Jesus the son of Josedek stood up and began to build the house of the Lord at Jerusalem, the prophets of the Lord being with them and helping them. ³ *At the same time ᶜSisinnes the governor of Syria and Phoenicia came to them, with ᵈSathrabuzanes and his companions, and said to them, ⁴"By whose authority do you build this house and this roof, and perform all the other things? Who are the builders who do these things?" ⁵ Nevertheless, the elders of the Jews obtained favor, because the Lord had visited the captives; ⁶ and they were not hindered from building until such time as communication was made to Darius concerning them, and his answer received. ⁷ A copy of the letter which Sisinnes, governor of Syria and Phoenicia, and Sathrabuzanes, with their companions, the rulers in Syria and Phoenicia, wrote and sent to Darius: ⁸"To King Darius, greetings. Let it be fully known to our lord the king, that having come into the country of Judea, and entered into the city of Jerusalem, we found in the city of Jerusalem the elders of the Jews that were of the captivity ⁹ building a great new house for the Lord of hewn and costly stones, with timber laid in the walls. ¹⁰ Those works are being done with great speed. The work goes on prosperously in their hands, and it is being accomplished with all glory and diligence. ¹¹ Then asked we these elders, saying, 'By whose authority are you building this house and laying the foundations of these works?' ¹² Therefore, to the intent that we might give knowledge to you by writing who were the leaders, we questioned them, and we required of them the names in writing of their principal men. ¹³ So they gave us this answer, 'We are the servants of the Lord who made heaven and earth. ¹⁴ As for this house, it was built many years ago by a great and strong king of Israel, and was finished. ¹⁵ But when our fathers sinned against the Lord of Israel who is in heaven, and provoked him to wrath, he gave them over into the hands of King Nabuchodonosor of Babylon, king of the Chaldeans. ¹⁶ They pulled down the house, burned it, and carried away the people captive to Babylon. ¹⁷ But in the first year that Cyrus reigned over the country of Babylon, King Cyrus wrote that this house should be rebuilt. ¹⁸ The holy vessels of gold and of silver that Nabuchodonosor had carried away out of the house at Jerusalem and had set up in his own temple, those King Cyrus brought out of the temple in Babylonia, and they were delivered to Zorobabel and to ᵉSanabassarus the governor, ¹⁹ with commandment that he should carry away all these vessels, and put them in the temple at Jerusalem, and that the Lord's temple should be built on its site. ²⁰ Then Sanabassarus, having come here, laid the foundations of the Lord's house which is in Jerusalem. From that time to this we are still building. It is not yet fully completed.' ²¹ Now therefore, if it seems good, O king, let a search be made among the royal archives of our lord the king that are in Babylon. ²² If it is found that the building of the house of the Lord which is in Jerusalem has been done with the consent of King Cyrus, and it seems good to our lord the king, let him send us directions concerning these things." ²³ *Then King Darius commanded that a search be made among the archives that were laid up at Babylon. So at Ekbatana the palace, which is in the country of Media, a scroll was found where these things were recorded: ²⁴"In the first year of the reign of Cyrus, King Cyrus commanded to build up the house of the Lord which is in Jerusalem, where they sacrifice with continual fire. ²⁵ Its height shall be sixty cubits, and the breadth sixty cubits, with three rows of hewn stones, and one row of new wood from that country. Its expenses are to be given out of the house of King Cyrus. ²⁶ The holy vessels of the house of the Lord, both gold and silver, that Nabuchodonosor took out of the house at Jerusalem and carried away to Babylon, should be restored to the house at Jerusalem, and be set in the place where they were before." ²⁷ Also he commanded that Sisinnes the governor of Syria and Phoenicia, and Sathrabuzanes, and their companions, and those who were appointed rulers in Syria and Phoenicia, should be careful not to meddle with the place, but allow Zorobabel, the servant of the Lord, and governor of Judea, and the elders of the Jews, to build that house of the Lord in its place. ²⁸"I also command to have it built up whole again; and that they look diligently to help those who are of the captivity of Judea, until the house of the Lord is finished, ²⁹ and that out of the tribute of Coelesyria and Phoenicia a portion shall be carefully given to these men for the sacrifices of the Lord, that is, to Zorobabel the governor for bulls, rams, and lambs, ³⁰ and also corn, salt, wine and oil, and that continually every year without further question, according as the priests who are in Jerusalem may direct to be daily spent, ³¹ that drink offerings may be made to the Most High God for the king and for his children, and that they may pray for their lives." ³² He commanded that whoever should transgress, yes, or neglect anything written here, a beam shall be taken out of his own house, and he shall be hanged on it, and all his goods seized for the king. ³³"Therefore may the Lord, whose name is called upon there, utterly destroy every king and nation that stretches out his hand to hinder or damage that house of the Lord in Jerusalem. ³⁴ I, King Darius have ordained that these things be done with diligence."

7

¹ Then * Sisinnes the governor of Coelesyria and Phoenicia, and Sathrabuzanes, with their companions, following the commandments of King Darius, ² very carefully supervised the holy work, assisting the elders of the Jews and rulers of the temple. ³ So the holy work prospered, while Aggaeus and Zacharias the prophets prophesied. ⁴ They finished these things by the commandment of the Lord, the God of Israel, and with the consent of Cyrus, Darius, and Artaxerxes, kings of the Persians. ⁵ So the holy house was finished by the twenty-third day of the month Adar, in the sixth year of King Darius. ⁶ The children of Israel, the priests, the Levites, and the others who returned from captivity who joined them did what was written in the book of Moses. ⁷ For the dedication of the Lord's temple, they offered one hundred bulls, two hundred rams, four hundred lambs, ⁸ and twelve male goats for the sin of all Israel, according to the number of the twelve princes of the tribes of Israel. ⁹ The priests and the Levites stood arrayed in their vestments, according to their kindred, for the services of the Lord, the God of Israel, according to the book of Moses. The gatekeepers were at every gate. ¹⁰ The children of Israel who came out of captivity held the Passover the fourteenth day of the first month, when the priests and the Levites were sanctified together, ¹¹ with all those who returned from captivity; for they were sanctified. For the Levites were all sanctified together, ¹² and they offered the Passover for all who returned from captivity, for their kindred the priests, and for themselves. ¹³ The children of Israel who came out of the captivity ate, even all those who had separated themselves from the abominations of the heathen of the land, and sought the Lord. ¹⁴ They kept the feast of unleavened bread seven days, rejoicing before the Lord, ¹⁵ because he had turned the counsel of the king of Assyria

---

* **5:58** Ezra 3:8- 9
* **5:63** Ezra 3:12- 13
* **5:66** Ezra 4:1
ᵃ *5:69* Another reading is, Asbacaphath.

* **6:1** Ezra 4:24; 5:1
ᵇ *6:1* Iddo. Another reading is, Eddin
* **6:3** Ezra 5:3
ᶜ *6:3* Tattenai.

ᵈ *6:3* Shetharbozenai
ᵉ *6:18* Another reading is, Sabunassarus.
* **6:23** Ezra 6:1
* **7:1** Ezra 6:13

toward them, to strengthen their hands in the works of the Lord, the God of Israel.

8

¹ * After these things, when Artaxerxes the king of the Persians reigned, Esdras came, who was the son of Azaraias, the son of Zechrias, the son of Helkias, the son of Salem, ² the son of Sadduk, the son of Ahitob, the son of Amarias, the son of Ozias,ᵃ the son of Memeroth, the son of Zaraias, the son of Savias, the son of Boccas, the son of Abisne, the son of Phinees, the son of Eleazar, the son of Aaron, the chief priest. ³ This Esdras went up from Babylon as a skilled scribe in the law of Moses, which was given by the God of Israel. ⁴ The king honored him, for he found favor in his sight in all his requests. ⁵ There went up with him also some of the children of Israel, and of the priests, Levites, holy singers, gatekeepers, and temple servants to Jerusalem ⁶ in the seventh year of the reign of Artaxerxes, in the fifth month (this was the king's seventh year); for they left Babylon on the new moon of the first month and came to Jerusalem, by the prosperous journey which the Lord gave themᵇ for his sake. ⁷ For Esdras had very great skill, so that he omitted nothing of the law and commandments of the Lord, but taught all Israel the ordinances and judgments. ⁸ Now the commission, which was written from King Artaxerxes, came to Esdras the priest and reader of the law of the Lord, was as follows: ⁹"King Artaxerxes to Esdras the priest and reader of the law of the Lord, greetings. ¹⁰ Having determined to deal graciously, I have given orders that those of the nation of the Jews, and of the priests and Levites, and of those within our realm who are willing and freely choose to, should go with you to Jerusalem. ¹¹ As many therefore as are so disposed, let them depart with you, as it has seemed good both to me and my seven friends the counselors, ¹² that they may look to the affairs of Judea and Jerusalem, in accordance with what is in the Lord's law, ¹³ and carry the gifts to the Lord of Israel to Jerusalem, which I and my friends have vowed, and that all the gold and silver that can be found in the country of Babylonia for the Lord in Jerusalem, ¹⁴ with that also which is given of the people for the temple of the Lord their God that is at Jerusalem, be collected: even the gold and silver for bulls, rams, and lambs, and what goes with them, ¹⁵ to the end that they may offer sacrifices to the Lord upon the altar of the Lord their God, which is in Jerusalem. ¹⁶ Whatever you and your kindred decide to do with gold and silver, do that according to the will of your God. ¹⁷ The holy vessels of the Lord, which are given you for the use of the temple of your God, which is in Jerusalem, ¹⁸ and whatever else you shall remember for the use of the temple of your God, you shall give it out of the king's treasury. ¹⁹ I, King Artaxerxes, have also commanded the keepers of the treasures in Syria and Phoenicia, that whatever Esdras the priest and reader of the law of the Most High God shall send for, they should give it to him with all diligence, ²⁰ to the sum of one hundred talents of silver, likewise also of wheat even to one hundred corsᶜ, and one hundred firkinsᵈ of wine, andᵉ salt in abundance. ²¹ Let all things be performed after God's law diligently to the most high God, that wrath come not upon the kingdom of the king and his sons. ²² I command you also that no tax, nor any other imposition, be laid upon any of the priests, or Levites, or holy singers, or gatekeepers, or temple servants, or any that have employment in this temple, and that no man has authority to impose any tax on them. ²³ You, Esdras, according to the wisdom of God, ordain judges and justices that they may judge in all Syria and Phoenicia all those who know the law of your God; and those who don't know it, you shall teach. ²⁴ Whoever transgresses the law of your God and of the king shall be punished diligently, whether it be by death, or other punishment, by penalty of money, or by imprisonment." ²⁵ Then Esdras the scribe said, "Blessed be the only Lord, the God of my fathers, who has put these things into the heart of the king, to glorify his house that is in Jerusalem, ²⁶ and has honored me in the sight of the king, his counselors, and all his friends and nobles. ²⁷ Therefore I was encouraged by the help of the Lord my God, and gathered together out of Israel men to go up with me. ²⁸ These are the chief according to their families and their several divisions, who went up with me from Babylon in the reign of King Artaxerxes: ²⁹ of the sons of Phinees, Gerson; of the sons of Ithamar, Gamael; of the sons of David,ᶠ Attusᵍ the son of Sechenias; ³⁰ of the sons of Phoros, Zacharais; and with him were counted one hundred fifty men; ³¹ of the sons of Phaath Moab, Eliaonias the son ofʰ Zaraias, and with him two hundred men; ³² ⁱof the sons of Zathoes, Sechenias the son of Jezelus, and with him three hundred men; of the sons of Adin, Obeth the son of Jonathan, and with him two hundred fifty men; ³³ of the sons of Elam, Jesias son of Gotholias, and with him seventy men; ³⁴ of the sons of Saphatias, Zaraias son of Michael, and with him seventy men; ³⁵ of the sons of Joab, Abadias son of Jehiel. Jezelus, and with him two hundred twelve men; ³⁶ ʲ of the sons of Banias, Salimoth son of Josaphias, and with him one hundred sixty men; ³⁷ of the sons of Babi, Zacharias son of Bebai, and with him twenty-eight men; ³⁸ of the sons of Azgad: Astath, Joannes son of Hakkatan Akatan, and with him one hundred ten men; ³⁹ of the sons of Adonikam, the last, and these are the names of them, Eliphalat, Jeuel, and Samaias, and with them seventy men; ⁴⁰ of the sons of Bago, Uthi the son of Istalcurus, and with him seventy men. ⁴¹ I gathered them together to the river called Theras. There we pitched our tents three days, and I inspected them. ⁴² When I had found there none of the priests and Levites, ⁴³ then sent I to Eleazar, Iduel, Maasmas, ⁴⁴ Elnathan, Samaias, Joribus, Nathan, Ennatan, Zacharias, and Mosollamus, principal men and men of understanding. ⁴⁵ I asked them to go to Loddeus the captain, who was in the place of the treasury, ⁴⁶ and commanded them that they should speak to Loddeus, to his kindred, and to the treasurers in that place, to send us such men as might execute the priests' office in our Lord's house. ⁴⁷ By the mighty hand of our Lord, they brought to us men of understanding of the sons ofᵏ Mooli the son of Levi, the son of Israel,ˡ Asebebias, and his sons, and his kindred, who were eighteen, ⁴⁸ andᵐ Asebias, Annuus, and Osaias his brother, of the sons of Chanuneus, and their sons were twenty men; ⁴⁹ and of the temple servants whom David and the principal men had appointed for the servants of the Levites, two hundred twenty temple servants. The list of all their names was reported. ⁵⁰ There I vowed a fast for the young men before our Lord, to seek from him a prosperous journey both for us and for our children and livestock that were with us; ⁵¹ for I was ashamed to ask of the king infantry, cavalry, and an escort for protection against our adversaries. ⁵² For we had said to the king that the power of our Lord would be with those who seek him, to support them in all ways. ⁵³ Again we prayed to our lord about these things, and found him to be merciful. ⁵⁴ Then I set apart twelve men of the chiefs of the priests,ⁿ Eserebias, Assamias, and ten men of their kindred with them. ⁵⁵ I weighed out to them the silver, the gold, and the holy vessels of the house of our Lord, which the king, his counselors, the nobles, and all Israel had given. ⁵⁶ When I had weighed it, I delivered to them six hundred fifty talents of silver, silver vessels weighing one hundred talents, one hundred talents of gold, ⁵⁷ twenty golden vessels, and twelve vessels of brass, even of fine brass, glittering like gold. ⁵⁸ I said to them, "You are holy to the Lord, the vessels are holy, and the gold and the silver are a vow to the Lord, the Lord of our fathers. ⁵⁹ Watch and keep them until you deliver them to the chiefs of the priests and Levites, and to the principal men of the families of Israel in Jerusalem, in the chambers of our Lord's house. ⁶⁰ So the priests and the Levites who received the silver, the gold, and the vessels which were in Jerusalem, brought them into the temple of the Lord. ⁶¹ We left the river Theras on the twelfth day of the first month. We came to Jerusalem by the mighty hand of our Lord which was upon us. The Lord delivered us from from every enemy on the way, and so we came to Jerusalem. ⁶² When we had been there three days, the silver and gold was weighed and delivered in our Lord's house on the fourth day toᵒ Marmoth the priest the son ofᵖ Urias. ⁶³ With him was Eleazar the son of Phinees, and with them were Josabdus the son of Jesus andᵠ Moeth the son of Sabannus, the Levites. All was delivered to them by number and weight. ⁶⁴ All the weight of them was recorded at the same hour. ⁶⁵ Moreover those who had come out of captivity offered sacrifices to the Lord, the God of Israel, even twelve bulls for all Israel, ninety-six rams, ⁶⁶ seventy-two lambs, and twelve goats for a peace offering–all of them a sacrifice to the Lord. ⁶⁷ They delivered the king's commandments to the king's stewards and to the governors of Coelesyria and Phoenicia; and they honored the people and the temple of the Lord. ⁶⁸ Now when these things were done, the principal men came to me and said, ⁶⁹"The nation of Israel, the princes, the priests, and the Levites haven't put away from themselves the foreign people of the land nor the uncleannesses of the Gentiles–the Canaanites, Hittites, Pherezites, Jebusites, Moabites,

---

* 8:1 Ezra 7:1
ᵃ 8:2 The Vatican MS. omits the son of Memeroth, the son of Zaraias, the son of Savias.
ᵇ 8:6 Some MSS. omit for his sake.
ᶜ 8:20 a cor is about 230 liters, so 100 cors is about 23 kiloliters or 652 bushels
ᵈ 8:20 a firkin is about 41 liters or 11 gallons.
ᵉ 8:20 So some authorities. See Ezra 7:22. The common reading is, other things.
ᶠ 8:29 Hattush.
ᵍ 8:29 Ezra 8:3, of the sons of Shecaniah; of the sons of Parosh.
ʰ 8:31 Zerehiah.
ⁱ 8:32 Ezra 8:5, of the sons of Shecaniah, the son of Jahaziel.
ʲ 8:36 Ezra 8:10, of the sons of Shelomith, the son of Josiphiah.
ᵏ 8:47 Mahli.
ˡ 8:47 Sherebiah.
ᵐ 8:48 Hashabiah.
ⁿ 8:54 Sherebiah, Hashabiah.
ᵒ 8:62 Meremoth.
ᵖ 8:62 Uriah.
ᵠ 8:63 Noadiah the son of Binnui.

Egyptians, and Edomites. ⁷⁰ For both they and their sons have married with their daughters, and the holy seed is mixed with the foreign people of the land. From the beginning of this matter the rulers and the nobles have been partakers of this iniquity." ⁷¹ And as soon as I had heard these things, I tore my clothes and my holy garment, and plucked the hair from off my head and beard, and sat down sad and full of heaviness. ⁷² So all those who were moved at the word of the Lord, the God of Israel, assembled to me while I mourned for the iniquity, but I sat still full of heaviness until the evening sacrifice. ⁷³ Then rising up from the fast with my clothes and my holy garment torn, and bowing my knees and stretching out my hands to the Lord, ⁷⁴ I said, "O Lord, I am ashamed and confounded before your face, ⁷⁵ for our sins are multiplied above our heads, and our errors have reached up to heaven ⁷⁶ ever since the time of our fathers. We are in great sin, even to this day. ⁷⁷ For our sins and our fathers' we with our kindred, our kings, and our priests were given up to the kings of the earth, to the sword, and to captivity, and for a prey with shame, to this day. ⁷⁸ Now in some measure mercy has been shown to us from you, O Lord, that there should be left us a root and a name in the place of your sanctuary, ⁷⁹ and to uncover a light in the house of the Lord our God, and to give us food in the time of our servitude. ⁸⁰ Yes, when we were in bondage, we were not forsaken by our Lord, but he gave us favor before the kings of Persia, so that they gave us food, ⁸¹ glorified the temple of our Lord, and raised up the desolate Zion, to give us a sure dwelling in Judea and Jerusalem. ⁸²"Now, O Lord, what shall we say, having these things? For we have transgressed your commandments which you gave by the hand of your servants the prophets, saying, ⁸³'The land, which you enter into to possess as an inheritance, is a land polluted with the pollutions of the foreigners of the land, and they have filled it with their uncleanness. ⁸⁴ Therefore now you shall not join your daughters to their sons, neither shall you take their daughters for your sons. ⁸⁵ You shall never seek to have peace with them, that you may be strong, and eat the good things of the land, and that you may leave it for an inheritance to your children for evermore.' ⁸⁶ All that has happened is done to us for our wicked works and great sins, for you, O Lord, made our sins light, ⁸⁷ and gave to us such a root; but we have turned back again to transgress your law in mingling ourselves with the uncleanness of the heathen of the land. ⁸⁸ You weren't angry with us to destroy us until you had left us neither root, seed, nor name. ⁸⁹ O Lord of Israel, you are true, for we are left a root this day. ⁹⁰ Behold, now we are before you in our iniquities, for we can't stand any longer before you because of these things." ⁹¹ *As Esdras in his prayer made his confession, weeping, and lying flat on the ground before the temple, a very great throng of men, women, and children gathered to him from Jerusalem; for there was great weeping among the multitude. ⁹² Then Jechonias the son of Jeelus, one of the sons of Israel, called out, and said, "O Esdras, we have sinned against the Lord God, we have married foreign women of the heathen of the land, but there is still hope for Israel. ⁹³ Let's make an oath to the Lord about this, that we will put away all our foreign wives with their children, ⁹⁴ as seems good to you, and to as many as obey the Lord's Law. ⁹⁵ Arise, and take action, for this is your task, and we will be with you to do valiantly." ⁹⁶ So Esdras arose, and took an oath from the chief of the priests and Levites of all Israel to do these things; and they swore to it.

9

¹ * Then Esdras rose up from the court of the temple and went to the chamber of Jonas the son of Eliasib, ² and lodged there, and ate no bread and drank no water, mourning for the great iniquities of the multitude. ³ A proclamation was made in all Judea and Jerusalem to all those who returned from captivity, that they should be gathered together at Jerusalem, ⁴ and that whoever didn't meet there within two or three days, in accordance with the ruling of the elders, that their livestock would be seized for the use of the temple, and they would be expelled from the multitude of those who returned from captivity. ⁵ Within three days, all those of the tribe of Judah and Benjamin gathered together at Jerusalem. This was the ninth month, on the twentieth day of the month. ⁶ All the multitude sat together shivering in the broad place before the temple because of the present foul weather. ⁷ So Esdras arose up and said to them, "You have transgressed the law and married foreign wives, increasing the sins of Israel. ⁸ Now make confession and give glory to the Lord, the God of our fathers, ⁹ and do his will, and separate yourselves from the heathen of the land, and from the foreign women." ¹⁰ Then the whole multitude cried out, and said with a loud voice, "Just as you have spoken, so we will do. ¹¹ But because the multitude is great, and it is foul weather, so that we can't stand outside, and this is not a work of one day or two, seeing our sin in these things has spread far, ¹² therefore let the rulers of the multitude stay, and let all those of our settlements that have foreign wives come at the time appointed, ¹³ and with them the rulers and judges of every place, until we turn away the wrath of the Lord from us for this matter." ¹⁴ So Jonathan the son of Azael andᵃ Ezekias the son of Thocanus took the matter on themselves. Mosollamus and Levis and Sabbateus were judges with them. ¹⁵ Those who returned from captivity did according to all these things. ¹⁶ Esdras the priest chose for himself principal men of their families, all by name. On the new moon of the tenth month they met together to examine the matter. ¹⁷ So their cases of men who had foreign wives was brought to an end by the new moon of the first month. ¹⁸ Of the priests who had come together and had foreign wives, there were found ¹⁹ of the sons of Jesus the son of Josedek, and his kindred,ᵇ Mathelas, Eleazar, andᶜ Joribus, andᵈ Joadanus. ²⁰ They gave their hands to put away their wives, and to offer rams to make reconciliation for their error. ²¹ Of the sons of Emmer: Ananias, Zabdeus, ᵉManes, ᶠSameus, ᵍHicreel, and ʰAzarias. ²² Of the sons of ⁱPhaisur: Elionas, Massias, Ishmael, Nathanael, ʲOcidelus, and ᵏSaloas. ²³ Of the Levites: Jozabdus, Semeis, ˡColius who was called ᵐCalitas, ⁿPatheus, Judas, and Jonas. ²⁴ Of the holy singers: ᵒEliasibus and Bacchurus. ²⁵ Of the gatekeepers: Sallumus andᵖ Tolbanes. ²⁶ Of Israel, of the sons of Phoros:ᑫ Hiermas,ʳ Ieddias,ˢ Melchias, Maelus,ᵗ Eleazar, Asibas, ᵘ and Banneas. ²⁷ Of the sons of Ela: Matthanias, Zacharias, ᵛ Jezrielus, Oabdius, Hieremoth, andʷ Aedias. ²⁸ Of the sons of ˣZamoth, ʸEliadas, ᶻEliasimus, ᵃᵃOthonias, Jarimoth, ᵇᵇSabathus, andᶜᶜ Zardeus. ²⁹ Of the sons of Bebai: Joannes, Ananias, ᵈᵈJozabdus, and ᵉᵉEmatheis. ³⁰ Of the sons of ᶠᶠ Mani: ᵍᵍOlamus, ʰʰMamuchus, ⁱⁱJedeus, Jasubas, ʲʲ Jasaelus, and Hieremoth. ³¹ Of the sons of Addi: Naathus, Moossias, Laccunus, Naidus, Matthanias, Sesthel, Balnuus, and Manasseas. ³² Of the sons of Annas: Elionas, Aseas, Melchias, Sabbeus, and Simon Chosameus. ³³ Of the sons of Asom: ᵏᵏMaltanneus, ˡˡMattathias, ᵐᵐSabanneus, Eliphalat, Manasses, and Semei. ³⁴ Of the sons of Baani: Jeremias, Momdis, Ismaerus, Juel, Mamdai, Pedias, Anos, Carabasion, Enasibus, Mamnitamenus, Eliasis, Bannus, Eliali, Someis, Selemias, and Nathanias. Of the sons of Ezora: Sesis, Ezril, Azaelus, Samatus, Zambri, and Josephus. ³⁵ Of the sons of Nooma: Mazitias, Zabadeas, Edos, Juel, and Banaias. ³⁶ All these had taken foreign wives, and they put them away with their children. ³⁷ The priests and Levites, and those who were of Israel, lived in Jerusalem and in the country, on the new moon of the seventh month, and the children of Israel in their settlements. ³⁸ *The whole multitude gathered together with one accord into the broad place before the porch of the temple toward the east. ³⁹ They said to Esdras the priest and reader, "Bring the law of Moses that was given by the Lord, the God of Israel." ⁴⁰ So Esdras the chief priest brought the law to the whole multitude both of men and women, and to all the priests, to hear the law on the new moon of the seventh month. ⁴¹ He read in the broad place before the porch of the temple from morning until midday, before both men and women; and all the multitude gave attention to the law. ⁴² Esdras the priest and reader of the law stood up upon the pulpit of wood which had been prepared. ⁴³ Beside him stood Mattathias, Sammus, Ananias, Azarias, Urias, ⁿⁿEzekias, and Baalsamus on the right hand, ⁴⁴ and on his left hand, ᵒᵒPhaldeus, Misael, Melchias, ᵖᵖLothasubus, Nabarias, and Zacharias. ⁴⁵ Then Esdras took the book of the law before the multitude, and sat honorably in the first place before all. ⁴⁶ When he opened the law, they all stood straight up. So Esdras blessed the Lord God Most High, the God of armies, the Almighty. ⁴⁷ All the people answered, "Amen." Lifting up their hands, they fell to the ground

---

* **8:91** Ezra **10:1**
* **9:1** Ezra **10:6**
a *9:14* Another reading is, Ezias.
b *9:19* Maaseiah.
c *9:19* Jarib.
d *9:19* Gedaliah.
e *9:21* Harim.
f *9:21* Maaseiah.
g *9:21* Jehiel.
h *9:21* Uzziah.
i *9:22* Pashhur.
j *9:22* Jozabad.
k *9:23* Elasah.
l *9:23* Kelaiah.
m *9:23* Kelita.
n *9:23* Pethahiah.
o *9:24* Eliashib.
p *9:25* Telem.
q *9:26* Parosh.
r *9:26* Ramiah.
s *9:26* Izziah. Another reading is, Iezias
t *9:26* Mijamin.
u *9:26* Malchijah.
v *9:27* Jehiel.
w *9:27* Abdi.
x *9:28* Zattu.
y *9:28* Elioenai.
z *9:28* Eliashib.
aa *9:28* Mattaniah.
bb *9:28* Zabad.
cc *9:28* Aziza.
dd *9:29* Zabbai.
ee *9:29* Athlai.
ff *9:30* Bani.
gg *9:30* Meshullam.
hh *9:30* Malluch.
ii *9:30* Adaiah.
jj *9:30* Sheal.
kk *9:33* Mattenai.
ll *9:33* Mattattah.
mm *9:33* Zabad.
* **9:38** Nehemiah **8:1**
nn *9:43* Hilkiah.
oo *9:44* Pedaiah.
pp *9:44* Hashuin.

and worshiped the Lord. ⁴⁸ Also Jesus, Annus, Sarabias, Iadinus, Jacubus, Sabateus, ᵃAuteas, Maiannas, Calitas, Azarias, Jozabdus, Ananias, and Phalias, the Levites, taught the law of the Lord, ᵇand read to the multitude the law of the Lord, explaining what was read. ⁴⁹ Then Attharates said to Esdras the chief priest and reader, and to the Levites who taught the multitude, even to all, ⁵⁰"This day is holy to the Lord–now they all wept when they heard the law– ⁵¹ go then, eat the fat, drink the sweet, and send portions to those who have nothing; ⁵² for the day is holy to the Lord. Don't be sorrowful, for the Lord will bring you to honor." ⁵³ So the Levites commanded all things to the people, saying, "This day is holy. Don't be sorrowful." ⁵⁴ Then they went their way, every one to eat, drink, enjoy themselves, to give portions to those who had nothing, and to rejoice greatly, ⁵⁵ because they ᶜunderstood the words they were instructed with, and for which they had been assembled.

The Second Book of Esdras, or Ezra Sutu'el

The Second Book of Esdras is included in the Slavonic Bible as *3 Esdras*, but is not found in the Greek Septuagint. It is included in the Appendix to the Latin Vulgate Bible as *4 Esdras*. It is considered to be Apocrypha by most church traditions. It is preserved here for its supplementary historical value.

1

¹ The second book of the prophet Esdras, the son of Saraias, the son of Azaraias, the son of Helkias, the son of Salemas, the son of Sadoc, the son of Ahitob, ² the son of Achias, the son of Phinees, the son of Heli, the son of Amarias, the son of Aziei, the son of Marimoth, the son of Arna, the son of Ozias, the son of Borith, the son of Abissei, the son of Phinees, the son of Eleazar, ³ the son of Aaron, of the tribe of Levi, who was captive in the land of the Medes, in the reign of Artaxerxes king of the Persians. ⁴ The Lord's word came to me, saying, ⁵"Go your way and show my people their sinful deeds, and their children their wickedness which they have done against me, that they may tell their children's children, ⁶ because the sins of their fathers have increased in them, for they have forgotten me, and have offered sacrifices to foreign gods. ⁷ Didn't I bring them out of the land of Egypt, out of the house of bondage? But they have provoked me to wrath and have despised my counsels. ⁸ So pull out the hair of your head and cast all evils upon them, for they have not been obedient to my law, but they are a rebellious people. ⁹ How long shall I endure them, to whom I have done so much good? ¹⁰ I have overthrown many kings for their sakes. I have struck down Pharoah with his servants and all his army. ¹¹ I have destroyed all the nations before them. In the east, I have scattered the people of two provinces, even of Tyre and Sidon, and have slain all their adversaries. ¹² Speak therefore to them, saying: ¹³"The Lord says, truly I brought you through the sea, and where there was no path I made highways for you. I gave you Moses for a leader and Aaron for a priest. ¹⁴ I gave you light in a pillar of fire. I have done great wonders among you, yet you have forgotten me, says the Lord. ¹⁵"The Lord Almighty says: The quails were for a token to you. I gave you a camp for your protection, but you complained there. ¹⁶ You didn't celebrate in my name for the destruction of your enemies, but even to this day you still complain. ¹⁷ Where are the benefits that I have given you? When you were hungry and thirsty in the wilderness, didn't you cry to me, ¹⁸ saying, 'Why have you brought us into this wilderness to kill us? It would have been better for us to have served the Egyptians than to die in this wilderness.' ¹⁹ I had pity on your mourning and gave you manna for food. You ate angels' bread. ²⁰ When you were thirsty, didn't I split the rock, and water flowed out in abundance? Because of the heat, I covered you with the leaves of the trees. ²¹ I divided fruitful lands among you. I drove out the Canaanites, the Pherezites, and the Philistines before you. What more shall I do for you?" says the Lord. ²² The Lord Almighty says, "When you were in the wilderness, at the bitter stream, being thirsty and blaspheming my name, ²³ I gave you not fire for your blasphemies, but threw a tree in the water, and made the river sweet. ²⁴ What shall I do to you, O Jacob? You, Judah, would not obey me. I will turn myself to other nations, and I will give my name to them, that they may keep my statutes. ²⁵ Since you have forsaken me, I also will forsake you. When you ask me to be merciful to you, I will have no mercy upon you. ²⁶ Whenever you call upon me, I will not hear you, for you have defiled your hands with blood, and your feet are swift to commit murder. ²⁷ It is not as though you have forsaken me, but your own selves," says the Lord. ²⁸ The Lord Almighty says, "Haven't I asked you as a father his sons, as a mother her daughters, and a nurse her young babies, ²⁹ that you would be my people, and I would be your God, that you would be my children, and I would be your father? ³⁰ I gathered you together, as a hen gathers her chicks under her wings. But now, what should I do to you? I will cast you out from my presence. ³¹ When you offer burnt sacrifices to me, I will turn my face from you, for I have rejected your solemn feast days, your new moons, and your circumcisions of the flesh. ³² I sent to you my servants the prophets, whom you have taken and slain, and torn their bodies in pieces, whose blood I will require from you," says the Lord. ³³ The Lord Almighty says, "Your house is desolate. I will cast you out as the wind blows stubble. ³⁴ Your children won't be fruitful, for they have neglected my commandment to you, and done that which is evil before me. ³⁵ I will give your houses to a people that will come, which not having heard of me yet believe me. Those to whom I have shown no signs will do what I have commanded. ³⁶ They have seen no prophets, yet they will remember their former condition. ³⁷ I call to witness the gratitude of the people who will come, whose little ones rejoice with gladness. Although they see me not with bodily eyes, yet in spirit they will

---

ᵃ *9:48* Hodiah.

ᵇ *9:48* Some authorities omit and read...Lord.

ᶜ *9:55* Or, were inspired by

believe what I say." ³⁸ And now, father, behold with glory, and see the people that come from the east: ³⁹ to whom I will give for leaders, Abraham, Isaac, and Jacob, Oseas, Amos, and Micheas, Joel, Abdias, and Jonas, ⁴⁰ Nahum, and Abacuc, Sophonias, Aggaeus, Zachary, and Malachy, who is also called the Lord's messenger.

2

¹ The Lord says, "I brought this people out of bondage. I gave them my commandments by my servants the prophets, whom they would not listen to, but made my counsels void. ² The mother who bore them says to them, 'Go your way, my children, for I am a widow and forsaken. ³ I brought you up with gladness, and I have lost you with sorrow and heaviness, for you have sinned before the Lord God, and done that which is evil before me. ⁴ But now what can I do for you? For I am a widow and forsaken. Go your way, my children, and ask for mercy from the Lord.' ⁵ As for me, O father, I call upon you for a witness in addition to the mother of these children, because they would not keep my covenant, ⁶ that you may bring them to confusion, and their mother to ruin, that they may have no offspring. ⁷ Let them be scattered abroad among the heathen. Let their names be blotted out of the earth, for they have despised my covenant. ⁸ Woe to you, Assur, you who hide the unrighteous with you! You wicked nation, remember what I did to Sodom and Gomorrah, ⁹ whose land lies in lumps of pitch and heaps of ashes. That is what I will also do to those who have not listened to me," says the Lord Almighty. ¹⁰ The Lord says to Esdras, "Tell my people that I will give them the kingdom of Jerusalem, which I would have given to Israel. ¹¹ I will also take their glory back to myself, and give these the everlasting tabernacles which I had prepared for them. ¹² They will have the tree of life for fragrant perfume. They will neither labor nor be weary. ¹³ Ask, and you will receive. Pray that your days may be few, that they may be shortened. The kingdom is already prepared for you. Watch! ¹⁴ Call heaven and earth to witness. Call them to witness, for I have left out evil, and created the good, for I live, says the Lord. ¹⁵ "Mother, embrace your children. I will bring them out with gladness like a dove does. Establish their feet, for I have chosen you, says the Lord. ¹⁶ I will raise those who are dead up again from their places, and bring them out from their tombs, for I recognize my name in them. ¹⁷ Don't be afraid, you mother of children, for I have chosen you, says the Lord. ¹⁸ For your help, I will send my servants Esaias and Jeremy, after whose counsel I have sanctified and prepared for you twelve trees laden with various fruits, ¹⁹ and as many springs flowing with milk and honey, and seven mighty mountains, on which roses and lilies grow, with which I will fill your children with joy. ²⁰ Do right to the widow. Secure justice for the fatherless. Give to the poor. Defend the orphan. Clothe the naked. ²¹ Heal the broken and the weak. Don't laugh a lame man to scorn. Defend the maimed. Let the blind man have a vision of my glory. ²² Protect the old and young within your walls. ²³ Wherever you find the dead, set a sign upon them and commit them to the grave, and I will give you the first place in my resurrection. ²⁴ Stay still, my people, and take your rest, for your rest will come. ²⁵ Nourish your children, good nurse, and establish their feet. ²⁶ As for the servants whom I have given you, not one of them will perish, for I will require them from among your number. ²⁷ Don't be anxious, for when the day of suffering and anguish comes, others will weep and be sorrowful, but you will rejoice and have abundance. ²⁸ The nations will envy you, but they will be able to do nothing against you, says the Lord. ²⁹ My hands will cover you, so that your children don't see Gehenna.[a] ³⁰ Be joyful, mother, with your children, for I will deliver you, says the Lord. ³¹ Remember your children who sleep, for I will bring them out of the secret places of the earth and show mercy to them, for I am merciful, says the Lord Almighty. ³² Embrace your children until I come, and proclaim mercy to them, for my wells run over, and my grace won't fail." ³³ I, Esdras, received a command from the Lord on Mount Horeb to go to Israel, but when I came to them, they rejected me and rejected the Lord's commandment. ³⁴ Therefore I say to you, O nations that hear and understand, "Look for your shepherd. He will give you everlasting rest, for he is near at hand who will come at the end of the age. ³⁵ Be ready for the rewards of the kingdom, for the everlasting light will shine on you forevermore. ³⁶ Flee the shadow of this world, receive the joy of your glory. I call to witness my savior openly. ³⁷ Receive that which is given to you by the Lord, and be joyful, giving thanks to him who has called you to heavenly kingdoms. ³⁸ Arise and stand up, and see the number of those who have been sealed at the Lord's feast. ³⁹ Those who withdrew themselves from the shadow of the world have received glorious garments from the Lord. ⁴⁰ Take again your full number, O Zion, and make up the reckoning of those of yours who are clothed in white, which have fulfilled the law of the Lord. ⁴¹ The number of your children, whom you long for, is fulfilled. Ask the power of the Lord, that your people, which have been called from the beginning, may be made holy." ⁴² I, Esdras, saw upon Mount Zion a great multitude, whom I could not number, and they all praised the Lord with songs. ⁴³ In the midst of them, there was a young man of a high stature, taller than all the rest, and upon every one of their heads he set crowns, and he was more exalted than they were. I marveled greatly at this. ⁴⁴ So I asked the angel, and said, "What are these, my Lord?" ⁴⁵ He answered and said to me, "These are those who have put off the mortal clothing, and put on the immortal, and have confessed the name of God. Now are they crowned, and receive palms." ⁴⁶ Then said I to the angel, "Who is the young man who sets crowns on them, and gives them palms in their hands?" ⁴⁷ So he answered and said to me, "He is the Son of God, whom they have confessed in the world." Then I began to praise those who stood so valiantly for the name of the Lord. ⁴⁸ Then the angel said to me, "Go your way, and tell my people what kind of things, and how great wonders of the Lord God you have seen."

3

¹ In the thirtieth year after the ruin of the city, I Salathiel, also called Esdras, was in Babylon, and lay troubled upon my bed, and my thoughts came up over my heart, ² for I saw the desolation of Zion and the wealth of those who lived at Babylon. ³ My spirit was very agitated, so that I began to speak words full of fear to the Most High, and said, ⁴ "O sovereign Lord, didn't you speak at the beginning when you formed the earth–and that yourself alone–and commanded the dust ⁵ and it gave you Adam, a body without a soul? Yet it was the workmanship of your hands, and you breathed into him the breath of life, and he was made alive in your presence. ⁶ You led him into the garden which your right hand planted before the earth appeared. ⁷ You gave him your one commandment, which he transgressed, and immediately you appointed death for him and his descendants. From him were born nations, tribes, peoples, and kindred without number. ⁸ Every nation walked after their own will, did ungodly things in your sight, and despised your commandments, and you didn't hinder them. ⁹ Nevertheless, again in process of time, you brought the flood on those who lived in the world and destroyed them. ¹⁰ It came to pass that the same thing happened to them. Just as death came to Adam, so was the flood to these. ¹¹ Nevertheless, you left one of them, Noah with his household, and all the righteous men who descended from him. ¹² "It came to pass that when those who lived upon the earth began to multiply, they also multiplied children, peoples, and many nations, and began again to be more ungodly than their ancestors. ¹³ It came to pass, when they did wickedly before you, you chose one from among them, whose name was Abraham. ¹⁴ You loved, and to him only you showed the end of the times secretly by night, ¹⁵ and made an everlasting covenant with him, promising him that you would never forsake his descendants. To him, you gave Isaac, and to Isaac you gave Jacob and Esau. ¹⁶ You set apart Jacob for yourself, but rejected Esau. Jacob became a great multitude. ¹⁷ It came to pass that when you led his descendants out of Egypt, you brought them up to Mount Sinai. ¹⁸ You bowed the heavens also, shook the earth, moved the whole world, made the depths tremble, and troubled the age. ¹⁹ Your glory went through four gates, of fire, of earthquake, of wind, and of ice, that you might give the law to the descendants of Jacob, and the commandment to the descendants of Israel. ²⁰ "Yet you didn't take away from them their wicked heart, that your law might produce fruit in them. ²¹ For the first Adam, burdened with a wicked heart transgressed and was overcome, as were all who are descended from him. ²² Thus disease was made permanent. The law was in the heart of the people along with the wickedness of the root. So the good departed away and that which was wicked remained. ²³ So the times passed away, and the years were brought to an end. Then you raised up a servant, called David, ²⁴ whom you commanded to build a city to your name, and to offer burnt offerings to you in it from what is yours. ²⁵ When this was done many years, then those who inhabited the city did evil, ²⁶ in all things doing as Adam and all his generations had done, for they also had a wicked heart. ²⁷ So you gave your city over into the hands of your enemies. ²⁸ "Then I said in my heart, 'Are their deeds of those who inhabit Babylon any better? Is that why it gained dominion over Zion?' ²⁹ For it came to pass when I came here, that I also saw impieties without number, and my soul saw many sinners in this thirtieth year, so that my heart failed me. ³⁰ For I have seen how you endure them sinning, and have spared those who act ungodly, and have destroyed your people, and have preserved your enemies; ³¹ and you have not shown how your way may be comprehended. Are the deeds of Babylon better than those of Zion? ³² Or is there any other nation that knows you beside Israel? Or what tribes have so believed your covenants as these tribes of Jacob? ³³ Yet their reward doesn't appear, and their labor has no fruit, for I have gone

---
[a] 2:29 or, Hell.

here and there through the nations, and I see that they abound in wealth, and don't think about your commandments. ³⁴ Weigh therefore our iniquities now in the balance, and theirs also who dwell in the world, and so will it be found which way the scale inclines. ³⁵ Or when was it that they who dwell on the earth have not sinned in your sight? Or what nation has kept your commandments so well? ³⁶ You will find some men by name who have kept your precepts, but you won't find nations."

4

¹ The angel who was sent to me, whose name was Uriel, gave me an answer, ² and said to me, "Your understanding has utterly failed you regarding this world. Do you think you can comprehend the way of the Most High?" ³ Then I said, "Yes, my Lord." He answered me, "I have been sent to show you three ways, and to set before you three problems. ⁴ If you can solve one for me, I also will show you the way that you desire to see, and I will teach you why the heart is wicked." ⁵ I said, "Say on, my Lord." Then said he to me, "Go, weigh for me the weight of fire, or measure for me blast of wind, or call back for me the day that is past." ⁶ Then answered I and said, "Who of the sons of men is able to do this, that you should ask me about such things?" ⁷ He said to me, "If I had asked you, 'How many dwellings are there in the heart of the sea? Or how many springs are there at the fountain head of the deep? Or how many streams are above the firmament? Or which are the exits ᵃof hell? Or which are the entrances of paradise?' ⁸ perhaps you would say to me, 'I never went down into the deep, or as yet into hell, neither did I ever climb up into heaven.' ⁹ Nevertheless now I have only asked you about the fire, wind, and the day, things which you have experienced, and from which you can't be separated, and yet have you given me no answer about them." ¹⁰ He said moreover to me, "You can't understand your own things that you grew up with. ¹¹ How then can your mind comprehend the way of the Most High? How can he who is already worn out with the corrupted world understand incorruption?" ᵇWhen I heard these things, I fell on my face ¹² and said to him, "It would have been better if we weren't here at all, than that we should come here and live in the midst of ungodliness, and suffer, and not know why." ¹³ He answered me, and said, "'A forest of the trees of the field went out, and took counsel together, ¹⁴ and said, 'Come! Let's go and make war against the sea, that it may depart away before us, and that we may make ourselves more forests.' ¹⁵ The waves of the sea also in like manner took counsel together, and said, 'Come! Let's go up and subdue the forest of the plain, that there also we may gain more territory.' ¹⁶ The counsel of the wood was in vain, for the fire came and consumed it. ¹⁷ Likewise also the counsel of the waves of the sea, for the sand stood up and stopped them. ¹⁸ If you were judge now between these two, which would you justify, or which would you condemn?" ¹⁹ I answered and said, "It is a foolish counsel that they both have taken, for the ground is given to the wood, and the place of the sea is given to bear its waves." ²⁰ Then answered he me, and said, "You have given a right judgment. Why don't you judge your own case? ²¹ For just as the ground is given to the wood, and the sea to its waves, even so those who dwell upon the earth may understand nothing but what is upon the earth. Only he who dwells above the heavens understands the things that are above the height of the heavens." ²² Then answered I and said, "I beg you, O Lord, why has the power of understanding been given to me? ²³ For it was not in my mind to be curious of the ways above, but of such things as pass by us daily, because Israel is given up as a reproach to the heathen. The people whom you have loved have been given over to ungodly nations. The law of our forefathers is made of no effect, and the written covenants are nowhere regarded. ²⁴ We pass away out of the world like locusts. Our life is like a vapor, and we aren't worthy to obtain mercy. ²⁵ What will he then do for his name by which we are called? I have asked about these things." ²⁶ Then he answered me, and said, "If you are alive you will see, and if you live long, you will marvel, for the world hastens quickly to pass away. ²⁷ For it is not able to bear the things that are promised to the righteous in the times to come; for this world is full of sadness and infirmities. ²⁸ For the evilᵈ about which you asked me has been sown, but its harvest hasn't yet come. ²⁹ If therefore that which is sown isn't reaped, and if the place where the evil is sown doesn't pass away, the field where the good is sown won't come. ³⁰ For a grain of evil seed was sown in the heart of Adam from the beginning, and how much wickedness it has produced to this time! How much more it will yet produce until the time of threshing comes! ³¹ Ponder now by yourself, how much fruit of wickedness a grain of evil seed has produced. ³² When the grains which are without number are sown, how great a threshing floor they will fill!" ³³ Then I answered and said, ᵉ"How long? When will these things come to pass? Why are our years few and evil?" ³⁴ He answered me, and said, "Don't hurry faster than the Most High; for your haste isᶠ for your own self, but he who is above hurries on behalf of many. ³⁵ Didn't the souls of the righteous ask question of these things in their chambers, saying, 'How long ᵍwill we be here? When does the fruit of the threshing floor come?' ³⁶ To them, Jeremiel the archangel answered, 'When the number is fulfilled of those who are like you. For he has weighed the world in the balance. ³⁷ By measure, he has measured the times. By number, he has counted the seasons. He won't ʰmove or stir them until that measure is fulfilled.'" ³⁸ Then I answered, "O sovereign Lord, all of us are full of ungodliness. ³⁹ Perhaps it is for our sakes that the threshing time of the righteous is kept back–because of the sins of those who dwell on the earth." ⁴⁰ So he answered me, "Go your way to a woman with child, and ask of her when she has fulfilled her nine months, if her womb may keep the baby any longer within her." ⁴¹ Then I said, "No, Lord, that can it not." He said to me, "In Hades, the chambers of souls are like the womb. ⁴² For just like a woman in labor hurries to escape the anguish of the labor pains, even so these places hurry to deliver those things that are committed to them from the beginning. ⁴³ Then you will be shown those things which you desire to see." ⁴⁴ Then I answered, "If I have found favor in your sight, and if it is possible, and if I am worthy, ⁴⁵ show me this also, whether there is more to come than is past, or whether the greater part has gone over us. ⁴⁶ For what is gone I know, but I don't know what is to come." ⁴⁷ He said to me, "Stand up on my right side, and I will explain the parable to you." ⁴⁸ So I stood, looked, and saw a hot burning oven passed by before me. It happened that when the flame had gone by I looked, and saw that the smoke remained. ⁴⁹ After this, a watery cloud passed in front of me, and sent down much rain with a storm. When the stormy rain was past, the drops still remained in it." ⁵⁰ Then said he to me, "Consider with yourself; as the rain is more than the drops, and the fire is greater than the smoke, so the quantity which is past was far greater; but the drops and the smoke still remained." ⁵¹ Then I prayed, and said, "Do you think that I will live until that time? Or who will be alive in those days?" ⁵² He answered me, "As for the signs you asked me about, I may tell you of them in part; but I wasn't sent to tell you about your life, for I don't know.

5

¹"Nevertheless, concerning the signs, behold, the days will come when those who dwell on earth will be taken ⁱwith great amazement, and the way of truth will be hidden, and the land will be barren of faith. ² Iniquity will be increased above what now you see, and beyond what you have heard long ago. ³ The land that you now see ruling will be a trackless waste, and men will see it desolate. ⁴ But if the Most High grants you to live, you will see what is after the third period will be troubled. The sun will suddenly shine in the night, and the moon in the day. ⁵ Blood will drop out of wood, and the stone will utter its voice. The peoples will be troubled, and the stars will fall. ⁶ He will rule whom those who dwell on the earth don't expect, and the birds will fly away together. ⁷ The Sodomite sea will cast out fish, and make a noise in the night, which many have not known; but all will hear its voice. ⁸ There will also be chaos in many places. Fires will break out often, and the wild animals will change their places, and women will bring forth monsters. ⁹ Salt waters will be found in the sweet, and all friends will destroy one another. Then reason will hide itself, and understanding withdraw itself into its chamber. ¹⁰ It will be sought by many, and won't be found. Unrighteousness and lack of restraint will be multiplied on earth. ¹¹ One country will ask another, 'Has righteousness, or a man that does righteousness, gone through you?' And it will say, 'No.' ¹² It will come to pass at that time that men will hope, but won't obtain. They will labor, but their ways won't prosper. ¹³ I am permitted to show you such signs. If you will pray again, and weep as now, and fast seven days, you will hear yet greater things than these." ¹⁴ Then I woke up, and an extreme trembling went through my body, and my mind was so troubled that it fainted. ¹⁵ So the angel who had come to talk with me held me, comforted me, and set me on my feet. ¹⁶ In the second night, it came to pass that ʲPhaltiel the captain of the people came to me, saying, "Where have you been? Why is your face sad? ¹⁷ Or don't you know that Israel is committed to you in the land of their captivity? ¹⁸ Get up then, and eat some bread, and don't forsake us, like a shepherd who leaves the flock in the power of cruel wolves." ¹⁹ Then said I

ᵃ *4:7* So the Syriac. The Latin omits of hell? or which are the paths.
ᵇ *4:11* So the Syriac and Aethiopic. The Latin is corrupt.
ᶜ *4:13* So the Oriental versions. The Latin is corrupt. See Judges **9:8**.
ᵈ *4:28* so the Syriac and Aethiopic.
ᵉ *4:33* So the chief oriental versions.
ᶠ *4:34* So the Syriac. The Latin is corrupt.
ᵍ *4:35* So the Syriac. The Latin has shall I hope on this fashion?
ʰ *4:37* Syr. rest.
ⁱ *5:1* So the syriac.
ʲ *5:16* The Syriac has Psaltiel.

to him, "Go away from me and don't come near me for seven days, and then you shall come to me." He heard what I said and left me. ²⁰ So I fasted seven days, mourning and weeping, like Uriel the angel had commanded me. ²¹ After seven days, the thoughts of my heart were very grievous to me again, ²² and my soul recovered the spirit of understanding, and I began to speak words before the Most High again. ²³ I said, "O sovereign Lord of all the woods of the earth, and of all the trees thereof, you have chosen one vine for yourself. ²⁴ Of all the lands of the world you have chosen one ᵃcountry for yourself. Of all the flowers of the world, you have chosen one lily for yourself. ²⁵ Of all the depths of the sea, you have filled one river for yourself. Of all built cities, you have consecrated Zion for yourself. ²⁶ Of all the birds that are created you have named for yourself one dove. Of all the livestock that have been made, you have provided for yourself one sheep. ²⁷ Among all the multitudes of peoples you have gotten yourself one people. To this people, whom you loved, you gave a law that is approved by all. ²⁸ Now, O Lord, why have you given this one people over to many, and ᵇhave dishonored the one root above others, and have scattered your only one among many? ²⁹ Those who opposed your promises have trampled down those who believed your covenants. ³⁰ If you really do hate your people so much, they should be punished with your own hands." ³¹ Now when I had spoken these words, the angel that came to me the night before was sent to me, ³² and said to me, "Hear me, and I will instruct you. Listen to me, and I will tell you more." ³³ I said, "Speak on, my Lord." Then said he to me, "You are very troubled in mind for Israel's sake. Do you love that people more than he who made them?" ³⁴ I said, "No, Lord; but I have spoken out of grief; for my heart is in agony every hour while I labor to comprehend the way of the Most High, and to seek out part of his judgment." ³⁵ He said to me, "You can't." And I said, "Why, Lord? Why was I born? Why wasn't my mother's womb my grave, that I might not have seen the travail of Jacob, and the wearisome toil of the people of Israel?" ³⁶ He said to me, "Count for me those who haven't yet come. Gather together for me the drops that are scattered abroad, and make the withered flowers green again for me. ³⁷ Open for me the chambers that are closed, and bring out the winds for me that are shut up in them. Or show me the image of a voice. Then I will declare to you the travail that you asked to see." ³⁸ And I said, "O sovereign Lord, who may know these things except he who doesn't have his dwelling with men? ³⁹ As for me, I lack wisdom. How can I then speak of these things you asked me about?" ⁴⁰ Then said he to me, "Just as you can do none of these things that I have spoken of, even so you can't find out my judgment, or the end of the love that I have promised to my people." ⁴¹ I said, "But, behold, O Lord, you have made the promise to those who are alive at the end. What should they do who have been before us, or we ourselves, or those who will come after us?" ⁴² He said to me, "I will compare my judgment to a ring. Just as there is no slowness of those who are last, even so there is no swiftness of those who be first." ⁴³ So I answered, "Couldn't you make them all at once that have been made, and that are now, and that are yet to come, that you might show your judgment sooner?" ⁴⁴ Then he answered me, "The creature may not move faster than the creator, nor can the world hold them at once who will be created in it." ⁴⁵ And I said, "How have you said to your servant, that ᶜyou will surely make alive at once the creature that you have created? ᵈIf therefore they will be alive at once, and the creation will sustain them, even so it might now also support them to be present at once." ⁴⁶ And he said to me, "Ask the womb of a woman, and say to her, 'If you bear ten children, why do you it at different times? Ask her therefore to give birth to ten children at once." ⁴⁷ I said, "She can't, but must do it each in their own time." ⁴⁸ Then said he to me, "Even so, I have given the womb of the earth to those who are sown in it in their own times. ⁴⁹ For just as a young child may not give birth, neither she who has grown old any more, even so have I organized the world which I created." ⁵⁰ I asked, "Seeing that you have now shown me the way, I will speak before you. Is our mother, of whom you have told me, still young? Or does she now draw near to old age?" ⁵¹ He answered me, "Ask a woman who bears children, and she will tell you. ⁵² Say to her, 'Why aren't they whom you have now brought forth like those who were before, but smaller in stature?' ⁵³ She also will answer you, 'Those who are born in the strength of youth are different from those who are born in the time of old age, when the womb fails.' ⁵⁴ Consider therefore you also, how you are shorter than those who were before you. ⁵⁵ So are those who come after you smaller than you, as born of the creature which now begins to be old, and is past the strength of youth." ⁵⁶ Then I said, "Lord, I implore you, if I have found favor in your sight, show your servant by whom you visit your creation."

6

¹ He said to me, "In the beginning, when the earth was made, before the portals of the world were fixed and before the gatherings of the winds blew, ² before the voices of the thunder sounded and before the flashes of the lightning shone, before the foundations of paradise were laid, ³ before the fair flowers were seen, before the powers of the earthquake were established, before the innumerable army of angels were gathered together, ⁴ before the heights of the air were lifted up, before the measures of the firmament were named, before the footstool of Zion ᵉwas established, ⁵ before the present years were reckoned, before the imaginations of those who now sin were estranged, and before they were sealed who have gathered faith for a treasure– ⁶ then I considered these things, and they all were made through me alone, and not through another; just as by me also they will be ended, and not by another." ⁷ Then I answered, "What will be the dividing of the times? Or when will be the end of the first and the beginning of the age that follows?" ⁸ He said to me, "From Abraham to Isaac, because Jacob and Esau were born to him, for Jacob's hand held Esau's heel from the beginning. ⁹ For Esau is the end of this age, and Jacob is the beginning of the one that follows. ¹⁰ ᶠThe beginning of a man is his hand, and the end of a man is his heel. Seek nothing else between the heel and the hand, Esdras!" ¹¹ Then I answered, "O sovereign Lord, if I have found favor in your sight, ¹² I beg you, show your servant the end of your signs which you showed me part on a previous night." ¹³ So he answered, "Stand up upon your feet, and you will hear a mighty sounding voice. ¹⁴ If the place you stand on is greatly moved ¹⁵ when it speaks don't be afraid, for the word is of the end, and the foundations of the earth will understand ¹⁶ that the speech is about them. They will tremble and be moved, for they know that their end must be changed." ¹⁷ It happened that when I had heard it, I stood up on my feet, and listened, and, behold, there was a voice that spoke, and its sound was like the sound of many waters. ¹⁸ It said, "Behold, the days come when I draw near to visit those who dwell upon the earth, ¹⁹ and when I investigate those who have caused harm unjustly with their unrighteousness, and when the affliction of Zion is complete, ²⁰ and when the seal will be set on the age that is to pass away, then I will show these signs: the books will be opened before the firmament, and all will see together. ²¹ The children a year old will speak with their voices. The women with child will deliver premature children at three or four months, and they will live and dance. ²² Suddenly the sown places will appear unsown. The full storehouses will suddenly be found empty. ²³ The trumpet will give a sound which when every man hears, they will suddenly be afraid. ²⁴ At that time friends will make war against one another like enemies. The earth will stand in fear with those who dwell in it. The springs of the fountains will stand still, so that for three hours they won't flow. ²⁵"It will be that whoever remains after all these things that I have told you of, he will be saved and will see my salvation, and the end of my world. ²⁶ They will see the men who have been taken up, who have not tasted death from their birth. The heart of the inhabitants will be changed and turned into a different spirit. ²⁷ For evil will be blotted out and deceit will be quenched. ²⁸ Faith will flourish. Corruption will be overcome, and the truth, which has been so long without fruit, will be declared." ²⁹ When he talked with me, behold, little by little, the place I stood on ᵍrocked back and forth. ³⁰ He said to me, "I came to show you these things ʰtonight. ³¹ If therefore you will pray yet again, and fast seven more days, I will ⁱagain tell you greater things than these. ³² For your voice has surely been heard before the Most High. For the Mighty has seen your righteousness. He has also seen your purity, which you have maintained ever since your youth. ³³ Therefore he has sent me to show you all these things, and to say to you, 'Believe, and don't be afraid! ³⁴ Don't be hasty to think vain things about the former times, that you may not hasten in the latter times.'" ³⁵ It came to pass after this, that I wept again, and fasted seven days in like manner, that I might fulfill the three weeks which he told me. ³⁶ On the eighth night, my heart was troubled within me again, and I began to speak in the presence of the Most High. ³⁷ For my spirit was greatly aroused, and my soul was in distress. ³⁸ I said, "O Lord, truly you spoke at the beginning of the creation, on the first day, and said this: 'Let heaven and earth be made,' and your word perfected the work. ³⁹ Then the spirit was hovering, and darkness and silence were on every side. The sound of man's voice was not yet there.ʲ ⁴⁰ Then you commanded a ray of light to be brought out of your treasuries, that your works might then appear. ⁴¹"On

---

ᵃ *5:24* After the Oriental versions. The Latin has pit.

ᵇ *5:28* After the Oriental versions. The Latin reads have prepared.

ᶜ *5:45* So the Syriac.

ᵈ *5:45* The Latin omits If...alive at once.

ᵉ *6:4* So the Syriac.

ᶠ *6:10* So the Syriac, etc. The Latin is defective.

ᵍ *6:29* After the Oriental versions. The Latin is corrupt.

ʰ *6:30* So the Syriac. The Latin is corrupt.

ⁱ *6:31* The Latin has tell you by day.

ʲ *6:39* The Latin adds from you.

the second day, again you made the spirit of the firmament and commanded it to divide and to separate the waters, that the one part might go up, and the other remain beneath. ⁴²"On the third day, you commanded that the waters should be gathered together in the seventh part of the earth. You dried up six parts and kept them, to the intent that of these some being both planted and tilled might serve before you. ⁴³ For as soon as your word went out, the work was done. ⁴⁴ Immediately, great and innumerable fruit grew, with many pleasant tastes, and flowers of inimitable color, and fragrances of most exquisite smell. This was done the third day. ⁴⁵"On the fourth day, you commanded that the sun should shine, the moon give its light, and the stars should be in their order; ⁴⁶ and gave them a command to serve mankind, who was to be made. ⁴⁷"On the fifth day, you said to the seventh part, where the water was gathered together, that it should produce living creatures, fowls and fishes; and so it came to pass ⁴⁸ that the mute and lifeless water produced living things as it was told, that the nations might therefore praise your wondrous works. ⁴⁹"Then you preserved two living creatures. The one you called Behemoth, and the other you called Leviathan. ⁵⁰ You separated the one from the other; for the seventh part, namely, where the water was gathered together, might not hold them both. ⁵¹ To Behemoth, you gave one part, which was dried up on the third day, that he should dwell in it, in which are a thousand hills; ⁵² but to Leviathan you gave the seventh part, namely, the watery part. You have kept them to be devoured by whom you wish, when you wish. ⁵³"But on the sixth day, you commanded the earth to produce before you cattle, animals, and creeping things. ⁵⁴ Over these, you ordained Adam as ruler over all the works that you have made. Of him came all of us, the people whom you have chosen. ⁵⁵"All this have I spoken before you, O Lord, because you have said that for our sakes you made ᵃthis world. ⁵⁶ As for the other nations, which also come from Adam, you have said that they are nothing, and are like spittle. You have likened the abundance of them to a drop that falls from a bucket. ⁵⁷ Now, O Lord, behold these nations, which are reputed as nothing, being rulers over us and devouring us. ⁵⁸ But we your people, whom you have called your firstborn, your only children, and your fervent lover, are given into their hands. ⁵⁹ Now if the world is made for our sakes, why don't we possess our world for an inheritance? How long will this endure?"

7

¹ When I had finished speaking these words, the angel which had been sent to me the nights before was sent to me. ² He said to me, "Rise, Esdras, and hear the words that I have come to tell you." ³ I said, "Speak on, my Lord." Then he said to me, "There is a sea set in a wide place, that it might be ᵇbroad and vast, ⁴ but its entrance is set in a narrow place so as to be like a river. ⁵ Whoever desires to go into the sea to look at it, or to rule it, if he didn't go through the narrow entrance, how could he come into the broad part? ⁶ Another thing also: There is a city built and set in a plain country, and full of all good things, ⁷ but its entrance is narrow, and is set in a dangerous place to fall, having fire on the right hand, and deep water on the left. ⁸ There is one only path between them both, even between the fire and the water, so that only one person can go there at once. ⁹ If this city is now given to a man for an inheritance, if the heir doesn't pass the danger before him, how will he receive his inheritance?" ¹⁰ I said, "That is so, Lord." Then said he to me, "Even so also is Israel's portion. ¹¹ I made the world for their sakes. What is now done was decreed when Adam transgressed my statutes. ¹² Then the entrances of this world were made narrow, sorrowful, and toilsome. They are but few and evil, full of perils, and involved in great toils. ¹³ For the entrances of the greater world are wide and safe, and produce fruit of immortality. ¹⁴ So if those who live don't enter these difficult and vain things, they can never receive those that are reserved for them. ¹⁵ Now therefore why are you disturbed, seeing you are but a corruptible man? Why are you moved, since you are mortal? ¹⁶ Why haven't you considered in your mind that which is to come, rather than that which is present?" ¹⁷ Then I answered and said, "O sovereign Lord, behold, you have ordained in your law that the righteous will inherit these things, but that the ungodly will perish. ¹⁸ The righteous therefore will suffer difficult things, and hope for easier things, but those who have done wickedly have suffered the difficult things, and yet will not see the easier things." ¹⁹ He said to me, "You are not a judge above God, neither do you have more understanding than the Most High. ²⁰ Yes, let many perish who now live, rather than that the law of God which is set before them be despised. ²¹ For God strictly commanded those who came, even as they came, what they should do to live, and what they should observe to avoid punishment. ²² Nevertheless, they weren't obedient to him, but spoke against him and imagined for themselves vain things. ²³ They made cunning plans of wickedness, and said moreover of the Most High that he doesn't exist, and they didn't know his ways. ²⁴ They despised his law and denied his covenants. They haven't been faithful to his statutes, and haven't performed his works. ²⁵ Therefore, Esdras, for the empty are empty things, and for the full are the full things. ²⁶ For behold, the time will come, and it will be, when these signs of which I told you before will come to pass, that the bride will appear, even the city coming forth, and she will be seen who now is withdrawn from the earth. ²⁷ Whoever is delivered from the foretold evils will see my wonders. ²⁸ For my son Jesus will be revealed with those who are with him, and those who remain will rejoice four hundred years. ²⁹ After these years my son Christᶜ will die, along with all of those who have the breath of lifeᵈ. ³⁰ Then the world will be turned into the old silence seven days, like as in the first beginning, so that no human will remain. ³¹ After seven days the world that is not yet awake will be raised up, and what is corruptible will die. ³² The earth will restore those who are asleep in it, and the dust those who dwell in it in silence, and the ᵉsecret places will deliver those souls that were committed to them. ³³ The Most High will be revealed on the judgment seat, ᶠ and compassion will pass away, and patience will be withdrawn. ³⁴ Only judgment will remain. Truth will stand. Faith will grow strong. ³⁵ Recompense will follow. The reward will be shown. Good deeds will awake, and wicked deeds won't sleep.ᵍ ³⁶ The ʰpit of torment will appear, and near it will be the place of rest. The furnace of hellⁱ will be shown, and near it the paradise of delight. ³⁷ Then the Most High will say to the nations that are raised from the dead, 'Look and understand whom you have denied, whom you haven't served, whose commandments you have despised. ³⁸ Look on this side and on that. Here is delight and rest, and there fire and torments.' Thus ʲhe will speak to them in the day of judgment. ³⁹ This is a day that has neither sun, nor moon, nor stars, ⁴⁰ neither cloud, nor thunder, nor lightning, neither wind, nor water, nor air, neither darkness, nor evening, nor morning, ⁴¹ neither summer, nor spring, nor heat, norᵏ winter, neither frost, nor cold, nor hail, nor rain, nor dew, ⁴² neither noon, nor night, nor dawn, neither shining, nor brightness, nor light, except only the splendor of the glory of the Most High, by which all will see the things that are set before them. ⁴³ It will endure as though it were a week of years. ⁴⁴ This is my judgment and its prescribed order; but I have only shown these things to you." ⁴⁵ I answered, "I said then, O Lord, and I say now: Blessed are those who are now alive and keep your commandments! ⁴⁶ But what about those for whom I prayed? For who is there of those who are alive who has not sinned, and who of the children of men hasn't transgressed your covenant? ⁴⁷ Now I see that the world to come will bring delight to few, but torments to many. ⁴⁸ For an evil heart has grown up in us, which has led us astray from these commandments and has brought us into corruption and into the ways of death. It has shown us the paths of perdition and removed us far from life–and that, not a few only, but nearly all who have been created." ⁴⁹ He answered me, "Listen to me, and I will instruct you. I will admonish you yet again. ⁵⁰ For this reason, the Most High has not made one world, but two. ⁵¹ For because you have said that the just are not many, but few, and the ungodly abound, hear the explanation. ⁵² If you have just a few precious stones, will you add them to lead and clay?" ⁵³ I said, "Lord, how could that be?" ⁵⁴ He said to me, "Not only that, but ask the earth, and she will tell you. Defer to her, and she will declare it to you. ⁵⁵ Say to her, 'You produce gold, silver, and brass, and also iron, lead, and clay; ⁵⁶ but silver is more abundant than gold, and brass than silver, and iron than brass, and lead than iron, and clay than lead.' ⁵⁷ Judge therefore which things are precious and to be desired, what is abundant or what is rare?" ⁵⁸ I said, "O sovereign Lord, that which is plentiful is of less worth, for that which is more rare is more precious." ⁵⁹ He answered me, "Weigh within yourself the things that you have thought, for he who has what is hard to get rejoices over him who has what is plentiful. ⁶⁰ So also is the judgment which I have promised; for I will rejoice over the few that will be saved, because these are those who have made my glory to prevail now, and through them, my name is now honored. ⁶¹ I won't grieve over the multitude of those who perish; for these are those who are now like mist, and have

---

ᵃ *6:55* So the Syriac. The Latin has the firstborn world.
ᵇ *7:3* So the chief Oriental versions. The Latin MSS. have deep.
ᶜ *7:29* "Christ" means "Anointed One".
ᵈ *7:29* Lat. man
ᵉ *7:32* Or, chambers See **2 Esdras 4:35**.
ᶠ *7:33* The Syriac adds and the end will come.
ᵍ *7:35* The passage from verse [**36**] to verse [**105**], formerly missing, has been restored to the text. See Preface, page ix.
ʰ *7:36* So the chief Oriental versions. The Latin MSS. have place.
ⁱ *7:36* Lat. Gehenna.
ʲ *7:38* So the chief Oriental versions. The Latin has will you speak.
ᵏ *7:41* Or, storm

become like flame and smoke; they are set on fire and burn hotly, and are extinguished." [62] I answered, "O earth, why have you produced, if the mind is made out of dust, like all other created things? [63] For it would have been better that the dust itself had been unborn, so that the mind might not have been made from it. [64] But now the mind grows with us, and because of this we are tormented, because we perish and we know it. [65] Let the race of men lament and the animals of the field be glad. Let all who are born lament, but let the four-footed animals and the livestock rejoice. [66] For it is far better with them than with us; for they don't look forward to judgment, neither do they know of torments or of salvation promised to them after death. [67] For what does it profit us, that we will be preserved alive, but yet be afflicted with torment? [68] For all who are born are defiled with iniquities, and are full of sins and laden with transgressions. [69] If after death we were not to come into judgment, perhaps it would have been better for us." [70] He answered me, "When the Most High made the world and Adam and all those who came from him, he first prepared the judgment and the things that pertain to the judgment. [71] Now understand from your own words, for you have said that the mind grows with us. [72] They therefore who dwell on the earth will be tormented for this reason, that having understanding they have committed iniquity, and receiving commandments have not kept them, and having obtained a law they dealt unfaithfully with that which they received. [73] What then will they have to say in the judgment, or how will they answer in the last times? [74] For how long a time has the Most High been patient with those who inhabit the world, and not for their sakes, but because of the times which he has foreordained!" [75] I answered, "If I have found grace in your sight, O Lord, show this also to your servant, whether after death, even now when every one of us gives up his soul, we will be kept in rest until those times come, in which you renew the creation, or whether we will be tormented immediately." [76] He answered me, "I will show you this also; but don't join yourself with those who are scorners, nor count yourself with those who are tormented. [77] For you have a treasure of works laid up with the Most High, but it won't be shown you until the last times. [78] For concerning death the teaching is: When the decisive sentence has gone out from the Most High that a man shall die, as the spirit leaves the body to return again to him who gave it, it adores the glory of the Most High first of all. [79] And if it is one of those who have been scorners and have not kept the way of the Most High, and that have despised his law, and who hate those who fear God, [80] these spirits won't enter into habitations, but will wander and be in torments immediately, ever grieving and sad, in seven ways. [81] The first way, because they have despised the law of the Most High. [82] The second way, because they can't now make a good repentance that they may live. [83] The third way, they will see the reward laid up for those who have believed the covenants of the Most High. [84] The fourth way, they will consider the torment laid up for themselves in the last days. [85] The fifth way, they will see the dwelling places of the others guarded by angels, with great quietness. [86] The sixth way, they will see how immediately some of them will pass into torment. [87] The seventh way, which is more grievous than all the aforesaid ways, because they will pine away in confusion and be consumed with shame, and will be withered up by fears, seeing the glory of the Most High before whom they have sinned while living, and before whom they will be judged in the last times. [88] "Now this is the order of those who have kept the ways of the Most High, when they will be separated from their mortal body. [89] In the time that they lived in it, they painfully served the Most High, and were in jeopardy every hour, that they might keep the law of the lawgiver perfectly. [90] Therefore this is the teaching concerning them: [91] First of all they will see with great joy the glory of him who takes them up, for they will have rest in seven orders. [92] The first order, because they have labored with great effort to overcome the evil thought which was fashioned together with them, that it might not lead them astray from life into death. [93] The second order, because they see the perplexity in which the souls of the ungodly wander, and the punishment that awaits them. [94] The third order, they see the testimony which he who fashioned them gives concerning them, that while they lived they kept the law which was given them in trust. [95] The fourth order, they understand the rest which, being gathered in their chambers, they now enjoy with great quietness, guarded by angels, and the glory that awaits them in the last days. [96] The fifth order, they rejoice that they have now escaped from that which is corruptible, and that they will inherit that which is to come, while they see in addition the difficulty and the pain from which they have been delivered, and the spacious liberty which they will receive with joy and immortality. [97] The sixth order, when it is shown to them how their face will shine like the sun, and how they will be made like the light of the stars, being incorruptible from then on. [98] The seventh order, which is greater than all the previously mentioned orders, because they will rejoice with confidence, and because they will be bold without confusion, and will be glad without fear, for they hurry to see the face of him whom in their lifetime they served, and from whom they will receive their reward in glory. [99] This is the order of the souls of the just, as from henceforth is announced to them. Previously mentioned are the ways of torture which those who would not give heed will suffer from after this." [100] I answered, "Will time therefore be given to the souls after they are separated from the bodies, that they may see what you have described to me?" [101] He said, "Their freedom will be for seven days, that for seven days they may see the things you have been told, and afterwards they will be gathered together in their habitations." [102] I answered, "If I have found favor in your sight, show further to me your servant whether in the day of judgment the just will be able to intercede for the ungodly or to entreat the Most High for them, [103] whether fathers for children, or children for parents, or kindred for kindred, or kinsfolk for their next of kin, or friends for those who are most dear." [104] He answered me, "Since you have found favor in my sight, I will show you this also. The day of judgment is[a] a day of decision, and displays to all the seal of truth. Even as now a father doesn't send his son, or a son his father, or a master his slave, or a friend him that is most dear, that in his place he may understand, or sleep, or eat, or be healed, [105] so no one will ever pray for another in that day, neither will one lay a burden on another, for then everyone will each bear his own righteousness or unrighteousness." [106] I answered, "How do we now find that first Abraham prayed for the people of Sodom, and Moses for the ancestors who sinned in the wilderness, [107] and Joshua after him for Israel in the days of *Achan, [108] and Samuel [b]in the days of Saul, and David for the plague, and Solomon for those who would worship in the sanctuary, [109] and Elijah for those that received rain, and for the dead, that he might live, [110] and Hezekiah for the people in the days of Sennacherib, and many others prayed for many? [111] If therefore now, when corruption has grown and unrighteousness increased, the righteous have prayed for the ungodly, why will it not be so then also?" [112] He answered me, "This present world is not the end. The full glory doesn't remain in it. Therefore those who were able prayed for the weak. [113] But the day of judgment will be the end of this age, and the beginning of the immortality to come, in which corruption has passed away, [114] intemperance is at an end, infidelity is cut off, but righteousness has grown, and truth has sprung up. [115] Then no one will be able to have mercy on him who is condemned in judgment, nor to harm someone who is victorious." [116] I answered then, "This is my first and last saying, that it would have been better if the earth had not produced Adam, or else, when it had produced him, to have restrained him from sinning. [117] For what profit is it for all who are in this present time to live in heaviness, and after death to look for punishment? [118] O Adam, what have you done? For though it was you who sinned, the evil hasn't fallen on you alone, but on all of us who come from you. [119] For what profit is it to us, if an immortal time is promised to us, but we have done deeds that bring death? [120] And that there is promised us an everlasting hope, but we have most miserably failed? [121] And that there are reserved habitations of health and safety, but we have lived wickedly? [122] And that the glory of the Most High will defend those who have led a pure life, but we have walked in the most wicked ways of all? [123] And that a paradise will be revealed, whose fruit endures without decay, in which is abundance and healing, but we won't enter into it, [124] for we have lived in perverse ways? [125] And that the faces of those who have practiced self-control will shine more than the stars, but our faces will be blacker than darkness? [126] For while we lived and committed iniquity, we didn't consider what we would have to suffer after death." [127] Then he answered, "This is the significance of the battle which humans born on the earth will fight: [128] if they are overcome, they will suffer as you have said, but if they get the victory, they will receive the thing that I say. [129] For this is the way that Moses spoke to the people while he lived, saying, 'Choose life, that you may live!' [130] Nevertheless they didn't believe him or the prophets after him, not even me, who have spoken to them. [131] Therefore there won't be such heaviness in their destruction, as there will be joy over those who are assured of salvation." [132] Then I answered, "I know, Lord, that the Most High is now called merciful, in that he has mercy upon those who have not yet come into the world; [133] and compassionate, in that he has compassion upon those who turn to his law; [134] and patient, in that he is patient with those who have sinned, since they are his creatures; [135] and bountiful, in that he is ready to give rather than to take away; [136] and very merciful, in that he multiplies more and more mercies to those who are present, and who are past, and also to those who are to come— [137] for if he

---

[a] *7:104* The Latin has a bold day
* *7:107* Joshua **7:1**

[b] *7:108* So the Syriac and other versions. The Latin omits in the days of Saul.

wasn't merciful, the world wouldn't continue with those who dwell in it– ¹³⁸ and one who forgives, for if he didn't forgive out of his goodness, that those who have committed iniquities might be relieved of them, not even one ten thousandth part of mankind would remain living; ¹³⁹ and a judge, for if he didn't pardon those who were created by his word, and blot out the multitude of sins, ¹⁴⁰ there would perhaps be very few left of an innumerable multitude."

8

¹ He answered me, "The Most High has made this world for many, but the world to come for few. ² Now I will tell you a parable, Esdras. Just as when you ask the earth, it will say to you that it gives very much clay from which earthen vessels are made, but little dust that gold comes from. Even so is the course of the present world. ³ Many have been created, but few will be saved." ⁴ I answered, "Drink your fill of understanding then, O my soul, and let my heart devour wisdom. ⁵ For you ᵃhave come here apart from your will, and depart against your will, for you have only been given a short time to live. ⁶ O Lord over us, grant to your servant that we may pray before you, and give us seed for our heart and cultivation for our understanding, that fruit may grow from it, by which everyone who is corrupt, who bears the ᵇlikeness of a man, may live. ⁷ For you alone exist, and we all one workmanship of your hands, just as you have said. ⁸ Because you give life to the body that is now fashioned in the womb, and give it members, your creature is preserved in fire and water, and your workmanship endures nine months as your creation which is created in it. ⁹ But that which keeps and that which is kept will both be kept ᶜby your keeping. When the womb gives up again what has grown in it, ¹⁰ you have commanded that out of the parts of the body, that is to say, out of the breasts, be given milk, which is the fruit of the breasts, ¹¹ that the body that is fashioned may be nourished for a time, and afterwards you guide it in your mercy. ¹² Yes, you have brought it up in your righteousness, nurtured it in your law, and corrected it with your judgment. ¹³ You put it to death as your creation, and make it live as your work. ¹⁴ If therefore you ᵈlightly and suddenly destroy him which with so great labor was fashioned by your commandment, to what purpose was he made? ¹⁵ Now therefore I will speak. About man in general, you know best, but about your people for whose sake I am sorry, ¹⁶ and for your inheritance, for whose cause I mourn, for Israel, for whom I am heavy, and for the seed of Jacob, for whose sake I am troubled, ¹⁷ therefore I will begin to pray before you for myself and for them; for I see the failings of us who dwell in the land; ¹⁸ but I have heard the swiftness of the judgment which is to come. ¹⁹ Therefore hear my voice, and understand my saying, and I will speak before you." The beginning of the words of Esdras, before he was taken up. He said, ²⁰"O Lord, you who remain forever, whose eyes are exalted, and whose chambers are in the air, ²¹ whose throne is beyond measure, whose glory is beyond comprehension, before whom the army of angels stand with trembling, ²² ᵉ at whose bidding they are changed to wind and fire, whose word is sure, and sayings constant, whose ordinance is strong, and commandment fearful, ²³ whose look dries up the depths, and whose indignation makes the mountains to melt away, and whose truth bears witness– ²⁴ hear, O Lord, the prayer of your servant, and give ear to the petition of your handiwork. ²⁵ Attend to my words, for as long as I live, I will speak, and as long as I have understanding, I will answer. ²⁶ Don't look at the sins of your people, but on those who have served you in truth. ²⁷ Don't regard the doings of those who act wickedly, but of those who have kept your covenants in affliction. ²⁸ Don't think about those who have lived wickedly before you, but remember those who have willingly known your fear. ²⁹ Let it not be your will to destroy those who have lived like cattle, but look at those who have ᶠclearly taught your law. ³⁰ Don't be indignant at those who are deemed worse than animals, but love those who have always put their trust in your glory. ³¹ For we and our fathers have ᵍpassed our lives in ʰways that bring death, but you are called merciful because of us sinners. ³² For if you have a desire to have mercy upon us who have no works of righteousness, then you will be called merciful. ³³ For the just, which have many good works laid up with you, will be rewarded for their own deeds. ³⁴ For what is man, that you should take displeasure at him? Or what is a corruptible race, that you should be so bitter toward it? ³⁵ For in truth, there is no man among those who are born who has not done wickedly, and among those who have lived, there is none which have not done wrong. ³⁶ For in this, O Lord, your righteousness and your goodness will be declared, if you are merciful to those who have no store of good works." ³⁷ Then he answered me, "Some things you have spoken rightly, and it will happen according to your words. ³⁸ For indeed I will not think about the fashioning of those who have sinned, or about their death, their judgment, or their destruction; ³⁹ but I will rejoice over the creation of the righteous and their pilgrimage, their salvation, and the reward that they will have. ⁴⁰ Therefore as I have spoken, so it will be. ⁴¹ For as the farmer sows many seeds in the ground, and plants many trees, and yet not all that is sown will ⁱcome up in due season, neither will all that is planted take root, even so those who are sown in the world will not all be saved." ⁴² Then I answered, "If I have found favor, let me speak before you. ⁴³ If the farmer's seed doesn't come up because it hasn't received your rain in due season, or if it is ruined by too much rain and perishes, ⁴⁴ likewise man, who is formed with your hands and is called your own image, because he is made like you, for whose sake you have formed all things, even him have you made like the farmer's seed. ⁴⁵ Don't be angry with us, but spare your people and have mercy upon your inheritance, for you have mercy upon your own creation." ⁴⁶ Then he answered me, "Things present are for those who live now, and things to come for those who will live hereafter. ⁴⁷ For you come far short of being able to love my creature more than I. But you have compared yourself to the unrighteous. Don't do that! ⁴⁸ Yet in this will you be admirable to the Most High, ⁴⁹ in that you have humbled yourself, as it becomes you, and have not judged yourself among the righteous, so as to be much glorified. ⁵⁰ For many grievous miseries will fall on those who dwell in the world in the last times, because they have walked in great pride. ⁵¹ But understand for yourself, and for those who inquire concerning the glory of those like you, ⁵² because paradise is opened to you. The tree of life is planted. The time to come is prepared. Plenteousness is made ready. A city is built. Rest is ʲallowed. Goodness is perfected, and wisdom is perfected beforehand. ⁵³ The root of evil is sealed up from you. Weakness is done away from you, and ᵏdeath is hidden. Hell and corruption have fled into forgetfulness. ⁵⁴ Sorrows have passed away, and in the end, the treasure of immortality is shown. ⁵⁵ Therefore ask no more questions concerning the multitude of those who perish. ⁵⁶ For when they had received liberty, they despised the Most High, scorned his law, and forsook his ways. ⁵⁷ Moreover they have trodden down his righteous, ⁵⁸ and said in their heart that there is no God–even knowing that they must die. ⁵⁹ For as the things I have said will welcome you, so thirst and pain which are prepared for them. For the Most High didn't intend that men should be destroyed, ⁶⁰ but those who are created have themselves defiled the name of him who made them, and were unthankful to him who prepared life for them. ⁶¹ Therefore my judgment is now at hand, ⁶² which I have not shown to all men, but to you, and a few like you." Then I answered, ⁶³"Behold, O Lord, now you have shown me the multitude of the wonders which you will do in the last times, but you haven't shown me when."

9

¹ He answered me, "Measure diligently within yourself. When you see that a certain part of the signs are past, which have been told you beforehand, ² then will you understand that it is the very time in which the Most High will visit the world which was made by him. ³ When earthquakes, tumult of peoples, plans of nations, wavering of leaders, and confusion of princes are seen in the world, ⁴ then will you understand that the Most High spoke of these things from the days that were of old, from the beginning. ⁵ For just as with everything that is made in the world, the beginning ˡis evident and the end manifest, ⁶ so also are the times of the Most High: the beginnings are manifest in wonders and mighty works, and the end in effects and signs. ⁷ Everyone who will be saved, and will be able to escape by his works, or by faith by which they have believed, ⁸ will be preserved from the said perils, and will see my salvation in my land and within my borders, which I have sanctified for myself from the beginning. ⁹ Then those who now have abused my ways will be amazed. Those who have cast them away despitefully will live in torments. ¹⁰ For as many as in their life have received benefits, and yet have not known me, ¹¹ and as many as have scorned my law, while they still had liberty and when an opportunity to repent was open to them, didn't understand, but despised ᵐ it, ¹² must know ⁿit in torment after death. ¹³ Therefore don't be curious any longer how the

---

ᵃ *8:5* So the Syriac. The Latin is incorrect.
ᵇ *8:6* So the Syriac. The Latin has place.
ᶜ *8:9* So the Syriac. The Latin is imperfect.
ᵈ *8:14* So the Syriac. The Latin is incorrect.
ᵉ *8:22* According to the chief Oriental versions. The Latin has, even they whose service takes the form of wind etc.
ᶠ *8:29* The Syriac has received the brightness of your law.
ᵍ *8:31* So the Syriac and Aethiopic versions.
ʰ *8:31* Lat. manners.
ⁱ *8:41* Lat. be saved.
ʲ *8:52* The Syriac has established.
ᵏ *8:53* After the chief Oriental versions.
ˡ *9:5* So the Syriac. The Latin is corrupt.
ᵐ *9:11* Or, me
ⁿ *9:12* Or, me

ungodly will be punished, but inquire how the righteous will be saved, ᵃthose who the world belongs to, and for whom the world was created." ¹⁴ I answered, ¹⁵"I have said before, and now speak, and will say it again hereafter, that there are more of those who perish than of those who will be saved, ¹⁶ like a wave is greater than a drop." ¹⁷ He answered me, "Just as the field is, so also the seed. As the flowers are, so are the colors. As the work is, so also is the ᵇjudgment on it. As is the farmer, so also is his threshing floor. For there was a time in the world ¹⁸ when I was preparing for those who now live, before the world was made for them to dwell in. Then no one spoke against me, ¹⁹ for ᶜno one existed. But now those who are created in this world that is prepared, both ᵈwith a table that doesn't fail and a law which is unsearchable, are corrupted in their ways. ²⁰ So I considered my world, and behold, it was destroyed, and my earth, and behold, it was in peril, because of the plans that had come into it. ²¹ I saw and spared them, but not greatly, and saved myself a grape out of a cluster, and a plant out of ᵉa great forest. ²² Let the multitude perish then, which were born in vain. Let my grape be saved, and my plant, for I have made them perfect with great labor. ²³ Nevertheless, if you will wait seven more days–however don't fast in them, ²⁴ but go into a field of flowers, where no house is built, and eat only of the flowers of the field, and you shall taste no flesh, and shall drink no wine, but shall eat flowers only– ²⁵ and pray to the Most High continually, then I will come and talk with you." ²⁶ So I went my way, just as he commanded me, into the field which is called ᶠArdat. There I sat among the flowers, and ate of the herbs of the field, and this food satisfied me. ²⁷ It came to pass after seven days that I lay on the grass, and my heart was troubled again, like before. ²⁸ My mouth was opened, and I began to speak before the Lord Most High, and said, ²⁹"O Lord, you showed yourself among us, to our fathers in the wilderness, when they went out of Egypt, and when they came into the wilderness, where no man treads and that bears no fruit. ³⁰ You said, 'Hear me, O Israel. Heed my words, O seed of Jacob. ³¹ For behold, I sow my law in you, and it will bring forth fruit in you, and you will be glorified in it forever.' ³² But our fathers, who received the law, didn't keep it, and didn't observe the statutes. The fruit of the law didn't perish, for it couldn't, because it was yours. ³³ Yet those who received it perished, because they didn't keep the thing that was sown in them. ³⁴ Behold, it is a custom that when the ground has received seed, or the sea a ship, or any vessel food or drink, and when it comes to pass that that which is sown, or that which is launched, ³⁵ or the things which have been received, should come to an end, these come to an end, but the receptacles remain. Yet with us, it doesn't happen that way. ³⁶ For we who have received the law will perish by sin, along with our heart which received it. ³⁷ Notwithstanding the law doesn't perish, but remains in its honor." ³⁸ When I spoke these things in my heart, I looked around me with my eyes, and on my right side I saw a woman, and behold, she mourned and wept with a loud voice, and was much grieved in mind. Her clothes were torn, and she had ashes on her head. ³⁹ Then let I my thoughts go in which I was occupied, and turned myself to her, ⁴⁰ and said to her, "Why are you weeping? Why are you grieved in your mind?" ⁴¹ She said to me, "Leave me alone, my Lord, that I may weep for myself and add to my sorrow, for I am very troubled in my mind, and brought very low." ⁴² I said to her, "What ails you? Tell me." ⁴³ She said to me, "I, your servant, was barren and had no child, though I had a husband thirty years. ⁴⁴ Every hour and every day these thirty years I made my prayer to the Most High day and night. ⁴⁵ It came to pass after thirty years that God heard me, your handmaid, and saw my low estate, and considered my trouble, and gave me a son. I rejoiced in him greatly, I and my husband, and all my ᵍneighbors. We gave great honor to the Mighty One. ⁴⁶ I nourished him with great care. ⁴⁷ So when he grew up, and I came to take him a wife, I made him a feast day.

10

¹"So it came to pass that when my son was entered into his wedding chamber, he fell down and died. ² Then we all put out the lamps, and all my ʰneighbors rose up to comfort me. I remained quiet until the second day at night. ³ It came to pass, when they had all stopped consoling me, encouraging me to be quiet, then rose I up by night, and fled, and came here into this field, as you see. ⁴ Now I don't intend to return into the city, but to stay here, and not eat or drink, but to continually mourn and fast until I die." ⁵ Then I left the reflections I was engaged in, and answered her in anger, ⁶"You most foolish woman, don't you see our mourning, and what has happened to us? ⁷ For Zion the mother of us all is full of sorrow, and much humbled. ⁸ ⁱIt is right now to mourn deeply, since we all mourn, and to be sorrowful, since we are all in sorrow, but you are mourning for one son. ⁹ Ask the earth, and she will tell you that it is she which ought to mourn for so many that grow upon her. ¹⁰ For out of her, all had their beginnings, and others will come; and, behold, almost all of them walk into destruction, and the multitude of them is utterly doomed. ¹¹ Who then should mourn more, ʲshe who has lost so great a multitude, or you, who are grieved but for one? ¹² But if you say to me, 'My lamentation is not like the earth's, for I have lost the fruit of my womb, which I brought forth with pains, and bare with sorrows;' ¹³ but it is with the earth after the manner of the earth. The multitude present in it has gone as it came. ¹⁴ Then say I to you, 'Just as you have brought forth with sorrow, even so the earth also has given her fruit, namely, people, ever since the beginning to him who made her.' ¹⁵ Now therefore keep your sorrow to yourself, and bear with a good courage the adversities which have happened to you. ¹⁶ For if you will acknowledge the decree of God to be just, you will both receive your son in time, and will be praised among women. ¹⁷ Go your way then into the city to your husband." ¹⁸ She said to me, "I won't do that. I will not go into the city, but I will die here." ¹⁹ So I proceeded to speak further to her, and said, ²⁰"Don't do so, but allow yourself to be persuaded by reason of the adversities of Zion; and be comforted by reason of the sorrow of Jerusalem. ²¹ For you see that our sanctuary has been laid waste, our altar broken down, our temple destroyed, ²² our lute has been brought low, our song is put to silence, our rejoicing is at an end, the light of our candlestick is put out, the ark of our covenant is plundered, our holy things are defiled, and the name that we are called is profaned. Our free men are despitefully treated, our priests are burned, our Levites have gone into captivity, our virgins are defiled and our wives ravished, our righteous men carried away, our little ones betrayed, our young men are brought into bondage, and our strong men have become weak. ²³ What is more than all, the seal of Zion has now lost the seal of her honor, and is delivered into the hands of those who hate us. ²⁴ Therefore shake off your great heaviness, and put away from yourself the multitude of sorrows, that the Mighty One may be merciful to you again, and the Most High may give you rest, even ease from your troubles." ²⁵ It came to pass while I was talking with her, behold, her face suddenly began to shine exceedingly, and her countenance glistered like lightning, so that I was very afraid of her, and wondered what this meant. ²⁶ Behold, suddenly she made a great and very fearful cry, so that the earth shook at the noise. ²⁷ I looked, and behold, the woman appeared to me no more, but there was a city built, and a place shown itself from large foundations. Then I was afraid, and cried with a loud voice, ²⁸"Where is Uriel the angel, who came to me at the first? For he has caused me to fall into this great trance, and my end has turned into corruption, and my prayer a reproach!" ²⁹ As I was speaking these words, behold, the angel who had come to me at first came to me, and he looked at me. ³⁰ Behold, I lay as one who had been dead, and my understanding was taken from me. He took me by the right hand, and comforted me, and set me on my feet, and said to me, ³¹"What ails you? Why are you so troubled? Why is your understanding and the thoughts of your heart troubled?" ³² I said, "Because you have forsaken me; yet I did according to your words, and went into the field, and, behold, I have seen, and still see, that which I am not able to explain." ³³ He said to me, "Stand up like a man, and I will instruct you." ³⁴ Then I said, "Speak on, my Lord; only don't forsake me, lest I die before my time. ³⁵ For I have seen what I didn't know, and hear what I don't know. ³⁶ Or is my sense deceived, or my soul in a dream? ³⁷ Now therefore I beg you to explain to your servant what this vision means." ³⁸ He answered me, "Listen to me, and I will inform you, and tell you about the things you are afraid of, for the Most High has revealed many secret things to you. ³⁹ He has seen that your way is righteous, because you are continually sorry for your people, and make great lamentation for Zion. ⁴⁰ This therefore is the meaning of the vision. ⁴¹ The woman who appeared to you a little while ago, whom you saw mourning, and began to comfort her, ⁴² but now you no longer see the likeness of the woman, but a city under construction appeared to you, ⁴³ and she told you of the death of her son, this is the interpretation: ⁴⁴ This woman, whom you saw, is Zion,ᵏ whom you now see as a city being built. ⁴⁵ She told you that she had been barren for thirty years because there were three thousand years in the world in which there was no offering as yet offered in her. ⁴⁶ And it came to pass after three thousand years that Solomon built the city and offered offerings. It was then that the barren bore a son. ⁴⁷ She told you that she nourished him with great care. That was the dwelling in Jerusalem. ⁴⁸ When she said to you, 'My son died when he entered into his

---

ᵃ *9:13* So the Syriac and other versions. The Latin has and whose... created, and when.
ᵇ *9:17* So the Aethiopic and Arabic. The Latin has creation.
ᶜ *9:19* So the Syriac.
ᵈ *9:19* So the Syriac.
ᵉ *9:21* So the Syriac and other versions. The Latin has great tribes.
ᶠ *9:26* The Syriac and Aethiopic have Arphad.
ᵍ *9:45* Lat. townsmen.
ʰ *10:2* Lat. townsmen.
ⁱ *10:8* See the Oriental versions. The Latin is corrupt.
ʲ *10:11* So the Syriac.
ᵏ *10:44* So the Syriac and other versions. The Latin is incorrect.

marriage chamber, and that misfortune befell her,' this was the destruction that came to Jerusalem. ⁴⁹ Behold, you saw her likeness, how she mourned for her son, and you began to comfort her for what has happened to her. These were the things to be opened to you. ⁵⁰ For now the Most High, seeing that you are sincerely grieved and suffer from your whole heart for her, has shown you the brightness of her glory and the attractiveness of her beauty. ⁵¹ Therefore I asked you to remain in the field where no house was built, ⁵² for I knew that the Most High would show this to you. ⁵³ Therefore I commanded you to come into the field, where no foundation of any building was. ⁵⁴ For no human construction could stand in the place in which the city of the Most High was to be shown. ⁵⁵ Therefore don't be afraid nor let your heart be terrified, but go your way in and see the beauty and greatness of the building, as much as your eyes are able to see. ⁵⁶ Then will you hear as much as your ears may comprehend. ⁵⁷ For you are more blessed than many, and are called by name to be with the Most High, like only a few. ⁵⁸ But tomorrow at night you shall remain here, ⁵⁹ and so the Most High will show you those visions in dreams of what the Most High will do to those who live on the earth in the last days." So I slept that night and another, as he commanded me.

11

¹ It came to pass the second night that I saw a dream, and behold, an eagle which had twelve feathered wings and three heads came up from the sea. ² I saw, and behold, she spread her wings over all the earth, and all the winds of heaven blew on her, ᵃand the clouds were gathered together against her. ³ I saw, and out of her wings there grew other wings near them; and they became little, tiny wings. ⁴ But her heads were at rest. The head in the middle was larger than the other heads, yet rested it with them. ⁵ Moreover I saw, and behold, the eagle flew with her wings to reign over the earth and over those who dwell therein. ⁶ I saw how all things under heaven were subject to her, and no one spoke against her–no, not one creature on earth. ⁷ I saw, and behold, the eagle rose on her talons, and uttered her voice to her wings, saying, ⁸"Don't all watch at the same time. Let each one sleep in his own place and watch in turn; ⁹ but let the heads be preserved for the last." ¹⁰ I saw, and behold, the voice didn't come out of her heads, but from the midst of her body. ¹¹ I counted ᵇher wings that were near the others, and behold, there were eight of them. ¹² I saw, and behold, on the right side one wing arose and reigned over all the earth. ¹³ When it reigned, the end of it came, and it disappeared, so that its place appeared no more. The next wing rose up and reigned, and it ruled a long time. ¹⁴ It happened that when it reigned, its end came also, so that it disappeared, like the first. ¹⁵ Behold, a voice came to it, and said, ¹⁶"Listen, you who have ruled over the earth all this time! I proclaim this to you, before you disappear, ¹⁷ none after you will rule as long as you, not even half as long." ¹⁸ Then the third arose, and ruled as the others before, and it also disappeared. ¹⁹ So it went with all the wings one after another, as every one ruled, and then disappeared. ²⁰ I saw, and behold, in process of time the ᶜwings that followed were set up on the ᵈright side, that they might rule also. Some of them ruled, but in a while they disappeared. ²¹ Some of them also were set up, but didn't rule. ²² After this I saw, and behold, the twelve wings disappeared, along with two of the little wings. ²³ There was no more left on the eagle's body, except the three heads that rested, and six little wings. ²⁴ I saw, and behold, two little wings divided themselves from the six and remained under the head that was on the right side; but four remained in their place. ²⁵ I saw, and behold, these ᵉunder wings planned to set themselves up and to rule. ²⁶ I saw, and behold, there was one set up, but in a while it disappeared. ²⁷ A second also did so, and it disappeared faster than the first. ²⁸ I saw, and behold, the two that remained also planned between themselves to reign. ²⁹ While they thought about it, behold, one of the heads that were at rest awakened, the one that was in the middle, for that was greater than the two other heads. ³⁰ I saw how it joined the two other heads with it. ³¹ Behold, the head turned with those who were with it, and ate the two ᶠunder wings that planned to reign. ³² But this head held the whole earth in possession, and ruled over those who dwell in it with much oppression. It had stronger governance over the world than all the wings that had gone before. ³³ After this I saw, and behold, the head also that was in the middle suddenly disappeared, like the wings. ³⁴ But the two heads remained, which also reigned the same way over the earth and over those who dwell in it. ³⁵ I saw, and behold, the head on the right side devoured the one that was on the left side. ³⁶ Then I heard a voice, which said to me, "Look in front of you, and consider the thing that you see." ³⁷ I saw, and behold, something like a lion roused out of the woods roaring. I heard how he sent out a man's voice to the eagle, and spoke, saying, ³⁸"Listen and I will talk with you. The Most High will say to you, ³⁹'Aren't you the one that remains of the four animals whom I made to reign in my world, that the end of my times might come through them? ⁴⁰ The fourth came and overcame all the animals that were past, and ruled the world with great trembling, and the whole extent of the earth with grievous oppression. He lived on the earth such a long time with deceit. ⁴¹ You have judged the earth, but not with truth. ⁴² For you have afflicted the meek, you have hurt the peaceful, you have hated those who speak truth, you have loved liars, destroyed the dwellings of those who produced fruit, and threw down the walls of those who did you no harm. ⁴³ Your insolence has come up to the Most High, and your pride to the Mighty. ⁴⁴ The Most High also has looked at his times, and behold, they are ended, and his ages are fulfilled. ⁴⁵ Therefore appear no more, you eagle, nor your horrible wings, nor your evil little wings, nor your cruel heads, nor your hurtful talons, nor all your worthless body, ⁴⁶ that all the earth may be refreshed and relieved, being delivered from your violence, and that she may hope for the judgment and mercy of him who made her.'"

12

¹ It came to pass, while the lion spoke these words to the eagle, I saw, ² and behold, the head that remained disappeared, and ᵍthe two wings which went over to it arose and set themselves up to reign; and their kingdom was brief and full of uproar. ³ I saw, and behold, they disappeared, and the whole body of the eagle was burned, so that the earth was in great fear. Then I woke up because of great perplexity of mind and great fear, and said to my spirit, ⁴"Behold, you have done this to me, because you search out the ways of the Most High. ⁵ Behold, I am still weary in my mind, and very weak in my spirit. There isn't even a little strength in me, because of the great fear with which I was frightened tonight. ⁶ Therefore I will now ask the Most High that he would strengthen me to the end." ⁷ Then I said, "O sovereign Lord, if I have found favor in your sight, and if I am justified with you more than many others, and if my prayer has indeed come up before your face, ⁸ strengthen me then, and show me, your servant, the interpretation and plain meaning of this fearful vision, that you may fully comfort my soul. ⁹ For you have judged me worthy to show me the end of time and the last events of the times." ¹⁰ He said to me, "This is the interpretation of this vision which you saw: ¹¹ The eagle, whom you saw come up from the sea, is the fourth kingdom which appeared in a vision to your brother Daniel. ¹² But it was not explained to him, as I now explain it to you or have explained it. ¹³ Behold, the days come that a kingdom will rise up on earth, and it will be feared more than all the kingdoms that were before it. ¹⁴ Twelve kings will reign in it, one after another. ¹⁵ Of those, the second will begin to reign, and will reign a longer time than others of the twelve. ¹⁶ This is the interpretation of the twelve wings which you saw. ¹⁷ As for when you heard a voice which spoke, not going out from the heads, but from the midst of its body, this is the interpretation: ¹⁸ That ʰafter the time of that kingdom, there will arise no small contentions, and it will stand in peril of falling. Nevertheless, it won't fall then, but will be restored again to its former power. ¹⁹ You saw the eight under wings sticking to her wings. This is the interpretation: ²⁰ That in it eight kings will arise, whose times will be short and their years swift. ²¹ Two of them will perish when the middle time approaches. Four will be kept for a while until the time of the ending of it will approach; but two will be kept to the end. ²² You saw three heads resting. This is the interpretation: ²³ In its last days, the Most High will raise up three ⁱkingdoms and renew many things in them. They will rule over the earth, ²⁴ and over those who dwell in it, with much oppression, more than all those who were before them. Therefore they are called the heads of the eagle. ²⁵ For these are those who will accomplish her wickedness, and who will finish her last actions. ²⁶ You saw that the great head disappeared. It signifies that one of them will die on his bed, and yet with pain. ²⁷ But for the two that remained, the sword will devour them. ²⁸ For the sword of the one will devour him that was with him, but he will also fall by the sword in the last days. ²⁹ You saw two under wings passing ʲover to the head that is on the right side. ³⁰ This is the interpretation: These are they whom the Most High has kept to his end. This is the brief reign that was full of trouble, as you saw. ³¹"The lion, whom you saw rising up out of the forest, roaring, speaking to the eagle, and rebuking her for her unrighteousness, and all her words which you have heard, ³² this is the anointed one, whom the Most High has kept to the end

---

ᵃ *11:2* So the chief Oriental versions. The Latin has only and were gathered together.
ᵇ *11:11* The Syriac has her little wings, and, etc.
ᶜ *11:20* The Syriac has little wings.
ᵈ *11:20* The Aethiopic has left.
ᵉ *11:25* The Syriac has little wings.
ᶠ *11:31* The Syriac has little wings.
ᵍ *12:2* So the chief Oriental versions.
ʰ *12:18* The Oriental versions havein the midst of.
ⁱ *12:23* The Oriental versions have kings
ʲ *12:29* So the Syriac. The Latin has over the head.

[of days, who will spring up out of the seed of David, and he will come and speak] to them and reprove them for their wickedness and unrighteousness, and will[b] heap up before them their contemptuous dealings. [33] For at first he will set them alive in his judgment, and when he has reproved them, he will destroy them. [34] For he will deliver the rest of my people with mercy, those who have been preserved throughout my borders, and he will make them joyful until the coming of the end, even the day of judgment, about which I have spoken to you from the beginning. [35] This is the dream that you saw, and this is its interpretation. [36] Only you have been worthy to know the secret of the Most High. [37] Therefore write all these things that you have seen in a book, and put it in a secret place. [38] You shall teach them to the wise of your people, whose hearts you know are able to comprehend and keep these secrets. [39] But wait here yourself seven more days, that you may be shown whatever it pleases the Most High to show you." Then he departed from me. [40] It came to pass, when all the people [c]saw that the seven days were past, and I had not come again into the city, they all gathered together, from the least to the greatest, and came to me, and spoke to me, saying, [41]"How have we offended you? What evil have we done against you, that you have utterly forsaken us, and sit in this place? [42] For of all the prophets, only you are left to us, like a cluster of the vintage, and like a lamp in a dark place, and like a harbor for a ship saved from the tempest. [43] Aren't the evils which have come to us sufficient? [44] If you will forsake us, how much better had it been for us if we also had been consumed in the burning of Zion! [45] For we are not better than those who died there." Then they wept with a loud voice. I answered them, [46]"Take courage, O Israel! Don't be sorrowful, you house of Jacob; [47] for the Most High remembers you. The Mighty has not forgotten you [d]forever. [48] As for me, I have not forsaken you. I haven't departed from you; but I have come into this place to pray for the desolation of Zion, and that I might seek mercy for the humiliation of your sanctuary. [49] Now go your way, every man to his own house, and after these days I will come to you." [50] So the people went their way into the city, as I told them to do. [51] But I sat in the field seven days, as the angel commanded me. In those days, I ate only of the flowers of the field, and my food was from plants.

13

[1] It came to pass after seven days, I dreamed a dream by night. [2] Behold, a wind arose from the sea that moved all its waves. [3] I saw, and behold, [e][this wind caused to come up from the midst of the sea something like the appearance of a man. I saw, and behold,] that man [f]flew with the clouds of heaven. When he turned his face to look, everything that he saw trembled. [4] Whenever the voice went out of his mouth, all who heard his voice melted, like the [g]wax melts when it feels the fire. [5] After this I saw, and behold, an innumerable multitude of people was gathered together from the four winds of heaven to make war against the man who came out of the sea. [6] I saw, and behold, he carved himself a great mountain, and flew up onto it. [7] I tried to see the region or place from which the mountain was carved, and I couldn't. [8] After this I saw, and behold, all those who were gathered together to fight against him were very afraid, and yet they dared to fight. [9] Behold, as he saw the assault of the multitude that came, he didn't lift up his hand, or hold a spear or any weapon of war; [10] but I saw only how he sent out of his mouth something like a flood of fire, and out of his lips a flaming breath, and out of his tongue he shot out a storm of sparks.[h] [11] These were all mixed together: the flood of fire, the flaming breath, and the great storm, and fell upon the assault of the multitude which was prepared to fight, and burned up every one of them, so that all of a sudden an innumerable multitude was seen to be nothing but dust of ashes and smell of smoke. When I saw this, I was amazed. [12] Afterward, I saw the same man come down from the mountain, and call to himself another multitude which was peaceful. [13] Many people came to him. Some of them were glad. Some were sorry. Some of them were bound, and some others brought some of those as offerings. Then through great fear I woke up and prayed to the Most High, and said, [14]"You have shown your servant these wonders from the beginning, and have counted me worthy that you should receive my prayer. [15] Now show me also the interpretation of this dream. [16] For as I conceive in my understanding, woe to those who will be left in those days! Much more woe to those who are not left! [17] For those who were not left will be in heaviness, [18] understanding the things that are laid up in the latter days, but not attaining to them. [19] But woe to them also who are left, because they will see great perils and much distress, like these dreams declare. [20] Yet is it [i]better for one to be in peril and to come into [j]these things, than to pass away as a cloud out of the world, and not to see the things that [k]will happen in the last days." He answered me, [21]"I will tell you the interpretation of the vision, and I will also open to you the things about which you mentioned. [22] You have spoken of those who are left behind. This is the interpretation: [23] He that will [l]endure the peril in that time will protect those who fall into danger, even those who have works and faith toward the Almighty. [24] Know therefore that those who are left behind are more blessed than those who are dead. [25] These are the interpretations of the vision: Whereas you saw a man coming up from the midst of the sea, [26] this is he whom the Most High has been keeping for many ages, who by his own self will deliver his creation. He will direct those who are left behind. [27] Whereas you saw that out of his mouth came wind, fire, and storm, [28] and whereas he held neither spear, nor any weapon of war, but destroyed the assault of that multitude which came to fight against him, this is the interpretation: [29] Behold, the days come when the Most High will begin to deliver those who are on the earth. [30] Astonishment of mind will come upon those who dwell on the earth. [31] One will plan to make war against another, city against city, place against place, people against people, and kingdom against kingdom. [32] It will be, when these things come to pass, and the signs happen which I showed you before, then my Son will be revealed, whom you saw as a man ascending. [33] It will be, when all the nations hear his voice, every man will leave his own land and the battle they have against one another. [34] An innumerable multitude will be gathered together, as you saw, desiring to come and to fight against him. [35] But he will stand on the top of Mount Zion. [36] Zion will come, and will be shown to all men, being prepared and built, like you saw the mountain carved without hands. [37] My Son will rebuke the nations which have come for their wickedness, with plagues that are like a storm, [38] and will rebuke them to their face with their evil thoughts, and the torments with which they will be tormented, which are like a flame. He will destroy them without labor by the law, which is like fire. [39] Whereas you saw that he gathered to himself another multitude that was peaceful, [40] these are the ten tribes which were led away out of their own land in the time of Osea the king, whom Salmananser the king of the Assyrians led away captive, and he carried them beyond the River, and they were taken into another land. [41] But they made this plan among themselves, that they would leave the multitude of the heathen, and go out into a more distant region, where mankind had never lived, [42] that there they might keep their statutes which they had not kept in their own land. [43] They entered by the narrow passages of the river Euphrates. [44] For the Most High then did signs for them, and stopped the springs of the River until they had passed over. [45] For through that country there was a long way to go, namely, of a year and a half. The same region is called [m]Arzareth. [46] Then they lived there until the latter time. Now when they begin to come again, [47] the Most High stops the springs of the River again, that they may go through. Therefore you saw the multitude gathered together with peace. [48] But those who are left behind of your people are those who are found within my holy border. [49] It will be therefore when he will destroy the multitude of the nations that are gathered together, he will defend the people who remain. [50] Then will he show them very many wonders." [51] Then I said, "O sovereign Lord, explain this to me: Why have I seen the man coming up from the midst of the sea?" [52] He said to me, as no one can explore or know what is in the depths of the sea, even so no man on earth can see my Son, or those who are with him, except in the time of [n]his day. [53] This is the interpretation of the dream which you saw, and for this only you are enlightened about this, [54] for you have forsaken your own ways, and applied your diligence to mine, and have searched out my law. [55] You have ordered your life in wisdom, and have called understanding your mother. [56] Therefore I have shown you this, for there is a reward laid up with the Most High. It will be, after another three days I will speak other things to you, and declare to you mighty and wondrous things." [57] Then I went out and passed into the field, giving praise and thanks greatly to the Most High because of his wonders, which he did from time to time, [58] and because he governs the time, and such things as happen in their seasons. So I sat there three days.

14

[1] It came to pass upon the third day, I sat under an oak, and, behold, a voice came out of a bush near me, and said, "Esdras, Esdras!" [2] I said, "Here I am, Lord," and I stood up on my feet. [3] Then he said to me, "I revealed myself in a bush and talked with Moses when my people were in bondage

---

[a] *12:32* The words in brackets are added from the Syriac.

[b] *12:32* The Syriac has set in order.

[c] *12:40* So the Syriac. The Latin has heard.

[d] *12:47* So the Syriac.

[e] *13:3* The words in brackets are added from the Syriac.

[f] *13:3* So the Syriac. The Latin has grew strong

[g] *13:4* So the Syriac and other Oriental versions.

[h] *13:10* So the Syriac and Arabic.

[i] *13:20* Lat. easier.

[j] *13:20* So the Syriac.

[k] *13:20* So the Syriac.

[l] *13:23* So the Syriac.

[m] *13:45* That is, another land. See Deuteronomy **29:28**.

[n] *13:52* So the Oriental versions. The Latin omits his.

in Egypt. ⁴ I sent him, and ᵃ he led my people out of Egypt. I brought him up to Mount Sinai, where I kept him with me for many days. ⁵ I told him many wondrous things, and showed him the secrets of the times and the end of the seasons. I commanded him, saying, ⁶ 'You shall publish these openly, and these you shall hide.' ⁷ Now I say to you: ⁸ Lay up in your heart the signs that I have shown, the dreams that you have seen, and the interpretations which you have heard; ⁹ for you will be taken away from men, and from now on you will live with my Son and with those who are like you, until the times have ended. ¹⁰ For the world has lost its youth, and the times begin to grow old. ¹¹ ᵇFor the age is divided into twelve parts, and ten parts of it are already gone, ᶜeven the half of the tenth part. ¹² There remain of it two parts after the middle of the tenth part. ¹³ Now therefore set your house in order, reprove your people, comfort the lowly among them, ᵈ and instruct those of them who are wise, and now renounce the life that is corruptible, ¹⁴ and let go of the mortal thoughts, cast away from you the burdens of man, put off now your weak nature, ¹⁵ lay aside the thoughts that are most grievous to you, and hurry to escape from these times. ¹⁶ For worse evils than those which you have seen happen will be done after this. ¹⁷ For look how much the world will be weaker through age, so much that more evils will increase on those who dwell in it. ¹⁸ For the truth will withdraw itself further off, and falsehood will be near. For now ᵉthe eagle which you saw in vision hurries to come." ¹⁹ Then I answered and said, ᶠ"Let me speak in your presence, O Lord. ²⁰ Behold, I will go, as you have commanded me, and reprove the people who now live, but who will warn those who will be born afterward? For the world is set in darkness, and those who dwell in it are without light. ²¹ For your law has been burned, therefore no one knows the things that are done by you, or the works that will be done. ²² But if I have found favor before you, send the Holy Spirit to me, and I will write all that has been done in the world since the beginning, even the things that were written in your law, that men may be able to find the path, and that those who would live in the latter days may live." ²³ He answered me and said, "Go your way, gather the people together, and tell them not to seek you for forty days. ²⁴ But prepare for yourself many tablets, and take with you Sarea, Dabria, Selemia, Ethanus, and Asiel, these five, which are ready to write swiftly; ²⁵ and come here, and I will light a lamp of understanding in your heart which will not be put out until the things have ended about which you will write. ²⁶ When you are done, some things you shall publish openly, and some things you shall deliver in secret to the wise. Tomorrow at this hour you will begin to write." ²⁷ Then went I out, as he commanded me, and gathered all the people together, and said, ²⁸ "Hear these words, O Israel! ²⁹ Our fathers at the beginning were foreigners in Egypt, and they were delivered from there, ³⁰ and received the law of life, which they didn't keep, which you also have transgressed after them. ³¹ Then the land of Zion was given to you for a possession; but you yourselves and your ancestors have done unrighteousness, and have not kept the ways which the Most High commanded you. ³² Because he is a righteous judge, in due time, he took from you what he had given you. ³³ Now you are here, and your kindred are among you. ³⁴ Therefore if you will rule over your own understanding and instruct your hearts, you will be kept alive, and after death you will obtain mercy. ³⁵ For after death the judgment will come, when we will live again. Then the names of the righteous will become manifest, and the works of the ungodly will be declared. ³⁶ Let no one therefore come to me now, nor seek me for forty days." ³⁷ So I took the five men, as he commanded me, and we went out into the field, and remained there. ³⁸ It came to pass on the next day that, behold, a voice called me, saying, "Esdras, open your mouth, and drink what I give you to drink." ³⁹ Then opened I my mouth, and behold, a full cup was handed to me. It was full of something like water, but its color was like fire. ⁴⁰ I took it, and drank. When I had drunk it, my heart uttered understanding, and wisdom grew in my chest, for my spirit retained its memory. ⁴¹ My mouth was opened, and shut no more. ⁴² The Most High gave understanding to the five men, and they wrote by course the things that were told them, in ᵍcharacters which they didn't know, and they sat forty days. Now they wrote in the day-time, and at night they ate bread. ⁴³ As for me, I spoke in the day, and by night I didn't hold my tongue. ⁴⁴ So in forty days, ninety-four books were written. ⁴⁵ It came to pass, when the forty days were fulfilled, that the Most High spoke to me, saying, "The first books that you have written, publish openly, and let the worthy and unworthy read them; ⁴⁶ but keep the last seventy, that you may deliver them to those who are wise among your people; ⁴⁷ for in them is the spring of understanding, the fountain of wisdom, and the stream of knowledge." ⁴⁸ I did so.

15

¹ "Behold, speak in the ears of my people the words of prophecy which I will put in your mouth," says the Lord. ² "Cause them to be written on paper, for they are faithful and true. ³ Don't be afraid of their plots against you. Don't let the unbelief of those who speak against you trouble you. ⁴ For all the unbelievers will die in their unbelief. ⁵ "Behold," says the Lord, "I bring evils on the whole earth: sword, famine, death, and destruction. ⁶ For wickedness has prevailed over every land, and their hurtful works have reached their limit. ⁷ Therefore," says the Lord, ⁸ "I will hold my peace no more concerning their wickedness which they profanely commit, neither will I tolerate them in these things, which they wickedly practice. Behold, the innocent and righteous blood cries to me, and the souls of the righteous cry out continually. ⁹ I will surely avenge them," says the Lord, "and will receive to me all the innocent blood from among them. ¹⁰ Behold, my people is led like a flock to the slaughter. I will not allow them now to dwell in the land of Egypt, ¹¹ but I will bring them out with a mighty hand and with a high arm, and will strike Egypt with plagues, as before, and will destroy all its land." ¹² Let Egypt and its foundations mourn, for the plague of the chastisement and the punishment that God will bring upon it. ¹³ Let the farmers that till the ground mourn, for their seeds will fail and their trees will be ruined through the blight and hail, and a terrible tempest. ¹⁴ Woe to the world and those who dwell in it! ¹⁵ For the sword and their destruction draws near, and nation will rise up against nation to battle with weapons in their hands. ¹⁶ For there will be sedition among men, and growing strong against one another. In their might, they won't respect their king or the chief of their great ones. ¹⁷ For a man will desire to go into a city, and will not be able. ¹⁸ For because of their pride the cities will be troubled, the houses will be destroyed, and men will be afraid. ¹⁹ A man will have no pity on his neighbors, but will assault their houses with the sword and plunder their goods, because of the lack of bread, and for great suffering. ²⁰ "Behold," says God, "I call together all the kings of the earth to stir up those who are from the rising of the sun, from the south, from the east, and Libanus, to turn themselves one against another, and repay the things that they have done to them. ²¹ Just as they do yet this day to my chosen, so I will do also, and repay into their bosom." The Lord God says: ²² "My right hand won't spare the sinners, and my sword won't cease over those who shed innocent blood on the earth. ²³ A fire has gone out from his wrath and has consumed the foundations of the earth and the sinners, like burnt straw. ²⁴ Woe to those who sin and don't keep my commandments!" says the Lord. ²⁵ "I will not spare them. Go your way, you rebellious children! Don't defile my sanctuary!" ²⁶ For the Lord knows all those who trespass against him, therefore he will deliver them to death and destruction. ²⁷ For now evils have come upon the whole earth, and you will remain in them; for God will not deliver you, because you have sinned against him. ²⁸ Behold, a horrible sight appearing from the east! ²⁹ The nations of the dragons of Arabia will come out with many chariots. From the day that they set out, their hissing is carried over the earth, so that all those who will hear them may also fear and tremble. ³⁰ Also the Carmonians, raging in wrath, will go out like the wild boars of the forest. They will come with great power and join battle with them, and will devastate a portion of the land of the Assyrians with their teeth. ³¹ Then the dragons will have the upper hand, remembering their nature. If they will turn themselves, conspiring together in great power to persecute them, ³² then these will be troubled, and keep silence through their power, and will turn and flee. ³³ From the land of the Assyrians, an enemy in ambush will attack them and destroy one of them. Upon their army will be fear and trembling, and indecision upon their kings. ³⁴ Behold, clouds from the east, and from the north to the south! They are very horrible to look at, full of wrath and storm. ³⁵ They will clash against one another. They will pour out a heavy storm on the earth, even their own storm. There will be blood from the sword to the horse's belly, ³⁶ and to the thigh of man, and to the camel's hock. ³⁷ There will be fearfulness and great trembling upon earth. They who see that wrath will be afraid, and trembling will seize them. ³⁸ After this, great storms will be stirred up from the south, from the north, and another part from the west. ³⁹ Strong winds will arise from the east, and will shut it up, even the cloud which he raised up in wrath; and the storm that was to cause destruction by the east wind will be violently driven toward the south and west. ⁴⁰ Great and mighty clouds, full of wrath, will be lifted up with the storm, that they may destroy all the earth and those who dwell in it. They will pour out over every high and lofty one a terrible storm, ⁴¹ fire, hail, flying swords, and many waters, that all plains may be full, and all rivers, with the abundance of those waters. ⁴² They will break

---

ᵃ 14:4 Another reading is. I.
ᵇ 14:11 Verses 11, 12 are omitted in the Syriac. The Aethiopic has For the age is divided into ten parts, and is come to the tenth: and half of the tenth remains. Now etc.
ᶜ 14:11 Lat. and.

ᵈ 14:13 The Latin alone omits and...wise.
ᵉ 14:18 So the Oriental versions.

ᶠ 14:19 The Latin omits I will speak.
ᵍ 14:42 So the Oriental versions.

down the cities and walls, mountains and hills, trees of the forest, and grass of the meadows, and their grain. ⁴³ They will go on steadily to Babylon and destroy her. ⁴⁴ They will come to it and surround it. They will pour out the storm and all wrath on her. Then the dust and smoke will go up to the sky, and all those who are around it will mourn for it. ⁴⁵ Those who remain will serve those who have destroyed it. ⁴⁶ You, Asia, who are partaker in the beauty of Babylon, and in the glory of her person– ⁴⁷ woe to you, you wretch, because you have made yourself like her. You have decked out your daughters for prostitution, that they might please and glory in your lovers, which have always lusted after you! ⁴⁸ You have followed her who is hateful in all her works and inventions. Therefore God says, ⁴⁹"I will send evils on you: widowhood, poverty, famine, sword, and pestilence, to lay waste your houses and bring you to destruction and death. ⁵⁰ The glory of your power will be dried up like a flower when the heat rises that is sent over you. ⁵¹ You will be weakened like a poor woman who is beaten and wounded, so that you won't be able to receive your mighty ones and your lovers. ⁵² Would I have dealt with you with such jealousy," says the Lord, ⁵³"if you had not always slain my chosen, exalting and clapping of your hands, and saying over their dead, when you were drunk? ⁵⁴"Beautify your face! ⁵⁵ The reward of a prostitute will be in your bosom, therefore you will be repaid. ⁵⁶ Just as you will do to my chosen," says the Lord, "even so God will do to you, and will deliver you to your adversaries. ⁵⁷ Your children will die of hunger. You will fall by the sword. Your cities will be broken down, and all your people in the field will perish by the sword. ⁵⁸ Those who are in the mountains will die of hunger, eat their own flesh, and drink their own blood, because of hunger for bread and thirst for water. ⁵⁹ You, unhappy above all others, will come and will again receive evils. ⁶⁰ In the passage, they will rush on the hateful city and will destroy some portion of your land, and mar part of your glory, and will return again to Babylon that was destroyed. ⁶¹ You will be cast down by them as stubble, and they will be to you as fire. ⁶² They will devour you, your cities, your land, and your mountains. They will burn all your forests and your fruitful trees with fire. ⁶³ They will carry your children away captive, and will plunder your wealth, and mar the glory of your face."

16

¹ Woe to you, Babylon, and Asia! Woe to you, Egypt and Syria! ² Put on sackcloth and garments of goats' hair, wail for your children and lament; for your destruction is at hand. ³ A sword has been sent upon you, and who is there to turn it back? ⁴ A fire has been sent upon you, and who is there to quench it? ⁵ Calamities are sent upon you, and who is there to drive them away? ⁶ Can one drive away a hungry lion in the forest? Can one quench a fire in stubble, once it has begun to burn? ⁷ Can one turn back an arrow that is shot by a strong archer? ⁸ The Lord God sends the calamities, and who will drive them away? ⁹ A fire will go out from his wrath, and who may quench it? ¹⁰ He will flash lightning, and who will not fear? He will thunder, and who wouldn't tremble? ¹¹ The Lord will threaten, and who will not be utterly broken in pieces at his presence? ¹² The earth and its foundations quake. The sea rises up with waves from the deep, and its waves will be troubled, along with the fish in them, at the presence of the Lord, and before the glory of his power. ¹³ For his right hand that bends the bow is strong, his arrows that he shoots are sharp, and will not miss when they begin to be shot into the ends of the world. ¹⁴ Behold, the calamities are sent out, and will not return again until they come upon the earth. ¹⁵ The fire is kindled and will not be put out until it consumes the foundations of the earth. ¹⁶ Just as an arrow which is shot by a mighty archer doesn't return backward, even so the calamities that are sent out upon earth won't return again. ¹⁷ Woe is me! Woe is me! Who will deliver me in those days? ¹⁸ The beginning of sorrows, when there will be great mourning; the beginning of famine, and many will perish; the beginning of wars, and the powers will stand in fear; the beginning of calamities, and all will tremble! What will they do when the calamities come? ¹⁹ Behold, famine and plague, suffering and anguish! They are sent as scourges for correction. ²⁰ But for all these things they will not turn them from their wickedness, nor be always mindful of the scourges. ²¹ Behold, food will be so cheap on earth that they will think themselves to be in good condition, and even then calamities will grow on earth: sword, famine, and great confusion. ²² For many of those who dwell on earth will perish of famine; and others who escape the famine, the sword will destroy. ²³ The dead will be cast out like dung, and there will be no one to comfort them; for the earth will be left desolate, and its cities will be cast down. ²⁴ There will be no farmer left to cultivate the earth or to sow it. ²⁵ The trees will give fruit, but who will gather it? ²⁶ The grapes will ripen, but who will tread them? For in all places there will be a great solitude; ²⁷ for one man will desire to see another, or to hear his voice. ²⁸ For of a city there will be ten left, and two of the field, who have hidden themselves in the thick groves, and in the clefts of the rocks. ²⁹ As in an orchard of olives upon every tree there may be left three or four olives, ³⁰ or as when a vineyard is gathered, there are some clusters left by those who diligently search through the vineyard, ³¹ even so in those days, there will be three or four left by those who search their houses with the sword. ³² The earth will be left desolate, and its fields will be for briers, and its roads and all her paths will grow thorns, because no sheep will pass along them. ³³ The virgins will mourn, having no bridegrooms. The women will mourn, having no husbands. Their daughters will mourn, having no helpers. ³⁴ Their bridegrooms will be destroyed in the wars, and their husbands will perish of famine. ³⁵ Hear now these things, and understand them, you servants of the Lord. ³⁶ Behold, the Lord's word: receive it. Don't doubt the things about which the Lord speaks. ³⁷ Behold, the calamities draw near, and are not delayed. ³⁸ Just as a woman with child in the ninth month, when the hour of her delivery draws near, within two or three hours great pains surround her womb, and when the child comes out from the womb, there will be no waiting for a moment, ³⁹ even so the calamities won't delay coming upon the earth. The world will groan, and sorrows will seize it on every side. ⁴⁰"O my people, hear my word: prepare for battle, and in those calamities be like strangers on the earth. ⁴¹ He who sells, let him be as he who flees away, and he who buys, as one who will lose. ⁴² Let he who does business be as he who has no profit by it, and he who builds, as he who won't dwell in it, ⁴³ and he who sows, as if he wouldn't reap, so also he who prunes the vines, as he who won't gather the grapes, ⁴⁴ those who marry, as those who will have no children, and those who don't marry, as the widowed. ⁴⁵ Because of this, those who labor, labor in vain; ⁴⁶ for foreigners will reap their fruits, plunder their goods, overthrow their houses, and take their children captive, for in captivity and famine they will conceive their children. ⁴⁷ Those who conduct business, do so only to be plundered. The more they adorn their cities, their houses, their possessions, and their own persons, ⁴⁸ the more I will hate them for their sins," says the Lord. ⁴⁹ Just as a respectable and virtuous woman hates a prostitute, ⁵⁰ so will righteousness hate iniquity, when she adorns herself, and will accuse her to her face, when he comes who will defend him who diligently searches out every sin on earth. ⁵¹ Therefore don't be like her or her works. ⁵² For yet a little while, and iniquity will be taken away out of the earth, and righteousness will reign over us. ⁵³ Don't let the sinner say that he has not sinned; for God will burn coals of fire on the head of one who says "I haven't sinned before God and his glory." ⁵⁴ Behold, the Lord knows all the works of men, their imaginations, their thoughts, and their hearts. ⁵⁵ He said, "Let the earth be made," and it was made, "Let the sky be made," and it was made. ⁵⁶ At his word, the stars were established, and he knows the number of the stars. ⁵⁷ He searches the deep and its treasures. He has measured the sea and what it contains. ⁵⁸ He has shut the sea in the midst of the waters, and with his word, he hung the earth over the waters. ⁵⁹ He has spread out the sky like a vault. He has founded it over the waters. ⁶⁰ He has made springs of water in the desert and pools on the tops of the mountains to send out rivers from the heights to water the earth. ⁶¹ He formed man, and put a heart in the midst of the body, and gave him breath, life, and understanding, ⁶² yes, the spirit of God Almighty. He who made all things and searches out hidden things in hidden places, ⁶³ surely he knows your imagination, and what you think in your hearts. Woe to those who sin, and try to hide their sin! ⁶⁴ Because the Lord will exactly investigate all your works, and he will put you all to shame. ⁶⁵ When your sins are brought out before men, you will be ashamed, and your own iniquities will stand as your accusers in that day. ⁶⁶ What will you do? Or how will you hide your sins before God and his angels? ⁶⁷ Behold, God is the judge. Fear him! Stop sinning, and forget your iniquities, to never again commit them. So will God lead you out, and deliver you from all suffering. ⁶⁸ For, behold, the burning wrath of a great multitude is kindled over you, and they will take away some of you, and feed you with that which is sacrificed to idols. ⁶⁹ Those who consent to them will be held in derision and in contempt, and be trodden under foot. ⁷⁰ For there will be in various places, and in the next cities, a great insurrection against those who fear the Lord. ⁷¹ They will be like mad men, sparing none, but spoiling and destroying those who still fear the Lord. ⁷² For they will destroy and plunder their goods, and throw them out of their houses. ⁷³ Then the trial of my elect will be made known, even as the gold that is tried in the fire. ⁷⁴ Hear, my elect ones, says the Lord: "Behold, the days of suffering are at hand, and I will deliver you from them. ⁷⁵ Don't be afraid, and don't doubt, for God is your guide. ⁷⁶ You who keep my commandments and precepts," says the Lord God, "don't let your sins weigh you down, and don't let your iniquities lift themselves up." ⁷⁷ Woe to those who are choked with their sins and covered with their iniquities, like a field is choked with bushes, and its path covered with thorns, that no one may travel through! ⁷⁸ It is shut off and given up to be consumed by fire.

The Book of Tobit

Tobit is recognized as Deuterocanonical Scripture by the Roman Catholic, Greek Orthodox, and Russian Orthodox Churches.

1

¹ The book of the words of Tobit, the son of Tobiel, the son of Ananiel, the son of Aduel, the son of Gabael, of the seed of Asiel, of the tribe of Naphtali; ² who in the days of Enemessar[a] king of the Assyrians was carried away captive out of Thisbe, which is on the right hand of Kedesh Naphtali in Galilee above Asher. ³ I, Tobit walked in the ways of truth and righteousness all the days of my life, and I did many alms deeds to my kindred and my nation, who went with me into the land of the Assyrians, to Nineveh. ⁴ When I was in my own country, in the land of Israel, while I was yet young, all the tribe of Naphtali my father fell away from the house of Jerusalem, which was chosen out of all the tribes of Israel, that all the tribes should sacrifice there, and the temple of the habitation of the Most High was hallowed and built therein for all ages. ⁵ All the tribes which fell away together sacrificed to the heifer Baal, and so did the house of Naphtali my father. ⁶ I alone went often to Jerusalem at the feasts, as it has been ordained to all Israel by an everlasting decree, having the first fruits and the tenths of my increase, and that which was first shorn; and I gave them at the altar to the priests the sons of Aaron. ⁷ I gave a tenth part of all my increase to the sons of Levi, who ministered at Jerusalem. A second tenth part I sold away, and went, and spent it each year at Jerusalem. ⁸ A third tenth I gave to them to whom it was appropriate, as Deborah my father's mother had commanded me, because I was left an orphan by my father. ⁹ When I became a man, I took as wife Anna of the seed of our own family. With her, I became the father of Tobias. ¹⁰ When I was carried away captive to Nineveh, all my kindred and my relatives ate of the bread of the Gentiles; ¹¹ but I kept myself from eating, ¹² because I remembered God with all my soul. ¹³ So the Most High gave me grace and favor[b] in the sight of Enemessar, and I was his purchasing agent. ¹⁴ And I went into Media, and left ten talents of silver in trust with Gabael, the brother of Gabrias, at Rages of Media. ¹⁵ And when Enemessar was dead, Sennacherib his son reigned in his place. In his time, the highways were troubled,[c] and I could no longer go into Media. ¹⁶ In the days of Enemessar, I did many alms deeds to my kindred: I gave my bread to the hungry, ¹⁷ and my garments to the naked. If I saw any of my race dead, and thrown out on[d] the wall of Ninevah, I buried him. ¹⁸ If Sennacherib the king killed any, when he came fleeing from Judea, I buried them privately; for in his wrath he killed many; and the bodies were sought for by the king, and were not found. ¹⁹ But one of the Ninevites went and showed to the king concerning me, how I buried them, and hid myself; and when I knew that I was sought for to be put to death, I withdrew myself for fear. ²⁰ And all my goods were forcibly taken away, and there was nothing left to me, save my wife Anna and my son Tobias. ²¹ No more than fifty five days passed before two of his sons killed him, and they fled into the mountains of Ararat. And Sarchedonus[e] his son reigned in his place; and he appointed Achiacharus my brother Anael's son over all the accounts of his kingdom, and over all his affairs. ²² Achiacharus requested me, and I came to Nineveh. Now Achiacharus was cupbearer, keeper of the signet, steward, and overseer of the accounts. Sarchedonus appointed him next to himself, but he was my brother's son.

2

¹ Now when I had come home again, and my wife Anna was restored to me, and my son Tobias, in the feast of Pentecost, which is the holy feast of the seven weeks, there was a good dinner prepared for me, and I sat down to eat. ² I saw abundance of meat, and I said to my son, "Go and bring whatever poor man you find of our kindred, who is mindful of the Lord. Behold, I wait for you." ³ Then he came, and said, "Father, one of our race is strangled, and has been cast out in the marketplace." ⁴ Before I had tasted anything, I sprang up, and took him up into a chamber until the sun had set. ⁵ Then I returned, washed myself, ate my bread in heaviness, ⁶ and remembered the prophecy of Amos, as he said, *"Your feasts will be turned into mourning, and all your mirth into lamentation." ⁷ So I wept: and when the sun had set, I went and dug a grave, and buried him. ⁸ My neighbors mocked me, and said, "He is no longer afraid to be put to death for this matter; and yet he fled away. Behold, he buries the dead again." ⁹ The same night I returned from burying him, and slept by the wall of my courtyard, being polluted; and my face was uncovered. ¹⁰ I didn't know that there were sparrows in the wall. My eyes were open and the sparrows dropped warm dung into my eyes, and white films came over my eyes. I went to the physicians, and they didn't help me; but Achiacharus nourished me, until I went[f] into Elymais. ¹¹ My wife Anna wove cloth in the women's chambers, ¹² and sent the work back to the owners. They on their part paid her wages, and also gave her a kid. ¹³ But when it came to my house, it began to cry, and I said to her, "Where did this kid come from? Is it stolen? Give it back to the owners; for it is not lawful to eat anything that is stolen." ¹⁴ But she said, "It has been given to me for a gift more than the wages." I didn't believe her, and I asked her to return it to the owners; and I was ashamed of her. But she answered and said to me, "Where are your alms and your righteous deeds? Behold, you and all your works are known.[g]"

3

¹ I was grieved and wept, and prayed in sorrow, saying, ²"O Lord, you are righteous, and all your works and all your ways are mercy and truth, and you judge true and righteous judgment forever. ³ Remember me, and look at me. Don't take vengeance on me for my sins and my ignorances, and the sins of my fathers who sinned before you. ⁴ For they disobeyed your commandments. You gave us as plunder, for captivity, for death, and for a proverb of reproach to all the nations among whom we are dispersed. ⁵ Now your judgments are many and true, that you should deal with me according to my sins and the sins of my fathers, because we didn't keep your commandments, for we didn't walk in truth before you. ⁶ Now deal with me according to that which is pleasing in your sight. Command my spirit to be taken from me, that I may be released, and become earth. For it is more profitable for me to die rather than to live, because I have heard false reproaches, and there is much sorrow in me. Command that I be released from my distress, now, and go to the everlasting place. Don't turn your face away from me." ⁷ The same day it happened to Sarah the daughter of Raguel in Ecbatana of Media, that she also was reproached by her father's maidservants; ⁸ because that she had been given to seven husbands, and Asmodaeus the evil spirit[h] killed them, before they had lain with her. And they said to her, "Do you not know that you strangle your husbands? You have had already seven husbands, and you haven't borne the name of any one of them. ⁹ Why do you scourge us? If they are dead, go your ways with them. Let us never see either son or daughter from you." ¹⁰ When she heard these things, she was grieved exceedingly, so that she thought about hanging herself. Then she said, "I am the only daughter of my father. If I do this, it will be a reproach to him, and I will bring down his old age with sorrow to the grave.[i]" ¹¹ Then she prayed by the window, and said, "Blessed are you, O Lord my God, and blessed is your holy and honorable name forever! Let all your works praise you forever! ¹² And now, Lord, I have set my eyes and my face toward you. ¹³ Command that I be released from the earth, and that I no longer hear reproach. ¹⁴ You know, Lord, that I am pure from all sin with man, ¹⁵ and that I never polluted my name or the name of my father in the land of my captivity. I am the only daughter of my father, and he has no child that will be his heir, nor brother near him, nor son belonging to him, that I should keep myself for a wife to him. Seven husbands of mine are dead already. Why should I live? If it doesn't please you to kill me, command some regard to be had of me, and pity taken of me, and that I hear no more reproach." ¹⁶ The prayer of both was heard before the glory of the great God. ¹⁷ Raphael also was sent to heal them both, to scale away the white films from Tobit's eyes, and to give Sarah the daughter of Raguel for a wife to Tobias the son of Tobit; and to bind Asmodaeus the evil spirit[j]; because it belonged to Tobias that he should inherit her. At that very time, Tobit returned and entered into his house, and Sarah the daughter of Raguel came down from her upper chamber.

4

¹ In that day Tobit remembered the money which he had left in trust with Gabael in Rages of Media, ² and he said to himself, I have asked for death; why do I not call my son Tobias, that I may explain to him about the money before I die? ³ And he called him, and said, "My child, if I die, bury me. Don't despise your mother. Honor her all the days of your life, and do that which is pleasing to her, and don't grieve her. ⁴ Remember, my child, that she has seen many dangers for you, when you were in her womb. When she is dead, bury her by me in one grave. ⁵ My child, be mindful of the Lord our God all your days, and don't let your will be set to sin and to transgress his commandments: do righteousness all the days of your life, and don't follow the ways of unrighteousness. ⁶ For if you do what is true, your deeds will prosperously succeed for you, and for all those who do righteousness. ⁷ Give

---

[a] *1:2* That is, Shalmaneser. Compare **2 Kings 17:3, 23**.
[b] *1:13* Gr. beauty.
[c] *1:15* Gr. his highways were troubled.
[d] *1:17* Some ancient authorities read behind.
[e] *1:21* That is, Esar-haddon, and so in verse **22**.
* *2:6* Amos **8:10**
[f] *2:10* Some authorities read until he went.
[g] *2:14* Gr. all things are known with you.
[h] *3:8* Gr. demon.
[i] *3:10* Gr. Hades.
[j] *3:17* Gr. demon.

alms from your possessions. When you give alms, don't let your eye be envious. Don't turn away your face from any poor man, and the face of God won't be turned away from you. ⁸ As your possessions are, give alms of it according to your abundance. If you have little, don't be afraid to give alms according to that little; ⁹ for you lay up a good treasure for yourself against the day of necessity; ¹⁰ because alms-giving delivers from death, and doesn't allow you to come into darkness. ¹¹ Alms is a good gift in the sight of the Most High for all that give it. ¹² Beware, my child, of all fornication, and take first a wife of the seed of your fathers. Don't take a strange wife, who is not of your father's tribe; for we are the descendants of the prophets. Remember, my child, that Noah, Abraham, Isaac, and Jacob, our fathers of old time, all took wives of their kindred, and were blessed in their children, and their seed will inherit the land. ¹³ And now, my child, love your kindred, and don't scorn your kindred and the sons and the daughters of your people in your heart, to take a wife of them; for in scornfulness is destruction and much trouble, and in idleness is decay and great lack; for idleness is the mother of famine. ¹⁴ Don't let the wages of any man who works for you wait with you, but give it to him out of hand. If you serve God, you will be rewarded. Take heed to yourself, my child, in all your works, and be discreet in all your behavior. ¹⁵ And what you yourself hate, do to no man. Don't drink wine to drunkenness, and don't let drunkenness go with you on your way. ¹⁶ Give of your bread to the hungry, and of your garments to those who are naked. Give alms from all your abundance. Don't let your eye be envious when you give alms. ¹⁷ Pour out your bread on the burial[a] of the just, and give nothing to sinners. ¹⁸ Ask counsel of every man who is wise, and don't despise any counsel that is profitable. ¹⁹ Bless the Lord your God at all times, and ask of him that your ways may be made straight, and that all your paths and counsels may prosper; for every nation has no counsel; but the Lord himself gives all good things, and he humbles whom he will, as he will. And now, my child, remember my commandments, and let them not be blotted out of your mind. ²⁰ And now I explain to you about the ten talents of silver, which I left in trust with Gabael the son of Gabrias at Rages of Media. ²¹ And fear not, my child, because we are made poor. You have much wealth, if you fear God, and depart from all sin, and do that which is pleasing in his sight."

5

¹ Then Tobias answered and said to him, "Father, I will do all things, whatever you have commanded me. ² But how could I receive the money, since I don't know him?" ³ He gave him the handwriting, and said to him, "Seek a man who will go with you, and I will give him wages, while I still live; and go and receive the money." ⁴ He went to seek a man, and found Raphael who was an angel; ⁵ and he didn't know it. He said to him, "Can I go with you to Rages of Media? Do you know those places well?" ⁶ The angel said to him, "I will go with you. I know the way well. I have lodged with our brother Gabael." ⁷ Tobias said to him, "Wait for me, and I will tell my father." ⁸ He said to him, "Go, and don't wait." And he went in and said to his father, "Behold, I have found someone who will go with me." But he said, "Call him to me, that I may know of what tribe he is, and whether he be a trustworthy man to go with you." ⁹ So he called him, and he came in, and they saluted one another. ¹⁰ And Tobit said to him, "Brother, of what tribe and of what family are you? Tell me." ¹¹ He said to him, "Do you seek a tribe and a family, or a hired man which will go with your son?" And Tobit said to him, "I want to know, brother, your kindred and your name." ¹² And he said, "I am Azarias, the son of Ananias the great, of your kindred." ¹³ And he said to him, "Welcome, brother. Don't be angry with me, because I sought to know your tribe and family. You are my brother, of an honest and good lineage; for I knew Ananias and Jathan, the sons of Shemaiah the great, when we went together to Jerusalem to worship, and offered the firstborn, and the tenths of our increase; and they didn't go astray in the error of our kindred. My brother, you are of a great stock. ¹⁴ But tell me, what wages shall I give you? A drachma a day, and those things that be necessary for you, as to my son? ¹⁵ And moreover, if you both return safe and sound, I will add something to your wages." ¹⁶ And so they agreed. And he said to Tobias, "Prepare yourself for the journey. May God prosper you." So his son prepared what was needful for the journey, and his father said to him, "Go with this man; but God, who dwells in heaven, will prosper your journey. May his angel go with you." Then they both departed, and the young man's dog went with them. ¹⁷ But Anna his mother wept, and said to Tobit, "Why have you sent away our child? Isn't he the staff of our hand, in going in and out before us? ¹⁸ Don't be greedy to add money to money; but let it be as refuse compared to our child. ¹⁹ For what the Lord has given us to live is enough for us." ²⁰ Tobit said to her, "Don't worry, my sister. He will return safe and sound, and your eyes will see him. ²¹ For a good angel will go with him. His journey will be prospered, and he will return safe and sound." ²² So she stopped weeping.

6

¹ Now as they went on their journey, they came at evening to the river Tigris, and they lodged there. ² But the young man went down to wash himself, and a fish leaped out of the river, and would have swallowed up the young man. ³ But the angel said to him, "Grab the fish!" So the young man grabbed the fish, and hauled it up onto the land. ⁴ And the angel said to him, "Cut the fish open, and take the heart, the liver, and the bile, and keep them with you." ⁵ And the young man did as the angel commanded him; but they roasted the fish, and ate it. And they both went on their way, till they drew near to Ecbatana. ⁶ The young man said to the angel, "Brother Azarias, of what use is the heart, the liver, and the bile of the fish?" ⁷ He said to him, "About the heart and the liver: If a demon or an evil spirit troubles anyone, we must burn those and make smoke of them before the man or the woman, and the affliction will flee. ⁸ But as for the bile, it is good to anoint a man that has white films in his eyes, and he will be healed." ⁹ But when they drew near to Rages, ¹⁰ the angel said to the young man, "Brother, today we will lodge with Raguel. He is your kinsman. He has an only daughter named Sarah. I will speak about her, that she should be given to you for a wife. ¹¹ For her inheritance belongs to you, and you only are of her kindred. ¹² The maid is fair and wise. And now hear me, and I will speak to her father. When we return from Rages we will celebrate the marriage; for I know that Raguel may in no way marry her to another according to the law of Moses, or else he would be liable to death, because it belongs to you to take the inheritance, rather than any other." ¹³ Then the young man said to the angel, "Brother Azarias, I have heard that this maid has been given to seven men, and that they all perished in the bride-chamber. ¹⁴ Now I am the only son of my father, and I am afraid, lest I go in and die, even as those before me. For a demon loves her, which harms no man, but those which come to her. Now I fear lest I die, and bring my father's and my mother's life to the grave with sorrow because of me. They have no other son to bury them." ¹⁵ But the angel said to him, "Don't you remember the words which your father commanded you, that you should take a wife of your own kindred? Now hear me, brother; for she will be your wife. Don't worry about the demon; for this night she will be given you as wife. ¹⁶ And when[b] you come into the bride-chamber, you shall take the ashes of incense, and shall lay upon them some of the heart and liver of the fish, and shall make smoke with them. ¹⁷ The demon will smell it, and flee away, and never come again any more. But when you go near to her, both of you rise up, and cry to God who is merciful. He will save you, and have mercy on you. Don't be afraid, for she was prepared for you from the beginning; and you will save her, and she will go with you. And I suppose that you will have children with her." When Tobias heard these things, he loved her, and his soul was strongly joined to her.

7

¹ They came to Ecbatana, and arrived at the house of Raguel. But Sarah met them; and she greeted them, and they her. Then she brought them into the house. ² Raguel said to Edna his wife, "This young man really resembles Tobit my cousin!" ³ And Raguel asked them, "Where are you two from, kindred?" They said to him, "We are of the sons of Naphtali, who are captives in Nineveh." ⁴ He said to them, "Do you know Tobit our brother?" They said, "We know him." Then he said to them, "Is he in good health?" ⁵ They said, "He is both alive, and in good health." Tobias said, "He is my father." ⁶ And Raguel sprang up, and kissed him, wept, ⁷ blessed him, and said to him, "You are the son of an honest and good man." When he had heard that Tobit had lost his sight, he was grieved, and wept; ⁸ and Edna his wife and Sarah his daughter wept. They received them gladly; and they killed a ram of the flock, and served them meat. But Tobias said to Raphael, "Brother Azarias, speak of those things of which you talked about in the way, and let the matter be finished." ⁹ So he communicated the thing to Raguel. Raguel said to Tobias, "Eat, drink, and make merry: ¹⁰ for it belongs to you to take my child. However I will tell you the truth. ¹¹ I have given my child to seven men of our relatives, and whenever they came in to her, they died in the night. But for the present be merry." And Tobias said, "I will taste nothing here, until you all make a covenant and enter into that covenant with me." ¹² Raguel said, "Take her to yourself from now on according to custom. You are her relative, and she is yours. The merciful God will give all good success to you." ¹³ And he called his daughter Sarah, and took her by the hand, and gave her to be wife of Tobias, and said, "Behold, take her to yourself after the law of Moses, and lead her away to your father." And he blessed them. ¹⁴ He called Edna his wife, then took a book, wrote a contract, and sealed it. ¹⁵ Then they began to eat. ¹⁶ And

---

[a] 4:17 Or, tomb   [b] 6:16 Gr. if.

Raguel called his wife Edna, and said to her, "Sister, prepare the other chamber, and bring her in there." ¹⁷ She did as he asked her, and brought her in there. She wept, and she received the tears of her daughter, and said to her, ¹⁸"Be comforted, my child. May the Lord of heaven and earth give you favor[a] for this your sorrow. Be comforted, my daughter."

8

¹ When they had finished their supper, they brought Tobias in to her. ² But as he went, he remembered the words of Raphael, and took the ashes of the incense, and put the heart and the liver of the fish on them, and made smoke with them. ³ When the demon smelled that smell, it fled into the uppermost parts of Egypt, and the angel bound him. ⁴ But after they were both shut in together, Tobias rose up from the bed, and said, "Sister, arise, and let's pray that the Lord may have mercy on us." ⁵ And Tobias began to say, "Blessed are you, O God of our fathers, and blessed is your holy and glorious name forever. Let the heavens bless you, and all your creatures. ⁶ You made Adam, and gave him Eve his wife for a helper and support. From them came the seed of men. You said, it is not good that the man should be alone. Let's make him a helper like him. ⁷ And now, O Lord, I take not this my sister for lust, but in truth. Command that I may find mercy and grow old with her." ⁸ She said with him, "Amen." And they both slept that night. ⁹ Raguel arose, and went and dug a grave, ¹⁰ saying, "Lest he also should die." ¹¹ And Raguel came into his house, ¹² and said to Edna his wife, "Send one of the maidservants, and let them see if he is alive. If not, we will bury him, and no man will know it." ¹³ So the maidservant opened the door, and went in, and found them both sleeping, ¹⁴ and came out, and told them that he was alive. ¹⁵ Then Raguel blessed God, saying, "Blessed are you, O God, with all pure and holy blessing! Let your saints bless you, and all your creatures! Let all your angels and your elect bless you forever! ¹⁶ Blessed are you, because you have made me glad; and it has not happened to me as I suspected; but you have dealt with us according to your great mercy. ¹⁷ Blessed are you, because you have had mercy on two that were the only begotten children of their parents. Show them mercy, O Lord. Fulfill their life in health with gladness and mercy. ¹⁸ He commanded his servants to fill the grave. ¹⁹ He kept the wedding feast for them fourteen days. ²⁰ Before the days of the wedding feast were finished, Raguel sware to him, that he should not depart till the fourteen days of the wedding feast were fulfilled; ²¹ and that then he should take half of his goods, and go in safety to his father; and the rest, said he, when my wife and I die.

9

¹ And Tobias called Raphael, and said to him, ²"Brother Azarias, take with you a servant and two camels, and go to Rages of Media to Gabael, and receive the money for me, and bring him to the wedding feast, ³ because Raguel has sworn that I must not depart. ⁴ My father counts the days; and if I wait long, he will be very grieved. ⁵ So Raphael went on his way, and lodged with Gabael, and gave him the handwriting; so he brought forth the bags with their seals, and gave them to him. ⁶ Then they rose up early in the morning together, and came to the wedding feast. Tobias blessed his wife.

10

¹ Tobit his father counted every day. When the days of the journey were expired, and they didn't come, ² he said, "Is he perchance detained?[b] Or is Gabael perchance dead, and there is no one to give him the money?" ³ He was very grieved. ⁴ But his wife said to him, "The child has perished, seeing he waits long." She began to bewail him, and said, ⁵"I care about nothing,[c] my child, since I have let you go, the light of my eyes." ⁶ Tobit said to her, "Hold your peace. Don't worry. He is in good health." ⁷ And she said to him, "Hold your peace. Don't deceive me. My child has perished." And she went out every day into the way by which they went, and ate no bread in the day-time, and didn't stop bewailing her son Tobias for whole nights, until the fourteen days of the wedding feast were expired, which Raguel had sworn that he should spend there. Then Tobias said to Raguel, "Send me away, for my father and my mother look no more to see me." ⁸ But his father-in-law said to him, "Stay with me, and I will send to your father, and they will declare to him how things go with you." ⁹ Tobias said, "No. Send me away to my father." ¹⁰ Raguel arose, and gave him Sarah his wife, and half his goods, servants and cattle and money; ¹¹ and he blessed them, and sent them away, saying, "The God of heaven will prosper you, my children, before I die." ¹² And he said to his daughter, "Honor your father-in-law and your mother-in-law. They are now your parents. Let me hear a good report of you." Then he kissed her. Edna said to Tobias, "May the Lord of heaven restore you, dear brother, and grant to me that I may see your children of my daughter Sarah, that I may rejoice before the Lord. Behold, I commit my daughter to you in special trust. Don't cause her grief.

11

¹ After these things Tobias also went his way, blessing God because he had prospered his journey; and he blessed Raguel and Edna his wife. Then he went on his way until they drew near to Nineveh. ² Raphael said to Tobias, "Don't you know, brother, how you left your father? ³ Let's run forward before your wife, and prepare the house. ⁴ But take in your hand the bile of the fish." So they went their way, and the dog went after them. ⁵ Anna sat looking around toward the path for her son. ⁶ She saw him coming, and said to his father, "Behold, your son is coming with the man that went with him!" ⁷ Raphael said, "I know, Tobias, that your father will open his eyes. ⁸ Therefore anoint his eyes with the bile, and being pricked with it, he will rub, and will make the white films fall away. Then he will see you." ⁹ Anna ran to him, and fell upon the neck of her son, and said to him, "I have seen you, my child! I am ready to die." They both wept. ¹⁰ Tobit rose toward the door and stumbled; but his son ran to him, ¹¹ and took hold of his father. He rubbed the bile on his father's eyes, saying, "Cheer up, my father." ¹² When his eyes began to hurt, he rubbed them. ¹³ Then the white films peeled away from the corners of his eyes; and he saw his son, and fell upon his neck. ¹⁴ He wept, and said, "Blessed are you, O God, and blessed is your name forever! Blessed are all your holy angels! ¹⁵ For you scourged, and had mercy on me. Behold, I see my son Tobias." And his son went in rejoicing, and told his father the great things that had happened to him in Media. ¹⁶ Tobit went out to meet his daughter-in-law at the gate of Nineveh, rejoicing and blessing God. Those who saw him go marveled, because he had received his sight. ¹⁷ Tobit gave thanks before them, because God had shown mercy on him. When Tobit came near to Sarah his daughter-in-law, he blessed her, saying, "Welcome, daughter! Blessed is God who has brought you to us, and blessed are your father and your mother." And there was joy among all his kindred who were at Nineveh. ¹⁸ Achiacharus and Nasbas his brother's son came. ¹⁹ Tobias' wedding feast was kept seven days with great gladness.

12

¹ And Tobit called his son Tobias, and said to him, "See, my child, that the man which went with you have his wages, and you must give him more." ² And he said to him, "Father, it is no harm to me to give him the half of those things which I have brought; ³ for he has led me for you in safety, and he cured my wife, and brought my money, and likewise cured you." ⁴ The old man said, "It is due to him." ⁵ And he called the angel, and said to him, "Take half of all that you have brought." ⁶ Then he called them both privately, and said to them, "Bless God, and give him thanks, and magnify him, and give him thanks in the sight of all that live, for the things which he has done with you. It is good to bless God and exalt his name, showing forth with honor the works of God. Don't be slack to give him thanks. ⁷ It is good to conceal the secret of a king, but to reveal gloriously the works of God. Do good, and evil won't find you. ⁸ Good is prayer with fasting, alms, and righteousness. A little with righteousness is better than much with unrighteousness. It is better to give alms than to lay up gold. ⁹ Alms delivers from death, and it purges away all sin. Those who give alms and do righteousness will be filled with life; ¹⁰ but those who sin are enemies to their own life. ¹¹ Surely I will conceal nothing from you. I have said, 'It is good to conceal the secret of a king, but to reveal gloriously the works of God.' ¹² And now, when you prayed, and Sarah your daughter-in-law, I brought the memorial of your prayer before the Holy One. When you buried the dead, I was with you likewise. ¹³ And when you didn't delay to rise up, and leave your dinner, that you might go and cover the dead, your good deed was not hidden from me. I was with you. ¹⁴ And now God sent me to heal you and Sarah your daughter-in-law. ¹⁵ I am Raphael, one of the seven holy angels which present the prayers of the saints and go in before the glory of the Holy One." ¹⁶ And they were both troubled, and fell upon their faces; for they were afraid. ¹⁷ And he said to them, "Don't be afraid. You will all have peace; but bless God forever. ¹⁸ For I came not of any favor of my own, but by the will of your God. Therefore bless him forever. ¹⁹ All these days I appeared to you. I didn't eat or drink, but you all saw a vision. ²⁰ Now give God thanks, because I ascend to him who sent me. Write in a book all the things which have been done." ²¹ Then they rose up, and saw him no more. ²² They confessed the great and wonderful works of God, and how the angel of the Lord had appeared to them.

---

[a] *7:18* Many ancient authorities read joy.

[b] *10:2* Many ancient authorities read "Are they perchance put to shame?"

[c] *10:5* Some authorities read "Woe is me."

13

¹ And Tobit wrote a prayer for rejoicing, and said, "Blessed is God who lives forever! Blessed is his kingdom! ² For he scourges, and shows mercy. He leads down to the grave,[a] and brings up again. There is no one who will escape his hand. ³ Give thanks to him before the Gentiles, all you children of Israel! For he has scattered us among them. ⁴ Declare his greatness, there. Extol him before all the living, because he is our Lord, and God is our Father forever. ⁵ He will scourge us for our iniquities, and will again show mercy, and will gather us out of all the nations among whom you are all scattered. ⁶ If you turn to him with your whole heart and with your whole soul, to do truth before him, then he will turn to you, and won't hide his face from you. See what he will do with you. Give him thanks with your whole mouth. Bless the Lord of righteousness. Exalt the everlasting King. I give him thanks in the land of my captivity, and show his strength and majesty to a nation of sinners. Turn, you sinners, and do righteousness before him. Who can tell if he will accept you and have mercy on you? ⁷ I exalt my God. My soul exalts the King of heaven, and rejoices in his greatness. ⁸ Let all men speak, and let them give him thanks in Jerusalem. ⁹ O Jerusalem, the holy city, he will scourge you for the works of your sons, and will again have mercy on the sons of the righteous. ¹⁰ Give thanks to the Lord with goodness, and bless the everlasting King, that his tabernacle may be built in you again with joy, and that he may make glad in you those who are captives, and love in you forever those who are miserable. ¹¹ Many nations will come from afar to the name of the Lord God with gifts in their hands, even gifts to the King of heaven. Generations of generations will praise you, and sing songs of rejoicing. ¹² All those who hate you are cursed. All those who love you forever will be blessed. ¹³ Rejoice and be exceedingly glad for the sons of the righteous; for they will be gathered together and will bless the Lord of the righteous. ¹⁴ Oh blessed are those who love you. They will rejoice for your peace. Blessed are all those who mourned for all your scourges; because they will rejoice for you when they have seen all your glory. They will be made glad forever. ¹⁵ Let my soul bless God the great King. ¹⁶ For Jerusalem will be built with sapphires, emeralds, and precious stones; your walls and towers and battlements with pure gold. ¹⁷ The streets of Jerusalem will be paved with beryl, carbuncle, and stones of Ophir. ¹⁸ All her streets will say, "Hallelujah!" and give praise, saying, "Blessed be God, who has exalted you forever!"

14

¹ Then Tobit finished giving thanks. ² He was fifty-eight years old when he lost his sight. After eight years, he received it again. He gave alms and he feared the Lord God more and more, and gave thanks to him. ³ Now he grew very old; and he called his son with the six sons of his son, and said to him, "My child, take your sons. Behold, I have grown old, and am ready to depart out of this life. ⁴ Go into Media, my child, for I surely believe all the things which Jonah the prophet spoke of Nineveh, that it will be overthrown, but in Media there will rather be peace for a season. Our kindred will be scattered in the earth from the good land. Jerusalem will be desolate, and the house of God in it will be burned up, and will be desolate for a time. ⁵ God will again have mercy on them, and bring them back into the land, and they will build the house, but not like to the former house, until the times of that age are fulfilled. Afterward they will return from the places of their captivity, and build up Jerusalem with honor. The house of God will be built in it forever with a glorious building, even as the prophets spoke concerning it. ⁶ And all the nations will turn to fear the Lord God truly, and will bury their idols. ⁷ All the nations will bless the Lord, and his people will give thanks to God, and the Lord will exalt his people; and all those who love the Lord God in truth and righteousness will rejoice, showing mercy to our kindred. ⁸ And now, my child, depart from Nineveh, because those things which the prophet Jonah spoke will surely come to pass. ⁹ But you must keep the law and the ordinances, and show yourself merciful and righteous, that it may be well with you. ¹⁰ Bury me decently, and your mother with me. Don't stay at Nineveh. See, my child, what Aman did to Achiacharus who nourished him, how out of light he brought him into darkness, and all the recompense that he made him. Achiacharus was saved, but the other had his recompense, and he went down into darkness. Manasses gave alms, and escaped the snare of death which he set for him; but Aman fell into the snare, and perished. ¹¹ And now, my children, consider what alms does, and how righteousness delivers." While he was saying these things, he gave up the ghost in the bed; but he was one hundred fifty eight years old. Tobias buried him magnificently. ¹² When Anna died, he buried her with his father. But Tobias departed with his wife and his sons to Ecbatana to Raguel his father-in-law, ¹³ and he grew old in honor, and he buried his father-in-law and mother-in-law magnificently, and he inherited their possessions, and his father Tobit's. ¹⁴ He died at Ecbatana of Media, being one hundred twenty seven years old. ¹⁵ Before he died, he heard of the destruction of Nineveh, which Nebuchadnezzar and Ahasuerus took captive. Before his death, he rejoiced over Nineveh.

---

[a] *13:2* Gr. Hades.

The Book of Judith

Judith is recognized as Deuterocanonical Scripture by the Roman Catholic, Greek Orthodox, and Russian Orthodox Churches.

1

[1] In the twelfth year of the reign of Nebuchadnezzar, who reigned over the Assyrians in Nineveh, the great city, in the days of Arphaxad, who reigned over the Medes in Ecbatana, [2] and built around Ecbatana walls of hewn stones three cubits broad and six cubits long, and made the height of the wall seventy cubits, and its breadth fifty cubits, [3] and set its towers at its gates one hundred cubits high, and its breadth in the foundation was sixty cubits, [4] and made its gates, even gates that were raised to the height of seventy cubits, and their breadth forty cubits, for his mighty army to go out of, and the setting in array of his footmen– [5] in those days King Nebuchadnezzar made war with King Arphaxad in the great plain. This plain is on the borders of Ragau. [6] There came to meet him all that lived in the hill country, and all that lived by Euphrates, Tigris, and Hydaspes, and in the plain of Arioch the king of the Elymaeans. Many nations of the sons of Chelod assembled themselves to the battle. [7] And Nebuchadnezzar king of the Assyrians sent to all who lived in Persia, and to all who lived westward, to those who lived in Cilicia, Damascus, Libanus, Antilibanus, and to all who lived along the sea coast, [8] and to those among the nations that were of Carmel and Gilead, and to the higher Galilee and the great plain of Esdraelon, [9] and to all who were in Samaria and its cities, and beyond Jordan to Jerusalem, Betane, Chellus, Kadesh, the river of Egypt, Tahpanhes, Rameses, and all the land of Goshen, [10] until you come above Tanis and Memphis, and to all that lived in Egypt, until you come to the borders of Ethiopia. [11] All those who lived in all the land made light of the commandment of Nebuchadnezzar king of the Assyrians, and didn't go with him to the war; for they were not afraid of him, but he was before them as one man. They turned away his messengers from their presence without effect, and with disgrace. [12] And Nebuchadnezzar was exceedingly angry with all this land, and he swore by his throne and kingdom that he would surely be avenged upon all the coasts of Cilicia, Damascus, and Syria, that he would kill with his sword all the inhabitants of the land of Moab, the children of Ammon, all Judea, and all who were in Egypt, until you come to the borders of the two seas. [13] And he set the battle in array with his army against King Arphaxad in the seventeenth year; and he prevailed in his battle, and turned to flight all the army of Arphaxad, with all his horses and all his chariots. [14] He took possession of his cities. He came to Ecbatana and took the towers, plundered its streets, and turned its beauty into shame. [15] He took Arphaxad in the mountains of Ragau, struck him through with his darts, and utterly destroyed him to this day. [16] He returned with them to Nineveh, he and all his company of sundry nations–an exceedingly great multitude of men of war. There he took his ease and banqueted, he and his army, for one hundred twenty days.

2

[1] In the eighteenth year, the twenty-second day of the first month, there was talk in the house of Nebuchadnezzar king of the Assyrians that he should be avenged on all the land, even as he spoke. [2] He called together all his servants and all his great men, and communicated with them his secret counsel, and with his own mouth, recounted the wickedness of all the land. [3] They decreed to destroy all flesh which didn't follow the word of his mouth. [4] It came to pass, when he had ended his counsel, Nebuchadnezzar king of the Assyrians called Holofernes the chief captain of his army, who was second to himself, and said to him, [5] "The great king, the lord of all the earth, says: 'Behold, you shall go out from my presence, and take with you men who trust in their strength, to one hundred twenty thousand footmen and twelve thousand horses with their riders. [6] And you shall go out against all the west country, because they disobeyed the commandment of my mouth. [7] You shall declare to them that they should prepare earth and water, because I will go out in my wrath against them, and will cover the whole face of the earth with the feet of my army, who will plunder them. [8] Their slain will fill their valleys and brooks, and the river will be filled with their dead until it overflows. [9] I will lead them as captives to the utmost parts of all the earth. [10] But you shall go forth, and take all their coasts for me first. If they will yield themselves to you,[a] then you must reserve them for me until the day of their reproof. [11] As for those who resist, your eye shall not spare; but you shall give them up to be slain and to be plundered in all your land. [12] For as I live, and by the power of my kingdom, I have spoken, and I will do this with my hand. [13] Moreover, you shall not transgress anything of the commandments of your lord, but you shall surely accomplish them, as I have commanded you. You shall not defer to do them.'" [14] So Holofernes went out from the presence of his lord, and called all the governors, the captains, and officers of the army of Asshur. [15] He counted chosen men for the battle, as his lord had commanded him, to one hundred twenty thousand, with twelve thousand archers on horseback. [16] He arranged them as a great multitude is ordered for the war. [17] He took camels, donkeys, and mules for their baggage, an exceedingly great multitude, and sheep, oxen, and goats without number for their provision, [18] and a large supply of rations for every man, and a huge amount of gold and silver out of the king's house. [19] He went out, he and all his army, on their journey, to go before King Nebuchadnezzar, and to cover all the face of the earth westward with their chariots, horsemen, and chosen footmen. [20] A great company of various nations went out with them like locusts and like the sand of the earth. For they could not be counted by reason of their multitude. [21] And they departed out of Nineveh three days' journey toward the plain of Bectileth, and encamped from Bectileth near the mountain which is at the left hand of the Upper Cilicia. [22] And he took all his army, his footmen, horsemen, and chariots, and went away from there into the hill country, [23] and destroyed Put and Lud, and plundered all the children of Rasses and the children of Ishmael, which were along the wilderness to the south of the land of the Chellians. [24] And he went over Euphrates, and went through Mesopotamia, and broke down all the high cities that were upon the river Arbonai, until you come to the sea. [25] And he took possession of the borders of Cilicia, and killed all who resisted him, and came to the borders of Japheth, which were toward the south, opposite Arabia. [26] He surrounded all the children of Midian, and set their tents on fire, and plundered their sheepfolds. [27] He went down into the plain of Damascus in the days of wheat harvest, and set all their fields on fire, and utterly destroyed their flocks and herds, plundered their cities, laid their plains waste, and struck all their young men with the edge of the sword. [28] And the fear and the dread of him fell upon those who lived on the sea coast, upon those who were in Sidon and Tyre, those who lived in Sur and Ocina, and all who lived in Jemnaan. Those who lived in Azotus and Ascalon feared him exceedingly.

3

[1] And they sent to him messengers with words of peace, saying, [2] "Behold, we the servants of Nebuchadnezzar the great king lie before you. Use us as it is pleasing in your sight. [3] Behold, our dwellings, and all our country, and all our fields of wheat, and our flocks and herds, and all the sheepfolds of our tents, lie before your face. Use them as it may please you. [4] Behold, even our cities and those who dwell in them are your servants. Come and deal with them as it is good in your eyes." [5] So the men came to Holofernes, and declared to him according to these words. [6] He came down toward the sea coast, he and his army, and set garrisons in the high cities, and took out of them chosen men for allies. [7] They received him, they and all the country round about them, with garlands and dances and timbrels. [8] He cast down all their borders, and cut down their sacred groves. It had been given to him to destroy all the gods of the land, that all the nations would worship Nebuchadnezzar only, and that all their tongues and their tribes would call upon him as a god. [9] Then he came toward Esdraelon near to Dotaea, which is opposite the great ridge of Judea. [10] He encamped between Geba and Scythopolis. He was there a whole month, that he might gather together all the baggage of his army.

4

[1] The children of Israel who lived in Judea heard all that Holofernes the chief captain of Nebuchadnezzar king of the Assyrians had done to the nations, and how he had plundered all their temples and destroyed them utterly. [2] They were exceedingly afraid at his approach, and were troubled for Jerusalem and for the temple of the Lord their God; [3] because they had newly come up from the captivity, and all the people of Judea were recently gathered together; and the vessels, the altar, and the house were sanctified after being profaned. [4] And they sent into every coast of Samaria, to Konae, to Beth-horon, Belmaim, Jericho, to Choba, Aesora, and to the valley of Salem; [5] and they occupied beforehand all the tops of the high mountains, fortified the villages that were in them, and stored supplies for the provision of war, for their fields were newly reaped. [6] Joakim the high priest, who was in those days at Jerusalem, wrote to those who lived in Bethulia and Betomesthaim, which is opposite Esdraelon toward the plain that is near to Dothaim, [7] charging them to seize upon the ascents of the hill country; because by them was the entrance into Judea, and it was easy to stop them from approaching, inasmuch as the approach was narrow, with space for two men at the most. [8] And the children of Israel did as Joakim the high priest had commanded them, as did the senate of all the people of Israel, which was in session at Jerusalem. [9] And every man of Israel cried to God

---

[a] *2:10* Gr. they will yield...and you shall reserve.

with great earnestness, and with great earnestness they humbled their souls. ¹⁰ They, their wives, their children, their cattle, and every sojourner, hireling, and servant bought with their money put sackcloth on their loins. ¹¹ Every man and woman of Israel, including the little children and the inhabitants of Jerusalem, fell prostrate before the temple, cast ashes upon their heads, and spread out their sackcloth before the Lord. They put sackcloth around the altar. ¹² They cried to the God of Israel earnestly with one consent, that he would not give their children as prey, their wives as plunder, the cities of their inheritance to destruction, and the sanctuary to being profaned and being made a reproach, for the nations to rejoice at. ¹³ The Lord heard their voice, and looked at their affliction. The people continued fasting many days in all Judea and Jerusalem before the sanctuary of the Lord Almighty. ¹⁴ And Joakim the high priest, and all the priests who stood before the Lord, and those who ministered to the Lord, had their loins dressed in sackcloth and offered the continual burnt offering, the vows, and the free gifts of the people. ¹⁵ They had ashes on their turbans. They cried to the Lord with all their power, that he would look upon all the house of Israel for good.

5

¹ Holofernes, the chief captain of the army of Asshur, was told that the children of Israel had prepared for war, had shut up the passages of the hill country, had fortified all the tops of the high hills, and had set up barricades in the plains. ² Then he was exceedingly angry, and he called all the princes of Moab, the captains of Ammon, and all the governors of the sea coast, ³ and he said to them, "Tell me now, you sons of Canaan, who are these people who dwell in the hill country? What are the cities that they inhabit? How large is their army? Where is their power and their strength? What king is set over them, to be the leader of their army? ⁴ Why have they turned their backs, that they should not come and meet me, more than all who dwell in the west?" ⁵ Then Achior, the leader of all the children of Ammon, said to him, "Let my lord now hear a word from the mouth of your servant, and I will tell you the truth concerning these people who dwell in this hill country, near to the place where you dwell. No lie will come out of the mouth of your servant. ⁶ These people are descended from the Chaldeans. ⁷ They sojourned before this in Mesopotamia, because they didn't want to follow the gods of their fathers, which were in the land of the Chaldeans. ⁸ They departed from the way of their parents, and worshiped the God of heaven, the God whom they knew. Their parents cast them out from the face of their gods, and they fled into Mesopotamia and sojourned there many days. ⁹ Then their God commanded them to depart from the place where they sojourned, and to go into the land of Canaan. They lived there, and prospered with gold and silver, and with exceedingly much cattle. ¹⁰ Then they went down into Egypt, for a famine covered all the land of Canaan. They sojourned there until they had grown up. They became a great multitude there, so that one could not count the population of their nation. ¹¹ Then the king of Egypt rose up against them, and dealt subtly with them, and brought them low, making them labor in brick,ᵃ and made them slaves. ¹² They cried to their God, and he struck all the land of Egypt with incurable plagues; so the Egyptians cast them out of their sight. ¹³ God dried up the Red sea before them, ¹⁴ and brought them into the way of Sinai Kadesh-Barnea and they cast out all that lived in the wilderness. ¹⁵ They lived in the land of the Amorites, and they destroyed by their strength everyone in Heshbon. Passing over Jordan, they possessed all the hill country. ¹⁶ They cast out before them the Canaanite, the Perizzite, the Jebusite, the Shechemite, and all the Girgashites, and they lived in that country many days. ¹⁷ And while they didn't sin before their God, they prospered, because God who hates iniquity was with them. ¹⁸ But when they departed from the way which he appointed them, they were destroyed in many severe battles, and were led captives into a land that was not theirs. The temple of their God was razed to the ground, and their cities were taken by their adversaries. ¹⁹ And now they have returned to their God, and have come up from the dispersion where they were dispersed, and have possessed Jerusalem, where their sanctuary is, and are settled in the hill country; for it was desolate. ²⁰ And now, my lord and master, if there is any error in this people, and they sin against their God, we will find out what this thing is in which they stumble, and we will go up and overcome them. ²¹ But if there is no lawlessness in their nation, let my lord now pass by, lest their Lord defend them, and their God be for them, and we will be a reproach before all the earth." ²² It came to pass, when Achior had finished speaking these words, all the people standing around the tent complained. The great men of Holofernes, and all who lived by the sea side and in Moab, said that he should be cut to pieces. ²³ For, they said, "We will not be afraid of the children of Israel, because, behold, they are a people that has no power nor might to make the battle strong. ²⁴ Therefore now we will go up, and they will be a prey to be devoured by all your army, Lord Holofernes."

6

¹ And when the disturbance of the men that were around the council had ceased, Holofernes the chief captain of the army of Asshur said to Achior and to all the children of Moab,ᵇ before all the people of the foreigners: ² "And who are you, Achior, and the mercenaries of Ephraim,ᶜ that you have prophesied among us as today, and have said that we should not make war with the race of Israel, because their God will defend them? And who is God but Nebuchadnezzar? ³ He will send forth his might, and will destroy them from the face of the earth, and their God will not deliver them; but we his servants will strike them as one man. They will not sustain the might of our cavalry. ⁴ For with them we will burn them up. Their mountains will be drunken with their blood. Their plains will be filled with their dead bodies. Their footsteps will not stand before us, but they will surely perish, says King Nebuchadnezzar, lord of all the earth; for he said, 'The words that I have spokenᵈ will not be in vain.' ⁵ But you, Achior, hireling of Ammon, who have spoken these words in the day of your iniquity, will see my face no more from this day, until I am avenged of the race of those that came out of Egypt. ⁶ And then the sword of my army, and the multitude of those who serve me, will pass through your sides, and you will fall among their slain when I return. ⁷ Then my servants will bring you back into the hill country, and will set you in one of the cities by the passes. ⁸ You will not perish until you are destroyed with them. ⁹ And if you hope in your heart that they will not be taken, don't let your countenance fall. I have spoken it, and none of my words will fall to the ground." ¹⁰ Then Holofernes commanded his servants who waited in his tent to take Achior, and bring him back to Bethulia, and deliver him into the hands of the children of Israel. ¹¹ So his servants took him, and brought him out of the camp into the plain, and they moved from the midst of the plains into the hill country, and came to the springs that were under Bethulia. ¹² When the men of the city saw them on the top of the hill, they took up their weapons, and went out of the city against them to the top of the hill. Every man that used a sling kept them from coming up, and threw stones at them. ¹³ They took cover under the hill, bound Achior, cast him down, left him at the foot of the hill, and went away to their lord. ¹⁴ But the children of Israel descended from their city, and came to him, untied him, led him away into Bethulia, and presented him to the rulers of their city, ¹⁵ which were in those days Ozias the son of Micah, of the tribe of Simeon, and Chabris the son of Gothoniel, and Charmis the son of Melchiel. ¹⁶ Then they called together all the elders of the city; and all their young men ran together, with their women, to the assembly. They set Achior in the midst of all their people. Then Ozias asked him what had happened. ¹⁷ He answered and declared to them the words of the council of Holofernes, and all the words that he had spoken in the midst of the princes of the children of Asshur, and all the great words that Holofernes had spoken against the house of Israel. ¹⁸ Then the people fell down and worshiped God, and cried, saying, ¹⁹ "O Lord God of heaven, behold their arrogance, and pity the low estate of our race. Look upon the face of those who are sanctified to you this day." ²⁰ They comforted Achior, and praised him exceedingly. ²¹ Then Ozias took him out of the assembly into his house, and made a feast for the elders. They called on the God of Israel for help all that night.

7

¹ The next day Holofernes commanded all his army and all the people who had come to be his allies, that they should move their camp toward Bethulia, seize the passes of the hill country, and make war against the children of Israel. ² Every mighty man of them moved that day. The army of their men of war was one hundred seventy thousand footmen, plus twelve thousand horsemen, besides the baggage and the men who were on foot among them— an exceedingly great multitude. ³ They encamped in the valley near Bethulia, by the fountain. They spread themselves in breadth over Dothaim even to Belmaim, and in length from Bethulia to Cyamon, which is near Esdraelon. ⁴ But the children of Israel, when they saw the multitude of them, were terrified, and everyone said to his neighbor, "Now these men will lick up the face of all the earth. Neither the high mountains, nor the valleys, nor the hills will be able to bear their weight. ⁵ Every man took up his weapons of war, and when they had kindled fires upon their towers, they remained and watched all that night. ⁶ But on the second day Holofernes led out all his cavalry in the sight of the children of Israel which were in Bethulia, ⁷ viewed the ascents to their city, and searched out the springs of the waters,

---

ᵃ *5:11* Some authorities read and he brought them low with clay and brick, etc.

ᵇ *6:1* Some authorities read Ammon. Compare ver. **5**.

ᶜ *6:2* Some authorities read Ammon. Compare ver. **5**.

ᵈ *6:4* Gr. he has spoken.

seized upon them, and set garrisons of men of war over them. Then he departed back to his people. **8** All the rulers of the children of Esau, all the leaders of the people of Moab, and the captains of the sea coast came to him and said, **9** "Let our lord now hear a word, that there not be losses in your army. **10** For this people of the children of Israel do not trust in their spears, but in the height of the mountains wherein they dwell, for it is not easy to come up to the tops of their mountains. **11** And now, my lord, don't fight against them as men fight who join battle, and there will not so much as one man of your people perish. **12** Remain in your camp, and keep every man of your army safe. Let your servants get possession of the water spring, which flows from the foot of the mountain, **13** because all the inhabitants of Bethulia get their water from there. Then thirst will kill them, and they will give up their city. Then we and our people will go up to the tops of the mountains that are near, and will camp upon them, to watch that not one man gets out of the city. **14** They will be consumed with famine–they, their wives, and their children. Before the sword comes against them they will be laid low in the streets where they dwell. **15** And you will pay them back with evil, because they rebelled, and didn't meet your face in peace." **16** Their words were pleasing in the sight of Holofernes and in the sight of all his servants; and he ordered them to do as they had spoken. **17** And the army of the children of Ammon moved, and with them five thousand of the children of Asshur, and they encamped in the valley. They seized the waters and the springs of the waters of the children of Israel. **18** The children of Esau went up with the children of Ammon, and encamped in the hill country near Dothaim. They sent some of them toward the south, and toward the east, near Ekrebel, which is near Chusi, that is upon the brook Mochmur. The rest of the army of the Assyrians encamped in the plain, and covered all the face of the land. Their tents and baggage were pitched upon it in a great crowd. They were an exceedingly great multitude. **19** The children of Israel cried to the Lord their God, for their spirit fainted; for all their enemies had surrounded them. There was no way to escape out from among them. **20** All the army of Asshur remained around them, their footmen and their chariots and their horsemen, for thirty-four days. All their vessels of water ran dry for all the inhabitants of Bethulia. **21** The cisterns were emptied, and they had no water to drink their fill for one day; for they rationed drink by measure. **22** Their young children were discouraged. The women and the young men fainted for thirst. They fell down in the streets of the city, and in the passages of the gates. There was no longer any strength in them. **23** All the people, including the young men, the women, and the children, were gathered together against Ozias, and against the rulers of the city. They cried with a loud voice, and said before all the elders, **24** "God be judge between all of you and us, because you have done us great wrong, in that you have not spoken words of peace with the children of Asshur. **25** Now we have no helper; but God has sold us into their hands, that we should be laid low before them with thirst and great destruction. **26** And now summon them, and deliver up the whole city as prey to the people of Holofernes, and to all his army. **27** For it is better for us to be captured by them. For we will be servants, and our souls will live, and we will not see the death of our babies before our eyes, and our wives and our children fainting in death. **28** We take to witness against you the heaven and the earth, and our God and the Lord of our fathers, who punishes us according to our sins and the sins of our fathers. Do what we have said today!" **29** And there was great weeping of all with one consent in the midst of the assembly; and they cried to the Lord God with a loud voice. **30** And Ozias said to them, "Brethren, be of good courage! Let us endure five more days, during which the Lord our God will turn his mercy toward us; for he will not forsake us utterly. **31** But if these days pass, and no help comes to us, I will do what you say." **32** Then he dispersed the people, every man to his own camp; and they went away to the walls and towers of their city. He sent the women and children into their houses. They were brought very low in the city.

8

1 In those days Judith heard about this. She was the daughter of Merari, the son of Ox, the son of Joseph, the son of Oziel, the son of Elkiah, the son of Ananias, the son of Gideon, the son of Raphaim, the son of Ahitub, the son of Elihu, the son of Eliab, the son of Nathanael, the son of Salamiel, the son of Salasadai, the son of Israel. **2** Her husband was Manasses, of her tribe and of her family. He died in the days of barley harvest. **3** For he stood over those who bound sheaves in the field, and was overcome by the burning heat, and he fell on his bed, and died in his city Bethulia. So they buried him with his fathers in the field which is between Dothaim and Balamon. **4** Judith was a widow in her house three years and four months. **5** She made herself a tent upon the roof of her house, and put on sackcloth upon her loins. The garments of her widowhood were upon her. **6** And she fasted all the days of her widowhood, except the eves of the Sabbaths, the Sabbaths, the eves of the new moons, the new moons, and the feasts and joyful days of the house of Israel. **7** She was beautiful in appearance, and lovely to behold. Her husband Manasses had left her gold, silver, menservants, maidservants, cattle, and lands. She remained on those lands. **8** No one said anything evil about her, for she feared God exceedingly. **9** She heard the evil words of the people against the governor, because they fainted for lack of water; and Judith heard all the words that Ozias spoke to them, how he swore to them that he would deliver the city to the Assyrians after five days. **10** So she sent her maid, who was over all things that she had, to summon Ozias, Chabris, and Charmis, the elders of her city. **11** They came to her, and she said to them, "Hear me now, O you rulers of the inhabitants of Bethulia! For your word that you have spoken before the people this day is not right. You have set the oath which you have pronounced between God and you, and have promised to deliver the city to our enemies, unless within these days the Lord turns to help you. **12** Now who are you that you have tested God this day, and stand in the place of God among the children of men? **13** Now try the Lord Almighty, and you will never know anything. **14** For you will not find the depth of the heart of man, and you will not perceive the things that he thinks. How will you search out God, who has made all these things, and know his mind, and comprehend his purpose? No, my kindred, don't provoke the Lord our God to anger! **15** For if he has not decided to help us within these five days, he has power to defend us in such time as he will, or to destroy us before the face of our enemies. **16** But don't you pledge the counsels of the Lord our God! For God is not like a human being, that he should be threatened, neither is he like a son of man, that he should be won over by pleading. **17** Therefore let's wait for the salvation that comes from him, and call upon him to help us. He will hear our voice, if it pleases him. **18** For there arose none in our age, neither is there any of us today, tribe, or kindred, or family, or city, which worship gods made with hands, as it was in the former days; **19** for which cause our fathers were given to the sword, and for plunder, and fell with a great destruction before our enemies. **20** But we know no other god beside him. Therefore we hope that he will not despise us, nor any of our race. **21** For if we are captured, all Judea will be captured and our sanctuary will be plundered; and he will require our blood for profaning it. **22** The slaughter of our kindred, the captivity of the land, and the desolation of our inheritance, he will bring on our heads among the Gentiles, wherever we will be in bondage. We will be an offense and a reproach to those who take us for a possession. **23** For our bondage will not be ordered to favor; but the Lord our God will turn it to dishonor. **24** And now, kindred, let's show an example to our kindred, because their soul depends on us, and the sanctuary, the house, and the altar depend on us. **25** Besides all this let's give thanks to the Lord our God, who tries us, even as he did our fathers also. **26** Remember all the things which he did to Abraham, and all the things in which he tried Isaac, and all the things which happened to Jacob in Mesopotamia of Syria, when he kept the sheep of Laban his mother's brother. **27** For he has not tried us in the fire, as he did them, to search out their hearts, neither has he taken vengeance on us; but the Lord scourges those who come near to him, to admonish them." **28** And Ozias said to her, "All that you have spoken, you have spoken with a good heart. There is no one who will deny your words. **29** For this is not the first day wherein your wisdom is manifested; but from the beginning of your days all the people have known your understanding, because the disposition of your heart is good. **30** But the people were exceedingly thirsty, and compelled us to do as we spoke to them, and to bring an oath upon ourselves, which we will not break. **31** And now pray for us, because you are a godly woman, and the Lord will send us rain to fill our cisterns, and we will faint no more." **32** Then Judith said to them, "Hear me, and I will do a thing, which will go down to all generations among the children of our race. **33** You shall all stand at the gate tonight. I will go out with my maid. Within the days after which you said that you would deliver the city to our enemies, the Lord will deliver Israel by my hand. **34** But you shall not inquire of my act; for I will not tell you until the things are finished that I will do." **35** Then Ozias and the rulers said to her, "Go in peace. May the Lord God be before you, to take vengeance on our enemies." **36** So they returned from the tent, and went to their stations.

9

1 But Judith fell upon her face, and put ashes upon her head, and uncovered the sackcloth with which she was clothed. The incense of that evening was now being offered at Jerusalem in the house of God, and Judith cried to the Lord with a loud voice, and said, **2** "O Lord God of my father Simeon, into whose hand you gave a sword to take vengeance on the strangers who loosened the belt of a virgin to defile her, uncovered her thigh to her shame, and profaned her womb to her reproach; for you said, 'It shall not be so;' and they did so. **3** Therefore you gave their rulers to be slain, and their bed, which was ashamed for her who was deceived,[a] to be dyed in blood, and struck the servants with their masters, and the masters upon their thrones; ⁴ and gave their wives for a prey, and their daughters to be captives, and all their spoils to be divided among your dear children; which were moved with zeal for you, and abhorred the pollution of their blood, and called upon you for aid. O God, O my God, hear me also who am a widow. ⁵ For you did the things that were before those things, and those things, and such as come after; and you planned the things which are now, and the things which are to come. The things which you planned came to pass. ⁶ Yes, the things which you determined stood before you, and said, 'Behold, we are here; for all your ways are prepared, and your judgment is with foreknowledge.' ⁷ For, behold, the Assyrians are multiplied in their power. They are exalted with horse and rider. They were proud of the strength of their footmen. They have trusted in shield, spear, bow, and sling. They don't know that you are the Lord who breaks the battles. 'The Lord' is your name. ⁸ Break their strength in your power, and bring down their force in your wrath; for they intend to profane your sanctuary, and to defile the tabernacle where your glorious name rests, and to destroy the horn of your altar with the sword. ⁹ Look at their pride, and send your wrath upon their heads. Give into my hand, which am a widow, the might that I have conceived. ¹⁰ Strike by the deceit of my lips the servant with the prince, and the prince with his servant. Break down their arrogance by the hand of a woman. ¹¹ For your power stands not in numbers, nor your might in strong men, but you are a God of the afflicted. You are a helper of the oppressed, a helper of the weak, a protector of the forsaken, a savior of those who are without hope. ¹² Please, please, God of my father, and God of the inheritance of Israel, Lord of the heavens and of the earth, Creator of the waters, King of all your creation, hear my prayer. ¹³ Make my speech and deceit to be their wound and bruise, who intend hard things against your covenant, your holy house, the top of Zion, and the house of the possession of your children. ¹⁴ Make every nation and tribe of yours to know that you are God, the God of all power and might, and that there is no other who protects the race of Israel but you."

10

¹ It came to pass, when she had ceased to cry to the God of Israel, and had finished saying all these words, ² that she rose up where she had fallen down, called her maid, and went down into the house that she lived on the Sabbath days and on her feast days. ³ She pulled off the sackcloth which she had put on, took off the garments of her widowhood, washed her body all over with water, anointed herself with rich ointment, braided the hair of her head, and put a tiara upon it. She put on her garments of gladness, which she used to wear in the days of the life of Manasses her husband. ⁴ She took sandals for her feet, and put on her anklet, bracelets, rings, earrings, and all her jewelry. She made herself very beautiful to deceive the eyes of all men who would see her. ⁵ She gave her maid a leather container of wine and a flask of oil, and filled a bag with roasted grain, lumps of figs, and fine bread. She packed all her vessels together, and laid them upon her. ⁶ They went out to the gate of the city of Bethulia, and found Ozias and the elders of the city, Chabris and Charmis standing by it. ⁷ But when they saw her, that her countenance was altered and her apparel was changed, they were greatly astonished by her beauty and said to her, ⁸"May the God of our fathers give you favor, and accomplish your purposes to the glory of the children of Israel, and to the exaltation of Jerusalem." Then she worshiped God, ⁹ and said to them, "Command that they open the gate of the city for me, and I will go out to accomplish the things you spoke with me about." And they commanded the young men to open to her, as she had spoken; ¹⁰ and they did so. Then Judith went out, she, and her handmaid with her. The men of the city watched her until she had gone down the mountain, until she had passed the valley, and they could see her no more. ¹¹ They went straight onward in the valley. The watch of the Assyrians met her; ¹² and they took her, and asked her, "Of what people are you? Where are you coming from? Where are you going?" She said, "I am a daughter of the Hebrews. I am fleeing away from their presence, because they are about to be given you to be consumed. ¹³ I am coming into the presence of Holofernes the chief captain of your army, to declare words of truth. I will show him a way that he can go and win all the hill country, and there will not be lacking of his men one person, nor one life." ¹⁴ Now when the men heard her words, and considered her countenance, the beauty thereof was exceedingly marvelous in their eyes. They said to her, ¹⁵"You have saved your life, in that you have hurried to come down to the presence of our master. Now come to his tent. Some of us will guide you until they deliver you into his hands. ¹⁶ But when[b] you stand before him, don't be afraid in your heart, but declare to him what you just said, and he will treat you well." ¹⁷ They chose out of them a hundred men, and appointed them to accompany her and her maid; and they brought them to the tent of Holofernes. ¹⁸ And there was great excitement throughout all the camp, for her coming was reported among the tents. They came and surrounded her as she stood outside Holofernes' tent, until they told him about her. ¹⁹ They marveled at her beauty, and marveled at the children of Israel because of her. Each one said to his neighbor, "Who would despise these people, who have among them such women? For it is not good that one man of them be left, seeing that, if they are let go, they will be able to deceive the whole earth. ²⁰ Then the guards of Holofernes and all his servants came out and brought her into the tent. ²¹ And Holofernes was resting upon his bed under the canopy, which was woven with purple, gold, emeralds, and precious stones. ²² And they told him about her; and he came out into the space before his tent, with silver lamps going before him. ²³ But when Judith had come before him and his servants, they all marveled at the beauty of her countenance. She fell down upon her face and bowed down to him, but his servants raised her up.

11

¹ Holofernes said to her, "Woman, take courage. Don't be afraid in your heart; for I never hurt anyone who has chosen to serve Nebuchadnezzar, the king of all the earth. ² And now, if your people who dwell in the hill country had not slighted me, I would not have lifted up my spear against them; but they have done these things to themselves. ³ And now tell me why you fled from them and came to us; for you have come to save yourself. Take courage! You will live tonight, and hereafter, ⁴ for there is no one that will wrong you, but all will treat you well, as is done to the servants of King Nebuchadnezzar my lord." ⁵ And Judith said to him, "Receive the words of your servant, and let your handmaid speak in your presence, and I won't lie to my lord tonight. ⁶ If you will follow the words of your handmaid, God will bring the thing to pass perfectly with you; and my lord will not fail to accomplish his purposes. ⁷ As Nebuchadnezzar king of all the earth lives, and as his power lives, who has sent you for the preservation of every living thing, not only do men serve him by you, but also the beasts of the field, the cattle, and the birds of the sky will live through your strength, in the time of Nebuchadnezzar and of all his house. ⁸ For we have heard of your wisdom and the subtle plans of your soul. It has been reported in all the earth that you only are brave in all the kingdom, mighty in knowledge, and wonderful in feats of war. ⁹ And now as concerning the matter which Achior spoke in your council, we have heard his words; for the men of Bethulia saved him, and he declared to them all that he had spoken before you. ¹⁰ Therefore, O lord and master, don't neglect his word, but lay it up in your heart, for it is true; for our race will not be punished, neither will the sword prevail against them, unless they sin against their God. ¹¹ And now, that my lord may not be defeated and frustrated in his purpose, and that death may fall upon them, their sin has overtaken them, wherewith they will provoke their God to anger, whenever they do wickedness. ¹² Since their food failed them, and all their water was scant, they took counsel to kill their livestock, and determined to consume all those things which God charged them by his laws that they should not eat. ¹³ They are resolved to spend the first fruits of the grain and the tithes of the wine and the oil, which they had sanctified and reserved for the priests who stand before the face of our God in Jerusalem, which it is not fitting for any of the people so much as to touch with their hands. ¹⁴ They have sent some to Jerusalem, because they also that dwell there have done this thing, to bring them permission from the council of elders. ¹⁵ When these instructions come to them and they do it, they will be given to you to be destroyed the same day. ¹⁶ Therefore I your servant, knowing all this, fled away from their presence. God sent me to work things with you, at which all the earth will be astonished, even as many as hear it. ¹⁷ For your servant is religious, and serves the God of heaven day and night. Now, my lord, I will stay with you; and your servant will go out by night into the valley. I will pray to God, and he will tell me when they have committed their sins. ¹⁸ Then I will come and tell you. Then you can go out with all your army, and there will be none of them that will resist you. ¹⁹ And I will lead you through the midst of Judea, until you come to Jerusalem. I will set your throne in the midst of it. You will drive them as sheep that have no shepherd, and a dog will not so much as open his mouth before you; for these things were told me according to my foreknowledge, and were declared to me, and I was sent to tell you." ²⁰ Her words were pleasing in the sight of Holofernes and of all his servants. They marveled at her wisdom, and said, ²¹"There is not such a woman from one end of the earth to the other, for beauty of face and wisdom of words." ²² Holofernes said to her, "God did well to send you before the people, that might would be in our hands, and destruction among those who slighted my

---

[a] *9:3* Some authorities read which was ashamed for their deceit that they practiced.

[b] *10:16* Gr. if.

lord. ²³ And now you are beautiful in your countenance, and wise in your words. If you will do as you have spoken, your God will be my God, and you will dwell in the palace of King Nebuchadnezzar, and will be renowned through the whole earth."

12

¹ He commanded that she should be brought in where his silver vessels were set, and asked that his servants should prepare some of his own delicacies for her, and that she should drink from his own wine. ² And Judith said, "I can't eat of it, lest there be an occasion of stumbling; but provision will be made for me from the things that have come with me." ³ And Holofernes said to her, "But if the things that are with you should run out, from where will we be able to give you more like it? For there is none of your race with us." ⁴ And Judith said to him, "As your soul lives, my lord, your servant will not use up those things that are with me until the Lord works by my hand the things that he has determined." ⁵ Then Holofernes' servants brought her into the tent, and she slept until midnight. Then she rose up toward the morning watch, ⁶ and sent to Holofernes, saying, "Let my lord now command that they allow your servant to go out to pray." ⁷ Holofernes commanded his guards that they should not stop her. She stayed in the camp three days, and went out every night into the valley of Bethulia and washed herself at the fountain of water in the camp. ⁸ And when she came up, she implored the Lord God of Israel to direct her way to the triumph of the children of his people. ⁹ She came in clean and remained in the tent until she ate her food toward evening. ¹⁰ It came to pass on the fourth day, that Holofernes made a feast for his own servants only, and called none of the officers to the banquet. ¹¹ And he said to Bagoas the eunuch, who had charge over all that he had, "Go now, and persuade this Hebrew woman who is with you that she come to us, and eat and drink with us. ¹² For behold, it would be a disgrace if we shall let such a woman go, not having had her company; for if we don't draw her to ourselves, she will laugh us to scorn." ¹³ Bagoas went from the presence of Holofernes, and came in to her, and said, "Let this fair lady not fear to come to my lord, and to be honored in his presence, and to drink wine and be merry with us, and to be made this day as one of the daughters of the children of Asshur who serve in Nebuchadnezzar's palace." ¹⁴ Judith said to him, "Who am I, that I should contradict my lord? For whatever would be pleasing in his eyes, I will do speedily, and this will be my joy to the day of my death." ¹⁵ She arose, and decked herself with her apparel and all her woman's attire; and her servant went and laid fleeces on the ground for her next to Holofernes, which she had received from Bagoas for her daily use, that she might sit and eat upon them. ¹⁶ Judith came in and sat down, and Holofernes' heart was ravished with her. His passion was aroused, and he exceedingly desired her company. He was watching for a time to deceive her from the day that he had seen her. ¹⁷ Holofernes said to her, "Drink now, and be merry with us." ¹⁸ Judith said, "I will drink now, my lord, because my life is magnified in me this day more than all the days since I was born." ¹⁹ Then she took and ate and drank before him what her servant had prepared. ²⁰ Holofernes took great delight in her, and drank exceedingly much wine, more than he had drunk at any time in one day since he was born.

13

¹ But when the evening had come, his servants hurried to depart. Bagoas shut the tent outside, and dismissed those who waited from the presence of his lord. They went away to their beds; for they were all weary, because the feast had been long. ² But Judith was left alone in the tent, with Holofernes lying along upon his bed; for he was drunk with wine. ³ Judith had said to her servant that she should stand outside her bedchamber, and wait for her to come out, as she did daily; for she said she would go out to her prayer. She spoke to Bagoas according to the same words. ⁴ All went away from her presence, and none was left in the bedchamber, small or great. Judith, standing by his bed, said in her heart, O Lord God of all power, look in this hour upon the works of my hands for the exaltation of Jerusalem. ⁵ For now is the time to help your inheritance, and to do the thing that I have purposed to the destruction of the enemies which have risen up against us. ⁶ She came to the bedpost which was at Holofernes' head, and took down his sword from there. ⁷ She drew near to the bed, took hold of the hair of his head, and said, "Strengthen me, O Lord God of Israel, this day." ⁸ She struck twice upon his neck with all her might and cut off his head, ⁹ tumbled his body down from the bed, and took down the canopy from the posts. After a little while she went out, and gave Holofernes' head to her maid; ¹⁰ and she put it in her bag of food. They both went out together to prayer, according to their custom. They passed through the camp, circled around that valley, and went up to the mountain of Bethulia, and came to its gates. ¹¹ Judith said afar off to the watchmen at the gates, "Open, open the gate, now. God is with us, even our God, to show his power yet in Israel, and his might against the enemy, as he has done even this day." ¹² It came to pass, when the men of her city heard her voice, they made haste to go down to the gate of their city, and they called together the elders of the city. ¹³ They all ran together, both small and great, for it seemed unbelievable to them that she had come. They opened the gate and received them, making a fire to give light, and surrounded them. ¹⁴ She said to them with a loud voice, "Praise God! Praise him! Praise God, who has not taken away his mercy from the house of Israel, but has destroyed our enemies by my hand tonight!" ¹⁵ Then she took the head out of the bag and showed it, and said to them, "Behold, the head of Holofernes, the chief captain of the army of Asshur, and behold, the canopy under which he laid in his drunkenness. The Lord struck him by the hand of a woman. ¹⁶ And as the Lord lives, who preserved me in my way that I went, my countenance deceived him to his destruction, and he didn't commit sin with me, to defile and shame me." ¹⁷ All the people were exceedingly amazed, and bowed themselves, and worshiped God, and said with one accord, "Blessed are you, O our God, who have this day humiliated the enemies of your people." ¹⁸ Ozias said to her, "Blessed are you, daughter, in the sight of the Most High God, above all the women upon the earth; and blessed is the Lord God, who created the heavens and the earth, who directed you to cut off the head of the prince of our enemies. ¹⁹ For your hope will not depart from the heart of men that remember the strength of God forever. ²⁰ May God turn these things to you for a perpetual praise, to visit you with good things, because you didn't spare your life by reason of the affliction of our race, but prevented our ruin, walking a straight way before our God." And all the people said, "Amen! Amen!"

14

¹ Judith said to them, "Hear me now, my kindred, and take this head, and hang it upon the battlement of your wall. ² It will be, so soon as the morning appears, and the sun comes up on the earth, you shall each take up his weapons of war, and every valiant man of you go out of the city. You shall set a captain over them, as though you would go down to the plain toward the watch of the children of Asshur; but you men shall not go down. ³ These will take up their full armor, and shall go into their camp and rouse up the captains of the army of Asshur. They will run together to Holofernes' tent. They won't find him. Fear will fall upon them, and they will flee before your face. ⁴ You men, and all that inhabit every border of Israel, shall pursue them and overthrow them as they go. ⁵ But before you do these things, summon Achior the Ammonite to me, that he may see and know him that despised the house of Israel, and that sent him to us, as it were to death. ⁶ And they called Achior out of the house of Ozias; but when he came, and saw the head of Holofernes in a man's hand in the assembly of the people, he fell upon his face, and his spirit failed. ⁷ But when they had recovered him,ᵃ he fell at Judith's feet, bowed down to her, and said, "Blessed are you in every tent of Judah! In every nation, those who hear your name will be troubled. ⁸ Now tell me all the things that you have done in these days." And Judith declared to him in the midst of the people all the things that she had done, from the day that she went out until the time that she spoke to them. ⁹ But when she finished speaking, the people shouted with a loud voice, and made a joyful noise in their city. ¹⁰ But when Achior saw all the things that the God of Israel had done, he believed in God exceedingly, and circumcised the flesh of his foreskin, and was joined to the house of Israel, to this day. ¹¹ But as soon as the morning arose, they hanged the head of Holofernes upon the wall, and every man took up his weapons, and they went forth by bands to the ascents of the mountain. ¹² But when the children of Asshur saw them, they sent word to their leaders, and they went to their captains and tribunes, and to every one of their rulers. ¹³ They came to Holofernes' tent, and said to him that was over all that he had, "Wake our lord up, now, for the slaves have been bold to come down against us to battle, that they may be utterly destroyed." ¹⁴ Bagoas went in, and knocked at the outer door of the tent; for he supposed that Holofernes was sleeping with Judith. ¹⁵ But when no one answered, he opened it, went into the bedchamber, and found him cast upon the threshold dead; and his head had been taken from him. ¹⁶ He cried with a loud voice, with weeping, groaning, and shouting, and tore his garments. ¹⁷ He entered into the tent where Judith lodged, and he didn't find her. He leaped out to the people, and cried aloud, ¹⁸"The slaves have dealt treacherously! One woman of the Hebrews has brought shame upon the house of King Nebuchadnezzar; for, behold, Holofernes lies upon the ground, and his head is not on him!" ¹⁹ But when the rulers of the army of Asshur heard this, they tore their tunics, and their souls were troubled exceedingly. There were cries and an exceedingly great noise in the midst of the camp.

ᵃ *14:7* Many authorities read he had recovered himself.

15

¹ When those who were in the tents heard, they were amazed at what happened. ² Trembling and fear fell upon them, and no man dared stay any more in the sight of his neighbor, but rushing out with one accord, they fled into every way of the plain and of the hill country. ³ Those who had encamped in the hill country round about Bethulia fled away. And then the children of Israel, every one who was a warrior among them, rushed out upon them. ⁴ Ozias sent to Betomasthaim, Bebai, Chobai, and Chola, and to every border of Israel, to tell about the things that had been accomplished, and that all should rush upon their enemies to destroy them. ⁵ But when the children of Israel heard this, they all fell upon them with one accord, and struck them to Chobai. Yes, and in like manner also, people from Jerusalem and from all the hill country came (for men had told them about what happened in their enemies' camp), and those who were in Gilead and in Galilee fell upon their flank with a great slaughter, until they were past Damascus and its borders. ⁶ The rest of the people who lived at Bethulia fell upon the camp of Asshur, and plundered them, and were enriched exceedingly. ⁷ The children of Israel returned from the slaughter, and got possession of that which remained. The villages and the cities that were in the hill country and in the plain country took many spoils; for there was an exceedingly great supply. ⁸ Joakim the high priest, and the elders of the children of Israel who lived in Jerusalem, came to see the good things which the Lord had showed to Israel, and to see Judith and to greet her. ⁹ When they came to her, they all blessed her with one accord, and said to her, "You are the exaltation of Jerusalem! You are the great glory of Israel! You are the great rejoicing of our race! ¹⁰ You have done all these things by your hand. You have done with Israel the things that are good, and God is pleased with it. May you be blessed by the Almighty Lord forever!" And all the people said, "Amen!" ¹¹ And the people plundered the camp for thirty days; and they gave Holofernes' tent to Judith, along with all his silver cups, his beds, his bowls, and all his furniture. She took them, placed them on her mule, prepared her wagons, and piled them on it. ¹² And all the women of Israel ran together to see her; and they blessed her, and made a dance among them for her. She took branches in her hand, and distributed them to the women who were with her.[a] ¹³ Then they made themselves garlands of olive, she and those who were with her, and she went before all the people in the dance, leading all the women. All the men of Israel followed in their armor with garlands, and with songs in their mouths.

16

¹ And Judith began to sing this song of thanksgiving in all Israel, and all the people sang with loud voices this song of praise. ² Judith said, "Begin a song to my God with timbrels. Sing to my Lord with cymbals. Make melody to him with psalm and praise. Exalt him, and call upon his name. ³ For the Lord is the God that crushes battles. For in his armies in the midst of the people, he delivered me out of the hand of those who persecuted me. ⁴ Asshur came out of the mountains from the north. He came with ten thousands of his army. Its multitude stopped the torrents. Their horsemen covered the hills. ⁵ He said that he would burn up my borders, kill my young men with the sword, throw my nursing children to the ground, give my infants up as prey, and make my virgins a plunder. ⁶ "The Almighty Lord brought them to nothing by the hand of a woman. ⁷ For their mighty one didn't fall by young men, neither did sons of the Titans strike him. Tall giants didn't attack him, but Judith the daughter of Merari made him weak with the beauty of her countenance. ⁸ "For she put off the apparel of her widowhood for the exaltation of those who were distressed in Israel. She anointed her face with ointment, bound her hair in a tiara, and took a linen garment to deceive him. ⁹ Her sandal ravished his eye. Her beauty took his soul prisoner. The sword passed through his neck. ¹⁰ "The Persians quaked at her daring. The Medes were daunted at her boldness. ¹¹ "Then my lowly ones shouted aloud. My oppressed people were terrified and trembled for fear. They lifted up their voices and the enemy fled. ¹² The children of slave-girls pierced them through, and wounded them as fugitives' children. They perished by the army of my Lord. ¹³ "I will sing to my God a new song: O Lord, you are great and glorious, marvelous in strength, invincible. ¹⁴ Let all your creation serve you; for you spoke, and they were made. You sent out your spirit, and it built them. There is no one who can resist your voice. ¹⁵ For the mountains will be moved from their foundations with the waters, and the rocks will melt as wax at your presence: But you are yet merciful to those who fear you. ¹⁶ For all sacrifice is little for a sweet savor, and all the fat is very little for a whole burnt offering to you; but he who fears the Lord is great continually. ¹⁷ "Woe to the nations who rise up against my race! The Lord Almighty will take vengeance on them in the day of judgment and put fire and worms in their flesh; and they will weep and feel their pain forever." ¹⁸ Now when they came to Jerusalem, they worshiped God. When the people were purified, they offered their whole burnt offerings, their free will offerings, and their gifts. ¹⁹ Judith dedicated all Holofernes' stuff, which the people had given her, and gave the canopy, which she had taken for herself out of his bedchamber, for a gift to the Lord. ²⁰ And the people continued feasting in Jerusalem before the sanctuary for three months, and Judith remained with them. ²¹ After these days, everyone departed to his own inheritance. Judith went away to Bethulia, and remained in her own possession, and was honorable in her time in all the land. ²² Many desired her, but no man knew her all the days of her life from the day that Manasses her husband died and was gathered to his people. ²³ She increased in greatness exceedingly; and she grew old in her husband's house, to one hundred five years. She let her maid go free. Then she died in Bethulia. They buried her in the cave of her husband Manasses. ²⁴ The house of Israel mourned for her seven days. She distributed her goods before she died to all those who were nearest of kin to Manasses her husband, and to those who were nearest of her own kindred. ²⁵ There was no one who made the children of Israel afraid any more in the days of Judith, nor for a long time after her death.

---

[a] *15:12* Compare **2 Maccabees 10:7**.

The First Book of the Maccabees

The First Book of the Maccabees is recognized as Deuterocanonical Scripture by the Roman Catholic, Greek Orthodox, and Russian Orthodox Churches.

1

[1] After Alexander the Macedonian, the son of Philip, who came out of the land of Chittim, and struck Darius king of the Persians and Medes, it came to pass, after he had struck him, that he reigned in his place, in former time, over[a] Greece. [2] He fought many battles, won many strongholds, killed the kings of the earth, [3] went through to the ends of the earth, and took spoils of a multitude of nations. The earth was quiet before him. He was exalted. His heart was lifted up. [4] He gathered together an exceedingly strong army and ruled over countries, nations, and principalities, and they paid him tribute. [5] After these things he fell sick, and perceived that he was going to die. [6] He called his honorable servants, which had been brought up with him from his youth, and he divided to them his kingdom while he was still alive. [7] Alexander reigned twelve years, then he died. [8] Then his servants ruled, each one in his place. [9] They all put crowns upon themselves after he was dead, and so did their sons after them many years; and they multiplied evils in the earth. [10] There came out of them a sinful root, Antiochus Epiphanes, son of Antiochus the king, who had been a hostage at Rome, and he reigned in[b] the one hundred thirty seventh year of the kingdom of the Greeks. [11] In those days transgressors of the law came out of Israel and persuaded many, saying, "Let's go make a covenant with the[c] Gentiles around us; for since we were separated from them many evils have befallen us." [12] That proposal was good in their eyes. [13] Some of the people eagerly went to the king, and he authorized them to observe the ordinances of the[d] Gentiles. [14] So[e] they built a gymnasium in Jerusalem according to the laws of the[f] Gentiles. [15] They made themselves uncircumcised, forsook the holy covenant, joined themselves to the[g] Gentiles, and sold themselves to do evil. [16] The kingdom was established in the sight of Antiochus, and he planned to reign over Egypt, that he might reign over both kingdoms. [17] He entered into Egypt with a[h] great multitude, with chariots, with elephants, with cavalry, and with a great[i] navy. [18] He made war against Ptolemy king of Egypt. Ptolemy was put to shame before him, and fled; and many fell wounded to death. [19] They took possession of the strong cities in the land of Egypt, and he took the spoils of Egypt. [20] Antiochus, after he had defeated Egypt, returned in[j] the one hundred forty third year, and went up against Israel and Jerusalem with a[k] great multitude, [21] and entered presumptuously into the sanctuary, and took the golden altar, the lampstand for the light, and all its utensils. [22] He took the table of the show bread, the cups for the drink offerings, the bowls, the golden censers, the veil, the crowns, and the gold decoration on the front of the temple. He peeled it all off. [23] He took the silver, the gold, and the precious vessels. He took the hidden treasures which he found. [24] When he had taken all of these, he went away into his own land. He made a great slaughter, and spoke very arrogantly. [25] Great mourning came upon Israel, in every place where they were. [26] The rulers and elders groaned. The virgins and young men were made feeble. The beauty of the women was changed. [27] Every bridegroom took up lamentation. She who sat in the marriage chamber was mourning. [28] The land was moved for its inhabitants, and all the house of Jacob was clothed with shame. [29] ¹After two full years, the king sent a chief collector of tribute to the cities of Judah, and he came to Jerusalem with a[m] great multitude. [30] He spoke words of peace to them in subtlety, and they believed him. Then he fell upon the city suddenly, struck it very severely, and destroyed many people of Israel. [31] He took the spoils of the city, set it on fire, and pulled down its houses and its walls on every side. [32] They led captive the women and the children, and seized the livestock. [33] Then they fortified the city of David with a large, strong wall and with strong towers, and it became their citadel. [34] They put a sinful nation, transgressors of the law, there, and they strengthened themselves in it. [35] They stored up weapons and food, and gathering together the spoils of Jerusalem, they stored them there, and they became a great menace. [36] It became a place to lie in wait against the sanctuary, and an evil adversary to Israel continually. [37] They shed innocent blood on every side of the sanctuary, and defiled the sanctuary. [38] The inhabitants of Jerusalem fled because of them. She became a habitation of foreigners. She became foreign to those who were born in her, and her children forsook her. [39] Her sanctuary was laid waste like a wilderness,[n] her feasts were turned into mourning, her Sabbaths into reproach, and her honor into contempt. [40] According to her glory, so was her dishonor multiplied, and her exaltation was turned into mourning. [41] King Antiochus wrote to his whole kingdom that all should be one people, [42] and that each should forsake his own laws. All the nations agreed according to the word of the king. [43] Many of Israel consented to his worship, sacrificed to the idols, and profaned the Sabbath. [44] The king sent letters by the hand of messengers to Jerusalem and the cities of Judah, that they should follow laws strange to the land, [45] and should forbid whole burnt offerings and sacrifice and drink offerings in the sanctuary; and should profane the Sabbaths and feasts, [46] and pollute the sanctuary and those who were holy; [47] that they should build altars, and temples, and shrines for idols, and should sacrifice swine's flesh and unclean animals; [48] and that they should leave their sons uncircumcised, that they should make their souls abominable with all manner of uncleanness and profanation; [49] so that they might forget the law, and change all the ordinances. [50] Whoever doesn't do according to the word of the king, he shall die. [51] According to all these words wrote he to his whole kingdom. He appointed overseers over all the people, and he commanded the cities of Judah to sacrifice, city by city. [52] From the people were gathered together to them many, everyone who had forsaken the law; and they did evil things in the land. [53] They made Israel to hide themselves in every place of refuge which they had. [54] On the fifteenth day of Chislev, in[o] the one hundred forty fifth year, they built an abomination of desolation upon the altar,[p] and in the cities of Judah on every side they built idol altars.[q] [55] At the doors of the houses and in the streets they burned incense. [56] They tore the books of the law which they found in pieces and set them on fire. [57] Anyone who was found with any a book of the covenant, and if any consented to the law, the king's sentence delivered him to death. [58] Thus did they in their might to Israel, to those who were found month by month in the cities. [59] On the twenty-fifth day of the month they sacrificed upon the idol altar that was on top of the altar of burnt offering. [60] ʳThey put to death women who had circumcised their children, according to the commandment. [61] They hung their babies around their necks, and their houses, and those who had circumcised them. [62] Many in Israel were fully resolved and confirmed in themselves not to eat unclean things. [63] ˢThey chose to die, that they might not be defiled with the food, and that they might not profane the holy covenant; and they died. [64] Exceedingly great wrath came upon Israel.

2

[1] In those days Mattathias the son of John, the son of Simeon, a priest of the sons of Joarib, from Jerusalem rose up; and he lived at Modin. [2] And he had five sons:[t] John, who was surnamed Gaddis; [3] Simon, who was called Thassi; [4] Judas, who was called Maccabaeus; [5] Eleazar, who was called Avaran; and Jonathan, who was called Apphus. [6] He saw the blasphemies that were committed in Judah and in Jerusalem, [7] and he said, "Woe is me! Why was I born to see the destruction of my people and the destruction of the holy city, and to dwell there when it was given into the hand of the enemy, the sanctuary into the hand of foreigners? [8] Her temple has become like a man who was glorious. [9] Her vessels of glory are carried away into captivity. Her infants are slain in her streets. Her young men are slain with the enemy's sword. [10] What nation has not inherited her palaces and taken possession of her spoils? [11] Her adornment has all been taken away. Instead of a free woman, she has become a slave. [12] Behold, our holy things, our beauty, and our glory are laid waste. The Gentiles have profaned them. [13] Why should we live any longer?" [14] Mattathias and his sons tore their clothes, put on sackcloth, and mourned exceedingly. [15] And the king's officers who were enforcing the apostasy came into the city Modin to sacrifice. [16] Many of Israel came to them, and Mattathias and his sons were

---

[a] 1:1 That is, the Greek Empire. Compare **1 Maccabees 1:10** and **1 Maccabees 6:2**.
[b] 1:10 circa B.C. **176**.
[c] 1:11 Or, nations: and so throughout this book.
[d] 1:13 Or, nations: and so throughout this book.
[e] 1:14 See **2 Maccabees 4:9, 12**.
[f] 1:14 Or, nations: and so throughout this book.
[g] 1:15 Or, nations: and so throughout this book
[h] 1:17 Gr. heavy.
[i] 1:17 Or, armament
[j] 1:20 circa B.C. **170**. See **2 Maccabees 5:11-16**.
[k] 1:20 Gr. heavy.
[l] 1:29 See **2 Maccabees 5:24**.
[m] 1:29 Gr. heavy.
[n] 1:39 See **2 Maccabees 6:6**.
[o] 1:54 circa B.C. **168**. See **2 Maccabees 5:11**.
[p] 1:54 The two words rendered altar are different in the Greek: and so in **1 Maccabees 1:59**.
[q] 1:54 The two words rendered altar are different in the Greek: and so in **1 Maccabees 1:59**.
[r] 1:60 See **2 Maccabees 6:10**.
[s] 1:63 See **2 Maccabees 6:19** and **7:1**, etc.
[t] 2:2 Gr. Joannes.

gathered together. ¹⁷ The king's officers answered and spoke to Mattathias, saying, "You are a ruler and an honorable and great man in this city, and strengthened with sons and kindred. ¹⁸ Now therefore come first and do the commandment of the king, as all the nations have done, including the men of Judah and those who remain in Jerusalem. You and your house will be numbered among the king's[a] friends, and you and your sons will be honored with silver and gold and many gifts." ¹⁹ And Mattathias answered and said with a loud voice, "If all the nations that are in the house of the king's dominion listen to him, to fall away each one from the worship of his fathers, and have made choice to follow his commandments, ²⁰ yet I and my sons and my kindred will walk in the covenant of our fathers. ²¹ Far be it from us that we should forsake the law and the ordinances. ²² We will not listen to the king's words, to turn aside from our worship, to the right hand, or to the left." ²³ When he had finished speaking these words, a Jew came in the sight of all to sacrifice on the altar which was at Modin, according to the king's commandment. ²⁴ Mattathias saw it, so his zeal was kindled, and his guts trembled, and he vented his wrath according to judgment, and ran and killed him upon the altar. ²⁵ He killed the king's officer, who compelled men to sacrifice, at the same time, and pulled down the altar. ²⁶ He was zealous for the law, even as Phinehas did to Zimri the son of Salu. ²⁷ Mattathias cried out in the city with a loud voice, saying, "Whoever is zealous for the law and maintains the covenant, let him follow me!" ²⁸ He and his sons fled into the mountains, and left all that they had in the city. ²⁹ Then many who sought justice and judgment went down into the wilderness to live there– ³⁰ they, their children, their wives, and their livestock–because evils were multiplied upon them. ³¹ It was told the king's officers and the forces that were in Jerusalem, the city of David, that certain men who had broken the king's commandment had gone down into the secret places in the wilderness; ³² and many pursued after them, and having overtaken them, they encamped against them and set the battle in array against them on the Sabbath day. ³³ They said to them, "Enough of this! Come out and do according to the word of the king, and you will all live!" ³⁴ They said, "We won't come out. We won't do the word of the king, to profane the Sabbath day." ³⁵ Then the enemy hurried to attack them. ³⁶ They didn't answer them. They didn't cast a stone at them, or block their secret places, ³⁷ saying, "Let's all die in our innocence. Heaven and earth testify for us, that you put us to death unjustly." ³⁸ So they attacked them on the Sabbath, and they died–they, their wives, their children, and their livestock–in number a thousand souls of men. ³⁹ When Mattathias and his friends found out about it, and they mourned over them exceedingly. ⁴⁰ One said to another, "If we all do as our kindred have done, and don't fight against the Gentiles for our lives and our ordinances, they will quickly destroy us from off the earth." ⁴¹ So they decided that day, saying, "Whoever comes against us to battle on the Sabbath day, let's fight against him, and we will in no way all die, as our kindred died in the secret places." ⁴² Then a company of the Hasidaeans,[b] mighty men of Israel, everyone who offered himself willingly for the law, were gathered together to them. ⁴³ All those who fled from the evils were added to them, and supported them. ⁴⁴ They mustered an army, and struck sinners in their anger, and lawless men in their wrath. The rest fled to the Gentiles for safety. ⁴⁵ And Mattathias and his friends went around and pulled down the altars. ⁴⁶ They forcibly circumcised the boys who were uncircumcised, as many as they found in the coasts of Israel. ⁴⁷ They pursued the arrogant, and the work prospered in their hand. ⁴⁸ They rescued the law out of the hand of the Gentiles and out of the hand of the kings. They never allowed the sinner to triumph. ⁴⁹ The days of Mattathias drew near that he should die, and he said to his sons, "Now pride and scorn have gained strength. It is a season of overthrow and indignant wrath. ⁵⁰ Now, my children, be zealous for the law, and give your lives for the covenant of your fathers. ⁵¹ Call to remembrance the deeds of our fathers which they did in their generations; and receive great glory and an everlasting name. ⁵² Wasn't Abraham found faithful in temptation, and it was reckoned to him for righteousness? ⁵³ Joseph in the time of his distress kept the commandment, and became lord of Egypt. ⁵⁴ Phinehas our father, because he was exceedingly zealous, obtained the covenant of an everlasting priesthood. ⁵⁵ Joshua became a judge in Israel for fulfilling the word. ⁵⁶ Caleb obtained a heritage in the land for testifying in the congregation. ⁵⁷ David inherited the throne of a kingdom forever and ever for being merciful. ⁵⁸ Elijah was taken up into heaven because he was exceedingly zealous for the law. ⁵⁹ Hananiah, Azariah, and Mishael believed, and were saved out of the flame. ⁶⁰ Daniel was delivered from the mouth of lions for his innocence. ⁶¹ "Thus consider from generation to generation that no one who put their trust in him will lack for strength. ⁶² Don't be afraid of the words of a sinful man; for his glory will be dung and worms. ⁶³ Today he will be lifted up, and tomorrow he will in no way be found, because he has returned to dust, and his thought has perished. ⁶⁴ You, my children, be strong, and show yourselves men on behalf of the law; for in it you will obtain glory. ⁶⁵ Behold, Simon your brother, whom I know to be a man of counsel. Always listen to him. He shall be a father to you. ⁶⁶ Judas Maccabaeus has been strong and mighty from his youth. He shall be your captain and shall fight[c] the battle of the people. ⁶⁷ Rally around all the doers of the law, and avenge the wrong done to your people. ⁶⁸ Repay the Gentiles, and obey the commandments of the law." ⁶⁹ He blessed them, and was gathered to his ancestors. ⁷⁰ He died in[d] the one hundred forty sixth year, and his sons buried him in the tombs of his ancestors at Modin. All Israel made great lamentation for him.

3

¹ His son Judas, who was called Maccabaeus, rose up in his place. ² All his kindred helped him, and so did all those who joined with his father, and they fought with gladness the battle of Israel. ³ He got his people great glory, and put on a breastplate like a giant, and bound his warlike harness around him, and set battles in array, protecting the army with his sword. ⁴ He was like a lion in his deeds, and like a lion's cub roaring for prey. ⁵ He hunted and pursued the lawless, and he burned up those who troubled his people. ⁶ The lawless shrunk back for fear of him, and all the workers of lawlessness were very troubled, and deliverance prospered in his hand. ⁷ He angered many kings and made Jacob glad with his acts. His memory is blessed forever. ⁸ He went through the cities of Judah, destroyed the ungodly[e] out of the land, and turned away wrath from Israel. ⁹ He was renowned to the utmost part of the earth. He gathered together those who were ready to perish. ¹⁰ Apollonius gathered the Gentiles together with a great army from Samaria to fight against Israel. ¹¹ Judas learned of it, and he went out to meet him, struck him, and killed him. Many fell wounded to death, and the rest fled. ¹² They took their spoils, and Judas took Apollonius' sword, and he fought with it all his days. ¹³ Seron, the commander of the army of Syria, heard that Judas had gathered a large company, including a body of faithful men who stayed with him, went out to war. ¹⁴ He said, "I will make myself a name and get myself glory in the kingdom. I will fight against Judas and those who are with him, who despise the king's command. ¹⁵ A mighty army of the ungodly went up with him to help him, to take vengeance on the children of Israel. ¹⁶ He came near to the ascent of Bethhoron, and Judas went out to meet him with a small company. ¹⁷ But when they saw the army coming to meet them, they said to Judas, "What? Shall we be able, being a small company, to fight against so great and strong a multitude? We for our part are faint, having tasted no food this day." ¹⁸ Judas said, "It is an easy thing for many to be hemmed in by the hands of a few. With[f] heaven it is all one, to save by many or by few; ¹⁹ for victory in battle stands not in the multitude of an army, but strength is from heaven. ²⁰ They come to us in fullness of insolence and lawlessness, to destroy us and our wives and our children, and to plunder us, ²¹ but we fight for our lives and our laws. ²² He himself will crush them before our face; but as for you, don't be afraid of them. ²³ Now when he had finished speaking, he rushed suddenly against Seron and his army, and they were defeated before him. ²⁴ They pursued them down the descent of Bethhoron to the plain, and about eight hundred men of them fell; but the rest fled into the land of the Philistines. ²⁵ The fear of Judas and his kindred, and the dread of them, began to fall on the nations around them. ²⁶ His fame reached the king, and every nation told of the battles of Judas. ²⁷ But when King Antiochus heard these words, he was full of indignation; and he sent and gathered together all the forces of his realm, an exceedingly strong army. ²⁸ He opened his treasury and gave his forces pay for a year, and commanded them to be ready for every need. ²⁹ He saw that the money was gone from his treasures, and that the tributes of the country were small, because of the dissension and disaster which he had brought upon the land, to the end that he might take away the laws which had been from the first days. ³⁰ He was afraid that he wouldn't have enough as at other times for the charges and the gifts which he used to give with a liberal hand, more abundantly than the kings who were before him. ³¹ And he was exceedingly perplexed in his mind, and he determined to go into Persia, and to take the tributes of those countries, and to gather much money. ³² He left Lysias, an honorable man, and one of royal lineage, to be over the affairs of the king from the river Euphrates to the borders of Egypt, ³³ and to bring up his son Antiochus, until he came again. ³⁴ He delivered to

---

[a] 2:18 See 1 Maccabees 3:38; 10:10, etc.; Compare 1 Maccabees 10:65; 11:27; 2 Maccabees 8:9.

[b] 2:42 That is, Chasidim.
[c] 2:66 Some ancient authorities read you shall fight.

[d] 2:70 circa B.C. **167**.
[e] 3:8 Gr. out of it.

[f] 3:18 Some ancient authorities read the God of heaven.

Lysias half of his forces and the elephants, and gave him charge of all the things that he would have done, and concerning those who lived in Judea and in Jerusalem, ³⁵ that he should send an army against them to root out and destroy the strength of Israel and the remnant of Jerusalem, and to take away their memory from the place, ³⁶ and that he should make foreigners live in all their territory, and should divide their land to them by lot. ³⁷ The king took the half that remained of the forces, and left Antioch, his royal city, in the one hundred forty seventh year;[a] and he passed over the river Euphrates, and went through the upper countries. ³⁸ Lysias chose Ptolemy the son of Dorymenes, Nicanor, and Gorgias, mighty men of the king's friends;[b] ³⁹ and with them, he sent forty thousand infantry and seven thousand cavalry to go into the land of Judah and to destroy it, according to the word of the king. ⁴⁰ They set out with all their army, and came and encamped near Emmaus in the plain country. ⁴¹ The merchants of the country heard of their fame, and took silver and gold in large quantities, and fetters,[c] and came into the camp to take the children of Israel for slaves. Forces of Syria and of the land of the Philistines[d] joined with them. ⁴² Judas and his kindred saw that evils were multiplied, and that the forces were encamping in their borders. They learned about the king's words which he had commanded, to destroy the people and make an end of them. ⁴³ Then they each said to his neighbor, "Let's repair the ruins of our people. Let's fight for our people and the holy place." ⁴⁴ The congregation was gathered together, that they might be ready for battle, and that they might pray and ask for mercy and compassion. ⁴⁵ Jerusalem was without inhabitant like a wilderness. There was none of her offspring who went in or went out. The sanctuary was trampled down. Children of foreigners were in the citadel. The Gentiles lived there. Joy was taken away from Jacob, and the pipe and the harp ceased. ⁴⁶ They gathered themselves together, and came to Mizpeh, near Jerusalem; for in Mizpeh there used to be a place of prayer for Israel. ⁴⁷ They fasted that day, put on sackcloth, put ashes on their heads, tore their clothes, ⁴⁸ and opened the book of the law, to learn about the things for which the Gentiles consulted the images of their idols. ⁴⁹ They brought the priests' garments, the first fruits, and the tithes. They stirred up the Nazarites, who had accomplished their days. ⁵⁰ They cried aloud toward heaven, saying, "What should we do with these men? Where should we carry them away? ⁵¹ Your holy place is trampled down and profaned. Your priests mourn in humiliation. ⁵² Behold, the Gentiles are assembled together against us to destroy us. You know what things they imagine against us. ⁵³ How will we be able to stand against them, unless you help us?" ⁵⁴ They sounded with the trumpets, and gave a loud shout. ⁵⁵ And after this Judas appointed leaders of the people: captains of thousands, captains of hundreds, captains of fifties, and captains of tens. ⁵⁶ He said to those who were building houses, were betrothing wives, were planting vineyards, and were fearful, that they should return, each man to his own house, according to the law. ⁵⁷ The army marched out and encamped upon the south side of Emmaus. ⁵⁸ Judas said, "Arm yourselves and be valiant men! Be ready in the morning to fight with these Gentiles who are assembled together against us to destroy us and our holy place. ⁵⁹ For it is better for us to die in battle than to see the calamities of our nation and the holy place. ⁶⁰ Nevertheless, as may be the will in heaven, so shall he do.

4

¹ Gorgias took five thousand infantry, a thousand chosen cavalry, and the army moved out at night, ² that it might fall upon the army of the Jews and strike them suddenly. The men of the citadel were his guides. ³ Judas heard of this, and he and the valiant men moved, that he might strike the king's army which was at Emmaus ⁴ while the forces were still dispersed from the camp. ⁵ Gorgias came into the camp of Judas at night and found no man. He sought them in the mountains; for he said, "These men are running away from us." ⁶ As soon as it was day, Judas appeared in the plain with three thousand men. However they didn't have the armor and swords they desired. ⁷ They saw the camp of the Gentiles strong and fortified, with cavalry all around it; and these were expert in war. ⁸ Judas said to the men who were with him, "Don't be afraid of their numbers, or when they charge. ⁹ Remember how our fathers were saved in the Red sea, when Pharaoh pursued them with an army. ¹⁰ Now let's cry to heaven, if he will have us, and will remember the covenant of our fathers, and destroy this army before our face today. ¹¹ Then all the Gentiles will know that there is one who redeems and saves Israel. ¹² The foreigners lifted up their eyes, and saw them coming near them. ¹³ They went out of the camp to battle. Those who were with Judas sounded their trumpets ¹⁴ and joined battle. The Gentiles were defeated, and fled into the plain. ¹⁵ But all those in the rear fell by the sword. They pursued them to[e] Gazara, and to the plains of Idumaea, Azotus, and Jamnia. About three thousand of those men fell. ¹⁶ Then Judas and his army returned from pursuing them; ¹⁷ and he said to the people, "Don't be greedy for the spoils, because there is a battle before us. ¹⁸ Gorgias and his army are near us on the mountain. But stand now against our enemies and fight against them, and afterwards take the spoils with boldness." ¹⁹ While Judas was finishing this speech, a part of them appeared looking out from the mountain. ²⁰ They saw that their army had been put to flight, and that the Jews were burning the camp; for the smoke that was seen declared what was done. ²¹ But when they perceived these things, they were very afraid. Perceiving also the army of Judas in the plain ready for battle, ²² they all fled into the land of the[f] Philistines. ²³ Judas returned to plunder the camp, and they took much gold, silver, blue, sea purple, and great riches. ²⁴ Then they returned home, and sang a song of thanksgiving, and gave praise to heaven, because he is good, because his mercy endures forever. ²⁵ Israel had a great deliverance that day. ²⁶ The foreigners who had escaped came and told Lysias all the things that had happened. ²⁷ When he heard of it, he was confounded and discouraged, because the things he desired had not been done to Israel, nor had such things happened as the king commanded him. ²⁸ In the next year, he gathered together sixty thousand chosen infantry and five thousand cavalry, that he might subdue them. ²⁹ They came into Idumaea and encamped at Bethsura. Judas met them with ten thousand men. ³⁰ He saw that the army was strong, and he prayed and said, "Blessed are you, O Savior of Israel, who defeated the attack of the mighty warrior by the hand of your servant David, and delivered the army of the[g] Philistines into the hands of Jonathan the son of Saul, and of his armor bearer. ³¹ Hem in this army in the hand of your people Israel, and let them be ashamed for their army and their cavalry. ³² Give them faintness of heart. Cause the boldness of their strength to melt away, and let them quake at their destruction. ³³ Strike them down with the sword of those who love you, and let all who know your name praise you with thanksgiving." ³⁴ They joined in battle; and about five thousand men of Lysias' army fell. They fell down near them. ³⁵ But when Lysias saw that his troops were put to flight, and the boldness that had come upon those who were with Judas, and how they were ready either to live or to die nobly, he withdrew to Antioch, and gathered together hired soldiers, that he might come again into Judea with an even greater army. ³⁶ But Judas and his kindred said, "Behold, our enemies are defeated. Let's go up to cleanse the holy place and to rededicate it." ³⁷ All the army was gathered together, and they went up to mount Zion. ³⁸ They saw the sanctuary laid desolate, the altar profaned, the gates burned up, shrubs growing in the courts as in a forest as on one of the mountains, and the priests' chambers pulled down; ³⁹ and they tore their clothes, made great lamentation, put ashes upon their heads, ⁴⁰ fell on their faces to the ground, [h] blew with the solemn trumpets,[i] and cried toward heaven. ⁴¹ Then Judas appointed certain men to fight against those who were in the citadel until he had cleansed the holy place. ⁴² He chose blameless priests who were devoted to the law; ⁴³ and they cleansed the holy place and carried the defiled stones out to an unclean place. ⁴⁴ They deliberated what to do with the altar of burnt offerings, which had been profaned. ⁴⁵ A good plan came into their mind, that they should pull it down, lest it would be a reproach to them, because the Gentiles had defiled it. So they pulled down the altar ⁴⁶ and laid up the stones on the temple hill in a convenient place, until a prophet would come to give an answer concerning them. ⁴⁷ They took whole stones according to the law, and built a new altar like the former. ⁴⁸ They built the holy place and the inner parts of the house; and they consecrated the courts. ⁴⁹ They made new holy vessels, and they brought the lampstand, the altar of incense, and the table into the temple. ⁵⁰ They burned incense on the altar, and they lit the lamps that were upon the lampstand, and they gave light in the temple. ⁵¹ They set loaves upon the table, hung up the curtains, and finished all the work which they had done. ⁵² They rose up early in the morning, on the twenty-fifth day of the ninth month, which is the month Chislev, in[j] the one hundred forty eighth year, ⁵³ and offered sacrifice according to the law on the new altar of burnt offerings which they had made. ⁵⁴ At the time and day the Gentiles had profaned it, even then it was dedicated with songs, harps, lutes, and with cymbals. ⁵⁵ All the people fell on their faces, worshiped, and gave praise toward heaven, which had given them good success. ⁵⁶ They celebrated the dedication of the altar eight days, and offered burnt offerings with gladness, and sacrificed a sacrifice of deliverance and praise. ⁵⁷ They decorated the front of the temple with crowns of gold and small shields. They dedicated the gates and the priests'

---

[a] 3:37 circa B.C. **166**.
[b] 3:38 See **1 Maccabees 2:18**.
[c] 3:41 Most of the authorities read servants.
[d] 3:41 Gr. foreigners.
[e] 4:15 Gr. Gazera.
[f] 4:22 Gr. foreigners.
[g] 4:30 Gr. foreigners.
[h] 4:40 Compare Numbers **31:6**.
[i] 4:40 Gr. trumpets of signals.
[j] 4:52 circa B.C. **165**.

chambers, and made doors for them. ⁵⁸There was exceedingly great gladness among the people, and the reproach of the Gentiles was turned away. ⁵⁹Judas and his kindred and the whole congregation of Israel ordained that the days of the dedication of the altar should be kept in their seasons from year to year for eight days, from the twenty-fifth day of the month Chislev, with gladness and joy. ⁶⁰At that time, they fortified mount Zion with high walls and strong towers around it, lest perhaps the Gentiles might come and trample them down, as they had done before. ⁶¹Judas stationed a garrison to guard it. They fortified Bethsura to keep it, that the people might have a stronghold near Idumaea.

5

¹It came to pass, when the Gentiles all around heard that the altar had been rebuilt and the sanctuary dedicated as before, they were exceedingly angry. ²They took counsel to destroy the race of Jacob that was in the midst of them, and they began to kill and destroy among the people. ³Judas fought against the children of Esau in Idumaea at Akrabattine, because they besieged Israel. He struck them with a great slaughter, humbled them, and took their spoils. ⁴He remembered the wickedness of the children of[a] Baean, who were a snare and a stumbling block to the people, lying in wait for them on the highways. ⁵They were shut up by him in the towers. He encamped against them, and destroyed them utterly, and burned with fire the towers of the place with all who were in them. ⁶He passed over to the children of Ammon, and found a mighty band and many people, with Timotheus for their leader. ⁷He fought many battles with them, and they were defeated before his face. He struck them, ⁸and took possession of Jazer and its villages,[b] and returned again into Judea. ⁹The Gentiles who were in Gilead gathered themselves together against the Israelites who were on their borders, to destroy them. They fled to the stronghold of Dathema, ¹⁰and sent letters to Judas and his kindred, saying, "The Gentiles who are around us are gathered together against us to destroy us. ¹¹They are preparing to come and get possession of the stronghold where we fled for refuge, and Timotheus is the leader of their army. ¹²Now therefore come and deliver us from their hand, for many of us have fallen. ¹³All our kindred who were in the land of[c]Tubias have been put to death. They have carried their wives, their children, and their stuff into captivity. They destroyed about a thousand men there." ¹⁴While the letters were still being read, behold, other messengers came from Galilee with their clothes torn, bringing a similar report, ¹⁵saying, "People of Ptolemais, of Tyre, of Sidon, and all Galilee of the[d] Gentiles have gathered together to destroy us." ¹⁶Now when Judas and the people heard these words, a great congregation assembled together to determine what they should do for their kindred who were in distress and under attack. ¹⁷Judas said to Simon his brother, "Choose men and go deliver your kindred who are in Galilee, but Jonathan my brother and I will go into the land of Gilead." ¹⁸He left Joseph the son of Zacharias, and Azarias, as leaders of the people, with the remnant of the army, in Judea, to guard it. ¹⁹He commanded them, saying, "Take charge of this people, and fight no battle with the Gentiles until we return." ²⁰Then three thousand men were assigned to go into Galilee with Simon, but eight thousand men were assigned to Judas to go into the land of Gilead. ²¹Simon went into Galilee and fought many battles with the Gentiles, and the Gentiles were defeated before him. ²²He pursued them to the gate of Ptolemais. About three thousand men of the Gentiles fell, and he took their spoils. ²³They took to them those who were in Galilee and in Arbatta, with their wives, their children, and all that they had, and brought them into Judea with great gladness. ²⁴Judas Maccabaeus and his brother Jonathan passed over the Jordan, and went three days' journey in the wilderness. ²⁵They met with the Nabathaeans, and these met them in a peaceful manner and told them all things that had happened to their kindred in the land of Gilead, ²⁶and how many of them were shut up in Bosora, Bosor, Alema,[e] Casphor, Maked, and[f] Carnaim–all these cities are strong and large– ²⁷and how they were shut up in the rest of the cities of the land of Gilead, and that tomorrow they planned to encamp against the strongholds, and to take them, and to destroy all these men in one day. ²⁸Judas and his army turned suddenly by the way of the wilderness to Bosora; and he took the city, and killed all the males with the edge of the sword, took all their spoils, and burned the city with fire. ²⁹He left there at night, and went until he came to the stronghold. ³⁰When the morning came, they lifted up their eyes and saw many people who couldn't be counted, bearing ladders and engines of war, to take the stronghold; and they were fighting against them. ³¹Judas saw that the battle had begun, and that the cry of the city went up to heaven, with trumpets and a great sound, ³²and he said to the men of his army, "Fight today for your kindred!" ³³Then he went out behind them in three companies. They sounded with their trumpets and cried out in prayer. ³⁴And the army of Timotheus perceived that it was Maccabaeus, and they fled from before him. He struck them with a great slaughter. About eight thousand men of them fell on that day. ³⁵He turned away to Mizpeh and fought against it, took it, killed all its males, took its spoils, and burned it with fire. ³⁶From there he marched and took[g] Casphor, Maked, Bosor, and the other cities of the land of Gilead. ³⁷Now after these things, Timotheus gathered another army and encamped near Raphon beyond the brook. ³⁸Judas sent men to spy on the army; and they brought him word, saying, "All the Gentiles who are around us are gathered together to them, an exceedingly great army. ³⁹They have hired Arabians to help them, and are encamped beyond the brook, ready to come against you to battle." So Judas went to meet them. ⁴⁰Timotheus said to the captains of his army when Judas and his army drew near to the brook of water, "If he crosses over to us first, we won't be able to withstand him, for he will certainly defeat us; ⁴¹but if he is afraid, and encamps beyond the river, we will cross over to him, and defeat him." ⁴²Now when Judas came near to the water brook, he caused the scribes of the people to remain by the brook, and commanded them, saying, "Allow no man to encamp, but let all come to the battle." ⁴³Then he crossed over the first against them, and all the people after him; and all the Gentiles were defeated before his face, and threw away their weapons, and fled to the temple at [h]Carnaim. ⁴⁴They took the city and burned the temple with fire, together with all who were in it. Carnaim was subdued. They couldn't stand any longer before the face of Judas. ⁴⁵Judas gathered together all Israel, those who were in the land of Gilead, from the least to the greatest, with their wives, their children, and their stuff, an exceedingly great army, that they might come into the land of Judah. ⁴⁶They came as far as Ephron, and this same city was large and very strong. It was on the road where they were going. They couldn't turn away from it on the right hand or on the left, but needed to pass through the middle of it. ⁴⁷The people of the city shut them out and blocked the gates with stones. ⁴⁸Judas sent to them with words of peace, saying, "We will pass through your land to go into our own land, and no one will harm you. We will only pass by on our feet." But they wouldn't open to him. ⁴⁹Then Judas commanded proclamation to be made in the army, that each man should encamp in the place where he was. ⁵⁰So the men of the army encamped, and fought against the city all that day and all that night, and the city was delivered into his hands. ⁵¹He destroyed all the males with the edge of the sword, razed the city, took its plunder, and passed through the city over those who were slain. ⁵²They went over the Jordan into the great plain near Bethshan. ⁵³And Judas gathered together those who lagged behind and encouraged the people all the way through, until he came into the land of Judah. ⁵⁴They went up to mount Zion with gladness and joy, and offered whole burnt offerings, because not so much as one of them was slain until they returned in peace. ⁵⁵In the days when Judas and Jonathan were in the land of Gilead, and Simon his brother in Galilee before Ptolemais, ⁵⁶Joseph the son of Zacharias, and Azarias, rulers of the army, heard of their exploits and of the war, and what things they had done. ⁵⁷They said, "Let's also get us a name, and let's go fight against the Gentiles who are around us." ⁵⁸So they gave orders to the men of the army that was with them, and went toward Jamnia. ⁵⁹Gorgias and his men came out of the city to meet them in battle. ⁶⁰Joseph and Azarias were put to flight, and were pursued to the borders of Judea. About two thousand men of Israel fell on that day. ⁶¹There was a great overthrow among the people, because they didn't listen to Judas and his kindred, thinking to do some exploit. ⁶²But they were not of the family of those men by whose hand deliverance was given to Israel. ⁶³The man Judas and his kindred were glorified exceedingly in the sight of all Israel, and of all the Gentiles, wherever their name was heard of. ⁶⁴Men gathered together to them, acclaiming them. ⁶⁵Judas and his kindred went out and fought against the children of Esau in the land toward the south. He struck Hebron and its villages,[i] pulled down its strongholds, and burned its towers all around. ⁶⁶He marched to go into the land of the[j] Philistines, and he went through[k] Samaria. ⁶⁷In that day certain priests, desiring to do exploits there, were slain in battle, when they went out to battle unadvisedly. ⁶⁸But Judas turned toward Azotus, to the land of the[l] Philistines, pulled down their

---

[a] 5:4 Compare **2 Maccabees 10:18- 23**.
[b] 5:8 Gr. daughters. Compare Numbers **21:25**.
[c] 5:13 Compare **2 Maccabees 12:17**.
[d] 5:15 Gr. foreigners.
[e] 5:26 Compare **2 Maccabees 12:13**.
[f] 5:26 compare **2 Maccabees 12:21**.
[g] 5:36 See **1 Maccabees 5:26**.
[h] 5:43 See **1 Maccabees 5:26**.
[i] 5:65 Gr. daughters. Compare Numbers **21:25**.
[j] 5:66 Gr. foreigners.
[k] 5:66 Or, Marisa See Josephus, Antiquities **12:8**, **6**, and **2 Maccabees 12:35**.
[l] 5:68 Gr. foreigners.

altars, burned the carved images of their gods with fire, took the plunder of their cities, and returned into the land of Judah.

6

¹ King Antiochus was traveling through the upper countries; and he heard that in Elymais in Persia there was a city renowned for riches, for silver and gold, ² and that the temple which was in it was exceedingly rich, and that in it were golden shields, breastplates, and weapons which Alexander, son of Philip, the Macedonian king, who reigned first among the Greeks, left behind there. ³ So he came and tried to take the city and to pillage it; and he was not able, because his plan was known to them of the city, ⁴ and they rose up against him in battle. He fled and returned to Babylon with great disappointment. ⁵ Then someone came into Persia bringing him news that the armies which went against the land of Judah had been put to flight, ⁶ and that Lysias went first with a strong army and was put to shame before them, and that they had grown strong because of weapons, power, and a supply of plunder which they took from the armies that they had cut off, ⁷ and that they had pulled down the abomination which he had built upon the altar that was in Jerusalem, and that they had surrounded the sanctuary with high walls, as before, and also Bethsura, his city. ⁸ It came to pass, when the king heard these words, he was astonished and moved exceedingly. He laid himself down on his bed, and fell sick for grief, because it had not turned out for him as he had planned. ⁹ He was there many days, because great grief continually gripped him, and he realized that he would die. ¹⁰ He called for all his[a] friends, and said to them, "Sleep departs from my eyes, and my heart fails because of worry. ¹¹ I said in my heart, 'To what suffering I have come! How great a flood it is that I'm in, now! For I was gracious and loved in my power.' ¹² But now I remember the evils which I did at Jerusalem, and that I took all the vessels of silver and gold that were in it, and sent out to destroy the inhabitants of Judah without a cause. ¹³ I perceive that it is because of this that these evils have come upon me. Behold, I am perishing through great grief in a strange land." ¹⁴ Then he called for Philip, one of his[b] friends, and set him over all his kingdom. ¹⁵ He gave him his crown, his robe, and his signet ring, so that he could guide Antiochus his son, and nourish him up that he might be king. ¹⁶ Then King Antiochus died there in the one hundred forty-ninth year.[c] ¹⁷ When Lysias learned that the king was dead, he set up Antiochus his son to reign, whom he had nourished up being young, and he called his name Eupator. ¹⁸ Those who were in the citadel kept hemming Israel in around the sanctuary, and always sought to harm them and to strengthen the Gentiles. ¹⁹ Judas planned to destroy them, and called all the people together to besiege them. ²⁰ They were gathered together, and besieged them in[d] the one hundred fiftieth year, and he made mounds to shoot from, and engines of war. ²¹ Some of those who were hemmed in came out, and some of the ungodly men of Israel joined to them. ²² They went to the king, and said, "How long will you not execute judgment, and avenge our kindred? ²³ We were willing to serve your father and to live by his words, and to follow his commandments. ²⁴ Because of this, the children of our people besieged the citadel[e] and were alienated from us; but as many of us as they could catch, they killed, and plundered our inheritances. ²⁵ Not against us only did they stretch out their hand, but also against all their borders. ²⁶ Behold, they are encamped this day against the citadel at Jerusalem to take it. They have fortified the sanctuary and Bethsura. ²⁷ If you don't quickly prevent them, they will do greater things than these, and you won't be able to control them." ²⁸ When the king heard this, he was angry, and gathered together all his[f] friends, the rulers of his army, and those who were over the cavalry. ²⁹ Bands of hired soldiers came to him from other kingdoms and from islands of the sea. ³⁰ The number of his forces was one hundred thousand infantry, and twenty thousand cavalry, and thirty-two elephants trained for war. ³¹ They went through Idumaea, and encamped against Bethsura, and fought against it many days, and made engines of war. The Jews came out and burned them with fire, and fought valiantly. ³² Judas marched away from the citadel and encamped at Bethzacharias, near the king's camp. ³³ The king rose early in the morning, and marched his army[g] at full speed along the road to Bethzacharias. His forces made themselves ready to battle and sounded their trumpets. ³⁴ They offered the elephants the juice of grapes and mulberries, that they might prepare them for the battle. ³⁵ They distributed the animals among the phalanxes. They set by each elephant a thousand men armed with coats of mail and helmets of brass on their heads. Five hundred chosen cavalry were appointed for each elephant. ³⁶ These were ready beforehand, wherever the elephant was. Wherever the elephant went, they went with it. They didn't leave it. ³⁷ Strong, covered wooden towers were upon them, one upon each elephant, fastened upon it with secure harnesses. Upon each were four valiant men who fought upon them, beside his Indian driver. ³⁸ The rest of the cavalry he set on this side and that side on the two flanks of the army, striking terror into the enemy, and protected by the phalanxes. ³⁹ Now when the sun shone upon the shields of gold and brass, the mountains lit up, and blazed like flaming torches. ⁴⁰ A part of the king's army was spread upon the high hills and some on the low ground, and they went on firmly and in order. ⁴¹ All who heard the noise of their multitude, the marching of the multitude, and the rattling of the weapons trembled; for the army was exceedingly great and strong. ⁴² Judas and his army drew near for battle, and six hundred men of the king's army fell. ⁴³ Eleazar, who was called Avaran, saw one of the animals armed with royal breastplates, and it was taller than all the animals, and the king seemed to be on it. ⁴⁴ He gave his life to deliver his people, and to get himself an everlasting name. ⁴⁵ He ran upon him courageously into the midst of the phalanx, and killed on the right hand and on the left, and they parted away from him on this side and on that. ⁴⁶ He crept under the elephant, and stabbed it from beneath, and killed it. The elephant fell to the earth upon him, and he died there. ⁴⁷ They saw the strength of the kingdom and the fierce attack of the army, and turned away from them. ⁴⁸ But the soldiers of the king's army went up to Jerusalem to meet them, and the king encamped toward Judea and toward mount Zion. ⁴⁹ He made peace with the people of Bethsura. He came out of the city because they had no food there to endure the siege, because it was a Sabbath to the land. ⁵⁰ The king took Bethsura, and appointed a garrison there to keep it. ⁵¹ He encamped against the sanctuary many days; and set there mounds to shoot from, and engines of war, and machines for throwing fire and stones, and weapons to throw darts, and slings. ⁵² The Jews also made engines of war against their engines, and fought for many days. ⁵³ But there was no food in the sanctuary, because it was the seventh year, and those who fled for safety into Judea from among the Gentiles had eaten up the rest of the stores. ⁵⁴ There were only a few people left in the sanctuary, because the famine prevailed against them, and they were scattered, each man to his own place. ⁵⁵ Lysias heard that Philip, whom Antiochus the king, while he was yet alive, appointed to raise his son Antiochus to be king, ⁵⁶ had returned from Persia and Media, and with him the forces that went with the king, and that he was seeking to take control of the government. ⁵⁷ He made haste, and gave orders to depart. He said to the king and the leaders of the army and to the men, "We get weaker daily, our food is scant, the place where we encamp is strong, and the affairs of the kingdom lie upon us. ⁵⁸ Now therefore let's negotiate with these men, and make peace with them and with all their nation, ⁵⁹ and covenant with them, that they may walk after their own laws, as before; for because of their laws which we abolished they were angered, and did all these things." ⁶⁰ The speech pleased the king and the princes, and he sent to them to make peace; and they accepted it. ⁶¹ The king and the princes swore to them. On these conditions, they came out from the stronghold. ⁶² Then the king entered into mount Zion. He saw the strength of the place, and broke the oath which he had sworn, and gave orders to pull down the wall all around. ⁶³ Then he left in haste and returned to Antioch, and found Philip master of the city. He fought against him, and took the city by force.

7

¹ In the one hundred fifty first year,[h] Demetrius the son of Seleucus came out of Rome, and went up with a few men to a city by the sea, and reigned there. ² It came to pass, when he would go into the house of the kingdom of his fathers, that the army laid hands on Antiochus and Lysias, to bring them to him. ³ The thing became known to him, and he said, "Don't show me their faces!" ⁴ So the army killed them. Then Demetrius sat upon the throne of his kingdom. ⁵ All the lawless and ungodly men of Israel came to him. Alcimus was their leader, desiring to be high priest. ⁶ They accused the people to the king, saying, "Judas and his kindred have destroyed all your friends, and have scattered us from our own land. ⁷ Now therefore send a man whom you trust, and let him go and see all the destruction which he has brought on us and the king's country, and how he has punished them and all who helped them." ⁸ So the king chose Bacchides, one of the king's[i] friends, who was ruler in the country beyond the river, and was a great man in the kingdom, and faithful to the king. ⁹ He sent him and that ungodly Alcimus, whom he made the high priest; and he commanded him to take vengeance upon the children of Israel. ¹⁰ They marched away and came with a great army into the land of Judah. He sent messengers to Judas and his

---

[a] 6:10 See 1 Maccabees 2:18.
[b] 6:14 See 1 Maccabees 2:18.
[c] 6:16 Circa B.C. 164.
[d] 6:20 circa B.C. 163.
[e] 6:24 Gr. it.
[f] 6:28 See 1 Maccabees 2:18.
[g] 6:33 Or, itself eager for the fight
[h] 7:1 circa B.C. 162.
[i] 7:8 See 1 Maccabees 2:18.

kindred with words of peace deceitfully. ¹¹ They paid no attention to their words; for they saw that they had come with a great army. ¹² A group of scribes gathered together to Alcimus and Bacchides to seek just terms. ¹³ The[a] Hasidaeans were the first among the children of Israel who sought peace from them, ¹⁴ for they said, "One who is a priest of the seed of Aaron has come with the army, and he will do us no wrong." ¹⁵ He spoke with them words of peace, and swore to them, saying, "We won't seek to harm you or your friends." ¹⁶ They trusted him. Then he seized sixty men of them, and killed them in one day, according to the word which was written, ¹⁷ [b] The flesh of your saints and their blood was shed all around Jerusalem, and there was no one to bury them. ¹⁸ The fear and the dread of them fell upon all the people, for they said, "There is neither truth nor justice in them; for they have broken the covenant and the oath which they swore." ¹⁹ Bacchides withdrew from Jerusalem, and encamped in Bezeth. He sent and seized many of the deserters who were with him, and some of the people, and he killed them, throwing them into a large pit. ²⁰ He placed Alcimus in charge of the country and left with him a force to aid him. Then Bacchides went away to the king. ²¹ Alcimus struggled to maintain his high priesthood. ²² All those who troubled their people joined him, and they took control of the land of Judah, and did great damage in Israel. ²³ Judas saw all the wrongs that Alcimus and his company had done among the children of Israel, even more than the Gentiles. ²⁴ He went out into all the borders of Judea and took vengeance on the men who had deserted from him, and they were restrained from going out into the country. ²⁵ But when Alcimus saw that Judas and his company had grown strong, and knew that he was not able to withstand them, he returned to the king, and brought evil accusations against them. ²⁶ [c] Then the king sent Nicanor, one of his honorable princes, a man who hated Israel and was their enemy, and commanded him to destroy the people. ²⁷ Nicanor came to Jerusalem with a great army. He sent to Judas and his kindred deceitfully with words of peace, saying, ²⁸ "Let there be no battle between me and you; I will come with a few men, that I may see your faces in peace." ²⁹ He came to Judas, and they saluted one another peaceably. The enemies were ready to seize Judas by violence. ³⁰ This was known to Judas, that he came to him with deceit, and he was very afraid of him, and would see his face no more. ³¹ Nicanor found out that his plan was disclosed; and he went out to meet Judas in battle beside Capharsalama. ³² About five hundred men of Nicanor's army fell, and the rest fled into the city of David. ³³ After these things, Nicanor went up to mount Zion. Some of the priests came out of the sanctuary, with some of the elders of the people, to salute him peaceably, and to show him the whole burned sacrifice that was being offered for the king. ³⁴ He mocked them, laughed at them, derided them shamefully,[d] spoke arrogantly, ³⁵ and swore in a rage, saying, "Unless Judas and his army are now delivered into my hands, it shall be that, if I return safely, I will burn up this house!" And he went out in a great rage. ³⁶ The priests entered in, and stood before the altar and the temple; and they wept, and said, ³⁷ "You chose this house to be called by your name, to be a house of prayer and supplication for your people. ³⁸ Take vengeance on this man and his army, and let them fall by the sword. Remember their blasphemies, and don't allow them to live any longer." ³⁹ Then Nicanor went out from Jerusalem and encamped in Bethhoron, and there the Syrian army met him. ⁴⁰ Judas encamped in Adasa with three thousand men. Judas prayed and said, ⁴¹ "When those who came from the king blasphemed, your angel went out, and struck among them one hundred eighty-five thousand. ⁴² Even so, crush this army before us today, and let all the rest know that he has spoken wickedly against your sanctuary. Judge him according to his wickedness." ⁴³ On the thirteenth day of the month Adar, the armies met in battle. Nicanor's army was defeated, and he himself was the first to fall in the battle. ⁴⁴ Now when his army saw that Nicanor had fallen, they threw away their weapons and fled. ⁴⁵ They pursued them a day's journey from Adasa until you come to[e] Gazara, and they sounded an alarm after them with the signal trumpets. ⁴⁶ Men came out of all the surrounding villages of Judea, and outflanked them. These turned them back on those, and they all fell by the sword. There wasn't one of them left. ⁴⁷ The Jews took the spoils and the booty, and they cut off Nicanor's head and his right hand, which he had stretched out so arrogantly, and brought them, and hung them up beside Jerusalem. ⁴⁸ The people were exceedingly glad, and they kept that day as a day of great gladness. ⁴⁹ [f] They ordained to keep this day year by year on the thirteenth day of Adar. ⁵⁰ So the land of Judah had rest a few days.

8

¹ Judas heard of the fame of the Romans, that they are valiant men, and have pleasure in all who join themselves to them, and make friends with all who come to them, ² and that they are valiant men. They told him of their wars and exploits which they do among the Gauls, and how they conquered them, and forced them to pay tribute; ³ and what things they did in the land of Spain, that they might take control of the silver and gold mines which were there; ⁴ and how by their policy and persistence they conquered all the place (and the place was exceedingly far from them), and the kings who came against them from the uttermost part of the earth, until they had defeated them, and struck them severely; and how the rest give them tribute year by year. ⁵ Philip, and Perseus, king of Chittim, and those who lifted up themselves against them, they defeated in battle, and conquered them. ⁶ Antiochus also, the great king of Asia, came against them to battle, having one hundred twenty elephants, with cavalry, chariots, and an exceedingly great army, and he was defeated by them. ⁷ They took him alive, and decreed that both he and those who reigned after him should give them a great tribute, and should give hostages, and a parcel of land from the best of their provinces: ⁸ the countries of India, Media, and Lydia. They took them from him, and gave them to King Eumenes. ⁹ Judas heard how the Greeks planned to come and destroy them, ¹⁰ but this became known to them, and they sent against them a general who fought against them, and many of them fell down wounded to death, and they made captive their wives and their children, and plundered them, and conquered their land, and pulled down their strongholds, and plundered them, and brought them into bondage to this day. ¹¹ The remaining kingdoms and islands, as many as rose up against them at any time, they destroyed and made them to be their servants; ¹² but with their friends and those who relied on them they stayed friends. They conquered the kingdoms that were near and those that were far off, and all that heard of their fame were afraid of them. ¹³ Moreover, whoever they desired to help and to make kings, these they make kings; and whoever they desired, they depose. They are exalted exceedingly. ¹⁴ For all this, none of them ever put on a crown, neither did they clothe themselves with purple, as a display of grandeur. ¹⁵ Judas heard how they had made for themselves a senate house, and day by day, three hundred twenty men sat in council, consulting always for the people, to the end they might be well governed, ¹⁶ and how they commit their government to one man year by year, that he should rule over them, and control all their country, and all are obedient to that one, and there is neither envy nor emulation among them. ¹⁷ So Judas chose Eupolemus the son of John, the son of Accos, and Jason the son of Eleazar, and sent them to Rome, to establish friendship and alliance with them, ¹⁸ and that they should free the yoke from themselves; for they saw that the kingdom of the Greeks kept Israel in bondage. ¹⁹ Then they went to Rome, a very long journey, and they entered into the senate house, and said, ²⁰ "Judas, who is also called Maccabaeus, and his kindred, and the people of the Jews, have sent us to you, to make an alliance and peace with you, and that we might be registered as your allies and friends." ²¹ This thing was pleasing to them. ²² This is the copy of the writing which they wrote back again on tables of brass, and sent to Jerusalem, that it might be with them there for a memorial of peace and alliance: ²³ "Good success be to the Romans, and to the nation of the Jews, by sea and by land forever. May the sword and the enemy be far from them. ²⁴ But if war arises for Rome first, or any of their allies in all their dominion, ²⁵ the nation of the Jews shall help them as allies, as the occasion shall indicate to them, with all their heart. ²⁶ To those who make war upon them, they shall not give supplies, food, weapons, money, or ships, as it has seemed good to Rome, and they shall keep their ordinances without taking anything in return. ²⁷ In the same way, moreover, if war comes first upon the nation of the Jews, the Romans shall willingly help them as allies, as the occasion shall indicate to them; ²⁸ and to those who are fighting with them, there shall not be given food, weapons, money, or ships, as it has seemed good to Rome. They shall keep these ordinances, and that without deceit. ²⁹ According to these terms, the Romans made a treaty with the Jewish people. ³⁰ But if hereafter the one party and the other shall determine to add or diminish anything, they shall do it at their pleasure, and whatever they add or take away shall be ratified. ³¹ Concerning the evils which King Demetrius is doing to them, we have written to him, saying, 'Why have you made your yoke heavy on our friends and allies the Jews? ³² If therefore they plead any more against you, we will do them justice, and fight with you on sea and on land.'"

9

¹ Demetrius heard that Nicanor had fallen with his forces in battle, and he sent Bacchides and Alcimus again into the land of Judah a second time, and the right wing of his army with them. ² They went by the way that leads to Gilgal, and encamped against Mesaloth, which is in Arbela, and took

---

[a] *7:13* That is, Chasidim.
[b] *7:17* Psalms **79:2**, **3**.
[c] *7:26* See **2 Maccabees 14:12**.
[d] *7:34* Gr. polluted them.
[e] *7:45* Gr. Gazera.
[f] *7:49* See **2 Maccabees 15:36**.

possession of it, and killed many people. ³ The first month of the one hundred fifty-second year, ᵃ they encamped against Jerusalem. ⁴ Then they marched away and went to Berea with twenty thousand infantry and two thousand cavalry. ⁵ Judas was encamped at Elasa with three thousand chosen men. ⁶ They saw the multitude of the forces, that they were many, and they were terrified. Many slipped away out of the army. There were not left of them more than eight hundred men. ⁷ Judas saw that his army slipped away and that the battle pressed upon him, and he was very troubled in spirit, because he had no time to gather them together, and he became faint. ⁸ He said to those who were left, "Let's arise and go up against our adversaries, if perhaps we may be able to fight with them." ⁹ They tried to dissuade him, saying, "There is no way we are able; but let's rather save our lives now. Let's return again with our kindred, and fight against them; but we are too few." ¹⁰ Judas said, "Let it not be so that I should do this thing, to flee from them. If our time has come, let's die in a manly way for our kindred's sake, and not leave a cause of reproach against our honor." ¹¹ The army marched out from the camp, and stood to encounter them. The cavalry was divided into two companies, and the slingers and the archers went before the army, and all the mighty men that fought in the front of the battle. ¹² Bacchides was in the right wing. The phalanx advanced on the two parts, and they blew with their trumpets. ¹³ The men by Judas' side sounded with their trumpets, and the earth shook with the shout of the armies, and the battle was joined, and continued from morning until evening. ¹⁴ Judas saw that Bacchides and the strength of his army were on the right side, and all that were brave in heart went with him, ¹⁵ and the right wing was defeated by them, and he pursued after them to the mount Azotus. ¹⁶ Those who were on the left wing saw that the right wing was defeated, and they turned and followed in the footsteps of Judas and of those who were with him. ¹⁷ The battle became desperate, and many on both sides fell wounded to death. ¹⁸ Judas fell, and the rest fled. ¹⁹ Jonathan and Simon took Judas their brother, and buried him in the tomb of his ancestors at Modin. ²⁰ They wept for him. All Israel made great lamentation for him, and mourned many days, and said, ²¹ "How is the mighty fallen, the savior of Israel!" ²² The rest of the acts of Judas, and his wars, and the valiant deeds which he did, and his greatness, are not written; for they were exceedingly many. ²³ It came to pass after the death of Judas, that the lawless emerged within all the borders of Israel. All those who did iniquity rose up. ²⁴ In those days there was an exceedingly great famine, and the country went over to their side. ²⁵ Bacchides chose the ungodly men and made them rulers of the country. ²⁶ They inquired and searched for the friends of Judas, and brought them to Bacchides, and he took vengeance on them and used them despitefully. ²⁷ There was great suffering in Israel, such as was not since the time prophets stopped appearing to them. ²⁸ All the friends of Judas were gathered together, and they said to Jonathan, ²⁹ "Since your brother Judas has died, we have no man like him to go out against our enemies and Bacchides, and among those of our nation who hate us. ³⁰ Now therefore we have chosen you this day to be our prince and leader in his place, that you may fight our battles." ³¹ So Jonathan took the governance upon him at that time, and rose up in the place of his brother Judas. ³² When Bacchides found out, he tried to kill him. ³³ Jonathan, and Simon his brother, and all who were with him, knew it; and they fled into the wilderness of Tekoah, and encamped by the water of the pool of Asphar. ³⁴ Bacchides found this out on the Sabbath day, and came–he and all his army–over the Jordan. ³⁵ Jonathan sent his brother, a leader of the multitude, and implored his friends the Nabathaeans, that they might store their baggage, which was much, with them. ³⁶ The children of Jambri came out of Medaba, and seized John and all that he had, and went their way with it. ³⁷ But after these things, they brought word to Jonathan and Simon his brother that the children of Jambri were celebrating a great wedding, and were bringing the bride, a daughter of one of the great nobles of Canaan, from Nadabath with a large escort. ³⁸ They remembered John their brother, and went up, and hid themselves under the cover of the mountain. ³⁹ They lifted up their eyes and looked, and saw a great procession with much baggage. The bridegroom came out with his friends and his kindred to meet them with timbrels, musicians, and many weapons. ⁴⁰ They rose up against them from their ambush and killed them, and many fell wounded to death. The remnant fled into the mountain, and the Jews took all their spoils. ⁴¹ So the wedding was turned into mourning, and the voice of their musicians into lamentation. ⁴² They avenged fully the blood of their brother, and turned back to the marshes of the Jordan. ⁴³ Bacchides heard it, and he came on the Sabbath day to the banks of Jordan with a great army. ⁴⁴ Jonathan said to his company, "Let's stand up now and fight for our lives, for things are different today than they were yesterday and the day before. ⁴⁵ For, behold, the battle is before us and behind us. Moreover the water of the Jordan is on this side and on that side, and marsh and thicket. There is no place to escape. ⁴⁶ Now therefore cry to heaven, that you may be delivered out of the hand of your enemies." ⁴⁷ So the battle was joined, and Jonathan stretched out his hand to strike Bacchides, and he turned away back from him. ⁴⁸ Jonathan and those who were with him leapt into the Jordan, and swam over to the other side. The enemy didn't pass over the Jordan against them. ⁴⁹ About a thousand men of Bacchides' company fell that day; ⁵⁰ and he returned to Jerusalem. They built strong cities in Judea, the stronghold that was in Jericho, and Emmaus, Bethhoron, Bethel, Timnath, Pharathon, and Tephon, with high walls and gates and bars. ⁵¹ He set garrisons in them to harass Israel. ⁵² He fortified the city Bethsura, Gazara, and the citadel, and put troops and stores of food in them. ⁵³ He took the sons of the chief men of the country for hostages, and put them under guard in the citadel at Jerusalem. ⁵⁴ And in the one hundred fifty-third year,ᵇ in the second month, Alcimus gave orders to pull down the wall of the inner court of the sanctuary. He also pulled down the works of the prophets. ⁵⁵ He began to pull down. At that time was Alcimus stricken, and his works were hindered; and his mouth was stopped, and he was taken with a palsy, and he could no more speak anything and give orders concerning his house. ⁵⁶ Alcimus died at that time with great torment. ⁵⁷ Bacchides saw that Alcimus was dead, and he returned to the king. Then the land of Judah had rest for two years. ⁵⁸ Then all the lawless men took counsel, saying, "Behold, Jonathan and his men are dwelling at ease and in security. Now therefore we will bring Bacchides, and he will capture them all in one night. ⁵⁹ They went and consulted with him. ⁶⁰ He marched out and came with a great army, and sent letters secretly to all his allies who were in Judea, that they should seize Jonathan and those who were with him; but they couldn't, because their plan was known to them. ⁶¹ Jonathan's men seized about fifty of the men of the country who were authors of the wickedness, and he killed them. ⁶² Jonathan, Simon, and those who were with him, went away to Bethbasi, which is in the wilderness, and he built up that which had been pulled down, and they made it strong. ⁶³ Bacchides found out about it, and he gathered together all his multitude, and sent orders to those who were of Judea. ⁶⁴ He went and encamped against Bethbasi and fought against it many days, and made engines of war. ⁶⁵ Jonathan left his brother Simon in the city, and went out into the country, and he went with a few men. ⁶⁶ He struck Odomera and his kindred, and the children of Phasiron in their tents. ⁶⁷ They began to strike them, and to go up with their forces. Then Simon and those who were with him went out of the city, and set the engines of war on fire, ⁶⁸ and fought against Bacchides, and he was defeated by them. They afflicted him severely; for his counsel and expedition was in vain. ⁶⁹ They were very angry with the lawless men who gave him counsel to come into the country, and they killed many of them. Then he decided to depart into his own land. ⁷⁰ Jonathan learned of this and sent ambassadors to him, to the end that they should make peace with him, and that he should restore to them the captives. ⁷¹ He accepted the thing, and did according to his words, and swore to him that he would not seek his harm all the days of his life. ⁷² He restored to him the captives which he had taken before out of the land of Judah, and he returned and departed into his own land, and didn't come any more into their borders. ⁷³ Thus the sword ceased from Israel. Jonathan lived at Michmash. Jonathan began to judge the people; and he destroyed the ungodly out of Israel.

10

¹ In the one hundred sixtieth year,ᶜ Alexander Epiphanes, the son of Antiochus, went up and took possession of Ptolemais. They received him, and he reigned there. ² King Demetrius heard about this, and he gathered together exceedingly great forces, and went out to meet him in battle. ³ Demetrius sent a letter to Jonathan with words of peace, so as to honor him. ⁴ For he said, "Let's go beforehand to make peace with them, before he makes peace with Alexander against us; ⁵ for he will remember all the evils that we have done against him, and to his kindred and to his nation." ⁶ So he gave him authority to gather together forces, and to provide weapons, and that he should be his ally. He also commanded that they should release the hostages that were in the citadel to him. ⁷ Jonathan came to Jerusalem, and read the letter in the hearing of all the people, and of those who were in the citadel. ⁸ They were very afraid when they heard that the king had given him authority to gather together an army. ⁹ Those in the citadel released the hostages to Jonathan, and he restored them to their parents. ¹⁰ Jonathan lived in Jerusalem and began to build and renew the city. ¹¹ He commanded those who did the work to build the walls and

---

ᵃ *9:3* circa B.C. **161**.   ᵇ *9:54* circa B.C. **160**.   ᶜ *10:1* circa B.C. **153**.

encircle Mount Zion with[a] square stones for defense; and they did so. ¹²The foreigners who were in the strongholds which Bacchides had built fled away. ¹³Each man left his place and departed into his own land. ¹⁴Only at Bethsura, there were left some of those who had forsaken the law and the commandments, for it was a place of refuge to them. ¹⁵King Alexander heard all the promises which Demetrius had sent to Jonathan. They told him of the battles and the valiant deeds which he and his kindred had done, and of the troubles which they had endured. ¹⁶So he said, "Could we find another man like him? Now we will make him our[b] friend and ally." ¹⁷He wrote a letter and sent it to him, in these words, saying, ¹⁸"King Alexander to his brother Jonathan, greetings. ¹⁹We have heard of you, that you are a mighty man of valour, and worthy to be our[c] friend. ²⁰Now we have appointed you this day to be high priest of your nation, and to be called the king's[d] friend, and to take our side, and to keep friendship with us." He also sent to him a purple robe and a golden crown. ²¹And Jonathan put on the holy garments in the seventh month of the one hundred sixtieth year,[e] at the feast of tabernacles; and he gathered together forces and provided weapons in abundance. ²²When Demetrius heard these things, he was grieved and said, ²³"What is this that we have done, that Alexander has gotten ahead of us in establishing friendship with the Jews to strengthen himself? ²⁴I also will write to them words of encouragement and of honor and of gifts, that they may be with me to aid me." ²⁵So he sent to them this message: "King Demetrius to the nation of the Jews, greetings. ²⁶Since as you have kept your covenants with us, and continued in our friendship, and have not joined yourselves to our enemies, we have heard of this, and are glad. ²⁷Now continue still to keep faith with us, and we will repay you with good in return for your dealings with us. ²⁸We will grant you many immunities and give you gifts. ²⁹"Now I free you and release all the Jews from the tributes, from the salt tax, and from the crown levies. ³⁰Instead of the third part of the seed, and instead of half of the fruit of the trees, which falls to me to receive, I release it from this day and henceforth, so that I will not take it from the land of Judah, and from the three districts which are added to it from the country of Samaria and Galilee, from this day forth and for all time. ³¹Let Jerusalem be holy and free, with her borders, tithes, and taxes. ³²I yield up also my authority over the citadel which is at Jerusalem, and give it to the high priest, that he may appoint in it men whom he chooses to keep it. ³³Every soul of the Jews who has been carried captive from the land of Judah into any part of my kingdom, I set at liberty without payment. Let officials also cancel the taxes on their livestock. ³⁴"All the feasts, the Sabbaths, new moons, appointed days, three days before a feast, and three days after a feast, let them all be days of immunity and release for all the Jews who are in my kingdom. ³⁵No man shall have authority to exact anything from any of them, or to trouble them concerning any matter. ³⁶"Let there be enrolled among the king's forces about thirty thousand men of the Jews, and pay shall be given to them, as is due to all the king's forces. ³⁷Of them, some shall be placed in the king's great strongholds, and some of them shall be placed over the affairs of the kingdom, which are positions of trust. Let those who are over them and their rulers be of themselves, and let them walk after their own laws, even as the king has commanded in the land of Judah. ³⁸"The three districts that have been added to Judea from the country of Samaria, let them be annexed to Judea, that they may be reckoned to be under one ruler, that they may not obey any other authority than the high priest's. ³⁹As for Ptolemais and its land, I have given it as a gift to the sanctuary that is at Jerusalem, for the expenses of the sanctuary. ⁴⁰I also give every year fifteen thousand shekels of silver from the king's revenues from the places that are appropriate. ⁴¹And all the additional funds which those who manage the king's affairs didn't pay as in the first years, they shall give from now on toward the works of the temple. ⁴²Besides this, the five thousand shekels of silver which they received from the uses of the sanctuary from the revenue year by year is also released, because it belongs to the priests who minister there. ⁴³Whoever flees to the temple that is at Jerusalem, and within all of its borders, whether one owe money to the king, or any other matter, let them go free, along with all that they have in my kingdom. ⁴⁴For the building and renewing of the structures of the sanctuary, the expense shall also be given out of the king's revenue. ⁴⁵For the building of the walls of Jerusalem and fortifying it all around, the expense shall also be given out of the king's revenue, also for the building of the walls in Judea." ⁴⁶Now when Jonathan and the people heard these words, they gave no credence to them, and didn't accept them, because they remembered the great evil which he had done in Israel, and that he had afflicted them very severely. ⁴⁷They were well pleased with Alexander, because he was the first who spoke words of peace to them, and they were allies with him always. ⁴⁸King Alexander gathered together great forces and encamped near Demetrius. ⁴⁹The two kings joined battle, and the army of Alexander fled; and Demetrius followed after him, and prevailed against them. ⁵⁰He strengthened the battle exceedingly until the sun went down; and Demetrius fell that day. ⁵¹Alexander sent ambassadors to Ptolemy king of Egypt with this message: ⁵²"Since I have returned to my kingdom, and am seated on the throne of my fathers, and have established my dominion, and have overthrown Demetrius, and have taken possession of our country– ⁵³yes, I joined the battle with him, and he and his army were defeated by us, and we sat on the throne of his kingdom– ⁵⁴now also let's make friends with one another. Give me now your daughter as my wife. I will be joined with you, and will give both you and her gifts worthy of you." ⁵⁵Ptolemy the king answered, saying, "Happy is the day you returned to the land of your ancestors and sat on the throne of their kingdom. ⁵⁶Now I will do to you as you have written, but meet me at Ptolemais, that we may see one another; and I will join with you, even as you have said." ⁵⁷So Ptolemy went out of Egypt, himself and Cleopatra his daughter, and came to Ptolemais in the one hundred sixty-second year.[f] ⁵⁸King Alexander met him, and he gave him his daughter Cleopatra, and celebrated her wedding at Ptolemais with great pomp, as kings do. ⁵⁹King Alexander wrote to Jonathan, that he should come to meet him. ⁶⁰He went with pomp to Ptolemais, and met the two kings. He gave them and their friends[g] silver and gold, and many gifts, and found favor in their sight. ⁶¹Some malcontents out of Israel, men who were transgressors of the law, gathered together against him to complain against him; but the king paid no attention to them. ⁶²The king commanded that they take off Jonathan's garments and clothe him in purple, and they did so. ⁶³The king made him sit with him, and said to his princes, "Go out with him into the midst of the city, and proclaim that no man may complain against him of any matter, and let no man trouble him for any reason." ⁶⁴It came to pass, when those who complained against him saw his honor according to the proclamation, and saw him clothed in purple, they all fled away. ⁶⁵The king gave him honor, and enrolled him among his chief friends,[h] and made him a captain and governor of a province. ⁶⁶Then Jonathan returned to Jerusalem with peace and gladness. ⁶⁷In the one hundred sixty-fifth year,[i] Demetrius, son of Demetrius, came out of Crete into the land of his ancestors. ⁶⁸When King Alexander heard of it, he grieved exceedingly and returned to Antioch. ⁶⁹Demetrius appointed Apollonius, who was over Coelesyria, and he gathered together a great army, and encamped against Jamnia, and sent to Jonathan the high priest, saying, ⁷⁰"You alone lift up yourself against us, but I am ridiculed and in reproach because of you. Why do you assume authority against us in the mountains? ⁷¹Now therefore, if you trust in your forces, come down to us into the plain, and let's match strength with each other there; for the power of the cities is with me. ⁷²Ask and learn who I am, and the rest who help us. They say, 'Your foot can't stand before our face; for your ancestors have been put to flight twice in their own land.' ⁷³Now you won't be able to withstand the cavalry and such an army as this in the plain, where is there is no stone or pebble, or place to flee." ⁷⁴Now when Jonathan heard the words of Apollonius, he was moved in his mind, and he chose ten thousand men, and went out from Jerusalem; and Simon his brother met him to help him. ⁷⁵Then he encamped against Joppa. The people of the city shut him out, because Apollonius had a garrison in Joppa. ⁷⁶So they fought against it. The people of the city were afraid, and opened to him; and Jonathan became master of Joppa. ⁷⁷Apollonius heard about that, and he gathered an army of three thousand cavalry, and a great army, and went to Azotus as though he were on a journey, and at the same time advanced onward into the plain, because he had a multitude of cavalry which he trusted. ⁷⁸He pursued him to Azotus, and the armies joined battle.[j] ⁷⁹Apollonius had secretly left a thousand cavalry behind them. ⁸⁰Jonathan learned that there was an ambush behind him. They surrounded his army, and shot their arrows at the people, from morning until evening; ⁸¹but the people stood fast, as Jonathan commanded them; and the enemy's horses grew tired. ⁸²Then Simon brought forward his army and joined battle with the phalanx (for the cavalry were exhausted), and they were defeated by him and fled.

---

[a] 10:11 So the versions and Josephus. Gr. four-foot stones.
[b] 10:16 See 1 Maccabees 2:18. Compare 1 Maccabees 10:65.
[c] 10:19 See 1 Maccabees 2:18. Compare 1 Maccabees 10:65.
[d] 10:20 See 1 Maccabees 2:18. Compare 1 Maccabees 10:65.
[e] 10:21 circa B.C. 153.
[f] 10:57 circa B.C. 151.
[g] 10:60 See 1 Maccabees 2:18. Compare 1 Maccabees 10:65.
[h] 10:65 See 1 Maccabees 11:27; 2 Maccabees 8:9. Compare 1 Maccabees 2:18; 10:16, etc.
[i] 10:67 circa B.C. 148.
[j] 10:78 Most of the authorities here repeat after him.

83 The cavalry were scattered in the plain. They fled to Azotus and entered into Beth-dagon, their idol's temple, to save themselves. 84 Jonathan burned Azotus and the cities around it and took their spoils. He burned the temple of Dagon and those who fled into it with fire. 85 Those who had fallen by the sword plus those who were burned were about eight thousand men. 86 From there, Jonathan left and encamped against Ascalon. The people of the city came out to meet him with great pomp. 87 Jonathan, with those who were on his side, returned to Jerusalem, having many spoils. 88 It came to pass, when King Alexander heard these things, he honored Jonathan even more. 89 He sent him a gold buckle, as the custom is to give to the king's kindred. He gave him Ekron and all its land for a possession.

11

1 Then the king of Egypt gathered together great forces, as the sand which is by the sea shore, and many ships, and sought to make himself master of Alexander's kingdom by deceit, and to add it to his own kingdom. 2 He went out into Syria with words of peace, and the people of the cities opened their gates to him and met him; for King Alexander's command was that they should meet him, because he was his father-in-law. 3 Now as he entered into the cities of Ptolemais, he set his forces for a garrison in each city. 4 But when he came near to Azotus, they showed him the temple of Dagon burned with fire, and Azotus and its pasture lands destroyed, and the bodies cast out, and those who had been burned, whom he burned in the war, for they had made heaps of them in his way. 5 They told the king what Jonathan had done, that they might cast blame on him; but the king kept silent. 6 Jonathan met the king with pomp at Joppa, and they greeted one another, and they slept there. 7 Jonathan went with the king as far as the river that is called Eleutherus, then returned to Jerusalem. 8 But King Ptolemy took control of the cities along the sea coast, to Selucia which is by the sea, and he devised evil plans concerning Alexander. 9 He sent ambassadors to King Demetrius, saying, "Come! Let's make a covenant with one another, and I will give you my daughter whom Alexander has, and you shall reign over your father's kingdom; 10 for I regret that I gave my daughter to him, for he tried to kill me. 11 He accused him, because he coveted his kingdom. 12 Taking his daughter from him, he gave her to Demetrius, and was estranged from Alexander, and their enmity was openly seen. 13 Ptolemy entered into Antioch, and put on himself the crown of Asia. He put two crowns upon his head, the crown of Egypt and that of Asia. 14 But King Alexander was in Cilicia at that time, because the people of that region were in revolt. 15 When Alexander heard of it, he came against him in war. Ptolemy marched out and met him with a strong force, and put him to flight. 16 Alexander fled into Arabia, that he might be sheltered there; but King Ptolemy was triumphant. 17 Zabdiel the Arabian took off Alexander's head, and sent it to Ptolemy. 18 King Ptolemy died the third day after, and those who were in his strongholds were slain by the inhabitants of the strongholds. 19 Demetrius became king in the one hundred sixty-seventh year.[a] 20 In those days Jonathan gathered together the Judeans to take the citadel that was at Jerusalem. He made many engines of war to use against it. 21 Some lawless men who hated their own nation went to the king and reported to him that Jonathan was besieging the citadel. 22 He heard, and was angry, but when he heard it, he set out immediately, and came to Ptolemais, and wrote to Jonathan, that he should not besiege it, and that he should meet him and speak with him at Ptolemais with all speed. 23 But when Jonathan heard this, he gave orders to continue the siege. He chose some of the elders of Israel and of the priests, and put himself in peril 24 by taking silver, gold, clothing, and various other presents, and went to Ptolemais to the king. Then he found favor in his sight. 25 Some lawless men of those who were of the nation made complaints against him, 26 and the king did to him even as his predecessors had done to him, and exalted him in the sight of all his[b] friends, 27 and confirmed to him the high priesthood, and all the other honors that he had before, and gave him preeminence among his[c] chief friends. 28 And Jonathan requested of the king that he would make Judea free from tribute, along with the three[d] provinces and the country of Samaria, and promised him three hundred talents. 29 The king consented, and wrote letters to Jonathan concerning all these things as follows: 30 "King Demetrius to his brother Jonathan, and to the nation of the Jews, greetings. 31 The copy of the letter which we wrote to Lasthenes our kinsman concerning you, we have written also to you, that you may see it. 32 'King Demetrius to Lasthenes his father, greetings. 33 We have determined to do good to the nation of the Jews, who are our friends, and observe what is just toward us, because of their good will toward us. 34 We have confirmed therefore to them the borders of Judea, and also the three governments of Aphaerema, Lydda, and Ramathaim (these were added to Judea from the country of Samaria), and all their territory to them, for all who do sacrifice in Jerusalem, instead of the king's dues which the king received of them yearly before from the produce of the earth and the fruits of trees. 35 As for the other payments to us from henceforth, of the tithes and the taxes that pertain to us, and the salt pits, and the crown taxes due to us, all these we will give back to them. 36 Not one of these grants shall be annulled from this time forth and forever. 37 Now therefore be careful to make a copy of these things, and let it be given to Jonathan, and let it be set up on the holy mountain in a suitable and conspicuous place.'" 38 When King Demetrius saw that the land was quiet before him, and that no resistance was made to him, he sent away all his troops, each man to his own place, except the foreign troops, which he had raised from the islands of the Gentiles. So all the troops of his fathers hated him. 39 Now Tryphon was one of those who previously had been on Alexander's side, and he saw that all the forces murmured against Demetrius. So he went to Imalcue the Arabian, who was raising up Antiochus the young child of Alexander, 40 and urgently insisted to him that he should deliver him to him, that he might reign in his father's place. He told him all that Demetrius had done, and the hatred with which his forces hated him; and he stayed there many days. 41 Now Jonathan sent to King Demetrius, that he should remove the troops of the citadel from Jerusalem, and the troops who were in the strongholds; for they fought against Israel continually. 42 Demetrius sent to Jonathan, saying, "I will not only do this for you and your nation, but I will greatly honor you and your nation, if I find an opportunity. 43 Now therefore you shall do well if you send me men who will fight for me; for all my forces have revolted." 44 So Jonathan sent him three thousand valiant men to Antioch. They came to the king, and the king was glad at their coming. 45 The people of the city gathered themselves together into the midst of the city, to the number of one hundred and twenty thousand men, and they wanted to kill the king. 46 The king fled into the court of the palace, and the people of the city seized the main streets of the city and began to fight. 47 The king called the Jews to help him, and they were gathered together to him all at once, and they dispersed themselves in the city, and killed that day about one hundred thousand. 48 They set the city on fire, and seized many spoils that day, and saved the king. 49 The people of the city saw that the Jews had taken control of the city as they pleased, and they became faint in their hearts, and they cried out to the king with supplication, saying, 50 "Give us your right hand, and let the Jews cease from fighting against us and the city." 51 They threw away their weapons and made peace. The Jews were glorified in the sight of the king, and before all who were in his kingdom. Then they returned to Jerusalem, having much plunder. 52 So King Demetrius sat on the throne of his kingdom, and the land was quiet before him. 53 He lied in all that he spoke, and estranged himself from Jonathan, and didn't repay him according to the benefits with which he had repaid him, and treated him very harshly. 54 Now after this, Tryphon returned, and with him the young child Antiochus, who reigned and put on a crown. 55 All the forces which Demetrius had sent away with disgrace were gathered to him, and they fought against him, and he fled and was routed. 56 Tryphon took the elephants, and took control of Antioch. 57 The young Antiochus wrote to Jonathan, saying, "I confirm to you the high priesthood, and appoint you over the four districts, and to be one of the king's[e] friends." 58 He sent to him golden vessels and furniture for the table, and gave him permission to drink in golden vessels, and to be clothed in purple, and to have a golden buckle. 59 He made his brother Simon governor from the Ladder of Tyre to the borders of Egypt. 60 Jonathan went out and took his journey beyond the river and through the cities. All the forces of Syria gathered themselves to him to be his allies. He came to Ascalon, and the people of the city met him honorably. 61 He departed from there to Gaza, and the people of Gaza shut him out. So he besieged it and burned its pasture lands with fire, and plundered them. 62 The people of Gaza pleaded with Jonathan, and he gave them his right hand, and took the sons of their princes for hostages, and sent them away to Jerusalem. Then he passed through the country as far as Damascus. 63 Then Jonathan heard that Demetrius' princes had come to Kedesh, which is in Galilee, with a great army, intending to remove him from his office. 64 He went to meet them, but he left Simon his brother in the country. 65 Simon encamped against Bethsura, and fought against it many days, and hemmed it in. 66 They asked him to give them his right hand, and he gave it to them. He removed them from there, took possession of the city, and set a garrison over it. 67 Jonathan and his army encamped at the water of Gennesareth, and early in the morning they marched to the plain of Hazor. 68 Behold, an army of foreigners met him in the plain. They laid

---

[a] 11:19 circa B.C. 146.
[b] 11:26 See 1 Maccabees 2:18.
[c] 11:27 See 1 Maccabees 10:65.
[d] 11:28 Gr. toparchies
[e] 11:57 See 1 Maccabees 2:18.

an ambush for him in the mountains, but they themselves met him face to face. ⁶⁹ But those who lay in ambush rose out of their places and joined battle. All those who were on Jonathan's side fled. ⁷⁰ Not one of them was left, except Mattathias the son of Absalom, and Judas the son of Chalphi, captains of the forces. ⁷¹ Jonathan tore his clothes, put dirt on his head, and prayed. ⁷² He turned again to them in battle, and routed them, and they fled. ⁷³ When the men on his side who had fled saw this, they returned to him and pursued with him to Kedesh to their camp, and they encamped there. ⁷⁴ About three thousand men of the foreigners fell on that day. Then Jonathan returned to Jerusalem.

12

¹ Jonathan saw that the time was favorable for him, so he chose men and sent them to Rome to confirm and renew the friendship that they had with them. ² He also sent similar letters to the Spartans, and to other places. ³ They went to Rome, entered into the senate house, and said, "Jonathan the high priest and the nation of the Jews have sent us to renew for them the friendship and the alliance, as in former time. ⁴ They gave them letters to the men in every place, that they should provide safe conduct for them on their way to the land of Judah. ⁵ This is the copy of the letters which Jonathan wrote to the Spartans: ⁶ "Jonathan the high priest, and the senate of the nation, and the priests, and the rest of the people of the Jews, to their kindred the Spartans, greetings. ⁷ Even before this time letters were sent to Onias the high priest from Arius,ᵃ who was reigning among you, to signify that you are our kindred, as the copy written below shows. ⁸ Onias welcomed honorably the man who was sent and received the letters, wherein declaration was made of alliance and friendship. ⁹ Therefore we also, even though we need none of these things, having for our encouragement the holy books which are in our hands, ¹⁰ have undertaken to send that we might renew our brotherhood and friendship with you, to the end that we should not become estranged from you altogether; for a long time has passed since you sent your letter to us. ¹¹ We therefore at all times without ceasing, both in our feasts, and on the other convenient days, remember you in the sacrifices which we offer, and in our prayers, as it is right and proper to be mindful of kindred. ¹² Moreover, we are glad for your glory. ¹³ But as for ourselves, many afflictions and many wars have encompassed us, and the kings who are around us have fought against us. ¹⁴ We were unwilling to be troublesome to you, and to the rest of our allies and friends, in these wars; ¹⁵ for we have the help which is from heaven to help us, and we have been delivered from our enemies, and our enemies have been humbled. ¹⁶ We chose therefore Numenius the son of Antiochus and Antipater the son of Jason, and have sent them to the Romans, to renew the friendship that we had with them, and the former alliance. ¹⁷ We commanded them therefore to go also to you, and to salute you, and to deliver you our letters concerning the renewing of friendship and our brotherhood. ¹⁸ And now you will do well if you give us a reply." ¹⁹ And this is the copy of the letters which they sent to Onias: ²⁰ "Arius king of the Spartans to Onias the chief priest, greetings. ²¹ It has been found in writing, concerning the Spartans and the Jews, that they are kindred, and that they are of the descendants of Abraham. ²² Now, since this has come to our knowledge, you will do well to write to us of yourᵇ prosperity. ²³ We moreover write on our part to you, that your livestock and goods are ours, and ours are yours. We do command therefore that they make report to you accordingly." ²⁴ Now Jonathan heard that Demetrius' princes had returned to fight against him with a greater army than before, ²⁵ so he marched away from Jerusalem, and met them in the country of Hamath; for he gave them no opportunity to set foot in his country. ²⁶ He sent spies into his camp, and they came again, and reported to him that they were preparing to attack them at night. ²⁷ But as soon as the sun was down, Jonathan commanded his men to watch, and to be armed, that all the night long they might be ready for battle. He stationed sentinels around the camp. ²⁸ The adversaries heard that Jonathan and his men were ready for battle, and they feared, and trembled in their hearts, and they kindled fires in their camp then withdrew. ²⁹ But Jonathan and his men didn't know it until the morning; for they saw the fires burning. ³⁰ Jonathan pursued after them, but didn't overtake them; for they had gone over the river Eleutherus. ³¹ Then Jonathan turned toward the Arabians, who are called Zabadaeans, and struck them, and took their spoils. ³² He came out from there, and came to Damascus, and took his journey through all the country. ³³ Simon went out, and took his journey as far as Ascalon, and the strongholds that were near it. Then he turned toward Joppa and took possession of it; ³⁴ for he had heard that they were planning to hand over the stronghold to Demetrius' men. He set a garrison there to guard it. ³⁵ Then Jonathan returned and called the elders of the people together. He planned with them to build strongholds in Judea, ³⁶ and to make the walls of Jerusalem higher, and to raise a great mound between the citadel and the city, to separate it from the city, that so it might be isolated, that its garrison might neither buy nor sell. ³⁷ They were gathered together to build the city. Part of the wall of the brook that is on the east side fell down, and he repaired the section called Chaphenatha. ³⁸ Simon also built Adida in theᶜ plain country, made it strong, and set up gates and bars. ³⁹ And Tryphon sought to reign over Asia and to crown himself, and to stretch out his hand against Antiochus the king. ⁴⁰ He was afraid that Jonathan wouldn't allow him, and that he would fight against him; and he sought a way to seize him, that he might destroy him. So he marched out and came to Bethshan. ⁴¹ Jonathan came out to meet him with forty thousand men chosen for battle, and came to Bethshan. ⁴² Tryphon saw that he came with a great army, and he was afraid to stretch out his hand against him. ⁴³ He received him honorably, and commended him to all hisᵈ friends, and gave him gifts, and commanded his forces to be obedient to him, as to himself. ⁴⁴ He said to Jonathan, "Why have you put all this people to so much trouble, seeing there is no war between us? ⁴⁵ Now send them away to their homes, but choose for yourself a few men who shall be with you, and come with me to Ptolemais, and I will give it to you, and the rest of the strongholds and the rest of the forces, and all the king's officers. Then I will turn around and depart; for this is why I came." ⁴⁶ He put his trust in him, and did even as he said, and sent away his forces, and they departed into the land of Judah. ⁴⁷ But he reserved to himself three thousand men, of whom he left two thousand in Galilee, but one thousand went with him. ⁴⁸ Now as soon as Jonathan entered into Ptolemais, the people of Ptolemais shut the gates and seized him. They killed all those who came in with him with the sword. ⁴⁹ Tryphon sent troops and cavalry into Galilee, and into the Great Plain, to destroy all Jonathan's men. ⁵⁰ They perceived that he had been seized and had perished, along with those who were with him. They encouraged one another and went on their way close together, prepared to fight. ⁵¹ Those who followed them saw that they were ready to fight for their lives, and turned back again. ⁵² They all came in peace into the land of Judah, and they mourned for Jonathan and those who were with him, and they were very afraid. All Israel mourned with a great mourning. ⁵³ And all the Gentiles who were around them sought to destroy them utterly; for they said, "They have no ruler nor anyone to help them. Now therefore let's fight against them, and take away their memory from among men."

13

¹ Simon heard that Tryphon had gathered together a mighty army to come into the land of Judah and destroy it utterly. ² He saw that the people were trembling in great fear. So he went up to Jerusalem and gathered the people together. ³ He encouraged them, and said to them, "You yourselves know all the things that I, my kindred, and my father's house have done for the laws and the sanctuary, and the battles and the distresses which we have seen. ⁴ Because of this, all my brothers have perished for Israel's sake, and I am left alone. ⁵ Now be it far from me, that I should spare my own life in any time of affliction, for I am not better than my kindred. ⁶ However, I will take vengeance for my nation, for the sanctuary, and for our wives and children, because all the Gentiles have gathered out of hatred to destroy us." ⁷ The spirit of the people revived as soon as they heard these words. ⁸ They answered with a loud voice, saying, "You are our leader in the place of Judas and Jonathan your brothers. ⁹ Fight our battles, and we will do all that you tell us to do." ¹⁰ He gathered together all the men of war, and hurried to finish the walls of Jerusalem. He fortified it all around. ¹¹ He sent Jonathan the son of Absalom, and with him a great army, to Joppa. He threw out those who were in it, and lived there. ¹² Tryphon left Ptolemais with a mighty army to enter into the land of Judah, and Jonathan was with him under guard. ¹³ But Simon encamped at Adida, near the plain. ¹⁴ Tryphon knew that Simon had risen up in the place of his brother Jonathan, and meant to join battle with him, so he sent ambassadors to him, saying, ¹⁵ "It is for money which Jonathan your brother owed to the king's treasury, by reason of the offices which he had, that we are detaining him. ¹⁶ Now send one hundred talents of silver and two of his sons for hostages, so that when he is released he may not revolt against us, and we will release him." ¹⁷ Simon knew that they spoke to him deceitfully, but he sent to get the money and the children, lest perhaps he would arouse great hostility among the people, ¹⁸ who might say, "Because I didn't send him the money and the children, he perished." ¹⁹ So he sent the children and the hundred talents, but Tryphon lied, and didn't release Jonathan. ²⁰ After this, Tryphon came

---

ᵃ *12:7* So the old Latin versions and Josephus: compare also ver. **20**. All the other authorities read Darius in this place.
ᵇ *12:22* Gr. peace
ᶜ *12:38* Gr. Sephela.
ᵈ *12:43* See **1 Maccabees 2:18**.

to invade the land and destroy it, and he went around by the way that leads to Adora. Simon and his army marched near him to every place, wherever he went. ²¹ Now the people of the citadel sent to Tryphon ambassadors, urging him to come to them through the wilderness, and to send them food. ²² So Tryphon prepared all his cavalry to come, but on that night a very heavy snow fell, and he didn't come because of the snow. He marched off and went into the land of Gilead. ²³ When he came near to Bascama, he killed Jonathan, and he was buried there. ²⁴ Then Tryphon turned back, and went away into his own land. ²⁵ Simon sent, and took the bones of Jonathan his brother, and buried him at Modin, the city of his fathers. ²⁶ All Israel made great lamentation over him, and mourned for him many days. ²⁷ Simon built a monument on the tomb of his father and his kindred, and raised it high so that it could be seen, with polished stone on the front and back. ²⁸ He also set up seven pyramids, one near another, for his father, his mother, and his four brothers. ²⁹ For these, he made an elaborate setting, erecting great pillars around them, and upon the pillars he made suits of armor for a perpetual memorial, and beside the suits of armor, he carved ships, so that they could be seen by all who sail on the sea. ³⁰ This is the tomb which he made at Modin. It remains to this day. ³¹ Now Tryphon deceived the young King Antiochus and killed him, ³² and reigned in his place. He put on himself the crown of Asia and brought a great calamity upon the land. ³³ Simon built up the strongholds of Judea, and walled them all around with high towers, great walls, gates, and bars; and he stored food in the strongholds. ³⁴ Simon chose men, and sent to King Demetrius with a request that he grant the country an immunity, because all that Tryphon did was to plunder. ³⁵ King Demetrius sent to him according to these words, and answered him, and wrote a letter to him, as follows: ³⁶ "King Demetrius to Simon the high priest and friend[a] of kings, and to the elders and nation of the Jews, greetings. ³⁷ The golden crown and the palm branch, which you sent, we have received. We are ready to make a steadfast peace with you, yes, and to write to our officers to release you from tribute. ³⁸ Whatever things we confirmed to you, they are confirmed. The strongholds, which you have built, let them be your own. ³⁹ As for any oversights and faults committed to this day, we forgive them, and the crown tax which you owed us. If there were any other tax collected in Jerusalem, let it be collected no longer. ⁴⁰ If any among you are qualified to be enrolled in our court, let them be enrolled, and let there be peace between us." ⁴¹ In the one hundred seventieth year,[b] the yoke of the Gentiles was taken away from Israel. ⁴² The people began to write in their instruments and contracts, "In the first year of Simon, the great high priest and captain and leader of the Jews." ⁴³ In those days Simon encamped against[c] Gazara, and surrounded it with troops. He made a seige engine, and brought it up to the city, and struck a tower, and captured it. ⁴⁴ Those who were in the engine leaped out into the city; and there was a great uproar in the city. ⁴⁵ The people of the city tore their clothes, and went up on the walls with their wives and children, and cried with a loud voice, asking Simon to give them[d] his right hand. ⁴⁶ They said, "Don't deal with us according to our wickednesses, but according to your mercy." ⁴⁷ So Simon was reconciled to them, and didn't fight against them; but he expelled them from the city and cleansed the houses where the idols were, and then entered into it with singing and giving praise. ⁴⁸ He removed all uncleanness out of it, and placed in it men who would keep the law, and made it stronger than it was before, and built a dwelling place for himself in it. ⁴⁹ But the people of the citadel in Jerusalem were hindered from going out and from going into the country, and from buying and selling. So they were very hungry, and a great number of them perished from famine. ⁵⁰ Then they cried out to Simon, that he should give them his right hand; and he gave it to them; but he expelled them from there, and he cleansed the citadel from its pollutions. ⁵¹ He entered into it on the twenty-third day of the second month, in the one hundred seventy-first year,[e] with praise and palm branches, with harps, with cymbals, and with stringed instruments, with hymns, and with songs, because a great enemy had been destroyed out of Israel. ⁵² Simon ordained that they should keep that day every year with gladness. He made the hill of the temple that was by the citadel stronger than before, and he lived there with his men. ⁵³ Simon saw that his son John was a man, so he made him leader of all his forces; and he lived in Gazara.

14

¹ In the one hundred seventy-second year,[f] King Demetrius gathered his forces together, and went into Media to get help, that he might fight against Tryphon. ² When Arsaces, the king of Persia and Media, heard that Demetrius had come into his borders, he sent one of his princes to take him alive. ³ He went and struck the army of Demetrius, and seized him and brought him to Arsaces, who put him under guard. ⁴ The land had rest all the days of Simon. He sought the good of his nation. His authority and his honor was pleasing to them all his days. ⁵ Amid all his honors, he took Joppa for a harbor, and made it an entrance for the islands of the sea. ⁶ He enlarged the borders of his nation and took possession of the country. ⁷ He gathered together a great number of captives, and took control of Gazara, Bethsura, and the citadel, and he removed its uncleannesses from it. There was no one who resisted him. ⁸ They tilled their land in peace, and the land gave her increase, and the trees of the plains gave their fruit. ⁹ The old men sat in the streets; they all conversed together about good things. The young men put on glorious and warlike apparel. ¹⁰ He provided food for the cities and furnished them with means of defense, until the glory of his name was known to the end of the earth. ¹¹ He made peace in the land, and Israel rejoiced with great joy. ¹² Each man sat under his vine and his fig tree, and there was no one to make them afraid. ¹³ No one was left in the land who fought against them. The kings were defeated in those days. ¹⁴ He strengthened all those of his people who were humble. He searched out the law, and every lawless and wicked person he took away. ¹⁵ He glorified the sanctuary, and added to the vessels of the temple. ¹⁶ It was heard at Rome that Jonathan was dead, and even in Sparta, and they were exceedingly grieved. ¹⁷ But as soon as they heard that his brother Simon was made high priest in his place, and ruled the country and the cities in it, ¹⁸ they wrote to him on brass tablets to renew with him the friendship and the alliance which they had confirmed with his brothers Judas and Jonathan. ¹⁹ These were read before the congregation at Jerusalem. ²⁰ This is the copy of the letters which the Spartans sent: "The rulers and the city of the Spartans, to Simon the high priest, to the elders, the priests, and the rest of the people of the Jews, our kindred, greetings. ²¹ The ambassadors who were sent to our people reported to us about your glory and honor. We were glad for their coming, ²² and we registered the things that were spoken by them in the public records[g] as follows: 'Numenius son of Antiochus, and Antipater son of Jason, the Jews' ambassadors, came to us to renew the friendship they had with us. ²³ It pleased the people to entertain the men honorably, and to put the copy of their words in the public records,[h] to the end that the people of the Spartans might have a record of them. Moreover they wrote a copy of these things to Simon the high priest.'" ²⁴ After this, Simon sent Numenius to Rome with a great shield of gold of weighing one thousand minas,[i] in order to confirm the alliance with them. ²⁵ But when the people heard these things, they said, "What thanks shall we give to Simon and his sons? ²⁶ For he and his brothers and the house of his father have made themselves strong, and have fought and chased away Israel's enemies, and confirmed liberty to Israel.[j]" ²⁷ So they wrote on tablets of brass, and set them on pillars on mount Zion. This is the copy of the writing: "On the eighteenth day of Elul, in the one hundred seventy-second year,[k] which is the third year of Simon the high priest, ²⁸ in Asaramel, in a great congregation of priests and people and princes of the nation, and of the elders of the country, it was proclaimed to us:[l] ²⁹ 'Since wars often occurred in the country, Simon the son of Mattathias, the son of the sons of Joarib, and his brothers, put themselves in jeopardy and withstood the enemies of their nation, that their sanctuary and the law might be established, and glorified their nation with great glory. ³⁰ Jonathan rallied the nation, became their high priest, and was gathered to his people. ³¹ Their enemies planned to invade their country, that they might destroy their country utterly, and stretch out their hands against their sanctuary. ³² Then Simon rose up and fought for his nation. He spent much of his own money to arm the valiant men of his nation and give them wages. ³³ He fortified the cities of Judea and Bethsura that lies on the borders of Judea, where the weapons of the enemies were had been stored, and there he placed a garrison of Jews. ³⁴ He fortified Joppa which is upon the sea, and Gazara which is upon the borders of Azotus, where the enemies used to live, and placed Jews there, and set in there all things necessary for their restoration. ³⁵ The people saw Simon's faith,[m] and the glory which he resolved to bring to his nation, and they made him their leader and high priest, because he had done all these things, and for the justice and the faith which he kept to his nation, and because he sought by all means to exalt his people. ³⁶ In his days, things prospered in his hands, so that the Gentiles

---

[a] 13:36 See 1 Maccabees 2:18.
[b] 13:41 circa B.C. 143.
[c] 13:43 See 1 Maccabees 13:53 (compare 1 Maccabees 13:48); 1 Maccabees 14:7, 34; 15:28;

16:1: also Josephus. All the authorities read Gaza in this verse.
[d] 13:45 Gr. right hands.
[e] 13:51 circa B.C. 142.
[f] 14:1 circa B.C. 141.

[g] 14:22 Gr. counsels of the people.
[h] 14:23 Gr. books that are appointed for the people.
[i] 14:24 1, 000 minas is about 499 kg or 1, 098 pounds.

[j] 14:26 Gr. him.
[k] 14:27 circa B.C. 141.
[l] 14:28 Gr. he made known.
[m] 14:35 Some authorities read acts.

were taken away out of their country, and they also who were in the city of David, those who were in Jerusalem, who had made themselves a citadel, out of which they used to go, and polluted everything around the sanctuary, and did great damage to its purity. ³⁷ He placed Jews in it and fortified it for the safety of the country and the city, and made high the walls of Jerusalem. ³⁸ King Demetrius confirmed to him the high priesthood according to these things, ³⁹ and made him one of his friends,ᵃ and honored him with great honor; ⁴⁰ for he had heard that the Jews had been called by the Romans friends, allies, and kindred, and that they had met the ambassadors of Simon honorably; ⁴¹ and that the Jews and the priests were well pleased that Simon should be their leader and high priest forever, until there should arise a faithful prophet; ⁴² and that he should be governor over them, and should take charge of the sanctuary, to set them over their works, and over the country, and over the weapons, and over the strongholds; and that he should take charge of the sanctuary, ⁴³ and that he should be obeyed by all, and that all contracts in the country should be written in his name, and that he should be clothed in purple, and wear gold; ⁴⁴ and that it should not be lawful for any of the people or of the priests to nullify any of these things, or to oppose the words that he should speak, or to gather an assembly in the country without him, or to be clothed in purple, or wear a buckle of gold; ⁴⁵ but whoever should do otherwise, or nullify any of these things, he will be liable to punishment.'" ⁴⁶ All the people consented to ordain for Simon that he should do according to these words. ⁴⁷ So Simon accepted this, and consented to be high priest, and to be captain and governorᵇ of the Jews and of the priests, and to be protector of all. ⁴⁸ They commanded to put this writing on tablets of brass, and to set them up within the precinct of the sanctuary in a conspicuous place, ⁴⁹ and moreover to put copies of them in the treasury, so that Simon and his sons might have them.

15

¹ Antiochus son of Demetrius the king sent a letter from the islands of the sea to Simon the priest andᶜ governor of the Jews, and to all the nation. ² Its contents follow: "King Antiochus to Simon the chief priest andᵈ governor, and to the nation of the Jews, greetings. ³ Whereas certain troublemakers have made themselves masters of the kingdom of our fathers, but my purpose is to claim the kingdom, that I may restore it as it was before; and moreover I have raised a multitude of foreign soldiers, and have prepared warships; ⁴ moreover I plan to land in the country, that I may punish those who have destroyed our country, and those who have made many cities in the kingdom desolate; ⁵ now therefore I confirm to you all the tax remissions which the kings who were before me remitted to you, and whatever gifts besides they remitted to you, ⁶ and I permit you to coin money for your country with your own stamp, ⁷ but that Jerusalem and the sanctuary should be free. All the weapons that you have prepared, and the strongholds that you have built, which you have in your possession, let them remain yours. ⁸ Every debt owed to the king, and the things that will be owed to the king from henceforth and for evermore, let them be remitted to you. ⁹ Moreover, when we have established our kingdom, we will glorify you and your nation and the temple with great glory, so that your glory will be made manifest in all the earth. ¹⁰ In the one hundred seventy-fourth year,ᵉ Antiochus went into the land of his fathers; and all the forces came together to him, so that there were few men with Tryphon. ¹¹ King Antiochus pursued him, and he came, as he fled, to Dor, which is by the sea; ¹² for he knew that troubles had come upon him all at once, and that his forces had deserted him. ¹³ Antiochus encamped against Dor, and with him one hundred twenty thousand men of war and eight thousand cavalry. ¹⁴ He surrounded the city, and the ships joined in the attack from the sea. He harassed the city by land and sea, and permitted no one to go out or in. ¹⁵ Numenius and his company came from Rome, having letters to the kings and to the countries, in which were written these things: ¹⁶ "Lucius, consul of the Romans, to King Ptolemy, greetings. ¹⁷ The Jews' ambassadors came to us as our friends and allies, to renew the old friendship and alliance, being sent from Simon the high priest, and from the people of the Jews. ¹⁸ Moreover they brought a shield of gold weighing one thousand minas.ᶠ ¹⁹ It pleased us therefore to write to the kings and to the countries, that they should not seek their harm or fight against them, their cities, and their country, or be allies with those who fight against them. ²⁰ Moreover, it seemed good to us to receive the shield from them. ²¹ If therefore any troublemakers have fled from their country to you, deliver them to Simon the high priest, that he may take vengeance on them according to their law." ²² He wrote the same things to King Demetrius, to Attalus, to Arathes, to Arsaces, ²³ to all the countries, toᵍ Sampsames, to the Spartans, to Delos, to Myndos, to Sicyon, to Caria, to Samos, to Pamphylia, to Lycia, to Halicarnassus, to Rhodes, to Phaselis, to Cos, to Side, to Aradus, Gortyna, Cnidus, Cyprus, and Cyrene. ²⁴ They also wrote this copy to Simon the high priest. ²⁵ But King Antiochus encamped against Dor the second day, bringing his forces up to it continually, and making engines of war; and he shut up Tryphon from going in or out. ²⁶ Simon sent him two thousand chosen men to fight on his side, with silver, gold, and instruments of war in abundance. ²⁷ He would not receive them, but nullified all the covenants which he had made with him before, and was estranged from him. ²⁸ He sent to him Athenobius, one of his friends,ʰ to confer with him, saying, "You hold possession of Joppa, Gazara, and the citadel that is in Jerusalem, cities of my kingdom. ²⁹ You have devastated their territory, and done great harm in the land, and control of many places in my kingdom. ³⁰ Now therefore hand over the cities which you have taken, and the tributes of the places which you have taken control of outside of the borders of Judea; ³¹ or else give me for them five hundred talents of silver; and for the harm that you have done, and the tributes of the cities, another five hundred talents. Otherwise we will come and subdue you." ³² Athenobius, the king's friend,ⁱ came to Jerusalem. When he saw the glory of Simon, the cupboard of gold and silver vessels, and his great attendance, he was amazed. He reported to him the king's words. ³³ Simon answered, and said to him, "We have not taken other men's land nor do we have possession of that which belongs to others, but of the inheritance of our fathers. However, it had been in possession of our enemies wrongfully for a while. ³⁴ But we, having opportunity, firmly hold the inheritance of our fathers. ³⁵ As for Joppa and Gazara, which you demand, they did great harm among the people throughout our country. We will give one hundred talents for them." Athenobius didn't answer even one word, ³⁶ but returned in a rage to the king, and reported to him these words, and the glory of Simon, and all that he had seen; and the king was exceedingly angry. ³⁷ Meanwhile, Tryphon embarked on board a ship, and fled to Orthosia. ³⁸ The king appointed Cendebaeus chief captain of the sea coast, and gave him troops of infantry and cavalry. ³⁹ He commanded him to encamp against Judea, and he commanded him to build up Kidron, and to fortify the gates, and that he should fight against the people; but the king pursued Tryphon. ⁴⁰ So Cendebaeus came to Jamnia and began to provoke the people, and to invade Judea, and to take the people captive and kill them. ⁴¹ He built Kidron and stationed cavalry and infantry there, to the end that going out they might make raids on the highways of Judea, as the king had commanded him.

16

¹ John went up from Gazara and told Simon his father what Cendebaeus was doing. ² Simon called his two oldest sons, Judas and John, and said to them, "I and my brothers and my father's house have fought the battles of Israel from our youth, even to this day; and things have prospered in our hands, that we have often delivered Israel. ³ But now I am old, and you moreover, by his mercy, are of a sufficient age. Take the place of me and my brother, and go out and fight for our nation; and let the help which is from heaven be with you. ⁴ He chose out of the country twenty thousand men of war and cavalry, and they went against Cendebaeus, and slept at Modin. ⁵ Rising up in the morning, they went into the plain, and, behold, a great army of infantry and cavalry came to meet them. There was a brook between them. ⁶ He encamped near them, he and his people. He saw that the people were afraid to pass over the brook, and he passed over first. When the men saw him, they passed over after him. ⁷ He divided the people, and placed the calvary in the midst of the infantry; but the enemies' cavalry were exceedingly many. ⁸ They sounded the trumpets; and Cendebaeus and his army were put to flight, and many of them fell wounded to death, but those who were left fled to the stronghold. ⁹ At that time Judas, John's brother, was wounded; but John pursued after them until he came to Kidron, which Cendebaeus had built. ¹⁰ They fled to the towers that are in the fields of Azotus; and he burned it with fire. About two thousand men men of them fell. Then he returned into Judea in peace. ¹¹ Ptolemy the son of Abubus had been appointed governor over the plain of Jericho, and he had much silver and gold; ¹² for he was the high priest's son-in-law. ¹³ His heart was lifted up, and he planned to make himself master of the country, and he made deceitful plans against Simon and his sons, to do away with them. ¹⁴ Now Simon was visiting the cities that were in the country, and attending to their

---

ᵃ *14:39* See **1 Maccabees 2:18**.
ᵇ *14:47* Gr. ethnarch.
ᶜ *15:1* Gr. ethnarch.
ᵈ *15:2* Gr. ethnarch.

ᵉ *15:10* circa B.C. **139**
ᶠ *15:18* **1,000** minas is about **499** kg. or about **1,098** pounds.

ᵍ *15:23* Some authorities read Sampsaces: the Latin versions have Lampsacus.
ʰ *15:28* See **1 Maccabees 2:18**.

ⁱ *15:32* See **1 Maccabees 2:18**.

needs. He went down to Jericho–himself with Mattathias and Judas his sons–in the one hundred seventy-seventh year,[a] in the eleventh month, which is the month Sebat. ¹⁵ The son of Abubus received them deceitfully into the little stronghold that is called Dok, which he had built, and made them a great banquet, and hid men there. ¹⁶ When Simon and his sons had drunk freely, Ptolemy and his men rose up, took their weapons, rushed in against Simon in the banqueting place, and killed him, his two sons, and some of his servants. ¹⁷ He committed a great iniquity, and repaid evil for good. ¹⁸ Ptolemy wrote these things and sent to the king, that he should send him forces to aid him, and should deliver him their country and the cities. ¹⁹ He sent others to Gazara to do away with John. To the captains of thousands, he sent letters to come to him, that he might give them silver, gold, and gifts. ²⁰ He sent others to take possession of Jerusalem and the temple hill. ²¹ One ran before to Gazara, and told John that his father and kindred had perished, and he has sent to kill you also. ²² When he heard, he was greatly shocked. He seized the men who came to destroy him and killed them; for he perceived that they were seeking to destroy him. ²³ And the rest of the acts of John and of his wars and of his valiant deeds which he did, and of the building of the walls which he built, and of his achievements, ²⁴ behold, they are written in the chronicles[b] of his high priesthood, from the time that he was made high priest after his father.

The Second Book of the Maccabees

The Second Book of the Maccabees is recognized as Deuterocanonical Scripture by the Roman Catholic, Greek Orthodox, and Russian Orthodox Churches.

1

¹ The kindred, the Jews who are in Jerusalem and those who are in the country of Judea, send greetings and good peace to the kindred, the Jews who are throughout Egypt. ² May God do good to you, and remember his covenant with Abraham, Isaac, and Jacob, his faithful servants, ³ and give you all a heart to worship him and do his will with a strong heart and a willing soul. ⁴ May God open your heart to his law and his statutes, and make peace, ⁵ and listen to your requests, and be reconciled with you, and not forsake you in an evil time. ⁶ Now we are praying for you here. ⁷ In the reign of Demetrius, in the one hundred sixty-ninth year, we the Jews have already written to you in the suffering and in the distress that has come upon us in these years, from the time that Jason and his company revolted from the holy land and the kingdom, ⁸ and set the gate on fire, and shed innocent blood. We prayed to the Lord, and were heard. We offered sacrifices and meal offerings. We lit the lamps. We set out the show bread.[c] ⁹ Now see that you keep the days of the feast of tabernacles in the month Chislev in the one hundred eighty-eighth year. ¹⁰ The people of Jerusalem and those who are in Judea, with the senate and Judas, to Aristobulus, King Ptolemy's teacher, who is also of the stock of the anointed priests, and to the Jews who are in Egypt, we send greetings and health. ¹¹ Having been saved by God out of great perils, as men arrayed against a king, we thank him greatly. ¹² For he threw out into Persia those who fought against us in the holy city. ¹³ For when the prince had come there, with an army that seemed irresistible, they were cut to pieces in the temple of Nanaea by the treachery of Nanaea's priests. ¹⁴ For Antiochus, on the pretense that he would marry her, came into the place, he and his friends who were with him, that they might take a large part of the treasures as a dowry. ¹⁵ And when the priests of Nanaea's temple had set the treasures out, and he had come there with a small company within the wall of the sacred precinct, they locked the temple when Antiochus had come in. ¹⁶ Opening the secret door of the panelled ceiling, they threw stones and struck down the prince. They cut him and his company in pieces, and cut off their heads, and threw them to the people who were outside. ¹⁷ Blessed be our God in all things, who handed over those who had committed impiety. ¹⁸ Since we are now about to celebrate the purification of the temple in the month Chislev, on the twenty-fifth day, we thought it necessary to notify you, so that you may also keep a feast of tabernacles, and remember the fire which was given when Nehemiah offered sacrifices, after he had built both the temple and the altar. ¹⁹ For indeed when our fathers were about to be led into the land of Persia, the godly priests of that time took some of the fire of the altar, and hid it secretly in the hollow of a well that was without water, where they made sure that the place was unknown to anyone. ²⁰ Now after many years, when it pleased God, Nehemiah, having received a charge from the king of Persia, sent in quest of the fire the descendants of the priests who hid it. When they declared to us that they had found no fire, but thick liquid, ²¹ he commanded them to draw some of it out and bring it to him. When the sacrifices had been offered, Nehemiah commanded the priests to sprinkle with that liquid both the wood and the things laid on it. ²² When that was done and some time had passed, and the sun shone out, which before was hidden with clouds, a great blaze was kindled, so that all men marveled. ²³ The priests made a prayer while the sacrifice was being consumed–both the priests and all the others. Jonathan led and the rest responded, as Nehemiah did. ²⁴ The prayer was like this: "O Lord, Lord God, the Creator of all things, who are awesome, strong, righteous, and merciful, who alone are King and gracious, ²⁵ who alone supply every need, who alone are righteous, almighty, and eternal, you who save Israel out of all evil, who chose the ancestors and sanctified them, ²⁶ accept the sacrifice for all your people Israel, and preserve your own portion, and consecrate it. ²⁷ Gather together our scattered people, set at liberty those who are in bondage among the heathen, look upon those who are despised and abhorred, and let the heathen know that you are our God. ²⁸ Punish those who oppress us and in arrogance shamefully entreat us. ²⁹ Plant your people in your holy place, even as Moses said." ³⁰ Then the priests sang the hymns. ³¹ As soon as the sacrifice was consumed, then Nehemiah commanded that the rest of the liquid be poured on large stones. ³² When this was done, a flame was kindled; but when the light from the altar shone back, it went out. ³³ When the matter became known, and it was told the king of the Persians that, in the place where the priests who were led away had hid the fire, the liquid appeared which Nehemiah and those who were with him purified the

---

[a] *16:14* circa B.C. **136**.

[b] *16:24* Gr. book of days.

[c] *1:8* Gr. loaves.

sacrifice, ³⁴ then the king enclosed the place and made it sacred after he had investigated the matter. ³⁵ When the king would show favor to any, he would exchange many presents and give them some of this liquid. ³⁶ Nehemiah and those who were with him called this thing "Nephthar", which is by interpretation, "Cleansing"; but most men call it Nephthai.

2

¹ It is also found in the records that Jeremiah the prophet commanded those who were carried away to take some of the fire, as has been mentioned, ² and how that the prophet charged those who were carried away, having given them the law, that they should not forget the statutes of the Lord or be led astray in their minds when they saw images of gold and silver, and their adornment. ³ With other such words exhorted he them, that the law should not depart from their hearts. ⁴ It was in the writing that the prophet, being warned by God, commanded that the tabernacle and the ark should follow with him,ᵃ when he went out to the mountain where Moses had gone up and saw God's inheritance. ⁵ Jeremiah came and found a cave, he brought the tabernacle, the ark, and the altar of incense into it; then he sealed the entrance. ⁶ Some of those who followed with him came there that they might mark the way, and could not find it. ⁷ But when Jeremiah learned about that, he rebuked them, saying, "The place shall be unknown until God gathers the people together again and shows mercy. ⁸ Then the Lord will disclose these things, and the glory of the Lord shall be seen with the cloud, as it was also shown to Moses, also as Solomon implored that the place might be consecrated greatly, ⁹ and it was also declared that he, having wisdom, offered a sacrifice of dedication, and of the finishing of the temple. ¹⁰ As Moses prayed to the Lord and fire came down out of heaven and consumed the sacrifice, even so Solomon also prayed, and the fire came down and consumed the burnt offerings. ¹¹ ᵇMoses said, 'Because the sin offering had not been eaten, it was consumed in like manner.' ¹² Likewise Solomon kept the eight days." ¹³ The same things were reported both in the public archives and in Nehemiah's records, and also how he, founding a library, gathered together the books about the kings and prophets, and the writings of David, and letters of kings about sacred gifts. ¹⁴ In like manner Judas also gathered together for us all those books that had been scattered by reason of the war, and they are still with us. ¹⁵ If therefore you have need of them, send some people to bring them to you. ¹⁶ Seeing then that we are about to celebrate the purification, we write to you. You will therefore do well if you celebrate the days. ¹⁷ Now God, who saved all his people, and restored the heritage to all, with the kingdom, the priesthood, and the consecration, ¹⁸ even as he promised through the law–in God have we hope, that he will soon have mercy upon us, and gather us together out of everywhere under heaven into his holy place; for he delivered us out of great evils, and purified the place. ¹⁹ Now the things concerning Judas Maccabaeus and his brothers, the purification of the greatest temple, the dedication of the altar, ²⁰ and further the wars against Antiochus Epiphanes and Eupator his son, ²¹ and the manifestations that came from heaven to those who fought with one another in brave deeds for the religion of the Jews; so that, being but a few, they seized the whole country, chased the barbarous multitudes, ²² recovered again the temple renowned all the world over, freed the city, and restored the laws which were about to be overthrown, seeing the Lord became gracious to them with all kindness. ²³ These things which have been declared by Jason of Cyrene in five books, we will attempt to abridge in one book. ²⁴ For having in view the confused mass of the numbers, and theᶜ difficulty which awaits those who would enter into the narratives of the history, by reason of the abundance of the matter, ²⁵ we were careful that those who choose to read may be attracted, and that those who wish us well may find it easy to recall, and that all readers may benefit. ²⁶ Although to us, who have taken upon ourselves the painful labor of the abridgement, the task is not easy, but a matter of sweat and sleeplessness, ²⁷ even as it is no light thing to him who prepares a banquet, and seeks the benefit of others. Nevertheless, for the sake of the gratitude of the many we will gladly endure the painful labor, ²⁸ leaving to the historian the exact handling of every particular, and again having no strength to fill in the outlines of our abridgement. ²⁹ For as the masterbuilder of a new house must care for the whole structure, and again he who undertakes to decorate and paint it must seek out the things fit for its adorning; even so I think it is also with us. ³⁰ To occupy the ground, and to indulge in long discussions, and to be curious in particulars, is fitting for the first author of the history; ³¹ but to strive after brevity of expression, and to avoid a labored fullness in the treatment, is to be granted to him who would bring a writing into a new form. ³² Here then let's begin the narration, only adding this much to that which has already been said; for it is a foolish thing to make a long prologue to the history, and to abridge the history itself.

3

¹ When the holy city was inhabited with unbroken peace and the laws were kept very well because of the godliness of Onias the high priest and his hatred of wickedness, ² it came to pass that even the kings themselves honored the place and glorified the temple with the noblest presents, ³ so that even King Seleucus of Asia bore all the costs belonging to the services of the sacrifices out of his own revenues. ⁴ But a man named Simon of the tribe of Benjamin, having been made guardian of the temple, disagreed with the high priest about the ruling of the market in the city. ⁵ When he couldn't overcome Onias, he went to Apollonius of ᵈTarsus, who at that time was governor of Coelesyria and Phoenicia. ⁶ He brought him word how that the treasury in Jerusalem was full of untold sums of money, so that the multitude of the funds was innumerable, and that they didn't pertain to the account of the sacrifices, but that it was possible that these should fall under the king's power. ⁷ When Apollonius met the king, he informed him of the money about which he had been told. So the king appointed Heliodorus, who was his chancellor, and sent him with a command to accomplish the removal of the reported money. ⁸ So Heliodorus set out on his journey at once, ostensibly to visit the cities of Coelesyria and Phoenicia, but in fact to execute the king's purpose. ⁹ When he had come to Jerusalem and had been courteously received by the high priest of the city, he told him about the information which had been given, and declared why he had come; and he inquired if in truth these things were so. ¹⁰ The high priest explained to him that there were in the treasury deposits of widows and orphans, ¹¹ and moreover some money belonging to Hyrcanus the son of Tobias, a man in very high place, not as that impious Simon falsely alleged; and that in all there were four hundred talents of silver and two hundred of gold, ¹² and that it was altogether impossible that wrong should be done to those who had put trust in the holiness of the place, and in the majesty and inviolable sanctity of the temple, honored over all the world. ¹³ But Heliodorus, because of the king's command given him, said that in any case this money must be confiscated for the king's treasury. ¹⁴ So having appointed a day, he entered in to direct the inquiry concerning these matters; and there was no small distress throughout the whole city. ¹⁵ The priests, prostrating themselves before the altar in their priestly garments, and called toward heaven upon him who gave the law concerning deposits, that he should preserve these treasures safe for those who had deposited them. ¹⁶ Whoever saw the appearance of the high priest was wounded in mind; for his countenance and the change of his color betrayed the distress of his soul. ¹⁷ For a terror and a shuddering of the body had come over the man, by which the pain that was in his heart was plainly shown to those who looked at him. ¹⁸ Those who were in the houses rushed out in crowds to make a universal supplication, because the place was about to come into dishonor. ¹⁹ The women, girded with sackcloth under their breasts, thronged the streets. The virgins who were kept indoors ran together, some to the gates, others to the walls, and some looked out through the windows. ²⁰ All, stretching out their hands toward heaven, made their solemn supplication. ²¹ Then it was pitiful to see the multitude prostrating themselves all mixed together, and the anxiety of the high priest in his great distress. ²² While therefore they called upon the Almighty Lord to keep the things entrusted to them ᵉ safe and secure for those who had entrusted them, ²³ Heliodorus went on to execute that which had been decreed. ²⁴ But when he was already present there with his guards near the treasury, the Sovereign of spirits and of all authority caused a great manifestation, so that all who had presumed to come with him, stricken with dismay at the power of God, fainted in terror. ²⁵ For they saw a horse with a frightening rider, adorned with beautiful trappings, and he rushed fiercely and struck at Heliodorus with his forefeet. It seemed like he who sat on the horse had complete armor of gold. ²⁶ Two others also appeared to him, young men notable in their strength, and beautiful in their glory, and splendid in their apparel, who stood by him on either side, and scourged him unceasingly, inflicting on him many sore stripes. ²⁷ When he had fallen suddenly to the ground, and great darkness had come over him, his guards picked him up and put him on a stretcher, ²⁸ and carried him–this man who had just now entered with a great retinue and all his guard into the aforesaid treasury, himself now brought to utter helplessness, manifestly made to recognize the sovereignty of God. ²⁹ So, while he, through the working of God, speechless and bereft of all hope and deliverance, lay prostrate, ³⁰ they blessed the Lord who acted

---

ᵃ *2:4* Gr. and when. The Greek text here is probably corrupt.

ᵇ *2:11* See Leviticus **10:16** and **9:24**.

ᶜ *2:24* Or, weariness

ᵈ *3:5* Greek Thraseas

ᵉ *3:22* Gr. safe with all security.

marvelously for his own place. The temple, which a little before was full of terror and alarm, was filled with joy and gladness after the Almighty Lord appeared. ³¹ But quickly some of Heliodorus's familiar friends implored Onias to call upon the Most High to grant life to him who lay quite at the last gasp. ³² The high priest, secretly fearing lest the king might come to think that some treachery toward Heliodorus had been perpetrated by the Jews, brought a sacrifice for the recovery of the man. ³³ But as the high priest was making the atoning sacrifice, the same young men appeared again to Heliodorus, arrayed in the same garments. They stood and said, "Give Onias the high priest great thanks, for for his sake the Lord has granted you life. ³⁴ See that you, since you have been scourged from heaven, proclaim to all men the sovereign majesty of God." When they had spoken these words, they vanished out of sight. ³⁵ So Heliodorus, having offered a sacrifice to the Lord and vowed [a]great vows to him who had saved his life, and having bidden Onias farewell, returned with his army to the king. ³⁶ He testified to all men the works of the greatest God, which he had seen with his eyes. ³⁷ When the king asked Heliodorus what sort of man was fit to be sent yet once again to Jerusalem, he said, ³⁸ "If you have any enemy or conspirator against the state, send him there, and you will receive him back well scourged, if he even escapes with his life; because truly there is some power of God in that place. ³⁹ For he who has his dwelling in heaven himself has his eyes on that place and helps it. Those who come to hurt it, he strikes and destroys." ⁴⁰ This was the history of Heliodorus and the keeping of the treasury.

4

¹ The previously mentioned Simon, who had given information about the money against his country, slandered Onias, saying that it was he who had incited Heliodorus and had been the real cause of these evils. ² He dared to call him a conspirator against the state who was actually the benefactor of the city, the guardian of his fellow countrymen, and a zealot for the laws. ³ When his hatred grew so great that even murders were perpetrated through one of Simon's approved agents, ⁴ Onias, seeing the danger of the contention, and that [b]Apollonius the son of Menestheus, the governor of Coelesyria and Phoenicia, was increasing Simon's malice, ⁵ appealed to the king, not to be an accuser of his fellow-citizens, but looking to the good of all the[c] people, both public and private; ⁶ for he saw that without the king's involvement it was impossible for the state to obtain peace any more, and that Simon would not cease from his madness. ⁷ When Seleucus was deceased, and Antiochus, who was called Epiphanes, succeeded to the kingdom, Jason the brother of Onias supplanted his brother in the high priesthood, ⁸ having promised to the king at an audience three hundred sixty talents of silver, and out of another fund eighty talents. ⁹ In addition to this, he undertook to assign one hundred fifty more, if it might be allowed him [d]through the king's authority to set him up a gymnasium and a body of youths to be trained in it, and to register the inhabitants of Jerusalem as citizens of Antioch. ¹⁰ When the king had assented, and Jason had taken possession of the office, he immediately shifted those of his own race to the Greek way of life. ¹¹ Setting aside the royal ordinances of special favor to the Jews, granted by the means of John the father of Eupolemus, who went on the mission to the Romans to establish friendship and alliance, and seeking to overthrow the lawful ways of living, he brought in new customs forbidden by the law. ¹² For he eagerly established a gymnasium under the citadel itself, and caused the noblest of the young men to wear the Greek hat. ¹³ Thus there was an extreme of hellenization, and an advance of a foreign religion, by reason of the exceeding profaneness of Jason, who was an ungodly man and not a high priest; ¹⁴ so that the priests had no more any zeal for the services of the altar; but despising the sanctuary and neglecting the sacrifices, they hastened to enjoy that which was unlawfully provided in the wrestling arena, after the summons to the discus-throwing. ¹⁵ They despised the honors of their fathers, and valued the prestige of the Greeks best of all. ¹⁶ For this reason, severe calamity overtook them. The men whose ways of living they earnestly followed, and to whom they desired to be made like in all things, these became their enemies and punished them. ¹⁷ For it is not a light thing to show irreverence to God's laws, but later events will make this clear. ¹⁸ Now when certain games that came every fifth year were kept at Tyre, and the king was present, ¹⁹ the vile Jason sent sacred envoys,[e] as being Antiochians of Jerusalem, bearing three hundred drachmas of silver to the sacrifice of Hercules, which even the bearers thereof thought not right to use for any sacrifice, because it was not fit, but to spend it for another purpose. ²⁰ Although the intended purpose of the sender this money was for the sacrifice of Hercules, yet on account of [f]present circumstances it went to the construction of trireme warships. ²¹ Now when Apollonius the son of Menestheus was sent into Egypt for the [g] enthronement of Philometor as king, Antiochus, learning that Philometor had shown himself hostile toward the government, took precautions for the security of his realm. Therefore, going to Joppa, he travelled on to Jerusalem. ²² Being magnificently received by Jason and the city, he was brought in with torches and shouting. Then he led his army down into Phoenicia. ²³ Now after a space of three years, Jason sent Menelaus, the previously mentioned Simon's brother, to carry the money to the king, and to make reports concerning some necessary matters. ²⁴ But he being commended to the king, and having been glorified by the display of his authority, secured the high priesthood for himself, outbidding Jason by three hundred talents of silver. ²⁵ After receiving the royal mandates, he returned bringing nothing worthy of the high priesthood, but having the passion of a cruel tyrant and the rage of a savage animal. ²⁶ So Jason, who had supplanted his own brother, was supplanted by another and driven as a fugitive into the country of the Ammonites, ²⁷ Menelaus had possession of the office; but of the money that had been promised to the king nothing was regularly paid, even though Sostratus the governor of the citadel demanded it– ²⁸ for his job was the gathering of the revenues–so they were both called by the king to his presence. ²⁹ Menelaus left his own brother Lysimachus for his[h] deputy in the high priesthood; and Sostratus left Crates, who was over the Cyprians. ³⁰ Now while this was the state of things, it came to pass that the people of Tarsus and Mallus revolted because they were to be given as a present to Antiochis, the king's concubine. ³¹ The king therefore quickly came to settle matters, leaving for his [i]deputy Andronicus, a man of high rank. ³² Then Menelaus, supposing that he had gotten a favorable opportunity, presented to Andronicus certain vessels of gold belonging to the temple, which he had stolen. He had already sold others into Tyre and the neighboring cities. ³³ When Onias had sure knowledge of this, he sharply reproved him, having withdrawn himself into a sanctuary at Daphne, that lies by Antioch. ³⁴ Therefore Menelaus, taking Andronicus aside, asked him to kill Onias. Coming to Onias, and being persuaded to use treachery, and being received as a friend, Andronicus gave him his right hand with oaths and, though he was suspicious, persuaded him to come out of the sanctuary. Then, with no regard for justice, he immediately put him to death. ³⁵ For this reason not only Jews, but many also of the other nations, had indignation and displeasure at the unjust murder of the man. ³⁶ And when the king had come back from the places in Cilicia, the Jews who were in the city appealed to him against Andronicus (the Greeks also joining with them in hatred of the wickedness), urging that Onias had been wrongfully slain. ³⁷ Antiochus therefore was heartily sorry, and was moved to pity, and wept, because of the sober and well ordered life of him who was dead. ³⁸ Being inflamed with anger, he immediately stripped off Andronicus's purple robe, and tore off his under garments, and when he had led him round through the whole city to that very place where he had committed the outrage against Onias, there he put the murderer out of the way, the Lord rendering to him the punishment he had deserved. ³⁹ Now when many sacrileges had been committed in the city by Lysimachus with the consent of Menelaus, and when the report of them had spread abroad outside, the people gathered themselves together against Lysimachus, after many vessels of gold had already been stolen. ⁴⁰ When the multitudes were rising against him and were filled with anger, Lysimachus armed about three thousand men, and with unrighteous violence began the attack under the leadership of Hauran, a man far gone in years and no less also in folly. ⁴¹ But when they perceived the assault of Lysimachus, some caught up stones, others logs of wood, and some took handfuls of the ashes that lay near, and they flung them all in wild confusion at Lysimachus and those who were with him. ⁴² As a result, they wounded many of them, they killed some, and they forced the rest of them to flee, but the author of the sacrilege himself they killed beside the treasury. ⁴³ But about these matters, there was an accusation laid against Menelaus. ⁴⁴ When the king had come to Tyre, the three men who were sent by the senate pleaded the cause before him. ⁴⁵ But Menelaus, seeing himself now defeated, promised much money to Ptolemy the son of Dorymenes, that he might win over the king. ⁴⁶ Therefore Ptolemy taking the king aside into a cloister, as if to get some fresh air, convinced him to change his mind. ⁴⁷ He who was the cause of all the evil, Menelaus, he discharged from the accusations; but these hapless men, who, if they had pleaded even before Scythians, would have been discharged

---

[a] 3:35 Gr. greatest.
[b] 4:4 Compare 2 Maccabees 4:21. See also 2 Maccabees 3:5. The Greek as commonly read means Apollonius, as being the governor...Phoenicia, did rage, and increase etc.
[c] 4:5 Gr. multitude.
[d] 4:9 Gr. through his.
[e] 4:19 See ver. 9.
[f] 4:20 Some authorities read the bearers.
[g] 4:21 The exact meaning of the Greek word is uncertain.
[h] 4:29 Gr. successor.
[i] 4:31 Gr. successor.

uncondemned, them he sentenced to death. ⁴⁸ Those who were spokesmen for the city and the families of Israel and the holy vessels soon suffered that unrighteous penalty. ⁴⁹ Therefore even certain Tyrians, moved with hatred of the wickedness, provided magnificently for their burial. ⁵⁰ But Menelaus, through the covetous dealings of those who were in power, remained still in his office, growing in wickedness, established as a great conspirator against his fellow-citizens.

5

¹ Now about this time Antiochus made his second invasion into Egypt. ² It happened that throughout all the city, for almost forty days, cavalry appeared in the midst of the sky in swift motion, wearing robes woven with gold and carrying spears, equipped with troops for battle– ³ drawing swords, squadrons of cavalry in array, encounters and pursuits of both armies, shaking shields, multitudes of lances, throwing of missiles, flashing of golden trappings, and putting on all sorts of armor. ⁴ Therefore everyone prayed that the manifestation might have been given for good. ⁵ When a false rumor had arisen that Antiochus was dead, Jason took not less than a thousand men, and suddenly made an assault upon the city. When those who were on the wall were being routed, and the city was at length nearly taken, Menelaus took refuge in the citadel. ⁶ But Jason slaughtered his own citizens without mercy, not considering that good success against kinsmen is the greatest misfortune, but supposing himself to be setting up trophies over enemies, and not over fellow-countrymen. ⁷ He didn't win control of the government, but receiving shame as the result of his conspiracy, he fled again as a fugitive into the country of the Ammonites. ⁸ At last therefore he met with a miserable end. Having been imprisoned at the court of Aretas the prince of the Arabians, fleeing from city to city, pursued by all men, hated as an rebel against the laws, and abhorred as the executioner of his country and his fellow citizens, he was cast ashore in Egypt. ⁹ He who had driven many from their own country into exile perished in exile, having crossed the sea to the Lacedaemonians, hoping to find shelter there because they were[a] near of kin. ¹⁰ He who had thrown out a multitude unburied had none to mourn for him. He didn't have any funeral at all and no place in the tomb of his ancestors. ¹¹ Now when news came to the king concerning that which was done, he thought that Judea was in revolt. So, setting out from Egypt in a rage, he took the city by force of weapons, ¹² and commanded his soldiers to cut down without mercy those who came in their way, and to kill those who went into their houses. ¹³ Then there was killing of young and old, destruction of boys, women, and children, and slaying of virgins and infants. ¹⁴ In a total of three days, eighty thousand were destroyed, of which forty thousand were slain in close combat, and no fewer were sold into slavery than slain. ¹⁵ Not content with this, he presumed to enter into the most holy temple of all the earth, having Menelaus for his guide (who had proved himself a traitor both to the laws and to his country), ¹⁶ even taking the sacred vessels with his polluted hands, and dragging down with his profane hands the offerings that had been dedicated by other kings to enhance the glory and honor of the place. ¹⁷ Antiochus was lifted up in mind, not seeing that because of the sins of those who lived in the city the Sovereign Lord had been provoked to anger a little while, and therefore his eye was turned away from the place. ¹⁸ But had it not been so that they were already bound by many sins, this man, even as Heliodorus who was sent by King Seleucus to view the treasury, would, as soon as he came forward, have been scourged and turned back from his daring deed. ¹⁹ However the Lord didn't choose the nation for the place's sake, but the place for the nation's sake. ²⁰ Therefore also the place itself, having shared in the calamities that happened to the nation, did afterward share in its benefits; and the place which was forsaken in the wrath of the Almighty was, at the reconciliation of the great Sovereign, restored again with all glory. ²¹ As for Antiochus, when he had carried away out of the temple one thousand eight hundred talents, he hurried away to Antioch, thinking in his arrogance that he could sail on land and walk on the sea, because his heart was lifted up. ²² Moreover he left governors to afflict the race: at Jerusalem, Philip, by race a Phrygian, and in character more barbarous than him who set him there; ²³ and at Gerizim, Andronicus; and besides these, Menelaus, who worse than all the rest, exalted himself against his fellow-citizens. Having a malicious mind[b] toward the Jews[c] whom he had made his citizens, ²⁴ he sent that[d] lord of pollutions Apollonius with an army of twenty-two thousand, commanding him to kill all those who were of full age, and to sell the women and the boys as slaves. ²⁵ He came to Jerusalem, and pretending to be a man of peace, waited till the holy day of the Sabbath, and finding the Jews at rest from work, he commanded his men to parade fully armed. ²⁶ He put to the sword all those who came out to the spectacle. Running into the city with the armed men, he killed great multitudes. ²⁷ But Judas, who is also called Maccabaeus, with about nine others, withdrew himself, and with his company kept himself alive in the mountains like wild animals do. They continued feeding on what grew wild, that they might not be partakers of the defilement.

6

¹ Not long after this, the king sent out [e]an old man of Athens to compel the Jews to depart from the laws of their fathers and not to live by the laws of God, ² and also to pollute the sanctuary in Jerusalem and to call it by the name of Olympian Zeus, and to call the sanctuary in Gerizim by the name of Zeus the Protector of foreigners, even as the people who lived in that place did. ³ The visitation of this evil was harsh and utterly grievous. ⁴ For the temple was filled with debauchery and reveling by the heathen, who [f] dallied with prostitutes, and had intercourse with women within the sacred precincts, and moreover brought inside things that were not appropriate. ⁵ The altar was filled with those abominable things which had been prohibited by the laws. ⁶ A man could neither keep the Sabbath, nor observe the feasts of their ancestors, nor so much as confess himself to be a Jew. ⁷ On the day of the king's birth every month, they were led along with bitter constraint to eat of the sacrifices. When the feast of Dionysia came, they were compelled to go in procession in honor of Dionysus, wearing wreaths of ivy. ⁸ A decree went out to the neighboring Greek cities, by the suggestion of Ptolemy, that they should observe the same conduct against the Jews, and should make them eat of the sacrifices, ⁹ and that they should kill those who didn't choose to go over to the Greek rites. So the present misery was for all to see. ¹⁰ For example, two women were brought in for having circumcised their children. These, when they had led them publicly around the city with the babes hung from their breasts, they threw down headlong from the wall. ¹¹ Others who had run together into the caves nearby to keep the seventh day secretly, were betrayed to Philip and were all burned together, because their piety kept them from defending themselves, in view of the honor of that most solemn day. ¹² I urge those who read this book to not be discouraged because of the calamities, but recognize that these punishments were not for the destruction, but for the chastening of our race. ¹³ For indeed it is a sign of great kindness that those who act impiously are not let alone for a long time, but immediately meet with retribution. ¹⁴ For in the case of the other nations, the Sovereign Lord waits patiently to punish them until they have attained to the full measure of their sins; but not with us, ¹⁵ that he may not take vengeance on us afterward,[g] when we have come to the[h] height of our sins. ¹⁶ Therefore he never withdraws his mercy from us; but though he chastens with calamity, he doesn't forsake his own people. ¹⁷ However let this that we have spoken suffice to remind you; but after a few words, we must come to the narrative. ¹⁸ Eleazar, one of the principal scribes, a man already well advanced in years, and of a noble countenance, was compelled to open his mouth to eat swine's flesh. ¹⁹ But he, welcoming death with honor rather than life with defilement, advanced of his own accord to the instrument of torture, but first spat out the flesh, ²⁰ as men ought to come who are resolute to repel such things as not even for the natural love of life is it lawful to taste. ²¹ But those who had the charge of that forbidden sacrificial feast took the man aside, for the acquaintance which of old times they had with him, and privately implored him to bring flesh of his own providing, such as was proper for him to use, and to make as if he did eat of the flesh from the sacrifice, as had been commanded by the king; ²² that by so doing he might be delivered from death, and so his ancient friendship with them might be treated kindly. ²³ But he, having formed a high resolve, and one that became his years, the dignity of old age, and the gray hairs[i] which he had reached with honor, and his excellent[j] education from a child, or rather the holy laws[k] of God's ordaining, declared his mind accordingly, bidding them to quickly send him to Hades. ²⁴ "For it doesn't become our years to dissemble," he said, "that many of the young should suppose that Eleazar, the man of ninety years, had gone over to an alien religion; ²⁵ and so they,

---

[a] 5:9 See 1 Maccabees 12:7.
[b] 5:23 Some authorities read toward the Jews, he sent. The Greek text of this sentence is uncertain.
[c] 5:23 Compare 2 Maccabees 4:9, 19; 9:19.

[d] 5:24 Gr. Μυσάρχην, which also may mean ruler of the Mysians.
[e] 6:1 Or, Geron an Athenian
[f] 6:4 Or, idled with their fellows

[g] 6:15 Or, when our sins have come to their height
[h] 6:15 Gr. end.
[i] 6:23 The Greek text appears to be corrupt.
[j] 6:23 Some authorities read manner of life.

[k] 6:23 Gr. legislation.

by reason of my deception, and for the sake of this brief and momentary life, would be led astray because of me, and I defile and disgrace myself in my old age. ²⁶ For even if for the present time I would remove from me the punishment of men, yet whether I live or die, I wouldn't escape the hands of the Almighty. ²⁷ Therefore, by bravely parting with my life now, I will show myself worthy of my old age, ²⁸ and ᵃleave behind a noble example to the young to die willingly and nobly a glorious death for the revered and holy laws." When he had said these words, he went immediately to the instrument of torture. ²⁹ ᵇ When they changed the good will they bore toward him a little before into ill will because these words of his were, as they thought, sheer madness, ³⁰ and when he was at the point to die with theᶜ blows, he groaned aloud and said, "To the Lord, who has the holy knowledge, it is manifest that, while I might have been delivered from death, I endure severe pains in my body by being scourged; but in soul I gladly suffer these things because of my fear of him." ³¹ So this man also died like this, leaving his death for an example of nobleness and a memorial of virtue, not only to the young but also to the great body of his nation.

7

¹ It came to pass that seven brothers and their mother were at the king's command taken and shamefully handled with scourges and cords, to compel them to taste of the abominable swine's flesh. ² One of them made himself the spokesman and said, "What would you ask and learn from us? For we are ready to die rather than transgress the laws of our ancestors." ³ The king fell into a rage, and commanded that pans and caldrons be heated. ⁴ When these were immediately heated, he gave orders to cut out the tongue of him who had been their spokesman, and to scalp him, and to cut off his extremities, with the rest of his brothers and his mother looking on. ⁵ And when he was utterlyᵈ maimed, the king gave orders to bring him to the fire, being yet alive, and to fry him in the pan. And as the smoke from the pan spread far, they and their mother also exhorted one another to die nobly, saying this: ⁶ "The Lord God sees, and in truth isᵉ entreated for us, as Moses declared in ᶠhis song, which witnesses against the people to their faces, saying, 'And he will have compassion on his servants.'" ⁷ And when the first had died like this, they brought the second to the mocking; and they pulled off the skin of his head with the hair and asked him, "Will you eat, before your body is punished in every limb?" ⁸ But he answered in the language of his ancestors and said to them, "No." Therefore he also underwent the next torture in succession, as the first had done. ⁹ When he was at the last gasp, he said, "You, miscreant, release us out of this present life, but the King of the world will raise us who have died for his laws up to an everlasting renewal of life." ¹⁰ After him, the third was made a victim of their mocking. When he was required, he quickly put out his tongue, and stretched out his hands courageously, ¹¹ and nobly said, "I got these from heaven. For his laws' sake I treat these with contempt. From him, I hope to receive these back again." ¹² As a result, the king himself and those who were with him were astonished at the young man's soul, for he regarded the pains as nothing. ¹³ When he too was dead, they shamefully handled and tortured the fourth in the same way. ¹⁴ Being near to death he said this: "It is good to die at the hands of men and look for the hope which is given by God, that we will be raised up again by him. For as for you, you will have no resurrection to life." ¹⁵ Next after him, they brought the fifth and shamefully handled him. ¹⁶ But he looked toward ᵍthe king and said, "Because you have authority among men, though you are corruptible, you do what you please. But don't think that our race has been forsaken by God. ¹⁷ But hold on to your ways, and see how his sovereign majesty will torture you and your descendants!" ¹⁸ After him they brought the sixth. When he was about to die, he said, "Don't be vainly deceived, for we suffer these things for our own doings, as sinning against our own God. Astounding things have come to pass; ¹⁹ but don't think you that you will be unpunished, having tried to fight against God!" ²⁰ But above all, the mother was marvelous and worthy of honorable memory; for when she watched seven sons perishing within the space of one day, she bore the sight with a good courage because of her hope in the Lord. ²¹ She exhorted each one of them in the language of their fathers, filled with a noble spirit and stirring up her woman's thoughts with manly courage, saying to them, ²² "I don't know how you came into my womb. It wasn't I who gave you your ʰspirit and your life. It wasn't I who brought into order the first elements of each one of you. ²³ Therefore the Creator of the world, who shaped the first origin of man and devised the first origin of all things, in mercy gives back to you again both your ⁱspirit and your life, as you now treat yourselves with contempt for his laws' sake." ²⁴ But Antiochus, thinking himself to be despised, and suspecting the reproachful voice, while the youngest was yet alive didn't only make his appeal to him by words, but also at the same time promised with oaths that he would enrich him andʲ raise him to high honor if he would turn from the ways of his ancestors, and that he would take him for his ᵏfriend and entrust him with public affairs. ²⁵ But when the young man would in no way listen, the king called to him his mother, and urged her to advise the youth to save himself. ²⁶ When he had urged her with many words, she undertook to persuade her son. ²⁷ But bending toward him, laughing the cruel tyrant to scorn, she spoke this in the language of her fathers: "My son, have pity upon me who carried you nine months in my womb, and nursed you three years, and nourished and brought you up to this age, and sustained you. ²⁸ I beg you, my child, to lift your eyes to the sky and the earth, and to see all things that are in it, and thus to recognize that God made them not of things that were, and that the race of men in this way comes into being. ²⁹ Don't be afraid of this butcher, but, proving yourself worthy of your brothers, accept your death, that in God's mercy I may receive you again with your brothers." ³⁰ But before she had finished speaking, the young man said, "What are you all waiting for? I don't obey the commandment of the king, but I listen to the commandment of the law that was given to our fathers through Moses. ³¹ But you, who have devised all kinds of evil against the Hebrews, will in no way escape God's hands. ³² For we are suffering because of our own sins. ³³ If for rebuke and chastening, our living Lord has been angered a little while, yet he will again be reconciled with his own servants. ³⁴ But you, O unholy man and of all most vile, don't be vainly lifted up in your wild pride with uncertain hopes, raising your hand against the heavenly children. ³⁵ For you have not yet escaped the judgment of the Almighty God who sees all things. ³⁶ For these our brothers, having endured a ˡ short pain that brings everlasting life, have now ᵐ died under God's covenant. But you, through God's judgment, will receive in just measure the penalties of your arrogance. ³⁷ But I, as my brothers, give up both body and soul for the laws of our fathers, calling upon God that he may speedily become ⁿgracious to the nation, and that you, amidst trials and plagues, may confess that he alone is God, ³⁸ and that in me and my brothers ᵒ you may bring to an end the wrath of the Almighty which has been justly brought upon our whole race." ³⁹ But the king, falling into a rage, handled him worse than all the rest, being exasperated at his mocking. ⁴⁰ So he also died pure, putting his whole trust in the Lord. ⁴¹ Last of all, after her sons, the mother died. ⁴² Let it then suffice to have said thus much concerning the sacrificial feasts and the extreme tortures.

8

¹ But Judas, who is also called Maccabaeus, and those who were with him, making their way secretly into the villages, called to them their kindred. Taking to them those who had continued in the Jews' religion, gathered together about six thousand. ² They called upon the Lord to look at the people who were oppressed by all, and to have compassion on the sanctuary that had been profaned by the ungodly men, ³ and to have pity on the city that was suffering ruin and ready to be leveled to the ground, and to listen to the blood that cried out to him, ⁴ and to remember the lawless destruction of the innocent infants, and concerning the blasphemies that had been committed against his name, and to show his hatred of wickedness. ⁵ When Maccabaeus had trained his men for service, the heathen at once found him irresistible, for the wrath of the Lord was turned into mercy. ⁶ ᵖComing without warning, he set fire to cities and villages. And in winning back the most important positions, putting to flight no small number of the enemies, ⁷ he especially took advantage of the nights for such assaults. His courage was loudly talked of everywhere. ⁸ But when Philip saw the man gaining ground little by little, and increasing more and more in his success, he wrote to Ptolemy, the governor of Coelesyria and Phoenicia, that he should support the king's cause. ⁹ Ptolemy quickly appointed Nicanor the son of Patroclus, one of the king's ᑫ chief friends, and sent him, in command of no fewer than twenty thousand of all nations, to destroy the whole race of

---

ᵃ *6:28* Gr. one that has left behind.
ᵇ *6:29* The Greek text of this verse is uncertain.
ᶜ *6:30* Or, blows
ᵈ *7:5* Gr. useless.
ᵉ *7:6* Or, comforted in
ᶠ *7:6* See Deuteronomy **31:21** and **32:36**.

ᵍ *7:16* Gr. him.
ʰ *7:22* Or, breath
ⁱ *7:23* Or, breath
ʲ *7:24* Gr. make him one that is counted happy.
ᵏ *7:24* See **2 Maccabees 8:9**.
ˡ *7:36* Gr. short pain of ever-flowing life.

ᵐ *7:36* Gr. fallen. By the omission of one Greek letter the words would signify having endured a short pain, have now drunk of ever-flowing life under God's covenant.
ⁿ *7:37* Gr. propitious.

ᵒ *7:38* Some authorities read may be stayed.
ᵖ *8:6* The Greek text of verses **6** and **7** is uncertain.
ᑫ *8:9* See **1 Maccabees 10:65**. Compare **2 Maccabees 1:14; 7:24; 10:13; 14:11; 1 Maccabees 2:18**.

Judea. With him he joined Gorgias also, a captain and one who had experience in matters of war. ¹⁰ Nicanor resolved by the sale of the captive Jews to make up for the king the tribute of two thousand talents which he was to pay to the Romans. ¹¹ Immediately he sent to the cities upon the sea coast, inviting them to buy Jewish ᵃslaves, promising to deliver seventy ᵇslaves for a talent, not expecting the judgment that was to overtake him from the Almighty. ¹² News came to Judas concerning Nicanor's invasion. When he communicated to those who were with him the presence of the army, ¹³ those who were cowardly and distrustful of God's judgment ᶜran away and left the country. ¹⁴ Others sold all that they had left, and at the same time implored the Lord to deliver those who had been sold as slaves by the impious Nicanor before he ever met them, ¹⁵ if not for their own sakes, then for the covenants made with their ancestors, and because he had called them by his holy and glorious name. ¹⁶ So Maccabaeus gathered his men together, six thousand in number, and exhorted them not to be frightened by the enemy, nor to fear the great multitude of the heathen who came wrongfully against them, but to fight nobly, ¹⁷ setting before their eyes the outrage that had been lawlessly perpetrated upon the holy place, and the torture of the city that had been turned to mockery, and further the overthrow of the way of life received from their ancestors. ¹⁸ "For they," he said, "trust their weapons and daring deeds, but we trust in the almighty God, since he is able at a nod to cast down those who are coming against us, and even the whole world." ¹⁹ Moreover, he recounted to them the help given from time to time in the days of their ancestors, both in the days of Sennacherib, when one hundred eighty-five thousand perished, ²⁰ and in the land of Babylon, in the battle that was fought against theᵈ Gauls, how they came to the battle with eight thousand in all, with four thousand Macedonians, and how, the Macedonians being hard pressed, the ᵉsix thousand destroyed the hundred and twenty thousand because of the help which they had from heaven, and took a great deal of plunder. ²¹ And when he had with these words filled them with courage and made them ready to die for the laws and their country, he divided his army into four parts. ²² He appointed his brothers, Simon, Joseph, and Jonathan, to be leaders of the divisions with him, giving each the command of one thousand five hundred men. ²³ Moreover Eleazer also, having read aloud the sacred book, and having given as watchword, "THE HELP OF GOD", leading the first band himself, joined battle with Nicanor. ²⁴ Since the Almighty fought on their side, they killed more than nine thousand of the enemy, and wounded andᶠ disabled most of Nicanor's army, and compelled them all to flee. ²⁵ They took the money of those who had come there to buy them as slaves. After they had pursued them for some ᵍdistance, they returned, being constrained by the time of the day; ²⁶ for it was the day before the Sabbath, and for this reason they made no effort to chase them far. ²⁷ ʰ When they had gathered ⁱthe weapons of the enemy together, and had stripped off their spoils, they kept the Sabbath, greatly blessing and thanking the Lord who had saved them to this day, because he had begun to show mercy to them. ²⁸ After the Sabbath, when they had given some of the spoils to the ʲ maimed, and to the widows and orphans, they distributed the rest among themselves and their children. ²⁹ When they had accomplished these things and had made a common supplication, they implored the merciful Lord to be wholly reconciled with his servants. ³⁰ Having had an encounter with the forces of Timotheus and Bacchides, they killed more than twenty thousand of them, and made themselves masters of exceedingly high strongholds, and divided very much plunder, giving the ᵏmaimed, orphans, widows, and the aged an equal share with themselves. ³¹ ˡ When they had gathered the weapons ᵐ of the enemy together, they stored them all up carefully in the most strategic positions, and they carried the rest of the spoils to Jerusalem. ³² They killed the ⁿphylarch of Timotheus's forces, a most unholy man, and one who had done the Jews much harm. ³³ ᵒ As they celebrated the feast of victory in the ᵖ city of their fathers, they burned those who had set the sacred ᵍgates on fire, including Callisthenes, who had fled into ʳa little house. So they received the proper reward for their impiety. ³⁴ The thrice-accursed Nicanor, who had brought the thousand merchants to buy the Jews as slaves, ³⁵ being through the help of the Lord humbled by them who in his eyes were held to be of least account, took off his glorious apparel, and passing through the country, ˢshunning all company like a fugitive slave, arrived at Antioch, ᵗ having, as he thought, had the greatest possible good fortune, though his army was destroyed. ³⁶ He who had taken upon himself to make tribute sure for the Romans by the captivity of the men of Jerusalem published abroad that the Jews had One who fought for them, and that ᵘbecause this was so, the Jews were invulnerable, because they followed the laws ordained by him.

9

¹ Now about that time, Antiochus retreated ᵛin disorder from the region of Persia. ² For he had entered into the city called Persepolis, and he attempted to rob ʷa temple and to control the city. Therefore the multitudes rushed in and the people of the country turned to defend themselves with weapons; and it came to pass that Antiochus was put to flight by the people of the country and broke his camp with disgrace. ³ While he was at Ecbatana, news was brought to him about what had happened to Nicanor and the forces of Timotheus. ⁴ Being overcome by his anger, he planned to make the Jews suffer for the evil deeds of those who had put him to flight. Therefore, with judgment from heaven even now accompanying him, he ordered his charioteer to drive without ceasing until he completed the journey; for he arrogantly said this: "I will make Jerusalem a common graveyard of Jews when I come there." ⁵ But the All-seeing Lord, the God of Israel, struck him with a ˣfatal and invisible stroke. As soon as he had finished speaking this word, an incurable pain of the bowels seized him, with bitter torments of the inner parts– ⁶ and that most justly, for he had tormented other men's bowels with many and strange sufferings. ⁷ But he in no way ceased from his rude insolence. No, he was filled with even more arrogance, breathing fire in his passion against the Jews, and giving orders to hasten the journey. But it came to pass moreover that he fell from his chariot as it rushed along, and having a grievous fall was tortured in all of the members of his body. ⁸ He who had just supposed himself to have the waves of the sea at his bidding because he was so superhumanly arrogant, and who thought to weigh the heights of the mountains in a balance, was now brought to the ground and carried in a litter, ʸshowing to all that the power was obviously God's, ⁹ so that worms swarmed out of the impious man's body, and while he was still living in anguish and pains, his flesh fell off, and by reason of the stench all the army turned with loathing from his decay. ¹⁰ The man who a little before supposed himself to touch the stars of heaven, no one could endure to carry because of his intolerable stench. ¹¹ Therefore he began in great part to cease from his arrogance, being broken in spirit, and to come to knowledge under the scourge of God, his pains increasing every moment. ¹² When he himself could not stand his own smell, he said these words: "It is right to be subject to God, and that one who is mortal should not think they are equal to God." ¹³ The vile man vowed to the sovereign Lord, who now no more would have pity upon him, saying ¹⁴ that the holy city, to which he was going in haste to lay it even with the ground and to ᶻmake it a common graveyard, he would declare free. ¹⁵ Concerning the Jews, whom he had decided not even to count worthy of burial, but to cast them out to the animals with their infants for the birds to devour, he would make them all equal to citizens of Athens. ¹⁶ The holy sanctuary, which before he had plundered, he would adorn with best offerings, and would restore all the sacred vessels many times multiplied, and out of his own revenues would defray the charges that were required for the sacrifices. ¹⁷ Beside all this, he said that he would become a Jew and would visit every inhabited place, proclaiming the power of God. ¹⁸ But when his sufferings did in no way cease, for the judgment of God had come upon him in righteousness, having given up all hope for himself, he wrote to the Jews the letter written below, having the nature of a supplication, to this effect: ¹⁹ "To the worthy Jewish citizens, Antiochus, king and general, wishes much joy and health and prosperity. ²⁰ May you and your children fare well, and may your affairs be as you wish. Having my hope in heaven, ²¹ I remembered with affection your honor and good will. Returning out of the region of Persia, and being

---

ᵃ *8:11* Gr. bodies.
ᵇ *8:11* Gr. bodies.
ᶜ *8:13* The Greek text here is uncertain.
ᵈ *8:20* Gr. Galatians.
ᵉ *8:20* Some authorities read eight.
ᶠ *8:24* Gr. disabled in their limbs.
ᵍ *8:25* Or, while
ʰ *8:27* The exact meaning of this clause is uncertain.

ⁱ *8:27* Gr. their weapons…the spoils of the enemy.
ʲ *8:28* Or, wounded Gr. shamefully handled.
ᵏ *8:30* Or, wounded Gr. shamefully handled.
ˡ *8:31* The exact meaning of this clause is uncertain.
ᵐ *8:31* Gr. of them.
ⁿ *8:32* That is, probably, the captain of an irregular auxiliary force. Some write

Phylarches, as a proper name.
ᵒ *8:33* The Greek text here is perhaps corrupt.
ᵖ *8:33* Or, country
ᵍ *8:33* Or, porches
ʳ *8:33* Or, a solitary hut
ˢ *8:35* Gr. having made himself solitary.
ᵗ *8:35* Or, having won the greatest possible favor by

reason of the destruction of his army
ᵘ *8:36* Or, because of this their way of life Gr. because of this manner.
ᵛ *9:1* Or, with dishonor
ʷ *9:2* Or, temples
ˣ *9:5* Gr. remediless.
ʸ *9:8* Or, showing manifestly to all the power of God
ᶻ *9:14* Gr. build.

taken with an annoying sickness, I deemed it necessary to take thought for the common safety of all, ²² not despairing of myself, but having great hope to escape from the sickness. ²³ But considering that my father also, at the time he led an army into the upper country, appointed his successor, ²⁴ to the end that, if anything fell out contrary to expectation, or if any unwelcome tidings were brought, the people in the country, knowing to whom the state had been left, might not be troubled, ²⁵ and, moreover, observing how the princes who are along the borders and neighbors to my kingdom watch for opportunities and look for the future event, I have appointed my son Antiochus to be king, whom I often entrusted and commended to most of you when I was hurrying to the upper provinces. I have written to him what is written below. ²⁶ I therefore urge you and beg you, having in your remembrance the benefits done to you in common and severally, to preserve your present good will, each of you, toward me and my son. ²⁷ For I am persuaded that he in gentleness and kindness will follow my purpose and treat you with moderation and kindness. ²⁸ So the murderer and blasphemer, having endured the most intense sufferings, even as he had dealt with other men, ended his life among the mountains by a most piteous fate in a strange land. ²⁹ Philip his foster brother took the body home and then, fearing the son of Antiochus, he withdrew himself to Ptolemy Philometor in Egypt.

10

¹ Then Maccabaeus and those who were with him, the Lord leading them on, recovered the temple and the city. ² They pulled down the altars that had been built in the marketplace by the foreigners, and also the sacred enclosures. ³ Having cleansed the sanctuary, they made another altar of sacrifice. ᵃStriking flint and starting a fire, they offered sacrifices after they had ceased for two years, burned incense, lit lamps, and set out the show bread. ⁴ When they had done these things, they fell prostrate and implored the Lord that they might fall no more into such evils; but that, if they ever did sin, they might be chastened by him with forbearance, and not be delivered to blaspheming and barbarous heathen. ⁵ Now on the same day that the sanctuary was profaned by foreigners, upon that very day it came to pass that the sanctuary was cleansed, even on the twenty-fifth day of the same month, which is Chislev. ⁶ They observed eight days with gladness in the manner of the feast of tabernacles, remembering how ᵇnot long before, during the feast of tabernacles, they were wandering in the mountains and in the caves like wild animals. ⁷ Therefore carrying wands wreathed with leaves, and beautiful branches, and palm fronds also, they offered up hymns of thanksgiving to him who had successfully brought to pass the cleansing of his own place. ⁸ They ordained also with a public statute and decree, for all the nation of the Jews, that they should observe these days every year. ⁹ Such were the events of the end of Antiochus, who was called Epiphanes. ¹⁰ Now we will declare what came to pass under Antiochus ᶜEupator, who proved himself a son of that ungodly man, and will summarize the main evils of the wars. ¹¹ For this man, when he succeeded to the kingdom, appointed one Lysias to be chancellor and supreme governor of Coelesyria and Phoenicia. ¹² For Ptolemy who was called Macron, setting an example of observing justice toward the Jews because of the wrong that had been done to them, endeavored to deal with them on peaceful terms. ¹³ Whereupon being accused by the king's ᵈfriends before Eupator, and hearing himself called traitor at every turn because he had abandoned Cyprus which Philometor had entrusted to him, and had withdrawn himself to Antiochus Epiphanes, and ᵉ failing to uphold the honor of his office, he took poison and did away with himself. ¹⁴ But when Gorgias was made governor of the district, he maintained a force of mercenaries, and at every turn kept up war with the Jews. ¹⁵ Together with him the Idumaeans also, being masters of important strongholds, harassed the Jews; and received those who had taken refuge from Jerusalem, they endeavored to keep up the war. ¹⁶ But Maccabaeus and his men, having made solemn supplication and having implored God to fight on their side, rushed upon the strongholds of the Idumaeans. ¹⁷ Assaulting them vigorously, they took control of the positions, and kept off all who fought upon the wall, and killed those whom they encountered, killing no fewer than twenty thousand. ¹⁸ Because no fewer than nine thousand had fled into two very strong towers having everything needed for a seige, ¹⁹ Maccabaeus, having left Simon and Joseph, and also Zacchaeus and those who were with him, a force sufficient to besiege them, departed himself to places where he was most needed. ²⁰ But Simon and those who were with him, yielding to covetousness, were bribed by some of those who were in the towers, and receiving seventy thousand drachmas, let some of them slip away. ²¹ But when word was brought to Maccabaeus of what was done, he gathered the leaders of the people together, and accused those men of having sold their kindred for money by setting their enemies free to fight against them. ²² So he killed these men for having turned traitors, and immediately took possession of the two towers. ²³ Prospering with his weapons in everything he undertook, he destroyed more than twenty thousand in the two strongholds. ²⁴ Now Timotheus, who had been defeated by the Jews before, having gathered together foreign forces in great multitudes, and having collected the cavalry which belonged to Asia, not a few, came as though he would take Judea by force of weapons. ²⁵ But as he drew near, Maccabaeus and his men sprinkled dirt on their heads and girded their loins with sackcloth, in supplication to God, ²⁶ and falling down upon the step in front of the altar, implored him to become ᶠgracious to them, and ᵍbe an enemy to their enemies and an adversary to their adversaries, as the law declares. ²⁷ Rising from their prayer they took up their weapons, and advanced some distance from the city. When they had come near to their enemies, theyʰ halted. ²⁸ When the dawn was now breaking, the two armies joined in battle, the one part having this, beside virtue, for a pledge of success and victory, that they had fled to the Lord for refuge, the others making their passion their leader in the fight. ²⁹ When the battle became strong, there appeared out of heaven to their adversaries five splendid men on horses with bridles of gold, ⁱand two of them, leading on the Jews, ³⁰ and taking Maccabaeus in the midst of them, and covering him with their own armor, guarded him from wounds, while they shot arrows and thunderbolts at the enemies. For this reason, they were blinded and thrown into confusion, and were cut to pieces, filled with bewilderment. ³¹ Twenty thousand five hundred were slain, beside six hundred cavalry. ³² Timotheus himself fled into a stronghold called Gazara, a fortress of great strength, ʲwhere Chaereas was in command. ³³ Then Maccabaeus and his men were glad and laid siege to the fortress for four days. ³⁴ Those who were within, trusting in the strength of the place, blasphemed exceedingly, and hurled out impious words. ³⁵ But at dawn of the fifth day, certain young men of Maccabaeus' company, inflamed with anger because of the blasphemies, assaulted the wall with masculine force and with ᵏfurious anger, and cut down whoever came in their way. ³⁶ Others climbing up in the same way, while the enemies were distracted with those who had made their way within, set fire to the towers, and kindled fires that burned the blasphemers alive, while others broke open the gates, and, having given entrance to the rest of the band, occupied the city. ³⁷ They killed Timotheus, who was hidden in a cistern, and his brother Chaereas, and Apollophanes. ³⁸ When they had accomplished these things, they blessed the Lord with hymns and thanksgiving, blessing him who provides great benefits to Israel and gives them the victory.

11

¹ Now after a very little time, Lysias, the king's guardian, kinsman, and chancellor, being very displeased about the things that had happened, ² collected about eighty thousand infantry and all his cavalry and came against the Jews, planing to make the city a home for Greeks, ³ and to levy tribute on the temple, as ˡon the other sacred places of the nations, and to put up the high priesthood for sale every year. ⁴ He took no account of God's power, but was puffed up with his ten thousands of infantry, his thousands of cavalry, and his eighty elephants. ⁵ Coming into Judea and approaching Bethsuron, which was a strong place and about five stadiaᵐ away from Jerusalem, he pressed it hard. ⁶ When Maccabaeus and his men learned that he was besieging the strongholds, they and all the people with lamentations and tears made supplication to the Lord to send a good angel to save Israel. ⁷ Maccabaeus himself took up weapons first, and exhorted the others to put themselves in jeopardy together with him and help their kindred; and they went out with him very willingly. ⁸ As they were there, close to Jerusalem, a horseman appeared at their head in white apparel, brandishingⁿ weapons

---

ᵃ *10:3* Gr. firing.
ᵇ *10:6* Or, not long before they kept the feast of tabernacles by wandering
ᶜ *10:10* That is, son of a good father.
ᵈ *10:13* See **2 Maccabees 8:9**
ᵉ *10:13* The Greek text here is corrupt.
ᶠ *10:26* Gr. propitious.
ᵍ *10:26* See Exodus **23:22**.
ʰ *10:27* Gr. were by themselves.
ⁱ *10:29* Some authorities read and leading on the Jews; who also, taking.
ʲ *10:32* See ver. **37**.
ᵏ *10:35* Gr. passion as of wild animals.
ˡ *11:3* Or, on all the sacred places of the heathen
ᵐ *11:5* One stadia was roughly **189** meters or **618** feet, so **5** stadia was about a little less than **1** km or a little more than half a mile.
ⁿ *11:8* Gr. a panoply.

of gold. ⁹They all together praised the merciful God, and were yet more strengthened in heart, being ready to ᵃassail not only men but the wildest animals and walls of iron, ¹⁰they advanced in array, having him who is in heaven to fight on their side, for the Lord had mercy on them. ¹¹Hurling themselves like lions against the enemy, they killed eleven thousand infantry and one thousand six hundred cavalry, and forced all the rest to flee. ¹²Most of them escaped wounded and naked. Lysias himself also escaped by shameful flight. ¹³But as he was a man not void of understanding, pondering the defeat which had befallen him, and considering that the Hebrews could not be overcome because the Almighty God fought on their side, he sent again ¹⁴and persuaded them to come to terms on condition that all their rights were acknowledged, and ᵇ promised that he would also persuade the king to become their friend. ¹⁵Maccabaeus gave consent upon all the conditions which Lysias proposed to him, being careful of the common good; for whatever requests Maccabaeus delivered in writing to Lysias concerning the Jews the king allowed. ¹⁶The letter written to the Jews from Lysias was to this effect: "Lysias to the ᶜpeople of the Jews, greetings. ¹⁷John and Absalom, who were sent from you, having delivered the document written below, made request concerning the things written therein. ¹⁸Whatever things therefore needed to be brought before the king I declared to him, and what things were possible he allowed. ¹⁹If then you will all preserve your good will toward the government, I will also endeavor in the future to contribute to your good. ²⁰Concerning this, I have given order in detail, both to these men and to those who are sent from me, to confer with you. ²¹Farewell. Written in the one hundred forty-eighth year, on the twenty-fourth day of the month ᵈDioscorinthius." ²²And the king's letter contained these words: "King Antiochus to his brother Lysias, greetings. ²³Seeing that our father passed to the gods having the wish that the subjects of his kingdom ᵉshould be undisturbed and give themselves to the care of their own affairs, ²⁴we, having heard that the Jews do not consent to our father's purpose to turn them to the customs of the Greeks, but choose rather their own way of living, and make request that the customs of their law be allowed to them– ²⁵choosing therefore that this nation also should be free from disturbance, we determine that their temple is to be restored to them, and that they live according to the customs that were in the days of their ancestors. ²⁶You will therefore do well to send messengers to them and give them the right hand of friendship, that they, knowing our mind, may be of good heart, and gladly occupy themselves with the conduct of their own affairs." ²⁷And to the nation, the king's letter was as follows: "King Antiochus to the senate of the Jews and to the other Jews, greetings. ²⁸If you are all well, it is as we desire. We ourselves also are in good health. ²⁹Menelaus informed us that your desire was to return home and follow your own business. ³⁰They therefore who depart home up to the thirtieth day of Xanthicus shall have our ᶠfriendship, with full permission ³¹that the Jews use their own foods and observe their own laws, even as formerly. None of them shall be in any way molested for the things that have been done in ignorance. ³²Moreover I have sent Menelaus also, that he may encourage you. ³³Farewell. Written in the one hundred forty-eighth year, on the fifteenth day of Xanthicus." ³⁴The Romans also sent to them a letter in these words: "Quintus Memmius and Titus Manius, ambassadors of the Romans, to the people of the Jews, greetings. ³⁵In regard to the things which Lysias the king's kinsman granted you, we also give consent. ³⁶But as for the things which he judged should be referred to the king, send someone promptly, after you have considered them, that we may publish such decrees as are appropriate for your case; for we are on our way to Antioch. ³⁷Therefore send someone with speed, that we also may learn what is your mind. ³⁸ ᵍFarewell. Written in the one hundred forty-eighth year, on the fifteenth day of Xanthicus.

12

¹So when this agreement had been made, Lysias departed to the king, and the Jews went about their farming. ²But some of the governors of districts, Timotheus and Apollonius the son of Gennaeus, and also Hieronymus and Demophon, and beside them Nicanor the governor of Cyprus, would not allow them to enjoy tranquillity and live in peace. ³Men of Joppa perpetrated this great impiety: they invited the Jews who lived among them to go with their wives and children into the boats which they had provided, as though they had no ill will toward them. ⁴Whenʰ the Jews,ⁱ relying on the public vote of the city, accepted the invitation, as men desiring to live in peace and suspecting nothing, they took them out to sea and drowned not less than two hundred of them. ⁵When Judas heard of the cruelty done to his fellow-countrymen, giving command to the men that were with him ⁶and calling upon God the righteous Judge, he came against the murderers of his kindred, and set the harbor on fire at night, burned the boats, and put to the sword those who had fled there. ⁷But when the town gates were closed, he withdrew, intending to come again to root out the whole community of the men of Joppa. ⁸But learning that the men of Jamnia intended to do the same thing to the Jews who lived among them, ⁹he attacked the Jamnites at night, and set fire to the harbor together with the fleet, so that the glare of the light was seen at Jerusalem, two hundred forty furlongsʲ distant. ¹⁰Now when they had drawn off nine furlongsᵏ from there, as they marched against Timotheus, an army of Arabians attacked him, no fewer than five thousand infantry and five hundred cavalry. ¹¹And when a hard battle had been fought, and Judas and his company, by the help of God, had good success, the nomads being overcome implored Judas to grant them friendship, promising to give him livestock, and to help ˡhis people in all other ways. ¹²So Judas, thinking that they would indeed be profitable in many things, agreed to live in peace with them; and receiving pledges of friendship they departed to their tents. ¹³He also attacked a certain city, strong and fenced with earthworks and walls, and inhabited by a mixed multitude of various nations. It was named Caspin. ¹⁴Those who were within, trusting in the strength of the walls and their store of provisions, behaved themselves rudely toward Judas and those who were with him, railing, and furthermore blaspheming and speaking impious words. ¹⁵But Judas and his company, calling upon the great Sovereign of the world, who without rams and cunning engines of war hurled down Jericho in the times of Joshua, rushed wildly against the wall. ¹⁶Having taken the city by the will of God, they made unspeakable slaughter, so much that the adjoining lake, which was two furlongsᵐ broad, appeared to be filled with the deluge of blood. ¹⁷When they had gone seven hundred fifty furlongsⁿ from there, they made their way to Charax, to the Jews that are called ᵒTubieni. ¹⁸They didn't find Timotheus in that district, for he had by then departed from the district without accomplishing anything, but had left behind a very strong garrison in one place. ¹⁹But Dositheus and Sosipater, who were captains under Maccabaeus, went out and destroyed those who had been left by Timotheus in the stronghold, more than ten thousand men. ²⁰Maccabaeus, arranging his own army in divisions, set ᵖthese two over the bands, and marched in haste against Timotheus, who had with him one hundred twenty thousand infantry and two thousand five hundred cavalry. ²¹When Timotheus heard of the approach of Judas, he at once sent away the women and the children with the baggage into the fortress called ᵍCarnion; for the place was hard to besiege and difficult of access by reason of the narrowness of the approaches on all sides. ²²When the band of Judas, who led the first division, appeared in sight, and when terror and fear came upon the enemy, because the manifestation of him who sees all things came upon them, they fled in every direction, carried this way and that, so that they were often injured by their own men, and pierced with the points of their own swords. ²³Judas continued the pursuit more vigorously, putting the wicked wretches to the sword, and he destroyed as many as thirty thousand men. ²⁴Timotheus himself, falling in with the company of Dositheus and Sosipater, implored them with much crafty guile to let him go with his life, because he had in his power the parents of many of them and the kindred of some. ʳ "Otherwise, he said, little regard will ˢ be shown to these." ²⁵So when he had with many words confirmed the agreement to restore them without harm, they let him go that they might save their kindred. ²⁶Then Judas, marching against ᵗCarnion and the temple of Atergatis, killed twenty-five thousand people. ²⁷After he had put these to flight and destroyed them,

---

ᵃ *11:9* Gr. wound.
ᵇ *11:14* The Greek text here is corrupt.
ᶜ *11:16* Gr. multitude.
ᵈ *11:21* This month name is not found elsewhere, and is perhaps corrupt.
ᵉ *11:23* Or, should not be disquieted but
ᶠ *11:30* Gr. right hand.
ᵍ *11:38* Gr. Be in good health.

ʰ *12:4* Gr. they also.
ⁱ *12:4* Gr. after.
ʲ *12:9* a furlong is about **201** meters or **220** yards, so **240** furlongs is about **48** km. or **30** miles
ᵏ *12:10* a furlong is about **201** meters or **220** yards, so **9** furlongs is about **1. 8** km. or **1 1/8** miles
ˡ *12:11* Gr. them.

ᵐ *12:16* a furlong is about **201** meters or **220** yards, so **2** furlongs is about **402** meters or 1/ 4 mile
ⁿ *12:17* a furlong is about **201** meters or **220** yards, so **750** furlongs is about **151** km. or **94** miles
ᵒ *12:17* That is, men of Tob: see Judges **11:3**, 2 Samuel **10:6**, and compare 1 Maccabees **5:13**.

ᵖ *12:20* Gr. them.
ᵍ *12:21* Compare Carnain, 1 Maccabees **5:26**, **43**, **44**.
ʳ *12:24* Gr. and the result will be that these be disregarded. The Greek text here is perhaps corrupt.
ˢ *12:24* Or, have been shown
ᵗ *12:26* Compare Carnain, 1 Maccabees **5:26**, **43**, **44**.

he marched against Ephron also, a strong city, [a]wherein were multitudes of people of all nations. Stalwart young men placed [b]on the walls made a vigorous defense. There were great stores of war engines and darts there. [28] But calling upon the Sovereign who with might shatters the [c]strength of [d]the enemy, they took the city into their hands, and killed as many as twenty-five thousand of those who were in it. [29] Setting out from there, they marched in haste against Scythopolis, which is six hundred furlongs[e] away from Jerusalem. [30] But when the Jews who were settled there testified of the good will that the Scythopolitans had shown toward them, and of their kind treatment of them in the times of their misfortune, [31] they gave thanks, and further exhorted them to remain well disposed toward the race for the future. Then they went up to Jerusalem, the feast of weeks being close at hand. [32] But after the feast called Pentecost, they marched in haste against Gorgias the governor of Idumaea. [33] He came out with three thousand infantry and four hundred cavalry. [34] When they had set themselves in array, it came to pass that a few of the Jews fell. [35] A certain Dositheus, one [f] of Bacenor's company, who was on horseback and was a strong man, pressed hard on Gorgias, and taking hold of his cloke dragged him along by main force. While he planned to take the accursed man alive, one of the Thracian cavalry bore down on him and disabled his shoulder, and so Gorgias escaped to [g]Marisa. [36] When those who were with Esdris had been fighting long and were weary, Judas called upon the Lord to show himself, fighting on their side and leading in the battle. [37] Then in the language of his ancestors he raised the battle cry joined with hymns. Then he rushed against Gorgias' troops when they were not expecting it, and put them to flight. [38] Judas gathered his army and came to the city of [h]Adullam. As the seventh day was coming on, they purified themselves according to the custom, and kept the Sabbath there. [39] On the following day, [i]when it had become necessary, Judas and his company came to take up the bodies of those who had fallen, [j]and in company with their kinsmen to bring them back to the sepulchres of their ancestors. [40] But under the garments of each one of the dead they found [k]consecrated tokens of the idols of Jamnia, which the law forbids the Jews to have anything to do with. It became clear to all that it was for this cause that they had fallen. [41] All therefore, blessing the ways of the Lord, the righteous Judge, who makes manifest the things that are hidden, [42] turned themselves to supplication, praying that the sin committed might be wholly blotted out. The noble Judas exhorted the multitude to keep themselves from sin, for they had seen with their own eyes what happened because of the sin of those who had fallen. [43] When he had made a collection man by man to the sum of two thousand drachmas of silver, he sent to Jerusalem to offer a sacrifice for sin, doing very well and honorably in this, in that he took thought for the resurrection. [44] For if he wasn't expecting that those who had fallen would rise again, it would be superfluous and idle to pray for the dead. [45] But if he was looking forward to an honorable memorial of gratitude laid up for those who [l]die [m]in godliness, then the thought was holy and godly. Therefore he made the atoning sacrifice for those who had died, that they might be released from their sin.

13

[1] In the one hundred forty-ninth year, news was brought to Judas and his company that Antiochus Eupator was coming with multitudes against Judea, [2] and with him Lysias his guardian and chancellor, each having a Greek force of one hundred ten thousand infantry, five thousand three hundred cavalry, twenty-two elephants, and three hundred chariots armed with scythes. [3] And Menelaus also joined himself with them, and with great hypocrisy encouraged Antiochus, not for the saving of his country, but because he thought that he would be set over the government. [4] But the King of kings stirred up the anger of Antiochus against the wicked wretch. When Lysias informed him that this man was the cause of all the evils, the king commanded to bring him to Beroea, and to put him to death in the way customary in that place. [5] Now there is in that place a tower that is fifty cubits high, full of ashes, and it had all around it a [n]circular rim sloping steeply on every side into the ashes. [6] Here one who is guilty of sacrilege or notorious for other crimes is pushed down to destruction. [7] By such a fate it happened that the breaker of the law, Menelaus, died, without obtaining so much as a grave in the earth, and that justly; [8] for inasmuch as he had perpetrated many sins [o] against the altar, whose fire and whose ashes were holy, he received his death in ashes. [9] Now the king,[p] infuriated in spirit, was coming with intent to inflict on the Jews the very worst of the sufferings that had been done in his father's time. [10] But when Judas heard of these things, he commanded the multitude to call upon the Lord day and night, if ever at any other time, so now to help those who were at the point of being deprived of the law, their country, and the holy temple, [11] and not to allow the people who had just begun to be revived to fall into the hands of those profane heathen. [12] So when they had all done the same thing together, [q] begging the merciful Lord with weeping and fastings and prostration for three days without ceasing, Judas exhorted them and commanded they should join him. [13] Having consulted privately with the elders, he resolved that before the king's army entered into Judea and made themselves masters of the city, they should go out and decide the matter by the help of [r]God. [14] And committing the decision to the [s]Lord of the world, and exhorting those who were with him to contend nobly even to death for laws, temple, city, country, and way of life, he pitched his camp by Modin. [15] He gave out to his men the watchword, "VICTORY IS GOD'S", with a chosen force of the bravest young men he attacked by the king's pavilion by night, and killed of his army as many as two thousand men, and [t]brought down the leading elephant with him who was in the [u]tower on him. [16] At last they filled the [v]army with terror and alarm, and departed with good success. [17] This had been accomplished when the day was just dawning, because of the Lord's protection that gave [w]Judas help. [18] But the king, having had a taste of the exceeding boldness of the Jews, made strategic attacks on their positions, [19] and on a strong fortress of the Jews at Bethsura. He advanced, was turned back, failed, and was defeated. [20] Judas sent the things that were necessary to those who were within. [21] But Rhodocus, from the Jewish ranks, made secrets known to the enemy. He was sought out, arrested, and shut up in prison. [22] The king negotiated with them in Bethsura the second time, gave his hand, took theirs, departed, attacked the forces of Judas, was put to the worse, [23] heard that Philip who had been left as chancellor in Antioch had become reckless, was confounded, made to the Jews an overture of peace, submitted himself and swore to acknowledge all their rights, came to terms with them and offered sacrifice, honored the sanctuary and the place, [24] showed kindness and graciously received Maccabaeus, left Hegemonides governor from Ptolemais even to the [x] Gerrenians, [25] and came to Ptolemais. The men of Ptolemais were displeased at the treaty, for they had exceedingly great indignation against the Jews. They desired to annul the articles of the agreement. [26] Lysias [y]came forward to speak, made the best defense that was possible, persuaded, pacified, gained their good will, and departed to Antioch. This was the issue of the attack and departure of the king.

14

[1] Three years later, news was brought to Judas and his company that Demetrius the son of Seleucus, having sailed into the harbor of Tripolis with a mighty army and a fleet, [2] had taken possession of the country, having made away with Antiochus and his guardian Lysias. [3] But one Alcimus, who had formerly been high priest, and had willfully polluted himself in the times when there was no mingling with the Gentiles, considering that there was no deliverance for him in any way, nor any more access to the holy altar, [4] came to King Demetrius in about the one hundred fifty-first year, presenting to him a crown of gold and a palm, and beside these some of the festal olive boughs of the temple. For that day, he held his peace; [5] but having gotten opportunity to further his own madness, being called by Demetrius into a meeting of his council, and asked how the Jews stood affected and what they intended, he answered: [6] "Those of the Jews called [z]Hasidaeans, whose leader is Judas Maccabaeus, keep up war and are seditious, not allowing the kingdom to find tranquillity. [7] Therefore, having

---

[a] *12:27* The Greek text here is perhaps corrupt.
[b] *12:27* Gr. in front of.
[c] *12:28* Some authorities read weight.
[d] *12:28* Or, his enemies
[e] *12:29* a furlong is about **201** meters or **220** yards, so **600** furlongs is about **121** km. or **75** miles
[f] *12:35* The Greek text is uncertain.
[g] *12:35* Compare **1 Maccabees 5:65**.
[h] *12:38* Gr. Odollam.
[i] *12:39* The Greek text here is uncertain.
[j] *12:39* Or, and to bring them back to be with their kinsmen in the sepulchres
[k] *12:40* Perhaps these were consecrated images of the idols.
[l] *12:45* Gr. fall asleep.
[m] *12:45* Or, on the side of godliness
[n] *13:5* Gr. contrivance or machine.
[o] *13:8* Gr. about.
[p] *13:9* Some authorities read indignant.
[q] *13:12* Gr. and implored.
[r] *13:13* Some authorities read the Lord.
[s] *13:14* Some authorities read Creator.
[t] *13:15* The Greek text here is probably corrupt.
[u] *13:15* Gr. house.
[v] *13:16* Gr. camp.
[w] *13:17* Gr. him.
[x] *13:24* The form of this word is uncertain. Compare Girzites (or Gizrites), **1 Samuel 27:8**. One manuscript reads Gerarenes.
[y] *13:26* Gr. came forward to the tribune or judgment seat.
[z] *14:6* That is, Chasidim.

laid aside my ancestral glory–I mean the high priesthood–I have now come [a]here, ⁸ first for the genuine care I have for the things that concern the king, and secondly because I have regard also to my own fellow citizens. For through the unadvised dealing of those of whom I spoke before, our whole race is in no small misfortune. ⁹ O king, having informed yourself of these things, take thought both for our country and for our race, which is surrounded by enemies, according to the gracious kindness with which you receive all. ¹⁰ For as long as Judas remains alive, it is impossible for the government to find peace. ¹¹ When he had spoken such words as these, at once [b]the rest of the king's [c]friends, having ill will against Judas, inflamed Demetrius yet more. ¹² He immediately appointed Nicanor, who had been master of the elephants, and made him governor of Judea. He sent him out, ¹³ giving him written instructions to kill Judas himself and to scatter those who were with him, and to set up Alcimus as high priest of the [d]great temple. ¹⁴ Those in Judea who [e]had driven Judas into exile thronged to Nicanor in flocks, supposing that the misfortunes and calamities of the Jews would be successes to themselves. ¹⁵ But when the Jews heard of Nicanor's advance and the assault of the heathen, they sprinkled dirt on their heads and made solemn prayers to him who had established his own people for evermore, and who always, making manifest his presence, upholds those who are his own heritage. ¹⁶ [f]When the leader had given orders, he immediately set out from there and joined battle with them at a village called Lessau. ¹⁷ But Simon, the brother of Judas, had encountered Nicanor, yet not till late, having been delayed by reason of the sudden consternation caused by his adversaries. ¹⁸ Nevertheless Nicanor, hearing of the valor of those who were with Judas, and their courage in fighting for their country, shrank from bringing the matter to the decision of the sword. ¹⁹ Therefore he sent Posidonius, Theodotus, and Mattathias to give and receive pledges of friendship. ²⁰ So when these proposals had been long considered, and the leader had made the [g]troops acquainted with them, and it appeared that they were all of like mind, they consented to the covenants. ²¹ They appointed a day on which to meet together by themselves. A chariot came forward from each army. They set up seats of honor. ²² Judas stationed armed men ready in convenient places, lest perhaps there should suddenly be treachery on the part of the enemy. They held a conference as was appropriate. ²³ Nicanor waited in Jerusalem, and did nothing to cause disturbance, but dismissed the flocks of people that had gathered together. ²⁴ He kept Judas always in his presence. He had gained a hearty affection for the man. ²⁵ He urged him to marry and have children. He married, settled quietly, and took part in common life. ²⁶ But Alcimus, perceiving the good will that was between them, [h]and having taken possession of the covenants that had been made, came to Demetrius and told him that Nicanor was disloyal to the government, for he had appointed that conspirator against his kingdom, Judas, to be his successor. ²⁷ The king, falling into a rage, and being exasperated by the false accusations of that most wicked man, wrote to Nicanor, signifying that he was displeased at the covenants, and commanding him to send Maccabaeus prisoner to Antioch in all haste. ²⁸ When this message came to Nicanor, he was confounded, and was very troubled at the thought of annulling the articles that had been agreed upon, the man having done no wrong; ²⁹ but because there was no opposing the king, he watched his time to execute this purpose by strategy. ³⁰ But Maccabaeus, when he perceived that Nicanor was behaving more harshly in his dealings with him, and that he had become ruler in his customary bearing, understanding that this harshness came not of good, gathered together not a few of his men, and concealed himself from Nicanor. ³¹ But the other,[i] when he became aware that he had been bravely defeated by the strategy of Judas,[j] came to the great[k] and holy temple, while the priests were offering the usual sacrifices, and commanded them to hand over the man. ³² When they declared with oaths that they had no knowledge where the man was whom he sought, ³³ he stretched out his right hand toward the sanctuary, and swore this oath: "If you won't deliver up to me Judas as a prisoner, I will level this [l]temple of God even with the ground, break down the altar, and I will erect here a temple to Dionysus for all to see. ³⁴ And having said this, he departed. But the priests, stretching forth their hands toward heaven, called upon him who always fights for our nation, in these words: ³⁵ "You, O Lord of the universe, who in yourself have need of nothing, were well pleased that a sanctuary of your habitation[m] should be set among us. ³⁶ So now, O holy Lord of all holiness, keep undefiled forever this house that has been recently cleansed." ³⁷ Now information was given to Nicanor against one Razis, an elder of Jerusalem, who was a lover of his countrymen and a man of very good report, and one called Father of the Jews for his good will. ³⁸ For in the former times when there was no mingling with the Gentiles, he had been accused of following the Jews' religion, and had risked body and life with all earnestness for the religion of the Jews. ³⁹ Nicanor, wishing to make evident the ill will that he bore against the Jews, sent above five hundred soldiers to seize him; ⁴⁰ for he thought by seizing him to inflict an injury on them. ⁴¹ But when the [n]troops were at the point of taking the tower, and were forcing the door of the court, and asked for fire to burn the doors, he, being surrounded on every side, fell upon his sword, ⁴² choosing rather to die nobly than to fall into the hands of the wicked wretches, and suffer outrage unworthy of his own nobleness. ⁴³ But since he missed his stroke through the excitement of the struggle, and the crowds were now rushing within the door, he ran bravely up to the wall and cast himself down bravely among the crowds. ⁴⁴ But as they quickly gave back, a space was made, and he fell on the middle of [o]his side. ⁴⁵ Still having breath within him, and being inflamed with anger, he rose up, and though his blood gushed out in streams and his wounds were grievous, he ran through the crowds, and standing upon a steep rock, ⁴⁶ when as his blood was now well near spent, he drew forth his bowels through the wound, and taking them in both his hands he shook them at the crowds. Calling upon him who is Lord of life and spirit to restore him [p]these again, he died like this.

15

¹ But Nicanor, hearing that Judas and his company were in the region of Samaria, resolved to attack them with complete safety on the day of rest. ² When the Jews who were compelled to follow him said, "Don't destroy so savagely and barbarously, but give due glory to the day which he who sees all things has honored and hallowed above other days." ³ Then the thrice-accursed wretch asked if there were a Sovereign in heaven who had commanded to keep the Sabbath day. ⁴ When they declared, "There is the Lord, living himself as Sovereign in heaven, who told us observe the seventh day." ⁵ He replied, "I also am a sovereign on the earth, who commands you to take up weapons and execute the king's business." Nevertheless he didn't prevail to execute his cruel plan. ⁶ And Nicanor, [q] in his utter boastfulness and arrogance, had determined to set up a monument of complete victory over Judas and all those who were with him. ⁷ But Maccabaeus still trusted unceasingly, with all hope that he should obtain help from the Lord. ⁸ He exhorted his company not to be fearful at the assault of the heathen, but keeping in mind the help which in former times they had often received from heaven, so now also to look for the victory which would come to them from the Almighty, ⁹ and encouraging them out of the law and the prophets, and reminding them of the conflicts that they had won, he made them more eager. ¹⁰ And when he had aroused their courage, he gave them orders, at the same time pointing out the faithlessness of the heathen and their breach of their oaths. ¹¹ Arming each one of them, not so much with the sure defense of shields and spears as with the encouragement of good words, and moreover relating to them a dream worthy to be believed, he made them all exceedingly glad. ¹² The vision of that dream was this: Onias, he who had been high priest, a noble and good man, modest in bearing, yet gentle in manner and well-spoken, and trained from a child in all points of virtue, with outstretched hands invoking blessings on the whole body of the Jews. ¹³ Then he saw a man appear, of venerable age and exceeding glory, and the dignity around him was wonderful and most majestic. ¹⁴ Onias answered and said, "This is the lover of the kindred, he who prays much for the people and the holy city: Jeremiah the prophet of God. ¹⁵ Jeremiah stretched out his right hand and delivered to Judas a gold sword, and in giving it addressed him thus: ¹⁶ "Take this holy sword, a gift from God, with which you shall strike down the adversaries." ¹⁷ Being encouraged by the words of Judas, which were noble and effective, and able to incite to virtue and to stir the souls of the young to manly courage, they determined not to carry on a campaign, but nobly to bear down upon the enemy, and fighting hand to hand with all

---

[a] 14:7 Some authorities read a second time.
[b] 14:11 Or, the king's friends likewise
[c] 14:11 See **2 Maccabees 8:9**.
[d] 14:13 Gr. greatest.
[e] 14:14 See **2 Maccabees 5:27**.

[f] 14:16 The Greek text of this verse and the next is corrupt.
[g] 14:20 Or, people Gr. multitudes.
[h] 14:26 Or, and the covenants that had been made, took occasion and came

[i] 14:31 Or, though he was conscious that he had been nobly defeated by
[j] 14:31 Gr. the man
[k] 14:31 Gr. greatest.
[l] 14:33 Or, chapel Gr. enclosure.
[m] 14:35 Gr. tabernacling.

[n] 14:41 Or, people Gr. multitudes.
[o] 14:44 Or, the void place
[p] 14:46 Some authorities read the same.
[q] 15:6 Gr. carrying his neck high.

courage bring the matter to a conclusion, because the city, the sanctuary, and the temple were in danger. ¹⁸ For their fear for wives and children, and furthermore for family and relatives, was less important to them; but greatest and first was their fear for the consecrated sanctuary. ¹⁹ Also those who were shut up in the city were in no light distress, being troubled because of the encounter in the open country. ²⁰ When all were now waiting for the decision of the issue, and the enemy had already joined battle, and the army had been set in array, and the elephants[a] brought back to a convenient post,[b] and the cavalry deployed on the flanks, ²¹ Maccabaeus, perceiving the presence of the [c]troops, and the various weapons with which they were equipped, and the savageness of the [d]elephants, holding up his hands to heaven called upon the Lord who works wonders, knowing that success comes not by weapons, but that, according to how the Lord judges, he gains the victory for those who are worthy. ²² And calling upon God, he said this: "You, O Sovereign Lord, sent your angel in the time of King Hezekiah of Judea, and he killed of the [e]army of Sennacherib as many as one hundred eighty-five thousand. ²³ So now also, O Sovereign of the heavens, send a good angel before us to bring terror and trembling. ²⁴ Through the greatness of your arm let them be stricken with dismay who with blasphemy have come here against your holy people." As he finished these words, ²⁵ Nicanor and his company advanced with trumpets and victory songs; ²⁶ but Judas and his company joined battle with the enemy with invocation and prayers. ²⁷ Fighting with their hands and praying to God with their hearts, they killed no less than thirty-five thousand men, being made exceedingly glad by the manifestation of God. ²⁸ When the engagement was over and they were returning again with joy, they recognized Nicanor lying dead in full armor. ²⁹ Then there was shouting and noise, and they blessed the Sovereign Lord in the language of their ancestors. ³⁰ He who in all things was in body and soul the foremost champion of his fellow-citizens, he who kept through life the good will of his youth toward his countrymen, ordered that Nicanor's head be cut off with his hand and arm, and that they be brought to Jerusalem. ³¹ When he had arrived there and had called his countrymen together and set the priests before the altar, he sent for those who were in the citadel. ³² Showing the head of the vile Nicanor and the hand of that profane man, which with proud brags he had stretched out against the holy house of the Almighty, ³³ and cutting out the tongue of the impious Nicanor, he said that he would give it in pieces to the birds, and hang up these rewards of his folly near the sanctuary. ³⁴ They all, looking up to heaven, blessed the Lord who had manifested himself, saying, "Blessed is he who has preserved his own place undefiled!" ³⁵ He hung Nicanor's head and shoulder from the citadel, a clear sign evident to all of the help of the Lord. ³⁶ They all ordained with a common decree to in no way let this day pass undistinguished, but to mark with honor the thirteenth day of the twelfth month (it is called Adar in the Syrian language), the day before the day of Mordecai. ³⁷ This then having been the account of the attempt of Nicanor, and the city having from those times been held by the Hebrews, I also will here make an end of my book. ³⁸ If I have written well and to the point in my story, this is what I myself desired; but if its poorly done and mediocre, this is the best I could do. ³⁹ For as it is [f]distasteful to drink wine alone and likewise to drink water alone, [g]while the mingling of wine with water at once gives full pleasantness to the flavor; so also the fashioning of the language delights the ears of those who read the story. Here is the end.

The Third Book of the Maccabees

The Third Book of the Maccabees is recognized as Deuterocanonical Scripture by the Greek Orthodox and Russian Orthodox Churches. It is considered to be apocrypha by most other church traditions.

1

¹ Now Philopater, on learning from those who came back that Antiochus had made himself master of the places which belonged to himself, sent orders to all his infantry and cavalry, took with him his sister Arsinoe, and marched out as far as the parts of Raphia, where Antiochus and his forces encamped. ² And one Theodotus, intending to carry out his design, took with him the bravest of the armed men who had been before committed to his trust by Ptolemy, and got through at night to the tent of Ptolemy, to kill him on his own responsibility, and so to end the war. ³ But Dositheus, called the son of Drimulus, by birth a Jew, afterward a renegade from the laws and observances of his country, conveyed Ptolemy away, and made an obscure person lie down in his stead in the tent. It turned out that this man received the fate which was meant for the other. ⁴ A fierce battle then took place. The men of Antiochus were prevailing. Arsinoe continually went up and down the ranks, and with dishevelled hair, with tears and entreaties, begged the soldiers to fight bravely for themselves, their children, and wives, and promised that if they proved conquerors, she would give them each two minas of gold. ⁵ It thus fell out that their enemies were defeated in hand-to-hand encounter, and that many of them were taken prisoners. ⁶ Having vanquished this attempt, the king then decided to proceed to the neighboring cities, and encourage them. ⁷ By doing this, and by making donations to their temples, he inspired his subjects with confidence. ⁸ The Jews sent some of their council and of their elders to him. The greetings, welcoming gifts, and congratulations of the past, given by them, filled him with the greater eagerness to visit their city. ⁹ Having arrived at Jerusalem, sacrificed, and offered thank-offerings to the Greatest God, and done whatever else was suitable to the sanctity of the place, and entered the inner court, ¹⁰ he was so impressed with the magnificence of the place, and so wondered at the orderly arrangements of the temple, that he considered entering the sanctuary itself. ¹¹ When they told him that this was not permissible, none of the nation, not even the priests in general, but only the supreme high priest of all, and he only once in a year, was allowed to go in, he would by no means give way. ¹² Then they read the law to him, but he persisted in intruding, exclaiming that he ought to be allowed. He said, "Even if they were deprived of this honor, I shouldn't be." ¹³ He asked why, when he entered all the other temples, did none of the priests who were present forbid him. ¹⁴ He was thoroughly answered by someone, that he did wrong to boast of this. ¹⁵ "Well, since I have done this," said he, "be the cause what it may, shall I not enter with or without your consent?" ¹⁶ When the priests fell down in their sacred vestments imploring the Greatest God to come and help in time of need, and to avert the violence of the fierce aggressor, and when they filled the temple with lamentations and tears, ¹⁷ then those who had been left behind in the city were scared, and rushed out, uncertain of the event. ¹⁸ Virgins, who had been shut up within their chambers, came out with their mothers, scattering dust and ashes on their heads, and filling the streets with outcries. ¹⁹ Women who had recently been arrayed for marriage left their bridal chambers, left the reserve that befitted them, and ran around the city in a disorderly manner. ²⁰ New-born babes were deserted by the mothers or nurses who waited upon them–some here, some there, in houses, or in fields; these now, with an ardor which could not be checked, swarmed into the Most High temple. ²¹ Various prayers were offered up by those who assembled in this place because of the unholy attempt of the king. ²² Along with these there were some of the citizens who took courage and would not submit to his obstinacy and his intention of carrying out his purpose. ²³ Calling out to arms, and to die bravely in defense of the law of their fathers, they created a great uproar in the place, and were with difficulty brought back by the aged and the elders to the station of prayer which they had occupied before. ²⁴ During this time, the multitude kept on praying. ²⁵ The elders who surrounded the king tried in many ways to divert his arrogant mind from the design which he had formed. ²⁶ He, in his hardened mood, insensible to all persuasion, was going onward with the view of carrying out this design. ²⁷ Yet even his own officers, when they saw this, joined the Jews in an appeal to Him who has all power to aid in the present crisis, and not wink at such haughty lawlessness. ²⁸ Such was the frequency and the vehemence of the cry of the assembled crowd, that an indescribable noise ensued. ²⁹ Not the men only,

---

[a] *15:20* Gr. animals.
[b] *15:20* Or, stationed for convenient action
[c] *15:21* Gr. multitudes.
[d] *15:21* Gr. animals.
[e] *15:22* Gr. camp.
[f] *15:39* Or, hurtful
[g] *15:39* Gr. but even as.

but the very walls and floor seemed to sound out, all things preferring death rather than to see the place defiled.

2

¹ Now it was that the high priest Simon bowed his knees near the holy place, spread out his hands in reverent form, and uttered the following prayer: ² "O Lord, Lord, King of the heavens, and Ruler of the whole creation, Holy among the holy, sole Governor, Almighty, give ear to us who are oppressed by a wicked and profane one, who celebrates in his confidence and strength. ³ It is you, the Creator of all, the Lord of the universe, who are a righteous Governor, and judge all who act with pride and insolence. ⁴ It was you who destroyed the former workers of unrighteousness, among whom were the giants, who trusted in their strength and daring, by covering them with a measureless flood. ⁵ It was you who made the Sodomites, those workers of exceedingly iniquity, men notorious for their vices, an example to later generations, when you covered them with fire and brimstone[a]. ⁶ You made known your power when you caused the bold Pharaoh, the enslaver of your people, to pass through the ordeal of many and diverse inflictions. ⁷ You rolled the depths of the sea over him when he pursued with chariots and with a multitude of followers, and gave a safe passage to those who put their trust in you, the Lord of the whole creation. ⁸ These saw and felt the works of your hands, and praised you, the Almighty. ⁹ You, O King, when you created the immeasurable and measureless earth, chose this city. You made this place sacred to your name, even though you need nothing. You glorified it with your illustrious presence, after constructing it to the glory of your great and honorable name. ¹⁰ You promised, out of love for the people of Israel, that if we fall away from you, become afflicted, and then come to this house and pray, you would hear our prayer. ¹¹ Truly you are faithful and true. ¹² When you often aided our fathers when hard pressed and humiliated, and delivered them out of great dangers, ¹³ see now, holy King, how through our many and great sins we are crushed and made subject to our enemies, and have become weak and powerless. ¹⁴ In our low condition, this bold and profane man seeks to dishonor this your holy place, consecrated out of the earth to the name of your Majesty. ¹⁵ Your dwelling place, the heaven of heavens, is indeed unapproachable to men. ¹⁶ But since it seemed good to you to exhibit your glory among your people Israel, you sanctified this place. ¹⁷ Don't punish us by means of the uncleanness of their men, and don't chastise us by means of their profanity, lest the lawless ones should boast in their rage, and exult in exuberant pride of speech, and say, ¹⁸ 'We have trampled upon the holy house, as idolatrous houses are trampled upon.' ¹⁹ Blot out our iniquities, do away with our errors, and show your compassion in this hour. ²⁰ Let your mercies quickly go before us. Grant us peace, that the downcast and broken hearted may praise you with their mouth." ²¹ At that time God, who sees all things, who is beyond all Holy among the holy, heard that prayer, so suitable, and scourged the man who was greatly uplifted with scorn and insolence. ²² Shaking him back and forth as a reed is shaken with the wind, he threw him down on the pavement, powerless, with limbs paralyzed, and by a righteous judgment deprived of the ability to speak. ²³ His friends and bodyguards, seeing the swift recompense which had suddenly overtaken him, struck with exceeding terror, and fearing that he would die, speedily removed him. ²⁴ When in course of time he had come to himself, this severe punishment caused no repentance within him, but he departed with bitter threatenings. ²⁵ He proceeded to Egypt, grew worse in wickedness through his previously mentioned companions in wine, who were lost to all goodness, ²⁶ and not satisfied with countless acts of impiety, his audacity so increased that he raised evil reports there, and many of his friends, watching his purpose attentively, joined in furthering his will. ²⁷ His purpose was to inflict a public stigma upon our race. Therefore he erected a stone pillar in the courtyard, and caused the following inscription to be engraved upon it: ²⁸ "Entrance to this temple is to be refused to all those who would not sacrifice. All the Jews were to be registered among the slaves. Those who resisted are to be forcibly seized and put to death. ²⁹ Those who are thus registered are to be marked on their persons by the ivy-leaf symbol of Dionysus, and to be reduced to these limited rights." ³⁰ To do away with the appearance of hating them all, he had it written underneath, that if any of them should elect to enter the community of those initiated in the rites, these should have equal rights with the Alexandrians. ³¹ Some of those who were over the city, therefore, abhorring any approach to the city of piety, unhesitatingly gave in to the king, and expected to derive some great honor from a future connection with him. ³² A nobler spirit, however, prompted the majority to cling to their religious observances, and by paying money that they might live unmolested, these sought to escape the registration, ³³ cheerfully looking forward to future aid, they abhorred their own apostates, considering them to be national foes, and depriving them of common fellowship and mutual help.

3

¹ On discovering this, so incensed was the wicked king, that he no longer confined his rage to the Jews in Alexandria. Laying his hand more heavily upon those who lived in the country, he gave orders that they should be quickly collected into one place, and most cruelly deprived of their lives. ² While this was going on, a hostile rumor was uttered abroad by men who had banded together to injure the Jewish race. The pretext of their charge was that the Jews kept them away from the ordinances of the law. ³ Now the Jews always maintained a feeling of unwavering loyalty toward the kings, ⁴ yet, as they worshiped God and observed his law, they made certain distinctions, and avoided certain things. Hence they appeared hateful to some people, ⁵ although, as they adorned their conversation with works of righteousness, they had established themselves in the good opinion of the world. ⁶ What all the rest of mankind said was, however, disregarded by the foreigners, ⁷ who said much of the exclusiveness of the Jews with regard to their worship and meats. They alleged that they were unsociable men, hostile to the king's interests, refusing to associate with him or his troops. By this way of speaking, they brought much hatred on them. ⁸ This unexpected uproar and sudden gathering of people was observed by the Greeks who lived in the city, concerning men who had never harmed them. Yet to aid them was not in their power, since all was oppression around, but they encouraged them in their troubles, and expected a favorable turn of affairs. ⁹ He who knows all things will not, they said, disregard so great a people. ¹⁰ Some of the neighbors, friends, and business associates of the Jews even called them secretly to an interview, pledged them their assistance, and promised to do their very utmost for them. ¹¹ Now the king, elated with his prosperous fortune, and not regarding the superior power of God, but thinking to persevere in his present purpose, wrote the following letter to the prejudice of the Jews: ¹² "King Ptolemy Philopater, to the commanders and soldiers in Egypt, and in all places, health and happiness! ¹³ I am doing well, and so, too, are my affairs. ¹⁴ Since our Asiatic campaign, the particulars of which you know, and which by the aid of the gods, not lightly given, and by our own vigor, has been brought to a successful conclusion according to our expectation, ¹⁵ we resolved, not with strength of spear, but with gentleness and much humanity, as it were to nurse the inhabitants of Coele-Syria and Phoenicia, and to be their willing benefactors. ¹⁶ So, having bestowed considerable sums of money upon the temples of the several cities, we proceeded even as far as Jerusalem, and went up to honor the temple of these wretched beings who never cease from their folly. ¹⁷ To outward appearance they received us willingly, but belied that appearance by their deeds. When we were eager to enter their temple, and to honor it with the most beautiful and exquisite gifts, ¹⁸ they were so carried away by their old arrogance as to forbid us the entrance, while we, out of our forbearance toward all men, refrained from exercising our power upon them. ¹⁹ Thus, exhibiting their enmity against us, they alone among the nations lift up their heads against kings and benefactors, as men unwilling to submit to any reasonable thing. ²⁰ We then, having endeavored to make allowance for the madness of these people, and on our victorious return treating all people in Egypt courteously, acted in a manner which was befitting. ²¹ Accordingly, bearing no ill will against their kinsmen, but rather remembering our connection with them, and the numerous matters with sincere heart from a remote period entrusted to them, we wished to venture a total alteration of their state, by giving them the rights of citizens of Alexandria, and to admit them to the everlasting rites of our solemnities. ²² All this, however, they have taken in a very different spirit. With their innate malignity, they have spurned the fair offer, and constantly inclining to evil, ²³ have rejected the inestimable rights. Not only so, but by using speech, and by refraining from speech, they abhor the few among them who are heartily disposed toward us, ever deeming that their infamous way of life will force us to do away with our reform. ²⁴ Having then received certain proofs that these Jews bear us every sort of ill will, we must look forward to the possibility of some sudden tumult among ourselves when these impious men may turn traitors and barbarous enemies. ²⁵ Therefore, as soon as the contents of this letter become known to you, in that same hour we order those Jews who dwell among you, with wives and children, to be sent to us, vilified and abused, in chains of iron, to undergo a cruel and shameful death, suitable to enemies. ²⁶ For by the punishment of them in one body we perceive that we have found the only means of establishing our affairs for the future on a firm and satisfactory basis. ²⁷ Whoever protects a Jew, whether it be old man, child, or nursing baby, shall with his whole house be tortured to death. ²⁸ Whoever informs against the Jews, besides receiving

---

[a] 2:5 or, sulfur

the property of the person charged, shall be presented with two thousand drachmas[a] from the royal treasury, shall be made free, and shall be crowned. ²⁹ Whatever place shelters a Jew shall be made unapproachable and shall be put under the ban of fire, and be forever rendered useless to every living being for all time to come." ³⁰ The king's letter was written in the above form.

4

¹ Wherever this decree was received, the people kept up a revelry of joy and shouting, as if their long-pent-up, hardened hatred would now show itself openly. ² The Jews suffered great throes of sorrow and wept much, while their hearts, all things around being lamentable, were set on fire as they bewailed the sudden destruction which was decreed against them. ³ What home, or city, or any inhabited place, or what streets were there, which their condition didn't fill with wailing and lamentation? ⁴ They were sent out unanimously by the generals in various cities, with such stern and pitiless feeling that the exceptional nature of the infliction moved even some of their enemies. These, influenced by sentiments of common humanity, and reflecting upon the uncertain issue of life, shed tears at their miserable expulsion. ⁵ A multitude of aged hoary-haired old men were driven along with halting bending feet, urged onward by the impulse of a violent, shameless force to quick speed. ⁶ Girls who had entered the bridal chamber quite lately, to enjoy the partnership of marriage, exchanged pleasure for misery; and with dust scattered upon their myrrh-anointed heads, were hurried along unveiled; and, in the midst of outlandish insults, set up with one accord a lamentable cry instead of the marriage hymn. ⁷ Bound and exposed to public gaze, they were hurried violently on board ship. ⁸ The husbands of these, in the prime of their youthful vigor, instead of crowns, wore ropes round their necks. Instead of feasting and youthful celebration, they spent the rest of their nuptial days in wailing, and saw only the grave at hand. ⁹ They were dragged along by unyielding chains, like wild animals. Of these, some had their necks thrust into the benches of the rowers, while the feet of others were enclosed in hard fetters. ¹⁰ The planks of the deck above them blocked out the light and shut out the day on every side, so that they might be treated like traitors during the whole voyage. ¹¹ They were carried like this in this vessel, and at the end of it arrived at Schedia. The king had ordered them to be cast into the vast hippodrome, which was built in front of the city. This place was well adapted by its situation to expose them to the gaze of all comers into the city, and of those who went from the city into the country. Thus they could hold no communication with his forces. They weren't deemed worthy of any civilized accommodation. ¹² When this was done, the king, hearing that their kindred in the city often went out and lamented the melancholy distress of these victims, ¹³ was full of rage, and commanded that they should be carefully subjected to the same–and not one bit milder–treatment. ¹⁴ The whole nation was now to be registered. Every individual was to be specified by name, not for that hard servitude of labor which we have a little before mentioned, but that he might expose them to the before-mentioned tortures; and finally, in the short space of a day, might exterminate them by his cruelties. ¹⁵ The registering of these men was carried on cruelly, zealously, assiduously, from the rising of the sun to its going down, and was not brought to an end in forty days. ¹⁶ The king was filled with great and constant joy, and celebrated banquets before the temple idols. His erring heart, far from the truth, and his profane mouth gave glory to idols, deaf and incapable of speaking or aiding, and uttered unworthy speech against the Greatest God. ¹⁷ At the end of the above-mentioned interval of time, the registrars brought word to the king that the multitude of the Jews was too great for registration, ¹⁸ inasmuch as there were many still left in the land, of whom some were in inhabited houses, and others were scattered about in various places, so that all the commanders in Egypt were insufficient for the work. ¹⁹ The king threatened them, and charged them with taking bribes, in order to contrive the escape of the Jews, but was clearly convinced of the truth of what had been said. ²⁰ They said, and proved, that paper and pens had failed them for the carrying out of their purpose. ²¹ Now this was an active interference of the unconquerable Providence which assisted the Jews from heaven.

5

¹ Then he called Hermon, who had charge of the elephants. Full of rage, altogether fixed in his furious design, ² he commanded him, with a quantity of unmixed wine with handfuls of incense infused, to drug the elephants early on the following day. These five hundred elephants were, when infuriated by the copious drinks of frankincense, to be led up to the execution of death upon the Jews. ³ The king, after issuing these orders, went to his feasting, and gathered together all those of his friends and of the army who hated the Jews the most. ⁴ The master of the elephants, Hermon, fulfilled his commission punctually. ⁵ The servants appointed for the purpose went out about evening and bound the hands of the miserable victims, and took other precautions for their security at night, thinking that the whole race would perish together. ⁶ The heathen believed the Jews to be destitute of all protection, for chains bound them. ⁷ They invoked the Almighty Lord, and ceaselessly implored with tears their merciful God and Father, Ruler of all, Lord of every power, ⁸ to overthrow the evil purpose which had gone out against them, and to deliver them by extraordinary manifestation from that death which was in store for them. ⁹ Their earnest entreaty went up to heaven. ¹⁰ Then Hermon, who had filled his merciless elephants with copious drinks of mixed wine and frankincense, came early to the palace to report on these preparations. ¹¹ He, however, who has sent his good creature sleep from all time by night or by day thus gratifying whom he wills, diffused a portion of it now upon the king. ¹² By this sweet and profound influence of the Lord, he was held fast, and thus his unjust purpose was quite frustrated, and his unflinching resolve greatly falsified. ¹³ But the Jews, having escaped the hour which had been fixed, praised their holy God, and again prayed him who is easily reconciled to display the power of his powerful hand to the arrogant Gentiles. ¹⁴ The middle of the tenth hour had nearly arrived, when the person who sent invitations, seeing the guests who were invited present, came and shook the king. ¹⁵ He gained his attention with difficulty, and hinting that the mealtime was getting past, talked the matter over with him. ¹⁶ The king listened to this, and then turning aside to his drinking, commanded the guests to sit down before him. ¹⁷ This done, he asked them to enjoy themselves, and to indulge in mirth at this somewhat late hour of the banquet. ¹⁸ Conversation grew on, and the king sent for Hermon, and inquired of him, with fierce denunciations, why the Jews had been allowed to outlive that day. ¹⁹ Hermon explained that he had done his bidding over night; and in this he was confirmed by his friends. ²⁰ The king, then, with a barbarity exceeding that of Phalaris, said, "They might thank his sleep of that day. Lose no time, and get ready the elephants against tomorrow, as you did before, for the destruction of these accursed Jews." ²¹ When the king said this, the company present were glad, and approved. Then each man went to his own home. ²² They didn't employ the night in sleep, but in contriving cruel mockeries for those deemed miserable. ²³ The morning cock had just crowed, and Hermon, having harnessed the brutes, was stimulating them in the great colonnade. ²⁴ The city crowds were collected together to see the hideous spectacle, and waited impatiently for the dawn. ²⁵ The Jews, breathless with momentary suspense, stretched out their hands and prayed the Greatest God, in mournful strains, again to help them speedily. ²⁶ The sun's rays were not yet shining and the king was waiting for his friends when Hermon came to him, calling him out, and saying that his desires could now be realized. ²⁷ The king, receiving him, was astonished at his unusual invitation. Overwhelmed with a spirit of oblivion about everything, inquired about the object of this earnest preparation. ²⁸ But this was the working of that Almighty God who had made him forget all his purpose. ²⁹ Hermon and all his friends pointed out the preparation of the animals. They are ready, O king, according to your own strict injunction. ³⁰ The king was filled with fierce anger at these words, for, by the Providence of God regarding these things, his mind had become entirely confused. He looked hard at Hermon, and threatened him as follows: ³¹ "Your parents, or your children, were they here, would have given a large meal to these wild animals, not these innocent Jews, who have loyally served me and my forefathers. ³² Had it not been for familiar friendship, and the claims of your office, your life should have gone for theirs." ³³ Hermon, being threatened in this unexpected and alarming manner, was troubled in his eyes, and his face fell. ³⁴ The friends, too, stole out one by one, and dismissed the assembled multitudes to their respective occupations. ³⁵ The Jews, having heard of these events, praised the glorious God and King of kings, because they had obtained this help, too, from him. ³⁶ Now the king arranged another banquet in the same way, and proclaimed an invitation to mirth. ³⁷ He summoned Hermon to his presence, and said, with threats, "How often, O wretch, must I repeat my orders to you about these same persons? ³⁸ Once more, arm the elephants for the extermination of the Jews tomorrow!" ³⁹ His kinsmen, who were reclining with him, wondered at his instability, and thus expressed themselves: ⁴⁰ "O king, how long do you test us, as of men bereft of reason? This is the third time that you have ordered their destruction. When the thing is to be done, you change your mind, and recall your instructions. ⁴¹ Because of this, the feeling of expectation causes tumult in the city. It swarms with factions,

---

[a] 3:28 a drachma was about a day's pay for an agricultural laborer

and is continually on the point of being plundered." ⁴² The king, just like another Phalaris, a prey to thoughtlessness, made no account of the changes which his own mind had undergone, issuing in the deliverance of the Jews. He swore a fruitless oath, and determined immediately to send them to hades, crushed by the knees and feet of the elephants. ⁴³ He would also invade Judea, level its towns with fire and the sword, destroy that temple which the heathen might not enter, and prevent sacrifices ever after being offered up there. ⁴⁴ Joyfully his friends broke up, together with his kinsmen; and, trusting in his determination, arranged their forces in guard at the most convenient places of the city. ⁴⁵ The master of the elephants urged the animals into an almost maniacal state, drenched them with incense and wine, and decked them with frightful devices. ⁴⁶ About early morning, when the city was filled with an immense number of people at the hippodrome, he entered the palace and called the king to the business in hand. ⁴⁷ The king's heart teemed with impious rage; and he rushed forth with the mass, along with the elephants. With unsoftened feelings and pitiless eyes, he longed to gaze at the hard and wretched doom of the previously mentioned Jews. ⁴⁸ But the Jews, when the elephants went out at the gate, followed by the armed force. When they saw the dust raised by the throng, and heard the loud cries of the crowd, ⁴⁹ thought that they had come to the last moment of their lives, to the end of what they had tremblingly expected. They gave way, therefore, to lamentations and moans. They kissed each other. Those nearest of kin to each other hung around one another's necks–fathers hugging their sons and mothers their daughters. Other women held their infants to their breasts, which drew what seemed their last milk. ⁵⁰ Nevertheless, when they reflected upon the help previously granted them from heaven, they prostrated themselves with one accord, removed even the sucking children from the breasts, and ⁵¹ sent up an exceedingly great cry asking the Lord of all power to reveal himself, and have mercy upon those who now lay at the gates of hades.

6

¹ Then Eleazar, an illustrious priest of the country, who had attained to length of days, and whose life had been adorned with virtue, caused the elders who were around him to cease to cry out to the holy God, and prayed this: ² "O king, mighty in power, most high, Almighty God, who regulates the whole creation with your tender mercy, ³ look at the seed of Abraham, at the children of the sanctified Jacob, your sanctified inheritance, O Father, now being wrongfully destroyed as foreigners in a foreign land. ⁴ You destroyed Pharaoh with his army of chariots when that lord of this same Egypt was uplifted with lawless daring and loud-sounding tongue. Shedding the beams of your mercy upon the race of Israel, you overwhelmed him and his proud army. ⁵ When Sennacherim, the grievous king of the Assyrians, exulting in his countless army, had subdued the whole land with his spear and was lifting himself against your holy city with boastings grievous to be endured, you, O Lord, demolished him and displayed your might to many nations. ⁶ When the three friends in the land of Babylon of their own will exposed their lives to the fire rather than serve vain things, you sent a moist coolness through the fiery furnace, and brought the fire on all their adversaries. ⁷ It was you who, when Daniel was hurled, through slander and envy, as a prey to lions down below, brought him back again unharmed to light. ⁸ When Jonah was pining away in the belly of the sea-born monster, you looked at him, O Father, and recovered him to the sight of his own. ⁹ Now, you who hate insolence, you who abound in mercy, you who are the protector of all things, appear quickly to those of the race of Israel, who are insulted by abhorred, lawless gentiles. ¹⁰ If our life during our exile has been stained with iniquity, deliver us from the hand of the enemy, and destroy us, O Lord, by the death which you prefer. ¹¹ Don't let the vain-minded congratulate vain idols at the destruction of your beloved, saying, 'Their god didn't deliver them.' ¹² You who are All-powerful and Almighty, O Eternal One, behold! Have mercy on us who are being withdrawn from life, like traitors, by the unreasoning insolence of lawless men. ¹³ Let the heathen cower before your invincible might today, O glorious One, who have all power to save the race of Jacob. ¹⁴ The whole band of infants and their parents ask you with tears. ¹⁵ Let it be shown to all the nations that you are with us, O Lord, and have not turned your face away from us, but as you said that you would not forget them even in the land of their enemies, so fulfill this saying, O Lord." ¹⁶ Now, at the time that Eleazar had ended his prayer, the king came along to the hippodrome with the wild animals, and with his tumultuous power. ¹⁷ When the Jews saw this, they uttered a loud cry to heaven so that the adjacent valleys resounded and caused an irrepressible lamentation throughout the army. ¹⁸ Then the all-glorious, all-powerful, and true God, displayed his holy countenance, and opened the gates of heaven, from which two angels, dreadful of form, came down and were visible to all but the Jews. ¹⁹ They stood opposite, and filled the enemies' army with confusion and cowardice, and bound them with immoveable shackles. ²⁰ A cold shudder came over the person of the king, and oblivion paralyzed the vehemence of his spirit. ²¹ They turned back the animals on the armed forces who followed them; and the animals trampled them and destroyed them. ²² The king's wrath was converted into compassion; and he wept at the things he had devised. ²³ For when he heard the cry, and saw them all on the verge of destruction, with tears he angrily threatened his friends, saying, ²⁴ "You have governed badly, and have exceeded tyrants in cruelty. You have labored to deprive me, your benefactor, at once of my dominion and my life, by secretly devising measures injurious to the kingdom. ²⁵ Who has gathered here, unreasonably removing each from his home, those who, in fidelity to us, had held the fortresses of the country? ²⁶ Who has consigned to unmerited punishments those who in good will toward us from the beginning have in all things surpassed all nations, and who often have engaged in the most dangerous undertakings? ²⁷ Loose, loose the unjust bonds! Send them to their homes in peace, begging pardon for what has been done. ²⁸ Release the sons of the almighty living God of heaven, who from our ancestors' times until now has granted a glorious and uninterrupted prosperity to our affairs." ²⁹ He said these things, and they, released the same moment, having now escaped death, praised God their holy Savior. ³⁰ The king then departed to the city, and called his financier to himself, and asked him provide a seven days' quantity of wine and other materials for feasting for the Jews. He decided that they should keep a cheerful festival of deliverance in the very place in which they expected to meet with their destruction. ³¹ Then they who were before despised and near to hades, yes, rather advanced into it, partook of the cup of salvation, instead of a grievous and lamentable death. Full of exultation, they apportioned the place intended for their fall and burial into banqueting booths. ³² Ceasing their miserable strain of woe, they took up the subject of their fatherland, singing in praise to God their wonder-working Savior. All groans and all wailing were laid aside. They formed dances as a sign of peaceful joy. ³³ So the king also collected a number of guests for the occasion, and returned unceasing thanks with much magnificence for the unexpected deliverance afforded him. ³⁴ Those who had marked them out as for death and for carrion, and had registered them with joy, howled aloud, and were clothed with shame, and had the fire of their rage ingloriously put out. ³⁵ But the Jews, as we just said, instituted a dance, and then gave themselves up to feasting, glad thanksgiving, and psalms. ³⁶ They made a public ordinance to commemorate these things for generations to come, as long as they should be sojourners. They thus established these days as days of mirth, not for the purpose of drinking or luxury, but because God had saved them. ³⁷ They requested the king to send them back to their homes. ³⁸ They were being enrolled from the twenty-fifth of Pachon to the fourth of Epiphi, a period of forty days. The measures taken for their destruction lasted from the fifth of Epiphi till the seventh, that is, three days. ³⁹ The Ruler over all during this time manifested his mercy gloriously, and delivered them all together unharmed. ⁴⁰ They feasted upon the king's provision up to the fourteenth day, then asked to be sent away. ⁴¹ The king commended them, and wrote the following letter, of magnanimous import for them, to the commanders of every city:

7

¹ "King Ptolemy Philopator to the commanders throughout Egypt, and to all who are set over affairs, joy and strength. ² We, too, and our children are well. God has directed our affairs as we wish. ³ Certain of our friends out of malice vehemently urged us to punish the Jews of our realm in a body, with the infliction of a monstrous punishment. ⁴ They pretended that our affairs would never be in a good state till this took place. Such, they said, was the hatred borne by the Jews to all other people. ⁵ They brought them fettered in grievous chains as slaves, no, as traitors. Without enquiry or examination they endeavored to annihilate them. They buckled themselves with a savage cruelty, worse than Scythian custom. ⁶ For this cause we severely threatened them; yet, with the clemency which we usually extend to all men, we at length permitted them to live. Finding that the God of heaven cast a shield of protection over the Jews so as to preserve them, and that he fought for them as a father always fights for his sons, ⁷ and taking into consideration their constancy and fidelity toward us and toward our ancestors, we have, as we ought, acquitted them of every sort of charge. ⁸ We have dismissed them to their several homes, telling all men everywhere to do them no wrong, or unrighteously revile them about the past. ⁹ For know this, that should we conceive any evil design, or in any way aggrieve them, we shall ever have as our adversary, not man, but the highest God, the ruler of all might. From Him there will be no escape, as the avenger of such deeds. Farewell." ¹⁰ When they had received this letter, they didn't hurry to depart immediately. They petitioned the king to be allowed to inflict fitting punishment upon those of their race who had willingly transgressed the holy god, and the law of God. ¹¹ They alleged that men who had for their

bellies' sake transgressed the ordinances of God, would never be faithful to the interests of the king. ¹²The king admitted the truth of this reasoning, and commended them. Full power was given them, without warrant or special commission, to destroy those who had transgressed the law of God boldly in every part of the king's dominions. ¹³Their priests, then, as it was appropriate, saluted him with good wishes, and all the people echoed with the "Hallelujah!" Then they joyfully departed. ¹⁴Then they punished and shamefully destroyed every polluted Jew that fell in their way, ¹⁵slaying this way, in that day, more than three hundred men, and esteeming this destruction of the wicked a season of joy. ¹⁶They themselves having held closely to their God to death, and having enjoyed a full deliverance, departed from the city garlanded with sweet-flowered wreaths of every kind. Uttering exclamations of joy, with songs of praise, and melodious hymns, they thanked the God of their fathers, the eternal Savior of Israel. ¹⁷Having arrived at Ptolemais, called from the specialty of that district "Rose-bearing", where the fleet, in accordance with the general wish, waited for them seven days, ¹⁸they partook of a banquet of deliverance, for the king generously granted them all the means of securing a return home. ¹⁹They were accordingly brought back in peace, while they gave utterance to appropriate thanks; and they determined to observe these days during their sojourn as days of joyfulness. ²⁰These they registered as sacred upon a pillar, when they had dedicated the place of their festivity to be one of prayer. They departed unharmed, free, abundant in joy, preserved by the king's command, by land, by sea, and by river, each to his own home. ²¹They had more weight than before among their enemies, and were honored and feared. No one in any way robbed them of their goods. ²²Every man received back his own, according to inventory, those who had obtained their goods, giving them up with the greatest terror. For the greatest God made perfect wonders for their salvation. ²³Blessed be the Redeemer of Israel forever! Amen.

Additions to Esther

The book of Esther in the Greek Septuagint contains 5 additions that the traditional Hebrew text doesn't have. These additions are recognized as Deuterocanonical Scripture by the Roman Catholic, Greek Orthodox, and Russian Orthodox Churches. Those additions are enclosed in [square brackets]. Because the additions by themselves make little sense without the broader context of the book, we present here a translation of the whole book of Esther from the Greek. We have chosen not to distract the reader with confusing out-of-order chapter numbers that would result from using the KJV versification, but rather merge these 5 additions as extensions at the beginning of 1:1 and after 3:13,4:17,8:12, and 10:3. This makes some verses (1:1,5:1, and 8:12) really long, but it also makes the verses line up with the same verse numbers in Esther as translated from the traditional Hebrew text. Some of the proper names in this book have been changed to the more familiar Hebrew form instead of the direct transliteration from the Greek.

1

¹[In the second year of the reign of Ahasuerus the great king, on the first day of Nisan, Mordecai the son of Jair, the son of Shimei, the son of Kish, of the tribe of Benjamin, a Jew dwelling in the city Susa, a great man, serving in the king's palace, saw a vision. Now he was one of the captives whom Nebuchadnezzar king of Babylon had carried captive from Jerusalem with Jeconiah the king of Judea. This was his dream: Behold, voices and a noise, thunders and earthquake, tumult upon the earth. And, behold, two great serpents came out, both ready for conflict. A great voice came from them. Every nation was prepared for battle by their voice, even to fight against the nation of the just. Behold, a day of darkness and blackness, suffering and anguish, affection and tumult upon the earth. And all the righteous nation was troubled, fearing their own afflictions. They prepared to die, and cried to God. Something like a great river from a little spring with much water, came from their cry. Light and the sun arose, and the lowly were exalted, and devoured the honorable. Mordecai, who had seen this vision and what God desired to do, having arisen, kept it in his heart, and desired by all means to interpret it, even until night. Mordecai rested quietly in the palace with Gabatha and Tharrha the king's two chamberlains, eunuchs who guarded the palace. He heard their conversation and searched out their plans. He learned that they were preparing to lay hands on King Ahasuerus; and he informed the king concerning them. The king examined the two chamberlains. They confessed, and were led away and executed. The king wrote these things for a record. Mordecai also wrote concerning these matters. The king commanded Mordecai to serve in the palace, and gave gifts for this service. But Haman the son of Hammedatha the Bougean was honored in the sight of the king, and he endeavored to harm Mordecai and his people, because of the king's two chamberlains.] [a] And it came to pass after these things[b] in the days of Ahasuerus, –(this Ahasuerus ruled over one hundred twenty-seven provinces from India)– ²in those days, when King Ahasuerus was on the throne in the city of Susa, ³in the third year of his reign, he made a feast for his friends, for people from the rest of the nations, for the nobles of the Persians and Medes, and for the chief of the local governors. ⁴After this–after he had shown them the wealth of his kingdom and the abundant glory of his wealth during one hundred eighty days– ⁵when the days of the wedding feast were completed, the king made a banquet lasting six days for the people of the nations who were present in the city, in the court of the king's house, ⁶which was adorned with fine linen and flax on cords of fine linen and purple, fastened to golden and silver studs on pillars of white marble and stone. There were golden and silver couches on a pavement of emerald stone, and of mother-of-pearl, and of white marble, with transparent coverings variously flowered, having roses arranged around it. ⁷There were gold and silver cups, and a small cup of carbuncle set out, of the value of thirty thousand talents, with abundant and sweet wine, which the king himself drank. ⁸This banquet was not according to the appointed law, but as the king desired to have it. He charged the stewards to perform his will and that of the company. ⁹Also Vashti the queen made a banquet for the women in the palace where King Ahasuerus lived. ¹⁰Now on the seventh day, the king, being merry, told Haman, Bazan, Tharrha, Baraze, Zatholtha, Abataza, and Tharaba, the seven chamberlains, servants of King Ahasuerus, ¹¹to bring in the queen to him, to[c] enthrone her, and crown her with the diadem, and to show her to the princes, and her beauty to the nations, for she was beautiful. ¹²But queen Vashti refused to come with the chamberlains; so the king was grieved and angered. ¹³And he said to his friends, "This is what Vashti said.

---

[a] *1:1* Note: In the Hebrew and some copies of LXX, Esther begins here.

[b] *1:1* Greek words.

[c] *1:11* Greek to make her queen.

Therefore pronounce your legal judgment on this case." ¹⁴ So Arkesaeus, Sarsathaeus, and Malisear, the princes of the Persians and Medes, who were near the king, who sat chief in rank by the king, drew near to him, ¹⁵ and reported to him according to the laws what it was proper to do to queen Vashti, because she had not done the things commanded by the king through the chamberlains. ¹⁶ And Memucan said to the king and to the princes, "Queen Vashti has not wronged the king only, but also all the king's rulers and princes; ¹⁷ for he has told them the words of the queen, and how she[a] disobeyed the king. As she then refused to obey King Ahasuerus, ¹⁸ so this day the other wives of the chiefs of the Persians and Medes, having heard what she said to the king, will dare in the same way to dishonor their husbands. ¹⁹ If then it seems good to the king, let him make a royal decree, and let it be written according to the laws of the Medes and Persians, and let him not alter it: 'Don't allow the queen to come in to him any more. Let the king give her royalty to a woman better than she.' ²⁰ Let the law of the king which he will have made be widely proclaimed in his kingdom. Then all the women will give honor to their husbands, from the poor even to the rich." ²¹ This advice pleased the king and the princes; and the king did as Memucan had said, ²² and sent into all his kingdom through the several provinces, according to their language, so that men might be feared in their own houses.

2

¹ After this, the king's anger was pacified, and he no more mentioned Vashti, bearing in mind what she had said, and how he had condemned her. ² Then the servants of the king said, "Let chaste, beautiful young virgins be sought for the king. ³ Let the king appoint local governors in all the provinces of his kingdom, and let them select beautiful, chaste young ladies and bring them to the city Susa, into the women's apartment. Let them be consigned to the king's chamberlain, the keeper of the women. Then let things for purification and other needs be given to them. ⁴ Let the woman who pleases the king be queen instead of Vashti." This thing pleased the king; and he did so. ⁵ Now there was a Jew in the city Susa, and his name was Mordecai, the son of Jairus, the son of Shimei, the son of Kish, of the tribe of Benjamin. ⁶ He had been brought as a prisoner from Jerusalem, whom Nebuchadnezzar king of Babylon had carried into captivity. ⁷ He had a foster child, daughter of Aminadab his father's brother. Her name was Esther. When her parents died, he brought her up to womanhood as his own. This lady was beautiful. ⁸ And because the king's ordinance was published, many ladies were gathered to the city of Susa under the hand of Hegai; and Esther was brought to Hegai, the keeper of the women. ⁹ The lady pleased him, and she found favor in his sight. He hurried to give her the things for purification, her portion, and the seven maidens appointed her out of the palace. He treated her and her maidens well in the women's apartment. ¹⁰ But Esther didn't reveal her family or her kindred, for Mordecai had charged her not to tell. ¹¹ But Mordecai used to walk every day by the women's court, to see what would become of Esther. ¹² Now this was the time for a virgin to go into the king, when she had completed twelve months; for so are the days of purification fulfilled, six months while they are anointing themselves with oil of myrrh, and six months with spices and women's purifications. ¹³ And then the lady goes in to the king. The officer that he commands to do so will bring her to come in with him from the women's apartment to the king's chamber. ¹⁴ She enters in the evening, and in the morning she departs to the second women's apartment, where Hegai the king's chamberlain is keeper of the women. She doesn't go in to the king again, unless she is called by name. ¹⁵ And when the time was fulfilled for Esther the daughter of Aminadab the brother of Mordecai's father to go in to the king, she neglected nothing which the chamberlain, the women's keeper, commanded; for Esther found grace in the sight of all who looked at her. ¹⁶ So Esther went in to King Ahasuerus in the twelfth month, which is Adar, in the seventh year of his reign. ¹⁷ The king loved Esther, and she found favor beyond all the other virgins. He put the queen's crown on her. ¹⁸ The king made a banquet for all his friends and great men for seven days, and he highly celebrated the marriage of Esther; and he granted a remission of taxes to those who were under his dominion. ¹⁹ Meanwhile, Mordecai served in the courtyard. ²⁰ Now Esther had not revealed her country, for so Mordecai commanded her, to fear God, and perform his commandments, as when she was with him. Esther didn't change her manner of life. ²¹ Two chamberlains of the king, the chiefs of the body-guard, were grieved, because Mordecai was promoted; and they sought to kill King Ahasuerus. ²² And the matter was discovered by Mordecai, and he made it known to Esther, and she declared to the king the matter of the conspiracy. ²³ And the king examined the two chamberlains and hanged them. Then the king gave orders to make a note for a memorial in the royal library of the goodwill shown by Mordecai, as a commendation.

3

¹ After this, King Ahasuerus highly honored Haman the son of Hammedatha, the Bugaean. He exalted him and set his seat above all his friends. ² All in the palace bowed down to him, for so the king had given orders to do; but Mordecai didn't bow down to him. ³ And they in the king's palace said to Mordecai, "Mordecai, why do you transgress the commands of the king?" ⁴ They questioned him daily, but he didn't listen to them; so they reported to Haman that Mordecai resisted the commands of the king; and Mordecai had shown to them that he was a Jew. ⁵ When Haman understood that Mordecai didn't bow down to him, he was greatly enraged, ⁶ and plotted to utterly destroy all the Jews who were under the rule of Ahasuerus. ⁷ In the twelfth year of the reign of Ahasuerus, Haman made a decision by casting lots by day and month, to kill the race of Mordecai in one day. The lot fell on the fourteenth day of the month of Adar. ⁸ So he spoke to King Ahasuerus, saying, "There is a nation scattered among the nations in all your kingdom, and their laws differ from all the other nations. They disobey the king's laws. It is not expedient for the king to tolerate them. ⁹ If it seem good to the king, let him make a decree to destroy them, and I will remit into the king's treasury ten thousand talents of silver." ¹⁰ So the king took off his ring, and gave it into the hands of Haman to seal the decrees against the Jews. ¹¹ The king said to Haman, "Keep the silver, and treat the nation as you will." ¹² So the king's recorders were called in the first month, on the thirteenth day, and they wrote as Haman commanded to the captains and governors in every province, from India even to Ethiopia, to one hundred twenty-seven provinces; and to the rulers of the nations according to their languages, in the name of King Ahasuerus. ¹³ The message was sent by couriers throughout the kingdom of Ahasuerus, to utterly destroy the race of the Jews on the first day of the twelfth month, which is Adar, and to plunder their goods.[b] [The following is the copy of the letter. "From the great King Ahasuerus to the rulers and the governors under them of one hundred twenty-seven provinces, from India even to Ethiopia, who hold authority under him: "Ruling over many nations and having obtained dominion over the whole world, I was determined (not elated by the confidence of power, but ever conducting myself with great moderation and gentleness) to make the lives of my subjects continually tranquil, desiring both to maintain the kingdom quiet and orderly to its utmost limits, and to restore the peace desired by all men. When I had asked my counselors how this should be brought to pass, Haman, who excels in soundness of judgment among us, and has been manifestly well inclined without wavering and with unshaken fidelity, and had obtained the second post in the kingdom, informed us that a certain ill-disposed people is scattered among the tribes throughout the world, opposed in their law to every other nation, and continually neglecting the commands of the king, so that the united government blamelessly administered by us is not quietly established. Having then conceived that this nation is continually set in opposition to every man, introducing as a change a foreign code of laws, and injuriously plotting to accomplish the worst of evils against our interests, and against the happy establishment of the monarchy, we instruct you in the letter written by Haman, who is set over the public affairs and is our second governor, to destroy them all utterly with their wives and children by the swords of the enemies, without pitying or sparing any, on the fourteenth day of the twelfth month Adar, of the present year; that the people aforetime and now ill-disposed to us having been violently consigned to death in one day, may hereafter secure to us continually a well constituted and quiet state of affairs."] ¹⁴ Copies of the letters were published in every province; and an order was given to all the nations to be ready for that day. ¹⁵ This business was hastened also in Susa. The king and Haman began to drink, but the city was confused.

4

¹ But Mordecai, having perceived what was done, tore his garments, put on sackcloth, and sprinkled dust upon himself. Having rushed forth through the open street of the city, he cried with a loud voice, "A nation that has done no wrong is going to be destroyed!" ² He came to the king's gate, and stood; for it was not lawful for him to enter into the palace wearing sackcloth and ashes. ³ And in every province where the letters were published, there was crying, lamentation, and great mourning on the part of the Jews. They wore sackcloth and ashes. ⁴ The queen's maids and chamberlains went in and told her; and when she had heard what was done, she was deeply troubled. She sent clothes to Mordecai to replace his sackcloth, but he refused. ⁵ So Esther called for her chamberlain Hathach,

---

[a] *1:17* Greek contradicted.

[b] *3:13* Note: The part in brackets is not in Hebrew

who waited upon her; and she sent to learn the truth from Mordecai. ⁷ Mordecai showed him what was done, and the promise which Haman had made the king of ten thousand talents to be paid into the treasury, that he might destroy the Jews. ⁸ And he gave him the copy of what was published in Susa concerning their destruction to show to Esther; and told him to charge her to go in and entreat the king, and to beg him for the people. "Remember, he said, the days of your humble condition, how you were nursed by my hand; because Haman, who holds the next place to the king, has spoken against us to cause our death. Call upon the Lord, and speak to the king concerning us, to deliver us from death." ⁹ So Hathach went in and told her all these words. ¹⁰ Esther said to Hathach, "Go to Mordecai, and say, ¹¹'All the nations of the empire know than any man or woman who goes in to the king into the inner court without being called, that person must die, unless the king stretches out his golden sceptre; then he shall live. I haven't been called to go into the king for thirty days.'" ¹² So Hathach reported to Mordecai all the words of Esther. ¹³ Then Mordecai said to Hathach, "Go, and say to her, 'Esther, don't say to yourself that you alone will escape in the kingdom, more than all the other Jews. ¹⁴ For if you keep quiet on this occasion, help and protection will come to the Jews from another place; but you and your father's house will perish. Who knows if you have been made queen for this occasion?'" ¹⁵ And Esther sent the messenger who came to her to Mordecai, saying, ¹⁶"Go and assemble the Jews that are in Susa, and all of you fast for me. Don't eat or drink for three days, night and day. My maidens and I will also fast. Then I will go in to the king contrary to the law, even if I must die." ¹⁷ So Mordecai went and did all that Esther commanded him.ᵃ ¹⁸[He prayed to the Lord, making mention of all the works of the Lord. ¹⁹ He said, "Lordᵇ God, you are king ruling over all, for all things are in your power, and there is no one who can oppose you in your purpose to save Israel; ²⁰ for you have made the heaven and the earth and every wonderful thing under heaven. ²¹ You are Lord of all, and there is no one who can resist you, Lord. ²² You know all things. You know, Lord, that it is not in insolence, nor arrogance, nor love of glory, that I have done this, to refuse to bow down to the arrogant Haman. ²³ For I would gladly have kissed the soles of his feet for the safety of Israel. ²⁴ But I have done this that I might not set the glory of man above the glory of God. I will not worship anyone except you, my Lord, and I will not do these things in arrogance. ²⁵ And now, O Lord God, the King, the God of Abraham, spare your people, for our enemies are planning our destruction, and they have desired to destroy your ancient inheritance. ²⁶ Do not overlook your people, whom you have redeemed for yourself out of the land of Egypt. ²⁷ Listen to my prayer. Have mercy on your inheritance and turn our mourning into gladness, that we may live and sing praise to your name, O Lord. Don't utterly destroy the mouth of those who praise you, O Lord." ²⁸ All Israel cried with all their might, for death was before their eyes. ²⁹ And queen Esther took refuge in the Lord, being taken as it were in the agony of death. ³⁰ Having taken off her glorious apparel, she put on garments of distress and mourning. Instead of grand perfumes she filled her head with ashes and dung. She greatly humbled her body, and she filled every place of her glad adorning with her tangled hair. ³¹ She implored the Lord God of Israel, and said, "O my Lord, you alone are our king. Help me. I am destitute, and have no helper but you, ³² for my danger is near at handᶜ. ³³ I have heard from my birth in the tribe of my kindred that you, Lord, took Israel out of all the nations, and our fathers out of all their kindred for a perpetual inheritance, and have done for them all that you have said. ³⁴ And now we have sinned before you, and you have delivered us into the hands of our enemies, ³⁵ because we honored their gods. You are righteous, O Lord. ³⁶ But now they have not been content with the bitterness of our slavery, but have laid their hands on the hands of their idols ³⁷ to abolish the decree of your mouth, and utterly to destroy your inheritance, and to stop the mouth of those who praise you, and to extinguish the glory of your house and your altar, ³⁸ and to open the mouth of the Gentiles to speak theᵈ praises of vanities, and that a mortal king should be admired forever. ³⁹ O Lord, don't surrender your sceptre to those who don't exist, and don't let them laugh at our fall, but turn their counsel against themselves, and make an example of him who has begun to injure us. ⁴⁰ Remember us, O Lord! Manifest yourself in the time of our affliction. Encourage me, O King of gods, and ruler of all dominion! ⁴¹ Put harmonious speech into my mouth before the lion, and turn his heart to hate him who fights against us, to the utter destruction of those who agree with him. ⁴² But deliver us by your hand, and help me who am alone and have no one but you, O Lord. ⁴³ You know all things, and know that I hate the glory of transgressors,ᵉ and that I abhor the bed of the uncircumcised and of every stranger. ⁴⁴ You know my necessity, for I abhor the symbol of my proud station, which is upon my head in the days of myᶠ splendor. I abhor it as a menstruous cloth, and I don't wear it in the days of my tranquility. ⁴⁵ Your handmaid has not eaten at Haman's table, and I have not honored the banquet of the king, neither have I drunk wine of libations. ⁴⁶ Neither has your handmaid rejoiced since the day of my promotion until now, except in you, O Lord God of Abraham. ⁴⁷ O god, who has power over all, listen to the voice of the desperate, and deliver us from the hand of those who devise mischief. Deliver me from my fear.]

5

¹ ᵍ It came to pass on the third day, when she had ceased praying, that she took off her servant's dress and put on her glorious apparel. Being splendidly dressed and having called upon God the Overseer and Preserver of all things, she took her two maids, and she leaned upon one, as a delicate female, and the other followed bearing her train. She was blooming in the perfection of her beauty. Her face was cheerful and looked lovely, but her heart was filled with fear. Having passed through all the doors, she stood before the king. He was sitting on his royal throne. He had put on all his glorious apparel, covered all over with gold and precious stones, and was very terrifying. And having raised his face resplendent with glory, he looked with intense anger. The queen fell, and changed her color as she fainted. She bowed herself upon the head of the maid who went before her. But God changed the spirit of the king to gentleness, and in intense feeling, he sprang from off his throne, and took her into his arms, until she recovered. He comforted her with peaceful words, and said to her, "What is the matter, Esther? I am your relative. Cheer up! You shall not die, for our command is openly declared to you: 'Draw near.'" ² And having raised the golden sceptre, he laid it upon her neck, and embraced her. He said, "Speak to me." So she said to him, "I saw you, my lord, as an angel of God, and my heart was troubled for fear of your glory; for you, my lord, are to be wondered at, and your face is full of grace." While she was speaking, she fainted and fell. Then the king was troubled, and all his servants comforted her. ³ The king said, "What do you desire, Esther? What is your request? Ask even to the half of my kingdom, and it shall be yours." ⁴ Esther said, "Today is a special day. So if it seems good to the king, let both him and Haman come to the feast which I will prepare this day." ⁵ The king said, "Hurry and bring Haman here, that we may do as Esther said." So they both came to the feast about which Esther had spoken. ⁶ At the banquet, the king said to Esther, "What is your request, queen Esther? You shall have all that you require." ⁷ She said, "My request and my petition is: ⁸ if I have found favor in the king's sight, let the king and Haman come again tomorrow to the feast which I shall prepare for them, and tomorrow I will do as I have done today." ⁹ So Haman went out from the king very glad and merry; but when Haman saw Mordecai the Jew in the court, he was greatly enraged. ¹⁰ Having gone into his own house, he called his friends, and his wife Zeresh. ¹¹ He showed them his wealth and the glory with which the king had invested him, and how he had promoted him to be chief ruler in the kingdom. ¹² Haman said, "The queen has called no one to the feast with the king but me, and I am invited tomorrow. ¹³ But these things don't please me while I see Mordecai the Jew in the court. ¹⁴ Then Zeresh his wife and his friends said to him, "Let a fifty cubit tallʰ gallows be made for you. In the morning you speak to the king, and let Mordecai be hanged on the gallows; but you go in to the feast with the king, and be merry." The saying pleased Haman, and the gallows was prepared.

6

¹ The Lord removed sleep from the king that night; so he told his servant to bring in theⁱ books, the registers of daily events, to read to him. ² And he found theʲ records written concerning Mordecai, how he had told the king about the king's two chamberlains, when they were keeping guard, and sought to lay hands on Ahasuerus. ³ The king said, "What honor or favor have we done for Mordecai?" The king's servants said, "You haven't done anything for him." ⁴ And while the king was enquiring about the kindness of Mordecai, behold, Haman was in the court. The king said, "Who is in the court? Now Haman had come in to speak to the king about hanging Mordecai on the gallows which he had prepared. ⁵ The king's servants said, "Behold, Haman stands in the court." And the king said, "Call him!" ⁶ The king said to Haman, "What should I do for the man whom I wish to honor?" Haman said within himself, "Whom would the king honor but myself?" ⁷ He said to the king, "As for the man whom the king wishes to honor, ⁸ let

---

ᵃ *4:17* Note: The part between brackets, i.e. to the end of chapter **5** is not in the Hebrew
ᵇ *4:19* See **3 Kings 8. 53.** ᴺᵒᵗᵉ·

ᶜ *4:32* ᴳʳᵉᵉᵏ in my hand.
ᵈ *4:38* ᴳʳᵉᵉᵏ virtues.
ᵉ *4:43* ᴼʳ· opinion.
ᶠ *4:44* ᴳʳᵉᵉᵏ vision.

ᵍ *5:1* From the first verse to the third, the ᴳʳᵉᵉᵏ widely differs from the Hebrew
ʰ *5:14* ᴳʳᵉᵉᵏ a tree cut.

ⁱ *6:1* ᴳʳᵉᵉᵏ letters.
ʲ *6:2* ᴳʳᵉᵉᵏ letters.

the king's servants bring the robe of fine linen which the king puts on, and the horse on which the king rides, ⁹and let him give it to one of the king's noble friends, and let him dress the man whom the king loves. Let him mount him on the horse, and proclaim through the[a] streets of the city, saying, "This is what will be done for every man whom the king honors!" ¹⁰Then the king said to Haman, "You have spoken well. Do so for Mordecai the Jew, who waits in the palace, and let not a word of what you have spoken be neglected!" ¹¹So Haman took the robe and the horse, dressed Mordecai, mounted him on the horse, and went through the streets of the city, proclaiming, "This is what will be done for every man whom the king wishes to honor." ¹²Then Mordecai returned to the palace; but Haman went home mourning, with his head covered. ¹³Haman related the events that had happened to him to Zeresh his wife and to his friends. His friends and his wife said to him, "If Mordecai is of the race of the Jews, and you have begun to be humbled before him, you will assuredly fall; and you will not be able to withstand him, for the living God is with him." ¹⁴While they were still speaking, the chamberlains arrived to rush Haman to the banquet which Esther had prepared.

7

¹So the king and Haman went in to drink with the queen. ²The king said to Esther at the banquet on the second day, "What is it, queen Esther? What is your request? What is your petition? It shall be done for you, up to half of my kingdom." ³She answered and said, "If I have found favor in the sight of the king, let my life be granted as my petition, and my people as my request. ⁴For both I and my people are sold for destruction, pillage, and genocide. If both we and our children were sold for male and female slaves, I would not have bothered you, for this[b] isn't worthy of the king's palace." ⁵The king said, "Who has dared to do this thing?" ⁶Esther said, "The enemy is Haman, this wicked man!" Then Haman was terrified in the presence of the king and the queen. ⁷The king rose up from the banquet to go into the garden. Haman began to beg the queen for mercy, for he saw that he was in serious trouble. ⁸The king returned from the garden; and Haman had fallen upon the couch, begging the queen for mercy. The king said, "Will you even assault my wife in my house?" And when Haman heard it, he changed countenance. ⁹And Bugathan, one of the chamberlains, said to the king, "Behold, Haman has also prepared a gallows for Mordecai, who spoke concerning the king, and a fifty cubit high gallows has been set up on Haman's property." The king said, "Let him be[c] hanged on it!" ¹⁰So Haman was hanged on the gallows that had been prepared for Mordecai. Then the king's wrath was abated.

8

¹On that day, King Ahasuerus gave to Esther all that belonged to Haman the slanderer. The king called Mordecai, for Esther had told that he was related to her. ²The king took the ring which he had taken away from Haman and gave it to Mordecai. Esther appointed Mordecai over all that had been Haman's. ³She spoke yet again to the king, and fell at his feet, and implored him to undo Haman's mischief and all that he had done against the Jews. ⁴Then the king extended the golden sceptre to Esther; and Esther arose to stand near the king. ⁵Esther said, "If it seems good to you, and I have found favor in your sight, let an order be sent that the letters sent by Haman may be reversed–letters that were written for the destruction of the Jews who are in your kingdom. ⁶For how could I see the affliction of my people, and how could I survive the destruction of my[d] kindred?" ⁷Then the king said to Esther, "If I have given and freely granted you all that was Haman's, and hanged him on a gallows because he laid his hands upon the Jews, what more do you seek? ⁸Write in my name whatever seems good to you, and seal it with my ring; for whatever is written at the command of the king, and sealed with my ring, cannot be countermanded. ⁹So the scribes were called in the first month, which is Nisan, on the twenty-third day of the same year; and orders were written to the Jews, whatever the king had commanded to the[e] local governors and chiefs of the local governors, from India even to Ethiopia–one hundred twenty-seven local governors, according to the several provinces, in their own languages. ¹⁰They were written by order of the king, sealed with his ring, and the letters were sent by the couriers. ¹¹In them, he charged them to use their own laws in every city, to help each other, and to treat their adversaries and those who attacked them as they pleased, ¹²on one day in all the kingdom of Ahasuerus, on the thirteenth day of the twelfth month, which is Adar. ¹³Let the copies be posted in conspicuous places throughout the kingdom. Let all the Jews be ready against this day, to fight against their enemies. The following is a copy of the letter containing orders: [f] [The great King Ahasuerus sends greetings to the rulers of provinces in one hundred twenty-seven local governance regions, from India to Ethiopia, even to those who are faithful to our interests. Many who have been frequently honored by the most abundant kindness of their[g] benefactors have conceived ambitious designs, and not only endeavor to hurt our subjects, but moreover, not being able to bear prosperity, they also endeavor to plot against their own benefactors. They not only would utterly abolish gratitude from among men, but also, elated by the boastings of men who are strangers to all that is good, they supposed that they would escape the sin-hating vengeance of the ever-seeing God. And oftentimes evil exhortation has made partakers of the guilt of shedding innocent blood, and has involved in irremediable calamities many of those who had been appointed to offices of authority, who had been entrusted with the management of their friends' affairs; while men, by the false sophistry of an evil disposition, have deceived the simple goodwill of the ruling powers. And it is possible to see this, not so much from more ancient traditional accounts, as it is immediately in your power to see it by examining what things have been wickedly[h] perpetrated by the baseness of men unworthily holding power. It is right to take heed with regard to the future, that we may maintain the government in undisturbed peace for all men, adopting needful changes, and ever judging those cases which come under our notice with truly equitable decisions. For whereas Haman, a Macedonian, the son of Hammedatha, in reality an alien from the blood of the Persians, and differing widely from our mild course of government, having been hospitably entertained by us, obtained so large a share of our universal kindness as to be called our father, and to continue the person next to the royal throne, reverenced of all; he however, overcome by[i] pride, endeavored to deprive us of our dominion, and our life;[j] having by various and subtle artifices demanded for destruction both Mordecai our deliverer and perpetual benefactor, and Esther the blameless consort of our kingdom, along with their whole nation. For by these methods he thought, having surprised us in a defenseless state, to transfer the dominion of the Persians to the Macedonians. But we find that the Jews, who have been consigned to destruction by the[k] most abominable of men, are not malefactors, but living according to the most just laws, and being the sons of the living God, the most high and[l] mighty, who maintains the kingdom, to us as well as to our forefathers, in the most excellent order. You will therefore do well in refusing to obey the letter sent by Haman the son of Hammedatha, because he who has done these things has been hanged with his whole family at the gates of Susa, Almighty God having swiftly returned to him a worthy punishment. We enjoin you then, having openly published a copy of this letter in every place, to give the Jews permission to use their own lawful customs and to strengthen them, that on the thirteenth of the twelfth month Adar, on the self-same day, they may defend themselves against those who attack them in a time of affliction. For in the place of the destruction of the chosen race, Almighty God has granted them this time of gladness. Therefore you also, among your notable feasts, must keep a distinct day with all festivity, that both now and hereafter it may be a day of deliverance to us and who are well disposed toward the Persians, but to those that plotted against us a memorial of destruction. And every city and province collectively, which shall not do accordingly, shall be consumed with vengeance by spear and fire. It shall be made not only inaccessible to men, but most hateful to wild beasts and birds forever.] Let the copies be posted in conspicuous places throughout the kingdom and let all the Jews be ready against this day, to fight against their enemies. ¹⁴So the horsemen went forth with haste to perform the king's commands. The ordinance was also published in Susa. ¹⁵Mordecai went out robed in royal apparel, wearing a golden crown and a diadem of fine purple linen. The people in Susa saw it and rejoiced. ¹⁶The Jews had light and gladness ¹⁷in every city and province where the ordinance was published. Wherever the proclamation took place, the Jews had joy and gladness, feasting and mirth. Many of the Gentiles were circumcised and became Jews for fear of the Jews.

9

¹Now in the twelfth month, on the thirteenth day of the month, which is Adar, the letters written by the king arrived. ²In that day, the adversaries of the Jews perished; for no one resisted, through fear of them. ³For the chiefs of the local governors, and the princes and the royal scribes, honored the Jews; for the fear of Mordecai was upon them. ⁴For the order of the king was in force, that he should be celebrated in all the kingdom. ⁶In the city Susa the Jews killed five hundred men, ⁷including Pharsannes, Delphon, Phasga, ⁸Pharadatha, Barea, Sarbaca, ⁹Marmasima, Ruphaeus, Arsaeus,

---

[a] *6:9* Or, wide space.
[b] *7:4* see Hebrew: slanderer
[c] *7:9* Or, impaled.
[d] *8:6* Greek country.
[e] *8:9* Greek stewards.
[f] *8:13* the passages in brackets are not in the Hebrew.
[g] *8:13* perhaps rulers, see Luke 22. 25.
[h] *8:13* Greek contrived.
[i] *8:13* Greek not having borne.
[j] *8:13* Greek spirit.
[k] *8:13* Greek thrice guilty.
[l] *8:13* Greek greatest.

and Zabuthaeus, [10] the ten sons of Haman the son of Hammedatha the Bugaean, the enemy of the Jews; and they plundered their property on the same day. [11] The number of those who perished in Susa was reported to the king. [12] Then the king said to Esther, "The Jews have slain five hundred men in the city Susa. What do you think they have done in the rest of the country? What more do you ask, that it may be done for you?" [13] Esther said to the king, "Let it be granted to the Jews to do the same to them tomorrow. Also, hang the bodies of the ten sons of Haman." [14] He permitted it to be done; and he gave up to the Jews of the city the bodies of the sons of Haman to hang. [15] The Jews assembled in Susa on the fourteenth day of Adar and killed three hundred men, but plundered no property. [16] The rest of the Jews who were in the kingdom assembled, and helped one another, and obtained rest from their enemies; for they destroyed fifteen thousand of them on the thirteenth day of Adar, but took no spoil. [17] They rested on the fourteenth of the same month, and kept it as a day of rest with joy and gladness. [18] The Jews in the city of Susa assembled also on the fourteenth day and rested; and they also observed the fifteenth with joy and gladness. [19] On this account then, the Jews dispersed in every foreign land keep the fourteenth of Adar as a[a] holy day with joy, each sending gifts of food to his neighbor. [20] Mordecai wrote these things in a book and sent them to the Jews, as many as were in the kingdom of Ahasuerus, both those who were near and those who were far away, [21] to establish these as joyful days and to keep the fourteenth and fifteenth of Adar; [22] for on these days the Jews obtained rest from their enemies; and in that month, which was Adar, in which a change was made for them from mourning to joy, and from sorrow to a holiday, to spend the whole of it in good days of[b] feasting and gladness, sending portions to their friends and to the poor. [23] And the Jews consented to this as Mordecai wrote to them, [24] showing how Haman the son of Hammedatha the Macedonian fought against them, how he made a decree and cast[c] lots to destroy them utterly; [25] also how he went in to the king, telling him to hang Mordecai; but all the calamities he tried to bring upon the Jews came upon himself, and he was hanged, along with his children. [26] Therefore these days were called Purim, because of the lots (for in their language they are called Purim) because of the words of this letter, and because of all they suffered on this account, and all that happened to them. [27] Mordecai established it, and the Jews took upon themselves, upon their offspring, and upon those who were joined to them to observe it, neither would they on any account behave differently; but these days were to be a memorial kept in every generation, city, family, and province. [28] These days of Purim shall be kept forever, and their memorial shall not fail in any generation. [29] Queen Esther the daughter of Aminadab and Mordecai the Jew wrote all that they had done, and gave the confirmation of the letter about Purim. [31] Mordecai and Esther the queen established this decision on their own, pledging their own well-being to their plan. [32] And Esther established it by a command forever, and it was written for a memorial.

10

[1] The king levied a tax upon his kingdom both by land and sea. [2] As for his strength and valour, and the wealth and glory of his kingdom, behold, they are written in the book of the Persians and Medes for a memorial. [3] Mordecai[d] was viceroy to King Ahasuerus, and was a great man in the kingdom, honored by the Jews, and lived his life loved by all his nation.[e] [4][Mordecai said, "These things have come from God. [5] For I remember the dream which I had concerning these matters; for not one detail of them has failed. [6] There was the little spring which became a river, and there was light, and the sun and much water. The river is Esther, whom the king married and made queen. [7] The two serpents are Haman and me. [8] The nations are those which combined to destroy the name of the Jews. [9] But as for my nation, this is Israel, even those who cried to God and were delivered; for the Lord delivered his people. The Lord rescued us out of all these calamities; and God worked such signs and great wonders as have not been done among the nations. [10] Therefore he ordained two lots. One for the people of God, and one for all the other nations. [11] And these two lots came for an appointed season, and for a day of judgment, before God, and for all the nations. [12] God remembered his people and vindicated his inheritance. [13] They shall observe these days in the month Adar, on the fourteenth and on the fifteenth day of the month, with an assembly, joy, and gladness before God, throughout the generations forever among his people Israel. [14] In the fourth year of the reign of Ptolemeus and Cleopatra, Dositheus, who said he was a priest and Levite, and Ptolemeus his son brought this letter of Purim, which they said was authentic, and that Lysimachus the son of Ptolemeus, who was in Jerusalem, had interpreted.]

Psalm 151

Psalm 151 is recognized as Deuterocanonical Scripture by the Greek Orthodox and Russian Orthodox Churches.

151

This Psalm is a genuine one of David, though extra,[f] composed when he fought in single combat with Goliath. [1] I was small among my brothers, and youngest in my father's house. I tended my father's sheep. [2] My hands formed a musical instrument, and my fingers tuned a lyre. [3] Who shall tell my Lord? The Lord himself, he himself hears. [4] He sent forth his angel and took me from my father's sheep, and he anointed me with his anointing oil. [5] My brothers were handsome and tall; but the Lord didn't take pleasure in them. [6] I went out to meet the Philistine, and he cursed me by his idols. [7] But I drew his own sword and beheaded him, and removed reproach from the children of Israel.

---

[a] *9:19* Greek good day.

[b] *9:22* Greek weddings.

[c] *9:24* Greek lot.

[d] *10:3* Greek succeeded to Or, came into the place of.

[e] *10:3* the passages in brackets are not in the Hebrew.

[f] *1:0* or, supernumerary

The Wisdom of Solomon

The *Wisdom of Solomon* is recognized as Deuterocanonical Scripture by the Roman Catholic, Greek Orthodox, and Russian Orthodox Churches.

1

[1] Love righteousness, all you who are judges of the earth. Think of the Lord[a] with a good mind. Seek him in singleness of heart, [2] because he is found by those who don't put him to the test, and is manifested to those who trust him. [3] for crooked thoughts separate from God. His Power convicts when it is tested, and exposes the foolish; [4] because wisdom will not enter into a soul that devises evil, nor dwell in a body that is enslaved by sin. [5] For a holy spirit of discipline will flee deceit, and will depart from thoughts that are without understanding, and will be ashamed when unrighteousness has come in. [6] For[b] wisdom is a spirit who loves man, and she will not hold a[c] blasphemer guiltless for his lips, because God is witness of his inmost self, and is a true overseer of his heart, and a hearer of his tongue. [7] Because the spirit of the Lord has filled[d] the world, and that which holds all things together knows what is said. [8] Therefore no one who utters unrighteous things will be unseen; neither will Justice, when it convicts, pass him by. [9] For in his counsels the ungodly will be searched out, and the sound of his words will come to the Lord to bring his lawless deeds to conviction; [10] because a jealous ear listens to all things, and the noise of murmurings is not hidden. [11] Beware then of unprofitable murmuring, and keep your tongue from slander; because no secret utterance will go on its way void, and a lying mouth destroys a soul. [12] Don't court death in the error of your life. Don't draw destruction upon yourselves by the works of your hands; [13] because God didn't make death, neither does he delight when the living perish. [14] For he created all things that they might have being. The generative powers of the world are wholesome, and there is no poison of destruction in them, nor has Hades[e] royal dominion upon earth; [15] for righteousness is immortal, [16] but ungodly men by their hands and their words summon death; deeming him a friend they[f] pined away. They made a covenant with him, because they are worthy to belong with him.

2

[1] For they said[g] within themselves, with unsound reasoning, "Our life is short and sorrowful. There is no healing when a man comes to his end, and no one was ever known who[h] was released from Hades. [2] Because we were born by mere chance, and hereafter we will be as though we had never been, because the breath in our nostrils is smoke, and reason is a spark kindled by the beating of our heart, [3] which being extinguished, the body will be turned into ashes, and the spirit will be dispersed as thin air. [4] Our name will be forgotten in time. No one will remember our works. Our life will pass away as the traces of a cloud, and will be scattered as is a mist, when it is chased by the rays of the sun, and[i] overcome by its heat. [5] For our allotted time is the passing of a shadow, and our end doesn't retreat, because it is securely sealed, and no one[j] turns it back. [6] "Come therefore and let's enjoy the good things that exist. Let's use the creation earnestly as in our youth. [7] Let's fill ourselves with costly wine and perfumes, and let no spring flower pass us by. [8] Let's crown ourselves with rosebuds before they wither. [9] Let none of us go without his share in our proud revelry. Let's leave tokens of mirth everywhere, because this is our portion, and this is our lot. [10] Let's oppress the righteous poor. Let's not spare the widow, nor regard the gray hair of the old man. [11] But let our strength be a law of righteousness; for that which is weak is proven useless. [12] But let's lie in wait for the righteous man, because he annoys us, is contrary to our works, reproaches us with sins against the law, and charges us with sins against our training. [13] He professes to have knowledge of God, and calls himself a child of the Lord. [14] He became to us a reproof of our thoughts. [15] He is grievous to us even to look at, because his life is unlike other men's, and his paths are strange. [16] We were regarded by him as something worthless, and he abstains from our ways as from uncleanness. He calls the latter end of the righteous happy. He boasts that God is his father. [17] Let's see if his words are true. Let's test what will happen at the end of his life. [18] For if the righteous man is God's son, he will uphold him, and he will deliver him out of the hand of his adversaries. [19] Let's test him with insult and torture, that we may find out how gentle he is, and test his patience. [20] Let's condemn him to a shameful death, for he will be protected, according to his words." [21] Thus they reasoned, and they were led astray; for their wickedness blinded them, [22] and they didn't know the mysteries of God, neither did they hope for wages of holiness, nor did they discern that there is a prize for blameless souls. [23] Because God created man for incorruption, and made him an image of his own everlastingness; [24] but death entered into the world by the envy of the devil, and those who belong to him experience it.

3

[1] But the souls of the righteous are in the hand of God, and no torment will touch them. [2] In the eyes of the foolish they seemed to have died. Their departure was considered a disaster, [3] and their travel away from us ruin, but they are in peace. [4] For even if in the sight of men they are punished, their hope is full of immortality. [5] Having borne a little chastening, they will receive great good; because God tested them, and found them worthy of himself. [6] He tested them like gold in the furnace, and he accepted them as a whole burnt offering. [7] In the time of their visitation they will shine. They will run back and forth like sparks among stubble. [8] They will judge nations and have dominion over peoples. The Lord will reign over them forever. [9] Those who trust him will understand truth. The faithful will live with him in love, because grace and mercy are with his chosen ones. [10] But the ungodly will be punished even as their reasoning deserves, those who neglected righteousness and revolted from the Lord; [11] for he who despises wisdom and discipline is miserable. Their hope is void and their toils unprofitable. Their works are useless. [12] Their wives are foolish and their children are wicked. [13] Their descendants are cursed. For the barren woman who is undefiled is happy, she who has not conceived in transgression. She will have fruit when God examines souls. [14] So is the eunuch which has done no lawless deed with his hands, nor imagined wicked things against the Lord; for a precious gift will be given to him for his faithfulness, and a delightful inheritance in the Lord's sanctuary. [15] For good labors have fruit of great renown. The root of understanding can't fail. [16] But children of adulterers will not come to maturity. The seed of an unlawful union will vanish away. [17] For if they live long, they will not be esteemed, and in the end, their old age will be without honor. [18] If they die young, they will have no hope, nor consolation in the day of judgment. [19] For the end of an unrighteous generation is always grievous.

4

[1] It is better to be childless with virtue, for immortality is in the memory of virtue, because it is recognized both before God and before men. [2] When it is present, people imitate it. They long after it when it has departed. Throughout all time it marches, crowned in triumph, victorious in the competition for the prizes that are undefiled. [3] But the multiplying brood of the ungodly will be of no profit, and their illegitimate offshoots won't take deep root, nor will they establish a sure hold. [4] For even if they grow branches and flourish for a season, standing unsure, they will be shaken by the wind. They will be uprooted by the violence of winds. [5] Their branches will be broken off before they come to maturity. Their fruit will be useless, never ripe to eat, and fit for nothing. [6] For unlawfully conceived children are witnesses of wickedness against parents when they are investigated. [7] But a righteous man, even if he dies before his time, will be at rest. [8] For honorable old age is not that which stands in length of time, nor is its measure given by number of years, [9] but understanding is gray hair to men, and an unspotted life is ripe old age. [10] Being found well-pleasing to God, someone was loved. While living among sinners he was transported. [11] He was caught away, lest evil should change his understanding, or guile deceive his soul. [12] For the fascination of wickedness obscures the things which are good, and the whirl of desire perverts an innocent mind. [13] Being made perfect quickly, he filled a long time; [14] for his soul was pleasing to the Lord. Therefore he hurried out of the midst of wickedness. [15] But the peoples saw and didn't understand, not considering this, that grace and mercy are with his chosen, and that he visits his holy ones; [16] but a righteous man who is dead will condemn the ungodly who are living, and youth who is quickly perfected will condemn the many years of an unrighteous man's old age. [17] For the ungodly will see a wise man's end, and won't understand what the Lord planned for him, and why he safely kept him. [18] They will see, and they will despise; but the Lord will laugh them to scorn. After this, they will become a dishonored carcass and a reproach among the dead forever; [19] because he will dash them speechless to the ground, and will shake them from the foundations. They will lie utterly waste. They will be in anguish and their memory will perish. [20] They will come with coward fear when their sins are counted. Their lawless deeds will convict them to their face.

5

[1] Then the righteous man will stand in great boldness before the face of those who afflicted him, and those who make his labors of no account. [2]

---

[a] 1:1 Gr. in goodness.
[b] 1:6 Some authorities read the spirit of wisdom is loving to man.
[c] 1:6 Or, reviler
[d] 1:7 Gr. the inhabited earth.
[e] 1:14 Or, a royal house
[f] 1:16 Or, were consumed with love of him
[g] 2:1 Or, among
[h] 2:1 Or, returned out of Hades
[i] 2:4 Gr. weighed down.
[j] 2:5 Or, comes again

When they see him, they will be troubled with terrible fear, and will be amazed at the marvel of salvation. ³ They will speak among themselves repenting, and for distress of spirit they will groan, "This was he whom we used to hold in derision, as a parable of reproach. ⁴ We fools considered his life madness, and his end without honor. ⁵ How was he counted among sons of God? How is his lot among saints? ⁶ Truly we went astray from the way of truth. The light of righteousness didn't shine for us. The sun didn't rise for us. ⁷ We[a] took our fill of the paths of lawlessness and destruction. We traveled through trackless deserts, but we didn't know the Lord's way. ⁸ What did our arrogance profit us? What good have riches and boasting brought us? ⁹ Those things all passed away as a shadow, like a rumor that runs by, ¹⁰ like a ship passing through the billowy water, which, when it has gone by, there is no trace to be found, no pathway of its keel in the waves. ¹¹ Or it is like when a bird flies through the air, no evidence of its passage is found, but the light wind, lashed with the stroke of its pinions, and torn apart with the violent rush of the moving wings, is passed through. Afterwards no sign of its coming remains. ¹² Or it is like when an arrow is shot at a mark, the air it divided closes up again immediately, so that men don't know where it passed through. ¹³ So we also, as soon as we were born, ceased to be; and we had no sign of virtue to show, but we were utterly consumed in our wickedness." ¹⁴ Because the hope of the ungodly man is like chaff carried by the wind, and[b] as[c] foam vanishing before a tempest; and is scattered like smoke by the wind, and passes by as the remembrance of a guest who stays just a day. ¹⁵ But the righteous live forever. Their reward is in the Lord, and the care for them with the Most High. ¹⁶ Therefore they will receive the crown of royal dignity and the diadem of beauty from the Lord's hand, because he will cover them with his right hand, and he will shield them with his arm. ¹⁷ He will take his zeal as complete armor, and will make the whole creation his weapons to punish his enemies: ¹⁸ He will put on righteousness as a breastplate, and will wear impartial judgment as a helmet. ¹⁹ He will take holiness as an invincible shield. ²⁰ He will sharpen stern wrath for a sword. The universe will go with him to fight against his frenzied foes. ²¹ Shafts of lightning will fly with true aim. They will leap to the mark from the clouds, as from a well-drawn bow. ²² Hailstones full of wrath will be hurled as from a catapult. The water of the sea will be angered against them. Rivers will sternly overwhelm them. ²³ A mighty wind will encounter them. It will winnow them away like a tempest. So lawlessness will make all the land desolate. Their evil-doing will overturn the thrones of princes.

6

¹ Hear therefore, you kings, and understand. Learn, you judges of the ends of the earth. ² Give ear, you rulers who have dominion over many people, and make your boast[d] in multitudes of nations, ³ because your dominion was given to you from the Lord, and your sovereignty from the Most High. He will search out your works, and will inquire about your plans, ⁴ because being officers of his kingdom, you didn't judge rightly, nor did you keep the law, nor did you walk according to God's counsel. ⁵ He will come upon you awfully and swiftly, because a stern judgment comes on those who are in high places. ⁶ For the man of low estate may be pardoned in mercy, but mighty men will be mightily tested. ⁷ For the Sovereign Lord of all will not be impressed with anyone, neither will he show deference to greatness; because it is he who made both small and great, and cares about them all; ⁸ but the scrutiny that comes upon the powerful is strict. ⁹ Therefore, my words are to you, O princes, that you may learn wisdom and not fall away. ¹⁰ For those who have kept the things that are holy in holiness will be made holy. Those who have been taught them will find what to say in defense. ¹¹ Therefore set your desire on my words. Long for them, and you princes will be instructed. ¹² Wisdom is radiant and doesn't fade away; and is easily seen by those who love her, and found by those who seek her. ¹³ She anticipates those who desire her, making herself known. ¹⁴ He who rises up early to seek her won't have difficulty, for he will find her sitting at his gates. ¹⁵ For to think upon her is perfection of understanding, and he who watches for her will quickly be free from care; ¹⁶ because she herself goes around, seeking those who are worthy of her, and in their paths she appears to them graciously, and in every purpose she meets them. ¹⁷ For her true beginning is desire for instruction; and desire for instruction is love. ¹⁸ And love is observance of her laws. To give heed to her laws confirms immortality. ¹⁹ Immortality brings closeness to God. ²⁰ So then desire for wisdom promotes to a kingdom. ²¹ If therefore you delight in thrones and sceptres, you princes of peoples, honor wisdom, that you may reign forever. ²² But what wisdom is, and how she came into being, I will declare. I won't hide mysteries from you; but I will explore from her first beginning, bring the knowledge of her into clear light, and I will not pass by the truth. ²³ Indeed, I won't travel with consuming envy, because envy will have no fellowship with wisdom. ²⁴ But a multitude of wise men is salvation to the world, and an understanding king is stability for his people. ²⁵ Therefore be instructed by my words, and you will profit.

7

¹ I myself am also[e] mortal, like everyone else, and am a descendant of one formed first and born of the earth. ² I molded into flesh in the time of ten months in my mother's womb, being compacted in blood from the seed of man and pleasure of marriage. ³ I also, when I was born, drew in the common air, and fell upon the kindred earth, uttering, like all, for my first voice, the same cry. ⁴ I was nursed with care in swaddling clothes. ⁵ For no king had a different beginning, ⁶ but all men have one entrance into life, and a common departure. ⁷ For this cause I prayed, and understanding was given to me. I asked, and a spirit of wisdom came to me. ⁸ I preferred her before sceptres and thrones. I considered riches nothing in comparison to her. ⁹ Neither did I liken to her any priceless gem, because all gold in her presence is a little sand, and silver will be considered as clay before her. ¹⁰ I loved her more than health and beauty, and I chose to have her rather than light, because her bright shining is never laid to sleep. ¹¹ All good things came to me with her, and innumerable riches are in her hands. ¹² And I rejoiced over them all because wisdom leads them; although I didn't know that she was their mother. ¹³ As I learned without guile, I impart without grudging. I don't hide her riches. ¹⁴ For she is a treasure for men that doesn't fail, and those who use it obtain friendship with God, commended by the gifts which they present through discipline. ¹⁵ But may God grant that I may speak his judgment, and to conceive thoughts worthy of what has been given me; because he is one who guides even wisdom and who corrects the wise. ¹⁶ For both we and our words are in his hand, with all understanding and skill in various crafts. ¹⁷ For he himself gave me an unerring knowledge of the things that are, to know the structure of the universe and the operation of the elements; ¹⁸ the beginning, end, and middle of times; the alternations of the solstices and the changes of seasons; ¹⁹ the circuits of years and the positions of stars; ²⁰ the natures of living creatures and the raging of wild beasts; the violence of[f] winds and the thoughts of men; the diversities of plants and the virtues of roots. ²¹ All things that are either secret or manifest I learned, ²² for wisdom, that is the architect of all things, taught me. For there is in her a spirit that is quick to understand, holy, unique, manifold, subtle, freely moving, clear in utterance, unpolluted, distinct, invulnerable, loving what is good, keen, unhindered, ²³ beneficent, loving toward man, steadfast, sure, free from care, all-powerful, all-surveying, and penetrating through all spirits that are quick to understand, pure, most subtle. ²⁴ For wisdom is more mobile than any motion. Yes, she pervades and penetrates all things by reason of her purity. ²⁵ For she is a breath of the power of God, and a pure emanation of the glory of the Almighty. Therefore nothing defiled can find entrance into her. ²⁶ For she is a reflection of everlasting light, an unspotted mirror of the working of God, and an image of his goodness. ²⁷ Although she is one, she has power to do all things. Remaining in herself, she renews all things. From generation to generation passing into holy souls, she makes friends of God and prophets. ²⁸ For God loves nothing as much as one who dwells with wisdom. ²⁹ For she is fairer than the sun, and above all the constellations of the stars. She is better than light. ³⁰ For daylight yields to night, but evil does not prevail against wisdom.

8

¹ But she reaches from one end to the other with full strength, and orders all things well. ² I loved her and sought her from my youth. I sought to take her for my bride. I became enamoured by her beauty. ³ She glorifies her noble birth by living with God. The Sovereign Lord of all loves her. ⁴ For she is initiated into the knowledge of God, and she chooses his works. ⁵ But if riches are a desired possession in life, what is richer than wisdom, which makes all things? ⁶ And if understanding is effective, who more than[g] wisdom is an architect of the things that exist? ⁷ If a man loves righteousness, the fruits of wisdom's labor[h] are virtues, for she teaches soberness, understanding, righteousness, and courage. There is nothing in life more profitable for people than these. ⁸ And if anyone longs for wide experience, she knows the things of old, and infers the things to come. She understands subtleties of speeches and interpretations of dark sayings. She foresees signs and wonders, and the issues of seasons and times. ⁹ Therefore I determined to take her to live with me, knowing that she is one who would

---

[a] 5:7 See Proverbs **14:14**.
[b] 5:14 Gr. like foam chased to thinness: or, as thin foam chased.
[c] 5:14 Most Greek authorities read hoar frost: some authorities, perhaps rightly, a spider's web.
[d] 6:2 Or, in the multitudes of your nations
[e] 7:1 Many authorities read a mortal man.
[f] 7:20 Or, spirits
[g] 8:6 Gr. she.
[h] 8:7 Gr. her labors

give me good counsel, and encourage me in cares and grief. ¹⁰ Because of her, I will have glory among multitudes, and honor in the sight of elders, though I am young. ¹¹ I will be found keen when I give judgment. I will be admired in the presence of rulers. ¹² When I am silent, they will wait for me. When I open my lips, they will heed what I say. If I continue speaking, they will put their hands on their mouths. ¹³ Because of her, I will have immortality, and leave behind an eternal memory to those who come after me. ¹⁴ I will govern peoples. Nations will be subjected to me. ¹⁵ Dreaded monarchs will fear me when they hear of me. Among the people, I will show myself to be good, and courageous in war. ¹⁶ When I come into my house, I will find rest with her. For conversation with her has no bitterness, and living with her has no pain, but gladness and joy. ¹⁷ When I considered these things in myself, and thought in my heart how immortality is in kinship to wisdom, ¹⁸ and in her friendship is good delight, and in the labors of her hands is wealth that doesn't fail, and understanding is in her companionship, and great renown in having fellowship with her words, I went about seeking how to take her to myself. ¹⁹ Now I was a clever child, and received a good soul. ²⁰ Or rather, being good, I came into an undefiled body. ²¹ But perceiving that I could not otherwise possess wisdom unless God gave her to me– yes, and to know and understand by whom the grace is given– I pleaded with the Lord and implored him, and with my whole heart I said:

9

¹ "O God of my ancestors and Lord of mercy, who made all things by your word; ² and by your wisdom you formed man, that he should have dominion over the creatures that were made by you, ³ and rule the world in holiness and righteousness, and execute judgment in uprightness of soul, ⁴ give me wisdom, her who sits by you on your thrones. Don't reject me from among your[a] servants, ⁵ because I am your servant and the son of your handmaid, a weak and short-lived man, with little power to understand judgment and laws. ⁶ For even if a man is perfect among the sons of men, if the wisdom that comes from you is not with him, he will count for nothing. ⁷ You chose me to be king of your people, and a judge for your sons and daughters. ⁸ You gave a command to build a sanctuary on your holy mountain, and[b] an altar in the city where you live, a copy of the holy tent which you prepared from the beginning. ⁹ Wisdom is with you and knows your works, and was present when you were making the world, and understands what is pleasing in your eyes, and what is right according to your commandments. ¹⁰ Send her from the holy heavens, and ask her to come from the throne of your glory, that being present with me she may work, and I may learn what pleases you well. ¹¹ For she knows all things and understands, and she will guide me prudently in my actions. She will guard me in her glory. ¹² So my works will be acceptable. I will judge your people righteously, and I will be worthy of my father's[c] throne. ¹³ For what man will know the counsel of God? Or who will conceive what the Lord wills? ¹⁴ For the thoughts of mortals are unstable, and our plans are prone to fail. ¹⁵ For a corruptible body weighs down the soul. The earthy tent burdens a mind that is full of cares. ¹⁶ We can hardly guess the things that are on earth, and we find the things that are close at hand with labor; but who has traced out the things that are in the heavens? ¹⁷ Who gained knowledge of your counsel, unless you gave wisdom, and sent your holy spirit from on high? ¹⁸ It was thus that the ways of those who are on earth were corrected, and men were taught the things that are pleasing to you. They were saved through wisdom."

10

¹ Wisdom[d] guarded to the end the first formed father of the world, who was created alone, and delivered him out of his own transgression, ² and gave him strength to rule over all things. ³ But when an unrighteous man fell away from her in his anger, he perished himself in the rage with which he killed his brother. ⁴ When for his cause the earth was drowning with a flood, wisdom again saved it, guiding the righteous man's course by a paltry piece of wood. ⁵ Moreover, when nations consenting together in wickedness had been confounded, wisdom[e] knew the righteous man, and preserved him blameless to God, and kept him strong when his heart yearned toward his child. ⁶ While the ungodly were perishing, wisdom[f] delivered a righteous man, when he fled from the fire that descended out of heaven on the five cities. ⁷ To whose wickedness a smoking waste still witnesses, and plants bearing fair fruit that doesn't ripen, a disbelieving soul has a memorial: a standing pillar of salt. ⁸ For having passed wisdom by, not only were they disabled from recognising the things which are good, but they also left behind them for their life a monument of their folly, to the end that where they stumbled, they might fail even to be unseen; ⁹ but wisdom delivered those who waited on her out of troubles. ¹⁰ When a righteous man was a fugitive from a brother's wrath,[g] wisdom guided him in straight paths. She showed him God's kingdom, and gave him knowledge of holy things. She prospered him in his toils, and multiplied the fruits of his labor. ¹¹ When in their covetousness men dealt harshly with him, she stood by him and made him rich. ¹² She guarded him from enemies, and she kept him safe from those who lay in wait. Over his severe conflict, she watched as judge, that he might know that godliness is more powerful than every one. ¹³ When a righteous man was sold,[h] wisdom didn't forsake him, but she delivered him from sin. She went down with him into a dungeon, ¹⁴ and in bonds she didn't depart from him, until she brought him the sceptre of a kingdom, and authority over those that dealt like a tyrant with him. She also showed those who had mockingly accused him to be false, and gave him eternal glory. ¹⁵ Wisdom[i] delivered a holy people and a blameless seed from a nation of oppressors. ¹⁶ She entered into the soul of a servant of the Lord, and withstood terrible kings in wonders and signs. ¹⁷ She rendered to holy men a reward of their toils. She guided them along a marvelous way, and became to them a covering in the day-time, and a starry flame through the night. ¹⁸ She brought them over the Red sea, and led them through much water; ¹⁹ but she drowned their enemies, and she cast them up from the bottom of the deep. ²⁰ Therefore the righteous plundered the ungodly, and they sang praise to your holy name, O Lord, and extolled with one accord your hand that fought for them, ²¹ because wisdom opened the mouth of the mute, and made the tongues of babes to speak clearly.

11

¹ Wisdom prospered their works in the hand of a holy prophet. ² They traveled through a desert without inhabitant, and they pitched their tents in trackless regions. ³ They withstood enemies and repelled foes. ⁴ They thirsted, and they called upon you, and water was given to them out of the[j] flinty rock, and healing of their thirst out of the hard stone. ⁵ For by what things their foes were punished, by these they in their need were benefited. ⁶ When enemies were troubled with clotted blood instead of a river's ever-flowing fountain, ⁷ to rebuke the decree for the slaying of babies, you gave them abundant water beyond all hope, ⁸ having shown by the thirst which they had suffered how you punished the adversaries. ⁹ For when they were tried, although chastened in mercy, they learned how the ungodly were tormented, being judged with wrath. ¹⁰ For you tested these as a father admonishing them; but you searched out those as a stern king condemning them. ¹¹ Yes and whether they were far off or near, they were equally distressed; ¹² for a double grief seized them, and a groaning at the memory of things past. ¹³ For when they heard that through their own punishments the others benefited, they recognized the Lord. ¹⁴ For him who long before was thrown out and exposed they stopped mocking. In the end of what happened, they marveled, having thirsted in another manner than the righteous. ¹⁵ But in return for the senseless imaginings of their unrighteousness, wherein they were led astray to worship irrational reptiles and wretched vermin, you sent upon them a multitude of irrational creatures to punish them, ¹⁶ that they might learn that by what things a man sins, by these he is punished. ¹⁷ For your all-powerful hand that created the world out of formless matter didn't lack means to send upon them a multitude of bears, fierce lions, ¹⁸ or newly-created and unknown wild beasts, full of rage, either breathing out a blast of fiery breath, or belching out smoke, or flashing dreadful sparks from their eyes; ¹⁹ which had power not only to consume them by their violence, but to destroy them even by the terror of their sight. ²⁰ Yes and without these they might have fallen by a single breath, being pursued by Justice, and scattered abroad by the breath of your power; but you arranged all things by measure, number, and weight. ²¹ For to be greatly strong is yours at all times. Who could withstand the might of your arm? ²² Because the whole world before you is as a grain in a balance, and as a drop of dew that comes down upon the earth in the morning. ²³ But you have mercy on all men, because you have power to do all things, and you overlook the sins of men to the end that they may repent. ²⁴ For you love all things that are, and abhor none of the things which you made; For you never would have formed anything if you hated it. ²⁵ How would anything have endured unless you had willed it? Or that which was not called by you, how would it have been preserved? ²⁶ But you spare all things, because they are yours, O Sovereign Lord, you who love the living.

12

¹ For your incorruptible spirit is in all things. ² Therefore you convict little by little those who fall from the right way, and, putting them in remembrance by the things wherein they sin, you admonish them, that

---

[a] 9:4 Or, children
[b] 9:8 Or, a place of sacrifice
[c] 9:12 Gr. thrones.
[d] 10:1 Gr. She.
[e] 10:5 Gr. she
[f] 10:6 Gr. she
[g] 10:10 Gr. she.
[h] 10:13 Gr. she.
[i] 10:15 Gr. she.
[j] 11:4 See Deuteronomy 8:15; Psalms 114:8.

escaping from their wickedness they may believe in you, O Lord. ³ For truly the old inhabitants of your holy land, ⁴ hating them because they practiced detestable works of enchantments and unholy rites– ⁵ merciless slaughters of children and sacrificial banquets of men's flesh and of blood– ⁶ allies in an impious fellowship, and murderers of their own helpless babes, it was your counsel to destroy by the hands of our fathers; ⁷ that the land which in your sight is most precious of all might receive a worthy colony of God's servants.ᵃ ⁸ Nevertheless you even spared these as men, and you sent hornetsᵇ as forerunners of your army, to cause them to perish little by little. ⁹ Not that you were unable to subdue the ungodly under the hand of the righteous in battle, or by terrible beasts or by a stern word to make away with them at once, ¹⁰ but judging them little by little you gave them a chance to repent, not being ignorant that their nature by birth was evil, their wickedness inborn, and that their manner of thought would never be changed. ¹¹ For they were a cursed seed from the beginning. It wasn't through fear of any that you left them unpunished for their sins. ¹² For who will say, "What have you done?" Or "Who will withstand your judgment?" Who will accuse you for the perishing of nations which you caused? Or who will come and stand before you as an avenger for unrighteous men? ¹³ For there isn't any God beside you that cares for all, that you might show that you didn't judge unrighteously. ¹⁴ No king or prince will be able to confront you about those whom you have punished. ¹⁵ But being righteous, you rule all things righteously, deeming it a thing alien from your power to condemn one who doesn't deserve to be punished. ¹⁶ For your strength is the source of righteousness, and your sovereignty over all makes you to forbear all. ¹⁷ For when men don't believe that you are perfect in power, you show your strength, and in dealing with those who think this, you confuse their boldness. ¹⁸ But you, being sovereign in strength, judge in gentleness, and with great forbearance you govern us; for the power is yours whenever you desire it. ¹⁹ But you taught your people by such works as these, how the righteous must be kind. You made your sons to have good hope, because you give repentance when men have sinned. ²⁰ For if on those who were enemies of your servantsᶜ and deserving of death, you took vengeance with so great deliberation and indulgence, giving them times and opportunities when they might escape from their wickedness, ²¹ with how great care you judged your sons, to whose fathers you gave oaths and covenants of good promises! ²² Therefore while you chasten us, you scourge our enemies ten thousand times more, to the intent that we may ponder your goodness when we judge, and when we are judged may look for mercy. ²³ Therefore also the unrighteous that lived in a life of folly, you tormented through their own abominations. ²⁴ For truly they went astray very far in the ways of error, Taking as gods those animalsᵈ which even among their enemies were held in dishonor, deceived like foolish babes. ²⁵ Therefore, as to unreasoning children, you sent your judgment to mock them. ²⁶ But those who would not be admonished by mild correction will experience the deserved judgment of God. ²⁷ For through the sufferings they were indignant of, being punished in these creatures which they supposed to be gods, they saw and recognized as the true God him whom they previously refused to know. Therefore also the result of extreme condemnation came upon them.

13

¹ For truly all men who had no perception of God were foolish by nature, and didn't gain power to know him who exists from the good things that are seen. They didn't recognize the architect from his works. ² But they thought that either fire, or wind, or swift air, or circling stars, or raging water, or luminaries of heaven were gods that rule the world. ³ If it was through delight in their beauty that they took them to be gods, let them know how much better their Sovereign Lord is than these, for the first author of beauty created them. ⁴ But if it was through astonishment at their power and influence, then let them understand from them how much more powerful he who formed them is. ⁵ For from the greatness of the beauty of created things, mankind forms the corresponding perception of their Maker.ᵉ ⁶ But yet for these men there is but small blame, for they too perhaps go astray while they are seeking God and desiring to find him. ⁷ For they diligently search while living among his works, and they trust their sight that the things that they look at are beautiful. ⁸ But again even they are not to be excused. ⁹ For if they had power to know so much, that they should be able to explore the world, how is it that they didn't find the Sovereign Lord sooner? ¹⁰ But they were miserable, and their hopes were in dead things, who called them gods which are works of men's hands, gold and silver, skillfully made, and likenesses of animals, or a useless stone, the work of an ancient hand. ¹¹ Yes and someᶠ woodcutter might saw down a tree that is easily moved, skillfully strip away all its bark, and fashion it in attractive form, make a useful vessel to serve his life's needs. ¹² Burning the scraps from his handiwork to cook his food, he eats his fill. ¹³ Taking a discarded scrap which served no purpose, a crooked piece of wood and full of knots, he carves it with the diligence of his idleness, and shapes it by the skill of his idleness. He shapes it in the image of a man, ¹⁴ or makes it like some worthless animal, smearing it with something red, painting it red, and smearing over every stain in it. ¹⁵ Having made a worthy chamber for it, he sets it in a wall, securing it with iron. ¹⁶ He plans for it that it may not fall down, knowing that it is unable to help itself (for truly it is an image, and needs help). ¹⁷ When he makes his prayer concerning goods and his marriage and children, he is not ashamed to speak to that which has no life. ¹⁸ Yes, for health, he calls upon that which is weak. For life, he implores that which is dead. For aid, he supplicates that which has no experience. For a good journey, he asks that which can't so much as move a step. ¹⁹ And for profit in business and good success of his hands, he asks ability from that which has hands with no ability.

14

¹ Again, one preparing to sail, and about to journey over raging waves, calls upon a piece of wood more fragile than the vessel that carries him. ² For the hunger for profit planned it, and wisdom was the craftsman who built it. ³ Your providence, O Father, guides it along, because even in the sea you gave a way, and in the waves a sure path, ⁴ showing that you can save out of every danger, that even a man without skill may put to sea. ⁵ It is your will that the works of your wisdom should not be ineffective. Therefore men also entrust their lives to a little piece of wood, and passing through the surge on a raft come safely to land. ⁶ Forᵍ in the old time also, when proud giants were perishing, the hope of the world, taking refuge on a raft, your hand guided the seed of generations of the race of men. ⁷ For blessed is wood through which comes righteousness; ⁸ but the idol made with hands is accursed, itself and he that made it; because his was the working, and the corruptible thing was called a god. ⁹ For both the ungodly and his ungodliness are alike hateful to God; ¹⁰ for truly the deed will be punished together with him who committed it. ¹¹ Therefore also there will be a visitation among the idols of the nation, because, though formed of things which God created, they were made an abomination, stumbling blocks to the souls of men, and a snare to the feet of the foolish. ¹² For the devising of idols was the beginning of fornication, and the invention of them the corruption of life. ¹³ For they didn't exist from the beginning, and they won't exist forever. ¹⁴ For by the boastfulness of men they entered into the world, and therefore a speedy end was planned for them. ¹⁵ For a father worn with untimely grief, making an image of the child quickly taken away, now honored him as a god which was then a dead human being, and delivered to those that were under him mysteries and solemn rites. ¹⁶ Afterward the ungodly custom, in process of time grown strong, was kept as a law, and the engraved images received worship by the commandments of princes. ¹⁷ And when men could not honor them in presence because they lived far off, imagining the likeness from afar, they made a visible image of the king whom they honored, that by their zeal they might flatter the absent as if present. ¹⁸ But worship was raised to a yet higher pitch, even by those who didn't know him, urged forward by the ambition of the architect; ¹⁹ for he, wishing perhaps to please his ruler, used his art to force the likeness toward a greater beauty. ²⁰ So the multitude, allured by reason of the grace of his handiwork, now consider an object of devotion him that a little before was honored as a man. ²¹ And this became an ambush, because men, in bondage either to calamity or to tyranny, invested stones and stocks with the Name that shouldn't be shared. ²² Afterward it was not enough for them to go astray concerning the knowledge of God, but also, while they live in a great war of ignorance, they call a multitude of evils peace. ²³ For either slaughtering children in solemn rites, or celebrating secret mysteries, or holding frenzied revels of strange customs, ²⁴ no longer do they guard either life or purity of marriage, but one brings upon another either death by treachery, or anguish by adultery. ²⁵ And all things confusedly are filled with blood and murder, theft and deceit, corruption, faithlessness, tumult, perjury, ²⁶ confusion about what is good, forgetfulness of favors, ingratitude for benefits, defiling of souls, confusion of sex, disorder in marriage, adultery and wantonness. ²⁷ For the worship of idols that may not be named * is a beginning and cause and end of every evil. ²⁸ For their worshipers either make merry to madness, or prophesy lies, or live unrighteously, or lightly commit perjury. ²⁹ For putting their trust in lifeless idols, when they

---

ᵃ 12:7 Or, children
ᵇ 12:8 Or, wasps
ᶜ 12:20 Or, children
ᵈ 12:24 Gr. living creatures: and so elsewhere in this book.
ᵉ 13:5 Gr. is the first maker of them seen.
ᶠ 13:11 Gr. carpenter who is a woodcutter.
ᵍ 14:6 The Greek text here may be corrupt.
* 14:27 Exodus 23:13; Psalms 16:4; Hosea 2:17; Wisdom 14:21

have sworn a wicked oath, they expect not to suffer harm. ³⁰ But on both counts, the just doom will pursue them, because they had evil thoughts of God by giving heed to idols, and swore unrighteously in deceit through contempt for holiness. ³¹ For it is not the power of things by which men swear, but it is the just penalty for those who sin that always visits the transgression of the unrighteous.

15

¹ But you, our God, are gracious and true, patient, and in mercy ordering all things. ² For even if we sin, we are yours, knowing your dominion; but we will not sin, knowing that we have been accounted yours. ³ For to be acquainted with you is[a] perfect righteousness, and to know your dominion is the root of immortality. ⁴ For we weren't led astray by any evil plan of men's, nor yet by painters' fruitless labor, a form stained with varied colors, ⁵ the sight of which leads fools into[b] lust. Their desire is for the breathless form of a dead image. ⁶ Lovers of evil things, and worthy of such hopes, are those who make, desire, and worship them. ⁷ For a potter, kneading soft earth, laboriously molds each article for our service. He fashions out of the same clay both the vessels that minister to clean uses, and those of a contrary sort, all in like manner. What shall be the use of each article of either sort, the potter is the judge. ⁸ Also, laboring to an evil end, he molds a vain god out of the same clay, he who, having but a little before been made of earth, after a short space goes his way to the earth out of which he was taken, when he is required to render back the[c] soul which was lent him. ⁹ However he has anxious care, not because his powers must fail, nor because his span of life is short; But he compares himself with goldsmiths and silversmiths, and he imitates molders in[d] brass, and considers it great that he molds counterfeit gods. ¹⁰ His heart is ashes. His hope is of less value than earth. His life is of less honor than clay, ¹¹ because he was ignorant of him who molded him, and of him that inspired into him[e] an active[f] soul, and breathed into him a vital spirit. ¹² But[g] he accounted our life to be a game, and our[h] lifetime a festival for profit; for, he says, one must get gain however one can, even if it is by evil. ¹³ For this man, beyond all others, knows that he sins, out of earthy matter making brittle vessels and engraved images. ¹⁴ But most foolish and more miserable than a baby, are the enemies of your people, who oppressed them; ¹⁵ because they even considered all the idols of the nations to be gods, which have neither the use of eyes for seeing, nor nostrils for drawing breath, nor ears to hear, nor fingers for handling, and their feet are helpless for walking. ¹⁶ For a man made them, and one whose own spirit is borrowed molded them; for no one has power as a man to mold a god like himself. ¹⁷ But, being mortal, he makes a dead thing by the work of lawless hands; for he is better than the objects of his worship, since he indeed had life, but they never did. ¹⁸ Yes, and they worship the creatures that are most hateful, for, being compared as to lack of sense, these are worse than all others; ¹⁹ Neither, as seen beside other creatures, are they beautiful, so that one should desire them, but they have escaped both the praise of God and his blessing.

16

¹ For this cause, they were deservedly punished through creatures like those which they worship, and tormented through a multitude of vermin. ² Instead of this punishment, you, giving benefits to your people, prepared quails for food, a delicacy to satisfy the desire of their appetite, ³ to the end that your enemies, desiring food, might for the hideousness of the creatures sent among them, loathe even the necessary appetite; but these, your people, having for a short time suffered lack, might even partake of delicacies. ⁴ For it was necessary that inescapable lack should come upon those oppressors, but that to these it should only be showed how their enemies were tormented. ⁵ For even when terrible raging of wild beasts came upon your people, and they were perishing by the bites of crooked serpents, your wrath didn't continue to the uttermost; ⁶ but for admonition were they troubled for a short time, having a token of salvation to put them in remembrance of the commandment of your law; ⁷ for he who turned toward it was not saved because of that which was seen, but because of you, the Savior of all. ⁸ Yes, and in this you persuaded our enemies that you are he who delivers out of every evil. ⁹ For the bites of locusts and flies truly killed them. No healing for their life was found, because they were worthy to be punished by such things. ¹⁰ But your children weren't overcome by the very fangs of venomous dragons, for your mercy passed by where they were and healed them. ¹¹ For they were bitten to put them in remembrance of your oracles, and were quickly saved, lest, falling into deep forgetfulness, they should become unable to respond to your kindness. ¹² For truly it was neither herb nor poultice that cured them, but your word, O Lord, which heals all people.

¹³ For you have authority over life and death, and you lead down to the gates of Hades, and lead up again. ¹⁴ But though a man kills by his wickedness, he can't retrieve the spirit that has departed or release the imprisoned soul. ¹⁵ But it is not possible to escape your hand; ¹⁶ for ungodly men, refusing to know you, were scourged in the strength of your arm, pursued with strange rains and hails and relentless storms, and utterly consumed with fire. ¹⁷ For, what was most marvelous, in the water which quenches all things, the fire burned hotter; for the world fights for the righteous. ¹⁸ For at one time the flame was restrained, that it might not burn up the creatures sent against the ungodly, but that these themselves as they looked might see that they were chased by the judgment of God. ¹⁹ At another time even in the midst of water it burns more intensely than fire, that it may destroy the produce of an unrighteous land. ²⁰ Instead of these things, you gave your people angels' food to eat, and you provided ready-to-eat bread for them from heaven without toil, having the virtue of every pleasant flavor, and agreeable to every taste. ²¹ For your nature showed your sweetness toward your children, while that bread, serving the desire of the eater, changed itself according to every man's choice. ²² But snow and ice endured fire, and didn't melt, that people might know that fire was destroying the fruits of the enemies, burning in the hail and flashing in the rains; ²³ and that this fire, again, in order that righteous people may be nourished, has even forgotten its own power. ²⁴ For the creation, ministering to you, its maker, strains its force against the unrighteous for punishment and in kindness, slackens it on behalf of those who trust in you. ²⁵ Therefore at that time also, converting itself into all forms, it ministered to your all-nourishing bounty, according to the desire of those who had need, ²⁶ that your children, whom you loved, O Lord, might learn that it is not the growth of crops that nourishes a man, but that your word preserves those who trust you. ²⁷ For that which was not destroyed by fire, melted away when it was simply warmed by a faint sunbeam, ²⁸ that it might be known that we must rise before the sun to give you thanks, and must pray to you at the dawning of the light; ²⁹ for the hope of the unthankful will melt as the winter's hoar frost, and will flow away as water that has no use.

17

¹ For your judgments are great, and hard to interpret; therefore undisciplined souls went astray. ² For when lawless men had supposed that they held a holy nation in their power, they, prisoners of darkness, and bound in the fetters of a long night, kept close beneath their roofs, lay exiled from the eternal providence. ³ For while they thought that they were unseen in their secret sins, they were divided from one another by a dark curtain of forgetfulness, stricken with terrible awe, and very troubled by apparitions. ⁴ For neither did the dark recesses that held them guard them from fears, but terrifying sounds rang around them, and dismal phantoms appeared with unsmiling faces. ⁵ And no power of fire prevailed to give light, neither were the brightest flames of the stars strong enough to illuminate that gloomy night; ⁶ but only the glimmering of a self-kindled fire appeared to them, full of fear. In terror, they considered the things which they saw to be worse than that sight, on which they could not gaze. ⁷ The mockeries of their magic arts were powerless, now, and a shameful rebuke of their boasted understanding: ⁸ For those who promised to drive away terrors and disorders from a sick soul, these were sick with a ludicrous fearfulness. ⁹ For even if no troubling thing frighted them, yet, scared with the creeping of vermin and hissing of serpents, ¹⁰ they perished trembling in fear, refusing even to look at the air, which could not be escaped on any side. ¹¹ For wickedness, condemned by a witness within, is a coward thing, and, being pressed hard by conscience, always has added forecasts of the worst. ¹² For fear is nothing else but a surrender of the help which reason offers; ¹³ and from within, the expectation of being less prefers ignorance of the cause that brings the torment. ¹⁴ But they, all through the night which was powerless indeed, and which came upon them out of the recesses of powerless Hades, sleeping the same sleep, ¹⁵ now were haunted by monstrous apparitions, and now were paralyzed by their soul's surrendering; for sudden and unexpected fear came upon them. ¹⁶ So then whoever it might be, sinking down in his place, was kept captive, shut up in that prison which was not barred with iron; ¹⁷ for whether he was a farmer, or a shepherd, or a laborer whose toils were in the wilderness, he was overtaken, and endured that inescapable sentence; for they were all bound with one chain of darkness. ¹⁸ Whether there was a whistling wind, or a melodious sound of birds among the spreading branches, or a measured fall of water running violently, ¹⁹ or a harsh crashing of rocks hurled down, or the swift course of animals bounding along unseen, or the voice of wild beasts harshly roaring, or an echo rebounding from the hollows of the

---

[a] *15:3* Gr. entire.
[b] *15:5* Some authorities read reproach.
[c] *15:8* Or, life
[d] *15:9* Or, copper
[e] *15:11* Gr. a soul that moves to activity.
[f] *15:11* Or, life
[g] *15:12* Some authorities read they accounted.
[h] *15:12* Or, way of life

mountains, all these things paralyzed them with terror. ²⁰ For the whole world was illuminated with clear light, and was occupied with unhindered works, ²¹ while over them alone was spread a heavy night, an image of the darkness that should afterward receive them; but to themselves, they were heavier than darkness.

18

¹ But for your holy ones there was great light. Their enemies, hearing their voice but not seeing their form, counted it a happy thing that they too had suffered, ² yet for that they do not hurt them, though wronged by them before, they are thankful; and because they had been at variance with them, they begged for pardon. ³ Therefore you provided a burning pillar of fire, to be a guide for your people's unknown journey, and a harmless sun for their glorious exile. ⁴ For the Egyptians well deserved to be deprived of light and imprisoned by darkness, they who had imprisoned your children, through whom the incorruptible light of the law was to be given to the race of men. ⁵ After they had taken counsel to kill the babes of the holy ones, and when a single child had been abandoned and saved to convict them of their sin, you took away from them their multitude of children, and destroyed all their army together in a mighty flood. ⁶ Our fathers were made aware of that night beforehand, that, having sure knowledge, they might be cheered by the oaths which they had trusted. ⁷ Salvation of the righteous and destruction of the enemies was expected by your people. ⁸ For as you took vengeance on the adversaries, by the same means, calling us to yourself, you glorified us. ⁹ For holy children of good men offered sacrifice in secret, and with one consent they agreed to the covenant of the divine law, that they would partake alike in the same good things and the same perils, the fathers already leading the sacred songs of praise. ¹⁰ But the discordant cry of the enemies echoed back, and a pitiful voice of lamentation for children was spread abroad. ¹¹ Both servant and master were punished with the same just doom, and the commoner suffering the same as king; ¹² Yes, they all together, under one form of death, had corpses without number. For the living were not sufficient even to bury them, Since at a single stroke, their most cherished offspring was consumed. ¹³ For while they were disbelieving all things by reason of the enchantments, upon the destruction of the firstborn they confessed the people to be God's children. ¹⁴ For while peaceful silence wrapped all things, and night in her own swiftness was half spent, ¹⁵ your all-powerful word leaped from heaven, from the royal throne, a stern warrior, into the midst of the doomed land, ¹⁶ bearing as a sharp sword your authentic commandment, and standing, it filled all things with death, and while it touched the heaven it stood upon the earth. ¹⁷ Then immediately apparitions in dreams terribly troubled them, and unexpected fears came upon them. ¹⁸ And each, one thrown here half dead, another there, made known why he was dying; ¹⁹ for the dreams, disturbing them, forewarned them of this, that they might not perish without knowing why they were afflicted. ²⁰ The experience of death also touched the righteous, and a multitude were destroyed in the wilderness, but the wrath didn't last long. ²¹ For a blameless man hurried to be their champion, bringing the weapon of his own ministry, prayer, and the atoning sacrifice of incense. He withstood the indignation and set an end to the calamity, showing that he was your servant. ²² And he overcame the anger, not by strength of body, not by force of weapons, but by his word, he subdued the avenger by bringing to remembrance oaths and covenants made with the fathers. ²³ For when the dead had already fallen in heaps one upon another, he intervened and stopped the wrath, and cut off its way to the living. ²⁴ For the whole world was pictured on his long robe, and the glories of the fathers were upon the engraving of the four rows of precious stones, and your majesty was upon the diadem on his head. ²⁵ The destroyer yielded to these, and they feared; for it was enough only to test the wrath.

19

¹ But indignation without mercy came upon the ungodly to the end; for God also foreknew their future, ² how, having changed their minds to let your people go, and having sped them eagerly on their way, they would change their minds and pursue them. ³ For while they were yet in the midst of their mourning, and lamenting at the graves of the dead, they made another foolish decision, and pursued as fugitives those whom they had begged to leave and driven out. ⁴ For the doom which they deserved was drawing them to this end, and it made them forget the things that had happened to them, that they might fill up the punishment which was yet lacking from their torments, ⁵ and that your people might journey on by a marvelous road, but they themselves might find a strange death. ⁶ For the whole creation, each part in its diverse kind, was made new again, complying with your commandments, that your servants might be kept unharmed. ⁷ Then the cloud that overshadowed the camp was seen, and dry land rising up out of what had been water, out of the Red sea an unhindered highway, and a grassy plain out of the violent surge, ⁸ by which they passed over with all their army, these who were covered with your hand, having seen strange marvels. ⁹ For like horses they roamed at large, and they skipped about like lambs, praising you, O Lord, who was their deliverer. ¹⁰ For they still remembered the things that happened in the time of their sojourning, how instead of bearing cattle, the land brought forth lice, and instead of fish, the river spewed out a multitude of frogs. ¹¹ But afterwards, they also saw a new kind of birds, when, led on by desire, they asked for luxurious dainties; ¹² for, to comfort them, quails came up for them from the sea. ¹³ Punishments came upon the sinners, not without the signs that were given beforehand by the violence of the thunder, for they justly suffered through their own wickednesses, for the hatred which they practiced toward guests was grievous indeed. ¹⁴ For while the others didn't receive the strangers when they came to them, the Egyptians made slaves of guests who were their benefactors. ¹⁵ And not only so, but while punishment of some sort will come upon the former, since they received as enemies those who were aliens; ¹⁶ because these first welcomed with feastings, and then afflicted with dreadful toils, those who had already shared with them in the same rights. ¹⁷ And moreover they were stricken with loss of sight (even as were those others at the righteous man's doors), when, being surrounded with yawning darkness, they each looked for the passage through his own door. ¹⁸ For as the notes of a lute vary the character of the rhythm, even so the elements, changing their order one with another, continuing always in its sound, as may clearly be conjectured from the sight of the things that have happened. ¹⁹ For creatures of the dry land were turned into creatures of the waters, and creatures that swim moved upon the land. ²⁰ Fire kept the mastery of its own power in water, and water forgot its quenching nature. ²¹ On the contrary, flames didn't consume flesh of perishable creatures that walked among them, neither did they melt the crystalline grains of ambrosial food that were melted easily. ²² For in all things, O Lord, you magnified your people, and you glorified them and didn't lightly regard them, standing by their side in every time and place.

The Wisdom of Jesus the Son of Sirach

The Wisdom of Jesus the Son of Sirach, also called *Ecclesiasticus*, is recognized as Deuterocanonical Scripture by the Roman Catholic, Greek Orthodox, and Russian Orthodox Churches.

1

¹ All wisdom comes from the Lord, and is with him forever. ² Who can count the sand of the seas, the drops of rain, and the days of eternity? ³ Who will search out the height of the sky, the breadth of the earth, the deep, and wisdom? ⁴ Wisdom has been created before all things, and the understanding of prudence from everlasting. ⁵ ᵃ ⁶ To whom has the root of wisdom been revealed? Who has known her shrewd counsels? ⁷ ᵇ ⁸ There is one wise, greatly to be feared, sitting upon his throne: the Lord. ⁹ He created her. He saw and measured her. He poured her out upon all his works. ¹⁰ She is with all flesh according to his gift. He gave her freely to those who love him. ¹¹ The fear of the Lord is glory, exultation, gladness, and a crown of rejoicing. ¹² The fear of the Lord will delight the heart, and will give gladness, joy, and length of days. ¹³ Whoever fears the Lord, it will go well with him at the last. He will be blessed in the day of his death. ¹⁴ To fear the Lord is the beginning of wisdom. It was created together with the faithful in the womb. ¹⁵ Sheᶜ laid an eternal foundation with men. She will be trusted among their offspring. ¹⁶ To fear the Lord is the fullness of wisdom. She inebriates men with her fruits. ¹⁷ She will fill all her house with desirable things, and her storehouses with her produce. ¹⁸ The fear of the Lord is the crown of wisdom, making peace andᵈ perfect health to flourish.ᵉ ¹⁹ He both saw and measured her. He rained down skill and knowledge of understanding, and exalted the honor of those who hold her fast. ²⁰ To fear the Lord is the root of wisdom. Her branches are length of days. ²¹ ᶠ ²² Unjust wrath can never be justified, for his wrath tips the scale to his downfall. ²³ A man that is patient will resist for a season, and afterward gladness will spring up to him. ²⁴ He will hide his words until the right moment, and the lips of many will tell of his understanding. ²⁵ A wise saying is in the treasures of wisdom; but godliness is an abomination to a sinner. ²⁶ If you desire wisdom, keep the commandments and the Lord will give her to you freely; ²⁷ for the fear of the Lord is wisdom and instruction. Faith and humility are his good pleasure. ²⁸ Don't disobey the fear of the Lord. Don't come to him with a double heart. ²⁹ Don't be a hypocrite in men's sight. Keep watch over your lips. ³⁰ Don't exalt yourself, lest you fall and bring dishonor upon your soul. The Lord will reveal your secrets and will cast you down in the midst of the congregation, because you didn't come to the fear of the Lord and your heart was full of deceit.

2

¹ My son, if you come to serve the Lord, prepare your soul for temptation. ² Set your heart aright, constantly endure, and don't make haste in time of calamity. ³ Cling to him, and don't depart, that you may be increased at your latter end. ⁴ Accept whatever is brought upon you, and be patient when you suffer humiliation. ⁵ For gold is tried in the fire, and acceptable men in the furnace of humiliation. ⁶ Put your trust in him, and he will help you. Make your ways straight, and set your hope on him. ⁷ All you who fear the Lord, wait for his mercy. Don't turn aside, lest you fall. ⁸ All you who fear the Lord, put your trust in him, and your reward will not fail. ⁹ All you who fear the Lord, hope for good things, and for eternal gladness and mercy. ¹⁰ Look at the generations of old, and see: Who ever put his trust in the Lord, and was ashamed? Or who remained in his fear, and was forsaken? Or who called upon him, and he neglected him? ¹¹ For the Lord is full of compassion and mercy. He forgives sins and saves in time of affliction. ¹² Woe to fearful hearts, to faint hands, and to the sinner who goes two ways! ¹³ Woe to the faint heart! For it doesn't believe. Therefore it won't be defended. ¹⁴ Woe to you who have lost your patience! And what will you all do when the Lord visits you? ¹⁵ Those who fear the Lord will not disobey his words. Those who love him will keep his ways. ¹⁶ Those who fear the Lord will seek his good pleasure. Those who love him will be filled with the law. ¹⁷ Those who fear the Lord will prepare their hearts, and will humble their souls in his sight. ¹⁸ We will fall into the hands of the Lord, and not into the hands of men; for as his majesty is, so also is his mercy.

3

¹ Hear me, your father, O my children, and do what you hear, that you all may be safe. ² For the Lord honors the father over the children, and has confirmed the judgment of the mother over her sons. ³ He who honors his father will make atonement for sins. ⁴ He who gives glory to his mother is as one who lays up treasure. ⁵ Whoever honors his father will have joy in his own children. He will be heard in the day of his prayer. ⁶ He who gives glory to his father will have length of days. He who listens to the Lord will bring rest to his mother, ⁷ ᵍ and will serve under his parents, as to masters. ⁸ Honor your father in deed and word, that a blessing may come upon you from him. ⁹ For the blessing of the father establishes the houses of children, but the curse of the mother roots out the foundations. ¹⁰ Don't glorify yourself in the dishonor of your father, for your father's dishonor is no glory to you. ¹¹ For the glory of a man is from the honor of his father, and a mother in dishonor is a reproach to her children. ¹² My son, help your father in his old age, and don't grieve him as long as he lives. ¹³ If he fails in understanding, have patience with him. Don't dishonor him in your full strength. ¹⁴ For the kindness to your father will not be forgotten. Instead of sins it will be added to build you up. ¹⁵ In the day of your affliction it will be remembered for you, as fair weather upon ice, so your sins will also melt away. ¹⁶ He who forsakes his father is as a blasphemer. He who provokes his mother is cursed by the Lord. ¹⁷ My son, go on with your business in humility; so you will be loved by an acceptable man. ¹⁸ The greater you are, humble yourself the more, and you will find favor before the Lord. ¹⁹ ʰ ²⁰ For the power of the Lord is great, and he is glorified by those who are lowly. ²¹ Don't seek things that are too hard for you, and don't search out things that are above your strength. ²² Think about the things that have been commanded you, for you have no need of the things that are secret. ²³ Don't be overly busy in tasks that are beyond you, for more things are shown to you than men can understand. ²⁴ For the conceit of many has led them astray. Evil opinion has caused their judgment to slip. ²⁵ ⁱThere is no light without eyes. There is no wisdom without knowledge. ²⁶ A stubborn heart will do badly at the end. He who loves danger will perish in it. ²⁷ A stubborn heart will be burdened with troubles. The sinner will heap sin upon sins. ²⁸ The calamity of the proud has no healing, for a weed of wickedness has taken root in him. ²⁹ The heart of the prudent will understand a proverb. A wise man desires the ear of a listener. ³⁰ Water will quench a flaming fire; almsgiving will make atonement for sins. ³¹ He who repays good turns is mindful of that which comes afterward. In the time of his falling he will find a support.

4

¹ My son, don't deprive the poor of his living. Don't make the needy eyes wait long. ² Don't make a hungry soul sorrowful, or provoke a man in his distress. ³ Don't add more trouble to a heart that is provoked. Don't put off giving to him who is in need. ⁴ Don't reject a suppliant in his affliction. Don't turn your face away from a poor man. ⁵ Don't turn your eye away from one who asks. Give no occasion to a man to curse you. ⁶ For if he curses you in the bitterness of his soul, he who made him will hear his supplication. ⁷ Endear yourself to the assembly. Bow your head to a great man. ⁸ Incline your ear to a poor man. Answer him with peaceful words in humility. ⁹ Deliver him who is wronged from the hand of him who wrongs him; Don't be hesitant in giving judgment. ¹⁰ Be as a father to the fatherless, and like a husband to their mother. So you will be as a son of the Most High, and he will love you more than your mother does. ¹¹ Wisdom exalts her sons, and takes hold of those who seek her. ¹² He who loves her loves life. Those who seek her early will be filled with gladness. ¹³ He who holds her fast will inherit glory. Whereʲ he enters, the Lord will bless. ¹⁴ Those who serve her minister to the Holy One. The Lord loves those who love her. ¹⁵ He who listens to her will judge the nations. He who heeds her will dwell securely. ¹⁶ If he trusts her, he will inherit her, and his generations will possess her. ¹⁷ For at the first she will walk with him in crooked ways, and will bring fear and dread upon him, and torment him with her discipline, until she may trust his soul, and try him by her judgments. ¹⁸ Then she will return him again to the straight way, and will gladden him, and reveal to him her secrets. ¹⁹ If he goes astray, she will forsake him, and

---

ᵃ *1:5* Verse **5** is omitted by the best authorities: The source of wisdom is God's word in the highest heaven, and her ways are the eternal commandments.

ᵇ *1:7* Verse **7** is omitted by the best authorities: To whom was the knowledge of wisdom manifested? Who has understood her abundant experience?

ᶜ *1:15* Gr. nested.

ᵈ *1:18* Gr. health of cure.

ᵉ *1:18* The remainder of this verse is omitted by the best authorities: Both are gifts of God for peace; glory opens out for those who love him. He saw her and took her measure.

ᶠ *1:21* Verse **21** is omitted by the best authorities: The fear of the Lord drives away sins. Where it resides, it will turn away all anger.

ᵍ *3:7* Some manuscripts add those who fear the Lord honor their father,

ʰ *3:19* Some manuscripts add Many are lofty and renowned, but he reveals his secrets to the humble.

ⁱ *3:25* Some manuscripts omit verse **25**.

ʲ *4:13* Or, she

hand him over to his fall. ²⁰ Watch for the opportunity, and beware of evil. Don't be ashamed of your soul. ²¹ For there is a shame that brings sin, and there is a shame that is glory and grace. ²² Don't show partiality, discrediting your soul. Don't revere any man to your falling. ²³ Don't refrain from speaking when it is for safety. ᵃDon't hide your wisdom for the sake of seeming fair. ²⁴ For wisdom will be known by speech, and instruction by the word of the tongue. ²⁵ Don't speak against the truth and be shamed for your ignorance. ²⁶ Don't be ashamed to confess your sins. Don't fight the river's current. ²⁷ Don't lay yourself down for a fool to tread upon. Don't be partial to one who is mighty. ²⁸ Strive for the truth to death, and the Lord God will fight for you. ²⁹ Don't be hasty with your tongue, or slack and negligent in your deeds. ³⁰ Don't be like a lion in your house, or suspicious of your servants. ³¹ Don't let your hand be stretched out to receive, and closed when you should repay.

5

¹ Don't set your heart upon your goods. Don't say, "They are sufficient for me." ² Don't follow your own mind and your strength to walk in the desires of your heart. ³ Don't say, "Who will have dominion over me?" for the Lord will surely take vengeance on you. ⁴ Don't say, "I sinned, and what happened to me?" for the Lord is patient. ⁵ Don't be so confident of atonement that you add sin upon sins. ⁶ Don't say, "His compassion is great. He will be pacified for the multitude of my sins," for mercy and wrath are with him, and his indignation will rest on sinners. ⁷ Don't wait to turn to the Lord. Don't put off from day to day; for suddenly the wrath of the Lord will come on you, and you will perish in the time of vengeance. ⁸ Don't set your heart upon unrighteous gains, for you will profit nothing in the day of calamity. ⁹ Don't winnow with every wind. Don't walk in every path. This is what the sinner who has a double tongue does. ¹⁰ Be steadfast in your understanding. Let your speech be consistent. ¹¹ Be swift to hear and answer with patience. ¹² If you have understanding, answer your neighbor; but if not, put your hand over your mouth. ¹³ Glory and dishonor is in talk. A man's tongue may be his downfall. ¹⁴ Don't be called a whisperer. Don't lie in wait with your tongue; for shame is on the thief, and an evil condemnation is on him who has a double tongue. ¹⁵ Don't be ignorant in a great or small matter.

6

¹ Don't become an enemy instead of a friend; for an evil name will inherit shame and reproach. So it is with the sinner who has a double tongue. ² Don't exalt yourself in the counsel of your soul, that your soul not be torn in pieces like a bull. ³ You will eat up your leaves, destroy your fruit, and leave yourself like a dry tree. ⁴ A wicked soul will destroy him who has it, and will make him a laughing stock to his enemies. ⁵ Sweet words will multiply a man's friends. A gracious tongue will multiply courtesies. ⁶ Let those that are at peace with you be many, but your advisers one of a thousand. ⁷ If you want to gain a friend, get him in a time of testing, and don't be in a hurry to trust him. ⁸ For there is a friend just for an occasion. He won't continue in the day of your affliction. ⁹ And there is a friend who turns into an enemy. He will discover strife to your reproach. ¹⁰ And there is a friend who is a companion at the table, but he won't continue in the day of your affliction. ¹¹ In your prosperity he will be as yourself, and will be bold over your servants. ¹² If you are brought low, he will be against you, and will hide himself from your face. ¹³ Separate yourself from your enemies, and beware of your friends. ¹⁴ A faithful friend is a strong defense. He who has found him has found a treasure. ¹⁵ There is nothing that can be taken in exchange for a faithful friend. His excellency is beyond price. ¹⁶ A faithful friend is a life-saving medicine. Those who fear the Lord will find him. ¹⁷ He who fears the Lord directs his friendship properly; for as he is, so is his neighbor also. ¹⁸ My son, gather instruction from your youth up. Even when you have gray hair you will find wisdom. ¹⁹ Come to her as one who plows and sows and wait for her good fruit; for your toil will be little in her cultivation, and you will soon eat of her fruit. ²⁰ How exceedingly harsh she is to the unlearned! He who is without understanding will not remain in her. ²¹ She will rest upon him as a mighty stone of trial. He won't hesitate to cast her from him. ²² For wisdom is according to her name. She isn't manifest to many. ²³ Give ear, my son, and accept my judgment. Don't refuse my counsel. ²⁴ Bring your feet into her fetters, and your neck into her chain. ²⁵ Put your shoulder under her and bear her. Don't be grieved with her bonds. ²⁶ Come to her with all your soul. Keep her ways with your whole power. ²⁷ Search and seek, and she will be made known to you. When you get hold of her, don't let her go. ²⁸ For at the last you will find her rest; and she will be turned for you into gladness. ²⁹ Her fetters will be to you for a covering of strength, and her chains for a robe of glory. ³⁰ For there is a golden ornament upon her, and her bands are * a purple cord. ³¹ You shall put her on as a robe of glory, and shall put her on as a crown of rejoicing. ³² My son, if you are willing, you will be instructed. If you will yield your soul, you will be prudent. ³³ If you love to hear, you will receive. If you incline your ear, you will be wise. ³⁴ Stand in the multitude of the elders. Attach yourself to whomever is wise. ³⁵ Be willing to listen to every godly discourse. Don't let the proverbs of understanding escape you. ³⁶ If you see a man of understanding, get to him early. Let your foot wear out the steps of his doors. ³⁷ Let your mind dwell on the ordinances of the Lord and meditate continually on his commandments. He will establish your heart and your desire for wisdom will be given to you.

7

¹ Do no evil, so no evil will overtake you. ² Depart from wrong, and it will turn away from you. ³ My son, don't sow upon the furrows of unrighteousness, and you won't reap them sevenfold. ⁴ Don't seek preeminence from the Lord, nor the seat of honor from the king. ⁵ Don't justify yourself in the presence of the Lord, and don't display your wisdom before the king. ⁶ Don't seek to be a judge, lest you not be able to take away iniquities, lest perhaps you fear the person of a mighty man, and lay a stumbling block in the way of your uprightness. ⁷ Don't sin against the multitude of the city. Don't disgrace yourself in the crowd. ⁸ Don't commit a sin twice, for even in one you will not be unpunished. ⁹ Don't say, "He will look upon the multitude of my gifts. When I make an offering to the Most High God, he will accept it." ¹⁰ Don't be faint-hearted in your prayer. Don't neglect to give alms. ¹¹ Don't laugh a man to scorn when he is in the bitterness of his soul, for there is one who humbles and exalts. ¹² Don't deviseᵇ a lie against your brother, or do the same to a friend. ¹³ Refuse to utter a lie, for that habit results in no good. ¹⁴ Don't babble in the assembly of elders. Don't repeat your words in your prayer. ¹⁵ Don't hate hard labor or farm work, which the Most High has created. ¹⁶ Don't number yourself among the multitude of sinners. Remember that wrath will not wait. ¹⁷ Humble your soul greatly, for the punishment of the ungodly man is fire and the worm. ¹⁸ Don't exchange a friend for something, neither a true brother for the gold of Ophir. ¹⁹ Don't deprive yourself of a wise and good wife, for her grace is worth more than gold. ²⁰ Don't abuse a servant who works faithfully, or a hireling who gives you his life. ²¹ Let your soul love a wise servant. Don't defraud him of liberty. ²² Do you have cattle? Look after them. If they are profitable to you, let them stay by you. ²³ Do you have children? Correct them, and make them obedient from their youth. ²⁴ Do you have daughters? Take care of their bodies, and don't be overly indulgent toward them. ²⁵ Give your daughter in marriage, and you will have accomplished a great matter. Give her to a man of understanding. ²⁶ Do you have a wife who pleases you? Don't cast her out. ᶜ But don't trust yourself to one who is hateful. ²⁷ Honor your father with your whole heart, and don't forget the birth pangs of your mother. ²⁸ Remember that you were born of them. What will you repay them for the things that they have done for you? ²⁹ Fear the Lord with all your soul; and revere his priests. ³⁰ With all your strength love him who made you. Don't forsake his ministers. ³¹ Fear the Lord and honor the priest. Give him his portion, even as it is commanded you: the first fruits, the trespass offering, the gift of the shoulders, the sacrifice of sanctification, and the first fruits of holy things. ³² Also stretch out your hand to the poor man, that your blessing may be complete. ³³ A gift has grace in the sight of every living man. Don't withhold grace for a dead man. ³⁴ Don't avoid those who weep, and mourn with those who mourn. ³⁵ Don't be slow to visit a sick man, for by such things you will gain love. ³⁶ In all your words, remember eternity, and you will never sin.

8

¹ Don't contend with a mighty man, lest perhaps you fall into his hands. ² Don't strive with a rich man, lest perhaps he overpower you; for gold has destroyed many, and turned away the hearts of kings. ³ Don't argue with a loudmouthed man. Don't heap wood upon his fire. ⁴ Don't make fun of a rude man, lest your ancestors be dishonored. ⁵ Don't reproach a man when he turns from sin. Remember that we are all worthy of punishment. ⁶ Don't dishonor a man in his old age, for some of us are also growing old. ⁷ Don't rejoice over anyone's death. Remember that we all die. ⁸ Don't neglect the discourse of the wise. Be conversant with their proverbs; for from them you will learn discipline and how to serve great men. ⁹ Don't miss the discourse of the aged, for they also learned from their parents, because from them you will learn understanding, and to give an answer in time of need. ¹⁰ Don't kindle the coals of a sinner, lest you be burned with the flame of his fire. ¹¹ Don't rise up from the presence of an insolent man, lest he lie in wait as an

---

ᵃ 4:23 Some manuscripts omit this line.

* 6:30 Numbers 15:38

ᵇ 7:12 Gr. Don't plow

ᶜ 7:26 Many authorities omit this line

ambush for your mouth. ¹² Don't lend to a man who is stronger than you; and if you lend, count it as a loss. ¹³ Don't be surety beyond your means. If you give surety, think as one who will have to pay. ¹⁴ Don't go to law with a judge; for according to his honor they will give judgment for him. ¹⁵ Don't travel with a reckless man, lest he be burdensome to you; for he will do as he pleases, and you will perish with his folly. ¹⁶ Don't fight with a wrathful man. Don't travel with him through the desert, for blood is as nothing in his sight. Where there is no help, he will overthrow you. ¹⁷ Don't consult with a fool, for he will not be able to keep a secret. ¹⁸ Do no secret thing before a stranger, for you don't know what it will cause. ¹⁹ Don't open your heart to every man. Don't let him return you a favor.

9

¹ Don't be jealous over the wife of your bosom, and don't teach her an evil lesson against yourself. ² Don't give your soul to a woman and let her trample down your strength. ³ Don't go to meet a woman who plays the prostitute, lest perhaps you fall into her snares. ⁴ Don't associate with a woman who is a singer, lest perhaps you be caught by her tricks. ⁵ Don't gaze at a virgin, lest perhaps you stumble and incur penalties for her. ⁶ Don't give your soul to prostitutes, that you not lose your inheritance. ⁷ Don't look around in the streets of the city. Don't wander in its deserted places. ⁸ Turn your eye away from a beautiful woman, and don't gaze at another's beauty. Many have been led astray by the beauty of a woman; and with this, passion is kindled like a fire. ⁹ Don't dine at all with a woman who has a husband, or revel with her at wine,ᵃ lest perhaps your soul turn away to her, and with your spirit you slide into destruction. ¹⁰ Don't forsake an old friend; for a new one is not comparable to him. A new friend is like new wine: if it becomes old, you will drink it with gladness. ¹¹ Don't envy the success of a sinner; for you don't know what his end will be. ¹² Don't delight in the delights of the ungodly. Remember they will not go unpunished toᵇ the grave. ¹³ Keep yourself far from the man who hasᶜ power to kill, and you will not be troubled by the fear of death. If you come to him, commit no fault, lest he take away your life. Know surely that you go about in the midst of snares, and walk upon the battlements of a city. ¹⁴ As well as you can, aim to know your neighbors, and take counsel with the wise. ¹⁵ Let your conversation be with men of understanding. Let all your discourse be in the law of the Most High. ¹⁶ Let righteous people be companions at your table. Let your glorying be in the fear of the Lord. ¹⁷ A work is commended because of the skill of the artisan; so he who rules the people will be considered wise for his speech. ¹⁸ A loudmouthed man is dangerous in his city. He who is reckless in his speech will be hated.

10

¹ A wise judge will instruct his people. The government of a man of understanding will be well ordered. ² As is the judge of his people, so are his officials. As the city's ruler is, so are all those who dwell in it. ³ An undisciplined king will destroy his people. A city will be established through the understanding of the powerful. ⁴ The government of the earth is in the Lord's hand. In due time, he will raise up over it the right person at the right time. ⁵ A man's prosperity is in the Lord's hand. He will lay his honor upon the person of the scribe. ⁶ Don't be angry with your neighbor for every wrong. Do nothing by works of violence. ⁷ Pride is hateful before the Lord and men. Arrogance is abhorrent in the judgment of both. ⁸ Sovereignty is transferred from nation to nation because of injustice, violence, and greed for money. ⁹ Why are dirt and ashes proud?ᵈ Because in life, my body decays. ¹⁰ A long disease mocks the physician. The king of today will die tomorrow. ¹¹ For when a man is dead, he will inherit maggots, vermin, and worms. ¹² It is the beginning of pride when a man departs from the Lord. His heart has departed from him who made him. ¹³ For the beginning of pride is sin. He who keeps it will pour out abomination. For this cause the Lord brought upon them strange calamities and utterly overthrew them. ¹⁴ The Lord cast down the thrones of rulers and set the lowly in their place. ¹⁵ The Lord plucked up the roots of nations and planted the lowly in their place. ¹⁶ The Lord overthrew the lands of nations and destroyed them to the foundations of the earth. ¹⁷ He took some of them away and destroyed them, and made their memory to cease from the earth. ¹⁸ Pride has not been created for men, nor wrathful anger for the offspring of women. ¹⁹ Whose offspring has honor? Human offspring who fear the Lord. Whose offspring has no honor? Human offspring who break the commandments. ²⁰ In the midst of kindred he who rules them has honor. Those who fear the Lord have honor in his eyes. ²¹ ᵉ ²² The rich man, the honorable, and the poor all glory in the fear of the Lord. ²³ It is not right to dishonor a poor man who has understanding. It is not fitting to glorify a man who is a sinner. ²⁴ The prince, the judge, and the mighty man will be honored. There is not one of them greater than he who fears the Lord. ²⁵ Free men will minister to a wise servant. A man who has knowledge will not complain. ²⁶ Don't flaunt your wisdom in doing your work. Don't boast in the time of your distress. ²⁷ Better is he who labors and abounds in all things, than he who boasts and lacks bread. ²⁸ My son, glorify your soul in humility, and ascribe to yourself honor according to your worthiness. ²⁹ Who will justify him who sins against his own soul? Who will honor him who dishonors his own life? ³⁰ A poor man is honored for his knowledge. A rich man is honored for his riches. ³¹ But he who is honored in poverty, how much more in riches? He who is dishonored in riches, how much more in poverty?

11

¹ The wisdom of the lowly will lift up his head, and make him sit in the midst of great men. ² Don't commend a man for his good looks. Don't abhor a man for his outward appearance. ³ The bee is little among flying creatures, but what it produces is the best of confections. ⁴ Don't boast about the clothes you wear, and don't exalt yourself in the day of honor; for the Lord's works are wonderful, and his works are hidden among men. ⁵ Manyᶠ kings have sat down upon the ground, but one who was never thought of has worn a crown. ⁶ Many mighty men have been greatly disgraced. Men of renown have been delivered into other men's hands. ⁷ Don't blame before you investigate. Understand first, and then rebuke. ⁸ Don't answer before you have heard. Don't interrupt while someone else is speaking. ⁹ Don't argue about a matter that doesn't concern you. Don't sit with sinners when they judge. ¹⁰ My son, don't be busy about many matters; for if you meddle much, you will not be unpunished. If you pursue, you will not overtake, and you will not escape by fleeing. ¹¹ There is one who toils, labors, and hurries, and is even more behind. ¹² There is one who is sluggish, and needs help, lacking in strength, and who abounds in poverty, but the Lord's eyes looked upon him for good, and he raised him up from his low condition, ¹³ and lifted up his head so that many marveled at him. ¹⁴ Good things and bad, life and death, poverty and riches, are from the Lord. ¹⁵⁻¹⁶ ᵍ ¹⁷ The Lord's gift remains with the godly. His good pleasure will prosper forever. ¹⁸ One grows rich by his diligence and self-denial, and this is the portion of his reward: ¹⁹ when he says, "I have found rest, and now I will eat of my goods!" he doesn't know how much time will pass until he leaves them to others and dies. ²⁰ Be steadfast in your covenant and be doing it, and grow old in your work. ²¹ Don't marvel at the works of a sinner, but trust the Lord and stay in your labor; for it is an easy thing in the sight of the Lord to swiftly and suddenly make a poor man rich. ²² The Lord's blessing is in the reward of the godly. He makes his blessing flourish in an hour that comes swiftly. ²³ Don't say, "What use is there of me? What further good things can be mine?" ²⁴ Don't say, "I have enough. What harm could happen to me now?" ²⁵ In the day of good things, bad things are forgotten. In the day of bad things, a man will not remember things that are good. ²⁶ For it is an easy thing in the sight of the Lord to reward a man in the day of death according to his ways. ²⁷ The affliction of an hour causes delights to be forgotten. In the end, a man's deeds are revealed. ²⁸ Call no man happy before his death. A man will be known in his children. ²⁹ Don't bring every man into your house, for many are the tricks of a deceitful man. ³⁰ Like a decoy partridge in a cage, so is the heart of a proud man. Like a spy, he looks for your weakness. ³¹ For he lies in wait to turn things that are good into evil, and assigns blame in things that are praiseworthy. ³² From a spark of fire, a heap of many coals is kindled, and a sinful man lies in wait to shed blood. ³³ Take heed of an evil-doer, for he plans wicked things, lest perhaps he ruin your reputation forever. ³⁴ Receive a stranger into your house, and he will distract you with arguments and estrange you from your own family.

12

¹ If you do good, know to whom you do it, and your good deeds will have thanks. ² Do good to a godly man, and you will find a reward– if not from him, then from the Most High. ³ No good will come to him who continues to do evil, nor to him who gives no alms. ⁴ Give to the godly man, and don't help the sinner. ⁵ Do good to one who is lowly. Don't give to an ungodly man. Keep back his bread, and don't give it to him, lest he subdue you with it; for you would receive twice as much evil for all the good you would have done to him. ⁶ For the Most High also hates sinners, and will repay

---

ᵃ *9:9* The preceding line of this verse is omitted by the best authorities.
ᵇ *9:12* Gr. Hades.
ᶜ *9:13* Or, authority

ᵈ *10:9* Two lines of this verse are here omitted by the best authorities.
ᵉ *10:21* Verse **21** is omitted by the best authorities: Fear of the Lord is the beginning of acceptance, but obstinance and pride are the beginning of rejection.
ᶠ *11:5* Gr. tyrants

ᵍ *11:15-16* Verses **15** and **16** are omitted by the best authorities.

vengeance to the ungodly.[a] ⁷ Give to the good man, and don't help the sinner. ⁸ A man's friend won't be[b] fully tried in prosperity. His enemy won't be hidden in adversity. ⁹ In a man's prosperity, his enemies are grieved. In his adversity, even his friend leaves. ¹⁰ Never trust your enemy, for his wickedness is like corrosion in copper. ¹¹ Though he humbles himself and walks bowed down, still be careful and beware of him. You will be to him as one who has wiped a mirror, to be sure it doesn't completely tarnish. ¹² Don't set him next to you, lest he overthrow you and stand in your place. Don't let him sit on your right hand, lest he seek to take your seat, and at the last you acknowledge my words, and be pricked with my sayings. ¹³ Who will pity a charmer that is bitten by a snake, or any who come near wild beasts? ¹⁴ Even so, who will pity him who goes to a sinner, and is associated with him in his sins? ¹⁵ For a while he will stay with you, and if you falter, he will not stay. ¹⁶ The enemy will speak sweetly with his lips, and in his heart plan to throw you into a pit. The enemy may weep with his eyes, but if he finds opportunity, he will want more blood. ¹⁷ If adversity meets you, you will find him there before you. Pretending to help you, he will trip you. ¹⁸ He will shake his head, clap his hands, whisper much, and change his countenance.

13

¹ He who touches pitch will be defiled. He who has fellowship with a proud man will become like him. ² Don't take up a burden above your strength. Have no fellowship with one who is mightier and richer than yourself. What fellowship would the earthen pot have with the kettle? The kettle will strike, and the pot will be dashed in pieces. ³ The rich man does a wrong and threatens. The poor is wronged and apologizes. ⁴ If you are profitable, he will exploit you. If you are in need, he will forsake you. ⁵ If you own something, he will live with you. He will drain your resources and will not be sorry. ⁶ Does he need you? Then he will deceive you, smile at you, and give you hope. He will speak kindly to you and say, "What do you need?" ⁷ He will shame you by his delicacies until he has made you bare twice or thrice, and in the end he will laugh you to scorn. Afterward he will see you, will forsake you, and shake his head at you. ⁸ Beware that you are not deceived and brought low in your enjoyment. ⁹ If a mighty man invites you, be reserved, and he will invite you more. ¹⁰ Don't press him, lest you be thrust back. Don't stand far off, lest you be forgotten. ¹¹ Don't try to speak with him as an equal, and don't believe his many words; for he will test you with much talk, and will examine you in a smiling manner. ¹² He who doesn't keep secrets to himself is unmerciful. He won't hesitate to harm and to bind. ¹³ Keep them to yourself and be careful, for you walk[c] in danger of falling. ¹⁴ [d] ¹⁵ Every living creature loves its own kind, and every man loves his neighbor. ¹⁶ All flesh associates with their own kind. A man will stick to people like himself. ¹⁷ What fellowship would the wolf have with the lamb? So is the sinner to the godly. ¹⁸ What peace is there between a hyena and a dog? What peace is there between a rich man and the poor? ¹⁹ Wild donkeys are the prey of lions in the wilderness; likewise poor men are feeding grounds for the rich. ²⁰ Lowliness is an abomination to a proud man; likewise a poor man is an abomination to the rich. ²¹ When a rich man is shaken, he is supported by his friends, but when the humble is down, he is pushed away even by his friends. ²² When a rich man falls, there are many helpers. He speaks things not to be spoken, and men justify him. A humble man falls, and men rebuke him. He utters wisdom, and is not listened to. ²³ A rich man speaks, and all keep silence. They extol what he says to the clouds. A poor man speaks, and they say, "Who is this?" If he stumbles, they will help to overthrow him. ²⁴ Riches are good if they have no sin. Poverty is evil only in the opinion of the ungodly. ²⁵ The heart of a man changes his countenance, whether it is for good or for evil.[e] ²⁶ A cheerful countenance is a sign of a prosperous heart. Devising proverbs takes strenuous thinking.

14

¹ Blessed is the man who has not slipped with his mouth, and doesn't suffer from sorrow for sins. ² Blessed is he whose soul does not condemn him, and who has not given up hope. ³ Riches are not appropriate for a stingy person. What would a miser do with money? ⁴ He who gathers by denying himself gathers for others. Others will revel in his goods. ⁵ If one is mean to himself, to whom will he be good? He won't enjoy his possessions. ⁶ There is none more evil than he who is grudging to himself. This is a punishment for his wickedness. ⁷ Even if he does good, he does it in forgetfulness. In the end, he reveals his wickedness. ⁸ A miser is evil. He turns away and disregards souls. ⁹ A covetous man's eye is not satisfied with his portion. Wicked injustice dries up his soul. ¹⁰ A miser begrudges bread, and it is lacking at his table. ¹¹ My son, according to what you have, treat yourself well, and bring worthy offerings to the Lord. ¹² Remember that death will not wait, and that the covenant of Hades hasn't been shown to you. ¹³ Do good to your friends before you die. According to your ability, reach out and give to them. ¹⁴ Don't deprive yourself of a good day. Don't let your share of a desired good pass you by. ¹⁵ Won't you leave your labors to another, and your toils be divided by lot? ¹⁶ Give, take, and treat yourself well, because there is no seeking of luxury in Hades. ¹⁷ All flesh grows old like a garment, for the covenant from the beginning is, "You must die!" ¹⁸ Like the leaves flourishing on a thick tree, some it sheds, and some grow, so also are the generations of flesh and blood: one comes to an end and another is born. ¹⁹ Every work rots and falls away, and its builder will depart with it. ²⁰ Blessed is the man who meditates on wisdom, and who reasons by his understanding. ²¹ He who considers her ways in his heart will also have knowledge of her secrets. ²² Go after her like a hunter, and lie in wait in her paths. ²³ He who peers in at her windows will also listen at her doors. ²⁴ He who lodges close to her house will also fasten a nail in her walls. ²⁵ He will pitch his tent near at hand to her, and will lodge in a lodging where good things are. ²⁶ He will set his children under her shelter, and will rest under her branches. ²⁷ By her he will be covered from heat, and will lodge in her glory.

15

¹ He who fears the Lord will do this. He who has possession of the law will obtain her. ² She will meet him like a mother, and receive him like a wife married in her virginity. ³ She will feed him with bread of understanding and give him water of wisdom to drink. ⁴ He will be stayed upon her, and will not be moved. He will rely upon her, and will not be confounded. ⁵ She will exalt him above his neighbors. She will open his mouth in the midst of the congregation. ⁶ He will inherit joy, a crown of gladness, and an everlasting name. ⁷ Foolish men will not obtain her. Sinners will not see her. ⁸ She is far from pride. Liars will not remember her. ⁹ Praise is not attractive in the mouth of a sinner; for it was not sent to him from the Lord. ¹⁰ For praise will be spoken in wisdom; The Lord will prosper it. ¹¹ Don't say, "It is through the Lord that I fell away;" for you shall not do the things that he hates. ¹² Don't say, "It is he that caused me to err;" for he has no need of a sinful man. ¹³ The Lord hates every abomination; and those who fear him don't love them. ¹⁴ He himself made man from the beginning and left him in the hand of his own counsel. ¹⁵ If you choose, you can keep the commandments. To be faithful is a matter of your choice. ¹⁶ He has set fire and water before you. You will stretch forth your hand to whichever you desire. ¹⁷ Before man is life and death. Whichever he likes, it will be given to him. ¹⁸ For the wisdom of the Lord is great. He is mighty in power, and sees all things. ¹⁹ His eyes are upon those who fear him. He knows every act of man. ²⁰ He has not commanded any man to be ungodly. He has not given any man license to sin.

16

¹ Don't desire a multitude of unprofitable children, neither delight in ungodly sons. ² If they multiply, don't delight in them unless the fear of the Lord is in them. ³ Don't trust in their life. Don't rely on their numbers; for one can be better than a thousand, and to die childless than to have ungodly children. ⁴ For from one who has understanding, a city will be populated, but a race of wicked men will be made desolate. ⁵ I have seen many such things with my eyes. My ear has heard mightier things than these. ⁶ In a congregation of sinners, a fire will be kindled. In a disobedient nation, wrath is kindled. ⁷ He was not pacified toward the giants of old time, who revolted in their strength. ⁸ He didn't spare Lot's neighbors, whom he abhorred for their pride. ⁹ He didn't pity the people of perdition who were taken away in their sins, ¹⁰ or in like manner, the six hundred thousand footmen who were gathered together in the hardness of their hearts. ¹¹ Even if there is one stiff-necked person, it is a marvel if he will be unpunished; for mercy and wrath are both with him who is mighty to forgive, and he pours out wrath. ¹² As his mercy is great, so is his correction also. He judges a man according to his works. ¹³ The sinner will not escape with plunder. The perseverance of the godly will not be frustrated. ¹⁴ He will make room for every work of mercy. Each man will receive according to his works. ¹⁵⁻¹⁶ [f] ¹⁷ Don't say, "I will be hidden from the Lord," and "Who will remember me from on high?" I will not be known among so many people, for what is my soul in a boundless creation? ¹⁸ Behold, the heaven, the heaven of heavens, the deep, and the earth, will be moved when he visits.

---

[a] *12:6* The remainder of this verse is omitted by the best authorities.

[b] *12:8* Or, punished

[c] *13:13* Gr. along with.

[d] *13:14* The remainder of verse 13, and verse 14, are omitted by the best authorities.

[e] *13:25* The remainder of this verse is omitted by the best authorities.

[f] *16:15-16* Verses 15 and 16 are omitted by the best authorities.

¹⁹ The mountains and the foundations of the earth together are shaken with trembling when he looks at them. ²⁰ No heart will think about these things. Who could comprehend his ways? ²¹ Like a tempest which no man can see, so, the majority of his works are[a] hidden. ²² Who will declare his works of righteousness? Who will wait for them? For his covenant is afar off.[b] ²³ He who is lacking in[c] understanding thinks about these things. An unwise and erring man thinks foolishly. ²⁴ My son, listen to me, learn knowledge, and heed my words with your heart. ²⁵ I will impart instruction with precision, and declare knowledge exactly. ²⁶ In the judgment of the Lord are his works from the beginning. From the making of them he determined their boundaries. ²⁷ He arranged his works for all time, and their beginnings to their generations. They aren't hungry or weary, and they don't cease from their works. ²⁸ No one pushes aside his neighbor. They will never disobey his word. ²⁹ After this also the Lord looked at the earth and filled it with his blessings. ³⁰ All manner of living things covered its surface, and they return into it.

17

¹ The Lord created mankind out of earth, and turned them back to it again. ² He gave them days by number, and a set time, and gave them authority over the things that are on it. ³ He endowed them with strength proper to them, and made them according to his own image. ⁴ He put the fear of man upon all flesh, and gave him dominion over beasts and birds. ⁵ [d] ⁶ He gave them counsel, tongue, eyes, ears, and heart to have understanding. ⁷ He filled them with the knowledge of wisdom, and showed them good and evil. ⁸ He set his eye upon their hearts, to show them the majesty of his works. ⁹ [e] ¹⁰ And they will praise his holy name, [f] that they may declare the majesty of his works. ¹¹ He added to them knowledge, and gave them a law of life for a heritage. ¹² He made an everlasting covenant with them, and showed them his decrees. ¹³ Their eyes saw the majesty of his glory. Their ears heard the glory of his voice. ¹⁴ He said to them, "Beware of all unrighteousness." So he gave them commandment, each man concerning his neighbor. ¹⁵ Their ways are ever before him. They will not be hidden from his eyes. ¹⁶ [g] ¹⁷ [h]For every nation he appointed a ruler, but Israel is the Lord's portion. ¹⁸ [i] ¹⁹ All their works are as clear as the sun before him. His eyes are continually upon their ways. ²⁰ Their iniquities are not hidden from him. All their sins are before the Lord. ²¹ [j] ²² With him the alms of a man is as a signet. He will keep a man's kindness as the pupil of the eye.[k] ²³ Afterwards he will rise up and repay them, and render their repayment upon their head. ²⁴ However to those who repent he grants a return. He comforts those who are losing hope. ²⁵ Return to the Lord, and forsake sins. Make your prayer before his face offend less. ²⁶ Turn again to the Most High, and turn away from iniquity.[l] Greatly hate the abominable thing. ²⁷ Who will give praise to the Most High in Hades, in place of the living who return thanks? ²⁸ Thanksgiving perishes from the dead, as from one who doesn't exist. He who is in life and health will praise the Lord. ²⁹ How great is the mercy of the Lord, and his forgiveness to those who turn to him! ³⁰ For humans are not capable of everything, because the son of man is not immortal. ³¹ What is brighter than the sun? Yet even this can be eclipsed. So flesh and blood devise evil. ³² He looks upon the power of the height of heaven, while all men are earth and ashes.

18

¹ He who lives forever created the whole universe. ² The Lord alone is just. ³ [m] ⁴ He has given power to declare his works to no one. Who could trace out his mighty deeds? ⁵ Who could measure the strength of his majesty? Who could also proclaim his mercies? ⁶ As for the wondrous works of the Lord, it is not possible to take from them nor add to them, neither is it possible to explore them. ⁷ When a man has finished, then he is just at the beginning. When he stops, then he will be perplexed. ⁸ What is mankind, and what purpose do they serve? What is their good, and what is their evil? ⁹ The number of man's days at the most are a hundred years. ¹⁰ As a drop of water from the sea, and a pebble from the sand, so are a few years in the day of eternity. ¹¹ For this cause the Lord was patient over them, and poured out his mercy upon them. ¹² He saw and perceived their end, that it is evil. Therefore he multiplied his forgiveness. ¹³ The mercy of a man is on his neighbor; but the mercy of the Lord is on all flesh: reproving, chastening, teaching, and bringing back, as a shepherd does his flock. ¹⁴ He has mercy on those who accept chastening, and that diligently seek after his judgments. ¹⁵ My son, don't add reproach to your good deeds, and no harsh words in any of your giving. ¹⁶ Doesn't the dew relieve the scorching heat? So a word is better than a gift. ¹⁷ Behold, isn't a word better than a gift? Both are with a gracious person. ¹⁸ A fool is ungracious and abusive. The gift of an grudging person consumes the eyes. ¹⁹ Learn before you speak. Take care of your health before you get sick. ²⁰ Before judgment, examine yourself, and in the hour of scrutiny you will find forgiveness. ²¹ Humble yourself before you get sick. In the time of sins, repent. ²² Let nothing hinder you to pay your vow in due time. Don't wait until death to be released. ²³ Before you make a vow, prepare yourself. Don't be like a man who tests the Lord. ²⁴ Think about the wrath coming in the days of the end, and the time of vengeance, when he turns away his face. ²⁵ In the days of fullness remember the time of hunger. Remember poverty and lack in the days of wealth. ²⁶ From morning until evening, the time changes. All things are speedy before the Lord. ²⁷ A wise man is cautious in everything. In days of sinning, he will beware of offense.[n] ²⁸ Every man of understanding knows wisdom. He will give thanks to him who found her. ²⁹ They who were of understanding in sayings also became wise themselves, and poured out apt proverbs. ³⁰ Don't go after your lusts. Restrain your appetites. ³¹ If you give fully to your soul the delight of her desire, she will make you[o] the laughing stock of your enemies. ³² Don't make merry in much luxury, and don't be tied to its expense. ³³ Don't be made a beggar by banqueting with borrowed money when you have nothing in your purse.[p]

19

¹ A worker who is a drunkard will not become rich. He who despises small things will fall little by little. ² Wine and women will make men of understanding go astray. He who joins with prostitutes is reckless. ³ Decay and worms will have him as their heritage. A reckless soul will be taken away. ⁴ He who is hasty to trust is shallow-hearted. He who sins offends against his own soul. ⁵ He who rejoices in wickedness will be condemned.[q] ⁶ [r] He who hates gossip has less wickedness. ⁷ Never repeat what is told you, and you won't lose anything. ⁸ Whether it is of friend or foe, don't tell it. Unless it is a sin to you, don't reveal it. ⁹ For if he has heard you and observed you, when the time comes, he will hate you. ¹⁰ Have you heard something? Let it die with you. Be brave: it will not make you burst! ¹¹ A fool will travail in pain with a word, as a woman in labor with a child. ¹² As an arrow that sticks in the flesh of the thigh, so is gossip in a fool. ¹³ Question a friend; it may be he didn't do it. If he did something, it may be that he may do it no more. ¹⁴ Question your neighbor; it may be he didn't say it. If he has said it, it may be that he may not say it again. ¹⁵ Question a friend; for many times there is slander. Don't trust every word. ¹⁶ There is one who slips, and not from the heart. Who is he who hasn't sinned with his tongue? ¹⁷ Reprove your neighbor before you threaten him; and give place to the law of the Most High. ¹⁸⁻¹⁹ [s] ²⁰ All wisdom is the fear of the Lord. In all wisdom is the doing of the law. ²¹ [t] ²² The knowledge of wickedness is not wisdom. The prudence of sinners is not counsel. ²³ There is a wickedness, and it is an abomination. There is a fool lacking in wisdom. ²⁴ Better is one who has little understanding, and fears God, than one who has much intelligence and transgresses the law. ²⁵ There is an exquisite subtlety, and it is unjust. And there is one who perverts favor to gain a judgment.[u] ²⁶ There is one who does wickedly, who hangs down his head with mourning; but inwardly he is full of deceit, ²⁷ bowing down his face, and pretending to be deaf in one ear. Where he isn't known, he will take

---

[a] *16:21* Gr. among hidden things.
[b] *16:22* The remainder of this verse is omitted by the best authorities.
[c] *16:23* Gr. heart.
[d] *17:5* Verse **5** is omitted by the best authorities.
[e] *17:9* Verse **9** is omitted by the best authorities.
[f] *17:10* This line is added by the best authorities.
[g] *17:16* Verses **16**, **18**, and **21** are omitted by the best authorities.
[h] *17:17* The preceding part of this verse is omitted by the best authorities.
[i] *17:18* Verses **16**, **18**, and **21** are omitted by the best authorities.
[j] *17:21* Verses **16**, **18**, and **21** are omitted by the best authorities.
[k] *17:22* The remainder of this verse is omitted by the best authorities.
[l] *17:26* A line is here omitted by the best authorities.
[m] *18:3* The remainder of verse **2**, and verse **3**, are omitted by the best authorities.
[n] *18:27* The remainder of this verse is omitted by the best authorities.
[o] *18:31* Or, a rejoicing to
[p] *18:33* The remainder of this verse is omitted by the best authorities.
[q] *19:5* The remainder of this verse is omitted by the best authorities.
[r] *19:6* The preceding part of this verse is omitted by the best authorities.
[s] *19:18-19* Verses **18** and **19** are omitted by the best authorities.
[t] *19:21* The remainder of verse **20** and verse **21** are omitted by the best authorities.
[u] *19:25* The remainder of this verse is omitted by the best authorities.

advantage of you. **28** And if for lack of power he is hindered from sinning, if he finds opportunity, he will do mischief. **29** A man will be known by his appearance. One who has understanding will be known by his face when you meet him. **30** A man's attire, grinning laughter, and the way he walks show what he is.

20

1 There is a reproof that is not timely; and there is a person who is wise enough to keep silent. **2** How good is it to reprove, rather than to be angry. He who confesses will be kept back from harm. **3** ᵃ **4** As is the lust of a eunuch to deflower a virgin, so is he who executes judgments with violence. **5** There is one who keeps silent and is found wise; and there is one who is hated for his much talk. **6** There is one who keeps silent, for he has no answer to make; And there is one who keeps silent, knowing when to speak. **7** A wise man will be silent until his time has come, but the braggart and fool will miss his time. **8** He who uses many words will be abhorred. He who takes authority for himself will be hated in it. **9** There is a prosperity that a man finds in misfortunes; and there is a gain that turns to loss. **10** There is a gift that will not profit you; and there is a gift that pays back double. **11** There are losses because of glory; and there is one who has lifted up his head from a low estate. **12** There is one who buys much for a little, and pays for it again sevenfold. **13** He who is wise in words will make himself beloved; but the pleasantries of fools will be wasted. **14** The gift of a fool will not profit you,ᵇ for he looks for repayment many times instead of one. **15** He will give little and insult much. He will open his mouth like a crier. Today he will lend, and tomorrow he will ask for it back. Such a one is a hateful man. **16** The fool will say, "I have no friend, and I have no thanks for my good deeds. Those who eat my bread have an evil tongue." **17** How often, and of how many, will he be laughed to scorn!ᶜ **18** A slip on a pavement is better than a slip with the tongue. So the fall of the wicked will come speedily. **19** A man without grace is a tale out of season. It will be continually in the mouth of the ignorant. **20** A parable from a fool's mouth will be rejected; for he won't tell it at the proper time. **21** There is one who is hindered from sinning through lack. When he rests, he will not be troubled. **22** There is one who destroys his soul through bashfulness. By a foolish countenance, he will destroy it. **23** There is one who for bashfulness makes promises to his friend; and he makes him his enemy for nothing. **24** A lie is an ugly blot on a person. It will be continually in the mouth of the ignorant. **25** A thief is better than a man who is continually lying, but they both will inherit destruction. **26** The destination of a liar is dishonor. His shame is with him continually. **27** He who is wise in words will advance himself. And one who is prudent will please great men. **28** He who tills his land will raise his harvest high. He who pleases great men will get pardon for iniquity. **29** Favors and gifts blind the eyes of the wise, and as a muzzle on the mouth, turn away reproofs. **30** Wisdom that is hidden, and treasure that is out of sight– what profit is in either of them? **31** Better is a man who hides his folly than a man who hides his wisdom. **32** ᵈ

21

1 My son, have you sinned? Do it no more; and ask forgiveness for your past sins. **2** Flee from sin as from the face of a snake; for if you go near, it will bite you. Its teeth are like lion's teeth, slaying people's souls. **3** All iniquity is as a two-edged sword. Its stroke has no healing. **4** Terror and violence will waste away riches. So the house of an arrogant man will be laid waste. **5** Supplication from a poor man's mouth reaches to the ears ofᵉ God, and his judgment comes speedily. **6** One who hates reproof is in the path of the sinner. He who fears the Lord will repent in his heart. **7** He who is mighty in tongue is known far away; but the man of understanding knows when he slips. **8** He who builds his house with other men's money is like one who gathers stones for his own tomb. **9** The congregation of wicked men is as a bundle of tow with a flame of fire at the end of them. **10** The way of sinners is paved with stones; and at the end of it is the pit of Hades. **11** He who keeps the law becomes master of its intent. The fulfilment of the fear of the Lord is wisdom. **12** He who is not clever will not be instructed. There is a cleverness which makes bitterness abound. **13** The knowledge of a wise man will be made to abound as a flood, and his counsel as a fountain of life. **14** The inward parts of a fool are like a broken vessel. He will hold no knowledge. **15** If a man of knowledge hears a wise word, he will commend it and add to it. The wanton man hears it, and it displeases him, so he throws it away behind his back. **16** The chatter of a fool is like a burden in the way, but grace will be found on the lips of the wise. **17** The utterance of the prudent man will be sought for in the congregation. They will ponder his words in their heart. **18** As a house that is destroyed, so is wisdom to a fool. The knowledge of an unwise man is talk without sense.ᶠ **19** Instruction is as fetters on the feet of an unwise man, and as manacles on the right hand. **20** A fool lifts up his voice with laughter, but a clever man smiles quietly. **21** Instruction is to a prudent man as an ornament of gold, and as a bracelet upon his right arm. **22** The foot of a fool rushes into a house, but a man of experience will be ashamed of entering. **23** A foolish man peers into the door of a house, but a man who is instructed will stand outside. **24** It is rude for someone to listen at a door, but a prudent person will be grieved with the disgrace. **25** The lips of strangers will be grieved at these things, but the words of prudent men will be weighed in the balance. **26** The heart of fools is in their mouth, but the mouth of wise men is their heart. **27** When the ungodly curses an adversary, he curses his own soul. **28** A whisperer defiles his own soul, and will be hated wherever he travels.

22

1 A slothful man is compared to a stone that is defiled. Everyone will at hiss at him in his disgrace. **2** A slothful man is compared to the filth of a dunghill. Anyone who picks it up will shake it out of his hand. **3** An undisciplined child is a disgrace to his father, and a foolish daughter is born to his loss. **4** A prudent daughter will inherit a husband of her own. She who brings shame is the grief of her father. **5** She who is arrogant brings shame on father and husband. She will be despised by both of them. **6** Ill-timed conversation is like music in mourning, but stripes and correction are wisdom in every season. **7** He who teaches a fool is like one who glues potsherds together, even like one who wakes a sleeper out of a deep sleep. **8** He who teaches a fool is as one who teaches a man who slumbers. In the end he will say, "What is it?" **9-10** ᵍ **11** Weep for the dead, for he lacks light. Weep for a fool, for he lacks understanding. Weep more sweetly for the dead, because he has found rest, but the life of the fool is worse than death. **12** Mourning for the dead lasts seven days, but for a fool and an ungodly man, it lasts all the days of his life. **13** Don't talk much with a foolish man, and don't go to one who has no understanding. Beware of him, lest you have trouble and be defiled in his onslaught. Turn away from him, and you will find rest, and you won't be wearied in his madness. **14** What would be heavier than lead? What is its name, but "Fool"? **15** Sand, salt, and a mass of iron is easier to bear than a man without understanding. **16** Timber girded and bound into a building will not be released with shaking. So a heart established in due season on well advised counsel will not be afraid. **17** A heart settled upon a thoughtful understanding is as an ornament of plaster on a polished wall. **18** Fences set on a high place will not stand against the wind; so a fearful heart in the imagination of a fool will not stand against any fear. **19** He who pricks the eye will make tears fall. He who pricks the heart makes it show feeling. **20** Whoever casts a stone at birds scares them away. He who insults a friend will dissolve friendship. **21** If you have drawn a sword against a friend, don't despair, for there may be a way back. **22** If you have opened your mouth against a friend, don't be afraid, for there may be reconciliation, unless it is for insulting, arrogance, disclosing of a secret, or a treacherous blow– for these things any friend will flee. **23** Gain trust with your neighbor in his poverty, that in his prosperity you may have gladness. Stay steadfast to him in the time of his affliction, that you may be heir with him in his inheritance.ʰ **24** Before fire is the vapor and smoke of a furnace, so insults precede bloodshed. **25** I won't be ashamed to shelter a friend. I won't hide myself from his face. **26** If any evil happens to me because of him, everyone who hears it will beware of him. **27** Who will set a watch over my mouth, and a seal of shrewdness upon my lips, that I may not fall from it, and that my tongue may not destroy me?

23

1 O Lord, Father and Master of my life, don't abandon me to their counsel. Don't let me fall because of them. **2** Who will set scourges over my thought, and a discipline of wisdom over my heart, that they spare me not for my errors, and not overlook their sins? **3** Otherwise my errors might be multiplied, and my sins abound, I fall before my adversaries, and my enemy rejoice over me.ⁱ **4** O Lord, Father and God of my life, don't give me a haughty eyes,ʲ **5** and turn away evil desire from me.ᵏ **6** Let neither gluttony

---

ᵃ *20:3* Verse **3** is omitted by the best authorities.

ᵇ *20:14* A line of this verse is here omitted by the best authorities.

ᶜ *20:17* The latter part of verse **17** is omitted by the best authorities.

ᵈ *20:32* Verse **32** is omitted by the best authorities.

ᵉ *21:5* Gr. him.

ᶠ *21:18* Gr. unexamined words.

ᵍ *22:9-10* Verses **9** and **10** are omitted by the best authorities.

ʰ *22:23* The remainder of this verse is omitted by the best authorities.

ⁱ *23:3* The remainder of this verse is omitted by the best authorities.

ʲ *23:4* The remainder of this verse is omitted by the best authorities.

ᵏ *23:5* The remainder of this verse is omitted by the best authorities.

nor lust overtake me. Don't give me over to a shameless mind. ⁷ Listen, my children, to the discipline of the mouth. He who keeps it will not be caught. ⁸ The sinner will be overpowered through his lips. By them, the insulter and the arrogant will stumble. ⁹ Don't accustom your mouth to an oath, and don't be accustomed to naming the Holy One, ¹⁰ for as a servant who is continually scourged will not lack bruises, so he also who swears and continually utters the Name will not be cleansed from sin. ¹¹ A man of many oaths will be filled with iniquity. The scourge will not depart from his house. If he offends, his sin will be upon him. If he disregards it, he has sinned doubly. If he has sworn falsely, he will not be justified, for his house will be filled with calamities. ¹² There is a manner of speech that is clothed with death. Let it not be found in the heritage of Jacob, for all these things will be far from the godly, and they will not wallow in sins. ¹³ Don't accustom your mouth to gross rudeness, for it involves sinful speech. ¹⁴ Remember your father and your mother, for you sit in the midst of great men, that you be not forgetful before them, and become a fool by your bad habit; so you may wish that you had not been born, and curse the day of your birth. ¹⁵ A man who is accustomed to abusive language won't be corrected all the days of his life. ¹⁶ Two sorts of people multiply sins, and the third will bring wrath: a hot passion, like a burning fire, will not be quenched until it is consumed; a fornicator in the body of his flesh will never cease until he has burned out the fire. ¹⁷ All bread is sweet to a fornicator. He will not cease until he dies. ¹⁸ A man who goes astray from his own marriage bed says in his heart, "Who sees me? Darkness is around me, and the walls hide me. No one sees me. Of whom am I afraid? The Most High will not remember my sins." ¹⁹ The eyes of men are his terror. He doesn't know that the eyes of the Lord are ten thousand times brighter than the sun, seeing all the ways of men, and looking into secret places. ²⁰ All things were known to him before they were created, and also after they were completed. ²¹ This man will be punished in the streets of the city. He will be seized where he least expects it. ²² So also is a wife who leaves her husband, and produces an heir by another man. ²³ For first, she was disobedient in the law of the Most High. Second, she trespassed against her own husband. Third, she played the adulteress in fornication, and had children by another man. ²⁴ She shall be brought out into the congregation. Her punishment will extend to her children. ²⁵ Her children will not take root. Her branches will bear no fruit. ²⁶ She will leave her memory for a curse. Her reproach won't be blotted out. ²⁷ And those who are left behind will know that there is nothing better than the fear of the Lord, and nothing sweeter than to heed the commandments of the Lord. ²⁸ ᵃ

24

¹ Wisdom will praise her own soul, and will proclaim her glory in the midst of her people. ² She will open her mouth in the congregation of the Most High, and proclaim her glory in the presence of his power. ³ "I came out of the mouth of the Most High, and covered the earth as a mist. ⁴ I lived in high places, and my throne is in the pillar of the cloud. ⁵ Alone I surrounded the circuit of heaven, and walked in the depth of the abyss. ⁶ In the waves of the sea, and in all the earth, and in every people and nation, I obtained a possession. ⁷ With all these I sought rest. In whose inheritance shall I lodge? ⁸ Then the Creator of all things gave me a command. He who created me made my tent to rest, and said, 'Let your dwelling be in Jacob, and your inheritance in Israel.' ⁹ He created me from the beginning, before the ages. For all ages, I will not cease to exist. ¹⁰ In the holy tabernacle, I ministered before him. So I was established in Zion. ¹¹ In the beloved city, likewise he gave me rest. In Jerusalem was my domain. ¹² I took root in a people that was honored, even in the portion of the Lord's own inheritance. ¹³ I was exalted like a cedar in Lebanon, And like a cypress tree on the mountains of Hermon. ¹⁴ I was exalted like a palm tree on the sea shore, like rose bushes in Jericho, and like a fair olive tree in the plain. I was exalted like a plane tree. ¹⁵ Like cinnamon and aspalathus, I have given a scent to perfumes. Like choice myrrh, I spread abroad a pleasant fragrance, likeᵇ galbanum, onycha, stacte, and as the smell of frankincense in the tabernacle. ¹⁶ Like the terebinth, I stretched out my branches. My branches are glorious and graceful. ¹⁷ Like the vine, I put forth grace. My flowers are the fruit of glory and riches. ¹⁸ ᶜ ¹⁹ "Come to me, all you who desire me, and be filled with my fruits. ²⁰ For my memory is sweeter than honey, and my inheritance than the honeycomb. ²¹ Those who eat me will be hungry for more. Those who drink me will be thirsty for more. ²² He who obeys me will not be ashamed. Those who work with me will not sin." ²³ All these things are the book of the covenant of the Most High God, the law which Moses commanded us for an inheritance for the assemblies of Jacob. ²⁴ ᵈ ²⁵ It is he who makes wisdom abundant, as Pishon, and as Tigris in the days of first fruits. ²⁶ He makes understanding full as the Euphrates, and as the Jordan in the days of harvest, ²⁷ who makes instruction shine forth as the light, as Gihon in the days of vintage. ²⁸ The first man didn't know her perfectly. In like manner, the last has not explored her. ²⁹ For her thoughts are filled from the sea, and her counsels from the great deep. ³⁰ I came out as a canal stream from a river, and as an irrigation ditch into a garden. ³¹ I said, "I will water my garden, and will drench my garden bed." Behold, my stream became a river, and my river became a sea. ³² I will yet bring instruction to light as the morning, and will make these things clear from far away. ³³ I will continue to pour out teaching like prophecy, and leave it to all generations. ³⁴ See that I have not labored for myself only, but for all those who diligently seek wisdom.

25

¹ I enjoy three things, and they are beautiful before the Lord and men: the agreement of kindred, the friendship of neighbors, and a woman and her husband who walk together in agreement. ² But my soul hates three sorts of people, and I am greatly offended at their life: a poor man who is arrogant, a rich man who is a liar, and an old fool who is an adulterer. ³ If you gathered nothing in your youth, how could you find anything in your old age? ⁴ How beautiful a thing is judgment in the gray-haired, and for elders to know good counsel! ⁵ How beautiful is the wisdom of old men, and understanding and counsel to men who are in honor! ⁶ Much experience is the crown of the aged. Their glory is the fear of the Lord. ⁷ There are nine things that I have thought of, and in my heart counted happy, and the tenth I will utter with my tongue: a man who has joy with his children, and a man who lives and sees the fall of his enemies. ⁸ Happy is he who dwells with a wife of understanding, he who has not slipped with his tongue, and he who has not served a man who is unworthy of him. ⁹ Happy is he who has found prudence, and he who speaks in the ears of those who listen. ¹⁰ How great is he who has found wisdom! Yet is there none above him who fears the Lord. ¹¹ The fear of the Lord surpasses all things. To whom shall he who holds it be likened? ¹² ᵉ ¹³ Any wound but a wound of the heart! Any wickedness but the wickedness of a woman! ¹⁴ Any calamity but a calamity from those who hate me! Any vengeance but the vengeance of enemies! ¹⁵ There is no venom worse than a snake's venom. There is no wrath worse than an enemy's wrath. ¹⁶ I would rather dwell with a lion and a dragon than keep house with a wicked woman. ¹⁷ The wickedness of a woman changes her appearance, and darkens her countenance like that of a bear. ¹⁸ Her husband will sit among his neighbors, and when he hears it, he sighs bitterly. ¹⁹ All malice is small compared to the malice of a woman. Let the portion of a sinner fall on her. ²⁰ As walking up a sandy hill is to the feet of the aged, so is a wife full of words to a quiet man. ²¹ Don't be ensnared by a woman's beauty. Don't desire a woman for her beauty. ²² There is anger, impudence, and great reproach if a woman supports her husband. ²³ A wicked woman is abasement of heart, sadness of countenance, and a wounded heart. A woman who won't make her husband happy is like hands that hang down, and weak knees. ²⁴ The beginning of sin came from a woman. Because of her, we all die. ²⁵ Don't give water an outlet, and don't give a wicked woman freedom of speech. ²⁶ If she doesn't go as you direct, cut her away from your flesh.ᶠ

26

¹ Happy is the husband of a good wife. The number of his days will be doubled. ² A faithful wife gives joy to her husband. He will fulfill his years in peace. ³ A good wife is a great gift. She will be given to those who fear the Lord. ⁴ Whether a man is rich or poor, a good heart makes a cheerful face at all times. ⁵ Of three things my heart was afraid, and concerning the fourthᵍ kind I made supplication: The slander of a city, the assembly of a mob, and a false accusation. All these are more grievous than death. ⁶ A grief of heart and sorrow is a woman who is jealous of another woman. Her tongue-lashing makes it known to all. ⁷ A wicked woman is like a chafing yoke. He who takes hold of her is like one who grasps a scorpion. ⁸ A drunken woman causes great wrath. She will not cover her own shame. ⁹ The fornication of a woman is in the lifting up of her eyes; it will be known by her eyelids. ¹⁰ Keep strict watch on a headstrong daughter, lest she find liberty for herself, and use it. ¹¹ Watch out for an impudent eye, and don't be surprised if it sins against you. ¹² She will open her mouth like a thirsty traveller, and drink from every water that is near. She will sit down at every post, and open her quiver to any arrow. ¹³ The grace of a wife will delight

---

ᵃ *23:28* Verse **28** is omitted by the best authorities.
ᵇ *24:15* See Exodus **30:34**.
ᶜ *24:18* Verse **18** is omitted by the best authorities.
ᵈ *24:24* Verse **24** is omitted by the best authorities.
ᵉ *25:12* Verse **12** is omitted by the best authorities.
ᶠ *25:26* The remainder of this verse is omitted by the best authorities.
ᵍ *26:5* Gr. countenance.

her husband. Her knowledge will strengthen[a] his bones. [14] A silent woman is a gift of the Lord. There is nothing worth so much as a well-instructed soul. [15] A modest woman is grace upon grace. There are no scales that can weigh the value of a self-controlled soul. [16] As the sun when it arises in the highest places of the Lord, so is the beauty of a good wife in her well-organized home. [17] As the lamp that shines upon the holy lampstand, so is the beauty of the face on a well-proportioned body. [18] As the golden pillars are upon a base of silver, so are beautiful feet with the breasts of one who is steadfast. [19-27] [b] [28] For two things my heart is grieved, and for the third anger comes upon me: a warrior who suffers for poverty, men of understanding who are counted as garbage, and one who turns back from righteousness to sin– the Lord will prepare him for the sword! [29] It is difficult for a merchant to keep himself from wrong doing, and for a retailer to be acquitted of sin.

27

[1] Many have sinned for profit. He who seeks to multiply wealth will turn his eye away. [2] As a nail will stick fast between the joinings of stones, so sin will thrust itself in between buying and selling. [3] Unless a person holds on diligently to the fear of the Lord, his house will be overthrown quickly. [4] In the shaking of a sieve, the refuse remains, so does the filth of man in his thoughts. [5] The furnace tests the potter's vessels; so the test of a person is in his thoughts. [6] The fruit of a tree discloses its cultivation, so is the utterance of the thought of a person's heart. [7] Praise no man before you hear his thoughts, for this is how people are tested. [8] If you follow righteousness, you will obtain it, and put it on like a long robe of glory. [9] Birds will return to their own kind, so truth will return to those who practice it. [10] The lion lies in wait for prey. So does sin for those who do evil. [11] The discourse of a godly man is always wise, but the fool changes like the moon. [12] Limit your time among people void of understanding, but persevere among the thoughtful. [13] The talk of fools is offensive. Their laughter is wantonly sinful. [14] Their talk with much swearing makes hair stand upright. Their strife makes others plug their ears. [15] The strife of the proud leads to bloodshed. Their abuse of each other is a grievous thing to hear. [16] He who reveals secrets destroys trust, and will not find a close friend. [17] Love a friend, and keep faith with him; but if you reveal his secrets, you shall not follow him; [18] for as a man has destroyed his enemy, so you have destroyed the friendship of your neighbor. [19] As a bird which you have released out of your hand, so you have let your neighbor go, and you will not catch him again. [20] Don't pursue him, for he has gone far away, and has escaped like a gazelle out of the snare. [21] For a wound may be bound up, and after abuse there may be reconciliation; but he who reveals secrets is without hope. [22] One who winks the eye contrives evil things; and those who know him will keep their distance. [23] When you are present, he will speak sweetly, and will admire your words; but afterward he will twist his speech and set a trap in your words. [24] I have hated many things, but nothing like him. The Lord will hate him. [25] One who casts a stone straight up casts it on his own head. A deceitful blow opens wounds. [26] He who digs a pit will fall into it. He who sets a snare will be caught in it. [27] He who does evil things, they will roll back upon him, and he will not know where they came from. [28] Mockery and reproach are from the arrogant. Vengeance lies in wait for them like a lion. [29] Those who rejoice at the fall of the godly will be caught in a snare. Anguish will consume them before they die. [30] Wrath and anger, these also are abominations. A sinner will possess them.

28

[1] He who takes vengeance will find vengeance from the Lord, and he will surely make his sins firm. [2] Forgive your neighbor the hurt that he has done, and then your sins will be pardoned when you pray. [3] Does anyone harbor anger against another and expect healing from the Lord? [4] Upon a man like himself he has no mercy, and does he make supplication for his own sins? [5] He himself, being flesh, nourishes wrath. Who will make atonement for his sins? [6] Remember your last end, and stop enmity. Remember corruption and death, and be true to the commandments. [7] Remember the commandments, and don't be angry with your neighbor. Remember the covenant of the Highest, and overlook ignorance. [8] Abstain from strife, and you will diminish your sins, for a passionate man will kindle strife. [9] A man who is a sinner will trouble friends and sow discord among those who are at peace. [10] As is the fuel of the fire, so it will burn; and as the stoutness of the strife is, so it will burn. As is the strength of the man, so will be his wrath; and as is his wealth, so he will exalt his anger. [11] A contention begun in haste kindles a fire; and hasty fighting sheds blood. [12] If you blow on a spark, it will burn; and if you spit upon it, it will be quenched. Both of these come out of your mouth. [13] Curse the whisperer and double-tongued, for he has destroyed many who were at peace. [14] A slanderer has shaken many, and dispersed them from nation to nation. It has pulled down strong cities and overthrown the houses of great men. [15] A slanderer has cast out brave women and deprived them of their labors. [16] He who listens to it will not find rest, nor will he live quietly. [17] The stroke of a whip makes a mark in the flesh, but the stroke of a tongue will break bones. [18] Many have fallen by the edge of the sword, yet not so many as those who have fallen because of the tongue. [19] Happy is he who is sheltered from it, who has not passed through its wrath, who has not drawn its yoke, and has not been bound with its bands. [20] For its yoke is a yoke of iron, and its bands are bands of brass. [21] Its death is an evil death, and Hades is better than it. [22] It will not have rule over godly men. They will not be burned in its flame. [23] Those who forsake the Lord will fall into it. It will burn among them, and won't be quenched. It will be sent against them like a lion. It will destroy them like a leopard. [24] As you hedge your possession about with thorns, and secure your silver and your gold, [25] so make a balance and a weight for your words, and make a door and a bar for your mouth. [26] Take heed lest you slip with it, lest you fall before one who lies in wait.

29

[1] He who shows mercy will lend to his neighbor. He who strengthens him with his hand keeps the commandments. [2] Lend to your neighbor in time of his need. Repay your neighbor on time. [3] Confirm your word, and keep faith with him; and at all seasons you will find what you need. [4] Many have considered a loan to be a windfall, and have given trouble to those who helped them. [5] Until he has received, he will kiss a man's hands. For his neighbor's money he will speak submissively. Then when payment is due, he will prolong the time, return excuses, and complain about the season. [6] If he prevails, the creditor will hardly receive half; and he will count it as a windfall. If not, he has deprived him of his money, and he has gotten him for an enemy without cause. He will pay him with cursing and railing. Instead of honor, he will pay him disgrace. [7] Many on account of fraud have turned away. They are afraid of being defrauded for nothing. [8] However be patient with a man in poor estate. Don't keep him waiting for your alms. [9] Help a poor man for the commandment's sake. According to his need don't send him empty away. [10] Lose your money for a brother and a friend. Don't let it rust under a stone and be lost. [11] Allocate your treasure according to the commandments of the Most High and it will profit you more than gold. [12] Store up almsgiving in your store-chambers and it will deliver you out of all affliction. [13] It will fight for you against your enemy better than a mighty shield and a ponderous spear. [14] A good man will be surety for his neighbor. He who has lost shame will fail him. [15] Don't forget the kindness of your guarantor, for he has given his life for you. [16] A sinner will waste the property of his guarantor. [17] He who is thankless will fail him who delivered him. [18] Being surety has undone many who were prospering and shaken them as a wave of the sea. It has driven mighty men from their homes. They wandered among foreign nations. [19] A sinner who falls into suretiship and undertakes contracts for work will fall into lawsuits. [20] Help your neighbor according to your power, and be careful not to fall yourself. [21] The essentials of life are water, bread, a garment, and a house for privacy. [22] Better is the life of a poor man under a shelter of logs than sumptuous fare in another man's house. [23] With little or with much, be well satisfied.[c] [24] It is a miserable life to go from house to house. Where you are a guest, you dare not open your mouth. [25] You will entertain, serve drinks, and have no thanks. In addition to this, you will hear bitter words. [26] "Come here, you sojourner, set a table, and if you have anything in your hand, feed me with it." [27] "Leave, you sojourner, for an honored guest is here. My brother has come to be my guest. I need my house." [28] These things are grievous to a man of understanding: The scolding about lodging and the insults of creditors.

30

[1] He who loves his son will continue to lay stripes upon him, that he may have joy from him in the end. [2] He who chastises his son will have profit from him, and will brag about him among his acquaintances. [3] He who teaches his son will provoke his enemy to jealousy. Before friends, he will rejoice in him. [4] His father dies, and is as though he had not died; for he has left one behind him like himself. [5] In his life, he saw his son and rejoiced. When he died, it was without regret. [6] He left behind him an avenger against his enemies, and one to repay kindness to his friends. [7] He who makes too much of his son will bind up his wounds. His heart will be troubled at every cry. [8] An unbroken horse becomes stubborn. An unrestrained son becomes

---

[a] *26:13* or, fatten
[b] *26:19-27* Verses **19- 27** are omitted by the best authorities.
[c] *29:23* The remainder of this verse is omitted by the best authorities.

headstrong. ⁹ Pamper your child, and he will make you afraid. Play with him, and he will grieve you. ¹⁰ Don't laugh with him, lest you have sorrow with him, and you gnash your teeth in the end. ¹¹ Give him no liberty in his youth, and don't ignore his follies.[a] ¹² [b]Bow down his neck in his youth, and beat him on the sides while he is a child, lest he become stubborn, and be disobedient to you, and there be sorrow to your soul.[c] ¹³ Chastise your son, and give him work, lest his shameless behavior be an offense to you. ¹⁴ Better is a poor man who is healthy and fit, than a rich man who is afflicted in his body. ¹⁵ Health and fitness are better than all gold, and a strong body better than wealth without measure. ¹⁶ There is no wealth better than health of body. There is no gladness above the joy of the heart. ¹⁷ Death is better than a bitter life, and eternal rest than a continual sickness. ¹⁸ Good things poured out upon a mouth that is closed are like food offerings laid upon a grave. ¹⁹ What does an offering profit an idol? For it can't eat or smell. So is he who is punished by the Lord, ²⁰ seeing with his eyes and groaning, like a eunuch embracing a virgin and groaning. ²¹ Don't give your soul to sorrow. Don't afflict yourself deliberately. ²² Gladness of heart is the life of a man. Cheerfulness of a man lengthens his days. ²³ Love your own soul, and comfort your heart. Remove sorrow far from you, for sorrow has destroyed many, and there is no profit in it. ²⁴ Envy and wrath shorten life. Anxiety brings old age before its time. ²⁵ Those who are cheerful and merry will benefit from their food.

31

¹ Wakefulness that comes from riches consumes the flesh, and anxiety about it takes away sleep. ² Wakeful anxiety will crave slumber. In a severe disease, sleep will be broken. ³ A rich man toils in gathering money together. When he rests, he is filled with his good things. ⁴ A poor man toils in lack of substance. When he rests, he becomes needy. ⁵ He who loves gold won't be justified. He who follows destruction will himself have his fill of it. ⁶ Many have been given over to ruin for the sake of gold. Their destruction meets them face to face. ⁷ It is a stumbling block to those who sacrifice to it. Every fool will be taken by it. ⁸ Blessed is the rich person who is found blameless, and who doesn't go after gold. ⁹ Who is he, that we may call him blessed? For he has done wonderful things among his people. ¹⁰ Who has been tried by it, and found perfect? Then let him boast. Who has had the power to transgress, and has not transgressed? And to do evil, and has not done it? ¹¹ His prosperity will be made sure. The congregation will proclaim his alms. ¹² Do you sit at a great table? Don't be greedy there. Don't say, "There is a lot of food on it!" ¹³ Remember that a greedy eye is a wicked thing. What has been created more greedy than an eye? Therefore it sheds tears from every face. ¹⁴ Don't stretch your hand wherever it looks. Don't thrust yourself with it into the dish. ¹⁵ Consider your neighbor's feelings by your own. Be discreet in every point. ¹⁶ Eat like a human being those things which are set before you. Don't eat greedily, lest you be hated. ¹⁷ Be first to stop for manners' sake. Don't be insatiable, lest you offend. ¹⁸ And if you sit among many, Don't reach out your hand before them. ¹⁹ How sufficient to a well-mannered man is a very little. He doesn't breathe heavily in his bed. ²⁰ Healthy sleep comes from moderate eating. He rises early, and his wits are with him. The pain of wakefulness, colic, and griping are with an insatiable man. ²¹ And if you have been forced to eat, rise up in the middle of it, and you shall have rest. ²² Hear me, my son, and don't despise me, and in the end you will appreciate my words. In all your works be skillful, and no disease will come to you. ²³ People bless him who is liberal with his food. The testimony of his excellence will be believed. ²⁴ The city will murmur at him who is a stingy with his food. The testimony of his stinginess will be accurate. ²⁵ Don't show yourself valiant in wine, for wine has destroyed many. ²⁶ The furnace tests the temper of steel by dipping; so does wine test hearts in the quarreling of the proud. ²⁷ Wine is as good as life to men, if you drink it in moderation. What life is there to a man who is without wine? It has been created to make men glad. ²⁸ Wine drunk in season and in moderation is joy of heart and gladness of soul: ²⁹ Wine drunk excessively is bitterness of soul, with provocation and conflict. ³⁰ Drunkenness increases the rage of a fool to his hurt. It diminishes strength and adds wounds. ³¹ Don't rebuke your neighbor at a banquet of wine. Don't despise him in his mirth. Don't speak a word of reproach to him. Don't distress him by making demands of him.

32

¹ Have they made you ruler of a feast? Don't be lifted up. Be among them as one of them. Take care of them first, and then sit down. ² And when you have done all your duties, take your place, that you may be gladdened on their account, and receive a wreath for your good service. ³ Speak, you who are older, for it's your right, but with sound knowledge; and don't interrupt the music. ⁴ Don't pour out talk where there is a performance of music. Don't display your wisdom at the wrong time. ⁵ As a ruby signet in a setting of gold, so is a music concert at a wine banquet. ⁶ As an emerald signet in a work of gold, so is musical melody with pleasant wine. ⁷ Speak, young man, if you are obliged to, but no more than twice, and only if asked. ⁸ Sum up your speech, many things in few words. Be as one who knows and yet holds his tongue. ⁹ When among great men, don't behave as their equal. When another is speaking, don't babble. ¹⁰ Lightning speeds before thunder. Approval goes before one who is modest. ¹¹ Rise up in good time, and don't be last. Go home quickly and don't loiter ¹² Amuse yourself there and do what is in your heart. Don't sin by proud speech. ¹³ For these things bless your Maker, who gives you to drink freely of his good things. ¹⁴ He who fears the Lord will receive discipline. Those who seek him early will find favor. ¹⁵ He who seeks the law shall be filled with it, but the hypocrite will stumble at it. ¹⁶ Those who fear the Lord will find true judgment, and will kindle righteous acts like a light. ¹⁷ A sinful man shuns reproof, and will find a judgment according to his will. ¹⁸ A sensible person won't neglect a thought. An insolent and proud man won't crouch in fear, even after he has done a thing by himself without counsel. ¹⁹ Do nothing without counsel, but when you have acted, don't regret it. ²⁰ Don't go in a way of conflict. Don't stumble in stony places. ²¹ Don't be overconfident on a smooth road. ²² Beware of your own children. ²³ In every work guard your own soul, for this is the keeping of the commandments. ²⁴ He who believes the law gives heed to the commandment. He who trusts in the Lord will suffer no loss.

33

¹ No evil will happen to him who fears the Lord, but in trials once and again he will deliver him. ² A wise man will not hate the law, but he who is a hypocrite about it is like a boat in a storm. ³ A man of understanding will put his trust in the law. And the law is faithful to him, as when one asks a divine oracle. ⁴ Prepare your speech, and so you will be heard. Bind up instruction, and make your answer. ⁵ The heart of a fool is like a cartwheel. His thoughts are like a rolling axle. ⁶ A stallion horse is like a mocking friend. He neighs under every one who sits upon him. ⁷ Why does one day excel another, when all the light of every day in the year is from the sun? ⁸ They were distinguished by the Lord's knowledge, and he varied seasons and feasts. ⁹ Some of them he exalted and hallowed, and some of them he has made ordinary days. ¹⁰ And all men are from the ground. Adam was created from dust. ¹¹ In the abundance of his knowledge the Lord distinguished them, and made their ways different. ¹² Some of them he blessed and exalted, and some of them he made holy and brought near to himself. Some of them he cursed and brought low, and overthrew them from their place. ¹³ As the clay of the potter in his hand, all his ways are according to his good pleasure, so men are in the hand of him who made them, to render to them according to his judgment. ¹⁴ Good is the opposite of evil, and life is the opposite of death; so[d] the sinner is the opposite of the godly. ¹⁵ Look upon all the works of the Most High like this, they come in pairs, one against another. ¹⁶ I was the last on watch, like one who gleans after the grape gatherers. ¹⁷ By the Lord's blessing I arrived before them, and filled my winepress like one who gathers grapes. ¹⁸ Consider that I labored not for myself alone, but for all those who seek instruction. ¹⁹ Hear me, you great men of the people, and listen with your ears, you rulers of the congregation. ²⁰ To son and wife, to brother and friend, don't give power over yourself while you live, and don't give your goods to another, lest you regret it and must ask for them. ²¹ While you still live and breath is in you, don't give yourself over to anybody. ²² For it is better that your children should ask from you than that you should look to the hand of your children. ²³ Excel in all your works. Don't bring a stain on your honor. ²⁴ In the day that you end the days of your life, in the time of death, distribute your inheritance. ²⁵ Fodder, a stick, and burdens are for a donkey. Bread, discipline, and work are for a servant. ²⁶ Set your slave to work, and you will find rest. Leave his hands idle, and he will seek liberty. ²⁷ Yoke and whip will bow the neck. For an evil slave there are racks and tortures. ²⁸ Send him to labor, that he not be idle, for idleness teaches much mischief. ²⁹ Set him to work, as is fit for him. If he doesn't obey, make his fetters heavy. ³⁰ Don't be excessive toward any. Do nothing unjust. ³¹ If you have a slave, treat him like yourself, because you have bought him with blood. ³² If you have a slave, treat him like yourself. For like your own soul, you will need him. If you treat him ill, and he departs and runs away, ³³ which way will you go to seek him?

---

[a] *30:11* This line and the previous two lines are absent from some older MSS.

[b] *30:12* These three lines are absent from the oldest MSS.

[c] *30:12* These three lines are absent from the oldest MSS.

[d] *33:14* A line of this verse is here omitted by the best authorities.

34

¹ Vain and false hopes are for a man void of understanding. Dreams give wings to fools. ² As one who grasps at a shadow and follows after the wind, so is he who sets his mind on dreams. ³ The vision of dreams is a reflection, the likeness of a face near a face. ⁴ From an unclean thing what can be cleansed? From that which is false what can be true? ⁵ Divinations, and soothsayings, and dreams, are vain. The heart has fantasies like a woman in labor. ⁶ If they are not sent in a visitation from the Most High, don't give your heart to them. ⁷ For dreams have led many astray. They have failed by putting their hope in them. ⁸ Without lying the law will be fulfilled. Wisdom is complete in a faithful mouth. ⁹ A well-instructed man knows many things. He who has much experience will declare understanding. ¹⁰ He who has no experience knows few things. But he who has traveled increases cleverness. ¹¹ I have seen many things in my travels. My understanding is more than my words. ¹² I was often in danger even to death. I was preserved because of these experiences. ¹³ The spirit of those who fear the Lord will live, for their hope is in him who saves them. ¹⁴ Whoever fears the Lord won't be afraid, and won't be a coward, for he is his hope. ¹⁵ Blessed is the soul of him who fears the Lord. To whom does he give heed? Who is his support? ¹⁶ The eyes of the Lord are on those who love him, a mighty protection and strong support, a cover from the hot blast, a shade from the noonday sun, a guard from stumbling, and a help from falling. ¹⁷ He raises up the soul, and enlightens the eyes. He gives health, life, and blessing. ¹⁸ He who sacrifices a thing wrongfully gotten, his offering is made in mockery. The mockeries of wicked men are not acceptable. ¹⁹ The Most High has no pleasure in the offerings of the ungodly, Neither is he pacified for sins by the multitude of sacrifices. ²⁰ Like one who kills a son before his father's eyes is he who brings a sacrifice from the goods of the poor. ²¹ The bread of the needy is the life of the poor. He who deprives him of it is a man of blood. ²² Like one who murders his neighbor is he who takes away his living. Like a shedder of blood is he who deprives a hireling of his hire. ²³ When one builds, and another pulls down, what profit do they have but toil? ²⁴ When one prays, and another curses, whose voice will the Lord listen to? ²⁵ He who washes himself after touching a dead body, and touches it again, what does he gain by his washing? ²⁶ Even so a man fasting for his sins, and going again, and doing the same, who will listen to his prayer? What profit does he have in his humiliation?

35

¹ He who keeps the law multiplies offerings. He who heeds the commandments sacrifices a peace offering. ² He who returns a kindness offers fine flour. He who gives alms sacrifices a thank offering. ³ To depart from wickedness pleases the Lord. To depart from unrighteousness is an atoning sacrifice. ⁴ See that you don't appear in the presence of the Lord empty. ⁵ For all these things are done because of the commandment. ⁶ The offering of the righteous enriches the altar. The sweet fragrance of it is before the Most High. ⁷ The sacrifice of a righteous man is acceptable. It won't be forgotten. ⁸ Glorify the Lord with generosity. Don't reduce the first fruits of your hands. ⁹ In every gift show a cheerful countenance, And dedicate your tithe with gladness. ¹⁰ Give to the Most High according as he has given. As your hand has found, give generously. ¹¹ For the Lord repays, and he will repay you sevenfold. ¹² Don't plan to bribe him with gifts, for he will not receive them. Don't set your mind on an unrighteous sacrifice, For the Lord is the judge, and with him is no respect of persons. ¹³ He won't accept any person against a poor man. He will listen to the prayer of him who is wronged. ¹⁴ He will in no way despise the supplication of the fatherless or the widow, when she pours out her tale. ¹⁵ Don't the tears of the widow run down her cheek? Isn't her cry against him who has caused them to fall? ¹⁶ He who serves God according to his good pleasure will be accepted. His supplication will reach to the clouds. ¹⁷ The prayer of the humble pierces the clouds. until it comes near, he will not be comforted. He won't depart until the Most High visits and he judges righteously and executes judgment. ¹⁸ And the Lord will not be slack, neither will he be patient toward them, until he has crushed the loins of the unmerciful. He will repay vengeance on the heathen until he has taken away the multitude of the arrogant and broken in pieces the sceptres of the unrighteous, ¹⁹ until he has rendered to every man according to his deeds, and repaid the works of men according to their plans, until he has judged the cause of his people, and he will make them rejoice in his mercy. ²⁰ Mercy is as welcome in the time of his affliction, as clouds of rain in the time of drought.

36

¹ Have mercy upon us, O Lord the God of all, and look at us with favor; ² and send your fear upon all the nations.[a] ³ Lift up your hand against the foreign nations and let them see your mighty power. ⁴ As you showed your holiness in us before them, so be magnified in them before us. ⁵ Let them know you, as we also have known you, that there is no God but only you, O God. ⁶ Show new signs, and work various wonders. Glorify your hand and your right arm.[b] ⁷ Raise up indignation and pour out wrath. Take away the adversary and destroy the enemy. ⁸ Hasten the time and remember your oath. Let them declare your mighty works. ⁹ Let him who escapes be devoured by raging fire. May those who harm your people find destruction. ¹⁰ Crush the heads of the rulers of the enemies who say, "There is no one but ourselves." ¹¹ Gather all the tribes of Jacob together, and[c] take them for your inheritance, as from the beginning. ¹² O Lord, have mercy upon the people that is called by your name, and upon Israel, whom you likened to a firstborn. ¹³ Have compassion upon the city of your sanctuary, Jerusalem, the place of your rest. ¹⁴ Fill Zion. Exalt your oracles and fill your people with your glory. ¹⁵ Give testimony to those who were your creatures in the beginning, and fulfill the prophecies that have been spoken in your name. ¹⁶ Reward those who wait for you, and men will put their trust in your prophets. ¹⁷ Listen, O Lord, to the prayer of your servants, according to the blessing of Aaron concerning your people; and all those who are on the earth will know that you are the Lord, the[d] eternal God. ¹⁸ The belly will eat any food, but one food is better than another. ¹⁹ The mouth tastes meats taken in hunting, so does an understanding heart detect false speech. ²⁰ A contrary heart will cause heaviness. A man of experience will pay him back. ²¹ A woman will receive any man, but one daughter is better than another. ²² The beauty of a woman cheers the countenance. A man desires nothing more. ²³ If kindness and humility are on her tongue, her husband is not like other sons of men. ²⁴ He who gets a wife gets his richest treasure, a help meet for him and a pillar of support. ²⁵ Where no hedge is, the property will be plundered. He who has no wife will mourn as he wanders. ²⁶ For who would trust a nimble robber who skips from city to city? Even so, who would trust a man who has no nest, and lodges wherever he finds himself at nightfall?

37

¹ Every friend will say, "I also am his friend"; but there is a friend which is only a friend in name. ² Isn't there a grief in it even to death when a companion and friend is turned into an enemy? ³ O wicked imagination, why were you formed to cover the dry land with deceit? ⁴ There is a companion who rejoices in the gladness of a friend, but in time of affliction will be against him. ⁵ There is a companion who for the belly's sake labors with his friend, yet in the face of battle will carry his buckler. ⁶ Don't forget a friend in your soul. Don't be unmindful of him in your riches. ⁷ Every counselor extols counsel, but some give counsel in their own interest. ⁸ Let your soul beware of a counselor, and know in advance what is his interest (for he will take counsel for himself), lest he cast the lot against you, ⁹ and say to you, "Your way is good." Then he will stand near you, to see what will happen to you. ¹⁰ Don't take counsel with one who looks askance at you. Hide your counsel from those who are jealous of you. ¹¹ Don't consult with a woman about her rival, with a coward about war, with a merchant about business, with a buyer about selling, with an envious man about thankfulness, with an unmerciful man about kindliness, with a sluggard about any kind of work, with a hireling in your house about finishing his work, or with an idle servant about much business. Pay no attention to these in any matter of counsel. ¹² But rather be continually with a godly man, whom you know to be a keeper of the commandments, who in his soul is as your own soul, and who will grieve with you, if you fail. ¹³ Make the counsel of your heart stand, for there is no one more faithful to you than it. ¹⁴ For a man's soul is sometimes inclined to inform him better than seven watchmen who sit on high on a watch-tower. ¹⁵ Above all this ask the Most High that he may direct your way in truth. ¹⁶ Let reason be the beginning of every work. Let counsel go before every action. ¹⁷ As a token of the changing of the heart, ¹⁸ four kinds of things rise up: good and evil, life and death. That which rules over them continually is the tongue. ¹⁹ There is one who is clever and the instructor of many, and yet is unprofitable to his own soul. ²⁰ There is one who is subtle in words, and is hated. He will be destitute of all food. ²¹ For grace was not given to him from the Lord, because he is deprived of all wisdom. ²² There is one who is wise to his own soul; and the fruits of his understanding are trustworthy in the mouth. ²³ A wise man will instruct his own people. The fruits of his understanding are trustworthy. ²⁴

---

[a] *36:2* The remainder of this verse is omitted by the best authorities.

[b] *36:6* The remainder of this verse is omitted by the best authorities.

[c] *36:11* The ancient authorities read I took them for my inheritance: but the Greek text is here very confused.

[d] *36:17* Gr. God of the ages.

A wise man will be filled with blessing. All those who see him will call him happy. ²⁵ The life of a man is counted by days. The days of Israel are innumerable. ²⁶ The wise man will inherit confidence among his people. His name will live forever. ²⁷ My son, test your soul in your life. See what is evil for it, and don't give in to it. ²⁸ For not all things are profitable for all men. Not every soul has pleasure in everything. ²⁹ Don't be insatiable in any luxury. Don't be greedy in the things that you eat. ³⁰ For overeating brings disease, and gluttony causes nausea. ³¹ Because of gluttony, many have perished, but he who takes heed shall prolong his life.

38

¹ Honor a physician according to your need with the honors due to him, for truly the Lord has created him. ² For healing comes from the Most High, and he shall receive a gift from the king. ³ The skill of the physician will lift up his head. He will be admired in the sight of great men. ⁴ The Lord created medicines out of the earth. A prudent man will not despise them. ⁵ Wasn't water made sweet with wood, that its power might be known? ⁶ He gave men skill that he might be glorified in his marvelous works. ⁷ With them he heals and takes away pain. ⁸ With these, the pharmacist makes a mixture. God's works won't be brought to an end. From him, peace is upon the face of the earth. ⁹ My son, in your sickness don't be negligent, but pray to the Lord, and he will heal you. ¹⁰ Put away wrong doing, and direct your hands in righteousness. Cleanse your heart from all sin. ¹¹ Give a sweet savor and a memorial of fine flour, and pour oil on your offering, according to your means. ¹² Then give place to the physician, for truly the Lord has created him. Don't let him leave you, for you need him. ¹³ There is a time when in recovery is in their hands. ¹⁴ For they also shall ask the Lord to prosper them in diagnosis and in healing for the maintenance of life. ¹⁵ He who sins before his Maker, let him fall into the hands of the physician. ¹⁶ My son, let your tears fall over the dead, and as one who suffers grievously, begin lamentation. Wind up his body with due honor. Don't neglect his burial. ¹⁷ Make bitter weeping and make passionate wailing. Let your mourning be according to his merit, for one day or two, lest you be spoken evil of; and so be comforted for your sorrow. ¹⁸ For from sorrow comes death. Sorrow of heart saps one's strength. ¹⁹ In calamity, sorrow also remains. A poor man's life is grievous to the heart. ²⁰ Don't give your heart to sorrow. Put it away, remembering the end. ²¹ Don't forget it, for there is no returning again. You do him no good, and you would harm yourself. ²² Remember his end, for so also will yours be: yesterday for me, and today for you. ²³ When the dead is at rest, let his remembrance rest. Be comforted for him when his spirit departs from him. ²⁴ The wisdom of the scribe comes by the opportunity of leisure. He who has little business can become wise. ²⁵ How could he become wise who holds the plow, who glories in the shaft of the goad, who drives oxen and is occupied in their labors, and who mostly talks about bulls? ²⁶ He will set his heart upon turning his furrows. His lack of sleep is to give his heifers their fodder. ²⁷ So is every craftsman and master artisan who passes his time by night as by day, those who cut engravings of signets. His diligence is to make great variety. He sets his heart to preserve likeness in his portraiture, and is careful to finish his work. ²⁸ So too is the smith sitting by the anvil and considering the unwrought iron. The smoke of the fire will waste his flesh. He toils in the heat of the furnace. The noise of the hammer deafens his ear. His eyes are upon the pattern of the object. He will set his heart upon perfecting his works. He will be careful to adorn them perfectly. ²⁹ So is the potter sitting at his work and turning the wheel around with his feet, who is always anxiously set at his work. He produces his handiwork in quantity. ³⁰ He will fashion the clay with his arm and will bend its strength in front of his feet. He will apply his heart to finish the glazing. He will be careful to clean the kiln. ³¹ All these put their trust in their hands. Each becomes skillful in his own work. ³² Without these no city would be inhabited. Men wouldn't reside as foreigners or walk up and down there. ³³ They won't be sought for in the council of the people. They won't mount on high in the assembly. They won't sit on the seat of the judge. They won't understand the covenant of judgment. Neither will they declare instruction and judgment. They won't be found where parables are. ³⁴ But they will maintain the fabric of the age. Their prayer is in the handiwork of their craft.

39

¹ Not so he who has applied his soul and meditates in the law of the Most High. He will seek out the wisdom of all the ancients and will be occupied with prophecies. ² He will keep the sayings of the men of renown and will enter in amidst the subtleties of parables. ³ He will seek out the hidden meaning of proverbs and be conversant in the dark sayings of parables. ⁴ He will serve among great men and appear before him who rules. He will travel through the land of foreign nations, for he has learned what is good and evil among men. ⁵ He will apply his heart to return early to the Lord who made him, and will make supplication before the Most High, and will open his mouth in prayer, and will ask for pardon for his sins. ⁶ If the great Lord wills, he will be filled with the spirit of understanding; he will pour forth the words of his wisdom and in prayer give thanks to the Lord. ⁷ He will direct his counsel and knowledge, and he will meditate in his secrets. ⁸ He will show the instruction which he has been taught and will glory in the law of the covenant of the Lord. ⁹ Many will commend his understanding. So long as the world endures, it won't be blotted out. His memory won't depart. His name will live from generation to generation. ¹⁰ Nations will declare his wisdom. The congregation will proclaim his praise. ¹¹ If he continues, he will leave a greater name than a thousand. If he finally rests, it is enough for him. ¹² Yet more I will utter, which I have thought about. I am filled like the full moon. ¹³ Listen to me, you holy children, and bud forth like a rose growing by a brook of water. ¹⁴ Give a sweet fragrance like frankincense. Put forth flowers like a lily. Scatter a sweet smell and sing a song of praise. Bless the Lord for all his works! ¹⁵ Magnify his name and give utterance to his praise with the songs on your lips and with harps! Say this when you utter his praise: ¹⁶ All the works of the Lord are exceedingly good, and every command will be done in its time. ¹⁷ No one can say, "What is this?" "Why is that?" for at the proper time they will all be sought out. At his word, the waters stood as a heap, as did the reservoirs of water at the word of his mouth. ¹⁸ At his command all his good pleasure is fulfilled. There is no one who can hinder his salvation. ¹⁹ The works of all flesh are before him. It's impossible to be hidden from his eyes. ²⁰ He sees from everlasting to everlasting. There is nothing too wonderful for him. ²¹ No one can say, "What is this?" "Why is that?" for all things are created for their own uses. ²² His blessing covered the dry land as a river and saturated it as a flood. ²³ As he has made the waters salty, so the heathen will inherit his wrath. ²⁴ His ways are plain to the holy. They are stumbling blocks to the wicked. ²⁵ Good things are created from the beginning for the good. So are evil things for sinners. ²⁶ The main things necessary for the life of man are water, fire, iron, salt, wheat flour, and honey, milk, the blood of the grape, oil, and clothing. ²⁷ All these things are for good to the godly, but for sinners, they will be turned into evils. ²⁸ There are winds that are created for vengeance, and in their fury they lay on their scourges heavily. In the time of reckoning, they pour out their strength, and will appease the wrath of him who made them. ²⁹ Fire, hail, famine, and death– all these are created for vengeance– ³⁰ wild beasts' teeth, scorpions, adders, and a sword punishing the ungodly to destruction. ³¹ They will rejoice in his commandment, and will be made ready upon earth when needed. In their seasons, they won't disobey his command. ³² Therefore from the beginning I was convinced, and I thought it through and left it in writing: ³³ All the works of the Lord are good. He will supply every need in its time. ³⁴ No one can say, "This is worse than that," for they will all be well approved in their time. ³⁵ Now with all your hearts and voices, sing praises and bless the Lord's name!

40

¹ Great travail is created for every man. A heavy yoke is upon the sons of Adam, from the day of their coming forth from their mother's womb, until the day for their burial in the mother of all things. ² The expectation of things to come, and the day of death, trouble their thoughts, and cause fear in their hearts. ³ From him who sits on a throne of glory, even to him who is humbled in earth and ashes, ⁴ from him who wears purple and a crown, even to him who is clothed in burlap, ⁵ there is wrath, jealousy, trouble, unrest, fear of death, anger, and strife. In the time of rest upon his bed, his night sleep changes his knowledge. ⁶ He gets little or no rest, and afterward in his sleep, as in a day of keeping watch, he is troubled in the vision of his heart, as one who has escaped from the front of battle. ⁷ In the very time of his deliverance, he awakens, and marvels that the fear is nothing. ⁸ To all creatures, human and animal, and upon sinners sevenfold more, ⁹ come death, bloodshed, strife, sword, calamities, famine, suffering, and plague. ¹⁰ All these things were created for the wicked, and because of them the flood came. ¹¹ All things that are of the earth turn to the earth again. All things that are of the waters return into the sea. ¹² All bribery and injustice will be blotted out. Good faith will stand forever. ¹³ The goods of the unjust will be dried up like a river, and like a great thunder in rain will go off in noise. ¹⁴ In opening his hands, a man will be made glad; so lawbreakers will utterly fail. ¹⁵ The children of the ungodly won't grow many branches, and are as unhealthy roots on a sheer rock. ¹⁶ The reeds by every water or river bank will be plucked up before all grass. ¹⁷ Kindness is like a garden of blessings. Almsgiving endures forever. ¹⁸ The life of one who labors and is content will be made sweet. He who finds a treasure is better than both. ¹⁹ Children and the building of a city establish a name. A blameless wife is better than both. ²⁰ Wine and music rejoice the heart. The love of wisdom is better than both. ²¹ The pipe and the lute make pleasant melody. A pleasant tongue is better than both. ²² Your eye desires grace and beauty,

but the green shoots of grain more than both. ²³ A friend and a companion is always welcome, and a wife with her husband is better than both. ²⁴ Relatives and helpers are for a time of affliction, but almsgiving rescues better than both. ²⁵ Gold and silver will make the foot stand sure, and counsel is esteemed better than both. ²⁶ Riches and strength will lift up the heart. The fear of the Lord is better than both. There is nothing lacking in the fear of the Lord. In it, there is no need to seek help. ²⁷ The fear of the Lord is like a garden of blessing and covers a man more than any glory. ²⁸ My son, don't lead a beggar's life. It is better to die than to beg. ²⁹ A man who looks to the table of another, his life is not to be considered a life. He will pollute his soul with another person's food, but a wise and well-instructed person will beware of that. ³⁰ Begging will be sweet in the mouth of the shameless, but it kindles a fire in his belly.

41

¹ O death, how bitter is the memory of you to a man who is at peace in his possessions, to the man who has nothing to distract him and has prosperity in all things, and who still has strength to enjoy food! ² O death, your sentence is acceptable to a man who is needy and who fails in strength, who is in extreme old age, is distracted about all things, is perverse, and has lost patience! ³ Don't be afraid of the sentence of death. Remember those who have been before you and who come after. This is the sentence from the Lord over all flesh. ⁴ And why do you refuse when it is the good pleasure of the Most High? Whether life lasts ten, or a hundred, or a thousand years, there is no inquiry about life in Hades.[a] ⁵ The children of sinners are abominable children and they frequent the dwellings of the ungodly. ⁶ The inheritance of sinners' children will perish and with their posterity will be a perpetual disgrace. ⁷ Children will complain of an ungodly father, because they suffer disgrace because of him. ⁸ Woe to you, ungodly men, who have forsaken the law of the Most High God![b] ⁹ If you are born, you will be born to a curse. If you die, a curse will be your portion. ¹⁰ All things that are of the earth will go back to the earth; so the ungodly will go from a curse to perdition. ¹¹ The mourning of men is about their bodies; but the evil name of sinners will be blotted out. ¹² Have regard for your name, for it continues with you longer than a thousand great treasures of gold. ¹³ A good life has its number of days, but a good name continues forever. ¹⁴ My children, follow instruction in peace. But wisdom that is hidden and a treasure that is not seen, what benefit is in them both? ¹⁵ Better is a man who hides his foolishness than a man who hides his wisdom. ¹⁶ Therefore show respect for my words; for it is not good to retain every kind of shame. Not everything is approved by all in good faith. ¹⁷ Be ashamed of sexual immorality before father and mother, of a lie before a prince and a mighty man, ¹⁸ of an offense before a judge and ruler, of iniquity before the congregation and the people, of unjust dealing before a partner and friend, ¹⁹ and of theft in the place where you sojourn. Be ashamed in regard of the truth of God and his covenant, of leaning on your elbow at dinner, of contemptuous behavior in the matter of giving and taking, ²⁰ of silence before those who greet you, of looking at a woman who is a prostitute, ²¹ of turning away your face from a kinsman, of taking away a portion or a gift, of gazing at a woman who has a husband, ²² of meddling with his maid–and don't come near her bed, of abusive speech to friends–and after you have given, don't insult, ²³ of repeating and speaking what you have heard, and of revealing of secrets. ²⁴ So you will be ashamed of the right things and find favor in the sight of every man.

42

¹ Don't be ashamed of these things, and don't sin to save face: ² of the law of the Most High and his covenant, of judgment to do justice to the ungodly, ³ of reckoning with a partner and with travellers, of a gift from the inheritance of friends, ⁴ of exactness of scales and weights, of getting much or little, ⁵ of bargaining dealing with merchants, of frequent correction of children, and of making the back of an evil slave to bleed. ⁶ A seal is good where an evil wife is. Where there are many hands, lock things up. ⁷ Whatever you hand over, let it be by number and weight. In giving and receiving, let all be in writing. ⁸ Don't be ashamed to instruct the unwise and foolish, and one of extreme old age who contends with those who are young. So you will be well instructed indeed and approved in the sight of every living man. ⁹ A daughter is a secret cause of wakefulness to a father. Care for her takes away sleep– in her youth, lest she pass the flower of her age; when she is married, lest she should be hated; ¹⁰ in her virginity, lest she should be defiled and be with child in her father's house; when she has a husband, lest she should transgress; and when she is married, lest she should be barren. ¹¹ Keep a strict watch over a headstrong daughter, lest she make you a laughingstock to your enemies, a byword in the city and notorious among the people, and shame you in public. ¹² Don't gaze at every beautiful body. Don't sit in the midst of women. ¹³ For from garments comes a moth, and from a woman comes a woman's wickedness. ¹⁴ Better is the wickedness of a man than a pleasant woman, a woman who puts you to shame and disgrace. ¹⁵ I will make mention now of the works of the Lord, and will declare the things that I have seen. The Lord's works are in his words. ¹⁶ The sun that gives light looks at all things. The Lord's work is full of his glory. ¹⁷ The Lord has not given power to the saints to declare all his marvelous works, which the Almighty Lord firmly settled, that the universe might be established in his glory. ¹⁸ He searches out the deep and the heart. He has understanding of their secrets. For the Most High knows all knowledge. He sees the signs of the world. ¹⁹ He declares the things that are past and the things that shall be, and reveals the traces of hidden things. ²⁰ No thought escapes him. There is not a word hidden from him. ²¹ He has ordered the mighty works of his wisdom. He is from everlasting to everlasting. Nothing has been added to them, nor diminished from them. He had no need of any counselor. ²² How desirable are all his works! One may see this even in a spark. ²³ All these things live and remain forever in all manner of uses. They are all obedient. ²⁴ All things are in pairs, one opposite the other. He has made nothing imperfect. ²⁵ One thing establishes the good things of another. Who could ever see enough of his glory?

43

¹ The pride of the heavenly heights is the clear sky, the appearance of heaven, in the spectacle of its glory. ² The sun, when it appears, bringing tidings as it rises, is a marvelous instrument, the work of the Most High. ³ At noon, it dries up the land. Who can stand against its burning heat? ⁴ A man tending a furnace is in burning heat, but the sun three times more, burning up the mountains, breathing out fiery vapors, and sending out bright beams, it blinds the eyes. ⁵ Great is the Lord who made it. At his word, he hastens on its course. ⁶ The moon marks the changing seasons, declares times, and is a sign for the world. ⁷ From the moon is the sign of feast days, a light that wanes when it completes its course. ⁸ The month is called after its name, increasing wonderfully in its changing– an instrument of the army on high, shining in the structure of heaven, ⁹ the beauty of heaven, the glory of the stars, an ornament giving light in the highest places of the Lord. ¹⁰ At the word of the Holy One, they will stand in due order. They won't faint in their watches. ¹¹ Look at the rainbow, and praise him who made it. It is exceedingly beautiful in its brightness. ¹² It encircles the sky with its glorious circle. The hands of the Most High have stretched it out. ¹³ By his commandment, he makes the snow fall and swiftly sends the lightnings of his judgment. ¹⁴ Therefore the storehouses are opened, and clouds fly out like birds. ¹⁵ By his mighty power, he makes the clouds strong and the hailstones are broken in pieces. ¹⁶ At his appearing, the mountains will be shaken. At his will, the south wind will blow. ¹⁷ The voice of his thunder rebukes the earth. So does the northern storm and the whirlwind. Like birds flying down, he sprinkles the snow. It falls down like the lighting of locusts. ¹⁸ The eye is dazzled at the beauty of its whiteness. The heart is amazed as it falls. ¹⁹ He also pours out frost on the earth like salt. When it is freezes, it has points like thorns. ²⁰ The cold north wind blows and ice freezes on the water. It settles on every pool of water. The water puts it on like it was a breastplate. ²¹ It will devour the mountains, burn up the wilderness, and consume the green grass like fire. ²² A mist coming speedily heals all things. A dew coming after heat brings cheerfulness. ²³ By his counsel, he has calmed the deep and planted islands in it. ²⁴ Those who sail on the sea tell of its dangers. We marvel when we hear it with our ears. ²⁵ There are also those strange and wondrous works in it– variety of all that has life and the huge creatures of the sea. ²⁶ Because of him, his messengers succeed. By his word, all things hold together. ²⁷ We may say many things, but couldn't say enough. The summary of our words is, "He is everything!" ²⁸ How could we have strength to glorify him? For he is himself the greater than all his works. ²⁹ The Lord is awesome and exceedingly great! His power is marvelous! ³⁰ Glorify the Lord and exalt him as much as you can! For even yet, he will surpass that. When you exalt him, summon your full strength. Don't be weary, because you can't praise him enough. ³¹ Who has seen him, that he may describe him? Who can magnify him as he is? ³² Many things greater than these are hidden, for we have seen just a few of his works. ³³ For the Lord made all things. He gave wisdom to the godly.

44

¹ Let us now praise famous men, our ancestors in their generations. ² The Lord created great glory in them– his mighty power from the beginning. ³

---

[a] *41:4* or, the place of the dead or, Sheol

[b] *41:8* The remainder of this verse is omitted by the best authorities.

Some ruled in their kingdoms and were men renowned for their power, giving counsel by their understanding. Some have spoken in prophecies, ⁴ leaders of the people by their counsels, and by their understanding, giving instruction for the people. Their words in their instruction were wise. ⁵ Some composed musical tunes, and set forth verses in writing, ⁶ rich men endowed with ability, living peaceably in their homes. ⁷ All these were honored in their generations, and were outstanding in their days. ⁸ Some of them have left a name behind them, so that others declare their praises. ⁹ But of others, there is no memory. They perished as though they had not been. They become as though they had not been born, they and their children after them. ¹⁰ But these were men of mercy, whose righteous deeds have not been forgotten. ¹¹ A good inheritance remains with their offspring. Their children are within the covenant. ¹² Their offspring stand fast, with their children, for their sakes. ¹³ Their offspring will remain forever. Their glory won't be blotted out. ¹⁴ Their bodies were buried in peace. Their name lives to all generations. ¹⁵ People will declare their wisdom. The congregation proclaims their praise. ¹⁶ Enoch pleased the Lord, and was taken up, an example of repentance to all generations. ¹⁷ Noah was found perfect and righteous. In the season of wrath, he kept the race alive. Therefore a remnant was left on the earth when the flood came. ¹⁸ Everlasting covenants were made with him, that all flesh should no more be blotted out by a flood. ¹⁹ Abraham was a great father of a multitude of nations. There was none found like him in glory, ²⁰ who kept the law of the Most High, and was taken into covenant with him. In his flesh he established the covenant. When he was tested, he was found faithful. ²¹ Therefore he assured him by an oath that the nations would be blessed through his offspring, that he would multiply him like the dust of the earth, exalt his offspring like the stars, and cause them to inherit from sea to sea, and from the Euphrates River to the utmost parts of the earth. ²² In Isaac also, he established the same assurance for Abraham his father's sake, the blessing of all men, and the covenant. ²³ He made it rest upon the head of Jacob. He acknowledged him in his blessings, gave to him by inheritance, and divided his portions. He distributed them among twelve tribes.

45

¹ He brought out of him a man of mercy, who found favor in the sight of all people, a man loved by God and men, even Moses, whose memory is blessed. ² He made him equal to the glory of the saints, and magnified him in the fears of his enemies. ³ By his words he caused the wonders to cease. God glorified him in the sight of kings. He gave him commandments for his people and showed him part of his glory. ⁴ He sanctified him in his faithfulness and meekness. He chose him out of all people. ⁵ He made him to hear his voice, led him into the thick darkness, and gave him commandments face to face, even the law of life and knowledge, that he might teach Jacob the covenant, and Israel his judgments. ⁶ He exalted Aaron, a holy man like Moses, even his brother, of the tribe of Levi. ⁷ He established an everlasting covenant with him, and gave him the priesthood of the people. He blessed him with stateliness, and dressed him in a glorious robe. ⁸ He clothed him in perfect splendor, and strengthened him with symbols of authority: the linen trousers, the long robe, and the ephod. ⁹ He encircled him with pomegranates; with many golden bells around him, to make a sound as he went, to make a sound that might be heard in the temple, for a reminder for the children of his people; ¹⁰ with a holy garment, with gold, blue, and purple, the work of the embroiderer; with an oracle of judgment–Urim and Thummim; ¹¹ with twisted scarlet, the work of the craftsman; with precious stones engraved like a signet, in a setting of gold, the work of the jeweller, for a reminder engraved in writing, after the number of the tribes of Israel; ¹² with a crown of gold upon the mitre, having engraved on it, as on a signet, "HOLINESS", an ornament of honor, the work of an expert, the desires of the eyes, goodly and beautiful. ¹³ Before him there never have been anything like it. No stranger put them on, but only his sons and his offspring perpetually. ¹⁴ His sacrifices shall be wholly burned, twice every day continually. ¹⁵ Moses consecrated him, and anointed him with holy oil. It was an everlasting covenant with him and to his offspring, all the days of heaven, to minister to the Lord, to serve as a priest, and to bless his people in his name. ¹⁶ He chose him out of all living to offer sacrifice to the Lord– incense, and a sweet fragrance, for a memorial, to make atonement for your people. ¹⁷ He gave to him in his commandments, authority in the covenants of judgments, to teach Jacob the testimonies, and to enlighten Israel in his law. ¹⁸ Strangers conspired against him and envied him in the wilderness: Dathan and Abiram with their company, and the congregation of Korah, with wrath and anger. ¹⁹ The Lord saw it, and it displeased him. In the wrath of his anger, they were destroyed.

He did wonders upon them, to consume them with flaming fire. ²⁰ He added glory to Aaron, and gave him a heritage. He divided to him the first fruits of the increase, and prepared bread of first fruits in abundance. ²¹ For they eat the sacrifices of the Lord, which he gave to him and to his offspring. ²² However, in the land of the people, he has no inheritance, and he has no portion among the people, for the Lord himself is your portion and inheritance. ²³ Phinehas the son of Eleazar is the third in glory, in that he was zealous in the fear of the Lord, and stood fast when the people turned away, and he made atonement for Israel. ²⁴ Therefore, a covenant of peace was established for him, that he should be leader of the sanctuary and of his people, that he and his offspring should have the dignity of the priesthood forever. ²⁵ Also he made a covenant with David the son of Jesse, of the tribe of Judah. The inheritance of the king is his alone from son to son. So the inheritance of Aaron is also to his seed. ²⁶ May God give you wisdom in your heart to judge his people in righteousness, that their good things may not be abolished, and that their glory may endure for all their generations.

46

¹ Joshua the son of Nun was valiant in war, and was the successor of Moses in prophecies. He was made great according to his name for the saving of[a] God's elect, to take vengeance on the enemies that rose up against them, that he might give Israel their inheritance. ² How was he glorified in the lifting up his hands, and in stretching out his sword against the cities! ³ Who before him stood so firm? For the Lord himself brought his enemies to him. ⁴ Didn't the sun go back by his hand? Didn't one day become as two? ⁵ He called upon the Most High, the Mighty One, when his foes pressed in all around him, and the great Lord heard him. ⁶ With hailstones of mighty power, he caused war to break violently upon the nation, and[b] on the slope he destroyed those who resisted, so that the nations might know his armor, how he fought in the sight of the Lord; for he followed the Mighty One. ⁷ Also in the time of Moses, he did a work of mercy– he and Caleb the son of Jephunneh– in that they withstood the adversary, hindered the people from sin, and stilled their wicked complaining. ⁸ And of six hundred thousand people on foot, they two alone were preserved to bring them into their inheritance, into a land flowing with milk and honey. ⁹ The Lord gave strength to Caleb, and it remained with him to his old age, so that he entered the hill country, and his offspring obtained it for an inheritance, ¹⁰ that all the children of Israel might see that it is good to follow the Lord. ¹¹ Also the judges, every one by his name, all whose hearts didn't engage in immorality, and who didn't turn away from the Lord– may their memory be blessed! ¹² May their bones flourish again out of their place. May the name of those who have been honored be renewed in their children. ¹³ Samuel, the prophet of the Lord, loved by his Lord, established a kingdom and anointed princes over his people. ¹⁴ By the law of the Lord he judged the congregation, and the Lord watched over Jacob. ¹⁵ By his faithfulness he was proved to be a prophet. By his words he was known to be faithful in vision. ¹⁶ When his enemies pressed on him on every side, he called upon the Lord, the Mighty One, with the offering of the suckling lamb. ¹⁷ Then the Lord thundered from heaven. He made his voice heard with a mighty sound. ¹⁸ He utterly destroyed the rulers of the Tyrians and all the princes of the Philistines. ¹⁹ Before the time of his age-long sleep, he testified in the sight of the lord and his anointed, "I have not taken any man's goods, so much as a sandal;" and no one accused him. ²⁰ Even after he fell asleep, he prophesied, and showed the king his end, and lifted up his voice from the earth in prophecy, to blot out the wickedness of the people.

47

¹ After him, Nathan rose up to prophesy in the days of David. ² As is the fat when it is separated from the peace offering, so was David separated from the children of Israel. ³ He played with lions as with kids, and with bears as with lambs of the flock. ⁴ In his youth didn't he kill a giant, and take away reproach from the people when he lifted up his hand with a sling stone, and beat down the boasting Goliath? ⁵ For he called upon the Most High Lord, and he gave him strength in his right hand to kill a man mighty in war, to exalt the horn of his people. ⁶ So they glorified him for his tens of thousands, and praised him for the blessings of the Lord, in that a glorious diadem was given to him. ⁷ For he destroyed the enemies on every side, and defeated the Philistines his adversaries. He broke their horn in pieces to this day. ⁸ In every work of his he gave thanks to the Holy One Most High with words of glory. He sang praise with his whole heart, and loved him who made him. ⁹ He set singers before the altar, to make sweet melody by their music.[c] ¹⁰ He gave beauty to the feasts, and set in order the seasons to completion while they praised his holy name, and the sanctuary resounded from early

---

[a] 46:1 Gr. his.
[b] 46:6 See Joshua **10:11**
[c] 47:9 The remainder of this verse is omitted by the best authorities.

morning. ¹¹ The Lord took away his sins, and exalted his horn forever. He gave him a covenant of kings, and a glorious throne in Israel. ¹² After him a wise son rose up, who because of him lived in security. ¹³ Solomon reigned in days of peace. God gave him rest all around, that he might set up a house for his name, and prepare a sanctuary forever. ¹⁴ How wise you were made in your youth, and filled as a river with understanding! ¹⁵ Your influence covered the earth, and you filled it with parables and riddles. ¹⁶ Your name reached to the far away islands, and you were loved for your peace. ¹⁷ For your songs, proverbs, parables, and interpretations, the countries marveled at you. ¹⁸ By the name of the Lord God, who is called the God of Israel, you gathered gold like tin, and multiplied silver like lead. ¹⁹ You bowed your loins to women, and in your body you were brought into subjection. ²⁰ You blemished your honor, and defiled your offspring, to bring wrath upon your children. I was grieved for your folly, ²¹ because the sovereignty was divided, and a disobedient kingdom ruled out of Ephraim. ²² But the Lord will never forsake his mercy. He won't destroy any of his works, nor blot out the posterity of his elect. He won't take away the offspring him who loved him. He gave a remnant to Jacob, and to David a root from his own family. ²³ So Solomon rested with his fathers. Of his offspring, he left behind him Rehoboam, the foolishness of the people, and one who lacked understanding, who made the people revolt by his counsel. Also Jeroboam the son of Nebat, who made Israel to sin, and gave a way of sin to Ephraim. ²⁴ Their sins were multiplied exceedingly, until they were removed from their land. ²⁵ For they sought out all manner of wickedness, until vengeance came upon them.

48

¹ Then Elijah arose, the prophet like fire. His word burned like a torch. ² He brought a famine upon them, and by his zeal made them few in number. ³ By the word of the Lord he shut up the heavens. He brought down fire three times. ⁴ How you were glorified, O Elijah, in your wondrous deeds! Whose glory is like yours? ⁵ You raised up a dead man from death, from Hades, by the word of the Most High. ⁶ You brought down kings to destruction, and honorable men from their sickbeds. ⁷ You heard rebuke in Sinai, and judgments of vengeance in Horeb. ⁸ You anointed kings for retribution, and prophets to succeed after you. ⁹ You were taken up in a tempest of fire, in a chariot of fiery horses. ¹⁰ You were recorded for reproofs in their seasons, to pacify anger, before it broke out into wrath, to turn the heart of the father to the son, and to restore the tribes of Jacob. ¹¹ Blessed are those who saw you, and those who have been beautified with love; for we also shall surely live. ¹² Elijah was wrapped in a whirlwind. Elisha was filled with his spirit. In his days he was not moved by the fear of any ruler, and no one brought him into subjection. ¹³ Nothing was too hard for him. When he was buried, his body prophesied. ¹⁴ As in his life he did wonders, so his works were also marvelous in death. ¹⁵ For all this the people didn't repent. They didn't depart from their sins, until they were carried away as a plunder from their land, and were scattered through all the earth. The people were left very few in number, but with a ruler from the house of David. ¹⁶ Some of them did that which was right, but some multiplied sins. ¹⁷ Hezekiah fortified his city, and brought water into its midst. He tunneled through rock with iron, and built cisterns for water. ¹⁸ In his days Sennacherib invaded, and sent Rabshakeh, and departed. He lifted up his hand against Zion, and boasted great things in his arrogance. ¹⁹ Then their hearts and their hands were shaken, and they were in pain, as women in labor. ²⁰ But they called upon the Lord who is merciful, spreading out their hands to him. The Holy One quickly heard them out of Heaven, and delivered them by the hand of Isaiah. ²¹ He struck the camp of the Assyrians, and his angel utterly destroyed them. ²² For Hezekiah did that which was pleasing to the Lord, and was strong in the ways of his ancestor David, which Isaiah the prophet commanded, who was great and faithful in his vision. ²³ In his days the sun went backward. He prolonged the life of the king. ²⁴ He saw by an excellent spirit what would come to pass in the future; and he comforted those who mourned in Zion. ²⁵ He showed the things that would happen through the end of time, and the hidden things before they came.

49

¹ The memory of Josiah is like the composition of incense prepared by the work of the perfumer. It will be sweet as honey in every mouth, and like music at a banquet of wine. ² He did what was right in the reforming of the people, and took away the abominations of iniquity. ³ He set his heart right toward the Lord. In lawless days, he made godliness prevail. ⁴ Except David, Hezekiah, and Josiah, all were wicked, because they abandoned the law of the Most High. The kings of Judah came to an end. ⁵ They gave their power to others, and their glory to a foreign nation. ⁶ They set the chosen city of the sanctuary on fire and made her streets desolate, as it was written by the hand of Jeremiah. ⁷ For they mistreated him; yet he was sanctified in the womb to be a prophet, to root out, to afflict, to destroy and likewise to build and to plant. ⁸ Ezekiel saw the vision of glory, which God showed him on the chariot of the cherubim. ⁹ For truly he remembered the enemies in rainstorm, and to do good to those who directed their ways aright. ¹⁰ Also of the twelve prophets,[a] may their bones flourish again out of their place. He comforted the people of Jacob, and delivered them by confident hope. ¹¹ How shall we magnify Zerubbabel? He was like a signet ring on the right hand. ¹² So was Jesus the son of Josedek, who in their days built the house, and exalted a[b] people holy to the Lord, prepared for everlasting glory. ¹³ Also of Nehemiah the memory is great. He raised up for us fallen walls, set up the gates and bars, and rebuilt our houses. ¹⁴ No man was created upon the earth like Enoch, for he was taken up from the earth. ¹⁵ Nor was there a man born like Joseph, a leader of his kindred, a supporter of the people. Even his bones were cared for. ¹⁶ Shem and Seth were honored among men, but above every living thing in the creation was Adam.

50

¹ It was Simon, the son of Onias, the high priest, who in his life repaired the house, and in his days strengthened the temple. ² The foundation was built by him to the height of the double walls, the lofty retaining walls of the temple enclosure. ³ In his days, a water cistern was dug, the brazen vessel like the sea in circumference. ⁴ He planned to save his people from ruin, and fortified the city against siege. ⁵ How glorious he was when the people gathered around him as he came out of the house of the veil! ⁶ He was like the morning star among clouds, like the full moon, ⁷ like the sun shining on the temple of the Most High, like the rainbow shining in clouds of glory, ⁸ like roses in the days of first fruits, like lilies by a water spring, like the shoot of the frankincense tree in summer time, ⁹ like fire and incense in the censer, like a vessel of beaten gold adorned with all kinds of precious stones, ¹⁰ like an olive tree loaded with fruit, and like a cypress growing high among the clouds. ¹¹ When he put on his glorious robe, and clothed himself in perfect splendor, ascending to the holy altar, he made the court of the sanctuary glorious. ¹² When he received the portions out of the priests' hands, as he stood by the hearth of the altar, with his kindred like a garland around him, he was like a young cedar in Lebanon surrounded by the trunks of palm trees. ¹³ All the sons of Aaron in their glory, held the Lord's offering in their hands before all the congregation of Israel. ¹⁴ Finishing the service at the altars, that he might arrange the offering of the Most High, the Almighty, ¹⁵ he stretched out his hand to the cup of libation, and poured out the cup of the grape. He poured it out at the foot of the altar, a sweet smelling fragrance to the Most High, the King of all. ¹⁶ Then the sons of Aaron shouted. They sounded the trumpets of beaten work. They made a great fanfare to be heard, for a reminder before the Most High. ¹⁷ Then all the people together hurried, and fell down to the ground on their faces to worship their Lord, the Almighty, God Most High. ¹⁸ The singers also praised him with their voices. There was a sweet melody in the whole house. ¹⁹ And the people implored the Lord Most High, in prayer before him who is merciful, until the worship of the Lord was finished, and so they accomplished his service. ²⁰ Then he went down, and lifted up his hands over the whole congregation of the children of Israel, to give blessing to the Lord with his lips, and to glory in his name. ²¹ He bowed himself down in worship the second time, to declare the blessing from the Most High. ²² Now bless the God of all, who everywhere does great things, who exalts our days from the womb, and deals with us according to his mercy. ²³ May he grant us joyfulness of heart, and that peace may be in our days in Israel for the days of eternity, ²⁴ to entrust his mercy with us, and let him deliver us in his time! ²⁵ With two nations my soul is vexed, and the third is no nation: ²⁶ Those who sit on the mountain of[c] Samaria, the Philistines, and the foolish people who live in Shechem. ²⁷ I have written in this book the instruction of understanding and knowledge, I Jesus, the son of Sirach Eleazar, of Jerusalem, who out of his heart poured forth wisdom. ²⁸ Blessed is he who will exercise these things. He who lays them up in his heart will become wise. ²⁹ For if he does them, he will be strong in all things, for the light of the Lord is his guide.[d]

51

A Prayer of Jesus the son of Sirach. ¹ I will give thanks to you, O Lord, O King, and will praise you, O God my Savior. I give thanks to your name, ² for you have been my protector and helper, and delivered my body out of destruction, and out of the snare of a slanderous tongue, from lips that

---

[a] 49:10 The remainder of this line is omitted by the best authorities.

[b] 49:12 Some ancient authorities read temple.

[c] 50:26 According to some ancient versions, Seir.

[d] 50:29 The remainder of this verse is omitted by the best authorities.

fabricate lies. You were my helper before those who stood by, ³ and delivered me, according to the abundance of your mercy and of your name, from the gnashings of teeth ready to devour, out of the hand of those seeking my life, out of the many afflictions I endured, ⁴ from the choking of a fire on every side, and out of the midst of fire that I hadn't kindled, ⁵ out of the depth of the belly of Hades, from an unclean tongue, and from lying words– ⁶ the slander of an unrighteous tongue to the king. My soul drew near to death. My life was near to Hades. ⁷ They surrounded me on every side. There was no one to help me. I was looking for human help, and there was none. ⁸ Then I remembered your mercy, O Lord, and your working which has been from everlasting, how you deliver those who wait for you, and save them out of the hand of their enemies. ⁹ I lifted up my prayer from the earth, and prayed for deliverance from death. ¹⁰ I called upon the Lord, the Father of my Lord, that he would not forsake me in the days of affliction, in the time when there was no help against the proud. ¹¹ I will praise your name continually. I will sing praise with thanksgiving. My prayer was heard. ¹² You saved me from destruction and delivered me from the evil time. Therefore I will give thanks and praise to you, and bless the name of the Lord. ¹³ When I was yet young, before I went abroad, I sought wisdom openly in my prayer. ¹⁴ Before the temple I asked for her. I will seek her out even to the end. ¹⁵ From the first flower to the ripening grape my heart delighted in her. My foot walked in uprightness. From my youth I followed her steps. ¹⁶ I inclined my ear a little, and received her, and found for myself much instruction. ¹⁷ I profited in her. I will give glory to him who gives me wisdom. ¹⁸ For I determined to practice her. I was zealous for that which is good. I will never be put to shame. ¹⁹ My soul has wrestled with her. In my conduct I was exact. I spread out my hands to the heaven above, and bewailed my ignorances of her. ²⁰ I directed my soul to her. In purity I found her. I got myself a heart joined with her from the beginning. Therefore I won't be forsaken. ²¹ My belly also was troubled to seek her. Therefore I have gained a good possession. ²² The Lord gave me a tongue for my reward. I will praise him with it. ²³ Draw near to me, all you who are uneducated, and live in the house of instruction. ²⁴ Why therefore are you all lacking in these things, and your souls are very thirsty? ²⁵ I opened my mouth and spoke, "Get her for yourselves without money." ²⁶ Put your neck under the yoke, and let your soul receive instruction. She is near to find. ²⁷ See with your eyes how that I labored just a little and found for myself much rest. ²⁸ Get instruction with a great sum of silver, and gain much gold by her. ²⁹ May your soul rejoice in his mercy, and may you all not be put to shame in praising him. ³⁰ Work your work before the time comes, and in his time he will give you your reward.

The Book of Baruch

The book of *Baruch* is recognized as Deuterocanonical Scripture by the Roman Catholic, Greek Orthodox, and Russian Orthodox Churches. In some Bibles, Baruch chapter **6** is listed as a separate book called *The Letter of Jeremiah*, reflecting its separation from Baruch in some copies of the Greek Septuagint.

1

¹ These are the words of the book which Baruch the son of Nerias, the son of Maaseas, the son of Sedekias, the son of Asadias, the son of Helkias, wrote in Babylon, ² in the fifth year, in the seventh day of the month, at the time when the Chaldeans took Jerusalem and burned it with fire. ³ Baruch read the words of this book in the hearing of Jechonias the son of Joakim king of Judah, and in the hearing of all the people who came to hear the book, ⁴ and in the hearing of the mighty men, and of the kings' sons, and in the hearing of the elders, and in the hearing of all the people, from the least to the greatest, even of all those who lived at Babylon by the river Sud. ⁵ Then they wept, fasted,[a] and prayed before the Lord. ⁶ They also made a collection of money according to every man's ability; ⁷ and they sent it to Jerusalem to Joakim the high priest, the son of Helkias, the son of Salom, and to the priests and to all the people who were found with him at Jerusalem, ⁸ at the same time when he took the vessels of the house of the Lord, that had been carried out of the temple, to return them into the land of Judah, the tenth day of Sivan–silver vessels which Sedekias the son of Josias king of Judah had made, ⁹ after Nabuchodonosor king of Babylon had carried away Jechonias, the princes, the captives, the mighty men, and the people of the land from Jerusalem, and brought them to Babylon. ¹⁰ And they said: Behold, we have sent you money; therefore buy with the money burnt offerings, sin offerings, and incense, and prepare an oblation, and offer upon the altar of the Lord our God; ¹¹ and pray for the life of Nabuchodonosor king of Babylon, and for the life of Baltasar his son, that their days may be[b] as the days of heaven above the earth. ¹² The Lord will give us strength and light to our eyes. We will live under the shadow of Nabuchodonosor king of Babylon and under the shadow of Baltasar his son, and we shall serve them many days, and find favor in their sight. ¹³ Pray for us also to the Lord our God, for we have sinned against the Lord our God. To this day the wrath of the Lord and his indignation is not turned from us. ¹⁴ You shall read this book which we have sent to you, to make confession in the house of the Lord upon the day of the feast and on the days of the solemn assembly. ¹⁵ You shall say: To the Lord our God belongs righteousness, but to us confusion of face, as at this day–to the men of Judah, to the inhabitants of Jerusalem, ¹⁶ to our kings, to our princes, to our priests, to our prophets, and to our fathers, ¹⁷ because we have sinned before the Lord. ¹⁸ We have disobeyed him and have not listened to the voice of the Lord our God, to walk in the commandments of the Lord that he has set before us. ¹⁹ Since the day that the Lord brought our fathers out of the land of Egypt to this present day, we have been disobedient to the Lord our God, and we have been negligent in not listening to his voice. ²⁰ Therefore the plagues have clung to us, along with the curse which the Lord declared through Moses his servant in the day that he brought our fathers out of the land of Egypt to give us a land that flows with milk and honey, as at this day. ²¹ Nevertheless we didn't listen to the voice of the Lord our God, according to all the words of the prophets whom he sent to us, ²² but we each walked in the imagination of his own wicked heart, to serve strange gods and to do what is evil in the sight of the Lord our God.

2

¹ Therefore the Lord has made good his word which he pronounced against us, and against our judges who judged Israel, and against our kings, and against our princes, and against the men of Israel and Judah, ² to bring upon us great plagues such as never happened before under the whole heaven,[c] as it came to pass in Jerusalem, according to the things that are written in the law of Moses, ³ that we should each eat the flesh of our own son, and each eat the flesh of our own daughter. ⁴ Moreover he has given them to be in subjection to all the kingdoms that are around us, to be a reproach and a desolation among all the people around us, where the Lord has scattered them. ⁵ Thus they were cast down and not exalted, because we sinned against the Lord our God in not listening to his voice. ⁶ To the Lord our God belongs righteousness, but to us and to our fathers confusion of face, as at this day. ⁷ All these plagues have come upon us which the Lord has pronounced against us. ⁸ Yet have we not entreated the favor of the Lord by everyone turning from the thoughts of his wicked heart. ⁹ Therefore the Lord has kept watch over the plagues. The Lord has brought them upon us, for the Lord is righteous in all his works which he has commanded us. ¹⁰

---

[a] *1:5* Another reading is, and vowed vows.

[b] *1:11* See Deuteronomy **11:21**.

[c] *2:2* Another reading is, even as he has done.

Yet we have not listened to his voice, to walk in the commandments of the Lord that he has set before us. ¹¹ And now, O Lord, you God of Israel who have brought your people out of the land of Egypt with a mighty hand, with signs, with wonders, with great power, and with a high arm, and have gotten yourself a name, as at this day: ¹² O Lord our God, we have sinned. We have been ungodly. We have done wrong in all your ordinances. ¹³ Let your wrath turn from us, for we are but a few left among the heathen where you have scattered us. ¹⁴ Hear our prayer, O Lord, and our petition, and deliver us for your own sake. Give us favor in the sight of those who have led us away captive, ¹⁵ that all the earth may know that you are the Lord our God, because Israel and his posterity is called by your name. ¹⁶ O Lord, look down from your holy house and consider us. Incline your ear, O Lord, and hear. ¹⁷ Open your eyes, and see; for the dead that are in Hades, whose breath is taken from their bodies, will give to the Lord neither glory nor righteousness; ¹⁸ but the soul who is greatly vexed, who goes stooping and feeble, and the eyes that fail, and the hungry soul, will declare your glory and righteousness, O Lord. ¹⁹ For we do not present our supplication before you, O Lord our God, for the righteousness of our fathers and of our kings. ²⁰ For you have sent your wrath and your indignation upon us, as you have spoken by your servants the prophets, saying, ²¹"The Lord says, 'Bow your shoulders to serve the king of Babylon, and remain in the land that I gave to your fathers. ²² But if you won't hear the voice of the Lord to serve the king of Babylon, ²³ I will cause to cease out of the cities of Judah and from the region near Jerusalem the voice of mirth, the voice of gladness, voice of the bridegroom, and the voice of the bride. The whole land will be desolate without inhabitant.'" ²⁴ But we wouldn't listen to your voice, to serve the king of Babylon. Therefore you have made good your words that you spoke by your servants the prophets, that the bones of our kings and the bones of our fathers would be taken out of their places. ²⁵ Behold, they are cast out to the heat by day and to the frost by night. They died in great miseries by famine, by sword, and by[a] pestilence. ²⁶ You have made the house that is called by your name as it is today because of the wickedness of the house of Israel and the house of Judah. ²⁷ Yet, O Lord our God, you have dealt with us after all your kindness and according to all your great mercy, ²⁸ as you spoke by your servant Moses in the day when you commanded him to write your law in the presence of the children of Israel, saying, ²⁹"If you won't hear my voice, surely this very great multitude will be turned into a small number among the nations where I will scatter them. ³⁰ For I know that they will not hear me, because they are a stiff-necked people; but in the land of their captivity they will take it to heart, ³¹ and will know that I am the Lord their God. I will give them a heart and ears to hear. ³² Then they will praise me in the land of their captivity, and think about my name, ³³ and will return from their stiff neck and from their wicked deeds; for they will remember the way of their fathers who sinned before the Lord. ³⁴ I will bring them again into the land which I promised to their fathers, to Abraham, to Isaac, and to Jacob, and they will rule over it. I will increase them, and they won't be diminished. ³⁵ And I will make an everlasting covenant with them to be their God, and they will be my people. I will no more remove my people Israel out of the land that I have given them."

3

¹ O Lord Almighty, you God of Israel, the soul in anguish and the troubled spirit cries to you. ² Hear, O Lord, and have mercy; for you are a merciful God. Yes, have mercy upon us, because we have sinned before you. ³ For you are enthroned forever, and we keep perishing. ⁴ O Lord Almighty, you God of Israel, hear now the prayer of the dead Israelites, and of the children of those who were sinners before you, who didn't listen to the voice of you their God; because of this, these plagues cling to us. ⁵ Don't remember the iniquities of our fathers, but remember your power and your name at this time. ⁶ For you are the Lord our God, and we will praise you, O Lord. ⁷ For this cause, you have put your fear in our hearts, to the intent that we should call upon your name. We will praise you in our captivity, for we have called to mind all the iniquity of our fathers who sinned before you. ⁸ Behold, we are yet this day in our captivity where you have scattered us, for a reproach and a curse, and to be subject to penalty according to all the iniquities of our fathers who departed from the Lord our God. ⁹ Hear, O Israel, the commandments of life! Give ear to understand wisdom! ¹⁰ How is it, O Israel, that you are in your enemies' land, that you have become old in a strange country, that you are defiled with the dead, ¹¹ that you are counted with those who are in Hades? ¹² You have forsaken the fountain of wisdom. ¹³ If you had walked in the way of God, you would have dwelled in peace forever. ¹⁴ Learn where there is wisdom, where there is strength, and where there is understanding, that you may also know where there is length of days and life, where there is the light of the eyes and peace. ¹⁵ Who has found out her place? Who has come into her treasuries? ¹⁶ Where are the princes of the heathen, and those who ruled the beasts that are on the earth, ¹⁷ those who had their pastime with the fowls of the air, and those who hoarded up silver and gold, in which people trust, and of their getting there is no end? ¹⁸ For those who diligently sought silver, and were so anxious, and whose works are past finding out, ¹⁹ they have vanished and gone down to Hades, and others have come up in their place. ²⁰ Younger men have seen the light and lived upon the earth, but they haven't known the way of knowledge, ²¹ nor understood its paths. Their children haven't embraced it. They are far off from their way. ²² It has not been heard of in Canaan, neither has it been seen in Teman. ²³ The sons also of Agar who seek understanding, which are in the land, the merchants of Merran and Teman, and the authors of fables, and the searchers out of understanding–none of these have known the way of wisdom or remembered her paths. ²⁴ O Israel, how great is the house of God! How large is the place of his possession! ²⁵ It is great and has no end. It is high and unmeasurable. ²⁶ Giants were born that were famous of old, great of stature, and expert in war. ²⁷ God didn't choose these, nor did he give the way of knowledge to them, ²⁸ so they perished, because they had no wisdom. They perished through their own foolishness. ²⁹ Who has gone up into heaven, taken her, and brought her down from the clouds? ³⁰ Who has gone over the sea, found her, and will bring her for choice gold? ³¹ There is no one who knows her way, nor any who comprehend her path. ³² But he that knows all things knows her, he found her out with his understanding. He who prepared the earth for all time has filled it with four-footed beasts. ³³ It is he who sends forth the light, and it goes. He called it, and it obeyed him with fear. ³⁴ The stars shone in their watches, and were glad. When he called them, they said, "Here we are." They shone with gladness to him who made them. ³⁵ This is our God. No other can be compared to him. ³⁶ He has found out all the way of knowledge, and has given it to Jacob his servant and to Israel who is loved by him. ³⁷ Afterward she appeared upon earth, and lived with men.

4

¹ This is the book of God's commandments and the law that endures forever. All those who hold it fast will live, but those who leave it will die. ² Turn, O Jacob, and take hold of it. Walk toward the shining of its light. ³ Don't give your glory to another, nor the things that are to your advantage to a foreign nation. ⁴ O Israel, we are happy; for the things that are pleasing to God are made known to us. ⁵ Be of good cheer, my people, the memorial of Israel. ⁶ You were not sold to the nations for destruction, but because you moved God to wrath, you were delivered to your adversaries. ⁷ For you provoked him who made you by sacrificing to demons and not to God. ⁸ You forgot the everlasting God who brought you up. You also grieved Jerusalem, who nursed you. ⁹ For she saw the wrath that came upon you from God, and said, "Listen, you who dwell near Zion; for God has brought upon me great mourning. ¹⁰ For I have seen the captivity of my sons and daughters, which the Everlasting has brought upon them. ¹¹ For with joy I nourished them, but sent them away with weeping and mourning. ¹² Let no man rejoice over me, a widow and forsaken by many. For the sins of my children, I am left desolate, because they turned away from the law of God ¹³ and had no regard for his statutes. They didn't walk in the ways of God's commandments or tread in the paths of discipline in his righteousness. ¹⁴ Let those who dwell near Zion come and remember the captivity of my sons and daughters, which the Everlasting has brought upon them. ¹⁵ For he has brought a nation upon them from afar, a shameless nation with a strange language, who didn't respect old men or pity children. ¹⁶ They have carried away the dear beloved sons of the widow, and left her who was alone desolate of her daughters." ¹⁷ But I–how can I help you? ¹⁸ For he who brought these calamities upon you will deliver you from the hand of your enemies. ¹⁹ Go your way, O my children. Go your way, for I am left desolate. ²⁰ I have put off the garment of peace, and put on the sackcloth of my petition. I will cry to the Everlasting as long as I live. ²¹ Take courage, my children. Cry to God, and he will deliver you from the power and hand of the enemies. ²² For I have trusted in the Everlasting, that he will save you; and joy has come to me from the Holy One, because of the mercy that will soon come to you from your Everlasting Savior. ²³ For I sent you out with mourning and weeping, but God will give you to me again with joy and gladness forever. ²⁴ For as now those who dwell near Zion have seen your captivity, so they will shortly see your salvation from our God which will come upon you with great glory and brightness of the Everlasting. ²⁵ My children, suffer patiently the wrath that has come upon you from God, for your enemy has persecuted you; but shortly you will see his destruction and will tread upon their necks. ²⁶ My delicate ones have traveled rough roads. They were taken away like a flock carried off by enemies. ²⁷ Take

---

[a] 2:25 See Jeremiah 32:36.

courage, my children, and cry to God; for you will be remembered by him who has brought this upon you. ²⁸ For as it was your decision to go astray from God, return and seek him ten times more. ²⁹ For he who brought these calamities upon you will bring you everlasting joy again with your salvation. ³⁰ Take courage, O Jerusalem, for he who called you by name will comfort you. ³¹ Miserable are those who afflicted you and rejoiced at your fall. ³² Miserable are the cities which your children served. Miserable is she who received your sons. ³³ For as she rejoiced at your fall and was glad of your ruin, so she will be grieved at her own desolation. ³⁴ And I will take away her pride in her great multitude and her boasting will be turned into mourning. ³⁵ For fire will come upon her from the Everlasting for many days; and she will be inhabited by demons for a long time. ³⁶ O Jerusalem, look around you toward the east, and behold the joy that comes to you from God. ³⁷ Behold, your sons come, whom you sent away. They come gathered together from the east to the west at the word of the Holy One, rejoicing in the glory of God.

5

¹ Take off the garment of your mourning and affliction, O Jerusalem, and put on forever the beauty of the glory from God. ² Put on the robe of the righteousness from God. Set on your head a diadem of the glory of the Everlasting. ³ For God will show your splendor everywhere under heaven. ⁴ For your name will be called by God forever "Righteous Peace, Godly Glory". ⁵ Arise, O Jerusalem, and stand upon the height. Look around you toward the east and see your children gathered from the going down of the sun to its rising at the word of the Holy One, rejoicing that God has remembered them. ⁶ For they went from you on foot, being led away by their enemies, but God brings them in to you carried on high with glory, on a royal throne. ⁷ For God has appointed that every high mountain and the everlasting hills should be made low, and the valleys filled up to make the ground level, that Israel may go safely in the glory of God. ⁸ Moreover the woods and every sweet smelling tree have shaded Israel by the commandment of God. ⁹ For God will lead Israel with joy in the light of his glory with the mercy and righteousness that come from him.

The Letter of Jeremiah
6

¹ A copy of a letter that Jeremy sent to those who were to be led captives into Babylon by the king of the Babylonians, to give them the message that God commanded him. ² Because of the sins which you have committed before God, you will be led away captives to Babylon by Nabuchodonosor king of the Babylonians. ³ So when you come to Babylon, you will remain there many years, and for a long season, even for seven generations. After that, I will bring you out peacefully from there. ⁴ But now you will see in Babylon gods of silver, gold, wood carried on shoulders, which cause the nations to fear. ⁵ Beware therefore that you in no way become like these foreigners. Don't let fear take hold of you because of them when you see the multitude before them and behind them, worshiping them. ⁶ But say in your hearts, "O Lord, we must worship you." ⁷ For my angel is with you, and I myself care for your souls. ⁸ For their tongue is polished by the workman, and they themselves are overlaid with gold and with silver; yet they are only fake, and can't speak. ⁹ And taking gold, as if it were for a virgin who loves to be happy, they make crowns for the heads of their gods. ¹⁰ Sometimes also the priests take gold and silver from their gods, and spend it on themselves. ¹¹ They will even give some of it to the common prostitutes. They dress them like men with garments, even the gods of silver, gods of gold, and gods of wood. ¹² Yet these gods can't save themselves from rust and moths, even though they are covered with purple garments. ¹³ They wipe their faces because of the dust of the temple, which is thick upon them. ¹⁴ And he who can't put to death one who offends against him holds a sceptre, as though he were judge of a country. ¹⁵ He has also a dagger in his right hand, and an axe, but can't deliver himself from war and robbers. ¹⁶ By this they are known not to be gods. Therefore don't fear them. ¹⁷ For like a vessel that a man uses is worth nothing when it is broken, even so it is with their gods. When they are set up in the temples, their eyes are full of dust through the feet of those who come in. ¹⁸ As the courts are secured on every side upon him who offends the king, as being committed to suffer death, even so the priests secure their temples with doors, with locks, and bars, lest they be carried off by robbers. ¹⁹ They light candles for them, yes, more than for themselves, even though they can't see one. ²⁰ They are like one of the beams of the temple. Men say their hearts are eaten out when things creeping out of the earth devour both them and their clothing. They don't feel it ²¹ when their faces are blackened through the smoke that comes out of the temple. ²² Bats, swallows, and birds land on their bodies and heads. So do the cats. ²³ By this you may know that they are no gods. Therefore don't fear them. ²⁴ Notwithstanding the gold with which they are covered to make them beautiful, unless someone wipes off the tarnish, they won't shine; for they didn't even feel it when they were molten. ²⁵ Things in which there is no breath are bought at any cost. ²⁶ Having no feet, they are carried upon shoulders. By this, they declare to men that they are worth nothing. ²⁷ Those who serve them are also ashamed, for if they fall to the ground at any time, they can't rise up again by themselves. If they are bowed down, they can't make themselves straight; but the offerings are set before them, as if they were dead men. ²⁸ And the things that are sacrificed to them, their priests sell and spend. In like manner, their wives also lay up part of it in salt; but to the poor and to the impotent they give none of it. ²⁹ The menstruous woman and the woman in childbed touch their sacrifices, knowing therefore by these things that they are no gods. Don't fear them. ³⁰ For how can they be called gods? Because women set food before the gods of silver, gold, and wood. ³¹ And in their temples the priests sit on seats, having their clothes torn and their heads and beards shaven, and nothing on their heads. ³² They roar and cry before their gods, as men do at the feast when one is dead. ³³ The priests also take off garments from them and clothe their wives and children with them. ³⁴ Whether it is evil or good what one does to them, they are not able to repay it. They can't set up a king or put him down. ³⁵ In like manner, they can neither give riches nor money. Though a man make a vow to them and doesn't keep it, they will never exact it. ³⁶ They can save no man from death. They can't deliver the weak from the mighty. ³⁷ They can't restore a blind man to his sight, or deliver anyone who is in distress. ³⁸ They can show no mercy to the widow, or do good to the fatherless. ³⁹ They are like the stones that are cut out of the mountain, these gods of wood that are overlaid with gold and with silver. Those who minister to them will be confounded. ⁴⁰ How could a man then think or say that they are gods, when even the Chaldeans themselves dishonor them? ⁴¹ If they shall see one mute who can't speak, they bring him and ask him to call upon Bel, as though he were able to understand. ⁴² Yet they can't perceive this themselves, and forsake them; for they have no understanding. ⁴³ The women also with cords around them sit in the ways, burning bran for incense; but if any of them, drawn by someone who passes by, lies with him, she reproaches her fellow, that she

was not thought as worthy as herself and her cord wasn't broken. ⁴⁴ Whatever is done among them is false. How could a man then think or say that they are gods? ⁴⁵ They are fashioned by carpenters and goldsmiths. They can be nothing else than what the workmen make them to be. ⁴⁶ And they themselves who fashioned them can never continue long. How then should the things that are fashioned by them? ⁴⁷ For they have left lies and reproaches to those who come after. ⁴⁸ For when there comes any war or plague upon them, the priests consult with themselves, where they may be hidden with them. ⁴⁹ How then can't men understand that they are no gods, which can't save themselves from war or from plague? ⁵⁰ For seeing they are only wood and overlaid with gold and silver, it will be known hereafter that they are false. ⁵¹ It will be manifest to all nations and kings that they are no gods, but the works of men's hands, and that there is no work of God in them. ⁵² Who then may not know that they are not gods? ⁵³ For they can't set up a king in a land or give rain to men. ⁵⁴ They can't judge their own cause, or redress a wrong, being unable; for they are like crows between heaven and earth. ⁵⁵ For even when fire falls upon the house of gods of wood overlaid with gold or with silver, their priests will flee away, and escape, but they themselves will be burned apart like beams. ⁵⁶ Moreover they can't withstand any king or enemies. How could a man then admit or think that they are gods? ⁵⁷ Those gods of wood overlaid with silver or with gold aren't able to escape from thieves or robbers. ⁵⁸ The gold, silver, and garments with which they are clothed–those who are strong will take from them, and go away with them. They won't be able to help themselves. ⁵⁹ Therefore it is better to be a king who shows his manhood, or else a vessel in a house profitable for whatever the owner needs, than such false gods– or even a door in a house, to keep the things safe that are in it, than such false gods; or better to be a pillar of wood in a palace than such false gods. ⁶⁰ For sun, moon, and stars, being bright and sent to do their jobs, are obedient. ⁶¹ Likewise also the lightning when it flashes is beautiful to see. In the same way, the wind also blows in every country. ⁶² And when God commands the clouds to go over the whole world, they do as they are told. ⁶³ And the fire sent from above to consume mountains and woods does as it is commanded; but these are to be compared to them neither in show nor power. ⁶⁴ Therefore a man shouldn't think or say that they are gods, seeing they aren't able to judge causes or to do good to men. ⁶⁵ Knowing therefore that they are no gods, don't fear them. ⁶⁶ For they can neither curse nor bless kings. ⁶⁷ They can't show signs in the heavens among the nations, or shine as the sun, or give light as the moon. ⁶⁸ The beasts are better than they; for they can get under a covert, and help themselves. ⁶⁹ In no way then is it manifest to us that they are gods. Therefore don't fear them. ⁷⁰ For as a scarecrow in a garden of cucumbers that keeps nothing, so are their gods of wood overlaid with gold and silver. ⁷¹ Likewise also their gods of wood overlaid with gold and with silver, are like a white thorn in an orchard that every bird sits upon. They are also like a dead body that is thrown out into the dark. ⁷² You will know them to be no gods by the bright purple that rots upon them. They themselves will be consumed afterwards, and will be a reproach in the country. ⁷³ Better therefore is the just man who has no idols; for he will be far from reproach.

The Book of Daniel with Greek Portions

1

¹ In the third year of the reign of Jehoiakim king of Judah, Nebuchadnezzar king of Babylon came to Jerusalem and besieged it. ² The Lord[a] gave Jehoiakim king of Judah into his hand, with part of the vessels of the house of God;[b] and he carried them into the land of Shinar to the house of his god. He brought the vessels into the treasure house of his god. ³ The king spoke to Ashpenaz the master of his eunuchs, that he should bring in some of the children of Israel, even of the royal offspring[c] and of the nobles– ⁴ youths in whom was no defect, but well-favored, and skillful in all wisdom, and endowed with knowledge, and understanding science, and who had the ability to serve in the king's palace; and that he should teach them the learning and the language of the Chaldeans. ⁵ The king appointed for them a daily portion of the king's delicacies, and of the wine which he drank, and that they should be nourished three years; that at its end they should serve the king. ⁶ Now among these were of the children of Judah: Daniel, Hananiah, Mishael, and Azariah. ⁷ The prince of the eunuchs gave names to them: to Daniel he gave the name Belteshazzar; to Hananiah, Shadrach; to Mishael, Meshach; and to Azariah, Abednego. ⁸ But Daniel purposed in his heart that he would not defile himself with the king's delicacies, nor with the wine which he drank. Therefore he requested of the prince of the eunuchs that he might not defile himself. ⁹ Now God made Daniel find kindness and compassion in the sight of the prince of the eunuchs. ¹⁰ The prince of the eunuchs said to Daniel, "I fear my lord the king, who has appointed your food and your drink. For why should he see your faces worse looking than the youths who are of your own age? Then you would endanger my head with the king." ¹¹ Then Daniel said to the steward whom the prince of the eunuchs had appointed over Daniel, Hananiah, Mishael, and Azariah: ¹²"Test your servants, I beg you, ten days; and let them give us vegetables to eat and water to drink. ¹³ Then let our faces be examined before you, and the face of the youths who eat of the king's delicacies; and as you see, deal with your servants." ¹⁴ So he listened to them in this matter, and tested them for ten days. ¹⁵ At the end of ten days, their faces appeared fairer, and they were fatter in flesh, than all the youths who ate of the king's delicacies. ¹⁶ So the steward took away their delicacies, and the wine that they would drink, and gave them vegetables. ¹⁷ Now as for these four youths, God gave them knowledge and skill in all learning and wisdom; and Daniel had understanding in all visions and dreams. ¹⁸ At the end of the days which the king had appointed for bringing them in, the prince of the eunuchs brought them in before Nebuchadnezzar. ¹⁹ The king talked with them; and among them all was found no one like Daniel, Hananiah, Mishael, and Azariah. Therefore they served the king. ²⁰ In every matter of wisdom and understanding concerning which the king inquired of them, he found them ten times better than all the magicians and enchanters who were in all his realm. ²¹ Daniel continued serving even to the first year of King Cyrus.

2

¹ In the second year of the reign of Nebuchadnezzar, Nebuchadnezzar dreamed dreams; and his spirit was troubled, and his sleep went from him. ² Then the king commanded that the magicians, the enchanters, the sorcerers, and the Chaldeans be called to tell the king his dreams. So they came in and stood before the king. ³ The king said to them, "I have dreamed a dream, and my spirit is troubled to know the dream." ⁴ Then the Chaldeans spoke to the king in the Syrian language, "O king, live forever! Tell your servants the dream, and we will show the interpretation." ⁵ The king answered the Chaldeans, "The thing has gone from me. If you don't make known to me the dream and its interpretation, you will be cut in pieces, and your houses will be made a dunghill. ⁶ But if you show the dream and its interpretation, you will receive from me gifts, rewards, and great honor. Therefore show me the dream and its interpretation." ⁷ They answered the second time and said, "Let the king tell his servants the dream, and we will show the interpretation." ⁸ The king answered, "I know of a certainty that you are trying to gain time, because you see the thing has gone from me. ⁹ But if you don't make known to me the dream, there is but one law for you; for you have prepared lying and corrupt words to speak before me, until the situation changes. Therefore tell me the dream, and I will know that you can show me its interpretation." ¹⁰ The Chaldeans answered before the king, and said, "There is not a man on the earth who can show the king's matter, because no king, lord, or ruler, has asked such a thing of any magician, enchanter, or Chaldean. ¹¹ It is a rare thing that the king requires, and there is no other who can show it before the king, except the gods, whose

---

[a] *1:2* The word translated "Lord" is "Adonai."

[b] *1:2* The Hebrew word rendered "God" is "אֱלֹהִים" (Elohim).

[c] *1:3* or, seed

dwelling is not with flesh." ¹² Because of this, the king was angry and very furious, and commanded that all the wise men of Babylon be destroyed. ¹³ So the decree went out, and the wise men were to be slain. They sought Daniel and his companions to be slain. ¹⁴ Then Daniel returned answer with counsel and prudence to Arioch the captain of the king's guard, who had gone out to kill the wise men of Babylon. ¹⁵ He answered Arioch the king's captain, "Why is the decree so urgent from the king?" Then Arioch made the thing known to Daniel. ¹⁶ Daniel went in, and desired of the king that he would appoint him a time, and he would show the king the interpretation. ¹⁷ Then Daniel went to his house and made the thing known to Hananiah, Mishael, and Azariah, his companions, ¹⁸ that they would desire mercies of the God of heaven concerning this secret, and that Daniel and his companions would not perish with the rest of the wise men of Babylon. ¹⁹ Then the secret was revealed to Daniel in a vision of the night. Then Daniel blessed the God of heaven. ²⁰ Daniel answered, "Blessed be the name of God forever and ever; for wisdom and might are his. ²¹ He changes the times and the seasons. He removes kings and sets up kings. He gives wisdom to the wise, and knowledge to those who have understanding. ²² He reveals the deep and secret things. He knows what is in the darkness, and the light dwells with him. ²³ I thank you and praise you, O God of my fathers, who have given me wisdom and might, and have now made known to me what we desired of you; for you have made known to us the king's matter." ²⁴ Therefore Daniel went in to Arioch, whom the king had appointed to destroy the wise men of Babylon. He went and said this to him: "Don't destroy the wise men of Babylon. Bring me in before the king, and I will show to the king the interpretation." ²⁵ Then Arioch brought in Daniel before the king in haste, and said this to him: "I have found a man of the children of the captivity of Judah who will make known to the king the interpretation." ²⁶ The king answered Daniel, whose name was Belteshazzar, "Are you able to make known to me the dream which I have seen, and its interpretation?" ²⁷ Daniel answered before the king, and said, "The secret which the king has demanded can't be shown to the king by wise men, enchanters, magicians, or soothsayers; ²⁸ but there is a God in heaven who reveals secrets, and he has made known to King Nebuchadnezzar what will be in the latter days. Your dream, and the visions of your head on your bed, are these: ²⁹"As for you, O king, your thoughts came on your bed, what should happen hereafter; and he who reveals secrets has made known to you what will happen. ³⁰ But as for me, this secret is not revealed to me for any wisdom that I have more than any living, but to the intent that the interpretation may be made known to the king, and that you may know the thoughts of your heart. ³¹"You, O king, saw, and behold,[a] a great image. This image, which was mighty, and whose brightness was excellent, stood before you; and its appearance was terrifying. ³² As for this image, its head was of fine gold, its chest and its arms of silver, its belly and its thighs of bronze, ³³ its legs of iron, its feet part of iron, and part of clay. ³⁴ You saw until a stone was cut out without hands, which struck the image on its feet that were of iron and clay, and broke them in pieces. ³⁵ Then the iron, the clay, the bronze, the silver, and the gold were broken in pieces together, and became like the chaff of the summer threshing floors. The wind carried them away, so that no place was found for them. The stone that struck the image became a great mountain, and filled the whole earth. ³⁶"This is the dream; and we will tell its interpretation before the king. ³⁷ You, O king, are king of kings, to whom the God of heaven has given the kingdom, the power, the strength, and the glory. ³⁸ Wherever the children of men dwell, he has given the animals of the field and the birds of the sky into your hand, and has made you rule over them all. You are the head of gold. ³⁹"After you, another kingdom will arise that is inferior to you; and a third kingdom of bronze, which will rule over all the earth. ⁴⁰ The fourth kingdom will be strong as iron, because iron breaks in pieces and subdues all things; and as iron that crushes all these, it will break in pieces and crush. ⁴¹ Whereas you saw the feet and toes, part of potters' clay, and part of iron, it will be a divided kingdom; but there will be in it of the strength of the iron, because you saw the iron mixed with miry clay. ⁴² As the toes of the feet were part of iron, and part of clay, so the kingdom will be partly strong, and partly brittle. ⁴³ Whereas you saw the iron mixed with miry clay, they will mingle themselves with the seed of men; but they won't cling to one another, even as iron does not mix with clay. ⁴⁴"In the days of those kings the God of heaven will set up a kingdom which will never be destroyed, nor will its sovereignty be left to another people; but it will break in pieces and consume all these kingdoms, and it will stand forever. ⁴⁵ Because you saw that a stone was cut out of the mountain without hands, and that it broke in pieces the iron, the bronze, the clay, the silver, and the gold. The great God has made known to the king what will happen hereafter. The dream is certain, and its interpretation sure." ⁴⁶ Then King Nebuchadnezzar fell on his face, worshiped Daniel, and commanded that they should offer an offering and sweet odors to him. ⁴⁷ The king answered to Daniel, and said, "Of a truth your God is the God of gods, and the Lord of kings, and a revealer of secrets, since you have been able to reveal this secret." ⁴⁸ Then the king made Daniel great, and gave him many great gifts, and made him rule over the whole province of Babylon, and to be chief governor over all the wise men of Babylon. ⁴⁹ Daniel requested of the king, and he appointed Shadrach, Meshach, and Abednego over the affairs of the province of Babylon; but Daniel was in the king's gate.

3

¹ Nebuchadnezzar the king made an image of gold, whose height was sixty cubits,[b] and its width six cubits. He set it up in the plain of Dura, in the province of Babylon. ² Then Nebuchadnezzar the king sent to gather together the local governors, the deputies, and the governors, the judges, the treasurers, the counselors, the sheriffs, and all the rulers of the provinces, to come to the dedication of the image which Nebuchadnezzar the king had set up. ³ Then the local governors, the deputies, and the governors, the judges, the treasurers, the counselors, the sheriffs, and all the rulers of the provinces, were gathered together to the dedication of the image that Nebuchadnezzar the king had set up; and they stood before the image that Nebuchadnezzar had set up. ⁴ Then the herald cried aloud, "To you it is commanded, peoples, nations, and languages, ⁵ that whenever you hear the sound of the horn, flute, zither, lyre, harp, pipe, and all kinds of music, you fall down and worship the golden image that Nebuchadnezzar the king has set up. ⁶ Whoever doesn't fall down and worship shall be cast into the middle of a burning fiery furnace the same hour." ⁷ Therefore at that time, when all the peoples heard the sound of the horn, flute, zither, lyre, harp, pipe, and all kinds of music, all the peoples, the nations, and the languages, fell down and worshiped the golden image that Nebuchadnezzar the king had set up. ⁸ Therefore at that time certain Chaldeans came near, and brought accusation against the Jews. ⁹ They answered Nebuchadnezzar the king, "O king, live for ever! ¹⁰ You, O king, have made a decree that every man who hears the sound of the horn, flute, zither, lyre, harp, pipe, and all kinds of music shall fall down and worship the golden image; ¹¹ and whoever doesn't fall down and worship shall be cast into the middle of a burning fiery furnace. ¹² There are certain Jews whom you have appointed over the affairs of the province of Babylon: Shadrach, Meshach, and Abednego. These men, O king, have not respected you. They don't serve your gods, and don't worship the golden image which you have set up." ¹³ Then Nebuchadnezzar in rage and fury commanded that Shadrach, Meshach, and Abednego be brought. Then these men were brought before the king. ¹⁴ Nebuchadnezzar answered them, "Is it on purpose, Shadrach, Meshach, and Abednego, that you don't serve my god, nor worship the golden image which I have set up? ¹⁵ Now if you are ready whenever you hear the sound of the horn, flute, zither, lyre, harp, pipe, and all kinds of music to fall down and worship the image which I have made, good; but if you don't worship, you shall be cast the same hour into the middle of a burning fiery furnace. Who is that god who will deliver you out of my hands?" ¹⁶ Shadrach, Meshach, and Abednego answered the king, "Nebuchadnezzar, we have no need to answer you in this matter. ¹⁷ If it happens, our God whom we serve is able to deliver us from the burning fiery furnace; and he will deliver us out of your hand, O king. ¹⁸ But if not, let it be known to you, O king, that we will not serve your gods or worship the golden image which you have set up." ¹⁹ Then Nebuchadnezzar was full of fury, and the form of his appearance was changed against Shadrach, Meshach, and Abednego. He spoke, and commanded that they should heat the furnace seven times more than it was usually heated. ²⁰ He commanded certain mighty men who were in his army to bind Shadrach, Meshach, and Abednego, and to cast them into the burning fiery furnace. ²¹ Then these men were bound in their pants, their tunics, their mantles, and their other clothes, and were cast into the middle of the burning fiery furnace. ²² Therefore because the king's commandment was urgent, and the furnace exceedingly hot, the flame of the fire killed those men who took up Shadrach, Meshach, and Abednego. ²³ These three men, Shadrach, Meshach, and Abednego, fell down bound into the middle of the burning fiery furnace.

---

[a] 2:31 "Behold", from "הִנֵּה", means look at, take notice, observe, see, or gaze at. It is often used as an interjection.

[b] 3:1 A cubit is the length from the tip of the middle finger to the elbow on a man's arm, or about 18 inches or 46 centimeters.

The Song of the Three Holy Children[a]
(or The Prayer of Azariah) Continuation of Daniel with Greek Portions

3

24 They walked in the midst of the fire, praising God, and blessing the Lord. 25 Then Azarias stood, and prayed like this. Opening his mouth in the midst of the fire he said, 26 "Blessed are you, O Lord, you God of our fathers! Your name is worthy to be praised and glorified for evermore; 27 for you are righteous in all the things that you have done. Yes, all your works are true. Your ways are right, and all your judgments are truth. 28 In all the things that you have brought upon us, and upon the holy city of our fathers, Jerusalem, you have executed true judgments. For according to truth and justice you have brought all these things upon us because of our sins. 29 For we have sinned and committed iniquity in departing from you. 30 In all things we have trespassed, and not obeyed your commandments or kept them. We haven't done as you have commanded us, that it might go well with us. 31 Therefore all that you have brought upon us, and everything that you have done to us, you have done in true judgment. 32 You delivered us into the hands of lawless enemies, most hateful rebels, and to an unjust king who is the most wicked in all the world. 33 And now we can't open our mouth. Shame and reproach have come on your servants and those who worship you. 34 Don't utterly deliver us up, for your name's sake. Don't annul your covenant. 35 Don't cause your mercy to depart from us, for the sake of Abraham who is loved by you, and for the sake of Isaac your servant, and Israel your holy one, 36 to whom you promised that you would multiply their offspring as the stars of the sky, and as the sand that is on the sea shore. 37 For we, O Lord, have become less than any nation, and are brought low this day in all the world because of our sins. 38 There isn't at this time prince, or prophet, or leader, or burnt offering, or sacrifice, or oblation, or incense, or place to offer before you, and to find mercy. 39 Nevertheless in a contrite heart and a humble spirit let us be accepted, 40 like the burnt offerings of rams and bullocks, and like ten thousands of fat lambs. So let our sacrifice be in your sight this day, that we may wholly go after you, for they shall not be ashamed who put their trust in you. 41 And now we follow you with all our heart. We fear you, and seek your face. 42 Put us not to shame; but deal with us after your kindness, and according to the multitude of your mercy. 43 Deliver us also according to your marvelous works, and give glory to your name, O Lord. Let all those who harm your servants be confounded. 44 Let them be ashamed of all their power and might, and let their strength be broken. 45 Let them know that you are the Lord, the only God, and glorious over the whole world." 46 The king's servants who put them in didn't stop making the furnace hot with naphtha, pitch, tinder, and small wood, 47 so that the flame streamed out forty nine cubits above the furnace. 48 It spread and burned those Chaldeans whom it found around the furnace. 49 But the angel of the Lord came down into the furnace together with Azarias and his fellows, and he struck the flame of the fire out of the furnace, 50 and made the midst of the furnace as it had been a moist whistling wind, so that the fire didn't touch them at all. It neither hurt nor troubled them. 51 Then the three, as out of one mouth, praised, glorified, and blessed God in the furnace, saying, 52 "Blessed are you, O Lord, you God of our fathers, to be praised and exalted above all forever! 53 Blessed is your glorious and holy name, to be praised and exalted above all forever! 54 Blessed are you in the temple of your holy glory, to be praised and glorified above all forever! 55 Blessed are you who see the depths and sit upon the cherubim, to be praised and exalted above all forever. 56 Blessed are you on the throne of your kingdom, to be praised and extolled above all forever! 57 Blessed are you in the firmament of heaven, to be praised and glorified forever! 58 O all you works of the Lord, bless the Lord! Praise and exalt him above all forever! 59 O you heavens, bless the Lord! Praise and exalt him above all for ever! 60 O you angels of the Lord, bless the Lord! Praise and exalt him above all forever! 61 O all you waters that are above the sky, bless the Lord! Praise and exalt him above all forever! 62 O all you powers of the Lord, bless the Lord! Praise and exalt him above all forever! 63 O you sun and moon, bless the Lord! Praise and exalt him above all forever! 64 O you stars of heaven, bless the Lord! Praise and exalt him above all forever! 65 O every shower and dew, bless the Lord! Praise and exalt him above all forever! 66 O all you winds, bless the Lord! Praise and exalt him above all forever! 67 O you fire and heat, bless the Lord! Praise and exalt him above all forever! 68 O you dews and storms of snow, bless the Lord! Praise and exalt him above all forever! 69 O you nights and days, bless the Lord! Praise and exalt him above all forever! 70 O you light and darkness, bless the Lord! Praise and exalt him above all forever! 71 O you cold and heat, bless the Lord! Praise and exalt him above all forever! 72 O you frost and snow, bless the Lord! Praise and exalt him above all forever! 73 O you lightnings and clouds, bless the Lord! Praise and exalt him above all forever! 74 O let the earth bless the Lord! Let it praise and exalt him above all forever! 75 O you mountains and hills, bless the Lord! Praise and exalt him above all forever! 76 O all you things that grow on the earth, bless the Lord! Praise and exalt him above all forever! 77 [b]O sea and rivers, bless the Lord! Praise and exalt him above all forever! 78 O you springs, bless the Lord! Praise and exalt him above all forever! 79 O you whales and all that move in the waters, bless the Lord! Praise and exalt him above all forever! 80 O all you birds of the air, bless the Lord! Praise and exalt him above all forever! 81 O all you beasts and cattle, bless the Lord! Praise and exalt him above all forever! 82 O you children of men, bless the Lord! Praise and exalt him above all forever! 83 O let Israel bless the Lord! Praise and exalt him above all forever! 84 O you priests of the Lord, bless the Lord! Praise and exalt him above all forever! 85 O you servants of the Lord, bless the Lord! Praise and exalt him above all forever! 86 O you spirits and souls of the righteous, bless the Lord! Praise and exalt him above all forever! 87 O you who are holy and humble of heart, bless the Lord! Praise and exalt him above all forever! 88 O Hananiah, Mishael, and Azariah, bless the Lord! Praise and exalt him above all forever; for he has rescued us from Hades, and saved us from the hand of death! He has delivered us out of the midst of the furnace and burning flame. He has delivered us out of the midst of the fire. 89 O give thanks to the Lord, for he is good; for his mercy is forever. 90 O all you who worship the Lord, bless the God of gods, praise him, and give him thanks; for his mercy is forever!"

Deliverance from the Furnace

91 [c] Then Nebuchadnezzar the king was astonished and rose up in haste. He spoke and said to his counselors, "Didn't we cast three men bound into the middle of the fire?" They answered the king, "True, O king." 92 He answered, "Look, I see four men loose, walking in the middle of the fire, and they are unharmed. The appearance of the fourth is like a son of the gods." 93 Then Nebuchadnezzar came near to the mouth of the burning fiery furnace. He spoke and said, "Shadrach, Meshach, and Abednego, you servants of the Most High God, come out, and come here!" Then Shadrach, Meshach, and Abednego came out of the middle of the fire. 94 The local governors, the deputies, and the governors, and the king's counselors, being gathered together, saw these men, that the fire had no power on their bodies. The hair of their head wasn't singed. Their pants weren't changed. The smell of fire wasn't even on them. 95 Nebuchadnezzar spoke and said, "Blessed be the God of Shadrach, Meshach, and Abednego, who has sent his angel and delivered his servants who trusted in him, and have changed the king's word, and have yielded their bodies, that they might not serve nor worship any god, except their own God. 96 Therefore I make a decree, that every people, nation, and language, who speak anything evil against the God of Shadrach, Meshach, and Abednego, shall be cut in pieces, and their houses shall be made a dunghill, because there is no other god who is able to deliver like this." 97 Then the king promoted Shadrach, Meshach, and Abednego in the province of Babylon.

4

1 Nebuchadnezzar the king, to all the peoples, nations, and languages, who dwell in all the earth: Peace be multiplied to you. 2 It has seemed good to me to show the signs and wonders that the Most High God has worked toward me. 3 How great are his signs! How mighty are his wonders! His kingdom is an everlasting kingdom. His dominion is from generation to generation. 4 I, Nebuchadnezzar, was at rest in my house, and flourishing in my palace. 5 I saw a dream which made me afraid; and the thoughts on my bed and the visions of my head troubled me. 6 Therefore I made a decree to bring in all the wise men of Babylon before me, that they might make known to me the interpretation of the dream. 7 Then the magicians, the enchanters, the Chaldeans, and the soothsayers came in; and I told the dream before them; but they didn't make known to me its interpretation. 8 But at the last Daniel came in before me, whose name was Belteshazzar,

---

[a] *3:24 The Song of the Three Holy Children* is an addition to *Daniel* found in the Greek Septuagint but not found in the traditional Hebrew text of *Daniel*. This portion is recognized as Deuterocanonical Scripture by the Roman Catholic, Greek Orthodox, and Russian Orthodox Churches. It is found inserted between Daniel **3:23** and Daniel **3:24** of the traditional Hebrew Bible. Here, the verses after **23** from the Hebrew Bible are numbered starting at **91** to make room for these verses.

[b] *3:77* Some authorities transpose this verse and the next one.

[c] *3:91* Verses **91**-**97** were numbered **24**-**30** in the traditional Hebrew text of Daniel.

according to the name of my god, and in whom is the spirit of the holy gods. I told the dream before him, saying, ⁹"Belteshazzar, master of the magicians, because I know that the spirit of the holy gods is in you, and no secret troubles you, tell me the visions of my dream that I have seen, and its interpretation. ¹⁰ These were the visions of my head on my bed: I saw, and behold, a tree in the middle of the earth; and its height was great. ¹¹ The tree grew, and was strong, and its height reached to the sky, and its sight to the end of all the earth. ¹² Its leaves were beautiful, and it had much fruit, and in it was food for all. The animals of the field had shade under it, and the birds of the sky lived in its branches, and all flesh was fed from it. ¹³"I saw in the visions of my head on my bed, and behold, a watcher and a holy one came down from the sky. ¹⁴ He cried aloud, and said this, 'Cut down the tree and cut off its branches! Shake off its leaves and scatter its fruit! Let the animals get away from under it, and the fowls from its branches. ¹⁵ Nevertheless leave the stump of its roots in the earth, even with a band of iron and bronze, in the tender grass of the field; and let it be wet with the dew of the sky. Let his portion be with the animals in the grass of the earth. ¹⁶ Let his heart be changed from man's, and let an animal's heart be given to him. Then let seven times pass over him. ¹⁷"The sentence is by the decree of the watchers, and the demand by the word of the holy ones, to the intent that the living may know that the Most High rules in the kingdom of men, and gives it to whomever he will, and sets up over it the lowest of men.' ¹⁸"This dream I, King Nebuchadnezzar, have seen; and you, Belteshazzar, declare the interpretation, because all the wise men of my kingdom are not able to make known to me the interpretation; but you are able, for the spirit of the holy gods is in you." ¹⁹ Then Daniel, whose name was Belteshazzar, was stricken mute for a while, and his thoughts troubled him. The king answered, "Belteshazzar, don't let the dream, or the interpretation, trouble you." Belteshazzar answered, "My lord, may the dream be for those who hate you, and its interpretation to your adversaries. ²⁰ The tree that you saw, which grew and was strong, whose height reached to the sky, and its sight to all the earth; ²¹ whose leaves were beautiful, and its fruit plentiful, and in it was food for all; under which the animals of the field lived, and on whose branches the birds of the sky had their habitation– ²² it is you, O king, who have grown and become strong; for your greatness has grown, and reaches to the sky, and your dominion to the end of the earth. ²³"Whereas the king saw a watcher and a holy one coming down from the sky, and saying, 'Cut down the tree, and destroy it; nevertheless leave the stump of its roots in the earth, even with a band of iron and bronze, in the tender grass of the field, and let it be wet with the dew of the sky. Let his portion be with the animals of the field, until seven times pass over him.' ²⁴"This is the interpretation, O king, and it is the decree of the Most High, which has come on my lord the king: ²⁵ that you shall be driven from men, and your dwelling shall be with the animals of the field. You shall be made to eat grass as oxen, and shall be wet with the dew of the sky, and seven times shall pass over you; until you know that the Most High rules in the kingdom of men, and gives it to whomever he will. ²⁶ Their command to leave the stump of the roots of the tree means your kingdom will be sure to you, after you will have known that the heavens do rule. ²⁷ Therefore, O king, let my counsel be acceptable to you, and break off your sins by righteousness, and your iniquities by showing mercy to the poor. Perhaps there may be a lengthening of your tranquility." ²⁸ All this came on the King Nebuchadnezzar. ²⁹ At the end of twelve months he was walking in the royal palace of Babylon. ³⁰ The king spoke and said, "Is not this great Babylon, which I have built for the royal dwelling place, by the might of my power and for the glory of my majesty?" ³¹ While the word was in the king's mouth, a voice came from the sky, saying, "O King Nebuchadnezzar, to you it is spoken: 'The kingdom has departed from you. ³² You shall be driven from men, and your dwelling shall be with the animals of the field. You shall be made to eat grass as oxen. Seven times shall pass over you, until you know that the Most High rules in the kingdom of men, and gives it to whomever he will.'" ³³ This was fulfilled the same hour on Nebuchadnezzar. He was driven from men, and ate grass as oxen, and his body was wet with the dew of the sky, until his hair had grown like eagles' feathers, and his nails like birds' claws. ³⁴ At the end of the days I, Nebuchadnezzar, lifted up my eyes to heaven, and my understanding returned to me, and I blessed the Most High, and I praised and honored him who lives forever. For his dominion is an everlasting dominion, and his kingdom from generation to generation. ³⁵ All the inhabitants of the earth are reputed as nothing; and he does according to his will in the army of heaven, and among the inhabitants of the earth; and no one can stop his hand, or ask him, "What are you doing?" ³⁶ At the same time my understanding returned to me; and for the glory of my kingdom, my majesty and brightness returned to me. My counselors and my lords sought me; and I was established in my kingdom, and excellent greatness was added to me. ³⁷ Now I, Nebuchadnezzar, praise and extol and honor the King of heaven; for all his works are right and his ways just; and those who walk in pride he is able to humble.

5

¹ Belshazzar the king made a great feast to a thousand of his lords, and drank wine before the thousand. ² Belshazzar, while he tasted the wine, commanded that the golden and silver vessels which Nebuchadnezzar his father had taken out of the temple which was in Jerusalem be brought to him, that the king and his lords, his wives and his concubines, might drink from them. ³ Then they brought the golden vessels that were taken out of the temple of God's house which was at Jerusalem; and the king and his lords, his wives and his concubines, drank from them. ⁴ They drank wine, and praised the gods of gold, and of silver, of bronze, of iron, of wood, and of stone. ⁵ In the same hour, the fingers of a man's hand came out and wrote near the lamp stand on the plaster of the wall of the king's palace. The king saw the part of the hand that wrote. ⁶ Then the king's face was changed in him, and his thoughts troubled him; and the joints of his thighs were loosened, and his knees struck one against another. ⁷ The king cried aloud to bring in the enchanters, the Chaldeans, and the soothsayers. The king spoke and said to the wise men of Babylon, "Whoever reads this writing and shows me its interpretation shall be clothed with purple, and have a chain of gold about his neck, and shall be the third ruler in the kingdom." ⁸ Then all the king's wise men came in; but they could not read the writing and couldn't make known to the king the interpretation. ⁹ Then King Belshazzar was greatly troubled. His face was changed in him, and his lords were perplexed. ¹⁰ The queen by reason of the words of the king and his lords came into the banquet house. The queen spoke and said, "O king, live forever; don't let your thoughts trouble you, nor let your face be changed. ¹¹ There is a man in your kingdom in whom is the spirit of the holy gods. In the days of your father, light, understanding, and wisdom like the wisdom of the gods were found in him. The king, Nebuchadnezzar, your father–yes, the king, your father–made him master of the magicians, enchanters, Chaldeans, and soothsayers ¹² because an excellent spirit, knowledge, understanding, interpreting of dreams, showing of dark sentences, and dissolving of doubts were found in the same Daniel, whom the king named Belteshazzar. Now let Daniel be called, and he will show the interpretation." ¹³ Then Daniel was brought in before the king. The king spoke and said to Daniel, "Are you that Daniel of the children of the captivity of Judah, whom the king my father brought out of Judah? ¹⁴ I have heard of you, that the spirit of the gods is in you, and that light, understanding, and excellent wisdom are found in you. ¹⁵ Now the wise men, the enchanters, have been brought in before me to read this writing, and make known to me its interpretation; but they could not show the interpretation of the thing. ¹⁶ But I have heard of you, that you can give interpretations and dissolve doubts. Now if you can read the writing, and make known to me its interpretation, you shall be clothed with purple, and have a chain of gold around your neck, and shall be the third ruler in the kingdom." ¹⁷ Then Daniel answered the king, "Let your gifts be to yourself, and give your rewards to another. Nevertheless, I will read the writing to the king, and make known to him the interpretation. ¹⁸"To you, king, the Most High God gave Nebuchadnezzar your father the kingdom, and greatness, and glory, and majesty. ¹⁹ Because of the greatness that he gave him, all the peoples, nations, and languages trembled and feared before him. He killed whom he wanted to, and he kept alive whom he wanted to. He raised up whom he wanted to, and he put down whom he wanted to. ²⁰ But when his heart was lifted up, and his spirit was hardened so that he dealt proudly, he was deposed from his kingly throne, and they took his glory from him. ²¹ He was driven from the sons of men and his heart was made like the animals', and his dwelling was with the wild donkeys. He was fed with grass like oxen, and his body was wet with the dew of the sky, until he knew that the Most High God rules in the kingdom of men, and that he sets up over it whomever he will. ²²"You, his son, Belshazzar, have not humbled your heart, though you knew all this, ²³ but have lifted up yourself against the Lord of heaven; and they have brought the vessels of his house before you, and you and your lords, your wives, and your concubines, have drunk wine from them. You have praised the gods of silver, gold, bronze, iron, wood, and stone, which don't see, hear, or know; and you have not glorified the God in whose hand is your breath and whose are all your ways. ²⁴ Then the part of the hand was sent from before him, and this writing was inscribed. ²⁵"This is the writing that was inscribed: 'MENE, MENE, TEKEL, UPHARSIN.' ²⁶"This is the interpretation of the thing: MENE: God has counted your kingdom, and brought it to an end. ²⁷ TEKEL: you are weighed in the balances, and are found wanting. ²⁸ PERES: your kingdom is divided, and given to the Medes and Persians." ²⁹ Then Belshazzar commanded, and they clothed Daniel with purple, and put a chain of gold about his neck, and proclaimed that he should be the third

highest ruler in the kingdom. ³⁰ In that night Belshazzar the Chaldean King was slain. ³¹ Darius the Mede received the kingdom, being about sixty-two years old.

6

¹ It pleased Darius to set over the kingdom one hundred twenty local governors, who should be throughout the whole kingdom; ² and over them three presidents, of whom Daniel was one; that these local governors might give account to them, and that the king should suffer no loss. ³ Then this Daniel was distinguished above the presidents and the local governors, because an excellent spirit was in him; and the king thought to set him over the whole realm. ⁴ Then the presidents and the local governors sought to find occasion against Daniel as touching the kingdom; but they could find no occasion or fault, because he was faithful. There wasn't any error or fault found in him. ⁵ Then these men said, "We won't find any occasion against this Daniel, unless we find it against him concerning the law of his God." ⁶ Then these presidents and local governors assembled together to the king, and said this to him, "King Darius, live forever! ⁷ All the presidents of the kingdom, the deputies and the local governors, the counselors and the governors, have consulted together to establish a royal statute, and to make a strong decree, that whoever asks a petition of any god or man for thirty days, except of you, O king, he shall be cast into the den of lions. ⁸ Now, O king, establish the decree, and sign the writing, that it not be changed, according to the law of the Medes and Persians, which doesn't alter." ⁹ Therefore King Darius signed the writing and the decree. ¹⁰ When Daniel knew that the writing was signed, he went into his house (now his windows were open in his room toward Jerusalem) and he kneeled on his knees three times a day, and prayed, and gave thanks before his God, as he did before. ¹¹ Then these men assembled together, and found Daniel making petition and supplication before his God. ¹² Then they came near, and spoke before the king concerning the king's decree: "Haven't you signed a decree that every man who makes a petition to any god or man within thirty days, except to you, O king, shall be cast into the den of lions?" The king answered, "This thing is true, according to the law of the Medes and Persians, which doesn't alter." ¹³ Then they answered and said before the king, "That Daniel, who is of the children of the captivity of Judah, doesn't respect you, O king, nor the decree that you have signed, but makes his petition three times a day." ¹⁴ Then the king, when he heard these words, was very displeased, and set his heart on Daniel to deliver him; and he labored until the going down of the sun to rescue him. ¹⁵ Then these men assembled together to the king, and said to the king, "Know, O king, that it is a law of the Medes and Persians, that no decree nor statute which the king establishes may be changed." ¹⁶ Then the king commanded, and they brought Daniel, and cast him into the den of lions. The king spoke and said to Daniel, "Your God whom you serve continually, he will deliver you." ¹⁷ A stone was brought, and laid on the mouth of the den; and the king sealed it with his own signet, and with the signet of his lords, that nothing might be changed concerning Daniel. ¹⁸ Then the king went to his palace, and passed the night fasting. No musical instruments were brought before him; and his sleep fled from him. ¹⁹ Then the king arose very early in the morning, and went in haste to the den of lions. ²⁰ When he came near to the den to Daniel, he cried with a troubled voice. The king spoke and said to Daniel, "Daniel, servant of the living God, is your God, whom you serve continually, able to deliver you from the lions?" ²¹ Then Daniel said to the king, "O king, live forever! ²² My God has sent his angel, and has shut the lions' mouths, and they have not hurt me; because I am innocent in his sight. Also before you, O king, I have done no harm." ²³ Then the king was exceedingly glad, and commanded that they should take Daniel up out of the den. So Daniel was taken up out of the den, and no kind of harm was found on him, because he had trusted in his God. ²⁴ The king commanded, and they brought those men who had accused Daniel, and they cast them into the den of lions–them, their children, and their wives; and the lions mauled them and broke all their bones in pieces before they came to the bottom of the den. ²⁵ Then King Darius wrote to all the peoples, nations, and languages, who dwell in all the earth: "Peace be multiplied to you. ²⁶"I make a decree that in all the dominion of my kingdom men tremble and fear before the God of Daniel; "for he is the living God, and steadfast forever. His kingdom is that which will not be destroyed. His dominion will be even to the end. ²⁷ He delivers and rescues. He works signs and wonders in heaven and in earth, who has delivered Daniel from the power of the lions." ²⁸ So this Daniel prospered in the reign of Darius, and in the reign of Cyrus the Persian.

7

¹ In the first year of Belshazzar king of Babylon, Daniel had a dream and visions of his head on his bed. Then he wrote the dream and told the sum of the matters. ² Daniel spoke and said, "I saw in my vision by night and behold, the four winds of the sky broke out on the great sea. ³ Four great animals came up from the sea, different from one another. ⁴"The first was like a lion, and had eagle's wings. I watched until its wings were plucked, and it was lifted up from the earth, and made to stand on two feet as a man. A man's heart was given to it. ⁵"Behold, there was another animal, a second, like a bear. It was raised up on one side, and three ribs were in its mouth between its teeth. They said this to it: 'Arise! Devour much flesh!' ⁶"After this I saw, and behold, another, like a leopard, which had on its back four wings of a bird. The animal also had four heads; and dominion was given to it. ⁷"After this I saw in the night visions, and, behold, there was a fourth animal, awesome and powerful, and exceedingly strong. It had great iron teeth. It devoured and broke in pieces, and stamped the residue with its feet. It was different from all the animals that were before it. It had ten horns. ⁸"I considered the horns, and behold, another horn came up among them, a little one, before which three of the first horns were plucked up by the roots: and behold, in this horn were eyes like the eyes of a man, and a mouth speaking great things. ⁹"I watched until thrones were placed, and one who was Ancient of Days sat. His clothing was white as snow, and the hair of his head like pure wool. His throne was fiery flames, and its wheels burning fire. ¹⁰ A fiery stream issued and came out from before him. Thousands of thousands ministered to him. Ten thousand times ten thousand stood before him. The judgment was set. The books were opened. ¹¹"I watched at that time because of the voice of the great words which the horn spoke. I watched even until the animal was slain, its body destroyed, and it was given to be burned with fire. ¹² As for the rest of the animals, their dominion was taken away; yet their lives were prolonged for a season and a time. ¹³"I saw in the night visions, and behold, one like a son of man came with the clouds, and he came to the Ancient of Days, and they brought him near before him. ¹⁴ Dominion was given him, with glory and a kingdom, that all the peoples, nations, and languages should serve him. His dominion is an everlasting dominion, which will not pass away, and his kingdom will not be destroyed. ¹⁵"As for me, Daniel, my spirit was grieved within my body, and the visions of my head troubled me. ¹⁶ I came near to one of those who stood by, and asked him the truth concerning all this. "So he told me, and made me know the interpretation of the things. ¹⁷"These great animals, which are four, are four kings, who will arise out of the earth. ¹⁸ But the saints of the Most High will receive the kingdom, and possess the kingdom forever, even forever and ever.' ¹⁹"Then I desired to know the truth concerning the fourth animal, which was different from all of them, exceedingly terrible, whose teeth were of iron, and its nails of bronze; which devoured, broke in pieces, and stamped the residue with its feet; ²⁰ and concerning the ten horns that were on its head, and the other horn which came up, and before which three fell, even that horn that had eyes, and a mouth that spoke great things, whose look was more stout than its fellows. ²¹ I saw, and the same horn made war with the saints and prevailed against them ²² until the Ancient of Days came, and judgment was given to the saints of the Most High, and the time came that the saints possessed the kingdom. ²³"So he said, 'The fourth animal will be a fourth kingdom on earth, which will be different from all the kingdoms, and will devour the whole earth, and will tread it down, and break it in pieces. ²⁴ As for the ten horns, ten kings will arise out of this kingdom. Another will arise after them; and he will be different from the former, and he will put down three kings. ²⁵ He will speak words against the Most High, and will wear out the saints of the Most High. He will plan to change the times and the law; and they will be given into his hand until a time and times and half a time. ²⁶"'But the judgment will be set, and they will take away his dominion, to consume and to destroy it to the end. ²⁷ The kingdom and the dominion, and the greatness of the kingdoms under the whole sky, will be given to the people of the saints of the Most High. His kingdom is an everlasting kingdom, and all dominions will serve and obey him.' ²⁸"Here is the end of the matter. As for me, Daniel, my thoughts troubled me greatly, and my face was changed in me; but I kept the matter in my heart."

8

¹ In the third year of the reign of King Belshazzar, a vision appeared to me, even to me, Daniel, after that which appeared to me at the first. ² I saw the vision. Now it was so, that when I saw, I was in the citadel of Susa, which is in the province of Elam. I saw in the vision, and I was by the river Ulai. ³ Then I lifted up my eyes, and saw, and behold, a ram which had two horns stood before the river. The two horns were high; but one was higher than the other, and the higher came up last. ⁴ I saw the ram pushing westward, northward, and southward. No animals could stand before him. There wasn't anyone who could deliver out of his hand; but he did according to his will, and magnified himself. ⁵ As I was considering, behold, a male goat came from the west over the surface of the whole earth, and didn't touch the ground. The goat had a notable horn between his eyes. ⁶ He came to the

ram that had the two horns, which I saw standing before the river, and ran on him in the fury of his power. ⁷ I saw him come close to the ram, and he was moved with anger against him, and struck the ram, and broke his two horns. There was no power in the ram to stand before him; but he cast him down to the ground, and trampled on him. There was no one who could deliver the ram out of his hand. ⁸ The male goat magnified himself exceedingly. When he was strong, the great horn was broken; and instead of it there came up four notable horns toward the four winds of the sky. ⁹ Out of one of them came out a little horn, which grew exceedingly great, toward the south, and toward the east, and toward the glorious land. ¹⁰ It grew great, even to the army of the sky; and it cast down some of the army and of the stars to the ground, and trampled on them. ¹¹ Yes, it magnified itself, even to the prince of the army; and it took away from him the continual burnt offering, and the place of his sanctuary was cast down. ¹² The army was given over to it together with the continual burnt offering through disobedience. It cast down truth to the ground, and it did its pleasure and prospered. ¹³ Then I heard a holy one speaking; and another holy one said to that certain one who spoke, "How long will the vision about the continual burnt offering, and the disobedience that makes desolate, to give both the sanctuary and the army to be trodden under foot be?" ¹⁴ He said to me, "To two thousand and three hundred evenings and mornings. Then the sanctuary will be cleansed." ¹⁵ When I, even I Daniel, had seen the vision, I sought to understand it. Then behold, there stood before me something like the appearance of a man. ¹⁶ I heard a man's voice between the banks of the Ulai, which called, and said, "Gabriel, make this man understand the vision." ¹⁷ So he came near where I stood; and when he came, I was frightened, and fell on my face; but he said to me, "Understand, son of man; for the vision belongs to the time of the end." ¹⁸ Now as he was speaking with me, I fell into a deep sleep with my face toward the ground; but he touched me, and set me upright. ¹⁹ He said, "Behold, I will make you know what will be in the latter time of the indignation; for it belongs to the appointed time of the end. ²⁰ The ram which you saw, that had the two horns, they are the kings of Media and Persia. ²¹ The rough male goat is the king of Greece. The great horn that is between his eyes is the first king. ²² As for that which was broken, in the place where four stood up, four kingdoms will stand up out of the nation, but not with his power. ²³"In the latter time of their kingdom, when the transgressors have come to the full, a king of fierce face, and understanding dark sentences, will stand up. ²⁴ His power will be mighty, but not by his own power. He will destroy awesomely, and will prosper in what he does. He will destroy the mighty ones and the holy people. ²⁵ Through his policy he will cause deceit to prosper in his hand. He will magnify himself in his heart, and he will destroy many in their security. He will also stand up against the prince of princes; but he will be broken without human power. ²⁶"The vision of the evenings and mornings which has been told is true; but seal up the vision, for it belongs to many days to come." ²⁷ I, Daniel, fainted, and was sick for some days. Then I rose up, and did the king's business. I wondered at the vision, but no one understood it.

9

¹ In the first year of Darius the son of Ahasuerus, of the offspring of the Medes, who was made king over the realm of the Chaldeans, ² in the first year of his reign I, Daniel, understood by the books the number of the years about which Yahweh's[a] word came to Jeremiah the prophet, for the accomplishing of the desolations of Jerusalem, even seventy years. ³ I set my face to the Lord God, to seek by prayer and petitions, with fasting in sackcloth and ashes. ⁴ I prayed to Yahweh my God, and made confession, and said, "Oh, Lord, the great and dreadful God, who keeps covenant and loving kindness with those who love him and keep his commandments, ⁵ we have sinned, and have dealt perversely, and have done wickedly, and have rebelled, even turning aside from your precepts and from your ordinances. ⁶ We haven't listened to your servants the prophets, who spoke in your name to our kings, our princes, and our fathers, and to all the people of the land. ⁷"Lord, righteousness belongs to you, but to us confusion of face, as it is today–to the men of Judah, and to the inhabitants of Jerusalem, and to all Israel, who are near, and who are far off, through all the countries where you have driven them, because of their trespass that they have trespassed against you. ⁸ Lord, to us belongs confusion of face, to our kings, to our princes, and to our fathers, because we have sinned against you. ⁹ To the Lord our God belong mercies and forgiveness; for we have rebelled against him. ¹⁰ We haven't obeyed Yahweh our God's voice, to walk in his laws, which he set before us by his servants the prophets. ¹¹ Yes, all Israel have transgressed your law, turning aside, that they wouldn't obey your voice. "Therefore the curse and the oath written in the law of Moses the servant of God has been poured out on us; for we have sinned against him. ¹² He has confirmed his words, which he spoke against us, and against our judges who judged us, by bringing on us a great evil; for under the whole sky, such has not been done as has been done to Jerusalem. ¹³ As it is written in the law of Moses, all this evil has come on us. Yet we have not entreated the favor of Yahweh our God, that we should turn from our iniquities and have discernment in your truth. ¹⁴ Therefore Yahweh has watched over the evil, and brought it on us; for Yahweh our God is righteous in all his works which he does, and we have not obeyed his voice. ¹⁵"Now, Lord our God, who has brought your people out of the land of Egypt with a mighty hand, and have gotten yourself renown, as it is today, we have sinned. We have done wickedly. ¹⁶ Lord, according to all your righteousness, please let your anger and your wrath be turned away from your city Jerusalem, your holy mountain, because for our sins, and for the iniquities of our fathers, Jerusalem and your people have become a reproach to all who are around us. ¹⁷"Now therefore, our God, listen to the prayer of your servant, and to his petitions, and cause your face to shine on your sanctuary that is desolate, for the Lord's sake. ¹⁸ My God, turn your ear and hear. Open your eyes and see our desolations and the city which is called by your name; for we don't present our petitions before you for our righteousness, but for your great mercies' sake. ¹⁹ Lord, hear. Lord, forgive. Lord, listen and do. Don't defer, for your own sake, my God, because your city and your people are called by your name." ²⁰ While I was speaking, praying, and confessing my sin and the sin of my people Israel, and presenting my supplication before Yahweh my God for the holy mountain of my God– ²¹ yes, while I was speaking in prayer, the man Gabriel, whom I had seen in the vision at the beginning, being caused to fly swiftly, touched me about the time of the evening offering. ²² He instructed me and talked with me, and said, "Daniel, I have now come to give you wisdom and understanding. ²³ At the beginning of your petitions the commandment went out and I have come to tell you, for you are greatly beloved. Therefore consider the matter and understand the vision. ²⁴"Seventy weeks are decreed on your people and on your holy city, to finish disobedience, to put an end to sin, to make reconciliation for iniquity, to bring in everlasting righteousness, to seal up vision and prophecy, and to anoint the most holy. ²⁵"Know therefore and discern that from the going out of the commandment to restore and to build Jerusalem to the Anointed One,[b] the prince, will be seven weeks and sixty-two weeks. It will be built again with street and moat, even in troubled times. ²⁶ After the sixty-two weeks the Anointed One[c] will be cut off and will have nothing. The people of the prince who come will destroy the city and the sanctuary. Its end will be with a flood, and war will be even to the end. Desolations are determined. ²⁷ He will make a firm covenant with many for one week. In the middle of the week he will cause the sacrifice and the offering to cease. On the wing of abominations will come one who makes desolate. Even to the full end that is decreed, wrath will be poured out on the desolate."

10

¹ In the third year of Cyrus king of Persia a revelation was revealed to Daniel, whose name was called Belteshazzar. The revelation was true, even a great warfare. He understood the revelation, and had understanding of the vision. ² In those days I, Daniel, was mourning three whole weeks. ³ I ate no pleasant bread. No meat or wine came into my mouth. I didn't anoint myself at all, until three whole weeks were fulfilled. ⁴ In the twenty-fourth day of the first month, as I was by the side of the great river, which is Hiddekel, ⁵ I lifted up my eyes and looked, and behold, there was a man clothed in linen, whose thighs were adorned with pure gold of Uphaz. ⁶ His body also was like beryl, and his face like the appearance of lightning, and his eyes like flaming torches. His arms and his feet were like burnished bronze. The voice of his words was like the voice of a multitude. ⁷ I, Daniel, alone saw the vision; for the men who were with me didn't see the vision; but a great quaking fell on them, and they fled to hide themselves. ⁸ So I was left alone, and saw this great vision. No strength remained in me; for my face grew deathly pale, and I retained no strength. ⁹ Yet I heard the voice of his words. When I heard the voice of his words, then I fell into a deep sleep on my face, with my face toward the ground. ¹⁰ Behold, a hand touched me, which set me on my knees and on the palms of my hands. ¹¹ He said to me, "Daniel, you greatly beloved man, understand the words that I speak to you. Stand upright, for I have been sent to you, now." When he had spoken this word to me, I stood trembling. ¹² Then he said to me, "Don't be afraid, Daniel; for from the first day that you set your heart to understand, and to humble yourself before your God, your words were heard. I have come for your words' sake. ¹³ But the prince of the kingdom of Persia

---

[a] 9:2 "Yahweh" is God's proper Name, sometimes rendered "LORD" (all caps) in other translations.

[b] 9:25 "Anointed One" can also be translated "Messiah" (same as "Christ").

[c] 9:26 "Anointed One" can also be translated "Messiah" (same as "Christ").

withstood me twenty-one days; but, behold, Michael, one of the chief princes, came to help me because I remained there with the kings of Persia. ¹⁴ Now I have come to make you understand what will happen to your people in the latter days; for the vision is yet for many days." ¹⁵ When he had spoken these words to me, I set my face toward the ground, and was mute. ¹⁶ Behold, one in the likeness of the sons of men touched my lips. Then I opened my mouth, and spoke and said to him who stood before me, "My lord, by reason of the vision my sorrows have overtaken me, and I retain no strength. ¹⁷ For how can the servant of my lord talk with my lord? For as for me, immediately there remained no strength in me. There was no breath left in me." ¹⁸ Then one like the appearance of a man touched me again, and he strengthened me. ¹⁹ He said, "Greatly beloved man, don't be afraid. Peace be to you. Be strong. Yes, be strong." When he spoke to me, I was strengthened, and said, "Let my lord speak; for you have strengthened me." ²⁰ Then he said, "Do you know why I have come to you? Now I will return to fight with the prince of Persia. When I go out, behold, the prince of Greece will come. ²¹ But I will tell you what is inscribed in the writing of truth. There is no one who supports me against these except Michael, your prince.

11

¹"As for me, in the first year of Darius the Mede, I stood up to confirm and strengthen him. ²"Now I will show you the truth. Behold, three more kings will stand up in Persia. The fourth will be far richer than all of them. When he has grown strong through his riches, he will stir up all against the realm of Greece. ³ A mighty king will stand up who will rule with great dominion, and do according to his will. ⁴ When he stands up, his kingdom will be broken, and will be divided toward the four winds of the sky, but not to his posterity, nor according to his dominion with which he ruled; for his kingdom will be plucked up, even for others besides these. ⁵"The king of the south will be strong. One of his princes will become stronger than him and have dominion. His dominion will be a great dominion. ⁶ At the end of years they will join themselves together. The daughter of the king of the south will come to the king of the north to make an agreement, but she will not retain the strength of her arm. He will also not stand, nor will his arm; but she will be given up, with those who brought her and he who became her father, and he who strengthened her in those times. ⁷"But out of a shoot from her roots one will stand up in his place who will come to the army and will enter into the fortress of the king of the north, and will deal against them and will prevail. ⁸ He will also carry their gods, with their molten images and their precious vessels of silver and of gold, captive into Egypt. He will refrain some years from the king of the north. ⁹ He will come into the realm of the king of the south, but he will return into his own land. ¹⁰ His sons will wage war and will assemble a multitude of great forces which will keep coming and overflow and pass through. They will return and wage war, even to his fortress. ¹¹"The king of the south will be moved with anger and will come out and fight with him, even with the king of the north. He will send out a great multitude, and the multitude will be given into his hand. ¹² The multitude will be lifted up, and his heart will be exalted. He will cast down tens of thousands, but he won't prevail. ¹³ The king of the north will return, and will send out a multitude greater than the former. He will come on at the end of the times, even of years, with a great army and with abundant supplies. ¹⁴"In those times many will stand up against the king of the south. Also the children of the violent among your people will lift themselves up to establish the vision; but they will fall. ¹⁵ So the king of the north will come and cast up a mound, and take a well-fortified city. The forces of the south won't stand, neither will his chosen people, neither will there be any strength to stand. ¹⁶ But he who comes against him will do according to his own will, and no one will stand before him. He will stand in the glorious land, and destruction will be in his hand. ¹⁷ He will set his face to come with the strength of his whole kingdom, and with him equitable conditions. He will perform them. He will give him the daughter of women to corrupt her; but she will not stand, and won't be for him. ¹⁸ After this he will turn his face to the islands, and will take many; but a prince will cause the reproach offered by him to cease. Yes, moreover, he will cause his reproach to turn on him. ¹⁹ Then he will turn his face toward the fortresses of his own land; but he will stumble and fall, and won't be found. ²⁰"Then one who will cause a tax collector to pass through the kingdom to maintain its glory will stand up in his place; but within few days he shall be destroyed, not in anger, and not in battle. ²¹"In his place, a contemptible person will stand up, to whom they had not given the honor of the kingdom; but he will come in time of security, and will obtain the kingdom by flatteries. ²² The overwhelming forces will be overwhelmed from before him, and will be broken. Yes, also the prince of the covenant. ²³ After the treaty is made with him, he will work deceitfully; for he will come up, and will become strong with a small people. ²⁴ In time of security, he will come even on the fattest places of the province. He will do that which his fathers have not done, nor his fathers' fathers. He will scatter among them prey, plunder, and substance. Yes, he will devise his plans against the strongholds, even for a time. ²⁵"He will stir up his power and his courage against the king of the south with a great army; and the king of the south will wage war in battle with an exceedingly great and mighty army; but he won't stand, for they will devise plans against him. ²⁶ Yes, those who eat of his delicacies will destroy him, and his army will be swept away. Many will fall down slain. ²⁷ As for both these kings, their hearts will be to do mischief, and they will speak lies at one table; but it won't prosper, for the end will still be at the appointed time. ²⁸ Then he will return into his land with great wealth. His heart will be against the holy covenant. He will take action and return to his own land. ²⁹"He will return at the appointed time and come into the south; but it won't be in the latter time as it was in the former. ³⁰ For ships of Kittim will come against him. Therefore he will be grieved, and will return, and have indignation against the holy covenant, and will take action. He will even return, and have regard to those who forsake the holy covenant. ³¹"Forces will stand on his part and they will profane the sanctuary, even the fortress, and will take away the continual burnt offering. Then they will set up the abomination that makes desolate. ³² He will corrupt those who do wickedly against the covenant by flatteries; but the people who know their God will be strong and take action. ³³"Those who are wise among the people will instruct many; yet they will fall by the sword and by flame, by captivity and by plunder, many days. ³⁴ Now when they fall, they will be helped with a little help; but many will join themselves to them with flatteries. ³⁵ Some of those who are wise will fall, to refine them, and to purify, and to make them white, even to the time of the end; because it is yet for the appointed time. ³⁶"The king will do according to his will. He will exalt himself, and magnify himself above every god, and will speak marvelous things against the God of gods. He will prosper until the indignation is accomplished; for what is determined will be done. ³⁷ He won't regard the gods of his fathers, or the desire of women, or regard any god; for he will magnify himself above all. ³⁸ But in his place he will honor the god of fortresses. He will honor a god whom his fathers didn't know with gold, silver, precious stones, and pleasant things. ³⁹ He will deal with the strongest fortresses by the help of a foreign god. He will increase with glory whoever acknowledges him. He will cause them to rule over many, and will divide the land for a price. ⁴⁰"At the time of the end, the king of the south will contend with him; and the king of the north will come against him like a whirlwind, with chariots, with horsemen, and with many ships. He will enter into the countries, and will overflow and pass through. ⁴¹ He will enter also into the glorious land, and many countries will be overthrown; but these will be delivered out of his hand: Edom, Moab, and the chief of the children of Ammon. ⁴² He will also stretch out his hand against the countries. The land of Egypt won't escape. ⁴³ But he will have power over the treasures of gold and of silver, and over all the precious things of Egypt. The Libyans and the Ethiopians will be at his steps. ⁴⁴ But news out of the east and out of the north will trouble him; and he will go out with great fury to destroy and utterly to sweep away many. ⁴⁵ He will plant the tents of his palace between the sea and the glorious holy mountain; yet he will come to his end, and no one will help him.

12

¹"At that time Michael will stand up, the great prince who stands for the children of your people. There will be a time of trouble, such as never was since there was a nation even to that same time. At that time, your people will be delivered–everyone who is found written in the book. ² Many of those who sleep in the dust of the earth will awake, some to everlasting life, and some to shame and everlasting contempt. ³ Those who are wise will shine as the brightness of the expanse. Those who turn many to righteousness will shine like the stars forever and ever. ⁴ But you, Daniel, shut up the words and seal the book, even to the time of the end. Many will run back and forth, and knowledge will be increased."
⁵ Then I, Daniel, looked, and behold, two others stood, one on the river bank on this side, and the other on the river bank on that side. ⁶ One said to the man clothed in linen, who was above the waters of the river, "How long will it be to the end of these wonders?" ⁷ I heard the man clothed in linen, who was above the waters of the river, when he held up his right hand and his left hand to heaven, and swore by him who lives forever that it will be for a time, times, and a half; and when they have finished breaking in pieces the power of the holy people, all these things will be finished. ⁸ I heard, but I didn't understand. Then I said, "My lord, what will be the outcome of these things?" ⁹ He said, "Go your way, Daniel; for the words are shut up and sealed until the time of the end. ¹⁰ Many will purify themselves, make themselves white, and be refined; but the wicked will do wickedly. None of the wicked will understand; but those who are wise will understand.

¹¹"From the time that the continual burnt offering is taken away and the abomination that makes desolate set up, there will be one thousand two hundred ninety days. ¹² Blessed is he who waits and comes to the one thousand three hundred thirty-five days. ¹³"But go your way until the end; for you will rest and will stand in your inheritance at the end of the days."

The History of Susanna
13

¹ ᵃA man lived in Babylon, and his name was Joakim. ² He took a wife, whose name was Susanna, the daughter of Helkias, a very fair woman, and one who feared the Lord. ³ Her parents were also righteous, and taught their daughter according to the law of Moses. ⁴ Now Joakim was a great rich man, and had a beautiful garden next to his house. The Jews used to come to him, because he was more honorable than all others. ⁵ The same year, two of the elders of the people were appointed to be judges, such as the Lord spoke of, that wickedness came from Babylon from elders who were judges, who were supposed to govern the people. ⁶ These were often at Joakim's house. All that had any lawsuits came to them. ⁷ When the people departed away at noon, Susanna went into her husband's garden to walk. ⁸ The two elders saw her going in every day and walking; and they were inflamed with lust for her. ⁹ They perverted their own mind and turned away their eyes, that they might not look to heaven, nor remember just judgments. ¹⁰ And although they both were wounded with lust for her, yet dared not show the other his grief. ¹¹ For they were ashamed to declare their lust, what they desired to do with her. ¹² Yet they watched eagerly from day to day to see her. ¹³ The one said to the other, "Let's go home, now; for it is dinner time." ¹⁴ So when they had gone out, they parted company, and turning back again, they came to the same place. After they had asked one another the cause, they acknowledged their lust. Then they appointed a time both together, when they might find her alone. ¹⁵ It happened, as they watched on an opportune day, she went in as before with only two maids, and she desired to wash herself in the garden; for it was hot. ¹⁶ There was nobody there except the two elders who had hid themselves and watched her. ¹⁷ Then she said to her maids, "Bring me olive oil and ointment, and shut the garden doors, that I may wash myself." ¹⁸ They did as she asked them and shut the garden doors, and went out themselves at the side doors to fetch the things that she had commanded them. They didn't see the elders, because they were hidden. ¹⁹ Now when the maids had gone out, the two elders rose up and ran to her, saying, ²⁰"Behold, the garden doors are shut, that no man can see us, and we are in love with you. Therefore consent to us, and lie with us. ²¹ If you will not, we will testify against you, that a young man was with you; therefore you sent your maids away from you." ²² Then Susanna sighed, and said, "I am trapped; for if I do this thing, it is death to me. If I don't do it, I can't escape your hands. ²³ It is better for me to fall into your hands, and not do it, than to sin in the sight of the Lord." ²⁴ With that Susanna cried with a loud voice; and the two elders cried out against her. ²⁵ Then one of them ran and opened the garden doors. ²⁶ So when the servants of the house heard the cry in the garden, they rushed in at the side door to see what had happened to her. ²⁷ But when the elders had told their tale, the servants were greatly ashamed; for there was never such a report made of Susanna. ²⁸ It came to pass on the next day, when the people assembled to her husband Joakim, the two elders came full of their wicked intent against Susanna to put her to death, ²⁹ and said before the people, "Send for Susanna, the daughter of Helkias, Joakim's wife." So they sent; ³⁰ and she came with her father and mother, her children, and all her kindred. ³¹ Now Susanna was a very delicate woman, and beautiful to behold. ³² These wicked men commanded her to be unveiled, for she was veiled, that they might be filled with her beauty. ³³ Therefore her friends and all who saw her wept. ³⁴ Then the two elders stood up in the midst of the people and laid their hands upon her head. ³⁵ She, weeping, looked up toward heaven; for her heart trusted in the Lord. ³⁶ The elders said, "As we walked in the garden alone, this woman came in with two maids, shut the garden doors, and sent the maids away. ³⁷ Then a young man who was hidden there came to her and lay with her. ³⁸ And we, being in a corner of the garden, saw this wickedness and ran to them. ³⁹ And when we saw them together, we couldn't hold the man; for he was stronger than we, and opened the doors, and leaped out. ⁴⁰ But having taken this woman, we asked who the young man was, but she would not tell us. We testify these things." ⁴¹ Then the assembly believed them, as those who were elders of the people and judges; so they condemned her to death. ⁴² Then Susanna cried out with a loud voice, and said, "O everlasting God, you know the secrets, and know all things before they happen. ⁴³ You know that they have testified falsely against me. Behold, I must die, even though I never did such things as these men have maliciously invented against me." ⁴⁴ The Lord heard her voice. ⁴⁵ Therefore when she was led away to be put to death, God raised up the holy spirit of a young youth, whose name was Daniel. ⁴⁶ He cried with a loud voice, "I am clear from the blood of this woman!" ⁴⁷ Then all the people

---

ᵃ *13:1 The History of Susanna* is translated from chapter **13** of *Daniel* in the Greek Septuagint. It is not found in the traditional Hebrew text of *Daniel*. The *History of Susanna* is recognized as Deuterocanonical Scripture by the Roman Catholic, Greek Orthodox, and Russian Orthodox Churches.

turned them toward him, and said, "What do these words that you have spoken mean?" ⁴⁸ So he, standing in the midst of them, said, "Are you all such fools, you sons of Israel, that without examination or knowledge of the truth you have condemned a daughter of Israel? ⁴⁹ Return again to the place of judgment; for these have testified falsely against her." ⁵⁰ Therefore all the people turned again in haste, and the elders said to him, "Come, sit down among us, and show it to us, seeing God has given you the honor of an elder." ⁵¹ Then Daniel said to them, "Put them far apart from each another, and I will examine them." ⁵² So when they were put apart one from another, he called one of them, and said to him, "O you who have become old in wickedness, now your sins have returned which you have committed before, ⁵³ in pronouncing unjust judgment, condemning the innocent, and letting the guilty go free; although the Lord says, 'You shall not kill the innocent and righteous.' ⁵⁴ Now then, if you saw her, tell me, under which tree did you see them companying together?" He answered, "Under a mastick tree." ⁵⁵ And Daniel said, "You have certainly lied against your own head; for even now the angel of God has received the sentence of God and will cut you in two." ⁵⁶ So he put him aside, and commanded to bring the other, and said to him, "O you seed of Canaan, and not of Judah, beauty has deceived you, and lust has perverted your heart. ⁵⁷ Thus you have dealt with the daughters of Israel, and they for fear were intimate with you; but the daughter of Judah would not tolerate your wickedness. ⁵⁸ Now therefore tell me, under which tree did you take them being intimate together?" He answered, "Under an evergreen oak tree." ⁵⁹ Then Daniel said to him, "You have also certainly lied against your own head; for the angel of God waits with the sword to cut you in two, that he may destroy you." ⁶⁰ With that, all the assembly cried out with a loud voice, and blessed God, who saves those who hope in him. ⁶¹ Then they arose against the two elders, for Daniel had convicted them of false testimony out of their own mouth. ⁶² According to the law of Moses they did to them what they maliciously intended to do to their neighbor. They put them to death, and the innocent blood was saved the same day. ⁶³ Therefore Helkias and his wife praised God for their daughter Susanna, with Joakim her husband, and all the kindred, because there was no dishonesty found in her. ⁶⁴ And from that day forth, Daniel had a great reputation in the sight of the people.

Bel and the Dragon
14

¹ ᵃKing Astyages was gathered to his fathers, and Cyrus the Persian received his kingdom. ² Daniel lived with the king, and was honored above all his friends. ³ Now the Babylonians had an idol called Bel, and every day twelve great measures of fine flour, forty sheep, and six firkinsᵇ of wine were spent on it. ⁴ The king honored it and went daily to worship it; but Daniel worshiped his own God. The king said to him, "Why don't you worship Bel?" ⁵ He said, "Because I may not honor idols made with hands, but only the living God, who has created the sky and the earth, and has sovereignty over all flesh." ⁶ Then the king said to him, "Don't you think that Bel is a living god? Don't you see how much he eats and drinks every day?" ⁷ Then Daniel laughed, and said, "O king, don't be deceived; for this is just clay inside, and brass outside, and never ate or drank anything." ⁸ So the king was angry, and called for his priests, and said to them, "If you don't tell me who this is who devours these expenses, you shall die. ⁹ But if you can show me that Bel devours them, then Daniel shall die; for he has spoken blasphemy against Bel." Daniel said to the king, "Let it be according to your word." ¹⁰ Now there were seventy priests of Bel, besides their wives and children. The king went with Daniel into Bel's temple. ¹¹ So Bel's priests said, "Behold, we will leave; but you, O king, set out the food, and mix the wine and set it out, shut the door securely, and seal it with your own signet. ¹² When you come in the morning, if you don't find that Bel has eaten everything, we will suffer death, or else Daniel, who speaks falsely against us." ¹³ They weren't concerned, for under the table they had made a secret entrance, by which they entered in continually, and consumed those things. ¹⁴ It happened, when they had gone out, the king set the food before Bel. Now Daniel had commanded his servants to bring ashes, and they scattered them all over the temple in the presence of the king alone. Then they went out, shut the door, sealed it with the king's signet, and so departed. ¹⁵ Now in the night, the priests came with their wives and children, as they usually did, and ate and drank it all. ¹⁶ In the morning, the king arose, and Daniel with him. ¹⁷ The king said, "Daniel, are the seals whole?" He said, "Yes, O king, they are whole." ¹⁸ And as soon as he had opened the door, the king looked at the table, and cried with a loud voice, "You are great, O Bel, and with you is no deceit at all!" ¹⁹ Then Daniel laughed, and held the king that he should not go in, and said, "Behold now the pavement, and mark well whose footsteps these are." ²⁰ The king said, "I see the footsteps of men, women, and children." Then the king was angry, ²¹ and took the priests with their wives and children, who showed him the secret doors, where they came in and consumed the things that were on the table. ²² Therefore the king killed them, and delivered Bel into Daniel's power, who overthrew it and its temple. ²³ In that same place there was a great dragon which the people of Babylon worshiped. ²⁴ The king said to Daniel, "Will you also say that this is of brass? Behold, he lives, eats and drinks. You can't say that he is no living god. Therefore worship him." ²⁵ Then Daniel said, "I will worship the Lord my God; for he is a living God. ²⁶ But allow me, O king, and I will kill this dragon without sword or staff." The king said, "I allow you." ²⁷ Then Daniel took pitch, fat, and hair, and melted them together, and made lumps of them. He put these in the dragon's mouth, so the dragon ate and burst apart. Daniel said, "Behold, these are the gods you all worship." ²⁸ When the people of Babylon heard that, they took great indignation, and conspired against the king, saying, "The king has become a Jew. He has pulled down Bel, slain the dragon, and put the priests to the sword." ²⁹ So they came to the king, and said, "Deliver Daniel to us, or else we will destroy you and your house." ³⁰ Now when the king saw that they trapped him, being constrained, the king delivered Daniel to them. ³¹ They cast him into the lion's den, where he was six days. ³² There were seven lions in the den, and they had been giving them two carcasses and two sheep every day, which then were not given to them, intending that they would devour Daniel. ³³ Now there was in Jewry the prophet Habakkuk,ᶜ who had made stew, and had broken bread into a bowl. He was going into the field to bring it to the reapers. ³⁴ But the angel of the Lord said to Habakkuk, "Go carry the dinner that you have into Babylon to Daniel, in the lions' den." ³⁵ Habakkuk said, "Lord, I never saw Babylon. I don't know where the den is." ³⁶ Then the angel of the Lord took him by the crown, and lifted him up by the hair of his head, and with the blast of his breath set him in Babylon over the den. ³⁷ Habakkuk cried, saying, "O Daniel, Daniel, take the dinner which God has sent you." ³⁸ Daniel said, "You have remembered me, O God! You haven't forsaken those who love

---

ᵃ *14:1 Bel and the Dragon* is translated from chapter **14** of *Daniel* in the Greek Septuagint. It is not found in the traditional Hebrew text of *Daniel*. *Bel and the Dragon* is recognized as Deuterocanonical Scripture by the Roman Catholic, Greek Orthodox, and Russian Orthodox Churches.

ᵇ *14:3* a firkin is about **41** liters or **11** gallons.

ᶜ *14:33* Gr. Ambakoum.

you!" ³⁹ So Daniel arose and ate; and the angel of God set Habakkuk in his own place again immediately. ⁴⁰ On the seventh day, the king came to mourn for Daniel. When he came to the den, he looked in, and, behold, Daniel was sitting. ⁴¹ Then the king cried with a loud voice, saying, "Great are you, O Lord, you God of Daniel, and there is none other beside you!" ⁴² So he drew him out, and cast those that were the cause of his destruction into the den; and they were devoured in a moment before his face.

ETHIOPIAN CANON

The Book of Jubilees, or The Little Genesis

Moses receives the tables of the law and instruction on past and future history which he is to inscribe in a book, 1-4. Apostasy of Israel, 5-9. Captivity of Israel and Judah, 10-13. Return of Judah and rebuilding of the temple, 15-18. Moses' prayer for Israel, 19-21. God's promise to redeem and dwell with them, 22-5,28. Moses bidden to write down the future history of the world (the Book of Jubilees?), 26. And an angel to write down the law, 27. This angel takes the heavenly chronological tablets to dictate therefrom to Moses, 29.

Prologue

THIS is the history of the division of the days of the law and of the testimony, of the events of the years, of their (year) weeks, of their Jubilees throughout all the years of the world, as the Lord spake to Moses on Mount Sinai when he went up to receive the tables of the law and of the commandment, according to the voice of God as he said unto him, 'Go up to the top of the Mount.'

God's Revelation to Moses on Mount Sinai (i. 1-26: cf. Ex. xxiv. 15-18).

1

¹ And it came to pass in the first year of the exodus of the children of Israel out of Egypt, in the third month, on the sixteenth day of the month, [2450 Anno Mundi] that God spake to Moses, saying: 'Come up to Me on the Mount, and I will give thee two tables of stone of the law and of the commandment, which I have written, that thou mayst teach them.' ² And Moses went up into the mount of God, and the glory of the Lord abode on Mount Sinai, and a cloud overshadowed it six days. ³ And He called to Moses on the seventh day out of the midst of the cloud, and the appearance of the glory of the Lord was like a flaming fire on the top of the mount. ⁴ And Moses was on the Mount forty days and forty nights, and God taught him the earlier and the later history of the division of all the days of the law and of the testimony. ⁵ And He said: 'Incline thine heart to every word which I shall speak to thee on this mount, and write them in a book in order that their generations may see how I have not forsaken them for all the evil which they have wrought in transgressing the covenant which I establish between Me and thee for their generations this day on Mount Sinai. ⁶ And thus it will come to pass when all these things come upon them, that they will recognise that I am more righteous than they in all their judgments and in all their actions, and they will recognise that I have been truly with them. ⁷ And do thou write for thyself all these words which I declare unto, thee this day, for I know their rebellion and their stiff neck, before I bring them into the land of which I sware to their fathers, to Abraham and to Isaac and to Jacob, saying: ' Unto your seed will I give a land flowing with milk and honey. ⁸ And they will eat and be satisfied, and they will turn to strange gods, to (gods) which cannot deliver them from aught of their tribulation: and this witness shall be heard for a witness against them. ⁹ For they will forget all My commandments, (even) all that I command them, and they will walk after the Gentiles, and after their uncleanness, and after their shame, and will serve their gods, and these will prove unto them an offence and a tribulation and an affliction and a snare. ¹⁰ And many will perish and they will be taken captive, and will fall into the hands of the enemy, because they have forsaken My ordinances and My commandments, and the festivals of My covenant, and My sabbaths, and My holy place which I have hallowed for Myself in their midst, and My tabernacle, and My sanctuary, which I have hallowed for Myself in the midst of the land, that I should set my name upon it, and that it should dwell (there). ¹¹ And they will make to themselves high places and groves and graven images, and they will worship, each his own (graven image), so as to go astray, and they will sacrifice their children to demons, and to all the works of the error of their hearts. ¹² And I will send witnesses unto them, that I may witness against them, but they will not hear, and will slay the witnesses also, and they will persecute those who seek the law, and they will abrogate and change everything so as to work evil before My eyes. ¹³ And I will hide My face from them, and I will deliver them into the hand of the Gentiles for captivity, and for a prey, and for devouring, and I will remove them from the midst of the land, and I will scatter them amongst the Gentiles. ¹⁴ And they will forget all My law and all My commandments and all My judgments, and will go astray as to new moons, and sabbaths, and festivals, and jubilees, and ordinances. ¹⁵ And after this they will turn to Me from amongst the Gentiles with all their heart and with all their soul and with all their strength, and I will gather them from amongst all the Gentiles, and they will seek me, so that I shall be found of them, when they seek me with all their heart and with all their soul. ¹⁶ And I will disclose to them

abounding peace with righteousness, and I will remove them the plant of uprightness, with all My heart and with all My soul, and they shall be for a blessing and not for a curse, and they shall be the head and not the tail. ¹⁷ And I will build My sanctuary in their midst, and I will dwell with them, and I will be their God and they shall be My people in truth and righteousness. ¹⁸ And I will not forsake them nor fail them; for I am the Lord their God.' ¹⁹ And Moses fell on his face and prayed and said, 'O Lord my God, do not forsake Thy people and Thy inheritance, so that they should wander in the error of their hearts, and do not deliver them into the hands of their enemies, the Gentiles, lest they should rule over them and cause them to sin against Thee. ²⁰ Let thy mercy, O Lord, be lifted up upon Thy people, and create in them an upright spirit, and let not the spirit of Beliar rule over them to accuse them before Thee, and to ensnare them from all the paths of righteousness, so that they may perish from before Thy face. ²¹ But they are Thy people and Thy inheritance, which thou hast delivered with thy great power from the hands of the Egyptians: create in them a clean heart and a holy spirit, and let them not be ensnared in their sins from henceforth until eternity.' ²² And the Lord said unto Moses: 'I know their contrariness and their thoughts and their stiffneckedness, and they will not be obedient till they confess their own sin and the sin of their fathers. ²³ And after this they will turn to Me in all uprightness and with all (their) heart and with all (their) soul, and I will circumcise the foreskin of their heart and the foreskin of the heart of their seed, and I will create in them a holy spirit, and I will cleanse them so that they shall not turn away from Me from that day unto eternity. ²⁴ And their souls will cleave to Me and to all My commandments, and they will fulfil My commandments, and I will be their Father and they shall be My children. ²⁵ And they all shall be called children of the living God, and every angel and every spirit shall know, yea, they shall know that these are My children, and that I am their Father in uprightness and righteousness, and that I love them. ²⁶ And do thou write down for thyself all these words which I declare unto thee on this mountain, the first and the last, which shall come to pass in all the divisions of the days in the law and in the testimony and in the weeks and the jubilees unto eternity, until I descend and dwell with them throughout eternity.'

God commands the Angel to write (i. 27-29).

²⁷ And He said to the angel of the presence: Write for Moses from the beginning of creation till My sanctuary has been built among them for all eternity. ²⁸ And the Lord will appear to the eyes of all, and all shall know that I am the God of Israel and the Father of all the children of Jacob, and King on Mount Zion for all eternity. And Zion and Jerusalem shall be holy.' ²⁹ And the angel of the presence who went before the camp of Israel took the tables of the divisions of the years -from the time of the creation- of the law and of the testimony of the weeks of the jubilees, according to the individual years, according to all the number of the jubilees [according, to the individual years], from the day of the [new] creation when the heavens and the earth shall be renewed and all their creation according to the powers of the heaven, and according to all the creation of the earth, until the sanctuary of the Lord shall be made in Jerusalem on Mount Zion, and all the luminaries be renewed for healing and for peace and for blessing for all the elect of Israel, and that thus it may be from that day and unto all the days of the earth.

The Angel dictates to Moses the Primæval History: the Creation of the World and Institution of the Sabbath (ii. 1-33; cf. Gen. i.-ii. 3).

2

¹ And the angel of the presence spake to Moses according to the word of the Lord, saying: Write the complete history of the creation, how in six days the Lord God finished all His works and all that He created, and kept Sabbath on the seventh day and hallowed it for all ages, and appointed it as a sign for all His works. ² For on the first day He created the heavens which are above and the earth and the waters and all the spirits which serve before him -the angels of the presence, and the angels of sanctification, and the angels [of the spirit of fire and the angels] of the spirit of the winds, and the angels of the spirit of the clouds, and of darkness, and of snow and of hail and of hoar frost, and the angels of the voices and of the thunder and of the lightning, and the angels of the spirits of cold and of heat, and of winter and of spring and of autumn and of summer and of all the spirits of his creatures which are in the heavens and on the earth, (He created) the abysses and the darkness, eventide <and night>, and the light, dawn and day, which He hath prepared in the knowledge of his heart. ³ And thereupon we saw His works, and praised Him, and lauded before Him on account of all His works; for seven great works did He create on the first day. ⁴ And on the second day He created the firmament in the midst of the waters, and the waters were divided on that day -half of them went up above and half of them went down below the firmament (that was) in the midst over the face of the whole earth. And this was the only work (God) created on the second day. ⁵ And on the third day He commanded the waters to pass from off the face of the whole earth into one place, and the dry land to appear. ⁶ And the waters did so as He commanded them, and they retired from off the face of the earth into one place outside of this firmament, and the dry land appeared. ⁷ And on that day He created for them all the seas according to their separate gathering-places, and all the rivers, and the gatherings of the waters in the mountains and on all the earth, and all the lakes, and all the dew of the earth, and the seed which is sown, and all sprouting things, and fruit-bearing trees, and trees of the wood, and the garden of Eden, in Eden and all plants after their kind. ⁸ These four great works God created on the third day. And on the fourth day He created the sun and the moon and the stars, and set them in the firmament of the heaven, to give light upon all the earth, and to rule over the day and the night, and divide the light from the darkness. ⁹ And God appointed the sun to be a great sign on the earth for days and for sabbaths and for months and for feasts and for years and for sabbaths of years and for jubilees and for all seasons of the years. ¹⁰ And it divideth the light from the darkness [and] for prosperity, that all things may prosper which shoot and grow on the earth. ¹¹ These three kinds He made on the fourth day. And on the fifth day He created great sea monsters in the depths of the waters, for these were the first things of flesh that were created by his hands, the fish and everything that moves in the waters, and everything that flies, the birds and all their kind. ¹² And the sun rose above them to prosper (them), and above everything that was on the earth, everything that shoots out of the earth, and all fruit-bearing trees, and all flesh. ¹³ These three kinds He created on the fifth day. And on the sixth day He created all the animals of the earth, and all cattle, and everything that moves on the earth. ¹⁴ And after all this He created man, a man and a woman created He them, and gave him dominion over all that is upon the earth, and in the seas, and over everything that flies, and over beasts and over cattle, and over everything that moves on the earth, and over the whole earth, and over all this He gave him dominion. ¹⁵ And these four kinds He created on the sixth day. And there were altogether two and twenty kinds. ¹⁶ And He finished all his work on the sixth day -all that is in the heavens and on the earth, and in the seas and in the abysses, and in the light and in the darkness, and in everything. ¹⁷ And He gave us a great sign, the Sabbath day, that we should work six days, but keep Sabbath on the seventh day from all work. ¹⁸ And all the angels of the presence, and all the angels of sanctification, these two great classes -He hath bidden us to keep the Sabbath with Him in heaven and on earth. ¹⁹ And He said unto us: 'Behold, I will separate unto Myself a people from among all the peoples, and these shall keep the Sabbath day, and I will sanctify them unto Myself as My people, and will bless them; as I have sanctified the Sabbath day and do sanctify (it) unto Myself, even so will I bless them, and they shall be My people and I will be their God. ²⁰ And I have chosen the seed of Jacob from amongst all that I have seen, and have written him down as My first-born son, and have sanctified him unto Myself for ever and ever; and I will teach them the Sabbath day, that they may keep Sabbath thereon from all work.' ²¹ And thus He created therein a sign in accordance with which they should keep Sabbath with us on the seventh day, to eat and to drink, and to bless Him who has created all things as He has blessed and sanctified unto Himself a peculiar people above all peoples, and that they should keep Sabbath together with us. ²² And He caused His commands to ascend as a sweet savour acceptable before Him all the days . . . ²³ There (were) two and twenty heads of mankind from Adam to Jacob, and two and twenty kinds of work were made until the seventh day; this is blessed and holy; and the former also is blessed and holy; and this one serves with that one for sanctification and blessing. ²⁴ And to this (Jacob and his seed) it was granted that they should always be the blessed and holy ones of the first testimony and law, even as He had sanctified and blessed the Sabbath day on the seventh day. ²⁵ He created heaven and earth and everything that He created in six days, and God made the seventh day holy, for all His works; therefore He commanded on its behalf that, whoever does any work thereon shall die, and that he who defiles it shall surely die. ²⁶ Wherefore do thou command the children of Israel to observe this day that they may keep it holy and not do thereon any work, and not to defile it, as it is holier than all other days. ²⁷ And whoever profanes it shall surely die, and whoever does thereon any work shall surely die eternally, that the children of Israel may observe this day throughout their generations, and not be rooted out of the land; for it is a holy day and a blessed day. ²⁸ And every one who observes it and keeps Sabbath thereon from all his work, will be holy and blessed throughout all days like unto us. ²⁹ Declare and say to the children of Israel the law of this day both that they should keep Sabbath thereon, and that they should not forsake it in the error of their hearts; (and) that it is not lawful to do any work thereon which is unseemly, to do thereon their own pleasure, and that they should not prepare thereon anything to be eaten or drunk, and (that it is not lawful) to draw

water, or bring in or take out thereon through their gates any burden, which they had not prepared for themselves on the sixth day in their dwellings. [30] And they shall not bring in nor take out from house to house on that day; for that day is more holy and blessed than any jubilee day of the jubilees; on this we kept Sabbath in the heavens before it was made known to any flesh to keep Sabbath thereon on the earth. [31] And the Creator of all things blessed it, but he did not sanctify all peoples and nations to keep Sabbath thereon, but Israel alone: them alone he permitted to eat and drink and to keep Sabbath thereon on the earth. [32] And the Creator of all things blessed this day which He had created for blessing and holiness and glory above all days. [33] This law and testimony was given to the children of Israel as a law for ever unto their generations.

Paradise and the Fall (iii. 1-35; cf. Gen. ii. 4-iii.).

3

[1] And on the six days of the second week we brought, according to the word of God, unto Adam all the beasts, and all the cattle, and all the birds, and everything that moves on the earth, and everything that moves in the water, according to their kinds, and according to their types: the beasts on the first day; the cattle on the second day; the birds on the third day; and all that which moves on the earth on the fourth day; and that which moves in the water on the fifth day. [2] And Adam named them all by their respective names, and as he called them, so was their name. [3] And on these five days Adam saw all these, male and female, according to every kind that was on the earth, but he was alone and found no helpmeet for him. [4] And the Lord said unto us: 'It is not good that the man should be alone: let us make a helpmeet for him.' [5] And the Lord our God caused a deep sleep to fall upon him, and he slept, and He took for the woman one rib from amongst his ribs, and this rib was the origin of the woman from amongst his ribs, and He built up the flesh in its stead, and built the woman. [6] And He awaked Adam out of his sleep and on awaking he rose on the sixth day, and He brought her to him, and he knew her, and said unto her: 'This is now bone of my bones and flesh of my flesh; she shall be called [my] wife; because she was taken from her husband.' [7] Therefore shall man and wife be one and therefore shall a man leave his father and his mother, and cleave unto his wife, and they shall be one flesh. [8] In the first week was Adam created, and the rib -his wife: in the second week He showed her unto him: and for this reason the commandment was given to keep in their defilement, for a male seven days, and for a female twice seven days. [9] And after Adam had completed forty days in the land where he had been created, we brought him into the garden of Eden to till and keep it, but his wife they brought in on the eightieth day, and after this she entered into the garden of Eden. [10] And for this reason the commandment is written on the heavenly tablets in regard to her that gives birth: 'if she bears a male, she shall remain in her uncleanness seven days according to the first week of days, and thirty and three days shall she remain in the blood of her purifying, and she shall not touch any hallowed thing, nor enter into the sanctuary, until she accomplishes these days which (are enjoined) in the case of a male child. [11] But in the case of a female child she shall remain in her uncleanness two weeks of days, according to the first two weeks, and sixty-six days in the blood of her purification, and they will be in all eighty days.' [12] And when she had completed these eighty days we brought her into the garden of Eden, for it is holier than all the earth besides and every tree that is planted in it is holy. [13] Therefore, there was ordained regarding her who bears a male or a female child the statute of those days that she should touch no hallowed thing, nor enter into the sanctuary until these days for the male or female child are accomplished. [14] This is the law and testimony which was written down for Israel, in order that they should observe (it) all the days. [15] And in the first week of the first jubilee, [1-7 A.M.] Adam and his wife were in the garden of Eden for seven years tilling and keeping it, and we gave him work and we instructed him to do everything that is suitable for tillage. [16] And he tilled (the garden), and was naked and knew it not, and was not ashamed, and he protected the garden from the birds and beasts and cattle, and gathered its fruit, and eat, and put aside the residue for himself and for his wife [and put aside that which was being kept]. [17] And after the completion of the seven years, which he had completed there, seven years exactly, [8 A.M.] and in the second month, on the seventeenth day (of the month), the serpent came and approached the woman, and the serpent said to the woman, 'Hath God commanded you, saying, Ye shall not eat of every tree of the garden?' [18] And she said to it, 'Of all the fruit of the trees of the garden God hath said unto us, Eat; but of the fruit of the tree which is in the midst of the garden God hath said unto us, Ye shall not eat thereof, neither shall ye touch it, lest ye die.' [19] And the serpent said unto the woman, 'Ye shall not surely die: for God doth know that on the day ye shall eat thereof, your eyes will be opened, and ye will be as gods, and ye will know good and evil. [20] And the woman saw the tree that it was agreeable and pleasant to the eye, and that its fruit was good for food, and she took thereof and eat. [21] And when she had first covered her shame with figleaves, she gave thereof to Adam and he eat, and his eyes were opened, and he saw that he was naked. [22] And he took figleaves and sewed (them) together, and made an apron for himself, and, covered his shame. [23] And God cursed the serpent, and was wroth with it for ever . . . [24] And He was wroth with the woman, because she harkened to the voice of the serpent, and did eat; and He said unto her: 'I will greatly multiply thy sorrow and thy pains: in sorrow thou shalt bring forth children, and thy return shall be unto thy husband, and he will rule over thee.' [25] And to Adam also he said, ' Because thou hast harkened unto the voice of thy wife, and hast eaten of the tree of which I commanded thee that thou shouldst not eat thereof, cursed be the ground for thy sake: thorns and thistles shall it bring forth to thee, and thou shalt eat thy bread in the sweat of thy face, till thou returnest to the earth from whence thou wast taken; for earth thou art, and unto earth shalt thou return.' [26] And He made for them coats of skin, and clothed them, and sent them forth from the Garden of Eden. [27] And on that day on which Adam went forth from the Garden, he offered as a sweet savour an offering, frankincense, galbanum, and stacte, and spices in the morning with the rising of the sun from the day when he covered his shame. [28] And on that day was closed the mouth of all beasts, and of cattle, and of birds, and of whatever walks, and of whatever moves, so that they could no longer speak: for they had all spoken one with another with one lip and with one tongue. [29] And He sent out of the Garden of Eden all flesh that was in the Garden of Eden, and all flesh was scattered according to its kinds, and according to its types unto the places which had been created for them. [30] And to Adam alone did He give (the wherewithal) to cover his shame, of all the beasts and cattle. [31] On this account, it is prescribed on the heavenly tablets as touching all those who know the judgment of the law, that they should cover their shame, and should not uncover themselves as the Gentiles uncover themselves. [32] And on the new moon of the fourth month, Adam and his wife went forth from the Garden of Eden, and they dwelt in the land of Elda in the land of their creation. [33] And Adam called the name of his wife Eve. [34] And they had no son till the first jubilee, [8 A.M.] and after this he knew her. [35] Now he tilled the land as he had been instructed in the Garden of Eden.

Cain and Abel (iv. 1-12; cf. Gen. iv.).

4

[1] And in the third week in the second jubilee [64-70 A.M.] she gave birth to Cain, and in the fourth [71-77 A.M.] she gave birth to Abel, and in the fifth [78-84 A.M.] she gave birth to her daughter Âwân. [2] And in the first (year) of the third jubilee [99-105 A.M.], Cain slew Abel because (God) accepted the sacrifice of Abel, and did not accept the offering of Cain. [3] And he slew him in the field: and his blood cried from the ground to heaven, complaining because he had slain him. [4] And the Lord reproved Cain because of Abel, because he had slain him, and he made him a fugitive on the earth because of the blood of his brother, and he cursed him upon the earth. [5] And on this account it is written on the heavenly tables, 'Cursed is ,he who smites his neighbour treacherously, and let all who have seen and heard say, So be it; and the man who has seen and not declared (it), let him be accursed as the other.' [6] And for this reason we announce when we come before the Lord our God all the sin which is committed in heaven and on earth, and in light and in darkness, and everywhere. [7] And Adam and his wife mourned for Abel four weeks of years, [99-127 A.M] and in the fourth year of the fifth week [130 A.M.] they became joyful, and Adam knew his wife again, and she bare him a son, and he called his name Seth; for he said 'GOD has raised up a second seed unto us on the earth instead of Abel; for Cain slew him.' [8] And in the sixth week [134-40 A.M.] he begat his daughter Azûrâ. [9] And Cain took Âwân his sister to be his wife and she bare him Enoch at the close of the fourth jubilee. [190-196 A.M.] And in the first year of the first week of the fifth jubilee, [197 A.M.] houses were built on the earth, and Cain built a city, and called its name after the name of his son Enoch. [10] And Adam knew Eve his wife and she bare yet nine sons. [11] And in the fifth week of the fifth jubilee [225-31 A.M.] Seth took Azûrâ his sister to be his wife, and in the fourth (year of the sixth week) [235 A.M.] she bare him Enos. [12] He began to call on the name of the Lord on the earth.

The Patriarchs from Adam to Noah (cf. Gen. v.); Life of Enoch; Death of Adam and Gain (iv. 13-33).

[13] And in the seventh jubilee in the third week [309-15 A.M.] Enos took Nôâm his sister to be his wife, and she bare him a son in the third year of the fifth week, and he called his name Kenan. [14] And at the close of the eighth jubilee [325,386-3992 A.M.] Kenan took Mûalêlêth his sister to be his wife, and she bare him a son in the ninth jubilee, in the first week in the third year of this week, [395 A.M] and he called his name Mahalalel. [15] And in the second week of the tenth jubilee [449-55 A.M.] Mahalalel took unto

him to wife DinaH, the daughter of Barakiel the daughter of his father's brother, and she bare him a son in the third week in the sixth year, [461 A.M.] and he called his name Jared, for in his days the angels of the Lord descended on the earth, those who are named the Watchers, that they should instruct the children of men, and that they should do judgment and uprightness on the earth. ¹⁶ And in the eleventh jubilee [512-18 A.M.] Jared took to himself a wife, and her name was Baraka, the daughter of Râsûjâl, a daughter of his father's brother, in the fourth week of this jubilee, [522 A.M.] and she bare him a son in the fifth week, in the fourth year of the jubilee, and he called his name Enoch. ¹⁷ And he was the first among men that are born on earth who learnt writing and knowledge and wisdom and who wrote down the signs of heaven according to the order of their months in a book, that men might know the seasons of the years according to the order of their separate months. ¹⁸ And he was the first to write a testimony and he testified to the sons of men among the generations of the earth, and recounted the weeks of the jubilees, and made known to them the days of the years, and set in order the months and recounted the Sabbaths of the years as we made (them), known to him. ¹⁹ And what was and what will be he saw in a vision of his sleep, as it will happen to the children of men throughout their generations until the day of judgment; he saw and understood everything, and wrote his testimony, and placed the testimony on earth for all the children of men and for their generations. ²⁰ And in the twelfth jubilee, [582-88] in the seventh week thereof, he took to himself a wife, and her name was Edna, the daughter of Danel, the daughter of his father's brother, and in the sixth year in this week [587 A.M.] she bare him a son and he called his name Methuselah. ²¹ And he was moreover with the angels of God these six jubilees of years, and they showed him everything which is on earth and in the heavens, the rule of the sun, and he wrote down everything. ²² And he testified to the Watchers, who had sinned with the daughters of men; for these had begun to unite themselves, so as to be defiled, with the daughters of men, and Enoch testified against (them) all. ²³ And he was taken from amongst the children of men, and we conducted him into the Garden of Eden in majesty and honour, and behold there he writes down the condemnation and judgment of the world, and all the wickedness of the children of men. ²⁴ And on account of it (God) brought the waters of the flood upon all the land of Eden; for there he was set as a sign and that he should testify against all the children of men, that he should recount all the deeds of the generations until the day of condemnation. ²⁵ And he burnt the incense of the sanctuary, (even) sweet spices acceptable before the Lord on the Mount. ²⁶ For the Lord has four places on the earth, the Garden of Eden, and the Mount of the East, and this mountain on which thou art this day, Mount Sinai, and Mount Zion (which) will be sanctified in the new creation for a sanctification of the earth; through it will the earth be sanctified from all (its) guilt and its uncleanness through- out the generations of the world. ²⁷ And in the fourteenth jubilee [652 A.M.] Methuselah took unto himself a wife, Edna the daughter of Azrial, the daughter of his father's brother, in the third week, in the first year of this week, [701-7 A.M.] and he begat a son and called his name Lamech. ²⁸ And in the fifteenth jubilee in the third week Lamech took to himself a wife, and her name was Betenos the daughter of Baraki'il, the daughter of his father's brother, and in this week she bare him a son and he called his name Noah, saying, 'This one will comfort me for my trouble and all my work, and for the ground which the Lord hath cursed.' ²⁹ And at the close of the nineteenth jubilee, in the seventh week in the sixth year [930 A.M.] thereof, Adam died, and all his sons buried him in the land of his creation, and he was the first to be buried in the earth. ³⁰ And he lacked seventy years of one thousand years; for one thousand years are as one day in the testimony of the heavens and therefore was it written concerning the tree of knowledge: 'On the day that ye eat thereof ye shall die.' For this reason he did not complete the years of this day; for he died during it. ³¹ At the close of this jubilee Cain was killed after him in the same year; for his house fell upon him and he died in the midst of his house, and he was killed by its stones; for with a stone he had killed Abel, and by a stone was he killed in righteous judgment. ³² For this reason it was ordained on the heavenly tablets: With the instrument with which a man kills his neighbour with the same shall he be killed; after the manner that he wounded him, in like manner shall they deal with him.' ³³ And in the twenty-fifth [1205 A.M.] jubilee Noah took to himself a wife, and her name was `Emzârâ, the daughter of Râkê'êl, the daughter of his father's brother, in the first year in the fifth week [1207 A.M.]: and in the third year thereof she bare him Shem, in the fifth year thereof [1209 A.M.] she bare him Ham, and in the first year in the sixth week [1212 A.M.] she bare him Japheth.

The Fall of the Angels and their Punishment; the Deluge foretold (v. 1-20; cf. Gen. vi. 1-12).

5

¹ And it came to pass when the children of men began to multiply on the face of the earth and daughters were born unto them, that the angels of God saw them on a certain year of this jubilee, that they were beautiful to look upon; and they took themselves wives of all whom they chose, and they bare unto them sons and they were giants. ² And lawlessness increased on the earth and all flesh corrupted its way, alike men and cattle and beasts and birds and everything that walks on the earth -all of them corrupted their ways and their orders, and they began to devour each other, and lawlessness increased on the earth and every imagination of the thoughts of all men (was) thus evil continually. ³ And God looked upon the earth, and behold it was corrupt, and all flesh had corrupted its orders, and all that were upon the earth had wrought all manner of evil before His eyes. ⁴ And He said that He would destroy man and all flesh upon the face of the earth which He had created. ⁵ But Noah found grace before the eyes of the Lord. ⁶ And against the angels whom He had sent upon the earth, He was exceedingly wroth, and He gave commandment to root them out of all their dominion, and He bade us to bind them in the depths of the earth, and behold they are bound in the midst of them, and are (kept) separate. ⁷ And against their sons went forth a command from before His face that they should be smitten with the sword, and be removed from under heaven. ⁸ And He said 'My spirit shall not always abide on man; for they also are flesh and their days shall be one hundred and twenty years'. ⁹ And He sent His sword into their midst that each should slay his neighbour, and they began to slay each other till they all fell by the sword and were destroyed from the earth. ¹⁰ And their fathers were witnesses (of their destruction), and after this they were bound in the depths of the earth for ever, until the day of the great condemnation, when judgment is executed on all those who have corrupted their ways and their works before the Lord. ¹¹ And He destroyed all from their places, and there was not left one of them whom He judged not according to all their wickedness. ¹² And he made for all his works a new and righteous nature, so that they should not sin in their whole nature for ever, but should be all righteous each in his kind alway. ¹³ And the judgment of all is ordained and written on the heavenly tablets in righteousness -even (the judgment of) all who depart from the path which is ordained for them to walk in; and if they walk not therein, judgment is written down for every creature and for every kind. ¹⁴ And there is nothing in heaven or on earth, or in light or in darkness, or in Sheol or in the depth, or in the place of darkness (which is not judged); and all their judgments are ordained and written and engraved. ¹⁵ In regard to all He will judge, the great according to his greatness, and the small according to his smallness, and each according to his way. ¹⁶ And He is not one who will regard the person (of any), nor is He one who will receive gifts, if He says that He will execute judgment on each: if one gave everything that is on the earth, He will not regard the gifts or the person (of any), nor accept anything at his hands, for He is a righteous judge. ¹⁷ [And of the children of Israel it has been written and ordained: If they turn to him in righteousness He will forgive all their transgressions and pardon all their sins. ¹⁸ It is written and ordained that He will show mercy to all who turn from all their guilt once each year.] ¹⁹ And as for all those who corrupted their ways and their thoughts before the flood, no man's person was accepted save that of Noah alone; for his person was accepted in behalf of his sons, whom (God) saved from the waters of the flood on his account; for his heart was righteous in all his ways, according as it was commanded regarding him, and he had not departed from aught that was ordained for him. ²⁰ And the Lord said that he would destroy everything which was upon the earth, both men and cattle, and

The Building of the Ark; the Flood (v. 21-32; cf. Gen. vi. 13-viii. 19).

²¹ beasts, and fowls of the air, and that which moveth on the earth. And He commanded Noah to make him an ark, that he might save himself from the waters of the flood. ²² And Noah made the ark in all respects as He commanded him, in the twenty-seventh jubilee of years, in the fifth week in the fifth year (on the new moon of the first month). [1307 A.M.] ²³ And he entered in the sixth (year) thereof, [1308 A.M.] in the second month, on the new moon of the second month, till the sixteenth; and he entered, and all that we brought to him, into the ark, and the Lord closed it from without on the seventeenth evening. ²⁴ And the Lord opened seven flood-gates of heaven, And the mouths of the fountains of the great deep, seven mouths in number. ²⁵ And the flood-gates began to pour down water from the heaven forty days and forty nights, And the fountains of the deep also sent up waters, until the whole world was full of water. ²⁶ And the waters increased upon the earth: Fifteen cubits did the waters rise above all the high mountains, And the ark was lift up above the earth, And it moved upon the face of the waters. ²⁷ And the water prevailed on the face of the earth five months -one hundred and fifty days. ²⁸ And the ark went and rested on the top of Lubar, one of the mountains of Ararat. ²⁹ And (on the new moon) in

the fourth month the fountains of the great deep were closed and the floodgates of heaven were restrained; and on the new moon of the seventh month all the mouths of the abysses of the earth were opened, and the water began to descend into the deep below. ³⁰ And on the new moon of the tenth month the tops of the mountains were seen, and on the new moon of the first month the earth became visible. ³¹ And the waters disappeared from above the earth in the fifth week in the seventh year [1309 A.M.] thereof, and on the seventeenth day in the second month the earth was dry. ³² And on the twenty-seventh thereof he opened the ark, and sent forth from it beasts, and cattle, and birds, and every moving thing.

Noah's Sacrifice; God's Covenant with him (cf. Gen. viii. 20-ix. 17). Instructions to Moses about eating of Blood, the Feast of Weeks, etc., and Division of the Year (vi. 1-38).

6

¹ And on the new moon of the third month he went forth from the ark, and built an altar on that mountain. ² And he made atonement for the earth, and took a kid and made atonement by its blood for all the guilt of the earth; for everything that had been on it had been destroyed, save those that were in the ark with Noah. ³ And he placed the fat thereof on the altar, and he took an ox, and a goat, and a sheep and kids, and salt, and a turtle-dove, and the young of a dove, and placed a burnt sacrifice on the altar, and poured thereon an offering mingled with oil, and sprinkled wine and strewed frankincense over everything, and caused a goodly savour to arise, acceptable before the Lord. ⁴ And the Lord smelt the goodly savour, and He made a covenant with him that there should not be any more a flood to destroy the earth; that all the days of the earth seed-time and harvest should never cease; cold and heat, and summer and winter, and day and night should not change their order, nor cease for ever. ⁵ 'And you, increase ye and multiply upon the earth, and become many upon it, and be a blessing upon it. The fear of you and the dread of you I will inspire in everything that is on earth and in the sea. ⁶ And behold I have given unto you all beasts, and all winged things, and everything that moves on the earth, and the fish in the waters, and all things for food; as the green herbs, I have given you all things to eat. ⁷ But flesh, with the life thereof, with the blood, ye shall not eat; for the life of all flesh is in the blood, lest your blood of your lives be required. At the hand of every man, at the hand of every (beast) will I require the blood of man. ⁸ Whoso sheddeth man's blood by man shall his blood be shed, for in the image of God made He man. ⁹ And you, increase ye, and multiply on the earth.' ¹⁰ And Noah and his sons swore that they would not eat any blood that was in any flesh, and he made a covenant before the Lord God for ever throughout all the generations of the earth in this month. ¹¹ On this account He spake to thee that thou shouldst make a covenant with the children of Israel in this month upon the mountain with an oath, and that thou shouldst sprinkle blood upon them because of all the words of the covenant, which the Lord made with them for ever. ¹² And this testimony is written concerning you that you should observe it continually, so that you should not eat on any day any blood of beasts or birds or cattle during all the days of the earth, and the man who eats the blood of beast or of cattle or of birds during all the days of the earth, he and his seed shall be rooted out of the land. ¹³ And do thou command the children of Israel to eat no blood, so that their names and their seed may be before the Lord our God continually. ¹⁴ And for this law there is no limit of days, for it is for ever. They shall observe it throughout their generations, so that they may continue supplicating on your behalf with blood before the altar; every day and at the time of morning and evening they shall seek forgiveness on your behalf perpetually before the Lord that they may keep it and not be rooted out. ¹⁵ And He gave to Noah and his sons a sign that there should not again be a flood on the earth. ¹⁶ He set His bow in the cloud for a sign of the eternal covenant that there should not again be a flood on the earth to destroy it all the days of the earth. ¹⁷ For this reason it is ordained and written on the heavenly tablets, that they should celebrate the feast of weeks in this month once a year, to renew the covenant every year. ¹⁸ And this whole festival was celebrated in heaven from the day of creation till the days of Noah -twenty-six jubilees and five weeks of years [1309-1659 A.M.]: and Noah and his sons observed it for seven jubilees and one week of years, till the day of Noah's death, and from the day of Noah's death his sons did away with (it) until the days of Abraham, and they eat blood. ¹⁹ But Abraham observed it, and Isaac and Jacob and his children observed it up to thy days, and in thy days the children of Israel forgot it until ye celebrated it anew on this mountain. ²⁰ And do thou command the children of Israel to observe this festival in all their generations for a commandment unto them: one day in the year in this month they shall celebrate the festival. ²¹ For it is the feast of weeks and the feast of first fruits: this feast is twofold and of a double nature: according to what is written and engraven concerning it, celebrate it. ²² For I have written in the book of the first law, in that which I have written for thee, that thou shouldst celebrate it in its season, one day in the year, and I explained to thee its sacrifices that the children of Israel should remember and should celebrate it throughout their generations in this month, one day in every year. ²³ And on the new moon of the first month, and on the new moon of the fourth month, and on the new moon of the seventh month, and on the new moon of the tenth month are the days of remembrance, and the days of the seasons in the four divisions of the year. These are written and ordained as a testimony for ever. ²⁴ And Noah ordained them for himself as feasts for the generations for ever, so that they have become thereby a memorial unto him. ²⁵ And on the new moon of the first month he was bidden to make for himself an ark, and on that (day) the earth became dry and he opened (the ark) and saw the earth. ²⁶ And on the new moon of the fourth month the mouths of the depths of the abyss beneath were closed. And on the new moon of the seventh month all the mouths of the abysses of the earth were opened, and the waters began to descend into them. ²⁷ And on the new moon of the tenth month the tops of the mountains were seen, and Noah was glad. ²⁸ And on this account he ordained them for himself as feasts for a memorial for ever, and thus are they ordained. ²⁹ And they placed them on the heavenly tablets, each had thirteen weeks; from one to another (passed) their memorial, from the first to the second, and from the second to the third, and from the third to the fourth. ³⁰ And all the days of the commandment will be two and fifty weeks of days, and (these will make) the entire year complete. Thus it is engraven and ordained on the heavenly tablets. ³¹ And there is no neglecting (this commandment) for a single year or from year to year. ³² And command thou the children of Israel that they observe the years according to this reckoning- three hundred and sixty-four days, and (these) will constitute a complete year, and they will not disturb its time from its days and from its feasts; for everything will fall out in them according to their testimony, and they will not leave out any day nor disturb any feasts. ³³ But if they do neglect and do not observe them according to His commandment, then they will disturb all their seasons and the years will be dislodged from this (order), [and they will disturb the seasons and the years will be dislodged] and they will neglect their ordinances. ³⁴ And all the children of Israel will forget and will not find the path of the years, and will forget the new moons, and seasons, and sabbaths and they will go wrong as to all the order of the years. ³⁵ For I know and from henceforth will I declare it unto thee, and it is not of my own devising; for the book (lies) written before me, and on the heavenly tablets the division of days is ordained, lest they forget the feasts of the covenant and walk according to the feasts of the Gentiles after their error and after their ignorance. ³⁶ For there will be those who will assuredly make observations of the moon -how (it) disturbs the seasons and comes in from year to year ten days too soon. ³⁷ For this reason the years will come upon them when they will disturb (the order), and make an abominable (day) the day of testimony, and an unclean day a feast day, and they will confound all the days, the holy with the unclean, and the unclean day with the holy; for they will go wrong as to the months and sabbaths and feasts and jubilees. ³⁸ For this reason I command and testify to thee that thou mayst testify to them; for after thy death thy children will disturb (them), so that they will not make the year three hundred and sixty-four days only, and for this reason they will go wrong as to the new moons and seasons and sabbaths and festivals, and they will eat all kinds of blood with all kinds of flesh.

Noah offers Sacrifice; the Cursing of Canaan (cf. Gen. ix. 20-28): Noah's Sons and Grandsons (cf. Gen. x.) and their Cities. Noah's Admonitions (vii. 1-39).

7

¹ And in the seventh week in the first year [1317 A.M.] thereof, in this jubilee, Noah planted vines on the mountain on which the ark had rested, named Lubar, one of the Ararat Mountains, and they produced fruit in the fourth year, [1320 A.M.] and he guarded their fruit, and gathered it in this year in the seventh month. ² And he made wine therefrom and put it into a vessel, and kept it until the fifth year, [1321 A.M.] until the first day, on the new moon of the first month. ³ And he celebrated with joy the day of this feast, and he made a burnt sacrifice unto the Lord, one young ox and one ram, and seven sheep, each a year old, and a kid of the goats, that he might make atonement thereby for himself and his sons. ⁴ And he prepared the kid first, and placed some of its blood on the flesh that was on the altar which he had made, and all the fat he laid on the altar where he made the burnt sacrifice, and the ox and the ram and the sheep, and he laid all their flesh upon the altar. ⁵ And he placed all their offerings mingled with oil upon it, and afterwards he sprinkled wine on the fire which he had previously made on the altar, and he placed incense on the altar and caused a sweet savour to ascend acceptable before the Lord his God. ⁶ And he rejoiced and drank of this wine, he and his children with joy. ⁷ And it was evening, and he went

into his tent, and being drunken he lay down and slept, and was uncovered in his tent as he slept. [8] And Ham saw Noah his father naked, and went forth and told his two brethren without. [9] And Shem took his garment and arose, he and Japheth, and they placed the garment on their shoulders and went backward and covered the shame of their father, and their faces were backward. [10] And Noah awoke from his sleep and knew all that his younger son had done unto him, and he cursed his son and said: 'Cursed be Canaan; an enslaved servant shall he be unto his brethren.' [11] And he blessed Shem, and said: 'Blessed be the Lord God of Shem, and Canaan shall be his servant. [12] God shall enlarge Japheth, and God shall dwell in the dwelling of Shem, and Canaan shall be his servant.' [13] And Ham knew that his father had cursed his younger son, and he was displeased that he had cursed his son. and he parted from his father, he and his sons with him, Cush and Mizraim and Put and Canaan. [14] And he built for himself a city and called its name after the name of his wife Ne'elatama'uk. [15] And Japheth saw it, and became envious of his brother, and he too built for himself a city, and he called its name after the name of his wife 'Adataneses. [16] And Shem dwelt with his father Noah, and he built a city close to his father on the mountain, and he too called its name after the name of his wife Sedeqetelebab. [17] And behold these three cities are near Mount Lubar; Sedeqetelebab fronting the mountain on its east; and Na'eltama'uk on the south; 'Adatan'eses towards the west. [18] And these are the sons of Shem: Elam, and Asshur, and Arpachshad -this (son) was born two years after the flood- and Lud, and Aram. [19] The sons of Japheth: Gomer and Magog and Madai and Javan, Tubal and Meshech and Tiras: these are the sons of Noah. [20] And in the twenty-eighth jubilee [1324-1372 A.M.] Noah began to enjoin upon his sons' sons the ordinances and commandments, and all the judgments that he knew, and he exhorted his sons to observe righteousness, and to cover the shame of their flesh, and to bless their Creator, and honour father and mother, and love their neighbour, and guard their souls from fornication and uncleanness and all iniquity. [21] For owing to these three things came the flood upon the earth, namely, owing to the fornication wherein the Watchers against the law of their ordinances went a whoring after the daughters of men, and took themselves wives of all which they chose: and they made the beginning of uncleanness. [22] And they begat sons the Naphidim, and they were all unlike, and they devoured one another: and the Giants slew the Naphil, and the Naphil slew the Eljo, and the Eljo mankind, and one man another. [23] And every one sold himself to work iniquity and to shed much blood, and the earth was filled with iniquity. [24] And after this they sinned against the beasts and birds, and all that moves and walks on the earth: and much blood was shed on the earth, and every imagination and desire of men imagined vanity and evil continually. [25] And the Lord destroyed everything from off the face of the earth; because of the wickedness of their deeds, and because of the blood which they had shed in the midst of the earth He destroyed everything. [26] 'And we were left, I and you, my sons, and everything that entered with us into the ark, and behold I see your works before me that ye do not walk in righteousness: for in the path of destruction ye have begun to walk, and ye are parting one from another, and are envious one of another, and (so it comes) that ye are not in harmony, my sons, each with his brother. [27] For I see, and behold the demons have begun (their) seductions against you and against your children and now I fear on your behalf, that after my death ye will shed the blood of men upon the earth, and that ye, too, will be destroyed from the face of the earth. [28] For whoso sheddeth man's blood, and whoso eateth the blood of any flesh, shall all be destroyed from the earth. [29] And there shall not be left any man that eateth blood, or that sheddeth the blood of man on the earth, Nor shall there be left to him any seed or descendants living under heaven; For into Sheol shall they go, And into the place of condemnation shall they descend, And into the darkness of the deep shall they all be removed by a violent death. [30] There shall be no blood seen upon you of all the blood there shall be all the days in which ye have killed any beasts or cattle or whatever flies upon the earth, and work ye a good work to your souls by covering that which has been shed on the face of the earth. [31] And ye shall not be like him who eats with blood, but guard yourselves that none may eat blood before you: cover the blood, for thus have I been commanded to testify to you and your children, together with all flesh. [32] And suffer not the soul to be eaten with the flesh, that your blood, which is your life, may not be required at the hand of any flesh that sheds (it) on the earth. [33] For the earth will not be clean from the blood which has been shed upon it; for (only) through the blood of him that shed it will the earth be purified throughout all its generations. [34] And now, my children, harken: work judgment and righteousness that ye maybe planted in righteousness over the face of the whole earth, and your glory lifted up before my God, who saved me from the waters of the flood. [35] And behold, ye will go and build for yourselves cities, and plant in them all the plants that are upon the earth, and moreover all fruit-bearing trees. [36] For three years the fruit of everything that is eaten will not be gathered: and in the fourth year its fruit will be accounted holy [and they will offer the first-fruits], acceptable before the Most High God, who created heaven and earth and all things. Let them offer in abundance the first of the wine and oil (as) first-fruits on the altar of the Lord, who receives it, and what is left let the servants of the house of the Lord eat before the altar which receives (it). [37] And in the fifth year make ye the release so that ye release it in righteousness and uprightness, and ye shall be righteous, and all that you plant shall prosper. [38] For thus did Enoch, the father of your father command Methuselah, his son, and Methuselah his son Lamech, and Lamech commanded me all the things which his fathers commanded him. [39] And I also will give you commandment, my sons, as Enoch commanded his son in the first jubilees: whilst still living, the seventh in his generation, he commanded and testified to his son and to his son's sons until the day of his death.'

Genealogy of the Descendants of Shem: Noah and his Sons divide the Earth (viii. 1-30; cf. Gen. x.).

8

[1] In the twenty-ninth jubilee, in the first week, [1373 A.M.] in the beginning thereof Arpachshad took to himself a wife and her name was Rasu'eja, the daughter of Susan, the daughter of Elam, and she bare him a son in the third year in this week, [1375 A.M.] and he called his name Kainam. [2] And the son grew, and his father taught him writing, and he went to seek for himself a place where he might seize for himself a city. [3] And he found a writing which former (generations) had carved on the rock, and he read what was thereon, and he transcribed it and sinned owing to it; for it contained the teaching of the Watchers in accordance with which they used to observe the omens of the sun and moon and stars in all the signs of heaven. [4] And he wrote it down and said nothing regarding it; for he was afraid to speak to Noah about it lest he should be angry with him on account of it. [5] And in the thirtieth jubilee, [1429 A.M.] in the second week, in the first year thereof, he took to himself a wife, and her name was Melka, the daughter of Madai, the son of Japheth, and in the fourth year [1432 A.M.] he begat a son, and called his name Shelah; for he said: 'Truly I have been sent.' [6] [And in the fourth year he was born], and Shelah grew up and took to himself a wife, and her name was Mu'ak, the daughter of Kesed, his father's brother, in the one and thirtieth jubilee, in the fifth week, in the first year [1499 A.M.] thereof. [7] And she bare him a son in the fifth year [1503 A.M.] thereof, and he called his name Eber: and he took unto himself a wife, and her name was 'Azûrâd, the daughter of Nebrod, in the thirty-second jubilee, in the seventh week, in the third year thereof. [1564 A.M.] [8] And in the sixth year [1567 A.M.] thereof, she bare him son, and he called his name Peleg; for in the days when he was born the children of Noah began to divide the earth amongst themselves: for this reason he called his name Peleg. [9] And they divided (it) secretly amongst themselves, and told it to Noah. [10] And it came to pass in the beginning of the thirty-third jubilee [1569 A.M.] that they divided the earth into three parts, for Shem and Ham and Japheth, according to the inheritance of each, in the first year in the first week, when one of us who had been sent, was with them. [11] And he called his sons, and they drew nigh to him, they and their children, and he divided the earth into the lots, which his three sons were to take in possession, and they reached forth their hands, and took the writing out of the bosom of Noah, their father. [12] And there came forth on the writing as Shem's lot the middle of the earth which he should take as an inheritance for himself and for his sons for the generations of eternity, from the middle of the mountain range of Rafa, from the mouth of the water from the river Tina, and his portion goes towards the west through the midst of this river, and it extends till it reaches the water of the abysses, out of which this river goes forth and pours its waters into the sea Me'at, and this river flows into the great sea. And all that is towards the north is Japheth's, and all that is towards the south belongs to Shem. [13] And it extends till it reaches Karaso: this is in the bosom of the tongue which looks towards the south. [14] And his portion extends along the great sea, and it extends in a straight line till it reaches the west of the tongue which looks towards the south: for this sea is named the tongue of the Egyptian Sea. [15] And it turns from here towards the south towards the mouth of the great sea on the shore of (its) waters, and it extends to the west to 'Afra, and it extends till it reaches the waters of the river Gihon, and to the south of the waters of Gihon, to the banks of this river. [16] And it extends towards the east, till it reaches the Garden of Eden, to the south thereof, [to the south] and from the east of the whole land of Eden and of the whole east, it turns to the east and proceeds till it reaches the east of the mountain named Rafa, and it descends to the bank of the mouth of the river Tina. [17] This portion came forth by lot for Shem and his sons, that they should possess it for ever unto his generations for evermore. [18] And Noah rejoiced that this portion came forth for Shem and for his sons, and he remembered all that he had spoken with his mouth in prophecy; for he had said: 'Blessed

be the Lord God of Shem And may the Lord dwell in the dwelling of Shem.' ¹⁹ And he knew that the Garden of Eden is the holy of holies, and the dwelling of the Lord, and Mount Sinai the centre of the desert, and Mount Zion -the centre of the navel of the earth: these three were created as holy places facing each other. ²⁰ And he blessed the God of gods, who had put the word of the Lord into his mouth, and the Lord for evermore. ²¹ And he knew that a blessed portion and a blessing had come to Shem and his sons unto the generations for ever -the whole land of Eden and the whole land of the Red Sea, and the whole land of the east and India, and on the Red Sea and the mountains thereof, and all the land of Bashan, and all the land of Lebanon and the islands of Kaftur, and all the mountains of Sanir and 'Amana, and the mountains of Asshur in the north, and all the land of Elam, Asshur, and Babel, and Susan and Ma'edai, and all the mountains of Ararat, and all the region beyond the sea, which is beyond the mountains of Asshur towards the north, a blessed and spacious land, and all that is in it is very good. ²² And for Ham came forth the second portion, beyond the Gihon towards the south to the right of the Garden, and it extends towards the south and it extends to all the mountains of fire, and it extends towards the west to the sea of 'Atel and it extends towards the west till it reaches the sea of Ma'uk -that (sea) into which everything which is not destroyed descends. ²³ And it goes forth towards the north to the limits of Gadir, and it goes forth to the coast of the waters of the sea to the waters of the great sea till it draws near to the river Gihon, and goes along the river Gihon till it reaches the right of the Garden of Eden. ²⁴ And this is the land which came forth for Ham as the portion which he was to occupy for ever for himself and his sons unto their generations for ever. ²⁵ And for Japheth came forth the third portion beyond the river Tina to the north of the outflow of its waters, and it extends north- easterly to the whole region of Gog, and to all the country east thereof. ²⁶ And it extends northerly to the north, and it extends to the mountains of Qelt towards the north, and towards the sea of Ma'uk, and it goes forth to the east of Gadir as far as the region of the waters of the sea. ²⁷ And it extends until it approaches the west of Fara and it returns towards 'Aferag, and it extends easterly to the waters of the sea of Me'at. ²⁸ And it extends to the region of the river Tina in a north-easterly direction until it approaches the boundary of its waters towards the mountain Rafa, and it turns round towards the north. ²⁹ This is the land which came forth for Japheth and his sons as the portion of his inheritance which he should possess for himself and his sons, for their generations for ever; five great islands, and a great land in the north. ³⁰ But it is cold, and the land of Ham is hot, and the land of Shem is neither hot nor cold, but it is of blended cold and heat.

Subdivision of the Three Portions amongst the Grandchildren: Oath taken by Noah's Sons (ix. 1-15; cf. Gen. x. partly).

9

¹ And Ham divided amongst his sons, and the first portion came forth for Cush towards the east, and to the west of him for Mizraim, and to the west of him for Put, and to the west of him [and to the west thereof] on the sea for Canaan. ² And Shem also divided amongst his sons, and the first portion came forth for Ham and his sons, to the east of the river Tigris till it approaches the east, the whole land of India, and on the Red Sea on its coast, and the waters of Dedan, and all the mountains of Mebri and Ela, and all the land of Susan and all that is on the side of Pharnak to the Red Sea and the river Tina. ³ And for Asshur came forth the second Portion, all the land of Asshur and Nineveh and Shinar and to the border of India, and it ascends and skirts the river. ⁴ And for Arpachshad came forth the third portion, all the land of the region of the Chaldees to the east of the Euphrates, bordering on the Red Sea, and all the waters of the desert close to the tongue of the sea which looks towards Egypt, all the land of Lebanon and Sanir and 'Amana to the border of the Euphrates. ⁵ And for Aram there came forth the fourth portion, all the land of Mesopotamia between the Tigris and the Euphrates to the north of the Chaldees to the border of the mountains of Asshur and the land of 'Arara. ⁶ And there came forth for Lud the fifth portion, the mountains of Asshur and all appertaining to them till it reaches the Great Sea, and till it reaches the east of Asshur his brother. ⁷ And Japheth also divided the land of his inheritance amongst his sons. ⁸ And the first portion came forth for Gomer to the east from the north side to the river Tina; and in the north there came forth for Magog all the inner portions of the north until it reaches to the sea of Me'at. ⁹ And for Madai came forth as his portion that he should posses from the west of his two brothers to the islands, and to the coasts of the islands. ¹⁰ And for Javan came forth the fourth portion every island and the islands which are towards the border of Lud. ¹¹ And for Tubal there came forth the fifth portion in the midst of the tongue which approaches towards the border of the portion of Lud to the second tongue, to the region beyond the second tongue unto the third tongue. ¹² And for Meshech came forth the sixth portion, all the region beyond the third tongue till it approaches the east of Gadir. ¹³ And for Tiras there came forth the seventh portion, four great islands in the midst of the sea, which reach to the portion of Ham [and the islands of Kamaturi came out by lot for the sons of Arpachshad as his inheritance]. ¹⁴ And thus the sons of Noah divided unto their sons in the presence of Noah their father, and he bound them all by an oath, imprecating a curse on every one that sought to seize the portion which had not fallen (to him) by his lot. ¹⁵ And they all said, 'So be it; so be it ' for themselves and their sons for ever throughout their generations till the day of judgment, on which the Lord God shall judge them with a sword and with fire for all the unclean wickedness of their errors, wherewith they have filled the earth with transgression and uncleanness and fornication and sin.

Noah's Sons led astray by Evil Spirits; Noah's Prayer; Mastêmâ; Death of Noah (x. 1-17; cf. Gen. ix. 28).

10

¹ And in the third week of this jubilee the unclean demons began to lead astray the children of the sons of Noah, and to make to err and destroy them. ² And the sons of Noah came to Noah their father, and they told him concerning the demons which were leading astray and blinding and slaying his sons' sons. ³ And he prayed before the Lord his God, and said: 'God of the spirits of all flesh, who hast shown mercy unto me And hast saved me and my sons from the waters of the flood, And hast not caused me to perish as Thou didst the sons of perdition; For Thy grace has been great towards me, And great has been Thy mercy to my soul; Let Thy grace be lift up upon my sons, And let not wicked spirits rule over them Lest they should destroy them from the earth. ⁴ But do Thou bless me and my sons, that we may increase and Multiply and replenish the earth. ⁵ And Thou knowest how Thy Watchers, the fathers of these spirits, acted in my day: and as for these spirits which are living, imprison them and hold them fast in the place of condemnation, and let them not bring destruction on the sons of thy servant, my God; for these are malignant, and created in order to destroy. ⁶ And let them not rule over the spirits of the living; for Thou alone canst exercise dominion over them. And let them not have power over the sons of the righteous from henceforth and for evermore.' ⁷ And the Lord our God bade us to bind all. ⁸ And the chief of the spirits, Mastêmâ, came and said: 'Lord, Creator, let some of them remain before me, and let them harken to my voice, and do all that I shall say unto them; for if some of them are not left to me, I shall not be able to execute the power of my will on the sons of men; for these are for corruption and leading astray before my judgment, for great is the wickedness of the sons of men.' ⁹ And He said: Let the tenth part of them remain before him, and let nine parts descend into the place of condemnation.' ¹⁰ And one of us He commanded that we should teach Noah all their medicines; for He knew that they would not walk in uprightness, nor strive in righteousness. ¹¹ And we did according to all His words: all the malignant evil ones we bound in the place of condemnation and a tenth part of them we left that they might be subject before Satan on the earth. ¹² And we explained to Noah all the medicines of their diseases, together with their seductions, how he might heal them with herbs of the earth. ¹³ And Noah wrote down all things in a book as we instructed him concerning every kind of medicine. Thus the evil spirits were precluded from (hurting) the sons of Noah. ¹⁴ And he gave all that he had written to Shem, his eldest son; for he loved him exceedingly above all his sons. ¹⁵ And Noah slept with his fathers, and was buried on Mount Lubar in the land of Ararat. ¹⁶ Nine hundred and fifty years he completed in his life, nineteen jubilees and two weeks and five years. [1659 A.M.] ¹⁷ And in his life on earth he excelled the children of men save Enoch because of the righteousness, wherein he was perfect. For Enoch's office was ordained for a testimony to the generations of the world, so that he should recount all the deeds of generation unto generation, till the day of judgment.

The Tower of Babel and the Confusion of Tongues (x. 18-27; cf. Gen. xi. 1-9).

¹⁸ And in the three and thirtieth jubilee, in the first year in the second week, Peleg took to himself a wife, whose name was Lomna the daughter of Sina'ar, and she bare him a son in the fourth year of this week, and he called his name Reu; for he said: 'Behold the children of men have become evil through the wicked purpose of building for themselves a city and a tower in the land of Shinar.' ¹⁹ For they departed from the land of Ararat eastward to Shinar; for in his days they built the city and the tower, saying, 'Go to, let us ascend thereby into heaven.' ²⁰ And they began to build, and in the fourth week they made brick with fire, and the bricks served them for stone, and the clay with which they cemented them together was asphalt which comes out of the sea, and out of the fountains of water in the land of Shinar. ²¹ And they built it: forty and three years [1645-1688 A.M.] were they building it; its breadth was 203 bricks, and the height (of a brick) was the

third of one; its height amounted to 5433 cubits and 2 palms, and (the extent of one wall was) thirteen stades (and of the other thirty stades). ²² And the Lord our God said unto us: Behold, they are one people, and (this) they begin to do, and now nothing will be withholden from them. Go to, let us go down and confound their language, that they may not understand one another's speech, and they may be dispersed into cities and nations, and one purpose will no longer abide with them till the day of judgment.' ²³ And the Lord descended, and we descended with him to see the city and the tower which the children of men had built. ²⁴ And he confounded their language, and they no longer understood one another's speech, and they ceased then to build the city and the tower. ²⁵ For this reason the whole land of Shinar is called Babel, because the Lord did there confound all the language of the children of men, and from thence they were dispersed into their cities, each according to his language and his nation. ²⁶ And the Lord sent a mighty wind against the tower and overthrew it upon the earth, and behold it was between Asshur and Babylon in the land of Shinar, and they called its name 'Overthrow'. ²⁷ In the fourth week in the first year [1688 A.M.] in the beginning thereof in the four and thirtieth jubilee, were they dispersed from the land of Shinar.

The Children of Noah enter their Districts Canaan seizes Palestine wrongfully; Madai receives Media (x. 28-36)

²⁸ And Ham and his sons went into the land which he was to occupy, which he acquired as his portion in the land of the south. ²⁹ And Canaan saw the land of Lebanon to the river of Egypt, that it was very good, and he went not into the land of his inheritance to the west (that is to) the sea, and he dwelt in the land of Lebanon, eastward and westward from the border of Jordan and from the border of the sea. ³⁰ And Ham, his father, and Cush and Mizraim his brothers said unto him: 'Thou hast settled in a land which is not thine, and which did not fall to us by lot: do not do so; for if thou dost do so, thou and thy sons will fall in the land and (be) accursed through sedition; for by sedition ye have settled, and by sedition will thy children fall, and thou shalt be rooted out for ever. ³¹ Dwell not in the dwelling of Shem; for to Shem and to his sons did it come by their lot. ³² Cursed art thou, and cursed shalt thou be beyond all the sons of Noah, by the curse by which we bound ourselves by an oath in the presence of the holy judge, and in the presence of Noah our father.' ³³ But he did not harken unto them, and dwelt in the land of Lebanon from Hamath to the entering of Egypt, he and his sons until this day. ³⁴ And for this reason that land is named Canaan. ³⁵ And Japheth and his sons went towards the sea and dwelt in the land of their portion, and Madai saw the land of the sea and it did not please him, and he begged a (portion) from Ham and Asshur and Arpachshad, his wife's brother, and he dwelt in the land of Media, near to his wife's brother until this day. ³⁶ And he called his dwelling-place, and the dwelling-place of his sons, Media, after the name of their father Madai.

The History of the Patriarchs from Reu to Abraham (cf. Gen. xi, 20-30); the Corruption of the Human Race (xi. 1-15).

11

¹ And in the thirty-fifth jubilee, in the third week, in the first year [1681 A.M.] thereof, Reu took to himself a wife, and her name was 'Ôrâ, the daughter of 'Ûr, the son of Kesed, and she bare him a son, and he called his name Sêrôh, in the seventh year of this week in this jubilee. [1687 A.M.] ² And the sons of Noah began to war on each other, to take captive and to slay each other, and to shed the blood of men on the earth, and to eat blood, and to build strong cities, and walls, and towers, and individuals (began) to exalt themselves above the nation, and to found the beginnings of kingdoms, and to go to war people against people, and nation against nation, and city against city, and all (began) to do evil, and to acquire arms, and to teach their sons war, and they began to capture cities, and to sell male and female slaves. ³ And 'Ûr, the son of Kesed, built the city of 'Ara of the Chaldees, and called its name after his own name and the name of his father. ⁴ And they made for themselves molten images, and they worshipped each the idol, the molten image which they had made for themselves, and they began to make graven images and unclean simulacra, and malignant spirits assisted and seduced (them) into committing transgression and uncleanness. ⁵ And the prince Mastêmâ exerted himself to do all this, and he sent forth other spirits, those which were put under his hand, to do all manner of wrong and sin, and all manner of transgression, to corrupt and destroy, and to shed blood upon the earth. ⁶ For this reason he called the name of Sêrôh, Serug, for every one turned to do all manner of sin and transgression. ⁷ And he grew up, and dwelt in Ur of the Chaldees, near to the father of his wife's mother, and he worshipped idols, and he took to himself a wife in the thirty-sixth jubilee, in the fifth week, in the first year thereof, [1744 A.M.] and her name was Melka, the daughter of Kaber, the daughter of his father's brother. ⁸ And she bare him Nahor, in the first year of this week, and he grew and dwelt in Ur of the Chaldees, and his father taught him the researches of the Chaldees to divine and augur, according to the signs of heaven. ⁹ And in the thirty-seventh jubilee in the sixth week, in the first year thereof, [1800 A.M.] he took to himself a wife, and her name was 'Ijaska, the daughter of Nestag of the Chaldees. ¹⁰ And she bare him Terah in the seventh year of this week. [1806 A.M.] ¹¹ And the prince Mastêmâ sent ravens and birds to devour the seed which was sown in the land, in order to destroy the land, and rob the children of men of their labours. Before they could plough in the seed, the ravens picked (it) from the surface of the ground. ¹² And for this reason he called his name Terah because the ravens and the birds reduced them to destitution and devoured their seed. ¹³ And the years began to be barren, owing to the birds, and they devoured all the fruit of the trees from the trees: it was only with great effort that they could save a little of all the fruit of the earth in their days. ¹⁴ And in this thirty-ninth jubilee, in the second week in the first year, [1870 A.M.] Terah took to himself a wife, and her name was 'Edna, the daughter of 'Abram, the daughter of his father's sister. ¹⁵ And in the seventh year of this week [1876 A.M.] she bare him a son, and he called his name Abram, by the name of the father of his mother; for he had died before his daughter had conceived a son.

Abram's Knowledge of God and wonderful Deeds (xi. 16-24).

¹⁶ And the child began to understand the errors of the earth that all went astray after graven images and after uncleanness, and his father taught him writing, and he was two weeks of years old, [1890 A.M.] and he separated himself from his father, that he might not worship idols with him. ¹⁷ And he began to pray to the Creator of all things that He might save him from the errors of the children of men, and that his portion should not fall into error after uncleanness and vileness. ¹⁸ And the seed time came for the sowing of seed upon the land, and they all went forth together to protect their seed against the ravens, and Abram went forth with those that went, and the child was a lad of fourteen years. ¹⁹ And a cloud of ravens came to devour the seed, and Abram ran to meet them before they settled on the ground, and cried to them before they settled on the ground to devour the seed, and said, ' Descend not: return to the place whence ye came,' and they proceeded to turn back. ²⁰ And he caused the clouds of ravens to turn back that day seventy times, and of all the ravens throughout all the land where Abram was there settled there not so much as one. ²¹ And all who were with him throughout all the land saw him cry out, and all the ravens turn back, and his name became great in all the land of the Chaldees. ²² And there came to him this year all those that wished to sow, and he went with them until the time of sowing ceased: and they sowed their land, and that year they brought enough grain home and eat and were satisfied. ²³ And in the first year of the fifth week [1891 A.M.] Abram taught those who made implements for oxen, the artificers in wood, and they made a vessel above the ground, facing the frame of the plough, in order to put the seed thereon, and the seed fell down therefrom upon the share of the plough, and was hidden in the earth, and they no longer feared the ravens. ²⁴ And after this manner they made (vessels) above the ground on all the frames of the ploughs, and they sowed and tilled all the land, according as Abram commanded them, and they no longer feared the birds.

Abram seeks to convert Terah from Idolatry; the Family of Terah (cf. Gen. xi. 27-30). Abram burns the Idols. Death of Haran (cf. Gen. xi. 28) (xii. 1-14).

12

¹ And it came to pass in the sixth week, in the seventh year thereof, [1904 A.M.] that Abram said to Terah his father, saying, 'Father!'
² And he said, 'Behold, here am I, my son.' And he said, 'What help and profit have we from those idols which thou dost worship, And before which thou dost bow thyself? ³ For there is no spirit in them, For they are dumb forms, and a misleading of the heart. Worship them not: ⁴ Worship the God of heaven, Who causes the rain and the dew to descend on the earth And does everything upon the earth, And has created everything by His word, And all life is from before His face. ⁵ Why do ye worship things that have no spirit in them? For they are the work of (men's) hands, And on your shoulders do ye bear them, And ye have no help from them, But they are a great cause of shame to those who make them, And a misleading of the heart to those who worship them: Worship them not.' ⁶ And his father said unto him, I also know it, my son, but what shall I do with a people who have made me to serve before them? ⁷ And if I tell them the truth, they will slay me; for their soul cleaves to them to worship them and honour them. ⁸ Keep silent, my son, lest they slay thee.' And these words he spake to his two brothers, and they were angry with him and he kept silent. ⁹ And in the fortieth jubilee, in the second week, in the seventh year thereof, [1925 A.M.] Abram took to himself a wife, and her name was Sarai, the daughter

of his father, and she became his wife. ¹⁰ And Haran, his brother, took to himself a wife in the third year of the third week, [1928 A.M.] and she bare him a son in the seventh year of this week, [1932 A.M.] and he called his name Lot. ¹¹ And Nahor, his brother, took to himself a wife. ¹² And in the sixtieth year of the life of Abram, that is, in the fourth week, in the fourth year thereof, [1936 A.M.] Abram arose by night, and burned the house of the idols, and he burned all that was in the house and no man knew it. ¹³ And they arose in the night and sought to save their gods from the midst of the fire. ¹⁴ And Haran hasted to save them, but the fire flamed over him, and he was burnt in the fire, and he died in Ur of the Chaldees before Terah his father, and they buried him in Ur of the Chaldees.

The Family of Terah in Haran; Abram's Experiences there; his Journey to Canaan (xii. 15-31; cf. Gen. xi, 31-xii. 3).

¹⁵ And Terah went forth from Ur of the Chaldees, he and his sons, to go into the land of Lebanon and into the land of Canaan, and he dwelt in the land of Haran, and Abram dwelt with Terah his father in Haran two weeks of years. ¹⁶ And in the sixth week, in the fifth year thereof, [1951 A.M.] Abram sat up throughout the night on the new moon of the seventh month to observe the stars from the evening to the morning, in order to see what would be the character of the year with regard to the rains, and he was alone as he sat and observed. ¹⁷ And a word came into his heart and he said: All the signs of the stars, and the signs of the moon and of the sun are all in the hand of the Lord. Why do I search (them) out? ¹⁸ If He desires, He causes it to rain, morning and evening; And if He desires, He withholds it, And all things are in his hand.' ¹⁹ And he prayed that night and said, 'My God, God Most High, Thou alone art my God, And Thee and Thy dominion have I chosen. And Thou hast created all things, And all things that are the work of thy hands. ²⁰ Deliver me from the hands of evil spirits who have dominion over the thoughts of men's hearts, And let them not lead me astray from Thee, my God. And stablish Thou me and my seed for ever That we go not astray from henceforth and for evermore.' ²¹ And he said, 'Shall I return unto Ur of the Chaldees who seek my face that I may return to them, am I to remain here in this place? The right path before Thee prosper it in the hands of Thy servant that he may fulfil (it) and that I may not walk in the deceitfulness of my heart, O my God.' ²² And he made an end of speaking and praying, and behold the word of the Lord was sent to him through me, saying: 'Get thee up from thy country, and from thy kindred and from the house of thy father unto a land which I will show thee, and I shall make thee a great and numerous nation. ²³ And I will bless thee And I will make thy name great, And thou shalt be blessed in the earth, And in Thee shall all families of the earth be blessed, And I will bless them that bless thee, And curse them that curse thee. ²⁴ And I will be a God to thee and thy son, and to thy son's son, and to all thy seed: fear not, from henceforth and unto all generations of the earth I am thy God.' ²⁵ And the Lord God said: 'Open his mouth and his ears, that he may hear and speak with his mouth, with the language which has been revealed'; for it had ceased from the mouths of all the children of men from the day of the overthrow (of Babel). ²⁶ And I opened his mouth, and his ears and his lips, and I began to speak with him in Hebrew in the tongue of the creation. ²⁷ And he took the books of his fathers, and these were written in Hebrew, and he transcribed them, and he began from henceforth to study them, and I made known to him that which he could not (understand), and he studied them during the six rainy months. ²⁸ And it came to pass in the seventh year of the sixth week [1953 A.M.] that he spoke to his father and informed him, that he would leave Haran to go into the land of Canaan to see it and return to him. ²⁹ And Terah his father said unto him; Go in peace: May the eternal God make thy path straight. And the Lord [(be) with thee, and] protect thee from all evil, And grant unto thee grace, mercy and favour before those who see thee, And may none of the children of men have power over thee to harm thee; Go in peace. ³⁰ And if thou seest a land pleasant to thy eyes to dwell in, then arise and take me to thee and take Lot with thee, the son of Haran thy brother as thine own son: the Lord be with thee. ³¹ And Nahor thy brother leave with me till thou returnest in peace, and we go with thee all together.'

Abram with Lot in Canaan and Egypt (cf. Gen. xii. 4-20). Abram separates from Lot (cf. Gen. xiii. 11-18) (xiii. 1-21).

13

¹ And Abram journeyed from Haran, and he took Sarai, his wife, and Lot, his brother Haran's son, to the land of Canaan, and he came into Asshur, and proceeded to Shechem, and dwelt near a lofty oak. ² And he saw, and, behold, the land was very pleasant from the entering of Hamath to the lofty oak. ³ And the Lord said to him: 'To thee and to thy seed will I give this land.' ⁴ And he built an altar there, and he offered thereon a burnt sacrifice to the Lord, who had appeared to him. ⁵ And he removed from thence unto the mountain . . . Bethel on the west and Ai on the east, and pitched his tent there. ⁶ And he saw and behold, the land was very wide and good, and everything grew thereon -vines and figs and pomegranates, oaks and ilexes, and terebinths and oil trees, and cedars and cypresses and date trees, and all trees of the field, and there was water on the mountains. ⁷ And he blessed the Lord who had led him out of Ur of the Chaldees, and had brought him to this land. ⁸ And it came to pass in the first year, in the seventh week, on the new moon of the first month, 1954 A.M.] that he built an altar on this mountain, and called on the name of the Lord: 'Thou, the eternal God, art my God.' ⁹ And he offered on the altar a burnt sacrifice unto the Lord that He should be with him and not forsake him all the days of his life. ¹⁰ And he removed from thence and went towards the south, and he came to Hebron and Hebron was built at that time, and he dwelt there two years, and he went (thence) into the land of the south, to Bealoth, and there was a famine in the land. ¹¹ And Abram went into Egypt in the third year of the week, and he dwelt in Egypt five years before his wife was torn away from him. ¹² Now Tanais in Egypt was at that time built- seven years after Hebron. ¹³ And it came to pass when Pharaoh seized Sarai, the wife of Abram that the Lord plagued Pharaoh and his house with great plagues because of Sarai, Abram's wife. ¹⁴ And Abram was very glorious by reason of possessions in sheep, and cattle, and asses, and horses, and camels, and menservants, and maidservants, and in silver and gold exceedingly. And Lot also his brother's son, was wealthy. ¹⁵ And Pharaoh gave back Sarai, the wife of Abram, and he sent him out of the land of Egypt, and he journeyed to the place where he had pitched his tent at the beginning, to the place of the altar, with Ai on the east, and Bethel on the west, and he blessed the Lord his God who had brought him back in peace. ¹⁶ And it came to pass in the forty-first jubilee in the third year of the first week, [1963 A.M.] that he returned to this place and offered thereon a burnt sacrifice, and called on the name of the Lord, and said: 'Thou, the most high God, art my God for ever and ever.' ¹⁷ And in the fourth year of this week [1964 A.M.] Lot parted from him, and Lot dwelt in Sodom, and the men of Sodom were sinners exceedingly. ¹⁸ And it grieved him in his heart that his brother's son had parted from him; for he had no children. ¹⁹ In that year when Lot was taken captive, the Lord said unto Abram, after that Lot had parted from him, in the fourth year of this week: 'Lift up thine eyes from the place where thou art dwelling, northward and southward, and westward and eastward. ²⁰ For all the land which thou seest I will give to thee and to thy seed for ever, and I will make thy seed as the sand of the sea: though a man may number the dust of the earth, yet thy seed shall not be numbered. ²¹ Arise, walk (through the land) in the length of it and the breadth of it, and see it all; for to thy seed will I give it.' And Abram went to Hebron, and dwelt there.

The Campaign of Chedorlaomer (xiii. 22-29; cf. Gen. xiv.).

²² And in this year came Chedorlaomer, king of Elam, and Amraphel, king of Shinar, and Arioch king of Sellasar, and Tergal, king of nations, and slew the king of Gomorrah, and the king of Sodom fled; and many fell through wounds in the vale of Siddim, by the Salt Sea. ²³ And they took captive Sodom and Adam and Zeboim, and they took captive Lot also, the son of Abram's brother, and all his possessions, and they went to Dan. ²⁴ And one who had escaped came and told Abram that his brother's son had been taken captive and (Abram) armed his household servants . . . ²⁵ . . . . for Abram, and for his seed, a tenth of the first fruits to the Lord, and the Lord ordained it as an ordinance for ever that they should give it to the priests who served before Him, that they should possess it for ever. ²⁶ And to this law there is no limit of days; for He hath ordained it for the generations for ever that they should give to the Lord the tenth of everything, of the seed and of the wine and of the oil and of the cattle and of the sheep. ²⁷ And He gave (it) unto His priests to eat and to drink with joy before Him. ²⁸ And the king of Sodom came to him and bowed himself before him, and said: 'Our Lord Abram, give unto us the souls which thou hast rescued, but let the booty be thine.' ²⁹ And Abram said unto him: 'I lift up my hands to the Most High God, that from a thread to a shoe-latchet I shall not take aught that is thine lest thou shouldst say, I have made Abram rich; save only what the young men have eaten, and the portion of the men who went with me -Aner, Eschol, and Mamre. These shall take their portion.'

God's Covenant with Abram (xiv. 1-20; cf. Gen. xv.).

14

¹ After these things, in the fourth year of this week, on the new moon of the third month, the word of the Lord came to Abram in a dream, saying: 'Fear not, Abram; I am thy defender, and thy reward will be exceeding great.' ² And he said: 'Lord, Lord, what wilt thou give me, seeing I go hence childless, and the son of Maseq, the son of my handmaid, is the Dammasek Eliezer: he will be my heir, and to me thou hast given no seed.' ³ And he said unto him: 'This (man) will not be thy heir, but one that will come out of thine own bowels; he will be thine heir.' ⁴ And He brought him forth abroad, and said: 'Look toward heaven and number the stars if thou art able to number them.' ⁵ And he looked toward heaven, and beheld

the stars. And He said unto him: 'So shall thy seed be.' ⁶ And he believed in the Lord, and it was counted to him for righteousness. ⁷ And He said unto him: 'I am the Lord that brought thee out of Ur of the Chaldees, to give thee the land of the Canaanites to possess it for ever; and I will be God unto thee and to thy seed after thee.' ⁸ And he said: 'Lord, Lord, whereby shall I know that I shall inherit (it)?' ⁹ And He said unto him: 'Take Me an heifer of three years, and a goat of three years, and a sheep of three years, and a turtle-dove, and a pigeon.' ¹⁰ And he took all these in the middle of the month and he dwelt at the oak of Mamre, which is near Hebron. ¹¹ And he built there an altar, and sacrificed all these; and he poured their blood upon the altar, and divided them in the midst, and laid them over against each other; but the birds divided he not. ¹² And birds came down upon the pieces, and Abram drove them away, and did not suffer the birds to touch them. ¹³ And it came to pass, when the sun had set, that an ecstasy fell upon Abram, and lo! an horror of great darkness fell upon him, and it was said unto Abram: 'Know of a surety that thy seed shall be a stranger in a land (that is) not theirs, and they shall bring them into bondage, and afflict them four hundred years. ¹⁴ And the nation also to whom they will be in bondage will I judge, and after that they shall come forth thence with much substance. ¹⁵ And thou shalt go to thy fathers in peace, and be buried in a good old age. ¹⁶ But in the fourth generation they shall return hither; for the iniquity of the Amorites is not yet full.' ¹⁷ And he awoke from his sleep, and he arose, and the sun had set; and there was a flame, and behold! a furnace was smoking, and a flame of fire passed between the pieces. ¹⁸ And on that day the Lord made a covenant with Abram, saying: 'To thy seed will I give this land, from the river of Egypt unto the great river, the river Euphrates, the Kenites, the Kenizzites, the Kadmonites, the Perizzites, and the Rephaim, the Phakorites, and the Hivites, and the Amorites, and the Canaanites, and the Girgashites, and the Jebusites. ¹⁹ And the day passed, and Abram offered the pieces, and the birds, and their fruit offerings, and their drink offerings, and the fire devoured them. ²⁰ And on that day we made a covenant with Abram, according as we had covenanted with Noah in this month; and Abram renewed the festival and ordinance for himself for ever.

The Birth of Ishmael (xiv. 21-24; cf. Gen. xvi. 1-4.11).
²¹ And Abram rejoiced, and made all these things known to Sarai his wife; and he believed that he would have seed, but she did not bear. ²² And Sarai advised her husband Abram, and said unto him: 'Go in unto Hagar, my Egyptian maid: it may be that I shall build up seed unto thee by her.' ²³ And Abram harkened unto the voice of Sarai his wife, and said unto her, 'Do (so).' And Sarai took Hagar, her maid, the Egyptian, and gave her to Abram, her husband, to be his wife. ²⁴ And he went in unto her, and she conceived and bare him a son, and he called his name Ishmael, in the fifth year of this week [1965 A.M.]; and this was the eighty-sixth year in the life of Abram.

The Feast of First-fruits Circumcision instituted. The Promise of Isaac's Birth. Circumcision ordained for all Israel (xv. 1-34; cf. Gen. xvii.).

15

¹ And in the fifth year of the fourth week of this jubilee, [1979 A.M.] in the third month, in the middle of the month, Abram celebrated the feast of the first-fruits of the grain harvest. ² And he offered new offerings on the altar, the first-fruits of the produce, unto the Lord, an heifer and a goat and a sheep on the altar as a burnt sacrifice unto the Lord; their fruit offerings and their drink offerings he offered upon the altar with frankincense. ³ And the Lord appeared to Abram, and said unto him: 'I am God Almighty; approve thyself before me and be thou perfect. ⁴ And I will make My covenant between Me and thee, and I will multiply thee exceedingly.' ⁵ And Abram fell on his face, and God talked with him, and said: ⁶ 'Behold my ordinance is with thee, And thou shalt be the father of many nations. ⁷ Neither shall thy name any more be called Abram, But thy name from henceforth, even for ever, shall be Abraham. For the father of many nations have I made thee. ⁸ And I will make thee very great, And I will make thee into nations, And kings shall come forth from thee. ⁹ And I shall establish My covenant between Me and thee, and thy seed after thee, throughout their generations, for an eternal covenant, so that I may be a God unto thee, and to thy seed after thee. ¹⁰ <And I will give to thee and to thy seed after thee> the land where thou hast been a sojourner, the land of Canaan, that thou mayst possess it for ever, and I will be their God.' ¹¹ And the Lord said unto Abraham: 'And as for thee, do thou keep my covenant, thou and thy seed after thee: and circumcise ye every male among you, and circumcise your foreskins, and it shall be a token of an eternal covenant between Me and you. ¹² And the child on the eighth day ye shall circumcise, every male throughout your generations, him that is born in the house, or whom ye have bought with money from any stranger, whom ye have acquired who is not of thy seed. ¹³ He that is born in thy house shall surely be circumcised, and those whom thou hast bought with money shall be circumcised, and My covenant shall be in your flesh for an eternal ordinance. ¹⁴ And the uncircumcised male who is not circumcised in the flesh of his foreskin on the eighth day, that soul shall be cut off from his people, for he has broken My covenant.' ¹⁵ And God said unto Abraham: 'As for Sarai thy wife, her name shall no more be called Sarai, but Sarah shall be her name. ¹⁶ And I will bless her, and give thee a son by her, and I will bless him, and he shall become a nation, and kings of nations shall proceed from him.' ¹⁷ And Abraham fell on his face, and rejoiced, and said in his heart: 'Shall a son be born to him that is a hundred years old, and shall Sarah, who is ninety years old, bring forth?' ¹⁸ And Abraham said unto God: 'O that Ishmael might live before thee!' ¹⁹ And God said: 'Yea, and Sarah also shall bear thee a son, and thou shalt call his name Isaac, and I will establish My covenant with him, an everlasting covenant, and for his seed after him. ²⁰ And as for Ishmael also have I heard thee, and behold I will bless him, and make him great, and multiply him exceedingly, and he shall beget twelve princes, and I will make him a great nation. ²¹ But My covenant will I establish with Isaac, whom Sarah shall bear to thee, in these days, in the next year.' ²² And He left off speaking with him, and God went up from Abraham. ²³ And Abraham did according as God had said unto him, and he took Ishmael his son, and all that were born in his house, and whom he had bought with his money, every male in his house, and circumcised the flesh of their foreskin. ²⁴ And on the selfsame day was Abraham circumcised, and all the men of his house, <and those born in the house>, and all those, whom he had bought with money from the children of the stranger, were circumcised with him. ²⁵ This law is for all the generations for ever, and there is no circumcision of the days, and no omission of one day out of the eight days; for it is an eternal ordinance, ordained and written on the heavenly tablets. ²⁶ And every one that is born, the flesh of whose foreskin is not circumcised on the eighth day, belongs not to the children of the covenant which the Lord made with Abraham, but to the children of destruction; nor is there, moreover, any sign on him that he is the Lord's, but (he is destined) to be destroyed and slain from the earth, and to be rooted out of the earth, for he has broken the covenant of the Lord our God. ²⁷ For all the angels of the presence and all the angels of sanctification have been so created from the day of their creation, and before the angels of the presence and the angels of sanctification He hath sanctified Israel, that they should be with Him and with His holy angels. ²⁸ And do thou command the children of Israel and let them observe the sign of this covenant for their generations as an eternal ordinance, and they will not be rooted out of the land. ²⁹ For the command is ordained for a covenant, that they should observe it for ever among all the children of Israel. ³⁰ For Ishmael and his sons and his brothers and Esau, the Lord did not cause to approach Him, and he chose them not because they are the children of Abraham, because He knew them, but He chose Israel to be His people. ³¹ And He sanctified it, and gathered it from amongst all the children of men; for there are many nations and many peoples, and all are His, and over all hath He placed spirits in authority to lead them astray from Him. ³² But over Israel He did not appoint any angel or spirit, for He alone is their ruler, and He will preserve them and require them at the hand of His angels and His spirits, and at the hand of all His powers in order that He may preserve them and bless them, and that they may be His and He may be theirs from henceforth for ever. ³³ And now I announce unto thee that the children of Israel will not keep true to this ordinance, and they will not circumcise their sons according to all this law; for in the flesh of their circumcision they will omit this circumcision of their sons, and all of them, sons of Beliar, will leave their sons uncircumcised as they were born. ³⁴ And there will be great wrath from the Lord against the children of Israel, because they have forsaken His covenant and turned aside from His word, and provoked and blasphemed, inasmuch as they do not observe the ordinance of this law; for they have treated their members like the Gentiles, so that they may be removed and rooted out of the land. And there will no more be pardon or forgiveness unto them [so that there should be forgiveness and pardon] for all the sin of this eternal error.

Angelic Visitation of Abraham in Hebron; Promise of Isaac's Birth repeated. The Destruction of Sodom and Lot's Deliverance (xvi. 1-9; cf. Gen. xviii.-xix.).

16

¹ And on the new moon of the fourth month we appeared unto Abraham, at the oak of Mamre, and we talked with him, and we announced to him that a son would be given to him by Sarah his wife. ² And Sarah laughed, for she heard that we had spoken these words with Abraham, and we admonished her, and she became afraid, and denied that she had laughed on account of the words. ³ And we told her the name of her son, as his name is ordained and written in the heavenly tablets (i.e.) Isaac, ⁴ And (that) when we returned to her at a set time, she would have conceived a son. ⁵ And in this month the Lord executed his judgments on Sodom, and Gomorrah, and

Zeboim, and all the region of the Jordan, and He burned them with fire and brimstone, and destroyed them until this day, even as [lo] I have declared unto thee all their works, that they are wicked and sinners exceedingly, and that they defile themselves and commit fornication in their flesh, and work uncleanness on the earth.⁶ And, in like manner, God will execute judgment on the places where they have done according to the uncleanness of the Sodomites, like unto the judgment of Sodom. ⁷ But Lot we saved; for God remembered Abraham, and sent him out from the midst of the overthrow. ⁸ And he and his daughters committed sin upon the earth, such as had not been on the earth since the days of Adam till his time; for the man lay with his daughters. ⁹ And, behold, it was commanded and engraven concerning all his seed, on the heavenly tablets, to remove them and root them out, and to execute judgment upon them like the judgment of Sodom, and to leave no seed of the man on earth on the day of condemnation.

Abraham at Beersheba. Birth and Circumcision of Isaac (cf. Gen. xxi. 1-4). Institution of the Feast of Tabernacles (xvi. 10-31).

¹⁰ And in this month Abraham moved from Hebron, and departed and dwelt between Kadesh and Shur in the mountains of Gerar. ¹¹ And in the middle of the fifth month he moved from thence, and dwelt at the Well of the Oath. ¹² And in the middle of the sixth month the Lord visited Sarah and did unto her as He had spoken and she conceived. ¹³ And she bare a son in the third month, and in the middle of the month, at the time of which the Lord had spoken to Abraham, on the festival of the first fruits of the harvest, Isaac was born. ¹⁴ And Abraham circumcised his son on the eighth day: he was the first that was circumcised according to the covenant which is ordained for ever. ¹⁵ And in the sixth year of the fourth week we came to Abraham, to the Well of the Oath, and we appeared unto him [as we had told Sarah that we should return to her, and she would have conceived a son. ¹⁶ And we returned in the seventh month, and found Sarah with child before us] and we blessed him, and we announced to him all the things which had been decreed concerning him, that he should not die till he should beget six sons more, and should see (them) before he died; but (that) in Isaac should his name and seed be called: ¹⁷ And (that) all the seed of his sons should be Gentiles, and be reckoned with the Gentiles; but from the sons of Isaac one should become a holy seed, and should not be reckoned among the Gentiles. ¹⁸ For he should become the portion of the Most High, and all his seed had fallen into the possession of God, that it should be unto the Lord a people for (His) possession above all nations and that it should become a kingdom and priests and a holy nation. ¹⁹ And we went our way, and we announced to Sarah all that we had told him, and they both rejoiced with exceeding great joy. ²⁰ And he built there an altar to the Lord who had delivered him, and who was making him rejoice in the land of his sojourning, and he celebrated a festival of joy in this month seven days, near the altar which he had built at the Well of the Oath. ²¹ And he built booths for himself and for his servants on this festival, and he was the first to celebrate the feast of tabernacles on the earth. ²² And during these seven days he brought each day to the altar a burnt offering to the Lord, two oxen, two rams, seven sheep, one he-goat, for a sin offering, that he might atone thereby for himself and for his seed. ²³ And, as a thank-offering, seven rams, seven kids, seven sheep, and seven he-goats, and their fruit offerings and their drink offerings; and he burnt all the fat thereof on the altar, a chosen offering unto the Lord for a sweet smelling savour. ²⁴ And morning and evening he burnt fragrant substances, frankincense and galbanum, and stackte, and nard, and myrrh, and spice, and costum; all these seven he offered, crushed, mixed together in equal parts (and) pure. ²⁵ And he celebrated this feast during seven days, rejoicing with all his heart and with all his soul, he and all those who were in his house, and there was no stranger with him, nor any that was uncircumcised. ²⁶ And he blessed his Creator who had created him in his generation, for He had created him according to His good pleasure; for He knew and perceived that from him would arise the plant of righteousness for the eternal generations, and from him a holy seed, so that it should become like Him who had made all things. ²⁷ And he blessed and rejoiced, and he called the name of this festival the festival of the Lord, a joy acceptable to the Most High God. ²⁸ And we blessed him for ever, and all his seed after him throughout all the generations of the earth, because he celebrated this festival in its season, according to the testimony of the heavenly tablets. ²⁹ For this reason it is ordained on the heavenly tablets concerning Israel, that they shall celebrate the feast of tabernacles seven days with joy, in the seventh month, acceptable before the Lord -a statute for ever throughout their generations every year. ³⁰ And to this there is no limit of days; for it is ordained for ever regarding Israel that they should celebrate it and dwell in booths, and set wreaths upon their heads, and take leafy boughs, and willows from the brook. ³¹ And Abraham took branches of palm trees, and the fruit of goodly trees, and every day going round the altar with the branches seven times [a day] in the morning, he praised and gave thanks to his God for all things in joy.

The Expulsion of Hagar and Ishmael (xvii. 1-14; cf. Gen. xxi. 8-21).

17

¹ And in the first year of the fifth week Isaac was weaned in this jubilee, [1982 A.M.] and Abraham made a great banquet in the third month, on the day his son Isaac was weaned. ² And Ishmael, the son of Hagar, the Egyptian, was before the face of Abraham, his father, in his place, and Abraham rejoiced and blessed God because he had seen his sons and had not died childless. ³ And he remembered the words which He had spoken to him on the day on which Lot had parted from him, and he rejoiced because the Lord had given him seed upon the earth to inherit the earth, and he blessed with all his mouth the Creator of all things. ⁴ And Sarah saw Ishmael playing and dancing, and Abraham rejoicing with great joy, and she became jealous of Ishmael and said to Abraham, 'Cast out this bondwoman and her son; for the son of this bondwoman will not be heir with my son, Isaac.' ⁵ And the thing was grievous in Abraham's sight, because of his maidservant and because of his son, that he should drive them from him. ⁶ And God said to Abraham 'Let it not be grievous in thy sight, because of the child and because of the bondwoman, in all that Sarah hath said unto thee, harken to her words and do (them); for in Isaac shall thy name and seed be called. ⁷ But as for the son of this bondwoman I will make him a great nation, because he is of thy seed.' ⁸ And Abraham rose up early in the morning, and took bread and a bottle of water, and placed them on the shoulders of Hagar and the child, and sent her away. ⁹ And she departed and wandered in the wilderness of Beersheba, and the water in the bottle was spent, and the child thirsted, and was not able to go on, and fell down. ¹⁰ And his mother took him and cast him under an olive tree, and went and sat her down over against him, at the distance of a bow-shot; for she said, 'Let me not see the death of my child,' and as she sat she wept. ¹¹ And an angel of God, one of the holy ones, said unto her, 'Why weepest thou, Hagar? Arise take the child, and hold him in thine hand; for God hath heard thy voice, and hath seen the child.' ¹² And she opened her eyes, and she saw a well of water, and she went and filled her bottle with water, and she gave her child to drink, and she arose and went towards the wilderness of Paran. ¹³ And the child grew and became an archer, and God was with him, and his mother took him a wife from among the daughters of Egypt. ¹⁴ And she bare him a son, and he called his name Nebaioth; for she said, 'The Lord was nigh to me when I called upon him.'

Mastêmâ proposes to God that Abraham shall be put to the Proof (xvi. 15-18).

¹⁵ And it came to pass in the seventh week, in the first year thereof, [2003 A.M.] in the first month in this jubilee, on the twelfth of this month, there were voices in heaven regarding Abraham, that he was faithful in all that He told him, and that he loved the Lord, and that in every affliction he was faithful. ¹⁶ And the prince Mastêmâ came and said before God, 'Behold, Abraham loves Isaac his son, and he delights in him above all things else; bid him offer him as a burnt-offering on the altar, and Thou wilt see if he will do this command, and Thou wilt know if he is faithful in everything wherein Thou dost try him. ¹⁷ And the Lord knew that Abraham was faithful in all his afflictions; for He had tried him through his country and with famine, and had tried him with the wealth of kings, and had tried him again through his wife, when she was torn (from him), and with circumcision; and had tried him through Ishmael and Hagar, his maid-servant, when he sent them away. ¹⁸ And in everything wherein He had tried him, he was found faithful, and his soul was not impatient, and he was not slow to act; for he was faithful and a lover of the Lord.

The Sacrifice of Isaac: Abraham returns to Beersheba (xviii. 1-19; Cf. Gen. xxii. 1-19).

18

¹ And God said to him, 'Abraham, Abraham'; and he said, Behold, (here) am I.' ² And he said, Take thy beloved son whom thou lovest, (even) Isaac, and go unto the high country, and offer him on one of the mountains which I will point out unto thee.' ³ And he rose early in the morning and saddled his ass, and took his two young men with him, and Isaac his son, and clave the wood of the burnt offering, and he went to the place on the third day, and he saw the place afar off. ⁴ And he came to a well of water, and he said to his young men, 'Abide ye here with the ass, and I and the lad shall go (yonder), and when we have worshipped we shall come again to you.' ⁵ And he took the wood of the burnt-offering and laid it on Isaac his son, and took in his hand the fire and the knife, and they went both of them together to that place. ⁶ And Isaac said to his father, 'Father;' and he said, 'Here am I, my son.' And he said unto him, 'Behold the fire, and the knife, and the wood;

but where is the sheep for the burnt-offering, father?' ⁷ And he said, 'God will provide for himself a sheep for a burnt-offering, my son.' And he drew near to the place of the mount of God. ⁸ And he built an altar, and he placed the wood on the altar, and bound Isaac his son, and placed him on the wood which was upon the altar, and stretched forth his hand to take the knife to slay Isaac his son. ⁹ And I stood before him, and before the prince Mastêmâ, and the Lord said, 'Bid him not to lay his hand on the lad, nor to do anything to him, for I have shown that he fears the Lord.' ¹⁰ And I called to him from heaven, and said unto him: 'Abraham, Abraham;' and he was terrified and said: 'Behold, (here) am I.' ¹¹ And I said unto him: 'Lay not thy hand upon the lad, neither do thou anything to him; for now I have shown that thou fearest the Lord, and hast not withheld thy son, thy first-born son, from me.' ¹² And the prince Mastêmâ was put to shame; and Abraham lifted up his eyes and looked, and, behold a ram caught . . . by his horns, and Abraham went and took the ram and offered it for a burnt-offering in the stead of his son. ¹³ And Abraham called that place 'The Lord hath seen', so that it is said in the mount the Lord hath seen: that is Mount Sion. ¹⁴ And the Lord called Abraham by his name a second time from heaven, as he caused us to appear to speak to him in the name of the Lord. ¹⁵ And he said: 'By Myself have I sworn, saith the Lord, Because thou hast done this thing, And hast not withheld thy son, thy beloved son, from Me, That in blessing I will bless thee, And in multiplying I will multiply thy seed As the stars of heaven, And as the sand which is on the seashore. And thy seed shall inherit the cities of its enemies, ¹⁶ And in thy seed shall all nations of the earth be blessed; Because thou hast obeyed My voice, And I have shown to all that thou art faithful unto Me in all that I have said unto thee: Go in peace.' ¹⁷ And Abraham went to his young men, and they arose and went together to Beersheba, and Abraham [2010 A.M.] dwelt by the Well of the Oath. ¹⁸ And he celebrated this festival every year, seven days with joy, and he called it the festival of the Lord according to the seven days during which he went and returned in peace. ¹⁹ And accordingly has it been ordained and written on the heavenly tablets regarding Israel and its seed that they should observe this festival seven days with the joy of festival.

The Death and Burial of Sarah (xix. 1-9; cf. Gen. xxiii.).

19

¹ And in the first year of the first week in the forty-second jubilee, Abraham returned and dwelt opposite Hebron, that is Kirjath Arba, two weeks of years.
² And in the first year of the third week of this jubilee the days of the life of Sarah were accomplished, and she died in Hebron. ³ And Abraham went to mourn over her and bury her, and we tried him [to see] if his spirit were patient and he were not indignant in the words of his mouth; and he was found patient in this, and was not disturbed. ⁴ For in patience of spirit he conversed with the children of Heth, to the intent that they should give him a place in which to bury his dead. ⁵ And the Lord gave him grace before all who saw him, and he besought in gentleness the sons of Heth, and they gave him the land of the double cave over against Mamre, that is Hebron, for four hundred pieces of silver. ⁶ And they besought him saying, We shall give it to thee for nothing; but he would not take it from their hands for nothing, for he gave the price of the place, the money in full, and he bowed down before them twice, and after this he buried his dead in the double cave. ⁷ And all the days of the life of Sarah were one hundred and twenty-seven years, that is, two jubilees and four weeks and one year: these are the days of the years of the life of Sarah. ⁸ This is the tenth trial wherewith Abraham was tried, and he was found faithful, patient in spirit. ⁹ And he said not a single word regarding the rumour in the land how that God had said that He would give it to him and to his seed after him, and he begged a place there to bury his dead; for he was found faithful, and was recorded on the heavenly tablets as the friend of God.

Marriage of Isaac and second Marriage of Abraham (cf. Gen. xxiv. 15, xxv. 1-4); the Birth of Esau and Jacob (cf. Gen. xxv. 19 ff.) (xix. 10-14).

¹⁰ And in the fourth year thereof he took a wife for his son Isaac and her name was Rebecca [2020 A.M.] [the daughter of Bethuel, the son of Nahor, the brother of Abraham] the sister of Laban and daughter of Bethuel; and Bethuel was the son of Melca, who was the wife of Nahor, the brother of Abraham. ¹¹ And Abraham took to himself a third wife, and her name was Keturah, from among the daughters of his household servants, for Hagar had died before Sarah. And she bare him six sons, Zimram, and Jokshan, and Medan, and Midian, and Ishbak, and Shuah, in the two weeks of years. ¹² And in the sixth week, in the second year thereof, Rebecca bare to Isaac two sons, Jacob and Esau, ¹³ and [2046 A.M.] Jacob was a smooth and upright man, and Esau was fierce, a man of the field, and hairy, and Jacob dwelt in tents. ¹⁴ And the youths grew, and Jacob learned to write; but Esau did not learn, for he was a man of the field and a hunter, and he learnt war, and all his deeds were fierce.

Abraham loves Jacob and blesses him (xix. 15-31).

¹⁵ And Abraham loved Jacob, but Isaac loved Esau. ¹⁶ And Abraham saw the deeds of Esau, and he knew that in Jacob should his name and seed be called; and he called Rebecca and gave commandment regarding Jacob, for he knew that she (too) loved Jacob much more than Esau. ¹⁷ And he said unto her: My daughter, watch over my son Jacob, For he shall be in my stead on the earth, And for a blessing in the midst of the children of men, And for the glory of the whole seed of Shem. ¹⁸ For I know that the Lord will choose him to be a people for possession unto Himself, above all peoples that are upon the face of the earth. ¹⁹ And behold, Isaac my son loves Esau more than Jacob, but I see that thou truly lovest Jacob. ²⁰ Add still further to thy kindness to him, And let thine eyes be upon him in love; For he shall be a blessing unto us on the earth from henceforth unto all generations of the earth. ²¹ Let thy hands be strong And let thy heart rejoice in thy son Jacob; For I have loved him far beyond all my sons. He shall be blessed for ever, And his seed shall fill the whole earth. ²² If a man can number the sand of the earth, His seed also shall be numbered. ²³ And all the blessings wherewith the Lord hath blessed me and my seed shall belong to Jacob and his seed alway. ²⁴ And in his seed shall my name be blessed, and the name of my fathers, Shem, and Noah, and Enoch, and Mahalalel, and Enos, and Seth, and Adam. ²⁵ And these shall serve To lay the foundations of the heaven, And to strengthen the earth, And to renew all the luminaries which are in the firmament. ²⁶ And he called Jacob before the eyes of Rebecca his mother, and kissed him, and blessed him, and said: ²⁷ 'Jacob, my beloved son, whom my soul loveth, may God bless thee from above the firmament, and may He give thee all the blessings wherewith He blessed Adam, and Enoch, and Noah, and Shem; and all the things of which He told me, and all the things which He promised to give me, may he cause to cleave to thee and to thy seed for ever, according to the days of heaven above the earth. ²⁸ And the Spirits of Mastêmâ shall not rule over thee or over thy seed to turn thee from the Lord, who is thy God from henceforth for ever. ²⁹ And may the Lord God be a father to thee and thou the first-born son, and to the people alway. ³⁰ Go in peace, my son.' And they both went forth together from Abraham. ³¹ And Rebecca loved Jacob, with all her heart and with all her soul, very much more than Esau; but Isaac loved Esau much more than Jacob.

Abraham's Last Words to his Children and Grandchildren (xx. i-ii).

20

¹ And in the forty-second jubilee, in the first year of the seventh week, Abraham called Ishmael, [2052 (2045?) A.M.] and his twelve sons, and Isaac and his two sons, and the six sons of Keturah, and their sons. ² And he commanded them that they should observe the way of the Lord; that they should work righteousness, and love each his neighbour, and act on this manner amongst all men; that they should each so walk with regard to them as to do judgment and righteousness on the earth. ³ That they should circumcise their sons, according to the covenant which He had made with them, and not deviate to the right hand or the left of all the paths which the Lord had commanded us; and that we should keep ourselves from all fornication and uncleanness, [and renounce from amongst us all fornication and uncleanness]. ⁴ And if any woman or maid commit fornication amongst you, burn her with fire and let them not commit fornication with her after their eyes and their heart; and let them not take to themselves wives from the daughters of Canaan; for the seed of Canaan will be rooted out of the land. ⁵ And he told them of the judgment of the giants, and the judgment of the Sodomites, how they had been judged on account of their wickedness, and had died on account of their fornication, and uncleanness, and mutual corruption through fornication. ⁶ 'And guard yourselves from all fornication and uncleanness, And from all pollution of sin, Lest ye make our name a curse, And your whole life a hissing, And all your sons to be destroyed by the sword, And ye become accursed like Sodom, And all your remnant as the sons of Gomorrah. ⁷ I implore you, my sons, love the God of heaven And cleave ye to all His commandments. And walk not after their idols, and after their uncleannesses, ⁸ And make not for yourselves molten or graven gods; For they are vanity, And there is no spirit in them; For they are work of (men's) hands, And all who trust in them, trust in nothing. ⁹ Serve them not, nor worship them, But serve ye the most high God, and worship Him continually: And hope for His countenance always, And work uprightness and righteousness before Him, That He may have pleasure in you and grant you His mercy, And send rain upon you morning and evening, And bless all your works which ye have wrought upon the earth, And bless thy bread and thy water, And bless the fruit of thy womb and the fruit of thy land, And the herds of thy cattle, and the flocks of thy sheep. ¹⁰ And ye will be for a

blessing on the earth, And all nations of the earth will desire you, And bless your sons in my name, That they may be blessed as I am.' ¹¹ And he gave to Ishmael and to his sons, and to the sons of Keturah, gifts, and sent them away from Isaac his son, and he gave everything to Isaac his son.

The Dwelling-places of the Ishmaelites and of the Sons of Keturah (xx. 12-13).

¹² And Ishmael and his sons, and the sons of Keturah and their sons, went together and dwelt from Paran to the entering in of Babylon in all the land which is towards the East facing the desert. ¹³ And these mingled with each other, and their name was called Arabs, and Ishmaelites.

Abraham's Last Words to Isaac (xxi. 1-25).

21

¹ And in the sixth year of the seventh week of this jubilee Abraham called Isaac his son, and [2057 (2050?) A.M.] commanded him: saying, 'I am become old, and know not the day of my death, and am full of my days. ² And behold, I am one hundred and seventy-five years old, and throughout all the days of my life I have remembered the Lord, and sought with all my heart to do His will, and to walk uprightly in all His ways. ³ My soul has hated idols, <and I have despised those that served them, and I have given my heart and spirit> that I might observe to do the will of Him who created me. ⁴ For He is the living God, and He is holy and faithful, and He is righteous beyond all, and there is with Him no accepting of (men's) persons and no accepting of gifts; for God is righteous, and executeth judgment on all those who transgress His commandments and despise His covenant. ⁵ And do thou, my son, observe His commandments and His ordinances and His judgments, and walk not after the abominations and after the graven images and after the molten images. ⁶ And eat no blood at all of animals or cattle, or of any bird which flies in the heaven. ⁷ And if thou dost slay a victim as an acceptable peace offering, slay ye it, and pour out its blood upon the altar, and all the fat of the offering offer on the altar with fine flour and the meat offering mingled with oil, with its drink offering -offer them all together on the altar of burnt offering; it is a sweet savour before the Lord. ⁸ And thou wilt offer the fat of the sacrifice of thank offerings on the fire which is upon the altar, and the fat which is on the belly, and all the fat on the inwards and the two kidneys, and all the fat that is upon them, and upon the loins and liver thou shalt remove, together with the kidneys. ⁹ And offer all these for a sweet savour acceptable before the Lord, with its meat-offering and with its drink- offering, for a sweet savour, the bread of the offering unto the Lord. ¹⁰ And eat its meat on that day and on the second day, and let not the sun on the second day go down upon it till it is eaten, and let nothing be left over for the third day; for it is not acceptable [for it is not approved] and let it no longer be eaten, and all who eat thereof will bring sin upon themselves; for thus I have found it written in the books of my forefathers, and in the words of Enoch, and in the words of Noah. ¹¹ And on all thy oblations thou shalt strew salt, and let not the salt of the covenant be lacking in all thy oblations before the Lord. ¹² And as regards the wood of the sacrifices, beware lest thou bring (other) wood for the altar in addition to these: cypress, bay, almond, fir, pine, cedar, savin, fig, olive, myrrh, laurel, aspalathus. ¹³ And of these kinds of wood lay upon the altar under the sacrifice, such as have been tested as to their appearance, and do not lay (thereon) any split or dark wood, (but) hard and clean, without fault, a sound and new growth; and do not lay (thereon) old wood, [for its fragrance is gone] for there is no longer fragrance in it as before. ¹⁴ Besides these kinds of wood there is none other that thou shalt place (on the altar), for the fragrance is dispersed, and the smell of its fragrance goes not up to heaven. ¹⁵ Observe this commandment and do it, my son, that thou mayst be upright in all thy deeds. ¹⁶ And at all times be clean in thy body, and wash thyself with water before thou approachest to offer on the altar, and wash thy hands and thy feet before thou drawest near to the altar; and when thou art done sacrificing, wash again thy hands and thy feet. ¹⁷ And let no blood appear upon you nor upon your clothes; be on thy guard, my son, against blood, be on thy guard exceedingly; cover it with dust. ¹⁸ And do not eat any blood for it is the soul; eat no blood whatever. ¹⁹ And take no gifts for the blood of man, lest it be shed with impunity, without judgment; for it is the blood that is shed that causes the earth to sin, and the earth cannot be cleansed from the blood of man save by the blood of him who shed it. ²⁰ And take no present or gift for the blood of man: blood for blood, that thou mayest be accepted before the Lord, the Most High God; for He is the defence of the good: and that thou mayest be preserved from all evil, and that He may save thee from every kind of death. ²¹ I see, my son, That all the works of the children of men are sin and wickedness, And all their deeds are uncleanness and an abomination and a pollution, And there is no righteousness with them. ²² Beware, lest thou shouldest walk in their ways And tread in their paths, And sin a sin unto death before the Most High God. Else He will [hide His face from thee And] give thee back into the hands of thy transgression, And root thee out of the land, and thy seed likewise from under heaven, And thy name and thy seed shall perish from the whole earth. ²³ Turn away from all their deeds and all their uncleanness, And observe the ordinance of the Most High God, And do His will and be upright in all things. ²⁴ And He will bless thee in all thy deeds, And will raise up from thee a plant of righteousness through all the earth, throughout all generations of the earth, And my name and thy name shall not be forgotten under heaven for ever. ²⁵ Go, my son in peace. May the Most High God, my God and thy God, strengthen thee to do His will, And may He bless all thy seed and the residue of thy seed for the generations for ever, with all righteous blessings, That thou mayest be a blessing on all the earth.' ²⁶ And he went out from him rejoicing.

Isaac, Ishmael and Jacob join in Festival with Abraham for the Last Time. Abraham's Prayer (xxii. 1-9).

22

¹ And it came to pass in the first week in the forty-fourth jubilee, in the second year, that is, the year in which Abraham died, that Isaac and Ishmael came from the Well of the Oath to celebrate the feast of weeks -that is, the feast of the first fruits of the harvest-to Abraham, their father, and Abraham rejoiced because his two sons had come. ² For Isaac had many possessions in Beersheba, and Isaac was wont to go and see his possessions and to return to his father. ³ And in those days Ishmael came to see his father, and they both came together, and Isaac offered a sacrifice for a burnt offering, and presented it on the altar of his father which he had made in Hebron. ⁴ And he offered a thank offering and made a feast of joy before Ishmael, his brother: and Rebecca made new cakes from the new grain, and gave them to Jacob, her son, to take them to Abraham, his father, from the first fruits of the land, that he might eat and bless the Creator of all things before he died. ⁵ And Isaac, too, sent by the hand of Jacob to Abraham a best thank offering, that he might eat and drink. ⁶ And he eat and drank, and blessed the Most High God, Who hath created heaven and earth, Who hath made all the fat things of the earth, And given them to the children of men That they might eat and drink and bless their Creator. ⁷ 'And now I give thanks unto Thee, my God, because thou hast caused me to see this day: behold, I am one hundred three score and fifteen years, an old man and full of days, and all my days have been unto me peace. ⁸ The sword of the adversary has not overcome me in all that Thou hast given me and my children all the days of my life until this day. ⁹ My God, may Thy mercy and Thy peace be upon Thy servant, and upon the seed of his sons, that they may be to Thee a chosen nation and an inheritance from amongst all the nations of the earth from henceforth unto all the days of the generations of the earth, unto all the ages.'

Abraham's Last Words to and Blessings of Jacob (xxii. 10-30).

¹⁰ And he called Jacob and said: 'My son Jacob, may the God of all bless thee and strengthen thee to do righteousness, and His will before Him, and may He choose thee and thy seed that ye may become a people for His inheritance according to His will alway. ¹¹ And do thou, my son, Jacob, draw near and kiss me.' And he drew near and kissed him, and he said: 'Blessed be my son Jacob And all the sons of God Most High, unto all the ages: May God give unto thee a seed of righteousness; And some of thy sons may He sanctify in the midst of the whole earth; May nations serve thee, And all the nations bow themselves before thy seed. ¹² Be strong in the presence of men, And exercise authority over all the seed of Seth. Then thy ways and the ways of thy sons will be justified, So that they shall become a holy nation. ¹³ May the Most High God give thee all the blessings Wherewith He has blessed me And wherewith He blessed Noah and Adam; May they rest on the sacred head of thy seed from generation to generation for ever. ¹⁴ And may He cleanse thee from all unrighteousness and impurity, That thou mayest be forgiven all the transgressions; which thou hast committed ignorantly. And may He strengthen thee, And bless thee. And mayest thou inherit the whole earth, ¹⁵ And may He renew His covenant with thee. That thou mayest be to Him a nation for His inheritance for all the ages, And that He may be to thee and to thy seed a God in truth and righteousness throughout all the days of the earth. ¹⁶ And do thou, my son Jacob, remember my words, And observe the commandments of Abraham, thy father: Separate thyself from the nations, And eat not with them: And do not according to their works, And become not their associate; For their works are unclean, And all their ways are a Pollution and an abomination and uncleanness. ¹⁷ They offer their sacrifices to the dead And they worship evil spirits, And they eat over the graves, And all their works are vanity and nothingness. ¹⁸ They have no heart to understand And their eyes do not see what their works are, And how they err in saying to a piece of wood: 'Thou art my God,' And to a stone: 'Thou art my Lord and thou art my deliverer.' [And they have no heart.] ¹⁹ And as for thee, my son Jacob, May the Most

High God help thee And the God of heaven bless thee And remove thee from their uncleanness and from all their error. ²⁰ Be thou ware, my son Jacob, of taking a wife from any seed of the daughters of Canaan; For all his seed is to be rooted out of the earth. ²¹ For, owing to the transgression of Ham, Canaan erred, And all his seed shall be destroyed from off the earth and all the residue thereof, And none springing from him shall be saved on the day of judgment. ²² And as for all the worshippers of idols and the profane (b) There shall be no hope for them in the land of the living; (c) And there shall be no remembrance of them on the earth; (c) For they shall descend into Sheol, (d) And into the place of condemnation shall they go, ²³ As the children of Sodom were taken away from the earth So will all those who worship idols be taken away. Fear not, my son Jacob, And be not dismayed, O son of Abraham: May the Most High God preserve thee from destruction, And from all the paths of error may he deliver thee. ²⁴ This house have I built for myself that I might put my name upon it in the earth: [it is given to thee and to thy seed for ever], and it will be named the house of Abraham; it is given to thee and to thy seed for ever; for thou wilt build my house and establish my name before God for ever: thy seed and thy name will stand throughout all generations of the earth.' ²⁵ And he ceased commanding him and blessing him. ²⁶ And the two lay together on one bed, and Jacob slept in the bosom of Abraham, his father's father and he kissed him seven times, and his affection and his heart rejoiced over him. ²⁷ And he blessed him with all his heart and said: 'The Most High God, the God of all, and Creator of all, who brought me forth from Ur of the Chaldees that he might give me this land to inherit it for ever, and that I might establish a holy seed-blessed be the Most High for ever.' ²⁸ And he blessed Jacob and said: 'My son, over whom with all my heart and my affection I rejoice, may Thy grace and Thy mercy be lift up upon him and upon his seed alway. ²⁹ And do not forsake him, nor set him at nought from henceforth unto the days of eternity, and may Thine eyes be opened upon him and upon his seed, that Thou mayst preserve him, and bless him, and mayest sanctify him as a nation for Thine inheritance; ³⁰ And bless him with all Thy blessings from henceforth unto all the days of eternity, and renew Thy covenant and Thy grace with him and with his seed according to all Thy good pleasure unto all the generations of the earth.'

The Death and Burial of Abraham (xxiii. 1-8; cf. Gen. xxv. 7-10).

23

¹ And he placed two fingers of Jacob on his eyes, and he blessed the God of gods, and he covered his face and stretched out his feet and slept the sleep of eternity, and was gathered to his fathers. ² And notwithstanding all this Jacob was lying in his bosom, and knew not that Abraham, his father's father, was dead. ³ And Jacob awoke from his sleep, and behold Abraham was cold as ice, and he said 'Father, father'; but there was none that spake, and he knew that he was dead. ⁴ And he arose from his bosom and ran and told Rebecca, his mother; and Rebecca went to Isaac in the night, and told him; and they went together, and Jacob with them, and a lamp was in his hand, and when they had gone in they found Abraham lying dead. ⁵ And Isaac fell on the face of his father and wept and kissed him. ⁶ And the voices were heard in the house of Abraham, and Ishmael his son arose, and went to Abraham his father, and wept over Abraham his father, he and all the house of Abraham, and they wept with a great weeping. ⁷ And his sons Isaac and Ishmael buried him in the double cave, near Sarah his wife, and they wept for him forty days, all the men of his house, and Isaac and Ishmael, and all their sons, and all the sons of Keturah in their places; and the days of weeping for Abraham were ended. ⁸ And he lived three jubilees and four weeks of years, one hundred and seventy-five years, and completed the days of his life, being old and full of days.

The decreasing Years and increasing Corruption of Mankind (xxiii. 9-17).

⁹ For the days of the forefathers, of their life, were nineteen jubilees; and after the Flood they began to grow less than nineteen jubilees, and to decrease in jubilees, and to grow old quickly, and to be full of their days by reason of manifold tribulation and the wickedness of their ways, with the exception of Abraham. ¹⁰ For Abraham was perfect in all his deeds with the Lord, and well-pleasing in righteousness all the days of his life; and behold, he did not complete four jubilees in his life, when he had grown old by reason of the wickedness, and was full of his days. ¹¹ And all the generations which shall arise from this time until the day of the great judgment shall grow old quickly, before they complete two jubilees, and their knowledge shall forsake them by reason of their old age Land all their know- ledge shall vanish away]. ¹² And in those days, if a man live a jubilee and a-half of years, they shall say regarding him: 'He has lived long, and the greater part of his days are pain and sorrow and tribulation, and there is no peace: ¹³ For calamity follows on calamity, and wound on wound, and tribulation on tribulation, and evil tidings on evil tidings, and illness on illness, and all evil judgments such as these, one with another, illness and overthrow, and snow and frost and ice, and fever, and chills, and torpor, and famine, and death, and sword, and captivity, and all kinds of calamities and pains.' ¹⁴ And all these shall come on an evil generation, which transgresses on the earth: their works are uncleanness and fornication, and pollution and abominations. ¹⁵ Then they shall say: 'The days of the forefathers were many (even), unto a thousand years, and were good; but behold, the days of our life, if a man has lived many, are three score years and ten, and, if he is strong, four score years, and those evil, and there is no peace in the days of this evil generation.' ¹⁶ And in that generation the sons shall convict their fathers and their elders of sin and unrighteousness, and of the words of their mouth and the great wickednesses which they perpetrate, and concerning their forsaking the covenant which the Lord made between them and Him, that they should observe and do all His commandments and His ordinances and all His laws, without departing either to the right hand or the left. ¹⁷ For all have done evil, and every mouth speaks iniquity and all their works are an uncleanness and an abomination, and all their ways are pollution, uncleanness and destruction.

The Messianic Woes (xxiii. 18-25). [Eschatological partly.]

¹⁸ Behold the earth shall be destroyed on account of all their works, and there shall be no seed of the vine, and no oil; for their works are altogether faithless, and they shall all perish together, beasts and cattle and birds, and all the fish of the sea, on account of the children of men. ¹⁹ And they shall strive one with another, the young with the old, and the old with the young, the poor with the rich, the lowly with the great, and the beggar with the prince, on account of the law and the covenant; for they have forgotten commandment, and covenant, and feasts, and months, and Sabbaths, and jubilees, and all judgments. ²⁰ And they shall stand <with bows and> swords and war to turn them back into the way; but they shall not return until much blood has been shed on the earth, one by another. ²¹ And those who have escaped shall not return from their wickedness to the way of righteousness, but they shall all exalt themselves to deceit and wealth, that they may each take all that is his neighbour's, and they shall name the great name, but not in truth and not in righteousness, and they shall defile the holy of holies with their uncleanness and the corruption of their pollution. ²² And a great punishment shall befall the deeds of this generation from the Lord, and He will give them over to the sword and to judgment and to captivity, and to be plundered and devoured. ²³ And He will wake up against them the sinners of the Gentiles, who have neither mercy nor compassion, and who shall respect the person of none, neither old nor young, nor any one, for they are more wicked and strong to do evil than all the children of men. And they shall use violence against Israel and transgression against Jacob, And much blood shall be shed upon the earth, And there shall be none to gather and none to bury. ²⁴ In those days they shall cry aloud, And call and pray that they may be saved from the hand of the sinners, the Gentiles; But none shall be saved. ²⁵ And the heads of the children shall be white with grey hair, And a child of three weeks shall appear old like a man of one hundred years, And their stature shall be destroyed by tribulation and oppression.

Renewed Study of the Law followed by a Renewal of Mankind. The Messianic Kingdom and the Blessedness of the Righteous (xxiii. 26-32; cf. Isa. lxv. 17 ff. [Eschatological.]

²⁶ And in those days the children shall begin to study the laws, And to seek the commandments, And to return to the path of righteousness. ²⁷ And the days shall begin to grow many and increase amongst those children of men Till their days draw nigh to one thousand years. And to a greater number of years than (before) was the number of the days. ²⁸ And there shall be no old man Nor one who is <not> satisfied with his days, For all shall be (as) children and youths. ²⁹ And all their days they shall complete and live in peace and in joy, And there shall be no Satan nor any evil destroyer; For all their days shall be days of blessing and healing. ³⁰ And at that time the Lord will heal His servants, And they shall rise up and see great peace, And drive out their adversaries. And the righteous shall see and be thankful, And rejoice with joy for ever and ever, And shall see all their judgments and all their curses on their enemies. ³¹ And their bones shall rest in the earth, And their spirits shall have much joy, And they shall know that it is the Lord who executes judgment, And shows mercy to hundreds and thousands and to all that love Him ³² And do thou, Moses, write down these words; for thus are they written, and they record (them) on the heavenly tablets for a testimony for the generations for ever.

Isaac at the Well of Vision: Esau sells his Birthright (xxiv. 1-7; cf. Gen. xxv. 11,29-34).

24

¹ And it came to pass after the death of Abraham, that the Lord blessed Isaac his son, and he arose from Hebron and went and dwelt at the Well of the Vision in the first year of the third week [2073 A.M.] of this jubilee, seven years. ² And in the first year of the fourth week a famine began in the land, [2080 A.M.] besides the first famine, which had been in the days of Abraham. ³ And Jacob sod lentil pottage, and Esau came from the field hungry. And he said to Jacob his brother: 'Give me of this red pottage.' And Jacob said to him: 'Sell to me thy [primogeniture, this] birthright and I will give thee bread, and also some of this lentil pottage.' ⁴ And Esau said in his heart: 'I shall die; of what profit to me is this birthright?' ⁵ 'And he said to Jacob: 'I give it to thee.' And Jacob said: 'Swear to me, this day,' and he sware unto him. ⁶ And Jacob gave his brother Esau bread and pottage, and he eat till he was satisfied, and Esau despised his birthright; for this reason was Esau's name called Edom, on account of the red pottage which Jacob gave him for his birthright. ⁷ And Jacob became the elder, and Esau was brought down from his dignity.

Isaac's Sojourn in Gerar and Dealings with Abimelech (xxiv. 8-27; cf. Gen. xxvi.).

⁸ And the famine was over the land, and Isaac departed to go down into Egypt in the second year of this week, and went to the king of the Philistines to Gerar, unto Abimelech. ⁹ And the Lord appeared unto him and said unto him: 'Go not down into Egypt; dwell in the land that I shall tell thee of, and sojourn in this land, and I will be with thee and bless thee. ¹⁰ For to thee and to thy seed will I give all this land, and I will establish My oath which I sware unto Abraham thy father, and I will multiply thy seed as the stars of heaven, and will give unto thy seed all this land. ¹¹ And in thy seed shall all the nations of the earth be blessed, because thy father obeyed My voice, and kept My charge and My commandments, and My laws, and My ordinances, and My covenant; and now obey My voice and dwell in this land.' ¹² And he dwelt in Gelar three weeks of years. ¹³ And Abimelech charged concerning him, [2080-2101 A.M.] and concerning all that was his, saying: 'Any man that shall touch him or aught that is his shall surely die.' ¹⁴ And Isaac waxed strong among the Philistines, and he got many possessions, oxen and sheep and camels and asses and a great household. ¹⁵ And he sowed in the land of the Philistines and brought in a hundred-fold, and Isaac became exceedingly great, and the Philistines envied him. ¹⁶ Now all the wells which the servants of Abraham had dug during the life of Abraham, the Philistines had stopped them after the death of Abraham, and filled them with earth. ¹⁷ And Abimelech said unto Isaac: 'Go from us, for thou art much mightier than we', and Isaac departed thence in the first year of the seventh week, and sojourned in the valleys of Gerar. ¹⁸ And they digged again the wells of water which the servants of Abraham, his father, had digged, and which the Philistines had closed after the death of Abraham his father, and he called their names as Abraham his father had named them. ¹⁹ And the servants of Isaac dug a well in the valley, and found living water, and the shepherds of Gerar strove with the shepherds of Isaac, saying: 'The water is ours'; and Isaac called the name of the well 'Perversity', because they had been perverse with us. ²⁰ And they dug a second well, and they strove for that also, and he called its name 'Enmity'. And he arose from thence and they digged another well, and for that they strove not, and he called the name of it 'Room', and Isaac said: 'Now the Lord hath made room for us, and we have increased in the land.' ²¹ And he went up from thence to the Well of the Oath in the first year of the first week in the [2108 A.M.] forty-fourth jubilee. ²² And the Lord appeared to him that night, on the new moon of the first month, and said unto him: 'I am the God of Abraham thy father; fear not, for I am with thee, and shall bless thee and shall surely multiply thy seed as the sand of the earth, for the sake of Abraham my servant.' ²³ And he built an altar there, which Abraham his father had first built, and he called upon the name of the Lord, and he offered sacrifice to the God of Abraham his father. ²⁴ And they digged a well and they found living water. ²⁵ And the servants of Isaac digged another well and did not find water, and they went and told Isaac that they had not found water, and Isaac said: 'I have sworn this day to the Philistines and this thing has been announced to us.' ²⁶ And he called the name of that place the Well of the Oath; for there he had sworn to Abimelech and Ahuzzath his friend and Phicol the prefect Or his host. ²⁷ And Isaac knew that day that under constraint he had sworn to them to make peace with them.

Isaac curses the Philistines (xxiv. 28-33).

²⁸ And Isaac on that day cursed the Philistines and said: 'Cursed be the Philistines unto the day of wrath and indignation from the midst of all nations; may God make them a derision and a curse and an object of wrath and indignation in the hands of the sinners the Gentiles and in the hands of the Kittim. ²⁹ And whoever escapes the sword of the enemy and the Kittim, may the righteous nation root out in judgment from under heaven; for they shall be the enemies and foes of my children throughout their generations upon the earth. ³⁰ And no remnant shall be left to them, Nor one that shall be saved on the day of the wrath of judgment; For destruction and rooting out and expulsion from the earth is the whole seed of the Philistines (reserved), And there shall no longer be left for these Caphtorim a name or a seed on the earth. ³¹ For though he ascend unto heaven, Thence shall he be brought down, And though he make himself strong on earth, Thence shall he be dragged forth, And though he hide himself amongst the nations, Even from thence shall he be rooted out; And though he descend into Sheol, There also shall his condemnation be great, And there also he shall have no peace. ³² And if he go into captivity, By the hands of those that seek his life shall they slay him on the way, And neither name nor seed shall be left to him on all the earth; For into eternal malediction shall he depart.' ³³ And thus is it written and engraved concerning him on the heavenly tablets, to do unto him on the day of judgment, so that he may be rooted out of the earth.

Rebecca admonishes Jacob not to marry a Canaanitish Woman. Rebecca's Blessing (xxv. 1-23; cf. Gen. xxviii. 1-4).

25

¹ And in the second year of this week in this jubilee, Rebecca called Jacob her son, and spake unto [2109 A.M.] him, saying: 'My son, do not take thee a wife of the daughters of Canaan, as Esau, thy brother, who took him two wives of the daughters of Canaan, and they have embittered my soul with all their unclean deeds: for all their deeds are fornication and lust, and there is no righteousness with them, for (their deeds) are evil. ² And I, my son, love thee exceedingly, and my heart and my affection bless thee every hour of the day and watch of the night. ³ And now, my son, hearken to my voice, and do the will of thy mother, and do not take thee a wife of the daughters of this land, but only of the house of my father, and of my father's kindred. Thou shalt take thee a wife of the house of my father, and the Most High God will bless thee, and thy children shall be a righteous generation and a holy seed.' ⁴ And then spake Jacob to Rebecca, his mother, and said unto her: 'Behold, mother, I am nine weeks of years old, and I neither know nor have I touched any woman, nor have I betrothed myself to any, nor even think of taking me a wife of the daughters of Canaan. ⁵ For I remember, mother, the words of Abraham, our father, for he commanded me not to take a wife of the daughters of Canaan, but to take me a wife from the seed of my father's house and from my kindred. ⁶ I have heard before that daughters have been born to Laban, thy brother, and I have set my heart on them to take a wife from amongst them. ⁷ And for this reason I have guarded myself in my spirit against sinning or being corrupted in all my ways throughout all the days of my life; for with regard to lust and fornication, Abraham, my father, gave me many commands. ⁸ And, despite all that he has commanded me, these two and twenty years my brother has striven with me, and spoken frequently to me and said: 'My brother, take to wife a sister of my two wives'; but I refuse to do as he has done. ⁹ I swear before thee, mother, that all the days of my life I will not take me a wife from the daughters of the seed of Canaan, and I will not act wickedly as my brother has done. ¹⁰ Fear not, mother; be assured that I shall do thy will and walk in uprightness, and not corrupt my ways for ever.' ¹¹ And thereupon she lifted up her face to heaven and extended the fingers of her hands, and opened her mouth and blessed the Most High God, who had created the heaven and the earth, and she gave Him thanks and praise. ¹² And she said: 'Blessed be the Lord God, and may His holy name be blessed for ever and ever, who has given me Jacob as a pure son and a holy seed; for he is Thine, and Thine shall his seed be continually and throughout all the generations for evermore. ¹³ Bless him, O Lord, and place in my mouth the blessing of righteousness, that I may bless him.' ¹⁴ And at that hour, when the spirit of righteousness descended into her mouth, she placed both her hands on the head of Jacob, and said: ¹⁵ Blessed art thou, Lord of righteousness and God of the ages And may He bless thee beyond all the generations of men. May He give thee, my Son, the path of righteousness, And reveal righteousness to thy seed. ¹⁶ And may He make thy sons many during thy life, And may they arise according to the number of the months of the year. And may their sons become many and great beyond the stars of heaven, And their numbers be more than the sand of the sea. ¹⁷ And may He give them this goodly land - as He said He would give it to Abraham and to his seed after him alway- And may they hold it as a possession for ever. ¹⁸ And may I see (born) unto thee, my son, blessed children during my life, And a blessed and holy seed may all thy seed be. ¹⁹ And as thou hast refreshed thy mother's spirit during her life, The womb of her that bare thee blesses thee thus, [My affection] and my breasts bless thee And my mouth and my tongue praise thee greatly. ²⁰ Increase and spread over the earth, And may thy seed be perfect in the joy of heaven and earth for ever; And may thy seed rejoice, And on the great day of peace may it have peace. ²¹ And may thy name and thy seed endure to all the ages, And may the Most High God be their God, And may the God

of righteousness dwell with them, And by them may His sanctuary be built unto all the ages. ²² Blessed be he that blesseth thee, And all flesh that curseth thee falsely, may it be cursed.' ²³ And she kissed him, and said to him; 'May the Lord of the world love thee As the heart of thy mother and her affection rejoice in thee and bless thee.' And she ceased from blessing.

Jacob obtains the Blessing of the Firstborn (xxvi. 1-35; cf. Gen. xxvii.).

26

¹ And in the seventh year of this week Isaac called Esau, his elder Son, and said unto him: ' I am [2114 A.M.] old, my son, and behold my eyes are dim in seeing, and I know not the day of my death. ² And now take thy hunting weapons thy quiver and thy bow, and go out to the field, and hunt and catch me (venison), my son, and make me savoury meat, such as my soul loveth, and bring it to me that I may eat, and that my soul may bless thee before I die.' ³ But Rebecca heard Isaac speaking to Esau. ⁴ And Esau went forth early to the field to hunt and catch and bring home to his father. ⁵ And Rebecca called Jacob, her son, and said unto him: 'Behold, I heard Isaac, thy father, speak unto Esau, thy brother, saying: "Hunt for me, and make me savoury meat, and bring (it) to me that ⁶ I may eat and bless thee before the Lord before I die." And now, my son, obey my voice in that which I command thee: Go to thy flock and fetch me two good kids of the goats, and I will make them savoury meat for thy father, such as he loves, and thou shalt bring (it) to thy father that he may eat and bless thee before the Lord before he die, and that thou mayst be blessed.' ⁷ And Jacob said to Rebecca his mother: 'Mother, I shall not withhold anything which my father would eat, and which would please him: only I fear, my mother, that he will recognise my voice and wish to touch me. ⁸ And thou knowest that I am smooth, and Esau, my brother, is hairy, and I shall appear before his eyes as an evildoer, and shall do a deed which he had not commanded me, and he will be wroth with me, and I shall bring upon myself a curse, and not a blessing.' ⁹ And Rebecca, his mother, said unto him: 'Upon me be thy curse, my son, only obey my voice.' ¹⁰ And Jacob obeyed the voice of Rebecca, his mother, and went and fetched two good and fat kids of the goats, and brought them to his mother, and his mother made them ~savoury meat~ such as he loved. ¹¹ And Rebecca took the goodly raiment of Esau, her elder son, which was with her in the house, and she clothed Jacob, her younger son, (with them), and she put the skins of the kids upon his hands and on the exposed parts of his neck. ¹² And she gave the meat and the bread which she had prepared into the hand of her son Jacob. ¹³ And Jacob went in to his father and said: 'I am thy son: I have done according as thou badest me: arise and sit and eat of that which I have caught, father, that thy soul may bless me.' ¹⁴ And Isaac said to his son: 'How hast thou found so quickly, my son? ¹⁵ 'And Jacob said: 'Because <the Lord> thy God caused me to find.' ¹⁶ And Isaac said unto him: Come near, that I may feel thee, my son, if thou art my son Esau or not.' ¹⁷ And Jacob went near to Isaac, his father, and he felt him and said: 'The voice is Jacob's voice, but the hands are the hands of Esau,' ¹⁸ and he discerned him not, because it was a dispensation from heaven to remove his power of perception and Isaac discerned not, for his hands were hairy as his brother Esau's, so that he blessed him. ¹⁹ And he said: 'Art thou my son Esau? ' and he said: 'I am thy son': and he said, 'Bring near to me that I may eat of that which thou hast caught, my son, that my soul may bless thee.' ²⁰ And he brought near to him, and he did eat, and he brought him wine and he drank. ²¹ And Isaac, his father, said unto him: 'Come near and kiss me, my son. ²² And he came near and kissed him. And he smelled the smell of his raiment, and he blessed him and said: 'Behold, the smell of my son is as the smell of a <full> field which the Lord hath blessed. ²³ And may the Lord give thee of the dew of heaven And of the dew of the earth, and plenty of corn and oil: Let nations serve thee, And peoples bow down to thee. ²⁴ Be lord over thy brethren, And let thy mother's sons bow down to thee; And may all the blessings wherewith the Lord hath blessed me and blessed Abraham, my father; Be imparted to thee and to thy seed for ever: Cursed be he that curseth thee, And blessed be he that blesseth thee.' ²⁵ And it came to pass as soon as Isaac had made an end of blessing his son Jacob, and Jacob had gone forth from Isaac his father he hid himself and Esau, his brother, came in from his hunting. ²⁶ And he also made savoury meat, and brought (it) to his father, and said unto his father: 'Let my father arise, and eat of my venison that thy soul may bless me.' ²⁷ And Isaac, his father, said unto him: 'Who art thou? 'And he said unto him: 'I am thy first born, thy son Esau: I have done as thou hast commanded me.' ²⁸ And Isaac was very greatly astonished, and said: 'Who is he that hath hunted and caught and brought (it) to me, and I have eaten of all before thou camest, and have blessed him: (and) he shall be blessed, and all his seed for ever.' ²⁹ And it came to pass when Esau heard the words of his father Isaac that he cried with an exceeding great and bitter cry, and said unto his father: 'Bless me, (even) me also, father.' ³⁰ And he said unto him: 'Thy brother came with guile, and hath taken away thy blessing.' And he said: 'Now I know why his name is named Jacob: behold, he hath supplanted me these two times: he took away my birth-right, and now he hath taken away my blessing.' ³¹ And he said: 'Hast thou not reserved a blessing for me, father?' and Isaac answered and said unto Esau: 'Behold, I have made him thy lord, And all his brethren have I given to him for servants, And with plenty of corn and wine and oil have I strengthened him: And what now shall I do for thee, my son?' ³² And Esau said to Isaac, his father: 'Hast thou but one blessing, O father? Bless me, (even) me also, father: ' ³³ And Esau lifted up his voice and wept. And Isaac answered and said unto him: 'Behold, far from the dew of the earth shall be thy dwelling, And far from the dew of heaven from above. ³⁴ And by thy sword wilt thou live, And thou wilt serve thy brother. And it shall come to pass when thou becomest great, And dost shake his yoke from off thy neck, Thou shalt sin a complete sin unto death, And thy seed shall be rooted out from under heaven.' ³⁵ And Esau kept threatening Jacob because of the blessing wherewith his father blessed him, and he: said in his heart: 'May the days of mourning for my father now come, so that I may slay my brother Jacob.'

Rebecca induces Isaac to send Jacob to Mesopotamia. Jacob's Dream and View at Bethel (xxvii. 1-27; cf. Gen. xxviii.).

27

¹ And the words of Esau, her elder son, were told to Rebecca in a dream, and Rebecca sent and called Jacob her younger son, ² and said unto him: 'Behold Esau thy brother will take vengeance on thee so as to kill thee. ³ Now, therefore, my son, obey my voice, and arise and flee thou to Laban, my brother, to Haran, and tarry with him a few days until thy brother's anger turns away, and he remove his anger from thee, and forget all that thou hast done; then I will send and fetch thee from thence.' ⁴ And Jacob said: 'I am not afraid; if he wishes to kill me, I will kill him.' ⁵ But she said unto him: 'Let me not be bereft of both my sons on one day.' ⁶ And Jacob said to Rebecca his mother: 'Behold, thou knowest that my father has become old, and does not see because his eyes are dull, and if I leave him it will be evil in his eyes, because I leave him and go away from you, and my father will be angry, and will curse me. I will not go; when he sends me, then only will I go.' ⁷ And Rebecca said to Jacob: 'I will go in and speak to him, and he will send thee away.' ⁸ And Rebecca went in and said to Isaac: 'I loathe my life because of the two daughters of Heth, whom Esau has taken him as wives; and if Jacob take a wife from among the daughters of the land such as these, for what purpose do I further live, for the daughters of Canaan are evil.' ⁹ And Isaac called Jacob and blessed him, and admonished him and said unto him: 'Do not take thee a wife of any of the daughters of Canaan; ¹⁰ arise and go to Mesopotamia, to the house of Bethuel, thy mother's father, and take thee a wife from thence of the daughters of Laban, thy mother's brother. ¹¹ And God Almighty bless thee and increase and multiply thee that thou mayest become a company of nations, and give thee the blessings of my father Abraham, to thee and to thy seed after thee, that thou mayest inherit the land of thy sojournings and all the land which God gave to Abraham: go, my son, in peace.' ¹² And Isaac sent Jacob away, and he went to Mesopotamia, to Laban the son of Bethuel the Syrian, the brother of Rebecca, Jacob's mother. ¹³ And it came to pass after Jacob had arisen to go to Mesopotamia that the spirit of Rebecca was grieved after her son, and she wept. ¹⁴ And Isaac said to Rebecca: 'My sister, weep not on account of Jacob, my son; for he goeth in peace, and in peace will he return. ¹⁵ The Most High God will preserve him from all evil, and will be with him; for He will not forsake him all his days; ¹⁶ For I know that his ways will be prospered in all things wherever he goes, until he return in peace to us, and we see him in peace. ¹⁷ Fear not on his account, my sister, for he is on the upright path and he is a perfect man: and he is faithful and will not perish. Weep not.' ¹⁸ And Isaac comforted Rebecca on account of her son Jacob, and blessed him. ¹⁹ And Jacob went from the Well of the Oath to go to Haran on the first year of the second week in the forty-fourth jubilee, and he came to Luz on the mountains, that is, Bethel, on the new moon of the first month of this week, [2115 A.M.] and he came to the place at even and turned from the way to the west of the road that night: and he slept there; for the sun had set. ²⁰ And he took one of the stones of that place and laid <it at his head> under the tree, and he was journeying alone, and he slept. ²¹ And he dreamt that night, and behold a ladder set up on the earth, and the top of it reached to heaven, and behold, the angels of the Lord ascended and descended on it: and behold, the Lord stood upon it. ²² And he spake to Jacob and said: 'I am the Lord God of Abraham, thy father, and the God of Isaac; the land whereon thou art sleeping, to thee will I give it, and to thy seed after thee. ²³ And thy seed shall be as the dust of the earth, and thou shalt increase to the west and to the east, to the north and the south, and in thee and in thy seed shall all the families of the nations be blessed. ²⁴ And behold, I will be

with thee, and will keep thee whithersoever thou goest, and I will bring thee again into this land in peace; for I will not leave thee until I do everything that I told thee of.' ²⁵ And Jacob awoke from his sleep, and said, 'Truly this place is the house of the Lord, and I knew it not.' And he was afraid and said: 'Dreadful is this place which is none other than the house of God, and this is the gate of heaven.' ²⁶ And Jacob arose early in the morning, and took the stone which he had put under his head and set it up as a pillar for a sign, and he poured oil upon the top of it. And he called the name of that place Bethel; but the name of the place was Luz at the first. ²⁷ And Jacob vowed a vow unto the Lord, saying: 'If the Lord will be with me, and will keep me in this way that I go, and give me bread to eat and raiment to put on, so that I come again to my father's house in peace, then shall the Lord be my God, and this stone which I have set up as a pillar for a sign in this place, shall be the Lord's house, and of all that thou givest me, I shall give the tenth to thee, my God.'

Jacob's Marriage to Leah and Rachel; his Children and Riches (xxviii. i- 30; cf. Gen. xxix., xxx., xxxi. 1-2).

28

¹ And he went on his journey, and came to the land of the east, to Laban, the brother of Rebecca, and he was with him, and served him for Rachel his daughter one week. ² And in the first year of the third week [2122 A.M.] he said unto him: 'Give me my wife, for whom I have served thee seven years '; and Laban said unto Jacob: 'I will give thee thy wife.' ³ And Laban made a feast, and took Leah his elder daughter, and gave (her) to Jacob as a wife, and gave her Zilpah his handmaid for an hand- maid; and Jacob did not know, for he thought that she was Rachel. ⁴ And he went in unto her, and behold, she was Leah; and Jacob was angry with Laban, and said unto him: 'Why hast thou dealt thus with me? Did not I serve thee for Rachel and not for Leah? Why hast thou wronged me? ⁵ Take thy daughter, and I will go; for thou hast done evil to me.' For Jacob loved Rachel more than Leah; for Leah's eyes were weak, but her form was very handsome; but Rachel had beautiful eyes and a beautiful and very handsome form. ⁶ And Laban said to Jacob: 'It is not so done in our country, to give the younger before the elder.' And it is not right to do this; for thus it is ordained and written in the heavenly tablets, that no one should give his younger daughter before the elder; but the elder, one gives first and after her the younger -and the man who does so, they set down guilt against him in heaven, and none is righteous that does this thing, for this deed is evil before the Lord. ⁷ And command thou the children of Israel that they do not this thing; let them neither take nor give the younger before they have given the elder, for it is very wicked. ⁸ And Laban said to Jacob: 'Let the seven days of the feast of this one pass by, and I shall give thee Rachel, that thou mayst serve me another seven years, that thou mayst pasture my sheep as thou didst in the former week.' ⁹ And on the day when the seven days of the feast of Leah had passed, Laban gave Rachel to Jacob, that he might serve him another seven years, and he gave to Rachel Bilhah, the sister of Zilpah, as a handmaid. ¹⁰ And he served yet other seven years for Rachel, for Leah had been given to him for nothing. ¹¹ And the Lord opened the womb of Leah, and she conceived and bare Jacob a son, and he called his name Reuben, on the fourteenth day of the ninth month, in the first year of the third week. [2122 A.M.] ¹² But the womb of Rachel was closed, for the Lord saw that Leah was hated and Rachel loved. ¹³ And again Jacob went in unto Leah, and she conceived, and bare Jacob a second son, and he called his name Simeon, on the twenty-first of the tenth month, and in the third year of this week. [2124 A.M.] ¹⁴ And again Jacob went in unto Leah, and she conceived, and bare him a third son, and he called his name Levi, in the new moon of the first month in the sixth year of this week. [2127 A.M.] ¹⁵ And again Jacob went in unto her, and she conceived, and bare him a fourth son, and he called his name Judah, on the fifteenth of the third month, in the first year of the fourth week. [2129 A.M.] ¹⁶ And on account of all this Rachel envied Leah, for she did not bear, and she said to Jacob: 'Give me children'; and Jacob said: 'Have I withheld from thee the fruits of thy womb? Have I forsaken thee?' ¹⁷ And when Rachel saw that Leah had borne four sons to Jacob, Reuben and Simeon and Levi and Judah, she said unto him: 'Go in unto Bilhah my handmaid, and she will conceive, and bear a son unto me.' (And she gave (him) Bilhah her handmaid to wife). ¹⁸ And he went in unto her, and she conceived, and bare him a son, and he called his name Dan, on the ninth of the sixth month, in the sixth year of the third week. [2127 A.M.] ¹⁹ And Jacob went in again unto Bilhah a second time, and she conceived, and bare Jacob another son, and Rachel called his name Napthali, on the fifth of the seventh month, in the second year of the fourth week. [2130 A.M.] ²⁰ And when Leah saw that she had become sterile and did not bear, she envied Rachel, and she also gave her handmaid Zilpah to Jacob to wife, and she conceived, and bare a son, and Leah called his name Gad, on the twelfth of the eighth month, in the third year of the fourth week.

[2131 A.M.] ²¹ And he went in again unto her, and she conceived, and bare him a second son, and Leah called his name Asher, on the second of the eleventh month, in the fifth year of the fourth week. [2133 A.M.] ²² And Jacob went in unto Leah, and she conceived, and bare a son, and she called his name Issachar, on the fourth of the fifth month, in the fourth year of the fourth week, [2132 A.M.] and she gave him to a nurse. ²³ And Jacob went in again unto her, and she conceived, and bare two (children), a son and a daughter, and she called the name of the son Zabulon, and the name of the daughter Dinah, in the seventh of the seventh month, in the sixth year of the fourth week. [2134 A.M.] ²⁴ And the Lord was gracious to Rachel, and opened her womb, and she conceived, and bare a son, and she called his name Joseph, on the new moon of the fourth month, in the sixth year in this fourth week. [2134 A.M.] ²⁵ And in the days when Joseph was born, Jacob said to Laban: 'Give me my wives and sons, and let me go to my father Isaac, and let me make me an house; for I have completed the years in which I have served thee for thy two daughters, and I will go to the house of my father.' ²⁶ And Laban said to Jacob: 'Tarry with me for thy wages, and pasture my flock for me again, and take thy wages.' ²⁷ And they agreed with one another that he should give him as his wages those of the lambs and kids which were born black and spotted and white, (these) were to be his wages. ²⁸ And all the sheep brought forth spotted and speckled and black, variously marked, and they brought forth again lambs like themselves, and all that were spotted were Jacob's and those which were not were Laban's. ²⁹ And Jacob's possessions multiplied exceedingly, and he possessed oxen and sheep and asses and camels, and menservants and maid-servants. ³⁰ And Laban and his sons envied Jacob, and Laban took back his sheep from him, and he observed him with evil intent.

Jacob's Flight with his Family: his Covenant with Laban (xxix. 1-12; cf. Gen, xxxi.).

29

¹ And it came to pass when Rachel had borne Joseph, that Laban went to shear his sheep; for they were distant from him a three days' journey. ² And Jacob saw that Laban was going to shear his sheep, and Jacob called Leah and Rachel, and spake kindly unto them that they should come with him to the land of Canaan. ³ For he told them how he had seen everything in a dream, even all that He had spoken unto him that he should return to his father's house, and they said: 'To every place whither thou goest we will go with thee.' ⁴ And Jacob blessed the God of Isaac his father, and the God of Abraham his father's father, and he arose and mounted his wives and his children, and took all his possessions and crossed the river, and came to the land of Gilead, and Jacob hid his intention from Laban and told him not. ⁵ And in the seventh year of the fourth week Jacob turned (his face) toward Gilead in the first month, on the twenty-first thereof. [2135 A.M.] And Laban pursued after him and overtook Jacob in the mountain of Gilead in the third month, on the thirteenth thereof. ⁶ And the Lord did not suffer him to injure Jacob; for he appeared to him in a dream by night. And Laban spake to Jacob. ⁷ And on the fifteenth of those days Jacob made a feast for Laban, and for all who came with him, and Jacob sware to Laban that day, and Laban also to Jacob, that neither should cross the mountain of Gilead to the other with evil purpose. ⁸ And he made there a heap for a witness; wherefore the name of that place is called: 'The Heap of Witness,' after this heap. ⁹ But before they used to call the land of Gilead the land of the Rephaim; for it was the land of the Rephaim, and the Rephaim were born (there), giants whose height was ten, nine, eight down to seven cubits. ¹⁰ And their habitation was from the land of the children of Ammon to Mount Hermon, and the seats of their kingdom were Karnaim and Ashtaroth, and Edrei, and Misur, and Beon. ¹¹ And the Lord destroyed them because of the evil of their deeds; for they were very malignant, and the Amorites dwelt in their stead, wicked and sinful, and there is no people to-day which has wrought to the full all their sins, and they have no longer length of life on the earth. ¹² And Jacob sent away Laban, and he departed into Mesopotamia, the land of the East, and Jacob returned to the land of Gilead.

Jacob, reconciled with Esau, dwells in Canaan and supports his Parents (xxix. 13-20; Cf. Gen. xxxii., xxxiii.).

¹³ And he passed over the Jabbok in the ninth month, on the eleventh thereof. And on that day Esau, his brother, came to him, and he was reconciled to him, and departed from him unto the land of Seir, but Jacob dwelt in tents. ¹⁴ And in the first year of the fifth week in this jubilee [2136 A.M.] he crossed the Jordan, and dwelt beyond the Jordan, and he pastured his sheep from the sea of the heap unto Bethshan, and unto Dothan and unto the forest of Akrabbim. ¹⁵ And he sent to his father Isaac of all his substance, clothing, and food, and meat, and drink, and milk, and butter, and cheese, and some dates of the valley. ¹⁶ And to his mother Rebecca also four times a year, between the times of the months, between ploughing and reaping, and between autumn and the rain (season) and between winter and spring,

to the tower of Abraham. [17] For Isaac had returned from the Well of the Oath and gone up to the tower of his father Abraham, and he dwelt there apart from his son Esau. [18] For in the days when Jacob went to Mesopotamia, Esau took to himself a wife Mahalath, the daughter of Ishmael, and he gathered together all the flocks of his father and his wives, and went Up and dwelt on Mount Seir, and left Isaac his father at the Well of the Oath alone. [19] And Isaac went up from the Well of the Oath and dwelt in the tower of Abraham his father on the mountains of Hebron, [20] And thither Jacob sent all that he did send to his father and his mother from time to time, all they needed, and they blessed Jacob with all their heart and with all their soul.

Dinah ravished. Slaughter of the Shechemites. Laws against Intermarriage between Israel and the Heathen. The Choice of Levi (xxx. 1-26; cf. Gen. xxxiv.).

30

[1] And in the first year of the sixth week [2143 A.M.] he went up to Salem, to the east of Shechem, in peace, in the fourth month. [2] And there they carried off Dinah, the daughter of Jacob, into the house of Shechem, the son of Hamor, the Hivite, the prince of the land, and he lay with her and defiled her, and she was a little girl, a child of twelve years. [3] And he besought his father and her brothers that she might be given to him to wife. And Jacob and his sons were wroth because of the men of Shechem; for they had defiled Dinah, their sister, and they spake to them with evil intent and dealt deceitfully with them and beguiled them. [4] And Simeon and Levi came unexpectedly to Shechem and executed judgment on all the men of Shechem, and slew all the men whom they found in it, and left not a single one remaining in it: they slew all in torments because they had dishonoured their sister Dinah. [5] And thus let it not again be done from henceforth that a daughter of Israel be defiled; for judgment is ordained in heaven against them that they should destroy with the sword all the men of the Shechemites because they had wrought shame in Israel. [6] And the Lord delivered them into the hands of the sons of Jacob that they might exterminate them with the sword and execute judgment upon them, and that it might not thus again be done in Israel that a virgin of Israel should be defiled. [7] And if there is any man who wishes in Israel to give his daughter or his sister to any man who is of the seed of the Gentiles he shall surely die, and they shall stone him with stones; for he hath wrought shame in Israel; and they shall burn the woman with fire, because she has dishonoured the name of the house of her father, and she shall be rooted out of Israel. [8] And let not an adulteress and no uncleanness be found in Israel throughout all the days of the generations of the earth; for Israel is holy unto the Lord, and every man who has defiled (it) shall surely die: they shall stone him with stones. [9] For thus has it been ordained and written in the heavenly tablets regarding all the seed of Israel: he who defileth (it) shall surely die, and he shall be stoned with stones. [10] And to this law there is no limit of days, and no remission, nor any atonement: but the man who has defiled his daughter shall be rooted out in the midst of all Israel, because he has given of his seed to Moloch, and wrought impiously so as to defile it. [11] And do thou, Moses, command the children of Israel and exhort them not to give their daughters to the Gentiles, and not to take for their sons any of the daughters of the Gentiles, for this is abominable before the Lord. [12] For this reason I have written for thee in the words of the Law all the deeds of the Shechemites, which they wrought against Dinah, and how the sons of Jacob spake, saying: 'We will not give our daughter to a man who is uncircumcised; for that were a reproach unto us.' [13] And it is a reproach to Israel, to those who live, and to those that take the daughters of the Gentiles; for this is unclean and abominable to Israel. [14] And Israel will not be free from this uncleanness if it has a wife of the daughters of the Gentiles, or has given any of its daughters to a man who is of any of the Gentiles. [15] For there will be plague upon plague, and curse upon curse, and every judgment and plague and curse will come upon him: if he do this thing, or hide his eyes from those who commit uncleanness, or those who defile the sanctuary of the Lord, or those who profane His holy name, (then) will the whole nation together be judged for all the uncleanness and profanation of this man. [16] And there will be no respect of persons [and no consideration of persons] and no receiving at his hands of fruits and offerings and burnt-offerings and fat, nor the fragrance of sweet savour, so as to accept it: and so fare every man or woman in Israel who defiles the sanctuary. [17] For this reason I have commanded thee, saying: 'Testify this testimony to Israel: see how the Shechemites fared and their sons: how they were delivered into the hands of two sons of Jacob, and they slew them under tortures, and it was (reckoned) unto them for righteousness, and it is written down to them for righteousness. [18] And the seed of Levi was chosen for the priesthood, and to be Levites, that they might minister before the Lord, as we, continually, and that Levi and his sons may be blessed for ever; for he was zealous to execute righteousness and judgment and vengeance on all those who arose against Israel. [19] And so they inscribe as a testimony in his favour on the heavenly tablets blessing and righteousness before the God of all: [20] And we remember the righteousness which the man fulfilled during his life, at all periods of the year; until a thousand generations they will record it, and it will come to him and to his descendants after him, and he has been recorded on the heavenly tablets as a friend and a righteous man. [21] All this account I have written for thee, and have commanded thee to say to the children of Israel, that they should not commit sin nor transgress the ordinances nor break the covenant which has been ordained for them, (but) that they should fulfil it and be recorded as friends. [22] But if they transgress and work uncleanness in every way, they will be recorded on the heavenly tablets as adversaries, and they will be destroyed out of the book of life, and they will be recorded in the book of those who will be destroyed and with those who will be rooted out of the earth. [23] And on the day when the sons of Jacob slew Shechem a writing was recorded in their favour in heaven that they had executed righteousness and uprightness and vengeance on the sinners, and it was written for a blessing. [24] And they brought Dinah, their sister, out of the house of Shechem, and they took captive everything that was in Shechem, their sheep and their oxen and their asses, and all their wealth, and all their flocks, and brought them all to Jacob their father. [25] And he reproached them because they had put the city to the sword for he feared those who dwelt in the land, the Canaanites and the Perizzites. [26] And the dread of the Lord was upon all the cities which are around about Shechem, and they did not rise to pursue after the sons of Jacob; for terror had fallen upon them.

Jacob's Journey to Bethel and Hebron. Isaac blesses Levi and Judah (xxxi. 1-25; cf. Gen. xxxv.).

31

[1] And on the new moon of the month Jacob spake to all the people of his house. saying: 'Purify yourselves and change your garments, and let us arise and go up to Bethel, where I vowed a vow to Him on the day when I fled from the face of Esau my brother, because he has been with me and brought me into this land in peace, and put ye away the strange gods that arc among you.' [2] And they gave up the strange gods and that which was in their ears and which was on their necks and the idols which Rachel stole from Laban her father she gave wholly to Jacob. And he burnt and brake them to pieces and destroyed them, and hid them under an oak which is in the land of Shechem. [3] And he went up on the new moon of the seventh month to Bethel. And he built an altar at the place where he had slept, and he set up a pillar there, and he sent word to his father Isaac to come to him to his sacrifice, and to his mother Rebecca. [4] And Isaac said: 'Let my son Jacob come, and let me see him before I die.' [5] And Jacob went to his father Isaac and to his mother Rebecca, to the house of his father Abraham, and he took two of his sons with him, Levi and Judah, and he came to his father Isaac and to his mother Rebecca. [6] And Rebecca came forth from the tower to the front of it to kiss Jacob and embrace him; for her spirit had revived when she heard: 'Behold Jacob thy son has come'; and she kissed him. [7] And she saw his two sons, and she recognised them, and said unto him: 'Are these thy sons, my son?' and she embraced them and kissed them, and blessed them, saying: 'In you shall the seed of Abraham become illustrious, and ye shall prove a blessing on the earth.' [8] And Jacob went in to Isaac his father, to the chamber where he lay, and his two sons were with him, and he took the hand of his father, and stooping down he kissed him, and Isaac clung to the neck of Jacob his son, and wept upon his neck. [9] And the darkness left the eyes of Isaac, and he saw the two sons of Jacob, Levi, and Judah, and he said: 'Are these thy sons, my son? for they are like thee.' [10] And he said unto him that they were truly his sons: 'And thou hast truly seen that they are truly my sons'. [11] And they came near to him, and he turned and kissed them and embraced them both together. [12] And the spirit of prophecy came down into his mouth, and he took Levi by his right hand and Judah by his left. [13] And he turned to Levi first, and began to bless him first, and said unto him: May the God of all, the very Lord of all the ages, bless thee and thy children throughout all the ages. [14] And may the Lord give to thee and to thy seed greatness and great glory, and cause thee and thy seed, from among all flesh, to approach Him to serve in His sanctuary as the angels of the presence and as the holy ones. (Even) as they, shall the seed of thy sons be for glory and greatness and holiness, and may He make them great unto all the ages. [15] And they shall be judges and princes, and chiefs of all the seed of the sons of Jacob; They shall speak the word of the Lord in righteousness, And they shall judge all His judgments in righteousness. And they shall declare My ways to Jacob And My paths to Israel. The blessing of the Lord shall be given in their mouths To bless all the seed of the beloved. [16] Thy mother has called thy name Levi, And justly has she called thy name; Thou shalt be joined to the Lord And be the companion of all the sons of Jacob; Let His table be thine, And do thou and thy sons eat thereof;

And may thy table be full unto all generations, And thy food fail not unto all the ages. ¹⁷ And let all who hate thee fall down before thee, And let all thy adversaries be rooted out and perish; And blessed be he that blesses thee, And cursed be every nation that curses thee.' ¹⁸ And to Judah he said: 'May the Lord give thee strength and power To tread down all that hate thee; A prince shalt thou be, thou and one of thy sons, over the sons of Jacob; May thy name and the name of thy sons go forth and traverse every land and region. Then shall the Gentiles fear before thy face, And all the nations shall quake [And all the peoples shall quake]. ¹⁹ In thee shall be the help of Jacob, And in thee be found the salvation of Israel. ²⁰ And when thou sittest on the throne of honour of thy righteousness There shall be great peace for all the seed of the sons of the beloved; Blessed be he that blesseth thee, And all that hate thee and afflict thee and curse thee Shall be rooted out and destroyed from the earth and be accursed.' ²¹ And turning he kissed him again and embraced him, and rejoiced greatly; for he had seen the sons of Jacob his son in very truth. ²² And he went forth from between his feet and fell down and bowed down to him, and he blessed them and rested there with Isaac his father that night, and they eat and drank with joy. ²³ And he made the two sons of Jacob sleep, the one on his right hand and the other on his left, and it was counted to him for righteousness. ²⁴ And Jacob told his father everything during the night, how the Lord had shown him great mercy, and how he had prospered (him in) all his ways, and protected him from all evil. ²⁵ And Isaac blessed the God of his father Abraham, who had not withdrawn his mercy and his righteousness from the sons of his servant Isaac.

Rebecca journeys with Jacob to Bethel (xxxi. 26-32).

²⁶ And in the morning Jacob told his father Isaac the vow which he had vowed to the Lord, and the vision which he had seen, and that he had built an altar, and that everything was ready for the sacrifice to be made before the Lord as he had vowed, and that he had come to set him on an ass. ²⁷ And Isaac said unto Jacob his son: 'I am not able to go with thee; for I am old and not able to bear the way: go, my son, in peace; for I am one hundred and sixty-five years this day; I am no longer able to journey; set thy mother (on an ass) and let her go with thee. ²⁸ And I know, my son, that thou hast come on my account, and may this day be blessed on which thou hast seen me alive, and I also have seen thee, my son. ²⁹ Mayest thou prosper and fulfil the vow which thou hast vowed; and put not off thy vow; for thou shalt be called to account as touching the vow; now therefore make haste to perform it, and may He be pleased who has made all things, to whom thou hast vowed the vow.' ³⁰ And he said to Rebecca: 'Go with Jacob thy son'; and Rebecca went with Jacob her son, and Deborah with her, and they came to Bethel. ³¹ And Jacob remembered the prayer with which his father had blessed him and his two sons, Levi and Judah, and he rejoiced and blessed the God of his fathers, Abraham and Isaac. ³² And he said: 'Now I know that I have an eternal hope, and my sons also, before the God of all'; and thus is it ordained concerning the two; and they record it as an eternal testimony unto them on the heavenly tablets how Isaac blessed them.

Levi's Dream at Bethel; he is appointed to the Priesthood. Jacob celebrates the Feast of Tabernacles and offers Tithes. The Institution of Tithes (xxxii. 1-15; cf. Gen. xxxv.).

32

¹ And he abode that night at Bethel, and Levi dreamed that they had ordained and made him the priest of the Most High God, him and his sons for ever; and he awoke from his sleep and blessed the Lord. ² And Jacob rose early in the morning, on the fourteenth of this month, and he gave a tithe of all that came with him, both of men and cattle, both of gold and every vessel and garment, yea, he gave tithes of all. ³ And in those days Rachel became pregnant with her son Benjamin. And Jacob counted his sons from him upwards and Levi fell to the portion of the Lord, and his father clothed him in the garments of the priesthood and filled his hands. ⁴ And on the fifteenth of this month, he brought to the altar fourteen oxen from amongst the cattle, and twenty-eight rams, and forty-nine sheep, and seven lambs, and twenty-one kids of the goats as a burnt-offering on the altar of sacrifice, well pleasing for a sweet savour before God. ⁵ This was his offering, in consequence of the vow which he had vowed that he would give a tenth, with their fruit-offerings and their drink- offerings. ⁶ And when the fire had consumed it, he burnt incense on the fire over the fire, and for a thank-offering two oxen and four rams and four sheep, four he-goats, and two sheep of a year old, and two kids of the goats; and thus he did daily for seven days. ⁷ And he and all his sons and his men were eating (this) with joy there during seven days and blessing and thanking the Lord, who had delivered him out of all his tribulation and had given him his vow. ⁸ And he tithed all the clean animals, and made a burnt sacrifice, but the unclean animals he gave (not) to Levi his son, and he gave him all the souls of the men. ⁹ And Levi discharged the priestly office at Bethel before Jacob his father in preference to his ten brothers, and he was a priest there, and Jacob gave his vow: thus he tithed again the tithe to the Lord and sanctified it, and it became holy unto Him. ¹⁰ And for this reason it is ordained on the heavenly tablets as a law for the tithing again the tithe to eat before the Lord from year to year, in the place where it is chosen that His name should dwell, and to this law there is no limit of days for ever. ¹¹ This ordinance is written that it may be fulfilled from year to year in eating the second tithe before the Lord in the place where it has been chosen, and nothing shall remain over from it from this year to the year following. ¹² For in its year shall the seed be eaten till the days of the gathering of the seed of the year, and the wine till the days of the wine, and the oil till the days of its season. ¹³ And all that is left thereof and becomes old, let it be regarded as polluted: let it be burnt with fire, for it is unclean. ¹⁴ And thus let them eat it together in the sanctuary, and let them not suffer it to become old. ¹⁵ And all the tithes of the oxen and sheep shall be holy unto the Lord, and shall belong to his priests, which they will eat before Him from year to year; for thus is it ordained and engraven regarding the tithe on the heavenly tablets.

Jacob's Visions. He celebrates the eighth day of Tabernacles. The Birth of Benjamin and Death of Rachel (xxxii. 16-34; cf. Gen. xxxv.).

¹⁶ And on the following night, on the twenty-second day of this month, Jacob resolved to build that place, and to surround the court with a wall, and to sanctify it and make it holy for ever, for himself and his children after him. ¹⁷ And the Lord appeared to him by night and blessed him and said unto him: 'Thy name shall not be called Jacob, but Israel shall they name thy name.' ¹⁸ And He said unto him again: 'I am the Lord who created the heaven and the earth, and I will increase thee and multiply thee exceedingly, and kings shall come forth from thee, and they shall judge everywhere wherever the foot of the sons of men has trodden. ¹⁹ And I will give to thy seed all the earth which is under heaven, and they shall judge all the nations according to their desires, and after that they shall get possession of the whole earth and inherit it for ever.' ²⁰ And He finished speaking with him, and He went up from him. And Jacob looked till He had ascended into heaven. ²¹ And he saw in a vision of the night, and behold an angel descended from heaven with seven tablets in his hands, and he gave them to Jacob, and he read them and knew all that was written therein which would befall him and his sons throughout all the ages. ²² And he showed him all that was written on the tablets, and said unto him: 'Do not build this place, and do not make it an eternal sanctuary, and do not dwell here; for this is not the place. Go to the house of Abraham thy father and dwell with Isaac thy father until the day of the death of thy father. ²³ For in Egypt thou shalt die in peace, and in this land thou shalt be buried with honour in the sepulchre of thy fathers, with Abraham and Isaac. ²⁴ Fear not, for as thou hast seen and read it, thus shall it all be; and do thou write down everything as thou hast seen and read.' ²⁵ And Jacob said: 'Lord, how can I remember all that I have read and seen? 'And he said unto him: 'I will bring all things to thy remembrance.' ²⁶ And he went up from him, and he awoke from his sleep, and he remembered everything which he had read and seen, and he wrote down all the words which he had read and seen. ²⁷ And he celebrated there yet another day, and he sacrificed thereon according to all that he sacrificed on the former days, and called its name 'Addition,' for this day was added and the former days he called 'The Feast '. ²⁸ And thus it was manifested that it should be, and it is written on the heavenly tablets: wherefore it was revealed to him that he should celebrate it, and add it to the seven days of the feast. ²⁹ And its name was called 'Addition,' because that it was recorded amongst the days of the feast days, according to the number of the days of the year. ³⁰ And in the night, on the twenty-third of this month, Deborah Rebecca's nurse died, and they buried her beneath the city under the oak of the river, and he called the name of this place, 'The river of Deborah,' and the oak, 'The oak of the mourning of Deborah.' ³¹ And Rebecca went and returned to her house to his father Isaac, and Jacob sent by her hand rams and sheep and he-goats that she should prepare a meal for his father such as he desired. ³² And he went after his mother till he came to the land of Kabratan, and he dwelt there. ³³ And Rachel bare a son in the night, and called his name 'Son of my sorrow '; for she suffered in giving him birth: but his father called his name Benjamin, on the eleventh of the eighth month in the first of the sixth week of this jubilee. [2143 A.M.] ³⁴ And Rachel died there and she was buried in the land of Ephrath, the same is Bethlehem, and Jacob built a pillar on the grave of Rachel, on the road above her grave.

Reuben's Sin with Bilhah. Laws regarding Incest. Jacob's Children (xxxiii. 1-23; Cf. Gen. xxxv. 21-27).

33

¹ And Jacob went and dwelt to the south of Magdaladra'ef. And he went to his father Isaac, he and Leah his wife, on the new moon of the tenth month.

² And Reuben saw Bilhah, Rachel's maid, the concubine of his father, bathing in water in a secret place, and he loved her. ³ And he hid himself at night, and he entered the house of Bilhah [at night], and he found her sleeping alone on a bed in her house. ⁴ And he lay with her, and she awoke and saw, and behold Reuben was lying with her in the bed, and she uncovered the border of her covering and seized him, and cried out, and discovered that it was Reuben. ⁵ And she was ashamed because of him, and released her hand from him, and he fled. ⁶ And she lamented because of this thing exceedingly, and did not tell it to any one. ⁷ And when Jacob returned and sought her, she said unto him: 'I am not clean for thee, for I have been defiled as regards thee; for Reuben has defiled me, and has lain with me in the night, and I was asleep, and did not discover until he uncovered my skirt and slept with me.' ⁸ And Jacob was exceedingly wroth with Reuben because he had lain with Bilhah, because he had uncovered his father's skirt. ⁹ And Jacob did not approach her again because Reuben had defiled her. And as for any man who uncovers his father's skirt his deed is wicked exceedingly, for he is abominable before the Lord. ¹⁰ For this reason it is written and ordained on the heavenly tablets that a man should not lie with his father's wife, and should not uncover his father's skirt, for this is unclean: they shall surely die together, the man who lies with his father's wife and the woman also, for they have wrought uncleanness on the earth. ¹¹ And there shall be nothing unclean before our God in the nation which He has chosen for Himself as a possession. ¹² And again, it is written a second time: 'Cursed be he who lieth with the wife of his father, for he hath uncovered his father's shame'; and all the holy ones of the Lord said 'So be it; so be it.' ¹³ And do thou, Moses, command the children of Israel that they observe this word; for it (entails) a punishment of death; and it is unclean, and there is no atonement for ever to atone for the man who has committed this, but he is to be put to death and slain, and stoned with stones, and rooted out from the midst of the people of our God. ¹⁴ For to no man who does so in Israel is it permitted to remain alive a single day on the earth, for he is abominable and unclean. ¹⁵ And let them not say: to Reuben was granted life and forgiveness after he had lain with his father's concubine, and to her also though she had a husband, and her husband Jacob, his father, was still alive. ¹⁶ For until that time there had not been revealed the ordinance and judgment and law in its completeness for all, but in thy days (it has been revealed) as a law of seasons and of days, and an everlasting law for the everlasting generations. ¹⁷ And for this law there is no consummation of days, and no atonement for it, but they must both be rooted out in the midst of the nation: on the day whereon they committed it they shall slay them. ¹⁸ And do thou, Moses, write (it) down for Israel that they may observe it, and do according to these words, and not commit a sin unto death; for the Lord our God is judge, who respects not persons and accepts not gifts. ¹⁹ And tell them these words of the covenant, that they may hear and observe, and be on their guard with respect to them, and not be destroyed and rooted out of the land; for an uncleanness, and an abomination, and a contamination, and a pollution are all they who commit it on the earth before our God. ²⁰ And there is no greater sin than the fornication which they commit on earth; for Israel is a holy nation unto the Lord its God, and a nation of inheritance, and a priestly and royal nation and for (His own) possession; and there shall no such uncleanness appear in the midst of the holy nation. ²¹ And in the third year of this sixth week [2145 A.M.] Jacob and all his sons went and dwelt in the house of Abraham, near Isaac his father and Rebecca his mother. ²² And these were the names of the sons of Jacob: the first-born Reuben, Simeon, Levi, Judah, Issachar, Zebulon, the sons of Leah; and the sons of Rachel, Joseph and Benjamin; and the sons of Bilhah, Dan and Naphtali; and the sons of Zilpah, Gad and Asher; and Dinah, the daughter of Leah, the only daughter of Jacob. ²³ And they came and bowed themselves to Isaac and Rebecca, and when they saw them they blessed Jacob and all his sons, and Isaac rejoiced exceedingly, for he saw the sons of Jacob, his younger son and he blessed them.

War of the Amorite Kings against Jacob and his Sons. Joseph sold into Egypt (cf. Gen. xxxvii.). The Death of Bilhah and Dinah (xxxiv. 1-19).

34

¹ And in the sixth year of this week of this forty-fourth jubilee [2148 A.M.] Jacob sent his sons to pasture their sheep, and his servants with them to the pastures of Shechem. ² And the seven kings of the Amorites assembled themselves together against them, to slay them, hiding themselves under the trees, and to take their cattle as a prey. ³ And Jacob and Levi and Judah and Joseph were in the house with Isaac their father; for his spirit was sorrowful, and they could not leave him: and Benjamin was the youngest, and for this reason remained with his father. ⁴ And there came the king[s] of Taphu and the king[s] of 'Aresa, and the king[s] of Seragan, and the king[s] of Selo, and the king[s] of Ga'as, and the king of Bethoron, and the king of Ma'anisakir, and all those who dwell in these mountains (and) who dwell in the woods in the land of Canaan. ⁵ And they announced this to Jacob saying: 'Behold, the kings of the Amorites have surrounded thy sons, and plundered their herds.' ⁶ And he arose from his house, he and his three sons and all the servants of his father, and his own servants, and he went against them with six thousand men, who carried swords. ⁷ And he slew them in the pastures of Shechem, and pursued those who fled, and he slew them with the edge of the sword, and he slew 'Aresa and Taphu and Saregan and Selo and 'Amani- sakir and Ga[ga]'as, and he recovered his herds. ⁸ And he prevailed over them, and imposed tribute on them that they should pay him tribute, five fruit products of their land, and he built Robel and Tamnatares. ⁹ And he returned in peace, and made peace with them, and they became his servants, until the day that he and his sons went down into Egypt. ¹⁰ And in the seventh year of this week [2149 A.M.] he sent Joseph to learn about the welfare of his brothers from his house to the land of Shechem, and he found them in the land of Dothan. ¹¹ And they dealt treacherously with him, and formed a plot against him to slay him, but changing their minds, they sold him to Ishmaelite merchants, and they brought him down into Egypt, and they sold him to Potiphar, the eunuch of Pharaoh, the chief of the cooks, priest of the city of 'Elew. ¹² And the sons of Jacob slaughtered a kid, and dipped the coat of Joseph in the blood, and sent (it) to Jacob their father on the tenth of the seventh month. ¹³ And he mourned all that night, for they had brought it to him in the evening, and he became feverish with mourning for his death, and he said: 'An evil beast hath devoured Joseph'; and all the members of his house [mourned with him that day, and they] were grieving and mourning with him all that day. ¹⁴ And his sons and his daughter rose up to comfort him, but he refused to be comforted for his son. ¹⁵ And on that day Bilhah heard that Joseph had perished, and she died mourning him, and she was living in Qafratef, and Dinah also, his daughter, died after Joseph had perished. ¹⁶ And there came these three mournings upon Israel in one month. And they buried Bilhah over against the tomb of Rachel, and Dinah also. his daughter, they buried there. ¹⁷ And he mourned for Joseph one year, and did not cease, for he said 'Let me go down to the grave mourning for my son'. ¹⁸ For this reason it is ordained for the children of Israel that they should afflict themselves on the tenth of the seventh month -on the day that the news which made him weep for Joseph came to Jacob his father- that they should make atonement for themselves thereon with a young goat on the tenth of the seventh month, once a year, for their sins; for they had grieved the affection of their father regarding Joseph his son. ¹⁹ And this day has been ordained that they should grieve thereon for their sins, and for all their transgressions and for all their errors, so that they might cleanse themselves on that day once a year.

The Wives of Jacob's Sons (xxxiv. 20-21).

²⁰ And after Joseph perished, the sons of Jacob took unto themselves wives. The name of Reuben's wife is 'Ada; and the name of Simeon's wife is 'Adlba'a, a Canaanite; and the name of Levi's wife is Melka, of the daughters of Aram, of the seed of the sons of Terah; and the name of Judah's wife, Betasu'el, a Canaanite; and the name of Issachar's wife, Hezaqa: and the name of Zabulon's wife, Ni'iman; and the name of Dan's wife, 'Egla; and the name of Naphtali's wife, Rasu'u, of Mesopotamia; and the name of Gad's wife, Maka; and the name of Asher's wife, 'Ijona; and the name of Joseph's wife, Asenath, the Egyptian; and the name of Benjamin's wife, 'Ijasaka. ²¹ And Simeon repented, and took a second wife from Mesopotamia as his brothers.

Rebecca's Last Admonitions and Death (xxxv. 1-27).

35

¹ And in the first year of the first week of the forty-fifth jubilee [2157 A.M.] Rebecca called Jacob, her son, and commanded him regarding his father and regarding his brother, that he should honour them all the days of his life. ² And Jacob said: 'I will do everything as thou hast commanded me; for this thing will be honour and greatness to me, and righteousness before the Lord, that I should honour them. ³ And thou too, mother, knowest from the time I was born until this day, all my deeds and all that is in my heart, that I always think good concerning all. ⁴ And how should I not do this thing which thou hast commanded me, that I should honour my father and my brother! ⁵ Tell me, mother, what perversity hast thou seen in me and I shall turn away from it, and mercy will be upon me.' ⁶ And she said unto him: 'My son, I have not seen in thee all my days any perverse but (only) upright deeds. And yet I will tell thee the truth, my son: I shall die this year, and I shall not survive this year in my life; for I have seen in a dream the day of my death, that I should not live beyond a hundred and fifty-five years: and behold I have completed all the days of my life which I am to live.' ⁷ And Jacob laughed at the words of his mother. because his mother had said unto him that she should die; and she was sitting opposite to him in possession of her strength, and she was not infirm in her strength; for she went in and

out and saw, and her teeth were strong, and no ailment had touched her all the days of her life. ⁸ And Jacob said unto her: 'Blessed am I, mother, if my days approach the days of thy life, and my strength remain with me thus as thy strength: and thou wilt not die, for thou art jesting idly with me regarding thy death.' ⁹ And she went in to Isaac and said unto him: 'One petition I make unto thee: make Esau swear that he will not injure Jacob, nor pursue him with enmity; for thou knowest Esau's thoughts that they are perverse from his youth, and there is no goodness in him; for he desires after thy death to kill him. ¹⁰ And thou knowest all that he has done since the day Jacob his brother went to Haran until this day: how he has forsaken us with his whole heart, and has done evil to us; thy flocks he has taken to himself, and carried off all thy possessions from before thy face. ¹¹ And when we implored and besought him for what was our own, he did as a man who was taking pity on us. ¹² And he is bitter against thee because thou didst bless Jacob thy perfect and upright son; for there is no evil but only goodness in him, and since he came from Haran unto this day he has not robbed us of aught, for he brings us everything in its season always, and rejoices with all his heart when we take at his hands and he blesses us, and has not parted from us since he came from Haran until this day, and he remains with us continually at home honouring us.' ¹³ And Isaac said unto her: 'I, too, know and see the deeds of Jacob who is with us, how that with all his heart he honours us; but I loved Esau formerly more than Jacob, because he was the firstborn; but now I love Jacob more than Esau, for he has done manifold evil deeds, and there is no righteousness in him, for all his ways are unrighteousness and violence, [and there is no righteousness around him.] ¹⁴ And now my heart is troubled because of all his deeds, and neither he nor his seed is to be saved, for they are those who will be destroyed from the earth and who will be rooted out from under heaven, for he has forsaken the God of Abraham and gone after his wives and after their uncleanness and after their error, he and his children. ¹⁵ And thou dost bid me make him swear that he will not slay Jacob his brother; even if he swear he will not abide by his oath, and he will not do good but evil only. ¹⁶ But if he desires to slay Jacob, his brother, into Jacob's hands will he be given, and he will not escape from his hands, [for he will descend into his hands.] ¹⁷ And fear thou not on account of Jacob; for the guardian of Jacob is great and powerful and honoured, and praised more than the guardian of Esau.' ¹⁸ And Rebecca sent and called Esau and he came to her, and she said unto him: 'I have a petition, my son, to make unto thee, and do thou promise to do it, my son.' ¹⁹ And he said: 'I will do everything that thou sayest unto me, and I will not refuse thy petition.' ²⁰ And she said unto him: 'I ask you that the day I die, thou wilt take me in and bury me near Sarah, thy father's mother, and that thou and Jacob will love each other and that neither will desire evil against the other, but mutual love only, and (so) ye will prosper, my sons, and be honoured in the midst of the land, and no enemy will rejoice over you, and ye will be a blessing and a mercy in the eyes of all those that love you.' ²¹ And he said: 'I will do all that thou hast told me, and I shall bury thee on the day thou diest near Sarah, my father's mother, as thou hast desired that her bones may be near thy bones. ²² And Jacob, my brother, also, I shall love above all flesh; for I have not a brother in all the earth but him only: and this is no great merit for me if I love him; for he is my brother, and we were sown together in thy body, and together came we forth from thy womb, and if I do not love my brother, whom shall I love? ²³ And I, myself, beg thee to exhort Jacob concerning me and concerning my sons, for I know that he will assuredly be king over me and my sons, for on the day my father blessed him he made him the higher and me the lower. ²⁴ And I swear unto thee that I shall love him, and not desire evil against him all the days of my life but good only.' ²⁵ And he sware unto her regarding all this matter. And she called Jacob before the eyes of Esau, and gave him commandment according to the words which she had spoken to Esau. ²⁶ And he said: 'I shall do thy pleasure; believe me that no evil will proceed from me or from my sons against Esau, and I shall be first in naught save in love only.' ²⁷ And they eat and drank, she and her sons that night, and she died, three jubilees and one week and one year old, on that night, and her two sons, Esau and Jacob, buried her in the double cave near Sarah, their father's mother.

Isaac's Last Words and Admonitions: his Death. The Death of Leah (xxxvi. 1-24).

36

¹ And in the sixth year of this week [2162 A.M.] Isaac called his two sons Esau and Jacob, and they came to him, and he said unto them: 'My sons, I am going the way of my fathers, to the eternal house where my fathers are. ² Wherefore bury me near Abraham my father, in the double cave in the field of Ephron the Hittite, where Abraham purchased a sepulchre to bury in; in the sepulchre which I digged for myself, there bury me. ³ And this I command you, my sons, that ye practise righteousness and uprightness on the earth, so that the Lord may bring upon you all that the Lord said that he would do to Abraham and to his seed. ⁴ And love one another, my sons, your brothers as a man who loves his own soul, and let each seek in what he may benefit his brother, and act together on the earth; and let them love each other as their own souls. ⁵ And concerning the question of idols, I command and admonish you to reject them and hate them, and love them not, for they are full of deception for those that worship them and for those that bow down to them. ⁶ Remember ye, my sons, the Lord God of Abraham your father, and how I too worshipped Him and served Him in righteousness and in joy, that He might multiply you and increase your seed as the stars of heaven in multitude, and establish you on the earth as the plant of righteousness which will not be rooted out unto all the generations for ever. ⁷ And now I shall make you swear a great oath -for there is no oath which is greater than it by the name glorious and honoured and great and splendid and wonderful and mighty, which created the heavens and the earth and all things together- that ye will fear Him and worship Him. ⁸ And that each will love his brother with affection and righteousness, and that neither will desire evil against his brother from henceforth for ever all the days of your life so that ye may prosper in all your deeds and not be destroyed. ⁹ And if either of you devises evil against his brother, know that from henceforth everyone that devises evil against his brother shall fall into his hand, and shall be rooted out of the land of the living, and his seed shall be destroyed from under heaven. ¹⁰ But on the day of turbulence and execration and indignation and anger, with flaming devouring fire as He burnt Sodom, so likewise will He burn his land and his city and all that is his, and he shall be blotted out of the book of the discipline of the children of men, and not be recorded in the book of life, but in that which is appointed to destruction, and he shall depart into eternal execration; so that their condemnation may be always renewed in hate and in execration and in wrath and in torment and in indignation and in plagues and in disease for ever. ¹¹ I say and testify to you, my sons, according to the judgment which shall come upon the man who wishes to injure his brother. ¹² And he divided all his possessions between the two on that day and he gave the larger portion to him that was the first-born, and the tower and all that was about it, and all that Abraham possessed at the Well of the Oath. ¹³ And he said: 'This larger portion I will give to the firstborn.' ¹⁴ And Esau said, 'I have sold to Jacob and given my birthright to Jacob; to him let it be given, and I have not a single word to say regarding it, for it is his.' ¹⁵ And Isaac said, May a blessing rest upon you, my sons, and upon your seed this day, for ye have given me rest, and my heart is not pained concerning the birthright, lest thou shouldest work wickedness on account of it. ¹⁶ May the Most High God bless the man that worketh righteousness, him and his seed for ever.' ¹⁷ And he ended commanding them and blessing them, and they eat and drank together before him, and he rejoiced because there was one mind between them, and they went forth from him and rested that day and slept. ¹⁸ And Isaac slept on his bed that day rejoicing; and he slept the eternal sleep, and died one hundred and eighty years old. He completed twenty-five weeks and five years; and his two sons Esau and Jacob buried him. ¹⁹ And Esau went to the land of Edom, to the mountains of Seir, and dwelt there. ²⁰ And Jacob dwelt in the mountains of Hebron, in the tower of the land of the sojournings of his father Abraham, and he worshipped the Lord with all his heart and according to the visible commands according as He had divided the days of his generations. ²¹ And Leah his wife died in the fourth year of the second week of the forty-fifth jubilee, [2167 A.M.] and he buried her in the double cave near Rebecca his mother to the left of the grave of Sarah, his father's mother ²² and all her sons and his sons came to mourn over Leah his wife with him and to comfort him regarding her, for he was lamenting her for he loved her exceedingly after Rachel her sister died; ²³ for she was perfect and upright in all her ways and honoured Jacob,and all the days that she lived with him he did not hear from her mouth a harsh word, for she was gentle and peaceable and upright and honourable. ²⁴ And he remembered all her deeds which she had done during her life and he lamented her exceedingly; for he loved her with all his heart and with all his soul.

Esau and his Sons wage War with Jacob (xxxvii. 1-25).

37

¹ And on the day that Isaac the father of Jacob and Esau died, [2162 A.M.] the sons of Esau heard that Isaac had given the portion of the elder to his younger son Jacob and they were very angry. ² And they strove with their father, saying 'Why has thy father given Jacob the portion of the elder and passed over thee, although thou art the elder and Jacob the younger?' ³ And he said unto them 'Because I sold my birthright to Jacob for a small mess of lentils, and on the day my father sent me to hunt and catch and bring him something that he should eat and bless me, he came with guile and brought my father food and drink, and my father blessed him and put me under his

hand. ⁴ And now our father has caused us to swear, me and him, that we shall not mutually devise evil, either against his brother, and that we shall continue in love and in peace each with his brother and not make our ways corrupt.' ⁵ And they said unto him, 'We shall not hearken unto thee to make peace with him; for our strength is greater than his strength, and we are more powerful than he; we shall go against him and slay him, and destroy him and his sons. And if thou wilt not go with us, we shall do hurt to thee also. ⁶ And now hearken unto us: Let us send to Aram and Philistia and Moab and Ammon, and let us choose for ourselves chosen men who are ardent for battle, and let us go against him and do battle with him, and let us exterminate him from the earth before he grows strong.' ⁷ And their father said unto them, 'Do not go and do not make war with him lest ye fall before him.' ⁸ And they said unto him, 'This too, is exactly thy mode of action from thy youth until this day, and thou art putting thy neck under his yoke. ⁹ We shall not hearken to these words.' And they sent to Aram, and to 'Aduram to the friend of their father, and they hired along with them one thousand fighting men, chosen men of war. ¹⁰ And there came to them from Moab and from the children of Ammon, those who were hired, one thousand chosen men, and from Philistia, one thousand chosen men of war, and from Edom and from the Horites one thousand chosen fighting men, and from the Kittim mighty men of war. ¹¹ And they said unto their father: Go forth with them and lead them, else we shall slay thee.' ¹² And he was filled with wrath and indignation on seeing that his sons were forcing him to go before (them) to lead them against Jacob his brother. ¹³ But afterward he remembered all the evil which lay hidden in his heart against Jacob his brother; and he remembered not the oath which he had sworn to his father and to his mother that he would devise no evil all his days against Jacob his brother. ¹⁴ And notwithstanding all this, Jacob knew not that they were coming against him to battle, and he was mourning for Leah, his wife, until they approached very near to the tower with four thousand warriors and chosen men of war. ¹⁵ And the men of Hebron sent to him saying, 'Behold thy brother has come against thee, to fight thee, with four thousand girt with the sword, and they carry shields and weapons'; for they loved Jacob more than Esau. So they told him; for Jacob was a more liberal and merciful man than Esau. ¹⁶ But Jacob would not believe until they came very near to the tower. ¹⁷ And he closed the gates of the tower; and he stood on the battlements and spake to his brother Esau and said, 'Noble is the comfort wherewith thou hast come to comfort me for my wife who has died. Is this the oath that thou didst swear to thy father and again to thy mother before they died? Thou hast broken the oath, and on the moment that thou didst swear to thy father wast thou condemned.' ¹⁸ And then Esau answered and said unto him, 'Neither the children of men nor the beasts of the earth have any oath of righteousness which in swearing they have sworn (an oath valid) for ever; but every day they devise evil one against another, and how each may slay his adversary and foe. ¹⁹ And thou dost hate me and my children for ever. And there is no observing the tie of brotherhood with thee. ²⁰ Hear these words which I declare unto thee, If the boar can change its skin and make its bristles as soft as wool, Or if it can cause horns to sprout forth on its head like the horns of a stag or of a sheep, Then will I observe the tie of brotherhood with thee And if the breasts separated themselves from their mother, for thou hast not been a brother to me. ²¹ And if the wolves make peace with the lambs so as not to devour or do them violence, And if their hearts are towards them for good, Then there shall be peace in my heart towards thee ²² And if the lion becomes the friend of the ox and makes peace with him And if he is bound under one yoke with him and ploughs with him, Then will I make peace with thee. ²³ And when the raven becomes white as the raza, Then know that I have loved thee And shall make peace with thee Thou shalt be rooted out, And thy sons shall be rooted out, And there shall be no peace for thee' ²⁴ And when Jacob saw that he was (so) evilly disposed towards him with his heart, and with all his soul as to slay him, and that he had come springing like the wild boar which comes upon the spear that pierces and kills it, and recoils not from it; ²⁵ then he spake to his own and to his servants that they should attack him and all his companions.

The War between Jacob and Esau at the Tower of Hebron. The Death of Esau and Overthrow of his Forces (xxxviii. 1-4).

38

¹ And after that Judah spake to Jacob, his father, and said unto him: 'Bend thy bow, father, and send forth thy arrows and cast down the adversary and slay the enemy; and mayst thou have the power, for we shall not slay thy brother, for he is such as thou, and he is like thee let us give him (this) honour.' ² Then Jacob bent his bow and sent forth the arrow and struck Esau, his brother (on his right breast) and slew him. ³ And again he sent forth an arrow and struck 'Adoran the Aramaean, on the left breast, and drove him backward and slew him. ⁴ And then went forth the sons of Jacob, they and their servants, dividing themselves into companies on the four sides of the tower. ⁵ And Judah went forth in front, and Naphtali and Gad with him and fifty servants with him on the south side of the tower, and they slew all they found before them, and not one individual of them escaped. ⁶ And Levi and Dan and Asher went forth on the east side of the tower, and fifty (men) with them, and they slew the fighting men of Moab and Ammon. ⁷ And Reuben and Issachar and Zebulon went forth on the north side of the tower, and fifty men with them, and they slew the fighting men of the Philistines. ⁸ And Simeon and Benjamin and Enoch, Reuben's son, went forth on the west side of the tower, and fifty (men) with them, and they slew of Edom and of the Horites four hundred men, stout warriors; and six hundred fled, and four of the sons of Esau fled with them, and left their father lying slain, as he had fallen on the hill which is in 'Aduram. ⁹ And the sons of Jacob pursued after them to the mountains of Seir. And Jacob buried his brother on the hill which is in 'Aduram, and he returned to his house. ¹⁰ And the sons of Jacob pressed hard upon the sons of Esau in the mountains of Seir, and bowed their necks so that they became servants of the sons of Jacob. ¹¹ And they sent to their father (to inquire) whether they should make peace with them or slay them. ¹² And Jacob sent word to his sons that they should make peace, and they made peace with them, and placed the yoke of servitude upon them, so that they paid tribute to Jacob and to his sons always. ¹³ And they continued to pay tribute to Jacob until the day that he went down into Egypt. ¹⁴ And the sons of Edom have not got quit of the yoke of servitude which the twelve sons of Jacob had imposed on them until this day.

The Kings of Edom (xxxviii. 15-24; cf. Gen. xxxvi. 31-39).

¹⁵ And these are the kings that reigned in Edom before there reigned any king over the children of Israel [until this day] in the land of Edom. ¹⁶ And Balaq, the son of Beor, reigned in Edom, and the name of his city was Danaba. ¹⁷ And Balaq died, and Jobab, the son of Zara of Boser, reigned in his stead. ¹⁸ And Jobab died, and 'Asam, of the land of Teman, reigned in his stead. ¹⁹ And 'Asam died, and 'Adath, the son of Barad, who slew Midian in the field of Moab, reigned in his stead, and the name of his city was Avith. ²⁰ And 'Adath died, and Salman, from 'Amaseqa, reigned in his stead. ²¹ And Salman died, and Saul of Ra'aboth (by the) river, reigned in his stead. ²² And Saul died, and Ba'elunan, the son of Achbor, reigned in his stead. ²³ And Ba'elunan, the son of Achbor died, and 'Adath reigned in his stead, and the name of his wife was Maitabith, the daughter of Matarat, the daughter of Metabedza'ab. ²⁴ These are the kings who reigned in the land of Edom.

Joseph's Service with Potiphar; his Purity and Imprisonment (xxxix. 1-13; cf. Gen. xxxix.).

39

¹ And Jacob dwelt in the land of his father's sojournings in the land of Canaan. These are the generations of Jacob. ² And Joseph was seventeen years old when they took him down into the land of Egypt, and Potiphar, an eunuch of Pharaoh, the chief cook bought him. ³ And he set Joseph over all his house and the blessing of the Lord came upon the house of the Egyptian on account of Joseph, and the Lord prospered him in all that he did. ⁴ And the Egyptian committed everything into the hands of Joseph; for he saw that the Lord was with him, and that the Lord prospered him in all that he did. ⁵ And Joseph's appearance was comely [and very beautiful was his appearance], and his master's wife lifted up her eyes and saw Joseph, and she loved him and besought him to lie with her. ⁶ But he did not surrender his soul, and he remembered the Lord and the words which Jacob, his father, used to read from amongst the words of Abraham, that no man should commit fornication with a woman who has a husband; that for him the punishment of death has been ordained in the heavens before the Most High God, and the sin will be recorded against him in the eternal books continually before the Lord. ⁷ And Joseph remembered these words and refused to lie with her. ⁸ And she besought him for a year, but he refused and would not listen. ⁹ But she embraced him and held him fast in the house in order to force him to lie with her, and closed the doors of the house and held him fast; but he left his garment in her hands and broke through the door, and fled without from her presence. ¹⁰ And the woman saw that he would not lie with her, and she calumniated him in the presence of his lord, saying 'Thy Hebrew servant, whom thou lovest, sought to force me so that he might lie with me; and it came to pass when I lifted up my voice that he fled and left his garment in my hands when I held him, and he brake through the door.' ¹¹ And the Egyptian saw the garment of Joseph and the broken door, and heard the words of his wife, and cast Joseph into prison into the place where the prisoners were kept whom the king imprisoned. ¹² And he was there in the prison; and the Lord gave Joseph favour in the sight of the chief of the prison guards and compassion before him, for he saw that the Lord was with him, and that the Lord made all that he did to prosper. ¹³ And he committed all things into his hands, and the chief of the prison guards

knew of nothing that was with him, for Joseph did every thing, and the Lord perfected it.

Joseph interprets the Dreams of the Chief Butler and the Chief Baker (xxxix. 14-18; cf. Gen. xl.).

[14] And he remained there two years. And in those days Pharaoh, king of Egypt was wroth against his two eunuchs, against the chief butler, and against the chief baker, and he put them in ward in the house of the chief cook, in the prison where Joseph was kept. [15] And the chief of the prison guards appointed Joseph to serve them; and he served before them. [16] And they both dreamed a dream, the chief butler and the chief baker, and they told it to Joseph. [17] And as he interpreted to them so it befell them, and Pharaoh restored the chief butler to his office and the (chief) baker he slew, as Joseph had interpreted to them. [18] But the chief butler forgot Joseph in the prison, although he had informed him what would befall him, and did not remember to inform Pharaoh how Joseph had told him, for he forgot.

Pharaoh's Dreams and their Interpretation. Joseph's Elevation and Marriage (xl. 1-13; cf. Gen. xli.).

40

[1] And in those days Pharaoh dreamed two dreams in one night concerning a famine which was to be in all the land, and he awoke from his sleep and called all the interpreters of dreams that were in Egypt, and magicians, and told them his two dreams, and they were not able to declare (them). [2] And then the chief butler remembered Joseph and spake of him to the king, and he brought him forth from the prison, and he to]d his two dreams before him. [3] And he said before Pharaoh that his two dreams were one, and he said unto him: 'Seven years shall come (in which there shall be) plenty over all the land of Egypt, and after that seven years of famine, such a famine as has not been in all the land. [4] And now let Pharaoh appoint overseers in all the land of Egypt, and let them store up food in every city throughout the days of the years of plenty, and there will be food for the seven years of famine, and the land will not perish through the famine, for it will be very severe.' [5] And the Lord gave Joseph favour and mercy in the eyes of Pharaoh, and Pharaoh said unto his servants. We shall not find such a wise and discreet man as this man, for the spirit of the Lord is with him.' [6] And he appointed him the second in all his kingdom and gave him authority over all Egypt, and caused him to ride in the second chariot of Pharaoh. [7] And he clothed him with byssus garments, and he put a gold chain upon his neck, and (a herald) proclaimed before him ' 'El 'El wa 'Abirer,' and placed a ring on his hand and made him ruler over all his house, and magnified him, and said unto him. 'Only on the throne shall I be greater than thou.' [8] And Joseph ruled over all the land of Egypt, and all the princes of Pharaoh, and all his servants, and all who did the king's business loved him, for he walked in uprightness, for he was without pride and arrogance, and he had no respect of persons, and did not accept gifts, but he judged in uprightness all the people of the land. [9] And the land of Egypt was at peace before Pharaoh because of Joseph, for the Lord was with him, and gave him favour and mercy for all his generations before all those who knew him and those who heard concerning him, and Pharaoh's kingdom was well ordered, and there was no Satan and no evil person (therein). [10] And the king called Joseph's name Sephantiphans, and gave Joseph to wife the daughter of Potiphar, the daughter of the priest of Heliopolis, the chief cook. [11] And on the day that Joseph stood before Pharaoh he was thirty years old [when he stood before Pharaoh]. [12] And in that year Isaac died. And it came to pass as Joseph had said in the interpretation of his two dreams, according as he had said it, there were seven years of plenty over all the land of Egypt, and the land of Egypt abundantly produced, one measure (producing) eighteen hundred measures. [13] And Joseph gathered food into every city until they were full of corn until they could no longer count and measure it for its multitude.

Judah's Incest with Tamar; his Repentance and Forgiveness (xli. 1-28; Cf. Gen. xxxviii.).

41

[1] And in the forty-fifth jubilee, in the second week, (and) in the second year, [2165 A.M.] Judah took for his first-born Er, a wife from the daughters of Aram, named Tamar. [2] But he hated, and did not lie with her, because his mother was of the daughters of Canaan, and he wished to take him a wife of the kinsfolk of his mother, but Judah, his father, would not permit him. [3] And this Er, the first-born of Judah, was wicked, and the Lord slew him. [4] And Judah said unto Onan, his brother 'Go in unto thy brother's wife and perform the duty of a husband's brother unto her, and raise up seed unto thy brother.' [5] And Onan knew that the seed would not be his, (but) his brother's only, and he went into the house of his brother's wife, and spilt the seed on the ground, and he was wicked in the eyes of the Lord, and He slew him. [6] And Judah said unto Tamar, his daughter-in-law: 'Remain in thy father's house as a widow till Shelah my son be grown up, and I shall give thee to him to wife.' [7] And he grew up; but Bedsu'el, the wife of Judah, did not permit her son Shelah to marry. And Bedsu'el, the wife of Judah, died [2168 A.M.] in the fifth year of this week. [8] And in the sixth year Judah went up to shear his sheep at Timnah. [2169 A.M.] And they told Tamar: 'Behold thy father-in-law goeth up to Timnah to shear his sheep.' [9] And she put off her widow's clothes, and put on a veil, and adorned herself, and sat in the gate adjoining the way to Timnah. [10] And as Judah was going along he found her, and thought her to be an harlot, and he said unto her: 'Let me come in unto thee'; and she said unto him Come in,' and he went in. [11] And she said unto him: 'Give me my hire'; and he said unto her: 'I have nothing in my hand save my ring that is on my finger, and my necklace, and my staff which is in my hand.' [12] And she said unto him 'Give them to me until thou dost send me my hire', and he said unto her: 'I will send unto thee a kid of the goats'; and he gave them to her, and he went in unto her, and she conceived by him. [13] And Judah went unto his sheep, and she went to her father's house. [14] And Judah sent a kid of the goats by the hand of his shepherd, an Adullamite, and he found her not; and he asked the people of the place, saying: 'Where is the harlot who was here?' And they said unto him; 'There is no harlot here with us.' [15] And he returned and informed him, and said unto him that he had not found her: 'I asked the people of the place, and they said unto me: "There is no harlot here." ' [16] And he said: 'Let her keep (them) lest we become a cause of derision.' And when she had completed three months, it was manifest that she was with child, and they told Judah, saying: 'Behold Tamar, thy daughter-in-law, is with child by whoredom.' [17] And Judah went to the house of her father, and said unto her father and her brothers: 'Bring her forth, and let them burn her, for she hath wrought uncleanness in Israel.' [18] And it came to pass when they brought her forth to burn her that she sent to her father-in-law the ring and the necklace, and the staff, saying: 'Discern whose are these, for by him am I with child.' [19] And Judah acknowledged, and said: 'Tamar is more righteous than I am. [20] And therefore let them burn her not' And for that reason she was not given to Shelah, and he did not again approach her. [21] And after that she bare two sons, Perez [2170 A.M.] and Zerah, in the seventh year of this second week. [22] And thereupon the seven years of fruitfulness were accomplished, of which Joseph spake to Pharaoh. [23] And Judah acknowledged that the deed which he had done was evil, for he had lain with his daughter-in-law, and he esteemed it hateful in his eyes, and he acknowledged that he had transgressed and gone astray, for he had uncovered the skirt of his son, and he began to lament and to supplicate before the Lord because of his transgression. [24] And we told him in a dream that it was forgiven him because he supplicated earnestly, and lamented, and did not again commit it. [25] And he received forgiveness because he turned from his sin and from his ignorance, for he transgressed greatly before our God; and every one that acts thus, every one who lies with his mother-in-law, let them burn him with fire that he may burn therein, for there is uncleanness and pollution upon them, with fire let them burn them. [26] And do thou command the children of Israel that there be no uncleanness amongst them, for every one who lies with his daughter-in-law or with his mother-in-law hath wrought uncleanness; with fire let them burn the man who has lain with her, and likewise the woman, and He will turn away wrath and punishment from Israel. [27] And unto Judah we said that his two sons had not lain with her, and for this reason his seed was stablished for a second generation, and would not be rooted out. [28] For in singleness of eye he had gone and sought for punishment, namely, according to the judgment of Abraham, which he had commanded his sons, Judah had sought to burn her with fire.

The Two Journeys of the Sons of Jacob to Egypt (xlii. 1-25; cf. Gen. xlii., xliii.).

42

[1] And in the first year of the third week of the forty-fifth jubilee the famine began to come into the [2171 A.M.] land, and the rain refused to be given to the earth, for none whatever fell. [2] And the earth grew barren, but in the land of Egypt there was food, for Joseph had gathered the seed of the land in the seven years of plenty and had preserved it. [3] And the Egyptians came to Joseph that he might give them food, and he opened the store-houses where was the grain of the first year, and he sold it to the people of the land for gold. [4] <Now the famine was very sore in the land of Canaan>, and Jacob heard that there was food in Egypt, and he sent his ten sons that they should procure food for him in Egypt; but Benjamin he did not send, and <the ten sons of Jacob> arrived <in Egypt> among those that went (there). [5] And Joseph recognised them, but they did not recognise him, and he spake unto them and questioned them, and he said unto them; 'Are ye not spies and have ye not come to explore the approaches of the land? 'And he put them in ward. [6] And after that he set them free again, and detained Simeon alone and sent off his nine brothers. [7] And he filled their sacks with corn, and he put their gold in their sacks, and they did not know. [8] And he

commanded them to bring their younger brother, for they had told him their father was living and their younger brother. ⁹ And they went up from the land of Egypt and they came to the land of Canaan; and they told their father all that had befallen them, and how the lord of the country had spoken roughly to them, and had seized Simeon till they should bring Benjamin. ¹⁰ And Jacob said: 'Me have ye bereaved of my children! Joseph is not and Simeon also is not, and ye will take Benjamin away. On me has your wickedness come. ¹¹ 'And he said: 'My son will not go down with you lest perchance he fall sick; for their mother gave birth to two sons, and one has perished, and this one also ye will take from me. If perchance he took a fever on the road, ye would bring down my old age with sorrow unto death.' ¹² For he saw that their money had been returned to every man in his sack, and for this reason he feared to send him. ¹³ And the famine increased and became sore in the land of Canaan, and in all lands save in the land of Egypt, for many of the children of the Egyptians had stored up their seed for food from the time when they saw Joseph gathering seed together and putting it in storehouses and preserving it for the years of famine. ¹⁴ And the people of Egypt fed themselves thereon during the first year of their famine. ¹⁵ But when Israel saw that the famine was very sore in the land, and that there was no deliverance, he said unto his sons: 'Go again, and procure food for us that we die not.' ¹⁶ And they said: 'We shall not go; unless our youngest brother go with us, we shall not go.' ¹⁷ And Israel saw that if he did not send him with them, they should all perish by reason of the famine ¹⁸ And Reuben said: 'Give him into my hand, and if I do not bring him back to thee, slay my two sons instead of his soul.' ¹⁹ And he said unto him: 'He shall not go with thee.' And Judah came near and said: 'Send him with me, and if I do not bring him back to thee, let me bear the blame before thee all the days of my life.' ²⁰ And he sent him with them in the second year of this week on the [2172 A.m.] first day of the month, and they came to the land of Egypt with all those who went, and (they had) presents in their hands, stacte and almonds and terebinth nuts and pure honey. ²¹ And they went and stood before Joseph, and he saw Benjamin his brother, and he knew him, and said unto them: Is this your youngest brother?' And they said unto him: 'It is he.' And he said The Lord be gracious to thee, my son!' ²² And he sent him into his house and he brought forth Simeon unto them and he made a feast for them, and they presented to him the gift which they had brought in their hands. ²³ And they eat before him and he gave them all a portion, but the portion of Benjamin was seven times larger than that of any of theirs. ²⁴ And they eat and drank and arose and remained with their asses. ²⁵ And Joseph devised a plan whereby he might learn their thoughts as to whether thoughts of peace prevailed amongst them, and he said to the steward who was over his house: 'Fill all their sacks with food, and return their money unto them into their vessels, and my cup, the silver cup out of which I drink, put it in the sack of the youngest, and send them away.'

Joseph finally tests his Brethren, and then makes himself known to them (xliii. 1-24; cf. Gen. xliv., xlv.).

43

¹ And he did as Joseph had told him, and filled all their sacks for them with food and put their money in their sacks, and put the cup in Benjamin's sack. ² And early in the morning they departed, and it came to pass that, when they had gone from thence, Joseph said unto the steward of his house: 'Pursue them, run and seize them, saying, "For good ye have requited me with evil; you have stolen from me the silver cup out of which my lord drinks." And bring back to me their youngest brother, and fetch (him) quickly before I go forth to my seat of judgment.' ³ And he ran after them and said unto them according to these words. ⁴ And they said unto him: 'God forbid that thy servants should do this thing, and steal from the house of thy lord any utensil, and the money also which we found in our sacks the first time, we thy servants brought back from the land of Canaan. ⁵ How then should we steal any utensil? Behold here are we and our sacks search, and wherever thou findest the cup in the sack of any man amongst us, let him be slain, and we and our asses will serve thy lord.' ⁶ And he said unto them: 'Not so, the man with whom I find, him only shall I take as a servant, and ye shall return in peace unto your house.' ⁷ And as he was searching in their vessels, beginning with the eldest and ending with the youngest, it was found in Benjamin's sack. ⁸ And they rent their garments, and laded their asses, and returned to the city and came to the house of Joseph, and they all bowed themselves on their faces to the ground before him. ⁹ And Joseph said unto them: 'Ye have done evil.' And they said: 'What shall we say and how shall we defend ourselves? Our lord hath discovered the transgression of his servants; behold we are the servants of our lord, and our asses also. ¹⁰ 'And Joseph said unto them: 'I too fear the Lord; as for you, go ye to your homes and let your brother be my servant, for ye have done evil. Know ye not that a man delights in his cup as I with this cup? And yet ye have stolen it from me.' ¹¹ And Judah said: 'O my lord, let thy servant, I pray thee, speak a word in my lord's ear two brothers did thy servant's mother bear to our father: one went away and was lost, and hath not been found, and he alone is left of his mother, and thy servant our father loves him, and his life also is bound up with the life of this (lad). ¹² And it will come to pass, when we go to thy servant our father, and the lad is not with us, that he will die, and we shall bring down our father with sorrow unto death. ¹³ Now rather let me, thy servant, abide instead of the boy as a bondsman unto my lord, and let the lad go with his brethren, for I became surety for him at the hand of thy servant our father, and if I do not bring him back, thy servant will hear the blame to our father for ever.' ¹⁴ And Joseph saw that they were all accordant in goodness one with another, and he could not refrain himself, and he told them that he was Joseph. ¹⁵ And he conversed with them in the Hebrew tongue and fell on their neck and wept. ¹⁶ But they knew him not and they began to weep. And he said unto them: 'Weep not over me, but hasten and bring my father to me; and ye see that it is my mouth that speaketh and the eyes of my brother Benjamin see. ¹⁷ For behold this is the second year of the famine, and there are still five years without harvest or fruit of trees or ploughing. ¹⁸ Come down quickly ye and your households, so that ye perish not through the famine, and do not be grieved for your possessions, for the Lord sent me before you to set things in order that many people might live. ¹⁹ And tell my father that I am still alive, and ye, behold, ye see that the Lord has made me as a father to Pharaoh, and ruler over his house and over all the land of Egypt. ²⁰ And tell my father of all my glory, and all the riches and glory that the Lord hath given me.' ²¹ And by the command of the mouth of Pharaoh he gave them chariots and provisions for the way, and he gave them all many-coloured raiment and silver. ²² And to their father he sent raiment and silver and ten asses which carried corn, and he sent them away. ²³ And they went up and told their father that Joseph was alive, and was measuring out corn to all the nations of the earth, and that he was ruler over all the land of Egypt. ²⁴ And their father did not believe it, for he was beside himself in his mind; but when he saw the wagons which Joseph had sent, the life of his spirit revived, and he said: 'It is enough for me if Joseph lives; I will go down and see him before I die.'

Jacob, celebrates the Feast of First-fruits and journeys to Egypt. List of his Descendants. (xliv. 1-34; cf. Gen. xlvi. 1-28).

44

¹ And Israel took his journey from Haran from his house on the new moon of the third month, and he went on the way of the Well of the Oath, and he offered a sacrifice to the God of his father Isaac on the seventh of this month. ² And Jacob remembered the dream that he had seen at Bethel, and he feared to go down into Egypt. ³ And while he was thinking of sending word to Joseph to come to him, and that he would not go down, he remained there seven days, if perchance he could see a vision as to whether he should remain or go down. ⁴ And he celebrated the harvest festival of the first-fruits with old grain, for in all the land of Canaan there was not a handful of seed [in the land], for the famine was over all the beasts and cattle and birds, and also over man. ⁵ And on the sixteenth the Lord appeared unto him, and said unto him, 'Jacob, Jacob'; and he said, 'Here am I.' And He said unto him: 'I am the God of thy fathers, the God of Abraham and Isaac; fear not to go down into Egypt, for I will there make of thee a great nation I will go down with thee, and I will bring thee up (again), and in this land shalt thou be buried, and Joseph shall put his hands upon thy eyes. ⁶ Fear not; go down into Egypt.' ⁷ And his sons rose up, and his sons' sons, and they placed their father and their possessions upon wagons. ⁸ And Israel rose up from the Well of the Oath on the sixteenth of this third month, and he went to the land of Egypt. ⁹ And Israel sent Judah before him to his son Joseph to examine the Land of Goshen, for Joseph had told his brothers that they should come and dwell there that they might be near him. ¹⁰ And this was the goodliest (land) in the land of Egypt, and near to him, for all (of them) and also for the cattle. ¹¹ And these are the names of the sons of Jacob who went into Egypt with Jacob their father. ¹² Reuben, the First-born of Israel; and these are the names of his sons Enoch, and Pallu, and Hezron and Carmi-five. ¹³ Simeon and his sons; and these are the names of his sons: Jemuel, and Jamin, and Ohad, and Jachin, and Zohar, and Shaul, the son of the Zephathite woman-seven. ¹⁴ Levi and his sons; and these are the names of his sons: Gershon, and Kohath, and Merari-four. ¹⁵ Judah and his sons; and these are the names of his sons: Shela, and Perez, and Zerah-four. ¹⁶ Issachar and his sons; and these are the names of his sons: Tola, and Phua, and Jasub, and Shimron-five. ¹⁷ Zebulon and his sons; and these are the names of his sons: Sered, and Elon, and Jahleel-four. ¹⁸ And these are the sons of Jacob and their sons whom Leah bore to Jacob in Mesopotamia, six, and their one sister, Dinah and all the souls of the sons of Leah, and their sons, who went with Jacob their father into Egypt, were twenty-nine, and Jacob their father being with them, they were thirty. ¹⁹ And the sons of

Zilpah, Leah's handmaid, the wife of Jacob, who bore unto Jacob Gad and Ashur. [20] And these are the names of their sons who went with him into Egypt. The sons of Gad: Ziphion, and Haggi, and Shuni, and Ezbon, <and Eri>, and Areli, and Arodi-eight. [21] And the sons of Asher: Imnah, and Ishvah, <and Ishvi>, and Beriah, and Serah, their one sister-six. [22] All the souls were fourteen, and all those of Leah were forty-four. [23] And the sons of Rachel, the wife of Jacob: Joseph and Benjamin. [24] And there were born to Joseph in Egypt before his father came into Egypt, those whom Asenath, daughter of Potiphar priest of Heliopolis bare unto him, Manasseh, and Ephraim-three. [25] And the sons of Benjamin: Bela and Becher and Ashbel, Gera, and Naaman, and Ehi, and Rosh, and Muppim, and Huppim, and Ard-eleven. [26] And all the souls of Rachel were fourteen. [27] And the sons of Bilhah, the handmaid of Rachel, the wife of Jacob, whom she bare to Jacob, were Dan and Naphtali. [28] And these are the names of their sons who went with them into Egypt. And the sons of Dan were Hushim, and Samon, and Asudi. and 'Ijaka, and Salomon-six. [29] And they died the year in which they entered into Egypt, and there was left to Dan Hushim alone. [30] And these are the names of the sons of Naphtali Jahziel, and Guni and Jezer, and Shallum, and 'Iv. [31] And 'Iv, who was born after the years of famine, died in Egypt. [32] And all the souls of Rachel were twenty-six. [33] And all the souls of Jacob which went into Egypt were seventy souls. These are his children and his children's children, in all seventy, but five died in Egypt before Joseph, and had no children. [34] And in the land of Canaan two sons of Judah died, Er and Onan, and they had no children, and the children of Israel buried those who perished, and they were reckoned among the seventy Gentile nations.

Joseph receives Jacob. The Land of Egypt is acquired for Pharaoh. Jacob's Death and Burial (xlv. 1-16; cf. Gen. xlvi. 28 ff., xlvii. 11 ff.).

45

[1] And Israel went into the country of Egypt, into the land of Goshen, on the new moon of the fourth [2172 A.M]. month, in the second year of the third week of the forty-fifth jubilee. [2] And Joseph went to meet his father Jacob, to the land of Goshen, and he fell on his father's neck and wept. [3] And Israel said unto Joseph: 'Now let me die since I have seen thee, and now may the Lord God of Israel be blessed the God of Abraham and the God of Isaac who hath not withheld His mercy and His grace from His servant Jacob. [4] It is enough for me that I have seen thy face whilst I am yet alive; yea, true is the vision which I saw at Bethel. Blessed be the Lord my God for ever and ever, and blessed be His name.' [5] And Joseph and his brothers eat bread before their father and drank wine, and Jacob rejoiced with exceeding great joy because he saw Joseph eating with his brothers and drinking before him, and he blessed the Creator of all things who had preserved him, and had preserved for him his twelve sons. [6] And Joseph had given to his father and to his brothers as a gift the right of dwelling in the land of Goshen and in Rameses and all the region round about, which he ruled over before Pharaoh. And Israel and his sons dwelt in the land of Goshen, the best part of the land of Egypt and Israel was one hundred and thirty years old when he came into Egypt. [7] And Joseph nourished his father and his brethren and also their possessions with bread as much as sufficed them for the seven years of the famine. [8] And the land of Egypt suffered by reason of the famine, and Joseph acquired all the land of Egypt for Pharaoh in return for food, and he got possession of the people and their cattle and everything for Pharaoh. [9] And the years of the famine were accomplished, and Joseph gave to the people in the land seed and food that they might sow (the land) in the eighth year, for the river had overflowed all the land of Egypt. [10] For in the seven years of the famine it had (not) overflowed and had irrigated only a few places on the banks of the river, but now it overflowed and the Egyptians sowed the land, and it bore much corn that year. [11] And this was the first year of [2178 A.M.] the fourth week of the forty-fifth jubilee. [12] And Joseph took of the corn of the harvest the fifth part for the king and left four parts for them for food and for seed, and Joseph made it an ordinance for the land of Egypt until this day. [13] And Israel lived in the land of Egypt seventeen years, and all the days which he lived were three jubilees, one hundred and forty-seven years, and he died in the fourth [2188 A.M.] year of the fifth week of the forty-fifth jubilee. [14] And Israel blessed his sons before he died and told them everything that would befall them in the land of Egypt; and he made known to them what would come upon them in the last days, and blessed them and gave to Joseph two portions in the land. [15] And he slept with his fathers, and he was buried in the double cave in the land of Canaan, near Abraham his father in the grave which he dug for himself in the double cave in the land of Hebron. [16] And he gave all his books and the books of his fathers to Levi his son that he might preserve them and renew them for his children until this day.

The Death of Joseph. The Bones of Jacob's Sons (except Joseph) interred at Hebron. The Oppression of Israel by Egypt (xlvi. 1-16; cf. Gen. l.; Exod. i.).

46

[1] And it came to pass that after Jacob died the children of Israel multiplied in the land of Egypt, and they became a great nation, and they were of one accord in heart, so that brother loved brother and every man helped his brother, and they increased abundantly and multiplied exceedingly, ten [2242 A.M.] weeks of years, all the days of the life of Joseph. [2] And there was no Satan nor any evil all the days of the life of Joseph which he lived after his father Jacob, for all the Egyptians honoured the children of Israel all the days of the life of Joseph. [3] And Joseph died being a hundred and ten years old; seventeen years he lived in the land of Canaan, and ten years he was a servant, and three years in prison, and eighty years he was under the king, ruling all the land of Egypt. [4] And he died and all his brethren and all that generation. [5] And he commanded the children of Israel before he died that they should carry his bones with them when they went forth from the land of Egypt. [6] And he made them swear regarding his bones, for he knew that the Egyptians would not again bring forth and bury him in the land of Canaan, for Makamaron, king of Canaan, while dwelling in the land of Assyria, fought in the valley with the king of Egypt and slew him there, and pursued after the Egyptians to the gates of 'Ermon. [7] But he was not able to enter, for another, a new king, had become king of Egypt, and he was stronger than he, and he returned to the land of Canaan, and the gates of Egypt were closed, and none went out and none came into Egypt. [8] And Joseph died in the forty-sixth jubilee, in the sixth week, in the second year, and they buried him in the land of Egypt, and [2242 A.M.] all his brethren died after him. [9] And the king of Egypt went forth to war with the king of Canaan [2263 A.M.] in the forty-seventh jubilee, in the second week in the second year, and the children of Israel brought forth all the bones of the children of Jacob save the bones of Joseph, and they buried them in the field in the double cave in the mountain. [10] And the most (of them) returned to Egypt, but a few of them remained in the mountains of Hebron, and Amram thy father remained with them. [11] And the king of Canaan was victorious over the king of Egypt, and he closed the gates of Egypt. [12] And he devised an evil device against the children of Israel of afflicting them and he said unto the people of Egypt: 'Behold the people of the children of Israel have increased and multiplied more than we. [13] Come and let us deal wisely with them before they become too many, and let us afflict them with slavery before war come upon us and before they too fight against us; else they will join themselves unto our enemies and get them up out of our land, for their hearts and faces are towards the land of Canaan.' [14] And he set over them taskmasters to afflict them with slavery; and they built strong cities for Pharaoh, Pithom, and Raamses and they built all the walls and all the fortifications which had fallen in the cities of Egypt. [15] And they made them serve with rigour, and the more they dealt evilly with them, the more they increased and multiplied. [16] And the people of Egypt abominated the children of Israel

The Birth and Early Years of Moses (xlvii. 1-12; cf. Exod. ii.).

47

[1] And in the seventh week, in the seventh year, in the forty-seventh jubilee, thy father went forth [2303 A.M.] from the land of Canaan, and thou wast born in the fourth week, in the sixth year thereof, in the [2330 A.M.] forty-eighth jubilee; this was the time of tribulation on the children of Israel. [2] And Pharaoh, king of Egypt, issued a command regarding them that they should cast all their male children which were born into the river. [3] And they cast them in for seven months until the day that thou wast born [4] And thy mother hid thee for three months, and they told regarding her. And she made an ark for thee, and covered it with pitch and asphalt, and placed it in the flags on the bank of the river, and she placed thee in it seven days, and thy mother came by night and suckled thee, and by day Miriam, thy sister, guarded thee from the birds. [5] And in those days Tharmuth, the daughter of Pharaoh, came to bathe in the river, and she heard thy voice crying, and she told her maidens to bring thee forth, and they brought thee unto her. [6] And she took thee out of the ark, and she had compassion on thee. [7] And thy sister said unto her: 'Shall I go and call unto thee one of the Hebrew women to nurse and suckle this babe for thee?' [8] And she said <unto her>: 'Go.' And she went and called thy mother Jochebed, and she gave her wages, and she nursed thee. [9] And afterwards, when thou wast grown up, they brought thee unto the daughter of Pharaoh, and thou didst become her son, and Amram thy father taught thee writing, and after thou hadst completed three weeks they brought thee into the royal court. [10] And thou wast three weeks of years at court until the time [2351-] when thou didst go forth from the royal court

and didst see an Egyptian smiting thy friend who was [2372 A.M.] of the children of Israel, and thou didst slay him and hide him in the sand. ¹¹ And on the second day thou didst and two of the children of Israel striving together, and thou didst say to him who was doing the wrong: 'Why dost thou smite thy brother?' ¹² And he was angry and indignant, and said: 'Who made thee a prince and a judge over us? Thinkest thou to kill me as thou killedst the Egyptian yesterday?' And thou didst fear and flee on account of these words.

From the Flight of Moses to the Exodus (xlviii. 1-19; cf. Exod. ii. 15 ff., iv. 19-24, vii-xiv.).

48

¹ And in the sixth year of the third week of the forty-ninth jubilee thou didst depart and dwell <in [2372 A.M.] the land of Midian>, five weeks and one year. And thou didst return into Egypt in the second week in the second year in the fiftieth jubilee. ² And thou thyself knowest what He spake unto thee on [2410 A.M.] Mount Sinai, and what prince Mastêmâ desired to do with thee when thou wast returning into Egypt <on the way when thou didst meet him at the lodging-place>. ³ Did he not with all his power seek to slay thee and deliver the Egyptians out of thy hand when he saw that thou wast sent to execute judgment and vengeance on the Egyptians? ⁴ And I delivered thee out of his hand, and thou didst perform the signs and wonders which thou wast sent to perform in Egypt against Pharaoh, and against all his house, and against his servants and his people. ⁵ And the Lord executed a great vengeance on them for Israel's sake, and smote them through (the plagues of) blood and frogs, lice and dog-flies, and malignant boils breaking forth in blains; and their cattle by death; and by hail-stones, thereby He destroyed everything that grew for them; and by locusts which devoured the residue which had been left by the hail, and by darkness; and <by the death> of the first-born of men and animals, and on all their idols the Lord took vengeance and burned them with fire. ⁶ And everything was sent through thy hand, that thou shouldst declare (these things) before they were done, and thou didst speak with the king of Egypt before all his servants and before his people. ⁷ And everything took place according to thy words; ten great and terrible judgments came on the land of Egypt that thou mightest execute vengeance on it for Israel. ⁸ And the Lord did everything for Israel's sake, and according to His covenant, which he had ordained with Abraham that He would take vengeance on them as they had brought them by force into bondage. ⁹ And the prince Mastêmâ stood up against thee, and sought to cast thee into the hands of Pharaoh, and he helped the Egyptian sorcerers, ¹⁰ and they stood up and wrought before thee the evils indeed we permitted them to work, but the remedies we did not allow to be wrought by their hands. ¹¹ And the Lord smote them with malignant ulcers, and they were not able to stand, for we destroyed them so that they could not perform a single sign. ¹² And notwithstanding all (these) signs and wonders the prince Mastêmâ was not put to shame because he took courage and cried to the Egyptians to pursue after thee with all the powers of the Egyptians, with their chariots, and with their horses, and with all the hosts of the peoples of Egypt. ¹³ And I stood between the Egyptians and Israel, and we delivered Israel out of his hand, and out of the hand of his people, and the Lord brought them through the midst of the sea as if it were dry land. ¹⁴ And all the peoples whom he brought to pursue after Israel, the Lord our God cast them into the midst of the sea, into the depths of the abyss beneath the children of Israel, even as the people of Egypt had cast their children into the river He took vengeance on 1,000,000 of them, and one thousand strong and energetic men were destroyed on account of one suckling of the children of thy people which they had thrown into the river. ¹⁵ And on the fourteenth day and on the fifteenth and on the sixteenth and on the seventeenth and on the eighteenth the prince Mastêmâ was bound and imprisoned behind the children of Israel that he might not accuse them. ¹⁶ And on the nineteenth we let them loose that they might help the Egyptians and pursue the children of Israel. ¹⁷ And he hardened their hearts and made them stubborn, and the device was devised by the Lord our God that He might smite the Egyptians and cast them into the sea. ¹⁸ And on the fourteenth we bound him that he might not accuse the children of Israel on the day when they asked the Egyptians for vessels and garments, vessels of silver, and vessels of gold, and vessels of bronze, in order to despoil the Egyptians in return for the bondage in which they had forced them to serve. ¹⁹ And we did not lead forth the children of Israel from Egypt empty handed.

Regulations regarding the Passover (xlix. 1-23; cf. Exod. xii.).

49

¹ Remember the commandment which the Lord commanded thee concerning the passover, that thou shouldst celebrate it in its season on the fourteenth of the first month, that thou shouldst kill it before it is evening, and that they should eat it by night on the evening of the fifteenth from the time of the setting of the sun. ² For on this night -the beginning of the festival and the beginning of the joy- ye were eating the passover in Egypt, when all the powers of Mastêmâ had been let loose to slay all the first-born in the land of Egypt, from the first-born of Pharaoh to the first-born of the captive maid-servant in the mill, and to the cattle. ³ And this is the sign which the Lord gave them: Into every house on the lintels of which they saw the blood of a lamb of the first year, into (that) house they should not enter to slay, but should pass by (it), that all those should be saved that were in the house because the sign of the blood was on its lintels. ⁴ And the powers of the Lord did everything according as the Lord commanded them, and they passed by all the children of Israel, and the plague came not upon them to destroy from amongst them any soul either of cattle, or man, or dog. ⁵ And the plague was very grievous in Egypt, and there was no house in Egypt where there was not one dead, and weeping and lamentation. ⁶ And all Israel was eating the flesh of the paschal lamb, and drinking the wine, and was lauding, and blessing, and giving thanks to the Lord God of their fathers, and was ready to go forth from under the yoke of Egypt, and from the evil bondage. ⁷ And remember thou this day all the days of thy life, and observe it from year to year all the days of thy life, once a year, on its day, according to all the law thereof, and do not adjourn (it) from day to day, or from month to month. ⁸ For it is an eternal ordinance, and engraven on the heavenly tablets regarding all the children of Israel that they should observe it every year on its day once a year, throughout all their generations; and there is no limit of days, for this is ordained for ever. ⁹ And the man who is free from uncleanness, and does not come to observe it on occasion of its day, so as to bring an acceptable offering before the Lord, and to eat and to drink before the Lord on the day of its festival, that man who is clean and close at hand shall be cut off: because he offered not the oblation of the Lord in its appointed season, he shall take the guilt upon himself. ¹⁰ Let the children of Israel come and observe the passover on the day of its fixed time, on the fourteenth day of the first month, between the evenings, from the third part of the day to the third part of the night, for two portions of the day are given to the light, and a third part to the evening. ¹¹ This is that which the Lord commanded thee that thou shouldst observe it between the evenings. ¹² And it is not permissible to slay it during any period of the light, but during the period bordering on the evening, and let them eat it at the time of the evening, until the third part of the night, and whatever is left over of all its flesh from the third part of the night and onwards, let them burn it with fire. ¹³ And they shall not cook it with water, nor shall they eat it raw, but roast on the fire: they shall eat it with diligence, its head with the inwards thereof and its feet they shall roast with fire, and not break any bone thereof; for of the children of Israel no bone shall be crushed. ¹⁴ For this reason the Lord commanded the children of Israel to observe the passover on the day of its fixed time, and they shall not break a bone thereof; for it is a festival day, and a day commanded, and there may be no passing over from day to day, and month to month, but on the day of its festival let it be observed. ¹⁵ And do thou command the children of Israel to observe the passover throughout their days, every year, once a year on the day of its fixed time, and it shall come for a memorial well pleasing before the Lord, and no plague shall come upon them to slay or to smite in that year in which they celebrate the passover in its season in every respect according to His command. ¹⁶ And they shall not eat it outside the sanctuary of the Lord, but before the sanctuary of the Lord, and all the people of the congregation of Israel shall celebrate it in its appointed season. ¹⁷ And every man who has come upon its day shall eat it in the sanctuary of your God before the Lord from twenty years old and upward; for thus is it written and ordained that they should eat it in the sanctuary of the Lord. ¹⁸ And when the children of Israel come into the land which they are to possess, into the land of Canaan, and set up the tabernacle of the Lord in the midst of the land in one of their tribes until the sanctuary of the Lord has been built in the land, let them come and celebrate the passover in the midst of the tabernacle of the Lord, and let them slay it before the Lord from year to year. ¹⁹ And in the days when the house has been built in the name of the Lord in the land of their inheritance, they shall go there and slay the passover in the evening, at sunset, at the third part of the day. ²⁰ And they shall offer its blood on the threshold of the altar, and shall place its fat on the fire which is upon the altar, and they shall eat its flesh roasted with fire in the court of the house which has been sanctified in the name of the Lord. ²¹ And they may not celebrate the passover in their cities, nor in any place save before the tabernacle of the Lord, or before His house where His name hath dwelt; and they shall not go astray from the Lord. ²² And do thou, Moses, command the children of Israel to observe the ordinances of the passover, as it was commanded unto thee; declare thou unto them every year and the day of its days, and the festival of unleavened bread, that they should eat unleavened bread seven days, (and) that they should observe its

festival, and that they bring an oblation every day during those seven days of joy before the Lord on the altar of your God. ²³ For ye celebrated this festival with haste when ye went forth from Egypt till ye entered into the wilderness of Shur; for on the shore of the sea ye completed it.

Laws regarding the Jubilees and the Sabbath (l. 1-13).

50

¹ And after this law I made known to thee the days of the Sabbaths in the desert of Sin[ai], which is between Elim and Sinai. ² And I told thee of the Sabbaths of the land on Mount Sinai, and I told thee of the jubilee years in the sabbaths of years: but the year thereof have I not told thee till ye enter the land which ye are to possess. ³ And the land also shall keep its sabbaths while they dwell upon it, and they shall know the jubilee year. ⁴ Wherefore I have ordained for thee the year-weeks and the years and the jubilees: there are forty-nine jubilees from the days of Adam until this day, [2410 A.M.] and one week and two years: and there are yet forty years to come (lit. 'distant') for learning the [2450 A.M.] commandments of the Lord, until they pass over into the land of Canaan, crossing the Jordan to the west. ⁵ And the jubilees shall pass by, until Israel is cleansed from all guilt of fornication, and uncleanness, and pollution, and sin, and error, and dwells with confidence in all the land, and there shall be no more a Satan or any evil one, and the land shall be clean from that time for evermore. ⁶ And behold the commandment regarding the Sabbaths -I have written (them) down for thee- and all the judgments of its laws. ⁷ Six days shalt thou labour, but on the seventh day is the Sabbath of the Lord your God. In it ye shall do no manner of work, ye and your sons, and your men-servants and your maid-servants, and all your cattle and the sojourner also who is with you. ⁸ And the man that does any work on it shall die: whoever desecrates that day, whoever lies with (his) wife, or whoever says he will do something on it, that he will set out on a journey thereon in regard to any buying or selling: and whoever draws water thereon which he had not prepared for himself on the sixth day, and whoever takes up any burden to carry it out of his tent or out of his house shall die. ⁹ Ye shall do no work whatever on the Sabbath day save what ye have prepared for yourselves on the sixth day, so as to eat, and drink, and rest, and keep Sabbath from all work on that day, and to bless the Lord your God, who has given you a day of festival and a holy day: and a day of the holy kingdom for all Israel is this day among their days for ever. ¹⁰ For great is the honour which the Lord has given to Israel that they should eat and drink and be satisfied on this festival day, and rest thereon from all labour which belongs to the labour of the children of men save burning frankincense and bringing oblations and sacrifices before the Lord for days and for Sabbaths. ¹¹ This work alone shall be done on the Sabbath-days in the sanctuary of the Lord your God; that they may atone for Israel with sacrifice continually from day to day for a memorial well-pleasing before the Lord, and that He may receive them always from day to day according as thou hast been commanded. ¹² And every man who does any work thereon, or goes a journey, or tills (his) farm, whether in his house or any other place, and whoever lights a fire, or rides on any beast, or travels by ship on the sea, and whoever strikes or kills anything, or slaughters a beast or a bird, or whoever catches an animal or a bird or a fish, or whoever fasts or makes war on the Sabbaths: ¹³ The man who does any of these things on the Sabbath shall die, so that the children of Israel shall observe the Sabbaths according to the commandments regarding the Sabbaths of the land, as it is written in the tablets, which He gave into my hands that I should write out for thee the laws of the seasons, and the seasons according to the division of their days. Herewith is completed the account of the division of the days.

The Book of Enoch

Abbreviations, Brackets, and Symbols

[ ] The use of these brackets means that the words so enclosed are found in Gg but not In E.
[[ ]] The use of these brackets means that the words so enclosed are found in E but not in Gg or Gs.
< > The use of these brackets means that the words so enclosed are restored.
[] The use of these brackets means that the words so enclosed are interpolations.
( ) The use of these brackets means that the words so enclosed are supplied by the editor.
The use of **thick type** denotes that the words so printed are emended.
† † corruption in the text.
. . . some words which have been lost.

The following abbreviations are used in the translation of Enoch:

E denotes the Ethiopic Version.
G^g denotes the large fragment of the Greek Version discovered at Akhmîm, and deposited in the Gizeh Museum, Cairo.

I-XXXVI

I-V. Parable of Enoch on the Future Lot of the Wicked and the Righteous.

1

¹ The words of the blessing of Enoch, wherewith he blessed the elect [[and]] righteous, who will be living in the day of tribulation, when all the wicked [[and godless]] are to be removed. ² And he took up his parable and said–Enoch a righteous man, whose eyes were opened by God, saw the vision of the Holy One in the heavens, [which] the angels showed me, and from them I heard everything, and from them I understood as I saw, but not for this generation, but for a remote one which is for to come. ³ Concerning the elect I said, and took up my parable concerning them: The Holy Great One will come forth from His dwelling, ⁴ And the eternal God will tread upon the earth, (even) on Mount Sinai, [And appear from His camp] And appear in the strength of His might from the heaven of heavens. ⁵ And all shall be smitten with fear And the Watchers shall quake, And great fear and trembling shall seize them unto the ends of the earth. ⁶ And the high mountains shall be shaken, And the high hills shall be made low, And shall melt like wax before the flame ⁷ And the earth shall be [wholly] rent in sunder, And all that is upon the earth shall perish, And there shall be a judgement upon all (men). ⁸ But with the righteous He will make peace. And will protect the elect, And mercy shall be upon them. And they shall all belong to God, And they shall be prospered, And they shall [all] be blessed. [And He will help them all], And light shall appear unto them, [And He will make peace with them]. ⁹ And behold! He cometh with ten thousands of [His] holy ones To execute judgement upon all, And to destroy [all] the ungodly: And to convict all flesh Of all the works [of their ungodliness] which they have ungodly committed, And of all the hard things which ungodly sinners [have spoken] against Him.

2

¹ Observe ye everything that takes place in the heaven, how they do not change their orbits, [and] the luminaries which are in the heaven, how they all rise and set in order each in its season, and transgress not against their appointed order. ² Behold ye the earth, and give heed to the things which take place upon it from first to last, [how **steadfast** they are], how [none of the things upon earth] change, [but] all the works of God appear [to you]. ³ Behold the summer and the winter, [[how the whole earth is filled with water, and clouds and dew and rain lie upon it]].

3

¹ Observe and see how (in the winter) all the trees [[seem as though they had withered and shed all their leaves, except fourteen trees, which do not lose their foliage but retain the old foliage from two to three years till the new comes.

4

¹ And again, observe ye the days of summer how the sun is above the earth over against it. And you seek shade and shelter by reason of the heat of the sun, and the earth also burns with growing heat, and so you cannot tread on the earth, or on a rock by reason of its heat.

5

¹ Observe [[ye]] how the trees cover themselves with green leaves and bear fruit: wherefore give ye heed [and know] with regard to all [His works], and recognize how He that liveth for ever hath made them so. ² And [all] His works go on [thus] from year to year for ever, and all the tasks [which

they accomplish for Him, and [their tasks] change not, but according as [[God]] hath ordained so is it done. ³ And behold how the sea and the rivers in like manner accomplish and [change not] their tasks [from His commandments]. ⁴ But ye–ye have not been steadfast, nor done the commandments of the Lord, But ye have turned away and spoken proud and hard words With your impure mouths against His greatness. Oh, ye hard-hearted, ye shall find no peace. ⁵ Therefore shall ye execrate your days, And the years of your life shall perish, And [the years of your destruction] shall be multiplied in eternal execration, And ye shall find no mercy. ⁶ a In those days ye shall make your names an eternal execration unto all the righteous, b And by you shall [all] who curse, curse, And all the sinners [and godless] shall imprecate by you, c And for you the godless there shall be a curse. d And all the . . . shall rejoice, e And there shall be forgiveness of sins, f And every mercy and peace and forbearance: g There shall be salvation unto them, a goodly light. i And for all of you sinners there shall be no salvation, j But on you all shall abide a curse. ⁷ a But for the elect there shall be light and joy and peace, b And they shall inherit the earth. ⁸ And then there shall be bestowed upon the elect wisdom, And they shall all live and never again sin, Either through ungodliness or through pride: But they who are wise shall be humble. ⁹ And they shall not again transgress, Nor shall they sin all the days of their life, Nor shall they die of (the divine) anger or wrath, But they shall complete the number of the days of their life. And their lives shall be increased in peace, And the years of their joy shall be multiplied, In eternal gladness and peace, All the days of their life.

VI-XI. The Fall of the Angels: the Demoralisation of Mankind: the Intercession of the Angels on behalf of Mankind. The Dooms pronounced by God on the Angels: the Messianic Kingdom (a Noah fragment).

6

¹ And it came to pass when the children of men had multiplied that in those days were born unto them beautiful and comely daughters. ² And the angels, the children of the heaven, saw and lusted after them, and said to one another: 'Come, let us choose us wives from among the children of men and beget us children.' ³ And Semjâzâ, who was their leader, said unto them: 'I fear ye will not indeed agree to do this deed, and I alone shall have to pay the penalty of a great sin.' ⁴ And they all answered him and said: 'Let us all swear an oath, and all bind ourselves by mutual imprecations not to abandon this plan but to do this thing.' ⁵ Then sware they all together and bound themselves by mutual imprecations upon it. ⁶ And they were in all two hundred; who descended [in the days] of **Jared** on the summit of Mount Hermon, and they called it Mount Hermon, because they had sworn and bound themselves by mutual imprecations upon it. ⁷ And these are the names of their leaders: Sêmîazâz, their leader, Arâkîba, Râmêêl, Kôkabîêl, Tâmîêl, Râmîêl, Dânêl, Êzêqêêl, Barâqîjâl, Asâêl, Armârôs, Batârêl, Anânêl, Zaqîêl, Samsâpêêl, Satarêl, Tûrêl, Jômjâêl, Sariêl. ⁸ These are their chiefs of tens.

7

¹ And all the others together with them took unto themselves wives, and each chose for himself one, and they began to go in unto them and to defile themselves with them, and they taught them charms and enchantments, and the cutting of roots, and made them acquainted with plants. ² And they became pregnant, and they bare great giants, whose height was three thousand ells: ³ Who consumed all the acquisitions of men. And when men could no longer sustain them, ⁴ the giants turned against them and devoured mankind. ⁵ And they began to sin against birds, and beasts, and reptiles, and fish, and to devour one another's flesh, and drink the blood. ⁶ Then the earth laid accusation against the lawless ones.

8

¹ And Azâzêl taught men to make swords, and knives, and shields, and breastplates, and made known to them **the metals** <of the earth> and the art of working them, and bracelets, and ornaments, and the use of antimony, and the beautifying of the eyelids, and all kinds of costly stones, and all colouring tinctures. ² And there arose much godlessness, and they committed fornication, and they were led astray, and became corrupt in all their ways. Semjâzâ taught enchantments, and root-cuttings, Armârôs the resolving of enchantments, Barâqîjâl, (taught) astrology, Kôkabêl the constellations, **Ezêqêêl the knowledge of the clouds,** <Araqiêl the signs of the earth, Shamsiêl the signs of the sun>, and Sariêl the course of the moon. And as men perished, they cried, and their cry went up to heaven . . .

9

¹ And then Michael, Uriel, Raphael, and Gabriel looked down from heaven and saw much blood being shed upon the earth, and all lawlessness being wrought upon the earth. ² And they said one to another: 'The earth made †without inhabitant cries the voice of their crying† up to the gates of heaven. ³ [[And now to you, the holy ones of heaven]], the souls of men make their suit, saying, "Bring our cause before the Most High.".' ⁴ And they said to the Lord **of the ages**: 'Lord of lords, God of gods, King of kings, <and God of the ages>, the throne of Thy glory (standeth) unto all the generations of the ages, and Thy name holy and glorious and blessed unto all the ages! ⁵ Thou hast made all things, and power over all things hast Thou: and all things are naked and open in Thy sight, and Thou seest all things, and nothing can hide itself from Thee. ⁶ Thou seest what Azâzêl hath done, who hath taught all unrighteousness on earth and revealed the eternal secrets which were (preserved) in heaven, which men were striving to **learn**: ⁷ And Semjâzâ, to whom Thou hast given authority to bear rule over his associates. ⁸ And they have gone to the daughters of men upon the earth, and have slept with the women, and have defiled themselves, and revealed to them all kinds of sins. ⁹ And the women have borne giants, and the whole earth has thereby been filled with blood and unrighteousness. ¹⁰ And now, behold, the souls of those who have died are crying and making their suit to the gates of heaven, and their lamentations have ascended: and cannot **cease** because of the lawless deeds which are wrought on the earth. ¹¹ And Thou knowest all things before they come to pass, and Thou seest these things and Thou dost suffer them, and Thou dost not say to us what we are to do to them in regard to these.'

10

¹ Then said the Most High, the Holy and Great One spake, and sent **Uriel** to the son of Lamech, and said to him: ² '<Go to Noah> and tell him in my name "Hide thyself!" and reveal to him the end that is approaching: that the whole earth will be destroyed, and a deluge is about to come upon the whole earth, and will destroy all that is on it. ³ And now instruct him that he may escape and his seed may be preserved for all the generations of the world.' ⁴ And again the Lord said to Raphael: 'Bind Azâzêl hand and foot, and cast him into the darkness: and make an opening in the desert, which is in Dûdâêl, and cast him therein. ⁵ And place upon him rough and jagged rocks, and cover him with darkness, and let him abide there for ever, and cover his face that he may not see light. ⁶ And on the day of the great judgement he shall be cast into the fire. ⁷ And heal the earth which the angels have corrupted, and proclaim the healing of the earth, that they may heal the plague, and that all the children of men may not perish through all the secret things that the Watchers have **disclosed** and have taught their sons. ⁸ And the whole earth has been corrupted through the works that were taught by Azâzêl: to him ascribe all sin.' ⁹ And to Gabriel said the Lord: 'Proceed against the bastards and the reprobates, and against the children of fornication: and destroy [the children of fornication and] the children of the Watchers from amongst men [and cause them to go forth]: send them one against the other that they may destroy each other in battle: for length of days shall they not have. ¹⁰ And no request that they (*i.e.* their fathers) make of thee shall be granted unto their fathers on their behalf; for they hope to live an eternal life, and that each one of them will live five hundred years.' ¹¹ And the Lord said unto Michael: 'Go, **bind** Semjâzâ and his associates who have united themselves with women so as to have defiled themselves with them in all their uncleanness. ¹² And when their sons have slain one another, and they have seen the destruction of their beloved ones, bind them fast for seventy generations in the **valleys** of the earth, till the day of their judgement and of their consummation, till the judgement that is for ever and ever is consummated. ¹³ In those days they shall be led off to the abyss of fire: <and> to the torment and the prison in which they shall be confined for ever. ¹⁴ And whosoever shall be **condemned** and destroyed will from thenceforth be bound together with them to the end of all generations. ¹⁵ And destroy all the spirits of the reprobate and the children of the Watchers, because they have wronged mankind. ¹⁶ Destroy all wrong from the face of the earth and let every evil work come to an end: and let the plant of righteousness and truth appear: [and it shall prove a blessing; the works of righteousness and truth] shall be planted in truth and joy for evermore. ¹⁷ And then shall all the righteous escape, And shall live till they beget thousands of children, And all the days of their youth and their **old age** Shall they complete in peace. ¹⁸ And then shall the whole earth be tilled in righteousness, and shall all be planted with trees and be full of blessing. ¹⁹ And all desirable trees shall be planted on it, and they shall plant vines on it: and the vine which they plant thereon shall yield wine in abundance, and as for all the seed which is sown thereon each measure (of it) shall bear a thousand, and each measure of olives shall yield ten presses of oil. ²⁰ And cleanse thou the earth from all oppression, and from all unrighteousness, and from all sin, and from all godlessness: and all the uncleanness that is wrought upon the earth destroy from off the earth. ²¹ [And all the children of men shall become righteous], and all nations shall offer adoration and shall praise Me, and all shall worship Me. And the earth shall be cleansed from all defilement, and from all sin, and from all punishment, and from all

torment, and I will never again send (them) upon it from generation to generation and for ever.

11

[1] And in those days I will open the store chambers of blessing which are in the heaven, so as to send them down [upon the earth] over the work and labour of the children of men. [2] And truth and peace shall be associated together throughout all the days of the world and throughout all the generations **of men**.'

XII-XVI. Dream Vision of Enoch: his intercession for Azâzêl and the fallen Angels: and his announcement to them of their first and final doom.

12

[1] Before these things Enoch was hidden, and no one of the children of men knew where he was hidden, and where he abode, and what had become of him. [2] And his activities had to do with the Watchers, and his days were with the holy ones. [3] And I, Enoch was blessing the Lord of **majesty** and the King of the ages, and lo! the Watchers called me–Enoch the scribe–and said to me: [4] 'Enoch, thou scribe of righteousness, go, †declare† to the Watchers of the heaven who have left the high heaven, the holy eternal place, and have defiled themselves with women, and have done as the children of earth do, and have taken unto themselves wives: "Ye have wrought great destruction on the earth: [5] And ye shall have no peace nor forgiveness of sin: and inasmuch as †they† delight themselves in †their† children, [6] The murder of †their† beloved ones shall †they† see, and over the destruction of †their† children shall †they† lament, and shall make supplication unto eternity, but mercy and peace shall ye not attain."'

13

[1] And Enoch went and said: 'Azâzêl, thou shalt have no peace: a severe sentence has gone forth against thee to put thee in bonds: [2] And thou shalt not have toleration nor †request† granted to thee, because of the unrighteousness which thou hast taught, and because of all the works of godlessness and unrighteousness and sin which thou hast shown to men.' [3] Then I went and spoke to them all together, and they were all afraid, and fear and trembling seized them. [4] And they besought me to draw up a petition for them that they might find forgiveness, and to read their petition in the presence of the Lord of heaven. [5] For from thenceforward they could not speak (with Him) nor lift up their eyes to heaven for shame of their sins for which they had been condemned. [6] Then I wrote out their petition, and the prayer in regard to their spirits and their deeds individually and in regard to their requests that they should have forgiveness and length <of days>. [7] And I went off and sat down at the waters of Dan, in the land of Dan, to the south of the west of Hermon: I read their petition till I fell asleep. [8] And behold a dream came to me, and visions fell down upon me, and I saw visions of chastisement, [and a voice came bidding (me)] I to tell it to the sons of heaven, and reprimand them. [9] And when I awaked, I came unto them, and they were all sitting gathered together, weeping in 'Abelsjâîl, which is between Lebanon and Sênêsêr, with their faces covered. [10] And I recounted before them all the visions which I had seen in sleep, and I began to speak the words of righteousness, and to reprimand the heavenly Watchers.

14

[1] The book of the words of righteousness, and of the reprimand of the eternal Watchers in accordance with the command of the Holy Great One in that vision. [2] I saw in my sleep what I will now say with a tongue of flesh and with the breath of my mouth: which the Great One has given to men to converse therewith and understand with the heart. [3] As He has created and given [[to man the power of understanding the word of wisdom, so hath He created me also and given]] me the power of reprimanding the Watchers, the children of heaven. [4] I wrote out your petition, and in my vision it appeared thus, that your petition will not be granted unto you [[throughout all the days of eternity, and that judgement has been finally passed upon you: yea (your petition) will not be granted unto you]]. [5] And from henceforth you shall not ascend into heaven unto all eternity, and [in bonds] of the earth the decree has gone forth to bind you for all the days of the world. [6] And (that) previously you shall have seen the destruction of your beloved sons and ye shall have no pleasure in them, but they shall fall before you by the sword. [7] And your petition on their behalf shall not be granted, nor yet on your own: even though you weep and pray and **speak all the words** contained in the writing which I have written. [8] And the vision was shown to me thus: Behold, in the vision clouds invited me and a mist summoned me, and the course of the stars and the lightnings sped and **hastened** me, and the winds in the vision caused me to fly and lifted me upward, and bore me into heaven. [9] And I went in till I drew nigh to a wall which is built of crystals and surrounded by tongues of fire: and it began to affright me. [10] And I went into the tongues of fire and drew nigh to a large house which was built of crystals: and the walls of the house were like a tesselated floor (made) of crystals, and its groundwork was of crystal. [11] Its ceiling was like the path of the stars and the lightnings, and between them were fiery cherubim, and their heaven was (clear as) water. [12] A flaming fire surrounded the walls, and its portals blazed with fire. [13] And I entered into that house, and it was hot as fire and cold as ice: there were no delights of life therein: fear covered me, and trembling got hold upon me. [14] And as I quaked and trembled, I fell upon my face. [15] And I beheld a vision, And lo! there was a second house, greater than the former, and the entire portal stood open before me, and it was built of flames of fire. [16] And in every respect it so excelled in splendour and magnificence and extent that I cannot describe to you its splendour and its extent. [17] And its floor was of fire, and above it were lightnings and the path of the stars, and its ceiling also was flaming fire. [18] And I looked and saw [[therein]] a lofty throne: its appearance was as crystal, and the wheels thereof as the shining sun, and there was the **vision** of cherubim. [19] And from underneath the throne came streams of flaming fire so that I could not look thereon. [20] And the Great Glory sat thereon, and His raiment shone more brightly than the sun and was whiter than any snow. [21] None of the angels could enter and could behold His face by reason of the magnificence and glory and no flesh could behold Him. [22] The flaming fire was round about Him, and a great fire stood before Him, and none around could draw nigh Him: ten thousand times ten thousand (stood) before Him, yet He needed no counselor. [23] And the most holy ones who were nigh to Him did not leave by night nor depart from Him. [24] And until then I had been prostrate on my face, trembling: and the Lord called me with His own mouth, and said to me: 'Come hither, Enoch, and hear my word.' [25] [And one of the holy ones came to me and waked me], and He made me rise up and approach the door: and I bowed my face downwards.

15

[1] And He answered and said to me, and I heard His voice: 'Fear not, Enoch, thou righteous man and scribe of righteousness: approach hither and hear my voice. [2] And go, say to [[the Watchers of heaven]], who have sent thee to intercede [[for them: "You should intercede"]] for men, and not men for you: [3] Wherefore have ye left the high, holy, and eternal heaven, and lain with women, and defiled yourselves with the daughters of men and taken to yourselves wives, and done like the children of earth, and begotten giants (as your) sons? [4] And though ye were holy, spiritual, living the eternal life, you have defiled yourselves with the blood of women, and have begotten (children) with the blood of flesh, and, **as the children** of men, have lusted after flesh and blood as those [also] do who die and perish. [5] Therefore have I given them wives also that they might impregnate them, and beget children by them, that thus nothing might be wanting to them on earth. [6] But you were [formerly] spiritual, living the eternal life, and immortal for all generations of the world. [7] And therefore I have not appointed wives for you; for as for the spiritual ones of the heaven, in heaven is their dwelling. [8] And now, the giants, who are produced from the spirits and flesh, shall be called evil spirits upon the earth, and on the earth shall be their dwelling. [9] Evil spirits have proceeded from their bodies; because they are born from **men**, [[and]] from the holy Watchers is their beginning and primal origin; [they shall be evil spirits on earth, and] evil spirits shall they be called. [10] [As for the spirits of heaven, in heaven shall be their dwelling, but as for the spirits of the earth which were born upon the earth, on the earth shall be their dwelling.] [11] And the spirits of the giants **afflict**, oppress, destroy, attack, do battle, and work destruction on the earth, and cause trouble: they take no food, [but nevertheless hunger] and thirst, and cause offences. And these spirits shall rise up against the children of men and against the women, because they have proceeded [from them].

16

[1] From the days of the slaughter and destruction and death [of the giants], from the souls of whose flesh the spirits, having gone forth, shall destroy without incurring judgement–thus shall they destroy until the day of the consummation, the great [judgement] in which the age shall be consummated, over the Watchers and the godless, yea, shall be wholly consummated." [2] And now as to the Watchers who have sent thee to intercede for them, who had been [[aforetime]] in heaven, (say to them): [3] "You have been in heaven, but [all] the mysteries had not yet been revealed to you, and you knew worthless ones, and these in the hardness of your hearts you have made known to the women, and through these mysteries women and men work much evil on earth." [4] Say to them therefore: "You have no peace."'

XVII-XXXVII. Enoch's Journeys through the Earth and Sheol.

XVII-XIX. The First Journey.

17

¹ And they took [and] brought me to a place in which those who were there were like flaming fire, and, when they wished, they appeared as men. ² And they brought me to the place of darkness, and to a mountain the point of whose summit reached to heaven. ³ And I saw the places of the luminaries [and the treasuries of the stars] and of the thunder [and] in the **uttermost depths**, where were a fiery bow and arrows and their quiver, and [[a fiery sword]] and all the lightnings. ⁴ And they took me to the living waters, and to the fire of the west, which receives every setting of the sun. ⁵ And I came to a river of fire in which the fire flows like water and discharges itself into the great sea towards the west. ⁶ I saw the great rivers and came to the great [river and to the great] darkness, and went to the place where no flesh walks. ⁷ I saw the mountains of the darkness of winter and the place whence all the waters of the deep flow. ⁸ I saw the mouths of all the rivers of the earth and the mouth of the deep.

18

¹ I saw the treasuries of all the winds: I saw how He had furnished with them the whole creation and the firm foundations of the earth. ² And I saw the corner-stone of the earth: I saw the four winds which bear [the earth and] the firmament of the heaven. ³ [[And I saw how the winds stretch out the vaults of heaven]], and have their station between heaven and earth: [[these are the pillars of the heaven]]. ⁴ I saw the winds of heaven which turn and bring the circumference of the sun and all the stars to their setting. ⁵ I saw the winds on the earth carrying the clouds: I saw [[the paths of the angels. I saw]] at the end of the earth the firmament of the heaven above. ⁶ And I proceeded and saw a place which burns day and night, where there are seven mountains of magnificent stones, three towards the east, and three towards the south. ⁷ And as for those towards the east, <one> was of coloured stone, and one of pearl, and one of **jacinth**, and those towards the south of red stone. ⁸ But the middle one reached to heaven like the throne of God, of alabaster, and the summit of the throne was of sapphire. ⁹ And I saw a flaming fire. And beyond these mountains ¹⁰ is a region the end of the great earth: there the heavens were completed. ¹¹ And I saw a deep abyss, with columns [[of heavenly fire, and among them I saw columns]] of fire fall, which were beyond measure alike towards the height and towards the depth. ¹² And beyond that abyss I saw a place which had no firmament of the heaven above, and no firmly founded earth beneath it: there was no water upon it, and no birds, but it was a waste and horrible place. ¹³ I saw there seven stars like great burning mountains, and to me, when I inquired regarding them, ¹⁴ The angel said: 'This place is the end of heaven and earth: this has become a prison for the stars and the host of heaven. ¹⁵ And the stars which roll over the fire are they which have transgressed the commandment of the Lord in the beginning of their rising, because they did not come forth at their appointed times. ¹⁶ And He was wroth with them, and bound them till the time when their guilt should be consummated (even) [for ten thousand years].'

19

¹ And Uriel said to me: 'Here shall stand the angels who have connected themselves with women, and their spirits assuming many different forms are defiling mankind and shall lead them astray into sacrificing to demons [[as gods]], (here shall they stand,) till [[the day of]] the great judgement in which they shall be judged till they are made an end of. ² And the women also of the angels who went astray shall become sirens.' ³ And I, Enoch, alone saw the vision, the ends of all things: and no man shall see as I have seen.

XX. Name and Functions of the Seven Archangels.

20

¹ And these are the names of the holy angels who watch. ² Uriel, one of the holy angels, who is over the world and over Tartarus. ³ Raphael, one of the holy angels, who is over the spirits of men. ⁴ Raguel, one of the holy angels who †takes vengeance on† the world of the luminaries. ⁵ Michael, one of the holy angels, to wit, he that is set over the best part of mankind [[and]] over chaos. ⁶ Saraqâêl, one of the holy angels, who is set over the spirits, who sin in the spirit. ⁷ Gabriel, one of the holy angels, who is over Paradise and the serpents and the Cherubim. ⁸ Remiel, one of the holy angels, whom God set over those who rise.

XXI. Preliminary and final place of punishment of the fallen angels (stars).

21

¹ And I proceeded to where things were chaotic. ² And I saw there something horrible: I saw neither a heaven above nor a firmly founded earth, but a place chaotic and horrible. ³ And there I saw seven stars of the heaven bound together in it, like great mountains and burning with fire. ⁴ Then I said: 'For what sin are they bound, and on what account have they been cast in hither?' ⁵ Then said Uriel, one of the holy angels, who was with me, and was chief over them, and said: 'Enoch, why dost thou ask, and why art thou eager for the truth? ⁶ These are of the number of the stars [of heaven], which have transgressed the commandment of the Lord, and are bound here till ten thousand years, the time entailed by their sins, are consummated.' ⁷ And from thence I went to another place, which was still more horrible than the former, and I saw a horrible thing: a great fire there which burnt and blazed, and the place was cleft as far as the abyss, being full of great descending columns of fire: neither its extent or magnitude could I see, nor could I conjecture. ⁸ Then I said: 'How fearful is the place and how terrible to look upon!' ⁹ Then Uriel answered me, one of the holy angels who was with me, and said unto me: 'Enoch, why hast thou such fear and affright?' And I answered: 'Because of this fearful place, and because of the spectacle of the pain.' ¹⁰ And he said [[unto me]]: 'This place is the prison of the angels, and here they will be imprisoned for ever.'

XXII. Sheol, or the Underworld.

22

¹ And thence I went to another place, and he showed me in the west [another] great and high mountain [and] of hard rock.

E	Gᵍ
² And there was in it †four† **hollow** places, deep and wide and very smooth. †How† smooth are **the hollow places** and deep and dark to look at.	² And there were †four† hollow places in it, deep and very smooth: †three† of them were dark and one and deep and bright; and there was a fountain of water in its midst. And I said: '†How† smooth are these hollow places, and deep and dark to view.'

³ Then Raphael answered, one of the holy angels who was with me, and said unto me: 'These hollow places have been created for this very purpose, that the spirits of the souls of the dead should assemble therein, yea that all the souls of the children of men should assemble here. ⁴ And these places **have been made** to receive them till the day of their judgement and till their appointed period [till the period appointed], till the great judgement (comes) upon them.'

E	Gᵍ
⁵ I saw the spirits of the children of men who were dead, and their voice went forth to heaven and made suit.	⁵ I saw (the spirit of) **a dead man** making suit, and his voice went forth to heaven and made suit.
⁶ Then I asked Raphael the angel who was with me, and I said unto him: 'This spirit–whose is it whose voice goeth forth and maketh suit?'	⁶ And I asked Raphael the angel who was with me, and I said unto him: 'This spirit which maketh suit, whose is it, whose voice goeth forth and maketh suit to heaven?'

⁷ And he answered me saying: 'This is the spirit which went forth from Abel, whom his brother Cain slew, and he makes his suit against him till his seed is destroyed from the face of the earth, and his seed is annihilated from amongst the seed of men.'

E	Gᵍ
⁸ Then I asked regarding it, and regarding all the **hollow places**: 'Why as one separated from the other?'	⁸ Then I asked regarding all the **hollow places**: 'Why is one separated from the other?'
⁹ And he answered me and said unto me: 'These three have been made that the spirits of the dead might be separated. And such a division has been made <for> the spirits of the righteous, in which there is the **bright** spring of **water**.	⁹ And he answered me saying: 'These three have been made that the spirits of the dead might be separated. And **this** division has been made for the spirits of the righteous, in which there is the bright spring of water.
¹⁰ **And** such has been made for sinners when they die and are buried in the earth and judgement has not been executed upon them in their lifetime.	¹⁰ And **this** has been made for sinners when they die and are buried in the earth and judgement has not been executed on them in their lifetime.
¹¹ Here their spirits shall be set apart in this great pain, till the great day of judgement and punishment and torments of the accursed for ever, retribution for their spirits. There He shall bind them for ever.	¹¹ Here their spirits shall be set apart in this great pain till the great day of judgement, scourgings, and torment of those who †curse† for ever, and retribution for their spirits. There He shall bind them for ever.
¹² And such a division has been made for the spirits of those who	¹² And **this** division has been made for the spirits of those who make

make their suit, who make disclosures concerning their destruction, when they were slain in the days of the sinners.	make their suit, who make their suit, who disclosures concerning their destruction, when they were slain in the days of the sinners.
¹³ Such has been made for the spirits of men who were not righteous but sinners, who were complete in transgression, and of transgressors. they shall be companions: but their spirits shall not be slain in the day of judgement nor shall they be raised from thence.	¹³ And **this** has been made for the spirits of men who shall not be righteous but sinners, who are godless, and of the lawless they shall be companions: but their spirits shall not be punished in the day of judgement nor shall they be raised from thence.
¹⁴ Then I blessed the Lord of glory and said: 'Blessed be my Lord, the Lord of righteousness, who ruleth for ever.'	¹⁴ Then I blessed the Lord of Glory and said: 'Blessed art Thou, Lord of righteousness, who rulest over the world.'

XXIII. The Fire that deals with the Luminaries of Heaven.

23

¹ From thence I went to another place to the west of the ends of the earth. ² And I saw a [[burning]] fire which ran without resting, and paused not from its course day or night but (ran) regularly. ³ And I asked saying: 'What is this which rests not?' ⁴ Then Raguel, one of the holy angels who was with me, answered me [[and said unto me]]: 'This course [of fire] [[which thou hast seen]] is the fire in the west which †persecutes† all the luminaries of heaven.'

XXIV. XXV. The Seven Mountains in the North-West and the Tree of Life.

24

¹ [[And from thence I went to another place of the earth]], and he showed me a mountain range of fire which burnt [[day and night]]. ² And I went beyond it and saw seven magnificent mountains all differing each from the other, and the stones (thereof) were magnificent and beautiful, magnificent as a whole, of glorious appearance and fair exterior: [[three towards]] the east, [[one]] founded on the other, and three towards the south, one upon the other, and deep rough ravines, no one of which joined with any other. ³ And the seventh mountain was in the midst of these, and it excelled them in height, resembling the seat of a throne: and fragrant trees encircled the throne. ⁴ And amongst them was a tree such as I had never yet smelt, neither was any amongst them nor were others like it: it had a fragrance beyond all fragrance, and its leaves and blooms and wood wither not for ever: and its fruit [[is beautiful, and its fruit]] resembles the dates of a palm. ⁵ Then I said: '[How] beautiful is this tree, and fragrant, and its leaves are fair, and its blooms [[very]] delightful in appearance.' ⁶ Then answered Michael, one of the holy [[and honoured]] angels who was with me, and was their leader.

25

¹ And he said unto me: 'Enoch, why dost thou ask me regarding the fragrance of the tree, and [why] dost thou wish to learn the truth?' ² Then I answered him [[saying]]: 'I wish to know about everything, but especially about this tree.' ³ And he answered saying: 'This high mountain [[which thou hast seen]], whose summit is like the throne of God, is His throne, where the Holy Great One, the Lord of Glory, the Eternal King, will sit, when He shall come down to visit the earth with goodness. ⁴ And as for this fragrant tree no mortal is permitted to touch it till the great judgement, when He shall take vengeance on all and bring (everything) to its consummation for ever. It shall then be given to the righteous and holy. ⁵ Its fruit **shall be** for food to the elect: it shall be transplanted to the holy place, to the temple of the Lord, the Eternal King. ⁶ Then shall they rejoice with joy and be glad, And into the holy place shall they enter; And its fragrance shall be in their bones, And they shall live a long life on earth, Such as thy fathers lived: And in their days shall no [[sorrow or]] plague Or torment or calamity touch them.' ⁷ Then blessed I the God of Glory, the Eternal King, who hath prepared such things for the righteous, and hath created them and promised to give to them.

XXVI. Jerusalem and the Mountains, Ravines and Streams.

26

¹ And I went from thence to the middle of the earth, and I saw a blessed place [in which there were trees] with branches abiding and blooming [of a dismembered tree]. ² And there I saw a holy mountain, [[and]] underneath the mountain to the east there was a stream and it flowed towards the south. ³ And I saw towards the east another mountain higher than this, and between them a deep and narrow ravine: in it also ran a stream [underneath] the mountain. ⁴ And to the west thereof there was another mountain, lower than the former and of small elevation, and a ravine [deep and dry] between them: and another deep and dry ravine was at the extremities of the three [mountains]. ⁵ And all the ravines were deep [[and narrow]], (being formed) of hard rock, and trees were not planted upon them. ⁶ And I marveled [[at the rocks, and I marveled]] at the ravine, yea, I marveled very much.

XXVII. The Purpose of the Accursed Valley.

27

¹ Then said I: 'For what object is this blessed land, which is entirely filled with trees, and this accursed valley [[between]]?' ² [[Then Uriel, one of the holy angels who was with me, answered and said: 'This]] accursed valley is for those who are accursed for ever: Here shall all [the accursed] be gathered together who utter with their lips against the Lord unseemly words and of His glory speak hard things.

E	G^g
Here shall they be gathered together, and here shall be their place of judgement.	Here shall they be gathered together, and here shall be the place of their habitation.
³ In the last days there shall be upon them the spectacle of righteous judgement in the presence of the righteous for ever: here shall the merciful bless the Lord of Glory, the Eternal King.	³ In the last times, in the days of true judgement in the presence of the righteous for ever: here shall the **godly** bless the Lord of Glory, the Eternal King.

⁴ In the days of judgement over the former, they shall bless Him for the mercy in accordance with which He has assigned them (their lot).' ⁵ Then I blessed the Lord of Glory and set forth His [glory] and lauded Him gloriously.

XXVIII-XXXIII. Further Journey to the East.

28

¹ And thence I went [[towards the east]], into the midst [[of the mountain range of the desert]], and I saw a wilderness and it was solitary, full of trees **and plants**. ² [[And]] water gushed forth from above. ³ Rushing like a copious watercourse [which flowed] towards the north-west it caused **clouds** and dew to ascend on every side.

29

¹ And thence I went to another place in the desert, and approached to the east of this mountain range. ² And [[there]] I saw **aromatic** trees exhaling the fragrance of frankincense and myrrh, and the trees also were similar to the almond tree.

30

¹ And beyond these, I went afar to the east, and I saw another place, a valley (full) of water. ² And [therein there was] a tree, the colour (?) of fragrant trees such as the mastic. ³ And on the sides of those valleys I saw fragrant cinnamon. And beyond these I proceeded to the east.

31

¹ And I saw other mountains, and amongst them were [groves of] trees, and there flowed forth from them nectar, which is named sarara and galbanum. ² And beyond these mountains I saw another mountain [to the east of the ends of the earth], [[whereon were aloe trees]], and all the trees were full **of stacte**, being like almond-trees. ³ And when one **burnt** it, it smelt sweeter than any fragrant odour.

32

E	G^g
¹ And after these fragrant odours, as I looked towards the north over the mountains I saw seven mountains full of choice nard and fragrant trees and cinnamon and pepper.	¹ To the north-east I beheld seven mountains full of choice nard and mastic and cinnamon and pepper.

² And thence I went over the summits of [all] these mountains, far towards the east [of the earth], and passed above the Erythraean sea and went far from it, and passed over [[the angel]] Zotîêl.

E	G^g
³ And I came to the Garden of Righteousness, and saw beyond those trees many large trees growing there and of goodly fragrance, large, and great–†two† trees there, very beautiful and glorious, and the tree of wisdom whereof they eat and know great wisdom.	³ And I came to the Garden of Righteousness, and from afar off trees more numerous than these trees and great, very beautiful and glorious, and the great, beautiful, and magnificent, and the tree of knowledge, whose holy fruit they eat and know great wisdom.

⁴ [That tree is in height like the fir, and its leaves are] like (those of) the Carob tree: and its fruit is like the clusters of the vine, very beautiful: and the fragrance of the tree penetrates afar. ⁵ Then I said: '[How] beautiful is the tree, and how attractive is its look!' ⁶ Then Raphael the holy angel, who was with me, answered me [[and said]]: 'This is the tree of wisdom, of which thy father old (in years) and thy aged mother, who were before thee, have eaten, and they learnt wisdom and their eyes were opened, and they knew that they were naked and they were driven out of the garden.'

33

¹ And from thence I went to the ends of the earth and saw there great beasts, and each differed from the other; and (I saw) birds also differing in appearance and beauty and voice, the one differing from the other. ² And to the east of those beasts I saw the ends of the earth whereon the heaven rests, and the portals of the heaven open. ³ And I saw how the stars of heaven come forth, and I counted the portals out of which they proceed, and wrote down all their outlets, of each individual star by itself, according to their number and their names, their courses and their positions, and their times and their months, as Uriel the holy angel who was with me showed me. ⁴ He showed all things to me and wrote them down for me: also their names he wrote for me, and their laws and their companies.

XXXIV. XXXV. Enoch's Journey to the North.

34

¹ And from thence I went towards the north to the ends of the earth, and there I saw a great and glorious device at the ends of the whole earth. ² And here I saw three portals of heaven open in the heaven: through each of them proceed north winds: when they blow there is cold, hail, frost, snow, dew, and rain. ³ And out of one portal they blow for good: but when they blow through the other two portals, it is with violence and affliction on the earth, and they blow with violence.

35

¹ And from thence I went towards the west to the ends of the earth, and saw there three portals of the heaven open such as I had seen in the †east†, the same number of portals, and the same number of outlets.

XXXVI. The Journey to the South.

36

¹ And from thence I went to the south to the ends of the earth, and saw there three open portals of the heaven: and thence there come dew, rain, †and wind†. ² And from thence I went to the east to the ends of the heaven, and saw here the three eastern portals of heaven open and small portals above them. ³ Through each of these small portals pass the stars of heaven and run their course to the west on the path which is shown to them. ⁴ And as often as I saw I blessed always the Lord of Glory, and I continued to bless the Lord of Glory who has wrought great and glorious wonders, to show the greatness of His work to the angels and to **spirits** and to men, that they might praise His work and all His creation: that they might see the work of His might and praise the great work of His hands and bless Him for ever.

XXXVII-LXXI. The Parables.

37

¹ The second vision which he saw, the vision of wisdom–which Enoch the son of Jared, the son of Mahalalel, the son of Cainan, the son of Enos, the son of Seth, the son of Adam, saw. ² And this is the beginning of the words of wisdom which I lifted up my voice to speak and say to those which dwell on earth: Hear, ye men of old time, and see, ye that come after, the words of the Holy One which I will speak before the Lord of Spirits. ³ It were better to declare (them only) to the men of old time, but even from those that come after we will not withhold the beginning of wisdom. ⁴ Till the present day such wisdom has never been given **by** the Lord of Spirits as I have received according to my insight, according to the good pleasure of the Lord of Spirits by whom the lot of eternal life has been given to me. ⁵ Now three parables were imparted to me, and I lifted up my voice and recounted them to those that dwell on the earth.

XXXVII-XLIV. The First Parable.
XXXVIII. The Coming Judgement of the Wicked.

38

¹ The First Parable. When the congregation of the righteous shall appear, And sinners shall be judged for their sins, And shall be driven from the face of the earth: ² And when the Righteous One shall appear before the eyes of the righteous, Whose elect works hang upon the Lord of Spirits, And light shall appear to the righteous and the elect who dwell on the earth, Where then will be the dwelling of the sinners, And where the resting-place of those who have denied the Lord of Spirits? It had been good for them if they had not been born. ³ When the secrets of the righteous shall be revealed and the sinners judged, And the godless driven from the presence of the righteous and elect, ⁴ From that time those that possess the earth shall no longer be powerful and exalted: And they shall not be able to behold the face of the holy, For the Lord of Spirits has **caused His light to appear** On the face of the holy, righteous, and elect. ⁵ Then shall the kings and the mighty perish And be given into the hands of the righteous and holy. ⁶ And thenceforward none shall seek for themselves mercy from the Lord of Spirits For their life is at an end.

XXXIX. The Abode of the Righteous and of the Elect One: the Praises of the Blessed.

39

¹ [And it †shall come to pass in those days that elect and holy children †will descend from the high heaven, and their seed will become one with the children of men. ² And in those days Enoch received books of zeal and wrath, and books of disquiet and expulsion.] And mercy shall not be accorded to them, saith the Lord of Spirits. ³ And in those days a whirlwind carried me off from the earth, And set me down at the end of the heavens. ⁴ And there I saw another vision, the dwelling-places of the holy, And the resting-places of the righteous. ⁵ Here mine eyes saw their dwellings with His righteous angels, And their resting-places with the holy. And they petitioned and interceded and prayed for the children of men, And righteousness flowed before them as water, And mercy like dew upon the earth: Thus it is amongst them for ever and ever. ⁶ a. And in that place mine eyes saw the Elect One of righteousness and of faith, ⁶ b. And I saw his dwelling-place under the wings of the Lord of Spirits. ⁷ a. And righteousness shall prevail in his days, And the righteous and elect shall be without number before Him for ever and ever. ⁷ b. And all the righteous and elect before Him shall be †strong† as fiery lights, And their mouth shall be full of blessing, And their lips extol the name of the Lord of Spirits, And righteousness before Him shall never fail, [And uprightness shall never fail before Him.] ⁸ There I wished to dwell, And my spirit longed for that dwelling-place: And there heretofore hath been my portion, For so has it been established concerning me before the Lord of Spirits. ⁹ In those days I praised and extolled the name of the Lord of Spirits with blessings and praises, because He hath destined me for blessing and glory according to the good pleasure of the Lord of Spirits. ¹⁰ For a long time my eyes regarded that place, and I blessed Him and praised Him, saying: 'Blessed is He, and may He be blessed from the beginning and for evermore. ¹¹ And before Him there is no ceasing. He knows before the world was created what is for ever and what will be from generation unto generation. ¹² Those who sleep not bless Thee: they stand before Thy glory and bless, praise, and extol, saying: "Holy, holy, holy, is the Lord of Spirits: He filleth the earth with spirits."' ¹³ And here my eyes saw all those who sleep not: they stand before Him and bless and say: 'Blessed be Thou, and blessed be the name of the Lord for ever and ever.' ¹⁴ And my face was changed; for I could no longer behold.

XL. XLI. 2. The Four Archangels.

40

¹ And after that I saw thousands of thousands and ten thousand times ten thousand, I saw a multitude beyond number and reckoning, who stood before the Lord of Spirits. ² And on the four sides of the Lord of Spirits I saw four presences, different from those that sleep not, and I learnt their names: for the angel that went with me made known to me their names, and showed me all the hidden things. ³ And I heard the voices of those four presences as they uttered praises before the Lord of glory. ⁴ The first voice blesses the Lord of Spirits for ever and ever. ⁵ And the second voice I heard blessing the Elect One and the elect ones who hang upon the Lord of Spirits. ⁶ And the third voice I heard **pray and intercede** for those who dwell on the earth and **supplicate** in the name of the Lord of Spirits. ⁷ And I heard the fourth voice fending off the Satans and forbidding them to come before the Lord of Spirits to accuse them who dwell on the earth. ⁸ After that I asked the angel of peace who went with me, who showed me everything that is hidden: 'Who are these four presences which I have seen and whose words I have heard and written down?' ⁹ And he said to me: 'This first is Michael, the merciful and long-suffering: and the second, who is set over all the diseases and all the wounds of the children of men, is Raphael: and the third, who is set over all the powers, is Gabriel: and the fourth, who is set over the repentance unto hope of those who inherit eternal life, is named Phanuel.' ¹⁰ And these are the four angels of the Lord of Spirits and the four voices I heard in those days.

41

¹ And after that I saw all the secrets of the heavens, and how the kingdom is divided, and how the actions of men are weighed in the balance. ² And there I saw the mansions of the elect and the mansions of the holy, and mine eyes saw there all the sinners being driven from thence which deny the

name of the Lord of Spirits, and being dragged off: and they could not abide because of the punishment which proceeds from the Lord of Spirits.

XLI. 3-9. Astronomical Secrets.

³ And there mine eyes saw the secrets of the lightning and of the thunder, and the secrets of the winds, how they are divided to blow over the earth, and the secrets of the clouds and dew, and there I saw from whence they proceed in that place and from whence they saturate the dusty earth. ⁴ And there I saw closed chambers out of which the winds are divided, the chamber of the hail and winds, the chamber of the mist, and of the clouds, and the cloud thereof hovers over the earth from the beginning of the world. ⁵ And I saw the chambers of the sun and moon, whence they proceed and whither they come again, and their glorious return, and how one is superior to the other, and their stately orbit, and how they do not leave their orbit, and they add nothing to their orbit and they take nothing from it, and they keep faith with each other, in accordance with the oath by which they are bound together. ⁶ And first the sun goes forth and traverses his path according to the commandment of the Lord of Spirits, and mighty is His name for ever and ever. ⁷ And after that I saw the hidden and the visible path of the moon, and she accomplishes the course of her path in that place by day and by night–the one holding a position opposite to the other before the Lord of Spirits. And they give thanks and praise and rest not; For unto them is their thanksgiving rest. ⁸ For the sun changes oft for a blessing or a curse, And the course of the path of the moon is light to the righteous And darkness to the sinners in the name of the Lord, Who made a separation between the light and the darkness, And divided the spirits of men, And strengthened the spirits of the righteous, In the name of His righteousness. ⁹ For no angel hinders and no power is able to hinder; for He appoints a judge for them all and He judges them all before Him.

XLII. The Dwelling-places of Wisdom and of Unrighteousness.

42

¹ Wisdom found no place where she might dwell; Then a dwelling-place was assigned her in the heavens. ² Wisdom went forth to make her dwelling among the children of men, And found no dwelling-place: Wisdom returned to her place, And took her seat among the angels. ³ And unrighteousness went forth from her chambers: Whom she sought not she found, And dwelt with them, As rain in a desert And dew on a thirsty land.

XLIII. XLIV. Astronomical Secrets.

43

¹ And I saw other lightnings and the stars of heaven, and I saw how He called them all by their names and they hearkened unto Him. ² And I saw how they are weighed in a righteous balance according to their proportions of light: (I saw) the width of their spaces and the day of their appearing, and how their revolution produces lightning: and (I saw) their revolution according to the number of the angels, and (how) they keep faith with each other. ³ And I asked the angel who went with me who showed me what was hidden: 'What are these?' ⁴ And he said to me: 'The Lord of Spirits hath showed thee their parabolic meaning (lit. 'their parable'): these are the names of the holy who dwell on the earth and believe in the name of the Lord of Spirits for ever and ever.'

44

¹ Also another phenomenon I saw in regard to the lightnings: how some of the stars arise and become lightnings and cannot part with their new form.

XLV-LVII. The Second Parable.
The Lot of the Apostates: the New Heaven and the New Earth.

45

¹ And this is the Second Parable concerning those who deny the name of the dwelling of the holy ones and the Lord of Spirits. ² And into the heaven they shall not ascend, And on the earth they shall not come: Such shall be the lot of the sinners Who have denied the name of the Lord of Spirits, Who are thus preserved for the day of suffering and tribulation. ³ On that day Mine Elect One shall sit on the throne of glory And shall **try** their works, And their places of rest shall be innumerable. And their souls shall grow strong within them when they see Mine Elect Ones, And those who have called upon My glorious name: ⁴ Then will I cause Mine Elect One to dwell among them. And I will transform the heaven and make it an eternal blessing and light ⁵ And I will transform the earth and make it a blessing: And I will cause Mine elect ones to dwell upon it: But the sinners and evil-doers shall not set foot thereon. ⁶ For I have provided and satisfied with peace My righteous ones And have caused them to dwell before Me: But for the sinners there is judgement impending with Me, So that I shall destroy them from the face of the earth.

XLVI. The Head of Days and the Son of Man.

46

¹ And there I saw One who had a head of days, And His head was white like wool, And with Him was another being whose countenance had the appearance of a man, And his face was full of graciousness, like one of the holy angels. ² And I asked the **angel** who went with me and showed me all the hidden things, concerning that Son of Man, who he was, and whence he was, (and) why he went with the Head of Days? ³ And he answered and said unto me: This is the son of Man who hath righteousness, With whom dwelleth righteousness, And who revealeth all the treasures of that which is hidden, Because the Lord of Spirits hath chosen him, And whose lot hath the pre-eminence before the Lord of Spirits in uprightness for ever. ⁴, And this Son of Man whom thou hast seen Shall †raise up† the kings and the mighty from their seats, [And the strong from their thrones] And shall loosen the reins of the strong, And break the teeth of the sinners. ⁵ [And he shall put down the kings from their thrones and kingdoms] Because they do not extol and praise Him, Nor humbly acknowledge whence the kingdom was bestowed upon them. ⁶ And he shall put down the countenance of the strong, And shall fill them with shame. And darkness shall be their dwelling, And worms shall be their bed, And they shall have no hope of rising from their beds, Because they do not extol the name of the Lord of Spirits. ⁷ And these are they who †judge† the stars of heaven, [And raise their hands against the Most High], †And tread upon the earth and dwell upon it†. And all their deeds manifest unrighteousness, And their power rests upon their riches, And their faith is in the †gods† which they have made with their hands, And they deny the name of the Lord of Spirits, ⁸ And they persecute the houses of His congregations, And the faithful who hang upon the name of the Lord of Spirits.

XLVII. The Prayer of the Righteous for Vengeance and their Joy at its coming.

47

¹ And in those days shall have ascended the prayer of the righteous, And the blood of the righteous from the earth before the Lord of Spirits. ² In those days the holy ones who dwell above in the heavens Shall unite with one voice And supplicate and pray [and praise, And give thanks and bless the name of the Lord of Spirits] On behalf of the blood of the righteous which has been shed, And that the prayer of the righteous may not be in vain before the Lord of Spirits, That judgement may be done unto them, And that they may not have to suffer for ever. ³ In those days I saw the Head of Days when He seated himself upon the throne of His glory, And the books of the living were opened before Him: And all His host which is in heaven above and His counselors stood before Him, ⁴ And the hearts of the holy were filled with joy; Because the number of the righteous **had been offered**, And the prayer of the righteous had been heard, And the blood of the righteous been required before the Lord of Spirits.

XLVIII. The Fount of Righteousness; the Son of Man–the Stay of the Righteous: Judgement of the Kings and the Mighty.

48

¹ And in that place I saw the fountain of righteousness Which was inexhaustible: And around it were many fountains of wisdom; And all the thirsty drank of them, And were filled with wisdom, And their dwellings were with the righteous and holy and elect. ² And at that hour that Son of Man was named In the presence of the Lord of Spirits, And his name before the Head of Days. ³ Yea, before the sun and the signs were created, Before the stars of the heaven were made, His name was named before the Lord of Spirits. ⁴ He shall be a staff to the righteous whereon to stay themselves and not fall, And he shall be the light of the Gentiles, And the hope of those who are troubled of heart. ⁵ All who dwell on earth shall fall down and worship before him, And will praise and bless and celebrate with song the Lord of Spirits. ⁶ And for this reason hath he been chosen and hidden before Him, Before the creation of the world and for evermore. ⁷ And the wisdom of the Lord of Spirits hath revealed him to the holy and righteous; For he hath preserved the lot of the righteous, Because they have hated and despised this world of unrighteousness, And have hated all its works and ways in the name of the Lord of Spirits: For in his name they are saved, And according to his good pleasure hath it been in regard to their life. ⁸ In these days downcast in countenance shall the kings of the earth have become, And the strong who possess the land because of the works of their hands; For on the day of their anguish and affliction they shall not (be able to) save themselves. ⁹ And I will give them over into the hands of Mine elect: As straw in the fire so shall they burn before the face of the holy: As lead in the water shall they sink before the face of the righteous, And no trace of them shall any more be found. ¹⁰ And on the day of their affliction

there shall be rest on the earth, And before them they shall fall and not rise again: And there shall be no one to take them with his hands and raise them: For they have denied the Lord of Spirits and His Anointed. The name of the Lord of Spirits be blessed.

XLIX. The Power and Wisdom of the Elect One.

49

1. For wisdom is poured out like water, And glory faileth not before him for evermore. ² For he is mighty in all the secrets of righteousness, And unrighteousness shall disappear as a shadow, And have no continuance; Because the Elect One standeth before the Lord of Spirits, And his glory is for ever and ever, And his might unto all generations. ³ And in him dwells the spirit of wisdom, And the spirit which gives insight, And the spirit of understanding and of might, And the spirit of those who have fallen asleep in righteousness. ⁴ And he shall judge the secret things, And none shall be able to utter a lying word before him; For he is the Elect One before the Lord of Spirits according to His good pleasure.

L. The Glorification and Victory of the Righteous: the Repentance of the Gentiles.

50

¹ And in those days a change shall take place for the holy and elect, And the light of days shall abide upon them, And glory and honour shall turn to the holy, ² On the day of affliction on which evil shall have been treasured up against the sinners. And the righteous shall be victorious in the name of the Lord of Spirits: And He will cause the others to witness (this) That they may repent And forgo the works of their hands. ³ They shall have no honour through the name of the Lord of Spirits, Yet through His name shall they be saved, And the Lord of Spirits will have compassion on them, For His compassion is great. ⁴ And He is righteous also in His judgement, And in the presence of His glory unrighteousness also shall not maintain itself: At His judgement the unrepentant shall perish before Him. ⁵ And from henceforth I will have no mercy on them, saith the Lord of Spirits.

LI. The Resurrection of the Dead, and the Separation by the Judge of the Righteous and the Wicked.

51

¹ And in those days shall the earth also give back that which has been entrusted to it, And Sheol also shall give back that which it has received, And hell shall give back that which it owes. ² And he shall choose the righteous and holy from among them: For the day has drawn nigh that they should be saved. ³ And the Elect One shall in those days sit on My throne, And his mouth shall **pour** forth all the secrets of wisdom and counsel: For the Lord of Spirits hath given (them) to him and hath glorified him. ⁴ And in those days shall the mountains leap like rams, And the hills also shall skip like lambs satisfied with milk, And the faces of [all] the angels in heaven shall be lighted up with joy. ⁵ a. For in those days the Elect One shall arise, ⁵ b. And the earth shall rejoice, c. And the righteous shall dwell upon it, d. And the elect shall walk thereon.

LII. The Seven Metal Mountains and the Elect One.

52

1. And after those days in that place where I had seen all the visions of that which is hidden–for I had been carried off in a whirlwind and they had borne me towards the west– ² There mine eyes saw all the secret things of heaven that shall be, a mountain of iron, and a mountain of copper, and a mountain of silver, and a mountain of gold, and a mountain of soft metal, and a mountain of lead. ³ And I asked the angel who went with me, saying, 'What things are these which I have seen in secret?' ⁴ And he said unto me: 'All these things which thou hast seen shall serve the dominion of His Anointed that he may be potent and mighty on the earth.' ⁵ And that angel of peace answered, saying unto me: 'Wait a little, and there shall be revealed unto thee all the secret things which surround the Lord of Spirits. ⁶ And these mountains which thine eyes have seen, The mountain of iron, and the mountain of copper, and the mountain of silver, And the mountain of gold, and the mountain of soft metal, and the mountain of lead, All these shall be in the presence of the Elect One As wax: before the fire, And like the water which streams down from above [upon those mountains], And they shall become powerless before his feet. ⁷ And it shall come to pass in those days that none shall be saved, Either by gold or by silver, And none be able to escape. ⁸ And there shall be no iron for war, Nor shall one clothe oneself with a breastplate. Bronze shall be of no service, And tin [shall be of no service and] shall not be esteemed, And lead shall not be desired. ⁹ And all these things shall be [denied and] destroyed from the surface of the earth, When the Elect One shall appear before the face of the Lord of Spirits.'

LIII. LVI. 6. The Valley of Judgement: the Angels of Punishment: the Communities of the Elect One.

53

¹ There mine eyes saw a deep valley with open mouths, and all who dwell on the earth and sea and islands shall bring to him gifts and presents and tokens of homage, but that deep valley shall not become full. ² And their hands commit lawless deeds, And the sinners devour all whom they lawlessly **oppress**: Yet the sinners shall be destroyed before the face of the Lord of Spirits, And they shall be banished from off the face of His earth, And they shall perish for ever and ever. ³ For I saw all the angels of punishment abiding (there) and preparing all the instruments of Satan. ⁴ And I asked the angel of peace who went with me: 'For whom are they preparing these instruments?' ⁵ And he said unto me: 'They prepare these for the kings and the mighty of this earth, that they may thereby be destroyed. ⁶ And after this the Righteous and Elect One shall cause the house of his congregation to appear: henceforth they shall be no more hindered in the name of the Lord of Spirits. ⁷ And these mountains shall not stand as the earth before his righteousness, But the hills shall be as a fountain of water, And the righteous shall have rest from the oppression of sinners.'

54

¹ And I looked and turned to another part of the earth, and saw there a deep valley with burning fire. ² And they brought the kings and the mighty, and began to cast them into this deep valley. ³ And there mine eyes saw how they made these their instruments, iron chains of immeasurable weight. ⁴ And I asked the angel of peace who went with me, saying: 'For whom are these chains being prepared?' ⁵ And he said unto me: 'These are being prepared for the hosts of Azâzêl, so that they may take them and cast them into the abyss of complete condemnation, and they shall cover their jaws with rough stones as the Lord of Spirits commanded. ⁶ And Michael, and Gabriel, and Raphael, and Phanuel shall take hold of them on that great day, and cast them on that day into the burning furnace, that the Lord of Spirits may take vengeance on them for their unrighteousness in becoming subject to Satan and leading astray those who dwell on the earth.'

LIV. 7.-LV 2. Noachic Fragment on the first World Judgement.

⁷ 'And in those days shall punishment come from the Lord of Spirits, and he will open all the chambers of waters which are above the heavens, and of the fountains which are beneath the earth. ⁸ And all the waters shall be joined with the waters: that which is above the heavens is the masculine, and the water which is beneath the earth is the feminine. ⁹ And they shall destroy all who dwell on the earth and those who dwell under the ends of the heaven. ¹⁰ And **when** they have recognized their unrighteousness which they have wrought on the earth, then by these shall they perish.

55

¹ And after that the Head of Days repented and said: 'In vain have I destroyed all who dwell on the earth.' ² And He sware by His great name: 'Henceforth I will not do so to all who dwell on the earth, and I will set a sign in the heaven: and this shall be a pledge of good faith between Me and them for ever, so long as heaven is above the earth. And this is in accordance with My command.'

LV. 3-LVI. 4. Final Judgement of Azâzêl, the Watchers and their children.

³ When I have desired to take hold of them by the hand of the angels on the day of tribulation and pain **because of** this, I will cause My chastisement and My wrath to abide upon them, saith God, the Lord of Spirits. ⁴ Ye †mighty kings† who dwell on the earth, ye shall have to behold Mine Elect One, how he sits on the throne of glory and judges Azâzêl, and all his associates, and all his hosts in the name of the Lord of Spirits.'

56

¹ And I saw there the hosts of the angels of punishment going, and they held scourges and chains of iron and bronze. ² And I asked the angel of peace who went with me, saying: 'To whom are these who hold the scourges going?' ³ And he said unto me: 'To their elect and beloved ones, that they may be cast into the chasm of the abyss of the valley. ⁴ And then that valley shall be filled with their elect and beloved, And the days of their lives shall be at an end, And the days of their leading astray shall not thenceforward be reckoned.

LVI. 5-8. Last struggle of heathen Powers against Israel.

⁵ And in those days the angels shall return And hurl themselves to the east upon the Parthians and Medes: They shall stir up the kings, so that a spirit of unrest shall come upon them, And they shall rouse them from their thrones, That they may break forth as lions from their lairs, And as hungry wolves among their flocks. ⁶ And they shall go up and tread under foot the land of His elect ones. [And the land of His elect ones shall be before them a threshing-floor and a highway:] ⁷ But the city of my righteous shall be a

hindrance to their horses. And they shall begin to fight among themselves, And their right hand shall be strong against themselves, And a man shall not know his brother, Nor a son his father or his mother, Till there be no number of the corpses through their slaughter, And their punishment be not in vain. ⁸ In those days Sheol shall open its jaws, And they shall be swallowed up therein And their destruction shall be at an end; Sheol shall devour the sinners in the presence of the elect.'

LVII. The Return from the Dispersion.

57

¹ And it came to pass after this that I saw another host of wagons, and men riding thereon, and coming on the winds from the east, and from the west to the south. ² And the noise of their wagons was heard, and when this turmoil took place the holy ones from heaven remarked it, and the pillars of the earth were moved from their place, and the sound thereof was heard from the one end of heaven to the other, in one day. ³ And they shall all fall down and worship the Lord of Spirits. And this is the end of the second Parable.

LVIII-LXXI. The Third Parable.
LVIII. The Blessedness of the Saints.

58

¹ And I began to speak the third Parable concerning the righteous and elect. ² Blessed are ye, ye righteous and elect, For glorious shall be your lot. ³ And the righteous shall be in the light of the sun. And the elect in the light of eternal life: The days of their life shall be unending, And the days of the holy without number. ⁴ And they shall seek the light and find righteousness with the Lord of Spirits: There shall be peace to the righteous in the name of the Eternal Lord. ⁵ And after this it shall be said to the holy in heaven That they should seek out the secrets of righteousness, the heritage of faith: For it has become bright as the sun upon earth, And the darkness is past. ⁶ And there shall be a light that never **endeth**, And to a limit (lit. 'number') of days they shall not come, For the darkness shall first have been destroyed, [And the light established before the Lord of Spirits] And the light of uprightness established for ever before the Lord of Spirits.

LIX. The Lights and the Thunder.

59

¹ [In those days mine eyes saw the secrets of the lightnings, and of the lights, and the judgements they execute (lit. 'their judgement'): and they lighten for a blessing or a curse as the Lord of Spirits willeth. ² And there I saw the secrets of the thunder, and how when it resounds above in the heaven, the sound thereof is heard, and he caused me to see the judgements executed on the earth, whether they be for well-being and blessing, or for a curse according to the word of the Lord of Spirits. ³ And after that all the secrets of the lights and lightnings were shown to me, and they lighten for blessing and for satisfying.]

LX. Book of Noah–a Fragment.
Quaking of Heaven: Behemoth and Leviathan: the Elements.

60

¹ In the year five hundred, in the seventh month, on the fourteenth day of the month in the life of †Enoch†. In that Parable I saw how a mighty quaking made the heaven of heavens to quake, and the host of the Most High, and the angels, a thousand thousands and ten thousand times **ten** thousand, were disquieted with a great disquiet. ² And the Head of Days sat on the throne of His glory, and the angels and the righteous stood around Him. ³ And a great trembling seized me, And fear took hold of me, And my loins gave way, And dissolved were my reins, And I fell upon my face. ⁴ And Michael sent another angel from among the holy ones and he raised me up, and when he had raised me up my spirit returned; for I had not been able to endure the look of this host, and the commotion and the quaking of the heaven. ⁵ And Michael said unto me: 'Why art thou disquieted with such a vision? Until this day lasted the day of His mercy; and He hath been merciful and long-suffering towards those who dwell on the earth. ⁶ And when the day, and the power, and the punishment, and the judgement come, which the Lord of Spirits hath prepared for those who worship not the righteous **law**, and for those who deny the righteous judgement, and for those who take His name in vain–that day is prepared, for the elect a covenant, but for sinners an inquisition. ⁷ And on that day were two monsters parted, a female monster named Leviathan, to dwell in the abysses of the ocean over the fountains of the waters. ⁸ But the male is named Behemoth, who occupied with his breast a waste wilderness named †Dûidâin†, on the east of the garden where the elect and righteous dwell, where my grandfather was taken up, the seventh from Adam, the first man whom the Lord of Spirits created. ⁹ And I besought the other angel that he should show me the might of those monsters, how they were parted on one day and cast, the one into the abysses of the sea, and the other unto the dry land of the wilderness. ¹⁰ And he said to me: 'Thou son of man, herein thou dost seek to know what is hidden.' ¹¹ And the other angel who went with me and showed me what was hidden told me what is first and last in the heaven in the height, and beneath the earth in the depth, and at the ends of the heaven, and on the foundation of the heaven. ¹² And the chambers of the winds, and how the winds are divided, and how they are weighed, and (how) the **portals** of the winds are reckoned, each according to the power of the wind, and the power of the lights of the moon, and according to the power that is fitting: and the divisions of the stars according to their names, and how all the divisions are divided. ¹³ And the thunders according to the places where they fall, and all the divisions that are made among the lightnings that it may lighten, and their host that they may at once obey. ¹⁴ For the thunder has †places of rest† (which) are assigned (to it) while it is waiting for its peal; and the thunder and lightning are inseparable, and although not one and undivided, they both go together through the spirit and separate not. ¹⁵ For when the lightning lightens, the thunder utters its voice, and the spirit enforces a pause during the peal, and divides equally between them; for the treasury of their peals is like the sand, and each one of them as it peals is held in with a bridle, and turned back by the power of the spirit, and pushed forward according to the many quarters of the earth. ¹⁶ And the spirit of the sea is masculine and strong, and according to the might of his strength he draws it back with a rein, and in like manner it is driven forward and disperses amid all the mountains of the earth. ¹⁷ And the spirit of the hoar-frost is his own angel, and the spirit of the hail is a good angel. ¹⁸ And the spirit of the snow has forsaken his chambers on account of his strength–There is a special spirit therein, and that which ascends from it is like smoke, and its name is frost. ¹⁹ And the spirit of the mist is not united with them in their chambers, but it has a special chamber; for its course is †glorious† both in light and in darkness, and in winter and in summer, and in its chamber is an angel. ²⁰ And the spirit of the dew has its dwelling at the ends of the heaven, and is connected with the chambers of the rain, and its course is in winter and summer: and its clouds and the clouds of the mist are connected, and the one gives to the other. ²¹ And when the spirit of the rain goes forth from its chamber, the angels come and open the chamber and lead it out, and when it is diffused over the whole earth it unites with the water on the earth. And whensoever it unites with the water on the earth . . . ²² For the waters are for those who dwell on the earth; for they are nourishment for the earth from the Most High who is in heaven: therefore there is a measure for the rain, and the angels take it in charge. ²³ And these things I saw towards the Garden of the Righteous. ²⁴ And the angel of peace who was with me said to me: 'These two monsters, prepared conformably to the greatness of God, shall feed . . . ²⁵ When the punishment of the Lord of Spirits shall rest upon them, it shall rest in order that the punishment of the Lord of Spirits may not come, in vain, and it shall slay the children with their mothers and the children with their fathers. Afterwards the judgement shall take place according to His mercy and His patience.'

LXI. Angels go off to measure Paradise: the Judgement of the Righteous by the Elect One: the Praise of the Elect One and of God.

61

¹ And I saw in those days how long cords were given to those angels, and they took to themselves wings and flew, and they went towards the north. ² And I asked the angel, saying unto him: 'Why have those (angels) taken these cords and gone off?' And he said unto me: 'They have gone to measure.' ³ And the angel who went with me said unto me: 'These shall bring the measures of the righteous, And the ropes of the righteous to the righteous, That they may stay themselves on the name of the Lord of Spirits for ever and ever. ⁴ The elect shall begin to dwell with the elect, And those are the measures which shall be given to faith And which shall strengthen righteousness. ⁵ And these measures shall reveal all the secrets of the depths of the earth, And those who have been destroyed by the desert, And those who have been devoured by the beasts, And those who have been devoured by the fish of the sea, That they may return and stay themselves On the day of the Elect One; For none shall be destroyed before the Lord of Spirits, And none can be destroyed. ⁶ And all who dwell above in the heaven received a command and power and one voice and one light like unto fire. ⁷ And that One (with) their first words they blessed, And extolled and lauded with wisdom, And they were wise in utterance and in the spirit of life. ⁸ And the Lord of Spirits placed the Elect one on the throne of glory. And he shall judge all the works of the holy above in the heaven, And in the balance shall their deeds be weighed ⁹ And when he shall lift up his countenance To judge their secret ways according to the word of the name

of the Lord of Spirits, And their path according to the way of the righteous judgement of the Lord of Spirits, Then shall they all with one voice speak and bless, And glorify and extol and sanctify the name of the Lord of Spirits. ¹⁰ And He will summon all the host of the heavens, and all the holy ones above, and the host of God, the Cherubic, Seraphin and Ophannin, and all the angels of power, and all the angels of principalities, and the Elect One, and the other powers on the earth (and) over the water. ¹¹ On that day shall raise one voice, and bless and glorify and exalt in the spirit of faith, and in the spirit of wisdom, and in the spirit of patience, and in the spirit of mercy, and in the spirit of judgement and of peace, and in the spirit of goodness, and shall all say with one voice: "Blessed is He, and may the name of the Lord of Spirits be blessed for ever and ever." ¹² All who sleep not above in heaven shall bless Him: All the holy ones who are in heaven shall bless Him, And all the elect who dwell in the garden of life: And every spirit of light who is able to bless, and glorify, and extol, and hallow Thy blessed name, And all flesh shall beyond measure glorify and bless Thy name for ever and ever. ¹³ For great is the mercy of the Lord of Spirits, and He is long-suffering, And all His works and all that He has created He has revealed to the righteous and elect In the name of the Lord of Spirits.

LXII. Judgement of the Kings and the Mighty: Blessedness of the Righteous.

62

¹ And thus the Lord commanded the kings and the mighty and the exalted, and those who dwell on the earth, and said: 'Open your eyes and lift up your horns if ye are able to recognize the Elect One.' ² And the Lord of Spirits seated him on the throne of His glory, And the spirit of righteousness was poured out upon him, And the word of his mouth slays all the sinners, And all the unrighteous are destroyed from before his face. ³ And there shall stand up in that day all the kings and the mighty, And the exalted and those who hold the earth, And they shall see and recognize How he sits on the throne of his glory, And righteousness is judged before him, And no lying word is spoken before him. ⁴ Then shall pain come upon them as on a woman in travail, [And she has pain in bringing forth] When her child enters the mouth of the womb, And she has pain in bringing forth. ⁵ And one portion of them shall look on the other, And they shall be terrified, And they shall be downcast of countenance, And pain shall seize them, When they see that Son of Man Sitting on the throne of his glory. ⁶ And the kings and the mighty and all who possess the earth shall bless and glorify and extol him who rules over all, who was hidden. ⁷ For from the beginning the Son of Man was hidden, And the Most High preserved him in the presence of His might, And revealed him to the elect. ⁸ And the congregation of the elect and holy shall be sown, And all the elect shall stand before him on that day. ⁹ And all the kings and the mighty and the exalted and those who rule the earth Shall fall down before him on their faces, And worship and set their hope upon that Son of Man, And petition him and supplicate for mercy at his hands. ¹⁰ Nevertheless that Lord of Spirits will so press them That they shall hastily go forth from His presence, And their faces shall be filled with shame, And the darkness grow deeper on their faces. ¹¹ And **He will deliver** them to the angels for punishment, To execute vengeance on them because they have oppressed His children and His elect ¹² And they shall be a spectacle for the righteous and for His elect: They shall rejoice over them, Because the wrath of the Lord of Spirits resteth upon them, And His sword is drunk with their blood. ¹³ And the righteous and elect shall be saved on that day, And they shall never thenceforward see the face of the sinners and unrighteous. ¹⁴ And the Lord of Spirits will abide over them, And with that Son of Man shall they eat And lie down and rise up for ever and ever. ¹⁵ And the righteous and elect shall have risen from the earth, And ceased to be of downcast countenance. And they shall have been clothed with garments of glory, ¹⁶ And these shall be the garments of life from the Lord of Spirits: And your garments shall not grow old, Nor your glory pass away before the Lord of Spirits.

LXIII. The unavailing Repentance of the Kings and the Mighty.

63

¹ In those days shall the mighty and the kings who possess the earth implore (Him) to grant them a little respite from His angels of punishment to whom they were delivered, that they might fall down and worship before the Lord of Spirits, and confess their sins before Him. ² And they shall bless and glorify the Lord of Spirits, and say: 'Blessed is the Lord of Spirits and the Lord of kings, And the Lord of the mighty and the Lord of the rich, And the Lord of glory and the Lord of wisdom, ³ And splendid in every secret thing is Thy power from generation to generation, And Thy glory for ever and ever: Deep are all Thy secrets and innumerable, And Thy righteousness is beyond reckoning. ⁴ We have now learnt that we should glorify And bless the Lord of kings and Him who is king over all kings.' ⁵ And they shall say: 'Would that we had rest to glorify and give thanks And confess our faith before His glory! ⁶ And now we long for a little rest but find it not: We follow hard upon and obtain (it) not: And light has vanished from before us, And darkness is our dwelling-place for ever and ever: ⁷ For we have not believed before Him Nor glorified the name of the Lord of Spirits, [nor glorified our Lord] But our hope was in the sceptre of our kingdom, And in our glory. ⁸ And in the day of our suffering and tribulation He saves us not, And we find no respite for confession That our Lord is true in all His works, and in His judgements and His justice, And His judgements have no respect of persons. ⁹ And we pass away from before His face on account of our works, And all our sins are reckoned up in righteousness.' ¹⁰ Now they shall say unto themselves: 'Our souls are full of unrighteous gain, but it does not prevent us from descending from the midst thereof into the †burden† of Sheol.' ¹¹ And after that their faces shall be filled with darkness And shame before that Son of Man, And they shall be driven from his presence, And the sword shall abide before his face in their midst. ¹² Thus spake the Lord of Spirits: 'This is the ordinance and judgement with respect to the mighty and the kings and the exalted and those who possess the earth before the Lord of Spirits.'

LXIV. Vision of the fallen Angels in the Place of Punishment.

64

¹ And other forms I saw hidden in that place. ² I heard the voice of the angel saying: 'These are the angels who descended to the earth, and revealed what was hidden to the children of men and seduced the children of men into committing sin.'

LXV. Enoch foretells to Noah the Deluge and his own Preservation.

65

¹ And in those days Noah saw the earth that it had sunk down and its destruction was nigh. ² And he arose from thence and went to the ends of the earth, and cried aloud to his grandfather Enoch: and Noah said three times with an embittered voice: Hear me, hear me, hear me.' ³ And I said unto him: 'Tell me what it is that is falling out on the earth that the earth is in such evil plight and shaken, lest perchance I shall perish with it?' ⁴ And thereupon there was a great commotion, on the earth, and a voice was heard from heaven, and I fell on my face. ⁵ And Enoch my grandfather came and stood by me, and said unto me: 'Why hast thou cried unto me with a bitter cry and weeping? ⁶ And a command has gone forth from the presence of the Lord concerning those who dwell on the earth that their ruin is accomplished because they have learnt all the secrets of the angels, and all the violence of the Satans, and all their powers–the most secret ones–and all the power of those who practice sorcery, and the power of witchcraft, and the power of those who make molten images for the whole earth: ⁷ And how silver is produced from the dust of the earth, and how soft metal originates in the earth. ⁸ For lead and tin are not produced from the earth like the first: it is a fountain that produces them, and an angel stands therein, and that angel is pre-eminent.' ⁹ And after that my grandfather Enoch took hold of me by my hand and raised me up, and said unto me: 'Go, for I have asked the Lord of Spirits as touching this commotion on the earth. ¹⁰ And He said unto me: "Because of their unrighteousness their judgement has been determined upon and shall not be **withheld** by Me for ever. Because of the **sorceries** which they have searched out and learnt, the earth and those who dwell upon it shall be destroyed." ¹¹ And these–they have no **place of repentance** for ever, because they have shown them what was hidden, and they are the damned: but as for thee, my son, the Lord of Spirits knows that thou art pure, and guiltless of this reproach concerning the secrets. ¹² And He has destined thy name to be among the holy, And will preserve thee amongst those who dwell on the earth, And has destined thy righteous seed both for kingship and for great honours, And from thy seed shall proceed a fountain of the righteous and holy without number for ever.

LXVI. The Angels of the Waters bidden to hold them in Check.

66

¹ And after that he showed me the angels of punishment who are prepared to come and let loose all the powers of the waters which are beneath in the earth in order to bring judgement and destruction on all who [abide and] dwell on the earth. ² And the Lord of Spirits gave commandment to the angels who were going forth, that they should not cause **the waters** to rise but should hold them in check; for those angels were over the powers of the waters. ³ And I went away from the presence of Enoch.

LXVII. God's Promise to Noah: Places of Punishment of the Angels and of the Kings.

67

¹ And in those days the word of God came unto me, and He said unto me: 'Noah, thy lot has come up before Me, a lot without blame, a lot of love and uprightness. ² And now the angels are making a wooden (building), and when they have completed that task I will place My hand upon it and preserve it, and there shall come forth from it the seed of life, and a change shall set in so that the earth will not remain without inhabitant. ³ And I will make fast thy seed before me for ever and ever, and I will spread abroad those who dwell with thee: it shall not **be unfruitful** on the face of the earth, but it shall be blessed and multiply on the earth in the name of the Lord.' ⁴ And He will imprison those angels, who have shown unrighteousness, in that burning valley which my grandfather Enoch had formerly shown to me in the west among the mountains of gold and silver and iron and soft metal and tin. ⁵ And I saw that valley in which there was a great convulsion and a convulsion of the waters. ⁶ And when all this took place, from that fiery molten metal and from the convulsion thereof in that place, there was produced a smell of sulphur, and it was connected with those waters, and that valley of the angels who had led astray (mankind) burned beneath that land. ⁷ And through its valleys proceed streams of fire, where these angels are punished who had led astray those who dwell upon the earth. ⁸ But those waters shall in those days serve for the kings and the mighty and the exalted, and those who dwell on the earth, for the healing of the body, but for the punishment of the spirit; now their spirit is full of lust, that they may be punished in their body, for they have denied the Lord of Spirits and see their punishment daily, and yet believe not in His name. ⁹ And in proportion as the burning of their bodies becomes severe, a corresponding change shall take place in their spirit for ever and ever; for before the Lord of Spirits none shall utter an idle word. ¹⁰ For the judgement shall come upon them, because they believe in the lust of their body and deny the Spirit of the Lord. ¹¹ And those same waters will undergo a change in those days; for when those angels are punished in these waters, these water-springs shall change their temperature, and when the angels ascend, this water of the springs shall change and become cold. ¹² And I heard Michael answering and saying: 'This judgement wherewith the angels are judged is a testimony for the kings and the mighty who possess the earth.' ¹³ Because these waters of judgement minister to the healing of the body of the **kings** and the lust of their body; therefore they will not see and will not believe that those waters will change and become a fire which burns for ever.

LXVIII. Michael and Raphael astonished at the Severity of the Judgement.

68

¹ And after that my grandfather Enoch gave me the teaching of all the secrets in the book in the Parables which had been given to him, and he put them together for me in the words of the book of the Parables. ² And on that day Michael answered Raphael and said: 'The power of the spirit transports and **makes me to tremble** because of the severity of the judgement of the secrets, the judgement of the angels: who can endure the severe judgement which has been executed, and before which they melt away?' ³ And Michael answered again, and said to Raphael: 'Who is he whose heart is not softened concerning it, and whose reins are not troubled by this word of judgement (that) has gone forth upon them because of those who have thus led them out?' ⁴ And it came to pass when he stood before the Lord of Spirits, Michael said thus to Raphael: 'I will not take their part under the eye of the Lord; for the Lord of Spirits has been angry with them because they do as if they were the Lord. ⁵ Therefore all that is hidden shall come upon them for ever and ever; for neither angel nor man shall have his portion (in it), but alone they have received their judgement for ever and ever.'

LXIX. The Names and Functions of the (fallen Angels and) Satans: the secret Oath.

69

¹ And after this judgement they shall terrify and **make** them **to tremble** because they have shown this to those who dwell on the earth. ² And behold the names of those angels [and these are their names: the first of them is Samjâzâ, the second Artâqîfâ, and the third Armên, the fourth Kôkabêl, the fifth †Tûrâêl†, the sixth Rûmjâl, the seventh Dânjâl, the eighth †Nêqâêl†, the ninth Barâqêl, the tenth Azâzêl, the eleventh Armârôs, the twelfth Batarjâl, the thirteenth †Busasêjal†, the fourteenth Hanânêl, the fifteenth †Tûrêl†, and the sixteenth Sîmâpêsîêl, the seventeenth Jetrêl, the eighteenth Tûmâêl, the nineteenth Tûrêl, the twentieth †Rumâêl†, the twenty-first †Azâzêl†. ³ And these are the chiefs of their angels and their names, and their chief ones over hundreds and over fifties and over tens]. ⁴ The name of the first Jeqôn: that is, the one who led astray [all] the sons of God, and brought them down to the earth, and led them astray through the daughters of men. ⁵ And the second was named Asbeêl: he imparted to the holy sons of **God** evil counsel, and led them astray so that they defiled their bodies with the daughters of men. ⁶ And the third was named Gâdreêl: he it is who showed the children of men all the blows of death, and he led astray Eve, and showed [the weapons of death to the sons of men] the shield and the coat of mail, and the sword for battle, and all the weapons of death to the children of men. ⁷ And from his hand they have proceeded against those who dwell on the earth from that day and for evermore. ⁸ And the fourth was named Pênêmûe: he taught the children of men the bitter and the sweet, and he taught them all the secrets of their wisdom. ⁹ And he instructed mankind in writing with ink and paper, and thereby many sinned from eternity to eternity and until this day. ¹⁰ For men were not created for such a purpose, to give confirmation to their good faith with pen and ink. ¹¹ For men were created exactly like the angels, to the intent that they should continue pure and righteous, and death, which destroys everything, could not have taken hold of them, but through this their knowledge they are perishing, and through this power it is consuming me†. ¹² And the fifth was named Kâsdejâ: this is he who showed the children of men all the wicked smitings of spirits and demons, and the smitings of the embryo in the womb, that it may pass away, and [the smitings of the soul] the bites of the serpent, and the smitings which befall through the noontide heat, the son of the serpent named Tabââ'ĕt. ¹³ And this is the **task** of Kâsbeêl, the chief of the oath which he showed to the holy ones when he dwelt high above in glory, and its name is Bîqâ. ¹⁴ This (angel) requested Michael to show him the hidden name, that he might enunciate it in the oath, so that those might quake before that name and oath who revealed all that was in secret to the children of men. ¹⁵ And this is the power of this oath, for it is powerful and strong, and he placed this oath Akâe in the hand of Michael. ¹⁶ And these are the secrets of this oath . . . And they are strong through his oath: And the heaven was suspended before the world was created, And for ever. ¹⁷ And through it the earth was founded upon the water, And from the secret recesses of the mountains come beautiful waters, From the creation of the world and unto eternity. ¹⁸ And through that oath the sea was created, And †as its foundation† He set for it the sand against the time of (its) anger, And it dare not pass beyond it from the creation of the world unto eternity. ¹⁹ And through that oath are the depths made fast, And abide and stir not from their place from eternity to eternity. ²⁰ And through that oath the sun and moon complete their course, And deviate not from their ordinance from eternity to eternity. ²¹ And through that oath the stars complete their course, And He calls them by their names, And they answer Him from eternity to eternity. ²² [And in like manner the spirits of the water, and of the winds, and of all zephyrs, and (their) paths from all the quarters of the winds. ²³ And there are preserved the voices of the thunder and the light of the lightnings: and there are preserved the chambers of the hail and the chambers of the hoarfrost, and the chambers of the mist, and the chambers of the rain and the dew. ²⁴ And all these believe and give thanks before the Lord of Spirits, and glorify (Him) with all their power, and their food is in every act of thanksgiving: they thank and glorify and extol the name of the Lord of Spirits for ever and ever.] ²⁵ And this oath is mighty over them And through it [they are preserved and] their paths are preserved, And their course is not destroyed.

Close of the Third Parable.

²⁶ And there was great joy amongst them, And they blessed and glorified and extolled Because the name of that Son of Man had been revealed unto them. ²⁷ And he sat on the throne of his glory, And the sum of judgement was given unto the Son of Man, And he caused the sinners to pass away and be destroyed from off the face of the earth, And those who have led the world astray. ²⁸ With chains shall they be bound, And in their assemblage-place of destruction shall they be imprisoned, And all their works vanish from the face of the earth. ²⁹ And from henceforth there shall be nothing corruptible; For that Son of Man has appeared, And has seated himself on the throne of his glory, And all evil shall pass away before his face, And the word of that Son of Man shall go forth And be strong before the Lord of Spirits. This is the Third Parable of Enoch.

LXX. The Final Translation of Enoch.

70

¹ And it came to pass after this that his name during his lifetime was raised aloft to that Son of Man and to the Lord of Spirits from amongst those who dwell on the earth. ² And he was raised aloft on the chariots of the spirit and his name vanished among them. ³ And from that day I was no longer numbered amongst them: and he set me between the two winds, between the North and the West, where the angels took the cords to measure for me the place for the elect and righteous. ⁴ And there I saw the first fathers and the righteous who from the beginning dwell in that place.

LXXI. Two earlier visions of Enoch.

71

[1] And it came to pass after this that my spirit was translated And it ascended into the heavens: And I saw the **holy sons of God**. They were stepping on flames of fire: Their garments were white [and their raiment], And their faces shone like snow. [2] And I saw two streams of fire, And the light of that fire shone like hyacinth, And I fell on my face before the Lord of Spirits. [3] And the angel Michael [one of the archangels] seized me by my right hand, And lifted me up and led me forth into all the secrets, And he showed me all the secrets of righteousness. [4] And he showed me all the secrets of the ends of the heaven, And all the chambers of all the stars, and all the luminaries, Whence they proceed before the face of the holy ones. [5] And he translated my spirit into the heaven of heavens, And I saw there as it were a structure built of crystals, And between those crystals tongues of living fire. [6] And my spirit saw the girdle which girt that house of fire, And on its four sides were streams full of living fire, And they girt that house. [7] And round about were Seraphin, Cherubic, and Ophannin: And these are they who sleep not And guard the throne of His glory. [8] And I saw angels who could not be counted, A thousand thousands, and ten thousand times ten thousand, Encircling that house. And Michael, and Raphael, and Gabriel, and Phanuel, And the holy angels who are above the heavens, Go in and out of that house. [9] And they came forth from that house, And Michael and Gabriel, Raphael and Phanuel, And many holy angels without number. [10] And with them the Head of Days, His head white and pure as wool, And His raiment indescribable. [11] And I fell on my face, And my whole body became relaxed, And my spirit was transfigured; And I cried with a loud voice, . . .with the spirit of power, And blessed and glorified and extolled. [12] And these blessings which went forth out of my mouth were well pleasing before that Head of Days. [13] And that Head of Days came with Michael and Gabriel, Raphael and Phanuel, thousands and ten thousands of angels without number. [Lost passage wherein the Son of Man was described as accompanying the Head of Days, and Enoch asked one of the angels (as in **46:3**) concerning the Son of Man as to who he was.] [14] And he (*i.e.* the angel) came to me and greeted me with His voice, and said unto me: 'This **is** the Son of Man who is born unto righteousness; And righteousness abides over him, And the righteousness of the Head of Days forsakes him not.' [15] And he said unto me: 'He proclaims unto thee peace in the name of the world to come; For from hence has proceeded peace since the creation of the world, And so shall it be unto thee for ever and for ever and ever. [16] And all shall walk in **his** ways since righteousness never forsaketh **him**: With **him** will be their dwelling-places, and with **him** their heritage, And they shall not be separated from him for ever and ever and ever. [17] And so there shall be length of days with that Son of Man, And the righteous shall have peace and an upright way In the name of the Lord of Spirits for ever and ever.'

LXXII-LXXXII. The Book of the Courses of the Heavenly Luminaries.
LXXII. The Sun.

72

[1] The book of the courses of the luminaries of the heaven, the relations of each, according to their classes, their dominion and their seasons, according to their names and places of origin, and according to their months, which Uriel, the holy angel, who was with me, who is their guide, showed me; and he showed me all their laws exactly as they are, and how it is with regard to all the years of the world and unto eternity, till the new creation is accomplished which dureth till eternity. [2] And this is the first law of the luminaries: the luminary the Sun has its rising in the eastern portals of the heaven, and its setting in the western portals of the heaven. [3] And I saw six portals in which the sun rises, and six portals in which the sun sets and the moon rises and sets in these portals, and the leaders of the stars and those whom they lead: six in the east and six in the west, and all following each other in accurately corresponding order: also many windows to the right and left of these portals. [4] And first there goes forth the great luminary, named the Sun, and his circumference is like the circumference of the heaven, and he is quite filled with illuminating and heating fire. [5] The chariot on which he ascends, the wind drives, and the sun goes down from the heaven and returns through the north in order to reach the east, and is so guided that he comes to the appropriate (lit. 'that') portal and shines in the face of the heaven. [6] In this way he rises in the first month in the great portal, which is the fourth [those six portals in the east]. [7] And in that fourth portal from which the sun rises in the first month are twelve window-openings, from which proceed a flame when they are opened in their season. [8] When the sun rises in the heaven, he comes forth through that fourth portal thirty mornings in succession, and sets accurately in the fourth portal in the west of the heaven. [9] And during this period the day becomes daily longer and the night nightly shorter to the thirtieth morning. [10] On that day the day is longer than the night by a ninth part, and the day amounts exactly to ten parts and the night to eight parts. [11] And the sun rises from that fourth portal, and sets in the fourth and returns to the fifth portal of the east thirty mornings, and rises from it and sets in the fifth portal. [12] And then the day becomes longer by †two† parts and amounts to eleven parts, and the night becomes shorter and amounts to seven parts. [13] And it returns to the east and enters into the sixth portal, and rises and sets in the sixth portal one-and-thirty mornings on account of its sign. [14] On that day the day becomes longer than the night, and the day becomes double the night, and the day becomes twelve parts, and the night is shortened and becomes six parts. [15] And the sun mounts up to make the day shorter and the night longer, and the sun returns to the east and enters into the sixth portal, and rises from it and sets thirty mornings. [16] And when thirty mornings are accomplished, the day decreases by exactly one part, and becomes eleven parts, and the night seven. [17] And the sun goes forth from that sixth portal in the west, and goes to the east and rises in the fifth portal for thirty mornings, and sets in the west again in the fifth western portal. [18] On that day the day decreases by †two† parts, and amounts to ten parts and the night to eight parts. [19] And the sun goes forth from that fifth portal and sets in the fifth portal of the west, and rises in the fourth portal for one-and-thirty mornings on account of its sign, and sets in the west. [20] On that day the day is equalized with the night, [and becomes of equal length], and the night amounts to nine parts and the day to nine parts. [21] And the sun rises from that portal and sets in the west, and returns to the east and rises thirty mornings in the third portal and sets in the west in the third portal. [22] And on that day the night becomes longer than the day, and night becomes longer than night, and day shorter than day till the thirtieth morning, and the night amounts exactly to ten parts and the day to eight parts. [23] And the sun rises from that third portal and sets in the third portal in the west and returns to the east, and for thirty mornings rises in the second portal in the east, and in like manner sets in the second portal in the west of the heaven. [24] And on that day the night amounts to eleven parts and the day to seven parts. [25] And the sun rises on that day from that second portal and sets in the west in the second portal, and returns to the east into the first portal for one-and-thirty mornings, and sets in the first portal in the west of the heaven. [26] And on that day the night becomes longer and amounts to the double of the day: and the night amounts exactly to twelve parts and the day to six. [27] And the sun has (therewith) traversed the divisions of his orbit and turns again on those divisions of his orbit, and enters that portal thirty mornings and sets also in the west opposite to it. [28] And on that night has the night decreased in length by a †ninth† part, and the night has become eleven parts and the day seven parts. [29] And the sun has returned and entered into the second portal in the east, and returns on those his divisions of his orbit for thirty mornings, rising and setting. [30] And on that day the night decreases in length, and the night amounts to ten parts and the day to eight. [31] And on that day the sun rises from that portal, and sets in the west, and returns to the east, and rises in the third portal for one-and-thirty mornings, and sets in the west of the heaven. [32] On that day the night decreases and amounts to nine parts, and the day to nine parts, and the night is equal to the day and the year is exactly as to its days three hundred and sixty-four. [33] And the length of the day and of the night, and the shortness of the day and of the night arise–through the course of the sun these distinctions are made (lit. 'they are separated'). [34] So it comes that its course becomes daily longer, and its course nightly shorter. [35] And this is the law and the course of the sun, and his return as often as he returns sixty times and rises, *i.e.* the great luminary which is named the sun, for ever and ever. [36] And that which (thus) rises is the great luminary, and is so named according to its appearance, according as the Lord commanded. [37] As he rises, so he sets and decreases not, and rests not, but runs day and night, and his light is sevenfold brighter than that of the moon; but as regards size they are both equal.

73

[1] And after this law I saw another law dealing with the smaller luminary, which is named the Moon. [2] And her circumference is like the circumference of the heaven, and her chariot in which she rides is driven by the wind, and light is given to her in (definite) measure. [3] And her rising and setting change every month: and her days are like the days of the sun, and when her light is uniform (*i.e.* full) it amounts to the seventh part of the light of the sun. [4] And thus she rises. And her first phase in the east comes forth on the thirtieth morning: and on that day she becomes visible, and constitutes for you the first phase of the moon on the thirtieth day together with the sun in the portal where the sun rises. [5] And the one half of her goes forth by a seventh part, and her whole circumference is empty, without light, with the exception of one-seventh part of it, (and) the fourteenth part

of her light. ⁶ And when she receives one-seventh part of the half of her light, her light amounts to one-seventh part and the half thereof. ⁷ And she sets with the sun, and when the sun rises the moon rises with him and receives the half of one part of light, and in that night in the beginning of her morning [in the commencement of the lunar day] the moon sets with the sun, and is invisible that night with the fourteen parts and the half of one of them. ⁸ And she rises on that day with exactly a seventh part, and comes forth and recedes from the rising of the sun, and in her remaining days she becomes bright in the (remaining) thirteen parts.

74

¹ And I saw another course, a law for her, (and) how according to that law she performs her monthly revolution. ² And all these Uriel, the holy angel who is the leader of them all, showed to me, and their positions, and I wrote down their positions as he showed them to me, and I wrote down their months as they were, and the appearance of their lights till fifteen days were accomplished. ³ In single seventh parts she accomplishes all her light in the east, and in single seventh parts accomplishes all her darkness in the west. ⁴ And in certain months she alters her settings, and in certain months she pursues her own peculiar course. ⁵ In two months the moon sets with the sun: in those two middle portals the third and the fourth. ⁶ She goes forth for seven days, and turns about and returns again through the portal where the sun rises, and accomplishes all her light: and she recedes from the sun, and in eight days enters the sixth portal from which the sun goes forth. ⁷ And when the sun goes forth from the fourth portal she goes forth seven days, until she goes forth from the fifth and turns back again in seven days into the fourth portal and accomplishes all her light: and she recedes and enters into the first portal in eight days. ⁸ And she returns again in seven days into the fourth portal from which the sun goes forth. ⁹ Thus I saw their position–how the moons rose and the sun set in those days. ¹⁰ And if five years are added together the sun has an overplus of thirty days, and all the days which accrue to it for one of those five years, when they are full, amount to 364 days. ¹¹ And the overplus of the sun and of the stars amounts to six days: in 5 years 6 days every year come to 30 days: and the moon falls behind the sun and stars to the number of 30 days. ¹² And **the sun** and the stars bring in all the years exactly, so that they do not advance or delay their position by a single day unto eternity; but **complete** the years with perfect justice in 364 days. ¹³ In ³ years there are 1092 days, and in 5 years 1820 days, so that in 8 years there are 2912 days. ¹⁴ For the moon alone the days amount in 3 years to 1062 days, and in 5 years she falls 50 days behind: [*i.e.* to the sum (of 1770) there is to be added (1000 and) 62 days.] ¹⁵ And in 5 years there are 1770 days, so that for the moon the days in 8 **years** amount to 2832 days. ¹⁶ [For in 8 years she falls behind to the amount of 80 days], all the days she falls behind in 8 years are 80. ¹⁷ And the year is accurately completed in conformity with their world-stations and the stations of the sun, which rise from the portals through which it (the sun) rises and sets 30 days.

75

¹ And the leaders of the heads of the thousands, who are placed over the whole creation and over all the stars, have also to do with the four intercalary days, being inseparable from their office, according to the reckoning of the year, and these render service on the four days which are not reckoned in the reckoning of the year. ² And owing to them men go wrong therein, for those luminaries truly render service on the world-stations, one in the first portal, one in the third portal of the heaven, one in the fourth portal, and one in the sixth portal, and the exactness of the year is accomplished through its separate three hundred and sixty-four stations. ³ For the signs and the times and the years and the days the angel Uriel showed to me, whom the Lord of glory hath set for ever over all the luminaries of the heaven, in the heaven and in the world, that they should rule on the face of the heaven and be seen on the earth, and be leaders for the day and the night, *i.e.* the sun, moon, and stars, and all the ministering creatures which make their revolution in all the chariots of the heaven. ⁴ In like manner twelve doors Uriel showed me, open in the circumference of the sun's chariot in the heaven, through which the rays of the sun break forth: and from them is warmth diffused over the earth, when they are opened at their appointed seasons. ⁵ [And for the winds and the spirit of the dew when they are opened, standing open in the heavens at the ends.] ⁶ As for the twelve portals in the heaven, at the ends of the earth, out of which go forth the sun, moon, and stars, and all the works of heaven in the east and in the west. ⁷ There are many windows open to the left and right of them, and one window at its (appointed) season produces warmth, corresponding (as these do) to those doors from which the stars come forth according as He has commanded them, and wherein they set corresponding to their number. ⁸ And I saw chariots in the heaven, running in the world, above those portals in which revolve the stars that never set. ⁹ And one is larger than all the rest, and it is that that makes its course through the entire world.

LXXVI. The Twelve Windows and their Portals.

76

¹ And at the ends of the earth I saw twelve portals open to all the **quarters** (of the heaven), from which the winds go forth and blow over the earth. ² Three of them are open on the face (*i.e.* the east) of the heavens, and three in the west, and three on the right (*i.e.* the south) of the heaven, and three on the left (*i.e.* the north). ³ And the three first are those of the east, and three are of †the north, and three [after those on the left] of the south†, and three of the west. ⁴ Through four of these come winds of blessing and prosperity, and from those eight come hurtful winds: when they are sent, they bring destruction on all the earth and on the water upon it, and on all who dwell thereon, and on everything which is in the water and on the land. ⁵ And the first wind from those portals, called the east wind, comes forth through the first portal which is in the east, inclining towards the south: from it come forth desolation, drought, heat, and destruction. ⁶ And through the second portal in the middle comes what is fitting, and from it there come rain and fruitfulness and prosperity and dew; and through the third portal which lies toward the north come cold and drought. ⁷ And after these come forth the south winds through three portals: through the first portal of them inclining to the east comes forth a hot wind. ⁸ And through the middle portal next to it there come forth fragrant smells, and dew and rain, and prosperity and health. ⁹ And through the third portal lying to the west come forth dew and rain, locusts and desolation. ¹⁰ And after these the north winds: from the seventh portal in the east come dew and rain, locusts and desolation. ¹¹ And from the middle portal come in a direct direction health and rain and dew and prosperity; and through the third portal in the west come cloud and hoar-frost, and snow and rain, and dew and locusts. ¹² And after these [four] are the west winds: through the first portal adjoining the north come forth dew and hoar-frost, and cold and snow and frost. ¹³ And from the middle portal come forth dew and rain, and prosperity and blessing; and through the last portal which adjoins the south come forth drought and desolation, and burning and destruction. ¹⁴ And the twelve portals of the four **quarters** of the heaven are therewith completed, and all their laws and all their plagues and all their benefactions have I shown to thee, my son Methuselah.

LXXVII. The Four Quarters of the World; the Seven Mountains, the Seven Rivers, etc.

77

¹ And the first **quarter** is called the east, because it is the first: and the second, the south, because the Most High **will descend** there, yea, there in quite a special sense will He who is blessed for ever **descend**. ² And the west **quarter** is named the diminished, because there all the luminaries of the heaven wane and go down. ³ And the fourth **quarter**, named the north, is divided into three parts: the first of them is for the dwelling of men: and the second contains seas of water, and the abysses and forests and rivers, and darkness and clouds; and the third part contains the garden of righteousness. ⁴ I saw seven high mountains, higher than all the mountains which are on the earth: and thence comes forth hoar-frost, and days, seasons, and years pass away. ⁵ I saw seven rivers on the earth larger than all the rivers: one of them coming from the west pours its waters into the Great Sea. ⁶ And these two come from the north to the sea and pour their waters into the Erythraean Sea in the east. ⁷ And the remaining four come forth on the side of the north to their own sea, <two of them> to the Erythraean Sea, and two into the Great Sea and discharge themselves there [and some say: into the desert]. ⁸ Seven great islands I saw in the sea and in the mainland: two in the mainland and five in the Great Sea.

LXXVIII. The Sun and Moon; the Waxing and Waning of the Moon.

78

¹ And the names of the sun are the following: the first Orjârês, and the second Tômâs. ² And the moon has four names: the first name is Asônjâ, the second Eblâ, the third Benâsê, and the fourth Erâe. ³ These are the two great luminaries: their circumference is like the circumference of the heaven, and the size of the circumference of both is alike. ⁴ In the circumference of the sun there are seven portions of light which are added to it more than to the moon, and in definite measures it is s transferred till the seventh portion of the sun is exhausted. ⁵ And they set and enter the portals of the west, and make their revolution by the north, and come forth through the eastern portals on the face of the heaven. ⁶ And when the moon rises one-fourteenth part appears in the heaven: [the light becomes full in her]: on the fourteenth day she accomplishes her light. ⁷ And fifteen parts of light are transferred to her till the fifteenth day (when) her light is

accomplished, according to the sign of the year, and she becomes fifteen parts, and the moon grows by (the addition of) fourteenth parts. ⁸ And in her waning (the moon) decreases on the first day to fourteen parts of her light, on the second to thirteen parts of light, on the third to twelve, on the fourth to eleven, on the fifth to ten, on the sixth to nine, on the seventh to eight, on the eighth to seven, on the ninth to six, on the tenth to five, on the eleventh to four, on the twelfth to three, on the thirteenth to two, on the fourteenth to the half of a seventh, and all her remaining light disappears wholly on the fifteenth. ⁹ And in certain months the month has twenty-nine days and once twenty-eight. ¹⁰ And Uriel showed me another law: when light is transferred to the moon, and on which side it is transferred to her by the sun. ¹¹ During all the period during which the moon is growing in her light, she is transferring it to herself when opposite to the sun during fourteen days [her light is accomplished in the heaven], and when she is illumined throughout, her light is accomplished full in the heaven. ¹² And on the first day she is called the new moon, for on that day the light rises upon her. ¹³ She becomes full moon exactly on the day when the sun sets in the west, and from the east she rises at night, and the moon shines the whole night through till the sun rises over against her and the moon is seen over against the sun. ¹⁴ On the side whence the light of the moon comes forth, there again she wanes till all the light vanishes and all the days of the month are at an end, and her circumference is empty, void of light. ¹⁵ And three months she makes of thirty days, and at her time she makes three months of twenty-nine days each, in which she accomplishes her waning in the first period of time, and in the first portal for one hundred and seventy-seven days. ¹⁶ And in the time of her going out she appears for three months (of) thirty days each, and for three months she appears (of) twenty-nine each. ¹⁷ At night she appears like a man for twenty days each time, and by day she appears like the heaven, and there is nothing else in her save her light.

LXXIX-LXXX. 1. Recapitulation of several of the Laws.

79

¹ And now, my son, I have shown thee everything, and the law of all the stars of the heaven is completed. ² And he showed me all the laws of these for every day, and for every season of bearing rule, and for every year, and for its going forth, and for the order prescribed to it every month and every week: ³ And the waning of the moon which takes place in the sixth portal: for in this sixth portal her light is accomplished, and after that there is the beginning of the waning: ⁴ <And the waning> which takes place in the first portal in its season, till one hundred and seventy-seven days are accomplished: reckoned according to weeks, twenty-five (weeks) and two days. ⁵ She falls behind the sun and the order of the stars exactly five days in the course of one period, and when this place which thou seest has been traversed. ⁶ Such is the picture and sketch of every luminary which Uriel the archangel, who is their leader, showed unto me.

80

¹ And in those days the angel Uriel answered and said to me: 'Behold, I have shown thee everything, Enoch, and I have revealed everything to thee that thou shouldst see this sun and this moon, and the leaders of the stars of the heaven and all those who turn them, their tasks and times and departures.

LXXX. 2-8. Perversion of Nature and the heavenly Bodies owning to the Sin of Men.

² And in the days of the sinners the years shall be shortened, And their seed shall be tardy on their lands and fields, And all things on the earth shall alter, And shall not appear in their time: And the rain shall be kept back And the heaven shall withhold (it). ³ And in those times the fruits of the earth shall be backward, And shall not grow in their time, And the fruits of the trees shall be withheld in their time. ⁴ And the moon shall alter her order, And not appear at her time. ⁵ [And in those days the **sun** shall be seen and he shall journey in the **evening** †on the extremity of the great chariot† in the west] And shall shine more brightly than accords with the order of light. ⁶ And many chiefs of the stars shall transgress the order (prescribed). And these shall alter their orbits and tasks, And not appear at the seasons prescribed to them. ⁷ And the whole order of the stars shall be concealed from the sinners, And the thoughts of those on the earth shall err concerning them, [And they shall be altered from all their ways], Yea, they shall err and take them to be gods. ⁸ And evil shall be multiplied upon them, And punishment shall come upon them So as to destroy all.'

LXXXI. The Heavenly Tablets and the Mission of Enoch.

81

¹ And he said unto me: 'Observe, Enoch, these heavenly tablets, And read what is written thereon, And mark every individual fact.' ² And I observed the heavenly tablets, and read everything which was written (thereon) and understood everything, and read the book of all the deeds of mankind, and of all the children of flesh that shall be upon the earth to the remotest generations. ³ And forthwith I blessed the great Lord the King of glory for ever, in that He has made all the works of the world, And I extolled the Lord because of His patience, And blessed Him because of the children of men. ⁴ And after that I said: 'Blessed is the man who dies in righteousness and goodness, Concerning whom there is no book of unrighteousness written, And against whom no day of judgement shall be found.' ⁵ And those seven holy ones brought me and placed me on the earth before the door of my house, and said to me: 'Declare everything to thy son Methuselah, and show to all thy children that no flesh is righteous in the sight of the Lord, for He is their Creator. ⁶ One year we will leave thee with thy son, till thou givest thy (last) commands, that thou mayest teach thy children and record (it) for them, and testify to all thy children; and in the second year they shall take thee from their midst. ⁷ Let thy heart be strong, For the good shall announce righteousness to the good; The righteous with the righteous shall rejoice, And shall offer congratulation to one another. ⁸ But the sinners shall die with the sinners, And the apostate go down with the apostate. ⁹ And those who practice righteousness shall die on account of the deeds of men, And be taken away on account of the doings of the godless.' ¹⁰ And in those days they ceased to speak to me, and I came to my people, blessing the Lord of the world.

LXXXII. Charge given to Enoch; the four Intercalary Days; the Stars which lead the Seasons and the Months.

82

¹ And now, my son Methuselah, all these things I am recounting to thee and writing down for thee, and I have revealed to thee everything, and given thee books concerning all these: so preserve, my son Methuselah, the books from thy father's hand, and (see) that thou deliver them to the generations of the world. ² I have given Wisdom to thee and to thy children, [And thy children that shall be to thee], That they may give it to their children for generations, This wisdom (namely) that passeth their thought. ³ And those who understand it shall not sleep, But shall listen with the ear that they may learn this wisdom, And it shall please those that eat thereof better than good food. ⁴ Blessed are all the righteous, blessed are all those who walk in the way of righteousness and sin not as the sinners, in the reckoning of all their days in which the sun traverses the heaven, entering into and departing from the portals for thirty days with the heads of thousands of the order of the stars, together with the four which are intercalated which divide the four portions of the year, which lead them and enter with them four days. ⁵ Owing to them men shall be at fault and not reckon them in the **whole reckoning of the year**: yea, men shall be at fault, and not recognize them accurately. ⁶ For they belong to the reckoning of the year and are truly recorded (thereon) for ever, one in the first portal and one in the third, and one in the fourth and one in the sixth, and the year is completed in three hundred and sixty-four days. ⁷ And the account thereof is accurate and the recorded reckoning thereof exact; for the luminaries, and months and festivals, and years and days, has Uriel shown and revealed to me, **to whom** the Lord of the whole creation of the world hath **subjected** the host of heaven. ⁸ And he has power over night and day in the heaven to cause the light to give light to men–sun, moon, and stars, and all the powers of the heaven which revolve in their circular chariots. ⁹ And these are the orders of the stars, which set in their places, and in their seasons and festivals and months. ¹⁰ And these are the names of those who lead them, who watch that they enter at their times, in their orders, in their seasons, in their months, in their periods of dominion, and in their positions. ¹¹ Their four leaders who divide the four parts of the year enter first; and after them the twelve leaders of the orders who divide the months; and for the three hundred and sixty (days) there are heads over thousands who divide the days; and for the four intercalary days there are the leaders which sunder the four parts of the year. ¹² And these heads over thousands are intercalated between leader and leader, each behind a station, but their leaders make the division. ¹³ And these are the names of the leaders who divide the four parts of the year which are ordained: Mîlkî'êl, Hel'emmêlêk, and Mêl'êjal, and Nârêl. ¹⁴ And the names of those who lead them: Adnâr'êl, and Îjâsûsa'êl, and 'Elômê'êl–these three follow the leaders of the orders, and there is one that follows the three leaders of the orders which follow those leaders of stations that divide the four parts of the year. ¹⁵ In the beginning of the year Melkejâl rises first and rules, who is named †Tam'âinî† and sun, and all the days of his dominion whilst he bears rule are ninety-one days. ¹⁶ And these are the signs of the days which are to be seen on earth in the days of his dominion: sweat, and heat, and calms; and all the trees bear fruit, and leaves are produced on all the trees, and the harvest of wheat, and the rose-flowers, and all the flowers which come forth in the field, but the trees of the winter season become withered. ¹⁷ And these are the names of the leaders which are under them: Berka'êl, Zêlebs'êl, and another who is added a head of a thousand, called Hîlûjâsĕph: and the days of the dominion of this (leader)

are at an end. ¹⁸ The next leader after him is Hêl'emmêlêk, whom one names the shining sun, and all the days of his light are ninety-one days. ¹⁹ And these are the signs of (his) days on the earth: glowing heat and dryness, and the trees ripen their fruits and produce all their fruits ripe and ready, and the sheep pair and become pregnant, and all the fruits of the earth are gathered in, and everything that is in the fields, and the winepress: these things take place in the days of his dominion. ²⁰ These are the names, and the orders, and the leaders of those heads of thousands: Gîdâ'îjal, Kê'êl, and Hê'êl, and the name of the head of a thousand which is added to them, Asfâ'êl': and the days of his dominion are at an end.

LXXXIII-XC. The Dream-Visions.
LXXXIII. LXXXIV. First Dream-Vision on the Deluge.

83

¹ And now, my son Methuselah, I will show thee all my visions which I have seen, recounting them before thee. ² Two visions I saw before I took a wife, and the one was quite unlike the other: the first when I was learning to write: the second before I took thy mother, (when) I saw a terrible vision. And regarding them I prayed to the Lord. ³ I had laid me down in the house of my grandfather Mahalalel, (when) I saw in a vision how the heaven collapsed and was borne off and fell to the earth. ⁴ And when it fell to the earth I saw how the earth was swallowed up in a great abyss, and mountains were suspended on mountains, and hills sank down on hills, and high trees were rent from their stems, and hurled down and sunk in the abyss. ⁵ And thereupon a word fell into my mouth, and I lifted up (my voice) to cry aloud, and said: 'The earth is destroyed.' ⁶ And my grandfather Mahalalel waked me as I lay near him, and said unto me: 'Why dost thou cry so, my son, and why dost thou make such lamentation?' ⁷ And I recounted to him the whole vision which I had seen, and he said unto me: 'A terrible thing hast thou seen, my son, and of grave moment is thy dream-vision as to the secrets of all the sin of the earth: it must sink into the abyss and be destroyed with a great destruction. ⁸ And now, my son, arise and make petition to the Lord of glory, since thou art a believer, that a remnant may remain on the earth, and that He may not destroy the whole earth. ⁹ My son, from heaven all this will come upon the earth, and upon the earth there will be great destruction.' ¹⁰ After that I arose and prayed and implored and besought, and wrote down my prayer for the generations of the world, and I will show everything to thee, my son Methuselah. ¹¹ And when I had gone forth below and seen the heaven, and the sun rising in the east, and the moon setting in the west, and a few stars, and the whole earth, and everything as †He had known† it in the beginning, then I blessed the Lord of judgement and extolled Him because He had made the sun to go forth from the windows of the east, and he ascended and rose on the face of the heaven, and set out and kept traversing the path shown unto him.

84

¹ And I lifted up my hands in righteousness and blessed the Holy and Great One, and spake with the breath of my mouth, and with the tongue of flesh, which God has made for the children of the flesh of men, that they should speak therewith, and He gave them breath and a tongue and a mouth that they should speak therewith: ² 'Blessed be Thou, O Lord, King, Great and mighty in Thy greatness, Lord of the whole creation of the heaven, King of kings and God of the whole world. And Thy power and kingship and greatness abide for ever and ever, And throughout all generations Thy dominion; And all the heavens are Thy throne for ever, And the whole earth Thy footstool for ever and ever. ³ For Thou hast made and Thou rulest all things, And nothing is too hard for Thee, Wisdom departs not **from the place of Thy throne, Nor turns away** from Thy presence. And Thou knowest and seest and hearest everything, And there is nothing hidden from Thee [for Thou seest everything]. ⁴ And now the angels of Thy heavens are guilty of trespass, And upon the flesh of men abideth Thy wrath until the great day of judgement. ⁵ And now, O God and Lord and Great King, I implore and beseech Thee to fulfil my prayer, To leave me a posterity on earth, And not destroy all the flesh of man, And make the earth without inhabitant, So that there should be an eternal destruction. ⁶ And now, my Lord, destroy from the earth the flesh which has aroused Thy wrath, But the flesh of righteousness and uprightness establish as a plant of the eternal seed, And hide not Thy face from the prayer of Thy servant, O Lord.'

85

LXXXV-XC. The Second Dream-Vision of Enoch: the History of the World to the Founding of the Messianic Kingdom.

¹ And after this I saw another dream, and I will show the whole dream to thee, my son. ² And Enoch lifted up (his voice) and spake to his son Methuselah: 'To thee, my son, will I speak: hear my words—incline thine ear to the dream-vision of thy father. ³ Before I took thy mother Edna, I saw in a vision on my bed, and behold a bull came forth from the earth, and that bull was white; and after it came forth a heifer, and along with this (latter) came forth two bulls, one of them black and the other red. ⁴ And that black bull gored the red one and pursued him over the earth, and thereupon I could no longer see that red bull. ⁵ But that black bull grew and that heifer went with him, and I saw that many oxen proceeded from him which resembled and followed him. ⁶ And that cow, that first one, went from the presence of that first bull in order to seek that red one, but found him not, and lamented with a great lamentation over him and sought him. ⁷ And I looked till that first bull came to her and quieted her, and from that time onward she cried no more. ⁸ And after that she bore another white bull, and after him she bore many bulls and black cows. ⁹ And I saw in my sleep that white bull likewise grow and become a great white bull, and from Him proceeded many white bulls, and they resembled him. And they began to beget many white bulls, which resembled them, one following the other, (even) many.

LXXXVI. The Fall of the Angels and the Demoralization of Mankind.

86

¹ And again I saw with mine eyes as I slept, and I saw the heaven above, and behold a star fell from heaven, and it arose and eat and pastured amongst those oxen. ² And after that I saw the large and the black oxen, and behold they all changed their stalls and pastures and their cattle, and began to live with each other. ³ And again I saw in the vision, and looked towards the heaven, and behold I saw many stars descend and cast themselves down from heaven to that first star, and they became bulls amongst those cattle and pastured with them [amongst them]. ⁴ And I looked at them and saw, and behold they all let out their privy members, like horses, and began to cover the cows of the oxen, and they all became pregnant and bare elephants, camels, and asses. ⁵ And all the oxen feared them and were affrighted at them, and began to bite with their teeth and to devour, and to gore with their horns. ⁶ And they began, moreover, to devour those oxen; and behold all the children of the earth began to tremble and quake before them and to flee from them.

LXXXVII. The Advent of the Seven Archangels.

87

¹ And again I saw how they began to gore each other and to devour each other, and the earth began to cry aloud. ² And I raised mine eyes again to heaven, and I saw in the vision, and behold there came forth from heaven beings who were like white men: and four went forth from that place and three with them. ³ And those three that had last come forth grasped me by my hand and took me up, away from the generations of the earth, and raised me up to a lofty place, and showed me a tower raised high above the earth, and all the hills were lower. ⁴ And one said unto me: 'Remain here till thou seest everything that befalls those elephants, camels, and asses, and the stars and the oxen, and all of them.'

LXXXVIII. The Punishment of the Fallen Angels by the Archangels.

88

¹ And I saw one of those four who had come forth first, and he seized that first star which had fallen from the heaven, and bound it hand and foot and cast it into an abyss: now that abyss was narrow and deep, and horrible and dark. ² And one of them drew a sword, and gave it to those elephants and camels and asses: then they began to smite each other, and the whole earth quaked because of them. ³ And as I was beholding in the vision, lo, one of those four who had come forth stoned (them) from heaven, and gathered and took all the great stars whose privy members were like those of horses, and bound them all hand and foot, and cast them in an abyss of the earth.

LXXXIX. 1-9. The Deluge and the Deliverance of Noah.

89

¹ And one of those four went to that white bull and instructed him in a secret, without his being terrified: he was born a bull and became a man, and built for himself a great vessel and dwelt thereon; and three bulls dwelt with him in that vessel and they were covered in. ² And again I raised mine eyes towards heaven and saw a lofty roof, with seven water torrents thereon, and those torrents flowed with much water into an enclosure. ³ And I saw again, and behold fountains were opened on the surface of that great enclosure, and that water began to swell and rise upon the surface, and I saw that enclosure till all its surface was covered with water. ⁴ And the water, the darkness, and mist increased upon it; and as I looked at the height of that water, that water had risen above the height of that enclosure, and was streaming over that enclosure, and it stood upon the earth. ⁵ And all the cattle of that enclosure were gathered together until I saw how they sank and were swallowed up and perished in that water. ⁶ But that vessel floated

on the water, while all the oxen and elephants and camels and asses sank to the bottom with all the animals, so that I could no longer see them, and they were not able to escape, (but) perished and sank into the depths. ⁷ And again I saw in the vision till those water torrents were removed from that high roof, and the chasms of the earth were levelled up and other abysses were opened. ⁸ Then the water began to run down into these, till the earth became visible; but that vessel settled on the earth, and the darkness retired and light appeared. ⁹ But that white bull which had become a man came out of that vessel, and the three bulls with him, and one of those three was white like that bull, and one of them was red as blood, and one black: and that white bull departed from them.

LXXXIX. 10-27. From the Death of Noah to the Exodus.

¹⁰ And they began to bring forth beasts of the field and birds, so that there arose different genera: lions, tigers, wolves, dogs, hyenas, wild boars, foxes, squirrels, swine, falcons, vultures, kites, eagles, and ravens; and among them was born a white bull. ¹¹ And they began to bite one another; but that white bull which was born amongst them begat a wild ass and a white bull with it, and the wild asses multiplied. ¹² But that bull which was born from him begat a black wild boar and a white sheep; and the former begat many boars, but that sheep begat twelve sheep. ¹³ And when those twelve sheep had grown, they gave up one of them to the asses, and those asses again gave up that sheep to the wolves, and that sheep grew up among the wolves. ¹⁴ And the Lord brought the eleven sheep to live with it and to pasture with it among the wolves: and they multiplied and became many flocks of sheep. ¹⁵ And the wolves began to fear them, and they oppressed them until they destroyed their little ones, and they cast their young into a river of much water: but those sheep began to cry aloud on account of their little ones, and to complain unto their Lord. ¹⁶ And a sheep which had been saved from the wolves fled and escaped to the wild asses; and I saw the sheep how they lamented and cried, and besought their Lord with all their might, till that Lord of the sheep descended at the voice of the sheep from a lofty abode, and came to them and pastured them. ¹⁷ And He called that sheep which had escaped the wolves, and spake with it concerning the wolves that it should admonish them not to touch the sheep. ¹⁸ And the sheep went to the wolves according to the word of the Lord, and another sheep met it and went with it, and the two went and entered together into the assembly of those wolves, and spake with them and admonished them not to touch the sheep from henceforth. ¹⁹ And thereupon I saw the wolves, and how they oppressed the sheep exceedingly with all their power; and the sheep cried aloud. ²⁰ And the Lord came to the sheep and they began to smite those wolves: and the wolves began to make lamentation; but the sheep became quiet and forthwith ceased to cry out. ²¹ And I saw the sheep till they departed from amongst the wolves; but the eyes of the wolves were blinded, and those wolves departed in pursuit of the sheep with all their power. ²² And the Lord of the sheep went with them, as their leader, and all His sheep followed Him: and his face was dazzling and glorious and terrible to behold. ²³ But the wolves began to pursue those sheep till they reached a sea of water. ²⁴ And that sea was divided, and the water stood on this side and on that before their face, and their Lord led them and placed Himself between them and the wolves. ²⁵ And as those wolves did not yet see the sheep, they proceeded into the midst of that sea, and the wolves followed the sheep, and [those wolves] ran after them into that sea. ²⁶ And when they saw the Lord of the sheep, they turned to flee before His face, but that sea gathered itself together, and became as it had been created, and the water swelled and rose till it covered those wolves. ²⁷ And I saw till all the wolves who pursued those sheep perished and were drowned.

LXXXIX. 28-40. Israel in the Desert, the Giving of the Law, the Entrance into Palestine.

²⁸ But the sheep escaped from that water and went forth into a wilderness, where there was no water and no grass; and they began to open their eyes and to see; and I saw the Lord of the sheep pasturing them and giving them water and grass, and that sheep going and leading them. ²⁹ And that sheep ascended to the summit of that lofty rock, and the Lord of the sheep sent it to them. ³⁰ And after that I saw the Lord of the sheep who stood before them, and His appearance was great and terrible and majestic, and all those sheep saw Him and were afraid before His face. ³¹ And they all feared and trembled because of Him, and they cried to that sheep with them [which was amongst them]: "We are not able to stand before our Lord or to behold Him." ³² And that sheep which led them again ascended to the summit of that rock, but the sheep began to be blinded and to wander from the way which he had showed them, but that sheep wot not thereof. ³³ And the Lord of the sheep was wrathful exceedingly against them, and that sheep discovered it, and went down from the summit of the rock, and came to the sheep, and found the greatest part of them blinded and fallen away. ³⁴ And when they saw it they feared and trembled at its presence, and desired to return to their folds. ³⁵ And that sheep took other sheep with it, and came to those sheep which had fallen away, and began to slay them; and the sheep feared its presence, and thus that sheep brought back those sheep that had fallen away, and they returned to their folds. ³⁶ And I saw in this vision till that sheep became a man and built a house for the Lord of the sheep, and placed all the sheep in that house. ³⁷ And I saw till this sheep which had met that sheep which led them fell asleep: and I saw till all the great sheep perished and little ones arose in their place, and they came to a pasture, and approached a stream of water. ³⁸ Then that sheep, their leader which had become a man, withdrew from them and fell asleep, and all the sheep sought it and cried over it with a great crying. ³⁹ And I saw till they left off crying for that sheep and crossed that stream of water, and there arose the two sheep as leaders in the place of those which had led them and fallen asleep (lit. "had fallen asleep and led them"). ⁴⁰ And I saw till the sheep came to a goodly place, and a pleasant and glorious land, and I saw till those sheep were satisfied; and that house stood amongst them in the pleasant land.

LXXXIX. 41-50. From the Time of the Judges till the Building of the Temple.

⁴¹ And sometimes their eyes were opened, and sometimes blinded, till another sheep arose and led them and brought them all back, and their eyes were opened. ⁴² And the dogs and the foxes and the wild boars began to devour those sheep till the Lord of the sheep raised up [another sheep] a ram from their midst, which led them. ⁴³ And that ram began to butt on either side those dogs, foxes, and wild boars till he had destroyed them †all†. ⁴⁴ And that sheep whose eyes were opened saw that ram, which was amongst the sheep, **till** it †forsook its glory† and began to butt those sheep, and trampled upon them, and behaved itself unseemly. ⁴⁵ And the Lord of the sheep sent the **lamb** to another **lamb** and raised it to being a ram and leader of the sheep instead of that ram which had †forsaken its glory†. ⁴⁶ And it went to it and spake to it alone, and raised it to being a ram, and made it the prince and leader of the sheep; but during all these things those dogs oppressed the sheep. ⁴⁷ And the first ram pursued that second ram, and that second ram arose and fled before it; and I saw till those dogs pulled down the first ram. ⁴⁸ And that second ram arose and led the [little] sheep. ⁴⁹ And those sheep grew and multiplied; but all the dogs, and foxes, and wild boars feared and fled before it, and that ram butted and killed the wild beasts, and those wild beasts had no longer any power among the sheep and robbed them no more of ought. ⁴⁸ ᵇ. And that ram begat many sheep and fell asleep; and a little sheep became ram in its stead, and became prince and leader of those sheep. ⁵⁰ And that house became great and broad, and it was built for those sheep: (and) a tower lofty and great was built on the house for the Lord of the sheep, and that house was low, but the tower was elevated and lofty, and the Lord of the sheep stood on that tower and they offered a full table before Him.

LXXXIX. 51-67. The Two Kingdoms of Israel and Judah, to the Destruction of Jerusalem.

⁵¹ And again I saw those sheep that they again erred and went many ways, and forsook that their house, and the Lord of the sheep called some from amongst the sheep and sent them to the sheep, but the sheep began to slay them. ⁵² And one of them was saved and was not slain, and it sped away and cried aloud over the sheep; and they sought to slay it, but the Lord of the sheep saved it from the sheep, and brought it up to me, and caused it to dwell there. ⁵³ And many other sheep He sent to those sheep to testify unto them and lament over them. ⁵⁴ And after that I saw that when they forsook the house of the Lord and His tower they fell away entirely, and their eyes were blinded; and I saw the Lord of the sheep how He wrought much slaughter amongst them in their herds until those sheep invited that slaughter and betrayed His place. ⁵⁵ And He gave them over into the hands of the lions and tigers, and wolves and hyenas, and into the hand of the foxes, and to all the wild beasts, and those wild beasts began to tear in pieces those sheep. ⁵⁶ And I saw that He forsook that their house and their tower and gave them all into the hand of the lions, to tear and devour them, into the hand of all the wild beasts. ⁵⁷ And I began to cry aloud with all my power, and to appeal to the Lord of the sheep, and to represent to Him in regard to the sheep that they were devoured by all the wild beasts. ⁵⁸ But He remained unmoved, though He saw it, and rejoiced that they were devoured and swallowed and robbed, and left them to be devoured in the hand of all the beasts. ⁵⁹ And He called seventy shepherds, and cast those sheep to them that they might pasture them, and He spake to the shepherds and their companions: "Let each individual of you pasture the sheep henceforward, and everything that I shall command you that do ye. ⁶⁰ And I will deliver them over unto you duly numbered, and tell you which of them are to be destroyed–and them destroy ye." And He gave over unto them those sheep. ⁶¹ And He called another and spake unto him: "Observe and mark everything that the shepherds will do to those sheep; for they will

destroy more of them than I have commanded them. ⁶² And every excess and the destruction which will be wrought through the shepherds, record (namely) how many they destroy according to my command, and how many according to their own caprice: record against every individual shepherd all the destruction he effects. ⁶³ And read out before me by number how many they destroy, and how many they deliver over for destruction, that I may have this as a testimony against them, and know every deed of the shepherds, that I may **comprehend** and see what they do, whether or not they abide by my command which I have commanded them. ⁶⁴ But they shall not know it, and thou shalt not declare it to them, nor admonish them, but only record against each individual all the destruction which the shepherds effect each in his time and lay it all before me." ⁶⁵ And I saw till those shepherds pastured in their season, and they began to slay and to destroy more than they were bidden, and they delivered those sheep into the hand of the lions. ⁶⁶ And the lions and tigers eat and devoured the greater part of those sheep, and the wild boars eat along with them; and they burnt that tower and demolished that house. ⁶⁷ And I became exceedingly sorrowful over that tower because that house of the sheep was demolished, and afterwards I was unable to see if those sheep entered that house.

LXXXIX. 68-71. First Period of the Angelic Rulers–from the Destruction of Jerusalem to the Return from the Captivity.

⁶⁸ And the shepherds and their associates delivered over those sheep to all the wild beasts, to devour them, and each one of them received in his time a definite number: it was written by the other in a book how many each one of them destroyed of them. ⁶⁹ And each one slew and destroyed many more than was prescribed; and I began to weep and lament on account of those sheep. ⁷⁰ And thus in the vision I saw that one who wrote, how he wrote down every one that was destroyed by those shepherds, day by day, and carried up and laid down and showed actually the whole book to the Lord of the sheep–(even) everything that they had done, and all that each one of them had made away with, and all that they had given over to destruction. ⁷¹ And the book was read before the Lord of the sheep, and He took the book from his hand and read it and sealed it and laid it down.

LXXXIX. 72-77. Second Period–from the time of Cyrus to that of Alexander the Great.

⁷² And forthwith I saw how the shepherds pastured for twelve hours, and behold three of those sheep turned back and came and entered and began to build up all that had fallen down of that house; but the wild boars tried to hinder them, but they were not able. ⁷³ And they began again to build as before, and they reared up that tower, and it was named the high tower; and they began again to place a table before the tower, but all the bread on it was polluted and not pure. ⁷⁴ And as touching all this the eyes of those sheep were blinded so that they saw not, and (the eyes of) their shepherds likewise; and they delivered them in large numbers to their shepherds for destruction, and they trampled the sheep with their feet and devoured them. ⁷⁵ And the Lord of the sheep remained unmoved till all the sheep were dispersed over the field and mingled with them (*i.e.* the beasts), and they (*i.e.* the shepherds) did not save them out of the hand of the beasts. ⁷⁶ And this one who wrote the book carried it up, and showed it and read it before the Lord of the sheep, and implored Him on their account, and besought Him on their account as he showed Him all the doings of the shepherds, and gave testimony before Him against all the shepherds. And he took the actual book and laid it down beside Him and departed.

XC. 1-5. Third Period–from Alexander the Great to the Graeco-Syrian Domination.

90

¹ And I saw till that in this manner thirty-five shepherds undertook the pasturing (of the sheep), and they severally completed their periods as did the first; and others received them into their hands, to pasture them for their period, each shepherd in his own period. ² And after that I saw in my vision all the birds of heaven coming, the eagles, the vultures, the kites, the ravens; but the eagles led all the birds; and they began to devour those sheep, and to pick out their eyes and to devour their flesh. ³ And the sheep cried out because their flesh was being devoured by the birds, and as for me I looked and lamented in my sleep over that shepherd who pastured the sheep. ⁴ And I saw until those sheep were devoured by the dogs and eagles and kites, and they left neither flesh nor skin nor sinew remaining on them till only their bones stood there: and their bones too fell to the earth and the sheep became few. ⁵ And I saw until that twenty-three had undertaken the pasturing and completed in their several periods fifty-eight times.

XC. 6-12. Fourth Period–from the Graeco-Syrian Domination to the Maccabæan Revolt.

⁶ But behold lambs were borne by those white sheep, and they began to open their eyes and to see, and to cry to the sheep. ⁷ Yea, they cried to them, but they did not hearken to what they said to them, but were exceedingly deaf, and their eyes were very exceedingly blinded. ⁸ And I saw in the vision how the ravens flew upon those lambs and took one of those lambs, and dashed the sheep in pieces and devoured them. ⁹ And I saw till horns grew upon those lambs, and the ravens cast down their horns; and I saw till there sprouted a great horn of one of those sheep, and their eyes were opened. ¹⁰ And it †looked at† them [and their eyes opened], and it cried to the sheep, and the rams saw it and all ran to it. ¹¹ And notwithstanding all this those eagles and vultures and ravens and kites still kept tearing the sheep and swooping down upon them and devouring them: still the sheep remained silent, but the rams lamented and cried out. ¹² And those ravens fought and battled with it and sought to lay low its horn, but they had no power over it.

XC. 13-19. The Last Assault of the Gentiles on the Jews (where vv. 13-15 and 16-18 are doublets).

¹³ And I saw till the †shepherds and† eagles and those vultures and kites came, and †they cried to the ravens† that they should break the horn of that ram, and they battled and fought with it, and it battled with them and cried that its help might come.

¹⁶ All the eagles and vultures and ravens and kites were gathered together, and there came with them all the sheep of the field, yea, they all came together, and helped each other to break that horn of the ram.

¹⁴ And I saw till that man, who wrote down the names of the shepherds [and] carried up into the presence of the Lord of the sheep [came and helped it and showed it everything: he had come down for the help of that ram].

¹⁷ And I saw that man, who wrote the book according to the command of the Lord, till he opened that book concerning the destruction which those twelve last shepherds had wrought, and showed that they had destroyed much more than their predecessors, before the Lord of the sheep.

¹⁵ And I saw till the Lord of the sheep came unto them in wrath, and all who saw Him fled, and they all fell †into His shadow† from before His face.

¹⁸ And I saw till a great sword was given to the sheep, and the sheep proceeded against all the beasts of the field to slay them, and all the beasts and the birds of the heaven fled before their face.

¹⁹ And I saw till the Lord of the sheep came unto them and took in His hand the staff of His wrath, and smote the earth, and the earth clave asunder, and all the beasts and all the birds of the heaven fell from among those sheep, and were swallowed up in the earth and it covered them.

XC. 20-27. Judgement of the Fallen Angels, the Shepherds, and the Apostates.

²⁰ And I saw till a throne was erected in the pleasant land, and the Lord of the sheep sat Himself thereon, and **the other** took the sealed books and opened those books before the Lord of the sheep. ²¹ And the Lord called those men the seven first white ones, and commanded that they should bring before Him, beginning with the first star which led the way, **all the** stars whose privy members were like those of horses, and they brought them all before Him. ²² And He said to that man who wrote before Him, being one of those seven white ones, and said unto him: "Take those seventy shepherds to whom I delivered the sheep, and who taking them on their own authority slew more than I commanded them." ²³ And behold they were all bound, I saw, and they all stood before Him. ²⁴ And the judgement was held first over the stars, and they were judged and found guilty, and went to the place of condemnation, and they were cast into an abyss, full of fire and flaming, and full of pillars of fire. ²⁵ And those seventy shepherds were judged and found guilty, and they were cast into that fiery abyss. ²⁶ And I saw at that time how a like abyss was opened in the midst of the earth, full of fire, and they brought those blinded sheep, and they were all judged and found guilty and cast into this fiery abyss, and they burned; now this abyss was to the right of that house. ²⁷ And I saw those sheep burning †and their bones burning†.

XC. 28-38. The New Jerusalem, the Conversion of the surviving Gentiles, the Resurrection of the Righteous, the Messiah.

²⁸ And I stood up to see till they folded up that old house; and carried off all the pillars, and all the beams and ornaments of the house were at the same time folded up with it, and they carried it off and laid it in a place in the south of the land. ²⁹ And I saw till the Lord of the sheep brought a new house greater and loftier than that first, and set it up in the place of the first which had beer folded up: all its pillars were new, and its ornaments were

new and larger than those of the first, the old one which He had taken away, and all the sheep were within it. ³⁰ And I saw all the sheep which had been left, and all the beasts on the earth, and all the birds of the heaven, falling down and doing homage to those sheep and making petition to and obeying them in every **thing**. ³¹ And thereafter those three who were clothed in white and had seized me by my hand [who had taken me up before], and the hand of that ram also seizing hold of me, they took me up and set me down in the midst of those sheep before the judgement took place. ³² And those sheep were all white, and their wool was abundant and clean. ³³ And all that had been destroyed and dispersed, and all the beasts of the field, and all the birds of the heaven, assembled in that house, and the Lord of the sheep rejoiced with great joy because they were all good and had returned to His house. ³⁴ And I saw till they laid down that sword, which had been given to the sheep, and they brought it back into the house, and it was sealed before the presence of the Lord, and all the sheep were invited into that house, but it held them not. ³⁵ And the eyes of them all were opened, and they saw the good, and there was not one among them that did not see. ³⁶ And I saw that that house was large and broad and very full. ³⁷ And I saw that a white bull was born, with large horns and all the beasts of the field and all the birds of the air feared him and made petition to him all the time. ³⁸ And I saw till all their generations were transformed, and they all became white bulls; and the first among them became a **lamb**, and that **lamb** became a great animal and had great black horns on its head; and the Lord of the sheep rejoiced over **it** and over all the oxen. ³⁹ And I slept in their midst: and I awoke and saw everything. ⁴⁰ This is the vision which I saw while I slept, and I awoke and blessed the Lord of righteousness and gave Him glory. ⁴¹ Then I wept with a great weeping and my tears stayed not till I could no longer endure it: when I saw, they flowed on account of what I had seen; for everything shall come and be fulfilled, and all the deeds of men in their order were shown to me. ⁴² On that night I remembered the first dream, and because of it I wept and was troubled–because I had seen that vision.'

XCI. 1-11. Enoch's Admonition to his Children.

91

¹ 'And now, my son Methuselah, call to me all thy brothers And gather together to me all the sons of thy mother; For the word calls me, And the spirit is poured out upon me, That I may show you everything That shall befall you for ever.' ² And there upon Methuselah went and summoned to him all his brothers and assembled his relatives. ³ And he spake unto all the children of righteousness and said: 'Hear, ye sons of Enoch, all the words of your father, And hearken aright to the voice of my mouth; For I exhort you and say unto you, beloved: Love uprightness and walk therein. ⁴ And draw not nigh to uprightness with a double heart, And associate not with those of a double heart, But walk in righteousness, my sons. And it shall guide you on good paths, And righteousness shall be your companion. ⁵ For I know that violence **must** increase on the earth, And a great chastisement be executed on the earth, And all unrighteousness come to an end: Yea, it shall be cut off from its roots, And its whole structure be destroyed. ⁶ And unrighteousness shall again be consummated on the earth, And all the deeds of unrighteousness and of violence And transgression shall prevail in a twofold degree. ⁷ And when sin and unrighteousness and blasphemy And violence in all kinds of deeds increase, And apostasy and transgression and uncleanness increase, A great chastisement shall come from heaven upon all these, And the holy Lord will come forth with wrath and chastisement To execute judgement on earth. ⁸ In those days violence shall be cut off from its roots, And the roots of unrighteousness together with deceit, And they shall be destroyed from under heaven. ⁹ And all the idols of the heathen shall be abandoned, And the temples burned with fire, And they shall remove them from the whole earth, And they (*i.e.* the heathen) shall be cast into the judgement of fire, And shall perish in wrath and in grievous judgement for ever. ¹⁰ And the righteous shall arise from their sleep, And wisdom shall arise and be given unto them. ¹¹ [And after that the roots of unrighteousness shall be cut off, and the sinners shall be destroyed by the sword . . . shall be cut off from the blasphemers in every place, and those who plan violence and those who commit blasphemy shall perish by the sword.]

XCI. 12.- 17 The Last Three Weeks.

¹² And after that there shall be another, the eighth week, that of righteousness, And a sword shall be given to it that a righteous judgement may be executed on the oppressors, And sinners shall be delivered into the hands of the righteous. ¹³ And at its close they shall acquire houses through their righteousness, And a house shall be built for the Great King in glory for evermore. ¹⁴ *a* And after that, in the ninth week, the righteous judgement shall be revealed to the whole world, *b* And all the works of the godless shall vanish from all the earth, *c* And the world shall be written down for destruction. *d*. And all mankind shall look to the path of uprightness. ¹⁵ And after this, in the tenth week in the seventh part, There shall be the great eternal judgement, In which He will execute vengeance amongst the angels. ¹⁶ And the first heaven shall depart and pass away, And a new heaven shall appear, And all the powers of the heavens shall give sevenfold light. ¹⁷ And after that there will be many weeks without number for ever, And all shall be in goodness and righteousness, And sin shall no more be mentioned for ever.

XCI. 18-19. Enoch's Admonition to his Children (continuation).

¹⁸ And now I tell you, my sons, and show you The paths of righteousness and the paths of violence. Yea, I will show them to you again That ye may know what will come to pass. ¹⁹ And now, hearken unto me, my sons, And walk in the paths of righteousness, And walk not in the paths of violence; For all who walk in the paths of unrighteousness shall perish for ever.'

92

XCII-CV. The Epistle of Enoch.

XCII. Enoch's Book of Admonition for his Children (continuation).

¹ The book written by Enoch–[Enoch indeed wrote this complete doctrine of wisdom, (which is) praised of all men and a judge of all the earth] for all my children who shall dwell on the earth. And for the future generations who shall observe uprightness and peace. ² Let not your spirit be troubled on account of the times; For the Holy and Great One has appointed days for all things. ³ And the righteous one shall arise from sleep, [Shall arise] and walk in the paths of righteousness, And all his path and conversation shall be in eternal goodness and grace. ⁴ He will be gracious to the righteous and give him eternal uprightness, And He will give him power so that he shall be (endowed) with goodness and righteousness. And he shall walk in eternal light. ⁵ And sin shall perish in darkness for ever, And shall no more be seen from that day for evermore.

XCIII. The Apocalypse of Weeks.

93

¹ And after that Enoch both †gave† and began to recount from the books. ² And Enoch said: 'Concerning the children of righteousness and concerning the elect of the world, And concerning the plant of uprightness, I will speak these things, Yea, I Enoch will declare (them) unto you, my sons: According to that which appeared to me in the heavenly vision, And which I have known through the word of the holy angels, And have learnt from the heavenly tablets.' ³ And Enoch began to recount from the books and said: 'I was born the seventh in the first week, While judgement and righteousness still endured. ⁴ And after me there shall arise in the second week great wickedness, And deceit shall have sprung up; And in it there shall be the first end. And in it a man shall be saved; And after it is ended unrighteousness shall grow up, And a law shall be made for the sinners. ⁵ And after that in the third week at its close A man shall be elected as the plant of righteous judgement, And **his posterity** shall become the plant of righteousness for evermore. ⁶ And after that in the fourth week, at its close, Visions of the holy and righteous shall be seen, And a law for all generations and an enclosure shall be made for them. ⁷ And after that in the fifth week, at its close, The house of glory and dominion shall be built for ever. ⁸ And after that in the sixth week all who live in it shall be blinded, And the hearts of all of them shall godlessly forsake wisdom. And in it a man shall ascend; And at its close the house of dominion shall be burnt with fire, And the whole race of the chosen root shall be dispersed. ⁹ And after that in the seventh week shall an apostate generation arise, And many shall be its deeds, And all its deeds shall be apostate. ¹⁰ And at its close shall be elected The elect righteous of the eternal plant of righteousness, To receive sevenfold instruction concerning all His creation. ¹¹ [For who is there of all the children of men that is able to hear the voice of the Holy One without being troubled? And who can think His thoughts? and who is there that can behold all the works of heaven? ¹² And how should there be one who could behold the heaven, and who is there that could understand the things of heaven and see a soul or a spirit and could tell thereof, or ascend and see all their ends and think them or do like them? ¹³ And who is there of all men that could know what is the breadth and the length of the earth, and to whom has been shown the measure of all of them? ¹⁴ Or is there any one who could discern the length of the heaven and how great is its height, and upon what it is founded, and how great is the number of the stars, and where all the luminaries rest?]

XCIV. 1-5. Admonitions to the Righteous.

94

¹ And now I say unto you, my sons, love righteousness and walk therein; For the paths of righteousness are worthy of acceptance, But the paths of

unrighteousness shall suddenly be destroyed and vanish. ² And to certain men of a generation shall the paths of violence and of death be revealed, And they shall hold themselves afar from them, And shall not follow them. ³ And now I say unto you the righteous: Walk not in the paths of wickedness, nor in the paths of death, And draw not nigh to them, lest ye be destroyed. ⁴ But seek and choose for yourselves righteousness and an elect life, And walk in the paths of peace, And ye shall live and prosper. ⁵ And hold fast my words in the thoughts of your hearts, And suffer them not to be effaced from your hearts; For I know that sinners will tempt men to **evilly-entreat** wisdom, So that no place may be found for her, And no manner of temptation may minish.

XCIV. 6-11. Woes for the Sinners.

⁶ Woe to those who build unrighteousness and oppression And lay deceit as a foundation; For they shall be suddenly overthrown, And they shall have no peace. ⁷ Woe to those who build their houses with sin; For from all their foundations shall they be overthrown, And by the sword shall they fall. [And those who acquire gold and silver in judgement suddenly shall perish.] ⁸ Woe to you, ye rich, for ye have trusted in your riches, And from your riches shall ye depart, Because ye have not remembered the Most High in the days of your riches. ⁹ Ye have committed blasphemy and unrighteousness, And have become ready for the day of slaughter, And the day of darkness and the day of the great judgement. ¹⁰ Thus I speak and declare unto you: He who hath created you will overthrow you, And for your fall there shall be no compassion, And your Creator will rejoice at your destruction. ¹¹ And your righteous ones in those days shall be A reproach to the sinners and the godless.

XCV. Enoch's Grief: fresh Woes against the Sinners.

95

¹ Oh that mine eyes were [a cloud of] waters That I might weep over you, And pour down my tears as a cloud †of† waters: That so I might rest from my trouble of heart! ² †Who has permitted you to practice reproaches and wickedness? And so judgement shall overtake you, sinners. † ³ Fear not the sinners, ye righteous; For again will the Lord deliver them into your hands, That ye may execute judgement upon them according to your desires. ⁴ Woe to you who fulminate anathemas which cannot be reversed: Healing shall therefore be far from you because of your sins. ⁵ Woe to you who requite your neighbour with evil; For ye shall be requited according to your works. ⁶ Woe to you, lying witnesses, And to those who weigh out injustice, For suddenly shall ye perish. ⁷ Woe to you, sinners, for ye persecute the righteous; For ye shall be delivered up and persecuted because of injustice, And heavy shall its yoke be upon you.

XCVI. Grounds of Hopefulness for the Righteous: Woes for the Wicked.

96

¹ Be hopeful, ye righteous; for suddenly shall the sinners perish before you, And ye shall have lordship over them according to your desires. ² [And in the day of the tribulation of the sinners, Your children shall mount and rise as eagles, And higher than the vultures will be your nest, And ye shall ascend and enter the crevices of the earth, And the clefts of the rock for ever as coneys before the unrighteous, And the sirens shall sigh because of you- and weep.] ³ Wherefore fear not, ye that have suffered; For healing shall be your portion, And a bright light shall enlighten you, And the voice of rest ye shall hear from heaven. ⁴ Woe unto you, ye sinners, for your riches make you appear like the righteous, But your hearts convict you of being sinners, And this fact shall be a testimony against you for a memorial of (your) evil deeds. ⁵ Woe to you who devour the finest of the wheat, And drink **wine in large bowls**, And tread under foot the lowly with your might. ⁶ Woe to you who drink water **from every fountain**, For suddenly shall ye be consumed and wither away, Because ye have forsaken the fountain of life. ⁷ Woe to you who work unrighteousness And deceit and blasphemy: It shall be a memorial against you for evil. ⁸ Woe to you, ye mighty, Who with might oppress the righteous; For the day of your destruction is coming. In those days many and good days shall come to the righteous–in the day of your judgement.

XCVII. The Evils in Store for Sinners and the Possessors of unrighteous Wealth.

97

¹ Believe, ye righteous, that the sinners will become a shame And perish in the day of unrighteousness. ² Be it known unto you (ye sinners) that the Most High is mindful of your destruction, And the angels of heaven rejoice over your destruction. ³ What will ye do, ye sinners, And whither will ye flee on that day of judgement, When ye hear the voice of the prayer of the righteous? ⁴ Yea, ye shall fare like unto them, Against whom this word shall be a testimony: "Ye have been companions of sinners." ⁵ And in those days the prayer of the righteous shall reach unto the Lord, And for you the days of your judgement shall come. ⁶ And all the words of your unrighteousness shall be read out before the Great Holy One, And your faces shall be covered with shame, And He will reject every work which is grounded on unrighteousness. ⁷ Woe to you, ye sinners, who live on the mid ocean and on the dry land, Whose remembrance is evil against you. ⁸ Woe to you who acquire silver and gold in unrighteousness and say: "We have become rich with riches and have possessions; And have acquired everything we have desired. ⁹ And now let us do what we purposed: For we have gathered silver, ¹⁰ And many are the husbandmen in our houses." ¹¹ And our granaries are (brim) full as with water, ¹² Yea and like water your lies shall flow away; For your riches shall not abide But speedily ascend from you;For ye have acquired it all in unrighteousness, And ye shall be given over to a great curse.

XCVIII. Self-indulgence of Sinners; Sin originated by Man; all Sin recorded in Heaven; Woes for the Sinners.

98

¹ And now I swear unto you, to the wise and to the foolish, For ye shall have manifold experiences on the earth. ² For ye men shall put on more adornments than a woman, And coloured garments more than a virgin: In royalty and in grandeur and in power, And in silver and in gold and in purple, And in splendour and in food they shall be poured out as water. ³ Therefore they shall be wanting in doctrine and wisdom, And they shall perish thereby together with their possessions; And with all their glory and their splendour, And in shame and in slaughter and in great destitution, Their spirits shall be cast into the furnace of fire. ⁴ I have sworn unto you, ye sinners, as a mountain has not become a slave, And a hill does not become the handmaid of a woman, Even so sin has not been sent upon the earth, But man of himself has created it, And under a great curse shall they fall who commit it. ⁵ And barrenness has not been given to the woman, But on account of the deeds of her own hands she dies without children. ⁶ I have sworn unto you, ye sinners, by the Holy Great One, That all your evil deeds are revealed in the heavens, And that none of your deeds of oppression are covered and hidden. ⁷ And do not think in your spirit nor say in your heart that ye do not know and that ye do not see that every sin is every day recorded in heaven in the presence of the Most High. ⁸ From henceforth ye know that all your oppression wherewith ye oppress is written down every day till the day of your judgement. ⁹ Woe to you, ye fools, for through your folly shall ye perish: and ye transgress against the wise, and so good hap shall not be your portion. ¹⁰ And now, know ye that ye are prepared for the day of destruction: wherefore do not hope to live, ye sinners, but ye shall depart and die; for ye know no ransom; for ye are prepared for the day of the great judgement, for the day of tribulation and great shame for your spirits. ¹¹ Woe to you, ye obstinate of heart, who work wickedness and eat blood: Whence have ye good things to eat and to drink and to be filled?From all the good things which the Lord the Most High has placed in abundance on the earth; therefore ye shall have no peace. ¹² Woe to you who love the deeds of unrighteousness: wherefore do ye hope for good hap unto yourselves? know that ye shall be delivered into the hands of the righteous, and they shall cut off your necks and slay you, and have no mercy upon you. ¹³ Woe to you who rejoice in the tribulation of the righteous; for no grave shall be dug for you. ¹⁴ Woe to you who set at nought the words of the righteous; for ye shall have no hope of life. ¹⁵ Woe to you who write down lying and godless words; for they write down their lies that men may hear them and act godlessly towards (their) neighbour. ¹⁶ Therefore they shall have no peace but die a sudden death.

XCIX. Woes pronounced on the Godless, the Lawbreakers; evil Plight of Sinners in the last Days; further Woes.

99

¹ Woe to you who work godlessness, And glory in lying and extol them: Ye shall perish, and no happy life shall be yours. ² Woe to them who pervert the words of uprightness, And transgress the eternal law, And transform themselves into what they were not [into sinners]: They shall be trodden under foot upon the earth. ³ In those days make ready, ye righteous, to raise your prayers as **a** memorial, And place them as a testimony before the angels, That they may place the sin of the sinners for a memorial before the Most High. ⁴ In those days the nations shall be stirred up, And the families of the nations shall arise on the day of destruction. ⁵ And in those days the destitute shall go forth and carry off their children, And they shall abandon them, so that their children shall perish through them: Yea, they shall abandon their children (that are still) sucklings, and not return to them, And shall have no pity on their beloved ones. ⁶ And again I swear to you, ye sinners, that sin is prepared for a day of unceasing bloodshed. ⁷ And they who worship stones, and grave images of gold and silver and wood <and

stone> and clay, and those who worship impure spirits and demons, and all kinds of idols not according to knowledge, shall get no manner of help from them. ⁸ And they shall become godless by reason of the folly of their hearts, And their eyes shall be blinded through the fear of their hearts And through visions in their dreams. ⁹ Through these they shall become godless and fearful; For they shall have wrought all their work in a lie, And shall have worshiped a stone: Therefore in an instant shall they perish. ¹⁰ But in those days blessed are all they who accept the words of wisdom, and understand them, And observe the paths of the Most High, and walk in the path of His righteousness, And become not godless with the godless; For they shall be saved. ¹¹ Woe to you who spread evil to your neighbours; For you shall be slain in Sheol. ¹² Woe to you who make deceitful and false measures, And (to them) who cause bitterness on the earth; For they shall thereby be utterly consumed. ¹³ Woe to you who build your houses through the grievous toil of others, And all their building materials are the bricks and stones of sin; I tell you ye shall have no peace. ¹⁴ Woe to them who reject the measure and eternal heritage of their fathers And whose souls follow after idols; For they shall have no rest. ¹⁵ Woe to them who work unrighteousness and help oppression, And slay their neighbours until the day of the great judgement. ¹⁶ For He shall cast down your glory, And bring affliction on your hearts, And shall arouse **His fierce indignation**, And destroy you all with the sword; And all the holy and righteous shall remember your sins.

C. The Sinners destroy each other; Judgement of the fallen Angels; the Safety of the Righteous; further Woes for the Sinners.

100

¹ And in those days in one place the fathers together with their sons shall be smitten And brothers one with another shall fall in death Till the streams flow with their blood. ² .For a man shall not withhold his hand from slaying his sons and his sons' sons, And the sinner shall not withhold his hand from his honoured brother: From dawn till sunset they shall slay one another. ³ And the horse shall walk up to the breast in the blood of sinners, And the chariot shall be submerged to its height. ⁴ In those days the angels shall descend into the secret places And gather together into one place all those who brought down sin And the Most High will arise on that day of judgement To execute great judgement amongst sinners. ⁵ And over all the righteous and holy He will appoint guardians from amongst the holy angels To guard them as the apple of an eye, Until He makes an end of all wickedness and all sin, And though the righteous sleep a long sleep, they have nought to fear. ⁶ And (then) the children of the earth shall see the wise **in security**, And shall understand all the words of this book, And recognize that their riches shall not be able to save them In the overthrow of their sins. ⁷ Woe to you, Sinners, on the day of strong anguish, **Ye who afflict** the righteous and burn them with fire: Ye shall be requited according to your works. ⁸ Woe to you, ye obstinate of heart, Who watch in order to devise wickedness: Therefore shall fear come upon you And there shall be none to help you. ⁹ Woe to you, ye sinners, on account of the words of your mouth, And on account of the deeds of your hands which your godlessness as wrought, In blazing flames burning worse than fire shall ye burn. ¹⁰ And now, know ye that from the angels He will inquire as to your deeds in heaven, from the sun and from the moon and from the stars in reference to your sins because upon the earth ye execute judgement on the righteous. ¹¹ And He will summon to testify against you every cloud and mist and dew and rain; for they shall all be withheld because of you from descending upon you, and they shall be mindful of your sins. ¹² And now give presents to the rain that it be not withheld from descending upon you, nor yet the dew, when it has received gold and silver from you that it may descend. ¹³ When the hoar-frost and snow with their chilliness, and all the snow-storms with all their plagues fall upon you, in those days ye shall not be able to stand before them.

CI. Exhortation to the Fear of God: all Nature fears Him, but not the Sinners.

101

¹ Observe the heaven, ye children of heaven, and every work of the Most High, and fear ye Him and work no evil in His presence. ² If He closes the windows of heaven, and withholds the rain and the dew from descending on the earth on your account, what will ye do then? ³ And if He sends His anger upon you because of your deeds, ye cannot petition Him; for ye spake proud and insolent words against His righteousness: therefore ye shall have no peace. ⁴ And see ye not the **sailors** of the ships, how their ships are tossed to and fro by the waves, and are shaken by the winds, and are in sore trouble? ⁵ And therefore do they fear because all their goodly possessions go upon the sea with them, and they have evil forebodings of heart that the sea will swallow them and they will perish therein. ⁶ Are not the entire sea and all its waters, and all its movements, the work of the Most High, and has He not set limits to its doings, and confined it throughout by the sand? ⁷ And at His reproof it is afraid and dries up, and all its fish die and all that is in it; But ye sinners that are on the earth fear Him not. ⁸ Has He not made the heaven and the earth, and all that is therein? Who has given understanding and wisdom to everything that moves on the earth and in the sea. ⁹ Do not the **sailors** of the ships fear the sea? Yet sinners fear not the Most High.

CII. Terrors of the Day of Judgement: the adverse Fortunes of the Righteous on the Earth.

102

¹ In those days when He hath brought a grievous fire upon you, Whither will ye flee, and where will ye find deliverance? And when He launches forth His Word against you Will you not be affrighted and fear? ² And all the luminaries shall be affrighted with great fear, And all the earth shall be affrighted and tremble and be alarmed. ³ And all the †angels shall execute their commands† And shall seek to hide themselves from the presence of the Great Glory, And the children of earth shall tremble and quake; And ye sinners shall be cursed for ever, And ye shall have no peace. ⁴ Fear ye not, ye souls of the righteous, And be hopeful ye that have died in righteousness. ⁵ And grieve not if your soul into Sheol has descended in grief, And that in your life your body fared not according to your goodness, But **wait for** the day of the **judgement** of sinners And for the day of cursing and chastisement. ⁶ And yet when ye die the sinners speak over you: "As we die, so die the righteous, And what benefit do they reap for their deeds? ⁷ Behold, even as we, so do they die in grief and darkness, And what have they more than we? From henceforth we are equal. ⁸ And what will they receive and what will they see for ever? Behold, they too have died, And henceforth for ever shall they see no light." ⁹ I tell you, ye sinners, ye are content to eat and drink, and rob and sin, and strip men naked, and acquire wealth and see good days. ¹⁰ Have ye seen the righteous how their end falls out, that no manner of violence is found in them till their death? ¹¹ "Nevertheless they perished and became as though they had not been, and their spirits descended into Sheol in tribulation."

CIII. Different Destinies of the Righteous and the Sinners: fresh Objections of the Sinners.

103

¹ Now, therefore, I swear to you, the righteous, by the glory of the Great and Honoured and Mighty One in dominion, and by His greatness I swear to you: ² I know a mystery And have read the heavenly tablets, And have seen the holy books, And have found written therein and inscribed regarding them: ³ That all goodness and joy and glory are prepared for them, And written down for the spirits of those who have died in righteousness, And that manifold good shall be given to you in recompense for your labours, And that your lot is abundantly beyond the lot of the living. ⁴ And the spirits of you who have died in righteousness shall live and rejoice, And their spirits shall not perish, nor their memorial from before the face of the Great One Unto all the generations of the world: wherefore no longer fear their contumely. ⁵ Woe to you, ye sinners, when ye have died, If ye die in the wealth of your sins, And those who are like you say regarding you: 'Blessed are the sinners: they have seen all their days. ⁶ And how they have died in prosperity and in wealth, And have not seen tribulation or murder in their life; And they have died in honour, And judgement has not been executed on them during their life." ⁷ Know ye, that their souls will be made to descend into Sheol And they shall be wretched in their great tribulation. ⁸ And into darkness and chains and a burning flame where there is grievous judgement shall your spirits enter; And the great judgement shall be for all the generations of the world. Woe to you, for ye shall have no peace. ⁹ Say not in regard to the righteous and good who are in life: "In our troubled days we have toiled laboriously and experienced every trouble, And met with much evil and been consumed, And have become few and our spirit small. ¹⁰ And we have been destroyed and have not found any to help us even with a word: We have been tortured [and destroyed], and not hoped to see life from day to day. ¹¹ We hoped to be the head and have become the tail: We have toiled laboriously and had no satisfaction in our toil; And we have become the food of the sinners and the unrighteous, And they have laid their yoke heavily upon us. ¹² They have had dominion over us that hated us †and smote us; And to those that hated us† we have bowed our necks But they pitied us not. ¹³ We desired to get away from them that we might escape and be at rest, But found no place whereunto we should flee and be safe from them. ¹⁴ And are complained to the rulers in our tribulation, And cried out against those who devoured us, But they did not attend to our cries And would not hearken to our voice. ¹⁵ And they helped those who robbed us and devoured us and those who made us few; and they

concealed their oppression, and they did not remove from us the yoke of those that devoured us and dispersed us and murdered us, and they concealed their murder, and remembered not that they had lifted up their hands against us.

CIV. Assurances given to the Righteous; Admonitions to Sinners and the Falsifiers of the Words of Uprightness.

104

¹ I swear unto you, that in heaven the angels remember you for good before the glory of the Great One: and your names are written before the glory of the Great One. ² Be hopeful; for aforetime ye were put to shame through ill and affliction; but now ye shall shine as the lights of heaven, ye shall shine and ye shall be seen, and the portals of heaven shall be opened to you. ³ And in your cry, cry for judgement, and it shall appear to you; for all your tribulation shall be visited on the rulers, and on all who helped those who plundered you. ⁴ Be hopeful, and cast not away your hopes for ye shall have great joy as the angels of heaven. ⁵ What shall ye be obliged to do? Ye shall not have to hide on the day of the great judgement and ye shall not be found as sinners, and the eternal judgement shall be far from you for all the generations of the world. ⁶ And now fear not, ye righteous, when ye see the sinners growing strong and prospering in their ways: be not companions with them, but keep afar from their violence; for ye shall become companions of the hosts of heaven. ⁷ And, although ye sinners say: "All our sins shall not be searched out and be written down," nevertheless they shall write down all your sins every day. ⁸ And now I show unto you that light and darkness, day and night, see all your sins. ⁹ Be not godless in your hearts, and lie not and alter not the words of uprightness, nor charge with lying the words of the Holy Great One, nor take account of your idols; for all your lying and all your godlessness issue not in righteousness but in great sin. ¹⁰ And now I know this mystery, that sinners will alter and pervert the words of righteousness in many ways, and will speak wicked words, and lie, and practice great deceits, and write books concerning their words. ¹¹ But when they write down truthfully all my words in their languages, and do not change or minish ought from my words but write them all down truthfully–all that I first testified concerning them. ¹² Then, I know another mystery, that books will be given to the righteous and the wise to become a cause of joy and uprightness and much wisdom. ¹³ And to them shall the books be given, and they shall believe in them and rejoice over them, and then shall all the righteous who have learnt therefrom all the paths of uprightness be recompensed.'

XCV. God and the Messiah to dwell with Man.

105

¹ In those days the Lord bade (them) to summon and testify to the children of earth concerning their wisdom: Show (it) unto them; for ye are their guides, and a recompense over the whole earth. ² For I and My son will be united with them for ever in the paths of uprightness in their lives; and ye shall have peace: rejoice, ye children of uprightness. Amen.

CVI-CVII. Fragment of the Book of Noah.

106

¹ And after some days my son Methuselah took a wife for his son Lamech, and she became pregnant by him and bore a son. ² And his body was white as snow and red as the blooming of a rose, and the hair of his head †and his long locks were white as wool, and his eyes beautiful†. And when he opened his eyes, he lighted up the whole house like the sun, and the whole house was very bright. ³ And thereupon he arose in the hands of the midwife, opened his mouth, and †conversed with† the Lord of righteousness. ⁴ And his father Lamech was afraid of him and fled, and came to his father Methuselah. ⁵ And he said unto him: 'I have begotten a strange son, diverse from and unlike man, and resembling the sons of the God of heaven; and his nature is different and he is not like us, and his eyes are as the rays of the sun, and his countenance is glorious. ⁶ And it seems to me that he is not sprung from me but from the angels, and I fear that in his days a wonder may be wrought on the earth. ⁷ And now, my father, I am here to petition thee and implore thee that thou mayest go to Enoch, our father, and learn from him the truth, for his dwelling-place is amongst the angels.' ⁸ And when Methuselah heard the words of his son, he came to me to the ends of the earth; for he had heard that I was there, and he cried aloud, and I heard his voice and I came to him. And ¹ said unto him: 'Behold, here am I, my son, **wherefore** hast thou come to me?' ⁹ And he answered and said: 'Because of a great cause of anxiety have I come to thee, and because of a disturbing vision have I approached. ¹⁰ And now, my father, hear me: unto Lamech my son there hath been born a son, the like of whom there is none, and his nature is not like man's nature, and the colour of his body is whiter than snow and redder than the bloom of a rose, and the hair of his head is whiter than white wool, and his eyes are like the rays of the sun, and he opened his eyes and thereupon lighted up the whole house. ¹¹ And he arose in the hands of the midwife, and opened his mouth and blessed the Lord of heaven. ¹² And his father Lamech became afraid and fled to me, and did not believe that he was sprung from him, but that he was in the likeness of the angels of heaven; and behold I have come to thee that thou mayest make known to me the truth.' ¹³ And I, Enoch, answered and said unto him: 'The Lord will do a new thing on the earth, and this I have already seen in a vision, and make known to thee that in the generation of my father Jared some of the **angels** of heaven transgressed the word of the Lord. ¹⁴ And behold they commit sin and transgress the law, and have united themselves with women and commit sin with them, and have married some of them, and have begot children by them. ¹⁵ Yea, there shall come a great destruction over the whole earth, and there shall be a deluge and a great destruction for one year. ¹⁶ And this son who has been born unto you shall be left on the earth, and his three children shall be saved with him: when all mankind that are on the earth shall die [he and his sons shall be saved]. ¹⁷ And they shall produce on the earth giants not according to the spirit, but according to the flesh, and there shall be a great punishment on the earth, and the earth shall be cleansed from all impurity. ¹⁸ And now make known to thy son Lamech that he who has been born is in truth his son, and call his name Noah; for he shall be left to you, and he and his sons shall be saved from the destruction, which shall come upon the earth on account of all the sin and all the unrighteousness, which shall be consummated on the earth in his days. ¹⁹ And after that there shall be still more unrighteousness than that which was first consummated on the earth; for I know the mysteries of the holy ones; for He, the Lord, has showed me and informed me, and I have read (them) in the heavenly tablets.

107

¹ And I saw written on them that generation upon generation shall transgress, till a generation of righteousness arises, and transgression is destroyed and sin passes away from the earth, and all manner of good comes upon it. ² And now, my son, go and make known to thy son Lamech that this son, which has been born, is in truth his son, and that (this) is no lie.' ³ And when Methuselah had heard the words of his father Enoch–for he had shown to him everything in secret–he returned and showed (them) to him and called the name of that son Noah; for he will comfort the earth after all the destruction.

CVIII. An Appendix to the Book of Enoch

108

¹ Another book which Enoch wrote for his son Methuselah and for those who will come after him, and keep the law in the last days. ² Ye who have done good shall wait for those days till an end is made of those who work evil; and an end of the might of the transgressors. ³ And wait ye indeed till sin has passed away, for their names shall be blotted out of the book of life and out of the holy books, and their seed shall be destroyed for ever, and their spirits shall be slain, and they shall cry and make lamentation in a place that is a chaotic wilderness, and **in the fire shall they burn**; for there is no earth there. ⁴ And I saw there something like an invisible cloud; for by reason of its depth I could not look over, and I saw a flame of fire blazing brightly, and things like shining mountains circling and sweeping to and fro. ⁵ And I asked one of the holy angels who was with me and said unto him: 'What is this shining thing? for it is not a heaven but only the flame of a blazing fire, and the voice of weeping and crying and lamentation and strong pain.' ⁶ And he said unto me: 'This place which thou seest–here are cast the spirits of sinners and blasphemers, and of those who work wickedness, and of those who pervert everything that the Lord hath spoken through the mouth of the prophets–(even) the things that shall be. ⁷ For some of them are written and inscribed above in the heaven, in order that the angels may read them and know that which shall befall the sinners, and the spirits of the humble, and of those who have afflicted their bodies, and been recompensed by God; and of those who have been put to shame by wicked men: ⁸ Who love God and loved neither gold nor silver nor any of the good things which are in the world, but gave over their bodies to torture. ⁹ Who, since they came into being, longed not after earthly food, but regarded everything as a passing breath, and lived accordingly, and the Lord tried them much, and their spirits were found pure so that they should bless His name. ¹⁰ And all the blessings destined for them I have recounted in the books. And he hath assigned them their recompense, because they have been found to be such as loved heaven more than their life in the world, and though they were trodden under foot of wicked men, and experienced abuse and reviling from them and were put to shame, yet they blessed Me. ¹¹ And now I will summon the spirits of the good who belong to the generation of light, and I will transform those who were born in darkness, who in the flesh were not recompensed with such honour as their faithfulness deserved. ¹² And I will bring forth in shining light those who

have loved My holy name, and I will seat each on the throne of his honour. **13** And they shall be resplendent for times without number; for righteousness is the judgement of God; for to the faithful He will give faithfulness in the habitation of upright paths. **14** And they shall see those who were, born in darkness led into darkness, while the righteous shall be resplendent. **15** And the sinners shall cry aloud and see them resplendent, and they indeed will go where days and seasons are prescribed for them.'

The Fourth Book of the Maccabees

The Fourth Book of the Maccabees appears in an appendix to the Greek Septuagint. It is considered to be apocrypha by most church traditions. It is preserved here for its supplementary historical value.

1

1 As I am going to demonstrate a most philosophical proposition, namely, that religious reasoning is absolute master of the emotions. I would willingly advise you to give the utmost heed to philosophy. **2** For reason is necessary to everyone as a step to science. In addition, it embraces the praise of self-control, the highest virtue. **3** If, then, reasoning appears to hold the mastery over the emotions which stand in the way of temperance, such as gluttony and lust, **4** it surely also and manifestly rules over the affections which are contrary to justice, such as malice, and of those which are hindrances to courage, such as wrath, pain, and fear. **5** Perhaps some may ask, "How is it, then, that reasoning, if it rules the emotions, isn't also master of forgetfulness and ignorance?" They attempt a ridiculous argument. **6** For reasoning does not rule over its own emotions, but over those that are contrary to justice, courage, temperance, and self-control; and yet over these, so as to withstand, without destroying them. **7** I might prove to you from many other considerations, that religious reasoning is sole master of the emotions; **8** but I will prove it with the greatest force from the fortitude of Eleazar, and seven kindred, and their mother, who suffered death in defense of virtue. **9** For all these, treating pains with contempt even to death, by this contempt, demonstrated that reasoning has command over the emotions. **10** For their virtues, then, it is right that I should commend those men who died with their mother at this time on behalf of nobility and goodness; and for their honors, I may count them blessed. **11** For they, winning admiration not only from men in general, but even from the persecutors, for their courage and endurance, became the means of the destruction of the tyranny against their nation, having conquered the tyrant by their endurance, so that by them their country was purified. **12** But we may now at once enter upon the question, having commenced, as is our custom, with laying down the doctrine, and so proceed to the account of these people, giving glory to the all-wise God. **13** Therefore the question whether reasoning is absolute master of the emotions. **14** Let's determine, then, what reasoning is and what emotion is, and how many forms of emotion there are, and whether reasoning rules over all of these. **15** Reasoning is intellect accompanied by a life of righteousness, putting foremost the consideration of wisdom. **16** Wisdom is a knowledge of divine and human things, and of their causes. **17** This is contained in the education of the law, by means of which we learn divine things reverently and human things profitably. **18** The forms of wisdom are self-control, justice, courage, and temperance. **19** The leading one of these is self-control, by whose means, indeed, it is that reasoning rules over the emotions. **20** Of the emotions, pleasure and pain are the two most comprehensive; and they also by nature refer to the soul. **21** There are many attendant affections surrounding pleasure and pain. **22** Before pleasure is lust; and after pleasure, joy. **23** Before pain is fear; and after pain is sorrow. **24** Wrath is an affection, common to pleasure and to pain, if any one will pay attention when it comes upon him. **25** There exists in pleasure a malicious disposition, which is the most complex of all the affections. **26** In the soul, it is arrogance, love of money, thirst for honor, contention, faithlessness, and the evil eye. **27** In the body, it is greediness, indiscriminate eating, and solitary gluttony. **28** As pleasure and pain are, therefore, two growths out of the body and the soul, so there are many offshoots of these emotions. **29** Reasoning, the universal farmer, purging and pruning each of these, tying up, watering, and transplanting, in every way improves the materials of the morals and affections. **30** For reasoning is the leader of the virtues, but it is the sole ruler of the emotions. Observe then first, through the very things which stand in the way of temperance, that reasoning is absolute ruler of the emotions. **31** Now temperance consists of a command over the lusts. **32** But of the lusts, some belong to the soul and others to the body. Reasoning appears to rule over both. **33** Otherwise, how is it that when urged on to forbidden meats, we reject the gratification which would come from them? Isn't it because reasoning is able to command the appetites? I believe so. **34** Hence it is, then, that when craving seafood, birds, four-footed animals, and all kinds of food which are forbidden to us by the law, we withhold ourselves through the mastery of reasoning. **35** For the affections of our appetites are resisted by the temperate understanding, and bent back again, and all the impulses of the body are reined in by reasoning.

2

1 Is it any wonder? If the lusts of the soul, after participation with what is beautiful, are frustrated, **2** on this ground, therefore, the temperate Joseph is praised in that by reasoning, he subdued, on reflection, the indulgence of the senses. **3** For, although young, and ripe for sexual intercourse, he nullified by reasoning the stimulus of his emotions. ⁴ It isn't merely the stimulus of sensual indulgence, but that of every desire, that reasoning is able to master. ⁵ For instance, the law says, "You shall not covet your neighbor's wife, nor anything that belongs to your neighbor." ⁶ Now, then, since it is the law which has forbidden us to desire, I shall much the more easily persuade you, that reasoning is able to govern our lusts, just as it does the affections which are impediments to justice. ⁷ Since in what way is a solitary eater, a glutton, and a drunkard reclaimed, unless it is clear that reasoning is lord of the emotions? ⁸ Therefore, a man who regulates his course by the law, even if he is a lover of money, immediately puts pressure on his own disposition by lending to the needy without interest, and cancelling the debt on the seventh year. ⁹ If a man is greedy, he is ruled by the law acting through reasoning, so that he doesn't glean his harvest crops or vintage. In reference to other points we may perceive that it is reasoning that conquers his emotions. ¹⁰ For the law conquers even affection toward parents, not surrendering virtue on their account. ¹¹ It prevails over love for one's wife, rebuking her when she breaks the law. ¹² It lords it over the love of parents toward their children, for they punish them for vice. It domineers over the intimacy of friends, reproving them when wicked. ¹³ Don't think it is a strange assertion that reasoning can on behalf of the law conquer even enmity. ¹⁴ It doesn't allow cutting down the fruit trees of an enemy, but preserves them from the destroyers, and collects their fallen ruins. ¹⁵ Reason appears to be master of the more violent emotions, like love of empire, empty boasting, and slander. ¹⁶ For the temperate understanding repels all these malignant emotions, as it does wrath; for it masters even this. ¹⁷ Thus Moses, when angered against Dathan and Abiram, did nothing to them in wrath, but regulated his anger by reasoning. ¹⁸ For the temperate mind is able, as I said, to be superior to the emotions, and to correct some and destroy others. ¹⁹ For why else did our most wise father Jacob blame Simeon and Levi for having irrationally slain the whole race of the Shechemites, saying, "Cursed be their anger!"? ²⁰ For if reasoning didn't possess the power of subduing angry affections, he would not have said this. ²¹ For at the time when God created man, he implanted within him his emotions and moral nature. ²² At that time he enthroned the mind above all as the holy leader, through the medium of the senses. ²³ He gave a law to this mind, by living according to which it will maintain a temperate, just, good, and courageous reign. ²⁴ How, then, a man may say, if reasoning is master of the emotions, has it no control over forgetfulness and ignorance?

3

¹ The argument is exceedingly ridiculous, for reasoning doesn't appear to rule over its own affections, but over those of the body, ² in such a way as that any one of you may not be able to root out desire, but reasoning will enable you to avoid being enslaved to it. ³ One may not be able to root out anger from the soul, but it is possible to withstand anger. ⁴ Any one of you may not be able to eradicate malice, but reasoning has force to work with you to prevent you yielding to malice. ⁵ For reasoning is not an eradicator, but an antagonist of the emotions. ⁶ This may be more clearly comprehended from the thirst of King David. ⁷ For after David had been attacking the Philistines the whole day, he with the soldiers of his nation killed many of them; ⁸ then when evening came, sweating and very weary, he came to the royal tent, around which the entire army of our ancestors was encamped. ⁹ Now all the rest of them were at supper; ¹⁰ but the king, being very much thirsty, although he had numerous springs, could not by their means quench his thirst; ¹¹ but a certain irrational longing for the water in the enemy's camp grew stronger and fiercer upon him, undid and consumed him. ¹² Therefore his bodyguards being troubled at this longing of the king, two valiant young soldiers, respecting the desire of the king, fully armed themselves, and taking a pitcher, got over the ramparts of the enemies. ¹³ Unperceived by the guardians of the gate, they went throughout the whole camp of the enemy in quest. ¹⁴ Having boldly discovered the fountain, they filled out of it the drink for the king. ¹⁵ But he, though parched with thirst, reasoned that a drink regarded of equal value to blood would be terribly dangerous to his soul. ¹⁶ Therefore, setting up reasoning in opposition to his desire, he poured out the drink to God. ¹⁷ For the temperate mind has power to conquer the pressure of the emotions, to quench the fires of excitement, ¹⁸ and to wrestle down the pains of the body, however excessive, and through the excellency of reasoning, to spurn all the assaults of the emotions. ¹⁹ But the occasion now invites us to give an illustration of temperate reasoning from history. ²⁰ For at a time when our fathers were in possession of undisturbed peace through obedience to the law and were prosperous, so that Seleucus Nicanor, the king of Asia, both assigned them money for divine service, and accepted their form of government, ²¹ then certain people, bringing in new things contrary to the public harmony, in various ways fell into calamities.

4

¹ For a certain man named Simon, who was in opposition to an honorable and good man who once held the high priesthood for life, named Onias. After slandering Onias in every way, Simon couldn't injure him with the people, so he went away as an exile, with the intention of betraying his country. ² When coming to Apollonius, the military governor of Syria, Phoenicia, and Cilicia, he said, ³ "Having good will to the king's affairs, I have come to inform you that tens of thousands in private wealth is laid up in the treasuries of Jerusalem which do not belong to the temple, but belong to King Seleucus." ⁴ Apollonius, acquainting himself with the particulars of this, praised Simon for his care of the king's interests, and going up to Seleucus informed him of the treasure. ⁵ Getting authority about it, and quickly advancing into our country with the accursed Simon and a very heavy force, ⁶ he said that he came with the commands of the king that he should take the private money of the treasury. ⁷ The nation, indignant at this proclamation, and replying to the effect that it was extremely unfair that those who had committed deposits to the sacred treasury should be deprived of them, resisted as well as they could. ⁸ But Appolonius went away with threats into the temple. ⁹ The priests, with the women and children, asked God to throw his shield over the holy, despised place, ¹⁰ and Appolonius was going up with his armed force to seize the treasure, when angels from heaven appeared riding on horseback, all radiant in armor, filling them with much fear and trembling. ¹¹ Apollonius fell half dead on the court which is open to all nations, and extended his hands to heaven, and implored the Hebrews, with tears, to pray for him, and take away the wrath of the heavenly army. ¹² For he said that he had sinned, so as to be consequently worthy of death, and that if he were saved, he would proclaim to all people the blessedness of the holy place. ¹³ Onias the high priest, induced by these words, although for other reasons anxious that King Seleucus wouldn't suppose that Apollonius was slain by human device and not by Divine punishment, prayed for him; ¹⁴ and he being thus unexpectedly saved, departed to report to the king what had happened to him. ¹⁵ But on the death of Seleucus the king, his son Antiochus Epiphanes succeeded to the kingdom–a terrible man of arrogant pride. ¹⁶ He, having deposed Onias from the high priesthood, appointed his brother Jason to be high priest, ¹⁷ who had made a covenant, if he would give him this authority, to pay yearly three thousand six hundred and sixty talents. ¹⁸ He committed to him the high priesthood and rulership over the nation. ¹⁹ He both changed the manner of living of the people, and perverted their civil customs into all lawlessness. ²⁰ So that he not only erected a gymnasium on the very citadel of our country, but neglected the guardianship of the temple. ²¹ Because of that, Divine vengeance was grieved and instigated Antiochus himself against them. ²² For being at war with Ptolemy in Egypt, he heard that on a report of his death being spread abroad, the inhabitants of Jerusalem had exceedingly rejoiced, and he quickly marched against them. ²³ Having subdued them, he established a decree that if any of them lived according to the ancestral laws, he should die. ²⁴ When he could by no means destroy by his decrees the obedience to the law of the nation, but saw all his threats and punishments without effect, ²⁵ for even women, because they continued to circumcise their children, were flung down a precipice along with them, knowing beforehand of the punishment. ²⁶ When, therefore, his decrees were disregarded by the people, he himself compelled by means of tortures every one of this race, by tasting forbidden meats, to renounce the Jewish religion.

5

¹ The tyrant Antiochus, therefore, sitting in public state with his assessors upon a certain lofty place, with his armed troops standing in a circle around him, ² commanded his spearbearers to seize every one of the Hebrews, and to compel them to taste swine's flesh and things offered to idols. ³ Should any of them be unwilling to eat the accursed food, they were to be tortured on the wheel and so killed. ⁴ When many had been seized, a foremost man of the assembly, a Hebrew, by name Eleazar, a priest by family, by profession a lawyer, and advanced in years, and for this reason known to many of the king's followers, was brought near to him. ⁵ Antiochus, seeing him, said, ⁶ "I would counsel you, old man, before your tortures begin, to taste the swine's flesh, and save your life; for I feel respect for your age and hoary head, which since you have had so long, you appear to me to be no philosopher in retaining the superstition of the Jews. ⁷ For therefore, since nature has conferred upon you the most excellent flesh of this animal, do you loathe it? ⁸ It seems senseless not to enjoy what is pleasant, yet not disgraceful; and from notions of sinfulness, to reject the gifts of nature. ⁹ You will be acting, I think, still more senselessly, if you follow vain conceits about the truth. ¹⁰ You will, moreover, be despising me to your own punishment. ¹¹ Won't you awake from your trifling philosophy, give up the folly of your notions, and regaining understanding worthy of your age,

search into the truth of an expedient course? ¹² Won't you respect my kindly admonition and have pity on your own years? ¹³ For bear in mind that if there is any power which watches over this religion of yours, it will pardon you for all transgressions of the law which you commit through compulsion." ¹⁴ While the tyrant incited him in this manner to the unlawful eating of meat, Eleazar begged permission to speak. ¹⁵ Having received permission to speak, he began to address the people as follows: ¹⁶ "We, O Antiochus, who are persuaded that we live under a divine law, consider no compulsion to be so forcible as obedience to that law. ¹⁷ Therefore we consider that we ought not to transgress the law in any way. ¹⁸ Indeed, were our law (as you suppose) not truly divine, and if we wrongly think it divine, we would have no right even in that case to destroy our sense of religion. ¹⁹ Don't think that eating unclean meat is a trifling offense. ²⁰ For transgression of the law, whether in small or great matters, is of equal importance; ²¹ for in either case the law is equally slighted. ²² But you deride our philosophy, as though we lived in it irrationally. ²³ Yet it instructs us in self-control, so that we are superior to all pleasures and lusts; and it trains us in courage, so that we cheerfully undergo every grievance. ²⁴ It instructs us in justice, so that in all our dealings we render what is due. It teaches us piety, so that we properly worship the one and only God. ²⁵ That is why we don't eat the unclean; for believing that the law was established by God, we are convinced that the Creator of the world, in giving his laws, sympathizes with our nature. ²⁶ Those things which are suitable for our souls, he has directed us to eat; but those which are not, he has forbidden. ²⁷ But, tyrant-like, you not only force us to break the law, but also to eat, that you may ridicule us as we thus profanely eat. ²⁸ But you won't have this cause of laughter against me, ²⁹ nor will I transgress the sacred oaths of my forefathers to keep the law. ³⁰ No, not if you pluck out my eyes, and consume my entrails. ³¹ I am not so old, and void of courage as to not be youthful in reason and in defense of my religion. ³² Now then, prepare your wheels, and kindle a fiercer flame. ³³ I will not so pity my old age, as on my account to break the law of my country. ³⁴ I will not play false to you, O law, my instructor, or forsake you, O beloved self-control! ³⁵ I will not put you to shame, O philosopher Reason, or deny you, O honored priesthood and knowledge of the law. ³⁶ Mouth! You shall not pollute my old age, nor the full stature of a perfect life. ³⁷ My ancestors will receive me as pure, not having feared your compulsion, even to death. ³⁸ For you will rule like a tyrant over the ungodly, but you will not lord it over my thoughts about religion, either by your arguments, or through deeds."

6

¹ When Eleazar had in this manner answered the exhortations of the tyrant, the spearbearers came up, and rudely dragged Eleazar to the instruments of torture. ² First, they stripped the old man, adorned as he was with the beauty of piety. ³ Then tying back his arms and hands, they disdainfully flogged him. ⁴ A herald opposite cried out, "Obey the commands of the king!" ⁵ But the high-minded and truly noble Eleazar, as one tortured in a dream, ignored it. ⁶ But raising his eyes on high to heaven, the old man's flesh was stripped off by the scourges, and his blood streamed down, and his sides were pierced through. ⁷ Falling on the ground from his body having no power to endure the pains, he still kept his reasoning upright and unbending. ⁸ Then one of the harsh spearbearers rushed at him and began to kick him in the side to force him to get up again after he fell. ⁹ But he endured the pains, despised the cruelty, and persevered through the indignities. ¹⁰ Like a noble athlete, the old man, when struck, vanquished his torturers. ¹¹ His face sweating, and he panting for breath, he was admired even by the torturers for his courage. ¹² Therefore, partly in pity for his old age, ¹³ partly from the sympathy of acquaintance, and partly in admiration of his endurance, some of the attendants of the king said, ¹⁴ "Why do you unreasonably destroy yourself, O Eleazar, with these miseries? ¹⁵ We will bring you some meat cooked by yourself, and you can save yourself by pretending that you have eaten swine's flesh." ¹⁶ Eleazar, as though the advice more painfully tortured him, cried out, ¹⁷ "Let us who are children of Abraham not be so evil advised as by giving way to make use of an unbecoming pretense. ¹⁸ For it would be irrational, if having lived up to old age in all truth, and having scrupulously guarded our character for it, we would now turn back ¹⁹ and ourselves become a pattern of impiety to the young, as being an example of eating pollution. ²⁰ It would be disgraceful if we would live on some short time, and that scorned by all men for cowardice, ²¹ and be condemned by the tyrant for cowardice by not contending to the death for our divine law. ²² Therefore you, O children of Abraham, die nobly for your religion. ²³ You spearbearers of the tyrant, why do you linger?" ²⁴ Beholding him so high-minded against misery, and not changing at their pity, they led him to the fire. ²⁵ Then with their wickedly contrived instruments they burned him on the fire, and poured stinking fluids down into his nostrils. ²⁶ He being at length burned down to the bones, and about to expire, raised his eyes Godward, and said, ²⁷ "You know, O God, that when I might have been saved, I am slain for the sake of the law by tortures of fire. ²⁸ Be merciful to your people, and be satisfied with the punishment of me on their account. ²⁹ Let my blood be a purification for them, and take my life in exchange for theirs." ³⁰ Thus speaking, the holy man departed, noble in his torments, and even to the agonies of death resisted in his reasoning for the sake of the law. ³¹ Confessedly, therefore, religious reasoning is master of the emotions. ³² For had the emotions been superior to reasoning, I would have given them the witness of this mastery. ³³ But now, since reasoning conquered the emotions, we befittingly award it the authority of first place. ³⁴ It is only fair that we should allow that the power belongs to reasoning, since it masters external miseries. ³⁵ It would be ridiculous if it weren't so. I prove that reasoning has not only mastered pains, but that it is also superior to the pleasures, and withstands them.

7

¹ The reasoning of our father Eleazar, like a first-rate pilot, steering the vessel of piety in the sea of emotions, ² and flouted by the threats of the tyrant, and overwhelmed with the breakers of torture, ³ in no way shifted the rudder of piety until it sailed into the harbor of victory over death. ⁴ No besieged city has ever held out against many and various war machines as that holy man did when his pious soul was tried with the fiery trial of tortures and rackings and moved his besiegers through the religious reasoning that shielded him. ⁵ For father Eleazar, projecting his disposition, broke the raging waves of the emotions as with a jutting cliff. ⁶ O priest worthy of the priesthood! You didn't pollute your sacred teeth, nor make your appetite, which had always embraced the clean and lawful, a partaker of profanity. ⁷ O harmonizer with the law, and sage devoted to a divine life! ⁸ Of such a character ought those to be who perform the duties of the law at the risk of their own blood, and defend it with generous sweat by sufferings even to death. ⁹ You, father, have gloriously established our right government by your endurance; and making of much account our past service, prevented its destruction, and by your deeds, have made credible the words of philosophy. ¹⁰ O aged man of more power than tortures, elder more vigorous than fire, greatest king over the emotions, Eleazar! ¹¹ For as father Aaron, armed with a censer, hastening through the consuming fire, vanquished the flame-bearing angel, ¹² so, Eleazar, the descendant of Aaron, wasted away by the fire, didn't give up his reasoning. ¹³ What is most wonderful is that though he was an old man, though the labors of his body were now spent, his muscles were relaxed, and his sinews worn out, he recovered youth. ¹⁴ By the spirit of reasoning, and the reasoning of Isaac, he rendered powerless the many-headed rack. ¹⁵ O blessed old age, and reverend hoar head, and life obedient to the law, which the faithful seal of death perfected. ¹⁶ If, then, an old man, through religion, despised tortures even to death, then certainly religious reasoning is ruler of the emotions. ¹⁷ But perhaps some might say, "It is not all who conquer emotions, as not all possess wise reasoning." ¹⁸ But those who have meditated upon religion with their whole heart, these alone can master the emotions of the flesh: ¹⁹ they who believe that to God they don't die; for, as our forefathers, Abraham, Isaac, and Jacob, they live to God. ²⁰ This circumstance, then, is by no means an objection, that some who have weak reasoning are governed by their emotions, ²¹ since what person, walking religiously by the whole rule of philosophy, and believing in God, ²² and knowing that it is a blessed thing to endure all kinds of hardships for virtue, would not, for the sake of religion, master his emotion? ²³ For only the wise and brave man is lord over his emotions. ²⁴ This is why even boys, trained with the philosophy of religious reasoning, have conquered still more bitter tortures; ²⁵ for when the tyrant was manifestly vanquished in his first attempt, in being unable to force the old man to eat the unclean thing,

8

¹ then, indeed, vehemently swayed with emotion, he commanded to bring others of the adult Hebrews, and if they would eat of the unclean thing, to let them go when they had eaten; but if they objected, to torment them more grievously. ² The tyrant having given this charge, seven kindred were brought into his presence, along with their aged mother. They were handsome, modest, well-born, and altogether comely. ³ When the tyrant saw them encircling their mother as in a dance, he was pleased with them. Being struck with their becoming and innocent manner, smiled at them, and calling them near, said, ⁴ "O youths, with favorable feelings, I admire the beauty of each of you. Greatly honouring so numerous a band of kindred, I not only counsel you not to share the madness of the old man who has been tortured before, ⁵ but I beg you to yield, and to enjoy my friendship; for I possess the power, not only of punishing those who disobey my commands, but of doing good to those who obey them. ⁶ Put confidence in me, then, and you will receive places of authority in my government, if you forsake your national way of life, ⁷ and, conforming to the Greek way of life, alter

your rule and revel in youth's delights. ⁸ For if you provoke me by your disobedience, you will compel me to destroy every one of you with terrible punishments by tortures. ⁹ Have mercy, then, upon your own selves, whom I, although an enemy, am compassionate for your age and attractive appearance. ¹⁰ Won't you consider this: that if you disobey, there will be nothing left for you but to die in torture?" ¹¹ When he had said this, he ordered the instruments of torture to be brought forward, that fear might prevail upon them to eat unclean meat. ¹² When the spearman brought forward the wheels, the racks, the hooks, racks, caldrons, pans, finger-racks, iron hands and wedges, and bellows, the tyrant continued: ¹³ "Fear, young men, and the righteousness which you worship will be merciful to you if you transgress because of compulsion." ¹⁴ Now they having listened to these words of persuasion, and seeing the fearful instruments, not only were not afraid, but even answered the arguments of the tyrant, and through their good reasoning destroyed his power. ¹⁵ Now let's consider the matter. Had any of them been weak-spirited and cowardly among them, what reasoning would they have employed but these? ¹⁶ "O wretched that we are, and exceedingly senseless! When the king exhorts us, and calls us to his bounty, should we not obey him? ¹⁷ Why do we cheer ourselves with vain counsels, and venture upon a disobedience bringing death? ¹⁸ Shall we not fear, O kindred, the instruments of torture and weigh the threatenings of torment and shun this vain-glory and destructive pride? ¹⁹ Let's have compassion upon our age and relent over the years of our mother. ²⁰ Let's bear in mind that we will be dying as rebels. ²¹ Divine Justice will pardon us if we fear the king through necessity. ²² Why withdraw ourselves from a most sweet life, and deprive ourselves of this pleasant world? ²³ Let's not oppose necessity, nor seek vain-glory by our own torture. ²⁴ The law itself wouldn't arbitrarily put us to death because we dread torture. ²⁵ Why has such angry zeal taken root in us, and such fatal obstinacy approved itself to us, when we might live unmolested by the king?" ²⁶ But the young men didn't say or think anything of this kind when about to be tortured. ²⁷ For they were well aware of the sufferings, and masters of the pains. ²⁸⁻²⁹ So that as soon as the tyrant had ceased counselling them to eat the unclean, they all with one voice, as from the same heart said,

9

¹ "Why do you delay, O tyrant? For we are more ready to die than to transgress the injunctions of our fathers. ² We would be disgracing our fathers if we didn't obey the law, and take knowledge for our guide. ³ O tyrant, counselor of law-breaking, do not, hating us as you do, pity us more than we pity ourselves. ⁴ For we consider your escape to be worse than death. ⁵ You try to scare us by threatening us with death by tortures, as though you had learned nothing by the death of Eleazar. ⁶ But if aged men of the Hebrews have died in the cause of religion after enduring torture, more rightly should we younger men die, scorning your cruel tortures, which our aged instructor overcame. ⁷ Make the attempt, then, O tyrant. If you put us to death for our religion, don't think that you harm us by torturing us. ⁸ For we through this ill-treatment and endurance will gain the rewards of virtue. ⁹ But you, for the wicked and despotic slaughter of us, will, from the Divine vengeance, endure eternal torture by fire." ¹⁰ When they had said this, the tyrant was not only exasperated against them for being disobedient, but enraged with them for being ungrateful. ¹¹ So, at his bidding, the torturers brought the oldest of them, and tearing through his tunic, bound his hands and arms on each side with thongs. ¹² When they had labored hard without effect in scourging him, they hurled him on the wheel. ¹³ The noble youth, extended upon this, became dislocated. ¹⁴ With every member disjointed, he denounced the tyrant, saying, ¹⁵ "O most accursed tyrant, and enemy of heavenly justice, and cruel-hearted, I am no murderer, nor sacrilegious man, whom you torture, but a defender of the Divine law." ¹⁶ And when the spearmen said, "Consent to eat, that you may be released from your tortures," ¹⁷ he answered, "Not so powerful, O accursed lackeys, is your wheel, as to stifle my reasoning. Cut my limbs, and burn my flesh, and twist my joints. ¹⁸ For through all my torments I will convince you that the children of the Hebrews are alone unconquered on behalf of virtue." ¹⁹ While he was saying this, they heaped up fuel, and setting fire to it, strained him on the wheel still more. ²⁰ The wheel was defiled all over with blood. The hot ashes were quenched by the droppings of gore, and pieces of flesh were scattered about the axles of the machine. ²¹ Although the framework of his bones was now destroyed, the high-minded and Abrahamic youth didn't groan. ²² But, as though transformed by fire into immortality, he nobly endured the rackings, saying, ²³ "Imitate me, O kindred. Never desert your station, nor renounce my brotherhood in courage. Fight the holy and honorable fight of religion, ²⁴ by which means our just and paternal Providence, becoming merciful to the nation, will punish the pestilent tyrant." ²⁵ Saying this, the revered youth abruptly closed his life. ²⁶ When all admired his courageous soul, the spearmen brought forward him who was second oldest, and having put on iron gauntlets with sharp hooks, bound him to the rack. ²⁷ When, on enquiring whether he would eat before he was tortured, they heard his noble sentiment. ²⁸ After they with the iron gauntlets had violently dragged all the flesh from the neck to the chin, the panther-like animals tore off the very skin of his head, but he, bearing with firmness this misery, said, ²⁹ "How sweet is every form of death for the religion of our fathers!" Then he said to the tyrant, ³⁰ "Don't you think, most cruel of all tyrants, that you are now tortured more than I, finding your arrogant conception of tyranny conquered by our perseverance in behalf of our religion? ³¹ For I lighten my suffering by the pleasures which are connected with virtue. ³² But you are tortured with threatenings for impiety. You won't escape, most corrupt tyrant, the vengeance of Divine wrath."

10

¹ Now this one endured this praiseworthy death. The third was brought along, and exhorted by many to taste and save his life. ² But he cried out and said, "Don't you know that the father of those who are dead is my father also, and that the same mother bore me, and that I was brought up in the same way? ³ I don't renounce the noble relationship of my kindred. ⁴ Now then, whatever instrument of vengeance you have, apply it to my body, for you aren't able to touch my soul, even if you want to." ⁵ But they, highly incensed at his boldness of speech, dislocated his hands and feet with racking engines, and wrenching them from their sockets, dismembered him. ⁶ They dragged around his fingers, his arms, his legs, and his ankles. ⁷ Not being able by any means to strangle him, they tore off his skin, together with the extreme tips of his fingers, and then dragged him to the wheel, ⁸ around which his vertebral joints were loosened, and he saw his own flesh torn to shreds, and streams of blood flowing from his entrails. ⁹ When about to die, he said, ¹⁰ "We, O accursed tyrant, suffer this for the sake of Divine education and virtue. ¹¹ But you, for your impiety and blood shedding, will endure unceasing torments." ¹² Thus having died worthily of his kindred, they dragged forward the fourth, saying, ¹³ "Don't share the madness of your kindred, but respect the king and save yourself." ¹⁴ But he said to them, "You don't have a fire so scorching as to make me play the coward. ¹⁵ By the blessed death of my kindred, and the eternal punishment of the tyrant, and the glorious life of the pious, I will not repudiate the noble brotherhood. ¹⁶ Invent, O tyrant, tortures, that you may learn, even through them, that I am the brother of those tormented before." ¹⁷ When he had said this, the blood-thirsty, murderous, and unholy Antiochus ordered his tongue to be cut out. ¹⁸ But he said, "Even if you take away the organ of speech, God still hears the silent. ¹⁹ Behold, my tongue is extended, cut it off; for in spite of that you won't silence our reasoning. ²⁰ We gladly lose our limbs on behalf of God. ²¹ But God will speedily find you, since you cut off the tongue, the instrument of divine melody."

11

¹ When he had died, disfigured in his torments, the fifth leaped forward, and said, ² "I don't intend, O tyrant, to get excused from the torment which is on behalf of virtue. ³ But I have come of my own accord, that by my death you may owe heavenly vengeance and punishment for more crimes. ⁴ O you hater of virtue and of men, what have we done that you thus revel in our blood? ⁵ Does it seem evil to you that we worship the Founder of all things, and live according to his surpassing law? ⁶ But this is worthy of honors, not torments, ⁷ if you had been capable of the higher feelings of men, and possessed the hope of salvation from God. ⁸ Behold now, being alien from God, you make war against those who are religious toward God." ⁹ As he said this, the spearbearers bound him and drew him to the rack, ¹⁰ to which binding him at his knees, and fastening them with iron fetters, they bent down his loins upon the wedge of the wheel; and his body was then dismembered, scorpion-fashion. ¹¹ With his breath thus confined, and his body strangled, he said, ¹² "A great favor you bestow upon us, O tyrant, by enabling us to manifest our adherence to the law by means of nobler sufferings." ¹³ He also being dead, the sixth, quite a youth, was brought out. On the tyrant asking him whether he would eat and be delivered, he said, ¹⁴ "I am indeed younger than my brothers, but in understanding I am as old; ¹⁵ for having been born and reared to the same end. We are bound to die also on behalf of the same cause. ¹⁶ So that if you think it is proper to torment us for not eating the unclean, then torment!" ¹⁷ As he said this, they brought him to the wheel. ¹⁸ Extended upon this, with limbs racked and dislocated, he was gradually roasted from beneath. ¹⁹ Having heated sharp spits, they approached them to his back; and having transfixed his sides, they burned away his entrails. ²⁰ He, while tormented, said, "O good and holy contest, in which for the sake of religion, we kindred have been called to the arena of pain, and have not been conquered. ²¹ For religious understanding, O tyrant, is unconquered. ²² Armed with upright virtue, I also will depart with my kindred. ²³ I, too, bearing with me a great avenger,

O inventor of tortures, and enemy of the truly pious. [24] We six youths have destroyed your tyranny. [25] For isn't your inability to overrule our reasoning, and to compel us to eat the unclean, your destruction? [26] Your fire is cold to us. Your racks are painless, and your violence harmless. [27] For the guards not of a tyrant but of a divine law are our defenders. Through this we keep our reasoning unconquered."

12

[1] When he, too, had undergone blessed martyrdom, and died in the cauldron into which he had been thrown, the seventh, the youngest of all, came forward, [2] whom the tyrant pitying, though he had been dreadfully reproached by his kindred, [3] seeing him already encompassed with chains, had him brought nearer, and endeavored to counsel him, saying, [4] "You see the end of the madness of your kindred, for they have died in torture through disobedience. You, if disobedient, having been miserably tormented, will yourself perish prematurely. [5] But if you obey, you will be my friend, and have a charge over the affairs of the kingdom." [6] Having thus exhorted him, he sent for the boy's mother, that, by showing compassion to her for the loss of so many sons, he might incline her, through the hope of safety, to render the survivor obedient. [7] He, after his mother had urged him on in the Hebrew tongue, (as we will soon relate) said, [8] "Release me that I may speak to the king and all his friends." [9] They, rejoicing exceedingly at the promise of the youth, quickly let him go. [10] He, running up to the pans, said, [11] "Impious tyrant, and most blasphemous man, were you not ashamed, having received prosperity and a kingdom from God, to kill His servants, and to rack the doers of godliness? [12] Therefore the divine vengeance is reserving you for eternal fire and torments, which will cling to you for all time. [13] Weren't you ashamed, man as you are, yet most savage, to cut out the tongues of men of like feeling and origin, and having thus abused to torture them? [14] But they, bravely dying, fulfilled their religion toward God. [15] But you will groan as you deserve for having slain without cause the champions of virtue. [16] Therefore," he continued, "I myself, being about to die, [17] will not forsake my kindred. [18] I call upon the God of my fathers to be merciful to my race. [19] But you, both living and dead, he will punish." [20] Thus having prayed, he hurled himself into the pans; and so expired.

13

[1] If then, the seven kindred despised troubles even to death, it is admitted on all sides that righteous reasoning is absolute master over the emotions. [2] For just as if they had eaten of the unholy as slaves to the emotions, we would have said that they had been conquered by them. [3] Now it is not so. But by means of the reasoning which is praised by God, they mastered their emotions. [4] It is impossible to overlook the leadership of reflection, for it gained the victory over both emotions and troubles. [5] How, then, can we avoid according to these men mastery of emotion through right reasoning, since they didn't withdraw from the pains of fire? [6] For just as by means of towers projecting in front of harbors men break the threatening waves, and thus assure a still course to vessels entering port, [7] so that seven-towered right-reasoning of the young men, securing the harbour of religion, conquered the tempest of emotions. [8] For having arranged a holy choir of piety, they encouraged one another, saying, [9] "Brothers, may we die brotherly for the law. Let us imitate the three young men in Assyria who despised the equally afflicting furnace. [10] Let's not be cowards in the manifestation of piety." [11] One said, "Courage, brother!" and another, "Nobly endure!" [12] Another said, "Remember of what stock you are;" and by the hand of our father Isaac endured to be slain for the sake of piety. [13] One and all, looking at each other serene and confident, said, "Let's sacrifice with all our heart our souls to God who gave them, and employ our bodies for the keeping of the law. [14] Let's not fear him who thinks he kills; [15] for great is the trial of soul and danger of eternal torment laid up for those who transgress the commandment of God. [16] Let's arm ourselves, therefore, in the self-control, which is divine reasoning. [17] If we suffer like this, Abraham, Isaac, and Jacob will receive us, and all the fathers will commend us. [18] As each one of the kindred was hauled away, the rest exclaimed, "Don't disgrace us, O brother, nor falsify those who died before you!" [19] Now you are not ignorant of the charm of brotherhood, which the Divine and all wise Providence has imparted through fathers to children, and has engendered through the mother's womb. [20] In which these brothers having remained an equal time, and having been formed for the same period, and been increased by the same blood, and having been perfected through the same principle of life, [21] and having been brought forth at equal intervals, and having sucked milk from the same springs, hence their brotherly souls are reared up lovingly together, [22] and increase the more powerfully by reason of this simultaneous rearing, and by daily companionship, and by other education, and exercise in the law of God. [23] Brotherly love being thus sympathetically constituted, the seven kindred had a more sympathetic mutual harmony. [24] For being educated in the same law, and practicing the same virtues, and reared up in a just course of life, they increased this harmony with each other. [25] For the same ardor for what is right and honorable increased their goodwill and harmony toward each other. [26] For it acting along with religion, made their brotherly feeling more desirable to them. [27] And yet, although nature, companionship, and virtuous morals increased their brotherly love, those who were left endured to see their kindred, who were mistreated for their religion, tortured even to death.

14

[1] More that this, they even urged them on to this mistreatment; so that they not only despised pains themselves, but they even got the better of their affections of brotherly love. [2] Reasoning is more royal than a king, and freer than freemen! [3] What a sacred and harmonious concert of the seven kindred as concerning piety! [4] None of the seven youths turned cowardly or shrank back from death. [5] But all of them, as though running the road to immortality, hastened to death through tortures. [6] For just as hands and feet are moved sympathetically with the directions of the soul, so those holy youths agreed to death for religion's sake, as through the immortal soul of religion. [7] O holy seven of harmonious kindred! For as the seven days of creation, about religion, [8] so the youths, circling around the number seven, annulled the fear of torments. [9] We now shudder at the recital of the affliction of those young men; but they not only saw, and not only heard the immediate execution of the threat, but undergoing it, persevered; and that through the pains of fire. [10] What could be more painful? For the power of fire, being sharp and quick, speedily dissolved their bodies. [11] Don't think it wonderful that reasoning ruled over those men in their torments, when even a woman's mind despised more manifold pains. [12] For the mother of those seven youths endured the rackings of each of her children. [13] Consider how comprehensive is the love of offspring, which draws every one to sympathy of affection, [14] where irrational animals possess a similar sympathy and love for their offspring with men. [15] The tame birds frequenting the roofs of our houses defend their fledglings. [16] Others build their nests, and hatch their young, on the tops of mountains and in the precipices of valleys, and the holes and tops of trees, and keep away the intruder. [17] If not able to do this, they fly circling round them in agony of affection, calling out in their own note, and save their offspring in whatever manner they are able. [18] But why should we point attention to the sympathy toward children shown by irrational animals? [19] Even bees, at the season of honey-making, attack all who approach, and pierce with their sting, as with a sword, those who draw near their hive, and repel them even to death. [20] But sympathy with her children didn't turn away the mother of the young men, who had a spirit kindred with that of Abraham.

15

[1] O reasoning of the sons, lord over the emotions, and religion more desirable to a mother than children! [2] The mother, when two things were set before her, religion and the safety of her seven sons for a time, on the conditional promise of a tyrant, [3] rather elected the religion which according to God preserves to eternal life. [4] In what way can I describe ethically the affections of parents toward their children, the resemblance of soul and of form impressed into the small type of a child in a wonderful manner, especially through the greater sympathy of mothers with the feelings of those born of them! [5] For by how much mothers are by nature weak in disposition and prolific in offspring, by so much the fonder they are of children. [6] Of all mothers, the mother of the seven was the fondest of children, who in seven childbirths had deeply engendered love toward them. [7] Through her many pains undergone in connection with each one, she was compelled to feel sympathy with them; [8] yet, through fear of God, she neglected the temporary salvation of her children. [9] Not only so, but on account of the excellent disposition to the law, her maternal affection toward them was increased. [10] For they were both just and temperate, and courageous, high-minded, fond of their kindred, and so fond of their mother that even to death they obeyed her by observing the law. [11] Yet, though there were so many circumstances connected with love of children to draw on a mother to sympathy, in the case of none of them were the various tortures able to pervert her principle. [12] But she inclined each one separately and all together to death for religion. [13] O holy nature and parental feeling, and reward of bringing up children, and unconquerable maternal affection! [14] At the racking and roasting of each one of them, the observant mother was prevented by religion from changing. [15] She saw her children's flesh dissolving around the fire, and their extremities quivering on the ground, and the flesh of their heads dropped forward down to their beards, like masks. [16] O you mother, who was tried at this time with bitterer pangs than those at birth! [17] O you only woman who have produced perfect holiness! [18] Your firstborn, expiring, didn't turn you, nor the second, looking miserable in his torments, nor the third, breathing out his soul. [19] You didn't weep when you saw each of their eyes looking sternly at their tortures, and

their nostrils foreboding death! ²⁰ When you saw children's flesh heaped upon children's flesh that had been torn off, heads decapitated upon heads, dead falling upon the dead, and a choir of children turned through torture into a burying ground, you didn't lament. ²¹ Not so do siren melodies or songs of swans attract the hearers to listening, O voices of children calling on your mother in the midst of torments! ²² With what and what manner of torments was the mother herself tortured, as her sons were undergoing the wheel and the fires! ²³ But religious reasoning, having strengthened her courage in the midst of sufferings, enabled her to forego, for the time, parental love. ²⁴ Although seeing the destruction of seven children, the noble mother, after one embrace, stripped off her feelings through faith in God. ²⁵ For just as in a council room, seeing in her own soul vehement counselors, nature and parentage and love of her children, and the racking of her children, ²⁶ she holding two votes, one for the death, the other for the preservation of her children, ²⁷ didn't lean to that which would have saved her children for the safety of a brief space. ²⁸ But this daughter of Abraham remembered his holy fortitude. ²⁹ O holy mother of a nation, avenger of the law, defender of religion, and prime bearer in the battle of the affections! ³⁰ O you nobler in endurance than males, and more courageous than men in perseverance! ³¹ For like Noah's ship, bearing the world in the world-filling flood, bore up against the waves, ³² so you, the guardian of the law, when surrounded on every side by the flood of emotions, and assaulted by violent storms which were the torments of your children, bore up nobly against the storms against religion.

16

¹ If, then, even a woman, and that an aged one, and the mother of seven children, endured to see her children's torments even to death, it must be admitted that religious reasoning is master even of the emotions. ² I have proved, then, that not only men have obtained the mastery of their emotions, but also that a woman despised the greatest torments. ³ The lions around Daniel were not so fierce, nor the furnace of Misael burning with most vehement fires as that natural love of children burned within her, when she saw her seven sons tortured. ⁴ But with the reasoning of religion the mother quenched emotions so great and powerful. ⁵ For we must consider also this: that, had the woman been faint hearted, as being their mother, she would have lamented over them, and perhaps might have spoken thus: ⁶ "Ah! I am wretched and many times miserable, who having born seven sons, have become the mother of none. ⁷ O seven useless childbirths, and seven profitless periods of labor, and fruitless givings of suck, and miserable nursings at the breast. ⁸ Vainly, for your sakes, O sons, have I endured many pangs, and the more difficult anxieties of rearing. ⁹ Alas, of my children, some of you unmarried, and some who have married to no profit, I will not see your children, nor have the joy of being a grandmother. ¹⁰ Ah, that I who had many and fair children, should be a lone widow full of sorrows! ¹¹ Nor, should I die, will I have a son to bury me." But with such a lament as this, the holy and God-fearing mother wept for none of them. ¹² Nor did she divert any of them from death, nor grieve for them as for the dead. ¹³ But as one possessed with an adamant mind, and as one bringing forth again her full number of sons to immortality, she rather urged them to death on behalf of religion. ¹⁴ O woman, soldier of God for religion, you, aged and a female, have conquered through endurance even a tyrant; and even though weak, have been found more powerful in deeds and words. ¹⁵ For when you were seized along with your children, you stood looking at Eleazar in torture, and said to your sons in the Hebrew tongue, ¹⁶ "O sons, the contest is noble, to which you being called as a witness for the nation, strive zealously for the laws of your country. ¹⁷ For it would be disgraceful if this old man endured pains for the sake of righteousness, and that you who are younger would be afraid of the tortures. ¹⁸ Remember that through God, you obtained existence and have enjoyed it. ¹⁹ Therefore, you ought to bear every affliction because of God. ²⁰ For him also our father Abraham was zealous to sacrifice Isaac our progenitor, and didn't shudder at the sight of his own paternal hand descending down with the sword upon him. ²¹ The righteous Daniel was cast to the lions; and Ananias, Azarias, and Misael were hurled into a fiery furnace, yet they endured through God. ²² You, then, having the same faith toward God, don't be troubled. ²³ For it is unreasonable that they who know religion wouldn't stand up against troubles. ²⁴ With these arguments, the mother of seven, exhorting each of her sons, encouraged and persuaded them not to transgress God's commandment. ²⁵ They saw this, too, that those who die for God, live to God, like Abraham, Isaac, Jacob, and all the patriarchs.

17

¹ Some of the spearbearers said that when she herself was about to be seized for the purpose of being put to death, she threw herself on the pile, rather than let them touch her body. ² O you mother, who together with seven children destroyed the violence of the tyrant, and rendered void his wicked intentions, and exhibited the nobleness of faith! ³ For you, like a house bravely built on the pillar of your children, bore the shock of tortures without swaying. ⁴ Cheer up, therefore, O holy-minded mother! Hold the firm hope of your steadfastness with God. ⁵ Not so gracious does the moon appear with the stars in heaven, as you are established as honorable before God, and fixed in the sky with your sons whom you illuminated with religion to the stars. ⁶ For your bearing of children was after the manner of a child of Abraham. ⁷ If it were lawful for us to paint as on a tablet the religion of your story, the spectators wouldn't shudder at seeing the mother of seven children enduring for the sake of religion various tortures even to death. ⁸ It would have been a worthwhile thing to have inscribed on the tomb itself these words as a memorial to those of the nation, ⁹ "Here an aged priest, and an aged woman, and seven sons, are buried through the violence of a tyrant, who wished to destroy the society of the Hebrews. ¹⁰ These also avenged their nation, looking to God, and enduring torments to death." ¹¹ For it was truly a divine contest which was carried through by them. ¹² For at that time virtue presided over the contest, approving the victory through endurance, namely, immortality, eternal life. ¹³ Eleazar was the first to contend. The mother of the seven children entered the contest, and the kindred contended. ¹⁴ The tyrant was the antagonist; and the world and living men were the spectators. ¹⁵ Reverence for God conquered, and crowned her own athletes. ¹⁶ Who didn't admire those champions of true legislation? Who were not amazed? ¹⁷ The tyrant himself, and all their council, admired their endurance, ¹⁸ through which, they also now stand beside the divine throne and live a blessed life. ¹⁹ For Moses says, "All the saints are under your hands." ²⁰ These, therefore, having been sanctified through God, have been honored not only with this honor, but that also by the fact that because of them, the enemy didn't overcome our nation. ²¹ That tyrant was punished and their country purified. ²² For they became the ransom to the sin of the nation. The Divine Providence saved Israel, which was afflicted before, by the blood of those pious ones and the death that appeased wrath. ²³ For the tyrant Antiochus, looking to their courageous virtue and to their endurance in torture, proclaimed that endurance as an example to his soldiers. ²⁴ They proved to be to him noble and brave for land battles and for sieges; and he conquered and stormed the towns of all his enemies.

18

¹ O Israelite children, descendants of the seed of Abraham, obey this law and in every way be religious, ² knowing that religious reasoning is lord of the emotions, and those not only inward but outward. ³ Therefore those people who gave up their bodies to pains for the sake of religion were not only admired by men, but were deemed worthy of a divine portion. ⁴ The nation through them obtained peace, and having renewed the observance of the law in their country, drove the enemy out of the land. ⁵ The tyrant Antiochus was both punished on earth, and is punished now that he is dead; for when he was quite unable to compel the Israelites to adopt foreign customs, and to desert the manner of life of their fathers, ⁶ then, departing from Jerusalem, he made war against the Persians. ⁷ The righteous mother of the seven children spoke also as follows to her offspring: "I was a pure virgin, and didn't go beyond my father's house, but I took care of the rib from which woman was made. ⁸ No destroyer of the desert or ravisher of the plain injured me, nor did the destructive, deceitful snake make plunder of my chaste virginity. I remained with my husband during the time of my maturity. ⁹ When these, my children, arrived at maturity, their father died. He was blessed! For having sought out a life of fertility in children, he was not grieved with a period of loss of children. ¹⁰ He used to teach you, when yet with you, the law and the prophets. ¹¹ He used to read to you about the slaying of Abel by Cain, the offering up of Isaac, and the imprisonment of Joseph. ¹² He used to tell you of the zealous Phinehas, and informed you of Ananias, Azarias, and Misael in the fire. ¹³ He used to glorify Daniel, who was in the den of lions, and pronounce him blessed. ¹⁴ He used to remind you of the scripture of Esaias, which says, "Even if you pass through the fire, it won't burn you." ¹⁵ He chanted to you David, the hymn writer, who says, "Many are the afflictions of the just." ¹⁶ He declared the proverbs of Solomon, who says, "He is a tree of life to all those who do His will." ¹⁷ He used to confirm what Ezekiel said: "Will these dry bones live?" ¹⁸ For he didn't forget the song which Moses taught, proclaiming, "I will kill, and I will make alive." ¹⁹ This is our life and the length of our days. ²⁰ O that bitter, and yet not bitter, day when the bitter tyrant of the Greeks, quenching fire with fire in his cruel caldrons, brought with boiling rage the seven sons of the daughter of Abraham to the rack, and to all his torments! ²¹ He pierced the balls of their eyes, and cut out their tongues, and put them to death with varied tortures. ²² Therefore divine retribution pursued and will pursue the pestilent wretch. ²³ But the children of Abraham, with their victorious mother, are assembled together to the choir of their father, having received

pure and immortal souls from God. ²⁴ To him be glory forever and ever. Amen.

The Book of Meqabyan I

This are the thing Meqabyan spoke on the Mo`abans and Miedonans kingdoms.

1

¹ There were one man whose name are called Tseerutsaydan and who love sin ~ him would boast in him horses abundance and him troops firmness beneath him authority. ² Him had many priests who serve him idols whom him worship and to whom him bow and sacrifice by night and by daylight. ³ But in him heart dullness it would seem to him that them give him firmness and Power. ⁴ and in him heart it would seem to him that them give him authority in all him Rule. ⁵ and again in formation time it would seem to him that them give him all the desired authority also. ⁶ and him would sacrifice to them day and night. ⁷ Him appointed priests who serve him idols. ⁸ While them ate from that defouled sacrifice - them would tell him pretendin that the idols eat night and day. ⁹ Again them would make other persons diligent like unto them - that them might sacrifice and eat. and again them would make other persons diligent that them might sacrifice - and sacrifice like unto them. ¹⁰ But him would trust in him idols that don't profit nor benefit. ¹¹ By him timeframe bein small - and in him heart dullness - it would seem to him that them Created him - that them feed him and that them crown him ~ it would seem to him that them Created him - to Satan have deafened him reasonin lest him know him Creator Who Created him bringin from not livin toward livin - or lest him with him kindreds know him Creator Who Created him bringin from not livin toward livin - that them might go toward *Gehannem* of fire forever - it bein judged on them with him who call them gods without them bein gods. ¹² As them aren't never well whenever - it are due that him might call them dead ones. ¹³ As Satan authority that mislead them will lodge in that idol image - and as him will tell them them reasonin accord - and as him will reveal to them like unto them loved - him will judge on the idols wherein them believed and wherein 'Adam childran trust - whose reasonin were like unto ashes. ¹⁴ and them will marvel on the time them sight up that him fulfilled what them thought to them - and them will do him accord to him reachin up til them sacrifice them daughter childran and them male childran birthed from them nature - up til them spill them daughter childran and male childran blood that were clean. ¹⁵ Them didn't sadden them - to Satan have savoured him sacrifice to them to fulfill them evil accord - that him might lower them toward *Gehannem* like unto him - where there are no exits up til Eternity - where him will raceive tribulation. ¹⁶ But that Tseerutsaydan were arrogant ~ him had fifty idols worked in males pattern and twenty worked in daughters pattern. ¹⁷ and him would boast in those idols that have no benefit ~ him would totally glorify them while him sacrificed sacrifice mornin and evenin. ¹⁸ and him would command persons that them might sacrifice to the idols - and him would eat from that defouled sacrifice - and him would command other persons that them might eat from the sacrifice ~ him would especially provoke to evil. ¹⁹ Him had five houses worked to him beaten worked idols that were iron and brass and lead. ²⁰ and him ornamanted them in silver and gold ~ him veiled curtains around the houses to them and planted a tent to them. ²¹ Him appointed keepers to them there ~ him would Continually sacrifice forty to him idols - ten fattened oxen - ten sterile cows - ten fattened sheep ewes - ten barren goats - with birds that have wings. ²² But it would seem to him that him idols ate ~ him would present to them fifty *feeqen* of grapes and fifty dishes of wheat kneaded with oil. ²³ and him told him priests: - "Take and give them ~ make mi creators eat what mi slaughtered to them - and make them drink the grape mi presented to them ~ as to if it aren't enough to them - mi will add to them." ²⁴ and him would command all that them might eat and drink from that defouled sacrifice. ²⁵ But in him evil malice him would send him troops who visit in all the kingdom - that as it were there were one who neither sacrifice nor bow - them might separate and know and bring him - and might punish him by fire and by sword before him - that them might plunder him money and might burn him house in fire - that them might destroy all him money him had on him. ²⁶ "To them are kind and great ones - and to them have Created we in them charity - and mi will show punishmant and tribulation to him unless him worshipped mi creators and sacrificed sacrifice to mi creators. ²⁷ and mi will show him punishmant and tribulation - to them have Created Earth and Heaven and the sea that were wide and moon and Sun and stars and rains and winds and all that live in this world to be food and to be satiety to wi." ²⁸ But persons who worship them shall be punished in firm tribulation - and them won't be nice to them.

2

¹ There were one man birthed from the tribe of Binyam whose name are called Meqabees ² him had three childran who were handsome and totally warriors ~ them had bein iloved alongside all persons in that Midyam and

Miedon country that are Tseerutsaydan Rule. ³ and like unto the king commanded them on the time him found them: - "Don't you bow to Tseerutsaydan creators? How about don't you sacrifice? ⁴ But if you refuse - we will seize and take you toward the king - and we will destroy all your money like unto the king commanded." ⁵ These youths who were handsome replied to him sayin - "As to Him to Whom I bow - there are I Father Creator Who Created Earth and Heaven and what are within she - and the sea - moon and Sun and clouds and stars ~ Him are the True Creator Whom I worship and in Whom I believe." ⁶ and these the king youths are four - and them servants who carry shield and spear are a hundred. ⁷ and on the time them loved that them might seize these hola ones - them escaped from them hands and there are none who touched them ~ as those youths are totally warriors in Power - them went seizin shields and them spears. ⁸ and there were from them one who strangle and kill panther - and at that time him would strangle it like unto a chicken. ⁹ and there were one from them who kill a lion with one rock or strikin at one time with a stick. ¹⁰ and there were one from them who kill a hundred persons - strikin in formation time with one sword - and them name and them hunt were thus ~ it were called in all Babilon and Mo`ab countries. ¹¹ and them were warriors in Power - and them had a thing bein iloved and attractiveness. ¹² and again them features attractiveness were wondrous - however because them worshipped JAH and because them didn't fear death - it are them reasonin attractiveness that surpass all. ¹³ and on the time them frightened the troops - there are none who could able to seize them - but them who were warriors escaped proceedin toward a lofty mountain. ¹⁴ and those troops returned toward the city and shut the fortress gate ~ them terrorized the people sayin - "Unless you brought those warriors the Meqabyans - we will burn your city in fire - and we will send toward the king and destroy your country." ¹⁵ and at that time the country persons - rich and poor ones and daughters and males - a child whose father and mother dead on him and old daughters - everyone proceeded and shouted together - and them straightened them necks toward the mountain and shouted toward them sayin - "Don't destroy I - and don't destroy I country on us." ¹⁶ At that time them wept together - and them feared - arisin from JAH. ¹⁷ Returnin them faces Eastward and streachin forth them hands them begged toward JAH together - "Lord - should I refuse these men who demolished Thy Command and Thy LAW? ¹⁸ Yet him believed in silver and gold and in the stone and wood that a person hands worked - but I don't love that I might hear that criminal word - who didn't believe Thy LAW" them said. ¹⁹ "When Thou are the Creator Who save and Who kill - him make him ras self like unto them Created him also ~ as to him - him are who spill a person blood and who eat a person flesh. ²⁰ But I don't love that I might sight up that criminal face nor hear him word" them said. ²¹ "However if Thou commanded I - I will go toward him ~ because I believe in Thee-I - I will pass and give I bodies to death - and on the time him said 'Sacrifice to mi creators' - I won't hear that criminal word. ²² But I believed Thee-I - Lord Who examine kidneys and reasonins - I Fathers Creator - 'Abriham and Yis'haq and Ya`iqob who did Thy Accord and lived firmed up in Thy LAW. ²³ Thou examine a person reasonin and help the sinner and the righteous one - and there be none hidden from Thee-I - and him who took refuge are revealed alongside Thee-I. ²⁴ But I have no other Creator apart from Thee-I. ²⁵ That I might give I bodies to death because Thy glorified Name - however be Power and Firmness and a Shelter to I in this Work that I are ruled to Thee-I. ²⁶ and on the time 'Isra'iel entered toward Gibts country Thou heard Ya`iqob plea - and now glorified God - I beg Thee-I." ²⁷ and on the time the two men whose features were quite handsome were sight up to them standin before them - on the time fire swords that frighten like unto lightnin alit and cut them necks and killed them - at that time them arose bein well like unto formerly. ²⁸ Them features attractiveness became totally handsome and them shone more than Sun - and them became more handsome than formerly.

3

¹ Like unto you sight up before you these the Most I JAH slaves - 'Abya - Seela - Fentos who dead and arose - you have that you might arise likewise after you dead - and your faces shall shine like unto the Sun in the Kingdom of Heaven. ² and them went with those men and raeceived martyrdom there. ³ At that time them begged - them praised - and them bowed to JAH ~ death didn't frighten them and the king punishmant didn't frighten them. ⁴ and them went toward those youths and became like unto a sheep that have no evil - yet them didn't frighten them - and on the time them arrived toward them - them seized and beat them and bound and whipped them - and them delivered them toward the king and stood them before him. ⁵ and the king answered to them sayin - "How won't you stubborn ones sacrifice and bow to mi creators?" ⁶ Those bredren who were cleansed from sin - who were honoured and chosen and Feeling good - and who shine like unto a jewel whose value were wondrous - Seela and 'Abya and Fentos answered to him in one word. ⁷ Them told that king who were a plague - "As to I - I won't bow nor sacrifice to defouled idols that have no knowledge nor reasonin." ⁸ and again them told him - "I won't bow to idols that were silver and gold that a person hand worked - that were stone and wood - that have no reasonin nor soul nor knowledge - that don't benefit them friends nor harm them enemies." ⁹ and the king answered to them sayin - "Why do you do thus - and as them know who insult them and who wrong them - why do you insult the glorified creators?" ¹⁰ Them answered to him sayin - "As them are like unto a trifle alongside I - as to I - I will insult them and won't glorify them." ¹¹ and the king answered to them sayin - "Mi will punish you like unto your Work evil measure ~ mi will destroy your features attractiveness with whippin and firm tribulation and fire. ¹² and now tell mi whether you will give or won't give sacrifice to mi creators - as to if this didn't happen - mi will punish you by sword and by whippin." ¹³ Them answered to him sayin - "As to I - I won't sacrifice nor bow to defouled idols" - and the king commanded them that them might beat them with a fat stick - and again that them might whip them with a whip - and after it - that them might splinter them up til them inner organs were sight up. ¹⁴ and after this them bound and made them while in jail house up til him counsel by money that punish and kill them. ¹⁵ Without niceness them took and bound them a firm imprisonmant in prison house - and them sat in prison house three nights and three daylights. ¹⁶ and after this third day the king commanded that a Proclamation speaker might turn and that counselors and nobles - country elders and officials - might be gathered. ¹⁷ and on the time the king Tseerutsaydan sat in square - him commanded that them might bring those honoured ones - Seela and 'Abya and Fentos ~ them stood before them bein wounded and bound. ¹⁸ and the king told them - "When you sat these three days - are there really the returnin that you returned - or are you in your former evil?" ¹⁹ and those honoured JAH Souljahs answered to him sayin - "As to that I were cruel - I won't agree that I might worship the idols filled of sin and evil that thou check up." ²⁰ and that criminal vexed and commanded that them might stand them up in lofty place and might renew them wounds ~ them blood flowed on Earth. ²¹ and again him commanded that them might burn them with a torch lamp and might char them flesh - and him servants did like unto him commanded them - and those honoured men told him - "Thou who forgot JAH LAW - speak ~ I reward shall abound in the measure whereby thou multiply I punishmant." ²² and again him commanded that them might bring and send on them bears and tigers and lions that were evil beasts before them eat them food that them might totally eat them flesh with them bones. ²³ and him commanded persons who keep the beasts that them might send the beasts on them - and them did like unto him commanded them - and them bound those honoured martyrs feet - and again them maliciously beat and bound them with tent-stakes. ²⁴ and those beasts were flung over them while them roared - and on the time them arrived toward the martyrs them hailed and bowed to them. ²⁵ Them returned toward them keepers while them roared - and them frightened them keepers ~ them took them toward the square up til them delivered them toward before the king. ²⁶ and them killed seventy five men from the criminals army there. ²⁷ Many persons panicked - the one anguishin on the one in fear - up til the king quit him throne and fled - and them seized the beasts with difficulty and took them toward them lodgin. ²⁸ Seela and 'Abya and Fentos two bredren came and released them from the imprisonmant them bound them and told them - "Come make I flee lest these skeptics and criminals find me. ²⁹ and those martyrs answered them bredren sayin - "It aren't procedure that I might flee after I set up to testimony ~ as it were you had feared - go fleein." ³⁰ and those them little bredren said - "I will stand with you before the king - and if you dead I will dead with you." ³¹ and after this the king were on him lordship hall balcany and sight up that these honoured men were released and that all the five bredren stood together ~ those chiefs who work and punish troops questioned that them were bredren and told the king - and the king vexed and shouted like unto a wilderness boar. ³² and up til the king counseled by money that punish all the five bredren - him commanded that them might seize and add them in prison house ~ them placed them in prison house bindin in firm imprisonmant without niceness with a hollow stalk. ³³ and the king Tseerutsaydan said - "These youths who erred wearied mi ~ what should these men reasonin firm up? and them Work evil are like unto them Power firmness ~ if mi say - "Them will return" - them will make them reasonin evil. ³⁴ and mi will bring the hardship on them like unto them Work evil measure - and mi will burn them flesh in fire that it might be charred ash - and on that mi will scattar them flesh ash like unto dust on mountains." ³⁵ and after him spoke this him waited three days and commanded that them might bring those honoured men - and on the time those honoured men approached him commanded that them might burn a fire within the great pit oven - and that them might add within it a malice Work that flame the fire and whereby them boil a yat - the fat and soapberries - sea foam and

resin and the sulfur. ³⁶ and on the time fire flamed in the pit the messengers went toward the king when them said - "We did what thou commanded we - send the men who will be added." ³⁷ and him commanded that them might receive and cast them in the fire pit - and the youths did like unto the king commanded them - and on the time those honoured men entered toward the fire them gave them souls to JAH. ³⁸ and when the persons who cast them sight up - Angels raceived and took them souls toward the Garden where Yis'haq and 'Abriham and Ya`iqob are - where Feeling good joy are found.

4

¹ and on the time that criminal sight up that them dead - him commanded that them might burn them flesh in fire up til it are ash and that them might scattar them in wind - but the fire couldn't able to burn the corpse hair from them corpses side - and them sent them forth from the pit. ² and again them flamed fire over them beginnin from mornin up til evenin ~ it didn't burn them ~ them said - "An now come make we cast them corpses seaward." ³ and them did like unto the king commanded them ~ them cast them on the sea ~ even if them cast them seaward addin great stones and iron hearthstones and a millstone whereby a donkey grind by turnin - there are no sinkin that the sea sank them ~ as JAH Spirit of Support have lodged in them - them floated on the sea yet them didn't sink ~ it failed him to destroy them by all the malice that were provoked on them. ⁴ "As this them death have made weary more than them Life - make mi cast them corpses to beasts that them might eat them - yet what will mi do?" him said. ⁵ and the youths did like unto him commanded them ~ vultures and beasts didn't touch them corpses ~ birds and vultures veiled them with them wings from burnin in Sun and the five martyrs corpses sat fourteen days. ⁶ and on the time them sight them up - them bodies shone up like unto Sun - and Angels incircled them corpses like unto light incircle the Tent. ⁷ Him counseled counsel ~ him lacked what him do - and after this him dug a grave and buried the five martyrs corpses. ⁸ and when that king who forgot JAH LAW had reclined on a bed at night the five martyrs were sight up to him standin before him at night vexin and seizin swords. ⁹ As it have seemed to him that them entered toward him house at night in crime - on the time him awoke from him slumber him feared and loved that him might flee from the bedchamber toward the hall - and as it have seemed to him that them kill him seemin that them committed crime on him - him feared and him knees trembled. ¹⁰ Because this thing him said - "Mi lords - what do you love? as to mi - what should mi do to you?" ¹¹ Them answered to him sayin - "Aren't I whom thou killed burnin in fire and I whom thou commanded that them might cast on the sea? As JAH have kept I bodies because I believed in Him - it failed thee to destroy I ~ as a person who believed in Him won't perish - make glory and praise due to JAH - and I also who believed in Him didn't shame in the tribulation. ¹² "As mi didn't know that a punishmant like unto this will find mi - what reward should mi give you because the stead wherefore mi did a evil thing on you? ¹³ and now separate to mi the reward mi give you - lest you take mi body in death and lest you lower mi body toward *See'ol* when mi are in Life. ¹⁴ As mi have wronged you - forgive mi mi sin - because it were your Father JAH LAW Niceness" him told them. ¹⁵ and those honoured martyrs answered to him sayin - "Because the stead wherefore thou did a evil thing on I - as to I - I won't pay thee a evil thing ~ as JAH are Who bring hardship on a soul - as to Him Who will pay thee hardship - there are JAH. ¹⁶ However I were sight up to thee bein revealed that I were well to thy timeframe bein small and because thy reasonin deafness ~ as to it seemin to thee that thou killed I - thou prepared welfare to me. ¹⁷ But thy idols priests and thou will descend toward *Gehannem* where are no exits forever. ¹⁸ Woe to thy idols to whom thou bow havin quit bowin to JAH Who Created you when you were scorned like unto spit - and to you who worship them - and you don't know JAH Who Created you bringin from not livin toward livin ~ aren't you who are sight up today like unto smoke and tomorrow who perish?" ¹⁹ and the king answered to them sayin - "What will you command mi that mi might do to you all that you loved?" ²⁰ "It are to save thy ras self lest thou enter toward the *Gehannem* of fire - yet it aren't to save I ras selves who teach thee. ²¹ to your idols are silver and gold - stone and wood - that have no reasonin nor soul knowledge - that a person hand worked. ²² But them don't kill ~ them don't save ~ them don't benefit them friend ~ them don't harm them enemy ~ them don't downbase ~ them don't honour ~ them don't make wealthy ~ them don't impoverish ~ them mislead you by demons authority - who don't love that the one from persons might be saved - yet them don't uproot nor plant. ²³ Them especially don't love that the persons like unto you might be saved from death - you dull-hearted ones to whom them seem that them Created you - when you are who worked them. ²⁴ As Satans and demons authority have lodged in them - them shall return a thing to you like unto you loved - that it might drown you within the sea of *Gehannem*. ²⁵ But thou - quit this thy error and make this also be I reward because I dead stead - that I might benefit I souls worshippin I Creator JAH" them told him. ²⁶ But him were alarmed and would totally astony - and as all five have been sight up to him drawin them swords - him feared - and because this thing him bowed to them. ²⁷ "Hence mi knew that after dead ones who were dust dead them will really arise ~ as to mi - only a little had remained to mi to dead." ²⁸ After this them were hidden from before that king face ~ from that day onward that Tseerutsaydan who are totally arrogant quit burnin them corpses. ²⁹ As them have misled them many eras - him would be Feeling good in him idols and him reasonin error - and him misled many persons like unto him up til them quit followin in Worship JAH Who Created them - yet it aren't only him who erred. ³⁰ and them would sacrifice them daughter childran and them male childran to demons - yet them work a seducin and disturbance that are them reasonin accord - that them father Satan taught them that him might make the seducin and disturbance that JAH don't love. ³¹ Them marry them mothers - and them abuse them aunts and them sistren ~ them abuse them bodies while them worked all that resemble this filthy Work ~ as Satan have firmed up those crooked persons reasonin - them said - "We won't return." ³² But that Tseerutsaydan - who don't know him Creator - were totally arrogant - and him would boast in him idols. ³³ If them say - "How will JAH give the Kingdom to the persons who don't know Him in LAW and in Worship?" - them will totally return toward Him in repentance ~ as Him test them thus - it are because this. ³⁴ But if them totally return in repentance Him would love them - and Him would keep them Kingdom - but if them refuse a fire will punish them in fire of *Gehannem* forever. ³⁵ But it would be due a king to fear him Creator JAH like unto him lordship fame - and it would be due a judge to be ruled to him Creator while him judged goodly judgemant like unto him Rule fame. ³⁶ and it would be due elders and chiefs and envoys and petty kings to be commanded to them Creator like unto them lordship abundance measure. ³⁷ As Him are Heaven and Earth Lord Who Created all the Creation - because there are no other Creator in Heavan nor Earth who impoverish and make rich - Him are Who honour and downbase.

5

¹ "The one warrior from the sixty warriors were proud ~ JAH made him body Beginnin from him foot up til him head to swell with one spoon of sulphur ~ him dead in one plague. ² and again Keeram who built a iron bed were proud arisin from him powerfulness abundance - and JAH hid him in death. ³ and again Nabukedenetsor were proud sayin - 'There are no other king without mi - and mi are Creator who make the Sun rise in this world' - and him said thus arisin from him arrogance abundance. ⁴ and JAH separated from persons and sent him toward a wilderness seven years - and him made him fortune with Heaven birds and wilderness beasts up til him knew that JAH were Who Created him. ⁵ and on the time him knew Him in worship - Him again returned him toward him kingdom ~ who are it who weren't of Earth - bein boldly proud on JAH Who Created him? ⁶ How about who are it demolished HIM LAW and Him Order and whom Earth didn't swallow? ⁷ and thou Tseerutsaydan love that thou might be proud on thy Creator - and again thou have that Him might destroy thee like unto them - and might lower thee toward a grave arisin from thy arrogance. ⁸ and again after them entered toward *See'ol* where are tooth grindin and mournin - that were darkness fulfillmant - thou have that Him might lower thee toward the deep pit *Gehannem* where are no exits forever. ⁹ As to thou - thou are a man who will dead and be demolished tomorrow like unto arrogant kings who were like unto thee - who quit this world livin. ¹⁰ As to I - I say - 'Thou are demolished ruins - but thou aren't JAH - to JAH are Who Created Earth and Heaven and thee.' ¹¹ Him downbase arrogant ones ~ Him honour them who were downbased ~ Him give firmness to persons who wearied. ¹² Him kill well ones ~ Him raise up the persons who were Earth - who dead buried in grave. ¹³ and Him send slaves forth free in Life from sin rulership. ¹⁴ O king Tseerutsaydan - why do thou boast in thy defouled idols who have no benefit? ¹⁵ But JAH Created Earth and Heaven and great seas ~ Him Created moon and Sun - and Him prepared eras. ¹⁶ Man graze toward him field - and him while when him plough up til it dusk - and Heaven stars live firmed up by Him Word. ¹⁷ and Him call all in Heaven ~ there are nothing done without JAH knowin it. ¹⁸ Him commanded Heaven Angels that them might serve Him and might praise Him glorified Name - and Angels are sent toward all persons who inherit Life. ¹⁹ Rufa'iel who were a servant were sent toward Thobeet - and him saved Thobya from death in Ragu'iel country. ²⁰ Hola Meeka'iel were sent toward Giediewon that him might draw him attention by money that him destroy 'Iloflee persons and him were sent toward the prophet Mussie on the time him made 'Isra'iel cross 'Eritra sea. ²¹ As only JAH have said him led them - there were no different idol with them. ²² and Him sent them forth toward crops on Earth. ²³ and Him fed them Him plantation grain ~ as Him have totally loved them - Him cherished them feedin the honey that firmed up like unto a rock. ²⁴ and that

thou might totally keep Him kindreds by what are due - and that thou might do JAH Accord Who Created thee - Him crowned thee givin Authority on the four kingdoms. ²⁵ to Him have crowned thee makin loftier than all - and thy Creator totally crowned thee that thou might love JAH. ²⁶ and it are procedure that thou might love thy Creator JAH like unto Him loved thee - like unto Him trusted thee on all the people - and thou - do JAH Accord that thy era might abound in this world and that Him might live with thee in Support. ²⁷ and do JAH Accord that Him might stand to thee bein a Guardian on thy enemies - and that Him might seat thee on thy throne - and that Him might hide thee in him Wing of Support. ²⁸ As to if thou don't know - JAH chose and crowned thee on 'Isra'iel like unto Him chose Sa'ol fron 'Isra'iel childran when him kept him father donkeys - and Him crowned him on him kindreds 'Isra'iel - and him sat with 'Isra'iel on him throne. ²⁹ and Him gave him a lofty fortune separatin from him kindreds ~ JAH crowned thee on Him kindreds ~ as to henceforth onward - check - keep Him kindreds. ³⁰ As JAH have Ipointed thee over them that thou might kill and might save - keep them in evil thing - them who work a goodly thing and them who work a evil thing on a goodly thing" him told him. ³¹ "An as JAH have Ipointed thee on all that thou might do Him Accord be it while thou whipped or while thou saved - pay them evil Work - them who work goodly Work and them who work goodly Work and evil Work. ³² to thou are a slave of JAH Who rule all in Heaven - and thou - do JAH Accord that Him might do thy accord to thee in all thou thought and in all thou begged while thou wheedled before Him. ³³ There are none who rule Him - but Him rule all. ³⁴ There are none who Ipoint Him - but Him Ipoint all. ³⁵ There are none who dismiss Him - but Him dismiss all. ³⁶ There are none who reproach Him - but Him reproach all. ³⁷ There are none who make Him diligent - but Him make all diligent ~ as Heaven and Earth rulership are to Him - there are none who escape from Him Authority all are revealed alongside Him - yet there are none hidden from Him Face. ³⁸ Him sight up all - but there are none who sight Him up ~ Him hear the person prayer who pray toward Him sayin 'Save I' - to Him have Created man in Him Pattern - and Him accept him plea. ³⁹. As Him are a King Who live up til the Eternity - Him feed all from Him unchangin Nature.

6

¹ As Him crown to true the kings who do Him Accord - the kings wrote a straight thing because Him. ² As them have done JAH Accord - Him shall shine up in Light that aren't examined Yis'haq and 'Abriham and Ya`iqob - Selomon and Daweet and Hiziqyas lodgins in the Garden where are all beautiful kings whose lodgin were Light. ³ Heaven Hall are what totally shone - yet Earth halls aren't like unto Heaven Hall ~ it floor - whose features are silver and gold and jewel features - are clean. ⁴ and it features that totally shine are unexamined by a person reasonin ~ Heaven Hall are what shine like unto jewels. ⁵ Like unto JAH knew - Who were a Nature Knower - the Heaven Hall that Him Created are what a person reasonin don't examine and what shine in total Light ~ it floor - that were worked in silver and gold - in jewels - in white silk and in blue silk - are clean. ⁶ It are quite totally beautiful like unto this. ⁷ Righteous ones who firmed up in religion and virtue are who shall inherit it in JAH Charity and to Pardon. ⁸ and there are welfare Water that flow from it - and it totally shine like unto Sun - and there are a Light tent within it - and it are incircled by grace perfume. ⁹ A Garden fruit that were beautiful and Iloved - whose features and taste were different - are around the house - and there are a oil and grape place there - and it are totally beautiful - and it fruit fragrance are sweet. ¹⁰ When a fleshly bloodly person enter toward it - him soul would have separated from him flesh from the Feeling good joy abundance that are in it arisin from it fragrance flavour. ¹¹ Beautiful kings who did JAH Accord shall be Feeling good there ~ them honour and them place are known in the Kingdom of Heaven that live firmed up forever - where welfare are found. ¹² Him showed that them lordship on Earth were famed and honoured - and that them lordship in Heaven were famed and honoured; them shall be honoured and lofty in Heaven like unto them honour them and bow to them in this world ~ if them work goodly Work in this world them shall be Feeling good. ¹³ But kings who were evil in them Rule and them kingdoms that JAH gave them - them don't judge to true by what are due ~ as them have ignored the destitute and poor ones cries - them don't judge Truth and save the refugee and the wronged child whose father and mother dead on him. ¹⁴ Them don't save destitute and poor ones from the wealthy hand that rob them ~ them don't divide and give from them food and satta them who hungered - and them don't divide and give from them drink and give to drink the persons who thirsted - and them didn't return them ears toward the poor one cry. ¹⁵ and Him shall take them toward *Gehannem* that were a dark endin ~ on the time that lofty Day arrived on them when JAH shall come - and on the time Him wrath were done on them like unto Daweet spoke in him Praises 'Lord - don't chastise I in Thy Judgemant and don't admonish I in Thy chastisemant' - them problems and them downbasemant shall abound like unto them fame abundance measure. ¹⁶ When nobles and kings are who rule this world in this world - there are persons who didn't keep thy law. ¹⁷ But JAH Who rule all are there in Heaven ~ all persons souls and all persons welfare have been seized by Him Authority ~ Him are Who give honour to persons who glorify Him - to Him totally rule all - and Him love the persons who love Him. ¹⁸ As Him are Earth and Heaven Lord - Him examine and know what kidneys transported and what a reasonin thought - and to a person who begged toward Him with a pure reasonin - Him shall give him him plea reward. ¹⁹ Him shall destroy powerful ones arrogance - who work evil Work on the child whose mother and father dead on him - and on old daughters. ²⁰ It aren't by thy Power that thou seized this kingdom ~ it aren't by thy bein able that thou sat on this throne ~ Him loved to test thee thus that it be possible to thee to rule like unto Sa'ol who ruled him kindreds in that season - and Him seated thee on a kingdom throne - yet it aren't by thy Power that thou seized this kingdom ~ it are when Him test thee like unto Sa'ol who ignored the prophet Samu'iel word and JAH Word and didn't serve him army nor 'Amalieq king - yet it aren't by thy bein able that thou seized this kingdom. ²¹ and JAH told the prophet Samu'iel - **Go - and as them have saddened I by demolishin LAW and worshippin the idols and bowin to the idol and by them mosques and by all them hated Works without benefit - tell Sa'ol - 'Go toward 'Amalieq country and destroy them hosts and all the kings Beginnin from persons up til livestock.'** ²² on them who saddened JAH - because this thing Him sent Sa'ol that him might destroy them. ²³ But him saved them king from death - and him saved many livestock and beauties and daughters and handsome youths from death ~ **As him have scorned I thing and as him didn't hear I Command - because this thing** - JAH told the prophet Samu'iel - **Go and divide him kingdom. ²⁴ Because him stead - Inoint `Issiey child Daweet that him might reign on 'Isra'iel. ²⁵ But on him adjourn a demon who will strangle and cast him. ²⁶ As him have refused if I-man gave him a kingdom that him might do I Accord - on the time him refused I to do I Accord I-man dismissed him from him kingdom that are due him - but thou - go and tell him sayin - 'Will thou thus ignore JAH Who crowned thee on Him kindreds 'Isra'iel - Who seated thee on Him Lordship Throne?' ²⁷ But thou - tell him - 'Thou didn't know JAH Who gave around this much honour and famousness'** Him told him. ²⁸ and the prophet Samu'iel went toward the king Sa'ol and entered toward him sittin at a dinnertable - and when 'Amalieq king 'Agag had sat on him left. ²⁹ 'Why did thou totally ignore JAH Who commanded thee that thou might destroy the livestock and persons?' him told him. ³⁰ and at that time the king feared and arose from him throne and tellin Samu'iel 'Return to wi' him seized him clothes - and Samu'iel refused to return ~ Samu'iel clothes were torn. ³¹ and Samu'iel told Sa'ol - 'JAH divided thy kingdom.' ³² and again Sa'ol told Samu'iel before the people - 'Honour mi and atone mi sin to mi before JAH that Him might forgive mi' ~ and as him have feared JAH Word Who Created him - but as him didn't fear the king who dead - Samu'iel refused to return in him word. ³³ Because this thing him pierced 'Amalieq king 'Agag before him swallowed what him chewed. ³⁴ and a demon seized that Sa'ol who demolished the LAW of JAH - and because Him were the King of Kings Who rule all - JAH struck on him head a king who worked sin - to it don't shame him. ³⁵ to Him are all the Creation Lord Who dismiss all the nobles and kings Authority who don't fear Him - but there are none who rule Him. ³⁶ Like unto Him spoke sayin - **Daweet kindred shall go while it were famed and honoured - but Sa'ol kindred shall go while it were downbased** - Him destroyed kingdom from him child and from Sa'ol. ³⁷ Because it saddened Him - and because Him destroyed the criminals who saddened Him by them evil Work - JAH revenged and destroyed Sa'ol kindred children - to a person who don't revenge JAH enemy - him are JAH enemy. ³⁸ When it are possible to him to revenge and destroy - and when him have Authority - a person who don't revenge and destroy the sinner and don't revenge and destroy a person who don't keep JAH LAW - as him are JAH enemy - Him destroyed Sa'ol kindred childran.

7

¹ and whether thou be a king or a ruler - what important thing are thou? ² Aren't it JAH Who Created thee bringin from not livin toward livin - that thou might do Him Accord and might live firmed up by Him Command and might fear Him Judgemant? Like unto thou vex on thy slaves and governed over them - all likewise there are also JAH Who vex on thee and govern over thee. ³ Like unto thou beat without niceness persons who worked sin - all likewise there are also JAH Who will strike thee and lower thee toward *Gehannem* where are no exits up til Eternity. ⁴ Like unto thou whip him who weren't ruled to thee and didn't bring a tribute to thee - to what are it that thou don't introduce a tribute to JAH? ⁵ As Him are Who Created thee in order that thou love that them might fear thee - and Who crowned

thee on all the Creation that thou might keep Him kindreds to true - to what are it that thou don't fear thy Creator JAH? ⁶ Judge by what are due and to true like unto JAH Ipointed thee - yet don't sight up a face and favour to small nor great ~ whom will thou fear without Him? keep Him Worship and the Nine Commands. ⁷ Like unto Mussie commanded 'Isra'iel childran sayin - 'I-man presented Water and fire to thee-I ~ add thy hand toward what thou loved' - don't go neither rightward nor leftward. ⁸ Hear Him Word that I-man tell thee - that thou might hear Him Word and might do Him Command - lest thou say - 'She are beyond the sea or beyond the deep or beyond the river ~ who will bring to mi that mi might sight she up and might hear Him Word and might do Him Command?' ⁹ Lest thou say - 'Who will proceed toward Heaven again and lower that JAH Word to mi that mi might hear and do she?' - JAH Word are what approached - check - to thou to teach she with thy mouth and give alms by she with thy hand. ¹⁰ and thou didn't hear thy Creator JAH unless thou heard Him Book - and thou didn't love Him nor keep Him Command unless thou kept Him LAW. ¹¹ and thou have that thou might enter toward *Gehannem* forever - and unless thou loved Him Command - and unless thou did JAH Accord - Who honoured and famed thee separatin from all thy kindreds that thou might keep them to true - thou have that thou might enter toward *Gehannem* forever. ¹² Him made thee above all - and Him crowned thee on all Him kindreds that thou might rule Him kindreds to true by what are due while thou thought of thy Creator Name Who Created thee and gave thee a kingdom. ¹³ There are them whom thou whip from persons who wronged thee - and there are him whom thou pardon while thou thought of JAH Work - and there are him to whom thou judge by what are due straightenin up thy reasonin. ¹⁴ and don't favour havin sight up a face on the time them argued before thee ~ as Earth physique are thy money - don't accept a bribe that thou might pardon the sinner person and wrong the clean person. ¹⁵ If thou did Him Accord - JAH shall multiply thy era in this world to thee - but if thou sadden Him - Him will diminish thy era. ¹⁶ Think that thou will rise after thou dead - and that thou will be examined standin before Him on all the Work thou worked whether it be goodly or evil. ¹⁷ If thou work goodly Work - thou will live in Garden in the Kingdom of Heaven - in houses where kind kings live and where Light filled. to JAH don't shame thy lordship authority - but if thou work evil Work - thou will live in *See'ol Gehannem* where evil kings live. ¹⁸ But on the time thou sight up thy bein feared famousness - thy warriors award - thy hangin shield and spear - and on the time thou sight up thy horses and thy troops beneath thy authority and them who beat drum and persons who play on a harp before thee... ¹⁹ But on the time thou sight up all this - thou make thy reasonin lofty - and thou firm up thy collar of reasonin - and thou don't think of JAH Who gave thee all this honour - however on the time Him told thee - **Quit all this** - thou aren't who quit it. ²⁰ to thou have totally neglected the Ipointmant Him Ipointed thee - and Him shall give thy lordship to another. ²¹ As death shall suddenly come on thee - and as Judgemant shall be done in Resurrection time - and as all man Work shall be examined - Him shall totally investigate and judge on thee. ²² There are none who will honour this world kings - to because Him were Truth Judge - in Judgemant time poor and wealthy will stand together. This world nobles crowns wherein them boast shall fall. ²³ Judgement are prepared - and a soul shall quake ~ at that time sinners and righteous ones Work shall be examined. ²⁴ and there are none who shall be hidden. on the time a daughter arrived to birthin - and on the time the fetus in she belly arrived to bein birthed - like unto she cyaan prevent the womb - Earth also cyaan prevent she lodgers that are on she ~ she will return. ²⁵ and like unto clouds cyaan prevent rain lest them take and rain toward the place JAH commanded them - to JAH Word have Created all bringin from not livin toward livin - and to JAH Word again have introduced all toward a grave and all likewise - after Resurrection time arrived - it aren't possible to be that dead persons won't rise. ²⁶ Like unto Mussie spoke sayin - 'It are by Words that proceed from JAH Tongue - yet it aren't only by grain that a person are saved'; and JAH Word again shall arouse all persons from graves. ²⁷ Check - it were known that dead persons shall arise by JAH Word. ²⁸ and again JAH said thus in Repeatin Law because persons who were nobles and kings who do Him Accord - **As the day have arrived when them are counted to destruction - I-man shall revenge and destroy them on the day when Judgemant are judged and at the time when them feet stumble** Him said. ²⁹ and again JAH told persons who know Him Judgemant - **Know know that I-man were your Creator JAH - and that I-man kill and I-man save.** ³⁰ **I-man chastise in the tribulation and I-man pardon ~ I-man lower toward *See'ol and* again I-man send forth toward the Garden - and there are none who shall escape from I Authority** Him told them. ³¹ JAH said thus because nobles and kings who didn't keep Him LAW - **As Earthly kingdoms are a passin - and as them pass from mornin up til evenin - keep I Order and I LAW that you might enter toward the Kingdom of Heaven that live firmed up forever** Him said. ³² to JAH callin Righteous ones are to glory - and sinners to tribulation ~ Him will make the sinner wretched but will honour righteous ones. ³³ Him will dismiss the person who didn't do Him Accord - but Him will Ipoint the person who did Him Accord.

8

¹ Hear I - make I tell thee the thing whereby dead persons shall arise ~ them shall plant a plant and be fertile and grapes shall send forth vines ~ as JAH shall bring the fruit *'imhibe 'albo* ~ them shall cast wine from it. ² Overstand that that plant thou planted were small - but that she sent forth tips fruit and leaves today. ³ JAH give she root to drink from Earth and Water - from both. ⁴ But Him feed she wood from fire and wind ~ roots give leaves Water to drink - and Earth give firmness to woods. ⁵ But the soul that JAH Created make them bear fruit amidst them - and dead persons arisin are likewise. ⁶ on the time soul were separated from flesh - as each of them ras selves have gone - Him said - **Gather souls from the four natures - from Earth and Water - wind and fire.** ⁷ But Earth nature lived firmed up in she nature and became Earth - and Water nature lived firmed up in she nature and became Water. ⁸ and wind nature lived firmed up in she nature and became wind - and fire nature lived firmed up in she nature and became a hot fire. ⁹ But a soul that JAH separated from flesh returned toward she Creator ~ up til Him raise she up inited with flesh on the time Him loved - Him place she in Garden in the place Him loved. ¹⁰ Him place righteous souls in Light house in Garden - but that Him might send way sinners souls - Him also place them in darkness house in *See'ol* up til the time when Him loved. ¹¹ JAH told the prophet Hiziq'iel - **Call souls from the four corners** - that them might be gathered and be one limb. ¹² on the time Him spoke in one Word sayin thus - the souls were gathered from the four corners. ¹³ and Water nature brought verdure - and again fire nature brought fire. ¹⁴ and again Earth nature brought Earth - and wind nature brought wind. ¹⁵ and JAH brought a soul from the Garden place where Him placed it ~ them were gathered by one Word - and a Resurrection were made. ¹⁶ and again I-man shall show thee the example that are alongside thee ~ the day dusk ~ thou sleep ~ the night dawn - and thou rise from thy beddin - but on the time thou slept it are thy death example. ¹⁷ and on the time thou awoke it are thy arisin example - but the night when all persons sleep whose physiques were dark - to darkness have covered them - are this world example. ¹⁸ But the mornin light - when darkness are eliminated and when light are in all the world and when persons arise and graze toward the field - are dead persons example. ¹⁹ and this Kingdom of Heaven where man are renewed are like unto this ~ dead persons Resurrection are like unto this ~ as this world are passin - it are the night example. ²⁰ and like unto Daweet spoke sayin - 'Him placed Him example in Sun' - as Sun shine on the time it rose - it are a Kingdom of Heaven example. ²¹ and like unto Sun shine in this world today - on the time Kristos come Him shall shine like unto Sun in Kingdom of Heaven that are new ~ as Him have said - **I-man am a Sun that don't set and a Torch that aren't extinguished** - Him JAH are she Light. ²² and Him shall quickly arouse the dead persons again ~ I-man shall bring one example to thee again from thy food that thou sow and whereby thou are saved - and whether it be a wheat kernel or a barley kernel or a lentil kernel or all man seeds sown on Earth - there are none that grow unless it were demolished and rotten. ²³ and like unto the person flesh thou sight up - on the time it were demolished and rotten - Earth eat stoutness with the hide. ²⁴ and on the time Earth ate it stoutness it grow bein around a kernel seventh ~ JAH give a cloud that seized rain like unto Him loved - and roots grow on Earth and send forth leaves. ²⁵ and if she were demolished and rotten she cyaan grow - but after she grew she send forth many buds. ²⁶ and by JAH Accord fruit are given to those buds that grew - and Him clothe it stoutness in straw. ²⁷ Sight up like unto the measure that the seed kernel thou sowed abounded - yet the silver and the leaf - the ear and the straw aren't counted to thee. ²⁸ Don't be a dull one who don't know - and sight up thy seed that it abounded - and all likewise - think that dead persons shall raceive the arisin that them will arise - and them hardship like unto them Work. ²⁹ Hear I - that if thou sow wheat - it won't grow bein barley - nor bein wheat if thou sow barley - and make I tell thee again that it won't grow ~ if thou sow wheat will thou gather barley? If thou sow watercress will thou gather linseed? ³⁰ How about from plants kind - if thou plant figs will it really grow to thee bein nuts? How about if thou plant almonds - will it grow to thee bein grapes? ³¹ If thou plant the sweet fruit will it grow to thee bein bitter? How about if thou plant the bitter fruit - are it possible to it to be sweet? ³² How about all likewise - if a sinner dead are it possible to arise bein righteous in Resurrection time? How about if a righteous person dead - are it possible to arise bein a sinner in Resurrection time? Every one shall raceive him hardship like unto him Work - yet him will raceive him hardship like unto him sin and him hand Work - yet there are none who will be convicted by him companion sin. ³³ A highland tree are planted and it

send forth long branches ~ it will totally dry up ~ yet unless Heaven rained rain it leaves won't be verdant. ³⁴ and the cedar will be uprooted from it roots unless summer rain alit on it. ³⁵ and all likewise - dead persons won't arise unless welfare dew alit to them bein commanded from JAH.

9

¹ Unless highland mountains and Gielabuhie regions rained a pardon rain to them bein commanded from JAH - them won't grow grass to beasts and animals. ² and 'Elam mountains and Gele`ad mountains won't give verdant leaves to sheeps and goats - nor to oribi and animals in wilderness - nor to ibexes and hartebeest. ³ and likewise - pardon and dew bein commanded from JAH didn't alight to doubters and criminals who made error and crime a money beforehand ~ dead persons won't arise ~ and Deemas and Qophros who worship idols and dig roots and work and instigate a thing... ⁴ and them who dig roots and practice sorcery and make persons battle... ⁵ and them who lust havin departed from LAW - and Miedon and 'Atiena persons who believe in them idols - and them who play and sing to them while them beat violins and drums and strummed harps - them won't arise unless pardon dew alit to them bein commanded from JAH. ⁶ These are who will be canvicted on the day when dead persons arise and when Definite Judgemant are done - yet persons who save them ras selves and who lust in them hands Work - them err by them idols. ⁷ Thou wasteful of heart dull one - do it seem to thee that dead persons won't arise? ⁸ on the time a trumpet were blown by the Angels Chief Hola Meeka'iel tongue - that dead ones arise then - as thou won't remain in grave without arisin - don't think a thing that are thus. ⁹ Hills and mountains shall be level and shall be a cleared path. ¹⁰ and Resurrection shall be done to all fleshly ones.

10

¹ However if it weren't thus - it are that former persons might be buried in them fathers grave Beginnin from 'Adam - Beginnin from Siet and 'Abiel - Siem and Noh - Yis'haq and 'Abriham - Yosief and Ya`iqob - and 'Aron and Mussie - yet to what are it that them didn't love that them might be buried in another place? ² Aren't it to them to arise together with them cousins in Resurrection time? How about aren't it lest them bones be counted with evil ones and pagans bones - them who worship idols? to what are it that them didn't love that them might be buried in another place? ³ But thou - don't mislead thy reasonin while thou said - 'How will dead persons arise after them dead - them who were buried in one grave bein tens of thousands and whose bodies were demolished and rotten?' ⁴ and on the time thou sight up toward a grave - thou speak this in thy reasonin dullness while thou said - 'A whole fistful of Earth won't be found ~ how will dead persons arise?' ⁵ Will thou say the seed thou sowed won't grow? Even the seed thou sowed shall grow. ⁶ and all likewise - the souls JAH sowed shall quickly arise - as Him have Created man in Him Truth bringin from not livin toward livin - Him shall arouse them quickly by Him Word that save ~ Him won't delay Him arousin. ⁷ and as Him have again returned him from livin - toward a grave in death - what about aren't it possible to Him again to return from death toward Life? ⁸ Savin and liftin up are possible to JAH.

11

¹ 'Armon perished and she fortress were demolished ~ as JAH have brought the hardship on them like unto them evil and the Work them worked by them hands - persons who worship the idols in 'Edomyas and Zablon shall be downbased at that time ~ as JAH have approached - Who shall canvict them who worked in them infancy and didn't quit up til them aged - because them idols and them evil - Seedona and Theeros shall weep.. ² Because them worked sin and seducin fornication and worshipped idols - because this thing JAH shall revenge and destroy them ~ to them didn't live firmed up in them Creator JAH Command - and Yihuda daughter childran shall be wretched. ³ She lived firmed up in killin prophets and in Feeling good joy - yet as she didn't live firmed up in the Nine Laws and the Worship - on the time when dead ones arise - 'Iyerusaliem sin shall be revealed. ⁴ At that time JAH shall examine she in Him Nature Wisdom ~ Him will revenge and destroy she on all she sin that she worked in she infancy era ~ she didn't quit workin she sin Beginnin from she beauty era up til she age. ⁵ She entered toward a grave and became dust like unto she former fathers who lived firmed up in them sin - and in Resurrection time Him shall revenge and destroy persons who demolished JAH LAW. ⁶ It shall be judged on them - to Mussie have spoken because them sayin - 'Them LAW lodgin - them reasonins - became Sedom law lodgin.' ⁷ and them kindred are Gemorra kindred - and them law are what destroy - and them Work are evil. ⁸ and them law are snake poison that destroy - and viper poison that destroy from alongside that.

12

¹ 'Iyerusaliem child - as this thy sin are like unto Gemorra and Sedom sin - 'Iyerusaliem child - this are thy tribulation that were spoken by a prophet. ² and thy tribulation are like unto Gemorra and Sedom tribulation - and them law lodgin reasonin firmed up in adultery and arrogance. ³ Aside from adultery and arrogance rain - pardon and humility rain didn't rain from them reasonins by money that them Law reasonin lodgin are fertile - apart from spillin man blood and robbin and forgettin them Creator JAH. ⁴ and them didn't know them Creator JAH - apart from them evil Work and them idols - and them are Feeling good in them hands Work - and them lust on males and on livestock. ⁵ As them eye of reasonin have been blinded lest them sight up secrets - and as them ears have deafened lest them hear or do JAH Accord that Him love - them didn't know JAH in them Work - and them reasonins are like unto Sedom law lodgin. and them kindred - Gemorra grapes kindred that bear sweet fruit. ⁶ and if them examine them Work - it are poison that kill - to it have firmed up in curse Beginnin from the day when it were worked - and to it grounation have been in destruction era. ⁷ As them Law lodgin - them reasonins - have firmed up in sin Work - as them bodies have firmed up in Satan burnin Work to build sin - them Law lodgin - them reasonins - have no goodly Work everytime. ⁸ and on the time him shame and were baptise (by one who is led) it were to chastisemant and destruction - and him will firm up the persons who drank and them reasonins - and him will make them who destroy I - disgustin persons who distanced from JAH. ⁹ to them have lived firmed up in them Work that were evil - and him will make them Deeyablos lodgin - and eatin what were sacrificed to the idols have been begun in the House of 'Isra'iel - and she proceed toward the mountains and the trees. ¹⁰ and she worship the idols that peoples in she area worship - and she daughter childran and she male childran to demons who don't know goodly Work separatin from evil. ¹¹ and them spill clean blood ~ them gush and spill grapes from Sedom to the idols forever. ¹² and she glorify and worship the Dagwon that the 'Iloflans worship - and she sacrifice to him from she flocks and she fattened cows - that she might be Feeling good in demons laziness that them taught she to sacrifice to them - and in them gushin and spillin the grapes - and that she might do them accord. ¹³ She sacrifice to him that she might be Feeling good in demons laziness that them taught she lest she know she Creator JAH Who feed she at each time and Who cherished and raised she Beginnin from she infancy up til she beauty - and again up til she age - and again up til she age day when she dead. ¹⁴ and **again I-man shall revenge and canvict him in Resurrection time - and as she didn't return toward I LAW - and as she didn't live firmed up in I Command - she time when she live in *Gehannem* shall be up til Eternity. ¹⁵ If them were Creators to true - make she idols arise with she and descend toward *Gehannem* and save she on the time I-man vexed and destroyed she - and on the time I-man distanced all the priests of the idols who lust with she. ¹⁶ Like unto she made sin and insult on the Hola Items and on I Lodgin the Temple - I-man made she wretched by all this. ¹⁷ When them told she - 'Check - this are JAH kindred - and she are 'Isra'iel Creator JAH Lodgin - and the famous King country 'Iyerusaliem who were separate from them who were separate - she are the Most I JAH Name Lodgin' - I-man made she wretched like unto she saddened I Name that were called in she. ¹⁸ She boast in I that she were I slave and that I-man were she Lord ~ she wink on I like unto a criminal - yet she aren't who fear I and do I Accord like unto I bein she Lord. ¹⁹ Them became a obstacle on she to mislead that them might distance she from I - yet she are ruled to other idols who don't feed she nor clothe she. ²⁰ She sacrifice to them - and she eat the sacrifice - and she spill blood to them - and she gush and drink from the grapes to them ~ she smoke up ishence to them - and she make the ishence fragrance smell to them ~ she idols command she - and she are commanded to them. ²¹ and again she sacrifice she daughter childran and she male childran to them - and as she present praises to them because them Love - she are Feeling good in the thing she spoke by she tongue and in she hands Work. ²² Woe to she on the day when Definite Judgemant are done - and woe to she idols whom she love and inite; and she shall descend with them toward *Gehannem* beneath *See'ol* - where the worm don't slumber and the fire aren't extinguished. ²³ Woe to thee wretched 'Iyerusaliem child - to thou have quit I Who Created thee and have worshipped different idols. ²⁴ and I-man shall bring the hardship on thee like unto thy Work ~ as thou have saddened I - and as thou have ignored I Word - and as thou didn't work goodly Work - I-man shall canvict thee toward thy pretensions. ²⁵ to thou have saddened I Word - and to thou didn't live firmed up in I LAW whereby thou swore with I - that thou might keep I LAW and that I-man might live with thee in Support and might save thee from all who fight thee - and also that thou might keep I Order that I-man commanded thee - and I-man shall ignore thee and won't quickly save thee from the tribulation. ²⁶ Thou didn't keep all this - and I-man ignored thee ~ as I-man have created thee - and as thou didn't keep I Command nor I Word - I-man shall canvict thee in**

Judgemant time - and I-man honoured thee that thou might be I kin. ²⁷ and **like unto Gemorra and Sedom were separated from I - thou were separated from I.** ²⁸ and **I-man judged and destroyed them - and like unto Sedom and Gemorra were separated from I - thou separated from I - and now like unto I-man vexed and destroyed them - I-man vexed and destroyed thee ~ as thou are from Sedom and Gemorra kindred whom I-man destroyed - I-man destroyed thee ~ as them whom I-man Created have saddened I by goin toward a youtmon wife and by lustin without LAW - with animals and males like unto arrivin with daughters - I-man destroyed them name invocation from this world lest them live in them Feeling good joy.** ²⁹ There are no fearin JAH in them faces Beginnin from a infant up til a elder ~ them help him in all them evil Work - yet Him don't vex on each one that them might quit workin she ~ as them Work are evil - them are sated of sin and iniquity. ³⁰ All evil Work - robbery and arrogance and greed - are prepared in them reasonins. ³¹ and because this thing JAH ignored them and destroyed them countries - and them are there that Him might burn them with fire up til them root grounation perish ~ them totally perished up til the Eternity - yet Him didn't make even one from them remain. ³² **As them have firmed up in sin - them shall wait in destruction forever up til the Day of Advent when Definite Judgemant are done - to them have saddened I with them evil Work - and I-man won't pardon them nor forgive them.** ³³ and **I-man ignored them ~ to thou won't find a reason on the time I-man vexed and seized thee because all thy Work were robbery and sin - adultery and greed and speakin lies - all error Work and the obstacle that I-man don't love - and thou 'Iyerusaliem child who were wretched - on the day when Judgemant are done thou will be seized in Judgemant like unto them.** ³⁴ I-man had made thee to honour - but thou downbased thy ras self ~ I-man had called thee I money - but thou became to another. ³⁵ I-man had betrothed thee to honour - but thou became to Deeyablos - and I-man shall revenge and destroy thee like unto thy evil Work. ³⁶ **Because thou didn't hear all I Word - and because thou didn't keep the Command I-man commanded thee on the time I-man loved thee - I-man shall multiply and bring firm vengeance on thee - to I-man am JAH Who Created thee - and I-man shall judge on all sinners like unto thee - and on the day when Judgemant are done I-man shall bring the hardship on them like unto them evil Work.** ³⁷ **As thou didn't keep I Word - and as thou have ignored I Judgemant - I-man shall canvict thee with them.** ³⁸ **Woe to you - Gemorra and Sedom - who have no fearin JAH in your reasonin.** ³⁹ **All likewise - woe to thy sista 'Iyerusaliem child on whom it shall be judged together with thee in fire of *Gehannem* - to you will descend together toward *Gehannem* that were prepared to you - where are no exits forever - and woe to all sinners who worked thy sin.** ⁴⁰ **As you didn't keep I Command nor I Word - thou and she who didn't keep I Command nor I Word shall descend toward *See'ol* together on the day when Judgemant are judged.** ⁴¹ **But kind persons who kept I Command and I Word shall eat the money that sinner persons accumulated - and like unto JAH commanded - kind persons shall share the loot that evil persons captured - and kind persons shall be totally Feeling good.** ⁴² **But wrongdoers and sinner persons shall weep - and them shall be sad because all them sin that them wronged havin departed from I Command.** ⁴³ Him who keep I Word and live firmed up in I Command - him are who find I blessin and are honoured alongside I. ⁴⁴ All person who keep I Word and live firmed up in I Command shall eat the fatness found from Earth - and shall live havin entered toward the Garden where enter kind kings who have straight reasonins.

13

¹ **As them shall be wretched and perish by I wrath on the time I-man seized them - woe to Theeros and Seedona and all Yihuda country regions who make them ras selves arrogant today.** ² Conquerin JAH said thus ~ Him have said - **Deeyablos child who are totally arrogant shall be birthed from them - the False *Messeeh* who to a Truth thing are she enemy - who firm up him collar of reasonin - who boast and don't know him Creator** - and Him said - **Woe to them** - and JAH Who rule all said - **I-man made him to I anger pattern that I-man might be revealed in him Power.** ³ and this Qifirnahom Semarya and Geleela and Demasqo and Sorya and 'Akeya and Qophros and all Yordanos region are kindreds who firmed up them collars of reasonin - who live firmed up in them sin - and whom death shadow and darkness covered - to Deeyablos have covered them reasonins in sin - and to them are commanded to that arrogant Deeyablos - and them didn't return toward fearin JAH. ⁴ At that time woe to persons who are commanded to demons and who sacrifice in them name to them ~ as them have denied JAH Who Created them - them resemble animals without minds - to the False *Messeeh* who forgot JAH LAW and are Deeyablos child shall set up him image in all the places (to him have said 'Mi are a god') - and he shall be Feeling good in him reasonin accord - in him hand Work and in robbery and all the sins and perfidy and iniquity - in robbery and all the adulteries that a person work. ⁵ to because it were counted alongside JAH that him work this - the era are known that them work sin. ⁶ Sun shall darken and moon shall be blood - and stars shall be shaken from Heaven - all the Work shall pass by the miracles that JAH shall bring in Fulfillmant Era that Him might make Earth pass - and that Him might make all pass who live in sin of persons who live within she. ⁷ As JAH have been proud on the Creation Him Created - and as Him have quickly made all Him loved in one hour - the Lord death shall destroy a small enemy Deeyablos. ⁸ to JAH Who rule all have said - **I-man shall judge and destroy** - but after Advent - Deeyablos have no authority. ⁹ and **on the day when him were seized by I anger - him shall descend toward *Gehannem* - to which him make application and where firm tribulation are ~ as him will take all who are with him toward chastisemant and destruction and perfidy - because I-man were Who send forth from *Gehannem* and Who introduce toward *Gehannem* - him will descend toward *Gehannem*.** ¹⁰ As Him give firmness and Power to weak persons - and again as Him give weakness to powerful and firm persons - make a powerful one not boast in him Power. ¹¹ As Him are a Ruler - and as Him judge and save the wronged persons from the persons hands who wrong them - Him will return the grudge of the widows and the child whose father and mother dead on him. ¹² **Woe to thee who boast and firm up thy collar of reasonin - to whom it seem that I-man won't rule thee nor judge and destroy thee - to in him boastin and him arrogance him have said - 'Mi will streach mi throne in stars and Heaven - and mi will be like unto JAH Who are lofty.'** ¹³ and like unto Him spoke sayin - **How Deeyablos fell from Heaven - him who shine like unto a mornin star that were Created precedin all** - woe to thee. ¹⁴ and thou dared and spoke this in thy arrogance - and thou didn't think of JAH Who totally Created thee by Him Authority ~ why did thou boast thy ras self that thou descend toward *Gehannem* in thy reasonin firmness? ¹⁵ Thou were downbased separate from all Angels like unto thee - to them praise them Creator with a humbled reasonin because them knew that Him were Who Created them from fire and wind - and to them don't depart from Him Command - and to them keep them reasonins from perfidy lest them totally depart from Him Command. ¹⁶ But thou did a firm perfidy in thy reasonin arrogance ~ thou became a wretched man separate from thy companions - to thou have cherished all the sin and iniquity - robbery and perfidy whereby persons who forgot JAH LAW and sinners like unto thee live firmed up - them who are from thy kindred and commit crime like unto thee - and who live firmed up by thy command and thy accord whereby thou teach sin. ¹⁷ Woe to thee - to the demons thou misled in thy malice and thou will descend toward *Gehannem* together. ¹⁸ O you JAH childran who erred by that misleadin criminal Deeyablos - woe to you ~ as you have erred like unto him by the money that him taught you and that him hosts taught you - you will descend toward *Gehannem* together - where are no exits forever. ¹⁹ and formerly when JAH slave Mussie were there - you saddened JAH by the Water where argumant were made and on Korieb - and by 'Amalieq and on Mount Seena. ²⁰ and moreover on the time you sent scouts toward Kene`an - on the time them told you this sayin 'The path are far - and them ramparts and them fortresses that reach up til Heaven are firm - and warriors live there' - you vexed that you might return towad Gibts country where you work worrisome Work - and you saddened JAH Word. ²¹ You didn't think of JAH Who firmed you up from the tribulation - and Who did great miracles in Gibts - and Who led you by Him Angel Authority. Him would veil you in cloud by day lest the Sun burn you and Him would shine a column of fire to you by night lest your feet stumble in darkness. ²² and on the time the army and Fer`on frightened you - you totally cried toward Mussie - and Mussie totally cried toward JAH - and Him lodged in Him Angel and kept you lest you meet with Fer`on. ²³ But Him introduced them toward 'Eritra in tribulation ~ JAH led only 'Isra'iel - to Him have said - **and there were no different idol with them** - but Him buried them enemies in sea at one time - and Him didn't preserve none who flee from them. ²⁴ and Him made 'Isra'iel cross amidst the sea by foot ~ there are no tribulation that found them arisin from the Gibtsans ~ Him delivered them toward Mount Seena - and there Him fed them *menna* forty eras. ²⁵ As 'Isra'iel childran sadden JAH everytime - Him did all this goodly thing to them and them neglected to worship JAH. ²⁶ Them placed evil in them reasonins Beginnin from them childhood up til them age - to JAH Mouth have spoken thus in *'Oreet* where the fathers birth were written ~ as Him have spoken sayin - **'Adam childran reasonin are ash - and all them Work are toward robbery and them run toward evil ~ there are none from them who love straight Work - apart from gatherin a person**

money in violence and swearin in lie and wrongin companions and robbin and stealin - them placed evil in them reasonins. ²⁷ and all go toward evil Work in the era when them live in Life ~ 'Isra'iel childran who demolished JAH LAW totally saddened JAH Beginnin from Antiquity up til fufillmant era.

14

¹ and on the time JAH destroyed Qayen childran - kindreds who preceded - in destruction Water because them sin - Him baptised Earth in Water of Destruction - and Him cleansed she from all Qayel childran sin. ² As Him have said - **I-man were sad because I-man Created man** - Him destroyed all wrongdoers ~ Him didn't preserve apart from eight persons ~ Him destroyed all ~ after this Him multiplied them and them filled Earth ~ them shared them father 'Adam inheritance. ³ But Noh swore with JAH a oath ~ them swore a oath with JAH lest JAH again destroy Earth in Destruction Water - and lest Noh childran eat what deceased nor what lodged dead - lest them worship different idols apart from JAH Who Created them - and that Him might be a Love Father to them - and lest Him destroy them at one time in them vain sin - and lest Him prevent them the first and the spring rain - and that Him might give to livestock and persons them food at each time - that Him might give them the grass and the grain fruit and plants - and that them might work goodly Work in all that JAH love. ⁴ and after Him gave them this Order - 'Isra'iel childran saddened JAH by them sin ~ them didn't live firmed up in Him LAW like unto them fathers Yis'haq and 'Abriham and Ya`iqob who didn't demolish them Creator JAH LAW. ⁵. and Beginnin from the small up til the great - those 'Isra'iel childran who didn't keep JAH LAW are crooked in them Work. ⁶ and whether them be them priests or them chiefs or them scribes - everyone demolish JAH LAW. ⁷ Them don't live firmed up in JAH Order and Him LAW that Mussie commanded them in Repeatin Law sayin - **'Love thy Creator JAH in thy complete body and thy complete reasonin.'** ⁸ Them don't firm up in JAH Order and Him LAW that Mussie commanded them in book where LAW were written sayin - **'Love thy companion like unto thy body - and don't worship him idols that were different - and don't go toward a youtmon wife ~ don't kill a soul ~ don't steal. ⁹ and don't witness in lie - and be it him donkey or be it him ox - don't love thy companion money nor all that thy bredda bought.'** ¹⁰ However after him commanded them all this - 'Isra'iel childran who were evil return toward treachery and sin - robbery and iniquity - toward a youtmon wife and toward lies and stealin and worshippin idols. ¹¹ 'Isra'iel childran saddened JAH on Korieb by workin a cow that graze toward grass ~ them bowed sayin - 'Check - these are we creators who sent we forth from Gibts.' ¹² and them were Feeling good in them hand Work ~ if them ate and drank and satta - them arose to sing. ¹³ As JAH have told him sayin - **Thy kindreds whom thou sent forth from Gibts country where rulership are - them have proceeded from LAW and wronged - and them worked a cow image and bowed to the idol** - because this thing Mussie vexed and alit from Seena mountain. ¹⁴ While Mussie vexed on him kindreds - him alit with him canfidante 'Iyasu - and on the time 'Iyasu heard - him said - 'Check - I-man hear warriors voice in 'Isra'iel camp.' ¹⁵ and Mussie told 'Iyasu - 'It are when 'Isra'iel play havin drunk the unboiled wine - yet as to a warrior voice - it aren't' - and him alit and broke them image and totally crushed it up til it were like unto dust ~ him mixed it within the Water that 'Isra'iel childran drink beside the mountain. ¹⁶ and after this him commanded the priests that them might slay one another because the sin them worked before JAH. ¹⁷ Them knew that defyin JAH surpass killin them and killin them fathers - and them did like unto him commanded them. ¹⁸ and Mussie told them - 'Because you saddened JAH Who fed you and cherished you and Who sent you forth from a rulership house and Who bequeathed to you the inheritance that Him swore to your fathers that Him might give to them and to them childran after them - because this thing you made JAH Feeling good.' ¹⁹ to them go toward sin and a evil thing - and them didn't quit saddenin JAH there. ²⁰ Them aren't like unto them fathers Yis'haq and 'Abriham and Ya`iqob who made JAH Feeling good with them goodly Work that Him might give them what are on Earth and what Him prepared to persons who love Him in Heaven Beginnin from them infancy up til them youthood and up til them age ~ them aren't like unto 'Abriham and Yis'haq and Ya`iqob who made Him Feeling good with them Work that Him might give them a Earth of inheritance where Feeling good joy are found in this world - and a garden that make Feeling good - prepared to kind persons in hereafter world - what Him prepared to 'Abriham and Yis'haq and Ya`iqob who made JAH Feeling good when them were in Life and who love Him - Whom a eye didn't sight up nor a ear hear and Who aren't thought of in reasonin. ²¹ and them childran who denied JAH and were evil and who live firmed up in them reasonin accord - them didn't hear JAH Command - Him Who fed them and cherished them and kept them Beginnin from them infancy. ²² Them didn't think of JAH - Who sent them forth from Gibts land and saved them from brick Work and a firm rulership. ²³ But them totally saddened Him - and Him would arouse peoples in them area on them - and them would arise on them in enmity and also tax them like unto them loved.

15

¹ and at that time Midyam persons arose on them in enmity - and them aroused them armies on 'Isra'iel that them might fight them - and them king name are called 'Akrandis ~ him quickly gathered many armies in Keeliqyas and Sorya and Demasqo. ² and campin beyond Yordanos him sent messengers sayin - 'An that mi might capture your money - pay tax toward 'Isra'iel to mi' ~ him told them - 'But if you don't pay tax - mi came that mi might punish you and might capture your livestocks and take your mares and capture your childran.' ³ 'Mi will capture and take you toward the country you don't know - and there mi will make you Water pourers and wood pickers' him told them. ⁴ 'Don't boast while you said - "I are JAH kindreds and there are nothing able to I" - aren't JAH Who sent mi that mi might destroy you and plunder your money? and aren't mi whom JAH sent that mi might gather all your kindreds? ⁵ Are there really a savin that them different idols saved the other kins that mi destroyed? Mi captured them mares and them horses and mi killed them and captured them childran. ⁶ and unless you introduced the tax that mi commanded you - mi will destroy you like unto them' him said - and him crossed Yordanos that him might plunder them livestocks and them money and capture them wives. ⁷ and after this 'Isra'iel childran wept a firm mournin toward JAH - and them totally cried - however them lacked one who help them. ⁸ and because this thing JAH gave firmness to the three bredren - and them names are like unto this: - and them are Yihuda and Mebikyas and Meqabees - whose features were handsome and who were warriors in them Power. ⁹ and 'Isra'iel childran totally wept there ~ on the time them heard - it saddened them in them heart arisin from all 'Isra'iel childran shout ~ the child whose mother and father dead on him - and widows - and them officials and them priests - all 'Isra'iel kindred - both daughters and males - and all childran - would weep sprinklin ash on them heads - and them nobles had worn sackcloth. ¹⁰ But those bredren - who were attractive and comely - went and agreed that them might save them ~ them counseled sayin - 'Make I go and give I bodies to death because these persons.' ¹¹ Tellin one another - 'Take heart - take heart' - them went girdin them swords on them waists and seizin them spears in them hands - and them went prepared that them might incriminate the warrior. ¹². and them arrived toward them camp ~ Mebikyus attacked the warrior (the king) when him had sat at a dinnertable ~ him cut him neck in one blow when food were in him mouth; and Meqabyus and Yihuda struck him armies on the king left and right by sword and killed them. ¹³ and on the time them king were defeated - them entered toward them spears in them companions hearts - and them all totally fled and them bows were broken and them were defeated. ¹⁴ But those bredren who are attractive and comely were saved from death ~ there are no evil thing that found them - but as JAH have returned chastisemant toward them - them sliced up one another and were depleted. ¹⁵ Them were defeated and dead and them crossed Yordanos - and up til them crossed them cast way all them money - and all them money remained - and pom the time 'Isra'iel childran sight up that them enemies fled - them went toward them camp and took both what them plundered and them money to them ras selves. ¹⁶ JAH saved 'Isra'iel doin thus by the bredren and Mebikyu hand. ¹⁷ 'Isra'iel sat a few days while them made JAH Feeling good. ¹⁸ But after that them again returned toward them sin ~ 'Isra'iel childran neglected worshippin JAH by what are due. ¹⁹ and Him shall again sadden them by kins who don't know them and who will gather them field crops and destroy them grape places and plunder them flocks and slaughter and feed them them livestocks before them... ²⁰ and who will capture them wives and them daughter childran and them male childran ~ because we sare that them sadden JAH everytime; as themare kindreds who demolished the LAW - them will hammer them childran before them on each of them heads ~ them won't save them.

16

¹ Them who do this are Theeros and Seedona and them who live beyond Yordanos river and on the sea edge - Keran and Gele`ad - 'Iyabuseewon and Kenaniewon - 'Edom and Giegiesiewon and 'Amalieq persons. ² All peoples do thus - who live firmed up in each of them tribes and countries and regions and in each of them Works and country languages - and all live firmed up like unto JAH worked them. ³ and there are persons from them who know JAH - and whose Work were beautiful. ⁴ and there are persons from them whose Work were evil and who don't know JAH Who Created them - and like unto them worked sin - Him ruled them in Sorya king Silminasor hand. ⁵ As him plunder and take Demasqo money - and as him share Semarya loot that are before Gibts king - Him ruled them in

Silminasor hand. ⁶ Gielabuhie region and also persons in Fars and Miedon - Qephedoqya and Sewseegya - who live in the West mountains - in Gele`ad fortress and Phasthos that are part of Yihuda land... ⁷ and these are who live in them region - and them are kindreds who don't know JAH nor keep Him Command - and whose collar of reasonin were firm. ⁸ and Him shall pay them them hardship like unto them Work evil and them hands Work. ⁹ to Gele`ad kindreds and Qeesarya region and 'Amalieq have become one there - that them might destroy JAH country that were filled of a Truth thing - and within which 'Isra'iel Creator are praised - Him Who are Most Glorified and Conquerin - and Whom Angels who are many many in Keerubiel chariots - them who stand before Him - serve fearin and tremblin - and Him shall pay them them hardship like unto them Work evil and them hands Work.

17

¹ 'Amalieq and 'Edomyas persons don't worship JAH by Whose Authority Earth and Heaven rulership were seized ~ as them are criminals who don't live firmed up in Truth Work - them don't fear to demolish Him Lodgin - the Temple. ² and there are no fearin JAH before them - apart from sheddin blood and adultery and eatin what were beaten and sacrificed to a idol and all that resemble what lodged dead - and these are scorned sinners. ³ Them have no virtue nor religion ~ as them are who hated goodly Work - and as them don't know JAH - and as them don't know Love Work - apart from robbin a person money and from sin - and apart from disturbin a person and all hated Work - apart from games and song like unto them father Deeyablos taught them - them have no virtue nor religion. ⁴ As him have ruled them with him host - demons - him teach them all evil Work that were to each of them ras selves - all robbery and sin - theft and falsehood - robbin money and eatin what were beaten and what lodged dead - and adultery Work. ⁵ and him teach them all that resemble this - and goin toward a youtmon wife - and sheddin blood - eatin what were sacrificed to idol and what lodged dead - and killin a person soul in violence - and envy and winkin and greed and all evil Work that JAH don't love ~ Deeyablos who were them enemy teach them this teachin that him might distance them from JAH LAW Who rule all the world. ⁶ But JAH Work are innocence and humility - not annoyin a bredren and lovin a companion - harmonisin and lovin with all persons. ⁷ Don't be hypocrites to favour to a person face - and don't be wrongdoers nor totally robbers nor persons who go toward a youtmon wife - nor persons who work iniquity and evil Work on them companion - nor who cajole that them might wrong them companion in violence. ⁸ Them wink and shake them heads and provoke to evil ~ them discourage to mislead that them might lower them toward Eternity Definite Judgemant.

18

¹ Think that thou will go in death toward JAH in Whose Hand all are - and thou will stand before Him that Him might canvict thee before Him on all the sin thou Worked. ² As them who are arrogant and evil - and powerful ones children who aren't strengthenin more than them - were likewise formerly - because them sight up them stature and them Power and them firm authority - them didn't make JAH before them - and them didn't know that Him were them Creator Who Created them bringin from not livin toward livin. ³ and when them fathers bein like unto "Angels" praised on Mount Hola with Angels - on the time them accord misled them - them alit toward this world where Definite Judgemant shall be done forever. ⁴ As JAH in the Antiquity have Created human flesh to them - that it might mislead them because them reasonin arrogance and might test them as it were them kept Him LAW and Him Command - them married wives from Qayel children. ⁵ But them didn't keep Him LAW ~ Him lowered them toward *Gehannem* fire with them father Deeyablos; to JAH have vexed on the offspring of Siet who wronged like unto persons - and persons era were diminished because them sin. ⁶ and them took 'Adam children toward sin with them ~ Him lowered them toward *See'ol* where them shall raceive a verdict. ⁷ As persons era have been divided because Siet children erred by Qayel children - when a person eras were nine hundred in the Antiquity - them returned toward livin a hundred twenty eras. ⁸ and as them are flesh and blood - JAH said - **I Spirit of Support won't live firmed up on them.** ⁹ and because this thing I era were divided - to because I sin and I iniquity - I era have been divided from I fathers who preceded - and when them are in them infancy again - them are dyin. ¹⁰ But I fathers era had abounded - because them kept Him LAW and because them didn't sadden JAH. ¹¹ But I fathers era had abounded - because them vexed on them daughter children that them might teach them - and because them vexed on them male childran lest them demolish JAH LAW. ¹² Because them didn't demolish JAH LAW with them daughter childran and them male children - because this thing them era had abounded to true.

19

¹ on the time Qayen childran abounded them worked drums and harps - *santee* and violins - and them made songs and all the games. ² Childran who are attractive and comely were birthed to Qayen from the wife of the kind man 'Abiel - whom him killed because she - to she were attractive - and after him killed him bredda him took that and she who were him money. ³ and separatin from him father - him seized them and went toward Qiefaz region that are toward the West - and that attractive one childran were attractive like unto them mother. ⁴ and because this thing Siet childran descended toward Qayen childran - and after them sight them up them didn't wait one hour - and them made the daughters whom them chose wives to them ras selves. ⁵ As them have taken I toward error together with them because them error - because this thing JAH vexed on I and vexed on them. ⁶ and Deeyablos havin cajoled sayin - 'You will become creators like unto your Creator JAH' - him took I mother Hiewan and I father 'Adam toward him error. ⁷ But it seemin Truth to them in them dullness - them demolished JAH LAW - Him Who Created them bringin from not-livin toward livin that them might bow and praise Him glorified Name. ⁸ But Him - them Creator - downbased those 'Adam and Hiewan who made godhood to them ras selves - and Him downbased him who are arrogant. ⁹ Like unto Daweet spoke sayin - ' 'Adam perish by the sinner Deeyablos arrogance' - Him abused them - to I father 'Adam have been convicted on Deeyablos arrogance by Him true Judgemant. ¹⁰ and Siet children who erred by Qayel childran took I toward them sin thus ~ because this thing I era that JAH gave I were less than I fathers eras. ¹¹ But them had worked goodly Work - to them had firmed up them reasonins in JAH - to them had taught them daughter children and them male children lest them depart from JAH LAW that them taught them - and there were no evil enemy who approach them. ¹² But if them worked goodly Work - there are nothing that benefit them if them didn't tell nor teach to them childran. ¹³ Like unto Daweet spoke sayin - 'Them didn't hide from them childran to another child - and teach JAH praise - the wondrous miracles Him did - and Him Power' - there are nothing that benefit them if them didn't teach to them childran that them might teach to them childran to make heart like unto them knew - and that them might know and do Him Accord - and that them might tell them JAH LAW Trust - and that them might keep Him LAW like unto them fathers who made JAH Feeling good with them beautiful Work. ¹⁴ and them who told them Trust from them fathers in them infancy didn't demolish Him Command - like unto them fathers learned JAH Worship and the Nine Laws from them fathers. ¹⁵ Them children learned from them fathers that them might work goodly Work and might present praise to them Creator - to them have kept Him LAW - and to them have loved Him. ¹⁶ and Him shall hear them in them prayer - and Him won't ignore them plea - but Him are a Forgiver. ¹⁷ Havin multiplied Him wrath - Him shall return it to them - and Him wouldn't destroy all in Him chastisemant.

20

¹ I bredren - think - don't forget what them told you formerly - that JAH keep the true Work of persons who work goodly Work. ² and Him multiply them childran in this world - and them name invocation shall live firmed up to a goodly thing up til the Eternity - and them children won't be troubled to grain in this world. ³ As Him shall dispute to them because them - and as Him won't cast them in them enemy hand - Him shall save them from them enemies hand who hate them. ⁴ and to persons who love Him Name - Him shall be them Helper in them tribulation time ~ Him shall guard them and pardon them all them sin.

21

¹ Daweet believed in JAH - to Him have believed in him - and Him saved him bein a Refuge from the king Sa'ol hand. ² and as him have believed in Him and kept Him LAW on the time when him child 'Abiesielom arose - and on the time when the 'Iloflans arose - and on the time when the 'Edomyans and the 'Amalieqans arose - on the time when the one from the four Rafayn arose - JAH saved Daweet from all this tribulation that enemies who disputed him brought on him. ³ As prevailin are by JAH Accord - them were defeated by them enemies hand - yet but JAH didn't save the evil kings who didn't believe in Him. ⁴ and Hiziqyas believed in JAH ~ Him saved him from Senakriem hand who were arrogant. ⁵ But him child Minassie were defeated by him enemy hand - to him didn't make him trustin in JAH ~ as him didn't make him trustin in JAH and as him didn't fear JAH Who totally honoured and famed him - them bound and took him toward them country - yet but those enemies who defeated Minassie weren't like unto him. ⁶ At that time Him denied him the kingdom Him gave him - to him didn't work goodly Work before him Creator JAH - that him era might abound and that Him might dispute him enemy to him and that him might have Power and firmness behind and in front. ⁷ to it are better to believe in JAH than in many armies - than believin in horses and bows and shields. ⁸ Believin in JAH surpass ~ a person who believed in Him shall firm up and

be honoured and totally lofty. ⁹ to JAH don't favour to a face - but persons who didn't believe in JAH - who believed in them money abundance - became them who departed from the grace and honour that Him gave them. ¹⁰ Him shall guard the persons who believe in Him - but Him shall make the persons ignorant who call Him ignorant - and as them didn't discipline them reasonins to follow JAH nor keep Him LAW - Him won't quickly help them in them tribulation time nor in the time them enemies disputed with them. ¹¹ But to a person who were disciplined in worshippin JAH and to keep Him LAW - Him shall be a Refuge in him tribulation time. ¹² By destroyin him enemy - and by plunderin him enemy livestock - and by capturin him enemy country persons - and by rainin eras rain - and by growin sprouts - and by introducin the grain pile - in the plant fruit... ¹³ and by rainin the first and the spring rains - and by makin the grass verdant - and by givin the rain that rain at each time that thy kindreds beneath thy Authority might be Feeling good - Him shall make him Feeling good. ¹⁴ Him shall make him Feeling good - that them might eat the other one money - that them might satta havin eaten the money them plundered from them enemy - that them might plunder animals and sheeps and cows - and that them might eat the other one dinnertable - and that them might take them enemies childran captive. ¹⁵ JAH shall do all this to the person whom Him love - but Him will make the person who hate Him to him enemy ransackery. ¹⁶ and Him shall bind him feet and him hands and shall cast him in him enemy hand - and Him shall make him to him enemies derision - and as him have become a blood shedder who demolished JAH LAW - Him won't make him Feeling good in him house seed. ¹⁷ and him won't firm up in Judgemant time - and that Him might bring the hardship to persons who work sin - Him will also give persons who work evil Work them sin hardship. ¹⁸ But it were commanded from alongside JAH to give persons who work goodly Work them reward - that Him might keep them in Him Authority. ¹⁹ to Him are empowered on all the Creation Him Created that Him might do goodly Work and might give them Iternal welfare and that them might praise JAH Who Created them - and Him commanded that him might keep Him LAW ~ apart from only man there are none from all the Creations Him Created that departed from Him Command. ²⁰ Like unto JAH commanded all who live firmed up in each of them Works - them all know and are kept in Him LAW. ²¹ But man are emboldened on JAH Who crowned all on each of them inventions - on animal and beasts and on Heaven birds. ²² Be it what are in sea or all on land - JAH gave all the Creation Him Created to them father 'Adam ~ JAH gave them that him might do what him loved - and that them might eat them like unto grain that grew on Earth - and that them might rule and tax them - and that be them beasts or animals them might be commanded to man - and Him Ipointed them on all Him Created that persons who reigned might be commanded to JAH Who gave them honour and that them might favour Him. ²³ But if them depart from Him LAW Him will separate them from the lordship Him gave them ~ as Him are Who rule Earth and Heaven - Him will give it to him who do Him Accord. ²⁴ Him Ipoint whom Him loved to Ipoint - but Him dismiss whom Him loved to dismiss ~ Him kill ~ Him save ~ Him whip in tribulation ~ Him forgive. ²⁵ There are no other Creator like unto Him ~ as Him are Ruler to all the Creation Him Created - as there are no other without Him - the Creator - in Heaven above Earth nor on Earth beneath Heaven - there are none who shall criticise Him. ²⁶ Him Ipoint ~ Him dismiss ~ Him kill ~ Him save ~ Him whip in tribulation ~ Him forgive ~ Him impoverish ~ Him honour. ²⁷ Him hear persons who beg Him in them plea ~ Him accept a person plea who do Him Accord with a clean reasonin; and Him hear them in them prayer - and Him do them accord to them in all that them begged Him. ²⁸ and Him make the great and the small to be commanded to them ~ all this are them money on hills and mountains and at trees roots and in caves and Earth wells and all them kindreds on both dry and sea. ²⁹ and to persons who do them Creator Accord all this are them money - and Him won't trouble them from them plenty - and Him shall give them them praise reward. ³⁰ and Him shall give them the honour Him prepared in Heaven to them fathers Yis'haq and 'Abriham and Ya`iqob ~ Him shall give them what Him prepared to Hiziqyas and Daweet and Samu'iel who didn't depart from Him LAW and Him Command. ³¹ That them might be Feeling good in Him Lordship - Him shall give them who served Him Beginnin from Antiquity the honour Him prepared to them fathers Yis'haq and 'Abriham and Ya`iqob - to whom Him swore to give them a inheritance.

22

¹ Please - think of persons name who work goodly Work - and don't forget them Work. ² Straighten up that thy name be called like unto them name - that thou might be Feeling good with them in the Kingdom of Heaven - that were Light Lodgin that Him prepared to nobles and kings who did JAH Accord and were kind persons. ³ and again - know and be canvinced of evil nobles and kings names - that Him shall canvict them and revile them alongside man after them dead. ⁴ to them didn't line up them Work while them sight up and heard - and know and be canvinced that unless them did JAH Accord - Him shall judge on them in the Kingdom of Heaven more than criminals and persons who forgot JAH LAW. ⁵ Be kindly - innocent - honest - yet don't thou also go on persons path who forgot JAH LAW - on whom JAH vexed because them evil Work. ⁶ Judge Truth and save the child whose mother and father dead on him - and the widow from sinner persons hand who rob them. ⁷ Be a guardian like unto him father to the child whose mother and father dead on him - that thou might save him from the wealthy one hand who rob him - and stand to him - and be alarmed on the time the child - whose mother and father dead on him - tears flowed before thee-I - lest thou be alarmed in fire sea where sinner persons who didn't enter repentance are punished. ⁸ and straighten up thy feet toward Love and Inity path ~ as JAH Eyes check up Him friends - and as Him Ears hear them plea - seek Love and follow she. ⁹ But JAH Face of Him Wrath are toward persons who work evil Work - that Him might destroy them name invocation from this world - and Him won't preserve a person who near on ramparts nor mountains. ¹⁰ **As I-man am JAH Who am jealous on I Godhood - as I-man am a Creator who revenge and destroy persons who hate I and don't keep I Word - I-man won't return I Face of Support reachin up til I-man destroy the person who don't keep I Word.** ¹¹ **and I-man shall honour persons who honour I and keep I Word.**

23

¹ Don't live firmed up in Qayel order - who killed him bredda who followed him in innocence - it seemin to him that him bredda love him. ² and him killed him bredda envyin on a daughter ~ persons who make envy and iniquity and betrayal on them companion are like unto him. ³ But as 'Abiel are innocent like unto a sheep - and as him blood are like unto the clean sheep blood that them sacrificed to JAH by a clean reasonin - them went on Qayel path that aren't on 'Abiel path. ⁴ to because all the persons who live in innocence were persons whom JAH love - like unto a kind man 'Abiel - them have been innocent ones like unto 'Abiel - but those persons who live firmed up in 'Abiel Work love JAH. ⁵ But JAH neglect evil ones - and them Definite Judgemant make application to them on them bodies - and it are written on the record of them reasonins - and on the time when Judgemant are judged - them shall read she before man and Angels and before all the Creation. ⁶ At that time them shall shame ~ wrongdoers and refusers who didn't do JAH Accord shall shame. ⁷ and a alarmin Word shall be given them that say - **Place them in *Gehannem* where are no exit up til Eternity.**

24

¹ But on the time Giediewon trusted JAH - him defeated uncircumcise peoples armies who were many many in army of a few tens of thousands and without number like unto locusts. ² **As there are no Creator without I - o nobles and kings - don't believe in the different idols.** ³ **As I-man am your Creator JAH Who sent you forth from your mothers wombs and raised you and fed you and clothed you - why do you pretext? How about why do you worship other idols without I?** ⁴ **I-man did all this to you ~ what did you give I? It are that you might live firmed up in I LAW and I Order and I Command and that I-man might give you your bodies welfare - yet what will I-man want from you?** ⁵ JAH Who rule all said thus ~ Him said - **Save your ras selves from worshippin idols and practisin sorcery and discouragin pessimism.** ⁶ As JAH chastisemant shall come on these who do this - and on them who hear them and do them accord and are them friends and who live firmed up in them command - save your ras selves from worshippin idols. ⁷ As peoples - who don't know you and aren't nice to you - shall arise on you - unless you who feared did JAH Accord - them will eat the money wherefor you wearied ~ like unto Him servants the prophets spoke and like unto Hienok spoke and like unto 'Asaf spoke - unless you did JAH Accord - them will eat the money wherefor you wearied. ⁸ **Evil persons will come havin changed them clothes** Him said ~ there are no other law alongside them apart from eatin and drinkin and adornin in silver and gold - and livin havin firmed up in sin all the Work JAH don't love. ⁹ But them are prepared to go toward drink and food ~ after them were aroused from them slumber Beginnin from mornin up til evenin them go toward evil Work; there are misery and tribulation in them path - yet them feet have no Love path. ¹⁰ and them don't know Love and Inity Work - and there are no fearin JAH in them faces ~ them are crooked evil ones without religion nor virtue ~ them are greedy ones who eat and drink alone ~ them are drunkards - and them sin are without LAW and without measure ~ them are who go toward seducin - sheddin blood - theft and perfidy and violently robbin him money who don't have it. ¹¹ and them are who criticise without Love and without LAW - to them don't fear JAH Who Created them - and there are no fear in them

faces. ¹² Them don't shame in the person face that them sight up - and them don't shame a grey-hair nor a elder face ~ on the time them heard when them said - 'An there are money in this world' - them make it them ras self money before them sight it up with them eyes - to there are no fearin JAH in them faces - and on the time them sight it up with them eyes it seem to them that them ate it. ¹³ and them nobles eat trust money ~ them are who eat ~ as them are negativists and as there are no straight thing in them tongues - them don't repeat in evenin what them spoke in mornin. ¹⁴ to them ignore sufferahs and poor ones cries - and them kings hasten to evil - them who disturb a person - him havin saved refugees from wealthy ones hands who rob them. ¹⁵ make them save him who were wronged and the refugee - yet make the kings not be them who begrudge justice because this thing. ¹⁶ But them are who exact tribute ~ them are who rob a person money - and them are criminals - and as them Work are evil - them aren't nice when them eat the newborn calf with she mother and a bird with she egg ~ them make all them sight up and heard them ras self money. ¹⁷ Them love that them might gather to them ras selves - yet them aren't nice to sick and poor ones - and them violently rob the money of a person who don't have it - and them gather all them found that them might be fattened and be Feeling good in it. ¹⁸ to them shall perish quickly like unto a scarab that proceeded from it pit and whose track aren't found and that don't return toward it house - and because them didn't work goodly Work when them are in them Life - woe to them bodies on the time JAH vexed and seized them. ¹⁹ on the time JAH neglected them - them will perish at one time like unto them are in one chastisemant - to Him indure them meanin as it were them returned toward repentance - yet Him don't quickly destroy them - and them shall perish on the time when them shall perish. ²⁰ But if them don't return toward repentance - Him will quickly destroy them like unto former persons who were precedin them - who didn't keep JAH LAW by what are due. ²¹ Them are who eat a person flesh and drink a person blood ~ as them gird and work violence to go toward sin - there are no fearin JAH in them faces everytime - and after them arose from them beddin them don't rest to work sin. ²² and them Work are drink and food - goin toward destruction and sin - that them might destroy many persons bodies in this world.

25

¹ As them Work are crooked - and as all are who live firmed up in Satan Work that mislead - JAH Who rule all said - **Woe to your body on the time I-man vexed and seized she.** ² **But to them don't know JAH Work - to them have returned it toward them rear - and to them have neglected I LAW.** ³ and **later in fulfillmant era I-man shall bring the hardship on them like unto them evil measure ~ like unto them sin were written alongside I - I-man shall revenge and destroy them on the day when Judgemant are judged.** ⁴ **As I-man JAH am full from horizon up til horizon - and as all the Creation have been seized in I Authority - there are none who escape from I Authority in Heaven nor Earth nor depth nor sea.** ⁵ **I-man command a snake that are beneath Earth - and I-man command a fish that are within sea - and I-man command birds in Heaven - and I-man command the desert donkey in wilderness - to it are I money Beginnin from horizon up til horizon.** ⁶ **As I-man am Who work wondrous Work and do miracles before I - there are none who escape from I Authority on Earth nor in Heaven ~ there are none who tell I - 'Where do Thou go? How about what do thou Work?'** ⁷ and **I-man command on Angels chiefs and hosts ~ all Creations whose name are called are I money - and beasts in wilderness and all birds in Heaven and livestocks are I moneys.** ⁸ It arise from 'Azieb wind and firm up in drought in Mesi` ~ later in fulfillmant era 'Eritra sea shall perish bein heard - arisin from JAH - Who shall come toward she - bein feared and famousness. ⁹ to Him rule them who dead and persons who are there - and she shall perish bein heard with Saba and Noba and Hindekie and 'Ityopphya limits and all them regions. ¹⁰ and Him watch all in lofty Authority and innocence - to Him Authority surpass all the authority - and Him keep cangregations in Him Authority. ¹¹ and to Him Authority firm up more than all the authority - and to Him Kingdom surpass all the kingdoms - and to Him Authority are what rule all the world - to Him able to all - and to there are nothing that fail Him. ¹² Him rule all clouds in Heaven ~ Him grow grass to livestocks on Earth - and Him give fruit on the buds. ¹³ Him feed to all in each of the kinds like unto Him loved ~ Him feed all that Him Created by each of the fruits and each of the foods - and Him feed ants and locusts beneath Earth and livestocks on Earth and beasts - and to a person who prayed Him give him him prayer - and Him don't ignore the plea of the child whose mother and father dead on him - nor widows. ¹⁴ As evil persons rebellion are like unto a swirlin wind and wrongdoers council like unto misty urine - Him shall rather accept the plea of them who beg toward Him at each time and clean ones. ¹⁵ and as them body are like unto a flyin bird - and as them features attractiveness that are silver and gold are perishable in this world - examination will benefit persons who forgot JAH LAW yet not them gold - and moths shall eat them clothes. ¹⁶ and weevils shall totally eat the wheat and the barley fatness - and all shall pass like unto the day that passed yesterday - and like unto a word that proceeded from a mouth don't return - sinner persons money also are like unto it - and them 'beautiful lifestyle' are like unto a passin shadow ~ sinner persons money before JAH are like unto a lie clothes. ¹⁷ But if kind persons are honoured JAH won't ignore them - to them have been honoured while them were nice to poor ones - and them hear justice of sufferahs and a child whose mother and father dead on him ~ JAH won't ignore them - to without neglectin them house childran - them honour Him while them clothe the naked from the clothes JAH gave them that them might give to the refugee sufferah. ¹⁸ Them don't favour loyal persons judgemant - and them don't make a hireling salary lodge ~ as JAH thing are Truth and honoured like unto a sword whose mouths were two - them won't do iniquity in them seasons number and in them balance measuremant.

26

¹ But poor ones will think again on them beddin - but if wealthy ones don't accept them - them will be like unto dry wood that have no verdure - and a root won't be fertile from alongside where no moisture are - and the leaf won't be fertile if there are no root. ² As a leaf serve a flower to be a ornamant to fruit - unless the leaf were fertile it won't bear fruit ~ as man fulfillmant are religion - a person without religion have no virtue. ³ If him firmed up religion him worked virtue - and JAH are Feeling good by a person who work Truth and straight Work. ⁴ and to the person who begged Him - Him shall give him him plea and him tongue reward - and Him won't wrong the true person because him true Work that him worked. ⁵ As JAH are true - and as Him have loved a Truth thing - Him won't justify the sinner person without repentance because the Work evil him worked - and as all persons souls have been seized in Him Authority because Him were Who ruled Earth and Heaven - as Him won't favour for the wealthy more than the poor in Judgemant time - Him won't justify him without repentance.

27

¹ Him Created havin brought all the world from not livin toward livin - and Him totally prepared hills and mountains - and Him firmed up Earth on Water - and lest sea be shaken Him delineated she by sand - to in Him first Word JAH have said make **Light be Created.** ² Light were Created when this world had been covered in darkness ~ JAH Created all the Creation - and Him prepared this world - and Him firmed up this world by what are due and by money that are straight ~ Him said - make **evenin be dark.** ³ and again JAH said make **Light be Created** ~ it dawned and there were Light - and Him Ilivated the upper Water toward Heaven. ⁴ and Him streached it forth like unto a tent - and Him firmed it up by a wind - and Him placed the lower Water within a pit. ⁵ and Him shut the sea lock in sand - and Him firmed them up in Him Authority lest them drown in Water - and Him placed animals and beasts within she - and Him placed within she Liewatan and Biehiemot who were great beasts - and Him placed within she the beasts without number - sight up and not sight up. ⁶ on the third day JAH Created on Earth plants - all the roots and woods and fruits that bear forth in each of them kinds - and a welfare wood beautiful to them to sight it up.. ⁷ and Him Created a welfare wood that were both beautiful to them to sight it up and sweet to them to eat it - and Him Created grass - and all plants whose seeds are found from within them - to be food to birds and livestocks and beasts. ⁸ It dusked ~ it dawned - and on the fourth day Him said - make **Light be Created in Heaven called cosmos** ~ JAH havin Created moon and Sun and stars - Him placed them in Heaven called cosmos that them might shine in this world and that them might feed them daylight and night. ⁹ and after this moon and Sun and stars alternated in night and daylight. ¹⁰ and on the fifth day JAH Created all animals and beasts that live within Water and all birds that fly on Heaven - all that are sight up and not sight up - all this. ¹¹ and on the sixth day Him Created livestocks and beasts and others - and havin Created and prepared all - Him Created 'Adam in Him Example and Him Appearance. ¹² Him gave him all animals and beasts Him Created that him might reign on them - and again - all animals and beasts and all fishes - and Liewatan and Biehiemot that are in sea. ¹³ and Him gave him all cows that live in this world and sheeps - the animals not sight up and them that are sight up. ¹⁴ and Him placed in Garden 'Adam whom Him Created in Him Example and Him Appearance - that him might eat and might cultivate plants and might praise JAH there. ¹⁵ and to lest him demolish Him Command - Him have said - on **the time when you ate from this Herb of Fig you will dead death.** ¹⁶ and Him commanded him lest him eat from the Herb of Fig that bring death - that draw attention to evil and good - that bring death. ¹⁷ I mother Hiewan were cajoled by a snake misleadin and she ate from that Herb of Fig and gave it to I father 'Adam. ¹⁸ and 'Adam havin eaten from that Herb of Fig brought

death on him childran and on him ras self. ¹⁹ As him have demolished Him Command - and as him have eaten from that Herb of Fig that JAH commanded sayin - **Don't eat from she** - JAH vexed on I father 'Adam and expelled and sent him way from the Garden - and Him gave him that Earth that grow thistle and thorn - that Him cursed because him on the time him demolished Him Command - that him might eat him weariness reward havin toiled and laboured that him might plow she. ²⁰ and on the time JAH sent him forth toward this land - 'Adam returned toward complete sadness - and havin toiled and laboured that him might plow Earth - him began to eat in weariness and also in struggles.

28

¹ and after him childran lived havin abounded - there were from them ones who praise and honour JAH and don't demolish Him Command. ² There were prophets who spoke what were done and what will be done henceforth - and from him childran there were sinners who speak lies and who wrong persons ~ 'Adam firstborn child Qayel became evil and killed him bredda 'Abiel. ³ JAH judged Judgemant on Qayel because him killed him bredda 'Abiel - and JAH vexed on Earth because she drank him blood. ⁴ and JAH told Qayel - **Where are thy bredda 'Abiel?** - and Qayel in him heart arrogance said - 'Are mi mi bredda 'Abiel keeper?' ⁵ 'Abiel became a clean man - but Qayel became a sinner man by killin a kind man - him bredda 'Abiel. ⁶ Again a kind child Siet were birthed ~ 'Adam birthed sixty childran ~ there are kind persons and evil persons from them. ⁷ and there are kind persons from them ~ and there are persons who were prophets and them who were traitors and sinners. ⁸ There are blessed persons who were kind persons - who fulfill them father 'Adam accord and all him told to him child Siet - Beginnin from 'Adam up til Noh who are a kind man who kept JAH LAW. ⁹ and him sanctioned JAH LAW to him childran ~ him told them - 'Guard' - lest them demolish JAH LAW - and that them might tell to them childran like unto them father Noh told them - and that them might keep JAH LAW. ¹⁰ and them lived while them taught them childran - persons birthed after them. ¹¹ But Satan lived when him spoke to them fathers - havin lodged in idols that reached to a grave and that have vows on them - and havin defeated the persons who told him alright - and when them did all that Satan - who are sin teacher - commanded them. ¹² and them lived when them worshipped the idols like unto them order - up til a kind man 'Abriham who fulfill JAH Accord. ¹³ to him have lived firmed up in the LAW beforehand separate from him cousins - and JAH swore a oath with him - havin lodged in wind and fire. ¹⁴ JAH swore to him that Him might give him a land of inheritance and that Him might give to him childran up til the Eternity. ¹⁵ and Him swore to Yis'haq like unto him that Him might give him him father 'Abriham inheritance - and Him swore to Ya`iqob that Him might give him him father Yis'haq inheritance ~ Him swore to him like yis'haq. ¹⁶ and Him separated childran - who were birthed after them from Ya`iqob - from the twelve tribes of 'Isra'iel - and made them priests and kings ~ Him blessed them sayin - **Abound and totally be many many.** ¹⁷ and Him gave them them father inheritance - however while Him fed them and loved them - them didn't quit saddenin JAH in all. ¹⁸ and on the time Him destroyed them - at that time them will seek Him in worship - and them will return from sin and go toward JAH - to Him love them - and JAH shall pardon them. ¹⁹ to bein nice to all Him Created - Him shall pardon them - and it are because them fathers Work that Him love them - yet it aren't because them ras selves Work. ²⁰ and Him streach forth Him Right Hand in plenty that Him might satta a hungry body - and Him reveal Him Eye to pardonin that Him might multiply grain to food. ²¹ Him give food to crows chicks and to beasts that beg Him ~ on the time them cried toward Him - Him will save 'Isra'iel childran from them enemies hands who delayed from the time. ²² and them will return toward sin again that them might sadden Him - and Him will arouse them enemies peoples in them area on them ~ them will destroy them and kill them and capture them. ²³ and again them will shout toward JAH in mournin and sadness - and there are the time when Him sent help and saved them by prophets hands. ²⁴ and there are the time when Him saved them by princes hands - and on the time them saddened JAH them enemies taxed them and captured them. ²⁵ and Daweet arose and saved them from the 'Iloflans hands; and again them saddened JAH - and JAH aroused on them peoples who worry them. ²⁶ and there are the time when Him saved them by Yoftahie hand - and again them forgot JAH Who saved them in them tribulation time. As JAH have brought the hardship on them - Him will arouse on them enemies who were evil and who will firm up tribulation on them and totally capture them. ²⁷ and on the time them were worried by tribulation them were seized and again cried toward Him - and Him saved them by Giediewon hand - and again them saddened JAH by them hands Work. ²⁸ and again Him aroused on them peoples who firm up tribulation on them - and them returned and wept and cried toward JAH. ²⁹ and again Him saved them from peoples by Somson hand - and them rested a little from the tribulation. and them arose that them might sadden JAH by them former sin. ³⁰ and again Him aroused on them other peoples who worry them - and again them cried and wept toward JAH that Him might send help to them - and Him saved them from peoples by Bariq and Deebora hands. ³¹ Again them lived a little season while them worshipped JAH - and again them forgot JAH in them former sin and saddened Him. ³² and Him aroused on them other peoples who worry them - and again Him saved them by Yodeet hand and havin sat again a little season them arose that them might sadden JAH by them sin like unto formerly. ³³ and Him aroused on them peoples who rule them - and them cried and wept toward JAH to Him have struck on him head 'Abiemieliek who were a warrior who came that him might fight Yihuda country. ³⁴ and Him saved them by the childran in the area and by Matatyu hand - and on the time that warrior dead him army fled and were scattared - and 'Isra'iel childran followed and fought them up til 'Iyabboq - and them didn't preserve even one person from them. ³⁵ After this them waited a little and arose that them might sadden JAH - and Him aroused on them peoples who rule them - and again them totally cried toward JAH and JAH ignored them cryin and them mournin - to them have saddened JAH everytime - and to them have demolished Him LAW. ³⁶ and them captured and took them with them priests toward Babilon persons country. ³⁷ and then 'Isra'iel childran who were traitors didn't quit saddenin JAH while them worked sin and worshipped idols. ³⁸ JAH vexed that Him might destroy them one time in them sin ~ Hama havin introduced ten thousand gold in the king box - on the day when it were known - him lodged anger in the king 'Arthieksis reasonin - lest him preserve them childran in Fars country Beginnin from Hindekie and up til 'Ityopphya on the time him told him that him might destroy them. ³⁹ Him did thus - and him wrote a letter where a message were written by the king authority - and him gave him a seal in him hand that him might deliver toward Fars country. ⁴⁰ Him gave him a seal that him might destroy them on one day when him loved them to destroy them like unto the king commanded - but him commanded that him might introduce them money - the gold and the silver - toward the king box. ⁴¹ and on the time 'Isra'iel childran heard this thing them totally cried and wept toward JAH - and them told it to Merdokyos - and Merdokyos told to 'Astier. ⁴² and 'Astier said - 'Fast - beg - and all 'Isra'iel childran kindreds - cry toward JAH in the place where you are.' ⁴³ and Merdokyos wore sackcloth and sprinkled dust on him ras self - and 'Isra'iel childran fasted - begged - and entered repentance in the country where them were. ⁴⁴ and 'Astier were totally sad - and bein a queen she wore sackcloth ~ she sprinkled dust and shaved she head - and she didn't anoint perfume like unto Fars queens anoint perfume - and in she deep reasonin she cried and wept toward she fathers Creator JAH. ⁴⁵ and because this thing Him gave she bein loved alongside Fars king 'Arthieksis - and she made a kind lunch to she fathers Creator. ⁴⁶ and Hama and the king entered toward the lunch that 'Astier prepared - and like unto him loved that him might do on Merdokyos - JAH paid the hardship on that Hama - and them hanged him on a tall wood. ⁴⁷ The king letter were commanded that them might quit 'Isra'iel like unto them were in all them accord - and lest them tax them nor rob them nor wrong them nor take them money on them. ⁴⁸ As JAH shall pardon 'Isra'iel doin thus on the time cried enterin repentance - it are that them might love them and honour them in Fars country where them lived - yet a king letter were commanded lest them destroy them country nor plunder them livestocks. ⁴⁹ and on them time them saddened Him - Him will arouse on them peoples who worry them ~ at that time them will totally weep and cry that Him might send them help to them and that Him might save them from peoples hand who firm up tribulation on them.

29

¹ and on the time Gibts persons also made 'Isra'iel childran work by makin them work bricks in difficulty - and on the time them worried them all the Work by kickin mud without straw and heatin bricks... ² and on the time them made them work havin appointed chiefs on them who rush workers - them cried toward JAH that Him might save them from workin all Gibts bricks. ³ At that time Him sent to them 'Aron and Mussie who help them - to JAH have sent them that them might send forth Him kindreds from Fer`on rulership house - and Him saved them from brick Work ~ because in him arrogance him refused to adjourn 'Isra'iel lest them be ruled and sacrifice to JAH in wilderness - JAH have sent them that them might send forth Him kindreds 'Isra'iel from Gibts king Fer`on rulership house - and them saved them. ⁴ to JAH neglect arrogant ones - and Him drowned Fer`on in 'Eritra sea with him army because him arrogance. ⁵ and like unto him - Him shall destroy them who didn't work goodly Work in all the kingdoms that Him I-pointed and crowned them - that them who ignore JAH Word when them are nobles and kings might fulfill Him Accord to Him - and that them might give persons who serve in goodly thing them wage - and that

them might honour Him famous Name. ⁶ JAH Who rule all said - **But if them will straighten up I Kingdom - I-man will straighten up them kingdom to them.** ⁷ **Work goodly Work to I - and I-man shall work goodly Work to you ~ keep I LAW - and I-man shall keep you your bodies ~ live firmed up in I LAW - and I-man shall live lodgin honesty in you like unto your reasonin.** ⁸ **Love I - and I-man shall love your welfare ~ near toward I - and I-man shall heal you.** ⁹ JAH Who rule all said - **Believe in I - and I-man shall save you from the tribulation.** ¹⁰ Don't live side by side ~ as JAH Who rule all love straight Work - Him said - **You - approach toward I - and I-man shall approach toward you ~ you persons who are sinners and traitors - cleanse your hands from sin - and distance your reasonins from evil.** ¹¹ and **I-man shall distance I anger from you - and I-man shall return to you in Charity and Forgiveness.** ¹² **I-man shall distance criminals and enemies who work iniquity from you - like unto I-man saved I slave Daweet from him enemies who met him - from them much malice - and from Gwolyad hand who were a warrior - and also from Sa'ol hand who sought that him might kill him - and from him child 'Abiesielom hand who loved that him might take him kingdom.** ¹³ **I-man shall save persons who keep I LAW and fulfill I Accord like unto him ~ I-man shall bequeath them honour - and them shall be Feeling good in the present world and yonder in the world that shall come ~ I-man shall crown them on all that them might be Feeling good.** ¹⁴ Them shall be one with kings who served JAH and were honoured in them beautiful way of Life - like unto the prophet Samu'iel served Him in him beautiful way of Life Beginnin from him infancy - whom JAH - Him bein LAW - chose. ¹⁵ Him told him that him might tell 'Elee who were a servant elder - and when him served in JAH Lodgin the Temple - Samu'iel Work also were merciful and I-loved. ¹⁶ and on the time him grew when him served in JAH Lodgin the Temple - Him made him to be Ipointed and Inointed - that him might Ipoint him people and that kings might be Inointed by JAH Accord. As JAH have loved him that the kindred him chose from 'Isra'iel children might be Ipointed - on the time him fulfilled JAH Accord Who Created him - Him gave him the Inointin of the Kingdom in him hand. ¹⁷ and when Sa'ol were in him kingdom JAH told Him prophet Samu'iel - **Go - and as I-man have loved `Issiey child Daweet who were birthed from Yihuda kin - Inoint him.**

30

¹ **I-man have hated Sa'ol kin - to him have saddened I because him violated I Word.** ² and **I-man neglected him - to him didn't keep I LAW - and I-man won't crown from him kin again.** ³ and **persons who didn't keep I LAW and I Word and I Order like unto him - I-man shall destroy I Kingdom and I gift from them childran up til the Eternity.** ⁴ and **as them didn't make I famous on the time I-man made them famous - I-man shall destroy them - yet I-man won't again return to lift them up ~ though I-man honour them - as them didn't honour I - I-man won't make them famous.** ⁵ **to them didn't do a goodly thing to I on the time I-man did a goodly thing to them - and to them didn't forgive I on the time I-man forgave them.** ⁶ and **as them didn't make I a Ruler on the time I-man made them rulers on all - as them didn't honour I on the time I-man honoured them more than all - I-man won't make them famous again nor honour them - and to them didn't keep I LAW.** ⁷ and **I-man withheld the gift I-man gave them - and I-man won't return the money I-man withheld from them like unto the measure I-man vexed and swore** ~ JAH Who rule all said thus ~ Him said - **I-man shall honour them who honoured I - and love them who loved I.** ⁸ **I-man shall separate them who didn't honour I nor keep I LAW from the gift I-man gave them.** ⁹ JAH Who rule all said; **I-man love them who loved I - and make famous him who made I famous** - Him said.. ¹⁰ **As I-man JAH am Who rule all - there are none who escape I Authority in Earth nor Heaven - to I-man am JAH Who kill and Who save and Who sadden and Who forgive.** ¹¹ **As famousness and honour are I money - I-man honour him whom I-man loved - to I-man am Who judge and Who revenge and destroy - and I-man make wretched him whom I-man hated.** ¹² **to I-man am Who forgive them who love I and call I Name everytime - to I-man am Who feed food to the wealthy and to the poor.** ¹³ and **I-man feed birds and animals - fishes in sea and beasts and flowers - yet I-man aren't Who feed only man.** ¹⁴ **I-man feed crocodiles and whales - gophers and hippos - and badgers...** ¹⁵ and **all that live within Water - all that fly on wind - yet I-man aren't Who feed only man ~ all this are I money.** ¹⁶ **I-man am Who feed all that seek I by all that are due and I-loved.**

31

¹ and **the kings don't reign without I Accord - and sufferahs are by I Command - yet them aren't poor without I Command - and powerful ones are by I Accord - yet them aren't strong without I Accord.** ² **I-man gave bein I-loved to Daweet and Wisdom to Selomon - and I-man added eras to Hiziqyas.** ³ **I-man diminished Gwolyad era - and I-man gave Power to Somson - and again I-man weakened him Power.** ⁴ and **I-man saved I slave Daweet from Gwolyad hand who were a warrior.** ⁵ and **again I-man saved him from the king Sa'ol hand and from the secand warrior who disputed him - and to him have kept I Command - and I-man saved him from the persons hand who dispute him and fight him.** ⁶ and **I-man loved him - and I-man love all the nobles and the kings who keep I LAW ~ as them have made I Feeling good - I-man shall give them prevailin and Power on them enemies.** ⁷ and **again that them might inherit them fathers land - I-man shall give them the cleansed and shinin land of inheritance that I-man swore to them fathers.**

32

¹ JAH Who rule all said - and **you the nobles and also the kings - hear I in I Word - and keep I Command ~ lest you sadden I and worship like unto 'Isra'iel childran saddened I and worshipped different idols - them whom I-man kept and saved when I-man JAH am them Creator** - JAH Who rule all said - **Hear I in I Word; and all whom I-man raised and loved and fed Beginnin that them were birthed from them mother and father.** ² and **whom I-man sent forth toward Earth crops - and whom I-man fed the fatness found from Earth makin like unto are due - and whom I-man gave the grape vine and the oil-tree fruit that them didn't plant and the clear Water well that them didn't dig.** ³ **Hear I in I Word lest you sadden I like unto 'Isra'iel childran saddened I worshippin other idols when I-man JAH am them Creator** - Him told them - **Who fed them the sheep milk and the honey comb with the hulled wheat - and Who clothed them clothes where ornamant are - and Who gave them all them love.** ⁴ and **without it livin that I-man deprived them all them begged I.**

33

¹ **Like unto Daweet spoke sayin - ''Isra'iel childran were fed the menna that Angels lowered' - and again hear I in I Word lest you sadden I like unto 'Isra'iel childran saddened I worshippin the idols when I-man am them Creator JAH Who fed them sweet *menna* in wilderness** - Him said ~ **I-man did all this to them that them might worship I by what are due and to true.** ² JAH Who rule all said - **But them didn't worship I - and I-man neglected them ~ them saddened I and lived firmed up in law of idols that weren't I LAW.** ³ and **I-man shall bring the hardship on them like unto them sin ~ as them have neglected I Worship and as them didn't firm up in I counsel and I Order - I-man neglected them in the sin measure that them worked by them hands - and I-man shall lower them toward *Gehannem* in Definite Judgemant that are done in Heaven.** ⁴ **to them didn't keep I LAW - and to I-man vex on them - and I-man shall diminish them era in this world.** ⁵ **If thou be a king - aren't thou a man who shall dead and be demolished and tomorrow who shall be worms and dust?** ⁶ **But today thou boast and are proud like unto a man who won't dead forever.** ⁷ JAH Who rule all said - **But thou who are sight up bein well today are a man who will dead tomorrow.** ⁸ **But if you keep I Command and I Word - I-man shall bequeath thee-I a honoured country with honoured kings who did I Accord - whose lodgin were Light and whose crowns were beautiful - and whose thrones were silver and gold and whom persons who sit on them adorned** - Him said. ⁹ and **them shall be Feeling good within Him country that are a place that approached to persons who worked goodly Work.** ¹⁰ **But to persons who work sin - as them didn't keep I LAW** - said JAH Who rule all... ¹¹ **it aren't due them that them might enter toward that country where honoured kings shall enter.**

34

¹ **Miedon kingdom shall perish - but Rom kingdom shall totally firm up on Meqiedonya kingdom - and Nenewie kingdom shall firm up on Fars kingdom.** ² and **'Ityopphya kingdom shall firm up on 'Iskindriya kingdom ~ as peoples shall arise - Mo`ab kingdom shall firm up on 'Amalieq kingdom.** ³ and **bredda shall arise on him bredda - and JAH shall revenge and destroy like unto Him spoke that it might perish.** ⁴ **Kingdom shall arise on kingdom - and the people on the people and country on country** - Him said. ⁵ and **argumants shall be done and there shall be formations - famine - plague - earthquake - drought ~ as Love have perished from this world - JAH chastisemant descended on she.** ⁶ **to the day have arrived suddenly when JAH shall come - Who frighten like unto lightnin that are sight up from East up til West.** ⁷ **on the day when HIM JAH judge Judgemant - at that time everyone shall raceive him hardship like unto him hand weakness and him sin firmness - to Him have said I-man shall revenge them on** the day when HIM JAH judge Judgemant and on the day when them feet are hindered - to the day when them are counted to destruction have arrived. ⁸

At that time JAH shall destroy in *Gehannem* forever persons who won't live firmed up in Him LAW - who work sin. ⁹ and **them who live in the West ilands and Noba and Hindekie - Saba and 'Ityopphya and Gibts persons - all persons who live in them...** ¹⁰ **at that time shall know I that I-man were JAH Who rule Earth and Heaven - and Who give bein I-loved and honour - and Who save and Who kill.** ¹¹ **I-man am Who send forth Sun - Who send it toward it settin - Who bring the evil and the good.** ¹² **I-man am Who bring peoples whom you don't know - who slaughter and eat the money whereby you wearied - your sheeps and your cows flocks.** ¹³ and **them shall capture your childran while them hammer them before you - and you cyaan save them**. Because JAH Spirit of Support didn't lodge in you - as you didn't fear JAH Command that you heard - Him shall destroy your lavishmants and your assignmants. ¹⁴ But a person in whom JAH Spirit of Support lodged will know all - like unto Nabukedenetsor told Dan'iel sayin - 'Mi sight up JAH Spirit of Support that lodged in thee-I.' ¹⁵ and a person in whom JAH Spirit of Support lodged will know all - and what were hidden will be revealed to him - and him will know all that were revealed and that were hidden - yet there are nothing hidden from a person in whom JAH Spirit of Support lodged. ¹⁶ But as I are persons who will dead tomorrow - I sins that I hid and worked shall be revealed. ¹⁷ and like unto them test silver and gold in fire - like unto there are sinners - later on the Day of Advent them shall be examined - to them didn't keep JAH Command. ¹⁸ At that time all peoples and all 'Isra'iel childran Works shall be examined.

35

¹ As JAH vex on you because you didn't judge a Truth Judgemant to the child whose mother and father dead on him - woe to you 'Isra'iel nobles. ² Woe to you persons who go toward a drinkin house mornin and evenin and get drunk - who are partial in judgemant - and who don't hear the widow justice nor the child whose mother and father dead on him - who live in sin and seducin. ³ JAH told 'Isra'iel nobles sayin thus: - **Unless you lived firmed up in I Command and kept I LAW and loved what I-man love - woe to you** - Him told them. ⁴ and **I-man shall bring destruction and chastisemant and tribulation on you - and you will perish like unto what weevils and moths ate - and your tracks and your region won't be found** - Him told them. ⁵ and your country will be a wilderness - and all persons who sight she up formerly shall clap them hands ~ them shall marvel on she while them said - 'Weren't this country filled of she plenty and all who love it?; JAH made she thus by persons sin who live in she.' ⁶ Them shall say - 'As she have made she heart proud - and as she have ilivated she ras self - and as she have firmed up she collar of reasonin up til JAH make she wretched on Earth - and as she shall be a desert by persons arrogance who live in she - and as thorns have grown on she with thistles - woe to she.' ⁷ and she grow weeds and nettles - and she became a wilderness and a desert - and beasts shall live within she. ⁸ to JAH Judgemant have firmed up on she - and to she shall raceive JAH Judgemant Chalice because she reasonin arrogance by persons sin who live in she - and she became frightenin to persons who go toward she.

36

¹ Meqiedon persons - don't boast ~ as JAH are there Who shall destroy you - 'Amalieqans - don't firm up your collar of reasonin. ² to you will be lofty up til Heaven and you will descend up til *Gehannem*. ³ on the time 'Isra'iel formerly entered toward Gibts country in Mo`ab and Miedon kingdom Him said - **Don't boast** - to it aren't due to pretend on JAH that you might pretend on Him. ⁴ Thou Yisma'iel kindred - slave child - why do thou firm up thy collar of reasonin by what weren't thy money? How about don't thou think that JAH shall judge on thee on the time Him arose that it might be judged on Earth - on the day when it are judged on thee? ⁵ JAH Who rule all said - **At that time thou will raceive thy hardship like unto thy hand Work - how about why do thou ilivate thy reasonin? How about why do thou firm up thy collar of reasonin?** ⁶ and **I-man shall pretend on thee like unto thou pretended on persons who weren't thy kindreds - to thou do what thou love that thou might work sin - and I-man shall neglect thee in the place where them sent thee.** ⁷ JAH Who rule all said - and **I-man shall do thus on thee** ~ Him said - **But if thou worked goodly Work and if thou love what I-man loved - I-man also shall hear thee-I in all that thou begged.** ⁸ and **if thou fulfill I Accord to I - I-man shall fulfill thy accord to thee-I - and I-man shall dispute thy enemies to thee-I - and I-man shall bless thy childran and thy seed to thee-I.** ⁹ and **I-man shall multiply thy sheeps and thy cows flocks to thee-I - and if thou lived firmed up in I Command and also if thou did what I-man love - JAH Who rule all said - I-man shall bless to thee-I all thou seized in thy hand.** ¹⁰ **But if thou don't do I Accord - if thou don't live firmed up in I LAW and I Command - all this tribulation that were told formerly shall find thee - to thou didn't indure tribulation firmed up in I Command - and to thou didn't live firmed up in I LAW - and thou cyaan escape from I anger that will come on thee everytime.** ¹¹ and **as thou didn't love what I-man loved - when I-man am Who Created thee bringin from not livin toward livin...** ¹² **all this were thy money - that thou might kill and heal to do all that thou loved - that thou might work and demolish - that thou might honour and abuse - that thou might ilivate and downbase - and as thou have neglected I Worship and I praise when I-man am Who gave thee lordship and also honour alongside persons who are beneath thy authority - thou cyaan escape from I anger that will come on thee.** ¹³ and **if thou did JAH Accord and if thou lived frmed up in Him Command - Him will love thee-I that thou might be Feeling good with Him in Him Lordship - and that thou might be a partaker with persons who inherited a honoured country.** ¹⁴ to Him have said - **If them indure I - I-man will bequeath them bein I-loved and honour - to I-man shall make them Feeling good in the Temple where prayer are prayed** - to JAH Who rule all have said - and **them shall be I-loved and chosen like unto a sacrifice.** ¹⁵ Don't neglect to do Work whereby welfare are done and a goodly thing that you might cross from death toward Life. ¹⁶ But persons who work goodly Work - JAH shall keep them in all Him goodly Work - that them might be Him slaves like unto 'Iyob whom JAH kept from all the tribulation ¹⁷ JAH shall keep them in all goodly Work - that them might be Him slaves to Him like unto 'Abriham whom Him saved on the time him killed the kings - and like unto Mussie whom Him saved from Kenaniewon hand and Fer`on hand - in whom 'Abriham lived - and who were also disturbin him body evenin and mornin night and day that them might make him worship idols. ¹⁸ But when them took him toward the idols that were them money - him would indure the tribulation while him refused. ¹⁹ to 'Abriham who believed Him Beginnin from him childhood were to JAH Him trusted friend - and while him refused him would worship JAH Who Created him. ²⁰ As him totally love JAH - him didn't quit worshippin JAH up til him dead - and him didn't depart from Him LAW up til when him dead - and him taught him childran that them might keep JAH LAW. ²¹ and like unto them father 'Abriham kept Him LAW - them didn't depart from JAH LAW ~ like unto Him told to Angels sayin - **I-man have a friend in this world called 'Abriham** - 'Abriham childran Ya`iqob and Yis'haq - who are Him slaves because whom JAH spoke - didn't depart from JAH LAW. ²² JAH Who were praised alongside them and Who rule all said - **'Abriham are I friend ~ Yis'haq are I canfidante - and Ya`iqob are I friend whom I Reasonin loved.** ²³ But when Him totally loved 'Isra'iel childran - them lived when them Continually saddened Him - and Him lived when Him indured them and when Him fed them *menna* in wilderness. ²⁴ Them clothes didn't age - to them have been fed *menna* that are knowledge *'injera* - and them feet didn't awaken. ²⁵ But them reasonins would distance from JAH everytime ~ as them were who work sin Beginnin from Antiquity - them had no hope to be saved. ²⁶ Them became like unto a crooked bow - yet them didn't become like unto them fathers Yis'haq and 'Abriham and Ya`iqob who served JAH in them beautiful way of Life ~ them would sadden Him everytime by them idols on the mountains and the hills ~ them would eat on the mountain and at the caves and the trees roots. ²⁷ Them would slaughter a steer ~ them would sacrifice a sacrifice - and them would be Feeling good in them hands Work ~ them would eat the rest of the sacrifice ~ them would drink of them sacrifice - and them would play with demons while them sang. ²⁸ and demons would admire all them games and them songs to them - and them would work them drunkenness and adultery without measure - and them would do the robbery and greed that JAH don't love. ²⁹ to Kene`an idols - and to Midyam idols and to Be`al - and to 'Aphlon and Dagon and Seraphyon and 'Arthiemadies who are 'Eloflee idols... ³⁰ and to all peoples idols in them area - them would sacrifice; and all 'Isra'iel would worship idols like unto peoples worship idols by money that them sight up and heard ~ them would make them games and them songs and them bluster that peoples make. ³¹ All 'Isra'iel kindreds do likewise - who say 'We will worship JAH' - without keepin Him Command and Him LAW that Mussie told them in 'Oreet that them might keep JAH LAW and might distance from worshippin idols. ³² Lest them worship separated idols - apart from them fathers Creator Who fed them the honey found from Maga who fed them the plantation grain and sent them forth toward the Earth crops - and Who fed them the *menna*... ³³ Mussie commanded them sayin 'Don't worship' - to Him are them Creator - and to Him feed them who loved Him - and Him won't deprive them who loved Him and desired Him. ³⁴ But them didn't quit saddenin JAH - and them would sadden JAH on the time Him made them Feeling good. ³⁵ and on the time Him saddened them - them would cry toward Him - and Him would save them from the tribulation that found them - and them would again be totally Feeling good and would live many eras. ³⁶ and at that time them would totally return them heart toward sin that them might sadden JAH like unto formerly - and Him would arouse

on them peoples in them area that them might destroy them - and them would worry and tax them. ³⁷ and again them would totally return and cry toward them Creator JAH. ³⁸ and Him would forgive them ~ it are because them fathers - Noh - Yis'haq and 'Abriham and Ya`iqob - who served JAH in them beautiful way of Life Iginnnin from Antiquity - to whom Him firmed up Him Oath - yet it aren't because them ras selves Work that Him forgive them. ³⁹ and Him loved persons who kept Him LAW lovin that them might multiply them childran like unto Heaven stars and sea sand. ⁴⁰ But on the time dead ones arose that them have like unto sea sand - them are sinner persons souls that will separate from 'Isra'iel childran and enter toward Gehannem. ⁴¹ As JAH have told 'Abriham - **Sight up toward Heaven at night and count Heaven stars as it were thou could count** - likewise as Him have told him - **Thy childran and righteous ones shall shine in Heaven like unto Heaven stars** - them are like unto stars that shine in Heaven - but what them have are kind persons souls birthed from 'Isra'iel. ⁴² and again as Him have told him - **Overstand toward the river edge and the sea - and sight up what are amidst the sand ~ count as it were thou could count - and thy sinner childran are likewise - who will descend toward *Gehannem* on the time dead ones arose** - them are sinner persons souls. ⁴³ and 'Abriham believed in JAH ~ because this thing it were counted to him bein Truth ~ him found him morale in this world - and after him wife Sora aged she birthed a child called Yis'haq. ⁴⁴ to him have believed that persons who worked goodly Work shall arise and go toward the Kingdom of Heaven that live firmed up forever - and again him shall find a Kingdom in Heaven. ⁴⁵ But to him have believed that persons who worked sin shall go toward *Gehannem* that live firmed up forever on the time dead ones arose - but that righteous ones who worked goodly Work shall reign with Him forever. ⁴⁶ But to him have believed that it shall be judged forever to true without falsehood on persons who worked sin - to him shall find Life Kingdom in Heaven." make glory and praise enter to JAH to true without falsehood - and the first book that speak the Meqabyans thing were filled and fulfilled.

The Book of Meqabyan II

1

¹ This are a book that speak that Meqabees found 'Isra'iel in Mesphiethomya that are Sorya part and killed them in them region beginnin from 'Iyabboq up til 'Iyerusaliem square - and that him destroyed the country. ² Because Sorya and 'Edomyas persons and the 'Amalieqans were one with the Mo`ab man Meqabees who destroyed 'Iyerusaliem country - as them have camped beginnin from Semarya up til 'Iyerusaliem square and up til all she region - them killed in war without preservin persons who fled apart from a few persons. ³ and on the time 'Isra'iel childran wronged - Him aroused Mo`ab man Meqabees on them - and him killed them by a sword. ⁴ and because this thing JAH enemies the peoples bragged on Him honoured country - and them swore in them crime. ⁵ and 'Iloflee and 'Idomyas persons camped - as Him have sent them because them pretended JAH Word - them began to revenge and destroy JAH country. ⁶ and that Meqabees country are Riemat that are Mo`ab part - and him arose from him country in Power and them swore also with persons with him. ⁷ and them camped in Gielabuhie region that are Mesphiethomya lot up til Sorya that them might destroy JAH country - and there him begged the 'Amalieqans and 'Iloflans ~ him gave them much silver and gold and chariots and horses that them might be one with him in crime. ⁸ Them came together and crushed the fortress ~ persons who lived in she shed blood like unto Water. ⁹ and them made 'Iyerusaliem like unto a plant keepin hut - and him made a voice heard within she ~ him worked all the sin Work that JAH don't love - and them also defouled JAH country that were filled of praise and honour. ¹⁰ Them made thy friends flesh and thy slaves corpses food to wilderness beasts and Heaven birds. ¹¹ and them robbed childran whose mother and father dead on them and widows - to without fearin JAH them have done like unto Satan taught them - and up til JAH Who examine kidneys and reasonins vexed - them took out the fetus in pregnant daughters belly. ¹² Them returned toward them country while them were Feeling good because them worked evil Work on JAH kindreds - and them took the plunder that them captured from a honoured country. ¹³ on the time them returned and entered toward them houses them made joy and song and clappin.

2

¹ The prophet whom them call Re`ay told him thus: - "Today be Feeling good a little on the time when Feeling good joy were made ~ JAH Whom 'Isra'iel glorified have that Him might revenge and destroy thee in the chastisemant thou didn't doubt. ² Will thou say - 'Mi horses are swift ~ because this mi will escape by runnin'? ³ As to I - I-man tell thee - Persons who will follow thee are swifter than vultures ~ thou won't escape from JAH Judgemant and destruction that shall come on thee. ⁴ Will thou say - 'Mi wear iron clothes - and spear flingin and bow stingin aren't able to mi'?; JAH Who honour 'Isra'iel said - **It aren't by spear flingin that I-man will revenge and destroy thee**" Him told him ~ "**I-man shall bring on thee heart sickness and itch and rheumatism sickness that were worse and firmer than spear flingin and bow stingin - yet it aren't by this that I-man shall revenge and destroy thee. ⁵ Thou have aroused I anger ~ I-man shall bring heart sickness on thee - and thou will lack one who help thee - and thou won't escape from I Authority up til I-man destroy thy name invocation from this world. ⁶ As thou have firmed up thy collar of reasonin - and as thou have ilivated thy ras self on I country - on the time I-man quickly did this thing like unto a eye wink - thou will know I that I-man were thy Creator ~ as thou are before I like unto grass before the wind that fire eat - and as thou are like unto the dust that winds spill and scattar from Earth - thou are like unto them alongside I. ⁷ to thou have aroused I anger - and to thou didn't know thy Creator - and I-man shall neglect all thy kindred - and neither will I-man preserve him who neared on thy fortress.** ⁸ and now return from all thy sin that thou worked ~ if thou return from thy sin and totally appease in mournin and sadness before JAH - and if thou beg toward him in clean reasonin - JAH will forgive thee all thy sin that thou worked before Him" - him told him. ⁹ At that time Meqabees wore dust and mourned before JAH because him sin - to JAH have vexed on him. ¹⁰ to Him eyes are revealed - to Him don't withhold - and to Him ears are opened - to Him don't neglect - and to Him don't make the word Him spoke false - and to Him quickly do she at one time - to JAH knew lest Him preserve the chastisemant Him spoke by the prophet Word. ¹¹ Him cast him clothes and wore sackcloth and sprinkled dust on him head and cried and wept before him Creator JAH because him sin that him worked.

3

¹ and the prophet came from Riemat and told him - to Riemat that are Mo`ab part are near to Sorya. ² Him dug a pit and entered up til him neck and wept firm tears - and him entered repentance because him sin that him worked

before JAH. ³ and JAH told the prophet thus: - **Return from Yihuda country Riemat toward the Mo`ab official Meqabees** Him told him. **Tell him - "JAH told thee thus" - Tell him - "Him told thee - I-man JAH Who am thy Creator sent thee by I Accord that thou might destroy I country - lest thou say - 'Mi destroyed the honoured country 'Iyerusaliem by mi Power firmness and mi army abundance' - yet it aren't thou who did this thing. ⁴ to she have saddened I by all she greed and she perfidy and she lustfulness. ⁵ and I-man neglected and cast she by thy hand - and now JAH forgave thee thy sin because thy childran whom thou birthed ~ it aren't because thou who firmed up thy collar of reasonin and say 'Mi incircled the country 'Iyerusaliem by mi authority firmness.' ⁶ As persons who doubt aren't disciplined to enter repentance - don't be a doubter - and now enter repentance bein disciplined in thy complete reasonin."** ⁷ However persons are admired who enter repentance in them complete reasonins and who don't again return toward thirst and sin by all that entered toward repentance because them sin. ⁸ Persons are admired who return toward them Creator JAH bein disciplined in mournin and sadness - in bowin and many pleas. Persons are admired who are disciplined and enter repentance - to Him have told them - **You are I moneys who entered repentance after you misled persons who entered repentance.** ⁹ Him told arrogant Meqabees on the time him returned toward Him in repentance after him misled - **I-man forgive thee thy sin because thy fright and thy alarm; to I-man am JAH thy Creator Who bring hardship on childran by a father sin up til seven generations if the child work the sin that the father worked - and Who do Charity up til ten thousand generations to persons who love I and keep I LAW.** ¹⁰ and now I-man will firm up I Oath with thee because these thy childran whom thou birthed - and JAH Who rule all and Who honoured 'Isra'iel said - **I-man will accept the repentance thou made because thy sin that thou worked.** ¹¹ At that time him proceeded from the pit and bowed to the prophet ~ him swore sayin - "As mi have saddened JAH - make mi what thou loved - yet make JAH do mi thus thus lest mi separate from thee-I ~ as we have no Law - mi didn't live firmed up in Him Command like unto mi fathers ~ thou know that we fathers taught we and that we worship idols. ¹² to mi are a sinner who lived firmed up in mi sin - who firmed up in mi collar of reasonin firmness and mi reasonin arrogance whereby mi saddened JAH Command - but up til now mi hadn't heard JAH servants the prophets Word - and mi didn't live firmed up in Him LAW and Him Command that Him commanded mi." ¹³ Him told him sayin - "As there are none from your kindred precedin you who trusted him sin - mi knew that the prophet received repentance today." ¹⁴ "But now quit thy worshippin idols and return toward knowin JAH that thou might have true repentance" him told him ~ him fell and bowed at the prophet feet - and the prophet lifted up and commanded him all the goodly Work that are due him. ¹⁵ and him returned toward him house doin also like unto JAH commanded him. ¹⁶ and that Meqabees returned him body toward worshippin JAH - and him destroyed from him house the idols and also the sorcery - persons who worship idols and pessimists and magicians. ¹⁷ and mornin and evenin like unto them fathers do - him would examine the childran him captured and brought from 'Iyerusaliem in all JAH Commands and Him Order and Him LAW. ¹⁸ and from the childran him captured - him appointed knowin ones on him house. ¹⁹ and again from the infants him appointed knowin childran who keep levelled childran who were small - who enter toward the beddin that them might teach them JAH LAW that 'Isra'iel childran do ~ him would hear from captured 'Isra'iel childran the Order and the LAW and the Nine Laws - that Mo`ab persons order and them mosques that them make were vain. ²⁰ Him destroyed them mosques - them idols and them sorcery - and the sacrifice and the grapes sacrificed to the idols mornin and evenin from the goat kids and fattened sheeps flocks. ²¹ and him destroyed him idols whom him worship and beg and believe in all him Work while him sacrificed sacrifice afternoon and at noon - and to all priests told him - and him idols to whom him do them accord. ²² As it would seem to him that them save him in all that them told - him wouldn't scorn all the thing them told him. ²³ But that Meqabees quit them Work. ²⁴ After him heard the Ra`ay thing - whom them call a prophet - him accomplished him Work in repentance ~ as 'Isra'iel childran would sadden Him at one time - and on the time Him chastised them in the tribulation - as them know and also cry toward JAH - all Him kindreds worked goodly Work more than 'Isra'iel childran in that season. ²⁵ on the time Him heard that them were seized and abused by peoples hand who firm up tribulation on them and that them cried toward Him - Him thought of them fathers oath and at that time Him would forgive them because them fathers Yis'haq - 'Abriham - and Ya`iqob. ²⁶ and on the time Him saved them - them would forget JAH Who saved them from tribulation - and them would return toward worshippin the idols. ²⁷ and at that time Him would arouse on them peoples who firm up tribulation on them - and on the time them firmed up tribulation on them and saddened them - them would cry toward JAH ~ as Him love them because them were Him Authority Creation - at that time Him would be nice and forgive them. ²⁸ and on the time Him kept them - them again returned toward sin that them might sadden Him by them hands Work that were firm and by worshippin idols in them councils. ²⁹ But Him would arouse on them Mo`ab and 'Iloflee - Sorya - Midyam and Gibts persons; and on the time them enemies defeated them - them would cry and weep ~ on the time them firmed up on them and taxed them and ruled them - JAH would arouse princes to them that Him might save them on the time Him loved.

4

¹ and in 'Iyasu time are a day when Him saved them. ² and in Giediewon time are a day when Him saved them. ³ and in Somson time and in Deebora and Bariq and Yodeet time are a day when Him saved them - and lodgin whether on male or on daughter - Him would arouse princes to them that them might save them from them enemies hands who firm up tribulation on them. ⁴ and like unto JAH loved - Him would save them from persons who firm up tribulation on them. ⁵ and them would be totally Feeling good in all the Work that Him accomplished to them ~ them would be Feeling good in them land seed and in multiplyin all them flocks in wilderness and them livestock. ⁶ and Him would bless them plants and them livestock to them - to Him sight them up in Eye of Mercy - and to Him wouldn't diminish them livestock on them - to them are kind persons childran and Him would totally love them. ⁷ But on the time them were evil in them Work - Him would cast them in them enemies hands. ⁸ and on the time Him destroyed them - them would seek Him in worship - and them would return from sin and march toward JAH in repentance. ⁹ and on the time them returned in them complete reasonin - Him would atone them sin to them ~ Him wouldn't think of them former sin on them - to Him know them that them were flesh and blood - to them have this world misleadin thoughts on them - and to them have demons in them. ¹⁰ But on the time that Meqabees heard this Order that JAH worked in Him worshippin place the Temple - him were slain in repentance. ¹¹ After him sight up and heard this - him didn't scorn workin goodly Work; him didn't scorn workin all the goodly Work that 'Isra'iel childran work on the time JAH forgave them - and after them trespassed from Him LAW - them weep and would cry on the time JAH whipped them - and again Him would forgive them - and them would keep Him LAW. ¹² and Meqabees likewise would straighten up him Work - and him would keep Him LAW - and him would live firmed up in 'Isra'iel Creator JAH Command. ¹³ At that time after him heard all the Work whereby 'Isra'iel childran boast - Him would boast like unto them in keepin JAH LAW. ¹⁴ Him would urge him kindred and childran that them might live firmed up in JAH Command and all Him LAW. ¹⁵ and him would forbid the order that 'Isra'iel forbid - and him would hear and keep the Law that 'Isra'iel keep - and when him kindred are another Mo`ab man - him would forbid the food that 'Isra'iel forbid. ¹⁶ and him would send forth tithes ~ him would give all that were first birthed and that him owned from him cows and him sheeps and him donkeys - and returnin him face toward 'Iyerusaliem him would sacrifice the sacrifice that 'Isra'iel sacrifice. ¹⁷ Him would sacrifice sin and vow sacrifice - a sacrifice whereby welfare are done and a accord sacrifice - and the Itinual sacrifice. ¹⁸ and him would give him first crops - and him would gush and pour the grapes that 'Isra'iel pour - and him would give this to him priest whom him I-pointed - and likewise him would do all that 'Isra'iel do - and him would sweeten him ishence. ¹⁹ Him built a candlestick and a bowl and a seat and a tent and the four links of rings - and diluted oil to the Hola of Holas lamps - and the curtain that 'Isra'iel make in the Hola of Holas on the time them served JAH. ²⁰ and like unto them worked goodly Work on the time them lived firmed up in Him Order and Him LAW and on the time JAH didn't neglect and cast them in them enemies hands - Meqabees also would work goodly Work like unto them. ²¹ Him would beg toward 'Isra'iel Creator JAH everytime that Him might be him Teacher and lest Him separate him from 'Isra'iel childran whom Him chose and who did Him Accord. ²² and again him would beg Him that Him might give him childran in Tsiyon and a house in 'Iyerusaliem - that Him might give them Heavenly Seed of Virtue in Tsiyon and a Heavenly House of Soul in 'Iyerusaliem - and that Him might save him from the destruction spoken by the prophet tongue - that Him might accept him repentance in all the mournin him wept before JAH bein sad and enterin repentance... ²³ and lest Him destroy childran in this world on him - and that Him might keep him in him proceedin and enterin. ²⁴ Kindreds from Mo`ab peoples beneath Meqabees Authority were Feeling good that them might believe - to them chief live firmed up in straight Work - and them would check up him judgemant and fulfill him accord - and them would scorn them country language and them country justice ~ them would overstand that Meqabees Work surpassed and were straight. ²⁵ and them would come and hear Meqabees charity and Truth judgemants. ²⁶ Him had

much money ~ him had daughter slaves and male slaves and camels and donkeys - and him had five hundred horses that wear breastplates ~ him would totally defeat the 'Amalieqans and 'Iloflans and Sorya persons - but formerly when him worshipped idols him lived when them defeated him. ²⁷ Him prevailed - yet but from him worshippin JAH onward - when him went toward battle there are none who defeated him. ²⁸ But them would come in them idols Power that them might fight him - and them would call them idols names and curse him - however there were none who defeat him - to him have made him faith on him Creator JAH. ²⁹ and when him did thus and when him defeated him enemies - him lived when him ruled peoples in him Authority. ³⁰ Him would revenge and destroy wronged persons enemy to them ~ him would judge Truth to a child whose mother and father dead on him. ³¹ and him would raceive widows in them trouble time - and him would give from him food and satta them who hungered - and him would clothe the naked from him clothes. ³² and him would be Feeling good in him hands Work - and him would give from the money him had without begrudgin - and him would give tithes to the Temple ~ Meqabees dead havin lived in Feeling good joy when him did this.

5

¹ and him dead quittin him childran who were small - and them grew up like unto them father taught them ~ them kept them house Order - and them would keep all them kindred - and them wouldn't make poor ones cry - nor widows nor a child whose mother and father dead on him. ² Them would fear JAH - and them would give them money alms to poor ones - and them would keep all the trust them father told them - and them would calm the child whose mother and father dead on them and widows in them trouble time - and them would be them mother and father ~ them would make them cast from persons hand who wrong them - and calm them from all the disturbance and sadness that found them. ³ Them lived five years while them did thus. ⁴ After this the Keledans king Tseerutsaydan came ~ him destroyed all them country - and him captured Meqabees childran and destroyed all them villages. ⁵ and him plundered all them money ~ them lived firmed up in all evil Work and sin - in adultery - insult and greed and not thinkin of them Creator - yet persons who don't live firmed up in JAH LAW and Him Command and who worship idols seized them also and took them toward them country. ⁶ Them eat what a beast bit and the blood and the carcass - and what a scavenger beat and cast - all that JAH don't love - yet them have no order from all the true Commands written in 'Oreet. ⁷ Them don't know JAH them Creator - Who sent them forth from them mothers wombs and fed them by what are due - were them Medicine. ⁸ Them marry from them aunt and them father wife - them step mother - and them go toward robbery and evil thing and sin and adultery - yet them have no order in Judgemant time - and them work all evil Work and them marry them aunts and them sistren and them have no LAW. ⁹ and all them roads are dark and slippery - and them Work are sin and adultery. ¹⁰ But those Meqabees childran would keep in all them Order ~ them wouldn't eat what a scavenger beat nor what dead and lodged ~ them wouldn't work all the Work that the Keledans childran work - to them many Works are evil that weren't written in this book - that sinners work - and doubters and criminals - betrayers totally filled of robbery and sin and pagans childran. ¹¹ All the Work them Creator JAH love aren't there alongside them. ¹² and again them would worship a idol called Bi'iel Fiegor ~ them would trust it like unto them Creator JAH when it were deaf and dumb. to it are the idol that a person hand worked - to it are the person hand Work that a smith worked who work silver and gold - that have no breath nor knowledge - and it had nothing that it sight up nor hear. ¹³ It don't eat nor drink. ¹⁴ It don't kill nor save. ¹⁵ It don't plant nor uproot. ¹⁶ It don't harm it enemy nor benefit it friend. ¹⁷ It don't impoverish nor honour. ¹⁸ It will be a hindrance to mislead the Keledans persons who were lazy - yet it don't chastise nor forgive.

6

¹ JAH enemy Tseerutsaydan who were arrogant appointed them who veil and falsehood priests to him idols. ² Him would sacrifice to them and pour the grapes to them. ³ and it would seem to him that them eat and drink. ⁴ and while it dawned him would give them cows and donkeys and heifers - and him would sacrifice mornin and evenin - and him would eat from that defouled sacrifice. ⁵ and again him would disturb and obligate other persons that them might sacrifice to him idols - yet it weren't that only them do it. ⁶ on the time them sight up Meqabees childran that them were handsome and that them worship them Creator JAH - the idols priests loved that them might mislead them to sacrifice and to eat from that hated sacrifice - but these honoured Meqabees childran refused them. ⁷ As them keep them father command - and as them have firmed up in workin goodly Work - and as them totally fear JAH - it failed them to agree... ⁸ on the time them bound them and insulted them and robbed them. ⁹ Them told to the king Tseerutsaydan that them refused sacrifice and bowin to him idols. ¹⁰ and because this thing the king vexed ~ him were sad and commanded that them might bring them - and them brought and stood them before him - and the king told them to him idols - "Sacrifice a sacrifice to mi idols." ¹¹ and them spoke and told him - "An I won't answer thee in this thing - and I won't sacrifice to thy defouled idols." ¹² Him frightened them by Works that abounded - yet him couldn't able to them - to them have disciplined them reasonins believin in JAH. ¹³ Him flamed a fire and cast them in fire - and them gave them bodies to JAH. ¹⁴ After them dead them arose and were sight up to him at night drawin them swords when him had reclined on him lordship throne - and him totally feared. ¹⁵ "Mi sirs - tell mi alright - what should mi do to you? Don't take mi body in death - that mi might do all what thou commanded mi." ¹⁶ Them told him all that are due to him while them said - "Think that JAH were thy Creator - and JAH are there Who shall dismiss from this thy kingdom where thou are arrogant - and Who shall lower thee toward *Gehannem* of fire with thy father Deeyablos ~ when I worshipped I Creator JAH without a iniquity livin that I wronged thee - and when I bowed to Him in fearin Him JAH-ness - like unto thou burned I in fire - thou will finish all thy hardship by that also. ¹⁷ to Him are Who Created all - Earth and Heaven and sea and all that are within she. ¹⁸ and to Him are Who Created moon and Sun and stars - and to Him Who Created all the Creation are JAH. ¹⁹ to there are no other creator withou Him in Earth nor Heaven - to Him are Who able to all - and to there are nothing that fail Him. As Him are Who kill and Who save - Who whip in tribulation and Who forgive - when I bowed to Him in fearin JAH - like unto thou burned I in fire - thou will finish thy hardship by that" them told him. ²⁰ "As Him are Who rule Earth and Heaven - there are none who escape from Him Authority. ²¹ There are none from the Creation Him Created who departed from Him Command - apart from thou who are a criminal - and criminals like unto thee whose reasonins thy father Satan hid - and thou and those thy priests and thy idols will descend together toward *Gehannem* where are no exits up til Eternity. ²² Thy teacher are Satan who taught thee this evil Work that thou might do a evil thing on I - yet as it aren't only thou who do this - you will descend toward *Gehannem* together. ²³ to thou make thy ras self like unto thy Creator JAH - yet thou didn't know JAH Who Created thee. ²⁴ and thou are arrogant in thy idols and thy hand Work up til JAH make thee wretched ~ Him shall canvict thee on all thy sin and iniquity that thou worked in this world.

7

¹ Woe to you who don't know JAH Who Created you - to thy idols who are like unto thee - and to thee - and to you have that you might regret a regrets that won't profit on the time you were sad bein seized in *See'ol* difficulty - and woe to thee - to you who don't keep Him Word and Him LAW. ² You will have no exit from she up til Eternity - thy priests and thou who sacrifice to them like unto your Creator JAH - to thy idols who have no breath nor soul - who won't revenge and destroy him who did a evil thing on them - nor do a goodly thing to him who did a goodly thing to them. ³ Woe to you who sacrifice to them - to them are a person hands Work where Satan live - lodgin there to mislead lazy ones reasonin like unto thee - that him might lower you toward *Gehannem* of fire - and the priests who serve demons commanded to you and your idols. ⁴ As you don't know that there are nothing that will profit you - you wrong and err. ⁵ As to the animals that JAH Created to be food to you - and dogs and beasts - them are better than you - to besides one death there are no more candemnation on them. ⁶ But as you will dead and raceive hardship in *Gehannem* fire where are no exits up til Eternity - animals are better." ⁷ Havin spoken this - them went and were hidden from him. ⁸ But that Tseerutsaydan lodged when him trembled - seized by a firm fright - and fright didn't quit him up til it dawned.

8

¹ and him lived firmed up in reasonin malice and arrogance. ² and as iron have been called firm - like unto Dan'iel sight it up on him kingdom - him turned in peoples countries in him area. ³ Him lived firmed up in evil and all him laziness and in disturbin persons. ⁴ and him totally destroy what I spoke formerly - and him eat a person money. ⁵ to him are diligent to evil like unto him father Deeyablos who firmed up in him collar of reasonin - and him destroy what remained with him army. ⁶ Him say - "Mi era became like unto the Sun era" - yet him don't know JAH that Him were him Creator. ⁷ and in him reasonin him think that the Sun are found from him. ⁸ Him arise in Power - him camp in Tribe of Zablon lot and begin a formation in Meqiedonya - and him receive him food from Semarya - and them give him presents from Semarya. ⁹ Him camp in nomads region - and him reach up til Seedona - and him cast a tax on 'Akayya - and him elevate him collar of reasonin up til the flowin sea - and him return and send messengers up til Hindekie sea. ¹⁰ and likewise him elevate him collar of reasonin up til Heaven. ¹¹ Him live firmed up in bein arrogant and in evil - yet him don't have humblin him ras self. ¹² and him path are toward darkness and

slipperiness - and toward crime and bein arrogant - and toward sheddin blood and tribulation. ¹³ and all him Work are what JAH hate ~ him do like unto robbery and evil and sin teacher Deeyablos taught him ~ him make a child cry whose mother and father dead on him - and him aren't nice to a poor one. ¹⁴ and him defeated and destroyed peoples kings by him authority. ¹⁵ and him ruled enemies chiefs - and him ruled many peoples - and him taxed them like unto him loved. ¹⁶ Even if him destroyed - him didn't quit ~ there are no person whom him didn't snatch Beginnin from Tersies sea up til 'Iyareeko sea. ¹⁷ Him would bow to idols ~ him would eat what dead and lodged - the blood - what a sword bloated and cut - and what were sacrificed to idols ~ all him Work are without justice - yet him have no justice ~ as him have been who alarm peoples beneath him authority - him would tax them tax like unto him loved. ¹⁸ As him do all that him loved before him - there are no fearin JAH before him - and him live in malice before JAH Who Created him. ¹⁹ Him didn't do it like unto him Creator - and like unto him did a evil thing on him companion on the time him vexed and seized him - JAH shall also pay him him hardship. ²⁰ As JAH have said - **I-man shall revenge and destroy sinner persons who don't live by I Command - that I-man might destroy them name invocation from this world** - like unto Him destroyed peoples who were precedin him - Him shall revenge and destroy him on the time when Him destroy. ²¹ and like unto evil persons did evil things - them shall raceive them hardship. ²² But bein commanded from JAH - goodly Work shall follow persons who work goodly Work. ²³ to like unto 'Iyasu destroyed the five Kene`an kings in cave in one day - and like unto him made Sun stand in Geba`on by him prayer that him might destroy them armies - Sun have stood amidst Heaven up til him destroyed 'Ewiewon and Kenaniewon - Fierziewon and Kiethiewon and 'Iyabusiewon armies - and like unto him killed around twenty thousand persons at one time - and like unto him killed them - and like unto him bound them makin foot from neck - and like unto him killed them in cave by spear - and like unto him fitted a stone on them... ²⁴ Tribulation like unto this shall find all persons who sadden JAH in them evil Work.

9

¹ "O thou weak man who aren't JAH - why are thou proud? thou who are sight up today bein a man are Earth ashes tomorrow - and thou will totally be worms in thy grave. ² to thy teacher are Deeyablos who return all persons sin hardship toward him ras self because him misled I father 'Adam - and *See'ol* will find thee again - and she will find persons who work thy sin. ³ to in firmin up him collar of reasonin and makin him ras self proud - like unto him refused to bow to 'Adam whom the Creator Created... ⁴ thou also have refused to bow to thy Creator JAH like unto thy teacher Deeyablos did. ⁵ Like unto thy precedin fathers - who don't know them Creator JAH in worship - will go toward *Gehannem* - thou also will go toward *Gehannem*. ⁶ Like unto Him revenged and destroyed them because them evil Work that them worked in this world - and like unto them descended toward *Gehannem*... ⁷ thou also will descend toward *Gehannem* like unto them. ⁸ As thou have aroused Him anger - and as thou have neglected to worship JAH Who gave thee Authority on the five kingdoms - do it seem to thee that thou will escape from JAH Authority? ⁹ Thou don't do thus that thou do Him Accord - thus Him examined thee - but if thou work goodly Work in this world - JAH will accomplish all thy Work to thee-I - and Him will accomplish and bless all the Work thou seized in thy hand to thee-I - and Him will subject thy Antiquity of enemies and thy day enemies to thee-I. ¹⁰ Thou will be Feeling good in thy enterins and thy proceedins and in thy child birthed from thy nature - and in thy flocks and thy fatnesses - and in all Work where thou placed thy hand - and in all that thou thought in thy heart ~ as Authority have been given thee-I from alongside JAH that thou might do thus and might work and plant and demolish - all will be commanded to thee-I. ¹¹ However if thou won't hear JAH Word nor live firmed up in Him LAW - like unto criminals who were precedin thee - and who don't worship JAH by what are due - and who didn't believe firmed up in HIM straight LAW - there are nothing whereby thou will escape from JAH Authority - to JAH Judgemant are Truth. ¹² All are totally revealed before Him - yet there are nothing hidden from before Him. ¹³ Him are Who seize the kings Authority and Who overturn powerful ones thrones. ¹⁴ Him are Who Ilivate them who were downbased and Who lift up them who fell. ¹⁵ Him are Who loose them who were bound and Who arouse them who dead ~ as pardon dew are found from alongside Him - on the time Him loved Him shall arouse persons whose flesh were demolished and rotten and were like unto dust. ¹⁶ and havin aroused and judged persons who worked evil Work - Him will take them toward *Gehannem* - to them have saddened Him. ¹⁷ to them are who demolished JAH Order and Him LAW - and Him will destroy them child from this world. ¹⁸ As kind persons Work are more difficult than sinner persons Work - sinner persons don't love that them might live in kind

persons counsel. ¹⁹ Like unto Heavens were distanced from Earth - likewise kind persons Work were distanced from evil persons Work. ²⁰ But sinner persons Work are robbery and sin - adultery and iniquity - greed and perfidy Work ~ it are bein drunk in iniquity and robbin a person money. ²¹ It are quickly goin toward sheddin a person blood - and it are goin toward destruction that don't benefit - and it are makin a child weep whose mother and father dead on him ~ it are eatin blood and what dead and lodged - and it are eatin camel and boar flesh - and it are goin toward a daughter in she blood before she are cleansed - and toward a daughter in childbirth. ²² All this are sinner persons Work ~ she are Satan trap that were a wide and prepared path - and that take toward *Gehannem* that live firmed up forever - and toward *See'ol*. ²³ But righteous ones path that were totally narrow are what take toward welfare - and innocence and humbleness - and Inity and Love - and prayer and fast - and flesh purity - toward keepin from what don't benefit - from eatin what a sword bloated and cut and what dead and lodged - and from goin toward a youtmon wife and from adultery. ²⁴ Them keep from what weren't commanded by LAW - from eatin disgustin food and from all hated Work - and from all the Work that JAH don't love - to sinner persons do all this. ²⁵ As to kind persons - them distance from all the Work that JAH don't love. ²⁶ Him love them and shall keep them from all them tribulation like unto Trust money. ²⁷ to them keep Him Order and Him LAW and all that Him love - but Satan rule sinner persons.

10

¹ Fear JAH Who Created you and kept you up til today - yet you the nobles and the kings - don't go on Satan path. ² Live in the LAW and Command of JAH Who rule all - yet don't go on Satan path. ³ As on the time 'Isra'iel childran came toward 'Amalieq that them might inherit Kiethiewon and Kenaniewon and Fierziewon country - Siefor child Balaq and Bele`am... ⁴ whom thou cursed are cursed - and him whom thou blessed blessed ~ don't go on Satan road - to him have said - "An mi will give thee much silver and gold that honour thee - that thou might curse to mi and - and havin cursed - that thou might destroy to mi." ⁵ and to Bele`am have come makin him sorcery reward a morale - and to Siefor child Balaq have shown him the place where 'Isra'iel childran camped. ⁶ to him have done him pessimism - and to him have sacrificed him sacrifice - and to him have slaughtered from him fattened cows and sheeps - and to him have loved that him might curse and destroy 'Isra'iel childran. ⁷ Him returned a curse toward a bless - yet but as JAH didn't love that him might curse them by Him Word - don't go on Satan road. ⁸ "As thou are the kindred that JAH chose - as thou are JAH Lodgin that shall come from Heaven - make persons be cursed who curse thee-I - and make persons who bless thee-I be blessed" him said. ⁹ on the time him blessed them before him - after this Siefor child Balaq were sad - and him totally vexed and commanded that him might curse them. ¹⁰ to the kindred that JAH blessed have come toward this country - and Bele`am told him - "Mi won't curse 'Isra'iel whom JAH blessed." ¹¹ and Siefor child Balaq told Bele`am - "As to mi - mi had loved that thou might curse to mi ~ thou blessed them before mi - yet but thou didn't curse them ~ if thou had cursed to mi and told mi 'Give mi' - as to mi - mi would have given thee a house full of silver and gold - but thou totally blessed them - and thou didn't do a goodly thing to mi - and mi won't do a goodly thing to thee." ¹² Bele`am said - "What JAH told mi **Speak** with mi tongue - mi will speak it - yet as to mi - mi cyaan dare to ignore JAH thing. ¹³ Lest mi curse a blessed kindred - as JAH shall vex on mi if mi love money - as to mi - mi don't love money more than mi soul. ¹⁴ As JAH have told them father Ya`iqob - make **persons who bless thee-I be blessed and make persons who curse thee-I be cursed** - lest mi curse blessed Ya`iqob - as to mi - mi don't love money more than mi soul" him said - and as JAH have told him - **Him who bless thee-I are blessed...** ¹⁵ and **a person who curse thee-I unjustly are cursed** - accomplish thy path and thy Work that JAH might love thee. ¹⁶ and don't be like unto former persons who saddened JAH in them sin and whom Him neglected - and there are them whom Him destroyed in Destruction Water. ¹⁷ and there are them whom Him destroyed by them haters hands ~ there are them whom Him destroyed by them enemies hands - bringin enemies who were evil persons who firmed up tribulation on them - and them captured them lords with them priests and them prophets. ¹⁸ and them delivered them toward the foreign country them don't know ~ them totally captured them - and them plundered them livestocks on them and destroyed them country. ¹⁹ to them have demolished the honoured country 'Iyerusaliem fences and ramparts - and them made 'Iyerusaliem like unto a field. ²⁰ and the priests were capture - and the LAW were demolished - and warriors fought in war and fell. ²¹ and widows were capture ~ as them have been capture - them wept to them ras selves - yet them didn't weep to them husbands who dead. ²² and the childran wept - and elders shamed - and them weren't nice to neither a grey haired person nor a elder. ²³ Them destroyed all them found in the country - yet them weren't nice to beauties nor to them

in LAW ~ as JAH have vexed on Him kindreds on the time Him loved that Him might beforehand destroy Him Lodgin the Temple - them captured and took them toward the country them don't know and toward peoples. [24] As them sadden them Creator everytime - because this thing on the time JAH neglected 'Isra'iel children - JAH made 'Iyerusaliem to be ploughed like unto a field. [25] to Him are nice to them because them fathers - but Him didn't destroy them at one time ~ as Him love them fathers Yis'haq and 'Abriham and Ya`iqob who reigned to true and lived firmed up in straight LAW before them Creator - it are because them fathers kindness - yet it aren't because them ras selves kindness that him forgive them. [26] and Him I-pointed them on honours that were twofold - and them found two Kingdoms - on Earth and in Heaven. [27] and you the kings and the nobles who live in this passin world - like unto your fathers who lived firmed up in Work that are due and who were precedin you likewise inherited the Kingdom of Heaven - and like unto them names were beautiful to a child children - think of them. [28] and thou - straighten up thy Work - that Him might straighten up thy Kingdom to thee - and that thy name might be called in goodly invocation like unto the kind kings who were precedin thee who served JAH in them beautiful lifestyle.

11

[1] Think of JAH slave Mussie who weren't annoyed when he kept around this kindred in him humbleness and him prayer and whom not even one person destroyed - and him begged toward JAH in him innocence to him sista and bredda who backbit him and loved that JAH might destroy them while him said - "As them have wronged Thee-I - Lord - pardon and don't neglect thy kindreds" - and him atoned them sin to them - yet Him thought of JAH servant Mussie who weren't annoyed. [2] "To I-man have wronged Thee-I - and forgive I Thy slave who am a sinner - to Thou are Merciful - and to Thou are a Pardoner - and forgive them them sin." [3] and Mussie likewise atoned them sin to him sista and bredda who backbit him. [4] and because this thing him were called innocent. [5] and JAH totally loved him more than all the priests children who were him bredren - to Him I-point the priests - and JAH made him like unto Him Ras Self alongside them. [6] But Him also sank beneath Earth Qorie children who challenged ~ Him lowered them toward *See'ol* with them livestocks and them tents when them said "We are there - we are there in flesh and soul" ~ as him Creator JAH have loved him - and as him didn't depart from Him Command - all the word him spoke would be done to him like unto JAH Word. [7] and unless thou demolished JAH Command likewise - JAH will do thy accord to thee-I and will love thy thing to thee-I - and Him will keep thy Kingdom to thee-I. [8] and 'Asaf and Qorie children who departed from Mussie command grumbled on him because him told them - "Straighten up your reasonins to be ruled to JAH." [9] Them grumbled sayin - "How about aren't we Liewee children who work priesthood Work in Tent that were special?" [10] Them went and smoked up ishence seizin them censers that them might smoke up - but JAH didn't accept them plea - and them were burnt by the fire in them censers - and them melted like unto the wax that fire melt - and not even one person remained from them ~ as Him have said - **Them censers were honoured by them bodies bein burnt** - apart from them censers that entered toward JAH Lodgin to JAH Command - neither them clothes nor them bones remained. [11] Because this thing JAH told 'Aron and Mussie - **Gather them censers toward the Tent ~ make it be a instrument to I Lodgin wherefor I-man prepared all I-ginnin from outside up til within.** [12] and him prepared the honoured Tent instrumants ~ him prepared the rings and the joiners - *Keerubiel* picture sea. [13] Him worked the cups - the curtains - the Tent area grounds to the mobilisation - the altar and the jugs whereby them sacrifice in the Tent that were special. [14] Them sacrificed the sacrifice that them sacrifice by them accord - the sacrifice whereby welfare are made - the sacrifice whereby Him atone sin - and the vow sacrifice and the mornin and the evenin sacrifice. [15] All that Him commanded to Mussie - him commanded them in the Tent that were special - that them might work Work in she. [16] Them didn't scorn bein ruled to them Creator JAH - that Him Name might be praised by them in the LAW Lodgin Tent of them Creator JAH Who gave them a promise that Him might give them to give them them fathers inheritance that produce honey and milk that Him swore to 'Abriham. [17] Them didn't scorn bein ruled to them Creator JAH - Who swore to Yis'haq and firmed up Him Worship to Ya`iqob... [18] and Who firmed up to 'Aron and Mussie the Tent where Him Worship are kept... [19] and Who firmed up Him Worship to both 'Elyas and Samu'iel in the Temple and Tent that Selomon worked up til it became JAH Lodgin in 'Iyerusaliem - and up til JAH Name Lodgin became JAH Lodgin that honoured 'Isra'iel. [20] to she are a supplication - and to she are a sin atonemant where it are overturned to them who live in innocence and to the priests. [21] and to she are a place to persons who do Him Accord where Him will hear them pleas... [22] and JAH LAW Canstruction that honoured 'Isra'iel. [23] to she are where sacrifice are sacrificed and where Ishence are smoked up that JAH Who honoured 'Isra'iel be in goodly Fragrance. [24] and Him would speak bein on the joiner where Him forgive in the Tent that were special ~ JAH Light would be revealed to Ya`iqob children whom Him chose and to friends who live firmed up in Him LAW and Him Command. [25] But persons who ignored JAH LAW will be like unto Qorie children whom Earth sank - and likewise sinner persons have that them might enter toward *Gehannem* that have no exits up til Eternity.

12

[1] You who didn't keep the LAW Him commanded you in Tent - woe to you 'Isra'iel nobles who also didn't do Him Accord - yet you did your ras selves accord - and this are bein arrogant and pride - greed and adultery - drink and bein drunk - and swearin in lie. [2] and **because this thing I anger - like unto chaff are burnt before a fire - and like unto fire burn the mountain - and like unto a whirl wind spill the crushed chaff from Earth and scattar it toward Heaven - lest it trace be found in it place - I anger will destroy you like unto that.** [3] JAH Who honoured 'Isra'iel said - **I-man shall likewise destroy all persons who work sin** - and think of JAH Who rule all and to Whom nothing fail. [4] Him love persons who love Him - and to persons who live firmed up in Him Command - Him will atone them iniquity and them sin to them ~ don't be dull and stingy of heart by not believin. [5] and make your reasonins straight to be ruled to JAH - and believe in Him that you might firm up your bodies - and **I-man shall save you from your enemy hand in your tribulation day.** [6] and **in your plea time I-man tell you - Check - I-man am there with you in Support ~ I-man shall save you from your enemy hand ~ as you have believed in I - and as you have done I Command - and as you didn't depart from I LAW - and as you have loved what I-man love** - JAH Who rule all said - **I-man won't neglect you on your tribulation day.** [7] Him love them who love Him - to Him are a Pardoner - and to Him are nice - and Him keep persons who keep Him LAW - like unto a trust money. [8] Him return Him anger to them many times ~ because Him were who know them that them are flesh and blood - as Him are a Pardoner - Him didn't destroy all in Him chastisemant - and on the time them souls were separated from them flesh - them will return toward them Earthliness. [9] As Him have Created them bringin from not livin toward livin - them won't know the place where them live up til JAH love that Him might bring them from not livin toward livin ~ again Him separated them souls from them flesh - and Earth nature returned toward it Earthliness. [10] and again Him Accord shall bring them from not livin toward livin." [11] But Tseerutsaydan who denied JAH multiplied bein arrogant before JAH ~ him made him ras self lofty up til the day that him loved on the time him quit Him. [12] "An mi era became like unto Heaven era - and mi are who send forth Sun - and mi won't dead up til Eternity" him said. [13] and before him finished speakin this thing the Angel of Death whose name are called Thilimyakos alit and struck him heart ~ him dead in that hour ~ as him didn't praise him Creator - him were separated from him beautiful lifestyle and him perished arisin from him arrogance abundance and him Work evil. [14] But when the Keledans king army had camped in the city and the country squares lovin to fight him - on the time him dead - them proceeded and destroyed him country ~ them plundered all him livestock - and them didn't preserve a elder who near and sight up ramparts. [15] Them plundered all him money - and them took him tiny money - and them burned him country in fire and returned toward them country.

13

[1] But these five Meqabees children who believed gave them bodies to death refusin to eat the sacrifice to idols. [2] to them have known that pretendin with JAH surpass from pretendin with persons - and JAH anger from the king anger. [3] Havin known that this world will totally pass and that the Feeling good joy won't live firmed up forever - them gave them bodies to fire that them might be saved from fire in Heaven. [4] and as them have known that bein made Feeling good in Garden one day are better than livin many eras in this world - and that findin Thy Pardon one hour Lord - are better than many eras - them gave them bodies to fire. [5] What are I era? Like unto a shadow - like unto passin wax melt and perish on a fire edge - aren't it like unto that? [6] But Thou Lord live forever - and Thy Era aren't fulfilled - and Thy Name invocation are to a child children. [7] and Meqabees children thought that it seemed all this ~ refusin to eat a disgustin sacrifice them chose believin in JAH. [8] Knowin that them will arise with persons who dead - and meanin because JAH - knowin that Judgemant shall be judged after Resurrection of Council - because this thing them gave them bodies to martyrdom. [9] You persons who don't know nor believe persons who dead risin - knowin that the Life them find later will surpass from this them passin Earthly Life - arisin from these five Meqabees children who gave them bodies together to the death and whose appearance were handsome -

after this them knew Resurrection. ¹⁰ Because them believed in Him knowin that all shall pass - and because them didn't bow to idols - because them didn't eat a disgustin sacrifice that don't give Support - them gave them bodies to death that them might find thanks from JAH. ¹¹ to because this thing knowin that Him will make them Feeling good in flesh and soul in later era - them didn't know this world flavour and death tribulation a serious thing to them who have child and wife - and knowin that Resurrection be made in flesh and soul on the Day of Advent - them gave them bodies to death. ¹² and knowin that persons who kept JAH LAW - with the nobles and the kings who believed JAH Word and were nice... ¹³ shall live reignin to a child childran many eras in Kingdom of Heaven where are no sadness and tribulation nor death - and knowin in them reasonins what will be done later - like unto wax melt amidst a fire - because this thing them gave them bodies to death. ¹⁴ Believin that them faces will shine seven hands more than the Sun - and that them will be Feeling good in Him Love on the time all arose in flesh and soul - them gave them bodies to death.

14

¹ But the Samrans and 'Ayhuds thing - the Seduqans who don't believe persons who dead risin - and the Fereesans thing quite totally sadden I - and it help I to I reasonin ~ "We will dead tomorrow" 'Ayhuds say - "Make we eat and drink ~ we will dead tomorrow ~ there are no Feeling good joy we will sight up in grave." ² But the Samrans say - "As we flesh will be dust - it won't arise. ³ Because she were invisible like unto wind and like unto iyunder voice - check - she are here - and because she were what them don't call and invisible - as soul won't arise if flesh dead - on the time Resurrection are done we will believe we souls arisin. ⁴ But as beasts will eat she and as worms will eat she in the grave - we flesh are sight up alongside all ~ she will become dust and ashes. ⁵ and those beasts who ate she will become dust - to them have been like unto grass - and to them have become dust like unto them weren't Created - and to them trace won't be found - but we flesh won't arise." ⁶ and the Fereesans say - "We believe as to persons who dead arisin - however Him will bring and Inite souls with another flesh that are in Heaven - that aren't on Earth ~ where will demolished and rotten fleshes be found?" ⁷ But the Seduqans say - "After we soul proceeded from we flesh - we won't arise with persons who dead - and flesh and soul have no arisin after them dead - and after we dead we won't arise." ⁸ and because this thing them totally err - and as them speak insult on JAH Lordship - them thing sadden I. ⁹ As them didn't believe JAH Who honour them - them have no hope to be saved - however them have no hope to dead and arise and be saved. ¹⁰ O 'Ayhudan who are blind of reasonin - when thou are whom Him Created bringin from not livin toward livin - and scorned like unto spit - will thou make JAH ignorant - Who made thee a person? Will it fail JAH Who Created thee in Him Example and Him Appearance to arouse Initin thy flesh and thy soul? ¹¹ As thou won't escape from JAH Authority - don't think a thing that are thus ~ thou will arise without thou lovin - to there are the hardship thou will raceive in *See'ol* where thou were seized on the time thou dead - and it shall be judged on thee without thou lovin. ¹² to the sin found from demons that demons place in thy reasonin are worked alongside thee after thou were birthed from thy mother womb - and to she are worked abundantly on the time thou grew up. ¹³ Them place she in thy body on the time thou dead - and she will bring hardship on them on the time them worked she. ¹⁴ Like unto there are sin in them collar of reasonin - as there are persons who work sin bein seized by she - she kindreds will present demons. ¹⁵ All sinner persons souls shall come from Heaven edge where them are - and thy sin likewise shall introduce thee toward *Gehannem* pullin and bringin thy soul from where thou are. ¹⁶ and after thy flesh lived separate from thy soul - JAH Charity dew shall arouse thee bein servant fold like unto I father 'Adam flesh. ¹⁷ Thou who live in grave - thou also err in thy error - yet make it not seem to thee that thou only mislead the others ~ thou say - "The arisin that persons who dead shall arise aren't there" - that them might depart from JAH Command and err. ¹⁸ Him shall arouse thee that Him might give thee thy hardship like unto thy Work that thou worked - yet who shall quit thee that thou might remain bein dust? ¹⁹ But at that time - whether wind in wind be thy nature - or if Water in Water be thy nature - or if Earth in Earth be thy nature - or if fire in fire be thy nature - it shall come. ²⁰ and if a soul that lodged in thee be what lived in *See'ol* - she shall come. ²¹ and righteous ones souls that live in Garden in joy shall come. ²² But thou 'Ayhudan - Samran - Fereesan - Seduqan - will live in *See'ol* up til it are judged on thee. ²³ At that time thou will sight up that JAH shall pay thee the hardship like unto thy sin because thou misled persons. ²⁴ "Persons who dead won't arise ~ as we will dead - make we eat and drink" - and because thou sat in Mussie chair and misled by thy words while thou said - "Persons who dead won't arise" - thou will sight up that Him shall pay thee thy hardship. ²⁵ and without thy knowin *'Oreet* Book - and when thou teach the books word - because this thing thou erred ~ it would be better had thou remained without learnin from thy misleadin a person. ²⁶ It would have been better if thou didn't know the books word - when thou promulgate JAH kindreds in thy evil teachin and thy worthless words. ²⁷ to JAH don't favour havin sight up a face - and to Him shall give the grace and glory Him prepared to Him friends - persons who teach goodly Work - but thou have that thou might raceive thy reward like unto thy Work and the things that thou spoke. ²⁸ But there are nothing whereby thou will escape from JAH Authority Who shall judge on thee - and Him have that Him might pay thee like unto thy Work - to them whom thou taught and thou together will receive a sentance. ²⁹ Know that persons who dead shall arise - and if them are persons who kept Him LAW them shall arise - and like unto Earth send forth grass on the time rain rained - as Him Command shall send them forth from a grave - it aren't possible to it to remain demolished and rotten. ³⁰ Like unto moist wood drink dew and send forth leaves on the time Him satta she rain to Earth - like unto wheat bear forth fruit - and like unto grain produce buds - like unto it aren't possible to she to withhold that she might prevent she fruit if JAH loved... ³¹ and like unto it aren't possible to a daughter who canceived to close and prevent she womb on the time labour seized she - like unto it aren't possible to she to escape without birthin... ³² as dew have alit toward she bein commanded from JAH - at that time she shall produce them at one time - yet after she heard JAH Word - a grave also likewise cyaan prevent the persons gathered alongside she from arisin. ³³ and fleshes shall be gathered in the place where them corpses fell - and them places where souls live shall be opened - and souls shall return toward the flesh where them were formerly separated. ³⁴ and on the time a drum were beaten - persons who dead shall quickly arise like unto a eye wink - and havin arisen them shall stand before JAH - and Him shall give them them reward like unto them hand Work. ³⁵ At that time thou will sight up that thou arise with dead ones - and thou will marvel at all the Work thou worked in this world - and on the time thou sight up all thy sins written before thee - at that time thou will regret a useless regret. ³⁶ Thou know that thou will arise with dead ones and that thou will receive thy hardship like unto the Work that thou worked.

15

¹ But persons who found them reward by them goodly Work shall be Feeling good at that time ~ persons who ignored while them said - "Persons who dead won't arise" shall be sad at that time on the time them sight up that persons who dead arose with them evil Work that don't benefit. ² That - them Work that them worked shall canvict them - and them ras selves shall know that it canvict them without one livin who will dispute them. ³ on the day when Judgemant and mournin are done - on the day when JAH shall come - on the day when Definite Judgemant are judged - persons who forgot JAH LAW shall stand in the place where them stand. ⁴ on the day when there shall be total darkness - and on the day when mist are pulled - on the day when flashes are sight up and when lightnin are heard... ⁵ and on the day when quakes and fright and heatwave and sleet frost are made... ⁶ on the day when a evil person who worked evil Work raceive hardship - and on the day when a clean person raceive him reward like unto him worked clean Work - and on the day when persons who forgot JAH LAW raceive the hardship like unto a sinner person worked sin - them shall stand in the place where them stand. ⁷ to on the day when a master aren't more honoured than him slave - and on the time when a mistress aren't more honoured than she slave... ⁸ and on the time when the king aren't more honoured than a poor one - and on the time when a elder aren't more honoured than a infant - on the time when a father aren't more honoured than him child - and on the time when a mother aren't more honoured than she child... ⁹ on the time when a wealthy one aren't more honoured than a poor one - and on the time when a arrogant one aren't more honoured than a downbased one - and on the time when the great aren't more honoured than the small - she are the day when Judgemant are judged - to she are the day when them raceive sentance and hardship - and to she are the day when all will raceive hardship like unto them worked sin. ¹⁰ and to she are the day when persons who worked goodly Work raceive them reward - and to she are the day when persons who worked sin raceive hardship. ¹¹ and as she are the day when persons who found them reward are made Feeling good - persons who forgot JAH LAW shall stand in the place where them stand. Persons who make liars - who digest books while them said - "Persons who dead won't arise" - them shall sight up Resurrection. ¹² At that time this world sinners - who didn't work goodly Work in this world - shall weep on them sin *'Oreet* them worked - because sadness found them without calmin. ¹³ and all likewise - kind persons who worked goodly Work - them Feeling good joy won't be fulfilled up til Eternity - to them have worked goodly Work when them were in this world. ¹⁴ to them have known that them will arise after them dead - and them didn't depart from them Creator LAW. ¹⁵

Because them didn't depart from Him LAW - them shall inherit two welfares ~ Him multiplied them seed in this world - and Him honoured them childran. [16] Him bequeathed them the Kingdom of Heaven where shall be found the welfare him swore to them fathers on the time when persons who dead arise - and on the time when rich ones become poor. [17] Persons shall weep who worked sin - who don't believe persons who dead arisin - who don't keep JAH LAW - and who don't think of Arisin Day. [18] At that time them will sight up the tribulation that shall find them and shall have no endin - and where are no calmin nor welfare - and it have the sadness that have no rest nor calmin in them reasonin. [19] and a fire that don't perish and worms that don't sleep shall find them. [20] and in the place where are them flesh are fire - sulphur - whirl wind - frost - hail - sleet ~ all this shall rain over them. [21] to persons who don't believe persons who dead arisin - there are fire of *Gehannem on* them.

16

[1] Thou - please think of what are on thy flesh - and thy feet and thy hands nails - and thy head hair - to them proceed quickly on the time thou cut them ~ know Resurrection by this - that thou have a reasonin - and that thou have religion and knowledge. [2] Thy feet and thy hands nails and thy head hair - thou say - "Where do these come from?" ~ aren't it JAH Who prepared it that them might proceed - that thou know arisin that shall be done on thy flesh that aren't on another flesh - that thou might know that thou will arise after thou dead? [3] Because thou misled persons while thou said - "There are no Resurrection of the dead ones" - on the time when dead ones arise thou will raceive thy hardship like unto thou worked sin and iniquity. [4] and as even what thou planted now won't remain refusin that it might grow - whether it be wheat or barley - thou will sight she up on the time the day arrived when thou raceive thy hardship. [5] and again - the plant thou planted won't say - "I-man won't grow" - and be it a fig wood or a grape vine - it fruit and it leaf won't be changed. [6] If thou plant grapes - it won't be changed that it might be a fig - and if thou plant figs - it won't be changed that it might be grapes - and if thou sow wheat it won't be changed that it might be barley. [7] All - in each of the seeds - in each of it kinds - each of the fruits - each of the woods - each of the leaves - each of the roots - send forth fruit havin raceived Pardon Dew blessin by what are found from JAH - yet if thou sow barley also it won't be changed that it might be wheat. [8] and all likewise - that a grave might produce flesh and soul - she shall produce persons like unto JAH sowed on she ~ the flesh and soul that JAH sowed shall arise bein Inited - yet persons who worked goodly Work won't be changed in persons who worked evil Work - and persons who worked evil Work also won't be changed in persons who worked goodly Work. [9] on the time the hour arrived when a drum are beaten - persons who dead shall arise by the Pardon Dew found from JAH ~ persons who worked goodly Work shall arise in Life Resurrection - and them reward are the Garden where are Feeling good joy that JAH prepared to kind persons - where are no tribulation nor disease - and that are clean ones lodgin where them won't again dead after this. [10] But persons who worked evil Work shall arise a Definite Judgemant arisin - and with Deeyablos who misled them... [11] and with him armies - demons who don't love that even one person might be saved from all 'Adam childran... [12] them shall descend toward *Gehannem* that were darkness edge - where are tooth grindin and mournin - where are no charity nor pardon - and where are no exits up til Eternity - that are beneath *See'ol* forever. to them didn't work goodly Work in them Life in this world when them were in them flesh. [13] Because this thing it shall be judged on them on the time when flesh and soul arise bein Inited. [14] Woe to persons who don't believe the flesh and soul arisin whereby JAH show Him miracles abundance together. [15] and all and each one shall raceive him reward like unto him Work and him hands weariness.

17

[1] A wheat kernel won't grow nor bear fruit unless she were demolished. But if a wheat kernel are demolished she will send roots toward Earth ~ she will send forth leaves ~ there will be buds ~ it will bear fruit. [2] You know that the one wheat kernel will become many kernels. [3] and all likewise - this kernel grow risin up from Water and wind and Earth dew - to wheat cyaan bear fruit without Sun - but Sun are because fire stead. [4] and wind are because a soul stead - and wheat cyaan bear fruit without wind - and the Water give Earth to drink and satta she. [5] and after Earth that are ashes drank Water - she produce roots - and she tips are lofty upward ~ she bear fruit around what JAH blessed she. [6] But a wheat kernel are 'Adam example - in whom lodged a resonatin soul that JAH Created - and likewise a grape wood drink Water and send forth roots - and the thin root kinds drink Water. [7] to Pardon Dew found from JAH give to drink vines tips that were long - and it send the Water upward toward the leaf tips ~ it bud up from the Sun heat - and by JAH Accord it bear fruit. [8] It shall be a goodly fragrance that make a reasonin Feeling good - and on the time them ate it - it shall satta like unto Water that don't make thirsty and grain that don't make hungry - and on the time them immersed it - it will be the cluster blood. [9] and like unto it were told in Psalm sayin - "Grapes make a person reasonin Feeling good" - on the time them drank it - it make a person heart Feeling good - and on the time a person who came loose opened him mouth and drank it - him are drunk ~ him drink and fill in him lungs - and the blood flow toward him heart. [10] As grapes drunkenness totally mislead - and as it deprive him him mind - it make the pit and the cliff like unto a wide meadow - and him don't know obstacles and thorns on him feet and hands. [11] JAH did thus on she fruit and grape wood that Him Name might be praised by persons who believe dead persons arisin and who do Him Accord. [12] in the Kingdom of Heaven Him shall make persons Feeling good who believe persons who dead arisin.

18

[1] You persons who don't believe persons who dead arisin - around what error you err! and on the time them took you toward the place you don't know - you will regret a useless regrets - and because you didn't believe the arisin that persons who dead shall arise Inited in soul and flesh - and on the time persons cast you toward *Gehannem*... [2] if you work whether the good or the evil - you will raceive your reward like unto your Work - to you have misled them companions reasonin while you said - "We know that persons who dead - who were dust and ashes - won't arise." [3] As them death have no exit - and as them have no Power to them chastisemant that shall come on them - and as them weren't firm in them tribulation - because this thing them mislead them companions ~ to them have that them might stand in JAH Square. [4] on the time Him vexed on them in Him wrath them will totally fear ~ because them didn't know that them were Created bringin from not livin toward livin - as them speak JAH LAW without knowin - it shall be judged on them all because them worked evil. [5] Them don't know *Gehannem* where them will go - to because them were angry and because them were crooked in them Work - them teach to them companions like unto them reasonin thirst measure - and to them are evil ones who teach a crooked thing while them said - "There are no Resurrection of dead ones." [6] At that time them shall know that persons who dead shall arise - and them shall know that it shall be judged on them because them didn't believe the persons who dead arisin that are to all 'Adam childran. [7] to all I are 'Adam childran - and to I have dead because 'Adam - and to death judgemant have found I all from alongside JAH because I father 'Adam error. [8] I will again arise there with I father 'Adam that I might raceive I hardship by I Work that I worked - to the world have been ruled to death by I father 'Adam ignorance. [9] By 'Adam infringin JAH Command - because this thing I raceived hardship ~ I flesh in grave melted like unto wax - and I bodies perished. [10] and Earth drank I marrow ~ I perished and I attractiveness perished in grave - and I flesh were buried in grave - and I beautiful words were buried in Earth. [11] and worms proceeded from I shinin eyes - and I features perished in grave and became dust. [12] Where are youtmons features attractiveness - who were attractive - whose stance were handsome and whose word thing succeeded? How about where are warriors firmness? [13] Where are the kings armies - or how about the nobles lordship? Where are adornin in horses and adornin in silver and gold and adornin in shinin weapons? Didn't it perish? [14] Where are sweet grape drink - and how about food flavour?

19

[1] O Earth who gathered the nobles and the kings and rich ones and elders and daughters who were attractive and beauties who were attractive - woe arisin from thee-I. [2] O Earth who gathered persons who were warriors - them who have attractiveness - and them who were fine of leg - and them who have reasonin and knowledge - and them whose words have words that were beautiful like unto a hummin harp and like unto a lyre and a violin beat... [3] and them who have a tune that make Feeling good like unto grape drink make Feeling good - and them whose eyes shine like unto a mornin star... and them who sketch what were firm like unto them right hands lift up what are given and withheld and like unto them were - and them whose feet were beautiful to sight up - and them who run like unto rushin wheels - woe arisin from thee-I. [5] O death who separated attractive persons souls from them flesh - woe arisin from thee-I - to thou have been sent by JAH Accord. [6] As thou have gathered many persons whom JAH produced from thee-I and returned toward thee-I - thou Earth - woe arisin from thee-I ~ I were found from thee-I ~ I returned toward thee-I by Accord of JAH ~ I were Feeling good over thee-I by JAH Accord. [7] Thou became a carpet to I corpses ~ I recurred over thee-I - and I were buried within thee-I ~ I ate thy fruit - and thou ate I flesh. [8] and I drank the Water found from thy springs - and thou drank I blood springs ~ I ate the fruit found from thy Earthliness - and thou ate I body flesh. [9] Like unto JAH commanded thee-I to be I food - I ate grain from thy Earthliness that have beautiful dew - and thou received

I fleh attractiveness and made it dust to thy food like unto JAH commanded thee-I. [10] O death who gathered the nobles and the kings who were powerful - woe arisin from thee-I ~ thou didn't fear arisin from them famousness and them frightenin - like unto JAH Who Created them commanded thee-I ~ o death - woe arisin from thee-I - and thou didn't scorn the sufferah. [11] and thou weren't nice to persons whose features are beautiful - and thou didn't quit powerful ones and warriors ~ thou didn't quit poor nor rich ones - neither kind nor evil ones - neither children nor elders - neither daughters nor males. [12] Thou didn't quit persons who think a goodly thing and who didn't depart from the LAW - and thou didn't quit them who were like unto animals in them Work - who think a evil thing - who were totally beautiful in them features attractiveness - in them thing flavour and in them words ~ o death - woe arisin from thee-I. [13] Thou didn't quit persons whose words were angry and whose mouths were full of curses ~ thou gathered persons who live in darkness and in light and them souls in thy places ~ o death - woe arisin from thee-I. [14] and Earth gathered the persons flesh who live whether in cave or in Earth - up til a drum are beaten and persons who dead arise. [15] As persons who dead shall arise quickly like unto a eye wink by JAH Command and on a drum bein beaten - persons who worked evil Work shall raceive them hardship in them sin abundance measure that them worked it - and persons who worked goodly Work shall be Feeling good.

20

[1] and believe I that all I Work that I worked in this world won't remain nor be hidden on the time I stood before Him fearin and tremblin. [2] and on the time I didn't seize provisions to I path - and on the time I won't have clothes to I bodies... [3] on the time I won't have a staff to I hands nor shoes to I feet... [4] and on the time I won't know the paths where demons take I - whether it be slippery or smooth - or be it dark - and whether it be thorns or nettles - or whether it be a Water depth or a pit depth - believe I that I Work that I worked in this world won't remain nor be hidden. [5] I won't know the demons who take I - and I won't hear them thing. [6] As them are black ones - and as them lead I toward darkness - I don't sight up them faces. [7] and like unto the prophet spoke sayin - "On the time I soul were separated from I flesh - Lord I Lord - Thou know I path - and them hid a trap on that path where I-man went - and I-man sight up returnin toward the right ~ I-man lacked one who know I - and I-man have nothing there whereby I-man will escape" - as them take I toward darkness - I won't sight up them faces. [8] As him know that demons ridicule on him - and as them will lead him toward the path him don't know - him speakin this are because this - and if him return leftward and rightward - there are no person who know him. [9] Him are alone amidst demons - and yet there are none who know him. [10] Angels of Light who are subtle are who are sent toward kind persons that them might raceive righteous ones souls - and might take toward a Light place - toward the Garden - where welfare are found. [11] Demons and Angels of darkness are who are sent that them might raceive them and might take them toward *Gehannem* that were prepared to them that them might raceive them hardship by them sin that them worked. [12] Woe to sinner persons souls who take them toward destruction - who have no welfare nor rest - nor escapin from the tribulation that found them - nor proceedin from *Gehannem* up til Eternity. [13] As them have lived firmed up in Qayel Work - and as them have perished by Bele`am iniquity price - and as them have lacked what them will do - woe to sinner persons - to them pretext to raceive interest and presents that in downgression them might take a foreigner money that weren't them money. [14] Them shall raceive them hardship in *Gehannem* by them sin that them worked.

21

[1] Where are persons who gather a foreigner money that weren't them hands Work nor them money? [2] to them take a person money for free - and to them shll be gathered without knowin the day when them dead that shall arrive on them - however them quit them money for a foreigner. [3] to like unto them fathers - them are sinners kindreds who worry and seize sinners like unto them whether it be by theft or by robbery - and them children won't be Feeling good by them fathers money. [4] As them have gathered to them in downgression - and as it are like unto misty urine and like unto the smoke that wind scattar and like unto wiltin grass - and like unto wax that melt arisin from before a fire - as sinners glory shall perish like unto that - there are none whom them fathers money will benefit ~ like unto Daweet spoke sayin - "I-man sight up a sinner man... [5] bein honoured and famed like unto a cordia and like unto a cypress - but on the time I-man returned I-man lacked him ~ I-man searched and didn't find him place" - there are none whom them fathers money will profit nor benefit. [6] Because them gathered a person money in downgression - it seemin to them that them won't dead - like unto persons who wrong them companions won't boast - sinner persons destruction are likewise at one time. [7] You lazy ones - think that you will perish and that your money will perish with you - and if your silver and your gold abound it shall be rusted. [8] and if you birth many children them shall be to many graves - and if you work many houses them shall be demolished. [9] to you didn't fulfill your Creator JAH Accord - and if you multiply livestock them shall be for your enemies capture - and all the money you seized in your hands won't be found - to it have been what weren't blessed. [10] Whether it be in house or in forest - and be it in wilderness or a pasture place - and be it in grape threshinfloor or in grain threshinfloor - it won't be found. [11] Because you didn't keep JAH Command - as JAH won't save you with all your house hold from the tribulation - there shall be sadness on you arisin from all your enemies - yet you won't be Feeling good in your children birthed from your nature. [12] But from Him plenty - Him won't trouble persons who kept Him Order and Him LAW ~ Him give all who begged Him - yet Him bless them children birthed from them nature and also them land fruit to them. [13] and Him make them rulers on all peoples in them area that them might rule lest them be who are ruled - and Him give them all Him plenty in them pasture place. [14] Him bless to them all them seized in them hand - all them field fruit - and all them livestocks places - and Him make them Feeling good in them children birthed from them nature. [15] and Him don't diminish them livestocks on them ~ Him save them from all them tribulation and from weariness and illness and destruction - and from them enemy them don't know and from him them know. [16] and Him will dispute to them in Judgemant time - and Him shall save them from a evil thing and from tribulation and from all who dispute them ~ in the first era if a priest lived who work the Tent Work - who keep the LAW and keep the Tent Order and live firmed up in JAH Accord - by the first Order and all the LAW as them would give him the tithe and what were birthed first Beginnin from man up til livestock - Him would save them from all the tribulation. [17] Like unto Mussie commanded Newie child 'Iyasu - there was a country of sanctuary in all them country ~ by not knowin and by knowin up til them judged judgemant on whom them canvicted and to whom them acquittin... [18] if a person lived who killed a soul - him would be measured there that him might be saved. [19] Him told them - "Examine in your reasonins that him have a quarrel with him formerly - and be it by axe or be it by a stone or be it by wood - as it have fallen from him hand by not knowin - if him say "That person on whom it fell dead on mi" - examine and save him ~ if him did it in not knowin make him be saved. [20] But if him do it knowin - him will raceive him hardship like unto him sin - and there are none who will pardon him; but if him kill him in not knowin - as him have done it in not knowin - examine and save him lest him dead. [21] Him worked to them that them might distance from all the sin - yet Mussie would work like unto this to 'Isra'iel children lest them depart from JAH LAW. [22] Him commanded them that 'Adam children - who live firmed up in JAH Command from worshippin idols and eatin what dead and lodged and what a sword bloated and cut - and who distance from all evil work like unto him worked to them - that them might work it and might totally distance from all that aren't due. [23] Him commanded them lest them depart from the Command Him worked to them in the Tent example in Heaven - that them might save them bodies and might find them lodgin with them fathers. [24] As them have been birthed from Siet and 'Adam who did JAH Accord - persons who believed in JAH Word and lived firmed up in Him Command will be called kind persons children. [25] As I are 'Adam children - as Him have Created I in Him Example and Him Appearance that I might work all goodly Work that make JAH Feeling good - Him won't scorn it. [26] As Him totally won't separate Him friends - if I work goodly Work - I shall inherit the Kingdom of Heaven where are welfare with persons who work goodly Work. [27] Him totally love persons who beg him cleanly - and Him hear them in them prayer - and Him accept the repentance of persons who are disciplined and enter repentance ~ Him give firmness and Power to persons who keep Him Order and Him LAW and Him Command. [28] Persons who did Him Accord shall be Feeling good with Him in Him Kingdom forever - and whether them be persons who preceded or who arose later - them will present praise to Him Beginnin from today up til Eternity. Make glory due to JAH forever - and the secand Meqabyan arrived and were fulfilled.

The Book of Meqabyan III

1

¹ Kristos shall rejoice Gibts persons - because Him shall come toward them in later era that Him will revenge and destroy Deeyablos - who wronged them who were kindly and innocent - and who misled persons - and who hate him Creator Work. ² Him shall revenge and destroy him ~ Him shall return him lordship toward wretchedness and bein downbased - to him have been arrogant in him reasonin. ³ Him shall return him lordship toward bein downbased - to him have said - "As mi will enter toward the sea midst - and as mi will proceed toward Heaven - and as mi will sight up depths - and as mi will grasp and seize 'Adam childran like unto bird chicks - who are it who are loftier than mi? ⁴ Because mi became by them reason that mi might distance them from the straight LAW of JAH - as mi will strengthen on persons who live in this world unless them did JAH Accord - there are none who will depose mi from mi authority" him said. ⁵ "To mi will be a reason to return them toward a path that were smooth to go toward Gehannem with mi. ⁶ Persons who loved Him and kept Him LAW hate mi because this thing - but persons who departed from them Lord LAW and who erred will come toward mi and love mi and keep mi oath ~ as mi will make them reasonin evil and change them thoughts lest them return toward them Creator JAH - them will do mi command like unto mi commanded them. ⁷ and on the time mi showed them this world money - mi will mislead them reasonin from straight LAW - and on the time mi showed them beautiful and attractive daughters - mi will distance them by these from straight LAW. ⁸ and on the time mi showed them shinin Hindekie jewels and silver and gold - mi will distance them by this also from straight LAW that them might return toward mi Work. ⁹ and on the time mi showed them thin clothes and red silk and white silk - and linens and white silk - mi will distance them by this also from straight LAW - and mi will return them toward mi thoughts ~ on the time mi multiplied money and livestocks like unto sand and showed them - by this also mi will return them toward mi Work. ¹⁰ and on the time mi showed them jealousy done in arrogance because daughters and because anger and quarrels - by all this mi will return them toward mi Work. ¹¹ and on the time mi showed them signs - mi will lodge in them companions reasonin - and mi will lodge a sign thing that were to each of the ras selves in them reasonin - and mi showed them words signs and misled them. ¹² and to persons in whom mi lodged mi lodgin - mi will show them signs - and be it in stars gait - or be it in cloud proceedin or in fire flickerin - or be it in beasts and birds cries - as them are mi lodgins - mi will lodge signs in them reasonin on them by all this. ¹³ Them will speak and give signs to them companions - and like unto those them naysayers told them - mi will precede and be a sign to them. ¹⁴ Mi will do them words signs to them - that persons who examined them might be misled - and that them might give a wage to magicians - and that them might tell to them companions sayin - 'There are no savants like unto so-an-so and so-an-so to whom it are done like unto them spoke - and who know prophecy - and who separate good and evil - and to whom all are like unto them spoke - and to whom it are done like unto them word.' ¹⁵ Mi will be Feeling good on the time them spoke this - that persons who perish and err by mi might totally abound and that 'Adam childran might perish - to JAH have downbased mi from mi rank because them father 'Adam - on mi sayin 'Mi won't bow to 'Adam who are downbased to mi.' ¹⁶ and mi will take toward destruction all him childran who live firmed up in mi command ~ mi have a Oath from JAH Who Created mi - that all persons whom mi misled might descend toward Gehannem with mi. ¹⁷ and on the time Him multiplied Him anger on mi - and on the time Him commanded that them might bind and cast mi toward Gehannem - on the time mi Creator commanded sayin thus - mi interceded with mi Lord ~ mi interceded before Him while mi said - 'As Thou have vexed on mi - and as Thou have admonished mi by Thy chastisemant - and as Thou have chastised mi by Thy wrath - Lord mi Lord - adjourn mi that mi might speak one thing before Thee-I.' ¹⁸ and mi Lord answered to mi sayin - **Speak - I-man will hear thee** ~ at that time mi began mi plea toward Him sayin - 'After mi were downbased from mi rank - make the persons whom mi misled be like unto mi in Gehannem where mi will raceive tribulation. ¹⁹ and make them be to Thy Lordship who refused mi - who didn't err by mi - who didn't keep mi command - that them might do Thy Command and might fulfill Thy Accord and might keep Thy Word - on the time them didn't err by mi like unto mi misled them havin refused like unto mi taught them - and on the time Thou loved mi - make them take the crown Thou gave to mi. ²⁰ Give them the crown of the authorities called Satans who were sent with mi ~ seat them on mi throne on Thy Right that were a wilderness from mi and mi hosts. ²¹ and make them praise Thee-I like unto Thou loved - and make them be like unto mi hosts and like unto mi ~ because Thou hated mi and loved them who were Created from ashes and Earth - as mi authority have perished - and as them authority have been lofty - make them praise Thee-I like unto Thou loved.' ²² Mi Lord answered to mi sayin - **As thou have misled them while them sight up and while them heard - if thou misled them without them lovin I Order - make them be to thee like unto thy accord and like unto thy word.** ²³ **If them quit the Books Word and I Command and came toward thee - and if thou misled them while them destruction also saddened mi - make them raceive tribulation in *Gehannem* like unto thee** - Him told mi. ²⁴ **You will raceive tribulation in *Gehannem* up til the Eternity - yet you will have no exits from *Gehannem* up til the Eternity - to them whom thou misled nor to thee.**

2

¹ **But I-man shall bequeath thy throne in lordship to them whom it failed thee to mislead - like unto I slave 'Iyob** ~ JAH Who rule all said - **I-man will give the Kingdom of Heaven to persons whom it failed thee to mislead.** ² and mi provoke on 'Adam childran in all ~ if it were possible to mi to mislead them - mi won't quit them that them might firm up in goodly Work ~ to mi provoke on all 'Adam childran - and mi sweeten this world Feeling good joy to them. ³ Be it by lovin drink and food and clothes - or by lovin things - or by withholdin and givin... ⁴ or be it by lovin to hear and sight up - or be it by lovin to caress and go - or be it by multiplyin arrogance and things - or be it by lovin dreams and slumber... ⁵ or be it by multiplyin drunkenness and drink - or be it by multiplyin insults and anger - be it by speakin games and useless things... ⁶ or be it by quarrels and by backbitin them companion - or be it by sightin up this world daughters who were attractive - be it by smellin perfumes fragrance that mislead them... ⁷ mi hate them by all this lest them able to be saved ~ mi distance them from JAH LAW that them might enter with mi toward the destruction whereby mi were downbased from mi rank." ⁸ and the prophet told him - "Thou who destroy persons - perish ~ on the time thou departed from JAH LAW and committed crime in thy reasonin firmness and thy arrogance - and by saddenin thy Creator and not worshippin thy Creator in thy reasonin firmness - will thou thus be arrogant on JAH Creation? ⁹ on the time thy Creator vexed on thee - Him downbased thee from thy rank because thy evil Work ~ why do thou take 'Adam toward sin - him whom him Creator Created from Earth - whom Him made like unto Him loved - and whom Him placed to Him praise?" him told him. ¹⁰ "On the time thou - who are subtle and were Created from wind and fire - were arrogant in sayin 'Mi are the Creator'... ¹¹ on the time thou boasted - as JAH have sight up thy evil Work and thou have denied JAH with thy hosts - Him Created 'Adam who will praise because thy stead - that him might praise Him Name without diminishin. ¹² As thou have made thy ras self prouder than all Angels hosts who are like unto thee - because thy arrogance JAH Created 'Adam with him childran that them might praise JAH Name because the praise that thou praise with thy hosts whom Him scorned. ¹³ and because this thing JAH destroyed thee separatin from all Angels chiefs like unto thee - and thy hosts Created in one counsel with thee - and thou - you proceeded and erred from JAH praise because your useless reasonin arrogance and because your reasonin firmness - and you were arrogant on your Creator - that aren't on another. ¹⁴ Because this thing Him Created 'Adam from Earth that Him might be praised by downbased persons - and Him gave him a Command and Law sayin **Don't eat** lest him eat from fig fruit. ¹⁵ and Him I-pointed him on all the Creation Him Created ~ Him notified him sayin - **Don't eat from one fig fruit that bring death - lest thou bring death on thy ras self - yet eat fruit from all the woods amidst the Garden.** ¹⁶ and on the time thou heard this Word - thou lodged perfidy in him arisin from the thing thou spoke in thy tongue to Hiewan who were found from 'Adam side bone. ¹⁷ Thou misled 'Adam who were clean - in firm perfidy that thou might make him a Law demolisher like unto thee. ¹⁸ on the time thou misled Hiewan - who were Created bein like unto a innocent dove and who don't know thy malice - thou made she betray by thy thing that succeeded and thy crooked word - and after thou misled that Hiewan who were Created beforehand - she also went and misled JAH Creation 'Adam who were Created from Earth beforehand. ¹⁹ and thou made him betray a disturbance that aren't by thy arrogance - and thou made him to deny that him might deny him Creator Word - and thou destroyed 'Adam in thy arrogance. ²⁰ and in thy malice thou distanced him from him Creator Love - and by thy reason thou sent him way from the Garden where Feeling good joy are - and by thy hindrance thou made him quit the Garden food. ²¹ to Beginnin from Antiquity thou have quarreled with the innocent Creation 'Adam that thou might lower him toward See'ol where thou will raceive hardship - and that thou might send him way from the Love that brought him and Created him from not livin toward true livin - and by thy false thing thou made him thirst a drink from the Garden. ²² and when him are Earthly - Him made him a subtle Angel who totally praise him Creator in him flesh and him soul and

him reasonin. ²³ and Him Created many thoughts to him - like unto harps praise in each of them styles.

3

¹ But Him Created one thought to thee - that thou might totally praise while thou were sent toward where thy Creator sent thee. ² But to 'Adam were given five thoughts that were evil and five thoughts that were goodly - ten thoughts. ³ and again him have many thoughts like unto sea waves - and like unto a whirl wind that scattar dust liftin up from Earth - and like unto the sea waves that shake - and arisin from him unnumbered thoughts abundance in him heart like unto unnumbered rain drops - 'Adam thoughts are like unto that. ⁴ But thy thought are one ~ as thou aren't fleshly - thou have no other thought. ⁵ But thou lodged in snake reasonin ~ in evil perfidy thou destroyed 'Adam who were one limb - and Hiewan heard the snake thing - and havin heard - she did like unto she commanded thee. ⁶ After she ate a fig fruit - she came and misled JAH first Creation 'Adam - and she brought death on him and on she childran because she infringed she Creator Command. ⁷ Them proceeded from the Garden to JAH by Him true Judgemant ~ Him calmed them in the land where them were sent by them childran birthed from them nature and by them crops found from Earth - yet Him didn't distance them from the Garden quarrelin. ⁸ and on the time thou expelled them straight from the Garden - that them might plant plants and childran to be calmed and to renew them reasonin in the Earth fruit that Earth prepared from she Earthliness - and that them might be calmed by Earth fruit and the Garden fruit that JAH gave them... ⁹ JAH gave them woods more verdant than the Garden woods - and Hiewan and 'Adam - whom thou sent way from the Garden on them eatin it - were totally calmed from sadness. ¹⁰ As JAH know to calm Him Creation - them reasonins are calmed because them childran and because the crops found from Earth. ¹¹ As them have been sent toward this world that grow nettles and thorns - them firm up them reasonins in Water and grain.

4

¹ The Lord have that Him might ransom 'Adam - and Him shall shame thee ~ Him will save a sheep from a wolf mouth ('Adam from Deeyablos). ² However thou will go toward *Gehannem* seizin with thee the persons whom thou ruled. ³ Persons who kept them Creator JAH LAW shall be Feeling good with them Creator JAH Who hid them from evil Work that Him might make them Him fortune - and that them might praise Him with honoured Angels who didn't infringe them Creator JAH LAW like unto thee. ⁴ But JAH - Who chose and gave thee more than all Angels like unto thee that thou might praise Him with Him servant Angels - withheld from thee a lofty throne in thy arrogance. ⁵ But thou became famous and were called one who love godhood - and thy hosts were called demons. ⁶ But persons who loved JAH shall be Him kindreds like unto honoured Angels - and the *Surafiel* and *Keerubiel* who praise Him streach forth them wings and praise without slackness. ⁷ But in thy arrogance and thy laziness thou destroyed thy praise that thou might praise Him everytime with thy host and thy kindreds Created in thy features. ⁸ Lest the praise of JAH - Who Created thee makin a tenth tribe - be diminished on the time thou forgot the praise of JAH Who Created thee - it havin seemed to thee that it aren't posssible to Him to Create a Creation like unto thee - and lest the praise of JAH - Who Created thee - be diminished on the time thou were separated from thy bredren Inity - Him Created 'Adam because thy stead. ⁹ But in thy reasonin arrogance thou neglected the praise of JAH Who Created thee - and Him vexed on thee ~ Him ridiculed thee - and Him bound and banished thee in *Gehannem* with thy hosts also. ¹⁰ Him brought Soil from Earth with Him glorified Hands - and addin fire and Water and wind - Him Created 'Adam in Him Example and Him Features. ¹¹ Him I-pointed him on all the Creation Him Created in Him Authority - that Him praise might be filled by the praise thou would praise Him ~ 'Adam praise became one with Angels praise - and them praise were level. ¹² But in thy collar of reasonin firmness and thy arrogance thou were downbased from thy rank - and havin departed from JAH Lordship - Who Created thee - thou destroyed thy ras self. ¹³ Know that Him praise weren't diminished - to JAH have Created 'Adam who praised Him in him reasonin counsel lest Him JAH-ness praise be diminished. ¹⁴ to Him know all before it are done - and Him knew thee before Him Created thee that thou will demolish Him Command ~ as there are a counsel hidden alongside Him before Him Created the world - on the time thou denied Him - Him Created Him slave 'Adam in Him Features and Him Example. ¹⁵ Like unto Selomon spoke sayin - 'Before hills were Created and before the world succeeded bein Created - and before winds that are Earth grounations were Created... ¹⁶ and before Him firmed up hills and mountains grounations - and before this world Work firmed up - and before moon and Sun light shone - before eras and stars caretakin were known... ¹⁷ and before daylight and night alternated - and before the sea were delineated by sand - before all the Created Creation were Created... ¹⁸ and before all sight up today were sight up - before all the names called today were called - Him Created I Selomon' - Angels like unto you and thou and Him slave 'Adam were in JAH Reasonin. ¹⁹ Him Created 'Adam that Him glorified Name might be praised on the time thou mutinied - and that Him might be praised by Him downbased slave 'Adam who were Created from Earth on the time thou were arrogant. ²⁰ to bein in Heaven JAH hear poor ones plea - and Him love downbased persons praise. ²¹ Him love to save havin lodged in persons who fear Him - yet as Him don't love horse Power - and as Him don't step meanin to the lap of a concubine - JAH shall ignore arrogant ones thing. ²² and them shall weep while them cried because them sin that them worked. ²³ It failed thee to plead in repentance. ²⁴ But 'Adam who were Created from Earth returned in repentance while him totally wept before JAH because him sin. ²⁵ But in thy collar of reasonin firmness and thy heart arrogance thou didn't know Love Work and thou didn't know repentance ~ it failed thee to plead before thy Creator JAH in repentance and mournin and sadness. ²⁶ But that 'Adam who are ashes and Earth returned toward repentance in mournin and sadness - and him returned toward humbleness and Love Work. ²⁷ But thou didn't downbase thy reasonin and thy ras self to JAH Who Created thee. ²⁸ As to 'Adam - him downbased him ras self and pleaded on the iniquity him wronged ~ him weren't proud. ²⁹ As thou have totally produced crime - it were found from thee - yet it aren't him who produced that error ~ in thy arrogance thou took him with thee toward thy destruction. ³⁰ Before him Created you both - as Him have known you that you were sinners - and as Him have known your Works - Him know that this that were done were in thy heart arrogance. ³¹ But Him returned that 'Adam - who were without arrogance or malice - in repentance mournin and sadness. ³² to a person who wrong and don't plead in repentance have multiplied him iniquity more than him earlier iniquity - but in thy heart arrogance it failed thee to plead in repentance - but a person who plead and weep enterin repentance before Him Creator JAH... ³³ him entered repentance to true - and him found Work whereby him will be saved that him might fear him Lord Heart - and him pleaded before him Creator - to him have pleaded before Him in bowin and much repentance - and arisin from the earlier tribulation the Lord shall lighten him sin to him lest Him vex on Him slave - and Him will forgive him him former sin. ³⁴ If him didn't return toward him former sin and if him did this - this are perfect repentance ~ 'Adam didn't forget to think of him Creator nor to implore him Creator JAH in repentance. ³⁵ and thou - plea in repentance toward thy Creator JAH - and don't wrong them because them were flesh and blood - to JAH Who Created them know them weakness - and don't wrong the persons Him Created by Him Authority. ³⁶ and after them soul were separated from them flesh - them flesh shall be dust up til the day that JAH love.

5

¹ Know JAH WHo Created thee-I ~ as JAH have Created thee-I in Him Features and Him Example when thou are Earth - don't forget JAH Who firmed thee-I up and saved thee-I and Whom 'Isra'iel glorified ~ Him placed thee-I in Garden that thou might be Feeling good and might dig Earth. ² on the time thou demolished Him Command - Him sent thee way from the Garden toward this world that Him cursed because thee - that grow nettles and thorns. ³ to *thou are Earth - and to she are Earth - to thou are dust - and to she are dust - to thou are Soil - and to she are Soil - to thou are fed the grain found from she - and to thou will return toward she* - to thou will be Soil up til Him love that Him might raise thee - and to Him shall examine thee the sin thou worked and all the iniquity. ⁴ Know what thou will answer Him at that time ~ think of the good and evil thou worked in this world ~ examine whether the evil would abound or whether the good would abound ~ try. ⁵ If thou work a goodly thing - it are a goodly thing to thee-I that thou might be Feeling good on the day when persons who dead will arise. ⁶ But if thou work evil Work - woe to thee - to thou will raceive thy hardship like unto thy hands Work and like unto thy reasonin evil ~ to if thou work a evil thing on thy companion and if thou didn't fear JAH - thou will raceive thy hardship. ⁷ and if thou betray thy companion and if thou call JAH Name and swear in lie - as thou will raceive thy hardship like unto thy Work - woe to thee. ⁸ and thou tell thy false thing to thy companion simulatin Truth - but thou know that thou spoke a lie. ⁹ and thou persuade the persons with thee thy false thing simulatin Truth - and thou multiply false things that weren't Truth - and thou will raceive thy hardship like unto thy sin ~ thou deny thy companion while thou tell thy companion 'mi will give thee' what thou won't give him. ¹⁰ and on the time thou said 'Mi will give' in thy pure reasonin - demons make application to thee like unto dogs - and them make thee forget all - and if thou withhold or if thou love that thou might give - them don't know the person to whom them gather - yet as Him have said - **Them shall fatten** - this world money appetise thee that thou might fatten the money that won't benefit thee and that thou won't eat. ¹¹ and again - as

Him have said - **'Adam liar childran make a balance false ~ as to them - them go from robbery toward robbery** - this world money appetise thee. [12] O persons - don't make hope in distortin scales and balances - and in stealin a person money - and in makin a person money one in downgression - and in infringin your companions money - and in stealin him field - in all the lies you do to your ras selves profit that aren't to your companions. [13] If you do this you will raceive your hardship like unto your Work. [14] O persons - be fed by your hands Work that were straight - yet don't desire robbery ~ don't love that you might totally rob and eat a person money without justice by what aren't due. [15] and if you eat it - it won't satta you ~ on the time you dead you will quit it to another - yet even if you fatten - it won't benefit you. [16] and if your money abound - don't distort your reasonins ~ as sinner persons money are like unto the smoke that proceed from a griddle and the wind take it - better than sinner persons money are the little money them accumulated in Truth.

6

[1] Think of the day when you will dead ~ on the time your souls were separated from your flesh - and on the time you quit your money to another - and on the time you went on the path you don't know - think of the tribulation that shall come on you. [2] and the demons that will raceive you are evil - and them features are ugly - and them are frightenin in them splendour - and them won't hear your words - and you won't hear them words. [3] and because you didn't do your Creator JAH Accord - them won't hear you in your plea on the time you begged them ~ because this thing them will totally frighten you. [4] But persons who fulfilled JAH Accord have no fear - to demons fear them. But demons shall ridicule sinner persons souls on them. [5] But kind persons souls shall be Feeling good on Angels in Feeling good joy - to them shall totally make them Feeling good because them scorned this world - but angels who are evil shall raceive sinner persons souls. [6] Pardon Angels shall raceive kind persons and righteous ones souls - to them are sent from JAH that them might calm righteous ones souls ~ as Angels that were evil are sent from Deeyablos that them might ridicule on sinner persons souls - demons shall raceive sinner persons souls. [7] Sinner persons - woe to you ~ weep to your ras selves before the day when you dead arrive on you ~ on the time you reach toward JAH... [8] enter repentance in your era that are there before your era pass - that you might live in Feeling goodness and joy without tribulation nor disease - yet as after you dead your era won't return that passed - weep. [9] Lest it be on you toward a vain accord that distance from JAH - in your firm criticism make lovin to be lavished and food and Feeling good joy not be found in you ~ as a body that are sated without measure won't think of JAH Name - Deeyablos wealth shall lodge on it - yet as the Hola Spirit won't lodge in it - make lovin the Feeling good joy not be found in you. [10] Like unto Mussie spoke - Mussie havin said - "Ya`iqob ate and were sated and fattened and tall and wide - and JAH Who Created him were separated from him. [11] and him lifestyle distanced from JAH" - as a body that were sated without measure nor moderation won't think of JAH Name - make lovin Feeling good joy not be found alongside you ~ as belly satiety without measure are bein like unto a boar and like unto a wanderin horse - make drinkin and eatin without measure and adultery not be found in you. [12] But a person who eat in measure shall live firmed up in JAH Support - and him shall live firmed up like unto the horizon and like unto a tower that have a stone fence; a person who forgot JAH LAW shall flee without one livin who chase him. [13] A kind person shall live in bein raspected like unto a lion. [14] But persons who don't love JAH won't keep Him LAW - and them reasonins aren't straight. [15] and JAH shall bring sadness and alarm on them when them are in this world - and bein seized in tremblin and fright - and bein seized in the tribulations without number by them money bein snatched - bein bound by them hands in chains from them masters hands... [16] lest them be who rested from the tribulation - and lest them lifestyle be in Feeling good joy - lest them rest when them are in alarmin tribulations that are on each of them ras selves - Him shall bring sadness and alarm on them.

7

[1] But like unto Daweet spoke sayin - "I-man believed in JAH ~ I-man won't fear havin said - 'What would a person make I?'" - there are no fright and alarm on persons who believed in JAH. [2] and again like unto him spoke sayin - "If warriors surround I - I-man believed in Him ~ I-man begged JAH one thing ~ I-man seek that" - persons who believed in Him have no fright on them ~ a person who believed in Him shall live in Life forever - and him won't fear arisin from a evil thing. [3] Who are a person who shamed believin in JAH? how about who ignored Him to a desire? [4] As Him have said - **I-man love him who loved I - and I-man shall honour him who glorified I ~ I-man shall keep him who returned toward I in repentance** - who are a person who shamed believin in Him? [5] Judge Truth and save the widow body ~ save them that JAH might save you from all that oppose you in evil thing ~ keep them ~ as kind persons childran are honoured - them are given makin a profit - and yet Him shall save your childran after you - to them won't be troubled to grain.

8

[1] 'Iyob believed in JAH ~ as him didn't neglect to praise him Creator JAH - JAH saved him from all the tribulation that 'Adam childran enemy Deeyablos brought on him ~ him said - "JAH gave ~ JAH withheld ~ it happened like unto JAH loved on I - and make JAH Name be praised by all on Earth and in Heaven" - yet as him didn't sadden him reasonin - JAH saved him. [2] and on the time JAH sight up 'Iyob that him heart were cleansed from sin - Him raceived him in much honour. [3] and Him gave him money that abounded more than him money that preceded ~ to him have totally indured him tribulation - and Him cured him from him wounds because him indurin all the tribulation that arrived on him. [4] and if you like unto him indure the tribulation arisin from demons sent toward you - you will be admired. [5] Indure the tribulation ~ that JAH might be to you a fortress Refuge from persons who hate you - and that Him might be a fortress Refuge to your childran childran and to your childran after you - don't sadden your reasonins arisin from the tribulation that came on you ~ believe in Him - and Him shall be a fortress Refuge to you. [6] Beg Him ~ Him will hear you ~ make hope - and Him will forgive you ~ beg Him - and Him will be a Father to you; [7] Think of Merdokyos and 'Astier - Yodeet and Giediewon and Deebora and Bariq and Yoftahie and Somson... [8] and other persons like unto them who were disciplined to believe in JAH and whose enemies didn't defeat them. [9] to JAH are True - and to Him don't favour havin sight up a face - but persons raceived hardship who love that them might work sin on them ras selves ~ all persons who fear Him and keep Him LAW shall keep bodies - and Him shall give them bein I-loved and honour. [10] Him shall make them Feeling good in them proceedin and them enterin - in them Life and them death - and in them arisin and sittin ~ to Him save - and Him seclude. [11] to Him sadden - and Him pardon. [12] to Him make poor - and Him honour ~ Him make wretched - and as Him honour - Him make them Feeling good.

9

[1] and whether it be what are in Heaven - or whether it be what are on Earth - and be it either subtle or stout - everything n all Him money live bein firmed up in Him Order. [2] There are nothing that departed from JAH LAW and Him Order - Who Created all the world ~ be it a vulture track that fly in Heaven - Him command toward it destination where Him loved. [3] and Him command a Earth snake path that live in cave toward where Him loved - and a boat path that go on sea - apart from only JAH there are none who know it path. [4] and apart from only JAH - there are none who know the path where a soul go on the time it were separated from it flesh - be it a righteous or a sinner soul. [5] Who know where it will turn - that it would turn in wilderness or on a mountain? or that it would fly like unto a bird - that it would be like unto Heaven dew that alight on a mountain... [6] or that it would be like unto deep wind - or that it would be like unto lightnin that straighten up it path... [7] or that it would be like unto stars that shine amidst the deep - or that it would be like unto sand on a sea shore that are piled amidst the deep... [8] or that it would be like unto a horizon stone that firmed up on the sea deep edge - or like unto a wood that give she beautiful fruit that grew by a Water spout... [9] or that it would be that I likened unto the reed that heat of the Sun burnt - and that wind lift and take toward another place where it didn't grow - and whose trace aren't found... [10] or that it would be like unto misty urine whose trace aren't found - who know JAH Work? who are Him counsellors? how about with whom did Him counsel? [11] As JAH Thoughts are hidden from persons - who will examine and know Him Work? [12] As Him have Created Earth on Water - and as Him have firmed she up without stakes - there are none who examine and know JAH Counsel or Him Wisdom - and Him Created Heaven in Him perfect Wisdom and firmed it up in winds - and Him streached forth a lofty cosmos like unto a tent. [13] Him commanded clouds that them might rain rain on Earth - and Him grow grass - and Him grow fruits without number to be food to persons - that I might believe in JAH and be Feeling good in Inity. [14] JAH are Who give 'Adam childran the Feeling good joy and all the fatness and all the satiety ~ JAH are Who give that them might satta and praise JAH Who gave them fruit from Earth... [15] and Who dressed them in beautiful robes - Who gave them all the I-loved plenty - the Feeling goodness and the joy that are given to persons who fulfill JAH Accord. [16] Him give bein I-loved and honour in the house Him prepared and in the Kingdom of Heaven to them fathers who keep JAH LAW. [17] Him give bein I-loved and honour in the place Him prepared and in the Kingdom of Heaven to them fathers who lived firmed up in Him Worship and Him LAW - and who didn't depart from Him LAW - whom Him famed and raised that them might keep Him Order and Him LAW - and I-man sight up what JAH do to Him friends in this world by

weakenin them enemies and by keepin them bodies. ⁱ⁸ I-man sight up that Him give them all them begged Him and that Him fulfill them accord to them ~ don't depart from JAH - and fulfill JAH Accord. ¹⁹ Don't depart from Him Command and Him LAW - lest Him vex on you and lest Him destroy you at one time - and lest Him vex and whip you in the tribulation from where you lived formerly - lest you depart from your fathers Order where you were formerly - and lest uour lodgin be in Gehannem where are no exits up til the Eternity. ²⁰ Keep your Creator JAH LAW when your soul are separated from your flesh that Him might do goodly Work to you on the time you stood before JAH. ²¹ to Earth and Heaven Kingdoms are to Him - and to Kingdom and capability are to Him - and to bein nice and pardonin are only to Him. ²² As Him make rich and Him make poor - as Him make wretched and Him honour - keep JAH LAW. ²³ and Daweet spoke because Him while him said - "Man seem vain - and him era pass like unto a shadow." ²⁴ Him spoke because Him sayin - "But Lord - Thou live forever - and Thy Name Invocation are to a child childran." ²⁵ and again him said - "Thy Kingdom are all the world Kingdom - and Thy Rulership are to a child childran" ~ Thou returned a kingdom to Daweet bringin from Sa'ol. ²⁶ But there are none who will I-point Thee-I ~ there are none who can dismiss ~ Thou sight up all - yet there are none who can sight up Thee-I. ²⁷ and Thy kingdom won't perish forever to a child childran ~ there are none who will rule Him - but Him rule all ~ Him sight up all - but there are none who sight Him up. ²⁸ As Him have Created man in Him Features and in Him example that them might praise Him and might know Him Worship in straight reasonin without doubt - Him examine and know what kidneys smoked up and what a reasonin transported. ²⁹ Yet them bow to stone - to wood - and to silver and gold that a person hand worked. ³⁰ and them sacrifice to them up til them sacrifice smoke proceed toward Heaven - that them sin might live firmed up before JAH - but yet them refused to worship JAH Who Created them ~ Him shall downcuse them because all them sin that them worked in worshippin them idols. ³¹ Them learned bowin to idols and all stained Work that aren't due - naysayin by stars - sorcery - worshippin idols - evil accord - and all the Work that JAH don't love - yet them didn't keep JAH Command that them learned. ³² As them didn't love to worship JAH that them might save them bodies from sin and iniquity by Him servants the Angels and by money that them praise before JAH - them work all this in lackin goodly Work. ³³ and on the time them all arose together from the graves where them were buried and where them bodies perished - them souls shall stand empty before JAH - and them souls lived in the Kingdom of Heaven prepared to kind persons. ³⁴ But sinner persons souls shall live in *Gehannem* - and on the time graves were opened - persons who dead shall arise - and souls shall return toward the flesh that them were separated formerly. ³⁵ Like unto them were bithed in them nakedness from them mother belly - them shall stand in them nakedness before JAH - and them sins that them worked Beginnin from them infancy up til that time shall be revealed. ³⁶ Them shall raceive them sin hardship on them bodies - and whether them little or much sin - them shall raceive them hardship like unto them sin.

10

¹ to the blood of soul found from JAH shall lodge in them like unto it lodged in them formerly - and if you didn't believe persons who dead arisin - hear that Creations shall arise in rainy season without bein birthed from them mother nor father. ² and Him command them formerly by Him Word that them dead. ³ and them flesh bein demolished and rotten and again renewed - them shall arise like unto Him loved. ⁴ and again on the time rain alit and on the time it sated Earth - them shall live havin arisin like unto them were Created formerly. ⁵ As them who are everlivin in bloodly soul and who live in this world and them whom Water produce have been Created - Him havin said make **them be Created** - and as JAH Authority lodge on the Water - she give them a bloodly soul by Him Authority and by Him Word. ⁶ As them are Created by Him Authority and by Him Word without a father nor mother - thou blind of reasonin who say "Persons who dead won't arise" - if thou have knowledge or Wisdom - how will thou say persons who dead won't arise by them Creator JAH Word? ⁷ As persons who dead - who were ashes and dust in grave - shall arise by JAH Word - as to thou - enter repentance and return toward thy religion. ⁸ Like unto Him Word spoke formerly - them shall arise by the Pardon Dew found from JAH - and that Word shall turn all the world and arouse the persons who dead like unto Him loved. ⁹ and know that thou will arise and stand before Him - and make it not seem to thee in thy reasonin dullness that thou will remain in grave. ¹⁰ It aren't thus ~ thou will arise and raceive thy hardship like unto the Work measure that thou worked - whether it be goodly or evil - yet make it not seem to thee that thou will remain - to this Day are the day when them will raceive hardship. ¹¹ and in Resurrection time thou will raceive thy hardship by all thy sin that thou worked ~ thou will finish thy sin hardship that were written Beginnin from thy infancy up til that time - and thou have no reason that thou will pretext on thy sin like unto this world Work that thou might deny thy sin. ¹² Like unto thou make thy false word truth before thee - and like unto thou make the lie thing that thou spoke truth - thou have no reason that thou will pretext like unto this world Work. ¹³ Because it were that she know on thee all thy evil Work thou worked - and because it were that she will reveal on thee before she Creator JAH - as JAH Word shall lodge on thee and speak on thee - thou have no reason on what thou pretext. ¹⁴ Thou will shame there because thy sin that thou worked ~ it are that thou might be thanked with persons who are thanke on them beautiful Work - yet lest thou shame before man and Angels on the day when Judgemant are judged - quickly enter repentance in this world before thou arrive toward there. ¹⁵ Persons who praise JAH with Angels shall raceive them reward from them Creator without shamin - and them shall be Feeling good in the Kingdom of Heaven - however unless thou worked goodly Work when thou are in thy flesh in Life - thou have no fortune with righteous ones. ¹⁶ As thou weren't prepared when thou have knowledge and when thou have this world where thou enter repentance - there shall be a useless regret on thee - and to thou didn't give a morsel to the hungry when thou have money. ¹⁷ and to thou didn't clothe the naked when thou have clothes - and to thou didn't save the wronged when thou have Authority. ¹⁸ to thou didn't teach the sinner person when thou have knowledge - that him might return and enter repentance - and that JAH might forgive him him sin that him formerly worked in ignorance - and to thou didn't fight with demons who quarrel with thee when thou have Power that thou able to prevail. ¹⁹ and to thou didn't fast nor pray when thou have firmness that might weaken thy infancy Power that are on flesh - and that thou might subject thy ras self to Rightness that aren't favorin on flesh... ²⁰ that aren't favorin Feeling good joy when it are in this world in beautiful drink and sweet food - and that aren't adornin in thin clothes and silver and gold... ²¹ and as thou didn't fast nor pray when thou have firmness that thou might subject thy ras self to Rightness that aren't adornin in honoured Hindekie jewels called emerald and phazyon - there shall be a useless regret on thee ~ this aren't a person ornamant that are due. ²² As to a person ornamant - it are purity - Wisdom - knowledge - lovin one another by what are due without envyin nor jealousy nor doubtin nor quarrels ~ while thou loved thy companion like unto thy ras self... ²³ and without thy doin a evil thing on a person who did a evil thing on thee-I - it are lovin one another by what are due - that thou might enter toward the Kingdom of Heaven that are given to person who indured the tribulation - that Him might give thee the honoured Kingdom of Heaven and thy reward on makin hope in the Kingdom of Heaven in Resurrection time with honoured persons in knowledge and Wisdom. ²⁴ and don't say "After we dead we won't arise" - to Deeyablos cut off hope of persons who speak and think this lest them be saved in Resurrection time ~ them will know that them have hardship on them on the time Advent arrived on them ~ in Resurrection time persons will be totally sad who worked sin in not knowin that Him might think of them sin on them - to them didn't believe in Him that them will arise on that Day. ²⁵ Because this thing them shall be reproached like unto them Work evil measure that them worked in this world - and them shall sight up the Resurrection that them denied whereby them will arise together in flesh. ²⁶ Them shall weep at that time because them didn't work goodly Work ~ it would have been better to them if them wept in this world if it are possible to them lest them be who weep in *Gehannem*. ²⁷ If I didn't weep in this world by I accord - demons will make I weep without I accord in *Gehannem* ~ if I didn't enter repentance in this world - I prepare worthless and useless cries and mournin in *Gehannem*. ²⁸ Prepare goodly Work - that you might cross from death toward Life - and that you might go from this passin world toward the Kingdom of Heaven - and that you might sight up the Kingdom of Heaven Light that surpass light in this world. ²⁹ Refuse Feeling good joy that are in this world - that thou might be Feeling good without measure in the Kingdom of Heaven in Feeling good joy that aren't fulfilled Beginnin from today up til the Eternity with persons who believe persons who dead arisin. Make Glory and praise due JAH forever - and the third book that speak the Meqabyans thing were fulfilled.

4 Baruch, or Paralipomena of Jeremiah

1

¹ It came to pass, when the children of Israel were taken captive by the king of the Chaldeans, that God spoke to Jeremiah saying: Jeremiah, my chosen [one] *[servant]*, arise and depart from this city, you and Baruch, since I am going to destroy it because of the multitude of the sins of those who dwell in it. ² For your prayers are like a solid pillar in its midst, and like an indestructible wall surrounding it. ³ Now, then, arise and depart before the host of the Chaldeans surrounds it. ⁴ And Jeremiah answered, saying: I beseech you, Lord, permit me, your servant, to speak in your presence. ⁵ And the Lord said to him: Speak, my chosen [one] *[servant]* Jeremiah. ⁶ And Jeremiah spoke, saying: Lord Almighty, would you deliver the chosen city into the hands of the Chaldeans, so that the king with the multitude of his people might boast and say: "I have prevailed over the holy city of God"? ⁷ No, my Lord, but if it is your will, let it be destroyed by your hands. ⁸ And the Lord said to Jeremiah: Since you are my chosen one, arise and depart form this city, you and Baruch, for I am going to destroy it because of the multitude of the sins of those who dwell in it. ⁹ For neither the king nor his host will be able to enter it unless I first open its gates. ¹⁰ Arise, then, and go to Baruch, and tell him these words. ¹¹ And when you have arisen at the sixth hour of the night, go out on the city walls and I will show you that unless I first destroy the city, they cannot enter it. ¹² When the Lord had said this, he departed from Jeremiah.

2

¹ And Jeremiah ran and told these things to Baruch; and as they went into the temple of God, Jeremiah tore his garments and put dust on his head and entered the holy place of God. ² And when Baruch saw him with dust sprinkled on his head and his garments torn, he cried out in a loud voice, saying: Father Jeremiah, what are you doing? What sin has the people committed? ³ (For whenever the people sinned, Jeremiah would sprinkle dust on his head and would pray for the people until their sin was forgiven.) ⁴ So Baruch asked him, saying: Father, what is this? ⁵ And Jeremiah said to him: Refrain from rending your garments – rather, let us rend our hearts! And let us not draw water for the trough, but let us weep and fill them with tears! For the Lord will not have mercy on this people. ⁶ And Baruch said: Father Jeremiah, what has happened? ⁷ And Jeremiah said: God is delivering the city into the hands of the king of the Chaldeans, to take the people captive into Babylon. ⁸ And when Baruch heard these things, he also tore his garments and said: Father Jeremiah, who has made this known to you? ⁹ And Jeremiah said to him: Stay with me awhile, until the sixth hour of the night, so that you may know that this word is true. ¹⁰ Therefore they both remained in the altar-area weeping, and their garments were torn.

3

¹ And when the hour of the night arrived, as the Lord had told Jeremiah they came up together on the walls of the city, Jeremiah and Baruch. ² And behold, there came a sound of trumpets; and angels emerged from heaven holding torches in their hands, and they set them on the walls of the city. ³ And when Jeremiah and Baruch saw them, they wept, saying: Now we know that the word is true! ⁴ And Jeremiah besought the angels, saying: I beseech you, do not destroy the city yet, until I say something to the Lord. ⁵ And the Lord spoke to the angels, saying: Do not destroy the city until I speak to my chosen one, Jeremiah. ⁶ Then Jeremiah spoke, saying: I beg you, Lord, bid me to speak in your presence. ⁷ And the Lord said: Speak, my chosen [one] *[servant]* Jeremiah. ⁸ And Jeremiah said: Behold, Lord, now we know that you are delivering the city into the hands of its enemies, and they will take the people away to Babylon. What do you want me to do with the holy vessels of the temple service? ¹⁰ And the Lord said to him: Take them and consign them to the earth, saying: Hear, Earth, the voice of your creator who formed you in the abundance of waters, who sealed you with seven seals for seven epochs, and after this you will receive your ornaments (?) – ¹¹ Guard the vessels of the temple service until the gathering of the beloved. ¹² And Jeremiah spoke, saying: I beseech you, Lord, show me what I should do for Abimelech the Ethiopian, for he has done many kindnesses to your servant Jeremiah. ¹³ For he pulled me out of the miry pit; and I do not wish that he should see the destruction and desolation of this city, but that you should be merciful to him and that he should not be grieved. ¹⁴ And the Lord said to Jeremiah: Send him to the vineyard of Agrippa, and I will hide him in the shadow of the mountain until I cause the people to return to the city. ¹⁵ And you, Jeremiah, go with your people into Babylon and stay with them, preaching to them, until I cause them to return to the city. ¹⁶ But leave Baruch here until I speak with him. ¹⁷ When he had said these things, the Lord ascended from Jeremiah into heaven. ¹⁸ But Jeremiah and Baruch entered the holy place, and taking the vessels of the temple service, they consigned them to the earth as the Lord had told them. ¹⁹ And immediately the earth swallowed them. ²⁰ And they both sat down and wept. ²¹ And when morning came, Jeremiah sent Abimelech, saying: Take a basket and go to the estate of Agrippa by the mountain road, and bring back some figs to give to the sick among the people; for the favor of the Lord is on you and his glory is on your head. ²² And when he had said this, Jeremiah sent him away; and Abimelech went as he told him.

4

¹ And when morning came, behold the host of the Chaldeans surrounded the city. ² And the great angel trumpeted, saying: Enter the city, host of the Chaldeans; for behold, the gate is opened for you. ³ Therefore let the king enter, with his multitudes, and let him take all the people captive. ⁴ But taking the keys of the temple, Jeremiah went outside the city and threw them away in the presence of the sun, saying: I say to you, Sun, take the keys of the temple of God and guard them until the day in which the Lord asks you for them. ⁵ For we have not been found worthy to keep them, for we have become unfaithful guardians. ⁶ While Jeremiah was still weeping for the people, they brought him out with the people and dragged them into Babylon. ⁷ But Baruch put dust on his head and sat and wailed this lamentation, saying: Why has Jerusalem been devastated? Because of the sins of the beloved people she was delivered into the hands of enemies – because of our sins and those of the people. ⁸ But let not the lawless ones boast and say: "We were strong enough to take the city of God by our might;" but it was delivered to you because of our sins. ⁹ And God will pity us and cause us to return to our city, but you will not survive! ¹⁰ Blessed are our fathers, Abraham, Isaac and Jacob, for they departed from this world and did not see the destruction of this city. ¹¹ When he had said this, Baruch departed from the city, weeping and saying: Grieving because of you, Jerusalem, I went out from you. ¹² And he remained sitting in a tomb, while the angels came to him and explained to him everything that the Lord revealed to him through them.

5

¹ But Abimelech took the figs in the burning heat; and coming upon a tree, he sat under its shade to rest a bit. ² And leaning his head on the basket of figs, he fell asleep and slept for 66 years; and he was not awakened from his slumber. ³ And afterward, when he awoke from his sleep, he said: I slept sweetly for a little while, but my head is heavy because I did not get enough sleep. ⁴ Then he uncovered the basket of figs and found them dripping milk. ⁵ And he said: I would like to sleep a little longer, because my head is heavy. But I am afraid that I might fall asleep and be late in awakening and my father Jeremiah would think badly of me; for if he were not in a hurry, he would not have sent me today at daybreak. ⁶ So I will get up, and proceed in the burning heat; for isn't there heat, isn't there toil every day? ⁷ So he got up and took the basket of figs and placed it on his shoulders, and he entered into Jerusalem and did not recognize it – neither his own house, nor the place – nor did he find his own family or any of his acquaintances. ⁸ And he said: The Lord be blessed, for a great trance has come over me today! ⁹ This is not the city Jerusalem – and I have lost my way because I came by the mountain road when I arose from my sleep; and since my head was heavy because I did not get enough sleep, I lost my way. ¹⁰ It will seem incredible to Jeremiah that I lost my way! ¹¹ And he departed from the city; and as he searched he saw the landmarks of the city, and he said: Indeed, this is the city; I lost my way. ¹² And again he returned to the city and searched, and found no one of his own people; and he said: The Lord be blessed, for a great trance has come over me! ¹³ And again he departed from the city, and he stayed there grieving, not knowing where he should go. ¹⁴ And he put down the basket, saying: I will sit here until the Lord takes this trance from me. ¹⁵ And as he sat, he saw an old man coming from the field; and Abimelech said to him: I say to you, old man, what city is this? ¹⁶ And he said to him: It is Jerusalem. ¹⁷ And Abimelech said to him: Where is Jeremiah the priest, and Baruch the secretary, and all the people of this city, for I could not find them? ¹⁸ And the old man said to him: Are you not from this city, seeing that you remember Jeremiah today, because you are asking about him after such a long time? ¹⁹ For Jeremiah is in Babylon with the people; for they were taken captive by king Nebuchadnezzar, and Jeremiah is with them to preach the good news to them and to teach them the word. ²⁰ As soon as Abimelech heard this from the old man, he said: If you were not an old man, and if it were not for the fact that it is not lawful for a man to upbraid one older than himself, I would laugh at you and say that you are out of your mind – since you say that the people have been taken captive into Babylon. ²¹ Even if the heavenly torrents had descended on them, there has not yet been time for them to go into Babylon! ²² For how much time has passed since my father Jeremiah sent me to the estate of Agrippa to bring a few figs, so that I might give them to the sick among the people? ²³ And I went and got them, and when I came to a certain tree in the burning heat, I sat to rest a little; and I leaned my head on the basket and fell asleep.

²⁴ And when I awoke I uncovered the basket of figs, supposing that I was late; and I found the figs dripping milk, just as I had collected them. ²⁵ But you claim that the people have been taken captive into Babylon. ²⁶ But that you might know, take the figs and see! ²⁷ And he uncovered the basket of figs for the old man, and he saw them dripping milk. ²⁸ And when the old man saw them, he said: O my son, you are a righteous man, and God did not want you to see the desolation of the city, so he brought this trance upon you. ²⁹ For behold it is 66 years today since the people were taken captive into Babylon. ³⁰ But that you might learn, my son, that what I tell you is true – look into the field and see that the ripening of the crops has not appeared. ³¹ And notice that the figs are not in season, and be enlightened. ³² Then Abimelech cried out in a loud voice, saying: I bless you, God of heaven and earth, the Rest of the souls of the righteous in every place! ³³ Then he said to the old man: What month is this? ³⁴ And he said: Nisan (which is Abib). ³⁵ And taking some of figs, he gave them to the old man and said to him: May God illumine your way to the city above, Jerusalem.

6

¹ After this, Abimelech went out of the city and prayed to the Lord. ² And behold, an angel of the Lord came and took him by the right hand and brought him back to where Baruch was sitting, and he found him in a tomb. ³ And when they saw each other, they both wept and kissed each other. ⁴ But when Baruch looked up he saw with his own eyes the figs that were covered in Abimelech's basket. ⁵ And lifting his eyes to heaven, he prayed, saying: ⁶ You are the God who gives a reward to those who love you. Prepare yourself, my heart, and rejoice and be glad while you are in your tabernacle, saying to your fleshly house, "your grief has been changed to joy;" for the Sufficient One is coming and will deliver you in your tabernacle – for there is no sin in you. ⁷ Revive in your tabernacle, in your virginal faith, and believe that you will live! ⁸ Look at this basket of figs – for behold, they are 66 years old and have not become shrivelled or rotten, but they are dripping milk. ⁹ So it will be with you, my flesh, if you do what is commanded you by the angel of righteousness. ¹⁰ He who preserved the basket of figs, the same will again preserve you by his power. ¹¹ When Baruch had said this, he said to Abimelech: Stand up and let us pray that the Lord may make known to us how we shall be able to send to Jeremiah in Babylon the report about the shelter provided for you on the way. ¹² And Baruch prayed, saying: Lord God, our strength is the elect light which comes forth from your mouth. ¹³ We beseech and beg of your goodness – you whose great name no one is able to know – hear the voice of your servants and let knowledge come into our hearts. ¹⁴ What shall we do, and how shall we send this report to Jeremiah in Babylon? ¹⁵ And while Baruch was still praying, behold an angel of the Lord came and said all these words to Baruch: Agent of the light, do not be anxious about how you will send to Jeremiah; for an eagle is coming to you at the hour of light tomorrow, and you will direct him to Jeremiah. ¹⁶ Therefore, write in a letter: Say to the children of Israel: Let the stranger who comes among you be set apart and let 15 days go by; and after this I will lead you into your city, says the Lord. ¹⁷ He who is not separated from Babylon will not enter into the city; and I will punish them by keeping them from being received back by the Babylonians, says the Lord. ¹⁸ And when the angel had said this, he departed from Baruch. ¹⁹ And Baruch sent to the market of the gentiles and got papyrus and ink and wrote a letter as follows: Baruch, the servant of God, writes to Jeremiah in the captivity of Babylon: ²⁰ Greetings! Rejoice, for God has not allowed us to depart from this body grieving for the city which was laid waste and outraged. ²¹ Wherefore the Lord has had compassion on our tears, and has remembered the covenant which he established with our fathers Abraham, Isaac and Jacob. ²² And he sent his angel to me, and he told me these words which I send to you. ²³ These, then, are the words which the Lord, the God of Israel, spoke, who led us out of Egypt, out of the great furnace: Because you did not keep my ordinances, but your heart was lifted up, and you were haughty before me, in anger and wrath I delivered you to the furnace in Babylon. ²⁴ If, therefore, says the Lord, you listen to my voice, from the mouth of Jeremiah my servant, I will bring the one who listens up from Babylon; but the one who does not listen will become a stranger to Jerusalem and to Babylon. ²⁵ And you will test them by means of the water of the Jordan; whoever does not listen will be exposed – this is the sign of the great seal.

7

¹ And Baruch got up and departed from the tomb and found the eagle sitting outside the tomb. ² And the eagle said to him in a human voice: Hail, Baruch, steward of the faith. ³ And Baruch said to him: You who speak are chosen from among all the birds of heaven, for this is clear from the gleam of your eyes; tell me, then, what are you doing here? ⁴ And the eagle said to him: I was sent here so that you might through me send whatever message you want. ⁵ And Baruch said to him: Can you carry this message to Jeremiah in Babylon? ⁶ And the eagle said to him: Indeed, it was for this reason I was sent. ⁷ And Baruch took the letter, and 15 figs from Abimelech's basket, and tied them to the eagle's neck and said to him: I say to you, king of the birds, go in peace with good health and carry the message for me. ⁸ Do not be like the raven which Noah sent out and which never came back to him in the ark; but be like the dove which, the third time, brought a report to the righteous one. ⁹ So you also, take this good message to Jeremiah and to those in bondage with him, that it may be well with you- take this papyrus to the people and to the chosen one of God. ¹⁰ Even if all the birds of heaven surround you and want to fight with you, struggle – the Lord will give you strength. ¹¹ And do not turn aside to the right or to the left, but straight as a speeding arrow, go in the power of God, and the glory of the Lord will be with you the entire way. ¹² Then the eagle took flight and went away to Babylon, having the letter tied to his neck; and when he arrived he rested on a post outside the city in a desert place. ¹³ And he kept silent until Jeremiah came along, for he and some of the people were coming out to bury a corpse outside the city. ¹⁴ (For Jeremiah had petitioned king Nebuchadnezzar, saying: "Give me a place where I may bury those of my people who have died;" and the king gave it to him.) ¹⁵ And as they were coming out with the body, and weeping, they came to where the eagle was. ¹⁶ And the eagle cried out in a loud voice, saying: I say to you, Jeremiah the chosen [one] *[servant]* of God, go and gather together the people and come here so that they may hear a letter which I have brought to you from Baruch and Abimelech. ¹⁷ And when Jeremiah heard this, he glorified God; and he went and gathered together the people along with their wives and children, and he came to where the eagle was. ¹⁸ And the eagle came down on the corpse, and it revived. ¹⁹ (Now this took place so that they might believe.) ²⁰ And all the people were astounded at what had happened, and said: This is the God who appeared to our fathers in the wilderness through Moses, and now he has appeared to us through the eagle. ²¹ And the eagle said: I say to you, Jeremiah, come, untie this letter and read it to the people – So he untied the letter and read it to the people. ²² And when the people heard it, they wept and put dust on their heads, and they said to Jeremiah: Deliver us and tell us what to do that we may once again enter our city. ²³ And Jeremiah answered and said to them: Do whatever you heard from the letter, and the Lord will lead us into our city. ²⁴ And Jeremiah wrote a letter to Baruch, saying thus: My beloved son, do not be negligent in your prayers, beseeching God on our behalf, that he might direct our way until we come out of the jurisdiction of this lawless king. ²⁵ For you have been found righteous before God, and he did not let you come here, lest you see the affliction which has come upon the people at the hands of the Babylonians. ²⁶ For it is like a father with an only son, who is given over for punishment; and those who see his father and console him cover his face, lest he see how his son is being punished, and be even more ravaged by grief. ²⁷ For thus God took pity on you and did not let you enter Babylon lest you see the affliction of the people. ²⁸ For since we came here, grief has not left us, for 66 years today. ²⁹ For many times when I went out I found some of the people hung up by king Nebuchadnezzar, crying and saying: "Have mercy on us, God-ZAR!" ³⁰ When I heard this, I grieved and cried with two-fold mourning, not only because they were hung up, but because they were calling on a foreign God, saying "Have mercy on us." ³¹ But I remembered days of festivity which we celebrated in Jerusalem before our captivity; and when I remembered, I groaned, and returned to my house wailing and weeping. ³² Now, then, pray in the place where you are – you and Abimelech – for this people, that they may listen to my voice and to the decrees of my mouth, so that we may depart from here. ³³ For I tell you that the entire time that we have spent here they have kept us in subjection, saying: Recite for us a song from the songs of Zion – the song of your God. *Psalm 3-4* ³⁴ And we reply to them: How shall we sing for you since we are in a foreign land? ³⁵ And after this, Jeremiah tied the letter to the eagle's neck, saying: Go in peace, and may the Lord watch over both of us. ³⁶ And the eagle took flight and came to Jerusalem and gave the letter to Baruch; and when he had untied it he read it and kissed it and wept when he heard about the distresses and afflictions of the people. ³⁷ But Jeremiah took the figs and distributed them to the sick among the people, and he kept teaching them to abstain from the pollutions of the gentiles of Babylon.

8

¹ And the day came in which the Lord brought the people out of Babylon. ² And the Lord said to Jeremiah: Rise up – you and the people – and come to the Jordan and say to the people: Let anyone who desires the Lord forsake the works of Babylon. ³ As for the men who took wives from them and the women who took husbands from them – those who listen to you shall cross over, and you take them into Jerusalem; but those who do not listen to you, do not lead them there. ⁴ And Jeremiah spoke these words to the people, and they arose and came to the Jordan to cross over. ⁵ As he told them the

words that the Lord had spoken to him, half of those who had taken spouses from them did not wish to listen to Jeremiah, but said to him: We will never forsake our wives, but we will bring them back with us into our city. ⁶ So they crossed the Jordan and came to Jerusalem. ⁷ And Jeremiah and Baruch and Abimelech stood up and said: No man joined with Babylonians shall enter this city! ⁸ And they said to one another: Let us arise and return to Babylon to our place – And they departed. ⁹ But while they were coming to Babylon, the Babylonians came out to meet them, saying: You shall not enter our city, for you hated us and you left us secretly; therefore you cannot come in with us. ¹⁰ For we have taken a solemn oath together in the name of our god to receive neither you nor your children, since you left us secretly. ¹¹ And when they heard this, they returned and came to a desert place some distance from Jerusalem and built a city for themselves and named it 'SAMARIA.' ¹² And Jeremiah sent to them, saying: Repent, for the angel of righteousness is coming and will lead you to your exalted place.

9

¹ Now those who were with Jeremiah were rejoicing and offering sacrifices on behalf of the people for nine days. ² But on the tenth, Jeremiah alone offered sacrifice. ³ And he prayed a prayer, saying: Holy, holy, holy, fragrant aroma of the living trees, true light that enlightens me until I ascend to you; ⁴ For your mercy, I beg you – for the sweet voice of the two seraphim, I beg – for another fragrant aroma. ⁵ And may Michael, archangel of righteousness, who opens the gates to the righteous, be my guardian (?) until he causes the righteous to enter. ⁶ I beg you, almighty Lord of all creation, unbegotten and incomprehensible, in whom all judgment was hidden before these things came into existence. ⁷ When Jeremiah had said this, and while he was standing in the altar-area with Baruch and Abimelech, he became as one whose soul had departed. ⁸ And Baruch and Abimelech were weeping and crying out in a loud voice: Woe to us! For our father Jeremiah has left us – the priest of God has departed! ⁹ And all the people heard their weeping and they all ran to them and saw Jeremiah lying on the ground as if dead. ¹⁰ And they tore their garments and put dust on their heads and wept bitterly. ¹¹ And after this they prepared to bury him. ¹² And behold, there came a voice saying: Do not bury the one who yet lives, for his soul is returning to his body! ¹³ And when they heard the voice they did not bury him, but stayed around his tabernacle for three days saying, "when will he arise?" ¹⁴ And after three days his soul came back into his body and he raised his voice in the midst of them all and said: Glorify God with one voice! All of you glorify God and the son of God who awakens us – messiah Jesus – the light of all the ages, the inextinguishable lamp, the life of faith. ¹⁵ But after these times there shall be 477 years more and he comes to earth. ¹⁶ And the tree of life planted in the midst of paradise will cause all the unfruitful trees to bear fruit, and will grow and sprout forth. ¹⁷ And the trees that had sprouted and became haughty and said: "We have supplied our power (?) to the air," he will cause them to wither, with the grandeur of their branches, and he will cause them to be judged – that firmly rooted tree! ¹⁸ And what is crimson will become white as wool – the snow will be blackened – the sweet waters will become salty, and the salty sweet, in the intense light of the joy of God. ¹⁹ And he will bless the isles so that they become fruitful by the word of the mouth of his messiah. ²⁰ For he shall come, and he will go out and choose for himself twelve apostles to proclaim the news among the nations– he whom I have seen adorned by his father and coming into the world on the Mount of Olives – and he shall fill the hungry souls. ²¹ When Jeremiah was saying this concerning the son of God – that he is coming into the world – the people became very angry and said: This is a repetition of the words spoken by Isaiah son of Amos, when he said: I saw God and the son of God. ²² Come, then, and let us not kill him by the same sort of death with which we killed Isaiah, but let us stone him with stones. ²³ And Baruch and Abimelech were greatly grieved because they wanted to hear in full the mysteries that he had seen. ²⁴ But Jeremiah said to them: Be silent and weep not, for they cannot kill me until I describe for you everything I saw. ²⁵ And he said to them: Bring a stone here to me. ²⁶ And he set it up and said: Light of the ages, make this stone to become like me in appearance, until I have described to Baruch and Abimelech everything I saw. ²⁷ Then the stone, by God's command, took on the appearance of Jeremiah. ²⁸ And they were stoning the stone, supposing that it was Jeremiah! ²⁹ But Jeremiah delivered to Baruch and to Abimelech all the mysteries he had seen, and forthwith he stood in the midst of the people desiring to complete his ministry. ³⁰ Then the stone cried out, saying: O foolish children of Israel, why do you stone me, supposing that I am Jeremiah? Behold, Jeremiah is standing in your midst! ³¹ And when they saw him, immediately they rushed upon him with many stones, and his ministry was fulfilled. ³² And when Baruch and Abimelech came, they buried him, and taking the stone they placed it on his tomb and inscribed it thus: This is the stone that was the ally of Jeremiah.

PSEUDEPIGRAPHA

The First Book of Adam and Eve
(or The Conflict of Adam and Eve with Satan)

1

The crystal sea. God commands Adam, expelled from Eden, to dwell in the Cave of Treasures.

¹ ON the third day, God planted the garden in the east of the earth, on the border of the world eastward, beyond which, towards the sun-rising, one finds nothing but water, that encompasses the whole world, and reaches unto the borders of heaven. ² And to the north of the garden there is a sea of wafer, clear and pure to the taste, like unto nothing else; so that, through the clearness thereof, one may look into the depths of the earth. ³ And when a man washes himself in it, becomes clean of the cleanness thereof, and white of its whiteness – even if he were dark. ⁴ And God created that sea of His own good pleasure, for He knew what would come of the man He should make; so that after he had left the garden, on account of his transgression, men should be born in the earth, from among whom righteous ones should die, whose souls God would raise at the last day; when they should return to their flesh; should bathe in the water of that sea, and all of them repent of their sins. ⁵ But when God made Adam go out of the garden, He did not place him on the border of it northward, lest he should draw near to the sea of water, and he and Eve wash themselves in it, be cleansed from their sins, forget the transgression they had committed, and he no longer reminded of it in the thought of their punishment. ⁶ Then, again, as to the southern side of the garden, God was not pleased to let Adam dwell there; because, when the wind blew from the north, it would bring him, on that southern side, the delicious smell of the trees of the garden. ⁷ Wherefore God did not put Adam there, lest he should smell the sweet smell of those trees forget his transgression, and find consolation for what he had done, take delight in the smell of the trees, and not be cleansed from his transgression. ⁸ Again, also, because God is merciful and of great pity, and governs all things in a way He alone knows – He made our father Adam dwell in the western border of the garden, because on that side the earth is very broad. ⁹ And God commanded him to dwell there in a cave in a rock – the Cave of Treasures below the garden.

2

Adam and Eve faint upon leaving the Garden. God sends His word to encourage them.

¹ BUT when our father Adam, and Eve, went out of the garden, they trod the ground on their feet, not knowing they were treading. ² And when they came to the opening of the gate of the garden, and saw the broad earth spread before them, covered with stones large and small, and with sand, they feared and trembled, and fell on their faces, from the fear that came upon them; and they were as dead. ³ Because – whereas they had hitherto been in the garden-land, beautifully planted with all manner of trees – they now saw themselves, in a strange land, which they knew not, and had never seen. ⁴ And because at that time they were filled with the grace of a bright nature, and they had not hearts turned towards earthly things. ⁵ Therefore had God pity on them; and when He saw them fallen before the gate of the garden, He sent His Word unto father Adam and Eve, and raised them from their fallen state.

3

Concerning the promise of the great five days and a half.

¹ GOD said to Adam, "I have ordained on this earth days and years, and thou and thy seed shall dwell and walk in it, until the days and years are fulfilled; when I shall send the Word that created thee, and against which thou hast transgressed, the Word that made thee come out of the garden and that raised thee when thou wast fallen. ² Yea, the Word that will again save thee when the five days and a half are fulfilled." ³ But when Adam heard these words from God, and of the great five days and a half, he did not understand the meaning of them. ⁴ For Adam was thinking that there would be but five days and a half for him, to the end of the world. ⁵ And Adam wept, and prayed God to explain it to him. ⁶ Then God in His mercy for Adam who was made after His own image and similitude, explained to him, that these were 5,000 and 500 years; and how One would then come and save him and his seed. ⁷ But God had before that made this covenant with our father, Adam, in the same terms, ere he came out of the garden, when he was by the tree whereof Eve took the fruit and gave it him to eat. ⁸ Inasmuch as when our father Adam came out of the garden, he passed by that tree, and saw how God had then changed the appearance of it into another form, and how it withered. ⁹ And as Adam went to it he feared, trembled and fell down; but God in His mercy lifted him up, and then made this covenant with him. ¹⁰ And, again, when Adam was by the gate of the

garden, and saw the cherub with a sword of flashing fire in his hand, and the cherub grew angry and frowned at him, both Adam and Eve became afraid of him, and thought he meant to put them to death. So they fell on their faces, and trembled with fear. **11** But he had pity on them, and showed them mercy; and turning from them went up to heaven, and prayed unto the Lord, and said: – **12** "Lord, Thou didst send me to watch at the gate of the garden, with a sword of fire. **13** "But when Thy servants, Adam and Eve, saw me, they fell on their faces, and were as dead. O my Lord, what shall we do to Thy servants?" **14** Then God had pity on them, and showed them mercy, and sent His Angel to keep the garden. **15** And the Word of the Lord came unto Adam and Eve, and raised them up. **16** And the Lord said to Adam, "I told thee that at the end of five days and a half, I will send my Word and save thee. **17** "Strengthen thy heart, therefore, and abide in the Cave of Treasures, of which I have before spoken to thee." **18** And when Adam heard this Word from God, he was comforted with that which God had told him. For He had told him how He would save him.

4

Adam laments the changed conditions. Adam and Eve enter the Cave of Treasures.

1 BUT Adam and Eve wept for having come out of the garden, their first abode. **2** And, indeed, when Adam looked at his flesh, that was altered, he wept bitterly, he and Eve, over what they had done. And they walked and went gently down into the Cave of Treasures. **3** And as they came to it Adam wept over himself and said to Eve, "Look at this cave that is to be our prison in this world, and a place of punishment! **4** "What is it compared with the garden? What is its narrowness compared with the space of the other? **5** "What is this rock, by the side of those groves? What is the gloom of this cavern, compared with the light of the garden? **6** "What is this overhanging ledge of rock to shelter us, compared with the mercy of the Lord that overshadowed us? **7** "What is the soil of this cave compared with the garden-land? This earth, strewed with stones; and that, planted with delicious fruit-trees?" **8** And Adam said to Eve, "Look at thine eyes, and at mine, which afore beheld angels in heaven, praising; and they, too, without ceasing. **9** "But now we do not see as we did: our eyes have become of flesh; they cannot see in like manner as they saw before." **10** Adam said again to Eve, "What is our body to-day, compared to what it was in former days, when we dwelt in the garden?" **11** After this Adam did not like to enter the cave, under the overhanging rock; nor would he ever have entered it. **12** But he bowed to God's orders; and said to himself, "Unless I enter the cave, I shall again be a transgressor."

5

In which Eve makes a noble and emotionable intercession, taking the blame on herself.

1 THEN Adam and Eve entered the cave, and stood praying, in their own tongue, unknown to us, but which they knew well. **2** And as they prayed, Adam raised his eyes, and saw the rock and the roof of the cave that covered him overhead, so that he could see neither heaven, nor God's creatures. So he wept and smote heavily upon his breast, until he dropped, and was as dead. **3** And Eve sat weeping; for she believed he was dead. **4** Then she arose, spread her hands towards God, suing Him for mercy and pity, and said, "O God, forgive me my sin, the sin which I committed, and remember it not against me. **5** "For I alone caused Thy servant to fall from the garden into this lost estate; from light into this darkness; and from the abode of joy into this prison. **6** "O God, look upon this Thy servant thus fallen, and raise him from his death, that he may weep and repent of his transgression which he committed through me. **7** "Take not away his soul this once; but let him live that he may stand after the measure of his repentance, and do Thy will, as before his death. **8** "But if Thou do not raise him up, then, O God, take away my own soul, that I be like him; and leave me not in this dungeon, one and alone; for I could not stand alone in this world, but with him only. **9** "For Thou, O God, didst cause a slumber to come upon him, and didst take a bone from his side, and didst restore the flesh in the place of it, by Thy divine power. **10** "And Thou didst take me, the bone, and make me a woman, bright like him, with heart, reason, and speech; and in flesh, like unto his own; and Thou didst make me after the likeness of his countenance, by Thy mercy and power. **11** "O Lord, I and he are one and Thou, O God, art our Creator, Thou are He who made us both in one day. **12** "Therefore, O God, give him life, that he may be with me in this strange land, while we dwell in it on account of our transgression. **13** "But if Thou wilt not give him life, then take me, even me, like him; that we both may die the same day." **14** And Eve wept bitterly, and fell upon our father Adam; from her great sorrow.

6

God's admonition to Adam and Eve in which he points out how and why they sinned.

1 BUT God looked upon them; for they had killed themselves through great grief. **2** But He would raise them and comfort them. **3** He, therefore, sent His Word unto them; that they should stand and be raised forthwith. **4** And the Lord said unto Adam and Eve, "You transgressed of your own free will, until you came out of the garden in which I had placed you. **5** "Of your own free will have you transgressed through your desire for divinity, greatness, and an exalted state, such as I have; so that I deprived you of the bright nature in which you then were, and I made you come out of the garden to this land, rough and full of trouble. **6** "If only you had not transgressed My commandment and had kept My law, and had not eaten of the fruit of the tree, near which I told you not to come! And there were fruit trees in the garden better than that one. **7** "But the wicked Satan who continued not in his first estate, nor kept his faith; in whom was no good intent towards Me, and who though I had created him, yet set Me at naught, and sought the Godhead, so that I hurled him down from heaven, – he it is who made the tree appear pleasant in your eyes, until you ate of it, by hearkening to him. **8** "Thus have you transgressed My commandment, and therefore have I brought upon you all these sorrows. **9** "For I am God the Creator, who, when I created My creatures, did not intend to destroy them. But after they had sorely roused My anger, I punished them with grievous plagues, until they repent. **10** "But, if on the contrary, they still continue hardened in their transgression, they shall be under a curse for ever."

7

The beasts are reconciled.

1 WHEN Adam and Eve heard these words from God, they wept and sobbed yet more; but they strengthened their hearts in God, because they now felt that the Lord was to them like a father and a mother; and for this very reason, they wept before Him, and sought mercy from Him. **2** Then God had pity on them, and said: "O Adam, I have made My covenant with thee, and I will not turn from it; neither will I let thee return to the garden, until My covenant of the great five days and a half is fulfilled." **3** Then Adam said unto God, "O Lord, Thou didst create us, and make us fit to be in the garden; and before I transgressed, Thou madest all beasts come to me, that I should name them. **4** "Thy grace was then on me; and I named every one according to Thy mind; and Thou madest them all subject unto me. **5** "But now, O Lord God, that I have transgressed Thy commandment, all beasts will rise against me and will devour me, and Eve Thy handmaid; and will cut off our life from the face of the earth. **6** "I therefore beseech Thee, O God, that, since Thou hast made us come out of the garden, and hast made us be in a strange land, Thou wilt not let the beasts hurt us." **7** When the Lord heard these words from Adam, He had pity on him, and felt that he had truly said that the beasts of the field would rise and devour him and Eve, because He, the Lord, was angry with them two on account of their transgression. **8** Then God commanded the beasts, and the birds, and all that moves upon the earth, to come to Adam and to be familiar with him, and not to trouble him and Eve; nor yet any of the good and righteous among their posterity. **9** Then the beasts did obeisance to Adam, according to the commandment of God; except the serpent, against which God was wroth. It did not come to Adam, with the beasts.

8

The "Bright Nature" of man is taken away.

1 THEN Adam wept and said, "O God, when we dwelt in the garden, and our hearts were lifted up, we saw the angels that sang praises in heaven, but now we do not see as we were used to do; nay, when we entered the cave, all creation became hidden from us." **2** Then God the Lord said unto Adam, "When thou wast under subjection to Me, thou hadst a bright nature within thee, and for that reason couldst thou see things afar off. But after thy transgression thy bright nature was withdrawn from thee; and it was not left to thee to see things afar off, but only near at hand; after the ability of the flesh; for it is brutish." **3** When Adam and Eve had heard these words from God, they went their way; praising and worshipping Him with a sorrowful heart. **4** And God ceased to commune with them.

9

Water from the Tree of Life. Adam and Eve near drowning.

1 THEN Adam and Eve came out of the Cave of Treasures, and drew near to the garden gate, and there they stood to look at it, and wept for having come away from it. **2** And Adam and Eve went from before the gate of the garden to the southern side of it, and found there the water that watered the garden, from the root of the Tree of Life, and that parted itself from thence into four rivers over the earth. **3** Then they came and drew near to that water, and looked at it; and saw that it was the water that came forth from under the root of the Tree of Life in the garden. **4** And Adam wept and wailed, and smote upon his breast, for being severed from the garden; and said to Eve: – **5** "Why hast thou brought upon me, upon thyself, and upon our seed, so many of these plagues and punishments?" **6** And Eve said unto him, "What is it thou hast seen, to weep and to speak to me in this wise?" ⁷ And he said to Eve, "Seest thou not this water that was with us in the garden, that watered the trees of the garden, and flowed out thence? ⁸ "And we, when we were in the garden, did not care about it; but since we came to this strange land, we love it, and turn it to use for our body." ⁹ But when Eve heard these words from him, she wept; and from the soreness of their weeping, they fell into that water; and would have put an end to themselves in it, so as never again to return and behold the creation; for when they looked upon the work of creation, they felt they must put an end to themselves.

10

Their bodies need water after they leave the Garden.

¹ THEN God, merciful and gracious, looked upon them thus lying in the water, and nigh unto death, and sent an angel, who brought them out of the water, and laid them on the seashore as dead. ² Then the angel went up to God, was welcome, and said, "O God, Thy creatures have breathed their last." ³ Then God sent His Word unto Adam and Eve, who raised them from their death. ⁴ And Adam said, after he was raised, "O God, while we were in the garden we did not require, or care for this water; but since we came to this land we cannot do without it." ⁵ Then God said to Adam, "While thou wast under My command and wast a bright angel, thou knewest not this water. ⁶ "But after that thou hast transgressed My commandment, thou canst not do without water, wherein to wash thy body and make it grow; for it is now like that of beasts, and is in want of water." ⁷ When Adam and Eve heard these words from God, they wept a bitter cry; and Adam entreated God to let him return into the garden, and look at it a second time. ⁸ But God said unto Adam, "I have made thee a promise; when that promise is fulfilled, I will bring thee back into the garden, thee and thy righteous seed." ⁹ And God ceased to commune with Adam.

11

A recollection of the glorious days in the Garden.

¹ THEN Adam and Eve felt themselves burning with thirst, and heat, and sorrow. ² And Adam said to Eve, "We shall not drink of this water, even if we were to die. O Eve, when this water comes into our inner parts, it will increase our punishments and that of our children, that shall come after us." ³ Both Adam and Eve then withdrew from the water, and drank none of it at all; but came and entered the Cave of Treasures. ⁴ But when in it Adam could not see Eve; he only heard the noise she made. Neither could she see Adam, but heard the noise he made. ⁵ Then Adam wept, in deep affliction, and smote upon his breast; and he arose and said to Eve, "Where art thou?" ⁶ And she said unto him, "Lo, I am standing in this darkness." ⁷ He then said to her, "Remember the bright nature in which we lived, while we abode in the garden! ⁸ "O Eve! remember the glory that rested on us in the garden. O Eve! remember the trees that overshadowed us in the garden while we moved among them. ⁹ "O Eve! remember that while we were in the garden, we knew neither night nor day. Think of the Tree of Life, from below which flowed the water, and that shed lustre over us! Remember, O Eve, the garden-land, and the brightness thereof! ¹⁰ "Think, oh think of that garden in which was no darkness, while we dwelt therein. ¹¹ "Whereas no sooner did we come into this Cave of Treasures than darkness compassed us round about; until we can no longer see each other; and all the pleasure of this life has come to an end."

12

How darkness came between Adam and Eve.

¹ THEN Adam smote upon his breast, he and Eve, and they mourned the whole night until dawn drew near, and they sighed over the length of the night in Miyazia. ² And Adam beat himself, and threw himself on the ground in the cave, from bitter grief, and because of the darkness, and lay there as dead. ³ But Eve heard the noise he made in falling upon the earth. And she felt about for him with her hands, and found him like a corpse. ⁴ Then she was afraid, speechless, and remained by him. ⁵ But the merciful Lord looked on the death of Adam, and on Eve's silence from fear of the darkness. ⁶ And the Word of God came unto Adam and raised him from his death, and opened Eve's mouth that she might speak. ⁷ Then Adam arose in the cave and said, "O God, wherefore has light departed from us, and darkness come over us? Wherefore dost Thou leave us in this long darkness? Why wilt Thou plague us thus? ⁸ "And this darkness, O Lord, where was it ere it came upon us? It is such, that we cannot see each other. ⁹ "For, so long as we were in the garden, we neither saw nor even knew what darkness is. I was not hidden from Eve, neither was she hidden from me, until now that she cannot see me; and no darkness came upon us, to separate us from each other. ¹⁰ "But she and I were both in one bright light. I saw her and she saw me. Yet now since we came into this cave, darkness has come upon us, and parted us asunder, so that I do not see her, and she does not see me. ¹¹ "O Lord, wilt Thou then plague us with this darkness?"

13

The fall of Adam. Why night and day were created.

¹ THEN when God, who is merciful and full of pity, heard Adam's voice, He said unto him: – ² "O Adam, so long as the good angel was obedient to Me, a bright light rested on him and on his hosts. ³ "But when he transgressed My commandment, I deprived him of that bright nature, and he became dark. ⁴ "And when he was in the heavens, in the realms of light, he knew naught of darkness. ⁵ "But he transgressed, and I made him fall from heaven upon the earth; and it was this darkness that came upon him. ⁶ "And on thee, O Adam, while in My garden and obedient to Me, did that bright light rest also. ⁷ "But when I heard of thy transgression, I deprived thee of that bright light. Yet, of My mercy, I did not turn thee into darkness, but I made thee thy body of flesh, over which I spread this skin, in order that it may bear cold and heat. ⁸ "If I had let My wrath fall heavily upon thee, I should have destroyed thee; and had I turned thee into darkness, it would have been as if I killed thee. ⁹ "But in My mercy, I have made thee as thou art; when thou didst transgress My commandment, O Adam, I drove thee from the garden, and made thee come forth into this land; and commanded thee to dwell in this cave; and darkness came upon thee, as it did upon him who transgressed My commandment. ¹⁰ "Thus, O Adam, has this night deceived thee. It is not to last for ever; but is only of twelve hours; when it is over, daylight will return. ¹¹ "Sigh not, therefore, neither be moved; and say not in thy heart that this darkness is long and drags on wearily; and say not in thy heart that I plague thee with it. ¹² "Strengthen thy heart, and be not afraid. This darkness is not a punishment. But, O Adam, I have made the day, and have placed the sun in it to give light; in order that thou and thy children should do your work. ¹³ "For I knew thou shouldest sin and transgress, and come out into this land. Yet would I not force thee, nor be heard upon thee, nor shut up; nor doom thee through thy fall; nor through thy coming out from light into darkness; nor yet through thy coming from the garden into this land. ¹⁴ "For I made thee of the light; and I willed to bring out children of light from thee and like unto thee. ¹⁵ "But thou didst not keep one day My commandment; until I had finished the creation and blessed everything in it. ¹⁶ "Then I commanded thee concerning the tree, that thou eat not thereof. Yet I knew that Satan, who deceived himself, would also deceive thee. ¹⁷ "So I made known to thee by means of the tree, not to come near him. And I told thee not to eat of the fruit thereof, nor to taste of it, nor yet to sit under it, nor to yield to it. ¹⁸ "Had I not been and spoken to thee, O Adam, concerning the tree, and had I left thee without a commandment, and thou hadst sinned – it would have been an offence on My part, for not having given thee any order; thou wouldst turn round and blame Me for it. ¹⁹ "But I commanded thee, and warned thee, and thou didst fall. So that My creatures cannot blame me; but the blame rests on them alone. ²⁰ "And, O Adam, I have made the day for thee and for thy children after thee, for them to work, and toil therein. And I have made the night for them to rest in it from their work; and for the beasts of the field to go forth by night and seek their food. ²¹ "But little of darkness now remains, O Adam; and daylight will soon appear."

14

The earliest prophecy of the coming of Christ.

¹ THEN Adam said unto God: "O Lord, take Thou my soul, and let me not see this gloom any more; or remove me to some place where there is no darkness." ² But God the Lord said to Adam, "Verily I say unto thee, this darkness will pass from thee, every day I have determined for thee, until the fulfilment of My covenant; when I will save thee and bring thee back again into the garden, into the abode of light thou longest for, wherein is no darkness. I will bring thee, to it – in the kingdom of heaven." ³ Again said God unto Adam, "All this misery that thou hast been made to take upon thee because of thy transgression, will not free thee from the hand of Satan, and will not save thee. ⁴ "But I will. When I shall come down from heaven, and shall become flesh of thy seed, and take upon Me the infirmity from which thou sufferest, then the darkness that came upon thee in this cave shall come upon Me in the grave, when I am in the flesh of thy seed. ⁵ "And I, who am without years, shall be subject to the reckoning of years, of times, of months, and of days, and I shall be reckoned as one of the sons of men, in order to save thee." ⁶ And God ceased to commune with Adam.

15

¹ THEN Adam and Eve wept and sorrowed by reason of God's word to them, that they should not return to the garden until the fulfilment of the days decreed upon them; but mostly because God had told them that He should suffer for their salvation.

16

The first sunrise. Adam and Eve think it is a fire coming to burn them.

¹ AFTER this Adam and Eve ceased not to stand in the cave, praying and weeping, until the morning dawned upon them. ² And when they saw the

light returned to them, they restrained from fear, and strengthened their hearts. [3] Then Adam began to come out of the cave. And when he came to the mouth of it, and stood and turned his face towards the east, and saw the sun rise in glowing rays, and felt the heat thereof on his body, he was afraid of it, and thought in his heart that this flame came forth to plague him. [4] He wept then, and smote upon his breast, and fell upon the earth on his face, and made his request, saying: – [5] "O Lord, plague me not, neither consume me, nor yet take away my life from the earth." [6] For he thought the sun was God. [7] Inasmuch as while he was in the garden and heard the voice of God and the sound He made in the garden, and feared Him, Adam never saw the brilliant light of the sun, neither did the flaming heat thereof touch his body. [8] Therefore was he afraid of the sun when flaming rays of it reached him. He thought God meant to plague him therewith all the days He had decreed for him. [9] For Adam also said in his thoughts, as God did not plague us with darkness, behold, He has caused this sun to rise and to plague us with burning heat. [10] But while he was thus thinking in his heart, the Word of God came unto him and said: – [11] "O Adam, arise and stand up. This sun is not God; but it has been created to give light by day, of which I spake unto thee in the cave saying, 'that the dawn would break forth, and there would be light by day.' [12] "But I am God who comforted thee in the night." [13] And God ceased to commune with Adam.

17

The Chapter of the Serpent.

[1] THEN Adam and Eve came out at the mouth of the cave, and went towards the garden. [2] But as they drew near to it, before the western gate, from which Satan came when he deceived Adam and Eve, they found the. serpent that became Satan coming at the gate, and sorrowfully licking the dust, and wriggling on its breast on the ground, by reason of the curse that fell upon it from God. [3] And whereas aforetime the serpent was the most exalted of all beasts, now it was changed and become slippery, and the meanest of them all, and it crept on its breast and went on its belly. [4] And whereas it was the fairest of all beasts, it had been changed, and was become the ugliest of them all. Instead of feeding on the best food, now it turned to eat the dust. Instead of dwelling, as before, in the best places, now it lived in the dust. [5] And, whereas it had been the most beautiful of all beasts, all of which stood dumb at its beauty, it was now abhorred of them. [6] And, again, whereas it dwelt in one beautiful abode, to which all other animals came from elsewhere; and where it drank, they drank also of the same; now, after it had become venomous, by reason of God's curse, all beasts fled from its abode, and would not drink of the water it drank; but fled from it.

18

The mortal combat with the serpent.

[1] WHEN the accursed serpent saw Adam and Eve, it swelled its head, stood on its tail, and with eyes blood-red, did as if it would kill them. [2] It made straight for Eve, and ran after her; while Adam standing by, wept because he had no stick in his hand wherewith to smite the serpent, and knew not how to put it to death. [3] But with a heart burning for Eve, Adam approached the serpent, and held it by the tail; when it turned towards him and said unto him: – [4] "O Adam, because of thee and of Eve, I am slippery, and go upon my belly." Then by reason of its great strength, it threw down Adam and Eve and pressed upon them, as if it would kill them. [5] But God sent an angel who threw the serpent away from them, and raised them up. [6] Then the Word of God came to the serpent, and said unto it, "In the first instance I made thee glib, and made thee to go upon thy belly; but I did not deprive thee of speech. [7] "Now, however, be thou dumb; and speak no more, thou and thy race; because in the first place, has the ruin of my creatures happened through thee, and now thou wishest to kill them." [8] Then the serpent was struck dumb, and spake no more. [9] And a wind came to blow from heaven by command of God that carried away the serpent from Adam and Eve, threw it on the sea shore, and it landed in India.

19

Beasts made subject to Adam.

[1] BUT Adam and Eve wept before God. And Adam said unto Him: – [2] "O Lord, when I was in the cave, I said this to Thee, my Lord, that the beasts of the field would rise and devour me, and cut off my life from the earth." [3] Then Adam, by reason of what had befallen him, smote upon his breast, and fell upon the earth like a corpse; then came to him the Word of God, who raised him, and said unto him, [4] "O Adam, not one of these beasts will be able to hurt thee; because when I made the beasts and other moving things come to thee in the cave, I did not let the serpent come with them, lest it should rise against you, make you tremble; and the fear of it should fall into your hearts. [5] "For I knew that that accursed one is wicked; therefore would I not let it come near you with the other beasts. [6] "But now strengthen thy heart and fear not. I am with thee unto the end of the days I have determined on thee."

20

Adam wishes to protect Eve.

[1] THEN Adam wept and said, "O God, remove us to some other place, that the serpent may not come again near us, and rise against us. Lest it find Thy handmaid Eve alone and kill her; for its eyes are hideous and evil." [2] But God said to Adam and Eve, "Henceforth fear not, I will not let it come near you; I have driven it away from you, from this mountain; neither will I leave in it aught to hurt you." [3] Then Adam and Eve worshipped before God 'and gave Him thanks, and praised Him for having delivered them from death.

21

Adam and Eve attempt suicide.

[1] THEN Adam and Eve went in search of the garden. [2] And the heat beat like a flame on their faces; and they sweated from the heat, and wept before the Lord. [3] But the place where they wept was nigh unto a high mountain, facing the western gate of the garden. [4] Then Adam threw himself down from the top of that mountain; his face was torn and his flesh was flayed; much blood flowed from him, and he was nigh unto death. [5] Meanwhile Eve remained standing on the mountain weeping over him, thus lying. [6] And she said, "I wish not to live after him; for all that he did to himself was through me." [7] Then she threw herself after him; and was torn and scotched by stones; and remained lying as dead. [8] But the merciful God, who looks upon His creatures, looked upon Adam and Eve as they lay dead, and He sent His Word unto them, and raised them. [9] And said to Adam, "O Adam, all this misery which thou hast wrought upon thyself, will not avail against My rule, neither will it alter the covenant of the 5500 years."

22

Adam in a chivalrous mood.

[1] THEN Adam said to God, "I wither in the heat; I am faint from walking, and am loth of this world. And I know not when Thou wilt bring me out of it, to rest." [2] Then the Lord God said unto him, "O Adam, it cannot be at present, not until thou hast ended thy days. Then shall I bring thee out of this wretched land." [3] And Adam said to God, "While I was in the garden I knew neither heat, nor languor, neither moving about, nor trembling, nor fear; but now since I came to this land, all this affliction has come upon me." [4] Then God said to Adam, "So long as thou wast keeping My commandment, My light and My grace rested on thee. But when thou didst transgress My commandment, sorrow and misery befell thee in this land." [5] And Adam wept and said, "O Lord, do not cut me off for this, neither smite me with heavy plagues, nor yet repay me according to my sin; For we, of our own will, did transgress Thy commandment, and forsook Thy law, and sought to become gods like unto Thee, when Satan the enemy deceived us." [6] Then God said again unto Adam, "Because thou hast borne fear and trembling in this land, languor and suffering treading and walking about, going upon this mountain, and dying from it, I will take all this upon Myself in order to save thee."

23

Adam and Eve gird themselves and make the first altar ever built.

[1] THEN Adam wept more and said, "O God, have mercy on me, so far as to take upon Thee, that which I will do." [2] But God took His Word from Adam and Eve. [3] Then Adam and Eve stood on their feet; and Adam said to Eve "Gird thyself, and I also will gird myself." And she girded herself, as Adam told her. [4] Then Adam and Eve took stones and placed them in the shape of an altar; and they took leaves from the trees outside the garden, with which they wiped, from the face of the rock, the blood they had spilled. [5] But that which had dropped on the sand, they took together with the dust wherewith it was mingled and offered it upon the altar as an offering unto God. [6] Then Adam and Eve stood under the altar and wept, thus entreating God, "Forgive us our trespass and our sin, and look upon us with Thine eye of mercy. For when we were in the garden our praises and our hymns went up before Thee without ceasing. [7] "But when we came into this strange land, pure praise was no longer ours, nor righteous prayer, nor understanding hearts, nor sweet thoughts, nor just counsels, nor long discernment, nor upright feelings, neither is our bright nature left us. But our body is changed from the similitude in which it was at first, when we were created. [8] "Yet now look upon our blood which is offered upon these stones, and accept it at our hands, like the praise we used to sing unto Thee at first, when in the garden." [9] And Adam began to make more requests unto God.

24

A vivid prophecy of the life and death of Christ.

[1] THEN the merciful God, good 'and lover of men, looked upon Adam and Eve, and upon their blood, which they had held up as an offering unto Him; without an order from Him for so doing. But He wondered at them; and accepted their offerings. [2] And God sent from His presence a bright fire, that consumed their offering. [3] He smelt the sweet savour of their offering,

and showed them mercy. ⁴ Then came the Word of God to Adam, and said unto him, "O Adam, as thou hast shed thy blood, so will I shed My own blood when I become flesh of thy seed; and as thou didst die, O Adam, so also will I die. And as thou didst build an altar, so also will I make for thee an altar on the earth; and as thou didst offer thy blood upon it, so also will I offer My blood upon an altar on the earth. ⁵ "And as thou didst sue for forgiveness through that blood, so also will I make My blood forgiveness of sins, and blot out transgressions in it. ⁶ "And now, behold, I have accepted thy offering, O Adam, but the days of the covenant, wherein I have bound thee, are not fulfilled. When they are fulfilled, then will I bring thee back into the garden. ⁷ "Now, therefore, strengthen thy heart; and when sorrow comes upon thee, make Me an offering, and I will be favourable to thee."

25

God represented as merciful and loving. The establishing of worship.

¹ BUT God knew that Adam had in his thoughts, that he should often kill himself and make an offering to Him of his blood. ² Therefore did He say unto him, "O Adam, do not again kill thyself as thou didst, by throwing thyself down from that mountain." ³ But Adam said unto God, "It was in my mind to put an end to myself at once, for having transgressed Thy commandments, and for my having come out of the beautiful garden; and for the bright light of which Thou hast deprived me; and for the praises which poured forth from my mouth without ceasing, and for the light that covered me. ⁴ "Yet of Thy goodness, O God, do not away with me altogether; but be favourable to me every time I die, and bring me to life. ⁵ "And thereby it will be made known that Thou art a merciful God, who willest not that one should perish; who lovest not that one should fall; and who dost not condemn any one cruelly, badly, and by whole destruction." ⁶ Then Adam remained silent. ⁷ And the Word of God came unto him, and blessed him, and comforted him, and covenanted with him, that He would save him at the end of the days determined upon him. ⁸ This, then, was the first offering Adam made unto God; and so it became his custom to do.

26

A beautiful prophecy of eternal life and joy (v. 15). The fall of night.

¹ THEN Adam took Eve, and they began to return to the Cave of Treasures where they dwelt. But when they neared it and saw it from afar, heavy sorrow fell upon Adam and Eve when they looked at it. ² Then Adam said to Eve, "When we were on the mountain we were comforted by the Word of God that conversed with us; and the light that came from the east, shone over us. ³ "But now the Word of God is hidden from us; and the light that shone over us is so changed as to disappear, and let darkness and sorrow come upon us. ⁴ "And we are forced to enter this cave which is like a prison, wherein darkness covers us, so that we are parted from each other; and thou canst not see me, neither can I see thee." ⁵ When Adam had said these words, they wept and spread their hands before God; for they were full of sorrow. ⁶ And they entreated God to bring the sun to them, to shine on them, so that darkness return not upon them, and they come not again under this covering of rock. And they wished to die rather than see the darkness. ⁷ Then God looked upon Adam and Eve and upon their great sorrow, and upon all they had done with a fervent heart, on account of all the trouble they were in, instead of their former well-being, and on account of all the misery that came upon them in a strange land. ⁸ Therefore God was not wroth with them; nor impatient with them; but He was longsuffering and forbearing towards them, as towards the children He had created. ⁹ Then came the Word of God to Adam, and said unto him, "Adam, as for the sun, if I were to take it and bring it to thee, days, hours, years and months would all come to naught, and the covenant I have made with thee, would never be fulfilled. ¹⁰ "But thou shouldest then be turned and left in a long plague, and no salvation would be left to thee for ever. ¹¹ "Yea, rather, bear long and calm thy soul while thou abidest night and day; until the fulfilment of the days, and the time of My covenant is come. ¹² "Then shall I come and save thee, O Adam, for I do not wish that thou be afflicted. ¹³ "And when I look at all the good things in which thou didst live, and why thou camest out of them, then would I willingly show thee mercy. ¹⁴ "But I cannot alter the covenant that has gone out of My mouth; else would I have brought thee back into the garden. ¹⁵ "When, however, the covenant is fulfilled, then shall I show thee and thy seed mercy, and bring thee into a land of gladness, where there is neither sorrow nor suffering; but abiding joy and gladness, and light that never fails, and praises that never cease; and a beautiful garden that shall never pass away." ¹⁶ And God said again unto Adam, "Be long-suffering and enter the cave, for the darkness, of which thou wast afraid, shall only be twelve hours long; and when ended, light shall arise." ¹⁷ Then when Adam heard these words from God, he and Eve worshipped before Him, and their hearts were comforted. They returned into the cave after their custom, while tears flowed from their eyes, sorrow and wailing came from their hearts, and they wished their soul would leave their body. ¹⁸ And Adam and Eve stood praying, until the darkness of night came upon them, and Adam was hid from Eve, and she from him. ¹⁹ And they remained standing in prayer.

27

The second tempting of Adam and Eve. The devil takes on the form of a beguiling light.

¹ WHEN Satan, the hater of all good, saw how they continued in prayer, and how God communed with them, and comforted them, and how He had accepted their offering – Satan made an apparition. ² He began with transforming his hosts; in his hands was a flashing fire, and they were in a great light. ³ He then placed his throne near the mouth of the cave because he could not enter into it by reason of their prayers. And he shed light into the cave, until the cave glistened over Adam and Eve; while his hosts began to sing praises. ⁴ And Satan did this, in order that when Adam saw the light, he should think within himself that it was a heavenly light, and that Satan's hosts were angels; and that God had sent them to watch at the cave, and to give him light in the darkness. ⁵ So that when Adam came out of the cave and saw them, and Adam and Eve bowed to Satan, then he would overcome Adam thereby, and a second time humble him before God. ⁶ When, therefore, Adam and Eve saw the light, fancying it was real, they strengthened their hearts; yet, as they were trembling, Adam said to Eve: – ⁷ "Look at that great light, and at those many songs of praise, and at that host standing outside that do not come in to us, do not tell us what they say, or whence they come, or what is the meaning of this light; what those praises are; wherefore they have been sent hither, and why they do not come in. ⁸ "If they were from God, they would come to us in the cave, and would tell us their errand." ⁹ Then Adam stood up and prayed unto God with a fervent heart, and said: – ¹⁰ "O Lord, is there in the world another god than Thou, who created angels and filled them with light, and sent them to keep us, who would come with them? ¹¹ "But, lo, we see these hosts that stand at the mouth of the cave; they are in a great light; they sing loud praises. If they are of some other god than Thou, tell me; and if they are sent by Thee, inform me of the reason for which Thou hast sent them." ¹² No sooner had Adam said this, than an angel from God appeared unto him in the cave, who said unto him, "O Adam, fear not. This is Satan and his hosts; he wishes to deceive you as he deceived you at first. For the first time, he was hidden in the serpent; but this time he is come to you in the similitude of an angel of light; in order that, when you worshipped him, he might enthrall you, in the very presence of God." ¹³ Then the angel went from Adam, and seized Satan at the opening of the cave, and stripped him of the feint he had assumed, and brought him in his own hideous form to Adam and Eve; who were afraid of him when they saw him. ¹⁴ And the angel said to Adam, "This hideous form has been his ever since God made him fall from heaven. He could not have come near you in it; therefore did he transform himself into an angel of light." ¹⁵ Then the angel drove away Satan and his hosts from Adam and Eve, and said unto them, "Fear not; God who created you, will strengthen you." ¹⁶ And the angel went from them. ¹⁷ But Adam and Eve remained standing in the cave; no consolation came to them; they were divided in their thoughts. ¹⁸ And when it was morning they prayed; and then went out to seek the garden. For their hearts were towards it, and they could get no consolation for having left it.

28

The Devil pretends to lead Adam and Eve to the water to bathe.

¹ BUT when the wily Satan saw them, that they were going to the garden, he gathered together his host, and came in appearance upon a cloud, intent on deceiving them. ² But when Adam and Eve saw him thus in a vision, they thought they were angels of God come to comfort them about their having left the garden, or to bring them back again into it. ³ And Adam spread his hands unto God, beseeching Him to make him understand what they were. ⁴ Then Satan, the hater of all good, said unto Adam, "O Adam, I am an angel of the great God; and, behold the hosts that surround me. ⁵ "God has sent me and them to take thee and bring thee to the border of the garden northwards; to the shore of the clear sea, and bathe thee and Eve in it, and raise you to your former gladness, that ye return again to the garden." ⁶ These words sank into the heart of Adam and Eve. ⁷ Yet God withheld His Word from Adam, and did not make him understand at once, but waited to see his strength; whether he would be overcome as Eve was when in the garden, or whether he would prevail. ⁸ Then Satan called to Adam and Eve, and said, "Behold, we go to the sea of water," and they began to go. ⁹ And Adam and Eve followed them at some little distance. ¹⁰ But when they came to the mountain to the north of the garden, a very high mountain, without any steps to the top of it, the Devil drew near to Adam and Eve, and made them go up to the top in reality, and not in a vision; wishing, as he did, to

throw them down and kill them, and to wipe off their name from the earth; so that this earth should remain to him and his hosts alone.

29

God tells Adam of the Devil's purpose. (v. 4).

¹ BUT when the merciful God saw that Satan wished to kill Adam with his manifold devices, and saw that Adam was meek and without guile, God spake unto Satan in a loud voice, and cursed him. ² Then he and his hosts fled, and Adam and Eve remained standing on the top of the mountain, whence they saw below them the wide world, high above which they were. But they saw none of the host which anon were by them. ³ They wept, both Adam and Eve, before God, and begged for forgiveness of Him. ⁴ Then came the Word from God to Adam, and said unto him, "Know thou and understand concerning this Satan, that he seeks to deceive thee and thy seed after thee." ⁵ And Adam wept before the Lord God, and begged and entreated Him to give him something from the garden, as a token to him, wherein to be comforted. ⁶ And God looked upon Adam's thought, and sent the angel Michael as far as the sea that reaches unto India, to take from thence golden rods and bring them to Adam. ⁷ This did God in His wisdom, in order that these golden rods, being with Adam in the cave, should shine forth with light in the night around him, and put an end to his fear of the darkness. ⁸ Then the angel Michael went down by God's order, took golden rods, as God had commanded him, and brought them to God.

30

Adam receives the first worldly goods.

¹ AFTER these things, God commanded the angel Gabriel to go down to the garden, and say to the cherub who kept it, "Behold, God has commanded me to come into the garden, and to take thence sweet smelling incense, and give it to Adam." ² Then the angel Gabriel went down by God's order to the garden, and told the cherub as God had commanded him. ³ The cherub then said, "Well." And Gabriel went in and took the incense. ⁴ Then God commanded His angel Raphael to go down to the garden, and speak to the cherub about some myrrh, to give to Adam. ⁵ And the angel Raphael went down and told the cherub as God had commanded him, and the cherub said, "Well." Then Raphael went in and took the myrrh. ⁶ The golden rods were from the Indian sea, where there are precious stones. The incense was from the eastern border of the garden; and the myrrh from the western border, whence bitterness came upon Adam. ⁷ And the angels brought these three things to God, by the Tree of Life, in the garden. ⁸ Then God said to the angels, "Dip them in the spring of water; then take them and sprinkle their water over Adam and Eve, that they be a little comforted in their sorrow, and give them to Adam and Eve. ⁹ And the angels did as God had commanded them, and they gave all those things to Adam and Eve on the top of the mountain upon which Satan had placed them, when he sought to make an end of them. ¹⁰ And when Adam saw the golden rods, the incense and the myrrh, he was rejoiced and wept because he thought that the gold was a token of the kingdom whence he had come, that the incense was a token of the bright light which had been taken from him, and that the myrrh was a token of the sorrow in which he was.

31

They make themselves more comfortable in the Cave of Treasures on the third day.

¹ AFTER these things God said unto Adam, "Thou didst ask of Me something from the garden, to be comforted therewith, and I have given thee these three tokens as a consolation to thee; that thou trust in Me and in My covenant with thee. ² "For I will come and save thee; and kings shall bring me when in the flesh, gold, incense and myrrh; gold as a token of My kingdom; incense as a token of My divinity; and myrrh as a token of My suffering and of My death. ³ "But, O Adam, put these by thee in the cave; the gold that it may shed light over thee by night; the incense, that thou smell its sweet savour; and the myrrh, to comfort thee in thy sorrow." ⁴ When Adam heard these words from God, he worshipped before Him. He and Eve worshipped Him and gave Him thanks, because He had dealt mercifully with them. ⁵ Then God commanded the three angels, Michael, Gabriel and Raphael, each to bring what he had brought, and give it to Adam. And they did so, one by one. ⁶ And God commanded Suriyel and Salathiel to bear up Adam and Eve, and bring them down from the top of the high mountain, and to take them to the Cave of Treasures. ⁷ There they laid the gold on the south side of the cave, the incense on the eastern side, and the myrrh on the western side. For the mouth of the cave was on the north side. ⁸ The angels then comforted Adam and Eve, and departed. ⁹ The gold was seventy rods; the incense, twelve pounds; and the myrrh, three pounds. ¹⁰ These remained by Adam in the House of Treasures; therefore was it called "of concealment." But other interpreters say it was called the "Cave of Treasures," by reason of the bodies of righteous men that were in it. ¹¹ These three things did God give to Adam, on the third day after he had come out of the garden, in token of the three days the Lord should remain in the heart of the earth. ¹² And these three things, as they continued with Adam in the cave, gave him light by night; and by day they gave him a little relief from his sorrow.

32

Adam and Eve go into the water to pray.

¹ AND Adam and Eve remained in the Cave of Treasures until the seventh day; they neither ate of the fruit of the earth, nor drank water. ² And when it dawned on the eighth day, Adam said to Eve, "O Eve, we prayed God to give us somewhat from the garden, and He sent His angels who brought us what we had desired. ³ "But now, arise, let us go to the sea of water we saw at first, and let us stand in it, praying that God will again be favourable to us and take us back to the garden; or give us something; or that He will give us comfort in some other land than this in which we are." ⁴ Then Adam and Eve came out of the cave, went and stood on the border of the sea in which they had before thrown themselves, and Adam said to Eve: – ⁵ "Come, go down into this place, and come not out of it until the end of thirty days, when I shall come to thee. And pray to God with fervent heart and a sweet voice, to forgive us. ⁶ "And I will go to another place, and go down into it, and do like thee." ⁷ Then Eve went down into the water, as Adam had commanded her. Adam also went down into the water; and they stood praying; and besought the Lord to forgive them their offence, and to restore them to their former state. ⁸ And they stood thus praying, unto the end of the five-and-thirty days.

33

Satan falsely promises the "bright light!"

¹ BUT Satan, the hater of all good, sought them in the cave, but found them not, although he searched diligently for them. ² But he found them standing in the water praying and thought within himself, "Adam and Eve are thus standing in that water beseeching God to forgive them their transgression, and to restore them to their former estate, and to take them from under my hand. ³ "But I will deceive them so that they shall come out of the water, and not fulfil their vow." ⁴ Then the hater of all good, went not to Adam, but he went to Eve, and took the form of an angel of God, praising and rejoicing, and said to her – ⁵ "Peace be unto thee! Be glad and rejoice! God is favourable unto you, and He sent me to Adam. I have brought him the glad tidings of salvation, and of his being filled with bright light as he was at first. ⁶ "And Adam, in his joy for his restoration, has sent me to thee, that thou come to me, in order that I crown thee with light like him. ⁷ "And he said to me, 'Speak unto Eve; if she does not come with thee, tell her of the sign when we were on the top of the mountain; how God sent His angels who took us and brought us to the Cave of Treasures; and laid the gold on the southern side; incense, on the eastern side; and myrrh on the western side.' Now come to him." ⁸ When Eve heard these words from him, she rejoiced greatly. And thinking that Satan's appearance was real, she came out of the sea. ⁹ He went before, and she followed him until they came to Adam. Then Satan hid himself from her, and she saw him no more. ¹⁰ She then came and stood before Adam, who was standing by the water and rejoicing in God's forgiveness. ¹¹ And as she called to him, he turned round, found her there and wept when he saw her, and smote upon his breast; and from the bitterness of his grief, he sank into the water. ¹² But God looked upon him and upon his misery, and upon his being about to breathe his last. And the Word of God came from heaven, raised him out of the water, and said unto him, "Go up the high bank to Eve." And when he came up to Eve he said unto her, "Who said to thee 'come hither'?" ¹³ Then she told him the discourse of the angel who had appeared unto her and had given her a sign. ¹⁴ But Adam grieved, and gave her to know it was Satan. He then took her and they both returned to the cave. ¹⁵ These things happened to them the second time they went down to the water, seven days after their coming out of the garden. ¹⁶ They fasted in the water thirty-five days; altogether forty-two days since they had left the garden.

34

Adam recalls the creation of Eve. He eloquently appeals for food and drink.

¹ AND on the morning of the forty-third day, they came out of the cave, sorrowful and weeping. Their bodies were lean, and they were parched from hunger and thirst, from fasting and praying, and from their heavy sorrow on account of their transgression. ² And when they had come out of the cave they went up the mountain to the west of the garden. ³ There they stood and prayed and besought God to grant them forgiveness of their sins. ⁴ And after their prayers Adam began to entreat God, saying, "O my Lord my God, and my Creator, thou didst command the four elements to be gathered together, and they were gathered together by Thine order. ⁵ "Then Thou spreadest Thy hand and didst create me out of one element, that of dust of the earth; and Thou didst bring me into the garden at the third hour, on a Friday, and didst inform me of it in the cave. ⁶ "Then, at first, I knew

neither night nor day, for I had a bright nature; neither did the light in which I lived ever leave me to know night or day. ⁷ "Then, again, O Lord, in that third hour in which Thou didst create me, Thou broughtest to me all beasts, and lions, and ostriches, and fowls of the air, and all things that move in the earth, which Thou hadst created at the first hour before me of the Friday. ⁸ "And Thy will was that I should name them all, one by one, with a suitable name. But Thou gavest me understanding and knowledge, and a pure heart and a right mind from Thee, that I should name them after Thine own mind regarding the naming of them. ⁹ "O God, Thou madest them obedient to me, and didst order that not one of them break from my sway, according to Thy commandment, and to the dominion which Thou hast given me over them. But now they are all estranged from me. ¹⁰ "Then it was in that third hour of Friday, in which Thou didst create me, and didst command me concerning the tree, to which I was neither to draw near, nor to eat thereof; for Thou saidst to me in the garden, 'When thou eatest of it, of death thou shalt die.' ¹¹ "And if Thou hadst punished me as Thou saidst, with death, I should have died that very moment. ¹² "Moreover, when Thou commandedst me regarding the tree, I was neither to approach nor to cat thereof, Eve was not with me; Thou hadst not Yet created her, neither hadst Thou yet taken her out of my side; nor had she yet heard this order from Thee. ¹³ "Then, at the end of the third hour of that Friday, O Lord, Thou didst cause a slumber and a sleep to come over me, and I slept, and was overwhelmed in sleep. ¹⁴ "Then Thou didst draw a rib out of my side, and created it after my own similitude and image. Then I awoke; and when I saw her and knew who she was, I said, 'This is bone of my bones, and flesh of my flesh; henceforth she shall be called woman.' ¹⁵ "It was of Thy good will, O God, that Thou broughtest a slumber and a sleep over me, and that Thou didst forthwith bring Eve out of my side, until she was out, so that I did not see how she was made; neither could I witness, O my Lord, how awful and great are Thy goodness and glory. ¹⁶ "And of Thy goodwill, O Lord, Thou madest us both with bodies of a bright nature, and Thou madest us two, one; and Thou gavest us Thy grace, and didst fill us with praises of the Holy Spirit; that we should be neither hungry nor thirsty, nor know what sorrow is, nor yet faintness of heart; neither suffering, fasting, nor weariness. ¹⁷ "But now, O God, since we transgressed Thy commandment and broke Thy law, Thou hast brought us out into a strange land, and has caused suffering, and faintness, hunger and thirst to come upon us. ¹S "Now, therefore, O God, we pray Thee, give us something to eat from the garden, to satisfy our hunger with it; and something wherewith to quench our thirst. ¹⁹ "For, behold, many days, O God, we have tasted nothing and drunk nothing, and our flesh is dried up, and our strength is wasted, and sleep is gone from our eyes from faintness and weeping. ²⁰ "Then, O God, we dare not gather aught of the fruit of trees, from fear of Thee. For when we transgressed at first Thou didst spare us, and didst not make us die. ²¹ "But now, we thought in our hearts, if we eat of the fruit of trees, without God's order, He will destroy us this time, and will wipe us off from the face of the earth. ²² "And if we drink of this water, without God's order, He will make an end of us, and root us up at once. ²³ "Now, therefore, O God, that I am come to this place with Eve, we beg Thou wilt give us of the fruit of the garden, that we may be satisfied with it. ²⁴ "For we desire the fruit that is on the earth, and all else that we lack in it."

35

God's reply.

¹ THEN God looked again upon Adam and his weeping and groaning, and the Word of God came to him, and said unto him: – ² "O Adam, when thou wast in My garden, thou knewest neither eating nor drinking; neither faintness nor suffering; neither leanness of flesh, nor change; neither did sleep depart from thine eyes. But since thou transgressedst, and camest into this strange land, all these trials are come upon thee."

36

Figs.

¹ THEN God commanded the cherub, who kept the gate of the garden with a sword of fire in his hand, to take some of the fruit of the fig-tree, and to give it to Adam. ² The cherub obeyed the command of the Lord God, and went into the garden and brought two figs on two twigs, each fig hanging to its leaf; they were from two of the trees among which Adam and Eve hid themselves when God went to walk in the garden, and the Word of God came to Adam and Eve and said unto them, "Adam, Adam, where art thou?" ³ And Adam answered, "O God, here am I. When I heard the sound of Thee and Thy voice, I hid myself, because I am naked." ⁴ Then the cherub took two figs and brought them to Adam and Eve. But he threw them to them from afar; for they might not come near the cherub by reason of their flesh, that could not come near the fire. ⁵ At first, angels trembled at the presence of Adam and were afraid of him. But now Adam trembled before the angels and was afraid of them. ⁶ Then Adam drew near and took one fig, and Eve also came in turn and took the other. ⁷ And as they took them up in their hands, they looked at them, and knew they were from the trees among which they had hidden them elves.

37

Forty-three days of penance do not redeem one hour of sin (v. 6).

¹ THEN Adam said to Eve, "Seest thou not these figs and their leaves, with which we covered ourselves when we were stripped of our bright nature? But now, we know not what misery and suffering may come upon us from eating them. ² "Now, therefore, O Eve, let us restrain ourselves and not eat of them, thou and I; and let us ask God to give us of the fruit of the Tree of Life." ³ Thus did Adam and Eve restrain themselves, and did not eat of these figs. ⁴ But Adam began to pray to God and to beseech Him to give him of the fruit of the Tree of Life, saying thus: "O God, when we transgressed Thy commandment at the sixth hour of Friday, we were stripped of the bright nature we had, and did not continue in the garden after our transgression, more than three hours. ⁵ "But on the evening Thou madest us come out of it. O God, we transgressed against Thee one hour, and all these trials and sorrows have come upon us until this day. ⁶ "And those days together with this the forty-third day, do not redeem that one hour in which we transgressed! ⁷ "O God, look upon us with an eye of pity, and do not requite us according to our transgression of Thy commandment, in presence of Thee. ⁸ "O, God, give us of the fruit of the Tree of Life, that we may eat of it, and live, and turn not to see sufferings and other trouble, in this earth; for Thou art God. ⁹ "When we transgressed Thy commandment, Thou madest us come out of the garden, and didst send a cherub to keep the Tree of Life, lest we should eat thereof, and live; and know nothing of faintness after we transgressed. ¹⁰ "But now, O Lord, behold, we have endured all these days, and have borne sufferings. Make these forty-three days an equivalent for the one hour in which we transgressed."

38

"When 5500 years are fulfilled . . . ."

¹ AFTER these things the Word of God came to Adam, and said unto him: – ² "O Adam, as to the fruit of the Tree of Life, for which thou askest, I will not give it thee now, but when the 5500 years are fulfilled. Then will I give thee of the fruit of the Tree of Life, and thou shalt eat, and live for ever, thou, and Eve, and thy righteous seed. ³ "But these forty-three days cannot make amends for the hour in which thou didst transgress My commandment. ⁴ "O Adam, I gave thee to eat of the fig-tree in which thou didst hide thyself. Go and eat of it, thou and Eve. ⁵ "I will not deny thy request, neither will I disappoint thy hope; therefore, bear up unto the fulfilment of the covenant I made with thee." ⁶ And God withdrew His Word from Adam.

39

Adam is cautious – but too late.

¹ THEN Adam returned to Eve, and said to her, "Arise, and take a fig for thyself, and I will take another; and let us go to our cave." ² Then Adam and Eve took each a fig and went towards the cave; the time was about the setting of the sun; and their thoughts made them long to eat of the fruit. ³ But Adam said to Eve, "I am afraid to eat of this fig. I know not what may come upon me from it." ⁴ So Adam wept, and stood praying before God, saying, "Satisfy my hunger, without my having to eat this fig; for after I have eaten it, what will it profit me? And what shall I desire and ask of Thee, O God, when it is gone?" ⁵ And he said again, "I am afraid to eat of it; for I know not what will befall me through it."

40

The first Human hunger.

¹ THEN the Word of God came to Adam, and said unto him, "O, Adam, why hadst thou not this dread, neither this fasting, nor this care ere this? And why hadst thou not this fear before thou didst transgress? ² "But when thou camest to dwell in this strange land, thy animal body could not be on earth without earthly food, to strengthen it and to restore its powers." ³ And God withdrew His Word from Adam.

41

The first Human thirst.

¹ THEN Adam took the fig, and laid it on the golden rods. Eve also took her fig, and put it upon the incense. ² And the weight of each fig was that of a water-melon; for the fruit of the garden was much larger than the fruit of this land. ³ But Adam and Eve remained standing and fasting the whole of that night, until the morning dawned. ⁴ When the sun rose they were at their prayers, and Adam said to Eve, after they had done praying: – ⁵ "O Eve, come, let us go to the border of the garden looking south; to the place whence the river flows, and is parted into four heads. There we will pray to God, and ask Him to give us to drink of the Water of Life. ⁶ "For God has not fed us with the Tree of Life, in order that we may not live. We will,

therefore, ask him to give us of the Water of Life, and to quench our thirst with it, rather than with a drink of water of this land." ⁷ When Eve heard these words from Adam, she agreed; and they both arose and came to the southern border of the garden, upon the brink of the river of water at some little distance from the garden. ⁸ And they stood and prayed before the Lord, and asked Him to look upon them this once, to forgive them, and to grant them their request. ⁹ After this prayer from both of them, Adam began to pray with his voice before God, and said: – ¹⁰ "O Lord, when I was in the garden and saw the water that flowed from under the Tree of Life, my heart did not desire, neither did my body require to drink of it; neither did I know thirst, for I was living; and above that which I am now. ¹¹ "So that in order to live I did not require any Food of Life, neither did I drink of the Water of Life. ¹² "But now, O God, I am dead; my flesh is parched with thirst. Give me of the Water of Life that I may drink of it and live. ¹³ "Of Thy mercy, O God, save me from these plagues and trials, and bring me into another land different from this, if Thou wilt not let me dwell in Thy garden."

42

A promise of the Water of Life. The third prophecy of the coming of Christ.
¹ THEN came the Word of God to Adam, and said unto him: – ² "O Adam, as to what thou sayest, 'Bring me into a land where there is rest,' it is not another land than this, but it is the kingdom of heaven where alone there is rest. ³ "But thou canst not make thy entrance into it at present; but only after thy judgment is past and fulfilled. ⁴ "Then will I make thee go up into the kingdom of heaven, thee and thy righteous seed; and I will give thee and them the rest thou askest for at present. ⁵ "And if thou saidst, 'Give me of the Water of Life that I may drink and live' – it cannot be this day, but on the day that I shall descend into hell, and break the gates of brass, and bruise in pieces the kingdoms of iron. ⁶ "Then will I in mercy save thy soul and the souls of the righteous, to give them rest in My garden. And that shall be when the end of the world is come. ⁷ "And, again, as regards the Water of Life thou seekest, it will not be granted thee this day; but on the day that I shall shed My blood upon thy head in the land of Golgotha. ⁸ "For My blood shall be the Water of Life unto thee, at that time, and not to thee alone, but unto all those of thy seed who shall believe in Me; that it be unto them for rest for ever." ⁹ The Lord said again unto Adam, "O Adam, when thou wast in the garden, these trials did not come to thee ¹⁰ "But since thou didst transgress My commandment, all these sufferings have come upon thee. ¹¹. "Now, also, does thy flesh require food and drink; drink then of that water that flows by thee on the face of the earth." ¹² Then God withdrew His Word from Adam. ¹³ And Adam and Eve worshipped the Lord, and returned from the river of water to the cave. It was noon-day; and when they drew near to the cave, they saw a large fire by it.

43

The Devil attempts arson.
¹ THEN Adam and Eve were afraid, and stood still. And Adam said to Eve, "What is that fire by our cave? We do nothing in it to bring about this fire. ² "We neither have bread to bake therein, nor broth to cook there. As to this fire, we know not the like, neither do we know what to call it. ³ "But ever since God sent the cherub with a sword of fire that flashed and lightened in his hand, from fear of which we fell down and were like corpses, have we not seen the like. ⁴ "But now O Eve, behold, this is the same fire that was in the cherub's hand, which God has sent to keep the cave in which we dwell. ⁵ "O Eve, it is because God is angry with us, and will drive us from it. ⁶ "O Eve, we have again transgressed His commandment in that cave, so that He had sent this fire to burn around it, and to prevent us from going into it. ⁷ "If this be really so, O Eve, where shall we dwell? And whither shall we flee from before the face of the Lord? Since, as regards the garden, He will not let us abide in it, and He has deprived us of the good things thereof; but He has placed us in this cave, in which we have borne darkness, trials and hardships, until at last we found comfort therein. ⁸ "But now that He has brought us out into another land, who knows what may happen in it? And who knows but that the darkness of that land may be far greater than the darkness of this land? ⁹ "Who knows what may happen in that land by day or by night? And who knows whether it will be far or near, O Eve? Where it will please God to put us, may be far from the garden, O Eve! or where God will prevent us from beholding Him, because we have transgressed His commandment, and because we have made requests unto Him at all times? ¹⁰ "O Eve, if God will bring us into a strange land other than this, in which we find consolation, it must be to put our souls to death, and blot out our name from the face of the earth. ¹¹ "O Eve, if we are farther estranged from the garden and from God, where shall we find Him again, and ask Him to give us gold, incense, myrrh, and some fruit of the fig-tree? ¹² "Where shall we find Him, to comfort us a second time? Where shall we find Him, that He may think of us, as regards the covenant He has made on our behalf T' ¹³ Then Adam said no more. And they kept looking, he and Eve, towards the cave, and at the fire that flared up around it. ¹⁴ But that fire was from Satan. For he had gathered trees and dry grasses, and had carried and brought them to the cave, and had set fire to them, in order to consume the cave and – what was in it. ¹⁵ So that Adam and Eve should be left in sorrow, and he should cut off their trust in God, and make them deny Him. ¹⁶ But by the mercy of God he could not burn the cave, for God sent His angel round the cave to guard it from such a fire, until it went out. ¹⁷ And this fire lasted from noon-day until the break of day. That was the forty-fifth day.

44

The power of fire over man.
¹ YET Adam and Eve were standing and looking at the fire, and unable to come near the cave from their dread of the fire. ² And Satan kept on bringing trees and throwing them into the fire, until the flame thereof rose up on high, and covered the whole cave, thinking, as he did in his own mind, to consume the cave with much fire. But the angel of the Lord was guarding it. ³ And yet he could not curse Satan, nor injure him by word, because he had no authority over him, neither did he take to doing so with words from his mouth. ⁴ Therefore did the angel bear with him, without saying one bad word until the Word of God came who said to Satan, "Go hence; once before didst thou deceive My servants, and this time thou seekest to destroy them. ⁵ "Were it not for My mercy I would have destroyed thee and thy hosts from off the earth. But I have had patience with thee, unto the end of the world." ⁶ Then Satan fled from before the Lord. But the fire went on burning around the cave like a coal-fire the whole day; which was the forty-sixth day Adam and Eve had spent since they came out of the garden. ⁷ And when Adam and Eve saw that the heat of the fire had somewhat cooled down, they began to walk towards the cave to get into it as they were wont; but they could not, by reason of the heat of the fire. ⁸ Then they both took to weeping because of the fire that made separation between them and the cave, and that drew towards them, burning. And they were afraid. ⁹ Then Adam said to Eve, "See this fire of which we have a portion in us: which formerly yielded to us, but no longer does so, now that we have transgressed the limit of creation, and changed our condition, and our nature is altered. But the fire is not changed in its nature, nor altered from its creation. Therefore has it now power over us; and when we come near it, it scorches our flesh."

45

Why Satan didn't fulfil his promises.
¹ THEN Adam rose and prayed unto God, saying, "See, this fire has made separation between us and the cave in which Thou hast commanded us to dwell; but now, behold, we cannot go into it." ² Then God heard Adam, and sent him His Word, that said: – ³ "O Adam, see this fire! how different the flame and heat thereof are from the garden of delights and the good things in it! ⁴ "When thou wast under My control, all creatures yielded to thee; but after thou hast transgressed My commandment, they all rise over thee." ⁵ Again said God unto him, "See, O Adam, how Satan has exalted thee! He has deprived thee of the Godhead, and of an exalted state like unto Me, and has not kept his word to thee; but, after all, is become thy foe. It is he who made this fire in which he meant to burn thee and Eve. ⁶ "Why, O Adam, has he not kept his agreement with thee, not even one day; but has deprived thee of the glory that was on thee – when thou didst yield to his command? ⁷ "Thinkest thou, Adam, that he loved thee when he made this agreement with thee? Or, that he loved thee and wished to raise thee on high? ⁸ "But no, Adam, he did not do all that out of love to thee; but he wished to make thee come out of light into darkness, and from an exalted state to degradation; from glory to abasement; from joy to sorrow; and from rest to fasting and fainting." ⁹ God said also to Adam, "See this fire kindled by Satan around thy cave; see this wonder that surrounds thee; and know that it will encompass about both thee and thy seed, when ye hearken to his behest; that he will plague you with fire; and that ye shall go down into hell after ye are dead. ¹⁰ "Then shall ye see the burning of his fire, that will thus be burning around you and your seed. There shall be no deliverance from it for you, but at My coming; in like manner as thou canst not now go into thy cave, by reason of the great fire around it; not until My Word shall come that will make a way for thee on the day My covenant is fulfilled. ¹¹ "There is no way for thee at present to come from hence to rest, not until My Word comes, who is My Word. Then will He make a way for thee, and thou shalt have rest." Then God called with His Word to that fire that burned around the cave, that it part itself asunder, until Adam had gone through it. Then the fire parted itself by God's order, and a way was made for Adam. ¹² And God withdrew His Word from Adam.

46

"How many times have I delivered thee out of his hand . . ."

¹ THEN Adam and Eve began again to come into the cave. And when they came to the way between the fire, Satan blew into the fire like a whirlwind, and made on Adam and Eve a burning coal-fire; so that their bodies were singed; and the coal-fire scorched them. ² And from the burning of the fire Adam and Eve cried aloud, and said, "O Lord, save us! Leave us not to be consumed and plagued by this burning fire; neither require us for having transgressed Thy commandment." ³ Then God looked upon their bodies, on which Satan had caused fire to burn, and God sent His angel that stayed the burning fire. But the wounds remained on their bodies. ⁴ And God said unto Adam, "See Satan's love for thee, who pretended to give thee the Godhead and greatness; and, behold, he burns thee with fire, and seeks to destroy thee from off the earth. ⁵ "Then look at Me, O Adam; I created thee, and how many times have I delivered thee out of his hand? If not, would he not have destroyed thee?" ⁶ God said again to Eve, "What is that he promised thee in the garden, saying, 'At the time ye shall eat of the tree, your eyes will be opened, and you shall become like gods, knowing good and evil.' But lo! he has burnt your bodies with fire, and has made you taste the taste of fire, for the taste of the garden; and has made you see the burning of fire, and the evil thereof, and the power it has over you. ⁷ "Your eyes have seen the good he has taken from you, and in truth he has opened your eyes; and you have seen the garden in which ye were with Me, and ye have also seen the evil that has come upon you from Satan. But as to the Godhead he cannot give it you, neither fulfil his speech to you. Nay, he was bitter against you and your seed, that will come after you." ⁸ And God withdrew His Word from them.

47
The Devil's own Scheming.
¹ THEN Adam and Eve came into the cave, yet trembling at the fire that had scorched their bodies. So Adam said to Eve: – ² "Lo, the fire has burnt our flesh in this world; but how will it be when we are dead, and Satan shall punish our souls? Is not our deliverance long and far off, unless God come, and in mercy to us fulfil His promise?" ³ Then Adam and Eve passed into the cave, blessing themselves for coming into it once more. For it was in their thoughts, that they never should enter it, when they saw the fire around it. ⁴ But as the sun was setting the fire was still burning and nearing Adam and Eve in the cave, so that they could not sleep in it. After the sun had set, they went out of it. This was the forty-seventh day after they came out of the garden. ⁵ Adam and Eve then came under the top of hill by the garden to sleep, as they were wont. ⁶ And they stood and prayed God to forgive them their sins, and then fell asleep under the summit of the mountain. ⁷ But Satan, the hater of all good, thought within himself: Whereas God has promised salvation to Adam by covenant, and that He would deliver him out of all the hardships that have befallen him-but has not promised me by covenant, and will not deliver me out of my hardships; nay, since He has promised him that He should make him and his seed dwell in the kingdom in which I once was – I will kill Adam. ⁸ The earth shall be rid of him; and shall be left to me alone; so that when he is dead he may not have any seed left to inherit the kingdom that shall remain my own realm; God will then be in want of me, and He will restore me to it with my hosts.

48
Fifth apparition of Satan to Adam and Eve.
¹ AFTER this Satan called to his hosts, all of which came to him, and said unto him: – ² "O, our Lord, what wilt thou do?" ³ He then said unto them, "Ye know that this Adam, whom God created out of the dust, is he who has taken our kingdom. Come, let us gather together and kill him; or hurl a rock at him and at Eve, and crush them under it." ⁴ When Satan's hosts heard these words, they came to the part of the mountain where Adam and Eve were asleep. ⁵ Then Satan and his hosts took a huge rock, broad and even, and without blemish, thinking within himself, "If there should be a hole in the rock, when it fell on them, the hole in the rock might come upon them, and so they would escape and not die." ⁶ He then said to his hosts, "Take up this stone, and throw it flat upon them, so that it roll not from them to somewhere else. And when ye have hurled it, flee and tarry not." ⁷ And they did as he bid them. But as the rock fell down from the mountain upon Adam and Eve, God commanded it to become a kind of shed over them, that did them no harm. And so it was by God's order. ⁸ But when the rock fell, the whole earth quaked with it, and. was shaken from the size of the rock. ⁹ And as it quaked and shook, Adam and Eve awoke from sleep, and found themselves under a rock like a shed. But they knew not how it was; for when they fell asleep they were under the sky, and not under a shed; and when they saw it, they were afraid. ¹⁰ Then Adam said to Eve, "Wherefore has the mountain bent itself, and the earth quaked and shaken on our account? And why has this rock spread itself over us like a tent? ¹¹ "Does God intend to plague us and to shut us up in this prison? Or will He close the earth upon us? ¹² "He is angry with us for our having come out of the cave without His order; and for our having done so of our own accord, without consulting Him, when we left the cave and came to this place." ¹³ Then Eve said, "If, indeed, the earth quaked for our sake, and this rock forms a tent over us because of our transgression, then woe be to us, O Adam, for our punishment will be long. ¹⁴ "But arise and pray Ito God to let us know concerning this, and what this rock is, that is spread over us like a tent." ¹⁵ Then Adam stood up and prayed before the Lord, to let him know about this strait. And Adam thus stood praying until the morning.

49
The first prophecy of the Resurrection.
¹ THEN the Word of God came and said: – ² "O Adam, who counselled thee, when thou earnest out of the cave, to come to this place?" ³ And Adam said unto God, "O Lord, we came to this place because of the heat of the fire, that came upon us inside the cave." ⁴ Then the Lord God said unto Adam, "O Adam, thou dreadest the heat of fire for one night, but how will it be when thou dwellest in hell? ⁵ "Yet, O Adam, fear not, neither say in thy heart that I have spread this rock as an awning over thee, to plague thee therewith. ⁶ "It came from Satan, who had promised thee the Godhead and majesty. It is he who threw down this rock to kill thee under it, and Eve with thee, and thus to prevent you from living upon the earth. ⁷ "But, in mercy for you, just as that rock was falling down upon you, I commanded it to form an awning over you; and the rock under you, to lower itself. ⁸ "And this sign, O Adam, will happen to Me at My coming upon earth: Satan will raise the people of the Jews Jo put Me to death; and they will lay Me in a rock, and seal a large stone upon Me, and I shall remain within that rock three days and three nights. ⁹ "But on the third day I shall rise again, and it shall be salvation to thee, O Adam, and to thy seed, to believe in Me. But, O Adam, I will not bring thee from under this rock until three days and three nights are passed." ¹⁰ And God withdrew His Word from Adam. ¹¹ But Adam and Eve abode under the rock three days and three nights, as God had told them. ¹² And God did so to them because they had left their cave and had come to this same place without God's order. ¹³ But, after three days and three nights, God opened the rock and brought them out from under it. Their flesh was dried up, and their eyes and their hearts were troubled from weeping and sorrow.

50
Adam and Eve seek to cover their nakedness.
¹ THEN Adam and Eve went forth and came into the Cave of Treasures, and they stood praying in it the whole of that day, until the evening. ² And this took place at the end of fifty days after they had left the garden. ³ But Adam and Eve rose again and prayed to God in the cave the whole of that night, and begged for mercy from Him. ⁴ And when the day dawned, Adam said unto Eve, "Come! let us go and do some work for our bodies." ⁵ So they went out of the cave, and came to the northern border of the garden, and they sought something to cover their bodies withal. But they found nothing, and knew not how to do the work. Yet their bodies were stained, and they were speechless from cold and heat. ⁶ Then Adam stood and asked God to show him something wherewith to cover their bodies. ⁷ Then came the Word of God and said unto him, "O Adam, take Eve and come to the seashore, where ye fasted before. There ye shall find skins of sheep, whose flesh was devoured by lions, and whose skins were left. Take them and make raiment for yourselves, and clothe yourselves withal."

51
"*What is his beauty that you should have followed him?*"
¹ WHEN Adam heard these words from God, he took Eve and removed from the northern end of the garden to the south of it, by the river of water, where they once fasted. ² But as they were going in the way, and before they reached that place, Satan, the wicked one, had heard the Word of God communing with Adam respecting his covering. ³ It grieved him, and he hastened to the place where the sheep-skins were, with the intention of taking them and throwing them into the sea, or of burning them with fire, that Adam and Eve should not find them. ⁴ But as he was about to take them, the Word of God came from heaven, and bound him by the side of those skins until Adam and Eve came near him. But as they neared him they were afraid of him, and of his hideous look. ⁵ Then came the Word of God to Adam and Eve, and said to them, "This is he who was hidden in the serpent, and who deceived you, and stripped you of the garment of light and glory in which you were. ⁶ "This is he who promised you majesty and divinity. Where, then, is the beauty that was on him? Where is his divinity? Where is his light? Where is the glory that rested on him? ⁷ "Now his figure is hideous; he is become abominable among angels; and he has come to be called Satan. ⁸ "O Adam I he wished to take from you this earthly garment of sheep-skins, and to destroy it, and not let you be covered with it. ⁹ "What, then, is his beauty that you should have followed him? And what have you gained by hearkening to him? See his evil works and then look at Me; at

Me, your Creator, and at the good deeds I do you. ¹⁰ "See, I bound him until you came and saw him and beheld his weakness, that no power is left with him." ¹¹ And God released him from his bonds.

52

Adam and Eve sew the first shirt.

¹ AFTER this Adam and Eve said no more, but wept before God on account of their creation, and of their bodies that required an earthly covering. ² Then Adam said unto Eve, "O Eve, this is the skin of beasts with which we shall be covered. But when we have put it on, behold, a token of death shall have come upon us, inasmuch as the owners of these skins have died, and have wasted away. So also shall we die, and pass away." ³ Then Adam and Eve took the skins, and went back to the Cave of Treasures; and when in it, they stood and prayed as they were wont. ⁴ And they thought how they could make garments of those skins; for they had no skill for it. ⁵ Then God sent to them His angel to show them how to work it out. And the angel said to Adam, "Go forth, and bring some palm-thorns." Then Adam went out, and brought some, as the angel had commanded him. ⁶ Then the angel began before them to work out the skins, after the manner of one who prepares a shirt. And he took the thorns and stuck them into the skins, before their eyes. ⁷ Then the angel again stood up and prayed God that the thorns in those skins should be hidden, so as to be, as it were, sewn with one thread. ⁸ And so it was, by God's order; they became garments for Adam and Eve, and He clothed them withal. ⁹ From that time the nakedness of their bodies was covered from the sight of each other's eyes. ¹⁰ And this happened at the end of the fifty-first day. ¹¹ Then when Adam's and Eve's bodies were covered, they stood and prayed, and sought mercy of the Lord, and forgiveness, and gave Him thanks for that He had had mercy on them, and had covered their nakedness. And they ceased not from prayer the whole of that night. ¹² Then when the mom dawned at the rising of the sun, they said their prayers after their custom; and then went out of the cave. ¹³ And Adam said unto Eve, "Since we know not what there is to the westward of this cave, let us go forth and see it to-day." Then they came forth and went towards the western border.

53

The prophecy of the Western Lands.

¹ THEY were not very far from the cave, when Satan came towards them, and hid himself between them and the cave, under the form of two ravenous lions three days without food, that came towards Adam and Eve, as if to break them in pieces and devour them. ² Then Adam and Eve wept, and prayed God to deliver them from their paws. ³ Then the Word of God came to them, and drove away the lions from them. ⁴ And God said unto Adam, "O Adam, what seekest thou on the western border? And why hast thou left of thine own accord the eastern border, in which was thy dwelling-place? ⁵ "Now, then, turn back to thy cave, and remain in it, that Satan do not deceive thee, nor work his purpose upon thee. ⁶ "For in this western border, O Adam, there will go from thee a seed, that shall replenish it; and that will defile themselves with their sins, and with their yielding to the behests of Satan, and by following his works. ⁷ "Therefore will I bring upon them the waters of a flood, and overwhelm them all. But I will deliver what is left of the righteous among them; and I will bring them to a distant land, and the land in which thou dwellest now shall remain desolate and without one inhabitant in it." ⁸ After God had thus discoursed to them, they went back to the Cave of Treasures. But their flesh was dried up, and their strength failed from fasting and praying, and from the sorrow they felt at having trespassed against God.

54

Adam and Eve go exploring.

¹ THEN Adam and Eve stood up in the cave and prayed the whole of that night until the morning dawned. And when the sun was risen they both went out of the cave; their heads wandering from heaviness of sorrow, and they not knowing whither they went. ² And they walked thus unto the southern border of the garden. And they began to go up that border until they came to the eastern border beyond which there was no farther space. ³ And the cherub who guarded the garden was standing at the western gate, and guarding it against Adam and Eve, lest they should suddenly come into the garden. And the cherub turned round, as if to put them to death; according to the commandment God had given him. ⁴ When Adam and Eve came to the eastern border of the garden – thinking in their hearts that the cherub was not watching – as they were standing by the gate as if wishing to go in, suddenly came the cherub with a flashing sword of fire in his hand; and when he saw them, he went forth to kill them. For he was afraid lest God should destroy him if they went into the garden without His order. ⁵ And the sword of the cherub seemed to flame afar off. But when he raised it over Adam and Eve, the flame thereof did not flash forth. ⁶ Therefore did the cherub think that God was favourable to them, and was bringing them back into the garden. And the cherub stood wondering. ⁷ He could not go up to Heaven to ascertain God's order regarding their getting into the garden; he therefore abode standing by them, unable as he was to part from them; for he was afraid lest they should enter the garden without leave from God, who then would destroy him. ⁸ When Adam and Eve saw the cherub coming towards them with a flaming sword of fire in his hand, they fell on their faces from fear, and were as dead. ⁹ At that time the heavens and the earth shook; and other cherubim came down from heaven to the cherub who guarded the garden, and saw him amazed and silent. ¹⁰ Then, again, other angels came down nigh unto the place where Adam and Eve were. They were divided between joy and sorrow. ¹¹ They were glad, because they thought that God was favourable to Adam, and wished him to return to the garden; and wished to restore him to the gladness he once enjoyed. ¹² But they sorrowed over Adam, because he was fallen like a dead man, he and Eve; and they said in their thoughts, "Adam has not died in this place; but God has put him to death, for his having come to this place, and wishing to get into the garden without His leave."

55

The Conflict of Satan.

¹ THEN came the Word of God to Adam and Eve, and raised them from their dead state, saying unto them, "Why came ye up hither? Dr, you intend to go into the garden, from which I brought you out? it can not be to-day; but only when the covenant I have made with you is fulfilled." ² Then Adam, when he heard the Word of God, and the fluttering of the angels whom he did not see, but only heard the sound of them with his ears, he and Eve wept, and said to the angels: – ³ "O Spirits, who wait upon God, look upon me, and upon my being unable to see you! For when I was in my former bright nature) then I could see you. I sang praises as you do; and my heart was far above you. ⁴ "But now, that I have transgressed, that bright nature is gone from me, and I am come to this miserable state. And now am I come to this, that I cannot see you, and you do not serve me As you were wont. For I am become animal flesh. ⁵ "Yet now O angels of God, ask God with me, to restore me to that wherein I was formerly; to rescue me from this misery, and to remove from me the sentence of death He passed upon me, for having trespassed against Him." ⁶ Then, when the angels heard these words, they all grieved over him; and cursed Satan who had beguiled Adam, until he came from the garden to misery; from life to death; from peace to trouble; and from gladness to a strange land. ⁷ Then the angels said unto Adam, "Thou didst hearken to Satan, and didst forsake the Word of God who created thee; and thou didst believe that Satan would fulfil all he had promised thee. ⁸ "But now, O Adam, we will make known to thee, what came upon us through him, before his fall from heaven. ⁹ "He gathered together his hosts, and deceived them, promising them to give them a great kingdom, a divine nature; and other promises he made them. ¹⁰ "His hosts believed that. his word was true, so they yielded to him, and renounced the glory of God. ¹¹ "He then sent for us according to the orders in which we were-to come under his command, and to hearken to his vain promise. But we would not, and we took not his advice. ¹² "Then after he had fought with God, and had dealt forwardly with Him, he gathered together his hosts, and made war with us. And if it had not been for God's strength that was with us, we could not have prevailed against him to hurl him from heaven. ¹³ "But when he fell from among us, there was great joy in heaven, because of his going down from us. For had he continued in heaven, nothing, not even one angel would have remained in it. ¹⁴ "But God in His mercy, drove him from among us to this dark earth; for he had become darkness itself and a worker of unrighteousness. ¹⁵ "And he has continued, O Adam, to make war against thee, until he beguiled thee and made thee come out of the garden, to this strange land, where all these trials have come to thee. And death, which God brought upon him he has also brought to thee, O Adam, because thou didst obey him, and didst transgress against God." ¹⁶ Then the angels rejoiced and praised God, and asked Him not to destroy Adam this time, for his having sought to enter the garden; but to bear with him until the fulfilment of the promise; and to help him in this world until he was free from Satan's hand.

56

A chapter of divine comfort.

¹ THEN came the Word of God to Adam, and said unto him: – ² "O Adam, look at that garden of joy and at this earth of toil, and behold the angels who are in the garden-that is full of them, and see thyself alone on this earth, with Satan whom thou didst obey. ³ "Yet, if thou hadst submitted, and been obedient to Me, and hadst kept My Word, thou wouldst be with My angels in My garden. ⁴ "But when thou didst transgress and hearken to Satan, thou didst become his guest among his angels, that are full of wickedness; and thou camest to this earth, that brings forth to thee thorns and thistles. ⁵ "O Adam, ask him who deceived thee, to give thee the divine nature he

promised thee, or to make thee a garden as I had made for thee; or to fill thee with that same bright nature with which I had filled thee. ⁶ "Ask him to make thee a body like the one I made thee, or to give thee a day of rest as I gave thee; or to create within thee a reasonable soul, as I did create for thee; or to remove thee hence to some other earth than this one which I gave thee. But, O Adam, he will not fulfil even one of the things he told thee. ⁷ "Acknowledge, then, My favour towards thee, and My mercy on thee, My creature; that I have not requited thee for thy transgression against Me, but in My pity for thee I have promised thee that at the end of the great five days and a half I will come and save thee." ⁸ Then God said again to Adam and Eve, "Arise, go down hence, lest the cherub with a sword of fire in his hand destroy you." ⁹ But Adam's heart was comforted by God's words to him, and he worshipped before Him. ¹⁰ And God commanded His angels to escort Adam and Eve to the cave with joy, instead of the fear that had come upon them. ¹¹ Then the angels took up Adam and Eve, and brought them down from the mountain by the garden, with songs and psalms, until they brought them to the cave. There the angels began to comfort and to strengthen them, and then departed from them towards heaven, to their Creator, who had sent them. ¹² But, after the angels were gone from Adam and Eve, came Satan, with shamefacedness, and stood at the entrance of the cave in which were Adam and Eve. He then called to Adam, and said, "O Adam, come, let me speak to thee." ¹³ Then Adam came out of the cave, thinking he was one of God's angels that was come to give him some good counsel.

57

"Therefore did I fall. . ."

¹ BUT when Adam came out and saw his hideous figure, he was afraid of him, and said unto him, "Who art thou?" ² Then Satan answered and said unto him, "It is I, who hid myself within the serpent, and who talked to Eve, and beguiled her until she hearkened to my command. I am he who sent her, through the wiles of my speech, to deceive thee, until thou and she ate of the fruit of the tree, and ye came away from under the command of God." ³ But when Adam heard these words from him, he said unto him, "Canst thou make me a garden as God made for me? Or canst thou clothe me in the same bright nature in which God had clothed me? ⁴ "Where is the divine nature thou didst promise to give me? Where is that fair speech of thine, thou didst hold with us at first, when we were in the garden?" ⁵ Then Satan said unto Adam, "Thinkest thou, that when I have spoken to one about anything, I shall ever bring it to him or fulfil my word? Not so. For I myself have never even thought of obtaining what I asked. ⁶ "Therefore did I fall, and did I make you fall by that for which I myself fell; and with you also, whosoever accepts my counsel, falls thereby. ⁷ "But now, O Adam, by reason of thy fall thou art under my rule, and I am king over thee; because thou hast hearkened to me, and hast transgressed against thy God. Neither will there be any deliverance from my hands until the day promised thee by thy God." ⁸ Again he said, "Inasmuch as we do not know the day agreed upon with thee by thy God, nor the hour in which thou shalt be delivered, for that reason will we multiply war and murder upon thee and thy seed after thee. ⁹ "This is our will and our good pleasure, that we may not leave one of the sons of men to inherit our orders in heaven. ¹⁰ "For as to our abode, O Adam, it is in burning fire; and we will not cease our evil doing no, not one day nor one hour. And I, O Adam, shall sow fire upon thee when thou comest into the cave to dwell there." ¹¹ When Adam heard these words he wept and mourned, and said unto Eve, "Hear what he said; that he will not fulfil aught of what he told thee in the garden. Did he really then become king over us? ¹² "But we will ask God, who created us, to deliver us out of his hands."

58

"About sunset on the 53rd day . . . ."

¹ THEN Adam and Eve spread their hands unto God, praying and entreating Him to drive Satan away from them; that he do them no violence, and do not force them to deny God. ² Then God sent to them at once His angel, who drove away Satan – from them. This happened about sunset, on the fifty-third day after they had come out of the garden. ³ Then Adam and Eve went into the cave, and stood up and turned their faces to the earth, to pray to God. ⁴ But ere they prayed Adam said unto Eve, "Lo, thou hast seen what temptations have befallen us in this land. Come, let us arise, and ask God to forgive us the sins we have committed; and we will not come out until the end of the day next to the fortieth. And if we die herein, He will save us." ⁵ Then Adam and Eve arose, and joined together in entreating God. ⁶ They abode thus praying in the cave; neither did they come out of it, by night or by day, until their prayers went up out of their mouths, like a flame of fire.

59

Eighth apparition of Satan to Adam and Eve.

¹ BUT Satan, the hater of all good, did not allow them to end their prayers. For he called to his hosts, and they came, all of them. He then said to them, "Since Adam and Eve, whom we beguiled, have agreed together to pray to God night and day, and to entreat Him to deliver them, and since they will not come out of the cave until the end of the fortieth day. ² "And since they will continue their prayers as they have both agreed to do, that He will deliver them out of our hands, and restore them to their former state, see what we shall do unto them." And his hosts said unto him, "Power is thine, O our Lord, to do what thou listest." ³ Then Satan, great in wickedness, took his hosts and came into the cave, in the thirtieth night of the forty days and one; and he smote Adam and Eve, until he left them dead. ⁴ Then came the Word of God unto Adam and Eve, who raised them from their suffering, and God said unto Adam, "Be strong, and be not afraid of him who has just come to thee." ⁵ But Adam wept and said, "Where wast Thou, O my God, that they should smite me with such blows, and that this suffering should come upon us; upon me and upon Eve, Thy handmaid?" ⁶ Then God said unto him, "O Adam, see, he is lord and master of all thou hast, he who said, he would give thee divinity. Where is this love for thee? And where is the gift he promised? ⁷ "For once has it pleased him, O Adam, to come to thee, to comfort thee, and to strengthen thee, and to rejoice with thee, and to send his hosts to guard thee; because thou hast hearkened to him, and hast yielded to his counsel; and hast transgressed My commandment but has followed his behest?" ⁸ Then Adam wept before the Lord, and said, "O Lord because I transgressed a little, Thou hast sorely plagued me in return for it, I ask Thee to deliver me out of his hands; or else have pity on me, and take my soul out of my body now in this strange land." ⁹ Then God said unto Adam, "If only there had been this sighing and praying before, ere thou didst transgress! Then wouldst thou have rest from the trouble in which thou art now." ¹⁰ But God had patience with Adam, and let him and Eve remain in the cave until they had fulfilled the forty days. ¹¹ But as to Adam and Eve, their strength and flesh withered from fasting and praying, from hunger and thirst; for they had not tasted either food or drink since they left the garden; nor were the functions of their bodies yet settled; and they had no strength left to continue in prayer from hunger, until the end of the next day to the fortieth. They were fallen down in the cave; yet what speech escaped from their mouths, was only in praises.

60

The Devil appears like an old man. He offers "a place of rest."

¹ THEN on the eighty-ninth day, Satan came to the cave, clad in a garment of light, and girt about with a bright girdle. ² In his hands was a staff of light, and he looked most awful: but his face was pleasant and his speech was sweet, ³ He thus transformed himself in order to deceive Adam and Eve, and to make them come out of the cave, ere they had fulfilled the forty days. ⁴ For he said within himself, "Now that when they had fulfilled the forty days' fasting and praying, God would restore them to their former estate; but if He did not do so, He would still be favourable to them; and even if He had not mercy on them, would He yet give them something from the garden to comfort them; as already twice before." ⁵ Then Satan drew near the cave in this fair appearance, and said: – ⁶ "O Adam, rise ye, stand up, thou and Eve, and come along with me, to a good land; and fear not. I am flesh and bones like you; and at first I was a creature that God created. ⁷ "And it was so, that when He had created me, He placed me in a garden in the north, on the border of the world. ⁸ "And He said to me, 'Abide here!' And I abode there according to His Word, neither did I transgress His commandment. ⁹ "Then He made a slumber to come over me, and He brought thee, O Adam, out of my side, but did not make thee abide by me. ¹⁰ "But God took thee in His divine hand, and placed thee in a garden to the eastward. ¹¹ "Then I grieved because of thee, for that while God had taken thee out of my side, He had not let thee abide with me. ¹² "But God said unto me: 'Grieve not because of Adam, whom I brought out of thy side; no harm will come to him. ¹³ "'For now I have brought out of his side a help-meet for him; and I have given him joy by so doing.'" ¹⁴ Then Satan said again, "I did not know how it is ye are in this cave, nor anything about this trial that has come upon you-until God said to me, 'Behold, Adam has transgressed, he whom I had taken out of thy side, and Eve also, whom I took out of his side; and I have driven them out of the garden; I have made them dwell in a land of sorrow and misery, because they transgressed against Me, and have hearkened to Satan. And lo, they are in suffering unto this day, the eightieth.' ¹⁵ "Then God said unto me, 'Arise, go to them, and make them come to thy place, and suffer not that Satan come near them, and afflict them. For they are now in great misery; and lie helpless from hunger.' ¹⁶ "He further said to me, 'When thou hast taken them to thyself, give them to eat of the fruit of the Tree of Life, and give them to drink of the water of peace; and clothe them in a garment of light, and restore them to their former state of grace, and leave them not in misery, for they came

from thee. But grieve not over them, nor repent of that which has come upon them.' ¹⁷ "But when I heard this, I was sorry; and my heart could not patiently bear it for thy sake, O my child. ¹⁸ "But, O Adam, when I heard the name of Satan, I was afraid, and I said within myself, I will not come out, lest he ensnare me, as he did my children, Adam and Eve. ¹⁹ "And I said, 'O God, when I go to my children, Satan will meet me in the way, and war against me, as he did against them.' ²⁰ "Then God said unto me, 'Fear not; when thou findest him, smite him with the staff that is in thine hand, and be not afraid of him for thou art of old standing, and he shall not prevail against thee.' ²¹ "Then I said, 'O my Lord, I am old, and cannot go. Send Thy angels to bring them.' ²² "But God said unto me, 'Angels, verily, are not like them; and they will not consent to come with them. But I have chosen thee, because they are thy offspring, and like thee, and will hearken to what thou sayest.' ²³ "God said further to me, 'If thou hast not strength to walk, I will send a cloud to carry thee and alight thee at the entrance of their cave; then the cloud will return and leave thee there. ²⁴ "'And if they will come with thee, I will send a cloud to carry thee and them.' ²⁵ "Then He commanded a cloud, and it bare me up and brought me to you; and then went back. ²⁶ "And now O my children, Adam and Eve, look at my hoar hairs and at my feeble estate, and at my coming from that distant place. Come, come with me, to a place of rest." ²⁷ Then he began to weep and to sob before Adam and Eve, and his tears poured upon the earth like water. ²⁸ And when Adam and Eve raised their eyes and saw his beard, and heard his sweet talk, their hearts softened towards him; they hearkened unto him, for they believed he was true. ²⁹ And it seemed to them that they really were his offspring, when they saw that his face was like their own; and they trusted him.

61

They begin to follow Satan.

¹ THEN he took Adam and Eve by the hand, and began to bring them out of the cave. ² But when they were come a little way out of it, God knew that Satan had overcome them, and had brought them out ere the forty days were ended, to take them to some distant place, and to destroy them. ³ Then the Word of the Lord God again came and cursed Satan, and drove him away from them. ⁴ And God began to speak unto Adam and Eve, saying to them, "What made you come out of the cave, unto this place?" ⁵ Then Adam said unto God, "Didst thou create a man before us? For when we were in the cave there suddenly came unto us a good old man who said to us, 'I am a messenger from God unto you, to bring you back to some place of rest.' ⁶ "And we did believe, O God, that he was a messenger from Thee; and we came out with him; and knew not whither we should go with him." ⁷ Then God said unto Adam, "See, that is the father of evil arts, who brought thee and Eve out of the Garden of Delights. And now, indeed, when he saw that thou and Eve both joined together in fasting and praying, and that you came not out of the cave before the end of the forty days, he wished to make your purpose vain, to break your mutual bond; to cut off all hope from you, and to drive you to some place where he might destroy you. ⁸ "Because he was unable to do aught to you, unless he showed himself in the likeness of you. ⁹ "Therefore did he come to you with a face like your own, and began to give you tokens as if they were all true. ¹⁰ "But I in mercy and with the favour I had unto you, did not allow him to destroy you; but I drove him away from you. ¹¹ "Now, therefore, O Adam, take Eve, and return to your cave, and remain in it until the morrow of the fortieth day. And when ye come out, go towards the eastern gate of the garden." ¹² Then Adam and Eve worshipped God, and praised and blessed Him for the deliverance that had come to them from Him. And they returned towards the cave. This happened at eventide of the thirty-ninth day. ¹³ Then Adam and Eve stood up and with great zeal, prayed to God, to be brought out of their want for strength; for their strength had departed from them, through hunger and thirst and prayer. But they watched the whole of that night praying, until morning. ¹⁴ Then Adam said unto Eve, "Arise, let us go towards the eastern gate of the garden as God told us." ¹⁵ And they said their prayers as they were wont to do every day; and they went out of the cave, to go near to the eastern gate of the garden. ¹⁶ Then Adam and Eve stood up and prayed, and besought God to strengthen them, and to send them something to satisfy their hunger. ¹⁷ But when they had ended their prayers, they remained where they were by reason of their failing strength. ¹⁸. Then came the Word of God again, and said unto them, "O Adam, arise, go and bring hither two figs." ¹⁹ Then Adam and Eve arose, and went until they drew near to the cave.

62

Two fruit trees.

¹ BUT Satan the wicked was envious, because of the consolation God had given them. ² So he prevented them, and went into the cave and took the two figs, and buried them outside the cave, so that Adam and Eve should not find them. He also had in his thoughts to destroy them. ³ But by God's mercy, as soon as those two figs were in the earth, God defeated Satan's counsel regarding them; and made them into two fruit-trees, that overshadowed the cave. For Satan had buried them on the eastern side of it. ⁴ Then when the two trees were grown, and were covered with fruit, Satan grieved and mourned, and said, "Better were it to have left those figs as they were; for now, behold, they have become two fruit-trees, whereof Adam will eat all the days of his life. Whereas I had in mind, when I buried them, to destroy them entirely, and to hide them for aye. ⁵ "But God has overturned my counsel; and would not that this sacred fruit should perish; and He has made plain my intention, and has defeated the counsel I had formed against His servants." ⁶ Then Satan went away ashamed, of not having wrought out his design.

63

The first joy of trees.

¹ BUT Adam and Eve, as they drew near to the cave, saw two fig-trees, covered with fruit, and overshadowing the cave. ² Then Adam said to Eve, "It seems to me we have gone astray. When did these two trees grow here? It seems to me that the enemy wishes to lead us astray, Sayest thou that there is in the earth another cave than this? ³ "Yet, O Eve, let us go into the cave, and find in it the two figs; for this is our cave, in which we were. But if we should not find the two figs in it, then it cannot be our cave." ⁴ They went then into the cave, and looked into the four corners of it, but found not the two figs. ⁵ And Adam wept and said to Eve, "Are we come to a wrong cave, then, O Eve? It seems to me these two fig-trees are the two figs that were in the cave." And Eve said, "I, for my part, do not know." ⁶ Then Adam stood up and prayed and said, "O God, Thou didst command us to come back to the cave, to take the two figs, and then to return to Thee. ⁷ "But now, we have not found them. O God, hast Thou taken them, and sown these two trees, or have we gone astray in the earth; or has the enemy deceived us? If it be real, then, O God, reveal to us the secret of these two trees and of the two figs." ⁸ Then came the Word of God to Adam, and said unto him, "O Adam, when I sent thee to fetch the figs, Satan went before thee to the cave, took the figs, and buried them outside, eastward of the cave, thinking to destroy them; and not sowing them with good intent. ⁹ "Not for his mere sake, then, have these trees grown up at once; but I had mercy on thee and I commanded them to grow. And they grew to be two large trees, that you be overshadowed by their branches, and find rest; and that I make you see My power and My marvellous works. ¹⁰ "And, also, to show you Satan's meanness, and his evil works, for ever since ye came out of the garden, he has not ceased, no, not one day, from doing you some harm. But I have not given him power over you." ¹¹ And God said, "Henceforth, O Adam, rejoice on account of the trees, thou and Eve; and rest under them when ye feel weary. But eat not of their fruit, nor come near them." ¹² Then Adam wept, and said, "O God, wilt Thou again kill us, or wilt Thou drive us away from before Thy face, and cut our life from off the face of the earth? ¹³ "O God, I beseech Thee, if Thou knowest that there be in these trees either death or some other evil, as at the first time, root them up from near our cave, and wither them; and leave us to die of the heat, of hunger and of thirst. ¹⁴ "For we know Thy marvellous works, O God, that they are great, and that by Thy power Thou canst bring one thing out of another, without one's wish. For Thy power can make rocks to become trees, and trees to become rocks."

64

Adam and Eve partake of the first earthly food.

¹ THEN God looked upon Adam and upon his strength of mind, upon his endurance of hunger and thirst, and of the heat. And he changed the two fig-trees into two figs, as they were at first, and then said to Adam and to Eve, "Each of you may take one fig." And they took them, as the Lord commanded them. ² And he said to them, "Go ye into the cave, and eat the figs, and satisfy your hunger, lest ye die." ³ So, as God commanded them, they went into the cave, about the time when the sun was setting. And Adam and Eve stood up and prayed at the time of the setting sun. ⁴ Then they sat down to eat the figs; but they knew not how to eat them; for they were not accustomed to eat earthly food. They feared also lest, if they ate, their stomach should be burdened and their flesh thickened, and their hearts take to liking earthly food. ⁵ But while they were thus seated, God, out of pity for them, sent them His angel, lest they should perish of hunger and thirst. ⁶ And the angel said unto Adam and Eve, "God says to you that ye have not strength to fast until death; eat, therefore, and strengthen your bodies; for ye are now animal flesh, that cannot subsist without food and drink." ⁷ Then Adam and Eve took the figs and began to eat of them. But God had put into them a mixture as of savoury bread and blood. ⁸ Then the angel went from Adam and Eve, who ate of the figs until they had satisfied their hunger. Then they put by what remained; but by the power of God, the figs became

full as before, because God blessed them. ⁹ After this Adam and Eve arose, and prayed with a joyful heart and renewed strength, and praised and rejoiced abundantly the whole of that night. And this was the end of the eighty-third day.

65

Adam and Eve acquire digestive organs. Final hope of returning to the Garden is quenched.

¹ AND when it was day, they rose and prayed, after their custom, and then went out of the cave. ² But as they felt great trouble from the food they had eaten, and to which they were not used, they went about in the cave saying to each other: – ³ "What has happened to us through eating, that this pain should have come upon us? Woe be to us, we shall die! Better for us to have died than to have eaten; and to have kept our bodies pure, than to have defiled them with food." ⁴ Then Adam said to Eve, "This pain did not come to us in the garden, neither did we eat such bad food there. Thinkest thou, O Eve, that God will plague us through the food that is in us, or that our inwards will come out; or that God means to kill us with this pain before He has fulfilled His promise to us?" ⁵ Then Adam besought the Lord and said, "O Lord, let us not perish through the food we have eaten. O Lord, smite us not; but deal with us according to Thy great mercy, and forsake us not until the day of the promise Thou hast made us." ⁶ Then God looked upon them, and at once fitted them for eating food; as unto this day; so that they should not perish. ⁷ Then Adam and Eve came back into the cave sorrowful and weeping because of the alteration in their nature. And they both knew from that hour that they were altered beings, that their hope of returning to the garden was now cut off; and that they could not enter it. ⁸ For that now their bodies had strange functions; and all flesh that requires food and drink for its existence, cannot be in the garden. ⁹ Then Adam said to Eve, "Behold, our hope is now cut off; and so is our trust to enter the garden. We no longer belong to the inhabitants of the garden; but henceforth we are earthy and of the dust, and of the inhabitants of the earth, We shall not return to the garden, until the day in which God has promised to save us, and to bring us again into the garden, as He promised us." ¹⁰ Then they prayed to God that He would have mercy on them; after which, their mind was quieted, their hearts were broken, and their longing was cooled down; and they were like strangers on earth. That night Adam and Eve spent in the cave, where they slept heavily by reason of the food they had eaten.

66

Adam does his first day's work.

¹ WHEN it was morning, the day after they had eaten food, Adam and Eve prayed in the cave, and Adam said unto Eve, "Lo, we asked for food of God, and He gave it. But now let us also ask Him to give us a drink of water." ² Then they arose, and went to the bank of the stream of water, that was on the south border of the garden, in which they had before thrown themselves. And they stood on the bank, and prayed to God that He would command them to drink of the water. ³ Then the Word of God came to Adam, and said unto him, "O Adam, thy body is become brutish, and requires water to drink. Take ye, and drink, thou and Eve; give thanks and praise." ⁴ Adam and Eve then drew near, and drank of it, until their bodies felt refreshed. After having drunk, they praised God, and then returned to their cave, after their former custom. This happened at the end of eighty-three days. ⁵ Then on the eighty-fourth day, they took two figs and hung them in the cave, together with the leaves thereof, to be to them a sign and a blessing from God. And they placed them there until there should arise a posterity to them, who should see the wonderful things God had done to them. ⁶ Then Adam and Eve again stood outside the cave, and besought God to show them some food wherewith to nourish their bodies. ⁷ Then the Word of God came and said unto him, "O Adam, go down to the westward of the cave, as far as a land of dark soil, and there thou shalt find food." ⁸ And Adam hearkened unto the Word of God, took Eve, and went down to a land of dark soil, and found there wheat growing, in the ear and ripe, and figs to eat; and Adam rejoiced over it. ⁹ Then the Word of God came again to Adam, and said unto him, "Take of this wheat and make thee bread of it, to nourish thy body withal." And God gave Adam's heart wisdom, to work out the corn until it became bread. ¹⁰ Adam accomplished all that, until he grew very faint and weary. He then returned to the cave; rejoicing at what he had learned of what is done with wheat, until it is made into bread for one's use.

67

"Then Satan began to lead astray Adam and Eve. . . ."

¹ BUT when Adam and Eve went down to the land of black mud, and came near to the wheat God had showed them, and saw it ripe and ready for reaping, as they had no sickle to reap it withal – they girt themselves, and began to pull up the wheat, until it was all done. ² Then they made it into a heap; and, faint from heat and from thirst, they went under a shady tree, where the breeze fanned them to sleep. ³ But Satan saw what Adam and Eve had done. And he called his hosts, and said to them, "Since God has shown to Adam and Eve all about this wheat, wherewith to strengthen their bodies – and, lo, they are come and have made a heap of it, and faint from the toil are now asleep – come, let us set fire to this heap of corn, and burn it, and let us take that bottle of water that is by them, and empty it out, so that they may find nothing to drink, and we kill them with hunger and thirst. ⁴ "Then, when they wake up from their sleep, and seek to return to the cave, we will come to them in the way, and will lead them astray; so that they die of hunger and thirst; when they may, perhaps, deny God, and He destroy them. So shall we be rid of them." ⁵ Then Satan and his hosts threw fire upon the wheat and consumed it. ⁶ But from the heat of the flame Adam and Eve awoke from their sleep, and saw the wheat burning, and the bucket of water by them, poured out. ⁷ Then they wept and went back to the cave. ⁸ But as they were going up from below the mountain where they were, Satan and his hosts met them in the form of angels, praising God. ⁹ Then Satan said to Adam, "O Adam, why art thou so pained with hunger and thirst? It seems to me that Satan has burnt up the wheat." And Adam said to him, "Ay." ¹⁰ Again Satan said to Adam, "Come back with us; we are angels of God. God sent us to thee, to show thee another field of corn, better than that; and beyond it is a fountain of good water, and many trees, where thou shalt dwell near it, and work the corn-field to better purpose than that which Satan has consumed." ¹¹ Adam thought that he was true, and that they were angels who talked with him; and he went back with them. ¹². Then Satan began to lead astray Adam and Eve eight days, until they both fell down as if dead, from hunger, thirst, and faintness. Then he fled with his hosts, and left them.

68

How destruction and trouble is of Satan when he is the master. Adam and Eve establish the custom of worship.

¹ THEN God looked upon Adam and Eve, and upon what had come upon them from Satan, and how he had made them perish. ² God, therefore, sent His Word, and raised up Adam and Eve from their state of death. ³ Then, Adam, when he was raised, said, "O God, Thou hast burnt and taken from us the corn Thou hadst given us, and Thou hast emptied out the bucket of water. And Thou hast sent Thy angels, who have waylaid us from the corn-field. Wilt Thou make us perish? If this be from Thee, O God, then take away our souls; but punish us not." ⁴ Then God said to Adam, "I did not burn down the wheat, and I did not pour the water out of the bucket, and I did not send My angels to lead thee astray. ⁵ "But it is Satan, thy master who did it; he to whom thou hast subjected thyself; My commandment being meanwhile set aside. He it is, who burnt down the corn, and poured out the water, and who has led thee astray; and all the promises he has made you, verily are but feint, and deceit, and a lie. ⁶ "But now, O Adam, thou shalt acknowledge My good deeds done to thee." ⁷ And God told His angels to take Adam and Eve, and to bear them up to the field of wheat, which they found as before, with the bucket full of water. ⁸ There they saw a tree, and found on it solid manna; and wondered at God's power. And the angels commanded them to eat of the manna when they were hungry. ⁹ And God adjured Satan with a curse, not to come again, and destroy the field of corn. ¹⁰ Then Adam and Eve took of the corn, and made of it an offering, and took it and offered it up on the mountain, the place where they had offered up their first offering of blood. ¹¹ And they offered this oblation again on the altar they had built at first. And they stood up and prayed, and besought the Lord saying, "Thus, O God, when we were in the garden, did our praises go up to Thee, like this offering; and our innocence went up to thee like incense. But now, O God, accept this offering from us, and turn us not back, reft of Thy mercy." ¹² Then God said to Adam and Eve, "Since ye have made this oblation and have offered it to Me, I shall make it My flesh, when I come down upon earth to save you; and I shall cause it to be offered continually upon an altar, for forgiveness and for mercy, unto those who partake of it duly." ¹³ And God sent a bright fire upon the offering of Adam and Eve, and filled it with brightness, grace, and light; and the Holy Ghost came down upon that oblation. ¹⁴ Then God commanded an angel to take fire-tongs, like a spoon, and with it to take an offering and bring it to Adam and Eve. And the angel did so, as God had commanded him, and offered it to them. ¹⁵ And the souls of Adam and Eve were brightened, and their hearts were filled with joy and gladness and with the praises of God. ¹⁶ And God said to Adam, "This shall be unto you a custom, to do so, when affliction and sorrow come upon you. But your deliverance and your entrance into the garden, shall not be until the days are fulfilled, as agreed between you and Me; were it not so, I would, of My mercy and pity for you, bring you back to My garden and to My favour for the sake of the offering you have just made to My name." ¹⁷ Adam rejoiced at these words which he heard

from God; and he and Eve worshipped before the altar, to which they bowed, and then went back to the Cave of Treasures. ¹⁸ And this took place at the end of the twelfth day after the eightieth day, from the time Adam and Eve came out of the garden. ¹⁹ And they stood up the whole night praying until morning; and then went out of the cave. ²⁰ Then Adam said to Eve, with joy of heart, because of the offering they had made to God, and that had been accepted of Him, "Let us do this three times every week, on the fourth day Wednesday, on the preparation day Friday, and on the Sabbath Sunday, all the days of our life." ²¹ And as they agreed to these words between themselves, God was pleased with their thoughts, and with the resolution they had each taken with the other. ²² After this, came the Word of God to Adam, and said, "O Adam, thou hast determined beforehand the days in which sufferings shall come upon Me, when I am made flesh; for they are the fourth Wednesday, and the preparation day Friday. ²³ "But as to the first day, I created in it all things, and I raised the heavens. And, again, through My rising again on this day, will I create joy, and raise them on high, who believe in Me; O Adam, offer this oblation, all the days of thy life." ²⁴ Then God withdrew His Word from Adam. ²⁵ But Adam continued to offer this oblation thus, every week three times, until, the end of seven weeks. And on the first day, which is the fiftieth, Adam made an offering as he was wont, and he and Eve took it and came to the altar before God, as He had taught them.

69

Twelfth apparition of Satan to Adam and Eve, while Adam was praying over the offering upon the altar; when Satan smote him.

¹ THEN Satan, the hater of all good, envious of Adam and of his offering through which he found favour with God, hastened and took a sharp stone from among sharp iron-stones; appeared in the form of a man, and went and stood by Adam and Eve. ² Adam was then offering on the altar, and had begun to pray, with his hands spread unto God. ³ Then Satan hastened with the sharp iron-stone he had with him, and with it pierced Adam on the right side, when flowed blood and water, then Adam fell upon the altar like a corpse. And Satan fled. ⁴ Then Eve came, and took Adam and placed him below the altar. And there she stayed, weeping over him; while a stream of blood flowed from Adam's side upon his offering. ⁵ But God looked upon the death of Adam. He then sent His Word, and raised him up and said unto him, "Fulfil thy offering, for indeed, Adam, it is worth much, and there is no shortcoming in it." ⁶ God said further unto Adam, "Thus will it also happen to Me, on the earth, when I shall be pierced and blood shall flow blood and water from My side and run over My body, which is the true offering; and which shall be offered on the altar as a perfect offering." ⁷ Then God commanded Adam to finish his offering, and when he had ended it he worshipped before God, and praised Him for the signs He had showed him. ⁸ And God healed Adam in one day, which is the end of the seven weeks; and that is the fiftieth day. ⁹ Then Adam and Eve returned from the mountain, and went into the Cave of Treasures, as they were used to do. This completed for Adam and Eve, one hundred and forty days since their coming out of the garden. ¹⁰ Then they both stood up that night and prayed to God. And when it was morning, they went out, and went down westward of the cave, to the place where their corn was, and there rested under the shadow of a tree, as they were wont. ¹¹ But when there a multitude of beasts came all round them. It was Satan's doing, in his wickedness; in order to wage war against Adam through marriage.

70

Thirteenth apparition of Satan to Adam and Eve, to make war against him, through his marriage with Eve.

¹ AFTER this Satan, the hater of all good, took the form n angel, and with him two others, so that they looked like the three angels who had brought to Adam gold, incense, and myrrh. ² They passed before Adam and Eve while they were under the tree, and greeted Adam and Eve with fair words that were full of guile. ³ But when Adam and Eve saw them with their comely mien, and heard their sweet speech, Adam rose, welcomed them, and brought them to Eve, and they remained all together; Adam's heart the while, being glad because he thought concerning them, that they were the same angels, who had brought him gold, incense, and myrrh. ⁴ Because, when they came to Adam the first time, there came upon him from them, peace and joy, through their bringing him good tokens; so Adam thought that they were come a second time to give him other tokens for him to rejoice withal. For he did not know it was Satan; therefore did he receive them with joy and companied with them. ⁵ Then Satan, the tallest of them, said, "Rejoice, O Adam, and be glad. Lo, God has sent us to thee to tell thee something." ⁶ And Adam said, "What is it?" Then Satan answered, "It is a light thing, yet it is a word of God, wilt thou hear it from us and do it? But if thou hearest not, we will return to God, and tell Him that thou wouldest not receive His word." And Satan said again to Adam, "Fear not, neither let a trembling come upon thee; dost not thou know us?" ⁸ But Adam said, "I know you not." ⁹ Then Satan said to him, "I am the angel who brought thee gold, and took it to the cave; this other one is he who brought thee incense; and that third one, is he who brought thee myrrh when thou wast on the top of the mountain, and who carried thee to the cave. ¹⁰ "But as to the other angels our fellows, who bare you to the cave, God has not sent them with us this time; for He said to us, 'You suffice.'" ¹¹ So when Adam heard these words he believed them, and said to these angels, "Speak the word of God, that I may receive it." ¹² And Satan said unto him "Swear, and promise me that thou wilt receive it." ¹³ Then Adam said, "I know not how to swear and promise." ¹⁴ And Satan said to him, "Hold out thy hand, and put it inside my hand." ¹⁵ Then Adam held out his hand, and put it into Satan's hand; when Satan said unto him, "Say, now – so true as God is living, rational, and speaking, who raised the heavens in the space, and established the earth upon the waters, and has created me out of the four elements, and out of the dust of the earth – I will not break my promise, nor renounce my word." ¹⁶ And Adam swore thus. ¹⁷ Then Satan said to him, "Lo, it is now some time since thou camest out of the garden, and thou knowest neither wickedness nor evil. But now God s says to thee, to take Eve who came out of thy side, and to wed her, that she bear thee children, to comfort thee, and to drive from thee trouble and sorrow; now this thing is not difficult, neither is there any scandal in it to thee."

71

Adam is troubled by his wedding with Eve.

¹ BUT when Adam heard these words from Satan, he sorrowed much, because of his oath and of his promise, and said, "Shall I commit adultery with my flesh and my bones, and shall I sin against myself, for God to destroy me, and to blot me out from off the face of the earth? ² "Since, when at first, I ate of the tree, He drove me out of the garden into this strange land, and deprived me of my bright nature, and brought death upon me. If, then, I should do this, He will cut off my life from the earth, and He will cast me into hell, and will plague me there a long time. ³ "But God never spoke the words thou hast told me; and ye are not God's angels, nor yet sent from Him. But ye are devils, come to me under the false appearance of angels . Away from me; ye cursed of God!" ⁴ Then those devils fled from before Adam. And he and Eve arose, and returned to the Cave of Treasures, and went into it. ⁵ Then Adam said to Eve, "If thou sawest what I did, tell it not; for I sinned against God n swearing by His great name, and I have placed my hand another time into that of Satan." Eve, then, held her peace, as Adam told her. ⁶ Then Adam arose, and spread his hands unto God, beseeching and entreating Him with tears, to forgive him what he had done. And Adam remained thus standing and praying forty days and forty nights. He neither ate nor drank until he dropped down upon the earth from hunger and thirst. ⁷ Then God sent His Word unto Adam, who raised him up from where he lay, and said unto him, "O Adam, why hast thou sworn by My name, and why hast thou made agreement with Satan another time?" ⁸ But Adam wept, and said, "O God, forgive me, for I did this unwittingly; believing they were God's angels." ⁹ And God forgave Adam, saying, to him, "Beware of Satan." ¹⁰ And He withdrew His Word from Adam. ¹¹ Then Adam's heart was comforted; and he took Eve, and they went out of the cave, to make some food for their bodies. ¹² But from that day Adam struggled in his mind about his wedding Eve; afraid as he was to do it, lest God should be wroth with him. ¹³ Then Adam and Eve went to the river of water, and sat on the bank, as people do when they enjoy themselves. ¹⁴ But Satan was jealous of them; and would destroy them.

72

Adam's heart is set on fire.

¹ THEN Satan, and ten from his hosts, transformed themselves into maidens, unlike any others in the whole world for grace. ² They came up out of the river in presence of Adam and Eve, and they said among themselves, "Come, we will look at the faces of Adam and of Eve, who are of the men upon earth. How beautiful they are, and how different is their look from our own faces." Then they came to Adam and Eve, and greeted them; and stood wondering at them. ³ Adam and Eve looked at them also, and wondered at their beauty, and said, "Is there, then, under us, another world, with such beautiful creatures as these in it" ⁴ And those maidens said to Adam and Eve, "Yes, indeed, we are an abundant creation." ⁵ Then Adam said to them, "But how do you multiply?" ⁶ And they answered him, "We have husbands who wedded us, and we bear them children, who grow up, and who in their turn wed and are wedded, and also bear children; and thus we increase. And if so be, O Adam, thou wilt not believe us, we will show thee our husbands and our children." ⁷ Then they shouted over the river as if to call their husbands and their children, who came up from the river, men and children; and every one came to his wife, his children being with him. ⁸ But when Adam and Eve saw them, they stood dumb, and wondered at

them. ⁹ Then they said to Adam and Eve, "You see our husbands and our children, wed Eve as we wed our wives, and you shall have children the same as we." This was a device of Satan to deceive Adam. ¹⁰ Satan also thought within himself, "God at first commanded Adam concerning the fruit of the tree, saying to him, 'Eat not of it; else of death thou shalt die.' But Adam ate of it, and yet God did not kill him; He only decreed upon him death, and plagues and trials, until the day he shall come out of his body. ¹¹ "Now, then, if I deceive him to do this thing, and to wed Eve without God's commandment, God will kill him then." ¹² Therefore did Satan work this apparition before Adam and Eve; because he sought to kill him, and to make him disappear from off the face of the earth. ¹³ Meanwhile the fire of sin came upon Adam, and he thought of committing sin. But he restrained himself, fearing lest if he followed this advice of Satan God would put him to death. ¹⁴ Then Adam and Eve arose, and prayed to God, while Satan and his hosts went down into the river, in presence of Adam and Eve; to let them see that they were going back to their own regions. ¹⁵ Then Adam and Eve went back to the Cave of Treasures, as they were wont; about evening time. ¹⁶ And they both arose and prayed to God that night. Adam remained standing in prayer, yet not knowing how to pray, by reason of the thoughts of his heart regarding his wedding Eve; and he continued so until morning. ¹⁷ And when light arose, Adam said unto Eve, "Arise, let us go below the mountain, where they brought us gold, and let us ask the Lord concerning this matter." ¹⁸ Then Eve said, "What is that matter, O Adam?" ¹⁹ And he answered her, "That I may request the Lord to inform me about wedding thee; for I will not do it without His order, lest He make us perish, thee and me. For those devils have set my heart on fire, with thoughts of what they showed us, in their sinful apparitions." ²⁰ Then Eve said to Adam, "Why need we go below the mountain? Let us rather stand up and pray in our cave to God, to let us know whether this counsel is good or not." ²¹ Then Adam rose up in prayer and said, "O God, thou knowest that we transgressed against Thee, and from the moment we transgressed, we were bereft of our bright nature; and our body became brutish, requiring food and drink; and with animal desires. ²² "Command us, O God, not to give way to them without Thy order, lest Thou bring us to nothing. For if Thou give us not the order, we shall be overpowered, and follow that advice of Satan; and Thou wilt again make us perish. ²³ "If not, then take our souls from us; let us be rid of this animal lust. And if Thou give us no order respecting this thing, then sever Eve from me, and me from her; and place us each far away from the other. ²⁴ "Yet again, O God, when Thou hast put us asunder from each other, the devils will deceive us with their apparitions, and destroy our hearts, and defile our thoughts towards each other. Yet if it is not each of us towards the other, it will, at all events, be through their appearance when they show themselves to us." Here Adam ended his prayer.

73

The betrothal of Adam and Eve.

¹ THEN God looked upon the words of Adam that they were true, and that he could long await His order, respecting the counsel of Satan. ² And God approved Adam in what he had thought concerning this, and in the prayer he had offered in His presence; and the Word of God came unto Adam and said to him, "O Adam, if only thou hadst had this caution at first, ere thou earnest out of the garden into this land!" ³ After that, God sent His angel who had brought gold, and the angel who had brought incense, and the angel who had brought myrrh to Adam, that they should inform him respecting his wedding Eve. ⁴ Then those angels said to Adam, "Take the gold and give it to Eve as a wedding gift, and betroth her; then give her some incense and myrrh as a present; and be ye, thou and she, one flesh." ⁵ Adam hearkened to the angels, and took the gold and put it into Eve's bosom in her garment; and bethrothed her with his hand. ⁶ Then the angels commanded Adam and Eve, to arise and pray forty days and forty nights; and after that, that Adam should come in to his wife; for then this would be an act pure and undefiled; and he should have children who would multiply, and replenish the face of the earth. ⁷ Then both Adam and Eve received the words of the angels; and the angels departed from them. ⁸ Then Adam and Eve began to fast and to pray, until the end of the forty days; and then they came together, as the angels had told them. And from the time Adam left the garden until he wedded Eve, were two hundred and twenty-three days, that is seven months and thirteen days. ⁹ Thus was Satan's war with Adam defeated.

74

The birth of Cain and Luluwa. Why they received those names.

¹ AND they dwelt on the earth working, in order to continue in the well-being of their bodies; and were so until the nine months of Eve's childbearing were ended, and the time drew near when she must be delivered. ² Then she said unto Adam, "This cave is a pure spot by reason of the signs wrought in it since we left the garden; and we shall again pray in it. It is not meet, then, that I should bring forth in it; let us rather repair to that of the sheltering rock, which Satan hurled at us, when he wished to kill us with it; but that was held up and spread as an awning over us by the command of God; and formed a cave." ³ Then Adam removed Eve to that cave; and when the time came that she should bring forth, she travailed much. So was Adam sorry, and his heart suffered for her sake; for she was nigh unto death; that the word of God to her should be fulfilled: "In suffering shalt thou bear a child, and in sorrow shalt thou bring forth thy child." ⁴ But when Adam saw the strait in which Eve was, he arose and prayed to God, and said, "O Lord, look upon me with the eye of Thy mercy, and bring her out of her distress." ⁵ And God looked at His maid-servant Eve, and delivered her, and she brought forth her first-born son, and with him a daughter. ⁶ Then Adam rejoiced at Eve's deliverance, and also over the children she had borne him. And Adam ministered unto Eve in the cave, until the end of eight days; when they named the son Cain, and the daughter Luluwa. ⁷ The meaning of Cain is "hater," because he hated his sister in their mother's womb; ere they came out of it. Therefore did Adam name him Cain. ⁸ But Luluwa means "beautiful," because she was more beautiful than her mother. ⁹ Then Adam and Eve waited until Cain and his sister were forty days old, when Adam said unto Eve, "We will make an offering and offer it up in behalf of the children." ¹⁰ And Eve said, "We will make one offering for the firstborn son; and afterwards we shall make one for the daughter."

75

The family revisits the Cave of Treasures. Birth of Abel and Aklemia.

¹ THEN Adam prepared an offering, and he and Eve offered it up for their children, and brought it to the altar they had built at first. ² And Adam offered up the offering, and besought God to accept his offering. ³ Then God accepted Adam's offering, and sent a light from heaven that shone upon the offering. And Adam and the son drew near to the offering, but Eve and the daughter did not approach unto it. ⁴ Then Adam came down from upon the altar, and they were joyful; and Adam and Eve waited until the daughter was eighty days old; then Adam prepared an offering and took it to Eve and to the children; and they went to the altar, where Adam offered it up, as he was wont, asking the Lord to accept his offering. ⁵ And the Lord accepted the offering of Adam and Eve. Then Adam, Eve, and the children, drew near together, and came down from the mountain, rejoicing. ⁶ But they returned not to the cave in which they were born; but came to the Cave of Treasures, in order that the children should go round it, and be blessed with the tokens brought from the garden. ⁷ But after they had been blessed with these tokens, they went back to the cave in which they were born. ⁸ However, before Eve had offered up the offering, Adam had taken her, and had gone with her to the river of water, in which they threw themselves at first; and there they washed themselves. Adam washed his body and Eve hers also clean, after the suffering and distress that had come upon them. ⁹ But Adam and Eve, after washing themselves in the river of water, returned every night to the Cave of Treasures, where they prayed and were blessed; and then went back to their cave where the children were born ¹⁰ So did Adam and Eve until the children had done sucking. Then, when they were weaned, Adam made an offering for the souls of his children; other than the three times he made an offering for them, every week. ¹¹ When the days of nursing the children were ended, Eve again conceived, and when her days were accomplished she brought forth another son and daughter; and they named the son Abel, and the daughter Aklia. ¹² Then at the end of forty days, Adam made an offering for the son, and at the end of eighty days he made another offering for the daughter, and did by them, as he had done before by Cain and his sister Luluwa. ¹³ He brought them to the Cave of Treasures, where they received a blessing, and then returned to the cave where they were born. After the birth of these, Eve ceased from childbearing.

76

Cain becomes jealous because of his sisters.

¹ AND the children began to wax stronger, and to grow in stature; but Cain was hardhearted, and ruled over his younger brother. ² And oftentimes when his father made an offering, he would remain behind and not go with them, to offer up. ³ But, as to Abel, he had a meek heart, and was obedient to his father and mother, whom he often moved to make an offering, because he loved it; and prayed and fasted much. ⁴ Then came this sign to Abel. As he was coming into the Cave of Treasures, and saw the golden rods, the incense and the myrrh, he inquired of his parents Adam and Eve concerning them, and said unto them, "How did you come by these?" ⁵ Then Adam told him all that had befallen them. And Abel felt deeply about what his father told him. ⁶ Furthermore his father Adam, told him of the works of God, and of the garden; and after that, he remained behind his father the whole of that night in the Cave of Treasures. ⁷ And that night, while he was

praying, Satan appeared unto him under the figure of a man, who said to him, "Thou hast oftentimes moved thy father to make an offering, to fast and to pray, therefore I will kill thee, and make thee perish from this world." ⁸ But as for Abel, he prayed to God, and drove away Satan from him; and believed not the words of the devil. Then when it was day, an angel of God appeared unto him, who said to him, "Shorten neither fasting, prayer, nor offering up an oblation unto thy God. For, lo, the Lord has accepted thy prayer. Be not afraid of the figure which appeared unto thee in the night, and who cursed thee unto death." And the angel departed from him. ⁹ Then when it was day, Abel came to Adam and Eve, and told them of the vision he had seen. But when they heard it, they grieved much over it, yet said nothing to him about it; they only comforted him. ¹⁰ But as to hard-hearted Cain, Satan came to him by night, showed himself and said unto him, "Since Adam and Eve love thy brother Abel much more than they love thee, and wish to join him in marriage to thy beautiful sister, because they love him; but wish to join thee in marriage to his ill-favoured sister, because they hate thee; ¹¹ "Now, therefore, I counsel thee, when they do that, to kill thy brother; then thy sister will be left for thee; and his sister will be cast, away." ¹² And Satan departed from him. But the wicked One remained behind in the heart of Cain, who sought many a time, to kill his brother.

77

Cain, 15 years old, and Abel 12 years old, grow apart.

¹ BUT when Adam saw that the elder brother hated the younger, he endeavoured to soften their hearts, and said unto Cain, "Take, O my son, of the fruits of thy sowing, and make an offering unto God, that He may forgive thee thy wickedness and thy sin." ² He said also to Abel, "Take thou of thy sowing and make an offering and bring it to God, that He may forgive thy wickedness and thy sin." ³ Then Abel hearkened unto his father's voice, and took of his sowing, and made a good offering, and said to his father, Adam, "Come with me, to show me how to offer it up." ⁴ And they went, Adam and Eve with him, and showed him how to offer up his gift upon the altar. Then after that, they stood up and prayed that God would accept Abel's offering. ⁵ Then God looked upon Abel and accepted his offering. And God was more pleased with Abel than with his offering, because of his good heart and pure body. There was no trace of guile in him. ⁶ Then they came down from the altar, and went to the cave in which they dwelt. But Abel, by reason of his joy at having made his offering, repeated it three times a week, after the example of his father Adam. ⁷ But as to Cain, he took no pleasure in offering; but after much anger on his father's part, he offered up his gift once; and when he did offer up, his eye was on the offering he made, and he took the smallest of his sheep for an offering, and his eye was again on it. ' ⁸ Therefore God did not accept his offering, because his heart was full of murderous thoughts. ⁹ And they all thus lived together in the cave in which Eve had brought forth, until Cain was fifteen years old, and Abel twelve years old.

78

Jealousy overcomes Cain. He makes trouble in the family. How the first murder was planned.

¹ THEN Adam said to Eve, "Behold the children are grown up; we must think of finding wives for them." ² Then Eve answered, "How can we do it?" ³ Then Adam said to her, "We will join Abel's sister in marriage to Cain, and Cain's sister to Abel." ⁴ Then said Eve to Adam, "I do not like Cain because he is hard-hearted; but let them bide until we offer up unto the Lord in their behalf." ⁵ And Adam said no more. ⁶ Meanwhile Satan came to Cain in the figure of a man of the field, and said to him, "Behold Adam and Eve have taken counsel together about the marriage of you two; and they have agreed to marry Abel's sister to thee, and thy sister to him. ⁷ "But if it was not that I love thee, I would not have told thee this thing. Yet if thou wilt take my advice, and hearken to me, I will bring: thee on thy wedding day beautiful robes, gold and silver in plenty, and my relations will attend thee." ⁸ Then Cain said with joy, "Where are thy relations?" ⁹ And Satan answered, "My relations are in a garden in the north, whither I once meant to bring thy father Adam; but he would not accept my offer. ¹⁰ "But thou, if thou wilt receive my words and if thou wilt come unto me after thy wedding, thou shalt rest from the misery in which thou art; and thou shalt rest and be better off than thy father Adam." ¹¹ At these words of Satan Cain opened his ears, and leant towards his speech. ¹² And he did not remain in the field, but he went to Eve, his mother, and beat her, and cursed her, and said to her, "Why are ye about taking my sister to wed her to my brother? Am I dead"" ¹³ His mother, however, quieted him, and sent him to the field where be had been. ¹⁴ Then when Adam came, she told him of what Cain had done. ¹⁵ But Adam grieved and held his peace, and said not a word. ¹⁶ Then on the morrow Adam said unto Cain his son, "Take of thy sheep, young and good, and offer them up unto thy God; and I will speak to thy brother, to make unto his God an offering of corn." ¹⁷ They both hearkened to their father Adam, and they took their offerings, and offered them up on the mountain by the altar. ¹⁸ But Cain behaved haughtily towards his brother, and thrust him from the altar, and would not let him offer up his gift upon the altar; but he offered his own upon it, with a proud heart, full of guile, and fraud. ¹⁹ But as for Abel, he set up stones that were near at hand, and upon that, he offered up his gift with a heart humble and free from guile. ²⁰ Cain was then standing by the altar on which he had offered up his gift; and he cried unto God to accept his offering; but God did not accept it from him; neither did a divine fire come down to consume his offering. ²¹ But he remained standing over against the altar, out of humour and wroth, looking towards his brother Abel, to see if God would accept his offering or not. ²² And Abel prayed unto God to accept his offering. Then a divine fire came down and consumed his offering. And God smelled the sweet savour of his offering; because Abel loved Him and rejoiced in Him. ²³ And because God was well pleased with him He sent him an angel of light in the figure of man who had partaken of his offering, because He had smelled the sweet savour of his offering, and they comforted Abel and strengthened his heart. ²⁴ But Cain was looking on all that took place at his brother's offering, and was wroth on account of it. ²⁵ Then he opened his mouth and blasphemed God, because He had not accepted his offering. ²⁶ But God said unto Cain, "Wherefore is thy countenance sad? Be righteous, that I may accept thy offering. Not against Me hast thou murmured, but against thyself." ²⁷ And God said this to Cain in rebuke, and because He abhorred him and his offering. ²⁸ And Cain came down from the altar, his colour changed and of a woeful countenance, and came to his father and mother and told them all that had befallen him. And Adam grieved much because God had not accepted Cain's offering. ²⁹ But Abel came down rejoicing, and with a gladsome heart, and told his father and mother how God had accepted his offering. And they rejoiced at it and kissed his face. ³⁰ And Abel said to his father, "Because Cain thrust me from the altar, and would not allow me to offer my gift upon it, I made an altar for myself and offered my gift upon it." ³¹ But when Adam heard this he was very sorry, because it was the altar he had built at first, and upon which he had offered his own gifts. ³² As to Cain, he was so sullen and so angry that he went into the field, where Satan came to him and said to him, "Since thy brother Abel has taken refuge with thy father Adam, because thou didst thrust him from the altar, they have kissed his face, and they rejoice over him, far more than over thee." ³³ When Cain heard these words of Satan, he was filled with rage; and he let no one know. But he was laying wait to kill his brother, until he brought him into the cave, and then said to him: – ³⁴ "O brother, the country is so beautiful, and there are such beautiful and pleasurable trees in it, and charming to look at! But brother, thou hast never been one day in the field to take thy pleasure therein. ³⁵ "To-day, O, my brother, I very much wish thou wouldest come with me into the field, to enjoy thyself and to bless our fields and our flocks, for thou art righteous, and I love thee much, O my brother! but thou hast estranged thyself from me." ³⁶ Then Abel consented to go with his brother Cain into the field. ³⁷ But before going out, Cain said to Abel, "Wait for me, until I fetch a staff, because of wild beasts." ³⁸ Then Abel stood waiting in his innocence. But Cain, the forward, fetched a staff and went out. ³⁹ And they began, Cain and his brother Abel, to walk in the way; Cain talking to him, and comforting him, to make him forget everything.

79

A wicked plan is carried to a tragic conclusion. Cain is frightened. "Am I my brother's keeper?" The seven punishments. Peace is shattered.

¹ AND so they went on, until they came to a lonely place, where there were no sheep; then Abel said to Cain, "Behold, my brother, we are weary of walking; for we see none of the trees, nor of the fruits, nor of the verdure, nor of the sheep, nor any one of the things of which thou didst tell me. Where are those sheep of thine thou didst tell me to bless?" ² Then Cain said to him, "Come on, and presently thou shalt see many beautiful things. but go before me, until I come up to thee." ³ Then went Abel forward, but Cain remained behind him. ⁴ And Abel was walking in his innocence, without guile; not believing his brother would kill him. ⁵ Then Cain, when he came up to him, comforted him with his talk, walking a little behind him; then he hastened, and smote him with the staff, blow upon blow, until he was stunned, ⁶ But when Abel fell down upon the ground, seeing that his brother meant to kill him, he said to Cain, "O, my brother, have pity on me. By the breasts we have sucked, smite me not! By the womb that bare us and that brought us into the world, smite me not unto death with that staff! If thou wilt kill me, take one of these large stones, and kill me outright." ⁷ Then Cain, the hard-hearted, and cruel murderer, took a large stone, and smote his brother with it upon the head, until his brains oozed out, and he weltered in his blood, before him. ⁸ And Cain repented not of what he had done. ⁹ But the earth, when the blood of righteous Abel fell upon it, trembled, as it drank his blood, and would have brought Cain to naught for

it. ¹⁰ And the blood of Abel cried mysteriously to God, to avenge him of his murderer. ¹¹ Then Cain began at once to dig the earth wherein to lay his brother; for he was trembling from the fear that came upon him, when he saw the earth tremble on his account. ¹² He then cast his brother into the pit he made, and covered him with dust. But the earth would not receive him; but it threw him up at once. ¹³ Again did Cain dig the earth and hid his brother in it; but again did the earth throw him up on itself; until three times did the earth thus throw up on itself the body of Abel. ¹⁴ The muddy earth threw him up the first time, because he was not the first creation; and it threw him up the second time and would not receive him, because he was righteous and good, and was killed without a cause; and the earth threw him up the third time and would not receive him, that there might remain before his brother a witness against him. ¹⁵ And so did the earth mock Cain, until the Word of God, came to him concerning his brother. ¹⁶ Then was God angry, and much displeased at Abel's death; and He thundered from heaven, and lightnings went before Him, and the Word of the Lord God came from heaven to Cain, and said unto him, "Where is Abel thy brother?" ¹⁷ Then Cain answered with a proud heart and a gruff voice, "How, O God? am I my brother's keeper?" ¹⁸ Then God said unto Cain, "Cursed be the earth that has drunk the blood of Abel thy brother; and thou, be thou trembling and shaking; and this will be a sign unto thee, that whosoever finds thee, shall kill thee." ¹⁹ But Cain wept because God had said those words to him; and Cain said unto Him "O God, whosoever finds me shall kill me, and I shall be blotted out from the face of the earth." ²⁰ Then God said unto Cain, "Whosoever shall find thee shall not kill thee;" because before this, God had been saying to Cain, "I shall forego seven punishments on him who kills Cain." For as to the word of God to Cain, "Where is thy brother?" God said it in mercy for him, to try and make him repent. ²¹ For if Cain had repented at that time, and had said, "O God, forgive me my sin, and the murder of my brother," God would then have forgiven him his sin. ²² And as to God saying to Cain, "Cursed be the ground that has drunk the blood of thy brother" that also, was God's mercy on Cain. For God did not curse him, but He cursed the ground; although it was not the ground that had killed Abel, and had committed iniquity. ²³ For it was meet that the curse should fall upon the murderer; yet in mercy did God so manage His thoughts as that no one should know it, and turn away from Cain. ²⁴ And He said to him, "Where is thy brother?" To which he answered and said, "I know not." Then the Creator said to him, "Be trembling and quaking." ²⁵ Then Cain trembled and became terrified; and through this sign did God make him an example before all the creation, as the murderer of his brother. Also did God bring trembling and terror upon him, that he might see the peace in which he was at first, and see also the trembling and terror he endured at the last; so that he might humble himself before God, and repent of his sin, and seek the peace he enjoyed at first. ²⁶ And in the word of God that said, "I will forego seven punishments on whomsoever kills Cain," God was not seeking to kill Cain with the sword, but He sought to make him die of fasting, and praying and weeping by hard rule, until the time that he was delivered from his sin. ²⁷ And the seven punishments are the seven generations during which God awaited Cain for the murder of his brother. ²⁸ But as to Cain, ever since he had killed his brother, he could find no rest in any place; but went back to Adam and Eve, trembling, terrified, and defiled with blood. . . .

The Second Book of Adam and Eve

1

The grief stricken family. Cain marries Luluwa and they move away.

¹ WHEN Luluwa heard Cain's words, she wept and went to her father and mother, and told them how that Cain had killed his brother Abel. ² Then they all cried aloud and lifted up their voices, and slapped their faces, and threw dust upon their heads, and rent asunder their garments, and went out and came to the place where Abel was killed. ³ And they found him lying on the earth, killed, and beasts around him; while they wept and cried because of this just one. From his body, by reason of its purity, went forth a smell of sweet spices. ⁴ And Adam carried him, his tears streaming down his face; and went to the Cave of Treasures, where he laid him, and wound him up with sweet spices and myrrh. ⁵ And Adam and Eve continued by the burial of him in great grief a hundred and forty days. Abel was fifteen and a half years old, and Cain seventeen years and a half. ⁶ As for Cain, when the mourning for his brother was ended, he took his sister Luluwa and married her, without leave from his father and mother; for they could not keep him from her, by reason of their heavy heart. ⁷ He then went down to the bottom of the mountain, away from the garden, near to the place where he had killed his brother. ⁸ And in that place were many fruit trees and forest trees. His sister bare him children, who in their turn began to multiply by degrees until they filled that place. ⁹ But as for Adam and Eve, they came not together after Abel's funeral, for seven years. After this, however, Eve conceived; and while she was with child, Adam said to her "Come, let us take an offering and offer it up unto God, and ask Him to give us a fair child, in whom we may find comfort, and whom we may join in marriage to Abel's sister." ¹⁰ Then they prepared an offering and brought it up to the altar, and offered it before the Lord, and began to entreat Him to accept their offering, and to give them a good offspring. ¹¹ And God heard Adam and accepted his offering. Then, they worshipped, Adam, Eve, and their daughter, and came down to the Cave of Treasures and placed a lamp in it, to burn by night and by day, before the body of Abel. ¹² Then Adam and Eve continued fasting and praying until Eve's time came that she should be delivered, when she said to Adam: "I wish to go to the cave in the rock, to bring forth in it." ¹³ And he said, "Go and take with thee thy daughter to wait on thee; but I will remain in this Cave of Treasures before the body of my son Abel." ¹⁴ Then Eve hearkened to Adam, and went, she and her daughter. But Adam remained by himself in the Cave of Treasures.

2

A third son is born to Adam and Eve.

¹ AND Eve brought forth a son perfectly beautiful in figure and in countenance. His beauty was like that of his father Adam, yet more beautiful. ² Then Eve was comforted when she saw him, and remained eight days in the cave; then she sent her daughter unto Adam to tell him to come and see the child and name him. But the daughter stayed in his place by the body of her brother, until Adam returned. So did she. ³ But when Adam came and saw the child's good looks, his beauty, and his perfect figure, he rejoiced over him, and was comforted for Abel. Then he named the child Seth, that means, "that God has heard my prayer, and has delivered me out of my affliction." But it means also "power and strength." ⁴ Then after Adam had named the child, he returned to the Cave of Treasures; and his daughter went back to her mother. ⁵ But Eve continued in her cave, until forty days were fulfilled, when she came to Adam, and brought with her the child and her daughter. ⁶ And they came to a river of water, where Adam and his daughter washed themselves, because of their sorrow for Abel; but Eve and the babe washed for purification. ⁷ Then they returned, and took an offering, and went to the mountain and offered it up, for the babe; and God accepted their offering, and sent His blessing upon them, and upon their son Seth; and they came back to the Cave of Treasures. ⁸ As for Adam, he knew not again his wife Eve, all the days of his life; neither was any more offspring born of them; but only those five, Cain, Luluwa, Abel, Aklia, and Seth alone. ⁹ But Seth waxed in stature and in strength; and began to fast and pray, fervently.

3

Satan appears as a beautiful woman tempting Adam, telling him he is still a youth. "Spend thy youth in mirth and pleasure." (12) The different forms which Satan takes (15).

¹ AS for our father Adam, at the end of seven years from the day he had been severed from his wife Eve, Satan envied him, when he saw him thus separated from her; and strove to make him live with her again. ² Then Adam arose and went up above the Cave of Treasures; and continued to sleep there night by night. But as soon as it was light every day he came down to the cave, to pray there and to receive a blessing from it. ³ But when it was evening he went up on the roof of the cave, where he slept by himself,

fearing lest Satan should overcome him. And he continued thus apart thirty-nine days. ⁴ Then Satan, the hater of all good, when he saw Adam thus alone, fasting and praying, appeared unto him in the form of a beautiful woman, who came and stood before him in the night of the fortieth day, and said unto him: – ⁵ "O Adam, from the time ye have dwelt in this cave, we have experienced great peace from you, and your prayers have reached us, and we have been comforted about you. ⁶ "But now, O Adam, that thou hast gone up over the roof of the cave to sleep, we have had doubts about thee, and a great sorrow has come upon us because of thy separation from Eve. Then again, when thou art on the roof of this cave, thy prayer is poured out, and thy heart wanders from side to side. ⁷ "But when thou wast in the cave thy prayer was like fire gathered together; it came down to us, and thou didst find rest. ⁸ "Then I also grieved over thy children who are severed from thee; and my sorrow is great about the murder of thy son Abel; for he was righteous; and over a righteous man every one will grieve. ⁹ "But I rejoiced over the birth of thy son Seth; yet after a little while I sorrowed greatly over Eve, because she is my sister. For when God sent a deep sleep over thee, and drew her out of thy side, He brought me out also with her. But He raised her by placing her with thee, while He lowered me. ¹⁰ "I rejoiced over my sister for her being with thee. But God had made me a promise before, and said, 'Grieve not; when Adam has gone up on the roof of the Cave of Treasures, and is separated from Eve his wife, I will send thee to him, thou shalt join thyself to him in marriage, and bear him five children, as Eve did bear him five.' ¹¹ "And now, lo! God's promise to me is fulfilled; for it is He who has sent me to thee for the wedding; because if thou wed me, I shall bear thee finer and better children than those of Eve. ¹² "Then again, thou art as yet but a youth; end not thy youth in this world in sorrow; but spend the days of thy youth in mirth and pleasure. For thy days are few and thy trial is great. Be strong; end thy days in this world in rejoicing. I shall take pleasure in thee, and thou shall rejoice with me in this wise, and without fear. ¹³ "Up, then, and fulfil the command of thy God," she then drew near to Adam, and embraced him. ¹⁴ But when Adam saw that he should be overcome by her, he prayed to God with a fervent heart to deliver him from her. ¹⁵ Then God sent His Word unto Adam, saying, "O Adam, that figure is the one that promised thee the Godhead, and majesty; he is not favourably disposed towards thee; but shows himself to thee at one time in the form of a woman; another moment, in the likeness of an angel; on another occasions, in the similitude of a serpent; and at another time, in the semblance of a god; but he does all that only to destroy thy soul. ¹⁶ "Now, therefore, O Adam, understanding thy heart, I have delivered thee many a time from his hands; in order to show thee that I am a merciful God; and that I wish thy good, and that I do not wish thy ruin."

4
Adam sees the Devil in his true colors.
¹ THEN God ordered Satan to show himself to Adam in plainly, in his own hideous form. ² But when Adam saw him, he feared, and trembled at the sight of him. ³ And God said to Adam, "Look at this devil, and at his hideous look, and know that he it is who made thee fall from brightness into darkness, from peace and rest to toil and misery. ⁴ And look, O Adam, at him, who said of himself that he is God! Can God be black? Would God take the form of a woman? Is there any one stronger than God? And can He be overpowered? ⁵ "See, then, O Adam, and behold him bound in thy presence, in the air, unable to flee away! Therefore, I say unto thee, be not afraid of him; henceforth take care, and beware of him, in whatever he may do to thee." ⁶ Then God drove Satan away from before Adam, whom He strengthened, and whose heart He comforted, saying to him, "Go down to the Cave of Treasures, and separate not thyself from Eve; I will quell in you all animal lust." ⁷ From that hour it left Adam and Eve, and they enjoyed rest by the commandment of God. But God did not the like to any one of Adam's seed; but only to Adam and Eve. ⁸ Then Adam worshipped before the Lord, for having delivered him, and for having layed his passions. And he came down from above the cave, and dwelt with Eve as aforetime. ⁹ This ended the forty days of his separation from Eve.

5
The devil paints a brilliant picture for Seth to feast his thoughts upon.
¹ AS for Seth, when he was seven years old, he knew good and evil, and was consistent in fasting and praying, and spent all his nights in entreating God for mercy and forgiveness. ² He also fasted when bringing up his offering every day, more than his father did; for he was of a fair countenance, likeunto an angel of God. He also had a good heart, preserved the finest qualities of his soul: and for this reason he brought up his offering every day. ³ And God was pleased with his offering; but He was also pleased with his purity. And he continued thus in doing the will of God, and of his father and mother, until he was seven years old. ⁴ After that, as he was coming down from the altar, having ended his offering, Satan appeared unto him in the form of a beautiful angel, brilliant with light; with a staff of light in his hand, himself girt about with a girdle of light. ⁵ He greeted Seth with a beautiful smile, and began to beguile him with fair words, saying to him, "O Seth, why abidest thou in this mountain? For it is rough, full of stones and of sand, and of trees with no good fruit on them; a wilderness without habitations and without towns; no good place to dwell in. But all is heat, weariness, and trouble." ⁶ He said further, "But we dwell in beautiful places, in another world than this earth. Our world is one of light and our condition is of the best; our women are handsomer than any others; and I wish thee, O Seth, to wed one of them; because I see that thou art fair to look upon, and in this land there is not one woman good enough for thee. Besides, all those who live in this world, are only five souls. ⁷ "But in our world there are very many men and many maidens, all more beautiful one than another. I wish, therefore, to remove thee hence, that thou mayest see my relations and be wedded to which ever thou likest. ⁸ "Thou shalt then abide by me and be at peace; thou shalt be filled with splendour and light, as we are. ⁹ "Thou shalt remain in our world. and rest from this world and the misery of it; thou shalt never again feel faint and weary; thou shalt never bring up an offering, nor sue for mercy; for thou shalt commit no more sin, nor be swayed by passions. ¹⁰ "And if thou wilt hearken to what I say, thou shalt wed one of my daughters; for with us it is no sin so to do; neither is it reckoned animal lust. ¹¹ "For in our world we have no God; but we all are gods; we all are of the light, heavenly, powerful, strong and glorious."

6
Seth's conscience helps him. He returns to Adam and Eve.
¹ WHEN Seth heard these words he was amazed, and inclined his heart to Satan's treacherous speech, and said to him, "Saidst thou there is another world created than this; and other creatures more beautiful than the creatures that are in this world?" ² And Satan said, "Yes; behold thou hast heard me; but I will yet praise them and their ways, in thy hearing." ³ But Seth said to him, "Thy speech has amazed me; and thy beautiful description of it all. ⁴ "Yet I cannot go with thee to-day; not until I have gone to my father Adam and to my mother Eve, and told them all thou hast said to me. Then if they give me leave to go with thee, I will come." ⁵ Again Seth said, "I am afraid of doing any thing without my father's and mother's leave, lest I perish like my brother Cain, and like my father Adam, who transgressed the commandment of God. But, behold, thou knowest this place; come, and meet me here to-morrow." ⁶ When Satan heard this, he said to Seth, "If thou tellest thy father Adam what I have told thee, he will not let thee come with me. ⁷ But hearken to me; do not tell thy father and mother what I have said to thee; but come with me to-day, to our world; where thou shalt see beautiful things and enjoy thyself there, and revel this day among my children, beholding them and taking thy fill of mirth; and rejoice ever more. Then I shall bring thee back to this place to-morrow; but if thou wouldest rather abide with me, so be it." ⁸ Then Seth answered, "The spirit of my father and of my mother, hangs on me; and if I hide from them one day, they will die, and God will hold me guilty of sinning against them. ⁹ "And except that they know I am come to this place to bring up to it my offering, they would not be separated from me one hour; neither should I go to any other place, unless they let me. But they treat me most kindly, because I come back to them quickly." ¹⁰ Then Satan said to him, "What will happen to thee if thou hide thyself from them one night, and return to them at break of day?" ¹¹ But Seth, when he saw how he kept on talking, and that he would not leave him-ran, and went up to the altar, and spread his hands unto God, and sought deliverance from Him. ¹² Then God sent His Word, and cursed Satan, who fled from Him. ¹³ But as for Seth, he had gone up to the altar, saying thus in his heart. "The altar is the place of offering, and God is there; a divine fire shall consume it; so shall Satan be unable to hurt me, and shall not take me away thence." ¹⁴ Then Seth came down from the altar and went to his father and mother, where he found in the way, longing to hear his voice; for he had tarried a while. ¹⁵ He then began to tell them what had befallen him from Satan, under the form of an angel. ¹⁶ But when Adam heard his account, he kissed his face, and warned him against that angel, telling him it was Satan who thus appeared to him. Then Adam took Seth, and they went to the Cave of Treasures, and rejoiced therein. ¹⁷ But from that day forth Adam and Eve never parted from him, to whatever place he might go, whether for his offering or for any thing else. ¹⁸ This sign happened to Seth, when he was nine years old.

7
Seth marries Aklia. Adam lives to see grand children and great-grand-children.
¹ WHEN our father Adam saw that Seth was of a perfect heart, he wished him to marry; lest the enemy should appear to him another time, and overcome him. ² So Adam said to his son Seth, "I wish, O my son, that thou wed thy sister Aklia, Abel's sister, that she may bear thee children, who

shall replenish the earth, according to God's promise to us. ³ "Be not afraid, O my son; there is no disgrace in it. I wish thee to marry, from fear lest the enemy overcome thee." ⁴ Seth, however, did not wish to marry; but in obedience to his father and mother, he said not a word. ⁵ So Adam married him to Aklia. And he was fifteen years old. ⁶ But when he was twenty years of age, he begat a son, whom he called Enos; and then begat other children than him. ⁷ Then Enos grew up, married, and begat Cainan. ⁸ Cainan also grew up, married, and begat Mahalaleel. ⁹ Those fathers were born during Adam's life-time, and dwelt by the Cave of Treasures. ¹⁰ Then were the days of Adam nine hundred and thirty years, and those of Mahalaleel one hundred. But Mahalaleel, when he was grown up, loved fasting, praying, and with hard labours, until the end of our father Adam's days drew near.

8

Adam's remarkable last words. He predicts the Flood. He exhorts his offspring to good. He reveals certain mysteries of life.

¹ WHEN our father Adam saw that his end was near, he called his son Seth, who came to him in the Cave of Treasures, and he said unto him: – ² "O Seth, my son bring me thy children and thy children's children, that I may shed my blessing on them ere I die." ³ When Seth heard these words from his father Adam, he went from him, shed a flood of tears over his face, and gathered together his children and his children's children, and brought them to his father Adam. ⁴ But when our father Adam saw them around him, he wept at having to be separated from them. ⁵ And when they saw him weeping, they all wept together, and fell upon his face saying, "How shalt thou be severed from us, O our father? And how shall the earth receive thee and hide thee from our eyes?" Thus did they lament much, and in like words. ⁶ Then our father Adam blessed them all, and said to Seth, after he had blessed them: – ⁷ "O Seth, my son, thou knowest this world – that it is full of sorrow, and of weariness; and thou knowest all that has come upon us, from our trials in it. I therefore now command thee in these words: to keep innocency, to be pure and just, and trusting in God; and lean not to the discourses of Satan, nor to the apparitions in which he will show himself to thee. ⁸ But keep the commandments that I give thee this day; then give the same to thy son Enos; and let Enos give it to his son Cainan; and Cainan to his son Mahalaleel; so that this commandment abide firm among all your children. ⁹ "O Seth, my son, the moment I am dead take ye my body and wind it up with myrrh, aloes, and cassia, and leave me here in this Cave of Treasures in which are all these tokens which God gave us from the garden. ¹⁰ "O my son, hereafter shall a flood come and overwhelm all creatures, and leave out only eight souls. ¹¹ "But, O my son, let those whom it will leave out from among your children at that time, take my body with them out of this cave; and when they have taken it with them, let the oldest among them command his children to lay my body in a ship until the flood has been assuaged, and they come out of the ship. ¹² Then they shall take my body and lay it in the middle of the earth, shortly after they have been saved from the waters of the flood. ¹³ "For the place where my body shall be laid, is the middle of the earth; God shall come from thence and shall save all our kindred. ¹⁴ "But now, O Seth, my son, place thyself at the head of thy people; tend them and watch over them in the fear of God; and lead them in the good way, Command them to fast unto God; and make them understand they ought not to hearken to Satan, lest he destroy them. ¹⁵ "Then, again, sever thy children and thy children's children from Cain's children; do not let them ever mix with those, nor come near them either in their words or in their deeds." ¹⁶ Then Adam let his blessing descend upon Seth, and upon his children, and upon all his children's children. ¹⁷ He then turned to his son Seth, and to Eve his wife, and said to them, "Preserve this gold, this incense, and this myrrh, that God has given us for a sign; for in days that are coming, a flood will overwhelm the whole creation. But those who shall go into the ark shall take with them the gold, the incense, and the myrrh, together with my body; and will lay the gold, the incense, and the myrrh, with my body in the midst of the earth. ¹⁸ "Then, after a long time, the city in which the gold, the incense, and the myrrh are found with my body, shall be plundered. But when it is spoiled, the gold the incense, and the myrrh shall be taken care of with the spoil that is kept; and naught of them shall perish, until the Word of God, made man shall come; when kings shall take them, and shall offer to Him, gold in token of His being King; incense, in token of His being God of heaven and earth; and myrrh, in token of His passion. ¹⁹ "Gold also, as a token of His overcoming Satan, and all our foes; incense as a token that He will rise from the dead, and be exalted above things in heaven and things in the earth; and myrrh, in token that He will drink bitter gall; and feel the pains of hell from Satan. ²⁰ "And now, O Seth, my son, behold I have revealed unto thee hidden mysteries, which God had revealed unto me. Keep my commandment, for thyself, and for thy people."

9

The death of Adam.

¹ WHEN Adam had ended his commandment to Seth, his limbs were loosened, his hands and feet lost all power, his mouth became dumb, and his tongue ceased altogether to speak. He closed his eyes and gave up the ghost. ² But when his children saw that he was dead, they threw themselves over him, men and women, old and young, weeping. ³ The death of Adam took place at the end of nine hundred and thirty years that be lived upon the earth; on the fifteenth day of Barmudeh, after the reckoning of an epact of the sun, at the ninth hour. ⁴ It was on a Friday, the very day on which he was created, and on which he rested; and the hour at which he died, was the same as that at which he came out of the garden. ⁵ Then Seth wound him up well, and embalmed him with plenty of sweet spices, from sacred trees and from the Holy Mountain; and be laid his body on the eastern side of the inside of the cave, the side of the incense; and placed in front of him a lamp-stand kept burning. ⁶ Then his children stood before him weeping and wailing over him the whole night until break of day. ⁷ Then Seth and big son Enos, and Cainan, the son of Enos, went out and took good offerings to present unto the Lord, and they came to the altar upon which Adam offered gifts to God, when he did offer. ⁸ But Eve said to them "Wait until we have first asked God to accept our offering, and to keep by Him the Soul of Adam His servant, and to take it up to rest." ⁹ And they all stood up and prayed.

10

"Adam was the first...."

¹ AND when they had ended their prayer, the Word of God came and comforted them concerning their father Adam. ² After this, they offered their gifts for themselves and for their father. ³ And when they had ended their offering, the Word of God came to Seth, the eldest among them, saying unto him, "O Seth, Seth, Seth, three times. As I was with thy father, so also shall I be with thee, until the fulfilment of the promise I made him-thy father saying, I will send My Word and save thee and thy seed. ⁴ But as to thy father Adam, keep thou the commandment he gave thee; and sever thy seed from that of Cain thy brother." ⁵ And God withdrew His Word from Seth. ⁶ Then Seth, Eve, and their children, came down from the mountain to the Cave of Treasures. ⁷ But Adam was the first whose soul died in the land of Eden, in the Cave of Treasures; for no one died before him, but his son Abel, who died murdered. ⁸ Then all the children of Adam rose up, and wept over their father Adam, and made offerings to him, one hundred and forty days.

11

Seth becomes head of the most happy and just tribe of people who ever lived.

¹ AFTER the death of Adam and of Eve, Seth severed his children, and his children's children, from Cain's children. Cain and his seed went down and dwelt westward, below the place where he had killed his brother Abel. ² But Seth and his children, dwelt northwards upon the mountain of the Cave of Treasures, in order to be near to their father Adam. ³ And Seth the elder, tall and good, with a fine soul, and of a strong mind, stood at the head of his people; and tended them in innocence, penitence, and meekness, and did not allow one of them to go down to Cain's children. ⁴ But because of their own purity, they were named "Children of God," and they were with God, instead of the hosts of angels who fell; for they continued in praises to God, and in singing psalms unto Him, in their cave – the Cave of Treasures. ⁵ Then Seth stood before the body of his father Adam, and of his mother Eve, and prayed night and day, and asked for mercy towards himself and his children; and that when he had some difficult dealing with a child, He would give him counsel. ⁶ But Seth and his children did not like earthly work, but gave themselves to heavenly things; for they had no other thought than praises, doxologies, and psalms unto God. ⁷ Therefore did they at all times hear the voices of angels, praising and glorifying God; from within the garden, or when they were sent by God on an errand, or when they were going up to heaven. ⁸ For Seth and his children, by reason of their own purity, heard and saw those angels. Then, again, the garden was not far above them, but only some fifteen spiritual cubits. ⁹ Now one spiritual cubit answers to three cubits of man, altogether forty-five cubits. ¹⁰ Seth and his children dwelt on the mountain below the garden; they sowed not, neither did they reap; they wrought no food for the body. not even wheat; but only offerings. They ate of the fruit and of trees well flavoured that grew on the mountain where they dwelt. ¹¹ Then Seth often fasted every forty days, as did also his eldest children. For the family of Seth smelled the smell of the trees in the garden, when the wind blew that way. ¹² They were happy, innocent, without sudden fear, there was no jealousy, no evil action, no hatred among them. There was no animal passion; from no mouth among them went forth either foul words or curse; neither evil counsel nor fraud. For the men of that time never swore, but under hard circumstances, when men must swear, they swore by the blood of Abel the just. ¹³ But they

constrained their children and their women every day in the cave to fast and pray, and to worship the most High God. They blessed themselves n the body of their father Adam, and anointed themselves with it. ¹⁴ And they did so until the end of Seth drew near.

12

Seth's family affairs. His death. The headship of Enos. How the outcast branch of Adam's family fared.

¹ THEN Seth, the just, called his son Enos, and Cainan, son of Enos, and Mahalaleel, son of Cainan, and said unto them: – ² "As my end is near, I wish to build a roof over the altar on which gifts are offered." ³ They hearkened to his commandment and went out, all of them, both old and young, and worked hard at it, and built a beautiful roof over the altar. ⁴ And Seth's thought in so doing, was that a blessing should come upon his children on the mountain; and that he should present an offering for them before his death. ⁵ Then when the building of the roof was completed, he commanded them to make offerings. They worked diligently at these, and brought them to Seth their father who took them and offered them upon the altar; and prayed God to accept their offerings, to have mercy on the souls of his children, and to keep them from the hand of Satan. ⁶ And God accepted his offering, and sent His blessing upon him and upon his children. And then God made a promise to Seth, saying, "At the end of the great five days and a half, concerning which I have made a promise to thee and to thy father, I will send My Word and save thee and thy seed." ⁷ Then Seth and his children, and his children's children, met together, and came down from the altar, and went to the Cave of Treasures – where they prayed, and blessed themselves in the body of our father Adam, and anointed themselves with it. ⁸ But Seth abode in the Cave of Treasures, a few days, and then suffered – sufferings unto death. ⁹ Then Enos, his first-born son, came to him, with Cainan, his son, and Mahalaleel, Cainan's son, and Jared, the son of Mahalaleel, and Enoch, Jared's son, with their wives and children to receive a blessing from Seth. ¹⁰ Then Seth prayed over them, and blessed them, and adjured them by the blood of Abel the just, saying, "I beg of you, my children, not to let one of you go down from this Holy and pure Mountain. ¹¹ Make no fellowship with the children of Cain the murderer and the sinner, who killed his brother; for ye know, O my children, that we flee from him, and from all his sin with all our might because he killed his brother Abel." ¹² After having said this, Seth blessed Enos, his first-born son, and commanded him habitually to minister in purity before the body of our father Adam, all the days of his life; then, also, to go at times to the altar which he Seth had built. And he commanded him to feed his people in righteousness, in judgment and purity all the days of his life. ¹³ Then the limbs of Seth were loosened; his hands and feet lost all power; his mouth became dumb and unable to speak; and he gave up the ghost and died the day after his nine hundred and twelfth year; on the twenty-seventh day of the month Abib; Enoch being then twenty years old. ¹⁴ Then they wound up the body of Seth, and embalmed him with sweet spices, and laid him in the Cave of Treasures, on the right side of our father Adam's body, and they mourned for him forty days. They offered gifts for him, as they had done for our father Adam. ¹⁵ After the death of Seth Enos rose at the head of his people, whom he fed in righteousness, and judgment, as his father had commanded him. ¹⁶ But by the time Enos was eight hundred and twenty years old, Cain had a large progeny; for they married frequently, being given to animal lusts; until the land below the mountain, was filled with them.

13

"Among the children of Cain there was much robbery, murder and sin."

¹ IN those days lived Lamech the blind, who was of the sons of Cain. He had a son whose name was Atun, and they two had much cattle. ² But Lamech was in the habit of sending them to feed with a young shepherd, who tended them; and who, when coming home in the evening wept before his grandfather, and before his father Atun and his mother Hazina, and said to them, "As for me, I cannot feed those cattle alone, lest one rob me of some of them, or kill me for the sake of them." For among the children of Cain, there was much robbery, murder, and sin. ³ Then Lamech pitied him, and he said, "Truly, he when alone, might be overpowered by the men of this place." ⁴ So Lamech arose, took a bow he had kept ever since he was a youth, ere he became blind, and he took large arrows, and smooth stones, and a sling which he had, and went to the field with the young shepherd, and placed himself behind the cattle; while the young shepherd watched the cattle. Thus did Lamech many days. ⁵ Meanwhile Cain, ever since God had cast him off, and had cursed him with trembling and terror, could neither settle nor find rest in any one place; but wandered from place to place. ⁶ In his wanderings he came to Lamech's wives, and asked them about him. They said to him, "He is in the field with the cattle." ⁷ Then Cain went to look for him; and as he came into the field, the young shepherd heard the noise he made, and the cattle herding together from before him. ⁸ Then said he to Lamech, "O my lord, is that a wild beast or a robber?" ⁹ And Lamech said to him, "Make me understand which way he looks, when he comes up." ¹⁰ Then Lamech bent his bow, placed an arrow on it, and fitted a stone in the sling, and when Cain came out from the open country, the shepherd said to Lamech, "Shoot, behold, he is coming." ¹¹ Then Lamech shot at Cain with his arrow and hit him in his side. And Lamech struck him with a stone from his sling, that fell upon his face, and knocked out both his eyes; then Cain fell at once and died. ¹² Then Lamech and the young shepherd came up to him, and found him lying on the ground. And the young shepherd said to him, "It is Cain our grandfather, whom thou hast killed, O my lord!" ¹³ Then was Lamech sorry for it, and from the bitterness of his regret, he clapped his hands together, and struck with his flat palm the head of the youth, who fell as if dead; but Lamech thought it was a feint; so he took up a stone and smote him, and smashed his head until he died.

14

Time, like an ever-rolling stream, bears away another generation of men.

¹ WHEN Enos was nine hundred years old, all the children of Seth, and of Cainan, and his first-born, with their wives and children, gathered around him, asking for a blessing from him. ² He then prayed over them and blessed them, and adjured them by the blood of Abel the just saying to them, "Let not one of your children go down from this Holy Mountain, and let them make no fellowship with the children of Cain the murderer." ³ Then Enos called his son Cainan and said to him, "See, O my son, and set thy heart on thy people, and establish them in righteousness, and in innocence; and stand ministering before the body of our father Adam, all the days of thy life." ⁴ After this Enos entered into rest, aged nine hundred and eighty-five years; and Cainan wound him up, and laid him in the Cave of Treasures on the left of his father Adam; and made offerings for him, after the custom of his fathers.

15

The offspring of Adam continue to keep the Cave of Treasures as a family shrine.

¹ AFTER the death of Enos, Cainan stood at the head of his people in righteousness and innocence, as his father had commanded him; he also continued to minister before the body of Adam, inside the Cave of Treasures. ² Then when he had lived nine hundred and ten years, suffering and affliction came upon him. And when he was about to enter into rest, all the fathers with their wives and children came to him, and he blessed them, and adjured them by the blood of Abel, the just, saying to them, "Let not one among you go down from this Holy Mountain; and make no fellowship with the children of Cain the murderer." ³ Mahalaleel, his first-born son, received this commandment from his father, who blessed him and died. ⁴ Then Mahalaleel embalmed him with sweet spices, and laid him in the Cave of Treasures, with his fathers; and they made offerings for him, after the custom of their fathers.

16

The good branch of the family is still afraid of the children of Cain.

¹ THEN Mahalaleel stood over his people, and fed them in righteousness and innocence, and watched them to see they held no intercourse with the children of Cain. ² He also continued in the Cave of Treasures praying and ministering before the body of our father Adam, asking God for mercy on himself and on his people; until he was eight hundred and seventy years old, when he fell sick. ³ Then all his children gathered unto him, to see him, and to ask for his blessing on them all, ere he left this world. ⁴ Then Mahalaleel arose and sat on his bed, his tears streaming down his face, and he called his eldest son Jared, who came to him. ⁵ He then kissed his face, and said to him, "O Jared, my son, I adjure thee by Him who made heaven and earth, to watch over thy people, and to feed them in righteousness and in innocence; and not to let one of them go down from this Holy Mountain to the children of Cain, lest he perish with them. ⁶ "Hear, O my son, hereafter there shall come a great destruction upon this earth on account of them; God will be angry with the world, and will destroy them with waters. ⁷ "But I also know that thy children will not hearken to thee, and that they will go down from this mountain and hold intercourse with the children of Cain, and that they shall perish with them. ⁸ "O my son! teach them, and watch over them, that no guilt attach to thee on their account." ⁹ Mahalaleel said, moreover, to his son Jared, "When I die, embalm my body and lay it in the Cave of Treasures, by the bodies of my fathers; then stand thou by my body and pray to God; and take care of them, and fulfil thy ministry before them, until thou enterest into rest thyself." ¹⁰ Mahalaleel then blessed all his children; and then lay down on his bed, and entered into rest like his fathers. ¹¹ But when Jared saw that his father Mahalaleel was dead, he wept, and sorrowed, and embraced and kissed his hands and his feet; and so did all his children. ¹² And his children embalmed him carefully, and laid him

by the bodies of his fathers. Then they arose, and mourned for him forty days.

17

Jared turns martinet. He is lured away to the land of Cain where he sees many voluptuous sights. Jared barely escapes with a clean heart.

[1] THEN Jared kept his father's commandment, and arose like a lion over his people. He fed them in righteousness and innocence, and commanded them to do nothing without his counsel. For he was afraid concerning them, lest they should go to the children of Cain. [2] Wherefore did he give them orders repeatedly; and continued to do so until the end of the four hundred and eighty-fifth year of his life. [3] At the end of these said years, there came unto him this sign. As Jared was standing like a lion before the bodies of his fathers, praying and warning his people, Satan envied him, and wrought a beautiful apparition, because Jared would not let his children do aught without his counsel. [4] Satan then appeared to him with thirty men of his hosts, in the form of handsome men; Satan himself being the elder and tallest among them, with a fine beard. [5] They stood at the mouth of the cave, and called out Jared, from within it. [6] He came out to them, and found them looking like fine men, full of light, and of great beauty. He wondered at their beauty and at their looks; and thought within himself whether they might not be of the children of Cain. [7] He said also in his heart, "As the children of Cain cannot come up to the height of this mountain, and none of them is so handsome as these appear to be; and among these men there is not one of my kindred – they must be strangers." [8] Then Jared and they exchanged a greeting and he said to the elder among them, "O my father, explain to me the wonder that is in thee, and tell me who these are, with thee; for they look to me like strange men." [9] Then the elder began to weep, and the rest wept with him; and he said to Jared: "I am Adam whom God made first; and this is Abel my son, who was killed by his brother Cain, into whose heart Satan put to murder him. [10] "Then this is my son Seth, whom I asked of the Lord, who gave him to me, to comfort me instead of Abel. [11] "Then this one is my son Enos, son of Seth, and that other one is Cainan, son of Enos, and that other one is Mahalaleel, son of Cainan, thy father." [12] But Jared remained wondering at their appearance, and at the speech of the elder to him. [13] Then the elder said to him, "Marvel not, O my son; we live in the land north of the garden, which God created before the world. He would not let us live there, but placed us inside the garden, below which ye are now dwelling. [14] "But after that I transgressed, He made me come out of it, and I was left to dwell in this cave; great and sore troubles came upon me; and when my death drew near, I commanded my son Seth to tend his people well; and this my commandment is to be handed from one to another, unto the end of the generations to come. [15] "But, O Jared, my son, we live in beautiful regions, while you live here in misery, as this thy father Mahalaleel informed me; telling me that a great flood will come and overwhelm the whole earth. [16] "Therefore, O my son, fearing for your sakes, I rose and took my children with me, and came hither for us to visit thee and thy children; but I found thee standing in this cave weeping, and thy children scattered about this mountain, in the heat and in misery. [17] "But, O my son, as we missed our way, and came as far as this, we found other men below this mountain; who inhabit a beautiful country, full of trees and of fruits, and of all manner of verdure; it is like a garden; so that when we found them we thought they were you; until thy father Mahalaleel told me they were no such thing. [18] "Now, therefore, O my son, hearken to my counsel, and go down to them, thou and thy children. Ye will rest from all this suffering in which ye are. But if thou wilt not go down to them, then, arise, take thy children, and come with us to our garden; ye shall live in our beautiful land, and ye shall rest from all this trouble, which thou and thy children are now bearing." [19] But Jared when he heard this discourse from the elder, wondered; and went hither and thither, but at that moment he found not one of his children. [20] Then he answered and said to the elder, "Why have you hidden yourselves until this day?" [21] And the elder replied, "If thy father had not told us, we should not have known it." [22] Then Jared believed his words were true. [23] So that elder said to Jared, "Wherefore didst thou turn about, so and so?" And he said, "I was seeking one of my children, to tell him about my going with you, and about their coming down to those about whom thou hast spoken to me." [24] When the elder heard Jared's intention, he said to him, "Let alone that purpose at present, and come with us; thou shalt see our country; if the land in which we dwell pleases thee, we and thou shall return hither and take thy family with us. But if our country does not please thee, thou shalt come back to thine own place." [25] And the elder urged Jared, to go before one of his children came to counsel him otherwise. [26] Jared, then, came out of the cave and went with them, and among them. And they comforted him, until they came to the top of the mountain of the sons of Cain. [27] Then said the elder to one of his companions, "We have forgotten something by the mouth of the cave, and that is the chosen garment we had brought to clothe Jared withal." [28] He then said to one of them, "Go back, thou some one; and we will wait for thee here, until thou come back. Then will we clothe Jared and he shall be like us, good, handsome, and fit to come with us into our country." [29] Then that one went back. [30] But when he was a short distance off, the elder called to him and said to him, "Tarry thou, until I come up and speak to thee." [31] Then he stood still, and the elder went up to him and said to him, "One thing we forgot at the cave, it is this – to put out the lamp that burns inside it, above the bodies that are therein. Then come back to us, quick." [32] That one went, and the elder came back to his fellows and to Jared. And they came down from the mountain, and Jared with them; and they stayed by a fountain of water, near the houses of the children of Cain, and waited for their companion until he brought the garment for Jared. [33] He, then, who went, back to the cave, put out the lamp, and came to them and brought a phantom with him and showed it them. And when Jared saw it he wondered at the beauty and grace thereof, and rejoiced in his heart believing it was all true. [34] But while they were staying there, three of them went into houses of the sons of Cain, and said to them, "Bring us to-day some food by the fountain of water, for us and our companions to eat." [35] But when the sons of Cain saw them, they wondered at them and thought: "These are beautiful to look at, and such as we never saw before." So they rose and came with them to the fountain of water, to see their companions. [36] They found them so very handsome, that they cried aloud about their places for others to gather together and come and look at these beautiful beings. Then they gathered around them both men and women. [37] Then the elder said to them, "We are strangers in your land, bring us some good food and drink you and your women, to refresh ourselves with you." [38] When those men heard these words of the elder, every one of Cain's sons brought his wife, and another brought his daughter, and so, many women came to them; every one addressing Jared either for himself or for his wife; all alike. [39] But when Jared saw what they did, his very soul wrenched itself from them; neither would he taste of their food or of their drink. [40] The elder saw hint as he wrenched himself from them, and said to him, "Be not sad; I am the great elder, as thou shalt see me do, do thyself in like manner." [41] Then he spread his hands and took one of the women, and five of his companions did the same before Jared, that he should do as they did. [42] But when Jared saw them working infamy he wept, and said in his mind, – My fathers never did the like. [43] He then spread his hands and prayed with a fervent heart, and with much weeping, and entreated God to deliver him from their hands. [44] No sooner did Jared begin to pray than the elder fled with his companions; for they could not abide in a place of prayer. [45] Then Jared turned round but could not see them, but found himself standing in the midst of the children of Cain. [46] He then wept and said, "O God, destroy me not with this race, concerning which my fathers have warned me; for now, O my Lord God, I was thinking that those who appeared unto me were my fathers; but I have found them out to be devils, who allured me by this beautiful apparition, until I believed them. [47] "But now I ask Thee, O God, to deliver me from this race, among whom I am now staying, as Thou didst deliver me from those devils. Send Thy angel to draw me out of the midst of them; for I have not myself power to escape from among them." [48] When Jared had ended his prayer, God sent His angel in the midst of them, who took Jared and set him upon the mountain, and showed him the way, gave him counsel, and then departed from him.

18

Confusion in the Cave of Treasures. Miraculous speech of the dead Adam.

[1] THE children of Jared were in the habit of visiting him hour after hour, to receive his blessing and to ask his advice for every thing they did; and when he had a work to do, they did it for him. [2] But this time when they went into the cave they found not Jared, but they found the lamp put out, and the bodies of the fathers thrown about, and voices came from them by the power of God, that said, "Satan in an apparition has deceived our son, wishing to destroy him, as he destroyed our son Cain." [3] They said also, "Lord God of heaven and earth, deliver our son from the hand of Satan, who wrought a great and false apparition before him," They also spake of other matters, by the power of God. [4] But when the children of Jared heard these voices they feared, and stood weeping for their father; for they knew not what had befallen him. [5] And they wept for him that day until the setting of the sun. [6] Then came Jared with a woeful countenance, wretched in mind and body, and sorrowful at having been separated from the bodies of his fathers. [7] But as he was drawing near to the cave, his children saw him, and hastened to the cave, and hung upon his neck, crying, and saying to him, "O father, where hast thou been, and why hast thou left us, as thou wast not wont to do?" And again, "O father, when thou didst disappear, the lamp over the bodies of our fathers went out, the bodies were thrown about, and voices came from them." [8] When Jared heard this he was sorry, and went

into the cave; and there found the bodies thrown about, the lamp put out, and the fathers themselves praying for his deliverance from the hand of Satan. ⁹ Then Jared fell upon the bodies and embraced them, and said, "O my fathers, through your intercession, let God deliver me from the hand of Satan! And I beg you will ask God to keep me and to bide me from him unto the day of my death." ¹⁰ Then all the voices ceased save the voice of our father Adam, who spake to Jared by the power of God, just as one would speak to his fellow, saying, "O Jared, my son, offer gifts to God for having delivered thee from the hand of Satan; and when thou bringest those offerings, so be it that thou offerest them on the altar on which I did offer. Then also, beware of Satan; for he deluded me many a time with his apparitions, wishing to destroy me, but God delivered me out of his hand. ¹¹ "Command thy people that they be on their guard against him; and never cease to offer up gifts to God." ¹² Then the voice of Adam also became silent; and Jared and his children wondered at this. Then they laid the bodies as they were it first; and Jared and his children stood praying the whole of that night, until break of day. ¹³ Then Jared made an offering and offered it up on the altar, as Adam had commanded him. And as he went up to the altar, he prayed to God for mercy and for forgiveness of his sin, concerning the lamp going out. ¹⁴ Then God appeared unto Jared on the altar and blessed him and his children, and accepted their offerings; and commanded Jared to take of the sacred fire from the altar, and with it to light the lamp that shed light on the body of Adam.

19

The children of Jared are led astray.

¹ THEN God revealed to him again the promise He had made to Adam; He explained to him the ⁵⁵⁰⁰ years, and revealed unto him the mystery of His coming upon the earth. ² And God said to Jared, "As to that fire which thou hast taken from the altar to light the lamp withal, let it abide with you to give light to the bodies; and let it not come out of the cave, until the body of Adam comes out of it. ³ But, O Jared, take care of the fire, that it burn bright in the lamp; neither go thou again out of the cave, until thou receivest an order through a vision, and not in an apparition, when seen by thee. ⁴ "Then command again thy people not to hold intercourse with the children of Cain, and not to learn their ways; for I am God who loves not hatred and works of iniquity." ⁵ God gave also many other commandments to Jared, and blessed him. And then withdrew His Word from him. ⁶ Then Jared drew near with his children, took some fire, and came down to the cave, and lighted the lamp before the body of Adam; and he gave his people commandments as God had told him to do. ⁷ This sign happened to Jared at the end of his four hundred and fiftieth year; as did also many other wonders, we do not record. But we record only this one for shortness sake, and in order not to lengthen our narrative. ⁸ And Jared continued to teach his children eighty years; but after that they began to transgress the commandments he had given them, and to do many things without his counsel. They began to go down from the Holy Mountain one after another, and to mix with the children of Cain, in foul fellowships. ⁹ Now the reason for which the children of Jared went down the Holy Mountain, is this, that we will now reveal unto you.

20

Ravishing music; strong drink loosed among the sons of Cain. They don colorful clothing. The children of Seth look on with longing eyes. They revolt from wise counsel; they descend the mountain into the valley of iniquity. They can not ascend the mountain again.

¹ AFTER Cain had gone down to the land of dark soil, and his children had multiplied therein, there was one of them, whose name was Genun, son of Lamech the blind who slew Cain. ² But as to this Genun, Satan came into him in his childhood; and he made sundry trumpets and horns, and string instruments, cymbals and psalteries, and lyres and harps, and flutes; and he played on them at all times and at every hour. ³ And when he played on them, Satan came into them, so that from among them were heard beautiful and sweet sounds, that ravished the heart. ⁴ Then he gathered companies upon companies to play on them; and when they played, it pleased well the children of Cain, who inflamed themselves with sin among themselves, and burnt as with fire; while Satan inflamed their hearts, one with another, and increased lust among them. ⁵ Satan also taught Genun to bring strong drink out of corn; and this Genun used to bring together companies upon companies in drink-houses; and brought into their hands all manner of fruits and flowers; and they drank together. ⁶ Thus did this Genun multiply sin exceedingly; he also acted with pride, and taught the children of Cain to commit all manner of the grossest wickedness, which they knew not; and put them up to manifold doings which they knew not before. ⁷ Then Satan, when he saw that they yielded to Genun and hearkened to him in every thing he told them, rejoiced greatly, increased Genun's understanding, until he took iron and with it made weapons of war. ⁸ Then when they were drunk, hatred and murder increased among them; one man used violence against another to teach him evil taking his children and defiling them before him. ⁹ And when men saw they were overcome, and saw others that were not overpowered, those who were beaten came to Genun, took refuge with him, and he made them his confederates. ¹⁰ Then sin increased among them greatly; until a man married his own sister, or daughter, or mother, and others; or the daughter of his father's sister, so that there was no more distinction of relationship, and they no longer knew what is iniquity; but did wickedly, and the earth was defiled with sin, and they angered God the Judge, who had created them. ¹¹ But Genun gathered together companies upon companies, that played on horns and on all the other instruments we have already mentioned, at the foot of the Holy Mountain; and they did so in order that the children of Seth who were on the Holy Mountain should hear it. ¹² But when the children of Seth heard the noise, they wondered, and came by companies, and stood on the top of the mountain to look at those below; and they did thus a whole year. ¹³ When, at the end of that year, Genun saw that they were being won over to him little by little, Satan entered into him, and taught him to make dyeing-stuffs for garments of divers patterns, and made him understand how to dye crimson and purple and what not. ¹⁴ And the sons of Cain who wrought all this, and shone in beauty and gorgeous apparel, gathered together at the foot of the mountain in splendour, with horns and gorgeous dresses, and horse races, committing all manner of abominations. ¹⁵ Meanwhile the children of Seth, who were on the Holy Mountain, prayed and praised God, in the place of the hosts of angels who had fallen; wherefore God had called them "angels," because He rejoiced over them greatly. ¹⁶ But after this, they no longer kept His commandment, nor held by the promise He had made to their fathers; but they relaxed from their fasting and praying, and from the counsel of Jared their father. And they kept on gathering together on the top of the mountain, to look upon the children of Cain, from morning until evening, and upon what they did, upon their beautiful dresses and ornaments. ¹⁷ Then the children of Cain looked up from below, and saw the children of Seth, standing in troops on the top of the mountain; and they called to them to come down to them. ¹⁸ But the children of Seth said to them from above, "We don't know the way." Then Genun, the son of Lamech, heard them say they did not know the way, and he bethought himself how he might bring them down. ¹⁹ Then Satan appeared to him by night, saying, "There is no way for them to come down from the mountain on which they dwell; but when they come to-morrow, say to them, 'Come ye to the western side of the mountain; there you will find the way of a stream of water, that comes down to the foot of the mountain, between two hills; come down that way to us.'" ²⁰ Then when it was day, Genun blew the horns and beat the drums below the mountain, as he was wont. The children of Seth heard it, and came as they used to do. ²¹ Then Genun said to them from down below, "Go to the western side of the mountain, there you will find the way to come down." ²² But when the children of Seth heard these words from him, they went back into the cave to Jared, to tell him all they had heard. ²³ Then when Jared heard it, he was grieved; for he knew that they would transgress his counsel. ²⁴ After this a hundred men of the children of Seth gathered together, and said among themselves, "Come, let us go down to the children of Cain, and see what they do, and enjoy ourselves with them." ²⁵ But when Jared heard this of the hundred men, his very soul was moved, and his heart was grieved. He then arose with great fervour, and stood in the midst of them, and adjured them by the blood of Abel the just, "Let not one of you go down from this holy and pure mountain, in which our fathers have ordered its to dwell." ²⁶ But when Jared saw that they did not receive his words, he said unto them, "O my good and innocent and holy children, know that when once you go down from this holy mountain, God will not allow you to return again to it." ²⁷ He again adjured them, saying, "I adjure by the death of our father Adam, and by the blood of Abel, of Seth, of Enos, of Cainan, and of Mahalaleel, to hearken to me, and not to go down from this holy mountain; for the moment you leave it, you will be reft of life and of mercy; and you shall no longer be called 'children of God,' but 'children of the devil.'" ²⁸ But they would not hearken to his words. ²⁹ Enoch at that time was already grown up, and in his zeal for God, be arose and said, "Hear me, O ye sons of Seth, small and great – when ye transgress the commandment of our fathers, and go down from this holy mountain – ye shall not come up hither again for ever." ³⁰ But they rose up against Enoch, and would not hearken to his words, but went down from the Holy Mountain. ³¹ And when they looked at the daughters of Cain, at their beautiful figures, and at their hands and feet dyed with colour, and tattooed in ornaments on their faces, the fire of sin was kindled in them. ³² Then Satan made them look most beautiful before the sons of Seth, as he also made the sons of Seth appear of the fairest in the eyes of the daughters of Cain, so that the daughters of Cain lusted after the sons of Seth like ravenous beasts, and the sons of Seth after the daughters of Cain, until they

committed abomination with them. ³³ But after they had thus fallen into this defilement, they returned by the way they had come, and tried to ascend the Holy Mountain. But they could not, because the stones of that holy mountain were of fire flashing before them, by reason of which they could not go up again. ³⁴ And God was angry with them, and repented of them because they had come down from glory, and had thereby lost or forsaken their own purity or innocence, and were fallen into the defilement of sin. ³⁵ Then God sent His Word to Jared, saying, "These thy children, whom thou didst call 'My children,' – behold they have transgressed My commandment, and have gone down to the abode of perdition, and of sin. Send a messenger to those that are left, that they may not go down, and be lost." ³⁶ Then Jared wept before the Lord, and asked of Him mercy and forgiveness. But he wished that his soul might depart from his body, rather than hear these words from God about the going down of his children from the Holy Mountain. ³⁷ But he followed God's order, and preached unto them not to go down from that holy mountain, and not to hold intercourse with the children of Cain. ³⁸ But they heeded not his message, and would not obey his counsel.

21

Jared dies in sorrow for his sons who had gone astray. A prediction of the Flood.

¹ AFTER this another company gathered together, and they went to look after their brethren; but they perished as well as they. And so it was, company after company, until only a few of them were left. ² Then Jared sickened from grief, and his sickness was such that the day of his death drew near. ³ Then he called Enoch his eldest son, and Methuselah Enoch's son, and Lamech the son of Methuselah, and Noah the son of Lamech. ⁴ And when they were come to him he prayed over them and blessed them, and said to them, "Ye are righteous, innocent sons; go ye not down from this holy mountain; for behold, your children and your children's children have gone down from this holy mountain, and have estranged themselves from this holy mountain, through their abominable lust and transgression of God's commandment. ⁵ "But I know, through the power of God, that He will not leave you on this holy mountain, because your children have transgressed His commandment and that of our fathers, which we had received from them. ⁶ "But, O my sons, God will take you to a strange land, and ye never shall again return to behold with your eyes this garden and this holy mountain. ⁷ "Therefore, O my sons, set your hearts on your own selves, and keep the commandment of God which is with you. And when you go from this holy mountain, into a strange land which ye know not, take with you the body of our father Adam, and with it these three precious, gifts and offerings, namely, the gold, the incense, and the myrrh; and let them be in the place where the body of our father Adam shall lay. ⁸ "And unto him of you who shall be left, O my sons, shall the Word of God come, and when he goes out of this land he shall take with him the body of our father Adam, and shall lay it in the middle of the earth the place in which salvation shall be wrought." ⁹ Then Noah said unto him, "Who is he of us that shall be left?" ¹⁰ And Jared answered, "Thou art he that shall be left. And thou shalt take the body of our father Adam from the cave, and place it with thee in the ark when the flood comes. ¹¹ "And thy son Shem, who shall come out of thy loins, he it is who shall lay the body of our father Adam in the middle of the earth, in the place whence salvation shall come." ¹² Then Jared turned to his son Enoch, and said unto him, "Thou, my son, abide in this cave, and minister diligently before the body of our father Adam all the days of thy life; and feed thy people in righteousness and innocence." ¹³ And Jared said no more. His hands were loosened, his eyes closed, and he entered into rest like his fathers. His death took place in the three hundred and sixtieth year of Noah, and in the nine hundred and eighty-ninth year of his own life; on the twelfth of Takhsas on a Friday. ¹⁴ But as Jared died, tears streamed down his face by reason of his great sorrow, for the children of Seth, who had fallen in his days. ¹⁵ Then Enoch, Methuselah, Lamech and Noah, these four, wept over him; embalmed him carefully, and then laid him in the Cave of Treasures. Then they rose and mourned for him forty days. ¹⁶ And when these days of mourning were ended, Enoch, Methuselah, Lamech and Noah remained in sorrow of heart, because their father had departed from them, and they saw him no more.

22

Only three righteous men left in the world. The evil conditions of men prior to the Flood.

¹ BUT Enoch kept the commandment of Jared his father, and continued to minister in the cave. ² It is this Enoch to whom many wonders happened, and who also wrote a celebrated book; but those wonders may not be told in this place. ³ Then after this, the children of Seth went astray and fell, they, their children and their wives. And when Enoch, Methuselah, Lamech and Noah saw them, their hearts suffered by reason of their fall into doubt full of unbelief; and they wept and sought of God mercy, to preserve them, and to bring them out of that wicked generation. ⁴ Enoch continued in his ministry before the Lord three hundred and eighty-five years, and at the end of that time he became aware through the grace of God, that God intended to remove him from the earth. ⁵ He then said to his son, "O my son, I know that God intends to bring the waters of the Flood upon the earth, and to destroy our creation. ⁶ "And ye are the last rulers over this people on this mountain; for I know that not one will be left you to beget children on this holy mountain; neither shall any one of you rule over the children of his people; neither shall any great company be left of you, on this mountain." ⁷ Enoch said also to them, "Watch over your souls, and hold fast by your fear of God and by your service of Him, and worship Him in upright faith, and serve Him in righteousness, innocence and judgment, in repentance and also in purity." ⁸ When Enoch had ended his commandments to them, God transported him from that mountain to the land of life, to the mansions of the righteous and of the chosen, the abode of Paradise of joy, in light that reaches up to heaven; light that is outside the light of this world; for it is the light of God, that fills the whole world, but which no place can contain. ⁹ Thus, because Enoch was in the light of God, he found himself out of the reach of death; until God would have him die. ¹⁰ Altogether, not one of our fathers or of their children, remained on that holy mountain, except those three, Methuselah, Lamech, and Noah. For all the rest went down from the mountain and fell into sin with the children of Cain. Therefore were they forbidden that mountain, and none remained on it but those three men.

Life of Adam and Eve, or Vita Adae et Evae

1

[1] When they were driven out from paradise, they made themselves a booth, and spent seven days mourning and lamenting in great grief.

2

[1] But after seven days, they began to be hungry and started to look for victual to eat, and they [2] found it not. Then Eve said to Adam: 'My lord, I am hungry. Go, look for (something) for us to eat. Perchance the Lord God will look back and pity us and recall us to the place in which we were before.

3

[1] And Adam arose and walked seven days over all that land, and found no victual such as they [2] used to have in paradise. And Eve said to Adam: 'Wilt thou slay me? that I may die, and perchance God the Lord will bring thee into paradise, for on my account hast thou been driven thence.' [3] Adam answered: 'Forbear, Eve, from such words, that peradventure God bring not some other curse upon us. How is it possible that I should stretch forth my hand against my own flesh? Nay, let us arise and look for something for us to live on, that we fail not.'

4

[1] And they walked about and searched for nine days, and they found none such as they were used to have in paradise, but found only animals' [2] food. And Adam said to Eve: 'This hath the Lord provided for animals and brutes to eat; [3] but we used to have angels' food. But it is just and right that we lament before the sight of God who made us. Let us repent with a great penitence: perchance the Lord will be gracious to us and will pity us and give us a share of something for our living.'

5

[1] And Eve said to Adam: 'What is penitence? Tell me, what sort of penitence am I to do? Let us not put too great a labour on ourselves, which we cannot endure, so that the Lord will not hearken to our prayers: and will turn away His countenance from us, because we have not [3] fulfilled what we promised. My lord, how much penitence hast thou thought (to do) for I have brought trouble and anguish upon thee?'

6

[1] And Adam said to Eve: 'Thou canst not do so much as I, but do only so much as thou hast strength for. For I will spend forty days fasting, but do thou arise and go to the river Tigris and lift up a stone and stand on it in the water up to thy neck in the deep of the river. And let no speech proceed out of thy mouth, since we are unworthy to address the Lord, for our lips are unclean from the unlawful and forbidden tree. [2] And do thou stand in the water of the river thirty-seven days. But I will spend forty days in the water of Jordan, perchance the Lord God will take pity upon us.'

7

[1] And Eve walked to the river Tigris and did [2] as Adam had told her. Likewise, Adam walked to the river Jordan and stood on a stone up to his neck in water.

8

[1] And Adam said: 'I tell thee, water of Jordan, grieve with me, and assemble to me all swimming (creatures), which are in thee, and let them surround me and mourn in company with me. Not for themselves let them lament, but for me; for it is not they that have sinned, but I.' [3] Forthwith, all living things came and surrounded him, and, from that hour, the water of Jordan stood (still) and its current was stayed.'

9

[1] And eighteen days passed by; then Satan was wroth and transformed himself into the brightness of angels, and went away to the river [2] Tigris to Eve, and found her weeping, and the devil himself pretended to grieve with her, and he began to weep and said to her: 'Come out of the river and lament no more. Cease now from sorrow and moans. Why art thou anxious [3] and thy husband Adam? The Lord God hath heard your groaning and hath accepted your penitence, and all we angels have entreated on your behalf, and made supplication to the Lord; [4] and he hath sent me to bring you out of the water and give you the nourishment which you had in paradise, and for which you are crying [5] out. Now come out of the water and I will conduct you to the place where your victual hath been made ready.'

10

[1] But Eve heard and believed and went out of the water of the river, and her flesh was (trembling) [2] like grass, from the chill of the water. And when she had gone out, she fell on the earth and the devil raised her up and led her to Adam. [3] But when Adam had seen her and the devil with her, he wept and cried aloud and said: 'O Eve, Eve, where is the labour of thy penitence? [4] How hast thou been again ensnared by our adversary, by whose means we have been estranged from our abode in paradise and spiritual joy?'

11

[1] And when she heard this, Eve understood that (it was) the devil (who) had persuaded her to go out of the river; and she fell on her face on the earth and her sorrow and groaning and wailing [2] was redoubled. And she cried out and said: 'Woe unto thee, thou devil. Why dost thou attack us for no cause? What hast thou to do with us? What have we done to thee? for thou pursuest us with craft? Or why doth thy malice [3] assail us? Have we taken away thy glory and caused thee to be without honour? Why dost thou harry us, thou enemy (and persecute us) to the death in wickedness and envy?'

12

[1] And with a heavy sigh, the devil spake: 'O Adam! all my hostility, envy, and sorrow is for thee, since it is for thee that I have been expelled from my glory, which I possessed in the heavens [2] in the midst of the angels and for thee was I cast out in the earth.' Adam answered, 'What dost [3] thou tell me? What have I done to thee or what is my fault against thee? Seeing that thou hast received no harm or injury from us, why dost thou pursue us?'

13

[1] The devil replied, 'Adam, what dost thou tell me? It is for thy sake that I have been hurled [2] from that place. When thou wast formed. I was hurled out of the presence of God and banished from the company of the angels. When God blew into thee the breath of life and thy face and likeness was made in the image of God, Michael also brought thee and made (us) worship thee in the sight of God; and God the Lord spake: Here is Adam. I have made thee in our image and likeness.'

14

[1] And Michael went out and called all the angels saying: 'Worship the image of God as the Lord God hath commanded.' [2] And Michael himself worshipped first; then he called me and said: 'Worship the image of God [3] the Lord.' And I answered, 'I have no (need) to worship Adam.' And since Michael kept urging me to worship, I said to him, 'Why dost thou urge me? I will not worship an inferior and younger being (than I). I am his senior in the Creation, before he was made was I already made. It is his duty to worship me.'

15

[1] When the angels, who were under me, heard this, they refused to worship him. [2] And Michael saith, 'Worship the image of God, but if thou wilt not worship him, the Lord God will be wrath [3] with thee.' And I said, 'If He be wrath with me, I will set my seat above the stars of heaven and will be like the Highest.'

16

[1] And God the Lord was wrath with me and banished me and my angels from our glory; and on [2] thy account were we expelled from our abodes into this world and hurled on the earth. And [3] straightway we were overcome with grief, since we had been spoiled of so great glory. And we [4] were grieved when we saw thee in such joy and luxury. And with guile I cheated thy wife and caused thee to be expelled through her (doing) from thy joy and luxury, as I have been driven out of my glory.

17

[1] When Adam heard the devil say this, he cried out and wept and spake: 'O Lord my God, my life is in thy hands. Banish this Adversary far from me, who seeketh to destroy my soul, and give [2,3] me his glory which he himself hath lost.' And at that moment, the devil vanished before him. But Adam endured in his penance, standing for forty days (on end) in the water of Jordan.

18

[1] And Eve said to Adam: 'Live thou, my Lord, to thee life is granted, since thou hast committed neither the first nor the second error. But I have erred and been led astray for I have not kept the commandment of God; and now banish me from the light of thy life and I will go to the sunsetting, [2] and there will I be, until I die.' And she began to walk towards the western parts and to mourn [3] and to weep bitterly and groan aloud. And she made there a booth, while she had in her womb offspring of three months old.

19

[1] And when the time of her bearing approached, she began to be distressed with pains, and she [2] cried aloud to the Lord and said: 'Pity me, O Lord, assist me.' And she was not heard and the [3] mercy of God did not encircle her. And she said to herself: 'Who shall tell my lord Adam? I implore you, ye luminaries of heaven, what time ye return to the east, bear a message to my lord Adam.'

20

[1] But in that hour, Adam said: 'The complaint of Eve hath come to me. Perchance, once more hath the serpent fought with her.' [2] And he went and found her in great distress. And Eve said: 'From the moment I saw thee, my lord, my grief-laden soul was refreshed. And now entreat the Lord God on my behalf to [3] hearken unto thee and look upon me and free me from my awful pains.' And Adam entreated the Lord for Eve.

21

[1] And behold, there came twelve angels and two 'virtues', standing on the right and on the left [2] of Eve; and Michael was standing on the right; and he stroked her on the face as far as to the breast and said to Eve: 'Blessed art thou, Eve, for Adam's sake. Since his prayers and intercessions are great, I have been sent that thou mayst receive our help. Rise up now, and [3] prepare thee to bear. And she bore a son and he was shining; and at once the babe rose up and ran and bore a blade of grass in his hands, and gave it to his mother, and his name was called Cain.

22

[1] And Adam carried Eve and the boy and led [2] them to the East. And the Lord God sent divers seeds by Michael the archangel and gave to Adam and showed him how to work and till the ground, that they might have fruit by which they and all their generations might live. [3] For thereafter Eve conceived and bare a son, whose name was Abel; and Cain and Abel used to stay together. [4] And Eve said to Adam: 'My lord, while I slept, I saw a vision, as it were the blood of our son Abel in the hand of Cain, who was gulping it down in his mouth. Therefore I have sorrow.' [5] And Adam said, 'Alas if Cain slew Abel. Yet let us separate them from each other mutually, and let us make for each of them separate dwellings.'

23

[1] And they made Cain an husbandman, (but) Abel they made a shepherd; in order that in this wise they might be mutually separated. [2] And thereafter, Cain slew Abel, but Adam was then one hundred and thirty years old, but Abel was slain when he was one hundred and twenty-two years. And thereafter Adam knew his wife and he begat a son and called his name Seth.

24

[1] And Adam said to Eve, 'Behold, I have begotten a son, in place of Abel, whom Cain slew.' [2] And after Adam had begotten Seth, he lived eight hundred years and begat thirty sons and thirty daughters; in all sixty-three children. And they were increased over the face of the earth in their nations.

25

[1] And Adam said to Seth, 'Hear, my son Seth, that I may relate to thee what I heard and [2] saw after your mother and I had been driven out of paradise. When we were at prayer, there [3] came to me Michael the archangel, a messenger of God. And I saw a chariot like the wind and its wheels were fiery and I was caught up into the Paradise of righteousness, and I saw the Lord sitting and his face was flaming fire that could not be endured. And many thousands of angels were on the right and the left of that chariot.

26

[1] When I saw this, I was confounded, and terror seized me and I bowed myself down before [2] God with my face to the earth. And God said to me, 'Behold thou diest, since thou hast transgressed the commandment of God, for thou didst hearken rather to the voice of thy wife, whom I gave into thy power, that thou mightst hold her to thy will. Yet thou didst listen to her and didst pass by My words.'

27

[1] And when I heard these words of God, I fell prone on the earth and worshipped the Lord and said, 'My Lord, All powerful and merciful God, Holy and Righteous One, let not the name that is mindful of Thy majesty be blotted out, but convert my soul, for I die and my [2] breath will go out of my mouth. Cast me not out from Thy presence, (me) whom Thou didst form of the clay of the earth. Do not banish from Thy favour him whom Thou didst nourish.' [3] And lo! a word concerning thee came upon me and the Lord said to me, 'Since thy days were fashioned, thou hast been created with a love of knowledge; therefore there shall not be taken from thy seed for ever the (right) to serve Me.'

28

[1] And when I heard these words. I threw myself on the earth and adored the Lord God and said, 'Thou art the eternal and supreme God; and all creatures give thee honour and praise. [2] 'Thou art the true Light gleaming above all light(s), the Living Life, infinite mighty Power. To Thee, the spiritual powers give honour and praise. Thou workest on the race of men the abundance of Thy mercy.' [3] After I had worshipped the Lord, straightway Michael, God's archangel, seized my hand and [4] cast me out of the paradise of 'vision' and of God's command. And Michael held a rod in his hand, and he touched the waters, which were round about paradise, and they froze hard.

29

[1] And I went across, and Michael the archangel went across with me, and he led me back to [2] the place whence he had caught me up. Hearken, my son Seth, even to the rest of the secrets [and sacraments] that shall be, which were revealed to me, when I had eaten of the tree of the [3] knowledge, and knew and perceived what will come to pass in this age; [what God intends to do [4] to his creation of the race of men. The Lord will appear in a flame of fire (and) from the mouth of His majesty He will give commandments and statutes [from His mouth will proceed a two-edged sword] and they will sanctify Him in the house of the habitation of His majesty. [5] And He will show them the marvellous place of His majesty. And then they will build a house to the Lord their God in the land which He shall prepare for them and there they will transgress His statutes and their sanctuary will be burnt up and their land will be deserted and they [6] themselves will be dispersed; because they have kindled the wrath of God. And once more He will cause them to come back from their dispersion; and again they will build the house of God; [7] and in the last time the house of God will be exalted greater than of old. And once more iniquity will exceed righteousness. And thereafter God will dwell with men on earth [in visible form]; and then, righteousness will begin to shine. And the house of God will be honoured in the age and their enemies will no more be able to hurt the men, who are believing in God; and God will stir up for Himself a faithful people, whom He shall save for eternity, and the impious shall be punished [8] by God their king, the men who refused to love His law. Heaven and earth, nights and days, and all creatures shall obey Him, and not overstep His commandment. Men shall not change their [9] works, but they shall be changed from forsaking the law of the Lord. Therefore the Lord shall repel from Himself the wicked, and the just shall shine like the sun, in the sight of God. And [10] in that time, shall men be purified by water from their sins. But those who are unwilling to be purified by water shall be condemned. And happy shall the man be, who hath ruled his soul, when the Judgement shall come to pass and the greatness of God be seen among men and their deeds be inquired into by God the just judge.

30

[1] After Adam was nine hundred and thirty years old, since he knew that his days were coming to an end, he said: 'Let all my sons assemble themselves to me, that I may bless them before I die, and speak with them.' [2] And they were assembled in three parts, before his sight, in the house of prayer, where they used [3] to worship the Lord God. And they asked him (saying): 'What concerns thee, Father, that thou shouldst assemble us, and why dost thou lie on [4] thy bed? 'Then Adam answered and said: 'My sons, I am sick and in pain.' And all his sons said to him: 'What does it mean, father, this illness and pain?'

31

[1] Then said Seth his son: 'O (my) lord, perchance thou hast longed after the fruit of paradise, which thou wast wont to eat, and therefore thou liest in sadness? Tell me and I will go to the nearest gates of paradise and put dust on my head and throw myself down on the earth before the gates of paradise and lament and make entreaty to God with loud lamentation; perchance he will hearken to me and send his angel to bring me the fruit, for which thou hast longed.' [2] Adam answered and said: 'No, my son, I do not long (for this), but I feel weakness and great [3] pain in my body.' Seth answered, 'What is pain, my lord father? I am ignorant; but hide it not from us, but tell us (about it).'

32

[1] And Adam answered and said: 'Hear me, my sons. When God made us, me and your mother, and placed us in paradise and gave us every tree bearing fruit to eat, he laid a prohibition on us concerning the tree of knowledge of good and evil, which is in the midst of paradise; (saying) [2] 'Do not eat of it.' But God gave a part of paradise to me and (a part) to your mother: the trees of the eastern part and the north, which is over against Aquilo he gave to me, and to your mother he gave the part of the south and the western part.

33

[1] (Moreover) God the Lord gave us two angels [2] to guard us. The hour came when the angels had ascended to worship in the sight of God; forthwith the adversary [the devil] found an opportunity while the angels were absent and the devil led your mother astray to eat of the [3] unlawful and forbidden tree. And she did eat and gave to me.

34

[1] And immediately, the Lord God was wrath with us, and the Lord said to me: 'In that thou hast left behind my commandment and hast not kept my

word, which I confirmed to thee; behold, I will bring upon thy body, seventy blows; with divers griefs, shalt thou be tormented, beginning at thy head and thine eyes and thine ears down to thy nails on thy toes, and in every [2] separate limb. These hath God appointed for chastisement. All these things hath the Lord sent to me and to all our race.'

35

[1] Thus spake Adam to his sons, and he was seized with violent pains, and he cried out with a loud voice, 'What shall I do? I am in distress. So cruel are the pains with which I am beset.' And when Eve had seen him weeping, she also began to weep herself, and said: 'O Lord my God, hand over to me his pain, for it is I who sinned.' [3] And Eve said to Adam: 'My lord, give me a part of thy pains, for this hath come to thee from fault of mine.'

36

[1] And Adam said to Eve: 'Rise up and go with my son Seth to the neighbourhood of paradise, and put dust on your heads and throw yourselves on the ground and lament in the sight of [2] God. Perchance He will have pity (upon you) and send His angel across to the tree of His mercy, whence floweth the oil of life, and will give you a drop of it, to anoint me with it, that I may have rest from these pains, by which I am being consumed.'

37

[1] Then Seth and his mother went off towards the gates of paradise. And while they were walking, lo! suddenly there came a beast [2] [a serpent] and attacked and bit Seth. And as soon as Eve saw it, she wept and said: 'Alas, wretched woman that I am. I am accursed since I have not kept the commandment of God.' [3] And Eve said to the serpent in a loud voice: 'Accursed beast! how (is it that) thou hast not feared to let thyself loose against the image of God, but hast dared to fight with it?'

38

[1] The beast answered in the language of men: 'Is it not against you, Eve, that our malice (is directed)? Are not ye the objects of our rage? [2] Tell me, Eve, how was thy mouth opened to eat of the fruit? But now if I shall begin to reprove thee thou canst not bear it.'

39

[1] Then said Seth to the beast: 'God the Lord revile thee. Be silent, be dumb, shut thy mouth, accursed enemy of Truth, confounder and destroyer. Avaunt from the image of God till the day when the Lord God shall order thee to be brought to the ordeal.' And the beast said to Seth: 'See, I leave the presence of the image of God, as thou hast said.' Forthwith he left Seth, wounded by his teeth.

40

[1] But Seth and his mother walked to the regions of paradise for the oil of mercy to anoint the sick Adam: and they arrived at the gates of paradise, (and) they took dust from the earth and placed it on their heads, and bowed themselves with their faces to the earth and began to lament and [2] make loud moaning, imploring the Lord God to pity Adam in his pains and to send His angel to give them the oil from the 'tree of His mercy'.

41

[1] But when they had been praying and imploring for many hours, behold, the angel Michael ap- [2] peared to them and said: 'I have been sent to you from the Lord -I am set by God over the [3] bodies of men- I tell thee, Seth, (thou) man of God, weep not nor pray and entreat on account of the oil of the tree of mercy to anoint thy father Adam for the pains of his body.

42

[1] 'For I tell thee that in no wise wilt thou be able to receive thereof save in the last days.' [2] [When five thousand five hundred years have been fulfilled, then will come upon earth the most beloved king Christ, the son of God, to revive the body of Adam and with him to revive [3] the bodies of the dead. He Himself, the Son of God, when He comes will be baptized in the river of Jordan, and when He hath come out of the water of Jordan, then He will anoint from the [4] oil of mercy all that believe in Him. And the oil of mercy shall be for generation to generation for those who are ready to be born again of [5] water and the Holy Spirit to life eternal. Then the most beloved Son of God, Christ, descending on earth shall lead thy father Adam to Paradise to the tree of mercy.]

43

[1] 'But do thou, Seth, go to thy father Adam, since the time of his life is fulfilled. Six days hence, his soul shall go off his body and when it shall have gone out, thou shalt see great marvels in the heaven and in the earth and the [2] luminaries of heaven. With these words, straightway Michael departed from Seth. [3] And Eve and Seth returned bearing with them herbs of fragrance, i.e. nard and crocus and calamus and cinnamon.

44

[1] And when Seth and his mother had reached Adam, they told him, how the beast [the serpent] [2] bit Seth. And Adam said to Eve: 'What hast thou done? A great plague hast thou brought upon us, transgression and sin for all our generations: and this which thou hast done, tell thy [3] children after my death, [for those who arise from us shall toil and fail but they shall be [4] wanting and curse us (and) say, All evils have our parents brought upon us, who were at the [5] beginning].' When Eve heard these words, she began to weep and moan.

45

[1] And just as Michael the archangel had fore- [2] told, after six days came Adam's death. When Adam perceived that the hour of his death was at hand, he said to all his sons: 'Behold, I am nine hundred and thirty years old, and if I die, [3] bury me towards the sunrising in the field of yonder dwelling.' And it came to pass that when he had finished all his discourse, he gave up the ghost. (Then) was the sun darkened and the moon

46

[1] and the stars for seven days, and Seth in his mourning embraced from above the body of his father, and Eve was looking on the ground with hands folded over her head, and all her children wept most bitterly. And behold, there appeared [2] Michael the angel and stood at the head of Adam and said to Seth: 'Rise up from the body of thy [3] father and come to me and see what is the doom of the Lord God concerning him. His creature is he, and God hath pitied him.' And all angels blew their trumpets, and cried:

47

[1] 'Blessed art thou, O Lord, for thou hast had pity on Thy creature.'

48

[1] Then Seth saw the hand of God stretched out holding Adam and he handed him over to [2] Michael, saying: 'Let him be in thy charge till the day of Judgement in punishment, till the last years when I will convert his sorrow into joy. [3] Then shall he sit on the throne of him who hath been his supplanter.' [4] And the Lord said again to the angels Michael and Uriel: 'Bring me three linen clothes of byssus and spread them out over Adam and other linen clothes over Abel his son and bury Adam and Abel his son.' [5] And all the 'powers' of angels marched before Adam, and the sleep of the dead was [6] consecrated. And the angels Michael and Uriel buried Adam and Abel in the parts of Paradise, before the eyes of Seth and his mother [7] [and no one else], and Michael and Uriel said: 'Just as ye have seen, in like manner, bury your dead.'

49

[1] Six days after, Adam died; and Eve perceived that she would die, (so) she assembled all her sons [2] and daughters, Seth with thirty brothers and thirty sisters, and Eve said to all, 'Hear me, my children, and I will tell you what the archangel Michael said to us when I and your father transgressed the command of God [3] On account of your transgression, Our Lord will bring upon your race the anger of his judgement, first by water, the second time by fire; by these two, will the Lord judge the whole human race

50

[1] But hearken unto me, my children. Make ye then tables of stone and others of clay, and write [2] on them, all my life and your father's (all) that ye have heard and seen from us. If by water the Lord judge our race, the tables of clay will be dissolved and the tables of stone will remain; but if by fire, the tables of stone will be broken up and the tables of clay will be baked (hard).' [3] When Eve had said all this to her children, she spread out her hands to heaven in prayer, and bent her knees to the earth, and while she worshipped the Lord and gave him thanks, she gave up the ghost. Thereafter, all her children buried her with loud lamentation.

51

[1] When they had been mourning four days, (then) Michael the archangel appeared and said [2] to Seth: 'Man of God, mourn not for thy dead more than six days, for on the seventh day is the sign of the resurrection and the rest of the age to come; on the seventh day the Lord rested from all His works.' [3] Thereupon Seth made the tables.

Slavonic Life of Adam and Eve

1

[1] And we sat together before the gate of paradise, Adam weeping with his face bent down to the earth, lay on the ground lamenting. And seven days passed by and we had nothing [2] to eat and were consumed with great hunger, and I Eve cried with a loud voice: 'Pity me, O Lord, My Creator; for my sake Adam suffereth thus!'

2

[1] And I said to Adam: 'Rise up! my lord, that we may seek us food; for now my spirit faileth me and my heart within me is brought low.' Then Adam spake to me: 'I have thoughts of [2] killing thee, but I fear since God created thine image and thou showest penitence and criest to God; hence my heart hath not departed from thee.'

3

[1] And Adam arose and we roamed through all lands and found nothing to eat save nettles (and) grass of the field. And we returned again to the gates of paradise and cried aloud and entreated: 'Have compassion on thy creature. [2] O Lord Creator, allow us food.'

4

[1] And for fifteen days continuously we entreated. Then we heard Michael the archangel and Joel [2] praying for us, and Joel the archangel was commanded by the Lord, and he took a seventh part of paradise and gave it to us. Then the [3] Lord said: 'Thorns and thistles shall spring up from under thy hands; and from thy sweat shalt thou eat (bread), and thy wife shall tremble when she looketh upon thee.'

5

[1] The archangel Joel said to Adam: 'Thus saith the Lord; I did not create thy wife to command thee, but to obey; why art thou obedient to thy wife?' [2] Again Joel the archangel bade Adam separate the cattle and all kinds of flying and creeping things and animals, both wild and tame; and to give names to all things. Then indeed [3] he took the oxen and began to plough.

6

[1] Then the devil approached and stood before the oxen, and hindered Adam in tilling the field and said to Adam: 'Mine are the things of [2] earth, the things of Heaven are God's; but if thou wilt be mine, thou shalt labour on the earth; but if thou wilt be God's, (pray) go away to paradise.' Adam said: 'The things [3] of Heaven are the Lord's, and the things of earth and Paradise and the whole Universe.'

7

[1] The devil said: 'I do not suffer thee to till the field, except thou write the bond that thou art mine.' Adam replied: 'Whosoever is lord of [2] the earth, to the same do I (belong) and my children.' Then the devil was overcome with joy. (But Adam was not ignorant that the Lord [3] would descend on earth and tread the devil under foot.) The devil said: 'Write me thy [4] bond.' And Adam wrote: 'Who is lord of the earth, to the same do I belong and my children.'

8

[1] Eve said to Adam, 'Rise up, my lord, let us pray to God in this cause that He set us free from that devil, for thou art in this strait on my account.' But Adam said: 'Eve, since thou repentest of [2] thy misdeed, my heart will hearken to thee, for the Lord created thee out of my ribs. Let us fast forty days perchance the Lord will have pity on us and will leave us understanding and life.' I, for my part, said: 'Do thou, (my) lord, [3] fast forty days, but I will fast forty-four.'

9

[1] And Adam said to me: 'Haste thee to the river, named Tigris, and take a great stone and place it under thy feet, and enter into the stream and clothe thyself with water, as with a cloak, up to the neck, and pray to God in thy heart and let no word proceed out of thy mouth.' And [2] I said: 'O (my) lord, with my whole heart will I call upon God.' And Adam said to me: [3] 'Take great care of thyself. Except thou seest me and all my tokens, depart not out of the water, nor trust in the words, which are said to thee, lest thou fall again into the snare.' And [4] Adam came to Jordan and he entered into the water and he plunged himself altogether into the flood, even (to) the hairs of his head, while he made supplication to God and sent (up) prayers to Him.

10

[1] And there, the angels came together and all living creatures, wild and tame, and all birds that fly, (and) they surrounded Adam, like a wall, praying to God for Adam.

11

[1] The devil came to me, wearing the form and brightness of an angel, and shedding big teardrops, (and) said to me: 'Come out of the water, [2] Eve, God hath heard thy prayers and (heard) us angels. God hath fulfilled the prayers of those who intercede on thy behalf. God hath sent me to thee, that thou mayst come out of the water.'

12

[1] But I (Eve) perceived that he was the devil and answered him nothing. But Adam (when) he returned from Jordan, saw the devil's footprints, and feared lest perchance he had deceived me; but when he had remarked me standing in the water he was overcome with joy (and) he took [2] me and led me out of the water.

13

[1] Then Adam cried out with a loud voice: 'Be silent, Eve, for already is my spirit straitened in my body; arise, go forth, utter prayers to God, till I deliver up my spirit to God.' (Passage follows exactly parallel to Apocalypsis Mosis chapter 32 sequence, but in abbreviated form.)

Five Psalms of David
(which are not written in the order of the Psalms)

1
A Thanksgiving of David.

¹ I was the youngest among my brethren, and a youth in my father's house. ² I used to feed my father's flock, and I found a lion and a wolf, and slew them and rent them. ³ My hands made an organ, and my fingers fashioned a harp. ⁴ Who will show me my Lord? He, my Lord, is become my God. ⁵ He sent His angel and took me away from my father's flock, and anointed me with the oil of anointing. ⁶ My brethren, the fair and the tall, in them the Lord had no pleasure. ⁷ And I went forth to meet the Philistine, and he cursed me by his idols. ⁸ But I drew his sword and cut off his head, and took away the reproach from the children of Israel.

2
The Prayer of Hezekiah when enemies surrounded him.

¹ With a loud voice glorify ye God; in the assembly of many proclaim ye His glory. ² Amid the multitude of the upright glorify His praise; and speak of His glory with the righteous. ³ Join yourselves *literally,* your soul to the good and to the perfect, to glorify the Most High. ⁴ Gather yourselves together to make known His strength; and be not slow in showing forth His deliverance [and His strength] and His glory to all babes. ⁵ That the honour of the Lord may be known, wisdom hath been given; and to tell of His works it hath been made known to men: ⁶ to make known unto babes His strength, and to make them that lack understanding *literally,* heart to comprehend His glory; ⁷ who are far from His entrances and distant from His gates: ⁸ because the Lord of Jacob is exalted, and His glory is upon all His works. ⁹ And a man who glorifies the Most High, in him will He take pleasure; as in one who offers fine meal, and as in one who offers he-goats and calves; ¹⁰ and as in one who makes fat the altar with a multitude of burnt offerings; and as the smell of incense from the hands of the just. ¹¹ From thy upright gates shall be heard His voice, and from the voice of the upright admonition. ¹² And in their eating shall be satisfying in truth, and in their drinking, when they share together. ¹³ Their dwelling is in the law of the Most High, and their speech is to make known His strength. ¹⁴ How far from the wicked is speech of Him, and from all transgressors to know Him! ¹⁵ Lo, the eye of the Lord taketh pity on the good, and unto them that glorify Him will He multiply mercy, and from the time of evil will He deliver their soul. ¹⁶ Blessed be the Lord, who hath delivered the wretched from the hand of the wicked; who raiseth up a horn out of Jacob and a judge of the nations out of Israel; ¹⁷ that He may prolong His dwelling in Zion, and may adorn our age in Jerusalem.

3
When the People obtained permission from Cyrus to return home.

¹ O Lord, I have cried unto Thee; hearken Thou unto me. ² I have lifted up my hands to Thy holy dwelling-place; incline Thine ear unto me. ³ And grant me my request; my prayer withhold not from me. ⁴ Build up my soul, and destroy it not; and lay it not bare before the wicked. ⁵ Them that recompense evil things turn Thou away from me, O judge of truth. ⁶ O Lord, judge me not according to my sins, because no flesh is innocent before Thee. ⁷ Make plain to me, O Lord, Thy law, and teach me Thy judgments; ⁸ and many shall hear of Thy works, and the nations shall praise Thine honour. ⁹ Remember me and forget me not; and lead me not into things that be too hard for me. ¹⁰ The sins of my youth make Thou to pass from me, and my chastisement let them not remember against me. ¹¹ Cleanse me, O Lord, from the evil leprosy, and let it no more come unto me. ¹² Dry up its roots in literally, *from* me, and let not its leaves sprout within me. ¹³ Great art Thou, O Lord; therefore my request shall be fulfilled from before Thee. ¹⁴ To whom shall I complain that he may give unto me? and what can the strength of men add [unto me]? ¹⁵ From before Thee, O Lord, is my confidence; I cried unto the Lord and He heard me, and healed the breaking of my heart. ¹⁶ I slumbered and slept; I dreamed and was helped, and the Lord sustained me. ¹⁷ They sorely pained my heart; I will return thanks because the Lord delivered me. ¹⁸ Now will I rejoice in their shame; I have hoped in Thee, and I shall not be ashamed. ¹⁹ Give Thou honour for ever, even for ever and ever. ²⁰ Deliver Israel Thine elect, and them of the house of Jacob Thy proved one.

4
Spoken by David when he was contending with the lion and the wolf which took a sheep from his flock.

¹ O God, O God, come to my aid; help Thou me and save me; deliver Thou my soul from the slayer. ² Shall I go down to Sheol by the mouth of the lion? or shall the wolf confound me? ³ Was it not enough for them that they lay in wait for my father's flock, and rent in pieces a sheep of my father's drove, but they were wishing also to destroy my soul? ⁴ Have pity, O Lord, and save Thy holy one from destruction; that he may rehearse Thy glories in all his times, and may praise Thy great name: ⁵ when Thou hast delivered him from the hands of the destroying lion and of the ravening wolf, and when Thou hast rescued my captivity from the hands of the wild beasts. ⁶ Quickly, O my Lord Adonai, send from before Thee a deliverer, and draw me out of the gaping pit, which imprisons me in its depths.

5
Spoken by David when returning thanks to God, who had delivered him from the lion and the wolf and he had slain both of them.

¹ Praise the Lord, all ye nations; glorify Him, and bless His name: ² Who rescued the soul of His elect from the hands of death, and delivered His holy one from destruction: ³ and saved me from the nets of Sheol, and my soul from the pit that cannot be fathomed. ⁴ Because, ere my deliverance could go forth from before Him, I was well nigh rent in two pieces by two wild beasts. ⁵ But He sent His angel, and shut up from me the gaping mouths, and rescued my life from destruction. ⁶ My soul shall glorify Him and exalt Him, because of all His kindnesses which He hath done and will do unto me.

The Psalms of Solomon

1

"They became insolent in their prosperity...."

I cried unto the Lord when I was in distress, Unto God when sinners assailed. Suddenly the alarm of war was heard before me; I said, He will hearken to me for I am full of righteousness. I thought in my heart that I was full of righteousness, Because I was well off and had become rich in children. Their wealth spread to the whole earth, And their glory unto the end of the earth. They were exalted unto the stars; They said they would never fan. But they became insolent in their prosperity, And they were without understanding, Their sins were in secret, And even I had no knowledge of them. Their transgressions went beyond those of the heathen before them; They utterly polluted the holy things of the Lord.

2

The desecration of Jerusalem; captivity, murder, and raping. A psalm of utter despair.

When the sinner waxed proud, with a battering-ram he cast down fortified walls, And thou didst not restrain him. Alien nations ascended Thine altar, They trampled it proudly with their sandals; Because the sons of Jerusalem had defiled the holy things of the Lord, Had profaned with iniquities the offerings of God. Therefore He said: Cast them far from Me; . . . . . . It was set at naught before God, It was utterly dishonoured; The sons and the daughters were m grievous captivity, Sealed was their neck, branded was it among the nations. According to their sins hath He done unto them, For He hath left them in the hands of them that prevailed. He hath turned away His face from pitying them, Young and old and their children together; For they had done evil one and all, in not hearkening. And the heavens were angry, And the earth abhorred them; For no man upon it had done what they did, And the earth recognized all Thy righteous judgements, O God. They set the sons of Jerusalem to be mocked at in return for the harlots in her; Every wayfarer entered in in the full light of day. They made mock with their transgressions, as they themselves were wont to do; In the full light of day they revealed their iniquities. And the daughters of Jerusalem were defiled in accordance with Thy judgement, Because they had defiled themselves with unnatural intercourse. I am pained in my bowels and my inward parts for these things. And yet I will justify Thee, O God, in uprightness of heart, For in Thy judgements is Thy righteousness displayed, O God. For Thou hast rendered to the sinners according to their deeds, Yea, according to their sins, which were very wicked. Thou hast uncovered their sins, that Thy judgement might be manifest; Thou hast wiped out their memorial from the earth. God is a righteous judge, And he is no respecter of persons. For the nations reproached Jerusalem, trampling it down; Her beauty was dragged down from the throne of glory. She girded on sackcloth instead of comely raiment, A rope was about her head instead of a crown. She put off the glorious diadem which God had set upon her, In dishonour was her beauty cast upon the ground. And I saw and entreated the Lord and said, Long enough, O Lord has Thine hand been heavy on Israel, in bringing the nations upon them. For they have made sport unsparingly in wrath and fierce anger; And they will make an utter end, unless Thou, O Lord, rebuke them in Thy wrath. For they have done. it not in zeal, but in lust of soul, Pouring out their wrath upon us with a view to rapine. Delay not, O God, to recompense them on their heads, To turn the pride of the dragon into dishonour. And I had not long to wait before God showed me the insolent one Slain on the mountains of Egypt, Esteemed of less account than the least, on land and sea; His body, too, borne hither and thither on the billows with much insolence, With none to bury him, because He had rejected him with dishonour. He reflected not that he was man, And reflected not on the latter end; He said: I will be lord of land and sea; And he recognized not that it is God who is great, Mighty in His great strength. He is king over the heavens, And judgeth kings and kingdoms. It is He who setteth me up in glory, And bringeth down the proud to eternal destruction in dishonour, Because they knew Him not. And now behold, ye princes of the earth, the judgement of the Lord, For a great king and righteous is He, judging all that is under heaven. Bless God, ye that fear the Lord with wisdom, For the mercy of the Lord will ~e upon them that fear Him, m the Judgement; So that He will distinguish between the righteous and the sinner, And recompense the sinners for ever according to their deeds; And have mercy on the righteous, delivering him from the affliction of the sinner, And recompensing the sinner for what he bath done to the righteous. For the Lord is good to them that call upon Him in patience, Doing according to His mercy to His pious ones, Establishing them at all times before Him in strength. Blessed be the Lord for ever before His servants.

3

Righteousness versus Sin.

Why sleepest thou, O my soul, And blessest not the Lord? Sing a new song, Unto God who is worthy to be praised. Sing and be wakeful against His awaking, For good is a psalm sung to God from a glad heart. The righteous remember the Lord at all times, With thanksgiving and declaration of the righteousness of the Lord's judgements. The righteous despiseth not the chastening of the Lord; His will is always before the Lord. The righteous stumbleth and holdeth the Lord righteous: He falleth and looketh out for what God will do to him; He seeketh out whence his deliverance will come. The steadfastness of the righteous is from God, their deliverer; There lodgeth not in the house of the righteous sin upon sin. The righteous continually searcheth his house, To remove utterly all iniquity done by him in error. He maketh atonement for sins of ignorance by fasting and afflicting his soul, And the Lord counteth guiltless every pious man and his house. The sinner stumbleth and curseth his life The day when he was begotten, and his mother's travail. He addeth sins to sins, while he liveth; He falleth–verily grievous is his fall–and riseth no more. The destruction of the sinner is for ever, And he shall not be remembered, when the righteous is visited. This is the portion of sinners for ever. But they that fear the Lord shall rise to life eternal, And their life shall be in the light of the Lord, and shall come to an end no more.

4

A conversation of Solomon with the Men-pleasers.

Wherefore sittest thou, O profane man, in the council of the pious, Seeing that thy heart is far removed from the Lord, Provoking with transgressions the God of Israel? Extravagant in speech, extravagant in outward seeming beyond all men, Is he that is severe of speech in condemning sinners in judgement. And his hand is first upon him as though he acted in zeal, And yet he is himself guilty in respect of manifold sins and of wantonness. His eyes are upon every woman without distinction; His tongue lieth when he maketh contract with an oath. By night and in secret he sinneth as though unseen, With his eyes he talketh to every woman of evil compacts. He is swift to enter every house with cheerfulness as though guileless. Let God remove those that live in hypocrisy in the company of the pious, Even the life of such an one with corruption of his flesh and penury. Let God reveal the deeds of the men-pleasers, The deeds of such an one with laughter and derision; That the pious may count righteous the judgement of their God, When sinners are removed from before the righteous, Even the man-pleaser who uttereth law guilefully. And their eyes are fixed upon any man's house that is still secure, That they may, like the Serpent, destroy the wisdom of . . . with words of transgressors, His words are deceitful that he may accomplish his wicked desire. He never ceaseth from scattering families as though they were orphans, Yea, he layeth waste a house on account of his lawless desire. He deceiveth with words, saying, There is none that seeth, or judgeth. He fills one house with lawlessness, And then his eyes are fixed upon the next house, To destroy it with words that give wing to desire. Yet with all these his soul like Sheol, is not sated. Let his portion, O Lord, be dishonoured before thee; Let him go forth groaning, and come home cursed. Let his life be spent in anguish, and penury, and want, O Lord; Let his sleep be beset with pains and his awaking with perplexities. Let sleep be withdrawn from his eyelids at night; Let him fail dishonourably in every work of his hands. Let him come home empty-handed to his house, And his house be void of everything wherewith he could sate his appetite. Let his old age be spent in childless loneliness until his removal by death. Let the flesh of the men-pleasers be rent by wild beasts, And let the bones of the lawless lie dishonoured in the sight of the sun. Let ravens peck out the eyes of the hypocrites. For they have laid waste many houses of men, in dishonour, And scattered them in their lust; And they have not remembered God, Nor feared God in all these things; But they have provoked God's anger and vexed Him. May He remove them from off the earth, Because with deceit they beguiled the souls of the flawless. Blessed are they that fear the Lord in their flawlessness; The Lord shall deliver them from guileful men and sinners, And deliver us from every stumbling-block of the lawless (men). Let God destroy them that insolently work all unrighteousness, For a great and mighty judge is the Lord our God in righteousness. Let Thy mercy, O Lord, be upon all them that love Thee.

5

A statement of the philosophy of the indestructibility of matter. One of the tenets of modern physics.

O Lord God, I will praise Thy name with joy, In the midst of them that know Thy righteous judgements. For Thou art good and merciful, the refuge of the poor; When I cry to Thee, do not silently disregard me. For no man taketh spoil from a mighty man; Who, then, can take aught of a that Thou hast made, except Thou Thyself givest? For man and his portion lie before Thee in the balance; He cannot add to, so as to enlarge, what has been prescribed by Thee. O God, when we are in distress we call upon Thee for help, And Thou dost not turn back our petition, for Thou art our God. Cause not Thy hand to be heavy upon us, Lest through necessity we sin. Even though Thou restore us not, we will not keep away; But unto Thee will we come. For if I hunger, unto Thee will I cry, O God; And *Thou* wilt give to me. Birds and fish dost Thou nourish, In that Thou givest rain to the steppes that green grass may spring up, So to prepare fodder in the steppe for every living thing; And if they hunger, unto Thee do they lift up their face. Kings and rulers and peoples *Thou* dost nourish, O God; And who is the help of the poor and needy, if not Thou, O Lord? And Thou wilt hearken–for who is good and gentle but thou?– Making glad the soul of the humble by opening Thine hand in mercy. Man's goodness is bestowed grudgingly and ...; And if he repeat it without murmuring, even that is marvellous. But Thy gift is great in goodness and wealth, And he whose hope is set on Thee shall have no lack of gifts. Upon the whole earth is Thy mercy, O Lord, in goodness. Happy is he whom God remembereth in granting to him a due sufficiency; If a man abound overmuch, he sinneth. Sufficient are moderate means with righteousness, And hereby the blessing of the Lord becomes abundance with righteousness. They that fear the Lord rejoice in good gifts, And thy goodness is upon Israel in Thy kingdom. Blessed is the glory of the Lord, for He is our king.

6

A song of hope and fearlessness and peace.

Happy is the man whose heart is fixed to call upon the name of the Lord; When he remembereth the name of the Lord, he will be saved. His ways are made even by the Lord, And the works of his hands are preserved by the Lord his God. At what he sees in his bad dreams, his soul shall not be troubled; When he passes through rivers and the tossing of the seas, he shall not be dismayed. He ariseth from his sleep, and blesseth the name of the Lord: When his heart is at peace, he singeth to the name of his God, And he entreateth the Lord for all his house. And the Lord heareth the prayer of every one that feareth God, And every request of the soul that hopes for Him doth the Lord accomplish. Blessed is the Lord, who showeth mercy to those who love Him in sincerity.

7

The fine old doctrine–"Thou art our Shield!"

Make not Thy dwelling afar from us, O God; Lest they assail us that hate us without cause. For Thou hast rejected them, O God; Let not their foot trample upon Thy holy inheritance. Chasten us Thyself in Thy good pleasure; But give us not up to the nations; For, if Thou sendest pestilence, Thou Thyself givest it charge concerning us; For Thou art merciful, And wilt not be angry to the point of consuming us.

While Thy name dwelleth in our midst, we shall find mercy; And the nations shall not prevail against us. For Thou art our shield, And when we call upon Thee, Thou hearkenest to us; For Thou wilt pity the seed of Israel for ever And Thou wilt not reject them: But we shall, be under Thy yoke for ever, And under the rod of Thy chastening. Thou wilt establish us in the time that Thou helpest us, Showing mercy to the house of Jacob on the day wherein Thou didst promise to help them.

8

Some remarkable similes of war creeping on Jerusalem. A survey of the sins that brought all this trouble.

Distress and the sound of war hath my ear heard, The sound of a trumpet announcing slaughter and calamity, The sound of much people as of an exceeding high wind, As a tempest with mighty fire sweeping through the Negeb. And I said in my heart, Surely God judgeth us; A sound I hear moving towards Jerusalem, the holy city My loins were broken at what I heard, my knees tottered; My heart was afraid, my bones were dismayed like flax. I said: They establish their ways in righteousness. I thought upon the judgments of God since the creation of heaven and earth; I held God righteous in His judgements which have been from of old. God bare their sins in the full light of day; All the earth came to know the righteous judgements of God. In secret places underground their iniquities were committed to provoke Him to anger; They wrought confusion, son with mother and father with daughter; They committed adultery, every man with his neighhour's wife. They concluded covenants with one another with an oath touching these things; They plundered the sanctuary of God, as though there was no avenger. They trode the altar of the Lord, coming straight from all manner of uncleanness; And with menstrual blood they defiled the sacrifices, as though these were common flesh. They left no sin undone, wherein they surpassed not the heathen. Therefore God mingled for them a spirit of wandering; And gave them to drink a cup of undiluted wine, that they might become drunken. He brought him that is from the end of the earth, that smiteth mightily; He decreed war against Jerusalem, and against her land. The princes of the land went to meet him with joy: they said unto him: Blessed be thy way! Come ye, enter ye in with peace. They made the rough ways even, before his entering in; They opened the gates to Jerusalem, they crowned its walls. As a father entereth the house of his sons, so he entered Jerusalem in peace; He established his feet there in great safety. He captured her fortresses and the wall of Jerusalem; For God Himself led him in safety, while they wandered. He destroyed their princes and every one wise in counsel; He poured out the blood of the inhabitants of Jerusalem, like the water of uncleanness. He led away their sons and daughters, whom they had begotten in defilement. They did according to their uncleanness, even as their fathers had done: They defiled Jerusalem and the things that had been hallowed to the name of God. But God hath shown Himself righteous in His judgements upon the nations of the earth; And the pious servants of God are like innocent lambs in their midst. Worthy to be praised is the Lord that judgeth the whole earth in His righteousness. Behold, now, O God, Thou hast shown us Thy judgement in Thy righteousness; Our eyes have seen Thy judgements, O God. We have justified Thy name that is honoured for ever; For Thou are the God of righteousness, judging Israel with chastening. Turn, O God, Thy mercy upon us, and have pity upon us; Gather together the dispersed of Israel, with mercy and goodness; For Thy faithfulness is with us, And though we have stiffened our neck, yet Thou art our chastener; Overlook us not, O our God, lest the nations swallow us up, as though there were none to deliver. But Thou art our God from the beginning, And upon Thee is our hope set, O Lord; And we will not depart from Thee, For good are Thy judgements upon us. Ours and our children's be Thy good pleasure for ever; O Lord, our Saviour, we shall never more be moved. The Lord is worthy to be praised for His judgements with the mouth of His pious ones; And blessed be Israel of the Lord for ever.

9

The exile of the tribes of Israel. A reference to the covenant which God made with Adam. (See the First Book of Adam and Eve, Chap. III, Verse 7).

When Israel was led away captive into a strange land, When they fell away from the Lord who redeemed them, They were cast away from the inheritance, which the Lord had given them. Among every nation were the dispersed of Israel according to the word of God, That Thou mightest be justified, O God, in Thy righteousness by reason of our transgressions: For Thou art a just judge over all the peoples of the earth. For from Thy knowledge none that doeth unjustly is hidden, And the righteous deeds of Thy pious ones are before Thee, O Lord; Where, then, can a man hide himself from Thy knowledge, O God? Our works are subject to our own choice and power To do right or wrong in the works of our hands; And in Thy righteousness Thou visitest the sons of men. He that doeth righteousness layeth up life for himself with the Lord; And he that doeth wrongly forfeits his life to destruction; For the judgements of the Lord are given in righteousness to every man and his house. Unto whom art Thou good, O God, except to them that call upon the Lord? He cleanseth from sins a soul when it maketh confession, when it maketh acknowledgement; For shame is upon us and u on our faces on account of all these things. And to whom doth He forgive sins, except to them that have sinned? Thou blessest the righteous, and dost not reprove them for the sins that they have committed; And Thy goodness is upon them that sin, when they repent. And, now, Thou art our God, and we the people whom Thou hast loved: Behold and show pity, O God of Israel, for we are Thine; And remove not Thy mercy from us, lest they assail us. For Thou didst choose the seed of Abraham before all the nations, And didst set Thy name upon us, O Lord, And Thou wilt not reject us for ever. Thou madest a covenant with our fathers concerning us; And we hope in Thee, when our soul turneth unto Thee. The mercy of the Lord be upon the house of Israel for ever and ever.

10

A glorious hymn. Further reference to the eternal covenant between God and Man.

Happy is the man whom the Lord remembereth with reproving, And whom He restraineth from the way of evil with strokes That he may be cleansed from sin, that it may not be multiplied. He that maketh ready his back for strokes shall be cleansed, For the Lord is good to them that endure chastening. For He maketh straight the ways of the righteous, And doth not pervert them by His chastening. And the mercy of the Lord is upon them that love Him in truth, And the Lord remembereth His servants in mercy. For the testimony is in the law of the eternal covenant, The testimony of the Lord is on the ways of men in His visitation. Just and kind is our Lord in His judgements for ever, And Israel shall praise the name of the Lord in gladness. And the pious shall give thanks in the assembly of the people; And on the poor shall God have mercy in the gladness of Israel; For good and merciful is God for ever, And the assemblies of Israel shall glorify the name of the Lord.

The salvation of the Lord be upon the house of Israel unto everlasting gladness!

11

Jerusalem hears a trumpet and stands on tiptoe to see her children returning from the North, East and West.

Blow ye in Zion on the trumpet to summon the saints, Cause ye to be heard in Jerusalem the voice of him that bringeth good tidings; For God hath had pity on Israel in visiting them. Stand on the height, O Jerusalem, and behold thy children, From the East and the West, gathered together by the Lord; From the North they come in the gladness of their God, From the isles afar off God hath gathered them. High mountains hath He abased into a plain for them; The hills fled at their entrance. The woods gave them shelter as they passed by; Every sweet-smelling tree God caused to spring up for them, That Israel might pass by in the visitation of the glory of their God. Put on, O Jerusalem, thy glorious garments; Make ready thy holy robe; For God hath spoken good concerning Israel, for ever and ever. Let the Lord do what He hath spoken concerning Israel and Jerusalem; Let the Lord raise up Israel by His glorious name. The mercy of the Lord be upon Israel for ever and ever.

12

An appeal for family tranquility and peace and quiet at home.

O Lord, deliver my soul from the lawless and wicked man, From the tongue that is lawless and slanderous, and speaketh lies and deceit. Manifoldly twisted are the words of the tongue of the wicked man, Even as among a people a fire that burneth up their beauty. So he delights to fill houses with a lying tongue, To cut down the trees of gladness which setteth on fire transgressors, To involve households in warfare by means of slanderous lips. May God remove far from the innocent the lips of transgressors by bringing them to want And may the bones of slanderers be scattered far away from them that fear the Lord! In flaming fire perish the slanderous tongue far away from the pious! May the Lord preserve the quiet soul that hateth the unrighteous; And may the Lord establish the man that followeth peace at home. The salvation of the Lord be upon Israel His servant for ever; And let the sinners perish together at the presence of the Lord; But let the Lord's pious ones inherit the promises of the Lord.

13

Of Solomon. A Psalm. Comfort for the righteous.

The right hand of the Lord hath covered me; The right hand of the Lord hath spared us. The arm of the Lord hath saved us from the sword that passed through, From famine and the death of sinners. Noisome beasts ran upon them: With their teeth they tore their flesh, And with their molars crushed their bones. But from all these things the Lord delivered us. The righteous was troubled on account of his errors, Lest he should be taken away along with the sinners; For terrible is the overthrow of the sinner; But not one of all these things toucheth the righteous. For not alike are the chastening of the righteous for sins done in ignorance, And the overthrow of the sinners. Secretly is the righteous chastened, Lest the sinner rejoice over the righteous. For He correcteth the righteous as a beloved son. And his chastisement is as that of a first-born. For the Lord spareth His pious ones, And blotteth out their errors by His chastening. For the life of the righteous shall be for ever; But sinners shall be taken away into destruction,, And their memorial shall be found no more. But upon the pious is the mercy of the Lord, And upon them that fear Him His mercy.

14

Sinners "love the brief day spent in companionship with their sin." Profound wisdom, beautifully expressed.

Faithful is the Lord to them that love Him in truth, To them that endure His chastening, To them that walk in the righteousness of His commandments, In the law which He commanded us that we might live. The pious of the Lord shall live by it for ever; The Paradise of the Lord, the trees of life, are His pious ones. Their planting is rooted for ever; They shall not be plucked up all the days of heaven: For the portion and the inheritance of God is Israel. But not so are the sinners and transgressors, Who love the brief day spent in companionship with their sin; Their delight is in fleeting corruption, And they remember not God. For the ways of men are known before Him at all times, And He knoweth the secrets of the heart before they come to pass. Therefore their inheritance is Sheol and darkness and destruction And they shall not be found in the day when the righteous obtain mercy; But the pious of the Lord shall inherit life in gladness.

15

The psalmist restates the great philosophy of Right and Wrong.

When I was in distress I called upon the name of the Lord, I hoped for the help of the God of Jacob and was saved; For the hope and refuge of the poor art Thou, O God. For who, O God, is strong except to give thanks unto Thee in truth? And wherein is a man powerful except in giving thanks to Thy name? A new psalm with song in gladness of heart, The fruit of the lips with the well-tuned instrument of the tongue, The first fruits of the lips from a pious and righteous heart– He that offereth these things shall never be shaken by evil; The flame of fire and the wrath against the unrighteous shall not touch him, When it goeth forth from the face of the Lord against sinners, To destroy all the substance of sinners, For the mark of God is upon the righteous that they may be saved. Famine and sword and pestilence shall be far from the righteous, For they shall flee away from the pious as men pursued in war; But they shall pursue sinners and overtake them, And they that do lawlessness shall not escape the judgement of God; As by enemies experienced in war shall they be overtaken, For the mark of destruction is upon their forehead. And the inheritance of sinners is destruction and darkness, And their iniquities shall pursue them unto Sheol beneath. Their inheritance shall not be found of their children, For sins shall lay waste the houses of sinners. And sinners shall perish for ever in the day of the Lord's judgement, When God visiteth the earth with His judgement. But they that fear the Lord shall find mercy therein, And shall live by the compassion of their God; But sinners shall perish for ever.

16

The psalmist again expresses profound truth–"For if Thou givest not strength, who can endure chastisement?"

When my soul slumbered being afar from the Lord, I had all but slipped down to the pit, When I was far from God, my soul had been well-nigh poured out unto death, I had been nigh unto the gates of Sheol with the sinner, When my soul departed from the Lord God of Israel– Had not the Lord helped me with His everlasting mercy. He pricked me, as a horse is pricked, that I might serve Him, My saviour and helper at all times saved me. I will give thanks unto Thee, O God, for Thou hast helped me to my salvation; And hast not counted me with sinners to my destruction. Remove not Thy mercy from me, O God, Nor Thy memorial from my heart until I die. Rule me, O God, keeping me back from wicked sin, And from every wicked woman that causeth the simple to stumble. And let not the beauty of a lawless woman beguile me, Nor any one that is subject to unprofitable sin. Establish the works of my hands before Thee, And preserve my goings in the remembrance of Thee. Protect my tongue and my lips with words of truth; Anger and unreasoning wrath put far from me. Murmuring, and impatience in affliction, remove far from me When, if I sin, Thou chastenest me that I may return unto Thee. But with goodwill and cheerfulness support my soul; When Thou strengthenest my soul, what is given to me will be sufficient for me. For if *Thou* givest not strength, Who can endure chastisement with poverty? When a man is rebuked by means of his corruption, Thy testing of him is in his flesh and in the affliction of poverty. If the righteous endureth in all these trials, he shall receive mercy from the Lord.

17

"They set a worldly monarchy . . . . they lay waste the Throne of David!" A poetic narrative about the utter disintegration of a great nation.

O Lord, Thou art our King for ever and ever, For in Thee, O God, doth our soul glory. How long are the days of man's life upon the earth? As are his days, so is the hope set upon him. But *we* hope in God, our deliverer; For the might of our God is for ever with mercy, And the kingdom of our God is for ever over the nations in judgement. Thou, O Lord, didst choose David to be king over Israel, And swaredst to him touching his seed that never should his kingdom fail before Thee. But, for our sins, sinners rose up against us; They assailed us and thrust us out; What Thou hadst not promised to them, they took away from us with violence. They in no wise glorified Thy honourable name; They set a worldly monarchy in place of that which was their excellency; They laid waste the throne of David in tumultuous arrogance. But Thou, O God, didst cast them down, and remove their seed from the earth, In that there rose up against them a man that was alien to our race. According to their sins didst Thou recompense them, O God; So that it befell them according to their deeds. God showed them no pity; He sought out their seed and let not one of them go free. Faithful is the Lord in all His judgements Which He doeth upon the earth. The lawless one laid waste our land so that none inhabited it, They destroyed young and old and their children together. In the heat of His anger He sent them away even unto the west, And He exposed the rulers of the land unsparingly to derision. Being an alien the enemy acted proudly, And his heart was alien from Our God. And all things whatsoever he did in Jerusalem, As also the nations in the cities to their gods. And the children of the covenant in the midst of the mingled peoples surpassed them in evil. There was not among them one that wrought in the midst of Jerusalem mercy and truth. They that loved the synagogues of the pious fled from them, As sparrows that fly from their nest. They wandered in deserts that their lives might be saved from harm, And precious in the eyes of them that lived abroad was any that escaped alive from them. Over the whole earth were they scattered by lawless men. For the heavens withheld the rain from dropping upon the earth, Springs were stopped that sprang perennially out of the deeps, that ran down from lofty mountains. For there was none among them that wrought righteousness and justice; From the chief of them to the least of them all were sinful; The king was a transgressor, and the judge disobedient, and the people sinful. Behold, O Lord, and raise up unto them their king, the son of David, At the time in the which Thou seest, O God, that he may reign over Israel Thy servant. And gird him with strength, that he may shatter unrighteous rulers, And that he may purge Jerusalem from nations that trample her down to destruction. Wisely, righteously he shall thrust out sinners from the inheritance, He shall destroy the pride of the sinner as a potter's vessel. With a rod of iron he shall break in pieces all their substance, He shall destroy the godless nations with the word of his mouth; At his rebuke nations shall flee before him, And he shall reprove sinners for the thoughts of their heart. And he shall gather together a holy people, whom he shall lead in righteousness, And he shall judge the tribes of the people that has been sanctified by the Lord his God. And he shall not suffer unrighteousness to lodge any more in their midst, Nor shall there dwell with them any man that knoweth wickedness, For he shall know them, that they are all sons of their God. And he shall divide them according to their tribes upon the land, And neither sojourner nor alien shall sojourn with them any more. He shall judge peoples and nations in the wisdom of his righteousness. *Selah*. And he shall have the heathen nations to serve him under his yoke; And he shall glorify the Lord in a place to be seen of all the earth; And he shall purge Jerusalem, making it holy as of old: So that nations shall come from the ends of the earth to see his glory, Bringing as gifts her sons who had fainted. And to see the glory of the Lord, wherewith God hath glorified her. And he shall be a righteous king, taught of God, over them, And there shall be no unrighteousness in his days in their midst, For all shall be holy and their king the anointed of the Lord. For he shall not put his trust in horse and rider and bow, Nor shall he multiply for himself gold and silver for war, Nor shall he gather confidence from a multitude for the day of battle. The Lord Himself is his king, the hope of him that is mighty through his hope in God. All nations shall be in fear before him, For he will smite the earth with the word of his mouth for ever. He will bless the people of the Lord with wisdom and gladness, And he himself will be pure from sin, so that he may rule a great people. He will rebuke rulers, and remove sinners by the might of his word; And relying upon his God, throughout his days he will not stumble; For God will make him mighty by means of His holy spirit, And wise by means of the spirit of understanding, with strength and righteousness. And the blessing of the Lord will be with him: he will be strong and stumble not; His hope will be in the Lord: who then can prevail against him? He will, be mighty in his works, and strong in the fear of God, He will be shepherding the flock of the Lord faithfully and righteously, And will suffer none among them to stumble in their pasture. He will lead them all aright, And there will be no pride among them that any among them should be oppressed. This will be the majesty of the king of Israel whom God knoweth; He will raise him up over the house of Israel to correct him. His words shall be more refined than costly gold, the choicest; In the assemblies he will judge the peoples, the tribes of the sanctified. His words shall be like the words of the holy ones in the midst of sanctified peoples. Blessed be they that shall be in those days, In that they shall see the good fortune of Israel which God shall bring to pass in the gathering together of the tribes. May the Lord hasten His mercy upon Israel! May He deliver us from the uncleanness of unholy enemies! The Lord Himself is our king for ever and ever.

18

With this psalm end the warlike Songs of Solomon.

Lord, Thy mercy is over the works of Thy hands for ever; Thy goodness is over Israel with a rich gift. Thine eyes look upon them, so that none of them suffers want; Thine ears listen to the hopeful prayer of the poor. Thy judgements are executed upon the whole earth in mercy; And Thy love is toward the seed of Abraham, the children of Israel. Thy chastisement is upon us as upon a first-born, only-begotten son, To turn back the obedient soul from folly that is wrought in ignorance. May God cleanse Israel against the day of mercy and blessing, Against the day of choice when Blessed shall they be that shall be in those days, He bringeth back His anointed. In that they shall see the goodness of the Lord which He shall perform for the generation that is to come, Under the rod of chastening of the Lord's anointed in the fear of his God, In the spirit of wisdom and righteousness and strength; That he may direct every man in the works of righteousness by the fear of God, That he may establish them all before the Lord, A good generation living in the fear of God in the days of mercy. Selah.

Great is our God and glorious, dwelling in the highest. It is He who hath established in their courses the lights of heaven for determining seasons from year to year, And they have not turned aside from the way which He appointed them. In the fear of God they pursue their path every day, From the day God created them and for evermore. And they have erred not since the day He created them. Since the generations of old they have not withdrawn from their path, Unless God commanded them so to do by the command of His servants.

The Martyrdom of Isaiah

1

1. AND it came to pass in the twenty-sixth year of the reign of Hezediah king of Judah that he called Manasseh his son. Now he was his only one. 2. And he called him into the presence of Isaiah the son of Amoz the prophet, and into the presence of Josab the son of Isaiah, in order to deliver unto him the words of righteousness which the king himself had seen: 3. And of the eternal judgments and torments of Gehenna, and of the prince of this world, and of his angels, and his authorities and his powers. 4. And the words of the faith of the Beloved which he himself had seen in the fifteenth year of his reign during his illness. 5. And he delivered unto him the written words which Samnas the scribe had written, and also those which Isaiah, the son of Amoz, had given to him, and also to the prophets, that they might write and store up with him what he himself had seen in the king's house regarding the judgment of the angels, and the destruction of this world, and regarding the garments of the saints and their going forth, and regarding their transformation and the persecution and ascension of the Beloved. 6. In the twentieth year of the reign of Hezekiah, Isaiah had seen the words of this prophecy and had delivered them to Josab his son. And whilst he (Hezekiah) gave commands, Josab the son of Isaiah standing by. 7. Isaiah said to Hezekiah the king, but not in the presence of Manasseh only did he say unto him: `As the Lord liveth, and th3e Spirit which speaketh in me liveth, all these commands and these words will be made of none effect by Manasseh thy son, and through the agency of his hands I shall depart mid the torture of my body. 8. And Sammael Malchira will serve Manasseh, and execute all his desire, and he will become a follower of Beliar rather than of me: 9. And many in Jerusalem and in Judea he will cause to abandon the true faith, and Beliar will dwell in Manasseh, and by his hands I shall be sawn asunder.' 10. And when Hezekiah heard these words he wept very bitterly, and rent his garments, and placed earth upon his head, and fell on his face. 11. And Isaiah said unto him: `The counsel of Sammael against Manasseh is consummated: nought will avail thee." 12. And on that day Hezekiah resolved in his heart to slay Manasseh his son. 13. And Isaiah said to Hezekiah: `The Beloved hath made of none effect thy design, and the purpose of thy heart will not be accomplished, for with this calling have I been called and I shall inherit the heritage of the Beloved.'

2

1. AND it came to pass after that Hezekiah died and Manasseh became king, that he did not remember the commands of Hezekiah his father, but forgat them, and Sammael abode in Manasseh and clung fast to him. 2. And Manasseh forsook the service of the God of his father, and he served Satan and his angels and his powers. 3. And he turned aside the house of his father, which had been before the face of Hezekiah (from) the words of wisdom and from the service of God. 4. And Manasseh turned aside his heart to serve Beliar; for the angel of lawlessness, who is the ruler of this world, is Beliar, whose name is Mantanbuchus. and he delighted in Jerusalem because of Manasseh, and he made him strong in apostatizing (Israel) and in the lawlessness which were spread abroad in Jerusalem. 5. And witchcraft and magic increased and divination and auguration, and fornication, a [and adultery], and the persecution of the righteous by Manasseh and [Belachira, and] Tobia the Canaanite, and John of Anathoth, an by (Zadok) the chief of the works. 6. And the rest of the acts, behold they are written in the book of the Kings of Judah and Israel. 7. And, when Isaiah, the son of Amoz, saw the lawlessness which was being perpetrated in Jerusalem and the worship of Satan and his wantonness, he withdrew from Jerusalem and settled in Bethlehem of Judah. 8. And there also there was much lawlessness, and withdrawing from Bethlehem he settled on a mountain in a desert place. 9. And Micaiah the prophet, and the aged Ananias, and Joel and Habakkuk, and his son Josab, and many of the faithful who believed in the ascension into heaven, withdrew and settled on the mountain. 10. They were all clothed with garments of hair, and they were all prophets. And they had nothing with them but were naked, and they all lamented with a great lamentation because of the going astray of Israel. 11. And these eat nothing save wild herbs which they gathered on the mountains, and having cooked them, they lived thereon together with Isaiah the prophet. And they spent two years of days on the mountains and hills. 12. And after this, whilst they were in the desert, there was a certain man in Samaria named Belchira, of the family of Zedekiah, the son of Chenaan, a false prophet, whose dwelling was in Bethlehem. Now Hezekiah the son of Chanani, who was the brother of his father, and in the days of Ahab, king of Israel, had been the teacher of the 400. prophets of Baal, had himself smitten and reproved Micaiah the son of Amada the prophet. 13. And he, Micaiah, had been reproved by Ahab and cast into prison. (And he was) with Zedekiah the prophet: they were with Ahaziah the son of Ahab, king in Samaria. 14. And Elijah the prophet of Tebon of Gilead was reproving Ahaziah and Samaria, and prophesied regarding Ahaziah that he should die on his bed of sickness, and that Samaria should be delivered into the had of Leba Nasr because he had slain the prophets of God. 15. And when the false prophets, who were with Ahaziah the son of Ahab and their teacher Jalerjas of Mount Joel, had heard- 16. Now he was a brother of Zedekiah - when they persuaded Ahaziah the king of Aguaron and (slew) Micaiah.

3

1. AND Belchira recognized and saw the place of Isaiah and the prophets who were with him; for he dwelt in the region of Bethlehem, and was an adherent of Manasseh. And he prophesied falsely in Jerusalem, and many belonging to Jerusalem were confederate with him, and he was a Samaritan. 2. And it came to pass when Alagar Zagar, king of Assyria, had come and captive, and led them away to the mountains of the medes and the rivers of Tazon; 3. This (Belchira), whilst still a youth, had escaped and come to Jerusalem in the days of Hezekiah king of Judah, but he walked not in the ways of his father of Samaria; for he feared Hezekiah. 4. And he was found in the days of Hezekiah speaking words of lawlessness in Jerusalem. 5. And the servants of Hezekiah accused him, and he made his escape to the region of Bethlehem. And they persuaded... 6. And Belchira accused Isaiah and the prophets who were with him, saying: `Isaiah and those who are with him prophesy against Jerusalem and against the cities of Judah that they shall be laid waste and (against the children of Judah and) Benjamin also that they shall go into captivity, and also against thee, O lord the king, that thou shalt go (bound) with hooks and iron chains'. 7. But they prophesy falsely against Israel and Judah. 8. And Isaiah himself hath said: `I see more than Moses the prophet.' 9. But Moses said: `No man can see God and live'; and Isaiah hath said: `I have seen God and behold I live.' 10. Know, therefore, O king, that he is lying. And Jerusalem also he hath called Sodom, and the princes of Judah and Jerusalem he hath declared to be the people of Gomorrah. And he brought many accusations against Isaiah and the prophets before Manasseh. 11. But Beliar dwelt in the heart of Manasseh and in the heart of the princes of Judah and Benjamin and of the eunuchs and of the councillors of the king. 12. And the words of Belchira pleased him [exceedingly], and he sent and seized Isaiah. 13. For Beliar was in great wrath against Isaiah by reason of the vision, and because of the exposure wherewith he had exposed Sammael, and because through him the going forth of the Beloved from the seventh heaven had been made known, and His transformation and His descent and the likeness into which He should be transformed (that is) the likeness of man, and the persecution wherewith he should be persecuted, and the torturers wherewith the children of Israel should torture Him, and the coming of His twelve disciples, and the teaching, and that He should before the sabbath be crucified upon the tree, and should be crucified together with wicked men, and that He should be buried in the sepulchre, 14. And the twelve who were with Him should be offended because of Him: and the watch of those who watched the sepulchre: 15. And the descent of the angel of the Christian Church, which is in the heavens, whom He will summon in the last days. 16. And that (Gabriel) the angel of the Holy Spirit, and Michael, the chief of the holy angels, on the third day will open the sepulchre: 17. And the Beloved sitting on their shoulders will come forth and send out His twelve disciples; 18. And they will teach all the nations and every tongue of the resurrection of the Beloved, and those who believe in His cross will be saved, and in His ascension into the seventh heaven whence He came: 19. And that many who believe in Him will speak through the Holy Spirit: 20. And many signs and wonders will be wrought in those days. 21. And afterwards, on the eve of His approach, His disciples will forsake the teachings of the Twelve Apostles, and their faith, and their love and their purity. 22. And there will be much contention on the eve of [His advent and] His approach. 23. And in those days many will love office, though devoid of wisdom. 24. And there will be many lawless elders, and shepherds dealing wrongly by their own sheep, and they will ravage (them) owing to their not having holy shepherds. 25. And many will change the honour of the garments of the saints for the garments of the covetous, and there will be much respect of persons in those days and lovers of the honour of this world. 26. And there will be much slander and vainglory at the approach of the Lord, and the Holy Spirit will withdraw from many. 27. And there will not be in those days many prophets, nor those who speak trustworthy words, save one here and there in divers places, 28. On account of the spirit of error and fornication and of vainglory, and of covetousness, which shall be in those, who will be called servants of that One and in those who will receive that One. 29. And there will be great hatred in the shepherds and elders towards each other. 30. For there will be great jealousy in the last days; for every one will say what is pleasing in his own eyes. 31. And they will make of none effect the prophecy of the prophets which were

before me, and these my visions also will they make of none effect, in order to speak after the impulse of their own hearts.

4

1. AND now Hezekiah and Josab my son, these are the days of the completion of the world. 2. After it is consummated, Beliar the great ruler, the king of this world, will descend, who hath ruled it since it came into being; yea, he will descent from his firmament in the likeness of a man, a lawless king, the slayer of his mother: who himself (even) this king. 3. Will persecute the plant which the Twelve Apostles of the Beloved have planted. Of the Twelve one will be delivered into his hands. 4. This ruler in the form of that king will come and there will come and there will come with him all the powers of this world, and they will hearken unto him in all that he desires. 5. And at his word the sun will rise at night and he will make the moon to appear at the sixth hour. 6. And all that he hath desired he will do in the world: he will do and speak like the Beloved and he will say: "I am God and before me there has been none." 7. And all the people in the world will believe in him. 8. And they will sacrifice to him and they will serve him saying: "This is God and beside him there is no other." 9. And they greater number of those who shall have been associated together in order to receive the Beloved, he will turn aside after him. 10. And there will be the power of his miracles in every city and region. 11. And he will set up his image before him in every city. 12. And he shall bear sway three years and seven months and twenty-seven days. 13. And many believers and saints having seen Him for whom they were hoping, who was crucified, Jesus the Lord Christ, [after that I, Isaiah, had seen Him who was crucified and ascended] and those also who were believers in Him - of these few in those days will be left as His servants, while they flee from desert to desert, awaiting the coming of the Beloved. 14. And after (one thousand) three hundred and thirty-two days the Lord will come with His angels and with the armies of the holy ones from the seventh heaven with the glory of the seventh heaven, and He will drag Beliar into Gehenna and also his armies. 15. And He will give rest of the godly whom He shall find in the body in this world, [and the sun wil be ashamed]: 16. And to all who because of (their) faith in Him have execrated Beliar and his kings. But the saints will come with the Lord with their garments which are (now) stored up on high in the seventh heaven: with the Lord they will come, whose spirits are clothed, they will descend and be present in the world, and He will strengthen those, who have been found in the body, together with the saints, in the garments of the saints, and the Lord will minister to those who have kept watch in this world. 17. And afterwards they will turn themselves upward in their garments, and their body will be left in the world. 18. Then the voice of the Beloved will in wrath rebuke the things of heaven and the things of earth and the things of earth and the mountains and the hills and the cities and the desert and the forests and the angel of the sun and that of the moon, and all things wherein Beliar manifested himself and acted openly in this world, and there will be [a resurrection and] a judgment in their midst in those days, and the Beloved will cause fire to go forth from Him, and it will consume all the godless, and they will be as though they had not been created. 19. And the rest of the words of the vision is written in the vision of Babylon. 20. And the rest of the vision regarding the Lord, behold, it is written in three parables according to my words which are written in the book which I publicly prophesied. 21. And the descent of the Beloved into Sheol, behold, it is written in the section, where the Lord says: "Behold my Son will understand." And all these things, behold they are written [in the Psalms] in the parables of David, the son of Jesse, and in the Proverbs of Solomon his son, and in the words of Korah, and Ethan the Israelite, and in the words of Asaph, and in the rest of the Psalms also which the angel of the Spirit inspired. 22. (Namely) in those which have not the name written, and in the words of my father Amos, and of Hosea the prophet, and of Micah and Joel and Nahum and Jonah and Obadiah and Habakkuk and Haggai and Malachi, and in the words of Joseph the Just and in the words of Daniel.

5

1. ON account of these visions, therefore, Beliar was wroth with Isaiah, and he dwelt in the heart of Manasseh and he sawed him in sunder with a wooden saw. 2. And when Isaiah was being sawn in sunder, Belchira stood up, accusing him, and all the false prophets stood up, laughing and rejoicing because of Isaiah. 3. And Belchira, with the aid of Mechembechus, stood up before Isaiah, [laughing] deriding; 4. And Belchira said to Isaiah: 'Say, "I have lied in all that I have spoken, and likewise the ways of Manasseh are good and right. 5. And the ways also of Belchira and of his associates are good." 6. And this he said to him when he began to be sawn in sunder. 7. But Isaiah was (absorbed) in a vision of the Lord, and though his eyes were open, he saw them (not). 8. And Belchira spake thus to Isaiah: "Say what I say unto thee and I will turn their hearts, and I will compel Manasseh and the princes of Judah and the people and all Jerusalem to reverence thee. 9. And Isaiah answered and said: "So far as I have utterance (I say): Damned and accused be thou and all they powers and all thy house. 10. For thou canst not take (from me) aught save the skin of my body." 11. And they seized and sawed in sunder Isaiah, the son of Amoz, with a wooden saw. 12. And Manasseh and Belchira and the false prophets and the princes and the people [and] all stood looking on. 13. And to the prophets who were with him he said before he had been sawn in sunder: "Go ye to the region of Tyre and Sidon; for for me only hath God mingled the cup." 14. And when Isaiah was being sawn in sunder, he neither cried aloud nor wept, but his lips spake with the Holy Spirit until he was sawn in twain. 15. This, Beliar did to Isaiah through Belchira and Manasseh; for Sammael was very wrathful against Isaiah from the days of Hezekiah, king of Judah, on account of the things which he had seen regarding the Beloved. 16. And on account of the destruction of Sammael, which he had seen through the Lord, while Hezekiah his father was still king. And he did according to the will of Satan.

The Ascension of Isaiah

6

1. The Vision Which Isaiah the Son of Amoz Saw: In the twentieth year of the reign of Hezekiah, king of Judah, came Isaiah the son of Amoz, and Josab the son of Isaiah to Hezekiah to Jerusalem from Galgala. 2. And (having entered) he sat down on the couch of the king, and they brought him a seat, but he would not sit (thereon). 3. And when Isaiah began to speak the words of faith and truth with King Hezekiah, all the princes of Israel were seated and the eunuchs and the councillors of the king. And there were there forty prophets and sons of the prophets: they had come from the villages and from the mountains and the plains when they had heard that Isaiah was coming from Galgala to Hezekiah. 4. And they had come to salute him and to hear his words. 5. And that he might place his hands upon them, and that they might prophesy and that he might hear their prophecy: and they were all before Isaiah. 6. And when Isaiah was speaking to Hezekiah the words of truth and faith, they all heard a door which one had opened and the voice of the Holy Spirit. 7. And the king summoned all the prophets and all the people who were found there, and they came. and Macaiah and the aged Ananias and Joel and Josab sat on his right hand (and on the left). 8. And it came to pass when they had all heard the voice of the Holy Spirit, they all worshipped on their knees, and glorified the God of truth, the Most High who is in the upper world and who sits on High the Holy One and who rest among His holy ones. 9. And they gave glory to Him who had thus bestowed a door in an alien world had bestowed (it) on a man. 10. And as he was speaking in the Holy Spirit in the hearing of all, he became silent and his mind was taken up from him and he saw not the men that stood before him. 11. Though his eyes indeed were open. Moreover his lips were silent and the mind in his body was taken up from him. 12. But his breath was in him; for he was seeing a vision. 13. And the angel who was sent to make him see was not of this firmament, nor was he of the angels of glory of this world, but he had come from the seventh heaven. 14. And the people who stood near did (not) think, but the circle of the prophets (did), that the holy Isaiah had been taken up. 15. And the vision which the holy Isaiah saw was not from this world but from the world which is hidden from the flesh. 16. And after Isaiah had seen this vision, he narrated it to Hezekiah, and to Josab his son and to the other prophets who had come. 17. But the leaders and the eunuchs and the people did not hear, but only Samna the scribe, and Ijoaqem, and Asaph the recorder; for these also were doers of righteousness, and the sweet smell of the Spirit was upon them. But the people had not heard; for Micaiah and Josab his son had caused them to go forth, when the wisdom of this world had been taken form him and he became as one dead.

7

1. AND the vision which Isaiah saw, he told to Hezekiah and Josab his son and Micaiah and the rest of the prophets, (and) said: 2. At this moment, when I prophesied according to the (words) heard which ye heard, I saw a glorious angel not like unto the glory of the angels which I used always to see, but possessing such glory ad position that I cannot describe the glory of that angel. 3. And having seized me by my hand he raised me on high, and I said unto him: "Who art thou, and what is thy name, and whither art thou raising me on high? for strength was given me to speak with him." 4. And he said unto me: "When I have raised thee on high [though the (various) degrees] and made thee see the vision, on account of which I have been sent, then thou wilt understand who I am: but my name thou dost not know. 5. Because thou wilt return into this thy body, but whither I am raising thee on high, thou wilt see; for for this purpose have I been sent." 6. And I rejoiced because he spake courteously to me. 7. And he said unto me: "Hast thou rejoiced because I have spoken courteously to thee?" And he said: "And thou wilt see how a grater also that I am will speak courteously and peaceably with thee." 8. And His Father also who is greater thou wilt see; for for this purpose have I been sent from the seventh heaven in order to explain all these things unto thee." 9. And we ascended to the firmament, I and he, and there I saw Sammael and his hosts, and there was great fighting therein and the angels of Satan were envying one another. 10. And as above so on the earth also; for the likeness of that which is in the firmament is here on he earth. 11. And I said unto the angel (who was with me): "(What is this war and) what is this envying?" 12. And he said unto me: "So has it been since this world was made until now, and this war (will continue) till He, whom thou shalt see will come and destroy him." 13. And afterwards he caused me to ascend (to that which is) above the firmament: which is the (first) heaven. 14. And there I saw a throne in the midst, and on his right and on his left were angels. 15. And (the angels on the left were) not like unto the angels who stood on the right, but those who stood on the right had the greater glory, and they all praised with one voice, and there was a throne in the midst, and those who were out he left gave praise after them; but their voice was not such as the voice of those on the right, nor their praise like the praise of those. 16. And I asked the angel who conducted me, and I said unto him: "To whom is this praise sent?" 17. And he said unto me: "(it is sent) to the praise of (Him who sitteth in) the seventh heaven: to Him who rests in the holy world, and to His Beloved, whence I have been sent to thee. [Thither is it sent.]" 18. And again, he made me to ascend to the second heaven. now the height of that heaven is the same as from the haven to the earth [and to the firmament]. 19. And (I saw there, as) in the first heaven, angels on the right and on the left, and a throne in the midst, and the praise of the angels in the second heaven; and he who sat on the throne in the second heaven was more glorious than all (the rest). 20. And there was great glory in the second heaven, and the praise also was not like the praise of those who were in the first heaven. 21. And I fell on my face to worship him, but he angel who conducted me did not permit me, but said unto me: "Worship neither throne nor angel which belongs to the six heavens - for for this cause I was sent to conduct thee j- until I tell thee in the seventh heaven. 22. For above all the heavens and their angels has thy throne been placed, and thy garments and thy crown which thou shalt see." 23. And I rejoiced with great joy, that those who love the Most High and His Beloved will afterwards ascend thither by the angel of the Holy Spirit. 24. And he raise me to the third heaven, and in like manner I saw those upon the right and upon the left, and there was a throne there in the midst; but the memorial of this world is there unheard of. 25. And I said to the angel who was with me; for the glory of my appearance was undergoing transformation as I ascended to each heaven in turn: "Nothing of the vanity of that world is here named." 26. And he answered me, and said unto me: "Nothing is named on account of its weakness, and nothing is hidden there of what is done." 27. And I wished to learn how it is know, and he answered me saying: "When I have raised thee to the seventh heaven whence I was sent, to that which is above these, then thou shalt know that there is nothing hidden from the thrones and from those who dwell in the heavens and from the angels. And the praise wherewith they praised and glory of him who sat on the throne was great, and the glory of the angels on the right hand and on the left was beyond that of the heaven which was below them. 28. And again he raised me to the fourth heaven, and the height from the third to the height from the third to the forth heaven was greater than from the earth to the firmament. 29. And there again I saw those who were on the right hand and those who were on the left, and him who sat on the throne was in the midst, and there also they were praising. 30. And the praise and glory of the angels on the right was greater than that of those on the left. 31. And again the glory of him who sat on the throne was greater than that of the angels on the right, and their glory was beyond that of those who were below. 32. And he raised me to the fifth heaven. 33. And again I saw those upon the right hand and on the left, and him who sat on the throne possessing greater glory that those of the forth heaven. 34. And the glory of those on the right hand was greater than that of those on the left [from the third to the fourth]. 35. And the glory of him who was on the throne was greater than that of the angels on the right hand. 36. And their praise was more glorious than that of the fourth heaven. 37. And I praised Him, who is not named and the Only-begotten who dwelleth in the heavens, whose name is not known to any flesh, who has bestowed such glory on the several heavens, and who makes great the glory of the angels, and more excellent the glory of Him who sitteth on the throne.

8

1. AND again he raised me into the air of the sixth heaven, and I saw such glory as I had not seen in the five heavens. 2. For I saw angels possessing great glory. 3. And the praise there was holy and wonderful. 4. And I said to the angel who conducted me: "What is this which I see, my Lord?" 5. And he said: "I am not thy lord, but thy fellow servant." 6. And again I asked him, and I said unto him: "Why are there not angelic fellow servants (on the left)?" 7. And he said: "From the sixth heaven there are no longer angels on the left, nor a throne set in the midst, but (they are directed) by the power of the seventh heaven, where dwelleth He that is not named and the Elect One, whose name has not been made known, and none of the heavens can learn His name. 8. For it is He alone to whose voice all the heavens and thrones give answer. I have therefore been empowered and sent to raise thee here that thou mayest see this glory. 9. And that thou mayest see the Lord of all those heavens and these thrones. 10. Undergoing (successive) transformation until He resembles your form and likeness. 11. I indeed say unto thee, Isaiah; No man about to return into a body of that world has ascended or seen what thou seest or perceived what thou hast perceived and what thou wilt see. 12. For it has been permitted to thee in the lot of the Lord to come hither. [And from thence comes the power of the sixth heaven and of the air]." 13. And I magnified my Lord with praise, in that through His lot I should come hither. 14. And he said: "Hear,

furthermore, therefore, this also from thy fellow servant: when from the body by the will of God thou hast ascended hither, then thou wilt receive the garment which thou seest, and likewise other numbered garments laid up (there) thou wilt see. 15. And then thou wilt become equal to the angels of the seventh heaven. 16. And he raised me up into the sixth heaven, and there were no (angels) on the left, nor a throne in the midst, but all had one appearance and their (power of) praise was equal. 17. And (power) was given to me also, and I also praised along with them and that angel also, and our praise was like theirs. 18. And there they all named the primal Father and His Beloved, the Christ, and the Holy Spirit, all with one voice. 19. And (their voice) was not like the voice of the angels in the five heavens. 20. [Nor like their discourse] but the voice was different there, and there was much light there. 21. And then, when I was in the sixth heaven I thought the light which I had seen in the five heavens to be but darkness. 22. And I rejoiced and praised Him who hath bestowed such lights on those who wait for His promise. 23. And I besought the angel who conducted me that I should not henceforth return to the carnal world. 24. I say indeed unto you, Hezekiah and Josab my son and Micaiah, that there is much darkness here. 25. And the angel who conducted me discovered what I thought and said: "If in this light thou dost rejoice, how much more wilt thou rejoice, when in the seventh heaven thou seest the light where is the Lord and His Beloved [whence I have been sent, who is to be called "Son" in this world. 26. Not (yet) hath been manifested he shall be in the corruptible world] and the garments, and the thrones, and the crowns which are laid up for the righteous, for those who trust in that Lord who will descend in your form. For the light which is there is great and wonderful. 27. And as concerning thy not returning into the body thy days are not yet fulfilled for coming here." 28. And when I heard (that) I was troubled, and he said: "Do not be troubled."

9

1. AND he took me into the air of the seventh heaven, and moreover I heard a voice saying: "How far will he ascend that dwelleth in the flesh?" And I feared and trembled. 2. And when I trembled, behold, I heard from hence another voice being sent forth, and saying: "It is permitted to the holy Isaiah to ascend hither; for here is his garment." 3. And I asked the angel who was with me and said: "Who is he who forbade me and who is he who permitted me to ascend?" 4. And he said unto me: "He who forbade thee, is he who is over the praise-giving of the sixth heaven. 5. And He who permitted thee, this is thy Lord God, the Lord Christ, who will be called "Jesus" in the world, but His name thou canst not hear till thou hast ascended out of thy body." 6. And he raised me up into the seventh heaven, and I saw there a wonderful light and angels innumerable. 7. And there I saw the holy Abel and all the righteous. 8. And there I saw Enoch and all who were with him, stript of the garments of the flesh, and I saw them in their garments of the upper world, and they were like angels, standing there in great glory. 9. And there I saw Enoch and all who were with him, stript of the garments of the flesh, and I saw them in their garments of the upper world, and they were like angels, standing there in great glory. 10. But they sat not on their thrones, nor were their crowns of glory on them. 11. And I asked the angel who was with me: "How is it that they have received the garments, but have not the thrones and the crowns?" 12. And he said unto me: "Crowns and thrones of glory they do not receive, till the Beloved will descent in the form in which you will see Him descent [will descent, I say] into the world in the last days the Lord, who will be called Christ. 13. Nevertheless they see and know whose will be thrones, and whose the crowns when He has descended and been made in your form, and they will think that He is flesh and is a man. 14. And the god of that world will stretch forth his hand against the Son, and they will crucify Him on a tree, and will slay Him not knowing who He is. 15. And thus His descent, as you will see, will be hidden even from the heavens, so that it will not be known who He is. 16. And when He hath plundered the angel of death, He will ascend on the third day, [and he will remain in that world five hundred and forty-five days]. 17. And then many of the righteous will ascend with Him, whose spirits do not receive their garments till the Lord Christ ascend and they ascend with Him. 18. Then indeed they will receive their [garments and] thrones and crowns, when He has ascended into the seventh heaven." 19. And I said unto him that which I had asked him in the third heaven: 20. "Show me how everything which is done in that world is here made known." 21. And whilst I was still speaking with him, behold one of the angels who stood nigh, more glorious than the glory of that angel, who had raised me up from the world. 22. Showed me a book, [but not as a book of this world] and he opened it, and the book was written, but not as a book of this world. And he gave (it) to me and I read it, and lo! the deeds of the children of Israel were written therein, and the deeds of those whom I know (not), my son Josab. 23. And I said: "In truth, there is nothing hidden in the seventh heaven, which is done in this world." 24. And I saw there many garments laid up, and many thrones and many crowns. 25. And I said to the angel: "Whose are these garments and thrones and crowns?" 26. And he said unto me: "These garments many from that world will receive, believing in the words of That One, who shall be named as I told thee, and they will observe those things, and believe in them, and believe in His cross: for them are these laid up." 27. And I saw a certain One standing, whose glory surpassed that of all, and His glory was great and wonderful. 28. And after I had seen Him, all the righteous whom I had seen and also the angels whom I had seen came to Him. And Adam and Abel and Seth and all the righteous first drew near and worshipped Him, and they all praised Him with one voice, and I myself also gave praise with them, and my giving of praise was as theirs. 29. And then all the angels drew nigh and worshipped and gave praise. 30. And I was (again) transformed and became like an angel. 31. And thereupon the angel who conducted me said to me: "Worship this One," and I worshipped and praised. 32. And the angel said unto me: "This is the Lord of all the praise-givings which thou hast seen." 33. And whilst he was still speaking, I saw another Glorious One who was like Him, and the righteous drew nigh and worshipped and praised, and I praised together with them. But my glory was not transformed into accordance with their form. 34. And thereupon the angels drew near and worshipped Him. 35. And I saw the Lord and the second angel, and they were standing. 36. And the second whom I saw was on he left of my Lord. And I asked: "Who is this?" and he said unto me: "Worship Him, for He is the angel of the Holy Spirit, who speaketh in thee and the rest of the righteous." 37. And I saw the great glory, the eyes of my spirit being open, and I could not thereupon see, nor yet could the angel who was with me, nor all the angels whom I had seen worshipping my Lord. 38. But I saw the righteous beholding with great power the glory of that One. 39. And my Lord drew nigh to me and the angel of the Spirit and He said: "See how it is given to thee to see God, and on thy account power is given to the angel who is with thee." 40. And I saw how my Lord and the angel of the Spirit worshipped, and they both together praised God. 41. And thereupon all the righteous drew near and worshipped. 42. And the angels drew near and worshipped and all the angels praised.

10

1. AND thereupon I heard the voices and the giving of praise, which I had heard in each of the six heavens, ascending and being heard there: 2. And all were being sent up to that Glorious One whose glory I could not behold. 3. And I myself was hearing and beholding the praise (which was given) to Him. 4. And the Lord and the angel of the Spirit were beholding all and hearing all. 5. And all the praises which are sent up from the six heavens are not only heard, but seen. 6. And I heard the angel who conducted me and he said: "This is the Most High of the high ones, dwelling in the holy world, and resting in His holy ones, who will be called by the Holy Spirit through the lips of the righteous the Father of the Lord." 7. And I heard the voice of the Most High, the Father of my Lord, saying to my Lord Christ who will be called Jesus: 8. "Go forth and descent through all the heavens, and thou wilt descent to the firmament and that world: to the angel in Sheol thou wilt descend, but to Haguel thou wilt not go. 9. And thou wilt become like unto the likeness of all who are in the five heavens. 10. And thou wilt be careful to become like the form of the angels of the firmament [and the angels also who are in Sheol]. 11. And none of the angels of that world shall know that Thou art with Me of the seven heavens and of their angels. 12. And they shall not know that Thou art with Me, till with a loud voice I have called (to) the heavens, and their angels and their lights, (even) unto the sixth heaven, in order that you mayest judge and destroy the princes and angels and gods of that world, and the world that is dominated by them: 13. For they have denied Me and said: "We alone are and there is none beside us." 14. And afterwards from the angels of death Thou wilt ascend to Thy place. And Thou wilt not be transformed in each heaven, but in glory wilt Thou ascend and sit on My right hand. 15. And thereupon the princes and powers of that world will worship Thee." 16. These commands I heard the Great Glory giving to my Lord. 17. And so I saw my Lord go forth from the seventh heaven into the sixth heaven. 18. And the angel who conducted me [from this world was with me and] said unto me: "Understand, Isaiah, and see the transformation and descent of the Lord will appear." 19. And I saw, and when the angels saw Him, thereupon those in the sixth heaven praised and lauded Him; for He had not been transformed after the shape of the angels there, and they praised Him and I also praised with them. 20. And I saw when He descended into the fifth heaven, that in the fifth heaven He made Himself like unto the form of the angels there, and they did not praise Him (nor worship Him); for His form was like unto theirs. 21. And then He descended into the forth heaven, and made Himself like unto the form of the angels there. 22. And when they saw Him, they did not praise

or laud Him; for His form was like unto their form. 23. And again I saw when He descended into the third heaven, and He made Himself like unto the form of the angels in the third heaven. 24. And those who kept the gate of the (third) heaven demanded the password, and the Lord gave (it) to them in order that He should not be recognized. And when they saw Him, they did not praise or laud Him; for His form was like unto their form. 25. And again I saw when He descended into the second heaven, and again He gave the password there; those who kept the gate proceeded to demand and the Lord to give. 26. And I saw when He made Himself like unto the form of the angels in the second heaven, and they saw Him and they did not praise Him; for His form was like unto their form. 27. And again I saw when He descended into the first heaven, and there also He gave the password to those who kept the gate, and He made Himself like unto the form of the angels who were on the left of that throne, and they neither praised nor lauded Him; for His form was like unto their form. 28. But as for me no one asked me on account of the angel who conducted me. 29. And again He descended into the firmament where dwelleth the ruler of this world, and He gave the password to those on the left, and His form was like theirs, and they did not praise Him there; but they were envying one another and fighting; for here there is a power of evil and envying about trifles. 30. And I saw when He descended and made Himself like unto the angels of the air, and He was like one of them. 31. And He gave no password; for one was plundering and doing violence to another.

11

1. AFTER this I saw, and the angel who spoke with me, who conducted me, said unto me: "Understand, Isaiah son of Amoz; for for this purpose have I been sent from God." 2. And I indeed saw a woman of the family of David the prophet, named Mary, and Virgin, and she was espoused to a man named Joseph, a carpenter, and he also was of the seed and family of the righteous David of Bethlehem Judah. 3. And he came into his lot. And when she was espoused, she was found with child, and Joseph the carpenter was desirous to put her away. 4. But the angel of the Spirit appeared in this world, and after that Joseph did not put her away, but kept Mary and did not reveal this matter to any one. 5. And he did not approach May, but kept her as a holy virgin, though with child. 6. And he did not live with her for two months. 7. And after two months of days while Joseph was in his house, and Mary his wife, but both alone. 8. It came to pass that when they were alone that Mary straight-way looked with her eyes and saw a small babe, and she was astonished. 9. And after she had been astonished, her womb was found as formerly before she had conceived. 10. And when her husband Joseph said unto her: "What has astonished thee?" his eyes were opened and he saw the infant and praised God, because into his portion God had come. 11. And a voice came to them: "Tell this vision to no one." 12. And the story regarding the infant was noised broad in Bethlehem. 13. Some said: "The Virgin Mary hath borne a child, before she was married two months." 14. And many said: "She has not borne a child, nor has a midwife gone up (to her), nor have we heard the cries of (labour) pains." And they were all blinded respecting Him and they all knew regarding Him, though they knew not whence He was. 15. And they took Him, and went to Nazareth in Galilee. 16. And I saw, O Hezekiah and Josab my son, and I declare to the other prophets also who are standing by, that (this) hath escaped all the heavens and all the princes and all the gods of this world. 17. And I saw: In Nazareth He sucked the breast as a babe and as is customary in order that He might not be recognized. 18. And when He had grown up he worked great signs and wonders in the land of Israel and of Jerusalem. 19. And after this the adversary envied Him and roused the children of Israel against Him, not knowing who He was, and they delivered Him to the king, and crucified Him, and He descended to the angel (of Sheol). 20. In Jerusalem indeed I was Him being crucified on a tree: 21. And likewise after the third day rise again and remain days. 22. And the angel who conducted me said: "Understand, Isaiah": and I saw when He sent out the Twelve Apostles and ascended. 23. And I saw Him, and He was in the firmament, but He had not changed Himself into their form, and all the angels of the firmament and the Satans saw Him and they worshipped. 24. And there was much sorrow there, while they said: "How did our Lord descend in our midst, and we perceived not the glory [which has been upon Him], which we see has been upon Him from the sixth heaven?" 25. And He ascended into the second heaven, and He did not transform Himself, but all the angels who were on the right and on the left and the throne in the midst. 26. Both worshipped Him and praised Him and said: "How did our Lord escape us whilst descending, and we perceived not?" 27. And in like manner He ascended into the third heaven, and they praised and said in like manner. 28. And in the fourth heaven and in the fifth also they said precisely after the same manner. 29. But there was one glory, and from it He did not change Himself. 30. And I saw when He ascended into the sixth heaven, and they worshipped and glorified Him. 31. But in all the heavens the praise increased (in volume). 32. And I saw how He ascended into the seventh heaven, and all the righteous and all the angels praised Him. And then I saw Him sit down on the right hand of that Great Glory whose glory I told you that I could not behold. 33. And also the angel of the Holy Spirit I saw sitting on the left hand. 34. And this angel said unto me: "Isaiah, son of Amoz, it is enough for thee;... for thou hast seen what no child of flesh has seen. 35. And thou wilt return into thy garment (of the flesh) until thy days are completed. Then thou wilt come hither." 36. These things Isaiah saw and told unto all that stood before him, and they praised. And he spake to Hezekiah the King and said: "I have spoken these things." 37. Both the end of this world; 38. And all this vision will be consummated in the last generations. 39. And Isaiah made him swear that he would not tell (it) to the people of Israel, nor give these words to any man to transcribe. 40. ...such things ye will read. and watch ye in the Holy Spirit in order they ye may receive your garments and thrones and crowns of glory which are laid up in the seventh heaven. 41. On account of these visions and prophecies Sammael Satan sawed in sunder Isaiah the son of Amoz, the prophet, by the hand of Manasseh. 42. And all these things Hezekiah delivered to Manasseh in the twenty-sixth year. 43. But Manasseh did not remember them nor place these things in his heart, but becoming the servant of Satan he was destroyed. Here endeth the vision of Isaiah the prophet with his ascension.

Fragments of a Zadokite Work
(or The Damascus Document)

1

Israel sent into Captivity, 3-4. A Root of God's Planting made to spring forth after 200 B.C. and a Teacher of Righteousness raised up, 5-8. Description of Israel's Wickedness in the First Century B.C. or at an earlier date, 9-17.

¹ Now, therefore, hearken (unto me) all ye who know righteousness, ² And have understanding in the works of God. For He hath a controversy with all flesh, And will execute judgment upon all who despise Him. ³ For because of the trespass of those who forsook Him, He hid His face from Israel and from His Sanctuary, And gave them over to the sword. ⁴ But when He remembered the covenant of the forefathers, He left a remnant to Israel, and gave them not over to destruction. ⁵ [And in the period of the wrath three hundred and ninety years after He had given them in the hand of Nebuchadnezzar, the King of Babylon He visited them], and He made to spring forth from Israel and Aaron, A root of His planting to inherit His land, And to grow fat through the goodness of His earth. ⁶ And they had understanding of their iniquity, And they knew that they were guilty men, And **had** like the blind **been groping** after the way twenty years. ⁷ And God considered their works; for they sought Him with a perfect heart And He raised them up a Teacher of righteousness To lead them in the way of His heart. ⁸ And He made known to later generations what He had done [to a later generation] to a congregation of treacherous men: Those who turned aside out of the way. ⁹ This was the time concerning which it was written: As a stubborn heifer So hath Israel behaved himself stubbornly: ¹⁰ When there arose the scornful man, Who talked to Israel lying words, And made them go astray in the wilderness where there was no way, [to bring low the pride of the world]. ¹¹ So that they should turn aside from the paths of righteousness, And remove the landmark which the forefathers had set in their inheritance: ¹² So as to make cleave unto them The curses of His covenant, To deliver them to the sword That avengeth with the vengeance of the covenant. ¹³ Because they sought after smooth things, And they chose deceits, And kept watch with a view to lawless deeds. ¹⁴ And they chose the best of the neck, And justified the wicked, And condemned the righteous: ¹⁵ And transgressed the covenant, And violated the statute, And attacked the soul of the righteous. ¹⁶ And all that walked uprightly their soul abhorred, And they pursued them with the sword, And rejoiced in the strife of the people. ¹⁷ And so the wrath of God was kindled against their congregation, So that He laid waste all their multitude, And their deeds were uncleanness before Him.

2

Wisdom is with God and Forgiveness of the repentant, but Wrath for the unrepentant, who are predestined to Destruction on the Ground of the Divine Foreknowledge, 1-7. But there is a Remnant whom He shall teach by the Messiah, 9-10.

¹ And now hearken unto me all ye who have entered into the covenant, And I will disclose to you the ways of the wicked. ² God loveth [knowledge] wisdom: And counsel He hath set before Him; Prudence and knowledge minister unto Him. ³ Longsuffering is with Him And plenteousness of forgivenesses To pardon those who repent of transgression. ⁴ And power and might and great fury with flames **of** fire [therein are all the angels of destruction] For them who turned aside out of the way, And abhorred the statute, ⁵ So that there should be no remnant, nor any to escape of them. ⁶ For God chose them not from the beginning of the world, And ere they were **formed** He knew their works. ⁷ And He abhorred their generations **from of old**, And hid His face from their land till they were consumed. ⁸ [And He knew the years of (their) office and the number and exact statement of their periods for all the things that belong to the ages and have been, moreover whatsoever shall come to pass in their periods for all the years of eternity.] ⁹ Yet in all of them He raised Him up men called by name, In order to leave a remnant to the earth, And to fill the face of the earth with their seed. ¹⁰ And through His Messiah He shall make them know His holy spirit. And he is true, and in the true interpretation of his name are their names: But them He hated He made to go astray.

3

Exhortation to choose God's Will and to shun the evil Inclination,1-2; through it fell the mighty Men of old, the Watchers and their Children 3-5; and all Flesh 6

¹ Now therefore, children, hearken unto me, And I will open your eyes to see, And to understand the works of God. And to choose what He approveth, And to reject what He hateth: ² To walk uprightly in all His ways, And not to go about in the thoughts of an evil imagination And (with) **eyes** (full) of fornication. ³ For many were led astray by them, And mighty men of valor stumbled by them from of old [and until this day]. ⁴ Because they walked in the stubbornness of their heart the **watchers** of heaven fell. By them were they caught because they kept not the commandment of God. ⁵ And their children whose height was like the loftiness of the cedars And whose bodies were like the mountains fell **thereby**. ⁶ All flesh that was on dry land perished **thereby**. And they were as though they had not been. ⁷ Because they did their own will, and kept not the commandment of their Maker, Until His wrath was kindled against them.

4

Also the Sons of Noah 1; Abraham, Isaac and Jacob walked not after the evil Inclination of the Heart, 2-3; but the Sons of Israel did in Egypt and in the Wilderness and were punished accordingly, 4-9.

¹ By **them** went astray the sons of Noah and their families: Because of **them** they were cut off. ² Abraham did not walk in **them**, And he was (recorded) friend because he kept the commandments of God, And chose not the will of his own spirit. ³ And he delivered (the commandment) to Isaac and Jacob, And they observed (it) and were recorded as friends of God, And members of the covenant forever. ⁴ The sons of Jacob went astray through them, And they were punished **according to** their error. ⁵ And their children in Egypt walked in the stubbornness of their heart, So that they took counsel against the commandments of God, And every man did that which was right in his own eyes. ⁶ [And they eat blood], and He cut off their males in the desert (when He said) to them in Kadesh: Go up and possess (the land, but they hardened) their spirit: ⁷ And they hearkened not unto the voice of their Maker [The commandments of their **Teacher**] but murmured in their tents, And so the wrath of God was kindled against their congregation ⁸ And their children [perished by it And their kings] were cut off by it, And their mighty men perished by it, And their land was made desolate by it. ⁹ By it the first that entered into the covenant incurred guilt, And they were delivered unto the sword, Because they forsook the covenant of God: ¹⁰ And they chose their own will, And went about after the stubbornness of their heart, Every man doing his own will.

5

God confirms the Covenant with the faithful through fresh Revelations, 1-3; when Israel transgressed again God forgave them, 4-6; and confirmed His Covenant with them through Ezekiel, 6-7.

¹ But with them that held fast by the commandments of God, [who were left of them], God confirmed the covenant of Israel forever, Revealing unto them the hidden things Wherein all Israel had erred: ² His holy Sabbaths and His glorious festivals, His righteous testimonies and His true ways, And the desires of His will [the which if a man do, he shall live by them] He opened before them. ³ And they digged a well of many waters: And he that despises them shall not live. ⁴ But they wallowed in the transgression of man, And in the ways of the unclean woman, And they said that it belongs to us. ⁵ But God **wondrously** pardoned their sins, And forgave their transgression, And He built them a sure house in Israel [the like of which never arose from of old nor until this day]. ⁶ They who hold fast to him are for the life of eternity, And all the glory of man is for them; As God confirmed it to them through Ezekiel the prophet, saying: ⁷ 'The priests and the Levites and the sons of Zadok, that kept the charge of **My** Sanctuary when the children of Israel went astray from them, they shall bring near unto Me fat and blood.'

6

Migration of the Penitents to Damascus. Sons of Zadok hold office in the end of the Days, 1-3. Law to be obeyed and relations with Judah broken of in the Period in which Belial is let loose. 4-12.

¹ The priests are the penitents of Israel who went forth out of the land of Judah: ² and (the Levites are) they who joined them. And the sons of Zadok are the elect of Israel called by ³ the name, that are holding office in the end of the days. Behold the statement of their names according to their generations, and the period of their office, and the number of their afflictions, and the years of their sojournings, and the statement of their works. ⁴ The **first saints** whom God pardoned, Both justified the righteous, and condemned the wicked. ⁵ And all they who come after them must do according to the interpretation of the Law, In which the forefathers were instructed until the consummation of the period of these years. ⁶ In

accordance with the covenant which God established with the forefathers in order to pardon their sins, so shall God make atonement for them. [7] And on the consummation of the period [of the number] of these years they shall no more join themselves to the house of Judah. But shall every one stand up against his net. [8] The wall shall have been built, the boundary been far removed. [9] And during all these years Belial shall be let loose against Israel, as God spake through Isaiah the prophet, the son of Amos, saying: 'Fear and the pit and the snare are upon thee, O inhabitant of the land.' [10] This means the three nets of Belial, concerning which Levi the son of Jacob spake, by which he caught Israel and directed their faces to three kinds of righteousness. [11] The first is fornication, the second is the wealth (of wickedness), the third is the pollution of the Sanctuary. [12] He that cometh up from this shall be caught by that, and he that escapeth from this shall be caught by that.

7

The Sin of Fornication. Divorce forbidden.

[1] The builders of the wall who walk after law-the law it is which talks, of which He said: Assuredly they shall talk-are caught [by two] by fornication in taking two wives during their lifetime. [2],[3] But the fundamental principle of the creation 'Male and Female created He them.' [4] And they who went into the Ark, 'Two and two went into the Ark.' And as to the prince it is written, [5] 'He shall not multiply wives unto himself.' But David read not in the Book of the Law that was sealed, which was in the Ark; for it was not opened in Israel from the day of the death of Eleazar and [6] Joshua, and the Elders who served Ashtaroth. And it was hidden (and was not) discovered until [7] Zadok arose: Now they glorified the deeds of David save only the blood of Uriah, and God abandoned them to him.

The Sin of polluting the Sanctuary.

[8] And they also pollute the Sanctuary since they separate not according to the Law, and lie with [9] her who sees the blood of her issue. And they take (to wife) each his brother's daughter or his [10] sister's daughter. But Moses said 'Thou shalt not approach thy mother's sister: she is thy is mother's near kin'. So the law of intercourse for males is written, and the same law holds for females; and let not the daughter of the brother uncover the nakedness of the brother of her father: he is near of kin. [12] They also polluted their holy spirit and with a tongue of blasphemies they opened the mouth [13] against the statutes of the covenant of God, saying: They are not established. But abominations they speak regarding them. [14] They are all 'kindlers of fire and setters aflame of firebrands': [15] 'The webs of spiders' are their weavings and 'the eggs of cockatrices' are their eggs: [16] He who comes near them shall not be innocent: **He that chooseth them** shall be held guilty [unless he was forced]. [17] Aforetime God visited their works, and His wrath was kindled because of their devices. [18] For 'it is a people of no understanding': 'They are a nation void of counsel,' (Because there is no understanding in them). [19] For aforetime arose Moses and Aaron through the prince of the Lights. But Belial raised Jochanneh and his brother with his evil device when the former delivered Israel.

8

When the Land was laid desolate God would raise up wise men who would restudy the Law and go in Exile to Damascus, 1-5; and according to its Precepts the repentant ones should walk till the Teacher of Righteousness arose (i.e. after 176 B.C.), 7-10.

[1] And during the period of the destruction of the land there arose those who removed the landmark [2] and led Israel astray. And the land became desolate because they spake rebellion against the commandments of God through Moses [and also through His holy anointed one], and they prophesied a lie to turn away Israel from God. [3] But God remembered the covenant with the forefathers: And He raised up from Aaron men of understanding. And from Israel wise men [4] And He made them to hearken, And they digged the well [5] 'A well the princes digged, The nobles of the people delved it By the order of the Lawgiver.' [6] The well is the Law, and they who digged it are the penitents of Israel who went forth out of the land of Judah and sojourned in the land of Damascus, all of whom God called princes. [7],[8] For they sought Him and **His glory** was not turned back in the mouth of one (of them). And the Lawgiver is he who studies the Law, in regard to whom Isaiah said,' He bringeth forth an instrument for his work.' And the nobles of the people are those who came to dig the well by the precepts in the which the Lawgiver ordained that they should walk throughout the full period of the **wickedness**. [10] And save them they shall get nothing until there arises the Teacher of Righteousness in the end of the days. *Conditions under which they can act as Priests* in *the Sanctuary.* [11] And none who **have** entered into the covenant shall enter into the Sanctuary to kindle His altar but they shall shut the doors concerning whom God said, [10] that there was one among you to shut the **doors**, So that ye might not vainly kindle the tire upon My altar,' [12] Unless they observe to do according to the true meaning of the Law until the period of the wickedness, and to sever themselves from the children of the pit, and to hold aloof from the polluted wealth of wickedness under a vow and a curse, and **from** the wealth of the Sanctuary: [13] And in respect to robbing the pool of His people, So that widows may be their spoil. And they may murder the fatherless: [14] And to make a difference between the clean and the unclean and to make men discern between, the holy and the profane: [15] And to observe the Sabbath according to its true meaning and the feasts and the day of the Fast according to the utterances of them who entered into the New Covenant in the land of Damascus: [16] To contribute their holy things according to the true interpretation: [17] To love every one his brother as himself, and to strengthen the hand of the poor and the needy and the stranger, and to seek every one the peace of his brother [18] To hold aloof from harlots according to the law: and that no man should commit a trespass against his next of kin: [19] To rebuke every one his brother according to the commandment, and not to bear a grudge from day to day, and to separate from all the pollutions according to their judgments [20] And no man shall make abominable (with these) his holy spirit, according as God separated (these) from them. [21] As for all those who walk in these things in the perfection of holiness according to all the ordinances, the covenant of God

9

A	B
Standeth fast unto them to preserve them to a thousand generations	Standeth fast unto them to preserve them for thousand s of generations. As it is written. 'Who keepeth covenant and mercy with them that love Him and keep His commandments to a thousand generations.

The Law as to binding and loosing

A	B
[1] And if they settle in camps according to the order of the land and take wives and beget children, they shall walk according to the Law, and according to the judgments of the ordinances according to the order of the Law as He spake, 'between a man and his wife, and between a father and his son'.	[1] And if they settle in camps according to the statues of the land which were from of old and take wives according to the custom of the Law and beget children, they shall walk according to the judgments of the ordinances according to the order of the Law as He spake, 'between a man and his wife, and between a father and his son.'

Threatened Judgment on those who rejected the Statues

A	B
[2] But as for all them that reject . . . when God will bring a visitation upon the land they shall be requited with the recompense of the wicked; when there shall come to pass the word which is written in the words of Isaiah the son of Amos [3] the prophet, who said : 'He will bring upon thee and upon thy people and upon thy father's house days that have (not) come from the day that Ephraim departed from Judah.'	[2] But as for all them that reject commandments and the statutes they shall be requited with the recompense of the wicked; when God will bring a visitation upon the land, when there shall come to pass the word which is written *by* the hand of Zechariah the prophet: '⁰ sword, awake against My shepherd and against the man that is My fellow, saith God; smite the shepherd and the sheep shall be scattered, and I will turn Mine hand against the little ones.'

Foundation of the Zadokite Party and its Expectations: the Law, the Prophets, and the Messiah.

[4] When the two houses of Israel separated, [Ephraim departed from Judah, and] all who proved faithless were delivered to the sword, and those who held fast escaped into the land of the North. [5] As He said, 'And I will cause to go into captivity Siccuth your King and Chiun your images, [6] (the star of your god which ye made for yourselves) beyond Damascus.' The books of the Law are the tabernacle of the King, as He said, 'And I will raise up the tabernacle of David that is [7] fallen.' The King is the congregation and Chiun the images are the books of the Prophets, whose [8] words Israel has despised. And the Star is he who studied the Law, who came to Damascus, as it is

written, 'There shall come forth a star out of Jacob, and a sceptre shall rise out of Israel.' The [9] scepter is the prince of all the congregation.

The Messiah will destroy those who were faithless to the New Covenant: their moral Derelictions through Hellenizing Influences.

A	B
And when 'he shall destroy all the sons of (battle) din'....These **shall** escape during the period of the (first) visitation, but those who proved faithless shall be delivered to the sword. [11] [Lost] [12] And this also shall be the judgment of all them who have entered into His covenant, who will not hold fast to these (statues): they shall be visited for destruction through the hand [13] of Belial. This is the day on which God shall visit (as He hath spoken)"' The princes of Judah were (like them that removed the landmark): Upon them **will I** pour out (My) wrath (like water).' [14] For they are too sick **to be healed** And they **have been at the head of** all the rebels. [15] Because they have not turned from the way or traitors, But have wallowed in the ways of harlots, And in the wealth of wickedness and (in) revenge. [16] And every man beareth a grudge against his Brother, And every man hateth his neighbor. [17] And the **committed trespass** every man against his next of kin. And drew near to unchastity: And exalted themselves with a view to wealth and unjust gain And every man did that which was right in his own eyes [18] And they chose every man the stubbornness of his heart, And they separated not from the people. [19] And they cast off restraint with a high hand To walk in the way of the wicked, concerning whom God said: 'Their wine is the poison of dragons And the cruel venom of asps'. [20] The dragons are the kings of the Gentiles and their wine is their ways, and the venom of asps is the head of the kings of Javan, who came to execute vengeance upon them.	[10] And they that give heed unto Him are the poor of the flock'. These shall escape during the period of the visitation, but the rest shall be handed over to the sword when the Messiah comes from Aaron and Israel: [11] Just as it was during the period of the first visitation, concerning which He spake through Ezekiel' to set a mark upon the foreheads of them that sigh and cry', but the rest were delivered to 'the sword that avengeth with the vengeance of the covenant'. [12] And this also shall be the judgment of all them that have entered into His covenant, who will not hold fast to these statutes: they shall be visited for destruction through the hand of belial. [13] This is the day on which God shall visit, as He hath spoken; The princes of Judah were like them that remove the landmark: Upon them will I pour out (My) wrath like water.' [15] Because they entered into the covenant of repentance and yet have not turned from the way of traitors: But have dealt wantonly in the ways of fornication, In the wealth of wickedness and in revenge. [16] And every man beareth a grudge against his brother, And every man hateth his neighbor [17] And they **committed trespass** every man against his next of kin, And drew near to unchastity: And they made themselves strong with a view to wealth and unjust gain, And every man did that which was right in his own eyes [18] And they chose every man the stubborness of his heart, And they separated not from the people and their sins. [19]And they cast off restraint with a high hand To walk in the ways of the wicked; concerning whom God said: 'Their wine is the poison of dragons and the cruel venom of asps.' [20] The dragons are the kings of the Gentiles and their wine is their ways, and the venom of asps is the head of the kings of Javen, who came to execute vengeance upon them.

Neither to these things nor to Moses did the Builders of the Wall give heed.

A	B
[21] But despite all these things they who built the wall and daubed it with untempered mortar percieved not- [22] For one who was perturbed of spirit and talked lies talked to them- that the wrath of God was kindled against all His congregation: [23] Nor that Moses	[21] But despite all these things they who built the wall and daubed it with untempered mortar perceived not- [22] For one who walked in wind and weighed storms, and talked lies to man (talked)-. That the wrath of God was kindled against all His congregation: [23] Nor Moses said to

said, 'Not for they righteousness or for the uprightness of thine heart dost thou go in to inherit these nations, but because He loved they fathes and because He would keep the oath.' | Israel,'Not for thy righteousness nor for the uprightness of thine heart dost thou go into inherit these nations, but because He loved they fathers and because He would keep the oath.

The Penitents like the Forefathers were loved of God for their Faithfulness to the Covenant, but as He judged the Builders of the Wall, so shall those faithless to the New Covenant be judged

A	B
[24] And such is the case of the penitents of Israel (who) turned aside from the way of the people. [25] Owing to the love of God for the forefathers who stirred up (the people to follow after Him, He loved them that came after them; for theirs is the covenant of the fathers. But since He hated the builders of the wall His wrath was kindled. [27] And such (will be) the case of all who reject the commandments of God, and forsake them and turn away in the stubbornness of their heart.	[24] Such is the case of the penitents of Israel (who) turned aside the way of the people. [25] Owing to the love of God for the forefathers who admonished the people (to follow) after God, He loved them that came after them, for theirs is the covenant of the fathers. [26] But God hates and abhors the builders of the wall and His wrath was kindled against them and against all who follow after them. [27] And such (will be) the case of all who reject the commandments of God, and forsake them and turn away in the stubbornness of their heart.

Excommunication of those who fall away from the New Covenant.

[28] This is the word which Jeremiah spake to Baruch the son of Neriah, and Elisha to his servant Gehazi. All the men who entered into the New Covenant in the land of Damascus. | [28] So are all the men who entered into the New Covenant in the land of Damascus and yet turned backward and acted treacherously and departed from the spring of living waters.

B

[29] They shall not be reckoned in the assembly of the people, and in its register they shall not be written, from the day when there was gathered in the Unique Teacher until there shall arise the Messiah from Aaron and from Israel. [30] And such is the case for all that enter into the congregation of the men of the perfection of holiness. [31] And **as for him** who abhors doing precepts of upright men [he is the man who is melted in the furnace], when his deeds **become known** he shalt be expelled from the congregation, as though his lot had not fallen among them that are taught of God. [32] According to his trespass they shall record him as a perverted man until he come back to stand in the office of the men of the perfection of holiness. [33] And when his deeds **become known** in accordance with the midrash of the Law in which walk the men of the perfection of holiness, no man shall consent (to be) with him in wealth and labor; for all the saints of the Most High have cursed him. [34] And such shall be the case of every one who rejects the first and the last, who have placed idols upon their hearts and walked in the stubbornness of their hearts. [35] They have no share in the House of the Law. [36] With a judgment like unto that of their neighbors who turned away with the scornful men, they shall be judged. [37] For they spake error against the statutes of righteousness, and rejected the covenant and the pledge of faith, which they had affirmed in the land of Damascus; and this is the New Covenant. [38] And there shall not be unto them nor unto their families a share in the House of the Law. [39]And from the day when there was gathered in the Unique Teacher until all the men of war were consumed who walked with the man of lies about forty years, [40] [And during this period there shall be kindled the wrath of God against Israel as He said, 'there is no king and no prince' and no judge, and none that rebuketh in righteousness.] [41] Those who repented of transgression (in Jacob) observed the covenant of God. [42] Then they spake each man with his neighbor (to strengthen one) another 'Let **our** steps hold fast to the way of God.' [43] And God hearkened to their words and heard, and a book of remembrance was written (before Him) for them that feared God (and) that thought upon His name until salvation and righteousness be revealed for (them that fear God. [44] Then shall ye return and discern) between the righteous and wicked, between him that serveth God and him that serveth Him not. [45] And He showeth mercy (unto thousands) of them that **love Him** and keep (His commandments) for a thousand generations. [46] From

the house of Peleg that have gone out from the holy city. ⁴⁷ And they trusted in God throughout the period that Israel trespassed and polluted the Sanctuary and returned again to molten images. ⁴⁸ The people with **few** words shall **all** be judged, each according to his spirit in the counsel of holiness. ⁴⁹ And as for all those who have broken down the landmark of the Law amongst those who entered into the covenant, when there shall shine forth the glory of God to Israel, they shall be cut off from the midst of the camp, and with all those who do wickedly of Judah in the days of its testing.

The faithful shall confess their sins and be forgiven and blessed.

⁵⁰ But all they who hold fast by these judgments in going out and coming in according to the Law, and listen to the voice of the Teacher and confess before God (saying) ⁵¹ 'We have done wickedly, we and our fathers, Because **we** have walked contrary to the statutes of the covenant, And true is thy judgment against us:' ⁵² And (who) lift not the hand against His holy statutes, His righteous judgment, and the testimony of His truth; ⁵³ and are chastised by the first judgments with which the children of men were judged: and give ear to the voice of the Unique Teacher of Righteousness: and reject not the statutes of righteousness when they hear them ⁵³ They shall rejoice and be glad, And their heart shall **exult,** And they shall make themselves strong against all the children of the world, And God will pardon them And they shall see His salvation; For they trust in His holy name.

10
A man is not to avenge himself or bear a Grudge.

¹ Every man who puts under the ban a man [amongst men] according to the ordinances of the Gentiles is to be put to death:² And as for that which He hath said: 'Thou shalt not take vengeance nor bear a grudge against the children of thy people,' every man of those who have entered into the covenant, who brings a charge against his neighbor whom he had not **rebuked** before witnesses, and yet brings it in his fierce wrath or recounts (it) to his elders in order to bring him into contempt, is taking vengeance and bearing a grudge. ³ But naught is written save that, 'He taketh vengeance on His adversaries, and He beareth a grudge against His enemies.' ⁴ If he held his peace with regard to him from day to day, but in his fierce wrath spake against him in a matter of death, he hath testified against himself because he did not give effect to the commandment of God, Who said to him, ⁵ 'Thou shalt surely rebuke thy neighbor and not bear sin because of him.' ⁶ As regards the oath, touching that which He said 'Thou shalt not avenge thee with thine own hand', the man who makes (another man) swear in the open field-that is, not in the presence of the judges, or owing to their commands-hath avenged himself with his own hand.

The law as to lost property.

⁷ And as for anything that is lost, should it not be known who has stolen it from the property of the camp in which the thing has been stolen, its owner shall **proclaim** (it) by the oath of cursing and whoso hears, if he knows and declares it not, shall be held guilty. ⁸ As for any restitution made by **him who returns** that which has [not] an owner, **he who returns (it)** shall confess to the priest, and (that which was lost) shall be **given back** to him, besides the ram of the guilt-offering **to the priest**; and so everything (that was) lost (and) found and has no owner shall **be given** to the priests for he who found it knows not its law. If its owner is not found they shall take charge (of it).

The Number of witnesses necessary in the case of Capital and other Offenses. The character of the Witnesses.

¹⁰ If a man in any matter trespasses against the Law and his neighbor and none but he sees it, if it be a matter of death, he shall make it known to the Censor in the presence of the accused in discharging the duty of reproof: and the Censor shall write it down with his own hand: ¹¹ If he do it again before **another**, he shall return and make it known to the Censor. ¹² If he shall be caught again before **another**, his judgment shall be executed. ¹³ And if they are two and they witness against him (each) on a different thing the man shall be only excluded from the Purity, provided that they are trustworthy, and that on the day on which they have seen the man they make it known to the Censor. ¹⁴ And according to the statute (they shall) accept two **trustworthy** witnesses, and not one to exclude the Purity. ¹⁵ And there shall arise no **witness** before the judges to cause a man to be put to death at his mouth, whose days have not been fulfilled so as to pass over unto those that are numbered (and who is not) a man who fears God. ¹⁶None shall be believed as a witness against his neighbor who transgresses a word of the commandment with a high hand until they are cleansed through repentance.

11
Regulations as to the Judges of the Zadokite Party.

¹ And this is the order in reference to the judges of the congregation. ² (They shall amount) to ten men selected from the congregation according to the time (defined); four of the tribe of Levi and Aaron, and six of Israel learned in the Book of the Hagu and in the Ordinances of the Covenant, from five and twenty years old even unto sixty years old. ³ But none shall be appointed when he is sixty years old and upward to judge the congregation. ⁴ For through the trespasses of man his days were minished, and when the wrath of God was kindled against the inhabitants of the earth, He commanded their intelligence to depart from them before they completed their days.

12
Levitical Law as to Bathing.

¹ As to being cleansed in water. No man shall wash in water (that is) filthy or insufficient for a man's **bath**. ² None shall cleanse himself in the waters of a vessel. And every pool in a rock in which there is not sufficient (water) for a **bath**, which an unclean person has touched, its waters shall be unclean like the waters of the vessel.

13
Laws regarding the Sabbath.

¹ As to the Sabbath, to observe it according to its law, no man shall do work on the sixth day from the time when the sun's orb in its fullness is still without the gate, for it is He who has said, 'Observe the Sabbath day to keep it holy.' ² And on the Sabbath day no man shall utter a word of folly and vanity. ³ No man shall lend aught, to his neighbor. ⁴ None shall dispute on matters of wealth and gain. ⁵ None shall speak on matters of work and labor to be done on the following morning. ⁶ No man shall walk in the field to do the work of his business. ⁷ On the Sabbath none shall walk outside his city more than a thousand cubits. ⁸ No man shall eat on the Sabbath day aught save that which is prepared or perishing (in the field). ⁹ Nor shall one eat or drink unless in the camp. ¹⁰ (If he was) on the way and went down to wash he may drink where he stands, but he shall not draw into any vessel. ¹¹ No man shall send the son of a stranger to do his business on the Sabbath day.

Laws as to unclean Garments.

¹² No man shall put on garments that are filthy or were brought by a Gentile unless they were washed in water or rubbed with frankincense.

Laws regarding the Sabbath.

¹³ No man shall **fast** of his own will on the Sabbath. ¹⁴ No man shall walk after the animal to pasture it outside his city more than two thousand cubits. ¹⁵ None shall lift his hand to smite it with (his) fist. ¹⁶ If it be stubborn he shall not remove it out of his house. No man shall carry anything from the house to the outside or from the outside into the house, and if he be in the vestibule he shall not **carry** anything out of it or **bring** in anything into it. ¹⁷ None shall **open** the cover of a vessel that is pasted on the Sabbath. ¹⁸ No man shall carry on him spices to go out or come in on the Sabbath. ¹⁹ None shall lift up in his **dwelling** house rock or earth. ²⁰ Let not the nursing father take the sucking child to go out or to come in on the Sabbath. ²¹ No man shall provoke his manservant or his maid-servant or his hireling on the Sabbath. ²² No man shall help an animal in its delivery on the Sabbath day. ²³ And if it falls into a pit or ditch, he shall not raise it on the Sabbath. ²⁴ No man shall rest in a place near to the Gentiles on the Sabbath. ²⁵ No man shall suffer himself to be polluted [the Sabbath] for the sake of wealth or gain on the Sabbath. ²⁶ And if any person falls into a place of water or into a place of… he shall not bring him up by a ladder or a cord or instrument. ²⁷ No man shall offer anything on the altar on the Sabbath, save the burnt-offering of the Sabbath, for so it is written 'Excepting your Sabbaths'.

Levitical Laws as to Uncleanness.

14

¹ **No** man shall send to the altar burnt-offering or meat-offering or frankincense or wood through the hand of a man (that is) unclean through any of the uncleannesses allowing him to defile the altar, for it is written: 'The sacrifice of the wicked is an abomination, but the prayer of the righteous' is like an offering of delight.' ² And none of those who enter into the house of worship shall enter when he is unclean even though washed. ³ And when the trumpets of the Congregation sound, it shall he (done) before or after, and they shall not put an end to the whole service: (the Sabbath) is holy. ⁴ No man shall lie with a woman in the city of the Sanctuary to defile the city of the Sanctuary by their impurity.

Law as to Necromancy.

⁵ Any man who is ruled by the spirits of Belial and speaks rebellion shall be judged by the judgement of the necromancer and wizard.

Law as to the Sabbath.

⁶ And he whom he leads astray into profaning the Sabbath and the Feasts shall not be put to death; but it shall be the duty of the sons of man to watch

him; and should he be healed of it, they shall watch him seven years and then he shall come into the Congregation.

Laws as to Intercourse with the Gentiles.
⁷ None shall stretch out his hand to shed the blood of any man from among the Gentiles for the sake of wealth or gain. ⁸ Nor shall he take aught of their wealth lest they blaspheme, unless by the counsel of the Community of Israel. ⁹ No man shall sell an animal or bird that is clean to the Gentiles, lest they sacrifice them. ¹⁰ Nor shall he sell them aught from his threshing-floor or his winepress for all his property. ¹¹ Nor shall he sell them his manservant or maidservant who entered with him into the covenant of Abraham.

Laws as to unclean Foods and Causes of Uncleanness.
¹² No man shall make himself abominable with any living creature or creeping thing, by eating of them: **or of the defilements** of bees or of any living creature that moveth in the waters. ¹³ Nor shall fish be eaten unless they were split alive and their blood was shed. ¹⁴ But all the locusts after their kind shall come into fire or into water whilst they are still living, for this is the manner of their creation. ¹⁵ And all wood and stones and dust which are polluted by the uncleanness of man are **polluted like them**. ¹⁶ According to their uncleanness shall be unclean he who toucheth them. And every instrument, nail, or peg in the wall which is with the dead in the house shall be unclean, **like** the uncleanness of an instrument of work.

15
Summary Reference to Laws of Uncleanness.
The regulation of the dwellers in the cities of Israel, according to these judgments, that a difference may be made between the unclean and the clean, and to make known (the difference) between the holy and the common. ² And these statutes are to give instruction so that the whole nation may walk in them according to the Law always. ³ And according to this law shall walk the seed of Israel, and they shall not be cursed.

The Ruler to be a Priest or a Levite.
⁴ And this is the regulation of the dwellers (according to which they should) act during the period of the wickedness until there arises the Messiah (from) Aaron and Israel, up to ten men at least, to thousands and hundreds and fifties and tens. ⁵ And when there arise ten, the man who is a priest learned in the Book of the Hagu shall not depart. According to his word shall they all be ruled. ⁶ And if he is not expert in all these, but a man of the Levites is expert in these, the lot shall be that all those that enter into the camp shall go out and come in according to his word.

Law as to Leprosy.
⁷ And if there be a judgment regarding the law of leprosy which is in a man, then the priest shall come and stand in the camp, and the Censor shall instruct him in the true meaning of the law. ⁸ And (even) if he is lacking in understanding He shall shut him up; for unto them (i.e. the priests) is the judgment.

16
The Duties of the Censor.
¹ And this is the regulation of the Censor of the camp. He shall instruct the many in the works of God, and shall make them understand His wondrous mighty acts, and shall narrate before them the things of the world **since its creation**. ² And he shall have mercy upon them as a father upon his children, and shall for(give) **all that have incurred guilt**. ³ As a shepherd with his flock he shall loose all the bonds of their knots…oppressed and crushed in his congregation. And every one who joins his congregation, he shall reckon him according to his works, his understanding, his might, his strength, and his wealth. ⁵ And they shall record him in his place in accordance with his **position** in a lot of the (camp). ⁶ No man of the children of the camp shall have power to bring a man into the congregation (without) the word of the Censor of the camp. ⁷ Nor shall any man of them who have entered into the covenant of God do business (with) the children of **the pit** (un)less hand to hand. ⁸ No man shall do (a thing as buy)ing and sell(ing) un(less he has spoken) to the Censor of the camp, and he shall do (it in the ca)mp and not… and so to him who casts forth…they, and he who is not connected with…⁹ And this is the settlement of the camps. ¹⁰ All shall not succeed to settle in the land…¹¹ that have not come from the day that Ephraim departed from Judah. ¹²And as for all who walk in these the covenant of God standeth fast unto them to save them from all the snares of the pit, for suddenly….

17
The Four Orders of the Community.
¹ And the regulation of the dwellers of all the camps is: ² They shall be numbered all by their names, the Priests first, the Levites second, the children of Israel third, and the proselyte fourth. ³ And they shall be recorded by their names one after another, the Priests *first*, the Levites second, the children of Israel third, and the proselyte fourth. ⁴ And so they shall be seated and so they shall ask with regard to every matter. ⁵ And the Priest who numbers the many (shall be) from thirty years old even unto sixty years old, learned in the Book (of the Hagu and) in all the judgements of the Law to direct them according to their judgments.

Duties of the Censor.
⁶ And the Censor who is over all the camps shall be from thirty years old even unto fifty years old, a **master** in every counsel of men, and in every tongue… ⁷ According to his word shall come in those who enter the congregation every man in his due order. ⁸ And as regards any matter on which it shall be incumbent for any man to speak, he shall speak to the Censor in regard to any suit or cause.

18
Almsgiving.
¹ And this is the regulation for the many in order to provide for all their needs. ² The wages of two days every month is the rule. And they shall give it into the hands of the Censor and the judges. ³ From it they shall give…and (from) it they shall strengthen the hand of the poor and the needy. ⁴ And to the aged man who…to the vagrant and him (who) was taken captive of a strange people. ⁵ And to the virgin who has (no dot) (and to Him whom) no man careth for: every work… and not… ⁶ And this is the explanation of the settlement… ⁷ And this is the explanation of the judgments which…⁸ (The Messiah from) Aaron and Israel. ⁹ And He will pardon our sins…in money and he shall know…punishment six days and who shall speak…¹⁰ against Mos(es)

19
Laws as to Oaths.
¹ …(Shall not swe)ar either by Aleph Lamed or by Aleph Daleth, but by the oath (written) in the curses of the covenant. ².But the Law of Moses he shall not mention, for…³ And if he swears and transgresses he profanes the Name. ⁴ And if by the curses of the covenant…the Judges. ⁵ And if he transgress he shall be held guilty but if he confess and make restitution he shall not bear (the penalty) of death. ⁶ And whosoever in all Israel shall enter into the covenant by a statute forever, together with their children who are (not of an age) to pass over into the number of those who are enrolled by the oath of the covenant, shall confirm it on their behalf. ⁷ And this is also the law throughout the entire period of the wickedness for every one who returns from his corrupt way. ⁸ On the day when he speaks with the Censor of the many they shall enrol him by the oath of the covenant that Moses established with Israel-¹⁰ the covenant to re(turn to the Law of M)oses…with all (his) heart…(and with all his) soul: as regards that which there is found to be done by them… ¹⁰ And no man shall make known to him the laws until he stand before the Censor (who) shall **search out** concerning him when he examines him. ¹¹ And when he imposes it upon him to return to the Law of Moses with all his heart and all his soul …of him if… ¹² And every thing that was revealed of the Law with regard to a suit… in him…the Censor him and shall command him…until…killed him…and the madman and all…*(loss of five lines)* ¹³ covenant with you and with the whole of Israel. ¹⁴ Therefore the man shall impose it upon himself to return to the Law of Moses; for in it everything is accurately treated.

20
Reference to the Book of Jubilees.
¹ And as for the exact statement of their periods to **put** Israel **in remembrance in regard to** all these, behold, it is treated accurately in the Book of the Divisions of the Seasons according to their Jubilees and their Weeks.

Laws as to Oaths and Vows.
² And on the day on which the man imposes it upon himself to return to the law of Moses the angel of Mastema will depart from him if he make good his word. ³ Therefore Abraham was circumcised on the day of his knowing it. ⁴ As to what he said, 'That which is gone forth from thy lips thou shalt keep' to make it good- ⁵ No binding oath, which a man imposes upon himself with a view to perform a commandment of the law, shall he **cancel** even at the risk of death. ⁶ Nothing which a man (imposes) upon himself with a view to (frustrate the la)w shall he make good even at the risk of death. ⁷ (As for) the oath of the woman, whose oath Mos(es sa)id should be disallowed, no man shall disa¹low an oath which no man knew. ⁸ It is to be confirmed. And whether it be to disallow or to transgress the covenant, he shall disallow it and not confirm it. ⁹ And so is also the law for her father. As to the law of the of(fer)ings no man shall vow anything for the altar under compulsion. ¹⁰ Nor shall the (pr)iests take anything from the Israelites… ¹¹ (Nor) shall a man dedicate the food…this is what he said, 'They hunt every man his brother with a net.' ¹² Nor shall de(vote)…of

all…his possession…holy…shall be punished he…who takes a vow… to the judge…

The Letter of Aristeas
1

At the time of the Jewish Captivity in Egypt, Ptolemy Philadelphus reveals himself as the first great bibliophile. He desires to have all the books in the world in his library; in order to get the Laws of Moses he offers to trade 100,000 captives for that work exclaiming, "It is a small boon indeed!"

[1] SINCE I have collected *material* for a memorable history of my visit to Eleazar the High Priest of the Jews, and because you, Philocrates, as you lose no opportunity of reminding me, have set great store upon receiving an account of the motives and object of my mission, I have attempted to draw up clear exposition of the matter for you, for I perceive that you possess a natural love of learning, a *quality* which is the highest possession of man–to be constantly attempting 'to add to his stock of knowledge and acquirements' whether through the study of history or by actually participating in the events themselves. [2] It is by this means, by taking up into itself the noblest elements, that the soul is established in purity, and having fixed its aim on piety, the noblest goal of all, it uses this as its infallible guide and so acquires a definite purpose. [3] It was my devotion to the pursuit of religious knowledge that led me to undertake the embassy to the man I have mentioned, who was held in the highest esteem by his own citizens and by others, both for his virtue and his majesty, and who had in his possession documents of the highest value to the Jews in his own country and in foreign lands for the interpretation of the divine law, for their laws are written on leather parchments in Jewish characters. [4] This embassy then I undertook with enthusiasm, having first of all found an opportunity of pleading with the king on behalf of the Jewish captives who had been transported from Judea to Egypt by the king's father, when he first obtained possession of this city and conquered the land of Egypt. [5] It is worth while that I should tell you this story, too, since I am convinced that you, with your disposition towards holiness and your sympathy with men who are living in accordance with the holy law, will all the more readily listen to the account which I purpose to set forth, since you yourself have lately come to us from the island and are anxious to hear everything that tends to build up the soul. [6] On a former occasion too, I sent you a record of the facts which I thought worth relating about the Jewish race,–the record which I had obtained from the most learned high priests of the most learned land of Egypt. [7] As you are so eager to acquire the knowledge of those things which can benefit the mind, I' feel it incumbent upon me to impart to you *all the information in my power*. [8] *I should feel the same duty* towards all who possessed the same disposition but I feel it especially towards you since you have aspirations which are so noble, and since you are not only my brother in character, no less than in blood, but are one with me as well in the pursuit of goodness. [9] For neither the pleasure derived from gold nor any other of the possessions which are prized by shallow minds confers the same benefit as the pursuit of culture and the study which we expend in securing it. [10] But that I may not weary you by a too lengthy introduction, I will proceed at once to the substance of my narrative. [11] Demetrius of Phalerum, the president of the king's library, received vast sum of money, for the purpose of collecting together, as far as he possibly could, all the books in the world. [12] By means of purchase and transcription, he carried out, to the best of his ability, the purpose of the king. [13] On one occasion when I was present he was asked, How many thousand books are there *in the library*? and he replied, 'More than two hundred thousand, O king, and I shall make endeavour in the immediate future *to gather together* the remainder also, so that the total of five hundred thousand may be reached. I am told that the laws of the Jews are worth transcribing and deserve a place in your library! [14] 'What is to prevent you from doing this?' replied the king. 'Everything that is necessary has been placed at your disposal! [15] 'They need to be translated,' answered Demetrius 'for in the country of the Jews they use a peculiar alphabet (just as the Egyptians, too, have a special form of letters) and speak a peculiar dialect. [16] They are supposed to use the Syriac tongue, but this is not the case; their language is quite different.' [17] And the king when he understood all the facts of the case ordered a letter to be written to the Jewish High Priest that his purpose (which has already been described) might be accomplished. [18] Thinking that the time had come to press the demand, which I had often laid before Sosibius of Tarentum and Andreas, the chief of the bodyguard, for the emancipation of the Jews who had been transported from Judea by the king's father–for when by a combination of good fortune and courage he had brought his attack on the whole district of Coele-Syria and Phoenicia to a successful issue, in the process of terrorising the country into subjection, he transported some of his foes and others he reduced to captivity. [19] The number of those whom he transported from the country of the Jews to Egypt amounted to no less than a hundred thousand. [20] Of these he armed thirty thousand picked men and settled them in garrisons in the country districts. [21] (And even before

this time large numbers of Jews had come into Egypt with the Persian, and in an earlier period still others had been sent *to Egypt* to help Psammetichus in his campaign against the king of the Ethiopians. But these were nothing like so numerous as the captives whom Ptolemy the son of Lagus transported.) [22] As I have already said Ptolemy picked out the best of these, the men who were in the prime of life and distinguished for their courage, and armed them, but the great mass of the others, those who were too old or too young for this purpose, and the women too, he reduced to slavery, not that he wished to do this of his own free will, but he was compelled by his soldiers who claimed them as a reward for the services which they had rendered in war. [23] Having, as has already been stated, obtained an opportunity for securing their emancipation, I addressed the king with the following arguments. 'Let us not be so unreasonable as to allow our deeds to give the lie to our words. [24] Since the law which we wish not only to transcribe but also to translate belongs to the whole Jewish race, what justification shall we be able to find for our embassy while such vast numbers of them remain in a state of slavery in your kingdom? [25] In the perfection and wealth of your clemency release those who are held in such miserable bondage, since as I have been at pains to discover, the God who gave them their law is the God who maintains your kingdom. [26] They worship the same God–the Lord and Creator of the Universe, as all other men, as we ourselves, O king, though we call him by different names, such as Zeus or Dis. [27] This name was very appropriately bestowed upon him by our first ancestors, in order to signify that He, through whom all things are endowed with life and come into being, is necessarily the Rider and Lord of the Universe. [28] Set all mankind an example of magnanimity by releasing those who are held in bondage.' [29] After a brief interval, while I was offering up an earnest prayer to God that He would so dispose the mind of the king that all the captives might be set at liberty–(for the human race, being the creation of God, is swayed and influenced by Him. [30] Therefore with many divers prayers I called upon Him who ruleth the heart that *the king* might be constrained to grant my request. [31] For I had great hopes with regard to the salvation of the men since I was assured that God would grant a fulfilment of my prayer. [32] For when men from pure motives plan some action in the interest of righteousness and the performance of noble deeds, Almighty God brings their efforts and purposes to a successful issue)–*the king* raised his head and looking up at me with a cheerful countenance asked, 'How many thousands do you think they will number?' [33] Andreas, who was standing near, replied, 'A little more than a hundred thousand.' [34] 'It is a small boon indeed,' said the king, 'that Aristeas asks of us!' [35] Then Sosibius and some others who were present said 'Yes, but it will be a fit tribute to your magnanimity for you to offer the enfranchisement of these men as an act of devotion to the supreme God. [36] You have been greatly honoured by Almighty God and exalted above all your forefathers in glory and it is only fitting that you should render to Him the greatest thank-offering in your power.' [37] Extremely pleased *with these arguments* he gave orders that an addition should be made to the wages *of the soldiers by the amount of the redemption money*, that twenty drachmae should be paid *to the owners* for every slave, that a public order should be issued and that registers of the captives should be attached to it. [38] He showed the greatest enthusiasm in the business, for it was God who had brought our purpose to fulfilment in its entirety and constrained him to redeem not only those who had come into Egypt with the army of his father but any who had come before that time or had been subsequently brought into the kingdom. [39] It was pointed out to him that the ransom money would exceed four hundred talents. [40] I think it will be useful to insert a copy of the decree, for in this way the magnanimity of the king, who was empowered by God to save such vast multitudes, will be made clearer and more manifest. [41] The decree of the king ran as follows: 'All who served in the army of our father in the campaign against Syria and Phoenicia and in the attack upon the country of the Jews and became possessed of Jewish captives and brought them back to the city of *Alexandria* and the land *of Egypt* or sold them to others–and in the same way any captives who were in our land before that time or were brought hither afterwards–all who possess such captives are required to set them at liberty at once, receiving twenty drachmae per head as ransom money. [42] The soldiers will receive this money as a gift added to their wages, the others from the king's treasury. [43] We think that it was against our father's will and against all propriety that they should have been made captives and that the devastation of their land and the transportation of the Jews to Egypt was an act of military wantonness. [44] The spoil which fell to the soldiers on the field *of battle* was all the booty which they should have claimed. [45] To reduce the people to slavery in addition was an act of absolute injustice. [46] Wherefore, since it is acknowledged that we are accustomed to render justice to all men and especially to those who are unfairly in a condition of servitude, and since we strive to deal fairly with all men according to the demands of justice and piety, we have decreed, in reference to the persons of the Jews who are in any condition of bondage in any part of our dominion, that those who possess them shall receive the stipulated sum of money and set them at liberty and that no man shall show any tardiness in discharging his obligations. [47] Within three days after the publication of this decree, they must make lists *of slaves* for the officers appointed to carry out our will, and immediately produce the persons *of the captives*. [48] For we consider that it will be advantageous to us and to our affairs that the matter should be brought to a conclusion. [49] Any one who likes may give information about any who disobey the decree, on condition that if the man is proved guilty he will become his slave; his property, however, will be handed over to the royal treasury.' [50] When the decree was brought to be read over to the king for his approval, it contained all the other provisions except the phrase 'any captives who were in the land before that time or were brought hither afterwards,' and in his magnanimity and the largeness of his heart the king inserted this clause and gave orders that the grant of money required for the redemption should be deposited in full with the paymasters of the forces and the royal bankers, and so the matter was decided and the decree ratified within seven days. [51] The grant for the redemption amounted to more than six hundred and sixty talents; for many infants at the breast were emancipated together with their mothers. [52] When the question was raised whether the sum of twenty talents was to be paid for these, the king ordered that it should be done, and thus he carried out his decision in the most comprehensive way.

2

Showing how the most careful records were kept of affairs of state. Government Red Tape. A committee of six is appointed to go to the High Priest in Jerusalem and arrange for the exchange. Aristeas is put in charge of the delegation.

[1] WHEN this had been done, he ordered Demetrius to draw up a memorial with regard to the transcription of the Jewish books. [2] For all affairs of state used to be carried out by means of decrees and with the most pains-taking accuracy by these *Egyptian* kings, and nothing was done in a slipshod or haphazard fashion. [3] And so I have inserted copies of the memorial and the letters, the number of the presents sent and the nature of each, since every one of them excelled in magnificence and technical skill. [4] The following is a copy of the memorial. *The Memory* of Demetrius to the great king. 'Since you have given me instructions O king, that the books which are needed to complete your library should be collected together, and that those which are defective should be repaired, I have devoted myself with the utmost care to the fulfilment of your wishes, and I now have the following proposal to lay before you. [5] The books of the law of the Jews (with some few others) are absent *from the library*. [6] They are written in the Hebrew characters and language and have been carelessly interpreted, and do not represent the original text as I am informed by those who know; for they have never had a king's care to protect them. [7] It is necessary that these should be made accurate for your library since the law which they contain, inasmuch as it is of divine origin, is full of wisdom and free from all blemish. [8] For this reason literary men and poets and the mass of historical writers have held aloof from referring to these books and the men who have lived and are living in accordance with them, because their conception of life is so sacred and religious, as Hecataeus of Abdera says. [9] If it please you, O king, a letter shall be written to the High Priest in Jerusalem, asking him to send six elders out of every tribe–men who have lived the noblest life and are most skilled in their law–that we may find out the points in which the majority of them are in agreement, and so having obtained an accurate translation may place it in a conspicuous place in a manner worthy of the work itself and your purpose. [10] May continual prosperity be yours!' [11] When this memorial had been presented, the king ordered a letter to be written to Eleazar on the matter, giving also an account of the emancipation of the *Jewish* captives. [12] And he gave fifty talents weight of gold and seventy talents of silver and a large quantity of precious stones to make bowls and vials and a table and libation cups. [13] He also gave orders to those who had the custody of his coffers to allow the artificers to make a selection of any materials they might require for the purpose, and that a hundred talents in money should be sent to provide sacrifices for the temple and for other needs. [14] I shall give you a full account of the workmanship after I have set before you copies of the letters. The letter of the king ran as follows: [15] 'King Ptolemy sends greeting and salutation to the High Priest Eleazar. [16] Since there are many Jews settled in our realm who were carried off from Jerusalem by the Persians at the time of their power and many more who came with my father into Egypt as captives–large numbers of these he placed in the army and paid them higher wages than usual, and when he had proved the loyalty of their leaders he built fortresses and placed them in their charge that the native Egyptians might be intimidated by them. [17] And I, when I ascended the throne, adopted a kindly attitude

towards all my subjects, and more particularly to those who were citizens of yours–I have set at liberty more than a hundred thousand captives, paying their owners the appropriate market price for them, and if ever evil has been done to your people through the passions of the mob, I have made them reparation. [18] The motive which prompted my action has been the desire to act piously and render unto the supreme God a thank-offering for maintaining my kingdom in peace and great glory in all the world. [19] Moreover those of your people who were in the prime of life I have drafted into my army, and those who were fit to be attached to my person and worthy of the confidence of the court, I have established in official positions. [20] Now since I am anxious to show my gratitude to these men and to the Jews throughout the world and to the generations yet to come, I have determined that your law shall be translated from the Hebrew tongue which is in use amongst you into the Greek language, that these books may be added to the other royal books in my library. [21] It will be a kindness on your part and a reward for my zeal if you will select six elders from each of your tribes, men of noble life and skilled in your law and able to interpret it, that *in questions of dispute* we may be able to discover the verdict in which the majority agree, for the investigation is of the highest possible importance. [22] I hope to win great renown by the accomplishment of this work. [23] I have sent Andreas, the chief of my bodyguard and Aristeas–men whom I hold in high esteem–to lay the matter before you and present you with a hundred talents of silver, the first-fruits of my offering for the temple and the sacrifices and other religious rites. [24] If you will write to me concerning your wishes in these matters, you will confer a great favour upon me and afford me a *new* pledge of friendship, for all your wishes shall be carried out as speedily as possible. Farewell! [25] To this letter Eleazar replied appropriately as follows: 'Eleazar the High Priest sends greetings to King Ptolemy his true friend. [26] My highest wishes are for your welfare and the welfare of Queen Arsinoe, your sister, and your children. [27] I also am well. I have received your letter and am greatly rejoiced by your purpose and your noble counsel. [28] I summoned together the whole people and read it to them that they might know of your devotion to our God. [29] I showed them too the cups which you sent, twenty of gold and thirty of silver, the five bowls and the table of dedication, and the hundred talents of silver for the offering of the sacrifices and providing the things of which the temple stands in need. [30] These gifts were brought to me by Andreas, one of your most honoured servants, and by Aristeas, both good men and true, distinguished by their learning, and worthy in every way to be the representatives of your high principles and righteous purposes. [31] These men imparted to me your message and received from me an answer in agreement with your letter. I will consent to everything which is advantageous to you even though your request is very unusual. [32] For you have bestowed upon our citizens great and never to be forgotten benefits in many ways. [33] Immediately therefore I offered sacrifices on behalf of you, your sister, your children, and your friends, and all the people prayed that your plans might prosper continually, and that Almighty God might preserve your kingdom in peace with honour, and that the translation of the holy law might prove advantageous to you and be carried out successfully. [34] In the presence of all the people I selected six elders from each tribe, good men and true, and I have sent them to you with a copy of our law. [35] It will be a kindness, O righteous king, if you will give instruction that as soon as the translation of the law is completed, the men shall be restored again to us in safety. Farewell! [36] *The following* are the names *of the elders*: Of the first tribe, Joseph, Ezekiah, Zachariah, John, Ezekiah, Elisha. [37] Of the second tribe, Judas, Simon, Samuel, Adaeus, Mattathias, Eschlemias. [38] Of the third tribe, Nehemia, Joseph, Theodosius, Baseas, Ornias, Dakis. [39] Of the fourth tribe, Jonathan, Abraeus, Elisha, Ananias, Chabrias. . . . [40] Of the fifth tribe, Isaac, Jacob, Jesus, Sabbataeus, Simon, Levi. [41] Of the sixth tribe, Judas, Joseph, Simon, Zacharias, Samuel, Selemas. [42] Of the seventh tribe, Sabbataeus, Zedekiah, Jacob, Isaac, Jesias, Natthaeus. [43] Of the eighth tribe, Theodosius, Jason, Jesus, Theodotus, John, Jonathan. [44] Of the ninth tribe, Theophilus, Abraham, Arsamos, Jason, Endemias, Daniel. [45] Of the tenth tribe, Jeremiah, Eleazar, Zachariah, Baneas, Elisha, Dathaeus. [46] Of the eleventh tribe, Samuel, Joseph, Judas, Jonathes, Chabu, Dositheus. [47] Of the twelfth tribe, Isaelus, John, Theodosius, Arsamos, Abietes, Ezekiel. [48] They were seventy-two in all. Such was the answer which Eleazar and his friends gave to the king's letter.

3

In which is described the most exquisite and beautiful table ever produced. Also other rich gifts, Interesting in the light of recent excavations in Egypt.

[1] I WILL now Proceed to redeem my promise and give a description of the works of art. [2] They were wrought with exceptional skill, for the king spared no expense and personally superintended the workmen individually. [3] They could not therefore scamp any part of the work or finish it off negligently. [4] First of all I will give you a description of the table. [5] The king was anxious that this piece of work should be of exceptionally large dimensions, and he caused enquiries to be made of the Jews in the locality with regard to the size of the table already in the temple at Jerusalem. [6] And when they described the measurements, he proceeded to ask whether he might make a larger structure. [7] And some of the priests and the other Jews replied that there was nothing to prevent him. [8] And he said that he was anxious to make it five times the size, but he hesitated lest it should prove useless for the temple services. [9] He was desirous that his gift should not merely be stationed in the temple, for it would afford him much greater pleasure if the men whose duty it was to offer the fitting sacrifices were able to do so appropriately on the table which he had made. [10] He did not suppose that it was owing to lack of gold that the former table had been made of small size, but there seems to have been, he said, some reason why it was made of–this dimension. [11] For had the order been given, there would have been no lack of means. [12] Wherefore we must not transgress or go beyond the proper measure. [13] At the same time he ordered them to press into service all the manifold forms of art, for he was a man of the most lofty conceptions and nature had endowed him with a keen imagination which enabled him to picture the appearance which would be presented *by the finished work*. [14] He gave orders too, that where there were no instructions laid down in the *Jewish* Scriptures, everything should be made as beautiful as possible.– [15] When such instructions were laid down, they were to be carried out to the letter. [16] They made the table two cubits long, one cubit broad, one and a half cubits high fashioning it of pure solid gold. [17] What I am describing was not thin gold laid over another foundation, but the whole structure was of massive gold welded together. [18] And they made a border of a hand's breadth round about it. [19] And there was a wreath of wave-work, engraved in relief in the form of ropes marvellously wrought on its three sides. [20] For it was triangular in shape and the style of the work was exactly the same on each of the sides, so that whichever side they were turned, they presented the same appearance. [21] Of the two sides under the border, the one which sloped down to the table was a very beautiful piece of work, but it was the outer side which attracted the gaze of the spectator. [22] Now the upper edge of the two sides, being elevated, was sharp since, as we have said, *the rim* was three-sided, from whatever point of view one approached it. [23] And there were layers of precious stones on it in the midst of the embossed cord-work, and they were interwoven with one another by an inimitable artistic device. [24] For the sake of security they were all fixed by golden needles which were inserted in perforations *in the stones*. [25] At the sides they were clamped together by fastenings to hold them firm. [26] On the part of the border round the table which slanted upwards and met the eyes, there was wrought a pattern of eggs in precious stones, elaborately engraved by a continuous piece of fluted relief-work, closely connected together round the whole table. [27] And under the stones which had been arranged to represent eggs the artists made a crown containing all kinds of fruits, having at its top clusters of grapes and ears of corn, dates also and apples, and pomegranates and the like, conspicuously arranged. [28] These fruits were wrought out of precious stones, of the same colour as the fruits themselves and they fastened them edgeways round all the sides of the table with a band of gold. [29] And after the crown *of fruit* had been put on, *underneath* there was inserted another pattern of eggs *in precious stones*, and other fluting and embossed work, that both sides of the table might be used, according to the wishes of the owners and for this reason the wave-work and the border were extended down to the feet of the table. [30] They made and fastened under the whole width of the table a massive plate four fingers thick, that the feet might be inserted into it, and clamped fast with linch-pins which fitted into sockets under the border, so that which ever side of the table people preferred, might be used. [31] Thus it became manifestly clear that the work was intended to be used either way. [32] On the table itself they engraved a 'maeander,' having precious stones standing out in the middle of it, rubies and emeralds and an onyx too and many other kinds of stones which excel in beauty. [33] And next to the 'maeander' there was placed a wonderful piece of network, which made the centre of the table appear like a rhomboid in shape, and on it a crystal and amber, as it is called, had been wrought, which produced an incomparable impression on the beholders. [34] They made the feet *of the table* with heads like lilies, so that they seemed to be like lilies bending down beneath the table, and the parts which were visible represented leaves which stood upright. [35] The basis of the foot on the ground consisted of a ruby and measured a hand's breadth *high* all round. [36] It had the appearance of a shoe and was eight fingers broad. [37] Upon it the whole expanse of the foot rested. [38] And they made *the foot appear like ivy* growing out of the stone, interwoven with akanthus and surrounded with a vine which encircled it with clusters of grapes, which were worked in stones, up to the top *of the foot*. [39] All the four feet were made in the same style, and everything was wrought and fitted so skilfully, and such

remarkable skill and knowledge were expended upon making it true to nature, that when the air was stirred by a breath of wind, movement was imparted to the leaves, and everything was fashioned to correspond with the actual reality *which it represented*. [40] And they made the top of the table in three parts like a triptychon, and they were so fitted and dovetailed together with spigots along the whole breadth of the work, that the meeting of the joints could not be seen or even discovered. [41] The thickness of the table was not less than half a cubit, so that the whole work must have cost many talents. [42] For since the king did not wish to add to its size he expended on the details the same sum of money which would have been required if the table could have been of larger dimensions. [43] And everything was completed in accordance with his plan, in a most wonderful and remarkable way, with inimitable art and incomparable beauty. [44] Of the mixing bowls, two were wrought in gold, and from the base to the middle were engraved with relief work in the pattern of scales, and between the scales Precious stones were inserted with great artistic skill. [45] Then there was a 'maeander' a cubit in height, with its surface. wrought out of precious stones of many colours, displaying great artistic effort and beauty. [46] Upon this there was a mosaic, worked in the form of a rhombus, having a net-like appearance and reaching right up to the brim. [47] In the middle, small shields which were made of different precious stones, placed alternately, and varying in kind, not less than four fingers broad, enhanced the beauty of their appearance. [48] On the top of the brim there was an ornament of lilies in bloom, and intertwining clusters of grapes were engraven all round. [49] Such then was the construction of the golden bowls, and they held more than two firkins each. [50] The silver bowls had a smooth surface, and were wonderfully made as if they were intended for looking-glasses, so that everything which was brought near to them was reflected even more clearly than in mirrors. [51] But it is impossible to describe the real impression which these works of art produced upon the mind when they were finished. [52] For, when these vessels had been completed and placed side by side, first a silver bowl and then a golden, then another silver, and then another golden, the appearance they presented is altogether indescribable, and those who came to see them were not able to tear themselves from the brilliant sight and entrancing spectacle. [53] The impressions produced by the spectacle were various in kind. [54] When men looked at the golden vessels, and their minds made a complete survey of each detail of workmanship, their souls were thrilled with wonder. [55] Again when a man wished to direct his gaze to the silver vessels, as they stood before him, everything seemed to flash with light round about the place where he was standing, and afforded a still greater delight to the onlookers. [56] So that it is really impossible to describe the artistic beauty of the works. [57] The golden vials they engraved in the centre with vine wreaths. [58] And about the rims they wove a wreath of ivy and myrtle and olive in relief work and inserted precious stones in it. [59] The other parts of the relief work they wrought in different patterns, since they made it a point of honour to complete everything in a way worthy of the majesty of the king. [60] In a word it may be said that neither in the king's treasury nor in any other, were there any works which equalled these in costliness or in artistic skill. [61] For the king spent no little thought upon them, for he loved to gain glory for the excellence of his *designs*. [62] For oftentimes he would neglect his official business, and spend his time with the artists in his anxiety that they should complete everything in a manner worthy of the place to which the gifts were to be sent. [63] So everything was carried out on a grand scale, in a manner worthy of the king who sent the gifts and of the high priest who was the ruler of the land. [64] There was no stint of precious stones, for not less than five thousand were used and they were all of large size. [65] The most exceptional artistic skill was employed, so that the cost of the stones and the workmanship was five times as much as that of the gold.

4

Vivid details of the sacrifice. The unerring accuracy of the priests is notable. A savage orgy. A description of the temple and its water-works.

[1] I HAVE given you this description of the presents because I thought it was necessary. [2] The next point in the narrative is an account of our journey to Eleazar, but I will first of all give you a description of the whole country. [3] When we arrived in the land of the Jews we saw the city situated in the middle of the whole of Judea on the top of a mountain of considerable altitude. [4] On the summit the temple had been built in all its splendour. [5] It was surrounded by three walls more than seventy cubits high and in length and breadth corresponding to the structure of the edifice. [6] All the buildings were characterised by a magnificence and costliness quite unprecedented. [7] It was obvious that no expense had been spared on the door and the fastenings, which connected it with the door-posts, and the stability of the lintel. [8] The style of the curtain too was thoroughly in proportion to that of the entrance. [9] Its fabric owing to the draught of wind was in perpetual motion, and as this motion was communicated from the bottom and the curtain bulged out to its highest extent, it afforded a pleasant spectacle from which a man could scarcely tear himself away. [10] The construction of the altar was in keeping with the place itself and with the burnt offerings which were consumed by fire upon it, and the approach to it was on a similar scale. [11] There was a *gradual* slope up to it, conveniently arranged for the purpose of decency, and the ministering priests were robed in linen garments, down to their ankles. [12] The Temple faces the east and its back is toward the west. [13] The whole of the floor is paved with stones and slopes down to the appointed places, that water may be conveyed to wash away the blood from the sacrifices, for many thousand beasts are sacrificed there on the feast days. [14] And there is an inexhaustible supply of water, because an abundant natural spring gushes up from within the temple area. [15] There are moreover wonderful and indescribable cisterns underground, as they pointed out to me, at a distance of five furlongs all round the site of the temple, and each of them has countless pipes so that the different streams converge together. [16] And all these were fastened with lead at the bottom and at the sidewalls, and over them a great quantity of plaster had been spread, and every part of the work had been most carefully carried out. [17] There are many openings for water at the base *of the altar* which are invisible to all except to those who are engaged in the ministration, so that all the blood of the sacrifices which is collected in great quantities is washed away in the twinkling of an eye. [18] Such is my opinion with regard to the character of the reservoirs and I will now show you how it was confirmed. [19] They led me more than four furlongs outside the city and bade me peer down towards a certain spot and listen to the noise that was made by the meeting of the waters, so that the great size of the reservoirs became manifest to me, as has already been pointed out. [20] The ministration of the priests is in every way unsurpassed both for its physical endurance and for its orderly and silent service. [21] For they all work spontaneously, though it entails much painful exertion, and each one has a special task allotted to him. [22] The service is carried on without interruption—some provide the wood, others the oil, others the fine wheat flour, others the spices; others again bring the pieces of flesh for the burnt offering, exhibiting a wonderful, degree of strength. [23] For they take up with both hands the limbs of a calf, each of them weighing more than two talents, and throw them with each hand in a wonderful way on to the high place *of the altar* and never miss placing them on the proper spot. [24] In the same way the pieces of the sheep and also of the goats are wonderful both for their weight and their fatness. [25] For those, whose business it is, always select *the beasts* which are without blemish and specially fat, and thus the sacrifice which I have described, is carried out. [26] There is a special place set apart for them to rest in, where those who are relieved from duty sit. [27] When this takes place, those who have already rested and are ready *to resume their duties* rise up *spontaneously* since there is no one to give orders with regard to the arrangement of the sacrifices. [28] The most complete silence reigns so that one might imagine that there was not a single person present, though there are actually seven hundred men engaged in the work, besides the vast number of those who are occupied in bringing up the sacrifices. [29] Everything is carried out with reverence and in a way worthy of the great God. [30] We were greatly astonished, when we saw Eleazar engaged in the ministration, at the mode of his dress, and the majesty *of his appearance*, which was revealed in the robe which he wore and the precious stones upon his person. [31] There were golden bells *upon the garment* which reached down to his feet, giving forth a peculiar kind of melody, and on both sides of them there were pomegranates with variegated flowers of a wonderful hue. [32] He was girded with a girdle of conspicuous beauty, woven in the most beautiful colours. [33] On his breast he wore the oracle of God, as it is called, on which twelve stones, of different kinds, were inset, fastened together with gold, containing the names of the leaders of the tribes, according to their original order, each one flashing forth in an indescribable way its own particular colour. [34] On his head he wore a tiara, as it is called, and upon this in the middle of his forehead an inimitable turban, the royal diadem full of glory with the name of God inscribed in sacred letters on a plate of gold . . . having been judged worthy to wear these *emblems* in the ministrations. [35] Their appearance created such awe and confusion *of mind* as to make one feel that one had come into the presence of a man who belonged to a different world. [36] I am convinced that any one who takes part in the spectacle which I have described will he filled with astonishment and indescribable wonder and be profoundly affected in his mind at the thought of the sanctity which is attached to each detail of the service. [37] But in order that we might gain complete information, we ascended to the summit of the neighboring citadel and looked around us. [38] It is situated in a very lofty spot, and is fortified with many towers, which have been built up to the very top, of immense stones, with the object, as we were informed, of guarding the temple precincts, so that if there were an attack, or an insurrection or an onslaught of the enemy, no one would be

able to force an entrance within the walls that surround the temple. ³⁹ On the towers of the citadel engines of war were placed and different kinds of machines, and the position was much higher than the circle of walls which I have mentioned. ⁴⁰ The towers were guarded too by most trusty men who had given the utmost proof of their loyalty to their country. ⁴¹ these men were never allowed to leave the citadel, except on feast days and then only in detachments, nor did they permit any stranger to enter it. ⁴² They were also very careful when any command came from the chief officer to admit any visitors to inspect the place, as our own experience taught us. ⁴³ They were very reluctant to admit us–though we were but two unarmed men–to view the offering of the sacrifices. ⁴⁴ And they asserted that they were bound by an oath when the trust was committed to them, for they had all sworn and were bound to carry out the oath sacredly to the letter, that though they were five hundred in number they would not permit more than five men to enter at one time. ⁴⁵ The citadel was the special protection of the temple and its founder had fortified it so strongly that it might efficiently protect it.

5

A description of the city and the countryside. Compare Verse 11 with conditions of today. Verses 89-41 reveal how the ancients estimate a scholar and a gentleman.

¹ THE size of the city is of moderate dimensions. ² It is about forty furlongs in circumference, as far as one could conjecture. ³ It has its towers arranged in the shape of a theatre, with thoroughfares leading between them now the crossroads of the lower towers are visible but those of the upper towers are more frequented. ⁴ For the ground ascends, since the city is built upon a mountain. ⁵ There are steps too which lead up to the crossroads, and some people are always going up, and others down and they keep as far apart from each other as possible on the road because of those who are bound by the rules of purity, lest they should touch anything which is unlawful. ⁶ It was not without reason that the original founders of the city built it in due proportions, for they possessed clear insight *with regard to what was required.* ⁷ For the country is extensive and beautiful. ⁸ Some parts of it are level, especially the districts which belong to Samaria, as it is called, and which border on the land of the Idumeans, other parts are mountainous, especially those which are contiguous to the land of Judea. ⁹ The people therefore are bound to devote themselves to agriculture and the cultivation of the soil that by this means they may have a plentiful supply of crops. ¹⁰ In this way cultivation of every kind is carried on and an abundant harvest reaped in the whole of the aforesaid land. ¹¹ The cities which are large and enjoy a corresponding prosperity are well-populated, but they neglect the country districts, since all men are inclined to a life of enjoyment, for every one has a natural tendency towards the pursuit of pleasure. ¹² The same thing happened in Alexandria, which excels all cities in size and prosperity. ¹³ Country people by migrating from the rural districts and settling in the city brought agriculture into disrepute: and so to prevent them from settling *in the city*, the king issued orders that they should not stay in it for more than twenty days. ¹⁴ And in the same way he gave the judges written instructions, that if it was necessary to issue a summons against *any one who lived in the country*, the case must be settled within five days. ¹⁵ And since he considered the matter one of great importance, he appointed also legal officers for every district with their assistants, that the farmers and their advocates might not in the interests of business empty the granaries of the city, I mean, of the produce of husbandry. ¹⁶ I have permitted this digression because it was Eleazar who pointed out with great clearness the points which have been mentioned. ¹⁷ For great is the energy which they expend on the tillage of the soil. ¹⁸ For the land is thickly planted with multitudes of olive trees, with crops of corn and pulse, with vines too, and there is abundance of honey. ¹⁹ Other kinds of fruit trees and dates do not count compared with these. ²⁰ There are cattle of all kinds in great quantities and a rich pasturage for them. ²¹ Wherefore they rightly recognise that the country districts need a large population, and the relations between the city and the villages are properly regulated. ²² A great quantity of spices and precious stones and gold is brought into the country by the Arabs. ²³ For the country is well adapted not only for agriculture but also for commerce, and the city is rich in the arts and lacks none of the merchandise which is brought across the sea. ²⁴ It possesses too suitable and commodious harbours at Askalon, Joppa, and Gaza, as well m at Ptolemais which was founded by the King and holds a central position compared with the other places named, being not far distant from any of them. ²⁵ The country produces everything in abundance, since it is well watered in all directions and well protected *from storms*. ²⁶ The river Jordan, as it is called, which never runs dry, flows through the land. ²⁷ Originally the country contained not less than ⁶⁰ million acres–though afterwards the neighbouring peoples made incursions against it–and 600,000 men were settled upon it in farms of a hundred acres each. ²⁸ The river like the Nile rises in harvest-time and irrigates a large portion of the land. ²⁹ Near the district belonging to the people of Ptolemais it issues into another river and this flows out into the sea. ³⁰ Other mountain torrents, as they are called, flow down into the plain and encompass the parts about Gaza and the district of Ashdod. ³¹ The country is encircled by a natural fence and is very difficult to attack and cannot be assailed by large forces, owing to the narrow passes, with theft overhanging precipices and deep ravines, and the rugged character of the mountainous regions which surround all the land. ³² We were told that from the neighbouring mountains of Arabia copper and iron were formerly obtained. ³³ This was stopped, however, at the time of the *Persian* rule, since the authorities of the time spread abroad a false report that the working of the mines was useless and expensive in order to prevent their country from being destroyed by the mining in these districts and possibly taken away from them owing to the Persian rule, since by the assistance of this false report they found an excuse for entering the district. ³⁴ I have now, my dear brother Philocrates, given you all the essential information upon this subject in brief form. ³⁵ I shall describe the work of translation in the sequel. ³⁶ The High Priest selected men of the finest character and the highest culture, such as one would expect from their noble parentage. ³⁷ They were men who had not only acquired proficiency in Jewish literature but had studied most carefully that of the Greeks as well. ³⁸ They were specially qualified therefore for serving on embassies and they undertook this duty whenever it was necessary. ³⁹ They possessed a great facility for conferences and the discussion of problems connected with the law. ⁴⁰ They espoused the middle course–and this is always the best course to pursue. ⁴¹ They abjured the rough and uncouth manner, but they were altogether above pride and never assumed an air of superiority over others, and in conversation they were ready to listen and give an appropriate answer to every question. ⁴² And all of them carefully observed this rule and were anxious above everything else to excel each other in its observance and they were all of them worthy of their leader and of his virtue. ⁴³ And one could observe how they loved Eleazar by their unwillingness to be torn away from him and how he loved them. ⁴⁴ Far besides the letter which he wrote to the king concerning their safe return, he also earnestly besought Andreas to work *for the same end* and urged me, too, to assist to the best of my ability. ⁴⁵ And although we promised to give our best attention to the matter, he said that he was still greatly distressed, for he knew that the king out of the goodness of his nature considered it his highest privilege, whenever he heard of a man who was superior to his fellows in culture and wisdom, to summon him to his court. ⁴⁶ For I have heard of a fine saying of his to the effect that by securing just and prudent men about his person he would secure the greatest protection for his kingdom, since such friends would unreservedly give him the most beneficial advice. ⁴⁷ And the men who were now being sent to him by Eleazar undoubtedly possessed these qualities. ⁴⁸ And he frequently asserted upon oath that he would never let the men go if it were merely some private interest of his own that constituted the impelling motive-but it was for the common advantage of all the citizens that he was sending them. ⁴⁹ For, *he explained*, the good life consists in the keeping of the enactments of the law, and this end is achieved much more by hearing than by reading. ⁵⁰ From this and other similar statements it was clear what his feelings towards them were.

6

Explanations of the customs of the people showing what is meant by the word, "Unclean." The essence and origin of the "God-Belief." Verses 48-44 give a picturesque description of the Divinity of physiology.

¹ IT is worth while to mention briefly the information which he gave in reply to our questions. ² For I suppose that most people feel a curiosity with regard to some of the enactments in the law, especially those about meats and drinks and animals recognised as unclean. ³ When we asked why, since there is but one form of creation, some animals are regarded as unclean for eating, and others unclean even to the touch (for though the law is scrupulous on most points, it is specially scrupulous on such matters as these) he began his reply as follows: ⁴ 'You observe,' he said, 'what an effect our modes of life and our associations produce upon us; by associating with the bad, men catch their depravities and become miserable throughout their life; but if they live with the wise and prudent, they find the means of escaping from ignorance and amending their lives. ⁵ Our lawgiver first of all laid down the principles of piety and righteousness and inculcated them point by point, not merely by prohibitions but by the use of examples as well, demonstrating the injurious effects *of sin* and the punishments inflicted by God upon the guilty. ⁶ For he proved first of all that there is only one God and that his power is manifested throughout the universe, since every place is filled with his sovereignty and none of the things which

are wrought in secret by men upon the earth escapes His knowledge. **7** For all that a man does and all that is to come to pass in the future are manifest to Him. **8** Working out these truths carefully and having made them plain, he showed that even if a man should think of doing evil–to say nothing of actually effecting it,–he would not escape detection, for he made it clear that the power of God pervaded the whole of the law. **9** Beginning from his starting point, he went on to show that all mankind except ourselves believe in the existence of many gods, though they themselves are much more powerful than the beings whom they vainly worship. **10** For when they have made statues of stone and wood, they say that they are the images of those who have invented something useful for life and they worship them, though they have clear proof that they possess no feeling. **11** For it would be utterly foolish to suppose that any one became a god in virtue of his inventions. **12** For *the inventors* simply took certain objects already created and by combining them together, showed that they possessed a fresh utility: they did not themselves create the substance of the thing, and so it is a vain and foolish thing for people to make gods of men like themselves. **13** For in our times there are many who are much more inventive and much more learned than the men of former days *who have been deified*, and yet they would never come to worship them. **14** The makers and authors of these myths think that they are the wisest of the Greeks. **15** Why need we speak of other infatuated people, Egyptians and the like, who place their reliance upon wild beasts and most kinds of creeping things and cattle, and worship them, and offer sacrifices to them both while living and when dead? **16** Now our Lawgiver being a wise man and specially endowed by God to understand all things, took a comprehensive view of each particular detail, and fenced us round with impregnable ramparts and walls of iron, that we might not mingle at all with any of the other nations, but remain pure in body and soul, free from all vain imaginations, worshipping the one Almighty God above the whole creation. **17** Hence the leading Egyptian priests having looked carefully into many matters, and being cognizant with our affairs, call us "men of God." **18** This is a title which does not belong to the rest of mankind but only to those who worship the true God. **19** The rest are men *not of God* but of meats and drinks and clothing. **20** For their whole disposition leads them to find solace in these things are reckoned of no account, but throughout their things. **21** Among our people such whole life their main consideration is the sovereignty of God. **22** Therefore lest we should be corrupted by any abomination, or our lives be perverted by evil communications, he hedged us round on all sides by rules of purity, affecting alike what we eat, or drink, or touch, or hear, or see. **23** For though, speaking generally, all things are alike in their natural constitution, since they are all governed by one and the same power, yet there is a deep reason in each individual case why we abstain from the use of certain things and enjoy the common use of others. **24** For the sake of illustration I will run over one or two points and explain them to you. **25** For you must not fall into the degrading idea that it was out of regard to mice and weasels and other such things that Moses drew up his laws with such exceeding care. **26** All these ordinances were made for the sake of righteousness to aid the quest for virtue and the perfecting of character. **27** For all the birds that we use are tame and distinguished by their cleanliness, feeding on various kinds of grain and pulse, such as for instance pigeons, turtle-doves, locusts, partridges, geese also, and all other birds of this class. **28** But the birds which are forbidden you will find to be wild and carnivorous, tyrannising over the others by the strength which they possess, and cruelly obtaining food by preying of the tame birds enumerated above. **29** And not only so, but they seize lambs and kids, and injure human beings too, whether dead or alive, and so by naming them unclean, he gave a sign by means of them that those, for whom the legislation was ordained, must practise righteousness in their hearts and not tyrannise over any one in reliance upon their own strength nor rob them of anything, but steer their course of life in accordance with justice, just as the tame birds, already mentioned, consume the different kinds of pulse that grow upon the earth and do not tyrannise to the destruction of their own kindred. **30** Our legislator taught us therefore that it is by such methods as these that indications are given to the wise, that they must be just and effect nothing by violence, and refrain from tyrannising over others in reliance upon their own strength. **31** For since it is *considered* unseemly even to touch such unclean animals, as have been mentioned, on account of their particular habits, ought we not to take every precaution lest our own characters should be destroyed to the same extent? **32** Wherefore all the rules which he has laid down with regard to what is permitted in the case of these *birds* and other animals, he has enacted with the object of teaching us a moral lesson. **33** For the division of the hoof and the separation of the claws are intended to teach us that we must discriminate between our individual actions with a view to the practice of virtue. **34** For the strength of our whole body and its activity depend upon our shoulders and limbs. **35** Therefore he compels us to recognise that we must perform all our actions with discrimination according to the standard of righteousness,–more especially because we have been distinctly separated from the rest of mankind. **36** For most other men defile themselves by promiscuous intercourse, thereby working great iniquity, and whole countries and cities pride themselves upon such vices. **37** For they not only have intercourse with men but they defile their own mothers and even their daughters. **38** But we have been kept separate from such sins. **39** And the people who have been separated in the aforementioned way are also characterised *by the Lawgiver* as possessing the *gift* of memory. **40** For all animals "which are cloven-footed and chew the cud" represent to the initiated the *symbol* of memory. **41** For the act of chewing the cud is nothing else than the reminiscence of life and existence. **42** For life is wont to be sustained by means of food, wherefor he exhorts us in the Scripture also in these words: "Thou shalt surely remember the Lord that wrought in thee those great and wonderful things." **43** For when they are properly conceived, they are manifestly great and glorious; first the construction of the body and the disposition of the food and the separation of each individual limb and, for more, the organisation of the senses, the operation and invisible movement of the mind, the rapidity of its particular actions and its discovery of the arts, display an infinite *resourcefulness*. **44** Wherefore he exhorts us to remember that the aforesaid parts are kept together by the divine power with consummate skill. **45** For he has marked out every time and place that we may continually remember the God who rules and preserves us. **46** For in the matter of meats and drinks he bids us first of all offer part as a sacrifice and then forthwith enjoy *our meal*. **47** Moreover, upon our garments he has given us a symbol of remembrance, and in like manner he has ordered us to put the divine oracles upon our gates and doors as a remembrance of God. **48** And upon our hands, too, he expressly orders the symbol to be fastened, clearly showing that we ought to perform every act in righteousness, remembering our own creation, and above all the fear of God. **49** He bids men also, when lying down to sleep and rising tip again, to meditate upon the works of God, not only in word, but by observing distinctly the change and impression produced upon them, when they are going to sleep, and also their waking, how divine and incomprehensible the change from one of these states to the other is. **50** The excellency of the analogy in regard to discrimination and memory has now been pointed out to you, according to our interpretation of "the cloven hoof and the chewing of the cud." **51** For our laws have not been drawn up at random or in accordance with the first casual thought that occurred to the mind, but with a view to truth and the indication of right reason. **52** For by means of the directions which he gives with regard to meats and drinks and particular cases of touching, he bids us neither to do nor listen to anything thoughtlessly nor to resort to injustice by the abuse of the power of reason. **53** In the case of the wild animals, too, the same principle may be discovered. **54** For the character of the weasel and of mice and such animals as these, which are expressly mentioned, is destructive. **55** Mice defile and damage everything, not only for their own food but even to the extent of rendering absolutely useless to man whatever it falls in their way to damage. **56** The weasel class, too, is peculiar: for besides what has been said, it has a characteristic which is defiling: It conceives through the ears and brings forth through the mouth. **57** And it is for this reason that a like practice is declared unclean in men. **58** For by embodying in speech all that they receive through the ears, they involve others in evils and work no ordinary impurity, being themselves altogether defiled by the pollution of impiety. **59** And your king, as we are informed, does quite right in destroying such men.' **60** Then I said 'I suppose you mean the informers, for he constantly exposes them to tortures and to painful forms of death.' **61** 'Yes,' he replied, 'these are the men I mean; for to watch for men's destruction is an unholy thing. **62** And our law forbids us to injure any one either by word or deed. **63** My brief account of these matters ought to have convinced you, that all our regulations have been drawn up with a view to righteousness, and that nothing has been enacted in the Scripture thoughtlessly or without due reason, but its purpose is to enable us throughout our whole life and in all our actions to practise righteousness before all men, being mindful of Almighty God. **64** And so concerning meats and things unclean, creeping things, and wild beasts, the whole system aims at righteousness and righteous relationships between man and man.' **65** He seemed to me to have made a good defence on all the points; for in reference also to the calves and rams and goats which are offered, he said that it was necessary to take them from the herds and flocks, and sacrifice tame animals and offer nothing wild, that the offerers of the sacrifices might understand the symbolic meaning of the lawgiver and not be under the influence of an arrogant self-consciousness. **66** For he, who offers a sacrifice, makes an offering also of his own soul in all its moods. **67** I think that these particulars with regard to our discussion are worth narrating, and on account of the sanctity and natural meaning of the law, I have been induced to explain them to you clearly, Philocrates, because of your own devotion to learning.

7

The arrival of the envoys with the manuscript of the precious book and gifts. Preparations for a royal banquet. The host immediately upon being seated at table entertains his guests with questions and answers. Some sage comments on sociology.

¹ AND Eleazar, after offering the sacrifice, and selecting the envoys, and preparing many gifts for the king, despatched us on our journey in great security. ² And when we reached Alexandria, the king was at once informed of our arrival. ³ On our admission to the palace, Andreas and I warmly greeted the king and handed over to him the letter written by Eleazar. ⁴ The king was very anxious to meet the envoys, and gave orders that all the other officials should be dismissed and the envoys summoned to his presence at once. ⁵ Now this excited general surprise, for it is customary for those who come to seek an audience with the king on matters of importance to be admitted to his presence on the fifth day, while envoys from kings or very important cities with difficulty secure admission to the Court in thirty days– but these men he counted worthy of greater honour, since he held their master in such high esteem, and so he immediately dismissed those whose presence he regarded as superfluous and continued walking about until they came in and he was able to welcome them. ⁶ When they entered with the gifts which had been sent with them and the valuable parchments, on which the law was inscribed in gold in Jewish characters, for the parchment was wonderfully prepared and the connexion *between the pages* had been so effected as to be invisible, the king as soon as he saw them began to ask them about the books. ⁷ And when they had taken the rolls out of their coverings and unfolded the pages, the king stood still for a long time and then making obeisance about seven times, he said: ⁸ 'I thank you, my friends, and I thank him that sent you still more, and most of all God, whose oracles these are.' ⁹ And when all, the envoys and the others who were present as well, shouted out at one time and with one voice: 'God save the King!' he burst into tears of joy. ¹⁰ For his exaltation of soul and the sense of the overwhelming honour which had been paid him compelled him to weep over his good fortune. ¹¹ He commanded them to put the rolls back in their places and then after saluting the men, said: 'It was right, men of God, that I should first of all pay my reverence to the books for the sake of which I summoned you here and then when I had done that, to extend the right-hand *of friendship to you*. ¹² It was for this reason that I did this first. ¹³ I have enacted that this day, on which you arrived, shall be kept as a great day and it will be celebrated annually throughout my life time. ¹⁴ It happens also that it is the anniversary of my naval victory over Antigonus. Therefore I shall be glad to feast with you to-day. ¹⁵ Everything that you may have occasion to use,' he said, 'shall be prepared for you in a befitting manner and for me also with you.' ¹⁶ After they had expressed their delight, he gave orders that the best quarters near the citadel should be assigned to them, and that preparations should be made for the banquet. ¹⁷ And Nicanor summoned the lord high steward, Dorotheus, who was the special officer appointed to look after *the Jews,* and commanded him to make the necessary preparation for each one. ¹⁸ For this arrangement had been made by the king and it is an arrangement which you see maintained to-day. ¹⁹ For as many cities as have special customs in the matter of drinking, eating, and reclining, have special officers appointed *to look after their requirements*. ²⁰ And whenever they come to visit the kings, preparations are made in accordance with their own customs, in order that there may be no discomfort to disturb the enjoyment of their visit. ²¹ The. same precaution was taken in the case of the Jewish envoys. ²² Now Dorotheus who was the patron appointed to look after *Jewish* guests was a very conscientious man. ²³ All the stores which were under his control and set apart for the reception of such guests, he brought out for the feast. ²⁴ He arranged the seats in two rows in accordance with the king's instructions. ²⁵ For he had ordered him to make half the men sit at his right hand and the rest behind him, in order that he might not withhold from them the highest possible honour. ²⁶ When they had taken their seats he instructed Dorotheus to carry out everything in accordance with the customs which were in use amongst his Jewish guests. ²⁷ Therefore he dispensed with the services of the sacred heralds and the sacrificing priests and the others who were accustomed to offer the prayers, and called upon one of our number, Eleazar, the oldest of the Jewish priests, to offer prayer instead. ²⁸ And he rose up and made a remarkable prayer. 'May Almighty God enrich you, O king, with all the good things which He has made and may He grant you and your wife and your children and your comrades the continual possession of them as long as you live!' ²⁹ At these words a loud and joyous applause broke out which lasted for a considerable time, and then they turned to the enjoyment of the banquet which had been prepared. ³⁰ All the arrangements for service at table were carried out in accordance with the injunction of Dorotheus. ³¹ Among the *attendants* were the royal pages and others who held places of honour at the king's court. ³² Taking an opportunity afforded by a pause *in the banquet* the king asked the envoy who sat in the seat of honour (for they were arranged according to seniority), how he could keep his kingdom unimpaired to the end? ³³ After pondering for a moment he replied, 'You could best establish its security if you were to imitate the unceasing benignity of God. For if you exhibit clemency and inflict mild punishments upon those who deserve them in accordance with their deserts, you will turn them from evil and lead them to repentance.' ³⁴ The king praised the answer and then asked the next man, how he could do everything for the best in all his actions? ³⁵ And he replied, 'If a man maintains a just bearing towards all, he will always act rightly on every occasion, remembering that every thought is known to God. If you take the fear of God as your starting-point, you will never miss the goal.' ³⁶ The king complimented this man, too, upon his answer and asked another, how he could have friends like-minded with himself? ³⁷ He replied, 'If they see you studying the interests of the multitudes over whom you rule; you will do well to observe how God bestows his benefits on the human race, providing for them health and food and–all other things in due season.' ³⁸ After expressing his agreement with the reply, the king asked the next guest, how in giving audiences and passing judgments he could gain the praise even of those who failed to win their suit? ³⁹ And he said, 'If you are fair in speech to all alike and never act insolently nor tyrannically in your treatment of offenders. And you will do this if you watch the method by which God acts. The petitions of the worthy are always fulfilled, while those who fail to obtain an answer to their prayers are informed by means of dreams or events of what was harmful *in their requests* and that God does not smite them according to their sins or the greatness of His strength, but acts with forbearance towards them.' ⁴⁰ The king praised the man warmly for his answer and asked the next in order, how he could be invincible in military affairs? ⁴¹ And he replied, 'If he did not trust entirely to his multitudes or his warlike forces, but called upon God continually to bring his enterprises to a successful issue, while he himself. discharged all his duties in the spirit of justice.' ⁴² Welcoming this answer, he asked another how he might become. an object of dread to his enemies. ⁴³ And he replied, 'If while maintaining a vast supply of arms and forces he remembered that these things were powerless to achieve a permanent and conclusive result. For even God instils fear into the minds of men by granting reprieves and making merely a display of the greatness of his power.' ⁴⁴ This man the king praised and then said to the next, 'What is the highest good in life?' ⁴⁵ And he answered, 'To know that God is Lord of the Universe, and that in our finest achievements it is not we who attain success but God who by his power brings all things to fulfilment and leads us *to the goal*.' ⁴⁶ The king exclaimed that the man had answered well and then asked the next how he could keep all his possessions intact and finally hand them down to his successors in the same condition? ⁴⁷ And he answered, 'By praying constantly to God that you may be inspired with high motives in all your undertakings and by warning your descendants not to be dazzled by fame or wealth, for it is God who bestows all these gifts and men never by themselves win the supremacy.' ⁴⁸ The king expressed his agreement with the answer and inquired of the next guest, how he could bear with equanimity whatever befell him? ⁴⁹ And he said, 'If you have a firm grasp of the thought that all men are appointed by God to share the greatest evil as well as the greatest good, since it is impossible for one who is a man to be exempt from these. But God to whom we ought always to pray, inspires us with courage to endure.' ⁵⁰ Delighted with the man's reply, the king said that all their answers had been good. 'I will put a question to one other,' *he added*, 'and then I will stop for the present: that we may turn our attention to the enjoyment *of the feast* and spend a pleasant time.' ⁵¹ Thereupon he asked the man, 'What is the true aim of courage?' ⁵² And he answered, 'If a right plan is carried out in the hour of danger in accordance with the original intention. For all things are accomplished by God to your advantage, O king, since your purpose is good.' ⁵³ When all had signified by their applause their agreement with the answer, the king said to the philosophers (for not a few of them were present), 'It is my opinion that these men excel in virtue and possess extraordinary knowledge, since on the spur of the moment they have given fitting answers to these questions which I have put to them, and have all made God the starting-point of their words.' ⁵⁴ And Menedemus, the philosopher of Eretria, said, 'True, O King–for since the universe is managed by providence and since we rightly perceive that man is the creation of God, it follows that all power and beauty of speech proceed from God.' ⁵⁵ When the king had nodded his assent to this sentiment, the speaking ceased and they proceeded to enjoy themselves. When evening came on, the banquet ended.

8

More questions and answers. Note Verse 20 with its reference to flying through the air written in 150 B. C.

¹ ON the following day they sat down to table again and continued the banquet according to the same arrangements. ² When the king thought that a fitting opportunity had arrived to put inquiries to his guests, he proceeded to ask further questions of the men who sat next in order to those who had given answers on the previous day. ³ He began to open the conversation with the eleventh man, for there were ten who had been asked questions on the former occasion. ⁴ When silence was established, he asked how he could continue to be rich? ⁵ After a brief reflection, the man who had been asked the question replied–'If he did nothing unworthy of his position, never acted licentiously, never lavished expense on empty and vain pursuits, but by acts of benevolence made all his subjects well disposed towards himself. For it is God who is the author of all good things and Him man must needs obey.' ⁶ The king bestowed praise upon him and then asked another how he could maintain the truth? ⁷ In reply to the question he said, 'By recognizing that a lie brings great disgrace upon all men, and more especially upon kings. For since they have the power to do whatever they wish, why should they resort to lies? In addition to this you must always remember, O King, that God is a lover of the truth. ⁸ The king received the answer with great delight and looking *at another* said, 'What is the teaching of wisdom?' ⁹ And the other replied, 'As you wish that no evil should befall you, but to be a partaker of all good things, so you should act on the same principle towards your subjects and offenders, and you should mildly admonish the noble and good. For God draws all men *to Himself* by his benignity.' ¹⁰ The king praised him and asked the next in order how he could be the friend of men? ¹¹ And he replied, 'By observing that the human race increases and is born with much trouble and great suffering: wherefore you must not lightly punish or inflict torments upon them, since you know that the life of men is made up of pains and penalties. For if you understood everything you would be filled with pity, for God also it pitiful! ¹² The king received the answer with approbation and inquired of the next, 'What is the most essential qualification for ruling?' ¹³ 'To keep oneself,' he answered, 'free from bribery and to practise sobriety during the greater part of one's life, to honour righteousness above all things, and to make friends of men of this type. For God, too, is a lover of justice! ¹³ Having signified his approval, the king said to another, 'What is the true mark of piety?' ¹⁴ And he replied, 'To perceive that God constantly works in the Universe and knows all things, and no man who acts unjustly and works wickedness can escape His notice. As God is the benefactor of the whole world, so you, too, must imitate Him and be void of offence! ¹⁵ The king signified his agreement and said to another, 'What is the essence of kingship?' ¹⁶ And he replied, 'To rule oneself well and not to be led astray by wealth or fame to immoderate or unseemly desires, this is the true way of ruling if you reason the matter well out. For all that you really need is yours, and God is free from need and benignant withal. Let your thoughts be such as become a man, and desire not many things but only such as are necessary for ruling! ¹⁷ The king praised him and asked another man, how his deliberations might be for the best? ¹⁸ And he replied, 'If he constantly set justice before him in everything and thought that injustice was equivalent to deprivation of life. For God always promises the highest blessings to the just!' ¹⁹ Having praised him, the king asked the next, how he could be free from disturbing thoughts in his sleep? ²⁰ And he replied, 'You have asked me a. question which is very difficult to answer, for we cannot bring our true selves into play during the hours for sleep, but are held fast in these by imaginations that cannot be controlled by reason. For our souls possess the feeling that they actually see the things that enter into our consciousness *during sleep*. But we make a mistake if we suppose that we are actually sailing on the sea in boats or flying through the air or travelling to other regions or anything else of the kind. And yet we actually do imagine such things to be taking place. ²¹ So far as it is possible for me to decide, I have reached the following conclusion. You must in every possible way, O King, govern your words and actions by the rule of piety that you may have the consciousness that you are maintaining virtue and that you never choose to gratify yourself at the expense of reason and never by abusing your power do despite to righteousness. ²² For the mind mostly busies itself in sleep with the same things with, which it occupies itself when awake. And he who has all his thoughts and actions set towards the noblest ends establishes himself *in righteousness* both when he is awake and when he is asleep. Wherefore. you must be steadfast in the constant discipline of self. ²³ The king bestowed praise on the man and said to another–'Since you are the tenth to answer, when you have spoken, we will devote ourselves to the banquet.' And then he put the question, how can I avoid doing anything unworthy of myself? ²⁴ And he replied, 'Look always to your own fame and your own supreme position, that you may speak and think only such things as are consistent therewith, knowing that all your subjects think and talk about you. For you must not appear to be worse than the actors, who study carefully the rôle, which it is necessary for them to play, and shape all their actions in accordance with it. You are not acting a part, but are really a king, since God has bestowed upon you a royal authority in keeping with your character.' ²⁵ When the king had applauded loud and long in the most, gracious way, the guests were urged to seek repose. So when the conversation ceased, they devoted themselves to the next course of the feast. ²⁶ On the following day, the same arrangement was observed, and when the king found an opportunity of putting questions to the men, he questioned the first of those who had been left over for the next interrogation, What is the highest form of government? ²⁷ And he replied, 'To rule oneself and not to be carried away by impulses. For all men possess a certain natural bent of mind. It is probable that most men have an inclination towards food and drink and pleasure, and kings a bent towards the acquisition of territory and great renown. But it is good that there should be moderation in all things. ²⁸ What God gives, that you must take and keep, but never yearn for things that are beyond your reach.' ²⁹ Pleased with these words, the king asked the next, how he could be free from envy? ³⁰ And he after a brief pause replied, 'If you consider first of all that it is God who bestows on all kings glory and great wealth and no one is king by his own power. All men wish to share this glory but cannot, since it is the gift of God! ³¹ The king praised the man in a long speech and then asked another, how he could despise his enemies? ³² And he replied, 'if you show kindness to all men and win their friendship, you need fear no one. To be popular with all men is the best of good gifts to receive from God! ³³ Having praised this answer the king ordered the next man to reply to the question, how he could maintain his great renown? ³⁴ And he replied that 'If you are generous and large-hearted in bestowing kindness and acts of grace upon others, you will never lose your renown, but if you wish the aforesaid graces to continue yours, you must call upon God continually.' ³⁵ The king expressed his approval and asked the next, To whom ought a man to show liberality? ³⁶ And he replied, 'All men acknowledge that we ought to show liberality to those who are well disposed towards us, but I think that we ought to show the same keen spirit of generosity to those who are opposed to us that by this means we may win them over to the right and to what is advantageous to ourselves. But we must pray to God that this may be accomplished, for he rules the minds of all men.' ³⁷ Having expressed his agreement with the answer, the king asked the sixth to reply to the question, to whom ought we to exhibit gratitude? ³⁸ And he replied, 'To our parents continually, for God has given us a most important commandment with regard to the honour due to parents. In the next place He reckons the attitude of friend towards friend for He speaks of "a friend which is as thine own soul." You do well in trying to bring all men into friendship with yourself.' ³⁹ The king spoke kindly to him and then asked the next, What is it that resembles beauty in value? ⁴⁰ And he said, 'Piety, for it is the pre-eminent form of beauty, and its power lies in love, which is the gift of God. This you have already acquired and with it all the blessings of life.' ⁴¹ The king in the most gracious way applauded the answer and asked another, how, if he were to fail, he could regain his reputation again in the same degree? ⁴² And he said, 'It is not possible for you to fail, for you have sown in all men the seeds of gratitude which produce a harvest of goodwill, and this is mightier than the strongest weapons and guarantees the greatest security. But if any man does fail, he must never again do those things which caused his failure, but he must form friendships and act justly. For it is the gift of God to be able to do good actions and not the contrary.' ⁴³ Delighted with these words, the king asked another, how he could be free from grief? ⁴⁴ And he replied, 'If he never injured any one, but did good to everybody and followed the pathway of righteousness, for its fruits bring freedom from grief. But we must pray to God that unexpected evils such as death or disease or pain or anything of this kind may not come upon us and injure us. But since you are devoted to piety, no such misfortune will ever come upon you.' ⁴⁵ The king bestowed great praise upon him and asked the tenth, What is the highest form of glory? ⁴⁶ And he said, 'To honour God, and this is done not with gifts and sacrifices but with purity of soul and holy conviction, since all things are fashioned and governed by God in accordance with His will. Of this purpose you are in constant possession as all men can she from your achievements in the past and in the present.' ⁴⁷ With loud voice the king greeted them all and spoke kindly to them, and all those who were present expressed their approval, especially the philosophers. For they were far superior to them [i. e. the philosophers] both in conduct and in argument, since they always made God their starting-point. ⁴⁸ After this the king to show his good feeling proceeded to drink the health of his guests.

9

Verse 8 epitomizes the value of knowledge. Verse 28, parental affection. Note especially the question in Verse 26 and the answer. Also note the question in Verse 47 and the answer. This is sage advice for business men.

¹ ON the following day the same arrangements were e for the banquet, and the king, as soon as an opportunity occurred, began to put questions to the men who sat next to those who had already responded, and he said to the first 'Is wisdom capable of being taught?' ² And he said, 'The soul is so constituted that it is able by the divine power to receive all the good and reject the contrary.' ³ The king expressed approval and asked the next man, What is it that is most beneficial to health? ⁴ And he said, 'Temperance, and it is not possible to acquire this unless God create a disposition towards it.' ⁵ The king spoke kindly to the man and said to another, 'How can a man worthily pay the debt of gratitude to his parents?' ⁶ And he said, 'By never causing them pain, and this is not possible unless God dispose the mind to the pursuit of the noblest ends.' ⁷ The king expressed agreement and asked the next, how he could become an eager listener? ⁸ And he said, 'By remembering that all knowledge is useful, because it enables you by the help of God in a time of emergency to select some of the things which you have learned and apply them to the crisis which confronts you. And so the efforts of men are fulfilled by the assistance of God.' ⁹ The king praised him and asked the next How he could avoid doing anything contrary to law? ¹⁰ And he said, 'If you recognize that it is God who has put the thoughts into the hearts of the lawgivers that the lives of men might be preserved, you will follow them.' ¹¹ The king acknowledged the man's answer and said to another, 'What is the advantage of kinship?' ¹² And he replied, 'If we consider that we ourselves are afflicted by the misfortunes which fall upon our relatives and if their sufferings become our own–then the strength of kinship is apparent at once, for it is only when such feeling is shown that we shall win honour and esteem in their eyes. For help, when it is linked with kindliness, is of itself a bond which is altogether indissoluble. And in the day of their prosperity we must not crave their possessions, but must pray God to bestow all manner of good upon them.' ¹³ And having accorded to him the same praise as to the rest, the king asked another, how he could attain freedom from fear? ¹⁴ And he said, 'When the mind is conscious that it has wrought no evil, and when God directs it to all noble counsels.' ¹⁵ The king expressed his approval and asked another, how he could always maintain a right judgement? ¹⁶ And he replied, 'If he constantly set before his eyes the misfortunes which befall men and recognized that it is God who takes away prosperity from some and brings others to great honour and glory.' ¹⁷ The king gave a kindly reception to the man and asked the next to answer the question, how he could avoid a life of ease and pleasure? ¹⁸ And he replied, 'If he continually remembered that he was the ruler of a great empire and the lord of vast multitudes, and that his mind ought not to be occupied with other things, but, he ought always to be considering how he could best promote their welfare. He must pray, too, to God that no duty might be neglected.' ¹⁹ Having bestowed praise upon him, the king asked the tenth, how he could recognize those who were dealing treacherously with him? ²⁰ And he replied to the question, 'If he observed whether the bearing of those about him was natural and whether they maintained the proper rule of precedence at receptions and councils, and in their general intercourse, never going beyond the bounds of propriety in congratulations or in other matters of deportment. But God will incline your mind, O King, to all that is noble.' ²¹ When the king had expressed his loud approval and praised them all individually (amid the plaudits of all who were present), they turned to the enjoyment of the feast. ²² And on the next day, when the opportunity offered, the king asked the next man, What is the grossest form of neglect? ²³ And he replied, 'If a man does not care for his children and devote every effort to their education. For we always pray to God not so much for ourselves as for our children that every blessing may be theirs. Our desire that our children may possess self-control is only realized by the power of God.' ²⁴ The king said that he had spoken well and then asked another, how he could be patriotic? ²⁵ 'By keeping before your mind,' he replied, 'the thought that it is good to live and die in one's own country. Residence abroad brings contempt upon the poor and shame upon the rich as though they had been banished for a crime. If you bestow benefits upon all, as you continually do, God will give you favour with all and you will be accounted patriotic." ²⁶ After listening to this man, the king asked the next in order, how he could live amicably with his wife? ²⁷ And he answered, 'By recognizing that womankind are by nature headstrong and energetic in the pursuit of their own desires, and subject to sudden changes of opinion through fallacious reasoning, and their nature is essentially weak. It is necessary to deal wisely with them and not to provoke strife. For the successful conduct of life. the steersman must know the goal toward which he ought to direct his course. It is only by calling upon the help of God that men can steer a true course of life at all times.' ²⁸ The king expressed his agreement and asked the next, how he could be free from error? ²⁹ And he replied, 'If you always act with deliberation and never give credence to slanders, but prove for yourself the things that are said to you and decide by your own judgement the requests which are made to you and carry out everything in the light of your judgement, you will be free from error, O King. But the knowledge and practice of these things is the work of the Divine power.' ³⁰ Delighted with these words, the king asked another, how he could be free from wrath? ³¹ And he said in reply to the question, 'If he recognized that he had power over all even to inflict death upon them, if he gave way to wrath, and that it would be useless and pitiful if he, just because he was lord, deprived many of life. ³² What need was there for wrath, when all men were in subjection and no one was hostile to him? It is necessary to recognize that God rules the whole world in the spirit of kindness and without wrath at all, and you,' said he, 'O King, must of necessity copy His example.' ³³ The king said that he had answered well and then inquired of the next man, What is good counsel? ³⁴ 'To act well at all times and with due reflection,' he explained, 'comparing what is advantageous to our own policy with the injurious effects that would result from the adoption of the opposite view, in order that by weighing every point we may be well advised and our purpose may be accomplished. And most important of all, by the power of God every plan of yours will find fulfilment because you practise piety.' ³⁵ The king said that this man had answered well, and asked another, What is philosophy? ³⁶ And he explained, 'To deliberate well in reference to any question that emerges and never to be carried away by impulses, but to ponder over the injuries that result from the passions, and to act rightly as the circumstances demand, practising moderation. But we must pray to God to instil into our mind a regard for these things.' ³⁷ The king signified his consent and asked another, how he could meet with recognition when traveling abroad? ³⁸ 'By being fair to all men,' he replied, 'and by appearing to be inferior rather than superior to those amongst whom he was traveling. For it is a recognized principle that God by His very nature accepts the humble. And the human race loves those who are willing to be in subjection to them.' ³⁹ Having expressed his approval at this reply, the king asked another, how he could build in such a way that his structures would endure after him? ⁴⁰ And he replied to the question, 'If his creations were on a great and noble scale, so that the beholders would spare them for their beauty, and if he never dismissed any of those who wrought such works and never compelled others to minister to his needs without wages. ⁴¹ For observing how God provides for the human race, granting them health and mental capacity and. all other gifts, he himself should follow His example by rendering to men a recompense for their arduous toil. For it is the deeds that are wrought in righteousness that abide continually! ⁴² The king said that this man, too, had answered well and asked the tenth, What is the fruit of wisdom? ⁴³ And he replied, 'That a man should be conscious in himself that he has wrought no evil and that he should live his life in the truth. Since it is from these, O mighty King, that the greatest joy and steadfastness of soul and strong faith in God accrue to you if you rule your realm in piety.' ⁴⁴ And when they heard the answer they all shouted with loud acclaim, and afterwards the king in the fullness of his joy began to drink their healths. ⁴⁵ And on the next day the banquet followed the same course as on previous occasions, and when the opportunity presented itself the king proceeded to put questions to the remaining guests, and he said to the first, 'How can a man keep himself from pride?' ⁴⁶ And he replied, 'If he maintains equality and remembers on all occasions that he is a man ruling over men. And God brings the proud to nought, and exalts the meek and humble! ⁴⁷ The king spoke kindly to him and asked the next, Whom ought a man to select as his counsellors? ⁴⁸ And he replied, 'Those who have been tested in many affairs and maintain unmingled goodwill towards him and partake of his own disposition. And God manifests Himself to those who are worthy that these ends may be attained.' ⁴⁹ The king praised him and asked another, What is the most necessary possession for a king? ⁵⁰ 'The friendship and love of his subjects,' he replied, 'for it is through this that the bond of goodwill is rendered indissoluble. And it is God who ensures that this may come to pass in accordance with *your* wish.' ⁵¹ The king praised him and inquired of another, What is goal of speech? And he replied, 'To convince your opponent by showing him his mistakes in a well-ordered army of *arguments*. ⁵² For in this way you will win your hearer, not by opposing him, but by bestowing praise upon him with a view to persuading him. And it is by the power of God that persuasion is accomplished.' ⁵³ The king said that he had given a good answer, and asked another, how he could live amicably with the many different races who formed the population of his kingdom? ⁵⁴ 'By acting the proper part towards each,' he replied, 'and taking righteousness as your guide, as you are now doing with the help of the insight which God bestows upon you.' ⁵⁵ The king was delighted by this reply, and asked another, 'Under what circumstances ought a man to suffer grief?' ⁵⁶ 'In the misfortunes that befall our friends,' he replied, 'when we

see that they are protracted and irremediable. Reason does not allow us to grieve for those who are dead and set free from evil, but all men do grieve *over them* because they think only of themselves and their own advantage. It is by the power of God alone that we can escape all evil!' ⁵⁷ The king said that he had given a fitting answer, and asked another, how is reputation lost? ⁵⁸ And he replied, 'When pride and unbounded self-confidence hold sway, dishonour and loss of reputation are engendered. For God is the Lord of all reputation and bestows it where He will.' ⁵⁹ The king gave his confirmation to the answer, and asked the next man, To whom ought men to entrust themselves? ⁶⁰ 'To those,' he replied, 'who serve you from goodwill and not from fear or self-interest, thinking only of their own gain. For the one is the sign of love, the other the mark of ill will and time-serving. ⁶¹ For the man who is always watching for his own gain is a traitor at heart. But you possess the affection of all your subjects by the help of the good counsel which God bestows upon you.' ⁶² The king said that he had answered wisely, and asked another, What is it that keeps a kingdom safe? ⁶³ And he replied to the question, 'Care and forethought that no evil may be wrought by those who are placed in a position of authority over the people, and this you always do by the help of God who inspires you with grave judgement.' ⁶⁴ The king spoke words of encouragement to him, and asked another, What is it that maintains gratitude and honour? ⁶⁵ And he replied, 'Virtue, for it is the creator of good deeds, and by it evil is destroyed, even as you exhibit nobility of character towards all by the gift which God bestows upon you.' ⁶⁶ The king graciously acknowledged the answer and asked the eleventh (since there were two more than seventy), how he could in time of war maintain tranquillity of soul? ⁶⁷ And he replied, 'By remembering that he had done no evil to any of his subjects, and that all would fight for him in return for the benefits which they had received, knowing that even if they lose their lives, you will care for those dependent on them. For you never fail to make reparation to any–such is the kind-heartedness with which God has inspired you.' ⁶⁸ The king loudly applauded them all and spoke very kindly to them and then drank a long draught to the health of each, giving himself up to enjoyment, and lavishing the most generous and joyous friendship upon his guests.

10

The questions and answers continue. Showing how the army officers ought to be selected. What man is worthy of admiration and other problems of daily life as true today as 2000 years ago. Verses 15-17 are notable for recommending the theatre. Verses 2i-22 describe the wisdom of electing a president or having a king.

¹ ON the seventh day much more extensive preparations were made, and many others were present from the different cities (among them a large number of ambassadors). ² When an opportunity occurred, the king asked the first of those who had not yet been questioned, how he could avoid being deceived *by fallacious reasoning*? ³ And he replied, 'By noticing carefully the speaker, the thing spoken, and the subject under discussion, and by putting the same questions again after an interval in different forms. But to possess an alert mind and to be able to form a sound judgement in every case is one of the good gifts of God, and you possess it, O King.' ⁴ The king loudly applauded the answer and asked another, Why is it that the majority of men never become virtuous? ⁵ 'Because,' he replied, 'all men are by nature intemperate and inclined to pleasure. Hence, injustice springs up and a flood of avarice. The habit of virtue is a hindrance to those who are devoted to a life of pleasure because it enjoins upon them the preference of temperance and righteousness. For it is God who is the master of these things.' ⁶ The king said that he had answered well, and asked, What ought kings to obey? And he said, 'The laws, in order that by righteous enactments they may restore the lives of men. Even as you by such conduct in obedience to the Divine command have laid up in store for yourself a perpetual memorial.' ⁷ The king said that this man, too, had spoken well, and asked the next, Whom ought we to appoint as governors? S And he replied, 'All who hate wickedness, and imitating your own conduct act righteously that they may maintain a good reputation constantly. For this is what you do, O mighty King,' he said, 'and it is God who has bestowed upon you the crown of righteousness.' ⁹ The king loudly acclaimed the answer and then looking at the next man said, 'Whom ought we to appoint as officers over the forces?' ¹⁰ And he explained, 'Those who excel in courage and righteousness and those who are more anxious about the safety of their men than to gain a victory by risking their lives through rashness. For as God acts well towards all men, so too you in imitation of Him are the benefactor of all your subjects.' ¹¹ The king said that he had given a good answer and asked another, What man is worthy of admiration? ¹² And he replied, 'The man who is furnished with reputation and wealth and power and possesses a soul equal to it all. You yourself show by your actions that you are most worthy of admiration through the help of God who makes you care for these things.' ¹ ¹³ The king expressed his approval and said to another, 'To what affairs ought kings to devote most time?' ¹⁴ And he replied, 'To reading and the *study of* the records of official journeys, which are written in reference to the *various* kingdoms, with a view to the reformation and preservation of the subjects. And it is by such activity that you have attained to a glory which has never been approached by others, through the help of God who fulfils all your desires.' ¹⁵ The king spoke enthusiastically to the man and asked another, how ought a man to occupy himself during his hours of relaxation and recreation? ¹⁶ And he replied, 'To watch those plays which can be acted with propriety and to set before one's eyes scenes taken from life and enacted with dignity and decency is profitable and appropriate. ¹⁷ For there is some edification to be found even in these amusements, for often some desirable lesson is taught by the most insignificant affairs of life. But by practising the utmost propriety in all your actions, you have shown that you are a philosopher and you are honoured by God on account of your virtue.' ¹⁸ The king, pleased with the words which had just been spoken, said to the ninth man, how ought a man to conduct himself at banquets? ¹⁹ And he replied, 'You should summon to your side men of learning and those who are able to give you useful hints with regard to the affairs of your kingdom and the lives of your subjects (for you could not find any theme more suitable or more educative than this) since such men are dear to God because they have trained their minds to contemplate the noblest themes–as you indeed are doing yourself, since all your actions are directed by God.' ²⁰ Delighted with the reply, the king inquired of the next man, What is best for the people? That a private citizen should be made king over them or a member of the royal family? ²¹ And he replied, 'He who is best by nature. For kings who come of royal lineage are often harsh and severe towards their subjects. And still more is this the case with some of those who have risen from the ranks of private citizens, who after having experienced evil and borne their share of poverty, when they rule over multitudes turn out to be more cruel than the godless tyrants. ²² But, as I have said, a good nature which has been properly trained is capable of ruling, and you are a great king, not so much because you excel in the glory of your rule and your wealth but rather because you have surpassed all men in clemency and philanthropy, thanks to God who has endowed you with these qualities.' ²³ The king spent some time in praising this man and then asked the last of all, What is the greatest achievement in ruling an empire? ²⁴ And he replied, 'That the subjects should continually dwell in a state of peace, and that justice should be speedily administered in cases of dispute.' ²⁵ These results are achieved through the influence of the ruler, when he is a man who hates evil and loves the good and devotes his energies to saving the lives of men, just as you consider injustice the worst form of evil and by your just administration have fashioned for yourself an undying reputation, since God bestows upon you a mind which is pure and untainted by any evil.' ²⁶ And when he ceased, loud and joyful applause broke out for some considerable time. When it stopped the king took a cup and gave a toast in honour of all his guests and the words which they had uttered. ²⁷ Then in conclusion he said, I have derived the greatest benefit from your presence. I have profited much by the wise caching which you have given me in reference to the art of ruling.' ²⁸ Then he ordered that three talents of silver should be presented to each of them, and *appointed* one of his slaves to deliver over the money. ²⁹ All at once shouted their approval, and the banquet became a scene of joy, while the king gave himself up to a continuous round of festivity.

11

For a comment on ancient stenography, see Verse 7. The translation is submitted for approval and accepted as read, and (Verse 23) a rising vote of approval is taken and unanimously carried.

¹ I HAVE written at length and must crave your pardon, Philocrates. ² I was astonished beyond measure at the men and the way in which on the spur of the moment they gave answers which really needed a long time to devise. ³ For though the questioner had given great thought to each particular question, those who replied one after the other had their answers to the questions *ready at once* and so they seemed to me and to all who were present and especially to the philosophers to be worthy of admiration. ⁴ And I suppose that the thing will seem incredible to those who will read my narrative in the future. ⁵ But it is unseemly to misrepresent facts which are recorded in the public archives. ⁶ And it would not be right for me to transgress in such a matter as this. I tell the story just as it happened, conscientiously avoiding any error. ⁷ I was so impressed by the force of their utterances, that I made an effort to consult those whose business it was to make a record of all that happened at the royal audiences and banquets. ⁸ For it is the custom, as you know, from the moment the king begins to transact business until the time when he retires to rest, for a record to be taken of all his sayings and doings–a most excellent and useful

arrangement. ⁹ For on the following day *the minutes of the* doings and sayings of the previous day are read over before business commence, and if there has been any irregularity, the matter is at once set right. ¹⁰ I obtained therefore, as has been said, accurate information from the public records, and I have set forth the facts in proper order since I know how eager you are to obtain useful information. ¹¹ Three days later Demetrius took the men and passing along the sea-wall, seven stadia long, to the island, crossed the bridge and made for the northern districts *of Pharos*. ¹² There he assembled them in a house, which had been built upon the sea-shore, of great beauty and in a secluded situation, and invited them to carry out the work of translation, since everything that they needed for the purpose was placed at their disposal. ¹³ So they set to work comparing their several results and making them agree, and whatever they agreed upon was suitably copied out under the direction of Demetrius. ¹⁴ And the session lasted until the ninth hour; after this they were set free to minister to their physical needs. ¹⁵ Everything they wanted was furnished for them on a lavish scale. In addition to this Dorotheus made the same preparations for them daily as were made for the king himself–for thus he had been commanded by the king. ¹⁶ In the early morning they appeared daily at the Court, and after saluting the king went back to their own place. ¹⁷ And as is the custom of all the Jews, they washed their hands in the sea and prayed to God and then devoted themselves to reading and translating the particular passage *upon which they were engaged*, and I put the question to them, Why it was that they washed their hands before they prayed? ¹⁸ And they explained that it was a token that they had done no evil (for every form of activity is wrought by means of the hands) since in their noble and holy way they regard everything as a symbol of righteousness and truth. ¹⁹ As I have already said, they met together daily in the place which was delightful for its quiet and its brightness and applied themselves to their task. ²⁰ And it so chanced that the work of translation was completed in seventy-two days, just as if this had been arranged of set purpose. ²¹ When the work was completed, Demetrius collected together the Jewish population in the place where the translation had been made, and read it over to all, in the presence of the translators, who met with a great reception also from the people, because of the great benefits which they had conferred upon them. ²² They bestowed warm praise upon Demetrius, too, and urged him to have the whole law transcribed and present a copy to their leaders. ²³ After the books had been read, the priests and the elders of the translators and the Jewish community and the leaders of the people stood up and said, that since so excellent and sacred and accurate a translation had been made, it was only right that it should remain as it was and no alteration should be made in it ²⁴ And when the whole company expressed their approval, they bade them pronounce a curse in accordance with their custom upon anyone who should make any alteration either by adding anything or changing in any way whatever any of the words which had been written or making any omission. ²⁵ This was a very wise precaution to ensure that the book might be preserved for all the future time unchanged. ²⁶ When the matter was reported to the king, he rejoiced greatly, for he felt that the design which he had formed had been safely carried out. ²⁷ The whole book was read over to him and he was greatly astonished at the spirit of the lawgiver. ²⁸ And he said to Demetrius, 'How is it that none of the historians or 'the poets have ever thought it worth their while to allude to such a wonderful achievement?' ²⁹ And he replied, 'Because the law is sacred and of divine origin. And some of those who formed the intention of *dealing with it* have been smitten by God and therefore desisted from their purpose.' ³⁰ He said that he had heard from Theopompus that he had been driven out of his mind for more than thirty days because he intended to insert in his history some of the incidents from the earlier and somewhat unreliable translations of the law. ³¹ When he had recovered a little, he besought God to make it clear to him why the misfortune had befallen him. ³² And it was revealed to him in a dream, that from idle curiosity he was wishing to communicate sacred truths to common men, and that if he desisted he would recover his health. ³³ I have heard, too, from the lips of Theodektes, one of the tragic poets, that when he was about to adapt some of the incidents recorded in the book for one of his plays, he was affected with cataract in both his eyes. ³⁴ And when he perceived the reason why the misfortune had befallen him, he prayed to God for many days and was afterwards restored. ³⁵ And after, the king, as I have already said, had received the explanation of Demetrius on this point, he did homage and ordered that great care should be taken of the books, and that they should be sacredly guarded. ³⁶ And he urged the translators to visit him frequently after their return to Judea, for it was only right, he said, that he should now send them home. ³⁷ But when they came back, he would treat them as friends, as was right, and they would receive rich presents from him. ³⁸ He ordered preparations to be made for them to return home, and treated them most munificently. ³⁹ He presented each one of them with three robes of the finest sort, two talents of gold, a sideboard weighing one talent, all the furniture for three couches. ⁴⁰ And with the escort he sent Eleazar ten couches with silver legs and all the necessary equipment, a sideboard worth thirty talents, ten robes, purple, and a magnificent crown, and a hundred pieces of the finest woven linen, also bowls and dishes, and two golden beakers to be dedicated to God. ⁴¹ He urged him also in a letter that if any of the men preferred to come back to him, not to hinder them. ⁴² For he counted it a great privilege to enjoy the society of such learned men, and he would rather lavish his wealth upon them than upon vanities. ⁴³ And now Philocrates, you have the complete story in accordance with my promise. ⁴⁴ I think that you find greater pleasure in these matters than in the writings of the mythologists. ⁴⁵ For you are devoted to the study of those things which can benefit the soul, and spend much time upon it. I shall attempt to narrate whatever other events are worth recording, that by perusing them you may secure the highest reward for your zeal.

The Story of Ahikar

1

Ahikar, Grand Vizier of Assyria, has 60 wives but is fated to have no son. Therefore he adopts his nephew. He crams him full of wisdom and knowledge more than of bread and water.

[1] THE story of Haiqâr the Wise, Vizier of Sennacherib the King, and of Nadan, sister's son to Haiqâr the Sage. [2] There was a Vizier in the days of King Sennacherib, son of Sarhadum, King of Assyria and Nineveh, a wise man named Haiqâr, and he was Vizier of the king Sennacherib. [3] He had a fine, fortune and much goods, and he was skilful, wise, a philosopher, in knowledge, in opinion and in government, and he had married sixty women, and had built a castle for each of them. [4] But with it all he had no child by any. of these women, who might be his heir. [5] And he was very sad on account of this, and one day he assembled the astrologers and the learned men and the wizards and explained to them his condition and the matter of his barrenness. [6] And they said to him, 'Go, sacrifice to the gods and beseech them that perchance they may provide thee with a boy.' [7] And he did as they told him and offered sacrifices to the idols, and besought them and implored them with request, and entreaty. [8] And they answered him not one word. And he went away sorrowful and dejected, departing with a pain at his heart. [9] And he returned, and implored the Most High God, and believed, beseeching Him with a burning in his heart, saying, 'O Most High God, O Creator of the Heavens and of the earth, O Creator of all created things! [10] I beseech Thee to give me a boy, that I may be consoled by him that he may be present at my heath, that he may close my eyes, and that he may bury me.' [11] Then there came to him a voice saying, 'Inasmuch as thou hast relied first of all on graven images, and hast offered sacrifices to them, for this reason thou shalt remain childless thy life long. [12] But take Nadan thy sister's son, and make him thy child and teach him thy learning and thy good breeding, and at thy death he shall bury thee.' [13] Thereupon he took Nadan his sister's son, who was a little suckling. And he handed him over to eight wet-nurses, that they might suckle him and bring him up. [14] And they brought him up with good food and gentle training and silken clothing, and purple and crimson. And he was seated upon couches of silk. [15] And when Nadan grew big and walked, shooting up like a tall cedar, he taught him good manners and writing and science and philosophy. [16] And after many days King Sennacherib looked at Haiqâr and saw that he had grown very old, and moreover he said to him. [17] 'O my honoured friend, the skilful, the trusty, the wise, the governor, my secretary, my vizier, my Chancellor and director; verily thou art grown very old and weighted with years; and thy departure from this world must be near. [18] Tell me who shall have a place in my service after thee.' And Haiqâr said to him, 'O my lord, may thy head live for ever! There is Nadan my sister's son, I have made him my child. [19] And I have brought him up and taught him my wisdom and my knowledge.' [20] And the king said to him, 'O Haiqâr! bring him to my presence, that I may see him, and if I find him suitable, put him in thy place; and thou shalt go thy way, to take a rest and to live the remainder of thy life in sweet repose.' [21] Then Haiqâr went and presented Nadan his sister's son. And he did homage and wished him power and honour. [22] And he looked at him and admired him and rejoiced in him and said to Haiqâr: 'Is this thy son, O Haiqâr? I pray that God may preserve him. And as thou hast served me and my father Sarhadum so may this boy of thine serve me and fulfil my undertakings, my needs, and my business, so that I may honour him and make him powerful for thy sake.' [23] And Haiqâr did obeisance to the king and said to him, 'May thy head live, O my lord the king, for ever! I seek from thee that thou mayst be patient with my boy Nadan and forgive his mistakes that he may serve thee as it is fitting.' [24] Then the king swore to him that he would make him the greatest of his favourites, and the most powerful of his friends, and that he should be with him in all honour and respect. And he kissed his hands and bade him farewell. [25] And he took Nadan. his sister's son with him and seated him in a parlour and set about teaching him night and day till he had crammed him with wisdom and knowledge more than with bread and water.

2

A "Poor Richard's Almanac" of ancient days. Immortal precepts of human conduct concerning money, women, dress, business, friends. Especially interesting proverbs are found in Verses 12, 17, 23, 37, 45, 47. Compare Verse 63 with some of the cynicism of today.

[1] THUS he taught him, saying: 'O my son! hear my speech and follow my advice and remember what I say. [2] O my son! if thou hearest a word, let it die in thy heart, and reveal it not to another, lest it become a live coal and burn thy tongue and cause a pain in thy body, and thou gain a reproach, and art shamed before God and man. [3] O my son! if thou hast heard a report, spread it not; and if thou hast seen something, tell it not. [4] O my son! make thy eloquence easy to the listener, and be not hasty to return an answer. [5] O my son! when thou hast heard anything, hide it not. [6] O my son! loose not a sealed knot, nor untie it, and seal not a loosened knot. [7] O my son! covet not outward beauty, for it wanes and passes away, but an honourable remembrance lasts for aye. [8] O my son! let not a silly woman deceive thee with her speech, lest thou die the most miserable of deaths, and she entangle thee in the net till thou art ensnared. [9] O my son! desire not a woman bedizened with dress and with ointments, who is despicable and silly in her soul. Woe o thee if thou bestow on her anything that is thine, or commit to her what is in thine hand and she entice thee into sin, and God be wroth with thee. [10] O my son! be not like the almond-tree, for it brings forth leaves before all the trees, and edible fruit after them all, but be like the mulberry-tree, which brings forth edible fruit before all the trees, and leaves after them all. [11] O my son! bend thy head low down, and soften thy voice, and be courteous, and walk in the straight path, and be not foolish. And raise not thy voice when thou laughest for if it were by a loud voice that a house was built, the ass would build many houses every day; and if it were by dint of strength that the plough were driven, the plough would never be removed from under the shoulders of the camels. [12] O m son! the removing of stones with a wise man is better than the drinking of wine with a sorry man. [13] O my son! pour out thy wine on the tombs of the just, and drink not with ignorant, contemptible people. [14] O my son! cleave to wise men who fear God and be like them, and go not near the ignorant, lest thou become like him and learn his ways. [15] O my son! when thou hast got thee a comrade or a friend, try him, and afterwards make him a comrade and a friend; and do not praise him without a trial; and do not spoil thy speech with a man who lacks wisdom. [16] O my son! while a shoe stays on thy foot, walk with it on the thorns, and make a road for thy son, and for thy household and thy children, and make thy ship taut before she goes on the sea and its waves and sinks and cannot be saved. [17] O my son! if the rich man eat a snake, they say,—"It is by his wisdom," and if a poor man eat it, the people say, "From his hunger." [18] O my son! he content with thy daily bread and thy goods, and covet not what is another's. [19] O my son! be not neighbour to the fool, and eat not bread with him, and rejoice not in the calamities of thy neighbours. If thine enemy wrong thee, show him kindness. [20] O my son! a man who fears God do thou fear him and honour him. [21] O my son! the ignorant man falls and stumbles, and the wise man, even if he stumbles, he is not shaken, and even if he falls he gets up quickly, and if he is sick, he can take care of his life. But as for the ignorant, stupid man, for his disease there is no drug. [22] O my son! if a man approach thee who is inferior to thyself, go forward to meet him, and remain standing, and if he cannot recompense thee, his Lord will recompense thee for him. [23] O my son! spare not to beat thy son, for the drubbing of thy son is like manure to the garden, and like tying the mouth of a purse, and like the tethering of beasts, and like the bolting of the door. [24] O my son! restrain thy son from wickedness, and teach him manners before he rebels against thee and brings thee into contempt amongst the people and thou hang thy head in the streets and the assemblies and thou be punished for the evil of his wicked deeds. [25] O my son! get thee a fat ox with a foreskin, and an ass great with its hoofs, and get not an ox with large horns, nor make friends with a tricky man, nor get a quarrelsome slave, nor a thievish handmaid, for everything which thou committest to them they will ruin. [26] O my son! let not thy parents curse thee, and the Lord be pleased with them; for it hath been said, "He who despiseth his father or his mother let him die the death (I mean the death of sin); and he who honoureth his parents shall prolong his days and his life and shall see all that is good." [27] O my son! walk not on the road without weapons, for thou knowest not when the foe may meet thee, so that thou mayst be ready for him. [28] O my son! be not like a bare, leafless tree that doth not grow, but be like a tree covered with its leaves and its boughs; for the man who has neither wife nor children is disgraced in the world and is hated by them, like a leafless and fruitless tree. [29] O my son! be like a fruitful tree on the roadside, whose fruit is eaten by all who pass by, and the beasts of the desert rest under its shade and eat of its leaves. [30] O my son! every sheep that wanders from its path and its companions becomes food for the wolf. [31] O my son! say not, "My lord is a fool and I am wise," and relate not the speech of ignorance and folly, lest thou be despised by him. [32] O my son! be not one of those servants, to whom their lords say, "Get away from us," but be one of those to whom they say, "Approach and come near to us." [33] O my son! caress not thy slave in the presence of his companion, for thou knowest not which of them shall be of most value to thee in the end. [34] O my son! be not afraid of thy Lord who created thee, lest He be silent to thee. [35] O my son! make thy speech fair and sweeten thy tongue; and permit not thy companion to tread on thy foot, lest he tread at another time on thy breast. [36] O my son! if thou beat a wise man with a word of wisdom, it will lurk in his breast like a subtle sense of shame; but if thou drub the ignorant with a stick he will neither understand nor hear. [37] O my son! if thou send a wise man for thy needs, do not give him many orders, for he will do thy

business as thou desirest: and if thou send a fool, do not order him, but go thyself and do thy business, for if thou order him, he will not do what thou desirest. If they send thee on business, hasten to fulfil it quickly. [38] O my son! make not an enemy of a man stronger than thyself, for he will take thy measure, and his revenge on thee. [39] O my son! make trial of thy son, and of thy servant, before thou committest thy belongings to them, lest they make away with them; for he who hath a full hand is called wise, even if he be stupid and ignorant, and he who hath an empty hand is called poor, ignorant, even if he be the prince of sages. [40] O my son! I have eaten a colocynth, and swallowed aloes, and I have found nothing more bitter than poverty and scarcity. [41] O my son! teach thy son frugality and hunger, that he may do well in the management of his household. [42] O my son! teach not to the ignorant the language of wise men, for it will be burdensome to him. [43] O my son! display not thy condition to thy friend, lest thou be despised by him. [44] O my son! the blindness of the heart is more grievous than the blindness of the eyes, for the blindness of the eyes may be guided little by little, but the blindness of the heart is not guided, and it leaves the straight path, and goes in a crooked way. [45] O my son! the stumbling of a man with his foot is better than the stumbling of a n with his tongue. [46] O my son! a friend who is near is better than a more excellent brother who is far away. [47] O my son! beauty fades but learning lasts, and the world wanes and becomes vain, but a good name neither becomes vain nor wanes. [48] O my son! the man who hath no rest, his death were better than his life; and the sound of weeping is better than the sound of singing; for sorrow and weeping, if the fear of God be in them, are better than the sound of singing and rejoicing. [49] O my child! the thigh of a frog in thy hand is better than a goose in the pot of thy neighbour; and a sheep near thee is better than an ox far away; and a sparrow in thy hand is better than a thousand sparrows flying; and poverty which gathers is better than the scattering of much provision; and a living fox is better than a dead lion; and a pound of wool is better than a pound of wealth, I mean of gold and silver; for the gold and the silver are hidden and covered up in the earth, and are not seen; but the wool stays in the markets and it is seen, and it is a beauty to him who wears it. [50] O my son! a small fortune is better than a scattered fortune. [51] O my son! a living dog is better than a dead poor man. [52] O my son! a poor man who does right is better than a rich man who is dead in sins. [53] O my son! keep a word in thy heart, and it shall be much to thee, and beware lost thou reveal the secret of thy friend. [54] O my son! let not a word issue from thy mouth till thou hast taken counsel with thy heart. And stand not betwixt persons quarrelling, because from a bad word there comes a quarrel, and from a quarrel there comes war, and from war there comes fighting, and thou wilt be forced to bear witness; but run from thence and rest thyself. [55] O my son! withstand not a man stronger than thyself, but get thee a patient spirit, and endurance and an upright conduct, for there is nothing more excellent than that. [56] O my son! hate not thy first friend, for the second one may not last. [57] O my son! visit the poor in his affliction, and speak of him in the Sultan's presence, and do thy diligence to save him from the mouth of the lion. [58] O my son! rejoice not in the death of thine enemy, for after a little while thou shalt be his neighbour, and him who mocks thee do thou respect and honour and be beforehand with him in greeting. [59] O my son! if water would stand still in heaven, and a black crow become white, and myrrh grow sweet as honey, then ignorant men and fools might understand and become wise. [60] O my son! if thou desire to be wise, restrain thy tongue from lying, and thy hand from stealing, and thine eyes from beholding evil; then thou wilt be called wise. [61] O my son! let the wise man beat thee with a rod, but let not the fool anoint thee with sweet salve. Be humble in thy youth and thou shalt be honoured in thine old age. [62] O my son! withstand not a man in the days of his power, nor a river in the days of its flood. [63] O my son! be not hasty in the wedding of a wife, for if it turns out well, she will say, 'My lord, make provision for me'; and if it turns out ill, she will rate at him who was the cause of it. [64] O my son! whosoever is elegant in his dress, he is the same in his speech; and he who has a mean appearance in his dress, he also is the same in his speech. [65] O my son! if thou hast committed a theft, make it known to the Sultan, and give him a share of it, that thou mayst be delivered from him, for otherwise thou wilt endure bitterness. [66] O my son! make a friend of the man whose hand is satisfied and filled, and make no friend of the man whose hand is closed and hungry. [67] There are four things in which neither the king nor his army can be secure: oppression by the vizier, and bad government, and perversion of the will, and tyranny over the subject; and four things which cannot be hidden: the prudent, and the foolish, and the rich, and the poor.'

3

Ahikar retires from active participation in affairs of state. He turns over his possessions to his treacherous nephew. Here is the amazing story of how a thankless profligate turns forgerer. A clever plot to entangle Ahikar results in his being condemned to death. Apparently the end of Ahikar.

[1] THUS spake Haiqâr, and when he had finished these injunctions and proverbs to Nadan, his sister's son, he imagined that he would keep them all, and he knew not that instead of that he was displaying to him weariness and contempt and mockery. [2] Thereafter Haiqâr sat still in his house and delivered over to Nadan all his goods, and the slaves, and the handmaidens, and the horses, and the cattle, and everything else that he had possessed and gained; and the power of bidding and of forbidding remained in the hand of Nadan. [3] And Haiqâr sat at rest in his house, and every now and then Haiqâr went and paid his respects to the king, and returned home. [4] Now when Nadan perceived that the power of bidding and of forbidding was in his own hand, he despised the position of Haiqâr and scoffed at him, and set about blaming him whenever he appeared, saying, 'My uncle Haiqâr is in his dotage, and he knows nothing now.' [5] And he began to beat the slaves and the handmaidens, and to sell the horses and the camels and be spendthrift with all that his uncle Haiqâr had owned. [6] And when Haiqâr saw that he had no compassion on his servants nor on his household, he arose and chased him from his house, and sent to inform the king that he had scattered his possessions and his provision. [7] And the king arose and called Nadan and said to him: 'Whilst Haiqâr remains in health, no one shall rule over his goods, nor over his household, nor over his possessions.' [8] And the hand of Nadan was lifted off from his uncle Haiqâr and from all his goods, and in the meantime he went neither in nor out, nor did he greet him. [9] Thereupon Haiqâr repented him of his toil with Nadan his sister's son, and he continued to be very sorrowful. [10] And Nadan had a younger brother named Benuzârdân, so Haiqâr took him to himself in place of Nadan, and brought up and honoured him with the utmost honour. And he delivered over to him all that he possessed, and made him governor of his house. [11] Now when Nadan perceived what had happened he was seized with envy and jealousy, and he began to complain to every one who questioned him, and to mock his, uncle Haiqâr, saying: 'My uncle has chased me from his house, and has preferred my brother to me, but if the Most High God give me the power, I shall bring upon him the misfortune of being killed.' [12] And Nadan continued to meditate as to the stumbling-block he might contrive for him. And after a while Nadan turned it over in his mind, and wrote a letter to Achish, son of Shah the Wise, king of Persia, saying thus: [13] 'Peace and health and might and honour from Sennacherib king of Assyria and Nineveh, and from his vizier and his secretary Haiqâr unto thee, O great king! Let there be pence between thee and me. [14] And when this letter reaches thee, if thou wilt arise and go quickly to the plain of Nisrîn, and to Assyria, and Nineveh, I will deliver up the kingdom to thee without war and without battle-array.' [15] And he wrote also another letter in the name of Haiqâr to Pharaoh king of Egypt, 'Let there be peace between thee and me, O mighty king! [16] If at the time of this letter reaching thee thou wilt arise and go to Assyria and Nineveh to the plain of Nisrîn, I will deliver up to thee the kingdom without war and without fighting.' [17] And the writing of Nadan was like to the writing of his uncle Haiqâr. [18] Then he folded the two letters, and sealed them with the seal of his uncle Haiqâr; they were nevertheless in the king's palace. [19] Then he went and wrote a letter likewise from the king to his uncle Haiqâr: 'Peace and health to my Vizier, my Secretary, my Chancellor, Haiqâr. [20] O Haiqâr, when this letter reaches thee, assemble all the soldiers who are with thee, and let them be perfect in clothing and in numbers, and bring them to me on the fifth day in the plain of Nisrîn. [21] And when thou shalt see me there coming towards thee, haste and make the army move against me as an enemy who would fight with me, for I have with me the ambassadors of Pharaoh king of Egypt, that they may see the strength of our army and may fear us, for they are our enemies and they hate us.' [22] Then he sealed the letter and sent it to Haiqâr by one of the king's servants. And he took the other letter which he had written and spread it before the king and read it to him and showed him the seal. [23] And when the king heard what was in the letter he was perplexed with a great perplexity and was wroth with a great and fierce wrath, and said, 'Ah, I have shown my wisdom! what have I done to Haiqâr that he has written these letters to my enemies? Is this my recompense from him for my benefits to him?' [24] And Nadan said to him, 'Be not grieved, O king! nor be wroth, but let us go to the plain of Nisrîn and see if the tale be true or not.' [25] Then Nadan arose on the fifth day and took the king and the soldiers and the vizier, and they went to the desert to the plain of Nisrîn. And the king looked, and lo! Haiqâr and the army were set in array. [26] And when Haiqâr saw that the king was there, he approached and signalled to the army to move as in war and to fight in array against the king as it had been found in the letter, he not knowing what a pit Nadan had digged for him. [27] And when the king saw the act of Haiqâr he was seized with anxiety and terror and perplexity, and was wroth with a great wrath. [28] And Nadan said to him, 'Hast thou seen, O my lord the king! what this wretch has done? but be not

thou wroth and be not grieved nor pained, but go to thy house and sit on thy throne, and I will bring Haiqâr to thee bound and chained with chains, and I will chase away thine enemy from thee without toil.' ²⁹ And the king returned to his throne, being provoked about Haiqâr, and did nothing concerning him. And Nadan went to Haiqâr and said to him, 'W'allah, O my uncle! The king verily rejoiceth in thee with great joy and thanks thee for having done what he commanded thee. ³⁰ And now he hath sent me to thee that thou mayst dismiss the soldiers to their duties and come thyself to him with thy hands bound behind thee, and thy feet chained, that the ambassadors of Pharaoh may see this, and that the king may be feared by them and by their king.' ³¹ Then answered Haiqâr and said, 'To hear is to obey.' And he arose straightway and bound his hands behind him, and chained his feet. ³² And Nadan took him and went with him to the king. And when Haiqâr entered the king's presence he did obeisance before him on the ground, and wished for power and perpetual life to the king. ³³ Then said the king, 'O Haiqâr, my Secretary, the Governor of my affairs, my Chancellor, the ruler of my State, tell me what evil have I done to thee that thou hast rewarded me by this ugly deed.' ³⁴ Then they showed him the letters in his writing and with his seal. And when Haiqâr saw this, his limbs trembled and his tongue was tied at once, and he was unable to speak a word from fear; but he hung his head towards the earth and was dumb. ³⁵ And when the king saw this, he felt certain that the thing was from him, and he straightway arose and commanded them to kill Haiqâr, and to strike his neck with the sword outside of the city. ³⁶ Then Nadan screamed and said, 'O Haiqâr, O blackface! what avails thee thy meditation or thy power in the doing of this deed to the king?' ³⁷ Thus says the story-teller. And the name of the swordsman was Abu Samîk. And the king said to him, 'O swordsman! arise, go, cleave the neck of Haiqâr at the door of his house, and cast away his head from his body a hundred cubits.' ³⁸ Then Haiqâr knelt before the king, and said, 'Let my lord the king live for ever! and if thou desire to slay me, let thy wish be fulfilled; and I know that I am not guilty, but the wicked man bas to give an account of his wickedness; nevertheless, O my lord the king! I beg of thee and of thy friendship, permit the swordsman to give my body to my slaves, that they may bury me, and let thy slave be thy sacrifice.' ³⁹ The king arose and commanded the swordsman to do with him according to his desire. ⁴⁰ And he straightway commanded his servants to take Haiqâr and the swordsman and go with him naked that they might slay him. ⁴¹ And when Haiqâr knew for certain that he was to be slain he sent to his wife, and said to her, 'Come out and meet me, and let there be with thee a thousand young virgins, and dress them in gowns of purple and silk that they may weep for me before my death. ⁴² And prepare a table for the swordsman and for his servants. And mingle plenty of wine, that they may drink.' ⁴³ And she did all that he commanded her. And she was very wise, clever, and prudent. And she united all possible courtesy and learning. ⁴⁴ And when the army of the king and the swordsman arrived the found the table set in order, and the wine and the luxurious viands, and they began eating and drinking till they were gorged and drunken. ⁴⁵ Then Haiqâr took the swordsman aside apart from the company and said, 'O Abu Samîk, dost thou not know that when Sarhadum the king, the father of Sennacherib, wanted to kill thee, I took thee and hid thee in a certain place till the king's anger subsided and he asked for thee? ⁴⁶ And when I brought thee into his presence he rejoiced in thee: and now remember the kindness I did thee. ⁴⁷ And I know that the king will repent him about me and will be wroth with a great wrath about my execution. ⁴⁸ For I am not guilty, and it shall be when thou shalt present me before him in his palace, thou shalt meet with great good fortune, and know that Nadan my sister's son has deceived me and has done this bad deed to me, and the king will repent of having slain me; and now I have a cellar in the garden of my house, and no one knows of it. ⁴⁹ Hide me in it with the knowledge of my wife. And I have a slave in prison who deserves to be killed. ⁵⁰ Bring him out and dress him in my clothes, and command the servants when they are drunk to slay him. They will not know who it is they are killing. ⁵¹ And cast away his head a hundred cubits from his body, and give his body to my slaves that they may bury it. And thou shalt have laid up a great treasure with me. ⁵² And then the swordsman did as Haiqâr had commanded him, and he went to the king and said to him, 'May thy head live for ever!' ⁵³ Then Haiqâr's wife let down to him in the hiding-place every week what sufficed for him, and no one knew of it but herself. ⁵⁴ And the story was reported and repeated and spread abroad in every place of how Haiqâr the Sage had been slain and was dead, and all the people of that city mourned for him. ⁵⁵ And they wept and said: 'Alas for thee, O Haiqâr! and for thy learning and thy courtesy! How sad about thee and about thy knowledge! Where can another like thee be found? and where can there be a man so intelligent, so learned, so skilled in ruling as to resemble thee that he may fill thy place?' ⁵⁶ But the king was repenting about Haiqâr, and his repentance availed him naught. ⁵⁷ Then he called for Nadan and said to him, 'Go and take thy friends with thee and make a mourning and a weeping for thy uncle Haiqâr, and lament for him as the custom is, doing honour to his memory.' ⁵⁸ But when Nadan, the foolish, the ignorant, the hardhearted, went to the house of his uncle, he neither wept nor sorrowed nor wailed, but assembled heartless and dissolute people and set about eating and drinking. ⁵⁹ And Nadan began to seize the maidservants and the slaves belonging to Haiqâr, and bound them and tortured them and drubbed them with a sore drubbing. ⁶⁰ And he did not respect the wife of his uncle, she who had brought him up like her own boy, but wanted her to fall into sin with him. ⁶¹ But Haiqâr had been cut into the hiding-place, and he heard the weeping of his slaves and his neighbours, and he praised the Most High God, the Merciful One, and gave thanks, and he always prayed and besought the Most High God. ⁶² And the swordsman came from time to time to Haiqâr whilst he was in the midst of the hiding-place: and Haiqâr came and entreated him. And he comforted him and wished him deliverance. ⁶³ And when the story was reported in other countries that Haiqâr the Sage had been slain, all the kings were grieved and despised king Sennacherib, and they lamented over Haiqâr the solver of riddles.

4

"The Riddles of the Sphinx." What really happened to Ahikar. His return.
¹ AND when the king of Egypt had made sure that Haiqâr was slain, he arose straightway and wrote a letter to king Sennacherib, reminding him in it 'of the peace and the health and the might and the honour which we wish specially for thee, my beloved brother, king Sennacherib. ² I have been desiring to build a castle between the heaven and the earth, and I want thee to send me a wise, clever man from thyself to build it for me, and to answer me all my questions, and that I may have the taxes and the custom duties of Assyria for three years.' ³ Then he sealed the letter and sent it to Sennacherib. ⁴ He took it and read it and gave it to his viziers and to the nobles of his kingdom, and they were perplexed and ashamed, and he was wroth with a great wrath, and was puzzled about how he should act. ⁵ Then he assembled the old men and the learned men and the wise men and the philosophers, and the diviners and the astrologers, and every one who was in his country, and read them the letter and said to them, 'Who amongst you will go to Pharaoh king of Egypt and answer him his questions?' ⁶ And they said to him, 'O our lord the king! know thou that there is none in thy kingdom who is acquainted with these questions except Haiqâr, thy vizier and secretary. ⁷ But as for us, we have no skill in this, unless it be Nadan, his sister's son, for he taught him all his wisdom and learning and knowledge. Call him to thee, perchance he may untie this hard knot.' ⁸ Then the king called Nadan and said to him, 'Look at this letter and understand what is in it.' And when Nadan read it, he said, 'O my lord! who is able to build a castle between the heaven and the earth?' ⁹ And when the king heard the speech of Nadan he sorrowed with a great and sore sorrow, and stepped down from his throne and sat in the ashes, and began to weep and wail over Haiqâr. ¹⁰ Saying, 'O my grief! O Haiqâr, who didst know the secrets and the riddles! woe is me for thee, O Haiqâr! O teacher of my country and ruler of my kingdom, where shall I find thy like? O Haiqâr, O teacher of my country, where shall I turn for thee? woe is me for thee! how did I destroy thee! and I listened to the talk of a stupid, ignorant boy without knowledge, without religion, without manliness. ¹¹ Ah! and again Ah for myself! who can give thee to me just for once, or bring me word that Haiqâr is alive? and I would give him the half of my kingdom. ¹² Whence is this to me? Ah, Haiqâr! that I might see thee just for once, that I might take my fill of gazing at thee, and delighting in thee. ¹³ Ah! O my grief for thee to all time! O Haiqâr, how have I killed thee! and I tarried not in thy case till I had seen the end of the matter.' ¹⁴ And the king went on weeping night and day. Now when the swordsman saw the wrath of the king and his sorrow for Haiqâr, his heart was softened towards him,, and he approached into his presence and said to him: ¹⁵ 'O my lord! command thy servants to cut off my head.' Then said the king to him: 'Woe to thee, Abu Samîk, what is thy fault?' ¹⁶ And the swordsman said unto him, 'O my master! every slave who acts contrary to the word of his master is killed, and I have acted contrary to thy command.' ¹⁷ Then the king said unto him. 'Woe unto thee, O Abu Samîk, in what hast thou acted contrary to my command?' ¹⁸ And the swordsman said unto him, 'O my lord! thou didst command me to kill Haiqâr, and I knew that thou wouldst repent thee concerning him, and that he had been wronged, and I hid him in a certain place, and I killed one of his slaves, and he is now safe in the cistern, and if thou command me I will bring him to thee.' ¹⁹ And the king said unto him. 'Woe to thee, O Abu Samîk! thou hast mocked me and I am thy lord.' ²⁰ And the swordsman said unto him, 'Nay, but by the life of thy head, O my lord! Haiqâr is safe and alive.' ²¹ And when the king heard that saying, he felt sure of the matter, and his head swam, and he fainted from joy, and he commanded them to bring Haiqâr. ²² And he said to the swordsman, 'O trusty servant! if thy speech be true, I would fain enrich thee, and exalt thy dignity above that of all thy friends.' ²³ And

the swordsman went along rejoicing till he came to Haiqâr's house. And he opened the door of the hiding-place, and went down and found Haiqâr sitting, praising God, and thanking Him. ²⁴ And he shouted to him, saying, 'O Haiqâr, I bring the greatest of joy, and happiness, and delight!' ²⁵ And Haiqâr said to him, 'What is the news, O Abu Samîk?' And he told him all about Pharaoh from the beginning to the end. Then he took him and went to the king. ²⁶ And when the king looked at him, he saw him in a state of want, and that his hair had grown long like the wild beasts' and his nails like the claws of an eagle, and that his body was dirty with dust, and the colour of his face had changed and faded and was now like ashes. ²⁷ And when the king saw him he sorrowed over him and rose at once and embraced him and kissed him, and wept over him and said: 'Praise be to God! who hath brought thee back to me.' ²⁸ Then he consoled him and comforted him. And he stripped off his robe, and put it on the swordsman, and was very gracious to him, and gave him great wealth, and made Haiqâr rest. ²⁹ Then said Haiqâr to the king, 'Let my lord the king live for ever! These be the deeds of the children of the world. I have reared me a palm-tree that I might lean on it, and it bent sideways, and threw me down. ³⁰ But, O my Lord! since I have appeared fore thee, let not care oppress thee!' And the king said to him: 'Blessed be God, who showed thee mercy, and knew that thou wast wronged, and saved thee and delivered thee from being slain. ³¹ But go to the warm bath, and shave thy head, and cut thy nails, and change thy clothes, and amuse thyself for the space of forty days, that thou mayst do good to thyself and improve thy condition and the colour of thy face may come back to thee.' ³² Then the king stripped off his costly robe, and put it on Haiqâr, and Haiqâr thanked God and did obeisance to the king, and departed to his dwelling glad and happy, praising the Most High God. ³³ And the people of his household rejoiced with him, and his friends and every one who heard that he was alive rejoiced also.

5

The letter of the "riddles" is shown to Ahikar. The boys on the eagles. The first "airplane" ride. Off to Egypt. Ahikar, being a man of wisdom also has a sense of humor. (Verse 27).

¹ AND he did as the king commanded him, and took rest for forty days. ² Then he dressed himself his gayest dress, and went riding to the king, with his slaves behind him and before him, rejoicing and delighted. ³ But when Nadan his sister's son perceived what was happening, fear took hold of him and terror, and he was perplexed, not knowing what to do. ⁴ And when Haiqâr saw it he entered into the king's presence and greeted him, and he returned the greeting, and made him sit down at his side, saying to him, 'O my darling Haiqâr! look at these letters which the, king of Egypt sent to us, after he had heard that thou wast slain. ⁵ They have provoked us and overcome us, and many of the people of our country have fled to Egypt for fear of the taxes that the king of Egypt hath sent to demand from us. ⁶ Then Haiqâr took the letter and read it and understood its contents. ⁷ Then he said to the king. 'Be not wroth, O my lord! I will go to Egypt, and I will return the answers to Pharaoh, and I will display this letter to him, and I will reply to him about the taxes, and I will send back all those who have run away; and I will put thy enemies to shame with the help of the Most High God, and for the Happiness of thy kingdom.' ⁸ And when the king heard this speech from Haiqâr he rejoiced with a great joy, and his heart was expanded and he showed him favour. ⁹ And Haiqâr said to the king: 'Grant me a delay of forty days that I may consider this question and manage it.' And the king permitted this. ¹⁰ And Haiqâr went to his dwelling, and he commanded the huntsmen to capture two young eaglets for him, and they captured them and brought them to him: and he commanded the weavers of ropes to weave two cables of cotton for him, each of them two thousand cubits long, and he had the carpenters brought and ordered them to make two great boxes, and they did this. ¹¹ Then he took two little lads, and spent every day sacrificing lambs and feeding the eagles and the boys, and making the boys ride on the backs of the eagles, and he bound them with a firm knot, and tied the cable to the feet of the eagles, and let them soar upwards little by little every day, to a distance of ten cubits, till they grew accustomed and were educated to it; and they rose all the length of the rope till they reached the sky; the boys being on their backs. Then he drew them to himself. ¹² And when Haiqâr saw that his desire was fulfilled he charged the boys that when they were borne aloft to the sky they were to shout, saying: ¹³ 'Bring us clay and stone, that we may build a castle for king Pharaoh, for we are idle.' ¹⁴ And Haiqâr was never done training them and exercising them till they had reached the utmost possible point (of skill). ¹⁵ Then leaving them he went to the king and said to him, 'O my lord! the work is finished according to thy desire. Arise with me that I may show thee the wonder.' ¹⁶ So the king sprang up and sat with Haiqâr and went to a wide place and sent to bring the eagles and the boys, and Haiqâr tied them and let them off into the air all the length of the ropes, and they began to shout as he had taught them. Then he drew them to himself and put them in their places. ¹⁷ And the king and those who were with him wondered with a great wonder: and the king kissed Haiqâr between his eyes and said to him, 'Go in peace, O my beloved! O pride of my kingdom! to Egypt and answer the questions of Pharaoh and overcome him by the strength of the Most High God.' ¹⁸ Then he bade him farewell, and took his troops and his army and the young men and the eagles, and went towards the dwellings of Egypt; and when he had arrived, he turned towards the country of the king. ¹⁹ And when the people of Egypt knew that Sennacherib had sent a man of his Privy Council to talk with Pharaoh and to answer his questions, they carried the news to king Pharaoh, and he sent a party of his Privy Councillors to bring him before him. ²⁰ And he came and entered into the presence of Pharaoh, and did obeisance to him as it is fitting to do to kings. ²¹ And he said to him: 'O my lord the king! Sennacherib the king hails thee with abundance of peace and might, and honour. ²² And he has sent me, who am one of his slaves, that I may answer thee thy questions, and may fulfil all thy desire: for thou hast sent to seek from my lord the king a man who will build thee a castle between the heaven and the earth. ²³ And I by the help of the Most High God and thy noble favour and the power of my lord the king will build it for thee as thou desirest. ²⁴ But, O my lord the king! what thou hast said in it about the taxes of Egypt for three years–now the stability of a kingdom is strict justice, and if thou winnest and my hand hath no skill in replying to thee, then my lord the king will send thee the taxes which thou hast mentioned. ²⁵ And if I shall have answered thee in thy questions, it shall remain for thee to send whatever thou hast mentioned to my lord the king.' ²⁶ And when Pharaoh heard that speech, he wondered and was perplexed by the freedom of his tongue and the pleasantness of his speech. ²⁷ And king Pharaoh said to him, 'O man! what is thy name?' And he said, 'Thy servant is Abiqâm, and I a little ant of the ants of king Sennacherib.' ²⁸ And Pharaoh said to him, 'Had thy lord no one of higher dignity than thee, that he has sent me a little ant to reply to me, and to converse with me?' ²⁹ And Haiqâr said to him, 'O my lord the king! I would to God Most High that I may fulfil what is on thy mind, for God is with the weak that He may confound the strong.' ³⁰ Then Pharaoh commanded that they should prepare a dwelling for Abiqâm and supply him with provender, meat, and drink, and all that he needed. ³¹ And when it was finished, three days afterwards Pharaoh clothed himself in purple and red and sat on his throne, and all his viziers and the magnates of his kingdom were standing with their hands crossed, their feet close together, and their heads bowed. ³² And Pharaoh sent to fetch Abiqâm, and when he was presented to him, he did obeisance before him, and kissed the ground in front of him. ³³ And king Pharaoh said to him, 'O Abiqâm, whom am I like? and the nobles of my kingdom, to whom are they like?' ³⁴ And Haiqâr said to him, 'O my lord the kin I thou art like the idol Bel, and the nobles of thy kingdom are like his servants.' ³⁵ He said to him, 'Go, and come back hither to-morrow.' So Haiqâr went as king Pharaoh had commanded him. ³⁶ And on the morrow Haiqâr went into the presence of Pharaoh, and did obeisance, and stood before the king. And Pharaoh was dressed in a red colour, and the nobles were dressed in white. ³⁷ And Pharaoh said to him 'O Abiqâm, whom am I like? and the nobles of my kingdom, to whom are they like?' ³⁸ And Abiqâm said to him, 'O my lord! thou art like the sun, and thy servants are like its beams.' And Pharaoh said to him, 'Go to thy dwelling, and come hither to-morrow.' ³⁹ Then Pharaoh commanded his Court to wear pure white, and Pharaoh was dressed like them and sat upon his throne, and he commanded them to fetch Haiqâr. And he entered and sat down before him. ⁴⁰ And Pharaoh said to him, 'O Abiqâm, whom am I like? and my nobles, to whom are they like?' ⁴¹ And Abiqâm said to him, 'O my lord! thou art like the moon, and thy nobles are like the planets and the stars.' And Pharaoh said to him, 'Go, and to-morrow be thou here.' ⁴² Then Pharaoh commanded his servants to wear robes of various colours, and Pharaoh wore a red velvet dress, and sat on his throne, and commanded them to fetch Abiqâm. And he entered and did obeisance before him. ⁴³ And he said, 'O Abiqâm, whom am I like? and my armies, to whom are they like?' And he said, 'O my lord! thou art like the month of April, and thy armies are like its flowers.' ⁴⁴ And when the king heard it he rejoiced with a great joy and said, 'O Abiqâm! the first time thou didst compare me to the idol Bel, and my nobles to his servants. ⁴⁵ And the second time thou didst compare me to the sun, and my nobles to the sunbeams. ⁴⁶ And the third time thou didst compare me to the moon, and my nobles to the planets and the stars. ⁴⁷ And the fourth time thou didst compare me to the month of April, and my nobles to its flowers. But now, O Abiqâm! tell me, thy lord, king Sennacherib, whom is he like? and his nobles, to whom are they like?' ⁴⁸ And Haiqâr shouted with a loud voice and said: 'Be it far from me to make mention of my lord the king and thou seated on thy throne. But get up on thy feet that I may tell thee whom my lord the king is like and to whom his nobles are like.' ⁴⁹ And Pharaoh was perplexed by the freedom of his tongue and his boldness in answering. Then Pharaoh arose from his

throne, and stood before Haiqâr, and said to him, 'Tell me now, that I may perceive whom thy lord the king is like, and his nobles, to whom they are like.' ⁵⁰ And Haiqâr said to him: 'My lord is the God of heaven, and his nobles are the lightnings and the thunder, and when he wills the winds blow and the rain falls. ⁵¹ And he commands the thunder, and it lightens and rains, and he holds the sun, and it gives not its light, and the moon and the stars, and they circle not. ⁵² And he commands the tempest, and it blows and the rain falls and it tramples on April and destroys its flowers and its houses.' ⁵³ And when Pharaoh heard this speech, he was greatly perplexed and was wroth with a great wrath, and said to him: 'O man! tell me the truth, and let me know who thou really art.' ⁵⁴ And he told him the truth. 'I am Haiqâr the scribe, greatest of the Privy Councillors of king Sennacherib, and I am his vizier and the Governor of his kingdom, and his Chancellor.' ⁵⁵ And he said to him, 'Thou hast told the truth in this saying. But we have heard of Haiqâr, that king Sennacherib has slain him, yet thou dost seem to be alive and well.' ⁵⁶ And Haiqâr said to him, 'Yes, so it was, but praise be to God, who knoweth what is hidden, for my lord the king commanded me to be killed, and he believed the word of profligate men, but the Lord delivered me, and blessed is he who trusteth in Him.' ⁵⁷ And Pharaoh said to Haiqâr, 'Go, and to-morrow be thou here, and tell me a word that I have never heard from my nobles nor from the people of my kingdom and my country.'

6

The ruse succeeds. Ahikar answers every question of Pharaoh. The boys on the eagles are the climax of the day. Wit, so rarely found in the ancient Scriptures, is revealed in Verses 34-45.

¹ AND Haiqâr went to his dwelling, and wrote a letter, saying in it on this wise: ² From Sennacherib king of Assyria. and Nineveh to Pharaoh king of Egypt. ³ 'Peace be to thee, O my brother! and what we make known to thee by this is that a brother has need of his brother, and kings of each other, and my hope from thee is that thou wouldst lend me nine hundred talents of gold, for I need it for the victualling of some of the soldiers, that, I may spend it upon them. And after a little while I will send it thee.' ⁴ Then he folded the letter, and presented it on the morrow to Pharaoh. ⁵ And when he saw it, he was perplexed and said to him, 'Verily I have never heard anything like this language from any one.' ⁶ Then Haiqâr said to him, 'Truly this is a debt which thou owest to my lord the king.' ⁷ And Pharaoh accepted this, saying, 'O Haiqâr, it is the like of thee who are honest in the service of kings. ⁸ Blessed be God who hath made thee perfect in wisdom and hath adorned thee with philosophy and knowledge. ⁹ And now, O Haiqâr, there remains what we desire from thee, that thou shouldst build as a castle between heaven and earth.' ¹⁰ Then said Haiqâr, 'To hear is to obey. I will build thee a castle according to thy wish and choice; but, O my lord I prepare us lime and stone and clay and workmen, and I have skilled builders who will build for thee as thou desirest.' ¹¹ And the king prepared all that for him, and they went to a wide place; and Haiqâr and his boys came to it, and he took the eagles and the young men with him; and the king and all his nobles went and the whole city assembled, that they might see what Haiqâr would do. ¹² Then Haiqâr let the eagles out of the boxes, and tied the young men on their backs, and tied the ropes to the eagles' feet, and let them go in the air. And they soared upwards, till they remained between heaven and earth. ¹³ And the boys began to shout, saying, 'Bring bricks, bring clay, that we may build the king's castle, for we are standing idle!' ¹⁴ And the crowd were astonished and perplexed, and they wondered. And the king and his nobles wondered. ¹⁵ And Haiqâr and his servants began to beat the workmen, and they shouted for the king's troops, saying to them, 'Bring to the skilled workmen what they want and do not hinder them from their work.' ¹⁶ And the king said to him, 'Thou art mad; who can bring anything up to that distance?' ¹⁷ And Haiqâr said to him, 'O my lord! how shall we build a castle in the air? and if my lord the king were here, he would have built several castles in a single day.' ¹⁸ And Pharaoh said to him, 'Go, O Haiqâr, to thy dwelling, and rest, for we have given up building the castle, and to-morrow come to me.' ¹⁹ Then Haiqâr went to his dwelling and on the morrow he appeared before Pharaoh. And Pharaoh said to him, 'O Haiqâr, what news is there of the horse of thy lord? for when he neighs in the country of Assyria and Nineveh, and our mares hear his voice, they cast their young.' ²⁰ And when Haiqâr heard this speech he went and took a cat, and bound her and began to flog her with a violent flogging till the Egyptians heard it, and they went and told the king about it. ²¹ And Pharaoh sent to fetch Haiqâr, and said to him, 'O Haiqâr, wherefore dost thou flog thus and beat that dumb beast?' ²² And Haiqâr said to him, my lord the king! verily she has done an ugly deed to me, and has deserved this drubbing and flogging, for my lord king Sennacherib had given me a fine cock, and he had a strong true voice and knew the hours of the day and the night. ²³ And the cat got up this very night and cut off its head and went away, and because of this deed I have treated her to this drubbing.' ²⁴ And Pharaoh said to him, 'O Haiqâr, I see from all this that thou art growing old and art in thy dotage, for between Egypt and Nineveh there are sixty-eight parasangs, and how did she go this very night and cut off the head of thy cock and come back?' ²⁵ And Haiqâr said to him, 'O my lord! if there were such a distance between Egypt and Nineveh how could thy mares hear when my lord the king's horse neighs and cast their young? and how could the voice of the horse reach to Egypt?' ²⁶ And when Pharaoh heard that, he knew that Haiqâr had answered his questions. ²⁷ And Pharaoh said, 'O Haiqâr, I want thee to make me ropes of the sea-sand.' ²⁸ And Haiqâr said to him, "O my lord the king! order them to bring me a rope out of the treasury that I may make one like it.' ²⁹ Then Haiqâr went to the back of the house, and bored holes in the rough shore of the sea, and took a handful of sand in his hand, sea-sand, and when the sun rose, and penetrated into the holes, he spread the sand in the sun till it became as if woven like ropes. ³⁰ And Haiqâr said, 'Command thy servants to take these ropes, and whenever thou desirest it, I will weave thee some like them.' ³¹ And Pharaoh said, 'O Haiqâr, we have a millstone here and it has been broken and I want thee to sew it up.' ³² Then Haiqâr looked at it, and found another stone. ³³ And he said to Pharaoh 'O my lord! I am a foreigner: and I have no tool for sewing. ³⁴ But I want thee to command thy faithful shoemakers to cut awls from this stone, that I may sew that millstone.' ³⁵ Then Pharaoh and all his nobles laughed. And he said, 'Blessed be the Most High God, who gave thee this wit and knowledge.' ³⁶ And when Pharaoh saw that Haiqâr had overcome him, and returned him his answers, he at once became excited, and commanded them to collect for him three years' taxes, and to bring them to Haiqâr. ³⁷ And he stripped off his robes and put them upon Haiqâr, and his soldiers, and his servants, and gave him the expenses of his journey. ³⁸ And he said to him, 'Go in peace, O strength of his lord and pride of his Doctors! have any of the Sultans thy like? give my greetings to thy lord king Sennacherib, and say to him how we have sent him gifts, for kings are content with little.' ³⁹ Then Haiqâr arose, and kissed king Pharaoh's hands and kissed the ground in front of him, and wished him strength and continuance, and abundance in his treasury, and said to him, 'O my lord! I desire from thee that not one of our countrymen may remain in Egypt.' ⁴⁰ And Pharaoh arose and sent heralds to proclaim in the streets of Egypt that not one of the people of Assyria or Nineveh should remain in the land of Egypt, but that they should go with Haiqâr. ⁴¹ Then Haiqâr went and took leave of king Pharaoh, and journeyed, seeking the land of Assyria and Nineveh; and he had some treasures and a great deal of wealth. ⁴² And when the news reached king Sennacherib that Haiqâr was coming, he went out to meet him and rejoiced over him exceedingly with great joy and embraced him and kissed him and said to him, 'Welcome home: O kinsman! my brother Haiqâr, the strength of my kingdom, and pride of my realm. ⁴³ Ask what thou would'st have from me, even if thou desirest the half of my kingdom and of my possessions.' ⁴⁴ Then said Haiqâr unto him, 'O my lord the king, live for ever! Show favour, O my lord the king! to Abu Samîk in my stead, for my life was in the hands of God and in his.' ⁴⁵ Then said Sennacherib the king, 'Honour be to thee, O my beloved Haiqâr! I will make the station of Abu Samîk the swordsman higher than all my Privy Councillors and my favourites.' ⁴⁶ Then the king began to ask him how he had got on with Pharaoh from his first arrival until he had come away from his presence, and how he had answered all his questions, and how he had received the taxes from him, and the changes of raiment and the presents. ⁴⁷ And Sennacherib the king rejoiced with a great joy, and said to Haiqâr, 'Take what thou wouldst fain have of this tribute, for it is all within the grasp of thy hand.' ⁴⁸ And Haiqâr mid: 'Let the king live for ever! I desire naught but the safety of my lord the king and the continuance of his greatness. ⁴⁹ O my lord! what can I do with wealth and its like? but if thou wilt show me favour, give me Nadan, my sister's son, that I may recompense him for what he has done to me, and grant me his blood and hold me guiltless of it.' ⁵⁰ And Sennacherib the king said, 'Take him, I have given him to thee.' And Haiqâr took Nadan, his sister's son, and bound his hands with chains of iron, and took him to his dwelling, and put a heavy fetter on his feet, and tied it with a tight knot, and after binding him thus he cast him into a dark room, beside the retiring-place, and appointed Nebuhal as sentinel over him to give him a loaf of bread and a little water every day.

7

The parables of Ahikar in which he completes his nephews education. Striking similes. Ahikar calls the boy picturesque names. Here ends the story of Ahikar.

¹ And whenever Haiqâr went in or out he scolded Nadan, his sister's son, saying to him wisely: ² 'O Nadan, my boy! I have done to thee all that is good and kind and thou hast rewarded me for it with what is ugly and bad and with killing. ³ 'O my son! it is said in the proverbs: He who listeneth not with his ear, they will make him listen with the scruff of his neck.' ⁴

And Nadan said, 'For what cause art thou wroth with me?' 5 And Haiqâr said to him, 'Because I brought thee up, and taught thee, and gave thee honour and respect and made thee great, and reared thee with the best of breeding, and seated thee in my place that thou mightest be my heir in the world, and thou didst treat me with killing and didst repay me with my ruin. 6 But the Lord knew that I was wronged, and He saved me from the ware which thou hadst set for me, for the Lord healeth the broken hearts and hindereth the envious and the haughty. 7 O my boy! thou hast been to me like the scorpion which when it strikes on brass, pierces it. 8 O my boy! thou art like the gazelle who was eating the roots of the madder, and it add me to-day and to-morrow they will tan thee hide in my roots." 9 O my boy! thou hast been to who saw his comrade naked in the chilly time of winter; and he took cold water and poured it on him. 10 O my boy! thou hast been to me like a man who took a stone, and threw it up to heaven to stone his Lord with it. And the stone did not hit, and did not reach high enough, but it became the cause of guilt and sin. 11 O my boy! if thou hadst honoured me and respected me and hadst listened to my words thou wouldst have been my heir and wouldst have reigned over my dominions. 12 O my son! know thou that if the tail of the dog or the pig were ten cubits long it would not approach to the worth of the horse's even if it were like silk. 13 O my boy! I thought that thou wouldst have been my heir at my death; and thou through thy envy and thy insolence didst desire to kill me. But the Lord delivered me from thy cunning. 14 O my son! thou hast been to me like a trap which was set up on the dunghill, and there came a sparrow and found the trap set up. And the sparrow said to the trap, "What doest thou here?" Said the trap, "I am praying here to God." 15 And the lark asked it also, "What is the piece of wood that thou holdest?" Said the trap, "That is a young oak-tree on which I lean at the time of prayer." 16 Said the lark: "And what is that thing in thy mouth?" Said the trap: "That is bread and victuals which I carry for all the hungry and the poor who come near to me." 17 Said the lark: "Now then may I come forward and eat, for I am hungry?" And the trap said to him, "Come forward." And the lark approached that it, might eat. 18 But the trap sprang up and seized the lark by its neck. 19 And the lark answered and said to the trap, "If that is thy bread for the hungry God accepteth not thine alms and thy kind deeds. 20 And if that is thy fasting and thy prayers, God accepteth from thee neither thy fast nor thy prayer, and God will not perfect what is good concerning thee." 21 O my boy! thou hast been to me (as) a lion who made friends with an ass, and the ass kept walking before the lion for a time; and one day the lion sprang upon the ass and ate it up. 22 O my boy! thou hast been to me like a weevil in the wheat, for it does no good to anything, but spoils the wheat and gnaws it. 23 O my boy! thou hast been like a man who sowed ten measures of wheat, and when it was harvest time, he arose and reaped it, and garnered it, and threshed it, and toiled over it to the very utmost, and it turned out to be ten measures, and its master said to it: "O thou lazy thing! thou hast not grown and thou hast not shrunk." 24 O my boy! thou hast been to me like the partridge that had been thrown into the net, and she could not save herself, but she called out to the partridges, that she might cast them with herself into the net. 25 O my son! thou hast been to me like the dog that was cold and it went into the potter's house to get warm. 26 And when it had got warm, it began to bark at them, and they chased it out and beat it, that it might not bite them. 27 O my son! thou hast been to me like the pig who went into the hot bath with people of quality, and when it came out of the hot bath, it saw a filthy hole and it went down and wallowed in it. 28 O my son! thou hast been to me like the goat which joined its comrades on their way to the sacrifice, and it was unable to save itself. 29 O my boy! the dog which is not fed from its hunting becomes food for flies. 30 O my son! the hand which does not labour and plough and (which) is greedy and cunning shall be cut away from its shoulder. 31 O my son! the eye in which light is not seen, the ravens shall pick at it and pluck it out. 32 O my boy! thou hast been to me like a tree whose branches they were cutting, and it said to them, "If something of me were not in your hands, verily you would be unable to cut me." 33 O my boy! thou art like the cat to whom they said: "Leave off thieving till we make for thee a chain of gold and feed thee with sugar and almonds." 34 And she said, "I am not forgetful of the craft of my father and my mother." 35 O my son! thou hast been like the serpent riding on a thorn-bush when he was in the midst of a river, and a wolf saw them and said, "Mischief upon mischief, and let him who is more mischievous than they direct both of them." 36 And the serpent said to the wolf, "The lambs and the goats and the sheep which thou hast eaten all thy life, wilt thou return them to their fathers and to their parents or no?" 37 Said the wolf, "No." And the serpent said to him, "I think that after myself thou art the worst of us." 38 O my boy! I fed thee with good food and thou didst not feed me with dry bread. 39 O my boy! I gave thee sugared water to. drink and good syrup, and thou didst not give me water from the well to drink. 40 O my boy! I taught thee, and brought thee up, and thou didst dig a hiding-place for me and didst conceal me. 41 O my boy! I brought thee up with the best upbringing and trained thee like a tall cedar; and thou hast twisted and bent me. 42 O my boy! it was my hope concerning thee that thou wouldst build me a fortified castle, that I might be concealed from my enemies in it, and thou didst become to me like one burying in the depth of the earth; but the Lord took pity on me and delivered me from thy cunning. 43 O my boy! I wished thee well, and thou didst reward me with evil and hatefulness, and now I would fain tear out thine eyes, and make thee food for dogs, and cut out thy tongue, and take off thy head with the edge of the sword, and recompense thee for thine abominable deeds.' 44 And when Nadan heard this speech from his uncle Haiqâr, he said: 'O my uncle! deal with me according to thy knowledge, and forgive me my sins, for who is there who hath sinned like me, or who is there who forgives like thee? 45 Accept me, O my uncle! Now I will serve in thy house, and groom thy horses and sweep up the dung of thy cattle, and feed thy sheep, for I am the wicked and thou art the righteous: I the guilty and thou the forgiving.' 46 And Haiqâr said to him, 'O my boy! thou art like the tree which was fruitless beside the water, and its master was fain to cut it down, and it said to him, "Remove me to another place, and if I do not bear fruit, cut me down." 47 And its master said to it, "Thou being beside the water hast not borne fruit, how shalt thou bear fruit when thou art in another place?" 48 O my boy! the old age of the eagle is better than the youth of the crow. 49 O my boy! they said to the wolf, "Keep away from the sheep lest their dust should harm thee." And the wolf said, "The dregs of the sheep's milk are good for my eyes." 50 O my boy! they made the wolf go to school that he might learn to read and they said to him, "Say A, B." He said, "Lamb and goat in my bell" 51 O my boy! they set the ass down at the table and he fell, and began to roll himself in the dust and one said, "Let him roll himself, for it is his nature, he will not change. 52 O my boy! the saying has been confirmed which runs: "If thou begettest a boy, call him thy son, and if thou rearest a boy, call him thy slave." 53 O my boy! he who doeth good shall meet with good; and he who doeth evil shall meet with evil, for the Lord requiteth a man according to the measure of his work. 54 O my boy! what shall I say more to thee than these sayings? for the Lord knoweth what is hidden, and is acquainted with the mysteries and the secrets. 55 And He will requite thee and will judge, betwixt me and thee, and will recompense thee according to thy desert.', 56 And when Nadan heard that speech from his uncle Haiqâr, he swelled up immediately and became like a blown-out bladder. 57 And his limbs swelled and his legs and his feet and his side, and he was torn and his belly burst asunder and his entrails were scattered, and he perished, and died. 58 And his latter end was destruction, and he went to hell. For he who digs a pit for his brother shall fall into it; and he who sets up traps shall be caught in them. 59 This is what happened and (what) we found about the tale of Haiqâr, and praise be to God for ever. Amen, and peace. 60 This chronicle is finished with the help of God, may He be exalted! Amen, Amen, Amen.

The Biblical Antiquities of Philo
(or the History of Philo from the Beginning of the World to King David)

Phrases and sentences in *italics* mark quotations from the Old Testament: single words in *italics*, and short phrases to which no Biblical reference is attached in the margin, are supplements of the translator. The following signs are also employed:

[ ] Words wrongly inserted into the text.
( ) Alternative readings of importance.
< > Words that have fallen out, restored by << >> conjecture.
† † Corrupt passages.

1

[1] The beginning of the world. Adam begat three sons and one daughter, Cain, Noaba, Abel and Seth. [2] And Adam *lived after he begat Seth* 700 *years, and begat* 12 *sons and* 8 *daughters.* [3] And these are the names of the males: Eliseel, Suris, Elamiel, Brabal, Naat, Zarama, Zasam, Maathal, and Anath. [4] And these are his daughters: Phua, Iectas, Arebica, Sifa, Tecia, Saba, Asin. [5] *And Seth lived* 105 *years and begat Enos. And Seth lived after he begat Enos* 707 *years, and begat* 3 *sons and* 2 *daughters.* [6] And these are the names of his sons: Elidia, Phonna, and Matha: and of his daughters, Malida and Thila. [7] *And Enos lived* 180 *years and begat Cainan. And Enos lived after he begat Cainan* 715 *years, and begat* 2 *sons and a daughter.* [8] And these are the names of his sons: Phoë and Thaal; and of the daughter, Catennath. [9] *And Cainan lived* 520 *years and begat Malalech. And Cainan lived after he begat Malalech* 730 *years, and begat* 3 *sons and* 2 *daughters.* [10] And these are the names of the males: Athach, Socer, Lopha: and of the names of the daughters, Ana and Leua. [11] *And Malalech lived* 165 *years and begat Jareth. And Malalech lived after he begat Jareth* 730 *years, and begat* 7 *sons and* 5 *daughters.* [12] And these are the names of the males: Leta, Matha, Cethar, Melie, Suriel, Lodo, Othim. And these are the names of the daughters: Ada and Noa, Iebal, Mada, Sella. [13] *And Jareth lived* 172 *years and begat Enoch. And Jareth lived after he begat Enoch* 800 *years and begat* 4 *sons and* 2 *daughters.* [14] And these are the names of the males: Lead, Anac, Soboac and Iectar: and of the daughters, Tetzeco, Lesse. [15] *And Enoch lived* 165 *years and begat Matusalam. And Enoch lived after he begat Matusalam* 200 *years, and begat* 5 *sons and* 3 *daughters.* [16] *But Enoch pleased God* at that time *and was not found, for God translated him.* [17] Now the names of his sons are: Anaz, Zeum, Achaun, Pheledi, Elith; and of the daughters, Theiz, Lefith, Leath. [18] *And Mathusalam lived* 187 *years and begot Lamech. And Mathusalam lived after he begat Lamech* 782 *years, and begot* 2 *sons and* 2 *daughters.* [19] And these are the names of the males: Inab and Rapho; and of the daughters, Aluma and Amuga. [20] *And Lamech lived* 182 *years and begot a son, and called him* according to his nativity *Noe, saying: This child will give rest to us* and to the earth from those who are therein, upon whom (*or* in the day when) a visitation shall be made because of the iniquity of their evil deeds. [21] *And Lamech lived after he begot Noe* 585 *years.* [22] *And Noe lived* 300 *years and begot* 3 *sons*, Sem, Cham, and Japheth.

2

[1] But Cain dwelt in the earth trembling, according as God appointed unto him after he slew Abel his brother; and the name of his wife was Themech. [2] *And Cain knew* Themech *his wife and she conceived and bare Enoch.* [3] Now Cain was 15 years old when he did these things; and from that time he began to build cities, until he had founded seven cities. And these are the names of the cities: The name of the first city according to the name of his son Enoch. The name of the second city Mauli, and of the third Leeth, and the name of the fourth Teze, and the name of the fifth Iesca; the name of the sixth Celeth, and the name of the seventh Iebbath. [4] And Cain lived after he begat Enoch 715 years and begat 3 sons and 2 daughters. And these are the names of his sons: Olad, Lizaph, Fosal; and of his daughters, Citha and Maac. And all the days of Cain were 730 years, and he died. [5] Then took Enoch a wife of the daughters of Seth, which bare him Ciram and Cuuth and Madab. But Ciram begat Matusael, and Matusael begat Lamech. [6] *But Lamech took unto himself two wives: the name of the one was Ada and the name of the other Sella.* [7] *And Ada bare him* Iobab: *he was the father of all that dwell in tents and herd flocks.* And again she bare him Iobal, *which was the first to teach all playing of instruments* (lit. every psalm of organs). [8] And at that time, when they that dwelt on the earth had begun to do evil, every one with his neighbour's wife, defiling them, God was angry. And he began to play upon the *lute* (kinnor) *and the harp* and on every instrument of sweet psalmody (lit. psaltery), and to corrupt the earth. [9] *But Sella bare Tubal* and Misa and Theffa, and this is that Tubal which showed unto men arts in lead and tin and iron and copper and silver and gold: and then began the inhabiters of the earth to make graven images and to worship them. [10] *Now Lamech said unto his two wives Ada and Sella: Hear my voice, ye wives of Lamech, give heed to my precept*: for I have corrupted men for myself, and *have taken away* sucklings from the breasts, that I might show my sons how to work evil, *and the inhabiters of the earth*. And now *shall vengeance be taken seven times of Cain, but of Lamech seventy times seven*.

3

[1] *And it came to pass when men had begun to multiply on the earth*, that beautiful *daughters were born unto them. And the sons of God saw the daughters of men that they were* exceeding *fair, and took them wives of all that they had chosen.* [2] *And God said: My spirit shall not* judge *among these men for ever, because they are of flesh; but their years shall be* 120 Upon whom he laid (*or* wherein I have set) the ends of the world, and in their hands wickednesses were not put out (or the law shall not be quenched). [3] *And God saw that in all the dwellers upon earth works of evil were fulfilled: and inasmuch as their thought was upon iniquity all their days*, God said: *I will blot out man* and all things that have budded upon the earth, *for it repenteth me that I have made him.* [4] *But Noe found grace* and mercy *before the Lord, and these are his generations. Noe, which was a righteous man and* undefiled *in his generation, pleased the Lord.* Unto whom God *said: The time of all men that dwell upon the earth is come, for their deeds are very evil. And now make thee an ark of* cedar wood, *and thus shalt thou make it.* 300 *cubits shall be the length thereof, and* 50 *cubits the breadth, and* 30 *cubits the height. And thou shall enter into the ark, thou and thy wife and thy sons and thy sons' wives with thee. And I will make my covenant with thee*, to destroy all the dwellers upon earth. *Now of clean beasts and of the fowls of the heaven that are clean thou shalt take by sevens male and female, that their seed may be saved alive upon the earth. But of unclean beasts and fowls thou shalt take to thee by twos male and female, and* shalt take provision for thee and for them also. [5] *And Noe did that which God commanded him and entered into the ark, he and all his sons with him. And it came to pass after* 7 *days that the water of the flood began to be upon the earth. And in that day all the depths were opened* and the great spring *of water and the windows of heaven, and there was rain upon the earth* 40 *days and* 40 *nights.* [6] And it was then the 1652nd (1656th) year from the time when God had made the heaven and the earth in the day when the earth was corrupted with the inhabiters thereof by reason of the iniquity of their works. [7] *And when the flood continued* 140 *days upon the earth*, Noe only and they that were with him in the ark remained alive: and when God remembered Noe, he made the water to diminish. [8] And it came to pass on the 90th day that God dried the earth, and said *unto Noe: Go out of the ark, thou* and all that are with thee, *and grow and multiply upon the earth. And Noe went out of the ark, he an d his sons and his sons' wives, and all the beasts and creeping things and fowls and cattle* brought he forth with him as God commanded him. *Then built Noe an altar unto the Lord, and took of all the cattle and of the clean fowls and offered burnt offerings on the altar*: and it was accepted of the Lord for a savour of rest. [9] *And God said: I will not again curse the earth for man's sake, for the guise of man's heart hath left off from his youth. And therefore I will not again destroy together all living as I have done.* But it shall be, when the dwellers upon earth have sinned, I will judge them by famine or by the sword or by fire or by pestilence (lit. death), and there shall be earthquakes, and they shall be scattered into places not inhabited (*or*, the places of *their* habitation shall be scattered). But I will not again spoil the earth with the water of a flood, and *in all the days of the earth seed time and harvest, cold and heat, summer and autumn, day and night shall not cease*, until I remember them that dwell on the earth, *even* until the times are fulfilled. [10] But when the years of the world shall be fulfilled, then shall the light cease and the darkness be quenched: and I will quicken the dead and raise up from the earth them that sleep: and Hell shall pay his debt and destruction give back that which was committed unto him, that I may render unto every man according to his works and according to the fruit of their imaginations, *even* until I judge between the soul and the flesh. And the world shall rest, and death shall be quenched, and Hell shall shut his mouth. And the earth shall not be without birth, neither barren for them that dwell therein: and none shall be polluted that hath been justified in me. And there shall be another earth and another heaven, even an everlasting habitation. [11] *And the Lord spake* further *unto Noe and to his sons saying: Behold I will make my covenant with you and with your seed after you, and will not again spoil the earth with the water of a flood. And all that liveth and moveth therein shall be to you for meal. Nevertheless the flesh with the blood of the soul shall ye not eat. For he that sheddeth man's blood, his blood shall be shed; for in the image of God was man made. And ye, grow ye and multiply and fill the earth* as the multitude of fishes that multiply in the waters. And God said: This is the covenant that I have made betwixt me and you; *and it shall be when I cover the heaven with clouds, that my bow shall appear in*

the cloud, and it shall be for a memorial of the covenant betwixt me and you, and all the dwellers upon earth.

4

¹ *And the sons of Noe which went forth of the ark were Sem, Cham, and Japheth.* ² *The sons of Japheth: Gomer, Magog, and Madai,* Nidiazech, *Tubal,* Mocteras, Cenez, *Riphath, and Thogorma, Elisa,* Dessin, Cethin, Tudant. And the sons of Gomer: Thelez, Lud, Deberlet. And the sons of Magog: Cesse, Thipha, Pharuta, Ammiel, Phimei, Goloza, Samanach. And the sons of Duden: Sallus, Phelucta Phallita. And the sons of Tubal: Phanatonova, Eteva. And the sons of Tyras: Maac, Tabel, Ballana, Samplameac, Elaz. And the sons of Mellech: Amboradat, Urach, Bosara. And the sons of <<As>>cenez: Jubal, Zaraddana, Anac. And the sons of Heri: Phuddet, Doad, Dephadzeat, Enoc. And the sons of Togorma: Abiud, Saphath, Asapli, Zepthir. And the sons of Elisa: Etzaac, Zenez, Mastisa, Rira. And the sons of Zepti: Macziel, Temna, Aela, Phinon. And the sons of Tessis: Meccul, Loon, Zelataban. And the sons of Duodennin: Itheb, Beath, Phenech. ³ And these are they that were scattered abroad, and dwelt in the earth with the Persians and Medes, and in the islands that are in the sea. And Phenech, the son of Dudeni, went up and commanded that ships of the sea should be made: and then was the third part of the earth divided. ⁴ Domereth and his sons took Ladech; and Magog and his sons took Degal; Madam and his sons took Besto; Iuban (*sc.* Javan) and his sons took Ceel; Tubal and his sons took Pheed; Misech and his sons took Nepthi; <<T>>iras and his sons took <<Rôô>>; Duodennut and his sons took Goda; Riphath and his sons took Bosarra; Torgoma and his sons took Fud; Elisa and his sons took Thabola; Thesis (*sc.* Tarshish) and his sons took Marecham; Cethim and his sons took Thaan; Dudennin and his sons took Caruba. ⁵ And then began they to till the earth and to sow upon it: and when the earth was athirst, the dwellers therein cried unto the Lord and he heard them and gave rain abundantly, and it was so, when the rain descended upon the earth, that the bow appeared in the cloud, and the dwellers upon earth saw the memorial of the covenant and fell upon their faces and sacrificed, offering burnt offerings unto the Lord. ⁶ *Now the sons of Cham were Chus, Mestra, and Phuni, and Chanaan. And the sons of Chus: Saba,* and . . . Tudan. And the sons of Phuni: [Effuntenus], Zeleutelup, Geluc, Lephuc. And the sons of Chanaan were Sydona, Endain, Racin, Simmin, Uruin, Nenugin, Amathin, Nephiti, Telaz, Elat, Cusin. ⁷ *And Chus begat Nembroth. He began to be* proud *before the Lord. But Mestram begat Ludin* and Megimin and Labin and Latuin and Petrosonoin and Ceslun: *thence came forth the Philistines* and the Cappadocians. ⁸ And then did they also begin to build cities: and these are the cities which they built: Sydon, and the parts that lie about it, that is Resun, Beosa, Maza, Gerara, Ascalon, Dabir, Camo, Tellun, Lacis, Sodom and Gomorra, Adama and Seboim. ⁹ *And the sons of Sem: Elam, Assur, Arphaxa, Luzi, Aram.* And the sons of Aram: Gedrum, Ese. *And Arphaxa begat Sale, Sale begat Heber, and unto Heber were born two sons: the name of the one was Phalech, for in his days the earth was divided, and the name of his brother was Jectan.* ¹⁰ *And Jectan begat Helmadam and Salastra and Mazaam, Rea, Dura, Uzia, Deglabal, Mimoel, Sabthphin, Evilac, Iubab.* And the sons of Phalech: Ragau, Rephuth, Zepheram, Aculon, Sachar, Siphaz, Nabi, Suri, Seciur, Phalacus, Rapho, Phalthia, Zaldephal, Zaphis, and Arteman, Heliphas. These are the sons of Phalech, and these are their names, and they took them wives of the daughters of Jectan and begat sons and daughters and filled the earth. ¹¹ But Ragau took him to wife Melcha the daughter of Ruth, and she begat him Seruch. And when the day of her delivery came she said: Of this child shall be born in the fourth generation one who shall set his dwelling on high, and shall be called perfect, and undefiled, and he shall be the father of nations, and his covenant shall not be broken, and his seed shall be multiplied for ever. ¹² *And Ragau lived after he begat Seruch* 119 *years and begat* 7 *sons and* 5 *daughters.* And these are the names of his sons: Abiel, Obed, Salma, Dedasal, Zeneza, Accur, Nephes. And these are the names of his daughters: Cedema, Derisa, Seipha, Pherita, Theila. ¹³ *And Seruch lived* 29 *years and begat Nachor. And Seruch lived after he begat Nachor* 67 *years and begat* 4 *sons and* 3 *daughters.* And these are the names of the males: Zela, Zoba, Dica and Phodde. And these are his daughters: Tephila, Oda, Selipha. ¹⁴ *And Nachor lived* 34 *years and begat Thara. And Nachor lived after he begat Thara* 200 *years and begat* 8 *sons and* 5 *daughters.* And these are the names of the males: Recap, Dediap, Berechap, Iosac, Sithal, Nisab, Nadab, Camoel. And these are his daughters: Esca, Thipha, Bruna, Ceneta. ¹⁵ *And Thara lived* 70 *years and begat Abram, Nachor, and Aram. And Aram begat Loth.* ¹⁶ Then began they that dwelt on the earth to look upon the stars, and began to prognosticate by them and to make divination, and to make their sons and daughters pass through the fire. But Seruch and his sons walked not according to them. ¹⁷ And these are the generations of Noe upon the earth according to their languages and their tribes, out of whom the nations were divided upon the earth after the flood.

V.

¹ Then came the sons of Cham, and made Nembroth a prince over themselves: but the sons of Japheth made Phenech their chief: *and* the sons of Sem gathered together and set over them Jectan to be their prince. ² And when these three had met together they took counsel that they would look upon and take account of the people of their followers. And this was done while Noe was yet alive, *even* that all men should be gathered together: and they lived at one with each other, and the earth was at peace. ³ Now in the 340th year of the going forth of Noe out of the ark, after that God dried up the flood, did the princes take account of their people. ⁴ And *first* Phenech the son of Japheth looked upon them. The sons of Gomer all of them passing by according to the sceptres of their captaincies were in number 5,800 But of the sons of Magog all of them passing by according to the sceptres of their leading the number was 6,200 And of the sons of Madai all of them passing by according to the sceptres of their captaincies were in number 5,700 And the sons of Tubal. all of them passing by according to the sceptres of their captaincies were in number 9,400 And the sons of Mesca all of them passing by according to the sceptres of their captaincies were in number 5,600 The sons of Thiras all of them passing by according to the sceptres of their captaincies were in number 12,300 And the sons of Ripha<<th>> passing by according to the sceptres of their captaincies were in number l4,500 And the sons of Thogorma passing by according to the sceptres of their captaincy were in number 14,400 But the sons of Elisa passing by according to the sceptres of their captaincy were in number 14,900 And the sons of Thersis all of them passing by according to the sceptres of their captaincy were in number 12,100 The sons of Cethin all of them passing by according to the sceptres of their captaincy were in number 17,300 And the sons of Doin passing by according to the sceptres of their captaincies were in number 17,700 And the number of the camp of the sons of Japheth, all of them men of might and all girt with their armour, which were set in the sight of their captains was 140,202 besides women and children. The account of Japheth in full was in number 142,000 ⁵ And Nembroth passed by, he and the son(s) of Cham all of them passing by according to the sceptres of their captaincies were found in number 24,800 The sons of Phua all of them passing by according to the sceptres of their captaincies were in number 27,700 And the sons of Canaan all of them passing by according to the sceptres of their captaincies were found in number 32,800 The sons of Soba all of them passing by according to the sceptres of their captaincies were found in number 4,300 The sons of Lebilla all of them passing by according to the sceptres of their captaincies were found in number 22,300 And the sons of Sata all of them passing by according to the sceptres of their captaincies were found in number 25,300 And the sons of Remma all of them passing by according to the sceptres of their captaincies were found in number 30,600 And the sons of Sabaca all of them passing by according to the sceptres of their captaincies were found in number 46,400 And the number of the camp of the sons of Cham, all of them mighty men, and furnished with armour, which were set in the sight of their captaincies was in number 244,900 besides women and children. ⁶ And Jectan the son of Sem looked upon the sons of Elam, and they were all of them passing by according to the number of the sceptres of their captaincies in number 47,000 And the sons of Assur all of them passing by according to the sceptres of their captaincies were found in number 73,000 And the sons of Aram all of them passing by according to the sceptres of their captaincies were found in number 87,300 The sons of Lud all of them passing by according to the sceptres of their captaincies were found in number 30,600 [The number of the sons of Cham was 73,000] But the sons of Arfaxat all of them passing by according to the sceptres of their captaincies were in number 114,600 And the whole number of them was 347,600 ⁷ The number of the camp of the sons of Sem, all of them setting forth in valour and in the commandment of war in the sight of their captaincies was † ix † besides women and children. ⁸ And these are the generations of Noe set forth separately, whereof the whole number together was 914,000 And all these were counted while Noe was yet alive, and in the presence of Noe 350 years after the flood. And all the days of Noe were 950 years, and he died.

VI.

¹ Then all they that had been divided and dwelt upon the earth gathered together there after, and dwelt together; *and they set forth from the East and found a plain in the land of Babylon: and there they dwelt, and they said every man to his neighbour*: Behold, it will come to pass that we shall be scattered every man. from his brother, and in the latter days we shall be fighting one against another. Now, therefore, come and let us build for ourselves a tower, the head whereof shall reach unto heaven, and we shall

make us a name and a renown upon the earth. ² And they said everyone to his neighbour: Let us take bricks (*lit.* stones), and let us, each one, write our names upon the bricks and burn them with fire: and that which is thoroughly burned shall be for mortar and brick. (*Perhaps*, that which is not thoroughly burned shall be for mortar, and that which is, for brick.) ³ And they took every man their bricks, saving 12 men, which would not take them, and these are their names: Abraham, Nachor, Loth, Ruge, Tenute, Zaba, Armodath, Iobab, Esar, Abimahel, Saba, Auphin. ⁴ And the people of the land laid hands on them and brought them before their princes and said: These are the men that have transgressed our counsels and will not walk in our ways. And the princes said unto them: Wherefore would ye not set every man your bricks with the people of the land? And they answered and said: We will not set bricks with you, neither will we be joined with your desire. One Lord know we, and him do we worship. And if ye should cast us into the fire with your bricks, we will not consent to you. ⁵ And the princes were wroth and said: As they have said, so do unto them, and if they consent not to set bricks with you, ye shall burn them with fire together with your bricks. ⁶ Then answered Jectan which was the first prince of the captains: Not so, but there shall be given them a space of 7 days. And it shall be, if they repent of their evil counsels, and will set bricks along with us, they shall live; but if not, let them be burned according to your word. But he sought how he might save them out of the hands of the people; for he was of their tribe, and he served God. ⁷ And when he had thus said he took them and shut them up in the king's house: and when it was evening the prince commanded 50 mighty men of valour to be called unto him, and said unto them: Go forth and take to-night these men that are shut up in mine house, and put provision for them from my house upon 10 beasts, and the men bring ye to me, and their provision together with the beasts take ye to the mountains and wait for them there: and know this, that if any man shall know what I have said unto you, I will burn you with fire. ⁸ And the men set forth and did all that their prince commanded them, and took the men from his house by night; and took provision and put it upon beasts and took them to the hill country as he commanded them. ⁹ And the prince called unto him those 12 men and said to them: Be of good courage and fear not, for ye shall not die. For God in whom ye trust is mighty, and therefore be ye stablished in him, for he will deliver you and save you. And now lo, I have commanded So men to take [you with] provision from my house, and go before you into the hill country and wait for you in the valley: and I will give you other 50 men which shall guide you thither: go ye therefore and hide yourselves there in the valley, having water to drink that floweth down from the rocks: hold yourselves *there* for 30 days, until the anger of the people of the land be appeased and until God send his wrath upon them and break them. For I know that the counsel of iniquity which they have agreed to perform shall not stand, for their thought is vain. And it shall be when 7 days are expired and they shall seek for you, I will say unto them: They have gone forth and have broken the door of the prison wherein they were shut up and have fled by night, and I have sent 100 men to seek them. So will I turn them from their madness that is upon them. ¹⁰ And there answered him 11 of the men saying: Thy servants have found favour in thy sight, in that we are set free out of the hands of these proud men. ¹¹ But Abram only kept silence, and the prince said unto him: Wherefore answerest thou not me, Abram, servant of God? Abram answered and said: Lo, I flee away to-day into the hill country, and if I escape the fire, wild beasts will come out of the mountains and devour us. Or our victuals will fail and we shall die of hunger; and we shall be found fleeing from the people of the land and shall fall in our sins. And now, as he liveth in whom I trust, I will not remove from my place wherein they have put me: and if there be any sin of mine so that I be indeed burned, the will of God be done. And the prince said unto him: Thy blood be upon thy head, if thou refuse to go forth with these. But if thou consent, thou shall be delivered. Yet if thou wilt abide, abide as thou art. And Abram said: I will not go forth, but I will abide here. ¹² And the prince took those 11 men and sent other 50 with them, and commanded them saying: Wait, ye also, in the hill country for 15 days with those 50 which were sent before you; and after that ye shall return and say We have not found them, as I said to the former ones. And know that if any man transgress one of all these words that I have spoken unto you, he shall be burned with fire. So the men went forth, and he took Abram by himself and shut him up where he had been shut up aforetime. ¹³ And after 7 days were passed, the people were gathered together and spake unto their prince saying: Restore us the men which would not consent unto us, that we may burn them with fire. And they sent captains to bring them, and they found them not, save Abram only. And they gathered all of them to their prince saying: The men whom ye shut up are fled and have escaped that which we counselled. ¹⁴ And Phenech and Nemroth said unto Jectan: Where are the men whom thou didst shut up? But he said: They have broken prison and fled by night: but I have sent 100 men to seek them, and commanded them if they find them that they should not only burn them with fire but give their bodies to the fowls of the heaven and so destroy them. ¹⁵ Then said they: This *fellow* which is found alone, let us burn him. And they took Abram and brought him before their princes and said to him: Where are they that were with thee? And he said: Verily at night I slept, and when I awaked I found them not. ¹⁶ And they took him and built a furnace and kindled it with fire, and put bricks burned with fire into the furnace. Then Jectan the prince being amazed (*lit.* melted) in his mind took Abram and put him with the bricks into the furnace of fire. ¹⁷ But God stirred up a great earthquake, and the fire gushed forth of the furnace and brake out into flames and sparks of fire and consumed all them that stood round about in sight of the furnace; and all they that were burned in that day were 83,500 But upon Abram was there not any the least hurt by the burning of the fire. ¹⁸ And Abram arose out of the furnace, and the fiery furnace fell down, and Abram was saved. And he went unto the 11 men that were hid in the hill country and told them all that had befallen him, and they came down with him out of the hill country rejoicing in the name of the Lord, and no man met them to affright them that day. And they called that place by the name of Abram, and in the tongue of the Chaldeans Deli, which is being interpreted, God.

VII.

¹ And it came to pass after these things, that the people of the land turned not from their evil thoughts: and they came together again unto their princes and said: The people shall not be overcome for ever: and now let us come together and build us a city and a tower which shall never be removed. ² And when they had begun to build, God saw the city and the tower which the children of men were building, *and he said: Behold, this is one people and their speech is one*, and this which they have begun to build the earth will not sustain, neither will the heaven suffer it, beholding it: and it shall be, if they be not now hindered, that they shall dare all things that they shall take in mind to do. ³ *Therefore, lo, I will divide their speech*, and scatter them over all countries, that they may not know every man his brother, neither every man understand the speech of his neighbour. And I will deliver them to the rocks, and they shall build themselves tabernacles of stubble and straw, and shall dig themselves caves and shall live therein like beasts of the field, and thus shall they continue before my face for ever, that they may never devise such things. And I will esteem them as a drop of water, and liken them unto spittle: and unto some of them their end shall come by water, and other of them shall be dried up with thirst. ⁴ And before all of them will I choose my servant Abram, and I will bring him out from their land, and lead him into the land which mine eye hath looked upon from the beginning when all the dwellers upon earth sinned before my face, and I brought *on them* the water of the flood: and *then* I destroyed not *that land*, but preserved it. Therefore the fountains of my wrath did not break forth therein, neither did the water of my destruction come down upon it. For there will I make my servant Abram to dwell, and I will make my covenant with him, and bless his seed, and will be called his God for ever. ⁵ Howbeit when the people that dwelt in the land had begun to build the tower, God divided their speech, and changed their likeness. And they knew not every man his brother, neither did each understand the speech of his neighbour. So it came to pass that when the builders commanded their helpers to bring bricks they brought water, and if they asked for water, the others brought them straw. And so their counsel was broken and they ceased building the city: and *God scattered them thence over the face of all the earth. Therefore was the name of that place called Confusion, because there God confounded their speech, and scattered them thence over the face of all the earth.*

VIII.

But Abram went forth thence and dwelt in the land of Chanaan, and took with him Loth his brothers son, and Sarai his wife.

¹ And because Sarai was barren and had no offspring, then Abram took Agar her maid, and she bare him Ismahel. And Ismahel begat 12 sons. ² Then Loth departed from Abram and dwelt in Sodom [but Abram dwelt in the land of Cam]. And the men of Sodom were very evil and sinners exceedingly. ³ And God appeared unto Abraham saying: Unto thy seed will I give this land; and thy name shall be called Abraham, and Sarai thy wife shall be called Sara. Ana I will give thee of her an eternal seed and make my covenant with thee. And Abraham knew Sara his wife, and she conceived and bare Isaac. ⁴ And Isaac took him a wife of Mesopotamia, the daughter of Bathuel, which conceived and bare him Esau and Jacob. ⁵ And Esau took to him for wives Judin the daughter of Bereu, and Basemath the daughter of Elon, and Elibema the daughter of Anan, and Manem the daughter of Samahel. And <<Basemath>> *bare him Adelifan, and the sons of Adelifan were Temar, Omar, Seffor, Getan, Tenaz, Amalec.* And Judin bare Tenacis, Ieruebemas, *Bassemen, Rugil: and the sons of Rugil were*

Naizar, Samaza; and Elibema bare Auz, Iollam, Coro. Manem bare Tenetde, Thenatela. ⁶ And Jacob took to him for wives the daughters Gen. of Laban the Syrian, Lia and Rachel, and two concubines, Bala and Zelpha. And Lia bare him Ruben, Simeon, Levi, Juda, Isachar, Zabulon, and Dina their sister. But Rachel bare Joseph and Benjamin. Bala bare Dan and Neptalim, and Zelpha bare Gad and Aser. These are the 12 sons of Jacob and one daughter. ⁷ And Jacob dwelt in the land of Chanaan, and Sichem the son of Emor the Correan forced his daughter Dina and humbled her. And Simeon and Levi the sons of Jacob went in and slew all their city with the edge of the sword, and took Dina their sister, and went out thence. ⁸ And thereafter Job took her to wife and begat of her 14 sons and 6 daughters, even 7 sons and 3 daughters before he was smitten with affliction, and thereafter when he was made whole 7 sons and 3 daughters. And these are their names: Eliphac, Erinoe, Diasat, Philias, Diffar, Zellud, Thelon: and his daughters Meru, Litaz, Zeli. And such as had been the names of the former, so were they also of the latter. ⁹ Now Jacob and his 12 sons dwelt in the land of Chanaan: and *his sons* hated their brother Joseph, whom also they delivered into Egypt, to Petephres the chief of the cooks of Pharao, and he abode with him 14 years. ¹⁰ And it came to pass after that the king of Egypt had seen a dream, that they told him of Joseph, and he declared him the dreams. And it was so after he declared his dreams, that Pharao made him prince over all the land of Egypt. At that time there was a famine in all the land, as Joseph had foreseen. And his brethren came down into Egypt to buy food, because in Egypt only was there food. And Joseph knew his brethren, and was made known to them, and dealt not evilly with them. And he sent and called his father out of the land of Chanaan, and he came down unto him. ¹¹ *And these are the names of the sons of Israel which came down into Egypt with Jacob*, each one with his house. *The sons of Reuben, Enoch and Phallud, Esrom and Carmin; the sons of Simeon, Namuhel and Iamin and Dot and Iachin, and Saul the son of a Canaanitish woman. The sons of Levi, Gerson, Caat and Merari: but the sons of Juda, Auna, Selon, Phares, Zerami. The sons of Isachar, Tola and Phua, Job and Sombram. The sons of Zabulon, Sarelon and Iaillil*. And Dina their sister bare 14 sons and 6 daughters. And these are the generations *of Lia whom she bare to Jacob. All the souls of sons and daughters were 72*. ¹² *Now the sons of Dan were Usinam. The sons of Neptalim*, Betaal, Neemmu, Surem, Optisariel. *And these are the generations of Balla which she bare to Jacob. All the souls were 8* ¹³ *But the sons of Gad*: . . . Sariel, Sua, Visui, Mophat *and Sar: their sister the daughter of Seriebel, Melchiel. These are the generations of Zelpha* the wife of Jacob *which she bare to him. And all the souls of sons and daughters were* in number 10 ¹⁴ *And the sons of Joseph, Ephraim and Manassen: and Benjamin* begat Gela, *Esbel, Abocmephec,* Utundeus. *And these were the souls which Rachel bare to Jacob,* ¹⁴ And they went down into Egypt and abode there 210 years.

IX.

¹ And it came to pass after the departure of Joseph, *the children of Israel were multiplied and increased greatly. And there arose another king in Egypt which knew not Joseph: and he said to his people: Lo, this people is multiplied more than we. Come let us take counsel against them that they multiply not. And the king of Egypt commanded all his people saying: Every son that shall be born to the He brews, cast into the river, but keep the females alive.*

¹ And the Egyptians answered their king saying: Let us slay their males and keep their females, to give them to our bondmen for wives: and he that is born of them shall be a bondman and serve us. And this is that that did appear most evil before the Lord. ² Then the elders of the people assembled the people with mourning and mourned and lamented saying: An untimely birth have the wombs of our wives suffered. Our fruit is delivered over to our enemies and now we are cut off. Yet let us appoint us an ordinance, that no man come near his wife, lest the fruit of their womb be defiled, and our bowels serve idols: for it is better to die childless, until we know what God will do. ³ And Amram answered and said: It will sooner come to pass that the age shall be utterly abolished and the immeasurable world fall, or the heart of the depths touch the stars, than that the race of the children of Israel should be diminished. And it shall be, when the covenant is fulfilled whereof God when he made it spake to Abraham saying: Surely thy sons shall dwell in a land that is not theirs, and shall be brought into bondage and afflicted 400 years.–And lo, since the word was passed which God spake to Abraham, there are 350 years. (And) since we have been in bondage in Egypt it is 130 years. ⁴ Now therefore I will not abide by that which ye ordain, but will go in and take my wife and beget sons, that we may be made many on the earth. For God will not continue in his anger, neither will he alway forget his people, nor cast forth the race of Israel to nought upon the earth, neither did he in vain make his covenant with our fathers: yea, when as yet we were not, God spake of these things. ⁵ Now therefore I will go and take my wife, neither will I consent to the commandment of this king. And if it be right in your eyes, so let us do all of us, for it shall be, when our wives conceive, they shall not be known to be great with child until 3 months are fulfilled, like as also our mother Thamar did, for her intent was not to fornication, but because she would not separate herself from the sons of Israel she took thought and said: It is better for me to die for sinning with my father-in-law than to be joined to Gentiles. And she hid the fruit of her womb till the 3rd month, for then was it perceived. And as she went to be put to death she affirmed it saying: The man whose is this staff and this ring and goatskin, of him have I conceived. And her device delivered her out of all peril. ⁶ Now therefore let us also do thus. And it shall be when the time of bringing forth is come, if it be possible, we will not cast forth the fruit of our womb. And who knoweth if thereby God will be provoked, to deliver us from our humiliation? ⁷ And the word which Amram had in his heart was pleasing before God: and God said: Because the thought of Amram is pleasing before me, and he hath not set at nought the covenant made between me and his fathers, therefore, lo now, that which is begotten of him shall serve me for ever, and by him will I do wonders in the house of Jacob, and will do by him signs and wonders for my people which I have done for none other, and will perform in them my glory and declare unto them my ways. ⁸ I the Lord will kindle for him my lamp to dwell in him, and will show him my covenant which no man hath seen, and manifest to him my great excellency, and my justice and judgments and will shine for him a perpetual light. For in ancient days I thought of him, saying: My spirit shall not be a mediator among these men for ever, for they are flesh, and their days shall be 120 years. ⁹ And Amram of the tribe of Levi went forth and took a wife of his tribe, and it was so when he took her, that the residue did after him and took their wives. Now he had one son and one daughter, and their names were Aaron and Maria, ¹⁰ And the spirit of God came upon Maria by night, and she saw a dream, and told her parents in the morning saying: I saw this night, and behold a man in a linen garment stood and said to me: Go and tell thy parents: behold, that which shall be born of you shall be cast into the water, for by him water shall be dried up, and by him will I do signs, and I will save my people, and he shall have the captaincy thereof alway. And when Maria had told her dream her parents believed her not. ¹¹ But the word of the king of Egypt prevailed against the children of Israel and they were humiliated and oppressed in the work of bricks. ¹² But Jochabeth conceived of Amram and hid *the child* in her womb 3 months, for she could not hide it longer: because the king of Egypt had appointed overseers of the region, that when the Hebrew women brought forth they should cast the males into the river straightway. And she took her child and made him an ark of the bark of a pine-tree and set the ark on the edge of the river. ¹³ Now the boy was born in the covenant of God and in the covenant of his flesh. ¹⁴ And it came to pass, when they cast him out, all the elders gathered together and chode with Amram saying: Are not these the words which we spake saying: "It is better for us to die childless than that our fruit should be cast into the water?" And when they said so, Amram hearkened not to them. ¹⁵ But the daughter of Pharao came down to wash in the river according as she had seen in a dream, and her maids saw the ark, and she sent one of them and took it and opened it. And when she saw the child and looked upon the covenant, that is, the testament in his flesh, she said: He is of the children of the Hebrews. ¹⁶ And she took him and nourished him and he became her son, and she called his name Moyses. But his mother called him Melchiel. And the child was nourished and became glorious above all men, and by him God delivered the children of Israel, as he had said.

X.

¹ Now when the king of Egypt was dead another king arose, and afflicted all the people of Israel. But they cried unto the Lord and he heard them, and sent Moses and delivered them out of the land of Egypt: and God sent also upon them 10 plagues and smote them. Now these were the plagues, namely, blood, and frogs, and all manner of flies, hail, and death of cattle, locusts and gnats, and darkness that might be felt, and the death of the firstborn. ² And when they had gone forth thence and were journeying, the heart of the Egyptians was yet again hardened, and they continued to pursue them, and found them by the Red Sea. And the children of Israel cried unto their God and spake to Moyses saying: Lo, now is come the time of our destruction, for the sea is before us and the multitude of enemies behind us, and we in the midst. Was it for this that God brought us out, or are these the covenants which he made with our fathers saying: To your seed will I give the land wherein ye dwell? and now let him do with us that which seemeth good in his sight. ³ Then did the children of Israel sever their counsels into three divisions of counsels, because of the fear of the time. For the tribe of Ruben and of Isachar and. of Zabulon and of Symeon said: Come, let us cast ourselves into the sea, for it is better for us to die in the water than to

be slain of our enemies. And the tribe of Gad and of Aser and of Dan and Neptalim said: Nay, but let us return with them, and if they will give us our lives, we will serve them. But the tribe of Levi and of Juda and Joseph and the tribe of Benjamin said: Not so, but let us take our weapons and fight them, and God will be with us. ⁴ Moses also cried unto the Lord and said: O Lord God of our fathers, didst thou not say unto me: Go and tell the sons of Lia, God hath sent me unto You? And now, behold, thou hast brought thy people to the brink of the sea, and the enemy follow after them: but thou, Lord, remember thy name. ⁵ And God said: Whereas thou hast cried unto me, take thy rod and smite the sea, and it shall be dried up. And when Moses did all this, God rebuked the sea, and the sea was dried up: the seas of waters stood still and the depths of the earth appeared, and the foundations of the dwelling-place were laid bare at the noise of the fear of God and at the breath of the anger of my Lord. ⁶ And Israel passed over on dry land in the midst of the sea. And the Egyptians saw and went on to pursue after them, and God hardened their mind, and they knew not that they were entering into the sea. And so it was that while the Egyptians were in the sea God commanded the sea yet again, and said to Moses: Smite the sea yet once again. And he did so. And the Lord commanded the sea and it returned unto his waves, and covered the Egyptians and their chariots and their horsemen unto this day. ⁷ But as for his own people, he led them forth into the wilderness: forty years did he rain bread from heaven for them, and he brought them quails from the sea, and a well of water following them brought he forth for them. And in a pillar of cloud he led them by day and in a pillar of fire by night did he give light unto them.

XI.

And in the 3rd month of the journeying of the children of Israel out of the land of Egypt, they came into the wilderness of Sinai.

¹ And God remembered his word and said: I will give light unto the world, and lighten the habitable places, and make my covenant with the children of men, and glorify my people above all nations, for unto them will I put forth an eternal exaltation which shall be unto them a light, but unto the ungodly a chastisement. ² And he said unto Moses: Behold, I will call thee to-morrow: be thou ready and tell my people: "For three days let not a man come near his wife," and on the 3rd day I will speak unto thee and unto them, and after that thou shalt come up unto me. And I will put my words in thy mouth and thou shalt enlighten my people. For I have given into thy hands an everlasting law whereby I will judge all the world. For this shall be for a testimony. For if men say: "We have not known thee, and therefore we have not served thee," therefore will I take vengeance upon them, because they have not known my law. ³ And Moses did as God commanded him, and sanctified the people and said unto them: *Be ye ready on the 3rd day*, for after 3 days will God make his covenant with you. And the people were sanctified. ⁴ *And it came to pass on the 3rd day that, lo, there were voices of thunderings (lit. them that sounded) and brightness of lightnings and the voice of instruments sounding aloud. And there was fear upon all the people that were in the camp. And Moses put forth the people to meet God.* ⁵ And behold the mountains burned with fire and the earth shook and the hills were removed and the mountains overthrown: the depths boiled, and all the habitable places were shaken: and the heavens were folded up and the clouds drew up water. And flames of fire shone forth and thunderings and lightnings were multiplied and winds and tempests made a roaring: the stars were gathered together and the angels ran before, until God established the law of an everlasting covenant with the children of Israel, and gave unto them an eternal commandment which should not pass away. ⁶ *And at that time the Lord spake unto his people all these words, saying: I am the Lord thy God which brought thee out of the land of Egypt, out of the house of bondage. Thou shalt not make to thyself graven gods, neither* shalt thou make any abominable image of the sun or the moon or any of the ornaments of the heaven, nor the *likeness of all things that are upon the earth* nor of such as creep in the waters or upon the earth. *I am the Lord thy God, a jealous God, requiting the sins of* them that sleep upon the living children of the ungodly, if they walk in the ways of their fathers; *unto the third and fourth generation, doing* (or *shewing*) *mercy unto* 1000 *generations to them that love me and keep my commandments.* ⁷ *Thou shall not take the name of the Lord thy God in vain*, that my ways be not made vain. *For God* abominateth *him that taketh his name in vain.* ⁸ *Keep the sabbath day to sanctify it. Six days do thy work, but the seventh day is the sabbath of the Lord. In it thou shall do no work, thou and all* thy labourers, saving that therein *ye praise the Lord in the congregation of the elders and glorify* the Mighty One *in the seat of the aged. For in six days the Lord made heaven and earth, the sea and all that are in them*, and all the world, the wilderness that is not inhabited, and all things that do labour, and all the order of the heaven, *and God rested the seventh day. Therefore God sanctified the seventh day*, because he rested therein. ⁹ *Thou shalt love thy father and my mother* and fear them: and then shall thy light rise, and I will command the heaven and it shall pay thee the rain thereof, and the earth shall hasten her fruit and thy days shall be many, and thou shalt dwell in thy land, and shalt not be childless, for thy seed shall not fail, even that of them that dwell therein. ¹⁰ *Thou shalt not commit adultery*, for thine enemies did not commit adultery with thee, but thou camest out with a high hand. ¹¹ *Thou shall not kill*: because thine enemies got not the mastery over thee to slay thee, but thou beheldest their death. ¹² *Thou shalt not bear false witness against thy neighbour*, speaking falsely, lest thy watchmen speak falsely against thee. ¹³ *Thou shall not covet thy neighbor's house, nor that which he hath*, lest others also covet thy land. ¹⁴ And when the Lord ceased speaking, the people feared with a great fear: and they saw the mountain burning with torches of fire, and they said to Moses: *Speak thou unto us, and let not God speak unto us, lest peradventure we die*. For, lo, to-day we know that God speaketh with man face to face, and man shall live. And now have we perceived of a truth how that the earth bare the voice of God with trembling. And Moses said unto them: Fear not, this cause came this voice unto you, that ye should not sin (or, for this cause, that he might prove. you, God came unto you, that ye might receive the fear of him unto you, that ye sin not). ¹⁵ *And all the people stood afar off, but Moses drew near unto the cloud*, knowing that God was there. And then God spake unto him his justice and judgements, and kept him by him 40 days and 40 nights. And there did he command him many things, and showed him the tree of life, whereof he cut and took and put it into Mara, and the water of Mara was made sweet and followed them in the desert 40 years, and went up into the hills with them and came down into the plain. Also he commanded him concerning the tabernacle and the ark of the Lord, and the sacrifice of burnt offerings and of incense, and the ordinance of the table and of the candlestick and concerning the laver and the base thereof, and the shoulder-piece and the breastplate, and the very precious stones, that the children of Israel should make them so: and he shewed him the likeness of them to make them according to the pattern which he saw. And said unto him: Make for me a sanctuary and the tabernacle of my glory shall be among you.

XII.

¹ And Moses came down: and whereas he was covered with invisible light–for he had gone down into the place where is the light of the sun and moon,–the light of his face overcame the brightness of the sun and moon, and he knew it not. And it was so, when he came down to the children of Israel, they saw him and knew him not. But when he spake, then they knew him. And this was like that which was done in Egypt when *Joseph knew his brethren but they knew not him*. And it came to pass after that, when Moses knew that his face was become glorious, he made him a veil to cover his face. ² But while he was in the mount, the heart of the people was corrupted, and *they came together to Aaron saying: Make us gods* that we may serve them, as the other nations also have. For this Moses by whom the wonders were done before us, is taken from us. And Aaron said unto them: Have patience, for Moses will come and bring judgement near to us, and light up a law for us, and set forth from his mouth the great excellency of God, and appoint judgements unto our people. ³ And when he said this, they hearkened not unto him, that the word might be fulfilled which was spoken in the day when the people sinned in building the tower, when God said: And now if I forbid them not, *they will adventure all that they take in mind to do*, and worse. But Aaron feared, because the people was greatly strengthened, and said to them: Bring us the earrings of your wives. And the men sought every one his wife, and they gave them straightway, and they put them in the fire and they were made into a figure, and there came out a molten calf. ⁴ And the Lord said to Moses: Make haste hence, for the people is corrupted and hath dealt deceitfully with my ways which I commanded them. What and if the promises are at an end which I made to their fathers when I said: To your seed will I give this land wherein ye dwell? For behold the people is not yet entered into the land, even though they bear *my* judgements, *yet* have they forsaken me. And therefore I know that if they enter the land they will do yet greater iniquities. Now therefore I also will forsake them: and I will turn again and make peace with them, that a house may be built for me among them; and that house also shall be done away, because they will sin against me, and the race of men shall be unto me as a drop of a pitcher, and shall be counted as spittle. ⁵ And Moses hasted and came down and saw the calf, and he looked upon the tables and saw that they were not written: and he hasted and brake them; and his hands were opened and he became like a woman travailing of her firstborn, which when she is taken in her pangs her hands are upon her bosom, and she shall have no strength to help her to bring forth. ⁶ And it came to pass after an hour he said within *himself*: Bitterness prevaileth not for ever, neither hath evil the dominion alway. Now therefore will I arise, and strengthen my

loins: for albeit they have sinned, *yet* shall not these things be in vain that were declared unto me above. ⁷ And he arose and brake the calf and cast it into the water, and made the people drink. And it was so, if any man's will in his mind were that the calf should be made, his tongue was cut off, but if any had been constrained thereto by fear, his face shone. ⁸ And then Moses went up into the mount and prayed the Lord, saying: Behold now, thou art God which hast planted this vineyard and set the roots thereof in the deep, and stretched out the shoots of it unto thy most high seat. Look upon it at this time, for the vineyard hath put forth her fruit and hath not known him that tilled her. And now if thou be wroth with thy vineyard and root it up out of the deep, and wither up the shoots from thy most high eternal seat, the deep will come no more to nourish it, neither thy throne to refresh that thy vineyard which thou hast burned. ⁹ For thou art he that art all light, and hast adorned thy house with precious stones and gold and perfumes and spices (*or* and jasper), and wood of balsam and cinnamon, and with roots of myrrh and costum hast thou strewed thine house, and with divers meats and sweetness of many drinks hast thou satisfied it. If therefore thou have not pity upon thy vineyard, all these things are done in vain, Lord, and thou wilt have none to glorify thee. For even if thou plant another vineyard, neither will that one trust in thee, because thou didst destroy the former. For if verily thou forsake the world, who will do for thee that that thou hast spoken as God? And now let thy wrath be restrained from thy vineyard the more <<because of>> that thou hast said and that which remaineth to be spoken, and let not thy labour be in vain, neither let thine heritage be torn asunder in humiliation. ¹⁰ And God said to him: Behold I am become merciful according to thy words. Hew thee out therefore two tables of stone from the place whence thou hewedst the former, and write upon them again my judgements which were on the first.

XIII.

¹ And Moses hasted and did all that God Ex. 34 commanded him, and came down and made the tables <<and the tabernacle>>, and the vessels thereof, and the ark and the lamps and the table and the altar of burnt offerings and the altar of incense and the shoulderpiece and the breastplate and the precious stones and the laver and the bases and all things that were shewn him. And he ordered all the vestures of the priests, the girdles and the *rest*, the mitre, the golden plate and the holy crown: he made also the anointing oil for the priests, and the priests themselves he sanctified. And when all things were finished the cloud covered all of them. ² Then Moses cried unto the Lord, and God spake to him from the tabernacle saying: This is the law of the altar, whereby ye shall sacrifice unto me and pray for your souls. But as concerning that which ye shall offer me, offer ye of cattle the calf, the sheep and the she goat: but of fowls the turtle and the dove. 3, And if there be leprosy in your land, and it so be that the leper is cleansed, let them take for the Lord two live young birds, and wood of cedar and hyssop and scarlet; and he shall come to the priest, and he shall kill one, and keep the other. And he shall order the leper according to all that I have commanded in my law. ⁴ And it shall be when the times come round to you, ye shall sanctify me with a feast-day and rejoice before me at the feast of the unleavened bread, and set bread before me, keeping a feast of remembrance because on that day ye came forth of the land of Egypt. ⁵ And in the feast of weeks ye shall set bread before me and make me an offering for your fruits. ⁶ But the feast of trumpets shall be for an offering for your watchers, because therein I oversaw my creation, that ye may be mindful of the whole world. In the beginning of the year, when ye show them me, I will acknowledge the number of the dead and of them that are born, and the fast of mercy. For ye shall fast unto me for your souls, that the promises of your fathers may be fulfilled. ⁷ Also the feast of tabernacles bring ye to me: ye shall take for me the pleasant fruit of the tree, and boughs of palm-tree and willows and cedars, and branches of myrrh: and I will remember the whole earth in rain, and the measure of the seasons shall be established, and I will order the stars and command the clouds, and the winds shall sound and the lightnings run abroad, and there shall be a storm of thunder, and this shall be for a perpetual sign. Also the nights shall yield dew, as I spake after the flood of the earth ⁸ when I (*or* Then he) gave him precept as concerning the year of the life of Noe, and said to him: These are the years which I ordained after the weeks wherein I visited the city of men, at what time I shewed them (*or* him) the place of birth and the colour (*or* and the serpent), and I (*or* he) said: This is. the place of which I taught the first man saying: If thou transgress not that I bade thee, all things shall be subject unto thee. But he transgressed my ways and was persuaded of his wife, and she was deceived by the serpent. And then was death ordained unto the generations of men. ⁹ And furthermore the Lord shewed (*or*, And the Lord said further: I shewed) him the ways of paradise and said unto him: These are the ways which men have lost by not walking in them, because they have sinned against me. ¹⁰ And the Lord commanded him concerning the salvation of the souls of the people and said: If they shall walk in my ways I will not forsake them, but will alway be merciful unto them, and will bless their seed, and the earth shall haste to yield her fruit, and there shall be rain for them to increase their gains, and the earth shall not be barren. Yet verily I know that they will corrupt their ways, and I shall forsake them, and they will forget the covenants which I made with their fathers. Yet will I not forget them for ever: for in the last days they shall know that because of their sins their seed was forsaken; for I am faithful in my ways.

XIV.

¹ *At that time God said unto him: Begin to number my people from* 20 *years and upwards* unto 40 years, that I may show your tribes all that I declared unto their fathers in a strange land. For by the 50th part *of them* did I raise them up out of the land of Egypt, but 40 and 9 parts of them died in the land of Egypt. ² When thou hast ordered them and numbered them (*or*, While ye abode there. And when thou hast numbered them, etc.), write the tale of them, till I fulfil all that I spake unto their fathers, and set them firmly in their own land: for I will not diminish any word of those I have spoken unto their fathers, even of those which I said to them: Your seed shall be as the stars of heaven for multitude. By number shall they enter into the land, and in a short time shall they become without number. ³ Then Moses went down and numbered them, and the number of the people was 604,550 *But the tribe of Levi numbered he not among them, for so was it commanded him*; only he numbered them that were upwards of 50 years, of whom the number was 47,300 Also he numbered them that were below 20 years, and the number of them was 850,850 And he looked over the tribe of Levi and the whole number of them was CXX. CCXD. DCXX. CC. DCCC. ⁴ And Moses declared the number of them to God; and God said to him: These are the words which I spake to their fathers in the land of Egypt, and appointed a number, even 210 years, unto all that saw my wonders. Now the number of them all was 9000 times 10,000, 200 times 95,000 men, besides women, and I put to death the whole multitude of them because they believed me not, and the 50th part of them I was left and I sanctified them unto me. Therefore do I command the generation of my people to give me tithes of their fruits, to be before me for a memorial of how great oppression I have removed from them. ⁵ And when Moses came down and declared these things to the people, they mourned and lamented and abode in the desert two years.

XV.

¹ And Moses sent spies to spy out the land, even 12 men, for so was it commanded him. And when they had gone up and seen the land, they returned to him bringing of the fruits of the land, and troubled the heart of the people, saying: Ye will not be able to inherit the land, for it is shut up with iron bars by their mighty men. ² But two men out of the 12 spake not so, but said: Like as hard iron can overcome the stars, or as weapons can conquer the lightnings, or the fowls of the air put out the thunder, so can these men resist the Lord. For they saw how that as they went up the lightnings of the stars shone and the thunders followed, sounding with them. ³ And these are the names of the men: Chaleb the son of Jephone, the son of Beri, the son of Batuel, the son of Galipha, the son of Zenen, the son of Selimun, the son of Selon, the son of Juda. The other, Jesus the son of Naue, the son of Eliphat, the son of Gal, the son of Nephelien, the son of Emon, the son of Saul, the son of Dabra, the son of Effrem, the son of Joseph. ⁴ But the people would not hear the voice of the twain, but were greatly troubled, and spake saying: Be these the words which God spake to us saying: I will bring you into a land flowing with milk and honey? And how now doth he bring us up that we may fall on the sword, and our women shall go into captivity? ⁵ And when they said thus, the glory of God appeared suddenly, and he said to Moses: Doth this people thus persevere to hearken unto me not at all? Lo now the counsel which hath gone forth from me shall not be in vain. I will send the angel of mine anger upon them to break up their bodies with fire in the wilderness. And I will give commandment to mine angels which watch over them that they pray not for them, for I will shut up their souls in the treasuries of darkness, and I will say to my servants their fathers: Behold, this is the seed unto which I spake saying: *Your seed shall come into a land that is not theirs*, *and the nation whom they shall serve I will judge*. And I fulfilled my words and made their enemies to melt away, and subjected angels under their feet, and put a cloud for a covering of their heads, and commanded the sea, and the depths were broken before their face and walls of water stood u. And there hath not been the like of this word since the day when I said: Let the waters under the heaven be gathered into one place, unto this day. And I brought them out, and slew their enemies and led them before me unto the Mount Sina. And I bowed the heavens and came down to kindle a lamp for my people, and to set bounds to all creatures. And I taught them to make me a sanctuary that I might dwell among them. But they have forsaken me and become

faithless in my words, and their mind hath fainted, and now behold the days shall come when I will do unto them as they have desired and I will cast forth their bodies in the wilderness. ⁷ And Moses said: Before thou didst take seed wherewith to make man upon the earth, did I order his ways? therefore now let thy mercy suffer us unto the end, and thy pity for the length of days.

XVI.

¹ At that time did he give him commandment concerning the fringes: and then did Choreb rebel and 200 men with him and spake saying: What if a law which we cannot bear is ordained for us? ² And God was wroth and said: I commanded the earth and it gave me man, and unto him were born at the first two sons. And the elder arose and slew the younger, and the earth hasted and swallowed his blood. But I drove forth Cain, and cursed the earth and spake unto Sion saying: Thou shalt not any more swallow up blood. And now are the thoughts of men greatly polluted. ³ Lo, I will command the earth, and it shall swallow up body and soul together, and their dwelling shall be in darkness and in destruction, and they shall not die but pine away until I remember the world and renew the earth. And then shall they die and not live, and their life shall be taken away out of the number of all men: neither shall Hell vomit them forth again, and destruction shall not remember them, and their departure shall be as that of the tribe of the nations of whom I said, "I will not remember them," that is, the camp of the Egyptians, and the people whom I destroyed with the water of the flood. And the earth shall swallow them, and I will not do any more *unto them*. ⁴ And when Moses spake all these words unto the people, Choreb, and his men were yet unbelieving. And Choreb sent to call his seven sons which were not of counsel with him. ⁵ But they sent to him in answer saying: As the painter showeth not forth an image made by his art unless he be first instructed, so we also when we received the law of the Most Mighty which teacheth us his ways, did not enter . therein save that we might walk therein. Our father begat us [not], but the Most Mighty formed us, and now if we walk in his ways we shall be his children. But if thou believe not, go thine own way. And they came not up unto him. ⁶ And it came to pass after this that the earth opened before them, and his sons sent unto him saying: If thy madness be still upon thee, who shall help thee in the day of thy destruction? and he hearkened not unto them. And the earth opened her mouth and swallowed them up, and their houses, and four times was the foundation of the earth moved to swallow up the men, as it was commanded her. And thereafter Choreb and his company groaned, until the firmament of the earth should be delivered back. ⁷ But the assemblies of the people said unto Moses: We cannot abide round about this place where Choreb and his men have been swallowed up. And he said to them. Take up your tents from round about them, neither be ye joined to their sins. And they did so.

XVII.

¹ Then was the lineage of the priests of God declared by the choosing of a tribe, and it was said unto Moses: *Take throughout every tribe one rod and put them in the tabernacle, and then shall the rod of him* to whomsoever my glory shall speak, *flourish, and I will take away the murmuring from my people*. ² And Moses did so and set 12 rods, and the rod of Aaron came out, and put forth *blossom and yielded seed of almonds*. ³ And this likeness which was born there was like unto the work which Israel wrought while he was in Mesopotamia with Laban the Syrian, when he took rods of almond, and put them at the gathering of waters, and the cattle came to drink and were divided among the peeled rods, and brought forth [kids] white and speckled and parti-coloured. ⁴ There fore was the synagogue of the people made like unto a flock of sheep, and as the cattle brought forth according to the almond rods, so was the priesthood established by means of the almond rods.

XVIII.

¹ At that time Moses slew Seon and Og, the kings of the Amorites, and divided all their land unto his people, and they dwelt therein. ² But Balac was the king of Moab, that lived over against them, and he was greatly afraid, and sent to Balaam the son of Beor the interpreter of dreams, which dwelt in Mesopotamia, and charged him saying: Behold I know how that in the reign of my father Sefor, when the Amorites fought against him, thou didst curse them and they were delivered up before him. And *now come and curse this people, for they are many, more than we, and will do thee great honour*. ³ And Balaam said: Lo, this is good in the sight of Balac, but he knoweth not that the counsel of God is not as man's counsel. And he knoweth not that the spirit which is given unto us is given for a time, and our ways are not guided except God will. *Now therefore abide ye here, and I will see what the Lord will say to me this night*. ⁴ And in the night *God said unto him: Who are the men that are come unto thee*? And Balaam said: Wherefore, Lord, dost thou tempt the race of man? They therefore cannot sustain it, for thou knewest more than they, all that was in the world, before thou foundedst it. And now enlighten thy servant if it be right that I go with them. ⁵ And God said to him: Was it not concerning this people that I spake unto Abraham in a vision saying: *Thy seed shall be as the stars of heaven*, when I raised him up above the firmament and showed him all the orderings of the stars, and required of him his son for a burnt offering? and he brought him to be laid upon the altar, but I restored him to his father. And because he resisted not, his offering was acceptable in my sight, and for the blood of him did I choose this people. And then I said unto the angels that work subtilly: Said I not of him: *To Abraham will I reveal all that I do*? ⁶ Jacob also, when he wrestled in the dust with the angel that was over the praises, did not let him go until he blessed him. And now, behold, thou thinkest to go with these, and curse them whom I have chosen. But if thou curse them, who is he that shall bless thee? ⁷ *And Balaam arose in the morning and said: Go your way, for God will not have me to come with you. And they went and told Balac* all that was said of Balaam. And *Balac sent yet again other men to Balaam* saying: Behold, I know that when thou offerest burnt offerings to God, God will be reconciled with man, and now ask yet again of thy Lord, and entreat by burnt offerings, as many as he will. For if peradventure he will be propitiated in my necessity, thou shalt have thy reward, if so be God accept thy offerings. ⁸ And Balaam said to them: Lo, the son of Sephor is foolish, and knoweth not that he dwelleth hard by (*lit.* round about) the dead: *And now tarry here this night and I will see what God will say unto me*. And God said to him: Go with them, and thy journey shall be an offence, and Balac himself shall go unto destruction. And he arose and went with them. ⁹ And his she-ass came by the way of the desert and saw the angel, and he opened the eyes of Balaam and he saw the angel and worshipped him on the earth. And the angel said to him: Haste and go on, for what thou sayest shall come to pass with him. ¹⁰ And he came unto the land of Moab and built an altar and offered sacrifices: and when he had seen a part of the people, the spirit of God abode not in him, and he took up his parable and said: Lo, Balac hath brought me hither unto the mount, saying: Come, run into the fire of these men. <<Lo>> I cannot abide that <<fire>> which waters quench, but that fire which consumeth water who shall endure? And he said to him: It is easier to take away the foundations and all the topmost part of them, and to quench the light of the sun and darken the shining of the moon, than for him who will to root up the planting of the Most Mighty or spoil his vineyard. And *Balac* himself hath not known it, because his mind is puffed up, to the intent his destruction may come swiftly. ¹¹ For behold, I see the heritage which the Most Mighty showed me in the night, and lo the days come when Moab shall be amazed at that which befalleth her, for Balac desired to persuade the Most Mighty with gifts and to purchase decision with money. Oughtest thou not to have asked what he sent upon Pharao and upon his land because he would bring them into bondage? Behold an overshadowing vine, desirable exceedingly, and who shall be jealous against it, for it withereth not? But if any say in his counsel that the Most Mighty hath laboured in vain or chosen them to no purpose, lo now I see the salvation of deliverance which is to come unto them. I am restrained in the speech of my voice and I cannot express that which I see with mine eyes, for but a little is left to me of the holy spirit which abideth in me, since I know that in that I was persuaded of Balac I have lost the days of my life: ¹² Lo, again I see the heritage of the abode of this people, and the light of it shineth above the brightness of lightning, and the running of it is swifter than arrows. And the time shall come when Moab shall groan, and they that serve Cham (Chemosh?) shall be weak, even such as took this counsel against them. But I shall gnash my teeth because I was deceived and did transgress that which was said to me in the night. Yet my prophecy shall remain manifest, and my words shall live, and the wise and prudent shall remember my words, for when I cursed I perished, and though I blessed I was not blessed. And when he had so said he held his peace. And Balac said: Thy God hath defrauded thee of many gifts from me. ¹³ Then Balaam said unto him: Come and let us advise what thou shalt do to them. Choose out the most comely women that are among you and that are in Midian and set them before them naked, and adorned with gold and jewels, and it shall be when they shall see them and lie with them, they will sin against their Lord and fall into your hands, for otherwise thou canst not subdue them. ¹⁴ And so saying Balaam turned away and returned to his place. And thereafter the people were led astray after the daughters of Moab, for Balac did all that Balaam had showed him.

XIX.

¹ At that time Moses slew the nations, and gave half of the spoils to the people, and he began to declare to them the words of the law which God spake to them in Oreb. ² And he spake to them, saying: Lo, I sleep with my fathers, and shall go unto my people. But I know that ye will arise and forsake the words that were ordained unto you by me, and God will be wroth with you and forsake you and depart out of your land, and bring

against you them that hate you, and they shall have dominion over you, but not unto the end, for he will remember the covenant which he made with your fathers. ³ But then both ye and your sons and all your generations after you will arise and seek the day of my death and will say in their heart: Who will give us a shepherd like unto Moses, or such another judge to the children of Israel, to pray for our sins at all times, and to be heard for our iniquities? ⁴ Howbeit, *this day I call heaven and earth to witness against you*, for the heaven shall hear this and the earth shall take it in with her ears, that God hath revealed the end of the world, that he might covenant with you upon his high places, and hath kindled an everlasting lamp among you. Remember, ye wicked, how that when I spake unto you, ye answered saying: All that God hath said unto us we will hear and do. But if we transgress or corrupt our ways, he shall call a witness against us and cut us off. ⁵ But know ye that ye did eat the bread of angels 40 years. And now behold I do bless your tribes, before my end come. But ye, know ye my labour wherein I have laboured with you since the day ye came up out of the land of Egypt. ⁶ And when he had so said, God spake unto him the third time, saying: Behold, thou goest to sleep with thy fathers, and this people will arise and seek me, and will forget my law wherewith I have enlightened them, and I shall forsake their seed for a season. ⁷ But unto thee will I show the land before thou die, but thou shall not enter therein in this age, lest thou see the graven images whereby this people will be deceived and led out of the way. I will show thee the place wherein they shall serve me 740 (*l*. 850) years. And thereafter it shall be delivered into the hand of their enemies, and they shall destroy it, and strangers shall compass it about, and it shall be in that day as it was in the day when I brake the tables of the covenant which I made with thee in Oreb: and when they sinned, that which was written therein vanished away. Now that day was the 17th day of the 4th month. ⁸ And Moses went up into Mount Oreb, as God had bidden him, and prayed, saying: Behold, I have fulfilled the time of my life, even 120 years. And now I pray thee let thy mercy be with thy people and let thy compassion be continued upon thine heritage, Lord, and thy long-suffering in thy place upon the race of thy choosing, for thou hast loved them more than all. ⁹ And thou knowest that I was a shepherd of sheep, and when I fed the flock in the desert, I brought them unto thy Mount Oreb, and then first saw I thine angel in fire out of the bush; but thou calledst me out of the bush, and I feared and turned away my face, and thou sentest me unto them, and didst deliver them out of Egypt, and their enemies thou didst sink in the water. And thou gavest them a law and judgements whereby they should live. *For what man is he that hath not sinned against thee*? How shall thine heritage be established except thou have mercy on them? Or who shall yet be born without sin? Yet wilt thou correct them for a season, but not in anger. ¹⁰ Then the Lord shewed him the land and all that is therein and said: This is the land which I will give to my people. And he shewed him the place from whence the clouds draw up water to water all the earth, and the place whence the river receiveth his water, and the land of Egypt, and the place of the firmament, from whence the holy land only drinketh. He shewed him also the place from whence it rained manna for the people, and even unto the paths of paradise. And he shewed him the measures of the sanctuary, and the number of the offerings, and the sign whereby men shall interpret (*lit.* begin to look; upon) the heaven, and said: These are the things which were forbidden to the sons of men because they sinned. ¹¹ And now, thy rod wherewith the signs were wrought shall be for a witness between me and my people. And when they sin I shall be wroth with them and remember my rod, and spare them according to my mercy, and thy rod shall be in my sight for a remembrance all the days, and shall be like unto the bow wherein I made a covenant with Noe when he came out of the ark, saying: I will set my bow in the cloud, and it shall be a sign between me and men that the water of a flood be no more upon the earth. ¹² But thee will I take hence and give thee sleep with thy fathers and give thee rest in thy slumber, and bury thee in peace, and all the angels shall lament for thee, and the hosts *of heaven* shall be sorrowful. But there shall not any, of angels or men, know thy sepulchre wherein thou art to be buried, but thou shalt rest therein until I visit the world, and raise thee up and thy fathers out of the earth [of Egypt] wherein ye shall sleep, and ye shall come together and dwell in an immortal habitation that is not subject unto time. ¹³ But this heaven shall be in my sight as a fleeting cloud, and like yesterday when it is past, and it shall be when I draw near to visit the world, I will command the years and charge the times, and they shall be shortened, and the stars shall be hastened, and the light of the sun make speed to set, neither shall the light of the moon endure, because I will hasten to raise up you that sleep, that in the place of sanctification which I shewed thee, all they that can live may dwell therein. ¹⁴ And Moses said: If I may ask yet one thing of thee, O Lord, according to the multitude of thy mercy, be not wroth with me. And shew me what measure of time hath passed by and what remaineth. ¹⁵ And the Lord said to him: An instant, the topmost part of a hand, the fulness of a moment, and the drop of a cup. And time hath fulfilled all. For 4½ have passed by, and 2½ remain. ¹⁶ And Moses when he heard was filled with under standing, and his likeness was changed gloriously: *and he died* in glory according *to the mouth of the Lord, and he buried him* as he had promised him, and the angels lamented at his death, and lightnings and torches and arrows went before him with one accord. And on that day the hymn of the hosts was not said because of the departure of Moses. Neither was there any day like unto it since the Lord made man upon earth, neither shall there be any such for ever, that he should make the hymn of the angels to cease because of a man; for he loved him greatly; and he buried him with his own hands on an high place of the earth, and in the light of the whole world.

XX.

¹ And at that time God made his covenant with Jesus the son of Naue which remained of the men that spied out the land: for the lot had fallen upon them that they should not see the land because they spake evil of it, and for this cause that generation died. ² Then said God unto Jesus the son of Naue: Wherefore mournest thou, and wherefore hopest thou in vain, thinking that Moses shall yet live? Now therefore thou waitest to no purpose, for Moses is dead. Take the garments of his wisdom and put them on thee, and gird thy loins with the girdle of his knowledge, and thou shalt be changed and become another man. Did I not speak for thee unto Moses my servant, saying: "He shall lead my people after thee, and into his hand will I deliver the kings of the Amorites"? ³ And Jesus took the garments of wisdom and put them on, and girded his loins with the girdle of understanding. And it came to pass when he put it on, that his mind was kindled and his spirit stirred up, and he said to the people: Lo, the former generation died in the wilderness because they spake against their God. And, behold now, know, all ye captains, this day that if ye go forth in the ways of your God, your paths shall be made straight. ⁴ But if ye obey not his voice, and are like your fathers, your works shall be spoiled, and ye yourselves broken, and your name shall perish out of the land, and then where shall be the words which God spake unto your fathers? For even if the heathen say: It may be God hath failed, because he hath not delivered his people, yet whereas they perceive that he hath chosen to himself other peoples, working for them great wonders, they shall understand that the Most Mighty accepteth not persons. But because ye sinned through vanity, therefore he took his power from you and subdued you. And now arise and set Your heart to walk in the ways of your Lord and he shall direct you. ⁵ And the people said unto him: Lo, this day see we that which Eldad and Modat prophesied in the days of Moses, saying: After that Moses resteth, the captainship of Moses shall be given unto Jesus the son of Naue. And Moses was not envious, but rejoiced when he heard them; and thenceforth all the people believed that thou shouldest lead them, and divide the land unto them in peace: and now also if there be conflict, be strong and do valiantly, for thou only shalt be leader in Israel. ⁶ And when he heard that, Jesus thought to send spies into Jericho. And he called Cenez and Seenamias his brother, the two sons of Caleph, and spake to them, saying: I and your father were sent of Moses in the wilderness and went up with other ten men: and they returned and spake evil of the lands and melted the heart of the people, and they were scattered and the heart of the people with them. But I and your father only fulfilled the word of the Lord, and lo, we are alive this day. And now will I send you to spy out the land of Jericho. Do like unto your father and ye also shall live. ⁷ And they went up and spied out the city. And when they brought back word, the people went up and besieged the city and burned it with fire. ⁸ And after that Moses was dead, the manna ceased to come down for the children of Israel, and then began they to eat the fruits of the land. And these are the three things which God gave his people for the sake of three persons, that is, the well of the water of Mara for Maria's sake, and the pillar of cloud for Aaron's sake, and the manna for the sake of Moses. And when these three came to an end, those three gifts were taken away from them. ⁹ Now the people and Jesus fought against the Amorites, and when the battle waxed strong against their enemies throughout all the days of Jesus, 30 and 9 kings which dwelt in the land were cut off. And Jesus gave the land by lot to the people, to every tribe according to the lots, according as he had received commandment. ¹⁰ Then came Caleph unto him and said: Thou knowest how that we two were sent by lot by Moses to go with the spies, and because we fulfilled the word of the Lord, behold we are alive at this day: and now if it be well-pleasing in thy sight, let there be given unto my son Cenez for a portion the territory of the three (*or* the tribe of the) towers. And Jesus blessed him, and did so.

XXI.

¹ And when Jesus was become old and well-stricken in years, God said to him: Behold, thou waxest old and well-stricken in days, and the land is become very great, and there is none to divide it (*or* take it by lot), and it

shall be after thy departure this people will mingle with the inhabitants of the land and go astray after other gods, and I shall forsake them as I testified in my word unto Moses; but do thou testify unto them before thou diest. ² And Jesus said: Thou knowest more than all, O Lord, what moveth the heart of the sea before it rageth, and thou hast tracked out the constellations and numbered the stars, and ordered the rain. Thou knowest the mind of all generations before they be born. And now, Lord, give unto thy people an heart of wisdom and a mind of prudence, and it shall be when thou givest these ordinances unto thine heritage, they shall not sin before thee and thou shall not be wroth with them. ³ Are not these the words which I spake before thee, Lord, when Achar stole of the curse, and the people were delivered up before thee, and I prayed in thy sight and said: Were it not better for us, O Lord, if we had died in the Red Sea, wherein thou drownedst our enemies? or if we had died in the wilderness, like our fathers, than to be delivered into the hand of the Amorites that we should be blotted out for ever? ⁴ Yet if thy word be about us, no evil shall befall us: for even though our end be removed unto death, thou livest which art before the world and after the world; and whereas a man cannot devise how to put one generation before another, he saith "God hath destroyed his people whom he chose": and behold, we shall be in Hell: yet thou wilt make thy word alive. And now let the fulness of thy mercies have patience with thy people, and choose for thine heritage a man which shall rule over thy people, he and his generation. ⁵ Was it not for this that our father Jacob spake, saying: *A prince shall not depart from Juda, nor a leader from his loins*. And now confirm the words spoken aforetime, that the nations of the earth and tribes of the world may learn that thou art everlasting. ⁶ And he said furthermore: O Lord, behold the days shall come and the house of Israel shall be like unto a brooding dove which setteth her young *in the nest* and will not forsake them nor forget her place. So, also, these shall turn from their deeds and fight against the salvation that shall be born unto them. ⁷ And Jesus went down from Galgala and built an altar of very great stones, and brought no iron upon them, as Moses had commanded, and set up great stones on mount Gebal, and whitened them and wrote on them the words of the law very plainly: and gathered all the people together and read in their ears all the words of the law. ⁸ And he came down with them and offered upon the altar peace-offerings, and they sang many praises, and lifted up the ark of the covenant of the Lord out of the tabernacle with timbrels and dances and lutes and harps and psalteries and all instruments of sweet sound. ⁹ And the priests and Levites were going up before the ark and rejoicing with psalms, and they set the ark before the altar, and lifted up on it yet again peace-offerings very many, and the whole house of Israel sang together with a loud voice saying: Behold, our Lord hath fulfilled that which he spake with our fathers saying: To your, seed will I give a land wherein to dwell, a land flowing with milk and honey. And lo, he hath brought us. into the land of our enemies and hath delivered them broken in heart before us, and he is the God which sent to our fathers in the secret places of souls, saying: Behold, the Lord hath done all that he spake unto us. And now know we of a truth that God hath confirmed all the words of the law which he spake to us in Oreb; and if our heart keep his ways it will be well with us, and with our sons after us. ¹⁰ And Jesus blessed them and said: The Lord grant your heart to continue therein (*or* in him) all the days, and if ye depart not from his name, the covenant of the Lord shall endure with you. And *he grant* that it be not corrupted, but that the dwelling-place of God be builded among you, as he spake when he sent you into his inheritance with mirth and gladness.

XXII.

¹ And it came to pass after these things, when Jesus and all Israel had heard that the children of Ruben and the children of Gad and the half tribe of Manasse which dwelt about Jordan had built them an altar and did offer sacrifices thereon and had made priests for the sanctuary, all the people were troubled above measure and came unto them to Silon. ² And Jesus and all the elders spake to them saying: What be these works which are done among you, while as yet we are not settled in our land? Are not these the words which Moses spake to you in the wilderness saying: See that when ye enter into the land ye spoil not your doings, and corrupt all the people? And now wherefore is it that our enemies have so much abounded, save because ye do corrupt your ways and have made all this trouble, and therefore will they assemble against us and overcome us. ³ And the children of Ruben and the children of Gad and the half tribe of Manasse said unto Jesus and all the people of Israel: Lo now hath God enlarged the fruit of the womb of men, and hath set up a light that that which is in darkness may see, for he knoweth what is in the secret places of the deep, and with him light abideth. Now the Lord God of our fathers knoweth if any of us or if we ourselves have done this thing in the way of iniquity, but only for our posterity's sake, that their heart be not separated from the Lord our God lest they say to us: Behold now, our brethren which be beyond Jordan have an altar, to make offerings upon it, but we in this place that have no altar, let us depart from the Lord our God, because our God hath set us afar off from his ways, that we should not serve him. ⁴ And then verily spake we among ourselves: Let us make us an altar, that they may have a zeal to seek the Lord. And verily there be some of us that stand by and know that we are your brothers and stand guiltless before your face. Do ye therefore that which is pleasing in the sight of the Lord. ⁵ And Jesus said: Is not the Lord our king mightier than woo sacrifices? And wherefore taught ye not your sons the words of the Lord which ye heard of us? For if your sons had been *occupied* in the meditation of the law of the Lord, their mind would not have been led aside after a sanctuary made with hands. Or know ye not that when the people were forsaken for a moment in the wilderness when Moses went up to receive the tables, their mind was led astray, and they made themselves idols? And except the mercy of the God of your fathers had kept *us*, all the synagogues should have become a byword, and all the sins of the people should have been blazed abroad because of your foolishness. ⁶ Therefore now go and dig down the sanctuaries that ye have builded you, and teach your sons the law, and they shall be meditating therein day and night, that the Lord may be with them for a witness and a judge unto them all the days of their life. And God shall be witness and judge between me and you, and between my heart and your heart, that if ye have done this thing in subtlety it shall be avenged upon you, because you would destroy your brothers: but if ye have done it ignorantly as ye say, God will be merciful unto you for your sons' sake. And all the people answered: Amen, Amen. ⁷ And Jesus and all the people of Israel offered for them 1,000 rams for a sin-offering (*lit.* the word of excusing), and prayed for them and sent them away in peace: and they went and destroyed the sanctuary, and fasted and wept, both they and their sons, and prayed and said: O God of our fathers, that knowest before the heart of all men, thou knowest that our ways were not wrought in iniquity in thy sight, neither have we swerved from thy ways, but have served thee all of us, for we are the work of thy hands: now *therefore* remember thy covenant with the sons of thy servants. ⁸ And after that Jesus went up unto Galgala, and reared up the tabernacle of the Lord, and the ark of the covenant and all the vessels thereof, and set it up in Silo, and put there the Demonstration and the Truth (*i.e.* the Urim and *Thummim*). And at that time Eleazar the priest which served the altar did teach by the Demonstration all them of the people that came to inquire of the Lord, for thereby it was shown unto them, but in the new sanctuary that was in Galgala, Jesus appointed even unto this day the burnt offerings that were offered by the children of Israel every year. ⁹ For until the house of the Lord was builded in Jerusalem, and so long as the offerings were made in the new sanctuary, the people were not forbidden to offer therein, because the Truth and the Demonstration revealed all things in Silo. And until the ark was set by Solomon in the sanctuary of the Lord they went on sacrificing there unto that day. But Eleazar the son of Aaron the priest of the Lord ministered in Silo.

XXIII.

¹ And Jesus the son of Naue ordered the people and divided unto them the land, being a mighty man of valour. And while yet the adversaries of Israel were in the land, the days of Jesus drew near that he should die, and he sent and called all Israel throughout all their land with their wives and their children, and said unto them: Gather yourselves together before the ark of the covenant of the Lord in Silo and I will make a covenant with you before I die. ² And when all the people were gathered together on the 16th day of the 3rd month before the face of the Lord in Silo with their wives and their children, Jesus said unto them: Hear, O Israel, behold I make with you the covenant of this law which the Lord ordained with our fathers in Oreb, and therefore tarry ye here this night and see what God will say unto me concerning You. ³ And as the people waited there that night, the Lord appeared unto Jesus in a vision and spake saying: According to all these words will I speak unto this people. ⁴ And Jesus came in the morning and assembled all the people and said unto them: Thus saith the Lord: One rock was there from whence I digged out your father, and the cutting of that rock brought forth two men, whose names were Abraham and Nachor, and out of the chiselling of that place were born two women whose names were Sara and Melcha. And they dwelled together beyond the river. And Abraham took Sara *to wife* and Nachor took Melcha. ⁵ And when the people of the land were led astray, every man after his own devices, Abraham believed in me and was not led aside after them. And I saved him out of the fire and took him and brought him over into all the land of Chanaan. And I spake unto him in a vision saying: Unto thy seed will I give this land. And he said unto me: Behold now thou hast given me a wife and she is barren. And how shall I have *seed* of that womb that is shut up? ⁶ And I said unto him: *Take for me a calf of three years old and a she-goat of three years and a ram of three years, a turtledove and a pigeon.* And he took them as I

commanded him. And *I sent a sleep upon him* and compassed him about with fear, and *I set* before him the place of fire wherein the works of them that commit iniquity against me shall be avenged, and I showed him the torches of fire whereby the righteous which have believed in me shall be enlightened. ⁷ And I said unto him: These shall be for a witness between me and thee that I will give thee seed of the womb that is shut up. And I will liken thee unto the dove, because thou hast received for me the city which thy sons shall (begin to) build in my sight. But the turtle-dove I will liken unto the prophets which shall be born of thee. And the ram will I liken unto the wise men which shall be born of thee and enlighten thy sons. But the calf I will liken unto the multitude of the peoples which shall be multiplied through thee. And the she-goat I will liken unto the women whose wombs I will open and they shall bring forth. These things shall be for a witness betwixt us that I will not transgress my words. ⁸ And I gave him Isaac and formed him in the womb of her that bare him, and commanded it that it should restore him quickly and render him unto me in the 7th month. And for this cause every woman that bringeth forth in the 7th month, her child shall live: because upon him did I call my glory, and showed forth the new age. ⁹ And I gave unto Isaac Jacob and Esau, and unto Esau I gave the land of Seir for an heritage. And Jacob and his sons went down into Egypt. And the Egyptians brought your fathers low, as ye know, and I remembered your fathers, and sent Moses my friend and delivered them from thence and smote their enemies. ¹⁰ And I brought them out with a high hand and led them through the Red Sea, and laid the cloud under their feet, and brought them out through the depth, and brought them beneath the mount Sina, and I *bowed the heavens and came down*, and I congealed the flame of the fire, and stopped up the springs of the deep, and impeded the course of the stars, and tamed the sound of the thunder, and quenched the fulness; of the wind, and rebuked the multitude of the clouds, and stayed their motions, and interrupted the storm of the hosts, that I should not break my covenant, for all things were moved at my coming down, and all things were quickened at my advent, and I suffered not my people to be scattered, but gave unto them my law, and enlightened them, that if they did these things they may live and have length of days and not die. ¹¹ And I have brought you into this land and given you vineyards. Ye dwell in cities which ye built not. And I have fulfilled the covenant which I spake unto your fathers. ¹² And now if ye obey your fathers, I will set my heart upon you for ever, and will overshadow you, and your enemies shall no more fight against you, and your land shall be renowned throughout all the world and your seed be elect in the midst of the peoples, which shall say: Behold the faithful people; because they believed the Lord, therefore hath the Lord delivered them and planted them. And therefore will I plant you as a desirable vineyard and will rule you as a beloved flock, and I will charge the rain and the dew, and they shall satisfy you all the days of your life. ¹³ And it shall be at the end that the lot of every one of you shall be in eternal life, both for you and your seed, and I will receive your souls and lay them up in peace, until the time of the age is fulfilled, and I restore you unto your fathers and your fathers unto you, and they shall know at your hand that it is not in vain that I have chosen you. These are the words that the Lord hath spoken unto me this night. ¹⁴ And all the people answered and said: The Lord is our God, and him only will we serve. And all the people made a great feast that day and a renewal thereof for 28 days.

XXIV.

¹ And after these days Jesus the son of Naue assembled all the people yet again, and said unto them: Behold now the Lord hath testified unto you this day: I have called heaven and earth to witness to you that if ye will continue to serve the Lord ye shall be unto him a peculiar people. But if ye will not serve him and will obey the gods of the Amorites in whose land ye dwell, say so this day before the Lord and go forth. *But I and my house will serve the Lord.* ² And all the people lifted up their voice and wept saying: Peradventure the Lord will account us worthy, and it is better for us to die in the fear of him, than to be destroyed out of the land. ³ And Jesus the son of Naue blessed the people and kissed them and said unto them: Let your words be for mercy before our Lord, and let him send his angel, and preserve you: Remember me after my death, and *remember ye* Moses the friend of the Lord. And let not the words of the covenant which he hath made with you depart from you all the days of your life. And he, sent them away and they departed every man to his inheritance. ⁴ But Jesus laid himself upon his bed, and sent and called Phineës the son of Eleazar the priest and said unto him: Behold now I see with mine eyes the transgression of this people wherein they will begin to deceive: but thou, strengthen thy hands in the time that thou art with them, And he kissed him and his father and his sons and blessed him and said: The Lord God of your fathers direct your ways and *the ways* of this people. ⁵ And when he ceased speaking unto them, *he drew up his feet into the bed* and slept with his fathers. And his sons *laid their hands upon his eyes*. ⁶ And then all Israel gathered together to bury him, and they lamented him with a great lamentation, and thus said they in their : Weep ye for the wing of this swift eagle, for he hath flown away from us. And weep ye for the strength of this lion's whelp, for he is hidden from us. Who now will go and report unto Moses the righteous, that we have had forty years a leader like unto him? And they fulfilled their mourning and *buried him* with their own hands *in the mount Effraim* and returned every man unto his tent. And after the death of Jesus the land of Israel was at rest.

XXV.

¹ And the Philistines sought to fight with the men of Israel: and they inquired of the Lord and said: Shall we go up and fight against the Philistines? and God said to them: If ye go up with a pure heart, fight; but if your heart is defiled, go not up. And they inquired yet again saying: How shall we know if all the heart of the people be alike? and God said to them: Cast lots among your tribes, and it shall be unto every tribe that cometh under the lot, that it shall be set apart into one lot, and then shall ye know whose heart is clean and whose is defiled. ² And the people said: Let us first appoint over us a prince, and so cast lots. And the angel of the Lord said to them: Appoint. And the people said: Whom shall we appoint that is worthy, Lord? And the angel of the Lord said to them: Cast the lot upon the tribe of Caleb, and he that is shown by the lot, even he shall be your prince. And they cast the lot for the tribe of Caleb and it came out upon Cenez, and they made him ruler over Israel. ³ And Cenez said to the people: Bring your tribes unto me and hear ye the word of the Lord. And the people gathered together and Cenez said to them: Ye know that which Moses the friend of the Lord charged you, that ye should not transgress the law to the right hand or to the left. And Jesus also who was after him gave you the same charge. And now, lo, we have heard of the mouth of the Lord that your heart is defiled. And the Lord hath charged us to cast lots among your tribes to know whose heart hath departed from the Lord our God. Shall not the fury of anger come upon the people? But I promise you this day that even if a man of mine own house come out in the lot of sin, he shall not be saved alive, but shall be burned with fire. And the people said: Thou hast spoken a good counsel, to perform it. ⁴ And the tribes were brought before him, and there were found of the tribe of Juda 345 men, and of the tribe of Ruben 560, and of the tribe of Simeon 775, and of the tribe of Levi 150, and of the tribe of Zabulon 655 (*or* 645), and of the tribe of Isachar 665, and of the tribe of Gad 380 Of the tribe of Aser 665, and of the tribe of Manasse 480, and of the tribe of Effraim 468, and of the tribe of Benjamin 267 And all the number of them that were found by the lot of sin was 6110 And Cenez took them all and shut them up in prison, till it should be known what should be done with them. ⁵ And Cenez said: Was it not of this that Moses the friend of the Lord spake saying: *There is a strong root among you bringing forth gall and bitterness*? Now blessed be the Lord who hath revealed all the devices of these men, neither hath he suffered them to corrupt his people by their evil works. Bring hither therefore the Demonstration and the Truth and call forth Eleazar the priest, and let us inquire of the Lord by him. ⁶ Then Cenez and Eleazar and all the elders and the whole synagogue prayed with one accord saying: Lord God of our fathers, reveal unto thy servants the truth, for we are found not believing in the wonders which thou didst for our fathers since thou broughtest them out of the land of Egypt unto this day. And the Lord answered and said: First ask them that were found, and let them confess their deeds which they did subtilly, and afterwards they shall be burned with fire. ⁷ And Cenez brought them forth and said to them: Behold now ye know how that Achiar confessed when the lot fell on him, and declared all that he had done. And now declare unto me all your wickedness and your inventions: who knoweth, if ye tell us the truth, even though ye die now, yet God will have mercy upon you when he shall quicken the dead? ⁸ And one of them named Elas said unto him: Shall not death come now upon us, that we shall die by fire? Nevertheless I tell thee, my Lord, there are none inventions like unto these which we have made wickedly. But if thou wilt search out the truth plainly, ask severally the men of every tribe, and so shall some one of them that stand by perceive the difference of their sins. ⁹ And Cenez asked them of his own tribe and they told him: We desired to imitate and make the calf that they made in the wilderness. And after that he asked the men of the tribe of Ruben, which said: We desired to sacrifice unto the gods of them that dwell in the land. And he asked the men of the tribe of Levi, which said: We would prove the tabernacle, whether it were holy. And he asked the remnant of the tribe of Isachar, which said: We would inquire by the evil spirits of the idols, to see whether they revealed plainly: and he asked the men of the tribe of Zabulon, which said: We desired to eat the flesh of our children and to learn whether God hath care for them. And he asked the remnant of the tribe of Dan, which said: The Amorites taught us that which they did, that we might teach our

children. And lo, they are hid under the tent of Elas, who told thee to inquire of us. Send therefore and thou shall find them. And Cenez sent and found them. ¹⁰ And thereafter asked he them that were left over of the tribe of Gad, and they said: We committed adultery with each other's wives. And he asked next the men of the tribe of Aser, which said: We found seven golden images which the Amorites called the holy Nymphs, and we took them with the precious stones that were set upon them, and hid them: and lo, now they are laid up under the top of the mount Sychem. Send therefore and thou shalt find them. And Cenez sent men and removed them thence. ¹¹ Now these are the Nymphs which when they were called upon did show unto the Amorites their works in every hour. For these are they which were devised by seven evil men after the flood, whose names are these: <? Cham> Chanaan, Phuth, Selath, Nembroth, Elath, Desuath. Neither shall there be again any like similitude in the world graven by the hand of the artificer and adorned with variety of painting, but they were set up and fixed for the consecration *(i.e.* the holy place?) of idols. *Now* the stones were precious, brought from the land of Euilath, among which was a crystal and a prase (*or* one crystalline and one green), and they shewed their fashion, being carved after the manner of a stone pierced with open-work, and another of them was graven on the top, and another as it were marked with spots (*or* like a spotted chrysoprase) so shone with its graving as if it shewed the water of the deep lying beneath. ¹² And these are the precious stones which the Amorites had in their holy places, and the price of them was above reckoning. For when any entered in by night, he needed not the light of a lantern, so much did the natural light of the stones shine forth. Wherein that one gave the greatest light which was cut after the form of a stone pierced with open-work, and was cleansed with bristles; for if any of the Amorites were blind, he went and put his eyes thereupon and recovered his sight. Now when Cenez found them, he set them apart and laid them up till he should know what should become of them. ¹³ And after that he asked them that were left of the tribe of Manasse, and they said: We did only defile the Lord's sabbaths. And he asked the forsaken of the tribe of Effraim, which said: We desired to pass our sons and our daughters through the fire, that we might know if that which was said were manifest. And he asked the forsaken of the tribe of Benjamin, which said: We desired at this time to examine the book of the law, whether God had plainly written that which was therein, or whether Moses had taught it of himself.

XXVI.

¹ And when Cenez had taken all these words and written them in a book and read them before the Lord, God said to him: Take the men and that which was found with them and all their goods and put them in the bed of the river Phison, and burn them with fire that mine anger may cease from them. ² And Cenez said: Shall we burn these precious stones also with fire, or sanctify them unto thee, for amoug us there are none like unto them? And God said to him: If God should receive in his own name any of the accursed thing, what should man do? Therefore now take these precious stones and all that was found, both books and men: and when thou dealest so with the men, set apart these stones with the books, for fire will not avail to burn them, and afterwards I will shew thee how thou must destroy them. But the men and all that was found thou shalt burn with fire. And thou shalt assemble all the people, and say to them: Thus shall it be done unto every man whose heart turneth away from his God. ³ And when the fire hath consumed those men, then the books and the precious stones which cannot be burned with fire, neither cut with iron, nor blotted out with water, lay them upon the top of the mount beside the new altar; and I will command a cloud, and it shall go and take up dew and shed it upon the books, and shall blot out that which is written therein, for they cannot be blotted out with any other water than such as hath never served men. And thereafter I will send my lightning, and it shall burn up the books themselves. ⁴ But as concerning the precious stones, I will command mine angel and he shall take them and go and cast them into the depths of the sea, and I will charge the deep and it shall swallow them up, for they may not continue in the world because they have been polluted by the idols of the Amorites, And I will command another angel, and he shall take for me twelve stones out of the place whence these seven were taken; and thou, when thou findest them in the top of the mount where he shall lay them, take and put them on the shoulder-piece over against the twelve stones which Moses set therein in the wilderness, and sanctify them in the breastplate (*lit.* oracle) according to the twelve tribes: and say not, How shall I know which stone I shall set for which tribe? Lo, I will tell thee the name of the tribe answering unto the name of the stone, and thou shalt find both one and other graven. ⁵ And Cenez went and took all that had been found and the men with it, and assembled all the people again, and said to them: Behold, ye have seen all the wonders which God hath shewed us unto this day, and lo, when we sought out all that had subtilly devised evil against the Lord and against Israel, God hath revealed them according to their works, and now cursed be every man that deviseth to do the like among you, brethren. And all the people answered Amen, Amen. And when he had so said, he burned all the men with fire, and all that was found with them, saving the precious stones. ⁶ And after that Cenez desired to prove whether the stones could be burned with fire, and cast them into the fire. And it was so, that when they fell therein, forthwith the fire was quenched. And Cenez took iron to break them, and when the sword touched them the iron thereof was melted; and thereafter he would at the least blot out the books with water; but it came to pass that the water when it fell upon them was congealed. And when he saw that, he said: Blessed be God who hath done so great wonders for the children of men, and made Adam the first-created and shewed him all things; that when Adam had sinned thereby, then he should deny him all these things, lest if he shewed them unto the race of men they should have the mastery over them. ⁷ And when he had so said, he took the books and the stones and laid them on the top of the mount by the new altar as the Lord had commanded him, and took a peace-offering and burnt-offerings, and offered upon the new altar 2000, offering them all for a burnt sacrifice. And on that day they kept a great feast, he and all the people together. ⁸ And God did that night as he spake unto Cenez, for he commanded a cloud, and it went and took dew from the ice of paradise and shed it upon the books and blotted them out. And after that an angel came and burned them up, and another angel took the precious stones and cast them into the heart of the sea, and he charged the depth of the sea, and it swallowed them up. And another angel went and brought twelve stones and laid them hard by the place whence he had taken those seven. And he graved thereon the names of the twelve tribes. ⁹ And Cenez arose on the morrow and found those twelve stones on the top of the mount where himself had laid those seven. And the graving of them was so as if the form of eyes was portrayed upon them. ¹⁰ And the first stone, whereon was written the name of the tribe of Ruben, was like a sardine stone. The second stone was graven with a tooth (*or* ivory), and therein was graven the name of the tribe of Simeon, and the likeness of a topaz was seen in it; and on the third stone was graven the name of the tribe of Levi, and it was like unto an emerald. But the fourth stone was called a crystal, wherein was graven the name of the tribe of Juda, and it was likened to a carbuncle. The fifth stone was green, and upon it was graven the name of the tribe of Isachar, and the colour of a sapphire stone was therein. And of the sixth stone the graving was as if it had been inscribed, (*or* as a chrysoprase) speckled with diverse markings, and thereon was written the tribe of Zabulon, And the jasper stone was likened unto it. ¹¹ Of the seventh stone the graving shone and shewed within itself, as it were, *enclosed* the water of the deep, and therein was written the name of the tribe of Dan, which stone was like a ligure. But the eighth stone was cut out with adamant, and therein was written the name of the tribe of Neptalim, and it was like an amethyst. And of the ninth stone the graving was pierced, and it *was* from Mount Ophir, and therein was written the tribe of Gad, and an agate stone was likened unto it. And of the tenth stone the graving was hollowed, and gave the likeness of a stone of Theman, and there was written the tribe of Aser, and a chrysolite was likened unto it. And the eleventh stone was an elect stone from Libanus, and thereon was written the name of the tribe of Joseph, and a beryl was. likened to it. And the twelfth stone was cut out of the height of Sion (*or* the quarry), and upon it was written the tribe of Benjamin; and the onyx stone was likened unto it. ¹² And God said to Cenez: Take these stones and put them in the ark of the covenant of the Lord with the tables of the covenant which I gave unto Moses in Oreb, and they shall be there with them until Jahel arise to build an house in my name, and then he shall set them before me upon the two cherubim, and they shall be in my sight for a memorial of the house of Israel. ¹³ And it shall be when the sins of my people are filled up, and their enemies have the mastery over their house, that I will take these stones and the former together with the tables, and lay them up in the place whence they were brought forth in the beginning, and they shall be there until I remember the world, and visit the dwellers upon earth. And then will I take them and many other better than they, from that *place* which *eye hath not seen nor ear heard neither hath it come up into the heart of man*, until the like cometh to pass unto the world, and the just shall have no need for the light of the sun nor of the shining of the moon, for the light of the precious stones shall be their light. ¹⁴ And Cenez arose and said: Behold what good things God hath done for men, and because of their sins have they been deprived of them all. And now know I this day that the race of men is weak, and their life shall be accounted as nothing. ¹⁵ And so saying, he took the stones from the place where they were laid, and as he took them there was as it were the light of the sun poured out upon them, and the earth shone with their light. And Cenez put them in the ark of the covenant of the Lord with the tables as it was commanded him, and there they are unto this day.

XXVII.

¹ And after this he armed of the people 300,000 men and went up to fight against the Amorites, and slew on the first day 800,000 men, and on the second day he slew about 500,000 ² And when the third day came, certain men of the people spake evil against Cenez, saying: Lo now, Cenez alone lieth in his house with his wife and his concubines, and sendeth us to battle, that we may be destroyed before our enemies. ³ And when the servants of Cenez heard, they brought him word. And he commanded a captain of fifty, and he brought of them thirty-seven men who spake against him and shut them up in ward. ⁴ And their names are these: Le and Uz, Betul, Ephal, Dealma, Anaph, Desac, Besac, Gethel, Anael, Anazim, Noac, Cehec, Boac, Obal, Iabal, Enath, Beath, Zelut, Ephor, Ezeth, Desaph, Abidan, Esar, Moab, Duzal, Azath, Phelac, Igat, Zophal, Eliesor, Ecar, Zebath, Sebath, Nesach and Zere. And when the captain of fifty had shut them up as Cenez commanded, Cenez said: When the Lord hath wrought salvation for his people by my hand, then will I punish these men. ⁵ And so saying, Cenez commanded the captain of fifty, saying: Go and choose of my servants 300 men, and as many horses, and let no man of the people know of the hour when I shall go forth to battle; but only in what hour I shall tell thee, prepare the men that they be ready this night. ⁶ And Cenez sent messengers, spies, to see where was the multitude of the camp of the Amorites. And the messengers went and spied, and saw that the multitude of the camp of the Amorites was moving among the rocks devising to come and fight against Israel. And the messengers returned and told him according to this word. And Cenez arose by night, he and 300 horsemen with him, and took a trumpet in his hand and began to go down with the 300 men. And it came to pass, when he was near to the camp of the Amorites, that he said to his servants: Abide here and I will go down alone and view the camp of the Amorites. And it shall be, if I blow with the trumpet ye shall come down, but if not, wait for me here. ⁷ And Cenez went down alone, and before he went down he prayed, and said: O Lord God of our fathers, thou hast shewn unto thy servant the marvellous things which thou hast prepared to do by thy covenant in the last days: and now, send unto thy servant one of thy wonders, and I will overcome thine adversaries, that they and all the nations and thy people may know that the Lord delivereth not by the multitude of an host, neither by the strength of horsemen, when they shall perceive the sign of deliverance which thou shalt work for me this day (*or* horsemen, and that thou, Lord, wilt perform a sign of salvation with me this day). Behold, I will draw my sword out of the scabbard and it shall glitter in the camp of the Amorites: and it shall be, if the Amorites perceive that it is I, Cenez, *then* I *shall* know that thou hast delivered them into mine hand. But if they perceive not that it is I, and think that it is another, then I *shall* know that thou hast not hearkened unto me, but hast delivered me unto mine enemies. But and if I be indeed delivered unto death, I shall know that because of mine iniquities the Lord hath not heard me, and hath delivered me unto mine enemies; but he will not destroy, his inheritance by my death. ⁸ And he set forth after he had prayed, and heard the multitude of the Amorites saying: Let us arise and fight against Israel: for we know that our holy Nymphs are there among them and will deliver them into our hands. ⁹ And Cenez arose, for the spirit of the Lord clothed him as *a garment*, and he drew his sword, and when the light of it shone upon the Amorites like sharp lightning, they saw it, and said: Is not this the sword of Cenez which hath made our wounded many? Now is the word justified which we spake, saying that our holy Nymphs have delivered them into our hands. Lo, now, this day shall there be feasting for the Amorites, when our enemy is delivered unto us. Now, therefore, arise and let everyone gird on his sword and begin the battle. ¹⁰ And it came to pass when Cenez heard their words, he was clothed with the spirit of might and changed into another man, and went down into the camp of the Amorites and began to smite them. And the Lord sent before his face the angel Ingethel (*or* Gethel), who is set over the hidden things, and worketh unseen, (and another) angel of might helping with him: and Ingethel smote the Amorites with blindness, so that every man that saw his neighbour counted them his adversaries, and they slew one another. And the angel Zeruel, who is set over strength, bare up the arms of Cenez lest they should perceive him; and Cenez smote of the Amorites forty and five thousand men, and they themselves smote one another, and fell forty and five thousand men. ¹¹ And when Cenez had smitten a great multitude, he would have loosened his hand from his sword, for the handle of the sword clave, that it could not be loosed, and his right hand had taken into it the strength of the sword. Then they that were left of the Amorites fled into the mountains; but Cenez sought how he might loose his hand: and he looked with his eyes and saw a man of the Amorites fleeing, and he caught him and said to him: I know that the Amorites are cunning: now therefore shew me how I may loose my hand from this sword, and I will let thee go. And the Amorite said: Go and take a man of the Hebrews and kill him, and while his blood is yet warm hold thine hand beneath and receive his blood, so shall thine hand be loosed. And (Zenez said: As the Lord liveth, if thou hadst said, Take a man of the Amorites, I would have taken one of them and saved thee alive: but forasmuch as thou saidest "of the Hebrews" that thou mightest show thine hatred, thy mouth shall be against thyself, and according as thou hast said, so will I do unto thee. And when he had thus said Cenez slew him, and while his blood was yet warm, he held his hand beneath and received it therein, and it was loosed. ¹² And Cenez departed and put off his garments, and cast himself into the river and washed, and came up again and changed his garments, and returned to his young men. Now the Lord cast upon them a heavy sleep in the night, and they slept and knew not any thing of all that Cenez had done. And Cenez came and awaked them out of sleep; and they looked [upon him] with their eyes and saw, and behold, the field was full of dead bodies: and they were astonished in their mind, and looked every man on his neighbour. And Cenez said unto them: Why marvel ye? Are the ways of the Lord as the way of men? For with men a multitude prevaileth, but with God that which he appointeth. And therefore if God hath willed to work deliverance for this people by my hands, wherefore marvel ye? Arise and gird on every man your swords, and we will go home to our brethren. ¹³ And when all Israel heard the deliverance that was wrought by the hands of Cenez, all the people came out with one accord to meet him, and said: Blessed be the Lord which hath made thee ruler over his people, and hath shown that those things are sure which he spake unto thee: that which we heard by speech we see now with our eyes, for the work of the word of God is manifest. ¹⁴ And Cenez said unto them: Ask now your brethren, and let them tell you how greatly they laboured with me in the battle. And the men that were with him said: As the Lord liveth, we fought not, neither knew we *anything*, save only when we awaked, we saw the field full of dead bodies. And the people answered: Now know we that when the Lord appointeth to work deliverance for his people, he hath no need of a multitude, but only of sanctification. ¹⁵ And Cenez said to the captain of fifty which had shut up those men in prison: Bring forth those men that we may hear their words. And when he had brought them forth, Cenez said to them: Tell me, what saw ye in me that ye murmured among the people? And they said: Why askest thou us? Why askest thou us? Now therefore command that we be burned with fire, for we die not for this sin that we have now spoken, but for that former one wherein those men were taken which were burned in their sins; for then we did consent unto their sin, saying: Peradventure the people will not perceive us; and then we did escape the people. But now have we been (rightly) made a public example by our sins in that we fell into slandering of thee. And Cenez said: If ye yourselves therefore witness against yourselves, how shall I have compassion upon you? And Cenez commanded them to be burned with fire, and cast their ashes into the place where they had burned the multitude of the sinners, even into the brook Phison. ¹⁶ And Cenez ruled over his people fifty and seven years, and there was fear upon all his enemies all his days.

XXVIII.

¹ And when the days of Cenez drew nigh that he should die, he sent and called all men (*or* all the elders), and the two prophets Jabis and Phinees, and Phinees the son of Eleazar the priest, and said to them: Behold now, the Lord hath showed me all his marvellous works which he hath prepared to do for his people in the last days. ² And now will I make my covenant with you this day, that ye forsake not the Lord your God after my departing. For ye have seen all the marvels *which came* upon them that sinned, and all that they declared, confessing their sins of their own accord, and how the Lord our God made an end of them for that they transgressed his covenant. Wherefore now spare ye them of your house and your sons, and abide in the ways of the Lord your God, that the Lord destroy not his inheritance. ³ And Phinees, the son of Eleazar the priest, said: If Cenez the ruler bid me, and the prophets and the people and the elders, I will speak a word which I heard of my father when he was a-dying, and will not keep silence concerning the commandment which he commanded me when his soul was being received. And Cenez the ruler and the prophets said: Let Phinees say on. Shall any other speak before the priest which keepeth the commandments of the Lord our God, and that, seeing that truth proceedeth out of his mouth, and out of his heart a shining light? ⁴ Then said Phinees: My father, when he was a-dying, commanded me saying: Thus shalt thou say unto the children of Israel when they, are gathered together unto the assembly: The Lord appeared unto me the third day before this in a dream in the night, and said unto me: Behold, thou hast seen, and thy father before thee, how greatly I have laboured for my people; and it shall be after thy death that this people shall arise and corrupt their ways, departing from my commandments, and I shall be exceeding wroth with them. Yet will I remember the time which was before the ages, *even* in the time when there

was not a man, and therein was no iniquity, when I said that the world should be, and they that should come should praise me therein, and I will plant a great vineyard, and out of it will I choose a plant, and order it and call it by my name, and it shall be mine for ever. But when I have done all that I have spoken, nevertheless my planting, which is called after me, will not know me, the planter thereof, but will corrupt his fruit, and will not yield me his fruit. These are the things which my father commanded me to speak unto this people. ⁵ And Cenez lifted up his voice, and the elders, and all the people with one accord, and wept with a great lamentation until the evening and said: Shall the shepherd destroy his flock to no purpose, except it continue in sin against him? And shall it not be he that shall spare according to the abundance of his mercy, seeing he hath spent great labour upon us? ⁶ Now while they were set, the holy spirit that dwelt in Cenez leapt upon him and took away from him his *bodily* sense, and he began to prophesy, saying: Behold now I see that which I looked not for, and perceive that I knew not. Hearken now, ye that dwell on the earth, even as they that sojourned therein prophesied before me, when they saw this hour, *even* before the earth was corrupted, that ye may know the prophecies appointed aforetime, all ye that dwell therein. ⁷ Behold now I see flames that burn not, and I hear springs of water awaked out of sleep, and they have no foundation, neither do I behold the tops of the mountains, nor the canopy of the firmament, but all things unappearing and invisible, which have no place whatsoever, and although mine eye knoweth not what it seeth, mine heart shall discover that which it may learn (or say). ⁸ Now out of the flame which I saw, and it burned not, I beheld, and lo a spark came up and as it were builded for itself a floor under heaven, and the likeness of the floor thereof was as a spider spinneth, in the fashion of a shield. And when the foundation was laid, I beheld, and from that spring there was stirred up as it were a boiling froth, and behold, it changed itself as it were into another foundation; and between the two foundations, even the upper and the lower, there drew near out of the light of the invisible place as it were forms of men, and they walked to and fro: and behold, a voice saying: These shall be for a foundation unto men and they shall dwell therein 7000 years. ⁹ And the lower foundation was a pavement and the upper was of froth, and they that came forth out of the light of the invisible place, they are those that shall dwell therein, and the name of that man is <Adam>. And it shall be, when he hath (*or* they have) sinned against me and the time is fulfilled, that the spark shall be quenched and the spring shall cease, and so they shall be changed. ¹⁰ And it came to pass after Cenez had spoken these words that he awaked and his sense returned unto him: but he knew not that which he had spoken neither that which he had seen, but this only he said to the people: If the rest of the righteous be such after they are dead, it is better for them to die to the corruptible world, that they see not sin. And when Cenez had so said, he died and slept with his fathers, and the people mourned for him 30 days.

XXIX.

¹ And after these things the people appointed Zebul ruler over them, and at that time he gathered the people together and said unto them: Behold now, we know all the labour wherewith Cenez laboured with us in the days of his life. Now if he had had sons, they should have been princes over the people, but inasmuch as his daughters are yet alive, let them receive a greater inheritance among the people, because their father in his life refused to give it unto them, lest he should be called covetous and greedy of gain. And the people said: Do all that is right in thine eyes. ² Now Cenez had three daughters whose names are these: Ethema the firstborn, the second Pheila, the third Zelpha. And Zebul gave to the firstborn all that was round about the land of the Phœnicians, and to the second he gave the olive yard of Accaron, and to the third all the tilled land that was about Azotus. And he gave them husbands, namely to the firstborn Elisephan, to the second Odiel, and to the third Doel. ³ Now in those days Zebul set up a treasury for the Lord and said unto the people: Behold, if any man will sanctify unto the Lord gold and silver, let him bring it to the Lord's treasury in Sylo: only let not any that hath stuff belonging to idols think to sanctify it to the Lord's treasures, for the Lord desireth not the abominations of the accursed things, lest ye disturb the synagogue of the Lord, for the wrath that is passed by sufficeth. And all the people brought that which their heart moved them to bring, both men and women, even gold and silver. And all that was brought was weighed, and it was 20 talents of gold, and 250 talents of silver. ⁴ And Zebul judged the people twenty and five years. And when he had accomplished his time, he sent and called all the people and said: Lo, now I depart to die. Look ye to the testimonies which they that went before us testified, and let not your heart be like unto the waves of the sea, but like as the wave of the sea under standeth not save only those things which are in the sea, so let your heart also think upon nothing save only those things which belong unto the law. And Zebul slept with his fathers, and was buried in the sepulchre of his father.

XXX.

¹ Then had the children of Israel no man whom they might appoint as judge over them: and their heart fell away, and they forgot the promise, and transgressed the ways which Moses and Jesus the servants of the Lord had commanded them, and were led away after the daughters of the Amorites, and served their gods. ² And the Lord was wroth with them, and sent his angel and said: Behold, I chose me one people out of all the tribes of the earth, and I said that my glory should abide with them in this world, and I sent unto them Moses my servant, to declare unto them my great majesty and my judgements, and they have transgressed my ways. Now therefore behold I will stir up their enemies and they shall rule over them, and then shall all *the* people[s] say: Because we have transgressed the ways of God and of our fathers, therefore are these things come upon us. Yet there shall a woman rule over them which shall give them light 40 years. ³ And after these things the Lord stirred up against them Jabin king of Asor, and he began to fight against them, and he had as captain of his might Sisara, who had 8000 chariots of iron. And he came unto the mount Effrem and fought against the people, and Israel feared him greatly, and the people could not stand all the days of Sisara. ⁴ And when Israel was brought very low, all the children of Israel gathered together with one accord unto the mount of Juda and said: We did call ourselves blessed more than *all* people, and now, lo, we are brought so low, more than all nations, that we cannot dwell in our land, and our enemies bear rule over us. And now who hath done all this unto us? Is it not our iniquities, because we have forsaken the Lord God of our fathers, and have walked in those things which could not profit us? Now therefore come let us fast seven days, both men and women, and from the least (*sic*) even to the sucking child. Who knoweth whether God will be reconciled unto his inheritance, that he destroy not the planting of his vineyard? ⁵ And after the people had fasted 7 days, sitting in sackcloth, the Lord sent unto them on the 7th day Debbora, who said unto them: Can the sheep that is appointed to the slaughter answer before him that slayeth it, when both he that slayeth <...> and he that is slain keepeth silence, when he is sometimes provoked against it? Now ye were born to be a flock before our Lord. And he led you into the height of the clouds, and subdued angels beneath your feet, and appointed unto you a law, and gave you commandments by prophets, and chastised you by rulers, and shewed you wonders not a few, and for your sake commanded the luminaries and they stood still in the places where they were bidden, and when your enemies came upon you he rained hailstones upon them and destroyed them, and Moses and Jesus and Cenez and Zebul gave you commandments. And ye have not obeyed them. ⁶ For while they lived, ye shewed yourselves as it were obedient unto your God, but when they died, your heart died also. And ye became like unto iron that is thrust into the fire, which when it is melted by the flame becometh as water, but when it is come out of the fire returneth unto its hardness. So ye also, while they that admonish you burn you, do show the effect, and when they are dead ye forget all things. ⁷ And now, behold, the Lord will have compassion upon you this day, not for your sakes, but for his covenant's sake which he made with your fathers and for his oath's sake which he sware, that he would not forsake you for ever. But know ye that after my decease ye will begin to sin in your latter days. Wherefore the Lord will perform marvellous things among you, and will deliver your enemies into your hands. For your fathers are dead, but God, which made a covenant with them, is life.

XXXI.

¹ And Debbora sent and called Barach and said to him: Arise and gird up thy loins as a man, and go down and fight against Sisara, For I see the constellations greatly moved in their ranks and preparing to fight for you. I see also the lightnings unmoveable in their courses, and setting forth to stay the wheels of the chariots of them that boast in the might of Sisara, who saith: I will surely go down in the arm of my might to fight against Israel, and will divide the spoil of them among my servants, and their fair women will I take unto me for concubines. Therefore hath the Lord spoken concerning him that the arm of a weak woman shall overcome him, and maidens shall take his spoil, and he also himself shall fall into the hands of a woman. ² And when Debbora and the people and Barach went down to meet their enemies, immediately the Lord disturbed the goings of his stars, and spake unto them saying: Hasten and go ye, for our (*or* your) enemies fall upon you: confound their arms and break the strength of their hearts, for I am come that my people may prevail. For though it be that my people have sinned, yet will I have mercy on them. And when this was said, the stars went forth as it was commanded them and burned up their enemies. And the number of them that were gathered (*or* burned) and slain in one hour was 90 times 97,000 men. But Sisara they destroyed not, for so it was

commanded them. ³ And when Sisara had fled on his horse to deliver his soul, Jahel the wife of Aber the Cinean decked herself with her ornaments and came out to meet him: now the woman was very fair: and when she saw him she said: Come in and take food, and sleep: and in. the evening I will send my servants with thee, for I know that thou wilt remember me and recompense me. And Sisara came in, and when he saw roses scattered upon the bed he said: If I be delivered, O Jahel, I will go unto my mother and thou shalt (*or* Jahel shall) be my wife. ⁴ And thereafter was Sisara athirst and he said to Jahel: Give me a little water, for I am faint and my soul burneth by reason of the flame which I beheld in the stars. And Jahel said unto him: Rest a little while and then thou shalt drink. ⁵ And when Sisara was fallen asleep, Jahel went to the flock and milked milk therefrom. And as she milked she said: Behold now, remember, O Lord, when thou didst divide every tribe and nation upon the earth, didst thou not choose out Israel only, and didst not liken him to any beast save only unto the ram that goeth before the flock and leadeth it? Behold therefore and see how Sisara hath thought *in his heart* saying: I will go and punish the flock of the Most Mighty. And lo, I will take of the milk of the beasts whereunto thou didst liken thy people, and will go and give him to drink, and when he hath drunk he shall become weak, and after that I will kill him. And this shall be the sign that thou shalt give me, O Lord, that, whereas Sisara sleepeth, when I go in, if he wake and ask me forthwith, saying: Give me water to drink, *then* I *shall* know that my prayer hath been heard. ⁶ So Jahel returned and entered in, and Sisara awaked and said to her: Give me to drink, for I burn mightily and my soul is inflamed. And Jahel took wine and mingled it with the milk and gave him to drink, and he drank and fell asleep. ⁷ But Jahel took a stake in her left hand and drew near unto him saying: If the Lord give me this sign I *shall* know that Sisara shall fall into my hands. Behold I will cast him upon the ground from off the bed whereon he sleepeth, and it shall be, if he perceive it not, that I shall know that he is delivered up. And Jahel took Sisara and pushed him from off the bed upon the earth, but he perceived it not, for he was exceeding faint. And Jahel said: Strengthen in me, O Lord, mine arm this day for thy sake and thy people's sake, and for them that put their trust in thee. And Jahel 'took the stake and set it upon his temple and smote with the hammer. And as he died Sisara' said to Jahel: Lo, pain hath come upon me, Jahel, and I die like a woman. And Jahel said unto him: Go boast thyself before thy father in hell, and tell him that thou hast fallen into (*or* say, I have been delivered into) the hands of a woman. And she made an end and slew him and laid his body *there* until Barach should return. ⁸ Now the mother of Sisara was called Themech, and she sent unto her friends saying: Come, let us go forth together to meet my son, and ye shall see the daughters of the Hebrews whom my son will bring hither to be his concubines. ⁹ But Barach returned from following after Sisara and was greatly vexed because he found him not, and Jahel came forth to meet him, and said: Come, enter in, thou blessed of God, and I will deliver thee thine enemy whom thou followedst after and hast not found. And Barach went in and found Sisara dead, and said: Blessed be the Lord which sent his spirit and said: Into the hands of a woman shall Sisara be delivered. And when he had so said he cut off the head of Sisara and sent it unto his mother, and gave her a message saying: Receive thy son whom thou didst look for to come with spoil.

XXXII.

¹ *Then Debbora and Barach the son of Abino* and all the people together *sang* an hymn unto the Lord *in that day*, saying: Behold, from on high hath the Lord shewn unto us his glory, even as he did aforetime when he sent forth his voice to confound the tongues of men. And he chose out our nation, and took Abraham our father out of the fire, and chose him before all his brethren, and kept him from the fire and delivered him from the bricks of the building of the tower, and gave him a son in the latter days of his old age, and brought him out of the barren womb, and all the angels were jealous against him, and the orderers of the hosts envied him. ² And it came to pass, when they were jealous against him, God said unto him: Slay for me the fruit of thy belly and offer for my sake that which I gave thee. And Abraham did not gainsay him and set forth immediately. And as he went forth he said to his son: Lo, now, my son, I offer thee for a burnt offering and deliver thee into his hands who gave thee unto me. ³ And the son said to his father: Hear me, father. If a lamb of the flock is accepted for an offering to the Lord for an odour of sweetness, and if for the iniquities of men sheep are appointed to the slaughter, but man is set to inherit the world, how then sayest thou now unto me: Come and inherit a life secure, and a time that cannot be measured? What and if I had not been born in the world to be offered a sacrifice unto him that made me? And it shall be my blessedness beyond all men, for there shall be no other *such thing*; and in me shall the generations be instructed, and by me the peoples shall understand that the Lord hath accounted the soul of a man worthy to be a sacrifice unto him. ⁴ And when his father had offered him upon the altar and had bound his feet to slay him, the Most Mighty hasted and sent forth his voice from on high saying: Kill not thy son, neither destroy the fruit of thy body: for now have I showed forth *myself* that I might appear to them that know me not, and have shut the mouths of them that always speak evil against thee. And thy memorial shall be before me for ever, and thy name and the name of this *thy son* from one generation to another. ⁵ And to Isaac he gave two sons, which also were from a womb shut up, for at that time their mother was in the third year of her marriage. And it shall not be so with any other woman, neither shall any wife boast herself so, that cometh near to her husband in the third year. And there were born to him two sons, even Jacob and Esau. And God loved Jacob, but Esau he hated because of his deeds. ⁶ And it came to pass in the old age of their father, that Isaac blessed Jacob and sent him into Mesopotamia, and there he begat 12 sons, and they went down into Egypt and dwelled there. ⁷ And when their enemies dealt evilly with them, the people cried unto the Lord, and their prayer was heard, and he brought them out thence, and led them unto the mount Sina, and brought forth unto them the foundation of understanding which he had prepared from the birth of the world; and then the foundation was moved, the hosts sped forth the lightnings upon their courses, and the winds sounded out of their storehouses, and the earth was stirred from her foundation, and the mountains and the rocks trembled in their fastenings, and the clouds lifted up their waves against the flame of the fire that it should not consume the world. ⁸ Then did the depth awake from his springs, and all the waves of the sea came together. Then did Paradise give forth the breath of her fruits, and the cedars of Libanus were moved from their roots. And the beasts of the field were terrified in the dwellings of the forests, and all his works gathered together to behold the Lord when he ordained a covenant with the children of Israel. And all things that the Most Mighty said, these hath he observed, having for witness Moses his beloved. ⁹ And when he was dying *God* appointed unto him the firmament, and shewed him these witnesses whom now we have, saying: Let the heaven whereinto thou hast entered and the earth wherein thou hast walked until now be a witness between me and thee and my people. For the sun and the moon and the stars shall be ministers unto us (*or* you). ¹⁰ And when Jesus arose to rule over the people, it came to pass in the day wherein he fought against the enemies, that the evening drew near, while yet the battle was strong, and Jesus said to the sun and the moon: O ye ministers that were appointed between the Most Mighty and his sons, lo now, the battle goeth on still, and do ye forsake your office? Stand still therefore to-day and give light unto his sons, and put darkness upon our enemies. And they did so. ¹¹ And now in these days Sisara arose to make us his bondmen, and we cried unto the Lord our God, and he commanded the stars and said: Depart out of your ranks, and burn mine enemies, that they may know my might. And the stars came down and overthrew their camp and kept us safe without any labour. ¹² Therefore will we not cease to sing praises, neither shall our mouths keep silence from telling of his marvellous works: for he hath remembered his promises both new and old, and hath shown us his deliverance,: and therefore doth Jahel boast herself among women, because she alone hath brought this good way to success, in that with her own hands she slew Sisara. ¹³ O earth, go thou, go, ye heavens and lightnings, go, ye angels and hosts, [go ye] and tell the fathers in the treasure-houses of their souls, and say: The Most Mighty hath not forgotten the least of all the promises which he made with us, saying: Many wonders will I perform for your sons. And now from this day forth it shall be known that whatsoever God hath said unto men that he will perform, he will perform it, even though man die. ¹⁴ Sing praises, sing praises, O Debbora (*or*, if man delay to sing praises to God, yet sing thou, O Debbora), and let the grace of an holy spirit awake in thee, and begin to praise the works of the Lord: for there shall not again arise such a day, wherein the stars shall bear tidings and overcome the enemies of Israel, as it was commanded them. From this time forth if Israel fall into a strait, let him call upon these his witnesses together with their ministers, and they shall go upon an embassy to the most High, and he will remember this day, and will send a deliverance to his covenant. ¹⁵ And thou, Debbora, begin to speak of that thou sawest in the field: how that the people walked and went forth safely, and the stars fought on their part (*or*, how that, like peoples walking, so went forth the stars and fought). Rejoice, O land, over them that dwell in thee, for in thee is the knowledge of the Lord which buildeth his stronghold in thee. For it was of right that God took out of thee the rib of him that was first formed, knowing that out of his rib Israel should be born. And thy forming shall be for a testimony of what the Lord hath done for his people. ¹⁶ Tarry, O ye hours of the day, and hasten not onward, that we may declare that which our understanding can bring forth, for night will come upon us. And it shall be like the night when God smote the firstborn of the Egyptians for the sake of his firstborn. ¹⁷ And then shall I cease from my hymn because the time will be hastened (*or* prepared) for

his righteous ones. For I will sing unto him as in the renewing of the creation, and the people shall remember this deliverance, and it shall be for a testimony unto them. Let the sea also bear witness, with the deeps thereof, for not only did God dry it up before the face of our fathers, but he did also overthrow the camp from its setting and overcame our enemies. [18] And when Debbora made an end of her words she went up with the people together unto Silo, and they offered sacrifices and burnt offerings and sounded upon the broad trumpets. And when they sounded and had offered the sacrifices, Debbora said: This shall be for a testimony of the trumpets between the stars and the Lord of them.

XXXIII.

[1] And Debbora went down thence, and judged Israel 40 years. And it came to pass when the day of her death drew near, that she sent and gathered all the people and said unto them: Hearken now, my people. Behold, I admonish you as a woman of God, and give you light as one of the race of women; obey me now as your mother, and give ear to my words, as men that shall yourselves die. [2] Behold, I depart to die by the way of all flesh, whereby ye also shall go: only direct your heart unto the Lord your God in the time of your life, for after your death ye will not be able to repent of those things wherein ye live. [3] For death is now sealed up, and accomplished, and the measure and the time and the years have restored that which was committed to them. For even if ye seek to do evil in hell after your death, ye will not be able, because the desire of sin shall cease, and the evil creation shall lose its power, and hell, which receiveth that that is committed to it, will not restore it unless it be demanded by him that committed it. Now, therefore, my sons, obey ye my voice while ye have the time of life and the light of the law, *and* direct your ways. [4] And when Debbora spake these words, all the people lifted up their voice together and wept, saying: Behold now mother, thou diest and forsakest thy sons; and to whom dost thou commit them? Pray thou, therefore, for us, and after thy departure thy soul shall be mindful of us for ever. [5] And Debbora answered and said to the people: While a man yet liveth he can pray for himself and for his sons; but after his end he will not be able to entreat nor to remember any man. Therefore, hope not in your fathers, for they will not profit you unless ye be found like unto them. But then your likeness shall be as the stars of the heaven, which have been manifested unto you at this time. [6] And Debbora died and slept with her fathers and was buried in the city of her fathers, and the people mourned for her 70 days. And as they bewailed her, thus they spake a lamentation, saying: Behold, a mother is perished out of Israel, and an holy one that bare rule in the house of Jacob, which made fast the fence about her generation, and her generation shall seek after her. And after her death the land had rest seven years.

XXXIV.

[1] And at that time there came up a certain Aod of the priests of Madian, and he was a wizard, and he spake unto Israel, saying: Wherefore give ye ear to your law? Come and I will shew you such a thing as your law is not. And the people said: What canst thou shew us that our law hath not? And he said to the people: Have ye ever seen the sun by night? And they said: Nay. And he said: Whensoever ye will, I will shew it unto you, that ye may know that our gods have power, and will not deceive them that serve them. And they said: Shew us. [2] And he departed and wrought with his magic, commanding the angels that were set over sorceries, because for a long time he did sacrifice unto them. [3] <<*For this was formerly in the power of the angels and was*>> performed by the angels before they were judged, and they would have destroyed the unmeasurable world; and because they transgressed, it came to pass that the angels had no longer the power. For when they were judged, then the power was not committed unto the rest: and by these *signs* (or *powers*) do they work who minister unto men in sorceries, until the unmeasurable age shall come. [4] And at that time Aod by art magic shewed unto the people the sun by night. And the people were astonished and said: Behold, what great things can the gods of the Madianites do, and we knew it not! [5] And God, willing to try Israel whether they were yet in iniquity, suffered *the angels*, and their work had good success, and the people of Israel were deceived and began to serve the gods of the Madianites. And God said: I will deliver them into the hands of the Madianites, inasmuch as by them are they deceived. And he delivered them into their hands, and the Madianites began to bring Israel into bondage.

XXXV.

[1] Now Gedeon was the son of Joath, the most mighty man among all his brethren. And when it was the time of summer, he came to the mountain, having sheaves with him, to thresh them there, and escape from the Madianites that pressed upon him. And the angel of the Lord met him, and said unto him: Whence comest thou and where is thine entering in? [2] He said to him: Why askest thou me whence I come? for straitness encompasseth me, for Israel is fallen into affliction, and they are verily delivered into the hands of the Madianites. And where are the wonders which our fathers have told us, saying: The Lord chose Israel alone before all the peoples of the earth? Lo, now he hath delivered us up, and hath forgotten the promises which he made to our fathers. For we should have chosen rather to be delivered unto death once for all, than that his people should be punished thus time after time. [3] And the angel of the Lord said unto him: It is not for nothing that ye are delivered up, but your own inventions have brought these things upon you, for like as ye have forsaken the promises which ye received of the Lord, these evils are come upon you, and ye have not been mindful of the commandments of God, which they commanded you that were before you. Therefore are ye come into the displeasure of your God. But he will have mercy upon you, as no man hath mercy, *even* upon the race of Israel, and that not for your sakes, but because of them that are fallen aslee. And now come, I will send thee, and thou shalt deliver Israel out of the hand of the Madianites. For thus saith the Lord: Though Israel be not righteous, yet because the Madianites are sinners, therefore, knowing the iniquity of my people, I will forgive them, and after that I will rebuke them for that they have done evil, but upon the Madianites I will be avenged presently. [5] And Gedeon said: Who am I and what is my father's house, that I should go against the Madianites to battle? And the angel said unto him: Peradventure thou thinkest that as is man's way so is the way of God. For men look upon the glory of the world and upon riches, but God looketh upon that which is upright and good, and upon meekness. Now therefore go, gird up thy loins, and the Lord shall be with thee, for thee hath he chosen to take vengeance of his enemies, like as, behold, he hath bidden thee. [6] And Gedeon said to him: *Let not my Lord be wroth if I speak* a word. Behold, Moses, the first of all the prophets, besought the Lord for a sign, and it was given him. But who am I, except the Lord that hath chosen me give me a sign that I may know that I go aright. And the angel of the Lord said unto him: Run and take for me water out of the pit yonder and pour it upon this rock, and I will give thee a sign. And he went and took it as he commanded him. [7] And the angel said unto him: Before thou pour the water upon the rock, ask what thou wouldst have it to become, either blood, or fire, or that it appear not at all. And Gedeon said: Let it become half of it blood and half fire. And Gedeon poured out the water upon the rock, and it came to pass when he had poured it out, that the half part became flame, and the half part blood, and they were mingled together, that is, the fire and the blood, yet the blood did not quench the fire, neither did the fire consume the blood. And when Gedeon saw that, he asked for yet. other signs, and they were given him. Are not these written in the book of the Judges?

XXXVI.

[1] And Gedeon took 300 men and departed and came unto the uttermost part of the camp of Madian, and he heard every man speaking to his neighbour and saying: Ye shall see a confusion above reckoning, of the sword of Gedeon, coming upon us, for God hath delivered into his hands the camp of the Madianites, and he will begin to make an end of us, even the mother with the children, because our sins are filled up, even as also our gods have shewed us and we believed them not. And now arise, let us succour our souls and fly. [2] And when Gedeon heard these words, immediately he was clothed with the spirit of the Lord, and, being endued with power, he said unto the 300 men: Arise and let every one of you gird on his sword, for the Madianites are delivered into our hands. And the men went down with him, and he drew near and began to fight. And they blew the trumpet and cried out together and said: The sword of the Lord is upon us. And they slew of the Madianites about 120,000 men, and the residue of the Madianites fled. [3] And after these things Gedeon came and gathered the people of Israel together and said unto them: Behold, the Lord sent me to fight your battle, and I went according as he commanded me. And now I ask one petition of you: turn not away your face; and let every man of you give me the golden armlets which ye have on your hands. And Gedeon spread out a coat, and every man cast upon it their armlets, and they were all weighed, and the weight of them was found to be 12 talents (*or* 12,000 shekels). And Gedeon took them., and of them he made idols and worshipped them. [4] And God said: One way is *verily* appointed, that I should not rebuke Gedeon in his lifetime, even because when he destroyed the sanctuary of Baal, then all men said: Let Baal avenge himself. Now, therefore, if I chastise him for that he hath done evil against me, ye will say: It was not God that chastised him, but Baal, because he sinned aforetime against him. Therefore now shall Gedeon die in a good old age, that they may not have whereof to speak. But after that Gedeon is dead I will punish him once, because he hath transgressed against me. And Gedeon died in a good old age and was buried in his own city.

XXXVII.

¹ And he had a son by a concubine whose name was Abimelech; the same slew all his brethren, desiring to be ruler over the people. [*A leaf gone.*] ² Then all the trees of the field came together unto the fig-tree and said: Come, reign over us. And the fig-tree said: Was I indeed born in the kingdom or in the rulership over the trees? or was I planted to that and that I should reign over you? And therefore even as I cannot reign over you, neither shall Abimelech obtain continuance in his rulership. After that the trees came together unto the vine and said: Come, reign over us. And the vine said: I was planted to give unto men the sweetness of wine, and I am preserved by rendering unto them my fruit. But like as I cannot reign over you, so shall the blood of Abimelech be required at your hand. And after that the trees came unto the apple and said: Come, reign over us. And he said: It was commanded me to yield unto men a fruit of sweet savour. Therefore I cannot reign over you, and Abimelech shall die by stones. ³ Then came the trees unto the bramble and said: Come, reign over us. And the bramble said: When the thorn was born, truth did shine forth in the semblance of a thorn. And when our first father was condemned to death, the earth was condemned to bring forth thorns and thistles. And when the truth enlightened Moses, it was by a thorn bush that it enlightened him. Now therefore it shall be that by me the truth shall be heard of you. Now if ye have spoken in sincerity unto the bramble that it should in truth reign over you, sit ye under the shadow of it: but if with dissembling, then let fire go forth and devour and consume the trees of the field. For the apple-tree was made for the chastisers, and the fig-tree was made for the people, and the vine[yard] was made for them that were before us. ⁴ And now shall *the bramble* be unto you even as Abimelech, which slew his brethren with wrong, and desireth to rule over you. If Abimelech be worthy of them (*or* Let Abimelech be a fire unto them) whom he desireth to rule, let him be as the bramble which was made to rebuke the foolish among the people. And there went forth fire out of the bramble and devoured the trees that are in the field. ⁵ After that Abimelech ruled over the people for one year and six months, and he died hard by a certain tower, whence a woman cast down upon him the half of a millstone. [*A gap of uncertain length in the text.*]

XXXVIII.

¹ (Then did Jair judge Israel 22 years.) The same built a sanctuary to Baal, and led the people astray saying: Every man that sacrificeth not unto Baal shall die. And when all the people sacrificed, seven men only would not sacrifice whose names are these: Dephal, Abiesdrel, Getalibal, Selumi, Assur, Jonadali, Memihel. ² The same answered and said unto Jair: Behold, we remember the precepts which they that were before us commanded us, and Debbora our mother, saying: Take heed that ye turn not away your heart to the right hand or to the left, but attend unto the law of the Lord day and night. Now therefore why dost thou corrupt the people of the Lord and deceive them, saying: Baal is God, let us worship him? And now if he be God as thou sayest, let him speak as a God, and then we will sacrifice unto him. ³ And Jair said: Burn them with fire, for they have blasphemed Baal. And his servants took them to burn them with fire. And when they cast them upon the fire there went forth Nathaniel, the angel which is over fire, and quenched the fire and burned up the servants of Jair: but the seven men he made to escape, so that no man of the people saw them, for he had smitten the people with blindness. ⁴ And when Jair came to the place (*or* it came to the place of Jair) he also was burned. But before he burned him, the angel of the Lord said unto him: Hear the word of the Lord before thou diest. Thus saith the Lord: I raised thee up out of the land of Egypt, and appointed thee ruler over my peoples. But thou hast risen and corrupted my covenant, and hast led them astray, and hast sought to burn my servants in the flame, because they reproved thee, which though they be burned with corruptible fire, yet now are they quickened with living fire and are delivered. But thou shalt die, saith the Lord, and in the fire wherein thou shalt die, therein shalt thou have thy dwelling. And thereafter he burned him, and came even unto the pillar of Baal and overthrew it, and burned up Baal with the people that stood by, even 1000 men.

XXXIX.

¹ And after these things came the children of Ammon and began to fight against Israel and took many of their cities. And when the people were greatly straitened, they gathered together in Masphath, saying every man to his neighbours: Behold now, we see the strait which encompasseth us, and the Lord is departed from us, and is no more with us, and our enemies have taken our cities, and there is no leader to go in and out before our face. Now therefore let us see whom we may set over us to fight our battle. ² *Now Jepthan the Galaadite was a mighty man of valour*, and because he was jealous of his brothers, they had cast him out of his land, *and he went and dwelt in the land of Tobi. And vagrant men gathered themselves unto him* and abode with him. ³ And it came to pass when Israel was overcome in battle, that they came into the land of Tobi to Jepthan and said unto him: Come, rule over the people. For who knoweth whether thou wast therefore preserved to this day or wast therefore delivered out of the hands of thy brethren that thou mightest at this time bear rule over thy people? ⁴ And Jepthan said unto them: Doth love so return after hatred, or doth time overcome all things? For ye did cast me out of my land and out of my father's house; and now are ye come unto me when ye are in a strait? And they said unto him: If the God of our fathers remembered not our sins, but delivered us when we had sinned against him and he had given us over before the face of our enemies, and we were oppressed by them, why wilt thou that art a mortal man remember the iniquities which happened unto us, in the time of our affliction? Therefore be it not so before thee, lord. ⁵ And Jepthan said: God indeed is able to be unmindful of our sins, seeing he hath time and place to repose himself of his long-suffering, for he is God; but I am mortal, made of the earth: whereunto I shall return, and where shall I cast away mine anger, and the wrong wherewith ye have injured me? And the people said unto him: Let the dove instruct thee, whereunto Israel was likened, for though her young be taken away from her, yet departeth she not out of her place, but spurneth away her wrong and forgetteth it as it were in the bottom of the deep. ⁶ And Jepthan arose and went with them and gathered all the people, and said unto them: Ye know how that when our princes were alive, they admonished us to follow our law. And Ammon and his sons turned away the people from their way wherein they walked, to serve other gods which should destroy them. Now therefore set your hearts in the law of the Lord your God, and let us entreat him with one accord. And so will we fight against our adversaries, and trust and hope in the Lord that he will not deliver us up for ever. *For* although our sins do overabound, nevertheless his mercy filleth *all* the earth. ⁷ And the whole people prayed with one accord, both men and women, boys and sucklings. And when they prayed they said: Look, O Lord, upon the people whom thou hast chosen, and spoil not the vine which thy right hand hath planted; that this people may be before thee for an inheritance, whom thou hast possessed from the beginning, and whom thou hast preferred alway, and for whose sake thou hast made the habitable places, and brought them into the land which thou swarest unto them; deliver us not up before them that hate thee, O Lord. ⁸ And God repented him of his anger and strengthened the spirit of Jepthan. And he sent a message unto Getal the king of the children of Ammon and said: Wherefore vexest thou our land and hast taken my cities, or wherefore afflictest thou us? Thou hast not been commanded of the God of Israel to destroy them that dwell in the land. Now therefore restore unto me my cities, and mine anger shall cease from thee. But if not, know that I will come up unto thee and repay thee for the former things, and recompense thy wickedness upon thine head: rememberest thou not how thou didst deal deceitfully with the people of Israel in the wilderness? And the messengers of Jepthan spake these words unto the king of the children of Ammon. ⁹ And Getal said: Did Israel take thought when he took the land of the Amorites? Say therefore: Know ye that now I will take from thee the remnant of thy cities and will repay thee thy wickedness and will take vengeance for the Amorites whom thou hast wronged. And Jepthan sent yet again to the king of the children of Ammon saying: Of a truth I perceive that God hath brought thee hither that I may destroy thee, unless thou rest from thine iniquity wherewith thou wilt vex Israel. And therefore I will come unto thee and show myself unto thee. For they are not, as ye say, gods which have given you the inheritance that ye possess. But because ye have been led astray after stones, fire shall follow after you unto vengeance. ¹⁰ And because the king of the children of Ammon would not hear the voice of Jepthan, Jepthan arose and armed all the people to go forth and fight in the borders saying: When the children of Ammon are delivered into my hands and I am returned, any that first meeteth with me shall be for a burnt offering unto the Lord. ¹¹ And the Lord was very wroth and said: Behold, Jepthan hath vowed that he will offer unto me that which meeteth with him first. Now therefore if a dog meet with Jepthan first, shall a dog be offered unto me? And now let the vow of Jepthan be upon his firstborn, even upon the fruit of his body, and his prayer upon his only begotten daughter. But I will verily deliver my people at this time, not for his sake, but for the prayer which Israel hath prayed.

XL.

¹ And Jepthan came and fought against the children of Ammon, and the Lord delivered them into his hand, and he smote threescore of their cities. And Jepthan returned in peace. And the women came out to meet him with dances. And he had an only begotten daughter; the same came out first in the dances to meet her father. And when Jepthan saw her he fainted and said: Rightly is thy name called Seila, that thou shouldest be offered for a sacrifice. And now who will put my heart in the balance and weigh my soul? and I will stand and see whether one will outweigh *the other*, the rejoicing that is come or the affliction which cometh upon me? for in that I

have opened my mouth unto my Lord in the song of *my* vows, I cannot call it back again. ² And Seila his daughter said unto him: And who is it that can be sorrowful in their death when they see the people delivered? Rememberest thou not that which was in the days of our fathers, when the father set his son for a burnt offering and he gainsaid him not, but consented unto him rejoicing? And he that was offered was ready, and he that offered was glad. ³ Now therefore annul not anything of that thou has vowed, but grant unto me one prayer. I ask of thee before I die a small request: I beseech thee that before I give up my soul, I may go into the mountains and wander (*or* abide) among the hills and walk about among the rocks, I and the virgins that are my fellows, and pour out my tears there and tell the affliction of my youth; and the trees of the field shall bewail me and the beasts of the field shall lament for me; for I am not sorrowful for that I die, neither doth it grieve me that I give up my soul: but whereas my father was overtaken in his vow, [and] if I offer not myself willingly for a sacrifice, I fear lest my death be not acceptable, and that I shall lose my life to no purpose. These things will I tell unto the mountains, and after that I will return. And her father said: Go. ⁴ And Seila the daughter of Jepthan went forth, she and the virgins that were her fellows, and came and told it to the wise men of the people. And no man could answer her words. And after that she went into the mount Stelac, and by night the Lord thought upon her, and said: Lo, now have I shut up the tongue of the wise among my people before this generation, that they could not answer the word of the daughter of Jepthan, that my word might be fulfilled, and my counsel not destroyed which I had devised: and I have seen that she is more wise than her father, and a maiden of understanding more than all the wise which are here. And now let her life be given her at her request, and her death shall be precious in my sight at all times. ⁵ And when the daughter of Jepthan came unto the mount Stelac, she began to lament. And this is her lamentation wherewith she mourned and bewailed herself before she departed, and she said: Hearken, O mountains, to my lamentation, and look, O hills, upon the tears of mine eyes, and be witness, O rocks, in the bewailing of my soul. Behold how I am accused, but my soul shall not be taken away in vain. Let my words go forth into the heavens, and let my tears be written before the face of the firmament, that the father overcome not (*or* fight not against) his daughter whom he hath vowed to offer up, that her ruler may hear that his only begotten daughter is promised for a sacrifice. ⁶ Yet I have not been satisfied with my bed of marriage, neither filled with the garlands of my wedding. For I have not been arrayed with brightness, sitting in my maidenhood; I have not used my precious ointment, neither hath my soul enjoyed the oil of anointing which was prepared for me. O my mother, to no purpose hast thou borne thine only begotten, and begotten her upon the earth, for hell is become my marriage chamber. Let all the mingling of oil which thou hast prepared for me be poured out, and the white robe which my mother wove for me, let the moth eat it, and the crown of flowers which my nurse plaited for me aforetime, let it wither, and the coverlet which she wove of violet and purple for my virginity, let the worm spoil it; and when the virgins, my fellows, tell of me, let them bewail me with groaning for *many* days. ⁷ Bow down your branches, O ye trees, and lament my youth. Come, ye beasts of the forest, and trample upon my virginity. For my years are cut off, and the days of my life are waxen old in darkness. ⁸ And when she had so said, Seila returned unto her father, and he did all that he had vowed, and offered burnt offerings. Then all the maidens of Israel gathered together and buried the daughter of Jepthan and bewailed her. And the children of Israel made a great lamentation and appointed in that month, on the 14th day of the month, that they should come together every year and lament for the daughter of Jepthan four days. And they called the name of her sepulchre according to her own name Seila. ⁹ And Jepthan judged the children of Israel ten years, and died, and was buried with his fathers.

XLI.

¹ And after him there arose a judge in Israel, Addo the son of Elech of Praton, and he also judged the children of Israel eight years. In his days the king of Moab sent messengers unto him saying: Behold now, thou knowest that Israel hath taken my cities: now therefore restore them in recompense. And Addo said: Are ye not yet instructed by that which hath befallen the children of Ammon, unless peradventure the sins of Moab be filled up? And Addo sent and took of the people 20,000 men and came against Moab, and fought against them and slew of them 45,000 men. And the remnant fled before him. And Addo returned in peace and offered burnt offerings and sacrifices unto his Lord, and died, and was buried in Ephrata his city. ² And at that time the people chose Elon and made him judge over them, and he judged Israel twenty years. In those days they fought against the Philistines and took of them twelve cities. And Elon died and was buried in his city. ³ But the children of Israel forgat the Lord their God and served the gods of the dwellers in the land. Therefore were they delivered unto the Philistines and served them forty years.

XLII.

¹ Now there was a man of the tribe of Dan, whose name was Manue, the son of Edoc, the son of Odo, the son of Eriden, the son of Phadesur, the son of Dema, the son of Susi, the son of Dan. And he had a wife whose name was Eluma, the daughter of Remac. And she was barren and bare him no child. And when Manue her husband said to her day by day: Lo, the Lord hath shut up thy womb, that thou shouldest not bear; set me free, therefore, that I may take an other wife lest I die without issue. And she said: The Lord hath not shut up me from bearing, but thee, that I should bear no fruit. And he said to her: Let the law make plain our trial. ² And as they contended day by day and both of them were sore grieved because they lacked fruit, upon a certain night the woman went up into the upper chamber and prayed saying: Do thou, O Lord God of all flesh, reveal unto me whether unto my husband or unto me it is not given to beget children, or to whom it is forbidden or to whom allowed to bear fruit, that to whom it is forbidden, the same may mourn for his sins, because he continueth without fruit. Or if both of us be deprived, reveal this also unto us, that we may bear our sin and keep silence before thee. ³ And the Lord hearkened to her voice and sent her his angel in the morning, and said unto her: Thou art the barren one that bringeth not forth, and thou art the womb which is forbidden, to bear fruit. But now hath the Lord heard thy voice and looked upon thy tears and opened thy womb. And behold thou shalt conceive and bear a son and shall call his name Samson, for he shall be holy unto thy Lord. But take heed that he taste not of any fruit of the vine, neither eat any unclean thing, for as himself hath said, he shall deliver Israel from the hand of the Philistines. And when the angel of the Lord had spoken these words he departed from her. ⁴ And she came unto her husband into the house and said unto him: Lo, I lay mine hand upon my mouth and will keep silence before thee all my days, because it was in vain that I boasted myself, and believed not thy words. For the angel of the Lord came unto me to-day, and showed me, saying: Eluma, thou art barren, but thou shalt conceive and bear a son. ⁵ And Manue believed not his wife. And he was ashamed and grieved and went up, he also, into the upper chamber and prayed saying: Lo, I am not worthy to hear the signs and wonders which God hath wrought in us, or to see the face of his messenger. ⁶ And it came to pass while he thus spake, the angel of the Lord came yet again unto his wife. Now she was in the field and Manue was in his house. And the angel said unto her: Run and call unto thine husband, for God hath accounted him worthy to hear my voice. ⁷ And the woman ran and called to her husband, and he hasted and came unto the angel in the field in Ammo (?), which said unto him: Go in unto thy wife and do quickly all these things. But he said to him: Yet see thou to it, Lord, that thy word be accomplished upon thy servant. And he said: It shall be so. ⁸ And Manue said unto him: If I were able, I would persuade thee to enter into mine house and eat bread with me, and know that when thou goest away I would give thee gifts to take with thee that thou mightest offer a sacrifice unto the Lord thy God. And the angel said unto him: I will not go in with thee into thine house, neither eat thy bread, neither will I receive thy gifts. For if thou offerest a sacrifice of that which is not thine, I can not show favour unto thee. ⁹ And Manue built an altar upon the rock, and offered sacrifices and burnt offerings. And it came to pass when he had cut up the flesh and laid it upon the holy place, the angel put forth *his hand* and touched it with the end of his sceptre. And there came forth fire out of the rock and consumed the burnt offerings and sacrifices. And the angel went up from him with the flame of the fire. ¹⁰ But Manue and his wife when they saw that, fell upon their faces and said: We shall surely die, because we have seen the Lord face to face. And it sufficed *me* not that I saw him, but I did also ask, his name, knowing not that he was the minister of God. Now the angel that came was called Phadahel.

XLIII.

¹ And it came to pass in the time of those days, that Eluma conceived and bare a son and called his name Samson. And the Lord was with him. And when he was begun to grow up, and sought to fight against the Philistines, he took him a wife of the Philistines. And the Philistines burned her with fire, for they were brought very low by Samson. ² And after that Samson entered into (*or* was enraged against) Azotus. And they shut him in and compassed the city about and said: Behold, now is our adversary delivered into our hands. Now therefore let us gather ourselves together and succour the souls one of another. And when Samson was arisen in the night and saw the city closed in he said: Lo, now, these fleas have shut me up in their city. And now shall the Lord be with me, and I will go forth by their gates and fight against them. ³ And he went and set his left hand under the bar of the gate and shook it and threw down the gate of the wall. One of the gates he held in his right hand for a shield, and the other he laid upon his shoulders

and bare it away, and because he had no sword he pursued after the Philistines with it, and killed therewith 25,000 men. And he lifted up all the purtenances of the gate and set them up on a mountain. ⁴ Now concerning the lion which he slew, and the jawbone of the ass wherewith he smote the Philistines, and the bands which he brake off from his arms as it were of themselves, and the foxes which he caught, are not these things written in the book of the Judges? ⁵ Then Samson went down unto Gerara, a city of the Philistines, and saw there an harlot whose name was Dalila, and was led away after her, and took her to him to wife. And God said: Behold, now Samson is led astray by his eyes and hath forgotten the mighty works which I have wrought with him, and is mingled with the daughters of the Philistines, and hath not considered my servant Joseph which was in a strange land and became a crown unto his brethren because he would not afflict his seed. Now therefore shall his concupiscence be a stumbling-block unto Samson, and his mingling shall be his destruction, and I will deliver him to his enemies and they shall blind him. Yet in the hour of his death will I remember him, and will avenge him yet once upon the Philistines. ⁶ And after these things his wife was importunate unto him, saying unto him: Show me thy strength, and wherein is thy might. So shall I know that thou lovest me. And when Samson had deceived her three times, and she continued importunate unto him every day, the fourth time he showed her his heart. But she made him drunk, and when he slumbered she called a barber, and he shaved the seven locks of his head, and his might departed from him, for so had himself revealed unto her. And she called the Philistines, and they smote Samson, and blinded him, and put him in prison. ⁷ And it came to pass in the day of their banqueting, that they called for Samson that they might mock him. And he being bound between two pillars prayed saying: O Lord God of my fathers, hear me yet this once, and strengthen me that I may die with these Philistines: for this sight of the eyes which they have taken from me was freely given unto me by thee. And Samson added saying: Go forth, O my soul, and be not grieved. Die, O my body, and weep not for thyself. ⁸ And he took hold upon the two pillars of the house and shook them. And the house fell and all that was in it and slew all them that were round about it, and the number of them was 40,000 men and women. And the brethren of Samson came down and all his father's house, and took him and buried him in the sepulchre of his father. And he judged Israel twenty years.

XLIV.

¹ And in those days there was no prince in Israel: but every man did that which was pleasing in his sight. ² At that time Michas arose, the son of Dedila the mother of Heliu, and he had 1000 drachms of gold and four wedges of molten gold, and 40 didrachms of silver. And his mother Dedila said unto him: My son, hear my voice and thou shalt make thee a name before thy death: take thou that gold and melt it, and thou shalt make thee idols, and they shall be to thee gods, and thou shalt become a priest to them. ³ And it shall be that whoso will inquire by them, they shall come to thee and thou shalt answer them. And there shall be in thine house an altar and a pillar built, and of that gold thou hast, thou shalt buy thee incense for burning and sheep for sacrifices. And it shall be that whoso will offer sacrifice, he shall give for sheep 7 didrachms, and for incense, if he will burn it, he shall give one didrachm of silver of *full* weight. And thy name shall be Priest, and thou shalt be called a worshipper of the gods. ⁴ And Michas said unto her: Thou hast well counselled me, my mother, how I may live: and now shall thy name be greater than my name, and in the last days these things shall be required of thee. ⁵ And Michas went and did all that his mother had commanded him. And he carved out and made for himself three images of boys, and of calves, and a lion and an eagle and a dragon and a dove. And it was so that all that were led astray came to him, and if any would ask for wives, they inquired of him by the dove; and if for sons, by the image of the boys: but he that would ask for riches took counsel by the likeness of the eagle, and he that asked for strength by the image of the lion: again, if they asked for men and maidens they inquired by the images of calves, but if for length of days, they inquired by the image of the dragon. And his iniquity was of many shapes, and his impiety was full of guile. ⁶ Therefore then, when the children of Israel departed from the Lord, the Lord said: Behold I will root out the earth and destroy all the race of men, because when I appointed great things upon mount Sina, I showed myself unto the children of Israel in the tempest and I said that they should not make idols, and they consented that they should not carve the likeness of gods. And I appointed to them they should not take my name in vain, and they chose this, even not to take my name in vain. And I commanded them to keep the sabbath day, and they consented unto me to sanctify themselves. And I said to them that they should honour their father and mother: and they promised that they would so do. And I appointed unto them not to steal, and they consented. And I bade them do no murder, and they received it, that they should not. And I commanded them not to commit adultery, and they refused not. And I appointed unto them to bear no false witness, and not to covet every man his neighbour's wife or his house or anything that is his: and they accepted it. ⁷ And now, whereas I spake unto them that they should not make idols, they have made the works of *all* those gods that are born of corruption by the name of *a* graven *image*. And also of them through whom all things have been corrupted. For mortal men made them, and the fire served in the melting of them: the act of men brought them forth, and hands have wrought them, and understanding contrived them. And whereas they have received them, they have taken my name in vain, and have given my name to graven images, and upon the sabbath day which they accepted, to keep it, they have wrought abominations therefrom. Because I said unto them that they should love their father and mother, they have dishonoured me their maker. And for that I said to them they should not steal, they have dealt thievishly in their understanding with graven images. And whereas I said they should not kill, they do kill them when they deceive. And when I had commanded them not to commit adultery, they have played the adulterer with their jealousy. And where they did choose not to bear false witness, they have received false witness from them whom they cast out, and have lusted after strange women. ⁸ Therefore, behold, I abhor the race of men, and to the end I may root out my creation, they that die shall be multiplied above the number of them that are born. For the house of Jacob is defiled with iniquities and the impieties of Israel are multiplied and I cannot [*some words lost*] wholly destroy the tribe of Benjamin, because that they first were led away after Michas. And the people of Israel also shall not be unpunished, but it shall be to them an offence for ever to the memory of all generations. ⁹ But Michas will I deliver unto the fire. And his mother shall pine away in his sight, living upon the earth, and worms shall issue forth out of her body. And when they shall speak one to the other, she shall say as it were a mother rebuking her son: Behold what a sin hast thou committed. And he shall answer as it were a son obedient to his mother and dealing craftily: And thou hast wrought yet greater iniquity. And the likeness of the dove which he made shall be to put out his eyes, and the likeness of the eagle shall be to shed fire from the wings of it, and the images of the boys he made shall be to scrape his sides, and for the image of the lion which he made, it shall be unto him as mighty ones tormenting him. ¹⁰ And thus will I do not only unto Michas but to all them also that sin against me. And now let the race of men know that they shall not provoke me by their own inventions. Neither unto them only that make idols shall this chastisement come, but it shall be to every man, that with what sin he hath sinned therewith shall he be judged. Therefore if they shall speak lies before me, I will command the heaven and it shall defraud them of rain. And if any will covet the goods of his, neighbour, I will command death and it shall deny them the fruit of their body. And if they swear by my name falsely I will not bear their prayer. And when the soul parteth from the body, then they shall say: Let us not mourn for the things which we have suffered, but because whatsoever we have devised, that shall we also receive.

XLV.

¹ And it came to pass at that time that a certain man of the tribe of Levi came to Gabaon, and when he desired to abide there, the sun set. And when he would enter in there, they that dwelt there suffered him not. And he said to his lad: Go on, lead the mule, and we will go to the city of Noba, peradventure they will suffer us to enter in there. And he came thither and sat in the street of the city. And no man said unto him: Come into my house. ² But there was there a certain Levite whose name was Bethac. The same saw him and said unto him: Art thou Beel of my tribe? And he said: I am. And he said to him: Knowest thou not the wickedness of them that dwell in this city? Who counselled thee to enter in hither? Haste and go out hence, and come into my house wherein I dwell, and abide there to-day, and the, Lord shall shut up their heart before us, as he shut up the men of Sodom before the face of Lot. And he entered into the city and abode there that night. ³ And all the dwellers in the city came together and said unto Bethac: Bring forth them that came unto thee this day, and if not we will burn them and thee with fire. And he went out unto them and said to them: Are not they our brethren? Let us not deal evilly with them, lest our sins be multiplied against us. And they answered: It was never so, that strangers should give commands to the indwellers. And they entered in with violence and took out him and his concubine and cast them forth, and they, 'Let the man go, but they abused his concubine until she died; for she had transgressed against her husband at one time by sinning with the Amalekites, and therefore did the Lord God deliver her into the hands of sinners. ⁴ And when it was day Beel went out and found his concubine dead. And he laid her upon the mule and hasted and went out and came to Gades. And he took her body and divided it and sent it into *all* parts (*or by portions*) throughout the twelve tribes, saying: These things were done unto

me in the city of Noba, for the dwellers therein rose up against me to slay me and took my concubine and shut me up and slew her. And if this is pleasing before your face) keep ye silence, and let the Lord be judge: but if ye will avenge it, the Lord shall help you. ⁵ And all the men, even the twelve tribes, were confounded. And they gathered together unto Silo and said every man to his neighbour: Hath such iniquity been done in Israel? ⁶ And the Lord said unto the Adversary: Seest thou how this foolish people is disturbed? In the hour when they should have died, even when Michas dealt craftily to deceive the people with these, *that is*, with the dove and the eagle and with the image of men and calves and of a lion and of a dragon, then were they not moved. And therefore because they were not provoked to anger, let their counsel *now* be vain and their heart moved, that they who allow evil may be consumed as well as the sinners.

XLVI.

¹ And when it was day the people of Israel were greatly moved and said: Let us go up and search out the sin that is done, that the iniquity may be taken away from us. And they spake thus, and said: Let us inquire first of the Lord and learn whether he will deliver our brethren into our hands. And if not, let us forbear. And Phinees said unto them: Let us offer the Demonstration and the Truth. And the Lord answered them and said: Go up, for I will deliver them into your hands. But he deceived them, that he might accomplish his word. ² And they went up to battle and came to the city of Benjamin and sent messengers saying: Send us the men that have done this wickedness and we will spare you, but requite to every man his evil doing. And the people of Benjamin hardened their heart and said unto the people of Israel: Wherefore should we deliver our brethren unto you? If ye spare *them* not, we will even fight against you. And the people of Benjamin came out against the children of Israel and pursued after them, and the children of Israel fell before them and they smote of them 45,000 men. ³ And the heart of the people was very sore vexed, and they came weeping and mourning unto Silo and said: Behold, the Lord hath delivered us up before the dwellers in Noba. Now let us inquire of the Lord which among us hath sinned. And they inquired of the Lord and he said unto them: If ye will, go up and fight, and they shall be delivered into your hands; and then it shall be told you wherefore ye fell before them. And they went tip the second day to fight against them. And the children of Benjamin came out and pursued after Israel and smote of them 46,000 men. ⁴ And the heart of the people was altogether melted and they said: Hath God willed to deceive his people? or hath he so ordained because of the evil that is done that as well the innocent should fall as they that do evil? And when they spake thus they fell down before the ark of the covenant of the Lord and rent their clothes and put ashes upon their heads both they and Phinees the son of Eleazar the priest, which prayed and said: What is this deceit wherewith thou hast deceived us, O Lord? If it be righteous before thy face which the children of Benjamin have done, wherefore didst thou not tell us, that we might consider it? But if it was not pleasing in thy sight, wherefore didst thou suffer us to fall before them?

XLVII.

¹ And Phinees added and said: O God of our fathers, hear my voice, and tell thy servant this day if it is well done in thy sight, or if peradventure the people have sinned and thou wouldest destroy their evil, that thou mightest correct among us also them that have sinned against thee. For I remember in my youth when Jambri sinned in the days of Moses thy servant, and I verily entered in, and was zealous in my soul, and lifted up both of them upon my sword, and the remnant would have risen against me to put me to death, and thou sentest thine angel and didst smite of them 24,000 men and deliver me out of their hands. ² And now thou hast sent the eleven tribes and brought them hither saying: Go and smite them. And when they went they were delivered up. And now they say that the declarations of thy truth are lying before thee. And now, O Lord God of our fathers, hide it not from thy servant, but tell us wherefore thou hast done this iniquity against us. ³ And when the Lord saw that Phinees prayed earnestly before him, he said to him: By myself have I sworn, saith the Lord, that had I not sworn, I would not have remembered thee in that thou hast spoken, neither would I have answered you this day. And now say unto the people: Stand up and hear the word of the Lord, ⁴ Thus saith the Lord: There was a certain mighty lion in the midst of the forest, and unto him all the beasts committed the forest that he should guard it by his power, lest perchance other beasts should come and lay it waste. And while the lion guarded it there came beasts of the field from another forest and devoured all the young of the beasts and laid waste the fruit of their body, and the lion saw it and held his peace. Now the beasts were at peace, because they had entrusted the forest unto the lion, and perceived not that their young were destroyed. ⁵ And after a time there arose a very small beast of those that had committed the forest unto the lion, and devoured the least of the whelps of another very evil beast. And lo, the lion cried out and stirred up all the beasts of the forest, and they fought among themselves, and every one fought against his neighbour. ⁶ And when many beasts were destroyed, another whelp out of another forest like unto it, saw *it*, and said: Hast thou not destroyed as many beasts? What iniquity is this, that in the beginning when many beasts and their young were destroyed unjustly by other evil beasts, and when all the beasts should have been moved to avenge themselves, seeing the fruit of their body was despoiled to no purpose, then thou didst keep silence and spakest not, but now one whelp of an evil beast hath perished, and thou hast stirred up the whole forest that all the beasts should devour one another without cause, and the forest be diminished. Now therefore thou oughtest first to be destroyed, and so the remnant be established. And when the young of the beasts heard that, they slew the lion first, and put over them the whelp in his stead, and so the rest of the beasts were subject together. ⁷ Michas arose and made you rich by that which he committed, both he and his mother. And there were evil things and wicked, which none devised before them, but in his subtlety he made graven images, which had not been made unto that day, and no man was provoked, but ye were all led astray, and did see the fruit of your body spoiled, and held your peace even as that evil lion. ⁸ And now when ye saw how that this man's concubine which suffered evil, died, ye were moved all of you and came unto me saying: Wilt thou deliver the children of Benjamin into our hands? Therefore did I deceive you and said: I will deliver them unto you. And now I have destroyed them which then held their peace, and so will I take vengeance on all that have done wickedly against me. But you, go ye up now, for I will deliver them unto you. ⁹ And all the people arose with one accord and went. And the children of Benjamin came out against them and thought that they would over come them as heretofore. And they knew not that their wickedness was fulfilled upon them. And when they had come on as at first, and were pursuing after them, the people fled from the face of them to give them place, and then they arose out of their ambushes, and the children of Benjamin were in the midst of them. ¹⁰ Then they which were fleeing turned back, and the men of the city of Noba were slain, both men and women, even 85,000 men, and the children of Israel burned the city and took the spoils and destroyed all things with the edge of the sword. And no man was left of the children of Benjamin save only 600 men which fled and were not found in the battle. And all the people returned unto Silo and Phinees the son of Eleazar the priest with them. ¹¹ Now these are they that were left of the race of Benjamin, the princes of the tribe, of ten families whose names are these: of the 1st family: Ezbaile, Zieb, Balac, Reindebac, Belloch; and of the 2nd family: Nethac, Zenip, Phenoch, Demech, Geresaraz; and of the 3rd family: Jerimuth, Veloth, Amibel, Genuth, Nephuth, Phienna; and of the 4th city: Gemuph, Eliel, Gemoth, Soleph, Raphaph, and Doffo; and of the 5th family: Anuel, Code, Fretan, Remmon, Peccan, Nabath; and of the 6th family: Rephaz, Sephet, Araphaz, Metach, Adhoc, Balinoc; and of the 7th family: Benin, Mephiz, Araph, Ruimel, Belon, Iaal, Abac; and (of) the (8th, 9th and) 10th family: Enophlasa, Melec, Meturia, Meac; and the rest of the princes of the tribe which were left, in number threescore. ¹² And at that time did the Lord requite unto Michas and unto his mother all the things that he had spoken. And Michas was melted with fire and his mother was pining away, even as the Lord had spoken concerning them.

XLVIII.

¹ At that time also Phinees laid himself down to die, and the Lord said unto him: Behold thou hast overpassed the 120 years that were ordained unto all men. And now arise and go hence and dwell in the mount Danaben and abide there many years, and I will command mine eagle and he shall feed thee there, and thou shalt not comedown any more unto men until the time come and thou be proved in the time. And then shalt thou shut the heaven, and at thy word it shall be opened. And after that thou shalt be lifted up into the place whither they that were before thee were lifted up, and shalt be there until I remember the world. And then will I bring you and ye shall taste what is death. ² And Phinees went up and did all that the Lord commanded him. Now in the days when he appointed him to be priest, he anointed him in Silo. ³ And at that time, when he went up, then it came to pass that the children of Israel when they kept the passover commanded the children of Benjamin saying: Go up and take wives for yourselves by force.. because we cannot give you our daughters, for we sware in the time of our anger: and it cannot be that a tribe perish out of Israel. And the children of Benjamin went up and seized for themselves wives and built Gabaon for them selves and began to dwell there. ⁴ And whereas in the meanwhile the children of Israel were at rest, they had no prince in those days, and every man did that which was right in his own eyes. ⁵ These are the commandments and the judgments and the testimonies and the manifestations that were in the days of the judges of Israel, before a king reigned over them.

XLIX.

1 And at that time the children of Israel began to inquire of the Lord, and said: Let us; all cast lots, that we may see who there is that can rule over us like Cenez, for peradventure we shall find a man that can deliver us from our afflictions, for it is not expedient that the people should be without a prince. **2** And they cast the lot and found no man; and the people were greatly grieved and said: The people is not worthy to be heard by the Lord, for he hath not answered us. Now therefore let us cast lots even by tribes, if perchance God will be appeased by a multitude, for we know that he will be reconciled unto them that are worthy *of him*. And they cast lots by tribes, and upon no tribe did the lot come forth. And Israel said: Let us choose one of ourselves, for we are in a strait, for we perceive that God abhorreth his people, and that his soul is displeased at us. **3** And one answered and said unto the people, whose name was Nethez: It is not he that hateth us, but we ourselves have made ourselves to be hated, that God should forsake us. And therefore, even though we die, let us not forsake him, but let us flee unto him *for refuge*; for we have walked in our evil ways and have not known him that made us, and therefore will our device be vain. For I know that God will not cast us off for ever, neither will he hate his people unto all generations: therefore now be ye strong and let us pray yet again and cast lots by cities, for although our sins be enlarged, yet will his long-suffering not fail. **4** And they cast lots by cities, and the lot came upon Armathem. And the people said: Is Armathem accounted righteous beyond all the cities of Israel, that he hath chosen her thus before all the cities? And every man said to his neighbour: In that same city which hath come forth by lot let us cast the lot by men, and let us see whom the Lord hath chosen out of her. **5** And they cast the lot by men, and it took no man save Elchana, for upon him the lot leapt out, and the people took him And said: Come and be ruler over us. And Elchana said unto the people: I cannot be a prince over this people, neither can I judge who can be a prince over you. But if my sins have found me out, that the lot should leap upon me, I will slay myself, that ye defile me not; for it is just that I should die for my *own* sins only and not have to bear the weight of the people. **6** And when the people saw that it was not the will of Elchana to take the leadership over them, they prayed again unto the Lord saying: O Lord God of Israel, wherefore hast thou forsaken thy people in the victory of the enemy and neglected thine heritage in the time of trouble? Behold even he that was taken by the lot hath not accomplished thy commandment; but only this *hath come about*, that the lot leapt out upon him, and we believed that we had a prince. And lo, he also contendeth against the lot. Whom shall we yet require, or unto whom shall we flee, and where is the place of our rest? For if the ordinances are true which thou madest with our fathers, saying: I will enlarge your seed, and they shall know of this, then it were better that thou saidst to us, I will cut off your seed, than that thou shouldest have no regard to our root. **7** And God said unto them: If indeed I recompensed you according to your evil deeds, I ought not to give ear unto your people; but what shall I do, because my name cometh to be called upon you? And now know ye that Elchana upon whom the lot hath fallen cannot rule over you, but it is rather his son that shall be born of him; he shall be prince over you and shall prophesy; and from henceforth there shall not be wanting unto you a prince for many years. **8** And the people said: Behold, Lord, Elchana hath ten sons, and which of them shall be a prince or shall prophesy? And God said: Not any of the sons of Phenenna can be a prince over the people, but he that is born of the barren woman whom I have given him to wife, he shall be a prophet before me, and I will love him even as I loved Isaac, and his name shall be before me for ever. And the people said: Behold now, it may be that God hath remembered us, to deliver us from the hand of them that hate us. And in that day they offered peace offerings and feasted in their orders.

L.

1 Now [whereas] Elchana had two wives, the name of the one was Anna and the name of the other Phenenna. And because Phenenna had sons, and Anna had none, Phenenna reproached her, saying: What profiteth it thee that Elchana thine husband loveth thee? but thou art a dry tree. I know moreover that he will love me, because he delighteth to see my sons standing about him like the planting of an oliveyard. **2** And so it was, when she reproached her every day, and Anna was very sore at heart, and she feared God from her youth, it came to pass when the good day of the passover drew on, and her husband went up to do sacrifice, that Phenenna reviled Anna saying: A woman is not *indeed* beloved even if her husband love her or her beauty. Let not Anna therefore boast herself of her beauty, but he that boasteth let him boast when he seeth his seed before his face; and when it is not so among women, even the fruit of their womb, then shall love become of no account. For what profit was it unto Rachel that Jacob loved her? except there had been given her the fruit of her womb, *surely* his love would have been to no purpose? And when Anna heard that, her soul was melted within her and *her eyes* ran down with tears. **3** And her husband saw her and said: *Wherefore art thou sad, and eatest not, and why is thy heart within thee cast down*? Is not thy behaviour better than the ten sons of Phenenna? And Anna hearkened to him and arose after she had eaten, and came unto Silo to the house of the Lord where Heli the priest abode, whom Phinees the son of Eleazar the priest had presented as it was commanded him. **4** And Anna prayed and said: Hast not thou, O Lord, examined the heart of all generations before thou formedst the world? But what is the womb that is born open, or what one that is shut up dieth, except thou will it? And now let my prayer go up before thee this day, lest I go down hence empty, for thou knowest my heart, how I have walked before thee from the days of my youth. **5** And Anna would not pray aloud as do all men, for she took thought at that time saying: Lest perchance I be not worthy to be heard, and it shall be that Phenenna will envy me yet more and reproach me as she daily saith: Where is thy God in whom thou trustest? And I know that it is not she that hath many sons that is enriched, neither she that lacketh them is poor, but whoso aboundeth in the will of God, she is enriched. For they that know for what I have prayed, if they perceive that I am not heard in my prayer, will blaspheme. And I shall not only have a witness in mine own soul, for my tears also are handmaidens of my prayers. **6** And as she prayed, Heli the priest, seeing that she was afflicted in her mind and carried herself like one drunken, said unto her: Go, put away thy wine from thee. And she said: Is my prayer so heard that I am called drunken? *Verily* I am drunken with sorrow and have drunk the cup of my weeping. **7** And Heli the priest said unto her: Tell me thy reproach. And she said unto him: I am the wife of Elchana, and because God hath surely shut up my womb, therefore I prayed before him that I might not depart out of this world unto him Without fruit, neither die without leaving mine own image. And Heli the priest said unto her: Go, for I know wherefore thou hast prayed, and. thy prayer is heard. **8** But Heli the priest would not tell her that a prophet was foreordained to be born of her: for he had heard when the Lord spake concerning him. And Anna came unto her house, and was consoled of her sorrow, *yet* she told no man of that for which she had prayed.

LI.

1 And in the time of those days she conceived and bare a son and called his name Samuel, which is interpreted Mighty, according as God called his name when he prophesied of him. And Anna sat and gave suck to the child until he was two years old, and when she had weaned him, she went up with him bearing gifts in her hands, and the child was very fair and the Lord was with him. **2** And Anna set the child before the face of Heli and said unto him: This is the desire which I desired, and this is the request which I sought. And Heli said unto her: Not thou only didst seek it, but the people *also* prayed for this. It is not thy request alone, but it was promised aforetime unto the tribes; and by this child is thy womb justified, that thou shouldest set up prophecy before the people, and appoint the milk of thy breasts for a fountain unto the twelve tribes. **3** And when Anna heard that, she prayed and said: Come ye at my voice, all ye peoples, and give ear unto my speech, all ye kingdoms, for my mouth is opened that I may speak, and my lips are commanded that I may sing praises unto the Lord. Drop, O my breasts, and give forth your testimonies, for it is appointed to you to give suck. For he shall be set up that is suckled by you, and by his words shall the people be enlightened, and he shall shew unto the nations their boundaries, and his horn shall be greatly exalted. **4** And therefore will I utter my words openly, for out of me shall arise the ordinance of the Lord, and all men shall find the truth. Haste ye not to talk proudly, neither to utter high words out of your mouth, but delight yourselves in boasting when the light shall come forth out of which wisdom shall be born, that they be not called rich which have most possessions, neither they that have borne abundantly be termed mothers: for the barren hath been satisfied, and she that was multi plied in sons is become empty; **5** For the Lord killeth with judgement, and quickeneth in mercy: for the ungodly are in this world: therefore quickeneth he the righteous when he will, but the ungodly he will shut up in darkness. But unto the righteous he preserveth their light, and when the ungodly are dead, then shall they perish, and when the righteous are fallen asleep, then shall they be delivered. And so shall all judgement endure until he be revealed which holdeth *it*. **6** Speak thou, speak thou, O Anna, and keep not silence: sing praises, O daughter of Bathuel, be cause of thy wonders which God hath wrought with thee. Who is Anna, that a prophet should come out of her? or who is the daughter of Bathuel, that she should bring forth a light foil the peoples? Arise thou also, Elchana, and gird up thy loins. Sing praises for the signs of the Lord: For of thy son did Asaph prophesy in the wilderness saying: *Moses and Aaron among his priests and Samuel among them*. Behold the word is accomplished and the prophecy come to pass. And these things endure thus, until they give an horn unto his anointed, and power cleaveth unto the throne of his king. Yet let my son stand here and minister, until there arise a light unto this people. ⁷ And they departed thence and set forth with mirth, rejoicing and exulting in heart for all the glory that God had wrought with them. But the people went down with one accord unto Silo with timbrels and dances, with lutes and harps, and came unto Heli the priest and offered Samuel unto him, whom they set before the face of the Lord and anointed him and said: Let the prophet live among the people, and let him be long a light unto this nation.

LII.

¹ But Samuel was a very young child and knew nothing of all these things. And whilst he served before the Lord, the two sons of Heli, which walked not in the ways of their fathers, began to do wickedly unto the people and multiplied their iniquities. And they dwelt hard by the house of Bethac, and when the people came together to sacrifice, Ophni and Phinees came and provoked the people to anger, seizing the oblations before the holy things were offered unto the Lord. ² And this thing pleased not the Lord, neither the people, nor their father. And their father spake thus unto them: What is this report that I hear of you? Know ye not that I have received the place that Phinees committed unto me? And if we waste that we have received, what shall we say if he that committed it require it again, and vex us for that which he committed *unto us*? Now therefore make straight your ways, and walk in good paths, and your deeds shall endure. But if ye gainsay *me* and refrain not from your evil devices, ye will destroy yourselves, and the priesthood will be in vain, and that which was sanctified will come to nought. And then will they say: To no purpose did the rod of Aaron spring up, and the flower that was born of it is come to nothing. ³ Therefore while ye are yet able, my sons, correct that ye have done ill, and the men against whom ye have sinned will pray for you. But if ye will not, but persist in your iniquities, I shall be guiltless, and I shall not only sorrow lest (*or* and now I shall not blot out these great evils in you, lest) I hear of the day of your death before I die, but also if this befall (or but even if this befall not) I shall be clear of blame: and though I be afflicted, ye shall nevertheless perish. ⁴ And his sons obeyed him not, for the Lord had given sentence concerning them that they should die, because they had sinned: for when *their father* said to them: Repent you of your evil way, they said: When we grow old, then will we repent. And for this cause it was not given unto them that they should repent when they were rebuked of their father, because they had always been rebellious, and had wrought very unjustly in despoiling Israel. But the Lord was angry with Heli.

LIII.

¹ But Samuel was ministering before the Lord and knew not as yet what were the oracles of the Lord: for he had not yet heard the oracles of the Lord, for he was 8 years old. ² But when God remembered Israel, he would reveal his words unto Samuel, and Samuel did sleep in the temple of the Lord. And it came to pass when God called unto him, that he considered first, and said: Be hold now, Samuel is young that he should be (or though he be) beloved in my sight; nevertheless because he hath not yet heard the voice of the Lord, neither is he confirmed unto the voice of the Most Highest, yet is he like unto Moses my servant: but unto Moses I spake when he was 80 years old, but Samuel is 8 years old. And Moses saw the fire first and his heart was afraid. And if Samuel shall see the fire now, how shall he abide it? There fore now shall there come unto him a voice as of a man, and not as of God. And when he under standeth, then I will speak unto him as God. ³ And at midnight a voice out of heaven called him: and Samuel awoke and perceived as it were the voice of Heli, and ran unto him and spake saying: Wherefore hast thou awaked me, father? For I was afraid, because thou didst never call me in the night. And Heli said: Woe is me, can it be that an unclean spirit hath deceived my son Samuel? And he said to him: Go and sleep, for I called thee not. Nevertheless, tell me if thou remember, how often he that called thee cried. And he said: Twice. And Heli said unto him: Say now, of whose voice wast thou aware, my son? And he said: Of thine, therefore ran I unto thee. ⁴ And Heli said: In thee do I behold the sign that men shall have from this day forward for ever, .that if one call unto another twice in the night or at noonday, they shall know that it is an evil spirit. But if he call a third time, they shall know that it is an angel. And Samuel went away and slept. ⁵ And he heard the second time a voice from heaven, and he arose and ran unto Heli and said unto him: Wherefore called he me, for I heard the voice of Elchana my father? Then did Heli under stand that God did begin to call him. And Heli said: In those two voices wherewith God hath called unto thee, he likened himself to thy father and to thy master, but now the third time *he will speak as* God. ⁶ And he said unto him: With thy right ear attend and with thy left refrain. For Phinees the priest commanded us, saying: The right ear heareth the Lord by night, and the left ear an angel. Therefore, if thou hear with thy right ear, say thus: Speak what thou wilt, for I hear thee, for thou hast formed me; but if thou hear with the left ear, come and tell me. And Samuel went away and slept as Heli had commanded him. ⁷ And the Lord added and spake yet a third time, and the right ear of Samuel was filled *with the voice*. And when he perceived that the speech of his father had come down unto him, Samuel turned upon his other side, and said: If I be able, speak, for thou hast formed me (*or* knowest well concerning me). ⁸ And God said unto him: Verily I enlightened the house of Israel in Egypt and chose unto me at that time Moses my servant for a prophet, and by him I wrought wonders for my people, and avenged them of mine enemies as I would, and I took my people into the wilderness, and enlightened them as they beheld. ⁹ And when one tribe rose up against another tribe, saying: Wherefore are the priests alone holy? I would not destroy them, but I said unto them: Give ye every one his rod, and it shall be that he whose rod flourisheth I have chosen him for the priesthood. And when they had all given their rods as I commanded, then did I command the earth of the tabernacle that the rod of Aaron should flourish, that his line might be manifested for many days. And now they which did flourish have abhorred my holy things. ¹⁰ Therefore, lo, the days shall come that I will cut off (*lit.* stop) the flower that came forth at that time, and I will go forth against them because they do transgress the word which I spake unto my servant Moses, saying: *If thou meet with a nest, thou shalt not take the mother with the young*, therefore it shall befall them that the mothers shall die with the children, and the fathers perish with the sons. ¹¹ And when Samuel heard these words his heart was melted, and he said: Hath it thus come against me in my youth that I should prophesy unto the destruction of him that fostered me? and how then was I granted at the request of my mother? and who is he that brought me up? how hath he charged me to bear evil tidings? ¹² And Samuel arose in the morning and would not tell it unto Heli. And Heli said unto him: Hear now, my son. Behold, before thou wast born God promised Israel that he would send thee unto them to prophesy. And now, when thy mother came hither and prayed, for she knew not that which had been done, I said unto her: Go forth, for that which shall be born of thee shall be a son unto me. Thus spake I unto thy mother, and thus hath the Lord directed thy way. And even if thou chasten thy nursing-father, as the Lord liveth, hide thou not from me the things that thou hast heard. ¹³ Then Samuel was, afraid, and told him all the words that he had heard. And he said: *Can the thing formed answer him tha*t *formed it*? So also can I not answer when he will take away that which he hath given, even the faithful giver, the holy one which hath prophesied, for I am subject unto his power.

LIV.

¹ And in those days the Philistines assembled their camp to fight against Israel, and the children of Israel went out to fight with them. And when the people of Israel had been put to flight in the first battle, they said: Let us bring up the ark of the covenant of the Lord, peradventure it Will fight with us, because in it are the testimonies of the Lord which he ordained unto our fathers in Oreb. ² And as the ark went up with them, when it was come into the camp, the Lord thundered and said: This time shall be likened unto that which was in the wilderness, when they took the ark without my commandment, and destruction befel them. So also, at this time, shall the people fall, and the ark shall be taken, that I may punish the adversaries of my people because of the ark, and rebuke my people because they have sinned. ³ And when the ark was come into the battle, the Philistines went forth to meet the children of Israel, and smote them. And there was there a certain Golia , a Philistine, which came even unto the ark, and Ophni and Phinees the sons of Heli and Saul the son of Cis held the ark. And Golia took *it* with his left hand and slew Ophni and Phinees. ⁴ But Saul, because he was light on his feet, fled from before him; and he rent his clothes, Sam. and put ashes on his head, and came unto Heli the priest. And Heli said unto him: Tell me what hath befallen in the camp? And Saul said unto him: Why askest thou me these things? for the people is overcome, and God hath forsaken Israel. Yea, and the priests also are slain with the sword, and the ark is delivered unto the Philistines. ⁵ And when Heli heard of the taking of the ark, he said: Behold, Samuel prophesied of me and my sons that we should die together, but the ark he named not unto me. And now the testimonies are delivered up unto the enemy, and what can I more say? Behold, Israel is perished from the truth, for the judgements are taken away from him. And because Heli despaired wholly, he fell off from his seat. And they died in one day, even Heli and Ophni and Phinees his sons. ⁶ And Heli's son's wife sat and travailed; and when she heard these things, all her bowels were melted. And the midwife said unto her: Be of good cheer, neither let thy soul faint, for a son is born to thee. And she said to her: Lo now is one soul born and we four die, that is, my father and his two sons and his daughter-in-law. And she called his name, Where is the glory? saying: The

glory of God is perished in Israel because the ark of the Lord is taken captive. And when she had thus said she gave up the ghost.

LV.

[1] But Samuel knew nothing of all these things, because three days before the battle God sent him *away*, saying unto him: Go and look upon the place of Arimatha, there shall be thy dwelling. And when Samuel heard what had befallen Israel, he came and prayed unto the Lord) saying: Behold, now, in vain is understanding denied unto me that I might see the destruction of my people. And now I fear lest my days grow old in evil and my years be ended in sorrow, for whereas the ark of the Lord is not with me, why should I yet live? [2] And the Lord said unto him: Be not grieved, Samuel, that the ark is taken away. I will bring it again, and them that have taken it will I overthrow, and will avenge my people of their enemies. And Samuel said: Lo, even if thou avenge them in time, according to thy longsuffering, yet what shall we do which die now? And God said to him: Before thou diest thou shalt see the end which I will bring upon mine enemies, whereby the Philistines shall perish *and shall be slain* by scorpions and by all manner of noisome creeping things. [3] And when the Philistines had set the ark of the Lord that was taken in the temple of Dagon their god, and were come to enquire of Dagon concerning their going forth, they found him fallen on his face and his hands and feet laid before the ark. And they went forth on the first morning, having crucified his priests. And on the second day they came and found as on the day before, and the destruction was greatly multiplied among them. [4] Therefore the Philistines gathered together in Accaron, and said every man to his neighbour: Behold now, we see that the destruction is enlarged among us, and the fruit of our body perisheth, for the creeping things that are sent upon us destroy them that are with child and the sucklings and them also that give suck. And they said: Let us see wherefore the hand of the Lord is strong against us. Is it for the ark's sake? for every day is our god found fallen upon his face before the ark, and we have slain our priests to no purpose once and again. [5] And the wise men of the Philistines said: Lo, now by this may we know if the Lord have sent destruction upon us for his ark's sake or if a chance affliction is come upon us for a season? [6] And now, whereas all that are with child and give suck die, and they that give suck are made childless, and they, that are suckled perish, we also will take kine that give suck and yoke them to a new cart, and set the ark upon it, and shut up the young of the kine. And it shall be, if the kine indeed go forth, and turn not back to their young, we shall know that we have suffered these things for the ark's sake; but if they refuse to go, yearning after their young, we shall know that the time of our fall is come upon us. [7] And certain of the wise men and diviners answered: Assay ye not only this, but let us set the kine at the head of the three ways that are about Accaron. For the middle way leadeth to Accaron, and the way on the right hand to Judæa, and the way on the left hand to Samaria. And direct ye the kine that bear the ark in the middle way. And if they set forth by the right-hand way straight unto Judæa, we shall know that of a truth the God of the Jews hath laid us waste; but if they go by those other ways, we shall know that an evil (*lit.* mighty) time hath befallen us, for now have we denied our gods. [8] And the Philistines took milch kine and yoked them to a new cart and set the ark thereon, and set them at the head of the three ways, and their young they shut up at home. And the kine, albeit they lowed and yearned for their young, went forward nevertheless by the right-hand way that leadeth to Judæa. And then they knew that for the ark's sake they were laid waste. [9] And all the Philistines assembled and brought the ark again unto Silo with timbrels and pipes and dances. And because of the noisome creeping things that laid them waste, they made seats of gold and sanctified the ark. [10] And in that plaguing of the Philistines, the number was of them that died being with child 75,000, and of the sucking children 65,000, and of them that gave suck 55,000, and of men 25,000 And the land had rest seven years.

LVI.

[1] And at that time the children of Israel required a king in their Just. And they gathered together unto Samuel, and said: Behold, now, thou art grown old, and thy sons walk not in the ways of the Lord; now, therefore, appoint a king over us to judge betwixt us, for the word is fulfilled which Moses spake unto our fathers in the wilderness, saying: Thou shalt surely appoint over thee a prince of your brethren. [2] And when Samuel heard mention of the kingdom, he was sore grieved in his heart, and said: Behold now I see that there is no more (*or* not yet) for us a time of a perpetual kingdom, neither of building the house of the Lord our God, inasmuch as these desire a king before the time. And now, if the Lord refuse it altogether (*or* But even if the Lord so will), it seemeth unto me that a king cannot be established. [3] And the Lord said unto him in the night: Be not grieved, for I will send them a king which shall lay them waste, and he himself shall be laid waste thereafter. Now he that shall come unto thee to-morrow at the sixth hour, he it is that shall reign over them. [4] And on the next day, Saul, the son of Cis, was coming from Mount Effrem, seeking the asses of his father; and when he was come to Armathem, he entered in to inquire of Samuel for the asses. Now he was walking hard by Baam, and Saul said unto him: Where is he that seeth? For at that time a prophet was called Seer. And Samuel said unto him: I am he that seeth. And he said: Canst thou tell me of the asses of my father? for they are lost. [5] And Samuel said unto him: Refresh thyself with me this day, and in the morning I will tell thee that whereof thou camest to inquire. And Samuel said unto the Lord: Direct, O Lord, thy people, and reveal unto me what thou hast determined concerning them. And Saul refreshed himself with Samuel that day and rose in the morning. And Samuel said unto him: Behold, know thou that the Lord hath chosen thee to be prince over his people at this time, and hath raised up thy ways, and thy time shall be directed. [6] And Saul said to Samuel: Who am I, and what is my father's house, that my lord should speak thus unto me? For I understand not what thou sayest, because I am a youth. And Samuel said to Saul: Who will grant that thy word should come even unto accomplishment of itself, that thou mayest live many days? but consider this, that thy words shall be likened unto the words of a prophet, whose name shall be Hieremias. [7] And as Saul went away that day, the people came unto Samuel, saying: Give us a king as thou didst promise us. And he said to them: Behold, the king shall come unto you after three days. And lo, Saul came. And there befell him all the signs which Samuel had told him. Are not these things written in the book of the Kings?

LVII.

[1] And Samuel sent and gathered all the people, and said unto them: Lo, ye and your king *are here*, and I am betwixt you, as the Lord commanded me. [2] And therefore I say unto you, before the face of your king, even as my lord Moses; the servant of God, said unto your fathers in the wilderness, when the synagogue of Core arose against him: Ye know that I have not taken aught of you, neither have I wronged any of you; and because certain lied at that time and said, Thou didst take, the earth swallowed them up. [3] Now, therefore, do ye whom the Lord hath not punished answer before the Lord and before his anointed, if it be for this cause that ye have required a king, because I have evil entreated you, and the Lord shall be your witness. But if, now the word of the Lord is fulfilled, I am free, and my father's house. [4] And the people answered: We are thy servants and our king with us; because we are unworthy to be judged by a prophet, therefore said we: Appoint a king over us to judge us. And all the people and the king wept with a great lamentation, and said: Let Samuel the prophet live. And when the king was appointed they offered sacrifices unto the Lord. [5] And after that Saul fought with the Philistines one year, and the battle prospered greatly.

LVIII.

[1] And at that time the Lord said unto Samuel: Go and say unto Saul: Thou art sent to destroy Amalech, that the words may be fulfilled which Moses my servant spake saying: I will destroy the name of Amalech out of the land whereof I spake in mine anger. And forget not to destroy every soul of them as it is commanded thee. [2] And Saul departed and fought against Amalech, and , saved alive Agag the king of Amalech because he said to him: I will shew thee hidden treasures. Therefore he spared him and saved him alive and brought him unto Armathem. [3] And God said unto Samuel: Hast thou seen how the king is corrupted with money even in a moment, and hath saved alive Agag king of Amalech and his wife? Now therefore suffer Agag and his wife to come together this night, and to-morrow thou shalt slay him; but his wife they shall preserve till she bring forth a male child, and then she also shall die, and he that is born of her shall be an offence unto Saul. But thou, arise on the morrow and slay Agag: for the sin of Saul is written before my face alway. 4 And when Samuel was risen on the morrow, Saul came forth to meet him and said unto him: The Lord hath delivered our enemies into our hands as he said. And Samuel said to Saul: Whom hath Israel wronged? for before the time was come that a king should rule over him, he demanded thee for his king, and thou, when thou wast sent to do the will of the Lord, hast transgressed it. Therefore he that was saved alive by thee shall die now, and those hidden treasures whereof he spake he shall not show thee, and he that is born of him shall be an offence unto thee. And Samuel came unto Agag with a sword and slew him, and returned unto his house.

LIX.

[1] And the Lord said unto him: Go, anoint him whom I shall tell thee, for the time is fulfilled wherein his kingdom shall come. And. Samuel said: Lo, wilt thou now blot out the kingdom of Saul? And he said: I will blot it out. [2] And Samuel went forth unto Bethel, and sanctified the elders, and Jesse, and his sons. And Eliab the firstborn of Jesse came. And Samuel said: Behold now the holy one, the anointed of the Lord. And the Lord said unto

him: Where is thy vision which thine heart hath seen? Art not thou he that saidst unto Saul: I am he that seeth? And how knowest thou not whom thou must anoint? And now let this rebuke suffice thee, and seek out the shepherd, the least of them all, and anoint him. ³ And Samuel said unto Jesse: Hearken, Jesse, send and bring hither thy son from the flock, for him hath God chosen. And Jesse sent and brought David, and Samuel anointed him in the midst of his brethren. And the Lord was with him from that day *forward*. ⁴ Then David began to sing this psalm, and said: In the ends of the earth will I begin to glorify *him*, and unto everlasting days will I sing praises. Abel at the first when he fed the sheep, his sacrifice was acceptable rather than his brother's. And his brother envied him and slew him. But it is not so with me, for God hath kept me, and hath delivered me unto his angels and his watchers to keep me, for my brethren envied me, and my father and my mother made me of no account, and when the prophet came they called not for me, and when the Lord's anointed was proclaimed they forgat me. But God came near unto me with his right hand, and with his mercy: therefore will I not cease to sing praises all the days of my life. ⁵ And as David yet spake, behold a fierce lion out of the wood and a she-bear out of the mountain took the bulls of David. And David said: Lo, this shall be a sign unto me for a mighty beginning of my victory in the battle. I will go out after them and deliver that which is carried off and will slay them. And David went out after them and took stones out of the wood and slew them. And God said unto him: Lo, by stones have I delivered thee these beasts in thy sight. And this shall be a sign unto thee that hereafter thou shalt slay with stones the adversary of my people.

LX.

¹ And at that time the spirit of the Lord was taken away from Saul, and an evil spirit oppressed (*lit.* choked) him. And Saul sent and fetched David, and he played a psalm upon his harp in the night. And this is the psalm which he sang unto Saul that the evil spirit might depart from him. ² There were darkness and silence before the world was, and the silence spake, and the darkness became visible. And then was thy name created, even at the drawing together of that which was stretched out, whereof the upper was called heaven and the lower was called earth. And it was commanded to the upper that it should rain according to its season, and to the lower that it should bring forth food for man that *should be* made. And after that was the tribe of your spirits made. ³ Now therefore, be not injurious, whereas thou art a second creation, but if not, then remember Hell (*lit.* be mindful of Tartarus) wherein thou walkedst. Or is it not enough for thee to hear that by that which resoundeth before thee I sing unto many? Or forgettest thou that out of a rebounding echo in the abyss (*or* chaos) thy creation was born? But that new womb shall rebuke thee, whereof I am born, of whom shall be born after a time of my loins he that shall subdue you. And when David sung praises, the spirit spared Saul.

LXI.

¹ And after these things the Philistines came to fight against Israel. And David was returned to the wilderness to feed his sheep, and the Madianites came and would have taken his sheep, and he came down unto them and fought against them and slew of them 15,000 men. This is the first battle that David fought, being in the wilderness. ² And there came a man out of the camp of the Philistines by name Golia, and he looked upon Saul and upon Israel and said: Art not thou Saul which fleddest before me when I took the ark from you and slew your priests? And now that thou reignest, wilt thou come down unto me like a man and a king and fight against us? If not, I will come unto thee, and will cause thee to be taken captive, and thy people to serve our gods. And when Saul and Israel heard that, they feared greatly. And the Philistine said: According to the number of the days wherein Israel feasted when they received the law in the wilderness, even 40 days, I will reproach them, and after that I will fight with them. ³ And it came to pass when the 40 days were fulfilled, and David was come to see the battle of his brethren, that he heard the words which the Philistine spake, and said: Is this *peradventure* the time whereof God said unto me: I will deliver the adversary of my people into thy hand by stones? ⁴ And Saul heard these words and sent and took him and said: What was the speech which thou spakest unto the people? And David said: Fear not, O king, for I will go and fight against the Philistine, and God will take away the hatred and reproach from Israel. ⁵ And David went forth and took 7 stones and wrote upon them the names of his fathers, Abraham, Isaac, and Jacob, Moses and Aaron, and his own name, and the name of the Most Mighty. And God sent Cervihel, the angel that is over strength. ⁶ And David went forth unto Golia and said unto him: Hear a word before thou diest. Were not the two women of whom I and thou were born sisters? and thy mother was Orpha and my mother was Ruth. And Orpha chose for herself the gods of the Philistines and went after them, but Ruth chose for herself the ways of the Most Mighty and walked in them. And now thou and thy brethren are born of Orpha, and as thou art arisen this day and come to lay Israel waste, behold, I also that am born of thy kindred am come to avenge my people. For thy three brethren also shall fall into my hands after thy death. And then shall ye say unto your mother: He that was born of thy sister hath not spared us. ⁷ And David put a stone in his sling and smote the Philistine in his forehead, and ran upon him and drew his sword out of the sheath and took his head from him. And Golia said unto him while his life was yet in him: Hasten and slay me and rejoice. ⁸ And David said unto him: Before thou diest, open thine eyes and behold thy slayer which hath killed thee. And the Philistine looked and saw the angel and said: Thou hast not killed me by thyself, but he that was with thee, whose form is not as the form of a man. And then David took his head from him. ⁹ And the angel of the Lord lifted up the face of David and no man knew him. And when Saul saw David he asked him who he was, and there was no man that knew him who he was.

LXII.

¹ And after these things Saul envied David and sought to kill him. But David and Jonathan, Saul's son, made a covenant together. And when David saw that Saul sought to kill him, he fled unto Armathem; and *Saul* went out after him. ² And the spirit abode in Saul, and he prophesied, saying: Why art thou deceived, O Saul, or whom dost thou persecute in vain? The time of thy kingdom is fulfilled. Go unto thy place, for thou shalt die and David shall reign. Shalt not thou and thy son die together? And then shall the kingdom of David appear. And the spirit departed from Saul, and he knew not what he had prophesied. ³ But David came unto Jonathan and said unto him: Come and let us make a covenant before we be parted one from the other. For Saul, thy father, seeketh to slay me without cause. And since he hath perceived that thou lovest me he telleth thee not what he deviseth concerning me. ⁴ But for this cause he hateth me, because thou lovest me, and lest I should reign in his stead. And whereas I have done him good he requiteth me with evil. And whereas I slew Golia by the word of the Most Mighty, see thou what an end he purposeth for me. For he hath determined concerning my father's house, to destroy it. And would that the judgement of truth might be put in the balance, that the multitude of the prudent might hear the sentence. ⁵ And now I fear lest he kill me and lose his own life for my sake. For he shall never shed innocent blood without punishment. Wherefore should my soul suffer persecution? For I was the, least among my brethren, feeding the sheep, and wherefore am I in peril of death? For I am righteous and have none iniquity. And wherefore doth thy father hate me? Yet the righteousness of my father shall help me that I fall not into thy father's hands. And seeing I am young and tender of age, it is to no purpose that Saul envieth me. ⁶ If I had wronged him, I would pray him to forgive me the sin. For if God forgiveth iniquity, how much more thy father who is flesh and blood? I have walked in his house with a perfect heart, yea, I grew up before his face like a swift eagle, I put mine hands unto the harp and blessed him in songs, and he hath devised to slay me, and like a sparrow that fleeth before the face of the hawk, so have I fled before his face. ⁷ Unto whom have I spoken this, or unto whom have I told the things that I have suffered save unto thee and Melchol thy sister? For as for both of us, let us go together in truth. ⁸ And it were better, my brother, that I should be slain in battle than that I should fall into the hands of thy father: for in the battle mine eyes were looking on every side that I might defend him from his enemies. O my brother Jonathan, hear my words, and if there be iniquity in me, reprove me. ⁹ And Jonathan answered and said: Come unto me, my brother David, and I will tell thee thy righteousness. My soul pineth away sore at thy sadness because now we are parted one from another. And this have our sins compelled, that we should be parted from one another. But let us remember one another day and night while we live. And even if death part us, yet I know that our souls will know one another. For thine is the kingdom in this world, and of thee shall be the beginning of the kingdom, and it cometh in its time. ¹⁰ And now, like a child that is weaned from its mother, even so shall be our separation. Let the heaven be witness and let the earth be witness of those things which we have spoken together. And let us weep each with the other and Jay up our tears in one vessel and commit the vessel to the earth, and it shall be a testimony unto us. ii. And they bewailed each one the other sore, and kissed one another. But Jonathan feared and said unto David: Let us remember, O my brother, the covenant that is made betwixt us, and the oath which is set in our heart. And if I die before thee and thou indeed reign, as the Lord hath spoken, be not mindful of the anger of my father, but of the covenant which is made betwixt me and thee. Neither think upon the hatred wherewith my father hateth thee in vain but upon my love wherewith I have loved thee. Neither think upon that wherein my father was unthankful unto thee, but remember the table whereat we have eaten together. Neither keep in mind the envy wherewith my father envied thee evilly, but the faith which I and thou keep. Neither

care thou for the lie wherewith Saul hath lied, but for the oaths that we have sworn one to another. And they kissed one another. And after that David departed into the wilderness, and Jonathan went into the city.

LXIII.

[1] At that time the priests that dwelt in Noba were polluting the holy things of the Lord and making the firstfruits a reproach unto the people. And God was wroth and said: Behold, I will wipe out the priests that dwell in Noba, because they walk in the ways of the sons of Heli. [2] And at that time came Doech the Syrian, which was over Saul's mules, unto Saul and said unto him: Knowest thou not that Abimelec the priest taketh counsel with David and hath given him a sword and sent him away in peace? And Saul sent and called Abimelec and said unto him: Thou shalt surely die, because thou hast taken counsel with mine enemy. And Saul slew Abimelec and all his father's house, and there was not so much as one of his tribe delivered save only Abiathar his son. The same came to David and told him all that had befallen him. [3] And God said: Behold, in the year when Saul began to reign, when Jonathan had sinned and he would have put him to death, this people rose up and suffered him not, and now when the priests were slain, even 385 men, they kept silence and said nothing. Therefore, lo, the days shall come quickly that I will deliver them into the hands of their enemies and they shall fall down wounded, they and their king. [4] And unto Doech the Syrian thus said the Lord: Behold, the days shall come quickly that the worm shall come up upon his tongue and shall cause him to pine away, and his dwelling shall be with Jair for ever in the fire that is not quenched. [5] Now all that Saul did, and the rest of his words, and how he pursued after David, are they not written in the book of the kings of Israel? [6] And after these things Samuel died, and all Israel gathered together and mourned him, and buried him.

LXIV.

[1] Then Saul took thought, saying: I will surely take away the sorcerers out of the land of Israel. So shall men remember me after my departure. And Saul scattered all the sorcerers out of the land. And God said: Behold, Saul hath taken away the sorcerers out of the land, not because of the fear of me, but that he might make himself a name. Behold, whom he hath scattered, unto them let him resort, and get divination from them, because he hath no prophets. [2] At that time the Philistines said every man to his neighbour: Behold, Samuel the prophet is dead and there is none that prayeth for Israel. David, also, which fought for them, is become Saul's adversary and is not with them. Now, therefore, let us arise and fight mightily against them, and avenge the blood of our fathers. And the Philistines assembled themselves and came *up* to battle. [3] And when Saul saw that Samuel was dead and David was not with him, his hands were loosened. And he inquired of the Lord, and he hearkened not unto him. And he sought prophets, and none appeared unto him. And Saul said unto the people: Let us seek out a diviner and inquire of him that which I have in mind. And the people answered him: Behold, now there is a woman named Sedecla, the daughter of Debin (*or* Adod) the Madianite, which deceived the people of Israel with sorceries: and lo she dwelleth in Endor. [4] And Saul put on vile raiment and went unto her, he and two men with him, by night and said unto her: Raise up unto me Samuel. And she said: I am afraid of the king Saul. And Saul said unto her: Thou shalt not be harmed of Saul in this matter. And Saul said within himself: When I was king in Israel, even though the Gentiles saw me not, yet knew they that I was Saul. And Saul asked the woman, saying: Hast thou seen Saul at any time? And she said: Oftentimes. And Saul went out and wept and said: Lo, now I know that my beauty is changed, and that the glory of my kingdom is passed from me. [5] And it came to pass, when the woman saw Samuel coming up, and beheld Saul with him, that she cried out and said: Behold, *thou art Saul, wherefore hast thou deceived me*? And he said unto her: *Fear not, but tell me what thou sawest*. And she said: Lo, these 40 years have I raised up the dead for the Philistines, but this appearance hath not been seen, neither shall it be seen hereafter. [6] And Saul said unto her: What is his form? And she said: Thou inquirest of meconcerning the gods. For, behold, his form is not the form of a man. For he is arrayed in a white robe and hath a mantle upon it, and two angels leading him. And Saul remembered the mantle which Samuel had rent while he lived, and he smote his hands together and cast himself upon the earth. [7] *And Samuel said unto him: Why hast thou disquieted me to bring me up*? I thought that the time was come for me to receive the reward of my deeds. Therefore boast not thyself, O king, neither thou, O woman. For it is not ye that have brought me up, but the precept which God spake unto me while I yet lived, that I should come and tell thee that thou hadst sinned yet the second time in neglecting God. For this cause are my bones disturbed after that I had rendered up my soul, that I should speak unto thee, and that being dead I should be heard as one living. [8] Now therefore *to-morrow shalt thou and thy sons be with me*, when the people are delivered into the hands of the Philistines. And because thy bowels have been moved with jealousy, therefore that that is thine shall be taken from thee. And Saul heard the words of Samuel, and his soul melted and he said: Behold, I depart to die with my sons, if perchance my destruction may be an atonement for mine iniquities. And Saul arose and departed thence.

LXV.

And the Philistines fought against Israel.
[1] And Saul went out to battle. *And Israel fled before the Philistines*: and when Saul saw that the battle waxed hard exceedingly, he said in his heart: Wherefore strengthenest thou thyself to live, seeing, Samuel hath proclaimed death unto thee and to thy sons? [2] *And Saul said to him that bare his armour: Take thy sword and slay me before the Philistines come and abuse me. And he that bare his armour would not lay hands upon him.* [3] *And he himself bowed upon his sword*, and he could not die. *And he looked behind him and saw* a man running and called unto him and said: Take my sword and slay me. *For my life is yet in me.* [4] And he came to slay him. And Saul said unto him: Before thou kill me, tell me, who art thou? And he said unto him: I am Edab, the son of Agag king of the Amalechites. And Saul said: Behold, now the words of Samuel are come upon me even as he said: He that shall be born of Agag shall be an offence unto thee. [5] But go thou and say unto David: I have slain thine enemy. And thou shalt say unto him: Thus saith Saul: Be not mindful of my hatred, neither of mine unrighteousness. . . .

The Book of Jasher

"Is not this written in the Book of Jasher?"–Joshua, x. 13.
"Behold it is written in the Book of Jasher."–II Samuel, i. 18.

This is the Book of the Generations of Man whom God Created upon the Earth on the day when the Lord God made Heaven and Earth.

1

[1] And God said, Let us make man in our image, after our likeness, and God created man in his own image. [2] And God formed man from the ground, and he blew into his nostrils the breath of life, and man became a living soul endowed with speech. [3] And the Lord said, It is not good for man to be alone; I will make unto him a helpmeet. [4] And the Lord caused a deep sleep to fall upon Adam, and he slept, and he took away one of his ribs, and he built flesh upon it, and formed it and brought it to Adam, and Adam awoke from his sleep, and behold a woman was standing before him. [5] And he said, This is a bone of my bones and it shall be called woman, for this has been taken from man; and Adam called her name Eve, for she was the mother of all living. [6] And God blessed them and called their names Adam and Eve in the day that he created them, and the Lord God said, Be fruitful and multiply and fill the earth. [7] And the Lord God took Adam and his wife, and he placed them in the garden of Eden to dress it and to keep it; and he commanded them and said unto them, From every tree of the garden you may eat, but from the tree of the knowledge of good and evil you shall not eat, for in the day that you eat thereof you shall surely die. [8] And when God had blessed and commanded them, he went from them, and Adam and his wife dwelt in the garden according to the command which the Lord had commanded them. [9] And the serpent, which God had created with them in the earth, came to them to incite them to transgress the command of God which he had commanded them. [10] And the serpent enticed and persuaded the woman to eat from the tree of knowledge, and the woman hearkened to the voice of the serpent, and she transgressed the word of God, and took from the tree of the knowledge of good and evil, and she ate, and she took from it and gave also to her husband and he ate. [11] And Adam and his wife transgressed the command of God which he commanded them, and God knew it, and his anger was kindled against them and he cursed them. [12] And the Lord God drove them that day from the garden of Eden, to till the ground from which they were taken, and they went and dwelt at the east of the garden of Eden; and Adam knew his wife Eve and she bore two sons and three daughters. [13] And she called the name of the first born Cain, saying, I have obtained a man from the Lord, and the name of the other she called Abel, for she said, In vanity we came into the earth, and in vanity we shall be taken from it. [14] And the boys grew up and their father gave them a possession in the land; and Cain was a tiller of the ground, and Abel a keeper of sheep. [15] And it was at the expiration of a few years, that they brought an approximating offering to the Lord, and Cain brought from the fruit of the ground, and Abel brought from the firstlings of his flock from the fat thereof, and God turned and inclined to Abel and his offering, and a fire came down from the Lord from heaven and consumed it. [16] And unto Cain and his offering the Lord did not turn, and he did not incline to it, for he had brought from the inferior fruit of the ground before the Lord, and Cain was jealous against his brother Abel on account of this, and he sought a pretext to slay him. [17] And in some time after, Cain and Abel his brother, went one day into the field to do their work; and they were both in the field, Cain tilling and ploughing his ground, and Abel feeding his flock; and the flock passed that part which Cain had ploughed in the ground, and it sorely grieved Cain on this account. [18] And Cain approached his brother Abel in anger, and he said unto him, What is there between me and thee, that thou comest to dwell and bring thy flock to feed in my land? [19] And Abel answered his brother Cain and said unto him, What is there between me and thee, that thou shalt eat the flesh of my flock and clothe thyself with their wool? [20] And now therefore, put off the wool of my sheep with which thou hast clothed thyself, and recompense me for their fruit and flesh which thou hast eaten, and when thou shalt have done this, I will then go from thy land as thou hast said? [21] And Cain said to his brother Abel, Surely if I slay thee this day, who will require thy blood from me? [22] And Abel answered Cain, saying, Surely God who has made us in the earth, he will avenge my cause, and he will require my blood from thee shouldst thou slay me, for the Lord is the judge and arbiter, and it is he who will requite man according to his evil, and the wicked man according to the wickedness that he may do upon earth. [23] And now, if thou shouldst slay me here, surely God knoweth thy secret views, and will judge thee for the evil which thou didst declare to do unto me this day. [24] And when Cain heard the words which Abel his brother had spoken, behold the anger of Cain was kindled against his brother Abel for declaring this thing. [25] And Cain hastened and rose up, and took the iron part of his ploughing instrument, with which he suddenly smote his brother and he slew him, and Cain spilt the blood of his brother Abel upon the earth, and the blood of Abel streamed upon the earth before the flock. [26] And after this Cain repented having slain his brother, and he was sadly grieved, and he wept over him and it vexed him exceedingly. [27] And Cain rose up and dug a hole in the field, wherein he put his brother's body, and he turned the dust over it. [28] And the Lord knew what Cain had done to his brother, and the Lord appeared to Cain and said unto him, Where is Abel thy brother that was with thee? [29] And Cain dissembled, and said, I do not know, am I my brother's keeper? And the Lord said unto him, What hast thou done? The voice of thy brother's blood crieth unto me from the ground where thou hast slain him. [30] For thou hast slain thy brother and hast dissembled before me, and didst imagine in thy heart that I saw thee not, nor knew all thy actions. [31] But thou didst this thing and didst slay thy brother for naught and because he spoke rightly to thee, and now, therefore, cursed be thou from the ground which opened its mouth to receive thy brother's blood from thy hand, and wherein thou didst bury him. [32] And it shall be when thou shalt till it, it shall no more give thee its strength as in the beginning, for thorns and thistles shall the ground produce, and thou shalt be moving and wandering in the earth until the day of thy death. [33] And at that time Cain went out from the presence of the Lord, from the place where he was, and he went moving and wandering in the land toward the east of Eden, he and all belonging to him. [34] And Cain knew his wife in those days, and she conceived and bare a son, and he called his name Enoch, saying, In that time the Lord began to give him rest and quiet in the earth. [35] And at that time Cain also began to build a city: and he built the city and he called the name of the city Enoch, according to the name of his son; for in those days the Lord had given him rest upon the earth, and he did not move about and wander as in the beginning. [36] And Irad was born to Enoch, and Irad begat Mechuyael and Mechuyael begat Methusael.

2

[1] And it was in the hundred and thirtieth year of the life of Adam upon the earth, that he again knew Eve his wife, and she conceived and bare a son in his likeness and in his image, and she called his name Seth, saying, Because God has appointed me another seed in the place of Abel, for Cain has slain him. [2] And Seth lived one hundred and five years, and he begat a son; and Seth called the name of his son Enosh, saying, Because in that time the sons of men began to multiply, and to afflict their souls and hearts by transgressing and rebelling against God. [3] And it was in the days of Enosh that the sons of men continued to rebel and transgress against God, to increase the anger of the Lord against the sons of men. [4] And the sons of men went and they served other gods, and they forgot the Lord who had created them in the earth: and in those days the sons of men made images of brass and iron, wood and stone, and they bowed down and served them. [5] And every man made his god and they bowed down to them, and the sons of men forsook the Lord all the days of Enosh and his children; and the anger of the Lord was kindled on account of their works and abominations which they did in the earth. [6] And the Lord caused the waters of the river Gihon to overwhelm them, and he destroyed and consumed them, and he destroyed the third part of the earth, and notwithstanding this, the sons of men did not turn from their evil ways, and their hands were yet extended to do evil in the sight of the Lord. [7] And in those days there was neither sowing nor reaping in the earth; and there was no food for the sons of men and the famine was very great in those days. [8] And the seed which they sowed in those days in the ground became thorns, thistles and briers; for from the days of Adam was this declaration concerning the earth, of the curse of God, which he cursed the earth, on account of the sin which Adam sinned before the Lord. [9] And it was when men continued to rebel and transgress against God, and to corrupt their ways, that the earth also became corrupt. [10] And Enosh lived ninety years and he begat Cainan; [11] And Cainan grew up and he was forty years old, and he became wise and had knowledge and skill in all wisdom, and he reigned over all the sons of men, and he led the sons of men to wisdom and knowledge; for Cainan was a very wise man and had understanding in all wisdom, and with his wisdom he ruled over spirits and demons; [12] And Cainan knew by his wisdom that God would destroy the sons of men for having sinned upon earth, and that the Lord would in the latter days bring upon them the waters of the flood. [13] And in those days Cainan wrote upon tablets of stone, what was to take place in time to come, and he put them in his treasures. [14] And Cainan reigned over the whole earth, and he turned some of the sons of men to the service of God. [15] And when Cainan was seventy years old, he begat three sons and two daughters. [16] And these are the names of the children of Cainan; the name of the first born Mahlallel, the second Enan, and the third Mered, and their sisters were Adah and Zillah; these are the five children of Cainan that were born to him. [17] And Lamech, the son of Methusael, became related to Cainan by marriage, and he took his two daughters for his wives, and Adah

conceived and bare a son to Lamech, and she called his name Jabal. ¹⁸ And she again conceived and bare a son, and called his name Jubal; and Zillah, her sister, was barren in those days and had no offspring. ¹⁹ For in those days the sons of men began to trespass against God, and to transgress the commandments which he had commanded to Adam, to be fruitful and multiply in the earth. ²⁰ And some of the sons of men caused their wives to drink a draught that would render them barren, in order that they might retain their figures and whereby their beautiful appearance might not fade. ²¹ And when the sons of men caused some of their wives to drink, Zillah drank with them. ²² And the child-bearing women appeared abominable in the sight of their husbands as widows, whilst their husbands lived, for to the barren ones only they were attached. ²³ And in the end of days and years, when Zillah became old, the Lord opened her womb. ²⁴ And she conceived and bare a son and she called his name Tubal Cain, saying, After I had withered away have I obtained him from the Almighty God. ²⁵ And she conceived again and bare a daughter, and she called her name Naamah, for she said, After I had withered away have I obtained pleasure and delight. ²⁶ And Lamech was old and advanced in years, and his eyes were dim that he could not see, and Tubal Cain, his son, was leading him and it was one day that Lamech went into the field and Tubal Cain his son was with him, and whilst they were walking in the field, Cain the son of Adam advanced towards them; for Lamech was very old and could not see much, and Tubal Cain his son was very young. ²⁷ And Tubal Cain told his father to draw his bow, and with the arrows he smote Cain, who was yet far off, and he slew him, for he appeared to them to be an animal. ²⁸ And the arrows entered Cain's body although he was distant from them, and he fell to the ground and died. ²⁹ And the Lord requited Cain's evil according to his wickedness, which he had done to his brother Abel, according to the word of the Lord which he had spoken. ³⁰ And it came to pass when Cain had died, that Lamech and Tubal went to see the animal which they had slain, and they saw, and behold Cain their grandfather was fallen dead upon the earth. ³¹ And Lamech was very much grieved at having done this, and in clapping his hands together he struck his son and caused his death. ³². And the wives of Lamech heard what Lamech had done, and they sought to kill him. ³³ And the wives of Lamech hated him from that day, because he slew Cain and Tubal Cain, and the wives of Lamech separated from him, and would not hearken to him in those days. ³⁴ And Lamech came to his wives, and he pressed them to listen to him about this matter. ³⁵ And he said to his wives Adah and Zillah, Hear my voice O wives of Lamech, attend to my words, for now you have imagined and said that I slew a man with my wounds, and a child with my stripes for their having done no violence, but surely know that I am old and grey-headed, and that my eyes are heavy through age, and I did this thing unknowingly. ³⁶ And the wives of Lamech listened to him in this matter, and they returned to him with the advice of their father Adam, but they bore no children to him from that time, knowing that God's anger was increasing in those days against the sons of men, to destroy them with the waters of the flood for their evil doings. ³⁷ And Mahlallel the son of Cainan lived sixty-five years and he begat Jared; and Jared lived sixty-two years and he begat Enoch.

3

¹ And Enoch lived sixty-five years and he begat Methuselah; and Enoch walked with God after having begot Methuselah, and he served the Lord, and despised the evil ways of men. ² And the soul of Enoch was wrapped up in the instruction of the Lord, in knowledge and in understanding; and he wisely retired from the sons of men, and secreted himself from them for many days. ³ And it was at the expiration of many years, whilst he was serving the Lord, and praying before him in his house, that an angel of the Lord called to him from Heaven, and he said, Here am I. ⁴ And he said, Rise, go forth from thy house and from the place where thou dost hide thyself, and appear to the sons of men, in order that thou mayest teach them the way in which they should go and the work which they must accomplish to enter in the ways of God. ⁵ And Enoch rose up according to the word of the Lord, and went forth from his house, from his place and from the chamber in which he was concealed; and he went to the sons of men and taught them the ways of the Lord, and at that time assembled the sons of men and acquainted them with the instruction of the Lord. ⁶ And he ordered it to be proclaimed in all places where the sons of men dwelt, saying, Where is the man who wishes to know the ways of the Lord and good works? let him come to Enoch. ⁷ And all the sons of men then assembled to him, for all who desired this thing went to Enoch, and Enoch reigned over the sons of men according to the word of the Lord, and they came and bowed to him and they heard his word. ⁸ And the spirit of God was upon Enoch, and he taught all his men the wisdom of God and his ways, and the sons of men served the Lord all the days of Enoch, and they came to hear his wisdom. ⁹ And all the kings of the sons of men, both first and last, together with their princes and judges, came to Enoch when they heard of his wisdom, and they bowed down to him, and they also required of Enoch to reign over them, to which he consented. ¹⁰ And they assembled in all, one hundred and thirty kings and princes, and they made Enoch king over them and they were all under his power and command. ¹¹ And Enoch taught them wisdom, knowledge, and the ways of the Lord; and he made peace amongst them, and peace was throughout the earth during the life of Enoch. ¹² And Enoch reigned over the sons of men two hundred and forty-three years, and he did justice and righteousness with all his people, and he led them in the ways of the Lord. ¹³ And these are the generations of Enoch, Methuselah, Elisha, and Elimelech, three sons; and their sisters were Melca and Nahmah, and Methuselah lived eighty-seven years and he begat Lamech. ¹⁴ And it was in the fifty-sixth year of the life of Lamech when Adam died; nine hundred and thirty years old was he at his death, and his two sons, with Enoch and Methuselah his son, buried him with great pomp, as at the burial of kings, in the cave which God had told him. ¹⁵ And in that place all the sons of men made a great mourning and weeping on account of Adam; it has therefore become a custom among the sons of men to this day. ¹⁶ And Adam died because he ate of the tree of knowledge; he and his children after him, as the Lord God had spoken. ¹⁷ And it was in the year of Adam's death which was the two hundred and forty-third year of the reign of Enoch, in that time Enoch resolved to separate himself from the sons of men and to secret himself as at first in order to serve the Lord. ¹⁸ And Enoch did so, but did not entirely secret himself from them, but kept away from the sons of men three days and then went to them for one day. ¹⁹ And during the three days that he was in his chamber, he prayed to, and praised the Lord his God, and the day on which he went and appeared to his subjects he taught them the ways of the Lord, and all they asked him about the Lord he told them. ²⁰ And he did in this manner for many years, and he afterward concealed himself for six days, and appeared to his people one day in seven; and after that once in a month, and then once in a year, until all the kings, princes and sons of men sought for him, and desired again to see the face of Enoch, and to hear his word; but they could not, as all the sons of men were greatly afraid of Enoch, and they feared to approach him on account of the Godlike awe that was seated upon his countenance; therefore no man could look at him, fearing he might be punished and die. ²¹ And all the kings and princes resolved to assemble the sons of men, and to come to Enoch, thinking that they might all speak to him at the time when he should come forth amongst them, and they did so. ²² And the day came when Enoch went forth and they all assembled and came to him, and Enoch spoke to them the words of the Lord and he taught them wisdom and knowledge, and they bowed down before him and they said, May the king live! May the king live! ²³ And in some time after, when the kings and princes and the sons of men were speaking to Enoch, and Enoch was teaching them the ways of God, behold an angel of the Lord then called unto Enoch from heaven, and wished to bring him up to heaven to make him reign there over the sons of God, as he had reigned over the sons of men upon earth. ²⁴ When at that time Enoch heard this he went and assembled all the inhabitants of the earth, and taught them wisdom and knowledge and gave them divine instructions, and he said to them, I have been required to ascend into heaven, I therefore do not know the day of my going. ²⁵ And now therefore I will teach you wisdom and knowledge and will give you instruction before I leave you, how to act upon earth whereby you may live; and he did so. ²⁶ And he taught them wisdom and knowledge, and gave them instruction, and he reproved them, and he placed before them statutes and judgments to do upon earth, and he made peace amongst them, and he taught them everlasting life, and dwelt with them some time teaching them all these things. ²⁷ And at that time the sons of men were with Enoch, and Enoch was speaking to them, and they lifted up their eyes and the likeness of a great horse descended from heaven, and the horse paced in the air; ²⁸ And they told Enoch what they had seen, and Enoch said to them, On my account does this horse descend upon earth; the time is come when I must go from you and I shall no more be seen by you. ²⁹ And the horse descended at that time and stood before Enoch, and all the sons of men that were with Enoch saw him. ³⁰ And Enoch then again ordered a voice to be proclaimed, saying, Where is the man who delighteth to know the ways of the Lord his God, let him come this day to Enoch before he is taken from us. ³¹ And all the sons of men assembled and came to Enoch that day; and all the kings of the earth with their princes and counsellors remained with him that day; and Enoch then taught the sons of men wisdom and knowledge, and gave them divine instruction; and he bade them serve the Lord and walk in his ways all the days of their lives, and he continued to make peace amongst them. ³² And it was after this that he rose up and rode upon the horse; and he went forth and all the sons of men went after him, about eight hundred thousand men; and they went with him one day's journey. ³³ And the second day he said to them, Return home to your tents, why will you go? perhaps you may die; and some of them went from

him, and those that remained went with him six day's journey; and Enoch said to them every day, Return to your tents, lest you may die; but they were not willing to return, and they went with him. ³⁴ And on the sixth day some of the men remained and clung to him, and they said to him, We will go with thee to the place where thou goest; as the Lord liveth, death only shall separate us. ³⁵ And they urged so much to go with him, that he ceased speaking to them; and they went after him and would not return; ³⁶ And when the kings returned they caused a census to be taken, in order to know the number of remaining men that went with Enoch; and it was upon the seventh day that Enoch ascended into heaven in a whirlwind, with horses and chariots of fire. ³⁷ And on the eighth day all the kings that had been with Enoch sent to bring back the number of men that were with Enoch, in that place from which he ascended into heaven. ³⁸ And all those kings went to the place and they found the earth there filled with snow, and upon the snow were large stones of snow, and one said to the other, Come, let us break through the snow and see, perhaps the men that remained with Enoch are dead, and are now under the stones of snow, and they searched but could not find him, for he had ascended into heaven.

4

¹ And all the days that Enoch lived upon earth, were three hundred and sixty-five years. ² And when Enoch had ascended into heaven, all the kings of the earth rose and took Methuselah his son and anointed him, and they caused him to reign over them in the place of his father. ³ And Methuselah acted uprightly in the sight of God, as his father Enoch had taught him, and he likewise during the whole of his life taught the sons of men wisdom, knowledge and the fear of God, and he did not turn from the good way either to the right or to the left. ⁴ But in the latter days of Methuselah, the sons of men turned from the Lord, they corrupted the earth, they robbed and plundered each other, and they rebelled against God and they transgressed, and they corrupted their ways, and would not hearken to the voice of Methuselah, but rebelled against him. ⁵ And the Lord was exceedingly wroth against them, and the Lord continued to destroy the seed in those days, so that there was neither sowing nor reaping in the earth. ⁶ For when they sowed the ground in order that they might obtain food for their support, behold, thorns and thistles were produced which they did not sow. ⁷ And still the sons of men did not turn from their evil ways, and their hands were still extended to do evil in the sight of God, and they provoked the Lord with their evil ways, and the Lord was very wroth, and repented that he had made man. ⁸ And he thought to destroy and annihilate them and he did so. ⁹ In those days when Lamech the son of Methuselah was one hundred and sixty years old, Seth the son of Adam died. ¹⁰ And all the days that Seth lived, were nine hundred and twelve years, and he died. ¹¹ And Lamech was one hundred and eighty years old when he took Ashmua, the daughter of Elishaa the son of Enoch his uncle, and she conceived. ¹² And at that time the sons of men sowed the ground, and a little food was produced, yet the sons of men did not turn from their evil ways, and they trespassed and rebelled against God. ¹³ And the wife of Lamech conceived and bare him a son at that time, at the revolution of the year. ¹⁴ And Methuselah called his name Noah, saying, The earth was in his days at rest and free from corruption, and Lamech his father called his name Menachem, saying, This one shall comfort us in our works and miserable toil in the earth, which God had cursed. ¹⁵ And the child grew up and was weaned, and he went in the ways of his father Methuselah, perfect and upright with God. ¹⁶ And all the sons of men departed from the ways of the Lord in those days as they multiplied upon the face of the earth with sons and daughters, and they taught one another their evil practices and they continued sinning against the Lord. ¹⁷ And every man made unto himself a god, and they robbed and plundered every man his neighbor as well as his relative, and they corrupted the earth, and the earth was filled with violence. ¹⁸ And their judges and rulers went to the daughters of men and took their wives by force from their husbands according to their choice, and the sons of men in those days took from the cattle of the earth, the beasts of the field and the fowls of the air, and taught the mixture of animals of one species with the other, in order therewith to provoke the Lord; and God saw the whole earth and it was corrupt, for all flesh had corrupted its ways upon earth, all men and all animals. ¹⁹ And the Lord said, I will blot out man that I created from the face of the earth, yea from man to the birds of the air, together with cattle and beasts that are in the field for I repent that I made them. ²⁰ And all men who walked in the ways of the Lord, died in those days, before the Lord brought the evil upon man which he had declared, for this was from the Lord, that they should not see the evil which the Lord spoke of concerning the sons of men. ²¹ And Noah found grace in the sight of the Lord, and the Lord chose him and his children to raise up seed from them upon the face of the whole earth.

5

¹ And it was in the eighty-fourth year of the life of Noah, that Enoch the son of Seth died, he was nine hundred and five years old at his death. ² And in the one hundred and seventy ninth year of the life of Noah, Cainan the son of Enosh died, and all the days of Cainan were nine hundred and ten years, and he died. ³ And in the two hundred and thirty fourth year of the life of Noah, Mahlallel the son of Cainan died, and the days of Mahlallel were eight hundred and ninety-five years, and he died. ⁴ And Jared the son of Mahlallel died in those days, in the three hundred and thirty-sixth year of the life of Noah; and all the days of Jared were nine hundred and sixty-two years, and he died. ⁵ And all who followed the Lord died in those days, before they saw the evil which God declared to do upon earth. ⁶ And after the lapse of many years, in the four hundred and eightieth year of the life of Noah, when all those men, who followed the Lord had died away from amongst the sons of men, and only Methuselah was then left, God said unto Noah and Methuselah, saying, ⁷ Speak ye, and proclaim to the sons of men, saying, Thus saith the Lord, return from your evil ways and forsake your works, and the Lord will repent of the evil that he declared to do to you, so that it shall not come to pass. ⁸ For thus saith the Lord, Behold I give you a period of one hundred and twenty years; if you will turn to me and forsake your evil ways, then will I also turn away from the evil which I told you, and it shall not exist, saith the Lord. ⁹ And Noah and Methuselah spoke all the words of the Lord to the sons of men, day after day, constantly speaking to them. ¹⁰ But the sons of men would not hearken to them, nor incline their ears to their words, and they were stiffnecked. ¹¹ And the Lord granted them a period of one hundred and twenty years, saying, If they will return, then will God repent of the evil, so as not to destroy the earth. ¹² Noah the son of Lamech refrained from taking a wife in those days, to beget children, for he said, Surely now God will destroy the earth, wherefore then shall I beget children? ¹³ And Noah was a just man, he was perfect in his generation, and the Lord chose him to raise up seed from his seed upon the face of the earth. ¹⁴ And the Lord said unto Noah, Take unto thee a wife, and beget children, for I have seen thee righteous before me in this generation. ¹⁵ And thou shalt raise up seed, and thy children with thee, in the midst of the earth; and Noah went and took a wife, and he chose Naamah the daughter of Enoch, and she was five hundred and eighty years old. ¹⁶ And Noah was four hundred and ninety-eight years old, when he took Naamah for a wife. ¹⁷ And Naamah conceived and bare a son, and he called his name Japheth, saying, God has enlarged me in the earth; and she conceived again and bare a son, and he called his name Shem, saying, God has made me a remnant, to raise up seed in the midst of the earth. ¹⁸ And Noah was five hundred and two years old when Naamah bare Shem, and the boys grew up and went in the ways of the Lord, in all that Methuselah and Noah their father taught them. ¹⁹ And Lamech the father of Noah, died in those days; yet verily he did not go with all his heart in the ways of his father, and he died in the hundred and ninety-fifth year of the life of Noah. ²⁰ And all the days of Lamech were seven hundred and seventy years, and he died. ²¹ And all the sons of men who knew the Lord, died in that year before the Lord brought evil upon them; for the Lord willed them to die, so as not to behold the evil that God would bring upon their brothers and relatives, as he had so declared to do. ²² In that time, the Lord said to Noah and Methuselah, Stand forth and proclaim to the sons of men all the words that I spoke to you in those days, peradventure they may turn from their evil ways, and I will then repent of the evil and will not bring it. ²³ And Noah and Methuselah stood forth, and said in the ears of the sons of men, all that God had spoken concerning them. ²⁴ But the sons of men would not hearken, neither would they incline their ears to all their declarations. ²⁵ And it was after this that the Lord said to Noah, The end of all flesh is come before me, on account of their evil deeds, and behold I will destroy the earth. ²⁶ And do thou take unto thee gopher wood, and go to a certain place and make a large ark, and place it in that spot. ²⁷ And thus shalt thou make it; three hundred cubits its length, fifty cubits broad and thirty cubits high. ²⁸ And thou shalt make unto thee a door, open at its side, and to a cubit thou shalt finish above, and cover it within and without with pitch. ²⁹ And behold I will bring the flood of waters upon the earth, and all flesh be destroyed, from under the heavens all that is upon earth shall perish. ³⁰ And thou and thy household shall go and gather two couple of all living things, male and female, and shall bring them to the ark, to raise up seed from them upon earth. ³¹ And gather unto thee all food that is eaten by all the animals, that there may be food for thee and for them. ³² And thou shalt choose for thy sons three maidens, from the daughters of men, and they shall be wives to thy sons. ³³ And Noah rose up, and he made the ark, in the place where God had commanded him, and Noah did as God had ordered him. ³⁴ In his five hundred and ninety-fifth year Noah commenced to make the ark, and he made the ark in five years, as the Lord had commanded. ³⁵ Then Noah took the three daughters of Eliakim, son of Methuselah, for wives for his sons, as the Lord had commanded Noah. ³⁶

And it was at that time Methuselah the son of Enoch died, nine hundred and sixty years old was he, at his death.

6

1 At that time, after the death of Methuselah, the Lord said to Noah, Go thou with thy household into the ark; behold I will gather to thee all the animals of the earth, the beasts of the field and the fowls of the air, and they shall all come and surround the ark. **2** And thou shalt go and seat thyself by the doors of the ark, and all the beasts, the animals, and the fowls, shall assemble and place themselves before thee, and such of them as shall come and crouch before thee, shalt thou take and deliver into the hands of thy sons, who shall bring them to the ark, and all that will stand before thee thou shalt leave. **3** And the Lord brought this about on the next day, and animals, beasts and fowls came in great multitudes and surrounded the ark. **4** And Noah went and seated himself by the door of the ark, and of all flesh that crouched before him, he brought into the ark, and all that stood before him he left upon earth. **5** And a lioness came, with her two whelps, male and female, and the three crouched before Noah, and the two whelps rose up against the lioness and smote her, and made her flee from her place, and she went away, and they returned to their places, and crouched upon the earth before Noah. **6** And the lioness ran away, and stood in the place of the lions. **7** And Noah saw this, and wondered greatly, and he rose and took the two whelps, and brought them into the ark. **8** And Noah brought into the ark from all living creatures that were upon earth, so that there was none left but which Noah brought into the ark. **9** Two and two came to Noah into the ark, but from the clean animals, and clean fowls, he brought seven couples, as God had commanded him. **10** And all the animals, and beasts, and fowls, were still there, and they surrounded the ark at every place, and the rain had not descended till seven days after. **11** And on that day, the Lord caused the whole earth to shake, and the sun darkened, and the foundations of the world raged, and the whole earth was moved violently, and the lightning flashed, and the thunder roared, and all the fountains in the earth were broken up, such as was not known to the inhabitants before; and God did this mighty act, in order to terrify the sons of men, that there might be no more evil upon earth. **12** And still the sons of men would not return from their evil ways, and they increased the anger of the Lord at that time, and did not even direct their hearts to all this. **13** And at the end of seven days, in the six hundredth year of the life of Noah, the waters of the flood were upon the earth. **14** And all the fountains of the deep were broken up, and the windows of heaven were opened, and the rain was upon the earth forty days and forty nights. **15** And Noah and his household, and all the living creatures that were with him, came into the ark on account of the waters of the flood, and the Lord shut him in. **16** And all the sons of men that were left upon the earth, became exhausted through evil on account of the rain, for the waters were coming more violently upon the earth, and the animals and beasts were still surrounding the ark. **17** And the sons of men assembled together, about seven hundred thousand men and women, and they came unto Noah to the ark. **18** And they called to Noah, saying, Open for us that we may come to thee in the ark–and wherefore shall we die? **19** And Noah, with a loud voice, answered them from the ark, saying, Have you not all rebelled against the Lord, and said that he does not exist? and therefore the Lord brought upon you this evil, to destroy and cut you off from the face of the earth. **20** Is not this the thing that I spoke to you of one hundred and twenty years back, and you would not hearken to the voice of the Lord, and now do you desire to live upon earth? **21** And they said to Noah, We are ready to return to the Lord; only open for us that we may live and not die. **22** And Noah answered them, saying, Behold now that you see the trouble of your souls, you wish to return to the Lord; why did you not return during these hundred and twenty years, which the Lord granted you as the determined period? **23** But now you come and tell me this on account of the troubles of your souls, now also the Lord will not listen to you, neither will he give ear to you on this day, so that you will not now succeed in your wishes. **24** And the sons of men approached in order to break into the ark, to come in on account of the rain, for they could not bear the rain upon them. **25** And the Lord sent all the beasts and animals that stood round the ark. And the beasts overpowered them and drove them from that place, and every man went his way and they again scattered themselves upon the face of the earth. **26** And the rain was still descending upon the earth, and it descended forty days and forty nights, and the waters prevailed greatly upon the earth; and all flesh that was upon the earth or in the waters died, whether men, animals, beasts, creeping things or birds of the air, and there only remained Noah and those that were with him in the ark. **27** And the waters prevailed and they greatly increased upon the earth, and they lifted up the ark and it was raised from the earth. **28** And the ark floated upon the face of the waters, and it was tossed upon the waters so that all the living creatures within were turned about like pottage in a cauldron. **29** And great anxiety seized all the living creatures that were in the ark, and the ark was like to be broken. **30** And all the living creatures that were in the ark were terrified, and the lions roared, and the oxen lowed, and the wolves howled, and every living creature in the ark spoke and lamented in its own language, so that their voices reached to a great distance, and Noah and his sons cried and wept in their troubles; they were greatly afraid that they had reached the gates of death. **31** And Noah prayed unto the Lord, and cried unto him on account of this, and he said, O Lord help us, for we have no strength to bear this evil that has encompassed us, for the waves of the waters have surrounded us, mischievous torrents have terrified us, the snares of death have come before us; answer us, O Lord, answer us, light up thy countenance toward us and be gracious to us, redeem us and deliver us. **32** And the Lord hearkened to the voice of Noah, and the Lord remembered him. **33** And a wind passed over the earth, and the waters were still and the ark rested. **34** And the fountains of the deep and the windows of heaven were stopped, and the rain from heaven was restrained. **35** And the waters decreased in those days, and the ark rested upon the mountains of Ararat. **36** And Noah then opened the windows of the ark, and Noah still called out to the Lord at that time and he said, O Lord, who didst form the earth and the heavens and all that are therein, bring forth our souls from this confinement, and from the prison wherein thou hast placed us, for I am much wearied with sighing. **37** And the Lord hearkened to the voice of Noah, and said to him, When though shalt have completed a full year thou shalt then go forth. **38** And at the revolution of the year, when a full year was completed to Noah's dwelling in the ark, the waters were dried from off the earth, and Noah put off the covering of the ark. **39** At that time, on the twenty-seventh day of the second month, the earth was dry, but Noah and his sons, and those that were with him, did not go out from the ark until the Lord told them. **40** And the day came that the Lord told them to go out, and they all went out from the ark. **41** And they went and returned every one to his way and to his place, and Noah and his sons dwelt in the land that God had told them, and they served the Lord all their days, and the Lord blessed Noah and his sons on their going out from the ark. **42** And he said to them, Be fruitful and fill all the earth; become strong and increase abundantly in the earth and multiply therein.

7

1 And these are the names of the sons of Noah: Japheth, Ham and Shem; and children were born to them after the flood, for they had taken wives before the flood. **2** These are the sons of Japheth; Gomer, Magog, Madai, Javan, Tubal, Meshech, and Tiras, seven sons. **3** And the sons of Gomer were Askinaz, Rephath and Tegarmah. **4** And the sons of Magog were Elichanaf and Lubal. **5** And the children of Madai were Achon, Zeelo, Chazoni and Lot. **6** And the sons of Javan were Elisha, Tarshish, Chittim and Dudonim. **7** And the sons of Tubal were Ariphi, Kesed and Taari. **8** And the sons of Meshech were Dedon, Zaron and Shebashni. **9** And the sons of Tiras were Benib, Gera, Lupirion and Gilak; these are the sons of Japheth according to their families, and their numbers in those days were about four hundred and sixty men. **10** And these are the sons of Ham; Cush, Mitzraim, Phut and Canaan, four sons; and the sons of Cush were Seba, Havilah, Sabta, Raama and Satecha, and the sons of Raama were Sheba and Dedan. **11** And the sons of Mitzraim were Lud, Anom and Pathros, Chasloth and Chaphtor. **12** And the sons of Phut were Gebul, Hadan, Benah and Adan. **13** And the sons of Canaan were Zidon, Heth, Amori, Gergashi, Hivi, Arkee, Seni, Arodi, Zimodi and Chamothi. **14** These are the sons of Ham, according to their families, and their numbers in those days were about seven hundred and thirty men. **15** And these are the sons of Shem; Elam, Ashur, Arpachshad, Lud and Aram, five sons; and the sons of Elam were Shushan, Machul and Harmon. **16** And the sons of Ashar were Mirus and Mokil, and the sons of Arpachshad were Shelach, Anar and Ashcol. **17** And the sons of Lud were Pethor and Bizayon, and the sons of Aram were Uz, Chul, Gather and Mash. **18** These are the sons of Shem, according to their families; and their numbers in those days were about three hundred men. **19** These are the generations of Shem; Shem begat Arpachshad and Arpachshad begat Shelach, and Shelach begat Eber and to Eber were born two children, the name of one was Peleg, for in his days the sons of men were divided, and in the latter days, the earth was divided. **20** And the name of the second was Yoktan, meaning that in his day the lives of the sons of men were diminished and lessened. **21** These are the sons of Yoktan; Almodad, Shelaf, Chazarmoveth, Yerach, Hadurom, Ozel, Diklah, Obal, Abimael, Sheba, Ophir, Havilah and Jobab; all these are the sons of Yoktan. **22** And Peleg his brother begat Yen, and Yen begat Serug, and Serug begat Nahor and Nahor begat Terah, and Terah was thirty-eight years old, and he begat Haran and Nahor. **23** And Cush the son of Ham, the son of Noah, took a wife in those days in his old age, and she bare a son, and they called his name Nimrod, saying, At that time the sons of men again began to rebel and transgress against God, and the child grew up, and his father loved him exceedingly, for he was the son of his old age. ²⁴ And the garments of skin which God made for Adam and his wife, when they went out of the garden, were given to Cush. ²⁵ For after the death of Adam and his wife, the garments were given to Enoch, the son of Jared, and when Enoch was taken up to God, he gave them to Methuselah, his son. ²⁶ And at the death of Methuselah, Noah took them and brought them to the ark, and they were with him until he went out of the ark. ²⁷ And in their going out, Ham stole those garments from Noah his father, and he took them and hid them from his brothers. ²⁸ And when Ham begat his first born Cush, he gave him the garments in secret, and they were with Cush many days. ²⁹ And Cush also concealed them from his sons and brothers, and when Cush had begotten Nimrod, he gave him those garments through his love for him, and Nimrod grew up, and when he was twenty years old he put on those garments. ³⁰ And Nimrod became strong when he put on the garments, and God gave him might and strength, and he was a mighty hunter in the earth, yea, he was a mighty hunter in the field, and he hunted the animals and he built altars, and he offered upon them the animals before the Lord. ³¹ And Nimrod strengthened himself, and he rose up from amongst his brethren, and he fought the battles of his brethren against all their enemies round about. ³² And the Lord delivered all the enemies of his brethren in his hands, and God prospered him from time to time in his battles, and he reigned upon earth. ³³ Therefore it became current in those days, when a man ushered forth those that he had trained up for battle, he would say to them, Like God did to Nimrod, who was a mighty hunter in the earth, and who succeeded in the battles that prevailed against his brethren, that he delivered them from the hands of their enemies, so may God strengthen us and deliver us this day. ³⁴ And when Nimrod was forty years old, at that time there was a war between his brethren and the children of Japheth, so that they were in the power of their enemies. ³⁵ And Nimrod went forth at that time, and he assembled all the sons of Cush and their families, about four hundred and sixty men, and he hired also from some of his friends and acquaintances about eighty men, and be gave them their hire, and he went with them to battle, and when he was on the road, Nimrod strengthened the hearts of the people that went with him. ³⁶ And he said to them, Do not fear, neither be alarmed, for all our enemies will be delivered into our hands, and you may do with them as you please. ³⁷ And all the men that went were about five hundred, and they fought against their enemies, and they destroyed them, and subdued them, and Nimrod placed standing officers over them in their respective places. ³⁸ And he took some of their children as security, and they were all servants to Nimrod and to his brethren, and Nimrod and all the people that were with him turned homeward. ³⁹ And when Nimrod had joyfully returned from battle, after having conquered his enemies, all his brethren, together with those who knew him before, assembled to make him king over them, and they placed the regal crown upon his head. ⁴⁰ And he set over his subjects and people, princes, judges, and rulers, as is the custom amongst kings. ⁴¹ And he placed Terah the son of Nahor the prince of his host, and he dignified him and elevated him above all his princes. ⁴² And whilst he was reigning according to his heart's desire, after having conquered all his enemies around, he advised with his counselors to build a city for his palace, and they did so. ⁴³ And they found a large valley opposite to the east, and they built him a large and extensive city, and Nimrod called the name of the city that he built Shinar, for the Lord had vehemently shaken his enemies and destroyed them. ⁴⁴ And Nimrod dwelt in Shinar, and he reigned securely, and he fought with his enemies and he subdued them, and he prospered in all his battles, and his kingdom became very great. ⁴⁵ And all nations and tongues heard of his fame, and they gathered themselves to him, and they bowed down to the earth, and they brought him offerings, and he became their lord and king, and they all dwelt with him in the city at Shinar, and Nimrod reigned in the earth over all the sons of Noah, and they were all under his power and counsel. ⁴⁶ And all the earth was of one tongue and words of union, but Nimrod did not go in the ways of the Lord, and he was more wicked than all the men that were before him, from the days of the flood until those days. ⁴⁷ And he made gods of wood and stone, and he bowed down to them, and he rebelled against the Lord, and taught all his subjects and the people of the earth his wicked ways; and Mardon his son was more wicked than his father. ⁴⁸ And every one that heard of the acts of Mardon the son of Nimrod would say, concerning him, From the wicked goeth forth wickedness; therefore it became a proverb in the whole earth, saying, From the wicked goeth forth wickedness, and it was current in the words of men from that time to this. ⁴⁹ And Terah the son of Nahor, prince of Nimrod's host, was in those days very great in the sight of the king and his subjects, and the king and princes loved him, and they elevated him very high. ⁵⁰ And Terah took a wife and her name was Amthelo the daughter of Cornebo; and the wife of Terah conceived and bare him a son in those days. ⁵¹ Terah was seventy years old when he begat him, and Terah called the name of his son that was born to him Abram, because the king had raised him in those days, and dignified him above all his princes that were with him.

8

¹ And it was in the night that Abram was born, that all the servants of Terah, and all the wise men of Nimrod, and his conjurors came and ate and drank in the house of Terah, and they rejoiced with him on that night. ² And when all the wise men and conjurors went out from the house of Terah, they lifted up their eyes toward heaven that night to look at the stars, and they saw, and behold one very large star came from the east and ran in the heavens, and he swallowed up the four stars from the four sides of the heavens. ³ And all the wise men of the king and his conjurors were astonished at the sight, and the sages understood this matter, and they knew its import. ⁴ And they said to each other, This only betokens the child that has been born to Terah this night, who will grow up and be fruitful, and multiply, and possess all the earth, he and his children for ever, and he and his seed will slay great kings, and inherit their lands. ⁵ And the wise men and conjurors went home that night, and in the morning all these wise men and conjurors rose up early, and assembled in an appointed house. ⁶ And they spoke and said to each other, Behold the sight that we saw last night is hidden from the king, it has not been made known to him. ⁷ And should this thing get known to the king in the latter days, he will say to us, Why have you concealed this matter from me, and then we shall all suffer death; therefore, now let us go and tell the king the sight which we saw, and the interpretation thereof, and we shall then remain clear. ⁸ And they did so, and they all went to the king and bowed down to him to the ground, and they said, May the king live, may the king live. ⁹ We heard that a son was born to Terah the son of Nahor, the prince of thy host, and we yesternight came to his house, and we ate and drank and rejoiced with him that night. ¹⁰ And when thy servants went out from the house of Terah, to go to our respective homes to abide there for the night, we lifted up our eyes to heaven, and we saw a great star coming from the east, and the same star ran with great speed, and swallowed up four great stars, from the four sides of the heavens. ¹¹ And thy servants were astonished at the sight which we saw, and were greatly terrified, and we made our judgment upon the sight, and knew by our wisdom the proper interpretation thereof, that this thing applies to the child that is born to Terah, who will grow up and multiply greatly, and become powerful, and kill all the kings of the earth, and inherit all their lands, he and his seed forever. ¹² And now our lord and king, behold we have truly acquainted thee with what we have seen concerning this child. ¹³ If it seemeth good to the king to give his father value for this child, we will slay him before he shall grow up and increase in the land, and his evil increase against us, that we and our children perish through his evil. ¹⁴ And the king heard their words and they seemed good in his sight, and he sent and called for Terah, and Terah came before the king. ¹⁵ And the king said to Terah, I have been told that a son was yesternight born to thee, and after this manner was observed in the heavens at his birth. ¹⁶ And now therefore give me the child, that we may slay him before his evil springs up against us, and I will give thee for his value, thy house full of silver and gold. ¹⁷ And Terah answered the king and said to him: My Lord and king, I have heard thy words, and thy servant shall do all that his king desireth. ¹⁸ But my lord and king, I will tell thee what happened to me yesternight, that I may see what advice the king will give his servant, and then I will answer the king upon what he has just spoken; and the king said, Speak. ¹⁹ And Terah said to the king, Ayon, son of Mored, came to me yesternight, saying, ²⁰ Give unto me the great and beautiful horse that the king gave thee, and I will give thee silver and gold, and straw and provender for its value; and I said to him, Wait till I see the king concerning thy words, and behold whatever the king saith, that will I do. ²¹ And now my lord and king, behold I have made this thing known to thee, and the advice which my king will give unto his servant, that will I follow. ²² And the king heard the words of Terah, and his anger was kindled and he considered him in the light of a fool. ²³ And the king answered Terah, and he said to him, Art thou so silly, ignorant, or deficient in understanding, to do this thing, to give thy beautiful horse for silver and gold or even for straw and provender? ²⁴ Art thou so short of silver and gold, that thou shouldst do this thing, because thou canst not obtain straw and provender to feed thy horse? and what is silver and gold to thee, or straw and provender, that thou shouldst give away that fine horse which I gave thee, like which there is none to be had on the whole earth? ²⁵ And the king left off speaking, and Terah answered the king, saying, Like unto this has the king spoken to his servant; ²⁶ I beseech thee, my lord and king, what is this which thou didst say unto me, saying, Give thy son that we may slay him, and I will give thee silver and gold for his value; what shall I do with silver and gold after the death of my son? who shall inherit me? surely then at my death, the silver and gold will return to my king who gave it. ²⁷ And when

the king heard the words of Terah, and the parable which he brought concerning the king, it grieved him greatly and he was vexed at this thing, and his anger burned within him. ²⁸ And Terah saw that the anger of the king was kindled against him, and he answered the king, saying, All that I have is in the king's power; whatever the king desireth to do to his servant, that let him do, yea, even my son, he is in the king's power, without value in exchange, he and his two brothers that are older than he. ²⁹ And the king said to Terah, No, but I will purchase thy younger son for a price. ³⁰ And Terah answered the king, saying, I beseech thee my lord and king to let thy servant speak a word before thee, and let the king hear the word of his servant, and Terah said, Let my king give me three days' time till I consider this matter within myself, and consult with my family concerning the words of my king; and he pressed the king greatly to agree to this. ³¹ And the king hearkened to Terah, and he did so and he gave him three days' time, and Terah went out from the king's presence, and he came home to his family and spoke to them all the words of the king; and the people were greatly afraid. ³² And it was in the third day that the king sent to Terah, saying, Send me thy son for a price as I spoke to thee; and shouldst thou not do this, I will send and slay all thou hast in thy house, so that thou shalt not even have a dog remaining. ³³ And Terah hastened, (as the thing was urgent from the king), and he took a child from one of his servants, which his handmaid had born to him that day, and Terah brought the child to the king and received value for him. ³⁴ And the Lord was with Terah in this matter, that Nimrod might not cause Abram's death, and the king took the child from Terah and with all his might dashed his head to the ground, for he thought it had been Abram; and this was concealed from him from that day, and it was forgotten by the king, as it was the will of Providence not to suffer Abram's death. ³⁵ And Terah took Abram his son secretly, together with his mother and nurse, and he concealed them in a cave, and he brought them their provisions monthly. ³⁶ And the Lord was with Abram in the cave and he grew up, and Abram was in the cave ten years, and the king and his princes, soothsayers and sages, thought that the king had killed Abram.

9

¹ And Haran, the son of Terah, Abram's oldest brother, took a wife in those days. ² Haran was thirty-nine years old when he took her; and the wife of Haran conceived and bare a son, and he called his name Lot. ³ And she conceived again and bare a daughter, and she called her name Milca; and she again conceived and bare a daughter, and she called her name Sarai. ⁴ Haran was forty-two years old when he begat Sarai, which was in the tenth year of the life of Abram; and in those days Abram and his mother and nurse went out from the cave, as the king and his subjects had forgotten the affair of Abram. ⁵ And when Abram came out from the cave, he went to Noah and his son Shem, and he remained with them to learn the instruction of the Lord and his ways, and no man knew where Abram was, and Abram served Noah and Shem his son for a long time. ⁶ And Abram was in Noah's house thirty-nine years, and Abram knew the Lord from three years old, and he went in the ways of the Lord until the day of his death, as Noah and his son Shem had taught him; and all the sons of the earth in those days greatly transgressed against the Lord, and they rebelled against him and they served other gods, and they forgot the Lord who had created them in the earth; and the inhabitants of the earth made unto themselves, at that time, every man his god; gods of wood and stone which could neither speak, hear, nor deliver, and the sons of men served them and they became their gods. ⁷ And the king and all his servants, and Terah with all his household were then the first of those that served gods of wood and stone. ⁸ And Terah had twelve gods of large size, made of wood and stone, after the twelve months of the year, and he served each one monthly, and every month Terah would bring his meat offering and drink offering to his gods; thus did Terah all the days. ⁹ And all that generation were wicked in the sight of the Lord, and they thus made every man his god, but they forsook the Lord who had created them. ¹⁰ And there was not a man found in those days in the whole earth, who knew the Lord (for they served each man his own God) except Noah and his household, and all those who were under his counsel knew the Lord in those days. ¹¹ And Abram the son of Terah was waxing great in those days in the house of Noah, and no man knew it, and the Lord was with him. ¹² And the Lord gave Abram an understanding heart, and he knew all the works of that generation were vain, and that all their gods were vain and were of no avail. ¹³ And Abram saw the sun shining upon the earth, and Abram said unto himself Surely now this sun that shines upon the earth is God, and him will I serve. ¹⁴ And Abram served the sun in that day and he prayed to him, and when evening came the sun set as usual, and Abram said within himself, Surely this cannot be God? ¹⁵ And Abram still continued to speak within himself, Who is he who made the heavens and the earth? who created upon earth? where is he? ¹⁶ And night darkened over him, and he lifted up his eyes toward the west, north, south, and east, and he saw that the sun had vanished from the earth, and the day became dark. ¹⁷ And Abram saw the stars and moon before him, and he said, Surely this is the God who created the whole earth as well as man, and behold these his servants are gods around him: and Abram served the moon and prayed to it all that night. ¹⁸ And in the morning when it was light and the sun shone upon the earth as usual, Abram saw all the things that the Lord God had made upon earth. ¹⁹ And Abram said unto himself Surely these are not gods that made the earth and all mankind, but these are the servants of God, and Abram remained in the house of Noah and there knew the Lord and his ways' and he served the Lord all the days of his life, and all that generation forgot the Lord, and served other gods of wood and stone, and rebelled all their days. ²⁰ And king Nimrod reigned securely, and all the earth was under his control, and all the earth was of one tongue and words of union. ²¹ And all the princes of Nimrod and his great men took counsel together; Phut, Mitzraim, Cush and Canaan with their families, and they said to each other, Come let us build ourselves a city and in it a strong tower, and its top reaching heaven, and we will make ourselves famed, so that we may reign upon the whole world, in order that the evil of our enemies may cease from us, that we may reign mightily over them, and that we may not become scattered over the earth on account of their wars. ²² And they all went before the king, and they told the king these words, and the king agreed with them in this affair, and he did so. ²³ And all the families assembled consisting of about six hundred thousand men, and they went to seek an extensive piece of ground to build the city and the tower, and they sought in the whole earth and they found none like one valley at the east of the land of Shinar, about two days' walk, and they journeyed there and they dwelt there. ²⁴ And they began to make bricks and burn fires to build the city and the tower that they had imagined to complete. ²⁵ And the building of the tower was unto them a transgression and a sin, and they began to build it, and whilst they were building against the Lord God of heaven, they imagined in their hearts to war against him and to ascend into heaven. ²⁶ And all these people and all the families divided themselves in three parts; the first said We will ascend into heaven and fight against him; the second said, We will ascend to heaven and place our own gods there and serve them; and the third part said, We will ascend to heaven and smite him with bows and spears; and God knew all their works and all their evil thoughts, and he saw the city and the tower which they were building. ²⁷ And when they were building they built themselves a great city and a very high and strong tower; and on account of its height the mortar and bricks did not reach the builders in their ascent to it, until those who went up had completed a full year, and after that, they reached to the builders and gave them the mortar and the bricks; thus was it done daily. ²⁸ And behold these ascended and others descended the whole day; and if a brick should fall from their hands and get broken, they would all weep over it, and if a man fell and died, none of them would look at him. ²⁹ And the Lord knew their thoughts, and it came to pass when they were building they cast the arrows toward the heavens, and all the arrows fell upon them filled with blood, and when they saw them they said to each other, Surely we have slain all those that are in heaven. ³⁰ For this was from the Lord in order to cause them to err, and in order; to destroy them from off the face of the ground. ³¹ And they built the tower and the city, and they did this thing daily until many days and years were elapsed. ³² And God said to the seventy angels who stood foremost before him, to those who were near to him, saying, Come let us descend and confuse their tongues, that one man shall not understand the language of his neighbor, and they did so unto them. ³³ And from that day following, they forgot each man his neighbor's tongue, and they could not understand to speak in one tongue, and when the builder took from the hands of his neighbor lime or stone which he did not order, the builder would cast it away and throw it upon his neighbor, that he would die. ³⁴ And they did so many days, and they killed many of them in this manner. ³⁵ And the Lord smote the three divisions that were there, and he punished them according to their works and designs; those who said, We will ascend to heaven and serve our gods, became like apes and elephants; and those who said, We will smite the heaven with arrows, the Lord killed them, one man through the hand of his neighbor; and the third division of those who said, We will ascend to heaven and fight against him, the Lord scattered them throughout the earth. ³⁶ And those who were left amongst them, when they knew and understood the evil which was coming upon them, they forsook the building, and they also became scattered upon the face of the whole earth. ³⁷ And they ceased building the city and the tower; therefore he called that place Babel, for there the Lord confounded the Language of the whole earth; behold it was at the east of the land of Shinar. ³⁸ And as to the tower which the sons of men built, the earth opened its mouth and swallowed up one third part thereof, and a fire also descended from heaven and burned another third, and the other third is left to this day, and it is of that part which was aloft,

and its circumference is three days' walk. ³⁹ And many of the sons of men died in that tower, a people without number.

10

¹ And Peleg the son of Eber died in those days, in the forty-eighth year of the life of Abram son of Terah, and all the days of Peleg were two hundred and thirty-nine years. ² And when the Lord had scattered the sons of men on account of their sin at the tower, behold they spread forth into many divisions, and all the sons of men were dispersed into the four corners of the earth. ³ And all the families became each according to its language, its land, or its city. ⁴ And the sons of men built many cities according to their families, in all the places where they went, and throughout the earth where the Lord had scattered them. ⁵ And some of them built cities in places from which they were afterward extirpated, and they called these cities after their own names, or the names of their children, or after their particular occurrences. ⁶ And the sons of Japheth the son of Noah went and built themselves cities in the places where they were scattered, and they called all their cities after their names, and the sons of Japheth were divided upon the face of the earth into many divisions and languages. ⁷ And these are the sons of Japheth according to their families, Gomer, Magog, Medai, Javan, Tubal, Meshech and Tiras; these are the children of Japheth according to their generations. ⁸ And the children of Gomer, according to their cities, were the Francum, who dwell in the land of Franza, by the river Franza, by the river Senah. ⁹ And the children of Rephath are the Bartonim, who dwell in the land of Bartonia by the river Ledah, which empties its waters in the great sea Gihon, that is, oceanus. ¹⁰ And the children of Tugarma are ten families, and these are their names: Buzar, Parzunac, Balgar, Elicanum, Ragbib, Tarki, Bid, Zebuc, Ongal and Tilmaz; all these spread and rested in the north and built themselves cities. ¹¹ And they called their cities after their own names, those are they who abide by the rivers Hithlah and Italac unto this day. ¹² But the families of Angoli, Balgar and Parzunac, they dwell by the great river Dubnee; and the names of their cities are also according to their own names. ¹³ And the children of Javan are the Javanim who dwell in the land of Makdonia, and the children of Medaiare are the Orelum that dwell in the land of Curson, and the children of Tubal are those that dwell in the land of Tuskanah by the river Pashiah. ¹⁴ And the children of Meshech are the Shibashni and the children of Tiras are Rushash, Cushni, and Ongolis; all these went and built themselves cities; those are the cities that are situate by the sea Jabus by the river Cura, which empties itself in the river Tragan. ¹⁵ And the children of Elishah are the Almanim, and they also went and built themselves cities; those are the cities situate between the mountains of Job and Shibathmo; and of them were the people of Lumbardi who dwell opposite the mountains of Job and Shibathmo, and they conquered the land of Italia and remained there unto this day. ¹⁶ And the children of Chittim are the Romim who dwell in the valley of Canopia by the river Tibreu. ¹⁷ And the children of Dudonim are those who dwell in the cities of the sea Gihon, in the land of Bordna. ¹⁸ These are the families of the children of Japheth according to their cities and languages, when they were scattered after the tower, and they called their cities after their names and occurrences; and these are the names of all their cities according to their families, which they built in those days after the tower. ¹⁹ And the children of Ham were Cush, Mitzraim, Phut and Canaan according to their generation and cities. ²⁰ All these went and built themselves cities as they found fit places for them, and they called their cities after the names of their fathers Cush, Mitzraim, Phut and Canaan. ²¹ And the children of Mitzraim are the Ludim, Anamim, Lehabim, Naphtuchim, Pathrusim, Casluchim and Caphturim, seven families. ²² All these dwell by the river Sihor, that is the brook of Egypt, and they built themselves cities and called them after their own names. ²³ And the children of Pathros and Casloch intermarried together, and from them went forth the Pelishtim, the Azathim, and the Gerarim, the Githim and the Ekronim, in all five families; these also built themselves cities, and they called their cities after the names of their fathers unto this day. ²⁴ And the children of Canaan also built themselves cities, and they called their cities after their names, eleven cities and others without number. ²⁵ And four men from the family of Ham went to the land of the plain; these are the names of the four men, Sodom, Gomorrah, Admah and Zeboyim. ²⁶ And these men built themselves four cities in the land of the plain, and they called the names of their cities after their own names. ²⁷ And they and their children and all belonging to them dwelt in those cities, and they were fruitful and multiplied greatly and dwelt peaceably. ²⁸ And Seir the son of Hur, son of Hivi, son of Canaan, went and found a valley opposite to Mount Paran, and he built a city there, and he and his seven sons and his household dwelt there, and he called the city which he built Seir, according to his name; that is the land of Seir unto this day. ²⁹ These are the families of the children of Ham, according to their languages and cities, when they were scattered to their countries after the tower. ³⁰ And some of the children of Shem son of Noah, father of all the children of Eber, also went and built themselves cities in the places wherein they were scattered, and they called their cities after their names. ³¹ And the sons of Shem were Elam, Ashur, Arpachshad, Lud and Aram, and they built themselves cities and called the names of all their cities after their names. ³² And Ashur son of Shem and his children and household went forth at that time, a very large body of them, and they went to a distant land that they found, and they met with a very extensive valley in the land that they went to, and they built themselves four cities, and they called them after their own names and occurrences. ³³ And these are the names of the cities which the children of Ashur built, Ninevah, Resen, Calach and Rehobother; and the children of Ashur dwell there unto this day. ³⁴ And the children of Aram also went and built themselves a city, and they called the name of the city Uz after their eldest brother, and they dwell therein; that is the land of Uz to this day. ³⁵ And in the second year after the tower a man from the house of Ashur, whose name was Bela, went from the land of Ninevah to sojourn with his household wherever he could find a place; and they came until opposite the cities of the plain against Sodom, and they dwelt there. ³⁶ And the man rose up and built there a small city, and called its name Bela, after his name; that is the land of Zoar unto this day. ³⁷ And these are the families of the children of Shem according to their language and cities, after they were scattered upon the earth after the tower. ³⁸ And every kingdom, city, and family of the families of the children of Noah built themselves many cities after this. ³⁹ And they established governments in all their cities, in order to be regulated by their orders; so did all the families of the children of Noah forever.

11

¹ And Nimrod son of Cush was still in the land of Shinar, and he reigned over it and dwelt there, and he built cities in the land of Shinar. ² And these are the names of the four cities which he built, and he called their names after the occurrences that happened to them in the building of the tower. ³ And he called the first Babel, saying, Because the Lord there confounded the language of the whole earth; and the name of the second he called Erech, because from there God dispersed them. ⁴ And the third he called Eched, saying there was a great battle at that place; and the fourth he called Calnah, because his princes and mighty men were consumed there, and they vexed the Lord, they rebelled and transgressed against him. ⁵ And when Nimrod had built these cities in the land of Shinar, he placed in them the remainder of his people, his princes and his mighty men that were left in his kingdom. ⁶ And Nimrod dwelt in Babel, and he there renewed his reign over the rest of his subjects, and he reigned securely, and the subjects and princes of Nimrod called his name Amraphel, saying that at the tower his princes and men fell through his means. ⁷ And notwithstanding this, Nimrod did not return to the Lord, and he continued in wickedness and teaching wickedness to the sons of men; and Mardon, his son, was worse than his father, and continued to add to the abominations of his father. ⁸ And he caused the sons of men to sin, therefore it is said, From the wicked goeth forth wickedness. ⁹ At that time there was war between the families of the children of Ham, as they were dwelling in the cities which they had built. ¹⁰ And Chedorlaomer, king of Elam, went away from the families of the children of Ham, and he fought with them and he subdued them, and he went to the five cities of the plain and he fought against them and he subdued them, and they were under his control. ¹¹ And they served him twelve years, and they gave him a yearly tax. ¹² At that time died Nahor, son of Serug, in the forty-ninth year of the life of Abram son of Terah. ¹³ And in the fiftieth year of the life of Abram son of Terah, Abram came forth from the house of Noah, and went to his father's house. ¹⁴ And Abram knew the Lord, and he went in his ways and instructions, and the Lord his God was with him. ¹⁵ And Terah his father was in those days, still captain of the host of king Nimrod, and he still followed strange gods. ¹⁶ And Abram came to his father's house and saw twelve gods standing there in their temples, and the anger of Abram was kindled when he saw these images in his father's house. ¹⁷ And Abram said, As the Lord liveth these images shall not remain in my father's house; so shall the Lord who created me do unto me if in three days' time I do not break them all. ¹⁸ And Abram went from them, and his anger burned within him. And Abram hastened and went from the chamber to his father's outer court, and he found his father sitting in the court, and all his servants with him, and Abram came and sat before him. ¹⁹ And Abram asked his father, saying, Father, tell me where is God who created heaven and earth, and all the sons of men upon earth, and who created thee and me. And Terah answered his son Abram and said, Behold those who created us are all with us in the house. ²⁰ And Abram said to his father, My lord, shew them to me I pray thee; and Terah brought Abram into the chamber of the inner court, and Abram saw, and behold the whole room was full of gods of wood and stone, twelve great images and others less than they without

number. ²¹ And Terah said to his son, Behold these are they which made all thou seest upon earth, and which created me and thee, and all mankind. ²² And Terah bowed down to his gods, and he then went away from them, and Abram, his son, went away with him. ²³ And when Abram had gone from them he went to his mother and sat before her, and he said to his mother, Behold, my father has shown me those who made heaven and earth, and all the sons of men. ²⁴ Now, therefore, hasten and fetch a kid from the flock, and make of it savory meat, that I may bring it to my father's gods as an offering for them to eat; perhaps I may thereby become acceptable to them. ²⁵ And his mother did so, and she fetched a kid, and made savory meat thereof, and brought it to Abram, and Abram took the savory meat from his mother and brought it before his father's gods, and he drew nigh to them that they might eat; and Terah his father, did not know of it. ²⁶ And Abram saw on the day when he was sitting amongst them, that they had no voice, no hearing, no motion, and not one of them could stretch forth his hand to eat. ²⁷ And Abram mocked them, and said, Surely the savory meat that I prepared has not pleased them, or perhaps it was too little for them, and for that reason they would not eat; therefore tomorrow I will prepare fresh savory meat, better and more plentiful than this, in order that I may see the result. ²⁸ And it was on the next day that Abram directed his mother concerning the savory meat, and his mother rose and fetched three fine kids from the flock, and she made of them some excellent savory meat, such as her son was fond of, and she gave it to her son Abram; and Terah his father did not know of it. ²⁹ And Abram took the savory meat from his mother, and brought it before his father's gods into the chamber; and he came nigh unto them that they might eat, and he placed it before them, and Abram sat before them all day, thinking perhaps they might eat. ³⁰ And Abram viewed them, and behold they had neither voice nor hearing, nor did one of them stretch forth his hand to the meat to eat. ³¹ And in the evening of that day in that house Abram was clothed with the spirit of God. ³² And he called out and said, Wo unto my father and this wicked generation, whose hearts are all inclined to vanity, who serve these idols of wood and stone which can neither eat, smell, hear nor speak, who have mouths without speech, eyes without sight, ears without hearing, hands without feeling, and legs which cannot move; like them are those that made them and that trust in them. ³³ And when Abram saw all these things his anger was kindled against his father, and he hastened and took a hatchet in his hand, and came unto the chamber of the gods, and he broke all his father's gods. ³⁴ And when he had done breaking the images, he placed the hatchet in the hand of the great god which was there before them, and he went out; and Terah his father came home, for he had heard at the door the sound of the striking of the hatchet; so Terah came into the house to know what this was about. ³⁵ And Terah, having heard the noise of the hatchet in the room of images, ran to the room to the images, and he met Abram going out. ³⁶ And Terah entered the room and found all the idols fallen down and broken, and the hatchet in the hand of the largest, which was not broken, and the savory meat which Abram his son had made was still before them. ³⁷ And when Terah saw this his anger was greatly kindled, and he hastened and went from the room to Abram. ³⁸ And he found Abram his son still sitting in the house; and he said to him, What is this work thou hast done to my gods? ³⁹ And Abram answered Terah his father and he said, Not so my lord, for I brought savory meat before them, and when I came nigh to them with the meat that they might eat, they all at once stretched forth their hands to eat before the great one had put forth his hand to eat. ⁴⁰ And the large one saw their works that they did before him, and his anger was violently kindled against them, and he went and took the hatchet that was in the house and came to them and broke them all, and behold the hatchet is yet in his hand as thou seest. ⁴¹ And Terah's anger was kindled against his son Abram, when he spoke this; and Terah said to Abram his son in his anger, What is this tale that thou hast told? Thou speakest lies to me. ⁴² Is there in these gods spirit, soul or power to do all thou hast told me? Are they not wood and stone, and have I not myself made them, and canst thou speak such lies, saying that the large god that was with them smote them? It is thou that didst place the hatchet in his hands, and then sayest he smote them all. ⁴³ And Abram answered his father and said to him, And how canst thou then serve these idols in whom there is no power to do any thing? Can those idols in which thou trustest deliver thee? can they hear thy prayers when thou callest upon them? can they deliver thee from the hands of thy enemies, or will they fight thy battles for thee against thy enemies, that thou shouldest serve wood and stone which can neither speak nor hear? ⁴⁴ And now surely it is not good for thee nor for the sons of men that are connected with thee, to do these things; are you so silly, so foolish or so short of understanding that you will serve wood and stone, and do after this manner? ⁴⁵ And forget the Lord God who made heaven and earth, and who created you in the earth, and thereby bring a great evil upon your souls in this matter by serving stone and wood? ⁴⁶ Did not our fathers in days of old sin in this matter, and the Lord God of the universe brought the waters of the flood upon them and destroyed the whole earth? ⁴⁷ And how can you continue to do this and serve gods of wood and stone, who cannot hear, or speak, or deliver you from oppression, thereby bringing down the anger of the God of the universe upon you? ⁴⁸ Now therefore my father refrain from this, and bring not evil upon thy soul and the souls of thy household. ⁴⁹ And Abram hastened and sprang from before his father, and took the hatchet from his father's largest idol, with which Abram broke it and ran away. ⁵⁰ And Terah, seeing all that Abram had done, hastened to go from his house, and he went to the king and he came before Nimrod and stood before him, and he bowed down to the king; and the king said, What dost thou want? ⁵¹ And he said, I beseech thee my lord, to hear me–Now fifty years back a child was born to me, and thus has he done to my gods and thus has he spoken; and now therefore, my lord and king, send for him that he may come before thee, and judge him according to the law, that we may be delivered from his evil. ⁵² And the king sent three men of his servants, and they went and brought Abram before the king. And Nimrod and all his princes and servants were that day sitting before him, and Terah sat also before them. ⁵³ And the king said to Abram, What is this that thou hast done to thy father and to his gods? And Abram answered the king in the words that he spoke to his father, and he said, The large god that was with them in the house did to them what thou hast heard. ⁵⁴ And the king said to Abram, Had they power to speak and eat and do as thou hast said? And Abram answered the king, saying, And if there be no power in them why dost thou serve them and cause the sons of men to err through thy follies? ⁵⁵ Dost thou imagine that they can deliver thee or do anything small or great, that thou shouldest serve them? And why wilt thou not sense the God of the whole universe, who created thee and in whose power it is to kill and keep alive? ⁵⁶ 0 foolish, simple, and ignorant king, woe unto thee forever. ⁵⁷ I thought thou wouldst teach thy servants the upright way, but thou hast not done this, but hast filled the whole earth with thy sins and the sins of thy people who have followed thy ways. ⁵⁸ Dost thou not know, or hast thou not heard, that this evil which thou doest, our ancestors sinned therein in days of old, and the eternal God brought the waters of the flood upon them and destroyed them all, and also destroyed the whole earth on their account? And wilt thou and thy people rise up now and do like unto this work, in order to bring down the anger of the Lord God of the universe, and to bring evil upon thee and the whole earth? ⁵⁹ Now therefore put away this evil deed which thou doest, and serve the God of the universe, as thy soul is in his hands, and then it will be well with thee. ⁶⁰ And if thy wicked heart will not hearken to my words to cause thee to forsake thy evil ways, and to serve the eternal God, then wilt thou die in shame in the latter days, thou, thy people and all who are connected with thee, hearing thy words or walking in thy evil ways. ⁶¹ And when Abram had ceased speaking before the king and princes, Abram lifted up his eyes to the heavens, and he said, The Lord seeth all the wicked, and he will judge them.

12

¹ And when the king heard the words of Abram he ordered him to be put into prison; and Abram was ten days in prison. ² And at the end of those days the king ordered that all the kings, princes and governors of different provinces and the sages should come before him, and they sat before him, and Abram was still in the house of confinement. ³ And the king said to the princes and sages, Have you heard what Abram, the son of Terah, has done to his father? Thus has he done to him, and I ordered him to be brought before me, and thus has he spoken; his heart did not misgive him, neither did he stir in my presence, and behold now he is confined in the prison. ⁴ And therefore decide what judgment is due to this man who reviled the king; who spoke and did all the things that you heard. ⁵ And they all answered the king saying, The man who revileth the king should be hanged upon a tree; but having done all the things that he said, and having despised our gods, he must therefore be burned to death, for this is the law in this matter. ⁶ If it pleaseth the king to do this, let him order his servants to kindle a fire both night and day in thy brick furnace, and then we will cast this man into it. And the king did so, and he commanded his servants that they should prepare a fire for three days and three nights in the king's furnace, that is in Casdim; and the king ordered them to take Abram from prison and bring him out to be burned. ⁷ And all the king's servants, princes, lords, governors, and judges, and all the inhabitants of the land, about nine hundred thousand men, stood opposite the furnace to see Abram. ⁸ And all the women and little ones crowded upon the roofs and towers to see what was doing with Abram, and they all stood together at a distance; and there was not a man left that did not come on that day to behold the scene. ⁹ And when Abram was come, the conjurors of the king and the sages saw Abram, and they cried out to the king, saying, Our sovereign lord, surely this is the man whom we know to have been the child at whose birth the great star swallowed the four stars, which we declared to the king now fifty years

since. ¹⁰ And behold now his father has also transgressed thy commands, and mocked thee by bringing thee another child, which thou didst kill. ¹¹ And when the king heard their words, he was exceedingly wroth, and he ordered Terah to be brought before him. ¹² And the king said, Hast thou heard what the conjurors have spoken? Now tell me truly, how didst thou; and if thou shalt speak truth thou shalt be acquitted. ¹³ And seeing that the king's anger was so much kindled, Terah said to the king, My lord and king, thou hast heard the truth, and what the sages have spoken is right. And the king said, How couldst thou do this thing, to transgress my orders and to give me a child that thou didst not beget, and to take value for him? ¹⁴ And Terah answered the king, Because my tender feelings were excited for my son, at that time, and I took a son of my handmaid, and I brought him to the king. ¹⁵ And the king said Who advised thee to this? Tell me, do not hide aught from me, and then thou shalt not die. ¹⁶ And Terah was greatly terrified in the king's presence, and he said to the king, It was Haran my eldest son who advised me to this; and Haran was in those days that Abram was born, two and thirty years old. ¹⁷ But Haran did not advise his father to anything, for Terah said this to the king in order to deliver his soul from the king, for he feared greatly; and the king said to Terah, Haran thy son who advised thee to this shall die through fire with Abram; for the sentence of death is upon him for having rebelled against the king's desire in doing this thing. ¹⁸ And Haran at that time felt inclined to follow the ways of Abram, but he kept it within himself. ¹⁹ And Haran said in his heart, Behold now the king has seized Abram on account of these things which Abram did, and it shall come to pass, that if Abram prevail over the king I will follow him, but if the king prevail I will go after the king. ²⁰ And when Terah had spoken this to the king concerning Haran his son, the king ordered Haran to be seized with Abram. ²¹ And they brought them both, Abram and Haran his brother, to cast them into the fire; and all the inhabitants of the land and the king's servants and princes and all the women and little ones were there, standing that day over them. ²² And the king's servants took Abram and his brother, and they stripped them of all their clothes excepting their lower garments which were upon them. ²³ And they bound their hands and feet with linen cords, and the servants of the king lifted them up and cast them both into the furnace. ²⁴ And the Lord loved Abram and he had compassion over him, and the Lord came down and delivered Abram from the fire and he was not burned. ²⁵ But all the cords with which they bound him were burned, while Abram remained and walked about in the fire. ²⁶ And Haran died when they had cast him into the fire, and he was burned to ashes, for his heart was not perfect with the Lord; and those men who cast him into the fire, the flame of the fire spread over them, and they were burned, and twelve men of them died. ²⁷ And Abram walked in the midst of the fire three days and three nights, and all the servants of the king saw him walking in the fire, and they came and told the king, saying, Behold we have seen Abram walking about in the midst of the fire, and even the lower garments which are upon him are not burned, but the cord with which he was bound is burned. ²⁸ And when the king heard their words his heart fainted and he would not believe them; so he sent other faithful princes to see this matter, and they went and saw it and told it to the king; and the king rose to go and see it, and he saw Abram walking to and fro in the midst of the fire, and he saw Haran's body burned, and the king wondered greatly. ²⁹ And the king ordered Abram to be taken out from the fire; and his servants approached to take him out and they could not, for the fire was round about and the flame ascending toward them from the furnace. ³⁰ And the king's servants fled from it, and the king rebuked them, saying, Make haste and bring Abram out of the fire that you shall not die. ³¹ And the servants of the king again approached to bring Abram out, and the flames came upon them and burned their faces so that eight of them died. ³² And when the king saw that his servants could not approach the fire lest they should be burned, the king called to Abram, O servant of the God who is in heaven, go forth from amidst the fire and come hither before me; and Abram hearkened to the voice of the king, and he went forth from the fire and came and stood before the king. ³³ And when Abram came out the king and all his servants saw Abram coming before the king, with his lower garments upon him, for they were not burned, but the cord with which he was bound was burned. ³⁴ And the king said to Abram, How is it that thou wast not burned in the fire? ³⁵ And Abram said to the king, The God of heaven and earth in whom I trust and who has all in his power, he delivered me from the fire into which thou didst cast me. ³⁶ And Haran the brother of Abram was burned to ashes, and they sought for his body, and they found it consumed. ³⁷ And Haran was eighty-two years old when he died in the fire of Casdim. And the king, princes, and inhabitants of the land, seeing that Abram was delivered from the fire, they came and bowed down to Abram. ³⁸ And Abram said to them, Do not bow down to me, but bow down to the God of the world who made you, and serve him, and go in his ways for it is he who delivered me from out of this fire, and it is he who created the souls and spirits of all men, and formed man in his mother's womb, and brought him forth into the world, and it is he who will deliver those who trust in him from all pain. ³⁹ And this thing seemed very wonderful in the eyes of the king and princes, that Abram was saved from the fire and that Haran was burned; and the king gave Abram many presents and he gave him his two head servants from the king's house; the name of one was Oni and the name of the other was Eliezer. ⁴⁰ And all the kings, princes and servants gave Abram many gifts of silver and gold and pearl, and the king and his princes sent him away, and he went in peace. ⁴¹ And Abram went forth from the king in peace, and many of the king's servants followed him, and about three hundred men joined him. ⁴² And Abram returned on that day and went to his father's house, he and the men that followed him, and Abram served the Lord his God all the days of his life, and he walked in his ways and followed his law. ⁴³ And from that day forward Abram inclined the hearts of the sons of men to serve the Lord. ⁴⁴ And at that time Nahor and Abram took unto themselves wives, the daughters of their brother Haran; the wife of Nahor was Milca and the name of Abram's wife was Sarai. And Sarai, wife of Abram, was barren; she had no offspring in those days. ⁴⁵ And at the expiration of two years from Abram's going out of the fire, that is in the fifty-second year of his life, behold king Nimrod sat in Babel upon the throne, and the king fell asleep and dreamed that he was standing with his troops and hosts in a valley opposite the king's furnace. ⁴⁶ And he lifted up his eyes and saw a man in the likeness of Abram coming forth from the furnace, and that he came and stood before the king with his drawn sword, and then sprang to the king with his sword, when the king fled from the man, for he was afraid; and while he was running, the man threw an egg upon the king's head, and the egg became a great river. ⁴⁷ And the king dreamed that all his troops sank in that river and died, and the king took flight with three men who were before him and he escaped. ⁴⁸ And the king looked at these men and they were clothed in princely dresses as the garments of kings, and had the appearance and majesty of kings. ⁴⁹ And while they were running, the river again turned to an egg before the king, and there came forth from the egg a young bird which came before the king, and flew at his head and plucked out the king's eye. ⁵⁰ And the king was grieved at the sight, and he awoke out of his sleep and his spirit was agitated; and he felt a great terror. ⁵¹ And in the morning the king rose from his couch in fear, and he ordered all the wise men and magicians to come before him, when the king related his dream to them. ⁵² And a wise servant of the king, whose name was Anuki, answered the king, saying, This is nothing else but the evil of Abram and his seed which will spring up against my Lord and king in the latter days. ⁵³ And behold the day will come when Abram and his seed and the children of his household will war with my king, and they will smite all the king's hosts and his troops. ⁵⁴ And as to what thou hast said concerning three men which thou didst see like unto thyself, and which did escape, this means that only thou wilt escape with three kings from the kings of the earth who will be with thee in battle. ⁵⁵ And that which thou sawest of the river which turned to an egg as at first, and the young bird plucking out thine eye, this means nothing else but the seed of Abram which will slay the king in latter days. ⁵⁶ This is my king's dream, and this is its interpretation, and the dream is true, and the interpretation which thy servant has given thee is right. ⁵⁷ Now therefore my king, surely thou knowest that it is now fifty-two years since thy sages saw this at the birth of Abram, and if my king will suffer Abram to live in the earth it will be to the injury of my lord and king, for all the days that Abram liveth neither thou nor thy kingdom will be established, for this was known formerly at his birth; and why will not my king slay him, that his evil may be kept from thee in latter days? ⁵⁸ And Nimrod hearkened to the voice of Anuki, and he sent some of his servants in secret to go and seize Abram, and bring him before the king to suffer death. ⁵⁹ And Eliezer, Abram's servant whom the king had given him, was at that time in the presence of the king, and he heard what Anuki had advised the king, and what the king had said to cause Abram's death. ⁶⁰ And Eliezer said to Abram, Hasten, rise up and save thy soul, that thou mayest not die through the hands of the king, for thus did he see in a dream concerning thee, and thus did Anuki interpret it, and thus also did Anuki advise the king concerning thee. ⁶¹ And Abram hearkened to the voice of Eliezer, and Abram hastened and ran for safety to the house of Noah and his son Shem, and he concealed himself there and found a place of safety; and the king's servants came to Abram's house to seek him, but they could not find him, and they searched through out the country and he was not to be found, and they went and searched in every direction and he was not to be met with. ⁶² And when the king's servants could not find Abram they returned to the king, but the king's anger against Abram was stilled, as they did not find him, and the king drove from his mind this matter concerning Abram. ⁶³ And Abram was concealed in Noah's house for one month, until the king had forgotten this matter, but Abram was still afraid of the king; and Terah came to see Abram his son secretly in the house of Noah, and Terah was very great in the eyes of the king. ⁶⁴ And Abram said to his father, Dost thou not know that the king thinketh to slay me, and to annihilate my name from the earth by the advice of his wicked counsellors? ⁶⁵ Now whom hast thou here and what hast thou in this land? Arise, let us go together to the land of Canaan, that we may be delivered from his hand, lest thou perish also through him in the latter days. ⁶⁶ Dost thou not know or hast thou not heard, that it is not through love that Nimrod giveth thee all this honor, but it is only for his benefit that he bestoweth all this good upon thee? ⁶⁷ And if he do unto thee greater good than this, surely these are only vanities of the world, for wealth and riches cannot avail in the day of wrath and anger. ⁶⁸ Now therefore hearken to my voice, and let us arise and go to the land of Canaan, out of the reach of injury from Nimrod; and serve thou the Lord who created thee in the earth and it will be well with thee; and cast away all the vain things which thou pursuest. ⁶⁹ And Abram ceased to speak, when Noah and his son Shem answered Terah, saying, True is the word which Abram hath said unto thee. ⁷⁰ And Terah hearkened to the voice of his son Abram, and Terah did all that Abram said, for this was from the Lord, that the king should not cause Abram's death.

13

¹ And Terah took his son Abram and his grandson Lot, the son of Haran, and Sarai his daughter-in-law, the wife of his son Abram, and all the souls of his household and went with them from Ur Casdim to go to the land of Canaan. And when they came as far as the land of Haran they remained there, for it was exceedingly good land for pasture, and of sufficient extent for those who accompanied them. ² And the people of the land of Haran saw that Abram was good and upright with God and men, and that the Lord his God was with him, and some of the people of the land of Haran came and joined Abram, and he taught them the instruction of the Lord and his ways; and these men remained with Abram in his house and they adhered to him. ³ And Abram remained in the land three years, and at the expiration of three years the Lord appeared to Abram and said to him; I am the Lord who brought thee forth from Ur Casdim, and delivered thee from the hands of all thine enemies. ⁴ And now therefore if thou wilt hearken to my voice and keep my commandments, my statutes and my laws, then will I cause thy enemies to fall before thee, and I will multiply thy seed like the stars of heaven, and I will send my blessing upon all the works of thy hands, and thou shalt lack nothing. ⁵ Arise now, take thy wife and all belonging to thee and go to the land of Canaan and remain there, and I will there be unto thee for a God, and I will bless thee. And Abram rose and took his wife and all belonging to him, and he went to the land of Canaan as the Lord had told him; and Abram was fifty years old when he went from Haran. ⁶ And Abram came to the land of Canaan and dwelt in the midst of the city, and he there pitched his tent amongst the children of Canaan, inhabitants of the land. ⁷ And the Lord appeared to Abram when he came to the land of Canaan, and said to him, This is the land which I gave unto thee and to thy seed after thee forever, and I will make thy seed like the stars of heaven, and I will give unto thy seed for an inheritance all the lands which thou seest. ⁸ And Abram built an altar in the place where God had spoken to him, and Abram there called upon the name of the Lord. ⁹ At that time, at the end of three years of Abram's dwelling in the land of Canaan, in that year Noah died, which was the fifty-eighth year of the life of Abram; and all the days that Noah lived were nine hundred and fifty years and he died. ¹⁰ And Abram dwelt in the land of Canaan, he, his wife, and all belonging to him, and all those that accompanied him, together with those that joined him from the people of the land; but Nahor, Abram's brother, and Terah his father, and Lot the son of Haran and all belonging to them dwelt in Haran. ¹¹ In the fifth year of Abram's dwelling in the land of Canaan the people of Sodom and Gomorrah and all the cities of the plain revolted from the power of Chedorlaomer, king of Elam; for all the kings of the cities of the plain had served Chedorlaomer for twelve years, and given him a yearly tax, but in those days in the thirteenth year, they rebelled against him. ¹² And in the tenth year of Abram's dwelling in the land of Canaan there was war between Nimrod king of Shinar and Chedorlaomer king of Elam, and Nimrod came to fight with Chedorlaomer and to subdue him. ¹³ For Chedorlaomer was at that time one of the princes of the hosts of Nimrod, and when all the people at the tower were dispersed and those that remained were also scattered upon the face of the earth, Chedorlaomer went to the land of Elam and reigned over it and rebelled against his lord. ¹⁴ And in those days when Nimrod saw that the cities of the plain had rebelled, he came with pride and anger to war with Chedorlaomer, and Nimrod assembled all his princes and subjects, about seven hundred thousand men, and went against Chedorlaomer, and Chedorlaomer went out to meet him with five thousand men, and they prepared for battle in the valley of Babel which is between Elam and Shinar. ¹⁵ And all those kings fought there, and Nimrod and his people were smitten before the people of Chedorlaomer, and there fell from Nimrod's men about six hundred thousand, and Mardon the king's son fell amongst them. ¹⁶ And Nimrod fled and returned in shame and disgrace to his land, and he was under subjection to Chedorlaomer for a long time, and Chedorlaomer returned to his land and sent princes of his host to the kings that dwelt around him, to Arioch king of Elasar, and to Tidal king of Goyim, and made a covenant with them, and they were all obedient to his commands. ¹⁷ And it was in the fifteenth year of Abram's dwelling in the land of Canaan, which is the seventieth year of the life of Abram, and the Lord appeared to Abram in that year and he said to him, I am the Lord who brought thee out from Ur Casdim to give thee this land for an inheritance. ¹⁸ Now therefore walk before me and be perfect and keep my commands, for to thee and to thy seed I will give this land for an inheritance, from the river Mitzraim unto the great river Euphrates. ¹⁹ And thou shalt come to thy fathers in peace and in good age, and the fourth generation shall return here in this land and shall inherit it forever; and Abram built an altar, and he called upon the name of the Lord who appeared to him, and he brought up sacrifices upon the altar to the Lord. ²⁰ At that time Abram returned and went to Haran to see his father and mother, and his father's household, and Abram and his wife and all belonging to him returned to Haran, and Abram dwelt in Haran five years. ²¹ And many of the people of Haran, about seventy-two men, followed Abram and Abram taught them the instruction of the Lord and his ways, and he taught them to know the Lord. ²² In those days the Lord appeared to Abram in Haran, and he said to him, Behold, I spoke unto thee these twenty years back saying, ²³ Go forth from thy land, from thy birth-place and from thy father's house, to the land which I have shown thee to give it to thee and to thy children, for there in that land will I bless thee, and make thee a great nation, and make thy name great, and in thee shall the families of the earth be blessed. ²⁴ Now therefore arise, go forth from this place, thou, thy wife, and all belonging to thee, also every one born in thy house and all the souls thou hast made in Haran, and bring them out with thee from here, and rise to return to the land of Canaan. ²⁵ And Abram arose and took his wife Sarai and all belonging to him and all that were born to him in his house and the souls which they had made in Haran, and they came out to go to the land of Canaan. ²⁶ And Abram went and returned to the land of Canaan, according to the word of the Lord. And Lot the son of his brother Haran went with him, and Abram was seventy-five years old when he went forth from Haran to return to the land of Canaan. ²⁷ And he came to the land of Canaan according to the word of the Lord to Abram, and he pitched his tent and he dwelt in the plain of Mamre, and with him was Lot his brother's son, and all belonging to him. ²⁸ And the Lord again appeared to Abram and said, To thy seed will I give this land; and he there built an altar to the Lord who appeared to him, which is still to this day in the plains of Mamre.

14

¹ In those days there was in the land of Shinar a wise man who had understanding in all wisdom, and of a beautiful appearance, but he was poor and indigent; his name was Rikayon and he was hard set to support himself. ² And he resolved to go to Egypt, to Oswiris the son of Anom king of Egypt, to show the king his wisdom; for perhaps he might find grace in his sight, to raise him up and give him maintenance; and Rikayon did so. ³ And when Rikayon came to Egypt he asked the inhabitants of Egypt concerning the king, and the inhabitants of Egypt told him the custom of the king of Egypt, for it was then the custom of the king of Egypt that he went from his royal palace and was seen abroad only one day in the year, and after that the king would return to his palace to remain there. ⁴ And on the day when the king went forth he passed judgment in the land, and every one having a suit came before the king that day to obtain his request. ⁵ And when Rikayon heard of the custom in Egypt and that he could not come into the presence of the king, he grieved greatly and was very sorrowful. ⁶ And in the evening Rikayon went out and found a house in ruins, formerly a bake house in Egypt, and he abode there all night in bitterness of soul and pinched with hunger, and sleep was removed from his eyes. ⁷ And Rikayon considered within himself what he should do in the town until the king made his appearance, and how he might maintain himself there. ⁸ And he rose in the morning and walked about, and met in his way those who sold vegetables and various sorts of seed with which they supplied the inhabitants. ⁹ And Rikayon wished to do the same in order to get a maintenance in the city, but he was unacquainted with the custom of the people, and he was like a blind man among them. ¹⁰ And he went and obtained vegetables to sell them for his support, and the rabble assembled about him and ridiculed him, and took his vegetables from him and left him nothing. ¹¹ And he rose up from there in bitterness of soul, and went sighing to the bake house in which he had remained all the night before, and he slept there the second night. ¹² And on that night again he reasoned within himself how he could save

himself from starvation, and he devised a scheme how to act. ¹³ And he rose up in the morning and acted ingeniously, and went and hired thirty strong men of the rabble, carrying their war instruments in their hands, and he led them to the top of the Egyptian sepulchre, and he placed them there. ¹⁴ And he commanded them, saying, Thus saith the king, Strengthen yourselves and be valiant men, and let no man be buried here until two hundred pieces of silver be given, and then he may be buried; and those men did according to the order of Rikayon to the people of Egypt the whole of that year. ¹⁵ And in eight months time Rikayon and his men gathered great riches of silver and gold, and Rikayon took a great quantity of horses and other animals, and he hired more men, and he gave them horses and they remained with him. ¹⁶ And when the year came round, at the time the king went forth into the town, all the inhabitants of Egypt assembled together to speak to him concerning the work of Rikayon and his men. ¹⁷ And the king went forth on the appointed day, and all the Egyptians came before him and cried unto him, saying, ¹⁸ May the king live forever. What is this thing thou doest in the town to thy servants, not to suffer a dead body to be buried until so much silver and gold be given? Was there ever the like unto this done in the whole earth, from the days of former kings yea even from the days of Adam, unto this day, that the dead should not be buried only for a set price? ¹⁹ We know it to be the custom of kings to take a yearly tax from the living, but thou dost not only do this, but from the dead also thou exactest a tax day by day. ²⁰ Now, O king, we can no more bear this, for the whole city is ruined on this account, and dost thou not know it? ²¹ And when the king heard all that they had spoken he was very wroth, and his anger burned within him at this affair, for he had known nothing of it. ²² And the king said, Who and where is he that dares to do this wicked thing in my land without my command? Surely you will tell me. ²³ And they told him all the works of Rikayon and his men, and the king's anger was aroused, and he ordered Rikayon and his men to be brought before him. ²⁴ And Rikayon took about a thousand children, sons and daughters, and clothed them in silk and embroidery, and he set them upon horses and sent them to the king by means of his men, and he also took a great quantity of silver and gold and precious stones, and a strong and beautiful horse, as a present for the king, with which he came before the king and bowed down to the earth before him; and the king, his servants and all the inhabitants of Egypt wondered at the work of Rikayon, and they saw his riches and the present that he had brought to the king. ²⁵ And it greatly pleased the king and he wondered at it; and when Rikayon sat before him the king asked him concerning all his works, and Rikayon spoke all his words wisely before the king, his servants and all the inhabitants of Egypt. ²⁶ And when the king heard the words of Rikayon and his wisdom, Rikayon found grace in his sight, and he met with grace and kindness from all the servants of the king and from all the inhabitants of Egypt, on account of his wisdom and excellent speeches, and from that time they loved him exceedingly. ²⁷ And the king answered and said to Rikayon, Thy name shall no more be called Rikayon but Pharaoh shall be thy name, since thou didst exact a tax from the dead; and he called his name Pharaoh. ²⁸ And the king and his subjects loved Rikayon for his wisdom, and they consulted with all the inhabitants of Egypt to make him prefect under the king. ²⁹ And all the inhabitants of Egypt and its wise men did so, and it was made a law in Egypt. ³⁰ And they made Rikayon Pharaoh prefect under Oswiris king of Egypt, and Rikayon Pharaoh governed over Egypt, daily administering justice to the whole city, but Oswiris the king would judge the people of the land one day in the year, when he went out to make his appearance. ³¹ And Rikayon Pharaoh cunningly usurped the government of Egypt, and he exacted a tax from all the inhabitants of Egypt. ³² And all the inhabitants of Egypt greatly loved Rikayon Pharaoh, and they made a decree to call every king that should reign over them and their seed in Egypt, Pharaoh. ³³ Therefore all the kings that reigned in Egypt from that time forward were called Pharaoh unto this day.

15

¹ And in that year there was a heavy famine throughout the land of Canaan, and the inhabitants of the land could not remain on account of the famine for it was very grievous. ² And Abram and all belonging to him rose and went down to Egypt on account of the famine, and when they were at the brook Mitzraim they remained there some time to rest from the fatigue of the road. ³ And Abram and Sarai were walking at the border of the brook Mitzraim, and Abram beheld his wife Sarai that she was very beautiful. ⁴ And Abram said to his wife Sarai, Since God has created thee with such a beautiful countenance, I am afraid of the Egyptians lest they should slay me and take thee away, for the fear of God is not in these places. ⁵ Surely then thou shalt do this, Say thou art my sister to all that may ask thee, in order that it may be well with me, and that we may live and not be put to death. ⁶ And Abram commanded the same to all those that came with him to Egypt on account of the famine; also his nephew Lot he commanded, saying, If the Egyptians ask thee concerning Sarai say she is the sister of Abram. ⁷ And yet with all these orders Abram did not put confidence in them, but he took Sarai and placed her in a chest and concealed it amongst their vessels, for Abram was greatly concerned about Sarai on account of the wickedness of the Egyptians. ⁸ And Abram and all belonging to him rose up from the brook Mitzraim and came to Egypt; and they had scarcely entered the gates of the city when the guards stood up to them saying, Give tithe to the king from what you have, and then you may come into the town; and Abram and those that were with him did so. ⁹ And Abram with the people that were with him came to Egypt, and when they came they brought the chest in which Sarai was concealed and the Egyptians saw the chest. ¹⁰ And the king's servants approached Abram, saying, What hast thou here in this chest which we have not seen? Now open thou the chest and give tithe to the king of all that it contains. ¹¹ And Abram said, This chest I will not open, but all you demand upon it I will give. And Pharaoh's officers answered Abram, saying, It is a chest of precious stones, give us the tenth thereof. ¹² Abram said, All that you desire I will give, but you must not open the chest. ¹³ And the king's officers pressed Abram, and they reached the chest and opened it with force, and they saw, and behold a beautiful woman was in the chest. ¹⁴ And when the officers of the king beheld Sarai they were struck with admiration at her beauty, and all the princes and servants of Pharaoh assembled to see Sarai, for she was very beautiful. And the king's officers ran and told Pharaoh all that they had seen, and they praised Sarai to the king; and Pharaoh ordered her to be brought, and the woman came before the king. ¹⁵ And Pharaoh beheld Sarai and she pleased him exceedingly, and he was struck with her beauty, and the king rejoiced greatly on her account, and made presents to those who brought him the tidings concerning her. ¹⁶ And the woman was then brought to Pharaoh's house, and Abram grieved on account of his wife, and he prayed to the Lord to deliver her from the hands of Pharaoh. ¹⁷ And Sarai also prayed at that time and said, O Lord God thou didst tell my Lord Abram to go from his land and from his father's house to the land of Canaan, and thou didst promise to do well with him if he would perform thy commands; now behold we have done that which thou didst command us, and we left our land and our families, and we went to a strange land and to a people whom we have not known before. ¹⁸ And we came to this land to avoid the famine, and this evil accident has befallen me; now therefore, O Lord God, deliver us and save us from the hand of this oppressor, and do well with me for the sake of thy mercy. ¹⁹ And the Lord hearkened to the voice of Sarai, and the Lord sent an angel to deliver Sarai from the power of Pharaoh. ²⁰ And the king came and sat before Sarai and behold an angel of the Lord was standing over them, and he appeared to Sarai and said to her, Do not fear, for the Lord has heard thy prayer. ²¹ And the king approached Sarai and said to her, What is that man to thee who brought thee hither? and she said, He is my brother. ²² And the king said, It is incumbent upon us to make him great, to elevate him and to do unto him all the good which thou shalt command us; and at that time the king sent to Abram silver and gold and precious stones in abundance, together with cattle, men servants and maid servants; and the king ordered Abram to be brought, and he sat in the court of the king's house, and the king greatly exalted Abram on that night. ²³ And the king approached to speak to Sarai, and he reached out his hand to touch her, when the angel smote him heavily, and he was terrified and he refrained from reaching to her. ²⁴ And when the king came near to Sarai, the angel smote him to the ground, and acted thus to him the whole night, and the king was terrified. ²⁵ And the angel on that night smote heavily all the servants of the king, and his whole household, on account of Sarai, and there was a great lamentation that night amongst the people of Pharaoh's house. ²⁶ And Pharaoh, seeing the evil that befell him, said, Surely on account of this woman has this thing happened to me, and he removed himself at some distance from her and spoke pleasing words to her. ²⁷ And the king said to Sarai, Tell me I pray thee concerning the man with whom thou camest here; and Sarai said, This man is my husband, and I said to thee that he was my brother for I was afraid, lest thou shouldst put him to death through wickedness. ²⁸ And the king kept away from Sarai, and the plagues of the angel of the Lord ceased from him and his household; and Pharaoh knew that he was smitten on account of Sarai, and the king was greatly astonished at this. ²⁹ And in the morning the king called for Abram and said to him, What is this thou hast done to me? Why didst thou say, She is my sister, owing to which I took her unto me for a wife, and this heavy plague has therefore come upon me and my household. ³⁰ Now therefore here is thy wife, take her and go from our land lest we all die on her account. And Pharaoh took more cattle, men servants and maid servants, and silver and gold, to give to Abram, and he returned unto him Sarai his wife. ³¹ And the king took a maiden whom he begat by his concubines, and he gave her to Sarai for a handmaid. ³² And the king said to his daughter, It is better for

thee my daughter to be a handmaid in this man's house than to be mistress in my house, after we have beheld the evil that befell us on account of this woman. ³³ And Abram arose, and he and all belonging to him went away from Egypt; and Pharaoh ordered some of his men to accompany him and all that went with him. ³⁴ And Abram returned to the land of Canaan, to the place where he had made the altar, where he at first had pitched his tent. ³⁵ And Lot the son of Haran, Abram's brother, had a heavy stock of cattle, flocks and herds and tents, for the Lord was bountiful to them on account of Abram. ³⁶ And when Abram was dwelling in the land the herdsmen of Lot quarrelled with the herdsmen of Abram, for their property was too great for them to remain together in the land, and the land could not bear them on account of their cattle. ³⁷ And when Abram's herdsmen went to feed their flock they would not go into the fields of the people of the land, but the cattle of Lot's herdsmen did otherwise, for they were suffered to feed in the fields of the people of the land. ³⁸ And the people of the land saw this occurrence daily, and they came to Abram and quarrelled with him on account of Lot's herdsmen. ³⁹ And Abram said to Lot, What is this thou art doing to me, to make me despicable to the inhabitants of the land, that thou orderest thy herdsman to feed thy cattle in the fields of other people? Dost thou not know that I am a stranger in this land amongst the children of Canaan, and why wilt thou do this unto me? ⁴⁰ And Abram quarrelled daily with Lot on account of this, but Lot would not listen to Abram, and he continued to do the same and the inhabitants of the land came and told Abram. ⁴¹ And Abram said unto Lot, How long wilt thou be to me for a stumbling block with the inhabitants of the land? Now I beseech thee let there be no more quarrelling between us, for we are kinsmen. ⁴² But I pray thee separate from me, go and choose a place where thou mayest dwell with thy cattle and all belonging to thee, but Keep thyself at a distance from me, thou and thy household. ⁴³ And be not afraid in going from me, for if any one do an injury to thee, let me know and I will avenge thy cause from him, only remove from me. ⁴⁴ And when Abram had spoken all these words to Lot, then Lot arose and lifted up his eyes toward the plain of Jordan. ⁴⁵ And he saw that the whole of this place was well watered, and good for man as well as affording pasture for the cattle. ⁴⁶ And Lot went from Abram to that place, and he there pitched his tent and he dwelt in Sodom, and they were separated from each other. ⁴⁷ And Abram dwelt in the plain of Mamre, which is in Hebron, and he pitched his tent there, and Abram remained in that place many years.

16

¹ At that time Chedorlaomer king of Elam sent to all the neighboring kings, to Nimrod, king of Shinar who was then under his power, and to Tidal, king of Goyim, and to Arioch, king of Elasar, with whom he made a covenant, saying, Come up to me and assist me, that we may smite all the towns of Sodom and its inhabitants, for they have rebelled against me these thirteen years. ² And these four kings went up with all their camps, about eight hundred thousand men, and they went as they were, and smote every man they found in their road. ³ And the five kings of Sodom and Gomorrah, Shinab king of Admah, Shemeber king of Zeboyim, Bera king of Sodom, Bersha king of Gomorrah, and Bela king of Zoar, went out to meet them, and they all joined together in the valley of Siddim. ⁴ And these nine kings made war in the valley of Siddim; and the kings of Sodom and Gomorrah were smitten before the kings of Elam. ⁵ And the valley of Siddim was full of lime pits and the kings of Elam pursued the kings of Sodom, and the kings of Sodom with their camps fled and fell into the lime pits, and all that remained went to the mountain for safety, and the five kings of Elam came after them and pursued them to the gates of Sodom, and they took all that there was in Sodom. ⁶ And they plundered all the cities of Sodom and Gomorrah, and they also took Lot, Abram's brother's son, and his property, and they seized all the goods of the cities of Sodom, and they went away; and Unic, Abram's servant, who was in the battle, saw this, and told Abram all that the kings had done to the cities of Sodom, and that Lot was taken captive by them. ⁷ And Abram heard this, and he rose up with about three hundred and eighteen men that were with him, and he that night pursued these kings and smote them, and they all fell before Abram and his men, and there was none remaining but the four kings who fled, and they went each his own road. ⁸ And Abram recovered all the property of Sodom, and he also recovered Lot and his property, his wives and little ones and all belonging to him, so that Lot lacked nothing. ⁹ And when he returned from smiting these kings, he and his men passed the valley of Siddim where the kings had made war together. ¹⁰ And Bera king of Sodom, and the rest of his men that were with him, went out from the lime pits into which they had fallen, to meet Abram and his men. ¹¹ And Adonizedek king of Jerusalem, the same was Shem, went out with his men to meet Abram and his people, with bread and wine, and they remained together in the valley of Melech. ¹² And Adonizedek blessed Abram, and Abram gave him a tenth from all that he had brought from the spoil of his enemies, for Adonizedek was a priest before God. ¹³ And all the kings of Sodom and Gomorrah who were there, with their servants, approached Abram and begged of him to return them their servants whom he had made captive, and to take unto himself all the property. ¹⁴ And Abram answered the kings of Sodom, saying, As the Lord liveth who created heaven and earth, and who redeemed my soul from all affliction, and who delivered me this day from my enemies, and gave them into my hand, I will not take anything belonging to you, that you may not boast tomorrow, saying, Abram became rich from our property that he saved. ¹⁵ For the Lord my God in whom I trust said unto me, Thou shalt lack nothing, for I will bless thee in all the works of thy hands. ¹⁶ And now therefore behold, here is all belonging to you, take it and go; as the Lord liveth I will not take from you from a living soul down to a shoetie or thread, excepting the expense of the food of those who went out with me to battle, as also the portions of the men who went with me, Anar, Ashcol, and Mamre, they and their men, as well as those also who had remained to watch the baggage, they shall take their portion of the spoil. ¹⁷ And the kings of Sodom gave Abram according to all that he had said, and they pressed him to take of whatever he chose, but he would not. ¹⁸ And he sent away the kings of Sodom and the remainder of their men, and he gave them orders about Lot, and they went to their respective places. ¹⁹ And Lot, his brother's son, he also sent away with his property, and he went with them, and Lot returned to his home, to Sodom, and Abram and his people returned to their home to the plains of Mamre, which is in Hebron. ²⁰ At that time the Lord again appeared to Abram in Hebron, and he said to him, Do not fear, thy reward is very great before me, for I will not leave thee, until I shall have multiplied thee, and blessed thee and made thy seed like the stars in heaven, which cannot be measured nor numbered. ²¹ And I will give unto thy seed all these lands that thou seest with thine eyes, to them will I give them for an inheritance forever, only be strong and do not fear, walk before me and be perfect. ²² And in the seventy-eighth year of the life of Abram, in that year died Reu, the son of Peleg, and all the days of Reu were two hundred and thirty-nine years, and he died. ²³ And Sarai, the daughter of Haran, Abram's wife, was still barren in those days; she did not bear to Abram either son or daughter. ²⁴ And when she saw that she bare no children she took her handmaid Hagar, whom Pharaoh had given her, and she gave her to Abram her husband for a wife. ²⁵ For Hagar learned all the ways of Sarai as Sarai taught her, she was not in any way deficient in following her good ways. ²⁶ And Sarai said to Abram, Behold here is my handmaid Hagar, go to her that she may bring forth upon my knees, that I may also obtain children through her. ²⁷ And at the end of ten years of Abram's dwelling in the land of Canaan, which is the eighty-fifth year of Abram's life, Sarai gave Hagar unto him. ²⁸ And Abram hearkened to the voice of his wife Sarai, and he took his handmaid Hagar and Abram came to her and she conceived. ²⁹ And when Hagar saw that she had conceived she rejoiced greatly, and her mistress was despised in her eyes, and she said within herself, This can only be that I am better before God than Sarai my mistress, for all the days that my mistress has been with my lord, she did not conceive, but me the Lord has caused in so short a time to conceive by him. ³⁰ And when Sarai saw that Hagar had conceived by Abram, Sarai was jealous of her handmaid, and Sarai said within herself, This is surely nothing else but that she must be better than I am. ³¹ And Sarai said unto Abram, My wrong be upon thee, for at the time when thou didst pray before the Lord for children why didst thou not pray on my account, that the Lord should give me seed from thee? ³² And when I speak to Hagar in thy presence, she despiseth my words, because she has conceived, and thou wilt say nothing to her; may the Lord judge between me and thee for what thou hast done to me. ³³ And Abram said to Sarai, Behold thy handmaid is in thy hand, do unto her as it may seem good in thy eyes; and Sarai afflicted her, and Hagar fled from her to the wilderness. ³⁴ And an angel of the Lord found her in the place where she had fled, by a well, and he said to her, Do not fear, for I will multiply thy seed, for thou shalt bear a son and thou shalt call his name Ishmael; now then return to Sarai thy mistress, and submit thyself under her hands. ³⁵ And Hagar called the place of that well Beer-lahai-roi, it is between Kadesh and the wilderness of Bered. ³⁶ And Hagar at that time returned to her master's house, and at the end of days Hagar bare a son to Abram, and Abram called his name Ishmael; and Abram was eighty-six years old when he begat him.

17

¹ And in those days, in the ninety-first year of the life of Abram, the children of Chittim made war with the children of Tubal, for when the Lord had scattered the sons of men upon the face of the earth, the children of Chittim went and embodied themselves in the plain of Canopia, and they built themselves cities there and dwelt by the river Tibreu. ² And the children of Tubal dwelt in Tuscanah, and their boundaries reached the river Tibreu, and

the children of Tubal built a city in Tuscanan, and they called the name Sabinah, after the name of Sabinah son of Tubal their father, and they dwelt there unto this day. ³ And it was at that time the children of Chittim made war with the children of Tubal, and the children of Tubal were smitten before the children of Chittim, and the children of Chittim caused three hundred and seventy men to fall from the children of Tubal. ⁴ And at that time the children of Tubal swore to the children of Chittim, saying, You shall not intermarry amongst us, and no man shall give his daughter to any of the sons of Chittim. ⁵ For all the daughters of Tubal were in those days fair, for no women were then found in the whole earth so fair as the daughters of Tubal. ⁶ And all who delighted in the beauty of women went to the daughters of Tubal and took wives from them, and the sons of men, kings and princes, who greatly delighted in the beauty of women, took wives in those days from the daughters of Tubal. ⁷ And at the end of three years after the children of Tubal had sworn to the children of Chittim not to give them their daughters for wives, about twenty men of the children of Chittim went to take some of the daughters of Tubal, but they found none. ⁸ For the children of Tubal kept their oaths not to intermarry with them, and they would not break their oaths. ⁹ And in the days of harvest the children of Tubal went into their fields to get in their harvest, when the young men of Chittim assembled and went to the city of Sabinah, and each man took a young woman from the daughters of Tubal, and they came to their cities. ¹⁰ And the children of Tubal heard of it and they went to make war with them, and they could not prevail over them, for the mountain was exceedingly high from them, and when they saw they could not prevail over them they returned to their land. ¹¹ And at the revolution of the year the children of Tubal went and hired about ten thousand men from those cities that were near them, and they went to war with the children of Chittim. ¹² And the children of Tubal went to war with the children of Chittim, to destroy their land and to distress them, and in this engagement the children of Tubal prevailed over the children of Chittim, and the children of Chittim, seeing that they were greatly distressed, lifted up the children which they had had by the daughters of Tubal, upon the wall which had been built, to be before the eyes of the children of Tubal. ¹³ And the children of Chittim said to them, Have you come to make war with your own sons and daughters, and have we not been considered your flesh and bones from that time till now? ¹⁴ And when the children of Tubal heard this they ceased to make war with the children of Chittim, and they went away. ¹⁵ And they returned to their cities, and the children of Chittim at that time assembled and built two cities by the sea, and they called one Purtu and the other Ariza. ¹⁶ And Abram the son of Terah was then ninety-nine years old. ¹⁷ At that time the Lord appeared to him and he said to him, I will make my covenant between me and thee, and I will greatly multiply thy seed, and this is the covenant which I make between me and thee, that every male child be circumcised, thou and thy seed after thee. ¹⁸ At eight days old shall it be circumcised, and this covenant shall be in your flesh for an everlasting covenant. ¹⁹ And now therefore thy name shall no more be called Abram but Abraham, and thy wife shall no more be called Sarai but Sarah. ²⁰ For I will bless you both, and I will multiply your seed after you that you shall become a great nation, and kings shall come forth from you.

18

¹ And Abraham rose and did all that God had ordered him, and he took the men of his household and those bought with his money, and he circumcised them as the Lord had commanded him. ² And there was not one left whom he did not circumcise, and Abraham and his son Ishmael were circumcised in the flesh of their foreskin; thirteen years old was Ishmael when he was circumcised in the flesh of his foreskin. ³ And in the third day Abraham went out of his tent and sat at the door to enjoy the heat of the sun, during the pain of his flesh. ⁴ And the Lord appeared to him in the plain of Mamre, and sent three of his ministering angels to visit him, and he was sitting at the door of the tent, and he lifted his eyes and saw, and lo three men were coming from a distance, and he rose up and ran to meet them, and he bowed down to them and brought them into his house. ⁵ And he said to them, If now I have found favor in your sight, turn in and eat a morsel of bread; and he pressed them, and they turned in and he gave them water and they washed their feet, and he placed them under a tree at the door of the tent. ⁶ And Abraham ran and took a calf, tender and good, and he hastened to kill it, and gave it to his servant Eliezer to dress. ⁷ And Abraham came to Sarah into the tent, and he said to her, Make ready quickly three measures of fine meal, knead it and make cakes to cover the pot containing the meat, and she did so. ⁸ And Abraham hastened and brought before them butter and milk, beef and mutton, and gave it before them to eat before the flesh of the calf was sufficiently done, and they did eat. ⁹ And when they had done eating one of them said to him, I will return to thee according to the time of life, and Sarah thy wife shall have a son. ¹⁰ And the men afterward departed and went their ways, to the places to which they were sent. ¹¹ In those days all the people of Sodom and Gomorrah, and of the whole five cities, were exceedingly wicked and sinful against the Lord and they provoked the Lord with their abominations, and they strengthened in aging abominably and scornfully before the Lord, and their wickedness and crimes were in those days great before the Lord. ¹² And they had in their land a very extensive valley, about half a day's walk, and in it there were fountains of water and a great deal of herbage surrounding the water. ¹³ And all the people of Sodom and Gomorrah went there four times in the year, with their wives and children and all belonging to them, and they rejoiced there with timbrels and dances. ¹⁴ And in the time of rejoicing they would all rise and lay hold of their neighbor's wives, and some, the virgin daughters of their neighbors, and they enjoyed them, and each man saw his wife and daughter in the hands of his neighbor and did not say a word. ¹⁵ And they did so from morning to night, and they afterward returned home each man to his house and each woman to her tent; so they always did four times in the year. ¹⁶ Also when a stranger came into their cities and brought goods which he had purchased with a view to dispose of there, the people of these cities would assemble, men, women and children, young and old, and go to the man and take his goods by force, giving a little to each man until there was an end to all the goods of the owner which he had brought into the land. ¹⁷ And if the owner of the goods quarreled with them, saying, What is this work which you have done to me, then they would approach to him one by one, and each would show him the little which he took and taunt him, saying, I only took that little which thou didst give me; and when he heard this from them all, he would arise and go from them in sorrow and bitterness of soul, when they would all arise and go after him, and drive him out of the city with great noise and tumult. ¹⁸ And there was a man from the country of Elam who was leisurely going on the road, seated upon his ass, which carried a fine mantle of divers colors, and the mantle was bound with a cord upon the ass. ¹⁹ And the man was on his journey passing through the street of Sodom when the sun set in the evening, and he remained there in order to abide during the night, but no one would let him into his house; and at that time there was in Sodom a wicked and mischievous man, one skillful to do evil, and his name was Hedad. ²⁰ And he lifted up his eyes and saw the traveler in the street of the city, and he came to him and said, Whence comest thou and whither dost thou go? ²¹ And the man said to him, I am traveling from Hebron to Elam where I belong, and as I passed the sun set and no one would suffer me to enter his house, though I had bread and water and also straw and provender for my ass, and am short of nothing. ²² And Hedad answered and said to him, All that thou shalt want shall be supplied by me, but in the street thou shalt not abide all night. ²³ And Hedad brought him to his house, and he took off the mantle from the ass with the cord, and brought them to his house, and he gave the ass straw and provender whilst the traveler ate and drank in Hedad's house, and he abode there that night. ²⁴ And in the morning the traveler rose up early to continue his journey, when Hedad said to him, Wait, comfort thy heart with a morsel of bread and then go, and the man did so; and he remained with him, and they both ate and drank together during the day, when the man rose up to go. ²⁵ And Hedad said to him, Behold now the day is declining, thou hadst better remain all night that thy heart may be comforted; and he pressed him so that he tarried there all night, and on the second day he rose up early to go away, when Hedad pressed him, saying, Comfort thy heart with a morsel of bread and then go, and he remained and ate with him also the second day, and then the man rose up to continue his journey. ²⁶ And Hedad said to him, Behold now the day is declining, remain with me to comfort thy heart and in the morning rise up early and go thy way. ²⁷ And the man would not remain, but rose and saddled his ass, and whilst he was saddling his ass the wife of Hedad said to her husband, Behold this man has remained with us for two days eating and drinking and he has given us nothing, and now shall he go away from us without giving anything? and Hedad said to her, Be silent. ²⁸ And the man saddled his ass to go, and he asked Hedad to give him the cord and mantle to tie it upon the ass. ²⁹ And Hedad said to him, What sayest thou? And he said to him, That thou my lord shalt give me the cord and the mantle made with divers colors which thou didst conceal with thee in thy house to take care of it. ³⁰ And Hedad answered the man, saying, This is the interpretation of thy dream, the cord which thou didst see, means that thy life will be lengthened out like a cord, and having seen the mantle colored with all sorts of colors, means that thou shalt have a vineyard in which thou wilt plant trees of all fruits. ³¹ And the traveler answered, saying, Not so my lord, for I was awake when I gave thee the cord and also a mantle woven with different colors, which thou didst take off the ass to put them by for me; and Hedad answered and said, Surely I have told thee the interpretation of thy dream and it is a good dream, and this is the interpretation thereof. ³² Now the sons of men give me four pieces of silver, which is my charge for interpreting dreams, and of thee only I require three

pieces of silver. ³³ And the man was provoked at the words of Hedad, and he cried bitterly, and he brought Hedad to Serak judge of Sodom. ³⁴ And the man laid his cause before Serak the judge, when Hedad replied, saying, It is not so, but thus the matter stands; and the judge said to the traveler, This man Hedad telleth thee truth, for he is famed in the cities for the accurate interpretation of dreams. ³⁵ And the man cried at the word of the judge, and he said, Not so my Lord, for it was in the day that I gave him the cord and mantle which was upon the ass, in order to put them by in his house; and they both disputed before the judge, the one saying, Thus the matter was, and the other declaring otherwise. ³⁶ And Hedad said to the man, Give me four pieces of silver that I charge for my interpretations of dreams; I will not make any allowance; and give me the expense of the four meals that thou didst eat in my house. ³⁷ And the man said to Hedad, Truly I will pay thee for what I ate in thy house, only give me the cord and mantle which thou didst conceal in thy house. ³⁸ And Hedad replied before the judge and said to the man, Did I not tell thee the interpretation of thy dream? the cord means that thy days shall be prolonged like a cord, and the mantle, that thou wilt have a vineyard in which thou wilt plant all kinds of fruit trees. ³⁹ This is the proper interpretation of thy dream, now give me the four pieces of silver that I require as a compensation, for I will make thee no allowance. ⁴⁰ And the man cried at the words of Hedad and they both quarreled before the judge, and the judge gave orders to his servants, who drove them rashly from the house. ⁴¹ And they went away quarreling from the judge, when the people of Sodom heard them, and they gathered about them and they exclaimed against the stranger, and they drove him rashly from the city. ⁴² And the man continued his journey upon his ass with bitterness of soul, lamenting and weeping. ⁴³ And whilst he was going along he wept at what had happened to him in the corrupt city of Sodom.

19

¹ And the cities of Sodom had four judges to four cities, and these were their names, Serak in the city of Sodom, Sharkad in Gomorrah, Zabnac in Admah, and Menon in Zeboyim. ² And Eliezer Abraham's servant applied to them different names, and he converted Serak to Shakra, Sharkad to Shakrura, Zebnac to Kezobim, and Menon to Matzlodin. ³ And by desire of their four judges the people of Sodom and Gomorrah had beds erected in the streets of the cities, and if a man came to these places they laid hold of him and brought him to one of their beds, and by force made him to lie in them. ⁴ And as he lay down, three men would stand at his head and three at his feet, and measure him by the length of the bed, and if the man was less than the bed these six men would stretch him at each end, and when he cried out to them they would not answer him. ⁵ And if he was longer than the bed they would draw together the two sides of the bed at each end, until the man had reached the gates of death. ⁶ And if he continued to cry out to them, they would answer him, saying, Thus shall it be done to a man that cometh into our land. ⁷ And when men heard all these things that the people of the cities of Sodom did, they refrained from coming there. ⁸ And when a poor man came to their land they would give him silver and gold, and cause a proclamation in the whole city not to give him a morsel of bread to eat, and if the stranger should remain there some days, and die from hunger, not having been able to obtain a morsel of bread, then at his death all the people of the city would come and take their silver and gold which they had given to him. ⁹ And those that could recognize the silver or gold which they had given him took it back, and at his death they also stripped him of his garments, and they would fight about them, and he that prevailed over his neighbor took them. ¹⁰ They would after that carry him and bury him under some of the shrubs in the deserts; so they did all the days to any one that came to them and died in their land. ¹¹ And in the course of time Sarah sent Eliezer to Sodom, to see Lot and inquire after his welfare. ¹² And Eliezer went to Sodom, and he met a man of Sodom fighting with a stranger, and the man of Sodom stripped the poor man of all his clothes and went away. ¹³ And this poor man cried to Eliezer and supplicated his favor on account of what the man of Sodom had done to him. ¹⁴ And he said to him, Why dost thou act thus to the poor man who came to thy land? ¹⁵ And the man of Sodom answered Eliezer, saying, Is this man thy brother, or have the people of Sodom made thee a judge this day, that thou speakest about this man? ¹⁶ And Eliezer strove with the man of Sodom on account of the poor man, and when Eliezer approached to recover the poor man's clothes from the man of Sodom, he hastened and with a stone smote Eliezer in the forehead. ¹⁷ And the blood flowed copiously from Eliezer's forehead, and when the man saw the blood he caught hold of Eliezer, saying, Give me my hire for having rid thee of this bad blood that was in thy forehead, for such is the custom and the law in our land. ¹⁸ And Eliezer said to him, Thou hast wounded me and requirest me to pay thee thy hire; and Eliezer would not hearken to the words of the man of Sodom. ¹⁹ And the man laid hold of Eliezer and brought him to Shakra the judge of Sodom for judgment. ²⁰ And the man spoke to the judge, saying, I beseech thee my lord, thus has this man done, for I smote him with a stone that the blood flowed from his forehead, and he is unwilling to give me my hire. ²¹ And the judge said to Eliezer, This man speaketh truth to thee, give him his hire, for this is the custom in our land; and Eliezer heard the words of the judge, and he lifted up a stone and smote the judge, and the stone struck on his forehead, and the blood flowed copiously from the forehead of the judge, and Eliezer said, If this then is the custom in your land give thou unto this man what I should have given him, for this has been thy decision, thou didst decree it. ²² And Eliezer left the man of Sodom with the judge, and he went away. ²³ And when the kings of Elam had made war with the kings of Sodom, the kings of Elam captured all the property of Sodom, and they took Lot captive, with his property, and when it was told to Abraham he went and made war with the kings of Elam, and he recovered from their hands all the property of Lot as well as the property of Sodom. ²⁴ At that time the wife of Lot bare him a daughter, and he called her name Paltith, saying, Because God had delivered him and his whole household from the kings of Elam; and Paltith daughter of Lot grew up, and one of the men of Sodom took her for a wife. ²⁵ And a poor man came into the city to seek a maintenance, and he remained in the city some days, and all the people of Sodom caused a proclamation of their custom not to give this man a morsel of bread to eat, until he dropped dead upon the earth, and they did so. ²⁶ And Paltith the daughter of Lot saw this man lying in the streets starved with hunger, and no one would give him any thing to keep him alive, and he was just upon the point of death. ²⁷ And her soul was filled with pity on account of the man, and she fed him secretly with bread for many days, and the soul of this man was revived. ²⁸ For when she went forth to fetch water she would put the bread in the water pitcher, and when she came to the place where the poor man was, she took the bread from the pitcher and gave it him to eat; so she did many days. ²⁹ And all the people of Sodom and Gomorrah wondered how this man could bear starvation for so many days. ³⁰ And they said to each other, This can only be that he eats and drinks, for no man can bear starvation for so many days or live as this man has, without even his countenance changing; and three men concealed themselves in a place where the poor man was stationed, to know who it was that brought him bread to eat. ³¹ And Paltith daughter of Lot went forth that day to fetch water, and she put bread into her pitcher of water, and she went to draw water by the poor man's place, and she took out the bread from the pitcher and gave it to the poor man and he ate it. ³² And the three men saw what Paltith did to the poor man, and they said to her, It is thou then who hast supported him, and therefore has he not starved, nor changed in appearance nor died like the rest. ³³ And the three men went out of the place in which they were concealed, and they seized Paltith and the bread which was in the poor man's hand. ³⁴ And they took Paltith and brought her before their judges, and they said to them, Thus did she do, and it is she who supplied the poor man with bread, therefore did he not die all this time; now therefore declare to us the punishment due to this woman for having transgressed our law. ³⁵ And the people of Sodom and Gomorrah assembled and kindled a fire in the street of the city, and they took the woman and cast her into the fire and she was burned to ashes. ³⁶ And in the city of Admah there was a woman to whom they did the like. ³⁷ For a traveler came into the city of Admah to abide there all night, with the intention of going home in the morning, and he sat opposite the door of the house of the young woman's father, to remain there, as the sun had set when be had reached that place; and the young woman saw him sitting by the door of the house. ³⁸ And he asked her for a drink of water and she said to him, Who art thou? and he said to her, I was this day going on the road, and reached here when the sun set, so I will abide here all night, and in the morning I will arise early and continue my journey. ³⁹ And the young woman went into the house and fetched the man bread and water to eat and drink. ⁴⁰ And this affair became known to the people of Admah, and they assembled and brought the young woman before the judges, that they should judge her for this act. ⁴¹ And the judge said, The judgment of death must pass upon this woman because she transgressed our law, and this therefore is the decision concerning her. ⁴² And the people of those cities assembled and brought out the young woman, and anointed her with honey from head to foot, as the judge had decreed, and they placed her before a swarm of bees which were then in their hives, and the bees flew upon her and stung her that her whole body was swelled. ⁴³ And the young woman cried out on account of the bees, but no one took notice of her or pitied her, and her cries ascended to heaven. ⁴⁴ And the Lord was provoked at this and at all the works of the cities of Sodom, for they had abundance of food, and had tranquility amongst them, and still would not sustain the poor and the needy, and in those days their evil doings and sins became great before the Lord. ⁴⁵ And the Lord sent for two of the angels that had come to Abraham's house, to destroy Sodom and its cities. ⁴⁶ And the angels rose up from the door of Abraham's tent, after they had eaten and

drunk, and they reached Sodom in the evening, and Lot was then sitting in the gate of Sodom, and when he saw them he rose to meet them, and he bowed down to the ground. ⁴⁷ And he pressed them greatly and brought them into his house, and he gave them victuals which they ate, and they abode all night in his house. ⁴⁸ And the angels said to Lot, Arise, go forth from this place, thou and all belonging to thee, lest thou be consumed in the iniquity of this city, for the Lord will destroy this place. ⁴⁹ And the angels laid hold upon the hand of Lot and upon the hand of his wife, and upon the hands of his children, and all belonging to him, and they brought him forth and set him without the cities. ⁵⁰ And they said to Lot, Escape for thy life, and he fled and all belonging to him. ⁵¹ Then the Lord rained upon Sodom and upon Gomorrah and upon all these cities brimstone and fire from the Lord out of heaven. ⁵² And he overthrew these cities, all the plain and all the inhabitants of the cities, and that which grew upon the ground; and Ado the wife of Lot looked back to see the destruction of the cities, for her compassion was moved on account of her daughters who remained in Sodom, for they did not go with her. ⁵³ And when she looked back she became a pillar of salt, and it is yet in that place unto this day. ⁵⁴ And the oxen which stood in that place daily licked up the salt to the extremities of their feet, and in the morning it would spring forth afresh, and they again licked it up unto this day. ⁵⁵ And Lot and two of his daughters that remained with him fled and escaped to the cave of Adullam, and they remained there for some time. ⁵⁶ And Abraham rose up early in the morning to see what had been done to the cities of Sodom; and he looked and beheld the smoke of the cities going up like the smoke of a furnace. ⁵⁷ And Lot and his two daughters remained in the cave, and they made their father drink wine, and they lay with him, for they said there was no man upon earth that could raise up seed from them, for they thought that the whole earth was destroyed. ⁵⁸ And they both lay with their father, and they conceived and bare sons, and the first born called the name of her son Moab, saying, From my father did I conceive him; he is the father of the Moabites unto this day. ⁵⁹ And the younger also called her son Benami; he is the father of the children of Ammon unto this day. ⁶⁰ And after this Lot and his two daughters went away from there, and he dwelt on the other side of the Jordan with his two daughters and their sons, and the sons of Lot grew up, and they went and took themselves wives from the land of Canaan, and they begat children and they were fruitful and multiplied.

20

¹ And at that time Abraham journeyed from the plain of Mamre, and he went to the land of the Philistines, and he dwelt in Gerar; it was in the twenty-fifth year of Abraham's being in the land of Canaan, and the hundredth year of the life of Abraham, that he came to Gerar in the land of the Philistines. ² And when they entered the land he said to Sarah his wife, Say thou art my sister, to any one that shall ask thee, in order that we may escape the evil of the inhabitants of the land. ³ And as Abraham was dwelling in the land of the Philistines, the servants of Abimelech, king of the Philistines, saw that Sarah was exceedingly beautiful, and they asked Abraham concerning her, and he said, She is my sister. ⁴ And the servants of Abimelech went to Abimelech, saying, A man from the land of Canaan is come to dwell in the land, and he has a sister that is exceeding fair. ⁵ And Abimelech heard the words of his servants who praised Sarah to him, and Abimelech sent his officers, and they brought Sarah to the king. ⁶ And Sarah came to the house of Abimelech, and the king saw that Sarah was beautiful, and she pleased him exceedingly. ⁷ And he approached her and said to her, What is that man to thee with whom thou didst come to our land? and Sarah answered and said He is my brother, and we came from the land of Canaan to dwell wherever we could find a place. ⁸ And Abimelech said to Sarah, Behold my land is before thee, place thy brother in any part of this land that pleases thee, and it will be our duty to exalt and elevate him above all the people of the land since he is thy brother. ⁹ And Abimelech sent for Abraham, and Abraham came to Abimelech. ¹⁰ And Abimelech said to Abraham, Behold I have given orders that thou shalt be honored as thou desirest on account of thy sister Sarah. ¹¹ And Abraham went forth from the king, and the king's present followed him. ¹² As at evening time, before men lie down to rest, the king was sitting upon his throne, and a deep sleep fell upon him, and he lay upon the throne and slept till morning. ¹³ And he dreamed that an angel of the Lord came to him with a drawn sword in his hand, and the angel stood over Abimelech, and wished to slay him with the sword, and the king was terrified in his dream, and said to the angel, In what have I sinned against thee that thou comest to slay me with thy sword? ¹⁴ And the angel answered and said to Abimelech, Behold thou diest on account of the woman which thou didst yesternight bring to thy house, for she is a married woman, the wife of Abraham who came to thy house; now therefore return that man his wife, for she is his wife; and shouldst thou not return her, know that thou wilt surely die, thou and all belonging to thee. ¹⁵ And on that night there was a great outcry in the land of the Philistines, and the inhabitants of the land saw the figure of a man standing with a drawn sword in his hand, and he smote the inhabitants of the land with the sword, yea he continued to smite them. ¹⁶ And the angel of the Lord smote the whole land of the Philistines on that night, and there was a great confusion on that night and on the following morning. ¹⁷ And every womb was closed, and all their issues, and the hand of the Lord was upon them on account of Sarah, wife of Abraham, whom Abimelech had taken. ¹⁸ And in the morning Abimelech rose with terror and confusion and with a great dread, and he sent and had his servants called in, and he related his dream to them, and the people were greatly afraid. ¹⁹ And one man standing amongst the servants of the king answered the king, saying, O sovereign king, restore this woman to her husband, for he is her husband, for the like happened to the king of Egypt when this man came to Egypt. ²⁰ And he said concerning his wife, She is my sister, for such is his manner of doing when he cometh to dwell in the land in which he is a stranger. ²¹ And Pharaoh sent and took this woman for a wife and the Lord brought upon him grievous plagues until he returned the woman to her husband. ²² Now therefore, O sovereign king, know what happened yesternight to the whole land, for there was a very great consternation and great pain and lamentation, and we know that it was on account of the woman which thou didst take. ²³ Now, therefore, restore this woman to her husband, lest it should befall us as it did to Pharaoh king of Egypt and his subjects, and that we may not die; and Abimelech hastened and called and had Sarah called for, and she came before him, and he had Abraham called for, and he came before him. ²⁴ And Abimelech said to them, What is this work you have been doing in saying you are brother and sister, and I took this woman for a wife? ²⁵ And Abraham said, Because I thought I should suffer death on account of my wife; and Abimelech took flocks and herds, and men servants and maid servants, and a thousand pieces of silver, and he gave them to Abraham, and he returned Sarah to him. ²⁶ And Abimelech said to Abraham, Behold the whole land is before thee, dwell in it wherever thou shalt choose. ²⁷ And Abraham and Sarah, his wife, went forth from the king's presence with honor and respect, and they dwelt in the land, even in Gerar. ²⁸ And all the inhabitants of the land of the Philistines and the king's servants were still in pain, through the plague which the angel had inflicted upon them the whole night on account of Sarah. ²⁹ And Abimelech sent for Abraham, saying, Pray now for thy servants to the Lord thy God, that he may put away this mortality from amongst us. ³⁰ And Abraham prayed on account of Abimelech and his subjects, and the Lord heard the prayer of Abraham, and he healed Abimelech and all his subjects.

21

¹ And it was at that time at the end of a year and four months of Abraham's dwelling in the land of the Philistines in Gerar, that God visited Sarah, and the Lord remembered her, and she conceived and bare a son to Abraham. ² And Abraham called the name of the son which was born to him, which Sarah bare to him, Isaac. ³ And Abraham circumcised his son Isaac at eight days old, as God had commanded Abraham to do unto his seed after him; and Abraham was one hundred, and Sarah ninety years old, when Isaac was born to them. ⁴ And the child grew up and he was weaned, and Abraham made a great feast upon the day that Isaac was weaned. ⁵ And Shem and Eber and all the great people of the land, and Abimelech king of the Philistines, and his servants, and Phicol, the captain of his host, came to eat and drink and rejoice at the feast which Abraham made upon the day of his son Isaac's being weaned. ⁶ Also Terah, the father of Abraham, and Nahor his brother, came from Haran, they and all belonging to them, for they greatly rejoiced on hearing that a son had been born to Sarah. ⁷ And they came to Abraham, and they ate and drank at the feast which Abraham made upon the day of Isaac's being weaned. ⁸ And Terah and Nahor rejoiced with Abraham, and they remained with him many days in the land of the Philistines. ⁹ At that time Serug the son of Reu died, in the first year of the birth of Isaac son of Abraham. ¹⁰ And all the days of Serug were two hundred and thirty-nine years, and he died. ¹¹ And Ishmael the son of Abraham was grown up in those days; he was fourteen years old when Sarah bare Isaac to Abraham. ¹² And God was with Ishmael the son of Abraham, and he grew up, and he learned to use the bow and became an archer. ¹³ And when Isaac was five years old he was sitting with Ishmael at the door of the tent. ¹⁴ And Ishmael came to Isaac and seated himself opposite to him, and he took the bow and drew it and put the arrow in it, and intended to slay Isaac. ¹⁵ And Sarah saw the act which Ishmael desired to do to her son Isaac, and it grieved her exceedingly on account of her son, and she sent for Abraham, and said to him, Cast out this bondwoman and her son, for her son shall not be heir with my son, for thus did he seek to do unto him this day. ¹⁶ And Abraham hearkened to the voice of Sarah, and he rose up early in the morning, and he took twelve loaves and a bottle of water

which he gave to Hagar, and sent her away with her son, and Hagar went with her son to the wilderness, and they dwelt in the wilderness of Paran with the inhabitants of the wilderness, and Ishmael was an archer, and he dwelt in the wilderness a long time. ¹⁷ And he and his mother afterward went to the land of Egypt, and they dwelt there, and Hagar took a wife for her son from Egypt, and her name was Meribah. ¹⁸ And the wife of Ishmael conceived and bare four sons and two daughters, and Ishmael and his mother and his wife and children afterward went and returned to the wilderness. ¹⁹ And they made themselves tents in the wilderness, in which they dwelt, and they continued to travel and then to rest monthly and yearly. ²⁰ And God gave Ishmael flocks and herds and tents on account of Abraham his father, and the man increased in cattle. ²¹ And Ishmael dwelt in deserts and in tents, traveling and resting for a long time, and he did not see the face of his father. ²² And in some time after, Abraham said to Sarah his wife, I will go and see my son Ishmael, for I have a desire to see him, for I have not seen him for a long time. ²³ And Abraham rode upon one of his camels to the wilderness to seek his son Ishmael, for he heard that he was dwelling in a tent in the wilderness with all belonging to him. ²⁴ And Abraham went to the wilderness, and he reached the tent of Ishmael about noon, and he asked after Ishmael, and he found the wife of Ishmael sitting in the tent with her children, and Ishmael her husband and his mother were not with them. ²⁵ And Abraham asked the wife of Ishmael, saying, Where has Ishmael gone? and she said, He has gone to the field to hunt, and Abraham was still mounted upon the camel, for he would not get off to the ground as he had sworn to his wife Sarah that he would not get off from the camel. ²⁶ And Abraham said to Ishmael's wife, My daughter, give me a little water that I may drink, for I am fatigued from the journey. ²⁷ And Ishmael's wife answered and said to Abraham, We have neither water nor bread, and she continued sitting in the tent and did not notice Abraham, neither did she ask him who he was. ²⁸ But she was beating her children in the tent, and she was cursing them, and she also cursed her husband Ishmael and reproached him, and Abraham heard the words of Ishmael's wife to her children, and he was very angry and displeased. ²⁹ And Abraham called to the woman to come out to him from the tent, and the woman came and stood opposite to Abraham, for Abraham was still mounted upon the camel. ³⁰ And Abraham said to Ishmael's wife, When thy husband Ishmael returneth home say these words to him, ³¹ A very old man from the land of the Philistines came hither to seek thee, and thus was his appearance and figure; I did not ask him who he was, and seeing thou wast not here he spoke unto me and said, When Ishmael thy husband returneth tell him thus did this man say, When thou comest home put away this nail of the tent which thou hast placed here, and place another nail in its stead. ³² And Abraham finished his instructions to the woman, and he turned and went off on the camel homeward. ³³ And after that Ishmael came from the chase he and his mother, and returned to the tent, and his wife spoke these words to him, ³⁴ A very old man from the land of the Philistines came to seek thee, and thus was his appearance and figure; I did not ask him who he was, and seeing thou wast not at home he said to me, When thy husband cometh home tell him, thus saith the old man, Put away the nail of the tent which thou hast placed here and place another nail in its stead. ³⁵ And Ishmael heard the words of his wife, and he knew that it was his father, and that his wife did not honor him. ³⁶ And Ishmael understood his father's words that he had spoken to his wife, and Ishmael hearkened to the voice of his father, and Ishmael cast off that woman and she went away. ³⁷ And Ishmael afterward went to the land of Canaan, and he took another wife and he brought her to his tent to the place where he then dwelt. ³⁸ And at the end of three years Abraham said, I will go again and see Ishmael my son, for I have not seen him for a long time. ³⁹ And he rode upon his camel and went to the wilderness, and he reached the tent of Ishmael about noon. ⁴⁰ And he asked after Ishmael, and his wife came out of the tent and she said, He is not here my lord, for he has gone to hunt in the fields, and to feed the camels, and the woman said to Abraham, Turn in my lord into the tent, and eat a morsel of bread, for thy soul must be wearied on account of the journey. ⁴¹ And Abraham said to her, I will not stop for I am in haste to continue my journey, but give me a little water to drink, for I have thirst; and the woman hastened and ran into the tent and she brought out water and bread to Abraham, which she placed before him and she urged him to eat, and he ate and drank and his heart was comforted and he blessed his son Ishmael. ⁴² And he finished his meal and he blessed the Lord, and he said to Ishmael's wife, When Ishmael cometh home say these words to him, ⁴³ A very old man from the land of the Philistines came hither and asked after thee, and thou wast not here; and I brought him out bread and water and he ate and drank and his heart was comforted. ⁴⁴ And he spoke these words to me: When Ishmael thy husband cometh home, say unto him, The nail of the tent which thou hast is very good, do not put it away from the tent. ⁴⁵ And Abraham finished commanding the woman, and he rode off to his home to the land of the Philistines; and when Ishmael came to his tent his wife went forth to meet him with joy and a cheerful heart. ⁴⁶ And she said to him, An old man came here from the land of the Philistines and thus was his appearance, and he asked after thee and thou wast not here, so I brought out bread and water, and he ate and drank and his heart was comforted. ⁴⁷ And he spoke these words to me, When Ishmael thy husband cometh home say to him, The nail of the tent which thou hast is very good, do not put it away from the tent. ⁴⁸ And Ishmael knew that it was his father, and that his wife had honored him, and the Lord blessed Ishmael.

22

¹ And Ishmael then rose up and took his wife and his children and his cattle and all belonging to him, and he journeyed from there and he went to his father in the land of the Philistines. ² And Abraham related to Ishmael his son the transaction with the first wife that Ishmael took, according to what she did. ³ And Ishmael and his children dwelt with Abraham many days in that land, and Abraham dwelt in the land of the Philistines a long time. ⁴ And the days increased and reached twenty six years, and after that Abraham with his servants and all belonging to him went from the land of the Philistines and removed to a great distance, and they came near to Hebron, and they remained there, and the servants of Abraham dug wells of water, and Abraham and all belonging to him dwelt by the water, and the servants of Abimelech king of the Philistines heard the report that Abraham's servants had dug wells of water in the borders of the land. ⁵ And they came and quarreled with the servants of Abraham, and they robbed them of the great well which they had dug. ⁶ And Abimelech king of the Philistines heard of this affair, and he with Phicol the captain of his host and twenty of his men came to Abraham, and Abimelech spoke to Abraham concerning his servants, and Abraham rebuked Abimelech concerning the well of which his servants had robbed him. ⁷ And Abimelech said to Abraham, As the Lord liveth who created the whole earth, I did not hear of the act which my servants did unto thy servants until this day. ⁸ And Abraham took seven ewe lambs and gave them to Abimelech, saying, Take these, I pray thee, from my hands that it may be a testimony for me that I dug this well. ⁹ And Abimelech took the seven ewe lambs which Abraham had given to him, for he had also given him cattle and herds in abundance, and Abimelech swore to Abraham concerning the well, therefore he called that well Beersheba, for there they both swore concerning it. ¹⁰ And they both made a covenant in Beersheba, and Abimelech rose up with Phicol the captain of his host and all his men, and they returned to the land of the Philistines, and Abraham and all belonging to him dwelt in Beersheba and he was in that land a long time. ¹¹ And Abraham planted a large grove in Beersheba, and he made to it four gates facing the four sides of the earth, and he planted a vineyard in it, so that if a traveler came to Abraham he entered any gate which was in his road, and remained there and ate and drank and satisfied himself and then departed. ¹² For the house of Abraham was always open to the sons of men that passed and repassed, who came daily to eat and drink in the house of Abraham. ¹³ And any man who had hunger and came to Abraham's house, Abraham would give him bread that he might eat and drink and be satisfied, and any one that came naked to his house he would clothe with garments as he might choose, and give him silver and gold and make known to him the Lord who had created him in the earth; this did Abraham all his life. ¹⁴ And Abraham and his children and all belonging to him dwelt in Beersheba, and he pitched his tent as far as Hebron. ¹⁵ And Abraham's brother Nahor and his father and all belonging to them dwelt in Haran, for they did not come with Abraham to the land of Canaan. ¹⁶ And children were born to Nahor which Milca the daughter of Haran, and sister to Sarah, Abraham's wife, bare to him. ¹⁷ And these are the names of those that were born to him, Uz, Buz, Kemuel, Kesed, Chazo, Pildash, Tidlaf, and Bethuel, being eight sons, these are the children of Milca which she bare to Nahor, Abraham's brother. ¹⁸ And Nahor had a concubine and her name was Reumah, and she also bare to Nahor, Zebach, Gachash, Tachash and Maacha, being four sons. ¹⁹ And the children that were born to Nahor were twelve sons besides his daughters, and they also had children born to them in Haran. ²⁰ And the children of Uz the first born of Nahor were Abi, Cheref, Gadin, Melus, and Deborah their sister. ²¹ And the sons of Buz were Berachel, Naamath, Sheva, and Madonu. ²² And the sons of Kemuel were Aram and Rechob. ²³ And the sons of Kesed were Anamlech, Meshai, Benon and Yifi; and the sons of Chazo were Pildash, Mechi and Opher. ²⁴ And the sons of Pildash were Arud, Chamum, Mered and Moloch. ²⁵ And the sons of Tidlaf were Mushan, Cushan and Mutzi. ²⁶ And the children of Bethuel were Sechar, Laban and their sister Rebecca. ²⁷ These are the families of the children of Nahor, that were born to them in Haran; and Aram the son of Kemuel and Rechob his brother went away from Haran, and they found a valley in the land by the river Euphrates. ²⁸ And they built a city there, and they called the name of the city after the

name of Pethor the son of Aram, that is Aram Naherayim unto this day. ²⁹ And the children of Kesed also went to dwell where they could find a place, and they went and they found a valley opposite to the land of Shinar, and they dwelt there. ³⁰ And they there built themselves a city, and they called the name at the city Kesed after the name of their father, that is the land Kasdim unto this day, and the Kasdim dwelt in that land and they were fruitful and multiplied exceedingly. ³¹ And Terah, father of Nahor and Abraham, went and took another wife in his old age, and her name was Pelilah, and she conceived and bare him a son and he called his name Zoba. ³² And Terah lived twenty-five years after he begat Zoba. ³³ And Terah died in that year, that is in the thirty-fifth year of the birth of Isaac son of Abraham. ³⁴ And the days of Terah were two hundred and five years, and he was buried in Haran. ³⁵ And Zoba the son of Terah lived thirty years and he begat Aram, Achlis and Merik. ³⁶ And Aram son of Zoba son of Terah, had three wives and he begat twelve sons and three daughters; and the Lord gave to Aram the son of Zoba, riches and possessions, and abundance of cattle, and flocks and herds, and the man increased greatly. ³⁷ And Aram the son of Zoba and his brother and all his household journeyed from Haran, and they went to dwell where they should find a place, for their property was too great to remain in Haran; for they could not stop in Haran together with their brethren the children of Nahor. ³⁸ And Aram the son of Zoba went with his brethren, and they found a valley at a distance toward the eastern country and they dwelt there. ³⁹ And they also built a city there, and they called the name thereof Aram, after the name of their eldest brother; that is Aram Zoba to this day. ⁴⁰ And Isaac the son of Abraham was growing up in those days, and Abraham his father taught him the way of the Lord to know the Lord, and the Lord was with him. ⁴¹ And when Isaac was thirty-seven years old, Ishmael his brother was going about with him in the tent. ⁴² And Ishmael boasted of himself to Isaac, saying, I was thirteen years old when the Lord spoke to my father to circumcise us, and I did according to the word of the Lord which he spoke to my father, and I gave my soul unto the Lord, and I did not transgress his word which he commanded my father. ⁴³ And Isaac answered Ishmael, saying, Why dost thou boast to me about this, about a little bit of thy flesh which thou didst take from thy body, concerning which the Lord commanded thee? ⁴⁴ As the Lord liveth, the God of my father Abraham, if the Lord should say unto my father, Take now thy son Isaac and bring him up an offering before me, I would not refrain but I would joyfully accede to it. ⁴⁵ And the Lord heard the word that Isaac spoke to Ishmael, and it seemed good in the sight of the Lord, and he thought to try Abraham in this matter. ⁴⁶ And the day arrived when the sons of God came and placed themselves before the Lord, and Satan also came with the sons of God before the Lord. ⁴⁷ And the Lord said unto Satan, Whence comest thou? and Satan answered the Lord and said, From going to and fro in the earth, and from walking up and down in it. ⁴⁸ And the Lord said to Satan, What is thy word to me concerning all the children of the earth? and Satan answered the Lord and said, I have seen all the children of the earth who serve thee and remember thee when they require anything from thee. ⁴⁹ And when thou givest them the thing which they require from thee, they sit at their ease, and forsake thee and they remember thee no more. ⁵⁰ Hast thou seen Abraham the son of Terah, who at first had no children, and he served thee and erected altars to thee wherever he came, and he brought up offerings upon them, and he proclaimed thy name continually to all the children of the earth. ⁵¹ And now that his son Isaac is born to him, he has forsaken thee, he has made a great feast for all the inhabitants of the land, and the Lord he has forgotten. ⁵² For amidst all that he has done he brought thee no offering; neither burnt offering nor peace offering, neither ox, lamb nor goat of all that he killed on the day that his son was weaned. ⁵³ Even from the time of his son's birth till now, being thirty-seven years, he built no altar before thee, nor brought any offering to thee, for he saw that thou didst give what he requested before thee, and he therefore forsook thee. ⁵⁴ And the Lord said to Satan, Hast thou thus considered my servant Abraham? for there is none like him upon earth, a perfect and an upright man before me, one that feareth God and avoideth evil; as I live, were I to say unto him, Bring up Isaac thy son before me, he would not withhold him from me, much more if I told him to bring up a burnt offering before me from his flock or herds. ⁵⁵ And Satan answered the Lord and said, Speak then now unto Abraham as thou hast said, and thou wilt see whether he will not this day transgress and cast aside thy words.

23

¹ At that time the word of the Lord came to Abraham, and he said unto him, Abraham, and he said, Here I am. ² And he said to him, Take now thy son, thine only son whom thou lovest, even Isaac, and go to the land of Moriah, and offer him there for a burnt offering upon one of the mountains which shall be shown to thee, for there wilt thou see a cloud and the glory of the Lord. ³ And Abraham said within himself, How shall I separate my son Isaac from Sarah his mother, in order to bring him up for a burnt offering before the Lord? ⁴ And Abraham came into the tent, and he sat before Sarah his wife, and he spoke these words to her, ⁵ My son Isaac is grown up and he has not for some time studied the service of his God, now tomorrow I will go and bring him to Shem, and Eber his son, and there he will learn the ways of the Lord, for they will teach him to know the Lord as well as to know that when he prayeth continually before the Lord, he will answer him, therefore there he will know the way of serving the Lord his God. ⁶ And Sarah said, Thou hast spoken well, go my lord and do unto him as thou hast said, but remove him not at a great distance from me, neither let him remain there too long, for my soul is bound within his soul. ⁷ And Abraham said unto Sarah, My daughter, let us pray to the Lord our God that he may do good with us. ⁸ And Sarah took her son Isaac and he abode all that night with her, and she kissed and embraced him, and gave him instructions till morning. ⁹ And she said to him, O my son, how can my soul separate itself from thee? And she still kissed him and embraced him, and she gave Abraham instructions concerning him. ¹⁰ And Sarah said to Abraham, O my lord, I pray thee take heed of thy son, and place thine eyes over him, for I have no other son nor daughter but him. ¹¹ O forsake him not. If he be hungry give him bread, and if he be thirsty give him water to drink; do not let him go on foot, neither let him sit in the sun. ¹² Neither let him go by himself in the road, neither force him from whatever he may desire, but do unto him as he may say to thee. ¹³ And Sarah wept bitterly the whole night on account of Isaac, and she gave him instructions till morning. ¹⁴ And in the morning Sarah selected a very fine and beautiful garment from those garments which she had in the house, that Abimelech had given to her. ¹⁵ And she dressed Isaac her son therewith, and she put a turban upon his head, and she enclosed a precious stone in the top of the turban, and she gave them provision for the road, and they went forth, and Isaac went with his father Abraham, and some of their servants accompanied them to see them off the road. ¹⁶ And Sarah went out with them, and she accompanied them upon the road to see them off, and they said to her, Return to the tent. ¹⁷ And when Sarah heard the words of her son Isaac she wept bitterly, and Abraham her husband wept with her, and their son wept with them a great weeping; also those who went with them wept greatly. ¹⁸ And Sarah caught hold of her son Isaac, and she held him in her arms, and she embraced him and continued to weep with him, and Sarah said, Who knoweth if after this day I shall ever see thee again? ¹⁹ And they still wept together, Abraham, Sarah and Isaac, and all those that accompanied them on the road wept with them, and Sarah afterward turned away from her son, weeping bitterly, and all her men servants and maid servants returned with her to the tent. ²⁰ And Abraham went with Isaac his son to bring him up as an offering before the Lord, as He had commanded him. ²¹ And Abraham took two of his young men with him, Ishmael the son of Hagar and Eliezer his servant, and they went together with them, and whilst they were walking in the road the young men spoke these words to themselves, ²² And Ishmael said to Eliezer, Now my father Abraham is going with Isaac to bring him up for a burnt offering to the Lord, as He commanded him. ²³ Now when he returneth he will give unto me all that he possesses, to inherit after him, for I am his first born. ²⁴ And Eliezer answered Ishmael and said, Surely Abraham did cast thee away with thy mother, and swear that thou shouldst not inherit any thing of all he possesses, and to whom will he give all that he has, with all his treasures, but unto me his servant, who has been faithful in his house, who has served him night and day, and has done all that he desired me? to me will he bequeath at his death all that he possesses. ²⁵ And whilst Abraham was proceeding with his son Isaac along the road, Satan came and appeared to Abraham in the figure of a very aged man, humble and of contrite spirit, and he approached Abraham and said to him, Art thou silly or brutish, that thou goest to do this thing this day to thine only son? ²⁶ For God gave thee a son in thy latter days, in thy old age, and wilt thou go and slaughter him this day because he committed no violence, and wilt thou cause the soul of thine only son to perish from the earth? ²⁷ Dost thou not know and understand that this thing cannot be from the Lord? for the Lord cannot do unto man such evil upon earth to say to him, Go slaughter thy child. ²⁸ And Abraham heard this and knew that it was the word of Satan who endeavored to draw him aside from the way of the Lord, but Abraham would not hearken to the voice of Satan, and Abraham rebuked him so that he went away. ²⁹ And Satan returned and came to Isaac; and he appeared unto Isaac in the figure of a young man comely and well favored. ³⁰ And he approached Isaac and said unto him, Dost thou not know and understand that thy old silly father bringeth thee to the slaughter this day for naught? ³¹ Now therefore, my son, do not listen nor attend to him, for he is a silly old man, and let not thy precious soul and beautiful figure be lost from the earth. ³² And Isaac heard this, and said unto Abraham, Hast thou heard, my father, that which this man has spoken? even thus has he spoken. ³³ And Abraham answered his son Isaac and said to him, Take heed of him and do not listen

to his words, nor attend to him, for he is Satan, endeavoring to draw us aside this day from the commands of God. ³⁴ And Abraham still rebuked Satan, and Satan went from them, and seeing he could not prevail over them he hid himself from them, and he went and passed before them in the road; and he transformed himself to a large brook of water in the road, and Abraham and Isaac and his two young men reached that place, and they saw a brook large and powerful as the mighty waters. ³⁵ And they entered the brook and passed through it, and the waters at first reached their legs. ³⁶ And they went deeper in the brook and the waters reached up to their necks, and they were all terrified on account of the water; and whilst they were going over the brook Abraham recognized that place, and he knew that there was no water there before. ³⁷ And Abraham said to his son Isaac, I know this place in which there was no brook nor water, now therefore it is this Satan who does all this to us, to draw us aside this day from the commands of God. ³⁸ And Abraham rebuked him and said unto him, The Lord rebuke thee, O Satan, begone from us for we go by the commands of God. ³⁹ And Satan was terrified at the voice of Abraham, and he went away from them, and the place again became dry land as it was at first. ⁴⁰ And Abraham went with Isaac toward the place that God had told him. ⁴¹ And on the third day Abraham lifted up his eyes and saw the place at a distance which God had told him of. ⁴² And a pillar of fire appeared to him that reached from the earth to heaven, and a cloud of glory upon the mountain, and the glory of the Lord was seen in the cloud. ⁴³ And Abraham said to Isaac, My son, dost thou see in that mountain, which we perceive at a distance, that which I see upon it? ⁴⁴ And Isaac answered and said unto his father, I see and lo a pillar of fire and a cloud, and the glory of the Lord is seen upon the cloud. ⁴⁵ And Abraham knew that his son Isaac was accepted before the Lord for a burnt offering. ⁴⁶ And Abraham said unto Eliezer and unto Ishmael his son, Do you also see that which we see upon the mountain which is at a distance? ⁴⁷ And they answered and said, We see nothing more than like the other mountains of the earth. And Abraham knew that they were not accepted before the Lord to go with them, and Abraham said to them, Abide ye here with the ass whilst I and Isaac my son will go to yonder mount and worship there before the Lord and then return to you. ⁴⁸ And Eliezer and Ishmael remained in that place, as Abraham had commanded. ⁴⁹ And Abraham took wood for a burnt offering and placed it upon his son Isaac, and he took the fire and the knife, and they both went to that place. ⁵⁰ And when they were going along Isaac said to his father, Behold, I see here the fire and wood, and where then is the lamb that is to be the burnt offering before the Lord? ⁵¹ And Abraham answered his son Isaac, saying, The Lord has made choice of thee my son, to be a perfect burnt offering instead of the lamb. ⁵² And Isaac said unto his father, I will do all that the Lord spoke to thee with joy and cheerfulness of heart. ⁵³ And Abraham again said unto Isaac his son, Is there in thy heart any thought or counsel concerning this, which is not proper? tell me my son, I pray thee, O my son conceal it not from me. ⁵⁴ And Isaac answered his father Abraham and said unto him, O my father, as the Lord liveth and as thy soul liveth, there is nothing in my heart to cause me to deviate either to the right or to the left from the word that he has spoken to thee. ⁵⁵ Neither limb nor muscle has moved or stirred at this, nor is there in my heart any thought or evil counsel concerning this. ⁵⁶ But I am of joyful and cheerful heart in this matter, and I say, Blessed is the Lord who has this day chosen me to be a burnt offering before Him. ⁵⁷ And Abraham greatly rejoiced at the words of Isaac, and they went on and came together to that place that the Lord had spoken of. ⁵⁸ And Abraham approached to build the altar in that place, and Abraham was weeping, and Isaac took stones and mortar until they had finished building the altar. ⁵⁹ And Abraham took the wood and placed it in order upon the altar which he had built. ⁶⁰ And he took his son Isaac and bound him in order to place him upon the wood which was upon the altar, to slay him for a burnt offering before the Lord. ⁶¹ And Isaac said to his father, Bind me securely and then place me upon the altar lest I should turn and move, and break loose from the force of the knife upon my flesh and thereof profane the burnt offering; and Abraham did so. ⁶² And Isaac still said to his father, O my father, when thou shalt have slain me and burnt me for an offering, take with thee that which shall remain of my ashes to bring to Sarah my mother, and say to her, This is the sweet smelling savor of Isaac; but do not tell her this if she should sit near a well or upon any high place, lest she should cast her soul after me and die. ⁶³ And Abraham heard the words of Isaac, and he lifted up his voice and wept when Isaac spake these words; and Abraham's tears gushed down upon Isaac his son, and Isaac wept bitterly, and he said to his father, Hasten thou, O my father, and do with me the will of the Lord our God as He has commanded thee. ⁶⁴ And the hearts of Abraham and Isaac rejoiced at this thing which the Lord had commanded them; but the eye wept bitterly whilst the heart rejoiced. ⁶⁵ And Abraham bound his son Isaac, and placed him on the altar upon the wood, and Isaac stretched forth his neck upon the altar before his father, and Abraham stretched forth his hand to take the knife to slay his son as a burnt offering before the Lord. ⁶⁶ At that time the angels of mercy came before the Lord and spake to him concerning Isaac, saying, ⁶⁷ ⁰ Lord, thou art a merciful and compassionate King over all that thou hast created in heaven and in earth, and thou supportest them all; give therefore ransom and redemption instead of thy servant Isaac, and pity and have compassion upon Abraham and Isaac his son, who are this day performing thy commands. ⁶⁸ Hast thou seen, O Lord, how Isaac the son of Abraham thy servant is bound down to the slaughter like an animal? now therefore let thy pity be roused for them, O Lord. ⁶⁹ At that time the Lord appeared unto Abraham, and called to him, from heaven, and said unto him, Lay not thine hand upon the lad, neither do thou any thing unto him, for now I know that thou fearest God in performing this act, and in not withholding thy son, thine only son, from me. ⁷⁰ And Abraham lifted up his eyes and saw, and behold, a ram was caught in a thicket by his horns; that was the ram which the Lord God had created in the earth in the day that he made earth and heaven. ⁷¹ For the Lord had prepared this ram from that day, to be a burnt offering instead of Isaac. ⁷² And this ram was advancing to Abraham when Satan caught hold of him and entangled his horns in the thicket, that he might not advance to Abraham, in order that Abraham might slay his son. ⁷³ And Abraham, seeing the ram advancing to him and Satan withholding him, fetched him and brought him before the altar, and he loosened his son Isaac from his binding, and he put the ram in his stead, and Abraham killed the ram upon the altar, and brought it up as an offering in the place of his son Isaac. ⁷⁴ And Abraham sprinkled some of the blood of the ram upon the altar, and he exclaimed and said, This is in the place of my son, and may this be considered this day as the blood of my son before the Lord. ⁷⁵ And all that Abraham did on this occasion by the altar, he would exclaim and say, This is in the room of my son, and may it this day be considered before the Lord in the place of my son; and Abraham finished the whole of the service by the altar, and the service was accepted before the Lord, and was accounted as if it had been Isaac; and the Lord blessed Abraham and his seed on that day. ⁷⁶ And Satan went to Sarah, and he appeared to her in the figure of an old man very humble and meek, and Abraham was yet engaged in the burnt offering before the Lord. ⁷⁷ And he said unto her, Dost thou not know all the work that Abraham has made with thine only son this day? for he took Isaac and built an altar, and killed him, and brought him up as a sacrifice upon the altar, and Isaac cried and wept before his father, but he looked not at him, neither did he have compassion over him. ⁷⁸ And Satan repeated these words, and he went away from her, and Sarah heard all the words of Satan, and she imagined him to be an old man from amongst the sons of men who had been with her son, and had come and told her these things. ⁷⁹ And Sarah lifted up her voice and wept and cried out bitterly on account of her son; and she threw herself upon the ground and she cast dust upon her head, and she said, O my son, Isaac my son, O that I had this day died instead of thee. And she continued to weep and said, It grieves me for thee, O my son, my son Isaac, O that I had died this day in thy stead. ⁸⁰ And she still continued to weep, and said, It grieves me for thee after that I have reared thee and have brought thee up; now my joy is turned into mourning over thee, I that had a longing for thee, and cried and prayed to God till I bare thee at ninety years old; and now hast thou served this day for the knife and the fire, to be made an offering. ⁸¹ But I console myself with thee, my son, in its being the word of the Lord, for thou didst perform the command of thy God; for who can transgress the word of our God, in whose hands is the soul of every living creature? ⁸² Thou art just, O Lord our God, for all thy works are good and righteous; for I also am rejoiced with thy word which thou didst command, and whilst mine eye weepeth bitterly my heart rejoiceth. ⁸³ And Sarah laid her head upon the bosom of one of her handmaids, and she became as still as a stone. ⁸⁴ She afterward rose up and went about making inquiries till she came to Hebron, and she inquired of all those whom she met walking in the road, and no one could tell her what had happened to her son. ⁸⁵ And she came with her maid servants and men servants to Kireath-arba, which is Hebron, and she asked concerning her Son, and she remained there while she sent some of her servants to seek where Abraham had gone with Isaac; they went to seek him in the house of Shem and Eber, and they could not find him, and they sought throughout the land and he was not there. ⁸⁶ And behold, Satan came to Sarah in the shape of an old man, and he came and stood before her, and he said unto her, I spoke falsely unto thee, for Abraham did not kill his son and he is not dead; and when she heard the word her joy was so exceedingly violent on account of her son, that her soul went out through joy; she died and was gathered to her people. ⁸⁷ And when Abraham had finished his service he returned with his son Isaac to his young men, and they rose up and went together to Beersheba, and they came home. ⁸⁸ And Abraham sought for Sarah, and could not find her, and he made inquiries concerning her, and they said unto him, She went as far as Hebron to seek you both where you had gone, for thus was she informed. ⁸⁹ And Abraham and Isaac went to her to Hebron, and when they found that she was dead they lifted up their voices and wept bitterly over her; and Isaac fell upon his mother's face and wept over her, and he said, O my mother, my mother, how hast thou left me, and where hast thou gone? O how, how hast thou left me! ⁹⁰ And Abraham and Isaac wept greatly and all their servants wept with them on account of Sarah, and they mourned over her a great and heavy mourning.

24

¹ And the life of Sarah was one hundred and twenty-seven years, and Sarah died; and Abraham rose up from before his dead to seek a burial place to bury his wife Sarah; and he went and spoke to the children of Heth, the inhabitants of the land, saying, ² I am a stranger and a sojourner with you in your land; give me a possession of a burial place in your land, that I may bury my dead from before me. ³ And the children of Heth said unto Abraham, behold the land is before thee, in the choice of our sepulchers bury thy dead, for no man shall withhold thee from burying thy dead. ⁴ And Abraham said unto them, If you are agreeable to this go and entreat for me to Ephron, the son of Zochar, requesting that he may give me the cave of Machpelah, which is in the end of his field, and I will purchase it of him for whatever he desire for it. ⁵ And Ephron dwelt among the children of Heth, and they went and called for him, and he came before Abraham, and Ephron said unto Abraham, Behold all thou requirest thy servant will do; and Abraham said, No, but I will buy the cave and the field which thou hast for value, In order that it may be for a possession of a burial place for ever. ⁶ And Ephron answered and said, Behold the field and the cave are before thee, give whatever thou desirest; and Abraham said, Only at full value will I buy it from thy hand, and from the hands of those that go in at the gate of thy city, and from the hand of thy seed for ever. ⁷ And Ephron and all his brethren heard this, and Abraham weighed to Ephron four hundred shekels of silver in the hands of Ephron and in the hands of all his brethren; and Abraham wrote this transaction, and he wrote it and testified it with four witnesses. ⁸ And these are the names of the witnesses, Amigal son of Abishna the Hittite, Adichorom son of Ashunach the Hivite, Abdon son of Achiram the Gomerite, Bakdil the son of Abudish the Zidonite. ⁹ And Abraham took the book of the purchase, and placed it in his treasures, and these are the words that Abraham wrote in the book, namely: ¹⁰ That the cave and the field Abraham bought from Ephron the Hittite, and from his seed, and from those that go out of his city, and from their seed for ever, are to be a purchase to Abraham and to his seed and to those that go forth from his loins, for a possession of a burial place for ever; and he put a signet to it and testified it with witnesses. ¹¹ And the field and the cave that was in it and all that place were made sure unto Abraham and unto his seed after him, from the children of Heth; behold it is before Mamre in Hebron, which is in the land of Canaan. ¹² And after this Abraham buried his wife Sarah there, and that place and all its boundary became to Abraham and unto his seed for a possession of a burial place. ¹³ And Abraham buried Sarah with pomp as observed at the interment of kings, and she was buried in very fine and beautiful garments. ¹⁴ And at her bier was Shem, his sons Eber and Abimelech, together with Anar, Ashcol and Mamre, and all the grandees of the land followed her bier. ¹⁵ And the days of Sarah were one hundred and twenty-seven years and she died, and Abraham made a great and heavy mourning, and he performed the rites of mourning for seven days. ¹⁶ And all the inhabitants of the land comforted Abraham and Isaac his son on account of Sarah. ¹⁷ And when the days of their mourning passed by Abraham sent away his son Isaac, and he went to the house of Shem and Eber, to learn the ways of the Lord and his instructions, and Abraham remained there three years. ¹⁸ At that time Abraham rose up with all his servants, and they went and returned homeward to Beersheba, and Abraham and all his servants remained in Beersheba. ¹⁹ And at the revolution of the year Abimelech king of the Philistines died in that year; he was one hundred and ninety-three years old at his death; and Abraham went with his people to the land of the Philistines, and they comforted the whole household and all his servants, and he then turned and went home. ²⁰ And it was after the death of Abimelech that the people of Gerar took Benmalich his son, and he was only twelve years old, and they made him lying in the place of his father. ²¹ And they called his name Abimelech after the name of his father, for thus was it their custom to do in Gerar, and Abimelech reigned instead of Abimelech his father, and he sat upon his throne. ²² And Lot the son of Haran also died in those days, in the thirty-ninth year of the life of Isaac, and all the days that Lot lived were one hundred and forty years and he died. ²³ And these are the children of Lot, that were born to him by his daughters, the name of the first born was Moab, and the name of the second was Benami. ²⁴ And the two sons of Lot went and took themselves wives from the land of Canaan, and they bare children to them, and the children of Moab were Ed, Mayon, Tarsus, and Kanvil, four sons, these are fathers to the children of Moab unto this day. ²⁵ And all the families of the children of Lot went to dwell wherever they should light upon, for they were fruitful and increased abundantly. ²⁶ And they went and built themselves cities in the land where they dwelt, and they called the names of the cities which they built after their own names. ²⁷ And Nahor the son of Terah, brother to Abraham, died in those days in the fortieth year of the life of Isaac, and all the days of Nahor were one hundred and seventy-two years and he died and was buried in Haran. ²⁸ And when Abraham heard that his brother was dead he grieved sadly, and he mourned over his brother many days. ²⁹ And Abraham called for Eliezer his head servant, to give him orders concerning his house, and he came and stood before him. ³⁰ And Abraham said to him, Behold I am old, I do not know the day of my death; for I am advanced in days; now therefore rise up, go forth and do not take a wife for my son from this place and from this land, from the daughters of the Canaanites amongst whom we dwell. ³¹ But go to my land and to my birthplace, and take from thence a wife for my son, and the Lord God of Heaven and earth who took me from my father's house and brought me to this place, and said unto me, To thy seed will I give this land for an inheritance for ever, he will send his angel before thee and prosper thy way, that thou mayest obtain a wife for my son from my family and from my father's house. ³² And the servant answered his master Abraham and said, Behold I go to thy birthplace and to thy father's house, and take a wife for thy son from there; but if the woman be not willing to follow me to this land, shall I take thy son back to the land of thy birthplace? ³³ And Abraham said unto him, Take heed that thou bring not my son hither again, for the Lord before whom I have walked he will send his angel before thee and prosper thy way. ³⁴ And Eliezer did as Abraham ordered him, and Eliezer swore unto Abraham his master upon this matter; and Eliezer rose up and took ten camels of the camels of his master, and ten men from his master's servants with him, and they rose up and went to Haran, the city of Abraham and Nahor, in order to fetch a wife for Isaac the son of Abraham; and whilst they were gone Abraham sent to the house of Shem and Eber, and they brought from thence his son Isaac. ³⁵ And Isaac came home to his father's house to Beersheba, whilst Eliezer and his men came to Haran; and they stopped in the city by the watering place, and he made his camels to kneel down by the water and they remained there. ³⁶ And Eliezer, Abraham's servant, prayed and said, O God of Abraham my master; send me I pray thee good speed this day and show kindness unto my master, that thou shalt appoint this day a wife for my master's son from his family. ³⁷ And the Lord hearkened to the voice of Eliezer, for the sake of his servant Abraham, and he happened to meet with the daughter of Bethuel, the son of Milcah, the wife of Nahor, brother to Abraham, and Eliezer came to her house. ³⁸ And Eliezer related to them all his concerns, and that he was Abraham's servant, and they greatly rejoiced at him. ³⁹ And they all blessed the Lord who brought this thing about, and they gave him Rebecca, the daughter of Bethuel, for a wife for Isaac. ⁴⁰ And the young woman was of very comely appearance, she was a virgin, and Rebecca was ten years old in those days. ⁴¹ And Bethuel and Laban and his children made a feast on that night, and Eliezer and his men came and ate and drank and rejoiced there on that night. ⁴² And Eliezer rose up in the morning, he and the men that were with him, and he called to the whole household of Bethuel, saying, Send me away that I may go to my master; and they rose up and sent away Rebecca and her nurse Deborah, the daughter of Uz, and they gave her silver and gold, men servants and maid servants, and they blessed her. ⁴³ And they sent Eliezer away with his men; and the servants took Rebecca, and he went and returned to his master to the land of Canaan. ⁴⁴ And Isaac took Rebecca and she became his wife, and he brought her into the tent. ⁴⁵ And Isaac was forty years old when he took Rebecca, the daughter of his uncle Bethuel, for a wife.

25

¹ And it was at that time that Abraham again took a wife in his old age, and her name was Keturah, from the land of Canaan. ² And she bare unto him Zimran, Jokshan, Medan, Midian, Ishbak and Shuach, being six sons. And the children of Zimran were Abihen, Molich and Narim. ³ And the sons of Jokshan were Sheba and Dedan, and the sons of Medan were Amida, Joab, Gochi, Elisha and Nothach; and the sons of Midian were Ephah, Epher, Chanoch, Abida and Eldaah. ⁴ And the sons of Ishbak were Makiro, Beyodua and Tator. ⁵ And the sons of Shuach were Bildad, Mamdad, Munan and Meban; all these are the families of the children of Keturah the Canaanitish woman which she bare unto Abraham the Hebrew. ⁶ And Abraham sent all these away, and he gave them gifts, and they went away from his son Isaac to dwell wherever they should find a place. ⁷ And all these went to the mountain at the east, and they built themselves six cities in which they dwelt unto this day. ⁸ But the children of Sheba and Dedan, children of Jokshan, with their children, did not dwell with their brethren in their cities, and they journeyed and encamped in the countries and

wildernesses unto this day. ⁹ And the children of Midian, son of Abraham, went to the east of the land of Cush, and they there found a large valley in the eastern country, and they remained there and built a city, and they dwelt therein, that is the land of Midian unto this day. ¹⁰ And Midian dwelt in the city which he built, he and his five sons and all belonging to him. ¹¹ And these are the names of the sons of Midian according to their names in their cities, Ephah, Epher, Chanoch, Abida and Eldaah. ¹² And the sons of Ephah were Methach, Meshar, Avi and Tzanua, and the sons of Epher were Ephron, Zur, Alirun and Medin, and the sons of Chanoch were Reuel, Rekem, Azi, Alyoshub and Alad. ¹³ And the sons of Abida were Chur, Melud, Kerury, Molchi; and the sons of Eldaah were Miker, and Reba, and Malchiyah and Gabol; these are the names of the Midianites according to their families; and afterward the families of Midian spread throughout the land of Midian. ¹⁴ And these are the generations of Ishmael the son Abraham, whom Hagar, Sarah's handmaid, bare unto Abraham. ¹⁵ And Ishmael took a wife from the land of Egypt, and her name was Ribah, the same is Meribah. ¹⁶ And Ribah bare unto Ishmael Nebayoth, Kedar, Adbeel, Mibsam and their sister Bosmath. ¹⁷ And Ishmael cast away his wife Ribah, and she went from him and returned to Egypt to the house of her father, and she dwelt there, for she had been very bad in the sight of Ishmael, and in the sight of his father Abraham. ¹⁸ And Ishmael afterward took a wife from the land of Canaan, and her name was Malchuth, and she bare unto him Nishma, Dumah, Masa, Chadad, Tema, Yetur, Naphish and Kedma. ¹⁹ These are the sons of Ishmael, and these are their names, being twelve princes according to their nations; and the families of Ishmael afterward spread forth, and Ishmael took his children and all the property that he had gained, together with the souls of his household and all belonging to him, and they went to dwell where they should find a place. ²⁰ And they went and dwelt near the wilderness of Paran, and their dwelling was from Havilah unto Shur, that is before Egypt as thou comest toward Assyria. ²¹ And Ishmael and his sons dwelt in the land, and they had children born to them, and they were fruitful and increased abundantly. ²² And these are the names of the sons of Nebayoth the first born of Ishmael; Mend, Send, Mayon; and the sons of Kedar were Alyon, Kezem, Chamad and Eli. ²³ And the sons of Adbeel were Chamad and Jabin; and the sons of Mibsam were Obadiah, Ebedmelech and Yeush; these are the families of the children of Ribah the wife of Ishmael. ²⁴ And the sons of Mishma the son of Ishmael were Shamua, Zecaryon and Obed; and the sons of Dumah were Kezed, Eli, Machmad and Amed. ²⁵ And the sons of Masa were Melon, Mula and Ebidadon; and the sons of Chadad were Azur, Minzar and Ebedmelech; and the sons of Tema were Seir, Sadon and Yakol. ²⁶ And the sons of Yetur were Merith, Yaish, Alyo, and Pachoth; and the sons of Naphish were Ebed-Tamed, Abiyasaph and Mir; and the sons of Kedma were Calip, Tachti, and Omir; these were the children of Malchuth the wife of Ishmael according to their families. ²⁷ All these are the families of Ishmael according to their generations, and they dwelt in those lands wherein they had built themselves cities unto this day. ²⁸ And Rebecca the daughter of Bethuel, the wife of Abraham's son Isaac, was barren in those days, she had no offspring; and Isaac dwelt with his father in the land of Canaan; and the Lord was with Isaac; and Arpachshad the son of Shem the son of Noah died in those days, in the forty-eighth year of the life of Isaac, and all the days that Arpachshad lived were four hundred and thirty-eight years, and he died.

26

¹ And in the fifty-ninth year of the life of Isaac the son of Abraham, Rebecca his wife was still barren in those days. ² And Rebecca said unto Isaac, Truly I have heard, my lord, that thy mother Sarah was barren in her days until my Lord Abraham, thy father, prayed for her and she conceived by him. ³ Now therefore stand up, pray thou also to God and he will hear thy prayer and remember us through his mercies. ⁴ And Isaac answered his wife Rebecca, saying, Abraham has already prayed for me to God to multiply his seed, now therefore this barrenness must proceed to us from thee. ⁵ And Rebecca said unto him, But arise now thou also and pray, that the Lord may hear thy prayer and grant me children, and Isaac hearkened to the words of his wife, and Isaac and his wife rose up and went to the land of Moriah to pray there and to seek the Lord, and when they had reached that place Isaac stood up and prayed to the Lord on account of his wife because she was barren. ⁶ And Isaac said, O Lord God of heaven and earth, whose goodness and mercies fill the earth, thou who didst take my father from his father's house and from his birthplace, and didst bring him unto this land, and didst say unto him, To thy seed will I give the land, and thou didst promise him and didst declare unto him, I will multiply thy seed as the stars of heaven and as the sand of the sea, now may thy words be verified which thou didst speak unto my father. ⁷ For thou art the Lord our God, our eyes are toward thee to give us seed of men, as thou didst promise us, for thou art the Lord our God and our eyes are directed toward thee only. ⁸ And the Lord heard the prayer of Isaac the son of Abraham, and the Lord was entreated of him and Rebecca his wife conceived. ⁹ And in about seven months after the children struggled together within her, and it pained her greatly that she was wearied on account of them, and she said to all the women who were then in the land, Did such a thing happen to you as it has to me? and they said unto her, No. ¹⁰ And she said unto them, Why am I alone in this amongst all the women that were upon earth? and she went to the land of Moriah to seek the Lord on account of this; and she went to Shem and Eber his son to make inquiries of them in this matter, and that they should seek the Lord in this thing respecting her. ¹¹ And she also asked Abraham to seek and inquire of the Lord about all that had befallen her. ¹² And they all inquired of the Lord concerning this matter, and they brought her word from the Lord and told her, Two children are in thy womb, and two nations shall rise from them; and one nation shall be stronger than the other, and the greater shall serve the younger. ¹³ And when her days to be delivered were completed, she knelt down, and behold there were twins in her womb, as the Lord had spoken to her. ¹⁴ And the first came out red all over like a hairy garment, and all the people of the land called his name Esau, saying, That this one was made complete from the womb. ¹⁵ And after that came his brother, and his hand took hold of Esau's heel, therefore they called his name Jacob. ¹⁶ And Isaac, the son of Abraham, was sixty years old when he begat them. ¹⁷ And the boys grew up to their fifteenth year, and they came amongst the society of men. Esau was a designing and deceitful man, and an expert hunter in the field, and Jacob was a man perfect and wise, dwelling in tents, feeding flocks and learning the instructions of the Lord and the commands of his father and mother. ¹⁸ And Isaac and the children of his household dwelt with his father Abraham in the land of Canaan, as God had commanded them. ¹⁹ And Ishmael the son of Abraham went with his children and all belonging to them, and they returned there to the land of Havilah, and they dwelt there. ²⁰ And all the children of Abraham's concubines went to dwell in the land of the east, for Abraham had sent them away from his son, and had given them presents, and they went away. ²¹ And Abraham gave all that he had to his son Isaac, and he also gave him all his treasures. ²² And he commanded him saying, Dost thou not know and understand the Lord is God in heaven and in earth, and there is no other beside him? ²³ And it was he who took me from my father's house, and from my birth place, and gave me all the delights upon earth; who delivered me from the counsel of the wicked, for in him did I trust. ²⁴ And he brought me to this place, and he delivered me from Ur Casdim; and he said unto me, To thy seed will I give all these lands, and they shall inherit them when they keep my commandments, my statutes and my judgments that I have commanded thee, and which I shall command them. ²⁵ Now therefore my son, hearken to my voice, and keep the commandments of the Lord thy God, which I commanded thee, do not turn from the right way either to the right or to the left, in order that it may be well with thee and thy children after thee forever. ²⁶ And remember the wonderful works of the Lord, and his kindness that he has shown toward us, in having delivered us from the hands of our enemies, and the Lord our God caused them to fall into our hands; and now therefore keep all that I have commanded thee, and turn not away from the commandments of thy God, and serve none beside him, in order that it may be well with thee and thy seed after thee. ²⁷ And teach thou thy children and thy seed the instructions of the Lord and his commandments, and teach them the upright way in which they should go, in order that it may be well with them forever. ²⁸ And Isaac answered his father and said unto him, That which my Lord has commanded that will I do, and I will not depart from the commands of the Lord my God, I will keep all that he commanded me; and Abraham blessed his son Isaac, and also his children; and Abraham taught Jacob the instruction of the Lord and his ways. ²⁹ And it was at that time that Abraham died, in the fifteenth year of the life of Jacob and Esau, the sons of Isaac, and all the days of Abraham were one hundred and seventy-five years, and he died and was gathered to his people in good old age, old and satisfied with days, and Isaac and Ishmael his sons buried him. ³⁰ And when the inhabitants of Canaan heard that Abraham was dead, they all came with their kings and princes and all their men to bury Abraham. ³¹ And all the inhabitants of the land of Haran, and all the families of the house of Abraham, and all the princes and grandees, and the sons of Abraham by the concubines, all came when they heard of Abraham's death, and they requited Abraham's kindness, and comforted Isaac his son, and they buried Abraham in the cave which he bought from Ephron the Hittite and his children, for the possession of a burial place. ³² And all the inhabitants of Canaan, and all those who had known Abraham, wept for Abraham a whole year, and men and women mourned over him. ³³ And all the little children, and all the inhabitants of the land wept on account of Abraham, for Abraham had been good to them all, and because he had been upright with God and men. ³⁴ And there arose not a man who feared God like unto Abraham, for he had feared his God

from his youth, and had served the Lord, and had gone in all his ways during his life, from his childhood to the day of his death. ³⁵ And the Lord was with him and delivered him from the counsel of Nimrod and his people, and when he made war with the four kings of Elam he conquered them. ³⁶ And he brought all the children of the earth to the service of God, and he taught them the ways of the Lord, and caused them to know the Lord. ³⁷ And he formed a grove and he planted a vineyard therein, and he had always prepared in his tent meat and drink to those that passed through the land, that they might satisfy themselves in his house. ³⁸ And the Lord God delivered the whole earth on account of Abraham. ³⁹ And it was after the death of Abraham that God blessed his son Isaac and his children, and the Lord was with Isaac as he had been with his father Abraham, for Isaac kept all the commandments of the Lord as Abraham his father had commanded him; he did not turn to the right or to the left from the right path which his father had commanded him.

27

¹ And Esau at that time, after the death of Abraham, frequently went in the field to hunt. ² And Nimrod king of Babel, the same was Amraphel, also frequently went with his mighty men to hunt in the field, and to walk about with his men in the cool of the day. ³ And Nimrod was observing Esau all the days, for a jealousy was formed in the heart of Nimrod against Esau all the days. ⁴ And on a certain day Esau went in the field to hunt, and he found Nimrod walking in the wilderness with his two men. ⁵ And all his mighty men and his people were with him in the wilderness, but they removed at a distance from him, and they went from him in different directions to hunt, and Esau concealed himself for Nimrod, and he lurked for him in the wilderness. ⁶ And Nimrod and his men that were with him did not know him, and Nimrod and his men frequently walked about in the field at the cool of the day, and to know where his men were hunting in the field. ⁷ And Nimrod and two of his men that were with him came to the place where they were, when Esau started suddenly from his lurking place, and drew his sword, and hastened and ran to Nimrod and cut off his head. ⁸ And Esau fought a desperate fight with the two men that were with Nimrod, and when they called out to him, Esau turned to them and smote them to death with his sword. ⁹ And all the mighty men of Nimrod, who had left him to go to the wilderness, heard the cry at a distance, and they knew the voices of those two men, and they ran to know the cause of it, when they found their king and the two men that were with him lying dead in the wilderness. ¹⁰ And when Esau saw the mighty men of Nimrod coming at a distance, he fled, and thereby escaped; and Esau took the valuable garments of Nimrod, which Nimrod's father had bequeathed to Nimrod, and with which Nimrod prevailed over the whole land, and he ran and concealed them in his house. ¹¹ And Esau took those garments and ran into the city on account of Nimrod's men, and he came unto his father's house wearied and exhausted from fight, and he was ready to die through grief when he approached his brother Jacob and sat before him. ¹² And he said unto his brother Jacob, Behold I shall die this day, and wherefore then do I want the birthright? And Jacob acted wisely with Esau in this matter, and Esau sold his birthright to Jacob, for it was so brought about by the Lord. ¹³ And Esau's portion in the cave of the field of Machpelah, which Abraham had bought from the children of Heth for the possession of a burial ground, Esau also sold to Jacob, and Jacob bought all this from his brother Esau for value given. ¹⁴ And Jacob wrote the whole of this in a book, and he testified the same with witnesses, and he sealed it, and the book remained in the hands of Jacob. ¹⁵ And when Nimrod the son of Cush died, his men lifted him up and brought him in consternation, and buried him in his city, and all the days that Nimrod lived were two hundred and fifteen years and he died. ¹⁶ And the days that Nimrod reigned upon the people of the land were one hundred and eighty-five years; and Nimrod died by the sword of Esau in shame and contempt, and the seed of Abraham caused his death as he had seen in his dream. ¹⁷ And at the death of Nimrod his kingdom became divided into many divisions, and all those parts that Nimrod reigned over were restored to the respective kings of the land, who recovered them after the death of Nimrod, and all the people of the house of Nimrod were for a long time enslaved to all the other kings of the land.

28

¹ And in those days, after the death of Abraham, in that year the Lord brought a heavy famine in the land, and whilst the famine was raging in the land of Canaan, Isaac rose up to go down to Egypt on account of the famine, as his father Abraham had done. ² And the Lord appeared that night to Isaac and he said to him, Do not go down to Egypt but rise and go to Gerar, to Abimelech king of the Philistines, and remain there till the famine shall cease. ³ And Isaac rose up and went to Gerar, as the Lord commanded him, and he remained there a full year. ⁴ And when Isaac came to Gerar, the people of the land saw that Rebecca his wife was of a beautiful appearance, and the people of Gerar asked Isaac concerning his wife, and he said, She is my sister, for he was afraid to say she was his wife lest the people of the land should slay him on account of her. ⁵ And the princes of Abimelech went and praised the woman to the king, but he answered them not, neither did he attend to their words. ⁶ But he heard them say that Isaac declared her to be his sister, so the king reserved this within himself. ⁷ And when Isaac had remained three months in the land, Abimelech looked out at the window, and he saw, and behold Isaac was sporting with Rebecca his wife, for Isaac dwelt in the outer house belonging to the king, so that the house of Isaac was opposite the house of the king. ⁸ And the king said unto Isaac, What is this thou hast done to us in saying of thy wife, She is my sister? how easily might one of the great men of the people have lain with her, and thou wouldst then have brought guilt upon us. ⁹ And Isaac said unto Abimelech, Because I was afraid lest I die on account of my wife, therefore I said, She is my sister. ¹⁰ At that time Abimelech gave orders to all his princes and great men, and they took Isaac and Rebecca his wife and brought them before the king. ¹¹ And the king commanded that they should dress them in princely garments, and make them ride through the streets of the city, and proclaim before them throughout the land, saying, This is the man and this is his wife; whoever toucheth this man or his wife shall surely die. And Isaac returned with his wife to the king's house, and the Lord was with Isaac and he continued to wax great and lacked nothing. ¹² And the Lord caused Isaac to find favor in the sight of Abimelech, and in the sight of all his subjects, and Abimelech acted well with Isaac, for Abimelech remembered the oath and the covenant that existed between his father and Abraham. ¹³ And Abimelech said unto Isaac, Behold the whole earth is before thee; dwell wherever it may seem good in thy sight until thou shalt return to thy land; and Abimelech gave Isaac fields and vineyards and the best part of the land of Gerar, to sow and reap and eat the fruits of the ground until the days of the famine should have passed by. ¹⁴ And Isaac sowed in that land, and received a hundred-fold in the same year, and the Lord blessed him. ¹⁵ And the man waxed great, and he had possession of flocks and possession of herds and great store of servants. ¹⁶ And when the days of the famine had passed away the Lord appeared to Isaac and said unto him, Rise up, go forth from this place and return to thy land, to the land of Canaan; and Isaac rose up and returned to Hebron which is in the land of Canaan, he and all belonging to him as the Lord commanded him. ¹⁷ And after this Shelach the son of Arpachshad died in that year, which is the eighteenth year of the lives of Jacob and Esau; and all the days that Shelach lived were four hundred and thirty-three years and he died. ¹⁸ At that time Isaac sent his younger son Jacob to the house of Shem and Eber, and he learned the instructions of the Lord, and Jacob remained in the house of Shem and Eber for thirty-two years, and Esau his brother did not go, for he was not willing to go, and he remained in his father's house in the land of Canaan. ¹⁹ And Esau was continually hunting in the fields to bring home what he could get, so did Esau all the days. ²⁰ And Esau was a designing and deceitful man, one who hunted after the hearts of men and inveigled them, and Esau was a valiant man in the field, and in the course of time went as usual to hunt; and he came as far as the field of Seir, the same is Edom. ²¹ And he remained in the land of Seir hunting in the field a year and four months. ²² And Esau there saw in the land of Seir the daughter of a man of Canaan, and her name was Jehudith, the daughter of Beeri, son of Epher, from the families of Heth the son of Canaan. ²³ And Esau took her for a wife, and he came unto her; forty years old was Esau when he took her, and he brought her to Hebron, the land of his father's dwelling place, and he dwelt there. ²⁴ And it came to pass in those days, in the hundred and tenth year of the life of Isaac, that is in the fiftieth year of the life of Jacob, in that year died Shem the son of Noah; Shem was six hundred years old at his death. ²⁵ And when Shem died Jacob returned to his father to Hebron which is in the land of Canaan. ²⁶ And in the fifty-sixth year of the life of Jacob, people came from Haran, and Rebecca was told concerning her brother Laban the son of Bethuel. ²⁷ For the wife of Laban was barren in those days, and bare no children, and also all his handmaids bare none to him. ²⁸ And the Lord afterward remembered Adinah the wife of Laban, and she conceived and bare twin daughters, and Laban called the names of his daughters, the name of the elder Leah, and the name of the younger Rachel. ²⁹ And those people came and told these things to Rebecca, and Rebecca rejoiced greatly that the Lord had visited her brother and that he had got children.

29

¹ And Isaac the son of Abraham became old and advanced in days, and his eyes became heavy through age; they were dim and could not see. ² At that time Isaac called unto Esau his son, saying, Get I pray thee thy weapons, thy quiver and thy bow, rise up and go forth into the field and get me some venison, and make me savory meat and bring it to me, that I may eat in

order that I may bless thee before my death, as I have now become old and gray-headed. ³ And Esau did so; and he took his weapon and went forth into the field to hunt for venison, as usual, to bring to his father as he had ordered him, so that he might bless him. ⁴ And Rebecca heard all the words that Isaac had spoken unto Esau, and she hastened and called her son Jacob, saying, Thus did thy father speak unto thy brother Esau, and thus did I hear, now therefore hasten thou and make that which I shall tell thee. ⁵ Rise up and go, I pray thee, to the flock and fetch me two fine kids of the goats, and I will get the savory meat for thy father, and thou shalt bring the savory meat that he may eat before thy brother shall have come from the chase, in order that thy father may bless thee. ⁶ And Jacob hastened and did as his mother had commanded him, and he made the savory meat and brought it before his father before Esau had come from his chase. ⁷ And Isaac said unto Jacob, Who art thou, my son? And he said, I am thy first born Esau, I have done as thou didst order me, now therefore rise up I pray thee, and eat of my hunt, in order that thy soul may bless me as thou didst speak unto me. ⁸ And Isaac rose up and he ate and he drank, and his heart was comforted, and he blessed Jacob and Jacob went away from his father; and as soon as Isaac had blessed Jacob and he had gone away from him, behold Esau came from his hunt from the field, and he also made savory meat and brought it to his father to eat thereof and to bless him. ⁹ And Isaac said unto Esau, And who was he that has taken venison and brought it me before thou camest and whom I did bless? And Esau knew that his brother Jacob had done this, and the anger of Esau was kindled against his brother Jacob that he had acted thus toward him. ¹⁰ And Esau said, Is he not rightly called Jacob? for he has supplanted me twice, he took away my birthright and now he has taken away my blessing; and Esau wept greatly; and when Isaac heard the voice of his son Esau weeping, Isaac said unto Esau, What can I do, my son, thy brother came with subtlety and took away thy blessing; and Esau hated his brother Jacob on account of the blessing that his father had given him, and his anger was greatly roused against him. ¹¹ And Jacob was very much afraid of his brother Esau, and he rose up and fled to the house of Eber the son of Shem, and he concealed himself there on account of his brother, and Jacob was sixty-three years old when he went forth from the land of Canaan from Hebron, and Jacob was concealed in Eber's house fourteen years on account of his brother Esau, and he there continued to learn the ways of the Lord and his commandments. ¹² And when Esau saw that Jacob had fled and escaped from him, and that Jacob had cunningly obtained the blessing, then Esau grieved exceedingly, and he was also vexed at his father and mother; and he also rose up and took his wife and went away from his father and mother to the land of Seir, and he dwelt there; and Esau saw there a woman from amongst the daughters of Heth whose name was Bosmath, the daughter of Elon the Hittite, and he took her for a wife in addition to his first wife, and Esau called her name Adah, saying the blessing had in that time passed from him. ¹³ And Esau dwelt in the land of Seir six months without seeing his father and mother, and afterward Esau took his wives and rose up and returned to the land of Canaan, and Esau placed his two wives in his father's house in Hebron. ¹⁴ And the wives of Esau vexed and provoked Isaac and Rebecca with their works, for they walked not in the ways of the Lord, but served their father's gods of wood and stone as their father had taught them, and they were more wicked than their father. ¹⁵ And they went according to the evil desires of their hearts, and they sacrificed and burnt incense to the Baalim, and Isaac and Rebecca became weary of them. ¹⁶ And Rebecca said, I am weary of my life because of the daughters of Heth; if Jacob take a wife of the daughters of Heth, such as these which are of the daughters of the land, what good then is life unto me? ¹⁷ And in those days Adah the wife of Esau conceived and bare him a son, and Esau called the name of the son that was born unto him Eliphaz, and Esau was sixty-five years old when she bare him. ¹⁸ And Ishmael the son of Abraham died in those days, in the sixty-forth year of the life of Jacob, and all the days that Ishmael lived were one hundred and thirty-seven years and he died. ¹⁹ And when Isaac heard that Ishmael was dead he mourned for him, and Isaac lamented over him many days. ²⁰ And at the end of fourteen years of Jacob's residing in the house of Eber, Jacob desired to see his father and mother, and Jacob came to the house of his father and mother to Hebron, and Esau had in those days forgotten what Jacob had done to him in having taken the blessing from him in those days. ²¹ And when Esau saw Jacob coming to his father and mother he remembered what Jacob had done to him, and he was greatly incensed against him and he sought to slay him. ²² And Isaac the son of Abraham was old and advanced in days, and Esau said, Now my father's time is drawing nigh that he must die, and when he shall die I will slay my brother Jacob. ²³ And this was told to Rebecca, and she hastened and sent and called for Jacob her son, and she said unto him, Arise, go and flee to Haran to my brother Laban, and remain there for some time, until thy brother's anger be turned from thee and then shalt thou come back. ²⁴ And Isaac called unto Jacob and said unto him, Take not a wife from the daughters of Canaan, for thus did our father Abraham command us according to the word of the Lord which he had commanded him, saying, Unto thy seed will I give this land; if thy children keep my covenant that I have made with thee, then will I also perform to thy children that which I have spoken unto thee and I will not forsake them. ²⁵ Now therefore my son hearken to my voice, to all that I shall command thee, and refrain from taking a wife from amongst the daughters of Canaan; arise, go to Haran to the house of Bethuel thy mother's father, and take unto thee a wife from there from the daughters of Laban thy mother's brother. ²⁶ Therefore take heed lest thou shouldst forget the Lord thy God and all his ways in the land to which thou goest, and shouldst get connected with the people of the land and pursue vanity and forsake the Lord thy God. ²⁷ But when thou comest to the land serve there the Lord, do not turn to the right or to the left from the way which I commanded thee and which thou didst learn. ²⁸ And may the Almighty God grant thee favor in the sight of the people of the earth, that thou mayest take there a wife according to thy choice; one who is good and upright in the ways of the Lord. ²⁹ And may God give unto thee and thy seed the blessing of thy father Abraham, and make thee fruitful and multiply thee, and mayest thou become a multitude of people in the land whither thou goest, and may God cause thee to return to this land, the land of thy father's dwelling, with children and with great riches, with joy and with pleasure. ³⁰ And Isaac finished commanding Jacob and blessing him, and he gave him many gifts, together with silver and gold, and he sent him away; and Jacob hearkened to his father and mother; he kissed them and arose and went to Padan-aram; and Jacob was seventy-seven years old when he went out from the land of Canaan from Beersheba. ³¹ And when Jacob went away to go to Haran Esau called unto his son Eliphaz, and secretly spoke unto him, saying, Now hasten, take thy sword in thy hand and pursue Jacob and pass before him in the road, and lurk for him, and slay him with thy sword in one of the mountains, and take all belonging to him and come back. ³² And Eliphaz the son of Esau was an active man and expert with the bow as his father had taught him, and he was a noted hunter in the field and a valiant man. ³³ And Eliphaz did as his father had commanded him, and Eliphaz was at that time thirteen years old, and Eliphaz rose up and went and took ten of his mother's brothers with him and pursued Jacob. ³⁴ And he closely followed Jacob, and he lurked for him in the border of the land of Canaan opposite to the city of Shechem. ³⁵ And Jacob saw Eliphaz and his men pursuing him, and Jacob stood still in the place in which he was going, in order to know what this was, for he did not know the thing; and Eliphaz drew his sword and he went on advancing, he and his men, toward Jacob; and Jacob said unto them, What is to do with you that you have come hither, and what meaneth it that you pursue with your swords. ³⁶ And Eliphaz came near to Jacob and he answered and said unto him, Thus did my father command me, and now therefore I will not deviate from the orders which my father gave me; and when Jacob saw that Esau had spoken to Eliphaz to employ force, Jacob then approached and supplicated Eliphaz and his men, saying to him, ³⁷ Behold all that I have and which my father and mother gave unto me, that take unto thee and go from me, and do not slay me, and may this thing be accounted unto thee a righteousness. ³⁸ And the Lord caused Jacob to find favor in the sight of Eliphaz the son of Esau, and his men, and they hearkened to the voice of Jacob, and they did not put him to death, and Eliphaz and his men took all belonging to Jacob together with the silver and gold that he had brought with him from Beersheba; they left him nothing. ³⁹ And Eliphaz and his men went away from him and they returned to Esau to Beersheba, and they told him all that had occurred to them with Jacob, and they gave him all that they had taken from Jacob. ⁴⁰ And Esau was indignant at Eliphaz his son, and at his men that were with him, because they had not put Jacob to death. ⁴¹ And they answered and said unto Esau, Because Jacob supplicated us in this matter not to slay him, our pity was excited toward him, and we took all belonging to him and brought it unto thee; and Esau took all the silver and gold which Eliphaz had taken from Jacob and he put them by in his house. ⁴² At that time when Esau saw that Isaac had blessed Jacob, and had commanded him, saying, Thou shalt not take a wife from amongst the daughters of Canaan, and that the daughters of Canaan were bad in the sight of Isaac and Rebecca, ⁴³ Then he went to the house of Ishmael his uncle, and in addition to his older wives he took Machlath the daughter of Ishmael, the sister of Nebayoth, for a wife.

30

¹ And Jacob went forth continuing his road to Haran, and he came as far as mount Moriah, and he tarried there all night near the city of Luz; and the Lord appeared there unto Jacob on that night, and he said unto him, I am the Lord God of Abraham and the God of Isaac thy father; the land upon which thou liest I will give unto thee and thy seed. ² And behold I am with

thee and will keep thee wherever thou goest, and I will multiply thy seed as the stars of Heaven, and I will cause all thine enemies to fall before thee; and when they shall make war with thee they shall not prevail over thee, and I will bring thee again unto this land with joy, with children, and with great riches. ³ And Jacob awoke from his sleep and he rejoiced greatly at the vision which he had seen; and he called the name of that place Bethel. ⁴ And Jacob rose up from that place quite rejoiced, and when he walked his feet felt light to him for joy, and he went from there to the land of the children of the East, and he returned to Haran and he set by the shepherd's well. ⁵ And he there found some men; going from Haran to feed their flocks, and Jacob made inquiries of them, and they said, We are from Haran. ⁶ And he said unto them, Do you know Laban, the son of Nahor? and they said, We know him, and behold his daughter Rachel is coming along to feed her father's flock. ⁷ Whilst he was yet speaking with them, Rachel the daughter of Laban came to feed her father's sheep, for she was a shepherdess. ⁸ And when Jacob saw Rachel, the daughter of Laban, his mother's brother, he ran and kissed her, and lifted up his voice and wept. ⁹ And Jacob told Rachel that he was the son of Rebecca, her father's sister, and Rachel ran and told her father, and Jacob continued to cry because he had nothing with him to bring to the house of Laban. ¹⁰ And when Laban heard that his sister's son Jacob had come, he ran and kissed him and embraced him and brought him into the house and gave him bread, and he ate. ¹¹ And Jacob related to Laban what his brother Esau had done to him, and what his son Eliphaz had done to him in the road. ¹² And Jacob resided in Laban's house for one month, and Jacob ate and drank in the house of Laban, and afterward Laban said unto Jacob, Tell me what shall be thy wages, for how canst thou serve me for nought? ¹³ And Laban had no sons but only daughters, and his other wives and handmaids were still barren in those days; and these are the names of Laban's daughters which his wife Adinah had borne unto him; the name of the elder was Leah and the name of the younger was Rachel; and Leah was tender-eyed, but Rachel was beautiful and well favored, and Jacob loved her. ¹⁴ And Jacob said unto Laban, I will serve thee seven years for Rachel thy younger daughter; and Laban consented to this and Jacob served Laban seven years for his daughter Rachel. ¹⁵ And in the second year of Jacob's dwelling in Haran, that is in the seventy ninth year of the life of Jacob, in that year died Eber the son of Shem, he was four hundred and sixty-four years old at his death. ¹⁶ And when Jacob heard that Eber was dead he grieved exceedingly, and he lamented and mourned over him many days. ¹⁷ And in the third year of Jacob's dwelling in Haran, Bosmath, the daughter of Ishmael, the wife of Esau, bare unto him a son, and Esau called his name Reuel. ¹⁸ And in the fourth year of Jacob's residence in the house of Laban, the Lord visited Laban and remembered him on account of Jacob, and sons were born unto him, and his first born was Beor, his second was Alib, and the third was Chorash. ¹⁹ And the Lord gave Laban riches and honor, sons and daughters, and the man increased greatly on account of Jacob. ²⁰ And Jacob in those days served Laban in all manner of work, in the house and in the field, and the blessing of the Lord was in all that belonged to Laban in the house and in the field. ²¹ And in the fifth year died Jehudith, the daughter of Beeri, the wife of Esau, in the land of Canaan, and she had no sons but daughters only. ²² And these are the names of her daughters which she bare to Esau, the name of the elder was Marzith, and the name of the younger was Puith. ²³ And when Jehudith died, Esau rose up and went to Seir to hunt in the field, as usual, and Esau dwelt in the land of Seir for a long time. ²⁴ And in the sixth year Esau took for a wife, in addition to his other wives, Ahlibamah, the daughter of Zebeon the Hivite, and Esau brought her to the land of Canaan. ²⁵ And Ahlibamah conceived and bare unto Esau three sons, Yeush, Yaalan, and Korah. ²⁶ And in those days, in the land of Canaan, there was a quarrel between the herdsmen of Esau and the herdsmen of the inhabitants of the land of Canaan, for Esau's cattle and goods were too abundant for him to remain in the land of Canaan, in his father's house, and the land of Canaan could not bear him on account of his cattle. ²⁷ And when Esau saw that his quarreling increased with the inhabitants of the land of Canaan, he rose up and took his wives and his sons and his daughters, and all belonging to him, and the cattle which he possessed, and all his property that he had acquired in the land of Canaan, and he went away from the inhabitants of the land to the land of Seir, and Esau and all belonging to him dwelt in the land of Seir. ²⁸ But from time to time Esau would go and see his father and mother in the land of Canaan, and Esau intermarried with the Horites, and he gave his daughters to the sons of Seir, the Horite. ²⁹ And he gave his elder daughter Marzith to Anah, the son of Zebeon, his wife's brother, and Puith he gave to Azar, the son of Bilhan the Horite; and Esau dwelt in the mountain, he and his children, and they were fruitful and multiplied.

31

¹ And in the seventh year, Jacob's service which he served Laban was completed, and Jacob said unto Laban, Give me my wife, for the days of my service are fulfilled; and Laban did so, and Laban and Jacob assembled all the people of that place and they made a feast. ² And in the evening Laban came to the house, and afterward Jacob came there with the people of the feast, and Laban extinguished all the lights that were there in the house. ³ And Jacob said unto Laban, Wherefore dost thou do this thing unto us? and Laban answered, Such is our custom to act in this land. ⁴ And afterward Laban took his daughter Leah, and he brought her to Jacob, and he came to her and Jacob did not know that she was Leah. ⁵ And Laban gave his daughter Leah his maid Zilpah for a handmaid. ⁶ And all the people at the feast knew what Laban had done to Jacob, but they did not tell the thing to Jacob. ⁷ And all the neighbors came that night to Jacob's house, and they ate and drank and rejoiced, and played before Leah upon timbrels, and with dances, and they responded before Jacob, Heleah, Heleah. ⁸ And Jacob heard their words but did not understand their meaning, but he thought such might be their custom in this land. ⁹ And the neighbors spoke these words before Jacob during the night, and all the lights that were in the house Laban had that night extinguished. ¹⁰ And in the morning, when daylight appeared, Jacob turned to his wife and he saw, and behold it was Leah that had been lying in his bosom, and Jacob said, Behold now I know what the neighbors said last night, Heleah, they said, and I knew it not. ¹¹ And Jacob called unto Laban, and said unto him, What is this that thou didst unto me? Surely I served thee for Rachel, and why didst thou deceive me and didst give me Leah? ¹² And Laban answered Jacob, saying, Not so is it done in our place to give the younger before the elder now therefore if thou desirest to take her sister likewise, take her unto thee for the service which thou wilt serve me for another seven years. ¹³ And Jacob did so, and he also took Rachel for a wife, and he served Laban seven years more, and Jacob also came to Rachel, and he loved Rachel more than Leah, and Laban gave her his maid Bilhah for a handmaid. ¹⁴ And when the Lord saw that Leah was hated, the Lord opened her womb, and she conceived and bare Jacob four sons in those days. ¹⁵ And these are their names, Reuben Simeon, Levi, and Judah, and she afterward left bearing. ¹⁶ And at that time Rachel was barren, and she had no offspring, and Rachel envied her sister Leah, and when Rachel saw that she bare no children to Jacob, she took her handmaid Bilhah, and she bare Jacob two sons, Dan and Naphtali. ¹⁷ And when Leah saw that she had left bearing, she also took her handmaid Zilpah, and she gave her to Jacob for a wife, and Jacob also came to Zilpah, and she also bare Jacob two sons, Gad and Asher. ¹⁸ And Leah again conceived and bare Jacob in those days two sons and one daughter, and these are their names, Issachar, Zebulon, and their sister Dinah. ¹⁹ And Rachel was still barren in those days, and Rachel prayed unto the Lord at that time, and she said, O Lord God remember me and visit me, I beseech thee, for now my husband will cast me off, for I have borne him no children. ²⁰ Now O Lord God, hear my supplication before thee, and see my affliction, and give me children like one of the handmaids, that I may no more bear my reproach. ²¹ And God heard her and opened her womb, and Rachel conceived and bare a son, and she said, The Lord has taken away my reproach, and she called his name Joseph, saying, May the Lord add to me another son; and Jacob was ninety-one years old when she bare him. ²² At that time Jacob's mother, Rebecca, sent her nurse Deborah the daughter of Uz, and two of Isaac's servants unto Jacob. ²³ And they came to Jacob to Haran and they said unto him, Rebecca has sent us to thee that thou shalt return to thy father's house to the land of Canaan; and Jacob hearkened unto them in this which his mother had spoken. ²⁴ At that time, the other seven years which Jacob served Laban for Rachel were completed, and it was at the end of fourteen years that he had dwelt in Haran that Jacob said unto Laban, give me my wives and send me away, that I may go to my land, for behold my mother did send unto me from the land at Canaan that I should return to my father's house. ²⁵ And Laban said unto him, Not so I pray thee; if I have found favor in thy sight do not leave me; appoint me thy wages and I will give them, and remain with me. ²⁶ And Jacob said unto him, This is what thou shalt give me for wages, that I shall this day pass through all thy flock and take away from them every lamb that is speckled and spotted and such as are brown amongst the sheep, and amongst the goats, and if thou wilt do this thing for me I will return and feed thy flock and keep them as at first. ²⁷ And Laban did so, and Laban removed from his flock all that Jacob had said and gave them to him. ²⁸ And Jacob placed all that he had removed from Laban's flock in the hands of his sons, and Jacob was feeding the remainder of Laban's flock. ²⁹ And when the servants of Isaac which he had sent unto Jacob saw that Jacob would not then return with them to the land of Canaan to his father, they then went away from him, and they returned home to the land of Canaan. ³⁰ And Deborah remained with Jacob in Haran, and she did not return with the servants of Isaac to the land of Canaan, and Deborah resided with Jacob's wives and children in Haran. ³¹ And Jacob served

Laban six years longer, and when the sheep brought forth, Jacob removed from them such as were speckled and spotted, as he had determined with Laban, and Jacob did so at Laban's for six years, and the man increased abundantly and he had cattle and maid servants and men servants, camels, and asses. ³² And Jacob had two hundred drove of cattle, and his cattle were of large size and of beautiful appearance and were very productive, and all the families of the sons of men desired to get some of the cattle of Jacob, for they were exceedingly prosperous. ³³ And many of the sons of men came to procure some of Jacob's flock, and Jacob gave them a sheep for a man servant or a maid servant or for an ass or a camel, or whatever Jacob desired from them they gave him. ³⁴ And Jacob obtained riches and honor and possessions by means of these transactions with the sons of men, and the children of Laban envied him of this honor. ³⁵ And in the course of time he heard the words of Laban's sons, saying, Jacob has taken away all that was our father's, and of that which was our father's has he acquired all this glory. ³⁶ And Jacob beheld the countenance of Laban and of his children, and behold it was not toward him in those days as it had been before. ³⁷ And the Lord appeared to Jacob at the expiration of the six years, and said unto him, Arise, go forth out of this land, and return to the land of thy birthplace and I will be with thee. ³⁸ And Jacob rose up at that time and he mounted his children and wives and all belonging to him upon camels, and he went forth to go to the land of Canaan to his father Isaac. ³⁹ And Laban did not know that Jacob had gone from him, for Laban had been that day sheep-shearing. ⁴⁰ And Rachel stole her father's images, and she took them and she concealed them upon the camel upon which she sat, and she went on. ⁴¹ And this is the manner of the images; in taking a man who is the first born and slaying him and taking the hair off his head, and taking salt and salting the head and anointing it in oil, then taking a small tablet of copper or a tablet of gold and writing the name upon it, and placing the tablet under his tongue, and taking the head with the tablet under the tongue and putting it in the house, and lighting up lights before it and bowing down to it. ⁴² And at the time when they bow down to it, it speaketh to them in all matters that they ask of it, through the power of the name which is written in it. ⁴³ And some make them in the figures of men, of gold and silver, and go to them in times known to them, and the figures receive the influence of the stars, and tell them future things, and in this manner were the images which Rachel stole from her father. ⁴⁴ And Rachel stole these images which were her father's, in order that Laban might not know through them where Jacob had gone. ⁴⁵ And Laban came home and he asked concerning Jacob and his household, and he was not to be found, and Laban sought his images to know where Jacob had gone, and could not find them, and he went to some other images, and he inquired of them and they told him that Jacob had fled from him to his father's, to the land of Canaan. ⁴⁶ And Laban then rose up and he took his brothers and all his servants, and he went forth and pursued Jacob, and he overtook him in mount Gilead. ⁴⁷ And Laban said unto Jacob, What is this thou hast done to me to flee and deceive me, and lead my daughters and their children as captives taken by the sword? ⁴⁸ And thou didst not suffer me to kiss them and send them away with joy, and thou didst steal my gods and didst go away. ⁴⁹ And Jacob answered Laban, saying, Because I was afraid lest thou wouldst take thy daughters by force from me; and now with whomsoever thou findest thy gods he shall die. ⁵⁰ And Laban searched for the images and he examined in all Jacob's tents and furniture, but could not find them. ⁵¹ And Laban said unto Jacob, We will make a covenant together and it shall be a testimony between me and thee; if thou shalt afflict my daughters, or shalt take other wives besides my daughters, even God shall be a witness between me and thee in this matter. ⁵² And they took stones and made a heap, and Laban said, This heap is a witness between me and thee, therefore he called the name thereof Gilead. ⁵³ And Jacob and Laban offered sacrifice upon the mount, and they ate there by the heap, and they tarried in the mount all night, and Laban rose up early in the morning, and he wept with his daughters and he kissed them, and he returned unto his place. ⁵⁴ And he hastened and sent off his son Beor, who was seventeen years old, with Abichorof the son of Uz, the son of Nahor, and with them were ten men. ⁵⁵ And they hastened and went and passed on the road before Jacob, and they came by another road to the land of Seir. ⁵⁶ And they came unto Esau and said unto him, Thus saith thy brother and relative, thy mother's brother Laban, the son of Bethuel, saying, ⁵⁷ Hast thou heard what Jacob thy brother has done unto me, who first came to me naked and bare, and I went to meet him, and brought him to my house with honor, and I made him great, and I gave him my two daughters for wives and also two of my maids. ⁵⁸ And God blessed him on my account, and he increased abundantly, and had sons, daughters and maid servants. ⁵⁹ He has also an immense stock of flocks and herds, camels and asses, also silver and gold in abundance; and when he saw that his wealth increased, he left me whilst I went to shear my sheep, and he rose up and fled in secrecy. ⁶⁰ And he lifted his wives and children upon camels, and he led away all his cattle and property which he acquired in my land, and he lifted up his countenance to go to his father Isaac, to the land of Canaan. ⁶¹ And he did not suffer me to kiss my daughters and their children, and he led my daughters as captives taken by the sword, and he also stole my gods and he fled. ⁶² And now I have left him in the mountain of the brook of Jabuk, him and all belonging to him; he lacketh nothing. ⁶³ If it be thy wish to go to him, go then and there wilt thou find him, and thou canst do unto him as thy soul desireth; and Laban's messengers came and told Esau all these things. ⁶⁴ And Esau heard all the words of Laban's messengers, and his anger was greatly kindled against Jacob, and he remembered his hatred, and his anger burned within him. ⁶⁵ And Esau hastened and took his children and servants and the souls of his household, being sixty men, and he went and assembled all the children of Seir the Horite and their people, being three hundred and forty men, and took all this number of four hundred men with drawn swords, and he went unto Jacob to smite him. ⁶⁶ And Esau divided this number into several parts, and he took the sixty men of his children and servants and the souls of his household as one head, and gave them in care of Eliphaz his eldest son. ⁶⁷ And the remaining heads he gave to the care of the six sons of Seir the Horite, and he placed every man over his generations and children. ⁶⁸ And the whole of this camp went as it was, and Esau went amongst them toward Jacob, and he conducted them with speed. ⁶⁹ And Laban's messengers departed from Esau and went to the land of Canaan, and they came to the house of Rebecca the mother of Jacob and Esau. ⁷⁰ And they told her saying, Behold thy son Esau has gone against his brother Jacob with four hundred men, for he heard that he was coming, and he is gone to make war with him, and to smite him and to take all that he has. ⁷¹ And Rebecca hastened and sent seventy two men from the servants of Isaac to meet Jacob on the road; for she said, Peradventure, Esau may make war in the road when he meets him. ⁷² And these messengers went on the road to meet Jacob, and they met him in the road of the brook on the opposite side of the brook Jabuk, and Jacob said when he saw them, This camp is destined to me from God, and Jacob called the name of that place Machnayim. ⁷³ And Jacob knew all his father's people, and he kissed them and embraced them and came with them, and Jacob asked them concerning his father and mother, and they said, They were well. ⁷⁴ And these messengers said unto Jacob, Rebecca thy mother has sent us to thee, saying, I have heard, my son, that thy brother Esau has gone forth against thee on the road with men from the children of Seir the Horite. ⁷⁵ And therefore, my son, hearken to my voice and see with thy counsel what thou wilt do, and when he cometh up to thee, supplicate him, and do not speak rashly to him, and give him a present from what thou possessest, and from what God has favored thee with. ⁷⁶ And when he asketh thee concerning thy affairs, conceal nothing from him, perhaps he may turn from his anger against thee and thou wilt thereby save thy soul, thou and all belonging to thee, for it is thy duty to honor him, for he is thy elder brother. ⁷⁷ And when Jacob heard the words of his mother which the messengers had spoken to him, Jacob lifted up his voice and wept bitterly, and did as his mother then commanded him.

32

¹ And at that time Jacob sent messengers to his brother Esau toward the land of Seir, and he spoke to him words of supplication. ² And he commanded them, saying, Thus shall ye say to my lord, to Esau, Thus saith thy servant Jacob, Let not my lord imagine that my father's blessing with which he did bless me has proved beneficial to me. ³ For I have been these twenty years with Laban, and he deceived me and changed my wages ten times, as it has all been already told unto my lord. ⁴ And I served him in his house very laboriously, and God afterward saw my affliction, my labor and the work of my hands, and he caused me to find grace and favor in his sight. ⁵ And I afterward through God's great mercy and kindness acquired oxen and asses and cattle, and men servants and maid servants. ⁶ And now I am coming to my land and my home to my father and mother, who are in the land of Canaan; and I have sent to let my lord know all this in order to find favor in the sight of my lord, so that he may not imagine that I have of myself obtained wealth, or that the blessing with which my father blessed me has benefited me. ⁷ And those messengers went to Esau, and found him on the borders of the land of Edom going toward Jacob, and four hundred men of the children of Seir the Horite were standing with drawn swords. ⁸ And the messengers of Jacob told Esau all the words that Jacob had spoken to them concerning Esau. ⁹ And Esau answered them with pride and contempt, and said unto them, Surely I have heard and truly it has been told unto me what Jacob has done to Laban, who exalted him in his house and gave him his daughters for wives, and he begat sons and daughters, and abundantly increased in wealth and riches in Laban's house through his means. ¹⁰ And when he saw that his wealth was abundant and his riches great he fled with all belonging to him, from Laban's house, and he led Laban's daughters

away from the face of their father, as captives taken by the sword without telling him of it. ¹¹ And not only to Laban has Jacob done thus but also unto me has he done so and has twice supplanted me, and shall I be silent? ¹² Now therefore I have this day come with my camps to meet him, and I will do unto him according to the desire of my heart. ¹³ And the messengers returned and came to Jacob and said unto him, We came to thy brother, to Esau, and we told him all thy words, and thus has he answered us, and behold he cometh to meet thee with four hundred men. ¹⁴ Now then know and see what thou shalt do, and pray before God to deliver thee from him. ¹⁵ And when he heard the words of his brother which he had spoken to the messengers of Jacob, Jacob was greatly afraid and he was distressed. ¹⁶ And Jacob prayed to the Lord his God, and he said, O Lord God of my fathers, Abraham and Isaac, thou didst say unto me when I went away from my father's house, saying, ¹⁷ I am the Lord God of thy father Abraham and the God of Isaac, unto thee do I give this land and thy seed after thee, and I will make thy seed as the stars of heaven, and thou shalt spread forth to the four sides of heaven, and in thee and in thy seed shall all the families of the earth be blessed. ¹⁸ And thou didst establish thy words, and didst give unto me riches and children and cattle, as the utmost wishes of my heart didst thou give unto thy servant; thou didst give unto me all that I asked from thee, so that I lacked nothing. ¹⁹ And thou didst afterward say unto me, Return to thy parents and to thy birth place and I will still do well with thee. ²⁰ And now that I have come, and thou didst deliver me from Laban, I shall fall in the hands of Esau who will slay me, yea, together with the mothers of my children. ²¹ Now therefore, O Lord God, deliver me, I pray thee, also from the hands of my brother Esau, for I am greatly afraid of him. ²² And if there is no righteousness in me, do it for the sake of Abraham and my father Isaac. ²³ For I know that through kindness and mercy have I acquired this wealth; now therefore I beseech thee to deliver me this day with thy kindness and to answer me. ²⁴ And Jacob ceased praying to the Lord, and he divided the people that were with him with the flocks and cattle into two camps, and he gave the half to the care of Damesek, the son of Eliezer, Abraham's servant, for a camp, with his children, and the other half he gave to the care of his brother Elianus the son of Eliezer, to be for a camp with his children. ²⁵ And he commanded them, saying, Keep yourselves at a distance with your camps, and do not come too near each other, and if Esau come to one camp and slay it, the other camp at a distance from it will escape him. ²⁶ And Jacob tarried there that night, and during the whole night he gave his servants instructions concerning the forces and his children. ²⁷ And the Lord heard the prayer of Jacob on that day, and the Lord then delivered Jacob from the hands of his brother Esau. ²⁸ And the Lord sent three angels of the angels of heaven, and they went before Esau and came to him. ²⁹ And these angels appeared unto Esau and his people as two thousand men, riding upon horses furnished with all sorts of war instruments, and they appeared in the sight of Esau and all his men to be divided into four camps, with four chiefs to them. ³⁰ And one camp went on and they found Esau coming with four hundred men toward his brother Jacob, and this camp ran toward Esau and his people and terrified them, and Esau fell off the horse in alarm, and all his men separated from him in that place, for they were greatly afraid. ³¹ And the whole of the camp shouted after them when they fled from Esau, and all the warlike men answered, saying, ³² Surely we are the servants of Jacob, who is the servant of God, and who then can stand against us? And Esau said unto them, O then, my lord and brother Jacob is your lord, whom I have not seen for these twenty years, and now that I have this day come to see him, do you treat me in this manner? ³³ And the angels answered him saying, As the Lord liveth, were not Jacob of whom thou speaketh thy brother, we had not let one remaining from thee and thy people, but only on account of Jacob we will do nothing to them. ³⁴ And this camp passed from Esau and his men and it went away, and Esau and his men had gone from them about a league when the second camp came toward him with all sorts of weapons, and they also did unto Esau and his men as the first camp had done to them. ³⁵ And when they had left it to go on, behold the third camp came toward him and they were all terrified, and Esau fell off the horse, and the whole camp cried out, and said, Surely we are the servants of Jacob, who is the servant of God, and who can stand against us? ³⁶ And Esau again answered them saying, O then, Jacob my lord and your lord is my brother, and for twenty years I have not seen his countenance and hearing this day that he was coming, I went this day to meet him, and do you treat me in this manner? ³⁷ And they answered him, and said unto him, As the Lord liveth, were not Jacob thy brother as thou didst say, we had not left a remnant from thee and thy men, but on account of Jacob of whom thou speakest being thy brother, we will not meddle with thee or thy men. ³⁸ And the third camp also passed from them, and he still continued his road with his men toward Jacob, when the fourth camp came toward him, and they also did unto him and his men as the others had done. ³⁹ And when Esau beheld the evil which the four angels had done to him and to his men, he became greatly afraid of his brother Jacob, and he went to meet him in peace. ⁴⁰ And Esau concealed his hatred against Jacob, because he was afraid of his life on account of his brother Jacob, and because he imagined that the four camps that he had lighted upon were Jacob's servants. ⁴¹ And Jacob tarried that night with his servants in their camps, and he resolved with his servants to give unto Esau a present from all that he had with him, and from all his property; and Jacob rose up in the morning, he and his men, and they chose from amongst the cattle a present for Esau. ⁴² And this is the amount of the present which Jacob chose from his flock to give unto his brother Esau: and he selected two hundred and forty head from the flocks, and he selected from the camels and asses thirty each, and of the herds he chose fifty kine. ⁴³ And he put them all in ten droves, and he placed each sort by itself, and he delivered them into the hands of ten of his servants, each drove by itself. ⁴⁴ And he commanded them, and said unto them, Keep yourselves at a distance from each other, and put a space between the droves, and when Esau and those who are with him shall meet you and ask you, saying, Whose are you, and whither do you go, and to whom belongeth all this before you, you shall say unto them, We are the servants of Jacob, and we come to meet Esau in peace, and behold Jacob cometh behind us. ⁴⁵ And that which is before us is a present sent from Jacob to his brother Esau. ⁴⁶ And if they shall say unto you, Why doth he delay behind you, from coming to meet his brother and to see his face, then you shall say unto them, Surely he cometh joyfully behind us to meet his brother, for he said, I will appease him with the present that goeth to him, and after this I will see his face, peradventure he will accept of me. ⁴⁷ So the whole present passed on in the hands of his servants, and went before him on that day, and he lodged that night with his camps by the border of the brook of Jabuk, and he rose up in the midst of the night, and he took his wives and his maid servants, and all belonging to him, and he that night passed them over the ford Jabuk. ⁴⁸ And when he passed all belonging to him over the brook, Jacob was left by himself, and a man met him, and he wrestled with him that night until the breaking of the day, and the hollow of Jacob's thigh was out of joint through wrestling with him. ⁴⁹ And at the break of day the man left Jacob there, and he blessed him and went away, and Jacob passed the brook at the break of day, and he halted upon his thigh. ⁵⁰ And the sun rose upon him when he had passed the brook, and he came up to the place of his cattle and children. ⁵¹ And they went on till midday, and whilst they were going the present was passing on before them. ⁵² And Jacob lifted up his eyes and looked, and behold Esau was at a distance, coming along with many men, about four hundred, and Jacob was greatly afraid of his brother. ⁵³ And Jacob hastened and divided his children unto his wives and his handmaids, and his daughter Dinah he put in a chest, and delivered her into the hands of his servants. ⁵⁴ And he passed before his children and wives to meet his brother, and he bowed down to the ground, yea he bowed down seven times until he approached his brother, and God caused Jacob to find grace and favor in the sight of Esau and his men, for God had heard the prayer of Jacob. ⁵⁵ And the fear of Jacob and his terror fell upon his brother Esau, for Esau was greatly afraid of Jacob for what the angels of God had done to Esau, and Esau's anger against Jacob was turned into kindness. ⁵⁶ And when Esau saw Jacob running toward him, he also ran toward him and he embraced him, and he fell upon his neck, and they kissed and they wept. ⁵⁷ And God put fear and kindness toward Jacob in the hearts of the men that came with Esau, and they also kissed Jacob and embraced him. ⁵⁸ And also Eliphaz, the son of Esau, with his four brothers, sons of Esau, wept with Jacob, and they kissed him and embraced him, for the fear of Jacob had fallen upon them all. ⁵⁹ And Esau lifted up his eyes and saw the women with their offspring, the children of Jacob, walking behind Jacob and bowing along the road to Esau. ⁶⁰ And Esau said unto Jacob, Who are these with thee, my brother? are they thy children or thy servants? and Jacob answered Esau and said, They are my children which God hath graciously given to thy servant. ⁶¹ And whilst Jacob was speaking to Esau and his men, Esau beheld the whole camp, and he said unto Jacob, Whence didst thou get the whole of the camp that I met yesternight? and Jacob said, To find favor in the sight of my lord, it is that which God graciously gave to thy servant. ⁶² And the present came before Esau, and Jacob pressed Esau, saying, Take I pray thee the present that I have brought to my lord, and Esau said, Wherefore is this my purpose? keep that which thou hast unto thyself. ⁶³ And Jacob said, It is incumbent upon me to give all this, since I have seen thy face, that thou still livest in peace. ⁶⁴ And Esau refused to take the present, and Jacob said unto him, I beseech thee my lord, if now I have found favor in thy sight, then receive my present at my hand, for I have therefore seen thy face, as though I had seen a god-like face, because thou wast pleased with me. ⁶⁵ And Esau took the present, and Jacob also gave unto Esau silver and gold and bdellium, for he pressed him so much that he took them. ⁶⁶ And Esau divided the cattle that were in the camp, and he gave the half to the men who had come with him, for they had come on hire, and the other half he delivered unto the hands of his children. ⁶⁷ And the silver and gold and bdellium he gave in the hands of Eliphaz his eldest son, and Esau said unto Jacob, Let us remain with thee, and we will go slowly along with thee until thou comest to my place with me, that we may dwell there together. ⁶⁸ And Jacob answered his brother and said, I would do as my lord speaketh unto me, but my lord knoweth that the children are tender, and the flocks and herds with their young who are with me, go but slowly, for if they went swiftly they would all die, for thou knowest their burdens and their fatigue. ⁶⁹ Therefore let my lord pass on before his servant, and I will go on slowly for the sake of the children and the flock, until I come to my lord's place to Seir. ⁷⁰ And Esau said unto Jacob, I will place with thee some of the people that are with me to take care of thee in the road, and to bear thy fatigue and burden, and he said, What needeth it my lord, if I may find grace in thy sight? ⁷¹ Behold I will come unto thee to Seir to dwell there together as thou hast spoken, go thou then with thy people for I will follow thee. ⁷² And Jacob said this to Esau in order to remove Esau and his men from him, so that Jacob might afterward go to his father's house to the land of Canaan. ⁷³ And Esau hearkened to the voice of Jacob, and Esau returned with the four hundred men that were with him on their road to Seir, and Jacob and all belonging to him went that day as far as the extremity of the land of Canaan in its borders, and he remained there some time.

33

¹ And in some time after Jacob went away from the borders of the land, and he came to the land of Shalem, that is the city of Shechem, which is in the land of Canaan, and he rested in front of the city. ² And he bought a parcel of the field which was there, from the children of Hamor the people of the land, for five shekels. ³ And Jacob there built himself a house, and he pitched his tent there, and he made booths for his cattle, therefore he called the name of that place Succoth. ⁴ And Jacob remained in Succoth a year and six months. ⁵ At that time some of the women of the inhabitants of the land went to the city of Shechem to dance and rejoice with the daughters of the people of the city, and when they went forth then Rachel and Leah the wives of Jacob with their families also went to behold the rejoicing of the daughters of the city. ⁶ And Dinah the daughter of Jacob also went along with them and saw the daughters of the city, and they remained there before these daughters whilst all the people of the city were standing by them to behold their rejoicings, and all the great people of the city were there. ⁷ And Shechem the son of Hamor, the prince of the land was also standing there to see them. ⁸ And Shechem beheld Dinah the daughter of Jacob sitting with her mother before the daughters of the city, and the damsel pleased him greatly, and he there asked his friends and his people, saying, Whose daughter is that sitting amongst the women, whom I do not know in this city? ⁹ And they said unto him, Surely this is the daughter of Jacob the son of Isaac the Hebrew, who has dwelt in this city for some time, and when it was reported that the daughters of the land were going forth to rejoice she went with her mother and maid servants to sit amongst them as thou seest. ¹⁰ And Shechem beheld Dinah the daughter of Jacob, and when he looked at her his soul became fixed upon Dinah. ¹¹ And he sent and had her taken by force, and Dinah came to the house of Shechem and he seized her forcibly and lay with her and humbled her, and he loved her exceedingly and placed her in his house. ¹² And they came and told the thing unto Jacob, and when Jacob heard that Shechem had defiled his daughter Dinah, Jacob sent twelve of his servants to fetch Dinah from the house of Shechem, and they went and came to the house of Shechem to take away Dinah from there. ¹³ And when they came Shechem went out to them with his men and drove them from his house, and he would not suffer them to come before Dinah, but Shechem was sitting with Dinah kissing and embracing her before their eyes. ¹⁴ And the servants of Jacob came back and told him, saying, When we came, he and his men drove us away, and thus did Shechem do unto Dinah before our eyes. ¹⁵ And Jacob knew moreover that Shechem had defiled his daughter, but he said nothing, and his sons were feeding his cattle in the field, and Jacob remained silent till their return. ¹⁶ And before his sons came home Jacob sent two maidens from his servants' daughters to take care of Dinah in the house of Shechem, and to remain with her, and Shechem sent three of his friends to his father Hamor the son of Chiddekem, the son of Pered, saying, Get me this damsel for a wife. ¹⁷ And Hamor the son of Chiddekem the Hivite came to the house of Shechem his son, and he sat before him, and Hamor said unto his son, Shechem, Is there then no woman amongst the daughters of thy people that thou wilt take an Hebrew woman who is not of thy people? ¹⁸ And Shechem said to him, Her only must thou get for me, for she is delightful in my sight; and Hamor did according to the word of his son, for he was greatly beloved by him. ¹⁹ And Hamor went forth to Jacob to commune with him concerning this matter, and when he had gone from the house of his son Shechem, before he came to Jacob to speak unto him, behold the sons of Jacob had come from the field, as soon as they heard the thing that Shechem the son of Hamor had done. ²⁰ And the men were very much grieved concerning their sister, and they all came home fired with anger, before the time of gathering in their cattle. ²¹ And they came and sat before their father and they spoke unto him kindled with wrath, saying, Surely death is due to this man and to his household, because the Lord God of the whole earth commanded Noah and his children that man shall never rob, nor commit adultery; now behold Shechem has both ravaged and committed fornication with our sister, and not one of all the people of the city spoke a word to him. ²² Surely thou knowest and understandest that the judgment of death is due to Shechem, and to his father, and to the whole city on account of the thing which he has done. ²³ And whilst they were speaking before their father in this matter, behold Hamor the father of Shechem came to speak to Jacob the words of his son concerning Dinah, and he sat before Jacob and before his sons. ²⁴ And Hamor spoke unto them, saying, The soul of my son Shechem longeth for your daughter; I pray you give her unto him for a wife and intermarry with us; give us your daughters and we will give you our daughters, and you shall dwell with us in our land and we will be as one people in the land. ²⁵ For our land is very extensive, so dwell ye and trade therein and get possessions in it, and do therein as you desire, and no one shall prevent you by saying a word to you. ²⁶ And Hamor ceased speaking unto Jacob and his sons, and behold Shechem his son had come after him, and he sat before them. ²⁷ And Shechem spoke before Jacob and his sons, saying, May I find favor in your sight that you will give me your daughter, and whatever you say unto me that will I do for her. ²⁸ Ask me for abundance of dowry and gift, and I will give it, and whatever you shall say unto me that will I do, and whoever he be that will rebel against your orders, he shall die; only give me the damsel for a wife. ²⁹ And Simeon and Levi answered Hamor and Shechem his son deceitfully, saying, All you have spoken unto us we will do for you. ³⁰ And behold our sister is in your house, but keep away from her until we send to our father Isaac concerning this matter, for we can do nothing without his consent. ³¹ For he knoweth the ways of our father Abraham, and whatever he sayeth unto us we will tell you, we will conceal nothing from you. ³² And Simeon and Levi spoke this unto Shechem and his father in order to find a pretext, and to seek counsel what was to be done to Shechem and to his city in this matter. ³³ And when Shechem and his father heard the words of Simeon and Levi, it seemed good in their sight, and Shechem and his father came forth to go home. ³⁴ And when they had gone, the sons of Jacob said unto their father, saying, Behold, we know that death is due to these wicked ones and to their city, because they transgressed that which God had commanded unto Noah and his children and his seed after them. ³⁵ And also because Shechem did this thing to our sister Dinah in defiling her, for such vileness shall never be done amongst us. ³⁶ Now therefore know and see what you will do, and seek counsel and pretext what is to be done to them, in order to kill all the inhabitants of this city. ³⁷ And Simeon said to them, Here is a proper advice for you: tell them to circumcise every male amongst them as we are circumcised, and if they do not wish to do this, we shall take our daughter from them and go away. ³⁸ And if they consent to do this and will do it, then when they are sunk down with pain, we will attack them with our swords, as upon one who is quiet and peaceable, and we will slay every male person amongst them. ³⁹ And Simeon's advice pleased them, and Simeon and Levi resolved to do unto them as it was proposed. ⁴⁰ And on the next morning Shechem and Hamor his father came again unto Jacob and his sons, to speak concerning Dinah, and to hear what answer the sons of Jacob would give to their words. ⁴¹ And the sons of Jacob spoke deceitfully to them, saying, We told our father Isaac all your words, and your words pleased him. ⁴² But he spoke unto us, saying, Thus did Abraham his father command him from God the Lord of the whole earth, that any man who is not of his descendants that should wish to take one of his daughters, shall cause every male belonging to him to be circumcised, as we are circumcised, and then we may give him our daughter for a wife. ⁴³ Now we have made known to you all our ways that our father spoke unto us, for we cannot do this of which you spoke unto us, to give our daughter to an uncircumcised man, for it is a disgrace to us. ⁴⁴ But herein will we consent to you, to give you our daughter, and we will also take unto ourselves your daughters, and will dwell amongst you and be one people as you have spoken, if you will hearken to us, and consent to be like us, to circumcise every male belonging to you, as we are circumcised. ⁴⁵ And if you will not hearken unto us, to have every male circumcised as we are circumcised, as we have commanded, then we will come to you, and take our daughter from you and go away. ⁴⁶ And Shechem and his father Hamor heard the words of the sons of Jacob, and the thing pleased them exceedingly, and Shechem and his father Hamor hastened to do the wishes of the sons of Jacob, for Shechem was very fond of Dinah, and his soul was riveted to her. ⁴⁷ And Shechem and his father Hamor hastened to the gate of the city, and they assembled all the men of their city

and spoke unto them the words of the sons of Jacob, saying, ⁴⁸ We came to these men, the sons of Jacob, and we spoke unto them concerning their daughter, and these men will consent to do according to our wishes, and behold our land is of great extent for them, and they will dwell in it, and trade in it, and we shall be one people; we will take their daughters, and our daughters we will give unto them for wives. ⁴⁹ But only on this condition will these men consent to do this thing, that every male amongst us be circumcised as they are circumcised, as their God commanded them, and when we shall have done according to their instructions to be circumcised, then will they dwell amongst us, together with their cattle and possessions, and we shall be as one people with them. ⁵⁰ And when all the men of the city heard the words of Shechem and his father Hamor, then all the men of their city were agreeable to this proposal, and they obeyed to be circumcised, for Shechem and his father Hamor were greatly esteemed by them, being the princes of the land. ⁵¹ And on the next day, Shechem and Hamor his father rose up early in the morning, and they assembled all the men of their city into the middle of the city, and they called for the sons of Jacob, who circumcised every male belonging to them on that day and the next. ⁵² And they circumcised Shechem and Hamor his father, and the five brothers of Shechem, and then every one rose up and went home, for this thing was from the Lord against the city of Shechem, and from the Lord was Simeon's counsel in this matter, in order that the Lord might deliver the city of Shechem into the hands of Jacob's two sons.

34

¹ And the number of all the males that were circumcised, were six hundred and forty-five men, and two hundred and forty-six children. ² But Chiddekem, son of Pered, the father of Hamor, and his six brothers, would not listen unto Shechem and his father Hamor, and they would not be circumcised, for the proposal of the sons of Jacob was loathsome in their sight, and their anger was greatly roused at this, that the people of the city had not hearkened to them. ³ And in the evening of the second day, they found eight small children who had not been circumcised, for their mothers had concealed them from Shechem and his father Hamor, and from the men of the city. ⁴ And Shechem and his father Hamor sent to have them brought before them to be circumcised, when Chiddekem and his six brothers sprang at them with their swords, and sought to slay them. ⁵ And they sought to slay also Shechem and his father Hamor and they sought to slay Dinah with them on account of this matter. ⁶ And they said unto them, What is this thing that you have done? are there no women amongst the daughters of your brethren the Canaanites, that you wish to take unto yourselves daughters of the Hebrews, whom ye knew not before, and will do this act which your fathers never commanded you? ⁷ Do you imagine that you will succeed through this act which you have done? and what will you answer in this affair to your brethren the Canaanites, who will come tomorrow and ask you concerning this thing? ⁸ And if your act shall not appear just and good in their sight, what will you do for your lives, and me for our lives, in your not having hearkened to our voices? ⁹ And if the inhabitants of the land and all your brethren the children of Ham, shall hear of your act, saying, ¹⁰ On account of a Hebrew woman did Shechem and Hamor his father, and all the inhabitants of their city, do that with which they had been unacquainted and which their ancestors never commanded them, where then will you fly or where conceal your shame, all your days before your brethren, the inhabitants of the land of Canaan? ¹¹ Now therefore we cannot bear up against this thing which you have done, neither can we be burdened with this yoke upon us, which our ancestors did not command us. ¹² Behold tomorrow we will go and assemble all our brethren, the Canaanitish brethren who dwell in the land, and we will all come and smite you and all those who trust in you, that there shall not be a remnant left from you or them. ¹³ And when Hamor and his son Shechem and all the people of the city heard the words of Chiddekem and his brothers, they were terribly afraid of their lives at their words, and they repented of what they had done. ¹⁴ And Shechem and his father Hamor answered their father Chiddekem and his brethren, and they said unto them, All the words which you spoke unto us are true. ¹⁵ Now do not say, nor imagine in your hearts that on account of the love of the Hebrews we did this thing that our ancestors did not command us. ¹⁶ But because we saw that it was not their intention and desire to accede to our wishes concerning their daughter as to our taking her, except on this condition, so we hearkened to their voices and did this act which you saw, in order to obtain our desire from them. ¹⁷ And when we shall have obtained our request from them, we will then return to them and do unto them that which you say unto us. ¹⁸ We beseech you then to wait and tarry until our flesh shall be healed and we again become strong, and we will then go together against them, and do unto them that which is in your hearts and in ours. ¹⁹ And Dinah the daughter of Jacob heard all these words which Chiddekem and his brothers had spoken, and what Hamor and his son Shechem and the people of their city had answered them. ²⁰ And she hastened and sent one of her maidens, that her father had sent to take care of her in the house of Shechem, to Jacob her father and to her brethren, saying: ²¹ Thus did Chiddekem and his brothers advise concerning you, and thus did Hamor and Shechem and the people of the city answer them. ²² And when Jacob heard these words he was filled with wrath, and he was indignant at them, and his anger was kindled against them. ²³ And Simeon and Levi swore and said, As the Lord liveth, the God of the whole earth, by this time tomorrow, there shall not be a remnant left in the whole city. ²⁴ And twenty young men had concealed themselves who were not circumcised, and these young men fought against Simeon and Levi, and Simeon and Levi killed eighteen of them, and two fled from them and escaped to some lime pits that were in the city, and Simeon and Levi sought for them, but could not find them. ²⁵ And Simeon and Levi continued to go about in the city, and they killed all the people of the city at the edge of the sword, and they left none remaining. ²⁶ And there was a great consternation in the midst of the city, and the cry of the people of the city ascended to heaven, and all the women and children cried aloud. ²⁷ And Simeon and Levi slew all the city; they left not a male remaining in the whole city. ²⁸ And they slew Hamor and Shechem his son at the edge of the sword, and they brought away Dinah from the house of Shechem and they went from there. ²⁹ And the sons of Jacob went and returned, and came upon the slain, and spoiled all their property which was in the city and the field. ³⁰ And whilst they were taking the spoil, three hundred men stood up and threw dust at them and struck them with stones, when Simeon turned to them and he slew them all with the edge of the sword, and Simeon turned before Levi, and came into the city. ³¹ And they took away their sheep and their oxen and their cattle, and also the remainder of the women and little ones, and they led all these away, and they opened a gate and went out and came unto their father Jacob with vigor. ³² And when Jacob saw all that they had done to the city, and saw the spoil that they took from them, Jacob was very angry at them, and Jacob said unto them, What is this that you have done to me? behold I obtained rest amongst the Canaanitish inhabitants of the land, and none of them meddled with me. ³³ And now you have done to make me obnoxious to the inhabitants of the land, amongst the Canaanites and the Perizzites, and I am but of a small number, and they will all assemble against me and slay me when they hear of your work with their brethren, and I and my household will be destroyed. ³⁴ And Simeon and Levi and all their brothers with them answered their father Jacob and said unto him, Behold we live in the land, and shall Shechem do this to our sister? why art thou silent at all that Shechem has done? and shall he deal with our sister as with a harlot in the streets? ³⁵ And the number of women whom Simeon and Levi took captives from the city of Shechem, whom they did not slay, was eighty-five who had not known man. ³⁶ And amongst them was a young damsel of beautiful appearance and well favored, whose name was Bunah, and Simeon took her for a wife, and the number of the males which they took captives and did not slay, was forty-seven men, and the rest they slew. ³⁷ And all the young men and women that Simeon and Levi had taken captives from the city of Shechem, were servants to the sons of Jacob and to their children after them, until the day of the sons of Jacob going forth from the land of Egypt. ³⁸ And when Simeon and Levi had gone forth from the city, the two young men that were left, who had concealed themselves in the city, and did not die amongst the people of the city, rose up, and these young men went into the city and walked about in it, and found the city desolate without man, and only women weeping, and these young men cried out and said, Behold, this is the evil which the sons of Jacob the Hebrew did to this city in their having this day destroyed one of the Canaanitish cities, and were not afraid of their lives of all the land of Canaan. ³⁹ And these men left the city and went to the city of Tapnach, and they came there and told the inhabitants of Tapnach all that had befallen them, and all that the sons of Jacob had done to the city of Shechem. ⁴⁰ And the information reached Jashub king of Tapnach, and he sent men to the city of Shechem to see those young men, for the king did not believe them in this account, saying, How could two men lay waste such a large town as Shechem? ⁴¹ And the messengers of Jashub came back and told him, saying, We came unto the city, and it is destroyed, there is not a man there; only weeping women; neither is any flock or cattle there, for all that was in the city the sons of Jacob took away. ⁴² And Jashub wondered at this, saying, How could two men do this thing, to destroy so large a city, and not one man able to stand against them? ⁴³ For the like has not been from the days of Nimrod, and not even from the remotest time, has the like taken place; and Jashub, king of Tapnach, said to his people, Be courageous and we will go and fight against these Hebrews, and do unto them as they did unto the city, and we will avenge the cause of the people of the city. ⁴⁴ And Jashub, king of Tapnach, consulted with his counsellors about this matter, and his advisers said unto him, Alone thou wilt not prevail over the Hebrews, for

they must be powerful to do this work to the whole city. ⁴⁵ If two of them laid waste the whole city, and no one stood against them, surely if thou wilt go against them, they will all rise against us and destroy us likewise. ⁴⁶ But if thou wilt send to all the kings that surround us, and let them come together, then we will go with them and fight against the sons of Jacob; then wilt thou prevail against them. ⁴⁷ And Jashub heard the words of his counsellors, and their words pleased him and his people, and he did so; and Jashub king of Tapnach sent to all the kings of the Amorites that surrounded Shechem and Tapnach, saying, ⁴⁸ Go up with me and assist me, and we will smite Jacob the Hebrew and all his sons, and destroy them from the earth, for thus did he do to the city of Shechem, and do you not know of it? ⁴⁹ And all the kings of the Amorites heard the evil that the sons of Jacob had done to the city of Shechem, and they were greatly astonished at them. ⁵⁰ And the seven kings of the Amorites assembled with all their armies, about ten thousand men with drawn swords, and they came to fight against the sons of Jacob; and Jacob heard that the kings of the Amorites had assembled to fight against his sons, and Jacob was greatly afraid, and it distressed him. ⁵¹ And Jacob exclaimed against Simeon and Levi, saying, What is this act that you did? why have you injured me, to bring against me all the children of Canaan to destroy me and my household? for I was at rest, even I and my household, and you have done this thing to me, and provoked the inhabitants of the land against me by your proceedings. ⁵² And Judah answered his father, saying, Was it for naught my brothers Simeon and Levi killed all the inhabitants of Shechem? Surely it was because Shechem had humbled our sister, and transgressed the command of our God to Noah and his children, for Shechem took our sister away by force, and committed adultery with her. ⁵³ And Shechem did all this evil and not one of the inhabitants of his city interfered with him, to say, Why wilt thou do this? surely for this my brothers went and smote the city, and the Lord delivered it into their hands, because its inhabitants had transgressed the commands of our God. Is it then for naught that they have done all this? ⁵⁴ And now why art thou afraid or distressed, and why art thou displeased at my brothers, and why is thine anger kindled against them? ⁵⁵ Surely our God who delivered into their hand the city of Shechem and its people, he will also deliver into our hands all the Canaanitish kings who are coming against us, and we will do unto them as my brothers did unto Shechem. ⁵⁶ Now be tranquil about them and cast away thy fears, but trust in the Lord our God, and pray unto him to assist us and deliver us, and deliver our enemies into our hands. ⁵⁷ And Judah called to one of his father's servants, Go now and see where those kings, who are coming against us, are situated with their armies. ⁵⁸ And the servant went and looked far off, and went up opposite Mount Sihon, and saw all the camps of the kings standing in the fields, and he returned to Judah and said, Behold the kings are situated in the field with all their camps, a people exceedingly numerous, like unto the sand upon the sea shore. ⁵⁹ And Judah said unto Simeon and Levi, and unto all his brothers, Strengthen yourselves and be sons of valor, for the Lord our God is with us, do not fear them. ⁶⁰ Stand forth each man, girt with his weapons of war, his bow and his sword, and we will go and fight against these uncircumcised men; the Lord is our God, He will save us. ⁶¹ And they rose up, and each girt on his weapons of war, great and small, eleven sons of Jacob, and all the servants of Jacob with them. ⁶² And all the servants of Isaac who were with Isaac in Hebron, all came to them equipped in all sorts of war instruments, and the sons of Jacob and their servants, being one hundred and twelve men, went towards these kings, and Jacob also went with them. ⁶³ And the sons of Jacob sent unto their father Isaac the son of Abraham to Hebron, the same is Kireath-arba, saying, ⁶⁴ Pray we beseech thee for us unto the Lord our God, to protect us from the hands of the Canaanites who are coming against us, and to deliver them into our hands. ⁶⁵ And Isaac the son of Abraham prayed unto the Lord for his sons, and he said, O Lord God, thou didst promise my father, saying, I will multiply thy seed as the stars of heaven, and thou didst also promise me, and establish thou thy word, now that the kings of Canaan are coming together, to make war with my children because they committed no violence. ⁶⁶ Now therefore, O Lord God, God of the whole earth, pervert, I pray thee, the counsel of these kings that they may not fight against my sons. ⁶⁷ And impress the hearts of these kings and their people with the terror of my sons and bring down their pride, and that they may turn away from my sons. ⁶⁸ And with thy strong hand and outstretched arm deliver my sons and their servants from them, for power and might are in thy hands to do all this. ⁶⁹ And the sons of Jacob and their servants went toward these kings, and they trusted in the Lord their God, and whilst they were going, Jacob their father also prayed unto the Lord and said, O Lord God, powerful and exalted God, who has reigned from days of old, from thence till now and forever; ⁷⁰ Thou art He who stirreth up wars and causeth them to cease, in thy hand are power and might to exalt and to bring down; O may my prayer be acceptable before thee that thou mayest turn to me with thy mercies, to impress the hearts of these kings and their people with the terror of my sons, and terrify them and their camps, and with thy great kindness deliver all those that trust in thee, for it is thou who canst bring people under us and reduce nations under our power.

35

¹ And all the kings of the Amorites came and took their stand in the field to consult with their counsellors what was to be done with the sons of Jacob, for they were still afraid of them, saying, Behold, two of them slew the whole of the city of Shechem. ² And the Lord heard the prayers of Isaac and Jacob, and he filled the hearts of all these kings' advisers with great fear and terror that they unanimously exclaimed, ³ Are you silly this day, or is there no understanding in you, that you will fight with the Hebrews, and why will you take a delight in your own destruction this day? ⁴ Behold two of them came to the city of Shechem without fear or terror, and they killed all the inhabitants of the city, that no man stood up against them, and how will you be able to fight with them all? ⁵ Surely you know that their God is exceedingly fond of them, and has done mighty things for them, such as have not been done from days of old, and amongst all the gods of nations, there is none can do like unto his mighty deeds. ⁶ Surely he delivered their father Abraham, the Hebrew, from the hand of Nimrod, and from the hand of all his people who had many times sought to slay him. ⁷ He delivered him also from the fire in which king Nimrod had cast him, and his God delivered him from it. ⁸ And who else can do the like? surely it was Abraham who slew the five kings of Elam, when they had touched his brother's son who in those days dwelt in Sodom. ⁹ And took his servant that was faithful in his house and a few of his men, and they pursued the kings of Elam in one night and killed them, and restored to his brother's son all his property which they had taken from him. ¹⁰ And surely you know the God of these Hebrews is much delighted with them, and they are also delighted with him, for they know that he delivered them from all their enemies. ¹¹ And behold through his love toward his God, Abraham took his only and precious son and intended to bring him up as a burnt offering to his God, and had it not been for God who prevented him from doing this, he would then have done it through his love to his God. ¹² And God saw all his works, and swore unto him, and promised him that he would deliver his sons and all his seed from every trouble that would befall them, because he had done this thing, and through his love to his God stifled his compassion for his child. ¹³ And have you not heard what their God did to Pharaoh king of Egypt, and to Abimelech king of Gerar, through taking Abraham's wife, who said of her, She is my sister, lest they might slay him on account of her, and think of taking her for a wife? and God did unto them and their people all that you heard of. ¹⁴ And behold, we ourselves saw with our eyes that Esau, the brother of Jacob, came to him with four hundred men, with the intention of slaying him, for he called to mind that he had taken away from him his father's blessing. ¹⁵ And he went to meet him when he came from Syria, to smite the mother with the children, and who delivered him from his hands but his God in whom he trusted? he delivered him from the hand of his brother and also from the hands of his enemies, and surely he again will protect them. ¹⁶ Who does not know that it was their God who inspired them with strength to do to the town of Shechem the evil which you heard of? ¹⁷ Could it then be with their own strength that two men could destroy such a large city as Shechem had it not been for their God in whom they trusted? he said and did unto them all this to slay the inhabitants of the city in their city. ¹⁸ And can you then prevail over them who have come forth together from your city to fight with the whole of them, even if a thousand times as many more should come to your assistance? ¹⁹ Surely you know and understand that you do not come to fight with them, but you come to war with their God who made choice of them, and you have therefore all come this day to be destroyed. ²⁰ Now therefore refrain from this evil which you are endeavoring to bring upon yourselves, and it will be better for you not to go to battle with them, although they are but few in numbers, because their God is with them. ²¹ And when the kings of the Amorites heard all the words of their advisers, their hearts were filled with terror, and they were afraid of the sons of Jacob and would not fight against them. ²² And they inclined their ears to the words of their advisers, and they listened to all their words, and the words of the counsellors greatly pleased the kings, and they did so. ²³ And the kings turned and refrained from the sons of Jacob, for they durst not approach them to make war with them, for they were greatly afraid of them, and their hearts melted within them from their fear of them. ²⁴ For this proceeded from the Lord to them, for he heard the prayers of his servants Isaac and Jacob, for they trusted in him; and all these kings returned with their camps on that day, each to his own city, and they did not at that time fight with the sons of Jacob. ²⁵ And the sons of Jacob kept their station that day till evening opposite mount Sihon, and

seeing that these kings did not come to fight against them, the sons of Jacob returned home.

36

¹ At that time the Lord appeared unto Jacob saying, Arise, go to Bethel and remain there, and make there an altar to the Lord who appeareth unto thee, who delivered thee and thy sons from affliction. ² And Jacob rose up with his sons and all belonging to him, and they went and came to Bethel according to the word of the Lord. ³ And Jacob was ninety-nine years old when he went up to Bethel, and Jacob and his sons and all the people that were with him, remained in Bethel in Luz, and he there built an altar to the Lord who appeared unto him, and Jacob and his sons remained in Bethel six months. ⁴ At that time died Deborah the daughter of Uz, the nurse of Rebecca, who had been with Jacob; and Jacob buried her beneath Bethel under an oak that was there. ⁵ And Rebecca the daughter of Bethuel, the mother of Jacob, also died at that time in Hebron, the same is Kireath-arba, and she was buried in the cave of Machpelah which Abraham had bought from the children of Heth. ⁶ And the life of Rebecca was one hundred and thirty-three years, and she died and when Jacob heard that his mother Rebecca was dead he wept bitterly for his mother, and made a great mourning for her, and for Deborah her nurse beneath the oak, and he called the name of that place Allon-bachuth. ⁷ And Laban the Syrian died in those days, for God smote him because he transgressed the covenant that existed between him and Jacob. ⁸ And Jacob was a hundred years old when the Lord appeared unto him, and blessed him and called his name Israel, and Rachel the wife of Jacob conceived in those days. ⁹ And at that time Jacob and all belonging to him journeyed from Bethel to go to his father's house, to Hebron. ¹⁰ And whilst they were going on the road, and there was yet but a little way to come to Ephrath, Rachel bare a son and she had hard labor and she died. ¹¹ And Jacob buried her in the way to Ephrath, which is Bethlehem, and he set a pillar upon her grave, which is there unto this day; and the days of Rachel were forty-five years and she died. ¹² And Jacob called the name of his son that was born to him, which Rachel bare unto him, Benjamin, for he was born to him in the land on the right hand. ¹³ And it was after the death of Rachel, that Jacob pitched his tent in the tent of her handmaid Bilhah. ¹⁴ And Reuben was jealous for his mother Leah on account of this, and he was filled with anger, and he rose up in his anger and went and entered the tent of Bilhah and he thence removed his father's bed. ¹⁵ At that time the portion of birthright, together with the kingly and priestly offices, was removed from the sons of Reuben, for he had profaned his father's bed, and the birthright was given unto Joseph, the kingly office to Judah, and the priesthood unto Levi, because Reuben had defiled his father's bed. ¹⁶ And these are the generations of Jacob who were born to him in Padan-aram, and the sons of Jacob were twelve. ¹⁷ The sons of Leah were Reuben the first born, and Simeon, Levi, Judah, Issachar, Zebulun, and their sister Dinah; and the sons of Rachel were Joseph and Benjamin. ¹⁸ The sons of Zilpah, Leah's handmaid, were Gad and Asher, and the sons of Bilhah, Rachel's handmaid, were Dan and Naphtali; these are the sons of Jacob which were born to him in Padan-aram. ¹⁹ And Jacob and his sons and all belonging to him journeyed and came to Mamre, which is Kireath-arba, that is in Hebron, where Abraham and Isaac sojourned, and Jacob with his sons and all belonging to him, dwelt with his father in Hebron. ²⁰ And his brother Esau and his sons, and all belonging to him went to the land of Seir and dwelt there, and had possessions in the land of Seir, and the children of Esau were fruitful and multiplied exceedingly in the land of Seir. ²¹ And these are the generations of Esau that were born to him in the land of Canaan, and the sons of Esau were five. ²² And Adah bare to Esau his first born Eliphaz, and she also bare to him Reuel, and Ahlibamah bare to him Jeush, Yaalam and Korah. ²³ These are the children of Esau who were born to him in the land of Canaan; and the sons of Eliphaz the son of Esau were Teman, Omar, Zepho, Gatam, Kenaz and Amalex, and the sons of Reuel were Nachath, Zerach, Shamah and Mizzah. ²⁴ And the sons of Jeush were Timnah, Alvah, Jetheth; and the sons of Yaalam were Alah, Phinor and Kenaz. ²⁵ And the sons of Korah were Teman, Mibzar, Magdiel and Eram; these are the families of the sons of Esau according to their dukedoms in the land of Seir. ²⁶ And these are the names of the sons of Seir the Horite, inhabitants of the land of Seir, Lotan, Shobal, Zibeon, Anah, Dishan, Ezer and Dishon, being seven sons. ²⁷ And the children of Lotan were Hori, Heman and their sister Timna, that is Timna who came to Jacob and his sons, and they would not give ear to her, and she went and became a concubine to Eliphaz the son of Esau, and she bare to him Amalek. ²⁸ And the sons of Shobal were Alvan, Manahath, Ebal, Shepho, and Onam, and the sons of Zibeon were Ajah, and Anah, this was that Anah who found the Yemim in the wilderness when he fed the asses of Zibeon his father. ²⁹ And whilst he was feeding his father's asses he led them to the wilderness at different times to feed them. ³⁰ And there was a day that he brought them to one of the deserts on the sea shore, opposite the wilderness of the people, and whilst he was feeding them, behold a very heavy storm came from the other side of the sea and rested upon the asses that were feeding there, and they all stood still. ³¹ And afterward about one hundred and twenty great and terrible animals came out from the wilderness at the other side of the sea, and they all came to the place where the asses were, and they placed themselves there. ³² And those animals, from their middle downward, were in the shape of the children of men, and from their middle upward, some had the likeness of bears, and some the likeness of the keephas, with tails behind them from between their shoulders reaching down to the earth, like the tails of the ducheephath, and these animals came and mounted and rode upon these asses, and led them away, and they went away unto this day. ³³ And one of these animals approached Anah and smote him with his tail, and then fled from that place. ³⁴ And when he saw this work he was exceedingly afraid of his life, and he fled and escaped to the city. ³⁵ And he related to his sons and brothers all that had happened to him, and many men went to seek the asses but could not find them, and Anah and his brothers went no more to that place from that day following, for they were greatly afraid of their lives. ³⁶ And the children of Anah the son of Seir, were Dishon and his sister Ahlibamah, and the children of Dishon were Hemdan, Eshban, Ithran and Cheran, and the children of Ezer were Bilhan, Zaavan and Akan, and the children of Dishon were Uz and Aran. ³⁷ These are the families of the children of Seir the Horite, according to their dukedoms in the land of Seir. ³⁸ And Esau and his children dwelt in the land of Seir the Horite, the inhabitant of the land, and they had possessions in it and were fruitful and multiplied exceedingly, and Jacob and his children and all belonging to them, dwelt with their father Isaac in the land of Canaan, as the Lord had commanded Abraham their father.

37

¹ And in the one hundred and fifth year of the life of Jacob, that is the ninth year of Jacob's dwelling with his children in the land of Canaan, he came from Padan-aram. ² And in those days Jacob journeyed with his children from Hebron, and they went and returned to the city of Shechem, they and all belonging to them, and they dwelt there, for the children of Jacob obtained good and fat pasture land for their cattle in the city of Shechem, the city of Shechem having then been rebuilt, and there were in it about three hundred men and women. ³ And Jacob and his children and all belonging to him dwelt in the part of the field which Jacob had bought from Hamor the father of Shechem, when he came from Padan-aram before Simeon and Levi had smitten the city. ⁴ And all those kings of the Canaanites and Amorites that surrounded the city of Shechem, heard that the sons of Jacob had again come to Shechem and dwelt there. ⁵ And they said, Shall the sons of Jacob the Hebrew again come to the city and dwell therein, after that they have smitten its inhabitants and driven them out? shall they now return and also drive out those who are dwelling in the city or slay them? ⁶ And all the kings of Canaan again assembled, and they came together to make war with Jacob and his sons. ⁷ And Jashub king of Tapnach sent also to all his neighboring kings, to Elan king of Gaash, and to Ihuri king of Shiloh, and to Parathon king of Chazar, and to Susi king of Sarton, and to Laban king of Bethchoran, and to Shabir king of Othnay-mah, saying, ⁸ Come up to me and assist me, and let us smite Jacob the Hebrew and his sons, and all belonging to him, for they are again come to Shechem to possess it and to slay its inhabitants as before. ⁹ And all these kings assembled together and came with all their camps, a people exceedingly plentiful like the sand upon the sea shore, and they were all opposite to Tapnach. ¹⁰ And Jashub king of Tapnach went forth to them with all his army, and he encamped with them opposite to Tapnach without the city, and all these kings they divided into seven divisions, being seven camps against the sons of Jacob. ¹¹ And they sent a declaration to Jacob and his son, saying, Come you all forth to us that we may have an interview together in the plain, and revenge the cause of the men of Shechem whom you slew in their city, and you will now again return to the city of Shechem and dwell therein, and slay its inhabitants as before. ¹² And the sons of Jacob heard this and their anger was kindled exceedingly at the words of the kings of Canaan, and ten of the sons of Jacob hastened and rose up, and each of them girt on his weapons of war; and there were one hundred and two of their servants with them equipped in battle array. ¹³ And all these men, the sons of Jacob with their servants, went toward these kings, and Jacob their father was with them, and they all stood upon the heap of Shechem. ¹⁴ And Jacob prayed to the Lord for his sons, and he spread forth his hands to the Lord, and he said, O God, thou art an Almighty God, thou art our father, thou didst form us and we are the works of thine hands; I pray thee deliver my sons through thy mercy from the hand of their enemies, who are this day coming to fight with them and save them from their hand, for in thy hand is power and might, to save the few from the many. ¹⁵ And give unto

my sons, thy servants, strength of heart and might to fight with their enemies, to subdue them, and make their enemies fall before them, and let not my sons and their servants die through the hands of the children of Canaan. ¹⁶ But if it seemeth good in thine eyes to take away the lives of my sons and their servants, take them in thy great mercy through the hands of thy ministers, that they may not perish this day by the hands of the kings of the Amorites. ¹⁷ And when Jacob ceased praying to the Lord the earth shook from its place, and the sun darkened, and all these kings were terrified and a great consternation seized them. ¹⁸ And the Lord hearkened to the prayer of Jacob, and the Lord impressed the hearts of all the kings and their hosts with the terror and awe of the sons of Jacob. ¹⁹ For the Lord caused them to hear the voice of chariots, and the voice of mighty horses from the sons of Jacob, and the voice of a great army accompanying them. ²⁰ And these kings were seized with great terror at the sons of Jacob, and whilst they were standing in their quarters, behold the sons of Jacob advanced upon them, with one hundred and twelve men, with a great and tremendous shouting. ²¹ And when the kings saw the sons of Jacob advancing toward them, they were still more panic struck, and they were inclined to retreat from before the sons of Jacob as at first, and not to fight with them. ²² But they did not retreat, saying, It would be a disgrace to us thus twice to retreat from before the Hebrews. ²³ And the sons of Jacob came near and advanced against all these kings and their armies, and they saw, and behold it was a very mighty people, numerous as the sand of the sea. ²⁴ And the sons of Jacob called unto the Lord and said, Help us O Lord, help us and answer us, for we trust in thee, and let us not die by the hands of these uncircumcised men, who this day have come against us. ²⁵ And the sons of Jacob girt on their weapons of war, and they took in their hands each man his shield and his javelin, and they approached to battle. ²⁶ And Judah, the son of Jacob, ran first before his brethren, and ten of his servants with him, and he went toward these kings. ²⁷ And Jashub, king of Tapnach, also came forth first with his army before Judah, and Judah saw Jashub and his army coming toward him, and Judah's wrath was kindled, and his anger burned within him, and he approached to battle in which Judah ventured his life. ²⁸ And Jashub and all his army were advancing toward Judah, and he was riding upon a very strong and powerful horse, and Jashub was a very valiant man, and covered with iron and brass from head to foot. ²⁹ And whilst he was upon the horse, he shot arrows with both hands from before and behind, as was his manner in all his battles, and he never missed the place to which he aimed his arrows. ³⁰ And when Jashub came to fight with Judah, and was darting many arrows against Judah, the Lord bound the hand of Jashub, and all the arrows that he shot rebounded upon his own men. ³¹ And notwithstanding this, Jashub kept advancing toward Judah, to challenge him with the arrows, but the distance between them was about thirty cubits, and when Judah saw Jashub darting forth his arrows against him, he ran to him with his wrath-excited might. ³² And Judah took up a large stone from the ground, and its weight was sixty shekels, and Judah ran toward Jashub, and with the stone struck him on his shield, that Jashub was stunned with the blow, and fell off from his horse to the ground. ³³ And the shield burst asunder out of the hand of Jashub, and through the force of the blow sprang to the distance of about fifteen cubits, and the shield fell before the second camp. ³⁴ And the kings that came with Jashub saw at a distance the strength of Judah, the son of Jacob, and what he had done to Jashub, and they were terribly afraid of Judah. ³⁵ And they assembled near Jashub's camp, seeing his confusion, and Judah drew his sword and smote forty-two men of the camp of Jashub, and the whole of Jashub's camp fled before Judah, and no man stood against him, and they left Jashub and fled from him, and Jashub was still prostrate upon the ground. ³⁶ And Jashub seeing that all the men of his camp had fled from him, hastened and rose up with terror against Judah, and stood upon his legs opposite Judah. ³⁷ And Jashub had a single combat with Judah, placing shield toward shield, and Jashub's men all fled, for they were greatly afraid of Judah. ³⁸ And Jashub took his spear in his hand to strike Judah upon his head, but Judah had quickly placed his shield to his head against Jashub's spear, so that the shield of Judah received the blow from Jashub's spear, and the shield was split in too. ³⁹ And when Judah saw that his shield was split, he hastily drew his sword and smote Jashub at his ankles, and cut off his feet that Jashub fell upon the ground, and the spear fell from his hand. ⁴⁰ And Judah hastily picked up Jashub's spear, with which he severed his head and cast it next to his feet. ⁴¹ And when the sons of Jacob saw what Judah had done to Jashub, they all ran into the ranks of the other kings, and the sons of Jacob fought with the army of Jashub, and the armies of all the kings that were there. ⁴² And the sons of Jacob caused fifteen thousand of their men to fall, and they smote them as if smiting at gourds, and the rest fled for their lives. ⁴³ And Judah was still standing by the body of Jashub, and stripped Jashub of his coat of mail. ⁴⁴ And Judah also took off the iron and brass that was about Jashub, and behold nine men of the captains of Jashub came along to fight against Judah. ⁴⁵ And Judah hastened and took up a stone from the ground, and with it smote one of them upon the head, and his skull was fractured, and the body also fell from the horse to the ground. ⁴⁶ And the eight captains that remained, seeing the strength of Judah, were greatly afraid and they fled, and Judah with his ten men pursued them, and they overtook them and slew them. ⁴⁷ And the sons of Jacob were still smiting the armies of the kings, and they slew many of them, but those kings daringly kept their stand with their captains, and did not retreat from their places, and they exclaimed against those of their armies that fled from before the sons of Jacob, but none would listen to them, for they were afraid of their lives lest they should die. ⁴⁸ And all the sons of Jacob, after having smitten the armies of the kings, returned and came before Judah, and Judah was still slaying the eight captains of Jashub, and stripping off their garments. ⁴⁹ And Levi saw Elon, king of Gaash, advancing toward him, with his fourteen captains to smite him, but Levi did not know it for certain. ⁵⁰ And Elon with his captains approached nearer, and Levi looked back and saw that battle was given him in the rear, and Levi ran with twelve of his servants, and they went and slew Elon and his captains with the edge of the sword.

38

¹ And Ihuri king of Shiloh came up to assist Elon, and he approached Jacob, when Jacob drew his bow that was in his hand and with an arrow struck Ihuri which caused his death. ² And when Ihuri king of Shiloh was dead, the four remaining kings fled from their station with the rest of the captains, and they endeavored to retreat, saying, We have no more strength with the Hebrews after their having killed the three kings and their captains who were more powerful than we are. ³ And when the sons of Jacob saw that the remaining kings had removed from their station, they pursued them, and Jacob also came from the heap of Shechem from the place where he was standing, and they went after the kings and they approached them with their servants. ⁴ And the kings and the captains with the rest of their armies, seeing that the sons of Jacob approached them, were afraid of their lives and fled till they reached the city of Chazar. ⁵ And the sons of Jacob pursued them to the gate of the city of Chazar, and they smote a great smiting amongst the kings and their armies, about four thousand men, and whilst they were smiting the army of the kings, Jacob was occupied with his bow confining himself to smiting the kings, and he slew them all. ⁶ And he slew Parathon king of Chazar at the gate of the city of Chazar, and he afterward smote Susi king of Sarton, and Laban king of Bethchorin, and Shabir king of Machnaymah, and he slew them all with arrows, an arrow to each of them, and they died. ⁷ And the sons of Jacob seeing that all the kings were dead and that they were broken up and retreating, continued to carry on the battle with the armies of the kings opposite the gate of Chazar, and they still smote about four hundred of their men. ⁸ And three men of the servants of Jacob fell in that battle, and when Judah saw that three of his servants had died, it grieved him greatly, and his anger burned within him against the Amorites. ⁹ And all the men that remained of the armies of the kings were greatly afraid of their lives, and they ran and broke the gate of the walls of the city of Chazar, and they all entered the city for safety. ¹⁰ And they concealed themselves in the midst of the city of Chazar, for the city of Chazar was very large and extensive, and when all these armies had entered the city, the sons of Jacob ran after them to the city. ¹¹ And four mighty men, experienced in battle, went forth from the city and stood against the entrance of the city, with drawn swords and spears in their hands, and they placed themselves opposite the sons of Jacob, and would not suffer them to enter the city. ¹² And Naphtali ran and came between them and with his sword smote two of them, and cut off their heads at one stroke. ¹³ And he turned to the other two, and behold they had fled, and he pursued them, overtook them, smote them and slew them. ¹⁴ And the sons of Jacob came to the city and saw, and behold there was another wall to the city, and they sought for the gate of the wall and could not find it, and Judah sprang upon the top of the wall, and Simeon and Levi followed him, and they all three descended from the wall into the city. ¹⁵ And Simeon and Levi slew all the men who ran for safety into the city, and also the inhabitants of the city with their wives and little ones, they slew with the edge of the sword, and the cries of the city ascended up to heaven. ¹⁶ And Dan and Naphtali sprang upon the wall to see what caused the noise of lamentation, for the sons of Jacob felt anxious about their brothers, and they heard the inhabitants of the city speaking with weeping and supplications, saying, Take all that we possess in the city and go away, only do not put us to death. ¹⁷ And when Judah, Simeon, and Levi had ceased smiting the inhabitants of the city, they ascended the wall and called to Dan and Naphtali, who were upon the wall, and to the rest of their brothers, and Simeon and Levi informed them of the entrance into the city, and all the sons of Jacob came to fetch the spoil. ¹⁸ And the sons of Jacob took the spoil of the city of Chazar, the flocks and herds, and the property, and they took all that could be captured, and went

away that day from the city. ¹⁹ And on the next day the sons of Jacob went to Sarton, for they heard that the men of Sarton who had remained in the city were assembling to fight with them for having slain their king, and Sarton was a very high and fortified city, and it had a deep rampart surrounding the city. ²⁰ And the pillar of the rampart was about fifty cubits and its breadth forty cubits, and there was no place for a man to enter the city on account of the rampart, and the sons of Jacob saw the rampart of the city, and they sought an entrance in it but could not find it. ²¹ For the entrance to the city was at the rear, and every man that wished to come into the city came by that road and went around the whole city, and he afterwards entered the city. ²² And the sons of Jacob seeing they could not find the way into the city, their anger was kindled greatly, and the inhabitants of the city seeing that the sons of Jacob were coming to them were greatly afraid of them, for they had heard of their strength and what they had done to Chazar. ²³ And the inhabitants of the city of Sarton could not go out toward the sons of Jacob after having assembled in the city to fight against them, lest they might thereby get into the city, but when they saw that they were coming toward them, they were greatly afraid of them, for they had heard of their strength and what they had done to Chazar. ²⁴ So the inhabitants of Sarton speedily took away the bridge of the road of the city, from its place, before the sons of Jacob came, and they brought it into the city. ²⁵ And the sons of Jacob came and sought the way into the city, and could not find it and the inhabitants of the city went up to the top of the wall, and saw, and behold the sons of Jacob were seeking an entrance into the city. ²⁶ And the inhabitants of the city reproached the sons of Jacob from the top of the wall, and they cursed them, and the sons of Jacob heard the reproaches, and they were greatly incensed, and their anger burned within them. ²⁷ And the sons of Jacob were provoked at them, and they all rose and sprang over the rampart with the force of their strength, and through their might passed the forty cubits' breadth of the rampart. ²⁸ And when they had passed the rampart they stood under the wall of the city, and they found all the gates of the city enclosed with iron doors. ²⁹ And the sons of Jacob came near to break open the doors of the gates of the city, and the inhabitants did not let them, for from the top of the wall they were casting stones and arrows upon them. ³⁰ And the number of the people that were upon the wall was about four hundred men, and when the sons of Jacob saw that the men of the city would not let them open the gates of the city, they sprang and ascended the top of the wall, and Judah went up first to the east part of the city. ³¹ And Gad and Asher went up after him to the west corner of the city, and Simeon and Levi to the north, and Dan and Reuben to the south. ³² And the men who were on the top of the wall, the inhabitants of the city, seeing that the sons of Jacob were coming up to them, they all fled from the wall, descended into the city, and concealed themselves in the midst of the city. ³³ And Issachar and Naphtali that remained under the wall approached and broke the gates of the city, and kindled a fire at the gates of the city, that the iron melted, and all the sons of Jacob came into the city, they and all their men, and they fought with the inhabitants of the city of Sarton, and smote them with the edge of the sword, and no man stood up before them. ³⁴ And about two hundred men fled from the city, and they all went and hid themselves in a certain tower in the city, and Judah pursued them to the tower and he broke down the tower, which fell upon the men, and they all died. ³⁵ And the sons of Jacob went up the road of the roof of that tower, and they saw, and behold there was another strong and high tower at a distance in the city, and the top of it reached to heaven, and the sons of Jacob hastened and descended, and went with all their men to that tower, and found it filled with about three hundred men, women and little ones. ³⁶ And the sons of Jacob smote a great smiting amongst those men in the tower and they ran away and fled from them. ³⁷ And Simeon and Levi pursued them, when twelve mighty and valiant men came out to them from the place where they had concealed themselves. ³⁸ And those twelve men maintained a strong battle against Simeon and Levi, and Simeon and Levi could not prevail over them, and those valiant men broke the shields of Simeon and Levi, and one of them struck at Levi's head with his sword, when Levi hastily placed his hand to his head, for he was afraid of the sword, and the sword struck Levi's hand, and it wanted but little to the hand of Levi being cut off. ³⁹ And Levi seized the sword of the valiant man in his hand, and took it forcibly from the man, and with it he struck at the head of the powerful man, and he severed his head. ⁴⁰ And eleven men approached to fight with Levi, for they saw that one of them was killed, and the sons of Jacob fought, but the sons of Jacob could not prevail over them, for those men were very powerful. ⁴¹ And the sons of Jacob seeing that they could not prevail over them, Simeon gave a loud and tremendous shriek, and the eleven powerful men were stunned at the voice of Simeon's shrieking. ⁴² And Judah at a distance knew the voice of Simeon's shouting, and Naphtali and Judah ran with their shields to Simeon and Levi, and found them fighting with those powerful men, unable to prevail over them as their shields were broken. ⁴³ And Naphtali saw that the shields of Simeon and Levi were broken, and he took two shields from his servants and brought them to Simeon and Levi. ⁴⁴ And Simeon, Levi and Judah on that day fought all three against the eleven mighty men until the time of sunset, but they could not prevail over them. ⁴⁵ And this was told unto Jacob, and he was sorely grieved, and he prayed unto the Lord, and he and Naphtali his son went against these mighty men. ⁴⁶ And Jacob approached and drew his bow, and came nigh unto the mighty men, and slew three of their men with the bow, and the remaining eight turned back, and behold, the war waged against them in the front and rear, and they were greatly afraid of their lives, and could not stand before the sons of Jacob, and they fled from before them. ⁴⁷ And in their flight they met Dan and Asher coming toward them, and they suddenly fell upon them, and fought with them, and slew two of them, and Judah and his brothers pursued them, and smote the remainder of them, and slew them. ⁴⁸ And all the sons of Jacob returned and walked about the city, searching if they could find any men, and they found about twenty young men in a cave in the city, and Gad and Asher smote them all, and Dan and Naphtali lighted upon the rest of the men who had fled and escaped from the second tower, and they smote them all. ⁴⁹ And the sons of Jacob smote all the inhabitants of the city of Sarton, but the women and little ones they left in the city and did not slay them. ⁵⁰ And all the inhabitants of the city of Sarton were powerful men, one of them would pursue a thousand, and two of them would not flee from ten thousand of the rest of men. ⁵¹ And the sons of Jacob slew all the inhabitants of the city of Sarton with the edge of the sword, that no man stood up against them, and they left the women in the city. ⁵² And the sons of Jacob took all the spoil of the city, and captured what they desired, and they took flocks and herds and property from the city, and the sons of Jacob did unto Sarton and its inhabitants as they had done to Chazar and its inhabitants, and they turned and went away.

39

¹ And when the sons of Jacob went from the city of Sarton, they had gone about two hundred cubits when they met the inhabitants of Tapnach coming toward them, for they went out to fight with them, because they had smitten the king of Tapnach and all his men. ² So all that remained in the city of Tapnach came out to fight with the sons of Jacob, and they thought to retake from them the booty and the spoil which they had captured from Chazar and Sarton. ³ And the rest of the men of Tapnach fought with the sons of Jacob in that place, and the sons of Jacob smote them, and they fled before them, and they pursued them to the city of Arbelan, and they all fell before the sons of Jacob. ⁴ And the sons of Jacob returned and came to Tapnach, to take away the spoil of Tapnach, and when they came to Tapnach they heard that the people of Arbelan had gone out to meet them to save the spoil of their brethren, and the sons of Jacob left ten of their men in Tapnach to plunder the city, and they went out toward the people of Arbelan. ⁵ And the men of Arbelan went out with their wives to fight with the sons of Jacob, for their wives were experienced in battle, and they went out, about four hundred men and women. ⁶ And all the sons of Jacob shouted with a loud voice, and they all ran toward the inhabitants of Arbelan, and with a great and tremendous voice. ⁷ And the inhabitants of Arbelan heard the noise of the shouting of the sons of Jacob, and their roaring like the noise of lions and like the roaring of the sea and its waves. ⁸ And fear and terror possessed their hearts on account of the sons of Jacob, and they were terribly afraid of them, and they retreated and fled before them into the city, and the sons of Jacob pursued them to the gate of the city, and they came upon them in the city. ⁹ And the sons of Jacob fought with them in the city, and all their women were engaged in slinging against the sons of Jacob, and the combat was very severe amongst them the whole of that day till evening. ¹⁰ And the sons of Jacob could not prevail over them, and the sons of Jacob had almost perished in that battle, and the sons of Jacob cried unto the Lord and greatly gained strength toward evening, and the sons of Jacob smote all the inhabitants of Arbelan by the edge of the sword, men, women and little ones. ¹¹ And also the remainder of the people who had fled from Sarton, the sons of Jacob smote them in Arbelan, and the sons of Jacob did unto Arbelan and Tapnach as they had done to Chazar and Sarton, and when the women saw that all the men were dead, they went upon the roofs of the city and smote the sons of Jacob by showering down stones like rain. ¹² And the sons of Jacob hastened and came into the city and seized all the women and smote them with the edge of the sword, and the sons of Jacob captured all the spoil and booty, flocks and herds and cattle. ¹³ And the sons of Jacob did unto Machnaymah as they had done to Tapnach, to Chazar and to Shiloh, and they turned from there and went away. ¹⁴ And on the fifth day the sons of Jacob heard that the people of Gaash had gathered against them to battle, because they had slain their king and their captains, for there had been fourteen captains in the city of Gaash, and the sons of Jacob had slain

them all in the first battle. ¹⁵ And the sons of Jacob that day girt on their weapons of war, and they marched to battle against the inhabitants of Gaash, and in Gaash there was a strong and mighty people of the people of the Amorites, and Gaash was the strongest and best fortified city of all the cities of the Amorites, and it had three walls. ¹⁶ And the sons of Jacob came to Gaash and they found the gates of the city locked, and about five hundred men standing at the top of the outer-most wall, and a people numerous as the sand upon the sea shore were in ambush for the sons of Jacob from without the city at the rear thereof. ¹⁷ And the sons of Jacob approached to open the gates of the city, and whilst they were drawing nigh, behold those who were in ambush at the rear of the city came forth from their places and surrounded the sons of Jacob. ¹⁸ And the sons of Jacob were enclosed between the people of Gaash, and the battle was both to their front and rear, and all the men that were upon the wall, were casting from the wall upon them, arrows and stones. ¹⁹ And Judah, seeing that the men of Gaash were getting too heavy for them, gave a most piercing and tremendous shriek and all the men of Gaash were terrified at the voice of Judah's cry, and men fell from the wall at his powerful shriek, and all those that were from without and within the city were greatly afraid of their lives. ²⁰ And the sons of Jacob still came nigh to break the doors of the city, when the men of Gaash threw stones and arrows upon them from the top of the wall, and made them flee from the gate. ²¹ And the sons of Jacob returned against the men of Gaash who were with them from without the city, and they smote them terribly, as striking against gourds, and they could not stand against the sons of Jacob, for fright and terror had seized them at the shriek of Judah. ²² And the sons of Jacob slew all those men who were without the city, and the sons of Jacob still drew nigh to effect an entrance into the city, and to fight under the city walls, but they could not for all the inhabitants of Gaash who remained in the city had surrounded the walls of Gaash in every direction, so that the sons of Jacob were unable to approach the city to fight with them. ²³ And the sons of Jacob came nigh to one corner to fight under the wall, the inhabitants of Gaash threw arrows and stones upon them like showers of rain, and they fled from under the wall. ²⁴ And the people of Gaash who were upon the wall, seeing that the sons of Jacob could not prevail over them from under the wall, reproached the sons of Jacob in these words, saying, ²⁵ What is the matter with you in the battle that you cannot prevail? can you then do unto the mighty city of Gaash and its inhabitants as you did to the cities of the Amorites that were not so powerful? Surely to those weak ones amongst us you did those things, and slew them in the entrance of the city, for they had no strength when they were terrified at the sound of your shouting. ²⁶ And will you now then be able to fight in this place? Surely here you will all die, and we will avenge the cause of those cities that you have laid waste. ²⁷ And the inhabitants of Gaash greatly reproached the sons of Jacob and reviled them with their gods, and continued to cast arrows and stones upon them from the wall. ²⁸ And Judah and his brothers heard the words of the inhabitants of Gaash and their anger was greatly roused, and Judah was jealous of his God in this matter, and he called out and said, O Lord, help, send help to us and our brothers. ²⁹ And he ran at a distance with all his might, with his drawn sword in his hand, and he sprang from the earth and by dint of his strength, mounted the wall, and his sword fell from his hand. ³⁰ And Judah shouted upon the wall, and all the men that were upon the wall were terrified, and some of them fell from the wall into the city and died, and those who were yet upon the wall, when they saw Judah's strength, they were greatly afraid and fled for their lives into the city for safety. ³¹ And some were emboldened to fight with Judah upon the wall, and they came nigh to slay him when they saw there was no sword in Judah's hand, and they thought of casting him from the wall to his brothers, and twenty men of the city came up to assist them, and they surrounded Judah and they all shouted over him, and approached him with drawn swords, and they terrified Judah, and Judah cried out to his brothers from the wall. ³² And Jacob and his sons drew the bow from under the wall, and smote three of the men that were upon the top of the wall, and Judah continued to cry and he exclaimed, O Lord help us, O Lord deliver us, and he cried out with a loud voice upon the wall, and the cry was heard at a great distance. ³³ And after this cry he again repeated to shout, and all the men who surrounded Judah on the top of the wall were terrified, and they each threw his sword from his hand at the sound of Judah's shouting and his tremor, and fled. ³⁴ And Judah took the swords which had fallen from their hands, and Judah fought with them and slew twenty of their men upon the wall. ³⁵ And about eighty men and women still ascended the wall from the city and they all surrounded Judah, and the Lord impressed the fear of Judah in their hearts, that they were unable to approach him. ³⁶ And Jacob and all who were with him drew the bow from under the wall, and they slew ten men upon the wall, and they fell below the wall, before Jacob and his sons. ³⁷ And the people upon the wall seeing that twenty of their men had fallen, they still ran toward Judah with drawn swords, but they could not approach him for they were greatly terrified at Judah's strength. ³⁸ And one of their mighty men whose name was Arud approached to strike Judah upon the head with his sword, when Judah hastily put his shield to his head, and the sword hit the shield, and it was split in two. ³⁹ And this mighty man after he had struck Judah ran for his life, at the fear of Judah, and his feet slipped upon the wall and he fell amongst the sons of Jacob who were below the wall, and the sons of Jacob smote him and slew him. ⁴⁰ And Judah's head pained him from the blow of the powerful man, and Judah had nearly died from it. ⁴¹ And Judah cried out upon the wall owing to the pain produced by the blow, when Dan heard him, and his anger burned within him, and he also rose up and went at a distance and ran and sprang from the earth and mounted the wall with his wrath-excited strength. ⁴² And when Dan came upon the wall near unto Judah all the men upon the wall fled, who had stood against Judah, and they went up to the second wall, and they threw arrows and stones upon Dan and Judah from the second wall, and endeavored to drive them from the wall. ⁴³ And the arrows and stones struck Dan and Judah, and they had nearly been killed upon the wall, and wherever Dan and Judah fled from the wall, they were attacked with arrows and stones from the second wall. ⁴⁴ And Jacob and his sons were still at the entrance of the city below the first wall, and they were not able to draw their bow against the inhabitants of the city, as they could not be seen by them, being upon the second wall. ⁴⁵ And Dan and Judah when they could no longer bear the stones and arrows that fell upon them from the second wall, they both sprang upon the second wall near the people of the city, and when the people of the city who were upon the second wall saw that Dan and Judah had come to them upon the second wall, they all cried out and descended below between the walls. ⁴⁶ And Jacob and his sons heard the noise of the shouting from the people of the city, and they were still at the entrance of the city, and they were anxious about Dan and Judah who were not seen by them, they being upon the second wall. ⁴⁷ And Naphtali went up with his wrath-excited might and sprang upon the first wall to see what caused the noise of shouting which they had heard in the city, and Issachar and Zebulun drew nigh to break the doors of the city, and they opened the gates of the city and came into the city. ⁴⁸ And Naphtali leaped from the first wall to the second, and came to assist his brothers, and the inhabitants of Gaash who were upon the wall, seeing that Naphtali was the third who had come up to assist his brothers, they all fled and descended into the city, and Jacob and all his sons and all their young men came into the city to them. ⁴⁹ And Judah and Dan and Naphtali descended from the wall into the city and pursued the inhabitants of the city, and Simeon and Levi were from without the city and knew not that the gate was opened, and they went up from there to the wall and came down to their brothers into the city. ⁵⁰ And the inhabitants of the city had all descended into the city, and the sons of Jacob came to them in different directions, and the battle waged against them from the front and the rear, and the sons of Jacob smote them terribly, and slew about twenty thousand of them men and women, not one of them could stand up against the sons of Jacob. ⁵¹ And the blood flowed plentifully in the city, and it was like a brook of water, and the blood flowed like a brook to the outer part of the city, and reached the desert of Bethchorin. ⁵² And the people of Bethchorin saw at a distance the blood flowing from the city of Gaash, and about seventy men from amongst them ran to see the blood, and they came to the place where the blood was. ⁵³ And they followed the track of the blood and came to the wall of the city of Gaash, and they saw the blood issue from the city, and they heard the voice of crying from the inhabitants of Gaash, for it ascended unto heaven, and the blood was continuing to flow abundantly like a brook of water. ⁵⁴ And all the sons of Jacob were still smiting the inhabitants of Gaash, and were engaged in slaying them till evening, about twenty thousand men and women, and the people of Chorin said, Surely this is the work of the Hebrews, for they are still carrying on war in all the cities of the Amorites. ⁵⁵ And those people hastened and ran to Bethchorin, and each took his weapons of war, and they cried out to all the inhabitants of Bethchorin, who also girt on their weapons of war to go and fight with the sons of Jacob. ⁵⁶ And when the sons of Jacob had done smiting the inhabitants of Gaash, they walked about the city to strip all the slain, and coming in the innermost part of the city and farther on they met three very powerful men, and there was no sword in their hand. ⁵⁷ And the sons of Jacob came up to the place where they were, and the powerful men ran away, and one of them had taken Zebulun, who he saw was a young lad and of short stature, and with his might dashed him to the ground. ⁵⁸ And Jacob ran to him with his sword and Jacob smote him below his loins with the sword, and cut him in two, and the body fell upon Zebulun. ⁵⁹ And the second one approached and seized Jacob to fell him to the ground, and Jacob turned to him and shouted to him, whilst Simeon and Levi ran and smote him on the hips with the sword and felled him to the ground. ⁶⁰ And the powerful man rose up from the ground with wrath-excited might, and Judah came to him before he had gained his footing, and struck him upon the head with the sword, and his head was split and he died. ⁶¹ And the third powerful man, seeing that his companions were killed, ran from before the sons of Jacob, and the sons of Jacob pursued him in the city; and whilst the powerful man was fleeing he found one of the swords of the inhabitants of the city, and he picked it up and turned to the sons of Jacob and fought them with that sword. ⁶² And the powerful man ran to Judah to strike him upon the head with the sword, and there was no shield in the hand of Judah; and whilst he was aiming to strike him, Naphtali hastily took his shield and put it to Judah's head, and the sword of the powerful man hit the shield of Naphtali and Judah escaped the sword. ⁶³ And Simeon and Levi ran upon the powerful man with their swords and struck at him forcibly with their swords, and the two swords entered the body of the powerful man and divided it in two, length-wise. ⁶⁴ And the sons of Jacob smote the three mighty men at that time, together with all the inhabitants of Gaash, and the day was about to decline. ⁶⁵ And the sons of Jacob walked about Gaash and took all the spoil of the city, even the little ones and women they did not suffer to live, and the sons of Jacob did unto Gaash as they had done to Sarton and Shiloh.

40

¹ And the sons of Jacob led away all the spoil of Gaash, and went out of the city by night. ² They were going out marching toward the castle of Bethchorin, and the inhabitants of Bethchorin were going to the castle to meet them, and on that night the sons of Jacob fought with the inhabitants of Bethchorin, in the castle of Bethchorin. ³ And all the inhabitants of Bethchorin were mighty men, one of them would not flee from before a thousand men, and they fought on that night upon the castle, and their shouts were heard on that night from afar, and the earth quaked at their shouting. ⁴ And all the sons of Jacob were afraid of those men, as they were not accustomed to fight in the dark, and they were greatly confounded, and the sons of Jacob cried unto the Lord, saying, Give help to us O Lord, deliver us that we may not die by the hands of these uncircumcised men. ⁵ And the Lord hearkened to the voice of the sons of Jacob, and the Lord caused great terror and confusion to seize the people of Bethchorin, and they fought amongst themselves the one with the other in the darkness of night, and smote each other in great numbers. ⁶ And the sons of Jacob, knowing that the Lord had brought a spirit of perverseness amongst those men, and that they fought each man with his neighbor, went forth from among the bands of the people of Bethchorin and went as far as the descent of the castle of Bethchorin, and farther, and they tarried there securely with their young men on that night. ⁷ And the people of Bethchorin fought the whole night, one man with his brother, and the other with his neighbor, and they cried out in every direction upon the castle, and their cry was heard at a distance, and the whole earth shook at their voice, for they were powerful above all the people of the earth. ⁸ And all the inhabitants of the cities of the Canaanites, the Hittites, the Amorites, the Hivites and all the kings of Canaan, and also those who were on the other side of the Jordan, heard the noise of the shouting on that night. ⁹ And they said, Surely these are the battles of the Hebrews who are fighting against the seven cities, who came nigh unto them; and who can stand against those Hebrews? ¹⁰ And all the inhabitants of the cities of the Canaanites, and all those who were on the other side of the Jordan, were greatly afraid of the sons of Jacob, for they said, Behold the same will be done to us as was done to those cities, for who can stand against their mighty strength? ¹¹ And the cries of the Chorinites were very great on that night, and continued to increase; and they smote each other till morning, and numbers of them were killed. ¹² And the morning appeared, and all the sons of Jacob rose up at daybreak and went up to the castle, and they smote those who remained of the Chorinites in a terrible manner, and they were all killed in the castle. ¹³ And the sixth day appeared, and all the inhabitants of Canaan saw at a distance all the people of Bethchorin lying dead in the castle of Bethchorin, and strewed about as the carcasses of lambs and goats. ¹⁴ And the sons of Jacob led all the spoil which they had captured from Gaash and went to Bethchorin, and they found the city full of people like the sand of the sea, and they fought with them, and the sons of Jacob smote them there till evening time. ¹⁵ And the sons of Jacob did unto Bethchorin as they had done to Gaash and Tapnach, and as they had done to Chazar, to Sarton and to Shiloh. ¹⁶ And the sons of Jacob took with them the spoil of Bethchorin and all the spoil of the cities, and on that day they went home to Shechem. ¹⁷ And the sons of Jacob came home to the city of Shechem, and they remained without the city, and they then rested there from the war, and tarried there all night. ¹⁸ And all their servants together with all the spoil that they had taken from the cities, they left without the city, and they did not enter the city, for they said, Peradventure there may be yet more fighting against us, and they may come to besiege us in Shechem. ¹⁹ And Jacob and his sons and their servants remained on that night and the next day in the portion of the field which Jacob had purchased from Hamor for five shekels, and all that they had captured was with them. ²⁰ And all the booty which the sons of Jacob had captured, was in the portion of the field, immense as the sand upon the sea shore. ²¹ And the inhabitants of the land observed them from afar, and all the inhabitants of the land were afraid of the sons of Jacob who had done this thing, for no king from the days of old had ever done the like. ²² And the seven kings of the Canaanites resolved to make peace with the sons of Jacob, for they were greatly afraid of their lives, on account of the sons of Jacob. ²³ And on that day, being the seventh day, Japhia king of Hebron sent secretly to the king of Ai, and to the king of Gibeon, and to the king of Shalem, and to the king of Adulam, and to the king of Lachish, and to the king of Chazar, and to all the Canaanitish kings who were under their subjection, saying, ²⁴ Go up with me, and come to me that we may go to the sons of Jacob, and I will make peace with them, and form a treaty with them, lest all your lands be destroyed by the swords of the sons of Jacob, as they did to Shechem and the cities around it, as you have heard and seen. ²⁵ And when you come to me, do not come with many men, but let every king bring his three head captains, and every captain bring three of his officers. ²⁶ And come all of you to Hebron, and we will go together to the sons of Jacob, and supplicate them that they shall form a treaty of peace with us. ²⁷ And all those kings did as the king of Hebron had sent to them, for they were all under his counsel and command, and all the kings of Canaan assembled to go to the sons of Jacob, to make peace with them; and the sons of Jacob returned and went to the portion of the field that was in Shechem, for they did not put confidence in the kings of the land. ²⁸ And the sons of Jacob returned and remained in the portion of the field ten days, and no one came to make war with them. ²⁹ And when the sons of Jacob saw that there was no appearance of war, they all assembled and went to the city of Shechem, and the sons of Jacob remained in Shechem. ³⁰ And at the expiration of forty days, all the kings of the Amorites assembled from all their places and came to Hebron, to Japhia, king of Hebron. ³¹ And the number of kings that came to Hebron, to make peace with the sons of Jacob, was twenty-one kings, and the number of captains that came with them was sixty-nine, and their men were one hundred and eighty-nine, and all these kings and their men rested by Mount Hebron. ³² And the king of Hebron went out with his three captains and nine men, and these kings resolved to go to the sons of Jacob to make peace. ³³ And they said unto the king of Hebron, Go thou before us with thy men, and speak for us unto the sons of Jacob, and we will come after thee and confirm thy words, and the king of Hebron did so. ³⁴ And the sons of Jacob heard that all the kings of Canaan had gathered together and rested in Hebron, and the sons of Jacob sent four of their servants as spies, saying, Go and spy these kings, and search and examine their men whether they are few or many, and if they are but few in number, number them all and come back. ³⁵ And the servants of Jacob went secretly to these kings, and did as the sons of Jacob had commanded them, and on that day they came back to the sons of Jacob, and said unto them, We came unto those kings, and they are but few in number, and we numbered them all, and behold, they were two hundred and eighty-eight, kings and men. ³⁶ And the sons of Jacob said, They are but few in number, therefore we will not all go out to them; and in the morning the sons of Jacob rose up and chose sixty two of their men, and ten of the sons of Jacob went with them; and they girt on their weapons of war, for they said, They are coming to make war with us, for they knew not that they were coming to make peace with them. ³⁷ And the sons of Jacob went with their servants to the gate of Shechem, toward those kings, and their father Jacob was with them. ³⁸ And when they had come forth, behold, the king of Hebron and his three captains and nine men with him were coming along the road against the sons of Jacob, and the sons of Jacob lifted up their eyes, and saw at a distance Japhia, king of Hebron, with his captains, coming toward them, and the sons of Jacob took their stand at the place of the gate of Shechem, and did not proceed. ³⁹ And the king of Hebron continued to advance, he and his captains, until he came nigh to the sons of Jacob, and he and his captains bowed down to them to the ground, and the king of Hebron sat with his captains before Jacob and his sons. ⁴⁰ And the sons of Jacob said unto him, What has befallen thee, O king of Hebron? why hast thou come to us this day? what dost thou require from us? and the king of Hebron said unto Jacob, I beseech thee my lord, all the kings of the Canaanites have this day come to make peace with you. ⁴¹ And the sons of Jacob heard the words of the king of Hebron, and they would not consent to his proposals, for the sons of Jacob had no faith in him, for they imagined that the king of Hebron had spoken deceitfully to them. ⁴² And the king of Hebron knew from the words of the sons of Jacob, that they did not believe his words, and the king of Hebron approached nearer to Jacob, and said unto him, I beseech thee, my lord, to be assured that all these kings have come to you on peaceable terms, for they have not come with all their men, neither did they bring their weapons of war with them, for they have come to seek peace from my lord

and his sons. ⁴³ And the sons of Jacob answered the king of Hebron, saying, Send thou to all these kings, and if thou speakest truth unto us, let them each come singly before us, and if they come unto us unarmed, we shall then know that they seek peace from us. ⁴⁴ And Japhia, king of Hebron, sent one of his men to the kings, and they all came before the sons of Jacob, and bowed down to them to the ground, and these kings sat before Jacob and his sons, and they spoke unto them, saying, ⁴⁵ We have heard all that you did unto the kings of the Amorites with your sword and exceedingly mighty arm, so that no man could stand up before you, and we were afraid of you for the sake of our lives, lest it should befall us as it did to them. ⁴⁶ So we have come unto you to form a treaty of peace between us, and now therefore contract with us a covenant of peace and truth, that you will not meddle with us, inasmuch as we have not meddled with you. ⁴⁷ And the sons of Jacob knew that they had really come to seek peace from them, and the sons of Jacob listened to them, and formed a covenant with them. ⁴⁸ And the sons of Jacob swore unto them that they would not meddle with them, and all the kings of the Canaanites swore also to them, and the sons of Jacob made them tributary from that day forward. ⁴⁹ And after this all the captains of these kings came with their men before Jacob, with presents in their hands for Jacob and his sons, and they bowed down to him to the ground. ⁵⁰ And these kings then urged the sons of Jacob and begged of them to return all the spoil they had captured from the seven cities of the Amorites, and the sons of Jacob did so, and they returned all that they had captured, the women, the little ones, the cattle and all the spoil which they had taken, and they sent them off, and they went away each to his city. ⁵¹ And all these kings again bowed down to the sons of Jacob, and they sent or brought them many gifts in those days, and the sons of Jacob sent off these kings and their men, and they went peaceably away from them to their cities, and the sons of Jacob also returned to their home, to Shechem. ⁵² And there was peace from that day forward between the sons of Jacob and the kings of the Canaanites, until the children of Israel came to inherit the land of Canaan.

41

¹ And at the revolution of the year the sons of Jacob journeyed from Shechem, and they came to Hebron, to their father Isaac, and they dwelt there, but their flocks and herds they fed daily in Shechem, for there was there in those days good and fat pasture, and Jacob and his sons and all their household dwelt in the valley of Hebron. ² And it was in those days, in that year, being the hundred and sixth year of the life of Jacob, in the tenth year of Jacob's coming from Padan-aram, that Leah the wife of Jacob died; she was fifty-one years old when she died in Hebron. ³ And Jacob and his sons buried her in the cave of the field of Machpelah, which is in Hebron, which Abraham had bought from the children of Heth, for the possession of a burial place. ⁴ And the sons of Jacob dwelt with their father in the valley of Hebron, and all the inhabitants of the land knew their strength and their fame went throughout the land. ⁵ And Joseph the son of Jacob, and his brother Benjamin, the sons of Rachel, the wife of Jacob, were yet young in those days, and did not go out with their brethren during their battles in all the cities of the Amorites. ⁶ And when Joseph saw the strength of his brethren, and their greatness, he praised them and extolled them, but he ranked himself greater than them, and extolled himself above them; and Jacob, his father, also loved him more than any of his sons, for he was a son of his old age, and through his love toward him, he made him a coat of many colors. ⁷ And when Joseph saw that his father loved him more than his brethren, he continued to exalt himself above his brethren, and he brought unto his father evil reports concerning them. ⁸ And the sons of Jacob seeing the whole of Joseph's conduct toward them, and that their father loved him more than any of them, they hated him and could not speak peaceably to him all the days. ⁹ And Joseph was seventeen years old, and he was still magnifying himself above his brethren, and thought of raising himself above them. ¹⁰ At that time he dreamed a dream, and he came unto his brothers and told them his dream, and he said unto them, I dreamed a dream, and behold we were all binding sheaves in the field, and my sheaf rose and placed itself upon the ground and your sheaves surrounded it and bowed down to it. ¹¹ And his brethren answered him and said unto him, What meaneth this dream that thou didst dream? dost thou imagine in thy heart to reign or rule over us? ¹² And he still came, and told the thing to his father Jacob, and Jacob kissed Joseph when he heard these words from his mouth, and Jacob blessed Joseph. ¹³ And when the sons of Jacob saw that their father had blessed Joseph and had kissed him, and that he loved him exceedingly, they became jealous of him and hated him the more. ¹⁴ And after this Joseph dreamed another dream and related the dream to his father in the presence of his brethren, and Joseph said unto his father and brethren, Behold I have again dreamed a dream, and behold the sun and the moon and the eleven stars bowed down to me. ¹⁵ And his father heard the words of Joseph and his dream, and, seeing that his brethren hated Joseph on account of this matter, Jacob therefore rebuked Joseph before his brethren on account of this thing, saying, What meaneth this dream which thou hast dreamed, and this magnifying thyself before thy brethren who are older than thou art? ¹⁶ Dost thou imagine in thy heart that I and thy mother and thy eleven brethren will come and bow down to thee, that thou speakest these things? ¹⁷ And his brethren were jealous of him on account of his words and dreams, and they continued to hate him, and Jacob reserved the dreams in his heart. ¹⁸ And the sons of Jacob went one day to feed their father's flock in Shechem, for they were still herdsmen in those days; and whilst the sons of Jacob were that day feeding in Shechem they delayed, and the time of gathering in the cattle was passed, and they had not arrived. ¹⁹ And Jacob saw that his sons were delayed in Shechem, and Jacob said within himself, Peradventure the people of Shechem have risen up to fight against them, therefore they have delayed coming this day. ²⁰ And Jacob called Joseph his son and commanded him, saying, Behold thy brethren are feeding in Shechem this day, and behold they have not yet come back; go now therefore and see where they are, and bring me word back concerning the welfare of thy brethren and the welfare of the flock. ²¹ And Jacob sent his son Joseph to the valley of Hebron, and Joseph came for his brothers to Shechem, and could not find them, and Joseph went about the field which was near Shechem, to see where his brothers had turned, and he missed his road in the wilderness, and knew not which way he should go. ²² And an angel of the Lord found him wandering in the road toward the field, and Joseph said unto the angel of the Lord, I seek my brethren; hast thou not heard where they are feeding? and the angel of the Lord said unto Joseph, I saw thy brethren feeding here, and I heard them say they would go to feed in Dothan. ²³ And Joseph hearkened to the voice of the angel of the Lord, and he went to his brethren in Dothan and he found them in Dothan feeding the flock. ²⁴ And Joseph advanced to his brethren, and before he had come nigh unto them, they had resolved to slay him. ²⁵ And Simeon said to his brethren, Behold the man of dreams is coming unto us this day, and now therefore come and let us kill him and cast him in one of the pits that are in the wilderness, and when his father shall seek him from us, we will say an evil beast has devoured him. ²⁶ And Reuben heard the words of his brethren concerning Joseph, and he said unto them, You should not do this thing, for how can we look up to our father Jacob? Cast him into this pit to die there, but stretch not forth a hand upon him to spill his blood; and Reuben said this in order to deliver him from their hand, to bring him back to his father. ²⁷ And when Joseph came to his brethren he sat before them, and they rose upon him and seized him and smote him to the earth, and stripped the coat of many colors which he had on. ²⁸ And they took him and cast him into a pit, and in the pit there was no water, but serpents and scorpions. And Joseph was afraid of the serpents and scorpions that were in the pit. And Joseph cried out with a loud voice, and the Lord hid the serpents and scorpions in the sides of the pit, and they did no harm unto Joseph. ²⁹ And Joseph called out from the pit to his brethren, and said unto them, What have I done unto you, and in what have I sinned? why do you not fear the Lord concerning me? am I not of your bones and flesh, and is not Jacob your father, my father? why do you do this thing unto me this day, and how will you be able to look up to our father Jacob? ³⁰ And he continued to cry out and call unto his brethren from the pit, and he said, O Judah, Simeon, and Levi, my brethren, lift me up from the place of darkness in which you have placed me, and come this day to have compassion on me, ye children of the Lord, and sons of Jacob my father. And if I have sinned unto you, are you not the sons of Abraham, Isaac, and Jacob? if they saw an orphan they had compassion over him, or one that was hungry, they gave him bread to eat, or one that was thirsty, they gave him water to drink, or one that was naked, they covered him with garments! ³¹ And how then will you withhold your pity from your brother, for I am of your flesh and bones, and if I have sinned unto you, surely you will do this on account of my father! ³² And Joseph spoke these words from the pit, and his brethren could not listen to him, nor incline their ears to the words of Joseph, and Joseph was crying and weeping in the pit. ³³ And Joseph said, O that my father knew, this day, the act which my brothers have done unto me, and the words which they have this day spoken unto me. ³⁴ And all his brethren heard his cries and weeping in the pit, and his brethren went and removed themselves from the pit, so that they might not hear the cries of Joseph and his weeping in the pit.

42

¹ And they went and sat on the opposite side, about the distance of a bow-shot, and they sat there to eat bread, and whilst they were eating, they held counsel together what was to be done with him, whether to slay him or to bring him back to his father. ² They were holding the counsel, when they lifted up their eyes, and saw, and behold there was a company of Ishmaelites coming at a distance by the road of Gilead, going down to

Egypt. ³ And Judah said unto them, What gain will it be to us if we slay our brother? peradventure God will require him from us; this then is the counsel proposed concerning him, which you shall do unto him: Behold this company of Ishmaelites going down to Egypt, ⁴ Now therefore, come let us dispose of him to them, and let not our hand be upon him, and they will lead him along with them, and he will be lost amongst the people of the land, and we will not put him to death with our own hands. And the proposal pleased his brethren and they did according to the word of Judah. ⁵ And whilst they were discoursing about this matter, and before the company of Ishmaelites had come up to them, seven trading men of Midian passed by them, and as they passed they were thirsty, and they lifted up their eyes and saw the pit in which Joseph was immured, and they looked, and behold every species of bird was upon him. ⁶ And these Midianites ran to the pit to drink water, for they thought that it contained water, and on coming before the pit they heard the voice of Joseph crying and weeping in the pit, and they looked down into the pit, and they saw and behold there was a youth of comely appearance and well favored. ⁷ And they called unto him and said, Who art thou and who brought thee hither, and who placed thee in this pit, in the wilderness? and they all assisted to raise up Joseph and they drew him out, and brought him up from the pit, and took him and went away on their journey and passed by his brethren. ⁸ And these said unto them, Why do you do this, to take our servant from us and to go away? surely we placed this youth in the pit because he rebelled against us, and you come and bring him up and lead him away; now then give us back our servant. ⁹ And the Midianites answered and said unto the sons of Jacob, Is this your servant, or does this man attend you? peradventure you are all his servants, for he is more comely and well favored than any of you, and why do you all speak falsely unto us? ¹⁰ Now therefore we will not listen to your words, nor attend to you, for we found the youth in the pit in the wilderness, and we took him; we will therefore go on. ¹¹ And all the sons of Jacob approached them and rose up to them and said unto them, Give us back our servant, and why will you all die by the edge of the sword? And the Midianites cried out against them, and they drew their swords, and approached to fight with the sons of Jacob. ¹² And behold Simeon rose up from his seat against them, and sprang upon the ground and drew his sword and approached the Midianites and he gave a terrible shout before them, so that his shouting was heard at a distance, and the earth shook at Simeon's shouting. ¹³ And the Midianites were terrified on account of Simeon and the noise of his shouting, and they fell upon their faces, and were excessively alarmed. ¹⁴ And Simeon said unto them, Verily I am Simeon, the son of Jacob the Hebrew, who have, only with my brother, destroyed the city of Shechem and the cities of the Amorites; so shall God moreover do unto me, that if all your brethren the people of Midian, and also the kings of Canaan, were to come with you, they could not fight against me. ¹⁵ Now therefore give us back the youth whom you have taken, lest I give your flesh to the birds of the skies and the beasts of the earth. ¹⁶ And the Midianites were more afraid of Simeon, and they approached the sons of Jacob with terror and fright, and with pathetic words, saying, ¹⁷ Surely you have said that the young man is your servant, and that he rebelled against you, and therefore you placed him in the pit; what then will you do with a servant who rebels against his master? Now therefore sell him unto us, and we will give you all that you require for him; and the Lord was pleased to do this in order that the sons of Jacob should not slay their brother. ¹⁸ And the Midianites saw that Joseph was of a comely appearance and well-favored; they desired him in their hearts and were urgent to purchase him from his brethren. ¹⁹ And the sons of Jacob hearkened to the Midianites and they sold their brother Joseph to them for twenty pieces of silver, and Reuben their brother was not with them, and the Midianites took Joseph and continued their journey to Gilead. ²⁰ They were going along the road, and the Midianites repented of what they had done, in having purchased the young man, and one said to the other, What is this thing that we have done, in taking this youth from the Hebrews, who is of comely appearance and well favored. ²¹ Perhaps this youth is stolen from the land of the Hebrews, and why then have we done this thing? and if he should be sought for and found in our hands we shall die through him. ²² Now surely hardy and powerful men have sold him to us, the strength of one of whom you saw this day; perhaps they stole him from his land with their might and with their powerful arm, and have therefore sold him to us for the small value which we gave unto them. ²³ And whilst they were thus discoursing together, they looked, and behold the company of Ishmaelites which was coming at first, and which the sons of Jacob saw, was advancing toward the Midianites, and the Midianites said to each other, Come let us sell this youth to the company of Ishmaelites who are coming toward us, and we will take for him the little that we gave for him, and we will be delivered from his evil. ²⁴ And they did so, and they reached the Ishmaelites, and the Midianites sold Joseph to the Ishmaelites for twenty pieces of silver which they had given for him to his brethren. ²⁵ And the Midianites went on their road to Gilead, and the Ishmaelites took Joseph and they let him ride upon one of the camels, and they were leading him to Egypt. ²⁶ And Joseph heard that the Ishmaelites were proceeding to Egypt, and Joseph lamented and wept at this thing that he was to be so far removed from the land of Canaan, from his father, and he wept bitterly whilst he was riding upon the camel, and one of their men observed him, and made him go down from the camel and walk on foot, and notwithstanding this Joseph continued to cry and weep, and he said, O my father, my father. ²⁷ And one of the Ishmaelites rose up and smote Joseph upon the cheek, and still he continued to weep; and Joseph was fatigued in the road, and was unable to proceed on account of the bitterness of his soul, and they all smote him and afflicted him in the road, and they terrified him in order that he might cease from weeping. ²⁸ And the Lord saw the ambition of Joseph and his trouble, and the Lord brought down upon those men darkness and confusion, and the hand of every one that smote him became withered. ²⁹ And they said to each other, What is this thing that God has done to us in the road? and they knew not that this befell them on account of Joseph. And the men proceeded on the road, and they passed along the road of Ephrath where Rachel was buried. ³⁰ And Joseph reached his mother's grave, and Joseph hastened and ran to his mother's grave, and fell upon the grave and wept. ³¹ And Joseph cried aloud upon his mother's grave, and he said, O my mother, my mother, O thou who didst give me birth, awake now, and rise and see thy son, how he has been sold for a slave, and no one to pity him. ³² O rise and see thy son, weep with me on account of my troubles, and see the heart of my brethren. ³³ Arouse my mother, arouse, awake from thy sleep for me, and direct thy battles against my brethren. O how have they stripped me of my coat, and sold me already twice for a slave, and separated me from my father, and there is no one to pity me. ³⁴ Arouse and lay thy cause against them before God, and see whom God will justify in the judgment, and whom he will condemn. ³⁵ Rise, O my mother, rise, awake from thy sleep and see my father how his soul is with me this day, and comfort him and ease his heart. ³⁶ And Joseph continued to speak these words, and Joseph cried aloud and wept bitterly upon his mother's grave; and he ceased speaking, and from bitterness of heart he became still as a stone upon the grave. ³⁷ And Joseph heard a voice speaking to him from beneath the ground, which answered him with bitterness of heart, and with a voice of weeping and praying in these words: ³⁸ My son, my son Joseph, I have heard the voice of thy weeping and the voice of thy lamentation; I have seen thy tears; I know thy troubles, my son, and it grieves me for thy sake, and abundant grief is added to my grief. ³⁹ Now therefore my son, Joseph my son, hope to the Lord, and wait for him and do not fear, for the Lord is with thee, he will deliver thee from all trouble. ⁴⁰ Rise my son, go down unto Egypt with thy masters, and do not fear, for the Lord is with thee, my son. And she continued to speak like unto these words unto Joseph, and she was still. ⁴¹ And Joseph heard this, and he wondered greatly at this, and he continued to weep; and after this one of the Ishmaelites observed him crying and weeping upon the grave, and his anger was kindled against him, and he drove him from there, and he smote him and cursed him. ⁴² And Joseph said unto the men, May I find grace in your sight to take me back to my father's house, and he will give you abundance of riches. ⁴³ And they answered him, saying, Art thou not a slave, and where is thy father? and if thou hadst a father thou wouldst not already twice have been sold for a slave for so little value; and their anger was still roused against him, and they continued to smite him and to chastise him, and Joseph wept bitterly. ⁴⁴ And the Lord saw Joseph's affliction, and Lord again smote these men, and chastised them, and the Lord caused darkness to envelope them upon the earth, and the lightning flashed and the thunder roared, and the earth shook at the voice of the thunder and of the mighty wind, and the men were terrified and knew not where they should go. ⁴⁵ And the beasts and camels stood still, and they led them, but they would not go, they smote them, and they crouched upon the ground; and the men said to each other, What is this that God has done to us? what are our transgressions, and what are our sins that this thing has thus befallen us? ⁴⁶ And one of them answered and said unto them, Perhaps on account of the sin of afflicting this slave has this thing happened this day to us; now therefore implore him strongly to forgive us, and then we shall know on whose account this evil befalleth us, and if God shall have compassion over us, then we shall know that all this cometh to us on account of the sin of afflicting this slave. ⁴⁷ And the men did so, and they supplicated Joseph and pressed him to forgive them; and they said, We have sinned to the Lord and to thee, now therefore vouchsafe to request of thy God that he shall put away this death from amongst us, for we have sinned to him. ⁴⁸ And Joseph did according to their words, and the Lord hearkened to Joseph, and the Lord put away the plague which he had inflicted upon those men on account of Joseph, and the beasts rose up from the ground and they conducted them, and they went on, and the raging storm abated and the earth became tranquilized, and the men proceeded on their journey to go down to Egypt, and the men knew that this evil had befallen them on account of Joseph. ⁴⁹ And they said to each other, Behold we know that it was on account of his affliction that this evil befell us; now therefore why shall we bring this death upon our souls? Let us hold counsel what to do to this slave. ⁵⁰ And one answered and said, Surely he told us to bring him back to his father; now therefore come, let us take him back and we will go to the place that he will tell us, and take from his family the price that we gave for him and we will then go away. ⁵¹ And one answered again and said, Behold this counsel is very good, but we cannot do so for the way is very far from us, and we cannot go out of our road. ⁵² And one more answered and said unto them, This is the counsel to be adopted, we will not swerve from it; behold we are this day going to Egypt, and when we shall have come to Egypt, we will sell him there at a high price, and we will be delivered from his evil. ⁵³ And this thing pleased the men and they did so, and they continued their journey to Egypt with Joseph.

43

¹ And when the sons of Jacob had sold their brother Joseph to the Midianites, their hearts were smitten on account of him, and they repented of their acts, and they sought for him to bring him back, but could not find him. ² And Reuben returned to the pit in which Joseph had been put, in order to lift him out, and restore him to his father, and Reuben stood by the pit, and he heard not a word, and he called out Joseph! Joseph! and no one answered or uttered a word. ³ And Reuben said, Joseph has died through fright, or some serpent has caused his death; and Reuben descended into the pit, and he searched for Joseph and could not find him in the pit, and he came out again. ⁴ And Reuben tore his garments and he said, The child is not there, and how shall I reconcile my father about him if he be dead? and he went to his brethren and found them grieving on account of Joseph, and counseling together how to reconcile their father about him, and Reuben said unto his brethren, I came to the pit and behold Joseph was not there, what then shall we say unto our father, for my father will only seek the lad from me. ⁵ And his brethren answered him saying, Thus and thus we did, and our hearts afterward smote us on account of this act, and we now sit to seek a pretext how we shall reconcile our father to it. ⁶ And Reuben said unto them, What is this you have done to bring down the grey hairs of our father in sorrow to the grave? the thing is not good, that you have done. ⁷ And Reuben sat with them, and they all rose up and swore to each other not to tell this thing unto Jacob, and they all said, The man who will tell this to our father or his household, or who will report this to any of the children of the land, we will all rise up against him and slay him with the sword. ⁸ And the sons of Jacob feared each other in this matter, from the youngest to the oldest, and no one spoke a word, and they concealed the thing in their hearts. ⁹ And they afterward sat down to determine and invent something to say unto their father Jacob concerning all these things. ¹⁰ And Issachar said unto them, Here is an advice for you if it seem good in your eyes to do this thing, take the coat which belongeth to Joseph and tear it, and kill a kid of the goats and dip it in its blood. ¹¹ And send it to our father and when he seeth it he will say an evil beast has devoured him, therefore tear ye his coat and behold his blood will be upon his coat, and by your doing this we shall be free of our father's murmurings. ¹² And Issachar's advice pleased them, and they hearkened unto him and they did according to the word of Issachar which he had counselled them. ¹³ And they hastened and took Joseph's coat and tore it, and they killed a kid of the goats and dipped the coat in the blood of the kid, and then trampled it in the dust, and they sent the coat to their father Jacob by the hand of Naphtali, and they commanded him to say these words: ¹⁴ We had gathered in the cattle and had come as far as the road to Shechem and farther, when we found this coat upon the road in the wilderness dipped in blood and in dust; now therefore know whether it be thy son's coat or not. ¹⁵ And Naphtali went and he came unto his father and he gave him the coat, and he spoke unto him all the words which his brethren had commanded him. ¹⁶ And Jacob saw Joseph's coat and he knew it and he fell upon his face to the ground, and became as still as a stone, and he afterward rose up and cried out with a loud and weeping voice and he said, It is the coat of my son Joseph! ¹⁷ And Jacob hastened and sent one of his servants to his sons, who went to them and found them coming along the road with the flock. ¹⁸ And the sons of Jacob came to their father about evening, and behold their garments were torn and dust was upon their heads, and they found their father crying out and weeping with a loud voice. ¹⁹ And Jacob said unto his sons, Tell me truly what evil have you this day suddenly brought upon me? and they answered their father Jacob, saying, We were coming along this day after the flock had been gathered in, and we came as far as the city of Shechem by the road in the wilderness, and we found this coat filled with blood upon the ground, and we knew it and we sent unto thee if thou couldst know it. ²⁰ And Jacob heard the words of his sons and he cried out with a loud voice, and he said, It is the coat of my son, an evil beast has devoured him; Joseph is rent in pieces, for I sent him this day to see whether it was well with you and well with the flocks and to bring me word again from you, and he went as I commanded him, and this has happened to him this day whilst I thought my son was with you. ²¹ And the sons of Jacob answered and said, He did not come to us, neither have we seen him from the time of our going out from thee until now. ²² And when Jacob heard their words he again cried out aloud, and he rose up and tore his garments, and he put sackcloth upon his loins, and he wept bitterly and he mourned and lifted up his voice in weeping and exclaimed and said these words, ²³ Joseph my son, O my son Joseph, I sent thee this day after the welfare of thy brethren, and behold thou hast been torn in pieces; through my hand has this happened to my son. ²⁴ It grieves me for thee Joseph my son, it grieves me for thee; how sweet wast thou to me during life, and now how exceedingly bitter is thy death to me. ²⁵ ⁰ that I had died in thy stead Joseph my son, for it grieves me sadly for thee my son, O my son, my son. Joseph my son, where art thou, and where hast thou been drawn? arouse, arouse from thy place, and come and see my grief for thee, O my son Joseph. ²⁶ Come now and number the tears gushing from my eyes down my cheeks, and bring them up before the Lord, that his anger may turn from me. ²⁷ ⁰ Joseph my son, how didst thou fall, by the hand of one by whom no one had fallen from the beginning of the world unto this day; for thou hast been put to death by the smiting of an enemy, inflicted with cruelty, but surely I know that this has happened to thee, on account of the multitude of my sins. ²⁸ Arouse now and see how bitter is my trouble for thee my son, although I did not rear thee, nor fashion thee, nor give thee breath and soul, but it was God who formed thee and built thy bones and covered them with flesh, and breathed in thy nostrils the breath of life, and then he gave thee unto me. ²⁹ Now truly God who gave thee unto me, he has taken thee from me, and such then has befallen thee ³⁰ And Jacob continued to speak like unto these words concerning Joseph, and he wept bitterly; he fell to the ground and became still. ³¹ And all the sons of Jacob seeing their father's trouble, they repented of what they had done, and they also wept bitterly. ³² And Judah rose up and lifted his father's head from the ground, and placed it upon his lap, and he wiped his father's tears from his cheeks, and Judah wept an exceeding great weeping, whilst his father's head was reclining upon his lap, still as a stone. ³³ And the sons of Jacob saw their father's trouble, and they lifted up their voices and continued to weep, and Jacob was yet lying upon the ground still as a stone. ³⁴ And all his sons and his servants and his servant's children rose up and stood round him to comfort him, and he refused to be comforted. ³⁵ And the whole household of Jacob rose up and mourned a great mourning on account of Joseph and their father's trouble, and the intelligence reached Isaac, the son of Abraham, the father of Jacob, and he wept bitterly on account of Joseph, he and all his household, and he went from the place where he dwelt in Hebron, and his men with him, and he comforted Jacob his son, and he refused to be comforted. ³⁶ And after this, Jacob rose up from the ground, and his tears were running down his cheeks, and he said unto his sons, Rise up and take your swords and your bows, and go forth into the field, and seek whether you can find my son's body and bring it unto me that I may bury it. ³⁷ Seek also, I pray you, among the beasts and hunt them, and that which shall come the first before you seize and bring it unto me, perhaps the Lord will this day pity my affliction, and prepare before you that which did tear my son in pieces, and bring it unto me, and I will avenge the cause of my son. ³⁸ And his sons did as their father had commanded them, and they rose up early in the morning, and each took his sword and his bow in his hand, and they went forth into the field to hunt the beasts. ³⁹ And Jacob was still crying aloud and weeping and walking to and fro in the house, and smiting his hands together, saying, Joseph my son, Joseph my son. ⁴⁰ And the sons of Jacob went into the wilderness to seize the beasts, and behold a wolf came toward them, and they seized him, and brought him unto their father, and they said unto him, This is the first we have found, and we have brought him unto thee as thou didst command us, and thy son's body we could not find. ⁴¹ And Jacob took the beast from the hands of his sons, and he cried out with a loud and weeping voice, holding the beast in his hand, and he spoke with a bitter heart unto the beast, Why didst thou devour my son Joseph, and how didst thou have no fear of the God of the earth, or of my trouble for my son Joseph? ⁴² And thou didst devour my son for naught, because he committed no violence, and didst thereby render me culpable on his account, therefore God will require him that is persecuted. ⁴³ And the Lord opened the mouth of the beast in order to comfort Jacob with its words, and it answered Jacob and spoke these words unto him, ⁴⁴ As God liveth who created us in the earth, and as thy soul liveth, my lord, I did not see thy son, neither did I tear him to pieces, but from a distant land I also came to seek my son who went from me this day, and I know not whether he be living or dead. ⁴⁵ And I came this day into the field to seek my son, and your sons found me, and seized me and increased my grief, and have

this day brought me before thee, and I have now spoken all my words to thee. ⁴⁶ And now therefore, O son of man, I am in thy hands, and do unto me this day as it may seem good in thy sight, but by the life of God who created me, I did not see thy son, nor did I tear him to pieces, neither has the flesh of man entered my mouth all the days of my life. ⁴⁷ And when Jacob heard the words of the beast he was greatly astonished, and sent forth the beast from his hand, and she went her way. ⁴⁸ And Jacob was still crying aloud and weeping for Joseph day after day, and he mourned for his son many days.

44

¹ And the sons of Ishmael who had bought Joseph from the Midianites, who had bought him from his brethren, went to Egypt with Joseph, and they came upon the borders of Egypt, and when they came near unto Egypt, they met four men of the sons of Medan the son of Abraham, who had gone forth from the land of Egypt on their journey. ² And the Ishmaelites said unto them, Do you desire to purchase this slave from us? and they said, Deliver him over to us, and they delivered Joseph over to them, and they beheld him, that he was a very comely youth and they purchased him for twenty shekels. ³ And the Ishmaelites continued their journey to Egypt and the Medanim also returned that day to Egypt, and the Medanim said to each other, Behold we have heard that Potiphar, an officer of Pharaoh, captain of the guard, seeketh a good servant who shall stand before him to attend him, and to make him overseer over his house and all belonging to him. ⁴ Now therefore come let us sell him to him for what we may desire, if he be able to give unto us that which we shall require for him. ⁵ And these Medanim went and came to the house of Potiphar, and said unto him, We have heard that thou seekest a good servant to attend thee, behold we have a servant that will please thee, if thou canst give unto us that which we may desire, and we will sell him unto thee. ⁶ And Potiphar said, Bring him before me, and I will see him, and if he please me I will give unto you that which you may require for him. ⁷ And the Medanim went and brought Joseph and placed him before Potiphar, and he saw him, and he pleased him exceedingly, and Potiphar said unto them, Tell me what you require for this youth? ⁸ And they said, Four hundred pieces of silver we desire for him, and Potiphar said, I will give it you if you bring me the record of his sale to you, and will tell me his history, for perhaps he may be stolen, for this youth is neither a slave, nor the son of a slave, but I observe in him the appearance of a goodly and handsome person. ⁹ And the Medanim went and brought unto him the Ishmaelites who had sold him to them, and they told him, saying, He is a slave and we sold him to them. ¹⁰ And Potiphar heard the words of the Ishmaelites in his giving the silver unto the Medanim, and the Medanim took the silver and went on their journey, and the Ishmaelites also returned home. ¹¹ And Potiphar took Joseph and brought him to his house that he might serve him, and Joseph found favor in the sight of Potiphar, and he placed confidence in him, and made him overseer over his house, and all that belonged to him he delivered over into his hand. ¹² And the Lord was with Joseph and he became a prosperous man, and the Lord blessed the house of Potiphar for the sake of Joseph. ¹³ And Potiphar left all that he had in the hand of Joseph, and Joseph was one that caused things to come in and go out, and everything was regulated by his wish in the house of Potiphar. ¹⁴ And Joseph was eighteen years old, a youth with beautiful eyes and of comely appearance, and like unto him was not in the whole land of Egypt. ¹⁵ At that time whilst he was in his master's house, going in and out of the house and attending his master, Zelicah, his master's wife, lifted up her eyes toward Joseph and she looked at him, and behold he was a youth comely and well favored. ¹⁶ And she coveted his beauty in her heart, and her soul was fixed upon Joseph, and she enticed him day after day, and Zelicah persuaded Joseph daily, but Joseph did not lift up his eyes to behold his master's wife. ¹⁷ And Zelicah said unto him, How goodly are thy appearance and form, truly I have looked at all the slaves, and have not seen so beautiful a slave as thou art; and Joseph said unto her, Surely he who created me in my mother's womb created all mankind. ¹⁸ And she said unto him, How beautiful are thine eyes, with which thou hast dazzled all the inhabitants of Egypt, men and women; and he said unto her, How beautiful they are whilst we are alive, but shouldst thou behold them in the grave, surely thou wouldst move away from them. ¹⁹ And she said unto him, How beautiful and pleasing are all thy words; take now, I pray thee, the harp which is in the house, and play with thy hands and let us hear thy words. ²⁰ And he said unto her, How beautiful and pleasing are my words when I speak the praise of my God and his glory; and she said unto him, How very beautiful is the hair of thy head, behold the golden comb which is in the house, take it I pray thee, and curl the hair of thy head. ²¹ And he said unto her, How long wilt thou speak these words? cease to utter these words to me, and rise and attend to thy domestic affairs. ²² And she said unto him, There is no one in my house, and there is nothing to attend to but to thy words and to thy wish; yet notwithstanding all this, she could not bring Joseph unto her, neither did he place his eye upon her, but directed his eyes below to the ground. ²³ And Zelicah desired Joseph in her heart, that he should lie with her, and at the time that Joseph was sitting in the house doing his work, Zelicah came and sat before him, and she enticed him daily with her discourse to lie with her, or ever to look at her, but Joseph would not hearken to her. ²⁴ And she said unto him, If thou wilt not do according to my words, I will chastise thee with the punishment of death, and put an iron yoke upon thee. ²⁵ And Joseph said unto her, Surely God who created man looseth the fetters of prisoners, and it is he who will deliver me from thy prison and from thy judgment. ²⁶ And when she could not prevail over him, to persuade him, and her soul being still fixed upon him, her desire threw her into a grievous sickness. ²⁷ And all the women of Egypt came to visit her, and they said unto her, Why art thou in this declining state? thou that lackest nothing; surely thy husband is a great and esteemed prince in the sight of the king, shouldst thou lack anything of what thy heart desireth? ²⁸ And Zelicah answered them, saying, This day it shall be made known to you, whence this disorder springs in which you see me, and she commanded her maid servants to prepare food for all the women, and she made a banquet for them, and all the women ate in the house of Zelicah. ²⁹ And she gave them knives to peel the citrons to eat them, and she commanded that they should dress Joseph in costly garments, and that he should appear before them, and Joseph came before their eyes and all the women looked on Joseph, and could not take their eyes from off him, and they all cut their hands with the knives that they had in their hands, and all the citrons that were in their hands were filled with blood. ³⁰ And they knew not what they had done but they continued to look at the beauty of Joseph, and did not turn their eyelids from him. ³¹ And Zelicah saw what they had done, and she said unto them, What is this work that you have done? behold I gave you citrons to eat and you have all cut your hands. ³² And all the women saw their hands, and behold they were full of blood, and their blood flowed down upon their garments, and they said unto her, this slave in your house has overcome us, and we could not turn our eyelids from him on account of his beauty. ³³ And she said unto them, Surely this happened to you in the moment that you looked at him, and you could not contain yourselves from him; how then can I refrain when he is constantly in my house, and I see him day after day going in and out of my house? how then can I keep from declining or even from perishing on account of this? ³⁴ And they said unto her, the words are true, for who can see this beautiful form in the house and refrain from him, and is he not thy slave and attendant in thy house, and why dost thou not tell him that which is in thy heart, and sufferest thy soul to perish through this matter? ³⁵ And she said unto them, I am daily endeavoring to persuade him, and he will not consent to my wishes, and I promised him everything that is good, and yet I could meet with no return from him; I am therefore in a declining state as you see. ³⁶ And Zelicah became very ill on account of her desire toward Joseph, and she was desperately lovesick on account of him, and all the people of the house of Zelicah and her husband knew nothing of this matter, that Zelicah was ill on account of her love to Joseph. ³⁷ And all the people of her house asked her, saying, Why art thou ill and declining, and lackest nothing? and she said unto them, I know not this thing which is daily increasing upon me. ³⁸ And all the women and her friends came daily to see her, and they spoke with her, and she said unto them, This can only be through the love of Joseph; and they said unto her, Entice him and seize him secretly, perhaps he may hearken to thee, and put off this death from thee. ³⁹ And Zelicah became worse from her love to Joseph, and she continued to decline, till she had scarce strength to stand. ⁴⁰ And on a certain day Joseph was doing his master's work in the house, and Zelicah came secretly and fell suddenly upon him, and Joseph rose up against her, and he was more powerful than she, and he brought her down to the ground. ⁴¹ And Zelicah wept on account of the desire of her heart toward him, and she supplicated him with weeping, and her tears flowed down her cheeks, and she spoke unto him in a voice of supplication and in bitterness of soul, saying, ⁴² Hast thou ever heard, seen or known of so beautiful a woman as I am, or better than myself, who speak daily unto thee, fall into a decline through love for thee, confer all this honor upon thee, and still thou wilt not hearken to my voice? ⁴³ And if it be through fear of thy master lest he punish thee, as the king liveth no harm shall come to thee from thy master through this thing; now, therefore pray listen to me, and consent for the sake of the honor which I have conferred upon thee, and put off this death from me, and why should I die for thy sake? and she ceased to speak. ⁴⁴ And Joseph answered her, saying, Refrain from me, and leave this matter to my master; behold my master knoweth not what there is with me in the house, for all that belongeth to him he has delivered into my hand, and how shall I do these things in my master's house? ⁴⁵ For he hath also greatly honored me in his house, and hath also made me overseer over his house, and he hath exalted me, and

there is no one greater in this house than I am, and my master hath refrained nothing from me, excepting thee who art his wife, how then canst thou speak these words unto me, and how can I do this great evil and sin to God and to thy husband? ⁴⁶ Now therefore refrain from me, and speak no more such words as these, for I will not hearken to thy words. But Zelicah would not hearken to Joseph when he spoke these words unto her, but she daily enticed him to listen to her. ⁴⁷ And it was after this that the brook of Egypt was filled above all its sides, and all the inhabitants of Egypt went forth, and also the king and princes went forth with timbrels and dances, for it was a great rejoicing in Egypt, and a holiday at the time of the inundation of the sea Sihor, and they went there to rejoice all the day. ⁴⁸ And when the Egyptians went out to the river to rejoice, as was their custom, all the people of the house of Potiphar went with them, but Zelicah would not go with them, for she said, I am indisposed, and she remained alone in the house, and no other person was with her in the house. ⁴⁹ And she rose up and ascended to her temple in the house, and dressed herself in princely garments, and she placed upon her head precious stones of onyx stones, inlaid with silver and gold, and she beautified her face and skin with all sorts of women's purifying liquids, and she perfumed the temple and the house with cassia and frankincense, and she spread myrrh and aloes, and she afterward sat in the entrance of the temple, in the passage of the house, through which Joseph passed to do his work, and behold Joseph came from the field, and entered the house to do his master's work. ⁵⁰ And he came to the place through which he had to pass, and he saw all the work of Zelicah, and he turned back. ⁵¹ And Zelicah saw Joseph turning back from her, and she called out to him, saying What aileth thee Joseph? come to thy work, and behold I will make room for thee until thou shalt have passed to thy seat. ⁵² And Joseph returned and came to the house, and passed from thence to the place of his seat, and he sat down to do his master's work as usual and behold Zelicah came to him and stood before him in princely garments, and the scent from her clothes was spread to a distance. ⁵³ And she hastened and caught hold of Joseph and his garments, and she said unto him, As the king liveth if thou wilt not perform my request thou shalt die this day, and she hastened and stretched forth her other hand and drew a sword from beneath her garments, and she placed it upon Joseph's neck, and she said, Rise and perform my request, and if not thou diest this day. ⁵⁴ And Joseph was afraid of her at her doing this thing, and he rose up to flee from her, and she seized the front of his garments, and in the terror of his flight the garment which Zelicah seized was torn, and Joseph left the garment in the hand of Zelicah, and he fled and got out, for he was in fear. ⁵⁵ And when Zelicah saw that Joseph's garment was torn, and that he had left it in her hand, and had fled, she was afraid of her life, lest the report should spread concerning her, and she rose up and acted with cunning, and put off the garments in which she was dressed, and she put on her other garments. ⁵⁶ And she took Joseph's garment, and she laid it beside her, and she went and seated herself in the place where she had sat in her illness, before the people of her house had gone out to the river, and she called a young lad who was then in the house, and she ordered him to call the people of the house to her. ⁵⁷ And when she saw them she said unto them with a loud voice and lamentation, See what a Hebrew your master has brought to me in the house, for he came this day to lie with me. ⁵⁸ For when you had gone out he came to the house, and seeing that there was no person in the house, he came unto me, and caught hold of me, with intent to lie with me. ⁵⁹ And I seized his garments and tore them and called out against him with a loud voice, and when I had lifted up my voice he was afraid of his life and left his garment before me, and fled. ⁶⁰ And the people of her house spoke nothing, but their wrath was very much kindled against Joseph, and they went to his master and told him the words of his wife. ⁶¹ And Potiphar came home enraged, and his wife cried out to him, saying, What is this thing that thou hast done unto me in bringing a He. brew servant into my house, for he came unto me this day to sport with me; thus did he do unto me this day. ⁶² And Potiphar heard the words of his wife, and he ordered Joseph to be punished with severe stripes, and they did so to him. ⁶³ And whilst they were smiting him, Joseph called out with a loud voice, and he lifted up his eyes to heaven, and he said, O Lord God, thou knowest that I am innocent of all these things, and why shall I die this day through falsehood, by the hand of these uncircumcised wicked men, whom thou knowest? ⁶⁴ And whilst Potiphar's men were beating Joseph, he continued to cry out and weep, and there was a child there eleven months old, and the Lord opened the mouth of the child, and he spake these words before Potiphar's men, who were smiting Joseph, saying, ⁶⁵ What do you want of this man, and why do you do this evil unto him? my mother speaketh falsely and uttereth lies; thus was the transaction. ⁶⁶ And the child told them accurately all that happened, and all the words of Zelicah to Joseph day after day did he declare unto them. ⁶⁷ And all the men heard the words of the child and they wondered greatly at the child's words, and the child ceased to speak and became still. ⁶⁸ And Potiphar was very much ashamed at the words of his son, and he commanded his men not to beat Joseph any more, and the men ceased beating Joseph. ⁶⁹ And Potiphar took Joseph and ordered him to be brought to justice before the priests, who were judges belonging to the king, in order to judge him concerning this affair. ⁷⁰ And Potiphar and Joseph came before the priests who were the king's judges, and he said unto them, Decide I pray you, what judgment is due to a servant, for thus has he done. ⁷¹ And the priests said unto Joseph, Why didst thou do this thing to thy master? and Joseph answered them, saying, Not so my lords, thus was the matter; and Potiphar said unto Joseph, Surely I entrusted in thy hands all that belonged to me, and I withheld nothing from thee but my wife, and how couldst thou do this evil? ⁷² And Joseph answered saying, Not so my lord, as the Lord liveth, and as thy soul liveth, my lord, the word which thou didst hear from thy wife is untrue, for thus was the affair this day. ⁷³ A year has elapsed to me since I have been in thy house; hast thou seen any iniquity in me, or any thing which might cause thee to demand my life? ⁷⁴ And the priests said unto Potiphar, Send, we pray thee, and let them bring before us Joseph's torn garment, and let us see the tear in it, and if it shall be that the tear is in front of the garment, then his face must have been opposite to her and she must have caught hold of him, to come to her, and with deceit did thy wife do all that she has spoken. ⁷⁵ And they brought Joseph's garment before the priests who were judges, and they saw and behold the tear was in front of Joseph, and all the judging priests knew that she had pressed him, and they said, The judgment of death is not due to this slave for he has done nothing, but his judgment is, that he be placed in the prison house on account of the report, which through him has gone forth against thy wife. ⁷⁶ And Potiphar heard their words, and he placed him in the prison house, the place where the king's prisoners are confined, and Joseph was in the house of confinement twelve years. ⁷⁷ And notwithstanding this, his master's wife did not turn from him, and she did not cease from speaking to him day after day to hearken to her, and at the end of three months Zelicah continued going to Joseph to the house of confinement day by day, and she enticed him to hearken to her, and Zelicah said unto Joseph, How long wilt thou remain in this house? but hearken now to my voice, and I will bring thee out of this house. ⁷⁸ And Joseph answered her, saying, It is better for me to remain in this house than to hearken to thy words, to sin against God; and she said unto him, If thou wilt not perform my wish, I will pluck out thine eyes, add fetters to thy feet, and will deliver thee into the hands of them whom thou didst not know before. ⁷⁹ And Joseph answered her and said, Behold the God of the whole earth is able to deliver me from all that thou canst do unto me, for he openeth the eyes of the blind, and looseth those that are bound, and preserveth all strangers who are unacquainted with the land. ⁸⁰ And when Zelicah was unable to persuade Joseph to hearken to her, she left off going to entice him; and Joseph was still confined in the house of confinement. And Jacob the father of Joseph, and all his brethren who were in the land of Canaan still mourned and wept in those days on account of Joseph, for Jacob refused to be comforted for his son Joseph, and Jacob cried aloud, and wept and mourned all those days.

45

¹ And it was at that time in that year, which is the year of Joseph's going down to Egypt after his brothers had sold him, that Reuben the son of Jacob went to Timnah and took unto him for a wife Eliuram, the daughter of Avi the Canaanite, and he came to her. ² And Eliuram the wife of Reuben conceived and bare him Hanoch, Palu, Chetzron and Carmi, four sons; and Simeon his brother took his sister Dinah for a wife, and she bare unto him Memuel, Yamin, Ohad, Jachin and Zochar, five sons. ³ And he afterward came to Bunah the Canaanitish woman, the same is Bunah whom Simeon took captive from the city of Shechem, and Bunah was before Dinah and attended upon her, and Simeon came to her, and she bare unto him Saul. ⁴ And Judah went at that time to Adulam, and he came to a man of Adulam, and his name was Hirah, and Judah saw there the daughter of a man from Canaan, and her name was Aliyath, the daughter of Shua, and he took her, and came to her, and Aliyath bare unto Judah, Er, Onan and Shiloh; three sons. ⁵ And Levi and Issachar went to the land of the east, and they took unto themselves for wives the daughters of Jobab the son of Yoktan, the son of Eber; and Jobab the son of Yoktan had two daughters; the name of the elder was Adinah, and the name of the younger was Aridah. ⁶ And Levi took Adinah, and Issachar took Aridah, and they came to the land of Canaan, to their father's house, and Adinah bare unto Levi, Gershon, Kehath and Merari; three sons. ⁷ And Aridah bare unto Issachar Tola, Puvah, Job and Shomron, four sons; and Dan went to the land of Moab and took for a wife Aphlaleth, the daughter of Chamudan the Moabite, and he brought her to the land of Canaan. ⁸ And Aphlaleth was barren, she had no offspring, and God afterward remembered Aphlaleth the wife of Dan, and she conceived and bare a son, and she called his name Chushim. ⁹ And Gad

and Naphtali went to Haran and took from thence the daughters of Amuram the son of Uz, the son of Nahor, for wives. ¹⁰ And these are the names of the daughters of Amuram; the name of the elder was Merimah, and the name of the younger Uzith; and Naphtali took Merimah, and Gad took Uzith; and brought them to the land of Canaan, to their father's house. ¹¹ And Merimah bare unto Naphtali Yachzeel, Guni, Jazer and Shalem, four sons; and Uzith bare unto Gad Zephion, Chagi, Shuni, Ezbon, Eri, Arodi and Arali, seven sons. ¹² And Asher went forth and took Adon the daughter of Aphlal, the son of Hadad, the son of Ishmael, for a wife, and he brought her to the land of Canaan. ¹³ And Adon the wife of Asher died in those days: she had no offspring; and it was after the death of Adon that Asher went to the other side of the river and took for a wife Hadurah the daughter of Abimael, the son of Eber, the son of Shem. ¹⁴ And the young woman was of a comely appearance, and a woman of sense, and she had been the wife of Malkiel the son of Elam, the son of Shem. ¹⁵ And Hadurah bare a daughter unto Malkiel, and he called her name Serach, and Malkiel died after this, and Hadurah went and remained in her father's house. ¹⁶ And after the death of the wife at Asher he went and took Hadurah for a wife, and brought her to the land of Canaan, and Serach her daughter he also brought with them, and she was three years old, and the damsel was brought up in Jacob's house. ¹⁷ And the damsel was of a comely appearance, and she went in the sanctified ways of the children of Jacob; she lacked nothing, and the Lord gave her wisdom and understanding. ¹⁸ And Hadurah the wife of Asher conceived and bare unto him Yimnah, Yishvah, Yishvi and Beriah; four sons. ¹⁹ And Zebulun went to Midian, and took for a wife Merishah the daughter of Molad, the son of Abida, the son of Midian, and brought her to the land of Canaan. ²⁰ And Merushah bare unto Zebulun Sered, Elon and Yachleel; three sons. ²¹ And Jacob sent to Aram, the son of Zoba, the son of Terah, and he took for his son Benjamin Mechalia the daughter of Aram, and she came to the land of Canaan to the house of Jacob; and Benjamin was ten years old when he took Mechalia the daughter of Aram for a wife. ²² And Mechalia conceived and bare unto Benjamin Bela, Becher, Ashbel, Gera and Naaman, five sons; and Benjamin went afterward and took for a wife Aribath, the daughter of Shomron, the son of Abraham, in addition to his first wife, and he was eighteen years old; and Aribath bare unto Benjamin Achi, Vosh, Mupim, Chupim, and Ord; five sons. ²³ And in those days Judah went to the house of Shem and took Tamar the daughter of Elam, the son of Shem, for a wife for his first born Er. ²⁴ And Er came to his wife Tamar, and she became his wife, and when he came to her he outwardly destroyed his seed, and his work was evil in the sight of the Lord, and the Lord slew him. ²⁵ And it was after the death of Er, Judah's first born, that Judah said unto Onan, go to thy brother's wife and marry her as the next of kin, and raise up seed to thy brother. ²⁶ And Onan took Tamar for a wife and he came to her, and Onan also did like unto the work of his brother, and his work was evil in the sight of the Lord, and he slew him also. ²⁷ And when Onan died, Judah said unto Tamar, Remain in thy father's house until my son Shiloh shall have grown up, and Judah did no more delight in Tamar, to give her unto Shiloh, for he said, Peradventure he will also die like his brothers. ²⁸ And Tamar rose up and went and remained in her father's house, and Tamar was in her father's house for some time. ²⁹ And at the revolution of the year, Aliyath the wife of Judah died; and Judah was comforted for his wife, and after the death of Aliyath, Judah went up with his friend Hirah to Timnah to shear their sheep. ³⁰ And Tamar heard that Judah had gone up to Timnah to shear the sheep, and that Shiloh was grown up, and Judah did not delight in her. ³¹ And Tamar rose up and put off the garments of her widowhood, and she put a vail upon her, and she entirely covered herself, and she went and sat in the public thoroughfare, which is upon the road to Timnah. ³² And Judah passed and saw her and took her and he came to her, and she conceived by him, and at the time of being delivered, behold, there were twins in her womb, and he called the name of the first Perez, and the name of the second Zarah.

46

¹ In those days Joseph was still confined in the prison house in the land of Egypt. ² At that time the attendants of Pharaoh were standing before him, the chief of the butlers and the chief of the bakers which belonged to the king of Egypt. ³ And the butler took wine and placed it before the king to drink, and the baker placed bread before the king to eat, and the king drank of the wine and ate of the bread, he and his servants and ministers that ate at the king's table. ⁴ And whilst they were eating and drinking, the butler and the baker remained there, and Pharaoh's ministers found many flies in the wine, which the butler had brought, and stones of nitre were found in the baker's bread. ⁵ And the captain of the guard placed Joseph as an attendant on Pharaoh's officers, and Pharaoh's officers were in confinement one year. ⁶ And at the end of the year, they both dreamed dreams in one night, in the place of confinement where they were, and in the morning Joseph came to them to attend upon them as usual, and he saw them, and behold their countenances were dejected and sad. ⁷ And Joseph asked them, Why are your countenances sad and dejected this day? and they said unto him, We dreamed a dream, and there is no one to interpret it; and Joseph said unto them, Relate, I pray you, your dream unto me, and God shall give you an answer of peace as you desire. ⁸ And the butler related his dream unto Joseph, and he said, I saw in my dream, and behold a large vine was before me, and upon that vine I saw three branches, and the vine speedily blossomed and reached a great height, and its clusters were ripened and became grapes. ⁹ And I took the grapes and pressed them in a cup, and placed it in Pharaoh's hand and he drank; and Joseph said unto him, The three branches that were upon the vine are three days. ¹⁰ Yet within three days, the king will order thee to be brought out and he will restore thee to thy office, and thou shalt give the king his wine to drink as at first when thou wast his butler; but let me find favor in thy sight, that thou shalt remember me to Pharaoh when it will be well with thee, and do kindness unto me, and get me brought forth from this prison, for I was stolen away from the land of Canaan and was sold for a slave in this place. ¹¹ And also that which was told thee concerning my master's wife is false, for they placed me in this dungeon for naught; and the butler answered Joseph, saying, If the king deal well with me as at first, as thou last interpreted to me, I will do all that thou desirest, and get thee brought out of this dungeon. ¹² And the baker, seeing that Joseph had accurately interpreted the butler's dream, also approached, and related the whole of his dream to Joseph. ¹³ And he said unto him, In my dream I saw and behold three white baskets upon my head, and I looked, and behold there were in the upper-most basket all manner of baked meats for Pharaoh, and behold the birds were eating them from off my head. ¹⁴ And Joseph said unto him, The three baskets which thou didst see are three days, yet within three days Pharaoh will take off thy head, and hang thee upon a tree, and the birds will eat thy flesh from off thee, as thou sawest in thy dream. ¹⁵ In those days the queen was about to be delivered, and upon that day she bare a son unto the king of Egypt, and they proclaimed that the king had gotten his first born son and all the people of Egypt together with the officers and servants of Pharaoh rejoiced greatly. ¹⁶ And upon the third day of his birth Pharaoh made a feast for his officers and servants, for the hosts of the land of Zoar and of the land of Egypt. ¹⁷ And all the people of Egypt and the servants of Pharaoh came to eat and drink with the king at the feast of his son, and to rejoice at the king's rejoicing. ¹⁸ And all the officers of the king and his servants were rejoicing at that time for eight days at the feast, and they made merry with all sorts of musical instruments, with timbrels and with dances in the king's house for eight days. ¹⁹ And the butler, to whom Joseph had interpreted his dream, forgot Joseph, and he did not mention him to the king as he had promised, for this thing was from the Lord in order to punish Joseph because he had trusted in man. ²⁰ And Joseph remained after this in the prison house two years, until he had completed twelve years.

47

¹ And Isaac the son of Abraham was still living in those days in the land of Canaan; he was very aged, one hundred and eighty years old, and Esau his son, the brother of Jacob, was in the land of Edom, and he and his sons had possessions in it amongst the children of Seir. ² And Esau heard that his father's time was drawing nigh to die, and he and his sons and household came unto the land of Canaan, unto his father's house, and Jacob and his sons went forth from the place where they dwelt in Hebron, and they all came to their father Isaac, and they found Esau and his sons in the tent. ³ And Jacob and his sons sat before his father Isaac, and Jacob was still mourning for his son Joseph. ⁴ And Isaac said unto Jacob, Bring me hither thy sons and I will bless them; and Jacob brought his eleven children before his father Isaac. ⁵ And Isaac placed his hands upon all the sons of Jacob, and he took hold of them and embraced them, and kissed them one by one, and Isaac blessed them on that day, and he said unto them, May the God of your fathers bless you and increase your seed like the stars of heaven for number. ⁶ And Isaac also blessed the sons of Esau, saying, May God cause you to be a dread and a terror to all that will behold you, and to all your enemies. ⁷ And Isaac called Jacob and his sons, and they all came and sat before Isaac, and Isaac said unto Jacob, The Lord God of the whole earth said unto me, Unto thy seed will I give this land for an inheritance if thy children keep my statutes and my ways, and I will perform unto them the oath which I swore unto thy father Abraham. ⁸ Now therefore my son, teach thy children and thy children's children to fear the Lord, and to go in the good way which will please the Lord thy God, for if you keep the ways of the Lord and his statutes the Lord will also keep unto you his covenant with Abraham, and will do well with you and your seed all the days. ⁹ And when Isaac had finished commanding Jacob and his children, he gave up the ghost and died, and was gathered unto his people. ¹⁰ And Jacob and Esau fell upon

the face of their father Isaac, and they wept, and Isaac was one hundred and eighty years old when he died in the land of Canaan, in Hebron, and his sons carried him to the cave of Machpelah, which Abraham had bought from the children of Heth for a possession of a burial place. ¹¹ And all the kings of the land of Canaan went with Jacob and Esau to bury Isaac, and all the kings of Canaan showed Isaac great honor at his death. ¹² And the sons of Jacob and the sons of Esau went barefooted round about, walking and lamenting until they reached Kireath-arba. ¹³ And Jacob and Esau buried their father Isaac in the cave of Machpelah, which is in Kireath-arba in Hebron, and they buried him with very great honor, as at the funeral of kings. ¹⁴ And Jacob and his sons, and Esau and his sons, and all the kings of Canaan made a great and heavy mourning, and they buried him and mourned for him many days. ¹⁵ And at the death of Isaac, he left his cattle and his possessions and all belonging to him to his sons; and Esau said unto Jacob, Behold I pray thee, all that our father has left we will divide it in two parts, and I will have the choice, and Jacob said, We will do so. ¹⁶ And Jacob took all that Isaac had left in the land of Canaan, the cattle and the property, and he placed them in two parts before Esau and his sons, and he said unto Esau, Behold all this is before thee, choose thou unto thyself the half which thou wilt take. ¹⁷ And Jacob said unto Esau, Hear thou I pray thee what I will speak unto thee, saying, The Lord God of heaven and earth spoke unto our fathers Abraham and Isaac, saying, Unto thy seed will I give this land for an inheritance forever. ¹⁸ Now therefore all that our father has left is before thee, and behold all the land is before thee; choose thou from them what thou desirest. ¹⁹ If thou desirest the whole land take it for thee and thy children forever, and I will take this riches, and it thou desirest the riches take it unto thee, and I will take this land for me and for my children to inherit it forever. ²⁰ And Nebayoth, the son of Ishmael, was then in the land with his children, and Esau went on that day and consulted with him, saying. ²¹ Thus has Jacob spoken unto me, and thus has he answered me, now give thy advice and we will hear. ²² And Nebayoth said, What is this that Jacob hath spoken unto thee? behold all the children of Canaan are dwelling securely in their land, and Jacob sayeth he will inherit it with his seed all the days. ²³ Go now therefore and take all thy father's riches and leave Jacob thy brother in the land, as he has spoken. ²⁴ And Esau rose up and returned to Jacob, and did all that Nebayoth the son of Ishmael had advised; and Esau took all the riches that Isaac had left, the souls, the beasts, the cattle and the property, and all the riches; he gave nothing to his brother Jacob; and Jacob took all the land of Canaan, from the brook of Egypt unto the river Euphrates, and he took it for an everlasting possession, and for his children and for his seed after him forever. ²⁵ Jacob also took from his brother Esau the cave of Machpelah, which is in Hebron, which Abraham had bought from Ephron for a possession of a burial place for him and his seed forever. ²⁶ And Jacob wrote all these things in the book of purchase, and he signed it, and he testified all this with four faithful witnesses. ²⁷ And these are the words which Jacob wrote in the book, saying: The land of Canaan and all the cities of the Hittites, the Hivites, the Jebusites, the Amorites, the Perizzites, and the Gergashites, all the seven nations from the river of Egypt unto the river Euphrates. ²⁸ And the city of Hebron Kireath-arba, and the cave which is in it, the whole did Jacob buy from his brother Esau for value, for a possession and for an inheritance for his seed after him forever. ²⁹ And Jacob took the book of purchase and the signature, the command and the statutes and the revealed book, and he placed them in an earthen vessel in order that they should remain for a long time, and he delivered them into the hands of his children. ³⁰ Esau took all that his father had left him after his death from his brother Jacob, and he took all the property, from man and beast, camel and ass, ox and lamb, silver and gold, stones and bdellium, and all the riches which had belonged to Isaac the son of Abraham; there was nothing left which Esau did not take unto himself, from all that Isaac had left after his death. ³¹ And Esau took all this, and he and his children went home to the land of Seir the Horite, away from his brother Jacob and his children. ³² And Esau had possessions amongst the children of Seir, and Esau returned not to the land of Canaan from that day forward. ³³ And the whole land of Canaan became an inheritance to the children of Israel for an everlasting inheritance, and Esau with all his children inherited the mountain of Seir.

48

¹ In those days, after the death of Isaac, the Lord commanded and caused a famine upon the whole earth. ² At that time Pharaoh king of Egypt was sitting upon his throne in the land of Egypt, and lay in his bed and dreamed dreams, and Pharaoh saw in his dream that he was standing by the side of the river of Egypt. ³ And whilst he was standing he saw and behold seven fat fleshed and well favored kine came up out of the river. ⁴ And seven other kine, lean fleshed and ill favored, came up after them, and the seven ill favored ones swallowed up the well favored ones, and still their appearance was ill as at first. ⁵ And he awoke, and he slept again and he dreamed a second time, and he saw and behold seven ears of corn came up upon one stalk, rank and good, and seven thin ears blasted with the east wind sprang, up after them, and the thin ears swallowed up the full ones, and Pharaoh awoke out of his dream. ⁶ And in the morning the king remembered his dreams, and his spirit was sadly troubled on account of his dreams, and the king hastened and sent and called for all the magicians of Egypt, and the wise men, and they came and stood before Pharaoh. ⁷ And the king said unto them, I have dreamed dreams, and there is none to interpret them; and they said unto the king, relate thy dreams to thy servants and let us hear them. ⁸ And the king related his dreams to them, and they all answered and said with one voice to the king, may the king live forever; and this is the interpretation of thy dreams. ⁹ The seven good kine which thou didst see denote seven daughters that will be born unto thee in the latter days, and the seven kine which thou sawest come up after them, and swallowed them up, are for a sign that the daughters which will be born unto thee will all die in the life-time of the king. ¹⁰ And that which thou didst see in the second dream of seven full good ears of corn coming up upon one stalk, this is their interpretation, that thou wilt build unto thyself in the latter days seven cities throughout the land of Egypt; and that which thou sawest of the seven blasted ears of corn springing up after them and swallowing them up whilst thou didst behold them with thine eyes, is for a sign that the cities which thou wilt build will all be destroyed in the latter days, in the life-time of the king. ¹¹ And when they spoke these words the king did not incline his ear to their words, neither did he fix his heart upon them, for the king knew in his wisdom that they did not give a proper interpretation of the dreams; and when they had finished speaking before the king, the king answered them, saying, What is this thing that you have spoken unto me? surely you have uttered falsehood and spoken lies; therefore now give the proper interpretation of my dreams, that you may not die. ¹² And the king commanded after this, and he sent and called again for other wise men, and they came and stood before the king, and the king related his dreams to them, and they all answered him according to the first interpretation, and the king's anger was kindled and he was very wroth, and the king said unto them, Surely you speak lies and utter falsehood in what you have said. ¹³ And the king commanded that a proclamation should be issued throughout the land of Egypt, saying, It is resolved by the king and his great men, that any wise man who knoweth and understandeth the interpretation of dreams, and will not come this day before the king, shall die. ¹⁴ And the man that will declare unto the king the proper interpretation of his dreams, there shall be given unto him all that he will require from the king. And all the wise men of the land of Egypt came before the king, together with all the magicians and sorcerers that were in Egypt and in Goshen, in Rameses, in Tachpanches, in Zoar, and in all the places on the borders of Egypt, and they all stood before the king. ¹⁵ And all the nobles and the princes, and the attendants belonging to the king, came together from all the cities of Egypt, and they all sat before the king, and the king related his dreams before the wise men, and the princes, and all that sat before the king were astonished at the vision. ¹⁶ And all the wise men who were before the king were greatly divided in their interpretation of his dreams; some of them interpreted them to the king, saying, The seven good kine are seven kings, who from the king's issue will be raised over Egypt. ¹⁷ And the seven bad kine are seven princes, who will stand up against them in the latter days and destroy them; and the seven ears of corn are the seven great princes belonging to Egypt, who will fall in the hands of the seven less powerful princes of their enemies, in the wars of our lord the king. ¹⁸ And some of them interpreted to the king in this manner, saying, The seven good kine are the strong cities of Egypt, and the seven bad kine are the seven nations of the land of Canaan, who will come against the seven cities of Egypt in the latter days and destroy them. ¹⁹ And that which thou sawest in the second dream, of seven good and bad ears of corn, is a sign that the government of Egypt will again return to thy seed as at first. ²⁰ And in his reign the people of the cities of Egypt will turn against the seven cities of Canaan who are stronger than they are, and will destroy them, and the government of Egypt will return to thy seed. ²¹ And some of them said unto the king, This is the interpretation of thy dreams; the seven good kine are seven queens, whom thou wilt take for wives in the latter days, and the seven bad kine denote that those women will all die in the lifetime of the king. ²² And the seven good and bad ears of corn which thou didst see in the second dream are fourteen children, and it will be in the latter days that they will stand up and fight amongst themselves, and seven of them will smite the seven that are more powerful. ²³ And some of them said these words unto the king, saying, The seven good kine denote that seven children will be born to thee, and they will slay seven of thy children's children in the latter days; and the seven good ears of corn which thou didst see in the second dream, are those princes against whom seven other less powerful princes will fight and destroy them in the latter

days, and avenge thy children's cause, and the government will again return to thy seed. ²⁴ And the king heard all the words of the wise men of Egypt and their interpretation of his dreams, and none of them pleased the king. ²⁵ And the king knew in his wisdom that they did not altogether speak correctly in all these words, for this was from the Lord to frustrate the words of the wise men of Egypt, in order that Joseph might go forth from the house of confinement, and in order that he should become great in Egypt. ²⁶ And the king saw that none amongst all the wise men and magicians of Egypt spoke correctly to him, and the king's wrath was kindled, and his anger burned within him. ²⁷ And the king commanded that all the wise men and magicians should go out from before him, and they all went out from before the king with shame and disgrace. ²⁸ And the king commanded that a proclamation be sent throughout Egypt to slay all the magicians that were in Egypt, and not one of them should be suffered to live. ²⁹ And the captains of the guards belonging to the king rose up, and each man drew his sword, and they began to smite the magicians of Egypt, and the wise men. ³⁰ And after this Merod, chief butler to the king, came and bowed down before the king and sat before him. ³¹ And the butler said unto the king, May the king live forever, and his government be exalted in the land. ³² Thou wast angry with thy servant in those days, now two years past, and didst place me in the ward, and I was for some time in the ward, I and the chief of the bakers. ³³ And there was with us a Hebrew servant belonging to the captain of the guard, his name was Joseph, for his master had been angry with him and placed him in the house of confinement, and he attended us there. ³⁴ And in some time after when we were in the ward, we dreamed dreams in one night, I and the chief of the bakers; we dreamed, each man according to the interpretation of his dream. ³⁵ And we came in the morning and told them to that servant, and he interpreted to us our dreams, to each man according to his dream, did he correctly interpret. ³⁶ And it came to pass as he interpreted to us, so was the event; there fell not to the ground any of his words. ³⁷ And now therefore my lord and king do not slay the people of Egypt for naught; behold that slave is still confined in the house by the captain of the guard his master, in the house of confinement. ³⁸ If it pleaseth the king let him send for him that he may come before thee and he will make known to thee, the correct interpretation of the dream which thou didst dream. ³⁹ And the king heard the words of the chief butler, and the king ordered that the wise men of Egypt should not be slain. ⁴⁰ And the king ordered his servants to bring Joseph before him, and the king said unto them, Go to him and do not terrify him lest he be confused and will not know to speak properly. ⁴¹ And the servants of the king went to Joseph, and they brought him hastily out of the dungeon, and the king's servants shaved him, and he changed his prison garment and he came before the king. ⁴² And the king was sitting upon his royal throne in a princely dress girt around with a golden ephod, and the fine gold which was upon it sparkled, and the carbuncle and the ruby and the emerald, together with all the precious stones that were upon the king's head, dazzled the eye, and Joseph wondered greatly at the king. ⁴³ And the throne upon which the king sat was covered with gold and silver, and with onyx stones, and it had seventy steps. ⁴⁴ And it was their custom throughout the land of Egypt, that every man who came to speak to the king, if he was a prince or one that was estimable in the sight of the king, he ascended to the king's throne as far as the thirty-first step, and the king would descend to the thirty-sixth step, and speak with him. ⁴⁵ If he was one of the common people, he ascended to the third step, and the king would descend to the fourth and speak to him, and their custom was, moreover, that any man who understood to speak in all the seventy languages, he ascended the seventy steps, and went up and spoke till he reached the king. ⁴⁶ And any man who could not complete the seventy, he ascended as many steps as the languages which he knew to speak in. ⁴⁷ And it was customary in those days in Egypt that no one should reign over them, but who understood to speak in the seventy languages. ⁴⁸ And when Joseph came before the king he bowed down to the ground before the king, and he ascended to the third step, and the king sat upon the fourth step and spoke with Joseph. ⁴⁹ And the king said unto Joseph, I dreamed a dream, and there is no interpreter to interpret it properly, and I commanded this day that all the magicians of Egypt and the wise men thereof, should come before me, and I related my dreams to them, and no one has properly interpreted them to me. ⁵⁰ And after this I this day heard concerning thee, that thou art a wise man, and canst correctly interpret every dream that thou hearest. ⁵¹ And Joseph answered Pharaoh, saying, Let Pharaoh relate his dreams that he dreamed; surely the interpretations belong to God; and Pharaoh related his dreams to Joseph, the dream of the kine, and the dream of the ears of corn, and the king left off speaking. ⁵² And Joseph was then clothed with the spirit of God before the king, and he knew all the things that would befall the king from that day forward, and he knew the proper interpretation of the king's dream, and he spoke before the king. ⁵³ And Joseph found favor in the sight of the king, and the king inclined his ears and his heart, and he heard all the words of Joseph. And Joseph said unto the king, Do not imagine that they are two dreams, for it is only one dream, for that which God has chosen to do throughout the land he has shown to the king in his dream, and this is the proper interpretation of thy dream: ⁵⁴ The seven good kine and ears of corn are seven years, and the seven bad kine and ears of corn are also seven years; it is one dream. ⁵⁵ Behold the seven years that are coming there will be a great plenty throughout the land, and after that the seven years of famine will follow them, a very grievous famine; and all the plenty will be forgotten from the land, and the famine will consume the inhabitants of the land. ⁵⁶ The king dreamed one dream, and the dream was therefore repeated unto Pharaoh because the thing is established by God, and God will shortly bring it to pass. ⁵⁷ Now therefore I will give thee counsel and deliver thy soul and the souls of the inhabitants of the land from the evil of the famine, that thou seek throughout thy kingdom for a man very discreet and wise, who knoweth all the affairs of government, and appoint him to superintend over the land of Egypt. ⁵⁸ And let the man whom thou placest over Egypt appoint officers under him, that they gather in all the food of the good years that are coming, and let them lay up corn and deposit it in thy appointed stores. ⁵⁹ And let them keep that food for the seven years of famine, that it may be found for thee and thy people and thy whole land, and that thou and thy land be not cut off by the famine. ⁶⁰ Let all the inhabitants of the land be also ordered that they gather in, every man the produce of his field, of all sorts of food, during the seven good years, and that they place it in their stores, that it may be found for them in the days of the famine and that they may live upon it. ⁶¹ This is the proper interpretation of thy dream, and this is the counsel given to save thy soul and the souls of all thy subjects. ⁶² And the king answered and said unto Joseph, Who sayeth and who knoweth that thy words are correct? And he said unto the king, This shall be a sign for thee respecting all my words, that they are true and that my advice is good for thee. ⁶³ Behold thy wife sitteth this day upon the stool of delivery, and she will bear thee a son and thou wilt rejoice with him; when thy child shall have gone forth from his mother's womb, thy first born son that has been born these two years back shall die, and thou wilt be comforted in the child that will be born unto thee this day. ⁶⁴ And Joseph finished speaking these words to the king, and he bowed down to the king and he went out, and when Joseph had gone out from the king's presence, those signs which Joseph had spoken unto the king came to pass on that day. ⁶⁵ And the queen bare a son on that day and the king heard the glad tidings about his son, and he rejoiced, and when the reporter had gone forth from the king's presence, the king's servants found the first born son of the king fallen dead upon the ground. ⁶⁶ And there was great lamentation and noise in the king's house, and the king heard it, and he said, What is the noise and lamentation that I have heard in the house? and they told the king that his first born son had died; then the king knew that all Joseph's words that he had spoken were correct, and the king was consoled for his son by the child that was born to him on that day as Joseph had spoken.

49

¹ After these things the king sent and assembled all his officers and servants, and all the princes and nobles belonging to the king, and they all came before the king. ² And the king said unto them, Behold you have seen and heard all the words of this Hebrew man, and all the signs which he declared would come to pass, and not any of his words have fallen to the ground. ³ You know that he has given a proper interpretation of the dream, and it will surely come to pass, now therefore take counsel, and know what you will do and how the land will be delivered from the famine. ⁴ Seek now and see whether the like can be found, in whose heart there is wisdom and knowledge, and I will appoint him over the land. ⁵ For you have heard what the Hebrew man has advised concerning this to save the land therewith from the famine, and I know that the land will not be delivered from the famine but with the advice of the Hebrew man, him that advised me. ⁶ And they all answered the king and said, The counsel which the Hebrew has given concerning this is good; now therefore, our lord and king, behold the whole land is in thy hand, do that which seemeth good in thy sight. ⁷ Him whom thou chooses, and whom thou in thy wisdom knowest to be wise and capable of delivering the land with his wisdom, him shall the king appoint to be under him over the land. ⁸ And the king said to all the officers: I have thought that since God has made known to the Hebrew man all that he has spoken, there is none so discreet and wise in the whole land as he is; if it seem good in your sight I will place him over the land, for he will save the land with his wisdom. ⁹ And all the officers answered the king and said, But surely it is written in the laws of Egypt, and it should not be violated, that no man shall reign over Egypt, nor be the second to the king, but one who has knowledge in all the languages of the sons of men. ¹⁰ Now therefore our lord and king, behold this Hebrew man can only speak the Hebrew

language, and how then can he be over us the second under government, a man who not even knoweth our language? ¹¹ Now we pray thee send for him, and let him come before thee, and prove him in all things, and do as thou see fit. ¹² And the king said, It shall be done tomorrow, and the thing that you have spoken is good; and all the officers came on that day before the king. ¹³ And on that night the Lord sent one of his ministering angels, and he came into the land of Egypt unto Joseph, and the angel of the Lord stood over Joseph, and behold Joseph was lying in the bed at night in his master's house in the dungeon, for his master had put him back into the dungeon on account of his wife. ¹⁴ And the angel roused him from his sleep, and Joseph rose up and stood upon his legs, and behold the angel of the Lord was standing opposite to him; and the angel of the Lord spoke with Joseph, and he taught him all the languages of man in that night, and he called his name Jehoseph. ¹⁵ And the angel of the Lord went from him, and Joseph returned and lay upon his bed, and Joseph was astonished at the vision which he saw. ¹⁶ And it came to pass in the morning that the king sent for all his officers and servants, and they all came and sat before the king, and the king ordered Joseph to be brought, and the king's servants went and brought Joseph before Pharaoh. ¹⁷ And the king came forth and ascended the steps of the throne, and Joseph spoke unto the king in all languages, and Joseph went up to him and spoke unto the king until he arrived before the king in the seventieth step, and he sat before the king. ¹⁸ And the king greatly rejoiced on account of Joseph, and all the king's officers rejoiced greatly with the king when they heard all the words of Joseph. ¹⁹ And the thing seemed good in the sight of the king and the officers, to appoint Joseph to be second to the king over the whole land of Egypt, and the king spoke to Joseph, saying, ²⁰ Now thou didst give me counsel to appoint a wise man over the land of Egypt, in order with his wisdom to save the land from the famine; now therefore, since God has made all this known to thee, and all the words which thou hast spoken, there is not throughout the land a discreet and wise man like unto thee. ²¹ And thy name no more shall be called Joseph, but Zaphnath Paaneah shall be thy name; thou shalt be second to me, and according to thy word shall be all the affairs of my government, and at thy word shall my people go out and come in. ²² Also from under thy hand shall my servants and officers receive their salary which is given to them monthly, and to thee shall all the people of the land bow down; only in my throne will I be greater than thou. ²³ And the king took off his ring from his hand and put it upon the hand of Joseph, and the king dressed Joseph in a princely garment, and he put a golden crown upon his head, and he put a golden chain upon his neck. ²⁴ And the king commanded his servants, and they made him ride in the second chariot belonging to the king, that went opposite to the king's chariot, and he caused him to ride upon a great and strong horse from the king's horses, and to be conducted through the streets of the land of Egypt. ²⁵ And the king commanded that all those that played upon timbrels, harps and other musical instruments should go forth with Joseph; one thousand timbrels, one thousand mecholoth, and one thousand nebalim went after him. ²⁶ And five thousand men, with drawn swords glittering in their hands, and they went marching and playing before Joseph, and twenty thousand of the great men of the king girt with girdles of skin covered with gold, marched at the right hand of Joseph, and twenty thousand at his left, and all the women and damsels went upon the roofs or stood in the streets playing and rejoicing at Joseph, and gazed at the appearance of Joseph and at his beauty. ²⁷ And the king's people went before him and behind him, perfuming the road with frankincense and with cassia, and with all sorts of fine perfume, and scattered myrrh and aloes along the road, and twenty men proclaimed these words before him throughout the land in a loud voice: ²⁸ Do you see this man whom the king has chosen to be his second? all the affairs of government shall be regulated by him, and he that transgresses his orders, or that does not bow down before him to the ground, shall die, for he rebels against the king and his second. ²⁹ And when the heralds had ceased proclaiming, all the people of Egypt bowed down to the ground before Joseph and said, May the king live, also may his second live; and all the inhabitants of Egypt bowed down along the road, and when the heralds approached them, they bowed down, and they rejoiced with all sorts of timbrels, mechol and nebal before Joseph. ³⁰ And Joseph upon his horse lifted up his eyes to heaven, and called out and said, He raiseth the poor man from the dust, He lifteth up the needy from the dunghill. O Lord of Hosts, happy is the man who trusteth in thee. ³¹ And Joseph passed throughout the land of Egypt with Pharaoh's servants and officers, and they showed him the whole land of Egypt and all the king's treasures. ³² And Joseph returned and came on that day before Pharaoh, and the king gave unto Joseph a possession in the land of Egypt, a possession of fields and vineyards, and the king gave unto Joseph three thousand talents of silver and one thousand talents of gold, and onyx stones and bdellium and many gifts. ³³ And on the next day the king commanded all the people of Egypt to bring unto Joseph offerings and gifts, and that he that violated the command of the king should die; and they made a high place in the street of the city, and they spread out garments there, and whoever brought anything to Joseph put it into the high place. ³⁴ And all the people of Egypt cast something into the high place, one man a golden ear-ring, and the other rings and ear-rings, and different vessels of gold and silver work, and onyx stones and bdellium did he cast upon the high place; every one gave something of what he possessed. ³⁵ And Joseph took all these and placed them in his treasuries, and all the officers and nobles belonging to the king exalted Joseph, and they gave him many gifts, seeing that the king had chosen him to be his second. ³⁶ And the king sent to Potiphera, the son of Ahiram priest of On, and he took his young daughter Osnath and gave her unto Joseph for a wife. ³⁷ And the damsel was very comely, a virgin, one whom man had not known, and Joseph took her for a wife; and the king said unto Joseph, I am Pharaoh, and beside thee none shall dare to lift up his hand or his foot to regulate my people throughout the land of Egypt. ³⁸ And Joseph was thirty years old when he stood before Pharaoh, and Joseph went out from before the king, and he became the king's second in Egypt. ³⁹ And the king gave Joseph a hundred servants to attend him in his house, and Joseph also sent and purchased many servants and they remained in the house of Joseph. ⁴⁰ Joseph then built for himself a very magnificent house like unto the houses of kings, before the court of the king's palace, and he made in the house a large temple, very elegant in appearance and convenient for his residence; three years was Joseph in erecting his house. ⁴¹ And Joseph made unto himself a very elegant throne of abundance of gold and silver, and he covered it with onyx stones and bdellium, and he made upon it the likeness of the whole land of Egypt, and the likeness of the river of Egypt that watereth the whole land of Egypt; and Joseph sat securely upon his throne in his house and the Lord increased Joseph's wisdom. ⁴² And all the inhabitants of Egypt and Pharaoh's servants and his princes loved Joseph exceedingly, for this thing was from the Lord to Joseph. ⁴³ And Joseph had an army that made war, going out in hosts and troops to the number of forty thousand six hundred men, capable of bearing arms to assist the king and Joseph against the enemy, besides the king's officers and his servants and inhabitants of Egypt without number. ⁴⁴ And Joseph gave unto his mighty men, and to all his host, shields and javelins, and caps and coats of mail and stones for slinging.

50

¹ At that time the children of Tarshish came against the sons of Ishmael, and made war with them, and the children of Tarshish spoiled the Ishmaelites for a long time. ² And the children of Ishmael were small in number in those days, and they could not prevail over the children of Tarshish, and they were sorely oppressed. ³ And the old men of the Ishmaelites sent a record to the king of Egypt, saying, Send I pray thee unto thy servants officers and hosts to help us to fight against the children of Tarshish, for we have been consuming away for a long time. ⁴ And Pharaoh sent Joseph with the mighty men and host which were with him, and also his mighty men from the king's house. ⁵ And they went to the land of Havilah to the children of Ishmael, to assist them against the children of Tarshish, and the children of Ishmael fought with the children of Tarshish, and Joseph smote the Tarshishites and he subdued all their land, and the children of Ishmael dwell therein unto this day. ⁶ And when the land of Tarshish was subdued, all the Tarshishites ran away, and came on the border of their brethren the children of Javan, and Joseph with all his mighty men and host returned to Egypt, not one man of them missing. ⁷ And at the revolution of the year, in the second year of Joseph's reigning over Egypt, the Lord gave great plenty throughout the land for seven years as Joseph had spoken, for the Lord blessed all the produce of the earth in those days for seven years, and they ate and were greatly satisfied. ⁸ And Joseph at that time had officers under him, and they collected all the food of the good years, and heaped corn year by year, and they placed it in the treasuries of Joseph. ⁹ And at any time when they gathered the food Joseph commanded that they should bring the corn in the ears, and also bring with it some of the soil of the field, that it should not spoil. ¹⁰ And Joseph did according to this year by year, and he heaped up corn like the sand of the sea for abundance, for his stores were immense and could not be numbered for abundance. ¹¹ And also all the inhabitants of Egypt gathered all sorts of food in their stores in great abundance during the seven good years, but they did not do unto it as Joseph did. ¹² And all the food which Joseph and the Egyptians had gathered during the seven years of plenty, was secured for the land in stores for the seven years of famine, for the support of the whole land. ¹³ And the inhabitants of Egypt filled each man his store and his concealed place with corn, to be for support during the famine. ¹⁴ And Joseph placed all the food that he had gathered in all the cities of Egypt, and he closed all the stores and placed sentinels over them. ¹⁵ And Joseph's

wife Osnath the daughter of Potiphera bare him two sons, Manasseh and Ephraim, and Joseph was thirty-four years old when he begat them. ¹⁶ And the lads grew up and they went in his ways and in his instructions, they did not deviate from the way which their father taught them, either to the right or left. ¹⁷ And the Lord was with the lads, and they grew up and had understanding and skill in all wisdom and in all the affairs of government, and all the king's officers and his great men of the inhabitants of Egypt exalted the lads, and they were brought up amongst the king's children. ¹⁸ And the seven years of plenty that were throughout the land were at an end, and the seven years of famine came after them as Joseph had spoken, and the famine was throughout the land. ¹⁹ And all the people of Egypt saw that the famine had commenced in the land of Egypt, and all the people of Egypt opened their stores of corn for the famine prevailed over them. ²⁰ And they found all the food that was in their stores, full of vermin and not fit to eat, and the famine prevailed throughout the land, and all the inhabitants of Egypt came and cried before Pharaoh, for the famine was heavy upon them. ²¹ And they said unto Pharaoh, Give food unto thy servants, and wherefore shall we die through hunger before thy eyes, even we and our little ones? ²² And Pharaoh answered them, saying, And wherefore do you cry unto me? did not Joseph command that the corn should be laid up during the seven years of plenty for the years of famine? and wherefore did you not hearken to his voice? ²³ And the people of Egypt answered the king, saying, As thy soul liveth, our lord, thy servants have done all that Joseph ordered, for thy servants also gathered in all the produce of their fields during the seven years of plenty and laid it in the stores unto this day. ²⁴ And when the famine prevailed over thy servants we opened our stores, and behold all our produce was filled with vermin and was not fit for food. ²⁵ And when the king heard all that had befallen the inhabitants of Egypt, the king was greatly afraid on account of the famine, and he was much terrified; and the king answered the people of Egypt, saying, Since all this has happened unto you, go unto Joseph, do whatever he shall say unto you, transgress not his commands. ²⁶ And all the people of Egypt went forth and came unto Joseph, and said unto him, Give unto us food, and wherefore shall we die before thee through hunger? for we gathered in our produce during the seven years as thou didst command, and we put it in store, and thus has it befallen us. ²⁷ And when Joseph heard all the words of the people of Egypt and what had befallen them, Joseph opened all his stores of the produce and he sold it unto the people of Egypt. ²⁸ And the famine prevailed throughout the land, and the famine was in all countries, but in the land of Egypt there was produce for sale. ²⁹ And all the inhabitants of Egypt came unto Joseph to buy corn, for the famine prevailed over them, and all their corn was spoiled, and Joseph daily sold it to all the people of Egypt. ³⁰ And all the inhabitants of the land of Canaan and the Philistines, and those beyond the Jordan, and the children of the east and all the cities of the lands far and nigh heard that there was corn in Egypt, and they all came to Egypt to buy corn, for the famine prevailed over them. ³¹ And Joseph opened the stores of corn and placed officers over them, and they daily stood and sold to all that came. ³² And Joseph knew that his brethren also would come to Egypt to buy corn, for the famine prevailed throughout the earth. And Joseph commanded all his people that they should cause it to be proclaimed throughout the land of Egypt, saying, ³³ It is the pleasure of the king, of his second and of their great men, that any person who wishes to buy corn in Egypt shall not send his servants to Egypt to purchase, but his sons, and also any Egyptian or Canaanite, who shall come from any of the stores from buying corn in Egypt, and shall go and sell it throughout the land, he shall die, for no one shall buy but for the support of his household. ³⁴ And any man leading two or three beasts shall die, for a man shall only lead his own beast. ³⁵ And Joseph placed sentinels at the gates of Egypt, and commanded them, saying, Any person who may come to buy corn, suffer him not to enter until his name, and the name of his father, and the name of his father's father be written down, and whatever is written by day, send their names unto me in the evening that I may know their names. ³⁶ And Joseph placed officers throughout the land of Egypt, and he commanded them to do all these things. ³⁷ And Joseph did all these things, and made these statutes, in order that he might know when his brethren should come to Egypt to buy corn; and Joseph's people caused it daily to be proclaimed in Egypt according to these words and statutes which Joseph had commanded. ³⁸ And all the inhabitants of the east and west country, and of all the earth, heard of the statutes and regulations which Joseph had enacted in Egypt, and the inhabitants of the extreme parts of the earth came and they bought corn in Egypt day after day, and then went away. ³⁹ And all the officers of Egypt did as Joseph had commanded, and all that came to Egypt to buy corn, the gate keepers would write their names, and their fathers' names, and daily bring them in the evening before Joseph.

¹ And Jacob afterward heard that there was corn in Egypt, and he called unto his sons to go to Egypt to buy corn, for upon them also did the famine prevail, and he called unto his sons, saying, ² Behold I hear that there is corn in Egypt, and all the people of the earth go there to purchase, now therefore why will you show yourselves satisfied before the whole earth? go you also down to Egypt and buy us a little corn amongst those that come there, that we may not die. ³ And the sons of Jacob hearkened to the voice of their father, and they rose up to go down to Egypt in order to buy corn amongst the rest that came there. ⁴ And Jacob their father commanded them, saying, When you come into the city do not enter together in one gate, on account of the inhabitants of the land. ⁵ And the sons of Jacob went forth and they went to Egypt, and the sons of Jacob did all as their father had commanded them, and Jacob did not send Benjamin, for he said, Lest an accident might befall him on the road like his brother; and ten of Jacob's sons went forth. ⁶ And whilst the sons of Jacob were going on the road, they repented of what they had done to Joseph, and they spoke to each other, saying, We know that our brother Joseph went down to Egypt, and now we will seek him where we go, and if we find him we will take him from his master for a ransom, and if not, by force, and we will die for him. ⁷ And the sons of Jacob agreed to this thing and strengthened themselves on account of Joseph, to deliver him from the hand of his master, and the sons of Jacob went to Egypt; and when they came near to Egypt they separated from each other, and they came through ten gates of Egypt, and the gate keepers wrote their names on that day, and brought them to Joseph in the evening. ⁸ And Joseph read the names from the hand of the gate-keepers of the city, and he found that his brethren had entered at the ten gates of the city, and Joseph at that time commanded that it should be proclaimed throughout the land of Egypt, saying, ⁹ Go forth all ye store guards, close all the corn stores and let only one remain open, that those who come may purchase from it. ¹⁰ And all the officers of Joseph did so at that time, and they closed all the stores and left only one open. ¹¹ And Joseph gave the written names of his brethren to him that was set over the open store, and he said unto him, Whosoever shall come to thee to buy corn, ask his name, and when men of these names shall come before thee, seize them and send them, and they did so. ¹² And when the sons of Jacob came into the city, they joined together in the city to seek Joseph before they bought themselves corn. ¹³ And they went to the walls of the harlots, and they sought Joseph in the walls of the harlots for three days, for they thought that Joseph would come in the walls of the harlots, for Joseph was very comely and well favored, and the sons of Jacob sought Joseph for three days, and they could not find him. ¹⁴ And the man who was set over the open store sought for those names which Joseph had given him, and he did not find them. ¹⁵ And he sent to Joseph, saying, These three days have passed, and those men whose names thou didst give unto me have not come; and Joseph sent servants to seek the men in all Egypt, and to bring them before Joseph. ¹⁶ And Joseph's servants went and came into Egypt and could not find them, and went to Goshen and they were not there, and then went to the city of Rameses and could not find them. ¹⁷ And Joseph continued to send sixteen servants to seek his brothers, and they went and spread themselves in the four corners of the city, and four of the servants went into the house of the harlots, and they found the ten men there seeking their brother. ¹⁸ And those four men took them and brought them before him, and they bowed down to him to the ground, and Joseph was sitting upon his throne in his temple, clothed with princely garments, and upon his head was a large crown of gold, and all the mighty men were sitting around him. ¹⁹ And the sons of Jacob saw Joseph, and his figure and comeliness and dignity of countenance seemed wonderful in their eyes, and they again bowed down to him to the ground. ²⁰ And Joseph saw his brethren, and he knew them, but they knew him not, for Joseph was very great in their eyes, therefore they knew him not. ²¹ And Joseph spoke to them, saying, From whence come ye? and they all answered and said, Thy servants have come from the land of Canaan to buy corn, for the famine prevails throughout the earth, and thy servants heard that there was corn in Egypt, so they have come amongst the other comers to buy corn for their support. ²² And Joseph answered them, saying, If you have come to purchase as you say, why do you come through ten gates of the city? it can only be that you have come to spy through the land. ²³ And they all together answered Joseph, and said, Not so my lord, we are right, thy servants are not spies, but we have come to buy corn, for thy servants are all brothers, the sons of one man in the land of Canaan, and our father commanded us, saying, When you come to the city do not enter together at one gate on account of the inhabitants of the land. ²⁴ And Joseph again answered them and said, That is the thing which I spoke unto you, you have come to spy through the land, therefore you all came through ten gates of the city; you have come to see the nakedness of the land. ²⁵ Surely every one that cometh to buy corn goeth his way, and you are already three days in the land, and what do you do in the walls of harlots in which you have been for these

three days? surely spies do like unto these things. ²⁶ And they said unto Joseph, Far be it from our lord to speak thus, for we are twelve brothers, the sons of our father Jacob, in the land of Canaan, the son of Isaac, the son of Abraham, the Hebrew, and behold the youngest is with our father this day in the land of Canaan, and one is not, for he was lost from us, and we thought perhaps he might be in this land, so we are seeking him throughout the land, and have come even to the houses of harlots to seek him there. ²⁷ And Joseph said unto them, And have you then sought him throughout the earth, that there only remained Egypt for you to seek him in? And what also should your brother do in the houses of harlots, although he were in Egypt? have you not said, That you are from the sons of Isaac, the son of Abraham, and what shall the sons of Jacob do then in the houses of harlots? ²⁸ And they said unto him, Because we heard that Ishmaelites stole him from us, and it was told unto us that they sold him in Egypt, and thy servant, our brother, is very comely and well favored, so we thought he would surely be in the houses of harlots, therefore thy servants went there to seek him and give ransom for him. ²⁹ And Joseph still answered them, saying, Surely you speak falsely and utter lies, to say of yourselves that you are the sons of Abraham; as Pharaoh liveth you are spies, therefore have you come to the houses of harlots that you should not be known. ³⁰ And Joseph said unto them, And now if you find him, and his master requireth of you a great price, will you give it for him? and they said, It shall be given. ³¹ And he said unto them, And if his master will not consent to part with him for a great price, what will you do unto him on his account? and they answered him, saying, If he will not give him unto us we will slay him, and take our brother and go away. ³² And Joseph said unto them, That is the thing which I have spoken to you; you are spies, for you are come to slay the inhabitants of the land, for we heard that two of your brethren smote all the inhabitants of Shechem, in the land of Canaan, on account of your sister, and you now come to do the like in Egypt on account of your brother. ³³ Only hereby shall I know that you are true men; if you will send home one from amongst you to fetch your youngest brother from your father, and to bring him here unto me, and by doing this thing I will know that you are right. ³⁴ And Joseph called to seventy of his mighty men, and he said unto them, Take these men and bring them into the ward. ³⁵ And the mighty men took the ten men, they laid hold of them and put them into the ward, and they were in the ward three days. ³⁶ And on the third day Joseph had them brought out of the ward, and he said unto them, Do this for yourselves if you be true men, so that you may live, one of your brethren shall be confined in the ward whilst you go and take home the corn for your household to the land of Canaan, and fetch your youngest brother, and bring him here unto me, that I may know that you are true men when you do this thing. ³⁷ And Joseph went out from them and came into the chamber, and wept a great weeping, for his pity was excited for them, and he washed his face, and returned to them again, and he took Simeon from them and ordered him to be bound, but Simeon was not willing to be done so, for he was a very powerful man and they could not bind him. ³⁸ And Joseph called unto his mighty men and seventy valiant men came before him with drawn swords in their hands, and the sons of Jacob were terrified at them. ³⁹ And Joseph said unto them, Seize this man and confine him in prison until his brethren come to him, and Joseph's valiant men hastened and they all laid hold of Simeon to bind him, and Simeon gave a loud and terrible shriek and the cry was heard at a distance. ⁴⁰ And all the valiant men of Joseph were terrified at the sound of the shriek, that they fell upon their faces, and they were greatly afraid and fled. ⁴¹ And all the men that were with Joseph fled, for they were greatly afraid of their lives, and only Joseph and Manasseh his son remained there, and Manassah the son of Joseph saw the strength of Simeon, and he was exceedingly wroth. ⁴² And Manassah the son of Joseph rose up to Simeon, and Manassah smote Simeon a heavy blow with his fist against the back of his neck, and Simeon was stilled of his rage. ⁴³ And Manassah laid hold of Simeon and he seized him violently and he bound him and brought him into the house of confinement, and all the sons of Jacob were astonished at the act of the youth. ⁴⁴ And Simeon said unto his brethren, None of you must say that this is the smiting of an Egyptian, but it is the smiting of the house of my father. ⁴⁵ And after this Joseph ordered him to be called who was set over the storehouse, to fill their sacks with corn as much as they could carry, and to restore every man's money into his sack, and to give them provision for the road, and thus did he unto them. ⁴⁶ And Joseph commanded them, saying, Take heed lest you transgress my orders to bring your brother as I have told you, and it shall be when you bring your brother hither unto me, then will I know that you are true men, and you shall traffic in the land, and I will restore unto you your brother, and you shall return in peace to your father. ⁴⁷ And they all answered and said, According as our lord speaketh so will we do, and they bowed down to him to the ground. ⁴⁸ And every man lifted his corn upon his ass, and they went out to go to the land of Canaan to their father, and they came to the inn and Levi spread his sack to give provender to his ass, when he saw and behold his money in full weight was still in his sack. ⁴⁹ And the man was greatly afraid, and he said unto his brethren, My money is restored, and lo, it is even in my sack, and the men were greatly afraid, and they said, What is this that God hath done unto us? ⁵⁰ And they all said, And where is the Lord's kindness with our fathers, with Abraham, Isaac, end Jacob, that the Lord has this day delivered us into the hands of the king of Egypt to contrive against us? ⁵¹ And Judah said unto them, Surely we are guilty sinners before the Lord our God in having sold our brother, our own flesh, and wherefore do you say, Where is the Lord's kindness with our fathers? ⁵² And Reuben said unto them, Said I not unto you, do not sin against the lad, and you would not listen to me? now God requireth him from us, and how dare you say, Where is the Lord's kindness with our fathers, whilst you have sinned unto the Lord? ⁵³ And they tarried over night in that place, and they rose up early in the morning and laded their asses with their corn, and they led them and went on and came to their father's house in the land of Canaan. ⁵⁴ And Jacob and his household went out to meet his sons, and Jacob saw and behold their brother Simeon was not with them, and Jacob said unto his sons, Where is your brother Simeon, whom I do not see? and his sons told him all that had befallen them in Egypt.

52

¹ And they entered their house, and every man opened his sack and they saw and behold every man's bundle of money was there, at which they and their father were greatly terrified. ² And Jacob said unto them, What is this that you have done to me? I sent your brother Joseph to inquire after your welfare and you said unto me. A wild beast did devour him. ³ And Simeon went with you to buy food and you say the king of Egypt hath confined him in prison, and you wish to take Benjamin to cause his death also, and bring down my grey hairs with sorrow to the grave on account of Benjamin and his brother Joseph. ⁴ Now therefore my son shall not go down with you, for his brother is dead and he is left alone, and mischief may befall him by the way in which you go, as it befell his brother. ⁵ And Reuben said unto his father, Thou shalt slay my two sons if I do not bring thy son and place him before thee; and Jacob said unto his sons, Abide ye here and do not go down to Egypt, for my son shall not go down with you to Egypt, nor die like his brother. ⁶ And Judah said unto them, refrain ye from him until the corn is finished, and he will then say, Take down your brother, when he will find his own life and the life of his household in danger from the famine. ⁷ And in those days the famine was sore throughout the land, and all the people of the earth went and came to Egypt to buy food, for the famine prevailed greatly amongst them, and the sons of Jacob remained in Canaan a year and two months until their corn was finished. ⁸ And it came to pass after their corn was finished, the whole household of Jacob was pinched with hunger, and all the infants of the sons of Jacob came together and they approached Jacob, and they all surrounded him, and they said unto him, Give unto us bread, and wherefore shall we all perish through hunger in thy presence? ⁹ Jacob heard the words of his son's children, and he wept a great weeping, and his pity was roused for them, and Jacob called unto his sons and they all came and sat before him. ¹⁰ And Jacob said unto them, And have you not seen how your children have been weeping over me this day, saying, Give unto us bread, and there is none? now therefore return and buy for us a little food. ¹¹ And Judah answered and said unto his father, If thou wilt send our brother with us we will go down and buy corn for thee, and if thou wilt not send him then we will not go down, for surely the king of Egypt particularly enjoined us, saying, You shall not see my face unless your brother be with you, for the king of Egypt is a strong and mighty king, and behold if we shall go to him without our brother we shall all be put to death. ¹² Dost thou not know and hast thou not heard that this king is very powerful and wise, and there is not like unto him in all the earth? behold we have seen all the kings of the earth and we have not seen one like that king, the king of Egypt; surely amongst all the kings of the earth there is none greater than Abimelech king of the Philistines, yet the king of Egypt is greater and mightier than he, and Abimelech can only be compared to one of his officers. ¹³ Father, thou hast not seen his palace and his throne, and all his servants standing before him; thou hast not seen that king upon his throne in his pomp and royal appearance, dressed in his kingly robes with a large golden crown upon his head; thou hast not seen the honor and glory which God has given unto him, for there is not like unto him in all the earth. ¹⁴ Father, thou hast not seen the wisdom, the understanding and the knowledge which God has given in his heart, nor heard his sweet voice when he spake unto us. ¹⁵ We know not, father, who made him acquainted with our names and all that befell us, yet he asked also after thee, saying, Is your father still living, and is it well with him? ¹⁶ Thou hast not seen the affairs of the government of Egypt regulated by him, without inquiring of Pharaoh his lord; thou hast not seen the awe and fear which he impressed

upon all the Egyptians. ¹⁷ And also when we went from him, we threatened to do unto Egypt like unto the rest of the cities of the Amorites, and we were exceedingly wroth against all his words which he spoke concerning us as spies, and now when we shall again come before him his terror will fall upon us all, and not one of us will be able to speak to him either a little or a great thing. ¹⁸ Now therefore father, send we pray thee the lad with us, and we will go down and buy thee food for our support, and not die through hunger. And Jacob said, Why have you dealt so ill with me to tell the king you had a brother? what is this thing that you have done unto me? ¹⁹ And Judah said unto Jacob his father, Give the lad into my care and we will rise up and go down to Egypt and buy corn, and then return, and it shall be when we return if the lad be not with us, then let me bear thy blame forever. ²⁰ Hast thou seen all our infants weeping over thee through hunger and there is no power in thy hand to satisfy them? now let thy pity be roused for them and send our brother with us and we will go. ²¹ For how will the Lord's kindness to our ancestors be manifested to thee when thou sayest that the king of Egypt will take away thy son? as the Lord liveth I will not leave him until I bring him and place him before thee; but pray for us unto the Lord, that he may deal kindly with us, to cause us to be received favorably and kindly before the king of Egypt and his men, for had we not delayed surely now we had returned a second time with thy son. ²² And Jacob said unto his sons, I trust in the Lord God that he may deliver you and give you favor in the sight of the king of Egypt, and in the sight of all his men. ²³ Now therefore rise up and go to the man, and take for him in your hands a present from what can be obtained in the land and bring it before him, and may the Almighty God give you mercy before him that he may send Benjamin and Simeon your brethren with you. ²⁴ And all the men rose up, and they took their brother Benjamin, and they took in their hands a large present of the best of the land, and they also took a double portion of silver. ²⁵ And Jacob strictly commanded his sons concerning Benjamin, Saying, Take heed of him in the way in which you are going, and do not separate yourselves from him in the road, neither in Egypt. ²⁶ And Jacob rose up from his sons and spread forth his hands and he prayed unto the Lord on account of his sons, saying, O Lord God of heaven and earth, remember thy covenant with our father Abraham, remember it with my father Isaac and deal kindly with my sons and deliver them not into the hands of the king of Egypt; do it I pray thee O God for the sake of thy mercies and redeem all my children and rescue them from Egyptian power, and send them their two brothers. ²⁷ And all the wives of the sons of Jacob and their children lifted up their eyes to heaven and they all wept before the Lord, and cried unto him to deliver their fathers from the hand of the king of Egypt. ²⁸ And Jacob wrote a record to the king of Egypt and gave it into the hand of Judah and into the hands of his sons for the king of Egypt, saying, ²⁹ From thy servant Jacob, son of Isaac, son of Abraham the Hebrew, the prince of God, to the powerful and wise king, the revealer of secrets, king of Egypt, greeting. ³⁰ Be it known to my lord the king of Egypt, the famine was sore upon us in the land of Canaan, and I sent my sons to thee to buy us a little food from thee for our support. ³¹ For my sons surrounded me and I being very old cannot see with my eyes, for my eyes have become very heavy through age, as well as with daily weeping for my son, for Joseph who was lost from before me, and I commanded my sons that they should not enter the gates of the city when they came to Egypt, on account of the inhabitants of the land. ³² And I also commanded them to go about Egypt to seek for my son Joseph, perhaps they might find him there, and they did so, and thou didst consider them as spies of the land. ³³ Have we not heard concerning thee that thou didst interpret Pharaoh's dream and didst speak truly unto him? how then dost thou not know in thy wisdom whether my sons are spies or not? ³⁴ Now therefore, my lord and king, behold I have sent my son before thee, as thou didst speak unto my sons; I beseech thee to put thy eyes upon him until he is returned to me in peace with his brethren. ³⁵ For dost thou not know, or hast thou not heard that which our God did unto Pharaoh when he took my mother Sarah, and what he did unto Abimelech king of the Philistines on account of her, and also what our father Abraham did unto the nine kings of Elam, how he smote them all with a few men that were with him? ³⁶ And also what my two sons Simeon and Levi did unto the eight cities of the Amorites, how they destroyed them on account of their sister Dinah? ³⁷ And also on account of their brother Benjamin they consoled themselves for the loss of his brother Joseph; what will they then do for him when they see the hand of any people prevailing over them, for his sake? ³⁸ Dost thou not know, O king of Egypt, that the power of God is with us, and that also God ever heareth our prayers and forsaketh us not all the days? ³⁹ And when my sons told me of thy dealings with them, I called not unto the Lord on account of thee, for then thou wouldst have perished with thy men before my son Benjamin came before thee, but I thought that as Simeon my son was in thy house, perhaps thou mightest deal kindly with him, therefore I did not this thing unto thee. ⁴⁰ Now therefore behold Benjamin my son cometh unto thee with my sons, take heed of him and put thy eyes upon him, and then will God place his eyes over thee and throughout thy kingdom. ⁴¹ Now I have told thee all that is in my heart, and behold my sons are coming to thee with their brother, examine the face of the whole earth for their sake and send them back in peace with their brethren. ⁴² And Jacob gave the record to his sons into the care of Judah to give it unto the king of Egypt.

53

¹ And the sons of Jacob rose up and took Benjamin and the whole of the presents, and they went and came to Egypt and they stood before Joseph. ² And Joseph beheld his brother Benjamin with them and he saluted them, and these men came to Joseph's house. ³ And Joseph commanded the superintendent of his house to give to his brethren to eat, and he did so unto them. ⁴ And at noon time Joseph sent for the men to come before him with Benjamin, and the men told the superintendent of Joseph's house concerning the silver that was returned in their sacks, and he said unto them, It will be well with you, fear not, and he brought their brother Simeon unto them. ⁵ And Simeon said unto his brethren, The lord of the Egyptians has acted very kindly unto me, he did not keep me bound, as you saw with your eyes, for when you went out from the city he let me free and dealt kindly with me in his house. ⁶ And Judah took Benjamin by the hand, and they came before Joseph, and they bowed down to him to the ground. ⁷ And the men gave the present unto Joseph and they all sat before him, and Joseph said unto them, Is it well with you, is it well with your children, is it well with your aged father? and they said, It is well, and Judah took the record which Jacob had sent and gave it into the hand of Joseph. ⁸ And Joseph read the letter and knew his father's writing, and he wished to weep and he went into an inner room and he wept a great weeping; and he went out. ⁹ And he lifted up his eyes and beheld his brother Benjamin, and he said, Is this your brother of whom you spoke unto me? And Benjamin approached Joseph, and Joseph placed his hand upon his head and he said unto him, May God be gracious unto thee my son. ¹⁰ And when Joseph saw his brother, the son of his mother, he again wished to weep, and he entered the chamber, and he wept there, and he washed his face, and went out and refrained from weeping, and he said, Prepare food. ¹¹ And Joseph had a cup from which he drank, and it was of silver beautifully inlaid with onyx stones and bdellium, and Joseph struck the cup in the sight of his brethren whilst they were sitting to eat with him. ¹² And Joseph said unto the men, I know by this cup that Reuben the first born, Simeon and Levi and Judah, Issachar and Zebulun are children from one mother, seat yourselves to eat according to your births. ¹³ And he also placed the others according to their births, and he said, I know that this your youngest brother has no brother, and I, like him, have no brother, he shall therefore sit down to eat with me. ¹⁴ And Benjamin went up before Joseph and sat upon the throne, and the men beheld the acts of Joseph, and they were astonished at them; and the men ate and drank at that time with Joseph, and he then gave presents unto them, and Joseph gave one gift unto Benjamin, and Manasseh and Ephraim saw the acts of their father, and they also gave presents unto him, and Osnath gave him one present, and they were five presents in the hand of Benjamin. ¹⁵ And Joseph brought them out wine to drink, and they would not drink, and they said, From the day on which Joseph was lost we have not drunk wine, nor eaten any delicacies. ¹⁶ And Joseph swore unto them, and he pressed them hard, and they drank plentifully with him on that day, and Joseph afterward turned to his brother Benjamin to speak with him, and Benjamin was still sitting upon the throne before Joseph. ¹⁷ And Joseph said unto him, Hast thou begotten any children? and he said, Thy servant has ten sons, and these are their names, Bela, Becher, Ashbal, Gera, Naaman, Achi, Rosh, Mupim, Chupim, and Ord, and I called their names after my brother whom I have not seen. ¹⁸ And he ordered them to bring before him his map of the stars, whereby Joseph knew all the times, and Joseph said unto Benjamin, I have heard that the Hebrews are acquainted with all wisdom, dost thou know anything of this? ¹⁹ And Benjamin said, Thy servant is knowing also in all the wisdom which my father taught me, and Joseph said unto Benjamin, Look now at this instrument and understand where thy brother Joseph is in Egypt, who you said went down to Egypt. ²⁰ And Benjamin beheld that instrument with the map of the stars of heaven, and he was wise and looked therein to know where his brother was, and Benjamin divided the whole land of Egypt into four divisions, and he found that he who was sitting upon the throne before him was his brother Joseph, and Benjamin wondered greatly, and when Joseph saw that his brother Benjamin was so much astonished, he said unto Benjamin, What hast thou seen, and why art thou astonished? ²¹ And Benjamin said unto Joseph, I can see by this that Joseph my brother sitteth here with me upon the throne, and Joseph said unto him, I am Joseph thy brother, reveal not this thing unto thy brethren; behold I will send thee with them when they go away, and I will command them to

be brought back again into the city, and I will take thee away from them. ²² And if they dare their lives and fight for thee, then shall I know that they have repented of what they did unto me, and I will make myself known to them, and if they forsake thee when I take thee, then shalt thou remain with me, and I will wrangle with them, and they shall go away, and I will not become known to them. ²³ At that time Joseph commanded his officer to fill their sacks with food, and to put each man's money into his sack, and to put the cup in the sack of Benjamin, and to give them provision for the road, and they did so unto them. ²⁴ And on the next day the men rose up early in the morning, and they loaded their asses with their corn, and they went forth with Benjamin, and they went to the land of Canaan with their brother Benjamin. ²⁵ They had not gone far from Egypt when Joseph commanded him that was set over his house, saying, Rise, pursue these men before they get too far from Egypt, and say unto them, Why have you stolen my master's cup? ²⁶ And Joseph's officer rose up and he reached them, and he spoke unto them all the words of Joseph; and when they heard this thing they became exceedingly wroth, and they said, He with whom thy master's cup shall be found shall die, and we will also become slaves. ²⁷ And they hastened and each man brought down his sack from his ass, and they looked in their bags and the cup was found in Benjamin's bag, and they all tore their garments and they returned to the city, and they smote Benjamin in the road, continually smiting him until he came into the city, and they stood before Joseph. ²⁸ And Judah's anger was kindled, and he said, This man has only brought me back to destroy Egypt this day. ²⁹ And the men came to Joseph's house, and they found Joseph sitting upon his throne, and all the mighty men standing at his right and left. ³⁰ And Joseph said unto them, What is this act that you have done, that you took away my silver cup and went away? but I know that you took my cup in order to know thereby in what part of the land your brother was. ³¹ And Judah said, What shall we say to our lord, what shall we speak and how shall we justify ourselves, God has this day found the iniquity of all thy servants, therefore has he done this thing to us this day. ³² And Joseph rose up and caught hold of Benjamin and took him from his brethren with violence, and he came to the house and locked the door at them, and Joseph commanded him that was set over his house that he should say unto them, Thus saith the king, Go in peace to your father, behold I have taken the man in whose hand my cup was found.

54

¹ And when Judah saw the dealings of Joseph with them, Judah approached him and broke open the door, and came with his brethren before Joseph. ² And Judah said unto Joseph, Let it not seem grievous in the sight of my lord, may thy servant I pray thee speak a word before thee? and Joseph said unto him, Speak. ³ And Judah spoke before Joseph, and his brethren were there standing before them; and Judah said unto Joseph, Surely when we first came to our lord to buy food, thou didst consider us as spies of the land, and we brought Benjamin before thee, and thou still makest sport of us this day. ⁴ Now therefore let the king hear my words, and send I pray thee our brother that he may go along with us to our father, lest thy soul perish this day with all the souls of the inhabitants of Egypt. ⁵ Dost thou not know what two of my brethren, Simeon and Levi, did unto the city of Shechem, and unto seven cities of the Amorites, on account of our sister Dinah, and also what they would do for the sake of their brother Benjamin? ⁶ And I with my strength, who am greater and mightier than both of them, come this day upon thee and thy land if thou art unwilling to send our brother. ⁷ Hast thou not heard what our God who made choice of us did unto Pharaoh on account of Sarah our mother, whom he took away from our father, that he smote him and his household with heavy plagues, that even unto this day the Egyptians relate this wonder to each other? so will our God do unto thee on account of Benjamin whom thou hast this day taken from his father, and on account of the evils which thou this day heapest over us in thy land; for our God will remember his covenant with our father Abraham and bring evil upon thee, because thou hast grieved the soul of our father this day. ⁸ Now therefore hear my words that I have this day spoken unto thee, and send our brother that he may go away lest thou and the people of thy land die by the sword, for you cannot all prevail over me. ⁹ And Joseph answered Judah, saying, Why hast thou opened wide thy mouth and why dost thou boast over us, saying, Strength is with thee? as Pharaoh liveth, if I command all my valiant men to fight with you, surely thou and these thy brethren would sink in the mire. ¹⁰ And Judah said unto Joseph, Surely it becometh thee and thy people to fear me; as the Lord liveth if I once draw my sword I shall not sheathe it again until I shall this day have slain all Egypt, and I will commence with thee and finish with Pharaoh thy master. ¹¹ And Joseph answered and said unto him, Surely strength belongeth not alone to thee; I am stronger and mightier than thou, surely if thou drawest thy sword I will put it to thy neck and the necks of all thy brethren. ¹² And Judah said unto him, Surely if I this day open my mouth against thee I would swallow thee up that thou be destroyed from off the earth and perish this day from thy kingdom. And Joseph said, Surely if thou openest thy mouth I have power and might to close thy mouth with a stone until thou shalt not be able to utter a word; see how many stones are before us, truly I can take a stone, and force it into thy mouth and break thy jaws. ¹³ And Judah said, God is witness between us, that we have not hitherto desired to battle with thee, only give us our brother and we will go from thee; and Joseph answered and said, As Pharaoh liveth, if all the kings of Canaan came together with you, you should not take him from my hand. ¹⁴ Now therefore go your way to your father, and your brother shall be unto me for a slave, for he has robbed the king's house. And Judah said, What is it to thee or to the character of the king, surely the king sendeth forth from his house, throughout the land, silver and gold either in gifts or expenses, and thou still talkest about thy cup which thou didst place in our brother's bag and sayest that he has stolen it from thee? ¹⁵ God forbid that our brother Benjamin or any of the seed of Abraham should do this thing to steal from thee, or from any one else, whether king, prince, or any man. ¹⁶ Now therefore cease this accusation lest the whole earth hear thy words, saying, For a little silver the king of Egypt wrangled with the men, and he accused them and took their brother for a slave. ¹⁷ And Joseph answered and said, Take unto you this cup and go from me and leave your brother for a slave, for it is the judgment of a thief to be a slave. ¹⁸ And Judah said, Why art thou not ashamed of thy words, to leave our brother and to take thy cup? Surely if thou givest us thy cup, or a thousand times as much, we will not leave our brother for the silver which is found in the hand of any man, that we will not die over him. ¹⁹ And Joseph answered, And why did you forsake your brother and sell him for twenty pieces of silver unto this day, and why then will you not do the same to this your brother? ²⁰ And Judah said, the Lord is witness between me and thee that we desire not thy battles; now therefore give us our brother and we will go from thee without quarreling. ²¹ And Joseph answered and said, If all the kings of the land should assemble they will not be able to take your brother from my hand; and Judah said, What shall we say unto our father, when he seeth that our brother cometh not with us, and will grieve over him? ²² And Joseph answered and said, This is the thing which you shall tell unto your father, saying, The rope has gone after the bucket. ²³ And Judah said, Surely thou art a king, and why speakest thou these things, giving a false judgment? woe unto the king who is like unto thee. ²⁴ And Joseph answered and said, There is no false judgment in the word that I spoke on account of your brother Joseph, for all of you sold him to the Midianites for twenty pieces of silver, and you all denied it to your father and said unto him, An evil beast has devoured him, Joseph has been torn to pieces. ²⁵ And Judah said, Behold the fire of Shem burneth in my heart, now I will burn all your land with fire; and Joseph answered and said, Surely thy sister-in-law Tamar, who killed your sons, extinguished the fire of Shechem. ²⁶ And Judah said, If I pluck out a single hair from my flesh, I will fill all Egypt with its blood. ²⁷ And Joseph answered and said, Such is your custom to do as you did to your brother whom you sold, and you dipped his coat in blood and brought it to your father in order that he might say an evil beast devoured him and here is his blood. ²⁸ And when Judah heard this thing he was exceedingly wroth and his anger burned within him, and there was before him in that place a stone, the weight of which was about four hundred shekels, and Judah's anger was kindled and he took the stone in one hand and cast it to the heavens and caught it with his left hand. ²⁹ And he placed it afterward under his legs, and he sat upon it with all his strength and the stone was turned into dust from the force of Judah. ³⁰ And Joseph saw the act of Judah and he was very much afraid, but he commanded Manassah his son and he also did with another stone like unto the act of Judah, and Judah said unto his brethren, Let not any of you say, this man is an Egyptian, but by his doing this thing he is of our father's family. ³¹ And Joseph said, Not to you only is strength given, for we are also powerful men, and why will you boast over us all? and Judah said unto Joseph, Send I pray thee our brother and ruin not thy country this day. ³² And Joseph answered and said unto them, Go and tell your father, an evil beast hath devoured him as you said concerning your brother Joseph. ³³ And Judah spoke to his brother Naphtali, and he said unto him, Make haste, go now and number all the streets of Egypt and come and tell me; and Simeon said unto him, Let not this thing be a trouble to thee; now I will go to the mount and take up one large stone from the mount and level it at every one in Egypt, and kill all that are in it. ³⁴ And Joseph heard all these words that his brethren spoke before him, and they did not know that Joseph understood them, for they imagined that he knew not to speak Hebrew. ³⁵ And Joseph was greatly afraid at the words of his brethren lest they should destroy Egypt, and he commanded his son Manasseh, saying, Go now make haste and gather unto me all the inhabitants of Egypt, and all the valiant men together, and let them come to me now upon horseback and on foot and with all sorts of musical instruments, and Manasseh went and

did so. ³⁶ And Naphtali went as Judah had commanded him, for Naphtali was lightfooted as one of the swift stags, and he would go upon the ears of corn and they would not break under him. ³⁷ And he went and numbered all the streets of Egypt, and found them to be twelve, and he came hastily and told Judah, and Judah said unto his brethren, Hasten you and put on every man his sword upon his loins and we will come over Egypt, and smite them all, and let not a remnant remain. ³⁸ And Judah said, Behold, I will destroy three of the streets with my strength, and you shall each destroy one street; and when Judah was speaking this thing, behold the inhabitants of Egypt and all the mighty men came toward them with all sorts of musical instruments and with loud shouting. ³⁹ And their number was five hundred cavalry and ten thousand infantry, and four hundred men who could fight without sword or spear, only with their hands and strength. ⁴⁰ And all the mighty men came with great storming and shouting, and they all surrounded the sons of Jacob and terrified them, and the ground quaked at the sound of their shouting. ⁴¹ And when the sons of Jacob saw these troops they were greatly afraid of their lives, and Joseph did so in order to terrify the sons of Jacob to become tranquilized. ⁴² And Judah, seeing some of his brethren terrified, said unto them, Why are you afraid whilst the grace of God is with us? and when Judah saw all the people of Egypt surrounding them at the command of Joseph to terrify them, only Joseph commanded them, saying, Do not touch any of them. ⁴³ Then Judah hastened and drew his sword, and uttered a loud and bitter scream, and he smote with his sword, and he sprang upon the ground and he still continued to shout against all the people. ⁴⁴ And when he did this thing the Lord caused the terror of Judah and his brethren to fall upon the valiant men and all the people that surrounded them. ⁴⁵ And they all fled at the sound of the shouting, and they were terrified and fell one upon the other, and many of them died as they fell, and they all fled from before Judah and his brethren and from before Joseph. ⁴⁶ And whilst they were fleeing, Judah and his brethren pursued them unto the house of Pharaoh, and they all escaped, and Judah again sat before Joseph and roared at him like a lion, and gave a great and tremendous shriek at him. ⁴⁷ And the shriek was heard at a distance, and all the inhabitants of Succoth heard it, and all Egypt quaked at the sound of the shriek, and also the walls of Egypt and of the land of Goshen fell in from the shaking of the earth, and Pharaoh also fell from his throne upon the ground, and also all the pregnant women of Egypt and Goshen miscarried when they heard the noise of the shaking, for they were terribly afraid. ⁴⁸ And Pharaoh sent word, saying, What is this thing that has this day happened in the land of Egypt? and they came and told him all the things from beginning to end, and Pharaoh was alarmed and he wondered and was greatly afraid. ⁴⁹ And his fright increased when he heard all these things, and he sent unto Joseph, saying, Thou hast brought unto me the Hebrews to destroy all Egypt; what wilt thou do with that thievish slave? send him away and let him go with his brethren, and let us not perish through their evil, even we, you and all Egypt. ⁵⁰ And if thou desirest not to do this thing, cast off from thee all my valuable things, and go with them to their land, if thou delightest in it, for they will this day destroy my whole country and slay all my people; even all the women of Egypt have miscarried through their screams; see what they have done merely by their shouting and speaking, moreover if they fight with the sword, they will destroy the land; now therefore choose that which thou desirest, whether me or the Hebrews, whether Egypt or the land of the Hebrews. ⁵¹ And they came and told Joseph all the words of Pharaoh that he had said concerning him, and Joseph was greatly afraid at the words of Pharaoh and Judah and his brethren were still standing before Joseph indignant and enraged, and all the sons of Jacob roared at Joseph, like the roaring of the sea and its waves. ⁵² And Joseph was greatly afraid of his brethren and on account of Pharaoh, and Joseph sought a pretext to make himself known unto his brethren, lest they should destroy all Egypt. ⁵³ And Joseph commanded his son Manasseh, and Manasseh went and approached Judah, and placed his hand upon his shoulder, and the anger of Judah was stilled. ⁵⁴ And Judah said unto his brethren, Let no one of you say that this is the act of an Egyptian youth for this is the work of my father's house. ⁵⁵ And Joseph seeing and knowing that Judah's anger was stilled, he approached to speak unto Judah in the language of mildness. ⁵⁶ And Joseph said unto Judah, Surely you speak truth and have this day verified your assertions concerning your strength, and may your God who delighteth in you, increase your welfare; but tell me truly why from amongst all thy brethren dost thou wrangle with me on account of the lad, as none of them have spoken one word to me concerning him. ⁵⁷ And Judah answered Joseph, saying, Surely thou must know that I was security for the lad to his father, saying, If I brought him not unto him I should bear his blame forever. ⁵⁸ Therefore have I approached thee from amongst all my brethren, for I saw that thou wast unwilling to suffer him to go from thee; now therefore may I find grace in thy sight that thou shalt send him to go with us, and behold I will remain as a substitute for him, to serve thee in whatever thou desirest, for wheresoever thou shalt send me I will go to serve thee with great energy. ⁵⁹ Send me now to a mighty king who has rebelled against thee, and thou shalt know what I will do unto him and unto his land; although he may have cavalry and infantry or an exceeding mighty people, I will slay them all and bring the king's head before thee. ⁶⁰ Dost thou not know or hast thou not heard that our father Abraham with his servant Eliezer smote all the kings of Elam with their hosts in one night, they left not one remaining? and ever since that day our father's strength was given unto us for an inheritance, for us and our seed forever. ⁶¹ And Joseph answered and said, You speak truth, and falsehood is not in your mouth, for it was also told unto us that the Hebrews have power and that the Lord their God delighteth much in them, and who then can stand before them? ⁶² However, on this condition will I send your brother, if you will bring before me his brother the son of his mother, of whom you said that he had gone from you down to Egypt; and it shall come to pass when you bring unto me his brother I will take him in his stead, because not one of you was security for him to your father, and when he shall come unto me, I will then send with you his brother for whom you have been security. ⁶³ And Judah's anger was kindled against Joseph when he spoke this thing, and his eyes dropped blood with anger, and he said unto his brethren, How doth this man this day seek his own destruction and that of all Egypt! ⁶⁴ And Simeon answered Joseph, saying, Did we not tell thee at first that we knew not the particular spot to which he went, and whether he be dead or alive, and wherefore speaketh my lord like unto these things? ⁶⁵ And Joseph observing the countenance of Judah discerned that his anger began to kindle when he spoke unto him, saying, Bring unto me your other brother instead of this brother. ⁶⁶ And Joseph said unto his brethren, Surely you said that your brother was either dead or lost, now if I should call him this day and he should come before you, would you give him unto me instead of his brother? ⁶⁷ And Joseph began to speak and call out, Joseph, Joseph, come this day before me, and appear to thy brethren and sit before them. ⁶⁸ And when Joseph spoke this thing before them, they looked each a different way to see from whence Joseph would come before them. ⁶⁹ And Joseph observed all their acts, and said unto them, Why do you look here and there? I am Joseph whom you sold to Egypt, now therefore let it not grieve you that you sold me, for as a support during the famine did God send me before you. ⁷⁰ And his brethren were terrified at him when they heard the words of Joseph, and Judah was exceedingly terrified at him. ⁷¹ And when Benjamin heard the words of Joseph he was before them in the inner part of the house, and Benjamin ran unto Joseph his brother, and embraced him and fell upon his neck, and they wept. ⁷² And when Joseph's brethren saw that Benjamin had fallen upon his brother's neck and wept with him, they also fell upon Joseph and embraced him, and they wept a great weeping with Joseph. ⁷³ And the voice was heard in the house of Joseph that they were Joseph's brethren, and it pleased Pharaoh exceedingly, for he was afraid of them lest they should destroy Egypt. ⁷⁴ And Pharaoh sent his servants unto Joseph to congratulate him concerning his brethren who had come to him, and all the captains of the armies and troops that were in Egypt came to rejoice with Joseph, and all Egypt rejoiced greatly about Joseph's brethren. ⁷⁵ And Pharaoh sent his servants to Joseph, saying, Tell thy brethren to fetch all belonging to them and let them come unto me, and I will place them in the best part of the land of Egypt, and they did so. ⁷⁶ And Joseph commanded him that was set over his house to bring out to his brethren gifts and garments, and he brought out to them many garments being robes of royalty and many gifts, and Joseph divided them amongst his brethren. ⁷⁷ And he gave unto each of his brethren a change of garments of gold and silver, and three hundred pieces of silver, and Joseph commanded them all to be dressed in these garments, and to be brought before Pharaoh. ⁷⁸ And Pharaoh seeing that all Joseph's brethren were valiant men, and of beautiful appearance, he greatly rejoiced. ⁷⁹ And they afterward went out from the presence of Pharaoh to go to the land of Canaan, to their father, and their brother Benjamin was with them. ⁸⁰ And Joseph rose up and gave unto them eleven chariots from Pharaoh, and Joseph gave unto them his chariot, upon which he rode on the day of his being crowned in Egypt, to fetch his father to Egypt; and Joseph sent to all his brothers' children, garments according to their numbers, and a hundred pieces of silver to each of them, and he also sent garments to the wives of his brethren from the garments of the king's wives, and he sent them. ⁸¹ And he gave unto each of his brethren ten men to go with them to the land of Canaan to serve them, to serve their children and all belonging to them in coming to Egypt. ⁸² And Joseph sent by the hand of his brother Benjamin ten suits of garments for his ten sons, a portion above the rest of the children of the sons of Jacob. ⁸³ And he sent to each fifty pieces of silver, and ten chariots on the account of Pharaoh, and he sent to his father ten asses laden with all the luxuries of Egypt, and ten she asses laden with corn and bread and nourishment for his father, and to all that were with him as provisions for the road. ⁸⁴ And he sent to his sister

Dinah garments of silver and gold, and frankincense and myrrh, and aloes and women's ornaments in great plenty, and he sent the same from the wives of Pharaoh to the wives of Benjamin. ⁸⁵ And he gave unto all his brethren, also to their wives, all sorts of onyx stones and bdellium, and from all the valuable things amongst the great people of Egypt, nothing of all the costly things was left but what Joseph sent of to his father's household. ⁸⁶ And he sent his brethren away, and they went, and he sent his brother Benjamin with them. ⁸⁷ And Joseph went out with them to accompany them on the road unto the borders of Egypt, and he commanded them concerning his father and his household, to come to Egypt. ⁸⁸ And he said unto them, Do not quarrel on the road, for this thing was from the Lord to keep a great people from starvation, for there will be yet five years of famine in the land. ⁸⁹ And he commanded them, saying, When you come unto the land of Canaan, do not come suddenly before my father in this affair, but act in your wisdom. ⁹⁰ And Joseph ceased to command them, and he turned and went back to Egypt, and the sons of Jacob went to the land of Canaan with joy and cheerfulness to their father Jacob. ⁹¹ And they came unto the borders of the land, and they said to each other, What shall we do in this matter before our father, for if we come suddenly to him and tell him the matter, he will be greatly alarmed at our words and will not believe us. ⁹² And they went along until they came nigh unto their houses, and they found Serach, the daughter of Asher, going forth to meet them, and the damsel was very good and subtle, and knew how to play upon the harp. ⁹³ And they called unto her and she came before them, and she kissed them, and they took her and gave unto her a harp, saying, Go now before our father, and sit before him, and strike upon the harp, and speak these words. ⁹⁴ And they commanded her to go to their house, and she took the harp and hastened before them, and she came and sat near Jacob. ⁹⁵ And she played well and sang, and uttered in the sweetness of her words, Joseph my uncle is living, and he ruleth throughout the land of Egypt, and is not dead. ⁹⁶ And she continued to repeat and utter these words, and Jacob heard her words and they were agreeable to him. ⁹⁷ He listened whilst she repeated them twice and thrice, and joy entered the heart of Jacob at the sweetness of her words, and the spirit of God was upon him, and he knew all her words to be true. ⁹⁸ And Jacob blessed Serach when she spoke these words before him, and he said unto her, My daughter, may death never prevail over thee, for thou hast revived my spirit; only speak yet before me as thou hast spoken, for thou hast gladdened me with all thy words. ⁹⁹ And she continued to sing these words, and Jacob listened and it pleased him, and he rejoiced, and the spirit of God was upon him. ¹⁰⁰ Whilst he was yet speaking with her, behold his sons came to him with horses and chariots and royal garments and servants running before them. ¹⁰¹ And Jacob rose up to meet them, and saw his sons dressed in royal garments and he saw all the treasures that Joseph had sent to them. ¹⁰² And they said unto him, Be informed that our brother Joseph is living, and it is he who ruleth throughout the land of Egypt, and it is he who spoke unto us as we told thee. ¹⁰³ And Jacob heard all the words of his sons, and his heart palpitated at their words, for he could not believe them until he saw all that Joseph had given them and what he had sent him, and all the signs which Joseph had spoken unto them. ¹⁰⁴ And they opened out before him, and showed him all that Joseph had sent, they gave unto each what Joseph had sent him, and he knew that they had spoken the truth, and he rejoiced exceedingly an account of his son. ¹⁰⁵ And Jacob said, It is enough for me that my son Joseph is still living, I will go and see him before I die. ¹⁰⁶ And his sons told him all that had befallen them, and Jacob said, I will go down to Egypt to see my son and his offspring. ¹⁰⁷ And Jacob rose up and put on the garments which Joseph had sent him, and after he had washed, and shaved his hair, he put upon his head the turban which Joseph had sent him. ¹⁰⁸ And all the people of Jacob's house and their wives put on the garments which Joseph had sent to them, and they greatly rejoiced at Joseph that he was still living and that he was ruling in Egypt, ¹⁰⁹ And all the inhabitants of Canaan heard of this thing, and they came and rejoiced much with Jacob that he was still living. ¹¹⁰ And Jacob made a feast for them for three days, and all the kings of Canaan and nobles of the land ate and drank and rejoiced in the house of Jacob.

55

¹ And it came to pass after this that Jacob said, I will go and see my son in Egypt and will then come back to the land of Canaan of which God had spoken unto Abraham, for I cannot leave the land of my birth-place. ² Behold the word of the Lord came unto him, saying, Go down to Egypt with all thy household and remain there, fear not to go down to Egypt for I will there make thee a great nation. ³ And Jacob said within himself, I will go and see my son whether the fear of his God is yet in his heart amidst all the inhabitants of Egypt. ⁴ And the Lord said unto Jacob, Fear not about Joseph, for he still retaineth his integrity to serve me, as will seem good in thy sight, and Jacob rejoiced exceedingly concerning his son. ⁵ At that time Jacob commanded his sons and household to go to Egypt according to the word of the Lord unto him, and Jacob rose up with his sons and all his household, and he went out from the land of Canaan from Beersheba, with joy and gladness of heart, and they went to the land of Egypt. ⁶ And it came to pass when they came near Egypt, Jacob sent Judah before him to Joseph that he might show him a situation in Egypt, and Judah did according to the word of his father, and he hastened and ran and came to Joseph, and they assigned for them a place in the land of Goshen for all his household, and Judah returned and came along the road to his father. ⁷ And Joseph harnessed the chariot, and he assembled all his mighty men and his servants and all the officers of Egypt in order to go and meet his father Jacob, and Joseph's mandate was proclaimed in Egypt, saying, All that do not go to meet Jacob shall die. ⁸ And on the next day Joseph went forth with all Egypt a great and mighty host, all dressed in garments of fine linen and purple and with instruments of silver and gold and with their instruments of war with them. ⁹ And they all went to meet Jacob with all sorts of musical instruments, with drums and timbrels, strewing myrrh and aloes all along the road, and they all went after this fashion, and the earth shook at their shouting. ¹⁰ And all the women of Egypt went upon the roofs of Egypt and upon the walls to meet Jacob, and upon the head of Joseph was Pharaoh's regal crown, for Pharaoh had sent it unto him to put on at the time of his going to meet his father. ¹¹ And when Joseph came within fifty cubits of his father, he alighted from the chariot and he walked toward his father, and when all the officers of Egypt and her nobles saw that Joseph had gone on foot toward his father, they also alighted and walked on foot toward Jacob. ¹² And when Jacob approached the camp of Joseph, Jacob observed the camp that was coming toward him with Joseph, and it gratified him and Jacob was astonished at it. ¹³ And Jacob said unto Judah, Who is that man whom I see in the camp of Egypt dressed in kingly robes with a very red garment upon him and a royal crown upon his head, who has alighted from his chariot and is coming toward us? and Judah answered his father, saying, He is thy son Joseph the king; and Jacob rejoiced in seeing the glory of his son. ¹⁴ And Joseph came nigh unto his father and he bowed to his father, and all the men of the camp bowed to the ground with him before Jacob. ¹⁵ And behold Jacob ran and hastened to his son Joseph and fell upon his neck and kissed him, and they wept, and Joseph also embraced his father and kissed him, and they wept and all the people of Egypt wept with them. ¹⁶ And Jacob said unto Joseph, Now I will die cheerfully after I have seen thy face, that thou art still living and with glory. ¹⁷ And the sons of Jacob and their wives and their children and their servants, and all the household of Jacob wept exceedingly with Joseph, and they kissed him and wept greatly with him. ¹⁸ And Joseph and all his people returned afterward home to Egypt, and Jacob and his sons and all the children of his household came with Joseph to Egypt, and Joseph placed them in the best part of Egypt, in the land of Goshen. ¹⁹ And Joseph said unto his father and unto his brethren, I will go up and tell Pharaoh, saying, My brethren and my father's household and all belonging to them have come unto me, and behold they are in the land of Goshen. ²⁰ And Joseph did so and took from his brethren Reuben, Issachar Zebulun and his brother Benjamin and he placed them before Pharaoh. ²¹ And Joseph spoke unto Pharaoh, saying, My brethren and my father's household and all belonging to them, together with their flocks and cattle have come unto me from the land of Canaan, to sojourn in Egypt; for the famine was sore upon them. ²² And Pharaoh said unto Joseph, Place thy father and brethren in the best part of the land, withhold not from them all that is good, and cause them to eat of the fat of the land. ²³ And Joseph answered, saying, Behold I have stationed them in the land of Goshen, for they are shepherds, therefore let them remain in Goshen to feed their flocks apart from the Egyptians. ²⁴ And Pharaoh said unto Joseph, Do with thy brethren all that they shall say unto thee; and the sons of Jacob bowed down to Pharaoh, and they went forth from him in peace, and Joseph afterward brought his father before Pharaoh. ²⁵ And Jacob came and bowed down to Pharaoh, and Jacob blessed Pharaoh, and he then went out; and Jacob and all his sons, and all his household dwelt in the land of Goshen. ²⁶ In the second year, that is in the hundred and thirtieth year of the life of Jacob, Joseph maintained his father and his brethren, and all his father's household, with bread according to their little ones, all the days of the famine; they lacked nothing. ²⁷ And Joseph gave unto them the best part of the whole land; the best of Egypt had they all the days of Joseph; and Joseph also gave unto them and unto the whole of his father's household, clothes and garments year by year; and the sons of Jacob remained securely in Egypt all the days of their brother. ²⁸ And Jacob always ate at Joseph's table, Jacob and his sons did not leave Joseph's table day or night, besides what Jacob's children consumed in their houses. ²⁹ And all Egypt ate bread during the days of the famine from the house of Joseph, for all the Egyptians sold all belonging to them on account of the famine. ³⁰ And Joseph purchased all the lands and fields of Egypt for bread on the account of Pharaoh, and

Joseph supplied all Egypt with bread all the days of the famine, and Joseph collected all the silver and gold that came unto him for the corn which they bought throughout the land, and he accumulated much gold and silver, besides an immense quantity of onyx stones, bdellium and valuable garments which they brought unto Joseph from every part of the land when their money was spent. ³¹ And Joseph took all the silver and gold that came into his hand, about seventy two talents of gold and silver, and also onyx stones and bdellium in great abundance, and Joseph went and concealed them in four parts, and he concealed one part in the wilderness near the Red sea, and one part by the river Perath, and the third and fourth part he concealed in the desert opposite to the wilderness of Persia and Media. ³² And he took part of the gold and silver that was left, and gave it unto all his brothers and unto all his father's household, and unto all the women of his father's household, and the rest he brought to the house of Pharaoh, about twenty talents of gold and silver. ³³ And Joseph gave all the gold and silver that was left unto Pharaoh, and Pharaoh placed it in the treasury, and the days of the famine ceased after that in the land, and they sowed and reaped in the whole land, and they obtained their usual quantity year by year; they lacked nothing. ³⁴ And Joseph dwelt securely in Egypt, and the whole land was under his advice, and his father and all his brethren dwelt in the land of Goshen and took possession of it. ³⁵ And Joseph was very aged, advanced in days, and his two sons, Ephraim and Manasseh, remained constantly in the house of Jacob, together with the children of the sons of Jacob their brethren, to learn the ways of the Lord and his law. ³⁶ And Jacob and his sons dwelt in the land of Egypt in the land of Goshen, and they took possession in it, and they were fruitful and multiplied in it.

56

¹ And Jacob lived in the land of Egypt seventeen years, and the days of Jacob, and the years of his life were a hundred and forty seven years. ² At that time Jacob was attacked with that illness of which he died and he sent and called for his son Joseph from Egypt, and Joseph his son came from Egypt and Joseph came unto his father. ³ And Jacob said unto Joseph and unto his sons, Behold I die, and the God of your ancestors will visit you, and bring you back to the land, which the Lord sware to give unto you and unto your children after you, now therefore when I am dead, bury me in the cave which is in Machpelah in Hebron in the land of Canaan, near my ancestors. ⁴ And Jacob made his sons swear to bury him in Machpelah, in Hebron, and his sons swore unto him concerning this thing. ⁵ And he commanded them, saying, Serve the Lord your God, for he who delivered your fathers will also deliver you from all trouble. ⁶ And Jacob said, Call all your children unto me, and all the children of Jacob's sons came and sat before him, and Jacob blessed them, and he said unto them, The Lord God of your fathers shall grant you a thousand times as much and bless you, and may he give you the blessing of your father Abraham; and all the children of Jacob's sons went forth on that day after he had blessed them. ⁷ And on the next day Jacob again called for his sons, and they all assembled and came to him and sat before him, and Jacob on that day blessed his sons before his death, each man did he bless according to his blessing; behold it is written in the book of the law of the Lord appertaining to Israel. ⁸ And Jacob said unto Judah, I know my son that thou art a mighty man for thy brethren; reign over them, and thy sons shall reign over their sons forever. ⁹ Only teach thy sons the bow and all the weapons of war, in order that they may fight the battles of their brother who will rule over his enemies. ¹⁰ And Jacob again commanded his sons on that day, saying, Behold I shall be this day gathered unto my people; carry me up from Egypt, and bury me in the cave of Machpelah as I have commanded you. ¹¹ Howbeit take heed I pray you that none of your sons carry me, only yourselves, and this is the manner you shall do unto me, when you carry my body to go with it to the land of Canaan to bury me, ¹² Judah, Issachar and Zebulun shall carry my bier at the eastern side; Reuben, Simeon and Gad at the south, Ephraim, Manasseh and Benjamin at the west, Dan, Asher and Naphtali at the north. ¹³ Let not Levi carry with you, for he and his sons will carry the ark of the covenant of the Lord with the Israelites in the camp, neither let Joseph my son carry, for as a king so let his glory be; howbeit, Ephraim and Manasseh shall be in their stead. ¹⁴ Thus shall you do unto me when you carry me away; do not neglect any thing of all that I command you; and it shall come to pass when you do this unto me, that the Lord will remember you favorably and your children after you forever. ¹⁵ And you my sons, honor each his brother and his relative, and command your children and your children's children after you to serve the Lord God of your ancestors all the days. ¹⁶ In order that you may prolong your days in the land, you and your children and your children's children for ever, when you do what is good and upright in the sight of the Lord your God, to go in all his ways. ¹⁷ And thou, Joseph my son, forgive I pray thee the prongs of thy brethren and all their misdeeds in the injury that they heaped upon thee, for God intended it for thine and thy children's benefit. ¹⁸ And O my son leave not thy brethren to the inhabitants of Egypt, neither hurt their feelings, for behold I consign them to the hand of God and in thy hand to guard them from the Egyptians; and the sons of Jacob answered their father saying, O, our father, all that thou hast commanded us, so will we do; may God only be with us. ¹⁹ And Jacob said unto his sons, So may God be with you when you keep all his ways; turn not from his ways either to the right or the left in performing what is good and upright in his sight. ²⁰ For I know that many and grievous troubles will befall you in the latter days in the land, yea your children and children's children, only serve the Lord and he will save you from all trouble. ²¹ And it shall come to pass when you shall go after God to serve him and will teach your children after you, and your children's children, to know the Lord, then will the Lord raise up unto you and your children a servant from amongst your children, and the Lord will deliver you through his hand from all affliction, and bring you out of Egypt and bring you back to the land of your fathers to inherit it securely. ²² And Jacob ceased commanding his sons, and he drew his feet into the bed, he died and was gathered to his people. ²³ And Joseph fell upon his father and he cried out and wept over him and he kissed him, and he called out in a bitter voice, and he said, O my father, my father. ²⁴ And his son's wives and all his household came and fell upon Jacob, and they wept over him, and cried in a very loud voice concerning Jacob. ²⁵ And all the sons of Jacob rose up together, and they tore their garments, and they all put sackcloth upon their loins, and they fell upon their faces, and they cast dust upon their heads toward the heavens. ²⁶ And the thing was told unto Osnath Joseph's wife, and she rose up and put on a sack and she with all the Egyptian women with her came and mourned and wept for Jacob. ²⁷ And also all the people of Egypt who knew Jacob came all on that day when they heard this thing, and all Egypt wept for many days. ²⁸ And also from the land of Canaan did the women come unto Egypt when they heard that Jacob was dead, and they wept for him in Egypt for seventy days. ²⁹ And it came to pass after this that Joseph commanded his servants the doctors to embalm his father with myrrh and frankincense and all manner of incense and perfume, and the doctors embalmed Jacob as Joseph had commanded them. ³⁰ And all the people of Egypt and the elders and all the inhabitants of the land of Goshen wept and mourned over Jacob, and all his sons and the children of his household lamented and mourned over their father Jacob many days. ³¹ And after the days of his weeping had passed away, at the end of seventy days, Joseph said unto Pharaoh, I will go up and bury my father in the land of Canaan as he made me swear, and then I will return. ³² And Pharaoh sent Joseph, saying, Go up and bury thy father as he said, and as he made thee swear; and Joseph rose up with all his brethren to go to the land of Canaan to bury their father Jacob as he had commanded them. ³³ And Pharaoh commanded that it should be proclaimed throughout Egypt, saying, Whoever goeth not up with Joseph and his brethren to the land of Canaan to bury Jacob, shall die. ³⁴ And all Egypt heard of Pharaoh's proclamation, and they all rose up together, and all the servants of Pharaoh, and the elders of his house, and all the elders of the land of Egypt went up with Joseph, and all the officers and nobles of Pharaoh went up as the servants of Joseph, and they went to bury Jacob in the land of Canaan. ³⁵ And the sons of Jacob carried the bier upon which he lay; according to all that their father commanded them, so did his sons unto him. ³⁶ And the bier was of pure gold, and it was inlaid round about with onyx stones and bdellium; and the covering of the bier was gold woven work, joined with threads, and over them were hooks of onyx stones and bdellium. ³⁷ And Joseph placed upon the head of his father Jacob a large golden crown, and he put a golden scepter in his hand, and they surrounded the bier as was the custom of kings during their lives. ³⁸ And all the troops of Egypt went before him in this array, at first all the mighty men of Pharaoh, and the mighty men of Joseph, and after them the rest of the inhabitants of Egypt, and they were all girded with swords and equipped with coats of mail, and the trappings of war were upon them. ³⁹ And all the weepers and mourners went at a distance opposite to the bier, going and weeping and lamenting, and the rest of the people went after the bier. ⁴⁰ And Joseph and his household went together near the bier barefooted and weeping, and the rest of Joseph's servants went around him; each man had his ornaments upon him, and they were all armed with their weapons of war. ⁴¹ And fifty of Jacob's servants went in front of the bier, and they strewed along the road myrrh and aloes, and all manner of perfume, and all the sons of Jacob that carried the bier walked upon the perfumery, and the servants of Jacob went before them strewing the perfume along the road. ⁴² And Joseph went up with a heavy camp, and they did after this manner every day until they reached the land of Canaan, and they came to the threshing floor of Atad, which was on the other side of Jordan, and they mourned an exceeding great and heavy mourning in that place. ⁴³ And all the kings of Canaan heard of this thing and they all went forth, each man from his house, thirty-one kings of Canaan, and they all came with their

men to mourn and weep over Jacob. ⁴⁴ And all these kings beheld Jacob's bier, and behold Joseph's crown was upon it, and they also put their crowns upon the bier, and encircled it with crowns. ⁴⁵ And all these kings made in that place a great and heavy mourning with the sons of Jacob and Egypt over Jacob, for all the kings of Canaan knew the valor of Jacob and his sons. ⁴⁶ And the report reached Esau, saying, Jacob died in Egypt, and his sons and all Egypt are conveying him to the land of Canaan to bury him. ⁴⁷ And Esau heard this thing, and he was dwelling in mount Seir, and he rose up with his sons and all his people and all his household, a people exceedingly great, and they came to mourn and weep over Jacob. ⁴⁸ And it came to pass, when Esau came he mourned for his brother Jacob, and all Egypt and all Canaan again rose up and mourned a great mourning with Esau over Jacob in that place ⁴⁹ And Joseph and his brethren brought their father Jacob from that place, and they went to Hebron to bury Jacob in the cave by his fathers. ⁵⁰ And they came unto Kireath-arba, to the cave, and as they came Esau stood with his sons against Joseph and his brethren as a hindrance in the cave, saying, Jacob shall not be buried therein, for it belongeth to us and to our father. ⁵¹ And Joseph and his brethren heard the words of Esau's sons, and they were exceedingly wroth, and Joseph approached unto Esau, saying, What is this thing which they have spoken? surely my father Jacob bought it from thee for great riches after the death of Isaac, now five and twenty years ago, and also all the land of Canaan he bought from thee and from thy sons, and thy seed after thee. ⁵² And Jacob bought it for his sons and his seed after him for an inheritance for ever, and why speakest thou these things this day? ⁵³ And Esau answered, saying, Thou speakest falsely and utterest lies, for I sold not anything belonging to me in all this land, as thou sayest, neither did my brother Jacob buy aught belonging to me in this land. ⁵⁴ And Esau spoke these things in order to deceive Joseph with his words, for Esau knew that Joseph was not present in those days when Esau sold all belonging to him in the land of Canaan to Jacob. ⁵⁵ And Joseph said unto Esau, Surely my father inserted these things with thee in the record of purchase, and testified the record with witnesses, and behold it is with us in Egypt. ⁵⁶ And Esau answered, saying unto him, Bring the record, all that thou wilt find in the record, so will we do. ⁵⁷ And Joseph called unto Naphtali his brother, and he said, Hasten quickly, stay not, and run I pray thee to Egypt and bring all the records; the record of the purchase, the sealed record and the open record, and also all the first records in which all the transactions of the birth-right are written, fetch thou. ⁵⁸ And thou shalt bring them unto us hither, that we may know from them all the words of Esau and his sons which they spoke this day. ⁵⁹ And Naphtali hearkened to the voice of Joseph and he hastened and ran to go down to Egypt, and Naphtali was lighter on foot than any of the stags that were upon the wilderness, for he would go upon ears of corn without crushing them. ⁶⁰ And when Esau saw that Naphtali had gone to fetch the records, he and his sons increased their resistance against the cave, and Esau and all his people rose up against Joseph and his brethren to battle. ⁶¹ And all the sons of Jacob and the people of Egypt fought with Esau and his men, and the sons of Esau and his people were smitten before the sons of Jacob, and the sons of Jacob slew of Esau's people forty men. ⁶² And Chushim the son of Dan, the son of Jacob, was at that time with Jacob's sons, but he was about a hundred cubits distant from the place of battle, for he remained with the children of Jacob's sons by Jacob's bier to guard it. ⁶³ And Chushim was dumb and deaf, still he understood the voice of consternation amongst men. ⁶⁴ And he asked, saying, Why do you not bury the dead, and what is this great consternation? and they answered him the words of Esau and his sons; and he ran to Esau in the midst of the battle, and he slew Esau with a sword, and he cut off his head, and it sprang to a distance, and Esau fell amongst the people of the battle. ⁶⁵ And when Chushim did this thing the sons of Jacob prevailed over the sons of Esau, and the sons of Jacob buried their father Jacob by force in the cave, and the sons of Esau beheld it. ⁶⁶ And Jacob was buried in Hebron, in the cave of Machpelah which Abraham had bought from the sons of Heth for the possession of a burial place, and he was buried in very costly garments. ⁶⁷ And no king had such honor paid him as Joseph paid unto his father at his death, for he buried him with great honor like unto the burial of kings. ⁶⁸ And Joseph and his brethren made a mourning of seven days for their father.

57

¹ And it was after this that the sons of Esau waged war with the sons of Jacob, and the sons of Esau fought with the sons of Jacob in Hebron, and Esau was still lying dead, and not buried. ² And the battle was heavy between them, and the sons of Esau were smitten before the sons of Jacob, and the sons of Jacob slew of the sons of Esau eighty men, and not one died of the people of the sons of Jacob; and the hand of Joseph prevailed over all the people of the sons of Esau, and he took Zepho, the son of Eliphaz, the son of Esau, and fifty of his men captive, and he bound them with chains of iron, and gave them into the hand of his servants to bring them to Egypt. ³ And it came to pass when the sons of Jacob had taken Zepho and his people captive, all those that remained were greatly afraid of their lives from the house of Esau, lest they should also be taken captive, and they all fled with Eliphaz the son of Esau and his people, with Esau's body, and they went on their road to Mount Seir. ⁴ And they came unto Mount Seir and they buried Esau in Seir, but they had not brought his head with them to Seir, for it was buried in that place where the battle had been in Hebron. ⁵ And it came to pass when the sons of Esau had fled from before the sons of Jacob, the sons of Jacob pursued them unto the borders of Seir, but they did not slay a single man from amongst them when they pursued them, for Esau's body which they carried with them excited their confusion, so they fled and the sons of Jacob turned back from them and came up to the place where their brethren were in Hebron, and they remained there on that day, and on the next day until they rested from the battle. ⁶ And it came to pass on the third day they assembled all the sons of Seir the Horite, and they assembled all the children of the east, a multitude of people like the sand of the sea, and they went and came down to Egypt to fight with Joseph and his brethren, in order to deliver their brethren. ⁷ And Joseph and all the sons of Jacob heard that the sons of Esau and the children of the east had come upon them to battle in order to deliver their brethren. ⁸ And Joseph and his brethren and the strong men of Egypt went forth and fought in the city of Rameses, and Joseph and his brethren dealt out a tremendous blow amongst the sons of Esau and the children of the east. ⁹ And they slew of them six hundred thousand men, and they slew amongst them all the mighty men of the children of Seir the Horite; there were only a few of them left, and they slew also a great many of the children of the east, and of the children of Esau; and Eliphaz the son of Esau, and the children of the east all fled before Joseph and his brethren. ¹⁰ And Joseph and his brethren pursued them until they came unto Succoth, and they yet slew of them in Succoth thirty men, and the rest escaped and they fled each to his city. ¹¹ And Joseph and his brethren and the mighty men of Egypt turned back from them with joy and cheerfulness of heart, for they had smitten all their enemies. ¹² And Zepho the son of Eliphaz and his men were still slaves in Egypt to the sons of Jacob, and their pains increased. ¹³ And when the sons of Esau and the sons of Seir returned to their land, the sons of Seir saw that they had all fallen into the hands of the sons of Jacob, and the people of Egypt, on account of the battle of the sons of Esau. ¹⁴ And the sons of Seir said unto the sons of Esau, You have seen and therefore you know that this camp was on your account, and not one mighty man or an adept in war remaineth. ¹⁵ Now therefore go forth from our land, go from us to the land of Canaan to the land of the dwelling of your fathers; wherefore shall your children inherit the effects of our children in latter days? ¹⁶ And the children of Esau would not listen to the children of Seir, and the children of Seir considered to make war with them. ¹⁷ And the children of Esau sent secretly to Angeas king of Africa, the same is Dinhabah, saying, ¹⁸ Send unto us some of thy men and let them come unto us, and we will fight together with the children of Seir the Horite, for they have resolved to fight with us to drive us away from the land. ¹⁹ And Angeas king of Dinhabah did so, for he was in those days friendly to the children of Esau, and Angeas sent five hundred valiant infantry to the children of Esau, and eight hundred cavalry. ²⁰ And the children of Seir sent unto the children of the east and unto the children of Midian, saying, You have seen what the children of Esau have done unto us, upon whose account we are almost all destroyed, in their battle with the sons of Jacob. ²¹ Now therefore come unto us and assist us, and we will fight them together, and we will drive them from the land and be avenged of the cause of our brethren who died for their sakes in their battle with their brethren the sons of Jacob. ²² And all the children of the east listened to the children of Seir, and they came unto them about eight hundred men with drawn swords, and the children of Esau fought with the children of Seir at that time in the wilderness of Paran. ²³ And the children of Seir prevailed then over the sons of Esau, and the children of Seir slew on that day of the children of Esau in that battle about two hundred men of the people of Angeas king of Dinhabah. ²⁴ And on the second day the children of Esau came again to fight a second time with the children of Seir, and the battle was sore upon the children of Esau this second time, and it troubled them greatly on account of the children of Seir. ²⁵ And when the children of Esau saw that the children of Seir were more powerful than they were, some men of the children of Esau turned and assisted the children of Seir their enemies. ²⁶ And there fell yet of the people of the children of Esau in the second battle fifty-eight men of the people at Angeas king of Dinhabah. ²⁷ And on the third day the children of Esau heard that some of their brethren had turned from them to fight against them in the second battle; and the children of Esau mourned when they heard this thing. ²⁸ And they said, What shall we do unto our brethren who turned from us to assist the children of Seir our enemies? and the children of Esau again sent to Angeas king of

Dinhabah, saying, ²⁹ Send unto us again other men that with them we may fight with the children of Seir, for they have already twice been heavier than we were. ³⁰ And Angeas again sent to the children of Esau about six hundred valiant men, and they came to assist the children of Esau. ³¹ And in ten days' time the children of Esau again waged war with the children of Seir in the wilderness of Paran, and the battle was very severe upon the children of Seir, and the children of Esau prevailed at this time over the children of Seir, and the children of Seir were smitten before the children of Esau, and the children of Esau slew from them about two thousand men. ³² And all the mighty men of the children of Seir died in this battle, and there only remained their young children that were left in their cities. ³³ And all Midian and the children of the east betook themselves to flight from the battle, and they left the children of Seir and fled when they saw that the battle was severe upon them, and the children of Esau pursued all the children of the east until they reached their land. ³⁴ And the children of Esau slew yet of them about two hundred and fifty men and from the people of the children of Esau there fell in that battle about thirty men, but this evil came upon them through their brethren turning from them to assist the children of Seir the Horite, and the children of Esau again heard of the evil doings of their brethren, and they again mourned on account of this thing. ³⁵ And it came to pass after the battle, the children of Esau turned back and came home unto Seir, and the children of Esau slew those who had remained in the land of the children of Seir; they slew also their wives and little ones, they left not a soul alive except fifty young lads and damsels whom they suffered to live, and the children of Esau did not put them to death, and the lads became their slaves, and the damsels they took for wives. ³⁶ And the children of Esau dwelt in Seir in the place of the children of Seir, and they inherited their land and took possession of it. ³⁷ And the children of Esau took all belonging in the land to the children of Seir, also their flocks, their bullocks and their goods, and all belonging to the children of Seir, did the children of Esau take, and the children of Esau dwelt in Seir in the place of the children of Seir unto this day, and the children of Esau divided the land into divisions to the five sons of Esau, according to their families. ³⁸ And it came to pass in those days, that the children of Esau resolved to crown a king over them in the land of which they became possessed. And they said to each other, Not so, for he shall reign over us in our land, and we shall be under his counsel and he shall fight our battles, against our enemies, and they did so. ³⁹ And all the children of Esau swore, saying, That none of their brethren should ever reign over them, but a strange man who is not of their brethren, for the souls of all the children of Esau were embittered every man against his son, brother and friend, on account of the evil they sustained from their brethren when they fought with the children of Seir. ⁴⁰ Therefore the sons of Esau swore, saying, From that day forward they would not choose a king from their brethren, but one from a strange land unto this day. ⁴¹ And there was a man there from the people of Angeas king of Dinhabah; his name was Bela the son of Beor, who was a very valiant man, beautiful and comely and wise in all wisdom, and a man of sense and counsel; and there was none of the people of Angeas like unto him. ⁴² And all the children of Esau took him and anointed him and they crowned him for a king, and they bowed down to him, and they said unto him, May the king live, may the king live. ⁴³ And they spread out the sheet, and they brought him each man earrings of gold and silver or rings or bracelets, and they made him very rich in silver and in gold, in onyx stones and bdellium, and they made him a royal throne, and they placed a regal crown upon his head, and they built a palace for him and he dwelt therein, and he became king over all the children of Esau. ⁴⁴ And the people of Angeas took their hire for their battle from the children of Esau, and they went and returned at that time to their master in Dinhabah. ⁴⁵ And Bela reigned over the children of Esau thirty years, and the children of Esau dwelt in the land instead of the children of Seir, and they dwelt securely in their stead unto this day.

58

¹ And it came to pass in the thirty-second year of the Israelites going down to Egypt, that is in the seventy-first year of the life of Joseph, in that year died Pharaoh king of Egypt, and Magron his son reigned in his stead. ² And Pharaoh commanded Joseph before his death to be a father to his son, Magron, and that Magron should be under the care of Joseph and under his counsel. ³ And all Egypt consented to this thing that Joseph should be king over them, for all the Egyptians loved Joseph as of heretofore, only Magron the son of Pharaoh sat upon, his father's throne, and he became king in those days in his father's stead. ⁴ Magron was forty-one years old when he began to reign, and forty years he reigned in Egypt, and all Egypt called his name Pharaoh after the name of his father, as it was their custom to do in Egypt to every king that reigned over them. ⁵ And it came to pass when Pharaoh reigned in his father's stead, he placed the laws of Egypt and all the affairs of government in the hand of Joseph, as his father had commanded him. ⁶ And Joseph became king over Egypt, for he superintended over all Egypt, and all Egypt was under his care and under his counsel, for all Egypt inclined to Joseph after the death of Pharaoh, and they loved him exceedingly to reign over them. ⁷ But there were some people amongst them, who did not like him, saying, No stranger shall reign over us; still the whole government of Egypt devolved in those days upon Joseph, after the death of Pharaoh, he being the regulator, doing as he liked throughout the land without any one interfering. ⁸ And all Egypt was under the care of Joseph, and Joseph made war with all his surrounding enemies, and he subdued them; also all the land and all the Philistines, unto the borders of Canaan, did Joseph subdue, and they were all under his power and they gave a yearly tax unto Joseph. ⁹ And Pharaoh king of Egypt sat upon his throne in his father's stead, but he was under the control and counsel of Joseph, as he was at first under the control of his father. ¹⁰ Neither did he reign but in the land of Egypt only, under the counsel of Joseph, but Joseph reigned over the whole country at that time, from Egypt unto the great river Perath. ¹¹ And Joseph was successful in all his ways, and the Lord was with him, and the Lord gave Joseph additional wisdom, and honor, and glory, and love toward him in the hearts of the Egyptians and throughout the land, and Joseph reigned over the whole country forty years. ¹² And all the countries of the Philistines and Canaan and Zidon, and on the other side of Jordan, brought presents unto Joseph all his days, and the whole country was in the hand of Joseph, and they brought unto him a yearly tribute as it was regulated, for Joseph had fought against all his surrounding enemies and subdued them, and the whole country was in the hand of Joseph, and Joseph sat securely upon his throne in Egypt. ¹³ And also all his brethren the sons of Jacob dwelt securely in the land, all the days of Joseph, and they were fruitful and multiplied exceedingly in the land, and they served the Lord all their days, as their father Jacob had commanded them. ¹⁴ And it came to pass at the end of many days and years, when the children of Esau were dwelling quietly in their land with Bela their king, that the children of Esau were fruitful and multiplied in the land, and they resolved to go and fight with the sons of Jacob and all Egypt, and to deliver their brother Zepho, the son of Eliphaz, and his men, for they were yet in those days slaves to Joseph. ¹⁵ And the children of Esau sent unto all the children of the east, and they made peace with them, and all the children of the east came unto them to go with the children of Esau to Egypt to battle. ¹⁶ And there came also unto them of the people of Angeas, king of Dinhabah, and they also sent unto the children of Ishmael and they also came unto them. ¹⁷ And all this people assembled and came unto Seir to assist the children of Esau in their battle, and this camp was very large and heavy with people, numerous as the sand of the sea, about eight hundred thousand men, infantry and cavalry, and all these troops went down to Egypt to fight with the sons of Jacob, and they encamped by Rameses. ¹⁸ And Joseph went forth with his brethren with the mighty men of Egypt, about six hundred men, and they fought with them in the land of Rameses; and the sons of Jacob at that time again fought with the children of Esau, in the fiftieth year of the sons of Jacob going down to Egypt, that is the thirtieth year of the reign of Bela over the children of Esau in Seir. ¹⁹ And the Lord gave all the mighty men of Esau and the children of the east into the hand of Joseph and his brethren, and the people of the children of Esau and the children of the east were smitten before Joseph. ²⁰ And of the people of Esau and the children of the east that were slain, there fell before the sons of Jacob about two hundred thousand men, and their king Bela the son of Beor fell with them in the battle, and when the children of Esau saw that their king had fallen in battle and was dead, their hands became weak in the combat. ²¹ And Joseph and his brethren and all Egypt were still smiting the people of the house of Esau, and all Esau's people were afraid of the sons of Jacob and fled from before them. ²² And Joseph and his brethren and all Egypt pursued them a day's journey, and they slew yet from them about three hundred men, continuing to smite them in the road; and they afterward turned back from them. ²³ And Joseph and all his brethren returned to Egypt, not one man was missing from them, but of the Egyptians there fell twelve men. ²⁴ And when Joseph returned to Egypt he ordered Zepho and his men to be additionally bound, and they bound them in irons and they increased their grief. ²⁵ And all the people of the children of Esau, and the children of the east, returned in shame each unto his city, for all the mighty men that were with them had fallen in battle. ²⁶ And when the children of Esau saw that their king had died in battle they hastened and took a man from the people of the children of the east; his name was Jobab the son of Zarach, from the land of Botzrah, and they caused him to reign over them instead of Bela their king. ²⁷ And Jobab sat upon the throne of Bela as king in his stead, and Jobab reigned in Edom over all the children of Esau ten years, and the children of Esau went no more to fight with the sons of Jacob from that day forward, for the sons of Esau knew the valor of the sons of Jacob, and they were greatly afraid of them. ²⁸ But from that day forward the children of

Esau hated the sons of Jacob, and the hatred and enmity were very strong between them all the days, unto this day. ²⁹ And it came to pass after this, at the end of ten years, Jobab, the son of Zarach, from Botzrah, died, and the children of Esau took a man whose name was Chusham, from the land of Teman, and they made him king over them instead of Jobab, and Chusham reigned in Edom over all the children of Esau for twenty years. ³⁰ And Joseph, king of Egypt, and his brethren, and all the children of Israel dwelt securely in Egypt in those days, together with all the children of Joseph and his brethren, having no hindrance or evil accident and the land of Egypt was at that time at rest from war in the days of Joseph and his brethren.

59

¹ And these are the names of the sons of Israel who dwelt in Egypt, who had come with Jacob, all the sons of Jacob came unto Egypt, every man with his household. ² The children of Leah were Reuben, Simeon, Levi, Judah, Issachar and Zebulun, and their sister Dinah. ³ And the sons of Rachel were Joseph and Benjamin. ⁴ And the sons of Zilpah, the handmaid of Leah, were Gad and Asher. ⁵ And the sons of Bilhah, the handmaid of Rachel, were Dan and Naphtali. ⁶ And these were their offspring that were born unto them in the land of Canaan, before they came unto Egypt with their father Jacob. ⁷ The sons of Reuben were Chanoch, Pallu, Chetzron and Carmi. ⁸ And the sons of Simeon were Jemuel, Jamin, Ohad, Jachin, Zochar and Saul, the son of the Canaanitish woman. ⁹ And the children of Levi were Gershon, Kehath and Merari, and their sister Jochebed, who was born unto them in their going down to Egypt. ¹⁰ And the sons of Judah were Er, Onan, Shelah, Perez and Zarach. ¹¹ And Er and Onan died in the land of Canaan; and the sons of Perez were Chezron and Chamul. ¹² And the sons of Issachar were Tola, Puvah, Job and Shomron. ¹³ And the sons of Zebulun were Sered, Elon and Jachleel, and the son of Dan was Chushim. ¹⁴ And the sons of Naphtali were Jachzeel, Guni, Jetzer and Shilam. ¹⁵ And the sons of Gad were Ziphion, Chaggi, Shuni, Ezbon, Eri, Arodi and Areli. ¹⁶ And the children of Asher were Jimnah, Jishvah, Jishvi, Beriah and their sister Serach; and the sons of Beriah were Cheber and Malchiel. ¹⁷ And the sons of Benjamin were Bela, Becher, Ashbel, Gera, Naaman, Achi, Rosh, Mupim, Chupim and Ord. ¹⁸ And the sons of Joseph, that were born unto him in Egypt, were Manasseh and Ephraim. ¹⁹ And all the souls that went forth from the loins of Jacob, were seventy souls; these are they who came with Jacob their father unto Egypt to dwell there: and Joseph and all his brethren dwelt securely in Egypt, and they ate of the best of Egypt all the days of the life of Joseph. ²⁰ And Joseph lived in the land of Egypt ninety-three years, and Joseph reigned over all Egypt eighty years. ²¹ And when the days of Joseph drew nigh that he should die, he sent and called for his brethren and all his father's household, and they all came together and sat before him. ²² And Joseph said unto his brethren and unto the whole of his father's household, Behold I die, and God will surely visit you and bring you up from this land to the land which he swore to your fathers to give unto them. ²³ And it shall be when God shall visit you to bring you up from here to the land of your fathers, then bring up my bones with you from here. ²⁴ And Joseph made the sons of Israel to swear for their seed after them, saying, God will surely visit you and you shall bring up my bones with you from here. ²⁵ And it came to pass after this that Joseph died in that year, the seventy-first year of the Israelites going down to Egypt. ²⁶ And Joseph was one hundred and ten years old when he died in the land of Egypt, and all his brethren and all his servants rose up and they embalmed Joseph, as was their custom, and his brethren and all Egypt mourned over him for seventy days. ²⁷ And they put Joseph in a coffin filled with spices and all sorts of perfume, and they buried him by the side of the river, that is Sihor, and his sons and all his brethren, and the whole of his father's household made a seven day's mourning for him. ²⁸ And it came to pass after the death of Joseph, all the Egyptians began in those days to rule over the children of Israel, and Pharaoh, king of Egypt, who reigned in his father's stead, took all the laws of Egypt and conducted the whole government of Egypt under his counsel, and he reigned securely over his people.

60

¹ And when the year came round, being the seventy-second year from the Israelites going down to Egypt, after the death of Joseph, Zepho, the son of Eliphaz, the son of Esau, fled from Egypt, he and his men, and they went away. ² And he came to Africa, which is Dinhabah, to Angeas king of Africa, and Angeas received them with great honor, and he made Zepho the captain of his host. ³ And Zepho found favor in the sight of Angeas and in the sight of his people, and Zepho was captain of the host to Angeas king of Africa for many days. ⁴ And Zepho enticed Angeas king of Africa to collect all his army to go and fight with the Egyptians, and with the sons of Jacob, and to avenge of them the cause of his brethren. ⁵ But Angeas would not listen to Zepho to do this thing, for Angeas knew the strength of the sons of Jacob, and what they had done to his army in their warfare with the children of Esau. ⁶ And Zepho was in those days very great in the sight of Angeas and in the sight of all his people, and he continually enticed them to make war against Egypt, but they would not. ⁷ And it came to pass in those days there was in the land of Chittim a man in the city of Puzimna, whose name was Uzu, and he became degenerately deified by the children of Chittim, and the man died and had no son, only one daughter whose name was Jania. ⁸ And the damsel was exceedingly beautiful, comely and intelligent, there was none seen like unto her for beauty and wisdom throughout the land. ⁹ And the people of Angeas king of Africa saw her and they came and praised her unto him, and Angeas sent to the children of Chittim, and he requested to take her unto himself for a wife, and the people of Chittim consented to give her unto him for a wife. ¹⁰ And when the messengers of Angeas were going forth from the land of Chittim to take their journey, behold the messengers of Turnus king of Bibentu came unto Chittim, for Turnus king of Bibentu also sent his messengers to request Jania for him, to take unto himself for a wife, for all his men had also praised her to him, therefore he sent all his servants unto her. ¹¹ And the servants of Turnus came to Chittim, and they asked for Jania, to be taken unto Turnus their king for a wife. ¹² And the people of Chittim said unto them, We cannot give her, because Angeas king of Africa desired her to take her unto him for a wife before you came, and that we should give her unto him, and now therefore we cannot do this thing to deprive Angeas of the damsel in order to give her unto Turnus. ¹³ For we are greatly afraid of Angeas lest he come in battle against us and destroy us, and Turnus your master will not be able to deliver us from his hand. ¹⁴ And when the messengers of Turnus heard all the words of the children of Chittim, they turned back to their master and told him all the words of the children of Chittim. ¹⁵ And the children of Chittim sent a memorial to Angeas, saying, Behold Turnus has sent for Jania to take her unto him for a wife, and thus have we answered him; and we heard that he has collected his whole army to go to war against thee, and he intends to pass by the road of Sardunia to fight against thy brother Lucus, and after that he will come to fight against thee. ¹⁶ And Angeas heard the words of the children of Chittim which they sent to him in the record, and his anger was kindled and he rose up and assembled his whole army and came through the islands of the sea, the road to Sardunia, unto his brother Lucus king of Sardunia. ¹⁷ And Niblos, the son of Lucus, heard that his uncle Angeas was coming, and he went out to meet him with a heavy army, and he kissed him and embraced him, and Niblos said unto Angeas, When thou askest my father after his welfare, when I shall go with thee to fight with Turnus, ask of him to make me captain of his host, and Angeas did so, and he came unto his brother and his brother came to meet him, and he asked him after his welfare. ¹⁸ And Angeas asked his brother Lucus after his welfare, and to make his son Niblos captain of his host, and Lucus did so, and Angeas and his brother Lucus rose up and they went toward Turnus to battle, and there was with them a great army and a heavy people. ¹⁹ And he came in ships, and they came into the province of Ashtorash, and behold Turnus came toward them, for he went forth to Sardunia, and intended to destroy it and afterward to pass on from there to Angeas to fight with him. ²⁰ And Angeas and Lucus his brother met Turnus in the valley of Canopia, and the battle was strong and mighty between them in that place. ²¹ And the battle was severe upon Lucus king of Sardunia, and all his army fell, and Niblos his son fell also in that battle. ²² And his uncle Angeas commanded his servants and they made a golden coffin for Niblos and they put him into it, and Angeas again waged battle toward Turnus, and Angeas was stronger than he, and he slew him, and he smote all his people with the edge of the sword, and Angeas avenged the cause of Niblos his brother's son and the cause of the army of his brother Lucus. ²³ And when Turnus died, the hands of those that survived the battle became weak, and they fled from before Angeas and Lucus his brother. ²⁴ And Angeas and his brother Lucus pursued them unto the highroad, which is between Alphanu and Romah, and they slew the whole army of Turnus with the edge of the sword. ²⁵ And Lucus king of Sardunia commanded his servants that they should make a coffin of brass, and that they should place therein the body of his son Niblos, and they buried him in that place. ²⁶ And they built upon it a high tower there upon the highroad, and they called its name after the name of Niblos unto this day, and they also buried Turnus king of Bibentu there in that place with Niblos. ²⁷ And behold upon the highroad between Alphanu and Romah the grave of Niblos is on one side and the grave of Turnus on the other, and a pavement between them unto this day. ²⁸ And when Niblos was buried, Lucus his father returned with his army to his land Sardunia, and Angeas his brother king of Africa went with his people unto the city of Bibentu, that is the city of Turnus. ²⁹ And the inhabitants of Bibentu heard of his fame and they were greatly afraid of him, and they went forth to meet him with weeping and supplication, and the inhabitants of Bibentu entreated of Angeas not to slay them nor destroy

their city; and he did so, for Bibentu was in those days reckoned as one of the cities of the children of Chittim; therefore he did not destroy the city. ³⁰ But from that day forward the troops of the king of Africa would go to Chittim to spoil and plunder it, and whenever they went, Zepho the captain of the host of Angeas would go with them. ³¹ And it was after this that Angeas turned with his army and they came to the city of Puzimna, and Angeas took thence Jania the daughter of Uzu for a wife and brought her unto his city unto Africa.

61

¹ And it came to pass at that time Pharaoh king of Egypt commanded all his people to make for him a strong palace in Egypt. ² And he also commanded the sons of Jacob to assist the Egyptians in the building, and the Egyptians made a beautiful and elegant palace for a royal habitation, and he dwelt therein and he renewed his government and he reigned securely. ³ And Zebulun the son of Jacob died in that year, that is the seventy-second year of the going down of the Israelites to Egypt, and Zebulun died a hundred and fourteen years old, and was put into a coffin and given into the hands of his children. ⁴ And in the seventy-fifth year died his brother Simeon, he was a hundred and twenty years old at his death, and he was also put into a coffin and given into the hands of his children. ⁵ And Zepho the son of Eliphaz the son of Esau, captain of the host to Angeas king of Dinhabah, was still daily enticing Angeas to prepare for battle to fight with the sons of Jacob in Egypt, and Angeas was unwilling to do this thing, for his servants had related to him all the might of the sons of Jacob, what they had done unto them in their battle with the children of Esau. ⁶ And Zepho was in those days daily enticing Angeas to fight with the sons of Jacob in those days. ⁷ And after some time Angeas hearkened to the words of Zepho and consented to him to fight with the sons of Jacob in Egypt, and Angeas got all his people in order, a people numerous as the sand which is upon the sea shore, and he formed his resolution to go to Egypt to battle. ⁸ And amongst the servants of Angeas was a youth fifteen years old, Balaam the son of Beor was his name and the youth was very wise and understood the art of witchcraft. ⁹ And Angeas said unto Balaam, Conjure for us, I pray thee, with the witchcraft, that we may know who will prevail in this battle to which we are now proceeding. ¹⁰ And Balaam ordered that they should bring him wax, and he made thereof the likeness of chariots and horsemen representing the army of Angeas and the army of Egypt, and he put them in the cunningly prepared waters that he had for that purpose, and he took in his hand the boughs of myrtle trees, and he exercised his cunning, and he joined them over the water, and there appeared unto him in the water the resembling images of the hosts of Angeas falling before the resembling images of the Egyptians and the sons of Jacob. ¹¹ And Balaam told this thing to Angeas, and Angeas despaired and did not arm himself to go down to Egypt to battle, and he remained in his city. ¹² And when Zepho the son of Eliphaz saw that Angeas despaired of going forth to battle with the Egyptians, Zepho fled from Angeas from Africa, and he went and came unto Chittim. ¹³ And all the people of Chittim received him with great honor, and they hired him to fight their battles all the days, and Zepho became exceedingly rich in those days, and the troops of the king of Africa still spread themselves in those days, and the children of Chittim assembled and went to Mount Cuptizia on account of the troops of Angeas king of Africa, who were advancing upon them. ¹⁴ And it was one day that Zepho lost a young heifer, and he went to seek it, and he heard it lowing round about the mountain. ¹⁵ And Zepho went and he saw and behold there was a large cave at the bottom of the mountain, and there was a great stone there at the entrance of the cave, and Zepho split the stone and he came into the cave and he looked and behold, a large animal was devouring the ox; from the middle upward it resembled a man, and from the middle downward it resembled an animal, and Zepho rose up against the animal and slew it with his swords. ¹⁶ And the inhabitants of Chittim heard of this thing, and they rejoiced exceedingly, and they said, What shall we do unto this man who has slain this animal that devoured our cattle? ¹⁷ And they all assembled to consecrate one day in the year to him, and they called the name thereof Zepho after his name, and they brought unto him drink offerings year after year on that day, and they brought unto him gifts. ¹⁸ At that time Jania the daughter of Uzu wife of king Angeas became ill, and her illness was heavily felt by Angeas and his officers, and Angeas said unto his wise men, What shall I do to Jania and how shall I heal her from her illness? And his wise men said unto him, Because the air of our country is not like the air of the land of Chittim, and our water is not like their water, therefore from this has the queen become ill. ¹⁹ For through the change of air and water she became ill, and also because in her country she drank only the water which came from Purmah, which her ancestors had brought up with bridges. ²⁰ And Angeas commanded his servants, and they brought unto him in vessels of the waters of Purmah belonging to Chittim, and they weighed those waters with all the waters of the land of Africa, and they found those waters lighter than the waters of Africa. ²¹ And Angeas saw this thing, and he commanded all his officers to assemble the hewers of stone in thousands and tens of thousands, and they hewed stone without number, and the builders came and they built an exceedingly strong bridge, and they conveyed the spring of water from the land of Chittim unto Africa, and those waters were for Jania the queen and for all her concerns, to drink from and to bake, wash and bathe therewith, and also to water therewith all seed from which food can be obtained, and all fruit of the ground. ²² And the king commanded that they should bring of the soil of Chittim in large ships, and they also brought stones to build therewith, and the builders built palaces for Jania the queen, and the queen became healed of her illness. ²³ And at the revolution of the year the troops of Africa continued coming to the land of Chittim to plunder as usual, and Zepho son of Eliphaz heard their report, and he gave orders concerning them and he fought with them, and they fled before him, and he delivered the land of Chittim from them. ²⁴ And the children of Chittim saw the valor of Zepho, and the children of Chittim resolved and they made Zepho king over them, and he became king over them, and whilst he reigned they went to subdue the children of Tubal, and all the surrounding islands. ²⁵ And their king Zepho went at their head and they made war with Tubal and the islands, and they subdued them, and when they returned from the battle they renewed his government for him, and they built for him a very large palace for his royal habitation and seat, and they made a large throne for him, and Zepho reigned over the whole land of Chittim and over the land of Italia fifty years.

62

¹ In that year, being the seventy-ninth year of the Israelites going down to Egypt, died Reuben the son of Jacob, in the land of Egypt; Reuben was a hundred and twenty-five years old when he died, and they put him into a coffin, and he was given into the hands of his children. ² And in the eightieth year died his brother Dan; he was a hundred and twenty years at his death, and he was also put into a coffin and given into the hands of his children. ³ And in that year died Chusham king of Edom, and after him reigned Hadad the son of Bedad, for thirty-five years; and in the eighty-first year died Issachar the son of Jacob, in Egypt, and Issachar was a hundred and twenty-two years old at his death, and he was put into a coffin in Egypt, and given into the hands of his children. ⁴ And in the eighty-second year died Asher his brother, he was a hundred and twenty-three years old at his death, and he was placed in a coffin in Egypt, and given into the hands of his children. ⁵ And in the eighty-third year died Gad, he was a hundred and twenty-five years old at his death, and he was put into a coffin in Egypt, and given into the hands of his children. ⁶ And it came to pass in the eighty-fourth year, that is the fiftieth year of the reign of Hadad, son of Bedad, king of Edom, that Hadad assembled all the children of Esau, and he got his whole army in readiness, about four hundred thousand men, and he directed his way to the land of Moab, and he went to fight with Moab and to make them tributary to him. ⁷ And the children of Moab heard this thing, and they were very much afraid, and they sent to the children of Midian to assist them in fighting with Hadad, son of Bedad, king of Edom. ⁸ And Hadad came unto the land of Moab, and Moab and the children of Midian went out to meet him, and they placed themselves in battle array against him in the field of Moab. ⁹ And Hadad fought with Moab, and there fell of the children of Moab and the children of Midian many slain ones, about two hundred thousand men. ¹⁰ And the battle was very severe upon Moab, and when the children of Moab saw that the battle was sore upon them, they weakened their hands and turned their backs, and left the children of Midian to carry on the battle. ¹¹ And the children of Midian knew not the intentions of Moab, but they strengthened themselves in battle and fought with Hadad and all his host, and all Midian fell before him. ¹² And Hadad smote all Midian with a heavy smiting, and he slew them with the edge of the sword, he left none remaining of those who came to assist Moab. ¹³ And when all the children of Midian had perished in battle, and the children at Moab had escaped, Hadad made all Moab at that time tributary to him, and they became under his hand, and they gave a yearly tax as it was ordered, and Hadad turned and went back to his land. ¹⁴ And at the revolution of the year, when the rest of the people of Midian that were in the land heard that all their brethren had fallen in battle with Hadad for the sake of Moab, because the children of Moab had turned their backs in battle and left Midian to fight, then five of the princes of Midian resolved with the rest of their brethren who remained in their land, to fight with Moab to avenge the cause of their brethren. ¹⁵ And the children of Midian sent to all their brethren the children of the east, and all their brethren, all the children of Keturah came to assist Midian to fight with Moab. ¹⁶ And the children of Moab heard this thing, and they were greatly afraid that all the children of the east had assembled together against them for battle, and they the children of Moab

sent a memorial to the land of Edom to Hadad the son of Bedad, saying, ¹⁷ Come now unto us and assist us and we will smite Midian, for they all assembled together and have come against us with all their brethren the children of the east to battle, to avenge the cause of Midian that fell in battle. ¹⁸ And Hadad, son of Bedad, king of Edom, went forth with his whole army and went to the land of Moab to fight with Midian, and Midian and the children of the east fought with Moab in the field of Moab, and the battle was very fierce between them. ¹⁹ And Hadad smote all the children of Midian and the children of the east with the edge of the sword, and Hadad at that time delivered Moab from the hand of Midian, and those that remained of Midian and of the children of the east fled before Hadad and his army, and Hadad pursued them to their land, and smote them with a very heavy slaughter, and the slain fell in the road. ²⁰ And Hadad delivered Moab from the hand of Midian, for all the children of Midian had fallen by the edge of the sword, and Hadad turned and went back to his land. ²¹ And from that day forth, the children of Midian hated the children of Moab, because they had fallen in battle for their sake, and there was a great and mighty enmity between them all the days. ²² And all that were found of Midian in the road of the land of Moab perished by the sword of Moab, and all that were found of Moab in the road of the land of Midian, perished by the sword of Midian; thus did Midian unto Moab and Moab unto Midian for many days. ²³ And it came to pass at that time that Judah the son of Jacob died in Egypt, in the eighty-sixth year of Jacob's going down to Egypt, and Judah was a hundred and twenty-nine years old at his death, and they embalmed him and put him into a coffin, and he was given into the hands of his children. ²⁴ And in the eighty-ninth year died Naphtali, he was a hundred and thirty-two years old, and he was put into a coffin and given into the hands of his children. ²⁵ And it came to pass in the ninety-first year of the Israelites going down to Egypt, that is in the thirtieth year of the reign of Zepho the son of Eliphaz, the son of Esau, over the children of Chittim, the children of Africa came upon the children of Chittim to plunder them as usual, but they had not come upon them for these thirteen years. ²⁶ And they came to them in that year, and Zepho the son of Eliphaz went out to them with some of his men and smote them desperately, and the troops of Africa fled from before Zepho and the slain fell before him, and Zepho and his men pursued them, going on and smiting them until they were near unto Africa. ²⁷ And Angeas king of Africa heard the thing which Zepho had done, and it vexed him exceedingly, and Angeas was afraid of Zepho all the days.

63

¹ And in the ninety-third year died Levi, the son of Jacob, in Egypt, and Levi was a hundred and thirty-seven years old when he died, and they put him into a coffin and he was given into the hands of his children. ² And it came to pass after the death of Levi, when all Egypt saw that the sons of Jacob the brethren of Joseph were dead, all the Egyptians began to afflict the children of Jacob, and to embitter their lives from that day unto the day of their going forth from Egypt, and they took from their hands all the vineyards and fields which Joseph had given unto them, and all the elegant houses in which the people of Israel lived, and all the fat of Egypt, the Egyptians took all from the sons of Jacob in those days. ³ And the hand of all Egypt became more grievous in those days against the children of Israel, and the Egyptians injured the Israelites until the children of Israel were wearied of their lives on account of the Egyptians. ⁴ And it came to pass in those days, in the hundred and second year of Israel's going down to Egypt, that Pharaoh king of Egypt died, and Melol his son reigned in his stead, and all the mighty men of Egypt and all that generation which knew Joseph and his brethren died in those days. ⁵ And another generation rose up in their stead, which had not known the sons of Jacob and all the good which they had done to them, and all their might in Egypt. ⁶ Therefore all Egypt began from that day forth to embitter the lives of the sons of Jacob, and to afflict them with all manner of hard labor, because they had not known their ancestors who had delivered them in the days of the famine. ⁷ And this was also from the Lord, for the children of Israel, to benefit them in their latter days, in order that all the children of Israel might know the Lord their God. ⁸ And in order to know the signs and mighty wonders which the Lord would do in Egypt on account of his people Israel, in order that the children of Israel might fear the Lord God of their ancestors, and walk in all his ways, they and their seed after them all the days. ⁹ Melol was twenty years old when he began to reign, and he reigned ninety-four years, and all Egypt called his name Pharaoh after the name of his father, as it was their custom to do to every king who reigned over them in Egypt. ¹⁰ At that time all the troops of Angeas king of Africa went forth to spread along the land of Chittim as usual for plunder. ¹¹ And Zepho the son of Eliphaz the son of Esau heard their report, and he went forth to meet them with his army, and he fought them there in the road. ¹² And Zepho smote the troops of the king of Africa with the edge of the sword, and left none remaining of them, and not even one returned to his master in Africa. ¹³ And Angeas heard of this which Zepho the son of Eliphaz had done to all his troops, that he had destroyed them, and Angeas assembled all his troops, all the men of the land of Africa, a people numerous like the sand by the sea shore. ¹⁴ And Angeas sent to Lucus his brother, saying, Come to me with all thy men and help me to smite Zepho and all the children of Chittim who have destroyed my men, and Lucus came with his whole army, a very great force, to assist Angeas his brother to fight with Zepho and the children of Chittim. ¹⁵ And Zepho and the children of Chittim heard this thing, and they were greatly afraid and a great terror fell upon their hearts. ¹⁶ And Zepho also sent a letter to the land of Edom to Hadad the son of Bedad king of Edom and to all the children of Esau, saying, ¹⁷ I have heard that Angeas king of Africa is coming to us with his brother for battle against us, and we are greatly afraid of him, for his army is very great, particularly as he comes against us with his brother and his army likewise. ¹⁸ Now therefore come you also up with me and help me, and we will fight together against Angeas and his brother Lucus, and you will save us out of their hands, but if not, know ye that we shall all die. ¹⁹ And the children of Esau sent a letter to the children of Chittim and to Zepho their king, saying, We cannot fight against Angeas and his people for a covenant of peace has been between us these many years, from the days of Bela the first king, and from the days of Joseph the son of Jacob king of Egypt, with whom we fought on the other side of Jordan when he buried his father. ²⁰ And when Zepho heard the words of his brethren the children of Esau he refrained from them, and Zepho was greatly afraid of Angeas. ²¹ And Angeas and Lucus his brother arrayed all their forces, about eight hundred thousand men, against the children of Chittim. ²² And all the children of Chittim said unto Zepho, Pray for us to the God of thy ancestors, peradventure he may deliver us from the hand of Angeas and his army, for we have heard that he is a great God and that he delivers all who trust in him. ²³ And Zepho heard their words, and Zepho sought the Lord and he said, ²⁴ ⁰ Lord God of Abraham and Isaac my ancestors, this day I know that thou art a true God, and all the gods of the nations are vain and useless. ²⁵ Remember now this day unto me thy covenant with Abraham our father, which our ancestors related unto us, and do graciously with me this day for the sake of Abraham and Isaac our fathers, and save me and the children of Chittim from the hand of the king of Africa who comes against us for battle. ²⁶ And the Lord hearkened to the voice of Zepho, and he had regard for him on account of Abraham and Isaac, and the Lord delivered Zepho and the children of Chittim from the hand of Angeas and his people. ²⁷ And Zepho fought Angeas king of Africa and all his people on that day, and the Lord gave all the people of Angeas into the hands of the children of Chittim. ²⁸ And the battle was severe upon Angeas, and Zepho smote all the men of Angeas and Lucus his brother, with the edge of the sword, and there fell from them unto the evening of that day about four hundred thousand men. ²⁹ And when Angeas saw that all his men perished, he sent a letter to all the inhabitants of Africa to come to him, to assist him in the battle, and he wrote in the letter, saying, All who are found in Africa let them come unto me from ten years old and upward; let them all come unto me, and behold if he comes not he shall die, and all that he has, with his whole household, the king will take. ³⁰ And all the rest of the inhabitants of Africa were terrified at the words of Angeas, and there went out of the city about three hundred thousand men and boys, from ten years upward, and they came to Angeas. ³¹ And at the end of ten days Angeas renewed the battle against Zepho and the children of Chittim, and the battle was very great and strong between them. ³² And from the army of Angeas and Lucus, Zepho sent many of the wounded unto his hand, about two thousand men, and Sosiphtar the captain of the host of Angeas fell in that battle. ³³ And when Sosiphtar had fallen, the African troops turned their backs to flee, and they fled, and Angeas and Lucus his brother were with them. ³⁴ And Zepho and the children of Chittim pursued them, and they smote them still heavily on the road, about two hundred men, and they pursued Azdrubal the son of Angeas who had fled with his father, and they smote twenty of his men in the road, and Azdrubal escaped from the children of Chittim, and they did not slay him. ³⁵ And Angeas and Lucus his brother fled with the rest of their men, and they escaped and came into Africa with terror and consternation, and Angeas feared all the days lest Zepho the son of Eliphaz should go to war with him.

64

¹ And Balaam the son of Beor was at that time with Angeas in the battle, and when he saw that Zepho prevailed over Angeas, he fled from there and came to Chittim. ² And Zepho and the children of Chittim received him with great honor, for Zepho knew Balaam's wisdom, and Zepho gave unto Balaam many gifts and he remained with him. ³ And when Zepho had returned from the war, he commanded all the children of Chittim to be

numbered who had gone into battle with him, and behold not one was missed. ⁴ And Zepho rejoiced at this thing, and he renewed his kingdom, and he made a feast to all his subjects. ⁵ But Zepho remembered not the Lord and considered not that the Lord had helped him in battle, and that he had delivered him and his people from the hand of the king of Africa, but still walked in the ways of the children of Chittim and the wicked children of Esau, to serve other gods which his brethren the children of Esau had taught him; it is therefore said, From the wicked goes forth wickedness. ⁶ And Zepho reigned over all the children of Chittim securely, but knew not the Lord who had delivered him and all his people from the hand of the king of Africa; and the troops of Africa came no more to Chittim to plunder as usual, for they knew of the power of Zepho who had smitten them all at the edge of the sword, so Angeas was afraid of Zepho the son of Eliphaz, and of the children of Chittim all the days. ⁷ At that time when Zepho had returned from the war, and when Zepho had seen how he prevailed over all the people of Africa and had smitten them in battle at the edge of the sword, then Zepho advised with the children of Chittim, to go to Egypt to fight with the sons of Jacob and with Pharaoh king of Egypt. ⁸ For Zepho heard that the mighty men of Egypt were dead and that Joseph and his brethren the sons at Jacob were dead, and that all their children the children of Israel remained in Egypt. ⁹ And Zepho considered to go to fight against them and all Egypt, to avenge the cause of his brethren the children of Esau, whom Joseph with his brethren and all Egypt had smitten in the land of Canaan, when they went up to bury Jacob in Hebron. ¹⁰ And Zepho sent messengers to Hadad, son of Bedad, king of Edom, and to all his brethren the children of Esau, saying, ¹¹ Did you not say that you would not fight against the king of Africa for he is a member of your covenant? behold I fought with him and smote him and all his people. ¹² Now therefore I have resolved to fight against Egypt and the children of Jacob who are there, and I will be revenged of them for what Joseph, his brethren and ancestors did to us in the land of Canaan when they went up to bury their father in Hebron. ¹³ Now then if you are willing to come to me to assist me in fighting against them and Egypt, then shall we avenge the cause of our brethren. ¹⁴ And the children of Esau hearkened to the words of Zepho, and the children of Esau gathered themselves together, a very great people, and they went to assist Zepho and the children of Chittim in battle. ¹⁵ And Zepho sent to all the children of the east and to all the children of Ishmael with words like unto these, and they gathered themselves and came to the assistance of Zepho and the children of Chittim in the war upon Egypt. ¹⁶ And all these kings, the king of Edom and the children of the east, and all the children of Ishmael, and Zepho the king of Chittim went forth and arrayed all their hosts in Hebron. ¹⁷ And the camp was very heavy, extending in length a distance of three days' journey, a people numerous as the sand upon the sea shore which can not be counted. ¹⁸ And all these kings and their hosts went down and came against all Egypt in battle, and encamped together in the valley of Pathros. ¹⁹ And all Egypt heard their report, and they also gathered themselves together, all the people of the land of Egypt, and of all the cities belonging to Egypt, about three hundred thousand men. ²⁰ And the men of Egypt sent also to the children of Israel who were in those days in the land of Goshen, to come to them in order to go and fight with these kings. ²¹ And the men of Israel assembled and were about one hundred and fifty men, and they went into battle to assist the Egyptians. ²² And the men of Israel and of Egypt went forth, about three hundred thousand men and one hundred and fifty men, and they went toward these kings to battle, and they placed themselves from without the land of Goshen opposite Pathros. ²³ And the Egyptians believed not in Israel to go with them in their camps together for battle, for all the Egyptians said, Perhaps the children of Israel will deliver us into the hand of the children of Esau and Ishmael, for they are their brethren. ²⁴ And all the Egyptians said unto the children of Israel, Remain you here together in your stand and we will go and fight against the children of Esau and Ishmael, and if these kings should prevail over us, then come you altogether upon them and assist us, and the children of Israel did so. ²⁵ And Zepho the son of Eliphaz the son of Esau king of Chittim, and Hadad the son of Bedad king of Edom, and all their camps, and all the children of the east, and children of Ishmael, a people numerous as sand, encamped together in the valley of Pathros opposite Tachpanches. ²⁶ And Balaam the son of Beor the Syrian was there in the camp of Zepho, for he came with the children of Chittim to the battle, and Balaam was a man highly honored in the eyes of Zepho and his men. ²⁷ And Zepho said unto Balaam, Try by divination for us that we may know who will prevail in the battle, we or the Egyptians. ²⁸ And Balaam rose up and tried the art of divination, and he was skillful in the knowledge of it, but he was confused and the work was destroyed in his hand. ²⁹ And he tried it again but it did not succeed, and Balaam despaired of it and left it and did not complete it, for this was from the Lord, in order to cause Zepho and his people to fall into the hand of the children of Israel, who had trusted in the Lord, the God of their ancestors,

in their war. ³⁰ And Zepho and Hadad put their forces in battle array, and all the Egyptians went alone against them, about three hundred thousand men, and not one man of Israel was with them. ³¹ And all the Egyptians fought with these kings opposite Pathros and Tachpanches, and the battle was severe against the Egyptians. ³² And the kings were stronger than the Egyptians in that battle, and about one hundred and eighty men of Egypt fell on that day, and about thirty men of the forces of the kings, and all the men of Egypt fled from before the kings, so the children of Esau and Ishmael pursued the Egyptians, continuing to smite them unto the place where was the camp of the children of Israel. ³³ And all the Egyptians cried unto the children of Israel, saying, Hasten to us and assist us and save us from the hand of Esau, Ishmael and the children of Chittim. ³⁴ And the hundred and fifty men of the children of Israel ran from their station to the camps of these kings, and the children of Israel cried unto the Lord their God to deliver them. ³⁵ And the Lord hearkened to Israel, and the Lord gave all the men of the kings into their hand, and the children of Israel fought against these kings, and the children of Israel smote about four thousand of the kings' men. ³⁶ And the Lord threw a great consternation in the camp of the kings, so that the fear of the children of Israel fell upon them. ³⁷ And all the hosts of the kings fled from before the children of Israel and the children of Israel pursued them continuing to smite them unto the borders of the land of Cush. ³⁸ And the children of Israel slew of them in the road yet two thousand men, and of the children of Israel not one fell. ³⁹ And when the Egyptians saw that the children of Israel had fought with such few men with the kings, and that the battle was so very severe against them, ⁴⁰ All the Egyptians were greatly afraid of their lives on account of the strong battle, and all Egypt fled, every man hiding himself from the arrayed forces, and they hid themselves in the road, and they left the Israelites to fight. ⁴¹ And the children of Israel inflicted a terrible blow upon the kings' men, and they returned from them after they had driven them to the border of the land of Cush. ⁴² And all Israel knew the thing which the men of Egypt had done to them, that they had fled from them in battle, and had left them to fight alone. ⁴³ So the children of Israel also acted with cunning, and as the children of Israel returned from battle, they found some of the Egyptians in the road and smote them there. ⁴⁴ And whilst they slew them, they said unto them these words: ⁴⁵ Wherefore did you go from us and leave us, being a few people, to fight against these kings who had a great people to smite us, that you might thereby deliver your own souls? ⁴⁶ And of some which the Israelites met on the road, they the children of Israel spoke to each other, saying, Smite, smite, for he is an Ishmaelite, or an Edomite, or from the children of Chittim, and they stood over him and slew him, and they knew that he was an Egyptian. ⁴⁷ And the children of Israel did these things cunningly against the Egyptians, because they had deserted them in battle and had fled from them. ⁴⁸ And the children of Israel slew of the men of Egypt in the road in this manner, about two hundred men. ⁴⁹ And all the men of Egypt saw the evil which the children of Israel had done to them, so all Egypt feared greatly the children of Israel, for they had seen their great power, and that not one man of them had fallen. ⁵⁰ So all the children of Israel returned with joy on their road to Goshen, and the rest of Egypt returned each man to his place.

65

¹ And it came to pass after these things, that all the counsellors of Pharaoh, king of Egypt, and all the elders of Egypt assembled and came before the king and bowed down to the ground, and they sat before him. ² And the counsellors and elders of Egypt spoke unto the king, saying, ³ Behold the people of the children of Israel is greater and mightier than we are, and thou knowest all the evil which they did to us in the road when we returned from battle. ⁴ And thou hast also seen their strong power, for this power is unto them from their fathers, for but a few men stood up against a people numerous as the sand, and smote them at the edge of the sword, and of themselves not one has fallen, so that if they had been numerous they would then have utterly destroyed them. ⁵ Now therefore give us counsel what to do with them, until we gradually destroy them from amongst us, lest they become too numerous for us in the land. ⁶ For if the children of Israel should increase in the land, they will become an obstacle to us, and if any war should happen to take place, they with their great strength will join our enemy against us, and fight against us, destroy us from the land and go away from it. ⁷ So the king answered the elders of Egypt and said unto them, This is the plan advised against Israel, from which we will not depart, ⁸ Behold in the land are Pithom and Rameses, cities unfortified against battle, it behooves you and us to build them, and to fortify them. ⁹ Now therefore go you also and act cunningly toward them, and proclaim a voice in Egypt and in Goshen at the command of the king, saying, ¹⁰ All ye men of Egypt, Goshen, Pathros and all their inhabitants! the king has commanded us to build Pithom and Rameses, and to fortify them for battle; who amongst you

of all Egypt, of the children of Israel and of all the inhabitants of the cities, are willing to build with us, shall each have his wages given to him daily at the king's order; so go you first and do cunningly, and gather yourselves and come to Pithom and Rameses to build. ¹¹ And whilst you are building, cause a proclamation of this kind to be made throughout Egypt every day at the command of the king. ¹² And when some of the children of Israel shall come to build with you, you shall give them their wages daily for a few days. ¹³ And after they shall have built with you for their daily hire, drag yourselves away from them daily one by one in secret, and then you shall rise up and become their task-masters and officers, and you shall leave them afterward to build without wages, and should they refuse, then force them with all your might to build. ¹⁴ And if you do this it will be well with us to strengthen our land against the children of Israel, for on account of the fatigue of the building and the work, the children of Israel will decrease, because you will deprive them from their wives day by day. ¹⁵ And all the elders of Egypt heard the counsel of the king, and the counsel seemed good in their eyes and in the eyes of the servants of Pharaoh, and in the eyes of all Egypt, and they did according to the word of the king. ¹⁶ And all the servants went away from the king, and they caused a proclamation to be made in all Egypt, in Tachpanches and in Goshen, and in all the cities which surrounded Egypt, saying, ¹⁷ You have seen what the children of Esau and Ishmael did to us, who came to war against us and wished to destroy us. ¹⁸ Now therefore the king commanded us to fortify the land, to build the cities Pithom and Rameses, and to fortify them for battle, if they should again come against us. ¹⁹ Whosoever of you from all Egypt and from the children of Israel will come to build with us, he shall have his daily wages given by the king, as his command is unto us. ²⁰ And when Egypt and all the children of Israel heard all that the servants of Pharaoh had spoken, there came from the Egyptians, and the children of Israel to build with the servants of Pharaoh, Pithom and Rameses, but none of the children of Levi came with their brethren to build. ²¹ And all the servants of Pharaoh and his princes came at first with deceit to build with all Israel as daily hired laborers, and they gave to Israel their daily hire at the beginning. ²² And the servants of Pharaoh built with all Israel, and were employed in that work with Israel for a month. ²³ And at the end of the month, all the servants of Pharaoh began to withdraw secretly from the people of Israel daily. ²⁴ And Israel went on with the work at that time, but they then received their daily hire, because some of the men of Egypt were yet carrying on the work with Israel at that time; therefore the Egyptians gave Israel their hire in those days, in order that they, the Egyptians their fellow-workmen, might also take the pay for their labor. ²⁵ And at the end of a year and four months all the Egyptians had withdrawn from the children of Israel, so that the children of Israel were left alone engaged in the work. ²⁶ And after all the Egyptians had withdrawn from the children of Israel they returned and became oppressors and officers over them, and some of them stood over the children of Israel as task masters, to receive from them all that they gave them for the pay of their labor. ²⁷ And the Egyptians did in this manner to the children of Israel day by day, in order to afflict in their work. ²⁸ And all the children of Israel were alone engaged in the labor, and the Egyptians refrained from giving any pay to the children of Israel from that time forward. ²⁹ And when some of the men of Israel refused to work on account of the wages not being given to them, then the exactors and the servants of Pharaoh oppressed them and smote them with heavy blows, and made them return by force, to labor with their brethren; thus did all the Egyptians unto the children of Israel all the days. ³⁰ And all the children of Israel were greatly afraid of the Egyptians in this matter, and all the children of Israel returned and worked alone without pay. ³¹ And the children of Israel built Pithom and Rameses, and all the children of Israel did the work, some making bricks, and some building, and the children of Israel built and fortified all the land of Egypt and its walls, and the children of Israel were engaged in work for many years, until the time came when the Lord remembered them and brought them out of Egypt. ³² But the children of Levi were not employed in the work with their brethren of Israel, from the beginning unto the day of their going forth from Egypt. ³³ For all the children of Levi knew that the Egyptians had spoken all these words with deceit to the Israelites, therefore the children of Levi refrained from approaching to the work with their brethren. ³⁴ And the Egyptians did not direct their attention to make the children of Levi work afterward, since they had not been with their brethren at the beginning, therefore the Egyptians left them alone. ³⁵ And the hands of the men of Egypt were directed with continued severity against the children of Israel in that work, and the Egyptians made the children of Israel work with rigor. ³⁶ And the Egyptians embittered the lives of the children of Israel with hard work, in mortar and bricks, and also in all manner of work in the field. ³⁷ And the children of Israel called Melol the king of Egypt "Meror, king of Egypt," because in his days the Egyptians had embittered their lives with all manner of work. ³⁸ And all the work wherein the Egyptians made the children of Israel labor, they exacted with rigor, in order to afflict the children of Israel, but the more they afflicted them, the more they increased and grew, and the Egyptians were grieved because of the children of Israel.

66

¹ At that time died Hadad the son of Bedad king of Edom, and Samlah from Mesrekah, from the country of the children of the east, reigned in his place. ² In the thirteenth year of the reign of Pharaoh king of Egypt, which was the hundred and twenty-fifth year of the Israelites going down into Egypt, Samlah had reigned over Edom eighteen years. ³ And when he reigned, he drew forth his hosts to go and fight against Zepho the son of Eliphaz and the children of Chittim, because they had made war against Angeas king of Africa, and they destroyed his whole army. ⁴ But he did not engage with him, for the children of Esau prevented him, saying, He was their brother, so Samlah listened to the voice of the children of Esau, and turned back with all his forces to the land of Edom, and did not proceed to fight against Zepho the son of Eliphaz. ⁵ And Pharaoh king of Egypt heard this thing, saying, Samlah king of Edom has resolved to fight the children of Chittim, and afterward he will come to fight against Egypt. ⁶ And when the Egyptians heard this matter, they increased the labor upon the children of Israel, lest the Israelites should do unto them as they did unto them in their war with the children of Esau in the days of Hadad. ⁷ So the Egyptians said unto the children of Israel, Hasten and do your work, and finish your task, and strengthen the land, lest the children of Esau your brethren should come to fight against us, for on your account will they come against us. ⁸ And the children of Israel did the work of the men of Egypt day by day, and the Egyptians afflicted the children of Israel in order to lessen them in the land. ⁹ But as the Egyptians increased the labor upon the children of Israel, so did the children of Israel increase and multiply, and all Egypt was filled with the children of Israel. ¹⁰ And in the hundred and twenty-fifth year of Israel's going down into Egypt, all the Egyptians saw that their counsel did not succeed against Israel, but that they increased and grew, and the land of Egypt and the land of Goshen were filled with the children of Israel. ¹¹ So all the elders of Egypt and its wise men came before the king and bowed down to him and sat before him. ¹² And all the elders of Egypt and the wise men thereof said unto the king, May the king live forever; thou didst counsel us the counsel against the children of Israel, and we did unto them according to the word of the king. ¹³ But in proportion to the increase of the labor so do they increase and grow in the land, and behold the whole country is filled with them. ¹⁴ Now therefore our lord and king, the eyes of all Egypt are upon thee to give them advice with thy wisdom, by which they may prevail over Israel to destroy them, or to diminish them from the land; and the king answered them saying, Give you counsel in this matter that we may know what to do unto them. ¹⁵ And an officer, one of the king's counsellors, whose name was Job, from Mesopotamia, in the land of Uz, answered the king, saying, ¹⁶ If it please the king, let him hear the counsel of his servant; and the king said unto him, Speak. ¹⁷ And Job spoke before the king, the princes, and before all the elders of Egypt, saying, ¹⁸ Behold the counsel of the king which he advised formerly respecting the labor of the children of Israel is very good, and you must not remove from them that labor forever. ¹⁹ But this is the advice counselled by which you may lessen them, if it seems good to the king to afflict them. ²⁰ Behold we have feared war for a long time, and we said, When Israel becomes fruitful in the land, they will drive us from the land if a war should take place. ²¹ If it please the king, let a royal decree go forth, and let it be written in the laws of Egypt which shall not be revoked, that every male child born to the Israelites, his blood shall be spilled upon the ground. ²² And by your doing this, when all the male children of Israel shall have died, the evil of their wars will cease; let the king do so and send for all the Hebrew midwives and order them in this matter to execute it; so the thing pleased the king and the princes, and the king did according to the word of Job. ²³ And the king sent for the Hebrew midwives to be called, of which the name of one was Shephrah, and the name of the other Puah. ²⁴ And the midwives came before the king, and stood in his presence. ²⁵ And the king said unto them, When you do the office of a midwife to the Hebrew women, and see them upon the stools, if it be a son, then you shall kill him, but if it be a daughter, then she shall live. ²⁶ But if you will not do this thing, then will I burn you up and all your houses with fire. ²⁷ But the midwives feared God and did not hearken to the king of Egypt nor to his words, and when the Hebrew women brought forth to the midwife son or daughter, then did the midwife do all that was necessary to the child and let it live; thus did the midwives all the days. ²⁸ And this thing was told to the king, and he sent and called for the midwives and he said to them, Why have you done this thing and have saved the children alive? ²⁹ And the midwives answered and spoke together before the king, saying, ³⁰ Let not the king think that the Hebrew women are as the

Egyptian women, for all the children of Israel are hale, and before the midwife comes to them they are delivered, and as for us thy handmaids, for many days no Hebrew woman has brought forth upon us, for all the Hebrew women are their own midwives, because they are hale. ³¹ And Pharaoh heard their words and believed them in this matter, and the midwives went away from the king, and God dealt well with them, and the people multiplied and waxed exceedingly.

67

¹ There was a man in the land of Egypt of the seed of Levi, whose name was Amram, the son of Kehath, the son of Levi, the son of Israel. ² And this man went and took a wife, namely Jochebed the daughter of Levi his father's sister, and she was one hundred and twenty-six years old, and he came unto her. ³ And the woman conceived and bare a daughter, and she called her name Miriam, because in those days the Egyptians had embittered the lives of the children of Israel. ⁴ And she conceived again and bare a son and she called his name Aaron, for in the days of her conception, Pharaoh began to spill the blood of the male children of Israel. ⁵ In those days died Zepho the son of Eliphaz, son of Esau, king of Chittim, and Janeas reigned in his stead. ⁶ And the time that Zepho reigned over the children of Chittim was fifty years, and he died and was buried in the city of Nabna in the land of Chittim. ⁷ And Janeas, one of the mighty men of the children of Chittim, reigned after him and he reigned fifty years. ⁸ And it was after the death of the king of Chittim that Balaam the son of Beor fled from the land of Chittim, and he went and came to Egypt to Pharaoh king of Egypt. ⁹ And Pharaoh received him with great honor, for he had heard of his wisdom, and he gave him presents and made him for a counsellor, and aggrandized him. ¹⁰ And Balaam dwelt in Egypt, in honor with all the nobles of the king, and the nobles exalted him, because they all coveted to learn his wisdom. ¹¹ And in the hundred and thirtieth year of Israel's going down to Egypt, Pharaoh dreamed that he was sitting upon his kingly throne, and lifted up his eyes and saw an old man standing before him, and there were scales in the hands of the old man, such scales as are used by merchants. ¹² And the old man took the scales and hung them before Pharaoh. ¹³ And the old man took all the elders of Egypt and all its nobles and great men, and he tied them together and put them in one scale. ¹⁴ And he took a milk kid and put it into the other scale, and the kid preponderated over all. ¹⁵ And Pharaoh was astonished at this dreadful vision, why the kid should preponderate over all, and Pharaoh awoke and behold it was a dream. ¹⁶ And Pharaoh rose up early in the morning and called all his servants and related to them the dream, and the men were greatly afraid. ¹⁷ And the king said to all his wise men, Interpret I pray you the dream which I dreamed, that I may know it. ¹⁸ And Balaam the son of Beor answered the king and said unto him, This means nothing else but a great evil that will spring up against Egypt in the latter days. ¹⁹ For a son will be born to Israel who will destroy all Egypt and its inhabitants, and bring forth the Israelites from Egypt with a mighty hand. ²⁰ Now therefore, O king, take counsel upon this matter, that you may destroy the hope of the children of Israel and their expectation, before this evil arise against Egypt. ²¹ And the king said unto Balaam, And what shall we do unto Israel? surely after a certain manner did we at first counsel against them and could not prevail over them. ²² Now therefore give you also advice against them by which we may prevail over them. ²³ And Balaam answered the king, saying, Send now and call thy two counsellors, and we will see what their advice is upon this matter and afterward thy servant will speak. ²⁴ And the king sent and called his two counsellors Reuel the Midianite and Job the Uzite, and they came and sat before the king. ²⁵ And the king said to them, Behold you have both heard the dream which I have dreamed, and the interpretation thereof; now therefore give counsel and know and see what is to be done to the children of Israel, whereby we may prevail over them, before their evil shall spring up against us. ²⁶ And Reuel the Midianite answered the king and said, May the king live, may the king live forever. ²⁷ If it seem good to the king, let him desist from the Hebrews and leave them, and let him not stretch forth his hand against them. ²⁸ For these are they whom the Lord chose in days of old, and took as the lot of his inheritance from amongst all the nations of the earth and the kings of the earth; and who is there that stretched his hand against them with impunity, of whom their God was not avenged? ²⁹ Surely thou knowest that when Abraham went down to Egypt, Pharaoh, the former king of Egypt, saw Sarah his wife, and took her for a wife, because Abraham said, She is my sister, for he was afraid, lest the men of Egypt should slay him on account of his wife. ³⁰ And when the king of Egypt had taken Sarah then God smote him and his household with heavy plagues, until he restored unto Abraham his wife Sarah, then was he healed. ³¹ And Abimelech the Gerarite, king of the Philistines, God punished on account of Sarah wife of Abraham, in stopping up every womb from man to beast. ³² When their God came to Abimelech in the dream of night and terrified him in order that he might restore to Abraham Sarah whom he had taken, and afterward all the people of Gerar were punished on account of Sarah, and Abraham prayed to his God for them, and he was entreated of him, and he healed them. ³³ And Abimelech feared all this evil that came upon him and his people, and he returned to Abraham his wife Sarah, and gave him with her many gifts. ³⁴ He did so also to Isaac when he had driven him from Gerar, and God had done wonderful things to him, that all the water courses of Gerar were dried up, and their productive trees did not bring forth. ³⁵ Until Abimelech of Gerar, and Ahuzzath one of his friends, and Pichol the captain of his host, went to him and they bent and bowed down before him to the ground. ³⁶ And they requested of him to supplicate for them, and he prayed to the Lord for them, and the Lord was entreated of him and he healed them. ³⁷ Jacob also, the plain man, was delivered through his integrity from the hand of his brother Esau, and the hand of Laban the Syrian his mother's brother, who had sought his life; likewise from the hand of all the kings of Canaan who had come together against him and his children to destroy them, and the Lord delivered them out of their hands, that they turned upon them and smote them, for who had ever stretched forth his hand against them with impunity? ³⁸ Surely Pharaoh the former, thy father's father, raised Joseph the son of Jacob above all the princes of the land of Egypt, when he saw his wisdom, for through his wisdom he rescued all the inhabitants of the land from the famine. ³⁹ After which he ordered Jacob and his children to come down to Egypt, in order that through their virtue, the land of Egypt and the land of Goshen might be delivered from the famine. ⁴⁰ Now therefore if it seem good in thine eyes, cease from destroying the children of Israel, but if it be not thy will that they shall dwell in Egypt, send them forth from here, that they may go to the land of Canaan, the land where their ancestors sojourned. ⁴¹ And when Pharaoh heard the words of Jethro he was very angry with him, so that he rose with shame from the king's presence, and went to Midian, his land, and took Joseph's stick with him. ⁴² And the king said to Job the Uzite, What sayest thou Job, and what is thy advice respecting the Hebrews? ⁴³ So Job said to the king, Behold all the inhabitants of the land are in thy power, let the king do as it seems good in his eyes. ⁴⁴ And the king said unto Balaam, What dost thou say, Balaam, speak thy word that we may hear it. ⁴⁵ And Balaam said to the king, Of all that the king has counselled against the Hebrews will they be delivered, and the king will not be able to prevail over them with any counsel. ⁴⁶ For if thou thinkest to lessen them by the flaming fire, thou canst not prevail over them, for surely their God delivered Abraham their father from Ur of the Chaldeans; and if thou thinkest to destroy them with a sword, surely Isaac their father was delivered from it, and a ram was placed in his stead. ⁴⁷ And if with hard and rigorous labor thou thinkest to lessen them, thou wilt not prevail even in this, for their father Jacob served Laban in all manner of hard work, and prospered. ⁴⁸ Now therefore, O King, hear my words, for this is the counsel which is counselled against them, by which thou wilt prevail over them, and from which thou shouldst not depart. ⁴⁹ If it please the king let him order all their children which shall be born from this day forward, to be thrown into the water, for by this canst thou wipe away their name, for none of them, nor of their fathers, were tried in this manner. ⁵⁰ And the king heard the words of Balaam, and the thing pleased the king and the princes, and the king did according to the word of Balaam. ⁵¹ And the king ordered a proclamation to be issued and a law to be made throughout the land of Egypt, saying, Every male child born to the Hebrews from this day forward shall be thrown into the water. ⁵² And Pharaoh called unto all his servants, saying, Go now and seek throughout the land of Goshen where the children of Israel are, and see that every son born to the Hebrews shall be cast into the river, but every daughter you shall let live. ⁵³ And when the children of Israel heard this thing which Pharaoh had commanded, to cast their male children into the river, some of the people separated from their wives and others adhered to them. ⁵⁴ And from that day forward, when the time of delivery arrived to those women of Israel who had remained with their husbands, they went to the field to bring forth there, and they brought forth in the field, and left their children upon the field and returned home. ⁵⁵ And the Lord who had sworn to their ancestors to multiply them, sent one of his ministering angels which are in heaven to wash each child in water, to anoint and swathe it and to put into its hands two smooth stones from one of which it sucked milk and from the other honey, and he caused its hair to grow to its knees, by which it might cover itself; to comfort it and to cleave to it, through his compassion for it. ⁵⁶ And when God had compassion over them and had desired to multiply them upon the face of the land, he ordered his earth to receive them to be preserved therein till the time of their growing up, after which the earth opened its mouth and vomited them forth and they sprouted forth from the city like the herb of the earth, and the grass of the forest, and they returned each to his family and to his father's house, and they remained with them. ⁵⁷ And the babes of the children of Israel were upon the earth like the herb

of the field, through God's grace to them. ⁵⁸ And when all the Egyptians saw this thing, they went forth, each to his field with his yoke of oxen and his ploughshare, and they ploughed it up as one ploughs the earth at seed time. ⁵⁹ And when they ploughed they were unable to hurt the infants of the children of Israel, so the people increased and waxed exceedingly. ⁶⁰ And Pharaoh ordered his officers daily to go to Goshen to seek for the babes of the children of Israel. ⁶¹ And when they had sought and found one, they took it from its mother's bosom by force, and threw it into the river, but the female child they left with its mother; thus did the Egyptians do to the Israelites all the days.

68

¹ And it was at that time the spirit of God was upon Miriam the daughter of Amram the sister of Aaron, and she went forth and prophesied about the house, saying, Behold a son will be born unto us from my father and mother this time, and he will save Israel from the hands of Egypt. ² And when Amram heard the words of his daughter, he went and took his wife back to the house, after he had driven her away at the time when Pharaoh ordered every male child of the house of Jacob to be thrown into the water. ³ So Amram took Jochebed his wife, three years after he had driven her away, and he came to her and she conceived. ⁴ And at the end of seven months from her conception she brought forth a son, and the whole house was filled with great light as of the light of the sun and moon at the time of their shining. ⁵ And when the woman saw the child that it was good and pleasing to the sight, she hid it for three months in an inner room. ⁶ In those days the Egyptians conspired to destroy all the Hebrews there. ⁷ And the Egyptian women went to Goshen where the children of Israel were, and they carried their young ones upon their shoulders, their babes who could not yet speak. ⁸ And in those days, when the women of the children of Israel brought forth, each woman had hidden her son from before the Egyptians, that the Egyptians might not know of their bringing forth, and might not destroy them from the land. ⁹ And the Egyptian women came to Goshen and their children who could not speak were upon their shoulders, and when an Egyptian woman came into the house of a Hebrew woman her babe began to cry. ¹⁰ And when it cried the child that was in the inner room answered it, so the Egyptian women went and told it at the house of Pharaoh. ¹¹ And Pharaoh sent his officers to take the children and slay them; thus did the Egyptians to the Hebrew women all the days. ¹² And it was at that time, about three months from Jochebed's concealment of her son, that the thing was known in Pharaoh's house. ¹³ And the woman hastened to take away her son before the officers came, and she took for him an ark of bulrushes, and daubed it with slime and with pitch, and put the child therein, and she laid it in the flags by the river's brink. ¹⁴ And his sister Miriam stood afar off to know what would be done to him, and what would become of her words. ¹⁵ And God sent forth at that time a terrible heat in the land of Egypt, which burned up the flesh of man like the sun in his circuit, and it greatly oppressed the Egyptians. ¹⁶ And all the Egyptians went down to bathe in the river, on account of the consuming heat which burned up their flesh. ¹⁷ And Bathia, the daughter of Pharaoh, went also to bathe in the river, owing to the consuming heat, and her maidens walked at the river side, and all the women of Egypt as well. ¹⁸ And Bathia lifted up her eyes to the river, and she saw the ark upon the water, and sent her maid to fetch it. ¹⁹ And she opened it and saw the child, and behold the babe wept, and she had compassion on him, and she said, This is one of the Hebrew children. ²⁰ And all the women of Egypt walking on the river side desired to give him suck, but he would not suck, for this thing was from the Lord, in order to restore him to his mother's breast. ²¹ And Miriam his sister was at that time amongst the Egyptian women at the river side, and she saw this thing and she said to Pharaoh's daughter, Shall I go and fetch a nurse of the Hebrew women, that she may nurse the child for thee? ²² And Pharaoh's daughter said to her, Go, and the young woman went and called the child's mother. ²³ And Pharaoh's daughter said to Jochebed, Take this child away and suckle it for me, and I will pay thee thy wages, two bits of silver daily; and the woman took the child and nursed it. ²⁴ And at the end of two years, when the child grew up, she brought him to the daughter of Pharaoh, and he was unto her as a son, and she called his name Moses, for she said, Because I drew him out of the water. ²⁵ And Amram his father called his name Chabar, for he said, It was for him that he associated with his wife whom he had turned away. ²⁶ And Jochebed his mother called his name Jekuthiel, Because, she said, I have hoped for him to the Almighty, and God restored him unto me. ²⁷ And Miriam his sister called him Jered, for she descended after him to the river to know what his end would be. ²⁸ And Aaron his brother called his name Abi Zanuch, saying, My father left my mother and returned to her on his account. ²⁹ And Kehath the father of Amram called his name Abigdor, because on his account did God repair the breach of the house of Jacob, that they could no longer throw their male children into the water. ³⁰ And their nurse called him Abi Socho, saying, In his tabernacle was he hidden for three months, on account of the children of Ham. ³¹ And all Israel called his name Shemaiah, son of Nethanel, for they said, In his days has God heard their cries and rescued them from their oppressors. ³² And Moses was in Pharaoh's house, and was unto Bathia, Pharaoh's daughter, as a son, and Moses grew up amongst the king's children.

69

¹ And the king of Edom died in those days, in the eighteenth year of his reign, and was buried in his temple which he had built for himself as his royal residence in the land of Edom. ² And the children of Esau sent to Pethor, which is upon the river, and they fetched from there a young man of beautiful eyes and comely aspect, whose name was Saul, and they made him king over them in the place of Samlah. ³ And Saul reigned over all the children of Esau in the land of Edom for forty years. ⁴ And when Pharaoh king of Egypt saw that the counsel which Balaam had advised respecting the children of Israel did not succeed, but that still they were fruitful, multiplied and increased throughout the land of Egypt, ⁵ Then Pharaoh commanded in those days that a proclamation should be issued throughout Egypt to the children of Israel, saying, No man shall diminish any thing of his daily labor. ⁶ And the man who shall be found deficient in his labor which he performs daily, whether in mortar or in bricks, then his youngest son shall be put in their place. ⁷ And the labor of Egypt strengthened upon the children of Israel in those days, and behold if one brick was deficient in any man's daily labor, the Egyptians took his youngest boy by force from his mother, and put him into the building in the place of the brick which his father had left wanting. ⁸ And the men of Egypt did so to all the children of Israel day by day, all the days for a long period. ⁹ But the tribe of Levi did not at that time work with the Israelites their brethren, from the beginning, for the children of Levi knew the cunning of the Egyptians which they exercised at first toward the Israelites.

70

¹ And in the third year from the birth of Moses, Pharaoh was sitting at a banquet, when Alparanith the queen was sitting at his right and Bathia at his left, and the lad Moses was lying upon her bosom, and Balaam the son of Beor with his two sons, and all the princes of the kingdom were sitting at table in the king's presence. ² And the lad stretched forth his hand upon the king's head, and took the crown from the king's head and placed it on his own head. ³ And when the king and princes saw the work which the boy had done, the king and princes were terrified, and one man to his neighbor expressed astonishment. ⁴ And the king said unto the princes who were before him at table, What speak you and what say you, O ye princes, in this matter, and what is to be the judgment against the boy on account of this act? ⁵ And Balaam the son of Beor the magician answered before the king and princes, and he said, Remember now, O my lord and king, the dream which thou didst dream many days since, and that which thy servant interpreted unto thee. ⁶ Now therefore this is a child from the Hebrew children, in whom is the spirit of God, and let not my lord the king imagine that this youngster did this thing without knowledge. ⁷ For he is a Hebrew boy, and wisdom and understanding are with him, although he is yet a child, and with wisdom has he done this and chosen unto himself the kingdom of Egypt. ⁸ For this is the manner of all the Hebrews to deceive kings and their nobles, to do all these things cunningly, in order to make the kings of the earth and their men tremble. ⁹ Surely thou knowest that Abraham their father acted thus, who deceived the army of Nimrod king of Babel, and Abimelech king of Gerar, and that he possessed himself of the land of the children of Heth and all the kingdoms of Canaan. ¹⁰ And that he descended into Egypt and said of Sarah his wife, she is my sister, in order to mislead Egypt and her king. ¹¹ His son Isaac also did so when he went to Gerar and dwelt there, and his strength prevailed over the army of Abimelech king of the Philistines. ¹² He also thought of making the kingdom of the Philistines stumble, in saying that Rebecca his wife was his sister. ¹³ Jacob also dealt treacherously with his brother, and took from his hand his birthright and his blessing. ¹⁴ He went then to Padan-aram to the house of Laban his mother's brother, and cunningly obtained from him his daughter, his cattle, and all belonging to him, and fled away and returned to the land of Canaan to his father. ¹⁵ His sons sold their brother Joseph, who went down into Egypt and became a slave, and was placed in the prison house for twelve years. ¹⁶ Until the former Pharaoh dreamed dreams, and withdrew him from the prison house, and magnified him above all the princes in Egypt on account of his interpreting his dreams to him. ¹⁷ And when God caused a famine throughout the land he sent for and brought his father and all his brothers, and the whole of his father's household, and supported them without price or reward, and bought the Egyptians for slaves. ¹⁸ Now therefore my lord king behold this child has risen up in their stead in Egypt, to do according to their deeds and to trifle with every king, prince and judge. ¹⁹ If it please

the king, let us now spill his blood upon the ground, lest he grow up and take away the government from thy hand, and the hope of Egypt perish after he shall have reigned. [20] And Balaam said to the king, Let us moreover call for all the judges of Egypt and the wise men thereof, and let us know if the judgment of death is due to this boy as thou didst say, and then we will slay him. [21] And Pharaoh sent and called for all the wise men of Egypt and they came before the king, and an angel of the Lord came amongst them, and he was like one of the wise men of Egypt. [22] And the king said to the wise men, Surely you have heard what this Hebrew boy who is in the house has done, and thus has Balaam judged in the matter. [23] Now judge you also and see what is due to the boy for the act he has committed. [24] And the angel, who seemed like one of the wise men of Pharaoh, answered and said as follows, before all the wise men of Egypt and before the king and the princes: [25] If it please the king let the king send for men who shall bring before him an onyx stone and a coal of fire, and place them before the child, and if the child shall stretch forth his hand and take the onyx stone, then shall we know that with wisdom has the youth done all that he has done, and we must slay him. [26] But if he stretch forth his hand upon the coal, then shall we know that it was not with knowledge that he did this thing, and he shall live. [27] And the thing seemed good in the eyes of the king and the princes, so the king did according to the word of the angel of the Lord. [28] And the king ordered the onyx stone and coal to be brought and placed before Moses. [29] And they placed the boy before them, and the lad endeavored to stretch forth his hand to the onyx stone, but the angel of the Lord took his hand and placed it upon the coal, and the coal became extinguished in his hand, and he lifted it up and put it into his mouth, and burned part of his lips and part of his tongue, and he became heavy in mouth and tongue. [30] And when the king and princes saw this, they knew that Moses had not acted with wisdom in taking off the crown from the king's head. [31] So the king and princes refrained from slaying the child, so Moses remained in Pharaoh's house, growing up, and the Lord was with him. [32] And whilst the boy was in the king's house, he was robed in purple and he grew amongst the children of the king. [33] And when Moses grew up in the king's house, Bathia the daughter of Pharaoh considered him as a son, and all the household of Pharaoh honored him, and all the men of Egypt were afraid of him. [34] And he daily went forth and came into the land of Goshen, where his brethren the children of Israel were, and Moses saw them daily in shortness of breath and hard labor. [35] And Moses asked them, saying, Wherefore is this labor meted out unto you day by day? [36] And they told him all that had befallen them, and all the injunctions which Pharaoh had put upon them before his birth. [37] And they told him all the counsels which Balaam the son of Beor had counselled against them, and what he had also counselled against him in order to slay him when he had taken the king's crown from off his head. [38] And when Moses heard these things his anger was kindled against Balaam, and he sought to kill him, and he was in ambush for him day by day. [39] And Balaam was afraid of Moses, and he and his two sons rose up and went forth from Egypt, and they fled and delivered their souls and betook themselves to the land of Cush to Kikianus, king of Cush. [40] And Moses was in the king's house going out and coming in, the Lord gave him favor in the eyes of Pharaoh, and in the eyes of all his servants, and in the eyes of all the people of Egypt, and they loved Moses exceedingly. [41] And the day arrived when Moses went to Goshen to see his brethren, that he saw the children of Israel in their burdens and hard labor, and Moses was grieved on their account. [42] And Moses returned to Egypt and came to the house of Pharaoh, and came before the king, and Moses bowed down before the king. [43] And Moses said unto Pharaoh, I pray thee my lord, I have come to seek a small request from thee, turn not away my face empty; and Pharaoh said unto him, Speak. [44] And Moses said unto Pharaoh, Let there be given unto thy servants the children of Israel who are in Goshen, one day to rest therein from their labor. [45] And the king answered Moses and said, Behold I have lifted up thy face in this thing to grant thy request. [46] And Pharaoh ordered a proclamation to be issued throughout Egypt and Goshen, saying, [47] To you, all the children of Israel, thus says the king, for six days you shall do your work and labor, but on the seventh day you shall rest, and shall not preform any work, thus shall you do all the days, as the king and Moses the son of Bathia have commanded. [48] And Moses rejoiced at this thing which the king had granted to him, and all the children of Israel did as Moses ordered them. [49] For this thing was from the Lord to the children of Israel, for the Lord had begun to remember the children of Israel to save them for the sake of their fathers. [50] And the Lord was with Moses and his fame went throughout Egypt. [51] And Moses became great in the eyes of all the Egyptians, and in the eyes of all the children of Israel, seeking good for his people Israel and speaking words of peace regarding them to the king.

71

[1] And when Moses was eighteen years old, he desired to see his father and mother and he went to them to Goshen, and when Moses had come near Goshen, he came to the place where the children of Israel were engaged in work, and he observed their burdens, and he saw an Egyptian smiting one of his Hebrew brethren. [2] And when the man who was beaten saw Moses he ran to him for help, for the man Moses was greatly respected in the house of Pharaoh, and he said to him, My lord attend to me, this Egyptian came to my house in the night, bound me, and came to my wife in my presence, and now he seeks to take my life away. [3] And when Moses heard this wicked thing, his anger was kindled against the Egyptian, and he turned this way and the other, and when he saw there was no man there he smote the Egyptian and hid him in the sand, and delivered the Hebrew from the hand of him that smote him. [4] And the Hebrew went to his house, and Moses returned to his home, and went forth and came back to the king's house. [5] And when the man had returned home, he thought of repudiating his wife, for it was not right in the house of Jacob, for any man to come to his wife after she had been defiled. [6] And the woman went and told her brothers, and the woman's brothers sought to slay him, and he fled to his house and escaped. [7] And on the second day Moses went forth to his brethren, and saw, and behold two men were quarreling, and he said to the wicked one, Why dost thou smite thy neighbor? [8] And he answered him and said to him, Who has set thee for a prince and judge over us? dost thou think to slay me as thou didst slay the Egyptian? and Moses was afraid and he said, Surely the thing is known? [9] And Pharaoh heard of this affair, and he ordered Moses to be slain, so God sent his angel, and he appeared unto Pharaoh in the likeness of a captain of the guard. [10] And the angel of the Lord took the sword from the hand of the captain of the guard, and took his head off with it, for the likeness of the captain of the guard was turned into the likeness of Moses. [11] And the angel of the Lord took hold of the right hand of Moses, and brought him forth from Egypt, and placed him from without the borders of Egypt, a distance of forty days' journey. [12] And Aaron his brother alone remained in the land of Egypt, and he prophesied to the children of Israel, saying, [13] Thus says the Lord God of your ancestors, Throw away, each man, the abominations of his eyes, and do not defile yourselves with the idols of Egypt. [14] And the children of Israel rebelled and would not hearken to Aaron at that time. [15] And the Lord thought to destroy them, were it not that the Lord remembered the covenant which he had made with Abraham, Isaac and Jacob. [16] In those days the hand of Pharaoh continued to be severe against the children of Israel, and he crushed and oppressed them until the time when God sent forth his word and took notice of them.

72

[1] And it was in those days that there was a great war between the children of Cush and the children of the east and Aram, and they rebelled against the king of Cush in whose hands they were. [2] So Kikianus king of Cush went forth with all the children of Cush, a people numerous as the sand, and he went to fight against Aram and the children of the east, to bring them under subjection. [3] And when Kikianus went out, he left Balaam the magician, with his two sons, to guard the city, and the lowest sort of the people of the land. [4] So Kikianus went forth to Aram and the children of the east, and he fought against them and smote them, and they all fell down wounded before Kikianus and his people. [5] And he took many of them captives and he brought them under subjection as at first, and he encamped upon their land to take tribute from them as usual. [6] And Balaam the son of Beor, when the king of Cush had left him to guard the city and the poor of the city, he rose up and advised with the people of the land to rebel against king Kikianus, not to let him enter the city when he should come home. [7] And the people of the land hearkened to him, and they swore to him and made him king over them, and his two sons for captains of the army. [8] So they rose up and raised the walls of the city at the two corners, and they built an exceeding strong building. [9] And at the third corner they dug ditches without number, between the city and the river which surrounded the whole land of Cush, and they made the waters of the river burst forth there. [10] At the fourth corner they collected numerous serpents by their incantations and enchantments, and they fortified the city and dwelt therein, and no one went out or in before them. [11] And Kikianus fought against Aram and the children of the east and he subdued them as before, and they gave him their usual tribute, and he went and returned to his land. [12] And when Kikianus the king of Cush approached his city and all the captains of the forces with him, they lifted up their eyes and saw that the walls of the city were built up and greatly elevated, so the men were astonished at this. [13] And they said one to the other, It is because they saw that we were delayed, in battle, and were greatly afraid of us, therefore have they done this thing and raised the city walls and fortified them so that the kings of Canaan might not come in battle against them. [14] So the king and the troops approached the city door and they looked up and behold, all the gates of the city were closed, and they

called out to the sentinels, saying, Open unto us, that we may enter the city. ¹⁵ But the sentinels refused to open to them by the order of Balaam the magician, their king, they suffered them not to enter their city. ¹⁶ So they raised a battle with them opposite the city gate, and one hundred and thirty men of the army at Kikianus fell on that day. ¹⁷ And on the next day they continued to fight and they fought at the side of the river; they endeavored to pass but were not able, so some of them sank in the pits and died. ¹⁸ So the king ordered them to cut down trees to make rafts, upon which they might pass to them, and they did so. ¹⁹ And when they came to the place of the ditches, the waters revolved by mills, and two hundred men upon ten rafts were drowned. ²⁰ And on the third day they came to fight at the side where the serpents were, but they could not approach there, for the serpents slew of them one hundred and seventy men, and they ceased fighting against Cush, and they besieged Cush for nine years, no person came out or in. ²¹ At that time that the war and the siege were against Cush, Moses fled from Egypt from Pharaoh who sought to kill him for having slain the Egyptian. ²² And Moses was eighteen years old when he fled from Egypt from the presence of Pharaoh, and he fled and escaped to the camp of Kikianus, which at that time was besieging Cush. ²³ And Moses was nine years in the camp of Kikianus king of Cush, all the time that they were besieging Cush, and Moses went out and came in with them. ²⁴ And the king and princes and all the fighting men loved Moses, for he was great and worthy, his stature was like a noble lion, his face was like the sun, and his strength was like that of a lion, and he was counsellor to the king. ²⁵ And at the end of nine years, Kikianus was seized with a mortal disease, and his illness prevailed over him, and he died on the seventh day. ²⁶ So his servants embalmed him and carried him and buried him opposite the city gate to the north of the land of Egypt. ²⁷ And they built over him an elegant strong and high building, and they placed great stones below. ²⁸ And the king's scribes engraved upon those stones all the might of their king Kikianus, and all his battles which he had fought, behold they are written there at this day. ²⁹ Now after the death of Kikianus king of Cush it grieved his men and troops greatly on account of the war. ³⁰ So they said one to the other, Give us counsel what we are to do at this time, as we have resided in the wilderness nine years away from our homes. ³¹ If we say we will fight against the city many of us will fall wounded or killed, and if we remain here in the siege we shall also die. ³² For now all the kings of Aram and of the children of the east will hear that our king is dead, and they will attack us suddenly in a hostile manner, and they will fight against us and leave no remnant of us. ³³ Now therefore let us go and make a king over us, and let us remain in the siege until the city is delivered up to us. ³⁴ And they wished to choose on that day a man for king from the army of Kikianus, and they found no object of their choice like Moses to reign over them. ³⁵ And they hastened and stripped off each man his garments and cast them upon the ground, and they made a great heap and placed Moses thereon. ³⁶ And they rose up and blew with trumpets and called out before him, and said, May the king live, may the king live! ³⁷ And all the people and nobles swore unto him to give him for a wife Adoniah the queen, the Cushite, wife of Kikianus, and they made Moses king over them on that day. ³⁸ And all the people of Cush issued a proclamation on that day, saying, Every man must give something to Moses of what is in his possession. ³⁹ And they spread out a sheet upon the heap, and every man cast into it something of what he had, one a gold earring and the other a coin. ⁴⁰ Also of onyx stones, bdellium, pearls and marble did the children of Cush cast unto Moses upon the heap, also silver and gold in great abundance. ⁴¹ And Moses took all the silver and gold, all the vessels, and the bdellium and onyx stones, which all the children of Cush had given to him, and he placed them amongst his treasures. ⁴² And Moses reigned over the children of Cush on that day, in the place of Kikianus king of Cush.

73

¹ In the fifty-fifth year of the reign of Pharaoh king of Egypt, that is in the hundred and fifty-seventh year of the Israelites going down into Egypt, reigned Moses in Cush. ² Moses was twenty-seven years old when he began to reign over Cush, and forty years did he reign. ³ And the Lord granted Moses favor and grace in the eyes of all the children of Cush, and the children of Cush loved him exceedingly, so Moses was favored by the Lord and by men. ⁴ And in the seventh day of his reign, all the children of Cush assembled and came before Moses and bowed down to him to the ground. ⁵ And all the children spoke together in the presence of the king, saying, Give us counsel that we may see what is to be done to this city. ⁶ For it is now nine years that we have been besieging round about the city, and have not seen our children and our wives. ⁷ So the king answered them, saying, If you will hearken to my voice in all that I shall command you, then will the Lord give the city into our hands and we shall subdue it. ⁸ For if we fight with them as in the former battle which we had with them before the death of Kikianus, many of us will fall down wounded as before. ⁹ Now therefore behold here is counsel for you in this matter; if you will hearken to my voice, then will the city be delivered into our hands. ¹⁰ So all the forces answered the king, saying, All that our lord shall command that will we do. ¹¹ And Moses said unto them, Pass through and proclaim a voice in the whole camp unto all the people, saying, ¹² Thus says the king, Go into the forest and bring with you of the young ones of the stork, each man a young one in his hand. ¹³ And any person transgressing the word of the king, who shall not bring his young one, he shall die, and the king will take all belonging to him. ¹⁴ And when you shall bring them they shall be in your keeping, you shall rear them until they grow up, and you shall teach them to dart upon, as is the way of the young ones of the hawk. ¹⁵ So all the children of Cush heard the words of Moses, and they rose up and caused a proclamation to be issued throughout the camp, saying, ¹⁶ Unto you, all the children of Cush, the king's order is, that you go all together to the forest, and catch there the young storks each man his young one in his hand, and you shall bring them home. ¹⁷ And any person violating the order of the king shall die, and the king will take all that belongs to him. ¹⁸ And all the people did so, and they went out to the wood and they climbed the fir trees and caught, each man a young one in his hand, all the young of the storks, and they brought them into the desert and reared them by order of the king, and they taught them to dart upon, similar to the young hawks. ¹⁹ And after the young storks were reared, the king ordered them to be hungered for three days, and all the people did so. ²⁰ And on the third day, the king said unto them, strengthen yourselves and become valiant men, and put on each man his armor and gird on his sword upon him, and ride each man his horse and take each his young stork in his hand. ²¹ And we will rise up and fight against the city at the place where the serpents are; and all the people did as the king had ordered. ²² And they took each man his young one in his hand, and they went away, and when they came to the place of the serpents the king said to them, Send forth each man his young stork upon the serpents. ²³ And they sent forth each man his young stork at the king's order, and the young storks ran upon the serpents and they devoured them all and destroyed them out of that place. ²⁴ And when the king and people had seen that all the serpents were destroyed in that place, all the people set up a great shout. ²⁵ And they approached and fought against the city and took it and subdued it, and they entered the city. ²⁶ And there died on that day one thousand and one hundred men of the people of the city, all that inhabited the city, but of the people besieging not one died. ²⁷ So all the children of Cush went each to his home, to his wife and children and to all belonging to him. ²⁸ And Balaam the magician, when he saw that the city was taken, he opened the gate and he and his two sons and eight brothers fled and returned to Egypt to Pharaoh king of Egypt. ²⁹ They are the sorcerers and magicians who are mentioned in the book of the law, standing against Moses when the Lord brought the plagues upon Egypt. ³⁰ So Moses took the city by his wisdom, and the children of Cush placed him on the throne instead of Kikianus king of Cush. ³¹ And they placed the royal crown upon his head, and they gave him for a wife Adoniah the Cushite queen, wife of Kikianus. ³² And Moses feared the Lord God of his fathers, so that he came not to her, nor did he turn his eyes to her. ³³ For Moses remembered how Abraham had made his servant Eliezer swear, saying unto him, Thou shalt not take a woman from the daughters of Canaan for my son Isaac. ³⁴ Also what Isaac did when Jacob had fled from his brother, when he commanded him, saying, Thou shalt not take a wife from the daughters of Canaan, nor make alliance with any of the children of Ham. ³⁵ For the Lord our God gave Ham the son of Noah, and his children and all his seed, as slaves to the children of Shem and to the children of Japheth, and unto their seed after them for slaves, forever. ³⁶ Therefore Moses turned not his heart nor his eyes to the wife of Kikianus all the days that he reigned over Cush. ³⁷ And Moses feared the Lord his God all his life, and Moses walked before the Lord in truth, with all his heart and soul, he turned not from the right way all the days of his life; he declined not from the way either to the right or to the left, in which Abraham, Isaac and Jacob had walked. ³⁸ And Moses strengthened himself in the kingdom of the children of Cush, and he guided the children of Cush with his usual wisdom, and Moses prospered in his kingdom. ³⁹ And at that time Aram and the children of the east heard that Kikianus king of Cush had died, so Aram and the children of the east rebelled against Cush in those days. ⁴⁰ And Moses gathered all the children of Cush, a people very mighty, about thirty thousand men, and he went forth to fight with Aram and the children of the east. ⁴¹ And they went at first to the children of the east, and when the children of the east heard their report, they went to meet them, and engaged in battle with them. ⁴² And the war was severe against the children of the east, so the Lord gave all the children of the east into the hand of Moses, and about three hundred men fell down slain. ⁴³ And all the children of the east turned back and retreated, so Moses and the children of Cush followed them and subdued them, and put a tax upon them, as was their custom. ⁴⁴ So Moses and all the people with him

passed from there to the land of Aram for battle. ⁴⁵ And the people of Aram also went to meet them, and they fought against them, and the Lord delivered them into the hand of Moses, and many of the men of Aram fell down wounded. ⁴⁶ And Aram also were subdued by Moses and the people of Cush, and also gave their usual tax. ⁴⁷ And Moses brought Aram and the children of the east under subjection to the children of Cush, and Moses and all the people who were with him, turned to the land of Cush. ⁴⁸ And Moses strengthened himself in the kingdom of the children of Cush, and the Lord was with him, and all the children of Cush were afraid of him.

74

¹ In the end of years died Saul king of Edom, and Baal Chanan the son of Achbor reigned in his place. ² In the sixteenth year of the reign of Moses over Cush, Baal Chanan the son of Achbor reigned in the land of Edom over all the children of Edom for thirty-eight years. ³ In his days Moab rebelled against the power of Edom, having been under Edom since the days of Hadad the son of Bedad, who smote them and Midian, and brought Moab under subjection to Edom. ⁴ And when Baal Chanan the son of Achbor reigned over Edom, all the children of Moab withdrew their allegiance from Edom. ⁵ And Angeas king of Africa died in those days, and Azdrubal his son reigned in his stead. ⁶ And in those days died Janeas king of the children of Chittim, and they buried him in his temple which he had built for himself in the plain of Canopia for a residence, and Latinus reigned in his stead. ⁷ In the twenty-second year of the reign of Moses over the children of Cush, Latinus reigned over the children of Chittim forty-five years. ⁸ And he also built for himself a great and mighty tower, and he built therein an elegant temple for his residence, to conduct his government, as was the custom. ⁹ In the third year of his reign he caused a proclamation to be made to all his skilful men, who made many ships for him. ¹⁰ And Latinus assembled all his forces, and they came in ships, and went therein to fight with Azdrubal son of Angeas king of Africa, and they came to Africa and engaged in battle with Azdrubal and his army. ¹¹ And Latinus prevailed over Azdrubal, and Latinus took from Azdrubal the aqueduct which his father had brought from the children of Chittim, when he took Janiah the daughter of Uzi for a wife, so Latinus overthrew the bridge of the aqueduct, and smote the whole army of Azdrubal a severe blow. ¹² And the remaining strong men of Azdrubal strengthened themselves, and their hearts were filled with envy, and they courted death, and again engaged in battle with Latinus king of Chittim. ¹³ And the battle was severe upon all the men of Africa, and they all fell wounded before Latinus and his people, and Azdrubal the king also fell in that battle. ¹⁴ And the king Azdrubal had a very beautiful daughter, whose name was Ushpezena, and all the men of Africa embroidered her likeness on their garments, on account of her great beauty and comely appearance. ¹⁵ And the men of Latinus saw Ushpezena, the daughter of Azdrubal, and praised her unto Latinus their king. ¹⁶ And Latinus ordered her to be brought to him, and Latinus took Ushpezena for a wife, and he turned back on his way to Chittim. ¹⁷ And it was after the death of Azdrubal son of Angeas, when Latinus had turned back to his land from the battle, that all the inhabitants of Africa rose up and took Anibal the son of Angeas, the younger brother of Azdrubal, and made him king instead at his brother over the whole land at Africa. ¹⁸ And when he reigned, he resolved to go to Chittim to fight with the children of Chittim, to avenge the cause of Azdrubal his brother, and the cause of the inhabitants of Africa, and he did so. ¹⁹ And he made many ships, and he came therein with his whole army, and he went to Chittim. ²⁰ So Anibal fought with the children of Chittim, and the children of Chittim fell wounded before Anibal and his army, and Anibal avenged his brother's cause. ²¹ And Anibal continued the war for eighteen years with the children of Chittim, and Anibal dwelt in the land of Chittim and encamped there for a long time. ²² And Anibal smote the children of Chittim very severely, and he slew their great men and princes, and of the rest of the people he smote about eighty thousand men. ²³ And at the end of days and years, Anibal returned to his land of Africa, and he reigned securely in the place of Azdrubal his brother.

75

¹ At that time, in the hundred and eightieth year of the Israelites going down into Egypt, there went forth from Egypt valiant men, thirty thousand on foot, from the children of Israel, who were all of the tribe of Joseph, of the children of Ephraim the son of Joseph. ² For they said the period was completed which the Lord had appointed to the children of Israel in the times of old, which he had spoken to Abraham. ³ And these men girded themselves, and they put each man his sword at his side, and every man his armor upon him, and they trusted to their strength, and they went out together from Egypt with a mighty hand. ⁴ But they brought no provision for the road, only silver and gold, not even bread for that day did they bring in their hands, for they thought of getting their provision for pay from the Philistines, and if not they would take it by force. ⁵ And these men were very mighty and valiant men, one man could pursue a thousand and two could rout ten thousand, so they trusted to their strength and went together as they were. ⁶ And they directed their course toward the land of Gath, and they went down and found the shepherds of Gath feeding the cattle of the children of Gath. ⁷ And they said to the shepherds, Give us some of the sheep for pay, that we may eat, for we are hungry, for we have eaten no bread this day. ⁸ And the shepherds said, Are they our sheep or cattle that we should give them to you even for pay? so the children of Ephraim approached to take them by force. ⁹ And the shepherds of Gath shouted over them that their cry was heard at a distance, so all the children of Gath went out to them. ¹⁰ And when the children of Gath saw the evil doings of the children of Ephraim, they returned and assembled the men of Gath, and they put on each man his armor, and came forth to the children of Ephraim for battle. ¹¹ And they engaged with them in the valley of Gath, and the battle was severe, and they smote from each other a great many on that day. ¹² And on the second day the children of Gath sent to all the cities of the Philistines that they should come to their help, saying, ¹³ Come up unto us and help us, that we may smite the children of Ephraim who have come forth from Egypt to take our cattle, and to fight against us without cause. ¹⁴ Now the souls of the children of Ephraim were exhausted with hunger and thirst, for they had eaten no bread for three days. And forty thousand men went forth from the cities of the Philistines to the assistance of the men of Gath. ¹⁵ And these men were engaged in battle with the children of Ephraim, and the Lord delivered the children of Ephraim into the hands of the Philistines. ¹⁶ And they smote all the children of Ephraim, all who had gone forth from Egypt, none were remaining but ten men who had run away from the engagement. ¹⁷ For this evil was from the Lord against the children of Ephraim, for they transgressed the word of the Lord in going forth from Egypt, before the period had arrived which the Lord in the days of old had appointed to Israel. ¹⁸ And of the Philistines also there fell a great many, about twenty thousand men, and their brethren carried them and buried them in their cities. ¹⁹ And the slain of the children of Ephraim remained forsaken in the valley of Gath for many days and years, and were not brought to burial, and the valley was filled with men's bones. ²⁰ And the men who had escaped from the battle came to Egypt, and told all the children of Israel all that had befallen them. ²¹ And their father Ephraim mourned over them for many days, and his brethren came to console him. ²² And he came unto his wife and she bare a son, and he called his name Beriah, for she was unfortunate in his house.

76

¹ And Moses the son of Amram was still king in the land of Cush in those days, and he prospered in his kingdom, and he conducted the government of the children of Cush in justice, in righteousness, and integrity. ² And all the children of Cush loved Moses all the days that he reigned over them, and all the inhabitants of the land of Cush were greatly afraid of him. ³ And in the fortieth year of the reign of Moses over Cush, Moses was sitting on the royal throne whilst Adoniah the queen was before him, and all the nobles were sitting around him. ⁴ And Adoniah the queen said before the king and the princes, What is this thing which you, the children of Cush, have done for this long time? ⁵ Surely you know that for forty years that this man has reigned over Cush he has not approached me, nor has he served the gods of the children of Cush. ⁶ Now therefore hear, O ye children of Cush, and let this man no more reign over you as he is not of our flesh. ⁷ Behold Menacrus my son is grown up, let him reign over you, for it is better for you to serve the son of your lord, than to serve a stranger, slave of the king of Egypt. ⁸ And all the people and nobles of the children of Cush heard the words which Adoniah the queen had spoken in their ears. ⁹ And all the people were preparing until the evening, and in the morning they rose up early and made Menacrus, son of Kikianus, king over them. ¹⁰ And all the children of Cush were afraid to stretch forth their hand against Moses, for the Lord was with Moses, and the children of Cush remembered the oath which they swore unto Moses, therefore they did no harm to him. ¹¹ But the children of Cush gave many presents to Moses, and sent him from them with great honor. ¹² So Moses went forth from the land of Cush, and went home and ceased to reign over Cush, and Moses was sixty-six years old when he went out of the land of Cush, for the thing was from the Lord, for the period had arrived which he had appointed in the days of old, to bring forth Israel from the affliction of the children of Ham. ¹³ So Moses went to Midian, for he was afraid to return to Egypt on account of Pharaoh, and he went and sat at a well of water in Midian. ¹⁴ And the seven daughters of Reuel the Midianite went out to feed their father's flock. ¹⁵ And they came to the well and drew water to water their father's flock. ¹⁶ So the shepherds of Midian came and drove them away, and Moses rose up and helped them and watered the flock. ¹⁷ And they came home to their father Reuel, and told him what Moses did for them. ¹⁸ And they said, An Egyptian man has

delivered us from the hands of the shepherds, he drew up water for us and watered the flock. ¹⁹ And Reuel said to his daughters, And where is he? wherefore have you left the man? ²⁰ And Reuel sent for him and fetched him and brought him home, and he ate bread with him. ²¹ And Moses related to Reuel that he had fled from Egypt and that he reigned forty years over Cush, and that they afterward had taken the government from him, and had sent him away in peace with honor and with presents. ²² And when Reuel had heard the words of Moses, Reuel said within himself, I will put this man into the prison house, whereby I shall conciliate the children of Cush, for he has fled from them. ²³ And they took and put him into the prison house, and Moses was in prison ten years, and whilst Moses was in the prison house, Zipporah the daughter of Reuel took pity over him, and supported him with bread and water all the time. ²⁴ And all the children of Israel were yet in the land of Egypt serving the Egyptians in all manner of hard work, and the hand of Egypt continued in severity over the children of Israel in those days. ²⁵ At that time the Lord smote Pharaoh king of Egypt, and he afflicted with the plague of leprosy from the sole of his foot to the crown of his head; owing to the cruel treatment of the children of Israel was this plague at that time from the Lord upon Pharaoh king of Egypt. ²⁶ For the Lord had hearkened to the prayer of his people the children of Israel, and their cry reached him on account of their hard work. ²⁷ Still his anger did not turn from them, and the hand of Pharaoh was still stretched out against the children of Israel, and Pharaoh hardened his neck before the Lord, and he increased his yoke over the children of Israel, and embittered their lives with all manner of hard work. ²⁸ And when the Lord had inflicted the plague upon Pharaoh king of Egypt, he asked his wise men and sorcerers to cure him. ²⁹ And his wise men and sorcerers said unto him, That if the blood of little children were put into the wounds he would be healed. ³⁰ And Pharaoh hearkened to them, and sent his ministers to Goshen to the children of Israel to take their little children. ³¹ And Pharaoh's ministers went and took the infants of the children of Israel from the bosoms of their mothers by force, and they brought them to Pharaoh daily, a child each day, and the physicians killed them and applied them to the plague; thus did they all the days. ³² And the number of the children which Pharaoh slew was three hundred and seventy-five. ³³ But the Lord hearkened not to the physicians of the king of Egypt, and the plague went on increasing mightily. ³⁴ And Pharaoh was ten years afflicted with that plague, still the heart of Pharaoh was more hardened against the children of Israel. ³⁵ And at the end of ten years the Lord continued to afflict Pharaoh with destructive plagues. ³⁶ And the Lord smote him with a bad tumor and sickness at the stomach, and that plague turned to a severe boil. ³⁷ At that time the two ministers of Pharaoh came from the land of Goshen where all the children of Israel were, and went to the house of Pharaoh and said to him, We have seen the children of Israel slacken in their work and negligent in their labor. ³⁸ And when Pharaoh heard the words of his ministers, his anger was kindled against the children of Israel exceedingly, for he was greatly grieved at his bodily pain. ³⁹ And he answered and said, Now that the children of Israel know that I am ill, they turn and scoff at us, now therefore harness my chariot for me, and I will betake myself to Goshen and will see the scoff of the children of Israel with which they are deriding me; so his servants harnessed the chariot for him. ⁴⁰ And they took and made him ride upon a horse, for he was not able to ride of himself; ⁴¹ And he took with him ten horsemen and ten footmen, and went to the children of Israel to Goshen. ⁴² And when they had come to the border of Egypt, the king's horse passed into a narrow place, elevated in the hollow part of the vineyard, fenced on both sides, the low, plain country being on the other side. ⁴³ And the horses ran rapidly in that place and pressed each other, and the other horses pressed the king's horse. ⁴⁴ And the king's horse fell into the low plain whilst the king was riding upon it, and when he fell the chariot turned over the king's face and the horse lay upon the king, and the king cried out, for his flesh was very sore. ⁴⁵ And the flesh of the king was torn from him, and his bones were broken and he could not ride, for this thing was from the Lord to him, for the Lord had heard the cries of his people the children of Israel and their affliction. ⁴⁶ And his servants carried him upon their shoulders, a little at a time, and they brought him back to Egypt, and the horsemen who were with him came also back to Egypt. ⁴⁷ And they placed him in his bed, and the king knew that his end was come to die, so Aparanith the queen his wife came and cried before the king, and the king wept a great weeping with her. ⁴⁸ And all his nobles and servants came on that day and saw the king in that affliction, and wept a great weeping with him. ⁴⁹ And the princes of the king and all his counselors advised the king to cause one to reign in his stead in the land, whomsoever he should choose from his sons. ⁵⁰ And the king had three sons and two daughters which Aparanith the queen his wife had borne to him, besides the king's children of concubines. ⁵¹ And these were their names, the firstborn Othri, the second Adikam, and the third Morion, and their sisters, the name of the elder Bathia and of the other Acuzi. ⁵² And Othri the first born of the king was an idiot, precipitate and hurried in his words. ⁵³ But Adikam was a cunning and wise man and knowing in all the wisdom of Egypt, but of unseemly aspect, thick in flesh, and very short in stature; his height was one cubit. ⁵⁴ And when the king saw Adikam his son intelligent and wise in all things, the king resolved that he should be king in his stead after his death. ⁵⁵ And he took for him a wife Gedudah daughter of Abilot, and he was ten years old, and she bare unto him four sons. ⁵⁶ And he afterward went and took three wives and begat eight sons and three daughters. ⁵⁷ And the disorder greatly prevailed over the king, and his flesh stank like the flesh of a carcass cast upon the field in summer time, during the heat of the sun. ⁵⁸ And when the king saw that his sickness had greatly strengthened itself over him, he ordered his son Adikam to be brought to him, and they made him king over the land in his place. ⁵⁹ And at the end of three years, the king died, in shame, disgrace, and disgust, and his servants carried him and buried him in the sepulcher of the kings of Egypt in Zoan Mizraim. ⁶⁰ But they embalmed him not as was usual with kings, for his flesh was putrid, and they could not approach to embalm him on account of the stench, so they buried him in haste. ⁶¹ For this evil was from the Lord to him, for the Lord had requited him evil for the evil which in his days he had done to Israel. ⁶² And he died with terror and with shame, and his son Adikam reigned in his place.

77

¹ Adikam was twenty years old when he reigned over Egypt, he reigned four years. ² In the two hundred and sixth year of Israel's going down to Egypt did Adikam reign over Egypt, but he continued not so long in his reign over Egypt as his fathers had continued their reigns. ³ For Melol his father reigned ninety-four years in Egypt, but he was ten years sick and died, for he had been wicked before the Lord. ⁴ And all the Egyptians called the name of Adikam Pharaoh like the name of his fathers, as was their custom to do in Egypt. ⁵ And all the wise men of Pharaoh called the name of Adikam Ahuz, for short is called Ahuz in the Egyptian language. ⁶ And Adikam was exceedingly ugly, and he was a cubit and a span and he had a great beard which reached to the soles of his feet. ⁷ And Pharaoh sat upon his father's throne to reign over Egypt, and he conducted the government of Egypt in his wisdom. ⁸ And whilst he reigned he exceeded his father and all the preceding kings in wickedness, and he increased his yoke over the children of Israel. ⁹ And he went with his servants to Goshen to the children of Israel, and he strengthened the labor over them and he said unto them, Complete your work, each day's task, and let not your hands slacken from our work from this day forward as you did in the days of my father. ¹⁰ And he placed officers over them from amongst the children of Israel, and over these officers he placed taskmasters from amongst his servants. ¹¹ And he placed over them a measure of bricks for them to do according to that number, day by day, and he turned back and went to Egypt. ¹² At that time the task-masters of Pharaoh ordered the officers of the children of Israel according to the command of Pharaoh, saying, ¹³ Thus says Pharaoh, Do your work each day, and finish your task, and observe the daily measure of bricks; diminish not anything. ¹⁴ And it shall come to pass that if you are deficient in your daily bricks, I will put your young children in their stead. ¹⁵ And the task-masters of Egypt did so in those days as Pharaoh had ordered them. ¹⁶ And whenever any deficiency was found in the children of Israel's measure of their daily bricks, the task-masters of Pharaoh would go to the wives of the children of Israel and take infants of the children of Israel to the number of bricks deficient, they would take them by force from their mother's laps, and put them in the building instead of the bricks; ¹⁷ Whilst their fathers and mothers were crying over them and weeping when they heard the weeping voices of their infants in the wall of the building. ¹⁸ And the task-masters prevailed over Israel, that the Israelites should place their children in the building, so that a man placed his son in the wall and put mortar over him, whilst his eyes wept over him, and his tears ran down upon his child. ¹⁹ And the task-masters of Egypt did so to the babes of Israel for many days, and no one pitied or had compassion over the babes of the children of Israel. ²⁰ And the number of all the children killed in the building was two hundred and seventy, some whom they had built upon instead of the bricks which had been left deficient by their fathers, and some whom they had drawn out dead from the building. ²¹ And the labor imposed upon the children of Israel in the days of Adikam exceeded in hardship that which they performed in the days of his father. ²² And the children of Israel sighed every day on account of their heavy work, for they had said to themselves, Behold when Pharaoh shall die, his son will rise up and lighten our work! ²³ But they increased the latter work more than the former, and the children of Israel sighed at this and their cry ascended to God on account of their labor. ²⁴ And God heard the voice of the children of Israel and their cry, in those days, and God remembered to them his covenant which he had made with Abraham, Isaac and Jacob. ²⁵ And God saw the burden of the children

of Israel, and their heavy work in those days, and he determined to deliver them. ²⁶ And Moses the son of Amram was still confined in the dungeon in those days, in the house of Reuel the Midianite, and Zipporah the daughter of Reuel did support him with food secretly day by day. ²⁷ And Moses was confined in the dungeon in the house of Reuel for ten years. ²⁸ And at the end of ten years which was the first year of the reign of Pharaoh over Egypt, in the place of his father, ²⁹ Zipporah said to her father Reuel, No person inquires or seeks after the Hebrew man, whom thou didst bind in prison now ten years. ³⁰ Now therefore, if it seem good in thy sight, let us send and see whether he is living or dead, but her father knew not that she had supported him. ³¹ And Reuel her father answered and said to her, Has ever such a thing happened that a man should be shut up in a prison without food for ten years, and that he should live? ³² And Zipporah answered her father, saying, Surely thou hast heard that the God of the Hebrews is great and awful, and does wonders for them at all times. ³³ He it was who delivered Abraham from Ur of the Chaldeans, and Isaac from the sword of his father, and Jacob from the angel of the Lord who wrestled with him at the ford of Jabbuk. ³⁴ Also with this man has he done many things, he delivered him from the river in Egypt and from the sword of Pharaoh, and from the children of Cush, so also can he deliver him from famine and make him live. ³⁵ And the thing seemed good in the sight of Reuel, and he did according to the word of his daughter, and sent to the dungeon to ascertain what became of Moses. ³⁶ And he saw, and behold the man Moses was living in the dungeon, standing upon his feet, praising and praying to the God of his ancestors. ³⁷ And Reuel commanded Moses to be brought out of the dungeon, so they shaved him and he changed his prison garments and ate bread. ³⁸ And afterward Moses went into the garden of Reuel which was behind the house, and he there prayed to the Lord his God, who had done mighty wonders for him. ³⁹ And it was that whilst he prayed he looked opposite to him, and behold a sapphire stick was placed in the ground, which was planted in the midst of the garden. ⁴⁰ And he approached the stick and he looked, and behold the name of the Lord God of hosts was engraved thereon, written and developed upon the stick. ⁴¹ And he read it and stretched forth his hand and he plucked it like a forest tree from the thicket, and the stick was in his hand. ⁴² And this is the stick with which all the works of our God were performed, after he had created heaven and earth, and all the host of them, seas, rivers and all their fishes. ⁴³ And when God had driven Adam from the garden of Eden, he took the stick in his hand and went and tilled the ground from which he was taken. ⁴⁴ And the stick came down to Noah and was given to Shem and his descendants, until it came into the hand of Abraham the Hebrew. ⁴⁵ And when Abraham had given all he had to his son Isaac, he also gave to him this stick. ⁴⁶ And when Jacob had fled to Padan-aram, he took it into his hand, and when he returned to his father he had not left it behind him. ⁴⁷ Also when he went down to Egypt he took it into his hand and gave it to Joseph, one portion above his brethren, for Jacob had taken it by force from his brother Esau. ⁴⁸ And after the death of Joseph, the nobles of Egypt came into the house of Joseph, and the stick came into the hand of Reuel the Midianite, and when he went out of Egypt, he took it in his hand and planted it in his garden. ⁴⁹ And all the mighty men of the Kinites tried to pluck it when they endeavored to get Zipporah his daughter, but they were unsuccessful. ⁵⁰ So that stick remained planted in the garden of Reuel, until he came who had a right to it and took it. ⁵¹ And when Reuel saw the stick in the hand of Moses, he wondered at it, and he gave him his daughter Zipporah for a wife.

78

¹ At that time died Baal Channan son of Achbor, king of Edom, and was buried in his house in the land of Edom. ² And after his death the children of Esau sent to the land of Edom, and took from there a man who was in Edom, whose name was Hadad, and they made him king over them in the place of Baal Channan, their king. ³ And Hadad reigned over the children of Edom forty-eight years. ⁴ And when he reigned he resolved to fight against the children of Moab, to bring them under the power of the children of Esau as they were before, but he was not able, because the children of Moab heard this thing, and they rose up and hastened to elect a king over them from amongst their brethren. ⁵ And they afterward gathered together a great people, and sent to the children of Ammon their brethren for help to fight against Hadad king of Edom. ⁶ And Hadad heard the thing which the children of Moab had done, and was greatly afraid of them, and refrained from fighting against them. ⁷ In those days Moses, the son of Amram, in Midian, took Zipporah, the daughter of Reuel the Midianite, for a wife. ⁸ And Zipporah walked in the ways of the daughters of Jacob, she was nothing short of the righteousness of Sarah, Rebecca, Rachel and Leah. ⁹ And Zipporah conceived and bare a son and he called his name Gershom, for he said, I was a stranger in a foreign land; but he circumcised not his foreskin, at the command of Reuel his father-in-law. ¹⁰ And she conceived again and bare a son, but circumcised his foreskin, and called his name Eliezer, for Moses said, Because the God of my fathers was my help, and delivered me from the sword of Pharaoh. ¹¹ And Pharaoh king of Egypt greatly increased the labor of the children of Israel in those days, and continued to make his yoke heavier upon the children of Israel. ¹² And he ordered a proclamation to be made in Egypt, saying, Give no more straw to the people to make bricks with, let them go and gather themselves straw as they can find it. ¹³ Also the tale of bricks which they shall make let them give each day, and diminish nothing from them, for they are idle in their work. ¹⁴ And the children of Israel heard this, and they mourned and sighed, and they cried unto the Lord on account of the bitterness of their souls. ¹⁵ And the Lord heard the cries of the children of Israel, and saw the oppression with which the Egyptians oppressed them. ¹⁶ And the Lord was jealous of his people and his inheritance, and heard their voice, and he resolved to take them out of the affliction of Egypt, to give them the land of Canaan for a possession.

79

¹ And in those days Moses was feeding the flock of Reuel the Midianite his father-in-law, beyond the wilderness of Sin, and the stick which he took from his father-in-law was in his hand. ² And it came to pass one day that a kid of goats strayed from the flock, and Moses pursued it and it came to the mountain of God to Horeb. ³ And when he came to Horeb, the Lord appeared there unto him in the bush, and he found the bush burning with fire, but the fire had no power over the bush to consume it. ⁴ And Moses was greatly astonished at this sight, wherefore the bush was not consumed, and he approached to see this mighty thing, and the Lord called unto Moses out of the fire and commanded him to go down to Egypt, to Pharaoh king of Egypt, to send the children of Israel from his service. ⁵ And the Lord said unto Moses, Go, return to Egypt, for all those men who sought thy life are dead, and thou shalt speak unto Pharaoh to send forth the children of Israel from his land. ⁶ And the Lord showed him to do signs and wonders in Egypt before the eyes of Pharaoh and the eyes of his subjects, in order that they might believe that the Lord had sent him. ⁷ And Moses hearkened to all that the Lord had commanded him, and he returned to his father-in-law and told him the thing, and Reuel said to him, Go in peace. ⁸ And Moses rose up to go to Egypt, and he took his wife and sons with him, and he was at an inn in the road, and an angel of God came down, and sought an occasion against him. ⁹ And he wished to kill him on account of his first born son, because he had not circumcised him, and had transgressed the covenant which the Lord had made with Abraham. ¹⁰ For Moses had hearkened to the words of his father-in-law which he had spoken to him, not to circumcise his first born son, therefore he circumcised him not. ¹¹ And Zipporah saw the angel of the Lord seeking an occasion against Moses, and she knew that this thing was owing to his not having circumcised her son Gershom. ¹² And Zipporah hastened and took of the sharp rock stones that were there, and she circumcised her son, and delivered her husband and her son from the hand of the angel of the Lord. ¹³ And Aaron the son of Amram, the brother of Moses, was in Egypt walking at the river side on that day. ¹⁴ And the Lord appeared to him in that place, and he said to him, Go now toward Moses in the wilderness, and he went and met him in the mountain of God, and he kissed him. ¹⁵ And Aaron lifted up his eyes, and saw Zipporah the wife of Moses and her children, and he said unto Moses, Who are these unto thee? ¹⁶ And Moses said unto him, They are my wife and sons, which God gave to me in Midian; and the thing grieved Aaron on account of the woman and her children. ¹⁷ And Aaron said to Moses, Send away the woman and her children that they may go to her father's house, and Moses hearkened to the words of Aaron, and did so. ¹⁸ And Zipporah returned with her children, and they went to the house of Reuel, and remained there until the time arrived when the Lord had visited his people, and brought them forth from Egypt from the hand at Pharaoh. ¹⁹ And Moses and Aaron came to Egypt to the community of the children of Israel, and they spoke to them all the words of the Lord, and the people rejoiced an exceeding great rejoicing. ²⁰ And Moses and Aaron rose up early on the next day, and they went to the house of Pharaoh, and they took in their hands the stick of God. ²¹ And when they came to the king's gate, two young lions were confined there with iron instruments, and no person went out or came in from before them, unless those whom the king ordered to come, when the conjurors came and withdrew the lions by their incantations, and this brought them to the king. ²² And Moses hastened and lifted up the stick upon the lions, and he loosed them, and Moses and Aaron came into the king's house. ²³ The lions also came with them in joy, and they followed them and rejoiced as a dog rejoices over his master when he comes from the field. ²⁴ And when Pharaoh saw this thing he was astonished at it, and he was greatly terrified at the report, for their appearance was like the appearance of the children of God. ²⁵ And Pharaoh said to Moses, What do you require? and they

answered him, saying, The Lord God of the Hebrews has sent us to thee, to say, Send forth my people that they may serve me. ²⁶ And when Pharaoh heard their words he was greatly terrified before them, and he said to them, Go today and come back to me tomorrow, and they did according to the word of the king. ²⁷ And when they had gone Pharaoh sent for Balaam the magician and to Jannes and Jambres his sons, and to all the magicians and conjurors and counsellors which belonged to the king, and they all came and sat before the king. ²⁸ And the king told them all the words which Moses and his brother Aaron had spoken to him, and the magicians said to the king, But how came the men to thee, on account of the lions which were confined at the gate? ²⁹ And the king said, Because they lifted up their rod against the lions and loosed them, and came to me, and the lions also rejoiced at them as a dog rejoices to meet his master. ³⁰ And Balaam the son of Beor the magician answered the king, saying, These are none else than magicians like ourselves. ³¹ Now therefore send for them, and let them come and we will try them, and the king did so. ³² And in the morning Pharaoh sent for Moses and Aaron to come before the king, and they took the rod of God, and came to the king and spoke to him, saying, ³³ Thus said the Lord God of the Hebrews, Send my people that they may serve me. ³⁴ And the king said to them, But who will believe you that you are the messengers of God and that you come to me by his order? ³⁵ Now therefore give a wonder or sign in this matter, and then the words which you speak will be believed. ³⁶ And Aaron hastened and threw the rod out of his hand before Pharaoh and before his servants, and the rod turned into a serpent. ³⁷ And the sorcerers saw this and they cast each man his rod upon the ground and they became serpents. ³⁸ And the serpent of Aaron's rod lifted up its head and opened its mouth to swallow the rods of the magicians. ³⁹ And Balaam the magician answered and said, This thing has been from the days of old, that a serpent should swallow its fellow, and that living things devour each other. ⁴⁰ Now therefore restore it to a rod as it was at first, and we will also restore our rods as they were at first, and if thy rod shall swallow our rods, then shall we know that the spirit of God is in thee, and if not, thou art only an artificer like unto ourselves. ⁴¹ And Aaron hastened and stretched forth his hand and caught hold of the serpent's tail and it became a rod in his hand, and the sorcerers did the like with their rods, and they got hold, each man of the tail of his serpent, and they became rods as at first. ⁴² And when they were restored to rods, the rod of Aaron swallowed up their rods. ⁴³ And when the king saw this thing, he ordered the book of records that related to the kings of Egypt, to be brought, and they brought the book of records, the chronicles of the kings of Egypt, in which all the idols of Egypt were inscribed, for they thought of finding therein the name of Jehovah, but they found it not. ⁴⁴ And Pharaoh said to Moses and Aaron, Behold I have not found the name of your God written in this book, and his name I know not. ⁴⁵ And the counsellors and wise men answered the king, We have heard that the God of the Hebrews is a son of the wise, the son of ancient kings. ⁴⁶ And Pharaoh turned to Moses and Aaron and said to them, I know not the Lord whom you have declared, neither will I send his people. ⁴⁷ And they answered and said to the king, The Lord God of Gods is his name, and he proclaimed his name over us from the days of our ancestors, and sent us, saying, Go to Pharaoh and say unto him, Send my people that they may serve me. ⁴⁸ Now therefore send us, that we may take a journey for three days in the wilderness, and there may sacrifice to him, for from the days of our going down to Egypt, he has not taken from our hands either burnt offering, oblation or sacrifice, and if thou wilt not send us, his anger will be kindled against thee, and he will smite Egypt either with the plague or with the sword. ⁴⁹ And Pharaoh said to them, Tell me now his power and his might; and they said to him, He created the heaven and the earth, the seas and all their fishes, he formed the light, created the darkness, caused rain upon the earth and watered it, and made the herbage and grass to sprout, he created man and beast and the animals of the forest, the birds of the air and the fish of the sea, and by his mouth they live and die. ⁵⁰ Surely he created thee in thy mother's womb, and put into thee the breath of life, and reared thee and placed thee upon the royal throne of Egypt, and he will take thy breath and soul from thee, and return thee to the ground whence thou wast taken. ⁵¹ And the anger of the king was kindled at their words, and he said to them, But who amongst all the Gods of nations can do this? my river is mine own, and I have made it for myself. ⁵² And he drove them from him, and he ordered the labor upon Israel to be more severe than it was yesterday and before. ⁵³ And Moses and Aaron went out from the king's presence, and they saw the children of Israel in an evil condition for the task-masters had made their labor exceedingly heavy. ⁵⁴ And Moses returned to the Lord and said, Why hast thou ill treated thy people? for since I came to speak to Pharaoh what thou didst send me for, he has exceedingly ill used the children of Israel. ⁵⁵ And the Lord said to Moses, Behold thou wilt see that with an outstretched hand and heavy plagues, Pharaoh will send the children of Israel from his land. ⁵⁶ And Moses and Aaron dwelt amongst their brethren the children of Israel in Egypt. ⁵⁷ And as for the children of Israel the Egyptians embittered their lives, with the heavy work which they imposed upon them.

80

¹ And at the end of two years, the Lord again sent Moses to Pharaoh to bring forth the children of Israel, and to send them out of the land of Egypt. ² And Moses went and came to the house of Pharaoh, and he spoke to him the words of the Lord who had sent him, but Pharaoh would not hearken to the voice of the Lord, and God roused his might in Egypt upon Pharaoh and his subjects, and God smote Pharaoh and his people with very great and sore plagues. ³ And the Lord sent by the hand of Aaron and turned all the waters of Egypt into blood, with all their streams and rivers. ⁴ And when an Egyptian came to drink and draw water, he looked into his pitcher, and behold all the water was turned into blood; and when he came to drink from his cup the water in the cup became blood. ⁵ And when a woman kneaded her dough and cooked her victuals, their appearance was turned to that of blood. ⁶ And the Lord sent again and caused all their waters to bring forth frogs, and all the frogs came into the houses of the Egyptians. ⁷ And when the Egyptians drank, their bellies were filled with frogs and they danced in their bellies as they dance when in the river. ⁸ And all their drinking water and cooking water turned to frogs, also when they lay in their beds their perspiration bred frogs. ⁹ Notwithstanding all this the anger of the Lord did not turn from them, and his hand was stretched out against all the Egyptians to smite them with every heavy plague. ¹⁰ And he sent and smote their dust to lice, and the lice became in Egypt to the height of two cubits upon the earth. ¹¹ The lice were also very numerous, in the flesh of man and beast, in all the inhabitants of Egypt, also upon the king and queen the Lord sent the lice, and it grieved Egypt exceedingly on account of the lice. ¹² Notwithstanding this, the anger of the Lord did not turn away, and his hand was still stretched out over Egypt. ¹³ And the Lord sent all kinds of beasts of the field into Egypt, and they came and destroyed all Egypt, man and beast, and trees, and all things that were in Egypt. ¹⁴ And the Lord sent fiery serpents, scorpions, mice, weasels, toads, together with others creeping in dust. ¹⁵ Flies, hornets, fleas, bugs and gnats, each swarm according to its kind. ¹⁶ And all reptiles and winged animals according to their kind came to Egypt and grieved the Egyptians exceedingly. ¹⁷ And the fleas and flies came into the eyes and ears of the Egyptians. ¹⁸ And the hornet came upon them and drove them away, and they removed from it into their inner rooms, and it pursued them. ¹⁹ And when the Egyptians hid themselves on account of the swarm of animals, they locked their doors after them, and God ordered the Sulanuth which was in the sea, to come up and go into Egypt. ²⁰ And she had long arms, ten cubits in length of the cubit of a man. ²¹ And she went upon the roofs and uncovered the raftering and flooring and cut them, and stretched forth her arm into the house and removed the lock and the bolt, and opened the houses of Egypt. ²² Afterward came the swarm of animals into the houses of Egypt, and the swarm of animals destroyed the Egyptians, and it grieved them exceedingly. ²³ Notwithstanding this the anger of the Lord did not turn away from the Egyptians, and his hand was yet stretched forth against them. ²⁴ And God sent the pestilence, and the pestilence pervaded Egypt, in the horses and asses, and in the camels, in herds of oxen and sheep and in man. ²⁵ And when the Egyptians rose up early in the morning to take their cattle to pasture they found all their cattle dead. ²⁶ And there remained of the cattle of the Egyptians only one in ten, and of the cattle belonging to Israel in Goshen not one died. ²⁷ And God sent a burning inflammation in the flesh of the Egyptians, which burst their skins, and it became a severe itch in all the Egyptians from the soles of their feet to the crowns of their heads. ²⁸ And many boils were in their flesh, that their flesh wasted away until they became rotten and putrid. ²⁹ Notwithstanding this the anger of the Lord did not turn away, and his hand was still stretched out over all Egypt. ³⁰ And the Lord sent a very heavy hail, which smote their vines and broke their fruit trees and dried them up that they fell upon them. ³¹ Also every green herb became dry and perished, for a mingling fire descended amidst the hail, therefore the hail and the fire consumed all things. ³² Also men and beasts that were found abroad perished of the flames of fire and of the hail, and all the young lions were exhausted. ³³ And the Lord sent and brought numerous locusts into Egypt, the Chasel, Salom, Chargol, and Chagole, locusts each of its kind, which devoured all that the hail had left remaining. ³⁴ Then the Egyptians rejoiced at the locusts, although they consumed the produce of the field, and they caught them in abundance and salted them for food. ³⁵ And the Lord turned a mighty wind of the sea which took away all the locusts, even those that were salted, and thrust them into the Red Sea; not one locust remained within the boundaries of Egypt. ³⁶ And God sent darkness upon Egypt, that the whole land of Egypt and Pathros became dark for three days, so that a man could not see his hand when he lifted it

to his mouth. ³⁷ At that time died many of the people of Israel who had rebelled against the Lord and who would not hearken to Moses and Aaron, and believed not in them that God had sent them. ³⁸ And who had said, We will not go forth from Egypt lest we perish with hunger in a desolate wilderness, and who would not hearken to the voice of Moses. ³⁹ And the Lord plagued them in the three days of darkness, and the Israelites buried them in those days, without the Egyptians knowing of them or rejoicing over them. ⁴⁰ And the darkness was very great in Egypt for three days, and any person who was standing when the darkness came, remained standing in his place, and he that was sitting remained sitting, and he that was lying continued lying in the same state, and he that was walking remained sitting upon the ground in the same spot; and this thing happened to all the Egyptians, until the darkness had passed away. ⁴¹ And the days of darkness passed away, and the Lord sent Moses and Aaron to the children of Israel, saying, Celebrate your feast and make your Passover, for behold I come in the midst of the night amongst all the Egyptians, and I will smite all their first born, from the first born of a man to the first born of a beast, and when I see your Passover, I will pass over you. ⁴² And the children of Israel did according to all that the Lord had commanded Moses and Aaron, thus did they in that night. ⁴³ And it came to pass in the middle of the night, that the Lord went forth in the midst of Egypt, and smote all the first born of the Egyptians, from the first born of man to the first born of beast. ⁴⁴ And Pharaoh rose up in the night, he and all his servants and all the Egyptians, and there was a great cry throughout Egypt in that night, for there was not a house in which there was not a corpse. ⁴⁵ Also the likenesses of the first born of Egypt, which were carved in the walls at their houses, were destroyed and fell to the ground. ⁴⁶ Even the bones of their first born who had died before this and whom they had buried in their houses, were raked up by the dogs of Egypt on that night and dragged before the Egyptians and cast before them. ⁴⁷ And all the Egyptians saw this evil which had suddenly come upon them, and all the Egyptians cried out with a loud voice. ⁴⁸ And all the families of Egypt wept upon that night, each man for his son and each man for his daughter, being the first born, and the tumult of Egypt was heard at a distance on that night. ⁴⁹ And Bathia the daughter of Pharaoh went forth with the king on that night to seek Moses and Aaron in their houses, and they found them in their houses, eating and drinking and rejoicing with all Israel. ⁵⁰ And Bathia said to Moses, Is this the reward for the good which I have done to thee, who have reared thee and stretched thee out, and thou hast brought this evil upon me and my father's house? ⁵¹ And Moses said to her, Surely ten plagues did the Lord bring upon Egypt; did any evil accrue to thee from any of them? did one of them affect thee? and she said, No. ⁵² And Moses said to her, Although thou art the first born to thy mother, thou shalt not die, and no evil shall reach thee in the midst of Egypt. ⁵³ And she said, What advantage is it to me, when I see the king, my brother, and all his household and subjects in this evil, whose first born perish with all the first born of Egypt? ⁵⁴ And Moses said to her, Surely thy brother and his household, and subjects, the families of Egypt, would not hearken to the words of the Lord, therefore did this evil come upon them. ⁵⁵ And Pharaoh king of Egypt approached Moses and Aaron, and some of the children of Israel who were with them in that place, and he prayed to them, saying, ⁵⁶ Rise up and take your brethren, all the children of Israel who are in the land, with their sheep and oxen, and all belonging to them, they shall leave nothing remaining, only pray for me to the Lord your God. ⁵⁷ And Moses said to Pharaoh, Behold though thou art thy mother's first born, yet fear not, for thou wilt not die, for the Lord has commanded that thou shalt live, in order to show thee his great might and strong stretched out arm. ⁵⁸ And Pharaoh ordered the children of Israel to be sent away, and all the Egyptians strengthened themselves to send them, for they said, We are all perishing. ⁵⁹ And all the Egyptians sent the Israelites forth, with great riches, sheep and oxen and precious things, according to the oath of the Lord between him and our Father Abraham. ⁶⁰ And the children of Israel delayed going forth at night, and when the Egyptians came to them to bring them out, they said to them, Are we thieves, that we should go forth at night? ⁶¹ And the children of Israel asked of the Egyptians, vessels of silver, and vessels of gold, and garments, and the children of Israel stripped the Egyptians. ⁶² And Moses hastened and rose up and went to the river of Egypt, and brought up from thence the coffin of Joseph and took it with him. ⁶³ The children of Israel also brought up, each man his father's coffin with him, and each man the coffins of his tribe.

81

¹ And the children of Israel journeyed from Rameses to Succoth, about six hundred thousand men on foot, besides the little ones and their wives. ² Also a mixed multitude went up with them, and flocks and herds, even much cattle. ³ And the sojourning of the children of Israel, who dwelt in the land of Egypt in hard labor, was two hundred and ten years. ⁴ And at the end of two hundred and ten years, the Lord brought forth the children of Israel from Egypt with a strong hand. ⁵ And the children of Israel traveled from Egypt and from Goshen and from Rameses, and encamped in Succoth on the fifteenth day of the first month. ⁶ And the Egyptians buried all their first born whom the Lord had smitten, and all the Egyptians buried their slain for three days. ⁷ And the children of Israel traveled from Succoth and encamped in Ethom, at the end of the wilderness. ⁸ And on the third day after the Egyptians had buried their first born, many men rose up from Egypt and went after Israel to make them return to Egypt, for they repented that they had sent the Israelites away from their servitude. ⁹ And one man said to his neighbor, Surely Moses and Aaron spoke to Pharaoh, saying, We will go a three days' journey in the wilderness and sacrifice to the Lord our God. ¹⁰ Now therefore let us rise up early in the morning and cause them to return, and it shall be that if they return with us to Egypt to their masters, then shall we know that there is faith in them, but if they will not return, then will we fight with them, and make them come back with great power and a strong hand. ¹¹ And all the nobles of Pharaoh rose up in the morning, and with them about seven hundred thousand men, and they went forth from Egypt on that day, and came to the place where the children of Israel were. ¹² And all the Egyptians saw and behold Moses and Aaron and all the children of Israel were sitting before Pi-hahiroth, eating and drinking and celebrating the feast of the Lord. ¹³ And all the Egyptians said to the children of Israel, Surely you said, We will go a journey for three days in the wilderness and sacrifice to our God and return. ¹⁴ Now therefore this day makes five days since you went, why do you not return to your masters? ¹⁵ And Moses and Aaron answered them, saying, Because the Lord our God has testified in us, saying, You shall no more return to Egypt, but we will betake ourselves to a land flowing with milk and honey, as the Lord our God had sworn to our ancestors to give to us. ¹⁶ And when the nobles of Egypt saw that the children of Israel did not hearken to them, to return to Egypt, they girded themselves to fight with Israel. ¹⁷ And the Lord strengthened the hearts of the children of Israel over the Egyptians, that they gave them a severe beating, and the battle was sore upon the Egyptians, and all the Egyptians fled from before the children of Israel, for many of them perished by the hand of Israel. ¹⁸ And the nobles of Pharaoh went to Egypt and told Pharaoh, saying, The children of Israel have fled, and will no more return to Egypt, and in this manner did Moses and Aaron speak to us. ¹⁹ And Pharaoh heard this thing, and his heart and the hearts of all his subjects were turned against Israel, and they repented that they had sent Israel; and all the Egyptians advised Pharaoh to pursue the children of Israel to make them come back to their burdens. ²⁰ And they said each man to his brother, What is this which we have done, that we have sent Israel from our servitude? ²¹ And the Lord strengthened the hearts of all the Egyptians to pursue the Israelites, for the Lord desired to overthrow the Egyptians in the Red Sea. ²² And Pharaoh rose up and harnessed his chariot, and he ordered all the Egyptians to assemble, not one man was left excepting the little ones and the women. ²³ And all the Egyptians went forth with Pharaoh to pursue the children of Israel, and the camp of Egypt was an exceedingly large and heavy camp, about ten hundred thousand men. ²⁴ And the whole of this camp went and pursued the children of Israel to bring them back to Egypt, and they reached them encamping by the Red Sea. ²⁵ And the children of Israel lifted up their eyes, and beheld all the Egyptians pursuing them, and the children of Israel were greatly terrified at them, and the children of Israel cried to the Lord. ²⁶ And on account of the Egyptians, the children of Israel divided themselves into four divisions, and they were divided in their opinions, for they were afraid of the Egyptians, and Moses spoke to each of them. ²⁷ The first division was of the children of Reuben, Simeon, and Issachar, and they resolved to cast themselves into the sea, for they were exceedingly afraid of the Egyptians. ²⁸ And Moses said to them, Fear not, stand still and see the salvation of the Lord which He will effect this day for you. ²⁹ The second division was of the children of Zebulun, Benjamin and Naphtali, and they resolved to go back to Egypt with the Egyptians. ³⁰ And Moses said to them, Fear not, for as you have seen the Egyptians this day, so shall you see them no more for ever. ³¹ The third division was of the children of Judah and Joseph, and they resolved to go to meet the Egyptians to fight with them. ³² And Moses said to them, Stand in your places, for the Lord will fight for you, and you shall remain silent. ³³ And the fourth division was of the children of Levi, Gad, and Asher, and they resolved to go into the midst of the Egyptians to confound them, and Moses said to them, Remain in your stations and fear not, only call unto the Lord that he may save you out of their hands. ³⁴ After this Moses rose up from amidst the people, and he prayed to the Lord and said, ³⁵ O Lord God of the whole earth, save now thy people whom thou didst bring forth from Egypt, and let not the Egyptians boast that power and might are theirs. ³⁶ So the Lord said to Moses, Why dost thou cry unto me? speak to the children of Israel that they shall proceed, and do thou stretch out thy rod upon the sea and divide

it, and the children of Israel shall pass through it. ³⁷ And Moses did so, and he lifted up his rod upon the sea and divided it. ³⁸ And the waters of the sea were divided into twelve parts, and the children of Israel passed through on foot, with shoes, as a man would pass through a prepared road. ³⁹ And the Lord manifested to the children of Israel his wonders in Egypt and in the sea by the hand of Moses and Aaron. ⁴⁰ And when the children of Israel had entered the sea, the Egyptians came after them, and the waters of the sea resumed upon them, and they all sank in the water, and not one man was left excepting Pharaoh, who gave thanks to the Lord and believed in him, therefore the Lord did not cause him to perish at that time with the Egyptians. ⁴¹ And the Lord ordered an angel to take him from amongst the Egyptians, who cast him upon the land of Ninevah and he reigned over it for a long time. ⁴² And on that day the Lord saved Israel from the hand of Egypt, and all the children of Israel saw that the Egyptians had perished, and they beheld the great hand of the Lord, in what he had performed in Egypt and in the sea. ⁴³ Then sang Moses and the children of Israel this song unto the Lord, on the day when the Lord caused the Egyptians to fall before them. ⁴⁴ And all Israel sang in concert, saying, I will sing to the Lord for He is greatly exalted, the horse and his rider has he cast into the sea; behold it is written in the book of the law of God. ⁴⁵ After this the children of Israel proceeded on their journey, and encamped in Marah, and the Lord gave to the children of Israel statutes and judgments in that place in Marah, and the Lord commanded the children of Israel to walk in all his ways and to serve him. ⁴⁶ And they journeyed from Marah and came to Elim, and in Elim were twelve springs of water and seventy date trees, and the children encamped there by the waters. ⁴⁷ And they journeyed from Elim and came to the wilderness of Sin, on the fifteenth day of the second month after their departure from Egypt. ⁴⁸ At that time the Lord gave the manna to the children of Israel to eat, and the Lord caused food to rain from heaven for the children of Israel day by day. ⁴⁹ And the children of Israel ate the manna for forty years, all the days that they were in the wilderness, until they came to the land of Canaan to possess it. ⁵⁰ And they proceeded from the wilderness of Sin and encamped in Alush. ⁵¹ And they proceeded from Alush and encamped in Rephidim. ⁵² And when the children of Israel were in Rephidim, Amalek the son of Eliphaz, the son of Esau, the brother of Zepho, came to fight with Israel. ⁵³ And he brought with him eight hundred and one thousand men, magicians and conjurers, and he prepared for battle with Israel in Rephidim. ⁵⁴ And they carried on a great and severe battle against Israel, and the Lord delivered Amalek and his people into the hands of Moses and the children of Israel, and into the hand of Joshua, the son of Nun, the Ephrathite, the servant of Moses. ⁵⁵ And the children of Israel smote Amalek and his people at the edge of the sword, but the battle was very sore upon the children of Israel. ⁵⁶ And the Lord said to Moses, Write this thing as a memorial for thee in a book, and place it in the hand of Joshua, the son of Nun, thy servant, and thou shalt command the children of Israel, saying, When thou shalt come to the land of Canaan, thou shalt utterly efface the remembrance of Amalek from under heaven. ⁵⁷ And Moses did so, and he took the book and wrote upon it these words, saying, ⁵⁸ Remember what Amalek has done to thee in the road when thou wentest forth from Egypt. ⁵⁹ Who met thee in the road and smote thy rear, even those that were feeble behind thee when thou wast faint and weary. ⁶⁰ Therefore it shall be when the Lord thy God shall have given thee rest from all thine enemies round about in the land which the Lord thy God giveth thee for an inheritance, to possess it, that thou shalt blot out the remembrance of Amalek from under heaven, thou shalt not forget it. ⁶¹ And the king who shall have pity on Amalek, or upon his memory or upon his seed, behold I will require it of him, and I will cut him off from amongst his people. ⁶² And Moses wrote all these things in a book, and he enjoined the children of Israel respecting all these matters.

82

¹ And the children of Israel proceeded from Rephidim and they encamped in the wilderness of Sinai, in the third month from their going forth from Egypt. ² At that time came Reuel the Midianite, the father-in-law of Moses, with Zipporah his daughter and her two sons, for he had heard of the wonders of the Lord which he had done to Israel, that he had delivered them from the hand of Egypt. ³ And Reuel came to Moses to the wilderness where he was encamped, where was the mountain of God. ⁴ And Moses went forth to meet his father-in-law with great honor, and all Israel was with him. ⁵ And Reuel and his children remained amongst the Israelites for many days, and Reuel knew the Lord from that day forward. ⁶ And in the third month from the children of Israel's departure from Egypt, on the sixth day thereof, the Lord gave to Israel the ten commandments on Mount Sinai. ⁷ And all Israel heard all these commandments, and all Israel rejoiced exceedingly in the Lord on that day. ⁸ And the glory of the Lord rested upon Mount Sinai, and he called to Moses, and Moses came in the midst of a cloud and ascended the mountain. ⁹ And Moses was upon the mount forty days and forty nights; he ate no bread and drank no water, and the Lord instructed him in the statutes and judgments in order to teach the children of Israel. ¹⁰ And the Lord wrote the ten commandments which he had commanded the children of Israel upon two tablets of stone, which he gave to Moses to command the children of Israel. ¹¹ And at the end of forty days and forty nights, when the Lord had finished speaking to Moses on Mount Sinai, then the Lord gave to Moses the tablets of stone, written with the finger of God. ¹² And when the children of Israel saw that Moses tarried to come down from the mount, they gathered round Aaron, and said, As for this man Moses we know not what has become of him. ¹³ Now therefore rise up, make unto us a god who shall go before us, so that thou shalt not die. ¹⁴ And Aaron was greatly afraid of the people, and he ordered them to bring him gold and he made it into a molten calf for the people. ¹⁵ And the Lord said to Moses, before he had come down from the mount, Get thee down, for thy people whom thou didst bring forth from Egypt have corrupted themselves. ¹⁶ They have made to themselves a molten calf, and have bowed down to it, now therefore leave me, that I may consume them from off the earth, for they are a stiffnecked people. ¹⁷ And Moses besought the countenance of the Lord, and he prayed to the Lord for the people on account of the calf which they had made, and he afterward descended from the mount and in his hands were the two tablets of stone, which God had given him to command the Israelites. ¹⁸ And when Moses approached the camp and saw the calf which the people had made, the anger of Moses was kindled and he broke the tablets under the mount. ¹⁹ And Moses came to the camp and he took the calf and burned it with fire, and ground it till it became fine dust, and strewed it upon the water and gave it to the Israelites to drink. ²⁰ And there died of the people by the swords of each other about three thousand men who had made the calf. ²¹ And on the morrow Moses said to the people, I will go up to the Lord, peradventure I may make atonement for your sins which you have sinned to the Lord. ²² And Moses again went up to the Lord, and he remained with the Lord forty days and forty nights. ²³ And during the forty days did Moses entreat the Lord in behalf of the children of Israel, and the Lord hearkened to the prayer of Moses, and the Lord was entreated of him in behalf of Israel. ²⁴ Then spake the Lord to Moses to hew two stone tablets and to bring them up to the Lord, who would write upon them the ten commandments. ²⁵ Now Moses did so, and he came down and hewed the two tablets and went up to Mount Sinai to the Lord, and the Lord wrote the ten commandments upon the tablets. ²⁶ And Moses remained yet with the Lord forty days and forty nights, and the Lord instructed him in statutes and judgments to impart to Israel. ²⁷ And the Lord commanded him respecting the children of Israel that they should make a sanctuary for the Lord, that his name might rest therein, and the Lord showed him the likeness of the sanctuary and the likeness of all its vessels. ²⁸ And at the end of the forty days, Moses came down from the mount and the two tablets were in his hand. ²⁹ And Moses came to the children of Israel and spoke to them all the words of the Lord, and he taught them laws, statutes and judgments which the Lord had taught him. ³⁰ And Moses told the children of Israel the word of the Lord, that a sanctuary should be made for him, to dwell amongst the children of Israel. ³¹ And the people rejoiced greatly at all the good which the Lord had spoken to them, through Moses, and they said, We will do all that the Lord has spoken to them. ³² And the people rose up like one man and they made generous offerings to the sanctuary of the Lord, and each man brought the offering of the Lord for the work of the sanctuary, and for all its service. ³³ And all the children of Israel brought each man of all that was found in his possession for the work of the sanctuary of the Lord, gold, silver and brass, and every thing that was serviceable for the sanctuary. ³⁴ And all the wise men who were practiced in work came and made the sanctuary of the Lord, according to all that the Lord had commanded, every man in the work in which he had been practiced; and all the wise men in heart made the sanctuary, and its furniture and all the vessels for the holy service, as the Lord had commanded Moses. ³⁵ And the work of the sanctuary of the tabernacle was completed at the end of five months, and the children of Israel did all that the Lord had commanded Moses. ³⁶ And they brought the sanctuary and all its furniture to Moses; like unto the representation which the Lord had shown to Moses, so did the children of Israel. ³⁷ And Moses saw the work, and behold they did it as the Lord had commanded him, so Moses blessed them.

83

¹ And in the twelfth month, in the twenty-third day of the month, Moses took Aaron and his sons, and he dressed them in their garments, and anointed them and did unto them as the Lord had commanded him, and Moses brought up all the offerings which the Lord had on that day commanded him. ² Moses afterward took Aaron and his sons and said to

them, For seven days shall you remain at the door of the tabernacle, for thus am I commanded. ³ And Aaron and his sons did all that the Lord had commanded them through Moses, and they remained for seven days at the door of the tabernacle. ⁴ And on the eighth day, being the first day of the first month, in the second year from the Israelites' departure from Egypt, Moses erected the sanctuary, and Moses put up all the furniture of the tabernacle and all the furniture of the sanctuary, and he did all that the Lord had commanded him. ⁵ And Moses called to Aaron and his sons, and they brought the burnt offering and the sin offering for themselves and the children of Israel, as the Lord had commanded Moses. ⁶ On that day the two sons of Aaron, Nadab and Abihu, took strange fire and brought it before the Lord who had not commanded them, and a fire went forth from before the Lord, and consumed them, and they died before the Lord on that day. ⁷ Then on the day when Moses had completed to erect the sanctuary, the princes of the children of Israel began to bring their offerings before the Lord for the dedication of the altar. ⁸ And they brought up their offerings each prince for one day, a prince each day for twelve days. ⁹ And all the offerings which they brought, each man in his day, one silver charger weighing one hundred and thirty shekels, one silver bowl of seventy shekels after the shekel of the sanctuary, both of them full of fine flour, mingled with oil for a meat offering. ¹⁰ One spoon, weighing ten shekels of gold, full of incense. ¹¹ One young bullock, one ram, one lamb of the first year for a burnt offering. ¹² And one kid of the goats for a sin offering. ¹³ And for a sacrifice of peace offering, two oxen, five rams, five he-goats, five lambs of a year old. ¹⁴ Thus did the twelve princes of Israel day by day, each man in his day. ¹⁵ And it was after this, in the thirteenth day of the month, that Moses commanded the children of Israel to observe the Passover. ¹⁶ And the children of Israel kept the Passover in its season in the fourteenth day of the month, as the Lord had commanded Moses, so did the children of Israel. ¹⁷ And in the second month, on the first day thereof, the Lord spoke unto Moses, saying, ¹⁸ Number the heads of all the males of the children of Israel from twenty years old and upward, thou and thy brother Aaron and the twelve princes of Israel. ¹⁹ And Moses did so, and Aaron came with the twelve princes of Israel, and they numbered the children of Israel in the wilderness of Sinai. ²⁰ And the numbers of the children of Israel by the houses of their fathers, from twenty years old and upward, were six hundred and three thousand, five hundred and fifty. ²¹ But the children of Levi were not numbered amongst their brethren the children of Israel. ²² And the number of all the males of the children of Israel from one month old and upward, was twenty-two thousand, two hundred and seventy-three. ²³ And the number of the children of Levi from one month old and above, was twenty-two thousand. ²⁴ And Moses placed the priests and the Levites each man to his service and to his burden to serve the sanctuary of the tabernacle, as the Lord had commanded Moses. ²⁵ And on the twentieth day of the month, the cloud was taken away from the tabernacle of testimony. ²⁶ At that time the children of Israel continued their journey from the wilderness of Sinai, and they took a journey of three days, and the cloud rested upon the wilderness of Paran; there the anger of the Lord was kindled against Israel, for they had provoked the Lord in asking him for meat, that they might eat. ²⁷ And the Lord hearkened to their voice, and gave them meat which they ate for one month. ²⁸ But after this the anger of the Lord was kindled against them, and he smote them with a great slaughter, and they were buried there in that place. ²⁹ And the children of Israel called that place Kebroth Hattaavah, because there they buried the people that lusted flesh. ³⁰ And they departed from Kebroth Hattaavah and pitched in Hazeroth, which is in the wilderness of Paran. ³¹ And whilst the children of Israel were in Hazeroth, the anger of the Lord was kindled against Miriam on account of Moses, and she became leprous, white as snow. ³² And she was confined without the camp for seven days, until she had been received again after her leprosy. ³³ The children of Israel afterward departed from Hazeroth, and pitched in the end of the wilderness of Paran. ³⁴ At that time, the Lord spoke to Moses to send twelve men from the children of Israel, one man to a tribe, to go and explore the land of Canaan. ³⁵ And Moses sent the twelve men, and they came to the land of Canaan to search and examine it, and they explored the whole land from the wilderness of Sin to Rechob as thou comest to Chamoth. ³⁶ And at the end of forty days they came to Moses and Aaron, and they brought him word as it was in their hearts, and ten of the men brought up an evil report to the children of Israel, of the land which they had explored, saying, It is better for us to return to Egypt than to go to this land, a land that consumes its inhabitants. ³⁷ But Joshua the son of Nun, and Caleb the son of Jephuneh, who were of those that explored the land, said, The land is exceedingly good. ³⁸ If the Lord delight in us, then he will bring us to this land and give it to us, for it is a land flowing with milk and honey. ³⁹ But the children of Israel would not hearken to them, and they hearkened to the words of the ten men who had brought up an evil report of the land. ⁴⁰ And the Lord heard the murmurings of the children of Israel and he was angry and swore, saying, ⁴¹ Surely not one man of this wicked generation shall see the land from twenty years old and upward excepting Caleb the son of Jephuneh and Joshua the son of Nun. ⁴² But surely this wicked generation shall perish in this wilderness, and their children shall come to the land and they shall possess it; so the anger of the Lord was kindled against Israel, and he made them wander in the wilderness for forty years until the end of that wicked generation, because they did not follow the Lord. ⁴³ And the people dwelt in the wilderness of Paran a long time, and they afterward proceeded to the wilderness by the way of the Red Sea.

84

¹ At that time Korah the son of Jetzer the son of Kehath the son of Levi, took many men of the children of Israel, and they rose up and quarreled with Moses and Aaron and the whole congregation. ² And the Lord was angry with them, and the earth opened its mouth, and swallowed them up, with their houses and all belonging to them, and all the men belonging to Korah. ³ And after this God made the people go round by the way of Mount Seir for a long time. ⁴ At that time the Lord said unto Moses, Provoke not a war against the children of Esau, for I will not give to you of any thing belonging to them, as much as the sole of the foot could tread upon, for I have given Mount Seir for an inheritance to Esau. ⁵ Therefore did the children of Esau fight against the children of Seir in former times, and the Lord had delivered the children of Seir into the hands of the children of Esau, and destroyed them from before them, and the children of Esau dwelt in their stead unto this day. ⁶ Therefore the Lord said to the children of Israel, Fight not against the children of Esau your brethren, for nothing in their land belongs to you, but you may buy food of them for money and eat it, and you may buy water of them for money and drink it. ⁷ And the children of Israel did according to the word of the Lord. ⁸ And the children of Israel went about the wilderness, going round by the way of Mount Sinai for a long time, and touched not the children of Esau, and they continued in that district for nineteen years. ⁹ At that time died Latinus king of the children of Chittim, in the forty-fifth year of his reign, which is the fourteenth year of the children of Israel's departure from Egypt. ¹⁰ And they buried him in his place which he had built for himself in the land of Chittim, and Abimnas reigned in his place for thirty-eight years. ¹¹ And the children of Israel passed the boundary of the children of Esau in those days, at the end of nineteen years, and they came and passed the road of the wilderness of Moab. ¹² And the Lord said to Moses, besiege not Moab, and do not fight against them, for I will give you nothing of their land. ¹³ And the children of Israel passed the road of the wilderness of Moab for nineteen years, and they did not fight against them. ¹⁴ And in the thirty-sixth year of the children of Israel's departing from Egypt the Lord smote the heart of Sihon, king of the Amorites, and he waged war, and went forth to fight against the children of Moab. ¹⁵ And Sihon sent messengers to Beor the son of Janeas, the son of Balaam, counsellor to the king of Egypt, and to Balaam his son, to curse Moab, in order that it might be delivered into the hand of Sihon. ¹⁶ And the messengers went and brought Beor the son of Janeas, and Balaam his son, from Pethor in Mesopotamia, so Beor and Balaam his son came to the city of Sihon and they cursed Moab and their king in the presence of Sihon king of the Amorites. ¹⁷ So Sihon went out with his whole army, and he went to Moab and fought against them, and he subdued them, and the Lord delivered them into his hands, and Sihon slew the king of Moab. ¹⁸ And Sihon took all the cities of Moab in the battle; he also took Heshbon from them, for Heshbon was one of the cities of Moab, and Sihon placed his princes and his nobles in Heshbon, and Heshbon belonged to Sihon in those days. ¹⁹ Therefore the parable speakers Beor and Balaam his son uttered these words, saying, Come unto Heshbon, the city of Sihon will be built and established. ²⁰ Woe unto thee Moab! thou art lost, O people of Kemosh! behold it is written upon the book of the law of God. ²¹ And when Sihon had conquered Moab, he placed guards in the cities which he had taken from Moab, and a considerable number of the children of Moab fell in battle into the hand of Sihon, and he made a great capture of them, sons and daughters, and he slew their king; so Sihon turned back to his own land. ²² And Sihon gave numerous presents of silver and gold to Beor and Balaam his son, and he dismissed them, and they went to Mesopotamia to their home and country. ²³ At that time all the children of Israel passed from the road of the wilderness of Moab, and returned and surrounded the wilderness of Edom. ²⁴ So the whole congregation came to the wilderness of Sin in the first month of the fortieth year from their departure from Egypt, and the children of Israel dwelt there in Kadesh, of the wilderness of Sin, and Miriam died there and she was buried there. ²⁵ At that time Moses sent messengers to Hadad king of Edom, saying, Thus says thy brother Israel, Let me pass I pray thee through thy land, we will not pass through field or vineyard, we will not drink the water of the well; we will walk in the king's

road. ²⁶ And Edom said to him, Thou shalt not pass through my country, and Edom went forth to meet the children of Israel with a mighty people. ²⁷ And the children of Esau refused to let the children of Israel pass through their land, so the Israelites removed from them and fought not against them. ²⁸ For before this the Lord had commanded the children of Israel, saying, You shall not fight against the children of Esau, therefore the Israelites removed from them and did not fight against them. ²⁹ So the children of Israel departed from Kadesh, and all the people came to Mount Hor. ³⁰ At that time the Lord said to Moses, Tell thy brother Aaron that he shall die there, for he shall not come to the land which I have given to the children of Israel. ³¹ And Aaron went up, at the command of the Lord, to Mount Hor, in the fortieth year, in the fifth month, in the first day of the month. ³² And Aaron was one hundred and twenty-three years old when he died in Mount Hor.

85

¹ And king Arad the Canaanite, who dwelt in the south, heard that the Israelites had come by the way of the spies, and he arranged his forces to fight against the Israelites. ² And the children of Israel were greatly afraid of him, for he had a great and heavy army, so the children of Israel resolved to return to Egypt. ³ And the children of Israel turned back about the distance of three days' journey unto Maserath Beni Jaakon, for they were greatly afraid on account of the king Arad. ⁴ And the children of Israel would not get back to their places, so they remained in Beni Jaakon for thirty days. ⁵ And when the children of Levi saw that the children of Israel would not turn back, they were jealous for the sake of the Lord, and they rose up and fought against the Israelites their brethren, and slew of them a great body, and forced them to turn back to their place, Mount Hor. ⁶ And when they returned, king Arad was still arranging his host for battle against the Israelites. ⁷ And Israel vowed a vow, saying, If thou wilt deliver this people into my hand, then I will utterly destroy their cities. ⁸ And the Lord hearkened to the voice of Israel, and he delivered the Canaanites into their hand, and he utterly destroyed them and their cities, and he called the name of the place Hormah. ⁹ And the children of Israel journeyed from Mount Hor and pitched in Oboth, and they journeyed from Oboth and they pitched at Ije-abarim, in the border of Moab. ¹⁰ And the children of Israel sent to Moab, saying, Let us pass now through thy land into our place, but the children of Moab would not suffer the children of Israel to pass through their land, for the children of Moab were greatly afraid lest the children of Israel should do unto them as Sihon king of the Amorites had done to them, who had taken their land and had slain many of them. ¹¹ Therefore Moab would not suffer the Israelites to pass through his land, and the Lord commanded the children of Israel, saying, That they should not fight against Moab, so the Israelites removed from Moab. ¹² And the children of Israel journeyed from the border of Moab, and they came to the other side of Arnon, the border of Moab, between Moab and the Amorites, and they pitched in the border of Sihon, king of the Amorites, in the wilderness of Kedemoth. ¹³ And the children of Israel sent messengers to Sihon, king of the Amorites, saying, ¹⁴ Let us pass through thy land, we will not turn into the fields or into the vineyards, we will go along by the king's highway until we shall have passed thy border, but Sihon would not suffer the Israelites to pass. ¹⁵ So Sihon collected all the people of the Amorites and went forth into the wilderness to meet the children of Israel, and he fought against Israel in Jahaz. ¹⁶ And the Lord delivered Sihon king of the Amorites into the hand of the children of Israel, and Israel smote all the people of Sihon with the edge of the sword and avenged the cause of Moab. ¹⁷ And the children of Israel took possession of the land of Sihon from Aram unto Jabuk, unto the children of Ammon, and they took all the spoil of the cities. ¹⁸ And Israel took all these cities, and Israel dwelt in all the cities of the Amorites. ¹⁹ And all the children of Israel resolved to fight against the children of Ammon, to take their land also. ²⁰ So the Lord said to the children of Israel, Do not besiege the children of Ammon, neither stir up battle against them, for I will give nothing to you of their land, and the children of Israel hearkened to the word of the Lord, and did not fight against the children of Ammon. ²¹ And the children of Israel turned and went up by the way of Bashan to the land of Og, king of Bashan, and Og the king of Bashan went out to meet the Israelites in battle, and he had with him many valiant men, and a very strong force from the people of the Amorites. ²² And Og king of Bashan was a very powerful man, but Naaron his son was exceedingly powerful, even stronger than he was. ²³ And Og said in his heart, Behold now the whole camp of Israel takes up a space of three parsa, now will I smite them at once without sword or spear. ²⁴ And Og went up Mount Jahaz, and took therefrom one large stone, the length of which was three parsa, and he placed it on his head, and resolved to throw it upon the camp of the children of Israel, to smite all the Israelites with that stone. ²⁵ And the angel of the Lord came and pierced the stone upon the head of Og, and the stone fell upon the neck of Og that Og fell to the earth on account of the weight of the stone upon his neck. ²⁶ At that time the Lord said to the children of Israel, Be not afraid of him, for I have given him and all his people and all his land into your hand, and you shall do to him as you did to Sihon. ²⁷ And Moses went down to him with a small number of the children of Israel, and Moses smote Og with a stick at the ankles of his feet and slew him. ²⁸ The children of Israel afterward pursued the children of Og and all his people, and they beat and destroyed them till there was no remnant left of them. ²⁹ Moses afterward sent some of the children of Israel to spy out Jaazer, for Jaazer was a very famous city. ³⁰ And the spies went to Jaazer and explored it, and the spies trusted in the Lord, and they fought against the men of Jaazer. ³¹ And these men took Jaazer and its villages, and the Lord delivered them into their hand, and they drove out the Amorites who had been there. ³² And the children of Israel took the land of the two kings of the Amorites, sixty cities which were on the other side of Jordan, from the brook of Arnon unto Mount Herman. ³³ And the children of Israel journeyed and came into the plain of Moab which is on this side of Jordan, by Jericho. ³⁴ And the children of Moab heard all the evil which the children of Israel had done to the two kings of the Amorites, to Sihon and Og, so all the men of Moab were greatly afraid of the Israelites. ³⁵ And the elders of Moab said, Behold the two kings of the Amorites, Sihon and Og, who were more powerful than all the kings of the earth, could not stand against the children of Israel, how then can we stand before them? ³⁶ Surely they sent us a message before now to pass through our land on their way, and we would not suffer them, now they will turn upon us with their heavy swords and destroy us; and Moab was distressed on account of the children of Israel, and they were greatly afraid of them, and they counselled together what was to be done to the children of Israel. ³⁷ And the elders of Moab resolved and took one of their men, Balak the son of Zippor the Moabite, and made him king over them at that time, and Balak was a very wise man. ³⁸ And the elders of Moab rose up and sent to the children of Midian to make peace with them, for a great battle and enmity had been in those days between Moab and Midian, from the days of Hadad the son of Bedad king of Edom, who smote Midian in the field of Moab, unto these days. ³⁹ And the children of Moab sent to the children of Midian, and they made peace with them, and the elders of Midian came to the land of Moab to make peace in behalf of the children of Midian. ⁴⁰ And the elders of Moab counselled with the elders of Midian what to do in order to save their lives from Israel. ⁴¹ And all the children of Moab said to the elders of Midian, Now therefore the children of Israel lick up all that are round about us, as the ox licks up the grass of the field, for thus did they do to the two kings of the Amorites who are stronger than we are. ⁴² And the elders of Midian said to Moab, We have heard that at the time when Sihon king of the Amorites fought against you, when he prevailed over you and took your land, he had sent to Beor the son of Janeas and to Balaam his son from Mesopotamia, and they came and cursed you; therefore did the hand of Sihon prevail over you, that he took your land. ⁴³ Now therefore send you also to Balaam his son, for he still remains in his land, and give him his hire, that he may come and curse all the people of whom you are afraid; so the elders of Moab heard this thing, and it pleased them to send to Balaam the son of Beor. ⁴⁴ So Balak the son of Zippor king of Moab sent messengers to Balaam, saying, ⁴⁵ Behold there is a people come out from Egypt, behold they cover the face of the earth, and they abide over against me. ⁴⁶ Now therefore come and curse this people for me, for they are too mighty for me, peradventure I shall prevail to fight against them, and drive them out, for I heard that he whom thou blessest is blessed, and whom thou cursest is cursed. ⁴⁷ So the messengers of Balak went to Balaam and brought Balaam to curse the people to fight against Moab. ⁴⁸ And Balaam came to Balak to curse Israel, and the Lord said to Balaam, Curse not this people for it is blessed. ⁴⁹ And Balak urged Balaam day by day to curse Israel, but Balaam hearkened not to Balak on account of the word of the Lord which he had spoken to Balaam. ⁵⁰ And when Balak saw that Balaam would not accede to his wish, he rose up and went home, and Balaam also returned to his land and he went from there to Midian. ⁵¹ And the children of Israel journeyed from the plain of Moab, and pitched by Jordan from Beth-jesimoth even unto Abel-shittim, at the end of the plains of Moab. ⁵² And when the children of Israel abode in the plain of Shittim, they began to commit whoredom with the daughters of Moab. ⁵³ And the children of Israel approached Moab, and the children of Moab pitched their tents opposite to the camp of the children of Israel. ⁵⁴ And the children of Moab were afraid of the children of Israel, and the children of Moab took all their daughters and their wives of beautiful aspect and comely appearance, and dressed them in gold and silver and costly garments. ⁵⁵ And the children of Moab seated those women at the door of their tents, in order that the children of Israel might see them and turn to them, and not fight against Moab. ⁵⁶ And all the children of Moab did this thing to the children of Israel, and every

man placed his wife and daughter at the door of his tent, and all the children of Israel saw the act of the children of Moab, and the children of Israel turned to the daughters of Moab and coveted them, and they went to them. ⁵⁷ And it came to pass that when a Hebrew came to the door of the tent of Moab, and saw a daughter of Moab and desired her in his heart, and spoke with her at the door of the tent that which he desired, whilst they were speaking together the men of the tent would come out and speak to the Hebrew like unto these words: ⁵⁸ Surely you know that we are brethren, we are all the descendants of Lot and the descendants of Abraham his brother, wherefore then will you not remain with us, and wherefore will you not eat our bread and our sacrifice? ⁵⁹ And when the children of Moab had thus overwhelmed him with their speeches, and enticed him by their flattering words, they seated him in the tent and cooked and sacrificed for him, and he ate of their sacrifice and of their bread. ⁶⁰ They then gave him wine and he drank and became intoxicated, and they placed before him a beautiful damsel, and he did with her as he liked, for he knew not what he was doing, as he had drunk plentifully of wine. ⁶¹ Thus did the children of Moab to Israel in that place, in the plain of Shittim, and the anger of the Lord was kindled against Israel on account of this matter, and he sent a pestilence amongst them, and there died of the Israelites twenty-four thousand men. ⁶² Now there was a man of the children of Simeon whose name was Zimri, the son of Salu, who connected himself with the Midianite Cosbi, the daughter of Zur, king of Midian, in the sight of all the children of Israel. ⁶³ And Phineas the son of Elazer, the son of Aaron the priest, saw this wicked thing which Zimri had done, and he took a spear and rose up and went after them, and pierced them both and slew them, and the pestilence ceased from the children of Israel.

86

¹ At that time after the pestilence, the Lord said to Moses, and to Elazer the son of Aaron the priest, saying, ² Number the heads of the whole community of the children of Israel, from twenty years old and upward, all that went forth in the army. ³ And Moses and Elazer numbered the children of Israel after their families, and the number of all Israel was seven hundred thousand, seven hundred and thirty. ⁴ And the number of the children of Levi, from one month old and upward, was twenty-three thousand, and amongst these there was not a man of those numbered by Moses and Aaron in the wilderness of Sinai. ⁵ For the Lord had told them that they would die in the wilderness, so they all died, and not one had been left of them excepting Caleb the son of Jephuneh, and Joshua the son of Nun. ⁶ And it was after this that the Lord said to Moses, Say unto the children of Israel to avenge upon Midian the cause of their brethren the children of Israel. ⁷ And Moses did so, and the children of Israel chose from amongst them twelve thousand men, being one thousand to a tribe, and they went to Midian. ⁸ And the children of Israel warred against Midian, and they slew every male, also the five princes ofMidian, and Balaam the son of Beor did they slay with the sword. ⁹ And the children of Israel took the wives of Midian captive, with their little ones and their cattle, and all belonging to them. ¹⁰ And they took all the spoil and all the prey, and they brought it to Moses and to Elazer to the plains of Moab. ¹¹ And Moses and Elazer and all the princes of the congregation went forth to meet them with joy. ¹² And they divided all the spoil of Midian, and the children of Israel had been revenged upon Midian for the cause of their brethren the children of Israel.

87

¹ At that time the Lord said to Moses, Behold thy days are approaching to an end, take now Joshua the son of Nun thy servant and place him in the tabernacle, and I will command him, and Moses did so. ² And the Lord appeared in the tabernacle in a pillar of cloud, and the pillar of cloud stood at the entrance of the tabernacle. ³ And the Lord commanded Joshua the son of Nun and said unto him, Be strong and courageous, for thou shalt bring the children of Israel to the land which I swore to give them, and I will be with thee. ⁴ And Moses said to Joshua, Be strong and courageous, for thou wilt make the children of Israel inherit the land, and the Lord will be with thee, he will not leave thee nor forsake thee, be not afraid nor disheartened. ⁵ And Moses called to all the children of Israel and said to them, You have seen all the good which the Lord your God has done for you in the wilderness. ⁶ Now therefore observe all the words of this law, and walk in the way of the Lord your God, turn not from the way which the Lord has commanded you, either to the right or to the left. ⁷ And Moses taught the children of Israel statutes and judgments and laws to do in the land as the Lord had commanded him. ⁸ And he taught them the way of the Lord and his laws; behold they are written upon the book of the law of God which he gave to the children of Israel by the hand of Moses. ⁹ And Moses finished commanding the children of Israel, and the Lord said to him, saying, Go up to the Mount Abarim and die there, and be gathered unto thy people as Aaron thy brother was gathered. ¹⁰ And Moses went up as the Lord had commanded him, and he died there in the land of Moab by the order of the Lord, in the fortieth year from the Israelites going forth from the land of Egypt. ¹¹ And the children of Israel wept for Moses in the plains of Moab for thirty days, and the days of weeping and mourning for Moses were completed.

88

¹ And it was after the death of Moses that the Lord said to Joshua the son of Nun, saying, ² Rise up and pass the Jordan to the land which I have given to the children of Israel, and thou shalt make the children of Israel inherit the land. ³ Every place upon which the sole of your feet shall tread shall belong to you, from the wilderness of Lebanon unto the great river the river of Perath shall be your boundary. ⁴ No man shall stand up against thee all the days of thy life; as I was with Moses, so will I be with thee, only be strong and of good courage to observe all the law which Moses commanded thee, turn not from the way either to the right or to the left, in order that thou mayest prosper in all that thou doest. ⁵ And Joshua commanded the officers of Israel, saying, Pass through the camp and command the people, saying, Prepare for yourselves provisions, for in three days more you will pass the Jordan to possess the land. ⁶ And the officers of the children of Israel did so, and they commanded the people and they did all that Joshua had commanded. ⁷ And Joshua sent two men to spy out the land of Jericho, and the men went and spied out Jericho. ⁸ And at the end of seven days they came to Joshua in the camp and said to him, The Lord has delivered the whole land into our hand, and the inhabitants thereof are melted with fear because of us. ⁹ And it came to pass after that, that Joshua rose up in the morning and all Israel with him, and they journeyed from Shittim, and Joshua and all Israel with him passed the Jordan; and Joshua was eighty-two years old when he passed the Jordan with Israel. ¹⁰ And the people went up from Jordan on the tenth day of the first month, and they encamped in Gilgal at the eastern corner of Jericho. ¹¹ And the children of Israel kept the Passover in Gilgal, in the plains of Jericho, on the fourteenth day at the month, as it is written in the law of Moses. ¹² And the manna ceased at that time on the morrow of the Passover, and there was no more manna for the children of Israel, and they ate of the produce of the land of Canaan. ¹³ And Jericho was entirely closed against the children of Israel, no one came out or went in. ¹⁴ And it was in the second month, on the first day of the month, that the Lord said to Joshua, Rise up, behold I have given Jericho into thy hand with all the people thereof; and all your fighting men shall go round the city, once each day, thus shall you do for six days. ¹⁵ And the priests shall blow upon trumpets, and when you shall hear the sound of the trumpet, all the people shall give a great shouting, that the walls of the city shall fall down; all the people shall go up every man against his opponent. ¹⁶ And Joshua did so according to all that the Lord had commanded him. ¹⁷ And on the seventh day they went round the city seven times, and the priests blew upon trumpets. ¹⁸ And at the seventh round, Joshua said to the people, Shout, for the Lord has delivered the whole city into our hands. ¹⁹ Only the city and all that it contains shall be accursed to the Lord, and keep yourselves from the accursed thing, lest you make the camp of Israel accursed and trouble it. ²⁰ But all the silver and gold and brass and iron shall be consecrated to the Lord, they shall come into the treasury of the Lord. ²¹ And the people blew upon trumpets and made a great shouting, and the walls of Jericho fell down, and all the people went up, every man straight before him, and they took the city and utterly destroyed all that was in it, both man and woman, young and old, ox and sheep and ass, with the edge of the sword. ²² And they burned the whole city with fire; only the vessels of silver and gold, and brass and iron, they put into the treasury of the Lord. ²³ And Joshua swore at that time, saying, Cursed be the man who builds Jericho; he shall lay the foundation thereof in his first-born, and in his youngest son shall he set up the gates thereof. ²⁴ And Achan the son of Carmi, the son of Zabdi, the son of Zerah, son of Judah, dealt treacherously in the accursed thing, and he took of the accursed thing and hid it in the tent, and the anger of the Lord was kindled against Israel. ²⁵ And it was after this when the children of Israel had returned from burning Jericho, Joshua sent men to spy out also Ai, and to fight against it. ²⁶ And the men went up and spied out Ai, and they returned and said, Let not all the people go up with thee to Ai, only let about three thousand men go up and smite the city, for the men thereof are but few. ²⁷ And Joshua did so, and there went up with him of the children of Israel about three thousand men, and they fought against the men of Ai. ²⁸ And the battle was severe against Israel, and the men of Ai smote thirty-six men of Israel, and the children of Israel fled from before the men of Ai. ²⁹ And when Joshua saw this thing, he tore his garments and fell upon his face to the ground before the Lord, he, with the elders of Israel, and they put dust upon their heads. ³⁰ And Joshua said, Why O Lord didst thou bring this people over the Jordan? what shall I say after the Israelites have turned their backs against their enemies? ³¹ Now

therefore all the Canaanites, inhabitants of the land, will hear this thing, and surround us and cut off our name. ³² And the Lord said to Joshua, Why dost thou fall upon thy face? rise, get thee off, for the Israelites have sinned, and taken of the accursed thing; I will no more be with them unless they destroy the accursed thing from amongst them. ³³ And Joshua rose up and assembled the people, and brought the Urim by the order of the Lord, and the tribe of Judah was taken, and Achan the son of Carmi was taken. ³⁴ And Joshua said to Achan, Tell me my son, what hast thou done, and Achan said, I saw amongst the spoil a goodly garment of Shinar and two hundred shekels of silver, and a wedge of gold of fifty shekels weight; I coveted them and took them, and behold they are all hid in the earth in the midst of the tent. ³⁵ And Joshua sent men who went and took them from the tent of Achan, and they brought them to Joshua. ³⁶ And Joshua took Achan and these utensils, and his sons and daughters and all belonging to him, and they brought them into the valley of Achor. ³⁷ And Joshua burned them there with fire, and all the Israelites stoned Achan with stones, and they raised over him a heap of stones, therefore did he call that place the valley of Achor, so the Lord's anger was appeased, and Joshua afterward came to the city and fought against it. ³⁸ And the Lord said to Joshua, Fear not, neither be thou dismayed, behold I have given into thy hand Ai, her king and her people, and thou shalt do unto them as thou didst to Jericho and her king, only the spoil thereof and the cattle thereof shall you take for a prey for yourselves; lay an ambush for the city behind it. ³⁹ So Joshua did according to the word of the Lord, and he chose from amongst the sons of war thirty thousand valiant men, and he sent them, and they lay in ambush for the city. ⁴⁰ And he commanded them, saying, When you shall see us we will flee before them with cunning, and they will pursue us, you shall then rise out of the ambush and take the city, and they did so. ⁴¹ And Joshua fought, and the men of the city went out toward Israel, not knowing that they were lying in ambush for them behind the city. ⁴² And Joshua and all the Israelites feigned themselves wearied out before them, and they fled by the way of the wilderness with cunning. ⁴³ And the men of Ai gathered all the people who were in the city to pursue the Israelites, and they went out and were drawn away from the city, not one remained, and they left the city open and pursued the Israelites. ⁴⁴ And those who were lying in ambush rose up out of their places, and hastened to come to the city and took it and set it on fire, and the men of Ai turned back, and behold the smoke of the city ascended to the skies, and they had no means of retreating either one way or the other. ⁴⁵ And all the men of Ai were in the midst of Israel, some on this side and some on that side, and they smote them so that not one of them remained. ⁴⁶ And the children of Israel took Melosh king of Ai alive, and they brought him to Joshua, and Joshua hanged him on a tree and he died. ⁴⁷ And the children of Israel returned to the city after having burned it, and they smote all those that were in it with the edge of the sword. ⁴⁸ And the number of those that had fallen of the men of Ai, both man and woman, was twelve thousand; only the cattle and the spoil of the city they took to themselves, according to the word of the Lord to Joshua. ⁴⁹ And all the kings on this side Jordan, all the kings of Canaan, heard of the evil which the children of Israel had done to Jericho and to Ai, and they gathered themselves together to fight against Israel. ⁵⁰ Only the inhabitants of Gibeon were greatly afraid of fighting against the Israelites lest they should perish, so they acted cunningly, and they came to Joshua and to all Israel, and said unto them, We have come from a distant land, now therefore make a covenant with us. ⁵¹ And the inhabitants of Gibeon over-reached the children of Israel, and the children of Israel made a covenant with them, and they made peace with them, and the princes of the congregation swore unto them, but afterward the children of Israel knew that they were neighbors to them and were dwelling amongst them. ⁵² But the children of Israel slew them not; for they had sworn to them by the Lord, and they became hewers of wood and drawers of water. ⁵³ And Joshua said to them, Why did you deceive me, to do this thing to us? and they answered him, saying, Because it was told to thy servants all that you had done to all the kings of the Amorites, and we were greatly afraid of our lives, and we did this thing. ⁵⁴ And Joshua appointed them on that day to hew wood and to draw water, and he divided them for slaves to all the tribes of Israel. ⁵⁵ And when Adonizedek king of Jerusalem heard all that the children of Israel had done to Jericho and to Ai, he sent to Hoham king of Hebron and to Piram king at Jarmuth, and to Japhia king of Lachish and to Deber king of Eglon, saying, ⁵⁶ Come up to me and help me, that we may smite the children of Israel and the inhabitants of Gibeon who have made peace with the children of Israel. ⁵⁷ And they gathered themselves together and the five kings of the Amorites went up with all their camps, a mighty people numerous as the sand of the sea shore. ⁵⁸ And all these kings came and encamped before Gibeon, and they began to fight against the inhabitants of Gibeon, and all the men of Gibeon sent to Joshua, saying, Come up quickly to us and help us, for all the kings of the Amorites have gathered together to fight against us. ⁵⁹ And Joshua and all the fighting people went up from Gilgal, and Joshua came suddenly to them, and smote these five kings with a great slaughter. ⁶⁰ And the Lord confounded them before the children at Israel, who smote them with a terrible slaughter in Gibeon, and pursued them along the way that goes up to Beth Horon unto Makkedah, and they fled from before the children of Israel. ⁶¹ And whilst they were fleeing, the Lord sent upon them hailstones from heaven, and more of them died by the hailstones, than by the slaughter of the children of Israel. ⁶² And the children of Israel pursued them, and they still smote them in the road, going on and smiting them. ⁶³ And when they were smiting, the day was declining toward evening, and Joshua said in the sight of all the people, Sun, stand thou still upon Gibeon, and thou moon in the valley of Ajalon, until the nation shall have revenged itself upon its enemies. ⁶⁴ And the Lord hearkened to the voice of Joshua, and the sun stood still in the midst of the heavens, and it stood still six and thirty moments, and the moon also stood still and hastened not to go down a whole day. ⁶⁵ And there was no day like that, before it or after it, that the Lord hearkened to the voice of a man, for the Lord fought for Israel.

89

¹ Then spoke Joshua this song, on the day that the Lord had given the Amorites into the hand of Joshua and the children of Israel, and he said in the sight of all Israel, ² Thou hast done mighty things, O Lord, thou hast performed great deeds; who is like unto thee? my lips shall sing to thy name. ³ My goodness and my fortress, my high tower, I will sing a new song unto thee, with thanksgiving will I sing to thee, thou art the strength of my salvation. ⁴ All the kings of the earth shall praise thee, the princes of the world shall sing to thee, the children of Israel shall rejoice in thy salvation, they shall sing and praise thy power. ⁵ To thee, O Lord, did we confide; we said thou art our God, for thou wast our shelter and strong tower against our enemies. ⁶ To thee we cried and were not ashamed, in thee we trusted and were delivered; when we cried unto thee, thou didst hear our voice, thou didst deliver our souls from the sword, thou didst show unto us thy grace, thou didst give unto us thy salvation, thou didst rejoice our hearts with thy strength. ⁷ Thou didst go forth for our salvation, with thine arm thou didst redeem thy people; thou didst answer us from the heavens of thy holiness, thou didst save us from ten thousands of people. ⁸ The sun and moon stood still in heaven, and thou didst stand in thy wrath against our oppressors and didst command thy judgments over them. ⁹ All the princes of the earth stood up, the kings of the nations had gathered themselves together, they were not moved at thy presence, they desired thy battles. ¹⁰ Thou didst rise against them in thine anger, and didst bring down thy wrath upon them; thou didst destroy them in thine anger, and cut them off in thine heart. ¹¹ Nations have been consumed with thy fury, kingdoms have declined because of thy wrath, thou didst wound kings in the day of thine anger. ¹² Thou didst pour out thy fury upon them, thy wrathful anger took hold of them; thou didst turn their iniquity upon them, and didst cut them off in their wickedness. ¹³ They did spread a trap, they fell therein, in the net they hid, their foot was caught. ¹⁴ Thine hand was ready for all thine enemies who said, Through their sword they possessed the land, through their arm they dwelt in the city; thou didst fill their faces with shame, thou didst bring their horns down to the ground, thou didst terrify them in thy wrath, and didst destroy them in thine anger. ¹⁵ The earth trembled and shook at the sound of thy storm over them, thou didst not withhold their souls from death, and didst bring down their lives to the grave. ¹⁶ Thou didst pursue them in thy storm, thou didst consume them in thy whirlwind, thou didst turn their rain into hail, they fell in deep pits so that they could not rise. ¹⁷ Their carcasses were like rubbish cast out in the middle of the streets. ¹⁸ They were consumed and destroyed in thine anger, thou didst save thy people with thy might. ¹⁹ Therefore our hearts rejoice in thee, our souls exalt in thy salvation. ²⁰ Our tongues shall relate thy might, we will sing and praise thy wondrous works. ²¹ For thou didst save us from our enemies, thou didst deliver us from those who rose up against us, thou didst destroy them from before us and depress them beneath our feet. ²² Thus shall all thine enemies perish O Lord, and the wicked shall be like chaff driven by the wind, and thy beloved shall be like trees planted by the waters. ²³ So Joshua and all Israel with him returned to the camp in Gilgal, after having smitten all the kings, so that not a remnant was left of them. ²⁴ And the five kings fled alone on foot from battle, and hid themselves in a cave, and Joshua sought for them in the field of battle, and did not find them. ²⁵ And it was afterward told to Joshua, saying, The kings are found and behold they are hidden in a cave. ²⁶ And Joshua said, Appoint men to be at the mouth of the cave, to guard them, lest they take themselves away; and the children of Israel did so. ²⁷ And Joshua called to all Israel and said to the officers of battle, Place your feet upon the necks of these kings, and Joshua said, So shall the Lord do to all your enemies. ²⁸ And Joshua commanded afterward

that they should slay the kings and cast them into the cave, and to put great stones at the mouth of the cave. ²⁹ And Joshua went afterward with all the people that were with him on that day to Makkedah, and he smote it with the edge of the sword. ³⁰ And he utterly destroyed the souls and all belonging to the city, and he did to the king and people thereof as he had done to Jericho. ³¹ And he passed from there to Libnah and he fought against it, and the Lord delivered it into his hand, and Joshua smote it with the edge of the sword, and all the souls thereof, and he did to it and to the king thereof as he had done to Jericho. ³² And from there he passed on to Lachish to fight against it, and Horam king of Gaza went up to assist the men of Lachish, and Joshua smote him and his people until there was none left to him. ³³ And Joshua took Lachish and all the people thereof, and he did to it as he had done to Libnah. ³⁴ And Joshua passed from there to Eglon, and he took that also, and he smote it and all the people thereof with the edge of the sword. ³⁵ And from there he passed to Hebron and fought against it and took it and utterly destroyed it, and he returned from there with all Israel to Debir and fought against it and smote it with the edge of the sword. ³⁶ And he destroyed every soul in it, he left none remaining, and he did to it and the king thereof as he had done to Jericho. ³⁷ And Joshua smote all the kings of the Amorites from Kadesh-barnea to Azah, and he took their country at once, for the Lord had fought for Israel. ³⁸ And Joshua with all Israel came to the camp to Gilgal. ³⁹ When at that time Jabin king of Chazor heard all that Joshua had done to the kings of the Amorites, Jabin sent to Jobat king of Midian, and to Laban king of Shimron, to Jephal king of Achshaph, and to all the kings of the Amorites, saying, ⁴⁰ Come quickly to us and help us, that we may smite the children of Israel, before they come upon us and do unto us as they have done to the other kings of the Amorites. ⁴¹ And all these kings hearkened to the words of Jabin, king of Chazor, and they went forth with all their camps, seventeen kings, and their people were as numerous as the sand on the sea shore, together with horses and chariots innumerable, and they came and pitched together at the waters of Merom, and they were met together to fight against Israel. ⁴² And the Lord said to Joshua, Fear them not, for tomorrow about this time I will deliver them up all slain before you, thou shalt hough their horses and burn their chariots with fire. ⁴³ And Joshua with all the men of war came suddenly upon them and smote them, and they fell into their hands, for the Lord had delivered them into the hands of the children of Israel. ⁴⁴ So the children of Israel pursued all these kings with their camps, and smote them until there was none left of them, and Joshua did to them as the Lord had spoken to him. ⁴⁵ And Joshua returned at that time to Chazor and smote it with the sword and destroyed every soul in it and burned it with fire, and from Chazor, Joshua passed to Shimron and smote it and utterly destroyed it. ⁴⁶ From there he passed to Achshaph and he did to it as he had done to Shimron. ⁴⁷ From there he passed to Adulam and he smote all the people in it, and he did to Adulam as he had done to Achshaph and to Shimron. ⁴⁸ And he passed from them to all the cities of the kings which he had smitten, and he smote all the people that were left of them and he utterly destroyed them. ⁴⁹ Only their booty and cattle the Israelites took to themselves as a prey, but every human being they smote, they suffered not a soul to live. ⁵⁰ As the Lord had commanded Moses so did Joshua and all Israel, they failed not in anything. ⁵¹ So Joshua and all the children of Israel smote the whole land of Canaan as the Lord had commanded them, and smote all their kings, being thirty and one kings, and the children of Israel took their whole country. ⁵² Besides the kingdoms of Sihon and Og which are on the other side Jordan, of which Moses had smitten many cities, and Moses gave them to the Reubenites and the Gadites and to half the tribe of Manasseh. ⁵³ And Joshua smote all the kings that were on this side Jordan to the west, and gave them for an inheritance to the nine tribes and to the half tribe of Israel. ⁵⁴ For five years did Joshua carry on the war with these kings, and he gave their cities to the Israelites, and the land became tranquil from battle throughout the cities of the Amorites and the Canaanites.

90

¹ At that time in the fifth year after the children of Israel had passed over Jordan, after the children of Israel had rested from their war with the Canaanites, at that time great and severe battles arose between Edom and the children of Chittim, and the children of Chittim fought against Edom. ² And Abianus king of Chittim went forth in that year, that is in the thirty-first year of his reign, and a great force with him of the mighty men of the children of Chittim, and he went to Seir to fight against the children of Esau. ³ And Hadad the king of Edom heard of his report, and he went forth to meet him with a heavy people and strong force, and engaged in battle with him in the field of Edom. ⁴ And the hand of Chittim prevailed over the children of Esau, and the children of Chittim slew of the children of Esau, two and twenty thousand men, and all the children of Esau fled from before them. ⁵ And the children of Chittim pursued them and they reached Hadad king of Edom, who was running before them and they caught him alive, and brought him to Abianus king of Chittim. ⁶ And Abianus ordered him to be slain, and Hadad king of Edom died in the forty-eighth year of his reign. ⁷ And the children of Chittim continued their pursuit of Edom, and they smote them with a great slaughter and Edom became subject to the children of Chittim. ⁸ And the children of Chittim ruled over Edom, and Edom became under the hand of the children of Chittim and became one kingdom from that day. ⁹ And from that time they could no more lift up their heads, and their kingdom became one with the children of Chittim. ¹⁰ And Abianus placed officers in Edom and all the children of Edom became subject and tributary to Abianus, and Abianus turned back to his own land, Chittim. ¹¹ And when he returned he renewed his government and built for himself a spacious and fortified palace for a royal residence, and reigned securely over the children of Chittim and over Edom. ¹² In those days, after the children of Israel had driven away all the Canaanites and the Amorites, Joshua was old and advanced in years. ¹³ And the Lord said to Joshua, Thou art old, advanced in life, and a great part of the land remains to be possessed. ¹⁴ Now therefore divide this land for an inheritance to the nine tribes and to the half tribe of Manasseh, and Joshua rose up and did as the Lord had spoken to him. ¹⁵ And he divided the whole land to the tribes of Israel as an inheritance according to their divisions. ¹⁶ But to the tribe at Levi he gave no inheritance, the offerings of the Lord are their inheritance as the Lord had spoken of them by the hand of Moses. ¹⁷ And Joshua gave Mount Hebron to Caleb the son of Jephuneh, one portion above his brethren, as the Lord had spoken through Moses. ¹⁸ Therefore Hebron became an inheritance to Caleb and his children unto this day. ¹⁹ And Joshua divided the whole land by lots to all Israel for an inheritance, as the Lord had commanded him. ²⁰ And the children of Israel gave cities to the Levites from their own inheritance, and suburbs for their cattle, and property, as the Lord had commanded Moses so did the children of Israel, and they divided the land by lot whether great or small. ²¹ And they went to inherit the land according to their boundaries, and the children of Israel gave to Joshua the son of Nun an inheritance amongst them. ²² By the word of the Lord did they give to him the city which he required, Timnath-serach in Mount Ephraim, and he built the city and dwelt therein. ²³ These are the inheritances which Elazer the priest and Joshua the son of Nun and the heads of the fathers of the tribes portioned out to the children of Israel by lot in Shiloh, before the Lord, at the door of the tabernacle, and they left off dividing the land. ²⁴ And the Lord gave the land to the Israelites, and they possessed it as the Lord had spoken to them, and as the Lord had sworn to their ancestors. ²⁵ And the Lord gave to the Israelites rest from all their enemies around them, and no man stood up against them, and the Lord delivered all their enemies into their hands, and not one thing failed of all the good which the Lord had spoken to the children of Israel, yea the Lord performed every thing. ²⁶ And Joshua called to all the children of Israel and he blessed them, and commanded them to serve the Lord, and he afterward sent them away, and they went each man to his city, and each man to his inheritance. ²⁷ And the children of Israel served the Lord all the days of Joshua, and the Lord gave them rest from all around them, and they dwelt securely in their cities. ²⁸ And it came to pass in those days, that Abianus king of Chittim died, in the thirty-eighth year of his reign, that is the seventh year of his reign over Edom, and they buried him in his place which he had built for himself, and Latinus reigned in his stead fifty years. ²⁹ And during his reign he brought forth an army, and he went and fought against the inhabitants of Britannia and Kernania, the children of Elisha son of Javan, and he prevailed over them and made them tributary. ³⁰ He then heard that Edom had revolted from under the hand of Chittim, and Latinus went to them and smote them and subdued them, and placed them under the hand of the children of Chittim, and Edom became one kingdom with the children of Chittim all the days. ³¹ And for many years there was no king in Edom, and their government was with the children of Chittim and their king. ³² And it was in the twenty-sixth year after the children of Israel had passed the Jordan, that is the sixty-sixth year after the children of Israel had departed from Egypt, that Joshua was old, advanced in years, being one hundred and eight years old in those days. ³³ And Joshua called to all Israel, to their elders, their judges and officers, after the Lord had given to all the Israelites rest from all their enemies round about, and Joshua said to the elders of Israel, and to their judges, Behold I am old, advanced in years, and you have seen what the Lord has done to all the nations whom he has driven away from before you, for it is the Lord who has fought for you. ³⁴ Now therefore strengthen yourselves to keep and to do all the words of the law of Moses, not to deviate from it to the right or to the left, and not to come amongst those nations who are left in the land; neither shall you make mention of the name of their gods, but you shall cleave to the Lord your God, as you have done to this day. ³⁵ And Joshua greatly exhorted the children of Israel to serve the Lord all their days. ³⁶ And all the Israelites

said, We will serve the Lord our God all our days, we and our children, and our children's children, and our seed for ever. ³⁷ And Joshua made a covenant with the people on that day, and he sent away the children of Israel, and they went each man to his inheritance and to his city. ³⁸ And it was in those days, when the children of Israel were dwelling securely in their cities, that they buried the coffins of the tribes of their ancestors, which they had brought up from Egypt, each man in the inheritance of his children, the twelve sons of Jacob did the children of Israel bury, each man in the possession of his children. ³⁹ And these are the names of the cities wherein they buried the twelve sons of Jacob, whom the children of Israel had brought up from Egypt. ⁴⁰ And they buried Reuben and Gad on this side Jordan, in Romia, which Moses had given to their children. ⁴¹ And Simeon and Levi they buried in the city Mauda, which he had given to the children of Simeon, and the suburb of the city was for the children of Levi. ⁴² And Judah they buried in the city of Benjamin opposite Bethlehem. ⁴³ And the bones of Issachar and Zebulun they buried in Zidon, in the portion which fell to their children. ⁴⁴ And Dan was buried in the city of his children in Eshtael, and Naphtali and Asher they buried in Kadesh-naphtali, each man in his place which he had given to his children. ⁴⁵ And the bones of Joseph they buried in Shechem, in the part of the field which Jacob had purchased from Hamor, and which became to Joseph for an inheritance. ⁴⁶ And they buried Benjamin in Jerusalem opposite the Jebusite, which was given to the children of Benjamin; the children of Israel buried their fathers each man in the city of his children. ⁴⁷ And at the end of two years, Joshua the son of Nun died, one hundred and ten years old, and the time which Joshua judged Israel was twenty-eight years, and Israel served the Lord all the days of his life. ⁴⁸ And the other affairs of Joshua and his battles and his reproofs with which he reproved Israel, and all which he had commanded them, and the names of the cities which the children of Israel possessed in his days, behold they are written in the book of the words of Joshua to the children of Israel, and in the book of the wars of the Lord, which Moses and Joshua and the children of Israel had written. ⁴⁹ And the children of Israel buried Joshua in the border of his inheritance, in Timnath-serach, which was given to him in Mount Ephraim. ⁵⁰ And Elazer the son of Aaron died in those days, and they buried him in a hill belonging to Phineas his son, which was given him in Mount Ephraim.

91

¹ At that time, after the death of Joshua, the children of the Canaanites were still in the land, and the Israelites resolved to drive them out. ² And the children of Israel asked of the Lord, saying, Who shall first go up for us to the Canaanites to fight against them? and the Lord said, Judah shall go up. ³ And the children of Judah said to Simeon, Go up with us into our lot, and we will fight against the Canaanites and we likewise will go up with you, in your lot, so the children of Simeon went with the children of Judah. ⁴ And the children of Judah went up and fought against the Canaanites, so the Lord delivered the Canaanites into the hands of the children of Judah, and they smote them in Bezek, ten thousand men. ⁵ And they fought with Adonibezek in Bezek, and he fled from before them, and they pursued him and caught him, and they took hold of him and cut off his thumbs and great toes. ⁶ And Adonibezek said, Three score and ten kings having their thumbs and great toes cut off, gathered their meat under my table, as I have done, so God has requited me, and they brought him to Jerusalem and he died there. ⁷ And the children of Simeon went with the children of Judah, and they smote the Canaanites with the edge of the sword. ⁸ And the Lord was with the children of Judah, and they possessed the mountain, and the children of Joseph went up to Bethel, the same is Luz, and the Lord was with them. ⁹ And the children of Joseph spied out Bethel, and the watchmen saw a man going forth from the city, and they caught him and said unto him, Show us now the entrance of the city and we will show kindness to thee. ¹⁰ And that man showed them the entrance of the city, and the children of Joseph came and smote the City with the edge of the sword. ¹¹ And the man with his family they sent away, and he went to the Hittites and he built a city, and he called the name thereof Luz, so all the Israelites dwelt in their cities, and the children at Israel dwelt in their cities, and the children of Israel served the Lord all the days of Joshua, and all the days of the elders, who had lengthened their days after Joshua, and saw the great work of the Lord, which he had performed for Israel. ¹² And the elders judged Israel after the death of Joshua for seventeen years. ¹³ And all the elders also fought the battles of Israel against the Canaanites and the Lord drove the Canaanites from before the children of Israel, in order to place the Israelites in their land. ¹⁴ And he accomplished all the words which he had spoken to Abraham, Isaac, and Jacob, and the oath which he had sworn, to give to them and to their children, the land of the Canaanites. ¹⁵ And the Lord gave to the children of Israel the whole land of Canaan, as he had sworn to their ancestors, and the Lord gave them rest from those around them, and the children of Israel dwelt securely in their cities. ¹⁶ Blessed be the Lord for ever, amen, and amen. ¹⁷ Strengthen yourselves, and let the hearts of all you that trust in the Lord be of good courage.

Bonus Guide

Use your phone's camera to scan the QR code below or insert the web address in your browser (peakquest.top/completeapocrypha-landing) … and **unlock your bonuses** on our website!

APOCALYPSES

The Second Book of Enoch
(or Slavonic Enoch, or The Book of the Secrets of Enoch)

1

¹ There was a wise man, a great artificer, and the Lord conceived love for him and received him, that he should behold the uppermost dwellings and be an eye-witness of the wise and great and inconceivable and immutable realm of God Almighty, of the very wonderful and glorious and bright and many-eyed station of the Lord's servants, and of the inaccessible throne of the Lord, and of the degrees and manifestations of the incorporeal hosts, and of the ineffable ministration of the multitude of the elements, and of the various apparition and inexpressible singing of the host of Cherubim, and of the boundless light. ² At that time, he said, when my one hundred and sixty-fifth year was completed, I begat my son Mathusal (Methuselah). ³ After this too I lived two hundred years and completed of all the years of my life three hundred and sixty-five years. ⁴ On the first day of the month I was in my house alone and was resting on my bed and slept. ⁵ And when I was asleep, great distress came up into my heart, and I was weeping with my eyes in sleep, and I could not understand what this distress was, or what would happen to me. ⁶ And there appeared to me two men, exceeding big, so that I never saw such on earth; their faces were shining like the sun, their eyes too (were) like a burning light, and from their lips was fire coming forth with clothing and singing of various kinds in appearance purple, their wings (were)brighter than gold, their hands whiter than snow. ⁷ They were standing at the head of my bed and began to call me by my name. ⁸ And I arose from my sleep and saw clearly those two men standing in front of me. ⁹ And I saluted them and was seized with fear and the appearance of my face was changed from terror, and those men said to me: ¹⁰ Have courage, Enoch, do not fear; the eternal God sent us to you, and lo! You shalt to-day ascend with us into heaven, and you shall tell your sons and all your household all that they shall do without you on earth in your house, and let no one seek you till the Lord return you to them. ¹¹ And I made haste to obey them and went out from my house, and made to the doors, as it was ordered me, and summoned my sons Mathusal (Methuselah) and Regim and Gaidad and made known to them all the marvels those (men) had told me.

2

¹ Listen to me, my children, I know not whither I go, or what will befall me; now therefore, my children, I tell you: turn not from God before the face of the vain, who made not Heaven and earth, for these shall perish and those who worship them, and may the Lord make confident your hearts in the fear of him. And now, my children, let no one think to seek me, until the Lord return me to you.

3

¹ It came to pass, when Enoch had told his sons, that the angels took him on to their wings and bore him up on to the first heaven and placed him on the clouds. And there I looked, and again I looked higher, and saw the ether, and they placed me on the first heaven and showed me a very great Sea, greater than the earthly sea.

4

¹ They brought before my face the elders and rulers of the stellar orders, and showed me two hundred angels, who rule the stars and (their) services to the heavens, and fly with their wings and come round all those who sail.

5

¹ And here I looked down and saw the treasure-houses of the snow, and the angels who keep their terrible store-houses, and the clouds whence they come out and into which they go.

6

¹ They showed me the treasure-house of the dew, like oil of the olive, and the appearance of its form, as of all the flowers of the earth; further many angels guarding the treasure-houses of these (things), and how they are made to shut and open.

7

¹ And those men took me and led me up on to the second heaven, and showed me darkness, greater than earthly darkness, and there I saw prisoners hanging, watched, awaiting the great and boundless judgment, and these angels (spirits) were dark-looking, more than earthly darkness, and incessantly making weeping through all hours. ² And I said to the men who were with me: Wherefore are these incessantly tortured? They answered me: These are God's apostates, who obeyed not God's commands, but took counsel with their own will, and turned away with their prince, who also (is) fastened on the fifth heaven. ³ And I felt great pity for them, and they saluted me, and said to me: Man of God, pray for us to the Lord; and I answered to them: Who am I, a mortal man, that I should pray for angels (spirits)? Who knows whither I go, or what will befall me? Or who will pray for me?

8

¹ And those men took me thence, and led me up on to the third heaven, and placed me there; and I looked downwards, and saw the produce of these places, such as has never been known for goodness. ² And I saw all the sweet-flowering trees and beheld their fruits, which were sweet-smelling, and all the foods borne (by them) bubbling with fragrant exhalation. ³ And in the midst of the trees that of life, in that place whereon the Lord rests, when he goes up into paradise; and this tree is of ineffable goodness and fragrance, and adorned more than every existing thing; and on all sides (it is) in form gold-looking and vermilion and fire-like and covers all, and it has produce from all fruits. ⁴ Its root is in the garden at the earth's end. ⁵ And paradise is between corruptibility and incorruptibility. ⁶ And two springs come out which send forth honey and milk, and their springs send forth oil and wine, and they separate into four parts, and go round with quiet course, and go down into the PARADISE OF EDEN, between corruptibility and incorruptibility. ⁷ And thence they go forth along the earth, and have a revolution to their circle even as other elements. ⁸ And here there is no unfruitful tree, and every place is blessed. ⁹ And (there are) three hundred angels very bright, who keep the garden, and with incessant sweet singing and never-silent voices serve the Lord throughout all days and hours. ¹⁰ And I said: How very sweet is this place, and those men said to me:

9

¹ This place, O Enoch, is prepared for the righteous, who endure all manner of offence from those that exasperate their souls, who avert their eyes from iniquity, and make righteous judgment, and give bread to the hungering, and cover the naked with clothing, and raise up the fallen, and help injured orphans, and who walk without fault before the face of the Lord, and serve him alone, and for them is prepared this place for eternal inheritance.

10

¹ And those two men led me up on to the Northern side, and showed me there a very terrible place, and (there were) all manner of tortures in that place: cruel darkness and unillumined gloom, and there is no light there, but murky fire constantly flaming aloft, and (there is) a fiery river coming forth, and that whole place is everywhere fire, and everywhere (there is) frost and ice, thirst and shivering, while the bonds are very cruel, and the angels (spirits) fearful and merciless, bearing angry weapons, merciless torture, and I said: ² Woe, woe, how very terrible is this place. ³ And those men said to me: This place, O Enoch, is prepared for those who dishonour God, who on earth practice sin against nature, which is child-corruption after the sodomitic fashion, magic-making, enchantments and devilish witchcrafts, and who boast of their wicked deeds, stealing, lies, calumnies, envy, rancour, fornication, murder, and who, accursed, steal the souls of men, who, seeing the poor take away their goods and themselves wax rich, injuring them for other men's goods; who being able to satisfy the empty, made the hungering to die; being able to clothe, stripped the naked; and who knew not their creator, and bowed to the soulless (and lifeless) gods, who cannot see nor hear, vain gods, (who also) built hewn images and bow down to unclean handiwork, for all these is prepared this place among these, for eternal inheritance.

11

¹ Those men took me, and led me up on to the fourth heaven, and showed me all the successive goings, and all the rays of the light of sun and moon. ² And I measure their goings, and compared their light, and saw that the sun's light is greater than the moon's. ³ Its circle and the wheels on which it goes always, like the wind going past with very marvellous speed, and day and night it has no rest. ⁴ Its passage and return (are accompanied by) four great stars, (and) each star has under it a thousand stars, to the right of the sun's wheel, (and by) four to the left, each having under it a thousand stars, altogether eight thousand, issuing with the sun continually. ⁵ And by day fifteen myriads of angels attend it, and by night A thousand. ⁶ And six-winged ones issue with the angels before the sun's wheel into the fiery flames, and a hundred angels kindle the sun and set it alight.

12

¹ And I looked and saw other flying elements of the sun, whose names (are) Phoenixes and Chalkydri, marvellous and wonderful, with feet and tails in the form of a lion, and a crocodile's head, their appearance (is) empurpled, like the rainbow; their size (is) nine hundred measures, their wings (are like) those of angels, each (has) twelve, and they attend and accompany the sun, bearing heat and dew, as it is ordered them from God. ² Thus (the sun)

revolves and goes, and rises under the heaven, and its course goes under the earth with the light of its rays incessantly.

13

[1] Those men bore me away to the east, and placed me at the sun's gates, where the sun goes forth according to the regulation of the seasons and the circuit of the months of the whole year, and the number of the hours day and night. [2] And I saw six gates open, each gate having sixty-one stadia and A quarter of one stadium, and I measured (them) truly, and understood their size (to be) so much, through which the sun goes forth, and goes to the west, and is made even, and rises throughout all the months, and turns back again from the six gates according to the succession of the seasons; thus (the period) of the whole year is finished after the returns of the four seasons.

14

[1] And again those men led me away to the western parts, and showed me six great gates open corresponding to the eastern gates, opposite to where the sun sets, according to the number of the days three hundred and sixty-five and A quarter. [2] Thus again it goes down to the western gates, (and) draws away its light, the greatness of its brightness, under the earth; for since the crown of its shining is in heaven with the Lord, and guarded by four hundred angels, while the sun goes round on wheel under the earth, and stands seven great hours in night, and spends half (its course) under the earth, when it comes to the eastern approach in the eighth hour of the night, it brings its lights, and the crown of shining, and the sun flames forth more than fire.

15

[1] Then the elements of the sun, called Phoenixes and Chalkydri break into song, therefore every bird flutters with its wings, rejoicing at the giver of light, and they broke into song at the command of the Lord. [2] The giver of light comes to give brightness to the whole world, and the morning guard takes shape, which is the rays of the sun, and the sun of the earth goes out, and receives its brightness to light up the whole face of the earth, and they showed me this calculation of the sun's going. [3] And the gates which it enters, these are the great gates of the calculation of the hours of the year; for this reason the sun is a great creation, whose circuit (lasts) twenty-eight years, and begins again from the beginning.

16

[1] Those men showed me the other course, that of the moon, twelve great gates, crowned from west to east, by which the moon goes in and out of the customary times. [2] It goes in at the first gate to the western places of the sun, by the first gates with (thirty)-one (days) exactly, by the second gates with thirty-one days exactly, the third with thirty days exactly, by the fourth with thirty days exactly, by the fifth with thirty-one days exactly, by the sixth with thirty-one days exactly, by the seventh with thirty days exactly, by the eighth with thirty-one days perfectly, by the ninth with thirty-one days exactly, by the tenth with thirty days perfectly, by the eleventh with thirty-one days exactly, by the twelfth with twenty-eight days exactly. [3] And it goes through the western gates in the order and number of the eastern, and accomplishes the three hundred and sixty-five and a quarter days of the solar year, while the lunar year has three hundred fifty-four, and there are wanting (to it) twelve days of the solar circle, which are the lunar epacts of the whole year. [4] Thus, too, the great circle contains five hundred and thirty-two years. [5] The quarter (of a day) is omitted for three years, the fourth fulfills it exactly. [6] Therefore they are taken outside of heaven for three years and are not added to the number of days, because they change the time of the years to two new months towards completion, to two others towards diminution. [7] And when the western gates are finished, it returns and goes to the eastern to the lights, and goes thus day and night about the heavenly circles, lower than all circles, swifter than the heavenly winds, and spirits and elements and angels flying; each angel has six wings. [8] It has a sevenfold course in nineteen years.

17

[1] In the midst of the heavens I saw armed soldiers, serving the Lord, with tympana and organs, with incessant voice, with sweet voice, with sweet and incessant (voice) and various singing, which it is impossible to describe, and (which) astonishes every mind, so wonderful and marvellous is the singing of those angels, and I was delighted listening to it.

18

[1] The men took me on to the fifth heaven and placed me, and there I saw many and countless soldiers, called Grigori, of human appearance, and their size (was) greater than that of great giants and their faces withered, and the silence of their mouths perpetual, and their was no service on the fifth heaven, and I said to the men who were with me: [2] Wherefore are these very withered and their faces melancholy, and their mouths silent, and (wherefore) is there no service on this heaven? [3] And they said to me: These are the Grigori, who with their prince Satanail (Satan) rejected the Lord of light, and after them are those who are held in great darkness on the second heaven, and three of them went down on to earth from the Lord's throne, to the place Ermon, and broke through their vows on the shoulder of the hill Ermon and saw the daughters of men how good they are, and took to themselves wives, and befouled the earth with their deeds, who in all times of their age made lawlessness and mixing, and giants are born and marvellous big men and great enmity. [4] And therefore God judged them with great judgment, and they weep for their brethren and they will be punished on the Lord's great day. [5] And I said to the Grigori: I saw your brethren and their works, and their great torments, and I prayed for them, but the Lord has condemned them (to be) under earth till (the existing) heaven and earth shall end for ever. [6] And I said: Wherefore do you wait, brethren, and do not serve before the Lord's face, and have not put your services before the Lord's face, lest you anger your Lord utterly? [7] And they listened to my admonition, and spoke to the four ranks in heaven, and lo! As I stood with those two men four trumpets trumpeted together with great voice, and the Grigori broke into song with one voice, and their voice went up before the Lord pitifully and affectingly.

19

[1] And thence those men took me and bore me up on to the sixth heaven, and there I saw seven bands of angels, very bright and very glorious, and their faces shining more than the sun's shining, glistening, and there is no difference in their faces, or behaviour, or manner of dress; and these make the orders, and learn the goings of the stars, and the alteration of the moon, or revolution of the sun, and the good government of the world. [2] And when they see evildoing they make commandments and instruction, and sweet and loud singing, and all (songs) of praise. [3] These are the archangels who are above angels, measure all life in heaven and on earth, and the angels who are (appointed) over seasons and years, the angels who are over rivers and sea, and who are over the fruits of the earth, and the angels who are over every grass, giving food to all, to every living thing, and the angels who write all the souls of men, and all their deeds, and their lives before the Lord's face; in their midst are six Phoenixes and six Cherubim and six six-winged ones continually with one voice singing one voice, and it is not possible to describe their singing, and they rejoice before the Lord at his footstool.

20

[1] And those two men lifted me up thence on to the seventh heaven, and I saw there a very great light, and fiery troops of great archangels, incorporeal forces, and dominions, orders and governments, Cherubim and seraphim, thrones and many-eyed ones, nine regiments, the Ioanit stations of light, and I became afraid, and began to tremble with great terror, and those men took me, and led me after them, and said to me: [2] Have courage, Enoch, do not fear, and showed me the Lord from afar, sitting on His very high throne. For what is there on the tenth heaven, since the Lord dwells there? [3] On the tenth heaven is God, in the Hebrew tongue he is called Aravat. [4] And all the heavenly troops would come and stand on the ten steps according to their rank, and would bow down to the Lord, and would again go to their places in joy and felicity, singing songs in the boundless light with small and tender voices, gloriously serving him.

21

[1] And the Cherubim and seraphim standing about the throne, the six-winged and many-eyed ones do not depart, standing before the Lord's face doing his will, and cover his whole throne, singing with gentle voice before the Lord's face: Holy, holy, holy, Lord Ruler of Sabaoth, heavens and earth are full of Your glory. [2] When I saw all these things, those men said to me: Enoch, thus far is it commanded us to journey with you, and those men went away from me and thereupon I saw them not. [3] And I remained alone at the end of the seventh heaven and became afraid, and fell on my face and said to myself: Woe is me, what has befallen me? [4] And the Lord sent one of his glorious ones, the archangel Gabriel, and (he) said to me: Have courage, Enoch, do not fear, arise before the Lord's face into eternity, arise, come with me. [5] And I answered him, and said in myself: My Lord, my soul is departed from me, from terror and trembling, and I called to the men who led me up to this place, on them I relied, and (it is) with them I go before the Lord's face. [6] And Gabriel caught me up, as a leaf caught up by the wind, and placed me before the Lord's face. [7] And I saw the eighth heaven, which is called in the Hebrew tongue Muzaloth, changer of the seasons, of drought, and of wet, and of the twelve constellations of the circle of the firmament, which are above the seventh heaven. [8] And I saw the ninth heaven, which is called in Hebrew Kuchavim, where are the heavenly homes of the twelve constellations of the circle of the firmament.

22

¹ On the tenth heaven, (which is called) Aravoth, I saw the appearance of the Lord's face, like iron made to glow in fire, and brought out, emitting sparks, and it burns. ² Thus (in a moment of eternity) I saw the Lord's face, but the Lord's face is ineffable, marvellous and very awful, and very, very terrible. ³ And who am I to tell of the Lord's unspeakable being, and of his very wonderful face? And I cannot tell the quantity of his many instructions, and various voices, the Lord's throne (is) very great and not made with hands, nor the quantity of those standing round him, troops of Cherubim and seraphim, nor their incessant singing, nor his immutable beauty, and who shall tell of the ineffable greatness of his glory. ⁴ And I fell prone and bowed down to the Lord, and the Lord with his lips said to me: ⁵ Have courage, Enoch, do not fear, arise and stand before my face into eternity. ⁶ And the architstratege Michael lifted me up, and led me to before the Lord's face. ⁷ And the Lord said to his servants tempting them: Let Enoch stand before my face into eternity, and the glorious ones bowed down to the Lord, and said: Let Enoch go according to Your word. ⁸ And the Lord said to Michael: Go and take Enoch from out (of) his earthly garments, and anoint him with my sweet ointment, and put him into the garments of My glory. ⁹ And Michael did thus, as the Lord told him. He anointed me, and dressed me, and the appearance of that ointment is more than the great light, and his ointment is like sweet dew, and its smell mild, shining like the sun's ray, and I looked at myself, and (I) was like (transfigured) one of his glorious ones. ¹⁰ And the Lord summoned one of his archangels by name Pravuil, whose knowledge was quicker in wisdom than the other archangels, who wrote all the deeds of the Lord; and the Lord said to Pravuil: Bring out the books from my store-houses, and a reed of quick-writing, and give (it) to Enoch, and deliver to him the choice and comforting books out of your hand.

23

¹ And he was telling me all the works of heaven, earth and sea, and all the elements, their passages and goings, and the thunderings of the thunders, the sun and moon, the goings and changes of the stars, the seasons, years, days, and hours, the risings of the wind, the numbers of the angels, and the formation of their songs, and all human things, the tongue of every human song and life, the commandments, instructions, and sweet-voiced singings, and all things that it is fitting to learn. ² And Pravuil told me: All the things that I have told you, we have written. Sit and write all the souls of mankind, however many of them are born, and the places prepared for them to eternity; for all souls are prepared to eternity, before the formation of the world. ³ And all double thirty days and thirty nights, and I wrote out all things exactly, and wrote three hundred and sixty-six books.

24

¹ And the Lord summoned me, and said to me: Enoch, sit down on my left with Gabriel. ² And I bowed down to the Lord, and the Lord spoke to me: Enoch, beloved, all (that) you see, all things that are standing finished I tell to you even before the very beginning, all that I created from non-being, and visible (physical) things from invisible (spiritual). ³ Hear, Enoch, and take in these my words, for not to My angels have I told my secret, and I have not told them their rise, nor my endless realm, nor have they understood my creating, which I tell you to-day. ⁴ For before all things were visible (physical), I alone used to go about in the invisible (spiritual) things, like the sun from east to west, and from west to east. ⁵ But even the sun has peace in itself, while I found no peace, because I was creating all things, and I conceived the thought of placing foundations, and of creating visible (physical) creation.

25

¹ I commanded in the very lowest (parts), that visible (physical) things should come down from invisible (spiritual), and Adoil came down very great, and I beheld him, and lo! He had a belly of great light. ² And I said to him: Become undone, Adoil, and let the visible (physical) (come) out of you. ³ And he came undone, and a great light came out. And I (was) in the midst of the great light, and as there is born light from light, there came forth a great age, and showed all creation, which I had thought to create. ⁴ And I saw that (it was) good. ⁵ And I placed for myself a throne, and took my seat on it, and said to the light: Go thence up higher and fix yourself high above the throne, and be A foundation to the highest things. ⁶ And above the light there is nothing else, and then I bent up and looked up from my throne.

26

¹ And I summoned the very lowest a second time, and said: Let Archas come forth hard, and he came forth hard from the invisible (spiritual). ² And Archas came forth, hard, heavy, and very red. ³ And I said: Be opened, Archas, and let there be born from you, and he came undone, an age came forth, very great and very dark, bearing the creation of all lower things, and I saw that (it was) good and said to him: ⁴ Go thence down below, and make yourself firm, and be a foundation for the lower things, and it happened and he went down and fixed himself, and became the foundation for the lower things, and below the darkness there is nothing else.

27

¹ And I commanded that there should be taken from light and darkness, and I said: Be thick, and it became thus, and I spread it out with the light, and it became water, and I spread it out over the darkness, below the light, and then I made firm the waters, that is to say the bottomless, and I made foundation of light around the water, and created seven circles from inside, and imaged (the water) like crystal wet and dry, that is to say like glass, (and) the circumcession of the waters and the other elements, and I showed each one of them its road, and the seven stars each one of them in its heaven, that they go thus, and I saw that it was good. ² And I separated between light and between darkness, that is to say in the midst of the water hither and thither, and I said to the light, that it should be the day, and to the darkness, that it should be the night, and there was evening and there was morning the first day.

28

¹ And then I made firm the heavenly circle, and (made) that the lower water which is under heaven collect itself together, into one whole, and that the chaos become dry, and it became so. ² Out of the waves I created rock hard and big, and from the rock I piled up the dry, and the dry I called earth, and the midst of the earth I called abyss, that is to say the bottomless, I collected the sea in one place and bound it together with a yoke. ³ And I said to the sea: Behold I give you (your) eternal limits, and you shalt not break loose from your component parts. ⁴ Thus I made fast the firmament. This day I called me the first-created [Sunday].

29

¹ And for all the heavenly troops I imaged the image and essence of fire, and my eye looked at the very hard, firm rock, and from the gleam of my eye the lightning received its wonderful nature, (which) is both fire in water and water in fire, and one does not put out the other, nor does the one dry up the other, therefore the lightning is brighter than the sun, softer than water and firmer than hard rock. ² And from the rock I cut off a great fire, and from the fire I created the orders of the incorporeal ten troops of angels, and their weapons are fiery and their raiment a burning flame, and I commanded that each one should stand in his order. ³ And one from out the order of angels, having turned away with the order that was under him, conceived an impossible thought, to place his throne higher than the clouds above the earth, that he might become equal in rank to my power. ⁴ And I threw him out from the height with his angels, and he was flying in the air continuously above the bottomless.

30

¹ On the third day I commanded the earth to make grow great and fruitful trees, and hills, and seed to sow, and I planted Paradise, and enclosed it, and placed as armed (guardians) flaming angels, and thus I created renewal. ² Then came evening, and came morning the fourth day. ³ [Wednesday]. On the fourth day I commanded that there should be great lights on the heavenly circles. ⁴ On the first uppermost circle I placed the stars, Kruno, and on the second Aphrodit, on the third Aris, on the fifth Zoues, on the sixth Ermis, on the seventh lesser the moon, and adorned it with the lesser stars. ⁵ And on the lower I placed the sun for the illumination of day, and the moon and stars for the illumination of night. ⁶ The sun that it should go according to each constellation, twelve, and I appointed the succession of the months and their names and lives, their thunderings, and their hour-markings, how they should succeed. ⁷ Then evening came and morning came the fifth day. ⁸ [Thursday]. On the fifth day I commanded the sea, that it should bring forth fishes, and feathered birds of many varieties, and all animals creeping over the earth, going forth over the earth on four legs, and soaring in the air, male sex and female, and every soul breathing the spirit of life. ⁹ And there came evening, and there came morning the sixth day. ¹⁰ [Friday]. On the sixth day I commanded my wisdom to create man from seven consistencies: one, his flesh from the earth; two, his blood from the dew; three, his eyes from the sun; four, his bones from stone; five, his intelligence from the swiftness of the angels and from cloud; six, his veins and his hair from the grass of the earth; seven, his soul from my breath and from the wind. ¹¹ And I gave him seven natures: to the flesh hearing, the eyes for sight, to the soul smell, the veins for touch, the blood for taste, the bones for endurance, to the intelligence sweetness [enjoyment]. ¹² I conceived a cunning saying to say, I created man from invisible (spiritual) and from visible (physical) nature, of both are his death and life and image, he knows speech like some created thing, small in greatness and again great in smallness, and I placed him on earth, a second angel, honourable, great and glorious, and I appointed him as ruler to rule on earth and to have my wisdom, and there was none like him of earth of all my existing creatures.

[superscript]13[/superscript] And I appointed him a name, from the four component parts, from east, from west, from south, from north, and I appointed for him four special stars, and I called his name Adam, and showed him the two ways, the light and the darkness, and I told him: [superscript]14[/superscript] This is good, and that bad, that I should learn whether he has love towards me, or hatred, that it be clear which in his race love me. [superscript]15[/superscript] For I have seen his nature, but he has not seen his own nature, therefore (through) not seeing he will sin worse, and I said After sin (what is there) but death? [superscript]16[/superscript] And I put sleep into him and he fell asleep. And I took from him A rib, and created him a wife, that death should come to him by his wife, and I took his last word and called her name mother, that is to say, Eva (Eve).

31

[superscript]1[/superscript] Adam has life on earth, and I created a garden in Eden in the east, that he should observe the testament and keep the command. [superscript]2[/superscript] I made the heavens open to him, that he should see the angels singing the song of victory, and the gloomless light. [superscript]3[/superscript] And he was continuously in paradise, and the devil understood that I wanted to create another world, because Adam was lord on earth, to rule and control it. [superscript]4[/superscript] The devil is the evil spirit of the lower places, as a fugitive he made Sotona from the heavens as his name was Satanail (Satan), thus he became different from the angels, (but his nature) did not change (his) intelligence as far as (his) understanding of righteous and sinful (things). [superscript]5[/superscript] And he understood his condemnation and the sin which he had sinned before, therefore he conceived thought against Adam, in such form he entered and seduced Eva (Eve), but did not touch Adam. [superscript]6[/superscript] But I cursed ignorance, but what I had blessed previously, those I did not curse, I cursed not man, nor the earth, nor other creatures, but man's evil fruit, and his works.

32

[superscript]1[/superscript] I said to him: Earth you are, and into the earth whence I took you you shalt go, and I will not ruin you, but send you whence I took you. [superscript]2[/superscript] Then I can again receive you at My second presence. [superscript]3[/superscript] And I blessed all my creatures visible (physical) and invisible (spiritual). And Adam was five and half hours in paradise. [superscript]4[/superscript] And I blessed the seventh day, which is the Sabbath, on which he rested from all his works.

33

[superscript]1[/superscript] And I appointed the eighth day also, that the eighth day should be the first-created after my work, and that (the first seven) revolve in the form of the seventh thousand, and that at the beginning of the eighth thousand there should be a time of not-counting, endless, with neither years nor months nor weeks nor days nor hours. [superscript]2[/superscript] And now, Enoch, all that I have told you, all that you have understood, all that you have seen of heavenly things, all that you have seen on earth, and all that I have written in books by my great wisdom, all these things I have devised and created from the uppermost foundation to the lower and to the end, and there is no counsellor nor inheritor to my creations. [superscript]3[/superscript] I am self-eternal, not made with hands, and without change. [superscript]4[/superscript] My thought is my counsellor, my wisdom and my word are made, and my eyes observe all things how they stand here and tremble with terror. [superscript]5[/superscript] If I turn away my face, then all things will be destroyed. [superscript]6[/superscript] And apply your mind, Enoch, and know him who is speaking to you, and take thence the books which you yourself have written. [superscript]7[/superscript] And I give you Samuil and Raguil, who led you up, and the books, and go down to earth, and tell your sons all that I have told you, and all that you have seen, from the lower heaven up to my throne, and all the troops. [superscript]8[/superscript] For I created all forces, and there is none that resists me or that does not subject himself to me. For all subject themselves to my monarchy, and labour for my sole rule. [superscript]9[/superscript] Give them the books of the handwriting, and they will read (them) and will know me for the creator of all things, and will understand how there is no other God but me. [superscript]10[/superscript] And let them distribute the books of your handwriting–children to children, generation to generation, nations to nations. [superscript]11[/superscript] And I will give you, Enoch, my intercessor, the archistratege Michael, for the handwritings of your fathers Adam, Seth, Enos, Cainan, Mahaleleel, and Jared your father.

34

[superscript]1[/superscript] They have rejected my commandments and my yoke, worthless seed has come up, not fearing God, and they would not bow down to me, but have begun to bow down to vain gods, and denied my unity, and have laden the whole earth with untruths, offences, abominable lecheries, namely one with another, and all manner of other unclean wickedness, which are disgusting to relate. [superscript]2[/superscript] And therefore I will bring down a deluge upon the earth and will destroy all men, and the whole earth will crumble together into great darkness.

35

[superscript]1[/superscript] Behold from their seed shall arise another generation, much afterwards, but of them many will be very insatiate. [superscript]2[/superscript] He who raises that generation, (shall) reveal to them the books of your handwriting, of your fathers, (to them) to whom he must point out the guardianship of the world, to the faithful men and workers of my pleasure, who do not acknowledge my name in vain. [superscript]3[/superscript] And they shall tell another generation, and those (others) having read shall be glorified thereafter, more than the first.

36

[superscript]1[/superscript] Now, Enoch, I give you the term of thirty days to spend in your house, and tell your sons and all your household, that all may hear from my face what is told them by you, that they may read and understand, how there is no other God but me. [superscript]2[/superscript] And that they may always keep my commandments, and begin to read and take in the books of your handwriting. [superscript]3[/superscript] And after thirty days I shall send my angel for you, and he will take you from earth and from your sons to me.

37

[superscript]1[/superscript] And the Lord called upon one of the older angels, terrible and menacing, and placed him by me, in appearance white as snow, and his hands like ice, having the appearance of great frost, and he froze my face, because I could not endure the terror of the Lord, just as it is not possible to endure A stove's fire and the sun's heat, and the frost of the air. [superscript]2[/superscript] And the Lord said to me: Enoch, if your face be not frozen here, no man will be able to behold your face.

38

[superscript]1[/superscript] And the Lord said to those men who first led me up: Let Enoch go down on to earth with you, and await him till the determined day. [superscript]2[/superscript] And they placed me by night on my bed. [superscript]3[/superscript] And Mathusal (Methuselah) expecting my coming, keeping watch by day and by night at my bed, was filled with awe when he heard my coming, and I told him, Let all my household come together, that I tell them everything.

39

[superscript]1[/superscript] Oh my children, my beloved ones, hear the admonition of your father, as much as is according to the Lord's will. [superscript]2[/superscript] I have been let come to you to-day, and announce to you, not from my lips, but from the Lord's lips, all that is and was and all that is now, and all that will be till judgment-day. [superscript]3[/superscript] For the Lord has let me come to you, you hear therefore the words of my lips, of a man made big for you, but I am one who has seen the Lord's face, like iron made to glow from fire it sends forth sparks and burns. [superscript]4[/superscript] You look now upon my eyes, (the eyes) of a man big with meaning for you, but I have seen the Lord's eyes, shining like the sun's rays and filling the eyes of man with awe. [superscript]5[/superscript] You see now, my children, the right hand of a man that helps you, but I have seen the Lord's right hand filling heaven as he helped me. [superscript]6[/superscript] You see the compass of my work like your own, but I have seen the Lord's limitless and perfect compass, which has no end. [superscript]7[/superscript] You hear the words of my lips, as I heard the words of the Lord, like great thunder incessantly with hurling of clouds. [superscript]8[/superscript] And now, my children, hear the discourses of the father of the earth, how fearful and awful it is to come before the face of the ruler of the earth, how much more terrible and awful it is to come before the face of the ruler of heaven, the controller (judge) of quick and dead, and of the heavenly troops. Who can endure that endless pain?

40

[superscript]1[/superscript] And now, my children, I know all things, for this (is) from the Lord's lips, and this my eyes have seen, from beginning to end. [superscript]2[/superscript] I know all things, and have written all things into books, the heavens and their end, and their plenitude, and all the armies and their marchings. [superscript]3[/superscript] I have measured and described the stars, the great countless multitude (of them). [superscript]4[/superscript] What man has seen their revolutions, and their entrances? For not even the angels see their number, while I have written all their names. [superscript]5[/superscript] And I measured the sun's circle, and measured its rays, counted the hours, I wrote down too all things that go over the earth, I have written the things that are nourished, and all seed sown and unsown, which the earth produces and all plants, and every grass and every flower, and their sweet smells, and their names, and the dwelling-places of the clouds, and their composition, and their wings, and how they bear rain and raindrops. [superscript]6[/superscript] And I investigated all things, and wrote the road of the thunder and of the lightning, and they showed me the keys and their guardians, their rise, the way they go; it is let out (gently) in measure by a chain, lest by A heavy chain and violence it hurl down the angry clouds and destroy all things on earth. [superscript]7[/superscript] I wrote the treasure-houses of the snow, and the store-houses of the cold and the frosty airs, and I observed their season's key-holder, he fills the clouds with them, and does not exhaust the treasure-houses. [superscript]8[/superscript] And I wrote the resting-places of the winds and observed and saw how their key-holders bear weighing-scales and measures; first, they put them in (one) weighing-scale, then in the other the weights and let them out according to measure cunningly over the whole earth, lest by heavy breathing they make the earth to rock. [superscript]9[/superscript] And I measured out the whole earth, its mountains, and all hills, fields, trees, stones, rivers, all existing things I wrote down, the height from earth to the seventh heaven, and downwards to the very lowest hell, and the judgment-place, and the very great, open and weeping hell. ¹⁰ And I saw how the prisoners are in pain, expecting the limitless judgment. ¹¹ And I wrote down all those being judged by the judge, and all their judgment (and sentences) and all their works.

41

¹ And I saw all forefathers from (all) time with Adam and Eva (Eve), and I sighed and broke into tears and said of the ruin of their dishonour: ² Woe is me for my infirmity and (for that) of my forefathers, and thought in my heart and said: ³ Blessed (is) the man who has not been born or who has been born and shall not sin before the Lord's face, that he come not into this place, nor bring the yoke of this place.

42

¹ I saw the key-holders and guards of the gates of hell standing, like great serpents, and their faces like extinguishing lamps, and their eyes of fire, their sharp teeth, and I saw all the Lord's works, how they are right, while the works of man are some (good), and others bad, and in their works are known those who lie evilly.

43

¹ I, my children, measured and wrote out every work and every measure and every righteous judgment. ² As (one) year is more honourable than another, so is (one) man more honourable than another, some for great possessions, some for wisdom of heart, some for particular intellect, some for cunning, one for silence of lip, another for cleanliness, one for strength, another for comeliness, one for youth, another for sharp wit, one for shape of body, another for sensibility, let it be heard everywhere, but there is none better than he who fears God, he shall be more glorious in time to come.

44

¹ The Lord with his hands having created man, in the likeness of his own face, the Lord made him small and great. ² Whoever reviles the ruler's face, and abhors the Lord's face, has despised the Lord's face, and he who vents anger on any man without injury, the Lord's great anger will cut him down, he who spits on the face of man reproachfully, will be cut down at the Lord's great judgment. ³ Blessed is the man who does not direct his heart with malice against any man, and helps the injured and condemned, and raises the broken down, and shall do charity to the needy, because on the day of the great judgment every weight, every measure and every makeweight (will be) as in the market, that is to say (they are) hung on scales and stand in the market, (and every one) shall learn his own measure, and according to his measure shall take his reward.

45

¹ Whoever hastens to make offerings before the Lord's face, the Lord for his part will hasten that offering by granting of his work. ² But whoever increases his lamp before the Lord's face and make not true judgment, the Lord will (not) increase his treasure in the realm of the highest. ³ When the Lord demands bread, or candles, or (the)flesh (of beasts), or any other sacrifice, then that is nothing; but God demands pure hearts, and with all that (only) tests the heart of man.

46

¹ Hear, my people, and take in the words of my lips. ² If any one bring any gifts to an earthly ruler, and have disloyal thoughts in his heart, and the ruler know this, will he not be angry with him, and not refuse his gifts, and not give him over to judgment? ³ Or (if) one man make himself appear good to another by deceit of tongue, but (have) evil in his heart, then will not (the other) understand the treachery of his heart, and himself be condemned, since his untruth was plain to all? ⁴ And when the Lord shall send a great light, then there will be judgment for the just and the unjust, and there no one shall escape notice.

47

¹ And now, my children, lay thought on your hearts, mark well the words of your father, which are all (come) to you from the Lord's lips. ² Take these books of your father's handwriting and read them. ³ For the books are many, and in them you will learn all the Lord's works, all that has been from the beginning of creation, and will be till the end of time. ⁴ And if you will observe my handwriting, you will not sin against the Lord; because there is no other except the Lord, neither in heaven, nor in earth, nor in the very lowest (places), nor in the (one) foundation. ⁵ The Lord has placed the foundations in the unknown, and has spread forth heavens visible (physical) and invisible (spiritual); he fixed the earth on the waters, and created countless creatures, and who has counted the water and the foundation of the unfixed, or the dust of the earth, or the sand of the sea, or the drops of the rain, or the morning dew, or the wind's breathings? Who has filled earth and sea, and the indissoluble winter? ⁶ I cut the stars out of fire, and decorated heaven, and put it in their midst.

48

¹ That the sun go along the seven heavenly circles, which are the appointment of one hundred and eighty-two thrones, that it go down on a short day, and again one hundred and eighty-two, that it go down on a big day, and he has two thrones on which he rests, revolving hither and thither above the thrones of the months, from the seventeenth day of the month Tsivan it goes down to the month Thevan, from the seventeenth of Thevan it goes up. ² And thus it goes close to the earth, then the earth is glad and makes grow its fruits, and when it goes away, then the earth is sad, and trees and all fruits have no florescence. ³ All this he measured, with good measurement of hours, and fixed A measure by his wisdom, of the visible (physical) and the invisible (spiritual). ⁴ From the invisible (spiritual) he made all things visible (physical), himself being invisible (spiritual). ⁵ Thus I make known to you, my children, and distribute the books to your children, into all your generations, and amongst the nations who shall have the sense to fear God, let them receive them, and may they come to love them more than any food or earthly sweets, and read them and apply themselves to them. ⁶ And those who understand not the Lord, who fear not God, who accept not, but reject, who do not receive the (books), a terrible judgment awaits these. ⁷ Blessed is the man who shall bear their yoke and shall drag them along, for he shall be released on the day of the great judgment.

49

¹ I swear to you, my children, but I swear not by any oath, neither by heaven nor by earth, nor by any other creature which God created. ² The Lord said: There is no oath in me, nor injustice, but truth. ³ If there is no truth in men, let them swear by the words, Yea, yea, or else, Nay, nay. ⁴ And I swear to you, yea, yea, that there has been no man in his mother's womb, (but that) already before, even to each one there is a place prepared for the repose of that soul, and a measure fixed how much it is intended that a man be tried in this world. ⁵ Yea, children, deceive not yourselves, for there has been previously prepared a place for every soul of man.

50

¹ I have put every man's work in writing and none born on earth can remain hidden nor his works remain concealed. ² I see all things. ³ Now therefore, my children, in patience and meekness spend the number of your days, that you inherit endless life. ⁴ Endure for the sake of the Lord every wound, every injury, every evil word and attack. ⁵ If ill-requitals befall you, return (them) not either to neighbour or enemy, because the Lord will return (them) for you and be your avenger on the day of great judgment, that there be no avenging here among men. ⁶ Whoever of you spends gold or silver for his brother's sake, he will receive ample treasure in the world to come. ⁷ Injure not widows nor orphans nor strangers, lest God's wrath come upon you.

51

¹ Stretch out your hands to the poor according to your strength. ² Hide not your silver in the earth. ³ Help the faithful man in affliction, and affliction will not find you in the time of your trouble. ⁴ And every grievous and cruel yoke that come upon you bear all for the sake of the Lord, and thus you will find your reward in the day of judgment. ⁵ It is good to go morning, midday, and evening into the Lord's dwelling, for the glory of your creator. ⁶ Because every breathing (thing) glorifies him, and every creature visible (physical) and invisible (spiritual) returns him praise.

52

¹ Blessed is the man who opens his lips in praise of God of Sabaoth and praises the Lord with his heart. ² Cursed every man who opens his lips for the bringing into contempt and calumny of his neighbour, because he brings God into contempt. ³ Blessed is he who opens his lips blessing and praising God. ⁴ Cursed is he before the Lord all the days of his life, who opens his lips to curse and abuse. ⁵ Blessed is he who blesses all the Lord's works. ⁶ Cursed is he who brings the Lord's creation into contempt. ⁷ Blessed is he who looks down and raises the fallen. ⁸ Cursed is he who looks to and is eager for the destruction of what is not his. ⁹ Blessed is he who keeps the foundations of his fathers made firm from the beginning. ¹⁰ Cursed is he who perverts the decrees of his forefathers. ¹¹ Blessed is he who imparts peace and love. ¹² Cursed is he who disturbs those that love their neighbours. ¹³ Blessed is he who speaks with humble tongue and heart to all. ¹⁴ Cursed is he who speaks peace with his tongue, while in his heart there is no peace but a sword. ¹⁵ For all these things will be laid bare in the weighing-scales and in the books, on the day of the great judgment.

53

¹ And now, my children, do not say: Our father is standing before God, and is praying for our sins, for there is there no helper of any man who has sinned. ² You see how I wrote all works of every man, before his creation, (all) that is done amongst all men for all time, and none can tell or relate my handwriting, because the Lord see all imaginings of man, how they are vain, where they lie in the treasure-houses of the heart. ³ And now, my children, mark well all the words of your father, that I tell you, lest you regret, saying: Why did our father not tell us?

54

¹ At that time, not understanding this let these books which I have given you be for an inheritance of your peace. ² Hand them to all who want them, and instruct them, that they may see the Lord's very great and marvellous works.

55

¹ My children, behold, the day of my term and time have approached. ² For the angels who shall go with me are standing before me and urge me to my departure from you; they are standing here on earth, awaiting what has been told them. ³ For to-morrow I shall go up on to heaven, to the uppermost Jerusalem to my eternal inheritance. ⁴ Therefore I bid you do before the Lord's face all (his) good pleasure.

56

¹ Mathosalam having answered his father Enoch, said: What is agreeable to your eyes, father, that I may make before your face, that you may bless our dwellings, and your sons, and that your people may be made glorious through you, and then (that) you may depart thus, as the Lord said? ² Enoch answered to his son Mathosalam (and) said: Hear, child, from the time when the Lord anointed me with the ointment of his glory, (there has been no) food in me, and my soul remembers not earthly enjoyment, neither do I want anything earthly.

57

¹ My child Methosalam, summon all your brethren and all your household and the elders of the people, that I may talk to them and depart, as is planned for me. ² And Methosalam made haste, and summoned his brethren, Regim, Riman, Uchan, Chermion, Gaidad, and all the elders of the people before the face of his father Enoch; and he blessed them, (and) said to them:

58

¹ Listen to me, my children, to-day. ² In those days when the Lord came down on to earth for Adam's sake, and visited all his creatures, which he created himself, after all these he created Adam, and the Lord called all the beasts of the earth, all the reptiles, and all the birds that soar in the air, and brought them all before the face of our father Adam. ³ And Adam gave the names to all things living on earth. ⁴ And the Lord appointed him ruler over all, and subjected to him all things under his hands, and made them dumb and made them dull that they be commanded of man, and be in subjection and obedience to him. ⁵ Thus also the Lord created every man lord over all his possessions. ⁶ The Lord will not judge a single soul of beast for man's sake, but adjudges the souls of men to their beasts in this world; for men have a special place. ⁷ And as every soul of man is according to number, similarly beasts will not perish, nor all souls of beasts which the Lord created, till the great judgment, and they will accuse man, if he feed them ill.

59

¹ Whoever defiles the soul of beasts, defiles his own soul. ² For man brings clean animals to make sacrifice for sin, that he may have cure of his soul. ³ And if they bring for sacrifice clean animals, and birds, man has cure, he cures his soul. ⁴ All is given you for food, bind it by the four feet, that is to make good the cure, he cures his soul. ⁵ But whoever kills beast without wounds, kills his own souls and defiles his own flesh. ⁶ And he who does any beast any injury whatsoever, in secret, it is evil practice, and he defiles his own soul.

60

¹ He who works the killing of a man's soul, kills his own soul, and kills his own body, and there is no cure for him for all time. ² He who puts a man in any snare, shall stick in it himself, and there is no cure for him for all time. ³ He who puts a man in any vessel, his retribution will not be wanting at the great judgment for all time. ⁴ He who works crookedly or speaks evil against any soul, will not make justice for himself for all time.

61

¹ And now, my children, keep your hearts from every injustice, which the Lord hates. Just as a man asks something for his own soul from God, so let him do to every living soul, because I know all things, how in the great time to come there is much inheritance prepared for men, good for the good, and bad for the bad, without number many. ² Blessed are those who enter the good houses, for in the bad houses there is no peace nor return from them. ³ Hear, my children, small and great! When man puts a good thought in his heart, brings gifts from his labours before the Lord's face and his hands made them not, then the Lord will turn away his face from the labour of his hand, and (that) man cannot find the labour of his hands. ⁴ And if his hands made it, but his heart murmur, and his heart cease not making murmur incessantly, he has not any advantage.

62

¹ Blessed is the man who in his patience brings his gifts with faith before the Lord's face, because he will find forgiveness of sins. ² But if he take back his words before the time, there is no repentance for him; and if the time pass and he do not of his own will what is promised, there is no repentance after death. ³ Because every work which man does before the time, is all deceit before men, and sin before God.

63

¹ When man clothes the naked and fills the hungry, he will find reward from God. ² But if his heart murmur, he commits a double evil; ruin of himself and of that which he gives; and for him there will be no finding of reward on account of that. ³ And if his own heart is filled with his food and his own flesh, clothed with his own clothing, he commits contempt, and will forfeit all his endurance of poverty, and will not find reward of his good deeds. ⁴ Every proud and magniloquent man is hateful to the Lord, and every false speech, clothed in untruth; it will be cut with the blade of the sword of death, and thrown into the fire, and shall burn for all time.

64

¹ When Enoch had spoken these words to his sons, all people far and near heard how the Lord was calling Enoch. They took counsel together: ² Let us go and kiss Enoch, and two thousand men came together and came to the place Achuzan where Enoch was, and his sons. ³ And the elders of the people, the whole assembly, came and bowed down and began to kiss Enoch and said to him: ⁴ Our father Enoch, (may) you (be) blessed of the Lord, the eternal ruler, and now bless your sons and all the people, that we may be glorified to-day before your face. ⁵ For you shalt be glorified before the Lord's face for all time, since the Lord chose you, rather than all men on earth, and designated you writer of all his creation, visible (physical) and invisible (spiritual), and redeemed of the sins of man, and helper of your household.

65

¹ And Enoch answered all his people saying: Hear, my children, before that all creatures were created, the Lord created the visible (physical) and invisible (spiritual) things. ² And as much time as there was and went past, understand that after all that he created man in the likeness of his own form, and put into him eyes to see, and ears to hear, and heart to reflect, and intellect wherewith to deliberate. ³ And the Lord saw all man's works, and created all his creatures, and divided time, from time he fixed the years, and from the years he appointed the months, and from the months he appointed the days, and of days he appointed seven. ⁴ And in those he appointed the hours, measured them out exactly, that man might reflect on time and count years, months, and hours, (their) alternation, beginning, and end, and that he might count his own life, from the beginning until death, and reflect on his sin and write his work bad and good; because no work is hidden before the Lord, that every man might know his works and never transgress all his commandments, and keep my handwriting from generation to generation. ⁵ When all creation visible (physical) and invisible (spiritual), as the Lord created it, shall end, then every man goes to the great judgment, and then all time shall perish, and the years, and thenceforward there will be neither months nor days nor hours, they will be adhered together and will not be counted. ⁶ There will be one aeon, and all the righteous who shall escape the Lord's great judgment, shall be collected in the great aeon, for the righteous the great aeon will begin, and they will live eternally, and then too there will be amongst them neither labour, nor sickness, nor humiliation, nor anxiety, nor need, nor brutality, nor night, nor darkness, but great light. ⁷ And they shall have a great indestructible wall, and a paradise bright and incorruptible (eternal), for all corruptible (mortal) things shall pass away, and there will be eternal life.

66

¹ And now, my children, keep your souls from all injustice, such as the Lord hates. ² Walk before his face with terror and trembling and serve him alone. ³ Bow down to the true God, not to dumb idols, but bow down to his similitude, and bring all just offerings before the Lord's face. The Lord hates what is unjust. ⁴ For the Lord sees all things; when man takes thought in his heart, then he counsels the intellects, and every thought is always before the Lord, who made firm the earth and put all creatures on it. ⁵ If you look to heaven, the Lord is there; if you take thought of the sea's deep and

all the under-earth, the Lord is there. ⁶ For the Lord created all things. Bow not down to things made by man, leaving the Lord of all creation, because no work can remain hidden before the Lord's face. ⁷ Walk, my children, in long-suffering, in meekness, honesty, in provocation, in grief, in faith and in truth, in (reliance on) promises, in illness, in abuse, in wounds, in temptation, in nakedness, in privation, loving one another, till you go out from this age of ills, that you become inheritors of endless time. ⁸ Blessed are the just who shall escape the great judgment, for they shall shine forth more than the sun sevenfold, for in this world the seventh part is taken off from all, light, darkness, food, enjoyment, sorrow, paradise, torture, fire, frost, and other things; he put all down in writing, that you might read and understand.

67

¹ When Enoch had talked to the people, the Lord sent out darkness on to the earth, and there was darkness, and it covered those men standing with Enoch, and they took Enoch up on to the highest heaven, where the Lord (is); and he received him and placed him before his face, and the darkness went off from the earth, and light came again. ² And the people saw and understood not how Enoch had been taken, and glorified God, and found a roll in which was traced The Invisible (spiritual) God; and all went to their dwelling places.

68

¹ Enoch was born on the sixth day of the month Tsivan, and lived three hundred and sixty-five years. ² He was taken up to heaven on the first day of the month Tsivan and remained in heaven sixty days. ³ He wrote all these signs of all creation, which the Lord created, and wrote three hundred and sixty-six books, and handed them over to his sons and remained on earth thirty days, and was again taken up to heaven on the sixth day of the month Tsivan, on the very day and hour when he was born. ⁴ As every man's nature in this life is dark, so are also his conception, birth, and departure from this life. ⁵ At what hour he was conceived, at that hour he was born, and at that hour too he died. ⁶ Methosalam and his brethren, all the sons of Enoch, made haste, and erected an altar at that place called Achuzan, whence and where Enoch had been taken up to heaven. ⁷ And they took sacrificial oxen and summoned all people and sacrificed the sacrifice before the Lord's face. ⁸ All people, the elders of the people and the whole assembly came to the feast and brought gifts to the sons of Enoch. ⁹ And they made a great feast, rejoicing and making merry three days, praising God, who had given them such a sign through Enoch, who had found favour with him, and that they should hand it on to their sons from generation to generation, from age to age. ¹⁰ Amen.

The Third Book of Enoch
(or Hebrew Enoch, or The Book of the Palaces)

1

R. Ishmael ascends to heaven to behold the vision of the Merkaba and is given in charge to Metatron. Rabbi Ishmael said:

¹ When I ascended on high to behold the vision of the Merkaba and had entered the six Halls, one within the other: ² as soon as I reached the door of the seventh Hall I stood still in prayer before the Holy One, blessed be He, and, lifting up my eyes on high (i.e. towards the Divine Majesty), I said: ³ "Lord of the Universe, I pray thee, that the merit of Aaron, the son of Amram, the lover of peace and pursuer of peace, who received the crown of priesthood from Thy Glory on the mount of Sinai, be valid for me in this hour, so that Qafsiel, the prince, and the angels with him may not get power over me nor throw me down from the heavens". ⁴ Forthwith the Holy One, blessed be He, sent to me Metatron, his Servant ('Ebed) the angel, the Prince of the Presence, and he, spreading his wings, with great joy came to meet me so as to save me from their hand. ⁵ And he took me by his hand in their sight, saying to me: "Enter in peace before the high and exalted King and behold the picture of the Merkaba". ⁶ Then I entered the seventh Hall, and he led me to the camp(s) of Shekina and placed me before the Holy One, blessed be He, to behold the Merkaba. ⁷ As soon as the princes of the Merkaba and the flaming Seraphim perceived me, they fixed their eyes upon me. Instantly trembling and shuddering seized me and I fell down and was benumbed by the radiant image of their eyes and the splendid appearance of their faces; until the Holy One, blessed be He, rebuked them, saying: ⁸ "My servants, my Seraphim, my Kerubim and my 'Ophannim Cover ye your eyes before Ishmael, my son, my friend, my beloved one and my glory, that he trembles not nor shudder!" ⁹ Forthwith Metatron the Prince of the Presence, came and restored my spirit and put me upon my feet. ¹⁰ After that (moment) there was not in me strength enough to say a song before the Throne of Glory of the glorious King, the mightiest of all kings, the most excellent of all princes, until after the hour had passed. ¹¹ After one hour (had passed) the Holy One, blessed be He, opened to me the gates of Shekina, the gates of Peace, the gates of Wisdom, the gates of Strength, the gates of Power, the gates of Speech (Dibbur), the gates of Song, the gates of Qedushsha, the gates of Chant. ¹² And he enlightened my eyes and my heart by words of psalm, song, praise, exaltation, thanksgiving, extolment, glorification, hymn and eulogy. And as I opened my mouth, uttering a song before the Holy One, blessed be He, the Holy Chayyoth beneath and above the Throne of Glory answered and said: "HOLY " and "BLESSED BE THE GLORY OF YHWH FROM HIS PLACE!" (i.e. chanted the Qedushsha).

2

The highest classes of angels make inquiries about R. Ishmael which are answered by Metatron. R. Ishmael said:

¹ In that hour the eagles of the Merkaba, the flaming 'Ophannim and the Seraphim of consuming fire asked Metatron, saying to him: ² "Youth! Why sufferest thou one born of woman to enter and behold the Merkaba? From which nation, from which tribe is this one? What is his character?" ³ Metatron answered and said to them: "From the nation of Israel whom the Holy One, blessed be He, chose for his people from among seventy tongues (nations), from the tribe of Levi, whom he set aside as a contribution to his name and from the seed of Aaron whom the Holy One, blessed be He, did choose for his servant and put upon him the crown of priesthood on Sinai". ⁴ Forthwith they spake and said: "Indeed, this one is worthy to behold the Merkaba ". And they said: "Happy is the people that is in such a case!".

3

Metatron has 70 names, but God calls him ' Youth '. R. Ishmael said:

¹ In that hour I asked Metatron, the angel, the Prince of the Presence: "What is thy name?" ² He answered me: "I have seventy names, corresponding to the seventy tongues of the world and all of them are based upon the name Metatron, angel of the Presence; but my King calls me Youth' (Na'ar)"

4

Metatron is identical with Enoch who was translated to heaven at the time of the Deluge. R. Ishmael said:

¹ I asked Metatron and said to him: "Why art thou called by the name of thy Creator, by seventy names? Thou art greater than all the princes, higher than all the angels, beloved more than all the servants, honoured above all the mighty ones in kingship, greatness and glory: why do they call thee 'Youth' in the high heavens?" ² He answered and said to me: "Because I am Enoch, the son of Jared. ³ For when the generation of the flood sinned and were confounded in their deeds, saying unto God: 'Depart from us, for we desire not the knowledge of thy ways' (Job xxi. 14), then the Holy One, blessed be He, removed me from their midst to be a witness against them

in the high heavens to all the inhabitants of the world, that they may not say: 'The Merciful One is cruel". ⁴ What sinned all those multitudes, their wives, their sons and their daughters, their horses, their mules and their cattle and their property, and all the birds of the world, all of which the Holy One, blessed be He, destroyed from the world together with them in the waters of the flood? ⁵ Hence the Holy One, blessed be He, lifted me up in their lifetime before their eyes to be a witness against them to the future world. And the Holy One, blessed be He, assigned me for a prince and a ruler among the ministering angels. ⁶ In that hour three of the ministering angels, 'UZZA, 'AZZA and 'AZZAEL came forth and brought charges against me in the high heavens, saying before the Holy One, blessed be He: "Said not the Ancient Ones (First Ones) rightly before Thee: Do not create man! ' " The Holy One, blessed be He, answered and said unto them: "I have made and I will bear, yea, I will carry and will deliver". (Is. xlvi. 4.) ⁷ As soon as they saw me, they said before Him: "Lord of the Universe! What is this one that he should ascend to the height of heights? Is not he one from among the sons of [the sons of] those who perished in the days of the Flood? "What doeth he in the Raqia'?" ⁸ Again, the Holy One, blessed be He, answered and said to them: "What are ye, that ye enter and speak in my presence? I delight in this one more than in all of you, and hence he shall be a prince and a ruler over you in the high heavens." ⁹ Forthwith all stood up and went out to meet me, prostrated themselves before me and said: "Happy art thou and happy is thy father for thy Creator doth favour thee". ¹⁰ And because I am small and a youth among them in days, months and years, therefore they call me "Youth" (Na'ar).

5

The idolatry of the generation of Enosh causes God to remove the Shekina from earth. The idolatry inspired by 'Azza, 'Uzza and 'Azziel. R. Ishmael said: Metatron, the Prince of the Presence, said to me:
¹ From the day when the Holy One, blessed be He, expelled the first Adam from the Garden of Eden (and onwards), Shekina was dwelling upon a Kerub under the Tree of Life. ² And the ministering angels were gathering together and going down from heaven in parties, from the Raqia in companies and from the heavens in camps to do His will in the whole world. ³ And the first man and his generation were sitting outside the gate of the Garden to behold the radiant appearance of the Shekina. ⁴ For the silendour of the Shekina traversed the world from one end to the other (with a splendour) 365,000 times (that) of the globe of the sun. And every one who made use of the splendour of the Shekina, on him no flies and no gnats did rest, neither was he ill nor suffered he any pain. No demons got power over him, neither were they able to injure him. ⁵ When the Holy One, blessed be He, went out and went in; from the Garden to Eden, from Eden to the Garden, from the Garden to Raqia and from Raqia to the Garden of Eden then all and every one beheld the splendour of His Shekina and they were not injured; ⁶ until the time of the generation of Enosh who was the head of all idol worshippers of the world. ⁷ And what did the generation of Enosh do? They went from one end of the world to the other, and each one brought silver, gold, precious stones and pearls in heaps like unto mountains and hills making idols out of them throughout all the world. And they erected the idols in every quarter of the world: the size of each idol was 1000 parasangs. ⁸ And they brought down the sun, the moon, planets and constellations, and placed them before the idols on their right hand and on their left, to attend them even as they attend the Holy One, blessed be He, as it is written (1 Kings xxii. 19): "And all the host of heaven was standing by him on his right hand and on his left". ⁹ What power was in them that they were able to bring them down? They would not have been able to bring them down but for 'Uzza, 'Azza and 'Azziel who taught them sorceries whereby they brought them down and made use of them ¹⁰ In that time the ministering angels brought charges (against them) before the Holy One, blessed be He, saying before him: "Master of the World! What hast thou to do with the children of men? As it is written (Ps. viii. 4) 'What is man (Enosh) that thou art mindful of him?' 'Mah Adam' is not written here, but 'Mah Enosh', for he (Enosh) is the head of the idol worshippers. ¹¹ Why hast thou left the highest of the high heavens, the abode of thy glorious Name, and the high and exalted Throne in 'Araboth Raqia' in the highest and art gone and dwellest with the children of men who worship idols and equal thee to the idols. ¹² Now thou art on earth and the idols likewise. What hast thou to do with the inhabitants of the earth who worship idols?" ¹³ Forthwith the Holy One, blessed be He, lifted up His Shekina from the earth, from their midst. ¹⁴ In that moment came the ministering angels, the troops of hosts and the armies of 'Araboth in thousand camps and ten thousand hosts: they fetched trumpets and took the horns in their hands and surrounded the Shekina with all kinds of songs. And He ascended to the high heavens, as it is written (Ps. xlvii. 5): "God is gone up with a shout, the Lord with the sound of a trumpet ".

6

Enoch lifted up to heaven together with the Shekina. Angels' protests answered by God. R. Ishmael said: Metatron, the Angel, the Prince of the Presence, said to me:
¹ When the Holy One, blessed be He, desired to lift me up on high, He first sent 'Anaphiel H (H = Tetragrammaton) the Prince, and he took me from their midst in their sight and carried me in great glory upon a fiery chariot with fiery horses, servants of glory. And he lifted me up to the high heavens together with the Shekina. ² As soon as I reached the high heavens, the Holy Chayyoth, the 'Ophannim, the Seraphim, the Kerubim, the Wheels of the Merkaba (the Galgallim), and the ministers of the consuming fire, perceiving my smell from a distance of 365,000 myriads of parasangs, said: "What smell of one born of woman and what taste of a white drop (is this) that ascends on high, and (lo, he is merely) a gnat among those who 'divide flames (of fire)'?" ³ The Holy One, blessed be He, answered and spake unto them: "My servants, my hosts, my Kerubim, my 'Ophannim, my Seraphim! Be ye not displeased on account of this! Since all the children of men have denied me and my great Kingdom and are gone worshipping idols, I have removed my Shekina from among them and have lifted it up on high. But this one whom I have taken from among them is an ELECT ONE among (the inhabitants of) the world and he is equal to all of them in faith, righteousness and perfection of deed and I have taken him for (as) a tribute from my world under all the heavens".

7

Enoch raised upon the wings of the Shekina to the place of the Throne, the Merkaba and the angelic hosts. R. Ishmael said: Metatron, the Angel, the Prince of the Presence, said to me:
¹ When the Holy One, blessed be He, took me away from the generation of the Flood, he lifted me on the wings of the wind of Shekina to the highest heaven and brought me into the great palaces of the 'Araboth Raqia' on high, where are the glorious Throne of Shekina, the Merkaba, the troops of anger, the armies of vehemence, the fiery Shin'anim', the flaming Kerubim, and the burning 'Ophannim, the flaming servants, the flashing Chashmattim and the lightening Seraphim. And he placed me (there) to attend the Throne of Glory day after day.

8

The gates (of the treasuries of heaven) opened to Metatron. R. Ishmael said: Metatron, the Prince of the Presence, said to me:
¹ Before He appointed me to attend the Throne of Glory, the Holy One, blessed be He, opened to me three hundred thousand gates of Understanding; three hundred thousand gates of Subtlety; three hundred thousand gates of Life; three hundred thousand gates of grace and loving-kindness; three hundred thousand gates of love; three hundred thousand gates of Tora; three hundred thousand gates of meekness; three hundred thousand gates of maintenance; three hundred thousand gates' of mercy; three hundred thousand gates of fear of heaven. ² In that hour the Holy One, blessed be He, added in me wisdom unto wisdom, understanding unto understanding, subtlety unto subtlety, knowledge unto knowledge, mercy unto mercy, instruction unto instruction, love unto love, loving-kindness unto loving-kindness, goodness unto goodness, meekness unto meekness, power unto power, strength unto strength, might unto might, brilliance unto brilliance, beauty unto beauty, splendour unto splendour, and I was honoured and adorned with all these good and praiseworthy things more than all the children of heaven.

9

Enoch receives blessings from the Most High and is adorned with angelic attributes. R. Ishmael said: Metatron, the Prince of the Presence, said to me:
¹ After all these things the Holy One, blessed be He, put His hand upon me and blessed me with 5360 blessings. ² And I was raised and enlarged to the size of the length and width of the world. ³ And He caused 72 wings to grow on me, 36 on each side. And each wing was as the whole world. ⁴ And He fixed on me 365 eyes: each eye was as the great luminary. ⁵ And He left no kind of splendour, brilliance, radiance, beauty in (of) all the lights of the universe that He did not fix on me.

10

God places Metatron on a throne at the door of the seventh Hall and announces through the Herald, that Metatron henceforth is God's representative and ruler over all the princes of kingdoms and all the children of heaven, save the eight high princes called YHWH by the name of their King. R. Ishmael said: Metatron, the Prince of the Presence, said to me:
¹ All these things the Holy One, blessed be He, made for me; He made me a Throne, similar to the Throne of Glory. And He spread over me a curtain

of splendour and brilliant appearance, of beauty, grace and mercy, similar to the curtain of the Throne of Glory; and on it were fixed all kinds of lights in the universe. ² And He placed it at the door of the Seventh Hall and seated me on it. ³ And the herald went forth into every heaven, saying; This is Metatron, my servant. I have made him into a prince and a ruler over all the princes of my kingdoms and over all the children of heaven, except the eight great princes, the honoured and revered ones who are called YHWH, by the name of their King. ⁴ And every angel and every prince who has a word to speak in my presence (before me) shall go into his presence (before him) and shall speak to him (instead). ⁵And every command that he utters to you in my name do ye observe and fulfil. For the Prince of Wisdom and the Prince of Understanding have I committed to him to instruct him in the wisdom of heavenly things and of earthly things, in the wisdom of this world and of the world to come. ⁶ Moreover, I have set him over all the treasuries of the palapes of Araboih and over all the stores of life that I have in the high heavens.

11

God reveals all mysteries and secrets to Metatron. R. Ishmael said: Metatron, the angel, the Prince of the Presence, said to me:

¹ Henceforth the Holy One, blessed be He, revealed to me all the mysteries of Tora and all the secrets of wisdom and all the depths of the Perfect Law; and all living beings' thoughts of heart and all the secrets of the universe and all the secrets of Creation were revealed unto me even as they are revealed unto the Maker of Creation. ² And I watched intently to behold the secrets of the depth and the wonderful mystery. Before a man did think in secret, I saw (it) and before a man made a thing I beheld it. ³ And there was no thing on high nor in the deep hidden from me.

12

God clothes Metatron in a garment of glory, puts a royal crown on his head and calls him "the Lesser YHWH". R. Ishmael said: Metatron, the Prince of the Presence, said to me:

¹ By reason of the love with which the Holy One, blessed be He, loved me more than all the children of heaven. He made me a garment of glory on which were fixed all kinds of lights, and He clad me in it. ²And He made me a robe of honour on which were fixed all kinds of beauty, splendour, brilliance and majesty. ³ And he made me a royal crown in which were fixed forty-nine costly stones like unto the light of the globe of the sun. ⁴ For its splendour went forth in the four quarters of the Araboth Raqia', and in (through) the seven heavens, and in the four quarters of the world. And he put it on my head. ⁵ And He called me THE LESSER YHWH in the presence of all His heavenly household; as it is written (Ex. xxiii. 21): "For my name is in him".

13

God writes with a flaming style on Metatron's crown the cosmic letters by which heaven and earth were created. R. Ishmael said: Metatron, the angel, the Prince of the Presence, the Glory of all heavens, said to me:

¹ Because of the great love and mercy with which the Holy One, blessed be He, loved and cherished me more than all the children of heaven. He wrote with his ringer with a flaming style upon the crown on my head the letters by which were created heaven and earth, the seas and rivers, the mountains and hills, the planets and constellations, the lightnings, winds, earthquakes and voices (thunders), the snow and hail, the storm-wind and the tempest; the letters by which were created all the needs of the world and all the orders of Creation. ² And every single letter sent forth time after time as it were lightnings, time after time as it were torches, time after time as it were flames of fire, time after time (rays) like [as] the rising of the sun and the moon and the planets.

14

All the highest princes, the elementary angels and the planetary and sideric angels fear and tremble at the sight of Metatron crowned. R. Ishmael said: Metatron, the Angel, the Prince of the Presence, said to me:

¹ When the Holy One, blessed be He, put this crown on my head, (then) trembled before me all the Princes of Kingdoms who are in the height of Araboth Raqiaf and all the hosts of every heaven; and even the princes (of) the 'Elim, the princes (of) the 'Er'ellim and the princes (of) the Tafsarim, who are greater than all the ministering angels who minister before the Throne of Glory, shook, feared and trembled before me when they beheld me. ² Even Sammael, the Prince of the Accusers, who is greater than all the princes of kingdoms on high; feared and trembled before me. ³ And even the angel of fire, and the angel of hail, and the angel of the wind, and the angel of the lightning, and the angel of anger, and the angel of the thunder, and the angel of the snow, and the angel of the rain; and the angel of the day, and the angel of the night, and the angel of the sun and the angel of the moon, and the angel of the planets and the angel of the constellations who rule the world under their hands, feared and trembled and were affrighted before me, when they beheld me. ⁴ These are the names of the rulers of the world: Gabriel, the angel of the fire, Baradiel, the angel of the hail, Ruchiel who is appointed over the wind, Baraqiel who is appointed over the lightnings, Za'amiel who is appointed over the vehemence, Ziqiel who is appointed over the sparks, Zi'iel who is appointed over the commotion, Zdaphiel who is appointed over the storm-wind, Ra'amiel who is appointed over the thunders, Rctashiel who is appointed over the earthquake, Shalgiel who is appointed over the snow, Matariel who is appointed over the rain, Shimshiel who is appointed over the day, Lailiel who is appointed over the night, Galgalliel who is appointed over the globe of the sun, 'Ophanniel who is appointed over the globe of the moon, Kokbiel who is appointed over the planets, Rahatiel who is appointed over the constellations. ⁵ And they all fell prostrate, when they saw me. And they were not able to behold me because of the majestic glory and beauty of the appearance of the shining light of the crown of glory upon my head.

15

Metatron transformed into fire. R. Ishmael said: Metatron, the angel, the Prince of the Presence, the Glory of all heavens, said to me:

¹ As soon as the Holy One, blessed be He, took me in (His) service to attend the Throne of Glory and the Wheels (Galgallim) of the Merkaba and the needs of Shekina, forthwith my flesh was changed into flames, my sinews into flaming fire, my bones into coals of burning juniper, the light of my eye-lids into splendour of lightnings, my eye-balls into fire-brands, the hair of my head into dot flames, all my limbs into wings of burning fire and the whole of my body into glowing fire. ² And on my right were divisions 6 of fiery flames, on my left fire-brands were burning, round about me stormwind and tempest were blowing and in front of me and behind me was roaring of thunder with earthquake.

FRAGMENT OF 'ASCENSION OF MOSES'

¹. R. Ishmael said: Said to me Metatron, the Prince of the Presence and the prince over all the princes and he stands before Him who is greater than all the Elohim. And he goes in under the Throne of Glory. And he has a great tabernacle of light on high. And he brings forth the fire of deafness and puts (it) into the ears of the Holy Chayyoth, that they may not hear the voice of the Word (Dibbur) that goes forth from the mouth of the Divine Majesty. ² And when Moses ascended on high, he fasted 121 fasts, till the habitations of the chashmal were opened to him; and he saw the heart within the heart of the Lion and he saw the innumerable companies of the hosts Around about him. And they desired to burn him. But Moses prayed for mercy, first for Israel and after that for himself: and He who sitteth on the Merkaba opened the windows that are above the heads of the Kerubim. And a host of 1800 advocates and the Prince of the Presence, Metatron, with them went forth to meet Moses. And they took the prayers of Israel and put them as a crown on the head of the Holy One, blessed be He. ³ And they said (Deut. vi. 4): "Hear, O Israel; the Lord our God is one Lord" and their face shone and rejoiced over Shekina and they said to Metatron: "What are these? And to whom do they give all this honour and glory?" And they answered: "To the Glorious Lord of Israel". And they spake: "Hear, O Israel: the Lord, our God, is one Lord. To whom shall be given abundance of honour and majesty but to Thee YHWH, the Divine Majesty, the King, living and eternal". ⁴ In that moment spake Akatriel Yah Yehod Sebaoth and said to Metatron, the Prince of the Presence: "Let no prayer that he prayeth before me return (to him) void. Hear thou his prayer and fulfil his desire whether (it be) great or small". ⁵ Forthwith Metatron, the Prince of the Presence, said to Moses: "Son of Amram! Fear not, for now God delights in thee. And ask thou u thy desire of the Glory and Majesty. For thy face shines from one end of the world to the other". But Moses answered him: "(I fear) lest I bring guiltiness upon myself". Metatron said to him: "Receive the letters of the oath, in (by) which there is no breaking the covenant" (which precludes any breach of the covenant).

16A

(Probably additional) Metatron divested of his privilege of presiding on a Throne of his own on account of Acher's misapprehension in taking him for a second Divine Power. R. Ishmael said: Metatron, the Angel, the Prince of the Presence, the Glory of all heaven, said to me:

¹ At first I was sitting upon a great Throne at the door of the Seventh Hall; and I was judging the children of heaven, the household on high by authority of the Holy One, blessed be He. And I divided Greatness, Kingship, Dignity, Rulership, Honour and Praise, and Diadem and Crown of Glory unto all the princes of kingdoms, while I was presiding (lit. sitting) in the Celestial Court (Yeshiba), and the princes of kingdoms were standing before me, on my right and on my left by authority of the Holy One, blessed be He. ² But when Acher came to behold the vision of the Merkaba and fixed his eyes on me, he feared and trembled before me and his soul was affrighted even unto departing from him, because of fear, horror and dread

of me, when he beheld me sitting upon a throne like a king with all the ministering angels standing by me as my servants and all the princes of kingdoms adorned with crowns surrounding me: ³ in that moment he opened his mouth and said: "Indeed, there are two Divine Powers in heaven!" ⁴ Forthwith Bath Qol (the Divine Voice) went forth from heaven from before the Shekina and said: "Return, ye backsliding children (Jer. iii. 22), except Acher!" ⁵ Then came 'Aniyel, the Prince, the honoured, glorified, beloved, wonderful, revered and fearful one, in commission from the Holy One, blessed be He and gave me sixty strokes with lashes of fire and made me stand on my feet.

17

The princes of the seven heavens, of the sun, moon, planets and constellations and their suites of angels. R. Ishmael said: Metatron, the angel, the Prince of the Presence, the glory of all heavens, said to me:

¹ Seven (are the) princes, the great, beautiful, revered, wonderful and honoured ones who are appointed over the seven heavens. And these are they: MIKAEL, GABRIEL, SHATQIEL, SHACHAQIEL, BAKARIEL, BAD ARIEL, PACHRIEL. ² And every one of them is the prince of the host of (one) heaven. And each one of them is accompanied by 496,000 myriads of ministering angels. ³ MIKAEL, the great prince, is appointed over the seventh heaven, the highest one, which is in the 'Araboth. GABRIEL, the prince of the host, is appointed over the sixth heaven which is in Makon. SHATAQIEL, prince of the host, is appointed over the fifth heaven which is in Ma'on. SHAHAQi'EL, prince of the host, is appointed over the fourth heaven which is in Zebul. BAD ARIEL, prince of the host, is appointed over the third heaven which is in Shehaqim. BARAKIEL, prince of the host, is appointed over the second heaven which is in the height of (Merom) Raqia. PAZRIEL, prince of the host, is appointed over the first heaven which is in Wilon, which is in Shamayim. ⁴ Under them is GALGALLIEL, the prince who is appointed over the globe (galgal) of the sun, and with him are 96 great and honoured angels who move the sun in Raqia'. ⁵ Under them is 'OPHANNIEL, the prince who is set over the globe ('ophari) of the moon. And with him are 88 angels who move the globe of the moon 354 thousand parasangs every night at the time when the moon stands in the East at its turning point. And when is the moon sitting in the East at its turning point? Answer: in the fifteenth day of every month. ⁶ Under them is RAHATIEL, the prince who is appointed over the constellations. And he is accompanied by 72 great and honoured angels. And why is he called RAHATIEL? Because he makes the stars run (marhit) in their orbits and courses 339 thousand parasangs every night from the East to the West, and from the West to the East. For the Holy One, blessed be He, has made a tent for all of them, for the sun, the moon, the planets and the stars in which they travel at night from the West to the East. ⁷ Under them is KOKBIEL, the prince who is appointed over all the planets. And with him are 365,000 myriads of ministering angels, great and honoured ones who move the planets from city to city and from province to province in the Raqia' of heavens. ⁸ And over them are SEVENTY-TWO PRINCES OF KINGDOMS on high corresponding to the 72 tongues of the world. And all of them are crowned with royal crowns and clad in royal garments and wrapped in royal cloaks. And all of them are riding on royal horses and they are holding royal sceptres in their hands. And before each one of them when he is travelling in Raqia', royal servants are running with great glory and majesty even as on earth they (princes) are travelling in chariot(s) with horsemen and great armies and in glory and greatness with praise, song and honour.

18

The order of ranks of the angels and the homage received by the higher ranks from the lower ones. R. Ishmael said: Metatron, the Angel, the Prince of the Presence, the glory of all heaven, said to me:

¹ THE ANGELS OF THE FIRST HEAVEN, when(ever) they see their prince, they dismount from their horses and fall on their faces. And THE PRINCE OF THE FIRST HEAVEN, when he sees the prince of the second heaven, he dismounts, removes the crown of glory from his head and falls on his face. And THE PRINCE OF THE SECOND HEAVEN, when he sees the Prince of the third heaven, he removes the crown of glory from his head and falls on his face. And THE PRINCE OF THE THIRD HEAVEN, when he sees the prince of the fourth heaven, he removes the crown of glory from his head and falls on his face. And THE PRINCE OF THE FOURTH HEAVEN, when he sees the prince of the fifth heaven, he removes the crown of glory from his head and falls on his face. And THE PRINCE OF THE FIFTH HEAVEN, when he sees the prince of the sixth heaven, he removes the crown of glory from his head and falls on his face. And THE PRINCE OF THE SIXTH HEAVEN, when he sees the prince of the seventh heaven, he removes the crown of glory from his head and falls on his face. ² And THE PRINCE OF THE SEVENTH HEAVEN, when he sees THE SEVENTY-TWO PRINCES OF KINGDOMS, he removes the crown of glory from his head and falls on his face. ³ And the seventy-two princes of kingdoms, when they see THE DOOR KEEPERS OF THE FIRST HALL IN THE ARABOTH RAQIA in the highest, they remove the royal crown from their head and fall on their faces. And THE DOOR KEEPERS OF THE FIRST HALL, when they see the door keepers of the second Hall, they remove the crown of glory from their head and fall on their faces. And THE DOOR KEEPERS OF THE SECOND HALL, when they see the door keepers of the third Hall, they remove the crown of glory from their head and fall on their faces. And THE DOOR KEEPERS OF THE THIRD HALL, when they see the door keepers of the fourth Hall, they remove the crown of glory from their head and fall on their faces. And THE DOOR KEEPERS OF THE FOURTH HALL, when they see the door keepers of the fifth Hall, they remove the crown of glory from their head and fall on their faces. And THE DOOR KEEPERS OF THE FIFTH HALL, when they see the door keepers of the sixth Hall, they remove the crown of glory from their head and fall on their faces. And THE DOOR KEEPERS OF THE SIXTH HALL, when they see the DOOR KEEPERS OF THE SEVENTH HALL, they remove the crown of glory from their head and fall on their faces. ⁴ And the door keepers of the seventh Hall, when they see THE FOUR GREAT PRINCES, the honoured ones, WHO ARE APPOINTED OVER THE FOUR CAMPS OF SHEKINA, they remove the crown(s) of glory from their head and fall on their faces. ⁵ And the four great princes, when they see TAG'AS, the prince, great and honoured with song (and) praise, at the head of all the children of heaven, they remove the crown of glory from their head and fall on their faces. ⁶ And Tag'as, the great and honoured prince, when he sees BARATTIEL, the great prince of three fingers in the height of 'Araboth, the highest heaven, he removes the crown of glory from his head and falls on his face. ⁷ And Barattiel, the great prince, when he sees HAMON, the great prince, the fearful and honoured, pleasant and terrible one who maketh all the children of heaven to tremble, when the time draweth nigh (that is set) for the saying of the '(Thrice) Holy', as it is written (Isa. xxxiii. 3): "At the noise of the tumult (hamon) the peoples are fled; at the lifting up of thyself the nations are scattered" he removes the crown of glory from his head and falls on his face. ⁸ And Hamon, the great prince, when he sees TUTRESIEL, the great prince, he removes the crown of glory from his head and falls on his face. ⁹ And Tutresiel H', the great prince, when he sees ATRUGIEL, the great prince, he removes the crown of glory from his head and falls on his face. ¹⁰ And Atrugiel the great prince, when he sees NA'ARIRIEL H', the great prince, he removes the crown of glory from his head and falls on his face. (n) And Na'aririel H', the great prince, when he sees SASNIGIEL H', the great prince, he removes the crown of glory from his head and falls on his face. ¹² And Sasnigiel H', when he sees ZAZRIEL H', the great prince, he removes the crown of glory from his head and falls on his face. ¹³ And Zazriel H', the prince, when he sees GEBURATIEL H', the prince, he removes the crown of glory from his head and falls on his face. ¹⁴ And Geburatiel H', the prince, when he sees 'ARAPHIEL H', the prince, he removes the crown of glory from his head and falls on his face. ¹⁵ And 'Araphiel H', the prince, when he sees 'ASHRUYLU, the prince, who presides in all the sessions of the children of heaven, he removes the crown of glory from his head and falls on his face. ¹⁶ And Ashruylu H, the prince, when he sees GALLISUR H', THE PRINCE, WHO REVEALS ALL THE SECRETS OF THE LAW (Tora), he removes the crown of glory from his head and falls on his face. ¹⁷ And Gallisur H', the prince, when he sees ZAKZAKIEL H', the prince who is appointed to write down the merits of Israel on the Throne of Glory, he removes the crown of glory from his head and falls on his face. ¹⁸ And Zakzakiel H', the great prince, when he sees 'ANAPHIEL H', the prince who keeps the keys of the heavenly Halls, he removes the crown of glory from his head and falls on his face. Why is he called by the name of 'Anaphiel? Because the bough of his honour and majesty and his crown and his splendour and his brilliance covers (overshadows) all the chambers of 'Araboth Raqia on high even as the Maker of the World (doth overshadow them). Just as it is written with regard to the Maker of the World (Hab. iii. 3): "His glory covered the heavens, and the earth was full of his praise", even so do the honour and majesty of 'Anaphiel cover all the glories of 'Araboth the highest. ¹⁹ And when he sees SOTHER 'ASHIEL H', the prince, the great, fearful and honoured one, he removes the crown of glory from his head and falls on his face. Why is he called Sother Ashiel? Because he is appointed over the four heads of the fiery river over against the Throne of Glory; and every single prince who goes out or enters before the Shekina, goes out or enters only by his permission. For the seals of the fiery river are entrusted to him. And furthermore, his height is 7000 myriads of parasangs. And he stirs up the fire of the river; and he goes out and enters before the Shekina to expound what is written (recorded) concerning the inhabitants of the world. According as it is written (Dan. vii. 10): "the judgement was

set, and the books were opened". ²⁰ And Sother 'Ashiel the prince, when he sees SHOQED CHOZI, the great prince, the mighty, terrible and honoured one, he removes the crown of glory from his head and falls upon his face. And why is he called Shoqed Chozi? Because he weighs all the merits (of man) in a balance in the presence of the Holy One, blessed be He. ²¹ And when he sees ZEHANPURYU H', the great prince, the mighty and terrible one, honoured, glorified and feared in all the heavenly household, he removes the crown of glory from his head and falls on his face. Why is he called Zehanpuryu? Because he rebukes the fiery river and pushes it back to its place. ²² And when he sees 'AZBUGA H', the great prince, glorified, revered, honoured, adorned, wonderful, exalted, beloved and feared among all the great princes who know the mystery of the Throne of Glory, he removes the crown of glory from his head and falls on his face. Why is he called 'Azbuga? Because in the future he will gird (clothe) the righteous and pious of the world with the garments of life and wrap them in the cloak of life, that they may live in them an eternal life. ²³ And when he sees the two great princes, the strong and glorified ones who are standing above him, he removes the crown of glory from his head and falls upon his face. And these are the names of the two princes: SOPHERIEL H' (WHO) KILLETH, (Sopheriel H' the Killer), the great prince, the honoured, glorified, blameless, venerable, ancient and mighty one; (and) SOPHERIEL H' (WHO) MAKETH ALIVE (Sopheriel H' the Lifegiver), the great prince, the honoured, glorified, blameless, ancient and mighty one. ²⁴ Why is he called Sopheriel H' who killeth (Sopheriel H' the Killer)? Because he is appointed over the books of the dead: [so that] every one, when the day of his death draws nigh, he writes him in the books of the dead. Why is he called Sopheriel H' who maketh alive (Sopheriel H' the Lifegiver)? Because he is appointed over the books of the living (of life), so that every one whom the Holy One, blessed be He, will bring into life, he writes him in the book of the living (of life), by authority of MAQOM. Thou might perhaps say: "Since the Holy One, blessed be He, is sitting on a throne, they also are sitting when writing". (Answer): The Scripture teaches us (1 Kings xxii. 19, 2 Chron. xviii. 18): "And all the host of heaven are standing by him ". "The host of heaven " (it is said) in order to show us, that even the Great Princes, none like whom there is in the high heavens, do not fulfil the requests of the Shekina otherwise than standing. But how is it (possible that) they (are able to) write, when they are standing? It is like this: ²⁵ One is standing on the wheels of the tempest and the other is standing on the wheels of the storm-wind. The one is clad in kingly garments, the other is clad in kingly garments. The one is wrapped in a mantle of majesty and the other is wrapped in a mantle of majesty. The one is crowned with a royal crown, and the other is crowned with a royal crown. The one's body is full of eyes, and the other's body is full of eyes. The appearance of one is like unto the appearance of lightnings, and the appearance of the other is like unto the appearance of lightnings. The eyes of the one are like the sun in its might, and the eyes of the other are like the sun in its might. The one's height is like the height of the seven heavens, and the other's height is like the height of the seven heavens. The wings of the one are as (many as) the days of the year, and the wings of the other are as (many as) the days of the year. The wings of the one extend over the breadth of Raqia', and the wings of the other extend over the breadth of Raqia. The lips of the one, are as the gates of the East, and the lips of the other are as the gates of the East. The tongue of the one is as high as the waves of the sea, and the tongue of the other is as high as the waves of the sea. From the mouth of the one a flame goes forth, and from the mouth of the other a flame goes forth. From the mouth of the one there go forth lightnings and from the mouth of the other there go forth lightnings. From the sweat of the one fire is kindled, and from the perspiration of the other fire is kindled. From the one's tongue a torch is burning, and from the tongue of the other a torch is burning. On the head of the one there is a sapphire stone, and upon the head of the other there is a sapphire stone. On the shoulders of the one there is a wheel of a swift cherub, and on the shoulders of the other there is a wheel of a swift cherub. One has in his hand a burning scroll, the other has in his hand a burning scroll. The one has in his hand a flaming style, the other has in his hand a flaming style. The length of the scroll is 3000 myriads of parasangs; the size of the style is 3000 myriads of parasangs; the size of every single letter that they write is 365 parasangs.

19

Rikbiel, the prince of the wheels of the Merkaba. The surroundings of the Merkaba. The commotion among the angelic hosts at the time of the Qedushsha. R. Ishmael said: Metatron, the Angel, the Prince of the Presence, said to me:

¹ Above these three angels, these great princes there is one Prince, distinguished, honoured, noble, glorified, adorned, fearful, valiant, strong, great, magnified, glorious, crowned, wonderful, exalted, blameless, beloved, lordly, high and lofty, ancient and mighty, like unto whom there is none among the princes. His name is RIKBIEL H', the great and revered Prince who is standing by the Merkaba. ² And why is he called RIKBIEL? Because he is appointed over the wheels of the Merkaba, and they are given in his charge. ³ And how many are the wheels? Eight; two in each direction. And there are four winds compassing them round about. And these are their names: "the Storm-Wind", "the Tempest", "the Strong Wind", and "the Wind of Earthquake". ⁴ And under them four fiery rivers are continually running, one fiery river on each side. And round about them, between the rivers, four clouds are planted (placed), and these they are: "clouds of fire", "clouds of lamps", "clouds of coal", "clouds of brimstone" and they are standing over against [their] wheels. ⁵ And the feet of the Chayyoth are resting upon the wheels. And between one wheel and the other earthquake is roaring and thunder is thundering. ⁶ And when the time draws nigh for the recital of the Song, (then) the multitudes of wheels are moved, the multitude of clouds tremble, all the chieftains (shallishim) are made afraid, all the horsemen (parashim) do rage, all the mighty ones (gibborim) are excited, all the hosts (seba'im) are afrighted, all the troops (gedudim) are in fear, all the appointed ones (memunnim) haste away, all the princes (sarim) and armies (chayyelim) are dismayed, all the servants (mesharetim) do faint and all the angels (mal'akim) and divisions (degalim) travail with pain. ⁷ And one wheel makes a sound to be heard to the other and one Kerub to another, one Chayya. to another, one Seraph to another (saying) (Ps. lxviii. 5) "Extol to him that rideth in 'Araboth, by his name Jah and rejoice before him!"

20

CHAYYLIEL, the prince of the Chayyoth. R. Ishmael said: Metatron, the angel, the Prince of the Presence, said to me:

¹ Above these there is one great and mighty prince. His name is CHAYYLIEL H', a noble and revered prince, a glorious and mighty prince, a great and revered prince, a prince before whom all the children of heaven do tremble, a prince who is able to swallow up the whole earth in one moment (at a mouthful). ² And why is he called CHAYYLIEL H'? Because he is appointed over the Holy Chayyoth and smites the Chayyoth with lashes of fire: and glorifies them, when they give praise and glory and rejoicing and he causes them to make haste to say "Holy" and "Blessed be the Glory of H' from his place!" (i.e. the Qedushshd).

21

The Chayyoth. R. Ishmael said: Metatron, the angel, the Prince of the Presence, said to me:

¹ Four (are) the Chayyoth corresponding to the four winds. Each Chayya is as the space of the whole world. And each one has four faces; and each face is as the face of the East. ² Each one has four wings and each wing is like the cover (roof) of the universe. ³ And each one has faces in the middle of faces and wings in the middle of wings. The size of the faces is (as the size of) 248 faces, and the size of the wings is (as the size of) 365 wings. ⁴ And every one is crowned with 2000 crowns on his head. And each crown is like unto the bow in the cloud. And its splendour is like unto the splendour of the globe of the sun. And the sparks that go forth from every one are like the splendour of the morning star (planet Venus) in the East.

22A

KERUBIEL, the Prince of the Kembim. Description of the Kerubim. R. Ishmael said: Metatron, the angel, the Prince of the Presence, said to me:

¹ Above these la there is one prince, noble, wonderful, strong, and praised with all kinds of praise. His name is KERUBIEL H', a mighty prince, full of power and strength a prince of highness, and Highness (is) with him, a righteous prince, and righteousness (is) with him, a holy prince, and holiness (is) with him, a prince glorified in (by) thousand hosts, exalted by ten thousand armies. ² At his wrath the earth trembles, at his anger the camps are moved, from fear of him the foundations are shaken, at his rebuke the Araboth do tremble. ³ His stature is full of (burning) coals. The height of his stature is as the height of the seven heavens the breadth of his stature is as the wideness of the seven heavens and the thickness of his stature is as the seven heavens. ⁴ The opening of his mouth is like a lamp of fire. His tongue is a consuming fire. His eyebrows are like unto the splendour of the lightning. His eyes are like sparks of brilliance. His countenance is like a burning fire. ⁵ And there is a crown of holiness upon his head on which (crown) the Explicit Name is graven, and lightnings go forth from it. And the bow of Shekina is between his shoulders. ⁶ And his sword is like unto a lightning; and upon his loins there are arrows like unto a flame, and upon his armour and shield there is a consuming fire, and upon his neck there are coals of burning juniper and (also) round about him (there are coals of burning juniper). ⁷ And the splendour of Shekina is on his face; and the horns of majesty on his wheels; and a royal diadem upon his skull. ⁸ And his body is full of eyes. And wings are covering the whole of his high

stature (lit. the height of his stature is all wings). ⁹ On his right hand a flame is burning, and on his left a fire is glowing; and coals are burning from it. And firebrands go forth from his body. And lightnings are cast forth from his face. With him there is always thunder upon (in) thunder, by his side there is ever earthquake upon (in) earthquake. ¹⁰ And the two princes of the Merkaba are together with him. ¹¹ Why is he called KERUBIEL H', the Prince. Because he is appointed over the chariot of the Kerubim. And the mighty Kerubim are given in his charge. And he adorns the crowns on their heads and polishes the diadem upon their skull. ¹² He magnifies the glory of their appearance. And he glorifies the beauty of their majesty. And he increases the greatness of their honour. He causes the song of their praise to be sung. He intensifies their beautiful strength. He causes the brilliance of their glory to shine forth. He beautifies their goodly mercy and lovingkindness. He frames the fairness of their radiance. He makes their merciful beauty even more beautiful. He glorifies their upright majesty. He extols the order of their praise, to stablish the dwelling place of him "who dwelleth on the Kerubim". ¹³ And the Kerubim are standing by the Holy Chayyoth, and their wings are raised up to their heads (lit. are as the height of their heads) and Shekina is (resting) upon them; and the brilliance of the Glory is upon their faces; and song and praise in their mouth; and their hands are under their wings; and their feet are covered by their wings; and horns of glory are upon their heads; and the splendour of Shekina on their face; and Shekina is (resting) upon them; and sapphire stones are round about them; and columns of fire on their four sides; and columns of firebrands beside them. ¹⁴ There is one sapphire on one side and another sapphire on another side and under the sapphires there are coals of burning juniper. ¹⁵ And one Kerub is standing in each direction but the wings of the Kerubim compass each other above their skulls in glory; and they spread them to sing with them a song to him that inhabiteth the clouds and to praise with them the fearful majesty of the king of kings. ¹⁶ And KERUBIEL H', the prince who is appointed over them, he arrays them in comely, beautiful and pleasant orders and he exalts them in all manner of exaltation, dignity and glory. And he hastens them in glory and might to do the will of their Creator every moment. For above their lofty heads abides continually the glory of the high king "who dwelleth on the Kerubim".

22B

(ADDITIONAL) ¹ And there is a court before the Throne of Glory, ² which no seraph nor angel can enter, and it is 36,000 myriads of parasangs, as it is written (Is.vi.2): "and the Seraphim are standing above him" (the last word of the scriptural passage being 'Lamech-Vav' [numerical value: 36]). ³ As the numerical value Lamech-Vav [36] the number of the bridges there. ⁴ And there are 24 myriads of wheels of fire. And the ministering angels are 12,000 myriads. And there are 12,000 rivers of hail, and 12,000 treasuries of snow. And in the seven Halls are chariots of fire and flames, without reckoning, or end or searching.. R. Ishmael said to me: Metatron, the angel, the Prince of the Presence, said to me: ¹ How are the angels standing on high? Pie said: Like a bridge that is placed over a river so that every one can pass over it, likewise a bridge is placed from the beginning of the entry to the end. ² And three ministering angels surround it and utter a song before YHWH, the God of Israel. And there are standing before its lords of dread and captains of fear, thousand times thousand and ten thousand times ten thousand in number and they sing praise and hymns before YHWH, the God of Israel. ³ Numerous bridges are there: bridges of fire and numerous bridges of hail. Also numerous rivers of hail, numerous treasuries of snow and numerous wheels of fire. ⁴ And how many are the ministering angels? 12,000 myriads: six (thousand myriads) above and six (thousand myriads) below. And 12,000 are the treasuries of snow, six above and six below. And 24 myriads of wheels of fire, 12 (myriads) above and 12 (myriads) below. And they surround the bridges and the rivers of fire and the rivers of hail. And there are numerous ministering angels, forming entries, for all the creatures that are standing in the midst thereof, corresponding to (over against) the paths of Raqia Shamayim. ⁵ What doeth YHWH, the God of Israel, the King of Glory? The Great and Fearful God, mighty in strength, doth cover his face. ⁶ In Araboth are 660,000 myriads of angels of glory standing over against the Throne of Glory and the divisions of flaming fire. And the King of Glory doth cover His face; for else the (Araboth Raqia would be rent asunder in its midst because of the majesty, splendour, beauty, radiance, loveliness, brilliancy, brightness and excellency of the appearance of (the Holy One,) blessed be He. ⁷ There are numerous ministering angels performing his will, numerous kings, numerous princes in the 'Araboth of his delight, angels who are revered among the rulers in heaven, distinguished, adorned with song and bringing love to remembrance: (who) are affrighted by the splendour of the Shekina, and their eyes are dazzled by the shining beauty of their King, their faces grow black and their strength doth fail. ⁸ There go forth rivers of joy, streams of gladness, rivers of rejoicing, streams of triumph, rivers of love, streams of friendship (another reading:) of commotion and they flow over and go forth before the Throne of Glory and wax great and go through the gates of the paths of 'Araboth Raqia at the voice of the shouting and music of the CHAYYOTH, at the voice of the rejoicing of the timbrels of his 'OPHANNIM and at the melody of the cymbals of His Kerubim. And they wax great and go forth with commotion with the sound of the hymn: "HOLY, HOLY, HOLY, IS THE LORD OF HOSTS; THE WHOLE EARTH IS FULL OF HIS GLORY!"

22C

R. Ishmael said: Metatron, the Prince of the Presence said to me:
¹ What is the distance between one bridge and another? 12 myriads of parasangs. Their ascent is 12 myriads of parasangs, and their descent 12 myriads of parasangs. ² (The distance) between the rivers of dread and the rivers of fear is 22 myriads of parasangs; between the rivers of hail and the rivers of darkness 36 myriads of parasangs; between the chambers of lightnings and the clouds of compassion 42 myriads of parasangs; between the clouds of compassion and the Merkaba 84 myriads of parasangs; between the Merkaba and the Kerubim 148 myriads of parasangs; between the Kerubim and the 'Ophannim 24 myriads of parasangs; between the Ophannim and the chambers of chambers 24 myriads of parasangs; between the chambers of chambers and the Holy Chayyoth 40,000 myriads of parasangs; between one wing (of the Chayyoth) and another 12 myriads of parasangs; and the breadth of each one wing is of that same measure; and the distance between the Holy Chayyoth and the Throne of Glory is 30,000 myriads of parasangs. ³ And from the foot of the Throne to the seat there are 40,000 myriads of parasangs. And the name of Him that sitteth on it: let the name be sanctified! ⁴ And the arches of the Bow are set above the 'Araboth, and they are 1000 thousands and 10,000 times ten thousands (of parasangs) high. Their measure is after the measure of the 'Irin and Qaddishin (Watchers and Holy Ones). As it is written (Gen. ix. 13) "My bow I have set in the cloud". It is not written here "I will set" but "I have set", (i.e.) already; clouds that surround the Throne of Glory. As His clouds pass by, the angels of hail (turn into) burning coal. ⁵ And a fire of the voice goes down from by the Holy Chayyoth. And because of the breath of that voice they "run" (Ezek. i. 14) to another place, fearing lest it command them to go; and they "return" lest it injure them from the other side. Therefore "they run and return" (Ezek. i. 14). ⁶ And these arches of the Bow are more beautiful and radiant than the radiance of the sun during the summer solstice. And they are whiter than a flaming fire and they are great and beautiful. ⁷ Above the arches of the Bow are the wheels of the 'Ophannim. Their height is 1000 thousand and 10,000 times 10,000 units of measure after the measure of the Seraphim and the Troops (Gedudim).

23

The winds blowing under the wings of the Kembim. R. Ishmael said: Metatron, the Angel, the Prince of the Presence, said to me:
¹ There are numerous winds blowing under the wings of the Kerubim. There blows "the Brooding Wind", as it is written (Gen. i. 2): " and the wind of God was brooding upon the face of the waters ". ² There blows "the Strong Wind", as it is said (Ex. xiv. 21): "and the Lord caused the sea to go back by a strong east wind all that night". ³ There blows "the East Wind" as it is written (Ex. x. 13): "the east wind brought the locusts". ⁴ There blows "the Wind of Quails" as it is written (Num. xi. 31): "And there went forth a wind from the Lord and brought quails". ⁵ There blows "the Wind of Jealousy" as it is written (Num. v. 14): "And the wind of jealousy came upon him". ⁶ There blows the "Wind of Earthquake" as it is written (i Kings .xix. 1): "and after that the wind of the earthquake; but the Lord was not in the earthquake". ⁷ There blows the "Wind of H' " as it is written (Ex. xxxvii. i): "and he carried me out by the wind of H' and set me down". ⁸ There blows the "Evil Wind" as it is written (i Sam. xvi. 23): "and the evil wind departed from him". ⁹ There blow the "Wind of Wisdom" Sand the "Wind of Understanding" and the "Wind of Knowledge" and the "Wind of the Fear of H'" as it is written (Is. xi. 2): "And the wind of H'shall rest upon him; the wind of wisdom and understanding, the wind of counsel and might, the wind of knowledge and of the fear. ¹⁰ There blows the "Wind of Rain", as it is written (Prov. xxv. 23): "the north wind bringeth forth rain". ¹¹ There blows the "Wind of Lightnings ", as it is written (Jer.x.l3, li. 16): "he maketh lightnings for the rain and bringeth forth the wind out of his treasuries ". ¹² There blows the "Wind, Breaking the Rocks", as it is written (i Kings xix. n): "the Lord passed by and a great and strong wind (rent the mountains and brake in pieces the rocks before the Lord)". ¹³ There blows the "Wind of Assuagement of the Sea", as it is written (Gen. viii. i): "and God made a wind to pass over the earth, and the waters assuaged". ¹⁴ There blows the "Wind of Wrath", as it is written (Job i. 19): "and behold there came a great wind from the wilderness and smote the four corners of the house and it

fell". ¹⁵ There blows the " Storm-Wind ", as it is written (Ps. cxlviii. 8): "Storm-wind, fulfilling his word". ¹⁶ And Satan is standing among these winds, for "storm-wind " is nothing else but "Satan", and all these winds do not blow but under the wings of the Kerubim, as it is written (Ps. xviii. n): "and he rode upon a cherub and did fly, yea, and he flew swiftly upon the wings of the wind". ¹⁷ And whither go all these winds? The Scripture teaches us, that they go out from under the wings of the Kerubim and descend on the globe of the sun, as it is written (Eccl. i. 6): " The wind goeth toward the south and turneth about unto the north; it turneth about continually in its course and the wind returneth again to its circuits ". And from the globe of the sun they return and descend upon the rivers and the seas, upon] the mountains and upon the hills, as it is written (Am.iv.13): "For lo, he that formeth the mountains and createth the wind". ¹⁸ And from the mountains and the hills they return and descend to the seas and the rivers; and from the seas and the rivers they return and descend upon (the) cities and provinces; and from the cities and provinces they return and descend into the Garden, and from the Garden they return and descend to Eden, as it is written (Gen.iii. 8): "walking in the Garden in the wind of day". And in the midst of the Garden they join together and blow from one side to the other and are perfumed with the spices of the Garden even from the remotest parts, until they separate from each other, and, filled with the scent of the pure spices, they bring the odour from the remotest parts of Eden and the spices of the Garden to the righteous and godly who in the time to come shall inherit the Garden of Eden and the Tree of Life, as it is written (Cant. iv. 16): "Awake, O north wind; and come thou south; blow upon my garden, that the spices thereof may flow out. Let my beloved come into his garden and eat his precious fruits".

24

The different chariots of the Holy One, blessed be He. R. Ishmael said: Metatron, the Angel, the Prince of the Presence, the glory of all heaven, said to me:

¹ Numerous chariots has the Holy One, blessed be He: He has the "Chariots of (the) Kerubim", as it is written (Ps.xviii.ll, 2 Sam.xxii.ll): "And he rode upon a cherub and did fly". ² He has the "Chariots of Wind", as it is written (ib.): "and he flew swiftly upon the wings of the wind ". ³ He has the "Chariots of (the) Swift Cloud", as it is written (Is. xix. i): "Behold, the Lord rideth upon a swift cloud". ⁴ He has "the Chariots of Clouds", as it is written (Ex. xix. 9): "Lo, I come unto thee in a cloud". ⁵ He has the "Chariots of the Altar", as it is written (Am. ix. i):"I saw the Lord standing upon the Altar". ⁶ He has the "Chariots of Ribbotaim", as it is written (Ps.Ixviii. 18): "The chariots of God are Ribbotaim; thousands of angels ". ⁷ He has the "Chariots of the Tent", as it is written (Deut.xxxi. 15): "And the Lord appeared in the Tent in a pillar of cloud ". ⁸ He has the "Chariots of the Tabernacle", as it is written (Lev. i. 1): "And the Lord spake unto him out of the tabernacle". ⁹ He has the "Chariots of the Mercy-Seat", as it is written (Num. vii. 89): "then he heard the Voice speaking unto him from upon the mercy-seat". ¹⁰ He has the "Chariots of Sapphire Stone", as it is written (Ex. xxiv. 10): "and there was under his feet as it were a paved work of sapphire stone". ¹¹ He has the "Chariots of Eagles ", as it is written (Ex. xix. 4):"I bare you on eagles' wings". Eagles literally are not meant here but "they that fly swiftly as eagles". ¹² He has the "chariots of Shout", as it is written (Ps. xlvii. 6):"God is gone up with a shout". ¹³ He has the "Chariots of Araboth", as it is written (Ps.Ixviii. 5): "Extol Him that rideth upon the Araboth". ¹⁴ He has the "Chariots of Thick Clouds", as it is written (Ps. civ. 3): "who maketh the thick clouds His chariot". ¹⁵ He has the "Chariots of the Chayyoth", as it is written (Ezek. i. 14): "and the Chayyoth ran and returned". They run by permission and return by permission, for Shekina is above their heads. ¹⁶ He has the "Chariots of Wheels (Galgallim)", as it is written (Ezek. x. 2): "And he said: Go in between the whirling wheels". ¹⁷ lie has the "Chariots of a Swift Kerub", as it is written (Ps.xviii.lO & Is.xix.l): "riding on a swift cherub". And at the time when He rides on a swift kerub, as he sets one of His feet upon him, before he sets the other foot upon his back, he looks through eighteen thousand worlds at one glance. And he discerns and sees into them all and knows what is in all of them and then he sets down the other foot upon him, according as it is written (Ezek. xlviii. 35): "Round about eighteen thousand". Whence do we know that He looks through every one of them every day? It is written (Ps. xiv. 2): "He looked down from heaven upon the children of men to see if there were any that did understand, that did seek after God". ¹⁸ He has the "Chariots of the 'Ophannim", as it is written (Ezek. X. 12): "and the 'Ophannim were full of eyes round about". ¹⁹ He has the "Chariots of His Holy Throne", as it is written (Ps. xlvii. 8):" God sitteth upon his holy throne ". ²⁰ He has the "chariots of the Throne of Yah", as it is written (Ex. xvii. 16): "Because a hand is lifted up upon the Throne of Jah". ²¹ He has the "Chariots of the Throne of Judgement", as it is written (Is. v. 16): "but the Lord of hosts shall be exalted in judgment". ²² He has the "Chariots of the Throne of Glory ", as it is written (Jer. xvii. 12): "The Throne of Glory, set on high from the beginning, is the place of our sanctuary". ²³ He has the "Chariots of the High and Exalted Throne", as it is written (Is. vi. i): "I saw the Lord sitting upon the high and exalted throne".

25

'Ophphanniel, the prince of the 'Ophannim. Description of the 'Ophannim. R. Ishmael said: Metatron, the Angel, the Prince of the Presence, said to me:

¹ Above these there is one great prince, revered, high, lordly, fearful, ancient and strong. 'OPHPHANNIEL H is his name. ² He has sixteen faces, four faces on each side, (also) hundred wings on each side. And he has 8466 eyes, corresponding to the days of the year. [2190 -and some say 2116- on each side.] [2191/2196 and sixteen on each side.] ³ And those two eyes of his face, in each one of them lightnings are flashing, and from each one of them firebrands are burning; and no creature is able to behold them: for anyone who looks at them is burnt instantly. ⁴ His height is (as) the distance of 2500 years journey. No eye can behold and no mouth can tell the mighty power of his strength save the King of kings, the Holy One, blessed be He, alone. ⁵ Why is he called 'OPHPHANNIEL? Because he is appointed over the 'Ophannim and the 'Ophannimare given in his charge. He stands every day and attends and beautifies them. And he exalts and orders their apartment and polishes their standing-place and makes bright their dwellings, makes their corners even and cleanses their seats. And he waits upon them early and late, by day and by night, to increase their beauty, to make great their dignity and to make them "diligent in praise of their Creator. ⁶ And all the 'Ophannim are full of eyes, and they are all full of brightness; seventy-two sapphire stones are fixed on their garments on their right side and seventy-two sapphire stones are fixed on their garments on their left side. ⁷ And four carbuncle stones are fixed on the crown of every single one, the splendour of which proceeds in the four directions of 'Araboth even as the splendour of the globe of the sun proceeds in all the directions of the universe. And why is it called Carbuncle (Bareqet)? Because its splendour is like the appearance of a lightning (Baraq). And tents of splendour, tents of brilliance, tents of brightness as of sapphire and carbuncle inclose them because of the shining appearance of their eyes.

26

SERAPHIEL, the Prince of the Seraphim. Description of the Seraphim. R. Ishmael said: Metatron, the Angel, the Prince of the Presence, said to me:

¹ Above these there is one prince, wonderful, noble, great, honourable, mighty, terrible, a chief and leader and a swift scribe, glorified, honoured and beloved. ² He is altogether filled with splendour, full of praise and shining; and he is wholly full of brilliance, of light and of beauty; and the whole of him is filled with goodliness and greatness. ³ His countenance is altogether like (that of) angels, but his body is like an eagle's body. ⁴ His splendour is like unto lightnings, his appearance like fire brands, his beauty like unto sparks, his honour like fiery coals, his majesty like chashmals, his radiance like the light of the planet Venus. The image of him is like unto the Greater Light. His height is as the seven heavens. The light from his eyebrows is like the sevenfold light. ⁵ The sapphire stone upon his head is as great as the whole universe and like unto the splendour of the very heavens in radiance. ⁶ His body is full of eyes like the stars of the sky, innumerable and unsearchable. Every eye is like the planet Venus. Yet, there are some of them like the Lesser Light and some of them like unto the Greater Light. From his ankles to his knees (they are) like unto stars of lightning, from his knees to his thighs like unto the planet Venus, from his thighs to his loins like unto the moon, from his loins to his neck like the sun, from his neck to his skull like unto the Light Imperishable. (Cf. Zeph. iii. 5.) ⁷ The crown on his head is like unto the splendour of the Throne of Glory. The measure of the crown is the distance of 502 years' journey. There is no kind of splendour, no kind of brilliance, no kind of radiance, no kind of light in the universe but is fixed on that crown. ⁸ The name of that prince is SERAPHIEL H". And the crown on his head, its name is "the Prince of Peace". And why is he called by the name of SERAPHIEL '? Because he is appointed over the Seraphim. And the flaming Seraphim are given in his charge. And he presides over them by day and by night and teaches them song, praise, proclamation of beauty, might and majesty; that they may proclaim the beauty of their King in all manner of Praise and Sanctification (Qedushsha). ⁹ How many are the Seraphim? Four, corresponding to the four winds of the world. And how many wings have they each one of them? Six, corresponding to the six days of Creation. And how many faces have they? Each one of them four faces. ¹⁰ The measure of the Seraphim and the height of each one of them correspond to the height of the seven heavens. The size of each wing is like the measure of all

Raqia'. The size of each face is like that of the face of the East. [11] And each one of them gives forth light like unto the splendour of the Throne of Glory: so that not even the Holy Chayyoth, the honoured 'Ophannim, nor the majestic KeruUm are able to behold it. For every one who beholds it, his eyes are darkened because of its great splendour. [12] Why are they called Seraphim? Because they burn (saraph) the writing tables of Satan: Every day Satan is sitting, together with SAMMAEL, the Prince of Rome, and with DUBBIEL, the Prince of Persia, and they write the iniquities of Israel on writing tables which they hand over to the Seraphim, in order that they may present them before the Holy One, blessed be He, so that He may destroy Israel from the world. But the Seraphim know from the secrets of the Holy One, blessed be He, that he desires not, that this people Israel should perish. What do the Seraphim? Every day do they receive (accept) them from the hand of Satan and burn them in the burning fire over against the high and exalted Throne in order that they may not come before the Holy One, blessed be He, at the time when he is sitting upon the Throne of Judgement, judging the whole world in truth.

27

RADWERIEL, the keeper of the Book of Records. R. Ishmael said: Metatron, the Angel of H', the Prince of the Presence, said to me:
[1] Above the Seraphim there is one prince, exalted above all the princes, wondrous more than all the servants. His name is RADWERIEL H' who is appointed over the treasuries of the books. [2] He fetches forth the Case of Writings (with) the Book of Records in it, and brings it before the Holy One, blessed be He. And he breaks the seals of the case, opens it, takes out the books and delivers them before the Holy One, blessed be He. And the Holy One, blessed be He, receives them of his hand and gives them in his sight to the Scribes, that they may read them in the Great Beth Din (The court of justice) in the height of 'Araboth Raqia', before the heavenly household. [3] And why is he called RADWERIEL? Because out of every word that goes forth from his mouth an angel is created: and he stands in the songs (in the singing company) of the ministering angels and utters a song before the Holy One, blessed be He when the time draws nigh for the recitation of the (Thrice) Holy.

28

The 'Irin and Qaddishin. R. Ishmael said: Metatron, the Angel, the Prince of the Presence, said to me:
[1] Above all these there are four great princes, Irin and Qaddishin by name; high, honoured, revered, beloved, wonderful and glorious ones, greater than all the children of heaven. There is none like unto them among all the celestial princes and none their equal among all the Servants. For each one of them is equal to all the rest together. [2] And their dwelling is over against the Throne of Glory, and their standing place over against the Holy One, blessed be He, so that the brilliance of their dwelling is a reflection of the brilliance of the Throne of Glory. And the splendour of their countenance is a reflection of the splendour of Shekina. [3] And they are glorified by the glory of 4the Divine Majesty (Gebura) and praised by (through) the praise of Shekina. [4] And not only that, but the Holy One, blessed be He, does nothing in his world without first consulting them, but after that he doeth it. As it is written (Dan. iv. 17): "The sentence is by the decree of the Irin and the demand by the word of the Qaddishin." [5] The Urin are two and the Qaddishin are two. And how are they standing before the Holy One, blessed be He? It is to be understood, that one 'Ir is standing on one side and the other 'Ir on the other side, and one Qaddish is standing on one side and the other on the other side. [6] And ever do they exalt the humble, and they abase to the ground those that are proud, and they exalt to the height those that are humble. [7] And every day, as the Holy One, blessed be He, is sitting upon the Throne of Judgement and judges the whole world, and the Books of the Living and the Books of the Dead are opened before Him, then all the children of heaven are standing before him in fear, dread, awe and trembling. At that time, (when) the Holy One, blessed be He, is sitting upon the Throne of Judgement to execute judgement, his garment is white as snow, the hair on his head as pure wool and the whole of his cloak is like the shining light. And he is covered with righteousness all over as with a coat of mail. [8] And those Irm and Qaddishin are standing before him like court officers before the judge. And they raise and argue every case and close the case that comes before the Holy One, blessed be He, in judgement, according as it is written (Dan. iv. 17): "The sentence is by the decree of the Irm and the demand by the word of the Qaddishin" [9] Some of them argue and others pass the sentence in the Great Beth Din in 'Araboth. Some of them make the requests from before the Divine Majesty and some close the cases before the Most High. Others finish by going down and (confirming) executing the sentences on earth below. According as it is written (Dan. iv. 13, 14): " Behold an Ir and a Qaddish came down from heaven and cried aloud and said thus. Hew down the tree, and cut off his branches, shake off his leaves, and scatter his fruit: let the beasts get away from under it, and the fowls from his branches ". [10] Why are they called 'Irin and Qaddishint By reason that they sanctify the body and the spirit with lashes of fire on the third day of the judgement, as it is written (Hos. vi. 2): "After two days will he revive us: on the third he will raise us up, and we shall live before him."

29

Description of a class of angels. R. Ishmael said: Metatron, the Angel, the Prince of the Presence, said to me:
[1] Each one of them has seventy names corresponding to the seventy tongues of the world. And all of them are (based) upon the name of the Holy One, blessed be He. And every several name is written with a flaming style upon the Fearful Crown (Keiher Nora) which is on the head of the high and exalted King. [2] And from each one of them there go forth sparks and lightnings. And each one of them is beset with horns of splendour round about. From each one lights are shining forth, and each one is surrounded by tents of brilliance so that not even the Seraphim and the Chayyoth who are greater than all the children of heaven are able to behold them.

30

The 72 princes of Kingdoms and the Prince of the World officiating at the Great Sanhedrin in heaven. R. Ishmael said: Metatron, the Angel, the Prince of the Presence, said to me:
[1] Whenever the Great Beth Din is seated in the Araboth Raqia' on high there is no opening of the mouth for anyone in the world save those great princes who are called H' by the name of the Holy One, blessed be He. [2] How many are those princes? Seventy-two princes of the kingdoms of the world besides the Prince of the World who speaks (pleads) in favour of the world before the Holy One, blessed be He, every day, at the hour when the book is opened in which are recorded all the doings of the world, according as it is written (Dan.vii.10): "The judgement was set and the books were opened."

31

(The attributes of) Justice, Mercy and Truth by the Throne of Judgement. R. Ishmael said: Metatron, the Angel, the Prince of the Presence, said to me:
[1] At the time when the Holy One, blessed be He, is sitting on the Throne, of Judgement, (then) Justice is standing on His right and Mercy on His left and Truth before His face. [2] And when man enters before Him to judgement, (then) there comes forth from the splendour of the Mercy towards him as (it were) a staff and stands in front of him. Forthwith man falls upon his face, (and) all the angels of destruction fear and tremble before him, according as it is written (Is.xvi. 5): "And with mercy shall the throne be established, and he shall sit upon it in truth."

32

The execution of judgement on the wicked. God's sword. R. Ishmael said: Metatron, the Angel, the Prince of the Presence, said to me:
[1] When the Holy One, blessed be He, opens the Book half of which is fire and half flame, (then) they go out from before Him in every moment to execute the judgement on the wicked by His sword (that is) drawn forth out of its sheath and the splendour of which shines like a lightning and pervades the world from one end to the other, as it is written (Is. Ixvi. 16): "For by fire will the Lord plead (and by his sword with all flesh)." [2] And all the inhabitants of the world (lit. those who come into the world) fear and tremble before Him, when they behold His sharpened sword like unto a lightning from one end of the world to the other, and sparks and flashes of the size of the stars of Raqia' going out from it; according as it is written (Deut. xxxii. 41):" If I whet the lightning of my sword".

33

The angels of Mercy, of Peace and of Destruction by the Throne of Judgement. The scribes, (vss. i, 2) The angels by the Throne of Glory and the fiery rivers under it. (vss. 3-5). R. Ishmael said: Metatron, the Angel, the Prince of the Presence, said to me:
[1] At the time that the Holy One, blessed be He, is sitting on the Throne of Judgement, (then) the angels of Mercy are standing on His right, the angels of Peace are standing on His left and the angels of Destruction are standing in front of Him. [2] And one scribe is standing beneath Him, and another scribe above Him. [3] And the glorious Seraphim surround the Throne on its four sides with walls of lightnings, and the 'Ophannim. surround them with fire-brands round about the Throne of Glory. And clouds of fire and clouds of flames compass them to the right and to the left; and the Holy Chayyoth carry the Throne of Glory from below: each one with three fingers. The measure of the fingers of each one is 800,000 and 700 times hundred, (and) 66,000 parasangs. [4] And underneath the feet of the Chayyoth seven fiery rivers are running and flowing. And the breadth of each river is 365

thousand parasangs and its depth is 248 thousand myriads of parasangs. Its length is unsearchable and immeasurable. ⁵ And each river turns round in a bow in the four directions of 'Araboth Raqict, and (from there) it falls down to Ma'on and is stayed, and from Mai on to Zebul, from Zebul to Shechaqim, from Shechaqim to Raqia', from Raqia' to Shamayim and from Shamayim upon the heads of the wicked who are in Gehenna, as it is written (Jer. xxiii. 19): "Behold a whirlwind of the Lord, even his fury, is gone, yea, a whirling tempest; it shall burst upon the head of the wicked".

34
The different concentric circles round the Chayyoth, consisting of fire, water, hailstones etc. and of the angels uttering the Qedushsha responsorium. R. Ishmael said: Metatron; the Angel, the Prince of the Presence, said to me:
¹ The hoofs of the Chayyoth are surrounded by seven clouds of burning coals. The clouds of burning coals are surrounded on the outside by seven walls of flame(s). The seven walls of flame(s) are surrounded on the outside by seven walls of hailstones (stones of 'Et-gabish, Ezek. xiii. 11,13, xxviii. 22). The hailstones are surrounded on the outside by stones of hail (stone of Barad). The stones of hail are surrounded on the outside by stones of "the wings of the tempest ". The stones of "the wings of the tempest" are surrounded on the outside by flames of fire. The flames of fire are surrounded by the chambers of the whirlwind. The chambers of the whirlwind are surrounded on the outside by the fire and the water. ² Round about the fire and the water are those who utter the "Holy". Round about those who utter the "Holy" are those who utter the "Blessed'". Round about those who utter the "Blessed" are the bright clouds. The bright clouds are surrounded on the outside by coals of burning jumper; and on the outside surrounding the coals of burning juniper there are thousand camps of fire and ten thousand hosts of flame(s). And between every several camp and every several host there is a cloud, so that they may not be burnt by the fire.

35
The camps of angels in 'Araboth Raqia: angels, performing the Qedushsha. R. Ishmael said: Metatron, the Angel, the Prince of the Presence, said to me:
¹ 506 thousand myriads of camps has the Holy One, blessed be He, in the height of Araboth Raqia. And each camp is (composed of) 496 thousand angels. ² And every single angel, the height of his stature is as the great sea; and the appearance of their countenance as the appearance of the lightning, and their eyes as lamps of fire, and their arms and their feet like in colour to polished brass and the roaring voice of their words like the voice of a multitude. ³ And they are all standing before the Throne of Glory in four rows. And the princes of the army are standing at the head of each row. ⁴ And some of them utter the "Holy" and others utter the "Blessed", some of them run as messengers, others are standing in attendance, according as it is written (Dan. vii. 10): "Thousand thousands ministered unto him, and ten thousand times ten thousand stood before him: the judgment was set and the books were opened ". ⁵ And in the hour, when the time draws nigh for to say the "Holy", (then) first there goes forth a whirlwind from before the Holy One, blessed be He, and bursts upon the camp of Shekina and there arises a great commotion among them, as it is written (Jer.xxx. 23): "Behold, the whirlwind of the Lord goeth forth with fury, a continuing commotion". ⁶ At that moment 4thousand thousands of them are changed into sparks, thousand thousands of them into firebrands, thousand thousands into flashes, thousand thousands into flames, thousand thousands into males, thousand thousands into females, thousand thousands into winds, thousand thousands into burning fires, thousand thousands into flames, thousand thousands into sparks, thousand thousands into chashmals of light; until they take upon themselves the yoke of the kingdom of heaven, the high and lifted up, of the Creator of them all with fear, dread, awe and trembling, with commotion, anguish, terror and trepidation. Then they are changed again into their former shape to have the fear of their King before them always, as they have set their hearts on saying the Song continually, as it is written (Is. vi. 3): "And one cried unto another and said (Holy, Holy, Holy, etc.)".

36
The angels bathe in the fiery river before reciting the 'Song'. R. Ishmael said: Metatron, the Angel, the Prince of the Presence, said to me:
¹ At the time when the ministering angels desire to say (the) Song, (then) Nehar di-Nur (the fiery stream) rises with many thousand thousands and myriads of myriads" (of angels) of power and strength of fire and it runs and passes under the Throne of Glory, between the camps of the ministering angels and the troops of Araboth. ² And all the ministering angels first go down into Nehar di-Nur, and they dip themselves in the fire and dip their tongue and their mouth seven times; and after that they go up and put on the garment of 'Machaqe Samal' and cover themselves with cloaks of chashmal and stand in four rows over against the Throne of Glory, in all the heavens.

37
The four camps of Shekina and their surroundings. R. Ishmael said: Metatron, the Angel, the Prince of the Presence, said to me:
¹ In the seven Halls there are standing four chariots of Shekina, and before each one are standing the four camps of Shekina. Between each camp a river of fire is continually flowing. ² Between each river there are bright clouds [surrounding them], and between each cloud there are put up pillars of brimstone. Between one pillar and another there are standing flaming wheels, surrounding them. And between one wheel and another there are flames of fire round about. Between one flame and another there are treasuries of lightnings; behind the treasuries of lightnings are the wings of the stormwind. Behind the wings of the storm-wind are the chambers of the tempest; behind the chambers of the tempest there are winds, voices, thunders, sparks [upon] sparks and earthquakes [upon] earthquakes.

38
The fear that befalls all the heavens at the sound of the 'Holy? esp. the heavenly bodies. These appeased by the Prince of the World. R. Ishmael said: Metatron, the Angel, the Prince of the Presence, said to me:
¹ At the time, when the ministering angels utter (the Thrice) Holy, then all the pillars of the heavens and their sockets do tremble, and the gates of the Halls of Araboth Raqia' are shaken and the foundations of Shechaqim and the Universe (Tebel) are moved, and the orders of Ma'on and the chambers of Makon quiver, and all the orders of Raqia and the constellations and the planets are dismayed, and the globes of the sun and the moon haste away and flee out of their courses and run 12,000 parasangs and seek to throw themselves down from heaven, ² by reason of the roaring voice of their chant, and the noise of their praise and the sparks and lightnings that go forth from their faces; as it is written (Ps. lxxvii. 18): "The voice of thy thunder was in the heaven (the lightnings lightened the world, the earth trembled and shook) ". ³ Until the prince of the world calls them, saying: "Be ye quiet in your place ! Fear not because of the ministering angels who sing the Song before the Holy One, blessed be He". As it is written (Job.xxxviii. 7): "When the morning stars sang together and all the children of heaven shouted for joy".

39
The explicit names fly off from the Throne and all the various angelic hosts prostrate themselves before it at the time of the Qedushsha. R. Ishmael said: Metatron, the Angel, the Prince of the Presence, said to me:
¹ When the ministering angels utter the "Holy" then all the explicit names that are graven with a flaming style on the Throne of Glory fly off like eagles, with sixteen wings. And they surround and compass the Holy One, blessed be He, on the four sides of the place of His Shekinal . ² And the angels of the host, and the flaming Servants, and the mighty 'Ophannim, and the Kerubim of the Shekina, and the Holy Chayyoth, and the Seraphim, and the 'Er'ellim, and the Taphsarim and the troops of consuming fire, and the fiery armies, and the flaming hosts, and the holy princes, adorned with crowns, clad in kingly majesty, wrapped in glory, girt with loftiness, fall upon their faces three times, saying: "Blessed be the name of His glorious kingdom for ever and ever".

40
The ministering angels rewarded with crowns, when uttering the "Holy" in its right order, and punished by consuming fire if not. New ones created in the stead of the consumed angels. R. Ishmael said: Metatron, the Angel, the Prince of the Presence, said to me:
¹ When the ministering angels say "Holy" before the Holy One, blessed be He, in the proper way, then the servants of His Throne, the attendants of His Glory, go forth with great mirth from under the Throne of Glory. ² And they all carry in their hands, each one of them thousand and ten thousand times ten thousand crowns of stars, similar in appearance to the planet Venus, and put them on the ministering angels and the great princes who utter the "Holy". Three crowns they put on each one of them: one crown because they say "Holy", another crown, because they say "Holy, Holy", and a third crown because they say "Holy, Holy, Holy, is the Lord of Hosts". ³ And in the moment that they do not utter the "Holy" in the right order, a consuming fire goes forth from the little finger of the Holy One, blessed be He, and falls down in the midst of their ranks and is divided into 496 thousand parts corresponding to the four camps of the ministering angels, and consumes them in one moment, as it is written (Ps. xcvii. 3): "A fire goeth before him and burneth up his adversaries round about". ⁴ After that the Holy One, blessed be He, opens His mouth and speaks one word and creates others in their stead, new ones like them. And each one stands before His Throne of Glory, uttering the "Holy", as it is written (Lam. iii. 23): "They are new every morning; great is thy faithfulness".

41

Metatron shows. R. Ishmael the letters engraved on the Throne of Glory by which letters everything in heaven and earth has been created. R. Ishmael said: Metatron, the Angel, the Prince of the Presence, said to me:
¹ Come and behold the letters by which the heaven and the earth were created, the letters by which were created the mountains and hills, the letters by which were created the seas and rivers, the letters by which were created the trees and herbs, the letters by which were created the planets and the constellations, the letters by which were created the globe of the moon and the globe of the sun, Orion, the Pleiades and all the different luminaries of Raqia' . ² the letters by which were created the Throne of Glory and the Wheels of the Merkaba, the letters by which were created the necessities of the worlds, ³ the letters by which were created wisdom, understanding, knowledge, prudence, meekness and righteousness by which the whole world is sustained. ⁴ And I walked by his side and he took me by his hand and raised me upon his wings and showed me those letters, all of them, that are graven with a flaming style on the Throne of Glory: and sparks go forth from them and cover all the chambers of 'Araboth.

42

Instances of polar opposites kept in balance by several Divine Names and other similar wonders. R. Ishmael said: Metatron, the Angel, the Prince of the Presence, said to me:
¹ Come and I will show thee, where the waters are suspended in the highest, where fire is burning in the midst of hail, where lightnings lighten out of the midst of snowy mountains, where thunders are roaring in the celestial heights, where a flame is burning in the midst of the burning fire and where voices make themselves heard in the midst of thunder and earthquake. ² Then I went by his side and he took me by his hand and lifted me up on his wings and showed me all those things. I beheld the waters suspended on high in Araboth Raqia' by (force of) the name YAH 'EHYE ASHER 'EHYE (Jah, I am that I am). And their fruits going down from heaven and watering the face of the world, as it is written (Ps.civ.13): "(He watereth the mountains from his chambers:) the earth is satisfied with the fruit of thy work". ³ And I saw fire and snow and hailstone that were mingled together within each other and yet were undamaged, by (force of) the name 'ESH 'OKELA (consuming fire), as it is written (Deut. iv. 24): "For the Lord, thy God, is a consuming fire". ⁴ And I saw lightnings that were lightning out of mountains of snow and yet were not damaged (quenched), by (force of) the name YAH SUR 'OLAMIM (Jah, the everlasting rock), as it is written (Is. xxvi. 4): "For in Jah, YHWH, the everlasting rock". ⁵ And I saw thunders and voices that were roaring in the midst of fiery flames and were not damaged (silenced), by (force of) the name 'EL-SHADDAI RABBA (the Great God Almighty) as it is written (Gen. xvii. i): "I am God Almighty". ⁶ And I beheld a flame (and) a glow (glowing flames) that were flaming and glowing in the midst of burning fire, and yet were not damaged (devoured), by (force of) the name YAD 'AL KES YAH (the hand upon the Throne of the Lord) as it is written (Ex. xvii. 16): " And he said: for the hand is upon the Throne of the Lord ". ⁷ And I beheld rivers of fire in the midst of rivers of water and they were not damaged (quenched) by (force of) the name 'OSE SHALOM (Maker of Peace) as it is written (Job xxv. 2): "He maketh peace in his high places". For he makes peace between the fire and the water, between the hail and the fire, between the wind and the cloud, between the earthquake and the sparks.

43

Metatron shows. R. Ishmael the abode of the unborn spirits and of the spirits of the righteous dead. R. Ishmael said: Metatron said to me:
¹ Come and I will show thee where are the spirits of the righteous that have been created and have returned, and the spirits of the righteous that have not yet been created. ² And he lifted me up to his side, took me by his hand and lifted me up near the Throne of Glory by the place of the Shekina; and he revealed the Throne of Glory to me, and he showed me the spirits that have been created and had returned: and they were flying above the Throne of Glory before the Holy One, blessed be He. ³ After that I went to interpret the following verse of Scripture and I found in what is written (Isa.lvii. 16): "for the spirit clothed itself before me, and the souls I have made" that ("for the spirit was clothed before me") means the spirits that have been created in the chamber of creation of the righteous and that have returned before the Holy One, blessed be He; (and the words:) "and the souls I have made" refer to the spirits of the righteous that have not yet been created in the chamber (GUPH).

44

Metatron shows. R. Ishmael the abode of the wicked and the intermediate in Sheol. (vss. 1-6) The Patriarchs pray for the deliverance of Israel (vss. 7-10). R. Ishmael said: Metatron, x the Angel, the Prince of the Presence, said to me:
¹ Come and I will show thee the spirits of the wicked and the spirits of the intermediate where they are standing, and the spirits of the intermediate, whither they go down, 3and the spirits of the wicked, where they go down. ² And he said to me: The spirits of the wicked go down to She'ol by the hands of two angels of destruction: ZAAPHIEL and SIMKIEL are their names. ³ SIMKIEL is appointed over the intermediate to support them and purify them because of the great mercy of the Prince of the Place (Maqom). ZAAPHIEL is appointed over the spirits of the wicked in order to cast them down from the presence of the Holy One, blessed be He, and from the splendour of the Shekina to She'ol, to be punished in the fire of Gehenna with staves of burning coal. ⁴ And I went by his side, and he took me by his hand and showed me all of them with his fingers. ⁵ And I beheld the appearance of their faces (and, lo, it was) as the appearance of children of men, and their bodies like eagles. And not only that but (furthermore) the colour of the countenance of the intermediate was like pale grey on account of their deeds, for there are stains upon them until they have become cleaned from their iniquity in the fire. ⁶ And the colour of the wicked was like the bottom of a pot on account of the wickedness of their doings. ⁷ And I saw the spirits of the Patriarchs Abraham Isaac and Jacob and the rest of the righteous whom they have brought up out of their graves and who have ascended to the Heaven (Raqirf). And they were praying before the Holy One, blessed be He, saying in their prayer: "Lord of the Universe! How long wilt thou sit upon (thy) Throne like a mourner in the days of his mourning with thy right hand behind thee and not deliver thy children and reveal thy Kingdom in the world? And for how long wilt thou have no pity upon thy children who are made slaves among the nations of the world? Nor upon thy right hand that is behind thee wherewith thou didst stretch out the heavens and the earth and the heavens of heavens? When wilt thou have compassion?" ⁸ Then the Holy One, blessed be He, answered every one of them, saying: "Since these wicked do sin so and so, and transgress with such and such transgressions against me, how could I deliver my great Right Hand in the downfall by their hands (caused by them). ⁹ In that moment Metatron called me and spake to me: "My servant! Take the books, and read their evil doings!" Forthwith I took the books and read their doings and there were to be found 36 transgressions (written down) with regard to each wicked one and besides, that they have transgressed all the letters in the Tora, as it is written (Dan. ix. u): "Yea, all Israel have transgressed thy Law". It is not written 'al torateka but 'et (JIN) torateka, for they have transgressed from 'Aleph to Taw, 40 statutes have they transgressed for each letter. ¹⁰ Forthwith Abraham, Isaac and Jacob wept. Then said to them the Holy One, blessed be He: "Abraham, my beloved, Isaac, my Elect one, Jacob, my firstborn! How can I now deliver them from among the nations of the world?" And forthwith MIKAEL, the Prince of Israel, cried and wept with a loud voice and said (Ps. x. i): "Why standest thou afar off, O Lord?".

45

Metatron shows. R. Ishmael past and future events recorded on the Curtain of the Throne. R. Ishmael said: Metatron said to me:
¹ Come, and I will show thee the Curtain of MAQOM (the Divine Majesty) which is spread before the Holy One, blessed be He, (and) whereon are graven all the generations of the world and all their doings, both what they have done and what they will do until the end of all generations. ² And I went, and he showed it to me pointing it out with his fingers Mike a father who teaches his children the letters of Tora. And I saw each generation, the rulers of each generation, and the heads of each generation, the shepherds of each generation, the oppressors (drivers) of each generation, the keepers of each generation, the scourgers of each generation, the overseers of each generation, the judges of each generation, the court officers of each generation , the teachers of each generation, the supporters of each generation, the chiefs of each generation, the presidents of academies of each generation, the magistrates of each generation, the princes of each generation, the counsellors of each generation, the nobles of each generation, and the men of might of each generation, the elders of each generation, and the guides of each generation. ³ And I saw Adam, his generation, their doings and their thoughts, Noah and his generation, their doings and their thoughts, and the generation of the flood, their doings and their thoughts, Shem and his generation, their doings and their thoughts, Nimrod and the generation of the confusion of tongues, and his generation, their doings and their thoughts, Abraham and his generation, their doings and their thoughts, Isaac and his generation, their doings and their thoughts, Ishmael and his generation, their doings and their thoughts, Jacob and his generation, their doings and their thoughts, Joseph and his generation, their doings and their thoughts, the tribes and their generation, their doings and their thoughts, Amram and his generation, their doings and their thoughts, Moses and his generation, their doings and their thoughts, ⁴ Aaron and Mirjam their works and their doings, the princes and the elders, their works

and doings, Joshua and his generation, their works and doings, the judges and their generation, their works and doings, Eli and his generation, their works and doings, "Phinehas, their works and doings, Elkanah and his generation, their works and their doings, Samuel and his generation, their works and doings, the kings of Judah with their generations, their works and their doings, the kings of Israel and their generations, their works and their doings, the princes of Israel, their works and their doings; the princes of the nations of the world, their works and their doings, the heads of the councils of Israel, their works and their doings; the heads of (the councils in) the nations of the world, their generations, their works and their doings; the rulers of Israel and their generation, their works and their doings; the nobles of Israel and their generation, their works and their doings; the nobles of the nations of the world and their generation(s), their works and their doings; the men of reputation in Israel, their generation, their works and their doings; the judges of Israel, their generation, their works and their doings; the judges of the nations of the world and their generation, their works and their doings; the teachers of children in Israel, their generations, their works and their doings; the teachers of children in the nations of the world, their generation, their works and their doings; the counsellors (interpreters) of Israel, their generation, their works and their doings; the counsellors (interpreters) of the nations of the world, their generation, their works and their doings; all the prophets of Israel, their generation, their works and their doings; all the prophets of the nations of the world, their generation, their works and their doings; [5] and all the fights and wars that the nations of the world wrought against the people of Israel in the time of their kingdom. And I saw Messiah, son of Joseph, and his generation "and their" works and their doings that they will do against the nations of the world. And I saw Messiah, son of David, and his generation, and all the fights and wars, and their works and their doings that they will do with Israel both for good and evil. And I saw all the fights and wars that Gog and Magog will fight in the days of Messiah, and all that the Holy One, blessed be He, will do with them in the time to come. [6] And all the rest of all the leaders of the generations and all the works of the generations both in Israel and in the nations of the world, both what is done and what will be done hereafter to all generations until the end of time, (all) were graven on the Curtain of MAQOM. And I saw all these things with my eyes; and after I had seen it, I opened my mouth in praise of MAQOM (the Divine Majesty) (saying thus, Eccl. viii. 4, 5): "For the King's word hath power (and who may say unto him: What doest thou?) Whoso keepeth the commandments shall know no evil thing". And I said: (Ps. civ. 24) "O Lord, how manifold are thy works!".

46
The place of the stars shown to. R. Ishmael. R. Ishmael said: Metatron said to me:
[1] (Come and I will show thee) the space of the stars a that are standing in Raqia' night by night in fear of the Almighty (MAQOM) and (I will show thee) where they go and where they stand. [2] I walked by his side, and he took me by his hand and pointed out all to me with his fingers. And they were standing on sparks of flames round the Merkaba of the Almighty (MAQOM). What did Metatron do? At that moment he clapped his hands and chased them off from their place. Forthwith they flew off on flaming wings, rose and fled from the four sides of the Throne of the Merkaba, and (as they flew) he told me the names of every single one. As it is written (Ps. cxlvii. 4):" He telleth the number of the stars; he giveth them all their names", teaching, that the Holy One, blessed be He, has given a name to each one of them. [3] And they all enter in counted order under the guidance of (lit. through, by the hands of) RAHATIEL to Raqia' ha-shSHamayim to serve the world. And they go out in counted order to praise the Holy One, blessed be He, with songs and hymns, according as it is written (Ps. xix. i): "The heavens declare the glory of God". [4] But in the time to come the Holy One, blessed be He, will create them anew, as it is written (Lam. iii. 23): "They are new every morning". And they open their mouth and utter a song. Which is the song that they utter? (Ps. viii. 3): "When I consider thy heavens".

47
Metatron shows. R. Ishmael the spirits of the punished angels. R. Ishmael said: Metatron said to me:
[1] Come and I will show thee the souls of the angels and the spirits of the ministering servants whose bodies have been burnt in the fire of MAQOM (the Almighty) that goes forth from his little finger. And they have been made into fiery coals in the midst of the fiery river (Nehar di-Nur). But their spirits and their souls are standing behind the Shekina. [2] Whenever the ministering angels utter a song at a wrong time or as not appointed to be sung they are burnt and consumed by the fire of their Creator and by a flame from their Maker, in the places (chambers) of the whirlwind, for it blows upon them and drives them into the Nehar di-Nur; and there they are made into numerous mountains of burning coal. But their spirit and their soul return to their Creator, and all are standing behind their Master. [3] And I went by his side and he took me by his hand; and he showed me all the souls of the angels and the spirits of the ministering servants who were standing behind the Shekina upon wings of the whirlwind and walls of fire surrounding them. [4] At that moment Metatron opened to me the gates of the walls within which they were standing behind the Shekina, And I lifted up my eyes and saw them, and behold, the likeness of every one was as (that of) angels and their wings the birds' (wings), made out of flames, the work of burning fire. In that moment I opened my mouth in praise of MAQOM and said (Ps. xcii. 5): "How great are thy works, O Lord ".

48A
Metatron shows. R. Ishmael the Right Hand of the Most High, now inactive behind Him, but in the future destined to work the deliverance of Israel. R. Ishmael said: Metatron said to me:
[1] Come, and I will show thee the Right Hand of MAQOM, laid behind (Him) because of the destruction of the Holy Temple; from which all kinds of splendour and light shine forth and by which the 955 heavens were created; and whom not even the Seraphim and the 'Ophannim are permitted (to behold), until the day of salvation shall arrive. [2] And I went by his side and he took me by his hand and showed me (the Right Hand of MAQOM), with all manner of praise, rejoicing and song: and no mouth can tell its praise, and no eye can behold it, because of its greatness, dignity, majesty, glory and beauty. [3] And not only that, but all the souls of the righteous who are counted worthy to behold the joy of Jerusalem, they are standing by it, praising and praying before it three times every day, saying (Is.li.9): "Awake, awake, put on strength, arm of the Lord" according as it is written (Is. Ixiii. 12): "He caused his glorious arm to go at the right hand of Moses". [4] In that moment the Right Hand of MAQOM was weeping. And there went forth from its five fingers five rivers of tears and fell down into the great sea and shook the whole world, according as it is written (Is. xxiv. 19, 20): "The earth is utterly broken [1], the earth is clean dissolved [2], the earth is moved exceedingly [3], the earth shall stagger like a drunken man [4] and shall be moved to and for like a hut [5]", five times corresponding to the fingers of his Great Right Hand. [5] But when the Holy One, blessed be He, sees, that there is no righteous man in the generation, and no pious man (Chasid] on earth, and no justice in the hands of men; and (that there is) no man like unto Moses, and no intercessor as Samuel who could pray before MAQOM for the salvation and for the deliverance, and for His Kingdom, that it be revealed in the whole world; and for His great Right Hand that He put it before Himself again to work great salvation by it for Israel, [6] then forthwith will the Holy One, blessed be He, remember His own justice, favour, mercy and grace: and He will deliver His great Arm by himself, and His righteousness will support Him. According as it is written (Is. lix. 16): "And he saw, that there was no man" (that is:) like unto Moses who prayed countless times for Israel in the desert and averted the (Divine) decrees from them" and he wondered, that there was no intercessor" like unto Samuel who intreated the Holy One, blessed be He, and called unto Him and he answered him and fulfilled his desire, even if it was not fit (in accordance with the Divine plan), according as it is written (i Sam. xii. 17): "Is it not wheat-harvest to-day? I will call unto the Lord". [7] And not only that, but He joined fellowship with Moses in every place, as it is written (Ps.xcix.6): "Moses and Aaron among His priests." And again it is written (Jer. xv. i): "Though Moses and Samuel stood before me" (Is. Ixiii. 5): "Mine own arm brought salvation unto me". [8] Said the Holy One, blessed be He in that hour: " How long shall I wait for the children of men to work salvation according to their righteousness for my arm? For my own sake and for the sake of my merit and righteousness will I deliver my arm and by it redeem my children from among the nations of the world. As it is written (Is. xlviii. n): "For my own sake will I do it. For how should my name be profaned". [9] In that moment will the Holy One, blessed be He, reveal His Great Arm and show it to the nations of the world: for its length is as the length of the world and its breadth is as the width of the world. And the appearance of its splendour is like unto the splendour of the sunshine in its might, in the summer solstice. [10] Forthwith Israel will be saved from among the nations of the world. And Messiah will appear unto them and He will bring them up to Jerusalem with great joy. And not only that but Israel will come from the four quarters of the World and eat with Messiah. But the nations of the world shall not eat with them, as it is written (Is. Hi. 10): "The Lord hath made bare his holy arm in the eyes of all the nations; and all the ends of the earth shall see the salvation of our God". And again (Deut. xxxii. 12): "The Lord alone did lead him, and there was no strange god with him". (Zech. xiv. 9): "And the Lord shall be king over all the earth".

48B

The Divine Names that go forth from the Throne of Glory, crowned and escorted by numerous angelic hosts through the heavens and back again to the Throne the angels sing the 'Holy' and the 'Blessed'

[1] These are the seventy-two names written on the heart of the Holy One, blessed be He: SS, SeDeQ {righteousness}, SaHPeL SUR {Is. xxvi. 4}, SBI, SaDdlQ{righteous}, STh, SHN, SeBa'oTh {Lord ofHostsKShaDdaY {God Almighty}, 'eLoHIM {God},YHWH, SH, DGUL, W'DOM, SSS", 'YW, 'F, 'HW, HB, YaH, HW, WWW, SSS, PPP, NN, HH, HaY {living}, HaY, ROKeB 'aRaBOTh {riding upon the 'Araboth', Ps. lxviii. 5}, YH, HH, WH, MMM, NNN, HWW, YH, YHH, HPhS, H'S, 1, W, S", Z', "', QQQ {Holy, Holy, Holy}, QShR, BW, ZK, GINUR, GINURYa', Y', YOD, 'aLePh, H'N, P'P, R'W, YYWy YYW, BBS, DDD, TTT, KKK, KLL, SYS, 'XT', BShKMLW { = blessed be the Name of His glorious kingdom for ever and ever}, completed for MeLeK HalOLaM {the King of the Universe], JBRH LB' {the beginning of Wisdom for the children of men}, BNLK W" Y {blessed be He who gives strength to the weary and increaseth strength to them that have no might. Is. xl. 29} that go forth (adorned) with numerous crowns of fire with numerous crowns of flame, with numerous crowns of chashmal, with numerous crowns of lightning from before the Throne of Glory. And with them (there are) thousand hundreds of power (i.e. powerful angels) who escort them like a king with trembling and dread, with awe and shivering, with honour and majesty and fear, with terror, with greatness and dignity, with glory and strength, with understanding and knowledge and with a pillar of fire and a pillar of flame and lightning and their light is as lightnings of light and with the likeness of the chashmal. [2] And they give glory unto them and they answer and cry before them: Holy, Holy, Holy. And they roll (convoy) them through every heaven as mighty and honoured princes. And when they bring them all back to the place of the Throne of Glory, then all the Chayyoth by the Merkaba open their mouth in praise of His glorious name, saying: "Blessed be the name of His glorious kingdom for ever and ever".

48C

An Enoch-Metatron piece
ALT 1

[1] "I seized him, and I took him and I appointed him" that is Enoch, the son of Jared, whose name is Metatron [2] and I took him from among the children of men [5] and made him a Throne over against my Throne. Which is the size of that Throne? Seventy thousand parasangs (all) of fire. [9] I committed unto him 70 angels corresponding to the nations (of the world) and I gave into his charge all the household above and below. [7] And I committed to him Wisdom and Intelligence more than (to) all the angels. And I called his name "the LESSER YAH", whose name is by Gematria 71. And I arranged for him all the works of Creation. And I made his power to transcend (lit. I made for him power more than) all the ministering angels.

ALT 2

[3] He committed unto Metatron that is Enoch, the son of Jared all treasuries. And I appointed him over all the stores that I have in every heaven. And I committed into his hands the keys of each heavenly store. [4] I made (of him) the prince over all the princes, and I made (of) him a minister of my Throne of Glory, to provide for and arrange the Holy Chayyoth, to wreathe crowns for them (to crown them with crowns), to clothe them with honour and majesty to prepare for them a seat when he is sitting on his throne to magnify his glory in the height. [5] The height of his stature among all those (that are) of high stature (is) seventy thousand parasangs. And I made his glory great as the majesty of my glory. [6] and the brilliance of his eyes as the splendour of the Throne of Glory. [7] his garment honour and majesty, his royal crown 500 by 500 parasangs.

ALT 3

[1] Aleph I made him strong, I took him, I appointed him: (namely) Metatron, my servant who is one (unique) among all the children of heaven. I made him strong in the generation of the first Adam. But when I beheld the men of the generation of the flood, that they were corrupt, then I went and removed my Shekina from among them. And lifted it up on high with the sound of a trumpet and with a shout, as it is written (Ps.xlvii. 6): "God is gone up with a shout, the Lord with the sound of a trumpet". [2] "And I took him": (that is) Enoch, the son of Jared, from among them. And I lifted him up with the sound of a trumpet and with a tera'a (shout) to the high heavens, to be my witness together with the Chayyoth by the Merkaba in the world to come. [3] I appointed him over all the treasuries and stores that I have in every heaven. And I committed into his hand the keys of every several one. [4] I made (of) him the prince over all the princes and a minister of the Throne of Glory (and) the Halls of 'Araboth: to open their doors to me, and (of) the Throne of Glory, to exalt an arrange it; (and I appointed him over) the Holy Chayyot to wreathe crowns upon their heads; the majestic 'Ophannim, to crown them with strength and glory; the; honoured Kerubim, to clothe them in majesty; over the radiant sparks, to make them to shine with splendour and brilliance; over the flaming Seraphim, to cover them with highness; the Chashmallim of light, to make them radiant with Light and to prepare the seat for me every morning as I sit upon the Throne of Glory. And to extol and magnify my glory in the height of my power; (and I have committed unto him) the secrets of above and the secrets of below (heavenly secrets and earthly secrets). [5] I made him higher than all. The height of his stature, in the midst of all (who are) high of stature (I made) seventy thousand parasangs. I made his Throne great by the majesty of my Throne. And I increased its glory by the honour of my glory. [6] I transformed his flesh into torches of fire, and all the bones of his body into fiery coals; and I made the appearance of his eyes as the lightning, and the light of his eyebrows as the imperishable light. I made his face bright as the splendour of the sun, and his eyes as the splendour of the Throne of Glory. [7] I made honour and majesty his clothing, beauty and highness his covering cloak and a royal crown of 500 by (times) 500 parasangs (his) diadem. And I put upon him of my honour, my majesty and the splendour, of my glory that is upon my Throne of Glory. I called him the LESSER YHWH, the Prince of the Presence, the Knower of Secrets: for every secret did I reveal to him as a father and all mysteries declared I unto him in uprightness. [8] I set up his throne at the door of my Hall that he may sit and judge the heavenly household on high. And I placed every prince before him, to receive authority from him, to perform his will. [9] Seventy names did I take from (my) names and called him by them to enhance his glory. Seventy princes gave I into his hand, to command unto them my precepts and my words in every language: to abase by his word the proud to the ground, and to exalt by the utterance of his lips the humble to the height; to smite kings by his speech, to turn kings away from their paths, to set up(the) rulers over their dominion as it is written (Dan.ii. 21): "and he changeth the times and the seasons, and to give wisdom unto all the set wise of the world and understanding (and) knowledge to all who understand knowledge, as it is written (Dan. ii. 21): " and knowledge to them that know understanding", to reveal to them the secrets of my words and to teach the decree of my righteous judgement, [10] as it is written (Is.Iv. n): "so shall my word be that goeth forth out of my mouth; it shall not return unto me void but shall accomplish (that which I please)". 'E'eseh' (I shall accomplish) is not written here, but "asdh" (he shall accomplish), meaning, that whatever word and whatever utterance goes forth from before the Holy One, blessed be He, Metatron stands and carries it out. And he establishes the decrees of the Holy One, blessed be He.

48D

The names of Metatron. The treasuries of Wisdom opened to Moses on mount Sinai. The angels protest against Metatron for revealing the secrets to Moses and are answered and rebuked by God. The chain of tradition and the power of the transmitted mysteries to heal diseases

[1] Seventy names has Metatron which the Holy One, blessed be He, took from his own name and put upon him. And these they are: YeHOEL, YaH, YeHOEL, YOPHIEL and Yophphiel, and APHPHIEL and MaRGeZIEL, GIPpUYEL, Pa'aZIEL, 'A'aH, PeRIEL, TaTRIEL, TaBKIEL,'W, YHWH, DH, WHYH, 'eBeD, DiBbURIEL, 'aPh'aPIEL, SPPIEL, PaSPaSIEL, SeNeGRON, MeTaTRON, SOGDIN, ADRIGON, ASUM, SaQPaM, SaQTaM, MIGON MITTON, MOTTRON, ROSPHIM, QINOTh, ChaTaTYaH, DeGaZYaH, PSPYaH, BSKNYH, MZRG, BaRaD.., MKRKK, MSPRD, ChShG, ChShB, MNRTTT, BSYRYM, MITMON, TITMON, PiSQON, SaPhSaPhYaH, ZRCh, ZRChYaH, B', BeYaH, HBH BeYaH, PeLeT, PLTYaH, RaBRaBYaH, ChaS, ChaSYaH, TaPhTaPhYaH, TaMTaMYaH, SeHaSYaH, IRURYaH, 'aL'aLYaH, BaZRIDYaH, SaTSaTKYaH, SaSDYaH, RaZRaZYAH, BaZRaZYaH, 'aRIMYaH, SBHYaH, SBIBKHYH, SiMKaM, YaHSeYaH, SSBIBYaH, SaBKaSBeYaH, QeLILQaLYaH, fKIHHH, HHYH, WH, WHYH, ZaKklKYaH, TUTRISYaH, SURYaH, ZeH, PeNIRHYaH, ZIZ'H, GaL RaZaYYa, MaMLIKYaH, TTYaH, eMeQ, QaMYaH, MeKaPpeRYaH, PeRISHYaH, SePhaM, GBIR, GiBbORYaH, GOR, GORYaH, ZIW, 'OKBaR, the LESSER YHWH, after the name of his Master, (Ex. xxiii. 21) "for my name is in him", RaBIBIEL, TUMIEL, Segansakkiel ('Sagnezagiel' / 'Neganzegael'), the Prince of Wisdom. [2] And why is he called by the name Sagnesakiel? Because all the treasuries of wisdom are committed in his hand. [3] And all of them were opened to Moses on Sinai, so that he learnt them during the forty days, while he was standing (remaining}: the Torah in the seventy aspects of the seventy tongues, the Prophets in the seventy aspects of the seventy tongues, the Writings in the seventy aspects of the seventy tongues, "the Halakas in the seventy aspects of the seventy tongues, the Traditions in the seventy aspects of the seventy tongues, the Haggadas in the seventy aspects of the seventy tongues and the Toseftas in the seventy aspects of the seventy tongues'. [4] But as soon as the forty days were ended,

he forgot all of them in one moment. Then the Holy One, blessed be He, called Yephiphyah, the Prince of the Law, and (through him) they were given to Moses as a gift. As it is written (Deut. x. 4): "and the Lord gave them unto me". And after that it remained with him. And whence do we know, that it remained (in his memory) ? Because it is written (Mai. iv. 4): " Remember ye the Law of Moses my servant which I commanded unto him in Horeb for all Israel, even my statutes and judgements". The Law of Moses': that is the Tora, the Prophets and the Writings, 'statutes': that is the Halakas and Traditions, 'judgements'; that is the Haggadas and the Toseftas. And all of them were given to Moses on high on Sinai. [5] These seventy names (are) a reflection of the Explicit Name(s) on the Merkaba which are graven upon the Throne of Glory. For the Holy One, blessed be He, took from His Explicit Name(s) and put upon the name of Metatron: Seventy Names of His by which the ministering angels call the King of the kings of kings, blessed be He, in the high heavens, and twenty-two letters that are on the ring upon his finger with which are sealed the destinies of the princes of kingdoms on high in greatness and power and with which are sealed the lots of the Angel of Death, and the destinies of every nation and tongue. [6] Said Metatron, the Angel, the Prince of the Presence; the Angel, the Prince of the Wisdom; the Angel, the Prince of the Understanding; the Angel, the Prince of the Kings; the Angel, the Prince of the Rulers; the angel, the Prince of the Glory; the angel, the Prince of the high ones, and of the princes, the exalted, great and honoured ones, in heaven and on earth: [7] "H, the God of Israel, is my witness in this thing, (that) when I revealed this secret to Moses, then all the hosts in every heaven on high raged against me and said to me: [8] Why dost thou reveal this secret to son of man, born of woman, tainted and unclean, a man of a putrefying drop, the secret by which were created heaven and earth, the sea and the dry land, the mountains and hills, the rivers and springs, Gehenna of fire and hail, the Garden of Eden and the Tree of Life; and by which were formed Adam and Eve, and the cattle, and the wild beasts, and the fowl of the air, and the fish of the sea, and Behemoth and Leviathan, and the creeping things, the worms, the dragons of the sea, and the creeping things of the deserts; and the Tora and Wisdom and Knowledge and Thought and the Gnosis of things above and the fear of heaven. Why dost thou reveal this to flesh and blood? I answered them: Because the Holy One, blessed be He, has given me authority. And furthermore, I have obtained permission from the high and exalted Throne, from which all the Explicit Names go forth with lightnings of fire and flaming chashmallim. [9] But they were not appeased, until the Holy One, blessed be He, rebuked them and drove them away with rebuke from before him, saying to them: "I delight in, and have set my love on, and have entrusted and committed unto Metatron, my Servant, alone, for he is One (unique) among all the children of heaven. [10] And Metatron brought them out from his house of treasuries and committed them to Moses, and Moses to Joshua, and Joshua to the elders, and the elders to the prophets and the prophets to the men of the Great Synagogue, and the men of the Great Synagogue to Ezra and Ezra the Scribe to Hillel the elder, and Hillel the elder to R. Abbahu and R. Abbahu to R. Zera, and R. Zera to the men of faith, and the men of faith (committed them) to give warning and to heal by them all diseases that rage in the world, as it is written (Ex. xv. 26): "If thou wilt diligently hearken to the voice of the Lord, thy God, and wilt do that which is right in his eyes, and wilt give ear to his commandments, and keep all his statutes, I will put none of the diseases upon thee, which I have put upon the Egyptians: for I am the Lord, that healeth thee". (Ended and finished. Praise be unto the Creator of the World.)

The Revelation of Esdras
(or Greek Apocalypse of Ezra)

Word and Revelation of Esdras, the Holy Prophet and Beloved of God.

IT came to pass in the thirtieth year, on the twenty-second of the month, I was in my house. And I cried out and said to the Most High: Lord, give the glory, in order that I may see Thy mysteries.

1

[1] And when it was night, there came an angel, Michael the archangel, and says to me: O Prophet Esdras, refrain from bread for seventy weeks. [2] And I fasted as he told me. And there came Raphael the commander of the host, and gave me a storax rod. And I fasted twice sixty weeks. [3] And I saw the mysteries of God and His angels. And I said to them: I wish to plead before God about the race of the Christians. It is good for a man not to be born rather than to come into the world. I was therefore taken up into heaven, and I saw in the first heaven a great army of angels; and they took me to the judgments. And I heard a voice saying to me: Have mercy on us, O thou chosen of God, Esdras. Then began I to say: Woe to sinners when they see one who is just more than the angels, and they themselves are in the Gehenna of fire! And Esdras said: Have mercy on the works of Thine hands, Thou who art compassionate, and of great mercy. Judge me rather than the souls of the sinners; for it is better that one soul should be punished, and that the whole world should not come to destruction. And God said: I will give rest in paradise to the righteous, and I have become merciful. [4] And Esdras said: Lord, why dost Thou confer benefits on the righteous? for just as one who has been hired out, and has served out his time, goes and again works as a slave when he come to his masters, so also the righteous has received his reward in the heavens. But have mercy on the sinners, for we know that Thou art merciful. And God said: I do not see how I can have mercy upon them. And Esdras said: They cannot endure Thy wrath. And God said: This is the fate of such. And God said: I wish to have thee like Paul and John, as thou hast given me uncorrupted the treasure that cannot be stolen, the treasure of virginity, the bulwark of men. [5] And Esdras said: It is good for a man not to be born. It is good not to be in life. The irrational creatures are better than man, because they have no punishment; but Thou hast taken us, and given us up to judgment. Woe to the sinners in the world to come! because their judgment is endless, and the flame unquenchable. And while I was thus speaking to him, there came Michael and Gabriel, and all the apostles; and they said: Rejoice, O faithful man of God! And Esdras said: [6] Arise, and come hither with me, O Lord, to judgment. And the Lord said: Behold, I give thee my covenant between me and thee, that you may receive it. And Esdras said: Let us plead in Thy hearing. [7] And God said: Ask Abraham your father how a son pleads with his father, and come plead with us. [8] And Esdras said: As the Lord liveth, I will not cease pleading with Thee in behalf of the race of the Christians. Where are Thine ancient compassions, O Lord? Where is Thy long-suffering? And God said: As I have made night and day, I have made the righteous and the sinner; and he should have lived like the righteous. And the prophet said: Who made Adam the first-formed? And God said: My undefiled hands. And I put him in paradise to guard the food of the tree of life; and thereafter he became disobedient. and did this in transgression. And the prophet said: Was he not protected by an angel? and was not his life guarded by the cherubim to endless ages? and how was he deceived who was guarded by angels? for Thou didst command all to be present, and to attend to what was said by Thee.

2

[1] But if Thou hadst not given him Eve, the serpent would not have deceived her; [2] but whom Thou wilt Thou savest, and whom Thou wilt Thou destroyest. [3] And the prophet said: Let us come, my Lord, to a second judgment. And God said: I cast fire upon Sodom and Gomorrah. And the prophet said: Lord, Thou dealest with us according to our deserts. And God said: Your sins transcend my clemency. And the prophet said: Call to mind the Scriptures, my Father, who hast measured out Jerusalem, and set her up again. Have mercy, O Lord, upon sinners; have mercy upon Thine own creatures; have pity upon Thy works. [4] Then God remembered those whom He had made, and said to the prophet: How can I have mercy upon them? Vinegar and gall did they give me to drink, and not even then did they repent. [5] And the prophet said: Reveal Thy cherubim, and let us go together to judgment; and show me the day of judgment, what like it is. And God said: Thou hast been deceived, Esdras; for such is the day of judgment as that in which there is no rain upon the earth; for it is a merciful tribunal as compared with that day. And the prophet said: I will not cease to plead with Thee, unless I see the day of the consummation. [6] And God said: Number the stars and the sand of the sea; and if thou shalt be able to number this, thou art also able to plead with me. And the prophet said: Lord, Thou knowest that I wear human flesh; and how can I count the stars of the

heaven, and the sand of the sea? And God said: My chosen prophet, no man will know that great day and the appearing that comes to judge the world. ⁷ For thy sake, my prophet, I have told thee the day; but the hour have I not told thee. And the prophet said: Lord, tell me also the years. And God said: If I see the righteousness of the world, that it has abounded, I will have patience with them; but if not, I will stretch forth my hand, and lay hold of the world by the four quarters, and bring them all together into the valley of Jehoshaphat, and I will wipe out the race of men, so that the world shall be no more. ⁸ And the prophet said: And how can Thy right hand be glorified? And God said: I shall be glorified by my angels. And the prophet said: Lord, if Thou hast resolved to do this, why didst Thou make man? Thou didst say to our father Abraham, ⁹ Multiplying I will multiply thy seed as the stars of the heaven, and as the sand that is by the sea-shore; and where is Thy promise? ¹⁰ And God said: First will I make an earthquake for the fall of four-footed beasts and of men; and when you see that brother gives up brother to death, and that children shall rise up against their parents, and that a woman forsakes her own husband, and when nation shall rise up against nation in war, then will you know that the end is near. ¹¹ For then neither brother pities brother, nor man wife, nor children parents, nor friends friends, nor a slave his master; for he who is the adversary of men shall come up from Tartarus, and shall show men many things. What shall I make of thee, Esdras? and wilt thou yet plead with me? And the prophet said: Lord, I shall not cease to plead with Thee. And God said: Number the flowers of the earth. If thou shalt be able to number them, thou art able also to plead with me. And the prophet said: Lord, I cannot number them. I wear human flesh; but I shall not cease to plead with Thee. I wish, Lord, to see also the under parts of Tartarus. And God said: Come down and see. And He gave me Michael, and Gabriel, and other thirty-four angels; and I went down eighty-five steps, and they brought me down five hundred steps, and I saw a fiery throne, and an old man sitting upon it; and his judgment was merciless. And I said to the angels: Who is this? and what is his sin? And they said to me: This is Herod, who for a time was a king, and ordered to put to death the children from two years old and under. ¹² And I said: Woe to his soul! And again they took me down thirty steps, and I there saw boilings up of fire, and in them there was a multitude of sinners; and I heard their voice, but saw not their forms. And they took me down lower many steps, which I could not measure. And I there saw old men, and fiery pivots turning in their ears. And I said: Who are these? and what is their sin? And they said to me: These are they who would not listen. ¹³ And they took me down again other five hundred steps, and I there saw the worm that sleeps not, and fire burning up the sinners. And they took me down to the lowest part of destruction, and I saw there the twelve plagues of the abyss. And they took me away to the south, and I saw there a man hanging by the eyelids; and the angels kept scourging him. And I asked: Who is this? and what is his sin? And Michael the commander said to me: This is one who lay with his mother; for having put into practice a small wish, he has been ordered to be hanged. And they took me away to the north, and I saw there a man bound with iron chains. And I asked: Who is this? And he said to me: This is he who said, I am the Son of God, that made stones bread, and water wine. And the prophet said: My lord, let me know what is his form, and I shall tell the race of men, that they may not believe in him. And he said to me: The form of his countenance is like that of a wild beast; his right eye like the star that rises in the morning, and the other without motion; his mouth one cubit; his teeth span long; his fingers like scythes; the track of his feet of two spans; and in his face an inscription, Antichrist. He has been exalted to heaven; he shall go down to Hades.

3

¹ At one time he shall become a child; at another, an old man. And the prophet said: Lord, and how dost Thou permit him, and he deceives the race of men? And God said: Listen, my prophet. He becomes both child and old man, and no one believes him that he is my beloved Son. And after this a trumpet, and the tombs shall be opened, and the dead shall be raised incorruptible. ² Then the adversary, hearing the dreadful threatening, shall be hidden in outer darkness. Then the heaven, and the earth, and the sea shall be destroyed. Then shall I burn the heaven eighty cubits, and the earth eight hundred cubits. And the prophet said: And how has the heaven sinned? And God said: Since... there is evil. ³ And the prophet said: Lord, and the earth, how has it sinned? And God said: Since the adversary, having heard the dreadful threatening, shall be hidden, even on account of this will I melt the earth, and with it the opponent of the race of men. And the prophet said: Have mercy, Lord, upon the race of the Christians. And I saw a woman hanging, and four wild beasts sucking her breasts. And the angels said to me: She grudged to give her milk, but even threw her infants into the rivers. And I saw a dreadful darkness, and a night that had no stars nor moon; nor is there there young or old, nor brother with brother, nor mother with child, nor wife with husband. And I wept, and said: O Lord God, have mercy upon the sinners. And as I said this, there came a cloud and snatched me up, and carried me away again into the heavens. And I saw there many judgments; and I wept bitterly, and said: It is good for a man not to have come out of his mother's womb. And those who were in torment cried out, saying: Since thou hast come hither, O holy one of God, we have found a little remission. And the prophet said: Blessed are they that weep for their sins. And God said: Hear, O beloved Esdras. ⁴ As a husbandman casts the seed of the corn into the ground, so also the man casts his seed into the parts of the woman. The first month it is all together; the second it increases in size; the third it gets hair; the fourth it gets nails; the fifth it is turned into milk; and the sixth it is made ready, and receives life; the seventh it is completely furnished; the ninth the barriers of the gate of the woman are opened; and it is born safe and sound into the earth. ⁵ And the prophet said: Lord, it is good for man not to have been born. Woe to the human race then, when Thou shall come to judgment! And I said to the Lord: Lord, why hast Thou created man, and delivered him up to judgment? And God said, with a lofty proclamation: I will not by any means have mercy on those who transgress my covenant. And the prophet said Lord, where is Thy goodness? And God said: I have prepared all things for man's sake, and man does not keep my commandments. And the prophet said: Lord, reveal to me the judgments and paradise. And the angels took me away towards the east, and I saw the tree of life. And I saw there Enoch, and Elias, and Moses, and Peter, and Paul, and Luke, and Matthias, and all the righteous, and the patriarchs. And I saw there the keeping of the air within bounds, and the blowing of the winds, and the storehouses of the ice, and the eternal judgments. And I saw there a man hanging by the skull. And they said to me: This man removed landmarks. And I saw there great judgments. ⁶ And I said to the Lord: O Lord God, and what man, then, who has been born has not sinned? And they took me lower down into Tartarus, and I saw all the sinners lamenting and weeping and mourning bitterly. And I also wept, seeing the race of men thus tormented. Then God says to me: Knowest thou, Esdras, the names of the angels at the end of the world? Michael, Gabriel, Uriel, Raphael, Gabuthelon, Aker, Arphugitonos, Beburos, Zebuleon. Then there came a voice to me: Come hither and die, Esdras, my beloved; give that which hath been entrusted to thee. ⁷ And the prophet said: And whence can you bring forth my soul? And the angels said: We can put it forth through the mouth. And the prophet said: Mouth to mouth have I spoken with God, and it comes not forth thence. ⁸ And the angels said: Let us bring it out through thy nostrils. And the prophet said: My nostrils have smelled the sweet savour of the glory of God. And the angels said: We can bring it out through thine eyes. And the prophet said: Mine eyes have seen the back parts of God. ⁹ And the angels said: We can bring it out through the crown of thy head. And the prophet said: I walked about with Moses also on the mountain, and it comes not forth thence. And the angels said: We can put it forth through the points of thy nails. And the prophet said: My feet also have walked about on the altar. And the angels went away without having done anything, saying: Lord, we cannot get his soul. Then He says to His only begotten Son: Go down, my beloved Son, with a great host of angels, and take the soul of my beloved Esdras. For the Lord, having taken a great host of angels, says to the prophet: Give me the trust which I entrusted to thee; the crown has been prepared for thee.

4

¹ And the prophet said: Lord, if Thou take my soul from me, who will be left to plead with Thee for the race of men And God said: As thou art mortal, and of the earth, do not plead with me. And the prophet said: I will not cease to plead. And God said: Give up just now the trust; the crown has been prepared for thee. Come and die, that thou mayst obtain it. Then the prophet began to say with tears: O Lord, what good have I done pleading with Thee, and I am going to fall down into the earth? Woe's me, woe's me, that I am going to be eaten up by worms! Weep, all ye saints and ye righteous, for me, who have pleaded much, and who am delivered up to death. Weep for me, all ye saints and ye righteous, because I have gone to the pit of Hades. And God said to him: Hear, Esdras, my beloved. I, who am immortal, endured a cross; I tasted vinegar and gall; I was laid in a tomb, and I raised up my chosen ones; I called Adam up out of Hades, that I might save the race of men. ² Do not therefore be afraid of death: for that which is from me–that is to say, the soul–goes to heaven; and that which is from the earth–that is to say, the body–goes to the earth, from which it was taken. ³ And the prophet said: Woe's me! woe's me! what shall I set about? what shall I do? I know not. And then the blessed Esdras began to say: ⁴ O eternal God, the Maker of the whole creation, who hast measured the heaven with a span, and who holdest the earth as a handful, who ridest upon the cherubim, who didst take the prophet Elias to the heavens in a chariot of fire, who givest food to all flesh, whom all things dread and tremble at from the face of Thy

power,– ⁵ listen to me, who have pleaded much, and give to all who transcribe this book, and have it, and remember my name, and honour my memory, give them a blessing from heaven; and bless him in all things, as Thou didst bless Joseph at last, and remember not his former wickedness in the day of his judgment. ⁶ And as many as have not believed this book shall be burnt up like Sodom and Gomorrah. And there came to him a voice, saying: Esdras, my beloved, all things whatever thou hast asked will I give to each one. And immediately he gave up his precious soul with much honour, in the month of October, on the twenty-eighth. And they prepared him for burial with incense and psalms; and his precious and sacred body dispenses strength of soul and body perpetually to those who have recourse to him from a longing desire. To whom is due glory, strength, honour, and adoration,–to the Father, and to the Son, and to the Holy Spirit, now and ever, and to ages of ages. Amen.

The Apocalypse of Sedrach

The Word of the holy and blessed Sedrach concerning love and concerning repentance and Orthodox Christians, and concerning the Second Coming of our Lord Jesus Christ. Lord give thy blessing.

1

Beloved, let us prefer nothing in honour except sincere love: for in many things we stumble every day and night and hour. And for this cause let us gain love, for it covereth a multitude of sins: for what is the profit, my children, if we have all things, and have not saving love…

O blessed love, supplier of all good things. Blessed is the man who has gained the true faith and sincere love, according as the Master said, there is no greater love than this that a man should lay down his life for his friend.

2

And invisibly he received a voice in his ears: Come hither, Sedrach, since thou wishest and desirest to converse with God and ask of him that he may reveal unto thee whatever thou wishest to ask. And Sedrach said: What, Sir? And the voice said to him: I was sent to thee to raise thee here into heaven. And he said: I desired to speak mouth to mouth with God: I am not fit, Sir, to come into heaven. And stretching out his wings he took him up and he came into heaven to the very flame, and he set him as high as the third heaven, and in it stood the flame of the divinity.

3

And the Lord saith to him: Welcome, my beloved Sedrach: What suit hast thou against God who created thee, that thou saidst, I desired to speak face to face with God? Sedrach saith to him: Yea, verily, the son hath a suit with the Father: my Lord, why didst thou make the earth? The Lord saith to him: For man's sake. Sedrach saith: And why didst Thou make the sea? Why didst Thou scatter every good thing on the earth? The Lord saith to him: For man's sake. Sedrach saith to him: If thou didst these things, why wilt Thou destroy him? And the Lord said: Man is my work and the creature of my hands, and I discipline him as I find good.

4

Sedrach saith to him: Chastisement and fire are thy discipline: they are bitter, my Lord: it were well for man if he had not been born: why then didst thou make him, my Lord? Why didst thou weary thine undefiled hands and create man, since thou didst not intend to have mercy on him? God saith to him: I made Adam the first creature and placed him in Paradise in the midst of the tree of life and said to him: Eat of all the fruits, but beware of the tree of life: for if thou eat of it, thou shalt die the death. But he transgressed my commandment, and being beguiled by the devil ate of the tree.

5

Sedrach saith to him: Of thy will Adam was beguiled, my Lord: Thou commandest thine angels to make approach to Adam, and the first of the angels himself transgressed thy commandment and did not make approach to him, and Thou didst banish him, because he transgressed thy commandment and did not make any approach to the work of thine hands: if thou lovedst man, why didst Thou not slay the devil, the worker of unrighteousness? Who is able to fight an invisible spirit? And he as a smoke enters into the hearts of men and teaches them every sin: he fights against thee, the immortal God, and what can wretched man then do to him? But have mercy, O Lord, and stop the chastisements: but if not, count me also with the sinners: if thou wilt have no mercy on the sinners, where are thy mercies, where is thy compassion, O Lord?

6

God saith to him: Be it known unto thee that I ordered all things to be placable to him: I gave him understanding and made him the heir of heaven and earth, and I subjected all things to him, and every living thing flees from him and from before his face: but he, having received of mine, became alien, adulterous, and sinful: tell me, what father, having given his son his portion, when he takes his substance and leaves his father and goes away and becomes an alien and serves an alien, when the father sees that the son has deserted him, does not darken his heart, and does not the father go and take his substance and banish him from his glory because he deserted his father? And how have I, the wonderful and jealous God, given him everything, and he having received these things has become an adulterer and a sinner?

7

Sedrach saith to him: Thou, O Lord, didst create man. Thou knewest of what sort of mind he was and of what sort of knowledge we are, and thou makest it a cause for chastisement: but cast him forth; for shall not I alone fill up the heavenly places? But if that is not to be so save man too, O Lord. He failed by thy will, wretched man. Why dost thou waste words on me,

Sedrach? I created Adam and his wife and the sun and said: Behold each other how bright he is, and the wife of Adam is brighter in the beauty of the moon and he was the giver of her life. Sedrach saith: but of what profit are beauties if they die away into the earth? How didst thou say, O Lord, Thou shalt not return evil for evil? How is it, O Lord? the word of Thy divinity never lies, and why dost Thou retaliate on man? or dost thou not in so doing render evil for evil? I know that among the quadrupeds there is no other so wily and unreasonable as the mule. But we strike it with the bridle when we wish: and thou hast angels: send them forth to guard them, and when man inclines towards sin, to take hold of his foot and not let him go whither he would.

8

God saith to him: If I catch him by the foot, he will say, Thou hast given me no joy in the world. But I have left him to his own will because I loved him. Wherefore I sent forth my righteous angels to guard him night and day. Sedrach saith: I know, O Lord, that of all thy creatures Thou chiefly lovedst man, of the quadrupeds the sheep, of woods the olive, of fruits the vine, of flying things the bee, of rivers the Jordan, of cities Jerusalem. And all these man also loves, my Lord. God saith to Sedrach: I will ask thee one thing, Sedrach: if thou answerest me, then I may fitly help thee, even though thou hast tempted thy creator. Sedrach saith: Speak. The Lord God saith: Since I made all things, how many men were born and how many died, and how many are to die and how many hairs have they? Tell me, Sedrach, since the heaven was created and the earth, how many trees grew in the world, and how many fell, and how many are to fall, and how many are to arise, and how many leaves have they? Tell me, Sedrach, since I made the sea, how many waves arose and how many fell, and how many are to arise, and how many winds blow along the margin of the sea? Tell me, Sedrach, from the creation of the world of the æons, when the air rained, how many drops fell upon the world, and how many are to fall? And Sedrach said: Thou alone knowest all these things, O Lord; thou only understandest all these things: only, I pray thee, deliver man from chastisement, and I shall not be separated from our race.

9

And God said to his only begotten Son: Go, take the soul of Sedrach my beloved, and place it in Paradise. The only begotten Son saith to Sedrach: Give me the trust which our Father deposited in the womb of thy mother in the holy tabernacle of thy body from a child. Sedrach saith: I will not give thee my soul. God saith to him: And wherefore was I sent to come hither, and thou pleadest against me? For I was commanded by my Father not to take thy soul with violence; but if not, (then) give me thy most greatly desired soul.

10

And Sedrach saith to God: And whence dost Thou intend to take my soul, and from which limb? And God saith to him: Dost thou not know that it is placed in the midst of thy lungs and thy heart and is dispersed into all thy limbs? It is brought up through the throat and gullet and the mouth and at whatever hour it is predestined to come forth, it is scattered, and brought together from the points of the nails and from all the limbs, and there is a great necessity that it should be separated from the body and parted from the heart. When Sedrach had heard all these things and had considered the memory of death he was greatly astounded, and Sedrach said to God: O Lord, give me a little respite that I may weep, for I have heard that tears are able to do much and much remedy comes to the lowly body of thy creature.

11

And weeping and bewailing he began to say: O marvellous head of heavenly adornment: O radiant as the sun which shines on heaven and earth: thy hairs are known from Teman, thine eyes from Bosor, thine ears from thunder, thy tongue from a trumpet, and thy brain is a small creation, thy head the energy of the whole body: O friendly and most fair beloved by all, and now falling into the earth it must become forgotten. O hands, mild, fair-fingered, worn with toil by which the body is nourished: O hands, deftest of all, heaping up from all quarters ye made ready houses. O fingers adorned and decked with gold and silver (rings): and great worlds are led by the fingers: the three joints enfold the palms, and heap up beautiful things: and now ye must become aliens to the world. O feet, skilfully walking about, self-running, most swift, unconquerable: O knees, fitted together, because without you the body does not move: the feet run along with the sun and the moon in the night and in the day, heaping up all things, foods and drinks, and nourishing the body: O feet, most swift and fair runners, moving on the face of the earth, getting ready the house with every good thing: O feet which bear up the whole body, that run up to the temples, making repentance and calling on the saints, and now ye are to remain motionless. O head and hands and feet, until now I have kept you. O soul, what sent thee into the humble and wretched body? and now being separated from it, thou art going up where the Lord calleth thee, and the wretched body goes away to judgment. O body well-adorned, hair clothed with stars, head of heavenly adornment and dress: O face well-anointed, light-bringing eyes, voice trumpet-like, tongue placable, chin fairly adorned, hairs like the stars, head high as heaven, body decked out, light-bringing eyes that know all things–and now you shall fall into the earth and under the earth your beauty shall disappear.

12

Christ saith to him: Stay, Sedrach; how long dost thou weep and groan? Paradise is opened to thee, and, dying, thou shalt live. Sedrach saith to him: Once more I will speak unto thee, O Lord: How long shall I live before I die? and do not disregard my prayer. The Lord saith to him: Speak, O Sedrach. Sedrach saith: If a man shall live eighty or ninety or an hundred years, and live these years in sin, and again shall turn, and the man live in repentance, in how many days dost thou forgive him his sins? God saith to him: If he shall live an hundred or eighty years and shall turn and repent for three years and do the fruit of righteousness, and death shall overtake him, I will not remember all his sins.

13

Sedrach saith to him: The three years are a long time, my Lord, lest death overtake him and he fulfil not his repentance: have mercy, Lord, on thine image and have compassion, for the three years are many. God saith to him: If a man live an hundred years and remember his death and confess before men and I find him, after a time I will forgive all his sins. Sedrach saith again: I will again beseech thy compassion for thy creature. The time is long lest death overtake him and snatch him suddenly. The Saviour saith to him: I will ask thee one word, Sedrach, my beloved, then thou shalt ask me in turn: if the man shall repent for forty days I will not remember all his sins which he did.

14

And Sedrach saith to the archangel Michael: Hearken to me, O powerful chief, and help thou me and be my envoy that God may have mercy on the world. And falling on their faces, they besought the Lord and said: O Lord, teach us how and by what sort of repentance and by what labour man shall be saved. God saith: By repentances, by intercessions, by liturgies, by tears in streams, in hot groanings. Dost thou not know that my prophet David was saved by tears, and the rest were saved in one moment? Thou knowest, Sedrach, that there are nations which have not the law and which do the works of the law: for if they are unbaptized and my divine spirit come unto them and they turn to my baptism, I also receive them with my righteous ones into Abraham's bosom. And there are some who have been baptized with my baptism and who have shared in my divine part and become reprobate in complete reprobation and will not repent: and I suffer them with much compassion and much pity and wealth in order that they may repent, but they do the things which my divinity hates, and did not hearken to the wise man asking (them), saying, we by no means justify a sinner. Dost thou not most certainly know that it is written: And those who repent never see chastisement? And they did not hearken to the Apostles or to my word in the Gospels, and they grieve my angels, and verily they do not attend to my messenger in the assemblies (for communion) and in my services, and they do not stand in my holy churches, but they stand and do not fall down and worship in fear and trembling, but boast things which I do not accept, or my holy angels.

15

Sedrach saith to God: O Lord, Thou alone art sinless and very compassionate, having compassion and pity for sinners, but thy divinity said: I am not come to call the righteous but sinners to repentance. And the Lord said to Sedrach: Dost thou not know, Sedrach, that the thief was saved in one moment to repent? Dost thou not know that my apostle and evangelist was saved in one moment? *"Peccatores enim non salvantur,"* for their hearts are like rotten stone: these are they who walk in impious ways and who shall be destroyed with Antichrist. Sedrach saith: O my Lord, Thou also saidst: My divine spirit entered into the nations which, not having the law, do the things of the law. So also the thief and the apostle and evangelist and the rest of those who have already got into thy Kingdom. O my Lord; so likewise do Thou pardon those who have sinned to the last: for life is very toilsome and there is no time for repentance.

16

The Lord saith to Sedrach: I made man in three stages: when he is young, I overlooked his stumblings as he was young: and again when he was a man I considered his purpose: and again when he grows old, I watch him till he repent. Sedrach saith: O Lord, Thou knowest and understandest all these things: but have sympathy for sinners. The Lord saith to him: Sedrach, my beloved, I promise to have sympathy and bring down the forty days to twenty: and whosoever shall remember thy name shall not see the place of chastisement, but shall be with the just in a place of refreshment and rest: and if anyone shall record this wonderful word his sins shall not be reckoned against him for ever and ever. And Sedrach saith: O Lord, and if anyone shall bring enlightenment to thy servant, save him, O Lord, from all evil. And Sedrach, the servant of the Lord, saith: Now take my soul, O Lord. And God took him and placed him in Paradise with all the saints. To whom be the glory and the power for ever and ever. Amen.

2 Baruch, or Syriac Apocalypse of Baruch

Announcement of the coming Destruction of Jerusalem to Baruch

1

[1] And it came to pass in the twenty-fifth year of Jeconiah, king of Judah, that the word of the Lord came to Baruch, the son of Neriah, and said to him: [2] 'Have you seen all that this people are doing to Me, that the evils which these two tribes which remained have done are greater than (those of) the ten tribes which were carried away captive? [3] For the former tribes were forced by their kings to commit sin, but these two of themselves have been forcing and compelling their kings to commit sin. [4] For this reason, behold I bring evil upon this city, and upon its inhabitants, and it shall be removed from before Me for a time, and I will scatter this people among the Gentiles that they may do good to the Gentiles. And My people shall be chastened, and the time shall come when they will seek for the prosperity of their times.

2

[1] For I have said these things to you that you may bid Jeremiah, and all those that are like you, to retire from this city. [2] For your works are to this city as a firm pillar, And your prayers as a strong wall.'

3

[1] And I said: 'O LORD, my Lord, have I come into the world for this purpose that I might see the evils of my mother? Not (so) my Lord. [2] If I have found grace in Your sight, first take my spirit that I may go to my fathers and not behold the destruction of my mother. For two things vehemently constrain me: for I cannot resist you, and my soul, moreover, cannot behold the evils of my mother. [4] But one thing I will say in Your presence, O Lord. [5] What, therefore, will there be after these things? for if you destroy Your city, and deliver up Your land to those that hate us, how shall the name of Israel be again remembered? [6] Or how shall one speak of Your praises? or to whom shall that which is in Your law be explained? Or shall the world return to its nature of aforetime), and the age revert to primeval silence? And shall the multitude of souls be taken away, and the nature of man not again be named? And where is all that which you did say regarding us?'

4

[1] And the Lord said unto me: 'This city shall be delivered up for a time, And the people shall be chastened during a time, And the world will not be given over to oblivion.

The heavenly Jerusalem

[2] [Dost you think that this is that city of which I said: "On the palms of My hands have I graven you"? [3] This building now built in your midst is not that which is revealed with Me, that which prepared beforehand here from the time when I took counsel to make Paradise, and showed Adam before he sinned, but when he transgressed the commandment it was removed from him, as also Paradise. [4] And after these things I showed it to My servant Abraham by night among the portions of the victims. [5] And again also I showed it to Moses on Mount Sinai when I showed to the likeness of the tabernacle and all its vessels. [6] And now, behold, it is preserved with Me, as Paradise. [7] Go, therefore, and do as I command you.']

Baruch's Complaint and God's Reassurance

5

[1] And I answered and said: 'So then I am destined to grieve for Zion, For your enemies will come to this place and pollute Your sanctuary, And lead your inheritance into captivity, And make themselves masters of those whom you have loved, And they will depart again to the place of their idols, And will boast before them: And what will you do for Your great name?' [2] And the Lord said unto me: 'My name and My glory are unto all eternity; And My judgment shall maintain its right in its own time. [3] And you shall see with your eyes That the enemy will not overthrow Zion, Nor shall they burn Jerusalem, But be the ministers of the Judge for the time. [4] But do you go and do whatsoever I have said unto you. [5] And I went and took Jeremiah, and Adu, and Seriah, and Jabish, and Gedaliah, and all the honorable men of the people, and I led them to the valley of Kidron, and I narrated to them all that had been said to me. [6] And they lifted up their voice, and they all wept. [7] And we sat there and fasted until the evening.

Invasion of the Chaldeans and their Entrance into the City after the Sacred Vessels were hidden and the City's Walls overthrown by Angels

6

[1] And it came to pass on the morrow that, lo! the army of the Chaldees surrounded the city, and at the time of the evening, I, Baruch, left the people, and I went forth and stood by the oak. [2] And I was grieving over Zion, and lamenting over the captivity which had come upon the people. [3] And lo! suddenly a strong spirit raised me, and bore me aloft over the wall

of Jerusalem. ⁴ And I beheld, and lo! four angels standing at the four corners of the city, each of them holding a torch of fire in his hands. ⁵ And another angel began to descend from heaven. and said unto them: 'Hold your lamps, and do not light them till I tell you. ⁶ For I am first sent to speak a word to the earth, and to place in it what the Lord the Most High has commanded me.' ⁷ And I saw him descend into the Holy of Holies, and take from there the veil, and holy ark, and the mercy-seat, and the two tables, and the holy raiment of the priests, and the altar of incense, and the forty-eight precious stones, wherewith the priest was adorned and all the holy vessels of the tabernacle. ⁸ And he spoke to the earth with a loud voice: 'Earth, earth, earth, hear the word of the mighty God, And receive what I commit to you, And guard them until the last times, So that, when you are ordered, you may restore them, So that strangers may not get possession of them. ⁹ For the time comes when Jerusalem also will be delivered for a time, Until it is said, that it is again restored for ever.' ¹⁰ And the earth opened its mouth and swallowed them up.

7

¹ And after these things I heard that angel saying unto those angels who held the lamps: 'Destroy, therefore, and overthrow its wall to its foundations, lest the enemy should boast and say: " We have overthrown the wall of Zion, And we have burnt the place of the mighty God."' ² And they have seized the place where I had been standing before.

8

¹ Now the angels did as he had commanded them, and when they had broken up the corners of the walls, a voice was heard from the interior of the temple, after the wall had fall saying: ² 'Enter, you enemies, And come, you adversaries; For he who kept the house has forsaken (it).' ³ And I, Baruch, departed. ⁴ And it came to pass after these things that the army of the Chaldees entered and seized the house, and all that was around it. And they led the people away captive and slew some of them, and bound Zedekiah the king, and sent him to the king of Babylon.

First Fast of seven Days: Baruch to remain amid the Ruins of Jerusalem and Jeremiah to accompany the Exiles to Babylon. Baruch's Dirge over Jerusalem

9

¹ And I, Baruch, came, and Jeremiah, whose heart was found pure from sins, who had not been captured in the seizure of the City. ² And we rent our garments, we wept, and mourned, and fasted seven days.

10

¹ And it came to pass after seven days, that the word of God carne to me, and said unto me: ² 'Tell Jeremiah to go and support the captivity of the people unto Babylon. But do you remain here amid the desolation of Zion, and I will show to you after these days 'what will befall at the end of days.' And I said to Jeremiah as the Lord commanded me. And he, indeed, departed with the people, but I, Baruch, returned and sat before the gates of the temple, and I lamented with the following lamentation over Zion and said: ⁶ 'Blessed is he who was not born, Or he, who having been born, has died. ⁷ But as for us who live, woe unto us, Because we see the afflictions of Zion, And what has befallen Jerusalem. ⁸ I will call the Sirens from the sea, And you Lilin, come you from the desert, And you Shedim and dragons from the forests: Awake and gird up your loins unto mourning, And take up with me the dirges, And make lamentation with me. ⁹ Ye husbandmen, sow not again; And, O earth, wherefore give you your harvest fruits? Keep within you the sweets of your sustenance. ¹⁰ And thou, vine, why further do you give your wine; For an offering will not again be made from there in Zion, Nor will first-fruits again be offered. ¹¹ And do ye, O heavens, 'withhold your dew, And open not the treasuries of rain: ¹² And do thou, O sun withhold the light of your rays. And do thou, O moon, extinguish the multitude of your light; For why should light rise again Where the light of Zion is darkened? ¹³ And you, you bridegrooms, enter not in, And let not the brides adorn themselves with garlands; And, you women, pray not that you may bear. ¹⁴ For the barren shall above all rejoice, And those who have no sons shall be glad, And those who have sons shall have anguish. ¹⁵ For why should they bear in pain, Only to bury in grief? ¹⁶ Or why, again, should mankind have sons? Or why should the seed of their kind again be named, Where this mother is desolate, And her sons are led into captivity? ¹⁷ From this time forward speak not of beauty, And discourse not of gracefulness. ¹⁸ Moreover, you priests) take you the keys of the sanctuary, And cast them into the height of heaven, And give them to the Lord and say: "Guard Your house Thyself, For lo! we are found false stewards." ¹⁹ And you, you virgins; who weave fine linen And silk with gold of Ophir, Take with haste all (these) things And cast (them) into the fire, That it may bear them to Him who made them, And the flame send them to Him who created them, Lest the enemy get possession of them.'

11

¹ Moreover, I, Baruch, say this against you, Babylon: 'If you had prospered, And Zion had dwelt in her glory, Yet the grief to us had been great That you should be equal to Zion. ² But now, lo! the grief is infinite, And the lamentation measureless, For lo! you are prospered And Zion desolate. ³ Who will be judge regarding these things? Or to whom shall we complain regarding that which has befallen us? Lord, how have you borne (it)? ⁴ Our fathers went to rest without grief, And lo! the righteous sleep in the earth in tranquility; ⁵ For they knew not this anguish, Nor yet had they heard of that which had befallen us. ⁶ Would that you had ears, O earth, And that you had a heart, O dust: That you might go and announce in Sheol, And say to the dead: ⁷ "Blessed are you more than we who live."'

12

¹ But I will say this as I think. And I will speak against you, O land, which alt prospering. ² The noonday does not always burn. Nor do the rays of the sun constantly give light. ³ Do not expect Land hope] that you will always he prosperous and rejoicing. And be not greatly up lifted and boastful. ⁴ For assuredly in its own season shall the (divine) wrath awake against you. Which now in long-suffering is held in as it were by reins.

Second Fast. Revelation as to the coming judgment on the Heathen.
⁵ And when I had said these things, I fasted seven days.

13

¹ And it came to pass after these things, that I, Baruch, was standing upon Mount Zion, and lo! a voice came from the height and said unto me: ² 'Stand upon your feet, Baruch, and hear the word of the mighty God.' ³ Because you have been astonished at what has befallen Zion, you shall therefore be assuredly preserved to the consummation of the times, that you may be for a testimony. ⁴ So that, if ever those prosperous cities say: ⁵ 'Why hath the mighty God brought upon us this retribution?' Say you to them, you and those like you who shall have seen this evil: '(This is the evil) and retribution which is coming upon you and upon your people in its (destined) time that the nations may be thoroughly smitten. ⁶ And then they shall be in anguish. ⁷ And if they say at that time: ⁸ For how long? you will say to them: "Ye who have drunk the strained wine, Drink you also of its dregs, The judgment of the Lofty One Who has no respect of persons."' ⁹ On this account he had aforetime no mercy on His own sons, But afflicted them as His enemies, because they sinned, ¹⁰ Then therefore were they chastened That they might be sanctified. ¹¹ But now, you peoples and nations, you are guilty Because you have always trodden down the earth, And used the creation unrighteously. ¹² For I have always benefited you. And you have always been ungrateful for the beneficence.

The Righteousness of the Righteous has profited neither them nor their City; God's Judgments are incomprehensible; the World was made for the Righteous, yet they pass and the World remains. Answer–Man knows God's Judgments and has sinned willingly. This World is a Weariness to the Righteous but the next is theirs, to be won through Character whether a Man's Time here be long or short. Final Weal or Woe–the supreme Question.

14

¹ And I answered and said: 'Lo! you have shown me the method of the times, and that which shall be after these things, and you have said unto me, that the retribution, which has been spoken of by you, shall come upon the nations. ² And now I know that those who have sinned are many, and they have lived in prosperity,' and departed from the world, but the few nations will be left in those times, to whom those words shall he said which you did say. ³ For what advantage is there in this, or what (evil), worse than what' we have seen befall us, are we to expect to see? ⁴ But again I will speak in Your presence: ⁵ What have they profited who had knowledge before you and have not walked in vanity as the rest of the nations, and have not said to the dead: "Give us life," but always feared you, and have not left Your ways? ⁶ And lo! they have been carried off, nor on their account have you had mercy on Zion. ⁷ And if others did evil, it was due to Zion that on account of the works of those who wrought good works she should be forgiven, and should not be overwhelmed on account of the works of those who wrought unrighteousness. ⁸ But who, O LORD, my Lord, will comprehend Your judgment, Or who will search out the profoundness of Your way? Or who will think out the weight of Your path? ⁹ Or who will be able to think out Your incomprehensible counsel? Or who of those that are born has ever found The beginning or end of Your wisdom? ¹⁰ For we have all been made like a breath. ¹¹ For as the breath ascends involuntarily, and again dies, so it is with the nature of men, who depart not according to their own will, and know not what will befall them in the end. ¹² For the righteous justly hope for the end, and without fear depart from this habitation, because they have with you a store of works preserved in

treasures. ¹³ On this account also these without fear leave this world, and trusting with joy they hope to receive the world which you have promised them. ¹⁴ But as for us–woe to us, who also are now shamefully entreated, and at that time look forward (only) to evils. ¹⁵ But you know accurately what you have done by means of Your servants; for we are not able to understand that which is good as you art, our Creator. ¹⁶ But again I will speak in Your presence, O LORD, my Lord. ¹⁷ When of old there was no world with its inhabitants, you did devise and speak with a word, and forthwith the works of creation stood before you. ¹⁸ And you did say that you wouldst make for Your world man as the administrator of Your works, that it might be known that he was by no means made on account of the world, but the world on account of him. ¹⁹ And now I see that as for the world which was made on account of us, lo! it abides; but we, on account of whom it was made, depart.'

15

¹ And the Lord answered and said unto me: 'You are rightly astonished regarding the departure of man, but you have not judged well regarding the evils which befall those who sin. ² And as regards what you have said, that the righteous are carried off and the impious are prospered, ³ And as regards what you have said: "Man knows not Your judgment "–On this account hear, and I will speak to you, and hearken, and I will cause you to hear My words. ⁵ Man would not rightly have understood My judgment, unless he had accepted the law, and I had instructed him in understanding. ⁶ But now, because he transgressed wittingly, yea, just on this ground that he knows (about it), he shall be tormented. ⁷ And as regards what you did say touching the righteous, that on account of them has this world come, so also again shall that, which is to come, come on their account. ⁸ For this world is to them a strife and a labor with much trouble; and that accordingly which is to come, a crown with great glory.'

16

¹ And I answered and said: '⁰ LORD, my Lord, lo! the years of this time are few and evil, and who is able in his little time to acquire that which is measureless?'

17

¹ And the Lord answered and said unto me: 'With the Most High account is not taken of time nor of a few years. ² For what did it profit Adam that he lived nine hundred and thirty years and transgressed that which he was commanded? Therefore the multitude of time that he lived did not profit him, but brought death and cut off the years of those who were born from him. wherein did Moses suffer loss in that he lived only one hundred and twenty years, and, inasmuch he was subject to Him who formed him, brought the law to the seed of Jacob, and lighted a lamp for the nation of Israel?'

18

¹ And I answered and said: 'He that lighted has taken from the light, and there are but few that have imitated him. But those many whom he has lighted have taken from the darkness of Adam and have not rejoiced in the light of the lamp.'

19

¹ And He answered and said unto me: 'Wherefore at that time he appointed for them a covenant and said: "Behold I have placed before you life and death," And he called heaven and earth to witness against them. ² For he knew that his time was but short, But that heaven and earth endure always. ³ But after his death they sinned and transgressed, Though they knew that they had the law reproving (them), And the light in which nothing could err, Also the spheres which testify, and Me. ⁴ Now regarding everything that is, it is I that judge, but do not you take counsel in your soul regarding these things, nor afflict thyself because of those which have been. ⁵ For now it is the consummation of time that should be considered, whether of business, or of prosperity, or of shame and not the beginning thereof. ⁶ Because if a man be prospered in his beginnings and shamefully entreated in his old age, he forgets all the prosperity that he had. ⁷ And again, if a man is shamefully entreated in his beginnings, and at his end is prospered, he remembers not again his evil entreatment. ⁸ And again hearken: though each one were prospered all that time–all the time from the day on which death was decreed against those who transgress–and in his end was destroyed, in vain would have been everything.'

Zion has been taken away to hasten the Advent of the Judgment

20

¹ 'Therefore, behold! the days come, And the times shall hasten more than the former, And the seasons shall speed on more than those that are past, And the years shall pass more quickly than the present (years). ² Therefore have I now taken away Zion, That I may the more speedily visit the world in its season. ³ Now therefore hold fast in your heart everything that I command you, And seal it in the recesses of your mind. ⁴ And then I will show you the judgment of My might, And My ways which are unsearchable. ⁵ Go therefore and sanctify thyself seven days, and eat no bread, nor drink water, nor speak to anyone. ⁶ And afterwards come to that place and I will reveal Myself to you, and speak true things with you, and I will give you commandment regarding the method of the times; for they are coming and tarry not.'

Fast of seven Days: Baruch's Prayer: God's Answer

The Prayer of Baruch the Son of Neriah.

21

¹ And I went there and sat in the valley of Kidron in a cave of the earth, and I sanctified my soul there, and I ate no bread, yet I was not hungry, and I drank no water, yet I thirsted not, and I was there till the seventh day, as He had commanded me. ² And afterwards I came to that place where He had spoken with me. ³ And it came to pass at sunset that my soul took much thought, and I began to speak in the presence of the Mighty One, and said: ⁴ 'O you that have made the earth, hear me, that have fixed the firmament by the word, and have made firm the height of the heaven by the spirit, that have called from the beginning of the world that which did not yet exist, and they obey you. ⁵ you that have commanded the air by Your nod, and have seen those things which are to be as those things which you are doing. ⁶ you that rule with great thought the hosts that stand before you: also the countless holy beings, which you did make from the beginning, of flame and fire, which stand around Your throne you rule with indignation. ⁷ To you only does this belong that you should do forthwith whatsoever you do wish. ⁸ Who causes the drops of rain to rain by number upon the earth, and alone knows the consummation of the times before they come; have respect unto my prayer. For ⁹ you alone are able to sustain all who are, and those who have passed away, and those who are to be, those who sin, and those who are to righteous [as living (and) being past finding out]. For you alone do live immortal and past finding out, and know the number of mankind. And if in time many have sinned, yet others not a few have been righteous.

Baruch's Depreciation of this Life.

¹² you know where you preserve the end of those who have sinned, or the consummation of those who have been righteous. ² For if there were this life only, which belongs to all men, nothing could be more bitter than this. ¹⁴ For of what profit is strength that turns to sickness, Or fullness of food that turns to famine, Or beauty that turns to ugliness. ¹⁵ For the nature of man is always changeable. ¹⁶ For what we were formerly now we no longer are and what we now are we shall not afterwards remain. ¹⁶ For if a consummation had not been prepared for all, in vain would have been their beginning. But regarding everything that comes from you do you inform me, and regarding everything about which I ask you, do you enlighten me.

Baruch prays to God to hasten the Judgment and fulfill His Promise

¹⁹ How long will that which is corruptible remain, and how long will the time of mortals be prospered, and until what time will those who transgress in the world be polluted with much wickedness? ²⁰ Command therefore in mercy and accomplish all that you saidst you wouldst bring, that Your might may be made known to those who think that Your long-suffering is weakness. ²¹ And show to those who know not, that everything that has befallen us and our city until now has been according to the long-suffering of Your power, because on account of Your name you have called us a beloved people. ²² Bring to an end therefore henceforth mortality. ²³ And reprove accordingly the angel of death, and let Your glory appear, and let the might of Your beauty be known, and let Sheol be sealed so that from this time forward it may not receive the dead, and let the treasuries of souls restore those which are enclosed in them. ²⁴ For there have been many years like those that are desolate from the days of Abraham and Isaac and Jacob, and of all those who are like them, who sleep in the earth, on whose account you did say that you had created the world. ²⁵ And now quickly show Your glory, and do not defer what has been promised by you.' ²⁶ And (when) I had completed the words of this prayer I was greatly weakened.

God's Reply to Baruch's Prayer. He will fulfill His Promise: Time needed for its Accomplishment: Things must be judged in the Light of their Consummation. Till all Souls are born the End cannot come.

22

¹ And it came to pass after these things that lo! the heavens were opened, and I saw, and power was given to me, and a voice was heard from on high, and it said unto me: ² Baruch, Baruch, why are you troubled? ³ He who travels by a road but does not complete it, or who departs by sea but does not arrive at the port, can he be comforted? ⁴ Or he who promises to give a present to another, but does not fulfill it, is it not robbery? ⁵ Or he who sows the earth, but does not reap its fruit in its season, does he not lose everything? ⁶ Or he who plants a plant unless it grows till the time suitable to it, does he who planted it expect to receive fruit from it? ⁷ Or a woman

who has conceived, if she bring forth untimely, does she not assuredly slay her infant? ⁸ Or he who builds a house, if he does not roof it and complete it, can it be called a house? Tell Me that first.'

23

¹ And I answered and said: Not so, O LORD, my Lord.' ² And He answered and said unto me: 'Why therefore are you troubled about that which you know not, and why are you ill at ease about things in which you are ignorant? ³ For as you have not forgotten the people who now are and those who have passed away, so I remember those who are appointed to come. ⁴ Because when Adam sinned and death was decreed against those who should be born, then the multitude of those who should be born was numbered, and for that number a place was prepared where the living might dwell and the dead might be guarded. Before therefore the number aforesaid is fulfilled, the creature will not live again [for My spirit is the creator of life], and Sheol will receive the dead. ⁶ And again it is given to you to hear what things are to come after these times. ⁷ For truly My redemption has drawn nigh, and is not far distant as aforetime.

The coming Judgment

24

¹ 'For behold! the days come and the books shall be opened in which are written the sins of all those who have sinned, and again also the treasuries in which the righteousness of all those who have been righteous in creation is gathered. ² For it shall come to pass at that time that you shall see–and the many that are with you–the long-suffering of the Most High, which has been throughout all generations, who has been long-suffering towards all who are born, (alike) those who sin and (those who) are righteous.' ³ And I answered and said: 'But, behold! O Lord, no one knows the number of those things which have passed nor yet of those things which are to come. ⁴ For I know indeed that which has befallen us, but what will happen to our enemies I know not, and when you will visit Your works.'

Sign of the coming Judgment

25

¹ And He answered and said unto me: 'You too shall be preserved till that time till that sign which the Most High will work for the inhabitants of the earth in the end of days. ² This therefore shall be the sign. ³ When a stupor shall seize the inhabitants of the earth, and they shall fall into many tribulations, and again when they shall fall into great torments. And it will come to pass when they say in their thoughts by reason of their much tribulation: "The Mighty 'One doth no longer remember the earth"–yes, it will come to pass when they abandon hope, that the time will then awake.'

26

¹ And I answered and said: 'Will that tribulation which is to be continue a long time, and will that necessity embrace many years?'

The Twelve Woes that are to Come upon the Earth: The Messiah and the temporary Messianic Kingdom

27

¹ And He answered and said unto me: 'Into twelve parts is that time divided, and each one of them is reserved for that which is appointed for it. ² In the first part there shall be the beginning of commotions. ³ And in the second part (there shall be) slayings of the great ones. ⁴ And in the third part the fall of many by death. ⁵ And in the fourth part the sending of the sword. ⁶ And in the fifth part famine and the withholding of rain. ⁷ And in the sixth part earthquakes and terrors. ⁸ [Wanting.] ⁹ And in the eighth part a multitude of specters and attacks of the Shedim. ¹⁰ And in the ninth part the fall of fire. ¹¹ And in the tenth part rapine and much oppression. ¹² And in the eleventh part wickedness and unchastity. ¹³ And in the twelfth part confusion from the mingling together of all those things aforesaid. ¹⁴ For these parts of that time are reserved, and shall be mingled one with another and minister one to another. ¹⁵ For some shall leave out some of their own, and receive (in its stead) from others, and some complete their own and that of others, so that those may not understand who are upon the earth in those days that this is the consummation of the times.

28

¹ Nevertheless, whoever understands shall then be wise. ² For the measure and reckoning of that time are two parts a week of seven weeks.' ³ And I answered and said: 'It is good for a man to come and behold, but it is better that he should not come lest he fall. ⁴ [But I will say this also: ⁵ Will he who is incorruptible despise those things which are corruptible, and whatever befalls in the case of those things which are corruptible, so that he might look only to those things which are not corruptible?] ⁶ But if; O Lord, those things shall assuredly come to pass which you have foretold to me, so do you show this also unto me if indeed I have found grace in Your sight. ⁷ Is it in one place or in one of the parts of the earth that those things are come to pass, or will the whole earth experience (them) ?'

29

¹ And He answered and said unto me: 'Whatever will then befall (will befall) the whole earth; therefore all who live will experience (them). ² For at that time I will protect only those who are found in those self-same days in this land. ³ And it shall come to pass when all is accomplished that was to come to pass in those parts, that the Messiah shall then begin to be revealed. ⁴ And Behemoth shall be revealed from his place and Leviathan shall ascend from the sea, those two great monsters which I created on the fifth day of creation, and shall have kept until that time; and then they shall be for food for all that are left. ⁵ The earth also shall yield its fruit ten-thousandfold and on each (?) vine there shall be a thousand branches, and each branch shall produce a thousand clusters, and each cluster produce a thousand grapes, and each grape produce a cor of wine. ⁶ And those who have hungered shall rejoice: moreover, also, they shall behold marvels every day. ⁷ For winds shall go forth from before Me to bring every morning the fragrance of aromatic fruits, and at the close of the day clouds distilling the dew of health. ⁸ And it shall come to pass at that self-same time that the treasury of manna shall again descend from on high, and they will eat of it in those years, because these are they who have come to the consummation of time.

30

¹ And it shall come to pass after these things, when the time of the advent of the Messiah is fulfilled, that He shall return in glory.

The Resurrection

² Then all who have fallen asleep in hope of Him shall rise again. And it shall come to pass at that time that the treasuries will be opened in which is preserved the number of the souls of the righteous, and they shall come forth, and a multitude of souls shall be seen together in one assemblage of one thought, and the first shall rejoice and the last shall not be grieved. ³ For they know that the time has come of which it is said, that it is the consummation of the times. ⁴ But the souls of the wicked, when they behold all these things, shall then waste away the more. ⁵ For they shall know that their torment has come and their perdition has arrived.'

Baruch exhorts the People to prepare themselves for worse Evils

31

¹ And it came to pass after these things: that I went to the people and said unto them: 'Assemble unto me all your elders and I will speak words unto them.' ² And they all assembled in the valley of the Kidron. ³ And I answered and said unto them: Hear, O Israel, and I will speak to you, And give ear, O seed of Jacob, and I will instruct you. ⁴ Forget not Zion, But hold in remembrance the anguish of Jerusalem. ⁵ For lo! the days come, When everything that is shall become the prey of corruption And be as though it had not been.

32

¹ 'But as for you, if you prepare your hearts, so as to sow in them the fruits of the law, it shall protect you in that time in which the Mighty One is to shake the whole creation. ² [Because after a little time the building of Zion will be shaken in order that it may be built again. But that building will not remain, but will again after a time be rooted out, and will remain desolate until the time. ⁴ And afterwards it must be renewed in glory, and perfected for evermore.] ⁵ Therefore we should not be distressed so much over the evil which has now come as over that which is still to be. ⁶ For there will be a greater trial than these two tribulations when the Mighty One will renew His creation. ⁷ And now do not draw near to me for a few days, nor seek me till I come to you.' ⁸ And it came to pass when I had spoken to them all these words, that I, Baruch, went my way, and when the people saw me setting out, they lifted up their voice and lamented and said : ⁹ To where are you departing from us, Baruch, and are you forsaking us as a father who forsakes his orphan children, and departs from them?

33

¹ 'Are these the commands which your companion, Jeremiah the prophet, commanded you, and said unto you: "Look to this people till I go and make ready the rest of the brethren in Babylon against whom has gone forth the sentence that they should be led into captivity"? And now if you also forsake us, it were good for us all to die before you, and then that you should withdraw from us.'

Lament of Baruch

34

¹ And I answered and said unto the people: 'Far be it from me to forsake you or to withdraw from you, but I will only go unto the Holy of Holies to inquire of the Mighty One concerning you and concerning Zion, if in some

respect I should receive more illumination: and after these things I will return to you.

35

¹ And I, Baruch, went to the holy place, and sat down upon the ruins and wept, and said: ² 'O that mine eyes were springs, And mine eyelids a fount of tears. ³ For how shall I lament for Zion, And how shall I mourn for Jerusalem? ⁴ Because in that place where I am now prostrate, Of old the high priest offered holy sacrifices, And placed thereon an incense of fragrant odors. ⁵ But now our glorying has been made into dust, And the desire of our soul into sand.'

The Vision of the Forest, the Vine, the Fountain and the Cedar

36

¹ And when I had said these things I fell asleep there, and I saw a vision in the night. ² And lo! a forest of trees planted on the plain, and lofty and rugged rocky mountains surrounded it, and that forest occupied much space. ³ And lo! over against it arose a vine, and from under it there went forth a fountain peacefully. ⁴ Now that fountain came to the forest and was (stirred) into great waves, and those waves submerged that forest, and suddenly they rooted out the greater part of that forest, and overthrew all the mountains which were round about it. ⁵ And the height of the forest began to be made low, and the top of the mountains was made low and that fountain prevailed greatly, so that it left nothing of that great forest save one cedar only. ⁶ Also when it had cast it down and had destroyed and rooted out the greater part of that forest, so that nothing was left of it, nor could its place be recognized, then that vine began to come with the fountain in peace and great tranquility, and it came to a place which was not far from that cedar, and they brought the cedar which had been cast down to it. ⁷ And I beheld and lo! that vine opened its mouth and spoke and said to that cedar: Art you not that cedar which was left of the forest of wickedness, and by whose means wickedness persisted, and was wrought all those years, and goodness never. ⁸ And you kept conquering that which was not yours, and to that which was your you did never show compassion, and you did keep extending your power over those who were far from you, and those who drew near you, you did hold fast in the toils of your wickedness, and you did uplift thyself always as one that could not be rooted out! ⁹ But now your time has sped and your hour is come. ¹⁰ Do you also therefore depart, O cedar, after the forest, which departed before you, and become dust with it, and let your ashes be mingled together. ¹¹ And now recline in anguish and rest in torment till your last time come, in which you will come again, and be tormented still more.'

37

¹ And after these things I saw that cedar burning, and the vine growing, itself and all around it, the plain full of unfading flowers. And I indeed awoke and arose.

Interpretation of the Vision

38

¹ And I prayed and said: 'O LORD, my Lord, you do always enlighten those who are led by understanding. ² Your law is life, and Your wisdom is right guidance. ³ Make known to me therefore the interpretation of this vision. ⁴ For you know that my soul hath always walked in Your law, and from my (earliest) days I departed not from Your wisdom.'

39

¹ And He answered and said unto me: 'Baruch, this is the interpretation of the vision which you have seen. ² As you have seen the great forest which lofty and rugged mountains surrounded, this is the word. ³ Behold! the days come, and this kingdom will be destroyed which once destroyed Zion, and it will be subjected to that which comes after it. ⁴ Moreover, that also again after a time will be destroyed, and another, a third, will arise, and that also will have dominion for its time, and will be destroyed. ⁵ And after these things a fourth kingdom will arise, whose power will be harsh and evil far beyond those which were before it, and it will rule many times as the forests on the plain, and it will hold fast for times, and will exalt itself more than the cedars of Lebanon. ⁶ And by it the truth will be hidden, and all those who are polluted with iniquity will flee to it, as evil beasts flee and creep into the forest. ⁷ And it will come to pass when the time of its consummation that it should fall has approached, then the principate of My Messiah will be revealed, which is like the fountain and the vine, and when it is revealed it will root out the multitude of its host. ⁸ And as touching that which you have seen, the lofty cedar, which was left of that forest, and the fact, that the vine spoke those words with it which you did hear, this is the word.

40

¹ The last leader of that time will be left alive, when the multitude of his hosts will be put to the sword, and he will be bound, and they will take him up to Mount Zion, and My Messiah will convict him of all his impieties, and will gather and set before him all the works of his hosts. ² And afterwards he will put him to death, and protect the rest of My people which shall be found in the place which I have chosen. ³ And his principate will stand for ever, until the world of corruption is at an end, and until the times aforesaid are fulfilled. ⁴ This is your vision, and this is its interpretation.'

The Destiny of the Apostates and of the Proselytes

41

¹ And I answered and said: 'For whom and for how many shall these things be? or who will be worthy to live at that time? ² For I will speak before you everything that I think, and I will ask of you regarding those things which I meditate. ³ For lo! I see many of Your people who have withdrawn from Your covenant, and cast from them the yoke of Your law. ⁴ But others again I have seen who have forsaken their vanity, and fled for refuge beneath Your wings. ⁵ What therefore will be to them? or how will the last time receive them? ⁶ Or perhaps the time of these will assuredly be weighed, and as the beam inclines will they be judged accordingly?'

42

¹ And He answered and said unto me: 'These things also will I show unto you. ² As for what you did say–"To whom will these things be, and how many (will they be)?"–to those who have believed there shall be the good which was spoken of aforetime, and to those who despise there shall be the contrary of these things. ³ And as for what you did say regarding those who have drawn near and those who have withdrawn this in the word. ⁴ As for those who were before subject, and afterwards withdrew and mingled themselves with the seed of mingled peoples, the time of these was the former, and was accounted as something exalted. ⁵ And as for those who before knew not but afterwards knew life, and mingled (only) with the seed of the people which had separated itself, the time of these (is) the latter, and is accounted as something exalted. ⁶ And time shall succeed to time and season to season, and one shall receive from another, and then with a view to the consummation shall everything be compared according to the measure of the times and the hours of the seasons. ⁷ For corruption shall take those that belong to it, and life those that belong to it. ⁸ And the dust shall be called, and there shall be said to it: "Give back that which is not yours, and raise up all that you have kept until its time".'

Baruch told of his Death and bidden to give his last Commands to the People

43

¹ But, do thou, Baruch, direct your heart to that which has been said to you, And understand those things which have been shown to you; For there are many eternal consolations for you. ² For you shall depart from this place, And you shall pass from the regions which are now seen by you, And you shall forget whatever is corruptible, And shall not again recall those things which happen among mortals. ³ Go therefore and command your people, and come to this place, and afterwards fast seven days, and then I will come to you and speak with you.'

Baruch tells the Elders of his impending Death, but encourages them to expect the Consolation of Zion

44

¹ And I, Baruch, went from thence, and came to my people, and I called my first-born son and [the Gedaliahs] my friends, and seven of the elders of the people, and I said unto them: Behold, I go unto my fathers According to the way of all the earth. ³ But withdraw you not from the way of the law, But guard and admonish the people which remain, Lest they withdraw from the commandments of the Mighty One. ⁴ For you see that He whom we serve is just, And our Creator is no respecter of persons. ⁵ And see you what hath befallen Zion, And what hath happened to Jerusalem. ⁶ For the judgment of the Mighty One shall (thereby) be made known, And His ways, which, though past finding out, are right. ⁷ For if you endure and persevere in His fear, And do not forget His law, The times shall change over you for good. And you shall see the consolation of Zion. ⁸, ⁹ Because whatever is now is nothing, But that which shall be is very great. For everything that is corruptible shall pass away, And everything that dies shall depart, And all the present time shall be forgotten, Nor shall there be any remembrance of the present time, which is defiled with evils. ¹⁰ For that which runs now runs unto vanity, And that which prospers shall quickly fall and be humiliated. ¹¹ For that which is to be shall be the object of desire, And for that which comes afterwards shall we hope; For it is a time that passes not away, ¹² And the hour comes which abides for ever. And the new world (comes) which does not turn to corruption those who depart to its blessedness, And has no mercy on those who depart to torment, And leads not to perdition those who live in it. ¹³ For these are they who shall inherit that time which has been spoken of, And theirs is the inheritance of the

promised time. ¹⁴ These are they who have acquired for themselves treasures of wisdom, And with them are found stores of understanding, And from mercy have they not withdrawn, And the truth of the law I have they preserved. ¹⁵ For to them shall be given the world to come, But the dwelling of the rest who are many shall be in the fire.'

45

¹ 'Do you therefore so far as you are able instruct the people, for that labor is ours. For if you teach them, you will quicken them.'

46

¹ And my son and the elders of the people answered and said unto me: 'Has the Mighty One humiliated us to such a degree As to take you from us quickly? ² And truly we shall be in darkness, And there shall be no light to the people who are left, ³ For where again shall we seek the law, Or who will distinguish for us between death and life?' ⁴ And I said unto them: 'The throne of the Mighty One I cannot resist; Nevertheless, there shall not be wanting to Israel a wise man Nor a son of the law to the race of Jacob. ⁵ But only prepare you your hearts, that you may obey the law, And be subject to those who in fear are wise and understanding; And prepare your souls that you may not depart from them. ⁶ For if you do these things, Good tidings shall come unto you. [Which I before told you of; nor shall you fall into the torment, of which I testified to you before.' ⁷ But with regard to the word that I was to be taken I did not make (it) known to them or to my son.]

47

¹ And when I had gone forth and dismissed them, I went there and said unto them: 'Behold! I go to Hebron: for thither the Mighty One hath sent me.' ² And I came to that place where the word had been spoken unto me, and I sat there, and fasted seven days.

Prayer of Baruch

48

¹ And it came to pass after the seventh day, that I prayed before the Mighty One and said ² 'O my Lord, you summon the advent of the times, And they stand before you; You cause the power of the ages to pass away, And they do not resist you; You arrange the method of the seasons, And they obey you. ³ You alone know the duration of the generations, And you reveal not Your mysteries to many. ⁴ You make known the multitude of the fire, And you weigh the lightness of the wind. ⁵ You explore the limit of the heights, And you scrutinize the depths of the darkness. ⁶ You care for the number which pass away that they may be preserved, And you prepare an abode for those that are to be. ⁷ You remember the beginning which you have made, And the destruction that is to be You forget not. ⁸ With nods of fear and indignation You command the flames, And they change into spirits, And with a word you quicken that which was not, And with mighty power you hold that which has not yet come. ⁹ You instruct created things in the understanding of you, And you make wise the spheres so as to minister in their orders. ¹⁰ Armies innumerable stand before you And minister in their orders quietly at Your nod. ¹¹ Hear Your servant And give ear to my petition. ¹² For in a little time are we born, And in a little time do we return. ¹³ But with you hours are as a time, And days as generations. ¹⁴ Be not therefore wroth with man; for he is nothing ¹⁵ And take not account of our works; For what are we? For lo! by Your gift do we come into the world, And we depart not of our own will. ¹⁶ For we said not to our parents, "Beget us, Nor did we send to Sheol and say, "Receive us." ¹⁷ What therefore is our strength that we should bear Your wrath, Or what are we that we should endure Your judgment? ¹⁸ Protect us in Your compassions, And in Your mercy help us. ¹⁹ Behold the little ones that are subject unto you, And save all that draw near unto you: And destroy not the hope of our people, And cut not short the times of our aid. ²⁰ For this is the nation which you have chosen, And these are the people, to whom you find no equal. ²¹ But I will speak now before you, And I will say as my heart thinks. ²² In you do we trust, for lo! Your law is with us, And we know that we shall not fall so long as we keep Your statutes. ²³ [To all time are we blessed at all events in this that we have not mingled with the Gentiles.] ²⁴ For we are all one celebrated people, Who have received one law from One: And the law which is amongst us will aid us, And the surpassing wisdom which is in us will help us.' ²⁵ And when I had prayed and said these things, I was greatly weakened. ²⁶ And He answered and said unto me: 'You have prayed simply, O Baruch, And all your words have been heard. ²⁷ But My judgment exacts its own And My law exacts its rights. ²⁸ For from your words I will answer you, And from your prayer I will speak to you. ²⁹ For this is as follows: he that is corrupted is not at all; he has both wrought iniquity so far as lie could do anything, and has not remembered My goodness, nor accepted My long-suffering. ³⁰ Therefore you shall surely be taken up, as I before told you. ³¹ For that time shall arise which brings affliction; for it shall come and pass by with quick vehemence, and it shall be turbulent coming in the heat of indignation. ³² And it shall come to pass in those days that all the inhabitants of the earth shall be moved one against another, because they know not that My judgment has drawn nigh. ³³ For there shall not be found many wise at that time, And the intelligent shall be but a few: Moreover, even those who know shall most of all be silent. ³⁴ And there shall be many rumors and tidings not a few, And the doing of phantasms shall be manifest, And promises not a few be recounted, Some of them (shall prove) idle, And some of them shall be confirmed. ³⁵ And honor shall be turned into shame, And strength humiliated into contempt, And probity destroyed, And beauty shall become ugliness. ³⁶ And many shall say to many at that time: "Where hath the multitude of intelligence hidden itself, And whither hath the multitude of wisdom removed itself?" ³⁷ And whilst they are meditating these things, Then envy shall arise in those who had not thought aught of themselves (?) And passion shall seize him that is peaceful, And many shall be stirred up in anger to injure many, And they shall rouse up armies in order to shed blood, And in the end they shall perish together with them. ³⁸ And it shall come to pass at the self-same time, That a change of times shall manifestly appeal to every man, Because in all those times they polluted themselves And they practiced oppression, And walked every man in his own works, And remembered not the law of the Mighty One. ³⁹ Therefore a fire shall consume their thoughts, And in flame shall the meditations of their reins be tried; For the Judge shall come and will not tarry. ⁴⁰ Because each of the inhabitants of the earth knew when he was transgressing. But My Law they knew not by reason of their pride. ⁴¹ But many shall then assuredly weep, Yea, over the living more than over the dead.' ⁴² And I answered and said: 'O Adam, what have you done to all those who are born from you? And what will be said to the first Eve who hearkened to the serpent? ⁴³ For all this multitude are going to corruption, Nor is there any numbering of those whom the fire devours. ⁴⁴ But again I will speak in Your presence. ⁴⁵ You, O LORD, my Lord, know what is in Your creature. ⁴⁶ For you did of old command the dust to produce Adam, and you know the number of those who are born from him, and how far they have sinned before you, who have existed and not confessed you as their Creator. ⁴⁷ And as regards all these their end shall convict them, and Your law which they have transgressed shall requite them on Your day.'

Fragment of an Address of Baruch to the People

⁴⁸ ['But now let us dismiss the wicked and inquire about the righteous. ⁴⁹ And I will recount their blessedness And not be silent in celebrating their glory, which is reserved for them. ⁵⁰ For assuredly as in a little time in this transitory world in which you live, you have endured much labor, So in that world to which there is no end, you shall receive great light.']

The Nature of the Resurrection Body: the final Destinies of the Righteous and the Wicked

49

¹ 'Nevertheless, I Will again ask from you, O Mighty One, yea, I will ask made all things. ² "In what shape will those live who live in Your day? Or how will the splendor of those who (are) after that time continue? ³ Will they then resume this form of the present, And put on these entrammelling members, Which are now involved in evils, And in which evils are consummated, Or will you perchance change these things which have been in the world As also the world?"

50

¹ And He answered and said unto me: 'Hear, Baruch, this word, And write in the remembrance of your heart all that you shall learn. ² For the earth shall then assuredly restore the dead, [Which it now receives, in order to preserve them]. It shall make no change in their form, But as it has received, so shall it restore them, And as I delivered them unto it, so also shall it raise them. ³ For then it will be necessary to show the living that the dead have come to life again, and that those who had departed have returned (again). ⁴ And it shall come to pass, when they have severally recognized those whom they now know, then judgment shall grow strong, and those things which before were spoken of shall come.

51

¹ And it shall come to pass, when that appointed day has gone by, that then shall the aspect of those who are condemned be afterwards changed, and the glory of those who are justified. ² For the aspect of those who now act wickedly shall become worse than it is, as they shall suffer torment. ³ Also (as for) the glory of those who have now been justified in My law, who have had understanding in their life, and who have planted in their heart the root of wisdom, then their splendor shall be glorified in changes, and the form of their face shall be turned into the light of their beauty, that they may be able to acquire and receive the world which does not die, which is then promised to them. ⁴ For over this above all shall those who come then lament, that they rejected My law, and stopped their ears that they might not hear wisdom or receive understanding. ⁵ When therefore they see those,

over whom they are now exalted, (but) who shall then be exalted and glorified more than they, they shall respectively be transformed, the latter into the splendor of angels, and the former shall yet more waste away in wonder at the visions and in the beholding of the forms. ⁶ For they shall first behold and afterwards depart to be tormented. ⁷ But those who have been saved by their works, And to whom the law has been now a hope, And understanding an expectation, And wisdom a confidence, Shall wonders appear in their time. ⁸ For they shall behold the world which is now invisible to them, And they shall behold the time which is now hidden from them: ⁹ And time shall no longer age them. ¹⁰ For in the heights of that world shall they dwell, And they shall be made like unto the angels, And be made equal to the stars, And they shall be changed into every form they desire, From beauty into loveliness, And from light into the splendor of glory. ¹¹ For there shall be spread before them the extents of Paradise, and there shall be shown to them the beauty of the majesty of the living creatures which are beneath the throne, and all the armies of the angels, who are now held fast by My word, lest they should appear, and] are held fast by a command, that they may stand in their places till their advent comes. ¹² Moreover, there shall then be excellency in the righteous surpassing that in the angels. ¹³ For the first shall receive the last, those whom they were expecting, and the last those of whom they used to hear that they had passed away. ¹⁴ For they have been delivered from this world of tribulation, And laid down the burthen of anguish. ¹⁵ For what then have men lost their life, And for what have those who were on the earth exchanged their soul? ¹⁶ For then they chose (not) for themselves this time, Which, beyond the reach of anguish, could not pass away: But they chose for themselves that time, Whose issues are full of lamentations and evils, And they denied the world which ages not those who come to it, And they rejected the time of glory, So that they shall not come to the honor of which I told you before.'

52

¹ And I answered and said: 'How can we forget those for whom woe is then reserved? ² And why therefore do we again mourn for those who die? Or why do we weep for those who depart to Sheol? ³ Let lamentations be reserved for the beginning of that coming torment, And let tears be laid up for the advent of the destruction of that time. ⁴ [But even in the face of these things will I speak. ⁵ And as for the righteous, what will they do now? ⁶ Rejoice you in the suffering which you now suffer: For why do you look for the decline of your enemies? ⁷ Make ready your soul for that which is reserved for you, And prepare your souls for the reward which is laid up for you.']

The Messiah Apocalypse
The Vision of the Cloud with black and white Waters

53

¹ And when I had said these things I fell asleep there, and I saw a vision, and lo! a cloud was ascending from a very great sea, and I kept gazing upon it) and lo! it was full of waters white and black, and there were many colors in those self-same waters, and as it were the likeness of great lightning was seen at its summit. ² And I saw the cloud passing swiftly in quick courses, and it covered all the earth. ³ And it came to pass after these things that that cloud began to pour upon the earth the waters that were in it. ⁴ And I saw that there was not one and the same likeness in the waters which descended from it. ⁵ For in the first beginning they were black and many (Or a time, and afterwards I saw that the waters became bright, but they were not many, and after these things again I saw black (waters), and after these things again bright, and again black and again bright. ⁶ Now this was done twelve times, but the black were always more numerous than the bright. ⁷ And it came to pass at the end of the cloud, that lo! it rained black waters, and they were darker than had been all those waters that were before, and fire was mingled with them, and where those waters descended, they wrought devastation and destruction. ⁸ And after these things I saw how that lightning which I had seen on the summit of the cloud, seized hold of it and hurled it to the earth. ⁹ Now that lightning shone exceedingly, so as to illuminate the whole earth, and it healed those regions where the last waters had descended and wrought devastation. ¹⁰ And it took hold of the whole earth, and had dominion over it. ¹¹ And I saw after these things, and lo! twelve rivers were ascending from the sea, and they began to surround that lightning and to become subject to it. ¹² And by reason of my fear I awoke.

Baruch's Prayer for an Interpretation of the Vision: Ramiel's advent for this Purpose

54

¹ And I besought the Mighty One, and said: 'You alone, O Lord, know of aforetime the deep things of the world, And the things which befall in their times You bring about by Your word, And against the works of the inhabitants of the earth you do hasten the beginnings of the times, And the end of the seasons you alone know. ² (You) for whom nothing is too hard, But who do everything easily by a nod: ³ (You) to whom the depths come as the heights, And whose word the beginnings of the ages serve: ⁴ (You) who reveal to those who fear you what is prepared for them, That thenceforth they may be comforted. ⁵ You show great acts to those who know not; You break up the enclosure of those who are ignorant, And lightest up what is dark, And reveal what is hidden to the pure, [Who in faith have submitted themselves to you and Your law.] ⁶ You have shown to Your servant this vision; Reveal to me also its interpretation. ⁷ For I know that as regards those things wherein I besought you, I have received a response, And as regards what I besought, you did reveal to me with what voice I should praise you, And from what members I should cause praises and hallelujahs to ascend to you. ⁸ For if my members were mouths, And the hairs of my head voices, Even so I could not give you the reward of praise, Nor laud you as is befitting, Nor could I recount Your praise, Nor tell the glory of Your beauty. ⁹ For what am I amongst men, Or why am I reckoned amongst those who are more excellent than I, That I have heard all these marvelous things from the Most High, And numberless promises from Him who created me? ¹⁰ Blessed be my mother among those that bear, And praised among women be she that bare me. ¹¹ For I will not be silent in praising the Mighty One, And with the voice of praise I will recount His marvelous deeds. ¹² For who doeth like unto Your marvelous deeds, O God, Or who comprehend Your deep thought of life. ¹³ For with Your counsel you do govern all the creatures which Your right hand has created And you have established every fountain of light beside you, And the treasures of wisdom beneath Your throne have you prepared. ¹⁴ And justly do they perish who have not loved Your law, And the torment of judgment shall await those who have not submitted themselves to Your power. ¹⁵ For though Adam first sinned And brought untimely death upon all, Yet of those who were born from him Each one of them has prepared for his own soul torment to come, And again each one of them has chosen for himself glories to come. ¹⁶ [For assuredly he who believeth will receive reward. ¹⁷ But now, as for you, you wicked that now are, turn you to destruction, because you shall speedily be visited, in that formerly you rejected the understanding of the Most High. ¹⁸ For His works have not taught you, Nor has the skill of His creation which is at all times persuaded you.] ¹⁹ Adam is therefore not the cause, save only of his own soul, But each of us has been the Adam of his own soul. ²⁰ But do You, O Lord, expound to me regarding those things which you have revealed to me, And inform me regarding that which I besought you. ²¹ For at the consummation of the world vengeance shall be taken upon those who have done wickedness according to their wickedness, And you will glorify the faithful according to their faithfulness. ²² For those who are amongst your own you rule, And those who sin you blot out from amongst your own.'

55

¹ And it came to pass when I had finished speaking the words of this prayer, that I sat there under a tree, that I might rest in the shade of the branches. ² And I wondered and was astonished, and pondered in my thoughts regarding the multitude of goodness which sinners who are upon the earth have rejected, and regarding the great torment which they have despised, though they knew that they should be tormented because of the sin they had committed. And when I was pondering on these things and the like, lo! the angel Ramiel who presides over true visions was sent to me, and he said unto me: ⁴ 'Why does your heart trouble you, Baruch, and why does your thought disturb you? ⁵ For if owing to the report which you have only heard of judgment you are so moved, What (wilt you be) when you shall see it manifestly with your eyes? ⁶ And if with the expectation wherewith you do expect the day of the Mighty One you are so overcome, What (wilt you be) when you shall come to its advent? ⁷ And, if at the word of the announcement of the torment of those who have done foolishly you are so wholly distraught, How much more when the event will reveal marvelous things? ⁸ And if you have heard tidings of the good and evil things which are then coming and are grieved, What (wilt you be) when you shall behold what the majesty will reveal, Which shall convict these and cause those to rejoice.'

Interpretation of the Vision. The black and bright Waters symbolize the World's History from Adam to the Advent of the Messiah.

56

¹ 'Nevertheless, because you have besought the Most High to reveal to you the interpretation of the vision which you have seen, I have been sent to tell you. ² And the Mighty One hath assuredly made known to you the methods of the times that have passed, and of those that are destined to pass in His world from the beginning of its creation even unto its consummation, of those things which (are) deceit and of those which (are) in truth. ³ For as you did see a great cloud which ascended from the sea, and went and

covered the earth, this is the duration of the world (= αιων) which the Mighty One made when he took counsel to make the world. ⁴ And it came to pass when the word had gone forth from His presence, that the duration of the world had come into being in a small degree, and was established according to the multitude of the intelligence of Him who sent it. ⁵ And as you did previously see on the summit of the cloud black waters which descended previously on the earth, this is the transgression wherewith Adam the first man transgressed. ⁶ For [since] when he transgressed Untimely death came into being, Grief was named And anguish was prepared, And pain was created, And trouble consummated, And disease began to be established, And Sheol kept demanding that it should be renewed in blood, And the begetting of children was brought about, And the passion of parents produced, And the greatness of humanity was humiliated, And goodness languished. ⁷ What therefore can be blacker or darker than these things? ⁸ This is the beginning of the black waters which you have seen. ⁹ And from these black (waters) again were black derived, and the darkness of darkness was produced. ¹⁰ For he became a danger to his own soul: even to the angels ¹¹ For, moreover, at that time when he was created, they enjoyed liberty. ¹² And became he a danger some of them descended, and mingled with the women. ¹³ And then those who did so were tormented in chains. ¹⁴ But the rest of the multitude of the angels, of which there is (no) number, restrained themselves. ¹⁵ And those who dwelt on the earth perished together (with them) through the waters of the deluge. ¹⁶ These are the black first waters.

57

¹ And after these (waters) you did see bright waters: this is the fount of Abraham, also his generations and advent of his son, and of his son's son, and of those like them. ² Because at that time the unwritten law was named amongst them, And the works of the commandments were then fulfilled, And belief in the coming judgment was then generated, And hope of the world that was to be renewed was then built up, And the promise of the life that should come hereafter was implanted. ³ These are the bright waters, which you have seen.

58

¹ 'And the black third waters which you have seen, these are the mingling of all sins, which the nations afterwards wrought after the death of those righteous men, and the wickedness of the land of Egypt, wherein they did wickedly in the service wherewith they made their sons to serve. ² Nevertheless, these also perished at last.

59

¹ 'And the bright fourth waters which you have seen are the advent of Moses and Aaron and Miriam and Joshua the son of Nun and Caleb and of all those like them. ² For at that time the lamp of the eternal law shone on all those who sat in darkness, which announced to them that believe the promise of their reward, and to them that deny, the torment of fire which is reserved for them. ³ But also the heavens at that time were shaken from their place, and those who were under the throne of the Mighty One were perturbed, when He was taking Moses unto Himself. ⁴ For He showed him many admonitions together with the principles of the law and the consummation of the times, as also to you, and likewise the pattern of Zion and its measures, in the pattern of which the sanctuary of the present time was to be made. ⁵ But then also He showed to him the measures of the fire, also the depths of the abyss, and the weight of the winds, and the number of the drops of rain: ⁶ And the suppression of anger, and the multitude of long-suffering, and the truth of judgment: ⁷ And the root of wisdom, and the riches of understanding, and the fount of knowledge: ⁸ And the height of the air, and the greatness of Paradise, and the consummation of the ages, and the beginning of the day of judgment: ⁹ And the number of the offerings, and the earths which have not yet come: ¹⁰ And the mouth of Gehenna, and the station of vengeance, and the place of faith, and the region of hope: And the likeness of future torment, and the multitude of innumerable angels, and the flaming hosts, and the splendor of the lightnings, and the voice of the thunders, and the orders of the chiefs of the angels, and the treasuries of light, and the changes of the times, and the investigations of the law. ¹² These are the bright fourth waters which you have seen.

60

¹ And the black fifth waters which you have seen raining are the works which the Amorites wrought, and the spells of their incantations which they wrought, and the wickedness of their mysteries, and the mingling of their pollution. ² But even Israel was then polluted by sins in the days of the judges, though they saw many signs which were from Him who made them.

61

¹ And the bright sixth waters which thru did see, this is the time in which David and Solomon were born. ² And there was at that time the building of Zion, And the dedication of the sanctuary, And the shedding of much blood of the nations that sinned then, And many offerings which were offered then in the dedication of the sanctuary. ³ And peace and tranquility existed at that time, ⁴ And wisdom was heard in the assembly: And the riches of understanding were magnified in the congregations, ⁵ And the holy festivals were fulfilled in blessedness and in much joy. ⁶ And the judgment of the rulers was then seen to be without guile, And the righteousness of the precepts of the Mighty One was accomplished with truth. ⁷ And the land [which] was then beloved by the Lord, And because its inhabitants sinned not, it was glorified beyond all lands, And the city Zion ruled then over all lands and regions. ⁸ These are the bright waters which you have seen.

62

¹ And the black seventh waters which you have seen, this is the perversion (brought about) by the counsel of Jeroboam, who took counsel to make two calves of gold: ² And all the iniquities which kings who were after him iniquitously wrought. ³ And the curse of Jezebel and the worship of idols which Israel practiced at that time. ⁴ And the withholding of rain, and the famines which occurred until women eat the fruit of their wombs. ⁵ And the time of their captivity which came upon the nine tribes and a half, because they were in many sins. ⁶ And Shalmanezzar king of Assyria came and led them away captive. ⁷ But regarding the Gentiles it were tedious to tell how they always wrought impiety and wickedness, and never wrought righteousness. ⁸ These are the black seventh waters which you have seen.

63

¹ 'And the bright eighth waters which you have seen, this is the rectitude and uprightness of Hezekiah king of Judah and the grace (of God) which came upon him. ² For when Sennacherib was stirred up in order that he might perish, and his wrath troubled him in order that he might thereby perish, for the multitude also of the nations which were with him. ³ When, moreover, Hezekiah the king heard those things which the king of Assyria was devising, (i.e.) to come and seize him and destroy his people, the two and a half tribes which remained: nay, more he wished to overthrow Zion also: then Hezekiah trusted in his works, and had hope in his righteousness, and spoke with the Mighty One and said: ⁴ "Behold, for lo! Sennacherib is prepared to destroy us, and he will be boastful and uplifted when he has destroyed Zion." ⁵ And the Mighty One heard him, for Hezekiah was wise, And He had respect unto his prayer, because he was righteous. ⁶ And thereupon the Mighty One commanded Ramiel His angel who speaks with you. ⁷ And I went forth and destroyed their multitude, the number of whose chiefs only was a hundred and eighty-five thousand, and each one of them had an equal number (at his command). ⁸ And at that time I burned their bodies within, but their raiment and arms I preserved outwardly, in order that the still more wonderful deeds of the Mighty One might appear, and that thereby His name might be spoken of throughout the whole earth. ⁹ And Zion was saved and Jerusalem delivered: Israel also was freed from tribulation. ¹⁰ And all those who were in the holy land rejoiced, and the name of the Mighty One was glorified so that it was spoken of ¹¹ These are the bright waters which you have seen.

64

¹ 'And the black ninth waters which you have seen, this is all the wickedness which was in the days of Manasseh the son of Hezekiah. ² For he wrought much impiety, and he slew the righteous, and he wrested judgment, and he shed the blood of the innocent, and wedded women he violently polluted, and he overturned the altars, and destroyed their offerings, and drove forth their priests lest they should minister in the sanctuary. ³ And he made an image with five faces: four of them looked to the four winds, and the fifth on the summit of the image as ah adversary of the zeal of the Mighty One. ⁴ And then wrath went forth from the presence of the Mighty One to the intent that Zion should be rooted out, as also it befell in your days. But also against the two tribes and a half went forth a decree that they should also be led away captive, as you have now seen. ⁵ And to such a degree did the impiety of Manasseh increase, that it removed the praise of the Most High from the sanctuary. ⁷ On this account Manasseh was at that time named 'the impious," and finally his abode was in the fire. ⁸ For though his prayer was heard with the Most High, finally, when he was cast into the brazen horse and the brazen horse was melted, it served as a sign unto him for the hour. ⁹ For he had not lived perfectly, for he was not worthy–but that thenceforward he might know by whom finally he should be tormented. ¹⁰ For he who is able to benefit is also able to torment.

65

¹ 'Thus, moreover, did Manasseh act impiously, and thought that in his time the Mighty One would not inquire into these things. ² These are the black ninth waters which you have seen.

66

¹ 'And the bright tenth waters which you have seen: this is the purity of the generations of Josiah king of Judah, who was the only one at the time who submitted himself to the Mighty One with all his heart and with all his soul. ² And he cleansed the land from idols, and hallowed all the vessels which had been polluted, and restored the offerings to the altar, and raised the horn of the holy, and exalted the righteous, and honored all that were wise in understanding, and brought back the priests to their ministry, and destroyed and removed the magicians and enchanters and necromancers from the land. ³ And not only did he slay the impious that were living, but they also took from the sepulchers the bones of the dead and burned them with fire. ⁴ [And the festivals and the Sabbaths he established in their sanctity], and their polluted ones he burnt in the fire, and the lying prophets which deceived the people, these also he burnt in the fire, and the people who listened to them when they were living, he cast them into the brook Kidron, and heaped stones upon them. ⁵ And he was zealous with zeal for the Mighty One with all his soul, and he alone was firm in the law at that time, so that he left none that was uncircumcised, or that wrought impiety in all the land, all the days of his life. ⁶ Therefore he shall receive an eternal reward, and he shall be glorified with the Mighty One beyond many at a later time. ⁷ For on his account and on account of those who are like him were the honorable glories, of which you were told before, created and prepared. These arc the bright waters which you have seen.

67

¹ 'And the black eleventh waters which you have seen: this is the calamity which is now befalling "Zion. ² Do you think that there is no anguish to the angels in the presence of the Mighty One, That Zion was so delivered up, And that lo! the Gentiles boast in their hearts, And assemble before their idols and say, "She is trodden down who oftentimes trod down, And she has been reduced to servitude who reduced (others)"? ³ Dost you think that in these things the Most High rejoices, Or that His name is glorified? ⁴ [But how will it serve towards His righteous judgment?] ⁵ Yet after these things shall the dispersed among the Gentiles be taken hold of by tribulation, And in shame shall they dwell in every place. ⁶ Because so far as Zion is delivered up And Jerusalem laid waste, Shall idols prosper in the cities of the Gentiles, And the vapor of the smoke of the incense of the righteousness which is by the law is extinguished in Zion, And in the region of Zion in every place lo! there is the smoke of impiety. ⁷ But the king of Babylon will arise who has now destroyed Zion, And he will boast over the people, And he will speak great things in his heart in the presence of the Most High. ⁸ But he also shall fall at last. These are the black waters.

68

¹ 'And the bright twelfth waters which you have seen: this is the word. For after these things time will come when your people shall fall into distress, so that they shall all run the risk of perishing together. ³ Nevertheless, they will be saved, and their enemies will fall in their presence. ⁴ And they will have in (due) time much joy. ⁵ And at that time after a little interval Zion will again be rebuilt, and its offerings will again be restored, and the priests will return to their ministry, and also the Gentiles will come to glorify it. ⁶ Nevertheless, not fully as in the beginning. ⁷ But it will come to pass after these things that there will be the fall of many nations. ⁸ These are the bright waters which you have seen.

69

¹ 'For the last waters which you have seen which were darker than all that were before them, those which were after the twelfth number, which were collected together, belong to the whole world. ² For the Most High made division from the beginning, because He alone knows what will befall. ³ For as to the enormities and the impieties which should be wrought before Him, He foresaw six kinds of them. ⁴ And of the good works of the righteous which should be accomplished before Him, He foresaw six kinds of them, beyond those which He should work at the consummation of the age. ⁵ On his account there were not black waters with black, nor bright with bright; for it is the consummation.

70

¹ 'Hear therefore the interpretation of the last black waters which are to come [after the black]: this the word. ² Behold! the days come, and it shall be when the time of the age has ripened, And the harvest of its evil and good seeds has come, That the Mighty One will bring upon the earth and its inhabitants and upon its rulers Perturbation of spirit and stupor of heart. ³ And they shall hate one another, And provoke one another to fight, And the mean shall rule over the honorable, And those of low degree shall be extolled above the famous. ⁴ And the many shall be delivered into the hands of the few, And those who were nothing shall rule over the strong, And the poor shall have abundance beyond the rich, And the impious shall exalt themselves above the heroic. ⁵ And the wise shall be silent, And the foolish shall speak, Neither shall the thought of men be then confirmed, Nor the counsel of the mighty, Nor the hope of those who hope be confirmed. ⁶ And when those things which were predicted have come to pass, Then shall confusion fall upon all men, And some of them shall fall in battle, And some of them shall perish in anguish, ⁷ And some of them shall be destroyed by their own. Then the Most High peoples whom He has prepared before, And they shall come and make war with the leaders that shall then be left. ⁸ And it shall come to pass that whoever gets safe out of the war shall die in the earthquake, And whoever gets safe out of the earthquake shall be burned by the fire, And whoever gets safe out of the fire shall be destroyed by famine. ⁹ [And it shall come to pass that whoever of the victors and the vanquished gets safe out of and escapes all these things aforesaid will be delivered into the hands of My servant Messiah.] ¹⁰ For all the earth shall devour its inhabitants.

71

¹ 'And the holy land shall have mercy on its own, And it shall protect its inhabitants at that time. ² This is the vision which you have seen, and this is the interpretation. ³ For I have come to tell you these things, because your prayer has been heard with the Most High.

72

¹ 'Hear now also regarding the bright lightning which is to come at the consummation after these black (waters): this is the word. ² After the signs have come, of which you were told before, when the nations become turbulent, and the time of My Messiah is come, he shall both summon all the nations, and some of them he shall spare, and some of them he shall slay. ³ These things therefore shall come upon the nations which are to be spared by Him. ⁴ Every nation, which knows not Israel and has not trodden down the seed of Jacob, shall indeed be spared. ⁵ And this because some out of every nation shall be subjected to your people. ⁶ But all those who have ruled over you, or have known you, shall be given up to the sword.

73

¹ 'And it shall come to pass, when He has brought low everything that is in the world, And has sat down in peace for the age on the throne of His kingdom, That joy shall then be revealed, And rest shall appear. ² And then healing shall descend in dew, And disease shall withdraw, And anxiety and anguish and lamentation pass from amongst men, And gladness proceed through the whole earth. ³ And no one shall again die untimely, Nor shall any adversity suddenly befall. ⁴ And judgments, and abusive talk, and contentions, and revenges, And blood, and passions, and envy, and hatred, And whatsoever things are like these shall go into condemnation when they are removed. ⁵ For it is these very things which have filled this world with evils, And on account of these the life of man has been greatly troubled. ⁶ And wild beasts shall come from the forest and minister unto men And asps and dragons shall come forth from their holes to submit themselves to a little child. ⁷ And women shall no longer then have pain when they bear, Nor shall they suffer torment when they yield the fruit of the womb.

74

¹ 'And it shall come to pass in those days that the reapers shall not grow weary, Nor those that build be toil-worn; For the works shall of themselves speedily advance Together with those who do them in much tranquility. ² For that time is the consummation of that which is corruptible, And the beginning of that which is not corruptible. ³ Therefore those things which were predicted shall belong to it: Therefore it is far away from evils, and near to those things which die not. ⁴ This is the bright lightning which came after the last dark waters.'

Baruch's Hymn on the Unsearchableness of God's Ways and on His Mercies through which the Faithful shall attain to a blessed Consummation

75

¹ And I answered and said: 'Who can understand, O Lord, Your goodness? For it is incomprehensible. ² Or who can search into your compassions, Which are infinite? ³ Or who can comprehend Your intelligence? ⁴ Or who is able to recount the thoughts of Your mind? ⁵ Or who of those who are born can hope to come to those things, Unless he is one to whom you are merciful and gracious? ⁶ Because, if assuredly you did not have compassion on man, Those who are under Your right hand, They could not come to those things, But those who are in the numbers named can be called. ⁷ But if, indeed, we who exist know wherefore we have come, And submit ourselves to Him who brought us out of Egypt, We shall come again and remember those things which have passed, And shall rejoice regarding that

which has been. ⁸ But if now we know not wherefore we have come, And recognize not the principate of Him who brought us up out of Egypt, We shall come again and seek after those things which have been now, And be grieved with pain because of those things which have befallen.'

Baruch bidden to instruct the People for forty days and then to hold himself ready for his Assumption on the Advent of the Messiah

76

¹ And He answered and said unto me: ['Inasmuch as the revelation of this vision has been interpreted to you as you requested], hear the word of the Most High that you may know what is to befall you after these things. ² For you shall surely depart from this earth, nevertheless not unto death, but you shall be preserved unto the consummation of the times. ³ Go up therefore to the top of that mountain, and there shall pass before you all the regions of that land, and the figure of the inhabited world, and the top(s) of the mountains, and the depth(s) of the valleys, and the depths of the seas, and the number of the rivers, that you may see what you are leaving, and whither you are going. ⁴ Now this shall befall after forty days. Go now therefore during these days and instruct the people so far as you are able, that they may learn so as not to die at the last time, but may learn in order that they may live at the last times.'

Baruch's Admonition to the People and his writing of two Letters–one to the nine and a half tribes in Assyria and the other to the two and a half in Babylon

77

¹ And I, Baruch, went there and came to the people, and assembled them together from the greatest to the least, and said unto them: ² 'Hear, you children of Israel, behold how many you are who remain of the twelve tribes of Israel. ³ For to you and to your fathers the Lord gave a law more excellent than to all peoples. ⁴ And because your brethren transgressed the commandments of the Most High, He brought vengeance upon you and upon them, And He spared not the former, And the latter also He gave into captivity: And He left not a residue of them, ⁵ But behold! you are here with me. ⁶ If, therefore, you direct your ways aright, Ye also shall not depart as your brethren departed, But they shall come to you. ⁷ For He is merciful whom you worship, And He is gracious in whom you hope, And He is true, so that He shall do good and not evil. ⁸ Have you not seen here what has befallen Zion? ⁹ Or do you perchance think that the place had sinned, And that on this account it was overthrown? Or that the land had wrought foolishness, And that therefore it was delivered up? ¹⁰ And know you not that on account of you who did sin, That which sinned not was overthrown, And, on account of those who wrought wickedly, That which wrought not foolishness was delivered up to (its) enemies?' ¹¹ And the whole people answered and said unto me: 'So far as we can recall the good things which the Mighty One has done unto us, we do recall them; and those things which we do not remember He in His mercy knows. ¹² Nevertheless, do this for us your people: write also to our brethren in Babylon an epistle of doctrine and a scroll of hope, that you may confirm them also before you do depart from us. ¹³ For the shepherds of Israel have perished, And the lamps which gave light are extinguished, And the fountains have withheld their stream whence we used to drink. ¹⁴ And we are left in the darkness, And amid the trees of the forest, And the thirst of the wilderness.' ¹⁵ And I answered and said unto them 'Shepherds and lamps and fountains come from the law: And though we depart, yet the law abides. ¹⁶ If therefore you have respect to the law, And are intent upon wisdom, A lamp will not be wanting, And a shepherd will not fail, And a fountain will not dry up. ¹⁷ Nevertheless, as you said unto me, I will write also unto your brethren in Babylon, and I will send by means of men, and I will write in like manner to the nine tribes and a half, and send by means of a bird.' ¹⁸ And it came to pass on the one and twentieth day in the eighth month that I, Baruch, came and sat down under the oak under the shadow of the branches, and no man was with me, but I was alone. ¹⁹ And I wrote these two epistles: one I sent by an eagle to the nine and a half tribes; and the other I sent to those that were at Babylon by means of three men. ²⁰ And I called the eagle and spoke these words unto it: ²¹ 'The Most High hath made you that you should be higher than all birds. ²² And now go and tarry not in (any) place, nor enter a nest, nor settle upon any tree, till you have passed over the breadth of the many waters of the river Euphrates, and have gone to the people that dwell there, and cast down to them this epistle. ²³ Remember, moreover, that, at the time of the deluge, Noah received from a dove the fruit of the olive, when he sent it forth from the ark. ²⁴ Yea, also the ravens ministered to Elijah, bearing him food, as they had been commanded. ²⁵ Solomon also, in the time of his kingdom, whithersoever he wished to send or seek for anything, commanded a bird (to go thither), and it obeyed him as he commanded it. ²⁶ And now let it not weary you, and turn not to the right hand nor the left, but fly and go by a direct way, that you may preserve the command of the Mighty One, according as I said unto you.'

The Epistle of Baruch the Son of Neriah which he erote to the Nine and a Half Tribes

78

¹ These are the words of that epistle which Baruch the son of Neriah sent to the nine and a half tribes, which were across the river Euphrates, in which these things were written. ² Thus says Baruch the son of Neriah to the brethren carried into captivity: 'Mercy and peace.' I bear in mind, my brethren, the love of Him who created us, who loved us from of old, and never hated us, but above all educated us. ³ And truly I know that behold all we the twelve tribes are bound by one bond, inasmuch as we are born from one father. ⁴ Wherefore I have been the more careful to leave you the words of this epistle before I die, that you may be comforted regarding the evils which have come upon you, and that you may be grieved also regarding the evil that has befallen your brethren; and again, also, that you may justify His judgment which ⁵ He has decreed against you that you should be carried away captive–for what you have suffered is disproportioned to what you have done–in order that, at the last times, you may be found worthy of your fathers. ⁶ Therefore, if you consider that ye have now suffered those things for your good, that you may not finally be condemned and tormented, then you will receive eternal hope; if above all you destroy from your heart vain error, on account of which you departed hence. ⁷ For if you so do these things, He will continually remember you, He who always promised on our behalf to those who were more excellent than we, that He will never forget or forsake us, but with much mercy will gather together again those who were dispersed.

79

¹ Now, my brethren, learn first what befell Zion: how that Nebuchadnezzar king of Babylon came up against us. ² For we have sinned against Him who made us, and we have not kept the commandments which he commanded us, yet he hath not chastened us as we deserved. ³ For what befell you we also suffer in a preeminent degree, for it befell us also.

80

¹ And now, my brethren, I make known unto you that when the enemy had surrounded the city, the angels of the Most High were sent, and they overthrew the fortifications of the strong wall, and they destroyed the firm iron corners, which could not be rooted out. ² Nevertheless, they hid all the vessels of the sanctuary, lest the enemy should get possession of them. ³ And when they had done these things, they delivered thereupon to the enemy the overthrown wall, and the plundered house, and the burnt temple, and the people who were overcome because they were delivered up, lest the enemy should boast and say: 'Thus by force have we been able to lay waste even the house of the Most High in war.' Your brethren also have they bound and led away to Babylon, and have caused them to dwell there. ⁵ But we have been left here, being very few. ⁶ This is the tribulation about which I wrote to you. ⁷ For assuredly I know that (the consolation of) the inhabitants of Zion consoles you : so far as you knew that it was prospered (your consolation) was greater than the tribulation which you endured in having to depart from it.

81

¹ But regarding consolation, hear the word. ² For I was mourning regarding Zion, and I prayed for mercy from the Most High, and I said: ³ 'How long will these things endure for us? And will these evils come upon us always?' ⁴ And the Mighty One did according to the multitude of His mercies, And the Most High according to the greatness of His compassion, And He revealed unto me the word, that I might receive consolation, And He showed me visions that I should not again endure anguish, And He made known to me the mystery of the times. And the advent of the hours he showed me.

82

¹ Therefore, my brethren, I have written to you, that you may comfort yourselves regarding the multitude of your tribulations. ² For know you that our Maker will assuredly avenge us on all our enemies, according to all that they have done to us, also that the consummation which the Most High will make is very nigh, and His mercy that is coming, and the consummation of His judgment, is by no means far off. ³ For lo! we see now the multitude of the prosperity of the Gentiles, though they act impiously, But they shall be like a vapor: ⁴ And we behold the multitude of their power, Though they do wickedly, But they shall be made like unto a drop: ⁵ And we see the firmness of their might. Though they resist the Mighty One every hour, But they shall be accounted as spittle. ⁶ And we consider the glory of their greatness, Though they do not keep the statutes of the Most High, But as

smoke shall they pass away. ⁷ And we meditate on the beauty of their gracefulness, Though they have to do with pollutions, But as grass that withers shall they fade away. ⁸ And we consider the strength of their cruelty, Though they remember not the end (thereof), But as a wave that passes shall they be broken. ⁹ And we remark the boastfulness of their might, Though they deny the beneficence of God, who gave (it) to them, But they shall pass away as a passing cloud.

83

¹ [For the Most High will assuredly hasten His times, And He will assuredly bring on His hours. ² And He will assuredly judge those who are in His world, And will visit in truth all things by means of all their hidden works. ³ And He will assuredly examine the secret thoughts, And that which is laid up in the secret chambers of all the members of mail. And will make (them) manifest in the presence of all with reproof. ⁴ Let none therefore of these present things ascend into your hearts, but above all let us be expectant, because that which is promised to us shall come. ⁵ And let us not now look unto the delights of the Gentiles in the present, but let us remember what has been promised to us in the end. ⁶ For the ends of the times and of the seasons and whatsoever is with them shall assuredly pass by together. ⁷ The consummation, moreover, of the age shall then show the great might of its ruler, when all things come to judgment. ⁸ Do you therefore prepare your hearts for that which before you believed, lest you come to be in bondage in both worlds, so that you be led away captive here and be tormented there. ⁹ For that which exists now or which has passed away, or which is to come, in all these things, neither is the evil fully evil, nor again the good fully good. ¹⁰ For all healthinesses of this time are turning into diseases, ¹¹ And all might of this time is turning into weakness, And all the force of this time is turning into impotence, ¹² And every energy of youth is turning into old age and consummation. And every beauty of gracefulness of this time is turning faded and hateful, ¹³ And every proud dominion of the present is turning into humiliation and shame, ¹⁴ And every praise of the glory of this time is turning into the shame of silence, And every vain splendor and insolence of this time is turning into voiceless ruin. ¹⁵ And every delight and joy of this time is turning to worms and corruption, ¹⁶ And every clamor of the pride of this time is turning into dust and stillness. ¹⁷ And every possession of riches of this time is being turned into Sheol alone, ¹⁸ And all the rapine of passion of this time is turning into involuntary death, And every passion of the lusts of this time is turning into a judgment of torment. ¹⁹ And every artifice and craftiness of this time is turning into a proof of the truth, ²⁰ And every sweetness of unguents of this time is turning into judgment and condemnation, ²¹ And every love of lying is turning to contumely through truth. ²² [Since therefore all these things are done now, does anyone think that they will not be avenged? But the consummation of all things will come to the truth.]

84

¹ Behold! I have therefore made known unto you (these things) whilst I live: for I have said (it) that you should learn the things that are excellent; for the Mighty One hath commanded me to instruct you: and I will set before you some of the commandments of His judgment before I die. ² Remember that formerly Moses assuredly called heaven and earth to witness against you and said: 'If you transgress the law you shall be dispersed, but if you keep it you shall be kept.' ³ And other things also he used to say unto you when you the twelve tribes were together in the desert. ⁴ And after his death you cast them away from you: on this account there came upon you what had been predicted. ⁵ And now Moses used to tell you before they befell you, and lo! they have befallen you: for you have forsaken the law. ⁶ Lo! I also say unto you after you have suffered, that if you obey those things which have been said unto you, you will receive from the Mighty One whatever has been laid up and reserved for you. ⁷ Moreover, let this epistle be for a testimony between me and you, that you may remember the commandments of the Mighty One, and that also there may be to me a defense in the presence of Him who sent me. ⁸ And remember you the law and Zion, and the holy land and your brethren, and the covenant of your fathers, and forget not the festivals and the Sabbaths. And deliver this epistle and the traditions of the law to your sons after you, as also your fathers delivered (them) to you. ¹⁰ And at all times make request perseveringly and pray diligently with your whole heart that the Mighty One may be reconciled to you, and that He may not reckon the multitude of your sins, but remember the rectitude of your fathers. ¹¹ For if He judge us not according to the multitude of His mercies, woe unto all us who are born.

85

¹ [Know, moreover, that in former times and in the generations of old our fathers had helpers, Righteous men and holy prophets: ² No more, we were in our own land [And they helped us when we sinned].

3 Baruch, or Greek Apocalypse of Baruch

Prologue.
¹ A narrative and revelation of Baruch, concerning those ineffable things which he saw by command of God. Bless Thou, O Lord.
² A revelation of Baruch, who stood upon the river Gel weeping over the captivity of ³ Jerusalem, when also Abimelech was preserved by the hand of God, at the farm of Agrippa. And he was sitting thus at the beautiful gates, where the Holy of holies lay.

1

¹ Verily I Baruch was weeping in my mind and sorrowing on account of the people, and that ² Nebuchadnezzar the king was permitted by God to destroy His city, saying: Lord, why didst Thou set on fire Thy vineyard, and lay it waste? Why didst Thou do this? And why, Lord, didst Thou not requite us with another chastisement, but didst deliver us to nations such as these, so that they ³ reproach us and say, Where is their God? And behold as I was weeping and saying such things, I saw an angel of the Lord coming and saying to me: Understand, O man, greatly beloved, and trouble not thyself so greatly concerning the salvation of Jerusalem, for thus saith the Lord God, ⁴ the Almighty. For He sent me before thee, to make known and to show to thee all (the things) of God. ⁵ For thy prayer was heard before Him, and entered into the ears of the Lord God. ⁶ And when he had said these things to me, I was silent. And the angel said to me: Cease to provoke ⁷ God, and I will show thee other mysteries, greater than these. And I Baruch said, As the Lord God liveth, if thou wilt show me, and I hear a word of thine, I will not continue to speak any longer. ⁸ God shall add to my judgement in the day of judgement, if I speak hereafter. And the angel of the powers said to me, Come, and I will show thee the mysteries of God.

The First Heaven.

2

¹ And he took me and led me where the firmament has been set fast, and where there was a river which no one can cross, nor any strange breeze of all those which God created. And he took me and led me to the first heaven, and showed me a door of great size. And he said to me, Let us enter ³ through it, and we entered as though borne on wings, a distance of about thirty days' journey. And he showed me within the heaven a plain ; and there were men dwelling thereon, with the faces of ⁴ oxen, and the horns of stags and the feet of goats, and the haunches of lambs. And I Baruch asked the angel, Make known to me, I pray thee, what is the thickness of the heaven in which we journeyed, ⁵ or what is its extent, or what is the plain, in order that I may also tell the sons of men? And the angel whose name is Phamael said to me: This door which thou seest is the door of heaven, and as great as is the distance from earth to heaven, so great also is its thickness; and again as great as is the distance (from North to South, so great) is the length of the plain which thou didst see. And again the angel of the powers said to me, Come, and I will show thee greater mysteries. ⁶ But I said, I pray thee show me what are these men. ⁷ And he said to me, These are they who built the tower of strife against God, and the Lord banished them.

The Second Heaven.

3

¹ And the angel of the Lord took me and led me to a second heaven. And he showed me there ² also a door like the first and said, Let us enter through it. And we entered, being borne on wings ³ a distance of about sixty days' journey. And he showed me there also a plain, and it was full of ⁴ men, whose appearance was like that of dogs, and whose feet were like those of stags. And I asked ⁵ the angel: I pray thee, Lord, say to me who are these. And he said, These are they who gave counsel to build the tower, for they whom thou seest drove forth multitudes of both men and women, to make bricks; among whom, a woman making bricks was not allowed to be released in the hour of child-birth, but brought forth while she was making bricks, and carried her child in her apron, and ⁶ continued to make bricks. And the Lord appeared to them and confused their speech, when they ⁷ had built the tower to the height of four hundred and sixty-three cubits. And they took a gimlet, and sought to pierce the heaven, saying, Let us see (whether) the heaven is made of clay, or of ⁸ brass, or of iron. When God saw this He did not permit them, but smote them with blindness and confusion of speech, and rendered them as thou seest.

The Third Heaven.

4

¹ And I Baruch said, Behold, Lord, Thou didst show me great and wonderful things; and now ² show me all things for the sake of the Lord. And the angel said to me, Come, let us proceed. (And I proceeded) with the angel from that place about one hundred and eighty-five days' ³ journey. And he showed me a plain and a serpent, which appeared to be two hundred plethra in length. ⁴ And he showed me Hades, and its appearance was dark

and abominable. And I said, [5] Who is this dragon, and who is this monster around him? And the angel said, The dragon is he [6] who eats the bodies of those who spend their life wickedly, and he is nourished by them. And this is Hades, which itself also closely resembles him, in that it also drinks about a cubit from [7] the sea, which does not sink at all. Baruch said, And how (does this happen)? And the angel said, Hearken, the Lord God made three hundred and sixty rivers, of which the chief of [8] all are Alphias, Abyrus, and the Gericus; and because of these the sea does not sink. And I said, I pray thee show me which is the tree which led Adam astray. And the angel said to me, It is the vine, which the angel Sammael planted, whereat the Lord God was angry, and He cursed him and his plant, while also on this account He did not permit Adam to touch it, and therefore [9] the devil being envious deceived him through his vine. [And I Baruch said, Since also the vine has been the cause of such great evil, and is under judgment of the curse of God, and was the [10] destruction of the first created, how is it now so useful? And the angel said, Thou askest aright. When God caused the deluge upon earth, and destroyed all flesh, and four hundred and nine thousand giants, and the water rose fifteen cubits above the highest mountains, then the water entered into paradise and destroyed every flower; but it removed wholly without the bounds the shoot [11] of the vine and cast it outside. And when the earth appeared out of the water, and Noah came out [12] of the ark, he began to plant of the plants which he found. But he found also the shoot of the vine; and he took it, and was reasoning in himself, What then is it? And I came and spake to [13] him the things concerning it. And he said, Shall I plant it, or what shall I do? Since Adam was destroyed because of it, let me not also meet with the anger of God because of it. And saying [14] these things he prayed that God would reveal to him what he should do concerning it. And when he had completed the prayer which lasted forty days, and having besought many things and wept, [15] he said: Lord, I entreat thee to reveal to me what I shall do concerning this plant. But God sent his angel Sarasael, and said to him, Arise, Noah, and plant the shoot of the vine, for thus saith the Lord: Its bitterness shall be changed into sweetness, and its curse shall become a blessing, and that which is produced from it shall become the blood of God; and as through it the human race obtained condemnation, so again through Jesus Christ the Immanuel will they receive in Him the [16] upward calling, and the entry into paradise]. Know therefore, [0] Baruch, that as Adam through this very tree obtained condemnation, and was divested of the glory of God, so also the men who now drink insatiably the wine which is begotten of it, transgress worse than Adam, and are far from the [17] glory of God, and are surrendering themselves to the eternal fire. For (no) good comes through it. For those who drink it to surfeit do these things: neither does a brother pity his brother, nor a father his son, nor children their parents, but from the drinking of wine come all evils, such as murders, adulteries, fornications, perjuries, thefts, and such like. And nothing good is established by it.

5

[1] And I Baruch said to the angel, [2] Let me ask thee one thing, Lord. Since thou didst say to me [3] that the dragon drinks one cubit out of the sea, say to me also, how great is his belly? And the angel said, His belly is Hades; and as far as a plummet is thrown (by) three hundred men, so great is his belly. Come, then, that I may show thee also greater works than these.

6

[1] And he took me and led me where the sun goes forth; [2] and he showed me a chariot and four, under which burnt a fire, and in the chariot was sitting a man, wearing a crown of fire, (and) the chariot (was) drawn by forty angels. And behold a bird circling before the sun, about nine [3] cubits away. And I said to the angel, What is this bird? And he said to me, This is the [4], [5] guardian of the earth. And I said, Lord, how is he the guardian of the earth? Teach me. And the angel said to me, This bird flies alongside of the sun, and expanding his wings receives its fiery [6] rays. For if he were not receiving them, the human race would not be preserved, nor any other [7] living creature. But God appointed this bird thereto. And he expanded his wings, and I saw on his right wing very large letters, as large as the space of a threshing-floor, the size of about four [8] thousand modii; and the letters were of gold. And the angel said to me, Read them. And I read [9] and they ran thus: Neither earth nor heaven bring me forth, but wings of fire bring me forth. And I said, Lord, what is this bird, and what is his name? And the angel said to me, His name is called [11] Phoenix. (And I said), And what does he eat? And he said to me, The manna of heaven and [12] the dew of earth. And I said, Does the bird excrete? And he said to me, He excretes a worm, and the excrement of the worm is cinnamon, which kings and princes use. But wait and thou shalt [13] see the glory of God. And while he was conversing with me, there was as a thunder-clap, and the place was shaken on which we were standing. And I asked the angel, My Lord, what is this sound? And the angel said to me, Even now the angels are opening the three hundred and sixty-five gates [14] of heaven, and the light is being separated from the darkness. And a voice came which said, Light [15] giver, give to the world radiance. And when I heard the noise of the bird, I said, Lord, what is this [16] noise? And he said, This is the bird who awakens from slumber the cocks upon earth. For as men do through the mouth, so also does the cock signify to those in the world, in his own speech. For the sun is made ready by the angels, and the cock crows.

7

[1] And I said, And where does the sun begin its labors, after the cock crows? [2] And the angel said to me, Listen, Baruch: All things whatsoever I showed thee are in the first and second heaven, and in the third heaven the sun passes through and gives light to the world. But wait, and thou [3] shalt see the glory of God. And while I was conversing with him, I saw the bird, and he appeared [4] in front, and grew less and less, and at length returned to his full size. And behind him I saw the shining sun, and the angels which draw it, and a crown upon its bead, the sight of which we were [5] not able to gaze Upon, and behold. And as soon as the sun shone, the Phoenix also stretched out his wings. But I, when I beheld such great glory, was brought low with great fear, and I fled and [6] hid in the wings of the angel. And the angel said to me, Fear not, Baruch, but wait and thou shalt also see their setting.

8

[1] And he took me and led me towards the west; and when the time of the, setting came, I saw again the bird coming before it, and as soon as lie came I saw the angels, and they lifted the crown [2], [3] from its head. But the bird stood exhausted and with wings contracted. And beholding these things, I said, Lord, wherefore did they lift the crown from the head of the sun, and wherefore is [4] the bird so exhausted? And the angel said to me, The crown of the sun, when it has run through the day-four angels take it, and bear it up to heaven, and renew it, because it and its rays have been defiled upon earth; moreover it is so renewed each day. And I Baruch said, Lord, and wherefore [5] are its beams defiled upon earth? And the angel said to me, Because it beholds the lawlessness and unrighteousness of men, namely fornications, adulteries, thefts, extortions, idolatries, drunkenness, murders, strife, jealousies, evil-speakings, murmurings, whisperings, divinations, and such like, which are not well-pleasing to God. On account of these things is it defiled, and therefore is it renewed. [6] But thou askest concerning the bird, how it is exhausted. Because by restraining the rays of the sun through the fire and burning heat of the whole day, it is exhausted thereby. For, as we said before, unless his wings were screening the rays of the sun, no living creature would be preserved.

9

[1] And they having retired, the night also fell, and at the same time came the chariot of the moon, along with the stars. [2] And I Baruch said, Lord, show me it also, I beseech thee, how [3] it goes forth, where it departs, and in what form it moves along. And the angel said, Wait' and thou shalt see it also shortly. And on the morrow I also saw it in the form of a woman, and sitting on a wheeled chariot. And there were before it oxen and lambs in the chariot, and a multitude of [4] angels in like manner. And I said, Lord, what are the oxen and the lambs? And he said to me, [5] They also are angels. And again I asked, Why is it that it at one time increases, but at another [6] time decreases? And (he said to me), Listen, [0] Baruch: This which thou seest had been written [7] by God beautiful as no other. And at the transgression of the first Adam, it was near to Sammael when he took the serpent as a garment. And it did not hide itself but increased, and God was [8] angry with it, and afflicted it, and shortened its days. And I said, And how does it not also shine always, but only in the night? And the angel said, Listen: as in the presence of a king, the courtiers cannot speak freely, so the moon and the stars cannot shine in the presence of the sun; for the stars are always suspended, but they are screened by the sun, and the moon, although it is uninjured, is consumed by the heat of the sun.

The Fourth Heaven.

10

[1] And when I had learnt all these things from the archangel, he took and led me into a fourth [2][3] heaven. And I saw a monotonous plain, and in the middle of it a pool of water. And there were in it multitudes of birds of all kinds, but not like those here on earth. But I saw a crane as great as [4] great oxen; and all the birds were great beyond those in the world. And I asked the angel, What [5] is the plain, and what the pool, and what the multitudes of birds around it? And the angel said, Listen, Baruch : The plain which contains in it the pool and other wonders is the place where the [6] souls of the righteous come, when they hold converse, living together in choirs. But the water is [7] that which the clouds receive, and rain upon the earth, and the fruits increase. And I said again to the angel of the Lord, But (what) are these birds? And he said to me, They are those which [8] continually sing praise to the Lord. And I said, Lord, and how do men say

that the water which [9] descends in rain is from the sea? And the angel said, The water which descends in rain-this also is from the sea, and from the waters upon earth; but that which stimulates the fruits is (only) from [10] the latter source. Know therefore henceforth that from this source is what is called the dew of heaven.

The Fifth Heaven.

11

[1] And the angel took me and led me thence to a fifth heaven. And the gate was closed. And I said, Lord, is not this gate-way open that we may enter? And the angel said to me, We cannot enter until Michael comes, who holds the keys of the Kingdom of Heaven; but wait and thou shalt see [3] the glory of God. And there was a great sound, as thunder. And I said, Lord, what is this sound? [4] And he said to me, Even now Michael, the commander of the angels, comes down to receive the [5] prayers of men. And behold a voice came, Let the gates be opened. And they opened them, and [6] there was a roar as of thunder. And Michael came, and the angel who was with me came face to [7] face with him and said, Hail, my commander, and that of all our order. And the commander Michael said, Hail thou also, our brother, and the interpreter of the revelations to those who pass through life [8] virtuously. And having saluted one another thus, they stood still. And I saw the commander Michael said, Hail thou also, our brother, and the interpreter of the revelations to those who pass through life [8] virtuously. And having saluted one another thus, they stood still. And I saw the commander Michael, holding an exceedingly great vessel; its depth was as great as the distance from heaven to [9] earth, and its breadth as great as the distance from north to south. And I said, Lord, what is that which Michael the archangel is holding? And he said to me, This is where the merits of the righteous enter, and such good works as they do, which are escorted before the heavenly God.

12

[1] And as I was conversing with them, behold angels came bearing baskets full of flowers. And [2] they gave them to Michael. And I asked the angel, Lord, who are these, and what are the things [3] brought hither from beside them? And he said to me, These are angels (who) are over the [4], [5] righteous. And the archangel took the baskets, and cast them into the vessel. And the angel [6] said to me, These flowers are the merits of the righteous. And I saw other angels bearing baskets which were (neither) empty-nor full. And they began to lament, and did not venture to draw near, [7] because they had not the prizes complete. And Michael cried and said, Come hither, also, ye [8] angels, bring what ye have brought. And Michael was exceedingly grieved, and the angel who was with me, because they did not fill the vessel.

13

[1] And then came in like manner other angels weeping and bewailing, and saying with fear, Behold how we are overclouded, [0] Lord, for we were delivered to evil men, and we wish to depart from [2] them. And Michael said, Ye cannot depart from them, in order that the enemy may not prevail to [3] the end; but say to me what ye ask. And they said, We pray thee, Michael our commander, transfer us from them, for we cannot abide with wicked and foolish men, for there is nothing good [4] in them, but every kind of unrighteousness and greed. For we do not behold them entering [into Church at all, nor among spiritual fathers, nor] into any good work. But where there is murder, there also are they in the midst, and where are fornications, adulteries, thefts, slanders, perjuries, jealousies, drunkenness, strife, envy, murmurings, whispering, idolatry, divination, and such like, [5] then are they workers of such works, and of others worse. Wherefore we entreat that we may depart from them. And Michael said to the angels, Wait till I learn from the Lord what shall come to pass.

14

[1] And in that very hour Michael departed, and the doors were closed. And there was a sound as [2] thunder. And I asked the angel, What is the sound? And he said to me, Michael is even now presenting the merits of men to God.

15

[1] And in that very hour Michael descended, and the gate was opened; and he brought oil. [2] And as for the angels which brought the baskets which were full, he filled them with oil, saying, Take it away, reward our friends a hundredfold, and those who have laboriously wrought good works. [3] For those who sowed virtuously, also reap virtuously. And he said also to those bringing the half-empty baskets, Come hither ye also; take away the reward according as ye brought, and [4] deliver it to the sons of men. [Then he said also to those who brought the full and to those who brought the half-empty baskets: Go and bless our friends, and say to them that thus saith the Lord, Ye are faithful over a few things, I will set you over many things; enter into the joy of your Lord.]

16

[1] And turning he said also to those who brought nothing: Thus saith the Lord, Be not sad of [2] countenance, and weep not, nor let the sons of men alone. But since they angered me in their works, go and make them envious and angry and provoked against a people that is no people, a [3] people that has no understanding. Further, besides these, send forth the caterpillar and the unwinged locust, and the mildew, and the common locust (and) hail with lightnings and anger, and [4] punish them severely with the sword and with death, and their children with demons. For they did not hearken to my voice, nor did they observe my commandments, nor do them, but were despisers of my commandments, and insolent towards the priests who proclaimed my words to them.

17

[1] And while he yet spake, the door was closed, and we withdrew. [2] And the angel took me and [3] restored me to the place where I was at the beginning. And having come to myself, I gave glory [4] to God, who counted me worthy of such honor. Wherefore do ye also, brethren, who obtained such a revelation, yourselves also glorify God, so that He also may glorify you, now and ever, and to all eternity. Amen.

The Apocalypse of Abraham
The Life and Death of our Father Abraham the Just, written according to the Apocalypse in nice words

1 Our father Abraham lived more than 175 years. In his lifetime he was vigorous, very gentle, compassionate and just towards all, and very hospitable. He dwelt not far from the place called *Dria the Black,* at the cross-road by which all strangers had to pass. He received the wayfarers and entertained them. Rich and poor, kings and princes, boyards and voyevods, all neighbours, the weak and the sick, all were treated with the greatest kindness, for Abraham was good and just, and loving all men, till he attained to extreme old age, and the time and the hour drew nigh when he was to taste the cup of death. **2** Then the Lord called the archangel *Mihail,* and said unto him: Go down, *Mihail,* to my friend Abraham, and remind him of death, for I have promised him to increase his property and to multiply his descendants like the stars of heaven and like the sand of the sea. And I have blessed him. Therefore he is now richer and more just than all in his goodness and hospitality which he displays until his end. **3** And the archangel *Mihail,* who sat before the Lord, went out of His presence and descended to Abraham in *Dria the Black,* And he found our father Abraham near the village with his servants and also other young men. And the archangel approached him. Abraham seeing him, thought he was a soldier, being so modest and fair in his appearance. **4** Then the aged Abraham arose in order to meet the archangel. And the archangel said, "Rejoice, venerable father, the chosen one of the Lord, righteous soul, friend of the Ruler of heaven." And Abraham said to the angel, "Rejoice, oh chief of the hosts (Arhistratig)! Thou, who art greater than any of the children of men, be welcome on my return home. Kindly relate me, oh young man, whence thou comest, and whence it is that thou art so beautiful?" **5** And the Arhistratig replied, "Oh, just man! I come from the Great City, and I am sent by the Great Ruler, to say to His chosen friend, that he should be prepared, because the Ruler calls him." And Abraham replied, " Well! Let us go back to the village."' And the Arhistratig said, "Let us go! " **6** And they went to the nearest village, and sat down to rest. And Abraham said to his servants, "Go to the field, where the horses are, and fetch two that are fit for riding, and get them ready, so that I may mount one, and the stranger the other one." But the Arhistratig said to Abraham, "Let them not bring the horses, because I do not ride on a beast with four legs. Oh, thou righteous soul, let us go on foot to thy pure abode." And Abraham replied, "Let it be so." And they walked from that village to his house. **7** On the way there grew a lofty and mighty cypress. And the tree exclaimed, by the will of God. with a loud voice of man: "Holy one! Holy one! Holy one! The Lord God calls thee!" And Abraham held his peace, and replied not, for he thought the Arhistratig had not heard the voice of the tree. **8** Then they approached the courtyard, and sat down. Isaac, the son of Abraham, saw the face of the angel, and said to his mother Sarah, "Look at the man who is sitting with my father, he does not appear to me to be born from a human being." And Isaac ran to the angel, and bowed down before him. And the angel blessed him, and said, "May God give thee what he has given to thy father and thy mother!" **9** And Abraham said to Isaac, "Take the basin and pour in some water, so that we may wash the feet of this stranger, who comes from afar to us, and who is weary." And Isaac ran to the well and poured water into the basin and brought it. And Abraham went to wash the feet of the angel, and Abraham sighed and wept on account of this stranger. And Isaac seeing his father weep, wept also, and his tears ran down. And the angel seeing them both weeping, wept with them, and his tears fell down into the basin. And these tears turned into precious stones. And when Abraham beheld this miracle, he took away the jewels and hid the secret in his heart. **10** And Abraham said to his beloved son, "Go into the room and get ready two beds, one for me and the other for the stranger, because he is a wayfarer; and prepare everything well and carefully, and put candles in the candlesticks, and prepare the table, and light the incense-burner, and bring sweet smelling herbs of the paradise and put them on the floor, so that they may scent the place, and light seven candles, and we will sit down and rejoice with the stranger, who is greater than any human being on the earth, and mightier than kings." And Isaac prepared everything carefully, according to the directions of his father. And Abraham went with the angel in the room, where the beds were ready, and they both sat down, one on one bed and one on the other, and between them stood the table with food. **11** And the Arhistratig arose and went out to take the air, and he ascended to heaven, and came before the Lord, and said to the Lord God, "Lord! Lord! know that Abraham is very powerful, so that I cannot mention to him of death, for I have never seen a man like unto him on the earth, just, compassionate, and avoiding all evil." **12** And the Lord spake to the Arhistratig, "Go to my friend Abraham, and eat of all that which will be put on the table; and I will send My Spirit unto his son Isaac, and I will show him the approach of his father's death, so that he may see all in a dream." **13** And the Arhistratig said, "The incorporeal beings of heaven do not eat, neither do they drink, and he has spread for me a table with all the good things of the earth; and now, O Lord, what shall I do? How can I become different, as we shall be all at one table?" **14** And the Lord answered him, "Go to My friend Abraham, and do not trouble thyself, for I will send spirits, who shall cause the food to disappear from thy hands and from thy mouth; all that is on the table shall disappear. And rejoice them with him. But thou shalt interpret Isaac's dreams unto him, so that Abraham may know the hour of his death. For he has numberless properties and lands and houses, because I have blessed him, and I have increased his possessions like the sands of the sea and like the stars in heaven." **15** Thereon the Artistratig descended to Abraham's table, and they sat down. And Isaac had provided the supper. And Abraham said his prayer, as it was his custom. And after the meal they arose, said a prayer, and sat down each one on his bed. **16** And Isaac said to his father, "I should like to sleep here also, because I love with all my heart to listen to the words of this stranger." But Abraham replied to his son, "No, my son! go thou to thy bed and rest, so that we may not inconvenience this stranger." Then Isaac received his father's blessing, and went to his bed to rest. **17** And the Lord showed Isaac in a dream the approaching death of his father. And after the third hour of the night Isaac awoke from his sleep, and arose from his bed, and ran quickly to his father, where he slept with the Arhistratig, and called aloud, "My father Abraham, open the door quickly, so that I may enter and cling to thy neck, and kiss thee before they take thee away from me." **18** And Abraham got up and opened the door. And Isaac entered, and he embraced his father, and wept aloud; and Abraham wept also; and the Arhistratig seeing this, wept with them. And Abraham said to Isaac, "My dear child, tell me truly what has appeared to thee, so that thou camest so frightened to me?" **19** And Isaac wept, and said to his father, 'I beheld the sun and the moon, with luminous and far-stretching rays, resting on my head, and seeing this I was glad; when suddenly the heaven opened and a luminous man descended from heaven. And he was brilliant. And he removed the sun from my head and ascended to heaven. And shortly afterwards, while I was still sad, I saw the luminous man again descending from heaven, and he removed the moon from my head. And I wept, and I said to him, "do not take from me my pride, but have pity on me and listen to me, for thou hast taken the sun from me. Do not also take away the moon!' And he replied, 'Let them go, because the Lord of heaven wishes that I should bring them to him.' And they left their rays upon me." **20** And the Arhistratig said to them, "Listen to me, oh Abraham the just! Thou art the sun, seen by thy son Isaac his father; and the luminous man, descending from heaven, will take away thy soul. And know, oh just Abraham! that thou wilt soon leave this world to go to the Lord." And Abraham replied, "Oh wonderful! I fear thou art the man who will take away my soul!" And the Arhistratig said to Abraham, "I am the angel *Mihail,* the greatest of the angels standing before the Lord; and I announce to thee the news of thy death. And thou wilt come to Him, according to thy covenant." And Abraham replied, "Now I understand that thou art he who will receive my soul—but I will not yield to thee!" **21** After these words of Abraham, the Arhistratig disappeared; for he went up to heaven and stood before the Lord, and related to him all that he had seen and heard in the house of Abraham, and how Abraham had said, "I will not yield to thee." **22** And the Lord replied to his Arhistratig, "Go to my friend Abraham, and say to him as follows: I am the Lord his God, who brought him out and led him to the Promised Land; and I have blessed him, so that his descendants shall become as numerous as the sands of the sea, and as the stars in the heaven. And say to him, How hast thou dared to oppose my Arhistratig Mihail, by saying that thou wouldst not follow him? "Does he not know that from the time of Adam and Eve all have died? That neither the kings, nor the forefathers have escaped death? because no one is immortal; but all have died and have gone down into hell. But to him I did not send either death, or sickness, or the scythe of death, which should mow him down; but I sent to him my Arhistratig. with a request, so that he might know my decision and put his house and lands in order. But why did he oppose my Arhistratig Mihail, saying that he would not follow? Does he not know, that I will send the angel of death, whose presence he could not endure?" **23** After receiving the command of the Lord, the Arhistratig descended to Abraham, fell at his feet, and repeated to him all that he had heard from the Lord. And Abraham the just said amidst many tears, "I entreat thee, Arhistratig of the heavenly powers, because thou had honoured me, a sinner, grant me one request. For the Lord God has always given me the things for which I have prayed, and has always fulfilled my wishes. And I know that I shall not escape death, but I shall certainly die. Know, therefore, that I expect that thou wilt fulfil this my request: I should like to see now, whilst still in the flesh, all the peoples and their deeds; then I will yield myself entirely." **24** And the Arhistratig ascended once more to heaven, and placed himself before the Lord, and told him all about Abraham. And the Lord replied to the Arhistratig, "Place Abraham the just in the chariot of the cherubim, and carry him to heaven." And the Arhistratig descended and took the just Abraham into the clouds and surrounded him with sixty angels. ²⁵ And Abraham walked on the clouds, and he beheld another chariot behind him, and also some who walked (?). And in another part he saw people who were suffering, and much wrong-doing. And he said, "Oh Lord! command that the earth may open and swallow them." And in another direction he saw people plundering and stealing, and despoiling the stranger. And he exclaimed, "Oh Lord I command that fire shall come down from heaven and destroy them." And fire came from heaven and consumed them. ²⁶ And instantly" there a voice came from heaven to the angels, and a thunder-clap reached the Arhistratig and he heard the words: "Turn round the chariot and depart with Abraham so that he may not see the people any more; for if he sees them living in sin he will destroy them all to the very last," because Abraham could not endure those who did evil. And the Lord continued: "I have created the world, and I do not wish that any human being shall be destroyed, for I do not desire the death of the wicked, but that he should repent and live. Lead the just Abraham to the first gate of heaven, so that he may see the last judgment, and that he also may repent even more than the sinners." ²⁷ And the Arhistratig turned round Abraham's chariot, and brought him to the first gate of heaven. And Abraham beheld two paths, one narrow and difficult to pursue, and the other wide and extended. And on the narrow path he saw a man sitting on a golden chair, and his face was terrible like unto God. And he saw many souls pursued by angels on the broad way, and but few souls conducted by the angels on the narrow path. And the marvellous man, when he saw all the wounded and sick souls on the wide way, tore out the hair of his head and of his beard, and he cast himself from his golden chair unto the ground and wept. But when he saw many souls in the narrow path, he rose and sat on his golden chair in joy. ²⁸ And Abraham asked the Arhistratig: "Lord! who is this marvellous man in such splendour? Sometimes he weeps, and sometimes he rejoices." The Arhistratig answered: "This is Adam, who was the first man created to adorn the world, for all are descended from him. And when he sees many souls traversing the narrow path he rejoices, because that is the entrance to heaven, by which the just go to paradise. And when he sees many souls going on the wide way he weeps and tears his hair, because that is the path of the sinners, by which they go to hell. In seven thousand years only one soul will be saved." ²⁹ And while they were speaking, two angels brought innumerable souls, and struck them with a whip of fire; and one poor soul was supported by their hands and led on the narrow way. ³⁰ And he beheld again at the doorway a golden chair, shining like fire; and on it there sat a man in the form of the Son of God. And in front of him stood a table of precious stones and pearls; and upon the table there lay a Bible, that is a big book of twelve yards in length, and eight yards in width. And there were two angels holding paper, ink, and pens. And at the head of the table there sat a luminous angel holding a scale in his hand; and at his left hand stood an angel of fire, who held in his hand a paper, and on it were inscribed the temptations and sins. And that man who sat there condemned or liberated the souls. And of the two angels who stood to the right and left, the one on the right wrote the virtues, and the one on the left hand wrote down the sins; and the one at the head of the table weighed the souls; and the angel of fire examined the souls. ³¹ And Abraham asked the Arhistratig: " What is it that I see? " And the angel replied, "That, which thou seest, oh just Abraham, is the judgment in the other world." And he saw the soul of a man brought before the judge by an angel. And the angel said to the judge, "Open the book and see the record of his sins and of his virtues .... and erase them, for he is neither to be condemned nor to be saved; therefore place him in the middle." ³² And Abraham said, "My lord! who are these judges, and these luminous angels?" And the Arhistratig replied, "Listen, oh just Abraham I He who sits in the chair and judges, is *Abel,* the son of Adam. He judges the righteous and the sinners. For the Lord hath said, that He will not judge mankind, but that they shall judge each other. And to him (Abel) he has given the power to judge men, till the last judgment. Then the Son of God will judge perfectly and finally and for ever; and no other will be able to judge. Because men are descended from Adam, they must be first judged by a son of Adam; but at the second resurrection they will all be judged by the twelve Apostles; but at the third resurrection, our Lord and Saviour will judge them. For at the third time, at that terrible judgment, all will be ended. As it is written, 'By three witnesses shall the judgment be fulfilled.' And of the two angels the angel on the left records the evil deeds, and the angel on the right records the good actions; and he shines like the sun." ³³ And Abraham asked his Arhistratig Mihail, "My lord! what is to be done with the soul which the angel brought in his hand, and which was placed in the middle?" The angel answered, "The judge has found that his good and his bad deeds shall be erased, and he is neither condemned nor saved, until the Lord, the Judge, shall come." ³⁴ And Abraham asked, "What is wanting to this soul that it should be saved? " The angel answered, "If he had performed one more good deed, he would had been saved." And Abraham said, "We will say a prayer for this soul perhaps God will save it!" And the Arhistratig said "Amen! so shall it be!" And they both prayed, and God listened to them and saved this soul. And Abraham said "I pray thee, Arhistratig, tell me where is the soul?" And the angel answered, "It hath been saved, in answer to the prayer of thy holiness! " ³⁵ And Abraham said, "Oh, Arhistratig, let us entreat God for the sins of those whom I cursed before! " And the Arhistratig listened to him, and they prayed for a long time, until there came a voice from heaven, saying, "Abraham! I have heard thy prayer for those whom it appeared to thee that I destroyed. But I have saved them, and have preserved them alive. At the last judgment I will separate them. For, even if I destroy some on earth, I do not deliver any one entirely to death; I wish that they may repent and live." ³⁶ And the Lord said to the Arhistratig, "My servant! Turn the chariot, and take him back to his dwelling, for the end of his life is approaching, and he must put his house in order." And the Arhistratig turned the chariot of clouds and brought him back to his house. And Abraham went and sat on his bed. ³⁷ And Sarah, the wife of Abraham, came and knelt at the angel's feet, and kissed them, and wept and thanked him, saying, "I thank thee, that thou hast brought back my lord, for it seemed to me, that he had withdrawn himself from our midst." And Isaac came and embraced his father; the servants also came and surrounded Abraham, thanking and blessing God. ³⁸ And the Arhistratig said to Abraham, "Set thy house in order, and settle all with thy servants which concerns them; for thy last day draws near, when thy soul will depart from thy body; because the Lord has ordered it so, and He is just." And Abraham replied to the Arhistratig, "I will not obey thee!" ³⁹ When the Arhistratig heard these words, he ascended at once to heaven, stood before the Lord, and said, "Lord! Sustainer of all! I fulfilled Thy will, and Thy friend Abraham has seen all the earth and the heaven, and whilst still living he beheld the Judgment from the chariot of clouds, and yet he says that he will not obey me. I would willingly give him time, because he has done so much good on the earth that no man is like unto him; he is like an immortal king, and he is worthy of immortality. Oh Lord! what dost Thou command?" ⁴⁰ And the Lord said, "Call Death hither!" And the Arhistratig Mihail went to Death, and said, "Go, for the Immortal King calls thee." "When Death heard this, he trembled and ground his teeth, and went to the Mighty Lord, and stood before Him with much fear and trembling. ⁴¹ And the Lord said unto Death, "Go and disguise thy fearful face and thy countenance, and clothe thyself with gentleness and beauty and splendour; and go to My friend Abraham and receive his soul and bring it to Me; and thou shalt not frighten him, but take it away in all tenderness." When Death heard this, he went away from the presence of the Lord, and changed his fearful countenance, and became gentle and luminous, and of great beauty. ⁴² And Abraham sat under a sweet smelling tree, resting his hand on his knees, awaiting hopefully the return of the Arhistratig Mihail. And he noticed the approach of a worthy and fine-looking man, and it appeared to him that it was the Arhistratig. And the angel beheld him, and bowed to him, and said, "Rejoice, venerable Abraham, just soul, friend of the Lord, like unto the angels!" And Abraham replied, "Rejoice, shining light, luminous man! From whence has this resplendent man come? " ⁴³ And Death answered, "I tell thee the truth. I am the poison of death!" And Abraham said, "Art thou the cup which poisonest? And art thou he who takest away the life of man and the beauty of woman? Art thou the poison of death?" And Death replied, "I am the poisoned cup of death; and I speak unto thee the truth, for thus has the Lord commanded me." ⁴⁴ And Abraham said, "Why hast thou come hither? " Death replied, "I have come for thy righteous soul." And Abraham said, "I understand! But, I do not wish to die!" And Death was silent, for he would not give any further answer. ⁴⁵ And Abraham arose and went in and seated himself on his bed. And Death seated himself also on the bed, at the feet of Abraham. And Abraham said, "Depart from me, for I would rest." And Death replied, "I shall not depart from thee until I have taken thy soul." And Abraham said, "Fulfil my wish: show me the bitterness of thy poison when thou takest the souls of mankind." And Death replied, "Thou could'st not in any case bear to see my fearful countenance." And Abraham said, "I will see it; in the Name of the Lord, for He is with me." ⁴⁶ Then Death cast off all his beauty, and he assumed a fierce and murderous and all-consuming expression, like unto the wild beasts; and (he assumed) a dragon's head with seven faces, and his countenance was as seventeen fiery faces; and he became like unto a fierce and dreadful lion and like a poisonous snake, and he had a mane like a lion, and he was like a thunderbolt, and like the waves of the sea, and like the stream of a rapid torrent, and like a very wild dragon with three wings. And from the fear of Death, seven thousand boys and girls died, and even Abraham the just was in danger of his life. ⁴⁷ All this Abraham saw, and he said to Death, "I pray thee, poisonous Death, hide thy fearful countenance, and appear in thy former beauty." And Death resumed his former beauty. And Abraham said, "What hast thou done to kill so many souls? Hast thou been sent to kill them also? " And Death replied, "No, my lord! I was sent only on thy account." ⁴⁸ Abraham said, "Indeed? How could'st thou kill them when the Lord did not command thee to do it?" And Death answered, "Believe me, my lord, it is a wonder thou did'st not die with them. But I swear to thee in very truth, that I have in this hour the power of killing thee, and thy strength, will not avail thee. Therefore put in order all that thou wishest to arrange." ⁴⁹ And Abraham said, "I acknowledge now that the weakness of death is upon me. and my soul grows faint. But, I pray thee, oh poisonous Death to tell me, why hast thou killed so many boys and girls? Let us now both entreat the Lord to restore these boys and girls to life, and perchance He may listen to us." And Death said, "Amen! so may it be." And Abraham arose and threw himself on the ground on his face, and Death also cast himself on the ground; and they both prayed to God for a long time. And God sent the spirit of life unto the dead, and they were restored to life again. ⁵⁰ And Abraham returned thanks unto God, and went to his bed. Death also went to the bed. And Abraham said to Death, "Depart from me; I would rest, for soon thou wilt take away my soul." And Death replied, "I will not leave thee, until I shall have taken thy soul." And the patriarch Abraham became cross with him, and spoke angry words, and said unto Death, "Who has sent thee to me? Dost thou really believe that I will die?" And Death repeated again, "I will not follow thee." ⁵¹ And Death said, "Listen to me, oh, just Abraham! In seven epochs I shall destroy the whole world, and I shall cause all human beings and kings to go down into the earth, and to descend into hell; the kings, princes, rich and poor, old and young. Therefore I have shown thee the seven heads of a lion and the fiery faces, so that thou mayest arrange thy property and leave everything in order." ⁵² And Abraham said, "Depart from me, for I will see, if having the favour of God, I must still die, as thou doest demand of me!" And Death said, "I tell thee the truth, by God, there are seventy-two kinds of death, and I mow whomsoever I like; put therefore away thy doubts, oh just Abraham, and obey me, according to the will of the Universal Judge!" And Abraham said, "Depart from me for a while, so that I may rest for a time on my bed; for I have lost, all strength since mine eyes have beheld thee; all parts of my body are weak, my head is heavy as lead, and my spirit is trembling within me, so that I can no longer see thy face." ⁵³ And Isaac came and cried bitterly; and all the servants gathered him and cried bitterly. And Abraham arose and set free all his servants and his maids. And he called his beloved son Isaac, and kissed him tenderly, and blessed him with the father's blessing. And he blessed his wife Sarah, and he took leave of her and of all. ⁵⁴ And the hour of his death approached; and Death said to Abraham, "Come and kiss my right hand, so that thou mayest revive for a while." And Abraham was deceived, and kissed the hand of Death. But Death, when he gave him his hand, gave him also the cup with the poison of death. And at the same moment the Arhistratig Mihail and numberless angels came and received in their holy hands the pure and holy soul, and brought into the holy hands of the Lord's. ⁵⁵ But the body was enveloped in clean and pure linen, and they sprinkled him with heavenly perfumes, and buried him with many heavenly songs. And all wept and lamented greatly. Isaac his beloved son, and Sarah, the mother of Isaac, and his servants, and his maids, and all his neighbours lamented for him, because they had lost their good and blessed father Abraham. ⁵⁶ And they buried him in "Dria the black," with many hymns and with great honour. And they heard the voice of the Lord saying from heaven, "Take My friend Abraham and lead him into the paradise of joy, the abode of all the righteous; and to the eternal life, which is everlasting and without end."

The Apocalyse of Daniel
The Fourteenth Vision of Daniel

¹ In the third year of Cyrus the Persian, who captured Babylon, a word was revealed to Daniel, whose name is Balthasar. This word is true. I, Daniel, fasted for twenty-one days until the evening; I had not eaten meat, I had not drunk wine, I had not anointed myself with oil. ² It happened, as I was on the bank of the Tigris, that this was revealed to me; I looked; and the four winds of heaven were blowing towards the great sea. ³ I saw four very frightening animals rising from the river. ⁴ The first animal resembled a bear, having wings like an eagle. I saw as I waited that it flew with its wings; a human heart was given to it and it stood on its feet. ⁵ The second animal resembled human flesh; excessively horrible, it stood to one side. I watched until three quarters of its face were broken and the fourth quarter remained firm. I looked at it until its teeth were torn out of its mouth. ⁶ The third animal resembled a panther; it had wings, four heads, devouring with speed and scattering what remained. ⁷ The fourth animal which I saw resembled a lion, an animal much more terrible than all the animals which had been before it. Power and great force were given to it; its hands were of iron, its nails of bronze; devouring, chewing, crushing with its feet what remained. I saw ten horns which came out from its head: I saw also another small horn, which came out beside these ten horns. And great power and a remarkable form were given to it. I saw four different (horns) which arose on its left, then four others which arose after all these; each of them was different from the others, and, between them all, they made nineteen (horns). ⁸ And I heard a voice which said to me: "Daniel, do you understand what you saw?" But I said: "How can I understand, if nobody guides me?". ⁹ I looked and I saw an angel of God standing on my right. Its wings were extremely bright. I was afraid and I fell to the ground. The angel seized me, made me stand on my feet and said to me: "Stand on your feet, so that I can proclaim to you what will happen in the last days. ¹⁰ The four animals which you saw are four kingdoms. The animal that you saw, similar to a bear, is the king of Persia. He will possess the land for five hundred fifty-five (555) years. Then he will perish with his kingdom; he will not be powerful for always. ¹¹ The second animal that you saw, similar to human flesh, it is the king of the Romans: he will seize the land as if by iron; he will extend himself over it; he will dominate by his armies as far as the land of the Ethiopians, and he will reign over it nine hundred and eleven years. But he will not possess the capital of the kingdom, until many days are completed. ¹² The third animal which you saw, who resembled a panther, it is the king of the Greeks. He will reign over it for a thousand years and thirty days; but his reign will not last. ¹³ The fourth animal which you saw, who resembles a lion, is the king of the sons of Ishmael. He will reign for a long time over the land and will be very powerful during many days. This realm will be of the race of Abraham and of the slave of Sara, the wife of Abraham. All the cities of the Persians, the Romans and the Greeks will be destroyed; nineteen kings of this race among the sons of Ishmael will reign over the land; they will reign until the time of their end. ¹⁴ The tenth of their kings will be like a prophet, the number of his name is 399. He will practise justice, will give bread to the famished, clothing to those which are naked. He will free those who are slaves. His mercy will spread over the whole land, and his justice up to heaven. ¹⁵ The eleventh of their kings will practise iniquity over all the land; he will ruin the old works. He will persecute those which are on the land, so that nobody is found who lives there or remains there. All men will groan for forty-two months. If the God of heaven treats him with indulgence, his reign will last forty months. ¹⁶ The reign of the twelfth of their kings will consequently be strengthened by the judgements of his mouth. He will carry out malicious actions in the land, so much that men will be astonished by what he did. There will be many wars during his reign. At the end of the time, a king will thoroughly disturb the kingdom of Ismaelites for one hundred and forty-seven years. In the hundred and tenth year of his reign, he will have a war with the Ethiopians. The Ismaelites will reign over them, until they have despoiled the city of the kingdom, which is Souban. They will send messengers to ask for peace; they will give them money and gold in great quantity, a tribute will be paid to them in Ethiopia. ¹⁷ The thirteenth of them will not live in this kingdom at all, and they will not fear him. His reign will be of a few days. ¹⁸ The fourteenth of their kings will receive gold and money in great quantity and he will judge the land with equity. He will engage in war with Lower Egypt, so that Egypt is in sorrow and groaning. The Ethiopians will not be subjected at all to him, they will not pay him tribute. In those days there will be war in the land of the Romans. The Ethiopians will make war with the southernmost regions of Egypt; they will plunder the boroughs and all the cities of lower Egypt, until they arrive at the town of Cleopatra that she built herself in Upper Egypt, which city is Schmoun. After these things, the king of Syria will learn of it, he will fear the end because the war is approaching him. In

the end, his reign will be established and he will enjoy a happy existence. ¹⁹ Then a child will arise among the Israelites will rise; this is the fifteenth of their kings. In his heart, he will be hard like iron; he will extend his sword to the Romans; his right hand will be on the Ethiopians. His face will be double (=cheating) and his language will be double (=crafty). During the days of his reign, there will be a great disorder over all the land, and his word will be violent like fire. The Ethiopians will bring gifts of gold to him, of silver, of pearls, and he will impose his work on everyone. He will make several nations captive in order to conscript them; throughout all his reign, there will not be enough bread; there will be no peace as long as he will reign, and in his time carnage will be frequent. ²⁰ As for the sixteenth of their kings, there will be no war in his kingdom, and he himself will not fight with anybody, and he will be granted a long time (which he will spend) in peace, and his reign will pass in uprightness. ²¹ As regards the seventeenth of their kings, a war will break out between him and his nation; it is him whose name makes the number 666. He will elevate from his nation a man who will make war for him; he will pursue him as far as Egypt with the riches of its kingdom. He will neglect his nation and its great people and will scatter riches in public places and highways. While moving in lower Egypt with his riches, he will go into Upper Egypt on the side of the North, with the intention to plunder Souban, the city of the Ethiopians, with the remainder of its riches. But a man of his own nation will kill him in the southernmost regions of lower Egypt, and will take what remains to him of his riches. ²² The eighteenth of their kings, at the beginning of his reign, will work great evils, for one thousand, two hundred and sixty days. He will wage war in the western countries, and he will gain the victory until the day of his death. ²³ Then among them a child will arise, who is his son. This one is the nineteenth of their kings. He will be the child of a double race, because his father is an Israelite, his mother is Roman. There will be war in Egypt and Syria for twenty-one months. Their swords will fall on themselves in this war. This is the king whose name makes the number 666; he will be called by these three names: Mametios, Khalle and Sarapidos. Being a child, he will reign in order to do much evil. He will order all the Jews which are in all places to gather in Jerusalem. All the land will be disturbed during his reign, until any man can be sold for a single dinar. He is without decency and he will forget the fear of God. He will not remember the law of Ishmael his father, nor of his mother, who is Roman; he will be arrogant, continuously drunk; he will make a great number of those who eat at his table die by poisoned beverages, and in these days there will be great devastations. He will free Syria and the territory of Jews, and will torment the East and Egypt. He will establish carriers of letters in Egypt. Two and three times in only one year, the East will be against itself in this reign which will be the nineteeth. He will seek neither justice, nor truth, but he will seek gold all the time. He will establish managers in the regions of Africa, and a great quantity of soldiers. War will break out between him and them; they will destroy the multitude which is with him; he will be established in the regions of Africa, with what will remain of his troops, for several years, and he will not overcome it (Africa). Then a foreign nation will rise against him; it is called Pitourgos (the Turk); it will make war on him. Sarapidos will dominate over many Romans, over Pentapolis, over the Medes; from them all he will take a tribute, will command their cities and will plunder the city which he built, and regions that his father had gathered. The Turk will prepare for war to remove the kingdom from the hands of Sarapidos; hitherto Sarapidos remained at home. He was looking for spoils, because Sarapidos had great riches before his eyes, gold, silver, all kinds of precious stones, and desirable utensils of every kind. But it will be proclaimed to him that the Turk has made himself Master of all Syria and his borders, and he will go out in great disorder with all his troops; he will leave all the water-skins, will not carry anything with him; but he will have a heart of an animal, reflecting and knowing not what to do. Then, when he flees, going up Egypt, the Turk will precede him with his troops. They will both land with their troops, they will fight until blood runs in floods. The Turk is of Roman race. There will be war at Eschmoun the city, until the water of the river is changed into blood because of the great quantity of those wounded to death. No-one will be able to drink the water any more. Many men will die by the sword, uncountable. Those who remain will plunder their own country from where they left. The Turk will make Sarapidos perish, in order to remove his kingdom from him, for fear he will not obtain the kingdom of the Ishmaelites; but this is here the end of their number. ²⁴ Then the king of the Romans will rise up against them, he will destroy them by the edge of the sword in the middle of the Ishmaelites in the territory of their fathers in the desert. The Ishmaelites will be governed always by the Romans; the Romans will dominate over Egypt for forty years. ²⁵ Then two nations will rise, by the name of Gog and Magog; they will shake the ground for several days; their number is as great as the grains of sand. ²⁶ Then Antichrist will appear who will deceive many of them. When he is strengthened, he will seduce even the elect. He will kill the two prophets Enoch and Elias, so that for three and a half days they will be dead in the public places of the great town of Jerusalem. ²⁷ Then the Ancient of Days will bring them back to life. It is He whom I see coming with the clouds from Heaven, similar to a son of man. His power is an eternal power and His reign will have no end. It is he which will put Antichrist to death and all the multitude which is with him. There will be misfortune then in truth to any soul who will live in that time over all the land, because there will be iniquity, a great affliction and groanings; but the salvation of man is between the hands of God in Heaven. This is the end of the speech." ²⁸ The angel said to me: "Daniel, Daniel, conceal these discourses, seal them up until the time when they will be fulfilled, because that is the end of all." I, Daniel, I arose, I put a seal to the discourse, and sealed them. I will glorify God, the father of all things and the lord of the universe, He who knows the dates and times. To him be glory and power forever. Amen.

The Apocalypse of Moses, or Revelation of Moses
Account and life of Adam and Eve, the first-created, revealed by God to His servant Moses, when he received from the hand of the Lord the tables of the law of the covenant, instructed by the archangel Michael.

¹ This is the account of Adam and Eve. After they went forth out of paradise, Adam took Eve his wife, and went up into the east. And he remained there eighteen years and two months; and Eve conceived and brought forth two sons, Diaphotus called Cain, and Amilabes called Abel. ² And after this, Adam and Eve were with one another; and when they lay down, Eve said to Adam her lord: My lord, I have seen in a dream this night the blood of my son Amilabes, who is called Abel, thrown into the mouth of Cain his brother, and he drank it without pity. And he entreated him to grant him a little of it, but he did not listen to him, but drank it all up; and it did not remain in his belly, but came forth out of his mouth. And Adam said to Eve: Let us arise, and go and see what has happened to them, lest perchance the enemy should be in any way warring against them. ³ And having both gone, they found Abel killed by the hand of Cain his brother. And God says to the archangel Michael: Say to Adam, Do not relate the mystery which thou knowest to thy son Cain, for he is a son of wrath. But grieve thyself not; for I will give thee instead of him another son, who shall show thee all things, as many as thou shalt do to him; but do thou tell him nothing. This God said to His angel; and Adam kept the word in his heart, and with him Eve also, having grief about Abel their son. ⁴ And after this, Adam knew his wife Eve, and she conceived and brought forth Seth. And Adam says to Eve: Behold, we have brought forth a son instead of Abel whom Cain slew; let us give glory and sacrifice to God. ⁵ And Adam had thirty sons and thirty daughters. And he fell into disease, and cried with a loud voice, and said: Let all my sons come to me, that I may see them before I die. And they were all brought together, for the earth was inhabited in three parts; and they all came to the door of the house into which he had entered to pray to God. ⁶ And his son Seth said: Father Adam, what is thy disease? And he says: My children, great trouble has hold of me. And they say: What is the trouble and disease? And Seth answered and said to him: Is it that thou rememberest the *fruits* of paradise of which thou didst eat, and grievest thyself because of the desire of them? If it is so, tell me, and I will go and bring thee fruit from paradise. For I will put dung upon my head, and weep and pray, and the Lord will hearken to me, and send his angel; and I shall bring *it* to thee, that thy trouble may cease from thee. ⁷ Adam says to him: No, my son Seth; but I have disease and trouble. Seth says to him: And how have they come upon thee? Adam said to him: When God made us, me and your mother, for whose sake also I die, He gave us every plant in paradise; but about one he commanded us not to eat of it, because on account of it we should die. And the hour was at hand for the angels who guarded your mother to go up and worship the Lord; and the enemy gave to her, and she ate of the tree, knowing that I was not near her, nor the holy angels; then she gave me also to eat. ⁸ And when we had both eaten, God was angry with us. And the Lord, coming into paradise, set His throne, and called with a dreadful voice, saying, Adam, where art thou? and why art thou hidden from my face? shall the house be hidden from him that built it? And He says, Since thou hast forsaken my covenant, I have brought upon thy body seventy strokes. The trouble of the first stroke is the injury of the eyes; the trouble of the second stroke, of the hearing; and so in succession, all the strokes shall overtake thee. ⁹ And Adam thus speaking to his sons, groaned out loud, and said: What shall I do? I am in great grief. And Eve also wept, saying: My lord Adam, arise, give me the half of thy disease, and let me bear it, because through me this has happened to thee; through me thou art in distresses and troubles. And Adam said to Eve: Arise, and go with our son Seth near paradise, and put earth upon your heads, and weep, beseeching the Lord that He may have compassion upon me, and send His angel to paradise, and give me of the tree in which flows the oil out of it, and that thou mayest bring it to me; and I shall anoint myself, and have rest, and show thee the manner in which we were deceived at first. ¹⁰ And Seth and Eve went into the regions of paradise. And as they were going along, Eve saw her son, and a wild beast fighting with him. And Eye wept, saying: Woe's me, woe's me; for if I come to the day of the resurrection, all who have sinned will curse me, saying, Eve did not keep the commandment of God. And Eve cried out to the wild beast, saying: O thou evil wild beast, wilt thou not be afraid to fight with the image of God? How has thy mouth been opened? how have thy teeth been strengthened? how hast thou not been mindful of thy subjection, that thou wast formerly subject to the image of God? ¹¹ Then the wild beast cried out, saying: O Eve, not against us thy upbraiding nor thy weeping, but against thyself, since the beginning of the wild beasts was from thee. How was thy mouth opened to eat of the tree about which God had commanded thee not to eat of it? For this reason also our nature has been changed. Now, therefore, thou shalt not be able to bear up, if I begin to reproach thee. ¹² And Seth says to the wild beast: Shut thy mouth and be silent, and stand off from the image of God till the day of judgment. Then the wild beast says to Seth: Behold, I stand off, Seth, from the image of God. Then the wild beast fled, and left him wounded, and went to his covert. ¹³ And Seth went with his mother Eve near paradise: and they wept there, beseeching God to send His angel, to give them the oil of compassion. And God sent to them the archangel Michael, and he said to them these words: Seth, man of God, do not weary thyself praying in this supplication about the tree in which flows the oil to anoint thy father Adam; for it will not happen to thee now, but at the last times. Then shall arise all flesh from Adam even to that great day, as many as shall be a holy people; then shall be given to them all the delight of paradise, and God shall be in the midst of them; and there shall not any more be sinners before Him, because the wicked heart shall be taken from them, and there shall be given to them a heart made to understand what is good, and to worship God only. Do thou again go to thy father, since the measure of his life has been fulfilled, equal to three days. And when his soul goes out, thou wilt behold its dreadful passage. ¹⁴ And the angel, having said this, went away from them. And Seth and Eve came to the tent where Adam was lying. And Adam says to Eve: Why didst thou work mischief against us, and bring upon us great wrath, which is death, holding sway over all our race? And he says to her: Call all our children, and our children's children, and relate to them the manner of our transgression. ¹⁵ Then Eve says to them: Listen, all my children, and my children's children, and I shall relate to you how our enemy deceived us. It came to pass, while we were keeping paradise, that we kept each the portion allotted to him by God. And I was keeping in my lot the south and west. And the devil went into the lot of Adam where were the male wild beasts; since God parted to us the wild beasts, and had given all the males to your father, and all the females He gave to me, and each of us watched his own. ¹⁶ And the devil spoke to the serpent, saying, Arise, come to me, and I shall tell you a thing in which thou mayst be of service. Then the serpent came to him, and the devil says to him, I hear that thou art more sagacious than all the wild beasts, and I have come to make thy acquaintance; and I have found thee greater than all the wild beasts, and they associate with thee; notwithstanding, thou doest reverence to one far inferior. Why eatest thou of the tares of Adam and his wife, and not of the fruit of paradise? Arise and come hither, and we shall make him be cast out of paradise through his wife, as we also were cast out through him. The serpent says to him, I am afraid lest the Lord be angry with me. The devil says to him, Be not afraid; only become my instrument, and I will speak through thy mouth a word by which thou shalt be able to deceive him. ¹⁷ Then straightway he hung by the walls of paradise about the hour when the angels of God went up to worship. Then Satan came in the form of an angel, and praised God as did the angels; and looking out from the wall, I saw him like an angel. And says he to me, Art thou Eve? And I said to him, I am. And says he to me, What doest thou in paradise? And I said to him, God has set us to keep it, and to eat of it. The devil answered me through the mouth of the serpent, Ye do well, but you do not eat of every plant. And I say to him, Yes, of every plant we eat, but one only which is in the midst of paradise, about which God has commanded us not to eat of it, since you will die the death. ¹⁸ Then says the serpent to me, As God liveth, I am grieved for you, because you are like cattle. For I do not wish you to be ignorant of this; but rise, come hither, listen to me, and eat, and perceive the value of the tree, as He told us. But I said to him, I am afraid lest God be angry with me. And he says to me, Be not afraid; for as soon as thou eatest, thine eyes shall be opened, and ye shall be as gods in knowing what is good and what is evil. And God, knowing this, that ye shall be like Him, has had a grudge against you, and said, Ye shall not eat of it. But do thou observe the plant, and thou shalt see great glory about it. And I observed the plant, and saw great glory about it. And I said to him, It is beautiful to the eyes to perceive; and I was afraid to take of the fruit. And he says to me, Come, I will give to thee: follow me. ¹⁹ And I opened to him, and he came inside into paradise, and went through it before me. And having walked a little, he turned, and says to me, I have changed my mind, and will not give thee to eat. And this he said, wishing at last to entice and destroy me. And he says to me, Swear to me that thou wilt give also to thy husband. And I said to him, I know not by what oath I shall swear to thee; but what I know I say to thee, By the throne of the Lord, and the cherubim, and the tree of life, I will give also to my husband to eat. And when he had taken the oath from me, then he went and ascended upon it. And he put upon the fruit which he gave me to eat the poison of his wickedness, that is, of his desire; for desire is the head of all sin. And I bent down the branch to the ground, and took of the fruit, and ate. ²⁰ And in that very hour mine eyes were opened. and I knew that I was stripped of the righteousness with which I had been clothed; and I wept, saying, What is this thou hast done to me, because I have been deprived of the glory with

which I was clothed? And I wept too about the oath. And he came down out of the tree, and went out of sight. And I sought leaves in my portion, that I might cover my shame; and I did not find them from the plants of paradise, since, at the time that I ate, the leaves of all the plants in my portion fell, except of the fig alone. And having taken leaves off it, I made myself a girdle, and it is from those plants of which I ate. [21] And I cried out with a loud voice, saying, Adam, Adam, where art thou? Arise, come to me, and I shall show thee a great mystery. And when your father came, I said to him words of wickedness, which brought us down from great glory. For as soon as he came I opened my mouth, and the devil spoke; and I began to advise him, saying, Come hither, my lord Adam, listen to me, and eat of the fruit of the tree of which God said to us not to eat of it, and thou shalt be as God. And your father answered and said, I am afraid lest God be angry with me. And I said to him, Be not afraid, for as soon as thou shalt eat thou shalt know good and evil. And then I quickly persuaded him, and he ate; and his eyes were opened, and he was aware, he also, of his nakedness. And he says to me, O wicked woman, why hast thou wrought mischief in us? Thou hast alienated me from the glory of God. [22] And that same hour we heard the archangel Michael sounding his trumpet, calling the angels, saying, Thus saith the Lord, Come with me to paradise, and hear the word in which I judge Adam. And when we heard the archangel sounding, we said, Behold, God is coming into paradise to judge us. And we were afraid, and hid ourselves. And God came up into paradise, riding upon a chariot of cherubim, and the angels praising Him. When God came into paradise, the plants both of Adam's lot and of my lot bloomed, and all lifted themselves up; and the throne of God was made ready where the tree of life was. [23] And God called Adam, saying, Adam, where art thou hidden, thinking that I shall not find thee? Shall the house be hidden from him that built it? Then your father answered and said, Not, Lord, did we hide ourselves as thinking that we should not be found by Thee; but I am afraid, because I am naked, and stand in awe of Thy power, O Lord. God says to him, Who hath shown thee that thou art naked, unless it be that thou hast forsaken my commandment which I gave thee to keep it? Then Adam remembered the word which I spake to him when I wished to deceive him, I will put thee out of danger from God. And he turned and said to me, Why hast thou done this? And I also remembered the word of the serpent, and said, The serpent deceived me. [24] God says to Adam, Since thou hast disobeyed my commandment, and obeyed thy wife, cursed be the ground in thy labours. For whenever thou labourest it, and it will not give its strength, thorns and thistles shall it raise for thee; and in the sweat of thy face shalt thou eat thy bread. And thou shalt be in distresses of many kinds. Thou shalt weary thyself, and rest not; thou shalt be afflicted by bitterness, and shall not taste of sweetness; thou shalt be afflicted by heat, and oppressed by cold; and thou shalt toil much, and not grow rich; and thou shalt make haste, and not attain thine end; and the wild beasts, of which thou wast lord, shall rise up against thee in rebellion, because thou hast not kept my commandment. [25] And having turned to me, the Lord says to me, Since thou hast obeyed the serpent, and disobeyed my commandment, thou shalt be in distresses and unbearable pains; thou shalt bring forth children with great tremblings; and in one hour shalt thou come *to bring them forth*, and lose thy life in consequence of thy great straits and pangs. And thou shalt confess, and say, Lord, Lord, save me; and I shall not return to the sin of the flesh. And on this account in thine own words I shall judge thee, on account of the enmity which the enemy hath put in thee; and thou shalt turn again to thy husband, and he shall be thy lord. [26] And after speaking thus to me, He spoke to the serpent in great wrath, saying to him, Since thou hast done this, and hast become an ungracious instrument until thou shouldst deceive those that were remiss in heart, cursed art thou of all the beasts. Thou shalt be deprived of the food which thou eatest; and dust shalt thou eat all the days of thy life; upon thy breast and belly shalt thou go, and thou shalt be deprived both of thy hands and feet; there shall not be granted thee ear, nor wing, nor one limb of all which those have whom thou hast enticed by thy wickedness, and hast caused them to be cast out of paradise. And I shall put enmity between thee and between his seed. He shall lie in wait for thy head, and thou for his heel, until the day of judgment. And having thus said, He commands His angels that we be cast out of paradise. And as we were being driven along, and were lamenting, your father Adam entreated the angels, saying, Allow me a little, that I may entreat God, and that He may have compassion upon me, and pity me, for I only have sinned. And they stopped driving him. And Adam cried out with weeping, saying, Pardon me, Lord, what I have done. Then says the Lord to His angels, Why have you stopped driving Adam out of paradise? It is not that the sin is mine, or that I have judged ill? Then the angels, falling to the ground, worshipped the Lord, saying, Just art Thou, Lord, and judgest what is right. [27] And turning to Adam, the Lord said, I will not permit thee henceforth to be in paradise. And Adam answered and said, Lord, give me of the tree of life, that I may eat before I am cast out. Then the Lord said to Adam, Thou shalt not now take of it, for it has been assigned to the cherubim and the flaming sword, which turneth to guard it on account of thee, that thou mayst not taste of it and be free from death for ever, but that thou mayst have the war which the enemy has set in thee. But when thou art gone out of paradise, if thou shalt keep thyself from all evil, as being destined to die, I will again raise thee up when the resurrection comes, and then there shall be given thee of the tree of life, and thou shalt be free from death for ever. [28] And having thus said, the Lord commanded us to be cast out of paradise. And your father wept before the angels over against paradise. And the angels say to him, What dost thou wish that we should do for thee, Adam? And your father answered and said to the angels, Behold, you cast me out. I beseech you, allow me to take sweet odours out of paradise, in order that, after I go out, I may offer sacrifice to God, that God may listen to me. And the angels, advancing, said to God, Jael, eternal King, order to be given to Adam sacrifices of sweet odour out of paradise. And God ordered Adam to go, that he might take perfumes of sweet odour out of paradise for his food. And the angels let him go, and he gathered both kinds–saffron and spikenard, and calamus and cinnamon, and other seeds for his food; and having taken them, he went forth out of paradise. And we came to the earth. [29] Now, then, my children, I have shown you the manner in which we were deceived. But do ye watch over yourselves, so as not to forsake what is good. [30] And when she had thus spoken in the midst of her sons, and Adam was lying in his disease, and he had one other day before going out of the body, Eve says to Adam: Why is it that thou diest, and I live? or how long time have I to spend after thou diest? tell me. Then says Adam to Eve: Do not trouble thyself about matters; for thou wilt not be long after me, but we shall both die alike, and thou wilt be laid into my place. And when I am dead you will leave me, and let no one touch me, until the angel of the Lord shall say something about me; for God will not forget me, but will seek His own vessel which He fashioned. Arise, rather, pray to God until I restore my spirit into the hands of Him who has given it; because we know not how we shall meet Him who made us, whether He shall be angry with us, or turn and have mercy upon us. [31] Then arose Eve, and went outside; and falling to the ground, she said: I have sinned, O God; I have sinned, O Father of all; I have sinned to Thee, I have sinned against Thy chosen angels, I have sinned against the cherubim, I have sinned against Thine unshaken throne; I have sinned, O Lord, I have sinned much, I have sinned before Thee, and every sin through me has come upon the creation. And while Eve was still praying, being on her knees, behold, there came to her the angel of humanity, and raised her up, saying: Arise, Eve, from thy repentance; for, behold, Adam thy husband has gone forth from his body; arise and see his spirit carried up to Him that made it, to meet Him. [32] And Eve arose, and covered her face with her hand; and the angel says to her: Raise thyself from the things of earth. And Eve gazed up into heaven, and she saw a chariot of light going along under four shining eagles–and it was not possible for any one born of woman to tell the glory of them, or to see the face of them–and angels going before the chariot. And when they came to the place where your father Adam was lying, the chariot stood still, and the seraphim between your father and the chariot. And I saw golden censers, and three vials; and, behold, all the angels with incense, and the censers, and the vials, came to the altar, and blew them up, and the smoke of the incense covered the firmaments. And the angels fell down and worshipped God, crying out and saying: Holy Jael, forgive; for he is Thine image, and the work of Thine holy hands. [33] And again, I Eve saw two great and awful mysteries standing before God. And I wept for fear, and cried out to my son Seth, saying: Arise, Seth, from the body of thy father Adam, and come to me, that thou mayst see what the eye of no one hath ever seen; and they are praying for thy father Adam. [34] Then Seth arose and went to his mother, and said to her: What has befallen thee? and why weepest thou? She says to him: Look up with thine eyes, and see the seven firmaments opened, and see with thine eyes how the body of thy father lies upon its face, and all the holy angels with him, praying for him, and saying: Pardon him, O Father of the universe; for he is Thine image. What then, my child Seth, will this be? and when will he be delivered into the hands of our invisible Father and God? And who are the two dark-faced ones who stand by at the prayer of thy father? [35] And Seth says to his mother: These are the sun and the moon, and they are falling down and praying for my father Adam. Eve says to him: And where is their light, and why have they become black-looking? And Seth says to her: They cannot shine in the presence of the Light of the universe, and for this reason the light from them has been hidden. [36] And while Seth was speaking to his mother, the angels lying upon their faces sounded their trumpets, and cried out with an awful voice, saying, Blessed be the glory of the Lord upon what He has made, for He has had compassion upon Adam, the work of His hands. When the angels had sounded this forth, there came one of the six-winged seraphim, and hurried Adam to the Acherusian lake, and washed him in presence of God. ³⁷ And he spent three hours lying, and thus the Lord of the universe, sitting upon His holy throne, stretched forth His hands, and raised Adam, and delivered him to the archangel Michael, saying to him: Raise him into paradise, even to the third heaven, and let him be there until that great and dreadful day which I am to bring upon the world. And the archangel Michael, having taken Adam, led him away, and anointed him, as God said to him at the pardoning of Adam. ³⁸ After all these things, therefore, the archangel asked about the funeral rites of the remains; and God commanded that all the angels should come together into His presence, each according to his rank. And all the angels were assembled, some with censers, some with trumpets. And the Lord of Hosts went up, and the winds drew Him, and cherubim riding upon the winds, and the angels of heaven went before Him; and they came to where the body of Adam was, and took it. And they came to paradise, and all the trees of paradise were moved so that all begotten from Adam hung their heads in sleep at the sweet smell, except Seth, because he had been begotten according to the appointment of God. The body of Adam, then, was lying on the ground in paradise, and Seth was grieved exceedingly about him. ³⁹ And the Lord God says: Adam, why hast thou done this? If thou hadst kept my commandment, those that brought thee down to this place would not have rejoiced. Nevertheless I say unto thee, that I will turn their joy into grief, but I will turn thy grief into joy; and having turned, I will set thee in thy kingdom, on the throne of him that deceived thee; and he shall be cast into this place, that thou mayst sit upon him. Then shall be condemned, he and those who hear him; and they shall be much grieved, and shall weep, seeing thee sitting upon his glorious throne. ⁴⁰ And then He said to the archangel Michael: Go into paradise, into the third heaven, and bring me three cloths of fine linen and silk. And God said to Michael, Gabriel, Uriel, and Raphael: Cover Adam's body with the cloths, and bring olive oil of sweet odour, and pour upon him. And having thus done, they prepared his body for burial. And the Lord said: Let also the body of Abel be brought. And having brought other cloths, they prepared it also for burial, since it had not been prepared for burial since the day on which his brother Cain slew him. For the wicked Cain, having taken great pains to hide it, had not been able; for the earth did not receive it, saying: I will not receive a body into companionship until that dust which was taken up and fashioned upon me come to me. And then the angels took it up, and laid it on the rock until his father died. And both were buried, according to the commandment of God, in the regions of paradise, in the place in which God found the dust. And God sent seven angels into paradise, and they brought many sweet-smelling herbs, and laid them in the earth; and thus they took the two bodies, and buried them in the place which they had dug and built. ⁴¹ And God called Adam, and said: Adam, Adam. And the body answered out of the ground, and said: Here am I, Lord. And the Lord says to him: I said to thee, Dust thou art, and unto dust thou shalt return. Again I promise thee the resurrection. I will raise thee up in the last day in the resurrection, with every man who is of thy seed. ⁴² And after these words God made a three-cornered seal, and sealed the tomb, that no one should do anything to him in the six days, until his rib should return to him. And the beneficent God and the holy angels having laid him in his place, after the six days Eve also died. And while she lived she wept about her falling asleep, because she knew not where her body was to be laid. For when the Lord was present in paradise when they buried Adam, both she and her children fell asleep, except Seth, as I said. And Eve, in the hour of her death, besought that she might be buried where Adam her husband was, saying thus: My Lord, Lord and God of all virtue, do not separate me, Thy servant, from the body of Adam, for of his members Thou madest me; but grant to me, even me, the unworthy and the sinner, to be buried by his body. And as I was along with him in paradise, and not separated from him after the transgression, so also let no one separate us. After having prayed, therefore, she looked up into heaven, and stood up, and said, beating her breast: God of all, receive my spirit. And straightway she gave up her spirit to God. ⁴³ And when she was dead, the archangel Michael stood beside her; and there came three angels, and took her body, and buried it where the body of Abel was. And the archangel Michael said to Seth: Thus bury every man that dies, until the day of the resurrection. And after having given this law, he said to him: Do not mourn beyond six days. And on the seventh day, rest, and rejoice in it, because in it God and we the angels rejoice in the righteous soul that has departed from earth. Having thus spoken, the archangel Michael went up into heaven, glorifying, and saying the Alleluia: Holy, holy, holy Lord, to the glory of God the Father, because to Him is due glory, honour, and adoration, with His unbeginning and life-giving Spirit, now and ever, and to ages of ages. Amen.

TESTAMENTS

The Testaments of the Twelve Patriarchs

Testament of Reuben

The First-Born Son of Jacob and Leah.

1

Reuben, the first-born son of Jacob and Leah. The man of experience counsels against fornication and points out the ways in. which men are most apt to fall into error.

¹ THE Copy of the Testament of Reuben, even the commands which he gave his sons before he died in the hundred and twenty-fifth year of his life. ² Two years after the death of Joseph his brother, when Reuben fell ill, his sons and his sons' sons were gathered together to visit him. ³ And he said to them: My children, behold I am dying, and go the way of my fathers. ⁴ And seeing there Judah, and Gad, and Asher, his brethren, he said to them: Raise me up that I may tell to my brethren and to my children what things I have hidden in my heart, for behold now at length I am passing away. ⁵ And he arose and kissed them, and said unto them: Hear, my brethren, and do ye my children, give ear to Reuben your father, in the commands which I give unto you. ⁶ And behold I call to witness against you this day the God of heaven, that ye walk not in the sins of youth and fornication, wherein I was poured out, and defiled the bed of my father Jacob. ⁷ And I tell you that he smote me with a sore plague in my loins for seven months; and had not my father Jamb prayed for me to the Lord, the Lord would have destroyed me. ⁸ For I was thirty years old when I wrought the evil thing before the Lord, and for seven months I was sick unto death. ⁹ And after this I repented with set purpose of my soul for seven years before the Lord. ¹⁰ And wine and strong drink I drank not, and flesh entered not into my mouth, and I ate no pleasant food; but I mourned over my sin, for it was great, such as had not been in Israel. ¹¹ And now hear me, my children, what things I saw concerning the seven spirits of deceit, when I repented. ¹² Seven spirits therefore are appointed against man, and they are the leaders in the works of youth. ¹³ And seven other spirits are given to him at his creation, that through them should be done every work of man. ¹⁴ The first is the spirit of life, with which the constitution of man is created. ¹⁵ The second is the sense of sight, with which ariseth desire. ¹⁶ The third is the sense of hearing, with which cometh teaching. ¹⁷ The fourth is the sense of smell, with which tastes are given to draw air and breath. ¹⁸ The fifth is the power of speech, with which cometh knowledge. ¹⁹ The sixth is the sense of taste, with which cometh the eating of meats and drinks; and by it strength is produced, for in food is the foundation. of strength. ²⁰ The seventh is the power of procreation and sexual intercourse, with which through love of pleasure sins enter in. ²¹ Wherefore it is the last in order of creation, and the first in that of youth, because it is filled with ignorance, and leadeth the youth as a blind man to a pit, and as a beast to a precipice. ²² Besides all these there is an eighth spirit of sleep, with which is brought about the trance of nature and the of death. ²³ With these spirits are mingled the spirits of error. ²⁴ First, the spirit of fornication is seated in the nature and in the senses; ²⁵ The second, the spirit of insatiableness in the belly; ²⁶ The third, the spirit of fighting, in the liver and gall. ²⁷ The fourth is the spirit of obsequiousness and chicanery, that through officious attention one may be fair in seeming. ²⁸ The fifth is the spirit of pride, that one may be boastful and arrogant. ²⁹ The sixth is the spirit of lying, in perdition and jealousy to practise deceits, and concealments from kindred and friends. ³⁰ The seventh is the spirit of injustice, with which are thefts and acts of rapacity, that a man may fulfil the desire of his heart; for injustice worketh together with the other spirits by the taking of gifts. ³¹ And with all these the spirit of sleep is joined which is that of error and fantasy. ³² And so perisheth every young man, darkening his mind from the truth, and not understanding the law of God, nor obeying the admonitions of his fathers, as befell me also in my youth. ³³ And now, my children, love the truth, and it will preserve you: hear ye the words of Reuben your father. ³⁴ Pay no heed to the face of a woman, ³⁵ Nor associate with another man's wife, ³⁶ Nor meddle with affairs of womankind. ³⁷ For had I not seen Bilhah bathing in a covered place, I had not fallen into this great iniquity. ³⁸ For my mind taking in the thought of the woman's nakedness, suffered me not to sleep until I had wrought the abominable thing. ³⁹ For while Jacob our father had gone to Isaac his father, when we were in Eder, near to Ephrath in Bethlehem, Bilhah became drunk and was asleep uncovered in her chamber. ⁴⁰ Having therefore gone in and beheld her nakedness, I wrought the impiety without her perceiving it, and leaving her sleeping departed. ⁴¹ And forthwith an angel of God revealed to my father concerning my impiety, and he came and mourned over me, and touched her no more.

2

Reuben continues with his experiences and his good advice.

1 PAY no heed, therefore, my children, to the beauty of women, nor set your mind on their affairs; but walk in singleness of heart in the fear of the Lord, and expend labour on good works, and on study and on your flocks, until the Lord give you a wife, whom He will, that ye suffer not as I did. **2** For until my father's death I had not boldness to look in his face, or to speak to any of my brethren, because of the reproach. **3** Even until now my conscience causeth me anguish on account of my impiety. **4** And yet my father comforted me much, and prayed for me unto the Lord, that the anger of the Lord might pass from me, even as the Lord showed. **5** And thenceforth until now I have been on my guard and sinned not. **6** Therefore, my children, I say unto you, observe all things whatsoever I command you, and ye shall not sin. **7** For a pit unto the soul is the sin of fornication, separating it from God, and bringing it near to idols, because it deceiveth the mind and understanding, and leadeth down young men into Hades before their time. **8** For many hath fornication destroyed; because, though a man be old or noble, or rich or poor, he bringeth reproach upon himself with the sons of men and derision with Beliar. **9** For ye heard regarding Joseph how he guarded himself from a woman, and purged his thoughts from all fornication, and found favour in the sight of God and men. **10** For the Egyptian woman did many things unto him, and summoned magicians, and offered him love potions, but the purpose of his soul admitted no evil desire. **11** Therefore the God of your fathers delivered him from every evil and hidden death. **12** For if fornication overcomes not your mind, neither can Beliar overcome you. **13** For evil are women, my children; and since they have no power or strength over man, they use wiles by outward attractions, that they may draw him to themselves. **14** And whom they cannot bewitch by outward attractions, him they overcome by craft. **15** For moreover, concerning them, the angel of the Lord told me, and taught me, that women are overcome by the spirit of fornication more than men, and in their heart they plot against men; and by means of their adornment they deceive first their minds, and by the glance of the eye instil the poison, and then through the accomplished act they take them captive. **16** For a woman cannot force a man openly, but by a harlot's bearing she beguiles him. **17** Flee, therefore, fornication, my children, and command your wives and your daughters, that they adorn not their heads and faces to deceive the mind: because every woman who useth these wiles bath been reserved for eternal punishment. **18** For thus they allured the Watchers who were before the flood; for as these continually beheld them, they lusted after them, and they conceived the act in their mind; for they changed themselves into the shape of men, and appeared to them when they were with their husbands. **19** And the women lusting in their minds after their forms, gave birth to giants, for the Watchers appeared to them as reaching even unto heaven. **20** Beware, therefore, of fornication; and if you wish to be pure in mind, guard your senses from every woman. **21** And command the women likewise not to associate with men, that they also may be pure in mind. **22** For constant meetings, even though the ungodly deed be not wrought, are to them an irremediable disease, and to us a destruction of Beliar and an eternal reproach. **23** For in fornication there is neither understanding nor godliness, and all jealousy dwelleth in the lust thereof. **24** Therefore, then I say unto you, ye will be jealous against the sons of Levi, and will seek to be exalted over them; but ye shall not be able. **25** For God will avenge them, and ye shall die by an evil death. For to Levi God gave the sovereignty and to Judah with him and to me also, and to Dan and Joseph, that we should be for rulers. **26** Therefore I command you to hearken to Levi, because he shall know the law of the Lord, and shall give ordinances for judgement and shall sacrifice for all Israel until the consummation of the times, as the anointed High Priest, of whom the Lord spake. **27** I adjure you by the God of heaven to do truth each one unto his neighbour and to entertain love each one for his brother. **28** And draw ye near to Levi in humbleness, of heart, that ye may receive a blessing from his mouth. **29** For he shall bless Israel and Judah, because him hath the Lord chosen to be king over all the nation. **30** And bow down before his seed, for on our behalf it will die in wars visible and invisible, and will be among you an eternal king. **31** And Reuben died, having given these commands to his sons. And they placed him in a coffin until they carried him up from Egypt, and buried him in Hebron in the cave where his father was.

Testament of Simeon
The Second Son of Jacob and Leah.

1

Simeon, the second son of Jacob and Leah. The strong man. He becomes jealous of Joseph and is an instigator of the plot against Joseph.

1 THE copy of the words of Simeon, the things which he spake to his sons before he died, in the hundred and twentieth year of his life, at which time Joseph, his brother, died. **2** For when Simeon was sick, his sons came to visit him. and he strengthened himself and sat up and kissed them, and said:– **3** Hearken, my children, to Simeon your father and I will declare unto you what things I have in my heart. **4** I was born of Jacob as my father's second son; and my mother Leah called me Simeon, because the Lord had heard her prayer. **5** Moreover, I became strong exceedingly; I shrank from no achievement nor was I afraid of ought. For my heart was hard, and my liver was immovable, and my bowels without compassion. **6** Because valour also has been given from the Most High to men in soul and body. **7** For in the time of my youth I was jealous in many things of Joseph, because my father loved him beyond all. **8** And I set my mind against him to destroy him because the prince of deceit sent forth the spirit of jealousy and blinded my mind, so that I regarded him not as a brother, nor did I spare even Jacob my father. **9** But his God and the God of his fathers sent forth His angel, and delivered him out of my hands. **10** For when I went to Shechem to bring ointment for the flocks, and Reuben to Dothan, where were our necessaries and all our stores, Judah my brother sold him to the Ishmaelites. **11** And when Reuben heard these things he was grieved, for he wished to restore him to his father. **12** But on hearing this I was exceedingly wroth against Judah in that he let him go away alive, and for five months I continued wrathful against him. **13** But the Lord restrained me, and withheld from me the power of my hands; for my right hand was half withered for seven days. **14** And I knew, my children, that because of Joseph this had befallen me, and I repented and wept; and I besought the Lord God that my hand might be restored and that I might hold aloof from all pollution and envy and from all folly. **15** For I knew that I had devised an evil thing before the Lord and Jacob my father, on account of Joseph my brother, in that I envied him. **16** And now, my children, hearken unto me and beware of the spirit of deceit and envy. **17** For envy ruleth over the whole mind of a man, and suffereth him neither to eat nor to drink, nor to do any good thing. But it ever suggesteth to him to destroy him that he envieth; and so long as he that is envied flourisheth, he that envieth fadeth away. **18** Two years therefore I afflicted my soul with fasting in the fear of the Lord, and I learnt that deliverance from envy cometh by the fear of God. **19** For if a man flee to the Lord, the evil spirit runneth away from him and his mind is lightened. **20** And henceforward he sympathiseth with him whom he envied and forgiveth those who are hostile to him, and so ceaseth from his envy.

2

Reuben counsels his hearers against envy.

1 AND my father asked concerning me, because he saw that I was sad; and I said unto him, I am pained in my liver. **2** For I mourned more than they all, because I was guilty of the selling of Joseph. **3** And when we went down into Egypt, and he bound me as a spy, I knew that I was suffering justly, and I grieved not. **4** Now Joseph was a good man, and had the Spirit of God within him: being compassionate and pitiful, he bore no malice against me; but loved me even as the rest of his brethren. **5** Beware, therefore, my children, of all jealousy and envy, and walk in singleness of heart, that God may give you also grace and glory, and blessing upon your heads, even as ye saw in Joseph's case. **6** All his days he reproached us not concerning this thing, but loved us as his own soul, and beyond his own sons glorified us, and gave us riches, and cattle and fruits. **7** Do ye also, my children, love each one his brother with a good heart, and the spirit of envy will withdraw from you. **8** For this maketh savage the soul and destroyeth the body; it causeth anger and war in the mind, and stirreth up unto deeds of blood, and leadeth the mind into frenzy, and causeth tumult to the soul and trembling to the body. **9** For even in sleep malicious jealousy gnaweth, and with wicked spirits disturbeth the soul, and causeth the body to be troubled, and waketh the mind from sleep in confusion; and as a wicked and poisonous spirit, so appeareth it to men. **10** Therefore was Joseph comely in appearance, and goodly to look upon, because no wickedness dwelt in him; for some of the trouble of the spirit the face manifesteth. **11** And now, my children, make your hearts good before the Lord, and your ways straight before men, and ye shall find grace before the Lord and men. **12** Beware, therefore, of fornication, for fornication is mother of all evils, separating from God, and bringing near to Beliar. **13** For I have seen it inscribed in the writing of Enoch that your sons shall be corrupted in fornication, and shall do harm to the sons of Levi with the sword. **14** But they shall not be able to withstand Levi; for he shall wage the war of the Lord, and shall conquer all your hosts. **15** And they shall be few in number, divided in Levi and Judah, and there shall be none of you for sovereignty, even as also our father prophesied in his blessings.

3

A prophecy of the coming of the Messiah.

1 BEHOLD I have told you all things, that I may be acquitted of your sin. **2** Now, if ye remove from you your envy and all stiff-neckedness, is a rose shall my bones flourish in Israel, and as a lily my flesh in Jacob, and my odour shall be as the odour of Libanus; and as cedars shall holy ones be multiplied from me for ever, and their branches shall stretch afar off. ³ Then shall perish the seed of Canaan, and a remnant shall not be unto Amalek, and all the Cappadocians shall perish, and all Hittites shall be utterly destroyed. ⁴ Then shall fail the land of Ham, and all the people shall perish. ⁵ Then shall all the earth rest from trouble, and all the world under heaven from war. ⁶ Then the Mighty One of Israel shall glorify Shem. ⁷ *For the Lord God shall appear on earth, and Himself save men*, ⁸ Then shall all the spirits of deceit be given to be trodden under foot, and men shall, rule over wicked spirits. ⁹ Then shall I arise in Joy and will bless the Most High because of his marvellous works, *because God hath taken a body and eaten with men and saved men*. ¹⁰ And now, my children,, and Judah, and obey Levi and Judah, and be not lifted up against these two tribes, for from them shall arise unto you the salvation of God. ¹¹ For the Lord shall raise up from Levi as it were a High Priest, and from Judah as it were a King, God and man, He shall save all the Gentiles and the race of Israel. ¹² Therefore I give you these commands that ye also may command your children, that they may observe them throughout their generations. ¹³ And when Simeon had made an end of commanding his sons, he slept with fathers, an hundred and twenty years old. ¹⁴ And they laid him in a wooden coffin, to take up his bones to Hebron. And they took them up secretly during a war of the Egyptians. For the bones of Joseph the Egyptians guarded in the tombs of the kings. ¹⁵ For the sorcerers told them, that on the departure of the bones of Joseph there should be throughout all the land darkness and gloom, and an exceeding great plague to the Egyptians, so that even with a lamp a man should not recognize his brother. ¹⁶ And the sons of Simeon bewailed their father. ¹⁷ And they were in Egypt until the day of their departure by the hand of Moses.

Testament of Levi
The Third Son of Jacob and Leah.

1

Levi, the third son of Jacob and Leah. A mystic and dreamer of dreams, a prophet.

¹ THE copy of the words of Levi, the things which he ordained unto his sons, according to all that they should do, and what things should befall them until the day of judgement. ² He was sound in health when he called them to him; for it had been revealed to him that he should die. ³ And when they were gathered together he said to them: ⁴ I, Levi, was born in Haran, and I came with my father to Shechem. ⁵ And I was young, about twenty years of age, when, with Simeon, I wrought vengeance on Hamor for our sister Dinah. ⁶ And when I was feeding the flocks in Abel-Maul, the spirit of understand of the Lord came upon me, and I saw all men corrupting their way, and that unrighteousness had built for itself walls, and lawlessness sat upon towers. ⁷ And I was grieving for the race of the sons of men, and I prayed to the Lord that I might be saved. ⁸ Then there fell upon me a sleep, and I beheld a high mountain, and I was upon it. ⁹ And behold the heavens were opened, and an angel of God said to me, Levi, enter. ¹⁰ And I entered from the first heaven, and I saw there a great sea hanging. ¹¹ And further I saw a second heaven far brighter and more brilliant, for there was a boundless light also therein, ¹² And I said to the angel, Why is this so? And the angel said to me, Marvel not at this, for thou shalt see another heaven more brilliant and incomparable. ¹³ And when thou hast ascended thither, Thou shalt stand near the Lord, and shalt be His minister, and shalt, declare His mysteries to men, and shalt proclaim concerning Him that shall redeem Israel. ¹⁴ And by thee and Judah shall the Lord appear among men, saving every race of men. ¹⁵ And from the Lord's portion shall be thy life, and He shall be thy field and vineyard, and fruits, gold, and silver. ¹⁶ Hear, therefore, regarding the heavens which have been shown to thee. ¹⁷ The lowest is for this cause gloomy unto thee, in that it beholds all the unrighteous deeds of men. ¹⁸ And it has fire, snow, and ice made ready for the day of judgement, in the righteous judgement of God; for in it are all the spirits of the retributions for vengeance on men. ¹⁹ And in the second are the hosts Of the armies which are ordained for the day of judgement, to work vengeance on the spirits of deceit and of Beliar. ²⁰ And above them are the holy ones. ²¹ And in the highest of all dwelleth the Great Glory, far above all holiness. ²² In the heaven next to it are the archangels, who minister and make propitiation to the Lord for all the sins of ignorance of the righteous; ²³ Offering to the Lord a sweet smelling savour, a reasonable and a bloodless offering. ²⁴ And in the heaven below this are the angels who bear answers to the angels of the presence of the Lord. ²⁵ And in the heaven next to this are thrones and dominions, in which always they offer praise to God. ²⁶ When, therefore, the Lord looketh upon us, all of us are shaken; yea, the heavens, and the earth, and the abysses are shaken at the presence of His majesty. ²⁷ But the sons of men, having no perception of these things, sin and provoke the Most High.

2

Levi urges piety and education.

¹ NOW, therefore, know that the Lord shall execute judgement upon the sons of men. ² Because when the rocks are being rent, and the sun quenched, and the waters dried up, and the fire cowering, and all creation troubled, and the invisible spirits melting away, and Hades taketh spoils through the visitations of the Most High, men will be unbelieving and persist in their iniquity. ³ On this account with punishment shall they be judged. ⁴ Therefore the Most High hath heard thy prayer, to separate thee from iniquity, and that thou shouldst become to Him a son, and a servant, and a minister of His presence. ⁵ The light of knowledge shalt thou light up in Jacob, and as the sun shalt thou be to all the seed of Israel. ⁶ And there shall be given to thee a blessing, and to all thy seed until the Lord shall visit all the Gentiles in His tender mercies for ever. ⁷ And therefore there have been given to thee counsel and understanding, that thou mightest instruct thy sons concerning this; ⁸ Because they that bless Him shall be blessed, and they that curse Him shall perish. ⁹ And thereupon the angel opened to me the gates of heaven, and I saw the holy temple, and upon a throne of glory the Most High. ¹⁰ And He said to me: Levi, I have given thee the blessing of the priesthood until I come and sojourn in the midst of Israel. ¹¹ Then the angel brought me down to the earth, and gave me a shield and a sword, and said to me: Execute vengeance on Shechem because of Dinah, thy sister, and I will be with thee because the Lord hath sent me. ¹² And I destroyed at that time the sons of Hamor, as it is written in the heavenly tables. ¹³ And I said to him: I pray thee, O Lord, tell me Thy name, that I may call upon Thee in a day of tribulation. ¹⁴ And he said: I am the angel who intercedeth for the nation of Israel that they may not be smitten utterly, for every evil spirit attacketh it. ¹⁵ And after these things I awaked, and blessed the Most High, and the angel who intercedeth for the nation of Israel and for all the righteous.

3

Levi has visions and shows what rewards are in store for the righteous.

¹ AND when I was going to my father, I found a brazen shield; wherefore also the name of the mountain is Aspis, which is near Gebal, to the south of Abila. ² And I kept these words in my heart. And after this I counselled my father, and Reuben my brother, to bid the sons of Hamor not to be circumcised; for I was zealous because of the abomination which they had wrought on my sister. ³ And I slew Shechem first, and Simeon slew Hamor. And after this my brothers came and smote that city with the edge of the sword. ⁴ And my father heard these things and was wroth, and he was grieved in that they had received the circumcision, and after that had been put to death, and in his blessings he looked amiss upon us. ⁵ For we sinned because we had done this thing against his will, and he was sick on that day. ⁶ But I saw that the sentence of God was for evil upon Shechem; for they sought to do to Sarah and Rebecca as they had done to Dinah our sister, but the Lord prevented them. ⁷ And they persecuted Abraham our father when he was a stranger, and they vexed his flocks when they were big with young; and Eblaen, who was born in his house, they most shamefully handled. ⁸ And thus they did to all strangers, taking away their wives by force, and they banished them. ⁹ But the wrath of the Lord came upon them to the uttermost. ¹⁰ And I said to my father Jacob: By thee will the Lord despoil the Canaanites, and will give their land to thee and to thy seed after thee. ¹¹ For from this day forward shall Shechem be called a city of imbeciles; for as a man mocketh a fool, so did we mock them. ¹² Because also they had wrought folly in Israel by defiling my sister. And we departed and came to Bethel. ¹³ And there again I saw a vision as the former, after we had spent there seventy days. ¹⁴ And I saw seven men in white raiment saying unto me: Arise, put on the robe of the priesthood, and the crown of righteousness, and the breastplate of understanding, and the garment of truth, and the late of faith, and the turban of the head, and the ephod of prophecy. ¹⁵ And they severally carried these things and put them on me, and said unto me: From henceforth become a priest of the Lord, thou and thy seed for ever. ¹⁶ And the first anointed me with holy oil, and gave to me the staff of judgement. ¹⁷ The second washed me with pure. water, and fed me with bread and wine even the most holy things, and clad me with a holy and glorious robe. ¹⁸ The third clothed me with a linen vestment like an ephod. ¹⁹ The fourth put round me a girdle like unto purple. ²⁰ The fifth gave me a branch of rich olive. ²¹ The sixth placed a crown on my head. ²² The seventh placed on my head a diadem of priesthood, and filled my hands with incense, that I might serve as priest to the Lord God. ²³ And they said to me: Levi, thy seed shall be divided into three offices, for a sign of the glory of the Lord who is to come. ²⁴ And the first portion shall be great; yea, greater than it shall none be. ²⁵ The second shall be in the priesthood. ²⁶ And the third shall be called by a new name, because a king shall arise in Judah, and shall establish a new priesthood, after the fashion of the

Gentiles. ²⁷ And His presence is beloved, as a prophet of the Most High, of the seed of Abraham our father. ²⁸ Therefore, every desirable thing in Israel shall be for thee and for thy seed, and ye shall eat everything fair to look upon, and the table of the Lord shall thy seed apportion. ²⁹ And some of them shall be high priests, and judges, and scribes; for by their mouth shall the holy place be guarded. ³⁰ And when I awoke, I understood that this dream was like the first dream. And I hid this also in my heart, and told it not to any man upon the earth. ³¹ And after two days I and Judah went up with our father Jacob to Isaac our father's father. ³² And my father's father blessed me according to all the words of the visions which I had seen. And he would not come with us to Bethel. ³³ And when we came to Bethel, my father saw a vision concerning me, that I should be their priest unto God. ³⁴ And he rose up early in the morning, and paid tithes of all to the Lord through me. And so we came to Hebron to dwell there. ³⁵ And Isaac called me continually to put me in remembrance of the law of the Lord, even as the angel of the Lord showed unto me. ³⁶ And he taught me the law of the priesthood of sacrifices, whole burnt-offerings, first-fruits, freewill-offerings, peace-offerings. ³⁷ And each day he was instructing me, and was busied on my behalf before the Lord, and said to me: Beware of the spirit of fornication; for this shall continue and shall by thy seed pollute the holy place. ³⁸ Take, therefore, to thyself a wife without blemish or pollution, while yet thou are young, and not of the race of strange nations. ³⁹ And before entering into the holy place, bathe; and when thou offerest the sacrifice, wash; and again, when thou finishest the sacrifice, wash. ⁴⁰ Of twelve trees having leaves offer to the Lord, as Abraham taught me also. ⁴¹ And of every clean beast and bird offer a sacrifice to the Lord. ⁴² And of all thy first-fruits and of wine offer the first, as a sacrifice to the Lord God; and every sacrifice thou shalt salt with salt. ⁴³ Now, therefore, observe whatsoever I command you, children; for whatsoever things I have heard from my fathers I have declared unto you. ⁴⁴ And behold I am clear from your ungodliness and transgression, which ye shall commit in the end of the ages against the Saviour of the world, Christ, acting godlessly, deceiving Israel, and stirring up against it great evils from the Lord. ⁴⁵ And ye shall deal lawlessly together with Israel, so He shall not bear with Jerusalem because of your wickedness; but the veil of the temple shall be rent, so as not to cover your shame. ⁴⁶ And ye shall be scattered as captives among the Gentiles, and shall be for a reproach and for a curse there. ⁴⁷ For the house which the Lord shall choose shall be called Jerusalem, as is contained in the book of Enoch the righteous. ⁴⁸ Therefore when I took a wife I was twenty-eight years old, and her name was Melcha. ⁴⁹ And she conceived and bare a son, and I called his name Gersam, for we were sojourners in our land. ⁵⁰ And I saw concerning him, that he would not be in the first rank. ⁵¹ And Kohath was born in the thirty-fifth year of my life, towards sunrise. ⁵² And I saw in a vision that he was standing on high in the midst of all the congregation. ⁵³ Therefore I called his name Kohath which is, beginning of majesty and instruction. ⁵⁴ And she bare me a third son, in the fortieth year of my life; and since his mother bare him with difficulty, I called him Merari, that is, 'my bitterness,' because he also was like to die. ⁵⁵ And Jochebed was born. in Egypt, in my sixty-fourth year, for I was renowned then in the midst of my brethren. ⁵⁶ And Gersam took a wife, and she bare to him Lomni and Semei. And the sons of Kohath, Ambram, Issachar, Hebron, and Ozeel. And the sons of Merari, Mooli, and Mouses. ⁵⁷ And in the ninety-fourth year Ambram took Jochebed my daughter to him to wife, for they were born in one day, he and my daughter. ⁵⁸ Eight years old was I when I went into the land of Canaan, and eighteen years when I slew Shechem, and at nineteen years I became priest, and at twenty-eight years I took a wife, and at forty-eight I went into Egypt. ⁵⁹ And behold, my children, ye are a third generation. In my hundred and eighteenth year Joseph died.

4

Levi shows how wisdom survives destruction. He has no use for scornful people.

¹ AND now, my children, I command you: Fear the Lord your God with your whole heart, and walk in simplicity according to all His law. ² And do ye also teach your children letters, that they may have understanding all their life, reading unceasingly the law of God. ³ For every one that knoweth the law of the Lord shall be honoured, and shall not be a stranger whithersoever he goeth. ⁴ Yea, many friends shall he gain more than his parents, and many men shall desire to serve him, and to hear the law from his mouth. ⁵ Work righteousness, therefore, my children, upon the earth, that ye may have it as a treasure in heaven. ⁶ And sow good things in your souls, that ye may find them in your life. ⁷ But if ye sow evil things, ye shall reap every trouble and affliction. ⁸ Get wisdom in the fear of God with diligence; for though there be a leading into captivity, and cities and lands be destroyed, and gold and silver and every possession perish, the wisdom of the wise nought can take away, save the blindness of ungodliness, and the callousness that comes of sin. ⁹ For if one keep oneself from these evil things, then even among his enemies shall wisdom be a glory to him, and in a strange country a fatherland, and in the midst of foes shall prove a friend. ¹⁰ Whosoever teaches noble things and does them, shall be enthroned with kings, as was also Joseph my brother. ¹¹ Therefore, my children, I have learnt that at the end of the ages ye will transgress against the Lord, stretching out hands to wickedness against Him; and to all the Gentiles shall ye become a scorn. ¹² For our father Israel is pure from the transgressions of the chief priests [who shall lay their hands upon the Saviour of the world]. ¹³ For as the heaven is purer in the Lord's sight than the earth, so also be ye, the lights of Israel, purer than all the Gentiles. ¹⁴ But if ye be darkened through transgressions, what, therefore, will all the Gentiles do living in blindness? ¹⁵ Yea, ye shall bring a curse upon our race, because the light of the law which was given for to lighten every man this ye desire to destroy by teaching commandments contrary to the ordinances of God. ¹⁶ The offerings of the Lord ye shall rob, and from His portion shall ye steal choice portions, eating them contemptuously with harlots. ¹⁷ And out of covetousness ye shall teach the commandments of the Lord, wedded women shall ye pollute, and the virgins of Jerusalem shall ye defile; and with harlots and adulteresses shall ye be joined, and the daughters of the Gentiles shall ye take to wife, purifying them with an unlawful purification; and your union shall be like unto Sodom and Gomorrah, ¹⁸ And ye shall be puffed up because of your priesthood, lifting yourselves up against men, and not only so, but also against the commands of God. ¹⁹ For ye shall contemn the holy things with jests and laughter. ²⁰ Therefore the temple, which the Lord shall choose, shall be laid waste through your uncleanness, and ye shall be captives throughout all nations. ²¹ And ye shall be an abomination unto them, and ye shall receive reproach and everlasting shame from the righteous judgement of God. ²² And all who hate you shall rejoice at your destruction. ²³ And if you were not to receive mercy through Abraham, Isaac, and Jacob, our fathers, not one of our seed should be left upon the earth. ²⁴ And now I have learnt that for seventy weeks ye shall go astray, and profane the priesthood, and pollute the sacrifices. ²⁵ And ye shall make void the law, and set at nought the words of the prophets by evil perverseness. ²⁶ And ye shall persecute righteous men, and hate the godly; the words of the faithful shall ye abhor. ²⁷ And a man who reneweth the law in the power of the Most High, ye shall call a deceiver; and at last ye shall rush upon him to slay him, not knowing his dignity, taking innocent blood through wickedness upon your heads. ²⁸ And your holy places shall be laid waste even to the ground because of him. ²⁹ And ye shall have no place that is clean; but ye shall be among the Gentiles a curse and a dispersion until He shall again visit you, and in pity shall receive you through faith and water.

5

He prophesies the coming of the Messiah. This was written 100 years before Christ.

¹ AND whereas ye have heard concerning the seventy weeks, hear also concerning the priesthood. For in each jubilee there shall be a priesthood. ² And in the first jubilee, the first who is anointed to the priesthood shall be great, and shall speak to God as to a father. ³ And his priesthood shall be perfect with the Lord, and in the day of his gladness shall he arise for the salvation of the world. ⁴ In the second jubilee, he that is anointed shall be conceived in the sorrow of beloved ones; and his priesthood shall be honoured and shall be glorified by all. ⁵ And the third priest shall he taken hold of by sorrow. ⁶ And the fourth shall be in pain, because unrighteousness shall gather itself against him exceedingly, and all Israel shall hate each one his neighbour. ⁷ The fifth shall be taken hold of by darkness. Likewise also the sixth and the seventh. ⁸ And in the seventh shall, be such pollution as I cannot express before men, for they shall know it who do these things. ⁹ Therefore shall they be taken captive and become a prey, and their land and their substance shall be destroyed. ¹⁰ And in the fifth week they shall return to their desolate country, and shall renew the house of the Lord. ¹¹ And in the seventh week shall become priests, who are idolaters, adulterers, lovers of money, proud, lawless, lascivious, abusers of children and beasts. ¹² And after their punishment shall have come from the Lord, the priesthood shall fail. ¹³ Then shall the Lord raise up a new priest. ¹⁴ And to him all the words of the Lord shall be revealed; and he shall execute a righteous judgement upon the earth for a multitude of days. ¹⁵ And his star shall arise in heaven as of a king. ¹⁶ Lighting up the light of knowledge as the sun the day, and he shall be magnified in the world. ¹⁷ He shall shine forth as the sun on the earth, and shall remove all darkness from under heaven, and there shall be peace in all the earth. ¹⁸ The heavens shall exult in his days, and the earth shall be glad, and the clouds shall rejoice; ¹⁹ And the knowledge of the Lord shall be poured forth upon the earth, as the

water of the seas; ²⁰ And the angels of the glory of the presence of the Lord shall be glad in him. ²¹ The heavens shall be opened, and from the temple of glory shall come upon him sanctification, with the Father's voice as from Abraham to Isaac. ²² And the glory of the Most High shall be uttered over him, and the spirit of understanding and sanctification shall rest upon him in the water. ²³ For he shall give the majesty of the Lord to His sons in truth for evermore; ²⁴ And there shall none succeed him for all generations for ever. ²⁵ And in his priesthood the Gentiles shall be multiplied in knowledge upon the earth, and enlightened through the grace of the Lord. In his priesthood shall sin come to an end, and the lawless shall cease to do evil. ²⁶ And he shall open the gates of paradise, and shall remove the threatening sword against Adam, and he shall give to the saints to eat from the tree of life, and the spirit of holiness shall be on them. ²⁷ And Beliar shall be bound by him, and he shall give power to His children to tread upon the evil spirits. ²⁸ And the Lord shall rejoice in His children, and be well pleased in His beloved ones for ever. ²⁹ Then shall Abraham and Isaac and Jacob exult, and I will be glad, and all the saints shall clothe themselves with joy. ³⁰ And now, my children, ye have heard all; choose, therefore, for yourselves either the light or the darkness, either the law of the Lord or the works of Beliar. ³¹ And his sons answered him., saying, Before the Lord we will walk according to His law. ³² And their father said unto them, The Lord is witness, and His angels are witnesses, and ye are witnesses, and I am witness, concerning the word of your mouth. ³³ And his sons said unto him: We are witnesses. ³⁴ And thus Levi ceased commanding his sons; and he stretched out his feet on the bed, and was gathered to his fathers, after he had lived a hundred and thirty-seven years. ³⁵ And they laid him in a coffin, and afterwards they buried him in Hebron, with I Abraham, Isaac, and Jacob.

Testament of Judah
The Fourth Son of Jacob and Leah.

1

Judah, the fourth son of Jacob and Leah. He is the giant, athlete, warrior; he recounts heroic deeds. He runs so fast that he can outstrip a hind.

¹ THE copy of the words of Judah, what things he spake to his sons before he died. ² They gathered themselves together, therefore, and came to him, and he said to them: Hearken, my children, to Judah your father. ³ I was the fourth son born to my father Jacob; and Leah my mother named me Judah, saying, I give thanks to the Lord, because He hath given me a fourth son also. ⁴ I was swift in my youth, and obedient to my father in everything. ⁵ And I honoured my mother and my mother's sister. ⁶ And it came to pass, when I became a man, that my father blessed me, saying, Thou shalt be a king, prospering in all things. ⁷ And the Lord showed me favour in all my works both in the field and in the house. ⁸ I know that I raced a hind, and caught it, and prepared the meat for my father, and he did eat. ⁹ And the roes I used to master in the chase, and overtake all that was in the plains. ¹⁰ A wild mare I overtook, and caught it and tamed it. ¹¹ I slew a lion and plucked a kid out of its mouth. ¹² I took a bear by its paw and hurled it down the cliff, and it was crushed. ¹³ I outran the wild boar, and seizing it as I ran, I tore it in sunder. ¹⁴ A leopard in Hebron leaped upon my dog, and I caught it by the tail, and hurled it on the rocks, and it was broken in twain ¹⁵ I found a wild ox feeding in the fields, and seizing it by the horns, and whirling it round and stunning it, I cast it from me and slew it. ¹⁶ And when the two kings of the Canaanites came sheathed, in armour against our flocks, and much people with them, single handed I rushed upon the king of Hazor, and smote him on the greives and dragged him down, and so I slew him. ¹⁷ And the other, the king of Tappuah, as he sat upon his horse, I slew, and so I scattered all his people. ¹⁸ Achor, the king, a man of giant stature, I found, hurling javelins before and behind as he sat on horseback, and I took up a stone of sixty pounds weight, and hurled it and smote his horse, and killed it. ¹⁹ And I fought with this other for two hours; and I clave his shield in twain, and I chopped off his feet, and killed him. ²⁰ And as I was stripping off his breastplate, behold nine men his companions began to fight with me, ²¹ And I wound my garment on my hand; and I slung stones at them, and killed four of them, and the rest fled. ²² And Jacob my father slew Beelesath, king of all the kings, a giant in strength, twelve cubits high. ²³ And fear fell upon them, and they ceased warring against us. ²⁴ Therefore my father was free from anxiety in the wars when I was with my brethren. ²⁵ For he saw in a vision concerning me that an angel of might followed me everywhere, that I should not be overcome. ²⁶ And in the south there came upon us a greater war than that in Shechem; and I joined in battle array with my brethren, and pursued a thousand men, and slew of them two hundred men and four kings. ²⁷ And I went up upon the wall, and I slew four mighty men. ²⁸ And so we captured Hazor, and took all the spoil. ²⁹ And the next day we departed to Aretan, a city strong and walled and inaccessible, threatening us with death. ³⁰ But I and Gad approached on the east side of the city, and Reuben and Levi on the west. ³¹ And they that were upon the wall, thinking that we were alone, were drawn down against us. ³² And so my brothers secretly climbed up the wall on both sides by stakes, and entered the city, while the men knew it not. ³³ And we took it with the edge of the sword. ³⁴ And as for those who had taken refuge in the tower, we set fire to the tower and took both it and, them. ³⁵ And as we were departing the men of Tappuah seized our spoil, and seeing this we fought with them. ³⁶ And we slew them. all and recovered our spoil. ³⁷ And when I was at the waters of Kozeba, the men of Jobel came against us to battle. ³⁸ And we fought with them and routed them; and their allies from Shiloh we slew, and we did not leave them power to come in against us. ³⁹ And the men of Makir came upon us the fifth day, to seize our spoil; and we attacked them and overcame them in fierce battle: for there was a host of mighty men amongst them, and we slew them before they had gone up the ascent. ⁴⁰ And when we came to their city their women rolled upon us stones from the brow of the hill on which the city stood. ⁴¹ And I and Simeon had ourselves behind the town, and seized upon the heights, and destroyed this city also. ⁴² And the next day it was told us that the king of the city of Gaash with. a mighty host was coming against us. ⁴³ I, therefore, and Dan feigned ourselves to be Amorites, and as allies went into their city. ⁴⁴ And in the depth of night our brethren came and we opened to them the gates; and we destroyed all the men and their substance, and we took for a prey all that was theirs, and their three walls we cast down. ⁴⁵ And we drew near to Thamna, where was all the substance of the hostile kings. ⁴⁶ Then being insulted by them, I was therefore wroth, and rushed against them to the summit; and they kept slinging against me stones and darts. ⁴⁷ And had not Dan my brother aided me, they would have slain me. ⁴⁸ We came upon them, therefore, with wrath, and they all fled; and passing by another way, they fought my father, and he made peace with them. ⁴⁹ And we did to them no hurt, and they became tributary to us, and we restored to them their spoil. ⁵⁰ And I built Thamna, and my father built Pabael. ⁵¹ I was twenty years old when this war befell. And the Canaanites feared me and my brethren. ⁵² And I had much cattle, and I had for chief herdsman Iram the Adullamite. ⁵³ And when I went to him I saw Parsaba, king of Adullam; and he spake unto us, and he made us a feast; and when I was heated he gave me his daughter Bathshua to wife. ⁵⁴ She bare me Er, and Onan and Shelah; and two of them the Lord smote: for Shelah lived, and his children are ye.

2

Judah describes some archeological findings, a city with walls of Iron and gates of brass. He has an encounter with an adventuress.

¹ AND eighteen years my father abode in peace with his brother Esau, and his sons with us, after that we came from Mesopotamia, from Laban. ² And when eighteen years were fulfilled, in the fortieth year of my life, Esau, the brother of my father, came upon us with a mighty and strong people. ³ And Jacob smote Esau with an arrow, and he was taken up wounded on Mount Seir, and as he went he died at Anoniram. ⁴ And we pursued after the sons of Esau. ⁵ Now they had a city with walls of iron and gates of brass; and we could not enter into it, and we encamped around, and besieged it. ⁶ And when they opened not to us in twenty days, I set up a ladder in the sight of all and with my shield upon my head I went up, sustaining the assault of stones, upwards of three talents weight; and I slew four of their mighty men. ⁷ And Reuben and Gad slew six others. ⁸ Then they asked from us terms of peace; and having taken counsel with our father, we received them as tributaries. ⁹ And they gave us five hundred cors of wheat, five hundred baths of oil, five hundred measures of wine, until the famine, when we went down into Egypt. ¹⁰ And after these things my son Er took to wife Tamar, from Mesopotamia, a daughter of Aram. ¹¹ Now Er was wicked, and he was in need concerning Tamar, because she was not of the land of Canaan. ¹² And on the third night an angel of the Lord smote him. ¹³ And he had not known her according to the evil craftiness of his mother, for he did not wish to have children by her. ¹⁴ In the days of the wedding feast I gave Onan to her in marriage; and he also in wickedness knew her not, though he spent with her a year. ¹⁵ And when I threatened him he went in unto her, but he spilled the seed on the ground, according to the command of his mother, and he also died through wickedness. ¹⁶ And I wished to give Shelah also to her, but his mother did not permit it; for she wrought evil against Tamar, because she was not the daughters of Canaan, as she also herself was. ¹⁷ And I knew that the race of the Canaanites was wicked, but the impulse of youth blinded my mind. ¹⁸ And when I saw her pouring out wine, owing to the intoxication of wine I was deceived, and took her although my father had not counselled it. ¹⁹ And while I was away she went and took for Shelah a wife from Canaan. ²⁰ And when I knew what she had done, I cursed her in the anguish of my soul. ²¹ And she also died through her wickedness together with her sons. ²² And after these things, while Tamar was a widow, she heard after two years that I was going up, to shear my sheep, and

adorned herself in bridal array, and sat in the city Enaim by the gate. ²³ For it was a law of the Amorites, that she who was about to marry should sit in fornication seven days by the gate. ²⁴ Therefore being drunk with wine, I did not recognize her; and her beauty deceived me, through the fashion of her adorning. ²⁵ And I turned aside to her, and said: Let me go in unto thee. ²⁶ And she said: What wilt thou give me? And I gave her my staff, and my girdle, and the diadem of my kingdom in pledge. ²⁷ And I went in unto her, and she conceived. ²⁸ And not knowing what I had done, I wished to slay her; but she privily sent my pledges, and put me to shame. ²⁹ And when I called her, I heard also the secret words which I spoke when lying with her in my drunkenness; and I could not slay her, because it was from the Lord. ³⁰ For I said, Lest haply she did it in subtlety, having received the pledge from another woman. ³¹ But I came not again near her while I lived, because I had done this abomination in all Israel. ³² Moreover, they who were in the city said there was no harlot in the gate, because she came from another place, and sat for a while in the gate. ³³ And I thought that no one knew that I had gone in to her. ³⁴ And after this we came into Egypt to Joseph, because of the famine. ³⁵ And I was forty and six years old, and seventy and three years lived I in Egypt.

3

He counsels against wine and lust as twin evils. "For he who is drunken reverenceth no man." (Verse 13).

¹ AND now I command you, my children, hearken to Judah your father, and keep my sayings to perform all the ordinances of the Lord, and to obey the commands of God. ² And walk not after your lusts, nor in the imaginations of your thoughts in haughtiness of heart; and glory not in the deeds and strength of your youth, for this also is evil in the eyes of the Lord. ³ Since I also gloried that in wars no comely woman's face ever enticed me, and reproved Reuben my brother concerning Bilhah, the wife of my father, the spirits of jealousy and of fornication arrayed themselves against me, until I lay with Bathshua the Canaanite, and Tamar, who was espoused to my sons. ⁴ For I said to my father-in-law: I will take counsel with my father, and so will I take thy daughter. ⁵ And he was unwilling but he showed me a boundless store of gold in his daughter's behalf; for be was a king. ⁶ And he adorned her with gold and pearls, and caused her to pour out wine for us at the feast with the beauty of women. ⁷ And the wine turned aside my eyes, and pleasure blinded my heart. ⁸ And I became enamoured of and I lay with her, and transgressed the commandment of the Lord and the commandment of my fathers, and I took her to wife. ⁹ And the Lord rewarded me according to the imagination of my heart, inasmuch as I had no joy in her children. ¹⁰ And now, my children, I say unto you, be not drunk with wine; for wine turneth the mind away from, the truth, and inspires the passion of lust, and leadeth the eyes into error. ¹¹ For the spirit of fornication hath wine as a minister to give pleasure to the mind; for these two also take away the mind of man. ¹² For if a man drink wine to drunkenness, it disturbeth the mind with filthy thoughts leading to fornication, and heateth the body to carnal union; and if the occasion of the lust be present, he worketh the sin, and is not ashamed. ¹³ Such is the inebriated man, my children; for he who is drunken reverenceth no man. ¹⁴ For, lo, it made me also to err, so that I was not ashamed of the multitude in the city, in that before the eyes of all I turned aside unto Tamar, and I wrought a great sin, and I uncovered the covering of my sons' shame. ¹⁵ After I had drunk wine I reverenced not the commandment of God, and I took a woman of Canaan to wife. ¹⁶ For much discretion needeth the man who drinketh wine, my children; and herein is discretion in drinking wine, a man may drink so long as he preserveth modesty. ¹⁷ But if he go beyond this limit the spirit of deceit attacketh his mind, and it maketh the drunkard to talk filthily, and to transgress and not to be ashamed, but even to glory in his shame, and to account himself honourable. ¹⁸ He that committeth fornication is not aware when he suffers loss, and is not ashamed when put to dishonour. ¹⁹ For even though a man be a king and commit fornication, he is stripped of his kingship by becoming the slave of fornication, as I myself also suffered. ²⁰ For I gave my staff, that is, the stay of my tribe; and my girdle, that is, my power; and my diadem, that is, the glory of my kingdom. ²¹ And indeed I repented of these things; wine and flesh I eat not until my old age, nor did I behold any joy. ²² And the angel of God showed me that for ever do women bear rule over king and beggar alike. ²³ And from the king they take away his glory, and from the valiant man his might, and from the beggar even that little which is the stay of his poverty. ²⁴ Observe, therefore, my children, the right limit in wine; for there are in it four evil spirits–of lust, of hot desire, of profligacy, of filthy lucre. ²⁵ If ye drink wine in gladness, be ye modest in the fear of God. ²⁶ For if in your gladness the fear of God departeth, then drunkenness ariseth and shamelessness stealeth in. ²⁷ But if ye would live soberly do not touch wine at all, lest ye sin in words of outrage, and in fightings and slanders, and the commandments of God, and ye perish before your time. ²⁸ Moreover, wine revealeth the mysteries of God and men, even as I also revealed the commandments of God and mysteries of Jacob my father to the Canaanitish woman Bathshua, which God bade me not to reveal. ²⁹ And wine is a cause both of war and confusion. ³⁰ And now, I command you, my children, not to love money, nor to gaze upon the beauty of women; because for the sake of money and beauty I was led astray to Bathshua the Canaanite. ³¹ For I know that because of these two things shall my race fall into wickedness. ³² For even wise men among my sons shall they mar, and shall cause the kingdom of Judah to be diminished, which the Lord gave me because of my obedience to my father. ³³ For I never caused grief to Jacob, my father; for all things whatsoever he commanded I did. ³⁴ And Isaac, the father of my father, blessed me to be king in Israel, and Jacob further blessed me in like manner. ³⁵ And I know that from me shall the kingdom be established. ³⁶ And I know what evils ye will do in the last days. ³⁷ Beware, therefore, my children, of fornication, and the love of money, and hearken to Judah your father. ³⁸ For these things withdraw au from the law of God, and blind the inclination of the soul, and teach arrogance, and suffer not a man to have compassion upon his neighbour. ³⁹ They rob his soul of all goodness, and oppress him with toils and troubles, and drive away sleep from him, and devour his flesh. ⁴⁰ And he hindereth the sacrifices of God; and he remembereth not the blessing of God, he hearkeneth not to a prophet when he speaketh, and resenteth the words of godliness. ⁴¹ For he is a slave to two contrary passions, and cannot obey God, because they have blinded his soul, and he walketh in the day as in the night. ⁴² My children, the love of money leadeth to idolatry; because, when led astray through money, men name as gods those who are not gods, and it causeth him who hath it to fall into madness. ⁴³ For the sake of money I lost my children, and had not my repentance, and my humiliation, and the prayers of my father been accepted, I should have died childless. ⁴⁴ But the God of my fathers had mercy on me, because I did it in ignorance. ⁴⁵ And the prince of deceit blinded me, and I sinned as a man and as flesh, being corrupted through sins; and I learnt my own weakness while thinking myself invincible. ⁴⁶ Know, therefore, my children, that two spirits wait upon man-the spirit of truth and the spirit of deceit. ⁴⁷ And in the midst is the spirit of understanding of the mind, to which it belongeth to turn whithersoever it will. And the works of truth and the works of deceit are written upon the hearts of men, and each one of them the Lord knoweth. ⁴⁹ And there is no time at which the works of men can be hid; for on the heart itself have they been written down before the Lord. ⁵⁰ And the spirit of truth testifieth all things, and accuseth all; and the sinner is burnt up by his own heart, and cannot raise his face to the judge.

4

Judah makes a vivid simile concerning tyranny and a dire prophecy concerning the morals of his listeners.

¹ AND now, my children, I command you, love Levi, that ye may abide, and exalt not yourselves against him, lest ye be utterly destroyed. ² For to me the Lord gave the kingdom, and to him the priesthood, and He set the kingdom beneath the priesthood. ³ To me He gave the things upon the earth; to him the things in the heavens. ⁴ As the heaven is higher than the earth, so is the priesthood of God higher than the earthly kingdom, unless it falls away through sin from the Lord and is dominated by the earthly kingdom. ⁵ For the angel of the Lord said unto me: The Lord chose him rather than thee, to draw near to Him, and to eat of His table and to offer Him the first-fruits of the choice things of the sons of Israel; but thou shalt be king of Jacob. ⁶ And thou shalt be amongst them as the sea. ⁷ For as, on the sea, just and unjust are tossed about, some taken into captivity while some are enriched, so also shall every race of men be in thee: some shall be impoverished, being taken captive, and others grow rich by plundering the possessions of others. ⁸ For the kings shall be as sea-monsters. ⁹ They shall swallow men like fishes: the sons and daughters of freemen shall they enslave; houses, lands, flocks, money shall they plunder: ¹⁰ And with the flesh of many shall they wrongfully feed the ravens and the cranes; and they shall advance in evil in covetousness uplifted, and there shall be false prophets like tempest, and they shall persecute all righteous men. ¹¹ And the Lord shall bring upon them divisions one against another. ¹² And there shall be continual wars in Israel; and among men of another race shall my kingdom be brought to an end, until the salvation of Israel shall come. ¹³ Until the appearing of the God of righteousness, that Jacob, and all the Gentiles may rest in peace. ¹⁴ And He shall guard the might of my kingdom for ever; for the Lord aware to me with an oath that He would not destroy the kingdom from my seed for ever. ¹⁵ Now I have much grief, my children, because of your lewdness and witchcrafts, and idolatries which ye shall practise against the kingdom, following them that have familiar spirits, diviners, and demons of error. ¹⁶ Ye shall make your daughters singing girls and harlots, and ye shall mingle in the abominations of the Gentiles. ¹⁷ For

which things' sake the Lord shall bring upon you famine and pestilence, death and the sword, beleaguering by enemies, and revilings of friends, the slaughter of children, the rape of wives, the plundering of possessions, the burning of the temple of God, the laying waste of the land, the enslavement of yourselves among the Gentiles. ¹⁸ And they shall make some of you eunuchs for their wives. ¹⁹ Until the Lord visit you, when with perfect heart ye repent and walk in all His commandments, and He bring you up from captivity among the Gentiles. ²⁰ And after these things shall a star arise to you from Jacob in peace, ²¹ And a man shall arise from my seed, like the sun of righteousness, ²² Walking with the sons of men in meekness and righteousness; ²³ And no sin shall be found in him. ²⁴ And the heavens shall be opened unto him, to pour out the spirit, even the blessing of the Holy Father; and He shall pour out the spirit of grace upon you; ²⁵ And ye shall be unto Him sons in truth, and ye shall walk in His commandments first and last. ²⁶ Then shall the sceptre of my kingdom shine forth; and from your root shall arise a stem; and from it shall grow a rod of righteousness to the Gentiles, to judge and to save all that call upon the Lord. ²⁷ And after these things shall Abraham and Isaac and Jacob arise unto life; and I and my brethren shall be chiefs of the tribes of Israel: ²⁸ Levi first, I the second, Joseph third, Benjamin fourth, Simeon fifth, Issachar sixth, and so all in order. ²⁹ And the Lord blessed Levi, and the Angel of the Presence, me; the powers of glory, Simeon; the heaven, Reuben; the earth, Issachar; the sea, Zebulun; the mountains, Joseph; the tabernacle, Benjamin; the luminaries, Dan; Eden, Naphtali; the sun, Gad; the moon, Asher. ³⁰ And ye shall be the people of the Lord, and have one tongue; and there shall be there no spirit of deceit of Beliar, for he shall be cast into the fire for ever. ³¹ And they who have died in grief shall arise in joy, and they who were poor for the Lord's sake shall be made rich, and they who are put to death for the Lord's sake shall awake to life. ³² And the harts of Jacob shall run in joyfulness, and the eagles of Israel shall fly in gladness; and all the people shall glorify the Lord for ever. ³³ Observe, therefore, my children, all the law of the Lord, for there is hope for all them who hold fast unto, His ways. ³⁴ And he said to them: Behold, I die before your eyes this day, a hundred and nineteen years old. ³⁵ Let no one bury me in costly apparel, nor tear open my bowels, for this shall they who are kings do; and carry me up to Hebron with you. ³⁶ And Judah, when he had said these things, fell asleep; and his sons did according to all whatsoever he commanded them, and they buried him in Hebron, with his fathers.

Testament of Issachar
The Fifth Son of Jacob and Leah.

1

Issachar, the fifth son of Jacob and Leah. The sinless child of hire for mandrakes. He appeals for simplicity.

¹ THE copy of the words of Issachar. ² For he called his sons and said to them: Hearken, my children, to Issachar your father; give ear to the words of him who is beloved of the Lord. ³ I was born the fifth son to Jacob, by way of hire for the mandrakes. ⁴ For Reuben my brother brought in mandrakes from the field, and Rachel met him and took them. ⁵ And Reuben wept, and at his voice Leah my mother came forth. ⁶ Now these mandrakes were sweet-smelling apples which were produced in the land of Haran below a ravine of water. ⁷ And Rachel said: I will not give them to thee, but they shall be to me instead of children. ⁸ For the Lord hath despised me, and I have not borne children to Jacob. ⁹ Now there were two apples; and Leah said to Rachel: Let it suffice thee that thou hast taken my husband: wilt thou take these also? ¹⁰ And Rachel said to her: Thou shalt have Jacob this night for the mandrakes of thy son, ¹¹ And Leah said to her: Jacob is mine, for I am the wife of his youth. ¹² But Rachel said: Boast not, and vaunt not thyself; for he espoused me before thee, and for my sake he served our father fourteen years. ¹³ And had not craft increased on the earth and the wickedness of men prospered, thou wouldst not now see the face of Jacob. ¹⁴ For thou art not his wife, but in craft wert taken to him in my stead. ¹⁵ And my father deceived me, and removed me on that night, and did not suffer Jacob to see me; for had I been there, this had not happened to him. ¹⁶ Nevertheless, for the mandrakes I am hiring Jacob to thee for one night. ¹⁷ And Jacob knew Leah, and she conceived and bare me, and on account of the hire I was called Issachar. ¹⁸ Then appeared to Jacob an angel of the Lord, saying: Two children shall Rachel bear, inasmuch as she hath refused company with her husband, and hath chosen continency. ¹⁹ And had not Leah my mother paid the two apples for the sake of his company, she would have borne eight sons; for this reason she bare six, and Rachel bare the two: for on account of the mandrakes the Lord visited her. ²⁰ For He knew that for the sake of children she wished to company with Jacob, and not for lust of pleasure. ²¹ For on the morrow also she again gave up Jacob. ²² Because of the mandrakes, therefore, the Lord hearkened to Rachel. ²³ For though she desired them, she cat them not, but offered them in the house of the Lord, presenting them to the priest of the Most High who was at that time. ²⁴ When, therefore, I grew up, my children, I walked in uprightness of heart, and I became a husbandman for my father and my brethren, and I brought in fruits from the field according to their season. ²⁵ And my father blessed me, for he saw that I walked in rectitude before him. ²⁶ And I was not a busybody in my doings, nor envious and malicious against my neighbour. ²⁷ I never slandered any one, nor did I censure the life of any man, walking as I did in singleness of eye. ²⁸ Therefore, when I was thirty-five years old, I took to myself a wife, for my labour wore away my strength, and I never thought upon pleasure with women; but owing to my toil, sleep overcame me. ²⁹ And my father always rejoiced in my rectitude, because I offered through the priest to the Lord all first-fruits; then to my father also. ³⁰ And the Lord increased ten thousandfold His benefits in my hands; and also Jacob, my father, knew that God aided my singleness. ³¹ For on all the poor and oppressed I bestowed the good things of the earth in the singleness of my heart. ³² And now, hearken to me, my children, and walk in singleness of your heart, for I have seen in it all that is well-pleasing to the Lord. ' ³³ The single-minded man coveteth not gold, he overreacheth not his neighbour, he longeth not after manifold dainties, he delighteth not in varied apparel. ³⁴ He doth not desire to live a long life, but only waiteth for the will of God. ³⁵ And the spirits of deceit have no power against him, for he looketh not on the beauty of women, lest he should pollute his mind with corruption. ³⁶ There is no envy in his thoughts, no malicious person maketh his soul to pine away, nor worry with insatiable desire in his mind. ³⁷ For he walketh in singleness of soul, and beholdeth all things in uprightness of heart, shunning eyes made evil through the error of the world, lest he should see the perversion of any of the commandments of the Lord. ³⁸ Keep, therefore, my children, the law of God, and get singleness, and walk in guilelessness, not playing the busybody with the business of your neighbour, but love the Lord and your neighbour, have compassion on the poor and weak. ³⁹ Bow down your back unto husbandry, and toil in labours in all manner of husbandry, offering gifts to the Lord with thanksgiving. ⁴⁰ For with the first-fruits of the earth will the Lord bless you, even as He blessed all the saints from Abel even until now. ⁴¹ For no other portion is given to you than of the fatness of the earth, whose fruits are raised by toil. ⁴² For our father Jacob blessed me with blessings of the earth and of first-fruits. ⁴³ And Levi and Judah were glorified by the Lord even among the sons of Jacob; for the Lord gave them an inheritance, and to Levi He gave the priesthood, and to Judah the kingdom. ⁴⁴ And do ye therefore obey them, and walk in the singleness of your father; for unto Gad hath it been given to destroy the troops that are coming upon Israel.

2

¹ KNOW ye therefore, my children, that in the last times your sons will forsake singleness, and will cleave unto insatiable desire. ² And leaving guilelessness, will draw near to malice; and forsaking the commandments of the Lord, they will cleave unto Beliar. ³ And leaving husbandry, they will follow after their own wicked devices, and they shall be dispersed among the Gentiles, and shall serve their enemies. ⁴ And do you therefore give these commands to your children, that, if they sin, they may the more quickly return to the Lord; For He is merciful, and will deliver them, even to bring them back into their land. ⁵ Behold, therefore, as ye see, I am a hundred and twenty-six years old and am not conscious of committing any sin. ⁶ Except my wife I have not known any woman. I never committed fornication by the uplifting of my eyes. ⁷ I drank not wine, to be led astray thereby; ⁸ I coveted not any desirable thing that was my neighbour's. ⁹ Guile arose not in my heart; ¹⁰ A lie passed not through my lips. ¹¹ If any man were in distress I joined my sighs with his, ¹² And I shared my bread with the poor. ¹³ I wrought godliness, all my days I kept truth. ¹⁴ I loved the Lord; likewise also every man with all my heart. ¹⁵ So do you also these things, my children, and every spirit of Beliar shall flee from you, and no deed of wicked men shall rule over you; ¹⁶ And every wild beast shall ye subdue, since you have with you the God of heaven and earth and walk with men in singleness of heart. ¹⁷ And having said these things, he commanded his sons that they should carry him up to Hebron, and bury him there in the cave with his fathers. ¹⁸ And he stretched out his feet and died, at a good old age; with every limb sound, and with strength unabated, he slept the eternal sleep.

Testament of Zebulun
The Sixth Son of Jacob and Leah.

1

Zebulun, the sixth son of Jacob and Leah. The inventor and philanthropist., What he learned as a result of the plot against Joseph.

¹ THE copy of the words of Zebulun, which he enjoined on his sons before he died in the hundred and fourteenth year of his life, two years after the death of Joseph. ² And he said to them: Hearken to me, ye sons of Zebulun

attend to the words of your father. ³ I, Zebulun, was born a good gift to my parents. ⁴ For when I was born my father was increased very exceedingly, both in flocks and herds, when with the straked rods he had his portion. ⁵ I am not conscious that I have sinned all my days, save in thought. ⁶ Nor yet do I remember that I have done any iniquity, except the sin of ignorance which I committed against Joseph; for I covenanted with my brethren not to tell my father what had been done. ⁷ But I wept in secret many days on account of Joseph, for I feared my brethren, because they had all agreed that if any one should declare the secret, he should be slain. ⁸ But when they wished to kill him, I adjured them much with tears not to be guilty of this sin. ⁹ For Simeon and Gad came against Joseph to kill him, and he said unto them with tears: Pity me, my brethren, have mercy upon the bowels of Jacob our father: lay not upon me your hands to shed innocent blood, for I have not sinned against you. ¹⁰ And if indeed I have sinned, with chastening chastise me, my brethren, but lay not upon your hand, for the sake of Jacob our father, ¹¹ And as he spoke these words, wailing as he did so, I was unable to bear his lamentations, and began to weep, and my liver was poured out, and all the substance of my bowels was loosened. ¹² And I wept with Joseph and my heart sounded, and the joints of my body trembled, and I was not able to stand. ¹³ And when Joseph saw me weeping with him, and them coming against him to slay him, he fled behind me, beseeching them. ¹⁴ But meanwhile Reuben arose and said: Come, my brethren, let us not slay him, but let us cast him into one of these dry pits, which our fathers digged and found no water. ¹⁵ For for this cause the Lord forbade that water should rise up in them in order that Joseph should be preserved. ¹⁶ And they did so, until they sold him to the Ishmaelites. ¹⁷ For in his price I had no share, my children. ¹⁸ But Simeon and Gad and six other of our brethren took the price of Joseph, and bought sandals for themselves, and their wives, and their children, saying: ¹⁹ We will not eat of it, for it is the price of our brother's blood, but we will assuredly tread it under foot, because he said that he would be king over us, and so let us see what will become of his dreams. ²⁰ Therefore it is written in the writing of the law of Moses, that whosoever will not raise up seed to his brother, his sandal should be unloosed, and they should spit in his face. ²¹ And the brethren of Joseph wished not that their brother should live, and the Lord loosed from them the sandal which they wore against Joseph their brother. ²² For when they came into Egypt they were unloosed by the servants of Joseph outside the gate, and so they made obeisance to Joseph after the fashion of King Pharaoh. ²³ And not only did they make obeisance to him, but were spit upon also, falling down before him forthwith, and so they were put to shame before. the Egyptians. ²⁴ For after this the Egyptians heard all the evils that they had done to Joseph. ²⁵ And after he was sold my brothers sat down to eat and drink. ²⁶ But I, through pity for Joseph, did not eat, but watched the pit, since Judah feared lest Simeon, Dan, and Gad should rush off and slay him. ²⁷ But when they saw that I did not eat, they set me to watch him, till he was sold to the Ishmaelites. ²⁸ And when Reuben came and heard that while he was away Joseph had been sold, he rent his garments, and mourning, said: ²⁹ How shall I look on the face of my father Jacob? And he took the money and ran after the merchants but as he failed to find them he returned grieving. ³⁰ But the merchants had left the broad road and marched through the Troglodytes by a short cut. ³¹ But Reuben was grieved, and ate no food that day. ³² Dan therefore came to him and said: Weep not, neither grieve; for we have found what we can say to our father Jacob. ³³ Let us slay a kid of the goats, and dip in it the coat of Joseph; and let us send it to Jacob, saying: Know, is this the coat of thy son? ³⁴ And they did so. For they stripped off from Joseph his coat when they were selling him, and put upon him the garment of a slave. ³⁵ Now Simeon took the coat, and would not give it up, for he wished to rend it with his sword, as he was angry that Joseph lived and that he had not slain him. ³⁶ Then we all rose up and said unto him: If thou givest not up the coat, we will say to our father that thou alone didst this evil thing in Israel. ³⁷ And so he gave it unto them, and they did even as Dan had said.

2

He urges human sympathy and understanding of one's fellow men.

¹ AND now children, I you (sic) to keep the commands of the Lord, and to show mercy to your neighbours, and to have compassion towards all, not towards men only, but also towards beasts. ² For all this thing's sake the Lord blessed me, and when all my brethren were sick, I escaped without sickness, for the Lord knoweth the purposes of each. ³ Have, therefore, compassion in your hearts, my children, because even as a man doeth to his neighbour, even so also will the Lord do to him. ⁴ For the sons of my brethren were sickening and were dying on account of Joseph, because they showed not mercy in their hearts; but my sons were preserved without sickness, as ye know. ⁵ And when I was in the land of Canaan, by the sea-coast, I made a catch of fish for Jacob my father; and when many were choked in the sea, I continued unhurt. ⁶ I was the first to make a boat to sail upon the sea, for the Lord gave me understanding and wisdom therein. ⁷ And I let down a rudder behind it, and I stretched a sail upon another upright piece of wood in the midst. ⁸ And I sailed therein along the shores, catching fish for the house of my father until we came to Egypt. ⁹ And through compassion I shared my catch with every stranger. ¹⁰ And if a man were a stranger, or sick, or aged, I boiled the fish, and dressed them well, and offered them to all men, as every man had need, grieving with and having compassion upon them. ¹¹ Wherefore also the Lord satisfied me with abundance of fish when catching fish; for he that shareth with his neighbour receiveth manifold more from the Lord. ¹² For five years I caught fish and gave thereof to every man whom I saw, and sufficed for all the house of my father. ¹³ And in the summer I caught fish, and in the winter I kept sheep with my brethren. ¹⁴ Now I will declare unto you what I did. ¹⁵ I saw a man in distress through nakedness in wintertime, and had compassion upon him, and stole away a garment secretly from my father's house, and gave it to him who was in distress. ¹⁶ Do you, therefore, my children, from that which God bestoweth upon you, show compassion and mercy without hesitation to all men, and give to every man with a good heart. ¹⁷ And if ye have not the wherewithal to give to him that needeth, have compassion for him in bowels of mercy. ¹⁸ I know that my hand found not the wherewithal to give to him that needed, and I walked with him weeping for seven furlongs, and my bowels yearned towards him in compassion. ¹⁹ Have, therefore, yourselves also, my children, compassion towards every man with mercy, that the Lord also may have compassion and mercy upon you. ²⁰ Because also in, the last days God will send His compassion on the earth, and wheresoever He findeth bowels of mercy He dwelleth in him. ²¹ For in the degree in which a man hath compassion upon his neighbours, in the same degree hath the Lord also upon him. ²² And when we went down into Egypt, Joseph bore no malice against us. ²³ To whom taking heed, do ye also, my children, approve yourselves without malice, and love one another; and do not set down in account, each one of you, evil against his brother. ²⁴ For this breaketh unity and divideth all kindred, and troubleth the soul, and weareth away the countenance. ²⁵ Observe, therefore, the waters, and know when they flow together, they sweep along stones, trees, earth, and other things. ²⁶ But if they are divided into many streams, the earth swalloweth them up, and they vanish away. ²⁷ So shall ye also be if ye be divided. Be not Ye, therefore, divided into two heads for everything which the Lord made .hath but one head, and two shoulders, two hands, two feet, and all the remaining members. ²⁸ For I have learnt in the writing of my fathers, that ye shall be divided in Israel, and ye shall follow two kings, and shall work every abomination. ²⁹ And your enemies shall lead you captive, and ye shall be evil entreated among the Gentiles, with many infirmities and tribulations. ³⁰ And after these things ye shall remember the Lord and repent, and He shall have mercy upon you, for He is merciful and compassionate. ³¹ And He setteth not down in account evil against the sons of men, because they are flesh, and are deceived through their own wicked deeds. ³² And after these things shall there arise unto you the Lord Himself, the light of righteousness, and ye shall return unto your land. ³³ And ye shall see Him in Jerusalem, for His name's sake. ³⁴ And again through the wickedness of your works shall ye provoke Him to anger, ³⁵ And ye shall be cast away by Him unto the time of consummation. ³⁶ And now, my children, grieve not that I am dying, nor be cast down in that I am coming to my end. ³⁷ For I shall rise again in the midst of you, as a ruler in the midst of his sons; and I shall rejoice in the midst of my tribe, as many as shall keep the law of the Lord, and the commandments of Zebulun their father. ³⁸ But upon the ungodly shall the Lord bring eternal fire, and destroy them throughout all generations. ³⁹ But I am now hastening away to my rest, as did also my fathers. ⁴⁰ But do ye fear the Lord our God with all your strength all the days of your life. ⁴¹ And when he had said these things he fell asleep, at a good old age. ⁴² And his sons laid him in a wooden coffin. And afterwards they carried him up and buried him in Hebron, with his fathers.

Testament of Dan

The Seventh Son of Jacob and Bilhah.

1

The seventh son of Jacob and Bilhah. The jealous one. He counsels against anger saying that "it giveth peculiar vision." This is a notable thesis on anger.

¹ THE copy of the words of Dan, which he spake to his sons in his last days, in the hundred and twenty-fifth year of his life. ² For he called together his I family, and said: Hearken to my words, ye sons of Dan; and give heed to the words of your father. ³ I have proved in my heart, and in my whole life, that truth with just dealing is good and well pleasing to God, and that lying and anger are evil, because they teach man all wickedness. ⁴ I confess, therefore, this day to you, my children, that in my heart I resolved on the death of Joseph my brother, the true and good man. . ⁵ And I rejoiced that

he was sold, because his father loved him more than us. ⁶ For the spirit of jealousy and vainglory said to me: Thou thyself also art his son. ⁷ And one of the spirits of Beliar stirred me up, saying: Take this sword, and with it slay Joseph: so shall thy father love thee when he is dead. ⁸ Now this is the spirit of anger that persuaded me to crush Joseph as a leopard crusheth a kid. ⁹ But the God of my fathers did not suffer him to fall into my hands, so that I should find him alone and slay him, and cause a second tribe to be destroyed in Israel. ¹⁰ And now, my children, behold I am dying, and I tell you of a truth, that unless ye keep yourselves from the spirit of lying and of anger, and love truth and longsuffering, ye shall perish. ¹¹ For anger is blindness, and does not suffer one to see the face of any man with truth. ¹² For though it be a father or a mother, he behaveth towards them as enemies; though it be a brother, he knoweth him not; though it be a prophet of the Lord, he disobeyeth him; though a righteous man, he regardeth him not; though a friend, he doth not acknowledge him. ¹³ For the spirit of anger encompasseth him with the net of deceit, and blindeth his eyes, and through lying darkeneth his mind, and giveth him its own peculiar vision. ¹⁴ And wherewith encompasseth it his eyes? With hatred of heart, so as to be envious of his brother. ¹⁵ For anger is an evil thing, my children, for it troubleth even the soul itself. ¹⁶ And the body of the angry man it maketh its own, and over his soul it getteth the mastery, and it bestoweth upon the body power that it may work all iniquity. ¹⁷ And when the body does all these things, the soul justifieth what is done, since it seeth not aright. ¹⁸ Therefore he that is wrathful, if he be a mighty man, hath a threefold power in his anger: one by the help of his servants; and a second by his wealth, whereby he persuadeth and overcometh wrongfully; and thirdly, having his own natural power he worketh thereby the evil. ¹⁹ And though the wrathful man be weak, yet hath he a power twofold of that which is by nature; for wrath ever aideth such in lawlessness. ²⁰ This spirit goeth always with lying at the right hand of Satan, that with cruelty and lying his works may be wrought. ²¹ Understand ye, therefore, the power of wrath, that it is vain. ²² For it first of all giveth provocation by word; then by deeds it strengtheneth him who is angry, and with sharp losses disturbeth his mind, and so stirreth up with great wrath his soul. ²³ Therefore, when any one. speaketh against you, be not ye moved to anger, and if any man praiseth you as holy men, be not uplifted: be not moved either to delight or to disgust. ²⁴ For first it pleaseth the hearing, and so maketh the mind keen to perceive the grounds for provocation; and then being enraged, he thinketh that he is justly angry. ²⁵ If ye fall into any loss or ruin, my children, be not afflicted; for this very spirit maketh a man desire that which is perishable, in order that he may be enraged through the affliction. ²⁶ And if ye suffer loss voluntarily, or involuntarily, be not vexed; for from vexation ariseth wrath with lying. ²⁷ Moreover, a twofold mischief is wrath with lying; and they assist one another in order to disturb the heart; and when the soul is continually disturbed, the Lord departeth from it, and Beliar ruleth over it.

2

A prophecy of the sins, captivity, plagues, and ultimate restitution of the nation. They still talk of Eden (See Verse 18). Verse 23 is remarkable in the light of prophecy.

¹ OBSERVE, therefore, my children, the commandments of the Lord, and keep His law; depart from wrath, and hate lying, that the Lord may dwell among you, and Beliar may flee from you. ² Speak truth each one with his neighbour. So shall ye not fall into wrath and confusion; but ye shall be in peace, having the God of peace, so shall no war prevail over you. ³ Love the Lord through all your life, and one another with a true heart. ⁴ I know that in the last days ye shall depart from the Lord, and ye shall provoke Levi unto anger, and fight against Judah; but ye shall not prevail against them, for an angel of the Lord shall guide them both; for by them shall Israel stand. ⁵ And whensoever ye depart from the Lord, ye shall walk in all evil and work the abominations of the Gentiles, going a-whoring after women of the lawless ones, while with all wickedness the spirits of wickedness work in you. ⁶ For I have read in the book of Enoch, the righteous, that your prince is Satan, and that all the spirits of wickedness and pride will conspire to attend constantly on the sons of Levi, to cause them to sin before the Lord. ⁷ And my sons will draw near to Levi, and sin with them in all things; and the sons of Judah will be covetous, plundering other men's goods like lions. ⁸ Therefore shall ye be led away with them into captivity, and there shall ye receive all the plagues of Egypt, and all the evils of the Gentiles. ⁹ And so when ye return to the Lord ye shall obtain mercy, and He shall bring you into His sanctuary, and He shall give you peace. ¹⁰ And there shall arise unto you from the tribe of Judah and of Levi the salvation of the Lord; and he shall make war against Beliar. ¹¹ And execute an everlasting vengeance on our enemies; and the captivity shall he take from Beliar the souls of the saints, and turn disobedient hearts unto the Lord, and give to them that call upon Him eternal peace. ¹² And the saints shall rest in Eden, and in the New Jerusalem shall the righteous rejoice, and it shall be unto the glory of God for ever. ¹³ And no longer shall Jerusalem endure desolation, nor Israel be led captive; for the Lord shall be in the midst of it [living amongst men], and the Holy One of Israel shall reign over it in humility and in poverty; and he who believeth on Him shall reign amongst men in truth. ¹⁴ And now, fear the Lord, my children, and beware of Satan and his spirits. ¹⁵ Draw near unto God and unto the angel that intercedeth for you, for he is a mediator between God and man, and for the peace of Israel he shall stand up against the kingdom of the enemy. ¹⁶ Therefore is the enemy eager to destroy all that call upon the Lord. ¹⁷ For he knoweth that upon the day on which Israel shall repent, the kingdom of the enemy shall be brought to an end. ¹⁸ For the very angel of peace shall strengthen Israel, that it fall not into the extremity of evil. ¹⁹ And it shall be in the time of the lawlessness of Israel, that the Lord will not depart from them, but will transform them into a nation that doeth His will, for none of the angels will be equal unto him. ²⁰ And His name shall be in every place in Israel, and among the Gentiles. ²¹ Keep, therefore, yourselves, my children, from every evil work, and cast away wrath and all lying, and love truth and long-suffering. ²² And the things which ye have heard from your father, do ye also impart to your children that the Saviour of the Gentiles may receive you; for he is true and long-suffering, meek and lowly, and teacheth by his works the law of God. ²³ Depart, therefore, from all unrighteousness, and cleave unto the righteousness of God, and your race will be saved for ever. ²⁴ And bury me near my fathers. ²⁵ And when he had said these things he kissed them, and fell asleep at a good old age. ²⁶ And his sons buried him, and after that they carried up his bones, and placed them near Abraham, and Isaac, and Jacob. ²⁷ Nevertheless, Dan prophesied unto them that they should forget their God, and should be alienated from the land of their inheritance and from the race of Israel, and from the family of their seed.

Testament of Naphtali
The Eighth Son of Jacob and Bilhah.

1

Naphtali, the eighth son of Jacob and Bilhah. The Runner. A lesson in physiology.

¹ THE copy of, the testament of Naphtali, which he ordained at the time of his death in the hundred and thirtieth year of his life. ² When his sons were gathered together in the seventh month, on the first day of the month, while still in good health, he made them a feast of food and wine. ³ And after he was awake in the morning, he said to them, I am dying; and they believed him not. ⁴ And as he glorified the Lord, he grew strong and said that after yesterday's feast he should die. ⁵ And he began then to say: Hear, my children, ye sons of Naphtali, hear the words of your father. ⁶ I was born from Bilhah, and because Rachel dealt craftly, and gave Bilhah in place of herself to Jacob, and she conceived and bare me upon Rachel's knees, therefore she called my name Naphtali. ⁷ For Rachel loved me very much because I was born upon her lap; and when I was still young she was wont to kiss me, and say: May I have a brother of thine from mine own womb, like unto thee. ⁸ Whence also Joseph was like unto me in all things, according to the prayers of Rachel. ⁹ Now my mother was Bilhah, daughter of Rotheus the brother of Deborah, Rebecca's nurse, who was born on one and the self-same day with Rachel. ¹⁰ And Rotheus was of the family of Abraham, a Chaldean, God-fearing, free-born, and noble. ¹¹ And he was taken captive and was bought by Laban; and he gave him Euna his handmaid to wife, and she bore a daughter, and called her name Zilpah, after the name of the village in which he had been taken captive. ¹² And next she bore Bilhah, saying: My daughter hastens after what is new, for immediately that she was born she seized the breast and hastened to suck it. ¹³ And I was swift on my feet like the deer, and my father Jacob appointed me for all messages, and as a deer did he give me his blessing. ¹⁴ For as the potter knoweth the vessel, how much it is to contain, and bringeth clay accordingly, so also doth the Lord make the body after the likeness of the spirit, and according to the capacity of the body doth He implant the spirit. ¹⁵ And the one does not fall short of the other by a third part of a hair; for by weight, and measure, and rule was all the creation made. ¹⁶ And as the potter knoweth the use of each vessel, what it is meet for, so also doth the Lord know the body, how far it will persist in goodness, and when it beginneth in evil. ¹⁷ For there is no inclination or thought which the Lord knoweth not, for He created every man after His own image. ¹⁸ For as a man's strength, so also in his work; as his eye, so also in his sleep; as his soul, so also in his word either in the law of the Lord or in the law of Beliar. ¹⁹ And as there is a division between light and darkness, between seeing and hearing, so also is there a division between man and man, and between woman and woman; and it is not to be said that the one is like the other either in face or in mind. ²⁰ For God made all things good in their order, the five senses in the head, and He joined on the neck to the head, adding to it

the hair also for comeliness and glory, then the heart for understanding, the belly for excrement, and the stomach for grinding, the windpipe for taking in the breath, the liver for wrath, the gall for bitterness, the spleen for laughter, the reins for prudence, the muscles of the loins for power, the lungs for drawing in, the loins for strength, and so forth. ²¹ So then, my children, let all your works be done in order with good intent in the fear of God, and do nothing disorderly in scorn or out of its due season. ²² For if thou bid the eye to hear, it cannot; so neither while ye are in darkness can ye do the works of light. ²³ Be ye, therefore, not eager to corrupt your doings through covetousness or with vain words to beguile your souls; because if ye keep silence in purity of heart, ye shall understand how to hold fast the will of God, and to cast away the will of Beliar. ²⁴ Sun and moon and stars, change not their order; so do ye also change not the law of God in the disorderliness of your doings. ²⁵ The Gentiles went astray, and forsook the Lord, and charged their order, and obeyed stocks and stones, spirits of deceit. ²⁶ But ye shall not be so, my children, recognizing in the firmament, in the earth, and in the sea, and in all created things, the Lord who made all things, that ye become not as Sodom, which changed the order of nature. ²⁷ In like manner the Watchers also changed the order of their nature, whom the Lord cursed at the flood, on whose account He made the earth without inhabitants and fruitless. ²⁸ These things I say unto you, my children, for I have read in the writing of Enoch that ye yourselves also shall depart from the Lord, walking according to all the lawlessness of the Gentiles, and ye shall do according to all the wickedness of Sodom. ²⁹ And the Lord shall bring captivity upon you, and there shall ye serve your enemies, and ye shall be bowed down with every affliction and tribulation, until the Lord have consumed you all. ³⁰ And after ye have become diminished and made few, ye return and acknowledge the Lord your God; and He shall bring you back into your land, according to His abundant mercy. ³¹ And it shall be, that after that they come into the land of their fathers, they shall again forget the Lord and become ungodly. ³² And the Lord shall scatter them upon the face of all the earth, until the compassion of the Lord shall come, a man working righteousness and working mercy unto all them that are afar off, and to them that are near.

2

He makes a plea for orderly living. Notable for their eternal wisdom are Verses 27-40.

¹ FOR in the fortieth year of my life, I saw a vision on the Mount of Olives, on the east of Jerusalem, that the sun and the moon were standing still. ² And behold Isaac, the father of my father, said to us; Run and lay hold of them, each one according to his strength; and to him that seizeth them will the sun and moon belong. ³ And we all of us ran together, and Levi laid hold of the sun, and Judah outstripped the others and seized the moon, and they were both of them lifted up with them. ⁴ And when Levi became as a sun, lo, a certain young man gave to him twelve branches of palm; and Judah was bright as the moon, and under their feet were twelve rays. ⁵ And the two, Levi and Judah, ran, and laid hold of them. ⁶ And lo, a bull upon the earth, with two great horns, and an eagle's wings upon its back; and we wished to seize him, but could not. ⁷ But Joseph came, and seized him, and ascended up with him on high. ⁸ And I saw, for I was there, and behold a holy writing appeared to us, saying: Assyrians, Medes, Persians, Chaldeans, Syrians, shall possess in captivity the twelve tribes of Israel. ⁹ And again, after seven days, I saw our father Jacob standing by the sea of Jamnia, and we were with him. ¹⁰ And behold, there came a ship sailing by, without sailors or pilot; and there was written upon the ship, The Ship of Jacob. ¹¹ And our father said to us: Come, let us embark on our ship. ¹² And when he had gone on board, there arose a vehement storm, and a mighty tempest of wind; and our father, who was holding the helm, departed from us. ¹³ And we, being tost with the tempest, were borne along over the sea; and the ship was filled with water, and was pounded by mighty waves, until it was broken up. ¹⁴ And Joseph fled away upon a little boat, and we were all divided upon nine planks, and Levi and Judah were together. ¹⁵ And we were all scattered unto the ends of the earth. ¹⁶ Then Levi, girt about with sackcloth, prayed for us all unto the Lord. ¹⁷ And when the storm ceased, the ship reached the land as it were in peace. ¹⁸ And, lo, our father came, and we all rejoiced with one accord. ¹⁹ These two dreams I told to my father; and he said to me: These things must be fulfilled in their season, after that Israel hath endured many things. ²⁰ Then my father saith unto me: I believe God that Joseph liveth, for I see always that the Lord numbereth him with you. ²¹ And he said, weeping: Ah me, my son Joseph, thou livest, though I behold thee not, and thou seest not Jacob that begat thee. ²² He caused me also, therefore, to weep by these words, and I burned in my heart to declare that Joseph had been sold, but I feared my brethren. ²³ And lo! my children, I have shown unto you the last times, how everything shall come to pass in Israel. ²⁴ Do ye also, therefore, charge your children that they be united to Levi and to Judah; for through them shall salvation arise unto Israel, and in them shall Jacob be blessed. ²⁵ For through their tribes shall God appear dwelling among men on earth, to save the race of Israel, and to gather together the righteous from amongst the Gentiles. ²⁶ If ye work that which is good, my children, both men and angels shall bless you; and God shall be glorified among the Gentiles through you, and the devil shall flee from you, and the wild beasts shall fear you, and the Lord shall love you, and the angels shall cleave to you. ²⁷ As a man who has trained a child well is kept in kindly remembrance; so also for a good work there is a good remembrance before God. ²⁸ But him that doeth not that which is good, both angels and men shall curse, and God shall be dishonoured among the Gentiles through him, and the devil shall make him as his own peculiar instrument, and every wild beast shall master him, and the Lord shall hate him. ²⁹ For the commandments of the law are twofold, and through prudence must they be fulfilled. ³⁰ For there is a season for a man to embrace his wife, and a season to abstain therefrom for his prayer. ³¹ So, then, there are two commandments; and, unless they be done in due order, they bring very great sin upon men. ³² So also is it with the other commandments. ³³ Be ye therefore wise in God, my children, and prudent, understanding the order of His commandments, and the laws of every word, that the Lord may love you, ³⁴ And when he had charged them with many such words, he exhorted them that they should remove his bones to Hebron, and that they should bury him with his fathers. ³⁵ And when he had eaten and drunken with a merry heart, he covered his face and died. ³⁶ And his sons did according to all that Naphtali their Father had commanded them.

Testament of Gad
The Ninth Son of Jacob and Zilpah.

1

Gad, the ninth son of Jacob and Zilpah. Shepherd and strong man but a murderer at heart. Verse 25 is a notable definition of hatred.

¹ THE copy of the testament of Gad, what things he spake unto his sons, in the hundred and twenty-fifth year of his life, saying unto them: ² Hearken, my children, I was the ninth son born to Jacob, and I was valiant in keeping the flocks. ³ Accordingly I guarded at night the flock; and whenever the lion came, or the wolf, or any wild beast against the fold, I pursued it, and overtaking it I seized its foot with my hand and hurled it about a stone's throw, and so killed it. ⁴ Now Joseph my brother was feeding the flock with us for upwards of thirty days, and being young, he fell sick by reason of the heat. ⁵ And he returned to Hebron to our father, who made him lie down near him, because he loved him greatly. ⁶ And Joseph told our father that the sons of Zilpah and Bilhah were slaying the best of the flock and eating them against the judgement of Reuben and Judah. ⁷ For he saw that I had delivered a lamb out of the mouth of a bear, and put the bear to death; but had slain the lamb, being grieved concerning it that it could not live, and that we had eaten it. ⁸ And regarding this matter I was wroth with Joseph until the day that he was sold. ⁹ And the spirit of hatred was in me, and I wished not either to hear of Joseph with the ears, or see him with the eyes, because he rebuked us to our faces saying that we were eating of the flock without Judah. ¹⁰ For whatsoever things he told our father, he believed him. ¹¹ I confess now my gin, my children, that oftentimes I wished to kill him, because I hated him from my heart. ¹² Moreover, I hated him yet more for his dreams; and I wished to lick him out of the land of the living, even as an ox licketh up the grass of the field. ¹³ And Judah sold him secretly to the Ishmaelites. ¹⁴ Thus the God of our fathers delivered him from our hands, that we should not work great lawlessness in Israel. ¹⁵ And now, my children, hearken to the words of truth to work righteousness, and all the law of the Most High, and go not astray through the spirit of hatred, for it is evil in all the doings of men. ¹⁶ Whatsoever a man doeth the hater abominateth him: and though a man worketh the law of the Lord, he praiseth him not; though a man feareth the Lord, and taketh pleasure in that which is righteous, he loveth him not. ¹⁷ He dispraiseth the truth, he envieth him that prospereth, he welcometh evil-speaking, he loveth arrogance, for hatred blindeth his soul; as I also then looked on Joseph. ¹⁸ Beware, therefore, my children of hatred, for it worketh lawlessness even against the Lord Himself. ¹⁹ For it will not hear the words of His commandments concerning the loving of one's–neighbour, and it sinneth against God. ²⁰ For if a brother stumble, it delighteth immediately to proclaim it to all men, and is urgent that he should be judged for it, and be punished and be put to death. ²¹ And if it be a servant it stirreth him up against his master, and with every affliction it deviseth against him, if possibly he can be put to death. ²² For hatred worketh with envy also against them that prosper: so long as it heareth of or seeth their success it always languisheth. ²³ For as love would quicken even the dead, and would call back them that are condemned to die, so hatred would slay the living, and those that had sinned venially it would not suffer to live. ²⁴ For the spirit of hatred worketh together with

Satan, through hastiness of spirits, in all things to men's death; but the spirit of love worketh together with the law of God in long-suffering unto the salvation of men. ²⁵ Hatred, therefore, is evil, for it constantly mateth with lying, speaking against the truth; and it maketh small things to be great, and causeth the light to be darkness, and calleth the sweet bitter, and teacheth slander, and kindleth wrath, and stirreth up war, and violence and all covetousness; it filleth the heart with evils and devilish poison. ²⁶ These things, therefore, I say to you from experience, my children, that ye may drive forth hatred, which is of the devil, and cleave to the love of God. ²⁷ Righteousness casteth out hatred, humility destroyeth envy. ²⁸ For he that is just and humble is ashamed to do what is unjust, being reproved not of another, but of his own heart, because the Lord looketh on his inclination. ²⁹ He speaketh not against a holy man, because the fear of God overcometh hatred. ³⁰ For fearing lest he should offend the Lord, he will not do wrong to any man, even in thought. ³¹ These things I learnt at last, after I had repented concerning Joseph. ³² For true repentance after a godly sort destroyeth ignorance, and driveth away the darkness, and enlighteneth the eyes, and giveth knowledge to the soul, and leadeth the mind to salvation. ³³ And those things which it hath not learnt from man, it knoweth through repentance. ³⁴ For God brought upon me a disease of the liver; and had not the prayers of Jacob my father succoured me, it had hardly failed but my spirit had departed. ³⁵ For by what things a man transgresseth by the same also is he punished. ³⁶ Since, therefore, my liver was set mercilessly against Joseph, in my liver too I suffered mercilessly, and was judged for eleven months, for so long a time as I had been angry against Joseph.

2

Gad exhorts his listeners against hatred showing how it has brought him into so much trouble. Verses 8-11 are memorable.

¹ AND now, my children, I exhort you, love ye each one his brother, and put away hatred from your hearts, love one another in deed, and in word, and in the inclination of the soul. ² For in the presence of my father I spake peaceably to Joseph; and when I had gone out, the spirit of hatred darkened my mind, and stirred up my soul to slay him. ³ Love ye one another from the heart; and if a man sin against thee, speak peaceably to him, and in thy soul hold not guile; and if he repent and confess, forgive him. ⁴ But if he deny it, do not get into a passion with him, lest catching the poison from thee he take to swearing and so thou sin doubly. ⁵ Let not another man hear thy secrets when engaged in legal strife, lest he come to hate thee and become thy enemy, and commit a great sin against thee; for ofttimes he addresseth thee guilefully or busieth himself about thee with wicked intent. ⁶ And though he deny it and yet have a sense of shame when reproved, give over reproving him. ⁷ For be who denieth may repent so as not again to wrong thee; yea, he may also honour thee, and fear and be at peace with thee. ⁸ And if he be shameless and persist in his wrong-doing, even so forgive him from the heart, and leave to God the avenging. ⁹ If a man prospereth more than you, do not be vexed, but pray also for him, that he may have perfect prosperity. ¹⁰ for so it is expedient for you. ¹¹ And if he be further exalted, be not envious of him, remembering that all flesh shall die; and offer praise to God, who giveth things good and profitable to all men. ¹² Seek out the judgments of the Lord, and thy mind will rest and be at peace. ¹³ And though a man become rich by evil means, even as Esau, the brother of my father, be not jealous; but wait for the end of the Lord. ¹⁴ For if he taketh away from a man wealth gotten by evil means He forgiveth him if he repent, but the unrepentant is reserved for eternal punishment. ¹⁵ For the poor man, if free from envy he pleaseth the Lord in all things, is blessed beyond all men, because he hath not the travail of vain men. ¹⁶ Put away, therefore, jealousy from your souls, and love one another with uprightness of heart. ¹⁷ Do ye also therefore tell these things to your children, that they honour Judah and Levi, for from them shall the Lord raise up salvation to Israel. ¹⁸ For I know that at the last your children shall depart from Him, and shall walk in O wickedness, and affliction and corruption before the Lord. ¹⁹ And when he had rested for a little while, he said again; My children, obey your father, and bury me near to my fathers. ²⁰ And he drew up his feet, and fell asleep in peace. ²¹ And after five years they carried him up to Hebron, and laid him with his fathers.

Testament of Asher
The Tenth Son of Jacob and Zilpah.

1

Asher, the tenth son of Jacob and Zilpah. An explanation of dual personality. The first Jekyll and Hyde story. For a statement of the Law of Compensation that Emerson would have enjoyed, see Verse 27.

¹ THE copy of the Testament To Asher, what things he spake to his sons in the hundred and twenty-fifth year of his life. ² For while he was still in health, he said to them: Hearken, ye children of Asher, to your father, and I will declare to you all that is upright in the sight of the Lord. ³ Two ways hath God given to the sons of men, and two inclinations, and two kinds of action, and two modes of action, and two issues. ⁴ Therefore all things are by twos, one over against the other. ⁵ For there are two ways of good and evil, and with these are the two inclinations in our breasts discriminating them. ⁶ Therefore if the soul take pleasure in the good inclination, all its actions are in righteousness; and if it sin it straightway repenteth. ⁷ For, having its thoughts set upon righteousness, and casting away wickedness, it straightway overthroweth the evil, and uprooteth the sin. ⁸ But if it incline to the evil inclination, all its actions are in wickedness, and it driveth away the good, and cleaveth to the evil, and is ruled by Beliar; even though it work what is good, he perverteth it to evil. ⁹ For whenever it beginneth to do good, he forceth the issue of the action into evil for him, seeing that the treasure of the inclination is filled with an evil spirit. ¹⁰ A person then may with words help the good for the sake of the evil, yet the issue of the action leadeth to mischief. ¹¹ There is a man who showeth no compassion upon him who serveth his turn in evil; and this thing bath two aspects, but the whole is evil. . ¹² And there is a man that loveth him that worketh evil, because he would prefer even to die in evil for his sake; and concerning this it is clear that it bath two aspects, but the whole is an evil work. ¹³ Though indeed he have love, yet is he wicked who concealeth what is evil for the sake of the good name, but the end of the action tendeth unto evil. ¹⁴ Another stealeth, doeth unjustly, plundereth, defraudeth, and withal pitieth the poor: this too bath a twofold aspect, but the whole is evil. ¹⁵ He who defraudeth his neighbour provoketh God, and sweareth falsely against the Most High, and yet pitieth the poor: the Lord who commanded the law he setteth at nought and provoketh, and yet he refresheth the poor. ¹⁶ He defileth the soul, and maketh gay the body; he killeth many, and pitieth a few: this, too, bath a twofold aspect, but the whole is evil. ¹⁷ Another committeth adultery and fornication, and abstaineth from meats, and when he fasteth he doeth evil, and by the power of his wealth overwhelmeth many; and notwithstanding his excessive wickedness he doeth the commandments: this, too, hath a twofold aspect, but the whole is evil. ¹⁸ Such men are hares; clean,–like those that divide the hoof, but in very deed are unclean. ¹⁹ For God in the tables of the commandments hath thus declared. ²⁰ But do not ye, my children, wear two faces like unto them, of goodness and of wickedness; but cleave unto goodness only, for God hath his habitation therein, and men desire it. ²¹ But from wickedness flee away, destroying the evil inclination by your good works; for they that are double-faced serve not God, but their own lusts, so that they may please Beliar and men like unto themselves. ²² For good men, even they that are of single face, though they be thought by them that are double-faced to sin, are just before God. ²³ For many in killing the wicked do two works, of good and evil; but the whole is good, because he hath uprooted and destroyed that which is evil. ²⁴ One man hateth the merciful and unjust man, and the man who committeth adultery and fasteth: this, too, hath a twofold aspect, but the whole work is good, because he followeth the Lord's example, in that he accepteth not the seeming good as the genuine good. ²⁵ Another desireth not to see good day with them that not, lest be defile his body and pollute his soul; this, too, is double-faced, but the whole is good. ²⁶ For such men are like to stags and to hinds, because in the manner of wild animals they seem to be unclean, but they are altogether clean; because they walk in zeal for the Lord and abstain from what God also hateth and forbiddeth by His commandments, warding off the evil from the good. ²⁷ Ye see, my children, how that there are two in all things, one against the other, and the one is hidden by the other: in wealth is hidden covetousness, in conviviality drunkenness, in laughter grief, in wedlock profligacy. ²⁸ Death succeedeth to life, dishonour to glory, night to day, and darkness to light; and all things are under the day, just things under life, unjust things under death; wherefore also eternal life awaiteth death. ²⁹ Nor may it be said that truth is a lie, nor right wrong; for all truth is under the light, even as all things are under God. ³⁰ All these things, therefore, I proved in my life, and I wandered not from the truth of the Lord, and I searched out the commandments of the Most High, walking according to all my strength with singleness of face unto that which is good. ³¹ Take heed, therefore, ye also, my children, to the commandments of the Lord, following the truth with singleness of face. ³² For they that are double-faced are guilty of a twofold sin; for they both do the evil thing and they have pleasure in them that do it, following the example of the spirits of deceit, and striving against mankind. ³³ Do ye, therefore, my children, keep the law of the Lord, and give not heed unto evil as unto good; but look unto the thing that is really good, and keep it in all commandments of the Lord, having your conversation therein, and resting therein. ³⁴ For the latter ends of men do show their righteousness or unrighteousness, when they meet the angels of the Lord and of Satan. ³⁵ for when the soul departs troubled, it is tormented by the evil spirit which also it served in lusts and evil works. ³⁶ But if he is peaceful with joy he meeteth the angel of peace, and he leadeth him into eternal life. ³⁷ Become not, my

children, as Sodom, which sinned against the angels of the Lord, and perished for ever. ³⁸ For I know that ye shall sin, and be delivered into the hands of your enemies; and your land shall be made desolate, and your holy places destroyed, and ye shall be scattered unto the four corners of the earth. ³⁹ And ye shall be set at nought in the dispersion vanishing away as water. ⁴⁰ Until the Most High shall visit the earth, coming Himself as man, with men eating and drinking, and breaking the head of the dragon in the water. ⁴¹ He shall save Israel and all the Gentiles, God speaking in the person of man. ⁴² Therefore do ye also, my children, tell these things to your children, that they disobey Him not. ⁴³ For I have known that ye shall assuredly be disobedient, and assuredly act ungodly, not giving heed to the law of God, but to the commandments of men, being corrupted through wickedness. ⁴⁴ And therefore shall ye be scattered as Gad and Dan my brethren, and ye shall know not your lands, tribe, and tongue. ⁴⁵ But the Lord will gather you together in faith through His tender mercy, and for the sake of Abraham, Isaac, and Jacob. ⁴⁶ And when he had said these things unto them, he commanded them, saying: Bury me in Hebron. ⁴⁷ And he fell asleep and died at a good old age. ⁴⁸ And his sons did as he had commanded them, and they carried him up to Hebron, and buried him with his fathers.

The Testament of Joseph
The Eleventh Son of Jacob and Rachel.

1

Joseph, the eleventh son of Jacob and Rachel, the beautiful and beloved. His struggle against the Egyptian temptress.

¹ THE copy of the Testament of Joseph. ² When he was about to die he called his sons and his brethren together, and said to them:– ³ My brethren and my children, hearken to Joseph the beloved of Israel; give ear, my sons, unto your father. ⁴ I have seen in my life envy and death, yet I went not astray, but persevered in the truth–of the Lord. ⁵ These my brethren hated me, but the Lord loved me: ⁶ They wished to slay me, but the God of my fathers guarded me: ⁷ They let me down into a pit, and the Most High brought me up again. ⁸ I was sold into slavery, and the Lord of all made me free: ⁹ I was taken into captivity, and His strong hand succoured me. ¹⁰ I was beset with hunger, and the Lord Himself nourished me. ¹¹ I was alone, and God comforted me: ¹² I was sick, and the Lord visited me. ¹³ I was in prison, and my God showed favour unto me; ¹⁴ In bonds, and He released me; ¹⁵ Slandered, and He pleaded my cause; ¹⁶ Bitterly spoken against by the Egyptians, and He delivered me; ¹⁷ Envied by my fellow-slaves, and He exalted me. ¹⁸ And this chief captain of Pharaoh entrusted to me his house. ¹⁹ And I struggled against a shameless woman, urging me to transgress with her; but the God of Israel my father delivered me from the burning flame. ²⁰ I was cast into prison, I was beaten, I was mocked; but the Lord granted me to find mercy, in the sight of the keeper of the prison. ²¹ For the Lord doth not forsake them that fear Him, neither in darkness, nor in bonds, nor in tribulations, nor in necessities. ²² For God is not put to shame as a man, nor as the son of man is he afraid, nor as one that is earth-born is He weak or affrighted. ²³ But in all those things doth He give protection, and in divers ways doth He comfort, though for a little space He departeth to try the inclination of the soul. ²⁴ In ten temptations He showed me approved, and in all of them I endured; for endurance is a mighty charm, and patience giveth many good things. ²⁵ How often did the Egyptian woman threaten me with death! ²⁶ How often did she give me over to punishment, and then call me back and threaten me, and when I was unwilling to company with her, she said to me: ²⁷ Thou shalt be lord of me, and all that is in my house, if thou wilt give thyself unto me, and thou shalt be as our master. ²⁸ But I remembered the words of my father, and going into my chamber, I wept and prayed unto the Lord. ²⁹ And I fasted in those seven years, and I appeared to the Egyptians as one living delicately, for they that fast for God's sake receive beauty of face. ³⁰ And if my lord were away from home, I drank no wine; nor for three days did I take my food, but I gave it to the poor and sick. ³¹ And I sought the Lord early, and I wept for the Egyptian woman of Memphis, for very unceasingly did she trouble me, for also at night she came to me under pretence of visiting me. ³² And because she had no male child she pretended to regard me as a son. ³³ And for a time she embraced me as a son, and I knew it not; but later, she sought to draw me into fornication. ³⁴ And when I perceived it I sorrowed unto death; and when she had gone out, I came to myself, and lamented for her many days, because I recognized her guile and her deceit. ³⁵ And I declared unto her the words of the Most High, if haply she would turn from her evil lust. ³⁶ Often, therefore, did she flatter me with words as a holy man, and guilefully in her talk praise my chastity before her husband, while desiring to ensnare me when we were alone. ³⁷ For she lauded me openly as chaste, and in secret she said unto me: Fear not my husband; for he is persuaded concerning thy chastity: for even should one tell him concerning us, he would not believe. ³⁸ Owing to all these things I lay upon the ground, and besought God that the Lord would deliver me from her deceit. ³⁹ And when she had prevailed nothing thereby, she came again to me under the plea of instruction, that she might learn the word of God. ⁴⁰ And she said unto me: If thou willest that I should leave my idols, lie with me, and I will persuade my husband to depart from his idols, and we will walk in the law by thy Lord. ⁴¹ And I said unto her: The Lord willeth not. that those who reverence Him should be in uncleanness, nor doth He take pleasure in them that commit adultery, but in those that approach Him with a pure heart and undefiled lips. ⁴² But she heed her peace, longing to accomplish her evil desire. ⁴³ And I gave myself yet more to fasting and prayer, that the Lord might deliver me from her. ⁴⁴ And again, at another time she said unto me: If thou wilt not commit adultery, I will kill my husband by poison; and take thee to be my husband. ⁴⁵ I therefore, when I heard this, rent my garments, and said unto her: ⁴⁶ Woman, reverence God, and do not this evil deed, lest thou be destroyed; for know indeed that I will declare this thy device unto all men. ⁴⁷ She therefore, being afraid, besought that I would not declare this device. ⁴⁸ And she departed soothing me with gifts, and sending to me every delight of the sons of men. ⁴⁹ And afterwards she sent me food mingled with enchantments. ⁵⁰ And when the eunuch who brought it came, I looked up and beheld a terrible man giving me with the dish a sword, and I perceived that her scheme was to beguile me. ⁵¹ And when he had gone out I wept, nor did I taste that or any other of her food. ⁵² So then after one day she came to me and observed the food, and said unto me: Why is it that thou hast not eaten of the food? ⁵³ And I said unto her: It is because thou hast filled it with deadly enchantments; and how saidst thou: I come not near to idols but to the Lord alone. ⁵⁴ Now therefore know that the God of my father hath revealed unto me by His angel thy wickedness, and I have kept it to convict thee, if haply thou mayst see and repent. ⁵⁵ But that thou mayst learn that the wickedness of the ungodly hath no power over them that worship God with chastity behold I will take of it and eat before thee. ⁵⁶ And having so said, I prayed thus: The God of my fathers and the angel of Abraham, be with me; and ate. ⁵⁷, And when she saw this she fell upon her face at my feet, weeping; and I raised her up and admonished her. ⁵⁸ And she promised to do this iniquity no more. ⁵⁹ But her heart was still set upon evil, and she looked around how to ensnare me, and sighing deeply she became downcast, though she was not sick. ⁶⁰ And when her husband saw her, he said unto her: Why is thy countenance fallen? ⁶¹ And she said unto him: I have a pain at my heart, and the groanings of my spirit oppress me; and so he comforted her who was not sick. ⁶² Then, accordingly seizing an opportunity, she rushed unto me while her husband was yet without, and said unto me: I will hang myself, or cast myself over a cliff, if thou wilt not lie with me. ⁶³ And when I saw the spirit of Beliar was troubling her, I prayed unto the Lord, and said unto her: ⁶⁴ Why, wretched woman, art thou troubled and disturbed, blinded through sins? ⁶⁵ Remember that if thou kill thyself, Asteho, the concubine of thy husband, thy rival, will beat thy children, and thou wilt destroy thy memorial from off the earth. ⁶⁶ And she said unto me: Lo, then thou lovest me; let this suffice me: only strive for my life and my children, and I expect that I shall enjoy my desire also. ⁶⁷ But she knew not that because of my lord I spake thus, and not because of her. ⁶⁸ For if a man hath fallen before the passion of a wicked desire and become enslaved by it, even as she, whatever good thing he may hear with regard to that passion, he receiveth it with a view to his wicked desire. ⁶⁹ I declare, therefore, unto you, my children, that it was about the sixth hour when she departed from me; and I knelt before the Lord all day, and all the night; and about dawn I rose up, weeping the while and praying for a release from her. ⁷⁰ At last, then, she laid hold of my garments, forcibly dragging me to have connexion with her. ⁷¹ When, therefore, I saw that in her madness she was holding fast to my garment, I left it behind, and fled away naked. ⁷² And holding fast to the garment she falsely accused me, and when her husband came he cast me into prison in his house; and on the morrow he scourged me and sent me into Pharaoh's prison. ⁷³ And when I was in bonds, the Egyptian woman was oppressed with grief, and she came and heard how I gave thanks unto the Lord and sang praises in the abode of darkness, and with glad voice rejoiced, glorifying my God that I was delivered from the lustful desire of the Egyptian woman. ⁷⁴ And often hath she sent unto me saying: Consent to fulfil my desire, and I will release thee from thy bonds, and I will free thee from the darkness. ⁷⁵ And not even in thought did I incline unto her. ⁷⁶ For God loveth him who in a den of wickedness combines fasting with chastity, rather than the man who in kings' chambers combines luxury with license. ⁷⁷ And if a man liveth in chastity, and desireth also glory, and the Most High knoweth that it is expedient for him, He bestoweth this also upon me. ⁷⁸ How often, though she were sick, did she come down to me at unlooked for times, and listened to my voice as I prayed! ⁷⁹ And when I heard her groanings I held my peace. ⁸⁰ For when I was in her house she was wont to bare her arms, and breasts, and legs, that I might lie with her; for she was very beautiful, splendidly

adorned in order to beguile me. ⁸¹ And the Lord guarded me from her devices.

2

Joseph is the victim of many plots by the wicked ingenuity of the Memphian woman. For an interesting prophetic parable, see Verses 73-74.

¹ YE see, therefore, my children, how great things patience worketh, and prayer with fasting. ² So ye too, if ye follow after chastity and purity with patience and prayer, with fasting in humility of heart, the Lord will dwell among you because He loveth chastity. ³ And wheresoever the Most High dwelleth, even though envy, or slavery, or slander befalleth a man, the Lord who dwelleth in him, for the sake of his chastity not only delivereth him from evil, but also exalteth him even as me. ⁴ For in every way the man is lifted up, whether in deed, or in word, or in thought. ⁵ My brethren knew how my father loved me, and yet I did not exalt myself in my mind: although I was a child, I had the fear of God in my heart; for I knew that all things would pass away. ⁶ And I did not raise myself against them with evil intent, but I honoured my brethren; and out of respect for them, even when I was being sold, I refrained from telling the Ishmaelites that I was a son of Jacob, a great man and a mighty. ⁷ Do ye also, my children, have the fear of God in all your works before your eyes, and honour your brethren. ⁸ For every one who doeth the law of the Lord shall be loved by Him. ⁹ And when I came to the Indocolpitae with the Ishmaelites, they asked me, saying: ¹⁰ Art thou a slave? And I said that I was a home-born slave, that I might not put my brethren to shame. ¹¹ And the eldest of them said unto me: Thou art not a slave, for even thy appearance doth make it manifest. ¹² But I said that I was their slave. ¹³ Now when we came into Egypt they strove concerning me, which of them should buy me and take me. ¹⁴ Therefore it seemed good to all that I should remain in Egypt with the merchant of their trade, until they should return bringing merchandise. ¹⁵ And the Lord gave me favour in the eyes of the merchant, and he entrusted unto me his house. ¹⁶ And God blessed him by my means, and increased him in gold and silver and in household servants. ¹⁷ And I was with him three months and five days. ¹⁸ And about that time the Memphian woman, the wife of Pentephris came down in a chariot, with great pomp, because she had heard from her eunuchs concerning me. ¹⁹ And she told her husband that the merchant had become rich by means of a young Hebrew, and they say that he had assuredly been stolen out of the land of Canaan. ²⁰ Now, therefore, render justice unto him, and take away the youth to thy house; so shall the God of the Hebrews bless thee, for grace from heaven is upon him. ²¹ And Pentephris was persuaded by her words, and commanded the merchant to be brought, and said unto him: ²² What is this that I hear concerning thee, that thou stealest persons out of the land of Canaan, and sellest them for slaves? ²³ But the merchant fell at his feet, and besought him, saying: I beseech thee, my lord, I know not what thou sayest. ²⁴ And Pentephris said unto him: Whence, then, is the Hebrew slave? ²⁵ And he said: The Ishmaelites entrusted him unto me until they should return. ²⁶ But he believed him not, but commanded him to be stripped and beaten. ²⁷ And when he persisted in this statement, Pentephris said: Let the youth be brought. ²⁸ And when I was brought in, I did obeisance to Pentephris for he was third in rank of the officers of Pharaoh. ²⁹ And he took me apart from him, and said unto me: Art thou a slave or free? ³⁰ And I said: A slave. ³¹ And he said: Whose? ³² And I said: The Ishmaelites'. ³³ And he said: How didst thou become their slave? ³⁴ And I said: They bought me out of the land of Canaan. ³⁵ And he said unto me: Truly thou liest; and straightway he commanded me to be stripped and beaten. ³⁶ Now, the Memphian woman was looking through a window at me while I was being beaten, for her house was near, and she sent unto him saying: ³⁷ Thy judgement is unjust; for thou dost punish a free man who hath been stolen, as though he were a transgressor. ³⁸ And when I made no change in my statement, though I was beaten, he ordered me to be imprisoned, until, he said, the owners of the boy should come. ³⁹ And the woman said unto her husband: Wherefore dost thou detain the captive and wellborn lad in bonds, who ought rather to be set at liberty, and be waited upon? ⁴⁰ For she wished to see me out of a desire of sin, but I was ignorant concerning all these things. ⁴¹ And he said to her: It is not the custom of the Egyptians to take that which belongeth to others before proof is given. ⁴² This, therefore, he said concerning the merchant; but as for the lad, he must be imprisoned. ⁴³ Now after four and twenty days came the Ishmaelites; for they had heard that Jacob my father was mourning much concerning me. ⁴⁴ And they came and said unto me: How is it that thou saidst that thou wast a slave? and lo, we have learnt that thou art the son of a mighty man in the land of Canaan, and thy father still mourneth for thee in sackcloth and ashes. ⁴⁵ When I heard this my bowels were dissolved and my heart melted, and I desired greatly to weep, but I restrained myself that I should not put my brethren to shame. ⁴⁶ And I said unto them, I know not, I am a slave. ⁴⁷ Then, therefore, they took counsel to sell me, that I should not be found in their hands. ⁴⁸ For they feared my father, lest he should come and execute upon them a grievous vengeance. ⁴⁹ For they had heard that he was mighty with God and with men. ⁵⁰ Then said the merchant unto them: Release me from the judgement of Pentiphri. ⁵¹ And they came and requested me, saying: Say that thou wast bought by us with money, and he will set us free. ⁵² Now the Memphian woman said to her husband: Buy the youth; for I hear, said she, that they are selling him. ⁵³ And straightway she sent a eunuch to the Ishmaelites, and asked them to sell me. ⁵⁴ But since the eunuch would not agree to buy me at their price he returned, having made trial of them, and he made known to his mistress that they asked a large price for their slave. ⁵⁵ And she sent another eunuch, saying: Even though they demand two minas, give them, do not spare the gold; only buy the boy, and bring him to me. ⁵⁶ The eunuch therefore went and gave them eighty pieces of gold, and he received me; but to the Egyptian woman he said I have given a hundred. ⁵⁷ And though I knew this I held my peace, lest the eunuch should be put to shame. ⁵⁸ Ye see, therefore, my children, what great things I endured that I should not put my brethren to shame. ⁵⁹ Do ye also, therefore, love one another, and with long-suffering hide ye one another's faults. ⁶⁰ For God delighteth in the unity of brethren, and in the purpose of a heart that takes pleasure in love. ⁶¹ And when my brethren came into Egypt they learnt that I had returned their money unto them, and upbraided them not, and comforted them. ⁶² And after the death of Jacob my father I loved them more abundantly, and all things whatsoever he commanded I did very abundantly for them. ⁶³ And I suffered them not to be afflicted in the smallest matter; and all that was in my hand I gave unto them. ⁶⁴ And their children were my children, and my children as their servants; and their life was my life, and all their suffering was my suffering, and all their sickness was my infirmity. ⁶⁵ My land was their land, and their counsel my counsel. ⁶⁶ And I exalted not myself among them in arrogance because of my worldly glory, but I was among them as one of the least. ⁶⁷ If ye also, therefore, walk in the commandments of the Lord, my children, He will exalt you there, and will bless you with good things for ever and ever. ⁶⁸ And if any one seeketh to do evil unto you, do well unto him, and pray for him, and ye shall be redeemed of the Lord from all evil. ⁶⁹ For, behold, ye see that out of my humility and longsuffering I took unto wife the daughter of the priest of Heliopolis. ⁷⁰ And a hundred talents of gold were given me with her, and the Lord made them to serve me. ⁷¹ And He gave me also beauty as a flower beyond the beautiful ones of Israel; and He preserved me unto old age in strength and in beauty, because I was like in all things to Jacob. ⁷² And hear ye, my children, also the vision which I saw. ⁷³ There were twelve harts feeding: and the nine were first dispersed over all the earth, and likewise also the three. ⁷⁴ And I saw that from Judah was born a virgin wearing a linen garment, and from her, was born a lamb, without spot; and on his left hand there was as it were a lion; and all the beasts rushed against him, and the lamb overcame them, and destroyed them and trod them under foot. ⁷⁵ And because of him the angels and men rejoiced, and all the land. ⁷⁶ And these things shall come to pass in their season, in the last days. ⁷⁷ Do ye therefore, my children, observe the commandments of the Lord, and honour Levi and Judah; for from them shall arise unto you the Lamb of God, who taketh away the sin of the world, one who saveth all the Gentiles and Israel. ⁷⁸ For His kingdom is an everlasting kingdom, which shall not pass away; but my kingdom among you shall come to an end as a watcher's hammock, which after the summer disappeareth. ⁷⁹ For I know that after my death the Egyptians will afflict you, but God will avenge you, and will bring you into that which He promised to your fathers. ⁸⁰ But ye shall carry up my bones with you; for when my bones are being taken up thither, the Lord shall be with you in light, and Beliar shall be in darkness with the Egyptians. ⁸¹ And carry ye up Asenath your mother to the Hippodrome, and near Rachel your mother bury her. ⁸² And when he had said these things he stretched out his feet, and died at a good old age. ⁸³ And all Israel mourned for him, and all Egypt, with a great mourning. ⁸⁴ And when the children of Israel went out of Egypt, they took with them the bones of Joseph, and they buried him in Hebron with his fathers, and the years of his life were one hundred and ten years.

The Testament of Benjamin

The Twelfth Son of Jacob and Rachel.

1

Benjamin, the twelfth son of Jacob and Rachel, the baby of the family, turns philosopher and philanthropist. ¹ THE copy of the words of Benjamin, which he commanded his sons to observe, after he had lived a hundred and twenty-five years. ² And he kissed them, and said: As Isaac was born to Abraham in his old age, so also was I to Jacob. ³ And since Rachel my mother died in giving me birth, I had no milk; therefore I was suckled by Bilhah her handmaid. ⁴ For Rachel remained barren for twelve years after she had borne Joseph; and she prayed the Lord with fasting twelve days, and she conceived and bare Me. ⁵ For my father loved Rachel dearly, and prayed that he might see two sons born from her. ⁶ Therefore was I called Benjamin, that is, a son of days. ⁷ And when I went into Egypt, to Joseph, and my brother recognized me, he said unto me: What did they tell my father when they sold me? ⁸ And I said unto him, They dabbled thy coat with blood and sent it, and said: Know whether this be thy son's coat. ⁹ And he said unto me: Even so, brother, when they had stripped me of my coat they gave me to the Ishmaelites, and they gave me a loin cloth, and scourged me, and bade me run. ¹⁰ And as for one of them that had beaten me with a rod, a lion met him and slew him. ¹¹ And so his associates were affrighted. ¹² Do ye also, therefore, my children, love the Lord God of heaven and earth, and keep His commandments, following the example of the good and holy man Joseph. ¹³ And let your mind be unto good, even as ye know me; for he that bath his mind right seeth all things rightly. ¹⁴ Fear ye the Lord, and love your neighbour; and even though the spirits of Beliar claim you to afflict you with every evil, yet shall they not have dominion over you, even as they had not over Joseph my brother., ¹⁵ How many men wished to slay him, and God shielded him! ¹⁶ For he that feareth God and loveth his neighbour cannot be smitten by the spirit of Beliar, being shielded by the fear of God. ¹⁷ Nor can he be ruled over by the device of men or beasts, for he is helped by the Lord through the love which he hath towards his neighbour. ¹⁸ For Joseph also besought our father that he would pray for his brethren, that the Lord would not impute to them as sin whatever evil they had done unto him. ¹⁹ And thus Jacob cried out: My good child, thou hast prevailed over the bowels of thy father Jacob. ²⁰ And he embraced him, and kissed him for two hours, saying: ²¹ In thee shall be fulfilled the prophecy of heaven concerning the Lamb of God, and Saviour of the world, and that a blameless one shall be delivered up for lawless men, and a sinless one shall die for ungodly men in the blood of the covenant, for the salvation of the Gentiles and of Israel, and shall destroy Beliar and his servants. ²² See ye, therefore, my children, the end of the good man? ²³ Be followers of his compassion, therefore, with a good mind, that ye also may wear crowns of glory. ²⁴ For the good man hath not a dark eye; for he showeth mercy to all men, even though they be sinners. ²⁵ And though they devise with evil intent. concerning him, by doing good he overcometh evil, being shielded by God; and he loveth the righteous as his own soul. ²⁶ If any one is glorified, he envieth him not; if any one is enriched, he is not jealous; if any one is valiant, he praiseth him; the virtuous man he laudeth; on the poor man he hath mercy; on the weak he hath compassion; unto God he singeth praises. ²⁷ And him that hath the grace of a good spirit he loveth as his own soul. ²⁸ If therefore, ye also have a good mind, then will both wicked men be at peace with you, and the profligate will reverence you and turn unto good; and the covetous will not only cease from their inordinate desire, but even give the objects of their covetousness to them that are afflicted. ²⁹ If ye do well, even the unclean spirits will flee from you; and the beasts will dread you. ³⁰ For where there is reverence for good works and light in the mind, even darkness fleeth away from him. ³¹ For if any one does violence to a holy man, he repenteth; for the holy man is merciful to his reviler, and holdeth his peace. ³² And if any one betrayeth a righteous man, the righteous man prayeth: though for a little he be humbled, yet not long after he appeareth far more glorious, as was Joseph my brother. ³³ The inclination of the good man is not in the power of the deceit of the spirit of Beliar, for the angel of peace guideth his soul. ³⁴ And he gazeth not passionately upon corruptible things, nor gathereth together riches through a desire of pleasure. ³⁵ He delighteth not in pleasure, he grieveth not his neighbour, he sateth not himself with luxuries, he erreth not in the uplifting of the eyes, for the Lord is his portion. ³⁶ The good inclination receiveth not glory nor dishonour from men, and it knoweth not any guile, or lie, or fighting or reviling; for the Lord dwelleth in him and lighteth up his soul, and he rejoiceth towards all men always. ³⁷ The good mind hath not two tongues, of blessing and of cursing, of contumely and of honour, of sorrow and of joy, of quietness and of confusion, of hypocrisy and of truth, of poverty and of wealth; but it hath one disposition, uncorrupt and pure, concerning all men. ³⁸ It hath no double sight, nor double hearing; for in everything which he doeth, or speaketh, or seeth, he knoweth that the Lord looketh on his soul. ³⁹ And he cleanseth his mind that he may not be condemned by men as well as by God. ⁴⁰ And in like manner the works of Beliar are twofold, and there is no singleness in them. ⁴¹ Therefore, my children, I tell you, flee the malice of Beliar; for he giveth a sword to them that obey him. ⁴² And the sword is the mother of seven evils. First the mind conceiveth through Beliar, and first there is bloodshed; secondly ruin; thirdly, tribulation; fourthly, exile; fifthly, dearth; sixthly, panic; seventhly, destruction. ⁴³ 'Therefore was Cain also delivered over to seven vengeances by God, for in every hundred years the Lord brought one plague upon him. ⁴⁴ And when he was two hundred years old he began to suffer, and in the nine-hundredth year he was destroyed. ⁴⁵ For on account of Abel, his brother, with -all the evils was he judged, but Lamech with seventy times seven. ⁴⁶ Because for ever those, who are like Cain in envy and hatred of brethren, shall be punished with the same judgement.

2

Verse 3 contains a striking example of the homeliness–yet vividness of the figures of speech of these ancient patriarchs.

¹ AND do ye, my children, flee evil-doing, envy, and hatred of brethren, and cleave to goodness and love. ² He that hath a pure mind in love, looketh not after a woman with a view to fornication; for he hath no defilement in his heart, because the Spirit of God resteth upon him. ³ For as the sun is not defiled by shining on dung and mire, but rather drieth up both and driveth away the evil smell; so also the pure mind, though encompassed by the defilements of earth, rather cleanseth them and is not itself defiled. ⁴ And I believe that there will be also evil-doings among you, from the words of Enoch the righteous: that ye shall commit fornication with the fornication of Sodom, and shall perish, all save a few, and shall renew wanton deeds with women; and the kingdom of the Lord shall not be among you, for straightway He shall take it away. ⁵ Nevertheless the temple of God shall be in your portion, and the last temple shall be more glorious than the first. ⁶ And the twelve tribes shall be gathered together there, and all the Gentiles, until the Most High shall send forth His salvation in the visitation of an only-begotten prophet. ⁷ And He shall enter into the first temple, and there shall the Lord be treated with outrage, and He shall be lifted up upon a tree. ⁸ And the veil of the temple shall be rent, and the Spirit of God shall pass on to the Gentiles as fire poured forth. ⁹ And He shall ascend from Hades and shall pass from earth into heaven. ¹⁰ And I know how lowly He shall be upon earth, and how glorious in heaven. ¹¹ Now when Joseph was in Egypt, I longed to see his figure and the form of his countenance; and through the prayers of Jacob my father I saw him, while awake in the daytime, even his entire figure exactly as he was. ¹² And when he had said these things, he said unto them: Know ye, therefore, my children, that I am dying. ¹³ Do ye, therefore, truth each one to his neighbour, and keep the law of the Lord and His commandments. ¹⁴ For these things do I leave you instead of inheritance. ¹⁵ Do ye also, therefore, give them to your children for an everlasting possession; for so did both Abraham, and Isaac, and Jacob. ¹⁶ For all these things they gave us for an inheritance, saying: Keep the commandments of God, until the Lord shall reveal His salvation to all Gentiles. ¹⁷ And then shall ye see Enoch, Noah, and Shem, and Abraham, and Isaac, and Jacob, rising on the right hand in gladness, ¹⁸ Then shall we also rise, each one over our tribe, worshipping the King of heaven, who appeared upon earth in the form of a man in humility. ¹⁹ And as many as believe on Him on the earth shall rejoice with Him. ²⁰ Then also all men shall rise, some unto glory and some unto shame. ²¹ And the Lord shall judge Israel first, for their unrighteousness; for when He appeared as God in the flesh to deliver them they believed Him not. ²² And then shall He judge all the Gentiles, as many as believed Him not when He appeared upon earth. ²³ And He shall convict Israel through the chosen ones of the Gentiles, even as He reproved Esau through the Midianites, who deceived their brethren, so that they fell into fornication, and idolatry; and they were alienated from God, becoming therefore children in the portion of them that fear the Lord. ²⁴ If ye therefore, my children, walk in holiness according to the commandments of the Lord, ye shall again dwell securely with me, and all Israel shall be gathered unto the Lord. ²⁵ And I shall no longer be called a ravening wolf on account of your ravages, but a worker of the Lord distributing food to them that work what is good. ²⁶ And there shall arise in the latter days one beloved of the Lord, of the tribe of Judah and Levi, a doer of His good pleasure in his mouth, with new knowledge enlightening the Gentiles. ²⁷ Until the consummation of the age shall he be in the synagogues of the Gentiles, and among their rulers, as a strain of music in the mouth of all. ²⁸ And he shall be inscribed in the holy books, both his work and his word, and he shall be a chosen one of God for ever. ²⁹ And through them he shall go to and fro as Jacob my father, saying: He shall fill up that which lacketh of thy tribe. ³⁰ And when he had said these things he stretched out his feet. ³¹ And died in a beautiful and good sleep. ³² And his sons did as he had enjoined them, and they took up his body and buried it in Hebron with his fathers. ³³ And the number of the days of his life was a hundred and twenty-five years.

The Testament of Abraham

¹ It came to pass, when the days of the death of Abraham drew near, that the Lord said to Michael: Arise and go to Abraham, my servant, and say to him, Thou shalt depart from life, for lo! the days of thy temporal life are fulfilled: so that he may set his house in order before he die. ² And Michael went and came to Abraham, and found him sitting before his oxen for ploughing, and he was exceeding old in appearance, and had his son in his arms. Abraham, therefore, seeing the archangel Michael, rose from the ground and saluted him, not knowing who he was, and said to him: The Lord preserve thee. May thy journey be prosperous with thee. And Michael answered him: Thou art kind, good father. Abraham answered and said to him: Come, draw near to me, brother, and sit down a little while, that I may order a beast to be brought that we may go to my house, and thou mayest rest with me, for it is toward evening, and in the morning arise and go whithersoever thou wilt, lest some evil beast meet thee and do thee hurt. And Michael enquired of Abraham, saying: Tell me thy name, before I enter thy house, lest I be burdensome to thee. Abraham answered and said, My parents called me Abram, and the Lord named me Abraham, saying: Arise and depart from thy house, and from thy kindred, and go into the land which I shall show unto thee. And when I went away into the land which the Lord showed me, he said to me: Thy name shall no more be called Abram, but thy name shall be Abraham. Michael answered and said to him: Pardon me, my father, experienced man of God, for I am a stranger, and I have heard of thee that thou didst go forty furlongs and didst bring a goat and slay it, entertaining angels in thy house, that they might rest there. Thus speaking together, they arose and went towards the house. And Abraham called one of his servants, and said to him: Go, bring me a beast that the stranger may sit upon it, for he is wearied with his journey. And Michael said: Trouble not the youth, but let us go lightly until we reach the house, for I love thy company. ³ And arising they went on, and as they drew nigh to the city, about three furlongs from it, they found a great tree having three hundred branches, like to a tamarisk tree. And they heard a voice from its branches singing, "Holy art thou, because thou hast kept the purpose for which thou wast sent." And Abraham heard the voice, and hid the mystery in his heart, saying within himself, What is the mystery that I have heard? As he came into the house, Abraham said to his servants, Arise, go out to the flocks, and bring three sheep, and slay them quickly, and make them ready that we may eat and drink, for this day is a feast for us. And the servants brought the sheep, and Abraham called his son Isaac, and said to him, My son Isaac, arise and put water in the vessel that we may wash the feet of this stranger. And he brought it as he was commanded, and Abraham said, I perceive, and so it shall be, that in this basin I shall never again wash the feet of any man coming to us as a guest. And Isaac hearing his father say this wept, and said to him, My father what is this that thou sayest, This is my last time to wash the feet of a stranger? And Abraham seeing his son weeping, also wept exceedingly, and Michael seeing them weeping, wept also, and the tears of Michael fell upon the vessel and became a precious stone. ⁴ When Sarah, being inside in her house, heard their weeping, she came out and said to Abraham, Lord, why is it that ye thus weep? Abraham answered, and said to her, It is no evil. Go into thy house, and do thy own work, lest we be troublesome to the man. And Sarah went away, being about to prepare the supper. And the sun came near to setting, and Michael went out of the house, and was taken up into the heavens to worship before God, for at sunset all the angels worship God and Michael himself is the first of the angels. And they all worshipped him, and went each to his own place, but Michael spoke before the Lord and said, Lord, command me to be questioned before thy holy glory! And the Lord said to Michael, Announce whatsoever thou wilt! And the Archangel answered and said, Lord, thou didst send me to Abraham to say to him, Depart from thy body, and leave this world; the Lord calls thee; and I dare not, Lord, reveal myself to him, for he is thy friend, and a righteous man, and one that receives strangers. But I beseech thee, Lord, command the remembrance of the death of Abraham to enter into his own heart, and bid not me tell it him, for it is great abruptness to say, Leave the world, and especially to leave one's own body, for thou didst create him from the beginning to have pity on the souls of all men. Then the Lord said to Michael, Arise and go to Abraham, and lodge with him, and whatever thou seest him eat, eat thou also, and wherever he shall sleep, sleep thou there also. For I will cast the thought of the death of Abraham into the heart of Isaac his son in a dream. ⁵ Then Michael went into the house of Abraham on that evening, and found them preparing the supper, and they ate and drank and were merry. And Abraham said to his son Isaac, Arise, my son, and spread the man's couch that he may sleep, and set the lamp upon the stand. And Isaac did as his father commanded him, and Isaac said to his father, I too am coming to sleep beside you. Abraham answered him, Nay, my son, lest we be troublesome to this man, but go to thy own chamber and sleep. And Isaac not wishing to disobey his father's command, went away and slept in his own chamber. ⁶ And it happened about the seventh hour of the night Isaac awoke, and came to the door of his father's chamber, crying out and saying, Open, father, that I may touch thee before they take thee away from me. Abraham arose and opened to him, and Isaac entered and hung upon his father's neck weeping, and kissed him with lamentations. And Abraham wept together with his son, and Michael saw them weeping and wept likewise. And Sarah hearing them weeping called from her bed-chamber, saying, My Lord Abraham, why is this weeping? Has the stranger told thee of thy brother's son Lot that he is dead? or has aught else befallen us? Michael answered and said to Sarah, Nay, Sarah, I have brought no tidings of Lot, but I knew of all your kindness of heart, that therein ye excel all men upon earth, and the Lord has remembered you. Then Sarah said to Abraham, How durst thou weep when the man of God has come in to thee, and why have thy eyes shed tears for today there is great rejoicing? Abraham said to her, How knowest thou that this is a man of God? Sarah answered and said, Because I say and declare that this is one of the three men who were entertained by us at the oak of Mamre, when one of the servants went and brought a kid and thou didst kill it, and didst say to me, Arise, make ready that we may eat with these men in our house. Abraham answered and said, Thou has perceived well, O woman, for I too, when I washed his feet knew in my heart that these were the feet which I had washed at the oak of Mamre, and when I began to enquire concerning his journey, he said to me, I go to preserve Lot thy brother from the men of Sodom, and then I knew the mystery. ⁷ And Abraham said to Michael, Tell me, man of God, and show to me why thou hast come hither. And Michael said, Thy son Isaac will show thee. And Abraham said to his son, My beloved son, tell me what thou hast seen in thy dream today, and wast frightened. Relate it to me. Isaac answered his father, I saw in my dream the sun and the moon, and there was a crown upon my head, and there came from heaven a man of great size, and shining as the light that is called the father of light. He took the sun from my head, and yet left the rays behind with me. And I wept and said, I beseech thee, my Lord, take not away the glory of my head, and the light of my house, and all my glory. And the sun and the moon and the stars lamented, saying, Take not away the glory of our power. And that shining man answered and said to me, Weep not that I take the light of thy house, for it is taken up from troubles into rest, from a low estate to a high one; they lift him up from a narrow to a wide place; they raise him from darkness to light. And I said to him, I beseech thee, Lord, take also the rays with it. He said to me, There are twelve hours of the day, and then I shall take all the rays. As the shining man said this, I saw the sun of my house ascending into heaven, but that crown I saw no more, and that sun was like thee my father. And Michael said to Abraham, Thy son Isaac has spoken truth, for thou shalt go, and be taken up into the heavens, but thy body shall remain on earth, until seven thousand ages are fulfilled, for then all flesh shall arise. Now therefore, Abraham, set thy house in order, and thy children, for thou hast heard fully what is decreed concerning thee. Abraham answered and said to Michael, I beseech thee, Lord, if I shall depart from my body, I have desired to be taken up in my body that I may see the creatures that the Lord my God has created in heaven and on earth. Michael answered and said, This is not for me to do, but I shall go and tell the Lord of this, and if I am commanded I shall show thee all these things. ⁸ And Michael went up into heaven, and spoke before the Lord concerning Abraham, and the Lord answered Michael, Go and take up Abraham in the body, and show him all things, and whatsoever he shall say to thee do to him as to my friend. So Michael went forth and took up Abraham in the body on a cloud, and brought him to the river of Ocean. ⁹ And after Abraham had seen the place of judgment, the cloud took him down upon the firmament below, and Abraham, looking down upon the earth, saw a man committing adultery with a wedded woman. And Abraham turning said to Michael, Seest thou this wickedness? but, Lord, send fire from heaven to consume them. And straightway there came down fire and consumed them, for the Lord had said to Michael, Whatsoever Abraham shall ask thee to do for him, do thou. Abraham looked again, and saw other men railing at their companions, and said, Let the earth open and swallow them, and as he spoke the earth swallowed them alive. Again the cloud led him to another place, and Abraham saw some going into a desert place to commit murder, and he said to Michael, Seest thou this wickedness? but let wild beasts come out of the desert, and tear them in pieces, and that same hour wild beasts came out of the desert, and devoured them. Then the Lord God spoke to Michael saying, Turn away Abraham to his own house, and let him not go round all the creation that I have made, because he has no compassion on sinners, but I have compassion on sinners that they may turn and live, and repent of their sins and be saved. ¹⁰ And Abraham looked and saw two gates, the one small and the other large, and between the two gates sat a man upon a throne of

great glory, and a multitude of angels round about him, and he was weeping, and again laughing, but his weeping exceeded his laughter seven-fold. And Abraham said to Michael, Who is this that sits between the two gates in great glory; sometimes he laughs, and sometimes he weeps, and his weeping exceeds his laughter seven-fold? And Michael said to Abraham, Knowest thou not who it is? And he said, No, Lord. And Michael said to Abraham, Seest thou these two gates, the small and the great? These are they which lead to life and to destruction. This man that sits between them is Adam, the first man whom the Lord created, and set him in this place to see every soul that departs from the body, seeing that all are from him. When, therefore, thou seest him weeping, know that he has seen many souls being led to destruction, but when thou seest him laughing, he has seen many souls being led into life. Seest thou how his weeping exceeds his laughter? Since he sees the greater part of the world being led away through the broad gate to destruction, therefore his weeping exceeds his laughter seven-fold. [11] And Abraham said, And he that cannot enter through the narrow gate, can he not enter into life? Then Abraham wept, saying, Woe is me, what shall I do? for I am a man broad of body, and how shall I be able to enter by the narrow gate, by which a boy of fifteen years cannot enter? Michael answered and said to Abraham, Fear not, father, nor grieve, for thou shalt enter by it unhindered, and all those who are like thee. And as Abraham stood and marveled, behold an angel of the Lord driving sixty thousand souls of sinners to destruction. And Abraham said to Michael, Do all these go into destruction? And Michael said to him, Yea, but let us go and search among these souls, if there is among them even one righteous. And when they went, they found an angel holding in his hand one soul of a woman from among these sixty thousand, because he had found her sins weighing equally with all her works, and they were neither in motion nor at rest, but in a state between; but the other souls he led away to destruction. Abraham said to Michael, Lord, is this the angel that removes the souls from the body or not? Michael answered and said, This is death, and he leads them into the place of judgment, that the judge may try them. [12] And Abraham said, My Lord, I beseech thee to lead me to the place of judgment so that I too may see how they are judged. Then Michael took Abraham upon a cloud, and led him into Paradise, and when he came to the place where the judge was, the angel came and gave that soul to the judge. And the soul said, Lord have mercy on me. And the judge said, How shall I have mercy upon thee, when thou hadst no mercy upon thy daughter which thou hadst, the fruit of thy womb? Wherefore didst thou slay her? It answered, Nay, Lord, slaughter has not been done by me, but my daughter has lied upon me. But the judge commanded him to come that wrote down the records, and behold cherubim carrying two books. And there was with them a man of exceeding great stature, having on his head three crowns, and the one crown was higher than the other two. These are called the crowns of witness. And the man had in his hand a golden pen, and the judge said to him, Exhibit the sin of this soul. And that man, opening one of the books of the cherubim, sought out the sin of the woman's soul and found it. And the judge said, O wretched soul, why sayest thou that thou hast not done murder? Didst thou not, after the death of thy husband, go and commit adultery with thy daughter's husband, and kill her? And he convicted her also of her other sins, whatsoever she had done from her youth. Hearing these things the woman cried out, saying, Woe is me, all the sins that I did in the world I forgot, but here they were not forgotten. Then they took her away also and gave her over to the tormentors. [13] And Abraham said to Michael, Lord, who is this judge, and who is the other, who convicts the sins? And Michael said to Abraham, Seest thou the judge? This is Abel, who first testified, and God brought him hither to judge, and he that bears witness here is the teacher of heaven and earth, and the scribe of righteousness, Enoch, for the Lord sent them hither to write down the sins and righteousnesses of each one. Abraham said, And how can Enoch bear the weight of the souls, not having seen death? or how can he give sentence to all the souls? Michael said, If he gives sentence concerning the souls, it is not permitted; but Enoch himself does not give sentence, but it is the Lord who does so, and he has no more to do than only to write. For Enoch prayed to the Lord saying, I desire not, Lord, to give sentence on the souls, lest I be grievous to anyone; and the Lord said to Enoch, I shall command thee to write down the sins of the soul that makes atonement and it shall enter into life, and if the soul make not atonement and repent, thou shalt find its sins written down and it shall be cast into punishment. And about the ninth hour Michael brought Abraham back to his house. But Sarah his wife, not seeing what had become of Abraham, was consumed with grief, and gave up the ghost, and after the return of Abraham he found her dead, and buried her. [14] But when the day of the death of Abraham drew nigh, the Lord God said to Michael, Death will not dare to go near to take away the soul of my servant, because he is my friend, but go thou and adorn Death with great beauty, and send him thus to Abraham, that he may see him with his eyes. And Michael straightway, as he was commanded, adorned Death with great beauty, and sent him thus to Abraham that he might see him. And he sat down near to Abraham, and Abraham seeing Death sitting near to him was afraid with a great fear. And Death said to Abraham, Hail, holy soul! hail, friend of the Lord God! hail, consolation and entertainment of travelers! And Abraham said, Thou art welcome, servant of the Most High. God. I beseech thee, tell me who thou art; and entering into my house partake of food and drink, and depart from me, for since I have seen thee sitting near to me my soul has been troubled. For I am not at all worthy to come near thee, for thou art an exalted spirit and I am flesh and blood, and therefore I cannot bear thy glory, for I see that thy beauty is not of this world. And Death said to Abraham, I tell thee, in all the creation that God has made, there has not been found one like thee, for even the Lord himself by searching has not found such an one upon the whole earth. And Abraham said to Death, How durst thou lie? for I see that thy beauty is not of this world. And Death said to Abraham, Think not, Abraham, that this beauty is mine, or that I come thus to every man. Nay, but if any one is righteous like thee, I thus take crowns and come to him, but if it is a sinner I come in great corruption, and out of their sin I make a crown for my head, and I shake them with great fear, so that they are dismayed. Abraham therefore said to him, And whence comes thy beauty? And Death said, There is none other more full of corruption than I am. Abraham said to him, And art thou indeed he that is called Death? He answered him and said, I am the bitter name. I am weeping.... [15] And Abraham said to Death, Show us thy corruption. And Death made manifest his corruption; and he had two heads, the one had the face of a serpent and by it some die at once by asps, and the other head was like a sword; by it some die by the sword as by bows. In that day the servants of Abraham died through fear of Death, and Abraham seeing them prayed to the Lord, and he raised them up. But God returned and removed the soul of Abraham as in a dream, and the archangel Michael took it up into the heavens. And Isaac buried his father beside his mother Sarah, glorifying and praising God, for to him is due glory, honor and worship, of the Father, Son and Holy Ghost, now and always and to all eternity. Amen.

The Testament of Job

1

1 On the day he became sick and (he) knew that he would have to leave his bodily abode, he called his seven sons and his three daughters together and spake to them as follows: **2** "Form a circle around me, children, and hear, and I shall relate to you what the Lord did for me and all that happened to me. **3** For I am Job your father. **4** Know ye then my children, that you are the generation of a chosen one and take heed of your noble birth. **5** For I am of the sons of Esau. My brother is Nahor, and your mother is Dinah. By her have I become your father. **6** For my first wife died with my other ten children in bitter death. **7** Hear now, children, and I will reveal unto you what happened to me. **8** I was a very rich man living in the East in the land Ausitis, (Utz) and before the Lord had named me Job, I was called Jobab. **9** The beginning of my trial was thus. Near my house there was the idol of one worshipped by the people; and I saw constantly burnt-offerings brought to him as a god. **10** Then I pondered and said to myself: "Is this he who made heaven and earth, the sea and us all How will I know the truth" **11** And in that night as I lay asleep, a voice came and called: "Jobab! Jobab! rise up, and I will tell thee who is the one whom thou wishest to know. **12** This, however, to whom the people bring burnt-offerings and libations, is not God, but this is the power and work of the Seducer (Satan) by which he beguiles the people". **13** And when I heard this, I fell upon the earth and I prostrated myself saying: **14** "O my Lord who speakest for the salvation of my soul. I pray thee, if this is the idol of Satan, I pray thee, let me go hence and destroy it and purify this spot. **15** For there is none that can forbid me doing this, as I am the king of this land, so that those that live in it will no longer be led astray". **16** And the voice that spoke out of the flame answered to me: "Thou canst purify this spot. **17** But behold I announce to thee what the Lord ordered me to tell thee, For I am the archangel of the God". **18** .And I said: "Whatever shall be told to his servant. I shall hear". **19** And the archangel, said to me: "Thus speaketh the Lord: If thou undertakest to destroy and takest away the image of Satan, he will set himself with wrath to wage war against thee, and he will display against thee all his malice. **21** He will bring upon thee many severe plagues, and take from thee all that thou hast. **21** He will take away thine children, and will inflict many evils upon thee. **22** Then thou must wrestle like an athlete and resist pain, sure of thy reward, overcome trials and afflictions. **23** But when thou endurest, I shall make thy name renowned throughout all generations of the earth until to the end of the world. **24** And I shall restore thee to all that thou hadst had, and the double part of what thou shalt lose will be given to thee in order that thou mayest know that God does not consider the person but giveth to each who deserveth the good. **25** And also to thee shall it be given, and thou shalt put on a crown of amarant. **26** And at the resurrection thou shalt awaken for eternal life. Then shalt thou know that he Lord is just, and true and mighty". **27** Whereupon, my children, I replied: "I shall from love of God endure until death all that will come upon me, and I shall not shrink back". **28** Then the angel put his seal upon me and left me.

2

1 After this I rose up in the night and took fifty slaves and went to the temple of the idol and destroyed it to the ground. **2**. And so I went back to my house and gave orders that the door should he firmly locked; saying to my doorkeepers: **3** "If somebody shall ask for me, bring no report to me, but tell him: He investigates urgent affairs. He is inside". **4** Then Satan disguised himself as a beggar and knocked heavily at the door, saying to the door-keeper: **5** "Report to Job and say that I desire to meet him", **6** And the door-keeper came in and told me that, but heard from me that I was studying. **7** The Evil One, having failed in this, went away and took upon his shoulder an old, torn basket and went in and spoke to the doorkeeper saying: "Tell Job: Give me bread from thine hands that I may eat". **8** And when I heard this, I gave her burnt bread to give it to him, and I made known to him: "Expect not to eat of my bread, for it is forbidden to thee". **9** But the door-keeper, being ashamed to hand him the burnt and ashy bread, as she did not know that it was Satan, took of her own fine bread and gave it to him. **10** But he took it and, knowing what occured, said to the maiden: "Go hence, bad servant, and bring me the bread that was given thee to hand to me". **11** And the servant cried and spoke in grief: "Thou speakest the truth, saying that I am a bad servant. because I have not done as I was instructed by my master". **12** And he turned back and brought him the burnt bread and said to him: "Thus says my lord: Thou shalt not eat of my bread anymore, for it is forbidden to thee. **13** And this he gave me [saying: This I give] in order that the charge may not be brought against me that I did not give to the enemy who asked".) **14** And when Satan heard this, he sent back the servant to me, saying: "As thou seest this bread all burnt, so shall I soon burn thy body to make it like this". **15** And I replied: "Do what thou desirest to do and accomplish whatever thou plottest. For I am ready to endure whatever thou bringest upon me". **16** And when the devil heard this, he left me, and walking up to under the [highest] heaven, he took from the Lord the oath that he might have power, over all my possessions. **17** And after having taken the power he went and instantly took away all my wealth.

3

1 For I had one hundred and thirty thousand sheep, and of these I separated seven thousand for the clothing of orphans and widows and of needy and sick ones. **2** I had a herd of eight hundred dogs who watched my sheep and besides these two hundred to watch my house. **3** And I had nine mills working for the whole city and ships to carry goods, and I seat them into every city and into the villages to the feeble and sick and to those that were unfortunate. **4** And I had three hundred and forty thousand nomadic asses, and of these I set aside five hundred, and the offspring of these I order to he sold and the proceeds to be given to the poor and the needy. **5** For from all the lands the poor came to meet me. **6** For the four doors of my house were opened, each, being in charge of a watchman who had to see whether there were any people coming asking alms, and whether they would see me sitting at one of the door's so that they could leave through the other and take whatever they needed. **7** I also had thirty immovable tables set at all hours for the strangers alone, and I also had twelve tables spread for the widows. **8** And if any one came asking for alms, he found food on my table to take all he needed, and I turned nobody away to leave my door with an empty stomach. **9** I also had three thousand five hundred yokes of oxen, and I selected of these five hundred and had them tend to the plowing. **10** And with these I had done all the work in each field by those who would, take it in charge and the income of their crops I laid aside for the poor on their table. **11** I also had fifty bakeries from which I sent [the bread] to the table for the poor. **12** And I had slaves selected for their service. **13** There were also some strangers who saw my good will; they wished to serve as waiters themselves. **14** Others, being in distress and unable to obtain a living, came with the request saying: **15** "We pray thee, since we also can fill this office of waiters (deacons) and have no possession, have pity upon us and advance money to us in order that we may go into the great cities and sell merchandise. **16** And the surplus of our profit we may give as help to the poor, and then shall we return to thee thine own (money). **17** And when I heard this, I was glad that they should take this altogether from me for the husbandry of charity for the poor. **18** And with a willing heart I gave them what they wanted, and I accepted their written bond, but would not take any other security from them except the written document. **19** And they went abroad and gave to time poor as far as they were successful. **20** Frequently, however, some of their goods were lost on the road or on the sea, or they would he robbed of them. **21** Then they would come and say: "We pray thee, act generously towards us in order that we may see how we can restore to you thine own". **22** And when I heard this, I had sympathy with them, and handed to them their bond, and often having read it before them tore it up and released them of their debt. saying to them: **23** "What I have consecrated for the benefit of the poor, I shall not take from you". **24** And so I accepted nothing from my debtor. **25** And when a man with cheerful heart came to me saying: I am not in need to be compelled to he a paid worker for the poor. **26** But I wish to serve the needy at thy table", and he consented to work, and he ate his share. **27** So I gave him his wages nevertheless, and I went home rejoicing. **28** And when he did not wish to take it, I forced him to do so, saying: "I know that thou art a laboring man who looks for and waits for his wages, and thou must take it." **29** Never did I defer paying the wages of the hireling or any other, nor keep back in my house for a single evening his hire that was due to him. **30** Those that milked the cows and the ewes signaled to the passersby that they should take their share. **31** For the milk flowed in such plenty that it curdled into butter on the hills and by the road side; and by the rocks and the hills the cattle lay which had given birth to their offspring. **32** For my servants grew weary keeping the meat of the widows and the poor and dividing it into small pieces. **33** For they would curse and say: "Oh that we had of his flesh that we could be satisfied", although I was very kind to them, **34** I also had six harps [and six slaves to play the harps] and also a cithara, a decachord, and I struck it during the day. **35** And I took the cithara, and the widows responded after their meals. **36** And with the musical instrument I reminded them of God that they should give praise to the Lord. **37** And when my female slaves would murmur, then I took the musical instruments and played as much as they would have done for their wages, and gave them respite from their labor and sighs.

4

1 And my children, after having taken charge of the service, took their meals each day along with their three sisters beginning with the older brother, and made a feast. **2** And I rose in the morning and offered as sin-offering for them fifty rams and nineteen sheep, and what remained as a residue was consecrated to the poor. **3** And I said to them: "Take these as residue and pray for my children. ⁴ Perchance my sons have sinned before the Lord, speaking in haughtiness of spirit: We are children of this rich man. Ours are all these goods; why should we be servants of the poor' ⁵ And speaking thus in a haughty spirit they may have provoked the anger of God, for overbearing pride is an abomination before the Lord." ⁶ So I brought oxen as offerings to the priest at the altar saying: "May my children never think evil towards God in their hearts." ⁷ While I lived in this manner, the Seducer could not bear to see the good [I did], and he demanded the warfare of God against me. ⁸ And he came upon me cruelly. ⁹ First he burnt up the large number of sheep, then the camels, then he burnt up the cattle and all my herds; or they were captured not only by enemies but also by such as had received benefits from me. ¹⁰ And the shepherds came and announced that to me. ¹¹ But when I heard it, I gave praise to God and did not blaspheme. ¹² And when the Seducer learned of my fortitude, he plotted new thing's against me. ¹³ He disguised himself as King of Persia and besieged my city, and after he had led off all that were therein, he spoke to them in malice, saying in boastful language: ¹⁴ "This man Job who has obtained all the goods of the earth and left nothing for others, he has destroyed and torn down the temple of god. ¹⁵ Therefore shall I repay to him what he has done to the house of the great god. ¹⁶ Now come with me and we shall pillage all that is left in his house." ¹⁷ And they answered and said to him: "He has seven sons and three daughters. ¹⁸ Take heed lest they flee into other lands and they may become our tyrants and then come over us with force and kill us." ¹⁹ And he said: Be not at all afraid. His flocks and his wealth have I destroyed by fire, and the rest have I captured, and behold, his children shall I kill." ²⁰ And having spoken thus, he went and threw the house upon my children and killed them. ²¹ And my fellow-citizens, seeing that what was said by him had become true, came and pursued me, and robbed me of all that was in my house. ²² And I saw with mine own eyes the pillage of my house, and men without culture and without honor sat at my table and on my couches, and I could not remonstrate against them. ²³ For I was exhausted like a woman with her loins let loose from multitude of pains, remembering chiefly that this warfare had been predicted to me by the Lord through His angel. ²⁴ And I became like one who, when seeing the rough sea and the adverse winds, while the lading of the vessel in mid-ocean is too heavy, casts the burden into the sea, saying: ²⁵ "I wish to destroy all this only in order to come safely into the city so that I may take as profit the rescued ship and the best of my things." ²⁶ Thus did I manage my own affairs. ²⁷ But there came another messenger and announced to me the ruin of my own children, and I was shaken with terror. ²⁸ And I tore my clothes and said: The Lord hath given, the Lord hath taken. As it hath deemed best to the Lord, thus it hath come to be. May the name of the Lord be blessed."

5

¹ And when Satan saw that he could riot put me to despair, he went and asked my body of the Lord in order to inflict plague on me, for the Evil one could not bear my patience. ² Then the Lord delivered me into his hands to use my body as he wanted, but he gave him no power over my soul. ³. And he came to me as I was sitting on my throne still mourning over my children. ⁴ And he resembled a great hurricane and turned over my throne and threw me upon the ground. ⁵ And I continued lying on the floor for three hours. and he smote me with a hard plague from the top of my head to the toes of my feet. ⁶ And I left the city in great terror and woe and sat down upon a dunghill my body being worm-eaten. ⁷ And I wet the earth with the moistness of my sore body, for matter flowed off my body, and many worms covered it. ⁸ And when a single worm crept off my body, I put it back saying: "Remain on the spot where thou hast been placed until He who hath sent thee will order thee elsewhere." ⁹ Thus I endured for sever years, sitting on a dung-hill outside of the city while being plague-stricken. ¹⁰ And I saw with mine own eyes my longed-for children [carried by angels to heaven] ¹¹ And my humbled wife who had been brought to her bridal chamber in such great luxuriousness and with spearmen as body-guards. I saw her do a water-carrier's work like a slave in the house of a common man in order to win some bread and bring it to me. ¹² And in my sore affliction I said: "Oh that these braggart city rulers whom I soul not have thought to be equal with my shepherd dogs should now employ my wife as servant!" ¹³ And after this I took courage again. ¹⁴ Yet afterwards they withheld even the bread that it should only have her own nourishment. ¹⁵ But she took it and divided it between herself and me, saying woefully: "Woe to me! Forthwith he may no longer feed on bread, and he cannot go to the market to ask bread of the bread-sellers in order to bring it to me that he may eat" ¹⁶ And when Satan learned this, he took the guise of a bread-seller, and it was as if by chance that my wife met him and asked him for bread thinking that it was that sort of man. ¹⁷ But Satan said to her: "Give me the value, and then take what thou wishest." ¹⁸ Whereupon she answered saying: Where shall I get money Dost thou not know what misfortune happened to me. If thou hast pity, show it to me; if not, thou shalt see." ¹⁹ And he replied saying: "If you did not deserve this misfortune, you would not have suffered all this. ²⁰ Now, if there is no silver piece in thine hand, give me the hair of thine head and take three loaves of bread for it, so that ye may live on there for three days. ²¹ Then she said to herself: "What is the hair of my head in comparison with my starving husband" ²² And so after having pondered over the matter, she said to him: "Rise and cut off my hair". ²³ Then he took a pair of scissors and took off the hair of her head in the presence of all, and gave her three loaves of bread. ²⁴ Then she took them and brought them to me. And Satan went behind her on the road, hiding himself as he walked and troubling her heart greatly.

6

¹ And immediately my wife came near me and crying aloud and weeping she said: "Job! Job! How long wilt thou sit upon the dung-hill outside of the city, pondering yet for a while and expecting to obtain your hoped-for salvation!" ² And I have been wandering from place to place, roaming about as a hired servant, behold they memory has already died away from earth. ³ And my sons and the daughters that I carried on my bosom and the labors and pains that I sustained have been for nothing ⁴ And thou sittest in the malodorous state of soreness and worms, passing the nights in the cold air. ⁵ And I have undergone all trials and troubles and pains, day and night until I succeeded in bringing bread to thee. ⁶ For your surplus of bread is no longer allowed to me; and as I can scarcely take my own food and divide it between us, I pondered in my heart that it was not right that thou shouldst be in pain and hunger for bread. ⁷ And so I ventured to go to the market without bashfulness. and when the bread-seller told me: "Give me money. and thou shalt have bread". I disclosed to him our state of distress. ⁸ Then I heard him say: "If thou hast no money, hand me the hair of thy head, and take three loaves of bread in order that ye may live on these for three days". ⁹ And I yielded to the wrong and said to him "Rise and cut off my hair !" and he rose and in disgrace cut off with the scissors the hair of my head on the market place while the crowd stood by and wondered. ¹⁰ Who would then not be astonished saying: "Is this Sitis, the wife of Job, who had fourteen curtains to cover her inner sitting room, and doors within doors so that he was greatly honored who would be brought near her, and now behold, she barters off her hair for bread! ¹¹ Who had camels laden with goods. and they were brought into remote lands to the poor, and now she sells her hair for bread! ¹² Behold her who had seven tables immovably set in her house at which each poor man and each stranger ate, and now she sells her hair for bread! ¹³ Behold her who had the basin wherewith to wash her feet made of gold and silver, and now she walks upon the ground and [sells her hair for bread !] ¹⁴ Behold her who had her garments made of byssus interwoven with gold, and now she exchanges her hair for bread! ¹⁵ Behold her who had couches of gold and of silver, and now she sells her hair for bread!" ¹⁶ In short then, Job, after the many things that have been said to me, I now say in one word to thee: ¹⁷ "Since the feebleness of my heart has crushed my bones, rise then and take these loaves of bread and enjoy them, and then speak some word against the Lord and die! ¹⁸ For I too, would exchange the torpor of death for the sustenance of my body". ¹⁹ But I replied to her "Behold I have been for these seven years plague-stricken, and I have stood the worms of my body, and I was not weighed down in my soul by all these pains. ²⁰ And as to the word which thou sayest: 'Speak some word against God and die!', together with thee I will sustain the evil which thou seest. and let us endure the ruin of all that we have. ²¹ Yet thou desirest that we should say some word against God and that He should be exchanged for the great Pluto [the god of the nether world.] ²² Why dost thou not remember those great goods which we possessed If these goods come from the lands of the Lord, should not we also endure evils and be high-minded in everything until the Lord will have mercy again and show pity to us ²³ Dost thou not see the Seducer stand behind thee and confound thy thoughts in order that thou shouldst beguile me ²⁴ And he turned to Satan and said: "Why dost thou not come openly to me Stop hiding thyself thou wretched one, ²⁵ Does the lion show his strength in the weasel cage Or does the bird fly in the basket I now tell thee: Go away and wage thy war against me". ²⁶ Then he went of from behind my wife and placed himself before me crying and he said: Behold, Job, I yield and give way to thee who art but flesh while I am a spirit. ²⁷ Thou art plague-stricken, but I am in great trouble. ²⁸ For I am like a wrestler contesting with a wrestler who has, in a single-handed combat, torn down his antagonist and covered him with dust and broken every limb of his, whereas the other one who lies beneath, having displayed his bravery, gives forth sounds of triumph testifying to his own superior excellence. ²⁹ Thus thou, O Job, art beneath and stricken with plague and pain, and yet thou hast carried the victory in the wrestling-match with me, and behold, I yield to thee". ³⁰. Then he left

me abashed. ³¹ Now my children, do you also show a firm heart in all the evil that happens to you, for greater than all things is firmness of heart.

7

¹ At this time the kings heard what had happened to me and they rose and came to me. each from his land to visit me and to comfort me. ². And when they came near me, they cried with a loud voice and each tore his clothes. ³ And after they had prostrated themselves, touching the earth with their heads, they sat down next to me for seven days and seven nights, and none spoke a word. ⁴ They were four in numbers: Eliplaz, the king of Teman, and Balad, and Sophar, and Elilhu. ⁵ And when they had taken their seat, they conversed about what had happened to me. ⁶ Now when for time first time they had come to me and I had shown them my precious stones, they were astonished and said: ⁷ "If of us three kings all our possessions would be brought together into one, it would not come up to the precious stones of .Jobab's kingdom (crown). For thou art of greater nobility than all the people of the East. ⁸ And when, therefore, they now came to the land of Ausitis "Uz" to visit me, they asked in the city: "Where is Jobab, the ruler of this whole land" ⁹ And they told them concerning me: "He sitteth upon the dung-hill outside of the city for he has not entered the city' for seven years". ¹⁰ And then again they- inquired concerning my possessions, and there was revealed to them all that happened to me. ¹¹ And when they had learned this, they went out of the city with the inhabitants, and my fellow-citizens pointed me out to them. ¹² But these remonstrated and said: "Surely, this is not Jobab". ¹³ And while they hesitated, there said Eliphaz. the King of Teman: "Come let us step near and see." ¹⁴ And when they came near I remembered them, and I wept very much when I learned the purpose of their journey. ¹⁵ And I threw earth upon my head, and while shaking my head I revealed unto them that I was [Job]. ¹⁶ And when they saw me shake my head they threw themselves down upon the ground, all overcome with emotion ¹⁷ And while their hosts were standing around, I saw the three kings lie upon the ground for three hours like dead. ¹⁸ Then they rose and said to each other: We cannot believe that this is Jobab". ¹⁹ And finally, after they had for seven day's inquired after everything concerning me and searched for my flocks and other possessions, they said: ²⁰ "Do we not know how many goods were sent by him to the cities and the villages round about to be given to the poor, aside from all that was given away by him within his own house How then could he have fallen into such a state of perdition and misery !" ²¹ And after the seven days Elihu said to the kings: "Come let us step near and examine him accurately, whether he truly is Jobab or not" ²² And they, being not half a mile (stadium) distant from his malodorous body, they rose and stepped near, carrying perfume in their hands, while their soldiers went with them and threw fragrant incense round about them so that they could come near me. ²³ And after they had thus passed three hours, covering the way with aroma, they drew nigh. ²⁴ And Eliphaz began and said: "Art thou, indeed, Job, our fellow-king Art thou the one who owned the great glory ²⁵ Art thou he who once shone like the sun of day upon the whole earth Art thou he who once resembled the moon and the stars effulgent throughout the night" ²⁶ And I answered him and said: "I am", and thereupon all wept and lamented, and they sang a royal song of lamentation, their whole army joining them in a chorus. ²⁷ And again Eliphaz said to me: "Art thou he who had ordered seven thousand sheep to be given for the clothing of the poor Whither, then hath gone the glory of thy throne ²⁸ Art thou he who had ordered three thousand cattle to do the plowing of the field for the poor Wither, then hath thy glory gone! ²⁹ Art thou he who had golden couches, and now thou sittest upon a dung hill [" Whither then hath thy glory gone !"] ³⁰ Art thou he who had sixty tables set for the poor Art thou he who had censer's for the fine perfume made of precious stones, and now thou art in a malodorous state Whither then hath thy glory gone! ³¹ Art thou he who had golden candelabras set upon silver stands; and now must thou long for the natural gleam of the moon ["Whither then hath thy glory gone !"] ³² Art thou the one who had ointment made of the spices of frankincense, and now thou art in a state of repulsiveness! [Whither then hath thy glory gone !"] ³³ Art thou he who laughed the wrong doers and sinners to scorn and now thou hast become a laughingstock to all !" [Whither then hath thine glory gone] ³⁴ And when Eliphaz had for a long time cried and lamented, while all the others joined him, so that the commotion was very great, I said to them: ³⁵ Be silent and I will show you my throne, and the glory of its splendor: My glory will be everlasting. ³⁶ The whole world shall perish, and its glory shall vanish, and all those who hold fast to it, will remain beneath, but my throne is in the upper world and its glory and splendor will be to the right of the Savior in the heavens. ³⁷ My throne exists in the life of the "holy ones" and its glory in the imperishable world. ³⁸ For rivers will be dried up and their arrogance shall go down to the depth of the abyss, but the streams of my land in which my throne is erected, shall not dry up, but shall remain unbroken in strength. ³⁹ The kings perish and the rulers vanish, and their glory and pride is as the shadow in a looking glass, but my Kingdom lasts forever and ever, and its glory and beauty is in the chariot of my Father).

8

I When I spoke thus to them, Ehiphaz. became angry and said to the other friends "For what purpose is it that we have come here with our hosts to comfort him ⁹ Behold, he upbraids us. Therefore let us return to our countries. ² This man sits here in misery worm-eaten amidst an unbearable state of putrefaction, and yet he challenges its saving: 'Kingdoms shall perish and their rulers, but my Kingdom, says he, shall last forever'". ³ Eliphaz, then, rose in great commotion, and, turning away from them in great fury, said': "I go hence. We have indeed come to comfort him, but he declares war to us in view of our armies". ⁴ But then Baldad seized him by the hand and said: "Not thus ought one to speak to an afflicted man, and especially to one stricken down with so many plagues. ⁵ Behold, we, being in good health, dared not approach him on account of the offensive odor, except with the help of plenty of fragrant aroma. But thou, Eliphaz. art forgetful of all this. ⁶ Let me speak plainly. Let us be magnanimous and learn what is the cause Must he in remembering his former days of happiness not become mad in his mind ⁷ Who should not be altogether perplexed seeing himself thus lapse into misfortune and plagues But let me step near him that I may find by what cause is he thus" ⁹ And Baldad rose and approached me saying: "Art thou Job" and he said: "Is thy heart still in good keeping ⁹ And I said: "I did not hold fast to the earthly things, since the earth with all that inhabit it is unstable. But my heart holds fast to the heaven, because there is no trouble in heaven". ¹⁰ Then Baldad rejoined and said: "We know that the earth is unstable, for it changes according to season. At times it is in a state of peace, and at times it is in a state of war. But of the heaven we hear that it is perfectly steady. ¹¹ But art thou truly in a state of calmness Therefore let me ask and speak, and when thou answerest me to my first word, I shall have a second question to ask, and if again thou answerest in well-set words, it will be manifest that thy heart has not been unbalanced". ¹² And I said: "Upon what dost thou set thy hope" And I said: "Upon the living God". ¹³. And he said to me: "Who deprived thee of all thou didst possess And who inflicted thee with these plagues ⁹" And I said: "God". ¹⁴ And he said: "If thou still placest thy hope upon God, how can He do wrong in judgment, having brought upon thee these plagues and misfortunes, and having taken from thee all thy possessions ¹⁵ And since He has taken these, it is clear that He has given thee nothing. No king will disgrace his soldier who has served him well as body-guard" ¹⁶ [And I answered saying]: "Who understands the depths of the Lord and of His wisdom to be able to accuse God of injustice" ¹⁷ [And Baldad said]: "Answer me, o Job, to this. Again I say to thee: 'If thou art in a state of calm reason, teach me if thou hast wisdom: ¹⁸ Why do we see the sun rise in the East and set in the West And again when rising in the morning we find him rise in the East Tell me thy- thought about this" ¹⁹ Then said I: "Why shall I betray (babble forth) the mighty mysteries of God And should my mouth stumble in revealing things belonging to the Master Never! ²⁰ Who are we that we should pry into matters concerning the upper world while we are only of flesh, nay, earth and ashes! ²¹ In order that you know that my heart is sound, hear what I ask you: ²² Through the stomach cometh food, and water you drink through the mouth, and then it flows through the same throat, and when the two go down to become excrement, they again part; who effects this separation". ²³ And Baldad said: "I do not know". And I rejoined and said to him: "If thou dost not understand even the exits of the body, how canst thou understand the celestial circuits" ²⁴ Then Sophar rejoined and said: "We do not inquire after our own affairs, but we desire to know whether thou art in a sound state, and behold, we see that thy reason has not been shaken. ²⁵. What now dost thou wish that we should do for thee Behold, we have come here and brought the physicians of three kings, and if thou wishest, thou mayest he cured by them". ²⁶ But I answered and said: "My cure and my restoration cometh from God, the Maker of physicians".

9

¹ And when I spoke thus to them, behold, there my wife Sitis came running, dressed in rags. from the service of the master by whom she was employed as slave though she had been forbidden to leave, lest the kings, on seeing her, might take her as captive. ² And when she came, she threw herself prostrate to their feet, crying and saying: "Remember'. Eliphaz and ye other friends, what I was once with you, and how I have changed, how I am now dressed to meet you" ³ Then the kings broke forth in great weeping and, being in double perplexity, they kept silent. But Eliphaz took his purple mantle and cast it about her to wrap herself up with it. ⁴ But she asked him saying: "I ask as favor of you, my Lords, that you order your soldiers that they should dig among the ruins of our house which fell upon my children,

so that their bones could be brought in a perfect state to the tombs. ⁵ Fir as we have, owing to our misfortune, no power at all, and so we may at least see their bones. ⁶ For have I like a brute the motherly feeling of wild beasts that my ten children should have perished on one day and not to one of them could I give a decent burial" ⁷ And the kings gave order that the ruins of my house should be dug up. But I prohibited it, saving ⁸ "Do not go to the trouble in vain; for my children will not he found, for they are in the keeping of their Maker and Ruler". ⁹ And the kings answered and said: "Who will gainsay that he is out of his mind and raves ¹⁰ For while we desire to bring the bones of his children back, he forbids us to do so saying: 'They have been taken and placed the keeping of their Maker'. Therefore prove unto us the truth". ¹¹ But I said to them: "Raise me that I may stand up, and they lifted me, holding up my arms from both sides. ¹² And I stood upright, and pronounced first the praise of God and after the prayer I said to them: "Look with your eyes to the East". ¹³ And they looked and saw my children with crowns near the glory of the King, the Ruler of heaven. ¹⁴ And when my wife Sitis saw this, she fell to the ground and prostrated [herself] before God, saying: "Now I know that my memory remains with the Lord". ¹⁵ And after she had spoken this, and the evening came, she went to the city, back to the master whom she served as slave, and lay herself down at the manger of the cattle and died there from exhaustion. ¹⁶ And when her despotic master searched for her and did not find her, he came to the fold of his herds, and there he saw her stretched out upon the manger dead, while all the animals around were crying about her. ¹⁷ And all who saw her wept and lamented, and the cry extended throughout the whole city. ¹⁸ And the people brought her down and wrapt her up and buried her by the house which had fallen upon her children. ¹⁹ And the poor of the city made a great mourning for her and said: "Behold this Sitis whose like in nobility and in glory is not found in any woman. Alas ! she was not found worthy of a proper tomb!" ²⁰ The dirge for her you will find in the record.

10

But Eliphaz and those that were with him were astonished at these things, and they sat down with me and replying to me, spoke in boastful words concerning me for twenty seven days. ² They repeated it again and again that I suffered deservedly thus for having committed many sins, and that there was no hope left for me, but I retorted to these men in zest of contention myself. ³ And they rose in anger, ready to part in wrathful spirit. But Elihu conjured them to stay yet a little while until he would have shown them what it was. ⁴ "For", said he, "so many days did you pass, allowing Job to boast that he is just. But I shall no longer suffer it. ⁵ For from the beginning did I continue crying over him, remembering his former happiness. But now he speaks boastfully and in overbearing pride he says that he has his throne in the heavens. ⁶ Therefore, hear me, and I will tell you what is the cause of his destiny. ⁷ Then, imbued with the spirit of Satan. Elihu spoke hard words which are written down in the records left of Elihu. ⁸ And after he had ended, God appeared to me in a storm and in clouds, and spoke. blaming Elihu and showing me that he who had spoken was not a man, but a wild beast. ⁹ And when God had finished speaking to me, the Lord spoke to Eliphaz: "Thou and thy friends have sinned in that ye have not spoken the truth concerning my servant Job. ¹⁰ Therefore rise up and make him bring a sin-offering for you in order that your sins may be forgiven; for were it not for him, I would have destroyed you". ¹¹ And so they brought to me all that belonged to a sacrifice, and I took it and brought for them a sin-offering, and the Lord received it favorably and forgave them their wrong. ¹² Then when Eliphaz, Baldad and Sophar saw that God had graciously pardoned their sin through His servant Job, but that He did not deign to pardon Elihu, then did Eliphaz begin to sing a hymn, while the others responded, their soldiers also joining while standing by the altar. ¹³ And Eliphaz spoke thus "Taken off is the sin and our injustice gone; ¹⁴ But Elihu, the evil one, shall have no remembrance among the living; his luminary is extinguished and has lost its light. ¹⁵ The glory of his lamp will announce itself for him, for he is the son of darkness. and not of light. ¹⁶ The doorkeepers of the place of darkness shall give him their glory and beauty as share; His Kingdom hath vanished, his throne hath moldered, and the honor of his stature is in (Sheol) Hades. ¹⁷ For he has loved the beauty of the serpent and the scales (skins) of" the dracon his gall and his venom belongs to the Northern One (Zphuni = Adder). ¹⁸ For he did not own himself unto the Lord nor did he fear him, but he hated those whom He hath chosen (known). ¹⁹ Thus God forgot him, and "the holy ones" forsook him, his wrath and anger shall be unto him desolation and he will have no mercy in his heart nor peace, because he, had the venom of an adder on his tongue. ²⁰ Righteous is the Lord, and His judgments are true, With him there is no preference of person, for He judgeth us all alike. ²¹ Behold, the Lord cometh! Behold, the "holy ones" have been prepared: The crowns and the prizes of the victors precede them! ²² Let the saints rejoice, and let their hearts exult in gladness; for they shall receive the glory which is in store for them. ²³ Our sins are forgiven, our injustice has been cleansed, but Elihu hath no remembrance among the living". ²⁴ After Eliphaz had finished the hymn, we rose and went back to the city, each to the house where they lived. ²⁵ And the people made a feast for me in gratitude and delight of God, and all my friends came back to me. ²⁶ And all those who had seen me in my former state of happiness, asked me saying: "What are those three things here amongst us".

11

¹ But I being desirous to take up again my work of benevolence for the poor, asked them saying: ² "Give me each a lamb for the clothing of the poor in their state of nakedness, and four drachmas (coins) of silver or gold" ³ Then the Lord blessed all that was left to me, and after a few days I became rich again in merchandise, in flocks and all things which I had lost, and I received all in double number again. ⁴ Then I also took as wife your mother and became the father of you ten in place of the ten children that had died. ⁵ And now, my children, let me admonish you: "Behold I die. You will take my place. ⁶ Only do not forsake the Lord. Be charitable towards the poor; Do not disregard the feeble. Take not unto yourselves wives from strangers. ⁷ Behold, my children, I shall divide among you what I possess, so that each may have control over his own and have full power to do good with his share". ⁸ And after he had spoken thus, he brought all his goods and divided them among his seven sons, but he gave nothing of his goods to his daughters. ⁹ Then they said to their father: "Our lord and father! Are we not also thy children Why, then, dost thou not also give us a share of thy possessions" ¹⁰ Then said Job to his daughters: "Do not become angry my daughters. I have not forgotten you. Behold, I have preserved for you a possession better than that which your brothers have taken". ¹¹ And he called his daughter whose name was Day (Yemima) and said to her: "Take this double ring used as a key and go to the treasure-house and bring me the golden casket, that I may give you your possession". ¹² And she went and brought it to him, and he opened it and took out three-stringed girdles about the appearance of which no man can speak. ¹³ For they were not earthly work, but celestial sparks of light flashed through them like the rays of the sun. ¹⁴ And he gave one string to each of His daughters and said: "Put these as girdles around you in order that all the days of your life they may encircle you and endow you with every thing good". ¹⁵ And the other daughter whose name was Kassiah said: "Is this the possession of which thou sayest it is better than that of our brothers What now Can we live on this" ¹⁶ And their father said to them: "Not only have you here sufficient to live on, but these bring you into a better world to live in, in the heavens. ¹⁷ Or do you not know my children, the value of these things here Hear then! When the Lord had deemed me worthy to have compassion on me and to take off my body the plagues and the worms, He called me and handed to me these three strings. ¹⁸ And He said to me: 'Rise and gird up thy loins like a man I will demand of thee and declare thou unto me'. ¹⁹ And I took them and girt them around my loins, and immediately did the worms leave my body, and likewise did the plagues, and my whole body took new strength through the Lord, and thus I passed on, as though I had never suffered. ²⁰ But also in my heart I forgot the pains. Then spoke the Lord unto me in His great power and showed to me all that was and will be. ²¹ Now then, my children, in keeping these, you will not have the enemy plotting against you nor [evil] intentions in your mind because this is a charm (Phylacterion) from the Lord. ²² Rise then and gird these around you before I die in order that you may see the angels come at my parting so that you may behold with wonder the powers of God". ²³ Then rose the one whose name was Day (Yemima) and girt herself; and immediately she departed her body, as her father had said, and she put on another heart, as if she never cared for earthly things. ²⁴ And she sang angelic hymns in the voice of angels, and she chanted forth the angelic praise of God while dancing. ²⁵ Then the other daughter, Kassia by name, put on the girdle, and her heart was transformed, so that she no longer wished for worldly things. ²⁶ And her mouth assumed the dialect of the heavenly rulers (Archonts) and she sang the donology of the work of the High Place and if any one wishes to know the work of the heavens he may take an insight into the hymns of Kassia. ²⁷ Then did the other daughter by the name of Amalthea's Horn (Keren Happukh) gird herself and her mouth spoke in the language of those on high; for her heart was transformed, being lifted above the worldly things. ²⁸ She spoke in the dialect of the Cherubim, singing the praise of the Ruler of the cosmic powers (virtues) and extolling their (His) glory. ²⁹ And he who desires to follow the vestiges of the "Glory of the Father" will find them written down in the Prayers of Amalthea's Horn.

12

¹ After these three had finished singing hymns. did I Nahor (Neros) brother of Job sit down next to him, as he lay down. ² And I heard the marvelous

(great) things of the three daughters of my brother, one always succeeding the other amidst awful silence. ³ And I wrote down this book containing the hymns except the hymns and signs of the [holy] Word, for these were the great things of God. ⁴ And Job lay down from sickness on his couch, yet without pain and suffering, because his pain did not take strong hold of him on account of, the charm of the girdle which he had wound around himself. ⁵ But after three days Job saw the holy angels come for his soul, and instantly he rose and took the cithara and gave it to his daughter Day (Yemima). ⁶ And to Kassia he gave a censer (with perfume = Kassia, and to Amalthea's horn (= music) he gave a timbrel in order that they might bless the holy angels who came for his soul. ⁷ And they took these, and sang, and played on the psaltery and praised and glorified God in the holy dialect. ⁸ And after this he came He who sitteth upon the great chariot and kissed Job, while his three daughters looked on, but the others saw it not. ⁹ And He took the soul of Job and He soared upward, taking her (the soul) by the arm and carrying her upon the chariot, and He went towards the East. ¹⁰ His body, however, was brought to the grave while the three daughters marched ahead, having put on their girdles and singing hymns in praise of God. ¹¹ Then held Nahor (Nereos) his brother and his seven sons, with the rest of the people and the poor, the orphans and the feeble ones, a great mourning over him, saying: ¹² "Woe unto us, for today has been taken from us the strength of the feeble, the light of the blind, the father of the orphans; ¹³ The receiver of strangers has been taken off the leader of the erring, the cover of the naked. the shield of the widows. Who would not mourn for the man of God! ¹⁴ And as they were mourning in this and in that form, they would not suffer him to be put into the grave. ¹⁵ After three days, however, he was finally put into the grave, like one in sweet slumber, and he received the name of the good (beautiful) who will remain renowned throughout all generations of the world. ¹⁶ He left seven sons and three daughters, and there were no daughters found on earth as fair as the daughters of Job. ¹⁷ The name of Job was formerly Jobab, and he was called Job by the Lord. ¹⁸ He had lived before his plague eighty five years, and after the plague he took the double share of all; hence also his year's he doubled, which is 170 years. Thus he lived altogether 255 years. ¹⁹ And, he saw sons of his sons unto the fourth generation. It is written that he will rise up with those whom the Lord will reawaken. To our Lord by glory. Amen.

The Testament of Solomon

Testament of Solomon, son of David, who was king in Jerusalem, and mastered and controlled all spirits of the air, on the earth, and under the earth. By means of them also he wrought all the transcendent works of the Temple. Telling also of the authorities they wield against men, and by what angels these demons are brought to naught.

¹ Blessed art thou, O Lord God, who didst give Solomon such authority. Glory to thee and might unto the ages. Amen. ² And behold, when the Temple of the city of Jerusalem was being built, and the artificers were working thereat, Ornias the demon came among them toward sunset; and he took away half of the pay of the chief-deviser's (?) little boy, as well as half his food. He also continued to suck the thumb of his right hand every day. And the child grew thin, although he was very much loved by the king. ³ So King Solomon called the boy one day, and questioned him, saying: "Do I not love thee more than all the artisans who are working in the Temple of God? Do I not give thee double wages and a double supply of food? How is it that day by day and hour by hour thou growest thinner?" ⁴ But the child said to the king: "I pray thee, O king. Listen to what has befallen all that thy child hath. After we are all released from our work on the Temple of God, after sunset, when I lie down to rest, one of the evil demons comes and takes away from me one half of my pay and one half of my food. Then he also takes hold of my right hand and sucks my thumb. And lo, my soul is oppressed, and so my body waxes thinner every day." ⁵ Now when I Solomon heard this, I entered the Temple of God, and prayed with all my soul, night and day, that the demon might be delivered into my hands, and that I might gain authority over him. And it came about through my prayer that grace was given to me from the Lord Sabaoth by Michael his archangel. [He brought me] a little ring, having a seal consisting of an engraved stone, and said to me: "Take, O Solomon, king, son of David, the gift which the Lord God has sent thee, the highest Sabaoth. With it thou shalt lock up all demons of the earth, male and female; and with their help thou shalt build up Jerusalem. [But] thou [must] wear this seal of God. And this engraving of the seal of the ring sent thee is a Pentalpha." ⁶ And I Solomon was overjoyed, and praised and glorified the God of heaven and earth. And on the morrow I called the boy, and gave him the ring, and said to him: "take this, and at the hour in which the demon shall come unto thee, throw this ring at the chest of the demon, and say to him: 'In the name of God, King Solomon calls thee hither.3' And then do thou come running to me, without having any misgivings or fear in respect of aught thou mayest hear on the part of the demon." ⁷ So the child took the ring, and went off; and behold, at the customary hour Ornias, the fierce demon, came like a burning fire to take the pay from the child. But the child according to the instructions received from the king, threw the ring at the chest of the demon, and said: "King Solomon calls thee hither." And then he went off at a run to the king. But the demon cried out aloud, saying: "Child, why hast thou done this to me? Take the ring off me, and I will render to thee the gold of the earth. Only take this off me, and forbear to lead me away to Solomon." ⁸ But the child said to the demon: "As the Lord God of Israel liveth, I will not brook thee. So come hither." And the child came at a run, rejoicing, to the king, and said: "I have brought the demon, O king, as thou didst command me, O my master. And behold, he stands before the gates of the court of thy palace, crying out, and supplicating with a loud voice; offering me the silver and gold of the earth if I will only bring him unto thee." ⁹ And when Solomon heard this, he rose up from his throne, and went outside into the vestibule of the court of his palace; and there he saw the demon, shuddering and trembling. And he said to him: "Who art thou?" And the demon answered: "I am called Ornias." ¹⁰ And Solomon said to him: "Tell me, O demon, to what zodiacal sign thou art subject." And he answered: "To the Water-pourer. And those who are consumed with desire for the noble virgins upon earth . . . . . [there appears to be a lacuna here], these I strangle. But in case there is no disposition to sleep, I am changed into three forms. Whenever men come to be enamoured of women, I metamorphose myself into a comely female; and I take hold of the men in their sleep, and play with them. And after a while I again take to my wings, and hie me to the heavenly regions. I also appear as a lion, and I am commanded by all the demons. I am offspring of the archangel Uriel, the power of God." ¹¹ I Solomon, having heard the name of the archangel, prayed and glorified God, the Lord of heaven and earth. And I sealed the demon and set him to work at stone-cutting, so that he might cut the stones in the Temple, which, lying along the shore, had been brought by the Sea of Arabia. But he, fearful of the iron, continued and said to me: "I pray thee, King Solomon, let me go free; and I will bring you all the demons." And as he was not willing to be subject to me, I prayed the archangel Uriel to come and succour me; and I forthwith beheld the archangel Uriel coming down to me from the heavens. ¹² And the angel bade the whales of the sea come out of the abyss.

And he cast his destiny upon the ground, and that [destiny] made subject [to him] the great demon. And he commanded the great demon and bold Ornias, to cut stones at the Temple. And accordingly I Solomon glorified the God of heaven and Maker of the earth. And he bade Ornias come with his destiny, and gave him the seal, saying: "Away with thee, and bring me hither the prince of all the demons." [13] So Ornias took the finger-ring, and went off to Beelzeboul, who has kingship over the demons. He said to him: "Hither! Solomon calls thee." But Beelzeboul, having heard, said to him: "Tell me, who is this Solomon of whom thou speakest to me?" Then Ornias threw the ring at the chest of Beelzeboul, saying: "Solomon the king calls thee." But Beelzeboul cried aloud with a mighty voice, and shot out a great burning flame of fire; and he arose, and followed Ornias, and came to Solomon. [14] And when I saw the prince of demons, I glorified the Lord God, Maker of heaven and earth, and I said: "Blessed art thou, Lord God Almighty, who hast given to Solomon thy servant wisdom, the assessor of the wise, and hast subjected unto me all the power of he devil." [15] And I questioned him, and said: "Who art thou?" The demon replied: "I am Beelzebub, the exarch of the demons. And all the demons have their chief seats close to me. And I it is who make manifest the apparition of each demon." And he promised to bring to me in bonds all the unclean spirits. And I again glorified the God of heaven and earth, as I do always give thanks to him. [16] I then asked of the demon if there were females among them. And when he told me that there were, I said that I desired to see them. So Beelzeboul went off at high speed, and brought unto me Onoskelis, that had a very pretty shape, and the skin of a fair-hued woman; and she tossed her head. [17] And when she was come, I said to her: "Tell me who art thou?" But she said to me: "I am called Onoskelis, a spirit wrought ...[?shabtai/Saturn?], lurking upon the earth. There is a golden cave where I lie. But I have a place that ever shifts. At one time I strangle men with a noose; at another, I creep up from the nature to the arms [in marg: "worms"]. But my most frequent dwelling-places are the precipices, caves, ravines. Oftentimes, however, do I consort with men in the semblance of a woman, and above all with those of a dark skin. For they share my star with me; since they it is who privily or openly worship my star, without knowing that they harm themselves, and but whet my appetite for further mischief. For they wish to provide money by means of memory (commemoration?), but I supply a little to those who worship me fairly." [18] And I Solomon questioned her about her birth, and she replied: "I was born of a voice untimely, the so-called echo of a man's ordure dropped in a wood." [19] And I said to her: "Under what star dost thou pass?" And she answered me: "Under the star of the full moon, for the reason that the moon travels over most things." Then I said to her: "And what angel is it that frustrates thee?" And she said to me: "He that in thee [or "through thee"] is reigning." And I thought that she mocked me, and bade a soldier strike her. But she cried aloud, and said: "I am [subjected] to thee, O king, by the wisdom of God given to thee, and by the angel Joel." [20] So I commanded her to spin the hemp for the ropes used in the building of the house of God; and accordingly, when I had sealed and bound her, she was so overcome and brought to naught as to stand night and day spinning the hemp. [21] And I at once bade another demon to be led unto me; and instantly there approached me the demon Asmodeus, bound, and I asked him: "Who art thou?" But he shot on me a glance of anger and rage, and said: "And who art thou?" And I said to him: "Thus punished as thou art, answerest thou me?" But he, with rage, said to me: "But how shall I answer thee, for thou art a son of man; whereas I was born an angel's seed by a daughter of man, so that no word of our heavenly kind addressed to the earth-born can be overweening. Wherefore also my star is bright in heaven, and men call it, some the Wain, and some the dragon's child. I keep near unto this star. So ask me not many things; for thy kingdom also after a little time is to be disrupted, and thy glory is but for a season. And short will be thy tyranny over us; and then we shall again have free range over mankind, so as that they shall revere us as if we were gods, not knowing, men that they are, the names of the angels set over us." [22] And I Solomon, on hearing this, bound him more carefully, and ordered him to be flogged with thongs of ox-hide, and to tell me humbly what was his name and what his business. And he answered me thus: "I am called Asmodeus among mortals, and my business is to plot against the newly wedded, so that they may not know one another. And I sever them utterly by many calamities, and I waste away the beauty of virgin women, and estrange their hearts." [23] And I said to him: "Is this thy only business?" And he answered me: "I transport men into fits of madness and desire, when they have wives of their own, so that they leave them, and go off by night and day to others that belong to other men; with the result that they commit sin, and fall into murderous deeds." [24] And I adjured him by the name of the Lord Sabaôth, saying: "Fear God, Asmodeus, and tell me by what angel thou art frustrated." But he said: "By Raphael, the archangel that stands before the throne of God. But the liver and gall of a fish put me to flight, when smoked over ashes of the tamarisk." I again asked him, and said: "Hide not aught from me. For I am Solomon, son of David, King of Israel. Tell me the name of the fish which thou reverest." And he answered: "It is the Glanos by name, and is found in the rivers of Assyria; wherefore it is that I roam about in those parts." [25] And I said to him: "Hast thou nothing else about thee, Asmodeus?" And he answered: "The power of God knoweth, which hath bound me with the indissoluble bonds of yonder one's seal, that whatever I have told thee is true. I pray thee, King Solomon, condemn me not to [go into] water." But I smiled, and said to him: "As the Lord God of my fathers liveth, I will lay iron on thee to wear. But thou shalt also make the clay for the entire construction of the Temple, treading it down with thy feet." And I ordered them to give him ten water-jars to carry water in. And the demon groaned terribly, and did the work I ordered him to do. And this I did, because that fierce demon Asmodeus knew even the future. And I Solomon glorified God, who gave wisdom to me Solomon his servant. And the liver of the fish and its gall I hung on the spike of a reed, and burned it over Asmodeus because of his being so strong, and his unbearable malice was thus frustrated. [26] And I summoned again to stand before me Beelzeboul, the prince of demons, and I sat him down on a raised seat of honour, and said to him: "Why art thou alone, prince of the demons?" And he said to me: "Because I alone am left of the angels of heaven that came down. For I was first angel in the first heaven being entitled Beelzeboul. And now I control all those who are bound in Tartarus. But I too have a child, and he haunts the Red Sea. And on any suitable occasion he comes up to me again, being subject to me; and reveals to me what he has done, and I support him. [27] I Solomon said unto him: "Beelzeboul, what is thy employment?" And he answered me: "I destroy kings. I ally myself with foreign tyrants. And my own demons I set on to men, in order that the latter may believe in them and be lost. And the chosen servants of God, priests and faithful men, I excite unto desires for wicked sins, and evil heresies, and lawless deeds; and they obey me, and I bear them on to destruction. And I inspire men with envy, and [desire for] murder, and for wars and sodomy, and other evil things. And I will destroy the world." [28] So I said to him: "Bring to me thy child, who is, as thou sayest, in the Red Sea." But he said to me: "I will not bring him to thee. But there shall come to me another demon called Ephippas. Him will I bind, and he will bring him up from the deep unto me." And I said to him: "How comes thy son to be in the depth of the sea, and what is his name? "And he answered me: "Ask me not, for thou canst not learn from me. However, he will come to thee by any command, and will tell thee openly." [29] I said to him: "Tell me by what angel thou art frustrated." And he answered: "By the holy and precious name of the Almighty God, called by the Hebrews by a row of numbers, of which the sum is 644, and among the Greeks it is Emmanuel. And if one of the Romans adjure me by the great name of the power Eleéth, I disappear at once." [30] I Solomon was astounded when I heard this; and I ordered him to saw up Theban marbles. And when he began to saw the marbles, the other demons cried out with a loud voice, howling because of their king Beelzeboul. [31] But I Solomon questioned him, saying: "If thou wouldst gain a respite, discourse to me about the things in heaven." And Beelzeboul said: "Hear, O king, if thou burn gum, and incense, and bulb of the sea, with nard and saffron, and light seven lamps in an earthquake, thou wilt firmly fix thy house. And if, being pure, thou light them at dawn in the sun alight, then wilt thou see the heavenly dragons, how they wind themselves along and drag the chariot of the sun." [32] And I Solomon, having heard this, rebuked him, and said: "Silence for this present, and continue to saw the marbles as I commanded thee." And I Solomon praised God, and commanded another demon to present himself to me. And one came before me who carried his face high up in the air, but the rest of the spirit curled away like a snail. And it broke through the few soldiers, and raised also a terrible dust on the ground, and carried it upwards; and then again hurled it back to frighten us, and asked what questions I could ask as a rule. And I stood up, and spat on the ground in that spot, and sealed with the ring of God. And forthwith the dust-wind stopped. Then I asked him, saying: "Who art thou, O wind?" Then he once more shook up a dust, and answered me: "What wouldst thou have, King Solomon?" I answered him: "Tell me what thou art called, and I would fain ask thee a question. But so far I give thanks to God who has made me wise to answer their evil plots." [33] But [the demon] answered me: "I am the spirit of the ashes (Tephras)." And I said to him: "What is thy pursuit?" And he said: "I bring darkness on men, and set fire to fields; and I bring homesteads to naught. But most busy am I in summer. However, when I get an opportunity, I creep into corners of the wall, by night and day. For I am offspring of the great one, and nothing less." Accordingly I said to him: "Under what star dost thou lie?" And he answered: "In the very tip of the moon's horn, when it is found in the south. There is my star. For I have been bidden to restrain the convulsions of the hemitertian fever; and this is why many men pray to the hemitertian fever, using these three names: Bultala, Thallal, Melchal. And I heal them." And I said to him: "I am Solomon; when therefore thou wouldst do harm, by whose aid dost thou do it?" But he said to me: "By the angel's, by whom also the third day's fever is lulled to rest." So I questioned him, and said: "And by what name?" And he answered: "That of the archangel Azael." And I summoned the archangel Azael, and set a seal on the demon, and commanded him to seize great stones, and toss them up to the workmen on the higher parts of the Temple. And, being compelled, the demon began to do what he was bidden to do. [34] And I glorified God afresh who gave me this authority, and ordered another demon to come before me. And there came seven spirits, females, bound and woven together, fair in appearance and comely. And I Solomon, seeing them, questioned them and said: "Who are ye?" But they, with one accord, said with one voice: "We are of the thirty-three elements of the cosmic ruler of the darkness." And the first said: "I am Deception." The second said: "I am Strife." The third: "I am Klothod, which is battle." The fourth: "I am Jealousy." The fifth: "I am Power." The sixth: "I am Error." The seventh: "I am the worst of all, and our stars are in heaven. Seven stars humble in sheen, and all together. And we are called as it were goddesses. We change our place all and together, and together we live, sometimes in Lydia, sometimes in Olympus, sometimes in a great mountain." [35] So I Solomon questioned them one by one, beginning with the first, and going down to the seventh. The first said: "I am Deception, I deceive and weave snares here and there. I whet and excite heresies. But I have an angel who frustrates me, Lamechalal." [36] Likewise also the second said: "I am Strife, strife of strifes. I bring timbers, stones, hangers, my weapons on the spot. But I have an angel who frustrates me, Baruchiachel." [37] Likewise also the third said: "I am called Klothod, which is Battle, and I cause the well-behaved to scatter and fall foul one of the other. And why do I say so much? I have an angel that frustrates me: "Marmarath." [38] Likewise also the fourth said: "I cause men to forget their sobriety and moderation. I part them and split them into parties; for Strife follows me hand in hand. I rend the husband from the sharer of his bed, and children from parents, and brothers from sisters. But why tell so much to my despite? I have an angel that frustrates me, the great Balthial." [39] Likewise also the fifth said: "I am Power. By power I raise up tyrants and tear down kings. To all rebels I furnish power. I have an angel that frustrates me, Asteraôth." [40] Likewise also the sixth said: "I am Error, O King Solomon. And I will make thee to err, as I have before made thee to err, when I caused thee to slay thy own brother. I will lead you into error, so as to pry into graves; and I teach them that dig, and I lead errant souls away from all piety, and many other evil traits are mine. But I have an angel that frustrates me, Uriel." [41] Likewise also the seventh said: "I am the worst, and I make thee worse off than thou wast; because I will impose the bonds of Artemis. But the locust will set me free, for by means thereof is it fated that thou shalt achieve my desire . . . . For if one were wise, he would not turn his steps toward me." [42] So I Solomon, having heard and wondered, sealed them with my ring; and since they were so considerable, I bade them dig the foundations of the Temple of God. For the length of it was 250 cubits. And I bade them be industrious, and with one murmur of joint protest they began to perform the tasks enjoined. [43] But I Solomon glorified the Lord, and bade another demon come before me. And there was brought to me a demon having all the limbs of a man, but without a head. And I, seeing him, said to him: "Tell me, who art thou?" And he answered: "I am a demon." So I said to him: "Which?" And he answered me: "I am called Envy. For I delight to devour heads, being desirous to secure for myself a head; but I do not eat enough, but am anxious to have such a head as thou hast." [44] I Solomon, on hearing this, sealed him, stretching out my hand against his chest. Whereon the demon leapt up, and threw himself down, and gave a groan, saying: "Woe is me! where am I come to? O traitor Ornias, I cannot see!" So I said to him: "I am Solomon. Tell me then how thou dost manage to see." And he answered me: "By means of my feelings." I then, Solomon, having heard his voice come up to me, asked him how he managed to speak. And he answered me: "I, O King Solomon, am wholly voice, for I have inherited the voices of many men. For in the case of all men who are called dumb, I it is who smashed their heads, when they were children and had reached their eighth day. Then when a child is crying in the night, I become a spirit, and glide by means of his voice. . . . In the crossways also I have many services to render, and my encounter is fraught with harm. For I grasp in an instant a man's head, and with my hands, as with a sword, I cut it off, and put it on to myself. And in this way, by means of the fire which is in me, through my neck it is swallowed up. I it is that sends grave mutilations and incurable on men's feet, and inflict sores." [45] And I Solomon, on hearing this, said to him: "Tell me how thou dost discharge forth the fire? Out of what sources dost thou emit it?" And the spirit said to me: "From the Day-star. For here hath not yet been found that Elburion, to whom men offer prayers and kindle lights. And his name is invoked by the seven demons before me. And he cherishes them." [46] But I said to him: "Tell me his name." But he answered: "I cannot tell thee. For if I tell his name, I render myself incurable. But he will come in response to his name." And on hearing this, I Solomon said to him: "Tell me then, by what angel thou art frustrated?" And he answered: "By the fiery flash of lightning." And I bowed myself before the Lord God of Israel, and bade him remain in the keeping of Beelzeboul until Iax should come. [47] Then I ordered another demon to come before me, and there came into my presence a hound, having a very large shape, and it spoke with a loud voice, and said, "Hail, Lord, King Solomon!" And I Solomon was astounded. I said to it: Who art thou, O hound?" And it answered: "I do indeed seem to thee to be a hound, but before thou wast, O King Solomon, I was a man that wrought many unholy deeds on earth. I was surpassingly learned in letters, and was so mighty that I could hold the stars of heaven back. And many divine works did I prepare. For I do harm to men who follow after our star, and turn them to . . . . And I seize the frenzied men by the larynx, and so destroy them." [48] And I Solomon said to him: "What is thy name?" And he answered: "Staff" (Rabdos). And I said to him: "What is thine employment? And what results canst thou achieve?" And he replied: "Give me thy man, and I will lead him away into a mountainous spot, and will show him a green stone tossed to and fro, with which thou mayest adorn the temple of the Lord God." [49] And I Solomon, on hearing this, ordered my servant to set off with him, and to take the finger-ring bearing the seal of God with him. And I said to him: "Whoever shall show thee the green stone, seal him with this finger-ring. And mark the spot with care, and bring me the demon hither. And the demon showed him the green stone, and he sealed it, and brought the demon to me. And I Solomon decided to confine with my seal on my right hand the two, the headless demon, likewise the hound, that was so huge; he should be bound as well. And I bade the hound keep safe the fiery spirit so that lamps as it were might by day and night cast their light through its maw on the artisans at work. [50] And I Solomon took from the mine of that stone 200 shekels for the supports of the table of incense, which was similar in appearance. And I Solomon glorified the Lord God, and then closed round the treasure of that stone. And I ordered afresh the demons to cut marble for the construction of the house of God. And I Solomon prayed to the Lord, and asked the hound, saying: "By what angel art thou frustrated?" And the demon replied: "By the great Brieus." [51] And I praised the Lord God of heaven and earth, and bade another demon come forward to me; and there came before me one in the form of a lion roaring. And he stood and answered me saying: "O king, in the form which I have, I am a spirit quite incapable of being perceived. Upon all men who lie prostrate with sickness I leap, coming stealthily along; and I render the man weak, so that his habit of body is enfeebled. But I have also another glory, O king. I cast out demons, and I have legions under my control. And I am capable of being received in my dwelling-places, along with all the demons belonging to the legions under me." But I Solomon, on hearing this, asked him: "What is thy name?" But he answered: "Lion-bearer, Rath in kind." And I said to him: "How art thou to be frustrated along with thy legions? What angel is it that frustrates thee?" And he answered: "If I tell thee my name, I bind not myself alone, but also the legions of demons under me." [52] So I said to him: "I adjure thee in the name of the God Sabaoth, to tell me by what name thou art frustrated along with thy host." And the spirit answered me: "The 'great among men,' who is to suffer many things at the hands of men, whose name is the figure 644, which is Emmanuel; he it is who has bound us, and who will then come and plunge us from the steep under water. He is noised abroad in the three letters which bring him down." [53] And I Solomon, on hearing this, glorified God, and condemned his legion to carry wood from the thicket. And I condemned the lion-shaped one himself to saw up the wood small with his teeth, for burning in the unquenchable furnace for the Temple of God. [54] And I worshipped the Lord God of Israel, and bade another demon come forward. And there came before me a dragon, three-headed, of fearful hue. And I questioned him: "Who art thou?" And he answered me: "I am a caltrop-like spirit, whose activity in three lines. But I blind children in women's wombs, and twirl their ears round. And I make them deaf and mute. And I have again in my third head means of slipping in. And I smite men in the limbless part of the body, and cause them to fall down, and foam, and grind their teeth. But I have my own way of being frustrated, Jerusalem being signified in writing, unto the place called 'of the head." For there is fore-appointed the angel of the great counsel, and now he will openly dwell on the cross. He doth frustrate me, and to him am I subject." [55] "But in the place where thou sittest, O King Solomon, standeth a column in the air, of purple... The demon called Ephippas hath brought [it] up from the Red Sea, from inner Arabia. He it is that shall be shut up in a skin-bottle and brought before thee. But at the entrance of the Temple, which thou hast begun to build, O King Solomon, lies stored much gold, which dig thou up and carry off." And I

Solomon sent my servant, and found it to be as the demon told me. And I sealed him with my ring, and praised the Lord God." **56** So I said to him: "What art thou called?" And the demon said: "I am the crest of dragons." And I bade him make bricks in the Temple. He had human hands. **57** And I adored the Lord God of Israel, and bade another demon present himself. And there came before me a spirit in woman's form, that had a head without any limbs, and her hair was dishevelled. And I said to her: "Who art thou?" But she answered: "Nay, who art thou? And why dost thou want to hear concerning me? But, as thou wouldst learn, here I stand bound before thy face. Go then into thy royal storehouses and wash thy hands. Then sit down afresh before thy tribunal, and ask me questions; and thou shalt learn, O king, who I am." **58** And I Solomon did as she enjoined me, and restrained myself because of the wisdom dwelling in me; in order that I might hear of her deeds, and reprehend them, and manifest them to men. And I sat down, and said to the demon: "What art thou?" And she said: "I am called among men Obizuth; and by night I sleep not, but go my rounds over all the world, and visit women in childbirth. And divining the hour I take my stand; and if I am lucky, I strangle the child. But if not, I retire to another place. For I cannot for a single night retire unsuccessful. For I am a fierce spirit, of myriad names and many shapes. And now hither, now thither I roam. And to westering parts I go my rounds. But as it now is, though thou hast sealed me round with the ring of God, thou hast done nothing. I am not standing before thee, and thou wilt not be able to command me. For I have no work other than the destruction of children, and the making their ears to be deaf, and the working of evil to their eyes, and the binding their mouths with a bond, and the ruin of their minds, and paining of their bodies." **59** When I Solomon heard this, I marvelled at her appearance, for I beheld all her body to be in darkness. But her glance was altogether bright and greeny, and her hair was tossed wildly like a dragon's; and the whole of her limbs were invisible. And her voice was very clear as it came to me. And I cunningly said: "Tell me by what angel thou art frustrated, O evil spirit?" By she answered me: "By the angel of God called Afarôt, which is interpreted Raphael, by whom I am frustrated now and for all time. His name, if any man know it, and write the same on a woman in childbirth, then I shall not be able to enter her. Of this name the number is **640**" And I Solomon having heard this, and having glorified the Lord, ordered her hair to be bound, and that she should be hung up in front of the Temple of God; that all the children of Israel, as they passed, might see it, and glorify the Lord God of Israel, who had given me this authority, with wisdom and power from God, by means of this signet. **60** And I again ordered another demon to come before me. And the came, rolling itself along, one in appearance like to a dragon, but having the face and hands of a man. And all its limbs, except the feet, were those of a dragon; and it had wings on its back. And when I beheld it, I was astonied, and said: "Who art thou, demon, and what art thou called? And whence hast thou come? Tell me." **61** And the spirit answered and said: "This is the first time I have stood before the, O King Solomon. I am a spirit made into a god among men, but now brought to naught by the ring and wisdom vouchsafed to thee by God. Now I am the so-called winged dragon, and I chamber not with many women, but only with a few that are of fair shape, which possess the name of xuli, of this star. And I pair with them in the guise of a spirit winged in form, coitum habens per nates. And she on whom I have leapt goes heavy with child, and that which is born of her becomes eros. But since such offspring cannot be carried by men, the woman in question breaks wind. Such is my role. Supposed then only that I am satisfied, and all the other demons molested and disturbed by thee will speak the whole truth. But those composed of fire will cause to be burned up by fire the material of the logs which is to be collected by them for the building in the Temple." **62** And as the demon said this, I saw the spirit going forth from his mouth, and it consumed the wood of the frankincense-tree, and burned up all the logs which we had placed in the Temple of God. And I Solomon saw what the spirit had done, and I marvelled. **63** And, having glorified God, I asked the dragon-shaped demon, and said: "Tell me, by what angel art thou frustrated?" And he answered: "By the great angel which has its seat in the second heaven, which is called in Hebrew Bazazeth. And I Solomon, having heard this, and having invoked his angel, condemned him to saw up marbles for the building of the Temple of God; and I praised God, and commanded another demon to come before me. **64** And there came before my face another spirit, as it were a woman in the form she had. But on her shoulders she had two other heads with hands. And I asked her, and said: "Tell me, who art thou?" And she said to me: "I am Enêpsigos, who also have a myriad names." And I said her: "By what angel art thou frustrated?" But she said to me: "What seekest, what askest thou? I undergo changes, like the goddess I am called. And I change again, and pass into possession of another shape. And be not desirous therefore to know all that concerns me. But since thou art before me for this much, hearken. I have my abode in the moon, and for that reason I possess three forms. At times I am magically invoked by the wise as Kronos. At other times, in connexion with those who bring me down, I come down and appear in another shape. The measure of the element is inexplicable and indefinable, and not to be frustrated. I then, changing into these three forms, come down and become such as thou seest me; but I am frustrated by the angel Rathanael, who sits in the third heaven. This then is why I speak to thee. Yonder temple cannot contain me." **65** I therefore Solomon prayed to my God, and I invoked the angel of whom Enépsigos spoke to me, and used my seal. And I sealed her with a triple chain, and (placed) beneath her the fastening of the chain. I used the seal of God, and the spirit prophesied to me, saying: "This is what thou, King Solomon, doest to us. But after a time thy kingdom shall be broken, and again in season this Temple shall be riven asunder; and all Jerusalem shall be undone by the King of the Persians and Medes and Chaldaeans. And the vessels of this Temple, which thou makest, shall be put to servile uses of the gods; and along with them all the jars, in which thou dost shut us up, shall be broken by the hands of men. And then we shall go forth in great power hither and thither, and be disseminated all over the world. And we shall lead astray the inhabited world for a long season, until the Son of God is stretched upon the cross. For never before doth arise a king like unto him, one frustrating us all, whose mother shall not have contact with man. Who else can receive such authority over spirits, except he, whom the first devil will seek to tempt, but will not prevail over? The number of his name is 644, which is Emmanuel. Wherefore, O King Solomon, thy time is evil, and thy years short and evil, and to thy servant shall thy kingdom be given." **66** And I Solomon, having heard this, glorified God. And though I marvelled at the apology of the demons, I did not credit it until it came true. And I did not believe their words; but when they were realized, then I understood, and at my death I wrote this Testament to the children of Israel, and gave it to them, so that they might know the powers of the demons and their shapes, and the names of their angels, by which these angels are frustrated. And I glorified the Lord God of Israel, and commanded the spirits to be bound with bonds indissoluble. **67** And having praised God, I commanded another spirit to come before me; and there came before my face another demon, having in front the shape of a horse, but behind of a fish. And he had a mighty voice, and said to me: "O King Solomon, I am a fierce spirit of the sea, and I am greedy of gold and silver. I am such a spirit as rounds itself and comes over the expanses of the water of the sea, and I trip up the men who sail thereon. For I round myself into a wave, and transform myself, and then throw myself on ships and come right in on them. And that is my business, and my way of getting hold of money and men. For I take the men, and whirl them round with myself, and hurl the men out of the sea. For I am not covetous of men's bodies, but cast them up out of the sea so far. But since Beelzeboul, ruler of the spirits of air and of those under the earth, and lord of earthly ones, hath a joint kingship with us in respect of the deeds of each one of us, therefore I went up from the sea, to get a certain outlook in his company. **68** "But I also have another character and role. I metamorphose myself into waves, and come up from the sea. And I show myself to men, so that those on earth call me Kuno[s]paston, because I assume the human form. And my name is a true one. For by my passage up into men, I send forth a certain nausea. I came then to take counsel with the prince Beelzeboul; and he bound me and delivered me into thy hands. And I am here before thee because of this seal, and thou dost now torment me. Behold now, in two or three days the spirit that converseth with thee will fail, because I shall have no water." **69** And I said to him: "Tell me by what angel thou art frustrated." And he answered: "By Iameth." And I glorified God. I commanded the spirit to be thrown into a phial along with ten jugs of sea-water of two measures each. And I sealed them round above the marbles and asphalt and pitch in the mouth of the vessel. And having sealed it with my ring, I ordered it to be deposited in the Temple of God. And I ordered another spirit to come before me. **70** And there came before my face another enslaved spirit, having obscurely the form of a man, with gleaming eyes, and bearing in his hand a blade. And I asked: "Who art thou? But he answered: "I am a lascivious spirit, engendered of a giant man who dies in the massacre in the time of the giants." I said to him: "Tell me what thou art employed on upon earth, and where thou hast thy dwelling." **71** And he said: "My dwelling is in fruitful places, but my procedure is this. I seat myself beside the men who pass along among the tombs, and in untimely season I assume the form of the dead; and if I catch any one, I at once destroy him with my sword. But if I cannot destroy him, I cause him to be possessed with a demon, and to devour his own flesh, and the hair to fall off his chin." But I said to him: "Do thou then be in fear of the God of heaven and of earth, and tell me by angel thou art frustrated." And he answered: "He destroys me who is to become Saviour, a man whose number, if any one shall write it on his forehead, he will defeat me, and in fear I shall quickly retreat. And, indeed, if any one write this sign on him, I shall be in fear." And I Solomon, on hearing this, and having glorified the Lord God, shut up this demon like the rest. [72] And I commanded another demon to come before me. And there came before my face thirty-six spirits, their heads shapeless like dogs, but in themselves they were human in form; with faces of asses, faces of oxen, and faces of birds. And I Solomon, on hearing and seeing them, wondered, and I asked them and said: "Who are you?" But they, of one accord with one voice, said: "We are the thirty-six elements, the world-rulers of this darkness. But, O King Solomon, thou wilt not wrong us nor imprison us, nor lay command on us; but since the Lord God has given thee authority over every spirit, in the air, and on the earth, and under the earth, therefore do we also present ourselves before thee like the other spirits, from ram and bull, from both twin and crab, lion and virgin, scales and scorpion, archer, goat-horned, water-pourer, and fish. [73] Then I Solomon invoked the name of the Lord Sabaoth, and questioned each in turn as to what was its character. And I bade each one come forward and tell of its actions. Then the first one came forward, and said: "I am the first decans of the zodiacal circle, and I am called the ram, and with me are these two." So I put to them the question: "Who are ye called?" The first said: "I, O Lord, am called Ruax, and I cause the heads of men to be idle, and I pillage their brows. But let me only hear the words, 'Michael, imprison Ruax,' and at once I retreat." [74] And the second said: "I am called Barsafael, and I cause those who are subject to my hour to feel the pain of migraine. If only I hear the words, 'Gabriel, imprison Barsafael,' at once I retreat." [75] The third said: "I am called Arôtosael. I do harm to eyes, and grievously injure them. Only let me hear the words, 'Uriel, imprison Aratosael' (sic), at once I retreat . . . . ." [76] The fifth said: "I am called Iudal, and I bring about a block in the ears and deafness of hearing. If I hear, 'Uruel Iudal,' I at once retreat." [77] The sixth said: "I am called Sphendonaêl. I cause tumours of the parotid gland, and inflammations of the tonsils, and tetanic recurvation. If I hear, 'Sabrael, imprison Sphendonaêl,' at once I retreat." [78] And the Seventh said: "I am called Sphandôr, and I weaken the strength of the shoulders, and cause them to tremble; and I paralyze the nerves of the hands, and I break and bruise the bones of the neck. And I, I suck out the marrow. But if I hear the words, 'Araêl, imprison Sphandôr,' I at once retreat." [79] And the eight said: "I am called Belbel. I distort the hearts and minds of men. If I hear the words, 'Araêl, imprison Belbel,' I at once retreat." [80] And the ninth said: "I am called Kurtaêl. I send colics in the bowels. I induce pains. If I hear the words, 'Iaôth, imprison Kurtaêl,' I at once retreat." [81] The tenth said: "I am called Metathiax. I cause the reins to ache. If I hear the words, 'Adônaêl, imprison Metathiax,' I at once retreat." [82] The eleventh said: "I am called Katanikotaêl. I create strife and wrongs in men's homes, and send on them hard temper. If any one would be at peace in his home, let him write on seven leaves of laurel the name of the angel that frustrates me, along with these names: Iae, Ieô, sons of Sabaôth, in the name of the great God let him shut up Katanikotaêl. Then let him wash the laurel-leaves in water, and sprinkle his house with the water, from within to the outside. And at once I retreat." [83] The twelfth said: "I am called Saphathoraél, and I inspire partisanship in men, and delight in causing them to stumble. If any one will write on paper these names of angels, Iacô, Iealô, Iôelet, Sabaôth, Ithoth, Bae, and having folded it up, wear it round his neck or against his ear, I at once retreat and dissipate the drunken fit." [84] The thirteenth said: "I am called Bobêl (sic), and I cause nervous illness by my assaults. If I hear the name of the great 'Adonaêl, imprison Bothothêl,' I at once retreat." [85] The fourteenth said: "I am called Kumeatêl, and I inflict shivering fits and torpor. If only I hear the words: 'Zôrôêl, imprison Kumentaêl,' I at once retreat." [86] The fifteenth said: "I am called Roêlêd. I cause cold and frost and pain in the stomach. Let me only hear the words: 'Iax, bide not, be not warmed, for Solomon is fairer than eleven fathers,' I at [once] retreat." [87] The sixteenth said: "I am called Atrax. I inflict upon men fevers, irremediable and harmful. If you would imprison me, chop up coriander and smear it on the lips, reciting the following charm: 'The fever which is from dirt. I exorcise thee by the throne of the most high God, retreat from dirt and retreat from the creature fashioned by God.' And at once I retreat." [88] The seventeenth said: "I am called Ieropaêl. On the stomach of men I sit, and cause convulsions in the bath and in the road; and wherever I be found, or find a man, I throw him down. But if any one will say to the afflicted into their ear these names, three times over, into the right ear: 'Iudarizê, Sabunê, Denôê,' I at once retreat." [89] The eighteenth said: "I am called Buldumêch. I separate wife from husband and bring about a grudge between them. If any one write down the names of thy sires, Solomon, on paper and place it in the ante-chamber of his house, I retreat thence. And the legend written shall be as follows: 'The God of Abram, and the God of Isaac, and the God of Jacob commands thee – retire from this house in peace.' And I at once retire." [90] The nineteenth said: "I am called Naôth, and I take my seat on the knees of men. If any one write on paper: 'Phnunoboêol, depart Nathath, and touch thou not the neck,' I at once retreat." [91] The twentieth said: "I am called Marderô. I send on men incurable fever. If any one write on the leaf of a book: 'Sphênêr, Rafael, retire, drag me not about, flay me not,' and tie it round his neck, I at once retreat." [92] The twenty-first said: "I am called Alath, and I cause coughing and hard-breathing in children. If any one write on paper: 'Rorêx, do thou pursue Alath,' and fasten it round his neck, I at once retire..." [93] The twenty-third said: "I am called Nefthada. I cause the reins to ache, and I bring about dysury. If any one write on a plate of tin the words: 'Iathôth, Uruêl, Nephthada,' and fasten it round the loins, I at once retreat." [94] The twenty-fourth said: "I am called Akton. I cause ribs and lumbic muscles to ache. If one engrave on copper material, taken from a ship which has missed its anchorage, this: 'Marmaraôth, Sabaôth, pursue Akton,' and fasten it round the loin, I at once retreat." [95] The twenty-fifth said: "I am called Anatreth, and I rend burnings and fevers into the entrails. But if I hear: 'Arara, Charara,' instantly do I retreat." [96] The twenty-sixth said: "I am called Enenuth. I steal away men's minds, and change their hearts, and make a man toothless (?). If one write: 'Allazoôl, pursue Enenuth,' and tie the paper round him, I at once retreat." [97] The twenty-seventh said: "I am called Phêth. I make men consumptive and cause hemorrhagia. ,If one exorcise me in wine, sweet-smelling and unmixed by the eleventh aeon, and say: 'I exorcise thee by the eleventh aeon to stop, I demand, Phêth (Axiôphêth),' then give it to the patient to drink, and I at once retreat." [98] The twenty-eighth said: "I am called Harpax, and I send sleeplessness on men. If one write 'Kokphnêdismos,' and bind it round the temples, I at once retire." [99] The twenty-ninth said: "I am called Anostêr. I engender uterine mania and pains in the bladder. If one powder into pure oil three seeds of laurel and smear it on, saying: 'I exorcise thee, Anostêr. Stop by Marmaraô,' at once I retreat." [100] The thirtieth said: "I am called Alleborith. If in eating fish one has swallowed a bone, then he must take a bone from the fish and cough, and at once I retreat." [101] The thirty-first said: "I am called Hephesimireth, and cause lingering disease. If you throw salt, rubbed in the hand, into oil and smear it on the patient, saying: 'Seraphim, Cherubim, help me!' I at once retire." [102] The thirty-second said: "I am called Ichthion. I paralyze muscles and contuse them. If I hear 'Adonaêth, help!' I at once retire." [103] The thirty-third said: "I am called Agchoniôn. I lie among swaddling-clothes and in the precipice. And if any one write on fig-leaves 'Lycurgos,' taking away one letter at a time, and write it, reversing the letters, I retire at once. 'Lycurgos, ycurgos, kurgos, yrgos, gos, os.'" [104] The thirty-fourth said: "I am called Autothith. I cause grudges and fighting. Therefore I am frustrated by Alpha and Omega, if written down." [105] The thirty-fifth said: "I am called Phthenoth. I cast evil eye on every man. Therefore, the eye much-suffering, if it be drawn. frustrates me." [106] The thirty-sixth said: "I am called Bianakith. I have a grudge against the body. I lay waste houses, I cause flesh to decay, and all else that is similar. If a man write on the front-door of his house: 'Mêltô, Ardu, Anaath,' I flee from that place." [107] And I Solomon, when I heard this, glorified the God of heaven and earth. And I commanded them to fetch water in the Temple of God. And I furthermore prayed to the Lord God to cause the demons without, that hamper humanity, to be bound and made to approach the Temple of God. Some of these demons I condemned to do the heavy work of the construction of the Temple of God. Others I shut up in prisons. Others I ordered to wrestle with fire in (the making of) gold and silver, sitting down by lead and spoon. And to make ready places for the other demons in which they should be confined. [108] And I Solomon had much quiet in all the earth, and spent my life in profound peace, honoured by all men and by all under heaven. And I built the entire Temple of the Lord God. And my kingdom was prosperous, and my army was with me. And for the rest the city of Jerusalem had repose, rejoicing and delighted. And all the kings of the earth came to me from the ends of the earth to behold the Temple which I builded to the Lord God. And having heard of the wisdom given to me, they did homage to me in the Temple, bringing gold and silver and precious stones, many and divers, and bronze, and iron, and lead, and cedar logs. And woods decay not they brought me, for the equipment of the Temple of God. [109] And among them also the queen of the South, being a witch, came in great concern and bowed low before me to the earth. And having heard my wisdom, she glorified the God of Israel, and she made formal trial of all my wisdom, of all love in which I instructed her, according to the wisdom imparted to me. And all the sons of Israel glorified God. [110] And behold, in those days one of the workmen, of ripe old age, threw himself down before me, and said: "King Solomon, pity me, because I am old." So I bade him stand up, and said: "Tell me, old man, all you will." And he answered: "I beseech you king, I have an only-born son, and he insults and beats me openly, and plucks out the hair of my head, and threatens me with a painful death. Therefore I beseech you avenge me. [111] And I Solomon, on hearing this, felt compunction as I looked at his old age; and I bade the child be brought to me. And when he was brought I questioned him whether it were true. And the youth said: "I was not so filled with madness as to strike my father with my hand. Be kind to me, O king. For I have not dared to commit such impiety, poor wretch that I am." But I Solomon on hearing this from the youth, exhorted the old man to reflect on the matter, and accept his son's apology. However, he would not, but said he would rather let him die. And as the old man would not yield, I was about to pronounce sentence on the youth, when I saw Ornias the demon laughing. I was very angry at the demon's laughing in my presence; and I ordered my men to remove the other parties, and bring forward Ornias before my tribunal. And when he was brought before me, I said to him: "Accursed one, why didst thou look at me and laugh?" And the demon answered: "Prithee, king, it was not because of thee I laughed, but because of this ill-starred old man and the wretched youth, his son. For after three days his son will die untimely; and lo, the old man desires to foully make away with him." [112] But I Solomon, having heard this, said to the demon: "Is that true that thou speakest?" And he answered: "It is true; O king." And I, on hearing that, bade them remove the demon, and that they should again bring before me the old man with his son. I bade them make friends with one another again, and I supplied them with food. And then I told the old man after three days to bring his son again to me here; "and," said I, "I will attend to him." And they saluted me, and went their way. [113] And when they were gone I ordered Ornias to be brought forward, and said to him: "Tell me how you know this;" and he answered: "We demons ascend into the firmament of heaven, and fly about among the stars. And we hear the sentences which go forth upon the souls of men, and forthwith we come, and whether by force of influence, or by fire, or by sword, or by some accident, we veil our act of destruction; and if a man does not die by some untimely disaster or by violence, then we demons transform ourselves in such a way as to appear to men and be worshipped in our human nature." [114] I therefore, having heard this, glorified the Lord God, and again I questioned the demon, saying: "Tell me how ye can ascend into heaven, being demons, and amidst the stars and holy angels intermingle." And he answered: "Just as things are fulfilled in heaven, so also on earth (are fulfilled) the types of all of them. For there are principalities, authorities, world-rulers, and we demons fly about in the air; and we hear the voices of the heavenly beings, and survey all the powers. And as having no ground (basis) on which to alight and rest, we lose strength and fall off like leaves from trees. And men seeing us imagine that the stars are falling from heaven. But it is not really so, O king; but we fall because of our weakness, and because we have nowhere anything to lay hold of; and so we fall down like lightnings in the depth of night and suddenly. And we set cities in flames and fire the fields. For the stars have firm foundations in the heavens like the sun and the moon." [115] And I Solomon, having heard this, ordered the demon to be guarded for five days. And after the five days I recalled the old man, and was about to question him. But he came to me in grief and with black face. And I said to him: "Tell me, old man, where is thy son? And what means this garb?" And he answered: "Lo, I am become childless, and sit by my son's grave in despair. For it is already two days that he is dead." But I Solomon, on hearing that, and knowing that the demon Ornias had told me the truth, glorified the God of Israel. [116] And the queen of the South saw all this, and marvelled, glorifying the God of Israel; and she beheld the Temple of the Lord being builded. And she gave a siklos of gold and one hundred myriads of silver and choice bronze, and she went into the Temple. And (she beheld) the altar of incense and the brazen supports of this altar, and the gems of the lamps flashing forth of different colours, and of the lamp-stand of stone, and of emerald, and hyacinth, and sapphire; and she beheld the vessels of gold, and silver, and bronze, and wood, and the folds of skins dyed red with madder. And she saw the bases of the pillars of the Temple of the Lord. All were of one gold ... apart from the demons whom I condemned to labour. And there was peace in the circle of my kingdom and over all the earth. [117] And it came to pass, which I was in my kingdom, the King of the Arabians, Adares, sent me a letter, and the writing of the letter was written as follows: – "To King Solomon, all hail! Lo, we have heard, and it hath been heard unto all the ends of the earth, concerning the wisdom vouchsafed in thee, and that thou art a man merciful from the Lord. And understanding hath been granted thee over all the spirits of the air, and on earth, and under the earth. Now, forasmuch as there is present in the land of Arabia a spirit of the following kind: at early dawn there begins to blow a certain wind until the third hour. And its blast is harsh and terrible, and it slays man and beast. And no spirit can live upon earth against this demon. I pray thee then, forasmuch as the spirit is a wind, contrive something according to the wisdom given in thee by the Lord thy God, and deign to send a man able to capture it. And behold, King Solomon, I and my people and all my land will serve thee unto death. And all Arabia shall be at peace with thee, if thou wilt perform this act of righteousness for us. Wherefore we pray thee, contemn not our humble prayer, and suffer not to be utterly brought to naught the eparchy subordinated to thy authority. Because we are suppliants, both I and my people and all my land. Farewell to my Lord. All health!" [118] And I Solomon read this epistle; and I folded it up and gave it to my people, and said to them: "After seven days shalt thou remind me of this epistle. And Jerusalem was built, and the Temple was being completed. And there was a stone, the end stone of the corner lying there, great, chosen out, one which I desired lay in the head of the corner of the completion of the Temple. And all the workmen, and all the demons helping them came to the same place to bring up the stone and lay it on the pinnacle of the holy Temple, and were not strong enough to stir it, and lay it upon the corner allotted to it. For that stone was exceedingly great and useful for the corner of the Temple." [119] And after seven days, being reminded of the epistle of Adares, King of Arabia, I called my servant and said to him: "Order thy camel and take for thyself a leather flask, and take also this seal. And go away into Arabia to the place in which the evil spirit blows; and there take the flask, and the signet-ring in front of the mouth of the flask, and (hold them) towards the blast of the spirit. And when the flask is blown out, thou wilt understand that the demon is (in it). Then hastily tie up the mouth of to flask, and seal it securely with the seal-ring, and lay it carefully on the camel and bring it me hither. And if on the way it offer thee gold or silver or treasure in return for letting it go, see that thou be not persuaded. But arrange without using oath to release it. And then if it point out to the places where are gold or silver, mark the places and seal them with this seal. And bring the demon to me. And now depart, and fare thee well." [120] Then the youth did as was bidden him. And he ordered his camel, and laid on it a flask, and set off into Arabia. And the men of that region would not believe that he would be able to catch the evil spirit. And when it was dawn, the servant stood before the spirit's blast, and laid the flask on the ground, and the finger-ring on the mouth of the flask. And the demon blew through the middle of the finger-ring into the mouth of the flask, and going in blew out the flask. But the man promptly stood up to it and drew tight with his hand the mouth of the flask, in the name of the Lord God of Sabaôth. And the demon remained within the flask. And after that the youth remained in that land three days to make trial. And the spirit no longer blew against that city. And all the Arabs knew that he had safely shut in the spirit. [121] Then the youth fastened the flask on the camel, and the Arabs sent him forth on his way with much honour and precious gifts, praising and magnifying the God of Israel. But the youth brought in the bag and laid it in the middle of the Temple. And on the next day, I King Solomon, went into the Temple of God and sat in deep distress about the stone of the end of the corner. And when I entered the Temple, the flask stood up and walked around some seven steps and then fell on its mouth and did homage to me. And I marvelled that even along with the bottle the demon still had power and could walk about; and I commanded it to stand up. And the flask stood up, and stood on its feet all blown out. And I questioned him, saying: "Tell me, who art thou?" And the spirit within said: "I am the demon called Ephippas, that is in Arabia." And I said to him: "Is this thy name?" And he answered: "Yes; wheresoever I will, I alight and set fire and do to death." [122] And I said to him: "By what angel art thou frustrated?" And he answered: "By the only-ruling God, that hath authority over me even to be heard. He that is to be born of a virgin and crucified by the Jews on a cross. Whom the angels and archangels worship. He doth frustrate me, and enfeeble me of my great strength, which has been given me by my father the devil." And I said to him: "What canst thou do?" And he answered: "I am able to remove mountains, to overthrow the oaths of kings. I wither trees and make their leaves to fall off." And I said to him: "Canst thou raise this stone, and lay it for the beginning of this corner which exists in the fair plan of the Temple?" And he said: "Not only raise this, O king; but also, with the help of the demon who presides over the Red Sea, I will bring up the pillar of air, and will stand it where thou wilt in Jerusalem." [123] Saying this, I laid stress on him, and the flask became as if depleted of air. And I placed it under the stone, and (the spirit) girded himself up, and lifted it up top of the flask. And the flask went up the steps, carrying the stone, and laid it down at the end of the entrance of the Temple. And I Solomon, beholding the stone raised aloft and placed on a foundation, said: "Truly the Scripture is fulfilled, which says: 'The stone which the builders rejected on trial, that same is become the head of the corner.' For this it is not mine to grant, but God's, that the demon should be strong enough to lift up so great a stone and deposit it in the place I wished." [124] And Ephippas led the demon of the Red Sea with the column. And they both took the column and raised it aloft from the earth. And I outwitted these two spirits, so that they could not shake the entire earth in a moment of time. And then I sealed round with my ring on this side and that, and said: "Watch." And the spirits have remained upholding it until this day, for proof of the wisdom vouchsafed to me. And there the pillar was hanging of enormous size, in mid air, supported by the winds. And thus the spirits appeared underneath, like air, supporting it. And if one looks fixedly, the pillar is a little oblique, being supported by the spirits; and it is so to day. ¹²⁵ And I Solomon questioned the other spirit which came up with the pillar from the depth of the Red Sea. And I said to him: "Who art thou, and what calls thee? And what is thy business? For I hear many things about thee." And the demon answered: "I, O King Solomon, am called Abezithibod. I am a descendant of the archangel. Once as I sat in the first heaven, of which the name is Ameleouth – I then am a fierce spirit and winged, and with a single wing, plotting against every spirit under heaven. I was present when Moses went in before Pharaoh, king of Egypt, and I hardened his heart. I am he whom Iannes and Iambres invoked homing with Moses in Egypt. I am he who fought against Moses with wonders with signs." ¹²⁶ I said therefore to him: "How wast thou found in the Red Sea?" And he answered: "In the exodus of the sons of Israel I hardened the heart of Pharaoh. And I excited his heart and that of his ministers. And I caused them to pursue after the children of Israel. And Pharaoh followed with (me) and all the Egyptians. Then I was present there, and we followed together. And we all came up upon the Red Sea. And it came to pass when the children of Israel had crossed over, the water returned and hid all the host of the Egyptians and all their might. And I remained in the sea, being kept under this pillar. But when Ephippas came, being sent by thee, shut up in the vessel of a flask, he fetched me up to thee." ¹²⁷ I, therefore, Solomon, having heard this, glorified God and adjured the demons not to disobey me, but to remain supporting the pillar. And they both sware, saying: "The Lord thy God liveth, we will not let go this pillar until the world's end. But on whatever day this stone fall, then shall be the end of the world." ¹²⁸ And I Solomon glorified God, and adorned the Temple of the Lord with all fair-seeming. And I was glad in spirit in my kingdom, and there was peace in my days. And I took wives of my own from every land, who were numberless. And I marched against the Jebusaeans, and there I saw Jebusaean, daughter of a man: and fell violently in love with her, and desired to take her to wife along with my other wives. And I said to their priests: "Give me the Sonmanites (i.e. Shunammite) to wife." But the priests of Moloch said to me: "If thou lovest this maiden, go in and worship our gods, the great god Raphan and the god called Moloch." I therefore was in fear of the glory of God, and did not follow to worship. And I said to them: "I will not worship a strange god. What is this proposal, that ye compel me to do so much?" But they said: ". . . . by our fathers." ¹²⁹ And when I answered that I would on no account worship strange gods, they told the maiden not to sleep with me until I complied and sacrificed to the gods. I then was moved, but crafty Eros brought and laid by her for me five grasshoppers, saying: "Take these grasshoppers, and crush them together in the name of the god Moloch; and then will I sleep with you." And this I actually did. And at once the Spirit of God departed from me, and I became weak as well as foolish in my words. And after that I was obliged by her to build a temple of idols to Baal, and to Rapha, and to Moloch, and to the other idols. ¹³⁰ I then, wretch that I am, followed her advice, and the glory of God quite departed from me; and my spirit was darkened, and I became the sport of idols and demons. Wherefore I wrote out this Testament, that ye who get possession of it may pity, and attend to the last things, and not to the first. So that ye may find grace for ever and ever. Amen.

The Testament of Moses
(or Assumption of Moses)

1

The Testament of Moses even the things which he commanded in the one hundred and twentieth year of his life, that is the two thousand five hundredth year from the creation of the world: [But according to oriental reckoning the two thousand and seven hundredth, and the four hundredth after the departure from Phoenicia], when the people had gone forth after the Exodus that was made by Moses to Amman beyond the Jordan, in the prophecy that was made by Moses in the book Deuteronomy: and he called to him Joshua the son of Nun, a man approved of the Lord, that he might be the minister of the people and of the tabernacle of the testimony with all its holy things, and that he might bring the people into the land given to their fathers, that it should be given to them according to the covenant and the oath, which He spoke in the tabernacle to give (it) by Joshua: saying to Joshua these words: '(Be strong) and of a good courage so as to do with thy might all that has been commanded that you may be blameless unto God.' So says the Lord of the world. For He has created the world on behalf of His people. But He was not pleased to manifest this purpose of creation from the foundation of the world, in order that the Gentiles might thereby be convicted, yea to their own humiliation might by (their) arguments convict one another. Accordingly He designed and devised me, and He prepared me before the foundation of the world, that I should be the mediator of His covenant. And now I declare unto you that the time of the years of my life is fulfilled and I am passing away to sleep with my fathers even in the presence of all the people And receive this writing that you may know how to preserve the books which I shall deliver unto you: and you shall set these in order and anoint them with oil of cedar and put them away in earthen vessels in the place which He made from the beginning of the creation of the world, that His name should be called upon until the day of repentance in the visitation wherewith the Lord will visit them in the consummation of the end of the days.

2

And now they shall go by means of you into the land which He determined and promised to give to their fathers, in the which you shall bless and give to them individually and confirm unto them their inheritance in me and establish for them the kingdom, and you shall appoint them local magistrates according to the good pleasure of their Lord in judgment and righteousness. And five years after they enter into the land, that thereafter they shall be ruled by chiefs and kings for eighteen years, and during nineteen years the ten tribes shall break away. And the twelve tribes shall go down and transfer the tabernacle of the testimony. Then the God of heaven will make the court of His tabernacle and the tower of His sanctuary, and the two holy tribes shall be (there) established: but the ten tribes shall establish kingdoms for themselves according to their own ordinances. And they shall offer sacrifices throughout twenty years: and seven shall entrench the walls, and I will protect nine, but four shall transgress the covenant of the Lord, and profane the oath which the Lord made with them. And they shall sacrifice their sons to strange gods, and they shall set up idols in the sanctuary, to worship them. And in the house of the Lord they shall work impiety and engrave every form of beast, even many abominations.

3

And in those days a king from the east shall come against them and his cavalry shall cover their land. And he shall burn their colony with fire together with the holy temple of the Lord, and he shall carry away all the holy vessels. And he shall cast forth all the people, and he shall take them to the land of his nativity, yea he shall take the two tribes with him. Then the two tribes shall call upon the ten tribes, and shall march as a lioness on the dusty plains, being hungry and thirsty. And they shall cry aloud: 'Righteous and holy is the Lord, for, inasmuch as ye have sinned, we too, in like manner, have been carried away with you, together with our children.' Then the ten tribes shall mourn on hearing the reproaches of the two tribes, and they shall say: 'What have we done unto you, brethren? Has not this tribulation come on all the house of Israel?' And all the tribes shall mourn, crying unto heaven and saying: 'God of Abraham God of Isaac and God of Jacob, remember Thy covenant which You made with them, and the oath which You didst swear unto them by Yourself, that their seed should never fail from the land which You hast given them.' Then they shall remember me, saying, in that day, tribe unto tribe and each man unto his neighbor: 'Is not this that which Moses did then declare unto us in prophecies, who suffered many things in Egypt and in the Red Sea and in the wilderness during forty years: and assuredly called heaven and earth to witness against us, that we should not transgress His commandments, in the which he was a mediator unto us? Behold these things have befallen us after his death according to his declaration, as he declared to us at that time, yes, behold these have taken place even to our being carried away captive into the country of the east.' Who shall be also in bondage for about seventy and seven years.

4

Then there shall enter one who is over them, and he shall spread forth his hands, and kneel upon his knees and pray on their behalf saying: 'Lord of all, King on the lofty throne, who rules the world, and did will that this people should be Your elect people, then (indeed) You didst will that You should be called their God, according to the covenant which You didst make with their fathers. 3 And yet they have gone in captivity in another land with their wives and their children, and around the gates of strange peoples and where there is great vanity. Regard and have compassion on them, O Lord of heaven.' Then God will remember them on account of the covenant which He made with their fathers. and He will manifest His compassion in those times also. And He will put it into the mind of a king to have compassion on them, and he shall send them off to their land and country. Then some portions of the tribes shall go up and they shall come to their appointed place, and they shall anew surround the place with walls. And the two tribes shall continue in their prescribed faith, sad and lamenting because they will not be able to offer sacrifices to the Lord of their fathers. And the ten tribes shall increase and multiply among the Gentiles during the time of their captivity.

5

And when the times of chastisement draw nigh and vengeance arises through the kings who share in their guilt and punish them, they themselves also shall be divided as to the truth. Wherefore it hath been said: 'They shall turn aside from righteousness and approach iniquity, and they shall defile with pollutions the house of their worship,' and [because] 'they shall prostitute themselves with strange gods.' For they shall not follow the truth of God, but some shall pollute the altar with the (very) gifts which they offer to the Lord, who are not priests but slaves, sons of slaves. And many in those times shall have respect unto desirable persons and receive gifts, and pervert judgment [on receiving presents]. And on this account the colony and the borders of their habitation shall be filled with lawless deeds and iniquities: those who wickedly depart from the Lord shall be judges: they shall be ready to judge for money as each may wish.

6

Then there shall be raised up unto them kings bearing rule, and they shall call themselves priests of the Most High God: they shall assuredly work iniquity in the holy of holies. And an insolent king shall succeed them, who will not be of the race of the priests, a man bold and shameless, and he shall judge them as they shall deserve. And he shall cut off their chief men with the sword, and shall destroy them in secret places, so that no one may know where their bodies are. He shall slay the old and the young, and he shall not spare. Then the fear of him shall be bitter unto them in their land. And he shall execute judgments on them as the Egyptians executed upon them, during thirty and four years, and he shall punish them. And he shall beget children, (who) succeeding him shall rule for shorter periods. Into their parts cohorts and a powerful king of the west shall come, who shall conquer them: and he shall take them captive, and burn a part of their temple with fire, (and) shall crucify some around their colony.

7

And when this is done the times shall be ended, in a moment the (second) course shall be (ended), the four hours shall come. They shall be forced.... And, in the time of these, destructive and impious men shall rule, saying that they are just. And these shall stir up the poison of their minds, being treacherous men, self-pleasers, dissemblers in all their own affairs and lovers of banquets at every hour of the day. gluttons, gourmands.... Devourers of the goods of the (poor) saying that they do so on the ground of their justice, but in reality to destroy them, complainers, deceitful, concealing themselves lest they should be recognized, impious, filled with lawlessness and iniquity from sunrise to sunset: saying: 'We shall have feastings and luxury, eating and drinking, and we shall esteem ourselves as princes.' And though their hands and their minds touch unclean things, yet their mouth shall speak great things, and they shall say furthermore: 'Do not touch me lest you should pollute me in the place (where I stand') . . .

8

And there shall come upon them a second visitation and wrath, such as has not befallen them from the beginning until that time, in which He will stir up against them the king of the kings of the earth and one that rules with great power, who shall crucify those who confess to their circumcision: and those who conceal (it) he shall torture and deliver them up to be bound and led into prison. And their wives shall be given to the gods among the Gentiles, and their young sons shall be operated on by the physicians in order to bring forward their foreskin. And others amongst them shall be punished by tortures and fire and sword, and they shall be forced to bear in public their idols, polluted as they are like those who keep. them. And they shall likewise be forced by those who torture them to enter their inmost sanctuary, and they shall be forced by goads to blaspheme with insolence the word, finally after these things the laws and what they had above their altar.

9

Then in that day there shall be a man of the tribe of Levi, whose name shall be Taxo, who having seven sons shall speak to them exhorting (them): 'Observe, my sons, behold a second ruthless (and) unclean visitation has come upon the people, and a punishment merciless and far exceeding the first. For what nation or what region or what people of those who are impious towards the Lord, who have done many abominations, have suffered as great calamities as have befallen us? Now, therefore, my sons, hear me: for observe and know that neither did the fathers nor their forefathers tempt God, so as to transgress His commands. And you know that this is our strength, and thus we will do. Let us fast for the space of three days and on the fourth let us go into a cave which is in the field, and let us die rather than transgress the commands of the Lord of Lords, the God of our fathers. For if we do this and die, our blood shall be avenged before the Lord.

10

And then His kingdom shall appear throughout all His creation, And then Satan shall be no more, And sorrow shall depart with him. Then the hands of the angel shall be filled; Who has been appointed chief, And he shall forthwith avenge them of their enemies. For the Heavenly One will arise from His royal throne, And He will go forth from His holy habitation; With indignation and wrath on account of His sons. And the earth shall tremble: to its confines shall it be shaken; And the high mountains shall be made low; And the hills shall be shaken and fall. And the horns of the sun shall be broken and he shall be turned into darkness; And the moon shall not give her light, and be turned wholly into blood. And the circle of the stars shall be disturbed. And the sea shall retire into the abyss, And the fountains of waters shall fail, And the rivers shall dry up. For the Most High will arise, the Eternal God alone, And He will appear to punish the Gentiles, And He will destroy all their idols. Then you, O Israel, shall be happy, And you shall mount upon the necks and wings of the eagle, And they shall be ended. And God will exalt you, And He will cause you to approach to the heaven of the stars, In the place of their habitation. And you will look from on high and see your enemies in Ge(henna) And you shall recognize them and rejoice, And you shall give thanks and confess thy Creator. And do you; Joshua (the son of) Nun, keep these words and this book; For from my death [assumption] until His advent there shall be 250 times [= year-weeks = 1750 years]. And this is the course of the times which they shall pursue till they are consummated. And I shall go to sleep with my fathers. Wherefore, Joshua you (son of) Nun, (be strong and) be of good courage; (for) God has chosen (you) to be minister in the same covenant.

11

And when Joshua had heard the words of Moses that were so written in his writing all that he had before said, he rent his clothes and cast himself at Moses' feet. And Moses comforted him and wept with him. And Joshua answered him and said: 'Why do you comfort me, (my) lord Moses ? And how shall I be comforted in regard to the bitter word which you hast spoken which has gone forth from thy mouth, which is full of tears and lamentation, in that you depart from this people? (But now) what place shall receive you? Or what shall be the sign that marks (your) sepulcher? Or who shall dare to move your body from there as that of a mere man from place to place? For all men when they die have according to their age their sepulchers on earth; but your sepulcher is from the rising to the setting sun, and from the south to the confines of the north: all the world is your sepulcher. My lord, you are departing, and who shall feed this people? Or who is there that shall have compassion on them and who shall be their guide by the way? Or who shall pray for them, not omitting a single day, in order that I may lead them into the land of their forefathers? How therefore am I to foster this people as a father (his) only son, or as a mistress her daughter, a virgin who is being prepared to be given to the husband whom she will revere, while she guards her person from the sun and (takes care) that her feet are not unshod for running upon the ground. (And how) shall I supply them with food and drink according to the pleasure of their will? For of them, there shall be 600,000 (men), for these have multiplied to this degree through your prayers, (my) lord Moses. And what wisdom or understanding have I that I should judge or answer by word in the house (of the Lord)? And the kings of the Amorites also when they hear that we are attacking them, believing that there is no longer among them the holy spirit who was worthy of the Lord, manifold and incomprehensible, the lord of the word, who was faithful in all things, God's chief prophet throughout the earth, the most perfect teacher in the world, [that he is no longer among them], shall say "Let us go against them. If the enemy have but once wrought impiously against their Lord, they have no advocate to offer prayers on their behalf to the Lord, like Moses the great messenger, who every hour day and night had his knees fixed to the earth, praying and looking for help to Him that rules all the world with compassion and righteousness, reminding Him of the covenant of the fathers and propitiating the Lord with the oath." For they shall say: "He is not with them: let us go therefore and destroy them from off the face of the earth." What shall then become of this people, my lord Moses?'

12

And when Joshua had finished (these) words, he cast himself again at the feet of Moses. And Moses took his hand and raised him into the seat before him, and answered and said unto him: Joshua, do not despise yourself; but set your mind at ease, and hear my words. All the nations which are in the earth God has created and us, He has foreseen them and us from the beginning of the creation of the earth unto the end of the age, and nothing has been neglected by Him even to the least thing, but all things He hath foreseen and caused all to come forth. (Yes) all things which are to be in this earth the Lord has foreseen and, look, they are brought forward (into the light. . . . The Lord) has on their behalf appointed me to (pray) for their sins and (make intercession) for them. For not for any virtue or strength of mine, but of His good pleasure have His compassion and longsuffering fallen to my lot. For I say unto you, Joshua: it is not on account of the godliness of this people that you shall root out the nations. The lights of the heaven, the foundations of the earth have been made and approved by God and are under the signet ring of His right hand. Those, therefore, who do and fulfill the commandments of God shall increase and be prospered: but those who sin and set at naught the commandments shall be without the blessings before mentioned, and they shall be punished with many torments by the nations. But wholly to root out and destroy them is not permitted. For God will go forth who has foreseen all things for ever, and His covenant has been established and by the oath which . . .

NEW TESTAMENT APOCRYPHA

APOSTOLIC FATHERS

The Didache, or Teaching of the Twelve Apostles

1

¹ There are two paths, one of life and one of death, and the difference is great between the two paths. ² Now the path of life is this – first, thou shalt love the God who made thee, thy neighbour as thyself, and all things that thou wouldest not should be done unto thee, do not thou unto another. ³ And the doctrine of these maxims is as follows. Bless them that curse you, and pray for your enemies. Fast on behalf of those that persecute you; for what thank is there if ye love them that love you? Do not even the Gentiles do the same? But do ye love them that hate you, and ye will not have an enemy. ⁴ Abstain from fleshly and worldly lusts. If any one give thee a blow on thy right cheek, turn unto him the other also, and thou shalt be perfect; if any one compel thee to go a mile, go with him two; if a man take away thy cloak, give him thy coat also; if a man take from thee what is thine, ask not for it again, for neither art thou able to do so. ⁵ Give to every one that asketh of thee, and ask not again; for the Father wishes that from his own gifts there should be given to all. Blessed is he who giveth according to the commandment, for he is free from guilt; but woe unto him that receiveth. For if a man receive being in need, he shall be free from guilt; but he who receiveth when not in need, shall pay a penalty as to why he received and for what purpose; and when he is in tribulation he shall be examined concerning the things that he has done, and shall not depart thence until he has paid the last farthing. ⁶ For of a truth it has been said on these matters, let thy almsgiving abide in thy hands until thou knowest to whom thou hast given.

2

¹ But the second commandment of the teaching is this. ² Thou shalt not kill; thou shalt not commit adultery; thou shalt not corrupt youth; thou shalt not commit fornication; thou shalt not steal; thou shalt not use soothsaying; thou shalt not practise sorcery; thou shalt not kill a child by abortion, neither shalt thou slay it when born; thou shalt not covet the goods of thy neighbour; ³ thou shalt not commit perjury; thou shalt not bear false witness; thou shalt not speak evil; thou shalt not bear malice; ⁴ thou shalt not be double-minded or double-tongued, for to be double tongued is the snare of death. ⁵ Thy speech shall not be false or empty, but concerned with action. ⁶ Thou shalt not be covetous, or rapacious, or hypocritical, or malicious, or proud; thou shalt not take up an evil design against thy neighbour; ⁷ thou shalt not hate any man, but some thou shalt confute, concerning some thou shalt pray, and some thou shalt love beyond thine own soul.

3

¹ My child, fly from everything that is evil, and from everything that is like to it. ² Be not wrathful, for wrath leadeth unto slaughter; be not jealous, or contentious, or quarrelsome, for from all these things slaughter ensues. ³ My child, be not lustful, for lust leadeth unto fornication; be not a filthy talker; be not a lifter up of the eye, for from all these things come adulteries. ⁴ My child, be not an observer of omens, since it leadeth to idolatry, nor a user of spells, nor an astrologer, nor a travelling purifier, nor wish to see these things, for from all these things idolatry ariseth. ⁵ My child, be not a liar, for lying leadeth unto theft; be not covetous or conceited, for from all these things thefts arise. ⁶ My child, be not a murmurer, since it leadeth unto blasphemy; be not self-willed or evil-minded, for from all these things blasphemies are produced; ⁷ but be thou meek, for the meek shall inherit the earth; ⁸ be thou longsuffering, and compassionate, and harmless, and peaceable, and good, and fearing alway the words that thou hast heard. ⁹ Thou shalt not exalt thyself, neither shalt thou put boldness into thy soul. Thy soul shall not be joined unto the lofty, but thou shalt walk with the just and humble. ¹⁰ Accept the things that happen to thee as good, knowing that without God nothing happens.

4

¹ My child, thou shalt remember both night and day him that speaketh unto thee the Word of God; thou shalt honour him as thou dost the Lord, for where the teaching of the Lord is given, there is the Lord; ² thou shalt seek out day by day the favour of the saints, that thou mayest rest in their words; ³ thou shalt not desire schism, but shalt set at peace them that contend; thou shalt judge righteously; thou shalt not accept the person of any one to convict him of transgression; ⁴ thou shalt not doubt whether a thing shall be or not. ⁵ Be not a stretcher out of thy hand to receive, and a drawer of it back in giving. ⁶ If thou hast, give by means of thy hands a redemption for

thy sins. ⁷ Thou shalt not doubt to give, neither shalt thou murmur when giving; for thou shouldest know who is the fair recompenser of the reward. ⁸ Thou shalt not turn away from him that is in need, but shalt share with thy brother in all things, and shalt not say that things are thine own; for if ye are partners in what is immortal, how much more in what is mortal? ⁹ Thou shalt not remove thine heart from thy son or from thy daughter, but from their youth shalt teach them the fear of God. ¹⁰ Thou shalt not command with bitterness thy servant or thy handmaid, who hope in the same God as thyself, lest they fear not in consequence the God who is over both; for he cometh not to call with respect of persons, but those whom the Spirit hath prepared. ¹¹ And do ye servants submit yourselves to your masters with reverence and fear, as being the type of God. ¹² Thou shalt hate all hypocrisy and everything that is not pleasing to God; ¹³ thou shalt not abandon the commandments of the Lord, but shalt guard that which thou hast received, neither adding thereto nor taking therefrom; ¹⁴ thou shalt confess thy transgressions in the Church, and shalt not come unto prayer with an evil conscience. This is the path of life.

5

¹ But the path of death is this. First of all, it is evil, and full of cursing; there are found murders, adulteries, lusts, fornication, thefts, idolatries, soothsaying, sorceries, robberies, false witnessings, hypocrisies, double-mindedness, craft, pride, malice, self-will, covetousness, filthy talking, jealousy, audacity, pride, arrogance; ² there are they who persecute the good – lovers of a lie, not knowing the reward of righteousness, not cleaving to the good nor to righteous judgment, watching not for the good but for the bad, from whom meekness and patience are afar off, loving things that are vain, following after recompense, having no compassion on the needy, nor labouring for him that is in trouble, not knowing him that made them, murderers of children, corrupters of the image of God, who turn away from him that is in need, who oppress him that is in trouble, unjust judges of the poor, erring in all things. From all these, children, may ye be delivered.

6

¹ See that no one make thee to err from this path of doctrine, since he who doeth so teacheth thee apart from God. ² If thou art able to bear the whole yoke of the Lord, thou wilt be perfect; but if thou art not able, what thou art able, that do. ³ But concerning meat, bear that which thou art able to do. But keep with care from things sacrificed to idols, for it is the worship of the infernal deities.

7

¹ But concerning baptism, thus baptize ye: having first recited all these precepts, baptize in the name of the Father, and of the Son, and of the Holy Spirit, in running water; ² but if thou hast not running water, baptize in some other water, and if thou canst not baptize in cold, in warm water; ³ but if thou hast neither, pour water three times on the head, in the name of the Father, and of the Son, and of the Holy Spirit. ⁴ But before the baptism, let him who baptizeth and him who is baptized fast previously, and any others who may be able. And thou shalt command him who is baptized to fast one or two days before.

8

¹ But as for your fasts, let them not be with the hypocrites, for they fast on the second and fifth days of the week, but do ye fast on the fourth and sixth days. ² Neither pray ye as the hypocrites, but as the Lord hath commanded in his gospel so pray ye: Our Father in heaven, hallowed be thy name. Thy kingdom come. Thy will be done as in heaven so on earth. Give us this day our daily bread. And forgive us our debt, as we also forgive our debtors. And lead us not into temptation, but deliver us from the evil: for thine is the power, and the glory, for ever. ³ Thrice a day pray ye in this fashion.

9

¹ But concerning the Eucharist, after this fashion give ye thanks. ² First, concerning the cup. We thank thee, our Father, for the holy vine, David thy Son, which thou hast made known unto us through Jesus Christ thy Son; to thee be the glory for ever. ³ And concerning the broken bread. We thank thee, our Father, for the life and knowledge which thou hast made known unto us through Jesus thy Son; to thee be the glory for ever. ⁴ As this broken bread was once scattered on the mountains, and after it had been brought together became one, so may thy Church be gathered together from the ends of the earth unto thy kingdom; for thine is the glory, and the power, through Jesus Christ, for ever. ⁵ And let none eat or drink of your Eucharist but such as have been baptized into the name of the Lord, for of a truth the Lord hath said concerning this, Give not that which is holy unto dogs.

10

¹ But after it has been completed, so pray ye. ² We thank thee, holy Father, for thy holy name, which thou hast caused to dwell in our hearts, and for the knowledge and faith and immortality which thou hast made known unto us through Jesus thy Son; to thee be the glory for ever. ³ Thou, Almighty Master, didst create all things for the sake of thy name, and hast given both meat and drink, for men to enjoy, that we might give thanks unto thee, but to us thou hast given spiritual meat and drink, and life everlasting, through thy Son. ⁴ Above all, we thank thee that thou art able to save; to thee be the glory for ever. ⁵ Remember, Lord, thy Church, to redeem it from every evil, and to perfect it in thy love, and gather it together from the four winds, even that which has been sanctified for thy kingdom which thou hast prepared for it; for thine is the kingdom and the glory for ever. ⁶ Let grace come, and let this world pass away. Hosanna to the Son of David. If any one is holy let him come (to the Eucharist); if any one is not, let him repent. Maranatha. Amen. ⁷ But charge the prophets to give thanks, so far as they are willing to do so.

11

¹ Whosoever, therefore, shall come and teach you all these things aforesaid, him do ye receive; ² but if the teacher himself turn and teach another doctrine with a view to subvert you, hearken not to him; but if he come to add to your righteousness, and the knowledge of the Lord, receive him as the Lord. ³ But concerning the apostles and prophets, thus do ye according to the doctrine of the Gospel. ⁴ Let every apostle who cometh unto you be received as the Lord. ⁵ He will remain one day, and if it be necessary, a second; but if he remain three days, he is a false prophet. ⁶ And let the apostle when departing take nothing but bread until he arrive at his resting-place; but if he ask for money, he is a false prophet. ⁷ And ye shall not tempt or dispute with any prophet who speaketh in the spirit; for every sin shall be forgiven, but this sin shall not be forgiven. ⁸ But not every one who speaketh in the spirit is a prophet, but he is so who hath the disposition of the Lord; by their dispositions they therefore shall be known, the false prophet and the prophet. ⁹ And every prophet who ordereth in the spirit that a table shall be laid, shall not eat of it himself, but if he do otherwise, he is a false prophet; ¹⁰ and every prophet who teacheth the truth, if he do not what he teacheth is a false prophet; ¹¹ and every prophet who is approved and true, and ministering in the visible mystery of the Church, but who teacheth not others to do the things that he doth himself, shall not be judged of you, for with God lieth his judgment, for in this manner also did the ancient prophets. ¹² But whoever shall say in the spirit, Give me money, or things of that kind, listen not to him; but if he tell you concerning others that are in need that ye should give unto them, let no one judge him.

12

¹ Let every one that cometh in the name of the Lord be received, but afterwards ye shall examine him and know his character, for ye have knowledge both of good and evil. ² If the person who cometh be a wayfarer, assist him so far as ye are able; but he will not remain with you more than two or three days, unless there be a necessity. ³ But if he wish to settle with you, being a craftsman, let him work, and so eat; ⁴ but if he know not any craft, provide ye according to you own discretion, that a Christian may not live idle among you; ⁵ but if he be not willing to do so, he is a trafficker in Christ. From such keep aloof.

13

¹ But every true prophet who is willing to dwell among you is worthy of his meat, ² likewise a true teacher is himself worthy of his meat, even as is a labourer. ³ Thou shalt, therefore, take the firstfruits of every produce of the wine-press and threshing-floor, of oxen and sheep, and shalt give it to the prophets, for they are your chief priests; ⁴ but if ye have not a prophet, give it unto the poor. ⁵ If thou makest a feast, take and give the firstfruits according to the commandment; ⁶ in like manner when thou openest a jar of wine or of oil, take the firstfruits and give it to the prophets; ⁷ take also the firstfruits of money, of clothes, and of every possession, as it shall seem good unto thee, and give it according to the commandment.

14

¹ But on the Lord's day, after that ye have assembled together, break bread and give thanks, having in addition confessed your sins, that your sacrifice may be pure. ² But let not any one who hath a quarrel with his companion join with you, until they be reconciled, that your sacrifice may not be polluted, ³ for it is that which is spoken of by the Lord. In every place and time offer unto me a pure sacrifice, for I am a great King, saith the Lord, and my name is wonderful among the Gentiles.

15

¹ Elect, therefore, for yourselves bishops and deacons worthy of the Lord, men who are meek and not covetous, and true and approved, for they perform for you the service of prophets and teachers. ² Do not, therefore, despise them, for they are those who are honoured among you, together with the prophets and teachers. ³ Rebuke one another, not in wrath but peaceably, as ye have commandment in the Gospel; and, but let no one

speak to any one who walketh disorderly with regard to his neighbour, neither let him be heard by you until he repent. ⁴ But your prayers and your almsgivings and all your deeds so do, as ye have commandment in the Gospel of our Lord.

16

¹ Watch concerning your life; let not your lamps be quenched or your loins be loosed, but be ye ready, for ye know not the hour at which our Lord cometh. ² But be ye gathered together frequently, seeking what is suitable for your souls; for the whole time of your faith shall profit you not, unless ye be found perfect in the last time. ³ For in the last days false prophets and seducers shall be multiplied, and the sheep shall be turned into wolves, and love shall be turned into hate; ⁴ and because iniquity aboundeth they shall hate each other, and persecute each other, and deliver each other up; and then shall the Deceiver of the world appear as the Son of God, and shall do signs and wonders, and the earth shall be delivered into his hands; and he shall do unlawful things, such as have never happened since the beginning of the world. ⁵ Then shall the creation of man come to the fiery trial of proof, and many shall be offended and shall perish; but they who remain in their faith shall be saved by the rock of offence itself. ⁶ And then shall appear the signs of the truth; first the sign of the appearance in heaven, then the sign of the sound of the trumpet, and thirdly the resurrection of the dead ⁷ – not of all, but as it has been said, The Lord shall come and all his saints with him; ⁸ then shall the world behold the Lord coming on the clouds of heaven.

The General Epistle of Barnabas
1

Preface to the Epistle.

¹ ALL happiness to you my sons and daughters, in the name of our Lord Jesus Christ, who loved us, in peace. ² Having perceived abundance of knowledge of the great and excellent laws of God to be in you, I exceedingly rejoice in your blessed and admirable souls, because ye have so worthily received the grace which was grafted in you. ³ For which cause I am full of joy, hoping the rather to he saved; inasmuch as I truly see a spirit infused into you, from the pure fountain of God: ⁴ Having this persuasion, and being fully convinced thereof, because that since I have begun to speak unto you, I have had a more than ordinary good success in the way of the law of the Lord which is in Christ. ⁵ For which cause brethren, I also think verily that I love you above my own soul: because that therein dwelleth the greatness of faith and charity, as also the hope of that life which is to come. ⁶ Wherefore considering this, that if I shall take care to communicate to you a part of what I have received, it shall turn to my reward, that I have served such good souls; I gave diligence to write in a few words unto you; that together with your faith, knowledge also may be perfect. ⁷ There are therefore three things ordained by the Lord; the hope of life; the beginning and the completion of it. ⁸ For the Lord hath both declared unto us, by the prophets those things that are past; and opened to us the beginnings of those that are to come. ⁹ Wherefore, it will behoove us, as he has spoken, to come more holily, and nearer to his altar. ¹⁰ I therefore, not as a teacher, but as one of you, will endeavour to lay before you a few things by which you may, on many accounts, become the more joyful.

2

That God has abolished the legal sacrifices to introduce the spiritual righteousness of the Gospel.

¹ SEEING then the days are exceeding evil, and the adversary has got the power of this present world we ought to give the more diligence to inquire into the righteous judgments of the Lord. ² Now the assistants of our faith are fear and patience; our fellow-combatants, long-suffering and continence. ³ Whilst these remain pure in what relates unto the Lord, wisdom, and understanding, and science, and knowledge, rejoice together with them. ⁴ For God has manifested to us by all the prophets, that he has no occasion for our sacrifices, or burnt-offerings, or oblations: saying thus; To what purpose is the multitude of your sacrifices unto me, saith the Lord. ⁵ I am full of the burnt-offerings of rams, and the fat of fed beasts; and I delight not in the blood of bullocks, or of he-goats ⁶ When ye come to appear before me; who hath required this at your hands? Ye shall no more tread my courts. ⁷ Bring no more vain oblations, incense is an abomination unto me; your new moons and sabbaths; the calling of assemblies I cannot away with, it is iniquity, even the solemn meeting; your new moons and your appointed feasts my soul hateth. ⁸ These things therefore hath God abolished, that the new law of our Lord Jesus Christ, which is without the yoke of any such necessity, might have the spiritual offering of men themselves. ⁹ For so the Lord saith again to those heretofore; Did I at all command your fathers when they came out of the land of Egypt concerning burnt-offerings of sacrifices? ¹⁰ But this I commanded them, saying, Let none of you imagine evil in your hearts against his neighbour, and love no false oath. ¹¹ Forasmuch then as we are not without understanding, we ought to apprehend the design of our merciful Father. For he speaks to us, being willing that we who have been in the same error about the sacrifices, should seek and find how to approach unto him. ¹² And therefore he thus bespeaks us, The sacrifice of God (is a broken spirit,) a broken and contrite heart God will not despise. ¹³ Wherefore brethren, we ought the more diligently to inquire after these things that belong to our salvation, that the adversary may not have any entrance into us, and deprive us of our spiritual life. ¹⁴ Wherefore he again speaketh to them, concerning these things; Ye shall not fast as ye do this day, to make your voice to be heard on high. ¹⁵ Is it such a fast that I have chosen? a day for a man to afflict his soul? Is it to bow down his head like a bulrush, and to spread sackcloth and ashes under him? Wilt thou call this a fast, and an acceptable day to the Lord? ¹⁶ But to us he saith on this wise. Is not this the fast that I have chosen, to loose the bands of wickedness, to undo the heavy burdens, and to let the oppressed go free; and that ye break every yoke? ¹⁷ Is it not to deal thy bread to the hungry, and that thou bring the poor that are cast out to thy house? When thou seest the naked that thou cover him, and that thou hide not thyself from thine own flesh. ¹⁸ Then shall thy light break forth as the morning, and thy health shall spring forth speedily; and thy righteousness shall go before thee, the glory of the Lord shall be thy reward. ¹⁹ Then shalt thou call and the Lord shall answer; thou shalt cry and he shall say, Here I am. If thou put away from the midst of thee the yoke, the putting forth of the finger, and speaking vanity; and if thou draw out thy soul to the hungry; and satisfy the afflicted

soul. ²⁰ In this therefore brethren, God has manifested his foreknowledge and love for us; because the people which he has purchased to his beloved Son were to believe in sincerity; and therefore he has shewn these things to all of us, that we should not run as proselytes to the Jewish law.

3

The prophecies of Daniel, concerning the ten kings, and the coming of Christ.

¹ WHEREFORE it is necessary that searching diligently into those things which are near to come to pass, we should write to you what may serve to keep you whole. ² To which end let us flee from every evil work and hate the errors of the present time, that we may be happy in that which is to come: ³ Let us not give ourselves the liberty of disputing with the wicked and sinners; lest we should chance in time to become like unto them. ⁴ For the consummation of sin is come, as it is written, as the prophet Daniel says. And for this end the Lord hath shortened the times and the days, that his beloved might hasten his coming to his inheritance. ⁵ For so the prophet speaks; There shall ten kings reign in the heart, and there shall rise last of all another little one, and he shall humble three kings. ⁶ And again Daniel speaks in like manner concerning the kingdoms; and I saw the fourth beast dreadful and terrible, and strong exceedingly; and it had ten horns. I considered the horns, and behold there came up among them another little horn, before which were three of the first horns plucked up by the roots. ⁷ We ought therefore to understand this also: And I beseech you as one of your own brethren, loving you all beyond my own life, that you look well to yourselves, and be not like to those who add sin to sin, and say: That their covenant is ours also. Nay, but it is ours only: for they have for ever lost that which Moses received. ⁸ For thus saith the Scripture: And Moses continued fasting forty days and forty nights in the Mount; and he received the covenant from the Lord, even the two tables of stone, written by the hand of God. ⁹ But having turned themselves to idols they lost it; as the Lord also said to Moses; Moses, go down quickly, for thy people which thou hast brought forth out of Egypt, have corrupted themselves, and turned aside from the way which I commanded them. And Moses cast the two tables out of his hands: and their covenant was broken; that the love of Jesus might be sealed in your hearts, unto the hope of his faith. ¹⁰ Wherefore let us give heed unto the last times. For all the time past of our life, and our faith will profit us nothing; unless we continue to hate what is evil, and to withstand the future temptations. So the Son of God tells us; Let us resist all iniquity and hate it. ¹¹ Wherefore consider the works of the evil way. Do not withdraw yourselves from others, as if you were already justified; but coming altogether into one place, inquire what is agreeable to and profitable for the beloved of God. For the Scripture saith; Wo unto them that are wise in their own eyes, and prudent in their sight. ¹² Let us become spiritual, a perfect temple to God. As much as in us lies let us meditate upon the fear of God; and strive to the utmost of our power to keep his commandments; that we may rejoice in his righteous judgments. ¹³ For God will judge the world without respect of persons: and every one shall receive according to his works. ¹⁴ If a man shall be good, his righteousness shall go before him; if wicked, the reward of his wickedness shall follow him. ¹⁵ Take heed therefore lest sitting still, now that we are called, we fall asleep in our sins; and the wicked one getting the dominion over us, stir us up, and shut us out of the kingdom of the Lord. ¹⁶ Consider this also: although you have seen so great signs and wonders done among the people of the Jews, yet this notwithstanding the Lord hath forsaken them. ¹⁷ Beware therefore, lest it happen to us; as it is written. There may be many called, but few chosen.

4

That Christ was to suffer: proved from the prophecies concerning him.

¹ FOR this cause did our Lord vouchsafe to give up his body to destruction, that through the forgiveness of our sins we might be sanctified; that is, by the sprinkling of his blood. ² Now for what concerns the things that are written about him, some belong to the people of the Jews, and some to us. ³ For thus saith the Scripture: He was wounded for our transgressions, he was bruised for our iniquities, and by his blood we are healed. He was led as a lamb to the slaughter, and as a sheep before his shearers is dumb, so he opened not his mouth. ⁴ Wherefore we ought the more to give thanks unto God, for that he hath both declared unto us what is passed, and not suffered us to be without understanding of those things that are to come. ⁵ But to them he saith; The nests are not unjustly spread for the birds. ⁶ This he spake, because a man will justly perish, if having the knowledge of the way of truth, he shall nevertheless not refrain himself from the way of darkness. ⁷ And for this cause the Lord was content to suffer for our souls, although he be the Lord of the whole earth; to whom God said before the beginning of the world, Let us make man after our own image and likeness. ⁸ Now how he suffered for us, seeing it was by men that he underwent it, I will shew you. ⁹ The prophets having received from him the gift of prophecy, spake before concerning him: ¹⁰ But he, that he might abolish death, and make known the resurrection from the dead, was content, as it was necessary, to appear in the flesh, that he might make good the promise before given to our fathers, and preparing himself a new people, might demonstrate to them whilst he was upon earth, that after the resurrection he would judge the world. ¹¹ And finally teaching the people of Israel, and doing many wonders and signs among them, he preached to them, and shewed the exceeding great love which he bare towards them. ¹² And when he chose his apostles, which were afterwards to publish his Gospel, he took men who had been very great sinners; that thereby he might plainly shew, That he came not to call the righteous but sinners to repentance. ¹³ Then he clearly manifested himself to be the Son of God. For had he not come in the flesh, how should men have been able to look upon him, that they might be saved? ¹⁴ Seeing if they beheld only the sun, which was the work of his hands, and shall hereafter cease to be, they are not able to endure steadfastly to look against the rays of it. ¹⁵ Wherefore the Son of God came in the flesh for this cause, that he might fill up the measure of their iniquity, who have persecuted his prophets unto death. And for the same reason also he suffered. ¹⁶ For God hath said of the stripes of his flesh, that they were from them. And, I will smite the shepherd, and the sheep of the flock shall be scattered. ¹⁷ Thus he would suffer, because it behooved him to suffer upon the cross. ¹⁸ For thus one saith, prophesying concerning him; Spare my soul from the sword. And again, Pierce my flesh from thy fear. ¹⁹ And again, the congregation of wicked doers rose up against me, (They have pierced my hands and my feet). ²⁰ And again he saith, I gave my back to the smiters, and my face I set as an hard rock.

5

The subject continued.

¹ AND when he had fulfilled the commandment of God, What says he? Who will contend with me? Let him stand against me: or who is he that will impede me? Let him draw near to the servant of the Lord. Wo be to you! Because ye shall all wax old as a garment, the moth shall eat you up. ² And again the prophet adds, He is put for a stone for stumbling. Behold I lay in Zion for a foundation, a precious stone, a choice corner stone; an honourable stone. And what follows? And he that hopeth in him shall live for ever. ³ What then? Is our hope built upon a stone? God forbid. But because the Lord hath hardened his flesh against sufferings, he saith, I have put me as a firm rock. ⁴ And again the prophet adds; The stone which the builders refused has become the head of the corner. And again he saith; This is the great and wonderful day which the Lord hath made. I write these things the more plainly to you that ye may understand: For indeed I could be content even to die for your sakes. ⁵ But what saith the prophet again? The counsel of the wicked encompassed me about. They came about me, as bees about the honey-comb: and, Upon my vesture they cast lots. ⁶ Forasmuch then as our Saviour was to appear in the flesh and suffer, his passion was hereby foretold. ⁷ For thus saith the prophet against Israel: Wo be to their soul, because they have taken wicked counsel against themselves, saying, let us lay snares for the righteous, because he is unprofitable to us. ⁸ Moses also in like manner speaketh to them; Behold thus saith the Lord God; Enter ye into the good land of which the Lord hath sworn to Abraham, and Isaac, and Jacob, that he would give it you, and possess it; a land flowing with milk and honey. ⁹ Now what the spiritual meaning of this is, learn; It is as if it had been said, Put your trust in Jesus, who shall be manifested to you in the flesh. For man is the earth which suffers: forasmuch as out of the substance of the earth Adam was formed. ¹⁰ What therefore does he mean when he says, Into a good land flowing with milk and honey? Blessed be our Lord, who has given us wisdom, and a heart to understand his secrets. For so says the prophet, Who shall understand the hard sayings of the Lord? But he that is wise, and intelligent, and that loves his Lord. ¹¹ Seeing therefore he has renewed us by the remission of our sins, he has put us into another frame, that we should have souls like those of children, forming us again himself by the spirit. ¹² For thus the Scripture saith concerning us, where it introduceth the Father speaking to the Son; Let us make man after our likeness and similitude; and let them have dominion over the beasts of the earth, and over the fowls of the air, and the fish of the sea. ¹³ And when the Lord saw the man which he had formed, that behold he was very good; he said, Increase and multiply, and replenish the earth. And this he spake to his son. ¹⁴ I will now shew you, how he made us a new creature, in the latter days. ¹⁵ The Lord saith; Behold I will make the last as the first. Wherefore the prophet thus spake, Enter into the land flowing with milk and honey, and have dominion over it. ¹⁶ Wherefore ye see how we are again formed anew; as also he speaks by another prophet; Behold saith the Lord, I will take from them, that is, from those whom the spirit of the Lord foresaw, their hearts of stone, and I will put into them hearts of flesh. ¹⁷ Because he was about to be made

manifest in the flesh and to dwell in us. ¹⁸ For, my brethren, the habitation of our heart is a holy temple unto the Lord. For the Lord saith again. In what place shall I appear before the Lord my God, and be glorified? ¹⁹ He answers I will confess unto thee in the congregation in the midst of my brethren; and will sing unto thee in the church of the saints. ²⁰ Wherefore we are they whom he has brought into that good land. ²¹ But what signifies the milk and honey? Because as the child is nourished first with milk, and then with honey; so we being kept alive by the belief of his promises, and his word, shall live and have dominion over the land. ²² For he foretold above, saying, increase and multiply, and have dominion over the fishes, etc. ²³ But who is there that is now able to have this dominion over the wild beasts, or fishes, or fowls of the air? For you know that to rule is to have power, that a man should be set over what he rules. ²⁴ But forasmuch as this we have not now, he tells us when we shall have it; namely, when we shall become perfect, that we may be made the inheritors of the covenant of the Lord.

6

The scape-goat an evident type of this.

¹ UNDERSTAND then my beloved children, that the good God hath before manifested all things unto us, that we might know to whom we ought always to give thanks and praise. ² If therefore the Son of God whet is the Lord of all, and shall come to judge both the quick and dead, hath suffered, that by his stripes we might live: let us believe that the Son of God could not have suffered but for us. But being crucified, they gave him vinegar and gall to drink. ³ Hear therefore how the priests of the temple did foreshew this also: the Lord by his command which was written, declared that whosoever did not fast the appointed fast he should die the death: because he also was himself one day to offer up his body for our sins; that so the type of what was done in Isaac might be fulfilled, who was offered upon the altar. ⁴ What therefore is it that he says by the prophet? And let them eat of the goat which is offered in the day of the fast for all their sins. Hearken diligently (my brethren,) and all the priests, and they only shall eat the inwards not washed with vinegar. ⁵ Why so? because I know that when I shall hereafter offer my flesh for the sins of a new people, ye will give me vinegar to drink mixed with gall; therefore do ye only eat, the people fasting the while, and lamenting in sackcloth and ashes. ⁶ And that he might foreshew that he was to suffer for them, hear then how he appointed it. ⁷ Take, says he, two goats, fair and alike, and offer them, and let the high priest take one of them for a burnt offering. And what must be done with the other? Let it says he be accursed. ⁸ Consider how exactly this appears to have been a type of Jesus. And let all the congregation spit upon it, and prick it; and put the scarlet wool about its head, and thus let it be carried forth into the wilderness. ⁹ And this being done, he that was appointed to convey the goat, led it into the wilderness, and took away the scarlet wool, and put it upon a thorn bush, whose young sprouts when we find them in the field we are wont to eat: so the fruit of that thorn only is sweet. ¹⁰ And to what end was this ceremony? Consider; one was offered upon the altar, the other was accursed. ¹¹ And why was that which was accursed crowned? Because they shall see Christ in that day having a scarlet garment about his body; and shall say: Is not this he whom we crucified; having despised him, pierced him, mocked him? Certainly, this is he, who then said, that he was the Son of God. ¹² As therefore he shall be then like to what he was on earth, so were the Jews heretofore commanded, to take two goats fair and equal. That when they shall see (our Saviour) hereafter coming (in the clouds of heaven), they may be amazed at the likeness of the goats. ¹³ Wherefore ye here again see a type of Jesus who was to suffer for us. ¹⁴ But what then signifies this. That the wool was to be put into the midst of the thorns? ¹⁵ This also is a figure of Jesus, sent out to the church. For as he who would take away the scarlet wool must undergo many difficulties, because that thorn was very sharp, and with difficulty get it: So they, says Christ, that will see me, and come to my kingdom, must through many afflictions and troubles attain unto me.

7

The red heifer, another type of Christ.

¹ BUT what type do ye suppose it to have been, where it is commanded to the people of Israel, that grown persons in whom sins are come to perfection, should offer an heifer, and after they had killed it should burn the same. ² But then young men should take up the ashes and put them in vessels; and tie a piece of scarlet wool and hyssop upon a stick, and so the young men should sprinkle every one of the people, and they should be clear from their sins. ³ Consider how all these are delivered in a figure to us. ⁴ This heifer is Jesus Christ; the wicked men that were to offer it are those sinners who brought him to death: who afterwards have no more to do with it; the sinners have no more the honour of handling of it: ⁵ But the young men that performed the sprinkling, signified those who preach to us the forgiveness of sins and the purification of the heart, to whom the Lord gave authority to preach his Gospel: being at the beginning twelve, to signify the tribes, because there were twelve tribes of Israel. ⁶ But why were there three young men appointed to sprinkle? To denote Abraham, and Isaac, and Jacob, because they were great before God. ⁷ And why was the wool put upon a stick? Because the kingdom of Jesus was founded upon the cross; and therefore they that put their trust in him, shall live for ever. ⁸ But why was the wool and hyssop put together? To signify that in the kingdom of Christ there shall be evil and filthy days, in which however we shall be saved; and because he that has any disease in the flesh by some filthy humours is cured by hyssop. ⁹ Wherefore these things being thus done, are to us indeed evident, but to the Jews they are obscure; because they hearkened not unto the voice of the Lord.

8

Of the circumcision of the ears; and how in the first institution of circumcision Abraham, mystically foretold Christ by name.

¹ AND therefore the Scripture again speaks concerning our ears, that God has circumcised them, together with our hearts For thus saith the Lord by the holy prophets: By the hearing of the ear they obeyed me. ² And again, whey who are afar off, shall hear and understand what things I have done. And again, Circumcise your hearts, saith the Lord. ³ And again he saith, Hear O Israel! For thus saith the Lord thy God. And again the Spirit of God prophesieth, saying: Who is there that would live for ever, let him hear the voice of my Son. ⁴ And again, Hear, O Heaven and give ear O Earth! Because the Lord has spoken these things for a witness. ⁵ And again he saith Hear the word of the Lord, ye princes of the people. And again Hear O Children! The voice of one crying in the wilderness. ⁶ Wherefore he has circumcised our ears that we should hear his word, and believe. But as for that circumcision, in which the Jews trust, it is abolished. For the circumcision of which God spake, was not of the flesh; ⁷ But they have transgressed his commands, because the evil one hath deceived them. For thus God bespeaks them; Thus saith the Lord your God (Here I find the new law) Sow not among thorns; but circumcise yourselves to the Lord your God. And what doth he mean by this saying? Hearken unto your Lord. ⁸ And again he saith, Circumcise the hardness of your heart, and harden not your neck. And again, Behold, saith the Lord, all the nations are uncircumcised, (they have not lost their fore-skin): but this people is uncircumcised in heart. ⁹ But you will say the Jews were circumcised for a sign. And so are all the Syrians and Arabians, and all the idolatrous priests: but are they therefore of the covenant of Israel? And even the Egyptians themselves are circumcised. ¹⁰ Understand therefore, children, these things more fully, that Abraham, who was the first that brought in circumcision, looking forward in the Spirit to Jesus, circumcised, having received the mystery of three letters. ¹¹ For the Scripture says that Abraham circumcised three hundred and eighteen men of his house. But what therefore was the mystery that was made known unto him? ¹² Mark, first the eighteen, and next the three hundred. For the numeral letters of ten and eight are I H. And these denote Jesus. ¹³ And because the cross was that by which we were to find grace; therefore he adds, three hundred; the note of which is T (the figure of his cross). Wherefore by two letters he signified Jesus, and by the third his cross. ¹⁴ He who has put the engrafted gift of his doctrine within us, knows that I never taught to any one a more certain truth; but I trust that ye are worthy of it.

9

That the commands of Moses concerning clean and unclean beasts, etc., were all designed for a spiritual signification.

¹ BUT why did Moses say Ye shall not eat of the swine, neither the eagle nor the hawk; nor the crow; nor any fish that has not a scale upon him?– answer, that in the spiritual sense, he comprehended three doctrines, that were to be gathered from thence. ² Besides which he says to them in the book of Deuteronomy, And I will give my statutes unto this people. Wherefore it is not the command of God that they should not eat these things; but Moses in the spirit spake unto them. ³ Now the sow he forbade them to eat; meaning thus much; thou shalt not join thyself to such persons as are like unto swine; who whilst they live in pleasure, forget their God; but when any want pinches them, then they know the Lord; as the sow when she is full knows not her master; but when she is hungry she makes a noise; and being again fed, is silent. ⁴ Neither, says he, shalt thou eat the eagle, nor the hawk, nor the kite, nor the crow; that is thou shalt not keep company with such kind of men as know not how by their labour and sweat to get themselves food: but injuriously ravish away the things of others; and watch how, to lay snares for them; when at the same time they appear to live in perfect innocence. ⁵ (So these birds alone seek not food for themselves, but) sitting idle seek how they may eat of the flesh others have provided; being destructive through their wickedness. ⁶ Neither, says he, shalt thou

eat the lamprey, nor the polypus, nor the cuttle-fish; that is, thou shalt not be like such men, by using to converse with them; who are altogether wicked and adjudged to death. For so those fishes are alone accursed, and wallow in the mire, nor swim as other fishes, but tumble in the dirt at the bottom of the deep. ⁷ But he adds, neither shalt thou eat of the hare. To what end?–To signify this to us; Thou shalt not be an adulterer; nor liken thyself to such persons. For the hare every year multiplies the places of its conception; and so many years as it lives, so many it has. ⁸ Neither shalt thou eat of the hyena; that is, again, be not an adulterer, nor a corruptor of others; neither be like to such. And wherefore so?–Because that creature every year changes its kind, and is sometimes male and sometimes female. ⁹ For which cause also he justly hated the weasel; to the end that they should not be like such persons who with their mouths commit wickedness by reason of their uncleanness; nor join themselves with those impure women, who with their mouths commit wickedness. Because that animal conceives with its mouth. ¹⁰ Moses, therefore, speaking as concerning meats, delivered indeed three great precepts to them in the spiritual signification of those commands. But they according to the desires of the flesh, understood him as if he had only meant it of meats. ¹¹ And therefore David took aright the knowledge of his threefold command, saying in like manner. ¹² Blessed is the man that hath not walked in the counsel of the ungodly; as the fishes before mentioned in the bottom of the deep in darkness. ¹³ Nor stood in the way of sinners, as they who seem to fear the Lord, but yet sin, as the sow. ¹⁴ And hath not sat in the seat of the scorners; as those birds who sit and watch that they may devour. ¹⁵ Here you have the law concerning meat perfectly set forth, and according to the true knowledge of it. ¹⁶ But, says Moses, ye shall eat all that divideth the hoof, and cheweth the cud. Signifying thereby such an one as having taken his food, knows him that nourisheth him; and resting upon him, rejoiceth in him. ¹⁷ And in this he spake well, having respect to the commandment. What, therefore, is it that he says?–That we should hold fast to them that fear the Lord; with those who meditate on the command of the word which they have received in their heart; with those that declare the righteous judgments of the Lord, and keep his commandments; ¹⁸ In short, with those who know that to meditate is a work of pleasure, and therefore exercise themselves in the word of the Lord. ¹⁹ But why might they eat those that clave the hoof?–Because the righteous liveth in this present world; but his expectation is fixed upon the other. See, brethren, how admirably Moses commanded these things. ²⁰ But how should we thus know all this, and understand it? We, therefore, understanding aright the commandments, speak as the Lord would have us. Wherefore he has circumcised our ears and our hearts, that we might know these things.

10

Baptism and the Cross of Christ foretold in figures under the law.

¹ LET us now inquire whether the Lord took care to manifest anything beforehand concerning water and the cross. ² Now for the former of these, it is written to the people of Israel how they shall not receive that baptism which brings to forgiveness of sins; but shall institute another to themselves that cannot. ³ For thus saith the prophet: Be astonished, O Heaven! and let the earth tremble at it, because this people have done two great and wicked things; they have left me, the fountain of living water, and have digged for themselves broken cisterns, that can hold no water. ⁴ Is my holy mountain a Zion, a desolate wilderness? For ye shall be as a young bird when its nest is taken away. ⁵ And again the prophet saith, I will go before thee, and will make plain the mountains, and will break the gates of brass, and will snap in sunder the bars of iron; and will give thee dark, and hidden, and invisible treasures, that they may know that I am the Lord God. ⁶ And again: He shall dwell in the high den of the strong rock. And then, what follows in the same prophet? His water is faithful; ye shall see the king with glory, and your soul shall learn the fear of the Lord. ⁷ And again he saith in another prophet: He that does these things; shall be like a tree, planted by the currents of water, which shall give its fruit in its season. Its leaf also shall not wither, and whatsoever he doth it shall prosper. ⁸ As for the wicked it is not so with them; but they are as the dust which the wind scattereth away from the face of the earth. ⁹ Therefore the ungodly shall not stand in the judgment, neither the sinners in the council of the righteous. For the Lord knoweth the way of the righteous and the way of the ungodly shall perish. ¹⁰ Consider how he has joined both the cross and the water together. ¹¹ For thus he saith: Blessed are they who put their trust in the cross, descend into the water; for they shall have their reward in due time; then, saith he, will I give it them. ¹² But as concerning the present time, he saith, their leaves shall not fall; meaning thereby that every word that shall go out of your mouth, shall through faith and charity be to the conversion and hope of many. ¹³ In like manner doth another prophet speak. And the land of Jacob was the praise of all the earth; magnifying thereby the vessel of his spirit. ¹⁴ And what follows?–And there was a river running on the right hand, and beautiful trees grew up by it; and he that shall eat of them shall live for ever. The signification of which is this: that we go down into the water full of sins and pollutions; but come up again, bringing forth fruit; having in our hearts the fear and hope which is in Jesus, by the spirit. And whosoever shall eat of them shall live for ever. ¹⁵ That is, whosoever shall hearken to those who call them, and shall believe, shall live for ever.

11

The subject continued.

¹ IN like manner he determines concerning the cross in another prophet, saying: And when shall these things be fulfilled? ² The Lord answers; When the tree that has fallen shall rise, and when blood shall drop down from the tree. Here you have again mention made, both of the cross, and of him that was to be crucified upon it. ³ And yet farther he saith by Moses; (when Israel was fighting with, and beaten by, a strange people; to the end that God might put them in mind how that for their sins they were delivered unto death) yea, the holy spirit put it into the heart of Moses, to represent both the sign of the cross, and of him that was to suffer; that so they might know that if they did not believe in him, they should be overcome for ever. ⁴ Moses therefore piled up armour upon armour in the middle of a rising ground, and standing up high above all of them, stretched forth his arms, and so Israel again conquered. ⁵ But no sooner did he let down his hands, but they were again slain. And why so?–To the end they might know, that except they trust in him they cannot be saved. ⁶ And in another prophet, he saith, I have stretched out my hands all the day long to a people disobedient, and speaking against my righteous way. ⁷ And again Moses makes a type of Jesus, to show that he was to die, and then that he, whom they thought to be dead, was to give life to others; in the type of those that fell in Israel. ⁸ For God caused all sorts of serpents to bite them, and they died; forasmuch as by a serpent transgression began in Eve: that so he might convince them that for their transgressions they shall be delivered into the pain of death. ⁹ Moses then himself, who had commanded them, saying, Ye shall not make to yourselves any graven or molten image, to be your God; yet now did so himself, that he might represent to them the figure of the Lord Jesus. ¹⁰ For he made a brazen serpent, and set it up on high, and called the people together by a proclamation; where being come, they entreated Moses that he would make an atonement for them, and pray that they might be healed. ¹¹ Then Moses spake unto them, saying: when any one among you shall be bitten, let him come unto the serpent that is set upon the pole; and let him assuredly trust in him, that though he be dead, yet he is able to give life, and presently he shall be saved; and so they did. See therefore how here also you have in this the glory of Jesus; and that in him and to him are all things. ¹² Again; What says Moses to Jesus the son of Nun, when he gave that name unto him, as being a prophet that all the people might hear him alone, because the father did manifest all things concerning his son Jesus, in Jesus the Son of Nun; and gave him that name when he sent him to spy out the land of Canaan; he said: Take a book in thine hands, and write what the Lord saith: Forasmuch as Jesus the Son of God shall in the last days cut off by the roots all the house of Amalek. See here again Jesus, not the son of man, but the Son of God, made manifest in a type and in the flesh. ¹³ But because it might hereafter be said, that Christ was the Son of David; therefore David fearing and well knowing the errors of the wicked, saith; the Lord saith unto my Lord, sit thou on my right hand until I make thine enemies thy footstool. ¹⁴ And again Isaiah speaketh on this wise. The Lord said unto Christ my Lord, I have laid hold on his right hand, that the nations should obey before him, and I will break the strength of kings. ¹⁵ Behold, how doth David and Isaiah call him Lord, and the Son of God.

12

The promise of God not made to the Jews only, but to the Gentiles also, and fulfilled to us by Jesus Christ.

¹ BUT let us go yet farther, and inquire whether this people be the heir, or the former; and whether the covenant be with us or with them. ² And first, as concerning the people, hear now what the Scripture saith. ³ Isaac prayed for his wife Rebekah, because she was barren; and she conceived. Afterwards Rebekah went forth to inquire of the Lord. ⁴ And the Lord said unto her; There are two nations in thy womb, and two people shall come from thy body; and the one shall have power over the other, and the greater shall serve the lesser. Understand here who was Isaac; who Rebekah; and of whom it was foretold, this people shall be greater than that. ⁵ And in another prophecy Jacob speaketh more clearly to his son Joseph saying; Behold the Lord hath not deprived me of seeing thy face, bring me thy sons that I may bless them. And he brought unto his father Manasseh and Ephraim, desiring that he should bless Manasseh, because he was the elder. ⁶ Therefore Joseph brought him to the right hand of his father Jacob. But Jacob by the spirit foresaw the figure of the of the people that was to come.

⁷ And what saith the Scripture? And Jacob crossed his hands, and put his right hand upon Ephraim, his second, and the younger son, and blessed him. And Joseph said unto Jacob; Put thy right hand upon the head of Manasseh, for he is my first-born son. And Jacob said unto Joseph; I know it, my son, I know it; but the greater shall serve the lesser; though he also shall be blessed. ⁸ Ye see of whom he appointed it, that they should be the first people, and heirs of the covenant. ⁹ If therefore God shall have yet farther taken notice of this by Abraham too; our understanding of it will then be perfectly established. ¹⁰ What then saith the Scripture to Abraham, when he believed, and it was imputed unto him for righteousness? Behold I have made thee a father of the nations, which without circumcision believe in the Lord. ¹¹ Let us therefore now inquire whether God has fulfilled the covenant, which he sware to our fathers, that he would give this people? Yes, verily, he gave it: but they were not worthy to receive it by reason of their sins. ¹² For thus saith the prophet: And Moses continued fasting in mount Sinai, to receive the covenant of the Lord with the people, forty days and forty nights. ¹³ And he received of the Lord two tables written with the finger of the Lord's hand in the Spirit. And Moses when he had received them brought them down that he might deliver them to the people. ¹⁴ And the Lord said unto Moses; Moses, Moses, get thee down quickly, for the people which thou broughtest out of the land of Egypt have done wickedly. ¹⁵ And Moses understood that they had again set up a molten image: and he cast the two tables out of his hands; and the tables of the covenant of the Lord were broken. Moses therefore received them, but they were not worthy. ¹⁶ Now then learn how we have received them. Moses, being a servant, took them; but the Lord himself has given them unto us, that we might be the people of his inheritance, having suffered for us. ¹⁷ He was therefore made manifest; that they should fill up the measure of their sins, and that we being made heirs by him, should receive the covenant of the Lord Jesus. ¹⁸ And again the prophet saith; Behold, I have set thee for a light unto the Gentiles, to be the saviour of all the ends of the earth, saith the Lord the God who hath redeemed thee. ¹⁹ Who for that very end was prepared, that by his own appearing he might redeem our hearts, already devoured by death, and delivered over to the irregularity of error, from darkness; and establish a covenant with us by his word. ²⁰ For so it is written that the father commanded him by delivering us from darkness, to prepare unto himself a holy people. ²¹ Wherefore the prophet saith: I the Lord thy God have called thee in righteousness, and I will take thee by thy hand and will strengthen thee. And give thee for a covenant of the people, for a light of the Gentiles. To open the eyes of the blind, to bring out the prisoners from the prison, and them that sit in darkness out of the prison house. ²² Consider therefore from whence we have been redeemed. And again the prophet saith: The spirit of the Lord is upon me, because he hath anointed me: he hath sent me to preach glad tidings to the lowly; to heal the broken in heart; to preach remission to the captives, and sight unto the blind; to proclaim the acceptable year of the Lord, and the day of restitution; to comfort all that mourn.

13

That the sabbath of the Jews was but a figure of a more glorious sabbath to come, and their temple, of the spiritual temples of God.

¹ FURTHERMORE it is written concerning the sabbath, in the Ten Commandments, which God spake in the Mount Sinai to Moses, face to face; Sanctify the sabbath of the Lord with pure hands, and with a clean heart. ² And elsewhere he saith; If thy children shall keep my sabbaths, then will I put my mercy upon them. ³ And even in the beginning of the creation he makes mention of the sabbath. And God made in six days the works of his hands; and he finished them on the seventh day, and he rested the seventh day, and sanctified it. ⁴ Consider, my children, what that signifies, he finished them in six days. The meaning of it is this; that in six thousand years the Lord God will bring all things to an end. ⁵ For with him one day is a thousand years; as himself testifieth, saying, Behold this day shall be as a thousand years. Therefore, children, in six days, that is, in six thousand years, shall all things be accomplished. ⁶ And what is that he saith, And he rested the seventh day: he meaneth this; that when his Son shall come, and abolish the season of the Wicked One, and judge the ungodly; and shall change the sun and the moon, and the stars; then he shall gloriously rest in that seventh day. ⁷ He adds lastly; Thou shalt sanctify it with clean hands and a pure heart. Wherefore we are greatly deceived if we imagine that any one can now sanctify that day which God has made holy, without having a heart pure in all things. ⁸ Behold therefore he will then truly sanctify it with blessed rest, when we (having received the righteous promise, when iniquity shall be no more, all things being renewed by the Lord) shall be able to sanctify it, being ourselves first made holy. ⁹ Lastly, he saith unto them: Your new moons and you: sabbaths I cannot bear them. Consider what he means by it; the sabbaths, says he, which ye now keep are not acceptable unto me, but those which I have made; when resting from all things I shall begin the eighth day, that is, the beginning of the other world. ¹⁰ For which cause we observe the eighth day with gladness, in which Jesus rose from the dead; and having manifested himself to his disciples, ascended into heaven. ¹¹ It remains yet that I speak to you concerning the temple how these miserable men being deceived have put their trust in the house, and not in God himself who made them, as if it were the habitation of God. ¹² For much after the same manner as the Gentiles, they consecrated him in the temple. ¹³ But learn therefore how the Lord speaketh, rendering the temple vain: Who has measured the heaven with a span, and the earth with his hand? Is it not I? Thus saith the Lord, Heaven is my throne, and the earth is my footstool. What is the house that ye will build me? Or what is the place of my rest? Know therefore that all their hope is vain. ¹⁴ And again he speaketh after this manner: Behold they that destroy this temple, even they shall again build it up. And so it came to pass; for through their wars it is now destroyed by their enemies; and the servants of their enemies built it up. ¹⁵ Furthermore it has been made manifest, how both the city and the temple, and the people of Israel should be given up. For the Scripture saith; And it shall come to pass in the last days, that the Lord will deliver up the sheep of his pasture, and their fold, and their tower into destruction. And it is come to pass, as the Lord hath spoken. ¹⁶ Let us inquire therefore, whether there be any temple of God? Yes there is; and that there, where himself declares that he would both make and perfect it. For it is written; And it shall be that as soon as the week shall be completed, the temple of the Lord shall be gloriously built in the name of the Lord. ¹⁷ I find therefore that there is a temple. But how shall it be built in the name of the Lord? I will shew you. ¹⁸ Before that we believed in God, the habitation of our heart was corruptible, and feeble, as a temple truly built with hands. ¹⁹ For it was a house full of idolatry, a house of devils; inasmuch as there was done in it whatsoever was contrary unto God. But it shall be built in the name of the Lord. ²⁰ Consider, how that the temple of the Lord shall be very gloriously built; and by what means that shall be, learn. ²¹ Having received remission of our sins, and trusting in the name of the Lord, we are become renewed, being again created as it were from the beginning. Wherefore God truly dwells in our house, that is, in us. ²² But how does he dwell in us? The word of his faith, the calling of his promise, the wisdom of his righteous judgments, the commands of his doctrine; he himself prophesies within us, he himself dwelleth in us, and openeth to us who were in bondage of death the gate of our temple, that is, the mouth of wisdom, having given repentance unto us; and by this means has brought us to be an incorruptible temple. ²³ He therefore that desires to be saved looketh not unto the man, but unto him that dwelleth in him, and speaketh by him; being struck with wonder, forasmuch as he never either heard him speaking such words out of his mouth, nor ever desired to hear them. ²⁴ This is that spiritual temple that is built unto the Lord.

14

Of the way of light; being a summary of what a Christian is to do, that he may be happy for ever.

¹ AND thus, I trust, I have declared to you as much, and with as great simplicity as I could, those things which make for your salvation, so as not to have omitted anything that might be requisite thereunto. ² For should I speak further of the things that now are, and of those that are to come, you would not yet understand them, seeing they lie in parables. This therefore shall suffice as to these things. ³ Let us now go on to the other kind of knowledge and doctrine There are two ways of doctrine and power; the one of light, the other of darkness. ⁴ But there is a great deal of difference between these two ways: for over one are appointed the angels of God, the leaders of the way of light; over the other, the angels of Satan. And the one is the Lord from everlasting to everlasting; the other is the prince of the time of unrighteousness. ⁵ Now the way of light is this, if any one desires to attain to the place that is appointed for him, and will hasten thither by his works. And the knowledge that has been given to us for walking in it, to this effect: Thou shalt love him that made thee: thou shalt glorify him that hath redeemed thee from death. ⁶ Thou shalt be simple in heart, and rich in the spirit. Thou shalt not cleave to those that walk in the way of death. Thou shalt hate to do anything that is not pleasing unto God. Thou shalt abhor all dissimulation. Thou shalt not neglect any of the commands of the Lord. ⁷ Thou shalt not exalt thyself, but shalt be humble. Thou shalt not take honour to thyself. Thou shalt not enter into any wicked counsel against thy neighbour. Thou shalt not be over-confident in thy heart. ⁸ Thou shalt not commit fornication, nor adultery. Neither shalt thou corrupt thyself with mankind. Thou shalt not make use of the word of God, to any impurity. ⁹ Thou shalt not accept any man's person, when thou reprovest any one's faults. Thou t shalt be gentle. Thou shalt be quiet. Thou shalt tremble at the words which thou hast heard. Thou shalt not keep any hatred in thy heart

against thy brother. Thou shalt not entertain any doubt whether it shall be or not. ¹⁰ Thou shalt not take the name of the Lord in vain. Thou shalt love thy neighbour above thy own soul. ¹¹ Thou shalt not destroy thy conceptions before they are brought forth; nor kill them after they are born. ¹² Thou shalt not withdraw thy hand from thy son, or from thy daughter; but shall teach them from their youth the fear of the Lord. ¹³ Thou shalt not covet thy neighbour's goods; neither shalt thou be an extortioner. Neither shall thy heart be joined to proud men; but thou shalt be numbered among the righteous and the lowly. Whatever events shall happen unto thee, thou shalt receive them as good. ¹⁴ Thou shalt not he double-minded, or double-tongued; for a double tongue is the snare of death. Thou shalt be subject unto the Lord and to inferior masters as to the representatives of God, in fear and reverence. ¹⁵ Thou shalt not be bitter in thy commands towards any of thy servants that trust in God; lest thou chance not to fear him who is over both; because he came not to call any with respect of persons, but whomsoever the spirit had prepared. ¹⁶ Thou shalt communicate to thy neighbour of all thou hast; thou shalt not call anything thine own: for if ye partake in such things as are incorruptible, how much more should you do it in those that are corruptible? ¹⁷ Thou shalt not be forward to speak; for the mouth is the snare of death. Strive for thy soul with all thy might. Reach not out thine hand to receive, and withhold it not when thou shouldest give. ¹⁸ Thou shalt love, as the apple of thine eye, every one that speaketh unto thee the Word of the Lord. Call to thy remembrance, day and night, the future judgment. ¹⁹ Thou shalt seek out every day the persons of the righteous: and both consider and go about to exhort others by the, word, and meditate how thou mayest save a soul. ²⁰ Thou shalt also labour with thy hands to give to the poor, that thy sins may be forgiven thee. Thou shalt not deliberate whether thou shouldst give: nor, having given, murmur at it. ²¹ Give to every one that asks: so shalt thou know who is the good rewarder of thy gifts. ²² Keep what thou hast received; thou shalt neither add to it nor take from it. ²³ Let the wicked be always thy aversion. Thou shalt judge righteous judgment. Thou shalt never cause divisions; but shalt make peace between those that are at variance, and bring them together. ²⁴ Thou shalt confess thy sins; and not come to thy prayer with an evil conscience. ²⁵ This is the way of light.

15

Of the way of darkness; that is, what kind of persons shall be for ever cast out of the kingdom of God.

¹ BUT the way of darkness is crooked and full of cursing. For it is the way of eternal death, with punishment; in which they that walk meet those things that destroy their own souls. ² Such are; idolatry, confidence, pride of power, hypocrisy, double-mindedness, adultery, murder, rapine, pride, transgression, deceit, malice, arrogance, witchcraft, covetousness, and the want of the fear of God. ³ In this walk those who are the persecutors of them that are good; haters of truth; lovers of lies; who know not the reward of righteousness, nor cleave to any thing that is good. ⁴ Who administer not righteous judgment to the widow and orphan; who watch for wickedness, and not for the fear of the Lord: ⁵ From whom gentleness and patience are far off; who love vanity, and follow after rewards; having no compassion upon the poor; nor take any pains for such as are heavy laden and oppressed. ⁶ Ready to evil speaking, not knowing him that made them; murderers of children; corrupters of the creatures of God; that turn away from the needy; oppress the afflicted; are the advocates of the rich, but unjust judges of the poor; being altogether sinners. ⁷ It is therefore fitting that learning the just commands of the Lord, which we have before mentioned, we should walk in them. For he who does such things shall be glorified in the kingdom of God. ⁸ But he that chooses the other part, shall be destroyed, together with his works. For this cause there shall be both a resurrection, and a retribution. ⁹ I beseech those that are in high estate among you, (if so be you will take the counsel which with a good intention I offer to you,) you have those with you towards whom you may do good; do not forsake them. ¹⁰ For the day is at hand in which all things shall be destroyed, together with the wicked one. The Lord is near, and his reward is with him. ¹¹ I beseech you, therefore, again, and again, be as good lawgivers to one another; continue faithful counsellors to each other; remove from among you all hypocrisy. ¹² And may God, the Lord of all the world give you wisdom, knowledge, counsel, and understanding of his judgments in patience. ¹³ Be ye taught of God; seeking what it is the Lord requires of you, and doing it; that ye may be saved in the day of judgment. ¹⁴ And if there be among you any remembrance of what is good, think of me; meditating upon these things, that both my desire and my watching for you may turn to a good account. ¹⁵ I beseech you; I ask it as a favour of you; whilst you are in this beautiful tabernacle of the body, be wanting in none of these things; but without ceasing seek them, and fulfil every command. For these things are fitting and worthy to be done. ¹⁶ Wherefore I have given the more diligence to write unto you, according to my ability, that you might rejoice. Farewell, children, of love and peace. ¹⁷ The Lord of glory and of all grace, be with your spirit, Amen.

The First Epistle of Clement to the Corinthians

1

¹ By reason of the sudden and repeated calamities and reverses which are befalling us, brethren, we consider that we have been somewhat tardy in giving heed to the matters of dispute that have arisen among you, dearly beloved, and to the detestable and unholy sedition, so alien and strange to the elect of God, which a few headstrong and self-willed persons have kindled to such a pitch of madness that your name, once revered and renowned and lovely in the sight of all men, hath been greatly reviled. ² For who that had sojourned among you did not approve your most virtuous and steadfast faith? Who did not admire your sober and forbearing piety in Christ? Who did not publish abroad your magnificent disposition of hospitality? Who did not congratulate you on your perfect and sound knowledge? ³ For ye did all things without respect of persons, and ye walked after the ordinances of God, submitting yourselves to your rulers and rendering to the older men among you the honor which is their due. On the young too ye enjoined modest and seemly thoughts; and the women ye charged to perform all their duties in a blameless and seemly and pure conscience, cherishing their own husbands, as is meet; and ye taught them to keep in the rule of obedience, and to manage the affairs of their household in seemliness, with all discretion.

2

¹ And ye were all lowly in mind and free from arrogance, yielding rather than claiming submission, *more glad to give than to receive*, and content with the provisions which God supplieth. And giving heed unto His words, ye laid them up diligently in your hearts, and His sufferings were before your eyes. ² Thus a profound and rich peace was given to all, and an insatiable desire of doing good. An abundant outpouring also of the Holy Spirit fell upon all; ³ and, being full of holy counsel, in excellent zeal and with a pious confidence ye stretched out your hands to Almighty God, supplicating Him to be propitious, if unwillingly ye had committed any sin. ⁴ Ye had conflict day and night for all the brotherhood, that the number of His elect might be saved with fearfulness and intentness of mind. ⁵ Ye were sincere and simple and free from malice one towards another. ⁶ Every sedition and every schism was abominable to you. Ye mourned over the transgressions of your neighbors: ye judged their shortcomings to be your own. ⁷ Ye repented not of any well-doing, but were *ready unto every good work*. ⁸ Being adorned with a most virtuous and honorable life, ye performed all your duties in the fear of Him. The commandments and the ordinances of the Lord were *written on the tablets of your hearts*.

3

¹ All glory and enlargement was given unto you, and that was fulfilled which is written *My beloved ate and drank and was enlarged and waxed fat and kicked*. ² Hence come jealousy and envy, strife and sedition, persecution and tumult, war and captivity. ³ So men were stirred up, *the mean against the honorable*, the ill reputed against the highly reputed, the foolish against the wise, the *young against the elder*. ⁴ For this cause *righteousness* and peace *stand aloof*, while each man hath forsaken the fear of the Lord and become purblind in the faith of Him, neither walketh in the ordinances of His commandments nor liveth according to that which becometh Christ, but each goeth after the lusts of his evil heart, seeing that they have conceived an unrighteous and ungodly jealousy, through which also *death entered into the world*.

4

¹ For so it is written, *And it came to pass after certain days that Cain brought of the fruits of the earth a sacrifice unto God, and Abel he also brought of the firstlings of the sheep and of their* fatness. ² *And God looked upon Abel and upon his gifts, but unto Cain and unto his sacrifices He gave no heed*. ³ *And Cain sorrowed exceedingly, and his countenance fell*. ⁴ *And God said unto Cain, Wherefore art thou very sorrowful and wherefore did thy countenance fall? If thou hast offered aright and hast not divided aright, didst thou not sin? Hold thy peace*. ⁵ *Unto thee shall he turn, and thou shalt rule over him*. {This last phrase has also been translated: *Be at peace: thine offering returns to thyself, and thou shalt again possess it.*} ⁶ *And Cain said unto Abel his brother, Let us go over unto the plain. And it came to pass, while they Were in the plain, that Cain rose up against Abel his brother and slew him*. ⁷ Ye see, brethren, jealousy and envy wrought a brother's murder. ⁸ By reason of jealousy our father Jacob ran away from the face of Esau his brother. ⁹ Jealousy caused Joseph to be persecuted even unto death, and to come even unto bondage. ¹⁰ Jealousy compelled Moses to flee from the face of Pharaoh king of Egypt while it was said to him by his own countryman, *Who made thee a judge or a decider over us, Wouldest thou slay me, even as yesterday thou slewest the Egyptian?* ¹¹ By reason of jealousy Aaron and Miriam were lodged outside the camp. ¹² Jealousy brought Dathan and Abiram down alive to hades, because they made sedition against Moses the servant of God. ¹³ By reason of jealousy David was envied not only by the Philistines, but was persecuted also by Saul [king of Israel].

5

¹ But, to pass from the examples of ancient days, let us come to those champions who lived nearest to our time. Let us set before us the noble examples which belong to our generation. ² By reason of jealousy and envy the greatest and most righteous pillars of the Church were persecuted, and contended even unto death. ³ Let us set before our eyes the good Apostles. ⁴ There was Peter who by reason of unrighteous jealousy endured not one not one but many labors, and thus having borne his testimony went to his appointed place of glory. ⁵ By reason of jealousy and strife Paul by his example pointed out the prize of patient endurance. After that he had been seven times in bonds, had been driven into exile, had been stoned, had preached in the East and in the West, he won the noble renown which was the reward of his faith, ⁶ having taught righteousness unto the whole world and having reached the farthest bounds of the West; and when he had borne his testimony before the rulers, so he departed from the world and went unto the holy place, having been found a notable pattern of patient endurance.

6

¹ Unto these men of holy lives was gathered a vast multitude of the elect, who through many indignities and tortures, being the victims of jealousy, set a brave example among ourselves. ² By reason of jealousy women being persecuted, after that they had suffered cruel and unholy insults as Danaids and Dircae, safely reached the goal in the race of faith, and received a noble reward, feeble though they were in body. ³ Jealousy hath estranged wives from their husbands and changed the saying of our father Adam, *This now is bone of my bones and flesh of my flesh*. ⁴ Jealousy and strife have overthrown great cities and uprooted great nations.

7

¹ These things, dearly beloved, we write, not only as admonishing you, but also as putting ourselves in remembrance. For we are in the same lists, and the same contest awaiteth us. ² Wherefore let us forsake idle and vain thoughts; and let us conform to the glorious and venerable rule which hath been handed down to us; ³ and let us see what is good and what is pleasant and what is acceptable in the sight of Him that made us. ⁴ Let us fix our eyes on the blood of Christ and understand how precious it is unto His Father, because being shed for our salvation it won for the whole world the grace of repentance. ⁵ Let us review all the generations in turn, and learn how from generation to generation the Master hath given a place for repentance unto them that desire to turn to Him. ⁶ Noah preached repentance, and they that obeyed were saved. ⁷ Jonah preached destruction unto the men of Nineveh; but they, repenting of their sins, obtained pardon of God by their supplications and received salvation, albeit they were aliens from God.

8

¹ The ministers of the grace of God through the Holy Spirit spake concerning repentance. ² Yea and the Master of the universe Himself spake concerning repentance with an oath: ³ *for, as I live saith the Lord, I desire not the death of the sinner, so much as his repentance*, ⁴ and He added also a merciful judgment: *Repent ye, O house of Israel, of your iniquity; say unto the sons of My people, Though your sins reach from the earth even unto the heaven, and though they be redder than scarlet and blacker than sackcloth, and ye turn unto Me with your whole heart and say Father, I will give ear unto you as unto a holy people*. ⁵ And in another place He saith on this wise, *Wash, be ye clean. Put away your iniquities from your souls out of My sight. Cease from your iniquities; learn to do good; seek out judgment; defend him that is wronged: give judgment for the orphan, and execute righteousness for the widow; and come and let us reason together, saith He; and though your sins be as crimson, I will make them white as snow; and though they be as scarlet, I will make them white as wool. And if ye be willing and will hearken unto Me, ye shall eat the good things of the earth; but if ye be not willing, neither hearken unto Me, a sword shall devour you; for the mouth of the Lord hath spoken these things*. ⁶ Seeing then that He desireth all His beloved to be partakers of repentance, He confirmed it by an act of His almighty will.

9

¹ Wherefore let us be obedient unto His excellent and glorious will; and presenting ourselves as suppliants of His mercy and goodness, let us fall down before Him and betake ourselves unto His compassions, forsaking the vain toil and the strife and the jealousy which leadeth unto death. ² Let us fix our eyes on them that ministered perfectly unto His excellent glory.

³ Let us set before us Enoch, who being found righteous in obedience was translated, and his death was not found. ⁴ Noah, being found faithful, by his ministration preached regeneration unto the world, and through him the Master saved the living creatures that entered into the ark in concord.

10

¹ Abraham, who was called the 'friend,' was found faithful in that he rendered obedience unto the words of God. ² He through obedience went forth from his land and from his kindred and from his father's house, that leaving a scanty land and a feeble kindred and a mean house he might inherit the promises of God. ³ For He saith unto him *Go forth from thy land and from thy kindred and from thy father's house unto the land which I shall show thee, and I will make thee into a great nation, and I will bless thee and will magnify thy name, and thou shalt be blessed. And I will bless them that bless thee, and I will curse them that curse thee; and in thee shall all the tribes of the earth be blessed.* ⁴ And again, when he was parted from Lot, God said unto him *Look up with thine eyes, and behold from the place where thou now art, unto the north and the south and the sunrise and the sea; for all the land which thou seest, I will give it unto thee and to thy seed for ever;* ⁵ *and I will make thy seed as the dust of the earth. If any man can count the dust of the earth, then shall thy seed also be counted.* ⁶ And again He saith; *God led Abraham forth and said unto him, Look up unto the heaven and count the stars, and see whether thou canst number them. So shall thy seed be. And Abraham believed God, and it was reckoned unto him for righteousness.* ⁷ For his faith and hospitality a son was given unto him in old age, and by obedience he offered him a sacrifice unto God on one of the mountains which He showed him.

11

¹ For his hospitality and godliness Lot was saved from Sodom, when all the country round about was judged by fire and brimstone; the Master having thus fore shown that He forsaketh not them which set their hope on Him, but appointeth unto punishment and torment them which swerve aside. ² For when his wife had gone forth with him, being otherwise minded and not in accord, she was appointed for a sign hereunto, so that she became a pillar of salt unto this day, that it might be known unto all men that they which are double-minded and they which doubt concerning the power of God are set for a judgment and for a token unto all the generations.

12

¹ For her faith and hospitality Rahab the harlot was saved. ² For when the spies were sent forth unto Jericho by Joshua the son of Nun, the king of the land perceived that they were come to spy out his country, and sent forth men to seize them, that being seized they might be put to death. ³ So the hospitable Rahab received them and hid them in the upper chamber under the flax stalks. ⁴ And when the messengers of the king came near and said, *The spies of our land entered in unto thee: bring them forth, for the king so ordereth:* then she answered, *The men truly, whom ye seek, entered in unto me, but they departed forthwith and are sojourning on the way;* and she pointed out to them the opposite road. ⁵ And she said unto the men, *Of a surety I perceive that the Lord your God delivereth this city unto you; for the fear and the dread of you is fallen upon the inhabitants thereof. When therefore it shall come to pass that ye take it, save me and the house of my father.* ⁶ And they said unto her, *It shall be even so as thou hast spoken unto us. Whensoever therefore thou perceivest that we are coming, thou shalt gather all thy folk beneath thy roof and they shall be saved; for as many as shall be found without the house shall perish.* ⁷ And moreover they gave her a sign, that she should hang out from her house a scarlet thread, thereby showing beforehand that through the blood of the Lord there shall be redemption unto all them that believe and hope on God. ⁸ Ye see, dearly beloved, not only faith, but prophecy, is found in the woman.

13

¹ Let us therefore be lowly minded, brethren, laying aside all arrogance and conceit and folly and anger, and let us do that which is written. For the Holy Ghost saith, *Let not the wise man boast in his wisdom, nor the strong in his strength, neither the rich in his riches; but he that boasteth let him boast in the Lord, that he may seek Him out, and do judgment and righteousness* most of all remembering the words of the Lord Jesus which He spake, teaching forbearance and long-suffering: ² for thus He spake *Have mercy, that ye may receive mercy: forgive, that it may be forgiven to you. As ye do, so shall it be done to you. As ye give, so shall it be given unto you. As ye judge, so shall ye be judged. As ye show kindness, so shall kindness be showed unto you. With what measure ye mete, it shall be measured withal to you.* ³ With this commandment and these precepts let us confirm ourselves, that we may walk in obedience to His hallowed words, with lowliness of mind. ⁴ For the holy word saith, *Upon whom shall I look, save upon him that is gentle and quiet and feareth Mine oracles?*

14

¹ Therefore it is right and proper, brethren, that we should be obedient unto God, rather than follow those who in arrogance and unruliness have set themselves up as leaders in abominable jealousy. ² For we shall bring upon us no common harm, but rather great peril, if we surrender ourselves recklessly to the purposes of men who launch out into strife and seditions, so as to estrange us from that which is right. ³ Let us be good one towards another according to the compassion and sweetness of Him that made us. For it is written: ⁴ *The good shall be dwellers in the land, and the innocent shall be left on it but they that transgress shall be destroyed utterly from it.* ⁵ And again He saith *I saw the ungodly lifted up on high and exalted as the cedars of Lebanon. And I passed by, and behold he was not; and sought out his place, and I found it not. Keep innocence and behold uprightness; for there is a remnant for the peaceful man.*

15

¹ Therefore let us cleave unto them that practice peace with godliness, and not unto them that desire peace with dissimulation. ² For He saith in a certain place *This people honoreth Me with their lips, but their heart is far from Me,* ³ and again, *they blessed with their mouth, but they cursed with their heart.* ⁴ And again He saith, *They loved Him with their mouth, and with their tongue they lied unto Him; and their heart was not upright with Him, neither were they steadfast in His covenant.* ⁵ *For this cause let the deceitful lips be made dumb which speak iniquity against the righteous.* And again *May the Lord utterly destroy all the deceitful lips, the tongue that speaketh proud things, even them that say, Let us magnify our tongue; our lips are our own; who is lord over us?* ⁶ *For the misery of the needy and for the groaning of the poor I will now arise, saith the Lord. I will set him in safety; I will deal boldly by him.*

16

¹ For Christ is with them that are lowly of mind, not with them that exalt themselves over the flock. ² The scepter of the majesty of God, even our Lord Jesus Christ, came not in the pomp of arrogance or of pride, though He might have done so, but in lowliness of mind, according as the Holy Spirit spake concerning Him. ³ For He saith *Lord, who believed our report? and to whom was the arm of the Lord revealed? We announced Him in His presence. As a child was He, as a root in a thirsty ground. There is no form in Him, neither glory. And we beheld Him, and He had no form nor comeliness, but His form was mean, lacking more than the form of men. He was a man of stripes and of toil, and knowing how to bear infirmity: for His face is turned away. He was dishonored and held of no account.* ⁴ *He beareth our sins and suffereth pain for our sakes: and we accounted Him to be in toil and in stripes and in affliction.* ⁵ *And He was wounded for our sins and hath been afflicted for our iniquities. The chastisement of our peace is upon Him. With His bruises we were healed.* ⁶ *We all went astray like sheep, each man went astray in his own path:* ⁷ *and the Lord delivered Him over for our sins. And He openeth not His mouth, because He is afflicted. As a sheep He was led to slaughter; and as a lamb before his shearer is dumb, so openeth He not His mouth. In His humiliation His judgment was taken away.* ⁸ *His generation who shall declare? For His life is taken away from the earth.* ⁹ *For the iniquities of my people He is come to death.* ¹⁰ *And I will give the wicked for His burial, and the rich for His death; for He wrought no iniquity, neither was guile found in His mouth. And the Lord desireth to cleanse Him from His stripes.* ¹¹ *If ye offer for sin, your soul shall see along lived seed.* ¹² *And the Lord desireth to take away from the toil of His soul, to show Him light and to mould Him with understanding, to justify a Just One that is a good servant unto many. And He shall bear their sins.* ¹³ *Therefore He shall inherit many, and shall divide the spoils of the strong; because His soul was delivered unto death, and He was reckoned unto the transgressors;* ¹⁴ *and He bare the sins of many, and for their sins was He delivered up.* ¹⁵ And again He Himself saith; *But I am a worm and no man, a reproach of men and an outcast of the people.* ¹⁶ *All they that beheld me mocked at me; they spake with their lips; they wagged their heads, saying, He hoped on the Lord; let Him deliver him, or let Him save him, for He desireth him.* ¹⁷ Ye see, dearly beloved, what is the pattern that hath been given unto us; for, if the Lord was thus lowly of mind, what should we do, who through Him have been brought under the yoke of His grace?

17

¹ Let us be imitators also of them which went about in goatskins and sheepskins, preaching the coming of Christ. We mean Elijah and Elisha and likewise Ezekiel, the prophets, and besides them those men also that obtained a good report. ² Abraham obtained an exceeding good report and was called the friend of God; and looking steadfastly on the glory of God, he saith in lowliness of mind, *But I am dust and ashes.* ³ Moreover concerning Job also it is thus written; *And Job was righteous and*

unblamable, one that was true and honored God and abstained from all evil. ⁴ Yet he himself accuseth himself saying, *No man from filth; no, not though his life be but for a day.* ⁵ Moses was called *faithful in all His house,* and through his ministration God judged Egypt with the plagues and the torments which befell them. Howbeit he also, though greatly glorified, yet spake no proud words, but said, when an oracle was given to him at the bush, *Who am I, that Thou sendest me?* ⁶ *Nay, I am feeble of speech and slow of tongue.* And again he saith, *But I am smoke from the pot.*

18

¹ But what must we say of David that obtained a good report? of whom God said, *I have found a man after My heart, David the son of Jesse: with eternal mercy have I anointed him.* ² Yet he too saith unto God *Have mercy upon me, O God, according to Thy great mercy; and according to the multitude of Thy compassions, blot out mine iniquity.* ³ *Wash me yet more from mine iniquity, and cleanse me from my sin. For I acknowledge mine iniquity, and my sin is ever before me. Against Thee only did I sin, and I wrought evil in Thy sight; that Thou mayest be justified in Thy words, and mayest conquer in Thy pleading.* ⁴ *For behold, in iniquities was I conceived, and in sins did my mother bear me. For behold Thou hast loved truth: the dark and hidden things of Thy wisdom hast Thou showed unto me.* ⁵ *Thou shalt sprinkle me with hyssop, and I shall be made clean. Thou shalt wash me, and I shall become whiter than snow.* ⁶ *Thou shalt make me to hear of joy and gladness. The bones which have been humbled shall rejoice.* ⁷ *Turn away Thy face from my sins, and blot out all mine iniquities.* ⁸ *Make a clean heart within me, O God, and renew a right spirit in mine inmost parts. Cast me not away from Thy presence, and take not Thy Holy Spirit from me.* ⁹ *Restore unto me the joy of Thy salvation, and strengthen me with a princely spirit.* ¹⁰ *I will teach sinners Thy ways, and godless men shall be converted unto Thee.* ¹¹ *Deliver me from blood guiltiness, O God, the God of my salvation. My tongue shall rejoice in Thy righteousness.* ¹² *Lord, Thou shalt open my mouth, and my lips shall declare Thy praise.* ¹³ *For, if Thou hadst desired sacrifice, I would have given it: in whole burnt offerings Thou wilt have no pleasure.* ¹⁴ *A sacrifice unto God is a contrite spirit; a contrite and humbled heart God will not despise.*

19

¹ The humility therefore and the submissiveness of so many and so great men, who have thus obtained a good report, hath through obedience made better not only us but also the generations which were before us, even them that received His oracles in fear and truth. ² Seeing then that we have been partakers of many great and glorious doings, let us hasten to return unto the goal of peace which hath been handed down to us from the beginning, and let us look steadfastly unto the Father and Maker of the whole world, and cleave unto His splendid and excellent gifts of peace and benefits. ³ Let us behold Him in our mind, and let us look with the eyes of our soul unto His long-suffering will. Let us note how free from anger He is towards all His creatures.

20

¹ The heavens are moved by His direction and obey Him in peace. ² Day and night accomplish the course assigned to them by Him, without hindrance one to another. ³ The sun and the moon and the dancing stars according to His appointment circle in harmony within the bounds assigned to them, without any swerving aside. ⁴ The earth, bearing fruit in fulfillment of His will at her proper seasons, putteth forth the food that supplieth abundantly both men and beasts and all living things which are thereupon, making no dissension, neither altering anything which He hath decreed. ⁵ Moreover, the inscrutable depths of the abysses and the unutterable statutes of the nether regions are constrained by the same ordinances. ⁶ The basin of the boundless sea, gathered together by His workmanship *into it's reservoirs*, passeth not the barriers wherewith it is surrounded; but even as He ordered it, so it doeth. ⁷ For He said, *So far shalt thou come, and thy waves shall be broken within thee.* ⁸ The ocean which is impassable for men, and the worlds beyond it, are directed by the same ordinances of the Master. ⁹ The seasons of spring and summer and autumn and winter give way in succession one to another in peace. ¹⁰ The winds in their several quarters at their proper season fulfill their ministry without disturbance; and the ever flowing fountains, created for enjoyment and health, without fail give their breasts which sustain the life for men. Yea, the smallest of living things come together in concord and peace. ¹¹ All these things the great Creator and Master of the universe ordered to be in peace and concord, doing good unto all things, but far beyond the rest unto us who have taken refuge in His compassionate mercies through our Lord Jesus Christ, ¹² to whom be the glory and the majesty for ever and ever. Amen.

21

¹ Look ye, brethren, lest His benefits, which are many, turn unto judgment to all of us, if we walk not worthily of Him, and do those things which are good and well pleasing in His sight with concord. ² For He saith in a certain place, *The Spirit of the Lord is a lamp searching the closets of the belly*. ³ Let us see how near He is, and how that nothing escapeth Him of our thoughts or our devices which we make. ⁴ It is right therefore that we should not be deserters from His will. ⁵ Let us rather give offense to foolish and senseless men who exalt themselves and boast in the arrogance of their words, than to God. ⁶ Let us fear the Lord Jesus [Christ], whose blood was given for us. Let us reverence our rulers; let us honor our elders; let us instruct our young men in the lesson of the fear of God. Let us guide our women toward that which is good: ⁷ let them show forth their lovely disposition of purity; let them prove their sincere affection of gentleness; let them make manifest the moderation of their tongue through their silence; let them show their love, not in factious preferences but without partiality towards all them that fear God, in holiness. Let our children be partakers of the instruction which is in Christ: ⁸ let them learn how lowliness of mind prevaileth with God, what power chaste love hath with God, how the fear of Him is good and great and saveth all them that walk therein in a pure mind with holiness. ⁹ For He is the searcher out of the intents and desires; whose breath is in us, and when He listeth, He shall take it away.

22

¹ Now all these things the faith which is in Christ confirmeth: for He Himself through the Holy Spirit thus invite thus: *Come, my children, hearken unto Me, I will teach you the fear of the Lord*. ² *What man is he that desireth life and loveth to see good days?* ³ *Make thy tongue to cease from evil, and thy lips that they speak no guile.* ⁴ *Turn aside from evil and do good.* ⁵ *Seek peace and ensue it.* ⁶ *The eyes of the Lord are over the righteous, and His ears are turned to their prayers. But the face of the Lord is upon them that do evil, to destroy their memorial from the earth.* ⁷ *The righteous cried out, and the Lord heard him, and delivered him from all his troubles. Many are the troubles of the righteous, and the Lord shall deliver him from them all.* ⁸ And again *Many are the stripes of the sinner, but them that set their hope on the Lord mercy shall compass about.*

23

¹ The Father, who is pitiful in all things, and ready to do good, hath compassion on them that fear Him, and kindly and lovingly bestoweth His favors on them that draw nigh unto Him with a single mind. ² Therefore let us not be double-minded, neither let our soul indulge in idle humors respecting His exceeding and glorious gifts. ³ Let this scripture be far from us where He saith *Wretched are the double-minded, Which doubt in their soul and say, These things we did hear in the days of our fathers also, and behold we have grown old, and none of these things hath befallen us.* ⁴ *Ye fools, compare yourselves unto a tree; take a vine. First it sheddeth its leaves, then a shoot cometh, then a leaf, then a flower, and after these a sour berry, then a full ripe grape. Ye see that in a little time the fruit of the tree attaineth unto mellowness.* ⁵ Of a truth quickly and suddenly shall His will be accomplished, the scripture also bearing witness to it, saying *He shall come quickly and shall not tarry; and the Lord shall come suddenly into His temple, even the Holy One, whom ye expect.*

24

¹ Let us understand, dearly beloved, how the Master continually showeth unto us the resurrection that shall be hereafter; whereof He made the Lord Jesus Christ the firstfruit, when He raised Him from the dead. ² Let us behold, dearly beloved, the resurrection which happeneth at its proper season. ³ Day and night show unto us the resurrection. The night falleth asleep, and day ariseth; the day departeth, and night cometh on. ⁴ Let us mark the fruits, how and in what manner the sowing taketh place. ⁵ *The sower goeth forth* and casteth into the earth each of the seeds; and these falling into the earth dry and bare decay: then out of their decay the mightiness of the Master's providence raiseth them up, and from being one they increase manifold and bear fruit.

25

¹ Let us consider the marvelous sign which is seen in the regions of the east, that is, in the parts about Arabia. ² There is a bird, which is named the phoenix. This, being the only one of its kind, liveth for five hundred years; and when it hath now reached the time of its dissolution that it should die, it maketh for itself a coffin of frankincense and myrrh and the other spices, into the which in the fullness of time it entereth, and so it dieth. ³ But, as the flesh rotteth, a certain worm is engendered, which is nurtured from the moisture of the dead creature and putteth forth wings. Then, when it is grown lusty, it taketh up that coffin where are the bones of its parent, and carrying them journeyeth from the country of Arabia even unto Egypt, to the place called the City of the Sun; ⁴ and in the daytime in the sight of all, flying to the altar of the Sun, it layeth them thereupon; and this done, it setteth forth to return. ⁵ So the priests examine the registers of the times, and they find that it hath come when the five hundredth year is completed.

26

¹ Do we then think it to be a great and marvelous thing, if the Creator of the universe shall bring about the resurrection of them that have served Him with holiness in the assurance of a good faith, seeing that He showeth to us even by a bird the magnificence of His promise? ² For He saith in a certain place *And Thou shalt raise me up, and I will praise Thee;* and; *I went to rest and slept, I was awaked, for Thou art with me.* ³ And again Job saith *And Thou shall raise this my flesh which hath endured all these things*.

27

¹ With this hope therefore let our souls be bound unto Him that is faithful in His promises and that is righteous in His judgments. ² He that commanded not to lie, much more shall He Himself not lie: for nothing is impossible with God save to lie. ³ Therefore let our faith in Him be kindled within us, and let us understand that all things are nigh unto Him. ⁴ By a word of His majesty He compacted the universe; and by a word He can destroy it. ⁵ *Who shall say unto Him, What hast thou done? or who shall resist the might of His strength?* When He listeth, and as He listeth, He will do all things; and nothing shall pass away of those things that He hath decreed. ⁶ All things are in His sight, and nothing escapeth His counsel, ⁷ seeing that *The heavens declare the glory of God, and the firmament proclaimeth His handiwork. Day uttereth word unto day, and night proclaimeth knowledge unto night; and there are neither words nor speeches, whose voices are not heard.*

28

¹ Since therefore all things are seen and heard, let us fear Him and forsake the abominable lusts of evil works, that we maybe shielded by His mercy from the coming judgments. ² For where can any of us escape from His strong hand? And what world will receive any of them that desert from His service? ³ For the holy writing saith in a certain place *Where shall I go, and where shall I be hidden from Thy face? If I ascend into the heaven, Thou art there; if I depart into the farthest parts of the earth, there is Thy right hand; if I make my bed in the depths, there is Thy Spirit.* ⁴ Whither then shall one depart, or where shall one flee, from Him that embraceth the universe?

29

¹ Let us therefore approach Him in holiness of soul, lifting up pure and undefiled hands unto Him, with love towards our gentle and compassionate Father who made us an elect portion unto Himself. ² For thus it is written: *When the Most High divided the nations, when He dispersed the sons of Adam, He fixed the boundaries of the nations according to the number of the angels of God. His people Jacob became the portion of the Lord, and Israel the measurement of His inheritance.* ³ And in another place He saith, *Behold, the Lord taketh for Himself a nation out of the midst of the nations, as a man taketh the first fruits of his threshing floor; and the holy of holies shall come forth from that nation.*

30

¹ Seeing then that we are the special portion of a Holy God, let us do all things that pertain unto holiness, forsaking evil speakings, abominable and impure embraces, drunkennesses and tumults and hateful lusts, abominable adultery, hateful pride. ² *For God,* He saith, *resisteth the proud, but giveth grace to the lowly.* ³ Let us therefore cleave unto those to whom grace is given from God. Let us clothe ourselves in concord, being lowlyminded and temperate, holding ourselves aloof from all back biting and evil speaking, being justified by works and not by words. ⁴ For He saith, *He that saith much shall hear also again. Doth the ready talker think to be righteous?* ⁵ *Blessed is the offspring of a woman that liveth but a short time. Be not thou abundant in words.* ⁶ Let our praise be with God, and not of ourselves: for God hateth them that praise themselves. ⁷ Let the testimony to our well doing be given by others, as it was given unto our fathers who were righteous. ⁸ Boldness and arrogance and daring are for them that are accursed of God; but forbearance and humility and gentleness are with them that are blessed of God.

31

¹ Let us therefore cleave unto His blessing, and let us see what are the ways of blessing. Let us study the records of the things that have happened from the beginning. ² Wherefore was our father Abraham blessed? Was it not because he wrought righteousness and truth through faith? ³ Isaac with confidence, as knowing the future, was led a willing sacrifice. ⁴ Jacob with humility departed from his land because of his brother, and went unto Laban and served; and the twelve tribes of Israel were given unto him.

32

¹ If any man will consider them one by one in sincerity, he shall understand the magnificence of the gifts that are given by Him. ² For of Jacob are all the priests and levites who minister unto the altar of God; of him is the Lord Jesus as concerning the flesh; of him are kings and rulers and governors in the line of Judah; yea and the rest of his tribes are held in no small honor, seeing that God promised saying, *Thy seed shall be as the stars of heaven.* ³ They all therefore were glorified and magnified, not through themselves or their own works or the righteous doing which they wrought, but through His will. ⁴ And so we, having been called through His will in Christ Jesus, are not justified through ourselves or through our own wisdom or understanding or piety or works which we wrought in holiness of heart, but through faith, whereby the Almighty God justified all men that have been from the beginning; to whom be the glory for ever and ever. Amen.

33

¹ What then must we do, brethren? Must we idly abstain from doing good, and forsake love? May the Master never allow this to befall us at least; but let us hasten with instancy and zeal to accomplish every good work. ² For the Creator and Master of the universe Himself rejoiceth in His works. ³ For by His exceeding great might He established the heavens, and in His incomprehensible wisdom He set them in order. And the earth He separated from the water that surroundeth it, and He set it firm on the sure foundation of His own will; and the living creatures which walk upon it He commanded to exist by His ordinance. Having before created the sea and the living creatures therein, He enclosed it by His own power. ⁴ Above all, as the most excellent and exceeding great work of His intelligence, with His sacred and faultless hands He formed man in the impress of His own image. ⁵ For thus saith God *Let us make man after our image and after our likeness. And God made man; male and female made He them.* ⁶ So having finished all these things, He praised them and blessed them and said, *Increase and multiply.* ⁷ We have seen that all the righteous were adorned in good works. Yea, and the Lord Himself having adorned Himself with worlds rejoiced. ⁸ Seeing then that we have this pattern, let us conform ourselves with all diligence to His will; let us with all our strength work the work of righteousness.

34

¹ The good workman receiveth the bread of his work with boldness, but the slothful and careless dareth not look his employer in the face. ² It is therefore needful that we should be zealous unto well doing, for of Him are all things: ³ since He forewarneth us saying, *Behold, the Lord, and His reward is before His face, to recompense each man according to his work.* ⁴ He exhorteth us therefore to believe on Him with our whole heart, and to be not idle nor careless unto every good work. ⁵ Let our boast and our confidence be in Him: let us submit ourselves to His will; let us mark the whole host of His angels, how they stand by and minister unto His will. ⁶ For the scripture saith, *Ten thousands of ten thousands stood by Him, and thousands of thousands ministered unto Him: and they cried aloud, Holy, holy, holy is the Lord of Sabaoth; all creation is full of His glory.* ⁷ Yea, and let us ourselves then, being gathered together in concord with intentness of heart, cry unto Him as from one mouth earnestly that we may be made partakers of His great and glorious promises. ⁸ For He saith, *Eye hath not seen and ear hath not heard, and it hath not entered into the heart of man what great things He hath prepared for them that patiently await Him.*

35

¹ How blessed and marvelous are the gifts of God, dearly beloved!! ² Life in immortality, splendor in righteousness, truth in boldness, faith in confidence, temperance in sanctification! And all these things fall under our apprehension. ³ What then, think ye, are the things preparing for them that patiently await Him? The Creator and Father of the ages, the All holy One Himself knoweth their number and their beauty. ⁴ Let us therefore contend, that we may be found in the number of those that patiently await Him, to the end that we may be partakers of His promised gifts. ⁵ But how shall this be, dearly beloved? If our mind be fixed through faith towards God; if we seek out those things which are well pleasing and acceptable unto Him; if we accomplish such things as beseem His faultless will, and follow the way of truth, casting off from ourselves all unrighteousness and iniquity, covetousness, strifes, malignities and deceits, whisperings and backbitings, hatred of God, pride and arrogance, vainglory and inhospitality. ⁶ For they that do these things are hateful to God; and not only they that do them, but they also that consent unto them. ⁷ For the scripture saith, *But unto the sinner said God, Wherefore dost thou declare Mine ordinances, and takest My covenant upon thy lips?* ⁸ *Yet Thou didst hate instruction and didst cast away My words behind thee. If thou sawest a thief thou didst keep company with him, and with the adulterers thou didst set thy portion. Thy mouth multiplied wickedness and thy tongue wove deceit. Thou sattest and spakest against thy brother, and against the son of thy mother thou didst lay a stumbling block.* ⁹ *These things Thou hast done, and I kept silence. Thou thoughtest, unrighteous man, that I should be like unto thee.* ¹⁰ *I will convict thee and will set thee face to face with thyself.* ¹¹ *Now understand ye these things, ye that forget God, lest at any time He seize you as a lion, and there*

be none to deliver. ¹² *The sacrifice of praise shall glorify Me, and there is the way wherein I will show him the salvation of God.*

36

¹ This is the way, dearly beloved, wherein we found our salvation, even Jesus Christ the High priest of our offerings, the Guardian and Helper of our weakness. ² Through Him let us look steadfastly unto the heights of the heavens; through Him we behold as in a mirror His faultless and most excellent visage; through Him the eyes of our hearts were opened; through Him our foolish and darkened mind springeth up unto the light; through Him the Master willed that we should taste of the immortal knowledge *Who being the brightness of His majesty is so much greater than angels, as He hath inherited a more excellent name.* ³ For so it is written *Who maketh His angels spirits and His ministers aflame of fire* ⁴ but of His Son the Master said thus, *Thou art My Son, I this day have begotten thee. Ask of Me, and I will give Thee the Gentiles for Thine inheritance, and the ends of the earth for Thy possession.* ⁵ And again He saith unto Him *Sit Thou on My right hand, until I make Thine enemies a footstool for Thy feet.* ⁶ Who then are these enemies? They that are wicked and resist His will.

37

¹ Let us therefore enlist ourselves, brethren, with all earnestness in His faultless ordinances. ² Let us mark the soldiers that are enlisted under our rulers, how exactly, how readily, how submissively, they execute the orders given them. ³ All are not prefects, nor rulers of thousands, nor rulers of hundreds, nor rulers of fifties, and so forth; but each man in his own rank executeth the orders given by the king and the governors. ⁴ The great without the small cannot exist, neither the small without the great. There is a certain mixture in all things, and therein is utility. ⁵ Let us take our body as an example. The head without the feet is nothing; so likewise the feet without the head are nothing: even the smallest limbs of our body are necessary and useful for the whole body: but all the members conspire and unite in subjection, that the whole body maybe saved.

38

¹ So in our case let the whole body be saved in Christ Jesus, and let each man be subject unto his neighbor, according as also he was appointed with his special grace. ² Let not the strong neglect the weak; and let the weak respect the strong. Let the rich minister aid to the poor; and let the poor give thanks to God, because He hath given him one through whom his wants may be supplied. Let the wise display his wisdom, not in words, but in good works. He that is lowly in mind, let him not bear testimony to himself, but leave testimony to be borne to him by his neighbor. He that is pure in the flesh, let him be so, and not boast, knowing that it is Another who bestoweth his continence upon him. ³ Let us consider, brethren, of what matter we were made; who and what manner of beings we were, when we came into the world; from what a sepulchre and what darkness He that molded and created us brought us into His world, having prepared His benefits aforehand ere ever we were born. ⁴ Seeing therefore that we have all these things from Him, we ought in all things to give thanks to Him, to whom be the glory for ever and ever. Amen.

39

¹ Senseless and stupid and foolish and ignorant men jeer and mock at us, desiring that they themselves should be exalted in their imaginations. ² For what power hath a mortal? or what strength hath a child of earth? ³ For it is written; *There was no form before mine eyes; only I heard a breath and a voice.* ⁴ *What then? Shall a mortal be clean in the sight of the Lord; or shall a man be unblamable for his works? seeing that He is distrustful against His servants and noteth some perversity against His angels.* ⁵ *Nay, the heaven is not clean in His sight. Away then, ye that dwell in houses of clay, whereof, even of the same clay, we ourselves are made. He smote them like a moth, and from morn to even they are no more. Because they could not succor themselves, they perished.* ⁶ *He breathed on them and they died, because they had no wisdom.* ⁷ *But call thou, if perchance one shall obey thee, or if thou shalt see one of the holy angels. For wrath killeth the foolish man, and envy slayeth him that has gone astray.* ⁸ *And I have seen fools throwing out roots, but forthwith their habitation was eaten up.* ⁹ *Far be their sons from safety. May they be mocked at the gates of inferiors, and there shall be none to deliver them. For the things which are prepared for them, the righteous shall eat; but they themselves shall not be delivered from evils.*

40

¹ Forasmuch then as these things are manifest beforehand, and we have searched into the depths of the Divine knowledge, we ought to do all things in order, as many as the Master hath commanded us to perform at their appointed seasons. ² Now the offerings and ministrations He commanded to be performed with care, and not to be done rashly or in disorder, but at fixed times and seasons. ³ And where and by whom He would have them performed, He Himself fixed by His supreme will: that all things being done with piety according to His good pleasure might be acceptable to His will. ⁴ They therefore that make their offerings at the appointed seasons are acceptable and blessed: for while they follow the institutions of the Master they cannot go wrong. ⁵ For unto the high priest his proper services have been assigned, and to the priests their proper office is appointed, and upon the levites their proper ministrations are laid. The layman is bound by the layman's ordinances.

41

¹ Let each of you, brethren, in his own order give thanks unto God, maintaining a good conscience and not transgressing the appointed rule of his service, but acting with all seemliness. ² Not in every place, brethren, are the continual daily sacrifices offered, or the freewill offerings, or the sin offerings and the trespass offerings, but in Jerusalem alone. And even there the offering is not made in every place, but before the sanctuary in the court of the altar; and this too through the high priest and the afore said ministers, after that the victim to be offered hath been inspected for blemishes. ³ They therefore who do any thing contrary to the seemly ordinance of His will receive death as the penalty. ⁴ Ye see, brethren, in proportion as greater knowledge hath been vouchsafed unto us, so much the more are we exposed to danger.

42

¹ The Apostles received the Gospel for us from the Lord Jesus Christ; Jesus Christ was sent forth from God. ² So then Christ is from God, and the Apostles are from Christ. Both therefore came of the will of God in the appointed order. ³ Having therefore received a charge, and having been fully assured through the resurrection of our Lord Jesus Christ and confirmed in the word of God with full assurance of the Holy Ghost, they went forth with the glad tidings that the kingdom of God should come. ⁴ So preaching everywhere in country and town, they appointed their firstfruits, when they had proved them by the Spirit, to be bishops and deacons unto them that should believe. ⁵ And this they did in no new fashion; for indeed it had been written concerning bishops and deacons from very ancient times; for thus saith the scripture in a certain place, *I will appoint their bishops in righteousness and their deacons in faith.*

43

¹ And what marvel, if they which were entrusted in Christ with such a work by God appointed the aforesaid persons? seeing that even the blessed Moses who was a *faithful servant in all His house* recorded for a sign in the sacred books all things that were enjoined upon him. And him also the rest of the prophets followed, bearing witness with him unto the laws that were ordained by him. ² For he, when jealousy arose concerning the priesthood, and there was dissension among the tribes which of them was adorned with the glorious name, commanded the twelve chiefs of the tribes to bring to him rods inscribed with the name of each tribe. And he took them and tied them and sealed them with the signet rings of the chiefs of the tribes, and put them away in the tabernacle of the testimony on the table of God. ³ And having shut the tabernacle he sealed the keys and likewise also the doors. ⁴ And he said unto them, Brethren, the tribe whose rod shall bud, this hath God chosen to be priests and ministers unto Him. ⁵ Now when morning came, he called together all Israel, even the six hundred thousand men, and showed the seals to the chiefs of the tribes and opened the tabernacle of the testimony and drew forth the rods. And the rod of Aaron was found not only with buds, but also bearing fruit. ⁶ What think ye, dearly beloved? Did not Moses know beforehand that this would come to pass? Assuredly he knew it. But that disorder might not arise in Israel, he did thus, to the end that the Name of the true and only God might be glorified: to whom he the glory for ever and ever. Amen...

44

¹ And our Apostles knew through our Lord Jesus Christ that there would be strife over the name of the bishop's office. ² For this cause therefore, having received complete foreknowledge, they appointed the aforesaid persons, and afterwards they provided a continuance, that if these should fall asleep, other approved men should succeed to their ministration. Those therefore who were appointed by them, or afterward by other men of repute with the consent of the whole Church, and have ministered unblamably to the flock of Christ in lowliness of mind, peacefully and with all modesty, and for long time have borne a good report with all these men we consider to be unjustly thrust out from their ministration. ³ For it will be no light sin for us, if we thrust out those who have offered the gifts of the bishop's office unblamably and holily. ⁴ Blessed are those presbyters who have gone before, seeing that their departure was fruitful and ripe: for they have no fear lest any one should remove them from their appointed place. ⁵ For we see that ye have displaced certain persons, though they were living

honorably, from the ministration which had been respected by them blamelessly.

45

¹ Be ye contentious, brethren, and jealous about the things that pertain unto salvation. ² Ye have searched the scriptures, which are true, which were given through the Holy Ghost; ³ and ye know that nothing unrighteous or counterfeit is written in them. Ye will not find that righteous persons have been thrust out by holy men. ⁴ Righteous men were persecuted, but it was by the lawless; they were imprisoned, but it was by the unholy. They were stoned by transgressors: they were slain by those who had conceived a detestable and unrighteous jealousy. ⁵ Suffering these things, they endured nobly. ⁶ For what must we say, brethren? Was Daniel cast into the lions' den by them that feared God? ⁷ Or were Ananias and Azarias and Misael shut up in the furnace of fire by them that professed the excellent and glorious worship of the Most High? Far be this from our thoughts. Who then were they that did these things? Abominable men and full of all wickedness were stirred up to such a pitch of wrath, as to bring cruel suffering upon them that served God in a holy and blameless purpose, not knowing that the Most High is the champion and protector of them that in a pure conscience serve His excellent Name: unto whom be the glory for ever and ever. Amen. ⁸ But they that endured patiently in confidence inherited glory and honor; they were exalted, and had their names recorded by God in their memorial for ever and ever. Amen.

46

¹ To such examples as these therefore, brethren, we also ought to cleave. ² For it is written; *Cleave unto the saints, for they that cleave unto them shall be sanctified.* ³ And again He saith in another place; *With the guiltless man thou shalt be guiltless, and with the elect thou shalt be elect, and with the crooked thou shalt deal crookedly.* ⁴ Let us therefore cleave to the guiltless and righteous: and these are the elect of God. ⁵ Wherefore are there strifes and wraths and factions and divisions and war among you? ⁶ Have we not one God and one Christ and one Spirit of grace that was shed upon us? And is there not one calling in Christ? ⁷ Wherefore do we tear and rend asunder the members of Christ, and stir up factions against our own body, and reach such a pitch of folly, as to forget that we are members one of another? ⁸ Remember the words of Jesus our Lord: for He said, *Woe unto that man; it were good for him if he had not been born, rather than that at he should offend one of Mine elect. It were better for him that a millstone were hanged about him, and be cast into the sea, than that he should pervert one of Mine elect.* ⁹ Your division hath perverted many; it hath brought many to despair, many to doubting, and all of us to sorrow. And your sedition still continueth.

47

¹ Take up the epistle of the blessed Paul the Apostle. ² What wrote he first unto you in the beginning of the Gospel? ³ Of a truth he charged you in the Spirit concerning himself and Cephas and Apollos, because that even then ye had made parties. ⁴ Yet that making of parties brought less sin upon you; for ye were partisans of Apostles that were highly reputed, and of a man approved in their sight. ⁵ But now mark ye, who they are that have perverted you and diminished the glory of your renowned love for the brotherhood. ⁶ It is shameful, dearly beloved, yes, utterly shameful and unworthy of your conduct in Christ, that it should be reported that the very steadfast and ancient Church of the Corinthians, for the sake of one or two persons, maketh sedition against its presbyters. ⁷ And this report hath reached not only us, but them also which differ from us, so that ye even heap blasphemies on the Name of the Lord by reason of your folly, and moreover create peril for yourselves.

48

¹ Let us therefore root this out quickly, and let us fall down before the Master and entreat Him with tears, that He may show Himself propitious and be reconciled unto us, and may restore us to the seemly and pure conduct which belongeth to our love of the brethren. ² For this is a gate of righteousness opened unto life, as it is written; *Open me the gates of righteousness, that I may enter in thereby and preach the Lord.* ³ *This is the gate of the Lord; the righteous shall enter in thereby.* ⁴ Seeing then that many gates are opened, this is that gate which is in righteousness, even that which is in Christ, whereby all are blessed that have entered in and direct their path in holiness and righteousness, performing all things without confusion. ⁵ Let a man be faithful, let him be able to expound a deep saying, let him be wise in the discernment of words, let him be strenuous in deeds, let him be pure; ⁶ for so much the more ought he to be lowly in mind, in proportion as he seemeth to be the greater; and he ought to seek the common advantage of all, and not his own.

49

¹ Let him that hath love in Christ fulfill the commandments of Christ. ² Who can declare the bond of the love of God? ³ Who is sufficient to tell the majesty of its beauty? ⁴ The height, where unto love exalteth, is unspeakable. ⁵ Love joineth us unto God; *love covereth a multitude of sins;* love endureth all things, is long-suffering in all things. There is nothing coarse, nothing arrogant in love. Love hath no divisions, love maketh no seditions, love doeth all things in concord. In love were all the elect of God made perfect; without love nothing is well pleasing to God: ⁶ in love the Master took us unto Himself; for the love which He had toward us, Jesus Christ our Lord hath given His blood for us by the will of God, and His flesh for our flesh and His life for our lives.

50

¹ Ye see, dearly beloved, how great and marvelous a thing is love, and there is no declaring its perfection. ² Who is sufficient to be found therein, save those to whom God shall vouchsafe it? Let us therefore entreat and ask of His mercy, that we may be found blameless in love, standing apart from the factiousness of men. All the generations from Adam unto this day have passed away: but they that by God's grace were perfected in love dwell in the abode of the pious; and they shall be made manifest in the visitation of the Kingdom of God. ³ For it is written; *Enter into the closet for a very little while until Mine anger and Mine wrath shall pass away, and I will remember a good day and will raise you from your tombs.* ⁴ Blessed were we, dearly beloved, if we should be doing the commandments of God in concord of love, to the end that our sins may through love be forgiven us. ⁵ For it is written; *Blessed are they whose iniquities are forgiven, and whose sins are covered. Blessed is the man to whom the Lord shall impute no sin, neither is guile in his mouth.* ⁶ This declaration of blessedness was pronounced upon them that have been elected by God through Jesus Christ our Lord, to whom be the glory for ever and ever. Amen.

51

¹ For all our transgressions which we have committed through any of the wiles of the adversary, let us entreat that we may obtain forgiveness. Yea and they also, who set themselves up as leaders of faction and division, ought to look to the common ground of hope. ² For such as walk in fear and love desire that they themselves should fall into suffering rather than their neighbors; and they pronounce condemnation against themselves rather than against the harmony which hath been handed down to us nobly and righteously. ³ For it is good for a man to make confession of his trespasses rather than to harden his heart, as the heart of those was hardened who made sedition against Moses the servant of God; whose condemnation was clearly manifest, ⁴ for they went down to hades alive, and *Death shall be their shepherd.* ⁵ Pharaoh and his host and all the rulers of Egypt, *their chariots and their horsemen,* were overwhelmed in the depths of the Red Sea, and perished for none other reason but because their foolish hearts were hardened after that the signs and the wonders had been wrought in the land of Egypt by the hand of Moses the servant of God.

52

¹ The Master, brethren, hath need of nothing at all. He desireth not anything of any man, save to confess unto Him. ² For the elect David saith; *I will confess unto the Lord, and it shall please Him more than a young calf that groweth horns and hoofs. Let the poor see it, and rejoice.* ³ For a sacrifice unto God is a broken spirit. **52:3** And again He saith; *Sacrifice to God a sacrifice of praise, and pay thy vows to the Most High: and call upon Me in the day of thine affliction, and I will deliver thee, and thou shalt glorify Me.* **52:4** *For a sacrifice unto God is a broken spirit.*

53

¹ For ye know, and know well, the sacred scriptures, dearly beloved, and ye have searched into the oracles of God. We write these things therefore to put you in remembrance. ² When Moses went up into the mountain and had spent forty days and forty nights in fasting and humiliation, God said unto him; *Moses, Moses, come down, quickly hence, for My people whom thou leadest forth from the land of Egypt have wrought iniquity: they have transgressed quickly out of the way which thou didst command unto them: they have made for themselves molten images.* ³ *And the Lord said unto him; I have spoken unto thee once and twice, saying, I have seen this people, and behold it is stiff-necked. Let Me destroy them utterly, and I will blot out their name from under heaven, and I will make of thee a nation great and wonderful and numerous more than this.* ⁴ And Moses said; *Nay, not so, Lord Forgive this people their sin, or blot me also out of the book of the living.* ⁵ O mighty love! O unsurpassable perfection! The servant is bold with his Master; he asketh forgiveness for the multitude, or he demandeth that himself also be blotted out with them.

54

¹ Who therefore is noble among you? Who is compassionate? Who is fulfilled with love? ² Let him say; If by reason of me there be faction and strife and divisions, I retire, I depart, whither ye will, and I do that which is ordered by the people: only let the flock of Christ be at peace with its duly appointed presbyters. ³ He that shall have done this, shall win for himself great renown in Christ, and every place will receive him: for *the earth is the Lord's and the fullness thereof*. ⁴ Thus have they done and will do, that live as citizens of that kingdom of God which bringeth no regrets.

55

¹ But, to bring forward examples of Gentiles also; many kings and rulers, when some season of pestilence pressed upon them, being taught by oracles have delivered themselves over to death, that they might rescue their fellow citizens through their own blood. Many have retired from their own cities, that they might have no more seditions. ² We know that many among ourselves have delivered themselves to bondage, that they might ransom others. Many have sold themselves to slavery, and receiving the price paid for themselves have fed others. ³ Many women being strengthened through the grace of God have performed many manly deeds. ⁴ The blessed Judith, when the city was beleaguered, asked of the elders that she might be suffered to go forth into the camp of the aliens. ⁵ So she exposed herself to peril and went forth for love of her country and of her people which were beleaguered; and the Lord delivered Holophernes into the hand of a woman. ⁶ To no less peril did Esther also, who was perfect in faith, expose herself, that she might deliver the twelve tribes of Israel, when they were on the point to perish. For through her fasting and her humiliation she entreated the all seeing Master, the God of the ages; and He, seeing the humility of her soul, delivered the people for whose sake she encountered the peril.

56

¹ Therefore let us also make intercession for them that are in any transgression, that forbearance and humility may be given them, to the end that they may yield not unto us, but unto the will of God. For so shall the compassionate remembrance of them with God and the saints be fruitful unto them, and perfect. ² Let us accept chastisement, whereat no man ought to be vexed, dearly beloved. The admonition which we give one to another is good and exceeding useful; for it joineth us unto the will of God. ³ For thus saith the holy word; *The Lord hath indeed chastened me, and hath not delivered me over unto death.* ⁴ *For whom the Lord loveth He chasteneth, and scourgeth every son whom He receiveth.* ⁵ *For the righteous,* it is said, *shall chasten me in mercy and shall reprove me, but let not the mercy of sinners anoint my head.* ⁶ And again He saith; *Blessed is the man whom the Lord hath reproved, and refuse not thou the admonition of the Almighty. For He causeth pain, and he restoreth again:* ⁷ *He hath smitten, and His hands have healed.* ⁸ *Six times shall He rescue thee from afflictions and at the seventh no evil shall touch thee.* ⁹ *In famine he shall deliver thee from death, and in war He shall release thee from the arm of the sword.* ¹⁰ *And from the scourge of the tongue He shall hide thee and thou shalt not be afraid when evils approach.* ¹¹ *Thou shalt laugh at the unrighteous and wicked, and of the wild beasts thou shalt not be afraid.* ¹² *For wild beasts shall be at peace with thee.* ¹³ *Then shalt thou know that thy house shall be at peace: and the abode of thy tabernacle shall not go wrong,* ¹⁴ *and thou shalt know that thy seed is many, and thy children as the plenteous herbage of the field.* ¹⁵ *And thou shalt come to the grave as ripe corn reaped in due season, or as the heap of the threshing floor gathered together at the right time.* ¹⁶ Ye see, dearly beloved, how great protection there is for them that are chastened by the Master: for being a kind father He chasteneth us to the end that we may obtain mercy through His holy chastisement.

57

¹ Ye therefore that laid the foundation of the sedition, submit yourselves unto the presbyters and receive chastisement unto repentance, bending the knees of your heart. ² Learn to submit yourselves, laying aside the arrogant and proud stubbornness of your tongue. For it is better for you to be found little in the flock of Christ and to have your name on God's roll, than to be had in exceeding honor and yet be cast out from the hope of Him. ³ For thus saith the All virtuous Wisdom; *Behold I will pour out for you a saying of My breath, and I will teach you My word.* ⁴ *Because I called and ye obeyed not, and I held out words and ye heeded not, but made My councils of none effect, and were disobedient unto My reproofs; therefore I also will laugh at your destruction, and will rejoice over you when ruin cometh upon you, and when confusion overtaketh you suddenly, and your overthrow is at hand like a whirlwind,* ⁵ *or when ye call upon Me, yet will I not here you. Evil men shall seek me and not find me: for they hated wisdom, and chose not the fear of the Lord, neither would they give head unto My councils, but mocked at My reproofs.* ⁶ *Therefore they shall eat the fruits of their own way, and shall be filled with their own ungodliness.* ⁷ *For because they wronged babes, they shall be slain, and inquisition shall destroy the ungodly. But he that heareth Me shall dwell safely trusting in hope, and shall be quiet from all fear of all evil.*

58

¹ Let us therefore be obedient unto His most holy and glorious Name, thereby escaping the threatenings which were spoken of old by the mouth of Wisdom against them which disobey, that we may dwell safely, trusting in the most holy Name of His majesty. ² Receive our counsel, and ye shall have no occasion of regret. For as God liveth, and the Lord Jesus Christ liveth, and the Holy Spirit, who are the faith and the hope of the elect, so surely shall he, who with lowliness of mind and instant in gentleness hath without regretfulness performed the ordinances and commandments that are given by God, be enrolled and have a name among the number of them that are saved through Jesus Christ, through whom is the glory unto Him for ever and ever. Amen.

59

¹ But if certain persons should be disobedient unto the words spoken by Him through us, let them understand that they will entangle themselves in no slight transgression and danger; ² but we shall be guiltless of this sin. And we will ask, with instancy of prayer and supplication, that the Creator of the universe may guard intact unto the end the number that hath been numbered of His elect throughout the whole world, through His beloved Son Jesus Christ, through whom He called us from darkness to light, from ignorance to the full knowledge of the glory of His Name. ³ [Grant unto us, Lord,] that we may set our hope on Thy Name which is the primal source of all creation, and open the eyes of our hearts, that we may know Thee, who alone abidest *Highest in the lofty, Holy in the holy;* who *layest low in the insolence of the proud,* who *settest the lowly on high*, and *bringest the lofty low;* who *makest rich and makest poor;* who *killest and makest alive;* who alone art the Benefactor of spirits and the God of all flesh; who *lookest into the abysses*, who scanest the works of man; the Succor of them that are in peril, the *Savior of them that are in despair*; The Creator and Overseer of every spirit; who multipliest the nations upon earth, and hast chosen out from all men those that love Thee through Jesus Christ, Thy beloved Son, through whom Thou didst instruct us, didst sanctify us, didst honor us. ⁴ We beseech Thee, Lord and Master, to be *our help and succor*. Save those among us who are in tribulation; have mercy on the lowly; lift up the fallen; show Thyself unto the needy; heal the ungodly; convert the wanderers of Thy people; feed the hungry; release our prisoners; raise up the weak; comfort the fainthearted. *Let all the Gentiles know that Thou art the God alone*, and Jesus Christ is Thy Son, and *we are Thy people and the sheep of Thy pasture.*

60

¹ Thou through Thine operations didst make manifest the everlasting fabric of the world. Thou, Lord, didst create the earth. Thou that art faithful throughout all generations, righteous in Thy judgments, marvelous in strength and excellence, Thou that art wise in creating and prudent in establishing that which Thou hast made, that art good in the things which are seen and faithful with them that trust on Thee, *pitiful and compassionate*, forgive us our iniquities and our unrighteousnesses and our transgressions and shortcomings. ² Lay not to our account every sin of Thy servants and Thine handmaids, but cleanse us with the cleansing of Thy truth, and *guide our steps to walk in holiness* and righteousness and singleness *of heart* and *to do such things as are good and well pleasing in Thy sight* and in the sight of our rulers. ³ Yea, Lord, *make Thy face to shine upon us* in peace for our good, that we may be sheltered *by Thy mighty hand and* delivered from every sin *by Thine uplifted arm.* And deliver us from them that hate us wrongfully. ⁴ Give concord and peace to us and to all that dwell on the earth, as Thou gavest to our fathers, *when they called on* Thee *in faith and truth* with holiness, [that we may be saved,] while we render obedience to Thine almighty and most excellent Name, and to our rulers and governors upon the earth.

61

¹ Thou, Lord and Master, hast given them the power of sovereignty through Thine excellent and unspeakable might, that we knowing the glory and honor which Thou hast given them may submit ourselves unto them, in nothing resisting Thy will. Grant unto them therefore, O Lord, health peace, concord, stability, that they may administer the government which Thou hast given them without failure. ² For Thou, O heavenly Master, King of the ages, givest to the sons of men glory and honor and power over all things that are upon the earth. Do Thou, Lord, direct their counsel according to that which is good and well pleasing in Thy sight, that, administering in peace and gentleness with Godliness the power which Thou hast given them, they may obtain Thy favor. ³ O Thou, who alone art able to do these things and things far more exceeding good than these for us, we praise Thee

through the High priest and Guardian of our souls, Jesus Christ, through whom be the glory and the majesty unto Thee both now and for all generations and for ever and ever. Amen.

62

¹ As touching those things which befit our religion and are most useful for a virtuous life to such as would guide [their steps] in holiness and righteousness, we have written fully unto you, brethren. ² For concerning faith and repentance and genuine love and temperance and sobriety and patience we have handled every argument, putting you in remembrance, that ye ought to please Almighty God in righteousness and truth and long suffering with holiness, laying aside malice and pursuing concord in love and peace, being instant in gentleness; even as our fathers, of whom we spake before, pleased Him, being lowly minded toward their Father and God and Creator and towards all men. ³ And we have put you in mind of these things the more gladly, since we knew well that we were writing to men who are faithful and highly accounted and have diligently searched into the oracles of the teaching of God.

63

¹ Therefore it is right for us to give heed to so great and so many examples and to submit the neck and occupying the place of obedience to take our side with them that are the leaders of our souls, that ceasing from this foolish dissension we may attain unto the goal which lieth before us in truthfulness, keeping aloof from every fault. ² For ye will give us great joy and gladness, if ye render obedience unto the things written by us through the Holy Spirit, and root out the unrighteous anger of your jealousy, according to the entreaty which we have made for peace and concord in this letter. ³ And we have also sent faithful and prudent men that have walked among us from youth unto old age unblamably, who shall also be witnesses between you and us. ⁴ And this we have done that ye might know that we have had, and still have, every solicitude that ye should be speedily at peace.

64

¹ Finally may the All seeing God and Master of spirits and Lord of all flesh, who chose the Lord Jesus Christ, and us through Him for a peculiar people, grant unto every soul that is called after His excellent and holy Name faith, fear, peace, patience, long-suffering, temperance, chastity and soberness, that they may be well pleasing unto His Name through our High priest and Guardian Jesus Christ, through whom unto Him be glory and majesty, might and honor, both now and for ever and ever. Amen.

65

¹ Now send ye back speedily unto us our messengers Claudius Ephebus and Valerius Bito, together with Fortunatus also, in peace and with joy, to the end that they may the more quickly report the peace and concord which is prayed for and earnestly desired by us, that we also may the more speedily rejoice over your good order. ² The grace of our Lord Jesus Christ be with you and with all men in all places who have been called by God and through Him, through whom be glory and honor, power and greatness and eternal dominion, unto Him, from the ages past and forever and ever. Amen.

The Second Epistle of Clement to the Corinthians

1

That we ought to value our salvation; and to skew that we do, by a sincere obedience.

¹ BRETHREN, we ought so to think of Jesus Christ as of God: as of the judge of the living, and the dead; nor should we think any less of our salvation. ² For if we think meanly of him, we shall hope only to receive some small things from him. ³ And if we do so; we shall sin; not considering from whence we have been called, and by whom, and to what place; and how much Jesus Christ vouchsafed to suffer for our sakes. ⁴ What recompense then shall we render unto him? Or what fruit that may be worthy of what he has given to us? ⁵ For indeed how great are those advantages which we owe to him in relation to our holiness? He has illuminated us: as a father, he has called us his children; he has saved us who were lost and undone. ⁶ What praise shall we give to him? Or what reward that may be answerable to those things which we have received? ⁷ We were defective in our understandings; worshipping stones and wood; gold, and silver, and brass, the works of men's hands; and our whole life was nothing else but death. ⁸ Wherefore being encompassed with darkness, and having such a mist before our eyes, we have looked up, and through his will have laid aside the cloud wherewith we were surrounded. ⁹ For he had compassion upon us, and being moved in his bowels towards us, he saved us; having beheld in us much error, and destruction; and seen that we had no hope of salvation, but only through him. ¹⁰ For he called us who were not; and was pleased from nothing to give us being.

2

1 That God had before prophesied by Isaiah, that the Gentiles should be saved. 8 That this ought to engage such especially to live well; without which they will still miscarry.

¹ REJOICE, thou barren, that bearest not, break forth and cry thou that travailest not; for she that is desolate hath many more children than she that hath an husband. ² In that he said, Rejoice thou barren that bearest not, he spake of us: for our church was barren before that children were given unto it. ³ And again; when he said, Cry thou that travailest not; he implied thus much: That after the manner of women in travail, we should not cease to put up our prayers unto God abundantly. ⁴ And for what follows, because she that is desolate hath more children than she that hath an husband: it was therefore added, because our people which seem to have been forsaken by God, now believing in him, are become more than they who seemed to have God. ⁵ And another Scripture saith, I came not to call the righteous but sinners (to repentance). The meaning of which is this: that those who were lost must be saved. ⁶ For that is, indeed, truly great and wonderful, not to confirm those things that are yet standing, but those which are falling. ⁷ Even so did it seem good to Christ to save what was lost; and when he came into the world, he saved many, and called us who were already lost. ⁸ Seeing then he has shewed so great mercy towards us; and chiefly for that, we who are alive, do now no longer sacrifice to dead Gods, nor pay any worship to them, but have by him been brought to the knowledge of the Father of truth. ⁹ Whereby shall we shew that we do indeed know him, but by not denying him by whom we have come to the knowledge of him? ¹⁰ For even he himself saith, Whosoever shall confess me before men, him will I confess before my Father. This therefore is our reward if we shall confess him by whom we have been saved. ¹¹ But, wherein must we confess him?–Namely, in doing those things which he saith, and not disobeying his commandments: by worshipping him not with our lips only, but with all our heart, and with all our mind. For he saith in Isaiah: This people honoureth me with their lips, but their heart is far from me. ¹² Let us then not only call him Lord; for that will not save us. For he saith: Not every one that saith unto me Lord, Lord, shall be saved, but he that doeth righteousness. ¹³ Wherefore, brethren, let us confess him by our works; by loving one another; in not committing adultery, not speaking evil against each other, not envying one another; but by being temperate, merciful, good. ¹⁴ Let us also have a mutual sense of one another's sufferings; and not be covetous of money: but let us, by our good works, confess God, and not by those that are otherwise. ¹⁵ Also let us not fear men: but rather God. Wherefore, if we should do such wicked things, the Lord hath said: Though ye should be joined unto me, even in my very bosom, and not keep my commandments, I would cast you off, and say unto you: Depart from me; I know not whence you are, ye workers of iniquity.

3

1 That whilst we secure the other world, we need not fear what can befal us in this. 5 That if we follow the interests of this present world, we cannot escape the punishment of the other. 10 Which ought to bring us to repentance and holiness, 14 and that presently: because in this world is the only time for repentance.

¹ WHEREFORE, brethren, leaving willingly for conscience sake our sojourning in this world, let us do the will of him who has called us, and not fear to depart out of this world. ² For the Lord saith, Ye shall be as sheep in the midst of wolves. Peter answered and said, What if the wolves shall tear in pieces the sheep? Jesus said unto Peter, Let not the sheep fear the wolves after death: And ye also fear not those that kill you, and after that have no more that they can do unto you; but fear him who after you are dead, has power to cast both soul and body into hell-fire. ³ For consider, brethren, that the sojourning of this flesh in the present world, is but little, and of a short continuance, but the promise of Christ is great and wonderful, even the rest of the kingdom that is to come, and of eternal life. ⁴ What then must we do that we may attain unto it?–We must order our conversation holily and righteously, and look upon all the things of this world as none of ours, and not desire them. For, if we desire to possess them we fall from the way of righteousness. ⁵ For thus saith the Lord, No servant can serve two masters. If therefore we shall desire to serve God and Mammon it will be without profit to us. For what will it profit, if one gain the whole world, and lose his own soul? ⁶ Now this world and that to come are two enemies. This speaketh of adultery and corruption, of covetousness and deceit; but renounces these things. ⁷ We cannot, therefore, be the friends of both; but we must resolve by forsaking the one, to enjoy the other. And we think it is better to hate the present things, as little, short-lived, and corruptible, and to love those which are to come, which are truly good and incorruptible. ⁸ For, if we do the will of Christ, we shall find rest: but if not, nothing shall deliver us from eternal punishment if we shall disobey his commands. For even thus saith the Scripture in the prophet Ezekiel, If Noah, Job, and Daniel should rise up, they shall not deliver their children in captivity. ⁹ Wherefore, if such righteous men are not able by their righteousness to deliver their children; how can we hope to enter into the kingdom of God, except we keep our baptism holy and undefiled? Or who shall be our advocate, unless we shall be found to have done what is holy and just? ¹⁰ Let us, therefore, my brethren, contend with all earnestness, knowing that our combat is at hand; and that many go long voyages to encounter for a corruptible reward. ¹¹ And yet all are not crowned, but they only that labour much, and strive gloriously. Let us, therefore, so contend, that we may all be crowned. Let us run in the straight road, the race that is incorruptible: and let us in great numbers pass unto it, and strive that we may receive the crown. But and if we cannot all be crowned, let us come as near to it as we are able. ¹² Moreover, we must consider, that he who contends in a corruptible combat, if he be found doing anything that is not fair, is taken away and scourged, and cast out of the lists. What think ye then that he shall suffer, who does anything that is not fitting in the combat of immortality? ¹³ Thus speaks the prophet concerning those who keep not their seal; Their worm shall not die, and their fire shall not be quenched; and they shall be for a spectacle unto all flesh. ¹⁴ Let us therefore repent, whilst we are yet upon the earth: for we are as clay in the hand of the artificer. For as the potter if he make a vessel, and it be turned amiss in his hands, or broken, again forms it anew; but if he have gone so far as to throw it into the furnace of fire, he can no more bring any remedy to it. ¹⁵ So we, whilst we are in this world, should repent with our whole heart for whatsoever evil we have done in the flesh; while we have yet the time of repentance, that we may be saved by the Lord. ¹⁶ For after we shall have departed out of this world, we shall no longer be able to confess our sins or repent in the other. ¹⁷ Wherefore, brethren, let us doing the will of the Father, and keeping our flesh pure, and observing the commandments of the Lord, lay hold on eternal life: for the Lord saith in the gospel, If ye have not kept that which was little, who will give you that which is great?–For I say unto you, he that is faithful in that which is least, is faithful also in much. ¹⁸ This, therefore, is what he saith; keep your bodies pure, and your seal without spot, that ye may receive eternal life.

4

1 We shall rise, and be judged in our bodies; therefore we must live well in them, 6 that we ought, for our own interest, to live well; though few seem to mind what really is for their advantage, 10 and not deceive ourselves: seeing God will certainly judge us, and render to all of us according to our works.

¹ AND let not any one among you say, that this very flesh is not judged, neither raised up. Consider, in what were you saved; in what did you look up, if not whilst you were in this flesh. ² We must, therefore, keep our flesh as the temple of God. For in like manner as ye were called in the flesh ye shall also come to judgment in the flesh. Our one Lord Jesus Christ, who has saved us, being first a spirit, was made flesh, and so called us; even so we also shall in this flesh receive the reward. ³ Let us, therefore, love one another, that we may attain unto the kingdom of God. Whilst we have time to be healed, let us deliver up ourselves to God our physician, giving our reward unto him. ⁴ And what reward shall we give?–Repentance out of a pure heart. For he knows all things before hand, and searches out our very hearts. ⁵ Let us, therefore, give praise unto him: not only with our mouths, but with all our souls; that he may receive us as children. For so the Lord hath said; They are my brethren, who do the will of my father. ⁶ Wherefore, my brethren, let us do the will of the Father, who hath called us, that we may live. Let us pursue virtue, and forsake wickedness, which leadeth us into sins; and let us flee all ungodliness, that evils overtake us not. ⁷ For, if we shall do our diligence to live well, peace shall follow us. And yet how hard is it to find a man that does this? For almost all are led by human fears, choosing rather the present enjoyments, than the future promise. ⁸ For they know not how great a torment the present enjoyments bring with them; nor what delights the future promise ⁹ And if they themselves only did this, it might the more easily be endured; but now they go on to infect innocent souls with their evil doctrines; not knowing that both themselves, and those that hear them, shall receive a double condemnation. ¹⁰ Let us, therefore, serve God with a pure heart, and we shall be righteous: but if we shall not serve him because we do not believe the promise of God, we shall be miserable. ¹¹ For thus saith the prophet; Miserable are the double minded who doubt in their heart, and say, these things we have heard, even in the time of our fathers, but we have seen none of them, though we have expected them from day to day. ¹² O ye fools! compare yourselves to a tree; take the vine for an example. First it sheds its leaves, then it buds, then come the sour grapes, then the ripe fruit; even so my people have borne its disorders and afflictions, but shall hereafter receive good things. ¹³ Wherefore my brethren, let us not doubt in our minds, but let us expect with hope, that we may receive our reward; for he is faithful, who has promised he will render to every one a reward according to his works. ¹⁴ If, therefore, we shall do what is just in the sight of God we shall enter into his kingdom, I and shall receive the promises; Which neither eye has seen, nor ear heard, nor have entered into the heart of man. ¹⁵ Wherefore let us every hour expect the kingdom of God in love and righteousness; because we know not the day of God's appearing.

5

A Fragment.
Of the Lord's kingdom.

¹ For the Lord himself, being asked by a certain person, When his kingdom should come? answered, When two shall be one, and that which is without as that which is within; and the male with the female, neither male nor female. ² Now *two are one*, when we speak the truth to each other, and there is (without hypocrisy) one soul in two bodies: ³ *And that which is without as that which is within;*–He means this: he calls the soul that which is within, and the body that which is without. As therefore thy body appears, so let thy soul be seen by its good works. ⁴ *And the male with the female neither male nor female;*–He means this; he calls our anger the male, our concupiscence the female. ⁵ When therefore a man is come to such a pass that he is subject neither to the one nor the other of these (both of which, through the prevalence of custom, and an evil education, cloud and darken the reason,) ⁶ But rather, having dispelled the mist arising from them, and being full of shame, shall by repentance have united both his soul and spirit in the obedience of reason; then, as Paul says, there is in us neither male nor female

The Shepherd of Hermas

Vision 1

1

[1] The master, who reared me, had sold me to one Rhoda in Rome. After many years, I met her again, and began to love her as a sister. [2] After a certain time I saw her bathing in the river Tiber; and I gave her my hand, and led her out of the river. So, seeing her beauty, I reasoned in my heart, saying, "Happy were I, if I had such an one to wife both in beauty and in character." I merely reflected on this and nothing more. [3] After a certain time, as I was journeying to Cumae, and glorifying God's creatures for their greatness and splendor and power, as I walked I fell asleep. And a Spirit took me, and bore me away through a pathless tract, through which no man could pass: for the place was precipitous, and broken into clefts by reason of the waters. When then I had crossed the river, I came into the level country, and knelt down, and began to pray to the Lord and to confess my sins. [4] Now, while I prayed, the heaven was opened, and I see the lady, whom I had desired, greeting me from heaven, saying, "Good morrow, Hermas." [5] And, looking at her, I said to her, "Lady, what doest thou here?" Then she answered me, "I was taken up, that I might convict thee of thy sins before the Lord." [6] I said to her, "Dost thou now convict me?" "Nay, not so," said she, "but hear the words, that I shall say to thee. God, Who dwelleth in the heavens, and created out of nothing the things which are, and increased and multiplied them for His holy Church's sake, is wroth with thee, for that thou didst sin against me." [7] I answered her and said, "Sin against thee? In what way? Did I ever speak an unseemly word unto thee? Did I not always regard thee as a goddess? Did I not always respect thee as a sister? How couldst thou falsely charge me, lady, with such villainy and uncleanness? [8] "Laughing she saith unto me, "The desire after evil entered into thine heart. Nay, thinkest thou not that it is an evil deed for a righteous man, if the evil desire should enter into his heart? It is indeed a sin and a great one too," saith she; "for the righteous man entertaineth righteous purposes. While then his purposes are righteous, his repute stands steadfast in the heavens, and he finds the Lord easily propitiated in all that he does. But they that entertain evil purposes in their hearts, bring upon themselves death an captivity, especially they that claim for themselves this present world and boast in its riches, and cleave not to the good things that are to come. [9] Their souls shall rue it, seeing that they have no hope, but have abandoned themselves and their life. But do thou pray unto God and He shall heal thine own sins, and those of thy whole house, and of all the saints."

2

[1] As soon as she had spoken these words the heavens were shut and I was given over to horror and grief Then I said within myself "If this sin is recorded against me, how can I be saved? Or how shall I propitiate God for my sins which are full-blown? Or with which words shall I entreat the Lord that He may be propitious unto me? [2] While I was advising and discussing these matters in my heart, I see, before me a great white chair of snow-white wool; and there came an aged lady in glistening raiment, having a book in her hands, and she sat down alone, and she saluted me, "Good morrow, Hermas." Then I grieved and weeping, said, "Good morrow, lady." [3] And she said to me "Why so gloomy, Hermas, thou that art patient and good-tempered and art always smiling? Why so downcast in thy looks, and far from cheerful?" And I said to her, "Because of an excellent lady's saying that I had sinned against her." [4] Then she said, "Far be this thing from the servant of God! Nevertheless the thought did enter into thy heart concerning her. Now to the servants of God such a purpose bringeth sin. For it is an evil and mad purpose to overtake a devout spirit that hath been already approved, that it should desire an evil deed, and especially if it be Hermas the temperate, who abstaineth from every evil desire, and is full of all simplicity and of great guilelessness.

3

[1] "Yet it is not for this that God is wroth with thee, but that thou mayest convert thy family, that hath done wrong against the Lord and against you their parents. But out of fondness for thy children thou didst not admonish thy family, but didst suffer it to become fearfully corrupt. Therefore the Lord is wroth with thee. But He will heal all thy past sins, which have been committed in thy family; for by reason of their sins and iniquities thou hast been corrupted by the affairs of this world. [2] But the great mercy of the Lord had pity on thee and thy family, and will strengthen thee, and establish thee in His glory. Only be not thou careless, but take courage, and strengthen thy family. For as the smith hammering his work conquers the task which he wills, so also doth righteous discourse repeated daily conquer all evil. Cease not therefore to reprove thy children; for I know that if they shall repent with all their heart, they shall be written in the books of life with the saints." [3] After these words of hers had ceased, she saith unto me, "Wilt thou listen to me as I read?" Then say I, "Yes, lady." She saith to me, "Be attentive, and hear the glories of God" I listened with attention and with wonder to that which I had no power to remember; for all the words were terrible, such as man cannot bear. The last words however I remembered, for they were suitable for us and gentle. [4] "Behold, the God of Hosts, Who by His invisible and mighty power and by His great wisdom created the world, and by His glorious purpose clothed His creation with comeliness, and by His strong word fixed the heaven, and founded the earth upon the waters, and by His own wisdom and providence formed His holy Church, which also He blessed-behold, He removeth the heavens and the mountains and the hills and the seas, and all things are made level for His elect, that He may fulfill to them the promise which He promised with great glory and rejoicing, if so be that they shall keep the ordinances of God, which they received, with great faith."

4

[1] When then she finished reading and arose from her chair, there came four young men, and they took away the chair, and departed towards the East. [2] Then she calleth me unto her, and she touched my breast, and saith to me, "Did my reading please thee?" And I say unto her, "Lady, these last words please me, but the former were difficult and hard." Then she spake to me, saying, "These last words are for the righteous, but the former are for the heathen and the rebellious." [3] While she yet spake with me, two men appeared, and took her by the arms, and they departed, whither the chair also had gone, towards the East. And she smiled as she departed and, as she was going, she saith to me, "Play the man, Hermas."

Vision 2

5

[1] I was on the way to Cumae, at the same season as last year, and called to mind my last year's vision as I walked; and again a Spirit taketh me, and carrieth me away to the same place as last year. [2] When then I arrived at the place, I fell upon my knees, and began to pray to the Lord, and to glorify His name, for that he counted me worthy, and made known unto me my former sins. [3] But after I had risen up from prayer, I behold before me the aged lady, whom also I had seen last year, walking and reading a little book. And she saith to me, "Canst thou report these things to the elect of God?" I say unto her, "Lady, I cannot recollect so much; but give me the little book, that I may copy it." "Take it," saith she, "and be sure and return it to me." [4] I took it, and retiring to a certain spot in the country I copied it letter for letter: for I could not make out the syllables. When then I had finished the letters of the book, suddenly the book was snatched out of my hand; but by whom I did not see.

6

[1] Now after fifteen days, when I had fasted and entreated the Lord earnestly, the knowledge of the writing was revealed to me. And this is what was written:– [2] "Thy seed, Hermas, have sinned against God, and have blasphemed the Lord, and have betrayed their parents through great wickedness, yea, they have got the name of betrayers of parents, and yet they did not profit by their betrayal; and they still further added to their sins wanton deeds and reckless wickedness; and so the measure of their transgressions was filled up. [3] But make these words known to all thy children, and to thy wife who shall be as thy sister; for she too refraineth not from using her tongue, wherewith she doeth evil. But, when she hears these words, she will refrain, and will find mercy. [4] After that thou hast made known unto them all these words, which the Master commanded me that they should be revealed unto thee, then all their sins which they sinned aforetime are forgiven to them; yea, and to all the saints that have sinned unto this day, if they repent with their whole heart, and remove double-mindedness from their heart. [5] For the Master sware by His own glory, as concerning His elect; that if, now that this day has been set as a limit, sin shall hereafter be committed, they shall not find salvation; for repentance for the righteous hath an end; the days of repentance are accomplished for all the saints; whereas for the Gentiles there is repentance until the last day. [6] Thou shalt therefore say unto the elders of the Church, that they direct their paths in righteousness, that they may receive in full the promises with abundant glory. [7] Ye therefore that work righteousness be steadfast, and be not double-minded, that ye may have admission with the holy angels. Blessed are ye, as many as endure patiently the great tribulation that cometh, and as many as shall not deny their life. [8] For the Lord swear concerning His Son, that those who denied their Lord should be rejected from their life, even they that are now about to deny Him in the coming days; but to those who denied Him aforetime, to them mercy was given of His great loving kindness.

7

[1] "But do thou, Hermas, no longer bear a grudge against thy children, neither suffer thy sister to have her way, so that they may be purified from their former sins. For they shall be chastised with a righteous chastisement, unless thou bear a grudge against them thyself. The bearing of a grudge worketh death. But thou, Hermas, hast had great tribulations of thine own, by reason of the transgressions of thy family, because thou hadst no care for them. For thou wast neglectful of them, and wast mixed up with thine evil transactions. [2] But herein is thy salvation, in that thou didst not depart from the living God, and in thy simplicity and thy great continence. These have saved thee, if thou abidest therein; and they save all who do such things, and walk in guilelessness and simplicity. These men prevail over all wickedness, and continue unto life eternal. [3] Blessed are all they that work righteousness. They shall never be destroyed. [4] But thou shalt say to Maximus, "Behold tribulation cometh (upon thee), if thou think fit to deny a second time. The Lord is nigh unto them that turn unto him, as it is written in Eldad and Modat, who prophesied to the people in the wilderness."

8

[1] Now, brethren, a revelation was made unto me in my sleep by a youth of exceeding fair form, who said to me, "Whom thinkest thou the aged woman, from whom thou receivedst the book, to be?" I say, "The Sibyl" "Thou art wrong," saith he, "she is not." "Who then is she?" I say. "The Church," saith he. I said unto him, "Wherefore then is she aged?" "Because," saith he, "she was created before all things; therefore is she aged; and for her sake the world was framed." [2] And afterwards I saw a vision in my house. The aged woman came, and asked me, if I had already given the book to the elders. I said that I had not given it. "Thou hast done well," she said, "for I have words to add. When then I shall have finished all the words, it shall be made known by thy means to all the elect. [3] Thou shalt therefore write two little books, and shalt send one to Clement, and one to Grapte. So Clement shall send to the foreign cities, for this is his duty; while Grapte shall instruct the widows and the orphans. But thou shalt read (the book) to this city along with the elders that preside over the Church.

Vision 3

9

[1] The third vision, which I saw, brethren, was as follows. [2] After fasting often, and entreating the Lord to declare unto me the revelation which He promised to show me by the mouth of the aged woman, that very night the aged woman was seen of me, and she said to me, "Seeing that thou art so importunate and eager to know all things, come into the country where thou abidest, and about the fifth hour I will appear, and will show thee what thou oughtest to see." [3] I asked her, saying, "Lady, to what part of the country?" "Where thou wilt," saith she. I selected a beautiful and retired spot; but before I spoke to her and named the spot, she saith to me, "I will come, whither thou willest." [4] I went then, brethren, into the country, and I counted up the hours, and came to the place where I appointed her to come, and I see an ivory couch placed there, and on the couch there lay a linen cushion, and on the cushion was spread a coverlet of fine linen of flax. [5] When I saw these things so ordered, and no one in the place, I was amazed, and a fit of trembling seized me, and my hair stood on end; and a fit of shuddering came upon me, because I was alone. When then I recovered myself, and remembered the glory of God, and took courage, I knelt down and confessed my sins to the Lord once more, as I had done on the former occasion. [6] Then she came with six young men, the same whom I had seen before, and she stood by me, and listened attentively to me, as I prayed and confessed my sins to the Lord. And she touched me, and said: "Hermas, make an end of constantly entreating for thy sins; entreat also for righteousness, that thou mayest take some part forthwith to thy family." [7] Then she raiseth me by the hand, and leadeth me to the couch, and saith to the young men, "Go ye, and build." [8] And after the young men had retired and we were left alone, she saith to me, "Sit down here." I say to her, "Lady, let the elders sit down first." "Do as I bid thee," saith she, "sit down." [9] When then I wanted to sit down on the right side, she would not allow me, but beckoned me with her hand that I should sit on the left side. As then I was musing thereon, and was sad because she would not permit me to sit on the right side, she saith to me, "Art thou sad, Hermas?" The place on the right side is for others, even for those who have already been well-pleasing to God, and have suffered for the Name's sake. But thou lackest much that thou shouldest sit with them; but as thou abidest in thy simplicity, even so, and thou shalt sit with them, thou and as many as shall have done their deeds, and have suffered what they suffered."

10

[1] "What did they suffer?" say I. "Listen," saith she. "Stripes, imprisonments, great tribulations, crosses, wild beasts, for the Name's sake. Therefore to them belongs the right side of the Holiness–to them, and to all who shall suffer for the Name. But for the rest is the left side. Howbeit, to both, to them that sit on the right, and to them that sit on the left, are the same gifts, and the same promises, only they sit on the right and have a certain glory. [2] Thou indeed art very desirous to sit on the right with them, but thy shortcomings are many; yet thou shalt be purified from thy shortcomings; yea, and all that are not double-minded shall be purified from all their sins unto this day." [3] When she had said this, she wished to depart; but, falling at her feet, I entreated her by the Lord that she would show me the vision which she promised. [4] Then she again took me by the hand, and raiseth me, and seateth me on the couch at the left hand, while she herself sat on the right. And lifting up a certain glistening rod, she saith to me, "Seest thou a great thing?" I say to her, "Lady, I see nothing." She saith to me, "Look thou; dost thou not see in front of thee a great tower being builded upon the waters, of glistening square stones?" [5] Now the tower was being builded foursquare by the six young men that came with her. And countless other men were bringing stones, some of them from the deep, and others from the land, and were handing them to the six young men. And they took them and builded. [6] The stones that were dragged from the deep they placed in every case, just as they were, into the building, for they had been shaped, and they fitted in their joining with the other stones; and they adhered so closely one with another that their joining could not possibly be detected; and the building of the tower appeared as if it were built of one stone. [7] But of the other stones which were brought from the dry land, some they threw away, and some they put into the building; and others they broke in pieces, and threw to a distance from the tower. [8] Now many other stones were lying round the tower, and they did not use them for the building; for some of them were mildewed, and others had cracks in them, and others were too short, and others were white and round, and did not fit into the building. [9] And I saw other stones thrown to a distance from the tower, and coming to the way, and yet not staying in the way, but rolling to where there was no way; and others falling into the fire and burning there; and others falling near the waters, and yet not able to roll into the water, although they desired to roll and to come to the water.

11

[1] When she had shown me these things, she wished to hurry away. I say to her, "Lady, what advantage is it to me to have seen these things, and yet not to know what the things mean? "She answered and said unto me, "Thou art an over-curious fellow, in desiring to know all that concerns the tower." "Yea, lady," I said, "that I may announce it to my brethren, and that they [may be the more gladdened and] when they hear [these things] they may know the Lord in great glory." Then said she, [2] "Many shall hear; but when they hear, some of them shall be glad, and others shall weep. Yet even these latter, if they hear and repent, shall likewise be glad. Hear thou therefore the parables of the tower; for I will reveal all things unto thee. And trouble me no more about revelation; for these revelations have an end, seeing that they have been completed. Nevertheless thou wilt not cease asking for revelations; for thou art shameless." [3] The tower, which thou seest building, is myself, the Church, which was seen of thee both now and aforetime. Ask, therefore, what thou willest concerning the tower, and I will reveal it unto thee, that thou mayest rejoice with the saints." [4] I say unto her, "Lady, since thou didst hold me worthy once for all, that thou shouldest reveal all things to me, reveal them." Then she saith to me, "Whatsoever is possible to be revealed to thee, shall be revealed. Only let thy heart be with God, and doubt not in thy mind about that which thou seest." [5] I asked her, "Wherefore is the tower builded upon waters, lady?" "I told thee so before," said she, "and indeed thou dost enquire diligently. So by thy enquiry thou discoverest the truth. Hear then why the tower is builded upon waters; it is because your life is saved and shall be saved by water. But the tower has been founded by the word of the Almighty and Glorious Name, and is strengthened by the unseen power of the Master."

12

[1] I answered and said unto her, "Lady, this thing is great and marvelous. But the six young men that build, who are they, lady?" "These are the holy angels of God, that were created first of all, unto whom the Lord delivered all His creation to increase and to build it, and to be masters of all creation. By their hands therefore the building of the tower will be accomplished." [2] "And who are the others who are bringing the stones in?" "They also are holy angels of God; but these six are superior to them. The building of the tower then shall be accomplished, and all alike shall rejoice in the (completed) circle of the tower, and shall glorify God that the building of the tower was accomplished." [3] I enquired of her, saying, "Lady, I could wish to know concerning the end of the stones, and their power, of what kind it is." She answered and said unto me, "It is not that thou of all men art especially worthy that it should be revealed to thee; for there are others before thee, and better than thou art, unto whom these visions ought to have been revealed. But that the name of God may be glorified, it hath been

revealed to thee, all shall be revealed, for the sake of the doubtful-minded, who question in their hearts whether these things are so or not. Tell them that all these things are true, and that there is nothing beside the truth, but that all are steadfast, and valid, and established on a firm foundation.

13

[1] "Hear now concerning the stones that go to the building The stones that are squared and white, and that fit together in their joints, these are the apostles and bishops and teachers and deacons, who walked after the holiness of God, and exercised their office of bishop and teacher and deacon in purity and sanctity for the elect of God, some of them already fallen on sleep, and others still living. And because they always agreed with one another, they both had peace among themselves and listened one to another. Therefore their joinings fit together in the building of the tower." [2] "But they that are dragged from the deep, and placed in the building, and that fit together in their joinings with the other stones that are already builded in, who are they?" "These are they that suffered for the name of the Lord." [3] "But the other stones that are brought from the dry land, I would fain know who these are, lady." She said, "Those that go to the building, and yet are not hewn, these the Lord hath approved because they walked in the uprightness of the Lord, and rightly performed His commandments." [4] "But they that are brought and placed in the building, who are they?" "They are young in the faith, and faithful; but they are warned by the angels to do good, because wickedness was found in them." [5] "But those whom they rejected and threw away, who are they?" "These have sinned, and desire to repent, therefore they were not cast to a great distance from the tower, because they will be useful for the building, if they repent. They then that shall repent, if they repent, will be strong in the faith, if they repent now while the tower is building. But if the building shall be finished, they have no more any place, but shall be castaways. This privilege only they have, that they lie near the tower.

14

[1] But wouldst thou know about them that are broken in pieces, and cast away far from the tower? These are the sons of lawlessness. They received the faith in hypocrisy, and no wickedness was absent from them. Therefore they have not salvation, for they are not useful for building by reason of their wickednesses. Therefore they were broken up and thrown far away by reason of the wrath of the Lord, for they excited Him to wrath. [2] But the rest whom thou hast seen lying in great numbers, not going to the building, of these they that are mildewed are they that knew the truth, but did not abide in it, nor cleave to the saints. Therefore they are useless." [3] "But they that have the cracks, who are they?" "These are they that have discord in their hearts against one another, and are not at peace among themselves; who have an appearance of peace, but when they depart from one another, their wickednesses abide in their hearts. These are the cracks which the stones have. [4] But they that are broken off short, these have believed, and have their greater part in righteousness, but have some parts of lawlessness; therefore they are too short, and are not perfect." [5] "But the white and round stones, which did not fit into the building, who are they, lady?" She answered and said to me, "How long art thou foolish and stupid, and enquirest everything, and understandest nothing? These are they that have faith, but have also riches of this world. When tribulation cometh, they deny their Lord by reason of their riches and their business affairs." [6] And I answered and said unto her, "When then, lady, will they be useful for the building?" "When," she replied, "their wealth, which leadeth their souls astray, shall be cut away, then will they be useful for God. For just as the round stone, unless it be cut away, and lose some portion of itself, cannot become square, so also they that are rich in this world, unless their riches be cut away, cannot become useful to the Lord. [7] Learn first from thyself When thou hadst riches, thou wast useless; but now thou art useful and profitable unto life. Be ye useful unto God, for thou thyself also art taken from the same stones.

15

[1] "But the other stones which thou sawest cast far away from the tower and falling into the way and rolling out of the way into the regions where there is no way, these are they that have believed, but by reason of their double heart they abandon their true way. Thus thinking that they can find a better way, they go astray and are sore distressed, as they walk about in the regions where there is no way. [2] But they that fall into the fire and are burned, these are they that finally rebelled from the living God, and it no more entered into their hearts to repent by reason of the lusts of their wantonness and of the wickednesses which they wrought. [3] But the others, which are near the waters and yet cannot roll into the water, wouldest thou know who are they? These are they that heard the word, and would be baptized unto the name of the Lord. Then, when they call to their remembrance the purity of the truth, they change their minds, and go back again after their evil desires." [4] So she finished the explanation of the tower. [5] Still importunate, I asked her further, whether for all these stones that were rejected and would not fit into the building of the tower that was repentance, and they had a place in this tower. "They can repent," she said, "but they cannot be fitted into this tower. [6] Yet they shall be fitted into another place much more humble, but not until they have undergone torments, and have fulfilled the days of their sins. And they shall be changed for this reason, because they participated in the Righteous Word; and then shall it befall them to be relieved from their torments, if the evil deeds, that they have done, come into their heart; but if these come not into their heart, they are not saved by reason of the hardness of their hearts."

16

[1] When then I ceased asking her concerning all these things, she saith to me; "Wouldest thou see something else?" Being very desirous of beholding, I was greatly rejoiced that I should see it. [2] She looked upon me, and smiled, and she saith to me, "Seest thou seven women round the tower?" "I see them, lady," say I. "This tower is supported by them by commandment of the Lord. [3] Hear now their employments. The first of them, the woman with the strong hands, is called Faith; through her are saved the elect of God. [4] And the second, that is girded about and looketh like a man, is called Continence; she is the daughter of Faith. Whosoever then shall follow her, becometh happy in his life, for he shall refrain from all evil deeds, believing that, if he refrain from every evil desire, he shall inherit eternal life." [5] "And the others, lady, who be they?" "They are daughters one of the other. The name of the one is Simplicity, of the next, Knowledge, of the next, Guilelessness, of the next, Reverence, of the next, Love. When then thou shalt do all the works of their mother, thou canst live." [6] "I would fain know, lady," I say, "what power each of them possesseth." "Listen then," saith she, "to the powers which they have. [7] Their powers are mastered each by the other, and they follow each other, in the order in which they were born. From Faith is born Continence, from Continence Simplicity, from Simplicity Guilelessness, from Guilelessness Reverence, from Reverence Knowledge, from Knowledge Love. Their works then are pure and reverent and divine. [8] Whosoever therefore shall serve these women, and shall have strength to master their works, shall have his dwelling in the tower with the saints of God." [9] Then I asked her concerning the seasons, whether the consummation is even now. But she cried aloud, saying, "Foolish man, seest thou not that the tower is still a-building? Whensoever therefore the tower shall be finished building, the end cometh; but it shall be built up quickly. Ask me no more questions: this reminder is sufficient for you and for the saints, and is the renewal of your spirits. [10] But it was not revealed to thyself alone, but in order that thou mightest show these things unto all. After three days– [11] for thou must understand first, and I charge thee, Hermas, first with these words, which I am about to speak to thee–(I charge thee to) tell all these things into the ears of the saints, that hearing them and doing them they may be purified from their wickednesses, and thyself also with them."

17

[1] "Hear me, my children. I brought you up in much simplicity and guilelessness and reverence, through the mercy of the Lord, Who instilled righteousness into you, that ye might be justified and sanctified from all wickedness and all crookedness. But ye will not to cease from your wickedness. [2] Now then hear me and be at peace among yourselves, and have regard one to another, and assist one another, and do not partake of the creatures of God alone in abundance, but share them also with those that are in want. [3] For some men through their much eating bring weakness on the flesh, and injure their flesh: whereas the flesh of those who have nought to eat is injured by their not having sufficient nourishment, and their body is ruined. [4] This exclusiveness therefore is hurtful to you that have and do not share with them that are in want. [5] Look ye to the judgment that cometh. Ye then that have more than enough, seek out them that are hungry, while the tower is still unfinished; for after the tower is finished, ye will desire to do good, and will find no place for it. [6] Look ye therefore, ye that exult in your wealth, lest they that are in want shall moan, and their moaning shall go up unto the Lord, and ye with your [abundance of good things be shut outside the door of the tower. [7] Now therefore I say unto you that are rulers of the Church, and that occupy the chief seats; be not ye like unto the sorcerers. The sorcerers indeed carry their drugs in boxes, but ye carry your drug and your poison in your heart. [8] Ye are case-hardened, and ye will not cleanse your hearts and mix your wisdom together in a clean heart, that ye may obtain mercy from the Great King. [9] Look ye therefore, children, lest these divisions of yours deprive you of your life. [10] How is it that ye wish to instruct the elect of the Lord, while ye yourselves have no instruction? Instruct one another therefore, and have peace among yourselves, that I also

may stand gladsome before the Father, and give an account concerning you all to your Lord."

18

[1] When then she ceased speaking with me, the six young men, who were building, came, and took her away to the tower, and other four lifted the couch, and took it also away to the tower. I saw not the face of these, for they were turned away. [2] And, as she went, I asked her to reveal to me concerning the three forms, in which she had appeared to me. She answered and said to me; "As concerning these things thou must ask another, that they may be revealed to thee." [3] Now she was seen of me, brethren, in my first vision of last year, as a very aged woman and seated on a chair. [4] In the second vision her face was youthful, but her flesh and her hair were aged, and she spake to me standing; and she was more gladsome than before. [5] But in the third vision she was altogether youthful and of exceeding great beauty, and her hair alone was aged; and she was gladsome exceedingly and seated on a couch. Touching these things I was very greatly anxious to learn this revelation. [6] And I see the aged woman in a vision of the night, saying to me, "Every enquiry needs humility. Fast therefore, and thou shalt receive what thou askest from the Lord." [7] So I fasted one day; and that very night there appeared unto me a young man, and he saith to me, "Seeing that thou askest me revelations offhand with entreaty, take heed lest by thy much asking thou injure thy flesh. [8] Sufficient for thee are these revelations. Canst thou see mightier revelations than those thou hast seen?" [9] I say unto him in reply, "Sir, this one thing alone I ask, concerning the three forms of the aged woman, that a complete revelation may be vouchsafed me." He saith to me in answer, How long are ye without understanding? It is your double-mindedness that maketh you of no understanding, and because your heart is not set towards the Lord." [10] I answered and said unto him again, "From thee, Sir, we shall learn the matters more accurately."

19

[1] Listen," saith he, "concerning the three forms, of which thou enquirest. [2] In the first vision wherefore did she appear to thee an aged woman and seated on a chair? Because your spirit was aged, and already decayed, and had no power by reason of your infirmities and acts of double-mindedness. [3] For as aged people, having no longer hope of renewing their youth, expect nothing else but to fall asleep, so ye also, being weakened with the affairs of this world gave yourselves over to repining, and cast not your cares on the Lord; but your spirit was broken, and ye were aged by your sorrows." [4] "Wherefore then she was seated on a chair, I would fain know, Sir." "Because every weak person sits on a chair by reason of his weakness, that the weakness of his body may be supported. So thou hast the symbolism of the first vision."

20

[1] "But in the second vision thou sawest her standing, and with her countenance more youthful and more gladsome than before; but her flesh and her hair aged. Listen to this parable also," saith he. [2] "Imagine an old man, who has now lost all hope of himself by reason of his weakness and his poverty, and expecteth nothing else save the last day of his life. Suddenly an inheritance is left him. He heareth the news, riseth up and full of joy clothes himself with strength, and no longer lieth down, but standeth up, and his spirit, which was now broken by reason of his former circumstances, is renewed again, and he no longer sitteth, but taketh courage; so also was it with you, when you heard the revelation which the Lord revealed unto you. [3] For He had compassion on you, and renewed your spirits, and ye laid aside your maladies, and strength came to you, and ye were made powerful in the faith, and the Lord rejoiced to see you put on your strength. And therefore He showed you the building of the tower; yea, and other things also shall He show you, if with your whole heart ye be at peace among yourselves.

21

[1] But in the third vision ye saw her younger and fair and gladsome, and her form fair. [2] For just as when to some mourner cometh some piece of good tidings, immediately he forgetteth his former sorrows, and admitteth nothing but the tidings which he hath heard, and is strengthened thenceforth unto that which is good, and his spirit is renewed by reason of the joy which he hath received; so also ye have received a renewal of your spirits by seeing these good things. [3] And whereas thou sawest her seated on a couch, the position is a firm on; for the couch has four feet and standeth firmly; for the world too Is upheld by means of four elements. [4] They then that have fully repented shall be young again, and founded firmly, seeing that they have repented with their whole heart. There thou hast the revelation entire and complete. Thou shalt ask nothing more as touching revelation– but if anything be lacking still, it shall be revealed unto thee."

Vision 4

22

[1] The fourth vision which I saw, brethren, twenty days after the former vision which came unto me, for a type of the impending tribulation. [2] I was going into the country by the Companion Way. From the high road, it is about ten stades; and the place is easy for traveling. [3] While then I am walking alone, I entreat the Lord that He will accomplish the revelations and the visions which He showed me through His holy Church, that He may strengthen me and may give repentance to His servants which have stumbled, that His great and glorious Name may be glorified, for that He held me worthy that He should show me His marvels. [4] And as I gave glory and thanksgiving to Him, there answered me as it were the sound of a voice, "Be not of doubtful mind, Hermas." I began to question in myself and to say, "How can I be of doubtful mind, seeing that I am so firmly founded by the Lord, and have seen glorious things?" [5] And I went on a little, brethren, and behold, I see a cloud of dust rising as it were to heaven, and I began to say within myself, "Can it be that cattle are coming, and raising a cloud of dust?" for it was just about a stade from me. [6] As the cloud of dust waxed greater and greater, I suspected that it was something supernatural. Then the sun shone out a little, and behold, I see a huge beast like some sea-monster, and from its mouth fiery locusts issued forth. And the beast was about a hundred feet in length, and its head was as it were of pottery. [7] And I began to weep, and to entreat the Lord that He would rescue me from it. And I remembered the word which I had heard, "Be not of doubtful mind, Hermas." [8] Having therefore, brethren, put on the faith of the Lord and called to mind the mighty works that He had taught me, I took courage and gave myself up to the beast. Now the beast was coming on with such a rush, that it might have ruined a city. [9] I come near it, and, huge monster as it was, it stretcheth itself on the ground, and merely put forth its tongue, and stirred not at all until I had passed by it. [10] And the beast had on its head four colors; black then fire and blood color, then gold, then white.

23

[1] Now after I had passed the beast, and had gone forward about thirty feet, behold, there meeteth me a virgin arrayed as if she were going forth from a bridal-chamber all in white and with white sandals, veiled up to her forehead, and her head-covering consisted of a turban, and her hair was white. [2] I knew from the former Visions that it was the Church, and I became more cheerful. She saluteth me, saying, "Good morrow, my good man"; and I saluted her in turn, "Lady, good morrow." [3] She answered and said unto me, "Did nothing meet thee? "I say unto her, Lady, such a huge beast, that could have destroyed whole peoples: but, by the power of the Lord and by His great mercy, I escaped it." [4] "Thou didst escape it well," saith she, "because thou didst cast thy care upon God, and didst open thy heart to the Lord, believing that thou canst be saved by nothing else but by His great and glorious Name. Therefore the Lord sent His angel, which is over the beasts, whose name is Segri, and shut his mouth that it might not hurt thee. Thou hast escaped a great tribulation by reason of thy faith, and because, though thou sawest so huge a beast, thou didst not doubt in thy mind. [5] Go therefore, and declare to the elect of the Lord His mighty works, and tell them that this beast is a type of the great tribulation which is to come. If therefore ye prepare yourselves beforehand, and repent (and turn) unto the Lord with your whole heart, ye shall be able to escape it, if your heart be made pure and without blemish, and if for the remaining days of your life ye serve the Lord blamelessly. Cast your cares upon the Lord and He will set them straight. [6] Trust ye in the Lord, ye men of doubtful mind, for He can do all things, yea, He both turneth away His wrath from you, and again He sendeth forth His plagues upon you that are of doubtful mind. Woe to them that hear these words and are disobedient; it were better for them that they had not been born."

24

[1] I asked her concerning the four colors, which the beast had upon its head. Then she answered me and said, "Again thou art curious about such matters." "Yes, lady," said I, "make known unto me what these things are." [2] "Listen," said she; "the black is this world in which ye dwell; [3] and the fire and blood color showeth that this world must perish by blood and fire; [4] and the golden part are ye that has escaped from this world. For as the gold is tested by the fire and is made useful, so ye also [that dwell in it] are being tested in yourselves. Ye then that abide and pass through the fire will be purified by it. For as the old loses its dross. so Ye also shall cast away all sorrow and tribulation, and shall be purified, and shall be useful for the building of the tower. [5] But the white portion is the coming age, in which the elect of God shall dwell; because the elect of God shall be without spot and pure unto life eternal. [6] Wherefore cease not thou to speak in the ears of the saints. Ye have now the symbolism also of the tribulation which is coming in power. But if ye be willing, it shall be nought. Remember ye the things that are written beforehand." [7] With these words she departed, and I

saw not in what direction she departed; for a noise was made: and I turned back in fear, thinking that the beast was coming.

Vision 5

25

¹ As I prayed in the house, and sat on the couch, there entered a man glorious in his visage, in the garb of a shepherd, with a white skin wrapped about him, and with a wallet on his shoulders and a staff in his hand. And he saluted me, and I saluted him in return. ² And he immediately sat down by my side, and he saith unto me, "I was sent by the most holy angel, that I might dwell with thee the remaining days of thy life." ³ I thought he came to tempt me, and I say unto him, "Why, who art thou? For I know," say I, "unto whom I was delivered." He saith to me, "Dost thou not recognize me?" "No," I say. "I," saith he, "am the shepherd, unto whom thou wast delivered." ⁴ While he was still speaking, his form was changed, and I recognized him as being the same, to whom I was delivered; and straightway I was confounded, and fear seized me, and I was altogether overwhelmed with distress that I had answered him so wickedly and senselessly. ⁵ But he answered and said unto me, "Be not confounded, but strengthen thyself in my commandments which I am about to command thee. For I was sent," saith he, "that I might show thee again all the things which thou didst see before, merely the heads which are convenient for you. First of all, write down my commandments and my parables; and the other matters thou shalt write down as I shall show them to thee. The reason why," saith he, "I command thee to write down first the commandments and parables is, that thou mayest read them off-hand, and mayest be able to keep them." ⁶ So I wrote down the commandments and parables, as he commanded me. ⁷ If then, when ye hear them, ye keep them and walk in them, and do them with a pure heart, ye shall receive from the Lord all things that He promised you; but if, when ye hear them, ye do not repent, but still add to your sins, ye shall receive from the Lord the opposite. All these the shepherd, the angel of repentance. commanded me to write.

Mandate 1

26

¹ "First of all, believe that God is One, even He who created all things and set them in order, and brought all things from non-existence into being, Who comprehendeth all things, being alone incomprehensible. ² Believe Him therefore, and fear Him, and in this fear be continent. Keep these things, and thou shalt cast off all wickedness from thyself, and shalt clothe thyself with every excellence of righteousness, and shalt live unto God, if thou keep this commandment."

Mandate 2

27

¹ He saith to me; "Keep simplicity and be guileless, and thou shalt be as little children, that know not the wickedness which destroyeth the life of men. ² First of all, speak evil of no man, neither take pleasure in listening to a slanderer. Otherwise thou that hearest too shalt be responsible for the sin of him that speaketh the evil, if thou believest the slander, which thou hearest; for in believing it thou thyself also wilt have a grudge against thy brother. So then shalt thou be responsible for the sin of him that speaketh the evil. ³ Slander is evil; it is a restless demon, never at peace, but always having its home among factions. Refrain from it therefore, and thou shalt have success at all times with all men. ⁴ But clothe thyself in reverence, wherein is no evil stumbling-block, but all things are smooth and gladsome. Work that which is good, and of thy labors, which God giveth thee, give to all that are in want freely, not questioning to whom thou shalt give, and to whom thou shalt not give. Give to all; for to all God desireth that there should be given of His own bounties. ⁵ They then that receive shall render an account to God why they received it, and to what end; for they that receive in distress shall not be judged, but they that receive by false pretence shall pay the penalty. ⁶ He then that giveth is guiltless; for as he received from the Lord the ministration to perform it, he hath performed it in sincerity, by making no distinction to whom to give or not to give. This ministration then, when sincerely performed, becomes glorious in the sight of God. He therefore that ministereth thus sincerely shall live unto God. ⁷ Therefore keep this commandment, as I have told thee, that thine own repentance and that of thy household may be found to be sincere, and [thy] heart pure and undefiled."

Mandate 3

28

¹ Again he saith to me; "Love truth, and let nothing but truth proceed out of thy mouth, that the Spirit which God made to dwell in this flesh, may be found true in the sight of all men; and thus shall the Lord, Who dwelleth in thee, be glorified; for the Lord is true in every word, and with Him there is no falsehood. ² They therefore that speak lies set the Lord at nought, and become robbers of the Lord, for they do not deliver up to Him the deposit which they received. For they received of Him a spirit free from lies. This if they shall return a lying spirit, they have defiled the commandment of the Lord and have become robbers." ³ When then I heard these things, I wept bitterly. But seeing me weep he saith, "Why weepest thou?" "Because, Sir," say I "I know not if I can be saved." "Why so?" saith he. "Because, Sir," I say, "never in my life spake I a true word, but I always lied deceitfully with all men and dressed up my falsehood as truth before all men; and no man ever contradicted me, but confidence was placed in my word. How then, Sir," say I, "can I live, seeing that I have done these things?" ⁴ "Your supposition," he saith, "is right and true, for it behoved thee as a servant of God to walk in truth, and no complicity with evil should abide with the Spirit of truth, nor bring grief to the Spirit which is holy and true." "Never, Sir," say I, "heard I clearly words such as these." ⁵ "Now then," saith he, "thou hearest. Guard them, that the former falsehoods also which thou spakest in thy business affairs may themselves become credible, now that these are found true; for they too can become trustworthy. If thou keep these things, and from henceforward speak nothing but truth, thou shalt be able to secure life for thyself And whosoever shall hear this command, and abstain from falsehood, that most pernicious habit, shall live unto God."

Mandate 4

29

¹ "I charge thee," saith he, "to keep purity, and let not a thought enter into thy heart concerning another's wife, or concerning fornication, or concerning any such like evil deeds; for in so doing thou commitest a great sin. But remember thine own wife always, and thou shalt never go wrong. ² For should this desire enter into thine heart, thou wilt go wrong, and should any other as evil as this, thou commitest sin. For this desire in a servant of God is a great sin; and if any man doeth this evil deed, he worketh out death for himself. ³ Look to it therefore. Abstain from this desire; for, where holiness dwelleth, there lawlessness ought not to enter into the heart of a righteous man." ⁴ I say to him, "Sir, permit me to ask thee a few more questions" "Say on," saith he. "Sir," say I, "if a man who has a wife that is faithful in the Lord detect her in adultery, doth the husband sin in living with her?" ⁵ "So long as he is ignorant," saith he, "he sinneth not; but if the husband know of her sin, and the wife repent not, but continue in her fornication, and her husband live with her, he makes himself responsible for her sin and an accomplice in her adultery." ⁶ "What then, Sir," say I, "shall the husband do, if the wife continue in this case?" "Let him divorce her," saith he, "and let the husband abide alone: but if after divorcing his wife he shall marry another, he likewise committeth adultery." ⁷ "If then, Sir," say I, "after the wife is divorced, she repent and desire to return to her own husband, shall she not be received?" ⁸ "Certainly," saith he, "if the husband receiveth her not, he sinneth and bringeth great sin upon himself; nay, one who hath sinned and repented must be received, yet not often; for there is but one repentance for the servants of God. For the sake of her repentance therefore the husband ought not to marry. This is the manner of acting enjoined on husband and wife. ⁹ Not only," saith he, "is it adultery, if a man pollute his flesh, but whosoever doeth things like unto the heathen committeth adultery. If therefore in such deeds as these likewise a man continue and repent not, keep away from him, and live not with him. Otherwise, thou also art a partaker of his sin. ¹⁰ For this cause ye were enjoined to remain single, whether husband or wife; for in such cases repentance is possible. ¹¹ I," said he, "am not giving an excuse that this matter should be concluded thus, but to the end that the sinner should sin no more. But as concerning his former sin, there is One Who is able to give healing; it is He Who hath authority over all things."

30

¹ I asked him again, saying, "Seeing that the Lord held me worthy that thou shouldest always dwell with me, suffer me still to say a few words, since I understand nothing, and my heart has been made dense by my former deeds. Make me to understand, for I am very foolish, and I apprehend absolutely nothing." ² He answered and said unto me, "I," saith he, "preside over repentance, and I give understanding to all who repent. Nay, thinkest thou not," saith he, "that this very act of repentance is understanding? To repent is great understanding," saith he. "For the man that hath sinned understandeth that he hath done evil before the Lord, and the deed which he hath done entereth into his heart, and he repenteth, and doeth no more evil, but doeth good lavishly, and humbleth his own soul and putteth it to torture because it sinned. Thou seest then that repentance is great understanding." ³ "It is on this account therefore, Sir," say I, "that I enquire everything accurately of thee; first, because I am a sinner; secondly, because I know not what deeds I must do that I may live, for my sins are many and various." ⁴ "Thou shalt live," saith he, "if thou keep my

commandments and walk in them and whosoever shall hear these commandments and keep them, shall live unto God."

31

[1] "I will still proceed, Sir," say I, "to ask a further question." "Speak on," saith he. "I have heard, Sir," say I, "from certain teachers, that there is no other repentance, save that which took place when we went down into the water and obtained remission of our former sins." [2] He saith to me; "Thou hast well heard; for so it is. For he that hath received remission of sins ought no longer to sin, but to dwell in purity. [3] But, since thou enquirest all things accurately, I will declare unto thee this also, so as to give no excuse to those who shall hereafter believe or those who have already believed, on the Lord. For they that have already believed, or shall hereafter believe, have not repentance for sins, but have only remission of their former sins. [4] To those then that were called before these days the Lord has appointed repentance. For the Lord, being a discerner of hearts and foreknowing all things, perceived the weakness of men and the manifold wiles of the devil, how that he will be doing some mischief to the servants of God, and will deal wickedly with them. [5] The Lord then, being very compassionate, had pity on His handiwork, and appointed this (opportunity of) repentance, and to me was given the authority over this repentance. [6] But I say unto you," saith he, "if after this great and holy calling any one, being tempted of the devil, shall commit sin, he hath only one (opportunity of) repentance. But if he sin off-hand and repent, repentance is unprofitable for such a man; for he shall live with difficulty." [7] I say unto him, "I was quickened unto life again, when I heard these things from thee so precisely. For I know that, if I shall add no more to my sins, I shall be saved." "Thou shalt be saved," he saith, "thou and all, as many as shall do these things."

32

[1] I asked him again, saying, "Sir, since once thou dost bear with me, declare unto me this further matter also." "Say on," saith he. "If a wife, Sir," say I, "or, it may be, a husband fall asleep, and one of them marry, doth the one that marrieth sin?" [2] "He sinneth not," saith he, "but if he remain single, he investeth himself with more exceeding honor and with great glory before the Lord; yet even if he should marry, he sinneth not. [3] Preserve purity and holiness therefore, and thou shalt live unto God. All these things, which I speak and shall hereafter speak unto thee, guard from this time forward, from the day when thou wast committed unto me, and I will dwell in thy house. [4] But for thy former transgressions there shall be remission, if thou keepest my commandments. Yea, and all shall have remission, if they keep these my commandments, and walk in this purity."

Mandate 5

33

[1] "Be thou long-suffering and understanding," he saith, "and thou shalt have the mastery over all evil deeds, and shalt work all righteousness. [2] For if thou art long-suffering, the Holy Spirit that abideth in thee shall be pure, not being darkened by another evil spirit, but dwelling in a large room shall rejoice and be glad with the vessel in which he dwelleth, and shall serve God with much cheerfulness, having prosperity in himself. [3] But if any angry temper approach, forthwith the Holy Spirit, being delicate, is straitened, not having [the] place clear, and seeketh to retire from the place; for he is being choked by the evil spirit, and has no room to minister unto the Lord, as he desireth, being polluted by angry temper. For the Lord dwelleth in long-suffering, but the devil in angry temper. [4] Thus that both the spirits then should be dwelling together is inconvenient and evil for that man in whom they dwell. [5] For if you take a little wormwood, and pour it into a jar of honey, is not the whole of the honey spoiled, and all that honey ruined by a very small quantity of wormwood? For it destroyeth the sweetness of the honey, and it no longer hath the same attraction for the owner, because it is rendered bitter and hath lost its use. But if the wormwood be not put into the honey, the honey is found sweet and becomes useful to its owner. [6] Thou seest [then] that long-suffering is very sweet, beyond the sweetness of honey, and is useful to the Lord, and He dwelleth in it. But angry, temper is bitter and useless. If then angry temper be mixed with long-suffering, long-suffering is polluted and the man's intercession is no longer useful to God." [7] "I would fain know, Sir," say I, "the working of angry temper, that I may guard myself from it." "Yea, verily," saith he, "if thou guard not thyself from it–thou and thy family–thou hast lost all thy hope. But guard thyself from it; for I am with thee. Yea, and all men shall hold aloof from it, as many as have repented with their whole heart. For I will be with them and will preserve them; for they all were justified by the most holy angel.

34

[1] "Hear now," saith he, "the working of angry temper, how evil it is, and how it subverteth the servants of God by its own working, and how it leadeth them astray from righteousness. But it doth not lead astray them that are full in the faith, nor can it work upon them, because the power of the Lord is with them; but them that are empty and double-minded it leadeth astray. [2] For when it seeth such men in prosperity it insinuates itself into the heart of the man, and for no cause whatever the man or the woman is embittered on account of worldly matters, either about meats, or some triviality, or about some friend, or about giving or receiving, or about follies of this kind. For all these things are foolish and vain and senseless and inexpedient for the servants of God. [3] But long-suffering is great and strong, and has a mighty and vigorous power, and is prosperous in great enlargement, gladsome, exultant, free from care, glorifying the Lord at every season, having no bitterness in itself, remaining always gentle and tranquil. This long-suffering therefore dwelleth with those whose faith is perfect. [4] But angry temper is in the first place foolish, fickle and senseless; then from foolishness is engendered bitterness, and from bitterness wrath, and from wrath anger, and from anger spite; then spite being composed of all these evil elements becometh a great sin and incurable. [5] For when all these spirits dwell in one vessel, where the Holy Spirit also dwelleth, that vessel cannot contain them, but overfloweth. [6] The delicate spirit therefore, as not being accustomed to dwell with an evil spirit nor with harshness, departeth from a man of that kind, and seeketh to dwell with gentleness and tranquillity. [7] Then, when it hath removed from that man, in whom it dwells, that man becometh emptied of the righteous spirit, and henceforward, being filled with the evil spirits, he is unstable in all his actions, being dragged about hither and thither by the evil spirits, and is altogether blinded and bereft of his good intent. Thus then it happeneth to all persons of angry temper. [8] Refrain therefore from angry temper, the most evil of evil spirits. But clothe thyself in long-suffering, and resist angry temper and bitterness, and thou shalt be round in company with the holiness which is beloved of the Lord. See then that thou never neglect this commandment; for if thou master this commandment, thou shalt be able likewise to keep the remaining commandments, which I am about to give thee. Be strong in them and endowed with power; and let all be endowed with power, as many as desire to walk in them."

Mandate 6

35

[1] I charged thee," saith he, "in my first commandment to guard faith and fear and temperance." "Yes, Sir," say I. "But now," saith he, "I wish to show thee their powers also, that thou mayest understand what is the power and effect of each one of them. For their effects are two fold. Now they are prescribed alike to the righteous and the unrighteous. [2] Do thou therefore trust righteousness, but trust not unrighteousness; for the way of righteousness is straight, but the way of unrighteousness is crooked. But walk thou in the straight [and level] path, and leave the crooked one alone. [3] For the crooked way has no tracks, but only pathlessness and many stumbling stones, and is rough and thorny. So it is therefore harmful to those who walk in it. [4] But those who walk in the straight way walk on the level and without stumbling: for it is neither rough nor thorny. Thou seest then that it is more expedient to walk in this way." [5] "I am pleased, Sir," say I, "to walk in this way." "Thou shalt walk," he saith, "yea, and whosoever shall turn unto the Lord with his whole heart shall walk in it.

36

[1] "Hear now," saith he, "concerning faith. There are two angels with a man, one of righteousness and one of wickedness." [2] "How then, Sir," say I, "shall I know their workings, seeing that both angels dwell with me?" [3] "Hear," saith he, "and understand their workings. The angel of righteousness is delicate and bashful and gentle and tranquil. When then this one enters into thy heart, forthwith he speaketh with thee of righteousness, of purity, of holiness, and of contentment, of every righteous deed and of every glorious virtue. When all these things enter into thy heart, know that the angel of righteousness is with thee. [These then are the works of the angel of righteousness.] Trust him therefore and his works. [4] Now see the works of the angel of wickedness also. First of all, he is quick tempered and bitter and senseless, and his works are evil, overthrowing the servants of God. Whenever then he entereth into thy heart, know him by his works." [5] "How I shall discern him, Sir," I reply, "I know not." Listen," saith he. "When a fit of angry temper or bitterness comes upon thee, know that he is in thee. Then the desire of much business and the costliness of many viands and drinking bouts and of many drunken fits and of various luxuries which are unseemly, and the desire of women, and avarice, and haughtiness and boastfulness, and whatsoever things are akin and like to these–when then these things enter into thy heart, know that the angel of wickedness is with thee. [6] Do thou therefore, recognizing his works, stand aloof from him, and trust him in nothing, for his works are evil and inexpedient for the servants of God. Here then thou hast the workings of both the angels. Understand

them, and trust the angel of righteousness. ⁷ But from the angel of wickedness stand aloof, for his teaching is evil in every matter; for though one be a man of faith, and the desire of this angel enter into his heart, that man, or that woman, must commit some sin. ⁸ And if again a man or a woman be exceedingly wicked, and the works of the angel of righteousness come into that man's heart, he must of necessity do something good. ⁹ Thou seest then," saith he, "that it is good to follow the angel of righteousness, and to bid farewell to the angel of wickedness. ¹⁰ This commandment declareth what concerneth faith, that thou mayest trust the works of the angel of righteousness, and doing them mayest live unto God. But believe that the works of the angel of wickedness are difficult; so by not doing them thou shalt live unto God."

Mandate 7

37

¹ "Fear the Lord," saith he, "and keep His commandments. So keeping the commandments of God thou shalt be powerful in every deed, and thy doing shall be incomparable. For whilst thou fearest the Lord, thou shalt do all things well. But this is the fear wherewith thou oughtest to be afraid, and thou shalt be saved. ² But fear not the devil; for, if thou fear the Lord, thou shalt be master over the devil, for there is no power in him. [For] in whom is no power, neither is there fear of him; but in whom power is glorious, of him is fear likewise. For every one that hath power hath fear, whereas he that hath no power is despised of all. ³ But fear thou the works of the devil, for they are evil. While then thou fearest the Lord, thou wilt fear the works of the devil, and wilt not do them, but abstain from them. ⁴ Fear therefore is of two kinds. If thou desire to do evil, fear the Lord, and thou shalt not do it. If again thou desire to do good, fear the Lord and thou shalt do it. Therefore the fear of the Lord is powerful and great and glorious. Fear the Lord then, and thou shalt live unto Him; yea, and as many of them that keep His commandments as shall fear Him, shall live unto God." ⁵ "Wherefore, Sir," say I, "didst thou say concerning those that keep His commandments, "They shall live unto God"?" "Because," saith he, "every creature feareth the Lord, but not every one keepeth His commandments. Those then that fear Him and keep His commandments, they have life unto God; but they that keep not His commandments have no life in them."

Mandate 8

38

¹ "I told thee," saith he, "that the creatures of God are twofold; for temperance also is twofold. For in some things it is right to be temperate, but in other things it is not right." ² "Make known unto me, Sir," say I, "in what things it is right to be temperate, and in what things it is not right." "Listen," saith he. "Be temperate as to what is evil, and do it not; but be not temperate as to what is good, but do it. For if thou be temperate as to what is good, so as not to do it, thou committest a great sin; but if thou be temperate as to what is evil, so as not to do it, thou doest great righteousness. Be temperate therefore in abstaining from all wickedness, and do that which is good." ³ "What kinds of wickedness, Sir," say I, "are they from which we must be temperate and abstain?" "Listen," saith he; "from adultery and fornication, from the lawlessness of drunkenness, from wicked luxury, from many viands and the costliness of riches, and vaunting and haughtiness and pride, and from falsehood and evil speaking and hypocrisy, malice and all blasphemy. ⁴ These works are the most wicked of all in the life of men. From these works therefore the servant of God must be temperate and abstain; for he that is not temperate so as to abstain from these cannot live unto God. Listen then to what follows upon these." ⁵ "Why, are there still other evil deeds, Sir," say I. "Aye, saith he, "there are many, from which the servant of God must be temperate and abstain; theft, falsehood, deprivation, false witness, avarice, evil desire, deceit, vainglory, boastfulness, and whatsoever things are like unto these. ⁶ Thinkest thou not that these things are wrong, yea, very wrong," [saith he,] "for the servants of God? In all these things he that serveth God must exercise temperance. Be thou temperate, therefore, and refrain from all these things, that thou mayest live unto God, and be enrolled among those who exercise self-restraint in them. These then are the things from which thou shouldest restrain thyself ⁷ Now hear," saith he, "the things, in which thou shouldest not exercise self restraint, but do them. Exercise no self-restraint in that which is good, but do it." ⁸ "Sir," say I, "show me the power of the good also, that I may walk in them and serve them, that doing them it may be possible for me to be saved." "Hear," saith he, "the works of the good likewise, which thou must do, and towards which thou must exercise no self-restraint. ⁹ First of all, there is faith, fear of the Lord, love, concord, words of righteousness, truth, patience; nothing is better than these in the life of men. If a man keep these, and exercise not self-restraint from them, he becomes blessed in his life. ¹⁰ Hear now what follow upon these; to minister to widows, to visit the orphans and the needy, to ransom the servants of God from their afflictions, to be hospitable (for in hospitality benevolence from time to time has a place), to resist no man, to be tranquil, to show yourself more submissive than all men, to reverence the aged, to practice righteousness, to observe brotherly feeling, to endure injury, to be long-suffering, to bear no grudge, to exhort those who are sick at soul, not to cast away those that have stumbled from the faith, but to convert them and to put courage Into them, to reprove sinners, not to oppress debtors and indigent persons, and whatsoever actions are like these. ¹¹ Do these things," saith he, "seem to thee to be good?" "Why, what, Sir," say I, "can be better than these?" "Then walk in them," saith he, "and abstain not from them, and thou shalt live unto God. ¹² Keep this commandment therefore. If thou do good and abstain not from it, thou shalt live unto God; yea, and all shalt live unto God who act so. And again if thou do not evil, and abstain from it, thou shalt live unto God; yea, and all shall live unto God, who shall keep these commandments, and walk in them."

Mandate 9

39

¹ He saith to me; "Remove from thyself a doubtful mind and doubt not at all whether to ask of God, saying within thyself, "How can I ask thing of the Lord and receive it, seeing that I have committed so many sins against Him?" ² Reason not thus, but turn to the Lord with thy whole heart, and ask of Him nothing wavering, and thou shalt know His exceeding compassion, that He will surely not abandon thee, but will fulfill the petition of thy soul. ³ For God is not as men who bear a grudge, but Himself is without malice and hath compassion on His creatures. ⁴ Do thou therefore cleanse thy heart from all the vanities of this life, and from the things mentioned before; and ask of the Lord, and thou shalt receive all things, and shalt lack nothing of all thy petitions, if thou ask of the Lord nothing wavering. ⁵ But if thou waver in thy heart, thou shalt surely receive none of thy petitions. For they that waver towards God, these are the doubtful-minded, and they never obtain any of their petitions. ⁶ But they that are complete in the faith make all their petitions trusting in the Lord, and they receive, because they ask without wavering, nothing doubting; for every doubtful-minded man, if he repent not, shall hardly be saved. ⁷ Cleanse therefore thy heart from doubtful-mindedness, and put on faith, for it is strong, and trust God that thou wilt receive all thy petitions which thou askest; and if after asking anything of the Lord, thou receive thy petition somewhat tardily, be not of doubtful mind because thou didst not receive the petition of thy soul at once. For assuredly it is by reason of some temptation or some transgression, of which thou art ignorant, that thou receivest thy petition so tardily. ⁸ Do thou therefore cease not to make thy soul's petition, and thou shalt receive it. But if thou grow weary, and doubt as thou askest, blame thyself and not Him that giveth unto thee. See to this doubtful-mindedness; for it is evil and senseless, and uprooteth many from the faith, yea, even very faithful and strong men. For indeed this doubtful-mindedness is a daughter of the devil, and worketh great wickedness against the servants of God. ⁹ Therefore despise doubtful-mindedness and gain the mastery over it in everything, clothing thyself with faith which is strong and powerful. For faith promiseth all things, accomplisheth all things; but doubtful-mindedness, as having no confidence in itself, fails in all the works which it doeth. ¹⁰ Thou seest then," saith he, "that faith is from above from the Lord, and hath great power; but doubtful-mindedness is an earthly spirit from the devil, and hath no power. ¹¹ Do thou therefore serve that faith which hath power, and hold aloof from the doubtful-mindedness which hath no power; and thou shalt live unto God; yea, and all those shall live unto God who are so minded."

Mandate 10

40

¹ "Put away sorrow from thyself," saith he, "for she is the sister of doubtful-mindedness and of angry temper." ² "How, Sir," say I, "is she the sister of these? For angry temper seems to me to be one thing, doubtful-mindedness another, sorrow another." "Thou art a foolish fellow," saith he, "[and] perceivest not that sorrow is more evil than all the spirits, and is most fatal to the servants of God, and beyond all the spirits destroys a man, and crushes out the Holy Spirit and yet again saves it." ³ "I, Sir," say I, "am without understanding, and I understand not these parables. For how it can crush out and again save, I do not comprehend." ⁴ "Listen," saith he. "Those who have never investigated concerning the truth, nor enquired concerning the deity, but have merely believed, and have been mixed up in business affairs and riches and heathen friendships, and many other affairs of this world–as many, I say, as devote themselves to these things, comprehend not the parables of the deity; for they are darkened by these actions, and are corrupted and become barren. ⁵ As good vineyards, when they are treated with neglect, are made barren by the thorns and weeds of various kinds, so men who after they have believed fall into these many occupations which were mentioned before, lose their understanding and comprehend nothing

at all concerning righteousness; for if they hear concerning the deity and truth, their mind is absorbed in their occupations, and they perceive nothing at all. [6] But they that have the fear of God, and investigate concerning deity and truth, and direct their heart towards the Lord, perceive and understand everything that is said to them more quickly, because they have the fear of the Lord in themselves; for where the Lord dwelleth, there too is great understanding. Cleave therefore unto the Lord, and thou shalt understand and perceive all things.

41

[1] "Hear now, senseless man," saith he, "How sorrow crusheth out the Holy Spirit, and again saveth it. [2] When the man of doubtful mind sets his hand to any action, and fails in it owing to his doubtful-mindedness, grief at this entereth into the man, and grieveth the Holy Spirit, and crusheth it out. [3] Then again when angry temper cleaveth to a man concerning any matter, and he is much embittered, again sorrow entereth into the heart of the man that was ill-tempered, and he is grieved at the deed which he hath done, and repenteth that he did evil. [4] This sadness therefore seemeth to bring salvation, because he repented at having done the evil. So both the operations sadden the Spirit; first, the doubtful mind saddens the Spirit, because it succeeded not in its business, and the angry temper again, because it did what was evil. Thus both are saddening to the Holy Spirit, the doubtful mind and the angry temper. [5] Put away therefore from thyself sadness, and afflict not the Holy Spirit that dwelleth in thee, lest haply He intercede with God [against thee], and depart from thee. [6] For the Spirit of God, that was given unto this flesh, endureth not sadness neither constraint.

42

[1] "Therefore clothe thyself in cheerfulness, which hath favor with Cod always, and is acceptable to Him, and rejoice in it. For every cheerful man worketh good, and thinketh good, and despiseth sadness; [2] but the sad man is always committing sin. In the first place he committeth sin, because he grieveth the Holy Spirit, which was given to the man being a cheerful spirit; and in the second place, by grieving the Holy Spirit he doeth lawlessness, in that he doth not intercede with neither confess unto God. For the intercession of a sad man hath never at any time power to ascend to the altar of God." [3] "Wherefore," say I, "doth not the intercession of him that is saddened ascend to the altar?" "Because," saith he, "sadness is seated at his heart. Thus sadness mingled with the intercession doth not suffer the intercession to ascend pure to the altar. For as vinegar when mingled with wine in the same (vessel) hath not the same pleasant taste, so likewise sadness mingled with the Holy Spirit hath not the same intercession. [4] Therefore cleanse thyself from this wicked sadness, and thou shalt live unto God; yea, and all they shall live unto God, who shall cast away sadness from themselves and clothe themselves in all cheerfulness."

Mandate 11

43

[1] He shewed me men seated on a couch, and another man seated on a chair. And he saith to me, "Seest thou those that are seated on the couch?" "I see them, Sir," say I. "These," saith he, "are faithful, but he that sitteth on the chair is a false prophet who destroyeth the mind of the servants of God–I mean, of the doubtful-minded, not of the faithful. [2] These doubtful-minded ones then come to him as to a soothsayer and enquire of him what shall befall them. And he, the false prophet, having no power of a divine Spirit in himself, speaketh with them according to their enquiries [and according to the lusts of their wickedness], and filleth their souls as they themselves wish. [3] For being empty himself he giveth empty answers to empty enquirers; for what-ever enquiry may be made of him, he answereth according to the emptiness of the man. But he speaketh also some true words; for the devil filleth him with his own spirit, if so be he shall be able to break down some of the righteous. [4] So many therefore as are strong in the faith of the Lord, clothed with the truth, cleave not to such spirits, but hold aloof from them; but as many as are doubters and frequently change their minds, practice soothsaying like the Gentiles, and bring upon themselves greater sin by their idolatries. For he that consulteth a false prophet on any matter is an idolater and emptied of the truth, and senseless. [5] For no Spirit given of God needeth to be consulted; but, having the power of deity, speaketh all things of itself, because it is from above, even from the power of the divine Spirit. [6] But the spirit which is consulted, and speaketh according to the desires of men, is earthly and fickle, having no power; and it speaketh not at all, unless it be consulted." [7] "How then, Sir," say I, "shall a man know who of them is a prophet, and who a false prophet?" "Hear," saith he, "concerning both the prophets; and, as I shall tell thee, so shalt thou test the prophet and the false prophet. By his life test the man that hath the divine Spirit. [8] In the first place, he that hath the [divine] Spirit, which is from above, is gentle and tranquil and humble-minded, and abstaineth from all wickedness and vain desire of this present world, and holdeth himself inferior to all men, and giveth no answer to any man when enquired of, nor speaketh in solitude (for neither doth the Holy Spirit speak when a man wisheth Him to speak); but the man speaketh then when God wisheth him to speak. [9] When then the man who hath the divine Spirit cometh into an assembly of righteous men, who have faith in a divine Spirit, and intercession is made to God by the gathering of those men, then the angel of the prophetic spirit, who is attached to him, filleth the man, and the man, being filled with the Holy Spirit, speaketh to the multitude, according as the Lord willeth. [10] In this way then the Spirit of the deity shall be manifest. This then is the greatness of the power as touching the Spirit of the deity of the Lord. [11] Hear now," saith he, "concerning the earthly and vain spirit, which hath no power but is foolish. [12] In the first place, that man who seemeth to have a spirit exalteth himself, and desireth to have a chief place, and straight-way he is impudent and shameless and talkative and conversant in many luxuries and in many other deceits and receiveth money for his prophesying, and if he receiveth not, he prophesieth not. Now can a divine Spirit receive money and prophesy? It is not possible for a prophet of God to do this, but the spirit of such prophets is earthly. [13] In the next place, it never approacheth an assembly of righteous men; but avoideth them, and cleaveth to the doubtful-minded and empty, and prophesieth to them in corners, and deceiveth them, speaking all things in emptiness to gratify their desires; for they too are empty whom it answereth. For the empty vessel placed together with the empty is not broken, but they agree one with the other. [14] But when he comes into an assembly full of righteous men who have a Spirit of deity, and intercession is made from them, that man is emptied, and the earthly spirit fleeth from him in fear, and that man is struck dumb and is altogether broken in pieces, being unable to utter a word. [15] For, if you pack wine or oil into a closet, and place an empty vessel among them, and again desire to unpack the closet, the vessel which you place there empty, empty in like manner you will find it. Thus also the empty prophets, whenever they come unto the spirits of righteous men, are found just such as they came. [16] I have given thee the life of both kinds of prophets. Therefore test, by his life and his works, the man who says that he is moved by the Spirit. [17] But do thou trust the Spirit that cometh from God, and hath power; but in the earthly and empty spirit put no trust at all; for in it there is no power, for it cometh from the devil. [18] Listen [then] to the parable which I shall tell thee. Take a stone, and throw it up to heaven– see if thou canst reach it; or again, take a squirt of water, and squirt it up to heaven–see if thou canst bore through the heaven." [19] "How, Sir," say I, "can these things be? For both these things which thou hast mentioned are beyond our power." "Well then," saith he, "just as these things are beyond our power, so likewise the earthly spirits have no power and are feeble. [20] Now take the power which cometh from above. The hail is a very, small grain, and yet, when it falleth on a man's head, what pain it causeth! Or again, take a drop which falls on the ground from the tiles, and bores through the stone. [21] Thou seest then that the smallest things from above falling on the earth have great power. So likewise the divine Spirit coming from above is powerful. This Spirit therefore trust, but from the other hold aloof."

Mandate 12

44

[1] He saith to me; "Remove from thyself all evil desire, and clothe thyself in the desire which is good and holy; for clothed with this desire thou shalt hate the evil desire, and shalt bridle and direct it as thou wilt. [2] For the evil desire is wild, and only tamed with difficulty; for it is terrible, and by its wildness is very costly to men; more especially if a servant of God get entangled in it, and have no understanding, he is put to fearful costs by it. But it is costly to such men as are not clothed in the good desire, but are mixed up with this life "These men then it hands over to death." [3] "Of what sort, Sir," say I, "are the works of the evil desire, which hand over men to death? Make them known to me, that I may hold aloof from them." Listen," [saith he,] "through what works the evil desire bringeth death to the servants of God.

45

[1] "Before all is desire for the wife or husband of another, and for extravagance of wealth, and for many needless dainties, and for drinks and other luxuries, many and foolish. For even luxury is foolish and vain for the servants of God. [2] These desires then are evil, and bring death to the servants of God. For this evil desire is a daughter of the devil. Ye must, therefore, abstain from the evil desires, that so abstaining ye may live unto God. [3] But as many as are mastered by them, and resist them not, are done to death utterly; for these desires are deadly. [4] But do thou clothe thyself in the desire of righteousness, and, having armed thyself with the fear of the Lord, resist them. For the fear of God dwelleth in the good desire. If the evil desire shall see thee armed with the fear of God and resisting itself, it shall flee far from

thee, and shall no more be seen of thee, being in fear of thine arms. ^{5} Do thou therefore, when thou art crowned for thy victory over it, come to the desire of righteousness, and deliver to her the victor's prize which thou hast received, and serve her, according as she herself desireth. If thou serve the good desire, and art subject to her, thou shalt have power to master the evil desire, and to subject her, according as thou wilt."

46

^{1} "I would fain know, Sir," say I, "in what ways I ought to serve the good desire." "Listen," saith he; "practice righteousness and virtue, truth and the fear of the Lord, faith and gentleness, and as many good deeds as are like these. Practicing these thou shalt be well-pleasing as a servant of God, and shalt live unto Him; yea, and every one who shall serve the good desire shall live unto God." ^{2} So he completed the twelve commandments, and he saith to me; Thou hast these commandments; walk in them, and exhort thy hearers that their repentance may become pure for the rest of the days of their life. ^{3} This ministration, which I give thee, fulfill thou with all diligence to the end, and thou shalt effect much. For thou shalt find favor among those who are about to repent, and they shall obey thy words. For I will be with thee, and will compel them to obey thee." ^{4} I say to him; "Sir, these commandments are great and beautiful and glorious, and are able to gladden the heart of the man who is able to observe them. But I know not whether these commandments can be kept by a man, for they are very hard." ^{5} He answered and said unto me; "If thou set it before thyself that they can be kept, thou wilt easily keep them, and they will not be hard; but if it once enter into thy heart that they cannot be kept by a man, thou wilt not keep them. ^{6} But now I say unto thee; if thou keep them not, but neglect them thou shalt not have salvation, neither thy children nor thy household, since thou hast already pronounced judgment against thyself that these commandments cannot be kept by a man."

47

^{1} And these things he said to me very angrily, so that I was confounded, and feared him exceedingly; for his form was changed, so that a man could not endure his anger. ^{2} And when he saw that I was altogether disturbed and confounded, he began to speak more kindly [and cheerfully] to me, and he saith; "Foolish fellow, void of understanding and of doubtful mind, perceivest thou not the glory of God, how great and mighty and marvelous it is, how that He created the world for man's sake, and subjected all His creation to man, and gave all authority to him, that he should be master over all things under the heaven? ^{3} If then," [he saith,] "man is lord of all the creatures of God and mastereth all things, cannot he also master these commandments Aye," saith he, "the man that hath the Lord in his heart can master [all things and] all these commandments. ^{4} But they that have the Lord on their lips, while their heart is hardened, and are far from the Lord, to them these commandments are hard and inaccessible. ^{5} Therefore do ye, who are empty and fickle in the faith, set your Lord in your heart, and ye shall perceive that nothing is easier than these commandments, nor sweeter, nor more gentle. ^{6} Be ye converted, ye that walk after the commandments of the devil, (the commandments which are so) difficult and bitter and wild and riotous; and fear not the devil, for there is no power in him against you. ^{7} For I will be with you, I, the angel of repentance, who have the mastery over him. The devil hath fear alone, but his fear hath no force. Fear him not therefore; and he will flee from you."

48

^{1} I say to him, "Sir, listen to a few words from me." "Say what thou wilt," saith he. "Man, Sir," I say, "is eager to keep the commandments of God, and there is no one that asketh not of the Lord that he may be strengthened in His commandments, and be subject to them; but the devil is hard and overmastereth them." ^{2} "He cannot," saith he, "overmaster the servants of God, who set their hope on Him with their whole heart. The devil can wrestle with them, but he cannot overthrow them. If then ye resist him, he will be vanquished and will flee from you disgraced. But as many," saith he, "as are utterly empty, fear the devil as if he had power. ^{3} When a man has filled amply sufficient jars with good wine, and among these jars a few are quite empty, he comes to the jars, and does not examine the full ones, for he knows that they are full; but he examineth the empty ones, fearing lest they have turned sour. For empty jars soon turn sour, and the taste of the wine is spoilt. ^{4} So also the devil cometh to all the servants of God tempting them. As many then as are complete in the faith, oppose him mightily, and he departeth from them, not having a place where he can find an entrance. So he cometh next to the empty ones, and finding a place goeth into them, and further he doeth what he willeth in them, and they become submissive slaves to him.

49

^{1} "But I, the angel of repentance, say unto you; Fear not the devil; for I was sent," saith he, "to be with you who repent with your whole heart, and to strengthen you in the faith. ^{2} Believe, therefore, on God, ye who by reason of your sins have despaired of your life, and are adding to your sins, and weighing down your life; for if ye turn unto the Lord with your whole heart, and work righteousness the remaining days of your life, and serve Him rightly according to His will, He will give healing to your former sins, and ye shall have power to master the works of the devil. But of the threatening of the devil fear not at all; for he is unstrung, like the sinews of a dead man. ^{3} Hear me therefore, and fear Him, Who is able to do all things, to save and to destroy, and observe these commandments, and ye shall live unto God." ^{4} I say to him, "Sir, now am I strengthened in all the ordinances of the Lord, because thou art with me; and I know that thou wilt crush all the power of the devil, and we shall be masters over him, and shall prevail over all his works. And I hope, Sir, that I am now able to keep these commandments which thou hast commanded, the Lord enabling me." ^{5} "Thou shalt keep them," saith he, "if thy heart be found pure with the Lord; yea, and all shall keep them, as many as shall purify their hearts from the vain desires of this world, and shall live unto God."

Parables Which He Spake With Me
Parable 1

50

^{1} He saith to me; "Ye know that ye, who are the servants of God, are dwelling in a foreign land; for your city is far from this city. If then ye know your city, in which ye shall dwell, why do ye here prepare fields and expensive displays and buildings and dwelling-chambers which are superfluous? ^{2} He, therefore, that prepareth these things for this city does not purpose to return to his own city. ^{3} O foolish and double-minded and miserable man, perceivest thou not that all these things are foreign, and are under the power of another For the lord of this city shall say, "I do not wish thee to dwell in my city; go forth from this city, for thou dost not conform to my laws." ^{4} Thou, therefor who hast fields and dwellings and many other possessions, when thou art cast out by him, what wilt thou do with thy field and thy house am all the other things that thou preparedst for thyself? For the lord of this country saith to thee justly, "Either conform to my laws, or depart from my country." ^{5} What then shalt thou do, who art under law in thine own city? For the sake of thy fields and the rest of thy possessions wilt thou altogether repudiate thy law, and walk according to the law of this city? Take heed, lest it be inexpedient to repudiate the law; for if thou shouldest desire to return again to thy city, thou shall surely not be received [because thou didst repudiate the law of the city], and shalt be shut out from it. ^{6} Take heed therefore; as dwelling in a strange land prepare nothing more for thyself but a competency which is sufficient for thee, and make ready that, whensoever the master of this city may desire to cast thee out for thine opposition to his law, thou mayest go forth from his city and depart into thine own city and use thine own law joyfully, free from all insult. ^{7} Take heed therefore, ye that serve God and have Him in your heart: work the "works of God being mindful of His commandments and of the promises which He made, and believe Him that He will perform them, if His commandments be kept. ^{8} Therefore, instead of fields buy ye souls that are in trouble, as each is able, and visit widows and orphans, and neglect them not; and spend your riches and all your displays, which ye received from God, on fields and houses of this kind. ^{9} For to this end the Master enriched you, that ye might perform these ministrations for Him. It is much better to purchase fields [and possessions] and houses of this kind, which thou wilt find in thine own city, when thou visitest it. ^{10} This lavish expenditure is beautiful and joyous, not bringing sadness or fear, but bringing joy. The expenditure of the heathen then practice not ye; for it is not convenient for you the servants of God. ^{11} But practice your own expenditure, in which ye can rejoice; and do not corrupt, neither touch that which is another man's, nor lust after it for it is wicked to lust after other men's possessions. But perform thine own task, and thou shalt be saved."

Parable 2

51

^{1} As I walked in the field, and noticed an elm and a vine, and was distinguishing them and their fruits, the shepherd appeareth to me and saith; "What art thou meditating within thyself?" "I am thinking, [Sir,]" say I, "about the elm and the vine, that they are excellently suited the one to the other." ^{2} "These two trees," saith he, "are appointed for a type to the servants of God." "I would fain know, [Sir,]" say I, "the type contained in these trees, of which thou speakest." "Seest thou," saith he, "the elm and the vine ?" "I see them, Sir," say I. ^{3} "This vine," saith he, "beareth fruit, but the elm is an unfruitful stock. Yet this vine, except it climb up the elm, cannot bear much fruit when it is spread on the ground; and such fruit as it beareth is rotten, because it is not suspended upon the elm. When then the vine is attached to the elm, it beareth fruit both from itself and from the elm. ^{4} Thou seest then that the elm also beareth [much] fruit, not less than the vine, but rather more." How more, Sir?" say I. "Because," saith he, "the vine, when hanging upon the elm, bears its fruit in abundance, and in good condition; but, when spread on the ground, it beareth little fruit, and that rotten. This parable therefore is applicable to the servants of God, to poor and to rich alike." [5] "How, Sir?" say I; "instruct me." "Listen," saith he; the rich man hath much wealth, but in the things of the Lord he is poor, being distracted about his riches, and his confession and intercession with the Lord is very scanty; and even that which he giveth is mall and weak and hath not power above. When then the rich man goeth up to the poor, and assisteth him in his needs, believing that for what he doth to the poor man he shall be able to obtain a reward with God—because the poor man is rich in intercession [and confession], and his intercession hath great power with God—the rich man then supplieth all things to the poor man without wavering. [6] But the poor man being supplied by the rich maketh intercession for him, thanking God for him that gave to him. And the other is still more zealous to assist the poor man, that he may be continuous in his life: for he knoweth that the intercession of the poor man is acceptable and rich before God. [7] They both then accomplish their work; the poor man maketh intercession, wherein he is rich [which he received of the Lord]; this he rendereth again to the Lord Who supplieth him with it. The rich man too in like manner furnisheth to the poor man, nothing doubting, the riches which he received from the Lord. And this work great and acceptable with God, because (the rich man) hath understanding concerning his riches, and worketh for the poor man from the bounties of the Lord, and accomplisheth the ministration of the Lord rightly. [8] In the sight of men then the elm seemeth not to bear fruit, and they know not, neither perceive, that if there cometh a drought the elm having water nurtureth the vine, and the vine having a constant supply of water beareth fruit two fold, both for itself and for the elm. So likewise the poor, by interceding with the Lord for the rich, establish their riches, and again the rich, supplying their needs to the poor, establish their souls. [9] So then both are made partners in the righteous work. He then that doeth these things shall not be abandoned of God, but shall be written in the books of the living. [10] Blessed are the rich, who understand also that they are enriched from the Lord. For they that have this mind shall be able to do some good work."

Parable 3

52

[1] He showed me many trees which had no leaves, but they seemed to me to be, as it were, withered; for they were all alike. And he saith to me; "Seest thou these trees?" "I see them, Sir," I say, "they are all alike, and are withered." He answered and said to me; "These trees that thou seest are they that dwell in this world." [2] "Wherefore then, Sir," say I, "are they as if they were withered, and alike?" "Because," saith he, "neither the righteous are distinguishable, nor the sinners in this world, but they are alike. For this world is winter to the righteous, and they are not distinguishable, as they dwell with the sinners. [3] For as in the winter the trees, having shed their leaves, are alike, and are not distinguishable, which are withered, and which alive, so also in this world neither the just nor the sinners are distinguishable, but they are all alike."

Parable 4

53

[1] He showed me many trees again, some of them sprouting, and others withered, and he saith to me; "Seest thou," saith he, "these trees?" "I see them, Sir," say I, "some of them sprouting, and others withered." [2] "These trees," saith he, "that are sprouting are the righteous, who shall dwell in the world to come; for the world to come is summer to the righteous, but winter to the sinners. When then the mercy of the Lord shall shine forth, then they that serve God shall be made manifest; yea, and all men shall be made manifest. [3] For as in summer the fruits of each several tree are made manifest, and are recognized of what sort they are, so also the fruits of the righteous shall be manifest, and all [even the very smallest] shall be known to be flourishing in that world. [4] But the Gentiles and the sinners, just as thou sawest the trees which were withered, even such shall they be found, withered and unfruitful in that world, and shall be burnt up as fuel, and shall be manifest, because their practice in their life hath been evil. For the sinners shall be burned, because they sinned and repented not; and the Gentiles shall be burned, because they knew not Him that created them. [5] Do thou therefore bear fruit, that in that summer thy fruit may be known. But abstain from overmuch business, and thou shalt never fill into any sin. For they that busy themselves overmuch, sin much also, being distracted about their business, and in no wise serving their own Lord. [6] How then," saith he, "can such a man ask anything of the Lord and receive it, seeing that he serveth not the Lord? [For] they that serve Him, these shall receive their petitions, but they that serve not the Lord, these shall receive nothing. [7] But if any one work one single action, he is able also to serve the Lord; for his mind shall not be corrupted from (following) the Lord, but he shall serve Him, because he keepeth his mind pure. [8] If therefore thou doest these things, thou shalt be able to bear fruit unto the world to come; yea, and whosoever shall do these things, shall bear fruit."

Parable 5

54

[1] As I was fasting and seated on a certain mountain, and giving thanks to the Lord for all that He had done unto me, I see the shepherd seated by me and saying; "Why hast thou come hither in the early morn?" "Because, Sir," say I, "I am keeping a station." [2] "What," saith he, "is a station?" "I am fasting, Sir," say I. "And what," saith he, "is this fast [that ye are fasting]?" "As I was accustomed, Sir," say I, "so I fast." [3] "Ye know not," saith he, "how to fast unto the Lord, neither is this a fast, this unprofitable fast which ye make unto Him." "wherefore, Sir," say I, "sayest thou this?" "I tell thee," saith he, "that this is not a fast, wherein ye think to fast; but I will teach thee what is a complete fast and acceptable to the Lord. Listen," saith he; [4] "God desireth not such a vain fast; for by so fasting unto God thou shalt do nothing for righteousness. But fast thou [unto God] such a fast as this; [5] do no wickedness in thy life, and serve the Lord with a pure heart; observe His commandments and walk in His ordinances, and let no evil desire rise up in thy heart; but believe God. Then, if thou shalt do these things, and fear Him, and control thyself from every evil deed, thou shalt live unto God; and if thou do these things, thou shalt accomplish a great fast, and one acceptable to God.

55

[1] "Hear the parable which I shall tell thee relating to fasting. [2] A certain man had an estate, and many slaves, and a portion of his estate he planted as a vineyard; and choosing out a certain slave who was trusty and well-pleasing (and) held in honor, he called him to him and saith unto him; "Take this vineyard [which I have planted], and fence it [till I come], but do nothing else to the vineyard. Now keep this my commandment, and thou shalt be free in my house." Then the master of the servant went away to travel abroad. [3] When then he had gone away, the servant took and fenced the vineyard; and having finished the fencing of the vineyard, he noticed that the vineyard was full of weeds. [4] So he reasoned within himself, saying, "This command of my lord I have carried out I will next dig this vineyard, and it shall be neater when it is digged; and when it hath no weeds it will yield more fruit, because not choked by the weeds." He took and digged the vineyard, and all the weeds that were in the vineyard he plucked up. And that vineyard became very neat and flourishing, when it had no weeds to choke it. [5] After a time the master of the servant [and of the estate] came, and he went into the vineyard. And seeing the vineyard fenced neatly, and digged as well, and [all] the weeds plucked up, and the vines flourishing, he rejoiced [exceedingly] at what his servant had done. [6] So he called his beloved son, who was his heir, and the friends who were his advisers, and told them what he had commanded his servant, and how much he had found done. And they rejoiced with the servant at the testimony which his master had borne to him. [7] And he saith to them; "I promised this servant his freedom, if he should keep the commandment which I commanded him; but he kept my commandment and did a good work besides to my vineyard, and pleased me greatly. For this work therefore which he has done, I desire to make him joint-heir with my son, because, when the good thought struck him, he did not neglect it, but fulfilled it." [8] In this purpose the son of the master agreed with him, that the servant should be made joint-heir with the son. [9] After some few days, his master made a feast, and sent to him many dainties from the feast. But when the servant received [the dainties sent to him by the master], he took what was sufficient for him, and distributed the rest to his fellow servants. [10] And his fellow-servants, when they received the dainties, rejoiced, and began to pray for him, that he might find greater favor with the master, because he had treated them so handsomely. [11] All these things which had taken place his master heard, and again rejoiced greatly at his deed. So the master called together again his friends and his son, and announced to them the deed that he had done with regard to his dainties which he had received; and they still more approved of his resolve, that his servant should be made joint-heir with his son."

56

[1] I say, "Sir, I understand not these parables, neither can I apprehend them, unless thou explain them for me." [2] "I will explain everything to thee," saith he; "and will show thee whatsoever things I shall speak with thee. Keep the commandments of the Lord, and thou shalt be well-pleasing to God, and shalt be enrolled among the number of them that keep His commandments. [3] But if thou do any good thing outside the commandment of God, thou shalt win for thyself more exceeding glory, and shalt be more glorious in the sight of God than thou wouldest otherwise have been. If then, while thou keepest the commandments of God, thou add these services likewise, thou

shalt rejoice, if thou observe them according to my commandment." ⁴ I say to him, "Sir, whatsoever thou commandest me, I will keep it; for I know that thou art with me." "I will be with thee," saith he, "because thou hast so great zeal for doing good; yea, and I will be with all," saith he, "whosoever have such zeal as this. ⁵ This fasting," saith he, "if the commandments of the Lord are kept, is very good. This then is the way, that thou shalt keep this fast which thou art about to observe]. ⁶ First of all, keep thyself from every evil word and every evil desire, and purify thy heart from all the vanities of this world. If thou keep these things, this fast shall be perfect for thee. ⁷ And thus shalt thou do. Having fulfilled what is written, on that day on which thou fastest thou shalt taste nothing but bread and water; and from thy meats, which thou wouldest have eaten, thou shalt reckon up the amount of that day's expenditure, which thou wouldest have incurred, and shalt give it to a widow, or an orphan, or to one in want, and so shalt thou humble thy soul, that he that hath received from thy humiliation may satisfy his own soul, and may pray for thee to the Lord. ⁸ If then thou shalt so accomplish this fast, as I have commanded thee, thy sacrifice shall be acceptable in the sight of God, and this fasting shall be recorded; and the service so performed is beautiful and joyous and acceptable to the Lord. ⁹ These things thou shalt so observe, thou and thy children and thy whole household; and, observing them, thou shalt be blessed; yea, and all those, who shall hear and observe them, shall be blessed, and whatsoever things they shall ask of the Lord, they shall receive."

57

¹ I entreated him earnestly, that he would show me the parable of the estate, and of the master, and of the vineyard, and of the servant that fenced the vineyard, [and of the fence,] and of the weeds which were plucked up out of the vineyard, and of the son, and of the friends, the advisers. For I understood that all these things are a parable. ² But he answered and said unto me; "Thou art exceedingly importunate in enquiries. Thou oughtest not," [saith he,] "to make any enquiry at all; for if it be right that a thing be explained unto thee, it shall be explained." I say to him; "Sir, whatsoever things thou showest unto me and dost not explain, I shall have seen them in vain, and without understanding what they are. In like manner also, if thou speak parables to me and interpret them not, I shall have heard a thing in vain from thee." ³ But he again answered, and said unto me; "Whosoever," saith he, "is a servant of God, and hath his own Lord in his heart, asketh understanding of Him, and receiveth it, and interpreteth every parable, and the words of the Lord which are spoken in parables are made known unto him. But as many as are sluggish and idle in intercession, these hesitate to ask of the Lord. ⁴ But the Lord is abundant in compassion, and giveth to them that ask of Him without ceasing. But thou who hast been strengthened by the holy angel, and hast received from him such (powers of intercession and art not idle, wherefore dost thou not ask understanding of the Lord, and obtain it from Him)." ⁵ I say to him, "Sir, I that have thee with me have (but) need to ask thee and enquire of thee; for thou showest me all things, and speakest with me; but if I had seen or heard them apart from thee I should have asked of the Lord, that they might be shown to me."

58

¹ "I told thee just now," saith he, "that thou art unscrupulous and importunate, in enquiring for the interpretations of the parables. But since thou art so obstinate, I will interpret to thee the parable of the estate and all the accompaniments thereof, that thou mayest make them known unto all. Hear now," saith he, "and understand them. ² The estate is this world, and the lord of the estate is He that created all things, and set them in order, and endowed them with power; and the servant is the Son of God, and the vines are this people whom He Himself planted; ³ and the fences are the [holy] angels of the Lord who keep together His people; and the weeds, which are plucked up from the vineyard, are the transgressions of the servants of God; and the dainties which He sent to him from the feast are the commandments which He gave to His people through His Son; and the friends and advisers are the holy angels which were first created; and the absence of the master is the time which remaineth over until His coming." ⁴ I say to him; "Sir, great and marvelous are all things and all things are glorious; was it likely then," say I, "that I could have apprehended them?" "Nay, nor can any other man, though he be full of understanding, apprehend them." "Yet again, Sir," say I, "explain to me what I am about to enquire of thee." ⁵ "Say on," he saith, "if thou desirest anything." "Wherefore, Sir,]" say I, "is the Son of God represented in the parable in the guise of a servant?"

59

¹ "Listen," said he; "the Son of God is not represented in the guise of a servant, but is represented in great power and lordship." "How, Sir?" say I; "I comprehend not." ² "Because," saith he, "God planted the vineyard, that is, He created the people, and delivered them over to His Son. And the Son placed the angels in charge of them, to watch over them; and the Son Himself cleansed their sins, by laboring much and enduring many toils; for no one can dig without toil or labor. ³ Having Himself then cleansed the sins of His people, He showed them the paths of life, giving them the law which He received from His Father. Thou seest," saith he, "that He is Himself Lord of the people, having received all power from His Father. ⁴ But how that the lord took his son and the glorious angels as advisers concerning the inheritance of the servant, listen. ⁵ The Holy Pre-existent Spirit. Which created the whole creation, God made to dwell in flesh that He desired. This flesh, therefore, in which the Holy Spirit dwelt, was subject unto the Spirit, walking honorably in holiness and purity, without in any way defiling the Spirit. ⁶ When then it had lived honorably in chastity, and had labored with the Spirit, and had cooperated with it in everything, behaving itself boldly and bravely, He chose it as a partner with the Holy Spirit; for the career of this flesh pleased [the Lord], seeing that, as possessing the Holy Spirit, it was not defiled upon the earth. ⁷ He therefore took the son as adviser and the glorious angels also, that this flesh too, having served the Spirit unblamably, might have some place of sojourn, and might not seem to hare lost the reward for its service; for all flesh, which is found undefiled and unspotted, wherein the Holy Spirit dwelt, shall receive a reward. ⁸ Now thou hast the interpretation of this parable also."

60

¹ "I was right glad, Sir," say I, "to hear this interpretation." "Listen now," saith he, "Keep this thy flesh pure and undefiled, that the Spirit which dwelleth in it may bear witness to it, and thy flesh may be justified. ² See that it never enter into thine heart that this flesh of thine is perishable, and so thou abuse it in some defilement. [For] if thou defile thy flesh, thou shalt defile the Holy Spirit also; but if thou defile the flesh, thou shalt not live." ³ "But if, Sir," say I, "there has been any ignorance in times past, before these words were heard, how shall a man who has defiled his flesh be saved?" "For the former deeds of ignorance," saith he, "God alone hath power to give healing; for all authority is His. ⁴ [But now keep thyself, and the Lord Almighty, Who is full of compassion, will give healing for thy former deeds of ignorance,] if henceforth thou defile not thy flesh, neither the Spirit; for both share in common, and the one cannot be defiled without the other. Therefore keep both pure, and thou shalt live unto God."

Parable 6

61

¹ As I sat in my house, and glorified the Lord for all things that I had seen, and was considering concerning the commandments, how that they were beautiful and powerful and gladsome and glorious and able to save a man's soul, I said within myself; "Blessed shall I be, if I walk in these commandments; yea, and whosoever shall walk in them shall be blessed." ² As I spake these things within myself, I see him suddenly seated by me, and saying as follows; "Why art thou of a doubtful mind concerning the commandments, which I commanded thee? They are beautiful. Doubt not at all; but clothe thyself in the faith of the Lord, and thou shalt walk in them. For I will strengthen thee in them. ³ These commandments are suitable for those who meditate repentance; for if they walk not in them, their repentance is in vain. ⁴ Ye then that repent, cast away the evil doings of this world which crush you; and, by putting on every excellence of righteousness, ye shall be able to observe these commandments, and to add no more to your sins. If then ye add no further sin at all, ye will depart from your former sins. Walk then in these my commandments, and ye shall live unto God. These things have [all] been told you from me." ⁵ And after he had told these things to me, he saith to me, "Let us go into the country, and I will show thee the shepherds of the sheep." "Let us go, Sir," say I. And we came to a certain plain, and he showeth me a young man, a shepherd, clothed in a light cloak, of saffron color; ⁶ and he was feeding a great number of sheep, and these sheep were, as it were, well fed and very frisky, and were gladsome as they skipped about hither and thither; and the shepherd himself was all gladsome over his flock; and the very visage of the shepherd was exceedingly gladsome; and he ran about among the sheep.

62

¹ And he saith to me; "Seest thou this shepherd?" "I see him Sir," I say. "This," saith he, "is the angel of self-indulgence and of deceit. He crusheth the souls of the servants of God, and perverteth them from the truth, leading them astray with evil desires, wherein they perish. ² For they forget the commandments of the living God, and walk in vain deceits and acts of self-indulgence, and are destroyed by this angel, some of them unto death, and others unto corruption." ³ I say to him, "Sir, I comprehend not what means "unto death," and what "unto corruption". "Listen," saith he; "the sheep which thou sawest gladsome and skipping about, these are they who have been turned asunder from God utterly, and have delivered themselves over to the lusts of this world. In these, therefore, there is not repentance unto life. For the Name of God is being blasphemed through them. The life of

such persons is death. ⁴ But the sheep, which thou sawest not skipping about, but feeding in one place, these are they that have delivered themselves over to acts of self-indulgence and deceit, but have not uttered any blasphemy against the Lord. These then have been corrupted from the truth. In these there is hope of repentance, wherein they can live. Corruption then hath hope of a possible renewal, but death hath eternal destruction." ⁵ Again we went forward a little way, and he showeth me a great shepherd like a wild man in appearance, with a white goatskin thrown about him; and he had a kind of wallet on his shoulders, and a staff very hard and with knots in it, and a great whip. And his look was very sour, so that I was afraid of him because of his look. ⁶ This shepherd then kept receiving from the young man, the shepherd, those sheep that were frisky and well fed, but not skipping about, and putting them in a certain spot, which was precipitous and covered with thorns and briars, so that the sheep could not disentangle themselves from the thorns and briars, but [became entangled among the thorns and briars. ⁷ And so they] pastured entangled in the thorns and briars, and were in great misery with being beaten by him; and he kept driving them about to and fro, and giving them no rest, and all together those sheep had not a happy time.

63

¹ When then I saw them so lashed with the whip and vexed, I was sorry for their sakes, because they were so tortured and had no rest at all. ² I say to the shepherd who was speaking with me; "Sir, who is this shepherd, who is [so] hard-hearted and severe, and has no compassion at all for these sheep?" "This," saith he, "is the angel of punishment, and he is one of the just angels, and presides over punishment. ³ So he receiveth those who wander away from God, and walk after the lusts and deceits of this life, and punisheth them, as they deserve, with fearful and various punishments." ⁴ "I would fain learn, Sir," said I, "of what sort are these various punishments." "Listen," saith he; "the various tortures and punishments are tortures belonging to the present life; for some are punished with losses, and others with want, and others with divers maladies, and others with [every kind] of unsettlement, and others with insults from unworthy persons and with suffering in many other respects. ⁵ For many, being unsettled in their plans, set their hands to many things, and nothing ever goes forward with them. And then they say that they do not prosper in their doings, and it doth not enter into their hearts that they have done evil deeds, but they blame the Lord. ⁶ When then they are afflicted with every kind of affliction, then they are delivered over to me for good instruction, and are strengthened in the faith of the Lord, and serve the Lord with a pure heart the remaining days of their life. But, if they repent, the evil works which they have done rise up in their hearts, and then they glorify God, saying that He is a just Judge, and that they suffered justly each according to his doings. And they serve the Lord thenceforward with a pure heart, and are prosperous in all their doings, receiving from the Lord whatsoever things they may ask; and then they glorify the Lord because they were delivered over unto me, and they no longer suffer any evil thing."

64

¹ I say unto him; "Sir, declare unto me this further matter." "What enquirest thou yet?" saith he. "Whether, Sir," say I, "they that live in self-indulgence and are deceived undergo torments during the same length of time as they live in self-indulgence and are deceived." He saith to me, "They undergo torments for the same length of time." ² "Then, Sir," say I, "they undergo very slight torments; for those who are living thus in self-indulgence and forget God ought to have been tormented seven-fold." ³ He saith to me, "Thou art foolish, and comprehendest not the power of the torment" "True," say I, "for if I had comprehended it, I should not have asked thee to declare it to me." "Listen," saith he, "to the power of both, [of the self-indulgence and of the torment]. ⁴ The time of the self-indulgence and deceit is one hour. But an hour of the torment hath the power of thirty days. If then one live in self indulgence and be deceived for one day, and be tormented for one day, the day of the torment is equivalent to a whole year. For as many days then as a man lives in self-indulgence, for so many years is he tormented. Thou seest then," saith he, "that the time of the self-indulgence and deceit is very short, but the time of the punishment and torment is long."

65

¹ "Inasmuch, Sir," say I, "as I do not quite comprehend concerning the time of the deceit and self-indulgence and torment, show me more clearly." ² He answered and said unto me; "Thy stupidity cleaveth to thee; and thou wilt not cleanse thy heart and serve God Take heed," [saith he,] "lest haply the time be fulfilled, and thou be found in thy foolishness. Listen then," [saith he,] "even as thou wishest, that thou mayest comprehend the matter. ³ He that liveth in self-indulgence and is deceived for one day, and doeth what he wisheth, is clothed in much folly and comprehendeth not the thing which he doeth; for on the morrow he forgetteth what he did the day before. For self-indulgence and deceit have no memories, by reason of the folly, wherewith each is clothed; but when punishment and torment cling to a man for a single day, he is punished and tormented for a whole year long; for punishment and torment have long memories. ⁴ So being tormented and punished for the whole year, the man remembers at length the self-indulgence and deceit, and perceiveth that it is on their account that he is suffering these ills. Every man, therefore, that liveth in self-indulgence and is deceived, is tormented in this way because, though possessing lire, they have delivered themselves over unto death." ⁵ "What kinds of self-indulgence, Sir," say I, "are harmful?" "Every action," saith he, "is self-indulgence to a man, which he does with pleasure; for the irascible man, when he gives the reins to his passion, is self-indulgent; and the adulterer and the drunkard and the slanderer and the liar and the miser and the defrauder and he that doeth things akin to these, giveth the reins to his peculiar passion; therefore he is self-indulgent in his action. ⁶ All these habits of self-indulgence are harmful to the servants of God; on account of these deceits therefore they so suffer who are punished and tormented. ⁷ But there are habits of self-indulgence like-wise which save men; for many are self-indulgent in doing good, being carried away by the pleasure it gives to themselves. This self-indulgence then is expedient for the servants of God, and bringeth life to a man of this disposition; but the harmful self-indulgences afore-mentioned bring to men torments and punishments; and if they continue in them and repent not, they bring death upon themselves."

Parable 7

66

¹ After a few days I saw him on the same plain, where also I had seen the shepherds, and he saith to me, "What seekest thou?" "I am here, Sir," say I, "that thou mayest bid the shepherd that punisheth go out of my house; for he afflicteth me much." "It is necessary for thee," saith he, "to be afflicted; for so," saith he, "the glorious angel ordered as concerning thee, for he wisheth thee to be proved." "Why, what so evil thing have I done, Sir," say I, "that I should be delivered over to this angel?" ² "Listen," saith he. "Thy sins are many, yet not so many that thou shouldest be delivered over to this angel; but thy house has committed great iniquities and sins, and the glorious angel was embittered at their deeds, and for this cause he bade thee be afflicted for a certain time, that they also might repent and cleanse themselves from every lust of this world. When therefore they shall repent and be cleansed, then shall the angel of punishment depart." ³ I say to him; "Sir, if they perpetrated such deeds that the glorious angel is embittered, what have I done?" "They cannot be afflicted otherwise," saith he, "unless thou, the head of the [whole] house, be afflicted; for if thou be afflicted, they also of necessity will be afflicted; but if thou be prosperous, they can suffer no affliction." ⁴ "But behold, Sir," say I, "they have repented with their whole heart." "I am quite aware myself," saith he, "that they have repented with their whole heart; well, thinkest thou that the sins of those who repent are forgiven forthwith? Certainly not; but the person who repents must torture his own soul, and must be thoroughly humble in his every action, and be afflicted with all the divers kinds of affliction; and if he endure the afflictions which come upon him, assuredly He Who created all things and endowed them with power will be moved with compassion and will bestow some remedy. ⁵ And this (will God do), if in any way He perceive the heart of the penitent pure from every evil thing. But it is expedient for thee and for thy house that thou shouldest be afflicted now. But why speak I many words to thee? Thou must be afflicted as the angel of the Lord commanded, even he that delivered thee unto me; and for this give thanks to the Lord, in that He deemed thee worthy that I should reveal unto thee beforehand the affliction, that foreknowing it thou might endure it with fortitude." ⁶ I say to him; "Sir, be thou with me, and I shall be able to endure all affliction [easily]." "I will be with thee," saith he; "and I will ask the angel that punisheth to afflict thee more lightly; but thou shalt be afflicted for a short time, and thou shalt be restored again to thy house. Only continue to be humble and to minister unto the Lord with a pure heart, thou and thy children and thy house, and walk in my commandments which I command thee, and thus it will be possible for thy repentance to be strong and pure. ⁷ And if thou keep these commandments with thy household, all affliction shall hold aloof from thee; yea, and affliction," saith he, "shall hold aloof from all whosoever shall walk in these my commandments."

Parable 8

67

¹ He showed me a [great] willow, overshadowing plains and mountains, and under the shadow of the willow all have come who are called by the name of the Lord. ² And by the willow there stood an angel of the Lord, glorious and very tall, having a great sickle, and he was lopping branches from the willow, and giving them to the people that sheltered beneath the willow; and he gave them little rods about a cubit long. ³ And after all had taken the

rods, the angel laid aside the sickle, and the tree was sound, just as I had seen it. ⁴ Then I marvelled within myself, saying, "How is the tree sound after so many branches have been lopped off?" The shepherd saith to me, "Marvel not that the tree remained sound, after so many branches were lopped off but wait until thou seest all things, and it shall be shown to thee what it is." ⁵ The angel who gave the rods to the people demanded them back from them again, and according as they had received them, so also they were summoned to him, and each of them returned the several rods. But the angel of the Lord took them, and examined them. ⁶ From some he received the rods withered and eaten as it were by grubs: the angel ordered those who gave up rods like these to stand apart. ⁷ And others gave them up withered, but not grub-eaten; and these again he ordered to stand apart. ⁸ And others gave them up half-withered; these also stood apart. ⁹ And others gave up their rods half-withered and with cracks; these also stood apart. ¹⁰ And others gave up their rods green and with cracks; these also stood apart. And others gave up their rods one half withered and one half green; these also stood apart. ¹¹ And others brought their rods two parts of the rod green, and the third part withered; these also stood apart. And others gave them up two parts withered, and the third part green; these also stood apart. ¹² And others gave up their rods nearly all green, but a very small portion of their rods was withered, just the end; but they had cracks in them; these also stood apart. ¹³ And in those of others there was a very small portion green, but the rest of the rods was withered; these also stood apart. ¹⁴ And others came bringing their rods green, as they received them from the angel; and the most part of the multitude gave up their rods in this state; and the angel rejoiced exceedingly at these; these also stood apart. ¹⁵ And others gave up their rods green and with shoots, these also stood apart; and at these again the angel rejoiced exceedingly. ¹⁶ And others gave up their rods green and with shoots; and their shoots had, as it were, a kind of fruit. And those men were exceeding gladsome, whose rods were found in this state. And over them the angel exulted, and the shepherd was very gladsome over them.

68

¹ And the angel of the Lord commanded crowns to be brought. And crowns were brought, made as it were of palm branches; and he crowned the men that had given up the rods which had the shoots and some fruit, and sent them away into the tower. ² And the others also he sent into the tower, even those who had given up the rods green and with shoots, but the shoots were without fruit; and he set a seal upon them. ³ And all they that went into the tower had the same raiment, white as snow. ⁴ And those that had given up their rods green as they received them, he sent away, giving them a [white] robe, and seals. ⁵ After the angel had finished these things, he saith to the shepherd; "I go away; but these thou shalt send away to (their places within) the walls, according as each deserveth to dwell; but examine their rods carefully), and so send them away. But be careful in examining them. Take heed lest any escape thee," saith he. "Still if any escape thee, I will test them at the altar." When he had thus spoken to the shepherd, he departed. ⁶ And, after the angel had departed, the shepherd saith to me; "Let us take the rods of all and plant them, to see whether any of them shall be able to live." I say unto him, "Sir, these withered things, how can they live?" ⁷ He answered and said unto me; "This tree is a willow, and this class of trees clingeth to life. If then the rods shall be planted and get a little moisture, many of them will live. And afterwards let us try to pour some water also over them. If any of them shall be able to live, I will rejoice with it; but if it live not, I at least shall not be found neglectful." ⁸ So the shepherd bade me call them, just as each one of them was stationed. And they came row after row, and they delivered up the rods to the shepherd. And the shepherd took the rods, and planted them in rows, and after he had planted them, he poured much water over them, so that the rods could not be seen for the water. ⁹ And after he had watered the rods, he saith to me; "Let us go now. and after days let us return and inspect all the rods; for He Who created this tree willeth that all those who have received rods from this tree should live. And I myself hope that these little rods, after they have got moisture and been watered, will live the greater part of them."

69

¹ I say to him; "Sir, inform me what this tree is. For I am perplexed herewith, because, though so many branches were cut off, the tree is sound, and nothing appears to have been cut from it; I am therefore perplexed thereat." ² "Listen," saith he; "this great tree which overshadows plains and mountains and all the earth is the law of God which was given to the whole world; and this law is the Son of Cod preached unto the ends of the earth. But the people that are under the shadow are they that have heard the preaching, and believed on Him; ³ but the great and glorious angel is Michael, who hath the power over this people and is their captain. For this is he that putteth the law into the hearts of the believers; therefore he himself inspecteth them to whom he gave it, to see whether they have observed it.

⁴ But thou seest the rods of every one; for the rods are the law. Thou seest these many rods rendered useless, and thou shalt notice all those that have not observed the law, and shalt see the abode of each severally." ⁵ I say unto him; "Sir, wherefore did he send away some into the tower, and leave others for thee?" "As many," saith he, "as transgressed the law which they received from him, these he left under my authority for repentance; but as many as already satisfied the law and have observed it, these he has under his own authority." ⁶ "Who then, Sir," say I, "are they that have been crowned and go into the tower?" ["As many," saith he, "as wrestled with the devil and overcame him in their wrestling, are crowned:] these are they that suffered for the law. ⁷ But the others, who likewise gave up their rods green and with shoots, though not with fruit, are they that were persecuted for the law, but did not suffer nor yet deny their law. ⁸ But they that gave them up green just as they received them, are sober and righteous men, who walked altogether in a pure heart and have kept the commandments of the Lord. But all else thou shalt know, when I have examined these rods that have been planted and watered."

70

¹ And after a few days we came to the place, and the shepherd sat down in the place of the angel, while I stood by him. And he saith to me; "Gird thyself with a garment of raw flax, and minister to me." So I girded myself with a clean garment of raw flax made of coarse material. ² And when he saw me girded and ready to minister to him "Call," saith he, "the men whose rods have been planted, according to the rank as each presented their rods." And I went away to the plain, and called them all; and they stood all of them according to their ranks. ³ He saith to them; "Let each man pluck out his own rod, and bring it to me." Those gave them up first, who had the withered and chipped rods, and they were found accordingly withered and chipped. He ordered them to stand apart. ⁴ Then those gave them up, who had the withered but not chipped; and some of them gave up the rods green, and others withered and chipped as by grubs. Those then that gave them up green he ordered to stand apart; but those that gave them up withered and chipped he ordered to stand with the first. ⁵ Then those gave them up who had the half-withered and with cracks; and many of them gave them up green and without cracks; and some gave them up green and with shoots, and fruits on the shoots, such as those had who went into the tower crowned; and some gave them up withered and eaten, and some withered and uneaten, and some such as they were, half-withered and with cracks. He ordered them to stand each one apart, some in their proper ranks, and others apart.

71

¹ Then those gave them up who had their rods green, but with cracks. These all gave them up green, and stood in their own company. And the shepherd rejoiced over these, because they all were changed and had put away their cracks. ² And those gave them up likewise who had the one half green and the other half withered. The rods of some were found entirely green, of some half-withered, of some withered and eaten, and of some green and with shoots. These were all sent away each to his company. ³ Then those gave them up who had two parts green and the third withered; many of them gave them up green, and many half-withered, and others withered and eaten. These all stood in their own company. ⁴ Then those gave them up who had two parts withered and the third part green. Many of them gave them up half-withered, but some withered and eaten, others half-withered and with cracks, and a few green. These all stood in their own company. ⁵ Then those gave them up who had their rods green, but a very small part [withered] and with cracks. Of these some gave them up green, and others green and with shoots. These also went away to their own company. ⁶ Then those gave them up who had a very small part green and the other parts withered. The rods of these were found for the most part green and with shoots and fruit on the shoots, and others altogether green. At these rods the shepherd rejoiced very [greatly], because they were found so. And these went away each to his own company.

72

¹ After [the shepherd] had examined the rods of all, he saith to me, "I told thee that this tree clingeth to life. Seest thou," saith he, "how many repented and were saved?" "I see, Sir," say I. "It is," saith he, that thou mayest see the abundant compassion of the Lord, how great and glorious it is, and He hath given (His) Spirit to those that are worthy of repentance." ² "Wherefore then, Sir," say I, "did they not all repent?" "To those, whose heart He saw about to become pure and to serve Him with all the heart, to them He gave repentance; but those whose craftiness and wickedness He saw, who intend to repent in hypocrisy, to them He gave not repentance, lest haply they should again profane His name." ³ I say unto him, "Sir, now then show me concerning those that have given up their rods, what manner of man each of them is, and their abode, that when they hear this, they that believed and

have received the seal and have broken it and did not keep it sound may fully understand what they are doing, and repent, receiving from thee a seal, and may glorify the Lord, that He had compassion upon them and sent thee to renew their spirits." ⁴ "Listen," saith he; "those whose rods were found withered and grub-eaten, these are the renegades and traitors to the Church, that blasphemed the Lord in their sins, and still further were ashamed of the Name of the Lord, which was invoked upon them. These then perished altogether unto God. But thou seest how not one of them repented, although they heard the words which thou spakest to them, which I commanded thee. From men of this kind life departed. ⁵ But those that gave up the _withered_ and undecayed (rods), these also are near them; for they were hypocrites, and brought in strange doctrines, and perverted the servants of God, especially them that had sinned, not permitting them to repent, but persuading them with their foolish doctrines. These then have hope of repenting. ⁶ But thou seest that many of them have indeed repented from the time when thou spakest to them my commandments; yea, and (others) still will repent. And as many as shall not repent, have lost their life; but as many of them as repented, became good; and their dwelling was placed within the first walls, and some of them even ascended into the tower. Thou seest then," [saith he,] "that repentance from sins bringeth life, but not to repent bringeth death.

73

¹ "But as many as gave up (the rods) half-withered, and with cracks in them, hear also concerning these. Those whose rods were half-withered throughout are the double-minded; for they neither live nor are dead. ² But those that have them half-withered and cracks in them, these are both double-minded and slanderers, and are never at peace among themselves but always causing dissensions. Yet even to these," [saith he,] "repentance is given. Thou seest," [saith he,] "that some of them have repented; and there is still," saith he, "hope of repentance among them. ³ And as many of them," saith he, "as have repented, have their abode within the tower; but as many of them as have repented tardily shall abide within the walls; and as many as repent not, but continue in their doings, shall die the death. ⁴ But they that have given up their rods green and with cracks, these were found faithful and good at all times, [but] they have a certain emulation one with another about first places and about glory of some kind or other; but all these are foolish in having (emulation) one with another about first places. ⁵ Yet these also, when they heard my commandments, being good, purified themselves and repented quickly. They have their habitation, therefore, within the tower. But if any one shall again turn to dissension, he shall be cast out from the tower and shall lose his life. ⁶ Life is for all those that keep the commandments of the Lord. But in the commandments there is nothing about first places, or about glory of any kind, but about long-suffering and humility in man. In such men, therefore, is the life of the Lord, but in factious and lawless men is death.

74

¹ "But they that gave up their rods half green and half withered, these are they that are mixed up in business and cleave not to the saints. Therefore the one half of them liveth, but the other half is dead. ² Many then when they heard my commandments repented. As many then as repented, have their abode within the tower. But some of them altogether stood aloof These then have no repentance; for by reason of their business affairs they blasphemed the Lord and denied Him. So they lost their life for the wickedness that they committed. ³ But many of them were doubtful-minded. These still have place for repentance, if they repent quickly, and their dwelling shall be within the tower; and if they repent tardily, they shall dwell within the walls; but if they repent not, they too have lost their life. ⁴ But they that have given up two parts green and the third part withered, these are they that have denied with manifold denials. ⁵ Many of them therefore repented and departed to dwell inside the tower; but many utterly rebelled from God; these lost their life finally. And some of them were double-minded and caused dissensions. For these then there is repentance, if they repent speedily and continue not in their pleasures; but if they continue in their doings, they likewise procure for themselves death.

75

¹ "But they that have given up their rods two thirds withered and one third green, these are men who have been believers, but grew rich and became renowned among the Gentiles. They clothed themselves with great pride and became high-minded, and abandoned the truth and did not cleave to the righteous, but lived together after the manner of the Gentiles, and this path appeared the more pleasant unto them; yet they departed not from God, but continued in the faith, though they wrought not the works of the faith. ² Many of them therefore repented, and they had their habitation within the tower. ³ But others at the last living with the Gentiles, and being corrupted by the vain opinions of the Gentiles, departed from God, and worked the works of the Gentiles. These therefore were numbered with the Gentiles. ⁴ But others of them were doubtful-minded, not hoping to be saved by reason of the deeds that they had done; and others were double-minded and made divisions among themselves. For these then that were double-minded by reason of their doings there is still repentance; but their repentance ought to be speedy, that their dwelling may be within the tower; but for those who repent not, but continue in their pleasures, death is nigh.

76

¹ "But they that gave up their rods green, yet with the extreme ends withered and with cracks; these were found at all times good and faithful and glorious in the sight of God, but they sinned to a very slight degree by reason of little desires and because they had somewhat against one another. But, when they heard my words, the greater part quickly repented, and their dwelling was assigned within the tower. ² But some of them were double-minded, and some being double-minded made a greater dissension. In these then there is still a hope of repentance, because they were found always good; and hardly shall one of them die. ³ But they that gave up their rods withered, yet with a very small part green, these are they that believed, but practiced the works of lawlessness. Still they never separated from God, but bore the Name gladly, and gladly received into their houses the servants of God. So hearing of this repentance they repented without wavering, and they practice all excellence and righteousness. ⁴ And some of them even suffer persecution willingly, knowing the deeds that they did. All these then shall have their dwelling within the tower."

77

¹ And after he had completed the interpretations of all the rods, he saith unto me; "Go, and tell all men to repent, and they shall live unto God; for the Lord in His compassion sent me to give repentance to all, though some of them do not deserve it for their deeds; but being long-suffering the Lord willeth them that were called through His Son to be saved." ² I say to him; "Sir, I hope that all when they hear these words will repent; for I am persuaded that each one, when he fully knows his own deeds and fears God, will repent." ³ He answered and said unto me; "As many," [saith he,] "as [shall repent] from their whole heart [and] shall cleanse themselves from all the evil deeds aforementioned, and shall add nothing further to their sins, shall receive healing from the Lord for their former sins, unless they be double-minded concerning these commandments, and they shall live unto God. [But as many," saith he, "as shall add to their sins and walk in the lusts of this world, shall condemn themselves to death.] ⁴ But do thou walk in my commandments, and live [unto God; yea, and as many as shall walk in them and shall do rightly, shall live unto God."] ⁵ Having shown me all these things [and told me them] he saith to me; "Now the rest will I declare (unto thee) after a few days."

Parable 9

78

¹ After I had written down the commandments and parables of the shepherd, the angel of repentance, he came to me and saith to me; "I wish to show thee all things that the Holy Spirit, which spake with thee in the form of the Church, showed unto thee. For that Spirit is the Son of God. ² For when thou wast weaker in the flesh, it was not declared unto thee through an angel; but when thou wast enabled through the Spirit, and didst grow mighty in thy strength so that thou couldest even see an angel, then at length was manifested unto thee, through the Church, the building of the tower. In fair and seemly manner hast thou seen all things, (instructed) as it were by a virgin; but now thou seest (being instructed) by an angel, though by the same Spirit; ³ yet must thou learn everything more accurately from me. For to this end also was I appointed by the glorious angel to dwell in thy house, that thou mightest see all things mightily, in nothing terrified, even as before." ⁴ And he took me away into Arcadia, to a certain rounded mountain, and set me on the top of the mountain, and showed me a great plain, and round the plain twelve mountains, the mountains having each a different appearance. ⁵ The first was black as soot; the second was bare, without vegetation; the third was thorny and full of briars; ⁶ the fourth had the vegetation half-withered, the upper part of the grass green, but the part by the roots withered, and some of the grass became withered, whenever the sun had scorched it; ⁷ the fifth mountain had green grass and was rugged; the sixth mountain was full with clefts throughout, some small and some great, and the clefts had vegetation, but the grass was not very luxuriant, but rather as if it had been withered; ⁸ the seventh mountain had smiling vegetation, and the whole mountain was in a thriving condition, and cattle and birds of every kind did feed upon that mountain; and the more the cattle and the birds did feed, so much the more did the herbage of that mountain flourish. The eighth mountain was full of springs, and every kind of creature of the Lord did drink of the springs on that mountain. ⁹ the ninth mountain had no water at all, and was entirely desert; and it had in it wild beasts and

deadly reptiles, which destroy mankind. The tenth mountain had very large trees and was umbrageous throughout, and beneath the shade lay sheep resting and feeding. ¹⁰ the eleventh mountain was thickly wooded all over, and the trees thereon were very productive, decked with divers kinds of fruits, so that one seeing them would desire to eat of their fruits. The twelfth mountain was altogether white and its aspect was cheerful; and the mountain was most beauteous in itself.

79

¹ And in the middle of the plain he showed me a great white rock, rising up from the plain. The rock was loftier than the mountains, being four-square, so that it could contain the whole world. ² Now this rock was ancient, and had a gate hewn out of it; but the gate seemed to me to have been hewed out quite recently. And the gate glistened beyond the brightness of the sun, so that I marvelled at the brightness of the gate. ³ And around the gate stood twelve virgins. The four then that stood at the corners seemed to me to be more glorious (than the rest); but the others likewise were glorious; and they stood at the four quarters of the gate, and virgins stood in pairs between them. ⁴ And they were clothed in linen tunics and girt about in seemly fashion, having their right shoulders free, as if they intended to carry some burden. Thus were they prepared, for they were very cheerful and eager. ⁵ After I had seen these things, I marvelled in myself at the greatness and the glory of what I was seeing And again I was perplexed concerning the virgins, that delicate as they were they stood up like men, as if they intended to carry the whole heaven. ⁶ And the shepherd saith unto me; "Why questionest thou within thyself and art perplexed, and bringest sadness on thyself? For whatsoever things thou canst not comprehend, attempt them not, if thou art prudent; but entreat the Lord, that thou mayest receive understanding to comprehend them. ⁷ What is behind thee thou canst not see, but what is before thee thou beholdest. The things therefore which thou canst not see, let alone, and trouble not thyself (about them; but the things which thou seest, these master, and be not over curious about the rest; but I will explain unto thee all things whatsoever I shall show thee. Have an eye therefore to what remaineth."

80

¹ I saw six men come, tall and glorious and alike in appearance and they summoned a multitude of men. And the others also which came were tall men and handsome and powerful. And the six men ordered them to build a tower above the gate. And there arose a great noise from those men who had come to build the tower, as they ran hither and thither round the gate. ² For the virgins standing round the gate told the men to hasten to build the tower. Now the virgins had spread out their hands, as if they would take something from the men. ³ And the six men ordered stones to come up from a certain deep place, and to go to the building of the tower. And there went up ten stones square and polished, [not] hewn from a quarry. ⁴ And the six men called to the virgins, and ordered them to carry all the stones which should go unto the building of the tower, and to pass through the gate and to hand them to the men that were about to build the tower. ⁵ And the virgins laid the first ten stones that rose out of the deep on each other, and they carried them together, stone by stone.

81

¹ And just as they stood together around the gate, in that order they carried them that seemed to be strong enough and had stooped under the corners of the stone, while the others stooped at the sides of the stone. And so they carried all the stones. And they carried them right through the gate, as they were ordered, and handed them to the men for the tower; and these took the stones and builded. ² Now the building of the tower was upon the great rock and above the gate. Those ten stones then were joined together, and they covered the whole rock. And these formed a foundation for the building of the tower. And [the rock and] the gate supported the whole tower. ³ And, after the ten stones, other twenty-five stones came up from the deep, and these were fitted into the building of the tower, being carried by the virgins, like the former. And after these thirty-five stones came up. And these likewise were fitted into the tower. And after these came up other forty stones. and these all were put into the building of the tower. So four rows were made in the foundations of the tower. ⁴ And (the stones) ceased coming up from the deep, and the builders likewise ceased for a little. And again the six men ordered the multitude of the people to bring in stones from the mountains for the building of the tower. ⁵ They were brought in accordingly from all the mountains, of various colors, shaped by the men, and were handed to the virgins; and the virgins carried them right through the gate, and handed them in for the building of the tower. And when the various stones were placed in the building, they became all alike and white, and they lost their various colors. ⁶ But some stones were handed in by the men for the building, and these did not become bright; but just as they were placed, such likewise were they found; for they were not handed in by the virgins, nor had they been carried in through the gate. These stones then were unsightly in the building of the tower. ⁷ Then the six men, seeing the stones that were unsightly in the building, ordered them to be removed and carried [below] into their own place whence they were brought. ⁸ And they say to the men who were bringing the stones in; "Abstain for your parts altogether from handing in stones for the building; but place them by the tower, that the virgins may carry them through the gate, and hand them in for the building. For if," [say they,] "they be not carried in through the gate by the hands of these virgins, they cannot change their colors. Labor not therefore," [say they,] "in vain."

82

¹ And the building was finished on that day, yet was not the tower finally completed, for it was to be carried up [still] higher; and there was a cessation in the building. And the six men ordered the builders to retire for a short time [all of them], and to rest; but the virgins they ordered not to retire from the tower. And methought the virgins were left to guard the tower. ² And after all had retired Land rested], I say to the shepherd; "How is it, Sir," say I, "that the building of the tower was not completed?" "The tower," he saith, "cannot yet be finally completed, until its master come and test this building, that if any stones be found crumbling, he may change them; for the tower is being built according to His will." ³ "I would fain know, Sir," say I, "what is this building of this tower, and concerning the rock and gate, and the mountains, and the virgins, and the stones that came up from the deep, and were not shaped, but went just as they were into the building; ⁴ and wherefore ten stones were first placed in the foundations, then twenty-five, then thirty-five, then forty, and concerning the stones that had gone to the building and were removed again and put away in their own place–concerning all these things set my soul at rest, Sir, and explain them to me." ⁵ "If," saith he, "thou be not found possessed of an idle curiosity, thou shalt know all things. For after a few days we shall come here, and thou shalt see the sequel that overtaketh this tower and shalt understand all the parables accurately." ⁶ And after a few days we came to the place where we had sat, and he saith to me, "Let us go to the tower; for the owner of the tower cometh to inspect it." And we came to the tower, and there was no one at all by it, save the virgins alone. ⁷ And the shepherd asked the virgins whether the master of the tower had arrived. And they said that he would be there directly to inspect the building.

83

¹ And, behold, after a little while I see an array of many men coming, and in the midst a man of such lofty stature that he overtopped the tower. ² And the six men who superintended the building walked with him on the right hand and on the left, and all they that worked at the building were with him, and many other glorious attendants around him. And the virgins that watched the tower ran up and kissed him, and they began to walk by his side round the tower. ³ And that man inspected the building so carefully, that he felt each single stone; and he held a rod in his hand and struck each single stone that was built in. ⁴ And when he smote, some of the stones became black as soot, others mildewed, others cracked, others broke off short, others became neither white nor black, others rough and not fitting in with the other stones, and others with many spots; these were the varied aspects of the stones which were found unsound for the building. ⁵ So he ordered all these to be removed from the tower, and to be placed by the side of the tower, and other stones to be brought and put into their place. ⁶ And the builders asked him from what mountain he desired stones to be brought and put into their place. And he would not have them brought from the mountains, but ordered them to be brought from a certain plain that was nigh at hand. ⁷ And the plain was dug, and stones were found there bright and square, but some of them too were round. And all the stones which there were anywhere in that plain were brought every one of them, and were carried through the gate by the virgins. ⁸ And the square stones were hewed, and set in the place of those which had been removed; but the round ones were not placed in the building, because they were too hard to be shaped, and to work on them was slow. So they were placed by the side of the tower, as though they were intended to be shaped and placed in the building; for they were very bright.

84

¹ So then, having accomplished these things, the glorious man who was lord of the whole tower called the shepherd to him, and delivered unto him all the stones which lay by the side of the tower, which were cast out from the building, and saith unto him; ² "Clean these stones carefully, and set them in the building of the tower, these, I mean, which can fit with the rest; but those which will not fit, throw far away from the tower." ³ Having given these orders to the shepherd, he departed from the tower with all those with whom he had come. And the virgins stood round the tower watching it. ⁴ I say to the shepherd, "How can these stones go again to the building of the

tower, seeing that they have been disapproved?" He saith unto me in answer; "Seest thou", saith he, "these stones ?" I see them, Sir," say I. "I myself," saith he, "will shape the greater part of these stones and put them into the building, and they shall fit in with the remaining stones." ⁵ "How, Sir," say I, "can they, when they are chiseled, fill the same space?" He saith unto me in answer, "As many as shall be found small, shall be put into the middle of the building; but as many as are larger, shall be placed nearer the outside, and they will bind them together." ⁶ With these words he saith to me, "Let us go away, and after two days let us come and clean these stones, and put them into the building; for all things round the tower must be made clean, lest haply the master come suddenly and find the circuit of the tower dirty, and he be wroth, and so these stones shall not go to the building of the tower, and I shall appear to be careless in my master's sight." ⁷ And after two days we came to the tower, and he saith unto me; "Let us inspect all the stones, and see those which can go to the building." I say to him, "Sir, let us inspect them."

85

¹ And so commencing first we began to inspect the black stones; and just as they were when set aside from the building, such also they were found. And the shepherd ordered them to be removed from the tower and to be put on one side. ² Then he inspected those that were mildewed, and he took and shaped many of them, and ordered the virgins to take them up and put them into the building. And the virgins took them up and placed them in the building of the tower in a middle position. But the rest he ordered to be placed with the black ones; for these also were found black. ³ Then he began to inspect those that had the cracks; and of these he shaped many, and he ordered them to be carried away by the hands of the virgins for the building. And they were placed towards the outside, because they were found to be sounder. But the rest could not be shaped owing to the number of the cracks. For this reason therefore they were cast aside from the building of the tower. ⁴ Then he proceeded to inspect the stunted (stones), and many among them were found black, and some had contracted great cracks; and he ordered these also to be placed with those that had been cast aside. But those of them which remained he cleaned and shaped, and ordered to be placed in the building So the virgins took them up, and fitted them into the middle of the building of the tower; for they were somewhat weak. ⁵ Then he began to inspect those that were half white and half black, and many of them were (now) found black; and he ordered these also to be taken up with those that had been cast aside. But all the rest were [found white, and were] taken up by the virgins; for being white they were fitted by [the virgins] them[selves] into the building. But they were placed towards the outside, because they were found sound, so that they could hold together those that were placed in the middle; for not a single one of them was too short. ⁶ Then he began to inspect the hard and rough; and a few of them were cast away, because they could not be shaped; but the rest of them were found very hard. But the rest of them were shaped [and taken up by the virgins] and fitted into the middle of the building of the tower; for they were somewhat weak. ⁷ Then he proceeded to inspect those that had the spots, and of these some few had turned black and were cast away among the rest; but the remainder were found bright and sound, and these were fitted by the virgins into the building; but they were placed towards the outside, owing to their strength.

86

¹ Then he came to inspect the white and round stones, and he saith unto me; "What shall we do with these stones?" "How do I know, Sir?" say I [And he saith to me,] "Perceivest thou nothing concerning them?" ² "I, Sir," say I, "do not possess this art, neither am I a mason, nor can I understand." Seest thou not," saith he, "that they are very round; and if I wish to make them square, very much must needs be chiseled off from them? Yet some of them must of necessity be placed into the building." ³ "If then, Sir," say I, "it must needs be so, why distress thyself, and why not choose out for the building those thou willest, and fit them into it?" He chose out from them the large and the bright ones, and shaped them; and the virgins took them up, and fitted them into the outer parts of the building. ⁴ But the rest, which remained over, were taken up, and put aside into the plain whence they were brought; they were not however cast away, "Because," saith he, there remaineth still a little of the tower to be builded. And the master of the tower is exceedingly anxious that these stones be fitted into the building, for they are very bright." ⁵ So twelve women were called, most beautiful in form, clad in black, [girded about and having the shoulders bare,] with their hair hanging loose. And these women, methought, had a savage look. And the shepherd ordered them to take up the stones which had been cast away from the building, and to carry them off to the same mountains from which also they had been brought; ⁶ and they took them up joyfully, and carried away all the stones and put them in the place whence they had been taken. And after all the stones had been taken up, and not a single stone still lay round the tower, the shepherd saith unto me; "Let us go round the tower, and see that there is no defect in it." And I proceeded to go round it with him. ⁷ And when the shepherd saw that the tower was very comely in the building, he was exceedingly glad; for the tower was so well builded, that when I saw it I coveted the building of it; for it was builded, as it were, of one stone, having one fitting in it. And the stone-work appeared as if hewn out of the rock; for it seemed to me to be all a single stone.

87

¹ And I, as I walked with him, was glad to see so brave a sight. And the shepherd saith to me; "Go and bring plaster and fine clay, that I may fill up the shapes of the stones that have been taken up and put into the building; for all the circuit of the tower must be made smooth." ² And I did as he bade, and brought them to him. "Assist me," saith he, "and the work will speedily be accomplished." So he filled in the shapes of the stones which had gone to the building, and ordered the circuit of the tower to be swept and made clean. ³ And the virgins took brooms and swept, and they removed all the rubbish from the tower, and sprinkled water, and the site of the tower was made cheerful and very seemly. ⁴ The shepherd saith unto me, "All," saith he, "hath now been cleaned. If the lord come to inspect the tower, he hath nothing for which to blame us." Saying this, he desired to go away. ⁵ But I caught hold of his wallet, and began to adjure him by the Lord that he would explain to me [all] what he had showed me. He saith to me; "I am busy for a little while, and then I will explain everything to thee. Await me here till I come." ⁶ I say to him; "Sir, when I am here alone what shall I do?" "Thou art not alone," saith he; "for these virgins are here with thee." "Commend me then to them," say I. The shepherd calleth them to him and saith to them; "I commend this man to you till I come," and he departed. ⁷ So I was alone with the virgins; and they were most cheerful, and kindly disposed to Me especially the four of them that were the more glorious in appearance.

88

¹ The virgins say to me; "Today the shepherd cometh not here." "What then shall I do?" say I. "Stay for him," say they, "till eventide; and if he come, he will speak with thee; but if he come not, thou shalt stay here with us till he cometh." ² I say to them; "I will await him till evening, and if he come not, I will depart home and return early in the morning." But they answered and said unto me; "To us thou wast entrusted; thou canst not depart from us." ³ "Where then," say I, "shall I remain?" "Thou shalt pass the night with us," say they as a brother, not as a husband; for thou art our brother, and henceforward we will dwell with thee; for we love thee dearly." But I was ashamed to abide with them. ⁴ And she that seemed to be the chief of them began to kiss and to embrace me; and the others seeing her embrace me, they too began to kiss me, and to lead me round the tower, and to sport with me. ⁵ And I had become as it were a younger man, and I commenced myself likewise to sport with them. For some of them began to dance, [others to skip,] others to sing. But I kept silence and walked with them round the tower, and was glad with them. ⁶ But when evening came I wished to go away home; but they would not let me go, but detained me. And I stayed the night with them, and I slept by the side of the tower. ⁷ For the virgins spread their linen tunics on the ground, and made me lie down in the midst of them, and they did nothing else but pray; and I prayed with them without ceasing, and not less than they. And the virgins rejoiced that I so prayed. And I stayed there with the virgins until the morning till the second hour. ⁸ Then came the shepherd, and saith to the virgins; "Have ye done him any injury?" "Ask him," say they. I say to him, "Sir, I was rejoiced to stay with them." "On what didst thou sup?" saith he "I supped, Sir," say I, "on the words of the Lord the whole night through." "Did they treat thee well?" saith he. "Yes, Sir," say I. ⁹ "Now," saith he, "what wouldest thou hear first?" "In the order as thou showedst to me, Sir, from the beginning," say I; "I request thee, Sir, to explain to me exactly in the order that I shall enquire of thee." According as thou desirest," saith he, "even so will I interpret to thee, and I will conceal nothing whatever from thee."

89

¹ "First of all, Sir," say I, "explain this to me. The rock and the gate, what is it?" "This rock," saith he, "and gate is the Son of God." "How, Sir," say I, "is the rock ancient, but the gate recent?" "Listen," saith he, "and understand, foolish man. ² The Son of God is older than all His creation, so that He became the Father's adviser in His creation. Therefore also He is ancient." "But the gate, why is it recent, Sir?" say I. ³ "Because," saith he, "He was made manifest in the last days of the consummation; therefore the gate was made recent, that they which are to be saved may enter through it into the kingdom of God. ⁴ Didst thou see," saith he, "that the stones which came through the gate have gone to the building of the tower, but those which came not through it were cast away again to their own place?" "I saw, Sir," say I. "Thus," saith he, "no one shall enter into the kingdom of God, except he receive the name of His Son. ⁵ For if thou wishest to enter

into any city, and that city is walled all round and has one gate only, canst thou enter into that city except through the gate which it hath?" "Why, how, Sir," say I, "is it possible otherwise?" "If then thou canst not enter into the city except through the gate itself, even so," saith he, "a man cannot enter into the kingdom of God except by the name of His Son that is beloved by Him. [6] Didst thou see," saith he, "the multitude that is building the tower?" "I saw it, Sir," say I. "They," saith he, are all glorious angels. With these then the Lord is walled around. But the gate is the Son of God; there is this one entrance only to the Lord. No one then shall enter in unto Him otherwise than through His Son. [7] Didst thou see," saith he, "the six men, and the glorious and mighty man in the midst of them, him that walked about the tower and rejected the stones from the building?" "I saw him, Sir," say I. [8] "The glorious man," saith he, "is the Son of God, and those six are the glorious angels who guard Him on the right hand and on the left. Of these glorious angels not one," saith he, "shall enter in unto God without Him; whosoever shall not receive His name, shall not enter into the kingdom of God."

90

[1] "But the tower," say I, "what is it?" "The tower," saith he, "why, this is the Church. [2] "And these virgins, who are they?" "They," saith he, "are holy spirits; and no man can otherwise be found in the kingdom of God, unless these shall clothe him with their garment; for if thou receive only the name, but receive not the garment from them, thou profitest nothing. For these virgins are powers of the Son of God. If [therefore] thou bear the Name, and bear not His power, thou shalt bear His Name to none effect. [3] And the stones," saith he, "which thou didst see cast away, these bare the Name, but clothed not themselves with the raiment of the virgins." "Of what sort, Sir," say I, "is their raiment?" "The names themselves," saith he, "are their raiment. Whosoever beareth the Name of the Son of God, ought to bear the names of these also; for even the Son Himself beareth the names of these virgins. [4] As many stones," saith he, "as thou sawest enter into the building of the tower, being given in by their hands and waiting for the building, they have been clothed in the power of these virgins. [5] For this cause thou seest the tower made a single stone with the rock. So also they that have believed in the Lord through His Son and clothe themselves in these spirits, shall become one spirit and one body, and their garments all of one color. But such persons as bear the names of the virgins have their dwelling in the tower." [6] "The stones then, Sir," say I, "which are cast aside, wherefore were they cast aside? For they passed through the gate and were placed in the building of the tower by the hands of the virgins." "Since all these things interest thee," saith he, "and thou enquirest diligently, listen as touching the stones that have been cast aside. [7] These all," [saith he,] "received the name of the Son of God, and received likewise the power of these virgins. When then they received these spirits, they were strengthened, and were with the servants of God, and they had one spirit and one body [and one garment]; for they had the same mind, and they wrought righteousness. [8] After a certain time then they were persuaded by the women whom thou sawest clad in black raiment, and having their shoulders bare and their hair loose, and beautiful in form. When they saw them they desired them, and they clothed themselves with their power, but they stripped off from themselves the power of the virgins. [9] They then were cast away from the house of God, and delivered to these (women). But they that were not deceived by the beauty of these women remained in the house of God. So thou hast," saith he, "the interpretation of them that were cast aside."

91

[1] What then, Sir," say I, "if these men, being such as they are, should repent and put away their desire for these women, and return unto the virgins, and walk in their power and in their works? Shall they not enter into the house of God?" [2] "They shall enter," saith he, "if they shall put away the works of these women, and take again the power of the virgins, and walk in their works. For this is the reason why there was also a cessation in the building, that, if these repent, they may go into the building of the tower; but if they repent not, then others will go, and these shall be cast away finally." [3] For all these things I gave thanks unto the Lord, because He had compassion on all that called upon His name, and sent forth the angel of repentance to us that had sinned against Him, and refreshed our spirit, and, when we were already ruined and had no hope of life, restored our life. [4] "Now, Sir," say I, "show me why the tower is not built upon the ground, but upon the rock and upon the gate." "Because thou art senseless," saith he, "and without understanding [thou askest the question]." "I am obliged, Sir," say I, "to ask all questions of thee, because I am absolutely unable to comprehend anything at all; for all are great and glorious and difficult for men to understand." [5] "Listen," saith he. "The name of the Son of God is great and incomprehensible, and sustaineth the whole world. If then all creation is sustained by the Son [of God], what thinkest thou of those that are called by Him, and bear the name of the Son of God, and walk according to His commandments? [6] Seest thou then what manner of men He sustaineth? Even those that bear His name with their whole heart. He Himself then is become their foundation, and He sustaineth them gladly, because they are not ashamed to bear His name."

92

[1] "Declare to me, Sir," say I, "the names of the virgins, and of the women that are clothed in the black garments." "Hear," saith he, "the names of the more powerful virgins, those that are stationed at the corners. [2] The first is Faith, and the second, Continence, and the third, Power, and the fourth, Long-suffering. But the others stationed between them have these names– Simplicity, Guilelessness, Purity, Cheerfulness, Truth, Understanding, Concord, Love. He that beareth these names and the name of the Son of God shall be able to enter into the kingdom of God. [3] Hear," saith he, "likewise the names of the women that wear the black garments. Of these also four are more powerful than the rest; the first is Unbelief; the second, Intemperance; the third, Disobedience; the fourth, Deceit; and their followers are called, Sadness, Wickedness, Wantonness, Irascibility, Falsehood, Folly, Slander, Hatred. The servant of God that beareth these names shall see the kingdom of God, but shall not enter into it." [4] "But the stones, Sir," say I, "that came from the deep, and were fitted into the building, who are they?" "The first," saith he, "even the ten, that were placed in the foundations, are the first generation; the twenty-five are the second generation of righteous men; the thirty-five are God's prophets and His ministers; the forty are apostles and teachers of the preaching of the Son of God." [5] "Wherefore then, Sir," say I, "did the virgins give in these stones also for the building of the tower and carry them through the gate?" [6] "Because these first," saith he, "bore these spirits, and they never separated the one from the other, neither the spirits from the men nor the men from the spirits, but the spirits abode with them till they fell asleep; and if they had not had these spirits with them, they would not have been found useful for the building of this tower."

93

[1] "Show me still further, Sir," say I. "What desirest thou to know besides?" saith he. "Wherefore, Sir," say I, "did the stones come up from the deep, and wherefore were they placed into the building, though they bore these spirits?" [2] "It was necessary for them," saith he, "to rise up through water, that they might be made alive; for otherwise they could not enter into the kingdom of God, except they had put aside the deadness of their [former] life. [3] So these likewise that had fallen asleep received the seal of the Son of God and entered into the kingdom of God. For before a man," saith he, "has borne the name of [the Son of] God, he is dead; but when he has received the seal, he layeth aside his deadness, and resumeth life. [4] The seal then is the water: so they go down into the water dead, and they come up alive. "thus to them also this seal was preached, and they availed themselves of it that they might enter into the kingdom of God." [5] "Wherefore, Sir," say I, "did the forty stones also come up with them from the deep, though they had already received the seal?" "Because," saith he, "these, the apostles and the teachers who preached the name of the Son of God, after they had fallen asleep in the power and faith of the Son of God, preached also to them that had fallen asleep before them, and themselves gave unto them the seal of the preaching. [6] Therefore they went down with them into the water, and came up again. But these went down alive [and again came up alive]; whereas the others that had fallen asleep before them went down dead and came up alive. [7] So by their means they were quickened into life, and came to the full knowledge of the name of the Son of God. For this cause also they came up with them, and were fitted with them into the building of the tower and were builded with them, without being shaped; for they fell asleep in righteousness and in great purity. Only they had not this seal. Thou hast then the interpretation of these things also." "I have, Sir," say I.

94

[1] "Now then, Sir, explain to me concerning the mountains. Wherefore are their forms diverse the one from the other, and various?" "Listen," saith he. "These twelve mountains are [twelve] tribes that inhabit the whole world. To these (tribes) then the Son of God was preached by the Apostles." [2] But explain to me, Sir, why they are various–these mountains–and each has a different appearance." "Listen," saith he. "These twelve tribes which inhabit the whole world are twelve nations; and they are various in understanding and in mind. As various, then, as thou sawest these mountains to be, such also are the varieties in the mind of these nations, and such their understanding. And I will show unto thee the conduct of each." [3] "First, Sir," say I, "show me this, why the mountains being so various, yet, when their stones were set into the building, became bright and of one color, just like the stones that had come up from the deep." [4] "Because," saith he, "all the nations that dwell under heaven, when they heard and believed, were

called by the one name of [the Son of] God. So having received the seal, they had one understanding and one mind, and one faith became theirs and [one] love, and they bore the spirits of the virgins along with the Name; therefore the building of the tower became of one color, even bright as the sun. ⁵ But after they entered in together, and became one body, some of them defiled themselves, and were cast out from the society of the righteous, and became again such as they were before, or rather even worse."

95

¹ "How, Sir," say I, "did they become worse, after they had fully known God?" "He that knoweth not God," saith he, "and committeth wickedness, hath a certain punishment for his wickedness; but he that knoweth God fully ought not any longer to commit wickedness, but to do good. ² If then he that ought to do good committeth wickedness, does he not seem to do greater wickedness than the man that knoweth not God? Therefore they that have not known God, and commit wickedness, are condemned to death; but they that have known God and seen His mighty works, and yet commit wickedness, shall receive a double punishment, and shall die eternally. In this way therefore shall the Church of God be purified. ³ And as thou sawest the stones removed from the tower and delivered over to the evil spirits, they too shall be cast out; and there shall be one body of them that are purified, just as the tower, after it had been purified, became made as it were of one stone. Thus shall it be with the Church of God also, after she hath been purified, and the wicked and hypocrites and blasphemers and double-minded and they that commit various kinds of wickedness have been cast out. ⁴ When these have been cast out, the Church of God shall be one body, one understanding, one mind, one faith, one love. And then the Son of God shall rejoice and be glad in them, for that He hath received back His people pure." "Great and glorious, Sir," say I, "are all these things. ⁵ Once more, Sir," [say I,] "show me the force and the doings of each one of the mountains, that every soul that trusteth in the Lord, when it heareth, may glorify His great and marvelous and glorious name." "Listen," saith he, "to the variety of the mountains and of the twelve nations.

96

¹ "From the first mountain, which was black, they that have believed are such as these; rebels and blasphemers against the Lord, and betrayers of the servants of God. For these there is no repentance, but there is death. For this cause also they are black; for their race is lawless. ² And from the second mountain, the bare one, they that believed are such as these; hypocrites and teachers of wickedness. And these then are like the former in not having the fruit of righteousness. For, even as their mountain is unfruitful, so likewise such men as these have a name indeed, but they are void of the faith, and there is no fruit of truth in them. For these then repentance is offered, if they repent quickly; but if they delay, they will have their death with the former." ³ "Wherefore, Sir," say I, "is repentance possible for them, but not for the former ? For their doings are almost the same." "On this account," he saith, "is repentance offered for them, because they blasphemed not their Lord, nor became betrayers of the servants of God; yet from desire of gain they played the hypocrite, and taught each other [after] the desires of sinful men. But they shall pay a certain penalty; yet repentance is ordained for them, because they are not become blasphemers or betrayers.

97

¹ "And from the third mountain, which had thorns and briars, they that believed are such as these; some of them are wealthy and others are entangled in many business affairs. The briars are the wealthy, and the thorns are they that are mixed up in various business affairs. ² These [then, that are mixed up in many and various business affairs,] cleave [not] to the servants of God, but go astray, being choked by their affairs, but the wealthy unwillingly cleave to the servants of God, fearing lest they may be asked for something by them. Such men therefore shall hardly enter into the kingdom of God. ³ For as it is difficult to walk on briars with bare feet, so also it is difficult for such men to enter the kingdom of God. ⁴ But for all these repentance is possible, but it must be speedy, that in respect to what they omitted to do in the former times, they may now revert to (past) days, and do some good. If then they shall repent and do some good, they shall live unto God; but if they continue in their doings, they shall be delivered over to those women, the which shall put them to death.

98

¹ "And from the fourth mountain, which had much vegetation, the upper part of the grass green and the part towards the roots withered, and some of it dried up by the sun, they that believed are such as these; the double-minded, and they that have the Lord on their lips, but have Him not in their heart. ² Therefore their foundations are dry and without power, and their words only live, but their works are dead. Such men are neither alive nor dead. They are, therefore, like unto the double-minded; for the double-minded are neither green nor withered; for they are neither alive nor dead. ³ For as their grass was withered up when it saw the sun, so also the double-minded, when they hear of tribulation, through their cowardice worship idols and are ashamed of the name of their Lord. ⁴ Such are neither alive nor dead. Yet these also, if they repent quickly, shall be able to live; but if they repent not, they are delivered over already to the women who deprive them of their life.

99

¹ "And from the fifth mountain, which had green grass and was rugged, they that believed are such as these; they are faithful, but slow to learn and stubborn and self-pleasers, desiring to know all things, and yet they know nothing at all. ² By reason of this their stubbornness, understanding stood aloof from them, and a foolish senselessness entered into them; and they praise themselves as having understanding, and they desire to be self-appointed teachers, senseless though they are. ³ Owing then to this pride of heart many, while they exalted themselves, have been made empty; for a mighty demon is stubbornness and vain confidence. Of these then many were cast away, but some repented and believed, and submitted themselves to those that had understanding, having learnt their own senselessness. ⁴ Yea, and to the rest that belong to this class repentance is offered; for they did not become wicked, but rather foolish and without understanding. If these then shall repent, they shall live unto God; but if they repent not, they shall have their abode with the women who work evil against them.

100

¹ "But they that believed from the sixth mountain, which had clefts great and small, and in the clefts herbage withered, are such as these; ² they that have the small clefts, these are they that have aught against one another, and from their backbitings they are withered in the faith; but many of these repented Yea, and the rest shall repent, when they hear my commandments; for their backbitings are but small, and they shall quickly repent. ³ But they that have great clefts, these are persistent in their backbitings and bear grudges, nursing wrath against one another. These then were thrown right away from the tower and rejected from its building. Such persons therefore shall with difficulty live. ⁴ If God and our Lord, Who ruleth over all things and hath the authority over all His creation, beareth no grudge against them that confess their sins, but is propitiated, doth man, who is mortal and full of sins, bear a grudge against man, as though he were able to destroy or save him? ⁵ I say unto you–I, the angel of repentance–unto as many as hold this heresy, put it away from you and repent, and the Lord shall heal your former sins, if ye shall purify yourselves from this demon; but if not, ye shall be delivered unto him to be put to death.

101

¹ "And from the seventh mountain, on which was herbage green and smiling, and the whole mountain thriving, and cattle of every kind and the fowls of heaven were feeding on the herbage on that mountain, and the green herbage, on which they fed, only grew the more luxuriant, they that believed are such as these; ² they were ever simple and guileless and blessed, having nothing against one another, but rejoicing always in the servants of God, and clothed in the Holy Spirit of these virgins, and having compassion always on every man, and out of their labors they supplied every man's need without reproach and without misgiving. ³ The Lord then seeing their simplicity and entire childliness made them to abound in the labors of their hands, and bestowed favor on them in all their doings. ⁴ But I say unto you that are such–I, the angel of repentance–remain to the end such as ye are, and your seed shall never be blotted out. For the Lord hath put you to the proof, and enrolled you among our number, and your whole seed shall dwell with the Son of God; for of His Spirit did ye receive.

102

¹ "And from the eighth mountain, where were the many springs, and all the creatures of the Lord did drink of the springs, they that believed are such as these; ² apostles and teachers, who preached unto the whole world, and who taught the word of the Lord in soberness and purity, and kept back no part at all for evil desire, but walked always in righteousness and truth, even as also they received the Holy Spirit. Such therefore shall have their entrance with the angels.

103

¹ "And from the ninth mountain, which was desert, which had [the] reptiles and wild beasts in it which destroy mankind, they that believed are such as these; ² they that have the spots are deacons that exercised their office ill, and plundered the livelihood of widows and orphans, and made gain for themselves from the ministrations which they had received to perform. If then they abide in the same evil desire, they are dead and there is no hope of life for them; but if they turn again and fulfill their ministrations in purity,

it shall be possible for them to live. ³ But they that are mildewed, these are they that denied and turned not again unto their Lord, but having become barren and desert, because they cleave not unto the servants of God but remain alone, they destroy their own souls. ⁴ For as a vine left alone in a hedge, if it meet with neglect, is destroyed and wasted by the weeds, and in time becometh wild and is no longer useful to its owner, so also men of this kind have given themselves up in despair and become useless to their Lord, by growing wild. ⁵ To these then repentance cometh, unless they be found to have denied from the heart; but if a man be found to have denied from the heart, I know not whether it is possible for him to live. ⁶ And this I say not in reference to these days, that a man after denying should receive repentance; for it is impossible for him to be saved who shall now deny his Lord; but for those who denied Him long ago repentance seemeth to be possible. If a man therefore will repent, let him do so speedily before the tower is completed; but if not, he shall be destroyed by the women and put to death. ⁷ And the stunted, these are the treacherous and backbiters; and the wild beasts which thou sawest on the mountain are these. For as wild beasts with their venom poison and kill a man, so also do the words of such men poison and kill a man. ⁸ These then are broken off short from their faith through the conduct which they have in themselves; but some of them repented and were saved; and the rest that are of this kind can be saved, if they repent; but if they repent not, they shall meet their death from those women of whose power they are possessed.

104

¹ "And from the tenth mountain, where were trees sheltering certain sheep, they that believed are such as these; ² bishops, hospitable persons, who gladly received into their houses at all times the servants of God without hypocrisy. [These bishops] at all times without ceasing sheltered the needy and the widows in their ministration and conducted themselves in purity at all times. ³ These [all] then shall be sheltered by the Lord for ever. They therefore that have done these things are glorious in the sight of God, and their place is even now with the angels, if they shall continue unto the end serving the Lord.

105

¹ "And from the eleventh mountain, where were trees full of fruit, decked with divers kinds of fruits, they that believed are such as these; ² they that suffered for the Name [of the Son of God], who also suffered readily with their whole heart, and yielded up their lives." ³ "Wherefore then, Sir," say I, "have all the trees fruits, but some of their fruits are more beautiful than others?" "Listen," saith he; "all as many as ever suffered for the Name's sake are glorious in the sight of God, and the sins of all these were taken away, because they suffered for the name of the Son of God. Now here why their fruits are various, and some surpassing others. ⁴ "As many," saith he, "as were tortured and denied not, when brought before the magistery, but suffered readily, these are the more glorious in the sight of the Lord; their fruit is that which surpasseth. But as many as become cowards, and were lost in uncertainty, and considered in their hearts whether they should deny or confess, and yet suffered, their fruits are less, because this design entered into their heart; for this design is evil, that a servant should deny his own lord. ⁵ See to it, therefore, ye who entertain this idea, lest this design remain in your hearts, and ye die unto God. But ye that suffer for the Name's sake ought to glorify God, because God deemed you worthy that ye should bear this name, and that all your sins should be healed. ⁶ Reckon yourselves blessed therefore; yea, rather think that ye have done a great work, if any of you shall suffer for God's sake. The Lord bestoweth life upon you, and ye percieved it not; for your sins weighed you down, and if ye had not suffered for the Name [of the Lord], ye had died unto God by reason of your sins. ⁷ These things I say unto you that waver as touching denial and confession. Confess that ye have the Lord, lest denying Him ye be delivered into prison. ⁸ If the Gentiles punish their slaves, if any one deny his lord, what think ye the Lord will do unto you, He who has authority over all things? Away with these designs from your hearts, that ye may live forever unto God."

106

¹ "And from the twelfth mountain, which was white, they that believed are such as these; they that are as very babes, into whose heart no guile entereth, neither lernt they what wickedness is, but they remained as babes forever. ² Such as these then dwell without doubt in the kingdom of God, because they defiled the commandments of God in nothing, but continued as babes all the days of their life in the same mind. ³ As many of you therefore as shall continue," saith he, "and shall be as infants not having guile, shall be glorious [even] than all them that have been mentioned before; for all infants are glorious in the sight of God, and stand first in His sight. Blessed then are ye, as many as have put away wickedness from you, and have clothed yourselves in guilelessness: ye shall live unto God chiefest of all."

⁴ After he had finished the parables of the mountains, I say unto him, "Sir, now explain to me concerning the stones that were taken from the plain and placed in the building in the room of the stoes that were taken from the tower, and concerning the round (stones) which were placed in the building, and concerning those that were still round".

107

¹ "Hear," saith he, "likewise concerning all these things. The stones which were taken from the plain and placed in the building of the tower in the room of those that were rejected, are the roots of this white mountain. ² When then they that believed from this mountain were all found guiltless, the lord of the tower ordered these from the roots of the mountain to be put into the building of the tower. For He knew that if these stones should go into the building [of the tower], they would remain bright and not one of them would turn black. ³ But if he added (stones) from other mountains, he would have been obliged to visit the tower again, and to purify it. Now all these have been found white, who have believed and who shall believe; for they are of the same kind. Blessed is this kind, for it is innocent! ⁴ Hear now likewise concerning those round and bright stones. All these are from the white mountain. Now here wherefore they have been found round. Their riches have darkened and obscured them a little from the truth. ⁵ When therefore the Lord percieved their mind, *that they could favor the truth,* and likewise remain good, He commanded their possessions to be cut off from them, yet not to be taken away altogether, so that they might be able to do some good with that which hath been left to them, and might live unto God for that they come of a good kind. So therefore they have been cut away a little, and placed in the building of this tower".

108

¹ "But the other (stones), which have remained round and have not been fitted into the building, because they have not yet received the seal, have been replaced in their own possession, for they were found very round. ² For this world and the vanities of their possessions must be cut off from them, and then they will fit into the kingdom of God. For it is necessary that they should enter into the kingdom of God; because the Lord hath blessed this innocent kind. Of this kind then not one shall perish. Yea, even though any one of them being tempted by the most wicked devil have committed any fault, he shall return speedily unto his Lord. ³ Blessed I pronounced you all to be–I the angel of repentance–whoever of you are guileless as infants, because your part is good and honorable in the sight of God. ⁴ Moreover I bid all of you, whoever have received this seal, keep guilelessness, and bear no grudge, and continue not in your wickedness nor in the memory of the offenses of bitterness; but become of one spirit, and heal these evil clefts and take them away from among you, that the owner of the flocks may rejoice concerning them. ⁵ For he will rejoice, if he find all things whole. But if he find any part of the flock scattered, woe unto the shepherds. ⁶ For if the shepherds themselves shall have been found scattered, how will they answer for the flocks? Will they say that they were harassed by the flock? No credence will be given them. For it is an incredible thing that a shepherd should be injured by his flock; and he will be punished the more because of his falsehood. And I am the shepherd, and it behoveth me most strongly to render an account for you.

109

¹ "Amend yourselves therefore, while the tower is still in course of building. ² The Lord dwelleth in men that love peace; for to Him peace is dear; but from the contentious and them that are given up to wickedness He keepeth afar off. Restore therefore to Him your spirit whole as ye received it. ³ For suppose thou hast given to a fuller a new garment whole, and desirest to receive it back again whole, but the fuller give it back to thee torn, wilt thou receive it thus? Wilt thou not at once blaze out and attack him with reproaches, saying; "The garment which I gave thee was whole; wherefore hast thou rent it and made it useless? See, by reason of the rent, which thou hast made in it, it cannot be of use." Wilt thou not then say all this to a fuller even about a rent which he has made in thy garment? ⁴ If therefore thou art thus vexed in the matter of thy garment, and complainest because thou receivest it not back whole, what thinkest thou the Lord will do to thee, He, Who gave thee the spirit whole, and thou hast made it absolutely useless, so that it cannot be of any use at all to its Lord? For its use began to be useless, when it was corrupted by thee. Will not therefore the Lord of this spirit for this thy deed punish [thee with death]?" ⁵ "Certainly," I said, "all those, whomsoever He shall find continuing to bear malice, He will punish." "Trample not," said he, "upon His mercy, but rather glorify Him, because He is so long-suffering with your sins, and is not like unto you. Practice then repentance which is expedient for you.

110

¹ "All these things which are written above I, the shepherd, the angel of repentance, have declared and spoken to the servants of God. If then ye

shall believe and hear my words, and walk in them, and amend your ways, ye shall be able to live. But if ye continue in wickedness and in bearing malice, no one of this kind shall live unto God. All things which were to be spoken by me have (now) been spoken to you." [2] The shepherd said to me, "Hast thou asked me all thy questions?" And I said, "Yes, Sir." "Why then hast thou not enquired of me concerning the shape of the stones placed in the building, in that we filled up their shapes?" And I said, "I forgot, Sir." [3] "Listen now," said he, "concerning them. These are they that have heard my commandments now, and have practiced repentance with their whole heart. So when the Lord saw that their repentance was good and pure, and that they could continue therein, he ordered their former sins to be blotted out. These shapes then were their former sins, and they have been chiseled away that they might not appear."

Parable 10

111

[1] After I had written out this book completely, the angel who had delivered me to the shepherd came to the house where I was, and sat upon a couch, and the shepherd stood at his right hand. Then he called me, and spake thus unto me; [2] "I delivered thee," said he, "and thy house to this shepherd, that thou mightest be protected by him." "True, Sir," I said "If therefore," said he, "thou desirest to be protected from all annoyance and all cruelty, to have also success in every good work and word, and all the power of righteousness, walk in his commandments, which I have given thee, and thou shalt be able to get the mastery over all wickedness. [3] For if thou keep his commandments, all evil desire and the sweetness of this world shall be subject unto thee; moreover success shall attend thee in every good undertaking. Embrace his gravity and self-restraint, and tell it out unto all men that he is held in great honor and dignity with the Lord, and is a ruler of great authority, and powerful in his office. To him alone in the whole world hath authority over repentance been assigned. Seemeth he to thee to be powerful? Yet ye despise the gravity and moderation which he useth towards you."

112

[1] I say unto him; "Ask him, Sir, himself, whether from the time that he hath been in my house, I have done ought out of order, whereby I have offended him." [2] "I myself know," said he, "that thou hast done nothing out of order, nor art about to do so. And so I speak these things unto thee, that thou mayest persevere. For he hath given a good account of thee unto me. Thou therefore shalt speak these words to others, that they too who have practiced or shall practice repentance may be of the same mind as thou art; and he may give a good report of them to me, and I unto the Lord." [3] "I too, Sir," I say, "declare to every man the mighty works of the Lord; for I hope that all who have sinned in the past, if they hear these things, will gladly repent and recover life." [4] "Continue therefore," said he, "in this ministry, and complete it unto the end. For whosoever fulfill his commandments shall have life; yea such a man (shall have) great honor with the Lord. But whosoever keep not his commandments, fly from their life, and oppose him, and follow not his commandments, but deliver themselves over to death; and each one becometh guilty of his own blood. But I bid thee obey these commandments, and thou shalt have a remedy for thy sins.

113

[1] "Moreover, I have sent these virgins unto thee, that they may dwell with thee; for I have seen that they are friendly towards thee. Thou hast them therefore as helpers, that thou mayest be the better able to keep his commandments; for it is impossible that these commandments be kept without the help of these virgins. I see too that they are glad to be with thee. But I will charge them that they depart not at all from thy house. [2] Only do thou purify thy house; for in a clean house they will gladly dwell. For they are clean and chaste and industrious, and have favor in the sight of the Lord. If, therefore, they shall find thy house pure, they will continue with thee; but if the slightest pollution arise, they will depart from thy house at once. For these virgins love not pollution in any form." [3] I said unto him, "I hope, Sir, that I shall please them, so that they may gladly dwell in my house for ever; and just as he to whom thou didst deliver me maketh no complaint against me, so they likewise shall make no complaint." [4] He saith unto the shepherd, "I perceive," saith he, "that he wishes to live as the servant of God, and that he will keep these commandments, and will place these virgins in a clean habitation." [5] With these words he again delivered me over to the shepherd, and called the virgins, and said to them; "Inasmuch as I see that ye are glad to dwell in this man's house, I commend to you him and his house, that ye depart not at all from his house." But they heard these words gladly.

114

[1] He said then to me, "Quit you like a man in this ministry; declare to every man the mighty works of the Lord, and thou shalt have favor in this ministry. Whosoever therefore shall walk in these commandments, shall live and be happy in his life; but whosoever shall neglect them, shall not live, and shall be unhappy in his life. [2] Charge all men who are able to do right, that they cease not to practice good works; for it is useful for them. I say moreover that every man ought to be rescued from misfortune; for he that hath need, and suffereth misfortune in his daily life, is in great torment and want. [3] Whosoever therefore rescueth from penury a life of this kind, winneth great joy for himself. For he who is harassed by misfortune of this sort is afflicted and tortured with equal torment as one who is in chains. For many men on account of calamities of this kind, because they can bear them no longer, lay violent hands on themselves. He then who knows the calamity of a man of this kind and rescueth him not, committeth great sin, and becometh guilty of the man's blood. [4] Do therefore good works, whoever of you have received (benefits) from the Lord, lest, while ye delay to do them, the building of the tower be completed. For it is on your account that the work of the building has been interrupted. Unless then ye hasten to do right, the tower will be completed, and ye shut out." [5] When then he had finished speaking with me, he rose from the couch and departed, taking with him the shepherd and the virgins. He said however unto me, that he would send the shepherd and the virgins back again to my house. . .

The Epistle of Ignatius to the Ephesians

1

1 Commends them for sending Onesimus, and other members of the church to him. 8 Exhorts them to unity, 13 by a due subjection to their bishop.

¹ IGNATIUS, who is also called Theophorus, to the church which is at Ephesus in Asia; most deservedly happy; being blessed through the greatness and fulness of God the Father, and predestinated before the world began, that it should be always unto an enduring and unchangeable glory; being united and chosen through his true passion, according to the will of the Father, and Jesus Christ our God; all happiness, by Jesus Christ, and his undefiled grace. ² I have heard of your name much beloved in God; which ye have very justly attained by a habit of righteousness, according to the faith and love which is in Jesus Christ our Saviour. ³ How that being followers of God, and stirring up yourselves by the blood of Christ ye have perfectly accomplished the work that was con-natural unto you. ⁴ For hearing that I came bound from Syria, for the common name and hope, trusting through your prayers to fight with beasts at Rome; so that by suffering I may become indeed the disciple of him who gave himself to God, an offering and sacrifice for us; (ye hastened to see me). I received, therefore, in the name of God, your whole multitude in Onesimus. ⁵ Who by inexpressible love is ours, but according to the flesh is your bishop; whom I beseech you, by Jesus Christ, to love; and that you would all strive to be like unto him. And blessed be God, who has granted unto you, who are so worthy of him, to enjoy such an excellent bishop. ⁶ For what concerns my fellow servant Burrhus, and your most blessed deacon in things pertaining to God; I entreat you that he may tarry longer, both for yours, and your bishop's honour. ⁷ And Crocus also worthy both our God and you, whom I have received as the pattern of your love, has in all things refreshed me, as the Father of our Lord Jesus Christ shall also refresh him; together with Onesimus, and Burrhus, and Euclus, and Fronto, in whom I have, as to your charity, seen all of you. And may I always, have joy of you, if I shall be worthy of it. ⁸ It is therefore fitting that you should by all means glorify Jesus Christ who hath glorified you: that by a uniform obedience ye may be perfectly joined together, in the same mind, and in the same judgment: and may all speak the same things concerning everything. ⁹ And that being subject to your bishop, and the presbytery, ye may be wholly and thoroughly sanctified. ¹⁰ These things I prescribe to you, not as if I were somebody extraordinary: for though I am bound for his name, I am not yet perfect in Christ Jesus. But now I begin to learn, and I speak to you as fellow disciples together with me. ¹¹ For I ought to have been stirred up by you, in faith, in admonition, in patience, in long-suffering; but forasmuch as charity suffers me not to be silent towards you, I have first taken upon me to exhort you, that ye would all run together according to the will of God. ¹² For even Jesus Christ, our inseparable life, is sent by the will of the Father; as the bishops, appointed unto the utmost bounds of the earth, are by the will of Jesus Christ. ¹³ Wherefore it will become you to run together according to the will of your bishop, as also ye do. ¹⁴ For your famous presbytery, worthy of God, is fitted as exactly to the bishop, as the strings are to the harp. ¹⁵ Therefore in your concord and agreeing charity, Jesus Christ is sung; and every single person among you makes up the chorus: ¹⁶ That so being all consonant in love, and taking up the song of God, ye may in a perfect unity with one voice, sing to the Father by Jesus Christ; to the end that he may both hear you, and perceive by your works, that ye are indeed the members of his son. ¹⁷ Wherefore it is profitable for you to live in an unblameable unity, that so ye may always have a fellowship with God.

2

1 The benefit of subjection. 4 The bishop not to be respected the less because he is not forward in exacting it: 8 warns them against heretics; bidding them cleave to Jesus, whose divine and human nature is declared; commends them for their care to keep themselves front false teachers; and shews them the way to God.

¹ FOR if I in this little time have had such a familiarity with your bishop, I mean not a carnal, but spiritual acquaintance with him; how much more must I think you happy who are so joined to him, as the church is to Jesus Christ, and Jesus Christ to the Father; that so all things may agree in the same unity? ² Let no man deceive himself; if a man be not within the altar, he is deprived of the bread of God. For if the prayers of one or two be of such force, as we are told; how much more powerful shall that of the bishop and the whole church be? ³ He therefore that does not come together in the same place with it, is proud, and has already condemned himself. For it is written, God resisteth the proud. Let us take heed therefore, that we do not set ourselves against the bishop, that we may be subject to God. ⁴ The more any one sees his bishop silent, the more let him revere him. For whomsoever the master of the house sends to be over his own household, we ought in like manner to receive him, as we would do him that sent him. It is therefore evident that we ought to look upon the bishop, even as we would do upon the Lord himself. ⁵ And indeed Onesimus himself does greatly commend your good order in God: that you all live according to the truth, and that no heresy dwells among you. For neither do ye hearken to any one more than to Jesus Christ speaking to you in truth. ⁶ For some there are who carry about the name of Christ in deceitfulness, but do things unworthy of God; whom ye must flee, as ye would do so many wild beasts. For they are ravening dogs, who bite secretly: against whom ye must guard yourselves, as men hardly to be cured. ⁷ There is one physician, both fleshly and spiritual; made and not made; God incarnate; true life in death; both of Mary and of God; first passable, then impassible; even Jesus Christ our Lord. ⁸ Wherefore let no man deceive you; as indeed neither are ye deceived. being wholly the servants of God. For inasmuch as there is no contention nor strife among you, to trouble you, ye must needs live according to God's will. My soul be for yours; and I myself the expiatory offering for your church of Ephesus, so famous throughout the world. ⁹ They that are of the flesh cannot do the works of the spirit; neither they that are of the spirit the works of the flesh. As he that has faith cannot be an infidel; nor he that is an infidel have faith. But even those things which ye do according to the flesh are spiritual; forasmuch as ye do all things in Jesus Christ. ¹⁰ Nevertheless I have heard of some who have passed by you, having perverse doctrine; whom ye did not suffer to sow among you; but stopped your ears, that ye might not receive those things that were sown by them; as becoming the stones of the temple of the Father, prepared for his building; and drawn up on high by the Cross of Christ, as by an engine. ¹¹ Using the Holy Ghost as the rope: your faith being your; and your charity the way that leads unto God. ¹² Ye are therefore, with all your companions in the same journey, full of God; his spiritual temples, full of Christ, full of holiness: adorned in all things with the commands of Christ. ¹³ In whom also I rejoice that I have been thought worthy by this present epistle to converse, and joy together with you; that with respect to the other life, ye love nothing but God only.

3

1 Exhorts them to prayer; to be unblameable. 5 To be careful of salvation; 11 frequent in public devotion; 13 and to live in charity.

¹ PRAY also without ceasing for other men: for there is hope of repentance in them, that they may attain unto God. Let them therefore at least be instructed by your works, if they will be no other way. ² Be ye mild at their anger; humble at their boasting; to their blasphemies return your prayers: to their error, your firmness in the faith: when they are cruel, be ye gentle; not endeavouring to imitate their ways. (³ Let us be their brethren in all kindness and moderation, but let us be followers of the Lord; for who was ever more unjustly used? More destitute? More despised?) ⁴ That so no herb of the devil may be found in you: but ye may remain in all holiness and sobriety both of body and spirit, in Christ Jesus. ⁵ The last times are come upon us: let us therefore be very reverent and fear the long-suffering of God, that it be not to us e unto condemnation. ⁶ For let us either fear the wrath that is to come, or let us love the grace that we at present enjoy: that by the one, or other, of these we may be found in Christ Jesus, unto true life. ⁷ Besides him, let nothing be worthy of you; for whom also I bear about these bonds, those spiritual jewels, in which I would to God that I might arise through your prayers. ⁸ Of which I entreat you to make me always partaker, that I may be found in the lot of the Christians of Ephesus, who have always agreed with the Apostles, through the power of Jesus Christ. ⁹ I know both who I am, and to whom I write; I, a person condemned: ye, such as have obtained mercy: I, exposed to danger; ye, confirmed against danger. ¹⁰ Ye are the passage of those that are killed for God; the companions of Paul in the mysteries of the Gospel; the Holy, the martyr, the deservedly most happy Paul: at whose feet may I be found, when I shall have attained unto God; who throughout all his epistle, makes mention of you in Christ Jesus. ¹¹ Let it be your care therefore to come more fully together, to the praise and glory of God. For when ye meet fully together in the same place, the powers of the devil are destroyed, and his mischief is dissolved by the unity of their faith. ¹² And indeed, nothing is better than peace, by which all war both spiritual and earthly is abolished. ¹³ Of all which nothing is hid from you, if ye have perfect faith and charity in Christ Jesus, which are the beginning and end of life. ¹⁴ For the beginning is faith; the end is charity. And these two joined together, are of God: but all other things which concern a holy life are the consequences of these. ¹⁵ No man professing a true faith, sinneth; neither does he who has charity hate any. ¹⁶ The tree is made manifest by its fruit; so they who profess themselves to be Christians are known by what they do. ¹⁷ For Christianity is not the work of an outward profession; but shows itself in the power of faith, if a man be found faithful unto the end. ¹⁸ It is better for a man to hold his peace, and be; than to say he is a Christian and not to be. ¹⁹ It is good to teach; if what

he says he does likewise. ²⁰ There is therefore one master who spake, and it was done; and even those things which he did without speaking, are worthy of the Father. ²¹ He that possesses the word of Jesus is truly able to hear his very silence, that he may be perfect; and both do according to what he speaks, and be known by those things of which he is silent. ²² There is nothing hid from God, but even our secrets are nigh unto him. ²³ Let us therefore do all things, as becomes those who have God dwelling in them; that we may be his temples, and he may be our God: as also he is, and will manifest himself before our faces, by those things for which we justly love him.

4

1 To have a care for the Gospel. 9 The virginity of Mary, the incarnation, and the death of Christ, were hid front the Devil. 11 How the birth of Christ was revealed. 16 Exhorts to unity.

¹ BE not deceived, my brethren: those that corrupt families inherit adultery, shall not inherit the kingdom of God. ² If therefore they who do this according to the flesh, have suffered death; how much more shall he die, who by his wicked doctrine corrupts the faith of God, for which Christ was crucified? ³ He that is thus defiled, shall depart into unquenchable fire, and so also shall he that hearkens to him. ⁴ For this cause did the Lord suffer the ointment to be poured on his head; that he might breathe the breath of immortality unto his church. ⁵ Be not ye therefore anointed with the evil savour of the doctrine of the prince of this world: let him not take you captive from the life that is set before you. ⁶ And why are we not all wise, seeing we have receive the knowledge of God, which is Jesus Christ? Why do we suffer ourselves foolishly to perish; not considering the gift which the Lord has truly sent to us? ⁷ Let my life be sacrificed for the doctrine of the cross; which is indeed a scandal to the unbelievers, but to us is salvation and life eternal. ⁸ Where is the wise man? Where is the disputer? Where is the boasting of those who are called wise? ⁹ For our God Jesus Christ was according to the dispensation of God conceived in the womb of Mary, of the seed of David, by the Holy Ghost; he was born and baptized, that through his passion he might purify water, to the washing away of sin. ¹⁰ Now the Virginity of Mary, and he who was born of her, was kept in secret from the prince of this world; as was also the death of our Lord: three of the mysteries the most spoken of throughout the world, yet done in secret by God. ¹¹ How then was our Saviour manifested to the world? A star shone in heaven beyond all the other stars, and its light was inexpressible, and its novelty struck terror into men's minds. All the rest of the stars, together with the sun and moon, were the chorus to this star; but that sent out its light exceedingly above them all. ¹² And men began to be troubled to think whence this new star came so unlike to all the others. ¹³ Hence all the power of magic became dissolved; and every bond of wickedness was destroyed: men's ignorance was taken away; and the old kingdom abolished; God himself appearing in the form of a man, for the renewal of eternal life. ¹⁴ From thence began what God had prepared: from thenceforth things were disturbed; forasmuch as he designed to abolish death. ¹⁵ But if Jesus Christ shall give me grace through your prayers, and it be his will, I purpose in a second epistle which I will suddenly write unto you to manifest to you more fully the dispensation of which I have now begun to speak, unto the new man, which is Jesus Christ; both in his faith, and charity; in his suffering, and in his resurrection. ¹⁶ Especially if the Lord shall make known unto me, that ye all by name come together in common in one faith, and in one Jesus Christ; who was of the race of David according to the flesh; the Son of man, and Son of God; obeying your bishop and the presbytery with an entire affection; breaking one and the same bread, which is the medicine of immortality; our antidote that we should not die, but live forever in Christ Jesus. ¹⁷ My soul be for yours, and theirs whom ye have sent to the glory of God, even unto Smyrna; from whence also I write to you; giving thanks unto the Lord and loving Polycarp even as I do you. Remember me, as Jesus Christ does remember you. ¹⁸ Pray for the church which is in Syria, from whence I am carried bound to Rome; being the least of all the faithful which are there, as I have been thought worthy to be found to the glory of God. ¹⁹ Fare ye well in God the Father, and in Jesus Christ, our common Hope. Amen.

The Epistle of Ignatius to the Magnesians

1

4 Mentions the arrival of Damon, their bishop, and others, 6 whom he exhorts them to reverence, notwithstanding he was a young man.

¹ IGNATIUS who is also called Theophorus; to the blessed (church) by the grace of God the Father in Jesus Christ our Saviour: in whom I salute the church which is at Magnesia near the Mæander: and wish it all joy in God the Father and in Jesus Christ. ² When I heard of your well ordered love and charity in God, being full of joy, I desired much to speak unto you in the faith of Jesus Christ. ³ For having been thought worthy to obtain a most excellent name, in the bonds which I carry about, I salute the churches; wishing in them a union both of the body and spirit of Jesus Christ, our eternal life: as also of faith and charity, to which nothing is preferred: but especially of Jesus and the Father in whom if we undergo all the injuries of the prince of this pre sent world, and escape, we shall enjoy God. ⁴ Seeing then I have been judged worthy to see you, by Damas your most excellent bishop; and by your very worthy presbyters, Bassus and Apollonius; and by my fellow-servant Sotio, the deacon; ⁵ In whom I rejoice, forasmuch as he is the subject unto his bishop as to the grace of God, and to the presbytery as to the law of Jesus Christ; I determined to write unto you. ⁶ Wherefore it will become you also not to use your bishop too familiarly upon the account of his youth; but to yield all reverence to him according to the power of God the Father; as also I perceive that your holy presbyters do: not considering is age, which indeed to appearance is young; but as becomes those who are prudent in God, submitting to him, or rather not to him, but to the Father of our Lord Jesus Christ, the bishop of us all. ⁷ It will therefore behoove you with all sincerity, to obey your bishop; in honour him whose pleasure it is that ye should do so. ⁸ Because he that does not do so, deceives not the bishop whom he sees, but affronts him that is invisible. For whatsoever of this kind is done, it reflects not upon man, but upon God, who knows the secrets of our hearts. ⁹ It is therefore fitting, that we should not only be called Christians, but be so. ¹⁰ As some call indeed their governor, bishop; but yet do all things without him. ¹¹ But I can never think that such as these have a good conscience, seeing that they are not gathered together thoroughly according to God's commandment.

2

1 That as all must die, 4 he exhorts them to live orderly and in unity.

¹ SEEING then all things have an end, there are these two indifferently set before us, death and life: and every one shall depart unto his proper place. ² For as there are two sorts of coins, the one of God, the other of the world; and each of these has its proper inscription engraven upon it; so also is it here. ³ The unbelievers are of this world; but the faithful, through charity, have the character of God the Father by Jesus Christ: by whom if we are not readily disposed to die after the likeness of his passion, his life is not in us. ⁴ Forasmuch, therefore, as I have in the persons before mentioned seen all of you in faith and charity; I exhort you that ye study to do all things in divine concord: ⁵ Your bishop presiding in the place of God; your presbyters in the place of the council of the Apostles; and your deacons most dear to me being entrusted with the ministry of Jesus Christ; who was the Father before all ages, and appeared in the end to us. ⁶ Wherefore taking the same holy course, see that ye all reverence one another: and let no one look upon his neighbour after the flesh; but do ye all mutually love each other in Jesus Christ. ⁷ Let there be nothing that may be able to make a division among you; but be ye united to your bishop, and those who preside over you, to be your pattern and direction in the way to immortality. ⁸ As therefore the Lord did nothing without the Father, being united to him; neither by himself nor yet by his Apostles, so neither do ye do anything without your bishop and presbyters: ⁹ Neither endeavour to let anything appear rational to yourselves apart; ¹⁰ But being come together into the same place have one common prayer; one supplication; one mind; one hope; one in charity, and in joy undefiled. ¹¹ There is one Lord Jesus Christ, than whom nothing is better. Wherefore come ye all together as unto one temple of God; as to one altar, as to one Jesus Christ; who proceeded from one Father, and exists in one, and is returned to one.

3

1 He cautions them against false opinions. 4 Especially those of Ebion and the Judaizing Christians.

¹ BE not deceived with strange doctrines; nor with old fables which are unprofitable. For if we still continue to live according to the Jewish law, we do confess ourselves not to have received grace. For even the most holy prophets lived according to Christ Jesus. ² And for this cause were they persecuted, being inspired by his grace, to convince the unbelievers and disobedient that there is one God who has manifested himself by Jesus Christ his Son; who is his eternal word, not coming forth from

silence, who in all things pleased him that sent him. ³ Wherefore if they who were brought up in these ancient laws came nevertheless to the newness of hope: no longer observing sabbaths, but keeping the Lord's day in which also our life is sprung up by him, and through his death, whom yet some deny: ⁴ (By which mystery we have been brought to believe and therefore wait that we may be found the disciples of Jesus Christ, our only master:) ⁵ How shall we be able to live different from him whose disciples the very prophets themselves being, did by the spirit expect him as their master. ⁶ And therefore he whom they justly waited for, being come, raised them up from the dead. ⁷ Let us not then be insensible of his goodness; for should he have dealt with us according to our works, we had not no had a being. ⁸ Wherefore being become his disciples, let us learn to live according to the rules of Christianity; for whosoever is called by any other name besides this, he is not of God. ⁹ Lay aside therefore the old and sour and evil leaven; and be ye changed into the new leaven, which is Jesus Christ. ¹⁰ Be ye salted in him, lest any one among you should be corrupted; for by your savour ye shall be judged. ¹¹ It is absurd to name Jesus Christ, and to Judaize. For the Christian religion did not embrace the Jewish, but the Jewish the Christian; that so every tongue that believed might be gathered together unto God. ¹² These things, my beloved, I write unto you; not that I know of any among you that lie under this error; but as one of the least among you, I am desirous to forewarn you, that ye fall not into the snares of false doctrine. ¹³ But that ye be fully instructed in the birth, and suffering, and resurrection of Jesus Christ, our hope; which was accomplished in the time of the government of Pontius Pilate, and that most truly and certainly and from which God forbid that any among you should be turned aside.

4

¹ *Commends their faith and piety; exhorts them to persevere;* ¹⁰ *desires their prayers for himself and the church at Antioch.* MAY I therefore have joy of you in all things, if I shall be worthy of it. For though I am bound, yet I am not worthy to be compared to one of you that are at liberty. ² I know that ye are not puffed up; for ye have Jesus Christ in your hearts. ³ And especially when I commend you, I know that ye are ashamed, as it is written, The just man condemneth himself. ⁴ Study therefore to be confirmed in the doctrine of our Lord, and of his Apostles; that so whatever ye do, ye may prosper both in body and spirit, in faith and charity, in the Son, and in the Father and in the Holy Spirit: in the beginning, and in the end. ⁵ Together with your most worthy bishop, and the well-wrought spiritual crown of your presbytery, and your deacons, which are according to God. ⁶ Be subject to your bishop, and to one another, as Jesus Christ to the Father, according to the flesh: and the Apostles both to Christ, and to the Father, and to the Holy Ghost: that so ye may be united both in body and spirit. ⁷ Knowing you to be full of God, I have the more briefly exhorted you. ⁸ Be mindful of me in your prayers, that I may attain unto God, and of the Church that is in Syria, from which I am not worthy to be called. ⁹ For I stand in need of your joint prayers in God, and of your charity, that the church which is in Syria may be thought worthy to be nourished by your church. ¹⁰ The Ephesians from Smyrna salute you, from which place I write unto you: (being present here to the glory of God, in like manner as you are,) who have in all things refreshed me, together with Polycarp, the bishop of the Smyrnæans. ¹¹ The rest of the churches in the honour of Jesus Christ, salute you. ¹² Farewell, and be ye strengthened in the concord of God: enjoying his inseparable spirit, which is Jesus Christ.

The Epistle of Ignatius to the Trallians

1

1 Acknowledges the coming of their bishop. 5 Commends them for their subjection to their bishop, priests, and deacons; and exhorts them to continue in it: 15 is afraid even of his over-great desire to suffer, lest it should be prejudicial to him.

¹ IGNATIUS, who is also called Theophorus, to the holy church which is at Tralles in Asia: beloved of God the Father of Jesus Christ, elect and worthy of God, having peace through the flesh and blood, and passion of Jesus Christ our hope, in the resurrection which is by him: which also I salute in its fulness, continuing in the apostolical character, wishing all joy and happiness unto it. ² I have heard of your blameless and constant disposition through patience, which not only appears in your outward conversation, but is naturally rooted and grounded in you. ³ In like manner as Polybius your bishop has declared unto me, who came to me to Smyrna, by the will of God and Jesus Christ, and so rejoiced together with me in my bonds for Jesus Christ, that in effect I saw your whole church in him. ⁴ Having therefore received testimony of your good will towards me for God's sake, by him; I seemed to find you, as also I knew that ye were the followers of God. ⁵ For whereas ye are subject to your bishop as to Jesus Christ, ye appear to me to live not after the manner of men, but according to Jesus Christ; who died for us, that so believing in his death, ye might escape death. ⁶ It is therefore necessary, that as ye do, so without your bishop, you should do nothing: also be ye subject to your presbyters, as to the Apostles of Jesus Christ our hope; in whom if we walk, we shall be found in him. ⁷ The deacons also, as being the ministers of the mysteries of Jesus Christ, must by all means please ye. For they are not the ministers of meat and drink, but of the church of God. Wherefore they must avoid all offences, as they would do fire. ⁸ In like manner let us reverence the deacons as Jesus Christ; and the bishop as the father; and the presbyters as the Sanhedrim of God, and college of the Apostles. ⁹ Without these there is no church. Concerning all which I am persuaded that ye think after the very same manner: for I have received, and even now have with me, the pattern of your love, in your bishop. ¹⁰ Whose very look is instructive; and whose mildness powerful: whom I am persuaded, the very Atheists themselves cannot but reverence. ¹¹ But because I have a love towards you, I will not write any more sharply unto you about this matter, though I very well might; but now I have done so; lest being a condemned man, I should seem to prescribe to you as an Apostle. ¹² I have great knowledge in God; but I refrain myself, lest I should perish in my boasting. ¹³ For now I ought the more to fear; and not to hearken to those that would puff me up. ¹⁴ For they that speak to me, in my praise, chasten me. ¹⁵ For I indeed desire to suffer, but I cannot tell whether I am worthy so to do. ¹⁶ And this desire, though to others it does not appear, yet to myself it is for that very reason the more violent. I have, therefore, need of moderation; by which the prince of this world is destroyed. ¹⁷ Am I not able to write to you of heavenly things?– But I fear lest I should harm you, who are yet but babes in Christ: (excuse me this care;) and lest per chance being not able to receive them, ye should be choken with them. ¹⁸ For even I myself, although I am in bonds, yet am not therefore able to understand heavenly things: ¹⁹ As the places of the angels, and the several companies of them, under their respective princes; things visible and invisible; but in these I am yet a learner. ²⁰ For many things are wanting to us, that we come not short of God.

2

1 Warns them against heretics, 4 exhorts them to humility and unity, 10 briefly sets before them the true doctrine concerning Christ.

¹ I EXHORT you therefore, or rather not I, but the love of Jesus Christ; that ye use none but Christian nourishment; abstaining from pasture which is of another kind, I mean heresy. ² For they that are heretics, confound together the doctrine of Jesus Christ, with their own poison: whilst they seem worthy of belief: ³ As men give a deadly potion mixed with sweet wine; which he who drinks of, does with the treacherous pleasure sweetly drink in his own death. ⁴ Wherefore guard yourselves against such persons. And that you will do if you are not puffed up; but continue inseparable from Jesus Christ our God, and from your bishop, and from the commands of the Apostles. ⁵ He that is within the altar is pure; but he that is without, that is, that does anything without the bishop, the presbyters, and deacons, is not pure in his conscience. ⁶ Not that I know there is any thing of this nature among you; but I fore-arm you, as being greatly beloved by me, foreseeing the snares of the devil. ⁷ Wherefore putting on meekness, renew yourselves in faith, that is, the flesh of the Lord; and in charity, that is, the blood of Jesus Christ. ⁸ Let no man have any grudge against his neighbour. Give no occasion to the Gentiles; lest by means of a few foolish men, the whole congregation of God be evil spoken of. ⁹ For woe to that man through whose vanity my name is blasphemed by any. ¹⁰ Stop your ears therefore, as often as any one

shall speak contrary to Jesus Christ; who was of the race of David, of the Virgin Mary. ¹¹ Who was truly born and did eat and drink; was truly persecuted under Pontius Pilate; was truly crucified and dead; both those in heaven and on earth, being spectators of it. ¹² Who was also truly raised from the dead by his Father. after the same manner as he will also raise up us who believe in him by Christ Jesus; without whom we have no true life. ¹³ But if, as some who are Atheists, that is to say infidels, pretend, that he only seemed to suffer: (they themselves only seeming to exist) why then am I bound?–Why do I desire to fight with beasts?–Therefore do I die in vain: therefore I will not speak falsely against the Lord. ¹⁴ Flee therefore these evil sprouts which bring forth deadly fruit; of which if any one taste, he shall presently die. ¹⁵ For these are not the plants of the Father; seeing if they were, they would appear to be the branches of the cross, and their fruit would be incorruptible; by which he invites you through his passion, who are members of him. ¹⁶ For the head cannot be without its members, God having promised a union, that is himself.

3

He again exhorts to unity: and desires their prayers for himself and for his church at Antioch.

¹ I SALUTE you from Smyrna, together with the churches of God that are present with me; who have refreshed me in all things, both in the flesh and in the spirit. ² My bonds, which I carry about me for the sake of Christ, beseeching him that I may attain unto God) exhort you, that you continue in concord among yourselves and in prayer with one another. ³ For it becomes every one of you, especially the presbyters, to refresh the bishop, to the honour of the Father of Jesus Christ and of the Apostles. ⁴ I beseech you, that you hearken to me in love; that I may not by those things which I write, rise up in witness against you. ⁵ Pray also for me; who through the mercy of God stand in need of your prayers, that I may be worthy of the portion which I am about to obtain that I be not found a reprobate. ⁶ The love of those who are at Smyrna and Ephesus salute you. Remember in your prayers the church of Syria, from which I am not worthy to be called, being one of the least of it. ⁷ Fare ye well in Jesus Christ; being subject to your bishop as to the command of God; and so likewise to the presbytery. ⁸ Love every one his brother with an unfeigned heart. My soul be your expiation, not only now, but when I shall have attained unto God; for I am yet under danger. ⁹ But the Father is faithful in Jesus Christ, to fulfil both mine and your petition; in whom may ye be found unblamable.

The Epistle of Ignatius to the Romans

1

He testifies his desire to see, and his hopes of suffering for Christ, 5 which he earnestly entreats them not to prevent, 10 but to pray for him, that God would strengthen him to the combat.

¹ IGNATIUS, who is also called Theophorus, to the church which has obtained mercy from the majesty of the Most High Father, and his only begotten Son Jesus Christ; beloved, and illuminated through the will of who willeth all things which are according to the love of Jesus Christ our God which also presides in the place of the region of the Romans; and which I salute in the name of Jesus Christ (as being) united both in flesh and spirit to all his commands, and filled with the grace of God; (all joy) in Jesus Christ our God. ² Forasmuch as I have at last obtained through my prayers to God, to see your faces, which I much desired to do; being bound in Jesus Christ, I hope ere long to salute you, if it shall be the will of God to grant me to attain unto the end I long for. ³ For the beginning is well disposed, if I shall but have grace, without hindrance, to receive what is appointed for me. ⁴ But I fear your love, lest it do me an injury. For it is easy for you to do what you please; but it will be hard for me to attain unto God, if you spare me. ⁵ But I would not that ye should please men, but God whom also ye do please. For neither shall I hereafter have such an opportunity of going unto God; nor will you if ye shall now be silent, ever be entitled to a better work. For if you shall be silent in my behalf, I shall be made partaker of God. ⁶ But if you shall love my body, I shall have my course again to run. Wherefore ye cannot do me a greater kindness, than to suffer me to be sacrificed unto God, now that the altar is already prepared: ⁷ That when ye shall be gathered together in love, ye may give thanks to the Father through Christ Jesus; that he has vouchsafed to bring a bishop of Syria unto you, being called from the east unto the west. ⁸ For it is good for me to set from the world, unto God; that I may rise again unto him. ⁹ Ye have never envied any one; ye have taught other. I would therefore that ye should now do those things yourselves, which in your instructions you have prescribed to others. ¹⁰ Only pray for me, that God would give me both inward and outward strength, that I may not only say, but will; nor be only called a Christian, but be found one. ¹¹ For if I shall be found a Christian, I may then deservedly be called one; and be thought faithful, when I shall no longer appear to the world. ¹² Nothing is good, that is seen. ¹³ For even our God, Jesus Christ, now that he is in the Father, does so much the more appear. ¹⁴ A Christian is not a work of opinion; but of greatness of mind, (especially when he is hated by the world.)

2

Expresses his great desire and determination to suffer martyrdom.

¹ I WRITE to the churches, and signify to them all, that am willing to die for God, unless hinder me. ² I beseech you that you shew not an unseasonable good will towards me. Suffer me to be food to the wild beasts; by whom I shall attain unto God. ³ For I am the wheat of God; and I shall be ground by the teeth of the wild beasts, that I may be found the pure bread of Christ. ⁴ Rather encourage the beasts, that they may become my sepulchre; and may leave nothing of my body; that being dead I mazy not be troublesome to any. ⁵ Then shall I be truly the disciple of Jesus Christ, when the world shall not see so much as my body, Pray therefore unto Christ for me, that by these instruments I may be made the sacrifice of God. ⁶ I do not, as Peter and Paul, command you. They were Apostles, I a condemned man; they were free, but I am even to this day a servant: ⁷ But if I shall suffer, I shall then become the freeman of Jesus Christ, and shall rise free. And now, being in bonds, I learn, not to desire anything. ⁸ From Syria even unto Rome, I fight with beasts both by sea and land; both night and day: being bound to ten leopards, that is to say, to such a band of soldiers; who, though treated with all manner of kindness, are the worse for it. ⁹ But I am the more instructed by their injuries; yet am I not therefore justified. ¹⁰ May I enjoy the wild beasts that are prepared for me; which also I wish may exercise all their fierceness upon me. ¹¹ And whom for that end I will encourage, that they may be sure to devour me, and not serve me as they have done some, whom out of fear they have not touched. But, and if they will not do it willingly, I will provoke them to it. ¹² Pardon me in this matter; I know what is profitable for me. Now I begin to be a disciple. Nor shall anything move me, whether visible or invisible, that I may attain to Jesus Christ. ¹³ Let fire, and the cross; let the companies of wild beasts; let breakings of bones and tearing of members; let the shattering in pieces of the whole body, and all the wicked torments of the devil come upon me; only let me enjoy Jesus Christ. ¹⁴ All the ends of the world, and the kingdoms of it, will profit me nothing: I would rather die for Jesus Christ, than rule to the utmost ends of the earth. Him I seek who died for us; him I desire, that rose again for us. This is the gain that is laid up for me. ¹⁵ Pardon me, my brethren, ye shall not hinder me from living. Nor seeing I desire to go to God, may you separate me from him, for the sake of this world; nor reduce me by any of the desires of it. Suffer me to enter into pure light: Where being come, I shall be indeed the servant of God. ¹⁶ Permit me to imitate the passion of my God. If any one has him within himself, let him consider what I desire; and let him have compassion on me, as knowing how I am straightened.

3

Further expresses his desire to suffer.

¹ THE prince of this world would fain carry me away, and corrupt my resolution towards my God. Let none of you therefore help him: Rather do ye join with me, that is, with God. ² Do not speak with Jesus Christ, and yet covet the world. Let not any envy dwell with you; No not though I myself when I shall be come unto you, should exhort you to it, yet do not ye hearken to me; but rather believe what I now write to you. ³ For though I am alive, at the writing this, yet my desire is to die. My love is crucified; (and the fire that is within me does not desire any water; but being alive and springing within me, says,) Come to the Father. ⁴ I take no pleasure in the food of corruption, nor in the pleasures of this life. ⁵ I desire the bread of God which is the flesh of Jesus Christ, (of the seed of David; and the drink that I long for) is his blood, which is incorruptible love. ⁶ I have no desire to live any longer after the manner of men, neither shall I, if you consent. Be ye therefore willing, that you yourselves also may be pleasing to God. I exhort you in a few words; I pray you believe me. ⁷ Jesus Christ will shew you that I speak truly. My mouth is without deceit, and the Father hath truly spoken by it. Pray therefore for me, that I may accomplish what I desire. ⁸ I have not written to you after the flesh, but according to the will of God. If I shall suffer, ye have loved me; but if I shall be rejected, ye have hated me. ⁹ Remember in your prayers the church of Syria, which now enjoys God for its shepherd instead of me: Let Jesus Christ only oversee it, and your charity. ¹⁰ But I am even ashamed to be reckoned as one of them: For neither am I worthy, being the least among them, and as one born out of due season. But through mercy I have obtained to be somebody, if I shall get unto God. ¹¹ My spirit salutes you; and the charity of the churches that have received me in the name of Jesus Christ; not as a passenger. For even they that were not near to me in the way, have gone before me to the next city to meet me. ¹² These things I write to you from Smyrna, by the most worthy of the

church of Ephesus. [13] There is now with me, together with many others, Crocus, most beloved of me. As for those which are come from Syria, and are gone before me to Rome, to the glory of God, I suppose you are not ignorant of them. [14] Ye shall therefore signify to them, that I draw near, for they are all worthy both of God and of you: Whom it is fit that you refresh in all things. [15] This have I written to you, the day before the ninth of the calends of September. Be strong unto the end, in the patience of Jesus Christ.

The Epistle of Ignatius to the Philadelphians

1

Commends their bishop whom they had sent unto him, 5 warns them against divisions and schism.

[1] IGNATIUS, who is also called Theophorus, to the church of God the Father, and our Lord Jesus Christ, which is at Philadelphia in Asia; which has obtained mercy, being fixed in the concord of God, and rejoicing evermore in the passion of our Lord, and being fulfilled in all mercy through his resurrection: Which also I salute in the blood of Jesus Christ, which is our eternal and undefiled joy; especially if they are at unity with the bishop, and presbyters who are with him, and the deacons appointed according to the mind of Jesus Christ; whom he has settled according to his own will in all firmness by his Holy Spirit: [2] Which bishop I know obtained that great ministry among you, not of himself, neither by men, nor out of vain glory; but by the love of God the Father, and our Lord Jesus Christ. [3] Whose moderation I admire; who by his silence is able to do more than others with all their vain talk. For he is fitted to the commands, as the harp to its strings. [4] Wherefore my soul esteems his mind towards God most happy, knowing it to be fruitful in all virtue, and perfect; full of constancy, free from passion, and according to all the moderation of the living God. [5] Wherefore as becomes the children both of the light and of truth; flee divisions and false doctrines; but where your shepherd is, there do ye, as sheep, follow after. [6] For there are many wolves who seem worthy of belief with a false pleasure lead captive those that run in the course of God; but in the concord they shall find no place. [7] Abstain therefore from evil herbs which Jesus does not dress; because such are not the plantation of the Father. Not that I have found any division among you, but rather all manner of purity. [8] For as many as are of God, and of Jesus Christ, are also with their bishop. And as many as shall with repentance return into the unity of the church, even these shall also be the servants of God, that they may live according to Jesus. [9] Be not deceived, brethren; if any one follows him that makes a schism in the church, he shall not inherit the kingdom of God. If any one walks after any other opinion, he agrees not with the passion of Christ. [10] Wherefore let it be your endeavour to partake all of the same holy eucharist. [11] For there is but one flesh of our Lord Jesus Christ; and one cup in the unity of his blood; one altar; [12] As also there is one bishop, together with his presbytery, and the deacons my fellow-servants: that so whatsoever ye do, ye may do it according to the will of God.

2

Desires their prayers, and to be united but not to Judaize.

[1] MY brethren, the love I have towards you makes me the more large; and having a great joy in you, I endeavour to secure you against danger; or rather not I, but Jesus Christ; in whom being bound I the more fear, as being yet only on the way to suffering. [2] But your prayer to God shall make me perfect, that I may attain to that portion, which by God's mercy is allotted to me: Fleeing to the Gospel as to the flesh of Christ; and to the Apostles as to the presbytery of the church. [3] Let us also love the prophets, forasmuch as they also have led us to the Gospel, and to hope in Christ, and to expect him. [4] In whom also believing they were saved in the unity of Jesus Christ; being holy men, worthy to be loved, and had in wonder; [5] Who have received testimony from Jesus Christ, and are numbered in the Gospel of our common hope. [6] But if any one shall preach the Jewish law unto you, hearken not unto him; for it is better to receive the doctrine of Christ from one that has been circumcised, than Judaism from one that has not. [7] But if either the one, or other, do not speak concerning Christ Jesus, they seem to me to be but as monuments and sepulchres of the dead, upon which are written only the names of men. [8] Flee therefore the wicked arts and snares of the prince of this world; lest at any time being oppressed by his cunning ye grow cold in your charity. But come all together into the same place with an undivided heart. [9] And I bless my God that I have a good conscience towards you, and that no one among you has whereof to boast either openly or privately, that I have been burthensome to him in much or little. [10] And I wish to all among whom I have conversed, that it may not turn to a witness against them. [11] For although some would have deceived me according to the flesh, yet the spirit, being from God, is not deceived; for it knows both whence it comes and whither it goes, and reproves the secrets of the heart. [12] I cried whilst I was among you; I spake with a loud voice: attend to the bishop, and to the presbytery, and to the deacons. [13] Now some supposed that I spake this as foreseeing the division that should come among you. [14] But he is my witness for whose sake I am in bonds that I knew nothing from any man. But the spirit spake, saying on this wise: Do nothing without the bishop: [15] Keep your bodies as the temples of God: Love unity; Flee divisions; Be the followers of Christ, as he was of his Father. [16] I therefore did as became me, as a man composed to unity. For where there is division, and wrath, God dwelleth not. [17] But the Lord forgives all that repent, if they

return to the unity of God, and to the council of the bishop. ¹⁸ For I trust in the grace of Jesus Christ that he will free you from every bond. ¹⁹ Nevertheless I exhort you that you do nothing out of strife, but according to the instruction of Christ. ²⁰ Because I have heard of some who say; unless I find it written in the originals, I will not believe it to be written in the Gospel. And when I said, It is written; they answered what lay before them in their corrupted copies. ²¹ But to me Jesus Christ is instead of all the uncorrupted monuments in the world; together with those undefiled monuments, his cross, and death, and resurrection, and the faith which is by him; by which I desire, through your prayers, to be justified. ²² The priests indeed are good; but much better is the High Priest to whom the Holy of Holies has been committed; and who alone has been entrusted with the secrets of God. ²³ He is the door of the Father; by which Abraham, and Isaac, and Jacob, and all the prophets, enter in; as well as the Apostles, and the church. ²⁴ And all these things tend to the unity which is of God. Howbeit the Gospel has some. what in it far above all other dispensations; namely, the appearance of our Saviour, the Lord Jesus Christ, his passion and resurrection. ²⁵ For the beloved prophets referred to him; but the gospel is the perfection of incorruption. All therefore together are good, if ye believe with charity.

3

Informs them he had heard that the persecution was stopped at Antioch, and directs them to send a messenger hitherto to congratulate with the church.

¹ NOW as concerning the church of Antioch which is in Syria, seeing I am told that through your prayers and the bowels which ye have towards it in Jesus Christ, it is in peace; it will become you, as the church of God, to ordain some deacon to go to them thither as the ambassador of God; that he may rejoice with them when they meet together, and glorify God's name. ² Blessed be that man in Jesus Christ, who shall be found worthy of such a ministry; and ye yourselves also shall be glorified. ³ Now if you be willing, it is not impossible for you to do this for the grace of God; as also the other neighbouring churches have sent them, some bishops, some priests and deacons. ⁴ As concerning Philo the deacon of Cilicia, a most worthy man, he still ministers unto me in the word of God: together with Rheus of Agathopolis, a singular good person, who has followed me even from Syria, not regarding his life: These also bear witness unto you. ⁵ And I myself give thanks to God for you that you receive them as the Lord shall receive you. But for those that dishonoured them, may they be forgiven through the grace of Jesus Christ. ⁶ The charity of the brethren that are at Troas salutes you: from whence also I now write by Burrhus, who was sent together with me by those of Ephesus and Smyrna, for respect sake. ⁷ May our Lord Jesus Christ honour them; in whom they hope, both in flesh, and soul, and spirit; in faith, in love, in unity. Farewell in Christ Jesus our common hope.

The Epistle of Ignatius to the Smyrnæans

1

1 Declares his joy for their firmness in the Gospel. 4 Enlarges on the person of Christ, against such as pretend that Christ did not really suffer.

¹ IGNATIUS, who is also called Theophorus, to the church of God the Father, and of the beloved Jesus Christ, which God hath mercifully blessed with every good gift; being filled with faith and charity, so that this is wanting in no gift; most worthy of God, and fruitful in saints: the church which is at Smyrna in Asia; all joy, through his immaculate spirit, and the word of God. ² I glorify God, even Jesus Christ, who has given you such wisdom. ³ For I have observed that you are settled in an immovable faith, as if you were nailed to the cross of our Lord Jesus Christ, both in the flesh and in the spirit; and are confirmed in love through the blood of Christ; being fully persuaded of those things which relate unto our Lord. ⁴ Who truly was of the race of David according to the flesh, but the Son of God according to the will and power of God; truly born of the Virgin, and baptized of John; that so all righteousness might be fulfilled by him. ⁵ He was also truly crucified by Pontius Pilate, and Herod the Tetrarch, being nailed for us in the flesh; by the fruits of which we are, even by his most blessed passion. ⁶ That he might set up a token for all ages through his resurrection, to all his holy and faithful servants, whether they be Jews or Gentiles, in one body of his church. ⁷ Now all these things he suffered for us that we might be saved. And he suffered truly, as he also truly raised up himself: And not, as some unbelievers say, that he only seemed to suffer, they themselves only seeming to be. ⁸ And as they believe so shall it happen unto them; when being divested of the body they shall become mere spirits. ⁹ But I know that even after his resurrection he was in the flesh; and I believed that he is still so. ¹⁰ And when he came to those who were with Peter, he said unto them, Take, handle me, and see that I am not an incorporeal dæmon. And straightway they felt and believed; being convinced both by his flesh and spirit. ¹¹ For this cause they despised death, and were found to be above it. ¹² But after his resurrection he did eat and drink with them, as he was flesh; although as to his Spirit he was united to the Father.

2

1 Exhorts them against heretics. 8 The danger of their doctrine.

¹ NOW these things, beloved, put you in mind of, not questioning but that you yourselves also believe that they are so. ² But I arm you before-hand against certain beasts in the shape of men whom you must not only not receive, but if it be possible must not meet with. ³ Only you must pray for them, that if it be the will of God they may repent; which yet will be very hard. But of this our Lord Jesus Christ has the power, who is our true life. ⁴ For if all these things were done only in shew by our Lord, then do I also seem only to be bound. ⁵ And why have I given up myself to death, to the fire, to the sword, to wild beasts! ⁶ But now the nearer I am to the sword, the nearer I am to God: when I shall come among the wild beasts, I shall come to God. ⁷ Only in the name of Jesus Christ, I undergo all, to suffer together with him; he who was made a perfect man strengthening me. ⁸ Whom some not knowing, do deny; or rather have been denied by him, being the advocates of death, rather than of the truth. Whom neither the prophecies, nor the law of Moses have persuaded; nor the Gospel itself even to this day, nor the sufferings of every one of us. ⁹ For they think also the same things of us. For what does a man profit me, if he shall praise me, and blaspheme my Lord; not confessing that he was truly made man? ¹⁰ Now he that doth not say this, does in effect deny him, and is in death. But for the names of such as do this, they being unbelievers, I thought it not fitting to write them unto you. ¹¹ Yea, God forbid that I should make any mention of them, till they shall repent to a true belief of Christ's passion, which is our resurrection. ¹² Let no man deceive himself; both the things which are in heaven and the glorious angels, and princes, whether visible or invisible, if they believe not in the blood of Christ, it shall be to them to condemnation. ¹³ He that is able to receive this, let him receive it. Let no man's place or state in the world puff him up: that which is worth all his faith and charity, to which nothing is to be preferred. ¹⁴ But consider those who are of a different opinion from us, as to what concerns the grace of Jesus Christ which is come unto us, how contrary they are to the design of God. ¹⁵ They have no regard to charity, no care of the widow, the fatherless, and the oppressed; of the bond or free, of the hungry or thirsty. ¹⁶ They abstain from the eucharist, and from the public offices; because they confess not the eucharist to be the flesh of our Saviour Jesus Christ; which suffered for our sins, and which the Father of his goodness, raised again from the dead. ¹⁷ And for this cause contradicting the gift of God, they die in their disputes: but much better would it be for them to receive it, that they might one day rise through it. ¹⁸ It will therefore become you to abstain from such persons; and not to speak with them neither in private nor in

public. ¹⁹ But to hearken to the prophets, and especially to the Gospel, in which both Christ's passion is manifested unto us, and his resurrection perfectly declared. ²⁰ But flee all divisions, as the beginning of evils.

3

1 Exhorts them to follow their bishop and pastors; but especially their bishop. 6 Thanks them for their kindness, 11 and acquaints them with the ceasing of the persecution at Antioch.

¹ SEE that ye all follow your bishop, as Jesus Christ, the Father; and the presbytery, as the Apostles. And reverence the deacons, as the command of God. ² Let no man do anything of what belongs to the church separately from the bishop. ³ Let that eucharist be looked upon as well established, which is either offered by the bishop, or by him to whom the bishop has given his consent. ⁴ Wheresoever the bishop shall appear, there let the people also be: as where Jesus Christ is, there is the Catholic church. ⁵ It is not lawful without the bishop, neither to baptize, nor to celebrate the Holy Communion; but whatsoever he shall approve of, that is also pleasing unto God; that so whatever is done, may be sure and well done. ⁶ For what remains, it is very reasonable that we should repent whilst there is yet time to return unto God. ⁷ It is a good thing to have a due regard both to God, and to the bishop: he that honours the bishop, shall be honoured of God. But he that does anything without his knowledge, ministers unto the devil. ⁸ Let all things therefore abound to you in charity; seeing that ye are worthy. ⁹ Ye have refreshed me in all things; so shall Jesus Christ you. Ye have loved me both when I was present with you, and now being absent, ye cease not to do so. ¹⁰ May God be your reward, from whom whilst ye undergo all things, ye shall attain unto him. ¹¹ Ye have done well in that ye have received Philo, and Rheus Agathopus, who followed me for the word of God, as the deacons of Christ our God. ¹² Who also gave thanks unto the Lord for you, forasmuch as ye have refreshed them in all things. Nor shall any thing that you have done be lost to you. ¹³ My soul be for yours, and my bonds which ye have not despised, nor been ashamed of. Wherefore neither shall Jesus Christ, our perfect faith, be ashamed of you. ¹⁴ Your prayer is come to the church of Antioch which is in Syria. From whence being sent bound with chains becoming God, I salute the churches; being not worthy to be called from thence, as being the least among them. ¹⁵ Nevertheless by the will of God I have been thought worthy of this honour; not for that I think I have deserved it, but by the grace of God. ¹⁶ Which I wish may be perfectly given unto me, that through your prayers I may attain unto God. ¹⁷ And therefore that your work may be fully accomplished both upon earth and in heaven; it will be fitting, and for the honour of God, that your church appoint some worthy delegate, who being come as far as Syria, may rejoice together with them that they are in peace; and that they are again restored to their former state, and have again received their proper body. ¹⁸ Wherefore I should think it a worthy action, to send some one from you with an epistle, to congratulate with them their peace in God; and that through your prayers they have now gotten to their harbor. ¹⁹ For inasmuch as ye are perfect yourselves, you ought to think those things that are perfect. For when you are desirous to do well, God is ready to enable you thereunto. ²⁰ The love of the brethren that are at Troas salute you; from whence I write to you by Burrhus whom you sent with me, together with the Ephesians your brethren; and who has in all things refreshed me. ²¹ And I would to God that all would imitate him, as being a pattern of the ministry of God. May his grace fully reward him. ²² I salute your very worthy bishop, and your venerable presbytery; and your deacons, my fellow-servants; and all of you in general, and every one in particular, in the name of Jesus Christ, and in his flesh and blood; in his passion and resurrection both fleshly and spiritually; and in the unity of God with you. ²³ Grace be with you, and mercy, and peace, and patience, for evermore. ²⁴ I salute the families of my brethren, with their wives and children; and the virgins that are called widows. Be strong in the power of the Holy Ghost. Philo, who is present with me salutes you. ²⁵ I salute the house of Tavias, and pray that it may be strengthened in faith and charity, both of flesh and spirit. ²⁶ I salute Alce my well-beloved, together with the incomparable Daphnus, and Eutechnus, and all by name. ²⁷ Farewell in the grace of God.

The Epistle of Ignatius to Polycarp

1

Blesses God for the firm establishment of Polycarp in the faith, and gives him particular directions for improving it.

¹ IGNATIUS, who is also called Theophorus, to Polycarp, bishop of the church which is at Smyrna; their overseer, but rather himself overlooked by God the Father, and the Lord Jesus Christ: all happiness. ² Having known that thy mind towards God, is fixed as it were upon an immovable rock; I exceedingly give thanks, that I have been thought worthy to behold thy blessed face, in which may I always rejoice in God. ³ Wherefore I beseech thee by the grace of God with which thou art clothed, to press forward in thy course, and to exhort all others that they may be saved. ⁴ Maintain thy place with all care both of flesh and spirit: Make it thy endeavour to preserve unity, than which nothing is better. Bear with all men, even as the Lord with thee. ⁵ Support all in love, as also thou dost. Pray without ceasing: ask more understanding than what thou already hast. Be watchful, having thy spirit always awake. ⁶ Speak to every one according as God shall enable thee. Bear the infirmities of all, as a perfect combatant; where the labour is great, the gain is the more. ⁷ If thou shalt love the good disciples, what thank is it? But rather do thou subject to thee those that are mischievous, in meekness. ⁸ Every wound is not healed with the same plaster: if the accessions of the disease be vehement, modify them with soft remedies: be in all things wise as a serpent, but harmless as a dove. ⁹ For this cause thou art composed of flesh and spirit; that thou mayest modify those things that appear before thy face. ¹⁰ And as for those that are not seen, pray to God that he would reveal them unto thee, that so thou mayest be wanting in nothing, but mayest abound in every gift. ¹¹ The times demand thee, as the pilots the winds; and he that is tossed in a tempest, the haven where he would be; that thou mayst attain unto God. ¹² Be sober as the combatant of God: the crown proposed to thee is immortality, and eternal life; concerning which thou art also fully persuaded. I will be thy surety in all things, and my bonds, which thou hast loved. ¹³ Let not those that seem worthy of credit, but teach other doctrines, disturb thee. Stand firm and immovable, as au anvil when it is beaten upon. ¹⁴ It is the part of a brave combatant to be wounded, and yet overcome. But especially we ought to endure all things for God's sake, that he may bear with us. ¹⁵ Be every day better than other: consider the times; and expect him, who is above all time, eternal, invisible, though for our sakes made visible: impalpable, and impassable, yet for us subjected to sufferings; enduring all manner of ways for our salvation.

2

1 Continues his advice, 6 and teaches him how to advise others. 12 Enforces unity and subjection to the bishop.

¹ LET not the widows be neglected: be thou after God, their guardian. ² Let nothing be done without thy knowledge and consent; neither do thou anything but according to the will of God; as also thou dost, with all constancy. ³ Let your assemblies be more full: inquire into all by name. ⁴ Overlook not the men and maid servants; neither let them be puffed up: but rather let them be the more subject to the glory of God, that they may obtain from him a better liberty. ⁵ Let them not desire to be set free at the public cost, that they be not slaves to their own lusts. ⁶ Flee evil arts; or rather, make not any mention of them. ⁷ Say to my sisters, that they love the Lord; and be satisfied with their own husbands, both in the flesh and spirit. ⁸ In like manner, exhort my brethren, in the name of Jesus Christ, that they love their wives, even as the Lord the Church. ⁹ If any man can remain in a virgin state, to the honour of the flesh of Christ, let him remain without boasting; but if he boast, he is undone. And if he desire to be more taken notice of than the bishop he is corrupted. ¹⁰ But it becomes all such as are married, whether men or women to come together with the consent of the bishop, that so their marriage may be according to godliness, and not in lust. ¹¹ Let all things be done to the honour of God. ¹² Hearken unto the bishop, that God also may hearken unto you. My soul be security for them that submit to their bishop, with their presbyters and deacons. And may my portion be together with theirs in God. ¹³ Labour with one another; contend together, run together, suffer together; sleep together, and rise together; as the stewards, and assessors, and ministers of God. ¹⁴ Please him under whom ye war, and from whom ye receive your wages. Let none of you be found a deserter; but let your baptism remain, as your arms; your faith, as your helmet; your charity, as your spear; your patience, as your whole armour. ¹⁵ Let your works be your charge, that so you may receive a suitable reward. Be longsuffering therefore towards each other in meekness: as God is towards you. ¹⁶ Let me have joy of you in all things.

3

1 Greets Polycarp on the peace of the church at Antioch: and desires him to write to that and other churches.

¹ NOW forasmuch as the church of Antioch in Syria, is, as I am told, [one word illegible] through your prayers; I also have been the more comforted and without care in God; if so be that by suffering, I shall attain unto God; that through your prayers I may be found a disciple of Christ. ² It will be very fit, O most worthy Polycarp, to call a select council, and choose some one whom ye particularly love, and who is patient of labour; that he may be the messenger of God; and that going unto Syria, he may glorify your incessant love, to the praise of Christ. ³ A Christian has not the power of himself: but must be always at leisure for God's service. Now this work is both God's and your's: when ye shall have perfected it. ⁴ For I trust through the grace of God that ye are ready to every good work that is fitting for you in the Lord. ⁵ Knowing therefore your earnest affection for the truth, I have exhorted you by these short letters. ⁶ But forasmuch as I have not been able to write to all the churches, because I must suddenly sail from Troas to Neapolis; (for so is the command of those to whose pleasure I am subject;) do you write to the churches that are near you, as being instructed in the will of God, that they also may do in like manner. ⁷ Let those that are able send messengers; and let the rest send their letters by those who shall be sent by you: that you may be glorified to all eternity, of which you are worthy. ⁸ I salute all by name, particularly the wife of Epitropus, with all her house and children. I salute Attalus my well-beloved. ⁹ I salute him who shall be thought worthy to be sent by you into Syria. Let grace be ever with him, and with Polycarp who sends him. ¹⁰ I wish you all happiness in our God, Jesus Christ; in whom continue, in the unity and protection of God. ¹¹ I salute Alce my well-beloved. Farewell in the Lord.

The Epistle of Ignatius to the Philippians

Ignatius, who is also called Theophorus, to the Church of God which is at Philippi, which has obtained mercy in faith, and patience, and love unfeigned: Mercy and peace from God the Father, and the Lord Jesus Christ, "who is the Saviour of all men, specially of them that believe."

1

Reason For Writing The Epistle

Being mindful of your love and of your zeal in Christ, which ye have manifested towards us we thought it fitting to write to you, who display such a godly and spiritual love to the brethren, to put you in remembrance of your Christian course, "that ye all speak the same thing, being of one mind, thinking the same thing, and walking by the same rule of faith," as Paul admonished you. For if there is one God of the universe, the Father of Christ, "of whom are all things;" and one Lord Jesus Christ, our [Lord], "by whom are all things;" and also one Holy Spirit, who wrought in Moses, and in the prophets and apostles; and also one baptism, which is administered that we should have fellowship with the death of the Lord; and also one elect Church; there ought likewise to be but one faith in respect to Christ. For "there is one Lord, one faith, one baptism; one God and Father of all, who is through all, and in all."

2

Unity Of The Three Divine Persons

There is then one God and Father, and not two or three; One who is; and there is no other besides Him, the only true [God]. For "the Lord thy God," saith [the Scripture], "is one Lord." And again, "Hath not one God created us? Have we not all one Father? And there is also one Son, God the Word. For "the only-begotten Son," saith [the Scripture], "who is in the bosom of the Father." And again, "One Lord Jesus Christ." And in another place, "What is His name, or what His Son's name, that we may know?" And there is also one Paraclete. For "there is also," saith [the Scripture], "one Spirit," since "we have been called in one hope of our calling." And again, "We have drunk of one Spirit," with what follows. And it is manifest that all these gifts [possessed by believers] "worketh one and the self-same Spirit." There are not then either three Fathers, or three Sons, or three Paracletes, but one Father, and one Son, and one Paraclete. Wherefore also the Lord, when He sent forth the apostles to make disciples of all nations, commanded them to "baptize in the name of the Father, and of the Son, and of the Holy Ghost," not unto one [person] having three names, nor into three [persons] who became incarnate, but into three possessed of equal honour.

3

Christ Was Truly Born, And Died

For there is but One that became incarnate, and that neither the Father nor the Paraclete, but the Son only, [who became so] not in appearance or imagination, but in reality. For "the Word became flesh." For "Wisdom builded for herself a house." And God the Word was born as man, with a body, of the Virgin, without any intercourse of man. For [it is written], "A virgin shall conceive in her womb, and bring forth a son." He was then truly born, truly grew up, truly ate and drank, was truly crucified, and died, and rose again. He who believes these things, as they really were, and as they really took place, is blessed. He who believeth them not is no less accursed than those who crucified the Lord. For the prince of this world rejoiceth when any one denies the cross, since he knows that the confession of the cross is his own destruction. For that is the trophy which has been raised up against his power, which when he sees, he shudders, and when he hears of, is afraid.

4

The Malignity And Folly Of Satan

And indeed, before the cross was erected, he (Satan) was eager that it should be so; and he "wrought" [for this end] "in the children of disobedience." He wrought in Judas, in the Pharisees, in the Sadducees, in the old, in the young, and in the priests. But when it was just about to be erected, he was troubled, and infused repentance into the traitor, and pointed him to a rope to hang himself with, and taught him [to die by] strangulation. He terrified also the silly woman, disturbing her by dreams; and he, who had tried every means to have the cross prepared, now endeavoured to put a stop to its erection; not that he was influenced by repentance on account of the greatness of his crime (for in that case he would not be utterly depraved), but because he perceived his own destruction [to be at hand]. For the cross of Christ was the beginning of his condemnation the beginning of his death, the beginning of his destruction. Wherefore, also, he works in some that they should deny the cross, be ashamed of the passion, call the death an appearance, mutilate and explain away the birth of the Virgin, and calumniate the [human] nature s itself as being abominable. He fights along with the Jews to a denial of the cross, and with the Gentiles to the calumniating of Mary, who are heretical in holding that Christ possessed a mere phantasmal body. For the leader of all wickedness assumes manifold forms, beguiler of men as he is, inconsistent, and even contradicting himself, projecting one course and then following another. For he is wise to do evil, but as to what good may be he is totally ignorant. And indeed he is full of ignorance, on account of his voluntary want of reason: for how can he be deemed anything else who does not perceive reason when it lies at his very feet?

5

Apostrophe To Satan

For if the Lord were a mere man, possessed of a soul and body only, why dost thou mutilate and explain away His being born with the common nature of humanity? Why dost thou call the passion a mere appearance, as if it were any strange thing happening to a [mere] man? And why dost thou reckon the death of a mortal to be simply an imaginary death? But if, [on the other hand,] He is both God and man, then why dost thou call it unlawful to style Him "the Lord of glory," who is by nature unchangeable? Why dost thou say that it is unlawful to declare of the Lawgiver who possesses a human soul, "The Word was made flesh," and was a perfect man, and not merely one dwelling in a man? But how came this magician into existence, who of old formed all nature that can be apprehended either by the senses or intellect, according to the will of the Father; and, when He became incarnate, healed every kind of disease and infirmity?

6

Continuation

And how can He be but God, who raises up the dead, sends away the lame sound of limb, cleanses the lepers, restores sight to the blind, and either increases or transmutes existing substances, as the five loaves and the two fishes, and the water which became wine, and who puts to flight thy whole host by a mere word? And why dost thou abuse the nature of the Virgin, and style her members disgraceful, since thou didst of old display such in public processions, and didst order them to be exhibited naked, males in the sight of females, and females to stir up the unbridled lust of males? But now these are reckoned by thee disgraceful, and thou pretendest to be full of modesty, thou spirit of fornication, not knowing that then only anything becomes disgraceful when it is polluted by wickedness. But when sin is not present, none of the things that have been created are shameful, none of them evil, but all very good. But inasmuch as thou art blind, thou revilest these things.

7

Continuation: Inconsistency Of Satan

And how, again, does Christ not at all appear to thee to be of the Virgin, but to be God over all, and the Almighty? Say, then, who sent Him? Who was Lord over Him? And whose will did He obey? And what laws did He fulfil, since He was subject neither to the will nor power of any one? And while you deny that Christ was born, you affirm that the unbegotten was begotten, and that He who had no beginning was nailed to the cross, by whose permission I am unable to say. But thy changeable tactics do not escape me, nor am I ignorant that thou art wont to walk with slanting and uncertain steps. And thou art ignorant who really was born, thou who pretendest to know everything.

8

Continuation: Ignorance Of Satan

For many things are unknown to thee; [such as the following]: the virginity of Mary; the wonderful birth; Who it was that became incarnate; the star which guided those who were in the east; the Magi who presented gifts; the salutation of the archangel to the Virgin; the marvellous conception of her that was betrothed; the announcement of the boy-forerunner respecting the son of the Virgin, and his leaping in the womb on account of what was foreseen; the songs of the angels over Him that was born; the glad tidings announced to the shepherds; the fear of Herod lest his kingdom should be taken from him; the command to slay the infants; the removal into Egypt, and the return from that country to the same region; the infant swaddling-bands; the human registration; the nourishing by means of milk; the name of father given to Him who did not beget; the manger because there was not room [elsewhere]; no human preparation [for the Child]; the gradual growth, human speech, hunger, thirst, journeyings, weariness; the offering of sacrifices and then also circumcision, baptism; the voice of God over Him that was baptized, as to who He was and whence [He had come]; the testimony of the Spirit and the Father from above; the voice of John the prophet when it signified the passion by the appellation of "the Lamb;" the performance of divers miracles, manifold healings; the rebuke of the Lord ruling both the sea and the winds; evil spirits expelled; thou thyself subjected to torture, and, when afflicted by the power of Him who had been manifested, not having it in thy power to do anything.

9

Continuation: Ignorance Of Satan

Seeing these things, thou wast in utter perplexity. And thou wast ignorant that it was a virgin that should bring forth; but the angels(1) song of praise struck thee with astonishment, as well as the adoration of the Magi, and the appearance of the star. Thou didst revert to thy state of [wilful] ignorance, because all the circumstances seemed to thee trifling; for thou didst deem the swaddling-bands, the circumcision, and the nourishment by means of milk contemptible: these things appeared to thee unworthy of God. Again, thou didst behold a man who remained forty days and nights without tasting human food, along with ministering gels at whose presence thou didst shudder, when first of all thou hadst seen Him baptized as a common man, and knewest not the reason thereof. But after His [lengthened] fast thou didst again assume thy wonted audacity, and didst tempt Him when hungry, as if He had been an ordinary man, not knowing who He was. For thou saidst, "If thou be the Son of God, command that these stones be made bread." Now, this expression, "If thou be the Son," is an indication of ignorance. For if thou hadst possessed real knowledge, thou wouldst have understood that the Creator can with equal ease both create what does not exist, and change that which already has a being. And thou temptedst by means of hunger Him who nourisheth all that require food. And thou temptedst the very "Lord of glory," forgetting in thy malevolence that "man shall not live by bread alone, but by every word that proceedeth out of the mouth of God." For if thou hadst known that He was the Son of God, thou wouldst also have understood that He who had kept his body from feeling any want for forty days and as many nights, could have also done the same for ever. Why, then, does He suffer hunger? In order to prove that He had assumed a body subject to the same feelings as those of ordinary men. By the first fact He showed that He was God, and by the second that He was also man.

10

Continuation: Audacity Of Satan

Darest thou, then, who didst fall "as lightning from the very highest glory, to say to the Lord, "Cast thyself down from hence [to Him] to whom the things that are not are reckoned as if they were,(and to provoke to a display of vainglory Him that was free from all ostentation? And didst thou pretend to read in Scripture concerning Him: "For He hath given His angels charge concerning Thee, and in their hands they shall bear Thee up, lest thou shouldest dash Thy foot against a stone?" At the same time thou didst pretend to be ignorant of the rest, furtively concealing what [the Scripture] predicted concerning thee and thy servants: "Thou shalt tread upon the adder and the basilisk; the lion and the dragon shalt thou trample under foot."

11

Continuation: Audacity Of Satan

If, therefore, thou art trodden down under the feet of the Lord, how dost thou tempt Him that cannot be tempted, forgetting that precept of the lawgiver, "Thou shall not tempt the Lord thy God?" Yea, thou even darest, most accursed one, to appropriate the works of God to thyself, and to declare that the dominion over these was delivered to thee. And thou dost set forth thine own fall as an example to the Lord, and dost promise to give Him what is really His own, if He would fall down and worship thee. And how didst thou not shudder, O thou spirit more wicked through thy malevolence than all other wicked spirits, to utter such words against the Lord? Through thine appetite was thou overcome, and through thy vainglory wast thou brought to dishonour: through avarice and ambition dost thou [now] draw on [others] to ungodliness. Thou, O Belial, dragon, apostate, crooked serpent, rebel against God, outcast from Christ, alien from the Holy Spirit, exile from the ranks of the angels, reviler of the laws of God, enemy of all that is lawful, who didst rise up against the first-formed of men, and didst drive forth [from obedience to] the commandment [of God] those who had in no respect injured thee; thou who didst raise up against Abel the murderous Cain; thou who didst take arms against Job: dost thou say to the Lord, "If Thou wilt fall down and worship me?" Oh what audacity! Oh what madness! Thou runaway slave, thou incorrigible slave, dost thou rebel against the good Lord? Dost thou say to so great a Lord, the God of all that either the mind or the senses can perceive, "If Thou wilt fall down and worship me?"

12

The Meek Reply Of Christ

But the Lord is long-suffering, and does not reduce to nothing him who in his ignorance dares [to utter] such words, but meekly replies, "Get thee hence, Satan." He does not say, "Get thee behind Me," for it is not possible that he should be converted; but, "Begone, Satan," to the course which thou hast chosen. "Begone" to those things to which, through thy malevolence, thou hast been called. For I know Who I am, and by Whom I have been sent, and Whom it behoves Me to worship. For "thou shall worship the Lord thy God, and Him only shalt thou serve." I know the one [God]; I am acquainted with the only [Lord] from whom thou hast become an apostate. I am not an enemy of God; I acknowledge His pre-eminence; I know the Father, who is the author of my generation.

13
Various Exhorations And Directions
These things, brethren, out of the affection which I entertain for you, I have felt compelled to write, exhorting you with a view to the glory of God, not as if I were a person of any consequence, but simply as a brother. Be ye subject to the bishop, to the presbyters, and to the deacons. Love one another in the Lord, as being the images of God. Take heed, ye husbands, that ye love your wives as your own members. Ye wives also, love your husbands, as being one with them in virtue of your union. If any one lives in chastity or continence, let him not be lifted up, lest he lose his reward. Do not lightly esteem the festivals. Despise not the period of forty days, for it comprises an imitation of the conduct of the Lord. After the week of the passion, do not neglect to fast on the fourth and sixth days, distributing at the same time of thine abundance to the poor. If any one fasts on the Lord's Day or on the Sabbath, except on the paschal Sabbath only, he is a murderer of Christ.

14
Farewells And Cautions
Let your prayers be extended to the Church of Antioch, whence also I as a prisoner am being led to Rome. I salute the holy bishop Polycarp; I salute the holy bishop Vitalius, and the sacred presbytery, and my fellow-servants the deacons; in whose stead may my soul be found. Once more I bid farewell to the bishop, and to the presbyters in the Lord. If any one celebrates the passover along with the Jews, or receives the emblems of their feast, he is a partaker with those that killed the Lord and His apostles.

15
Salutations And Conclusion
Philo and Agathopus the deacons salute you. I salute the company of virgins, and the order of widows; of whom may I have joy! I salute the people of the Lord, from the least unto the greatest. I have sent you this letter through Euphanius the reader, a man honoured of God, and very faithful, happening to meet with me at Rhegium, just as he was going on board ship. Remember my bonds that I may be made perfect in Christ. Fare ye well in the flesh, the soul, and the spirit, while ye think of things perfect, and turn yourselves away from the workers of iniquity, who corrupt the word of truth, and are strengthened inwardly by the grace of our Lord Jesus Christ.

The Martyrdom of Ignatius

1
Desire Of Ignatius For Martyrdom
When Trajan, not long since, succeeded to the empire of the Romans, Ignatius, the disciple of John the apostle, a man in all respects of an apostolic character, governed the Church of the Antiochians with great care, having with difficulty escaped the former storms of the many persecutions under Domitian, inasmuch as, like a good pilot, by the helm of prayer and fasting, by the earnestness of his teaching, and by his [constant spiritual labour, he resisted the flood that rolled against him, fearing [only] lest he should lose: any of those who were deficient in courage, or apt to suffer from their simplicity. Wherefore he rejoiced over the tranquil state of the Church, when the persecution ceased for a little time, but was grieved as to himself, that he had not yet attained to a true love to Christ, nor reached the perfect rank of a disciple. For he inwardly reflected, that the confession which is made by martyrdom, would bring him into a yet more intimate relation to the Lord. Wherefore, continuing a few years longer with the Church, and, like a divine lamp, enlightening every one's understanding by his expositions of the [Holy] Scriptures, he [at length] attained the object of his desire.

2
Ignatius Is Condemned By Trajan
For Trajan, in the ninth year of his reign, being lifted up [with pride], after the victory he had gained over the Scythians and Dacians, and many other nations, and thinking that the religious body of the Christians were yet wanting to complete the subjugation of all things to himself, and [thereupon] threatening them with persecution unless they should agree to worship daemons, as did all other nations, thus compelled all who were living godly lives either to sacrifice [to idols] or die. Wherefore the noble soldier of Christ [Ignatius], being in fear for the Church of the Antiochians, was, in accordance with his own desire, brought before Trajan, who was at that time staying at Antioch, but was in haste [to set forth] against Armenia and the Parthians. And when he was set before the emperor Trajan, [that prince] said unto him, "Who art thou, eked wretch, who settest thyself to transgress our commands, and persuadest others to do the same, so that they should miserably perish?" Ignatius replied, "No one ought to call Theophorus wicked; for all evil spirits have departed from the servants of God. But if, because I am an enemy to these [spirits], you call me wicked in respect to them, I quite agree with you; for inasmuch as I have Christ the King of heaven [within me], I destroy all the devices of these [evil spirits]." Trajan answered, "And who is Theophorus?" Ignatius replied, "He who has Christ within his breast." Trajan said, "Do we not then seem to you to have the gods in our mind, whose assistance we enjoy in fighting against our enemies?" Ignatius answered, "Thou art in error when thou callest the daemons of the nations gods. For there is but one God, who made heaven, and earth, and the sea, and all that are in them; and one Jesus Christ, the only-begotten Son of God, whose kingdom may I enjoy." Trajan said, "Do you mean Him who was crucified under Pontius Pilate?" Ignatius replied, "I mean Him who crucified my sin, with him who was the inventor of it, and who has condemned [and cast down] all the deceit and malice of the devil under the feet of those who carry Him in their heart." Trajan said, "Dost thou then carry within thee Him that was crucified?" Ignatius replied, "Truly so; for it is written, 'I will dwell in them, and walk in them.'" Then Trajan pronounced sentence as follows: "We command that Ignatius, who affirms that he carries about within him Him that was crucified, be bound by soldiers, and carried to the great [city] Rome, there to be devoured by the beasts, for the gratification of the people." When the holy martyr heard this sentence, he cried out with joy, "I thank thee, O Lord, that Thou hast vouchsafed to honour me with a perfect love towards Thee, and hast made me to be bound with iron chains, like Thy Apostle Paul." Having spoken thus, he then, with delight, clasped the chains about him; and when he had first prayed for the Church, and commended it with tears to the Lord, he was hurried away by the savage cruelty of the soldiers, like a distinguished ram the leader of a goodly flock, that he might be carried to Rome, there to furnish food to the bloodthirsty beasts.

3
Ignatius Sails To Smyrna
Wherefore, with great alacrity and joy, through his desire to suffer, he came down from Antioch to Seleucia, from which place he set sail. And after a great deal of suffering he came to Smyrna, where he disembarked with great joy, and hastened to see the holy Polycarp, [formerly] his fellow-disciple, and [now] bishop of Smyrna. For they had both, in old times, been disciples of St. John the Apostle. Being then brought to him, and having communicated to him some spiritual gifts, and glorying in his bonds, he

entreated of him to labour along with him for the fulfilment of his desire; earnestly indeed asking this of the whole Church (for the cities and Churches of Asia had welcomed the holy man through their bishops, and presbyters, and deacons, all hastening to meet him, if by any means they might receive from him some spiritual gift), but above all, the holy Polycarp, that, by means of the wild beasts, he soon disappearing from this world, might be manifested before the face of Christ.

4

Ignatius Writes To The Churches

And these things he thus spake, and thus testified, extending his love to Christ so far as one who was about to secure heaven through his good confession, and the earnestness of those who joined their prayers to his in regard to his [approaching] conflict; and to give a recompense to the Churches, who came to meet him through their rulers, sending letters of thanksgiving to them, which dropped spiritual grace, along with prayer and exhortation. Wherefore, seeing all men so kindly affected towards him, and fearing lest the love of the brotherhood should hinder his zeal towards the Lord, while a fair door of suffering martyrdom was opened to him, he wrote to the Church of the Romans the Epistle which is here subjoined.
(See the Epistle as formerly given.)

5

Ignatius Is Brought To Rome

Having therefore, by means of this Epistle, settled, as he wished, those of the brethren at Rome who were unwilling [for his martyrdom]; and setting sail from Smyrna (for Christophorus was pressed by the soldiers to hasten to the public spectacles in the mighty [city] Rome, that, being given up to the wild beasts in the sight of the Roman people, he might attain to the crown for which he strove), he [next] landed at Troas. Then, going on from that place to Neapolis, he went [on foot] by Philippi through Macedonia, and on to that part of Epirus which is near Epidamnus; and finding a ship in one of the seaports, he sailed over the Adriatic Sea, and entering from it on the Tyrrhene, he passed by the various islands and cities, until, when Puteoli came in sight, he was eager there to disembark, having a desire to tread in the footsteps of the Apostle Paul. But a violent wind arising did not suffer him to do so, the ship being driven rapidly forwards; and, simply expressing his delight over the love of the brethren in that place, he sailed by. Wherefore, continuing to enjoy fair winds, we were reluctantly hurried on in one day and a night, mourning [as we did] over the coming departure from us of this righteous man. But to him this happened just as he wished, since he was in haste as soon as possible to leave this world, that he might attain to the Lord whom he loved. Sailing then into the Roman harbour, and the unhallowed sports being just about to close, the soldiers began to be annoyed at our slowness, but the bishop rejoicingly yielded to their urgency.

6

Ignatius Is Devoured By The Beasts At Rome

They pushed forth therefore from the place which is called Portus; and (the fame of all relating to the holy martyr being already spread abroad) we met the brethren full of fear and joy; rejoicing indeed because they were thought worthy to meet with Theophorus, but struck with fear because so eminent a man was being led to death. Now he enjoined some to keep silence who, in their fervent zeal, were saying that they would appease the people, so that they should not demand the destruction of this just one. He being immediately aware of this through the Spirit, and having saluted them all, and begged of them to show a true affection towards him, and having dwelt [on this point] at greater length than in his Epistle, and having persuaded them not to envy him hastening to the Lord, he then, after he had, with all the brethren kneeling [beside him], entreated the Son of God in behalf of the Churches, that a stop might be put to the persecution, and that mutual love might continue among the brethren, was led with all haste into the amphitheatre. Then, being immediately thrown in, according to the command of Caesar given some time ago, the public spectacles being just about to close (for it was then a solemn day, as they deemed it, being that which is called the thirteenth in the Roman tongue, on which the people were wont to assemble in more than ordinary numbers), he was thus cast to the wild beasts close, beside the temple, that so by them the desire of the holy martyr Ignatius should be fulfilled, according to that which is written, "The desire of the righteous is acceptable [to God]," to the effect that he might not be troublesome to any of the brethren by the gathering of his remains, even as he had in his Epistle expressed a wish beforehand that so his end might be. For only the harder portions of his holy remains were left, which were conveyed to Antioch and wrapped in linen, as an inestimable treasure left to the holy Church by the grace which was in the martyr.

7

Ignatius Appears In A Vision After His Death

Now these things took place on the thirteenth day before the Kalends of January, that is, on the twentieth of December, Sun and Senecio being then the consuls of the Romans for the second time. Having ourselves been eye-witnesses of these things, and having spent the whole night in tears within the house, and having entreated the Lord, with bended knees and much prayer, that He would give us weak men full assurance respecting the things which were done, it came to pass, on our filling into a brief slumber, that some of us saw the blessed Ignatius suddenly standing by us and embracing us, while others beheld him again praying for us, and others still saw him dropping with sweat, as if he had just come from his great labour, and standing by the Lord. When, therefore, we had with great joy witnessed these things, and had compared our several visions together, we sang praise to God, the giver of all good things, and expressed our sense of the happiness of the holy [martyr]; and now we have made known to you both the day and the time [when these things happened], that, assembling ourselves together according to the time of his martyrdom, we may have fellowship with the champion and noble martyr of Christ, who trode under foot the devil, and perfected the course which, out of love to Christ, he had desired, in Christ Jesus our Lord; by whom, and with whom, be glory and power to the Father, with the Holy Spirit, for evermore! Amen.

The Epistle of Polycarp to the Philippians

1

Commends the Philippians for their respect to those who suffered for the Gospel; and for their own faith.

¹ POLYCARP, and the presbyters that are with him, to the church of God which is at Philippi: mercy unto you and peace from God Almighty; and the Lord Jesus Christ, our Saviour, be multiplied. ² I rejoiced greatly with you in our Lord Jesus Christ, that ye received the images of a true love, and accompanied, as it is behooved you, those who were in bonds, becoming saints; which are the crowns of such as are truly chosen by God and our Lord: ³ As also that the root of the faith which was preached from ancient times, remains firm in you to this day; and brings forth fruit to our Lord Jesus Christ, who suffered himself to be brought even to the death for our sins. ⁴ Whom God hath raised up, having loosed the pains of death, whom having not seen, ye love; in whom though now ye see him not, yet believing ye rejoice with joy unspeakable and full of glory. ⁵ Into which many desire to enter; knowing that by grace ye are saved; not by works, but by the will of God through Jesus Christ. ⁶ Wherefore girding up the loins of your minds; serve the Lord with fear, and in truth: laying aside all empty and vain speech, and the error of many; believing in him that raised up our Lord Jesus Christ from the dead, and hath given him glory and a throne at his right hand. ⁷ To whom all things are made subject, both that are in heaven, and that are in earth; whom every living creature shall worship; who shall come to be the judge of the quick and dead.: whose blood God shall require of them that believe in him. ⁸ But he that raised up Christ from the dead, shall also raise up us in like manner, if we do his will and walk according to his commandments; and love those things which he loved: ⁹ Abstaining from all unrighteousness; inordinate affection, and love of money; from evil speaking; false witness; not rendering evil for evil, or railing for railing, or striking for striking, or cursing for cursing. ¹⁰ But remembering what the Lord has taught us saying, Judge not, and ye shall not be judged; forgive and ye shall be forgiven; be ye merciful, and ye shall obtain mercy; for with the same measure that ye mete withal, it shall be measured to you again. ¹¹ And again, that blessed are the poor, and they that are persecuted for righteousness' sake; for theirs is the kingdom of God.

2

2 Exhorts to Faith, Hope, and Charity. 5 Against covetousness, and as to the duties of husbands, wives, widows, 6 deacons, young men, virgins, and presbyters.

¹ THESE things, my brethren, I took not the liberty of myself to write unto you concerning righteousness, but you yourselves before encouraged me to it. ² For neither can I, nor any other such as I am, come up to the wisdom of the blessed and renowned Paul: who being himself in person with those who then lived, did with all exactness and soundness teach the word of truth; and being gone from you wrote an epistle to you. ³ Into which if you look, you will be able to edify yourselves in the faith that has been delivered unto you; which is the mother of us all; being followed with hope, and led on by a general love, both towards God and towards Christ, and towards our neighbour. ⁴ For if any man has these things he has fulfilled the law of righteousness: for he that has charity is far from all sin. ⁵ But the love of money is the root of all evil. Knowing therefore that as we brought nothing into this world, so neither may we carry any thing out; let us arm ourselves with the armour of righteousness. ⁶ And teach ourselves first to walk according to the commandments of the Lord; and then your wives to walk likewise according to the faith that is given to them; in charity, and in purity; loving their own husbands with all sincerity, and all others alike with all temperance; and to bring up their children in the instruction and fear of the Lord. ⁷ The widows likewise teach that they be sober as to what concerns the faith of the Lord: praying always for all men; being far from all detraction, evil speaking, false witness; from covetousness, and from all evil. ⁸ Knowing that they are the altars of God, who sees all blemishes, and from whom nothing is hid; who searches out the very reasonings, and thoughts, and secrets of our hearts. ⁹ Knowing therefore that God is not mocked, we ought to walk worthy both of his command and of his glory. ¹⁰ Also the deacons must be blameless before him, as the ministers of God in Christ, and not of men. Not false accusers; not double tongued; not lovers of money; but moderate in all things; compassionate, careful; walking according to the truth of the Lord, who was the servant of all. ¹¹ Whom if we please in this present world we shall also be made partakers of that which is to come, according as he has promised to us, that he will raise us from the dead; and that if we shall walk worthy of him, we shall also reign together with him, if we believe. ¹² In like manner the younger men must be unblameable in all things; above all, taking care of their purity, and to restrain themselves from all evil. For it is good to be cut off from the lusts that are in the world; because every such lust warreth against the spirit: and neither fornicators, nor effeminate, nor abusers of themselves with mankind, shall inherit the kingdom of God; nor they who do such things as are foolish and unreasonable. ¹³ Wherefore ye must needs abstain from all these things, being subject to the priests and deacons, as unto God and Christ. ¹⁴ The virgins admonish to walk in a spotless and pure conscience. ¹⁵ And let the elders be compassionate and merciful towards all; turning them from their errors; seeking out those that are weak; not forgetting the widows, the fatherless, and the poor; but always providing what is good both in the sight of God and man. ¹⁶ Abstaining from all wrath, respect of persons, and unrighteous judgment: and especially being free from all covetousness. ¹⁷ Not easy to believe any thing against any; not severe in judgment; knowing that we are all debtors in point of sin. ¹⁸ If therefore we pray to the Lord that he would forgive us, we ought also to forgive others; for we are all in the sight of our Lord and God; and must all stand before the judgment seat of Christ; and shall every one give an account of himself. ¹⁹ Let us therefore serve him in fear, and with all reverence as both himself hath commanded; and as the Apostles who have preached the Gospel unto us, and the prophets who have foretold the coming of our Lord have taught us. ²⁰ Being zealous of what is good; abstaining from all offence, and from false brethren; and from those who bear the name of Christ in hypocrisy; who deceive vain men.

3

1 As to faith in our Saviour Christ: his nature and sufferings, the resurrection and judgment. 3 Exhorts to prayer 5 and steadfastness in the faith, from the examples of Christ, 7 and Apostles and saints, and exhorts to carefulness in all well-doing.

¹ FOR whosoever does not confess that Jesus Christ is come in the flesh, he is Antichrist: and whoever does not confess his suffering upon the cross, is from the devil. ² And whosoever perverts the oracles of the Lord to his own lusts; and says that there shall neither be any resurrection, nor judgment, he is the first-born of Satan. ³ Wherefore leaving the vanity of many, and their false doctrines; let us return to the word that was delivered to us from the beginning; Watching unto prayer; and persevering in fasting. ⁴ With supplication beseeching the all seeing God not to lead us into temptation; as the Lord hath said, The spirit is truly willing, but the flesh is weak. ⁵ Let us therefore without ceasing hold steadfastly to him who is our hope, and the earnest of our righteousness, even Jesus Christ; Who his own self bare our sins in his own body on the tree: who did no sin, neither was guile found in his mouth. But suffered all for us that we might live through him. ⁶ Let us therefore imitate his patience; and if we suffer for his name, let us glorify him; for this example he has given us by himself, and so have we believed. ⁷ Wherefore I exhort all of you that ye obey the word of righteousness, and exercise all patience; which ye have seen set forth before our eyes, not only in the blessed Ignatius, and Zozimus, and Rufus; but in others among yourselves; and in Paul himself, and the rest of the Apostles: ⁸ Being confident of this, that all, these have not run in vain; but in faith and righteousness, and are gone to the place that was due to them from the Lord; with whom they also suffered. ⁹ For they loved not this present world; but him who died, and was raised again by God for us. ¹⁰ Stand therefore in these things, and follow the example of the Lord; being firm and immutable in the faith, lovers of the brotherhood, lovers of one another: companions together in the truth, being kind and gentle towards each other, despising none. ¹¹ When it is in your power to do good, defer it not, for charity delivered from death. ¹² Be all of you subject one to another, having your conversation honest among the Gentiles; that by your good works, both ye yourselves may receive praise, and the Lord may not be blasphemed through you. But wo be to him by whom the name of the Lord is blasphemed. ¹³ Therefore teach all men sobriety; in which do ye also exercise yourselves.

4

Valens, a presbyter, having fallen into the sin of covetousness, he exhorts them against it.

¹ I AM greatly afflicted for Valens, who was once a presbyter among you; that he should so little understand the place that was given to him in the church. Wherefore I admonish you that ye abstain from covetousness; and that ye be chaste, and true of speech. ² Keep yourselves from all evil. For he that in these things cannot govern himself how shall he be able to prescribe them to another? ³ If a man does not keep himself from covetousness, he shall be polluted with idolatry and be judged as if he were a Gentile. ⁴ But who of you are ignorant of the judgment of God? Do we not know that the saints shall judge the world, as Paul teaches? ⁵ But I have neither perceived nor heard any thing of this kind in you, among whom the blessed Paul laboured; and who are named in the beginning of his Epistle. ⁶ For he glories of you in all the churches who then only knew God; for we did not then know him. Wherefore, my brethren, I am exceedingly sorry

both for him, and for his wife; to whom God grant a true repentance. ⁷ And be ye also moderate upon this occasion; and look not upon such as enemies, but call them back as suffering, and erring members, that ye may save your whole body: for by so doing, ye shall edify your own selves. ⁸ For I trust that ye are well exercised in the Holy Scriptures, and that nothing is hid from you; but at present it is not granted unto me to practice that which is written, Be angry and sin not; and again, Let not the sun go down upon your wrath. ⁹ Blessed be he that believeth and remembereth these things; which also I trust you do. ¹⁰ Now the God and Father of our Lord Jesus Christ; and he himself who is our everlasting high-priest, the Son of God, even Jesus Christ, build you up in faith and in truth and in all meekness and lenity; in patience and long-suffering, in forbearance and chastity. ¹¹ And grant unto you a lot and portion among his saints; and us with you, and to all that are under the heavens, who shall believe in our Lord Jesus Christ, and in his Father who raised him from the dead. ¹² Pray for all the saints: pray also for kings, and all that are in authority; and for those who persecute you, and hate you, and for the enemies of the cross; that your fruit may be manifest in all; and that ye may be perfect in Christ. ¹³ Ye wrote to me, both ye, and also Ignatius, that if any one went from hence into Syria, he should bring your letters with him; which also I will take care of, as soon as I shall have a convenient opportunity; either by myself, or him whom I shall send upon your account. ¹⁴ The Epistles of Ignatius which he wrote unto us, together with what others of his have come to our hands, we have sent to you, according to your order; which are subjoined to this epistle. ¹⁵ By which we may be greatly profited; for they treat of faith and patience, and of all things that pertain to edification in the Lord Jesus. ¹⁶¹ What you know certainly of Ignatius, and those that are with him signify to us. ¹⁷ If These things have I written unto you by Crescens, whom by this present epistle I have recommended to you, and do now again commend. ¹⁸ For he has had his conversation without blame among us; and I suppose also with you. ¹⁹ Ye will also have regard unto his sister when she shall come unto you. ²⁰ Be ye safe in the Lord Jesus Christ; and in favour with all yours. Amen.

The Martyrdom of Polycarp

The Church of God which sojourns at Smyrna, to the Church of God sojourning in Philomelium, and to all the congregations of the Holy and Catholic Church in every place: Mercy, peace, and love from God the Father, and our Lord Jesus Christ, be multiplied.

1
Subject Of Which We Write
We have written to you, brethren, as to what relates to the martyrs, and especially to the blessed Polycarp, who put an end to the persecution, having, as it were, set a seal upon it by his martyrdom. For almost all the events that happened previously [to this one], took place that the Lord might show us from above a martyrdom becoming the Gospel. For he waited to be delivered up, even as the Lord had done, that we also might become his followers, while we look not merely at what concerns ourselves but have regard also to our neighbours. For it is the part of a true and well-founded love, not only to wish one's self to be saved, but also all the brethren.

2
The Wonderful Constancy Of The Martyrs
All the martyrdoms, then, were blessed and noble which took place according to the will of God. For it becomes us who profess greater piety than others, to ascribe the authority over all things to God. And truly, who can fail to admire their nobleness of mind, and their patience, with that love towards their Lord which they displayed?–who, when they were so torn with scourges, that the frame of their bodies, even to the very inward veins and arteries, was laid open, still patiently endured, while even those that stood by pitied and bewailed them. But they reached such a pitch of magnanimity, that not one of them let a sigh or a groan escape them; thus proving to us all that those holy martyrs of Christ, at the very time when they suffered such torments, were absent from the body, or rather, that the Lord then stood by them, and communed with them. And, looking to the grace of Christ, they despised all the torments of this world, redeeming themselves from eternal punishment by [the suffering of] a single hour. For this reason the fire of their savage executioners appeared cool to them. For they kept before their view escape from that fire which is eternal and never shall be quenched, and looked forward with the eyes of their heart to those good things which are laid up for such as endure; things "which ear hath not heard, nor eye seen, neither have entered into the heart of man," but were revealed by the Lord to them, inasmuch as they were no longer men, but had already become angels. And, in like manner, those who were condemned to the wild beasts endured dreadful tortures, being stretched out upon beds full of spikes, and subjected to various other kinds of torments, in order that, if it were possible, the tyrant might, by their lingering tortures, lead them to a denial [of Christ].

3
The Constancy Of Germanicus; The Death Of Polycarp Is Demanded
For the devil did indeed invent many things against them; but thanks be to God, he could not prevail over all. For the most noble Germanicus strengthened the timidity of others by his own patience, and fought heroically with the wild beasts. For, when the proconsul sought to persuade him, and urged him to take pity upon his age, he attracted the wild beast towards himself, and provoked it, being desirous to escape all the more quickly from an unrighteous and impious world. But upon this the whole multitude, marvelling at the nobility of mind displayed by the devout and godly race of Christians, cried out, "Away with the Atheists; let Polycarp be sought out!"

4
Quintus The Apostate
Now one named Quintus, a Phrygian, who was but lately come from Phrygia, when he saw the wild beasts, became afraid. This was the man who forced himself and some others to come forward voluntarily [for trial]. Him the proconsul, after many entreaties, persuaded to swear and to offer sacrifice. Wherefore, brethren, we do not commend those who give themselves up [to suffering], seeing the Gospel does not teach so to do.

5
The Departure And Vision Of Polycarp
But the most admirable Polycarp, when he first heard [that he was sought for], was in no measure disturbed, but resolved to continue in the city. However, in deference to the wish of many, he was persuaded to leave it. He departed, therefore, to a country house not far distant from the city. There he stayed with a few [friends], engaged in nothing else night and day than praying for all men, and for the Churches throughout the world, according to his usual custom. And while he was praying, a vision presented itself to him three days before he was taken; and, behold, the pillow under

his head seemed to him on fire. Upon this, turning to those that were with him, he said to them prophetically," I must be burnt alive."

6
Polycarp Is Betrayed By A Servant
And when those who sought for him were at hand, he departed to another dwelling, whither his pursuers immediately came after him. And when they found him not, they seized upon two youths [that were there], one of whom, being subjected to torture, confessed. It was thus impossible that he should continue hid, since those that betrayed him were of his own household. The Irenarch then (whose office is the same as that of the Cleronomus), by name Herod, hastened to bring him into the stadium. [This all happened] that he might fulfil his special lot, being made a partaker of Christ, and that they who betrayed him might undergo the punishment of Judas himself.

7
Polycarp Is Found By His Pursuers
His pursuers then, along with horsemen, and taking the youth with them, went forth at supper-time on the day of the preparation? with their usual weapons, as if going out against a robber. And being come about evening [to the place where he was], they found him lying down in the upper room of a certain little house, from which he might have escaped into another place; but he refused, saying, "The will of God be done." So when he heard that they were come, he went down and spake with them. And as those that were present marvelled at his age and constancy, some of them said. "Was so much effort made to capture such a venerable man? Immediately then, in that very hour, he ordered that something to eat and drink should be set before them, as much indeed as they cared for, while he besought them to allow him an hour to pray without disturbance. And on their giving him leave, he stood and prayed, being full of the grace of God, so that he could not cease for two full hours, to the astonishment of them that heard him, insomuch that many began to repent that they had come forth against so godly and venerable an old man.

8
Polycarp Is Brought Into The City
Now, as soon as he had ceased praying, having made mention of all that had at any time come in contact with him, both small and great, illustrious and obscure, as well as the whole Catholic Church throughout the world, the time of his departure having arrived, they set him upon an ass, and conducted him into the city, the day being that of the great Sabbath. And the Irenarch Herod, accompanied by his father Nicetes (both riding in a chariot), met him, and taking him up into the chariot, they seated themselves beside him, and endeavoured to persuade him, saying, "What harm is there in saying, Lord Caesar, and in sacrificing, with the other ceremonies observed on such occasions, and so make sure of safety?" But he at first gave them no answer; and when they continued to urge him, he said, "I shall not do as you advise me." So they, having no hope of persuading him, began to speak bitter words unto him, and cast him with violence out of the chariot, insomuch that, in getting down from the carriage, he dislocated his leg [by the fall]. But without being disturbed, and as if suffering nothing, he went eagerly forward with all haste, and was conducted to the stadium, where the tumult was so great, that there was no possibility of being heard.

9
Polycarp Refuses To Revile Christ
Now, as Polycarp was entering into the stadium, there came to him a voice from heaven, saying, "Be strong, and show thyself a man, O Polycarp!" No one saw who it was that spoke to him; but those of our brethren who were present heard the voice. And as he was brought forward, the tumult became great when they heard that Polycarp was taken. And when he came near, the proconsul asked him whether he was Polycarp. On his confessing that he was, [the proconsul] sought to persuade him to deny [Christ], saying, "Have respect to thy old age," and other similar things, according to their custom, [such as], "Swear by the fortune of Caesar; repent, and say, Away with the Atheists." But Polycarp, gazing with a stern countenance on all the multitude of the wicked heathen then in the stadium, and waving his hand towards them, while with groans he looked up to heaven, said, "Away with the Atheists." Then, the proconsul urging him, and saying, "Swear, and I will set thee at liberty, reproach Christ;" Polycarp declared, "Eighty and six years have I served Him, and He never did me any injury: how then can I blaspheme my King and my Saviour?"

10
Polycarp Confesses Himself A Christian
And when the proconsul yet again pressed him, and said, "Swear by the fortune of Caesar," he answered, "Since thou art vainly urgent that, as thou sayest, I should swear by the fortune of Caesar, and pretendest not to know who and what I am, hear me declare with boldness, I am a Christian. And if you wish to learn what the doctrines of Christianity are, appoint me a day, and thou shalt hear them." The proconsul replied, "Persuade the people." But Polycarp said, "To thee I have thought it right to offer an account [of my faith]; for we are taught to give all due honour (which entails no injury upon ourselves) to the powers and authorities which are ordained of God. But as for these, I do not deem them worthy of receiving any account from me."

11
No Threats Have Any Effect On Polycarp
The proconsul then said to him, "I have wild beasts at hand ; to these will I cast thee, except thou repent." But he answered, "Call them then, for we are not accustomed to repent of what is good in order to adopt that which is evil; and it is well for me to be changed from what is evil to what is righteous." But again the proconsul said to him, "I will cause thee to be consumed by fire, seeing thou despisest the wild beasts, if thou wilt not repent." But Polycarp said, "Thou threatenest me with fire which burneth for an hour, and after a little is extinguished, but art ignorant of the fire of the coming judgment and of eternal punishment, reserved for the ungodly. But why tarriest thou? Bring forth what thou wilt."

12
Polycarp Is Sentenced To Be Burned
While he spoke these and many other like things, he was filled with confidence and joy, and his countenance was full of grace, so that not merely did it not fall as if troubled by the things said to him, but, on the contrary, the proconsul was astonished, and sent his herald to proclaim in the midst of the stadium thrice, "Polycarp has confessed that he is a Christian." This proclamation having been made by the herald, the whole multitude both of the heathen and Jews, who dwelt at Smyrna, cried out with uncontrollable fury, and in a loud voice, "This is the teacher of Asia, the father of the Christians, and the overthrower of our gods, he who has been teaching many not to sacrifice, or to worship the gods." Speaking thus, they cried out, and besought Philip the Asiarch to let loose a lion upon Polycarp. But Philip answered that it was not lawful for him to do so, seeing the shows of wild beasts were already finished. Then it seemed good to them to cry out with one consent, that Polycarp should be burnt alive. For thus it behooved the vision which was revealed to him in regard to his pillow to be fulfilled, when, seeing it on fire as he was praying, he turned about and said prophetically to the faithful that were with him," I must be burnt alive."

13
The Funeral Pile Is Erected
This, then, was carried into effect with greater speed than it was spoken, the multitudes immediately gathering together wood and fagots out of the shops and baths; the Jews especially, according to custom, eagerly assisting them in it. And when the funeral pile was ready, Polycarp, laying aside all his garments, and loosing his girdle, sought also to take off his sandals,–a thing he was not accustomed to do, inasmuch as every one of the faithful was always eager who should first touch his skin. For, on account of his holy life, he was, even before his martyrdom, adorned with every kind of good. Immediately then they surrounded him with those substances which had been prepared for the funeral pile. But when they were about also to fix him with nails, he said, "Leave me as I am; for He that giveth me strength to endure the fire, will also enable me, without your securing me by nails, to remain without moving in the pile."

14
The Prayer Of Polycarp
They did not nail him then, but simply bound him. And he, placing his hands behind him, and being bound like a distinguished ram [taken] out of a great flock for sacrifice, and prepared to be an acceptable burnt-offering unto God, looked up to heaven, and said, "O Lord God Almighty, the Father of thy beloved and blessed Son Jesus Christ, by whom we have received the knowledge of Thee, the God of angels and powers, and of every creature, and of the whole race of the righteous who live before thee, I give Thee thanks that Thou hast counted me, worthy of this day and this hour, that I should have a part in the number of Thy martyrs, in the cup of thy Christ, to the resurrection of eternal life, both of soul and body, through the incorruption [imparted] by the Holy Ghost. Among whom may I be accepted this day before Thee as a fat and acceptable sacrifice, according as Thou, the ever-truthful God, hast fore-ordained, hast revealed beforehand to me, and now hast fulfilled. Wherefore also I praise Thee for all things, I bless Thee, I glorify Thee, along with the everlasting and heavenly Jesus Christ, Thy beloved Son, with whom, to Thee, and the Holy Ghost, be glory both now and to all coming ages. Amen."

15
Polycarp Is Not Injured By The Fire
When he had pronounced this amen, and so finished his prayer, those who were appointed for the purpose kindled the fire. And as the flame blazed forth in great fury, we, to whom it was given to witness it, beheld a great miracle, and have been preserved that we might report to others what then took place. For the fire, shaping itself into the form of an arch, like the sail of a ship when filled with the wind, encompassed as by a circle the body of the martyr. And he appeared within not like flesh which is burnt, but as bread that is baked, or as gold and silver glowing in a furnace. Moreover, we perceived such a sweet odour [coming from the pile], as if frankincense or some such precious spices had been smoking there.

16
Polycarp Is Pierced By A Dagger
At length, when those wicked men perceived that his body could not be consumed by the fire, they commanded an executioner to go near and pierce him through with a dagger. And on his doing this, there came forth a dove, and a great quantity of blood, so that the fire was extinguished; and all the people wondered that there should be such a difference between the unbelievers and the elect, of whom this most admirable Polycarp was one, having in our own times been an apostolic and prophetic teacher, and bishop of the Catholic Church which is in Smyrna. For every word that went out of his mouth either has been or shall yet be accomplished.

17
The Christians Are Refused Polycarp's Body
But when the adversary of the race of the righteous, the envious, malicious, and wicked one, perceived the impressive nature of his martyrdom, and [considered] the blameless life he had led from the beginning, and how he was now crowned with the wreath of immortality, having beyond dispute received his reward, he did his utmost that not the least memorial of him should be taken away by us, although many desired to do this, and to become possessors of his holy flesh. For this end he suggested it to Nicetes, the father of Herod and brother of Alce, to go and entreat the governor not to give up his body to be buried, "lest," said he, "forsaking Him that was crucified, they begin to worship this one. "This he said at the suggestion and urgent persuasion of the Jews, who also watched us, as we sought to take him out of the fire, being ignorant of this, that it is neither possible for us ever to forsake Christ, who suffered for the salvation of such as shall be saved throughout the whole world (the blameless one for sinners), nor to worship any other. For Him indeed, as being the Son of God, we adore; but the martyrs, as disciples and followers of the Lord, we worthily love on account of their extraordinary affection towards their own King and Master, of whom may we also be made companions and fellow-disciples!

18
The Body Of Polycarp Is Burned
The centurion then, seeing the strife excited by the Jews, placed the body in the midst of the fire, and consumed it. Accordingly, we afterwards took up his bones, as being more precious than the most exquisite jewels, and more purified than gold, and deposited them in a fitting place, whither, being gathered together, as opportunity is allowed us, with joy and rejoicing, the Lord shall grant us to celebrate the anniversary of his martyrdom, both in memory of those who have already finished their course, and for the exercising and preparation of those yet to walk in their steps.

19
Praise Of The Martyr Polycarp
This, then, is the account of the blessed Polycarp, who, being the twelfth that was martyred in Smyrna (reckoning those also of Philadelphia), yet occupies a place of his own in the memory of all men, insomuch that he is everywhere spoken of by the heathen themselves. He was not merely an illustrious teacher, but also a pre-eminent martyr, whose martyrdom all desire to imitate, as having been altogether consistent with the Gospel of Christ. For, having through patience overcome the unjust governor, and thus acquired the crown of immortality, he now, with the apostles and all the righteous[in heaven], rejoicingly glorifies God, even the Father, and blesses our Lord Jesus Christ, the Saviour of our souls, the Governor of our bodies, and the Shepherd of the Catholic Church throughout the world.

20
This Epistle Is To Be Transmitted To The Brethren
Since, then, ye requested that we would at large make you acquainted with what really took place, we have for the present sent you this summary account through our brother Marcus. When, therefore, ye have yourselves read this Epistle, be pleased to send it to the brethren at a greater distance, that they also may glorify the Lord, who makes such choice of His own servants. To Him who is able to bring us all by His grace and goodness into his everlasting kingdom, through His only-begotten Son Jesus Christ, to Him be glory, and honour, and power, and majesty, for ever. Amen. Salute all the saints. They that are with us salute you, and Evarestus, who wrote this Epistle, with all his house.

21
The Date Of The Martyrdom
Now, the blessed Polycarp suffered martyrdom on the second day of the month Xanthicus just begun, the seventh day before the Kalends of May, on the great Sabbath, at the eighth hour. He was taken by Herod, Philip the Trallian being high priest, Statius Quadratus being proconsul, but Jesus Christ being King for ever, to whom be glory, honour, majesty, and an everlasting throne, from generation to generation. Amen.

22
Salutation
We wish you, brethren, all happiness, while you walk according to the doctrine of the Gospel of Jesus Christ; with whom be glory to God the Father and the Holy Spirit, for the salvation of His holy elect, after whose example the blessed Polycarp suffered, following in whose steps may we too be found in the kingdom of Jesus Christ! These things Caius transcribed from the copy of Irenaeus (who was a disciple of Polycarp), having himself been intimate with Irenaeus. And I Socrates transcribed them at Corinth from the copy of Caius. Grace be with you all. And I again, Pionius, wrote them from the previously written copy, having carefully searched into them, and the blessed Polycarp having manifested them to me through a revelation, even as I shall show in what follows. I have collected these things, when they had almost faded away through the lapse of time, that the Lord Jesus Christ may also gather me along with His elect into His heavenly kingdom, to whom, with the Father and the Holy Spirit, be glory for ever and ever. Amen.

The Epistle of Mathetes to Diognetus

1

¹ Since I see, most excellent Diognetus, that thou art exceedingly anxious to understand the religion of the Christians, and that thy enquiries respecting them are distinctly and carefully made, as to what God they trust and how they worship Him, that they all disregard the world and despise death, and take no account of those who are regarded as gods by the Greeks, neither observe the superstition of the Jews, and as to the nature of the affection which they entertain one to another, and of this new development or interest, which has entered into men's lives now and not before: I gladly welcome this zeal in thee, and I ask of God, Who supplieth both the speaking and the hearing to us, that it may be granted to myself to speak in such a way that thou mayest be made better by the hearing, and to thee that thou mayest so listen that I the speaker may not be disappointed.

2

¹ Come then, clear thyself of all the prepossessions which occupy thy mind, and throw off the habit which leadeth thee astray, and become a new man, as it were, from the beginning, as one who would listen to a new story, even as thou thyself didst confess. See not only with thine eyes, but with thine intellect also, of what substance or of what form they chance to be whom ye call and regard as gods. ² Is not one of them stone, like that which we tread under foot, and another bronze, no better than the vessels which are forged for our use, and another wood, which has already become rotten, and another silver, which needs a man to guard it lest it be stolen, and another iron, which is corroded with rust, and another earthenware, not a whit more comely than that which is supplied for the most dishonourable service? ³ Are not all these of perishable matter? Are they not forged by iron and fire? Did not the sculptor make one, and the brass-founder another, and the silversmith another, and the potter another? Before they were moulded into this shape by the crafts of these several artificers, was it not possible for each one of them to have been changed in form and made to resemble these several utensils? Might not the vessels which are now made out of the same material, if they met with the same artificers, be made like unto such as these? ⁴ Could not these things which are now worshipped by you, by human hands again be made vessels like the rest? Are not they all deaf and blind, are they not soul-less, senseless, motionless? Do they not all rot and decay? ⁵ These things ye call gods, to these ye are slaves, these ye worship; and ye end by becoming altogether like unto them. ⁶ Therefore ye hate the Christians, because they do not consider these to be gods. ⁷ For do not ye yourselves, who now regard and worship them, much more despise them? Do ye not much rather mock and insult them, worshipping those that are of stone and earthenware unguarded, but shutting up those that are of silver and gold by night, and setting guards over them by day, to prevent their being stolen? ⁸ And as for the honours which ye think to offer to them, if they are sensible of them, ye rather punish them thereby, whereas, if they are insensible, ye reproach them by propitiating them with the blood and fat of victims. ⁹ Let one of yourselves undergo this treatment, let him submit to these things being done to him. Nay, not so much as a single individual will willingly submit to such punishment, for he has sensibility and reason; but a stone submits, because it is insensible. Therefore ye convict his sensibility. ¹⁰ Well, I could say much besides concerning the Christians not being enslaved to such gods as these; but if any one should think what has been said insufficient, I hold it superfluous to say more.

3

¹ In the next place, I fancy that thou art chiefly anxious to hear about their not practising their religion in the same way as the Jews. ² The Jews then, so far as they abstain from the mode of worship described above, do well in claiming to reverence one God of the universe and to regard Him as Master; but so far as they offer Him this worship in methods similar to those already mentioned, they are altogether at fault. ³ For whereas the Greeks, by offering these things to senseless and deaf images, make an exhibition of stupidity, the Jews considering that they are presenting them to God, as if He were in need of them, ought in all reason to count it folly and not religious worship. ⁴ For He that made the heaven and the earth and all things that are therein, and furnisheth us all with what we need, cannot Himself need any of these things which He Himself supplieth to them that imagine they are giving them to Him. ⁵ But those who think to perform sacrifices to Him with blood and fat and whole burnt offerings, and to honour Him with such honours, seem to me in no way different from those who show the same respect towards deaf images; for the one class think fit to make offerings to things unable to participate in the honour, the other class to One Who is in need of nothing.

4

¹ But again their scruples concerning meats, and their superstition relating to the sabbath and the vanity of their circumcision and the dissimulation of their fasting and new moons, I do [not] suppose you need to learn from me, are ridiculous and unworthy of any consideration. ² For of the things created by God for the use of man to receive some as created well, but to decline others as useless and superfluous, is not this impious? ³ And again to lie against God, as if He forbad us to do any good thing on the sabbath day, is not this profane? ⁴ Again, to vaunt the mutilation of the flesh as a token of election as though for this reason they were particularly beloved by God, is not this ridiculous? ⁵ And to watch the stars and the moon and to keep the observance of months and of days, and to distinguish the arrangements of God and the changes of the seasons according to their own impulses, making some into festivals and others into times of mourning, who would regard this as an exhibition of godliness and not much more of folly? ⁶ That the Christians are right therefore in holding aloof from the common silliness and error of the Jews and from their excessive fussiness and pride, I consider that thou hast been sufficiently instructed; but as regards the mystery of their own religion, expect not that thou canst be instructed by man.

5

¹ For Christians are not distinguished from the rest of mankind either in locality or in speech or in customs. ² For they dwell not somewhere in cities of their own, neither do they use some different language, nor practise an extraordinary kind of life. ³ Nor again do they possess any invention discovered by any intelligence or study of ingenious men, nor are they masters of any human dogma as some are. ⁴ But while they dwell in cities of Greeks and barbarians as the lot of each is cast, and follow the native customs in dress and food and the other arrangements of life, yet the constitution of their own citizenship, which they set forth, is marvellous, and confessedly contradicts expectation. ⁵ They dwell in their own countries, but only as sojourners; they bear their share in all things as citizens, and they endure all hardships as strangers. Every foreign country is a fatherland to them, and every fatherland is foreign. ⁶ They marry like all other men and they beget children; but they do not cast away their offspring. ⁷ They have their meals in common, but not their wives. ⁸ They find themselves in the flesh, and yet they live not after the flesh. ⁹ Their existence is on earth, but their citizenship is in heaven. ¹⁰ They obey the established laws, and they surpass the laws in their own lives. ¹¹ They love all men, and they are persecuted by all. ¹² They are ignored, and yet they are condemned. They are put to death, and yet they are endued with life. ¹³ They are in beggary, and yet they make many rich. They are in want of all things, and yet they abound in all things. ¹⁴ They are dishonoured, and yet they are glorified in their dishonour. They are evil spoken of, and yet they are vindicated. ¹⁵ They are reviled, and they bless; they are insulted, and they respect. ¹⁶ Doing good they are punished as evil-doers; being punished they rejoice, as if they were thereby quickened by life. ¹⁷ War is waged against them as aliens by the Jews, and persecution is carried on against them by the Greeks, and yet those that hate them cannot tell the reason of their hostility.

6

¹ In a word, what the soul is in a body, this the Christians are in the world. ² The soul is spread through all the members of the body, and Christians through the divers cities of the world. ³ The soul hath its abode in the body, and yet it is not of the body. So Christians have their abode in the world, and yet they are not of the world. ⁴ The soul which is invisible is guarded in the body which is visible: so Christians are recognised as being in the world, and yet their religion remaineth invisible. ⁵ The flesh hateth the soul and wageth war with it, though it receiveth no wrong, because it is forbidden to indulge in pleasures; so the world hateth Christians, though it receiveth no wrong from them, because they set themselves against its pleasures. ⁶ The soul loveth the flesh which hateth it, and the members: so Christians love those that hate them. ⁷ The soul is enclosed in the body, and yet itself holdeth the body together; so Christians are kept in the world as in a prison-house, and yet they themselves hold the world together. ⁸ The soul though itself immortal dwelleth in a mortal tabernacle; so Christians sojourn amidst perishable things, while they look for the imperishability which is in the heavens. ⁹ The soul when hardly treated in the matter of meats and drinks is improved; and so Christians when punished increase more and more daily. ¹⁰ So great is the office for which God hath appointed them, and which it is not lawful for them to decline.

7

¹ For it is no earthly discovery, as I said, which was committed to them, neither do they care to guard so carefully any mortal invention, nor have they entrusted to them the dispensation of human mysteries. ² But truly the Almighty Creator of the Universe, the Invisible God Himself from heaven

planted among men the truth and the holy teaching which surpasseth the wit of man, and fixed it firmly in their hearts, not as any man might imagine, by sending (to mankind) a subaltern, or angel, or ruler, or one of those that direct the affairs of earth, or one of those who have been entrusted with the dispensations in heaven, but the very Artificer and Creator of the Universe Himself, by Whom He made the heavens, by Whom He enclosed the sea in its proper bounds, Whose mysteries all the elements faithfully observe, from Whom [the sun] hath received even the measure of the courses of the day to keep them, Whom the moon obeys as He bids her shine by night, Whom the stars obey as they follow the course of the moon, by Whom all things are ordered and bounded and placed in subjection, the heavens and the things that are in the heavens, the earth and the things that are in the earth, the sea and the things that are in the sea, fire, air, abyss, the things that are in the heights, the things that are in the depths, the things that are between the two. Him He sent unto them. ³ Was He sent, think you, as any man might suppose, to establish a sovereignty, to inspire fear and terror? ⁴ Not so. But in gentleness [and] meekness has He sent Him, as a king might send his son who is a king. He sent Him, as sending God; He sent Him, as [a man] unto men; He sent Him, as Saviour, as using persuasion, not force: for force is no attribute of God. ⁵ He sent Him, as summoning, not as persecuting; He sent Him, as loving, not as judging. ⁶ For He will send Him in judgment, and who shall endure His presence? ... ⁷ [Dost thou not see] them thrown to wild beasts that so they may deny the Lord, and yet not overcome? ⁸ Dost thou not see that the more of them are punished, just so many others abound? ⁹ These look not like the works of a man; they are the power of God; they are proofs of His presence.

8

¹ For what man at all had any knowledge what God was, before He came? ² Or dost thou accept the empty and nonsensical statements of those pretentious philosophers: of whom some said that God was fire (they call that God, whereunto they themselves shall go), and others water, and others some other of the elements which were created by God? ³ And yet if any of these statements is worthy of acceptance, any one other created thing might just as well be made out to be God. ⁴ Nay, all this is the quackery and deceit of the magicians; ⁵ and no man has either seen or recognised Him, but He revealed Himself. ⁶ And He revealed (Himself) by faith, whereby alone it is given to see God. ⁷ For God, the Master and Creator of the Universe, Who made all things and arranged them in order, was found to be not only friendly to men, but also long-suffering. ⁸ And such indeed He was always, and is, and will be, kindly and good and dispassionate and true, and He alone is good. ⁹ And having conceived a great and unutterable scheme He communicated it to His Son alone. ¹⁰ For so long as He kept and guarded His wise design as a mystery, He seemed to neglect us and to be careless about us. ¹¹ But when He revealed it through His beloved Son, and manifested the purpose which He had prepared from the beginning, He gave us all these gifts at once, participation in His benefits, and sight and understanding of (mysteries) which none of us ever would have expected.

9

¹ Having thus planned everything already in His mind with His Son, He permitted us during the former time to be borne along by disorderly impulses as we desired, led astray by pleasures and lusts, not at all because He took delight in our sins, but because He bore with us, not because He approved of the past season of iniquity, but because He was creating the present season of righteousness, that, being convicted in the past time by our own deeds as unworthy of life, we might now be made deserving by the goodness of God, and having made clear our inability to enter into the kingdom of God of ourselves, might be enabled by the ability of God. ² And when our iniquity had been fully accomplished, and it had been made perfectly manifest that punishment and death were expected as its recompense, and the season came which God had ordained, when henceforth He should manifest His goodness and power (O the exceeding great kindness and love of God), He hated us not, neither rejected us, nor bore us malice, but was long-suffering and patient, and in pity for us took upon Himself our sins, and Himself parted with His own Son as a ransom for us, the holy for the lawless, the guileless for the evil, _the just for the unjust,_ the incorruptible for the corruptible, the immortal for the mortal. ³ For what else but His righteousness would have covered our sins? ⁴ In whom was it possible for us lawless and ungodly men to have been justified, save only in the Son of God? ⁵ O the sweet exchange, O the inscrutable creation, O the unexpected benefits; that the iniquity of many should be concealed in One Righteous Man, and the righteousness of One should justify many that are iniquitous! ⁶ Having then in the former time demonstrated the inability of our nature to obtain life, and having now revealed a Saviour able to save even creatures which have no ability, He willed that for both reasons we should believe in His goodness and should regard Him as nurse, father, teacher, counsellor, physician, mind, light, honour, glory, strength and life.

10

¹ This faith if thou also desirest, apprehend first full knowledge of the Father. ² _For God loved_ men for whose sake He made the world, to whom He subjected all things that are in the earth, to whom He gave reason and mind, whom alone He permitted to look up to heaven, whom He created after His own image, to whom _He sent His only begotten Son,_ to whom He promised the kingdom which is in heaven, and will give it to those that have loved Him. ³ And when thou hast attained to this full knowledge, with what joy thinkest thou that thou wilt be filled, or how wilt thou love Him that so loved thee before? ⁴ And loving Him thou wilt be an imitator of His goodness. And marvel not that a man can be an imitator of God. He can, if God willeth it. ⁵ For happiness consisteth not in lordship over one's neighbours, nor in desiring to have more than weaker men, nor in possessing wealth and using force to inferiors; neither can any one imitate God in these matters; nay, these lie outside His greatness. ⁶ But whosoever taketh upon himself the burden of his neighbour, whosoever desireth to benefit one that is worse off in that in which he himself is superior, whosoever by supplying to those that are in want possessions which he received from God becomes a God to those who receive them from him, he is an imitator of God. ⁷ Then, though thou art placed on earth, thou shalt behold that God liveth in heaven; then shalt thou begin to declare the mysteries of God; then shalt thou both love and admire those that are punished because they will not deny God; then shalt thou condemn the deceit and error of the world; when thou shalt perceive the true life which is in heaven, when thou shalt despise the apparent death which is here on earth, when thou shalt fear the real death, which is reserved for those that shall be condemned to the eternal fire that shall punish those delivered over to it unto the end. ⁸ Then shalt thou admire those who endure for righteousness' sake the fire that is for a season, and shalt count them blessed when thou perceivest that fire. . .

11

¹ Mine are no strange discourses nor perverse questionings, but having been a disciple of Apostles I come forward as a teacher of the Gentiles, ministering worthily to them, as they present themselves disciples of the truth, the lessons which have been handed down. ² For who that has been rightly taught and has entered into friendship with the Word does not seek to learn distinctly the lessons revealed openly by the Word to the disciples; to whom the Word appeared and declared them, speaking plainly, not perceived by the unbelieving, but relating them to disciples who being reckoned faithful by Him were taught the mysteries of the Father? ³ For which cause He sent forth the Word, that He might appear unto the world, Who being dishonoured by the people, and preached by the Apostles, was believed in by the Gentiles. ⁴ This Word, Who was from the beginning, Who appeared as new and yet was proved to be old, and is engendered always young in the hearts of saints, ⁵ He, I say, Who is eternal, Who to-day was accounted a Son, through Whom the Church is enriched and grace is unfolded and multiplied among the saints, grace which confers understanding, which reveals mysteries, which announces seasons, which rejoices over the faithful, which is bestowed upon those who seek her, even those by whom the pledges of faith are not broken, nor the boundaries of the fathers overstepped. ⁶ Whereupon the fear of the law is sung, and the grace of the prophets is recognised, and the faith of the gospels is established, and the tradition of the apostles is preserved, and the joy of the Church exults. ⁷ If thou grieve not this grace, thou shalt understand the discourses which the Word holds by the mouth of those whom He desires when He wishes. ⁸ For in all things, that by the will of the commanding Word we were moved to utter with much pains, we become sharers with you, through love of the things revealed unto us.

12

¹ Confronted with these truths and listening to them with attention, ye shall know how much God bestoweth on those that love (Him) rightly, who become a Paradise of delight, a tree bearing all manner of fruits and flourishing, growing up in themselves and adorned with various fruits. ² For in this garden a tree of knowledge and a tree of life hath been planted; yet the tree of knowledge does not kill, but disobedience kills; ³ for the scriptures state clearly how God from the beginning planted a tree [of knowledge and a tree] of life in the midst of Paradise, revealing life through knowledge; and because our first parents used it not genuinely they were made naked by the deceit of the serpent. ⁴ For neither is there life without knowledge, nor sound knowledge without true life; therefore the one (tree) is planted near the other. ⁵ Discerning the force of this and blaming the knowledge which is exercised apart from the truth of the injunction which leads to life, the apostle says, Knowledge puffeth up, but charity edifieth._

[6] For the man who supposes that he knows anything without the true knowledge which is testified by the life, is ignorant, he is deceived by the serpent, because he loved not life; whereas he who with fear recognises and desires life plants in hope expecting fruit. [7] Let your heart be knowledge, and your life true reason, duly comprehended. [8] Whereof if thou bear the tree and pluck the fruit, thou shalt ever gather the harvest which God looks for, which serpent toucheth not, nor deceit infecteth, neither is Eve corrupted, but is believed on as a virgin, [9] and salvation is set forth, and the apostles are filled with understanding, and the passover of the Lord goes forward, and the congregations are gathered together, and [all things] are arranged in order, and as He teacheth the saints the Word is gladdened, through Whom the Father is glorified, to Whom be glory for ever and ever. Amen.

The Fragments of Papias

Fragments of Papias from the Exposition of the Oracles of the Lord.

1

THE writings of Papias in common circulation are five in number, and these are called an Exposition of the Oracles of the Lord. Irenaeus makes mention of these as the only works written by him, in the following words: "Now testimony is borne to these things in writing by Papias, an ancient man, who was a hearer of John, and a friend of Polycarp, in the fourth of his books; for five books were composed by him." Thus wrote Irenaeus. Moreover, Papias himself, in the introduction to his books, makes it manifest that he was not himself a hearer and eye-witness of the holy apostles; but he tells us that he received the truths of our religion from those who were aquainted with them the apostles in the following words:

But I shall not be unwilling to put down, along with my interpretations, whatsoever instructions I received with care at any time from the elders, and stored up with care in my memory, assuring you at the same time of their truth. For I did not, like the multitude, take pleasure in those who spoke much, but in those who taught the truth; nor in those who related strange commandments, but in those who rehearsed the commandments given by the Lord to faith, and proceeding from truth itself. If, then, any one who had attended on the elders came, I asked minutely after their sayings,–what Andrew or Peter said, or what was said by Philip, or by Thomas, or by James, or by John, or by Matthew, or by any other of the Lord's disciples: which things Aristion and the presbyter John, the disciples of the Lord, say. For I imagined that what was to be got from books was not so profitable to me as what came from the living and abiding voice.

2

The early Christians called those who practised a godly guilelessness, children, as is stated by Papias in the first book of the Lord's Expositions, and by Clemens Alexandrinus in his Paedagogue.

3

Judas walked about in this world a sad example of impiety; for his body having swollen to such an extent that he could not pass where a chariot could pass easily, he was crushed by the chariot, so that his bowels gushed out.

4

As the elders who saw John the disciple of the Lord remembered that they had heard from him how the Lord taught in regard to those times, and said: "The days will come in which vines shall grow, having each ten thousand branches, and in each branch ten thousand twigs, and in each true twig ten thousand shoots, and in every one of the shoots ten thousand clusters, and on every one of the clusters ten thousand grapes, and every grape when pressed will give five-and-twenty metretes of wine. And when any one of the saints shall lay hold of a cluster, another shall cry out, 'I am a better cluster, take me; bless the Lord through me.' In like manner, He said that a grain of wheat would produce ten thousand ears, and that every ear would have ten thousand grains, and every grain would yield ten pounds of clear, pure, fine flour; and that apples, and seeds, and grass would produce in similar proportions; and that all animals, feeding then only on the productions of the earth, would become peaceable and harmonious, and be in perfect subjection to man." Testimony is borne to these things in writing by Papias, an ancient man, who was a hearer of John and a friend of Polycarp, in the fourth of his books; for five books were composed by him. And he added, saying, "Now these things are credible to believers. And Judas the traitor," says he, "not believing, and asking, 'How shall such growths be accomplished by the Lord?' the Lord said, 'They shall see who shall come to them.' These, then, are the times mentioned by the prophet Isaiah: 'And the wolf shall lie, down with the lamb,' etc. (Isa. xi. 6 ff.)."

5

As the presbyters say, then those who are deemed worthy of an abode in heaven shall go there, others shah enjoy the delights of Paradise, and others shall possess the splendour of the city; for everywhere the Saviour will be seen, according as they shall be worthy who see Him. But that there is this distinction between the habitation of those who produce an hundredfold, and that of those who produce sixty-fold, and that of those who produce thirty-fold; for the first will be taken up into the heavens, the second class will dwell in Paradise, and the last will inhabit the city; and that on this account the Lord said, "In my Father's house are many mansions:" for all things belong to God, who supplies all with a suitable dwelling-place, even as His word says, that a share is given to all by the Father, according as each one is or shall be worthy. And this is the couch in which they shall recline who feast, being invited to the wedding. The presbyters, the disciples of the apostles, say that this is the gradation and arrangement of those who are saved, and that they advance through steps of this nature; and that, moreover, they ascend through the Spirit to the Son, and through the Son to the Father; and that in due time the Son will yield up His work to the Father, even as it is said by the apostle, "For He must reign till He hath put all enemies under His feet. The last enemy that shall be destroyed is death." For in the times of the kingdom the just man who is on the earth shall forget to die. "But when He saith all things are put under Him, it is manifest that He is excepted which did put all things under Him. And when all things shall be subdued unto Him, then shall the Son also Himself be subject unto Him that put all things under Him, that God may be all in all."

6

Papias, who is now mentioned by us, affirms that he received the sayings of the apostles from those who accompanied them, and he moreover asserts that he heard in person Aristion and the presbyter John. Accordingly he mentions them frequently by name, and in his writings gives their traditions. Our notice of these circumstances may not be without its use. It may also be worth while to add to the statements of Papias already given, other passages of his in which he relates some miraculous deeds, stating that he acquired the knowledge of them from tradition. The residence of the Apostle Philip with his daughters in Hierapolis has been mentioned above. We must now point out how Papias, who lived at the same time, relates that he had received a wonderful narrative from the daughters of Philip. For he relates that a dead man was raised to life in his day. He also mentions another miracle relating to Justus, surnamed Barsabas, how he swallowed a deadly poison, and received no harm, on account of the grace of the Lord. The same person, moreover, has set down other things as coming to him from unwritten tradition, amongst these some strange parables and instructions of the Saviour, and some other things of a more fabulous nature. Amongst these he says that there will be a millennium after the resurrection from the dead, when the personal reign of Christ will be established on this earth. He moreover hands down, in his own writing, other narratives given by the previously mentioned Aristion of the Lord's sayings, and the traditions of the presbyter John.

For information on these points, we can merely refer our readers to the books themselves; but now, to the extracts already made, we shall add, as being a matter of primary importance, a tradition regarding Mark who wrote the Gospel, which he Papias has given in the following words: And the presbyter said this. Mark having become the interpreter of Peter, wrote down accurately whatsoever he remembered. It was not, however, in exact order that he related the sayings or deeds of Christ. For he neither heard the Lord nor accompanied Him. But afterwards, as I said, he accompanied Peter, who accommodated his instructions to the necessities of his hearers, but with no intention of giving a regular narrative of the Lord's sayings. Wherefore Mark made no mistake in thus writing some things as he remembered them. For of one thing he took especial care, not to omit anything he had heard, and not to put anything fictitious into the statements. This is what is related by Papias regarding Mark; but with regard to Matthew he has made the following statements: Matthew put together the oracles of the Lord in the Hebrew language, and each one interpreted them as best he could. The same person uses proofs from the First Epistle of John, and from the Epistle of Peter in like manner. And he also gives another story of a woman who was accused of many sins before the Lord, which is to be fount in the Gospel according to the Hebrews.

7

Papias thus speaks, word far word: To some of them angels He gave dominion over the arrangement of the world, and He commissioned them to exercise their dominion well. And he says, immediately after this: but it happened that their arrangement came to nothing.

8

With regard to the inspiration of the book (Revelation), we deem it superfluous to add another word; for the blessed Gregory Theologus and Cyril, and even men of still older date, Papias, Irenaeus, Methodius, and Hippolytus, bore entirely satisfactory testimony to it.

9

Taking occasion from Papias of Hierapolis, the illustrious, a disciple of the apostle who leaned on the bosom of Christ, and Clemens, and Pantaenus the priest of the Church of the Alexandrians, and the wise Ammonius, the ancient and first expositors, who agreed with each other, who understood the work of the six days as referring to Christ and the whole Church.

10

Mary the mother of the Lord; Mary the wife of Cleophas or Alphaeus, who was the mother of James the bishop and apostle, and of Simon and Thaddeus, and of one Joseph; Mary Salome, wife of Zebedee, mother of John the evangelist and James; Mary Magdalene. These four are found in the Gospel. James and Judas and Joseph were sons of an aunt of the Lord's. James also and John were sons of another aunt of the Lord's. Mary, mother of James the Less and Joseph, wife of Alphaeus was the sister of Mary the mother of the Lord, whom John names of Cleophas, either from her father or from the family of the clan, or for some other reason. Mary Salome is called Salome either from her husband or her village. Some affirm that she is the same as Mary of Cleophas, because she had two husbands.

INFANCY GOSPELS

The Gospel of the Birth of Mary
(or The Gospel of Pseudo-Matthew)

1

1 The parentage of Mary. 7 Joachim her father, and Anna her mother, go to Jerusalem to the feast of the dedication. 9 Issachar the high priest reproaches Joachim for being childless.

[1] THE blessed and ever glorious Virgin Mary, sprung from the royal race and family of David, was born in the city of Nazareth, and educated at Jerusalem, in the temple of the Lord. [2] Her father's name was Joachim, and her mother's Anna. The family of her father was of Galilee and the city of Nazareth. The family of her mother was of Bethlehem. [3] Their lives were plain and right in the sight of the Lord, pious and faultless before men. For they divided all their substance into three parts: [4] One of which they devoted to the temple and officers of the temple; another they distributed among strangers, and persons in poor circumstances; and the third they reserved for themselves and the uses of their own family. [5] In this manner they lived for about twenty years chastely, in the favour of God, and the esteem of men, without any children. [6] But they vowed, if God should favour them with any issue, they would devote it to the service of the Lord; on which account they went at every feast in the year to the temple of the Lord [7] And it came to pass, that when the feast of the dedication drew near, Joachim, with some others of his tribe, went up to Jerusalem, and at that time, Issachar was high-priest; [8] Who, when he saw Joachim along with the rest of his neighbours, bringing his offering, despised both him and his offerings, and asked him, [9] Why he, who had no children, would presume to appear among those who had? Adding, that his offerings could never be acceptable to God, who judged him unworthy to have children; the Scripture having said, Cursed is every one who shall not beget a male in Israel. [10] He further said, that he ought first to be free from that curse by begetting some issue, and then come with his offerings into the presence of God. [11] But Joachim being much confounded with the shame of such reproach, retired to the shepherds, who were with the cattle in their pastures; [12] For he was not inclined to return home, lest his neighbours, who were present and heard all this from the high-priest, should publicly reproach him in the same manner.

2

1 An angel appears to Joachim, 9 and informs him that Anna shall conceive and bring forth a daughter, who shall be called Mary, 11 be brought up in the temple, 12 and while yet a virgin, in a way unparalleled, bring forth the Son of God: 13 gives him a sign, 14 and departs.

[1] BUT when he had been there for some time, on a certain day when he was alone, the angel of the Lord stood by him with a prodigious light. [2] To whom, being troubled at the appearance, the angel who had appeared to him, endeavouring to compose him said: [3] Be not afraid, Joachim, nor troubled at the sight of me, for I am an angel of the Lord sent by him to you, that I might inform you, that your prayers are heard, and your alms ascended in the sight of God. [4] For he hath surely seen your shame, and heard you unjustly reproached for not having children: for God is the avenger of sin, and not of nature; [5] And so when he shuts the womb of any person, he does it for this reason, that he may in a more wonderful manner again open it, and that which is born appear to be not the product of lust, but the gift of God. [6] For the first mother of your nation Sarah, was she not barren even till her eightieth year: And yet even in the end of her old age brought forth Isaac, in whom the promise was made a blessing to all nations. [7] Rachel also, so much in favour with God, and beloved so much by holy Jacob, continued barren for a long time, yet afterwards was the mother of Joseph, who was not only governor of Egypt, but delivered many nations from perishing with hunger. [8] Who among the judges was more valiant than Samson, or more holy than Samuel? And yet both their mothers were barren. [9] But if reason will not convince you of the truth of my words, that there are frequent conceptions in advanced years, and that those who were barren have brought forth to their great surprise; therefore Anna your wife shall bring you a daughter, and you shall call her name Mary; [10] She shall, according to your vow, be devoted to the Lord from her infancy, and be filled with the Holy Ghost from her mother's womb; [11] She shall neither eat nor drink anything which is unclean, nor shall her conversation be without among the common people, but in the temple of the Lord; that so she may not fall under any slander or suspicion of what is bad. [12] So in the process of her years, as she shall be in a miraculous manner born of one that was barren, so she shall, while yet a virgin, in a way unparalleled, bring forth the Son of the most High God, who shall, be called Jesus, and, according to the signification of his name, be the Saviour of all nations. [13] And this shall be a sign to you of the things which I declare, namely, when you come to the golden gate of Jerusalem, you shall there meet your wife Anna, who being very much troubled that you returned no sooner, shall then rejoice to see you. [14] When the angel had said this he departed from him.

3

1 The angel appears to Anna; 2 tells her a daughter shall be born unto her, 3 devoted to the service of the Lord in the temple, 5, who, being a virgin and not knowing man, shall bring forth the Lord, 6 and gives her a sign therefore. 8 Joachim and Anna meet and rejoice, 10 and praise the Lord. 11 Anna conceives, and brings forth a daughter called Mary.

[1] AFTERWARDS the angel appeared to Anna his wife saying: Fear not, neither think that which you see is a spirit. [2] For I am that angel who hath offered up your prayers and alms before God, and am now sent to you, that I may inform you, that a daughter will be born unto you, who shall be called Mary, and shall be blessed above all women. [3] She shall be, immediately upon her birth, full of the grace of the Lord, and shall continue during the three years of her weaning in her father's house, and afterwards, being devoted to the service of the Lord, shall not depart from the temple, till she arrives to years of discretion. [4] In a word, she shall there serve the Lord night and day in fasting and prayer, shall abstain from every unclean thing, and never know any man; [5] But, being an unparalleled instance without any pollution or defilement, and a virgin not knowing any man, shall bring forth a son, and a maid shall bring forth the Lord, who both by his grace and name and works, shall be the Saviour of the world. [6] Arise therefore, and go up to Jerusalem, and when you shall come to that which is called the golden gate (because it is gilt with gold), as a sign of what I have told you, you shall meet your husband, for whose safety you have been so much concerned. [7] When therefore you find these things thus accomplished, believe that all the rest which I have told you, shall also undoubtedly be accomplished. [8] According therefore to the command of the angel, both of them left the places where they were, and when they came to the place specified in the angel's prediction, they met each other. [9] Then, rejoicing at each other's vision, and being fully satisfied in the promise of a child, they gave due thanks to the Lord, who exalts the humble. [10] After having praised the Lord, they returned home, and lived in a cheerful and assured expectation of the promise of God. [11] So Anna conceived, and brought forth a daughter, and, according to the angel's command, the parents did call her name Mary.

4

1 Mary brought to the temple at three years old. 6 Ascends the stairs of the temple by miracle. 8 Her parents sacrificed and returned home.

[1] AND when three years were expired, and the time of her weaning complete, they brought the Virgin to the temple of the Lord with offerings. [2] And there were about the temple, according to the fifteen Psalms of degrees, fifteen stairs to ascend. [3] For the temple being built in a mountain, the altar of burnt-offering, which was without, could not be come near but by stairs; [4] The parents of the blessed Virgin and infant Mary put her upon one of these stairs; [5] But while they were putting off their clothes, in which they had travelled, and according to custom putting on some that were more neat and clean, [6] In the mean time the Virgin of the Lord in such a manner went up all the stairs one after another, without the help of any to lead or lift her, that any one would have judged from hence that she was of perfect age. [7] Thus the Lord did, in the infancy of his Virgin, work this extraordinary work, and evidence by this miracle how great she was like to be hereafter. [8] But the parents having offered up their sacrifice, according to the custom of the law, and perfected their vow, left the Virgin with other virgins in the apartments of the temple, who were to be brought up there, and they returned home.

5

2 Mary ministered unto by angels. 4 The high-priest orders all virgins of fourteen years old to quit the temple and endeavour to be married. 5 Mary refuses, 6 having vowed her virginity to the Lord. 7 The high-priest commands a meeting of the chief persons of Jerusalem, 11 who seek the Lord for counsel in the matter. 13 A voice from the mercy-seat. 15 The high priest obeys it by ordering all the unmarried men of the house of David to bring their rods to the altar, 17 that his rod which should flower, and on which the Spirit of God should sit, should betroth the Virgin.

[1] BUT the Virgin of the Lord, as she advanced in fears, increased also in perfections, and according to the saying of the Psalmist, her father and mother forsook her, but the Lord took care of her. [2] For she every day had the conversation of angels, and every day received visitors from God, which preserved her from all sorts of evil, and caused her to abound with all good things; [3] So that when at length she arrived to her fourteenth year, as the wicked could not lay anything to her charge worthy of reproof, so all good persons, who were acquainted with her, admired her life and conversation.

⁴ At that time the high-priest made a public order. That all the virgins who had public settlements in the temple, and were come to this age, should return home, and, as they were now of a proper maturity, should, according to the custom of their country, endeavour to be married. ⁵ To which command, though all the other virgins readily yielded obedience, Mary the Virgin of the Lord alone answered, that she could not comply with it. ⁶ Assigning these reasons, that both she and her parents had devoted her to the service of the Lord; and besides, that she had vowed virginity to the Lord, which vow she was resolved never to break through by lying with a man. ⁷ The high priest being hereby brought into a difficulty, ⁸ Seeing he durst neither on the one hand dissolve the vow, and disobey the Scripture, which says, Vow and pay, ⁹ Nor on the other hand introduce a custom, to which the people were strangers, commanded, ¹⁰ That at the approaching feast all the principal persons both of Jerusalem and the neighbouring places should meet together, that he might have their advice, how he had best proceed in so difficult a case. ¹¹ When they were accordingly met, they unanimously agreed to seek the Lord, and ask counsel from him on this matter. ¹² And when they were all engaged in prayer, the high-priest, according to the usual way, went to consult God. ¹³ And immediately there was a voice from the ark, and the mercy seat, which all present heard, that it must be inquired or sought out by a prophecy of Isaiah to whom the Virgin should be given and be betrothed; ¹⁴ For Isaiah saith, there shall come forth a rod out of the stem of Jesse, and a flower shall spring out of its root, ¹⁵ And the Spirit of the Lord shall rest upon him, the Spirit of Wisdom and Understanding, the Spirit of Counsel and Might, the Spirit of Knowledge and Piety, and the Spirit of the fear of the Lord shall fill him. ¹⁶ Then, according to this prophecy, he appointed, that all the men of the house and family of David, who were marriageable, and not married, should bring their several rods to the altar, ¹⁷ And out of whatsoever person's rod after it was brought, a flower should bud forth, and on the top of it the Spirit of the Lord should sit in the appearance of a dove, he should be the man to whom the Virgin should be given and be betrothed.

6

1 Joseph draws back his rod. 5 The dove pitches on it. He betroths Mary and returns to Bethlehem. 7 Mary returns to her parents' house at Galilee.

¹ AMONG the rest there was a man named Joseph, of the house and family of David, and a person very far advanced in years, who drew back his rod, when every one besides presented his. ² So that when nothing appeared agreeable to the heavenly voice, the high-priest judged it proper to consult God again, ³ Who answered that he to whom the Virgin was to be betrothed was the only person of those who were brought together, who had not brought his rod. ⁴ Joseph therefore was betrayed. ⁵ For, when he did bring his rod, and a dove coming from Heaven pitched upon the top of it, every one plainly saw, that the Virgin was to be betrothed to him: ⁶ Accordingly, the usual ceremonies of betrothing being over, he returned to his own city of Bethlehem, to set his house in order, and make the needful for the marriage. ⁷ But the Virgin of the Lord, Mary, with seven other virgins of the same age, who had been weaned at the same time, and who had been appointed to attend her by the priest, returned to her parents' house in Galilee.

7

7 The salutation of the Virgin by Gabriel, who explains to her that she shall conceive, without lying with a man, while a Virgin, 19 by the Holy Ghost coming upon her without the heats of lust. 21 She submits.

¹ NOW at this time of her first coming into Galilee, the angel Gabriel was sent to her from God, to declare to her the conception of our Saviour, and the manner and way of her conceiving him. ² Accordingly going into her, he filled the chamber where she was with a prodigious light, and in a most courteous manner saluting her, he said, ³ Hail, Mary! Virgin of the Lord most acceptable! O Virgin full of Grace! The Lord is with you, you are blessed above all women, you are blessed above all men, that. Have been hitherto born. ⁴ But the Virgin, who had before been well acquainted with the countenances of angels, and to whom such light from heaven was no uncommon thing, ⁵ Was neither terrified with the vision of the angel, nor astonished at the greatness of the light, but only troubled about the angel's words: ⁶ And began to consider what so extraordinary a salutation should mean, what it did portend, or what sort of end it would have. ⁷ To this thought the angel, divinely inspired, replies; ⁸ Fear not, Mary, as though I intended anything inconsistent with your chastity in this salutation: ⁹ For you have found favour with the Lord, because you made virginity your choice. ¹⁰ Therefore while you are a Virgin, you shall conceive without sin, and bring forth a son. ¹¹ He shall be great, because he shall reign from sea to sea, and from the rivers to the ends of the earth. ¹² And he shall be called the Son of the Highest; for he who is born in a mean state on earth reigns in an exalted one in heaven. ¹³ And the Lord shall give him the throne of his father David, and he shall reign over the house of Jacob for ever, and of his kingdom there shall be no end. ¹⁴ For he is the King of Kings, and Lord of Lords, and his throne is for ever and ever. ¹⁵ To this discourse of the angel the Virgin replied not, as though she were unbelieving, but willing to know the manner of it. ¹⁶ She said, How can that be? For seeing, according to my vow, I have never known any man, how can I bear a child without the addition of a man's seed? ¹⁷ To this the angel replied and said, Think not, Mary, that you shall conceive in the ordinary way. ¹⁸ For, without lying with a man, while a Virgin, you shall conceive; while a Virgin, you shall bring forth; and while a Virgin shall give suck. ¹⁹ For the Holy Ghost shall come upon you, and the power of the Most High shall overshadow you, without any of the heats of lust. ²⁰ So that which shall be born of you shall be only holy, be. Cause it only is conceived without sin, and being born, shall be called the Son of God. ²¹ Then Mary stretching forth her hands, and lifting her eyes to heaven, said, Behold the handmaid of the Lord! Let it be unto me according to thy word.

8

1 Joseph returns to Galilee to marry the Virgin he had betrothed. 4 perceives she is with child, 5 is uneasy, 7 purposes to put her away privily, 8 is told by the angel of the Lord it is not the work of man but the Holy Ghost, 12 Marries her, but keeps chaste, 13 removes with her to Bethlehem, 15 where she brings forth Christ.

¹ JOSEPH therefore went from Judæa to Galilee, with intention to marry the Virgin who was betrothed to him: ² For it was now near three months since she was betrothed to him. ³ At length it plainly appeared she was with child, and it could not be hid from Joseph: ⁴ For going to the Virgin in a free manner, as one espoused, and talking familiarly with her, he perceived her to be with child. ⁵ And thereupon began to be uneasy and doubtful, not knowing what course it would be best to take; ⁶ For being a just man, he was not willing to expose her, nor defame her by the suspicion of being a whore, since he was a pious man. ⁷ He purposed therefore privately to put an end to their agreement, and as privately to put her away. ⁸ But while he was meditating these things, behold the angel of the Lord appeared to him in his sleep, and said Joseph, son of David, fear not; ⁹ Be not willing to entertain any suspicion of the Virgin's being guilty of fornication, or to think any thing amiss of her, neither be afraid to take her to wife; ¹⁰ For that which is begotten In her and now distresses your mind, is not the work of man, but the Holy Ghost. ¹¹ For she of all women is that only Virgin who shall bring forth the Son of God, and you shall call his name Jesus, that is, Saviour: for he will save his people from their sins. ¹² Joseph thereupon, according to the command of the angel, married the Virgin, and did not know her, but kept her in chastity. ¹³ And now the ninth month from her conception drew near, when Joseph took his wife and what other things were necessary to Bethlehem, the city from whence he came. ¹⁴ And it came to pass, while they were there, the days were fulfilled for her bringing forth. ¹⁵ And she brought forth her first-born son, as the holy Evangelists have taught, even our Lord Jesus Christ, who with the Father, Son, and Holy Ghost, lives and reigns to everlasting ages.

The Protoevangelium of James, or The Gospel of James

1

¹ In the history of the twelve tribes of Israel we read there was a certain person called Joachim, who being very rich, made double offerings to the Lord God, having made this resolution: "My substance shall be for the benefit of the whole people, and that I may find mercy from the Lord God for the forgiveness of my sins." ² But at a certain great feast of the Lord, when the children of Israel offered their gifts, and Joachim also offered his, Reuben the high priest opposed him, saying, "It is not lawful for you to offer your gifts, seeing you have not begotten any issue in Israel." ³ At this Joachim, being concerned very much, went away to consult the registries of the twelve tribes, to see whether he was the only person who had begotten no issue. ⁴ But upon inquiry he found that all the righteous had raised up seed in Israel: ⁵ Then he called to mind the patriarch Abraham, how God in the end of his life had given him his son Isaac; and upon this he was exceedingly distressed, and would not be seen by his wife, ⁶ but retired into the wilderness, and fixed his tent there, and fasted forty days and forty nights, saying to himself, "I will not go down either to eat or drink, till the Lord my God shall look down upon me, but prayer shall be my meat and drink."

2

¹ In the meantime his wife Anna was distressed and perplexed on a double account, and said, "I will mourn both for my widowhood and my barrenness." ² Then drew near a great feast of the Lord, and Judith her maid said, "How long will you thus afflict your soul? The feast of the Lord is now come, when it is unlawful for anyone to mourn. ³ Take therefore this hood which was given by one who makes such things, for it is not fit that I, who am a servant, should wear it, but it well suits a person of your greater character." ⁴ But Anna replied, "Depart from me, I am not used to such things; besides, the Lord has greatly humbled me. ⁵ I fear some ill-designing person has given you this, and you have come to pollute me with my sin." ⁶ Then Judith her maid answered, "What evil shall I wish you when you will not hearken to me? ⁷ I cannot wish you a greater curse than you are under, in that God has shut up your womb, that you should not be a mother in Israel." ⁸ At this Anna was exceedingly troubled, and having on her wedding garment, went about the ninth hour to walk in her garden. ⁹ And she saw a laurel tree, and sat under it, and prayed to the Lord, saying, ¹⁰ "O God of my fathers, bless me and regard my prayer as you did bless the womb of Sarah, and gave her a son, Isaac."

3

¹ And as she was looking towards heaven she perceived a sparrow's nest in the laurel, ² and mourning within herself, she said, "Woe is me! Who begot me? And what womb did bear me, that I should be thus accursed before the children of Israel, and that they should reproach and deride me in the temple of my God? Woe is me! To what can I be compared? ³ I am not comparable to the very beasts of the earth, for even the beasts of the earth are fruitful before You, O Lord! Woe is me! To what can I be compared? ⁴ I am not comparable to the brute animals, for even the brute animals are fruitful before You, O Lord! Woe is me! To what am I comparable ⁵ I cannot be compared to these waters, for even the waters are fruitful before You, O Lord! Woe is me! to what can I be compared? ⁶ I am not comparable to the waves of the sea; for these, whether they are calm or in motion, with the fishes which are in them, praise You, O Lord! Woe is me! To what can I be compared? ⁷ I am not comparable to the very earth, for the earth produces its fruits, and praises You, O Lord!"

4

¹ Then an angel of the Lord stood by her and said, "Anna, Anna, the Lord has heard your prayer. You shall conceive and bring forth, and your progeny shall be spoken of in all the world." ² And Anna answered, "As the Lord my God lives, whatever I bring forth, whether it is male or female, I will devote it to the Lord my God, and it shall minister to Him in holy things, during its whole life." ³ And behold, there appeared two angels, saying to her, "Behold, Joachim you husband is coming with his shepherds. ⁴ For an angel of the Lord has also come down to him, and said, 'The Lord God has heard your prayer; make haste and go from here, for behold, Anna your wife shall conceive.'" ⁵ (And Joachim went down and called his shepherds, saying, "Bring me hither ten she-lambs without spot or blemish, and they shall be for the Lord my God. ⁶ And bring me twelve calves without blemish, and the twelve calves shall be for the priests and the elders. ⁷ Bring me also a hundred goats, and the hundred goats shall be for the whole people.") ⁸ And Joachim went down with the shepherds, and Anna stood by the gate and saw Joachim coming with the shepherds. ⁹ And she ran and, hanging about his neck, said, "Now I know that the Lord has greatly blessed me; ¹⁰ for behold, I who was a widow am no longer a widow, and I who was barren shall conceive."

5

¹ And Joachim abode the first day in his house, but on the morrow he brought his offerings and said, ² "If the Lord is propitious to me, let the plate which is on the priest's forehead make it manifest." ³ And he consulted the plate which the priest wore, and saw it, and behold, sin was not found in him. ⁴ And Joachim said, "Now I know that the Lord is propitious to me, and has taken away all my sins." ⁵ And he went down from the temple of the Lord justified, and he went to his own house. ⁶ And when nine months were fulfilled to Anna, she brought forth, and said to the midwife, "What have I brought forth?" ⁷ And she told her, "A girl." ⁸ Then Anna said, "The Lord has this day magnified my soul." And she lay in her bed. ⁹ And when the days of her purification were accomplished, she gave suck to the child, and called her name Mary.

6

¹ And the child increased in strength every day, so that when she was nine months old, her mother put her upon the ground to try if she could stand, and when she had walked nine steps, she came again to her mother's lap. ² then her mother caught her up, and said, "As the Lord my God lives, you shall not walk again on the earth till I bring you into the temple of the Lord." ³ Accordingly she made her chamber a holy place, and allowed nothing uncommon or unclean to come near her, but invited certain undefiled daughters of Israel, and they drew her aside. ⁴ But when the child was a year old, Joachim made a great feast, and invited the priests, scribes, elders, and all the people of Israel. ⁵ And Joachim then made an offering of the girl to the chief priests, and they blessed her, saying, "The God of our fathers bless this girl, and give her a name famous and lasting through all generations." And all the people replied, "So be it. Amen." ⁶ Then Joachim a second time offered her to the priests, and they blessed her, saying, "O Most HighGod, regard this girl and bless her with an everlasting blessing." ⁷ Upon this, her mother took her up and gave her the breast and sung the following song to the Lord: ⁸ I will sing a new song to the Lord, my God, for He has visited me, and taken away from me the reproach of my enemies, and has given me the fruit of His righteousness, that it may now be told the sons of Reuben, that Anna gives suck." ⁹ Then she put the child to rest in the room which she had consecrated, and she went out and served them. ¹⁰ And when the feast was ended, they went away rejoicing and praising the God of Israel.

7

¹ But the child grew, and when she was two years old, Joachim said to Anna, "Let us lead her to the temple of the Lord, that we may perform our vow, which we have vowed to the Lord God, lest He should be angry with us, and our offering be unacceptable." ² But Anna said, "Let us wait the third year, lest she should be at a loss to know her father." And Joachim said, "Let us then wait." ³ And when the child was three years old, Joachim said, "Let us invite the daughters of the Hebrews, who are undefiled, and let them take each a lamp, and let them be lighted, that the child may not turn back again, and her mind be set against the temple of the Lord." ⁴ And they did thus till they ascended into the temple of the Lord. And the high priest received her, and blessed her, and said, "Mary, the Lord God has magnified your name to all generations. And to the very end of time, the Lord by you will show his redemption to the children of Israel." ⁵ And he placed her on the third step of the altar, and the Lord gave to her grace, and she danced with her feet, and all the house of Israel loved her.

8

¹ And her parents went away filled with wonder, and praising God, because the girl did not return back to them. ² But Mary continued in the temple as a dove educated there, and received her food from the hand of an angel. ³ And when she was twelve years of age, the priests met in a council, and said, "Behold, Mary is twelve years of age. What shall we do with her, for fear lest the holy place of the Lord our God should be defiled?" ⁴ Then the priests replied to Zachary the high priest, "Stand at the altar of the Lord, and enter into the holy place, and make petitions concerning her, and whatever the Lord shall manifest to you, do that." ⁵ Then the high priest entered into the Holy of Holies and, taking away with him the breastplate of judgment, made prayers concerning her. ⁶ And behold, an angel of the Lord came to him and said, "Zachary, Zachary, go forth and call together all the widowers among the people, and let every one of them bring his rod, and he by whom the Lord shall show a sign shall be the husband of Mary." ⁷ And the criers went out throughout all Judaea, and the trumpet of the Lord sounded, and all the people ran and met together. ⁸ Joseph also, throwing away the hatchet, went out to meet them, and when they were met, they went to the high priest, taking every man his rod. ⁹ After the high priest had received their rods, he went into the temple to pray. ¹⁰ And when he

had finished his prayer, he took the rods, and went forth and distributed them, and there was no miracle attending them. ¹¹ The last rod was taken by Joseph, and behold, a dove proceeded out of the rod, and flew upon the head of Joseph. ¹² And the high priest said, "Joseph, you are the person chosen to take the Virgin of the Lord, to keep her for him." ¹³ But Joseph refused, saying, "I am an old man, and have children, but she is young, and I fear lest I should appear ridiculous in Israel." ¹⁴ then the high priest replied, "Joseph, fear the Lord your God, and remember how God dealt with Dathan, Korah, and Abiram, how the earth opened and swallowed them up, because of their contradiction. ¹⁵Now therefore, Joseph, fear God, lest the like things should happen in your family." ¹⁶ Joseph then, being afraid, took her to his house, and Joseph said to Mary, "Behold, I have taken you from the temple of the Lord, and now I will leave you in my house. I must go to mind my trade of building. The Lord be with you."

9

¹ And it came to pass, in a council of priests, that it was said, "Let us make a new veil for the temple." ² And the high priest said, "Call together to me seven undefiled virgins of the tribe of David." ³ And the servants went and brought them into the temple of the Lord, and the high priest said to them, "Cast lots before me now, who of you shall spin the gold thread, who the blue, who the scarlet,, who the fine linen, and who the true purple." ⁴ then the high priest knew Mary, that she was of the tribe of David, and he called her, and the true purple fell to her lot to spin, and she went away to her own home. ⁵ But from that time Zachary the high priest became dumb, and Samuel was placed in his stead till Zachary spoke again. ⁶ But Mary took the true purple, and spun it. ⁷ And she took a pot, and went out to draw water, and heard a voice saying to her, "Hail, you who are full of grace, the Lord is with you. You are blessed among women." ⁸ And she looked around to the right and to the left to see from where the voice came, and then, trembling, went into her house, and laying down the water-pot she took the purple, and sat down in her seat to work it. ⁹ And behold, the angel of the Lord stood by her, and said, "Fear not, Mary, for you have found favor in the sight of God." ¹⁰ When she heard it, she reasoned within herself what that sort of greeting meant. ¹¹ And the angel said to her, "The Lord is with you, and you shall conceive," ¹² to which she replied, "What! Shall I conceive by the living God, and bring forth as all other women do?" ¹³ But the angel replied, "Not so, Mary, but the Holy Spirit shall come upon you, and the power of the Most High shall overshadow you; ¹⁴ therefore, that which shall be born of you shall be holy, and shall be called the Son of the Living God, and you shall call his name Jesus, for He shall save His people from their sins. ¹⁵ And behold, your cousin Elizabeth, she also has conceived a son in her old age, ¹⁶ and this is now the sixth month with her, who was called barren, for nothing is impossible with God." ¹⁷ And Mary said, "Behold the handmaid of the Lord; let it be to me according to your word." ¹⁸ And when she had wrought her purple, she carried it to the high priest, and the high priest blessed her, saying, "Mary, the Lord God has magnified your name, and you shall be blessed in all the ages of the world." ¹⁹ Then Mary, filled with joy, went away to her cousin Elizabeth, and knocked at the door. ²⁰ When Elizabeth heard it, she ran and opened to her, and blessed her, and said, "How is this come to me, that the mother of my Lord should come to me? ²¹ For lo! as soon as the voice of your greeting reached my ears, that which is in me leaped, and blessed you." ²² But Mary, being ignorant of all those mysterious things which the archangel Gabriel had spoken to her, lifted up her eyes to heaven, and said, "Lord! What am I, that all the generations of the earth should call me blessed?" ²³ But perceiving herself daily to grow big, and being afraid, she went home, and hid herself from the children of Israel. And she was sixteen years old when all these things happened.

10

¹ And when her sixth month was come, Joseph returned from his building houses abroad, which was his trade, and entering into the house, found the Virgin grown big. ² Then, smiting upon his face, he said, "With what face can I look up to the Lord my God? Or what shall I say concerning this young woman? ³ For I received her a Virgin from the temple of the Lord my God, and have not preserved her such! Who has thus deceived me? ⁴ Who has committed this evil in my house and, seducing the Virgin from me, has defiled her? ⁵ Is not the history of Adam exactly accomplished in me? ⁶ For in the very instant of his glory, the serpent came and found Eve alone, and seduced her. ⁷ Just after the same manner it has happened to me." ⁸ Then Joseph, arising from the ground, called her and said, "O you who have been so much favored by God, why have you done this? ⁹ Why have you thus debased your soul, who were educated in the Holy of Holies, and received your food from the hand of angels?" ¹⁰ But she, with a flood of tears, replied, "I am innocent, and have known no man." ¹¹ Then said Joseph, "How does it come to pass that you are with child?" ¹² Mary answered, "As the Lord my God lives, I do not know by what means." ¹³Then Joseph was exceedingly afraid, and went away from her, considering what he should do with her. And thus he reasoned with himself: ¹⁴ "If I conceal her crime, I shall be found guilty by the law of the Lord; ¹⁵ and if I reveal her to the children of Israel, I fear lest – she being with child by an angel – I shall be found to betray the life of an innocent person. ¹⁶ What, therefore, shall I do? I will privately dismiss her." ¹⁷ Then the night was come upon him, when behold an angel of the Lord appeared to him in a dream, and said, ¹⁸ "Do not be afraid to take that young woman, for That which is within her is of the Holy Spirit, ¹⁹ and she shall bring forth a Son, and you shall call His name Jesus, for He shall save His people from their sins. ²⁰ Then Joseph arose from his sleep, and glorified the God of Israel, who had shown him such favor, and preserved the Virgin.

11

¹ Then came Annas the scribe, and said to Joseph, "Why have we not seen you since your return?" ² And Joseph replied, "Because I was weary after my journey, and rested the first day." ³ But Annas, turning about, perceived the Virgin big with child. ⁴ And he went away to the priest and told him, "Joseph in whom you placed so much confidence is guilty of a notorious crime, in that he has defiled the Birgin whom he received out of the temple of the Lord, and has privately married her, not revealing it to the children of Israel." ⁵ Then said the priest, "Has Joseph done this?" ⁶ Annas replied, "If you send any of your servants, you will find that she is with child." ⁷ And the servants went, and found it as he said. ⁸ Upon this, both she and Joseph were brought to their trial, and the priest said to her, "Mary, what have you done? ⁹ Why have you debased your soul, and forgotten your God, seeing you were brought up in the Holy of Holies, and received your food from the hands of angels, and heard their songs? ¹⁰ Why have you done this?" ¹¹ To which, with a flood of tears, she answered, "As the Lord my God lives, I am innocent in His sight, seeing I know no man." ¹² Then the priest said to Joseph, "Why have you done this?" ¹³ And Joseph answered, "As the Lord my God lives, I have not been concerned with her." ¹⁴ But the priest said, "Do not lie, but declare the truth. You have privately married her, and not revealed it to the children of Israel, and humbled yourself under the Mighty Hand, that your seed might be blessed." ¹⁵ And Joseph was silent. ¹⁶ Then said the priest, "You must restore to the temple of the Lord the Virgin whom you took from there." ¹⁷ But he wept bitterly. And the priest added, "I will cause you both to drink the water of the Lord, which is for trial, and so your iniquity shall be laid open before you." ¹⁸ Then the priest took the water, and made Joseph drink, and sent him to a mountainous place. ¹⁹ And he returned perfectly well, and all the people marveled that his guilt was not revealed. ²⁰ So the priest said, "Since the Lord has not made your sins evident, neither do I condemn you." ²¹ So he sent them away. ²² Then Joseph took Mary, and went to his house, rejoicing and praising the God of Israel.

12

¹ And it came to pass that there went forth a decree from the Emperor Augustus, that all the Jews should be taxed, who were of Bethlehem in Judaea. ² And Joseph said, "I will take care that my children are taxed, but what shall I do with this young woman? ³ To have her taxed as my wife I am ashamed, and if I tax her as my daughter, all Israel knows she is not my daughter. ⁴ When the time of the Lord's appointment shall come, let Him do as seems good to Him." ⁵ And he saddled the ass, and put her upon it, and Joseph and Simon followed after her, and came near Bethlehem, within three miles. ⁶ Then Joseph, turning about, saw Mary sorrowful, and said within himself, "Perhaps she is in pain through That which is within her." ⁷ But when he turned about again, he saw her laughing, and said to her, ⁸ "Mary, how does it happen that I sometimes see sorrow and sometimes laughter and joy in your face?" ⁹ And Mary replied to him, "I see two people with my eyes, the one weeping and mourning, the other laughing and rejoicing." ¹⁰ And he went again across the way, and Mary said to Joseph, "Take me down from the ass, for That which is in me presses to come forth." ¹¹ But Joseph replied, "Where shall I take you? For the place is desolate." ¹² Then Mary said again to Joseph, "Take me down, for That which is within me mightily presses me." ¹³ And Joseph took her down. ¹⁴ And he found a cave there, and led her into it.

13

¹ And leaving her and his sons in the cave, Joseph went forth to seek a Hebrew midwife in the village of Bethlehem. ² "But as I was going," said Joseph, I looked up into the air, and I saw the clouds astonished, and the fowls of the air stopping in the midst of their flight. ³ And I looked down towards the earth, and saw a table spread, and working people sitting around it, but their hands were upon the table, and they did not move to eat. ⁴ They who had meat in their mouths did not eat. ⁵ They who lifted their hands up

to their heads did not draw them back, ⁶ and they who lifted them up to their mouths did not put anything in, ⁷ but all their faces were fixed upwards. ⁸ And I beheld the sheep dispersed, and yet the sheep stood still. ⁹ And the shepherd lifted up his hand to smite them, and his hand continued up. ¹⁰ And I looked to a river, and saw the kids with their mouths close to the water, and touching it, but they did not drink."

14

¹ "Then I beheld a woman coming down from the mountains, and she said, 'Where are you going, O man?' ² And I said to her, 'I go to inquire for a Hebrew midwife.' ³ She replied to me, 'Where is the woman who is to be delivered?' ⁴ And I answered, 'In the cave, and she is betrothed to me.'" ⁵ Then said the midwife, "Is she not your wife?" ⁶ Joseph answered, "It is Mary, who was educated in the Holy of Holies, in the house of the Lord, and she fell to my lot, and is not my wife, but has conceived by the Holy Spirit." ⁷ The midwife said, "Is this true?" ⁸ He answered, "Come and see." ⁹ And the midwife went along with him, and stood in the cave. ¹⁰ Then a bright cloud overshadowed the cave, and the midwife said, "This day my soul is magnified, for my eyes have seen surprising things, and salvation is brought forth to Israel." ¹¹ But of a sudden the cloud became a great light in the cave, so that their eyes could not bear it. ¹² But the light gradually decreased, until the infant appeared, and sucked the breast of his mother Mary. ¹³ Then the midwife cried out, and said, "How glorious a day is this, wherein my eyes have seen this extraordinary sight! ¹⁴ And the midwife went out from the cave, and Salome met her. ¹⁵ And the midwife said to her, "Salome, Salome, I will tell you a most surprising thing, which I saw. ¹⁶ A virgin has brought forth, which is a thing contrary to nature." ¹⁷ To which Salome replied, "As the Lord my God lives, unless I receive particular proof of this matter, I will not believe that a virgin has brought forth." ¹⁸ Then Salome went in, and the midwife said, "Mary, show yourself, for a great controversy has arisen about you." ¹⁹ And Salome tested her with her finger. ²⁰ But her hand was withered, and she groaned bitterly, ²¹ and said, "Woe to me, because of my iniquity! For I have tempted the living God, and my hand is ready to drop off." ²² Then Salome made her supplication to the Lord, and said, "O God of my fathers, remember me, for I am of the seed of Abraham, and Isaac, and Jacob. ²³ Make me not a reproach among the children of Israel, but restore me sound to my parents. ²⁴ For You well know, O Lord, that I have performed many works of charity in Your name, and have received my reward from You." ²⁵ Upon this an angel of the Lord stood by Salome and said, "The Lord God has heard your prayer; reach forth your hand to the Child, and carry Him, and by that means you shall be restored." ²⁶ Salome, filled with exceeding joy, went to the child, and said, "I will touch Him." ²⁷ And she purposed to worship Him, for she said, "This is a great King who is born in Israel." ²⁸ And straightway Salome was cured. ²⁹ Then the midwife went out of the cave, being approved by God. ³⁰ And lo! a voice came to Salome, "Declare not the strange things which you have seen, till the Child shall come to Jerusalem." So Salome also departed, approved by God.

15

¹ Then Joseph was preparing to go away, because there arose a great disorder in Bethlehem by the coming of some wise men from the east, ² who said, "Where is the king of the Jews born? For we have seen his star in the east, and have come to worship him." ³ When Herod heard this, he was exceedingly troubled, and sent messengers to the wise men, and to the priests, and inquired of his officials, ⁴ and said to them, "Where do you have it written concerning Christ the King, or where should He be born?" ⁵ Then they say to him, "In Bethlehem of Judaea, for so it is written: 'And you, Bethlehem in the land of Judah, are not the least among the princes of Judah, for out of you shall come a Ruler who shall rule my people Israel.'" ⁶ And having sent away the chief priests, he inquired of the wise men, and said to them, "What sign was it you saw, concerning the King who is born?" ⁷ They answered him, "We saw an extraordinarily large star shining among the stars of heaven, and so outshining all the other stars that they became invisible, and we knew thereby that a great King was born in Israel, and therefore we have come to worship him." ⁸ Then Herod said to them, "Go and make diligent inquiry, and if you find the Child, bring me word again, that I may come and worship Him also." ⁹ So the wise men went forth, and behold, the star which they saw in the east went before them, till it came and stood over the cave where the young Child was with Mary His mother. ¹⁰ Then they brought forth out of their treasures, and offered to Him gold and frankincense, and myrrh. ¹¹ And being warned in a dream by an angel that they should not return to Herod through Judaea, they departed into their own country by another way.

16

¹ Then Herod, perceiving that he was being mocked by the wise men, and being very angry, commanded certain men to go and to kill all the children who were in Bethlehem, from two years old and under. ² But Mary, hearing that the children were to be killed, being under much fear, took the Child, and wrapped Him up in swaddling clothes, and laid Him in an ox-manger, because there was no roiom for them in the inn. ³ Elizabeth also, hearing that her son John was about to be searched for, took him and went up into the mountains, and looked around for a place to hide him; ⁴ and there was no place to be found. ⁵ Then she groaned within herself, and said, "O mountain of the Lord, receive the mother with the child." ⁶ For Elizabeth could not climb up. ⁷ And instantly the mountain was divided and received them. ⁸ And there appeared to them an angel of the Lord, to preserve them. ⁹ But Herod made search after John, and sent servants to Zachary, when he was at the altar, and said to him, "Where have you hidden your son?" ¹⁰ He replied to them, "I am a servant of God, and a servant at the altar; how should I know where my son is?" ¹¹ So the servants went back, and told Herod everything, at which he was incensed, and said, "Is ot this son of his likely to be king in Israel?" ¹² Therefore he sent his servants again to Zachary, saying, "Tell us the truth, where is your son? For you know that your life is in my hand." ¹³ So the servants went and told him all this. ¹⁴ But Zachary replied to them, "I am a martyr for God, and if he shed my blood, the Lord will receive my soul. ¹⁵ Besides, know that you shed innocent blood." ¹⁶ However, Zachary was murdered at the entrance of the temple and altar, and about the partition. ¹⁷ But the children of Israel knew not when he was killed. ¹⁸ Then at the hour of salutation the priests went into the temple, but Zachary did not, according to custom, meet them and bless them, ¹⁹ But still they continued waiting for him to salute them. ²⁰ And when they found he did not come in a long time, one of them ventured into the holy place where the altar was, and he saw blood lying upon the ground, congealed. ²¹ Then, behold, a voice from heaven said, "Zachary is murdered, and his blood shall not be wiped away, until the avenger of his blood comes." ²² And when he heard this, he was afraid, and went forth and told the priests what he had seen and heard. And they all went in, and saw the fact. ²³ Then the roofs of the temple howled, and were rent from the top to the bottom, ²⁴ and they could not find the body, but only blood made hard like stone. ²⁵ And they went away, and told the people that Zachary was murdered, and all the tribes of Israel heard of it, and mourned for him, and lamented three days. ²⁶ Then the priests took counsel together concerning a person to succeed him. ²⁷ And Simeon and the other priests cast lots, and the lot fell upon Simeon. ²⁸ For he had been assured by the Holy Spirit, that he should not die, till he had seen Christ come in the flesh.

I, James, wrote this history in Jerusalem. And when the disturbance was, I retired into a desert place until the death of Herod. And the disturbances ceased at Jerusalem. That which remains is, that I glorify God that He has given me such wisdom to write to you who are spiritual, and who love God, to whom be glory and dominion for ever and ever. Amen.

The Arabic Infancy Gospel, or Syriac Infancy Gospel

[1] We find what follows in the book of Joseph the high priest, who lived in the time of Christ. Some say that he is Caiaphas. He has said that Jesus spoke, and, indeed, when He was lying in His cradle said to Mary His mother: I am Jesus, the Son of God, the Logos, whom thou hast brought forth, as the Angel Gabriel announced to thee; and my Father has sent me for the salvation of the world. [2] In the three hundred and ninth year of the era of Alexander, Augustus put forth an edict, that every man should be enrolled in his native place. Joseph therefore arose, and taking Mary his spouse, went away to Jerusalem, and came to Bethlehem, to be enrolled along with his family in his native city. And having come to a cave, Mary told Joseph that the time of the birth was at hand, and that she could not go into the city; but, said she, let us go into this cave. This took place at sunset. And Joseph went out in haste to go for a woman to be near her. When, therefore, he was busy about that, he saw an Hebrew old woman belonging to Jerusalem, and said: Come hither, my good woman, and go into this cave, in which there is a woman near her time. [3] Wherefore, after sunset, the old woman, and Joseph with her, came to the cave, and they both went in. And, behold, it was filled with lights more beautiful than the gleaming of lamps and candles, and more splendid than the light of the sun. The child, enwrapped in swaddling clothes, was sucking the breast of the Lady Mary His mother, being placed in a stall. And when both were wondering at this light, the old woman asks the Lady Mary: Art thou the mother of this Child? And when the Lady Mary gave her assent, she says: Thou art not at all like the daughters of Eve. The Lady Mary said: As my son has no equal among children, so his mother has no equal among women. The old woman replied: My mistress, I came to get payment; I have been for a long time affected with palsy. Our mistress the Lady Mary said to her: Place thy hands upon the child. And the old woman did so, and was immediately cured. Then she went forth, saying: Henceforth I will be the attendant and servant of this child all the days of my life. [4] Then came shepherds; and when they had lighted a fire, and were rejoicing greatly, there appeared to them the hosts of heaven praising and celebrating God Most High. And while the shepherds were doing the same, the cave was at that time made like a temple of the upper world, since both heavenly and earthly voices glorified and magnified God on account of the birth of the Lord Christ. And when that old Hebrew woman saw the manifestation of those miracles, she thanked God, saying: I give Thee thanks, O God, the God of Israel, because mine eyes have seen the birth of the Saviour of the world. [5] And the time of circumcision, that is, the eighth day, being at hand, the child was to be circumcised according to the law. Wherefore they circumcised Him in the cave. And the old Hebrew woman took the piece of skin; but some say that she took the navel-string, and laid it past in a jar of old oil of nard. And she had a son, a dealer in unguents, and she gave it to him, saying: See that thou do not sell this jar of unguent of nard, even although three hundred denarii should be offered thee for it. And this is that jar which Mary the sinner bought and poured upon the head and feet of our Lord Jesus Christ, which thereafter she wiped with the hair of her head. Ten days after, they took Him to Jerusalem; and on the fortieth day after His birth they carried Him into the temple, and set Him before the Lord, and offered sacrifices for Him, according to the command-meet of the law of Moses, which is: Every male that openeth the womb shall be called the holy of God. [6] Then old Simeon saw Him shining like a pillar of light, when the Lady Mary, His virgin mother, rejoicing over Him, was carrying Him in her arms. And angels, praising Him, stood round Him in a circle, like life guards standing by a king. Simeon therefore went up in haste to the Lady Mary, and, with hands stretched out before her, said to the Lord Christ: Now, O my Lord, let Thy servant depart in peace, according to Thy word; for mine eyes have seen Thy compassion, which Thou hast prepared for the salvation of all peoples, a light to all nations, and glory to Thy people Israel. Hanna also, a prophetess, was present, and came up, giving thanks to God, and calling the Lady Mary blessed. [7] And it came to pass, when the Lord Jesus was born at Bethlehem of Judaea, in the time of King Herod, behold, magi came from the east to Jerusalem, as Zeraduscht had predicted; and there were with them gifts, gold, and frankincense, and myrrh. And they adored Him, and presented to Him their gifts. Then the Lady Mary took one of the swaddling-bands, and, on account of the smallness of her means, gave it to them; and they received it from her with the greatest marks of honour. And in the same hour there appeared to them an angel in the form of that star which had before guided them on their journey; and they went away, following the guidance of its light, until they arrived in their own country. [8] And their kings and chief men came together to them, asking what they had seen or done, how they had gone and come back, what they had brought with them. And they showed them that swathing-cloth which the Lady Mary had given them. Wherefore they celebrated a feast, and, according to their custom, lighted a fire and worshipped it, and threw that swathing-cloth into it; and the fire laid hold of it, and enveloped it. And when the fire had gone out, they took out the swathing-cloth exactly as it had been before, just as if the fire had not touched it. Wherefore they began to kiss it, and to put it on their heads and their eyes, saying: This verily is the truth without doubt. Assuredly it is a great thing that the fire was not able to burn or destroy it. Then they took it, and with the greatest honour laid it up among their treasures. [9] And when Herod saw that the magi had left him, and not come back to him, he summoned the priests and the wise men, and said to them: Show me where Christ is to be born. And when they answered, In Bethlehem of Judaea, he began to think of putting the Lord Jesus Christ to death. Then appeared an angel of the Lord to Joseph in his sleep, and said: Rise, take the boy and His mother, and go away into Egypt. He rose, therefore, towards cockcrow, and set out. [10] While he is reflecting how be is to set about his journey, morning came upon him after he had gone a very little way. And now he was approaching a great city, in which there was an idol, to which the other idols and gods of the Egyptians offered gifts and vows. And there stood before this idol a priest ministering to him, who, as often as Satan spoke from that idol, reported it to the inhabitants of Egypt and its territories. This priest had a son, three years old, beset by several demons; and he made many speeches and utterances; and when the demons seized him, he tore his clothes, and remained naked, and threw stones at the people. And there was a hospital in that city dedicated to that idol. And when Joseph and the Lady Mary had come to the city, and had turned aside into that hospital, the citizens were very much afraid; and all the chief men and the priests of the idols came together to that idol, and said to it: What agitation and commotion is this that has arisen in our land? The idol answered them: A God has come here in secret, who is God indeed; nor is any god besides Him worthy of divine worship, because He is truly the Son of God. And when this land became aware of His presence, it trembled at His arrival, and was moved and shaken; and we are exceedingly afraid from the greatness of His power. And in the same hour that idol fell down, and at its fall all, inhabitants of Egypt and others, ran together. [11] And the son of the priest, his usual disease having come upon him, entered the hospital, and there came upon Joseph and the Lady Mary, from whom all others had fled. The Lady Mary had washed the cloths of the Lord Christ, and had spread them over some wood. That demoniac boy, therefore, came and took one of the cloths, and put it on his head. Then the demons, fleeing in the shape of ravens and serpents, began to go forth out of his mouth. The boy, being immediately healed at the command of the Lord Christ, began to praise God, and then to give thanks to the Lord who had healed him. And when his father saw him restored to health, My son, said he, what has happened to thee? and by what means hast thou been healed? The son answered: When the demons had thrown me on the ground, I went into the hospital, and there I found an august woman with a boy, whose newly-washed cloths she had thrown upon some wood: one of these I took up and put upon my head, and the demons left me and fled. At this the father rejoiced greatly, and said: My son, it is possible that this boy is the Son of the living God who created the heavens and the earth: for when he came over to us, the idol was broken, and all the gods fell, and perished by the power of his magnificence. [12] Here was fulfilled the prophecy which says, Out of Egypt have I called my son. Joseph indeed, and Mary, when they heard that that idol had fallen down and perished, trembled, and were afraid. Then they said: When we were in the land of Israel, Herod thought to put Jesus to death, and on that account slew all the children of Bethlehem and its confines; and there is no doubt that the Egyptians, as soon as they have heard that this idol has been broken, will burn us with fire. [13] Going out thence, they came to a place where there were robbers who had plundered several men of their baggage and clothes, and had bound them. Then the robbers heard a great noise, like the noise of a magnificent king going out of his city with his army, and his chariots and his drums; and at this the robbers were terrified, and left all their plunder. And their captives rose up, loosed each other's bonds, recovered their baggage, and went away. And when they saw Joseph and Mary coming up to the place, they said to them: Where is that king, at the hearing of the magnificent sound of whose approach the robbers have left us, so that we have escaped safe? Joseph answered them: He will come behind us. [14] Thereafter they came into another city, where there was a demoniac woman whom Satan, accursed and rebellious, had beset, when on one occasion she had gone out by night for water. She could neither bear clothes, nor live in a house; and as often as they tied her up with chains and thongs, she broke them, and fled naked into waste places; and, standing in cross-roads and cemeteries, she kept throwing stones at people, and brought very heavy calamities upon her friends. And when the Lady Mary saw her, she pitied her; and upon this Satan immediately left her, and fled away in the form of a young man,

saying: Woe to me from thee, Mary, and from thy son. So that woman was cured of her torment, and being restored to her senses, she blushed on account of her nakedness; and shunning the sight of men, went home to her friends. And after she put on her clothes, she gave an account of the matter to her father and her friends; and as they were the chief men of the city, they received the Lady Mary and Joseph with the greatest honour and hospitality.[15] On the day after, being supplied by them with provision for their journey, they went away, and on the evening of that day arrived at another town, in which they were celebrating a marriage; but, by the arts of accursed Satan and the work of enchanters, the bride had become dumb, and could not speak a word. And after the Lady Mary entered the town, carrying her son the Lord Christ, that dumb bride saw her, and stretched out her hands towards the Lord Christ, and drew Him to her, and took Him into her arms, and held Him close and kissed Him, and leaned over Him, moving His body back and forwards. Immediately the knot of her tongue was loosened, and her ears were opened; and she gave thanks and praise to God, because He had restored her to health. And that night the inhabitants of that town exulted with joy, and thought that God and His angels had come down to them.[16] There they remained three days, being held in great honour, and living splendidly. Thereafter, being supplied by them with provision for their journey, they went away and came to another city, in which, because it was very populous, they thought of passing the night. And there was in that city an excellent woman: and once, when she had gone to the river to bathe, lo, accursed Satan, in the form of a serpent, had leapt upon her, and twisted himself round her belly; and as often as night came on, he tyrannically tormented her. This woman, seeing the mistress the Lady Mary, and the child, the Lord Christ, in her bosom, was struck with a longing for Him, and said to the mistress the Lady Mary: O mistress, give me this child, that I may carry him, and kiss him. She therefore gave Him to the woman; and when He was brought to her, Satan let her go, and fled and left her, nor did the woman ever see him after that day. Wherefore all who were present praised God Most High, and that woman bestowed on them liberal gifts[17] On the day after, the same woman took scented water to wash the Lord Jesus; and after she had washed Him, she took the water with which she had done it, and poured part of it upon a girl who was living there, whose body was white with leprosy, and washed her with it. And as soon as this was done, the girl was cleansed from her leprosy. And the towns- people said: There is no doubt that Joseph and Mary and that boy are gods, not men. And when they were getting ready to go away from them, the girl who had laboured under the leprosy came up to them, and asked them to let her go with them.[18] When they had given her permission, she went with them. And afterwards they came to a city, in which was the castle of a most illustrious prince, who kept a house for the entertainment of strangers. They turned into this place; and the girl went away to the prince's wife; and she found her weeping and sorrowful, and she asked why she was weeping. Do not be surprised, said she, at my tears; for I am overwhelmed by a great affliction, which as yet I have not endured to tell to any one. Perhaps, said the girl, if you reveal it and disclose it to me, I may have a remedy for it. Hide this secret, then, replied the princess, and tell it to no one. I was married to this prince, who is a king and ruler over many cities, and I lived long with him, but by me he had no son. And when at length I produced him a son, he was leprous; and as soon as he saw him, he turned away with loathing, and said to me: Either kill him, or give him to the nurse to be brought up in some place from which we shall never hear of him more. After this I can have nothing to do with thee, and I will never see thee more. On this account I know not what to do, and I am overwhelmed with grief. Alas! my son. Alas! my husband. Did I not say so? said the girl. I have found a cure for thy disease, and I shall tell it thee. For I too was a leper; but I was cleansed by God, who is Jesus, the son of the Lady Mary. And the woman asking her where this God was whom she had spoken of, Here, with thee, said the girl; He is living in the same house. But how is this possible? said she. Where is he? There, said the girl, are Joseph and Mary; and the child who is with them is called Jesus; and He it is who cured me of my disease and my torment. But by what means, said she, wast thou cured of thy leprosy? Wilt thou not tell me that? Why not? said the girl. I got from His mother the water in which He had been washed, and poured it over myself; and so I was cleansed from my leprosy. Then the princess rose up, and invited them to avail themselves of her hospitality. And she prepared a splendid banquet for Joseph in a great assembly of the men of the place. And on the following day she took scented water with which to wash the Lord Jesus, and thereafter poured the same water over her son, whom she had taken with her; and immediately her son was cleansed from his leprosy. Therefore, singing thanks and praises to God, she said: Blessed is the mother who bore thee, O Jesus; dost thou so cleanse those who share the same nature with thee with the water in which thy body has been washed? Besides, she bestowed great gifts upon the mistress the Lady Mary, and sent her away with great honour.[19] Coming thereafter to another city, they wished to spend the night in it. They turned aside, therefore, to the house of a man newly married, but who, under the influence of witchcraft, was not able to enjoy his wife; and when they had spent that night with him, his bond was loosed. And at daybreak, when they were girding themselves for their journey, the bridegroom would not let them go, and prepared for them a great banquet.[20] They set out, therefore, on the following day; and as they came near another city, they saw three women weeping as they came out of a cemetery. And when the Lady Mary beheld them, she said to the girl who accompanied her: Ask them what is the matter with them, or what calamity has befallen them. And to the girl's questions they made no reply, but asked in their turn: Whence are you, and whither are you going? for the day is already past, and night is coming on apace. We are travellers, said the girl, and are seeking a house of entertainment in which we may pass the night. They said: Go with us, and spend the night with us. They followed them, therefore, and were brought into a new house with splendid decorations and furniture. Now it was winter; and the girl, going into the chamber of these women, found them again weeping and lamenting. There stood beside them a mule, covered with housings of cloth of gold, and sesame was put before him; and the women were kissing him, and giving him food. And the gift said: What is all the ado, my ladies, about this mule? They answered her with tears, and said: This mule, which thou seest, was our brother, born of the same mother with ourselves. And when our father died, and left us great wealth, and this only brother, we did our best to get him married, and were preparing his nuptials for him, after the manner of men. But some women, moved by mutual jealousy, bewitched him unknown to us; and one night, a little before daybreak, when the door of our house was shut, we saw that this our brother had been turned into a mule, as thou now beholdest him. And we are sorrowful, as thou seest, having no father to comfort us: there is no wise man, or magician, or enchanter in the world that we have omitted to send for; but nothing has done us any good. And as often as our hearts are overwhelmed with grief, we rise and go away with our mother here, and weep at our father's grave, and come back again.[21] And when the girl heard these things, Be of good courage, said she, and weep not: for the cure of your calamity is near; yea, it is beside you, and in the middle of your own house. For I also was a leper; but when I saw that woman, and along with her that young child, whose name is Jesus, I sprinkled my body with the water with which His mother had washed Him, and I was cured. And I know that He can cure your affliction also. But rise, go to Mary my mistress; bring her into your house, and tell her your secret; and entreat and supplicate her to have pity upon yon. After the woman had heard the girl's words, they went in haste to the Lady Mary, and brought her into their chamber, and sat down before her weeping, and saying: O our mistress, Lady Mary, have pity on thy hand-maidens; for no one older than ourselves, and no head of the family, is left- -neither father nor brother–to live with us; but this mule which thou seest was our brother, and women have made him such as thou seest by witchcraft. We beseech thee, therefore, to have pity upon us. Then, grieving at their lot, the Lady Mary took up the Lord Jesus, and put Him on the mule's back; and she wept as well as the women, and said to Jesus Christ: Alas! my son, heal this mule by Thy mighty power, and make him a man endowed with reason as he was before. And when these words were uttered by the Lady Mary, his form was changed, and the mule became a young man, free from every defect. Then he and his mother and his sisters adored the Lady Mary, and lifted the boy above their heads, and began to kiss Him, saying: Blessed is she that bore Thee, O Jesus, O Saviour of the world; blessed are the eyes which enjoy the felicity of seeing Thee.[22] Moreover, both the sisters said to their mother: Our brother indeed, by the aid of the Lord Jesus Christ, and by the salutary intervention of this girl, who pointed out to us Mary and her son, has been raised to human form. Now, indeed, since our brother is unmarried, it would do very well for us to give him as his wife this girl, their servant. And having asked the Lady Mary, and obtained her consent, they made a splendid wedding for the girl; and their sorrow being changed into joy, and the beating of their breasts into dancing, they began to be glad, to rejoice, to exult, and sing–adorned, on account of their great joy, in most splendid and gorgeous attire. Then they began to recite songs and praises, and to say: O Jesus, son of David, who turnest sorrow into gladness, and lamentations into joy! And Joseph and Mary remained there ten clays. Thereafter they set out, treated with great honours by these people, who bade them farewell, and from bidding them farewell returned weeping, especially the girl.[23] And turning away from this place, they came to a desert; and hearing that it was infested by robbers, Joseph and the Lady Mary resolved to cross this region by night. But as they go along, behold, they see two robbers lying in the way, and along with them a great number of robbers, who were their associates, sleeping. Now those two robbers, into whose hands they had fallen, were

Titus and Dumachus. Titus therefore said to Dumachus: I beseech thee to let these persons go freely, and so that our comrades may not see them. And as Dumachus refused, Titus said to him again: Take to thyself forty drachmas from me, and hold this as a pledge. At the same time he held out to him the belt which he had about his waist, to keep him from opening his mouth or speaking. And the Lady Mary, seeing that the robber had done them a kindness, said to him: The Lord God will sustain thee by His right hand, and will grant thee remission of thy sins. And the Lord Jesus answered, and said to His mother: Thirty years hence, O my mother, the Jews will crucify me at Jerusalem, and these two robbers will be raised upon the cross along with me, Titus on my right hand and Dumachus on my left; and after that day Titus shall go before me into Paradise. And she said: God keep this from thee, my son. And they went thence towards a city of idols, which, as they came near it, was changed into sand-hills.[24] Hence they turned aside to that sycamore which is now called Matarea,[1] and the Lord Jesus brought forth in Matarea a fountain in which the Lady Mary washed His shirt. And from the sweat of the Lord Jesus which she sprinkled there, balsam was produced in that region.[25] Thence they came down to Memphis, and saw Pharaoh, and remained three years in Egypt; and the Lord Jesus did in Egypt very many miracles which are recorded neither in the Gospel of the Infancy nor in the perfect Gospel.[26] And at the end of the three years He came back out of Egypt, and returned. And when they had arrived at Judaea, Joseph was afraid to enter it; but hearing that Herod was dead, and that Archelaus his son had succeeded him, he was afraid indeed, but he went into Judaea. And an angel of the Lord appeared to him, and said: O Joseph, go into the city of Nazareth, and there abide. Wonderful indeed, that the Lord of the world should be thus borne and carried about through the world![27] Thereafter, going into the city of Bethlehem, they saw there many and grievous diseases infesting the eyes of the children, who were dying in consequence. And a woman was there with a sick son, whom, now very near death, she brought to the Lady Mary, who saw him as she was washing Jesus Christ. Then said the woman to her: O my Lady Mary, look upon this son of mine, who is labouring under a grievous disease. And the Lady Mary listened to her, and said: Take a little of that water in which I have washed my son, and sprinkle him with it. She therefore took a little of the water, as the Lady Mary had told her, and sprinkled it over her son. And when this was done his illness abated; and after sleeping a little, he rose up from sleep safe and sound. His mother rejoicing at this, again took him to the Lady Mary. And she said to her: Give thanks to God, because He hath healed this thy son.[28] There was in the same place another woman, a neighbour of her whose son had lately been restored to health. And as her son was labouring under the same disease, and his eyes were now almost blinded, she wept night and day. And the mother of the child that had been cured said to her: Why dost thou not take thy son to the Lady Mary, as I did with mine when he was nearly dead? And he got well with that water with which the body of her son Jesus had been washed. And when the woman heard this from her, she too went and got some of the same water, and washed her son with it, and his body and his eyes were instantly made well. Her also, when she had brought her son to her, and disclosed to her all that had happened, the Lady Mary ordered to give thanks to God for her son's restoration to health, and to tell nobody of this matter.[29] There were in the same city two women, wives of one man, each having a son ill with fever. The one was called Mary, and her son's name was Cleopas. She rose and took up her son, and went to the Lady Mary, the mother of Jesus, and offering her a beautiful mantle, said: O my Lady Mary, accept this mantle, and for it give me one small bandage. Mary did so, and the mother of Cleopas went away, and made a shirt of it, and put it on her son. So he was cured of his disease; but the son of her rival died. Hence there sprung up hatred between them; and as they did the house-work week about, and as it was the turn of Mary the mother of Cleopas, she heated the oven to bake bread; and going away to bring the lump that she had kneaded, she left her son Cleopas beside the oven. Her rival seeing him alone–and the oven was very hot with the fire blazing under it–seized him and threw him into the oven, and took herself off. Mary coming back, and seeing her son Cleopas lying in the oven laughing, and the oven quite cold, as if no fire had ever come near it, knew that her rival had thrown him into the fire. She drew him out, therefore, and took him to the Lady Mary, and told her of what had happened to him. And she said: Keep silence, and tell nobody of the affair; for I am afraid for you if you divulge it. After this her rival went to the well to draw water; and seeing Cleopas playing beside the well, and nobody near, she seized him and threw him into the well, and went home herself. And some men who had gone to the well for water saw the boy sitting on the surface of the water; and so they went down and drew him out. And they were seized with a great admiration of that boy, and praised God. Then came his mother, and took him up, and went weeping to the Lady Mary, and said: O my lady, see what my rival has done to my son, and how she has thrown him into the well; she will be sure to destroy him some day or other. The Lady Mary said to her: God will avenge thee upon her. Thereafter, when her rival went to the well to draw water, her feet got entangled in the rope, and she fell into the well. Some men came to draw her out, but they found her skull fractured and her bones broken. Thus she died a miserable death, and in her came to pass that saying: They have digged a well deep, but have fallen into the pit which they had prepared.[1][30] Another woman there had twin sons who had fallen into disease, and one of them died, and the other was at his last breath. And his mother, weeping, lifted him up, and took him to the Lady Mary, and said: O my lady, aid me and succour me. For I had two sons, and I have just buried the one, and the other is at the point of death. See how I am going to entreat and pray to God. And she began to say: O Lord, Thou art compassionate, and merciful, and full of affection. Thou gavest me two sons, of whom Thou hast taken away the one: this one at least leave to me. Wherefore the Lady Mary, seeing the fervour of her weeping, had compassion on her, and said: Put thy son in my son's bed, and cover him with his clothes. And when she had put him in the bed in which Christ was lying, he had already closed his eyes in death; but as soon as the smell of the clothes of the Lord Jesus Christ reached the boy, he opened his eyes, and, calling upon his mother with a loud voice, he asked for bread, and took it and sucked it. Then his mother said: O Lady Mary, now I know that the power of God dwelleth in thee, so that thy son heals those that partake of the same nature with himself, as soon as they have touched his clothes. This boy that was healed is he who in the Gospel is called Bartholomew.[31] Moreover, there was there a leprous woman, and she went to the Lady Mary, the mother of Jesus, and said: My lady, help me. And the Lady Mary answered: What help dost thou seek? Is it gold or silver? or is it that thy body be made clean from the leprosy? And that woman asked: Who can grant me this? And the Lady Mary said to her: Wait a little, until I shall have washed my son Jesus, and put him to bed. The woman waited, as Mary had told her; and when she had put Jesus to bed, she held out to the woman the water in which she had washed His body, and said: Take a little of this water, and pour it over thy body. And as soon as she had done so, she was cleansed, and gave praise and thanks to God.[32] Therefore, after staying with her three days, she went away; and coming to a city, saw there one of the chief men, who had married the daughter of another of the chief men. But when he saw the woman, he beheld between her eyes the mark of leprosy in the shape of a star; and so the marriage was dissolved, and became null and void. And when that woman saw them in this condition, weeping and overwhelmed with sorrow, she asked the cause of their grief. But they said: Inquired not into our condition, for to no one living can we tell our grief, and to none but ourselves can we disclose it. She urged them, however, and entreated them to entrust it to her, saying that she would perhaps be able to tell them of a remedy. And when they showed her the girl, and the sign of leprosy which appeared between her eyes, as soon as she saw it, the woman said: I also, whom you see here, laboured under the same disease, when, upon some business which happened to come in my way, I went to Bethlehem. There going into a cave, I saw a woman named Mary, whose son was he who was named Jesus; and when she saw that I was a leper. she took pity on me, and handed me the water with which she had washed her son's body. With it I sprinkled my body, and came out clean. Then the woman said to her: Wilt thou not, O lady, rise and go with us, and show us the Lady Mary? And she assented; and they rose and went to the Lady Mary, carrying with them splendid gifts. And when they had gone in, and presented to her the gifts, they showed her the leprous girl whom they had brought. The Lady Mary therefore said: May the compassion of the Lord Jesus Christ descend upon you; and handling to them also a little of the water in which she had washed the body of Jesus Christ, she ordered the wretched woman to be bathed in it. And when this had been done, she was immediately cured; and they, and all standing by, praised God. Joyfully therefore they returned to their own city, praising the Lord for what He had done. And when the chief heard that his wife had been cured, he took her home, and made a second marriage, and gave thanks to God for the recovery of his wife's health.[33] There was there also a young woman afflicted by Satan; for that accursed wretch repeatedly appeared to her in the form of a huge dragon, and prepared to swallow her. He also sucked out all her blood, so that she was left like a corpse. As often as he came near her, she, with her hands clasped over her head, cried out, and said: Woe, woe's me, for nobody is near to free me from that accursed dragon. And her father and mother, and all who were about her or saw her, bewailed her lot; and men stood round her in a crowd, and all wept and lamented, especially when she wept, and said: Oh, my brethren and friends, is there no one to free me from that murderer? And the daughter of the chief who had been healed of her leprosy, hearing the girl's voice, went up to the roof of her castle, and saw her with her hands clasped over her head weeping, and all the crowds standing round her weeping as wall. She therefore asked the demoniac's husband whether his wife's mother were alive. And when he answered that both her parents were living, she said: Send for her mother to come to me. And when she saw that he had sent for her, and she had come, she said: Is that distracted girl thy daughter? Yes, O lady, said that sorrowful and weeping woman, she is my daughter. The chiefs daughter answered: Keep my secret, for I confess to thee that I was formerly a leper; but now the Lady Mary, the mother of Jesus Christ, has healed me. But if thou wishest thy daughter to be healed, take her to Bethlehem, and seek Mary the mother of Jesus, and believe that thy daughter will be healed; I indeed believe that thou wilt come back with joy, with thy daughter healed. As soon as the woman heard the words of the chief's daughter, she led away her daughter in haste; and going to the place indicated, she went to the Lady Mary, and revealed to her the state of her daughter. And the Lady Mary hearing her words, gave her a little of the water in which she had washed the body of her son Jesus, and ordered her to pour it on the body of her daughter. She gave her also from the clothes of the Lord Jesus a swathing-cloth, saying: Take this cloth, and show it to thine enemy as often as thou shalt see him. And she saluted them, and sent them away.[34] When, therefore, they had gone away from her, and returned to their own district, and the time was at hand at which Satan was wont to attack her, at this very time that accursed one appeared to her in the shape of a huge dragon, and the girl was afraid at the sight of him. And her mother said to her: Fear not, my daughter; allow him to come near thee, and then show him the cloth which the Lady Mary hath given us, and let us see what will happen. Satan, therefore, having come near in the likeness of a terrible dragon, the body of the girl shuddered for fear of him; but as soon as she took out the cloth, and placed it on her head, and covered her eyes with it, flames and live coals began to dart forth from it, and to be cast upon the dragon. O the great miracle which was done as soon as the dragon saw the cloth of the Lord Jesus, from which the fire darted, and was cast upon his head and eyes! He cried out with a loud voice: What have I to do with thee, O Jesus, son of Mary? Whither shall I fly from thee? And with great fear he turned his back and departed from the girl, and never afterwards appeared to her. And the girl now had rest from him, and gave praise and thanks to God, and along with her all who were present at that miracle.[35] Another woman was living in the same place, whose son was tormented by Satan. He, Judas by name, as often as Satan seized him, used to bite all who came near him; and if he found no one near him, he used to bite his own hands and other limbs. The mother of this wretched creature, then, hearing the fame of the Lady Mary and her son Jesus, rose up and brought her son Judas with her to the Lady Mary. In the meantime, James and Joses had taken the child the Lord Jesus with them to play with the other children; and they had gone out of the house and sat down, and the Lord Jesus with them. And the demoniac Judas came up, and sat down at Jesus' right hand: then, being attacked by Satan in the same manner as usual, he wished to bite the Lord Jesus, but was not able; nevertheless he struck Jesus on the right side, whereupon He began to weep. And immediately Satan went forth out of that boy, fleeing like a mad dog. And this boy who struck Jesus, and out of whom Satan went forth in the shape of a dog, was Judas Iscariot, who betrayed Him to the Jews; and that same side on which Judas struck Him, the Jews transfixed with a lance.[36] Now, when the Lord Jesus had completed seven years from His birth, on a certain day He was occupied with boys of His own age. For they were playing among clay, from which they were making images of asses, oxen, birds, and other animals; and each one boasting of his skill, was praising his own work. Then the Lord Jesus said to the boys: The images that I have made I will order to walk. The boys asked Him whether then he were the son of the Creator; and the Lord Jesus bade them walk. And they immediately began to leap; and then, when He had given them leave, they again stood still. And He had made figures of birds and sparrows, which flew when He told them to fly, and stood still when He told them to stand, and ate and drank when He handed them food and drink. After the boys had gone away and told this to their parents, their fathers said to them: My sons, take care not to keep company with him again, for he is a wizard: flee from him, therefore, and avoid him, and do not play with him again after this.[37] On a certain day the Lord Jesus, running about and playing with the boys, passed the shop of a dyer, whose name was Salem; and he had in his shop many pieces of cloth which he was to dye. The Lord Jesus then, going into his shop, took up all the pieces of cloth, and threw them into a tub full of indigo. And when Salem came and saw his cloths destroyed, he began to cry out with a loud voice, and to reproach Jesus, saying: Why hast thou done this to me, O son of Mary? Thou hast disgraced me before all my townsmen: for, seeing that every one wished the colour that suited himself, thou indeed hast come and destroyed them all. The Lord Jesus answered: I shall change for thee the colour of any piece of cloth which thou shalt wish to be changed. And immediately He began to take the pieces of cloth out of the tub, each of them of that colour which the dyer wished, until He had taken them all out. When the Jews saw this miracle and prodigy, they praised God.[38] And Joseph used to go about through the whole city, and take the Lord Jesus with him, when people sent for him in the way of his trade to make for them doors, and milk-pails, and beds, and chests; and the Lord Jesus was with him wherever he went. As often, therefore, as Joseph had to make anything a cubit or a span longer or shorter, wider or narrower, the Lord Jesus stretched His hand towards it; and as soon as He did so, it became such as Joseph wished. Nor was it necessary for him to make anything with his own hand, for Joseph was not very skilful in carpentry.[39] Now, on a certain day, the king of Jerusalem sent for him, and said: I wish thee, Joseph, to make for me a throne to fit that place in which I usually sit. Joseph obeyed, and began the work immediately, and remained in the palace two years, until he finished the work of that throne. And when he had it carried to its place, he perceived that each side wanted two spans of the prescribed measure. And the king, seeing this, was angry with Joseph; and Joseph, being in great fear of the king, spent the night without supper, nor did he taste anything at all. Then, being asked by the Lord Jesus why he was afraid, Joseph said: Because I have spoiled all the work that I have been two years at. And the Lord Jesus said to him: Fear not, and do not lose heart; but do thou take hold of one side of the throne; I shall take the other; and we shall put that to rights. And Joseph, having done as the Lord Jesus had said and each having drawn by his own side, the throne was put to rights, and brought to the exact measure of the place. And those that stood by and saw this miracle were struck with astonishment, and praised God. And the woods used in that throne were of those which are celebrated in the time of Solomon the son of David; that is, woods of many and various kinds.[40] On another day the Lord Jesus went out into the road, and saw the boys that had come together to play, and followed them; but the boys hid themselves from Him. The Lord Jesus, therefore, having come to the door of a certain house, and seen some women standing there, asked them where the boys had gone; and when they answered that there was no one there, He said again: Who are these whom you see in the furnace?' They replied that they were kids of three years old. And the Lord Jesus cried out, and said: Come out hither, O kids, to your Shepherd. Then the boys, in the form of kids, came out, and began to dance round Him; and the women, seeing this, were very much astonished, and were seized with trembling, and speedily, supplicated and adored the Lord Jesus, saying: O our Lord Jesus, son of Mary, Thou art of a truth that good Shepherd of Israel; have mercy on Thy handmaidens who stand before Thee, and who have never doubted: for Thou hast come, O our Lord, to heal, and not to destroy. And when the Lord Jesus answered that the sons of Israel were like the Ethiopians among the nations, the women said: Thou, O Lord, knowest all things, nor is anything hid from Thee; now, indeed, we beseech Thee, and ask Thee of Thy affection to restore these boys Thy servants to their former condition. The Lord Jesus therefore said: Come, boys, let us go and play. And immediately, while these women were standing by, the kids were changed into boys.[41] Now in the month Adar, Jesus, after the manner of a king, assembled the boys together. They spread their clothes on the ground, and He sat down upon them. Then they put on His head a crown made of flowers, and, like chamber-servants, stood in His presence, on the right and on the left, as if He were a king. And whoever passed by that way was forcibly dragged by the boys, saying: Come hither, and adore the king; then go thy way.[42] In the meantime, while these things were going on, some men came up carrying a boy. For this boy had gone into the mountain with those of his own age to seek wood, and there he found a partridge's nest; and when he stretched out his hand to take the eggs from it, a venomous serpent bit him from the middle of the nest, so that he called out for help. His comrades accordingly went to him with haste, and found him lying on the ground like one dead. Then his relations came and took hun up to carry him back to the city. And after they had come to that place where the Lord Jesus was sitting like a king, and the rest of the boys standing round Him like His servants, the boys went hastily forward to meet him who had been bitten by the serpent, and said to his relations: Come and salute the king. Bat when they were unwilling to go, on account of the sorrow in I which they were, the boys dragged them by force against their will. And when they had come up to the Lord Jesus, He asked them why they were carrying the boy. And when they answered that a serpent had bitten him, the Lord Jesus said to the boys: Let us go and kill that serpent. And the parents of the boy asked leave to go away, because their son was in the agony of death; but the boys answered them, saying: Did you not hear the king saying: Let us go kill the serpent? and will yon not obey him? And so, against their will the could was carried back. And when they came to the nest, the Lord Jesus said to the boys: Is this the serpent's place? They saint that it was; and the serpent, at the call of the Lord, came forth without delay, and submitted itself to Him. And He said to it: Go away, and suck out all the poison which thou hast infused into this boy. And so the serpent crawled to the boy, and sucked out all its poison. Then the Lord Jesus cursed it, and immediately on this being done it burst asunder; and the Lord Jesus stroked the boy with his hand, and he was healed. And he began to weep; but Jesus said: Do not weep, for by and by thou shalt be my disciple. And this is Simon the Cananite, of whom mention is made in the Gospel.[43] On another day, Joseph sent his son James to gather wood, and the Lord Jesus went with him as his companion. And when they had come to the place where the wood was, and James had begun to gather it, behold, a venomous viper bit his band, so that he began to cry out and weep. The Lord Jesus then, seeing him in this condition, went up to him, and blew upon the place where the viper had bitten him; and this being done, he was healed immediately.[44] One day, when the Lord Jesus was again with the boys playing on the roof of a house, one of the boys fell down from above, and immediately expired. And the rest of the boys fled in all directions, and the Lord Jesus was left alone on the roof. And the relations of the boy came up and said to the Lord Jesus: It was thou who didst throw our son headlong from the roof. And when He denied it, they cried out, saying: Our son is dead, and here is he who has killed him. And the Lord Jesus said to them: Do not bring an evil report against me; but if you do not believe me, come and let us ask the boy himself, that be may bring the truth to light. Then the Lord Jesus went down, and standing over the dead body, said, with a loud voice: Zeno, Zeno, who threw thee down from the roof? Then the dead boy answered and said: My lord, it was not thou who didst throw me down, but such a one cast me down from it. And when the Lord commanded those who were standing by to attend to His words, all who were present praised God for this miracle.[45] Once upon a time the Lady Mary bad ordered the Lord Jesus to go and bring her water from the well. And when He had gone to get the water, the pitcher already full was knocked against something, and broken. And the Lord Jesus stretched out His handkerchief, and collected the water, and carried it to His mother; and she was astonished at it. And she hid and preserved in her heart all that she saw.[46] Again, on another day, the Lord Jesus was with the boys at a stream of water, and they had again made little fish-ponds. And the Lord Jesus had made twelve sparrows, and had arranged them round His fish-pond, three on each side. And it was the Sabbath-day. Wherefore a Jew, the son of Hanan, coming up, and seeing them thus engaged, said in anger and great indignation: Do you make figures of clay on the Sabbath-day? And he ran quickly, and destroyed their fish-ponds. But when the Lord Jesus clapped His hands over the sparrows which He had made, they flew away chirping. Then the son of Hanan came up to the fish-pond of Jesus also, and kicked it with his shoes, and the water of it vanished away. And the Lord Jesus said to him: As that water has vanished away, so thy life shall likewise vanish away. And immediately that boy dried up.[47] At another time, when the Lord Jesus was returning home with Joseph in the evening. He met a boy, who ran up against Him with so much force that He fell. And the Lord Jesus said to him: As thou hast thrown me down, so thou shall fall and not rise again. And the same hour the boy fell down, and expired.[48] There was, moreover, at Jerusalem, a certain man named Zacchaeus, who taught boys. He said to Joseph: Why, O Joseph, dost thou not bring Jesus to the to learn his letters? Joseph agreed to do so, and reported the matter to the Lady Mary. They therefore took Him to the master; and he, as soon as he saw Him, wrote out the alphabet for Him, and told Him to say Aleph. And when he had said Aleph, the master ordered Him to pronounce Beth. And the Lord Jesus said to him: Tell me first the meaning of the letter Aleph, and then I shall pronounce Beth. And when the master threatened to flog Him, the Lord Jesus explained to him the meanings of the letters Aleph and Beth; also which figures of the letter were straight, which crooked, which drawn round into a spiral, which marked with points, which without them, why one letter went before another; and many other things He began to recount and to elucidate which the master himself had never either heard or read in any book. The Lord Jesus, moreover, said to the master: Listen, and I shall say them to thee. And He began clearly and distinctly to repeat Aleph, Beth, Gimel, Daleth, on to Tau. And the master was astonished, and said: I think that this boy was born before Noah. And turning to Joseph, be said: Thou hast brought to me to be taught a boy more learned than all the masters. To the Lady Mary also be said: This son of thine has no need of instruction.[49] Thereafter they took Him to another and a more learned master, who, when be saw Him, said: Say Aleph. And when He had said Aleph, the master ordered him to pronounce Beth. And the Lord Jesus answered him, and said: First tell me the meaning of the letter Aleph, and then I shall pronounce Beth. And when the master hereupon raised his hand and flogged Him, immediately his hand dried up, and he died. Then said Joseph, to the Lady Mary: From this time we shall not let him go out of the house, since every one who opposes him is struck dead.[50] And when He was twelve years old, they took Him to Jerusalem to the feast. And when the feast was finished, they indeed returned; but the Lord Jesus remained in the temple among the teachers and elders and learned men of the sons of Israel, to whom He put various questions upon the sciences, and gave answers in His turn. For He said to them: Whose son is the Messias? They answered Him: The son of David. Wherefore then, said He, does he in the Spirit call him his lord, when he says, The Lord said to my lord, Sit at my right hand, that I may put thine enemies under thy footsteps? Again the chief of the teachers said to Him: Hast thou read the books? Both the books, said the Lord Jesus, and the things contained in the books. And He explained the books, and the law, and the precepts, and the statutes, and the mysteries, which are contained in the books of the prophets–things which the understanding of no creature attains to. That teacher therefore said: I hitherto have neither attained to nor heard of such knowledge: Who, pray, do you think that boy will be?[51] And a philosopher who was there present, a skilful astronomer, asked the Lord Jesus whether He had studied astronomy. And the Lord Jesus answered him, and explained the number of the spheres, and of the heavenly bodies, their natures and operations; their opposition; their aspect, triangular, square, and sextile; their course, direct and retrograde; the twenty-fourths, and sixtieths of twenty-fourths; and other things beyond the reach of reason.[52] There was also among those philosophers one very skilled in treating of natural science, and he asked the Lord Jesus whether He had studied medicine. And He, in reply, explained to him physics and metaphysics, hyperphysics and hypophysics, the powers likewise and humours of the body, and the effects of the same; also the number of members and bones, of veins, arteries, and nerves; also the effect of heat and dryness, of cold and moisture, and what these give rise to; what was the operation of the soul upon the body, and its perceptions and powers; what was the operation of the faculty of speech, of anger, of desire; lastly, their conjunction and disjunction, and other things beyond the reach of any created intellect. Then that philosopher rose up, and adored the Lord Jesus, and said: O Lord, from this time I will be thy disciple and slave.[53] While they were speaking to each other of these and other things, the Lady Mary came, after having gone about seeking Him for three days along with Joseph. She therefore, seeing Him sitting among the teachers asking them questions, and answering in His turn, said to Him: My son, why hast thou treated us thus? Behold, thy father and I have sought thee with great trouble. But He said: Why do you seek me? Do you not know that I ought to occupy myself in my Father's house? But they did not understand the words that He spoke to them. Then those teachers asked Mary whether He were her son; and when she signified that He was, they said: Blessed art thou, O Mary, who hast brought forth such a son. And returning with them to Nazareth, He obeyed them in all things. And His mother kept all these words of His in her heart. And the Lord Jesus advanced in stature, and in wisdom, and in favour with God and man.[54] And from this day He began to hide His miracles and mysteries and secrets, and to give attention to the law, until He completed His thirtieth year, when His Father publicly declared Him at the Jordan by this voice sent down from heaven: This is my beloved Son, in whom I am well pleased; the Holy Spirit being present in the form of a white dove.[55] This is He whom we adore with supplications, who hath given us being and life, and who hath brought us from our mothers' wombs; who for our sakes assumed a human body, and redeemed us, that He might embrace us in eternal compassion, and show to us His mercy according to His liberality, and beneficence, and generosity, and benevolence. To Him is glory, and beneficence, and power, and dominion from this time forth for evermore. Amen. Here endeth the whole Gospel of the Infancy, with the aid of God Most High, according to what we have found in the original.

Thomas's Gospel of the Infancy of Jesus Christ

1

2 Jesus miraculously dears the water after rain. 4 plays with clay sparrows, which he animates on the sabbath day.

¹ I THOMAS, an Israelite, judged it necessary to make known to our brethren among the Gentiles, the actions and miracles of Christ in his childhood, which our Lord and God Jesus Christ wrought after his birth in Bethlehem in our country, at which I myself was astonished; the beginning of which was as followeth. ² When the child Jesus was five years of age and there had been a shower of rain, which was now over, Jesus was playing with other Hebrew boys by a running stream; and the water running over the banks, stood in little lakes; ³ But the water instantly became clear and useful again; he having smote them only by his word, they readily obeyed him. ⁴ Then he took from the bank of the stream some soft clay, and formed out of it twelve sparrows; and there were other boys playing with him. ⁵ But a certain Jew seeing the things which he was doing, namely, his forming clay into the figures of sparrows on the sabbath day, went presently away, and told his father Joseph, and said, ⁶ Behold, thy boy is playing by the river side, and has taken clay, and formed it into twelve sparrows, and profaneth the sabbath. ⁷ Then Joseph came to the place where he was, and when he saw him, called to him, and said, Why doest thou that which it is not lawful to do on the sabbath day? ⁸ Then Jesus clapping together the palms of his hands, called to the sparrows, and said to them: Go, fly away; and while ye live remember me. ⁹ So the sparrows fled away, making a noise. ¹⁰ The Jews seeing this, were astonished, and went away, and told their chief persons what a strange miracle they had seen wrought by Jesus.

2

2 Causes a boy to wither who broke down his fish pools, 6 partly restores him, 7 dills another boy, 16 causes blindness to fall on his accusers, 18 for which Joseph pulls him by the ear.

¹ BESIDES this, the son of Anna the scribe was standing there with Joseph, and took a bough of a willow tree, and scattered the waters which Jesus had gathered into lakes. ² But the boy Jesus seeing what he had done, became angry, and said to him, Thou fool, what harm did the lake do thee, that thou shouldest scatter the water? ³ Behold, now thou shalt wither as a tree, and shalt not bring forth either leaves, or branches, or fruit. ⁴ And immediately he became withered all over. ⁵ Then Jesus went away home. But the parents of the boy who was withered, lamenting the misfortune of his youth, took and carried him to Joseph, accusing him, and said, Why dost thou keep a son who is guilty of such actions? ⁶ Then Jesus at the request of all who were present did heal him, leaving only some small member to continue withered, that they might take warning. ⁷ Another time Jesus went forth into the street, and a boy running by, rushed upon his shoulder; ⁸ At which Jesus being angry, said to him, thou shalt go no farther. ⁹ And he instantly fell down dead: ¹⁰ Which when some persons saw, they said, Where was this boy born, that everything which he says presently cometh to pass? ¹¹ Then the parents of the dead buy going to Joseph complained, saying, You are not fit to live with us, in our city, having such a boy as that: ¹² Either teach him that he bless and not curse, or else depart hence with him, for he kills our children. ¹³ Then Joseph calling the boy Jesus by himself, instructed him saying, Why doest thou such things to injure the people so, that they hate us and prosecute us? ¹⁴ But Jesus replied, I know that what thou sayest is not of thyself, but for thy sake I will say nothing; ¹⁵ But they who have said these things to thee, shall suffer everlasting punishment. ¹⁶ And immediately they who had accused him became blind. ¹⁷ And all they who saw it were exceedingly afraid and confounded, and said concerning him, Whatsoever he saith, whether good or bad, immediately cometh to pass: and they were amazed. ¹⁸ And when they saw this action of Christ, Joseph arose, and plucked him by the ear, at which the boy was angry, and said to him, Be easy; ¹⁹ For if they seek for us, they shall not find us: thou hast done very imprudently. ²⁰ Dost thou not know that I am thine? Trouble me no more.

3

1 Astonishes his schoolmaster by his learning.

¹ A CERTAIN schoolmaster named Zacchæus, standing in a certain place, heard Jesus speaking these things to his father. ² And he was much surprised, that being a child, he should speak such things; and after a few days he came to Joseph, and said, ³ Thou hast a wise and sensible child, send him to me, that he may learn to read. ⁴ When he sat down to teach the letters to Jesus, he began with the first letter Aleph; ⁵ But Jesus pronounced the second letter Mpeth (Beth) Cghimel (Gimel), and said over all the letters to him to the end. ⁶ Then opening a book, he taught his master the prophets: but be was ashamed, and was at a loss to conceive how he came to know the letters. ⁷ And he arose and went home, wonderfully surprised at so strange a thing.

4

1 Fragment of an adventure at a dyer's.

¹ AS Jesus was passing by a certain shop, he saw a young man dipping (or dyeing) some cloths and stockings in a furnace, of a sad colour, doing them according to every person's particular order; ² The boy Jesus going to the young man who was doing this, took also some of the cloths.

The History of Joseph the Carpenter

IN the name of God, of one essence and three persons. The History of the death of our father, the holy old man, Joseph the carpenter. May his blessings and prayers preserve us all, O brethren! Amen. His whole life was one hundred and eleven years, and his departure from this world happened on the twenty-sixth of the month Abib, which answers to the month Ab. May his prayer preserve us! Amen. And, indeed, it was our Lord Jesus Christ Himself who related this history to His holy disciples on the Mount of Olives, and all Joseph's labour, and the end of his days. And the holy apostles have preserved this conversation, and have left it written down in the library at Jerusalem. May their prayers preserve us! Amen.

[1] It happened one day, when the Saviour, our Master, God, and Saviour Jesus Christ, was sitting along with His disciples, and they were all assembled on the Mount of Olives, that He said to them: O my brethren and friends, sons of the Father who has chosen you from all men, you know that I have often told you that I must be crucified, and must die for the salvation of Adam and his posterity, and that I shall rise from the dead. Now I shall commit to you the doctrine of the holy gospel formerly announced to you, that you may declare it. throughout the whole world. And I shall endow you with power from on high, and fill you with the Holy Spirit. And you shall declare to all nations repentance and remission of sins. For a single cup of water, if a man shall find it in the world to come, is greater and better than all the wealth of this whole world. And as much ground as one foot can occupy in the house of my Father, is greater and more excellent than all the riches of the earth. Yea, a single hour in the joyful dwelling of the pious is more blessed and more precious than a thousand years among sinners: inasmuch as their weeping and lamentation shall not come to an end, and their tears shall not cease, nor shall they find for themselves consolation and repose at any time for ever. And now, O my honoured members, go declare to all nations, tell them, and say to them: Verily the Saviour diligently inquires into the inheritance which is due, and is the administrator of justice. And the angels will cast down their enemies, and will fight for them in the day of conflict. And He will examine every single foolish and idle word which men speak, and they shall give an account of it. For as no one shall escape death, so also the works of every man shall be laid open on the day of judgment, whether they have been good or evil. Tell them also this word which I have said to you to-day: Let not the strong man glory in his strength, nor the rich man in his riches; but let him who wishes to glory, glory in the Lord. [2] There was a man whose name was Joseph, sprung from a family of Bethlehem, a town of Judah, and the city of King David. This same man, being well furnished with wisdom and learning, was made a priest in the temple of the Lord. He was, besides. skilful in his trade, which was that of a carpenter; and after the manner of all men, he married a wife. Moreover, he begot for himself sons and daughters, four sons, namely, and two daughters. Now these are their names–Judas, Justus, James, and Simon. The names of the two daughters were Assia and Lydia. At length the wife of righteous Joseph, a woman intent on the divine glory in all her works, departed this life. But Joseph, that righteous man, my father after the flesh, and the spouse of my mother Mary, went away with his sons to his trade, practising the art of a carpenter. [3] Now when righteous Joseph became a widower, my mother Mary, blessed, holy, and pure, was already twelve years old. For her parents offered her in the temple when she was three years of age, and she remained in the temple of the Lord nine years. Then when the priests saw that the virgin, holy and God-fearing, was growing up, they spoke to each other, saying: Let us search out a man, righteous and pious, to whom Mary may be entrusted until the time of her marriage; lest, if she remains in the temple, it happens to her as is wont to happen to women, and lest on that account we sin, and God be angry with us. [4] Therefore they immediately sent out, and assembled twelve old men of the tribe of Judah. And they wrote down the names of the twelve tribes of Israel. And the lot fell upon the pious old man, righteous Joseph. Then the priests answered, and said to my blessed mother: Go with Joseph, and be with him till the time of your marriage. Righteous Joseph therefore received my mother, and led her away to his own house. And Mary found James the Less in his father's house, broken-hearted and sad on account of the loss of his mother, and she brought him up. Hence Mary was called the mother of James. Thereafter Joseph left her at home, and went away to the shop where he wrought at his trade of a carpenter. And after the holy virgin had spent two years in his house her age was exactly fourteen years, including the time at which he received her. [5] And I chose her of my own will, with the concurrence of my Father, and the counsel of the Holy Spirit. And I was made flesh of her, by a mystery which transcends the grasp of created reason. And three months after her conception the righteous man Joseph returned from the place where he worked at his trade; and when he found my virgin mother pregnant, he was greatly perplexed, and thought of sending her away secretly. But from fear, and sorrow, and the anguish of his heart, he could endure neither to eat nor drink that day. [6] But at mid-day there appeared to him in a dream the prince of the angels, the holy Gabriel, furnished with a command from my Father; and he said to him: Joseph, son of David, fear not to take Mary as thy wife: for she has conceived of the Holy Spirit; and she will bring forth a son, whose name shall be called Jesus. He it is who shall rule all nations with a rod of iron. Having thus spoken, the angel departed from him. And Joseph rose from his sleep, and did as the angel of the Lord had said to him; and Mary abode with him. [7] Some time after that, there came forth an order from Augustus Caesar the king, that all the habitable world should be enrolled, each man in his own city. The old man therefore, righteous Joseph, rose up and took the virgin Mary and came to Bethlehem, because the time of her bringing forth was at hand. Joseph then inscribed his name in the list; for Joseph the son of David, whose spouse Mary was, was of the tribe of Judah. And indeed Mary, my mother, brought me forth in Bethlehem, in a cave near the tomb of Rachel the wife of the patriarch Jacob, the mother of Joseph and Benjamin. [8] But Satan went and told this to Herod the Great, the father of Archelaus. And it was this same Herod who ordered my friend and relative John to be beheaded. Accordingly he searched for me diligently, thinking that my kingdom was to be of this world. But Joseph, that pious old man, was warned of this by a dream. Therefore he rose and took Mary my mother, and I lay in her bosom. Salome also was their fellow-traveller. Having therefore set out from home, he retired into Egypt, and remained there the space of one whole year, until the hatred of Herod passed away. [9] Now Herod died by the worst form of death, atoning for the shedding of the blood of the children whom he wickedly cut off, though there was no sin in them. And that impious tyrant Herod being dead, they returned into the land of Israel, and lived in a city of Galilee which is called Nazareth. And Joseph, going back to his trade of a carpenter, earned his living by the work of his hands; for, as the law of Moses had commanded, he never sought to live for nothing by another's labour. [10] At length, by increasing years, the old man arrived at a very advanced age. He did not, however, labour under any bodily weakness, nor had his sight failed, nor had any tooth perished from his mouth. In mind also, for the whole time of his life, he never wandered; but like a boy he always in his business displayed youthful vigour, and his limbs remained unimpaired, and free from all pain. His life, then, in all, amounted to one hundred and eleven years, his old age being prolonged to the utmost limit. [11] Now Justus and Simeon, the eider sons of Joseph, were married, and had families of their own. Both the daughters were likewise married, and lived in their own houses. So there remained in Joseph's house, Judas and James the Less, and my virgin mother. I moreover dwelt along with them, not otherwise than if I had been one of his sons. But I passed all my life without fault. Mary I called my mother, and Joseph father, and I obeyed them in all that they said; nor did I ever contend against them, but complied with their commands, as other men whom earth produces are wont to do; nor did I at any time arouse their anger, or give any word or answer in opposition to them. On the contrary, I cherished them with great love, like the pupil of my eye. [12] It came to pass, after these things, that the death of that old man, the pious Joseph, and his departure from this world, were approaching, as happens to other men who owe their origin to this earth. And as his body was verging on dissolution, an angel of the Lord informed him that his death was now close at hand. Therefore fear and great perplexity came upon him. So he rose up and went to Jerusalem; and going into the temple of the Lord, he poured out his prayers there before the sanctuary, and said: [13] O God! author of all consolation, God of all compassion, and Lord of the whole human race; God of my soul, body, and spirit; with supplications I reverence thee, O Lord and my God. If now my days are ended, and the time draws near when I must leave this world, send me, I beseech Thee, the great Michael, the prince of Thy holy angels: let him remain with me, that my wretched soul may depart from this afflicted body without trouble, without terror and impatience. For great fear and intense sadness take hold of all bodies on the day of their death, whether it be man or woman, beast wild or tame, or whatever creeps on the ground or flies in the air. At the last all creatures under heaven in whom is the breath of life are struck with horror, and their souls depart from their bodies with strong fear and great depression. Now therefore, O Lord and my God, let Thy holy angel be present with his help to my soul and body, until they shall be dissevered from each other. And let not the face of the angel, appointed my guardian from the day of my birth, be turned away from me; but may he be the companion of my journey even until he brings me to Thee: let his countenance be pleasant and gladsome to me, and let him accompany me in peace. And let not demons of frightful aspect come near me in the way in which I am to go, until I come to Thee in bliss. And let not the doorkeepers hinder my soul from entering paradise. And do not uncover my sins, and expose me to condemnation before Thy terrible

tribunal. Let not the lions rush in upon me; nor let the waves of the sea of fire overwhelm my soul–for this must every soul pass through –before I have seen the glory of Thy Godhead. O God, most righteous Judge, who in justice and equity wilt judge mankind, and wilt render unto each one according to his works, O Lord and my God, I beseech Thee, be present to me in Thy compassion, and enlighten my path that I may come to Thee; for Thou art a fountain overflowing with all good things, and with glory for evermore. Amen. ¹⁴ It came to pass thereafter, when he returned to his own house in the city of Nazareth, that he was seized by disease, and had to keep his bed. And it was at this time that he died, according to the destiny of all mankind. For this disease was very heavy upon him, and he had never been ill, as he now was, from the day of his birth. And thus assuredly it pleased Christ to order the destiny of righteous Joseph. He lived forty years unmarried; thereafter his wife remained under his care forty-nine years, and then died. And a year after her death, my mother, the blessed Mary, was entrusted to him by the priests, that he should keep her until the time of her marriage. She spent two years in his house; and in the third year of her stay with Joseph, in the fifteenth year of her age, she brought me forth on earth by a mystery which no creature can penetrate or understand, except myself, and my Father and the Holy Spirit, constituting one essence with myself. ¹⁵ The whole age of my father, therefore, that righteous old man, was one hundred and eleven years, my Father in heaven having so decreed. And the day on which his soul left his body was the twenty-sixth of the month Abib. For now the fine gold began to lose its splendour, and the silver to be worn down by use–I mean his understanding and his wisdom. He also loathed food and drink, and lost all his skill in his trade of carpentry, nor did he any more pay attention to it. It came to pass, then, in the early dawn of the twenty-sixth day of Abib, that Joseph, that righteous old man, lying in his bed, was giving up his unquiet soul. Wherefore he opened his mouth with many sighs, and struck his hands one against the other, and with a loud voice cried out, and spoke after the following manner:– ¹⁶ Woe to the day on which I was born into the world! Woe to the womb which bare me! Woe to the bowels which admitted me! Woe to the breasts which suckled me! Woe to the feet upon which I sat and rested! Woe to the hands which carried me and reared me until I grew up! For I was conceived in iniquity, and in sins did my mother desire me. Woe to my tongue and my lips, which have brought forth and spoken vanity, detraction, falsehood, ignorance, derision, idle tales, craft, and hypocrisy! Woe to mine eyes, which have looked upon scandalous things! Woe to mine ears, which have delighted in the words of slanderers! Woe to my hands, which have seized what did not of right belong to them! Woe to my belly and my bowels, which have lusted after food unlawful to be eaten! Woe to my throat, which like a fire has consumed all that it found! Woe to my feet, which have too often walked in ways displeasing to God! Woe to my body; and woe to my miserable soul, which has already turned aside from God its Maker! What shall I do when I arrive at that place where I must stand before the most righteous Judge, and when He shall call me to account for the works which I have heaped up in my youth? Woe to every man dying in his sins! Assuredly that same dreadful hour, which came upon my father Jacob, when his soul was flying forth from his body, is now, behold, near at hand for me. Oh! how wretched I am this day, and worthy of lamentation! But God alone is the disposer of my soul and body; He also will deal with them after His own good pleasure. ¹⁷ These are the words spoken by Joseph, that righteous old man. And I, going in beside him, found his soul exceedingly troubled, for he was placed in great perplexity. And I said to him: Hail! my father Joseph, thou righteous man; how is it with thee? And he answered me: All hail! my well-beloved son. Indeed, the agony and fear of death have already environed me; but as soon as I heard Thy voice, my soul was at rest. O Jesus of Nazareth! Jesus, my Saviour! Jesus, the deliverer of my soul! Jesus, my protector! Jesus! O sweetest name in my mouth, and in the mouth of all those that love it! O eye which seest, and ear which hearest, hear me! I am Thy servant; this day I most humbly reverence Thee, and before Thy face I pour out my tears. Thou art altogether my God; Thou art my Lord, as the angel has told me times without number, and especially on that day when my soul was driven about with perverse thoughts about the pure and blessed Mary, who was carrying Thee in her womb, and whom I was thinking of secretly sending away. And while I was thus meditating, behold, there appeared to me in my rest angels of the Lord, saying to me in a wonderful mystery: O Joseph, thou son of David, fear not to take Mary as thy wife; and do not grieve thy soul, nor speak unbecoming words of her conception, because she is with child of the Holy Spirit, and shall bring forth a son, whose name shall be called Jesus, for He shall save His people from their sins. Do not for this cause wish me evil, O Lord! for I was ignorant of the mystery of Thy birth. I call to mind also, my Lord, that day when the boy died of the bite of the serpent. And his relations wished to deliver Thee to Herod, saying that Thou hadst killed him; but Thou didst raise him from the dead, and restore him to them. Then I went up to Thee, and took hold of Thy hand, saying: My son, take care of thyself. But Thou didst say to me in reply: Art thou not my father after the flesh? I shall teach thee who I am. Now therefore, O Lord and my God, do not be angry with me, or condemn me on account of that hour. I am Thy servant, and the son of Thine handmaiden; but Thou art my Lord, my God and Saviour, most surely the Son of God. ¹⁸ When my father Joseph had thus spoken, he was unable to weep more. And I saw that death now had dominion over him. And my mother, virgin undefiled, rose and came to me, saying: O my beloved son, this pious old man Joseph is now dying. And I answered: Oh my dearest mother, assuredly upon all creatures produced in this world the same necessity of death lies; for death holds sway over the whole human race. Even thou, O my virgin mother, must look for the same end of life as other mortals. And yet thy death, as also the death of this pious man, is not death, but life enduring to eternity. Nay more, even I must die, as concerns the body which I have received from thee. But rise, O my venerable mother, and go in to Joseph, that blessed old man, in order that thou mayst see what will happen as his soul ascends from his body. ¹⁹ My undefiled mother Mary, therefore, went and entered the place where Joseph was. And I was sitting at his feet looking at him, for the signs of death already appeared in his countenance. And that blessed old man raised his head, and kept his eyes fixed on my face; but he had no power of speaking to me, on account of the agonies of death, which held him in their grasp. But he kept fetching many sighs. And I held his hands for a whole hour; and he turned his face to me, and made signs for me not to leave him. Thereafter I put my hand upon his breast, and perceived his soul now near his throat, preparing to depart from its receptacle. ²⁰ And when my virgin mother saw me touching his body, she also touched his feet. And finding them already dead and destitute of heat, she said to me: O my beloved son, assuredly his feet are already beginning to stiffen, and they are as cold as snow. Accordingly she summoned his sons and daughters, and said to them: Come, as many as there are of you, and go to your father; for assuredly he is now at the very point of death. And Assia, his daughter, answered and said: Woe's me, O my brothers, this is certainly the same disease that my beloved mother died of. And she lamented and shed tears; and all Joseph's other children mourned along with her. I also, and my mother Mary, wept along with them. ²¹ And turning my eyes towards the region of the south, I saw Death already approaching, and all Gehenna with him, closely attended by his army and his satellites; and their clothes, their faces, and their mouths poured forth flames. And when my father Joseph saw them coming straight to him, his eyes dissolved in tears, and at the same time he groaned after a strange manner. Accordingly, when I saw the vehemence of his sighs, I drove back Death and all the host of servants which accompanied him. And I called upon my good Father, saying:– ²² O Father of all mercy, eye which seest, and ear which hearest, hearken to my prayers and supplications in behalf of the old man Joseph; and send Michael, the prince of Thine angels, and Gabriel, the herald of light, and all the light of Thine angels, and let their whole array walk with the soul of my father Joseph, until they shall have conducted it to Thee. This is the hour in which my father has need of compassion. And I say unto you, that all the saints, yea, as many men as are born in the world, whether they be just or whether they be perverse, must of necessity taste of death. ²³ Therefore Michael and Gabriel came to the soul of my father Joseph, and took it, and wrapped it in a shining wrapper. Thus he committed his spirit into the hands of my good Father, and He bestowed upon him peace. But as yet none of his children knew that he had fallen asleep. And the angels preserved his soul from the demons of darkness which were in the way, and praised God even until they conducted it into the dwelling-place of the pious. ²⁴ Now his body was lying prostrate and bloodless; wherefore I reached forth my hand, and put right his eyes and shut his mouth, and said to the virgin Mary: O my mother, where is the skill which he showed in all the time that he lived in this world? Lo! it has perished, as if it had never existed. And when his children heard me speaking with my mother, the pure virgin, they knew that he had already breathed his last, and they shed tears, and lamented. But I said to them: Assuredly the death of your father is not death, but life everlasting: for he has been freed from the troubles of this life, and has passed to perpetual and everlasting rest. When they heard these words, they rent their clothes, and wept. ²⁵ And, indeed, the inhabitants of Nazareth and of Galilee, having heard of their lamentation, flocked to them, and wept from the third hour even to the ninth. And at the ninth hour they all went together to Joseph's bed. And they lifted his body, after they had anointed it with costly unguents. But I entreated my Father in the prayer of the celestials–that same prayer which with any own hand I made before I was carried in the womb of the virgin Mary, my mother. And as soon as I had finished it, and pronounced the amen, a great multitude of angels came up; and I ordered two of them to stretch out their shining garments, and to wrap in them the body of Joseph, the blessed old man. [26] And I spoke to Joseph, and said: The smell or corruption of death shall not have dominion over thee, nor shall a worm ever come forth from thy body. Not a single limb of it shall be broken, nor shall any hair on thy head be changed. Nothing of thy body shall perish, O my father Joseph, but it will remain entire and uncorrupted even until the banquet of the thousand years. And whosoever shall make an offering on the day of thy remembrance, him will I bless and recompense in the congregation of the virgins; and whosoever shall give food to the wretched, the poor, the widows, and orphans from the work of his hands, on the day on which thy memory shall be celebrated, and in thy name, shall not be in want of good things all the days of his life. And whosoever shall have given a cup of water, or of wine, to drink to the widow or orphan in thy name, I will give him to thee, that thou mayst go in with him to the banquet of the thousand years. And every man who shall present an offering on the day of thy commemoration will I bless and recompense in the church of the virgins: for one I will render unto him thirty, sixty, and a hundred. And whosoever shall write the history of thy life, of thy labour, and thy departure from this world, and this narrative that has issued from my mouth, him shall I commit to thy keeping as long as he shall have to do with this life. And when his soul departs from the body, and when he must leave this world, I will burn the book of his sins, nor will I torment him with any punishment in the day of judgment; but he shall cross the sea of flames, and shall go through it without trouble or pain. And upon every poor man who can give none of those things which I have mentioned this is incumbent: viz., if a son is born to him, he shall call his name Joseph. So there shall not take place in that house either poverty or any sudden death for ever. [27] Thereafter the chief men of the city came together to the place where the body of the blessed old man Joseph had been laid, bringing with them burial-clothes; and they wished to wrap it up in them after the manner in which the Jews are wont to arrange their dead bodies. And they perceived that he kept his shroud fast; for it adhered to the body in such a way, that when they wished to take it off, it was found to be like iron–impossible to be moved or loosened. Nor could they find any ends in that piece of linen, which struck them with the greatest astonishment. At length they carried him out to a place where there was a cave, and opened the gate, that they might bury his body beside the bodies of his fathers. Then there came into my mind the day on which he walked with me into Egypt, and that extreme trouble which he endured on my account. Accordingly, I bewailed his death for a long time; and lying upon his body, I said:– [28] O Death! who makest all knowledge to vanish away, and raisest so many tears and lamentations, surely it is God my Father Himself who hath granted thee this power. For men die for the transgression of Adam and his wife Eve, and Death spares not so much as one. Nevertheless, nothing happens to any one, or is brought upon him, without the command of my Father. There have certainly been men who have prolonged their life even to nine hundred years; but they died. Yea, though some of them have lived longer, they have, notwithstanding, succumbed to the same fate; nor has any one of them ever said: I have not tasted death. For the Lord never sends the same punishment more than once, since it hath pleased my Father to bring it upon men. And at the very moment when it, going forth, beholds the command descending to it from heaven, it says: I will go forth against that man, and will greatly move him. Then, without delay, it makes an onset on the soul, and obtains the mastery of it, doing with it whatever it will. For, because Adam did not the will of my Father, but transgressed His commandment, the wrath of my Father was kindled against him, and He doomed him to death; and thus it was that death came into the world. But if Adam had observed my Father's precepts, death would never have fallen to his lot. Think you that I can ask my good Father to send me a chariot of fire, which may take up the body of my father Joseph, and convey it to the place of rest, in order that it may dwell with the spirits? But on account of the transgression of Adam, that trouble and violence of death has descended upon all the human race. And it is for this cause that I must die according to the flesh, for my work which I have created, that they may obtain grace. [29] Having thus spoken, I embraced the body of my father Joseph, and wept over it; and they opened the door of the tomb, and placed his body in it, near the body of his father Jacob. And at the time when he fell asleep he had fulfilled a hundred and eleven years. Never did a tooth in his mouth hurt him, nor was his eyesight rendered less sharp, nor his body bent, nor his strength impaired; but he worked at his trade of a carpenter to the very last day of his life; and that was the six-and-twentieth of the month Abib. [30] And we apostles, when we heard these things from our Saviour, rose up joyfully, and prostrated ourselves in honour of Him, and said: O our Saviour, show us Thy grace. Now indeed we have heard the word of life: nevertheless we wonder, O our Saviour, at the fate of Enoch and Elias, inasmuch as they had not to undergo death. For truly they dwell in the habitation of the righteous even to the present day, nor have their bodies seen corruption. Yet that old man Joseph the carpenter was, nevertheless, Thy father after the flesh. And Thou hast ordered us to go into all the world and preach the holy Gospel; and Thou hast said: Relate to them the death of my father Joseph, and celebrate to him with annual solemnity a festival and sacred day. And whosoever shall take anything away from this narrative, or add anything to it, commits sin. We wonder especially that Joseph, even from that day on which Thou wast born in Bethlehem, called Thee his son after the flesh. Wherefore, then, didst Thou not make him immortal as well as them, and Thou sayest that he was righteous and chosen? [31] And our Saviour answered and said: Indeed, the prophecy of my Father upon Adam, for his disobedience, has now been fulfilled. And all things are arranged according to the will and pleasure of my Father. For if a man rejects the commandment of God, and follows the works of the devil by committing sin, his life is prolonged; for be is preserved in order that he may perhaps repent, and reflect that he must be delivered into the hands of death. But if any one has been zealous of good works, his life also is prolonged, that, as the fame of his old age increases, upright men may imitate him. But when you see a man whose mind is prone to anger, assuredly his days are shortened; for it is these that are taken away in the flower of their age. Every prophecy, therefore, which my Father has pronounced concerning the sons of men, must be fulfilled in every particular. But with reference to Enoch and Elias, and how they remain alive to this day, keeping the same bodies with which they were born; and as to what concerns my father Joseph, who has not been allowed as well as they to remain in the body: indeed, though a man live in the world many myriads of years, nevertheless at some time or other he is compelled to exchange life for death. And I say to you, O my brethren, that they also, Enoch and Elias, must towards the end of time return into the world and die–in the day, namely, of commotion, of terror, of perplexity, and affliction. For Antichrist will slay four bodies, and will pour out their blood like water, because of the reproach to which they shall expose him, and the ignominy with which they, in their lifetime, shall brand him when they reveal his impiety. [32] And we said: O our Lord, our God and Saviour, who are those four whom Thou hast said Antichrist will cut off from the reproach they bring upon him? The Lord answered: They are Enoch, Elias, Schila, and Tabitha. When we heard this from our Saviour, we rejoiced and exulted; and we offered all glory and thanksgiving to the Lord God, and our Saviour Jesus Christ. He it is to whom is due glory, honour, dignity, dominion, power, and praise, as well as to the good Father with Him, and to the Holy Spirit that giveth life, henceforth and in all time for evermore. Amen.

GNOSTICS

[ ] Gap in the text
( ) Editorial insertion
/ \ Editorial correction of a scribal error

The Gospel of Thomas

Prologue
These are the hidden sayings that the living Jesus spoke and Didymos Judas Thomas wrote down.

Saying 1: True Meaning
And he said, "Whoever discovers the meaning of these sayings won't taste death."

Saying 2: Seek and Find
Jesus said, "Whoever seeks shouldn't stop until they find. When they find, they'll be disturbed. When they're disturbed, they'll be […] amazed, and reign over the All."

Saying 3: Seeking Within
Jesus said, "If your leaders tell you, 'Look, the kingdom is in heaven,' then the birds of heaven will precede you. If they tell you, 'It's in the sea,' then the fish will precede you. Rather, the kingdom is within you and outside of you. "When you know yourselves, then you'll be known, and you'll realize that you're the children of the living Father. But if you don't know yourselves, then you live in poverty, and you are the poverty."

Saying 4: First and Last
Jesus said, "The older person won't hesitate to ask a little seven-day-old child about the place of life, and they'll live, because many who are first will be last, and they'll become one."

Saying 5: Hidden and Revealed
Jesus said, "Know what's in front of your face, and what's hidden from you will be revealed to you, because there's nothing hidden that won't be revealed."

Saying 6: Public Ritual
His disciples said to him, "Do you want us to fast? And how should we pray? Should we make donations? And what food should we avoid?" Jesus said, "Don't lie, and don't do what you hate, because everything is revealed in the sight of heaven; for there's nothing hidden that won't be revealed, and nothing covered up that will stay secret."

Saying 7: The Lion and the Human
Jesus said, "Blessed is the lion that's eaten by a human and then becomes human, but how awful for the human who's eaten by a lion, and the lion becomes human."

Saying 8: The Parable of the Fish
He said, "The human being is like a wise fisher who cast a net into the sea and drew it up from the sea full of little fish. Among them the wise fisher found a fine large fish and cast all the little fish back down into the sea, easily choosing the large fish. Anyone who has ears to hear should hear!"

Saying 9: The Parable of the Sower
Jesus said, "Look, a sower went out, took a handful of seeds, and scattered them. Some fell on the roadside; the birds came and gathered them. Others fell on the rock; they didn't take root in the soil and ears of grain didn't rise toward heaven. Yet others fell on thorns; they choked the seeds and worms ate them. Finally, others fell on good soil; it produced fruit up toward heaven, some sixty times as much and some a hundred and twenty."

Saying 10: Jesus and Fire (1)
Jesus said, "I've cast fire on the world, and look, I'm watching over it until it blazes."

Saying 11: Those Who Are Living Won't Die (1)
Jesus said, "This heaven will disappear, and the one above it will disappear too. Those who are dead aren't alive, and those who are living won't die. In the days when you ate what was dead, you made it alive. When you're in the light, what will you do? On the day when you were one, you became divided. But when you become divided, what will you do?"

Saying 12: James the Just
The disciples said to Jesus, "We know you're going to leave us. Who will lead us then?" Jesus said to them, "Wherever you are, you'll go to James the Just, for whom heaven and earth came into being."

Saying 13: Thomas' Confession
Jesus said to his disciples, "If you were to compare me to someone, who would you say I'm like?" Simon Peter said to him, "You're like a just angel." Matthew said to him, "You're like a wise philosopher." Thomas said to him, "Teacher, I'm completely unable to say whom you're like." Jesus said, "I'm not your teacher. Because you've drunk, you've become intoxicated by the bubbling spring I've measured out." He took him aside and told him three things. When Thomas returned to his companions, they asked, "What did Jesus say to you?" Thomas said to them, "If I tell you one of the things he said to me, you'll pick up stones and cast them at me, and fire will come out of the stones and burn you up."

Saying 14: Public Ministry
Jesus said to them, "If you fast, you'll bring guilt upon yourselves; and if you pray, you'll be condemned; and if you make donations, you'll harm your spirits. "If they welcome you when you enter any land and go around in the countryside, heal those who are sick among them and eat whatever they give you, because it's not what goes into your mouth that will defile you. What comes out of your mouth is what will defile you."

Saying 15: Worship
Jesus said, "When you see the one who wasn't born of a woman, fall down on your face and worship that person. That's your Father."

Saying 16: Not Peace, but War
Jesus said, "Maybe people think that I've come to cast peace on the world, and they don't know that I've come to cast divisions on the earth: fire, sword, and war. Where there are five in a house, there'll be three against two and two against three, father against and son and son against father. They'll stand up and be one."

Saying 17: Divine Gift
Jesus said, "I'll give you what no eye has ever seen, no ear has ever heard, no hand has ever touched, and no human mind has ever thought."

Saying 18: Beginning and End
The disciples said to Jesus, "Tell us about our end. How will it come?" Jesus said, "Have you discovered the beginning so that you can look for the end? Because the end will be where the beginning is. Blessed is the one who will stand up in the beginning. They'll know the end, and won't taste death."

Saying 19: Five Trees in Paradise
Jesus said, "Blessed is the one who came into being before coming into being. If you become my disciples and listen to my message, these stones will become your servants; because there are five trees in paradise which don't change in summer or winter, and their leaves don't fall. Whoever knows them won't taste death."

Saying 20: The Parable of the Mustard Seed
The disciples asked Jesus, "Tell us, what can the kingdom of heaven be compared to?" He said to them, "It can be compared to a mustard seed. Though it's the smallest of all the seeds, when it falls on tilled soil it makes a plant so large that it shelters the birds of heaven."

Saying 21: The Parables of the Field, the Bandits, and the Reaper
Mary said to Jesus, "Whom are your disciples like?" He said, "They're like little children living in a field which isn't theirs. When the owners of the field come, they'll say, 'Give our field back to us.' They'll strip naked in front of them to let them have it and give them their field. "So I say that if the owner of the house realizes the bandit is coming, they'll watch out beforehand and won't let the bandit break into the house of their domain and steal their possessions. You, then, watch out for the world! Prepare to defend yourself so that the bandits don't attack you, because what you're expecting will come. May there be a wise person among you! "When the fruit ripened, the reaper came quickly, sickle in hand, and harvested it. Anyone who has ears to hear should hear!"

Saying 22: Making the Two into One
Jesus saw some little children nursing. He said to his disciples, "These nursing children can be compared to those who enter the kingdom." They said to him, "Then we'll enter the kingdom as little children?" Jesus said to them, "When you make the two into one, and make the inner like the outer and the outer like the inner, and the upper like the lower, and so make the male and the female a single one so that the male won't be male nor the female female; when you make eyes in the place of an eye, a hand in the place of a hand, a foot in the place of a foot, and an image in the place of an image; then you'll enter [the kingdom]."

Saying 23: Those Who are Chosen (1)
Jesus said, "I'll choose you, one out of a thousand and two out of ten thousand, and they'll stand as a single one."

Saying 24: Light
His disciples said, "Show us the place where you are, because we need to look for it." He said to them, "Anyone who has ears to hear should hear! Light exists within a person of light, and they light up the whole world. If they don't shine, there's darkness."

Saying 25: Love and Protect
Jesus said, "Love your brother as your own soul. Protect them like the pupil of your eye."

Saying 26: Speck and Beam
Jesus said, "You see the speck that's in your brother's eye, but you don't see the beam in your own eye. When you get the beam out of your own eye, then you'll be able to see clearly to get the speck out of your brother's eye."

Saying 27: Fasting and Sabbath

"If you don't fast from the world, you won't find the kingdom. If you don't make the Sabbath into a Sabbath, you won't see the Father."

Saying 28: The World is Drunk
Jesus said, "I stood in the middle of the world and appeared to them in the flesh. I found them all drunk; I didn't find any of them thirsty. My soul ached for the children of humanity, because they were blind in their hearts and couldn't see. They came into the world empty and plan on leaving the world empty. Meanwhile, they're drunk. When they shake off their wine, then they'll change."

Saying 29: Spirit and Body
Jesus said, "If the flesh came into existence because of spirit, that's amazing. If spirit came into existence because of the body, that's really amazing! But I'm amazed at how [such] great wealth has been placed in this poverty."

Saying 30: Divine Presence
Jesus said, "Where there are three deities, they're divine. Where there are two or one, I'm with them."

Saying 31: Prophet and Doctor
Jesus said, "No prophet is welcome in their own village. No doctor heals those who know them."

Saying 32: The Parable of the Fortified City
Jesus said, "A city built and fortified on a high mountain can't fall, nor can it be hidden."

Saying 33: The Parable of the Lamp
Jesus said, "What you hear with one ear, listen to with both, then proclaim from your rooftops. No one lights a lamp and puts it under a basket or in a hidden place. Rather, they put it on the stand so that everyone who comes and goes can see its light."

Saying 34: The Parable of Those Who Can't See
Jesus said, "If someone who's blind leads someone else who's blind, both of them fall into a pit."

Saying 35: The Parable of Binding the Strong
Jesus said, "No one can break into the house of the strong and take it by force without tying the hands of the strong. Then they can loot the house."

Saying 36: Anxiety
Jesus said, "Don't be anxious from morning to evening or from evening to morning about what you'll wear."

Saying 37: Seeing Jesus
His disciples said, "When will you appear to us? When will we see you?" Jesus said, "When you strip naked without being ashamed, and throw your clothes on the ground and stomp on them as little children would, then [you'll] see the Son of the Living One and won't be afraid."

Saying 38: Finding Jesus
Jesus said, "Often you've wanted to hear this message that I'm telling you, and you don't have anyone else from whom to hear it. There will be days when you'll look for me, but you won't be able to find me."

Saying 39: The Keys of Knowledge
Jesus said, "The Pharisees and the scholars have taken the keys of knowledge and hidden them. They haven't entered, and haven't let others enter who wanted to. So be wise as serpents and innocent as doves."

Saying 40: A Grapevine
Jesus said, "A grapevine has been planted outside of the Father. Since it's malnourished, it'll be pulled up by its root and destroyed."

Saying 41: More and Less
Jesus said, "Whoever has something in hand will be given more, but whoever doesn't have anything will lose even what little they do have."

Saying 42: Passing By
Jesus said, "Become passersby."

Saying 43: The Tree and the Fruit
His disciples said to him, "Who are you to say these things to us?"
"You don't realize who I am from what I say to you, but you've become like those Judeans who either love the tree but hate its fruit, or love the fruit but hate the tree."

Saying 44: Blasphemy
Jesus said, "Whoever blasphemes the Father will be forgiven, and whoever blasphemes the Son will be forgiven, but whoever blasphemes the Holy Spirit will not be forgiven, neither on earth nor in heaven."

Saying 45: Good and Evil
Jesus said, "Grapes aren't harvested from thorns, nor are figs gathered from thistles, because they don't produce fruit. [A person who's good] brings good things out of their treasure, and a person who's [evil] brings evil things out of their evil treasure. They say evil things because their heart is full of evil."

Saying 46: Greater than John the Baptizer
Jesus said, "From Adam to John the Baptizer, no one's been born who's so much greater than John the Baptizer that they shouldn't avert their eyes. But I say that whoever among you will become a little child will know the kingdom and become greater than John."

Saying 47: The Parables of Divided Loyalties, New Wine in Old Wineskins, and New Patch on Old Cloth
Jesus said, "It's not possible for anyone to mount two horses or stretch two bows, and it's not possible for a servant to follow two leaders, because they'll respect one and despise the other. "No one drinks old wine and immediately wants to drink new wine. And new wine isn't put in old wineskins, because they'd burst. Nor is old wine put in new wineskins, because it'd spoil. "A new patch of cloth isn't sewn onto an old coat, because it'd tear apart."

Saying 48: Unity (1)
Jesus said, "If two make peace with each other in a single house, they'll say to the mountain, 'Go away,' and it will."

Saying 49: Those Who Are Chosen (2)
Jesus said, "Blessed are those who are one – those who are chosen, because you'll find the kingdom. You've come from there and will return there."

Saying 50: Our Origin and Identity
Jesus said, "If they ask you, 'Where do you come from?' tell them, 'We've come from the light, the place where light came into being by itself, [established] itself, and appeared in their image.' "If they ask you, 'Is it you?' then say, 'We are its children, and we're chosen by our living Father.' "If they ask you, 'What's the sign of your Father in you?' then say, 'It's movement and rest.'"

Saying 51: The New World
His disciples said to him, "When will the dead have rest, and when will the new world come?" He said to them, "What you're looking for has already come, but you don't know it."

Saying 52: Twenty-Four Prophets
His disciples said to him, "Twenty-four prophets have spoken in Israel, and they all spoke of you." He said to them, "You've ignored the Living One right in front of you, and you've talked about those who are dead."

Saying 53: True Circumcision
His disciples said to him, "Is circumcision useful, or not?" He said to them, "If it were useful, parents would have children who are born circumcised. But the true circumcision in spirit has become profitable in every way."

Saying 54: Those Who Are Poor
Jesus said, "Blessed are those who are poor, for yours is the kingdom of heaven."

Saying 55: Discipleship (1)
Jesus said, "Whoever doesn't hate their father and mother can't become my disciple, and whoever doesn't hate their brothers and sisters and take up their cross like I do isn't worthy of me."

Saying 56: The World is a Corpse
Jesus said, "Whoever has known the world has found a corpse. Whoever has found a corpse, of them the world isn't worthy."

Saying 57: The Parable of the Weeds
Jesus said, "My Fathers' kingdom can be compared to someone who had [good] seed. Their enemy came by night and sowed weeds among the good seed. The person didn't let anyone pull out the weeds, 'so that you don't pull out the wheat along with the weeds,' they said to them. 'On the day of the harvest, the weeds will be obvious. Then they'll be pulled out and burned.'"

Saying 58: Finding Life
Jesus said, "Blessed is the person who's gone to a lot of trouble. They've found life."

Saying 59: The Living One
Jesus said, "Look for the Living One while you're still alive. If you die and then try to look for him, you won't be able to."

Saying 60: Don't Become a Corpse
They saw a Samaritan carrying a lamb to Judea. He said to his disciples, "What do you think he's going to do with that lamb?" They said to him, "He's going to kill it and eat it." He said to them, "While it's living, he won't eat it, but only after he kills it and it becomes a corpse." They said, "He can't do it any other way." He said to them, "You, too, look for a resting place, so that you won't become a corpse and be eaten."

Saying 61: Jesus and Salome
Jesus said, "Two will rest on a couch. One will die, the other will live." Salome said, "Who are you, Sir, to climb onto my couch and eat off my table as if you're from someone?" Jesus said to her, "I'm the one who exists in equality. Some of what belongs to my Father was given to me." "I'm your disciple." "So I'm telling you, if someone is /equal\, they'll be full of light; but if they're divided, they'll be full of darkness."

Saying 62: Mysteries
Jesus said, "I tell my mysteries to [those who are worthy of my] mysteries. Don't let your left hand know what your right hand is doing."

Saying 63: The Parable of the Rich Fool

Jesus said, "There was a rich man who had much money. He said, 'I'll use my money to sow, reap, plant, and fill my barns with fruit, so that I won't need anything.' That's what he was thinking to himself, but he died that very night. Anyone who has ears to hear should hear!"

Saying 64: The Parable of the Dinner Party
Jesus said, "Someone was planning on having guests. When dinner was ready, they sent their servant to call the visitors. "The servant went to the first and said, 'My master invites you.' "They said, 'Some merchants owe me money. They're coming tonight. I need to go and give them instructions. Excuse me from the dinner.' "The servant went to another one and said, 'My master invites you.' "They said, 'I've just bought a house and am needed for the day. I won't have time.' "The servant went to another one and said, 'My master invites you.' "They said, 'My friend is getting married and I'm going to make dinner. I can't come. Excuse me from the dinner.' "The servant went to another one and said, 'My master invites you.' "They said, "I've just bought a farm and am going to collect the rent. I can't come. Excuse me.' "The servant went back and told the master, 'The ones you've invited to the dinner have excused themselves.' "The master said to their servant, 'Go out to the roads and bring whomever you find so that they can have dinner.' "Buyers and merchants won't [enter] the places of my Father."

Saying 65: The Parable of the Sharecroppers
He said, "A [creditor] owned a vineyard. He leased it out to some sharecroppers to work it so he could collect its fruit. "He sent his servant so that the sharecroppers could give him the fruit of the vineyard. They seized his servant, beat him, and nearly killed him. "The servant went back and told his master. His master said, 'Maybe he just didn't know them.' He sent another servant, but the tenants beat that one too. "Then the master sent his son, thinking, 'Maybe they'll show some respect to my son.' "Because they knew that he was the heir of the vineyard, the sharecroppers seized and killed him. Anyone who has ears to hear should hear!"

Saying 66: The Rejected Cornerstone
Jesus said, "Show me the stone the builders rejected; that's the cornerstone."

Saying 67: Knowing Isn't Everything
Jesus said, "Whoever knows everything, but is personally lacking, lacks everything."

Saying 68: Persecution
Jesus said, "Blessed are you when you're hated and persecuted, and no place will be found where you've been persecuted."

Saying 69: Those Who Are Persecuted
Jesus said, "Blessed are those who've been persecuted in their own hearts. They've truly known the Father. Blessed are those who are hungry, so that their stomachs may be filled."

Saying 70: Salvation is Within
Jesus said, "If you give birth to what's within you, what you have within you will save you. If you don't have that within [you], what you don't have within you [will] kill you."

Saying 71: Destroying the Temple
Jesus said, "I'll destroy [this] house, and no one will be able to build it […]"

Saying 72: Not a Divider
[Someone said to him], "Tell my brothers to divide our inheritance with me." He said to him, "Who made me a divider?" He turned to his disciples and said to them, "Am I really a divider?"

Saying 73: Workers for the Harvest
Jesus said, "The harvest really is plentiful, but the workers are few. So pray that the Lord will send workers to the harvest."

Saying 74: The Empty Well
He said, "Lord, many are gathered around the well, but there's nothing to drink."

Saying 75: The Bridal Chamber
Jesus said, "Many are waiting at the door, but those who are one will enter the bridal chamber."

Saying 76: The Parable of the Pearl
Jesus said, "The Father's kingdom can be compared to a merchant with merchandise who found a pearl. The merchant was wise; they sold their merchandise and bought that single pearl for themselves. "You, too, look for the treasure that doesn't perish but endures, where no moths come to eat and no worms destroy."

Saying 77: Jesus is the All
Jesus said, "I'm the light that's over all. I am the All. The All has come from me and unfolds toward me. "Split a log; I'm there. Lift the stone, and you'll find me there."

Saying 78: Into the Desert
Jesus said, "What did you go out into the desert to see? A reed shaken by the wind? A [person] wearing fancy clothes, [like your] rulers and powerful people? They (wear) fancy [clothes], but can't know the truth."

Saying 79: Listening to the Message
A woman in the crowd said to him, "Blessed is the womb that bore you, and the breasts that nourished you." He said to [her], "Blessed are those who have listened to the message of the Father and kept it, because there will be days when you'll say, 'Blessed is the womb that didn't conceive and the breasts that haven't given milk.'"

Saying 80: The World is a Body
Jesus said, "Whoever has known the world has found the body; but whoever has found the body, of them the world isn't worthy."

Saying 81: Riches and Renunciation (1)
Jesus said, "Whoever has become rich should become a ruler, and whoever has power should renounce it."

Saying 82: Jesus and Fire (2)
Jesus said, "Whoever is near me is near the fire, and whoever is far from me is far from the kingdom."

Saying 83: Light and Images
Jesus said, "Images are revealed to people, but the light within them is hidden in the image of the Father's light. He'll be revealed, but his image will be hidden by his light."

Saying 84: Our Previous Images
Jesus said, "When you see your likeness, you rejoice. But when you see your images that came into being before you did – which don't die, and aren't revealed – how much you'll have to bear!"

Saying 85: Adam Wasn't Worthy
Jesus said, "Adam came into being from a great power and great wealth, but he didn't become worthy of you. If he had been worthy, [he wouldn't have tasted] death."

Saying 86: Foxes and Birds
Jesus said, "[The foxes have dens] and the birds have nests, but the Son of Humanity has nowhere to lay his head and rest."

Saying 87: Body and Soul
Jesus said, "How miserable is the body that depends on a body, and how miserable is the soul that depends on both."

Saying 88: Angels and Prophets
Jesus said, "The angels and the prophets will come to you and give you what belongs to you. You'll give them what you have and ask yourselves, 'When will they come and take what is theirs?'"

Saying 89: Inside and Outside
Jesus said, "Why do you wash the outside of the cup? Don't you know that whoever created the inside created the outside too?"

Saying 90: Jesus' Yoke is Easy
Jesus said, "Come to me, because my yoke is easy and my requirements are light. You'll be refreshed."

Saying 91: Reading the Signs
They said to him, "Tell us who you are so that we may trust you." He said to them, "You read the face of the sky and the earth, but you don't know the one right in front of you, and you don't know how to read the present moment."

Saying 92: Look and Find
Jesus said, "Look and you'll find. I didn't answer your questions before. Now I want to give you answers, but you aren't looking for them."

Saying 93: Don't Throw Pearls to Pigs
"Don't give what's holy to the dogs, or else it might be thrown on the manure pile. Don't throw pearls to the pigs, or else they might […]"

Saying 94: Knock and It Will Be Opened
Jesus [said], "Whoever looks will find, [and whoever knocks], it will be opened for them."

Saying 95: Giving Money
[Jesus said], "If you have money, don't lend it at interest. Instead, give [it to] someone from whom you won't get it back."

Saying 96: The Parable of the Yeast
Jesus [said], "The Father's kingdom can be compared to a woman who took a little yeast and [hid] it in flour. She made it into large loaves of bread. Anyone who has ears to hear should hear!"

Saying 97: The Parable of the Jar of Flour
Jesus said, "The Father's kingdom can be compared to a woman carrying a jar of flour. While she was walking down [a] long road, the jar's handle broke and the flour spilled out behind her on the road. She didn't know it, and didn't realize there was a problem until she got home, put down the jar, and found it empty."

Saying 98: The Parable of the Assassin
Jesus said, "The Father's kingdom can be compared to a man who wanted to kill someone powerful. He drew his sword in his house and drove it into the wall to figure out whether his hand was strong enough. Then he killed the powerful one."

Saying 99: Jesus' True Family

The disciples said to him, "Your brothers and mother are standing outside." He said to them, "The people here who do the will of my Father are my brothers and mother; they're the ones who will enter my Father's kingdom."

Saying 100: Give to Caesar What Belongs to Caesar
They showed Jesus a gold coin and said to him, "Those who belong to Caesar demand tribute from us." He said to them, "Give to Caesar what belongs to Caesar, give to God what belongs to God, and give to me what belongs to me."

Saying 101: Discipleship (2)
"Whoever doesn't hate their [father] and mother as I do can't become my [disciple], and whoever [doesn't] love their [father] and mother as I do can't become my [disciple]. For my mother […], but [my] true [Mother] gave me Life."

Saying 102: The Dog in the Feeding Trough
Jesus said, "How awful for the Pharisees who are like a dog sleeping in a feeding trough for cattle, because the dog doesn't eat, and [doesn't let] the cattle eat either."

Saying 103: The Parable of the Bandits
Jesus said, "Blessed is the one who knows where the bandits are going to enter. [They can] get up to assemble their defenses and be prepared to defend themselves before they arrive."

Saying 104: Prayer and Fasting
They said to [Jesus], "Come, let's pray and fast today." Jesus said, "What have I done wrong? Have I failed? "Rather, when the groom leaves the bridal chamber, then people should fast and pray."

Saying 105: Knowing Father and Mother
Jesus said, "Whoever knows their father and mother will be called a bastard."

Saying 106: Unity (2)
Jesus said, "When you make the two into one, you'll become Children of Humanity, and if you say 'Mountain, go away!', it'll go."

Saying 107: The Parable of the Lost Sheep
Jesus said, "The kingdom can be compared to a shepherd who had a hundred sheep. The largest one strayed. He left the ninety-nine and looked for that one until he found it. Having gone through the trouble, he said to the sheep: 'I love you more than the ninety-nine.'"

Saying 108: Becoming Like Jesus
Jesus said, "Whoever drinks from my mouth will become like me, and I myself will become like them; then, what's hidden will be revealed to them."

Saying 109: The Parable of the Hidden Treasure
Jesus said, "The kingdom can be compared to someone who had a treasure [hidden] in their field. [They] didn't know about it. After they died, they left it to their son. The son didn't know it either. He took the field and sold it. "The buyer plowed the field, [found] the treasure, and began to loan money at interest to whomever they wanted."

Saying 110: Riches and Renunciation (2)
Jesus said, "Whoever has found the world and become rich should renounce the world."

Saying 111: Those Who are Living Won't Die (2)
Jesus said, "The heavens and the earth will roll up in front of you, and whoever lives from the Living One won't see death." Doesn't Jesus say, "Whoever finds themselves, of them the world isn't worthy"?

Saying 112: Flesh and Soul
Jesus said, "How awful for the flesh that depends on the soul. How awful for the soul that depends on the flesh."

Saying 113: The Kingdom is Already Present
His disciples said to him, "When will the kingdom come?" "It won't come by looking for it. They won't say, 'Look over here!' or 'Look over there!' Rather, the Father's kingdom is already spread out over the earth, and people don't see it."

Saying 114: Peter and Mary
Simon Peter said to them, "Mary should leave us, because women aren't worthy of life." Jesus said, "Look, am I to make her a man? So that she may become a living spirit too, she's equal to you men, because every woman who makes herself manly will enter the kingdom of heaven."

Apocryphon of James, or The Secret Book of James

Prologue
Since you asked me to send you a secret book revealed to Peter and me by the Lord, and I could neither turn you down nor talk to you (directly), [I've written] it in Hebrew letters and have sent it to you – and to you alone. But as a minister of the salvation of the saints, take care not to tell too many people about this book, which the Savior didn't want to tell all twelve of us, the disciples. But blessed are those who will be saved through the faith of this message. Ten months ago, I sent you another secret book that the Savior revealed to me. But think of that one as revealed to me, James. And this one […]

The Savior Appears
Now all twelve disciples [were] sitting together [at the same time] recalling what the Savior had told each of them, whether privately or publicly, and organizing it in books. [But I] was writing what went into [my book]. Look! The Savior appeared, [after] he had left [us, while we were watching] for him. Five hundred and fifty days after he had risen from the dead, we told him, "You went away and left us!" But Jesus said, "No, but I'll return to the place from which I came. If you want to come with me, come on!" They all replied and said, "We'll come if you tell us to." He said, "Truly I tell you, no one will ever enter the kingdom of heaven because I ordered it, but because you yourselves are full. Leave James and Peter to me so that I may fill them." After he called these two, he took them aside and told the rest to keep doing what they were doing.

Being Filled
The Savior said, "You've received mercy. […] they [haven't] understood. Don't you want to be filled? Your hearts are drunk. Don't you, then, want to be sober? Then be ashamed! From now on, awake or asleep, remember that you've seen the Son of Humanity, and have talked to him in person, and have heard him in person. Woe to those who've seen the Son of Humanity! Blessed are those who haven't seen that man, mingled with him, spoken to him, or heard a thing he's said. Yours is life! Know, then, that he healed you when you were sick, so that you might reign. Woe to those who've found relief from their sickness, because they'll relapse into sickness. Blessed are those who haven't been sick and have found relief before getting sick. Yours is the kingdom of God! So I tell you, be full and leave no space within you empty, because the one who is coming will be able to mock you." Then Peter replied, "Three times you've told us to be [full, but] we are full." In [response the Savior said], "That's why I [told] you ['be full'] – so that you won't [be lacking. Those who are lacking] won't [be saved]. It's good to be full [and] bad [to be lacking]. So just as it's good for you to be lacking and bad for you to be full, whoever is full is also lacking. One who's lacking isn't filled the same way that someone who's lacking is filled, and anyone who's full gets everything they need. So it's right to be lacking while it's possible to fill you, and to be filled while it's possible to be lacking, so that you can [fill] yourselves more. So [be] full of the Spirit but lacking in reason, because reason is of the soul – in fact, it is soul."

The Cross and Death
In response I told him, "Lord, we can obey you if you want us to, because we've abandoned our fathers, our mothers, and our villages, and have followed you. So help us not to be tempted by the devil, the evil one." In response the Lord said, "What good is it to you if you do the will of the Father, and he doesn't give it to you as a gift when you're tempted by Satan? But if you're oppressed by Satan and persecuted and do (God's) will, I [say] that he'll love you, make you equal, and regard [you] as having become beloved through his forethought by your own choice. So won't you stop loving the flesh and being afraid of sufferings? Or don't you know that you haven't yet been abused, unjustly accused, locked up in prison, illegally condemned, crucified by reason, nor buried in the sand as I myself was by the evil one? Do you dare to spare the flesh, you for whom the Spirit is a surrounding wall? If you consider how long the world existed <before> you, and how long it will exist after you, you'll find that your life is a single day and your sufferings a single hour. For the good won't come into the world. So scorn death and take thought for life! Remember my cross and my death, and you'll live!" But in response I told him, "Lord, don't teach us about the cross and death, because they're far from you." In response the Lord said, "Truly I tell you, no one will be saved unless they [believe] in my cross, [because] the kingdom of God belongs to those who've believed in my cross. So become those who seek death, like the dead who seek life; because what they seek is revealed to them. So what do they have to worry about? When you turn to the subject of death, it will teach you about election. Truly I tell you, no one who's afraid of death will be saved,

because the kingdom of <God> belongs to those who are put to death. Become better than I; be like the child of the Holy Spirit."

Prophecies and Parables
Then I asked him, "Lord, how can we prophesy to those who ask us to prophesy to them? Because there are many who ask us, and who look to us to hear a message from us." In response the Lord said, "Don't you know that the head of prophecy was cut off with John?" But I said, "Lord, is it possible to remove the head of prophecy? The Lord told me, "When you realize what 'head' means, and that prophecy comes from the head, understand what 'its head was removed' means. At first I spoke to you in parables, and you didn't understand. Now I speak to you openly, and you still don't perceive. But to me you were a parable among parables and something visible out in the open. "Be eager to be saved without being urged. Rather, be ready on your own and, if possible, get there before me, because the Father will love you. "Come to hate hypocrisy and evil intention, because intention is what produces hypocrisy, and hypocrisy is far from the truth. "Don't let the kingdom of heaven wither, because it's like a date palm shoot whose fruit has poured down around it. It sent out some leaves, and after they sprouted, they made their productivity dry up. This is also what happened with the fruit that came from this single root; when it was picked, many acquired fruit. Wouldn't it truly be good if you could produce the new plants now? <You> would find it. "Since I've already been glorified like this, why do you hold me back in my eagerness to go? For after the [labor], you've made me stay with you another eighteen days because of the parables. For some people, it was enough <to listen> to the teaching and understand 'The Shepherds,' 'The Seed,' 'The Building,' 'The Lamps of the Young Women,' 'The Wage of the Workers,' and 'The Silver Coins and the Woman.' "Be eager about the message! The first stage of the message is faith, the second is love, and the third is works, because from these comes life. "The message is like a grain of wheat. When someone sowed it, they believed in it, and when it sprouted, they loved it, because they saw many grains in place of one. And after they worked, they were saved because they prepared it as food, then kept enough left over to be sown. This is also how you yourselves can receive the kingdom of heaven. Unless you receive it through knowledge, you won't be able to find it.

Be Saved
"So I tell you, be sober! Don't be deceived. And many times I told you all together – and also to you alone, James, I've said – 'Be saved!' And I've commanded you to follow me, and I've taught you what to do in the face of the rulers. "See that I've come down, spoken, been torn, and taken my crown when I saved you, because I came down to dwell with you so that you'll dwell with me. And when I found your houses without ceilings, I lived in the houses that could receive me at the time I came down. "Trust me about this, my brothers (i.e., Peter and James). Understand what the great light is. The Father doesn't need me, because a father doesn't need a son, but it's the son who needs the father. I'm going to him, because the Father of the Son doesn't need you. "Listen to the message, understand knowledge, love life, and no one will persecute or oppress you other than yourselves. "You wretches! You poor devils! You hypocrites of the truth! You falsifiers of knowledge! You sinners against the Spirit! Can you still bear to listen, when you should've been speaking from the beginning? Can you still bear to sleep, when you should've been awake from the beginning so that the kingdom of heaven might receive you? "Truly I tell you, it's easier for a holy person to fall into defilement, and for an enlightened person to fall into darkness, than for you to reign – or not reign. "I've remembered your tears, your grief, and your pain. They're far from us. But now, you who are outside of the Father's inheritance, weep where it's necessary, grieve, and proclaim what's good as the Son is ascending as he should. "Truly I tell you, if I had been sent (only) to those who would listen to me and had spoken to them (alone), I wouldn't ever have gone up from the earth. Now, then, be ashamed for these things! "Look, I'll leave you and go away. I don't want to continue with you anymore, just as you yourselves don't want that. Now, then, follow me eagerly. That's why I tell you that I came down for you. You're beloved; you'll bring life for many. Call on the Father. Pray to God often, and (God) will be generous with you. "Blessed is the one who has seen you with (God) when (God) was proclaimed among the angels and given glory among the holy ones; yours is life. Rejoice and be glad as children of God. Keep (God's) will so that you may be saved. Accept my warning and save yourselves. I'm pleading for you with the Father, who will forgive you much."

Few Have Found the Kingdom
And when we heard these things, we were delighted, because we had been depressed about the things we mentioned before. But when he saw us rejoicing, he said, "Woe to you who need an advocate! Woe to you who need grace! Blessed will be those who've spoken out and acquired grace for themselves! "Be like foreigners. How are they viewed in your city? Why are you disturbed when you cast yourselves out on your own and separate yourselves from your city? Why do you leave your dwelling on your own and make it available for those who want to live in it? You outcasts and runaways! Woe to you, because you'll be caught! "Or do you think that the Father is a lover of humanity, or is persuaded by prayers, or grants grace to one on behalf of another, or puts up with one who seeks? "(God) knows about desire and what the flesh needs. It's not this (flesh) which desires the soul, because without the soul, the body doesn't sin, just as the soul isn't saved without the spirit. But if the soul is saved without evil, and the spirit is also saved, then the body becomes sinless. For it's the spirit that raises the soul, but the body that kills it; that is, (the soul) kills itself. "Truly I tell you, (God) won't ever forgive the sin of the soul or the guilt of the flesh, because no one who's worn the flesh will be saved. Do you think that many have found the kingdom of heaven? Blessed is the one who's seen oneself (at) the fourth (stage) in heaven."

Know Yourselves
When we heard these things, we felt depressed. But when he saw that we were depressed, he said, "I'm telling you this so that you may know yourselves. For the kingdom of heaven is like an ear of grain after it had sprouted in a field. And when it had ripened, it scattered its fruit, and again it filled the field with ears of grain for another year. You, too, be eager to reap an ear of the grain of life for yourselves so that you may be filled with the kingdom! "And as long as I'm with you, pay attention to me and trust in me, but when I leave you, remember me. And remember me because when I was with you, you didn't know me. Blessed are those who've known me. Woe to those who've heard and haven't believed! Blessed will be those who haven't seen, [but …]! "And once again I [appeal to] you, because I'm revealed to you building a house very valuable to you when you take shelter under it, just as it will be able to support your neighbors' house when it threatens to fall. Truly I tell you, woe to those for whom I was sent down to this place! Blessed will be those who go up to the Father. Again I warn you, you who are. Be like those who are not so that you may be with those who are not. "Don't let the kingdom of heaven become a desert within you. Don't be haughty because of the light that enlightens, but behave toward yourselves the way that I've behaved toward you. I've put myself under the curse for you, so that you may be saved."

Final Words
But in response to these comments Peter said, "Sometimes you urge us on to the kingdom of heaven, and again at other times you turn us away, Lord. Sometimes you persuade and draw us to faith and promise us life, and again at other times you cast us out of the kingdom of heaven." But in response the Lord told us, "I've given you faith many times. Moreover, I've revealed myself to you, James, and you haven't known me. Now again, I see you rejoicing often. And when you're delighted about the promise of life, nevertheless you're sad and depressed when you're taught about the kingdom. "But through faith and knowledge, you've received life. Despise rejection when you hear it, but when you hear the promise, rejoice all the more. Truly I tell you, whoever will receive life and believe the kingdom will never leave it – not even if the Father wants to banish them! "This is all I'm going to tell you up to this point, but now I'll go up to the place from which I came. But when I was eager to go, you cast me out, and instead of accompanying me, you've chased me away. But be attentive to the glory that awaits me, and when you've opened your hearts, listen to the hymns that await me up in heaven, because today I need to sit at the right hand of the Father. "Now I've spoken (my) last word to you, and I'll leave you, because a chariot of the Spirit has taken me up, and from now on I'll strip myself so that I may clothe myself. But pay attention: Blessed are those who've proclaimed the Son before his coming down so that when I've come, I might go up. Blessed three times over are those who [were] proclaimed by the Son before they came to be, so that you may have a portion with them."

Heavenly Ascent
When he said these things, he left. But Peter and I knelt down, gave thanks, and sent our hearts up to heaven. We heard with our ears, and saw with our eyes, the cacophony of wars and a trumpet blare and a great commotion. And when we passed beyond that place, we sent our minds up higher and heard with our ears hymns and angelic praises and angelic rejoicing. And heavenly majesties were singing hymns, and we rejoiced too. After this again, we wanted to send our spirit up to the Majesty. And after we went up, we weren't allowed to see or hear anything, because the other disciples called us and asked us, "What did you hear from the Teacher?" And, "What did he tell you?" And, "Where did he go?" But we responded, "He went up." And, "He's given us his right hand and promised us all life, and he revealed to us children who are to come after us, after telling [us] to love them, as we'd be [saved] because of them."

The Gospel of Mary

[Pages 1 through 6 are missing.]

An Eternal Perspective

"Then will [matter] be [destroyed], or not?" The Savior said, "Every nature, every form, every creature exists in and with each other, but they'll dissolve again into their own roots, because the nature of matter dissolves into its nature alone. Anyone who has ears to hear should hear!" Peter said to him, "Since you've explained everything to us, tell us one more thing. What's the sin of the world?" The Savior said, "Sin doesn't exist, but you're the ones who make sin when you act in accordance with the nature of adultery, which is called 'sin.' That's why the Good came among you, up to the things of every nature in order to restore it within its root." Then he continued and said, "That's why you get sick and die, because [you love what tricks you. Anyone who] can understand should understand! "Matter [gave birth to] a passion that has no image because it comes from what's contrary to nature. Then confusion arises in the whole body. That's why I told you to be content at heart. If you're discontented, find contentment in the presence of the various images of nature. Anyone who has ears to hear should hear!"

The Gospel

When the Blessed One said these things, he greeted them all and said, "Peace be with you! Acquire my peace. Be careful not to let anyone mislead you by saying, 'Look over here!' or 'Look over there!' Because the Son of Humanity exists within you. Follow him! Those who seek him will find him. "Go then and preach the gospel about the kingdom. Don't lay down any rules beyond what I've given you, nor make a law like the lawgiver, lest you be bound by it." When he said these things, he left. But they grieved and wept bitterly. They said, "How can we go up to the Gentiles to preach the gospel about the kingdom of the Son of Humanity? If they didn't spare him, why would they spare us?"

Mary and Jesus

Then Mary arose and greeted them all. She said to her brothers (and sisters), "Don't weep and grieve or let your hearts be divided, because his grace will be with you all and will protect you. Rather we should praise his greatness because he's prepared us and made us Humans." When Mary said these things, she turned their hearts [toward] the Good and they [started] to debate the words of [the Savior]. Peter said to Mary, "Sister, we know the Savior loved you more than all other women. Tell us the words of the Savior that you remember – the things which you know that we don't, and which we haven't heard." In response Mary said, "I'll tell you what's hidden from you." So she started to tell them these words: "I," she said, "I saw the Lord in a vision and I said to him, 'Lord, I saw you in a vision today.' "In response he said to me, 'You're blessed because you didn't waver at the sight of me. For where the mind is, there is the treasure.' "I said to him, 'Lord, now does the one who sees the vision see it /in\ the soul /or\ in the spirit?' "In response the Savior said, 'They don't see in the soul or in the spirit, but the mind which [exists] between the two is [what] sees the vision [and] it [that …]

[Pages 11 through 14 are missing.]

Overcoming the Powers

"And Desire said, 'I didn't see you going down, but now I see you're going up. So why are you lying, since you belong to me?' "In response the soul said, 'I saw you, but you didn't see me or know me. I was to you just a garment, and you didn't recognize me.' When it said these things, it left, rejoicing greatly. "Again, it came to the third power, which is called 'Ignorance.' [It] interrogated the soul and [said], 'Where are you going? In wickedness you're bound. Since you're bound, don't judge!' "[And] the soul said, 'Why do you judge me, since I haven't judged? I was bound, even though I haven't bound. They didn't recognize me, but I've recognized that everything will dissolve – both the things of the [earth] and the things of [heaven].' "When the soul had overcome the third power, it went up and saw the fourth power, which took seven forms: The first form is Darkness; The second, Desire; The third, Ignorance; The fourth, Zeal for Death; The fifth, the Kingdom of the Flesh; The sixth, the Foolish 'Wisdom' of Flesh; The seventh, the 'Wisdom' of Anger. "These are the seven powers of Wrath. "They ask the soul, 'Where do you come from, you murderer, and where are you going, conqueror of space?' "In response the soul said, 'What binds me has been killed, what surrounds me has been overcome, my desire is gone, and ignorance has died. In a [world] I was released from a world, [and] in a type from a type which is above, and from the chain of forgetfulness which exists only for a time. From now on I'll receive the rest of the time of the season of the age in silence.'" When Mary said these things, she fell silent because the Savior had spoken with her up to this point.

Conflict over Authority

In response Andrew said to the brothers (and sisters), 'Say what you will about what she's said, I myself don't believe that the Savior said these

Conclusion

And when they heard, they believed the revelation indeed, but were angry about those to be born. So, not wanting to give them a scandal, I sent each of them to a different place. But I myself went up to Jerusalem, praying to acquire a portion with the beloved ones who will be revealed. And I pray that the beginning may come from you, because this is how I can be saved, since they'll be enlightened through me, by my faith – and through another (faith) that's even better than mine, because I want mine to be the lesser. So do your best to be like them, and pray that you acquire a portion with them. Apart from what I've said, the Savior didn't disclose a revelation to us for them. We do indeed proclaim a portion with those for whom the proclamation was made – those whom the Lord has (accepted as) children.

things, because these teachings seem like different ideas." In response Peter spoke out with the same concerns. He asked them concerning the Savior: "He didn't speak with a woman without our knowledge and not publicly with us, did he? Will we turn around and all listen to her? Did he prefer her to us?" Then Mary wept and said to Peter, "My brother Peter, what are you thinking? Do you really think that I thought this up by myself in my heart, or that I'm lying about the Savior?" In response Levi said to Peter, "Peter, you've always been angry. Now I see you debating with this woman like the adversaries. But if the Savior made her worthy, who are you then to reject her? Surely the Savior knows her very well. That's why he loved her more than us. "Rather we should be ashamed, clothe ourselves with perfect Humanity, acquire it for ourselves as he instructed us, and preach the gospel, not laying down any other rule or other law beyond what the Savior said." When [Levi said these things], they started to go out to teach and to preach.

The Book of Marcion, or The Gospel of the Lord
The written account of the life of Jesus Christ, preserved in its original Greek by Marcion, son of Philologus, bishop of Sinope. (Anno Domine 130)

1

[1] In the fifteenth year of the reign of Tiberius Caesar, [2] [Pontius Pilatus being the Governor of Judaea,] Jesus came down to Capernaum, a city in Galilee, and was [3] teaching on the sabbath days: and they were astonished at his doctrine: for his word was in authority. [4] And in the synagogue there was a man which had a spirit of an unclean demon, and he cried out with a loud [5] voice, Saying, "let *us* alone; what have we to do with thee, Jesus? art thou come to destroy us? I know thee [6] who thou art: the Holy One of God." And Jesus rebuked him, saying; "Hold thy peace, and come out of him." And when the demon had thrown him into the midst, [7] he came out of him, having done no hurt. And amazement came upon all, and they spake together saying to one another, what is this word? For in authority and power he commandeth the unclean spirits, [8] and they come out. And a rumour of him went out into every place of the country round about, [9] And he arose out of the synagogue, and entered into the house of Simon. And Simon`s mother in law was taken with a great fever: and they besought him for her. [10] And he stood over her, and rebuked the fever: and it left her: and immidately she arose and ministered unto them. [11] And he came to Nazareth, and went into the [12] synagogue [on the Sabbath day] and sat down. And the eyes of all in the synagogue fastened on him, [13] And he began to speak to them; [14] and all wondered [15] at the words which proceedeth from his mouth. And he said unto them, " Ye will surely say unto me this parable, *Physician, heal thyself*; whatsoever we have [16] heard done at Capernaum, do also here. But I tell you of a truth, many widows were in Israel in the days of Elijah, when the heaven was shut up three years and six months, [17] when great famine occured throughout all the land: and unto none of them was Elijah sent, but only to Sarepta, [18] a *city* of Sidon, unto a woman *that was* a widow. And many lepers were in Israel in the time of Elisha the prophet: and none of them was cleansed, but only [19] Naaman the syrian". And they were all filled with wrath [20] in the synagogue, when they heard these things, and rose up, and thrust him out of the city, and led him unto the brow of the hill whereon their city was built, to cast [21] him down headlong. But he passing through the midst of them went his way. [22] And when the sun was setting, all as many as had any sick with divers diseases brought them unto him; and he laid his hands on every one of them, and healed them. [23] And demons also came out of many, crying out, saying, "Thou art Son of God" and he rebuked *them* suffered them not to speak; for they knew that he was the Christ. [24] And when it was day, he departed and went into a desert place: and the multitudes sought him, and came unto him, and stayed him, that he should not depart from [25] them. And he said unto them, "I must announce as good tidings the kingdom of God to the other cities also: for therefore am i sent. [26] And he was preaching in the synagogues of Galilee.

2

[1] Now it came to pass, that, as the multitude pressed upn him to hear the word of God, he was standing by [2] the lake of Gennesaret, and saw two boats standing by the lake: but the fdishermen were gone out of them, [3] and were washing *their* nets. And he entered into one of the boats, which was Simon`s, and asked him to thrust out a litle from land. And he sat down, and [4] taught the multitudes out of the boat. Now when he had left speaking, he said unto Simon, "Put put into the [5] deep, and let down your nets a draught". And Simon answering said unto him, "Master, we have toiled all the night, and taken nothing; but at thy word I will let down [6] the net." When they had this done, they inclosed a [7] great multitude of fishes: and their nets were breaking. And they beckoned unto *their* partners, in the other boat, that they should come and help them out. And they came, and [8] filled both the boats, so that they began to sink. When Simon Peter saw *it*, he fell down at Jesus` knees, saying, [9] "Depart from me; for I am a sinful man, O Lord." For amazement overcame him, and all that were with him, at [10] the draught of the fishes which they had taken: which were partners with Simon. And Jesus said unto Simon, "fear not; from henceforth thou shalt be taking men [11] alive." And when they had brought their boats to land, they left all, and followed him. [12] And it came to pass, when he was in one of the cities, behold a man full of leprosy: who seeing Jesus fell on *his* face, and besought him, saying; "Lord, if thou wilt, thou [13] canst make me clean." And he put forth *his* hand, and touched him, saying, " I will: be thou cleansed" And [14] immediately the leprosy departed from the man. And he charged him to tell no man; but go, and shew thyself to the priest, and offer for thy cleansing, according as Moses [15] commanded, that this may be a testimony to you. But so much the more went there a fame abroad of him: and many multitidues came together to hear, and to be healed [16] by him for

their infirmities. And he himself was withdrawing in the wilderness, praying. ¹⁷ And it came to pass on one of the days that he was teaching, and there were Pharisees and doctors of the law sitting vtm which were come out of every village of Galilee, Judaea, and Jerusalem: and the power of the ¹⁸ Lord was *with Him* toheal them. And behold, men brought in a bed a man that was palsied; and they sought ¹⁹ to bring him in, and to lay *him* before him. And not finding by what *way* they might bring him in because of the multitude, they went up to the housetop, and let him down through the tiles with *his* couch into the midst before ²⁰ Jesus. And seeing their faith, he said unto him, "Man, thy ²¹ sins are forgiven thee." And the scribes and the Pharisees began to reason, saying, "Who is this which speaketh blasphemies? Who can forgive sin, but God alone? ²² But Jesus perceiving their reasoning answered and said unto them, "What reasen ye in your hearts? ²³ Whether is easier, to say, Thy sins are forgiven thee; or ²⁴ to say; Rise up and walk? But that ye may know that the Son of man hath authority upon earth to forgive sins (he said unto the palsied man) I say unto thee, Arise ²⁵ and take up they couch, and go to thine house. And immediately he rose up before them, and took up that whereon he lay, and departed to his house, glorifying ²⁶ God. And amazement took hold on all, and they glorified God, and were filled with fear, saying, "We have seen strange things today". ²⁷ And after these things he went forth, and saw a publican, named Levi, sitting at the place of toll: and he ²⁸ said unto him, "Follow me." And he left all, rose up, and ²⁹ followed him. And Levi made him a great feast in his hourse: and there was a great company of publicans ³⁰ of others that were reclining with them. And their scribes and the Pharisees murmured against his disciples, ³⁰ saying, "Why do ye year and drink with publicans and ³¹ sinners?" And Jesus answering said unto them, "They that are whole have no need of a physiciian; but they ³² that are sick. I am not come to call the righteous, but ³³ sinners to repentance. And they said unto him, "Why do the disciples of John fast often, and make prayers, and likewise the *disciples* of the Pharisees; but thine eat and ³⁴ drink? And he said unto them, "Can ye make the sons of the bridal chamber fast, while the bridegroom is with ³⁵ them? But the days will come; and when the bridegroom shall be taken away from them, then will they fast in ³⁶ those days." And he spake also a parable unto them; "No man putteth a piece of new garment upon an old garment; else both the new maketh a rent, and the piece that was *taken* out of the new agreeth not with the ³⁷ old. And no man puttteth new wine into old wine-skins, else the new wine will burst the skins; and itself will be ³⁸ spilled, and the skins will perish. But new wine must be put into new wine-skins, and both are preserved. ³⁹ No man also having drunk old *wine* straigtway desireth new; for he saith, the old is better.

3

¹ And it came to pass on the second sabbath after the first, that he was going through the corn fields: and his disciples plucked the ears of cornm and did eat, rubbing *them* in ² their hands. And certain of the Pharisees said unto them, "Why do ye that which is not lawful to do ³ on the sabbath day?" And Jesus answering them, said, "Have ye not read even this what David did, when himself was ⁴ an hungered, and they which were with him; how they went into the house of God, and did take and eat the shewbread, and gave also to them that were with him; which it is not lawful to eat but for the priests alone?" ⁵ And he said unto them, "That the Son of man is Lord even of the sabbath" ⁶ And it came to pass also on another Sabbath, that he entered into the synagogue and taught; and there were a ⁷ a man there and his right hand was withered. And the scribes and Pharisees watched him, whether he would heal on the sabbath day; that they might find an ⁸ accusation against him. But he knew their reasonings, and said to the man which had the withered man, "Rise up, and stand forth in the midst. And he rose and stood ⁹ forth. Then said Jesus unto them, "I will ask you something; Is it lawful on the sabbath to do good ¹⁰ or to do evil? To save life, or to destroy *it*?" And looking round about upon them all, he said unto the man, "stretch forth thy hand." and he did so: and his hand was ¹¹ restored as the other. And they were filled with madness; and commanded one with another what they might do to Jesus. ¹² And it came to pass in those days, that he went out into the mountains to pray, and was passing the whole night ¹³ in prayer to God. And when it was day, he called *unto him* his disciples: and he chose from them twelve. ¹⁴ whom he also named; apostles; Simon (whom was also named Peter), and Andrew his brother, James and John, Phillip ¹⁵ and Bartholomew, Matthew and Thomas, James the *son* ¹⁶ of Alphaeas, and Simon whom they called Zelotes, and Judas *the brother* of James, and Judas Iscarioth, which also became a ¹⁷ traitor. And he came down among them, and stood on a level place, and the multitude of his disciples, and a great number of people out of all Judaea and Jerusalem, and from the sea coast of Tyre and Sidon, which came to hear ¹⁸ him, and to be healed of their diseases; and they that were troubled by unclean spirits: and they were healed. ¹⁹ And the whole multitude sought to touch him: for power went out of him, and healed *them* all. ²⁰ And he lifted up his eyes on his disciples, and said: "Blessed *are ye* poor: for your`s is the kingdom of God. ²¹ Blessed *are ye* that hunger now: for ye shall be filled. Blessed *are ye* that weep now: for ye shall laught. ²² Blessed *are ye*, when men shall hate you, and when they shall separate you *from their company*, and shall reproach *you*, and cast out your name as evil, for the Son of man`s ²³ sake. Rejoice ye in that day, and leap *for you*: for, behold, your reward *is* great in heaven: for according to ²⁴ these things did their fathers unto the prophets. But woe unto you that are rich! for ye have consolation ²⁵ in full. Woe unto you that are full! for ye shall hunger. Woe unto you that laugh now! for ye ²⁶ shall mourn and weep. Woe unto you, when all men shall speak well of you! for according to these things did their fathers to the false prophets. ²⁷ But I say unto you that hear, Love your enemies, do ²⁸ good to them which hate you, bless them that curse you, ²⁹ and pray for them which despitefully use you.Unto him that smiteth thee on the *one* cheek, offer also the other; and from him that taketh away thy cloke, withhold ³⁰ not thy coat also. Give every man that asketh of thee: and of him that taketh away thy goods ask *them*. ³¹ not again. and as ye would that men should do to you, ³² do ye also to them likewise. And if ye love them which love you, what thank have ye? for sinners also love those ³³ that love them. And if ye do good to them which do good to you, what thank have ye? for sinners also do ³⁴ the same. And if ye lend to *them* of whom ye hope to receive, what thank have ye? for sinners also lend to ³⁵ sinners, to receive equal things.But love ye your enemies, and do good, and lend, hoping for nothing again: and your reward shall be great, and ye shall be sons of the Highest: for he is kind unto the unthankful and *to* ³⁶ the evil. Be ye therefore merciful, as your Father also is ³⁷ merciful. And Judge not, and ye shall not be judged: condemn not, and ye shall not be condemned: release ³⁸ and ye shall be released: Give, and it shall be given unto you; good measure, pressed down, and shaken together, and running over, shall they give into your bosom. For with the same measure that ye mete withal it shall be measured to you again." ³⁹ And he spake a parable unto them, "Can the blind lead ⁴⁰ the blind? shall they not both fall into the ditch? The disciple is not above his teacher: but every one that is 41 perfect shall be as his teacher. And why beholdest thou the mote that is in thy brothers eye, but perceivest ⁴² not the beam that is in thine won eye? Either how canst thou say to thy brother, Brother, let me pull the mote that is in thine eye, when thou thyself beholdest not the beam in thine own eye? Thou hypocrite, cast out first the beam out of thine own eye, and then shall you see clearly to pull out the mote that is in thy brother`s eye!. ⁴³ For there is no good tree that maketh corrupt fruit; nor ⁴⁴ corrupt tree that maketh good fruit. For each tree is known by its fruit. For of thorns do they not gather figs, nor of a bramble bush gather they grapes. ⁴⁵ The good man out of the good treasure of his heart bringeth forth that which is truely good: and the evil man out of the evil treasure of his heart bringeth forth that which is evil: for out of the abundance of the heart his ⁴⁶ mouth speaketh. And why call ye me, Lord, Lord, and ⁴⁷ do not do the things which I say? Everyone that cometh to me, and heareth my sayings, and doeth them, I will ⁴⁸ shew you to whom he is like: He is like a man building a house, who digged and went deep, and laid a foundation on the rock: and when the flood arose, the stream beat vehemtly upon the house, and had not strenght to shake it: for it was founded upon the ⁴⁹ rock. But he that heareth, and doeth not, is like a man that without a foundation built a house upon the earth; against which the stream did beat vehemently, and immediately it fell, and the ruin of that house was great.

4

¹ Now when he had completed all his sayings in the ears of the people, he entered into Capernaum. ² And a certain centurion`s servant was sick, and going to ³ die; and he was precious unto him. And when he heard of Jesus, he sent unto him elders of the Jews ⁴ asking him that he would come and save his servant. And when they came to Jesus, they besought him earnestly, saying, That he was worthy for whom he should do this: ⁵ "For he loveth our nation, and he hath built us the ⁶ synagogue". Then Jesus went with them. And when he was now not far from the house, the centurion sent friends to him,saying unto him: "Lord, trouble not thyself; for I am not worthy that thou shouldest enter under my roof. ⁷ Wherefore neither thoughtr I myself worthy to come unto thee: but say in a word, and my boy shall be healed. ⁸ For I aslo am a man set under authority, having under me soliders, and I say unto this one, Go, and he goeth; and to another, Come, and he cometh; and to my servant, Do ⁹ this, and he doeth *it*". And when Jesus heard these things, he marveled at him, and turned, and said unto the multitude that followed him, "I say unto you, not even in ¹⁰ Israel have I found so great faith." And they that were sent, returned to the house, and found the sick servant whole. ¹¹ And it came to pass the day after, that he was going into a city called Nain,; and many of his disciples were ¹² going

with him, and a great multitude. Now when he came night to the gate of the city, behold, a dead man was being carried out, the only son of his mother, and she was a widow: and a considerable multitude of the [13] city was with her. And when the Lord saw her, he had [14] compassion on her, and said unto her, "Weep not." And he came and touched the bier: and they that bare *him* stood still. And he said, "Young man, I say unto thee, Arise!" [15] And the *dead man* sat up, and began to speak. And [16] he delivered him to his mother. And fear took hold on all: and they glorified God, saying, That a great prophet is risen up among us; and, That God hath [17] visited his people. And this rumour of him went forth in the whole of Judaea, and in all region round about. [18] And the disciples of John told him of all these [19] things. And John calling *unto him* a certain two of his disciples sent *them* to Jesus, saying, "Art thou he that [20] cometh? or are we to look for another?" And when the men were come unto him, they said, "John the Baptist hath sent us unto thee, saying; Art thou he that cometh? [21] or are we to look for another?" And in that same hour he cured many infirmities and plagues and of evil spirits; [22] and unto many blind he gave sight. And Jesus answering said unto them, "Go your way, and tell John what things ye have seen and heard: that the blind receive their sight, the lame walk, the lepers are cleansed, the deaf hear, the dead are raised, the poor have good tidings [23] announced to them. And blessed is *he*, whosoever shall not be offended in me." [24] And when the messengers of John were departed, he began to say unto the multitudes concerning John What are ye come into the wilderness to gaze at? A reed [25] shaken with the wind? But what are ye come out to see? A man clothed in soft rainment? Behold, they which are in gorgeous apparel, and delicacy, are kings` [26] courts. But what are ye come out to see? A Prophet? Yea, I say unto you, and much more than a prophet. [27] This is *he*, of whom it is written, "Behold, I send my messenger before thy face, which shall prepare thy way [28] before thee." For I say unto you, Among those that are born from women, a greater prophet than John the Baptist, there is none: but he that is less in the Kingdom of God [29] is greater than he". And all the people when they heard it, and the publicans, justified God, being baptised with [30] the baptism of John. But the Pharisees and lawyer rejected the counsel of God unto themselves, being not [31] baptised of him. And the Lord said, "Whereunto then shall I liken the men of this generation? and to what are [32] they like? They are like unto children sitting in the marketplace, and calling to one another, and saying: We piped unto you, and ye did not dance, we mourned [33] you, and ye did not weep. For John the Baptist is come neither eating bread nor drinking wine, and ye say, He [34] hath a demon. The Son of man is coming eating and drinking, and ye say, Behold a gluttonous man, and a [35] winebibber, a friend of publicans and sinners! And wisdom was justified of all her children". [36] And one of the Pharisees desired him that he would eat with him. And he went into the Pharisee`s house, and [37] reclined *to meat*. And behold, a woman of the city, which was a sinner, when she knew that he was reclining in the Pharisee`s house, brought an alabaster box of ointment [38] and stood at his feet behind *him* weeping, and began to wet his feet with the tears,, and did wipe *them* with the hairs of her head, and kissed his feet, and anointed [39] *them* with the ointment. Now when the Pharisee which had bidden him saw *it*, he spake to himself, saying, "This man, if he were a prophet, would have known who and what manner manner of woman *this is* that touched him: [40] for she is a sinner. And Jesus answering said unto him, "Simon, I have somewhat to say unto thee." And he saith, [41] "Teacher, say on." "A certain money-lender had two debtors: the one owed five hundred denarii, and [42] the other fifty. And when they had not whewewith to pay, he forgave them both. Tell me therefore, which [43] of them will love him more?" Simon answered and said, "I suppose that *he*, to whom he forgave the more." And he said unto [44] him, "Thou hast rightly judged"And he turned to the woman, and said unto Simon, "Seest thou this woman? I entered into thine house: water for my feet thou gavest me not: but she hath wetted my feet with tears, and wiped [45] them with the hairs of her head. A kiss thou gavest me not: but she since the time I came hath not ceased [46] kissing my feet. My head with oil thou didst not anoint: but this woman hath anointed my feet with ointment. [47] For the sake of which I say unto thee; Her sins which are many are forgiven; for she loved much: but to [48] whom little is forgiven, *the same* loveth little". And he [49] said unto her, " Thy sins are forgiven." And they that were reclining with him began to say among themselves, [50] "Who is this that even forgiveth sins?" And he said to the woman "Thy faith has saved thee, go in peace."

5

[1] And it came to pass afterward, that he made his way through city and village, preaching and announcing as good tidings the kingdom of God: and the twelve *were* [2] with him. And certain women, which had been healed of evil spirits and infirmities, Mary called Magdalene, from [3] whom seven demons had gone out, and Joannah the wife of Chuza, Herod`s steward, and Susanna, and many others, which ministered unto him of their possessions. [4] And when a great multitude were coming together, and they of every city were come to him, he spake by a [5] parable: "The sower went out to sow his seed: and as he sowed, some fell by the way side: and it was trodden [6] down, and the fowls of the heaven devoured it. And other fell upon the rock, and when sprung up, it withered away, [7] because it lacked moisture. And other fell in the midst of the thorns; and the thorns sprang up with it, and [8] choked it. And other fell on the good ground, and when sprung up, it made fruit and hundredfold". And when he said these things, he cried," He that hath ears to hear, let him hear!" [9] And his disciples asked him, saying, "What might this [10] parable be?" And he said, "Unto you it is given to know the mysteries of the Kingdom of God: but to the rest in parables; that seeing they may not see, and hearing [11] that they may not understand. Now the parable is this: [12] The seed is the word of God. Those by the way side are they that hear; then cometh the devil, and taketh away the word from their hearts, lest they should believe and [13] be saved. Those on the rock *are they*, which, when they hear, receive the word with joy; and these have no root, which for a while believe, and in time of temptation fall [14] away. And that which fell among thorns, these are they, which, when they have heard, go, and are choked with cares and riches and pleasures of *this* life, and bring [15] no fruit of perfection. But that on the good ground, these are, whoever in an honest and good heart, having heard the word, keep hold *of it*, and bring forth fruit in patience. [16] No man, when he hath lighted a lamp, covereth it with a vessel, or putteth *it* under a bed; but setteth *it* on a lamp-stand, that they which enter in may see the light. [17] For there is no secret *thing*, that shall not be made manifest; nor hidden, that shall not be known and come [18] into view. Take heed therefore how ye hear: for whosoever hath, to him shall be given: and whosoever hath not, even what he seemed to have shall be taken from him." [19] And it was told him *by certain* which said, "Thy mother and thy brethren stand without, desiring to see thee" [20] And he answered and said unto them, " Who is my mother and who is *my* brethren? My mother and my brethren are these, which hear the word of God, and do it!" [21] Now it came to pass on one of the days, that he went into a boat and his disciples: and he said unto them, "Let us go over unto the other side of the lake". And they [22] launched forth. But as they sailed he fell asleep: and there came down a storm of wind on the lake; and they were filling *with water*, and were in jeopardy, [23] And they came to him, and awoke him, saying, "Master, master, we perish" And he arose, and rebuked the wind and the raging of the water: and they ceased, and there [24] was a calm. And he said unto them, " Where is your faith?" And they were frightened and wondered, saying one to another, "Who then is this? for he commandeth even the winds and water, and they obey him?" [25] And they sailed down to the country of the Gandarenes, [26] which is over against Galilee. And when he went forth to land, there met him out of the city a certain man, which had demons long time, and wore no cloke, neither abode [27] in a house, but among the tombs. When he saw Jesus, he cried out, and fell down before him, and with a loud voice said, "What have I to do with thee, Jesus, *thou* Son of [28] God most high? I beseech thee, torment me not." (For he had commanded the unclean spirit to come out of the man. For oftentimes it had caught him: and he was guarded and bound with chains and in fetters: and he brake the bands asunder, and was driven of the demon [29] into the deserts) And Jesus asked him, saying, "What is [30] thy name?" And he said, "Legion" because many demons were entered into him. And they besought him that he [31] would not command them to go out into the abyss. And there was an herd of many swine feeding of the mountain: and they besought him that he would suffer them to enter into them. And he suffered them. [32] Then went the demons out of the man, and entered into the swine: and the herd ran violently down the [33] steep place into the lake, and were drowned. When they that fed *them* saw what was done, they fled, and went and told *it* [34] in the city and in the country. Then they went out to see what was done; and came to Jesus, and found the man, from whom the demons were departed, sitting at the feet of Jesus, clothed, and in his right mind: and they [35] were afraid. They also which saw *it* told them by what means he that was possessed of the demons was saved. [36] Then the whole multitude of the country of the Gandarenes round about him asked him to depart from them; for they were holden with great fear: and he entered into the [37] boat, and returned back again. Now the man, from whom the demons had departed, besought him that he might be with him: but Jesus sent him away, saying [38] "Return to thine house, and recount how great things God hath done unto thee." And he went his way, publishing throughout the whole city how great things Jesus had done unto him. [39] And it came to pass, that, when Jesus returned, the multitude welcomed him: for they were all waiting for [40] him. And, behold, there came a man whose name was Jairus, and he was a ruler of the synagogue: and he fell down at Jesus` feet, and besought him that he would [41] come into his house: For he had an only daughter, about twelve years of age, and she was dying. But as he went the multitudes thronged him. [42] And

a woman having an issue of blood twelve years, which had spent all her living upon physicians, neither [43] could be healed if any, came behind *him*, and touched the border of his garment; and immediately her issue of [44] blood stanched. And Jesus said, "Who touched me?" When all denied, Peter and they that were with him said, "Master, the multitude throng thee, and press *thee*, and [45] sayest thou, "Who touched me?" And Jesus said, "Somebody touched me: for I perceived that power had gone [46] out of me." And when the woman saw that shw was not hid, she came trembling, and falling down before him, she declared unto him before all the people for what reason she touched him, and how she was healed immediately. [47] And he said unto her, "Daughter, be of good comfort: thy faith hath saved thee; go into peace" [48] While he yet spake, theere cometh one from the ruler of the synagogue`s *house*, saying to him, "The daughter is [49] dead; trouble not the Teacher." But when Jesus heard *it*, he answered him, saying, "Fear not, believe only, [50] and she shall be saved." And when he came into the house, he suffered no man to go in, save Peter, and James, and John, and the father and the mother of the maiden. [51] And all were weeping, and bewailing her, but he said: [52] "Weep not: she is not dead, but sleepeth." And they [53] laughed to scorn him, knowing that she was dead. And he put them all out, and took her by the hand, and called [54] saying, "Maid, arise". And her spirit came again, and she arose staightway; and he commanded that *something* be [55] given her to eat. And her parents were astonished: but he charged them to tell no man what was done.

The Gospel of Philip

Gentiles, Hebrews, and Christians

A Hebrew creates a Hebrew, and [those] of this kind are called "a proselyte." But a [proselyte] doesn't create (another) proselyte. They're like […] and they create others […] it's good enough for them that they come into being. The slave seeks only freedom; they don't seek their master's property. But the son isn't just a son; he claims his father's inheritance for himself. Those who inherit the dead are themselves dead, and they inherit the dead. Those who inherit the living are themselves alive, and they inherit (both) the living and the dead. The dead can't inherit anything, because how can the dead inherit? If the dead inherits the living they won't die, but the dead will live even more! A gentile doesn't die, because they've never lived in order that they may die. Whoever has believed in the Truth has lived, and is at risk of dying, because they're alive since the day Christ came. The world is created, the cities gentrified, and the dead carried out. When we were Hebrews, we were fatherless – we had (only) our mother. But when we became Christians, we gained both father and mother.

Life, Death, Light, and Darkness

Those who sow in the winter reap in the summer. The winter is the world, the summer the other age. Let's sow in the world so that we may reap in the summer. Because of this, it's not right for us to pray in the winter. The summer follows the winter. But if someone reaps in the winter they won't reap, but uproot, as this kind won't produce fruit […] it doesn't just come out […] but in the other Sabbath […] it's fruitless. Christ came to buy some, but to save others, and to redeem yet others. He bought those who were strangers, made them his own, and set them apart as a pledge as he wanted to. It wasn't just when he appeared that he laid down his life when he wanted to, but since the day the world came into being he laid down his life when he wanted to. Then he came first to take it, since it had been pledged. It was dominated by the robbers that had captured it, but he saved it; and those who are good in the world he redeemed, as well as those who are bad. The light and the darkness, the right and the left, are brothers of each other. They're inseparable. So, those who are good aren't good, those who are bad aren't bad, nor is life (really) life, nor is death (really) death. Because of this, each one will be dissolved into its origin from the beginning. But those who are exalted above the world are indissoluble and eternal.

Names

The names that are given to those who are worldly are very deceptive, because they turn the heart away from what's right to what's not right, and someone who hears "God" doesn't think of what's right but thinks of what's not right. So also with "the Father," "the Son," "the Holy Spirit," "the life," "the light," "the resurrection," "the church," and all the others – they don't think of [what's right] but think of what's [not] right, [unless] they've learned what's right. The [names that were heard] exist in the world […] [deceive. If they existed] in the (eternal) age they wouldn't have been used as names in the world, nor would they have been placed among worldly things. They have an end in the (eternal) age. There's one name that isn't uttered in the world: the name which the Father gave to the Son. It's exalted over everything; it's the Father's name, because the Son wouldn't have become father unless he had taken the name of the Father. Those who have this name know it, but don't say it; and those who don't have it, don't know it. But Truth brought names into the world for us, because it's impossible for us to learn it (Truth) without these names. There's only one Truth, but it's many things for us, to teach this one thing in love through many things.

The Rulers

The rulers wanted to deceive humanity, because they (the rulers) saw that they (humanity) had a kinship with those that are truly good. They took the name of those that are good and gave it to those that aren't good, to deceive them (humanity) by the names and bind them to those that aren't good; and then, what a favor they do for them! They take them from those that aren't good and place them among those that are good. They knew what they were doing, because they wanted to take those who were free and place them in slavery forever. There are powers that exist […] humanity, not wanting them to be [saved], so that they may be […] because if humanity [was saved], sacrifices [wouldn't] happen […] and animals offered up to the powers, because those to whom offerings were made were animals. They were offered up alive, but when they were offered up they died. A human was offered up to God dead, and he lived. Before Christ came, there wasn't any bread in the world – just as Paradise, where Adam was, had many trees to feed the animals but no wheat to feed humanity. Humanity used to eat like the animals, but when Christ, the perfect human, came, he brought bread from heaven so that humanity would be fed with the food of humanity. The rulers thought they did what they did by their own power and will, but the Holy Spirit was secretly accomplishing everything it wanted to through them. Truth, which has existed from the beginning, is sown everywhere; and many see it being sown, but few see it being reaped.

The Virgin Birth

Some say that "Mary conceived by the Holy Spirit." They're wrong; they don't know what they're saying. When did a woman ever conceive by a woman? "Mary is the virgin whom no power defiled" is the great testimony of those Hebrews who became (the first) apostles and (the) apostolic (successors). The virgin whom no power defiled […] the powers defiled themselves. And the Lord [wouldn't] have said, "my [Father who is in] heaven" unless [he] had another father. Instead, he would simply have said ["my Father."] The Lord said to the [disciples, "…] [from] every [house] and bring into the Father's house, but don't steal (anything) from the Father's house or carry it away."

Jesus, Christ, Messiah, Nazarene

"Jesus" is a hidden name; "Christ" is a revealed name. So "Jesus" is not translated, but he's called by his name "Jesus." But the name "Christ" in Syriac is "Messiah," in Greek "Christ," and all the others have it according to their own language. "The Nazarene" reveals what's hidden. Christ has everything within himself, whether human or angel or mystery, and the Father.

The Resurrection

Those who say that the Lord died first and then arose are wrong, because he arose first and (then) he died. Anyone who doesn't first acquire the resurrection won't die. As God lives, that one would /die\! No one will hide something great and valuable in a great thing, but often someone has put countless thousands into something worth (only) a penny. It's the same with the soul; a valuable thing came to be in a contemptible body. Some are afraid that they'll arise naked. So they want to arise in the flesh, and [they] don't know that those who wear the [flesh] are naked. Those […] to strip themselves naked [are] not naked. "Flesh [and blood won't] inherit [God's] kingdom." What is it that won't inherit? That which is on us. But what is it, too, that will inherit? It is Jesus' (flesh) and blood. Because of this, he said, "Whoever doesn't eat my flesh and drink my blood doesn't have life in them." What's his flesh? It's the Word, and his blood is the Holy Spirit. Whoever has received these have food, drink, and clothing. (So) I myself disagree with the others who say, "It won't arise." Both (sides) are wrong. You who say, "the flesh won't arise," tell me what will arise, so that we may honor you. You say, "the spirit in the flesh and this other light in the flesh." (But) this saying is in the flesh too, because whatever you say, you can't say apart from the flesh. It's necessary to arise in this flesh, since everything exists in it. In this world, people are better than the clothes they wear. In the kingdom of heaven, the clothes are better than the people who wear them. Everything is purified by water and fire – the visible by the visible, the hidden by the hidden. Some things are hidden by things that are visible. There's water in water, and fire in chrism.

Seeing Jesus

Jesus took all of them by stealth, because he didn't appear as he was, but he appeared as [they'd] be able to see him. He appeared to them (in) [all these] (ways): he [appeared] to [the] great as great. He [appeared] to the small as small. He [appeared] [to the] angels as an angel, and to humans as a human. So his Word hid itself from everyone. Some did see him, thinking they were seeing themselves. But when he appeared to his disciples in glory on the mountain, he wasn't small. He became great, but he made the disciples great (too) so that they would be able to see him as great. He said on that day in the Eucharist, "You who've united the perfect light with the Holy Spirit, unite the angels with us too, with the images!" Don't despise the lamb, because without him it's impossible to see the door. No one will be able to approach the king naked.

Father, Son, and Holy Spirit

The children of the heavenly human are more numerous than those of the earthly human. If Adam has so many children, even though they die, how many children does the perfect human have – those who don't die, but are begotten all the time? The father makes a son, but it's impossible for a son to make a son, because it's impossible for someone who's been born to beget (sons); the son begets brothers, not sons. All who are begotten in the world are begotten physically, and the others in […] are begotten by him […] out there to the human […] in the […] heavenly place […] it from the mouth […] the Word came out from there they would be nourished from the mouth [and] become perfect. The perfect are conceived and begotten through a kiss. Because of this we kiss each other too, conceiving from the grace within each other. There were three who traveled with the Lord all the time: His mother Mary, her sister, and Magdalene, who is called his companion; because Mary is his sister, his mother, and his partner. "The Father" and "The Son" are single names; "the Holy Spirit" is a double name, because they're everywhere. They're in heaven, they're below, they're hidden, and they're revealed. The Holy Spirit is revealed below and hidden in heaven.

Those who are holy are served through the evil powers, because the Holy Spirit has blinded them so that they think they're serving a (regular) human when they're (really) working for the holy ones. So a disciple asked the Lord one day about a worldly thing. He told him, "Ask your Mother, and she'll give you from someone else." The apostles said to the disciples, "May our entire offering acquire salt." They called […] "salt." Without it, the offering doesn't [become] acceptable. But Wisdom [is] childless; because of this [she's] called […], this of salt, the place they'll […] in their own way. The Holy Spirit […] […] many children. What belongs to the father belongs to the son, and he himself – the son – as long as he's little, is not entrusted with what's his. When he becomes a man, his father gives him everything that belongs to him. Those who've been begotten by the Spirit and go astray, go astray through it too. Because of this, through this one Spirit it blazes, that is, the fire, and it's extinguished. Echamoth is one thing and Echmoth another. Echamoth is simply Wisdom, but Echmoth is the Wisdom of Death, which knows death. This is called "the little Wisdom."

Humans and Animals

There are animals that submit to humans, like the calf, the donkey, and others of this kind. Others are not submissive, and live alone in the wilderness. Humanity ploughs the field with the submissive animals, and consequently nourishes itself and the animals, whether submissive or not. That's what it's like with the perfect human: they plough with the submissive powers, preparing for everyone that will exist. So because of this the whole place stands, whether the good or the evil, and the right and the left. The Holy Spirit shepherds everyone and rules all the powers – those that are submissive, those that [aren't], and those that are alone – because truly it […] confines them [so that …] want to, they won't be able to [leave]. [The one who's been] formed [is beautiful, but] you'd find his children being noble forms. If he weren't formed but begotten, you'd find that his seed was noble. But now he was formed, and he begot. What nobility is this? First there was adultery, and then murder; and he (Cain) was begotten in adultery, because he was the son of the serpent. Because of this he became a murderer like his father too, and he killed his brother (Abel). Every partnership between those who are dissimilar is adultery.

Becoming Christians

God is a dyer. Like the good dyes – they're called true – die with what's been dyed in them, so it is with those who were dyed by God. Because his dyes are immortal, they become immortal by means of his colors. But God baptizes in water. It's impossible for anyone to see anything that really exists unless they become like them. It's not like the person in the world who sees the sun without becoming a sun, and who sees heaven and earth and everything else without becoming them. That's the way it is. But you've seen something of that place, and have become them. You saw the Spirit, you became spirit; you saw Christ, you became Christ; you saw [the Father, you] will become father. Because of this, [here] you see everything and don't [see yourself], but you see yourself [there], because you'll [become] what you see. Faith receives; love gives. [No one will be able to] [receive] without faith, and no one will be able to give without love. So we believe in order that we may receive, but we give in order that we may love, since anyone who doesn't give with love doesn't get anything out of it. Whoever hasn't received the Lord is still a Hebrew. The apostles before us called (him) "Jesus the Nazarene Messiah," that is, "Jesus the Nazarene Christ." The last name is "Christ," the first is "Jesus," the middle one is "the Nazarene." "Messiah" has two meanings: both "Christ" and "the measured." "Jesus" in Hebrew is "the redemption." "Nazara" is "the truth." So "the Nazarene" is "the truth." "Christ" is the one who was measured. "The Nazarene" and "Jesus" are the ones who were measured. A pearl doesn't become less valuable if it's cast down into the mud, nor will it become more valuable if it's anointed with balsam; but it's valuable to its owner all the time. That's what it's like with God's children: no matter where they are, they're still valuable to their Father. If you say, "I'm a Jew," no one will be moved. If you say, "I'm a Roman," no one will be disturbed. If you say, "I'm a Greek," "a Barbarian," "a slave," ["a free person,"] no one will be troubled. [If] you [say,] "I'm a Christian," the […] will tremble. If only […] of] this kind, this one [who …] won't be able to endure [hearing] his name. God is a human-eater. Because of this, the human is [sacrificed] to him. Before the human was sacrificed, animals were sacrificed, because those to whom they were sacrificed weren't gods. Vessels of glass and pottery come into being by means of fire. But if glass vessels break they're remade, because they came into being by means of a breath, but if pottery vessels break they're destroyed, because they came into being without breath. A donkey turning a millstone traveled a hundred miles. When it was released, it still found itself in the same place. Many people travel, but don't get anywhere. When evening came, they saw neither city nor village, nor anything created or natural, nor power nor angel. The wretches worked in vain. The Eucharist is Jesus, because in Syriac he's called "Pharisatha," that is, "the one who's spread out," because Jesus came to crucify the world. The Lord went into Levi's place of dyeing. He took seventy-two colors and threw them into the vat. He brought all of them out white and said, "That's the way the Son of Humanity has come [as] a dyer." The Wisdom who is called "the barren" is the Mother [of the angels] and [the] companion of the [… Mary] Magdalene [… loved her] more than the disciples [… he] kissed her on her [… many] times. The rest of […] […] they said to him, "Why do you love her more than all of us?" The Savior said to them in reply, "Why don't I love you like her? When a person who's blind and one who sees are both in the dark, they're no different from one another. When the light comes, the one who sees will see the light, and the one who's blind will remain in the dark." The Lord said, "Blessed is the one who exists before existing, because they who exist did exist, and will exist." The superiority of humanity isn't revealed, but exists in what's hidden. So it (humanity) masters animals that are stronger, that are greater in terms of that which is revealed and that which is hidden. This allows them to survive; but if humanity separates from them (the animals), they kill, bite, and eat each other, because they didn't find food. But now they've found food because humanity has worked the earth. If someone goes down into the water and comes up without having received anything, and says, "I'm a Christian," they've borrowed the name at interest. But if they receive the Holy Spirit, they have the gift of the name. Whoever has received a gift doesn't have it taken away, but whoever has borrowed it at interest has to give it back. That's what it's like when someone comes into being in a mystery.

The Mystery of Marriage
[The] mystery of marriage [is] great, because [without] it the world would [not exist]; because [the] structure of [the world …], but the structure [… the marriage]. Think about the [intimate …] defiled, because it has […] power. Its image exists in a [defilement]. The impure spirits take male and female [forms]. The males are those that are intimate with the souls which dwell in a female form, and the females are those that mingle with those in a male form through disobedience. No one will be able to escape being bound by them without receiving a male power and a female one – the groom and the bride – in the image of the bridal chamber. When the foolish females see a male sitting alone, they jump on him, play with him, and defile him. In the same way, when the foolish males see a beautiful female sitting alone, they seduce and coerce her, wanting to defile her. But if they see the husband and his wife sitting together, the females can't go inside the husband, nor the males inside the wife. That's what it's like when the image unites with the angel; no one will be able to dare to go inside the [male] or the female.

Overcoming the World
Whoever comes out of the world can no longer be bound because they were in the world. They're revealed to be above the desire of the [… and] fear. They're master over […] they're better than envy. If […] come, they (the powers) bind and choke [them]. How will [they] be able to escape the [great powers …]? How will they be able to […]? There are some who [say], "We're faithful," in order that […] [impure spirit] and demon, because if they had the Holy Spirit, no impure spirit would cling to them. Don't fear the flesh, nor love it. If you fear it, it'll master you; if you love it, it'll swallow and choke you. Someone exists either in this world, or in the resurrection, or in the middle places. May I never be found there! There's both good and evil in this world. Its good things aren't good, and its evil things aren't evil. But there's an evil after this world which is truly evil: that which is called "the middle." It's death. While we're in this world, it's right for us to acquire the resurrection for ourselves, so that when we're stripped of the flesh we'll be found in the rest and not travel in the middle, because many stray on the way. It's good to come out of the world before one sins. There are some who neither want to nor can, but others who, if they wanted to, (still) wouldn't benefit, because they didn't act. The wanting makes them sinners. But (even) if they don't want, justice will (still) be hidden from them. It's not the will, and it's not the act. An apostle saw [in a] vision some people confined in a burning house, and bound with burning […], thrown […] of the burning […] them in […] and they said to them [… able] to be saved […] they didn't want to, and they received […] punishment, which is called "the [outer] darkness," because it […]. The soul and the spirit came into being from water and fire. The offspring of the bridal chamber was from water and fire and light. The fire is the chrism, the light is the fire. I'm not talking about that formless fire, but of the other one whose form is white, which is bright and beautiful, and which gives beauty. Truth didn't come into the world naked, but it came in types and images. It (the world) won't receive it in any other way. There's a rebirth, and an image of rebirth. It's truly necessary to be begotten again through the image. What's the resurrection and the image? Through the image it's necessary for it to arise. The bridal chamber and the image? Through the image it's necessary for them to enter the truth, which is the restoration. It's not only necessary for those who acquire the name of the Father and the Son and the Holy Spirit, but they too have been acquired for you. If someone doesn't acquire them, the name will also be taken from them. But they're received in the chrism of the […] of the power of the cross. The apostles called this "[the] right and the left," because this person is no longer a [Christian], but a Christ. The Lord [did] everything in a mystery: a baptism, a chrism, a Eucharist, a redemption, a bridal chamber […] he [said], "I came to make [the below] like the [above and the outside] like the [inside, and to unite] them in the place." […] here through [types …] Those who say, "[…] there's one above […]," they're wrong, because] what's revealed is that […], that [which] is called "what's below," and what's hidden is to it what's above it, because it's good, and they say "inside and what's outside and what's outside the outside." So the Lord called destruction "the outer darkness." There's nothing outside it. He said, "My Father who's hidden." He said, "Enter your closet, shut the door behind you, and pray to your Father who's hidden," that is, the one who's within all of them. But the one who's within all of them is the fullness. Beyond that, there's nothing else within. This is what's called "that which is above them." Before Christ, some came from where they were no longer able to enter, and they went where they were no longer able to come out. Then Christ came. He brought out those who entered, and brought in those who went out.

Adam, Eve, and the Bridal Chamber
When Eve was [in] Adam, death didn't exist. When she separated from him, death came into being. If he [enters] again and receives it for himself, there will be no death. "[My] God, my God, why, Lord, [have] you forsaken me?" He said this on the cross, because he was divided in that place. […] that he was begotten through that which […] from God. The […] from the dead […] exists, but […] he's perfect […] of flesh, but this […] is true flesh […] isn't true, [but …] image of the true. A bridal chamber isn't for the animals, nor for the slaves, nor for the impure, but it's for free people and virgins. We're begotten again through the Holy Spirit, but we're begotten through Christ by two things. We're anointed through the Spirit. When we were begotten, we were united. Without light, no one can see themselves in water or in a mirror; nor again will you be able to see in light without water or mirror. Because of this, it's necessary to baptize in both: in the light and in the water, but the light is the chrism. There were three houses of offering in Jerusalem. The one which opens to the west is called "the Holy." The other one, which opens to the south, is called "the Holy of the Holy." The third, which opens to the east, is called "the Holy of the Holies," the place where the high priest enters alone. Baptism is "the Holy" house. [Redemption] is "the Holy of the Holy." "The [Holy] of the Holies" is the bridal chamber. The [baptism] includes the resurrection [with] the redemption. The redemption is in the bridal chamber. But [the] bridal chamber is better than […] You won't find its […] those who pray […] Jerusalem. […] Jerusalem who [… Jerusalem], being seen […] these that are called "[the Holies] of the Holies" [… the] veil torn […] bridal chamber except the image [… which] [is above. So] its veil was torn from top to bottom, because it was necessary for some from below to go up above. The powers can't see those who have put on the perfect light, and they can't bind them. But one will put on that light in the mystery of the union. If the female wouldn't have been separated from the male, she wouldn't have died with the male. His separation was the beginning of death. Because of this, Christ came to repair the separation that existed since the beginning by uniting the two again. He'll give life to those who died as a result of the separation by uniting them. Now, the wife unites with her husband in the bridal chamber, and those who have united in the bridal chamber won't be separated any longer. Because of this, Eve separated from Adam, because she didn't unite with him in the bridal chamber. It was through a breath that Adam's soul came into being. Its partner was the spirit. That which was given to him was his mother. His soul was [taken] and he was given [life] (Eve) in its place. When he was united […] words that were better than the powers, and they envied him […] spiritual partner […] hidden […] that is, the […] themselves […] bridal chamber so that […] Jesus appeared [… the] Jordan, the [fullness of the kingdom] of heaven. He who [was begotten] before everything was begotten again. He [who was anointed] first was anointed again. He who was redeemed, redeemed again. If it's necessary to speak of a mystery: the Father of everything united with the virgin who came down, and a fire enlightened him on that day. He revealed the great bridal chamber, so his body came into being on that day. He came out of the bridal chamber like the one who came into being from the groom and the bride. That's the way Jesus established everything within himself. It's also necessary for each of the disciples to enter into his rest through these things. Adam came into being from two virgins: from the Spirit and from the virgin earth. So Christ was begotten from a virgin, to rectify the fall that occurred in the beginning. There are two trees growing in Paradise. One begets [animals], the other begets humans. Adam [ate] from the tree that begot

animals, [and he] became an animal, and he begot [animals]. So Adam's children worship the [animals]. The tree [...] is fruit [...] this they [...] ate the [...] fruit of the [...] beget humans [...] of the human of [...] God makes the human, [... humans] make [God]. That's what it's like in the world: humans make gods and worship their creation. It would be better for the gods to worship humans! The truth is that the work of humankind comes from their power, so they're called "the powers." Their works are their children, who come into being through rest; so their power exists in their works, but the rest is revealed in their children. And you'll find that this extends to the image. And this is the person in the image: they do their works through their power, but they beget their children through rest. In this world, the slaves work for the free. In the kingdom of heaven, the free will serve the slaves. The children of the bridal chamber will serve the children of the [marriage. The] children of the bridal chamber have a [single] name: "Rest." [Being] together they don't need to take form, [because they have] contemplation [...] they're many [...] with those who are in the [...] the glories of the [...] not [...] them [...] go down to the [water ...] they'll redeem themselves [...] that is, those who have [...] in his name, because he said: "[That's the way] we'll fulfill all righteousness."

Baptism, Chrism, Eucharist, Bridal Chamber
Those who say that they'll die first and (then) they'll rise are wrong. If they don't first receive the resurrection while they're living, they won't receive anything when they die. It's the same when they talk about baptism and they say "Baptism is a great thing," because those who receive it will live. Philip the apostle said, "Joseph the carpenter planted a garden because he needed wood for his trade. It was he who made the cross from the trees he planted, and his offspring hung from what he planted. His offspring was Jesus, and the plant was the cross." But the Tree of Life is in the middle of Paradise, and from the olive tree came the chrism, and from that the resurrection. This world eats corpses. All that are eaten in it die also. Truth eats life, so no one nourished by [Truth] will die. Jesus came from that place, he brought food from there, and to those who wanted, he gave them [to eat, so that] they won't die. [God ...] a Paradise, [human ...] Paradise, there are [...] and [...] of God [...] those in [it ...] I wish that [Paradise ...] they'll say to me, "[... eat] this," or "don't eat [that ...] wish." The tree of knowledge is the place where I'll eat everything. It killed Adam, but here it makes humanity live. The Law was the tree. It has the power to give the knowledge of good and evil. It neither kept them from evil nor placed them in the good, but it created death for those who ate from it; because when it said, "Eat this, don't eat that," it became the beginning of death. The chrism is better than baptism, since we're called "Christians" because of the chrism, not because of baptism. And it was because of the chrism that Christ was named, because the Father anointed the Son, and the Son anointed the apostles, and the apostles anointed us. Whoever is anointed has everything: the resurrection, the light, the cross, the Holy Spirit. The Father gave this to him in the bridal chamber, and he received it. The Father was in the Son and the Son in the Father. This is [the kingdom] of heaven. The Lord said [it] well: "Some went to the kingdom of heaven laughing and they came out [...] a Christian [...] and as soon as [... went down] into the water and he [...] everything about [...] it's [a] game, [but ... disregard] this [...] to the kingdom of [heaven ...] if they disregard [...] and if they scorn it as a game, [... out] laughing. It's the same way with the bread and the cup and the oil, though there's one better than these. The world came into being through a transgression, because the one who created it wanted to create it imperishable and immortal. He fell away and didn't get what he wanted, because the world wasn't imperishable, and the one who created it wasn't imperishable; because things aren't imperishable, but rather children. Nothing will be able to receive imperishability without becoming a child. But whoever can't receive, how much more will they be unable to give? The cup of prayer has wine and water, since it's laid down as the type of the blood over which they give thanks. It fills with the Holy Spirit, and it belongs to the completely perfect human. Whenever we drink this, we'll receive the perfect human. The living water is a body. It's necessary for us to put on the living human. So coming down to the water, they strip themselves so that they'll put on that one. A horse begets a horse, a human begets a human, and a god begets god. It's the same way with [the groom] and [brides too]. They [come into being] from the [...] No Jew [...] from [...] exists and [...] from the Jews [...] the Christians [...] called these [...] "the chosen race of [...]" and "the true human" and "the Son of the Human" and "the seed of the Son of the Human." This true race is known in the world. These are the places where the children of the bridal chamber exist. In this world, union is between male and female, the place of power and weakness; in the (eternal) age, the union is like something else, but we refer to them by the same names. There are other names, however, that are above every name that's named, and they're better than the strong, because where there's force, there are those who are even more powerful. They're not (two) different things, but they're both the same thing. This is what won't be able to come down upon the fleshly heart. Isn't it necessary for everyone who has everything to know themselves completely? Some who don't know themselves won't be able to enjoy what they have, but those who've come to understand themselves will enjoy them. Not only won't they be able to bind the perfect human, they won't be able to see them (the perfect human), because if they see them they'll bind them. There's no other way for someone to acquire this grace for themselves [except by] putting on the perfect light [and] becoming the perfect [light. Whoever has put it on] themselves will go [...] this is the perfect [...] for us to become [...] before we came to [...] whoever receives everything [...] these places, they'll be able to [...] that place, but they'll [... the middle] as incomplete. Only Jesus knows the end of this one. The holy man (priest) is completely holy, down to his (very) body, because if he receives the bread he'll make it holy, or the cup, or anything else that he takes and purifies. Why won't he purify the body too? As Jesus perfected the water of baptism, that's the way he poured out death. So we go down into the water, but we don't go down into death, so that we won't be poured out into the spirit of the world. When it blows, the winter comes. When the Holy Spirit breathes, the summer comes. Whoever knows the truth is a free person, and the free person doesn't sin, because "whoever sins is the slave of sin." Truth is the Mother, but knowledge is the joining. Those who aren't given to sin are called "free" by the world. These who aren't given to sin are made proud by the knowledge of the truth. That's what makes them free and exalts them over everything. But "love builds up," and whoever has been made free through knowledge is a slave because of love for those who aren't yet able to attain [the] freedom of knowledge, [but] knowledge makes them able [to] become free. Love [...] anything its own [...] it [...] its own. It never [says "..."] or "this is mine," [but "...] are yours." Spiritual love is wine with fragrance. All those who will anoint themselves with it enjoy it. While those who are anointed stay around, those who are nearby also enjoy it. If those who are anointed with ointment leave them and go, those who aren't anointed but are only nearby remain in their stench. The Samaritan didn't give anything to the wounded man except wine with oil. It wasn't anything but the ointment, and it healed the wounds, because "love covers a multitude of sins." The children to whom a woman gives birth will look like the man she loves. If it's her husband, they look like her husband; if it's an adulterer, they look like the adulterer. Often, if a woman sleeps with her husband because she has to, but her heart is with the adulterer with whom she is intimate and she bears a child, the child she bears looks like the adulterer. But you who exist with the Son of God, don't love the world; rather, love the Lord, so that those you'll beget may not come to look like the world, but will come to look like the Lord. The human unites with the human, the horse unites with the horse, the donkey unites with the donkey. Species unite [with] similar species. That's what it's like when spirit unites with spirit, the [Word] is intimate with the Word, [and light is] intimate [with light. If you] become human, [it's the human who will] love you. If you become [spirit], it's the Spirit who will unite with you. [If] you become Word, it's the Word that will unite with you. If [you] become light, it's the light which will be intimate with you. If you become one of those from above, those from above will rest upon you. If you become horse or donkey or calf or dog or sheep or any other of the animals which are outside or below, neither human nor spirit nor Word nor light nor those from above nor those inside will be able to love you. They won't be able to rest within you, and you'll have no part in them. Whoever is an unwilling slave will be able to be made free. Whoever has become free by the grace of their master and has sold themselves (back) into slavery won't be able to be made free any longer.

Spiritual Growth
The world is farmed through four things. They gather into barns through water, earth, wind, and light. And in the same way, God farms through four things too: through faith, hope, love, and knowledge. Our earth is the faith in which we're rooted. [And] the [water] is the hope through which [we're] nourished. The wind is the love through which we grow. And the light [is] the knowledge through which we [ripen]. Grace exists in [four kinds. It's] earthly, it's [heavenly, ...] the heaven of the heaven [...] through [....] Blessed is the one who hasn't [...] a soul. This one is Jesus Christ. He went all over the place and didn't burden anyone. So, blessed is someone like this; they're a perfect person, because the Word tells us about how hard it is to keep up. How will we be able to achieve such a great thing? How will he give rest to everyone? First and foremost, it's not right to cause anyone grief – whether great or small, or faithless or faithful – and then give rest to those who are (already) at rest among those who are well off. There are some who benefit from giving rest to the one who's well off. Whoever does good can't give rest to them because they can't just do whatever they want; they can't cause grief because they can't cause distress, but sometimes the

one who's well off causes them grief. They're not like that, but it's their (own) evil that causes them grief. Whoever has the nature (of the perfect person) gives joy to the one who's good, but some grieve terribly at this. A householder acquired everything, whether child or slave or cattle or dog or pig or wheat [or] barley or straw or hay or […] or meat and acorn. [But they're] wise and understand what to feed each [one]. To the children they served bread […] but [… the] slaves they served […], and to the cattle [they threw barley] and straw and hay. To [the] dogs they threw bones [and] to [the pigs] they threw acorns and slops. That's what it's like with the disciple of God. If they're wise, they understand what it means to be a disciple. The bodily forms won't deceive them, but they'll look at the condition of the soul of each one and speak with them. There are many animals in the world that are made in human form. They (the disciple) recognizes them. To the pigs they'll throw acorns, but to the cattle they'll throw barley with straw and hay. To the dogs they'll throw bones, to the slaves they'll give the appetizer, and to the children they'll give the perfect (food). There's the Son of Humanity, and there's the son of the Son of Humanity. The Lord is the Son of Humanity, and the son of the Son of Humanity is the one who creates through the Son of Humanity. The Son of Humanity received from God the ability to create. He (also) has the ability to beget. The one who received the ability to create is a creature; the one who received the ability to beget is begotten. The one who creates can't beget; the one who begets can create. They say, "The one who creates, begets." But what they beget is a creature. [So] their begotten aren't their children, but they're […]. The one who creates works [publicly], and are themselves [revealed]. The one who begets, begets [secretly], and they're hidden […] the image. [Again], the one who [creates, creates] publicly, but the one who begets, [begets] children secretly. No [one will be able to] know [when the husband] and the wife are intimate with each other, except they themselves, because the marriage of the world is a mystery for those who have married. If the defiled marriage is hidden, how much more is the undefiled marriage a true mystery! It's not fleshly, but pure. It isn't of desire, but of the will. It isn't of the darkness or the night, but it's of the day and the light. If a marriage is stripped naked, it becomes pornography – not only if the bride receives the seed of another man, but even if she leaves the chamber and is seen, she commits adultery. Let her reveal herself to her father, her mother, the best man, and the groom's children. They're allowed to enter the bridal chamber every day. But let the others yearn just to hear her voice and enjoy her perfume, and, like dogs, let them eat the crumbs that fall from the table. Grooms and brides belong to the bridal chamber. No one will be able to see the groom and the bride unless [they become] such.

Uprooting Evil
When Abraham […] to see what he was going to see, [he] circumcised the flesh of the foreskin, [telling] us that it's necessary to destroy the flesh. [Most (things)] of [the] world can stand up and live as long as their [insides are hidden. If they're revealed], they die, as [illustrated] by the visible human. [As long as] the human's guts are hidden, the human is alive. If their guts are exposed and come out of them, the human will die. It's the same way with the tree. While its root is hidden, it blossoms and grows. If its root is exposed, the tree dries up. That's what it's like with everything that's born in the world, not only the revealed, but also the hidden; because as long as the root of evil is hidden, it's strong. But if it's recognized, it dissolves, and if it's revealed, it dies. So the Word says, "Already the axe is laid at the root of the trees." It won't (just) cut, (because) that which will be cut blossoms again. Rather, the axe digs down into the ground until it brings up the root. Jesus plucked out the root completely, but others did so partially. As for us, let every one of us dig down to the root of the evil within and pluck it out from its root in us. It'll be uprooted if we recognize it. But if we don't recognize it, it takes root within us and bears its fruit in us. It masters us, and we're forced to serve it. It captures us so that we do what we do [not] want to; and we do [not] do what we want to. [It's] powerful because we haven't recognized it. It's active as long as [it exists]. [Ignorance] is the mother of [all evil]. Ignorance will cause [death, because] what exists from [ignorance] neither did exist nor [does exist], nor will they come into being […] they'll be perfected when the whole truth is revealed, because the truth is like ignorance. When it's hidden, it rests within itself, but if it's revealed and recognized, it's glorified inasmuch as it's stronger than ignorance and error. It gives freedom. The Word says, "If you'll know the truth, the truth will make you free." Ignorance is slavery; knowledge is freedom. If we know the truth, we'll find the fruits of truth within us. If we unite with it, it'll receive our fullness. Now we have what's revealed of creation. We say, "Those who are strong are honorable, but those who are hidden are weak and scorned." That's what it's like with those who are revealed of the truth; they're weak and scorned, but the hidden are strong and honorable. But the mysteries of the truth are revealed in types and images. The chamber is hidden, however; it's the Holy in the Holy. At first, the veil concealed how God managed the creation, but when the veil is torn and what's inside is revealed, then this house will be left behind [like] a desert, or rather, will be [destroyed]. And all divinity will flee [from] these places, not into the Holies [of the] Holies, because it won't be able to unite with the pure [light] and the [flawless] fullness, [but] it'll come to be under the wings of the cross [and under] its arms. This ark will [become their] salvation when the flood of water surges over them. If some belong to the priesthood, they'll be able to enter inside the veil with the high priest. So the veil wasn't torn only at the top, since it would've been open only to those at the top; nor was it torn only at the bottom, since it would've been revealed only to those at the bottom; but it was torn from the top to the bottom. Those at the top opened to us the bottom, so that we'll enter the secret of the truth. This truly is what's honorable, what's strong, but we'll enter there through scorned types and weaknesses. They're humbled in the presence of the perfect glory. There's glory that's better than glory; there's power that's better than power. So the perfect was opened to us with the secrets of the truth, and the Holies of the Holies were revealed, and the chamber invited us in. As long as it's hidden, evil is inactive, but it hasn't been removed from among the Holy Spirit's seed. They're slaves of evil. But whenever it's revealed, then the perfect light will flow out upon everyone, and all of them who are in it will [receive the chrism]. Then the slaves will be made free and the captives will be redeemed. "[Every] plant [which] my Father who's in heaven [hasn't] planted [will be] uprooted." Those who are separated will unite […] will be filled.

Conclusion
Everyone who will [enter] the chamber will kindle their [lamp], because [it's] like the marriages which are […] happen at night, the fire […] at night and is put out. But the mysteries of this marriage are fulfilled in the day and the light. Neither that day nor its light ever sets. If anyone becomes a child of the bridal chamber, they'll receive the light. If anyone doesn't receive it while they're here, they won't be able to receive it in the other place. Whoever will receive that light won't be seen or bound, and no one will be able to trouble someone like this even while they dwell in the world. Moreover, when they leave the world, they've already received the Truth in the images. The world has become the (eternal) ages, because the (eternal) age is the fullness for them, and it's like this: it's revealed to them alone. It's not hidden in the darkness and the night, but it's hidden in a perfect day and a holy light.

The Secret Gospel of Mark

From the letters of the most holy Clement, the author of the Stromateis. To Theodore.

You did well in silencing the unspeakable teachings of the Carpocrations. For these are the *"wandering stars"* referred to in the prophecy, who wander from the narrow road of the commandments into a boundless abyss of the carnal and bodily sins. For, priding themselves in knowledge, as they say, *"of the deep things of Satan"*, they do not know that they are casting themselves away into *"the nether world of the darkness"* of falsity, and boasting that they are free, they have become slaves of servile desires. Such men are to be opposed in all ways and altogether. For, even if they should say something true, one who loves the truth should not, even so, agree with them. For not all true things are the truth, nor should that truth which merely seems true according to human opinions be preferred to the true truth, that according to the faith.

Now of the things they keep saying about the divinely inspired Gospel according to Mark, some are altogether falsifications, and others, even if they do contain some true elements, nevertheless are not reported truly. For the true things, being mixed with inventions, are falsified, so that, as the saying goes, even the salt loses its savor.

As for Mark, then, during Peter's stay in Rome he wrote an account of the Lord's doings, not, however, declaring all of them, nor yet hinting at the secret ones, but selecting what he thought most useful for increasing the faith of those who were being instructed. But when Peter died a martyr, Mark came over to Alexandria, bringing both his own notes and those of Peter, from which he transferred to his former book the things suitable to whatever makes for progress toward knowledge. Thus he composed a more spiritual Gospel for the use of those who were being perfected. Nevertheless, he yet did not divulge the things not to be uttered, nor did he write down the hierophantic teaching of the Lord, but to the stories already written he added yet others and, moreover, brought in certain sayings of which he knew the interpretation would, as a mystagogue, lead the hearers into the innermost sanctuary of that truth hidden by seven veils. Thus, in sum, he prepared matters, neither grudgingly nor incautiously, in my opinion, and, dying, he left his composition to the church in 1, verso Alexandria, where it even yet is most carefully guarded, being read only to those who are being initiated into the great mysteries.

But since the foul demons are always devising destruction for the race of men, Carpocrates, instructed by them and using deceitful arts, so enslaved a certain presbyter of the church in Alexandria that he got from him a copy of the secret Gospel, which he both interpreted according to his blasphemous and carnal doctrine and, moreover, polluted, mixing with the spotless and holy words utterly shameless lies. From this mixture is drawn off the teaching of the Carpocratians.

To them, therefore, as I said above, one must never give way; nor, when they put forward their falsifications, should one concede that the secret Gospel is by Mark, but should even deny it on oath. For, *"Not all true things are to be said to all men"*. For this reason the Wisdom of God, through Solomon, advises, *"Answer the fool from his folly"*, teaching that the light of the truth should be hidden from those who are mentally blind. Again it says, *"From him who has not shall be taken away"*, and *"Let the fool walk in darkness"*. But we are *"children of Light"*, having been illuminated by *"the dayspring"* of the spirit of the Lord *"from on high"*, and *"Where the Spirit of the Lord is"*, it says, *"there is liberty"*, for *"All things are pure to the pure"*.

To you, therefore, I shall not hesitate to answer the questions you have asked, refuting the falsifications by the very words of the Gospel. For example, after *"And they were in the road going up to Jerusalem"* and what follows, until *"After three days he shall arise"*, the secret Gospel brings the following material word for word:

"And they come into Bethany. And a certain woman whose brother had died was there. And, coming, she prostrated herself before Jesus and says to him, 'Son of David, have mercy on me.' But the disciples rebuked her. And Jesus, being angered, went off with her into the garden where the tomb was, and straightway a great cry was heard from the tomb. And going near, Jesus rolled away the stone from the door of the tomb. And straightaway, going in where the youth was, he stretched forth his hand and raised him, seizing his hand. But the youth, looking upon him, loved him and began to beseech him that he might be with him. And going out of the tomb, they came into the house of the youth, for he was rich. And after six days Jesus told him what to do, and in the evening the youth comes to him, wearing a linen cloth over his naked body. And he remained with him that night, for Jesus taught him the mystery of the Kingdom of God. And thence, arising, he returned to the other side of the Jordan."

After these words follows the text, *"And James and John come to him"*, and all that section. But *"naked man with naked man,"* and the other things about which you wrote, are not found.

And after the words, *"And he comes into Jericho,"* the secret Gospel adds only, *"And the sister of the youth whom Jesus loved and his mother and Salome were there, and Jesus did not receive them."* But the many other things about which you wrote both seem to be, and are, falsifications.

Now the true explanation, and that which accords with the true philosophy ...

Apocalypse of Adam

The revelation which Adam taught his son Seth in the seven hundreth year, saying:

Listen to my words, my son Seth. When God had created me out of the earth, along with Eve, your mother, I went about with her in a glory which she had seen in the aeon from which we had come forth. She taught me a word of knowledge of the eternal God. And we resembled the great eternal angels, for we were higher than the god who had created us and the powers with him, whom we did not know.

Then God, the ruler of the aeons and the powers, divided us in wrath. Then we became two aeons. And the glory in our heart(s) left us, me and your mother Eve, along with the first knowledge that breathed within us. And it (glory) fled from us; it entered into [...] great [...] which had come forth, not from this aeon from which we had come forth, I and Eve your mother. But it (knowledge) entered into the seed of great aeons. For this reason I myself have called you by the name of that man who is the seed of the great generation or from whom (it comes). After those days, the eternal knowledge of the God of truth withdrew from me and your mother Eve. Since that time, we learned about dead things, like men. Then we recognized the God who had created us. For we were not strangers to his powers. And we served him in fear and slavery. And after these things, we became darkened in our heart(s). Now I slept in the thought of my heart.

And I saw three men before me whose likeness I was unable to recognize, since they were not the powers of the God who had created us. They surpassed [...] glory, and [...] men [...] saying to me, "Arise, Adam, from the sleep of death, and hear about the aeon and the seed of that man to whom life has come, who came from you and from Eve, your wife."

When I had heard these words from the great men who were standing before me, then we sighed, I and Eve, in our heart(s). And the Lord, the God who had created us, stood before us. He said to us, "Adam, why were you (both) sighing in your hearts? Do you not know that I am the God who created you? And I breathed into you a spirit of life as a living soul." Then darkness came upon our eyes.

Then the God who created us, created a son from himself and Eve, your mother. I knew sweet desire for your mother, for [...] in the thought of my [...] I knew a sweet desire for your mother. Then the vigor of our eternal knowledge was destroyed in us, and weakness pursued us. Therefore the days of our life became few. For I knew that I had come under the authority of death.

Now then, my son Seth, I will reveal to you the things which those men whom I saw before me at first revealed to me: after I have completed the times of this generation and the years of the generation have been accomplished, then [...] slave [...].

For rain-showers of God the almighty will be poured forth, so that he might destroy all flesh [of God the almighty, so that he might destroy all flesh] from the earth on account of the things that it seeks after, along with those from the seed of the men to whom passed the life of the knowledge which came from me and Eve, your mother. For they were strangers to him. Afterwards, great angels will come on high clouds, who will bring those men into the place where the spirit of life dwells [...] glory [...] there, [...] come from heaven to earth. Then the whole multitude of flesh will be left behind in the waters.

Then God will rest from his wrath. And he will cast his power upon the waters, and he will give power to his sons and their wives by means of the ark along with the animals, whichever he pleased, and the birds of heaven, which he called and released upon the earth. And God will say to Noah - whom the generations will call 'Deucalion' - "Behold, I have protected <you> in the ark, along with your wife and your sons and their wives and their animals and the birds of heaven, which you called and released upon the earth. Therefore I will give the earth to you - you and your sons. In kingly fashion you will rule over it - you and your sons. And no seed will come from you of the men who will not stand in my presence in another glory."

Then they will become as the cloud of the great light. Those men will come who have been cast forth from the knowledge of the great aeons and the angels. They will stand before Noah and the aeons. And God will say to Noah, "Why have you departed from what I told you? You have created another generation so that you might scorn my power." Then Noah will say, "I shall testify before your might that the generation of these men did not come from me nor from my sons. [...] knowledge.

And he will [...] those men and bring them into their proper land, and build them a holy dwelling place. And they will be called by that name and dwell there six hundred years in a knowledge of imperishability. And the angels of the great Light will dwell with them. No foul deed will dwell in their heart(s), but only the knowledge of God.

Then Noah will divide the whole earth among his sons, Ham and Japheth and Shem. He will say to them, "My sons, listen to my words. Behold, I have divided the earth among you. But serve him in fear and slavery all the days of your life. Let not your seed depart from the face of God the Almighty. [...] I and your [...] son of Noah, "My seed will be pleasing before you and before your power. Seal it by your strong hand, with fear and commandment, so that the whole seed which came forth from me may not be inclined away from you and God the Almighty, but it will serve in humility and fear of its knowledge."

Then others from the seed of Ham and Japheth will come, four hundred thousand men, and enter into another land and sojourn with those men who came forth from the great eternal knowledge. For the shadow of their power will protect those who have sojourned with them from every evil thing and every unclean desire. Then the seed of Ham and Japheth will form twelve kingdoms, and their seed also will enter into the kingdom of another people. Then [...] will take counsel [...] who are dead, of the great aeons of imperishability. And they will go to Sakla, their God. They will go in to the powers, accusing the great men who are in their glory.

They will say to Sakla, "What is the power of these men who stood in your presence, who were taken from the seed of Ham and Japheth, who will number four hundred <thousand> men? They have been received into another aeonfrom which they had come forth, and they have overturned all the glory of your power and the dominion of your hand. For the seed of Noah through his sons has done all your will, and (so have) all the powers in the aeons over which your might rules, while both those men and the ones who are sojourners in their glory have not done your will. But they have turned (aside) your whole throng."

Then the god of the aeons will give them (some) of those who serve him [...]. They will come upon that land where the great men will be who have not been defiled, nor will be defiled, by any desire. For their soul did not come from a defiled hand, but it came from a great commandment of an eternal angel. Then fire and sulphur and asphalt will be cast upon those men, and fire and (blinding) mist will come over those aeons, and the eyes of the powers of the illuminators will be darkened, and the aeons will not see them in those days. And great clouds of light will descend, and other clouds of light will come down upon them from the great aeons.

Abrasax and Sablo and Gamaliel will descend and bring those men out of the fire and the wrath, and take them above the aeons and the rulers of the powers, and take them away [...] of life [...] and take them away [...] aeons [...] dwelling place of the great [...] there, with the holy angels and the aeons. The men will be like those angels, for they are not strangers to them. But they work in the imperishable seed.

Once again, for the third time, the illuminator of knowledge will pass by in great glory, in order to leave (something) of the seed of Noah and the sons of Ham and Japheth - to leave for himself fruit-bearing trees. And he will redeem their souls from the day of death. For the whole creation that came from the dead earth will be under the authority of death. But those who reflect upon the knowledge of the eternal God in their heart(s) will not perish. For they have not received spirit from this kingdom alone, but they have received (it) from a [...] eternal angel. [...] illuminator [...] will come upon [...] that is dead [...] of Seth. And he will perform signs and wonders in order to scorn the powers and their ruler.

Then the god of the powers will be disturbed, saying, "What is the power of this man who is higher than we?" Then he will arouse a great wrath against that man. And the glory will withdraw and dwell in holy houses which it has chosen for itself. And the powers will not see it with their eyes, nor will they see the illuminator either. Then they will punish the flesh of the man upon whom the holy spirit came.

Then the angels and all the generations of the powers will use the name in error, asking, "Where did it (the error) come from?" or "Where did the words of deception, which all the powers have failed to discover, come from?"

Now the first kingdom says of him that he came from [...]. A spirit [...] to heaven. He was nourished in the heavens. He received the glory of that one and the power. He came to the bosom of his mother. And thus he came to the water.

And the second kingdom says about him that he came from a great prophet. And a bird came, took the child who was born, and brought him onto a high mountain. And he was nourished by the bird of heaven. An angel came forth there. He said to him "Arise! God has given glory to you." He received glory and strength. And thus he came to the water.

The third kingdom says of him that he came from a virgin womb. He was cast out of his city, he and his mother. He was brought to a desert place. He was nourished there. He came and received glory and strength. And thus he came to the water.

The fourth kingdom says of him that he came from a virgin. [...] Solomon sought her, he and Phersalo and Sauel and his armies, which had been sent out. Solomon himself sent his army of demons to seek out the virgin. And they did not find the one whom they sought, but the virgin who was given them. It was she whom they fetched. Solomon took her. The virgin became pregnant and gave birth to the child there. She nourished him on a border of the desert. When he had been nourished, he received glory and power from the seed from which he was begotten. And thus he came to the water.

And the fifth kingdom says of him that he came from a drop from heaven. He was thrown into the sea. The abyss received him, gave birth to him, and brought him to heaven. He received glory and power. And thus he came to the water.

And the sixth kingdom says that [...] down to the aeonwhich is below, in order to gather flowers. She became pregnant from the desire of the flowers. She gave birth to him in that place. The angels of the flower garden nourished him. He received glory there, and power. And thus he came to the water.

And the seventh kingdom says of him that he is a drop. It came from heaven to earth. Dragons brought him down to caves. He became a child. A spirit came upon him and brought him on high to the place where the drop had come forth. He received glory and power there. And thus he came to the water.

And the eighth kingdom says of him that a cloud came upon the earth and enveloped a rock. He came from it. The angels who were above the cloud nourished him. He received glory and power there. And thus he came to the water.

And the ninth kingdom says of him that from the nine Muses one separated away. She came to a high mountain and spent (some) time seated there, so that she desired herself alone in order to become androgynous. She fulfilled her desire and became pregnant from her desire. He was born. The angels who were over the desire nourished him. And he received glory there, and power. And thus he came to the water.

The tenth kingdom says of him that his god loved a cloud of desire. He begot him in his hand and cast upon the cloud above him (some) of the drop, and he was born. He received glory and power there. And thus he came to the water.

And the eleventh kingdom says that the father desired his own daughter. She herself became pregnant from her father. She cast [...] tomb out in the desert. The angel nourished him there. And thus he came to the water.

The twelfth kingdom says of him that he came from two illuminators. He was nourished there. He received glory and power. And thus he came to the water.

And the thirteenth kingdom says of him that every birth of their ruler is a word. And this word received a mandate there. He received glory and power. And thus he came to the water, in order that the desire of those powers might be satisfied.

But the generation without a king over it says that God chose him from all the aeons. He caused a knowledge of the undefiled one of truth to come to be in him. He said, "Out of a foreign air, from a great aeon, the great illuminator came forth. And he made the generation of those men whom he had chosen for himself shine, so that they could shine upon the whole aeon" Then the seed, those who will receive his name upon the water and (that) of them all, will fight against the power. And a cloud of darkness will come upon them.

Then the peoples will cry out with a great voice, saying, "Blessed is the soul of those men because they have known God with a knowledge of the truth! They shall live forever, because they have not been corrupted by their desire, along with the angels, nor have they accomplished the works of the powers, but they have stood in his presence in a knowledge of God like light that has come forth from fire and blood.

"But we have done every deed of the powers senselessly. We have boasted in the transgression of all our works. We have cried against the God of truth because all his works [...] is eternal. These are against our spirits. For now we have known that our souls will die the death."

Then a voice came to them, saying "Micheu and Michar and Mnesinous, who are over the holy baptism and the living water, why were you crying out against the living God with lawless voices and tongues without law over them, and souls full of blood and foul deeds? You are full of works that are not of the truth, but your ways are full of joy and rejoicing. Having defiled the water of life, you have drawn it within the will of the powers to whom you have been given to serve them.

"And your thought is not like that of those men whom you persecute [...] desire [...]. Their fruit does not wither. But they will be known up to the great aeons, because the words they have kept, of the God of the aeons, were not committed to the book, nor were they written. But angelic (beings) will bring them, whom all the generations of men will not know. For they will be on a high mountain, upon a rock of truth. Therefore they will be named "The Words of Imperishability and Truth," for those who know the eternal God in wisdom of knowledge and teaching of angels forever, for he knows all things."

These are the revelations which Adam made known to Seth, his son, And his son taught his seed about them. This is the hidden knowledge of Adam, which he gave to Seth, which is the holy baptism of those who know the eternal knowledge through those born of the word and the imperishable illuminators, who came from the holy seed: Yesseus, Mazareus, Yessedekeus, the Living Water.

The Odes of Solomon

Ode 1

[1] The Lord is on my head like a crown, and I shall not be without Him. [2] They wove for me a crown of truth, and it caused thy branches to bud in me. [3] For it is not like a withered crown which buddeth not: but thou livest upon my head, and thou hast blossomed upon my head. [4] Thy fruits are full-grown and perfect, they are full of thy salvation.

Ode 2

(*No part of this Ode has ever been identified.*)

Ode 3

The first words of this Ode have disappeared.

[1] . . . I put on: [2] And his members are with him. And on them do I stand, and He loves me: [3] For I should not have known how to love the Lord, if He had not loved me. [4] For who is able to distinguish love, except the one that is loved? [5] I love the Beloved, and my soul loves Him: [6] And where His rest is, there also am I; [7] And I shall be no stranger, for with the Lord Most High and Merciful there is no grudging. [8] I have been united to I-run, for the Lover has found the Beloved, [9] And because I shall love Him that, is the Son, I shall become a son; [10] For he that is joined to Him that is immortal, will also himself become immortal; [11] And he who has pleasure in the Living One, will become living. [12] This is the Spirit of the Lord, which doth not lie, which teacheth the sons of men to know His ways. [13] Be wise and understanding and vigilant. Hallelujah.

Ode 4

This Ode is important because of the historical allusion with which it commences. This may refer to the closing of the temple at Leontopolis in Egypt which would date this writing about 73 A. D.

[1] No man, O my God, changeth thy holy place; [2] And it is not (possible) that he should change it and put it in another place: because he hath no power over it: [3] For thy sanctuary thou hast designed before thou didst make (other) places: [4] That which is the older shall not be altered by those that are younger than itself. [5] Thou has given thy heart, O Lord, to thy believers: never wilt thou fail, nor be without fruits: [6] For one hour of thy Faith is more precious than all days and years. [7] For who is there that shall put on thy grace, and be hurt? [8] For thy seal is known: and thy creatures know it: and thy (heavenly) hosts possess it: and the elect archangels are clad with it. [9] Thou hast given us thy fellowship: it was not that thou wast in need of us: but that we are in need of thee: [10] Distill thy dews upon us and open thy rich fountains that pour forth to us milk and honey: [11] For there is no repentance with thee that thou shouldest repent of anything that thou hast promised: [12] And the end was revealed before thee: for what thou gavest, thou gavest freely: [13] So that thou mayest, not draw them back and take them again: [14] For all was revealed before thee as God, and ordered from the beginning before thee: and thou, O God, hast made all things. Hallelujah.

Ode 5

This Ode has strangely appeared in a speech by Salome in another ancient work called the Pistis Sophia.

[1] I will give thanks unto thee, O Lord, because I love thee; [2] O Most High, thou wilt not forsake me, for thou art my hope: [3] Freely I have received thy grace, I shall live thereby: [4] My persecutors will come and not see me: [5] A cloud of darkness shall fall on their eyes; and an air of thick gloom shall darken them: [6] And they shall have no light to see: they may not take hold upon me. [7] Let their counsel become thick darkness, and what I have cunningly devised, let it return upon their own heads: [8] For they have devised a counsel, and it did not succeed: [9] For my hope is upon the Lord, and I will not fear, and because the Lord is my salvation, I will not fear: [10] And He is as a garland on my head and I shall not be moved; even if everything should be shaken, I stand firm; [11] And if all things visible should perish, I shall not die; because the Lord is with me and I am with Him. Hallelujah.

Ode 6

First century universalism is revealed in an interesting way in verse 10.

[1] As the hand moves over the harp, and the strings speak. [2] So speaks in my members the Spirit of the Lord, and I speak by His love. [3] For it destroys what is foreign, and everything that is bitter: [4] For thus it was from the beginning and will be to the end, that nothing should be His adversary, and nothing should stand up against Him. [5] The Lord has multiplied the knowledge of Himself, and is zealous that these things should be known, which by His grace have been given to us. [6] And the praise of His name He gave us: our spirits praise His holy Spirit. [7] For there went forth a stream and became a river great and broad; [8] For it flooded and broke up everything and it brought (water) to the Temple: [9] And the restrainers of the children of men were not able to restrain it, nor the arts of those whose business it is to restrain waters; [10] For it spread over the face of the whole earth, and filled everything: and all the thirsty upon earth were given to drink of it; [11] And thirst was relieved and quenched: for from the Most High the draught was given. [12] Blessed then are the ministers of that draught who are entrusted with that water of His: [13] They have assuaged the dry lips, and the will that had fainted they have raised up; [14] And souls that were near departing they have caught back from death: [15] And limbs that had fallen they straightened and set up: [16] They gave strength for their feebleness and light to their eyes: [17] For everyone knew them in the Lord, and they lived by the water of life for ever. Hallelujah.

Ode 7

A wonderfully, simple and joyful psalm on the Incarnation.

[1] As the impulse of anger against evil, so is the impulse of joy over what is lovely, and brings in of its fruits without restraint: [2] My joy is the Lord and my impulse is toward Him: this path of mine is excellent: [3] For I have a helper, the Lord. [4] He hath caused me to know Himself, without grudging, by His simplicity: His kindness has humbled His greatness. [5] He became like me, in order that I might receive Him: [6] He was reckoned like myself in order that I might put Him on; [7] And I trembled not when I saw Him: because He was gracious to me: [8] Like my nature He became that I might learn Him and like my form, that I might not turn back from Him: [9] The Father of knowledge is the word of knowledge: [10] He who created wisdom is wiser than His works: [11] And He who created me when yet I was not knew what I should do when I came into being: [12] Wherefore He pitied me in His abundant grace: and granted me to ask from Him and to receive from His sacrifice: [13] Because He it is that is incorrupt, the fulness of the ages and the Father of them. [14] He hath given Him to be seen of them that are His, in order that they may recognize Him that made them: and that they might not suppose that they came of themselves: [15] For knowledge He hath appointed as its way, He hath widened it and extended it; and brought to all perfection; [16] And set over it the traces of His light, and I walked therein from the beginning even to the end. [17] For by Him it was wrought, and He was resting in the Son, and for its salvation He will take hold of everything; [18] And the Most High shall be known in His Saints, to announce to those that have songs of the coming of the Lord; [19] That they may go forth to meet Him, and may sing to Him with joy and with the harp of many tones: [20] The seers shall come before Him and they shall be seen before Him, [21] And they shall praise the Lord for His love: because He is near and beholdeth. [22] And hatred shall be taken from the earth, and along with jealousy it shall be drowned: [23] For ignorance hath been destroyed, because the knowledge of the Lord hath arrived. [24] They who make songs shall sing the grace of the Lord Most High; [25] And they shall bring their songs, and their heart shall be like the day: and like the excellent beauty of the Lord their pleasant song: [26] And there shall neither be anything that breathes without knowledge, nor any that is dumb: [27] For He hath given a mouth to His creation, to open the voice of the mouth towards Him, to praise Him: [28] Confess ye His power, and show forth His grace. Hallelujah.

Ode 8

Note the sudden transition from the person of the Psalmist to the person of the Lord (v. 10). This is like the canonical Psalter in style.

[1] Open ye, open ye your hearts to the exultation of the Lord: [2] And let your love be multiplied from the heart and even to the lips, [3] To bring forth fruit to the Lord [fruit], holy [fruit], and to talk with watchfulness in His light. [4] Rise up, and stand erect, ye who sometime were brought low: [5] Tell forth ye who were in silence, that your mouth hath been opened. [6] Ye, therefore, that were despised, be henceforth lifted up, because your righteousness hath been exalted. [7] For the right hand of the Lord is with you: and He is your helper: [8] And peace was prepared for you, before ever your war was. [9] Hear the word of truth, and receive the knowledge of the Most High. [10] Your flesh has not known what I am saying to you neither have your hearts known what I am showing to you. [11] Keep my secret, ye who are kept by it: [12] Keep my faith, ye who are kept by it. [13] And understand my knowledge, ye who know me in truth. [14] Love me with affection, ye who love: [15] For I do not turn away my face from them that are mine; [16] For I know them, and before they came into being I took knowledge of them, and on their faces I set my seal: [17] I fashioned their members: my own breasts I prepared for them, that they might drink my holy milk and live thereby. [18] I took pleasure in them and am not ashamed of them: [19] For my workmanship are they and the strength of my thoughts: [20] Who then shall rise up against my handiwork, or who is there that is not subject to them? [21] I willed and fashioned mind and heart: and they are mine, and by my own right hand I set my elect ones: [22] And my righteousness goeth before them and they shall not be deprived of my name, for it is with them. [23] Ask, and abound and abide in the love of the Lord, [24] And yet beloved ones in the Beloved: those

who are kept, in Him that liveth: ²⁵ And they that are saved in Him that was saved; ²⁶ And ye shall be found incorrupt in all ages to the name of your Father. Hallelujah.

Ode 9

We shall never know surely whether the wars referred to here are spiritual or actual outward wars.

¹ Open your ears and I will speak to you. Give me your souls that I may also give you my soul, ² The word of the Lord and His good pleasures, the holy thought which He has devised concerning his Messiah. ³ For in the will of the Lord is your salvation, and His thought is everlasting life; and your end is immortality. q Be enriched in God the Father, and receive the thought of the Most High. ⁵ Be strong and be redeemed by His grace. ⁶ For I announce to you peace, to you His saints; ⁷ That none of those who hear may fall in war, and that those again who have known Him may not perish, and that those who receive may not be ashamed. ⁸ An everlasting crown for ever is Truth. Blessed are they who set it on their heads: ⁹ A stone of great price is it; and there have been wars on account of the crown. ¹⁰ And righteousness hath taken it and hath given it to you. ¹¹ Put on the crown in the true covenant of the Lord. ¹² And all those who have conquered shall be written in His book. ¹³ For their book is victory which is yours. And she (Victory) sees you before her and wills that you shall be saved. Hallelujah.

Ode 10

A vigorous little Ode in which Christ Himself is the speaker.

¹ The Lord hath directed my mouth by His word: and He hath opened my heart by His light: and He hath caused to dwell in me His deathless life; ² And gave me that I might speak the fruit of His peace: ³ To convert the souls of them who are willing to come to Him; and to lead captive a good captivity for freedom. ⁴ I was strengthened and made mighty and took the world captive; ⁵ And it became to me for the praise of the Most High, and of God my Father. ⁶ And the Gentiles were gathered together who were scattered abroad. ⁷ And I was unpolluted by my love for them, because they confessed me in high places: and the traces of the light were set upon their heart: ⁸ And they walked in my life and were saved and became my people for ever and ever. Hallelujah.

Ode 11

A beautiful sketch of Paradise regained and the blessedness of those who have returned to the privileges of the fallen Adam.

¹ My heart was cloven and its flower appeared; and grace sprang up in it: and it brought forth fruit to the Lord, ² For the Most High clave my heart by His Holy Spirit and searched my affection towards Him: and filled me with His love. ³ And His opening of me became my salvation; and I ran in His way in His peace, even in the way of truth: ⁴ From the beginning and even to the end I acquired His knowledge: ⁵ And I was established upon the rock of truth, where He had set me up: ⁶ And speaking waters touched my lips from the fountain of the Lord plenteously: ⁷ And I drank and was inebriated with the living water that doth not die; ⁸ And my inebriation was not one without knowledge, but I forsook vanity and turned to the Most High my God, ⁹ And I was enriched by His bounty, and I forsook the folly which is diffused over the earth; and I stripped it off and cast it from me: ¹⁰ And the Lord renewed me in His raiment, and possessed me by His light, and from above He gave me rest in incorruption; ¹¹ And I became like the land which blossoms and rejoices in its fruits: ¹² And the Lord was like the sun shining on the face of the land; ¹³ He lightened my eyes, and my face received the dew; and my nostrils enjoyed the pleasant odour of the Lord; ¹⁴ And He carried me to His Paradise; where is the abundance of the pleasure of the Lord; ¹⁵ And I worshipped the Lord on account of His glory; and I said, Blessed, O Lord, are they who are planted in thy land! and those who have a place in thy Paradise; ¹⁶ And they grow by the fruits of the trees. And they have changed from darkness to light. ¹⁷ Behold! all thy servants are fair, who do good works, and turn away from wickedness to the pleasantness that is thine: ¹⁸ And they have turned back the bitterness of the trees from them, when they were planted in thy, land; ¹⁹ And everything became like a relic of thyself, and memorial for ever of thy faithful works. ²⁰ For there is abundant room in thy Paradise, and nothing is useless therein; ²¹ But everything is filled with fruit; glory be to thee, O God, the delight of Paradise for ever. Hallelujah.

Ode 12

An exceptionally high level of spiritual thought.

¹ He hath filled me with words of truth; that I may speak the same; ² And like the flow of waters flows truth from my mouth, and my lips show forth His fruit. ³ And He has caused His knowledge to abound in me, because the mouth of the Lord is the true Word, and the door of His light; ⁴ And the Most High hath given it to His words, which are the interpreters of His own beauty, and the repeaters of His praise, and the confessors of His counsel, and the heralds of His thought, and the chasteners of His servants. ⁵ For the swiftness of the Word is inexpressible, and like its expression is its swiftness and force; ⁶ And its course knows no limit. Never doth it fail, but it stands sure, and it knows not descent nor the way of it. ⁷ For as its work is, so is its end: for it is light and the dawning of thought; ⁸ And by it the worlds talk one to the other; and in the Word there were those that were silent; ⁹ And from it came love and concord; and they spake one to the other whatever was theirs; and they were penetrated by the Word; ¹⁰ And they knew Him who made them, because they were in concord; for the mouth of the Most High spake to them; and His explanation ran by means of it: ¹¹ For the dwelling-place of the Word is man: and its truth is love. ¹² Blessed are they who by means thereof have understood everything, and have known the Lord in His truth. Hallelujah.

Ode 13

A strange little Ode.

¹ Behold! the Lord is our mirror: open the eyes and see them in Him: and learn the manner of your face: ² And tell forth praise to His spirit: and wipe off the filth from your face: and love His holiness and clothe yourselves therewith: ³ And be without stain at all times before Him. Hallelujah.

Ode 14

This Ode is as beautiful in style as the canonical Psalter.

¹ As the eyes of a son to his father, so are my eyes, O Lord, at all times towards thee. ² For with thee are my consolations and my delight. ³ Turn not away thy mercies from me, O Lord: and take not thy kindness from me. ⁴ Stretch out to me, O Lord, at all times thy right hand: and be my guide even unto the end, according to thy good pleasure. ⁵ Let me be well-pleasing before thee, because of thy glory and because of thy name: ⁶ Let me be preserved from evil, and let thy meekness, O Lord, abide with me, and the fruits of thy love. ⁷ Teach me the Psalms of thy truth, that I may bring forth fruit in thee: ⁸ And open to me the harp of thy Holy Spirit, that with all its notes I may praise thee, O Lord. ⁹ And according to the multitude of thy tender mercies, so thou shalt give to me; and hasten to grant our petitions; and thou art able for all our needs. Hallelujah.

Ode 15

One of the loveliest Odes in this unusual collection.

¹ As the sun is the joy to them that seek for its daybreak, so is my joy the Lord; ² Because He is my Sun and His rays have lifted me up; and His light hath dispelled all darkness from my face. ³ In Him I have acquired eyes and have seen His holy day: ⁴ Ears have become mine and I have heard His truth. ⁵ The thought of knowledge hath been mine, and I have been delighted through Him. ⁶ The way of error I have left, and have walked towards Him and have received salvation from Him, without grudging. ⁷ And according to His bounty He hath given to me, and according to His excellent beauty He hath made me. ⁸ I have put on incorruption through His name: and have put oft corruption by His grace. ⁹ Death hath been destroyed before my face: and Sheol hath been abolished by my word: ¹⁰ And there hath gone up deathless life in the Lord's land, ¹¹ And it hath been made known to His faithful ones, and hath been given without stint to all those that trust in Him. Hallelujah.

Ode 16

The beauty of God's creation.

¹ As the work of the husbandman is the ploughshare: and the work of the steersman is the guidance of the ship: ² So also my work is the Psalm of the Lord: my craft and my occupation are in His praises: ³ Because His love bath nourished my heart, and even to my lips His fruits He poured out. ⁴ For my love is the Lord, and therefore I will sing unto Him: ⁵ For I am made strong in His praise, and I have faith in Him. ⁶ I will open my mouth and His spirit utter in me the glory of the Lord and His beauty; the work of His hands and the operation of His fingers: ⁷ The multitude of His mercies and the strength of His word. ⁸ For the word of the Lord searches out all things, both the invisible and that which reveals His thought; ⁹ For the eye sees His works, and the ear hears His thought; ¹⁰ He spread out the earth and He settled the waters in the sea: ¹¹ He measured the heavens and fixed the stars: and He established the creation and set it up: ¹² And He rested from His works: ¹³ And created things run in their courses, and do their works: ¹⁴ And they know not how to stand and be idle; and His heavenly hosts are subject to His word. ¹⁵ The treasure-chamber of the light is the sun, and the treasury of the darkness is the night: ¹⁶ And He made the sun for the day that it may be bright, but night brings darkness over the face of the land; ¹⁷ And their alternations one to the other speak the beauty of God: IS And there is nothing that is without the Lord; for He was before any thing came into being: ¹⁹ And the worlds were made by His word, and by the thought of His heart. Glory and honour to His name. Hallelujah.

Ode 17

A peculiar change of personality, scarcely realized until the return from it in the last verse.

¹ I was crowned by my God: my crown is living: ² And I was justified in my Lord: my incorruptible salvation is He. ³ I was loosed from vanity, and I was not condemned: ⁴ The choking bonds were cut off by her hands: I received the face and the fashion of a new person: and I walked in it and was saved; ⁵ And the thought of truth led me on. And I walked after it and did not wander: ⁶ And all that have seen me were amazed: and I was regarded by them as a strange person: ⁷ And He who knew and brought me up is the Most High in all His perfection. And He glorified me by His kindness, and raised my thoughts to the height of His truth. ⁸ And from thence He gave me the way of His precepts and I opened the doors that were closed, ⁹ And brake in pieces the bars of iron; but my iron melted and dissolved before me; ¹⁰ Nothing appeared closed to me: because I was the door of everything. ¹¹ And I went over all my bondmen to loose them; that I might not leave any man bound or binding: ¹² And I imparted my knowledge without grudging: and my prayer was in my love: ¹³ And I sowed my fruits in hearts, and transformed them into myself: and they received my blessing and lived; ¹⁴ And they were gathered to me and were saved; because they were to me as my own members and I was their head. Glory to thee our head, the Lord Messiah. Hallelujah.

Ode 18

A man who had a spiritual experience brings a message.

¹ My heart was lifted up in the love of the Most High and was enlarged: that I might praise Him for His name's sake. ² My members were strengthened that they might not fall from His strength. ³ Sicknesses removed from my body, and it stood to the Lord by His will. For His kingdom is true. ⁴ O Lord, for the sake of them that are deficient do not remove thy word from me! ⁵ Neither for the sake of their works do thou restrain from me thy perfection! ⁶ Let not the luminary be conquered by the darkness; nor let truth flee away from falsehood. ⁷ Thou wilt appoint me to victory; our Salvation is thy right hand. And thou wilt receive men from all quarters. ⁸ And thou wilt preserve whosoever is held in evils: ⁹ Thou art my God. Falsehood and death are not in thy mouth: ¹⁰ For thy will is perfection; and vanity thou knowest not, ¹¹ Nor does it know thee. ¹² And error thou knowest not, ¹³ Neither does it know thee. ¹⁴ And ignorance appeared like a blind man; and like the foam of the sea, ¹⁵ And they supposed of that vain thing that it was something great; ¹⁶ And they too came in likeness of it and became vain; and those have understood who have known and meditated; ¹⁷ And they have not been corrupt in their imagination; for such were in the mind of the Lord; ¹⁸ And they mocked at them that were walking in error; ¹⁹ And they spake truth from the inspiration which the Most High breathed into them; Praise and great comeliness to His name Hallelujah.

Ode 19

Fantastic and not in harmony with the other Odes. The reference to a painless Virgin Birth is notable.

¹ A cup of milk was offered to me: and I drank it in the sweetness of the delight of the Lord. ² The Son is the cup, and He who was milked is the Father: ³ And the Holy Spirit milked Him: because His breasts were full, and it was necessary for Him that His milk should be sufficiently released; ⁴ And the Holy Spirit opened His bosom and mingled the milk from the two breasts of the Father; and gave the mixture to the world without their knowing: ⁵ And they who receive in its fulness are the ones on the right hand. ⁶ The Spirit opened the womb of the Virgin and she received conception and brought forth; and the Virgin became a Mother with many mercies; ⁷ And she travailed and brought forth a Son, without incurring pain; ⁸ And because she was not sufficiently prepared, and she had not sought a midwife (for He brought her to bear) she brought forth, as if she were a man, of her own will; ⁹ And she brought Him forth openly, and acquired Him with great dignity, ¹⁰ And loved Him in His swaddling clothes and guarded Him kindly, and showed Him in Majesty. Hallelujah.

Ode 20

A mixture of ethics and mysticism; of the golden rule and the tree of life.

¹ I am a priest of the Lord, and to Him I do priestly service: and to Him I offer the sacrifice of His thought. ² For His thought is not like the thought of the world nor the thought of the flesh, nor like them that serve carnally. ³ The sacrifice of the Lord is righteousness, and purity of heart and lips. ⁴ Present your reins before Him blamelessly: and let not thy heart do violence to heart, nor thy soul to soul. ⁵ Thou shalt not acquire a stranger by the price of thy silver, neither shalt thou seek to devour thy neighbour, ⁶ Neither shalt thou deprive him of the covering of his nakedness. ⁷ But put on the grace of the Lord without stint; and come into His Paradise and make thee a garland from its tree, ⁸ And put it on thy head and be glad, and recline on His rest, and glory shall go before thee, ⁹ And thou shalt receive of His kindness and of His grace; and thou shalt be flourishing in truth in the praise of His holiness. Praise and honour be to His name. Hallelujah.

Ode 21

A remarkable explanation of the "coats of skin" in the third chapter of Genesis.

¹ My arms I lifted up to the Most High, even to the grace of the Lord: because He had cast off my bonds from me: and my Helper had lifted me up to His grace and to His salvation: ² And I put off darkness and clothed myself with light, ³ And my soul acquired a body free from sorrow or affliction or pains. ⁴ And increasingly helpful to me was the thought of the Lord, and His fellowship in incorruption: ⁵ And I was lifted up in His light; and I served before Him, ⁶ And I became near to Him, praising and confessing Him; ⁷ My heart ran over and was found in my mouth: and it arose upon my lips; and the exultation of the Lord increased on my face, and His praise likewise. Hallelujah.

Ode 22

Like the Psalms of David in their exultation because of freedom.

¹ He who brought me down from on high, also brought me up from the regions below; ² And He who gathers together the things that are betwixt is He also who cast me down: ³ He who scattered my enemies had existed from ancient and my adversaries: ⁴ He who gave me authority over bonds that I might loose them; ⁵ He that overthrew by my hands the dragon with seven heads: and thou hast set me over his roots that I might destroy his seed. ⁶ Thou wast there and didst help me, and in every place thy name was a rampart me ⁷ Thy right hand destroyed his wicked poison; and thy hand levelled the way for those who believe in thee. ⁸ And thou didst choose them from the graves and didst separate them from the dead. ⁹ Thou didst take dead bones and didst cover them with bodies. ¹⁰ They were motionless, and thou didst give them energy for life. ¹¹ Thy way was without corruption, and thy face; thou didst bring thy world to corruption: that everything might be dissolved, and then renewed, ¹² And that the foundation for everything might be thy rock: and on it thou didst build thy kingdom; and it became the dwelling place of the saints. Hallelujah.

Ode 23

The reference to the sealed document sent by God is one of the great mysteries of the collection.

¹ Joy is of the saints! and who shall put it on, but they alone? ² Grace is of the elect! and who shall receive it except those who trust in it from the beginning? ³ Love is of the elect? And who shall put it on except those who have possessed it from the beginning? ⁴ Walk ye in the knowledge of the Most High without grudging: to His exultation and to the perfection of His knowledge. ⁵ And His thought was like a letter; His will descended from on high, and it was sent like an arrow which is violently shot from the bow: ⁶ And many hands rushed to the letter to seize it and to take and read it: ⁷ And it escaped their fingers and they were affrighted at it and at the seal that was upon it. ⁸ Because it was not permitted to them to loose its seal: for the power that was over the seal was greater than they. ⁹ But those who saw it went after the letter that they might know where it would alight, and who should read it and who should hear it. ¹⁰ But a wheel received it and came over it: ¹¹ And there was with it a sign of the Kingdom and of the Government: ¹² And everything which tried to move the wheel it mowed and cut down: ¹³ And it gathered the multitude of adversaries, and bridged the rivers and crossed over and rooted up many forests and made a broad path. ¹⁴ The head went down to the feet, for down to the feet ran the wheel, and that which was a sign upon it. ¹⁵ The letter was one of command, for there were included in it all districts; ¹⁶ And there was seen at its head, the head which was revealed even the Son of Truth from the Most High Father, ¹⁷ And He inherited and took possession of everything. And the thought of many was brought to nought. ¹⁸ And all the apostates hasted and fled away. And those who persecuted and were enraged became extinct. ¹⁹ And the letter was a great volume, which was wholly written by the. finger of God: ²⁰ And the name of the Father was on it, and of the Son and of the Holy Spirit, to rule for ever and ever. Hallelujah.

Ode 24

The mention of the Dove refers to a lost Gospel to which there are rare references in ancient writings.

¹ The Dove fluttered over the Messiah, because He was her head; and she sang over Him and her voice was heard: ² And the inhabitants were afraid and the sojourners were moved: ³ The birds dropped their wings and all creeping things died in their holes: and the abysses were opened which had been hidden; and they cried to the Lord like women in travail: ⁴ And no food was given to them, because it did not belong to them; ⁵ And they sealed up the abysses with the seal of the Lord. And they perished, in the thought, those that had existed from ancient times; ⁶ For they were corrupt from the

beginning; and the end of their corruption was life: ⁷ And every one of them that was imperfect perished: for it was not possible to give them a word that they might remain: ⁸ And the Lord destroyed the imaginations of all them that had not the truth with them. ⁹ For they who in their hearts were lifted up were deficient in wisdom, and so they were rejected, because the truth was not with them. ¹⁰ For the Lord disclosed His way, and spread abroad His grace: and those who understood it, know His holiness. Hallelujah.

Ode 25
Back again to personal experience.
¹ I was rescued from my bonds and unto thee, my God, I fled: ² For thou art the right hand of my Salvation and my helper. ³ Thou hast restrained those that rise up against me, ⁴ And I shall see him no more: because thy face was with me, which saved me by thy grace. ⁵ But I was despised and rejected in the eye of many: and I was in their eyes like lead, ⁶ And strength was mine from thyself and help. ⁷ Thou didst set me a lamp at my right hand and at my left: and in me there shall be nothing that is not bright: ⁸ And I was clothed with the covering of thy Spirit, and thou didst remove from me my raiment of skin; ⁹ For thy right hand lifted me up and removed sickness from me: ¹⁰ And I became mighty in: the truth, and holy by thy righteousness; and all my adversaries were afraid of me; ¹¹ And I became admirable by the name of the Lord, and was justified by His gentleness, and His rest is for ever and ever. Hallelujah.

Ode 26
Remarkable praise.
¹ I poured out praise to the Lord, for I am His: ² And I will speak His holy song, for my heart is with Him. ³ For His harp is in my hands, and the Odes of His rest shall not be silent. ⁴ I will cry unto him from my whole heart: I will praise and exalt Him with all my members. ⁵ For from the east and even to the west is His praise: ⁶ And from the south and even to the north is the confession of Him: ⁷ And from the top of the hills to their utmost bound is His perfection. ⁸ Who can write the Psalms of the Lord, or who read them? ⁹ Or who can train his soul for life, that his soul may be saved, ¹⁰ Or who can rest on the Most High, so that with His mouth he may speak? ¹¹ Who is able to interpret the wonders of the Lord? ¹² For he who could interpret would be dissolved and would become that which is interpreted. ¹³ For it suffices to know and to rest: for in rest the singers stand, ¹⁴ Like a river which has an abundant fountain, and flows to the help of them that seek it. Hallelujah.

Ode 27
The human body makes a cross when a man stands erect in prayer with arms outstretched.
¹ I stretched out my hands and sanctified my Lord: ² For the extension of my hands is His sign: ³ And my expansion is the upright tree [or cross].

Ode 28
This Ode is a musical gem.
¹ As the wings of doves over their nestlings; and the mouth of their nestlings towards their mouths. ² So also are the wings of the Spirit over my heart: ³ My heart is delighted and exults: like the babe who exults in the womb of his mother: ⁴ I believed; therefore I was at rest; for faithful is He in whom I have believed: ⁵ He has richly blessed me and my head is with Him: and the sword shall not divide me from Him, nor the scimitar; ⁶ For I am ready before destruction comes; and I have been set on His immortal pinions: ⁷ And He showed me His sign: forth and given me to drink, and from that life is the spirit within me, and it cannot die, for it lives. ⁸ They who saw me marvelled at me, because I was persecuted, and they supposed that I was swallowed up: for I seemed to them as one of the lost; ⁹ And my oppression became my salvation; and I was their reprobation because there was no zeal in me; ¹⁰ Because I did good to every man I was hated, ¹¹ And they came round me like mad dogs, who ignorantly attack their masters, ¹² For their thought is corrupt and their understanding perverted. ¹³ But I was carrying water in my right hand, and their bitterness I endured by my sweetness; ¹⁴ And I did not perish, for I was not their brother nor was my birth like theirs. ¹⁵ And they sought for my death and did not find it: for I was older than the memorial of them; ¹⁶ And vainly did they make attack upon me and those who, without reward, came after me: ¹⁷ They sought to destroy the memorial of him who was before them. ¹⁸ For the thought of the Most High cannot be anticipated; and His heart is superior to all wisdom. Hallelujah.

Ode 29
Again reminiscent of the Psalms, of David.
¹ The Lord is my hope: in Him I shall not be confounded. ² For according to His praise He made me, and according to His goodness even so He gave unto me: ³ And according to His mercies He exalted me: and according to His excellent beauty He set me on high: ⁴ And brought me up out of the depths of Sheol: and from the mouth of death He drew me: ⁵ And thou didst lay my enemies low, and He justified me by His grace. ⁶ For I believed in the Lord's Messiah: and it appeared to me that He is the Lord; ⁷ And He showed him His sign: and He led me by His light, and gave me the rod of His power; ⁸ That I might subdue the imaginations of the peoples; and the power of the men of might to bring them low: ⁹ To make war by His word, and to take victory by His power. ¹⁰ And the Lord overthrew my enemy by His word: and he became like the stubble which the wind carries away; ¹¹ And I gave praise to the Most High because He exalted me His servant and the son of His handmaid. Hallelujah.

Ode 30
An invitation to the thirsty.
¹ Fill ye waters for yourselves from the living fountain of the Lord, for it is opened to you: ² And come all ye thirsty, and take the draught; and rest by the fountain of the Lord. ³ For fair it is and pure and gives rest to the soul. Much more pleasant are its waters than honey; ⁴ And the honeycomb of bees is not to be compared with it. ⁵ For it flows forth from the lips of the Lord and from the heart of the Lord is its name. ⁶ And it came infinitely and invisibly: and until it was set in the midst they did not know it: ⁷ Blessed are they who have drunk therefrom and have found rest thereby. Hallelujah.

Ode 31
A song that Marcus Aurelius might have known when he said "Be like the promontory against which the waves continually break."
¹ The abysses were dissolved before the Lord: and darkness was destroyed by His appearance: ² Error went astray and perished at His hand: and folly found no path to walk in, and was submerged by the truth of the Lord. ³ He opened His mouth and spake grace and joy: and He spake a new song of praise to His name: ⁴ And He lifted up His voice to the Most High, and offered to Him the sons that were with Him. ⁵ And His face was justified, for thus His holy Father had given to Him. ⁶ Come forth, ye that have been afflicted and receive joy, and possess your souls by His grace; and take to you immortal life. ⁷ And they made me a debtor when I rose up, me who had been a debtor: and they divided my spoil, though nothing was due to them. ⁸ But I endured and held my peace and was silent, as if not, moved by them. ⁹ But I stood unshaken like a firm rock which is beaten by the waves and endures. ¹⁰ And I bore their bitterness for humility's sake: ¹¹ In order, that I might redeem my people, and inherit it and that I might not make void my promises to the fathers, to whom I promised the salvation of their seed. Hallelujah.

Ode 32
Joy and light.
¹ To the blessed there is joy from their hearts, and light from Him that dwells in them: ² And words from the Truth, who was self-originate: for He is strengthened by the holy power of the Most High: and He is unperturbed for ever and ever. Hallelujah.

Ode 33
A virgin stands and proclaims (v. 5).
¹ Again Grace ran and forsook corruption, and came down in Him to bring it to nought; ² And He destroyed perdition from before Him, and devastated all its order; ³ And He stood on a lofty summit and uttered His voice from one end of the earth to the other: ⁴ And drew to Him all those who obeyed Him; and there did not appear as it were an evil person. ⁵ But there stood a perfect virgin who was proclaiming and calling and saying, ⁶ O ye sons of men, return ye, and ye daughters of men, come ye: ⁷ And forsake the ways of that corruption and draw near unto me, and I will enter into you, and will bring you forth from perdition, ⁸ And make you wise in the ways of truth: that you be not destroyed nor perish: ⁹ Hear ye me and be redeemed. For the grace of God I am telling among you: and by my means you shall be redeemed and become blessed. ¹⁰ I am your judge; and they who have put me on shall not be injured: but they shall possess the new world that is incorrupt: ¹¹ My chosen ones walk in me, and my ways I will make known to them that seek me, and I will make them trust in my name. Hallelujah.

Ode 34
True poetry–pure and simple.
¹ No way is hard where there is a simple heart. ² Nor is there any wound where the thoughts are upright: ³ Nor is there any storm in the depth of the illuminated thought: ⁴ Where one is surrounded on every side by beauty, there is nothing that is divided. ⁵ The likeness of what is below is that which is above; for everything is above: what is below is nothing but the imagination of those that are without knowledge. ⁶ Grace has been revealed for your salvation. Believe and live and be saved. Hallelujah.

Ode 35
"No cradled child more softly lies than I: come soon, eternity."

[1] The dew of the Lord in quietness He distilled upon me: [2] And the cloud of peace He caused to rise over my head, which guarded me continually; [3] It was to me for salvation: everything was shaken and they were affrighted; [4] And there came forth from them a smoke and a judgment; and I was keeping quiet in the order of the Lord: [5] More than shelter was He to me, and more than foundation. [6] And I was carried like a child by his mother: and He gave me milk, the dew of the Lord: [7] And I grew great by His bounty, and rested in His perfection, [8] And I spread out my hands in the lifting up of my soul: and I was made right with the Most High, and I was redeemed with Him. Hallelujah.

Ode 36

Theologians have never agreed on an explanation of this perplexing Ode.
[1] I rested in the Spirit of the Lord: and the Spirit raised me on high: [2] And made me stand on my feet in the height of the Lord, before His perfection and His glory, while I was praising Him by the composition of His songs. [3] The Spirit brought me forth before the face of the Lord: and, although a son of man, I was named the Illuminate, the Son of God: [4] While I praised amongst the praising ones, and great was I amongst the mighty ones. [5] For according to the greatness of the Most High, so He made me: and like His own newness He renewed me; and He anointed me from His own perfection: [6] And I became one of His Neighbours; and my mouth was opened, like a cloud of dew, [7] And my heart poured out as it were a gushing stream of righteousness, [8] And my access to Him was in peace; and I was established by the Spirit of His government. Hallelujah.

Ode 37

An elementary Ode.
[1] I stretched out my hands to my Lord: and to the Most I High I raised my voice: [2] And I spake with the lips of my heart; and He heard me, when my voice reached I Him: [3] His answer came to me, and gave me the fruits of my labours; [4] And it gave me rest by the grace of the Lord. Hallelujah.

Ode 38

A beautiful description of the power of truth.
[1] I went up to the light of truth as if into a chariot: [2] And the Truth took me and led me: and carried me across pits and gulleys; and from the rocks and the waves it preserved me: [3] And it became to me a haven of Salvation: and set me on the arms of immortal life: [4] And it went with me and made me rest, and suffered me not to wander, because it was the Truth; [5] And I ran no risk, because I walked with Him; [6] And I did not make an error in anything because I obeyed the Truth. [7] For Error flees away from it, and meets it not: but the Truth proceeds in the right path, and [8] Whatever I did not know, it made clear to me, all the poisons of error, and the plagues of death which they think to be sweetness: [9] And I saw the destroyer of destruction, when the bride who is corrupted is adorned: and the bridegroom who corrupts and is corrupted; [10] And I asked the Truth 'Who are these?'; and He said to me, 'This is the deceiver and the error: [11] And they are alike in the beloved and in his bride: and they lead astray and corrupt the whole world: [12] And they invite many to the banquet, [13] And give them to drink of the wine of their intoxication, and remove their wisdom and knowledge, and so they make them without intelligence; [14] And then they leave them; and then these go about like madmen corrupting: seeing that-they are without heart, nor do they seek for it! [15] And I was made wise so as not to fall into the hands of the deceiver; and I congratulated myself because the Truth went with me, [16] And I was established and lived and was redeemed, [17] And my foundations were laid on the hand of the Lord: because He established me. [18] For He set the root and watered it and fixed it and blessed it; and its fruits are for ever. [19] It struck deep and sprung up and spread out, and was full and enlarged; [20] And the Lord alone was glorified in His planting and in His husbandry: by His care and by the blessing of His lips, [21] By the beautiful planting of His right hand: and by the discovery of His planting, and by the thought of His mind. Hallelujah.

Ode 39

One of the few allusions to events in the Gospels–that of our Lord walking on the Sea of Galilee.
[1] Great rivers are the power of the Lord: [2] And they carry headlong those who despise Him: and entangle their paths: [3] And they sweep away their fords, and catch their bodies and destroy their lives. [4] For they are more swift than lightning and more rapid, and those who cross them in faith are not moved; [5] And those who walk on them without blemish shall not be afraid. [6] For the sign in them is the Lord; and the sign is the way of those who cross in the name of the Lord; [7] Put on, therefore, the name of the Most High, and know Him, and you shall cross without danger, for the rivers will be subject to you. [8] The Lord has bridged them by His word; and He walked and crossed them on foot: [9] And His footsteps stand firm on the water, and are not injured; they are as firm as a tree that is truly set up. [10] And the waves were lifted up on this side and on that, but the footsteps of our Lord Messiah stand firm and are not obliterated and are not defaced. [11] And a way has been appointed for those who cross after Him and for those who adhere to the course of faith in Him and worship His name. Hallelujah.

Ode 40

A song of praise without equal.
[1] As the honey distills from the comb of the bees, [2] And the milk flows from the woman that loves her children; [3] So also is my hope on Thee, my God. [4] As the fountain gushes out its water, [5] So my heart gushes out the praise of the Lord and my lips utter praise to Him, and my tongue His psalms. [6] And my face exults with His gladness, and my spirit exults in His love, and my soul shines in Him: [7] And reverence confides in Him; and redemption in Him stands assured: [8] And His inheritance is immortal life, and those who participate in it are incorrupt. Hallelujah.

Ode 41

We discover that the writer may be a Gentile (v. 8).
[1] All the Lord's children will praise Him, and will collect the truth of His faith. [2] And His children shall be known to Him. Therefore we will sing in His love: [3] We live in the Lord by His grace: and life we receive in His Messiah: [4] For a great day has shined upon us: and marvellous is He who has given us of His glory. [5] Let us, therefore, all of us unite together in the name of the Lord, and let us honour Him in His goodness, [6] And let our faces shine in His light: and let our hearts meditate in His love by night and by day. [7] Let us exult with the joy of the Lord. [8] All those will be astonished that see me. For from another race am I: [9] For the Father of truth remembered me: He who possessed me from the beginning: [10] For His bounty begat me, and the thought of His heart: [11] And His Word is with us in all our way; [12] The Saviour who makes alive and does not reject our souls-; [13] The man who was humbled, and exalted by His own righteousness, [14] The Son of the Most High appeared in the perfection of His Father; [15] And light dawned from the Word that was beforetime in Him; [16] The Messiah is truly one; and He was known before the foundation of the world, [17] That He might save souls for ever by the truth of His name: a new song arises from those who love Him. Hallelujah.

Ode 42

The Odes of Solomon, the Son of David, are ended with the following exquisite verses.
[1] I stretched out my hands and approached my Lord: [2] For the stretching of my hands is His sign: [3] My expansion is the outspread tree which was set up on the way of the Righteous One. [4] And I became of no account to those who did not take hold of me; and I shall be with those who love me. [5] All my persecutors are dead; and they sought after me who hoped in me, because I was alive: [6] And I rose up and am with them; and I will speak by their mouths. [7] For they have despised those who persecuted them; [8] And I lifted up over them the yoke of my love; [9] Like the arm of the bridegroom over the bride, [10] So was my yoke over those that know me: [11] And as the couch that is spread in the house of the bridegroom and bride, [12] So is my love over those that believe in me. [13] And I was not rejected though I was reckoned to be so. [14] I did not perish, though they devised it against me. [15] Sheol saw me and was made miserable: [16] Death cast me up, and many along with me. [17] I had gall and bitterness, and I went down with him to the utmost of his depth: [18] And the feet and the head he let go, for they were not able to endure my face: [19] And I made a congregation of living men amongst his dead men, and I spake with them by living lips: [20] Because my word shall not be void: [21] And those who had died ran towards me: and they cried and said, Son of God, have pity on us, and do with us according to thy kindness, [22] And bring us out from the bonds of darkness: and open to us the door by which we shall come out to thee. [23] For we see that our death has not touched thee. [24] Let us also be redeemed with thee: for thou art our Redeemer. [25] And I heard their voice; and my name I sealed upon their heads: [26] For they are free men and they are mine. Hallelujah.

PASSION GOSPELS

The Gospel of Peter

¹ BUT of the Jews none washed his hands, neither Herod nor any one of his judges. And when they had refused to wash them, Pilate rose up. And then Herod the king commandeth that the Lord be taken saying to them, What things soever I commanded you to do unto him, do. ² And there was standing there Joseph the friend of Pilate and of the Lord; and, knowing that they were about to crucify him, he came to Pilate and asked the body of the Lord for burial. And Pilate sent to Herod and asked his body. And Herod said, Brother Pilate, even if no one has asked for him, we purposed to bury him, especially as the sabbath draweth on: for it is written in the law, that the sun set not upon one that hath been put to death. ³ And he delivered him to the people on the day before the unleavened bread, their feast. And they took the Lord and pushed him as they ran, and said, Let us drag away the Son of God, having obtained power over him. And they clothed him with purple, and set him on the seat of judgment, saying, Judge righteously, O king of Israel. And one of them brought a crown of thorns and put it on the head of the Lord. And others stood and spat in his eyes, and others smote his cheeks: others pricked him with a reed; and some scourged him, saying, With this honor let us honor the Son of God. ⁴ And they brought two malefactors, and they crucified the Lord between them. But he held his peace, as though having no pain. And when they had raised the cross, they wrote the title: This is the king of Israel. And having set his garments before him they parted them among them, and cast lots for them. And one of those malefactors reproached them, saying, We for the evils that we have done have suffered thus, but this man, who hath become the Saviour of men, what wrong hath he done to you? And they, being angered at him, commanded that his legs should not be broken, that he might die in torment. ⁵ And it was noon, and darkness came over all Judæa: and they were troubled and distressed, lest the sun had set, whilst he was yet alive: [for] it is written for them, that the sun set not on him that hath been put to death. And one of them said, Give him to drink gall with vinegar. And they mixed and gave him to drink, and fulfilled all things, and accomplished their sins against their own head. And many went about with lamps, supposing that it was night, and fell down. And the Lord cried out, saying, My power, my power, thou hast forsaken me. And when he had said it he was taken up. And in that hour the vail of the temple of Jerusalem was rent in twain. ⁶ And then they drew out the nails from the hands of the Lord, and laid him upon the earth, and the whole earth quaked, and great fear arose. Then the sun shone, and it was found the ninth hour: and the Jews rejoiced, and gave his body to Joseph that he might bury it, since he had seen what good things he had done. And he took the Lord, and him, and rolled him in a linen cloth, and brought him to his own tomb, which was called the Garden of Joseph. ⁷ Then the Jews and the elders and the priests, perceiving what evil they had done to themselves, began to lament and to say, Woe for our sins: the judgment hath drawn nigh, and the end of Jerusalem. And I with my companions was grieved; and being wounded in mind we hid ourselves: for we were being sought for by them as malefactors, and as wishing to set fire to the temple. And upon all these things we fasted and sat mourning and weeping night and day until the sabbath. ⁸ But the scribes and Pharisees and elders being gathered together one with another, when they heard that all the people murmured and beat their breasts saying, If by his death these most mighty signs have come to pass, see how righteous he is,–the elders were afraid and came to Pilate beseeching him and saying, Give us soldiers, that we may guard his sepulchre for three days, lest his disciples come and steal him away, and the people suppose that he is risen from the dead and do us evil. And Pilate gave them Petronius the centurion with soldiers to guard the tomb. And with them came elders and scribes to the sepulchre, and having rolled a great stone together with the centurion and the soldiers, they all together who were there set it at the door of the sepulchre; and they affixed seven seals, and they pitched a tent there and guarded it. And early in the morning as the sabbath was drawing on, there came a multitude from Jerusalem and the region round about, that they might see the sepulchre that was sealed. ⁹ And in the night in which the Lord's day was drawing on, as the soldiers kept guard two by two in a watch, there was a great voice in the heaven; and they saw the heavens opened, and two men descend from thence with great light and approach the tomb. And that stone which was put at the door rolled of itself and made way in part; and the tomb was opened, and both the young men entered in. ¹⁰ When therefore those soldiers saw it, they awakened the centurion and the elders; for they too were hard by keeping guard. And as they declared what things they had seen, again they see three men come forth from the tomb, and two of them supporting one, and a cross following them: and of the two the head reached unto the heaven, but the head of him who was lead by them overpassed the heavens. And they heard a voice from the heavens, saying, Thou hast preached to them that sleep. And a response was heard from the cross, Yea. ¹¹ They therefore considered one with another whether to go away and shew these things to Pilate. And while they yet thought thereon, the heavens again are seen to open, and a certain man to descend and enter into the sepulchre. When the centurion and they that were with him saw these things, they hastened in the night to Pilate, leaving the tomb which they were watching, and declared all things which they had seen, being greatly distressed and saying, Truly he was the Son of God. Pilate answered and said, I am pure from the blood of the Son of God: but it was ye who determined this. Then they all drew near and besought him and entreated him to command the centurion and the soldiers to say nothing of the things which they had seen: For it is better, say they, for us to be guilty of the greatest sin before God, and not to fall into the hands of the people of the Jews and to be stoned. Pilate therefore commanded the centurion and the soldiers to say nothing. ¹² And at dawn upon the Lord's day Mary Magdalene, a disciple of the Lord, fearing because of the Jews, since they were burning with wrath, had not done at the Lord's sepulchre the things which women are wont to do for those that die and for those that are beloved by them–she took her friends with her and came to the sepulchre where he was laid. And they feared lest the Jews should see them, and they said, Although on that day on which he was crucified we could not weep and lament, yet now let us do these things at his sepulchre. But who shall roll away for us the stone that was laid at the door of the sepulchre, that we may enter in and sit by him and do the things that are due? For the stone was great, and we fear lest some one see us. And if we cannot, yet if we but set at the door the things which we bring as a memorial of him, we will weep and lament, until we come unto our home. ¹³ And they went and found the tomb opened, and coming near they looked in there; and they see there a certain young man sitting in the midst of the tomb, beautiful and clothed in a robe exceeding bright; who said to them, Wherefore are ye come? Whom seek ye? Him that was crucified? He is risen and gone. But if ye believe not, look in and see the place where he lay, that he is not [here]; for he is risen and gone thither, whence he was sent. Then the women feared and fled. ¹⁴ Now it was the last day of the unleavened bread, and many were going forth, returning to their homes, as the feast was ended. But we, the twelve disciples of the Lord, wept and were grieved: and each one, being grieved for that which was come to pass, departed to his home. But I Simon Peter and Andrew my brother took our nets and went to the sea; and there was with us Levi the son of Alphæus, whom the Lord . . .

The Gospel of Bartholomew

1

(The opening 3 verses are given from each of the three texts)

[Greek]. **1** After the resurrection from the dead of our Lord Jesus Christ, Bartholomew came unto the Lord and questioned him, saying: Lord, reveal unto me the mysteries of the heavens. **2** Jesus answered and said unto him: If I put off the body of the flesh, I shall not be able to tell them unto thee. **3** Om. *[Slavonic].* **1** Before the resurrection of our Lord Jesus Christ from the dead, the apostles said: Let us question the Lord: Lord, reveal unto us the wonders. **2** And Jesus said unto them: If I put off the body of the flesh, I cannot tell them unto you. **3** But when he was buried and risen again, they all durst not question him, because it was not to look upon him, but the fullness of his Godhead was seen. **4** But Bartholomew, etc. *[Latin].* **2.** At that time, before the Lord Jesus Christ suffered, all the disciples were gathered together, questioning him and saying: Lord, show us the mystery in the heavens. **2** But Jesus answered and said unto them: If I put not off the body of flesh I cannot tell you. **3** But after that he had suffered and risen again, all the apostles, looking upon him, durst not question him, because his countenance was not as it had been aforetime, but showed forth the fullness of power. *[Greek].* **4** Bartholomew therefore drew near unto the Lord and said: I have a word to speak unto thee, Lord. **5** And Jesus said to him: I know what thou art about to say; say then what thou wilt, and I will answer thee. **6** And Bartholomew said: Lord, when thou wentest to be hanged upon the cross, I followed thee afar off and saw thee hung upon the cross, and the angels coming down from heaven and worshipping thee. And when there came darkness, **7** I beheld, and I saw thee that thou wast vanished away from the cross and I heard only a voice in the parts under the earth, and great wailing and gnashing of teeth on a sudden. Tell me, Lord, whither wentest thou from the cross? **8** And Jesus answered and said: Blessed art thou, Bartholomew, my beloved, because thou sawest this mystery, and now will I tell thee all things whatsoever thou askest me. **9** For when I vanished away from the cross, then went I down into Hades that I might bring up Adam and all them that were with him, according to the supplication of Michael the archangel. **10** Then said Bartholomew: Lord, what was the voice which was heard? **11** Jesus said unto him: Hades said unto Beliar: As I perceive, a God cometh hither. *[Slavonic and Latin continue:]* And the angels cried unto the powers, saying: Remove your gates, ye princes, remove the everlasting doors, for behold the King of glory cometh down. **12** Hades said: Who is the King of glory, that cometh down from heaven unto us? **13** And when I had descended five hundred steps, Hades was troubled, saying: I hear the breathing of the Most High, and I cannot endure it. (*[Latin].* He cometh with great fragrance and I cannot bear it.) **14** But the devil answered and said: Submit not thyself, O Hades, but be strong: for God himself hath not descended upon the earth. **15** But when I had descended yet five hundred steps, the angels and the powers cried out: Take hold, remove the doors, for behold the King of glory cometh down. And Hades said: O, woe unto me, for I hear the breath of God.] *[Greek].* **16-17** And Beliar said unto Hades: Look carefully who it is that , for it is Elias, or Enoch, or one of the prophets that this man seemeth to me to be. But Hades answered Death and said: Not yet are six thousand years accomplished. And whence are these, O Beliar; for the sum of the number is in mine hands. *[Slavonic].* **16** And the devil said unto Hades: Why affrightest thou me, Hades? it is a prophet, and he hath made himself like unto God: this prophet will we take and bring him hither unto those that think to ascend into heaven. **17** And Hades said: Which of the prophets is it? Show me: Is it Enoch the scribe of righteousness? But God hath not suffered him to come down upon the earth before the end of the six thousand years. Sayest thou that it is Elias, the avenger? But before he cometh not down. What shall I do, whereas the destruction is of God: for surely our end is at hand? For I have the number (of the years) in mine hands.] *[Greek].* **18** Be not troubled, make safe thy gates and strengthen thy bars: consider, God cometh not down upon the earth. **19** Hades saith unto him: These be no good words that I hear from thee: my belly is rent, and mine inward parts are pained: it cannot be but that God cometh hither. Alas, whither shall I flee before the face of the power of the great king? Suffer me to enter into myself (thyself, *Latin*): for before (of, *Latin*) thee was I formed. **20** Then did I enter in and scourged him and bound him with chains that cannot be loosed, and brought forth thence all the patriarchs and came again unto the cross. **21** Bartholomew saith unto him: [*Latin*, I saw thee again, hanging upon the cross, and all the dead arising and worshipping thee, and going up again into their sepulchres.] Tell me, Lord, who was he whom the angels bare up in their hands, even that man that was very great of stature? [*Slavonic, Latin*, And what spakest thou unto him that he sighed so sore?] **22** Jesus answered and said unto him: It was Adam the first-formed, for whose sake I came down from heaven upon earth. And I said unto him: I was hung upon the cross for thee and for thy children's sake. And he, when he heard it, groaned and said: So was thy good pleasure, O Lord. **23** Again Bartholomew said: Lord, I saw the angels ascending before Adam and singing praises. **24** But one of the angels which was very great, above the rest, would not ascend up with them: and there was in his hand a sword of fire, and he was looking steadfastly upon thee only. [*Slavonic*] **25** And all the angels besought him that he would go up with them, but he would not. But when thou didst command him to go up, I beheld a flame of fire issuing out of his hands and going even unto the city of Jerusalem. **26** And Jesus said unto him: Blessed art thou, Bartholomew my beloved because thou sawest these mysteries. This was one of the angels of vengeance which stand before my Father's throne: and this angel sent he unto me. **27** And for this cause he would not ascend up, because he desired to destroy all the powers of the world. But when I commanded him to ascend up, there went a flame out of his hand and rent asunder the veil of the temple, and parted it in two pieces for a witness unto the children of Israel for my passion because they crucified me. (*Latin.* But the flame which thou sawest issuing out of his hands smote the house of the synagogue of the Jews, for a testimony of me wherein they crucified me.)]. *[Greek].* **28** And when he had thus spoken, he said unto the apostles: Tarry for me in this place, for today a sacrifice is offered in paradise. **29** And Bartholomew answered and said unto Jesus: Lord, what is the sacrifice which is offered in paradise? And Jesus said: There be souls of the righteous which to-day have departed out of the body and go unto paradise, and unless I be **30** And Bartholomew said: Lord, how many souls depart out of the world daily? Jesus saith unto him: Thirty thousand. **31** Bartholomew saith unto him: Lord, when thou wast with us teaching the word, didst thou receive the sacrifices in paradise? Jesus answered and said unto him: Verily I say unto thee, my beloved, that I both taught the word with you and continually sat with my Father, and received the sacrifices in paradise everyday. **32** Bartholomew answered and said unto him: Lord, if thirty thousand souls depart out of the world every day, how many souls out of them are found righteous? Jesus saith unto him: Hardly fifty [three] my beloved. **33** Again Bartholomew saith: And how do three only enter into paradise? Jesus saith unto him: The [fifty] three enter into paradise or are laid up in Abraham's bosom: but the others go into the place of the resurrection, for the three are not like unto the fifty. **34** Bartholomew saith unto him: Lord, how many souls above the number are born into the world daily? Jesus saith unto him: One soul only is born above the number of them that depart.[**30**, etc., *Latin*. Bartholomew said: How many are the souls which depart out of the body every day? Jesus said: Verily I say unto thee, twelve (thousand) eight hundred, four score and three souls depart out of the body every day.] **35** And when he had said this he gave them the peace, and vanished away from them.

2

1 Now the apostles were in the place [Cherubim, Cheltoura, Chritir] with Mary. **2** And Bartholomew came and said unto Peter and Andrew and John: Let us ask her that is highly favoured how she conceived the incomprehensible, or how she bare him that cannot be carried, or how she brought forth so much greatness. But they doubted to ask her. **3** Bartholomew therefore said unto Peter: Thou that art the chief, and my teacher, draw near and ask her. But Peter said to John: Thou art a virgin and undefiled (and beloved) and thou must ask her. **4** And as they all doubted and disputed, Bartholomew came near unto her with a cheerful countenance and said to her: Thou that art highly favoured, the tabernacle of the Most High, unblemished we, even all the apostles, ask thee (or All the apostles have sent me to ask thee) to tell us how thou didst conceive the incomprehensible, or how thou didst bear him that cannot be **5** But Mary said unto them: Ask me not (or Do ye indeed ask me) concerning this mystery. If I should begin to tell you, fire will issue forth out of my mouth and consume all the world. **6** But they continued yet the more to ask her. And she, for she could not refuse to hear the apostles, said: Let us stand up in prayer. **7** And the apostles stood behind Mary: but she said unto Peter: Peter, thou chief, thou great pillar, standest thou behind us? Said not our Lord: the head of the man is Christ ? now therefore stand ye before me and pray. **8** But they said unto her: In thee did the Lord set his tabernacle, and it was his good pleasure that thou shouldest contain him, and thou oughtest to be the leader in the prayer (al. to go with us to). **9** But she said unto them: Ye are shining stars, and as the prophet said, 'I did lift up mine eyes unto the hills, from whence shall come mine help'; ye, therefore, are the hills, and it behoveth you to pray. **10** The apostles say unto her: Thou oughtest to pray, thou art the mother of the heavenly king. **11** Mary saith unto them: In your likeness did God form the sparrows, and sent them forth into the four corners of the world. **12** But they say unto her: He that is scarce contained by the **13** Then Mary stood up before them and spread out her hands toward the heaven and began to speak thus: Elphue Zarethra Charboum Nemioth

Melitho Thraboutha Mephnounos Chemiath Aroura Maridon Elison Marmiadon Section Hesaboutha Ennouna Saktinos Athoor Belelam Opheoth Abo Chrasar (this is the reading of one *[Greek]* copy: the others and the *Slavonic* have many differences as in all such cases: but as the original words-assuming them to have once had a meaning-are hopelessly corrupted, the matter is not of importance), which is in the *Greek* tongue(Hebrew, *Slavonic*): O God the exceeding great and all-wise and king of the worlds (ages), that art not to be described, the ineffable, that didst establish the greatness of the heavens and all things by a word, that out of darkness (or the unknown) didst constitute and fasten together the poles of heaven in harmony, didst bring into shape the matter that was in confusion, didst bring into order the things that were without order, didst part the misty darkness from the light, didst establish in one place the foundations of the waters, thou that makest the beings of the air to tremble, and art the fear of them that are on (or under) the earth, that didst settle the earth and not suffer it to perish, and filledst it, which is the nourisher of all things, with showers of blessing: (Son of) the Father, thou whom the seven heavens hardly contained, but who wast well-pleased to be contained without pain in me, thou that art thyself the full word of the Father in whom all things came to be: give glory to thine exceeding great name, and bid me to speak before thy holy [14] And when she had ended the prayer she began to say unto them: Let us sit down upon the ground; and come thou, Peter the chief, and sit on my right hand and put thy left hand beneath mine armpit; and thou, Andrew, do so on my left hand; and thou, John, the virgin, hold together my bosom; and thou, Bartholomew, set thy knees against my back and hold my shoulders, lest when I begin to speak my bones be loosed one from another. [15] And when they had so done she began to say: When I abode in the temple of God and received my food from an angel, on a certain day there appeared unto me one in the likeness of an angel, but his face was incomprehensible, and he had not in his hand bread or a cup, as did the angel which came to me aforetime. [16] And straightway the robe (veil) of the temple was rent and there was a very great earthquake, and I fell upon the earth, for I was not able to endure the sight of him. [17] But he put his hand beneath me and raised me up, and I looked up into heaven and there came a cloud of dew and sprinkled me from the head to the feet, and he wiped me with his robe. [18] And said unto me: Hail, thou that art highly favoured, the chosen vessel, grace inexhaustible. And he smote his garment upon the right hand and there came a very great loaf, and he set it upon the altar of the temple and did eat of it first himself, and gave unto me also. [19] And again he smote his garment upon the left hand and there came a very great cup full of wine: and he set it upon the altar of the temple and did drink of it first himself, and gave also unto me. And I beheld and saw the bread and the cup whole as they were. [20] And he said unto me: Yet three years, and I will send my word unto thee and then shalt conceive my (or a) son, and through him shall the whole creation be saved. Peace be unto [21] And when he had so said he vanished away from mine eyes, and the temple was restored as it had been before. [22] And as she was saying this, fire issued out of her mouth; and the world was at the point to come to an end: but Jesus appeared quickly (*Latin*, and laid his hand upon her mouth) and said unto Mary: Utter not this mystery, or this day my whole creation will come to an end (*Latin*, and the flame from her mouth ceased). And the apostles were taken with fear lest haply the Lord should be wroth with them.

3

[1] And he departed with them unto the mount Mauria (*Latin*, Mambre), and sat in the midst of them. [2] But they doubted to question him, being afraid. [3] And Jesus answered and said unto them: Ask me what ye will that I should teach you, and I will show it you. For yet seven days, and I ascend unto my Father, and I shall no more be seen of you in this likeness. [4] But they, yet doubting, said unto him: Lord, show us the deep (abyss) according unto thy promise. [5] And Jesus said unto them: It is not good (*Latin*, is good) for you to see the deep: notwithstanding, if ye desire it, according to my promise, come, follow me and behold. [6] And he led them away into a place that is called Cherubim (Cherukt *Slavonic*, Chairoudee Gr., *Latin* omits), that is the place of truth. [7] And he beckoned unto the angels of the West and the earth was rolled up like a volume of a book and the deep was revealed unto them. [8] And when the apostles saw it they fell on their faces upon the earth. [9] But Jesus raised them up, saying: Said I not unto you, 'It is not good for you to see the deep'. And again he beckoned unto the angels, and the deep was covered up.

4

[1] And he took them and brought them again unto the Mount of olives. [2] And Peter said unto Mary: Thou that art highly favoured, entreat the Lord that he would reveal unto us the things that are in the heavens. [3] And Mary said unto Peter: O stone hewn out of the rock, did not the Lord build his church upon thee? Go thou therefore first and ask him. [4] Peter saith again: O tabernacle that art spread abroad. [5] Mary saith: Thou art the image of Adam: was not he first formed and then Eve? Look upon the sun, that according to the likeness of Adam it is bright. and upon the moon, that because of the transgression of Eve it is full of clay. For God did place Adam in the east and Eve in the west, and appointed the lights that the sun should shine on the earth unto Adam in the east in his fiery chariots, and the moon in the west should give light unto Eve with a countenance like milk. And she defiled the commandment of the Lord. Therefore was the moon stained with clay (*Latin*, is cloudy) and her light is not bright. Thou therefore, since thou art the likeness of Adam, oughtest to ask him: but in me was it contained that I might recover the strength of the female. [6] Now when they came up to the top of the mount, and the Master was withdrawn from them a little space, Peter saith unto Mary: Thou art she that hast brought to nought the transgression of Eve, changing it from shame into joy; it is lawful, therefore, for thee to ask. [7] When Jesus appeared again, Bartholomew saith unto him: Lord, show us the adversary of men that we may behold him, of what fashion he is, and what is his work, and whence he cometh forth, and what power he hath that he spared not even thee, but caused thee to be hanged upon the tree. [8] But Jesus looked upon him and said: Thou bold heart! thou askest for that which thou art not able to look upon. [9] But Bartholomew was troubled and fell at Jesus' feet and began to speak thus: O lamp that cannot be quenched, Lord Jesus Christ, maker of the eternal light that hast given unto them that love thee the grace that beautifieth all, and hast given us the eternal light by thy coming into the world, that hast accomplished the work of the Father, hast turned the shame-facedness of Adam into mirth, hast done away the sorrow of Eve with a cheerful countenance by thy birth from a virgin: remember not evil against me but grant me the word of mine asking. (*Latin*, who didst come down into the world, who hast confirmed the eternal word of the Father, who hast called the sadness of joy, who hast made the shame of Eve glad, and restored her by vouchsafing to be contained in the womb.) [10] And as he thus spake, Jesus raised him up and said unto him: Bartholomew, wilt thou see the adversary of men? I tell thee that when thou beholdest him, not thou only but the rest of [11] But they all said unto him: Lord, let us behold him. [12] And he led them down from the Mount of Olives and looked wrathfully upon the angels that keep hell (Tartarus), and beckoned unto Michael to sound the trumpet in the height of the heavens. And Michael sounded, and the earth shook, and Beliar came up, being held by 660 (560 Gr., 6,064 *Latin*, 6,060 *Latin*) angels and bound with fiery chains. 12 And the length of him was 1,600 cubits and his breadth 40 (*Latin*, 300, *Slavonic* 17) cubits (*Latin*, his length 1,900 cubits, his breadth 700, one wing of him 80), and his face was like a lightning of fire and his eyes full of darkness (like sparks, *Slavonic*). And out of his nostrils came a stinking smoke; and his mouth was as the gulf of a precipice, and the one of his wings was four-score cubits. [14] And straightway when the apostles saw him, they fell to the earth on their faces and became as dead. [15] But Jesus came near and raised the apostles and gave them a spirit of power, and he saith unto Bartholomew: Come near, Bartholomew, and trample with thy feet on his neck, and he will tell thee his work, what it is, and how he deceiveth men. [16] And Jesus stood afar off with the rest of the apostles. [17] And Barthololmew feared, and raised his voice and said: Blessed be the name of thine immortal kingdom from henceforth even for ever. And when he had spoken, Jesus permitted him, saying: Go and tread upon the neck of Beliar: and Bartholomew ran quickly upon him and trode upon his neck: and Beliar trembled. (For this verse the Vienna MS. has: And Bartholomew raised his voice and said thus: O womb more spacious than a city, wider than the spreading of the heavens, that contained him whom the seven heavens contain not, but thou without pain didst contain sanctified in thy bosom, etc.: evidently out of place. *Latin* has only: Then did Antichrist tremble and was filled with fury.) [18] And Bartholomew was afraid, and fled, and said unto Jesus: Lord, give me an hem of thy garments (*Latin*, the kerchief (?) from thy shoulders) that I may have courage to draw near unto him. [19] But Jesus said unto him: Thou canst not take an hem of my garments, for these are not my garments which I wore before I was crucified. [20] And Bartholomew said: Lord, I fear lest, like as he spared not thine angels, he swallow me up also. [21] Jesus saith unto him: Were not all things made by my word, and by the will of my Father the spirits were made subject unto Solomon? thou, therefore, being commanded by my word, go in my name and ask him what thou wilt. (*Latin* omits [20].) [22] [And Bartholomew made the sign of the cross and prayed unto Jesus and went behind him. And Jesus said to him: Draw near. And as Bartholomew drew near, fire was kindled on every side, so that his garments appeared fiery. Jesus saith to Bartholomew: As I said unto thee, tread upon his neck and ask him what is his power.] And Bartholomew went and trode upon his neck, and pressed down his face into the earth as far as his ears. [23] And Bartholomew saith unto him: Tell me who thou art and what is thy name. And he said to him: Lighten me a little, and I will tell thee who

I am and how I came hither, and what my work is and what my power is. 24 And he lightened him and saith to him: Say all that thou hast done and all that thou doest. 25 And Beliar answered and said: If thou wilt know my name, at the first I was called Satanael, which is interpreted a messenger of God, but when I rejected the image of God my name was called Satanas, that is, an angel that keepeth hell (Tartarus). 26 And again Bartholomew saith unto him: Reveal unto me all things and hide nothing from me. 27 And he said unto him: I swear unto thee by the power of the glory of God that even if I would hide aught I cannot, for he is near that would convict me. For if I were able I would have destroyed you like one of them that were before you. 28 For, indeed, I was formed (al. called) the first angel: for when God made the heavens, he took a handful of fire and formed me first, Michael second [Vienna MS. here has these sentences: for he had his Son before the heavens and the earth and we were formed (for when he took thought to create all things, his Son spake a word), so that we also were created by the will of the Son and the consent of the Father. He formed, I say, first me, next Michael the chief captain of the hosts that are above], Gabriel third, Uriel fourth, Raphael fifth, Nathanael sixth, and other angels of whom I cannot tell the names. [Jerusalem MS., Michael, Gabriel, Raphael, Uriel, Xathanael, and other 6,000 angels. *Latin* I, Michael the honour of power, third Raphael, fourth Gabriel, and other seven. *Latin*, Raphael third, Gabriel fourth, Uriel fifth, Zathael sixth, and other six.] For they are the rod-bearers (lictors) of God, and they smite me with their rods and pursue me seven times in the night and seven times in the day, and leave me not at all and break in pieces all my power. These are the (twelve, *Latin*) angels of vengeance which stand before the throne of God: these are the angels that were first formed. 30 And after them were formed all the angels. In the first heaven are an hundred myriads, and in the second an hundred myriads, and in the third an hundred myriads, and in the fourth an hundred myriads, and in the fifth an hundred myriads, and in the sixth an hundred myriads, and in the seventh (an hundred myriads, and outside the seven heavens, Jerusalem MS.) is the first firmament (flat surface) wherein are the powers which work upon men. 31 For there are four other angels set over the winds. The first angel is over the north, and he is called Chairoum (... broil, Jerusalem MS.; *Latin*, angel of the north, Mauch), and hath in his hand a rod of fire, and restraineth the super-fluity of moisture that the earth be not overmuch wet. 32 And the angel that is over the north is called Oertha (*Latin*, Alfatha): he hath a torch of fire and putteth it to his sides, and they warm the great coldness of him that he freeze not the world. 33 And the angel that is over the south is called Kerkoutha (*Latin*, Cedar) and they break his fierceness that he shake not the earth. 34 And the angel that is over the south-west is called Naoutha, and he hath a rod of snow in his hand and putteth it into his mouth, and quencheth the fire that cometh out of his mouth. And if the angel quenched it not at his mouth it would set all the world on fire. 35 And there is another angel over the sea which maketh it rough with the waves thereof. 36 But the 37 Bartholomew saith unto him: How chastisest thou the souls of men? 38 Beliar saith unto him: Wilt thou that I declare unto thee the punishment of the hypocrites, of the back-biters, of the jesters, of the idolaters, and the covetous, and the adulterers, and the wizards, and the diviners, and of them that believe in us, and of all whom I look upon (deceive?)? (38 *Latin*: When I will show any illusion by them. But they that do these things, and they that consent unto them or follow them, do perish with me.) 39 Bartholomew said unto him: Declare quickly how thou persuadest men not to follow God and thine evil arts, that are slippery and dark, that they should leave the straight and shining paths of the Lord.) 39 Bartholomew saith unto him: I will that thou declare it in few words. 40 And he smote his teeth together, gnashing them, and there came up out of the bottomless pit a wheel having a sword flashing with fire, and in the sword were pipes. 41 And I (he) asked him, saying: What is this sword? 42 And he said: This sword is the sword of the gluttonous: for into this pipe are sent they that through their gluttony devise all manner of sin; into the second pipe are sent the backbiters which backbite their neighbour secretly; into the third pipe are sent the hypocrites and the rest whom I overthrow by my contrivance. (*Latin*: 40 And Antichrist said: I will tell thee. And a wheel came up out of the abyss, having seven fiery knives. The first knife hath twelve pipes (canales) ... 42 Antichrist answered: The pipe of fire in the first knife, in it are put the casters of lots and diviners and enchanters, and they that believe in them or have sought them, because in the iniquity of their heart they have invented false divinations. In the second pipe of fire are first the blasphemers ... suicides ... idolaters.... In the rest are first perjurers ... (long enumeration).) 43 And Bartholomew said: Dost thou then do these things by thyself alone? 44 And Satan said: If I were able to go forth by myself, I would have destroyed the whole world in three days: but neither I nor any of the six hundred go forth. For we have other swift ministers whom we command, and we furnish them with an hook of many points and send them forth to hunt, and they catch for us souls of men, enticing them with sweetness of divers baits, that is by drunkenness and laughter, by backbiting, hypocrisy, pleasures, fornication, and the rest of the 45 And I will tell thee also the rest of the names of the angels. The angel of the hail is called Mermeoth, and he holdeth the hail upon his head, and my ministers do adjure him and send him whither they will. And other angels are there over the snow, and other over the thunder, and other over the lightning, and when any spirit of us would go forth either by land or by sea, these angels send forth fiery stones and set our limbs on fire. (*Latin* enumerates all the transgressions 46 Bartholomew saith: Be still (be muzzled) thou dragon of the pit. 47 And Beliar said: Many things will I tell thee of the angels. They that run together throughout the heavenly places and the earthly are these: Mermeoth, Onomatath, Douth, Melioth, Charouth, Graphathas, Oethra, Nephonos, Chalkatoura. With them do fly (are administered?) the things that are in heaven and on earth and under the earth. 48 Bartholomew saith unto him: Be still (be muzzled) and be faint, that I may entreat my Lord. 49 And Bartholomew fell upon his face and cast earth upon his head and began to say: O Lord Jesu Christ, the great and glorious name. All the choirs of the angels praise thee, O Master, and I that am unworthy with my lips ... do praise thee, O Master. Hearken unto me thy servant, and as thou didst choose me from the receipt of custom and didst not suffer me to have my conversation unto the end in my former deeds, O Lord Jesu Christ, hearken unto me and have mercy upon the sinners. 50 And when he had so said, the Lord saith unto him: Rise up, suffer him that groaneth to arise: I will declare the rest unto thee. 51 And Bartholomew raised up Satan and said unto him: Go unto thy place, with thine angels, but the Lord hath mercy upon all his world. (50, 51, again enormously amplified in *Latin*. Satan complains that he has been tricked into telling his secrets before the time. The interpolation is to some extent dated by this sentence: ' Simon Magus and Zaroes and Arfaxir and Jannes and Mambres are my brothers.' Zaroes and Arfaxatare wizards who figure in the *Latin* Acts of Matthew and of Simon and Jude (see below). 52 But the devil said: Suffer me, and I will tell thee how I was cast down into this place and how the Lord did make man. 53 I was going to and fro in the world, and God said unto Michael: Bring me a clod from the four corners of the earth, and water out of the four rivers of paradise. And when Michael brought them God formed Adam in the regions of the east, and shaped the clod which was shapeless, and stretched sinews and veins upon it and established it with Joints; and he worshipped him, himself for his own sake first, because he was the image of God, therefore he worshipped him. 54 And when I came from the ends of the earth Michael said: Worship thou the image of God, which he hath made according to his likeness. But I said: I am fire of fire, I was the first angel formed, and shall worship clay and matter? 55 And Michael saith to me: Worship, lest God be wroth with thee. But I said to him: God will not be wroth with me; but I will set my throne over against his throne, and I will be as he is. Then was God wroth with me and cast me down, having commanded the windows of heaven to be opened. 56 And when I was cast down, he asked also the six hundred that were under me, if they would worship: but they said: Like as we have seen the first angel do, neither will we worship him that is less than ourselves. Then were the six hundred also cast down by him with me. 57 And when we were cast down upon the earth we were senseless for forty years, and when the sun shone forth seven times brighter than fire, suddenly I awaked; and I looked about and saw the six hundred that were under me senseless. 58 And I awaked my son Salpsan and took him to counsel how I might deceive the man on whose account I was cast out of the heavens. 59 And thus did I contrive it. I took a vial in mine hand and scraped the sweat from off my breast and the hair of mine armpits, and washed myself (*Latin*, I took fig leaves in my hands and wiped the sweat from my bosom and below mine arms and cast it down beside the streams of waters. 69 is greatly prolonged in this text) in the springs of the waters whence the four rivers flow out, and Eve drank of it and desire came upon her: for if she had not drunk of that water I should not have been able to deceive her. 61 And Bartholomew came and fell at Jesus' feet and began with tears to say thus: Abba, Father, that art past finding out by us, Word of the Father, whom the seven heavens hardly contained, but who wast pleased to be contained easily and without pain within the body of the Virgin: whom the Virgin knew not that she bare: thou by thy thought hast ordained all things to be: thou givest us that which we need before thou art entreated. 62 Thou that didst wear a crown of thorns that thou mightest prepare for us that repent the precious crown from heaven; that didst hang upon the tree, that (a clause gone): (*Latin*, that thou mightest turn from us the tree of lust and concupiscence (etc., etc.). The verse is prolonged for over 40 lines) (that didst drink wine mingled with gall) that thou mightest give us to drink of the wine of compunction, and wast pierced in the side with a spear that thou mightest fill us with thy body and thy blood: 63 Thou that gavest names unto the four rivers: to the first Phison, because of the faith (pistis) which thou didst appear in the world to preach; to the second Geon, for that man was made of earth (ge); to the third Tigris, because by thee was revealed unto us the consubstantial Trinity in the heavens (to make anything of this we must read Trigis); to the fourth Euphrates, because by thy presence in the world thou madest every soul to rejoice (euphranai) through the word of immortality. ⁶⁴ My God, and Father, the greatest, my King: save, Lord, the sinners. ⁶⁵ When he had thus prayed Jesus said unto him: Bartholomew, my Father did name me Christ, that I might come down upon earth and anoint every man that cometh unto me with the oil of life: and he did call me Jesus that I might heal every sin of them that know not . . . and give unto men (several corrupt words: the ⁶⁶ And again Bartholomew saith unto him: Lord, is it lawful for me to reveal these mysteries unto every man? Jesus saith unto him: Bartholomew, my beloved, as many as are faithful and are able to keep them unto themselves, to them mayest thou entrust these things. For some there are that be worthy of them, but there are also other some unto whom it is not fit to entrust them: for they are vain (swaggerers), drunkards, proud, unmerciful, partakers in idolatry, authors of fornication, slanderers, teachers of foolishness, and doing all works that are of the devil, and therefore are they not worthy that these should be entrusted to them. ⁶⁸ And also they are secret, because of those that cannot contain them; for as many as can contain them shall have a part in them. Herein (Hitherto?) therefore, my beloved, have I spoken unto thee, for blessed art thou and all thy kindred which of their choice have this word entrusted unto them; for all they that of my judgement. ⁶⁹ Then I, Bartholomew, which wrote these things in mine heart, took hold on the hand of Glory be to thee, O Lord Jesus Christ, that givest unto all thy grace which all we have perceived. Alleluia. Glory be to thee, O Lord, the life of sinners. Glory be to thee, O Lord, death is put to shame. Glory be to thee, O Lord, the treasure of righteousness. For unto God do we sing. ⁷⁰ And as Bartholomew thus spake again, Jesus put off his mantle and took a kerchief from the neck of Bartholomew and began to rejoice and say (⁷⁰ *Latin*, Then Jesus took a kerchief (?) I and said: I am good: mild and gracious and merciful, strong and righteous, wonderful and holy): I am good. Alleluia. I am meek and gentle. Alleluia. Glory be to thee, O Lord: for I give gifts unto all them that desire me. Alleluia. Glory be to thee, O Lord, world without end. Amen. Alleluia. ⁷¹ And when he had ceased, the apostles kissed him, and he gave them the peace of love.

5

¹ Bartholomew saith unto him: Declare unto us, Lord what sin is heavier than all sins? ² Jesus saith unto him: Verily I say unto thee that hypocrisy and backbiting is heavier than all sins: for because of them, the prophet said in the psalm, that 'the ungodly shall not rise in the judgement, neither sinners in the council of the righteous', neither the ungodly in the judgement of my Father. Verily, verily, I say unto you, that every sin shall be forgiven unto every man, but the sin against the Holy Ghost shall not be forgiven. ³ And Bartholomew saith unto him: What is the sin against the Holy Ghost? ⁴ Jesus saith unto him: Whosoever shall decree against any man that hath served my holy Father hath blasphemed against the Holy Ghost: For every man that serveth God worshipfully is worthy of the Holy Ghost, and he that speaketh anything evil against him shall not be forgiven. ⁵ Woe unto him that sweareth by the head of God, yea woe (?) to him that sweareth falsely by him truly. For there are twelve heads of God the most high: for he is the truth, and in him is no lie, neither forswearing. ⁶ Ye, therefore, go ye and preach unto all the world the word of truth, and thou, Bartholomew, preach this word unto every one that desireth it; and as many as ⁷ Bartholomew saith: O Lord, and if any sin with sin of the body, what is their reward? ⁸ And Jesus said: It is good if he that is baptized present his baptism blameless: but the pleasure of the flesh will become a lover. For a single marriage belongeth to sobriety: for verily I say unto thee, he that sinneth after the third marriage (wife) is unworthy of God. (⁸ *Latin* is to this effect: . . . But if the lust of the flesh come upon him, he ought to be the husband of one wife. The married, if they are good and pay tithes, will receive a hundredfold. A second marriage is lawful, on condition of the diligent performance of good works, and due payment of tithes: but a third marriage is reprobated: and virginity is best.) ⁹ But ye, preach ye unto every man that they keep themselves from such things: for I depart not from you and I do supply you with the Holy Ghost. (*Latin*, At the end of ⁹, Jesus ascends in the clouds, and two angels appear and say: 'Ye men of Galilee', and the rest) ¹⁰ And Bartholomew worshipped him with the apostles, and glorified God earnestly, saying: Glory be to thee, Holy Father, Sun unquenchable, incomprehensible, full of light. Unto thee be glory, unto thee honour and adoration, world without end. Amen. (*Latin*, End of the questioning of the most blessed Bartholomew and (or) the other apostles with the Lord Jesus Christ.)

The Gospel of Nicodemus, or Acts of Pontius Pilate

1

1 Christ accused to Pilate by the Jews of healing on the sabbath, 9 summoned before Pilate by a messenger who does him honour, 20 worshipped by the standards bowing down to him.

¹ ANNAS and Caiaphas, and Summas, and Datam, Gamaliel, Judas, Levi, Nepthalim, Alexander, Cyrus, and other Jews, went to Pilate about Jesus, accusing him with many bad crimes. ² And said, We are assured that Jesus is the son of Joseph the carpenter, land born of Mary, and that he declares himself the Son of God, and a king; and not only so, but attempts the dissolution of the sabbath, and the laws of our fathers. ³ Pilate replied; What is it which he declares? And what is it which he attempts dissolving? ⁴ The Jews told him, We have a law which forbids doing cures on the sabbath day; but he cures both the lame and the deaf, those afflicted with the palsy, the blind, and lepers, and demoniacs, on that day by wicked methods. ⁵ Pilate replied, How can he do this by wicked methods? They answered, He is a conjurer, and casts out devils by the prince of the devils; and so all things become subject to him. ⁶ Then said Pilate, Casting out devils seems not to be the work of an unclean spirit, but to proceed from the power of God. ⁷ The Jews replied to Pilate, We entreat your highness to summon him to appear before your tribunal, and hear him yourself. ⁸ Then Pilate called a messenger and said to him, By what means will Christ be brought hither? ⁹ Then went the messenger forth, and knowing Christ, worshipped him; and having spread the cloak which he had in his hand upon the ground, he said, Lord, walk upon this, and go in, for the governor calls thee. ¹⁰ When the Jews perceived what the messenger had done they exclaimed (against him) to Pilate, and said, Why did you not give him his summons by a beadle, and not by a messenger?–For the messenger, when he saw him, worshipped him, and spread the cloak which he had in his hand upon the ground before him, and said to him, Lord, the governor calls thee. ¹¹ Then Pilate called the messenger, and said, Why hast thou done thus? ¹² The messenger replied, When thou sentest me from Jerusalem to Alexander, I saw Jesus sitting in a mean figure upon a she-ass, and the children of the Hebrews cried out, Hosannah, holding boughs of trees in their hands. ¹³ Others spread their garments in the way, and said, Save us, thou who art in heaven; blessed is he who cometh in the name of the Lord. ¹⁴ Then the Jews cried out, against the messenger, and said, The children of the Hebrews made their acclamations in the Hebrew language; and how couldst thou, who art a Greek, understand the Hebrew? ¹⁵ The messenger answered them and said, I asked one of the Jews and said, What is this which the children do cry out in the Hebrew language? ¹⁶ And he explained it to me, saying, they cry out Hosannah, which being interpreted, is, O, Lord, save me; or, O Lord, save. ¹⁷ Pilate then said to them, Why do you yourselves testify to the words spoken by the children, namely, by your silence? In what has the messenger done amiss? And they were silent. ¹⁸ Then the governor said unto the messenger, Go forth and endeavour by any means to bring him in. ¹⁹ But the messenger went forth, and did as before; and said, Lord, come in, for the governor calleth thee. ²⁰ And as Jesus was going in by the ensigns, who carried the standards, the tops of them bowed down and worshipped Jesus. ²¹ Whereupon the Jews exclaimed more vehemently against the ensigns. ²² But Pilate said to the Jews, I know it is not pleasing to you that the tops of the standards did of themselves bow and worship Jesus; but why do ye exclaim against the ensigns, as if they had bowed and worshipped? ²³ They replied to Pilate, We saw the ensigns themselves bowing and worshipping Jesus. ²⁴ Then the governor called the ensigns and said unto them, Why did you do thus? ²⁵ The ensigns said to Pilate, We are all Pagans and worship the gods in temples; and how should we think anything about worshipping him? We only held the standards in our hands and they bowed themselves and worshipped him. ²⁶ Then said Pilate to the rulers of the synagogue, Do ye yourselves choose some strong men, and let them hold the standards, and we shall see whether they will then bend of themselves. ²⁷ So the elders of the Jews sought out twelve of the most strong and able old men, and made them hold the standards and they stood in the presence of the governor. ²⁸ Then Pilate said to the messenger, Take Jesus out, and by some means bring him in again. And Jesus and the messenger went out of the hall. ²⁹ And Pilate called the ensigns who before had borne the standards, and swore to them, that if they had not borne the standards in that manner when Jesus before entered in, he would cut off their heads. ³⁰ Then the governor commanded Jesus to come in again. ³¹ And the messenger did as he had done before, and very much entreated Jesus that he would go upon his cloak, and walk on it, and he did walk upon it, and went in. ³² And when Jesus went in, the standards bowed themselves as before, and worshipped him.

2

2 Is compassionated by Pilate's wife, 7 charged with being born in fornication. 12 Testimony to the betrothing of his parents. Hatred of the Jews to him.

[1] NOW when Pilate saw this, he was afraid, and was about to rise from his seat. [2] But while he thought to rise, his own wife who stood at a distance, sent to him, saying Have thou nothing to do with that just man; for I have suffered much concerning him in a vision this night. [3] When the Jews heard this they said to Pilate, Did we not say unto thee, He is a conjuror? Behold, he hath caused thy wife to dream. [4] Pilate then calling Jesus, said, thou hast heard what they testify against thee, and makest no answer? [5] Jesus replied, If they had not a power of speaking, they could not have spoke; but because every one has the command of his own tongue, to speak both good and bad, let him look to it. [6] But the elders of the Jews answered, and said to Jesus, What shall we look to? [7] In the first place, we know this concerning thee, that thou wast born through fornication; secondly, that upon the account of thy birth the infants were slain in Bethlehem; thirdly, that thy father and mother Mary fled into Egypt, because they could not trust their own people. [8] Some of the Jews who stood by spake more favourably, We cannot say that he was born through fornication; but we know that his mother Mary was betrothed to Joseph, and so he was not born through fornication. [9] Then said Pilate to the Jews who affirmed him to be born through fornication, This your account is not true, seeing there was a betrothment, as they testify who are of your own nation. [10] Annas and Caiaphas spake to Pilate, All this multitude of people is to be regarded, who cry out, that he was born through fornication, and is a conjuror; but they who deny him to be born through fornication, are his proselytes and disciples. [11] Pilate answered Annas and Caiaphas, Who are the proselytes? They answered, They are those who are the children of Pagans, and are not become Jews, but followers of him. [12] Then replied Eleazer, and Asterius, and Antonius, and James, Caras and Samuel, Isaac and Phinees, Crispus and Agrippa, Annas and Judas, We are not proselytes, but children of Jews, and speak the truth, and were present when Mary was betrothed. [13] Then Pilate addressing himself to the twelve men who spake this, said to them, I conjure you by the life of Cæsar, that ye faithfully declare whether he was born through fornication, and those things be true which ye have related. [14] They answered Pilate, We have a law, whereby we are forbid to swear, it being a sin: Let them swear by the life of Cæsar that it is not as we have said, and we will be contented to be put to death. [15] Then said Annas and Caiaphas to Pilate, Those twelve men will not believe that we know him to be basely born, and to be a conjuror, although he pretends that he is the son of God, and a king: which we are so far from believing, that we tremble to hear. [16] Then Pilate commanded every one to go out except the twelve men who said he was not born through fornication, and Jesus to withdraw to a distance, and said to them, Why have the Jews a mind to kill Jesus? [17] They answered him, They are angry because he wrought cures on the Sabbath day. Pilate said, Will they kill him for good work? They say unto him, Yes, Sir.

3

1 Is exonerated by Pilate. 11 Disputes with Pilate concerning Truth.

[1] THEN Pilate, filled with anger, went out of the hall, and said to the Jews, I call the whole world to witness that I find no fault in that man. [2] The Jews replied to Pilate, If he had not been a wicked person, we had not brought him before thee. [3] Pilate said to them, Do ye take him and try him by your law. [4] Then the Jews said, It is not lawful for us to put any one to death. [5] Pilate said to the Jews, The command, therefore thou shalt not kill, belongs to you, but not to me. [6] And he went again into the hall, and called Jesus by himself, and said to him, Art thou the king of the Jews? [7] And Jesus answering, said to Pilate, Dost thou speak this of thyself, or did the Jews tell it thee concerning me? [8] Pilate answering, said to Jesus, Am I a Jew? The whole nation and rulers of the Jews have delivered thee up to me. What hast thou done? [9] Jesus answering, said, My kingdom is not of this world: if my kingdom were of this world, then would my servants fight, and I should not have been delivered to the Jews; but now my kingdom is not from hence. [10] Pilate said, Art thou a king then? Jesus answered, Thou sayest that I am a king: to this end was I born, and for this end came I into the world; and for this purpose I came, that I should bear witness to the truth; and every one who is of the truth, heareth my voice. [11] Pilate saith to him, What is truth? [12] Jesus said, Truth is from heaven. [13] Pilate said, Therefore truth is not on earth. [14] Jesus said to Pilate, Believe that truth is on earth among those, who when they have the power of judgment, are governed by truth, and form right judgment.

4

1 Pilate finds no fault in Jesus. 16 The Jews demand his crucifixion.

[1] THEN Pilate left Jesus in the hall, and went out to the Jews, and said, I find not any one fault in Jesus. [2] The Jews say unto him, But he said, I can destroy the temple of God, and in three days build it up again. [3] Pilate saith unto them, What sort of temple is that of which he speaketh? [4] The Jews say unto him, That which Solomon was forty-six years in building, he said he would destroy, and in three days build up. [5] Pilate said to them again, I am innocent from the blood of that man; do ye look to it. [6] The Jews say to him, His blood be upon us and our children. Then Pilate calling together the elders and scribes, priests and Levites, saith to them privately, Do not act thus; I have found nothing in your charge (against him) concerning his curing sick persons, and breaking the sabbath, worthy of death. [7] The Priests and Levites replied to Pilate, By the life of Cæsar, if any one be a blasphemer, he is worthy of death; but this man hath blasphemed against the Lord. [8] Then the governor again commanded the Jews to depart out of the hall; and calling Jesus, said to him, What shall I do with thee? [9] Jesus answered him, Do according as it is written. [10] Pilate said to him, How is it written? [11] Jesus saith to him, Moses and the prophets have prophesied concerning my suffering and resurrection. [12] The Jews hearing this, were provoked, and said to Pilate, Why wilt thou any longer hear the blasphemy of that man? [13] Pilate saith to them, If these words seem to you blasphemy, do ye take him, bring him to your court, and try him according to your law. [14] The Jews reply to Pilate, Our law saith, he shall be obliged to receive nine and thirty stripes, but if after this manner he shall blaspheme against the Lord, he shall be stoned. [15] Pilate saith unto them, If that speech of his was blasphemy, do ye try him according to your law. [16] The Jews say to Pilate, Our law commands us not to put any one to death: we desire that he may be crucified, because he deserves the death of the cross. [17] Pilate saith to them, It is not fit he should be crucified: let him be only whipped and sent away. [18] But when the governor looked upon the people that were present and the Jews, he saw many of the Jews in tears, and said to the chief priests of the Jews, All the people do not desire his death. [19] The elders of the Jews answered to Pilate, We and all the people came hither for this very purpose, that he should die. [20] Pilate saith to them, Why should he die? [21] They said to him, Because he declares himself to be the Son of God, and a King.

5

1 Nicodemus speaks in defence of Christ, and relates his miracles. 12 Another Jew, 26 with Veronica, 34 Centurio, and others, testify of other miracles.

[1] BUT Nicodemus, a certain Jew, stood before the governor, and said, I entreat thee, O righteous judge, that thou wouldst favour me with the liberty of speaking a few words. [2] Pilate said to him, Speak on. [3] Nicodemus said, I spake to the elders of the Jews, and the scribes, and priests and Levites, and all the multitude of the Jews, in their assembly; What is it ye would do with this man? [4] He is a man who hath wrought many useful and glorious miracles, such as no man on earth ever wrought before, nor will ever work. Let him go, and do him no harm; if he cometh from God, his miracles, (his miraculous cures) will continue; but if from men, they will come to nought. [5] Thus Moses, when he was sent by God into Egypt, wrought the miracles which God commanded him, before Pharaoh king of Egypt; and though the magicians of that country, Jannes and Jambres, wrought by their magic the same miracles which Moses did, yet they could not work all which he did; [6] And the miracles which the magicians wrought, were not of God, as ye know, O Scribes and Pharisees; but they who wrought them perished, and all who believed them. [7] And now let this man go; because the very miracles for which ye accuse him, are from God; and he is not worthy of death. [8] The Jews then said to Nicodemus, Art thou become his disciple, and making speeches in his favour? [9] Nicodemus said to them, Is the governor become his disciple also, and does he make speeches for him? Did not Cæsar place him in that high post? [10] When the Jews heard this they trembled, and gnashed their teeth at Nicodemus, and said to him, Mayest thou receive his doctrine for truth, and have thy lot with Christ! [11] Nicodemus replied, Amen; I will receive his doctrine, and my lot with him, as ye have said. [12] Then another certain Jew rose up, and desired leave of the governor to hear him a few words. [13] And the governor said, Speak what thou hast a mind. [14] And he said, I lay for thirty-eight years by the sheep-pool at Jerusalem, labouring under a great infirmity, and waiting for a cure which should be wrought by the coming of an angel, who at a certain time troubled the water; and whosoever first after the troubling of the water stepped in, was made whole of whatsoever disease he had. [15] And when Jesus saw me languishing there, he said to me, Wilt thou be made whole? And I answered, Sir, I have no man, when the water is troubled, to put me into the pool. [16] And he said unto me, Rise, take up thy bed and walk. And I was immediately made whole, and took up my bed and walked. [17] The Jews then said to Pilate, Our Lord Governor, pray ask him what day it was on which he was cured of his infirmity. [18] The infirm person replied, It was on the sabbath. [19] The Jews said to Pilate, Did we not say that he wrought his cures on the sabbath, and

cast out devils by the prince of devils? ²⁰ Then another certain Jew came forth, and said, I was blind, could hear sounds, but could not see any one; and as Jesus was going along, I heard the multitude passing by, and I asked what was there? ²¹ They told me that Jesus was passing by: then I cried out, saying, Jesus, Son of David, have mercy on me. And he stood still, and commanded that I should be brought to him, and said to me, What wilt thou? ²² I said, Lord, that I may receive my sight. ²³ He said to me, Receive thy sight: and presently I saw, and followed him, rejoicing and giving thanks. ²⁴ Another Jew also came forth, and said, I was a leper, and he cured me by his word only, saying, I will, be thou clean; and presently I was cleansed from my leprosy. ²⁵ And another Jew came forth, and said, I was crooked, and he made me straight by his word. ²⁶ And a certain woman named Veronica, said, I was afflicted with an issue of blood twelve years, and I touched the hem of his garments, and presently the issue of my blood stopped. ²⁷ The Jews then said, We have a law, that a woman shall not be allowed as an evidence. ²⁸ And, after other things, another Jew said, I saw Jesus invited to a wedding with his disciples, and there was a want of wine in Cana of Galilee; ²⁹ And when the wine was all drank, he commanded the servants that they should fill six pots which were there with water, and they filled them up to the brim, and he blessed them, and turned the water into wine, and all the people drank, being surprised at this miracle. ³⁰ And another Jew stood forth, and said, I saw Jesus teaching in the synagogue at Capernaum; and there was in the synagogue a certain man who had a devil; and he cried out, saying, let me alone; what have we to do with thee, Jesus of Nazareth? Art thou come to destroy us? I know that thou art the Holy One of God. ³¹ And Jesus rebuked him, saying, Hold thy peace, unclean spirit, and come out of the man; and presently he came out of him, and did not at all hurt him. ³² The following things were also said by a Pharisee; I saw that a great company came to Jesus from Galilee and Judaea, and the sea-coast, and many countries about Jordan, and many infirm persons came to him, and he healed them all. ³³ And I heard the unclean spirits crying out, and saying, Thou art the Son of God. And Jesus strictly charged them, that they should not make him known. ³⁴ After this another person, whose name was Centurio, said, I saw Jesus in Capernaum, and I entreated him, saying, Lord, my servant lieth at home sick of the palsy. ³⁵ And Jesus said to me, I will come and cure him. ³⁶ But I said, Lord, I am not worthy that thou shouldst come under my roof; but only speak the word, and my servant shall be healed. ³⁷ And Jesus said unto me, Go thy way; and as thou hast believed, so be it done unto thee. And my servant was healed from that same hour. ³⁸ Then a certain nobleman said, I had a son in Capernaum, who lay at the point of death; and when I heard that Jesus was come into Galilee, I went and besought him that he would come down to my house, and heal my son, for he was at the point of death. ³⁹ He said to me, Go thy way, thy son liveth. ⁴⁰ And my son was cured from that hour. ⁴¹ Besides these, also many others of the Jews, both men and women, cried out and said, He is truly the Son of God, who cures all diseases only by his word, and to whom the devils are altogether subject. ⁴² Some of them farther said,, This power can proceed fro none but God. ⁴³ Pilate said to the Jews Why are not the devils subject your doctors? ⁴⁴ Seine of them said, The power of subjecting devils can not proceed but from God. ⁴⁵ But others said to Pilate That he had raised Lazarus from the dead, after he had been four days in his grave. ⁴⁶ The governor hearing this, trembling said to the multitude of the Jews, What will it profit you to shed innocent blood?

6

1 Pilate dismayed by the turbulence of the Jews, 5 who demand Barabbas to be released, and Christ to be crucified, 9 Pilate warmly expostulates with them, 20 washes his hands of Christ's blood, 23 and sentences him to be whipped and crucified.

¹ THEN Pilate having called together Nicodemus, and the fifteen men who said that Jesus was not born through fornication, said to them, What shall I do, seeing there is like to be a tumult among the people. ² They said unto him, We know not; let them look to it who raise the tumult. ³ Pilate then called the multitude again, and said to them, Ye know that ye have a custom, that I should release to you one prisoner at the feast of the assover; ⁴ I have a noted prisoner, a murderer, who is called Barabbas, and Jesus who is called Christ, in whom I find nothing that deserves death; which of them therefore have you a mind that I should release to you? ⁵ They all cry out, and say, Release to us Barabbas. ⁶ Pilate saith to them, What then shall I do with Jesus who, is called Christ? ⁷ They all answer, Let him be crucified. ⁸ Again they cry out and say to Pilate, You are not the friend of Cæsar, if you release this man? For he hath declared that he is the Son of God, and a king. But are you inclined that he should be king, and not Cæsar? ⁹ Then Pilate filled with anger said to them, Your nation hath always been seditious, and you are always against those who have been serviceable to you? ¹⁰ The Jews replied, Who are those who have been serviceable to us? ¹¹ Pilate answered them, Your God who delivered you from the hard bondage of the Egyptians, and brought you over the Red Sea as though it had been dry land, and fed you in the wilderness with manna and the flesh of quails, and brought water out of the rock, and gave you a law from heaven: ¹² Ye provoked him all ways, and desired for yourselves a molten calf, and worshipped it, and sacrificed to it, and said, These are Thy Gods, O Israel, which brought thee out of the land of Egypt ¹³ On account of which your God was inclined to destroy you; but Moses interceded for you, and your God heard him, and forgave your iniquity. ¹⁴ Afterwards ye were enraged against, and would have killed your prophets, Moses and Aaron, when they fled to the tabernacle, and ye were always murmuring against God and his prophets. ¹⁵ And arising from his judgment seat, he would have gone out; but the Jews all cried out, We acknowledge Cæsar to be king, and not Jesus. ¹⁶ Whereas this person, as soon as he was born, the wise men came and offered gifts unto him; which when Herod heard, he was exceedingly troubled, and would have killed him. ¹⁷ When his father knew this, he fled with him and his mother Mary into Egypt. Herod, when he heard he was born, would have slain him; and accordingly sent and slew all the children which were in Bethlehem, and in all the coasts thereof, from two years old and under. ¹⁸ When Pilate heard this account, he was afraid; and commanding silence among the people, who made a noise, he said to Jesus, Art thou therefore a king? ¹⁹ All the Jews replied to Pilate, he is the very person whom Herod sought to have slain. ²⁰ Then Pilate taking water, washed his hands before the people and said, I am innocent of the blood of this just person; look ye to it . ²¹ The Jews answered and said, His blood be upon us and our children. ²² Then Pilate commanded Jesus to be brought before him, and spake to him in the following words: ²³ Thy own nation hath charged thee as making thyself a king; wherefore I, Pilate, sentence thee to be whipped according to the laws of former governors; and that thou be first bound, then hanged upon a cross in that place where thou art now a prisoner; and also two criminals with thee, whose names are Dimas and Gestas.

7

1 Manner of Christ's crucifixion with the two thieves.

¹ THEN Jesus went out of the hall, and the two thieves with him. ² And when they came to the place which is called Golgotha, they stript him of his raiment, and girt him about with a linen cloth, and put a crown of thorns upon his head, and put a reed in his hand. ³ And in like manner did they to the two thieves who were crucified with him, Dimas on his right hand and Gestas on his left. ⁴ But Jesus said, My Father, forgive them; For they know not what they do. ⁵ And they divided his garments, and upon his vesture they cast lots. ⁶ The people in the mean time stood by, and the chief priests and elders of the Jews mocked him, saying, he saved others, let him now save himself if he can; if he be the son of God, let him now come down from the cross. ⁷ The soldiers also mocked him, and taking vinegar and gall offered it to him to drink, and said to him, If thou art king of the Jews deliver thyself. ⁸ Then Longinus, a certain soldier, taking a spear, pierced his side, and presently there came forth blood and water. ⁹ And Pilate wrote the title upon the cross in Hebrew, Latin, and Greek letters, viz. This is the king of the Jews. ¹⁰ But one of the two thieves who were crucified with Jesus, whose name was Gestas, said to Jesus, If thou art the Christ, deliver thyself and us. ¹¹ But the thief who was crucified on his right hand, whose name was Dimas, answering, rebuked him, and said, Dost not thou fear God, who art condemned to this punishment? We indeed receive rightly and justly the demerit of our actions; but this Jesus, what evil hath he done? ¹² After this groaning, he said to Jesus, Lord, remember me when thou comest into thy kingdom. ¹³ Jesus answering, said to him, Verily I say unto thee, that this day thou shalt be with me in Paradise.

8

1 Miraculous appearance at his death. 10 The Jews say the eclipse was natural. 12 Joseph of Arimathæa embalms Christ's body and buries it.

¹ AND it was about the sixth hour, and darkness was upon the face of the whole earth until the ninth hour. ² And while the sun was eclipsed, behold the vail of the temple was rent from the top to the bottom; and the rocks also were rent, and the graves opened, and many bodies of saints, which slept, arose. ³ And about the ninth hour Jesus cried out with a loud voice, saying, Hely, Hely, lama zabacthani? Which being interpreted, is, My God, My God, why hast thou forsaken me? ⁴ And after these things, Jesus said, Father, into thy hands I commend my spirit; and having said this, he gave up the ghost. ⁵ But when the centurion saw that Jesus thus crying out gave up the ghost, he glorified God, and said, Of a truth this was a just man. ⁶ And all the people who stood by, were exceedingly troubled at the sight; and reflecting upon what had passed, smote upon their breasts, and then returned to the city of Jerusalem. ⁷ The centurion went to the governor, and related to him all that had passed; ⁸ And when he had heard all these things,

he was exceeding sorrowful; ⁹ And calling the Jews together, said to them, Have ye seen the miracle of the sun's eclipse, and the other things which came to pass, while Jesus was dying? ¹⁰ Which when the Jews heard, they answered to the governor, The eclipse of the sun happened according to its usual custom. ¹¹ But all those who were the acquaintance of Christ, stood at a distance, as did the women who had followed Jesus from Galilee, observing all these things. ¹² And behold a certain man of Arimathæa, named Joseph, who also was a disciple of Jesus, but not openly so, for fear of the Jews, came to the governor, and entreated the governor that he would give him leave to take away the body of Jesus from the cross. ¹³ And the governor gave him leave. ¹⁴ And Nicodemus came, bringing with him a mixture of myrrh and aloes about a hundred pound weight; and they took down Jesus from the cross with tears, and bound him with linen cloths with spices, according to the custom of burying among the Jews, ¹⁵ And placed him in a new tomb, which Joseph had built, and caused to be cut out of a rock, in which never any man had been put; and they rolled a great stone to the door of the sepulchre.

9

1 The Jews angry with Nicodemus; 5 and with Joseph of Arimathæa, 7 whom they imprison.

¹ WHEN the unjust Jews heard that Joseph had begged and buried the body of Jesus, they sought after Nicodemus; and those fifteen men who had testified before the Governor, that Jesus was not born through fornication, and other good persons who had shewn any good actions towards him. ² But when they all concealed themselves through fear of the Jews Nicodemus alone shewed himself to them, and said, How can such persons as these enter into the synagogue? ³ The Jews answered him, But how durst thou enter into the synagogue who wast a confederate with Christ? Let thy lot be along with him in the other world. ⁴ Nicodemus answered, Amen; so may it be, that I may have my lot with him in his kingdom. ⁵ In like manner Joseph, when he came to the Jews, said to them Why are ye angry with me for desiring the body of Jesus of Pilate? Behold, I have put him in my tomb, and wrapped him up in clean linen, and put a stone at the door of the sepulchre: ⁶ I have acted rightly towards him; but ye have acted unjustly aghast that just person, in crucifying him, giving him vinegar to drink, crowning him with thorns, tearing his body with whips, and prayed down the guilt of his blood upon you. ⁷ The Jews at the hearing of this were disquieted, and troubled; and they seized Joseph, and commanded him to be put in custody before the sabbath, and kept there till the sabbath was over. ⁸ And they said to him, Make confession; for at this time it is not lawful to do thee any harm, till the first day of the week come. But we know that thou wilt not be thought worthy of a burial; but we will give thy flesh to the birds of the air, and the beasts of the earth. ⁹ Joseph answered, That speech is like the speech of proud Goliath, who reproached the living God in speaking against David. But ye scribes and doctors know that God saith by the prophet, Vengeance is mine, and I will repay to you evil equal to that which ye have threatened to me. ¹⁰ The God whom you have hanged upon the cross, is able to deliver me out of your hands. All your wickedness will return upon you. ¹¹ For the governor, when he washed his hands, said, I am clear from the blood of this just person. But ye answered and cried out, His blood be upon us and our children. According as ye have said, may ye perish for ever. ¹² The elders of the Jews hearing these words, were exceedingly enraged; and seizing Joseph, they put him into a chamber where there was no window; they fastened the door, and put a seal upon the lock; ¹³ And Annas and Caiaphas placed a guard upon it, and took counsel with the priests and Levites, that they should all meet after the sabbath, and they contrived to what death they should put Joseph. ¹⁴ When they had done this, the rulers, Annas and Caiaphas, ordered Joseph to be brought forth. *In this place there is a portion of the Gospel lost or omitted, which cannot be supplied.*

10

1 Joseph's escape. 2 The soldiers relate Christ's resurrection. 18 Christ is seen preaching in Galilee. 21 The Jews repent of their cruelty to him.

¹ WHEN all the assembly heard this, they admired and were astonished, because they found the same seal upon the lock of the chamber, and could not find Joseph. ² Then Annas and Caiaphas went forth, and while they were all admiring at Joseph's being gone, behold one of the soldiers, who kept the sepulchre of Jesus, spake in the assembly. ³ That while they were guarding the sepulchre of Jesus, there was an earthquake; and we saw an angel of God roll away the stone of the sepulchre and sit upon it; ⁴ And his countenance was like lightning and his garment like snow; and we became through fear like persons dead. ⁵ And we heard an angel saying to the women at the sepulchre of Jesus, Do not fear; I know that you seek Jesus who was crucified; he is risen as he foretold. ⁶ Come and see the place where he was laid; and go presently, and tell his disciples that he is risen from the dead, and he will go before you into Galilee; there ye shall see him as he told you. ⁷ Then the Jews called together all the soldiers who kept the sepulchre of Jesus, and said to them, Who are those women, to whom the angel spoke? Why did ye not seize them? ⁸ The soldiers answered and said, We know not whom the women were; besides we became as dead persons through fear, and how could we seize those women? ⁹ The Jews said to them, As the Lord liveth we do not believe you. ¹⁰ The soldiers answering said to the Jews, when ye saw and heard Jesus working so many miracles, and did not believe him, how should ye believe us? Ye well said, As the Lord liveth, for the Lord truly does live. ¹¹ We have heard that ye shut up Joseph, who buried the body of Jesus, in a chamber, under a lock which was sealed; and when ye opened it, found him not there. ¹² Do ye then produce Joseph whom ye put under guard in the chamber, and we will produce Jesus whom we guarded in the sepulchre. ¹³ The Jews answered and said, We will produce Joseph, do ye produce Jesus. But Joseph is in his own city of Arimathæa. ¹⁴ The soldiers replied, If Joseph be in Arimathæa, and Jesus in Galilee, we heard the angel inform the women. ¹⁵ The Jews hearing this, were afraid, and said among themselves, If by any means these things should become public, then every body will believe in Jesus. ¹⁶ Then they gathered a large sum of money, and gave it to the soldiers, saying, Do ye tell the people that the disciples of Jesus came in the night when ye were asleep and stole away the body of Jesus; and if Pilate the governor should hear of this, we will satisfy him and secure you. ¹⁷ The soldiers accordingly took the money, and said as they were instructed by the Jews; and their report was spread abroad among the people. ¹⁸ But a certain priest Phinees, Ada a schoolmaster, and a Levite, named Ageus, they three came from Galilee to Jerusalem, and told the chief priests and all who were in the synagogues, saying, ¹⁹ We have seen Jesus, whom ye crucified, talking with his eleven disciples, and sitting in the midst of them in Mount Olivet, and saying to them, ²⁰ Go forth into the whole world, preach the Gospel to all nations, baptizing them in the name of the Father, and the Son, and the Holy Ghost; and whosoever shall believe and be baptized, shall be saved. ²¹ And when he had said these things to his disciples, we saw him ascending up to heaven. ²² When the chief priests, and elders, and Levites heard these things, they said to these three men, Give glory to the God of Israel, and make confession to him, whether those things are true, which ye say ye have seen and heard. ²³ They answering said, As the Lord of our fathers liveth, the God of Abraham, and the God of Isaac, and the God of Jacob, according as we heard Jesus talking with his disciples, and according as we saw him ascending up to heaven, so we have related the truth to you. ²⁴ And the three men farther answered, and said, adding these words, If we should not own the words which we heard Jesus speak, and that we saw him ascending into heaven, we should be guilty of sin. ²⁵ Then the chief priests immediately rose up, and holding the book of the law in their hands, conjured these men, saying, Ye shall no more hereafter declare those things which ye have spoke concerning Jesus. ²⁶ And they gave them a large sum of money, and sent other persons along with them, who should conduct them to their own country, that they might not by any means make any stay at Jerusalem. ²⁷ Then the Jews did assemble all together, and having expressed the most lamentable concern, said, What is this extraordinary thing which is come to pass in Jerusalem? ²⁸ But Annas and Caiaphas comforted them, saying, Why should we believe the soldiers who guarded the sepulchre of Jesus, in telling us, that an angel rolled away the stone from the door of the sepulchre? ²⁹ Perhaps his own disciples told them this, and gave them money that they should say so, and they themselves took away the body of Jesus. ³⁰ Besides, consider this, that there is no credit to be given to foreigners, because they also took a large sum of us, and they have declared to us according to the instructions which we gave them. They must either be faithful to us, or to the disciples of Jesus.

11

1 Nicodemus counsels the Jews. 6 Joseph found. 11 Invited by the Jews to return. 19 Relates the manner of his miraculous escape.

¹ THEN Nicodemus arose, and said, Ye say right, O sons of Israel, ye have heard what those three men have sworn by the Law of God, who said, We have seen Jesus speaking with his disciples upon Mount Olivet, and we saw him ascending up to heaven. ² And the scripture teacheth us that the blessed prophet Elijah was taken up to heaven; and Elisha being asked by the sons of the prophets, Where is our father Elijah? He said to them, that he is taken up to heaven. ³ And the sons of the prophets said to him, Perhaps the spirit hath carried him into one of the mountains of Israel, there perhaps we shall find him. And they besought Elisha, and he walked about with them three days, and they could not find him. ⁴ And now hear me, O sons of Israel, and let us send men into the mountains of Israel, lest perhaps the spirit hath carried away Jesus, and there perhaps we shall find him, and be satisfied. ⁵ And the counsel of Nicodemus pleased all the people; and they sent forth

men who sought for Jesus, but could not find him: and they returning, said, We went all about, but could not find Jesus, but we have found Joseph in his city of Arimathæa. ⁶ The rulers hearing this, and all the people, were glad, and praised the God of Israel, because Joseph was found, whom they had shut up in a chamber, and could not find. ⁷ And when they had formed a large assembly, the chief priests said, By what means shall we bring Joseph to us to speak with him? ⁸ And taking a piece of paper, they wrote to him, and said, Peace be with thee, and all thy family. We know that we have offended against God and thee. Be pleased to give a visit to us your fathers, for we were perfectly surprised at your escape from prison. ⁹ We know that it was malicious counsel which we took against thee, and that the Lord took care of thee, and the Lord himself delivered thee from our designs. Peace be unto thee, Joseph, who art honourable among all the people. ¹⁰ And they chose seven of Joseph's friends, and said to them, When ye come to Joseph, salute him in peace, and give him this letter. ¹¹ Accordingly, when the men came to Joseph, they did salute him in peace, and gave him the letter. ¹² And when Joseph had read it, he said, Blessed be the Lord God, who didst deliver me from the Israelites, that they could not shed my blood. Blessed be God, who has protected me under thy wings. ¹³ And Joseph kissed them, and took them into his house. And on the morrow, Joseph mounted his ass, and went along with them to Jerusalem. ¹⁴ And when all the Jews heard these things, they went out to meet him, and cried out, saying, Peace attend thy coming hither, father Joseph. ¹⁵ To which he answered, Prosperity from the Lord attend all the people. ¹⁶ And they all kissed him; and Nicodemus took him to his house, having prepared a large entertainment. ¹⁷ But on the morrow, being a preparation-day, Annas, Caiaphas, and Nicodemus, said to Joseph, Make confession to the God of Israel, and answer to us all those questions which we shall ask thee; ¹⁸ For we have been very much troubled, that thou didst bury the body of Jesus; and that' when we had locked thee in a chamber, we could not find thee; and we have been afraid ever since, till this time of thy appearing among us. Tell us therefore before God, all that came to pass. ¹⁹ Then Joseph answering, said, Ye did indeed put me under confinement, on the day of preparation, till the morning. ²⁰ But while I was standing at prayer in the middle of the night, the house was surrounded with four angels; and I saw Jesus as the brightness of the sun, and fell down upon the earth for fear. ²¹ But Jesus laying hold on my hand, lifted me from the ground, and the dew was then sprinkled upon me; but he, wiping my face, kissed me, and said unto me, Fear not, Joseph; look upon me, for it is I. ²² Then I looked upon him, and said, Rabboni Elias! He answered me, I am not Elias, but Jesus of Nazareth, whose body thou didst bury. ²³ I said to him, Shew me the tomb in which I laid thee. ²⁴ Then Jesus, taking me by the hand, led me unto the place where I laid him, and shewed me the linen clothes, and napkin which I put round his head. Then I knew that it was Jesus, and worshipped him, and said, Blessed be he who cometh in the name of the Lord. ²⁵ Jesus again taking me by the hand, led me to Arimathæa to my own house, and said to me, Peace be to thee; but go not out of thy house till the fortieth day; but I must go to my disciples.

12

1 The Jews astonished and confounded. 17 Simeon's two sons, Charinus and Lenthius, rise from the dead at Christ's crucifixion. 19 Joseph proposes to get them to relate the mysteries of their resurrection. 21 They are sought and found, 22 brought to the synagogue, 23 privately sworn to secrecy, 25 and undertake to write what they had seen.

¹ WHEN the chief priests and heard all these things, they were astonished, and fell down with their faces on the ground as dead men, and crying out to one another said, What is this extraordinary sign which is come to pass in Jerusalem? We know the father and mother of Jesus. ² And a certain Levite said, I know many of his relations, religious persons, who are wont to offer sacrifices and burnt-offerings to the God of Israel, in the temple, with prayers. ³ And when the high priest Simeon took him up in his arms. He said to him, Lord, now lettest thou thy servant depart in peace, according to thy word; for mine eyes have seen thy salvation, which thou hast prepared before the face of all people: a light to enlighten the Gentiles, and the glory of thy people Israel. ⁴ Simeon in like manner blessed Mary the mother of Jesus, and said to her, I declare to thee concerning that child; He is appointed for the fall and rising again of many, and for a sign which shall be spoken against. ⁵ Yea, a sword shall pierce through thine own soul also, and the thoughts of many hearts shall be revealed. ⁶ Then said all the Jews, Let us send to those three men, who said they saw him talking with his disciples in Mount Olivet. ⁷ After this, they asked them what they had seen; who answered with one accord, In the presence of the God of Israel we affirm, that we plainly saw Jesus talking with his disciples in Mount Olivet, and ascending up to heaven. ⁸ Then Annas and Caiaphas took them into separate places, and examined them separately; who unanimously confessed the truth, and said, they had seen Jesus. ⁹ Then Annas and Caiaphas said "Our law saith, By the mouth of two or three witnesses every word shall be established." ¹⁰ But what have we said? The blessed Enoch pleased God, and was translated by the word of God; and the burying-place of the blessed Moses is known. ¹¹ But Jesus was delivered to Pilate, whipped, crowned with thorns, spit upon, pierced with a spear, crucified, died upon the cross, and was buried, and his body the honorable Joseph buried in a new sepulchre, and he testifies that he saw him alive. ¹² And besides these men have declared, that they saw him talking with his disciples in Mount Olivet, and ascending up to heaven. ¹³ Then Joseph rising up. Said to Annas and Caiaphas, Ye may be justly under a great surprise, that you have been told, that Jesus is alive, and gone up to heaven. ¹⁴ It is indeed a thing really surprising, that he should not only himself arise from the dead, but also raise others from their graves, who have been seen by many in Jerusalem. ¹⁵ And now hear me a little: We all knew the blessed Simeon, the high-priest, who took Jesus when an infant into his arms in the temple. ¹⁶ This same Simeon had two sons of his own, and we were all present at their death and funeral. ¹⁷ Go therefore and see their tombs, for these are open, and they are risen: and behold, they are in the city of Arimathæa, spending their time together in offices of devotion. ¹⁸ Some, indeed, have heard the sound of their voices in prayer, but they will not discourse with any one, but they continue as mute as dead men. ¹⁹ But come, let us go to them, and behave ourselves towards them with all due respect and caution. And if we can bring them to swear, perhaps they will tell us some of the mysteries of their resurrection. ²⁰ When the Jews heard this, they were exceedingly rejoiced. ²¹ Then Annas and Caiaphas, Nicodemus, Joseph, and Gamaliel, went to Arimathæa, but did not find them in their graves; but walking about the city, they bound them on their bended knees at their devotions: ²² Then saluting them with all respect and deference to God, they brought them to the synagogue at Jerusalem: and having shut the gates, they took the book of the law of the Lord, ²³ And putting it in their hands, swore them by God Adonai, and the God of Israel, who spake to our fathers by the law and the prophets, saying, If ye believe him who raised you from the dead, to be Jesus, tell us what ye have seen, and how ye were raised from the dead. ²⁴ Charinus and Lenthius, the two sons of Simeon, trembled when they heard these things, and were disturbed, and groaned; and at the same time looking up to heaven, they made the sign of the cross with their fingers on their tongues. ²⁵ And immediately they spake, and said, Give each of us some paper, and we will write down for you all those things which we have seen. And they each sat down and wrote, saying,

13

1 The narrative of Charinus and Lenthius commences. 3 A great light in hell. 7 Simeon arrives, and announces the coming of Christ.

¹ O LORD Jesus and Father, who art God, also the resurrection and life of the dead, give us leave to declare thy mysteries, which we saw after death, belonging to thy cross; for we are sworn by thy name. ² For thou hast forbid thy servants to declare the secret things, which were wrought by thy divine power in hell. ³ When we were placed with our fathers in the depth of hell, in the blackness of darkness, on a sudden there appeared the colour of the sun like gold, and a substantial purple-coloured light enlightening the place. ⁴ Presently upon this, Adam, the father of all mankind, with all the patriarchs and prophets, rejoiced and said, That light is the author of everlasting light, who hath promised to translate us to everlasting light. ⁵ Then Isaiah the prophet cried out, and said, This is the light of the Father, and the Son of God, according to my prophecy, when I was alive upon earth. ⁶ The land of Zabulon, and the land of Nephthalim beyond Jordan, a people who walked in darkness, saw a great light; and to them who dwelled in the region of the shadow of death, light is arisen. And now he is come, and hath enlightened us who sat in death. ⁷ And while we were all rejoicing in the light which shone upon us, our father Simeon came among us, and congratulating all the company, said, Glorify the Lord Jesus Christ the Son of God. ⁸ Whom I took up in my arms when an infant in the temple, and being moved by the Holy Ghost, said to him, and acknowledged, That now mine eyes have seen thy salvation, which thou hast prepared before the face of all people, a light to enlighten the Gentiles and the glory of thy people Israel. ⁹ All the saints who were in the depth of hell, hearing this, rejoiced the more. ¹⁰ Afterwards there came forth one like a little hermit, and was asked by every one, Who art thou? ¹¹ To which he replied, I am the voice of one crying in the wilderness, John the Baptist, and the prophet of the Most High, who went before his coming to prepare his way, to give the knowledge of salvation to his people for the forgiveness of sins. ¹² And I John, when I saw Jesus coming to me, being moved by the Holy Ghost, I said, Behold the Lamb of God, behold him who takes away the sins of the world. ¹³ And I baptized him in the river Jordan, and saw the Holy Ghost descending upon him in the form of a dove, and heard a voice from heaven,

saying, This is my beloved Son, in whom I am well pleased. ¹⁴ And now while I was going before him, I came down hither to acquaint you, that the Son of God will next visit us, and, as the day-spring from on high, will come to us, who are in darkness and the shadow of death.

14

1 Adam causes Seth to relate what he heard from Michael the archangel, when he sent him to Paradise to entreat God to anoint his head in his sickness.

¹ BUT when the first man our father Adam heard these things, that Jesus was baptized in Jordan, he called out to his son, Seth, and said, ² Declare to your sons, the patriarchs and prophets, all those things, which thou didst hear from Michael, the archangel, when I sent thee to the gates of Paradise, to entreat God that he would anoint my head when I was sick. ³ Then Seth, coming near to the patriarchs and prophets, said, I Seth, when I was praying to God at the gates of Paradise, beheld the angel of the Lord, Michael appear unto me saying, I am sent unto thee from the Lord; I am appointed to preside over human bodies. ⁴ I tell thee Seth, do not pray to God in tears, and entreat him for the oil of the tree of mercy wherewith to anoint thy father Adam for his head-ache; ⁵ Because thou canst not by any means obtain it till the last day and times, namely, till five thousand and five hundred years be past. ⁶ Then will Christ, the most merciful Son of God, come on earth to raise again the human body of Adam, and at the same time to raise the bodies of the dead, and when he cometh he will be baptized in Jordan: ⁷ Then with the oil of his mercy he will anoint all those who believe on him; and the oil of his mercy will continue to future generations, for those who shall be born of the water and the Holy Ghost unto eternal life. ⁸ And when at that time the most merciful Son of God, Christ Jesus, shall come down on earth, he will introduce our father Adam into Paradise, to the tree of mercy. ⁹ When all the patriarchs and prophets heard all these things from Seth, they rejoiced more.

15

1 Quarrel between Satan and the prince of hell concerning the expected arrival of Christ in hell.

¹ WHILE all the saints were rejoicing, behold Satan, the prince and captain of death, said to the prince of hell, ² Prepare to receive Jesus of Nazareth himself, who boasted that he was the Son of God, and yet was a man afraid of death, and said, My soul is sorrowful even to death. ³ Besides he did many injuries to me and to many others; for those whom I made blind and lame and those also whom I tormented with several devils, he cured by his word; yea, and those whom I brought dead to thee, he by force takes away from thee. ⁴ To this the prince of hell replied to Satan, Who is that so-powerful prince, and yet a man who is afraid of death? ⁵ For all the potentates of the earth are subject to my power, whom thou broughtest to subjection by thy power. ⁶ But if be be so powerful in his human nature, I affirm to thee for truth, that he is almighty in his divine nature, and no man can resist his power. ⁷ When therefore he said be was afraid of death, he designed to ensnare thee, and unhappy it will be to thee for everlasting ages. ⁸ Then Satan replying, said to the prince of hell, Why didst thou express a doubt, and wast afraid to receive that Jesus of Nazareth, both thy adversary and mine? ⁹ As for me, I tempted him and stirred up my old people the Jews with zeal and anger against him? ¹⁰ I sharpened the spear for his suffering; I mixed the gall and vinegar, and commanded that he should drink it; I prepared the cross to crucify him, and the nails to pierce through Ibis hands and feet; and now his death is near at hand, I will bring him hither, subject both to thee and me. ¹¹ Then the prince of hell answering, said, Thou saidst to me just now, that he took away the dead from me by force. ¹² They who have been kept here till they should live again upon earth, were taken away hence, not by their own power, but by prayers made to God, and their almighty God took them from me. ¹³ Who then is that Jesus of Nazareth that by his word hath taken away the dead from me without prayer to God? ¹⁴ Perhaps it is the same who took away from me Lazarus, after he had been four days dead, and did both stink and was rotten, and of whom I had possession as a dead person, yet he brought him to life again by his power. ¹⁵ Satan answering, replied to the prince of hell, It is the very same person, Jesus of Nazareth. ¹⁶ Which when the prince of hell heard, he said to him, I adjure thee by the powers which belong to thee and me, that thou bring him not to me. ¹⁷ For when I heard of the power of his word, I trembled for fear, and all my impious company were at the same time disturbed; ¹⁸ And we were not able to detain Lazarus, but he gave himself a shake, and with all the signs of malice, he immediately went away from us; and the very earth, in which the dead body of Lazarus was lodged, presently turned him out alive. ¹⁹ And I know now that he is Almighty God who could perform such things, who is mighty in his dominion, and mighty in his human nature, who is the Saviour of mankind. ²⁰ Bring not therefore this person hither, for he will set at liberty all those whom I hold in prison under unbelief, and bound with the fetters of their sins, and will conduct them to everlasting life.

16

1 Christ's arrival at hell-gates; the confusion thereupon. 10 He descends into hell.

¹ AND while Satan and the prince of hell were discoursing thus to each other, on a sudden there was a voice as of thunder and the rushing of winds, saying, Lift up your gates, O ye princes; and be ye lift up, O everlasting gates, and the King of Glory shall come in. ² When the prince of hell heard this, he said to Satan, Depart from me, and begone out of my habitations; if thou art a powerful warrior, fight with the King of Glory. But what hast thou to do with him? ³ And he cast him forth from his habitations. ⁴ And the prince said to his impious officers, Shut the brass gates of cruelty, and make them fast with iron bars, and fight courageously, lest we be taken captives. ⁵ But when all the company of the saints heard this they spake with a loud voice of anger to the prince of hell: ⁶ Open thy gates that the King of Glory may come in. ⁷ And the divine prophet David, cried out saying, Did not I when on earth truly prophesy and say, O that men would praise the Lord for his goodness, and for his wonderful works to the children of men. ⁸ For he hath broken the gates of brass, and cut the bars of iron in sunder. He hath taken them because of their iniquity, and because of their unrighteousness they are afflicted. ⁹ After this another prophet, namely, holy Isaiah, spake in like manner to all the saints, did not I rightly prophesy to you when I was alive on earth? ¹⁰ The dead men shall live, and they shall rise again who are in their graves, and they shall rejoice who are in earth; for the dew which is from the Lord shall bring deliverance to them. ¹¹ And I said in another place, O death, where is thy victory? O death, where is thy sting? ¹² When all the saints heard these things spoken by Isaiah, they said to the prince of hell, Open now thy gates, and take away thine iron bars; for thou wilt now be bound, and have no power. ¹³ Then there was a great voice, as of the sound of thunder saying, Lift up your gates, O princes; and be ye lifted up, ye gates of hell, and the King of Glory will enter in. ¹⁴ The prince of hell perceiving the same voice repeated, cried out as though he had been ignorant, Who is that King of Glory? ¹⁵ David replied to the prince of hell, and said, I understand the words of that voice, because I spake them by his spirit. And now, as I have above said, I say unto thee, the Lord strong and powerful, the Lord mighty in battle: he is the King of Glory, and he is the Lord in heaven and in earth; ¹⁶ He hath looked down to hear the groans of the prisoners, and to set loose those that are appointed to death. ¹⁷ And now, thou filthy and stinking prince of hell, open thy gates, that the King of Glory may enter in; for he is the Lord of heaven and earth. ¹⁸ While David was saying this, the mighty Lord appeared in the form of a man, and enlightened those places which had ever before been in darkness, ¹⁹ And broke asunder the fetters which before could not be broken; and with his invincible power visited those who sate in the deep darkness by iniquity, and the shadow of death by sin.

17

1 Death and the devils in great horror at Christ's coming. 13 He tramples on death, seizes the prince of hell, and takes Adam with him to heaven.

¹ ¹IMPIOUS Death and her cruel officers hearing these things, were seized with fear in their several kingdoms, when they saw the clearness of the light, ² And Christ himself on a sudden appearing in their habitations; they cried out therefore, and said, We are bound by thee; thou seemest to intend our confusion before the Lord. ³ Who art thou, who hast no sign of corruption, but that bright appearance which is a full proof of thy greatness, of which yet thou seemest to take no notice? ⁴ Who art thou, so powerful and so weak, so great and so little, a mean and yet a soldier of the first rank, who can command in the form of a servant as a common soldier? ⁵ The King of Glory, dead and alive, though once slain upon the cross? ⁶ Who layest dead in the grave, and art come down alive to us, and in thy death all the creatures trembled, and all the stars were moved, and now hast thou thy liberty among the dead, and givest disturbance to our legions? ⁷ Who art thou, who dost release the captives that were held in chains by original sin, and bringest them into their former liberty ⁸ Who art thou, who dost spread so glorious and divine a light over those who were made blind by the darkness of sin? ⁹ In like manner all the legions of devils were seized with the like horror, and with the most submissive fear cried out, and said, ¹⁰ Whence comes it, O thou Jesus Christ, that thou art a man so powerful and glorious in majesty, so bright as to have no spot, and so pure as to have no crime? For that lower world of earth, which was ever till now subject to us, and from whence we received tribute, never sent us such a dead man before, never sent such presents as these to the princes of hell. ¹¹ Who therefore art thou, who with such courage enterest among our abodes, and art not only not afraid to threaten us with the greatest punishments, but also endeavourest to rescue all others from the chains in which we hold them?

¹² Perhaps thou art that Jesus, of whom Satan just now spoke to our prince, that by the death of the cross thou wert about to receive the power of death. ¹³ Then the King of Glory trampling upon death, seized the prince of hell, deprived him of all his power, and took our earthly father Adam with him to his glory.

18

1 Beelzebub, prince of hell, vehemently upbraids Satan for persecuting Christ and bringing him to hell. 4 Christ gives Beelzebub dominion over Satan for ever, as a recompense for taking away Adam and his sons.

¹ THEN the prince of hell took Satan, and with great indication said to him, O thou prince of destruction, author of Beelzebub's defeat and banishment, the scorn of God's angels and loathed by all righteous persons! What inclined thee to act thus? ² Thou wouldst crucify the King of Glory, and by his destruction, hast made us promises of very large advantages, but as a fool wert ignorant of what thou wast about. ³ For behold now that Jesus of Nazareth, with the brightness of his glorious divinity, puts to flight all the horrid powers of darkness and death; ⁴ He has broke down our prisons from top to bottom, dismissed all the captives, released all who were bound, and all who were wont formerly to groan under the weight of their torments have now insulted us, and we are like to be defeated by their prayers. ⁵ Our impious dominions are subdued, and no part of mankind is now left in our subjection, but on the other hand, they all boldly defy us; ⁶ Though, before, the dead never durst behave themselves insolently towards us, nor, being prisoners, could ever on any occasion be merry. ⁷ O Satan, thou prince of all the wicked, father of the impious and abandoned, why wouldest thou attempt this exploit, seeing our prisoners were hitherto always without the least hopes of salvation and life? ⁸ But now there is not one of them does ever groan, nor is there the least appearance of a tear in any of their faces. ⁹ O prince Satan, thou great keeper of the infernal regions, all thy advantages which thou didst acquire by the forbidden tree, and the loss of Paradise, thou hast now lost by the wood of the cross; ¹⁰ And thy happiness all then expired, when thou didst crucify Jesus Christ the King of Glory. ¹¹ Thou hast acted against thine own interest and mine, as thou wilt presently perceive by those large torments and infinite punishments which thou art about to suffer. ¹² O Satan, prince of all evil, author of death, and source of all pride, thou shouldest first have inquired into the evil crimes of Jesus of Nazareth, and then wouldest have found that he was guilty of no fault worthy of death. ¹³ Why didst thou venture, without either reason or justice, to crucify him, and hast brought down to our regions a person innocent and righteous, and thereby hast lost all the sinners, impious and unrighteous persons in the whole world? ¹⁴ While the prince of hell was thus speaking to Satan, the King of Glory said to Beelzebub, the prince of hell, Satan, the prince shall be subject to thy dominion for ever, in the room of Adam and his righteous sons, who are mine.

19

1 Christ takes Adam by the hand, the rest of the saints join hands, and they all ascend with him to Paradise.

¹ THEN Jesus stretched forth his hand, and said, Come to me, all ye my saints, who were created in my image, who were condemned by the tree of forbidden fruit, and by the devil and death; ² Live now by the wood of my cross; the devil, the prince of this world, is overcome, and death is conquered. ³ Then presently all the saints were joined together under the hand of the most high God; and the Lord Jesus laid hold on Adam's hand and said to him, Peace be to thee, and all thy righteous posterity, which is mine. ⁴ Then Adam, casting himself at the feet of Jesus, addressed himself to him, with tears, in humble language, and a loud voice, saying, ⁵ I will extol thee, O Lord, for thou hast lifted me up, and hast not made my foes to rejoice over me. O Lord my God, I cried unto thee, and thou hast healed me. ⁶ O Lord thou hast brought up my soul from the grave; thou hast kept me alive, that I should not go down to the pit. ⁷ Sing unto the Lord, all ye saints of his, and give thanks at the remembrance of his holiness. For his anger endureth but for a moment; in his favour is life. ⁸ In like manner all the saints, prostrate at the feet of Jesus, said with one voice, Thou art come, O Redeemer of the world, and hast actually accomplished all things, which thou didst foretell by the law and thy holy prophets. ⁹ Thou hast redeemed the living by thy cross, and art come down to us, that by the death of the cross thou mightest deliver us from hell, and by thy power from death. ¹⁰ O, Lord, as thou hast put the ensigns of thy glory in heaven, and hast set up the sign of thy redemption, even thy cross on earth! so, Lord, set the sign of the victory of thy cross in hell, that death may have dominion no longer. ¹¹ Then the Lord stretching forth his hand, made the sign of the cross upon Adam, and upon all his saints. ¹² And taking hold of Adam by his right hand, he ascended from hell, and all the saints of God followed him. ¹³ Then the royal prophet David boldly cried, and said, O sing unto the Lord a new song, for he hath done marvellous things; his right hand and his holy arm have gotten him the victory. ¹⁴ The Lord hath made known his salvation, his righteousness hath he openly shewn in the sight of the heathen. ¹⁵ And the whole multitude of saints answered, saying, This honour have all his saints, Amen, Praise ye the Lord. ¹⁶ Afterwards, the prophet Habakkuk cried out, and said, Thou wentest forth for the salvation of thy people, even for the salvation of thy people. ¹⁷ And all the saints said, Blessed is he who cometh in the name of the Lord; for the Lord hath enlightened us. This is our God for ever and ever; he shall reign over us to everlasting ages, Amen. ¹⁸ In like manner all the prophets spake the sacred things of his praise, and followed the Lord.

20

1 Christ delivers Adam to Michael the archangel. 3 They meet Enoch and Elijah in heaven, 5 and also the blessed thief, who relates how he cares to Paradise.

¹ THEN the Lord holding Adam by the hand, delivered him to Michael the archangel; and he led them into Paradise, filled with mercy and glory; ² And two very ancient men met them, and were asked by the saints, Who are ye, who have not yet been with us in hell, and have had your bodies placed in Paradise? ³ One of them answering, said, I am Enoch, who was translated by the word of God: and this man who is with me, is Elijah the Tishbite, who was translated in a fiery chariot. ⁴ Here we have hitherto been, and have not tasted death, but are now about to return at the coming of Antichrist, being armed with divine signs and miracles, to engage with him in battle, and to be slain by him at Jerusalem, and to be taken up alive again into the clouds, after three days and a half. ⁵ And while the holy Enoch and Elias were relating this, behold there came another man in a miserable figure carrying the sign of the cross upon his shoulders. ⁶ And when all the saints saw him, they said to him, Who art thou? For thy countenance is like a thief's; and why dost thou carry a cross upon thy shoulders? ⁷ To which he answering, said, Ye say right, for I was a thief who committed all sorts of wickedness upon earth. ⁸ And the Jews crucified me with Jesus; and I observed the surprising things which happened in the creation at the crucifixion of the Lord Jesus. ⁹ And I believed him to be the Creator of all things, and the Almighty King; and I prayed to him, saying, Lord, remember me, when thou comest into thy kingdom. ¹⁰ He presently regarded my supplication, and said to me, Verily I say unto thee, this day thou shalt be with me in Paradise. ¹¹ And he gave me this sign of the cross saying, Carry this, and go to Paradise; and if the angel who is the guard of Paradise will not admit thee, shew him the sign of the cross, and say unto him: Jesus Christ who is now crucified, hath sent me hither to thee. ¹² When I did this, and told the angel who is the guard of Paradise all these things, and he heard them, he presently opened the gates, introduced me, and placed me on the right-hand in Paradise, ¹³ Saying, Stay here a little time, till Adam, the father of all mankind, shall enter in, with all his sons, who are the holy and righteous servants of Jesus Christ, who was crucified. ¹⁴ When they heard all this account from the thief, all the patriarchs said with one voice, Blessed be thou, O Almighty God, the Father of everlasting goodness, and the Father of mercies, who hast shewn such favour to those who were sinners against him, and hast brought us to the mercy of Paradise, and hast placed us amidst thy large and spiritual provisions, in a spiritual and holy life. Amen.

21

1 Charinus and Lenthius being only allowed three days to remain on earth, 7 deliver in their narratives, which miraculously correspond; they vanish, 13 and Pilate records these transactions.

¹ THESE are the divine and sacred mysteries which we saw and heard. I, Charinus and Lenthius are not allowed to declare the other mysteries of God, as the archangel Michael ordered us, ² Saying, ye shall go with my brethren to Jerusalem, and shall continue in prayers, declaring and glorifying the resurrection of Jesus Christ, seeing he hath raised you from the dead at the same time with himself. ³ And ye shall not talk with any man, but sit as dumb persons till the time come when the Lord will allow you to relate the mysteries of his divinity. ⁴ The archangel Michael farther commanded us to go beyond Jordan, to an excellent and fat country, where there are many who rose from the dead along with us for the proof of the resurrection of Christ. ⁵ For we have only three days allowed us from the dead, who arose to celebrate the assover of our Lord with our parents, and to bear our testimony for Christ the Lord, and we have been baptized in the holy river of Jordan. And now they are not seen by any one. ⁶ This is as much as God allowed us to relate to you; give ye therefore praise and honour to him, and repent, and he will have mercy upon you. Peace be to you from the Lord God Jesus Christ, and the Saviour of us all. Amen, Amen, Amen. ⁷ And after they had made an end of writing and had wrote in two distinct pieces of paper, Charinus gave what he wrote into the hands of Annas, and Caiaphas, and Gamaliel. ⁸ Lenthius likewise gave what he

wrote into the hands of Nicodemus and Joseph; and immediately they were changed into exceeding white forms and were seen no more. ⁹ But what they had wrote was found perfectly to agree, the one not containing one letter more or less than the other. ¹⁰ When all the assembly of the Jews heard all these surprising relations of Charinus and Lenthius, they said to each other, Truly all these things were wrought by God, and blessed be the Lord Jesus for ever and ever, Amen. ¹¹ And they went about with great concern, and fear, and trembling, and smote upon their breasts and went away every one to his home. ¹² But immediately all these things which were related by the Jews in their synagogues concerning Jesus, were presently told by Joseph and Nicodemus to the governor. ¹³ And Pilate wrote down all these transactions, and placed all these accounts in the public records of his hall.

22

1 Pilate goes to the temple; calls together the rulers, and scribes, and doctors. 2 Commands the gates to be shut; orders the book of the Scripture; and causes the Jews to relate what they really knew concerning Christ. 14 They declare that they crucified Christ in ignorance, and that they now know him to be the Son of God, according to the testimony of the Scriptures; which, after they put him to death, they are examined.

¹ AFTER these things Pilate went to the temple of the Jews, and called together all the rulers and scribes, and doctors of the law, and went with them into a chapel of the temple. ² And commanding that all the gates should be shut, said to them, I have heard that ye have a certain large book in this temple; I desire you therefore, that it may be brought before me. ³ And when the great book, carried by four ministers of the temple, and adorned with gold and precious stones, was brought, Pilate said to them all, I adjure you by the God of your Fathers, who made and commanded this temple to be built, that ye conceal not the truth from me. ⁴ Ye know all the things which are written in that book; tell me therefore now, if ye in the Scriptures have found any thing of that Jesus whom ye crucified, and at what time of the world he ought to have come: shew it me. ⁵ Then having sworn Annas and Caiaphas, they commanded all the rest who were with them to go out of the chapel. ⁶ And they shut the gates of the temple and of the chapel, and said to Pilate, Thou hast made us to swear, O judge, by the building of this temple, to declare to thee that which is true and right. ⁷ After we had crucified Jesus, not knowing that he was the Son of God, but supposing he wrought his miracles by some magical arts, we summoned a large assembly in this temple. ⁸ And when we were deliberating among one another about the miracles which Jesus had wrought, we found many witnesses of our own country, who declared that they had seen him alive after his death, and that they heard him discoursing with his disciples, and saw him ascending unto the height of the heavens, and entering into them; ⁹ And we saw two witnesses, whose bodies Jesus raised from the dead, who told us of many strange things which Jesus did among the dead, of which we have a written account in our hands. ¹⁰ And it is our custom annually to open this holy book before an assembly, and to search there for the counsel of God. ¹¹ And we found in the first of the seventy books, where Michael the archangel is speaking to the third son of Adam the first man, an account that after five thousand five hundred years, Christ the most beloved Son of God was come on earth, ¹² And we further considered, that perhaps he was the very God of Israel who spoke to Moses, Thou shalt make the ark of the testimony; two cubits and a half shall be the length thereof, and a cubit and a half the breadth thereof, and a cubit and a half the height thereof. ¹³ By these five cubits and a half for the building of the ark of the Old Testament, we perceived and knew that in five thousand years and a half (one thousand) years, Jesus Christ was to come in the ark or tabernacle of a body; ¹⁴ And so our scriptures testify that he is the son of God, and the Lord and King of Israel. ¹⁵ And because after his suffering, our chief priests were surprised at the signs which were wrought by his means, we opened that book to search all the generations down to the generation of Joseph and Mary the mother of Jesus, supposing him to be of the seed of David; ¹⁶ And we found the account of the creation, and at what time he made the heaven and the earth and the first man Adam, and that from thence to the flood, were two thousand, two hundred and twelve years. ¹⁷ And from the flood to Abraham, nine hundred and twelve. And from Abraham to Moses, four hundred and thirty. And from Moses to David the king, five hundred and ten. ¹⁸ And from David to the Babylonish captivity, five hundred years. And from the Babylonish captivity to the incarnation of Christ, four hundred years. ¹⁹ The sum of all which amounts to five thousand and half (a thousand). ²⁰ And so it appears, that Jesus whom we crucified, is Jesus Christ the Son of God, and true and Almighty God. Amen.

In the name of the Holy Trinity, thus end the Acts of our Saviour Jesus Christ, which the Emperor Theodosius the Great found at Jerusalem, in the hall of Pontius Pilate among the public records; the things were acted in the nineteenth year of Tiberius Cæsar, Emperor of the Romans, and in the seventeenth year of the government of Herod the son of Herod king of Galilee, on the eighth of the calends of April, which is the twenty-third day of the month of March, in the CCIId Olympiad, when Joseph and Caiaphas were Rulers of the Jews; being a History written in Hebrew by Nicodemus, of what happened after our Saviour's crucifixion.

Letters of Herod and Pilate

Herod to Pontius Pilate the Governor of Jerusalem: Peace.

[1] I AM in great anxiety. I write these things unto thee, that when thou hast heard them thou mayest be grieved for me. For as my daughter Herodias, who is dear to me, was playing upon a pool of water which had ice upon it, it broke under her, and all her body went down, and her head was cut off and remained on the surface of the ice. And behold, her mother is holding her head upon her knees in her lap, and my whole house is in great sorrow. [2] For I, when I heard of the man Jesus, wished to come to thee, that I might see him alone, and hear his word, whether it was like that of the sons of men. And it is certain that because of the many evil things which were done by me to John the Baptist, and because I mocked the Christ, behold I receive the reward of righteousness, for I have shed much blood of others' children upon the earth. Therefore the judgments of God are righteous; for every man receives according to his thought. But since thou wast worthy to see that God-man, therefore it becometh you to pray for me. My son Azbonius also is in the agony of the hour of death. [3] And I too am in affliction and great trial, because I have the dropsy; and am in great distress, because I persecuted the introducer of baptism by water, which was John. Therefore, my brother, the judgments of God are righteous. And my wife, again, through all her grief for her daughter, is become blind in her left eye, because we desired to blind the Eye of righteousness. [4] There is no peace to the doers of evil, saith the Lord. For already great affliction cometh upon the priests and upon the writers of the law; because they delivered unto thee the Just One. For this is the consummation of the world, that they consented that the Gentiles should become heirs. For the children of light shall be cast out, for they have not observed the things which were preached concerning the Lord, and concerning his Son. Therefore gird up thy loins, and receive righteousness, thou with thy wife remembering Jesus night and day; and the kingdom shall belong to you Gentiles, for we the (chosen) people have mocked the Righteous One. [5] Now if there is place for our request, O Pilate, because we were at one time in power, bury my household carefully; for it is right that we should be buried by thee, rather than by the priests, whom, after a little time, as the Scriptures say, at the coming of Jesus Christ, vengeance shall overtake. [6] Fare thee well, with Procla thy wife. [7] I send thee the earrings of my daughter and my own ring, that they may be unto thee a memorial of my decease. For already do worms begin to issue from my body, and lo, I am receiving temporal judgment, and I am afraid of the judgment to come. For in both we stand before the works of the living God; but this judgment, which is temporal, is for a time, while that to come is judgment for ever.

Letters of Pilate to Herod

Pilate to Herod the Tetrarch: Peace.

[1] KNOW and see, that in the day when thou didst deliver Jesus unto me, I took pity on myself, and testified by washing my hands (that I was innocent), concerning him who rose from the grave after three days, and had performed thy pleasure in him, for thou didst desire me to be associated with thee in his crucifixion. [2] But I now learn from the executioners and from the soldiers who watched his sepulchre that he rose from the dead. And I have especially confirmed what was told me, that he appeared bodily in Galilee, to the same form, and with the same voice, and with the same doctrine, and with the sane disciples, not having changed in anything, but preaching with boldness his resurrection, and an everlasting kingdom. [3] And behold, heaven and earth rejoice; and behold, Procla my wife is believing in the visions which appeared unto her, when thou sentest that I should deliver Jesus to the people of Israel, because of the ill-will they had. [4] Now when Procla, my wife, heard that Jesus was risen, and had appeared in Galilee, she took with her Longinus the centurion and twelve soldiers, the same that had watched at the sepulchre, and went to greet the face of Christ, as if to a great spectacle, and saw him with his disciples. [5] Now while they were standing, and wondering, and gazing at him, he looked at them, and said to them, What is it? Do ye believe in me? Procla, know that in the covenant which God gave to the fathers, it is said that every body which had perished should live by means of my death, which ye have seen. And now, ye see that I live, whom ye crucified. And I suffered many things, till that I was laid in the sepulchre. But now, hear me, and believe in my Father–God who is in me. For I loosed the cords of death, and brake the gates of Sheol; and my coming shall be hereafter. [6] And when Procla my wife and the Romans heard these things, they came and told me, weeping; for they also were against him, when they devised the evils which they had done unto him. So that, I also was on the couch of my bed in affliction, and put on a garment of mourning, and took unto me fifty Romans with my wife and went into Galilee. [7] And when I was going in the way I testified these things; that Herod did these things by me, that he took counsel with me, and constrained me to arm my hands against him, and to judge him that judgeth all, and to scourge the Just One, Lord of the just. And when we drew nigh to him, O Herod, a great voice was heard from heaven, and dreadful thunder, and the earth trembled, and gave forth a sweet smell, like unto which was never perceived even in the temple of Jerusalem. [8] Now while I stood in the way, our Lord saw me as he stood and talked with his disciples. But I prayed in my heart, for I knew that it was he whom ye delivered unto me, that he was Lord of created things and Creator of all. But we, when we saw him, all of us fell upon our faces before his feet. And I said with a loud voice, I have sinned, O Lord, in that I sat and judged thee, who avengest all in truth. [9] And lo, I know that thou art God, the Son of God, and I beheld thy humanity and not thy divinity. But Herod, with the children of Israel, constrained me to do evil unto thee. Have pity, therefore, upon me, O God of Israel! [10] And my wife, in great anguish, said, God of heaven and of earth, God of Israel, reward me not according to the deeds of Pontius Pilate, nor according to the will of the children of Israel, nor according to the thought of the sons of the priests; but remember my husband in thy glory! [11] Now our Lord drew near and raised up me and my wife, and the Romans; and I looked at him and saw there were on him the scars of his cross. And he said, That which all the righteous fathers hoped to receive, and saw not–in thy time the Lord of Time, the Son of Man, the Son of the Most High, who is for ever, arose from the dead, and is glorified on high by all that he created, and established for ever and ever. [12] Justinus, one of the writers that were in the days of Augustus and Tiberius and Gains, wrote in his third discourse: Now Mary the Galilæan, who bare the Christ that was crucified in Jerusalem, had not been with a husband. And Joseph did not abandon her; but Joseph continued in sanctity without a wife, he and his five sons by a former wife; and Mary continued without a husband. [13] Theodorus wrote to Pilate the Governor: Who was the man, against whom there was a complaint before thee, that he was crucified by the men of Palestine? If the many demanded this righteously, why didst thou not consent to their righteousness? And if they demanded this unrighteously, how didst thou transgress the law and command what was far from righteousness? [14] Pilate sent to him:–Because he wrought signs I did not wish to crucify him: and since his accusers said, He calleth himself a king, I crucified him. [15] Josephus saith: Agrippa, the king, was clothed in a robe woven with silver, and saw the spectacle in the theatre of Cæsarea. When the people saw that his raiment flashed, they said to him, Hitherto we feared thee as a man: henceforth thou art exalted above the nature of mortals. And he saw an angel standing over him, and he smote him as unto death.

The Epistle of Pontius Pilate

Which he Wrote to the Roman Emperor Concerning our Lord Jesus Christ.

Pontius Pilate to Tiberius Cæsar–Greeting:

[1] UPON Jesus Christ, whom I fully made known to thee in my last, a bitter punishment hath at length been inflicted by the will of the people, although I was unwilling and apprehensive. In good truth, no age ever had or will have a man so good and strict. But the people made a wonderful effort, and all their scribes, chiefs and elders agreed to crucify this ambassador of truth, their own prophets, like the Sibyls with us, advising the contrary; and when he was hanged supernatural signs appeared, and in the judgment of philosophers menaced the whole world with ruin. His disciples flourish, not belying their master by their behavior and continence of life; nay, in his name they are most beneficent. Had I not feared a sedition might arise among the people, who were almost furious, perhaps this man would have yet been living with us. Although, being rather compelled by fidelity to thy dignity, than led by my own inclination, I did not strive with all my might to prevent the sale and suffering of righteous blood, guiltless of every accusation, unjustly, indeed, through the maliciousness of men, and yet, as the Scriptures interpret, to their own destruction. Farewell. The fifth of the Calends of April.

The Report of Pilate The Governor

Concerning our Lord Jesus Christ; which was Sent to Augustus Cæsar, in Rome.

[1] IN those days, when our Lord Jesus Christ was crucified under Pontius Pilate, the governor of Palestine and Phoenicia, the things here recorded came to pass in Jerusalem, and were done by the Jews against the Lord. Pilate therefore sent the same to Cæsar in Rome, along with his private report, writing thus: [2] To the most potent, august, divine and awful Augustus Cæsar, Pilate, the administrator of the Eastern Province: [3] I have received information, most excellent one, in consequence of which I am seized with fear and trembling. For in this province which I administer, one of whose cities is called Jerusalem, the whole multitude of Jews delivered unto me a certain man called Jesus, and brought many accusations against him, which they were unable to establish by consistent evidence. [4] But they charged him with one heresy in particular, namely, That Jesus said the Sabbath was not a rest, nor to be observed by them. For he performed many

cures on that day, and made the blind see, and the lame walk, raised the dead, cleansed lepers, healed the paralytic who were wholly unable to move their body or brace their nerves, but could only speak and discourse, and he gave them power to walk and run, removing their infirmity by his word alone. ⁵ There is another very mighty deed which is strange to the gods we have: he raised up a man who had been four days dead, summoning him by his word alone, when the dead man had begun to decay, and his body was corrupted by the worms which had been bred, and had the stench of a dog; but, seeing him lying in the tomb he commanded him to run, nor did the dead man at all delay, but as a bridegroom out of his chamber, so did he go forth from his tomb, filled with abundant perfume. ⁶ Moreover, even such as were strangers, and clearly demoniacs, who had their dwelling in deserts, and devoured their own flesh, and wandered about like cattle and creeping things, he turned into inhabiters of cities, and by a word rendered them rational, and prepared them to become wise and powerful, and illustrious, taking their food with all the enemies of the unclean spirits which were destructive in them, and which he cast into the depth of the sea. ⁷ And, again, there was another who had a withered hand, and not only the hand but rather the half of the body of the man was like a stone, and he had neither the shape of a man nor the symmetry of a body: even him He healed with a word and rendered whole. ⁸ And a woman also, who had an issue of blood for a long time, and whose veins and arteries were exhausted, and who did not bear a human body, being like one dead, and daily speechless, so that all the physicians of the district were unable to cure her, for there remained unto her not a hope of life; but as Jesus passed by she mysteriously received strength by his shadow falling on her, from behind she touched the hem of his garment, and immediately, in that very hour, strength filled her exhausted limbs, and as if she had never suffered anything, she began to run along towards Capernaum, her own city, so that she reached it in a six days' journey. ⁹ And I have made known these things which I have recently been informed of, and which Jesus did on the Sabbath. And he did other miracles greater than these, so that I have observed greater works of wonder done by him than by the gods whom we worship. ¹⁰ But Herod and Archelaus and Philip, Annas and Caiaphas, with all the people, delivered him to me, making a great tumult against me in order that I might try him. Therefore, I commanded him to be crucified, when I had first scourged him, though I found no cause in him for evil accusations or dealings. ¹¹ Now when he was crucified, there was darkness over all the world, and the sun was obscured for half a day, and the stars appeared, but no lustre was seen in them; and the moon lost its brightness, as though tinged with blood; and the world of the departed was swallowed up; so that the very sanctuary of the temple, as they call it, did not appear to the Jews themselves at their fall, but they perceived a chasm in the earth, and the rolling of successive thunders. ¹² And amid this terror the dead appeared rising again, as the Jews themselves bore witness, and said that it was Abraham, and Isaac, and Jacob, and the twelve patriarchs, and Moses, and Job, who had died before, as they say, some three thousand five hundred years. And there were very many whom I myself saw appearing in the body, and they made lamentation over the Jews, because of the transgression which was committed by them, and because of the destruction of the Jews and of their law. ¹³ And the terror of the earthquake continued from the sixth hour of the preparation until the ninth hour; and when it was evening on the first day of the week, there came a sound from heaven, and the heaven became seven times more luminous than on all other days. And at the third hour of the night the sun appeared more luminous than it had ever shone, lighting up the whole hemisphere. ¹⁴ And as lightning-flashes suddenly come forth in a storm, so there were seen men, lofty in stature, and surpassing in glory, a countless host, crying out, and their voice was heard as that of exceedingly loud thunder, Jesus that was crucified is risen again: come up from Hades ye that were enslaved in the subterraneous recesses of Hades. ¹⁵ And the chasm in the earth was as if it had no bottom; but it was so that the very foundations of the earth appeared, with those that shouted in heaven, and walked in the body among the dead that were raised. And He that raised up all the dead and bound Hades said, Say to my disciples He goeth before you into Galilee, there shall ye see Him. ¹⁶ And all that night the light ceased not shining. And many of the Jews died in the chasm of the earth, being swallowed up, so that on the morrow most of those who had been against Jesus were not to be found. Others saw the apparition of men rising again whom none of us had ever seen. One synagogue of the Jews was alone left in Jerusalem itself, for they all disappeared in that ruin. ¹⁷ Therefore being astounded by that terror, and being possessed with the most dreadful trembling, I have written what I saw at that time and sent it to thine excellency; and I have inserted what was done against Jesus by the Jews, and sent it to thy divinity, my lord.

The Report of Pontius Pilate to Tiberius Cæsar

Governor of Judea; Which was sent to Tiberius Cæsar in Rome. To the most potent, august, dreadful, and divine Augustus, Pontius Pilate, administrator of the Eastern Province.

¹ I HAVE undertaken to communicate to thy goodness by this my writing, though possessed with much fear and trembling, most excellent king, the present state of affairs, as the result hath shown. For as I administered this province, my lord, according to the command of thy serenity, which is one of the eastern cities called Jerusalem, wherein the temple of the nation of the Jews is erected, all the multitude of the Jews, being assembled, delivered up to me a certain man called Jesus, bringing many and endless accusations against him; but they could not convict him in anything. But they had one heresy against him, that he said the sabbath was not their proper rest. ² Now that man wrought many cures and good works: he caused the blind to see, he cleansed lepers, he raised the dead, he healed paralytics, who could not move at all, but had only voice, and all their bones in their places; and he gave them strength to walk and run, enjoining it by his word alone. And he did another yet more mighty work, which had been strange even among our gods, he raised from the dead one Lazarus, who had been dead four days, commanding by a word alone that the dead man should be raised, when his body was already corrupted by worms which bred in his wounds. And he commanded the fetid body, which lay in the grave, to run, and as bridegroom from his chamber so he went forth from his grave, full of sweet perfume. ³ And some that were grievously afflicted by demons, and had their dwellings in desert places, and devoured the flesh of their own limbs, and went up and down among creeping things and wild beasts, he caused to dwell in cities in their own houses, and by a word made them reasonable, and caused to become wise and honorable those that were vexed by unclean spirits, and the demons that were in them he sent out into a herd of swine into the sea and drowned them. ⁴ Again, another who had a withered hand, and lived in suffering, and had not even the half of his body sound, he made whole by a word alone. And a woman who had an issue of blood for a long time, so that because of the discharge all the joints of her bones were seen and shone through like glass, for all the physicians had dismissed her without hope, and had not cleansed her, for there was in her no hope of health at all; but once, as Jesus was passing by she touched from behind the hem of his garments, and in that very hour the strength of her body was restored, and she was made whole, as if she had no affliction, and began to run fast towards her own city of Paneas. ⁵ And these things happened thus: but the Jews reported that Jesus did these things on the sabbath. And I saw that greater marvels had been wrought by him than by the gods whom we worship. Him then Herod and Archelaus and Philip, and Annas and Caiaphas, with all the people, delivered to me, to put him on his trial. And because many raised a tumult against me, I commanded that he should be crucified. ⁶ Now when he was crucified darkness came over all the world; the sun was altogether hidden, and the sky appeared dark while it was yet day, so that the stars were seen, though still they had their lustre obscured, wherefore, I suppose your excellency is not unaware that in all the world they lighted their lamps from the sixth hour until evening. ⁷ And the moon, which was like blood, did not shine all night long, although it was at the full, and the stars and Orion made lamentation over the Jews, because of the transgression committed by them. ⁸ And on the first day of the week, about the third hour of the night, the sun appeared as it never shone before, and the whole heaven became bright. And as lightnings come in a storm, so certain men of lofty stature, in beautiful array, and of indescribable glory, appeared in the air, and a countless host of angels, crying out and saying, Glory to God in the highest, and on earth peace, good will among men: Come up from Hades, ye who are in bondage in the depths of Hades. And at their voice all the mountains and hills were moved, and the rocks were rent, and great chasms were made in the earth, so that the very places of the abyss were visible. ⁹ And amid the terror dead men were seen rising again, so that the Jews who saw it said, We beheld Abraham and Isaac, and Jacob, and the twelve patriarchs, who died some two thousand five hundred years before, and we beheld Noah clearly in the body. And all the multitude walked about and sang hymns to God with a loud voice, saying, The Lord our God, who hath risen from the dead, hath made alive all the dead, and Hades he hath spoiled and slain. ¹⁰ Therefore, my lord king, all that night the light ceased not. But many of the Jews died, and were sunk and swallowed up in the chasms that night, so that not even their bodies were to be seen. Now I mean, that those of the Jews suffered who spake against Jesus. And but one synagogue remained in Jerusalem, for all the synagogues which had been against Jesus were overwhelmed. ¹¹ Through that terror, therefore, being amazed and being seized with great trembling, in that very hour, I ordered what had been done by them all to be written, and I have sent it to thy mightiness.

The Trial and Condemnation of Pilate

¹ NOW when the letters came to the city of the Romans, and were read to Cæsar with no few standing there, they were all terrified, because, through the transgression of Pilate, the darkness and the earthquake had happened to all the world. And Cæsar, being filled with anger, sent soldiers and commanded that Pilate should be brought as a prisoner. ² And when he was brought to the city of the Romans, and Cæsar heard that he was come, he sat in the temple of the gods, above all the senate, and with all the army, and with all the multitude of his power, and commanded that Pilate should stand in the entrance. And Cæsar said to him, Most impious one, when thou sawest so great signs done by that man, why didst thou dare to do thus? By daring to do an evil deed thou hast ruined all the world. ³ And Pilate said, King and Autocrat, I am not guilty of these things, but it is the multitude of the Jews who are precipitate and guilty. And Cæsar said, And who are they? Pilate saith, Herod, Archelaus, Philip, Annas and Caiaphas, and all the multitude of the Jews. Cæsar saith, For what cause didst thou execute their purpose? ⁴ And Pilate said, Their nation is seditious and insubordinate, and not submissive to thy power. And Cæsar said, When they delivered him to thee thou oughtest to have made him secure and sent him to me, and not consented to them to crucify such a man, who was just and wrought such great and good miracles, as thou saidst in thy report. For by such miracles Jesus was manifested to be the Christ, the King of the Jews. ⁵ And when Cæsar said this and himself named the name of Christ, all the multitude of the gods fell down together, and became like dust where Cæsar sat with the senate. And all the people that stood near Cæsar were filled with trembling because of the utterance of the word and the fall of their gods, and being seized with fear they all went away, every man to his house, wondering at what had happened. And Cæsar commanded Pilate to be safely kept, that he might know the truth about Jesus. ⁶ And on the morrow when Cæsar sat in the capitol with all the senate, he undertook to question Pilate again. And Cæsar said, Say the truth, most impious one, for through thy impious deed which thou didst commit against Jesus, even here the doing of thy evil works were manifested, in that the gods were brought to ruin. Say then, who is he that was crucified, for his name hath destroyed all the gods? Pilate said, ⁷ And verily his records are true; for even I myself was convinced by his works that he was greater than all the gods whom we venerate. And Cæsar said, For what cause then didst thou perpetrate against him such daring and doing, not being ignorant of him, or assuredly designing some mischief to my government? And Pilate said, I did it because of the transgression and sedition of the lawless and ungodly Jews. ⁸ And Cæsar was filled with anger, and held a council with all his senate and officers, and ordered a decree to be written against the Jews thus:– ⁹ To Licianus who holdeth the first place in the East Country. Greeting: I have been informed of the audacity perpetrated very recently by the Jews inhabiting Jerusalem and the cities round about, and their lawless doing, how they compelled Pilate to crucify a certain god called Jesus, through which great transgression of theirs the world was darkened and drawn into ruin. Determine therefore, with a body of soldiers, to go to them there at once and proclaim their subjection to bondage by this decree. By obeying and proceeding against them, and scattering them abroad in all nations, enslave them, and by driving their nation from all Judea as soon as possible show, wherever this hath not yet appeared, that they are full of evil. ¹⁰ And when this decree came into the East Country, Licianus obeyed, through fear of the decree, and laid waste all the nation of the Jews, and caused those that were left in Judea, to go into slavery with them that were scattered among the Gentiles, that it might be known by Cæsar that these things had been done by Licianus against the Jews in the East Country, and to please him. ¹¹ And again Cæsar resolved to have Pilate questioned, and commanded a captain, Albius by name, to cut off Pilate's head, saying, As he laid hands upon the just man, that is called Christ, he also shall fall in like manner, and find no deliverance. ¹² And when Pilate came to the place he prayed in silence, saying, O Lord, destroy not me with the wicked Hebrews, for I should not have laid hands upon thee, but for the nation of lawless Jews, because they provoked sedition against mss but thou knowest that I did it in ignorance. Destroy me not, therefore, for this my sin, nor be mindful of the evil that is in me, O Lord, and in thy servant Procla who standeth with me in this the hour of my death, whom thou taughtest to prophecy that thou must be nailed to the cross. Do not punish her too in my sin, but forgive us, and number us in the portion of thy just ones. ¹³ And behold, when Pilate had finished his prayer, there came a voice from heaven, saying, All generations and the families of the Gentiles shall call thee blessed, because under thee were fulfilled all these things that were spoken by the prophets concerning me; and thou thyself must appear as my witness at my second coming, when I shall judge the twelve tribes of Israel, and them that have not confessed my name. ¹⁴ And the Prefect cut off the head of Pilate, and behold an angel of the Lord received it. And when his wife Procla saw the angel coming and receiving his head, she also, being filled with joy, forthwith gave up the ghost, and was buried with her husband.

The Death of Pilate
Who Condemned Jesus.

¹ NOW whereas Tiberius Cæsar emperor of the Romans was suffering from a grievous sickness, and hearing that there was at Jerusalem a certain physician, Jesus by name, who healed all diseases by his word alone; not knowing that the Jews and Pilate had put him to death, he thus bade one of his attendants, Volusianus by name, saying, Go as quickly as thou canst across the sea, and tell Pilate, my servant and friend, to send me this physician to restore me to my original health. ² And Volusianus, having heard the order of the emperor, immediately departed, and came to Pilate, as it was commanded him. And he told the same Pilate what had been committed to him by Tiberius Cæsar, saying, Tiberius Cæsar, emperor of the Romans, thy Lord, having heard that in this city there is a physician who healeth diseases by his word alone, earnestly entreateth thee to send him to him to heal his disease. ³ And Pilate was greatly terrified on hearing this, knowing that through envy he had caused him to be slain. Pilate answered the messenger, saying thus, This man was a malefactor, and a man who drew after himself all the people; so, after counsel taken of the wise men of the city, I caused him to be crucified. ⁴ And as the messenger returned to his lodgings he met a certain woman named Veronica, who had been acquainted with Jesus, and he said, O woman, there was a certain physician in this city, who healed the sick by his word alone, why have the Jews slain him? ⁵ And she began to weep, saying, Ah, me, my lord, it was my God and my Lord whom Pilate through envy delivered up, condemned, and commanded to be crucified. Then he, grieving greatly, said, I am exceedingly sorry that I cannot fulfil that for which my lord hath sent me. ⁶ Veronica said to him, When my Lord went about preaching, and I was very unwillingly deprived of his presence, I desired to have his picture painted for me, that while I was deprived of his presence, at least the figure of his likeness might give me consolation. And when I was taking the canvas to the painter to be painted, my Lord met me and asked whither I was going. ⁷ And when I had made known to him the cause of my journey, He asked me for the canvas, and gave it back to me printed with the likeness of his venerable face. Therefore, if thy lord will devoutly look upon the sight of this, he will straightway enjoy the benefit of health. Is a likeness of this kind to be procured with gold or silver? he asked. No, said she, but with a pious sentiment of devotion. Therefore, I will go with thee, and carry the likeness to Cæsar to look upon, and will return. ⁸ So Volusianus came with Veronica to Rome, and said to Tiberius the emperor, Jesus, whom thou hast long desired, Pilate and the Jews have surrendered to an unjust death, and through envy fastened to the wood of the cross. Therefore, a certain matron hath come with me bringing the likeness of the same Jesus, and if thou wilt devoutly gaze upon it, thou wilt presently obtain the benefit of thy health. So Cæsar caused the way to be spread with cloths of silk, and ordered the portrait to be presented to him; and as soon as he had looked upon it he regained his original health. ⁹ Then Pontius Pilate was apprehended by command of Cæsar and brought to Rome. Cæsar, hearing that Pilate had come to Rome, was filled with exceeding wrath against him, and caused him to be brought to him. Now Pilate brought with him the seamless coat of Jesus, and wore it when before the emperor. As soon as the emperor saw him he laid aside all his wrath, and forthwith rose to him, and was unable to speak harshly to him in anything: and he who in his absence seemed so terrible and fierce now in his presence is found comparatively gentle. ¹⁰ And when he had dismissed him, he soon became terribly inflamed against him, declaring himself wretched, because he had not expressed to him the anger of his bosom. And immediately he had him recalled, swearing and protesting that he was a child of death, and unfitted to live upon earth. And when he saw him he instantly greeted him, and laid aside all the fury of his mind. ¹¹ All were astonished, and he was astonished himself, that he was so enraged against Pilate while absent, and could say nothing to him sharply while he was present. At length, by Divine suggestion, or perhaps by the persuasion of some Christian, he had him stripped of the coat, and soon resumed against him his original fury of mind. ¹² And when the emperor was wondering very much about this, they told him it had been the coat of the Lord Jesus. Then the emperor commanded him to be kept in prison till he should take counsel with the wise men what ought to be done with him. And after a few days sentence was given against Pilate that he should be condemned to the most ignominious death. When Pilate heard this he slew himself with his own dagger, and by such a death put an end to his life. ¹³ When Pilate's death was made known Cæsar said, Truly he has died a most ignominious death, whose own hand has not spared him. He was therefore fastened to a great block of stone and sunk in the river Tiber. But wicked and unclean spirits, rejoicing in his wicked and unclean body, all moved about in the water, and caused in the air dreadful lightning and tempests,

thunder and hail, so that all were seized with horrible fear. ¹⁴ On which account the Romans dragged him out of the river Tiber, bore him away in derision to Vienne, and sunk him in the river Rhone. For Vienne means, as it were, Way of Gehenna, because it was then a place of cursing. And evil spirits were there and did the same things. ¹⁵ Those men, therefore, not enduring to be so harassed by demons, removed the vessel of cursing from them and sent it to be buried in the territory of Losania. But when they were troubled exceedingly by the aforesaid vexations, they put it away from them and sunk it in a certain pool surrounded by mountains, where even yet, according to the account of some, sundry diabolical contrivances are said to issue forth.

The Avenging of the Saviour
IN the days of the Emperor Tiberius Caesar, when Herod was tetrarch, Christ was delivered under Pontius Pilate by the Jews, and revealed by Tiberius.

¹ In those days Titus was a prince under Tiberius in the region of Equitania, in a city of Libia which is called Burgidalla. And Titus had a sore in his right nostril, on account of a cancer, and he had his face torn even to the eye. There went forth a certain man from Judaea, by name Nathan the son of Nahum; for he was an Ishmaelite who went from land to land, and from sea to sea, and in all the ends of the earth. Now Nathan was sent from Judaea to the Emperor Tiberius, to carry their treaty to the city of Rome. And Tiberius was ill, and full of ulcers and fevers, and had nine kinds of leprosy. And Nathan wished to go to the city of Rome. But the north wind blew and hindered his sailing, and carried him down to the harbour of a city of Libia. Now Titus, seeing the ship coming, knew that it was from Judaea; and they all wondered, and said that they had never seen any vessel so coming from that quarter. And Titus ordered the captain to come to him, and asked him who he was. And he said: I am Nathan the son of Nahum, of the race of the Ishmaelites, and I am a subject of Pontius Pilate in Judaea. And I have been sent to go to Tiberius the Roman emperor, to carry a treaty from Judaea. And a strong wind came down upon the sea, and has brought me to a country that I do not know. ² And Titus says: If thou couldst at any time find anything either of cosmetics or herbs which could cure the wound that I have in my face, as thou seest, so that I should become whole, and regain my former health, I should bestow upon thee many good things. And Nathan said to him: I do not know, nor have I ever known, of such things as thou speakest to me about. But for all that, if thou hadst been some time ago in Jerusalem, there thou wouldst have found a choice prophet, whose name was Emanuel, for He will save His people from their sins. And He, as His first miracle in Cana of Galilee, made wine from water; and by His word He cleansed lepers, He enlightened the eyes of one born blind, He healed paralytics, He made demons flee, He raised up three dead; a woman caught in adultery, and condemned by the Jews to be stoned, He set free; and another woman, mined Veronica, who suffered twelve years from an issue of blood, and came up to Him behind, and touched the fringe of His garment, He healed; and with five loaves and two fishes He satisfied five thousand men, to say nothing of little ones and women, and there remained of the fragments twelve baskets. All these things, and many others, were accomplished before His passion. ³ After His resurrection we saw Him in the flesh as He had been before. And Titus said to Him: How did he rise again from the dead, seeing that he was dead? And Nathan answered and said: He was manifestly dead, and hung up on the cross, and again taken down from the cross, and for three days He lay in the tomb: thereafter He rose again from the dead, and went down to Hades, and freed the patriarchs and the prophets, and the whole human race; thereafter He appeared to His disciples, and ate with them; thereafter they saw Him going up into heaven. And so it is the truth, all this that I tell you. For I saw it with my own eyes, and all the house of Israel. And Titus said in his own words: ⁴ Woe to thee, O Emperor Tiberius, full of ulcers, and enveloped in leprosy, because such a scandal has been committed in thy kingdom; because thou hast made such laws in Judaea, in the land of the birth of our Lord Jesus Christ, and they have seized the King, and put to death the Ruler of the peoples; and they have not made Him come to us to cure thee of thy leprosy, and cleanse me from mine infirmity: on which account, if they had been before my face, with my own hands I should have slain the carcases of those Jews, and hung them up on the cruel tree, because they have destroyed my Lord, and mine eyes have not been worthy to see His face. And when he had thus spoken, immediately the wound fell from the face of Titus, and his flesh and his face were restored to health. And all the sick who were in the same place were made whole in that hour. And Titus cried out, and all the rest with him, in a loud voice, saying: My King and my God, because I have never seen Thee, and Thou hast made me whole, bid me go with the ship over the waters to the land of Thy birth, to take vengeance on Thine enemies; and help me, O Lord, that I may be able to destroy them, and avenge Thy death: do Thou, Lord, deliver them into my hand. And having thus spoken, he ordered that he should be baptized. And he called Nathan to him, and said to him: How hast thou seen those baptized who believe in Christ? Come to me, and baptize me in the name of the Father, and of the Son, and of the Holy Ghost. Amen. For I also firmly believe in the Lord Jesus Christ with all my heart, and with all my soul; because nowhere in the whole world is there another who has created me, and made me whole from my wounds. ⁵ And having thus spoken, he sent messengers to Vespasian to come with all haste with his bravest men, so prepared as if for war. ⁶ Then Vespasian brought with him five thousand armed men, and they went to meet Titus. And when they had come to the city of Libia, he said to Titus: Why is it

that thou hast made me come hither? And he said: Know that Jesus has come into this world, and has been born in Judaea, in a place which is called Bethlehem, and has been given up by the Jews, and scourged, and crucified on Mount Calvary, and has risen again from the dead on the third day. And His disciples have seen Him in the same flesh in which he was born, and He has shown Himself to His disciples, and they have believed in Him. And we indeed wish to become His disciples. [7] Now, let us go and destroy His enemies from the earth, that they may now know that there is none like the Lord our God on the face of the earth. [8] With this design, then, they went forth from the city of Libia which is called Burgidalla, and went on board a ship, and proceeded to Jerusalem, and surrounded the kingdom of the Jews, and began to send them to destruction. And when the kings of the Jews heard of their doings, and the wasting of their land, fear came upon them, and they were in great perplexity. Then Archelaus was perplexed in his words, and said to his son: [9] My son, take my kingdom and judge it; and take counsel with the other kings who are in the land of Judah, that you may be able to escape from our enemies. And having thus said, he unsheathed his sword and leant upon it; and turned his sword, which was very sharp, and thrust it into his breast, and died. And his son allied himself with the other kings who were under him, and they took counsel among themselves, and went into Jerusalem with their chief men who were in their counsel, and stood in the same place seven years. And Titus and Vespasian took counsel to surround their city. And they did so. And the seven years being fulfilled, there was a very sore famine, and for want of bread they began to eat earth. [10] Then all the soldiers who were of the four kings took counsel among themselves, and said: Now we are sure to die: what will God do to us? or of what good is our life to us, because the Romans have come to take our place and nation? It is better for us to kill each other, than that the Romans should say that they have slain us, and gained the victory over us. And they drew their swords and smote themselves, and died, to the number of twelve thousand men of them. Then there was a great stench in that city from the corpses of those dead men. And their kings feared with a very great fear even unto death; and they could not bear the stench of them, nor bury them, nor throw them forth out of the city. And they said to each other: What shall we do? We indeed gave up Christ to death, and now we given up to death ourselves. Let us bow our heads, and give up the keys of the city to the Romans, because God has already given us up to death. And immediately they went up upon the walls of the city, and all cried out with a loud voice, saying: Titus and Vespasian, take the keys of the city, which have been given to you by Messiah, who is called Christ. [11] Then they gave themselves up into the hands of Titus and Vespasian, and said: Judge us, seeing that we ought to die, because we judged Christ; and he was given up without cause. Titus and Vespasian seized them, and some they stoned, and some they hanged on a tree, feet up and head down, and struck them through with lances; and others they gave up to be sold, and others they divided among themselves, and made four parts of them, just as they had done of the garments of the Lord. And they said: They sold Christ for thirty pieces of silver, and we shall sell thirty of them for one denarius. And so they did. And having done so, they seized all the lands of Judaea and Jerusalem. [12] Then they made a search about the face or portrait of Jesus, how they might find it. And they found a woman named Veronica who had it. Then they seized Pilate, and sent him to prison, to be guarded by four quaternions of soldiers at the door of the prison. Then they forthwith sent their messengers to Tiberius, the emperor of the city of Rome, that he should send Velosianus to them. And he said to him: Take all that is necessary for thee in the sea, and go down into Judaea, and seek out one of the disciples of him who is called Christ and Lord, that he may come to me, and in the name of his God cure me of the leprosy and the infirmities by which I am daily exceedingly burdened, and of my wounds, because I am ill at ease. And send upon the kings of the Jews, who are subject to my authority, thy forces and terrible engines, because they have put to death Jesus Christ our Lord, and condemn them to death. And if thou shalt there find a man as may be able to free me from this infirmity of mine, I will believe in Christ the Son of God, and will baptize myself in his name. And Velosianus said: My lord emperor, if I find such a man as may be able to help and free us, what reward shall I promise him? Tiberius said to him: The half of my kingdom, without fail, to be in his hand. [13] Then Velosianus immediately went forth, and went on board the ship, and hoisted the sail in the vessel, and went on sailing through the sea. And he sailed a year and seven days, after which he arrived at Jerusalem. And immediately he ordered some of the Jews to come to his power, and began carefully to ask what had been the acts of Christ. Then Joseph, of the city of Arimathaea, and Nicodemus, came at the same time. And Nicodemus said: I saw Him, and I know indeed that He is the Saviour of the world. And Joseph said to him: And I took Him down from the cross, and laid Him in a new tomb, which had been cut out of the rock. And the Jews kept me shut up on the day of the preparation, at evening; and while I was standing in prayer on the Sabbath-day, the house was hung up by the four corners, and I saw the Lord Jesus Christ like a gleam of light, and for fear I fell to the ground. And He said to me, Look upon me, for I am Jesus, whose body thou buriedst in thy tomb. And I said to Him, Show me the sepulchre where I laid Thee. And Jesus, holding my hand in His right hand, led me to the place where I buried Him. [14] And there came also the woman named Veronica, and said to him: And I touched in the crowd the fringe of His garment, because for twelve years I had suffered from an issue of blood; and He immediately healed me. Then Velosianus said to Pilate: Thou, Pilate, impious and cruel, why hast thou slain the Son of God? And Pilate answered: His own nation, and the chief priests Annas and Caiaphas, gave him to me. Volosianus said: Impious and cruel, thou art worthy of death and cruel punishment. And he sent him back to prison. And Velosianus at last sought for the face or the countenance of the Lord. And all who were in that same place said: It is the woman called Veronica who has the portrait of the Lord in her house. And immediately he ordered her to be brought before his power. And he said to her: Hast thou the portrait of the Lord in thy house? But she said, No. Then Velosianus ordered her to be put to the torture, until she should give up the portrait of the Lord. And she was forced to say: I have it in clean linen, my lord, and I daily adore it. Velosianus said: Show it to me. Then she showed the portrait of the Lord. [15] When Velosianus saw it, he prostrated himself on the ground; and with a ready heart and true faith he took hold of it, and wrapped it in cloth of gold, and placed it in a casket, and sealed it with his ring. And he swore with an oath, and said: As the Lord God liveth, and by the health of Caesar, no man shall any more see it upon the face of the earth, until I see the face of my lord Tiberius. And when he had thus spoken, the princes, who were the chief men of Judaea, seized Pilate to take him to a seaport. And he took the portrait of the Lord, with all His disciples, and all in his pay, and they went on board the ship the same day. Then the woman Veronica, for the love of Christ, left all that she possessed, and followed Velosianus. And Velosianus said to her: What dost thou wish, woman, or what dost thou seek? And she answered: I am seeking the portrait of our Lord Jesus Christ, who enlightened me, not for my own merits, but through His own holy affection. Give back to me the portrait of my Lord Jesus Christ; for because of this I die with a righteous longing. But if thou do not give it back to me, I will not leave it until I see where thou wilt put it, because I, most miserable woman that I am, will serve Him all the days of my life; because I believe that He, my Redeemer, liveth for everlasting. [16] Then Velosianus ordered the woman Veronica to be taken down with him into the ship And the sails being hoisted. they began to go in the vessel in the name of the Lord, and they sailed through the sea. But Titus, along with Vespasian, went up into Judaea, avenging all nations upon their land. At the end of a year Velosianus came to the city of Rome, brought his vessel into the river which is called Tiberis, or Tiber, and entered the city which is called Rome. And he sent his messenger to his lord Tiberius the emperor in the Lateran about his prosperous arrival. [17] Then Tiberius the emperor, when he heard the message of Velosianus, rejoiced greatly, and ordered him to come before his face. And when he had come, he called him, saying: Velosianus, how hast thou come, and what hast thou seen in the region of Judaea of Christ the Lord and his disciples? Tell me, I beseech thee, that he is going to cure me of mine infirmity, that I may be at once cleansed from that leprosy which I have over my body, and I give up my whole kingdom into thy power and his. [18] And Velosianus said: My lord emperor, I found thy servants Titus and Vespasian in Judaea fearing the Lord, and they were cleansed from all their ulcers and sufferings. And I found that all the kings and rulers of Judaea have been hanged by Titus; Annas and Caiaphas have been stoned, Archelaus has killed himself with his own lance; and I have sent Pilate to Damascus in bonds, and kept him in prison under safe keeping. But I have also found out about Jesus, whom the Jews most wickedly attacked with swords, and staves, and weapons; and they crucified him who ought to have freed and enlightened us, and to have come to us, and they hanged him on a tree. And Joseph came from Arimathaea, and Nicodemus with him, bringing a mixture of myrrh and aloes, about a hundred pounds, to anoint the body of Jesus; and they took him down from the cross, and laid him in a new tomb. And on the third day he most assuredly rose again froth the dead, and showed himself to his disciples in the same flesh in which he had been born. [19] At length, after forty days, they saw him going up into heaven. Many, indeed, and other miracles did Jesus before his passion and after. First, of water he made wine; he raised the dead, he cleansed lepers, he enlightened the blind, he cured paralytics, he put demons to flight; he made the deaf hear, the dumb speak; Lazarus, when four days dead, he raised from the tomb; the woman Veronica, who suffered from an issue of blood twelve years, and touched the fringe of his garment, he made whole. Then it pleased the Lord in the heavens, that the Son of God, who, sent into this world as the first-created, had died upon earth, should send his angel; and he commanded Titus and Vespasian, whom I knew in that place where thy throne is. And it pleased God Almighty that they went into Judaea and Jerusalem, and seized thy subjects, and put them under that sentence, as it were, in the same manner as they did when thy subjects seized Jesus and bound him. [20] And Vespasian afterwards said: What shall we do about those who shall remain? Titus answered: They hanged our Lord on a green tree, and struck him with a lance; now let us hang them on a dry tree, and pierce their bodies through and through with the lance. And they did so. And Vespasian said: What about those who are left? [21] Titus answered: They seized the tunic of our Lord Jesus Christ, and of it made four parts; now let us seize them, and divide them into four parts,–to thee one, to me one, to thy men another, and to my servants the fourth part. And they did so. And Vespasian said: But what shall we do about those who are left? Titus answered him: The Jews sold our Lord for thirty pieces of silver: now let us sell thirty of them for one piece of silver. And they did so. And they seized Pilate, and gave him up to me, and I put him in prison, to be guarded by four quaternions of soldiers in Damascus. Then they made a search with great diligence to seek the portrait of the Lord; and they found a woman named Veronica who had the portrait of the Lord. Then the [22] Emperor Tiberius said to Velosianus: How hast thou it? And he answered: I have it in clean cloth of gold, rolled up in a shawl. And the Emperor Tiberius said: Bring it to me, and spread it before my face, that I, falling to the ground and bending my knees, may adore it on the ground. Then Velosianus spread out his shawl with the cloth of gold on which the portrait of the Lord had been imprinted; and the Emperor Tiberius saw it. [23] And he immediately adored the image of the Lord with a pure heart, and his flesh was cleansed as the flesh of a little child. And all the blind, the lepers, the lame, the dumb, the deaf, and those possessed by various diseases, who were there present, were healed, and cured, and cleansed. And the Emperor Tiberius bowed his head and bent his knees, considering that saying: Blessed is the womb which bore Thee, and the breasts which Thou hast sucked; and he groaned to the Lord, saying with tears: [24] God of heaven and earth, do not permit me to sin, but confirm my soul and my body, and place me in Thy kingdom, because in Thy name do I trust always: free me from all evils, as Thou didst free the three children from the furnace of blazing fire. [25] Then said the Emperor Tiberius to Velosianus: Velosianus, hast thou seen any of those men who saw Christ? Velosianus answered: I have. He said: Didst thou ask how they baptize those who believed in Christ? Velosianus said: Here, my Lord, we have one of the disciples of Christ himself. Then he ordered Nathan to be summoned to come to him. Nathan therefore came and baptized him in the name of the Father, and of the Son, and of the Holy Ghost. Amen. Immediately the Emperor Tiberius, made whole from all his diseases, ascended upon his throne, and said: Blessed art Thou, O Lord God Almighty, and worthy to be praised, who hast freed me from the snare of death, and cleansed me from all mine iniquities; because I have greatly sinned before Thee, O Lord my God, and I am not worthy to see Thy face. And then the Emperor Tiberius was instructed in all the articles of the faith, fully, and with strong faith. [26] May that same God Almighty, who is King of kings and Lord of lords, Himself shield us in His faith, and defend us, and deliver us from all danger and evil, and deign to bring us to life everlasting, when this life, which is temporary, shall fail; who is blessed for ever and ever. Amen.

The Narrative of Joseph of Arimathaea

Narrative of Joseph of Arimathaea, that Begged the Lord's Body; In which also he brings in the Cases of the Two Robbers.

1

[1] I am Joseph of Arimathaea, who begged from Pilate the body of the Lord Jesus for burial, and who for this cause was kept close in prison by the murderous and God-fighting Jews, who also, keeping to the law, have by Moses himself become partakers in tribulation and having provoked their Lawgiver to anger, and not knowing that He was God, crucified Him and made Him manifest to those that knew God. in those days in which they condemned the Son of God to be crucified, seven days before Christ suffered, two condemned robbers were sent from Jericho to the procurator Pilate; and their case was as follows: [2] The first, his name Gestas, put travellers to death, murdering them with the sword, and others he exposed naked. And he hung up women by the heels, head down, and cut off their breasts, and drank the blood of infants limbs, never having known God, not obeying the laws, being violent from the beginning, and doing such deeds. And the case of the other was as follows: He was called Demas, and was by birth a Galilaean, and kept an inn. He made attacks upon the rich, but was good to the poor a thief like Tobit, for he buried the bodies of the poor. And he set his hand to robbing the multitude of the Jews, and stole the law itself in Jerusalem, and stripped naked the daughter of Caiaphas, who was priestess of the sanctuary, and took away from its place the mysterious deposit itself placed there by Solomon. Such were his doings. [3] And Jesus also was taken on the third day before the passover, in the evening. And to Caiaphas and the multitude of the Jews it was not a passover, but it was a great mourning to them, on account of the plundering of the sanctuary by the robber. And they summoned Judas Iscariot, and spoke to him, for he was son of the brother of Caiaphas the priest. He was not a disciple before the face of Jesus; but all the multitude of the Jews craftily supported him, that he might follow Jesus, not that he might be obedient to the miracles done by Him, nor that he might confess Him, but that he might betray Him to them, wishing to catch up some lying word of Him, giving him gifts for such brave, honest conduct to the amount of a half shekel, of gold each day. And he did this for two years with Jesus, as says one of His disciples called John. [4] And on the third day, before Jesus was laid hold of, Judas says to the Jews: Come, let us hold a council; for perhaps it was not the robber that stole the law, but Jesus himself, and I accuse him. And when these words had been spoken, Nicodemus, who kept the keys of the sanctuary, came in to us, and said to all: Do not do such a deed. For Nicodemus was true, more than all the multitude of the Jews. And the daughter of Caiaphas, Sarah by name, cried out, and said: He himself said before all against this holy place, I am able to destroy this temple, and in three days to raise it. The Jews say to her: Thou hast credit with all of us. For they regarded her as a prophetess. And assuredly, after the council had been held, Jesus was laid hold of.

2

[1] And on the following day, the fourth day of the week, they brought Him at the ninth hour into the hall of Caiaphas. And Annas and Caiaphas say to Him: Tell us, why hast thou stolen our law, and renounced the ordinances of Moses and the prophets? And Jesus answered nothing. And again a second time, the multitude also being present, they say to Him: The sanctuary which Solomon built in forty and six years, why dost thou wish to destroy in one moment? And to these things Jesus answered nothing. For the sanctuary of the synagogue had been plundered by the robber. [2] And the evening of the fourth day being ended, all the multitude sought to burn the daughter of Caiaphas, on account of the loss of the law; for they did not know how they were to keep the passover. And she said to them: Wait, my children, and let us destroy this Jesus, and the law will be found, and the holy feast will be fully accomplished. And secretly Annas and Caiaphas gave considerable money to Judas Iscariot, saying: Say as thou saidst to us before, I know that the law has been stolen by Jesus, that the accusation may be turned against him, and not against this maiden, who is free from blame. And Judas having received this command, said to them: Let not all the multitude know that I have been instructed by you to do this against Jesus; but release Jesus, and I persuade the multitude that it is so. And craftily they released Jesus. [3] And Judas, going into the sanctuary at the dawn of the fifth day, says to all the people: What will you give me, and I will give up to you the overthrower of the law, and the plunderer of the prophets? The Jews say to him: If thou wilt give him up to us, we will give thee thirty pieces of gold. And the people did not know that Judas was speaking about Jesus, for many of them confessed that he was the Son of God. And Judas received the thirty pieces of gold. [4] And going out at the fourth hour, and at the fifth, he finds Jesus walking in the street. And as evening was coming on, Judas says to the Jews: Give me the aid of soldiers with swords and staves, and I will give him up to you. They therefore gave

him officers for the purpose of seizing Him. And as they were going along, Judas says to them: Lay hold of the man whom I shall kiss, for he has stolen the law and the prophets. Going up to Jesus, therefore, he kissed Him, saying: Hail, Rabbi! it being the evening of the fifth day. And having laid hold of Him, they gave Him up to Caiaphas and the chief priests, Judas saying: This is he who stole the law and the prophets. And the Jews gave Jesus an unjust trial, saying: Why hast thou done these things? And be answered nothing. [5] And Nicodemus and I Joseph, seeing the seat of the plagues, stood off from them, not wishing to perish along with the counsel of the ungodly.

3

[1] Having therefore done many and dreadful things against Jesus that night, they gave Him up to Pilate the procurator at the dawn of the preparation, that he might crucify Him; and for this purpose they all came together. After a trial, therefore, Pilate the procurator ordered Him to be nailed to the cross, along with the two robbers. And they were nailed up along with Jesus, Gestas on the left. and Demas on the right. [2] And he that was on the left began to cry out, saying to Jesus: See how many evil deeds I have done in the earth; and if I had known that thou wast the king, I should have cut off thee also. And why dost thou call thyself Son of God, and canst not help thyself in necessity? how canst thou afford it to another one praying for help? If thou art the Christ, come down from the cross, that I may believe in thee. But now I see thee perishing along with me, not like a man, but like a wild beast. And many other things he began to say against Jesus, blaspheming and gnashing his teeth upon Him. For the robber was taken alive in the snare of the devil. [3] But the robber on the right hand, whose name was Demas, seeing the Godlike grace of Jesus, thus cried out: I know Thee, Jesus Christ, that Thou art the Son of God. I see Thee, Christ, adored by myriads of myriads of angels. Pardon me my sins which I have done. Do not in my trial make the stars come against me, or the moon, when Thou shall judge all the world; because in the night I have accomplished my wicked purposes. Do not urge the sun, which is now darkened on account of Thee, to tell the evils of my heart, for no gift can I give Thee for the remission of my sins. Already death is coming upon me because of my sins; but Thine is the propitiation. Deliver me, O Lord of all, from Thy fearful judgment. Do not give the enemy power to swallow me up, and to become heir of my soul, as of that of him who is hanging on the left; for I see how the devil joyfully takes his soul, and his body disappears. Do not even order me to go away into the portion of the Jews; for I see Moses and the patriarchs in great weeping, and the devil rejoicing over them. Before, then, O Lord, my spirit departs, order my sins to be washed away, and remember me the sinner in Thy kingdom, when upon the great most lofty throne thou shalt judge the twelve tribes of Israel. For Thou hast prepared great punishment for Thy world on account of Thyself. [4] And the robber having thus spoken, Jesus says to him: Amen, amen; I say to thee, Demas, that to-day thou shalt be with me in paradise. And the sons of the kingdom, the children of Abraham, and Isaac, and Jacob, and Moses, shall be cast out into outer darkness; there shall be weeping and gnashing of teeth. And thou alone shalt dwell in paradise until my second appearing, when I am to judge those who do not confess my name. And He said to the robber: Go away, and tell the cherubim and the powers, that turn the flaming sword, that guard paradise from the time that Adam, the first created, was in paradise, and sinned, and kept not my commandments, and I cast him out thence. And none of the first shall see paradise until I am to come the second time to judge living and dead. And He wrote thus: Jesus Christ the Son of God, who have come down from the heights of the heavens, who have come forth out of the bosom of the invisible Father without being separated from Him, and who have come down into the world to be made flesh, and to be nailed to a cross, in order that I might save Adam, whom I fashioned, to my archangelic powers, the gatekeepers of paradise, to the officers of my Father: I will and order that he who has been crucified along with me should go in, should receive remission of sins through me; and that he, having put on an incorruptible body, should go in to paradise, and dwell where no one has ever been able to dwell. [5] And, behold, after He had said this, Jesus gave up the ghost, on the day of the preparation, at the ninth hour. And there was darkness over all the earth; and from a great earthquake that happened, the sanctuary fell down, and the wing of the temple.

4

[1] And I Joseph begged the body of Jesus, and put it in a new tomb, where no one had been put. And of the robber on the right the body was not found; but of him on the left, as the form of a dragon, so was his body. [2] And after I had begged the body of Jesus to bury, the Jews, carried away by hatred and rage, shut me up in prison, where evil-doers were kept under restraint. And this happened to me on the evening of the Sabbath, whereby our nation transgressed the law. And, behold, that same nation of ours endured fearful tribulations on the Sabbath. [3] And now, on the evening of the first of the week, at the fifth hour of the night, Jesus comes to me in the prison, along with the robber who had been crucified with Him on the right, whom He sent into paradise. And there was a great light in the building. And the house was hung up by the four corners, and the place was opened, and I came out. Then I first recognised Jesus, and again the robber, bringing a letter to Jesus. And as we were going into Galilee, there shone a great light, which the creation did not produce. And there was also with the robber a great fragrance out of paradise. [4] And Jesus, having sat down in a certain place, thus read: We, the cherubim and the six-winged, who have been ordered by Thy Godhead to watch the garden of paradise, make the following statement through the robber who was crucified along with Thee, by Thy arrangement: When we saw the print of the nails of the robber crucified along with Thee, and the shining light of the letter of Thy Godhead, the fire indeed was extinguished, not being able to bear the splendour of the print; and we crouched down, being in great fear. For we heard that the Maker of heaven and earth, and of the whole creation, had come down from on high to dwell in the lower parts of the earth, on account of Adam, the first created. And when we beheld the undefiled cross shining like lightning from the robber, gleaming with sevenfold the light of the sun, trembling fell upon us. We felt a violent shaking of the world below; and with a loud voice, the ministers of Hades said, along with us: Holy, holy, holy is He who in the beginning was in the highest. And the powers sent up a cry: O Lord, Thou hast been made manifest in heaven and in earth, bringing joy to the world; and, a greater gift than this, Thou hast freed Thine own image from death by the invisible purpose of the ages. CHAP. [5]. [1] After I had beheld these things, as I was going into Galilee with Jesus and the robber, Jesus was transfigured, and was not as formerly, before He was crucified, but was altogether light; and angels always ministered to Him, and Jesus spoke with them. And I remained with Him three days. And no one of His disciples was with Him, except the robber alone. [2] And in the middle of the feast of unleavened bread, His disciple John comes, and we no longer beheld the robber as to what took place. And John asked Jesus: Who is this, that Thou hast not made me to be seen by him? But Jesus answered him nothing. And falling down before Him, he said: Lord, I know that Thou hast loved me from the beginning, and why dost Thou not reveal to me that man? Jesus says to him: Why dost thou seek what is hidden? Art thou still without understanding? Dost thou not perceive the fragrance of paradise filling the place? Dost thou not know who it is? The robber on the cross has become heir of paradise. Amen, amen; I say to thee, that it shall belong to him alone until that the great day shall come. And John said: Make me worthy to behold him. [3] And while John was yet speaking, the robber suddenly appeared; and John, struck with astonishment, fell to the earth. And the robber was not in his first form, as before John came; but he was like a king in great power, having on him the cross. And the voice of a great multitude was sent forth: Thou hast come to the place prepared for thee in paradise. We have been commanded by Him that has sent thee, to serve thee until the great day. And after this voice, both the robber and I Joseph vanished, and I was found in my own house; and I no longer saw Jesus. [4] And I, having seen these things, have written them down, in order that all may believe in the crucified Jesus Christ our Lord, and may no longer obey the law of Moses, but may believe in the signs and wonders that have happened through Him, and in order that we who have believed may inherit eternal life, and be found in the kingdom of the heavens. For to Him are due glory, strength, praise, and majesty for ever and ever. Amen.

The Book of John the Evangelist

1 I, John, your brother and partaker in tribulation, and that shall be also a partaker in the kingdom of heaven, when I lay upon breast of our Lord Jesus Christ and said unto him: Lord, who is he that shall betray thee? [and] he answered and said: He that dippeth his hand with me in the dish: then Satan entered unto him and he sought how he might betray me. **2** And I said: Lord, before Satan fell, in what glory abode he with thy Father? And he said unto me: In such glory was he that he commanded the powers of the heavens: but I sat with my Father, and he did order all the followers of the Father, and went down from heaven unto the deep and ascended up out of the deep unto the throne of the invisible Father. And he saw the glory of him that moveth the heavens, and he thought to set his seat above the clouds of heaven and desired to be like unto the Most High. **3** And when he had descended into the air, he said unto the angel of the air: Open unto me the gates of the air. And he opened them unto him. And he sought to go further downward and found the angel which held the waters, and said unto him: Open unto me the gates of the waters. And he opened to him. And he passed through and found all the face of the earth covered with waters. And he passed through beneath the earth and found two fishes lying upon the waters, and they were as oxen yoked for ploughing, holding the whole earth by the commandment of the invisible Father, from the west even unto the sunrising. And when he had gone down he found clouds hanging which held the waters of the sea. And he went down yet further and found hell, that is the gehenna of fire and thereafter he could go down no further because of the flame of the burning fire. And Satan returned back and filled up (passed over again) the paths and entered in unto the angel of the air and to him that was over the waters, and said unto them: All these things are mine: if ye will hearken unto me, I will set my seat in the clouds and be like the Most High, and I will take the waters from this upper firmament and gather together the other parts (places) of the sea, and thereafter there shall be no water upon the face of all the earth, and I will reign with you world without end. **4** And when he had said thus unto the angels, he went up unto the other angels, even unto the fifth heaven, and thus spake he unto each of them: How much owest thou unto thy lord? He said: An hundred measures (cors) of wheat. And he said unto him: Take pen and ink and write sixty. And unto others he said: And thou, how much owest thou unto thy lord? and he answered: An hundred jars of oil. And he said: Sit down and write fifty. And as he went up through all the heavens he said thus, even unto the fifth heaven, seducing the angels of the invisible Father. And there came forth a voice out of the throne of the Father, saying: What doest thou, O denier of the Father, seducing the angels? doer of iniquity, that thou hast devised do quickly. **5** Then the Father commanded his angels, saying: Take away their garments. And the angels took away their garments and their thrones and their crowns from all the angels that hearkened unto him. **6** And I asked of the Lord: When Satan fell, in what place dwelt he? And he answered me: My Father changed his appearance because of his pride, and the light was taken from him, and his face became like unto heated iron, and his face became wholly like that of a man: and he drew with his tail the third part of the angels of God, and was cast out from the seat of God and from the stewardship of the heavens. And Satan came down into this firmament, and he could find (make) no rest for himself nor for them that were with him. And he asked the Father saying: Have patience with me and I will pay thee all. And the Father had mercy on him and gave him rest and them that were with him, as much as they would even unto seven days. **7** And so sat he in the firmament and commanded the angel that was over the air and him that was over the waters, and they raised the earth up and it appeared dry: and he took the crown of the angel that was over the waters, and of the half thereof he made the light of the moon and of the half the light of the stars: and of the precious stones he made all the hosts of the stars. **8** And thereafter he made the angels his ministers according to the order of the form of the Most High, and by the commandment of the invisible Father he made thunder, rain, hail, and snow. **9** And he sent forth angels to be ministers over them. And he commanded the earth to bring forth every beast for food (fatling), and every creeping thing, and trees and herbs: and he commanded the sea to bring forth fishes, and the fowls of the heaven. **10** And he devised furthermore and made man in his likeness, and commanded the (or an) angel of the third heaven to enter into the body of clay. And he took thereof and made another body in the form of a woman, and commanded the (or an) angel of the second heaven to enter into the body of the woman. But the angel lamented when they beheld a mortal shape upon them and that they were unlike in shape. And he commanded them to do the deed of the flesh in the bodies of clay, and they knew not how to commit sin. **11** Then did the contriver of evil devise in his mind to make paradise, and he brought the man and woman into it. And he Commanded to bring a reed, and the devil planted it in the midst of paradise, and so did the wicked devil hide his device that they knew not his deceit. And he came in and spake unto them, saying: Of every fruit which is in paradise eat ye, but of the fruit of the knowledge of good and evil eat not. Notwithstanding, the devil entered into a wicked serpent and seduced the angel that was in the form of the woman, and he wrought his lust with Eve in the Song of the serpent. And therefore are they called sons of the devil and sons of the serpent that do the lust of the devil their father, even unto the end of this world. And again the devil poured out upon the angel that was in Adam the poison of his lust, and it begetteth the sons of the serpent and the sons of the devil even unto the end of this world. **12** And after that I, John, asked of the Lord, saying: How say men that Adam and Eve were created by God and set in paradise to keep the commandments of the Father, and were delivered unto death? And the Lord said to me: Hearken, John, beloved of my Father; foolish men say thus in their deceitfulness that my Father made bodies of clay: but by the Holy Ghost made he all the powers of the heavens, and holy ones were found having bodies of clay because of their transgression, and therefore were delivered unto death. **13** And again I, John, asked the Lord: How beginneth a man to be in the Spirit (to have a spirit) in a body of flesh? And the Lord said unto me: Certain of the angels which fell do enter unto the bodies of women, and receive flesh from the lust of the flesh, and so is a spirit born of spirit, and flesh of flesh, and so is the kingdom of Satan accomplished in this world and among all nations. **14** And he said to me: My Father hath suffered him to reign seven days, which are seven ages. **15** And I asked the Lord and said: What shall be in that time? And he said to me: From the time when the devil fell from the glory of the Father and (lost) his own glory, he sat upon the clouds, and sent his ministers, even angels flaming with fire, unto men from Adam even unto Henoch his servant. And he raised up Henoch upon the firmament and showed him his godhead and commanded pen and ink to be given him: and he sat down and wrote threescore and seven books. And he commanded that he should take them to the earth and deliver them unto his sons. And Henoch let his books down upon the earth and delivered them unto his sons, and began to teach them to perform the custom of sacrifice, and unrighteous mysteries, and so did he hide the kingdom of heaven from men. And he said unto them: Behold that I am your god and beside me is none other god. And therefore did my Father send me into the world that I might make it known unto men, that they might know the evil device of the devil. **16** And then when he perceived that I had come down out of heaven into the world, he sent an angel and took of three sorts of wood and gave them unto Moses that I might be crucified, and now are they reserved for me. But then (now) did the devil proclaim unto him (Moses) his godhead, and unto his people, and commanded a law to be given unto the children of Israel, and brought them out through the midst of the sea which was dried up. **17** When my Father thought to send me into the world, he sent his angel before me, by name Mary, to receive me. And I when I came down entered in by the ear and came forth by the ear. **18** And Satan the prince of this world perceived that I was come to seek and save them that were lost, and sent his angel, even Helias the prophet, baptizing with water: who is called John the Baptist. And Helias asked the prince of this world: How can I know him? Then his lord said: On whom soever thou shalt see the spirit descending like a dove and resting upon him, he it is that baptizeth with the Holy Ghost unto forgiveness of sins: thou wilt be able to destroy him and to save. And again I, John, asked the Lord: Can a man be saved by the baptism of John without thy baptism? And the Lord answered: Unless I have baptized him unto forgiveness of sins, by the baptism of water can no man see the kingdom of heaven: for I am the bread of life that came down from the seventh heaven and they that eat my flesh and drink my blood, they shall be called the sons of God. **19** And I asked the Lord and said: What meaneth it, to eat my flesh and drink my blood? (An answer and question seem to have fallen out.) And the Lord said unto me: Before the falling of the devil with all his host from the glory of the Father [in prayer], they did glorify the Father in their prayers thus, saying: Our Father, which art in heaven; and so did all their songs come up before the throne of the Father. But when they had fallen, after that they are not able to glorify God with that prayer. **20** And I asked the Lord: How do all men receive the baptism of John, but thine not at all? And the Lord answered: Because their deeds are evil and they come not unto the light. **21** The disciples of John marry and are given in marriage; but my disciples neither marry nor are given in marriage, but are as the angels of God in heaven. But I said: If, then, it be sin to have to do with a woman, it is not good to marry. And the Lord said unto me: Not every one can receive this saying (etc., Matt. xix.11, 12). **22** I asked the Lord concerning the day of judgement: What shall be the sign of thy coming? And he answered and said unto me: When the numbers of the righteous shall be accomplished that is, the number of the righteous that are crowned, that have fallen, then shall Satan be loosed out of his prison, having great wrath, and shall make war with the righteous, and they shall cry unto the

Lord with a loud voice. And immediately the Lord shall command an angel to blow with the trumpet, and the voice of the archangel shall be heard in the trumpet from heaven even unto hell. ²³ And then shall the sun be darkened and the moon shall not give her light, and the stars shall fall, and the four winds shall be loosed from their foundations, and shall cause the earth and the sea and the mountains to quake together. And the heaven shall immediately shake and the sun shall be darkened, and it shall shine even to the fourth hour. Then shall appear the sign of the Son of man, and all the holy angels with him, and he shall set his seat upon the clouds, and sit on the throne of his majesty with the twelve apostles on the twelve seats of their glory. And the books shall be opened and he shall judge the whole world and the faith which he proclaimed. And then shall the Son of man send his angels, and they shall gather his elect from the four winds from the heights of the heavens unto the boundaries of them, and shall bring them to seek. ²⁴ Then shall the Son of God send the evil spirits, to bring all nations before him, and shall say unto them: Come, ye that did say: We have eaten and drunk and received the gain of this world. And after that they shall again be brought, and shall all stand before the judgement seat, even all nations, in fear. And the books of life shall be opened and all nations shall show forth their ungodliness. And he shall glorify the righteous for their patience: and glory and honour and incorruption shall be the reward of their good works: but as for them that kept the commandments of the angels and obeyed unrighteously, indignation and trouble and anguish shall take hold on then. ²⁵ And the Son of God shall bring forth the elect out of the midst of the sinners and say unto them: Come, ye blessed of my Father, inherit the kingdom prepared for you from the foundation of the world. Then shall he say unto the sinners: Depart from me, ye cursed, into everlasting fire, which was prepared for the devil and his angels. And the rest, beholding the last cutting off, shall cast the sinners into hell by the commandment of the invisible Father. Then shall the spirits of them that believe not go forth out of the prisons, and then shall my voice be heard, and there shall be one fold and one shepherd: and the darkness and obscurity shall come forth out of the lower parts of the earth -that is to say, the darkness of the gehenna of fire- and shall burn all things from below even to the air of the firmament. And the Lord shall be in the firmament and even to the lower parts of the earth. (read And the distance from the firmament unto the lower parts of the earth shall be) as if a man of thirty years old should take up a stone and cast it down, hardly in three years would it reach the bottom: so great is the depth of the pit and of the fire wherein the sinners shall dwell. ²⁶ And then shall Satan and all his host be bound and cast into the lake of fire. And the Son of God shall walk with his elect above the firmament and shall shut up the devil, binding him with strong chains that cannot be loosed. At that time the sinners, weeping and mourning, shall say: O earth, swallow us up and cover us in death. And then shall the righteous shine as the sun in the kingdom of their Father. And he shall bring them before the throne of the invisible Father, saying: Behold, I and my children whom God hath given me. O righteous one, the world hath not known thee, but I have known thee in truth, because thou hast sent me. And then shall the Father answer his Son and say: My beloved Son, sit thou on my right hand until I make thine enemies the footstool of thy feet, which have denied me and said: We are gods, and beside us there is none other god: which have slain thy prophets and persecuted thy righteous ones, and thou hast persecuted them even unto the outer darkness: there shall be weeping and gnashing of teeth. ²⁷ And then shall the Son of God sit on the right hand of his Father, and the Father shall command his angels, and they shall minister unto them (i.e. the righteous) and set them among the choirs of the angels, to clothe them with incorruptible garments, and shall give them crowns that fade not and seats that cannot be moved. And God shall be in the midst of them; and they shall not hunger nor thirst any more, neither shall the sun light on them nor any heat. And God shall wipe away every tear from their eyes. And he shall reign with his holy Father, and of his kingdom there shall be no end for ever and ever.

EPISTLES

The Epistles of Jesus Christ and Abgarus King of Edessa

1

A copy of a letter written by King Abgarus to Jesus, and sent to him by Ananias, his footman, to Jerusalem, 5 inviting him to Edessa.

¹ ABGARUS, king of Edessa, to Jesus the good Saviour, who appears at Jerusalem, greeting. ² I have been informed concerning you and your cures, which are performed without the use of medicines and herbs. ³ For it is reported, that you cause the blind to see, the lame to walk, do both cleanse lepers, and cast out unclean spirits and devils, and restore them to health who have been long diseased, and raisest up the dead; ⁴ All which when I heard, I was persuaded of one of these two, viz: either that you are God himself descended from heaven, who do these things, or the son of God. ⁵ On this account therefore I have wrote to you, earnestly to desire you would take the trouble of a journey hither, and cure a disease which I am under. ⁶ For I hear the Jews ridicule you, and intend you mischief. ⁷ My city is indeed small, but neat, and large enough for us both.

2

The answer of Jesus by Ananias the footman to Abgarus the king, 3 declining to visit Edessa.

¹ ABGARUS, you are happy, forasmuch as you have believed on me, whom ye have not seen. ² For it is written concerning me, that those who have seen me should not believe on me, that they who have not seen might believe and live. ³ As to that part of your letter, which relates to my giving you a visit, I must inform you, that I must fulfil all the ends of my mission in this country, and after that be received up again to him who sent me. ⁴ But after my ascension I will send one of my disciples, who will cure your disease, and give life to you, and all that are with you.

The Epistle of Paul to the Laodiceans

1 He salutes the brethren. 3 exhorts them to persevere in good works, 4 and not to be moved by vain speaking. 6 Rejoices in his bonds, 10 desires them to live in the fear of the Lord.

[1] PAUL an Apostle, not of men, neither by man, but by Jesus Christ, to the brethren which are at Laodicea. [2] Grace be to you, and Peace, from God the Father and our Lord Jesus Christ. [3] I thank Christ in every prayer of mine, that ye may continue and persevere in good works looking for that which is promised in the day of judgment. [4] Let not the vain speeches of any trouble you who pervert the truth, that they may draw you aside from the truth of the Gospel which I have preached. [5] And now may God grant, that my converts may attain to a perfect knowledge of the truth of the Gospel, be beneficent, and doing good works which accompany salvation. [6] And now my bonds, which I suffer in Christ, are manifest, in which I rejoice and am glad. [7] For I know that this shall turn to my salvation for ever, which shall be through your prayer, and the supply of the Holy Spirit. [8] Whether I live or die; (for) to me to live shall be a life to Christ, to die will be joy. [9] And our Lord will grant us his mercy, that ye may have the same love, and be like-minded. [10] Wherefore, my beloved, as ye have heard of the coming of the Lord, so think and act in fear, and it shall be to you life eternal; [11] For it is God who worketh in you; [12] And do all things without sin. [13] And what is best, my beloved, rejoice in the Lord Jesus Christ, and avoid all filthy lucre. [14] Let all your requests be made known to God, and be steady in the doctrine of Christ. [15] And whatsoever things are sound and true, and of good report, and chaste, and just, and lovely, these things do. [16] Those things which ye have heard, and received, think on these things, and peace shall be with you. [17] All the saints salute you. [18] The grace of our Lord Jesus Christ be with your spirit. Amen. [19] Cause this Epistle to be read to the Colossians, and the Epistle of the Colossians to be read among you.

The Epistles of Paul to Seneca, with Seneca's to Paul

1

Annæus Seneca to Paul Greeting.

[1] I SUPPOSE, Paul, you have been informed of that conversation, which passed yesterday between me and my Lucilius, concerning hypocrisy and other subjects; for there were some of your disciples in company with us; [2] For when we were retired into the Sallustian gardens, through which they were also passing, and would have gone another way, by our persuasion they joined company with us. [3] I desire you to believe, that we much wish for your conversation: [4] We were much delighted with your book of many Epistles, which you have wrote to some cities and chief towns of provinces, and contain wonderful instructions for moral conduct: [5] Such sentiments, as I suppose you were not the author of, but only the instrument of conveying, though sometimes both the author and the instrument. [6] For such is the sublimity of those doctrines, and their grandeur, that I suppose the age of a man is scarce sufficient to be instructed and perfected in the knowledge of them. I wish your welfare, my brother. Farewell.

2

Paul to Seneca Greeting.

[1] I RECEIVED your letter yesterday with pleasure: to which I could immediately have wrote an answer, had the young man been at home, whom I intended to have sent to you: [2] For you know when, and by whom, at what seasons, and to whom I must deliver every thing which I send. [3] I desire therefore you would not charge me with negligence, if I wait for a proper person. [4] I reckon myself very happy in having the judgment of so valuable a person, that you are delighted with my Epistles: [5] For you would not be esteemed a censor, a philosopher, or be the tutor of so great a prince, and a master of every thing, if you were not sincere. I wish you a lasting prosperity.

3

Annæus Seneca to Paul Greeting.

[1] I HAVE completed some volumes, and divided them into their proper parts. [2] I am determined to read them to Cæsar, and if any favourable opportunity happens, you also shall be present, when they are read; [3] But if that cannot be, I will appoint and give you notice of a day, when we will together read over the performance. [4] I had determined, if I could with safety, first to have your opinion of it, before I published it to Cæsar, that you might be convinced of my affection to you. Farewell, dearest Paul.

4

Paul to Seneca Greeting.

[1] AS often as I read your letters, I imagine you present with me; nor indeed do I think any other, than that you are always with us. [2] As soon therefore as you begin to come, we shall presently see each other. I wish you all prosperity.

5

Annæus Seneca to Paul Greeting.

[1] WE are very much concerned at your too long absence from us. [2] What is it, or what affairs are they, which obstruct your coming? [3] If you fear the anger of Cæsar, because you have abandoned your former religion, and made proselytes also of others, you have this to plead, that your acting thus proceeded not from inconstancy, but judgment. Farewell.

6

Paul to Seneca and Lucilius Greeting.

[1] CONCERNING those things about which ye wrote to me it is not proper for me to mention anything in writing with pen and ink: the one of which leaves marks, and the other evidently declares things. [2] Especially since I know that there are near you, as well as me, those who will understand my meaning. [3] Deference is to be paid to all men, and so much the more, as they are more likely to take occasions of quarrelling. [4] And if we show a submissive temper, we shall overcome effectually in all points, if so be they are, who are capable of seeing and acknowledging themselves to have been in the wrong. Farewell.

7

Annæus Seneca to Paul Greeting.

[1] I PROFESS myself extremely pleased with the reading your letters to the Galatians, Corinthians, and people of Achaia. [2] For the Holy Ghost has in them by you delivered those sentiments which are very lofty, sublime, deserving of all respect, and beyond your own invention. [3] I could wish therefore, that when you are writing things so extraordinary, there might not be wanting an elegancy of speech agreeable to their majesty. [4] And I must own my brother, that I may not at once dishonestly conceal anything from you, and be unfaithful to my own conscience, that the emperor is

extremely pleased with the sentiments of your Epistles; ⁵ For when he heard the beginning of them read, he declared, That he was surprised to find such notions in a person, who had not had a regular education. ⁶ To which I replied, That the Gods sometimes made use of mean (innocent) persons to speak by, and gave him an instance of this in a mean countryman, named Vatienus, who, when he was in the country of Reate, had two men appeared to him, called Castor and Pollux, and received a revelation from the gods. Farewell.

8

Paul to Seneca Greeting.
¹ ALTHOUGH I know the emperor is both an admirer and favourer of our (religion), yet give me leave to advise you against your suffering any injury, (by shewing favour to us.) ² I think indeed you ventured upon a very dangerous attempt, when you would declare to the emperor) that which is so very contrary to his religion, and way of worship; seeing he is a worshipper of the heathen gods. ³ I know not what you particularly had in view, when you told him of this; but I suppose you did it out of too great respect for me. ⁴ But I desire that for the future you would not do so; for you had need be careful, lest by shewing your affection for me, you should offend your master: ⁵ His anger indeed will do us no harm, if he continue a heathen; nor will his not being angry be of any service to us: ⁶ And if the empress act worthy of her character, she will not be angry; but if she acts as a woman, she will be affronted. Farewell.

9

Annæus Seneca to Paul Greeting.
¹ I KNOW that my letter, wherein I acquainted you, that I had read to the Emperor your Epistles, does not so much affect of as the nature of the things (contained in them), ² Which do so powerfully divert men's minds from their former manners and practices, that I have always been surprised, and have been fully convinced of it by many arguments heretofore. ³ Let us therefore begin afresh; and if any thing heretofore has been imprudently acted, do you forgive. ⁴ I have sent you a book *de copia verborum*. Farewell, dearest Paul.

10

Paul to Seneca Greeting.
¹ AS often as I write to you, and place my name before yours, I do a thing both disagreeable to myself; and contrary to our religion: ² For I ought, as I have often declared, to become all things to all men, and to have that regard to your quality, which the Roman law has honoured all senators with; namely, to put my name last in the (inscription of the) Epistle, that I may not at length with uneasiness and shame be obliged to do that which it was always my inclination to do. Farewell, most respected master. Dated the fifth of the calends of July, in the fourth consulship of Nero, and Messala.

11

Annæus Seneca to Paul Greeting.
¹ ALL happiness to you, my dearest Paul. ² If a person so great, and every way agreeable as you are, become not only a common, but a most intimate friend to me, how happy will be the case of Seneca! ³ You therefore, who are so eminent, and so far exalted above all, even the greatest, do not think yourself unfit to be first named in the inscription of an Epistle; ⁴ Lest I should suspect you intend not so much to try me, as to banter me; for you know yourself to be a Roman citizen. ⁵ And I could wish to be in that circumstance or station which you are, and that you were in the same that I am. Farewell, dearest Paul. Dated the tenth of the calends of April, in the consulship of Aprianus and Capito.

12

Annæus Seneca to Paul Greeting.
¹ ALL happiness to you, my dearest Paul. Do you not suppose I am extremely concerned and grieved that your innocence should bring you into sufferings? ² And that all the people should suppose you (Christians) so criminal, and imagine all the misfortunes that happen to the city, to be caused by you? ³ But let us bear the charge with a patient temper, appealing (for our innocence) to the court (above), which is the only one our hard fortune will allow us to address to, till at length our misfortunes shall end in unalterable happiness. ⁴ Former ages have produced (tyrants) Alexander the son of Philip, and Dionysius; ours also has produced Caius Cæsar; whose inclinations were their only laws. ⁵ As to the frequent burnings of the city of Rome, the cause is manifest; and if a person in my mean circumstances might be allowed to speak, and one might declare these dark things without danger, every one should see the whole of the matter. ⁶ The Christians and Jews are indeed commonly punished for the crime of burning the city; but that impious miscreant, who delights in murders and butcheries, and disguises his villanies with lies, is appointed to, or reserved till, his proper time. ⁷ And as the life of every excellent person is now sacrificed instead of that one person (who is the author of the mischief), so this one shall be sacrificed for many, and he shall be devoted to be burnt with fire instead of all. ⁸ One hundred and thirty-two houses, and four whole squares (or islands) were burnt down in six days: the seventh put an end to the burning. I wish you all happiness. ⁹ Dated the fifth of the calends of April, in the consulship of Frigius and Bassus.

13

Annæus Seneca to Paul *Greeting.*
¹ ALL happiness to you, my dearest Paul. ² You have wrote many volumes in an allegorical and mystical style, and therefore such mighty matters and business being committed to you, require not to be set off with any rhetorical flourishes of speech, but only with some proper elegance. ³ I remember you often say, that many by affecting such a style do injury to their subjects, and lose the force of the matters they treat of. ⁴ But in this I desire you to regard me, namely, to have respect to true Latin, and to choose just words, that so you may the better manage the noble trust which is reposed in you. ⁵ Farewell. Dated the fifth of the names of July, Leo and Savinus consuls.

14

Paul to Seneca Greeting.
¹ YOUR serious consideration requited with these discoveries, which the Divine Being has granted but to few. ² I am thereby assured that I sow the most strong seed in a fertile soil, not anything material, which is subject to corruption, but the durable word of God, which shall increase and bring forth fruit to eternity. ³ That which by your wisdom you have attained to, shall abide without decay for ever. ⁴ Believe that you ought to avoid the superstitions of Jews and Gentiles. ⁵ The things which you have in some measure arrived to, prudently make known to the emperor, his family, and to faithful friends; ⁶ And though your sentiments will seem disagreeable, and not be comprehended by them, seeing most of them will not regard your discourses, yet the Word of God once infused into them, will at length make them become new men, aspiring towards God. ⁷ Farewell Seneca, who art most dear to us. Dated on the Calends of August, in the consulship of Leo and Savinus.

The Epistula Apostolorum, or Epistle of the Apostles

Some pages of the Coptic MS. are lost, so we rely on the Ethiopic texts.

¹ The book which Jesus Christ revealed unto his disciples: and how that Jesus Christ revealed the book for the company (college) of the apostles, the disciples of Jesus Christ, even the book which is for all men. Simon and Cerinthus, the false apostles, concerning whom it is written that no man shall cleave unto them for there is in them deceit wherewith they bring men to destruction. (The book hath been written) that ye may be steadfast and not flinch nor be troubled, and depart not from the word of the Gospel which ye have heard. Like as we heard it, we keep it in remembrance and have written it for the whole world. We commend you our sons and our daughters in joy in the name of God the Father the Lord of the world, and of Jesus Christ. Let grace be multiplied upon you. ² We, John, Thomas, Peter, Andrew, James, Philip, Bartholomew, Matthew, Nathanael, Judas Zelotes, and Cephas, write unto the churches of the east and the west, of the north and the south declaring and imparting unto you that which concerneth our Lord Jesus Christ: we do write according as we have seen and heard and touched him, after that he was risen from the dead: and how that he revealed unto us things mighty and wonderful and true. ³ This know we: that our Lord and Redeemer Jesus Christ is God the Son of God, who was sent of God the Lord of the whole world, the maker and creator of it, who is named by all names and high above all powers, Lord of lords, King of kings, Ruler of rulers, the heavenly one, that sitteth above the cherubim and seraphim at the right hand of the throne of the Father: who by his word made the heavens, and formed the earth and that which is in it, and set bounds to the sea that it should not pass: the deeps also and fountains, that they should spring forth and flow over the earth: the day and the night, the sun and the moon, did he establish, and the stars in the heaven: that did separate the light from the darkness: that called forth hell, and in the twinkling of an eye ordained the rain of the winter, the snow (cloud), the hail, and the ice, and the days in their several seasons: that maketh the earth to quake and again establisheth it: that created man in his own image, after his likeness, and by the fathers of old and the prophets is it declared (or, and spake in parables with the fathers of old and the prophets in verity), of whom the apostles preached, and whom the disciples did touch. In God, the Lord, the Son of God, do we believe, that he is the word become flesh: that of Mary the holy virgin he took a body, begotten of the Holy Ghost, not of the will (lust) of the flesh, but by the will of God: that he was wrapped in swaddling clothes in Bethlehem and made manifest, and grew up and came to ripe age, when also we beheld it. ⁴ This did our Lord Jesus Christ, who was sent by Joseph and Mary his mother to be taught. [And] when he that taught him said unto him: Say Alpha: then answered he and said: Tell thou me first what is Beta (probably: Tell thou me first what is Beta. Cf. the Marcosian story quoted by Irenaeus (see above, Gospel of Thomas)- The story is in our texts of the Gospel of Thomas, and runs through all the Infancy Gospels). This thing which then came to pass Is true and of verity. ⁵ Thereafter was there a marriage in Cana of Galilee; and they bade him with his mother and his brethren, and he changed water into wine. He raised the dead, he caused the lame to walk: him whose hand was withered he caused to stretch it out, and the woman which had suffered an issue of blood twelve years touched the hem of his garment and was healed in the same hour. And when we marvelled at the miracle which was done, he said: Who touched me? Then said we: Lord, the press of men hath touched thee. But he answered and said unto us: I perceive that a virtue is gone out of me. Straightway that woman came before him, and answered and said unto him: Lord, I touched thee. And he answered and said unto her: Go, thy faith hath made thee whole. Thereafter he made the deaf to hear and the blind to see; out of them that were possessed he cast out the unclean spirits, and cleansed the lepers. The spirit which dwelt in a man, whereof the name was Legion, cried out against Jesus, saying: Before the time of our destruction is come, thou art come to drive us out. But the Lord Jesus rebuked him, saying: Go out of this man and do him no hurt. And he entered into the swine and drowned them in the water and they were choked. Thereafter he did walk upon the sea, and the winds blew, and he cried out against them (rebuked them), and the waves of the sea were made calm. And when we his disciples had no money, we asked him: What shall we do because of the tax-gatherer? And he answered and told us: Let one of you cast an hook into the deep, and take out a fish, and he shall find therein a penny: that give unto the tax-gatherer for me and you. And thereafter when we had no bread, but only five loaves and two fishes, he commanded the people to sit them down, and the number of them was five thousand, besides children and women. We did set pieces of bread before them, and they ate and were filled, and there remained over, and we filled twelve baskets full of the fragments, asking one another and saying: What mean these five loaves? They are the symbol of our faith in the Lord of the Christians (in the great christendom), even in the Father, the Lord Almighty, and in Jesus Christ our redeemer, in the Holy Ghost the comforter, in the holy church, and in the remission of sins. ⁶ These things did our Lord and Saviour reveal unto us and teach us. And we do even as he, that ye may become partakers in the grace of our Lord and in our ministry and our giving of thanks (glory), and think upon life eternal. Be ye steadfast and waver not in the knowledge and confidence of our Lord Jesus Christ, and he will have mercy on you and save you everlastingly, world without end.

Here begins the Coptic text.

⁷ Cerinthus and Simon are come to go to and fro in the world, but they are enemies of our Lord Jesus Christ, for they do pervert the word and the true thing, even (faith in) Jesus Christ. Keep yourselves therefore far from them, for death is in them, and great pollution and corruption, even in these on whom shall come judgement and the end and everlasting destruction. ⁸ Therefore have we not shrunk from writing unto you concerning the testimony of Christ our Saviour, of what he did, when we followed with him, how he enlightened our understanding . . . . ⁹ Concerning whom we testify that the Lord is he who was crucified by Pontius Pilate and Archelaus between the two thieves (and with them he was taken down from the tree of the cross, Ethiopian), and was buried in a place which is called the place of a skull (Kranion). And thither went three women, Mary, she that was kin to Martha, and Mary Magdalene (Sarrha, Martha, and Mary, Ethiopian), and took ointments to pour upon the body, weeping and mourning over that which was come to pass. And when they drew near to the sepulchre, they looked in and found not the body (Ethiopian they found the stone rolled away and opened the entrance). ¹⁰ And as they mourned and wept, the Lord showed himself unto them and said to them: For whom weep ye? weep no more I am he whom ye seek. But let one of you go to your brethren and say: Come ye, the Master is risen from the dead. Martha (Mary, Ethiopian) came and told us. We said unto her: What have we to do with thee, woman? He that is dead and buried, is it possible that he should live? And we believed her not that the Saviour was risen from the dead. Then she returned unto the Lord and said unto him: None of them hath believed me, that thou livest. He said: Let another of you go unto them and tell them again. Mary (Sarrha, Ethiopian) came and told us again, and we believed her not; and she returned unto the Lord and she also told him. ¹¹ Then said the Lord unto Mary and her sisters: Let us go unto them. And he came and found us within (sitting veiled or fishing, Ethiopian), and called us out, but we thought that it was a phantom and believed not that it was the Lord. Then said he unto us: Come, fear ye not. I am your master, even he, O Peter, whom thou didst deny thrice; and dost thou now deny again? And we came unto him, doubting in our hearts whether it were he. Then said he unto us: Wherefore doubt ye still, and are unbelieving? I am he that spake unto you of my flesh and my death and my resurrection. But that ye may know that I am he, do thou, Peter, put thy finger into the print of the nails in mine hands, and thou also, Thomas, put thy finger into the wound of the spear in my side; but thou, Andrew, look on my feet and see whether they press the earth; for it is written in the prophet: A phantom of a devil maketh no footprint on the earth. ¹² And we touched him, that we might learn of a truth whether he were risen in the flesh; and we fell on our faces (and worshipped him) confessing our sin, that we had been unbelieving. Then said our Lord and Saviour unto us: Rise up, and I will reveal unto you that which is above the heaven and in the heaven, and your rest which is in the kingdom of heaven. For my Father hath given me power (sent me, Ethiopian) to take you up thither, and them also that believe on me. ¹³ Now that which he revealed unto us is this, which he spake: It came to pass when I was about (minded) to come hither from the Father of all things, and passed through the heavens, then did I put on the wisdom of the Father, and I put on the power of his might. I was in heaven, and I passed by the archangels and the angels in their likeness, like as if I were one of them, among the princedoms and powers. I passed through them because I possessed the wisdom of him that had sent me. Now the chief captain of the angels, [is] Michael, and Gabriel and Uriel and Raphael followed me unto the fifth firmament (heaven), for they thought in their heart that I was one of them; such power was given me of my Father. And on that day did I adorn the archangels with a wonderful voice (so Coptic: Ethiopian, Lat., I made them quake -amazed them), so that they should go unto the altar of the Father and serve and fulfil the ministry until I should return unto him. And so wrought I the likeness by my wisdom; for I became all things in all, that I might praise the dispensation of the Father and fulfil the glory of him that sent me (the verbs might well be transposed) and return unto him. (Here the Latin omits a considerable portion of text without notice, to near the beginning of c. 17.) ¹⁴ For ye know that the angel Gabriel brought the message unto Mary. And we answered: Yea, Lord. He answered and said unto us: Remember ye not, then, that I said unto you a little while ago: I became an angel among the

angels, and I became all things in all? We said unto him: Yea, Lord. Then answered he and said unto us: On that day whereon I took the form of the angel Gabriel, I appeared unto Mary and spake with her. Her heart accepted me, and she believed (She believed and laughed, Ethiopian), and I formed myself and entered into her body. I became flesh, for I alone was a minister unto myself in that which concerned Mary (I was mine own messenger, Ethiopian) in the appearance of the shape of an angel. For so must I needs (or, was I wont to) do. Thereafter did I return to my Father (Coptic After my return to the Father, and run on). [15] But do ye commemorate my death. Now when the Passover (Easter, pascha) cometh, one of you shall be cast into prison for my names sake; and he will be in grief and sorrow, because ye keep the Easter while he is in prison and separated from you, for he will be sorrowful because he keepeth not Easter with you. And I will send my power in the form of mine angel Gabriel, and the doors of the prison shall open. And he shall come forth and come unto you and keep the night-watch with you until the cock crow. And when ye have accomplished the memorial which is made of me, and the Agape (love-feast), he shall again be cast into prison for a testimony, until he shall come out thence and preach that which I have delivered unto you. And we said unto him: Lord, is it then needful that we should again take the cup and drink? (Lord, didst not thou thyself fulfil the drinking of the Passover? is it then needful that we should accomplish it again? Ethiopian) He said unto us: Yea, it is needful, until the day when I come again, with them that have been put to death for my sake (come with my wounds, Ethiopian). [16] Then said we to him: Lord, that which thou hast revealed unto us (revealest, Ethiopian) is great. Wilt thou come in the power of any creature or in an appearance of any kind? (In what power or form wilt thou come? Ethiopian) He answered and said unto us: Verily I say unto you, I shall come like the sun when it is risen, and my brightness will be seven times the brightness thereof! The wings of the clouds shall bear me in brightness, and the sign of the cross shall go before me, and I shall come upon earth to judge the quick and the dead. [17] We said unto him: Lord, after how many years shall this come to pass? He said unto us: When the hundredth part and the twentieth part is fulfilled, between the Pentecost and the feast of unleavened bread, then shall the coming of my Father be (so Coptic: When an hundred and fifty years are past, in the days of the feast of Passover and Pentecost, &c., Ethiopian: . . . (imperfect word) year is fulfilled, between the unleavened bread and Pentecost shall be the coming of my Father, lat.). We said unto him: Now sayest thou unto us: I will come; and how sayest thou: He that sent me is he that shall come? Then said he to us: I am wholly in the Father and my Father is in me. Then said we to him: Wilt thou indeed forsake us until thy coming? Where can we find a master? But he answered and said unto us: Know ye not, then, that like as until now I have been here, so also was I there, with him that sent me? And we said to him: Lord, is it then possible that thou shouldest be both here and there? But he answered us: I am wholly in the Father and the Father in me, because of (in regard of) the likeness of the form and the power and the fullness and the light and the full measure and the voice. I am the word, I am become unto him a thing, that is to say (word gone) of the thought, fulfilled in the type (likeness); I have come into the Ogdoad (eighth number), which is the Lord's day. [The Lord's day considered as the eighth day of the week.] (In place of these sentences Ethiopian has: I am of his resemblance and form, of his power and completeness, and of his light. I am his complete (fulfilled, entire) word. [18] But it came to pass after he was crucified, and dead and arisen again, when the work was fulfilled which was accomplished in the flesh, and he was crucified and the ascension come to pass at the end of the days, then said he thus, &c. It is an interpolation, in place of words which the translator did not understand, or found heretical.) But the whole fulfilment of the fulfilment shall ye see after the redemption which hath come to pass by me, and ye shall see me, how I go up unto my Father which is in heaven. But behold, now, I give unto you a new commandment: Love one another and [a leaf lost in Coptic] obey one another, that peace may rule always among you. Love your enemies, and what ye would not that man do unto you, that do unto no man. [19] And this preach ye also and teach them that believe on me and preach the kingdom of heaven of my Father, and how my Father hath given me the power, that ye may bring near the children of my heavenly Father. Preach ye, and they shall obtain faith, that ye may be they for whom it is ordained that they shall bring his children unto heaven. And we said unto him: Lord, unto thee it is possible to accomplish that whereof thou tellest us, but how shall we be able to do it? He said to us: Verily I say unto you, preach and proclaim as I command you, for I will be with you, for it is my good pleasure to be with you, that ye may be heirs with me in the kingdom of heaven, even the kingdom of him that sent me. Verily I say unto you, ye shall be my brethren and my friends for my Father hath found pleasure in you: and so also shall they be that believe on me by your means. Verily I say unto you such and so great joy hath my Father prepared for you that the angels and the powers desired and do desire to see it and look upon it; but it is not given unto them to behold the glory of my Father. We said unto him: Lord, what is this whereof thou speakest to us?

Coptic begins again: words are missing.
He answered us: Ye shall behold a light, more excellent than that which shineth . . . (shineth more brightly than the light, and is more perfect than perfection. And the Son shall become perfect through the Father who is Light, for the Father is perfect which bringeth to pass death and resurrection, and ye shall see a perfection more perfect than the perfect. And I am wholly at the right hand of the Father, even in him that maketh perfect. So Ethiopian: Coptic has gaps). And we said unto him: Lord, in all things art thou become salvation and life unto us, for that thou makest known such a hope unto us. And he said to us: Be of good courage and rest in me. Verily I say unto you, your rest shall be above (?), in the place where is neither eating nor drinking, nor care (Coptic joy) nor sorrow, nor passing away of them that are therein: for ye shall have no part in (the things of earth, Ethiopian) but ye shall be received in the everlastingness of my Father. Like as I am in him, so shall ye also be in me. Again we said unto him: In what form? in the fashion of angels, or in flesh? And he answered and said unto us: Lo, I have put on your flesh, wherein I was born and crucified, and am risen again through my Father which is in heaven, that the prophecy of David the prophet might be fulfilled, in regard of that which was declared concerning me and my death and resurrection, saying: Lord, they are increased that fight with me, and many are they that are risen up against me. Many there be that say to my soul: There is no help for him in his God.But thou, O Lord, art my defender: thou art my worship, and the lifter up of my head.I did call upon the Lord with my voice and he heard me (out of the high place of his temple, Ethiopian). I laid me down and slept,and rose up again: for thou,O Lord, art my defender. I will not be afraid for ten thousands of the people, that have set themselves against me round about. Up, Lord, and help me, O my God: for thou hast smitten down all them that without cause are mine enemies: thou hast broken the teeth of the ungodly. Salvation belongeth unto the Lord, and his good pleasure is upon his people (Ps. iii. 1-8). If, therefore, all the words which were spoken by the prophets have been fulfilled in me (for I myself was in them), how much more shall that which I say unto you come to pass indeed, that he which sent me may be glorified by you and by them that believe on me? [20] And when he had said this unto us, we said to him: In all things hast thou had mercy on us and saved us, and hast revealed all things unto us; but yet would we ask of thee somewhat if thou give us leave. And he said unto us: I know that ye pay heed, and that your heart is well-pleased when ye hear me: now concerning that which ye desire, I will speak good words unto you. [21] For verily I say unto you: Like as my Father hath raised me from the dead, so shall ye also rise (in the flesh, Ethiopian) and be taken up into the highest heaven, unto the place whereof I have told you from the beginning, unto the place which he who sent me hath prepared for you. And so will I accomplish all dispensations (all grace, Ethiopian), even I who am unbegotten and yet begotten of mankind, who am without flesh and yet have borne flesh : for to that end am I come, that (gap in Coptic: Ethiopian continues) ye might rise from the dead in your flesh, in the second birth, even a vesture that shall not decay, together with all them that hope and believe in him that sent me: for so is the will of my Father that I would give unto you, and unto them whom it pleaseth me, the hope of the kingdom. Then said we unto him: Great is that which thou sufferest us to hope, and tellest us. And he answered and said: Believe ye that every thing that I tell you shall come to pass? We answered and said: Yea, Lord. (Coptic resumes for a few lines: then another gap. Follow Ethiopian) He said unto us: Verily I say unto you, that I have obtained the whole power of my Father, that I may bring back into light them that dwell in darkness, them that are in corruption into incorruption, them that are in death into life and that I may loose them that are in fetters. For that which is impossible with men, is possible with the Father. I am the hope of them that despair, the helper of them that have no saviour, the wealth of the poor, the health of the sick, and the resurrection of the dead. [22] When he had thus said, we said unto him: Lord, is it true that the flesh shall be judged together with the soul and the spirit and that the one part shall rest in heaven and the other part be punished everlastingly yet living? And he said unto us: (Coptic resumes) How long will ye inquire and doubt? [23] Again we said unto him: Lord, there is necessity upon us to inquire of thee -because thou hast commanded us to preach- that we ourselves may learn assuredly of thee and be profitable preachers, and that they which are instructed by us may believe in thee. Therefore must we needs inquire of thee. [24] He answered us and said: Verily I say unto you, the resurrection of the flesh shall come to pass with the soul therein and the spirit. And we said unto him: Lord, is it then possible that that which is dissolved and brought to nought should become whole? and we ask thee not as unbelieving, neither as if it were impossible unto thee;

but verily we believe that that which thou sayest shall come to pass. And he was wroth with us and said: O ye of little faith, how long will ye ask questions? But what ye will, tell it me, and I myself will tell you without grudging: only keep ye my commandments and do that which I bid you, and turn not away your face from any man, that I turn not my face away from you, but without shrinking and fear and without respect of persons, minister ye in the way that is direct and narrow and strait. So shall my Father himself rejoice over you. 25 Again we said unto him: Lord, already are we ashamed that we question thee oft-times and burden thee. And he answered and said unto us: I know that in faith and with your whole heart ye do question me, therefore do I rejoice over you for verily I say unto you: I rejoice, and my Father that is in me, because ye question me; and your importunity (shamelessness) is unto me rejoicing and unto you it giveth life. And when he had so said unto us, we were glad that we had questioned him and we said to him: Lord, in all things thou makest us alive and hast mercy on us. Wilt thou now declare unto us that which we shall ask thee? Then said he unto us: Is it the flesh that passeth away, or is it the spirit? We said unto him: The flesh is it that passeth away. Then said he unto us: That which hath fallen shall rise again, and that which was lost shall be found, and that which was weak shall recover, that in these things that are so created the glory of my Father may be revealed. As he hath done unto me, so will I do unto all that believe in me. 26 Verily I say unto you: the flesh shall arise, and the soul, alive, that their defence may come to pass on that day in regard of that that they have done, whether it be good or evil: that there may be a choosing-out of the faithful who have kept the commandments of my Father that sent me; and so shall the judgement be accomplished with strictness. For my Father said unto me: My Son, in the day of judgement thou shalt have no respect for the rich, neither pity for the poor, but according to the sins of every man shalt thou deliver him unto everlasting torment. But unto my beloved that have done the commandments of my Father that sent me will I give the rest of life in the kingdom of my Father which is in heaven, and they shall behold that which he hath given me. And he hath given me authority to do that which I will, and to give that which I have promised and determined to give and grant unto them. 27 For to that end went I down unto the place of Lazarus, and preached unto the righteous and the prophets, that they might come out of the rest which is below and come up into that which is above; and I poured out upon them with my right hand the water (?) (baptism, Ethiopian) of life and forgiveness and salvation from all evil, as I have done unto you and unto them that believe on me. But if any man believe on me and do not my commandments, although he have confessed my name, he hath no profit therefrom but runneth a vain race: for such will find themselves in perdition and destruction, because they have despised my commandments. 28 But so much the more have I redeemed you, the children of light, from all evil and from the authority of the rulers (archons), and every one that believeth on me by your means. For that which I have promised unto you will I give unto them also, that they may come out of the prison-house and the fetters of the rulers. We answered and said: Lord thou hast given unto us the rest of life and hast given us <Joy? by wonders, unto the confirmation of faith: wilt thou now preach the same unto us, seeing that thou hast preached it unto the and the prophets? Then said he unto us: Verily I say unto you, all that have believed on me and that believe in him that sent me will I take up into the heaven, unto the place which my Father hath prepared for the elect, and I will give you the kingdom, the chosen kingdom, in rest, and everlasting life. 29 But all they that have offended against my commandments and have taught other doctrine, (perverting) the Scripture and adding thereto, striving after their own glory, and that teach with other words them that believe on me in uprightness, ie they make them fall thereby, shall receive everlasting punishment. We said unto him: Lord, shall there then be teaching by others, diverse from that which thou hast spoken unto us? He said unto us: It must needs be, that the evil and the good may be made manifest; and the judgement shall be manifest upon them that do these things, and according to their works shall they be judged and shall be delivered unto death. Again we said unto him: Lord, blessed are we in that we see thee and hear thee declaring such things, for our eyes have beheld these great wonders that thou hast done. He answered and said unto us: Yea, rather blessed are they that have not seen and yet have believed for they shall be called children of the kingdom, and they shall be perfect among the perfect, and I will be unto them life in the kingdom of my Father. Again we said unto him: Lord, how shall men be able to believe that thou wilt depart and leave us; for thou sayest unto us: There shall come a day and an hour when I shall ascend unto my Father? 30 But he said unto us: Go ye and preach unto the twelve tribes, and preach also unto the heathen, and to all the land of Israel from the east to the west and from the south unto the north, and many shall believe on the Son of God. But we said unto him: Lord, who will believe us, or hearken unto us, or (how shall we be able, Ethiopian) to teach the powers and signs and wonders which thou hast done? Then answered he and said to us: Go ye and preach the mercifulness of my Father, and that which he hath done through me will I myself do through you, for I am in you, and I will give you my peace, and I will give you a power of my spirit, that ye may prophesy to them unto life eternal. And unto the others also will I give my power, that they may teach the residue of the peoples.

(Six leaves lost in Coptic: Ethiopian continues.)
31 And behold a man shall meet you, whose name is Saul which being interpreted is Paul: he is a Jew, circumcised according to the law, and he shall receive my voice from heaven with fear and terror and trembling. And his eyes shall be blinded and by your hands by the sign of the cross shall they be protected (healed: other Ethiopian MSS. with spittle by your hands shall his eyes &c.). Do ye unto him all that I have done unto you. Deliver it (? the word of God) unto the other. And at the same time that man shall open his eyes and praise the Lord, even my Father which is in heaven. He shall obtain power among the people and shall preach and instruct; and many that hear him shall obtain glory and be redeemed. But thereafter shall men be wroth with him and deliver him into the hands of his enemies, and he shall bear witness before kings that are mortal, and his end shall he that he shall turn unto me, whereas he persecuted me at the first. He shall preach and teach and abide with the elect, as a chosen vessel and a wall that shall not be overthrown, yea, the last of the last shall become a preacher unto the Gentiles, made perfect by the will of my Father. Like as ye have learned from the Scripture that your fathers the prophets spake of me, and in me it is indeed fulfilled. And he said unto us: Be ye also therefore guides unto them; and all things that I said unto you, and that ye write concerning me (tell ye them), that I am the word of the Father and that the Father is in me. Such also shall ye be unto that man, as becometh you. Instruct him and bring to his mind that which is spoken of me in the Scripture and is fulfilled, and thereafter shall he become the salvation of the Gentiles. 32 And we asked him: Lord, is there for us and for them the self-same expectation of the inheritance? He answered and said unto us: Are then the fingers of the hand like unto each other, or the ears of corn in the field, or do all fruit-trees bear the same fruit? Doth not every one bear fruit according to its nature? And we said unto him: Lord, wilt thou again speak unto us in parables? Then said he unto us: Lament not. Verily I say unto you, ye are my brethren, and my companions in the kingdom of heaven unto my Father, for so is his good pleasure. Verily I say unto you, unto them also whom ye teach and who believe on me will I give that expectation. 33 And we asked him again: When shall we meet with that man, and when wilt thou depart unto thy Father and our God and Lord? He answered and said unto us: That man will come out of the land of Cilicia unto Damascus of Syria, to root up the church which ye must found there. It is I that speak through you; and he shall come quickly: and he shall become strong in the faith, that the word of the prophet may be fulfilled, which saith: Behold, out of Syria will I begin to call together a new Jerusalem, and Sion will I subdue unto me, and it shall be taken, and the place which is childless shall be called the son and daughter of my Father, and my bride. For so hath it pleased him that sent me. But that man will I turn back, that he accomplish not his evil desire, and the praise of my Father shall be perfected in him, and after that I am gone home and abide with my Father, I will speak unto him from heaven, and all things shall be accomplished which I have told you before concerning him. 34 And we said unto him again: Lord, so many great things hast thou told us and revealed unto us as never yet were spoken, and in all hast thou given us rest and been gracious unto us. After thy resurrection thou didst reveal unto us all things that we might be saved indeed; but thou saidst unto us only: There shall be wonders and strange appearances in heaven and on earth before the end of the world come. Tell us now, how shall we perceive it? And he answered us: I will teach it you; and not that which shall befall you only, but them also whom ye shall teach and who shall believe, as well as them who shall hear that man and believe on me. In those years and days shall it come to pass. And we said again unto him: Lord, what shall come to pass? And he said unto us: Then shall they that believe and they that believe not hear (see Ethiopian) a trumpet in the heaven, a vision of great stars which shall be seen in the day, wonderful sights in heaven reaching down to the earth; stars which fall upon the earth like fire, and a great and mighty hail of fire (a star shining from the east unto this place, like unto fire, Ethiopian). The sun and the moon fighting one with the other, a continual rolling and noise of thunders and lightnings, thunder and earthquake; cities falling and men perishing in their overthrow, a continual dearth for lack of rain, a terrible pestilence and great mortality, mighty and untimely, so that they that die lack burial: and the bearing forth of brethren and sisters and kinsfolk shall be upon one bier. The kinsman shall show no favour to his kinsman, nor any man to his neighbour. And they that were overthrown shall rise up and behold them that overthrew them, that they lack burial, for the pestilence shall be full of hatred and pain

and envy: and men shall take from one and give to another. And thereafter shall it wax yet worse than before. (Bewail ye them that have not hearkened unto my commandments, Ethiopian.) ³⁵ Then shall my Father be wroth at the wickedness of men, for many are their transgressions, and the abomination of their uncleanness weigheth heavy upon them in the corruption of their life. And we asked him: What of them that trust in thee? He answered and said unto us: Ye are yet slow of heart; and how long? Verily I say unto you, as the prophet David spake of me and of my people, so shall it be (?) for them also that believe on me. But they that are deceivers in the world and enemies of righteousness, upon them shall come the fulfilment of the prophecy of David, who said: Their feet are swift to shed blood, their tongue uttereth slander, adders' poison is under their lips. I behold thee companying with thieves, and partaking with adulterers, thou continuest speaking against thy brother and puttest stumbling blocks before thine own mother's son. What thinkest thou that I shall be like unto thee? Behold now how the prophet of God hath spoken of all, that all things may be fulfilled which he said aforetime. ³⁶ And again we said unto him: Lord, will not then the nations say: Where is their God? And he answered and said unto us: Thereby shall the elect be known, that they being plagued with such afflictions, come forth. We said: Will then their departure out of the world be by a pestilence which giveth them pain? He answered us: Nay, but if they suffer such affliction, it will be a proving of them, whether they have faith and remember these my sayings, and fulfil my commandments. These shall arise, and short will be their expectation, that he may be glorified that sent me, and I with him. For he hath sent me unto you to tell you these things; and that ye may impart them unto Israel and the Gentiles and they may hear, and they also be redeemed and believe on me and escape the woe of the destruction. But whoso escapeth from the destruction of death, him will they take and hold him fast in the prison-house in torments like the torments of a thief. And we said unto him: Lord, will they that believe be treated like the unbelievers, and wilt thou punish them that have escaped from the pestilence? And he said unto us: If they that believe in my name deal like the sinners, then have they done as though they had not believed. And we said again to him: Lord, have they on whom this lot hath fallen no life? He answered and said unto us: Whoso hath accomplished the praise of my Father, he shall abide in the resting-place of my Father. ³⁷ Then said we unto him: Lord, teach us what shall come to pass thereafter? And he answered us: In those years and days shall war be kindled upon war; the four ends of the earth shall be in commotion and fight against each other. Thereafter shall be quakings of clouds (or, clouds of locusts), darkness, and dearth, and persecutions of them that believe on me and against the elect. Thereupon shall come doubt and strife and transgressions against one another. And there shall be many that believe on my name and yet follow after evil and spread vain doctrine. And men shall follow after them and their riches, and be subject unto their pride, and lust for drink, and bribery, and there shall be respect of persons among them. ³⁸ But they that desire to behold the face of God and respect not the persons of the rich sinners, and are not ashamed before the people that lead them astray, but rebuke (?) them, they shall be crowned by the Father. And they also shall be saved that rebuke their neighbours, for they are sons of wisdom. and of faith. But if they become not children of wisdom, whoso hateth his brother and persecuteth him and showeth him no favour, him will God despise and reject.

(Coptic resumes.)
But they that walk in truth and in the knowledge of the faith, and have love towards me -for they have endured insult- they shall be praised for that they walk in poverty and endure them that hate them and put them to shame. Men have stripped them naked, for they despised them because they continued in hunger and thirst, but after they have endured patiently, they shall have the blessedness of heaven, and they shall be with me for ever. But woe unto them that walk in pride and boasting, for their end is perdition. ³⁹ And we said unto him: Lord, is this thy purpose, that thou leavest us, to come upon them? (Will all this come to pass, Ethiopian) He answered and said unto us: After what manner shall he judgement be? whether righteous or unrighteous? (In Coptic and Ethiopian the general sense is the same: but the answer of Jesus in the form of a question is odd, and there is probably a corruption.) We said unto him: Lord, in that day they will say unto thee: Thou hast not distinguished between (probably: will they not say unto thee: Thou hast distinguished between) righteousness and unrighteousness, between the light and the darkness, and evil and good? Then said he: I will answer them and say: Unto Adam was power given to choose one of the two: he chose the light and laid his hand thereon, but the darkness he left behind him and cast away from him. Therefore have all men power to believe in the light which is life, and which is the Father that hath sent me. And every one that believeth and doeth the works of the light shall live in them, but if there be any that confesseth that he belongeth unto the light,
and doeth the works of darkness, such an one hath no defence to utter, neither can he lift up his face to look upon the Son of God, which Son am I. For I will say unto him: As thou soughtest, so hast thou found, and as thou askedst, so hast thou received. Wherefore condemnest thou me, O man? Wherefore hast thou departed from me and denied me? And wherefore hast thou confessed me and yet denied me? hath not every man power to live and to die? Whoso then hath kept my commandments shall be a son of the light, that is, of the Father that is in me. But because of them that corrupt my words am I come down from heaven. I am the word: I became flesh, and I wearied myself (or, suffered) and taught, saying: The heavy laden shall be saved, and they that are gone astray shall go astray for ever. They shall be chastised and tormented in their flesh and in their soul. ⁴⁰ And we said unto him: O Lord, verily we are sorrowful for their sake. And he said unto us: Ye do rightly, for the righteous are sorry for the sinners, and pray for them, making prayer unto my Father. Again we said unto him: Lord, is there none that maketh intercession unto thee (so Ethiopian)? And he said unto us: Yea, and I will hearken unto the prayer of the righteous which they make for them. When he had so said unto us, we said to him: Lord, in all things hast thou taught us and had mercy on us and saved us that we might preach unto them that are worthy to be saved, and that we might obtain a recompense with thee. (Shall we be partakers of a recompense from thee? Ethiopian) ⁴¹ He answered and said unto us: Go and preach, and ye shall be labourers, and fathers, and ministers. We said unto him: Thou art he (or, Art thou he) that shalt preach by us. (Lord, thou art our father. Ethiopian) Then answered he us, saying: Be not (or, Are not ye) all fathers or all masters. (Are then all fathers, or all servants, or all masters? Ethiopian) We said unto him: Lord, thou art he that saidst unto us: Call no man your father upon earth, for one is your Father, which is in heaven, and your master. Therefore sayest thou now unto us: Ye shall be fathers of many children, and servants and masters? He answered and said unto us: According as ye have said (Ye have rightly said, Ethiopian). For verily I say unto you: whosoever shall hear you and believe on me, shall receive of you the light of the seal through me, and baptism through me: ye shall be fathers and servants and masters. ⁴² But we said unto him: Lord, how may it be that every one of us should be these three? He said unto us: Verily I say unto you: Ye shall be called fathers, because with praiseworthy heart and in love ye have revealed unto them the things of the kingdom of heaven. And ye shall be called servants, because they shall receive the baptism of life and the remission of their sins at my hand through you. And ye shall be called masters because ye have given them the word without grudging, and have admonished them, and when ye admonished them, they turned themselves (were converted). Ye were not afraid of their riches, nor ashamed before their face, but ye kept the commandments of my Father and fulfilled them. And ye shall have a great reward with my Father which is in heaven, and they shall have forgiveness of sins and everlasting life, and be partakers in the kingdom of heaven. And we said unto him: Lord, even if every one of us had ten thousand tongues to speak withal, we could not thank thee, for that thou promisest such things unto us. Then answered he us, saying: Only do ye that which I say unto you, even as I myself also have done it. ⁴³ And ye shall be like the wise virgins which watched and slept not, but went forth unto the lord into the bride chamber: but the foolish virgins were not able to watch, but slumbered. And we said unto him: Lord, who are the wise and who are the foolish? He said unto us: Five wise and five foolish; for these are they of whom the prophet hath spoken: Sons of ; God are they. Hear now their names. But we wept and were troubled for them that slumbered. He said unto us: The five wise are Faith and Love and Grace and Peace and Hope. Now they of the faithful which possess this (these) shall be guides unto them that have believed on me and on him that sent me. For I am the Lord and I am the bridegroom whom they have received, and they have entered in to the house of the bridegroom and are laid down with me in the bridal chamber rejoicing. But the five foolish, when they had slept and had awaked, came unto the door of the bridal chamber and knocked, for the doors were shut. Then did they weep and lament that no man opened unto them. We said unto him: Lord, and their wise sisters that were within in the bridegroom's house, did they continue without opening unto them, and did they not sorrow for their sakes nor entreat the bridegroom to open unto them? He answered us saying: They were not yet able to obtain favour for them. We said unto him: Lord, on what day shall they enter in for their sisters' sake? Then said he unto us: He that is shut out, is shut out. And we said unto him: Lord, is this word (determined?). Who then are the foolish? He said unto us: Hear their names. They are Knowledge, Understanding (Perception) Obedience, Patience, and Compassion. These are they that slumbered in them that have believed and confessed me but have not fulfilled my commandments. ⁴⁴ On account of them that have slumbered, they shall remain outside the kingdom and the fold of the shepherd and his sheep. But whoso shall abide outside the

sheepfold, him will the wolves devour, and he shall be (condemned?) and die in much affliction: in him shall be no rest nor endurance, and (Ethiopian) although he be hardly punished, and rent in pieces and devoured in long and evil torment, yet shall he not be able to obtain death quickly. ⁴⁵ And we said unto him: Lord, well hast thou revealed all this unto us. Then answered he us, saying: Understand ye not (or. Ye understand not) these words? We said unto him: Yea Lord. By five shall men enter into thy kingdom : notwithstanding, they that watched were with thee the Lord and bridegroom, even though they rejoiced not because of them that slumbered (yet will they have no pleasures because of, Ethiopian). He said unto us: They will indeed rejoice that they have entered in with the bridegroom the Lord; and they are sorrowful because of them that slumbered, for they are their sisters. For all ten are daughters of God, even the Father. Then said we unto him: Lord is it then for thee to show them favour on account of their sisters? (It becometh thy majesty to show them favour, Ethiopian) He said unto us: but his that sent me, and I am consenting with him (It is not yours, &c., Ethiopian). ⁴⁶ But be ye upright and preach rightly and teach, and be not abashed by any man and fear not any man, and especially the rich, for they do not my commandments, but boast themselves (swell) in their riches. And we said unto him: Lord, tell us if it be the rich only. He answered, saying unto us: If any man who is not rich and possesseth a small livelihood giveth unto the poor and needy, men will call him a benefactor. ⁴⁷ But if any man fall under the load of sin that he hath committed, then shall his neighbour correct him because of the good that he hath done unto his neighbour. And if his neighbour correct him and he return, he shall be saved, and he that corrected him shall receive a reward and live for ever. For a needy man, if he see him that hath done him good sin and correct him not, shall be judged with severe judgement. Now if a blind man lead a blind, they both fall into a ditch: and whoso respecteth persons for their sake, shall be as the two , as the prophet hath said: Woe unto them that respect persons and justify the ungodly for reward, even they whose God is their belly. Behold that judgement shall be their portion. For verily I say unto you: On that day will I neither have respect unto the rich nor pity for the poor. ⁴⁸ If thou behold a sinner, admonish him betwixt him and thee: (if he hear thee, thou hast gained thy brother, Ethiopian) and if he hear thee not, then take to thee another, as many as three, and instruct thy brother: again, if he hear thee not, let him be unto thee

(Coptic defective from this point.)

as an heathen man or a publican. ⁴⁹ If thou hear aught against thy brother, give it no credence; slander not, and delight not in hearing slander. For thus it is written: Suffer not thine ear to receive aught against thy brother: but if thou seest aught correct him, rebuke him and convert him. And we said unto him: Lord, thou hast in ail things taught us and warned us. But, Lord, concerning the believers, even them to whom it belongeth to believe in the preaching of thy name: is it determined that among them also there shall be doubt and division, jealousy confusion, hatred, and envy? For thou sayest: They shall find fault with one another and respect the person of them that sin, and hate them that rebuke them. And he answered and said unto us: How then shall the judgement come about, that the corn should be gathered into the garner and the chaff thereof cast into the fire? ⁵⁰ They that hate such things, and love me and rebuke them that fulfil not my commandments, shall be hated and persecuted and despised and mocked. Men will of purpose speak of them that which is not true, and will band themselves together against them that love me. But these will rebuke them, that they may be saved. But them that will rebuke and chasten and warn them, them will they (the others) hate, and thrust them aside, and despise them, and hold themselves far from them that wish them good. But they that endure such things shall be like unto the martyrs with the Father, because they have striven for righteousness, and have not striven for corruption. And we asked him: Lord, shall such things be among us? And he answered us: Fear not; it shall not be in many, but in a few. We said unto him: Yet tell us, in what manner it shall come to pass. And he said unto us: There shall come forth another doctrine, and a confusion, and because they shall strive after their own advancement, they shall bring forth an unprofitable doctrine. And therein shall be a deadly corruption (of uncleanness), and they shall teach it, and shall turn away them that believe on me from my commandments and cut them off from eternal life. But woe unto them that falsify this my word and commandment, and draw away them that hearken to them from the life of the doctrine and separate themselves from the commandment of life: for together with them they shall come into everlasting judgement. ⁵¹ And when he had said this, and had finished his discourse with us, he said unto us again: Behold, on the third day and at the third hour shall he come which hath sent me, that I may depart with him. And as he so spake, there was thunder and lightning and an earthquake, and the heavens parted asunder and there appeared a light (bright) cloud which bore him up. And there came voices of many angels, rejoicing and singing praises and saying: Gather us, O Priest, unto the light of the majesty. And when they drew nigh unto the firmament, we heard his voice saying unto us: Depart hence in peace.

ACTS AND OTHER APOCRYPHAS

The Acts of Andrew

The famous triumphs of the apostles are, I believe, not unknown to any of the faithful, for some of them are taught us in the pages of the gospel, others are related in the Acts of the Apostles, and about some of them books exist in which the actions of each apostle are recorded; yet of the more part we have nothing but their Passions in writing. Now I have come upon a book on the miracles (virtues, great deeds) of St. Andrew the apostle, which, because of its excessive verbosity, was called by some apocryphal. And of this I thought good to extract and set out the 'virtues' only, omitting all that bred weariness, and so include the wonderful miracles within the compass of one small volume, which might both please the reader and ward off the spite of the adverse critic: for it is not the multitude of words, but the soundness of reason and the purity of mind that produce unblemished faith.

1

[1] After the Ascension the apostles dispersed to preach in various countries. Andrew began in the province of Achaia, but Matthew went to the city of Mermidona. [2] Andrew left Mermidona and came back to his own allotted district. Walking with his disciples he met a blind man who said: 'Andrew, apostle of Christ, I know you can restore my sight, but I do not wish for that: only bid those with you to give me enough money to clothe and feed myself decently.' Andrew said: 'This is the devil's voice, who will not allow the man to recover his sight.' He touched his eyes and healed him. Then, as be had but a vile rough garment, Andrew said: 'Take the filthy garment off him and clothe him afresh.' All were ready to strip themselves, and Andrew said: 'Let him have what will suffice him.' He returned home thankful. [3] Demetrius of Amasea had an Egyptian boy of whom he was very fond, who died of a fever. Demetrius hearing of Andrew's miracles, came, fell at his feet, and besought help. Andrew pitied him, came to the house, held a very long discourse, turned to the bier, raised the boy, and restored him to his master. All believed and were baptized. [4] A Christian lad named Sostratus came to Andrew privately and told him: 'My mother cherishes a guilty passion for me: I have repulsed her, and she has gone to the proconsul to throw the guilt on me. I would rather die than expose her.' The officers came to fetch the boy, and Andrew prayed and went with him. The mother accused him. The proconsul bade him defend himself. He was silent, and so continued, until the proconsul retired to take counsel. The mother began to weep. Andrew said: 'Unhappy woman, that dost not fear to cast thine own guilt on thy son.' She said to the proconsul: 'Ever since my son entertained his wicked wish he has been in constant company with this man.' The proconsul was enraged, ordered the lad to be sewn into the leather bag of parricides and drowned in the river, and Andrew to be imprisoned till his punishment should be devised. Andrew prayed, there was an earthquake, the proconsul fell from his seat, every one was prostrated, and the mother withered up and died. The proconsul fell at Andrew's feet praying for mercy. The earthquake and thunder ceased, and he healed those who had been hurt. The proconsul and his house were baptized. [5] The son of Cratinus (Gratinus) of Sinope bathed in the women's bath and was seized by a demon. Cratinus wrote to Andrew for help: he himself had a fever and his wife dropsy. Andrew went there in a vehicle. The boy tormented by the evil spirit fell at his feet. He bade it depart and so it did, with outcries. He then went to Cratinus' bed and told him he well deserved to suffer because of his loose life, and bade him rise and sin no more. He was healed. The wife was rebuked for her infidelity. 'If she is to return to her former sin, let her not now be healed: if she can keep from it, let her be healed.' The water broke out of her body and she was cured. The apostle brake bread and gave it her. She thanked God, believed with all her house, and relapsed no more into sin. Cratinus afterwards sent Andrew great gifts by his servants, and then, with his wife, asked him in person to accept them, but he refused saying: 'It is rather for you to give them to the needy.' [6] After this he went to Nicaea where were seven devils living among the tombs by the wayside, who at noon stoned passersby and had killed many. And all the city came out to meet Andrew with olive branches, crying: 'Our salvation is in thee, O man of God.' When they had told him all, he said: 'If you believe in Christ you shall be freed.' They cried: 'We will.' He thanked God and commanded the demons to appear; they came in the form of dogs. Said he: 'These are your enemies: if you profess your belief that I can drive them out in Jesus' name, I will do so.' They cried out: 'We believe that Jesus Christ whom thou preachest is the Son of God.' Then he bade the demons go into dry and barren places and hurt no man till the last day. They roared and vanished. The apostle baptized the people and made Callistus bishop. [7] At the gate of Nicomedia he met a dead man borne on a bier, and his old father supported by slaves, hardly able to walk, and his old mother with hair torn, bewailing.

'How has it happened?' he asked. 'He was alone in his chamber and seven dogs rushed on him and killed him.' Andrew sighed and said: 'This is an ambush of the demons I banished from Nicaea. What will you do, father, if I restore your son?' 'I have nothing more precious than him, I will give him.' He prayed: 'Let the spirit of this lad return.' The faithful responded, 'Amen'. Andrew bade the lad rise, and he rose, and all cried: 'Great is the God of Andrew.' The parents offered great gifts which he refused, but took the lad to Macedonia, instructing him. [8] Embarking in a ship he sailed into the Hellespont, on the way to Byzantium. There was a great storm. Andrew prayed and there was calm. They reached Byzantium. [9] Thence proceeding through Thrace they met a troop of armed men who made as if to fall on them. Andrew made the sign of the cross against them, and prayed that they might be made powerless. A bright angel touched their swords and they all fell down, and Andrew and his company passed by while they worshipped him. And the angel departed in a great light. [10] At Perinthus he found a ship going to Macedonia, and an angel told him to go on board. As he preached the captain and the rest heard and were converted, and Andrew glorified God for making himself known on the sea. [11] At Philippi were two brothers, one of whom had two sons, the other two daughters. They were rich and noble, and said: 'There is no family as good as ours in the place: let us marry our sons to our daughters.' It was agreed and the earnest paid by the father of the sons. On the wedding-day a word from God came to them: 'Wait till my servant Andrew comes: he will tell you what you should do.' All preparations had been made, and guests bidden, but they waited. On the third day Andrew came: they went out to meet him with wreaths and told him how they had been charged to wait for him, and how things stood. His face was shining so that they marvelled at him. He said: 'Do not, my children, be deceived: rather repent, for you have sinned in thinking to join together those who are near of kin. We do not forbid or shun marriage [this cannot be the author's original sentiment: it is contradicted by all that we know of the Acts]. It is a divine institution: but we condemn incestuous unions.' The parents were troubled and prayed for pardon. The young people saw Andrew's face like that of an angel, and said: 'We are sure that your teaching is true.' The apostle blessed them and departed. [12] At Thessalonica was a rich noble youth, Exoos, who came without his parents' knowledge and asked to be shown the way of truth. He was taught, and believed, and followed Andrew taking no care of his worldly estate. The parents heard that he was at Philippi and tried to bribe him with gifts to leave Andrew. He said: 'Would that you had not these riches, then would you know the true God, and escape his wrath.' Andrew, too, came down from the third storey and preached to them, but in vain: he retired and shut the doors of the house. They gathered a band and came to burn the house, saying: 'Death to the son who has forsaken his parents': and brought torches, reeds, and faggots, and set the house on fire. It blazed up. Exoos took a bottle of water and prayed: 'Lord Jesu Christ, in whose hand is the nature of all the elements, who moistenest the dry and driest the moist, coolest the hot and kindlest the quenched, put out this fire that thy servants may not grow evil, but be more enkindled unto faith.' He sprinkled the flames and they died. 'He is become a sorcerer,' said the parents, and got ladders, to climb up and kill them, but God blinded them. They remained obstinate, but one Lysimachus, a citizen, said: 'Why persevere? God is fighting for these. Desist, lest heavenly fire consume you.' They were touched, and said: 'This is the true God.' It was now night, but a light shone out, and they received sight. They went up and fell before Andrew and asked pardon, and their repentance made Lysimachus say: 'Truly Christ whom Andrew preaches is the Son of God.' All were converted except the youth's parents, who cursed him and went home again, leaving all their money to public uses. Fifty days after they suddenly died, and the citizens, who loved the youth, returned the property to him. He did not leave Andrew, but spent his income on the poor. [13] The youth asked Andrew to go with him to Thessalonica. All assembled in the theatre, glad to see their favourite. The youth preached to them, Andrew remaining silent, and all wondered at his wisdom. The people cried out: 'Save the son of Carpianus who is ill, and we will believe.' Carpianus went to his house and said to the boy: 'You shall be cured to-day, Adimantus.' He said: 'Then my dream is come true: I saw this man in a vision healing me.' He rose up, dressed, and ran to the theatre, outstripping his father, and fell at Andrew's feet. The people seeing him walk after twenty-three years, cried: 'There is none like the God of Andrew.' [14] A citizen had a son possessed by an unclean spirit and asked for his cure. The demon, foreseeing that he would be cast out, took the son aside into a chamber and made him hang himself. The father said: 'Bring him to the theatre: I believe this stranger is able to raise him.' He said the same to Andrew. Andrew said to the people: 'What will it profit you if you see this accomplished and do not believe?' They said: 'Fear not, we will believe.' The lad was raised and they said: 'It is enough, we do believe.' And they escorted Andrew to the house with torches and lamps, for it was night, and he taught them for three days. [15] Medias of Philippi came and prayed for his sick son. Andrew wiped his cheeks and stroked his head, saying: 'Be comforted, only believe,' and went with him to Philippi. As they entered the city an old man met them and entreated for his sons, whom for an unspeakable crime Medias had imprisoned, and they were putrefied with sores. Andrew said: 'How can you ask help for your son when you keep these men bound? Loose their chains first, for your unkindness obstructs my prayers.' Medias, penitent, said: 'I will loose these two and seven others of whom you have not been told.' They were brought, tended for three days, cured, and freed. Then the apostle healed the son, Philomedes, who had been ill twenty-two years. The people cried: 'Heal our sick as well.' Andrew told Philomedes to visit them in their houses and bid them rise in the name of Jesus Christ, by which he had himself been healed. This was done, and all believed and offered gifts, which Andrew did not accept. [16] A citizen, Nicolaus, offered a gilt chariot and four white mules and four white horses as his most precious possession for the cure of his daughter. Andrew smiled. 'I accept your gifts, but not these visible ones: if you offer this for your daughter, what will you for your soul? That is what I desire of you, that the inner man may recognize the true God, reject earthly things and desire eternal . . .' He persuaded all to forsake their idols, and healed the girl. His fame went through all Macedonia. [17] Next day as he taught, a youth cried out: 'What hast thou to do with us. Art thou come to turn us out of our own place?' Andrew summoned him: 'What is your work?' 'I have dwelt in this boy from his youth and thought never to leave him: but three days since I heard his father say, "I shall go to Andrew": and now I fear the torments thou bringest us and I shall depart.' The spirit left the boy. And many came and asked: 'In whose name dost thou cure our sick?' Philosophers also came and disputed with him, and no one could resist his teaching. [18] At this time, one who opposed him went to the proconsul Virinus and said: 'A man is arisen in Thessalonica who says the temples should be destroyed and ceremonies done away, and all the ancient law abolished, and one God worshipped, whose servant he says he is.' The proconsul sent soldiers and knights to fetch Andrew. They found his dwelling: when they entered, his face so shone that they fell down in fear. Andrew told those present the proconsul's purpose. The people armed themselves against the soldiers, but Andrew stopped them. The proconsul arrived; not finding Andrew in the appointed place, he raged like a lion and sent twenty more men. They, on arrival, were confounded and said nothing. The proconsul sent a large troop to bring him by force. Andrew said: 'Have you come for me?' 'Yes, if you are the sorcerer who says the gods ought not to be worshipped.' 'I am no sorcerer, but the apostle of Jesus Christ whom I preach.' At this, one of the soldiers drew his sword and cried: 'What have I to do with thee, Virinus, that thou sendest me to one who can not only cast me out of this vessel, but burn me by his power? Would that you would come yourself! you would do him no harm.' And the devil went out of the soldier and he fell dead. On this came the proconsul and stood before Andrew but could not see him. 'I am he whom thou seekest.' His eyes were opened, and he said in anger: 'What is this madness, that thou despisest us and our officers? Thou art certainly a sorcerer. Now will I throw thee to the beasts for contempt of our gods and us, and we shall see if the crucified whom thou preachest will help thee.' Andrew: 'Thou must believe, proconsul, in the true God and his Son whom he hath sent, specially now that one of thy men is dead.' And after long prayer he touched the soldier: 'Rise up: my God Jesus Christ raiseth thee.' He arose and stood whole. The people cried: 'Glory be to our God.' The proconsul: 'Believe not, O people, believe not the sorcerer.' They said: 'This is no sorcery but sound and true teaching.' The proconsul: 'I shall throw this man to the beasts and write about you to Caesar, that ye may perish for contemning his laws.' They would have stoned him, and said: 'Write to Caesar that the Macedonians have received the word of God, and forsaking their idols, worship the true God.' Then the proconsul in wrath retired to the praetorium, and in the morning brought beasts to the stadium and had the Apostle dragged thither by the hair and beaten with clubs. First they sent in a fierce boar who went about him thrice and touched him not. The people praised God. A bull led by thirty soldiers and incited by two hunters, did not touch Andrew but tore the hunters to pieces, roared, and fell dead. 'Christ is the true God,' said the people. An angel was seen to descend and strengthen the apostle. The proconsul in rage sent in a fierce leopard, which left every one alone but seized and strangled the proconsul's son; but Virinus was so angry that he said nothing of it nor cared. Andrew said to the people: 'Recognize now that this is the true God, whose power subdues the beasts, though Virinus knows him not. But that ye may believe the more, I will raise the dead son, and confound the foolish father.' After long prayer, he raised him. The people would have slain Virinus, but Andrew restrained them, and Virinus went to the praetorium, confounded. [19] After this a youth who followed the apostle sent for his mother to meet Andrew. She came, and after being instructed, begged him to come to their house, which was devastated by a great serpent. As Andrew approached, it hissed loudly and with raised head came to meet him; it was fifty cubits long: every one fell down in fear. Andrew said: 'Hide thy head, foul one, which thou didst raise in the beginning for the hurt of mankind, and obey the servants of God, and die.' The serpent roared, and coiled about a great oak near by and vomited poison and blood and died. Andrew went to the woman's farm, where a child killed by the serpent lay dead. He said to the parents: 'Our God who would have you saved hath sent me here that you may believe on him. Go and see the slayer slain.' They said: 'We care not so much for the child's death, if we be avenged.' They went, and Andrew said to the proconsul's wife (her conversion has been omitted by Gregory): 'Go and raise the boy.' She went, nothing doubting, and said: 'In the name of my God Jesus Christ, rise up whole.' The parents returned and found their child alive, and fell at Andrew's feet. [20] On the next night he saw a vision which he related. 'Hearken, beloved, to my vision. I beheld, and lo, a great mountain raised up on high, which had on it nothing earthly, but only shone with such light, that it seemed to enlighten all the world. And lo, there stood by me my beloved brethren the apostles Peter and John; and John reached his hand to Peter and raised him to the top of the mount, and turned to me and asked me to go up after Peter, saying: "Andrew, thou art to drink Peter's cup." And he stretched out his hands and said: "Draw near to me and stretch out thy hands so as to join them unto mine, and put thy head by my head." When I did so I found myself shorter than John. After that he said to me: "Wouldst thou know the image of that which thou seest, and who it is that speaketh to thee?" and I said: "I desire to know it." And he said to me: "I am the word of the cross whereon thou shalt hang shortly, for his name's sake whom thou preachest." And many other things said he unto me, of which I must now say nothing, but they shall be declared when I come unto the sacrifice. But now let all assemble that have received the word of God, and let me commend them unto the Lord Jesus Christ, that he may vouchsafe to keep them unblemished in his teaching. For I am now being loosed from the body, and go unto that promise which he hath vouchsafed to promise me, who is the Lord of heaven and earth, the Son of God Almighty, very God with the Holy Ghost, continuing for everlasting ages.' All the brethren wept and smote their faces. When all were gathered, Andrew said: 'Know, beloved, that I am about to leave you, but I trust in Jesus whose word I preach, that he will keep you from evil, that this harvest which I have sown among you may not be plucked up by the enemy, that is, the knowledge and teaching of my Lord Jesus Christ. But do ye pray always and stand firm in the faith, that the Lord may root out all tares of offence and vouchsafe to gather you into his heavenly garner as pure wheat.' So for five days he taught and confirmed them: then he spread his hands and prayed: 'Keep, I beseech thee, O Lord, this flock which hath now known thy salvation, that the wicked one may not prevail against it, but that what by thy command and my means it hath received, it may be able to preserve inviolate for ever.' And all responded 'Amen'. He took bread, brake it with thanksgiving, gave it to all, saying: 'Receive the grace which Christ our Lord God giveth you by me his servant.' He kissed every one and commended them to the Lord, and departed to Thessalonica, and after teaching there two days, he left them. [21] Many faithful from Macedonia accompanied him in two ships. And all were desirous of being on Andrew's ship, to hear him. He said: 'I know your wish, but this ship is too small. Let the servants and baggage go in the larger ship, and you with me in this.' He gave them Anthimus to comfort them, and bade them go into another ship which he ordered to keep always near . . . that they might see him and hear the word of God. And as he slept a little, one fell overboard. Anthimus roused him, saying: 'Help us, good master; one of thy servants perisheth.' He rebuked the wind, there was a calm, and the man was borne by the waves to the ship. Anthimus helped him on board and all marvelled. On the twelfth day they reached Patrae in Achaia, disembarked, and went to an inn. [22] Many asked him to lodge with them, but he said he could only go where God bade him. That night he had no revelation, and the next night, being distressed at this, he heard a voice saying: 'Andrew, I am alway with thee and forsake thee not,' and was glad. Lesbius the proconsul was told in a vision to take him in, and sent a messenger for him. He came, and entering the proconsul's chamber found him lying as dead with closed eyes; he struck him on the side and said: 'Rise and tell us what hath befallen thee.' Lesbius said: 'I abominated the way which you teach and sent soldiers in ships to the proconsul of Macedonia to send you bound to me, but they were wrecked and could not reach their destination. As I continued in my purpose of destroying your Way, two black men (Ethiopes) appeared and scourged me, saying: "We can no longer prevail here, for the man is coming whom you mean to persecute. So to-night, while we still have the power, we will avenge ourselves on you." And they beat me sorely and left me. But now do you pray that I may be pardoned and healed.' Andrew preached the word and all believed, and the proconsul was healed and confirmed in the faith.

23 Now Trophima, once the proconsul's mistress, and now married to another, left her husband and clave to Andrew. Her husband came to her lady (Lesbius' wife) and said she was renewing her liaison with the proconsul. The wife, enraged, said: 'This is why my husband has left me these six months.' She called her steward (procurator) and had Trophima sentenced as a prostitute and sent to the brothel. Lesbius knew nothing, and was deceived by his wife, when he asked about her. Trophima in the brothel prayed continually, and had the Gospel on her bosom, and no one could approach her. One day one offered her violence, and the Gospel fell to the ground. She cried to God for help and an angel came, and the youth fell dead. After that, she raised him, and all the city ran to the sight. Lesbius' wife went to the bath with the steward, and as they bathed an ugly demon came and killed them both. Andrew heard and said: 'It is the judgement of God for their usage of Trophima.' The lady's nurse, decrepit from age, was carried to the spot, and supplicated for her. Andrew said to Lesbius: 'Will you have her raised?' 'No, after all the ill she has done.' 'We ought not to be unmerciful.' Lesbius went to the praetorium; Andrew raised his wife, who remained shamefaced: he bade her go home and pray. 'First', she said, 'reconcile me to Trophima whom I have injured.' 'She bears you no malice.' He called her and they were reconciled. Callisto was the wife. Lesbius, growing in faith, came one day to Andrew and confessed all his sins. Andrew said: 'I thank God, my son, that thou fearest the judgement to come. Be strong in the Lord in whom thou believest.' And he took his hand and walked with him on the shore. **24** They sat down, with others, on the sand, and he taught. A corpse was thrown up by the sea near them. 'We must learn', said Andrew, 'what the enemy has done to him.' So he raised him, gave him a garment, and bade him tell his story. He said: 'I am the son of Sostratus, of Macedonia, lately come from Italy. On returning home I heard of a new teaching, and set forth to find out about it. On the way here we were wrecked and all drowned.' And after some thought, he realized that Andrew was the man he sought, and fell at his feet and said: 'I know that thou art the servant of the true God. I beseech thee for my companions, that they also may be raised and know him.' Then Andrew instructed him, and thereafter prayed God to show the bodies of the other drowned men: thirty-nine were washed ashore, and all there prayed for them to be raised. Philopator, the youth, said: 'My father sent me here with a great sum. Now he is blaspheming God and his teaching. Let it not be so.' Andrew ordered the bodies to be collected, and said: 'Whom will you have raised first?' He said: 'Warus my foster-brother.' So he was first raised and then the other thirty-eight. Andrew prayed over each, and then told the brethren each to take the hand of one and say: 'Jesus Christ the son of the living God raiseth thee.' Lesbius gave much money to Philopator to replace what he had lost, and he abode with Andrew. **25** A woman, Calliopa, married to a murderer, had an illegitimate child and suffered in travail. She told her sister to call on Diana for help; when she did so the devil appeared to her at night and said: 'Why do you trouble me with vain prayers? Go to Andrew in Achaia.' She came, and he accompanied her to Corinth, Lesbius with him. Andrew said to Calliopa: 'You deserve to suffer for your evil life: but believe in Christ, and you will be relieved, but the child will be born dead.' And so it was. **26** Andrew did many signs in Corinth. Sostratus the father of Philopator, warned in a vision to visit Andrew, came first to Achaia and then to Corinth. He met Andrew walking with Lesbius, recognized him by his vision, and fell at his feet. Philopator said: 'This is my father, who seeks to know what he must do.' Andrew: 'I know that he is come to learn the truth; we thank God who reveals himself to believers.' Leontius the servant of Sostratus, said to him: 'Seest thou, sir, how this man's face shineth?' 'I see, my beloved,' said Sostratus; 'let us never leave him, but live with him and hear the words of eternal life.' Next day they offered Andrew many gifts, but he said: 'It is not for me to take aught of you but your own selves. Had I desired money, Lesbius is richer.' **27** After some days he bade them prepare him a bath; and going there saw an old man with a devil, trembling exceedingly. As he wondered at him, another, a youth, came out of the bath and fell at his feet, saying: 'What have we to do with thee, Andrew? Hast thou come here to turn us out of our abodes?' Andrew said to the people: 'Fear not,' and drove out both the devils. Then, as he bathed, he told them: 'The enemy of mankind lies in wait everywhere, in baths and in rivers; therefore we ought always to invoke the Lord's name, that he may have w power over us.' They brought their sick to him to be healed, and so they did from other cities. **28** An old man, Nicolaus, came with clothes rent and said: 'I am seventy-four years old and have always been a libertine. Three days ago I heard of your miracles and teaching. I thought I would turn over a new leaf, and then again that I would not. in this doubt, I took a Gospel and prayed God to make me forget my old devices. A few days after, I forgot the Gospel I had about me, and went to the brothel. The woman said: "Depart, old man, depart: thou art an angel of God, touch me not nor approach me, for I see in thee a great mystery." Then I remembered the Gospel, and am come to you for help and pardon.' Andrew discoursed long against incontinence, and prayed from the sixth to the ninth hour. He rose and washed his face and said: 'I will not eat till I know if God will have mercy on this man.' A second day he fasted, but had no revelation until the fifth day, when he wept vehemently and said: 'Lord, we obtain mercy for the dead, and now this man that desireth to know thy greatness, wherefore should he not return and thou heal him?' A voice from heaven said: 'Thou hast prevailed for the old man; but like as thou art worn with fasting, let him also fast, that he may be saved.' And he called him and preached abstinence. On the sixth day he asked the brethren all to pray for Nicolaus, and they did. Andrew then took food and permitted the rest to eat. Nicolaus went home, gave away all his goods, and lived for six months on dry bread and water. Then he died. Andrew was not there, but in the place where he was he heard a voice: 'Andrew, Nicolaus for whom thou didst intercede, is become mine.' And he told the brethren that Nicolaus was dead, and prayed that he might rest in peace. **29** And while he abode in that place (probably Lacedaemon) Antiphanes of Megara came and said: 'If there be in thee any kindness, according to the command of the Saviour whom thou preachest, show it now.' Asked what his story was, he told it. Returning from a journey, I heard the porter of my house crying out. They told me that he and his wife and son were tormented of a devil. I went upstairs and found other servants gnashing their teeth, running at me, and laughing madly. I went further up and found they had beaten my wife: she lay with her hair over her face unable to recognize me. Cure her, and I care nothing for the others.' Andrew said: 'There is no respect of persons with God. Let us go there.' They went from Lacedaemon to Megara, and when they entered the house, all the devils cried out: 'What dost thou here, Andrew? Go where thou art permitted: this house is ours.' He healed the wife and all the possessed persons, and Antiphanes and his wife became firm adherents. **30** He returned to Patrae where Egeas was now proconsul, and one Iphidamia, who had been converted by a disciple, Sosias, came and embraced his feet and said: 'My lady Maximilla who is in a fever has sent for you. The proconsul is standing by her bed with his sword drawn, meaning to kill himself when she expires.' He went to her, and said to Egeas: 'Do thyself no harm, but put up thy sword into his place. There will be a time when thou wilt draw it on me.' Egeas did not understand, but made way. Andrew took Maximilla's hand, she broke into a sweat, and was well: he bade them give her food. The proconsul sent him a hundred pieces of silver, but he would not look at them. **31** Going thence he saw a sick man lying in the dirt begging, and healed him. **32** Elsewhere he saw a blind man with wife and son, and said: 'This is indeed the devil's work: he has blinded them in soul and body.' He opened their eyes and they believed. **33** One who saw this said: 'I beg thee come to the harbour; there is a man, the son of a sailor, sick fifty years, cast out of the house, lying on the shore, incurable, full of ulcers and worms.' They went to him. The sick man said: 'Perhaps you are the disciple of that God who alone can save.' Andrew said: 'I am he who in the name of my God can restore thee to health,' and added: 'In the name of Jesus Christ, rise and follow me.' He left his filthy rags and followed, the pus and worms flowing from him. They went into the sea, and the apostle washed him in the name of the Trinity and he was whole, and ran naked through the city proclaiming the true God. **34** At this time the proconsul's brother Stratocles arrived from Italy. One of his slaves, Alcman, whom he loved, was taken by a devil and lay foaming in the court. Stratocles hearing of it said: 'Would the sea had swallowed me before I saw this.' Maximilla and Iphidamia said: 'Be comforted: there is here a man of God, let us send for him.' When he came he took the boy's hand and raised him whole. Stratocles believed and clave to Andrew. **35** Maximilla went daily to the praetorium and sent for Andrew to teach there. Egeas was away in Macedonia, angry because Maximilla had left him since her conversion. As they were all assembled one day, he returned, to their great terror. Andrew prayed that he might not be suffered to enter the place till all had dispersed. And Egeas was at once seized with indisposition, and in the interval the apostle signed them all and sent them away, himself last. But Maximilla on the first opportunity came to Andrew and received the word of God and went home. **36** After this Andrew was taken and imprisoned by Egeans, and all came to the prison to be taught. After a few days he was scourged and crucified; he hung for three days, preaching, and expired, as is fully set forth in his Passion. Maximilla embalmed and buried his body. **37** From the tomb comes manna like flour, and oil: the amount shows the barrenness or fertility of the coming season -as I have told in my first book of Miracles. I have not set out his Passion at length, because I find it well done by some one else. **38** This much have I presumed to write, unworthy, unlettered, &c. The author's prayer for himself ends the book. May Andrew, on whose death-day he was born, intercede to save him.

(The Passion to which Gregory alludes is that which begins Conversante et docente'.)

Of the detached fragments and quotations which precede the Passion there are three: [a] One is in the Epistle of Titus. When, finally, Andrew also [John has been cited shortly before] had come to a wedding, he too, to manifest the glory of God, disjoined certain who were intended to marry each other, men and women, and instructed them to continue holy in the single state. No doubt this refers to the story in Gregory, ch. 11 Gregory, it may be noted, has altered the story (or has used an altered text), for the marriage of cousins was not forbidden till Theodosius' time (so Flamion). He or his source has imagined the relationship between the couples; in the original Acts none need have existed: the mere fact of the marriage was enough. [b] The next are in a tract by Evodius, bishop of Uzala, against the Manichees: Observe, in the Acts of Leucius which he wrote under the name of the apostles, what manner of things you accept about Maximilla the wife of Egetes: who, refusing to pay her due to her husband (though the apostle has said: Let the husband pay the due to the wife and likewise the wife to the husband: 1 Cor. vii. 3), imposed her maid Euclia upon her husband, decking her out, as is there written, with wicked (lit. hostile) enticements and paintings, and substituted her as deputy for herself at night, so that he in ignorance used her as his wife. There also is it written, that when this same Maximilla and Iphidamia were gone together to hear the apostle Andrew, a beautiful child, who, Leucius would have us understand, was either God or at least an angel, escorted them to the apostle Andrew and went to the praetorium of Egetes, and entering their chamber feigned a woman's voice, as of Maximilla, complaining of the sufferings of womankind, and of Iphidamia replying. When Egetes heard this dialogue, he went away. [c] Evodius quotes another sentence, not certainly from the Acts of Andrew, but more in their manner than in that of John or Peter: In the Acts written by Leucius, which the Manichees receive, it is thus written: For the deceitful figments and pretended shows and collection (force, compelling) of visible things do not even proceed from their own nature, but from that man who of his own will has become worse through seduction. It is obscure enough, in original and version: but is the kind of thing that would appeal to those who thought of material things and phenomena as evil. We do not wonder that such narratives as that which Evodius quotes have been expunged, either by Gregory or his source, from the text.

The next passage is a fragment of some pages in length found by M. Bonnet in a Vatican MS. (Gr. 808) of tenth to eleventh century. There is no doubt that it is a piece of the original Acts. It is highly tedious in parts. Andrew in prison discourses to the brethren.

1

[1] . . . is there in you altogether slackness? are ye not yet convinced of yourselves that ye do not yet bear his goodness? let us be reverent, let us rejoice with ourselves in the bountiful (ungrudging) fellowship which cometh of him. Let us say unto ourselves: Blessed is our race! by whom hath it been loved? blessed is our state! of whom hath it obtained mercy? we are not cast on the ground, we that have been recognized by so great highness: we are not the offspring of time, afterward to be dissolved by time; we are not a contrivance (product) of motion, made to be again destroyed by itself, nor things of earthly birth. ending again therein. We belong, then, to a greatness, unto which we aspire, of which we are the property, and peradventure to a greatness that hath mercy upon us. We belong to the better; therefore we flee from the worse: we belong to the beautiful, for whose sake we reject the foul; to the righteous, by whom we cast away the unrighteous, to the merciful, by whom we reject the unmerciful; to the Saviour, by whom we recognize the destroyer; to the light, by whom we have cast away the darkness; to the One, by whom we have turned away from the many; to the heavenly, by whom we have learned to know the earthly; to the abiding, by whom we have seen the transitory. If we desire to offer unto God that hath had mercy on us a worthy thanksgiving or confidence or hymn or boasting, what better cause (theme) have we than that we have been recognized by him? [2] And having discoursed thus to the brethren, he sent them away every one to his house, saying to them: Neither are ye ever forsaken of me, ye that are servants of Christ, because of the love that is in him: neither again shall I be forsaken of you because of his intercession (mediation). And every one departed unto his house: and there was among them rejoicing after this sort for many days, while Aegeates took not thought to prosecute the accusation against the Apostle. Every one of them then was confirmed at that time in hope toward the Lord, and they assembled without fear in the prison, with Maximilla, Iphidamia, and the rest, continually, being sheltered by the protection and grace of the Lord. [3] But one day Aegeates, as he was hearing causes, remembered the matter concerning Andrew: and as one seized with madness, he left the cause which he had in hand, and rose up from the judgement seat and ran quickly to the praetorium, inflamed with love of Maximilla and desiring to persuade her with flatteries. And Maximilla was beforehand with him, coming from the prison and entering the house. And he went in and said to her: [4] Maximilla, thy parents counted me worthy of being thy consort, and gave me thine hand in marriage, not looking to wealth or descent or renown, but it may be to my good disposition of soul: and, that I may pass over much that I might utter in reproach of thee, both of that which I have enjoyed at thy parents' hands and thou from me during all our life, I am come, leaving the court, to learn of thee this one thing: answer me then reasonably, if thou wert as the wife of former days, living with me in the way we know, sleeping, conversing, bearing offspring with me, I would deal well with thee in all points; nay more, I would set free the stranger whom I hold in prison: but if thou wilt not to thee I would do nothing harsh, for indeed I cannot; but him, whom thou affectionest more than me, I will afflict yet more. Consider, then, Maximilla, to whether of the two thou inclinest, and answer me to-morrow; for I am wholly armed for this emergency. [5] And with these words he went out; but Maximilla again at the accustomed hour, with Iphidamia, went to Andrew: and putting his hands before her own eyes, and then putting them to her mouth, she began to declare to him the whole rmatter of the demand of Aegeates. And Andrew answered her: I know, Maximilla my child, that thou thyself art moved to resist the whole attraction (promise) of nuptial union, desiring to be quit of a foul and polluted way of life: and this hath long been firmly held in thine (MS. mine) intention; but now thou wishest for the further testimony of mine opinion. I testify, O Maximilla: do it not; be not vanquished by the threat of Aegeates: be not overcome by his discourse: fear not his shameful counsels: fall not to his artful flatteries: consent not to surrender thyself to his impure spells, but endure all his torments looking unto us for a little space, and thou shalt see him wholly numbed and withering away from thee and from all that are akin to thee. But (For) that which I most needed to say to thee -for I rest not till I fulfil the business which is seen, and which cometh to pass in thy person- hath escaped me: and rightly in thee do I behold Eve repenting, and in myself Adam returning; for that which she suffered in ignorance, thou now (for whose soul I strive) settest right by returning: and that which the spirit suffered which was overthrown with her and slipped away from itself, is set right in me, with thee who seest thyself being brought back. For her defect thou hast remedied by not suffering like her; and his imperfection I have perfected by taking refuge with God, that which she disobeyed thou hast obeyed: that whereto he consented I flee from: and that which they both transgressed we have been aware of, for it is ordained that every one should correct (and raise up again) his own fall. [6] I, then, having said this as I have said it, would go on to speak as followeth: Well done, O nature that art being saved for thou hast been strong and hast not hidden thyself (from God like Adam)! Well done, O soul that criest out of what thou hast surfered, and returnest unto thyself ! Well done, O man that understandest what is thine and dost press on to what is thine! Well done, thou that hearest what is spoken, for I see thee to be greater than things that are thought or spoken! I recognize thee as more powerful than the things which seemed to overpower thee; as more beautiful than those which cast thee down into foulness, which brought thee down into captivity. Perceiving then, O man, all this in thyself, that thou art immaterial, holy light, akin to him that is unborn, that thou art intellectual, heavenly, translucent, pure, above the flesh, above the world, above rulers, above principalities, over whom thou art in truth, then comprehend thyself in thy condition and receive full knowledge and understand wherein thou excellest: and beholding thine own face in thine essence, break asunder all bonds -I say not only those that are of thy birth, but those that are above birth, whereof we have set forth to thee the names which are execeding great -desire earnestly to see him that is revealed unto thee, him who doth not come into being, whom perchance thou alone shalt recognize with confidence. [7] These things have I spoken of thee, Maximilla, for in their meaning the things I have spoken reach unto thee. Like as Adam died in Eve because he consented unto her confession, so do I now live in thee that keepest the Lord's commandment and stablishest thyself in the rank (dignity) of thy being. But the threats of Aegeates do thou trample down, Maximilla, knowing that we have God that hath mercy on us. And let not his noise move thee, but continue chaste- and let him punish me not only with such torments as bonds, but let him cast me to the beasts or burn me with fire, and throw me from a precipice. And what need I say? there is but this one body; let him abuse that as he will, for it is akin to himself. [8] And yet again unto thee is my speech, Maximilla: I say unto thee, give not thyself over unto Aegeates: withstand his ambushes- for indeed, Maximilla, I have seen my Lord saying unto me: Andrew, Aegeates' father the devil will loose thee from this prison. Thine,

therefore, let it be henceforth to keep thyself chaste and pure, holy, unspotted, sincere, free from adultery, not reconciled to the discourses of our enemy, unbent, unbroken, tearless, unwounded, not storm-tossed, undivided, not stumbling without fellow-feeling for the works of Cain. For if thou give not up thyself, Maximilla, to what is contrary to these, I also shall rest, though I be thus forced to leave this life for thy sake that is, for mine own. But if I were thrust out hence, even I, who, it may be, might avail through thee to profit others that are akin to me, and if thou wert persuaded by the discourse of Aegeates and the flatteries of his father the serpent, so that thou didst turn unto thy former works, know thou that on thine account I should be tormented until thou thyself sawest that I had contemned life for the sake of a soul which was not worthy. [9] I entreat, therefore, the wise man that is in thee that thy mind continue clear seeing. I entreat thy mind that is not seen, that it be preserved whole: I beseech thee, love thy Jesus, and yield not unto the worse. Assist me, thou whom I entreat as a man, that I may become perfect: help me also, that thou mayest recognize thine own true nature: feel with me in my suffering, that thou mayest take knowledge of what I suffer, and escape suffering see that which I see, and thou shalt be blind to what thou seest: see that which thou shouldst, and thou shalt not see that thou shouldst not: hearken to what I say, and cast away that which thou hast heard. [10] These things have I spoken unto thee and unto every one that heareth, if he will hear. But thou, O Stratocles, said he, looking toward him, Why art thou so oppressed, with many tears and groanings to be heard afar off? what is the lowness of spirit that is on thee? why thy much pain and thy great anguish? dost thou take note of what is said, and wherefore I pray thee to be disposed in mind as my child? (or, my child, to be composed in mind): dost thou perceive unto whom my words are spoken? hath each of them taken hold on thine understanding? have they whetted (MS. touched) thine intellectual part? have I thee as one that hath hearkened to me? do I find myself in thee? is there in thee one that speaketh whom I see to be mine own? doth he love him that speaketh in me and desire to have fellowship with him? doth he wish to be made one with him? doth lie hasten to become his friend? doth he yearn to be joined with him? doth he find in him any rest? hath he where to lay his head? doth nought oppose him there? nought that is wroth with him, resisteth him, hateth him, fleeth from him, is savage, avoideth, turneth away, starteth off, is burdened, maketh war, talketh with others, is flattered by others, agreeth with others? Doth nothing else disturb him? Is there one within that is strange to me? an adversary, a breaker of peace, an enemy, a cheat, a sorcerer, a crooked dealer, unsound, guileful, a hater of men, a hater of the word, one like a tyrant, boastful, puffed up, mad, akin to the serpent, a weapon of the devil, a friend of the fire, belonging to darkness? Is there in thee any one, Stratocles, that cannot endure my saying these things? Who is it? Answer: do I talk in vain? have I spoken in vain? Nay, saith the man in thee, Stratocles, who now again weepeth. [11] And Andrew took the band of Stratocles and said: I have him whom I loved; I shall rest on him whom I look for; for thy yet groaning, and weeping without restraint, is a sign unto me that I have already found rest, that I have not spoken to thee these words which are akin to me, in vain. [12] And Stratocles answered him: Think not, most blessed Andrew, that there is aught else that afflicteth me but thee; for the words that come forth of thee are like arrows of fire shot against me, and every one of them reacheth me and verily burneth me up. That part of my soul which inclineth to what I hear is tormented, divining the affliction that is to follow, for thou thyself departest, and, I know, nobly: but hereafter when I seek thy care and affection, where shall I find it, or in whom? I have received the seeds of the words of salvation, and thou wast the sower: but that they should sprout up and grow needs none other but thee, most blessed Andrew. And what else have I say to thee but this? I need much mercy and help from thee, to become worthy of the seed I have from thee, which will not otherwise increase perpetually or grow up into the light except thou willest it, and prayest for them and for the whole of me. [13] And Andrew answered him: This, my child, was what I beheld in thee myself. And I glorify my Lord that my thought of thee walked not on the void, but knew what it said. But that ye may know the truth, to-morrow doth Aegeates deliver me up to be crucified: for Maximilla the servant of the Lord will enrage the enemy that is in him, unto whom he belongeth, by not consenting to that which is hateful to her; and by turning against me he will think to console himself. [14] Now while the apostle spake these things, Maximilla was not there, for she having heard throughout the words wherewith he answered her, and being in part composed by them, and of such a mind as the words pointed out, set forth not inadvisedly nor without purpose and went to the praetorium. And she bade farewell to all the life of the flesh, and when Aegeates brought to her the same demand which he had told her to consider, whether she would lie with him, she rejected it- and thenceforth he bent himself to putting Andrew to death, and thought to what death he should expose him. And when of all deaths crucifixion alone prevailed with him, he went away with his like and dined; and Maximilla, the Lord going before her in the likeness of Andrew, with Iphidamia came back to the prison- and there being therein a great gathering of the brethren, she found Andrew discoursing thus: [15] I, brethren, was sent forth by the Lord as an apostle unto these regions whereof my Lord thought me worthy, not to teach any man, but to remind every man that is akin to such words that they live in evils which are temporal, delighting in their injurious delusions: wherefrom I have always exhorted you also to depart, and encouraged you to press toward things that endure, and to take flight from all that is transitory (flowing)- for ye see that none of you standeth, but that all things, even to the customs of men, are easily changeable. And this befalleth because the soul is untrained and erreth toward nature and holdeth pledges toft its error. I therefore account them blessed who have become obedient unto the word preached, and thereby see the mysteries of their own nature; for whose sake all things have been builded up. [16] I enjoin you therefore, beloved children, build yourselves firmly upon the foundation that hath been laid for you, which is unshaken, and against which no evil- willer can conspire. Be then, rooted upon this foundation: be established, remembering what ye have seen (or heard) and all that hath come to pass while I walked with you all. Ye have seen works wrought through me which ye have no power to disbelieve, and such signs come to pass as perchance even dumb nature will proclaim aloud; I have delivered you words which I pray may so be received by you as the words themselves would have it. Be established then, beloved upon all that ye have seen, and heard, and partaken of. And God on whom ye have believed shall have mercy on you and present you lmto himself, giving you rest unto all ages. [17] Now as for that which is to befall me, let it not really trouble you as some strange spectacle, that the servant of God unto whom God himself hath granted much in deeds and words, should by an evil man be driven out of this temporal life: for not only unto me will this come to pass, but unto all them that have loved and believed on him and confess him. The devil that is wholly shameless will arm his own children against them, that they may consent unto him; and he will not have his desire. And wherefore he essayeth this I will tell you. From the beginning of all things, and if I may so say, since he that hath no beginning came down to be under his rule, the enemy that is a foe to peace driveth away from (God) such a one as doth not belong indeed to him, but is some one of the weaker sort and not fully enlightened (?), nor yet able to recognize himself. And because he knoweth him not, therefore must he be fought against by him (the devil). For he, thinking that he possesseth him and is his master for ever, opposeth him so much, that he maketh his enmity to be a kind of friendship: for suggesting to him his own thoughts, he often portrayeth them as pleasurable and specious (MS. deceitful), by which he thinketh to prevail over him. He was not, then, openly shown to be an enemy, for he feigned a friendship that was worthy of him. [18] And this his work he carried on so long that he (man) forgat to recognize it, but he (the devil) knew it himself: that is, he, because of his gifts. But when the mystery of grace was lighted up, and the counsel of rest manifested, and the light of the word shown, and the race of them that were saved was proved, warring against many pleasures, the enemy himself despised, and himself, through the goodness of him that had mercy on us, derided because of his own gifts, by which he had thought to triumph over man- he began to plot against us with hatred and enmity and assaults; and this hath he dctcrmined, not to cease from us till he thinketh to separate us (from God). For before, our enemy was without care, and offered us a feigned friendship which was worthy of him, and was able not to fear that we, deceived by him, should depart from him. But when the light of dispensation was kindled, it made , I say not stronger, . For it exposed that part of his nature which was hidden and which thought to escape notice, and made it confess what it is. Knowing therefore, brethren, that which shall be, let us be vigilant, not discontented, not making a proud figure, not carrying upon our souls marks of him which are not our own: but wholly lifted upward by the whole word, let us all gladly await the end, and take our flight away from him, that he may be henceforth shown as he is, who our nature unto (or against) our . . .

The Martydom

1

[1] And after he had thus discoursed throughout the night to the brethren, and prayed with them and committed them unto the Lord, early in the morning Aegeates the proconsul sent for the apostle Andrew out of the prison and said to him: The end of thy judgement is at hand, thou stranger, enemy of this present life and foe of all mine house. Wherefore hast thou thought good to intrude into places that are not thine, and to corrupt my wife who was of old obedient unto me? why hast thou done this against me and against all Achaia? Therefore shalt thou receive from me a gift in recompense of that thou hast wrought against me. [2] And he commanded

him to be scourged by seven men and afterward to be crucified: and charged the executioners that his legs should be left unpierced, and so he should be hanged up: thinking by this means to torment him the more. **3** Now the report was noised throughout all Patrae that the stranger, the righteous man, the servant of Christ whom Aegeates held prisoner, was being crucified, having done nothing amiss: and they ran together with one accord unto the sight, being wroth with the proconsul because of his impious judgement. **4** And as the executioners led him unto the place to fulfil that which was commanded them, Stratocles heard what was come to pass, and ran hastily and overtook them, and beheld the blessed Andrew violently haled by the executioners like a malefactor. And he spared them not, but beating every one of them soundly and tearing their coats from top to bottom, he caught Andrew away from them, saying: Ye may thank the blessed man who hath instructed me and taught me to refrain from extremity of wrath: for else I would have showed you what Stratocles is able to do, and what is the power of the foul Aegeates. For we have learnt to endure that which others inflict upon us. And he took the hand of the apostle and went with him to the place by the sea-shore where he was to be crucified. **5** But the soldiers who had received him from the proconsul left him with Stratocles, and returned and told Aegeates, saying: As we went with Andrew Stratocles prevented us, and rent our coats and pulled him away from us and took him with him, and lo, here we are as thou seest. And Aegeates answered them: Put on other raiment and go and fulfil that which I commanded you, upon the condemned man: but be not seen of Stratocles, neither answer him again if he ask aught of you; for I know the rashness of his soul, what it is, and if he were provoked he would not even spare me. And they did as Aegeates said unto them. **6** But as Stratocles went with the apostle unto the place appointed, Andrew perceived that he was wroth with Aegeates and was reviling him in a low voice, and said unto him: My child Stratocles, I would have thee henceforth possess thy soul unmoved, and remove from thyself this temper, and neither be inwardly disposed thus toward the things that seem hard to thee, nor be inflamed outwardly: for it becometh the servant of Jesus to be worthy of Jesus. And another thing will I say unto thee and to the brethren that walk with me: that the man that is against us, when he dareth aught against us and findeth not one to consent unto him, is smitten and beaten and wholly deadened because he hath not accomplished that which he undertook; let us therefore, little children, have him alway before our eyes, lest if we fall asleep he slaughter us (you) like an adversary. **7** And as he spake this and yet more unto Stratocles and them that were with him, they came to the place where he was to be crucified: and (seeing the cross set up at the edge of the sand by the sea-shore) he left them all and went to the cross and spake unto it (as unto a living creature, with a loud voice): **8** Hail, O cross, yea be glad indeed! Well know I that thou shalt henceforth be at rest, thou that hast for a long time been wearied, being set up and awaiting me. I come unto thee whom I know to belong to me. I come unto thee that hast yearned after me. I know thy mystery, for the which thou art set up: for thou art planted in the world to establish the things that are unstable: and the one part of thee stretcheth up toward heaven that thou mayest signify the heavenly word (or, the word that is above) (the head of all things): and another part of thee is spread out to the right hand and the left that it may put to flight the envious and adverse power of the evil one, and gather into one the things that are scattered abroad (or, the world): And another part of thee is planted in the earth, and securely set in the depth, that thou mayest join the things that are in the earth and that are under the earth unto the heavenly things. **9** O cross, device (contrivance) of the salvation of the Most High! O cross, trophy of the victory [of Christ] over the enemies! O cross, planted upon the earth and having thy fruit in the heavens! O name of the cross, filled with all things (lit. a thing filled with all). **10** Well done, O cross, that hast bound down the mobility of the world (or, the circumference)! Well done, O shape of understanding that hast shaped the shapeless (earth?)! Well done, O unseen chastisement that sorely chastisest the substance of the knowledge that hath many gods, and drivest out from among mankind him that devised it! Well done, thou that didst clothe thyself with the Lord, and didst bear the thief as a fruit, and didst call the apostle to repentance, and didst not refuse to accept us! **11** But how long delay I, speaking thus, and embrace not the cross, that by the cross I may be made alive, and by the cross (win) the common death of all and depart out of life? **12** Come hitller ye ministers of joy unto me, ye servants of Aegeates: accomplish the desire of us both, and bind the lamb unto the wood of suffering, the man unto the maker, the soul unto the Saviour. **13** And the blessed Andrew having thus spoken, standing upon the earth, looked earnestly upon the cross, and bade the brethren that the executioners should come and do that which was commanded them; for they stood afar off. **14** And they came and bound his hands and his feet and nailed them not; for such a charge had they from Aegeates; for he wished to afflict him by hanging him up, and that in the night he might be devoured alive by dogs.

And they left him hanging and departed from him. **15** And when the multitudes that stood by of them that had been made disciples in Christ by him saw that they had done unto him none of the things accustomed with them that are crucified, they hoped to hear something again from him. For as he hung, he moved his head and smiled. And Stratocles asked him, saying: Wherefore smilest thou, servant of God? thy laughter maketh us to mourn and weep because we are bereaved of thee. And the blessed Andrew answered him: Shall I not laugh, my son Stratocles, at the vain assault (ambush) of Aegeates, whereby he thinketh to punish us? we are strangers unto him and his conspiracies. He hath not to hear; for if he had, he would have heard that the man of Jesus cannot be punished, because he is henceforth known of him. **16** And thereafter he spake unto them all in common, for the heathen also were come together, being wroth at the unjust judgement of Aegeates. **17** Ye men that are here present, and women and children, old and young, bond and free, and all that will hear, take ye no heed of the vain deceit of this present life, but heed us rather who hang here for the Lord's sake and are about to depart out of this body: and renounce all the lusts of the world and contemn (spit upon) the worship of the abominable idols, and run unto the true worshipping of our God that lieth not, and make yourselves a temple pure and ready to receive the word. **18** And the multitudes hearing the things which he spake departed not from the place; and Andrew continued speaking yet more unto them, for a day and a night. And on the day following, beholding his endurance and constancy of soul and wisdom of spirit and strength of mind, they were wroth, and hastened with one accord unto Aegeates, to the judgement-seat where he sat, and cried out against him, saying: What is this judgement of thine, O proconsul? thou hast ill judged! thou hast condemned unjustly: thy court is against law! What evil hath this man done? wherein hath he offended? The city is troubled: thou injurest us all! destroy not Caesar's city! give us the righteous man! restore us the holy man! slay not a man dear to God! destroy not a man gentle and pious! lo, two days is he hanged up and yet liveth, and hath tasted nothing, and yet refresheth us all with his words, and lo, we believe in the God whom he preacheth. Take down the righteous man and we will all turn philosophers; loose the chaste man and all Patrae will be at peace, set free the wise man and all Achaia shall be set free by him! (or, obtain mercy.) **19** But when at the first Aegeates would not hear them, but beckoned with the hand to the people that they should depart, they were filled with rage and were at the point to do him violence, being in number about two thousand. **20** And when the proconsul saw them to be after a sort mad, he feared lest there should be a rising against him, and rose up from the judgement-seat and went with them, promising to release Andrew. And some went before and signified to the apostle and to the rest of the people that were there, wherefore the proconsul was coming. And all the multitude of the disciples rejoiced together with Maximilla and Iphidamia and Stratocles. **21** But when Andrew heard it, he began to say: O the dullness and disobedience and simplicity of them whom I have taught! how much have I spoken, and even to this day I have not persuaded them to flee from the love of earthly things! but they are yet bound unto them and continue in them, and will not depart from them. What meaneth this affection and love and sympathy with the flesh? how long heed ye worldly and temporal things? how long understand ye not the things that be above us, and press not to overtake them? leave me henceforth to be put to death in the manner which ye behold, and let no man by any means loose me from these bonds, for so is it appointed unto me to depart out of the body and be present with the Lord, with whom also I am crucified. And this shall be accomplished. **22** And he turned unto Aegeates and said with a loud voice: Wherefore art thou come, Aegeates, that art an alien unto me? what wilt thou dare afresh, what contrive, or what fetch? tell us that thou hast repented and art come to loose us? nay, not if thou repentest, indeed, Aegeates, will I now consent unto thee, not if thou promise me all thy substance will I depart from myself, not if thou say that thou art mine will I trust thee. And dost thou, proconsul, loose him that is bound? him that hath been set free? that hath been recognized by his kinsman? that hath obtained mercy and is beloved of him? dost thou loose him that is alien to thee? the stranger? that only appeareth to thee? I have one with whom I shall be for ever, with whom I shall converse for unnumbered ages. Unto him do I go, unto him do I hasten, who made thee also known unto me, who said to me: Understand thou Aegeates and his gifts let not that fearful one afright thee, nor think that he holdeth thee who art mine. He is thine enemy: he is pestilent, a deceiver, a corrupter, a madman, a sorcerer, a cheat, a murderer, wrathful, without compassion. Depart therefore from me, thou worker of all iniquity. **23** And the Proconsul hearing this stood speechless and as it were beside himself; but as all the city made an e uproar that he should loose Andrew, he drew near to the cross to loose him and take him down. But the blessed Andrew cried out with a loud voice: Suffer not Lord, thine Andrew that hath been bound upon thy cross, to be loosed again; give not me that am upon thy mystery to the shameless devil; O Jesu Christ, let not thine adversary loose him that is hung upon thy grace; O Father, let not this mean (little) one humble any more him that hath known thy greatness. But do thou, Jesu Christ, whom I have seen, whom I hold, whom I love, in whom I am and shall be, receive me in peace into thine everlasting tabernacles, that by my going out there may be an entering in unto thee of many that are akin to me, and that they may rest in thy majesty. And having so said, and yet more glorified the Lord, he gave up the ghost, while we all wept and lamented at our parting from him. [24] And after the decease of the blessed Andrew, Maximilla together with Stratocles, caring nought for them that stood by, drew near and herself loosed his body: and when it was evening she paid it the accustomed care and buried it (hard by the sea-shore). And she continued separate from Aegeates because of his brutal soul and his wicked manner of life: and she led a reverend and quiet life, filled with the love of Christ, among the brethren. Whom Aegeates solicited much, and promised that she should have the rule over his affairs; but being unable to persuade her, he arose in the dead of night and unknown to them of his house cast himself down from a great height and perished. [25] But Stratocles, which was his brother after the flesh, would not touch aught of the things that were left of his substance; for the wretched man died without offspring: but said: Let thy goods go with thee, Aegeates. [26] For of these things we have no need, for they are polluted; but for me, let Christ be my friend and I his servant, and all my substance do I offer unto him in whom I have believed, and I pray that by worthy hearing of the blessed teaching of the apostle I may appear a partaker with him in the ageless and unending kingdom. And so the uproar of the people ceased, and all were glad at the amazing and untimely and sudden fall of the impious and lawless Aegeates.

The Apostles' Creed

It is affirmed by Ambrose "that the twelve Apostles, as skilful artificers assembled together, and made a key by their common advice, that is, the Creed; by which the darkness of the devil is disclosed, that the light of Christ may appear." Others fable that every Apostle inserted an article, by which the creed is divided into twelve articles; and a sermon, fathered upon St. Austin, and quoted by the Lord Chancellor King, fabricates that each particular article was thus inserted by each particular Apostle

"*Peter*–[1] I believe in God the Father Almighty; "*John*–[2] Maker of heaven and earth; "*James*–[3] And in Jesus Christ his only Son, our Lord; "*Andrew*–[4] Who was conceived by the Holy Ghost, born of the Virgin Mary; "*Philip*–[5] Suffered under Pontius Pilate, was crucified, dead and buried; "*Thomas*–[6] He descended into hell, the third day he rose again from the dead; "*Bartholomew*–[7] He ascended into heaven, sitteth at the right hand of God the Father Almighty; "*Matthew*–[8] From thence he shall come to judge the quick and the dead; "*James, the son of Alpheus*–[9] I believe in the Holy Ghost, the holy Catholic Church; "*Simon Zelotes*–[10] The communion of saints, the forgiveness of sins; "*Jude the brother of James*–[11] The resurrection of the body; "*Matthias*–[12] Life everlasting. Amen."

As it stood An. Dom. 600. Copied from Mr. Justice Bailey's Edition of the book of Common Prayer.

[1] I Believe in God the Father Almighty: [2] And in Jesus Christ his only begotten Son, our Lord; [3] Who was born of the Holy Ghost and Virgin Mary, [4] And was crucified under Pontius Pilate, and was buried; [5] And the third day rose again from the dead. [6] Ascended into heaven, sitteth on the right hand of the Father; [7] Whence he shall come to judge the quick and the dead; [8] And in the Holy Ghost; [9] The Holy Church; [10] The remission of sins; [11] And the resurrection of the flesh, Amen.

As it stands in the book of Common Prayer of the United Church of England and Ireland as by law established.

[1] I Believe in God the Father Almighty, maker of heaven and earth: [2] And in Jesus Christ his only Son, our Lord: [3] Who was conceived by the Holy Ghost, born of the Virgin Mary, [4] Suffered under Pontius Pilate, was crucified, dead and buried; [5] He descended into hell; [6] The third day he rose again from the dead; [7] He ascended into heaven, and sitteth on the right hand of God the Father Almighty; [8] From thence he shall come to judge the quick and the dead. [9] I believe in the Holy Ghost; [10] The holy Catholic Church; the communion of saints; [11] The forgiveness of sins; [12] The resurrection of the body and the life everlasting, Amen.

The Acts of Paul and Thecla

The Martyrdom of the holy and glorious first Martyr and Apostle Thecla.

1

1 Demas and Hermogenes become Paul's companions. 4 Paul visits Onesiphorus. 8 Invited by Demas and Hermogenes. 11 Preaches to the household of Onesiphorus. 12 His sermon.

¹ WHEN Paul went up to Iconium, after his flight from Antioch, Demas and Hermogenes became his companions, who were then full of hypocrisy. ² But Paul looking only at the goodness of God, did them no harm, but loved them greatly. ³ Accordingly he endeavoured to make agreeable to them, all the oracles and doctrines of Christ, and the design of the Gospel of God's well-beloved Son, instructing them in the knowledge of Christ, as it was revealed to him. ⁴ And a certain man named Onesiphorus, hearing that Paul was come to Iconium, went out speedily to meet him, together with his wife Lectra, and his sons Simmia and Zeno, to invite him to their house. ⁵ For Titus had given them a description of Paul's personage, they as yet not knowing him in person, but only being acquainted with his character. ⁶ They went in the king's highway to Lystra, and stood there waiting for him, comparing all who passed by, with that description which Titus had given them. ⁷ At length they saw a man coming (namely Paul), of a low stature, bald (or shaved) on the head, crooked thighs, handsome legs, hollow-eyed; had a crooked nose; full of grace; for sometimes he appeared as a man, sometimes he had the countenance of an angel. And Paul saw Onesiphorus, and was glad. ⁸ And Onesiphorus said: Hail, thou servant of the blessed God. Paul replied, The grace of God be with thee and thy family. ⁹ But Demos and Hermogenes were moved with envy, and, under a show of great religion, Demas said, And are not we also servants of the blessed God? Why didst thou not salute us? ¹⁰ Onesiphorus replied, Because I have not perceived in, you the fruits of righteousness; nevertheless, if ye are of that sort, ye shall be welcome to my house also. ¹¹ Then Paul went into the house of Onesiphorus, and there was great joy among the family on that account: and they employed themselves in prayer, breaking of bread, and hearing Paul preach the word of God concerning temperance and the resurrection, in the following manner: ¹² Blessed are the pure in heart; for they shall see God. ¹³ Blessed are they who keep their flesh undefiled (or pure); for they shall be the temple of God. ¹⁴ Blessed are the temperate (or chaste); for God will reveal himself to them. ¹⁵ Blessed are they who abandon their secular enjoyments; for they shall be accepted of God. ¹⁶ Blessed are they who have wives, as though they had them not; for they shall be made angels of God. ¹⁷ Blessed are they who tremble at the word of God; for they shall be comforted. ¹⁸ Blessed are they who keep their baptism pure; for they shall find peace with the Father, Son, and Holy Ghost. ¹⁹ Blessed are they who pursue the wisdom (or doctrine) of Jesus Christ; for they shall be called the sons of the Most High. ²⁰ Blessed are they who observe the instructions of Jesus Christ; for they shall dwell in eternal light. ²¹ Blessed are they, who for the love of Christ abandon the glories of the world; for they shall judge angels, and be placed at the right hand of Christ, and shall not suffer the bitterness of the last judgment. ²² Blessed are the bodies and souls of virgins; for they are acceptable to God, and shall not lose the reward of their virginity; for the word of their (heavenly) Father shall prove effectual to their salvation in the day of his Son, and they shall enjoy rest for evermore.

2

1 Thecla listens anxiously to Paul's preaching. 5 Thamyris, her admirer, concerts with Theoclia her mother to dissuade her, 12 in vain. 14 Demos and Hermogenes viler Paul to Thamyria.

¹ WHILE Paul was preach this sermon in the church which was in the house of Onesiphorus, a certain virgin, named Thecla (whose mother's name was Theoclia, and who was betrothed to a man named Thamyris) sat at a certain window in her house. ² From whence, by the advantage of a window in the house where Paul was, she both night and day heard Paul's sermons concerning God, concerning charity, concerning faith in Christ, and concerning prayer; ³ Nor would she depart from the window, till with exceeding joy she was subdued to the doctrines of faith. ⁴ At length, when she saw many women and virgins going in to Paul, she earnestly desired that she might be thought worthy to appear in his presence, and hear the word of Christ; for she had not yet seen Paul's person, but only heard his sermons, and that alone. ⁵ But when she would not be prevailed upon to depart from the window, her mother sent to Thamyris, who came with the greatest pleasure, as hoping now to marry her. Accordingly he said to Theoclia, Where is my Thecla? ⁶ Theoclia replied, Thamyris, I have something very strange to tell you; for Thecla, for the space of three days, will not move from the window not so much as to eat or drink, but is so intent in hearing the artful and delusive discourses of a certain foreigner, that I perfectly admire, Thamyris, that a young woman of her known modesty, will suffer herself to be so prevailed upon. ⁷ For that man has disturbed the whole city of Iconium, and even your Thecla, among others, All the women and young men flock to him to receive his doctrine; who, besides all the rest, tells them that there is but one God, who alone is to be worshipped, and that we ought to live in chastity. ⁸ Notwithstanding this, my daughter Thecla, like a spider's web fastened to the window, is captivated by the discourses of Paul, and attends upon them with prodigious eagerness, and vast delight; and thus, by attending on what he says, the young woman is seduced. Now then do you go, and speak to her, for she is betrothed to you. ⁹ Accordingly Thamyris went, and having saluted her, and taking care not to surprise her, he said, Thecla, my spouse, why sittest thou in this melancholy posture? What strange impressions are made upon thee? Turn to Thamyris, and blush. ¹⁰ Her mother also spake to her after the same manner, and said, Child, why dost thou sit so melancholy, and, like one astonished, makest no reply? ¹¹ Then they wept exceedingly, Thamyria, that he had lost his spouse; Theoclia, that she had lost her daughter; and the maids, that they had lost their mistress; and there was an universal mourning in the family. ¹² But all these things made no impression upon Thecla, so as to incline her so much as to turn to them, and take notice of them; for she still regarded the discourses of Paul. ¹³ Then Thamyris ran forth into the street to observe who they were who went into Paul, and came out from him; and he saw two men engaged in a very warm dispute, and said to them; ¹⁴ Sirs, what business have you here? And who is that man within, belonging to you, who deludes the minds of men, both young men and virgins, persuading them, that they ought not to marry, but continue as they are? ¹⁵ I promise to give you a considerable sum, if you will give me a just account of him; for I am the chief person of this city. ¹⁶ Demas and Hermogenes replied, We cannot so exactly tell who he is; but this we know, that he deprives young men of their (intended) wives, and virgins of their (intended) husbands, by teaching, There can be no future resurrection, unless ye continue in chastity, and do not defile your flesh.

3

1 They betray Paul. 7 Thamyris arrests him with officers.

¹ THEN said Thamyris, Come along with me to my house, and refresh yourselves. So they went to a very splendid entertainment, where there was wine in abundance, and very rich provision. ² They were brought to a table richly spread, and made to drink plentifully by Thamyris, on account of the love he had for Thecla and his desire to marry her. ³ Then Thamyris said, I desire ye would inform me what the doctrines of this Paul are, that I may understand them; for I am under no small concern about Thecla, seeing she so delights in that stranger's discourses, that I am in danger of losing my intended wife. ⁴ Then Demas and Hermogenes answered both together, and said, Let him be brought before the governor Castellius, as one who endeavours to persuade the people into the new religion of the Christians, and he, according to the order of Cæsar, will put him to death, by which means you will obtain your wife; ⁵ While we at the same time will teach her, that the resurrection which he speaks of is already come, and consists in our having children; and that we then arose again, when we came to the knowledge of God. ⁶ Thamyris having this account from them, was filled with hot resentment: ⁷ And rising early in the morning he went to the house of Onesiphorus, attended by the magistrates, the jailor, and a great multitude of people with staves, and said to Paul; ⁸ Thou hast perverted the city of Iconium, and among the rest, Thecla, who is betrothed to me, so that now she will not marry me. Thou shalt therefore go with us to the governor Castellius. ⁹ And all the multitude cried out, Away with this impostor (magician), for he has perverted the minds of our wives, and all the people hearken to him.

4

1 Paul accused before the governor by Thamyris. 5 Defends himself. 9 Is committed to Prison, 10 and visited by Thecla.

¹ THEN Thamyris standing before the governor's judgment-seat, spake with a loud voice in the following manner. ² O governor, I know not whence this man cometh; but he is one who teaches that matrimony is unlawful. Command him therefore to declare before you for what reason he publishes such doctrines. ³ While he was saying thus, Demas and Hermogenes (whispered to Thamyris, and) said; Say that he is a Christian, and he will presently be put to death. ⁴ But the governor was more deliberate, and calling to Paul, he said, Who art thou? What dost thou teach? They seem to lay gross crimes to thy charge. ⁵ Paul then spake with a loud voice, saying, As I am now called to give an account, O governor, of my doctrines, I desire your audience. ⁶ That God, who is a God of vengeance, and who stands in need of nothing but the salvation of his creatures, has sent me to reclaim them from their wickedness and corruptions, from all (sinful) pleasures, and from death; and to persuade them to sin no more. ⁷ On this account, God sent his Son Jesus Christ, whom I preach, and in whom I instruct men to

place their hopes as that l person who only had such compassion on the deluded world, that it might not, O governor, be condemned, but have faith, the fear of God, the knowledge of religion, and the love of truth. ⁸ So that if I only teach those things which I have received by revelation from God, where is my crime? ⁹ When the governor heard this, he ordered Paul to be bound, and to be put in prison, till he should be more at leisure to hear him more fully. ¹⁰ But in the night, Thecla taking off her ear-rings, gave them to the turnkey of the prison, who then opened the doors to her, and let her in; ¹¹ And when she made a present of a silver looking-glass to the jailor, was allowed to go into the room where Paul was; then she sat down at his feet, and heard from him the great things of God. ¹² And as she perceived Paul not to be afraid of suffering, but that by divine assistance he behaved himself with courage, her faith so far increased that she kissed his chains.

5

1 Thecla sought and found by her relations. 4 Brought with Paul before the governor. 9 Ordered to be burnt, and Paul to be whipt. 15 Thecla miraculously saved.

¹ AT length Thecla was missed, and sought for by the family and by Thamyris in every street, as though she had been lost, but one of the porter's fellow-servants told them, that she had gone out in the night-time. ² Then they examined the porter, and he told them, that she was gone to the prison to the strange man. ³ They went therefore according to his direction, and there found her; and when they came out, they got a mob together, and went and told the governor all that happened. ⁴ Upon which he ordered Paul to be brought before his judgment seat. ⁵ Thecla in the mean time lay wallowing on the ground in the prison, in that same place where Paul had sat to teach her; upon which the governor also ordered her to be brought before his judgment-seat; which summons she received with joy, and went. ⁶ When Paul was brought thither, the mob with more vehemence cried out, He is a magician, let him die. ⁷ Nevertheless the governor attended with pleasure upon Paul's discourses of the holy works of Christ; and, after a council called, he summoned Thecla, and said to her, Why do you not, according to the law of the Iconians, marry Thamyris? ⁸ She stood still, with her eyes fixed upon Paul; and finding she made no reply, Theoclia, her mother, cried out, saying, Let the unjust creature be burnt; let her be burnt in the midst of the theatre, for refusing Thamyris, that all women may learn from her to avoid such practices. ⁹ Then the governor was exceedingly concerned, and ordered Paul to be whipt out of the city, and Thecla to be burnt. ¹⁰ So the governor arose, and went immediately into the theatre; and all the people went forth to see the dismal sight. ¹¹ But Thecla, just as a lamb in the wilderness looks every way to see her shepherd, looked around for Paul; ¹² And as she was looking upon the multitude, she saw the Lord Jesus in the likeness of Paul, and said to herself, Paul is come to see me in my distressed circumstances. And she fixed her eyes upon him; but he instantly ascended up to heaven, while she looked on him. ¹³ Then the young men and women brought wood and straw for the burning of Thecla; who, being brought naked to the stake, extorted tears from the governor, with surprise beholding the greatness of her beauty. ¹⁴ And when they had placed the wood in order, the people commanded her to go upon it; which she did, first making the sign of the cross. ¹⁵ Then the people set fire to the pile; though the flame was exceeding large, it did not touch her, for God took compassion on her, and caused a great eruption from the earth beneath, and a cloud from above to pour down great quantities of rain and hail; ¹⁶ Insomuch that by the rupture of the earth, very many were in great danger, and some were killed, the fire was extinguished, and Thecla preserved.

6

1 Paul with Onesiphorus in a cave. 7 Thecla discovers Paul; 12 proffers to follow him: 13 he exhorts her not for fear of fornication.

¹ IN the mean time Paul, together with Onesiphorus, his wife and children, was keeping a fast in a certain cave, which was in the road from Iconium to Daphne. ² And when they had fasted for several days, the children said to Paul, Father, we are hungry, and have not wherewithal to buy bread; for Onesiphorus had left all his substance to follow Paul with his family. ¹ Entrance to the confines of Hell. ² Charon in his bark. ³ The Minotaur roaring at the approach of condemned souls. ⁴ Souls agitated by the impure breath of evil spirits. ⁵ Cerberus devouring the souls of gourmands. ⁶ The avaricious and prodigal condemned to carry burdens. ⁷ The envious and angry cast into the Styx. ⁸ Tower and wall of the evil city. ⁹ In this ditch are those who have sinned against their neighbors; Centaurs shoot arrows at them. ¹⁰ Those who have sinned against themselves are here tormented by Harpies. ¹¹ Rain of fire for those who have sinned against God. ¹² Soul of the tyrant Gerion cast into the flames. ¹³ Debauchees and corruptors of youth flogged by devils. ¹⁴ Poisonous gulf into which flatterers are plunged. ¹⁵ Lake of fire in the caldrons into which Simoniacs are cast. ¹⁶ Sorcerers and diviners, their faces turned backward. ¹⁷ Bog of boiling pitch for cheats, thieves, and deceivers. ¹⁸ Hypocrite crucified. ¹⁹ Perfidious advisers plunged into a flaming ditch. ²⁰ For scandalous persons: one holds his head in his hand. ²¹ Robbers and other criminals tormented by a centaur armed with serpents. ²² Alchemists and quacks a prey to leprosy. ²³ Well of ice, for traitors and the ungrateful. ²⁴ Pluto in the midst of a glacier devouring the damned. ²⁵ The holy city of Jerusalem. ³ Then Paul, taking off his coat, said to the boy, Go, child, and buy bread, and bring it hither. ⁴ But while the boy was buying the bread, he saw his neighbour Thecla and was surprised, and said to her. Thecla, where are you going? ⁵ She replied, I am in pursuit of Paul, having been delivered from the flames. ⁶ The boy then said, I will bring you to him, for he is under great concern on your account, and has been in prayer and fasting these six days. ⁷ When Thecla came to the cave, she found Paul upon his knees praying and saying, O holy Father, O Lord Jesus Christ, grant that the fire may not touch Thecla; but be her helper, for she is thy servant. ⁸ Thecla then standing behind him, cried out in the following words: O sovereign Lord, Creator of heaven and earth, the Father of thy beloved and holy Son, I praise thee that thou hast preserved me from the fire, to see Paul again. ⁹ Paul then arose, and when he saw her, said, O God, who searchest the heart, Father of my Lord Jesus Christ, I praise thee that thou hast answered my prayer. ¹⁰ And there prevailed among them in the cave an entire affection to each other; Paul, Onesiphorus, and all that were with them being filled with joy. ¹¹ They had five loaves, some herbs and water, and they solaced each other in reflections upon the holy works of Christ. ¹² Then said Thecla to Paul, If you be pleased with it, I will follow you whithersoever you go. ¹³ He replied to her, Persons are now much given to fornication, and you being handsome, I am afraid lest you should meet with greater temptation than the former, and should not withstand, but be overcome by it. ¹⁴ Thecla replied, Grant me only the seal of Christ, and no temptation shall affect me. ¹⁵ Paul answered, Thecla, wait with patience, and you shall receive the gift of Christ.

7

1 Paul and Thecla go to Antioch. 2 Alexander, a magistrate, falls in love with Thecla: kisses her by force: 5 she resists him: 6 is carried before the governor, and condemned to be thrown to wild beasts.

¹ THEN Paul sent back Onesiphorus and his family to their own home, and taking Thecla along with him, went for Antioch; ² And as soon as they came into the city, a certain Syrian, named Alexander, a magistrate, in the city, who had done many considerable services for the city during his magistracy, saw Thecla and fell in love with her, and endeavoured by many rich presents to engage Paul m his interest. ³ But Paul told him, I know not the woman of whom you speak, nor does she belong to me. ⁴ But he being a person of great power in Antioch, seized her in the street and kissed her; which Thecla would not bear, but looking about for Paul, cried out in a distressed loud tone, Force me not, who am a stranger; force me not, who am a servant of God; I am one of the principal persons of Iconium, and was obliged to leave that city because I would not be married to Thamyris. ⁵ Then she laid hold on Alexander, tore his coat, and took his crown off his head, and made him appear ridiculous before all the people. ⁶ But Alexander, partly as he loved her, and partly being ashamed of what had been done, led her to the governor, and upon her confession of what she had done,' he condemned her to be thrown among the beasts.

8

2 Thecla entertained by Trifina; 3 brought out to the wild beasts; a she-lion licks her feet. 5 Trifina upon a vision of her deceased daughter, adopts Thecla, 11 who is taken to the amphitheatre again.

¹ WHICH when the people saw, they said: The judgments passed in this city are unjust. But Thecla desired the favour of the governor, that her chastity might not be attacked, but preserved till she should be cast to the beasts. ² The governor then inquired, Who would entertain her; upon which a certain very rich widow, named Trifina, whose daughter was lately dead, desired that she might have the keeping of her; and she began to treat her in her house as her own daughter. ³ At length a day came, when the beasts were to be brought forth to be seen; and Thecla was brought to the amphitheatre, and put into a den in which was an exceeding fierce she-lion, in the presence of a multitude of spectators. ⁴ Trifina, without any surprise, accompanied Thecla, and the she-lion licked the feet of Thecla. The title written which denotes her crime, was, Sacrilege. Then the woman cried out, O God, the judgments of this city are unrighteous. ⁵ After the beasts had been shewn, Trifina took Thecla home with her, and they went to bed; and behold, the daughter of Trifina, who was dead, appeared to her mother, and said; Mother, let the young woman, Thecla, be reputed by you as your daughter in my stead; and desire her that she should pray for me, that I may be translated to a state of happiness. ⁶ Upon which Trifina, with a mournful air, said, My daughter Falconilla has appeared to me, and ordered me to receive you in her room; wherefore I desire, Thecla, that you would pray

for my daughter, that she may be translated into a state of happiness, and to life eternal. ⁷ When Thecla heard this, she immediately prayed to the Lord, and said: O Lord God of heaven and earth, Jesus Christ, thou Son of the Most High, grant that her daughter Falconilla may live forever. Trifina hearing this groaned again, and said: O unrighteous judgments! O unreasonable wickedness! That such a creature should (again) be cast to the beasts! ⁸ On the morrow, at break of day, Alexander came to Trifina's house, and said: The governor and the people are waiting; bring the criminal forth. ⁹ But Trifina ran in so violently upon him, that he was affrighted, and ran away. Trifina was one of the royal family; and she thus expressed her sorrow, and said; Alas! I have trouble in my house' nn two accounts, and there is no one who will relieve me, either under the loss of my daughter, or my being unable to save Thecla. But now, O Lord God, be thou the helper of Thecla thy servant. ¹⁰ While she was thus engaged, the governor sent one of his own officers to bring Thecla. Trifina took her by the hand, and, going with her, said: I went with Falconilla to her grave, and. Now must go with Thecla to the beasts. ¹¹ When Thecla heard this, she weeping prayed, and said: O Lord God, whom I have made my confidence and refuge, reward Trifina for her compassion to me, and preserving my chastity. ¹² Upon this there was a great noise in the amphitheatre; the beasts roared, and the people cried out, Bring in the criminal. ¹³ But the woman cried out, and said: Let the whole city suffer for such crimes; and order all of us, O governor, to the same punishment. O unjust judgment! O cruel sight! ¹⁴ Others said, Let the whole city be destroyed for this vile action. Kill us all, O governor. O cruel sight! O unrighteous judgment.

9

1 Thecla thrown naked to the wild beasts; 2 they all refuse to attack her; 8 throws herself into a pit of water. 10 other wild beasts refuse her. 11 Tied to wild bulls. 13 Miraculously saved. 15 Released. 24 Entertained by Trifina.

¹ THEN Thecla was taken out of the hand of Trifina, stripped naked, had a girdle put on, and thrown into the place appointed for fighting with the beasts: and the lions and the bears were let loose upon her. ² But a she-lion, which was of all the most fierce, ran to Thecla, and fell down at her feet. Upon which the multitude of women shouted aloud. ³ Then a she-bear ran fiercely towards her; but the she-lion met the bear, and tore it to pieces. ⁴ Again, a he-lion, who had been wont to devour men, and which belonged to Alexander, ran towards her; but the she-lion encountered the he-lion, and they killed each other. ⁵ Then the women were under a greater concern, because the she-lion, which had helped Thecla, was dead. ⁶ Afterwards they brought out many other wild beasts; but Thecla stood with her hands stretched towards heaven, and prayed; and when she had done praying, she turned about, and saw a pit of water, and said, Now it is a proper time for me to be baptized. ⁷ Accordingly she threw herself into the water, and said, In thy name, O my Lord Jesus Christ, I am this last day baptized. The women and the people seeing this, cried out, and said, Do not throw yourself into the water. And the governor himself cried out, to think that the fish (sea-calves) were like to devour so much beauty. ⁸ Notwithstanding all this, Thecla threw herself into the water, in the name of our Lord Jesus Christ. ⁹ But the fish (sea-calves,) when they saw the lighting and fire, were killed, and swam dead upon the surface of the water, and a cloud of fire surrounded Thecla, so that as the beasts could not come near her, so the people could not see her nakedness. ¹⁰ Yet they turned other wild beasts upon her; upon which they made a very mournful outcry; and some of them scattered spikenard, others cassia, others amomus (a sort of spikenard, or the herb of Jerusalem, or ladies-rose) others ointment; so that the quantity of ointment was large, in proportion to the number of people; and upon this all the beasts lay as though they had been fast asleep, and did not touch Thecla. ¹¹ Whereupon Alexander said to the Governor, I have some very terrible bulls; let us bind her to them. To which the governor, with concern, replied, You may do what you think fit. ¹² Then they put a cord round Thecla's waist, which bound also her feet, and with it tied her to the bulls, to whose privy-parts they applied red-hot irons, that so they being the more tormented, might more violently drag Thecla about, till they had killed her. ¹³ The bulls accordingly tore about, making a most hideous noise; but the flame which was about Thecla, burnt off the cords which were fastened to the members of the bulls, and she stood in the middle of the stage, as unconcerned as if she had not been bound. ¹⁴ But in the mean time Trifina, who sat upon one of the benches, fainted away and died; upon which the whole city was under a very great concern. ¹⁵ And Alexander himself was afraid, and desired the governor, saying: I entreat you, take compassion on me and the city, and release this woman, who has fought with the beasts; lest, both you and I, and the whole city be destroyed ¹⁶ For if Cæsar should have any account of what has passed now, he will certainly immediately destroy the city, because Trifina, a person of royal extract, and a relation of his, is dead upon her seat. ¹⁷ Upon this the governor called Thecla from among the beasts to him, and said to her, Who art thou? And what are thy circumstances, that not one of the beasts will touch thee? ¹⁸ Thecla replied to him; I am a servant of the living God; and as to my state, I am a believer on Jesus Christ his Son, in whom God is well pleased; and for that reason none of the beasts could touch me. ¹⁹ He alone is the way to eternal salvation, and the foundation of eternal life. He is a refuge to those who are in distress; a support to the afflicted, hope and defence to those who are hopeless; and, in a word, all those who do not believe on him, shall not live, but suffer eternal death. ²⁰ When the govern or heard these things, he ordered her clothes to be brought, and said to her put on your clothes. ²¹ Thecla replied: May that God who clothed me when I was naked among the beasts, in the day of judgment clothe your soul with the robe of salvation. Then she took her clothes, and put them on; and the governor immediately published an order in these words; I release to you Thecla the servant of God. ²² Upon which the women cried out together with a loud voice, and with one accord gave praise unto God, and said; There is but one God, who is the God of Thecla; the one God who delivered Thecla. ²³ So loud were their voices that the whole city seemed to be shaken; and Trifina herself heard the glad tidings, and arose again, and ran with the multitude to meet Thecla; and embracing her, said: Now I believe there shall be a resurrection of the dead; now I am persuaded that my daughter is alive. Come therefore home with me, my daughter Thecla, and I will make over all that I have to you. ²⁴ So Thecla went with Trifina, and was entertained there a few days, teaching her the word of the Lord, whereby many young women were converted; and there was great joy in the family of Trifina. ²⁵ But Thecla longed to see Paul, and inquired and sent everywhere to find him; and when at length she was informed that he was at Myra, in Lycia, she took with her many young men and women; and putting on a girdle, and dressing herself in the habit of a man, she went to him to Myra in Lycia, and there found Paul preaching the word of God; and she stood by him among the throng.

10

1 Thecla visits Paul. 8 Visits Onesiphorus. 8 Visits her mother. 9 Who repulses her. 12 Is tempted by the devil. Works miracles.

¹ BUT it was no small surprise to Paul when he saw her and the people with her; for he imagined some fresh trial was coining upon them; ² Which when Thecla perceived, she said to him: I have been baptized, O Paul; for he who assists you in preaching, has assisted me to baptize. ³ Then Paul took her, and led her to the house of Hermes; and Thecla related to Paul all that had befallen her in Antioch, insomuch that Paul exceedingly wondered, and all who heard were confirmed in the faith, and prayed for Trifina's happiness. ⁴ Then Thecla arose, and said to Paul, I am going to Iconium. Paul replied to her: Go, and teach the word of the Lord. ⁵ But Trifina had sent large sums of money to Paul, and also clothing by the hands of Thecla, for the relief of the poor. ⁶ So Thecla went to Iconium. And when she came to the house of Onesiphorus, she fell down upon the floor where Paul had sat and preached, and, mixing tears with her prayers, she praised and glorified God in the following words: ⁷ O Lord the God of this house, in which I was first enlightened by thee; O Jesus, son of the living God, who wast my helper before the governor, my helper in the fire, and my helper among the beasts; thou alone art God forever and ever. Amen. ⁸ Thecla now (on her return) found Thamyris dead, but her mother living. So calling her mother, she said to her: Theoclia, my mother, is it possible for you to be brought to a belief, that there is but one Lord God, who dwells in the heavens? If you desire great riches, God will give them to you by me; if you want your daughter again, here I am. ⁹ These and many other things she represented to her mother, (endeavouring) to persuade her (to her own opinion). But her mother Theoclia gave no credit to the things which were said by the martyr Thecla. ¹⁰ So that Thecla perceiving she discoursed to no purpose, signing her whole body with the sign (of the cross), left the house and went to Daphine; and when she came there, she went to the cave, where she had found Paul with Onesiphorus, and fell down on the ground; and wept before God. ¹¹ When she departed thence, she went to Seleucia, and enlightened many in the knowledge of Christ. ¹² And a bright cloud conducted her in her journey. ¹³ And after she had arrived at Seleucia she went to a place out of the city, about the distance of a furlong, being afraid of the inhabitants, because they were worshippers of idols. ¹⁴ And she was led (by the cloud) into a mountain called Calamon, or Rodeon. There she abode many years, and underwent a great many grievous temptations of the devil, which she bore in a becoming manner, by the assistance which she had from Christ. ¹⁵ At length certain gentlewomen hearing of the virgin Thecla, went to her, and were instructed by her in the oracles of God, and many of them abandoned this world, and led a monastic life with her. ¹⁶ Hereby a good report was spread everywhere of Thecla, and she wrought several (miraculous) cures, so that all the city and adjacent countries brought their

sick to that mountain, and before they came as far as the door of the cave, they were instantly cured of whatsoever distemper they had. [17] The unclean spirits were cast out, making a noise; all received their sick made whole, and glorified God, who had bestowed such power on the virgin Thecla; [18] Insomuch that the physicians of Seleucia were now of no more account, and lost all the profit of their trade, because no one regarded them; upon which they were filled with envy, and began to contrive what methods to take with this servant of Christ.

11

1 Is attempted to be ravished, 12 escapes by a rock opening, 17 and closing miraculously.

[1] THE devil then suggested bad advice to their minds; and being on a certain day met together to consult, they reasoned among each other thus: The virgin is a priestess of the great goddess Diana, and whatsoever she requests from her, is granted, because she is a virgin, and so is beloved by all the gods. [2] Now then let us procure some rakish fellows, and after we have made them sufficiently drunk, and given them a good sum of money, let us order them to go and debauch this virgin, promising them, if they do it, a larger reward. [3] (For they thus concluded among themselves, that if they be able to debauch her, the gods will no more regard her, nor Diana cure the sick for her.) [4] They proceeded according to this resolution, and the fellows went to the mountain, and as fierce as lions to the cave, knocking at the door. [5] The holy martyr Thecla, relying upon the God in whom she believed, opened the door, although she was before apprized of their design, and said to them, Young men, what is your business? [6] They replied, Is there any one within, whose name is Thecla? She answered, What would you have with her? They said, We have a mind to lie with her. [7] The blessed Thecla answered: Though I am a mean old woman, I am the servant of my Lord Jesus Christ; and though you have a vile design against me, ye shall not be able to accomplish it. They replied: It is impossible but we must be able to do with you what we have a mind. [8] And while they were saying this, they laid hold on her by main force, and would have ravished her. Then she with the (greatest) mildness said to them: Young men have patience, and see the glory of the Lord. [9] And while they held her, she looked up to heaven and said; O God most reverend, to whom none can be likened; who makest thyself glorious over thine enemies; who didst deliver me from the fire, and didst not give me up to Thamyris, didst not give me up to Alexander; who deliveredst me from the wild beasts; who didst preserve me in the deep waters; who hast everywhere been my helper, and hast glorified thy name in me; [10] Now also deliver me from the hands of these wicked and unreasonable men, nor suffer them to debauch my chastity which I have hitherto preserved for thy honour; for I love thee and long for thee, and worship thee, O Father, Son, and Holy Ghost, for evermore. Amen. [11] Then came a voice from heaven, saying, Fear not, Thecla, my faithful servant, for I am with thee. Look and see the place which is opened for thee: there thy eternal abode shall be; there thou shalt receive the beatific vision. [12] The blessed Thecla observing, saw the rock opened to as large a degree as that a man might enter in; she did as she was commanded, bravely fled from the vile crew, and went into the rock, which instantly so closed, that there was not any crack visible where it had opened. [13] The men stood perfectly astonished at so prodigious a miracle, and had no power to detain the servant of God; but only, catching hold of her veil, or hood, they tore off a piece of it; [14] And even that was by the permission of God, for the confirmation of their faith who should come to see this venerable place, and to convey blessings to those in succeeding ages, who should believe on our Lord Jesus Christ from a pure heart. [15] Thus suffered that first martyr and apostle of God, and virgin, Thecla; who came from Iconium at eighteen years of age; afterwards, partly in journeys and travels, and partly in a monastic life in the cave, she lived seventy-two years; so that she was ninety years old when the Lord translated her. [16] Thus ends her life. [17] The day which is kept sacred to her memory, is the twenty-fourth of September, to the glory of the Father, and the Son, and the Holy Ghost, now and for evermore. Amen.

Tertullian On Specticals
1

[1] Learn, O you servants of God who are just now entering upon His service, and you who have already solemnly sworn allegiance to Him recall what principle of faith, what reason inherent in truth, what rule in our way of life forbid, along with the other errors of the world, also the pleasures of the spectacles, lest by ignorance or self-deception anyone fall into sin. [2] For so strong is the appeal of pleasure that it can bring about a prolongation of ignorance with a resulting facility for sin, or a perversion of conscience leading to self-deception. [3] In addition, some may perhaps be allured to either error by the opinions of the heathens who commonly use the following arguments against us in this matter: such comforting and merely external pleasures of the eyes and ears are not opposed to religion which is founded in man's mind and conscience; neither is God offended by a man's enjoying himself, nor is taking delight in such enjoyment in its proper time and place a sin as long as the fear of God and God's honor remain unimpaired. [4] But this is precisely what we intend to prove: that these things are not compatible with true religion and true obedience to the true God. [5] There are some who think that the Christians, a sort of people ever ready to die, are trained in that stubbornness of theirs that they more easily despise life, once its ties have been cut, as it were, and lose their craving for that which, as far as they themselves are concerned, they have already made empty of everything desirable; and thus it is considered a rule laid down by human design and forethought rather than by divine command. [6] It would, indeed, be loathsome for people continuing in the enjoyment of such delightful pleasures to die for God. On the other hand, if what they say were true, stubbornness in a rule of life so strict as ours might well submit to a plan so apt.

2

[1] Moreover, there is no one of our adversaries who will not offer this excuse, too: that all things have been created by God and handed over to man–just as we Christians teach–and that they are undoubtedly good, as coming from a good Creator; and among them we must count all the various components that make up the spectacles, the horse, for instance, and the lion, the strength of body and the sweetness of voice. [2] Accordingly, they say that a thing which exists by God's creation cannot be considered either foreign or opposed to God, nor must a thing which is not opposed to God, because it is not foreign to Him, be considered opposed to God's worshipers. [3] Obviously, they continue, the very structures of the places–the squared stones, unhewn stones, marble slabs and columns–also are all the handiwork of God who gave them to furnish the earth; indeed, the performances themselves take place under God's heaven. How clever in adducing proofs does human ignorance think itself, especially when it is afraid of losing some of these delights and enjoyments of the world! [4] Accordingly, you will find more people turned away from our religion by the danger to their pleasures than by the danger to their lives. For of death even a fool is not particularly afraid, feeling that it is a debt he owes to nature; but pleasure, inasmuch as it is born with man, even a sage does not despise, since both fool and sage have no other gratification in life but pleasure. [5] No one denies– because everyone knows what nature of its own accord tells us–that God is the Creator of the universe, and that this universe is good and has been made over to man by its Creator. [6] But because they have no real knowledge of God–knowing Him only by natural law and not by right of friendship, knowing Him only from afar and not from intimate association–it is inevitable that they prove ignorant of His commands regarding the use of His creation. Likewise, must they be unaware of the rival power that by its hostile actions seeks to pervert to wrong uses the things of divine creation. For with such defective knowledge of God one cannot know either His will or His adversary. [7] We must, then, consider not only by whom all things were created, but also by whom they were perverted. For in this way it will become clear for what use they were created, once it is evident for what use they were not. [8] The state of corruption differs vastly from that of innocence, because there is an enormous difference between the Creator and the perverter. Why, every form of evil-doing–misdeeds which also the heathens forbid and punish as such–comes from things created by God. [9] You see murder committed by iron dagger, poison, or magic incantation: but iron, poisonous herbs, demons are all equally creatures of God. Yet, did the Creator design those creatures of His for man's destruction? Certainly not. He forbids man-slaying by the one summary commandment: 'Thou shalt not kill.' [10] In like manner, gold, brass, silver, ivory, wood, and any other material used in the manufacture of idols–who has brought them into the world if, not God, the Maker of the world? Yet, has He done this that they may be made into objects of worship set up in opposition to Himself? Certainly not. For the most grievous sin in His eyes is idolatry. What is there that offends God

and is not His own? But, when it offends God, it has ceased to be His; and when it has ceased to be His, it offends Him. ¹¹ Man himself, the perpetrator of every kind of villainy, is not only the work of God, but also His likeness–yet, both in body and spirit he has fallen away from his Creator. For we did not receive the eyes for gratifying carnal appetite, the tongue for speaking evil, the ears for listening to slander, the gullet for indulging in the sin of gluttony, the belly to be the gullet's partner, the organs of sex for immodest excesses, the hands for committing acts of violence, and the feet to lead a roving life; nor was the spirit implanted in the body that it might become a workshop for contriving acts of treachery and fraud and injustice. I think not. ¹² For if God, who demands innocence of us, hates all wickedness, even if it be only in thought, then it is certain beyond all doubt that it was never His intention in creation that whatever He created should lead to acts He condemns, even if those acts are done through the medium of His handiwork. The whole reason for condemnation is, rather, the misuse of God's creation by God's creatures. ¹³ We, therefore, in coming to know the Lord, have also looked upon His rival, and in learning the Creator, we have likewise detected the perverter; we ought, then, to feel neither surprise nor doubt. For man himself, God's handiwork and image, the lord of the whole universe, was hurled down in the very beginning from his state of innocence by the power of that angel, perverter of God's creation and His rival; at the same time, that same perverter corrupted along with man the whole material world, man's possession, created like man for innocence, and turned it against the Creator. And in his anger that God had given it to man and not to him he intended to make man in this very possession guilty before God as well as establish his own power in it.

3

¹ Armed with this knowledge against heathen opinion, let us now turn, instead, to the same excuses put forward by people in our own ranks. For there are some brethren who, being either too naive or overparticular in their faith, demand a testimony from holy Scripture, when faced with giving up the spectacles, and declare the matter an open question, because such a renunciation is neither specifically nor in so many words enjoined upon the servants of God. ² Now, to be sure, nowhere do we find it laid down with the same precision as 'Thou shalt not kill,' 'Thou shalt not worship an idol,' 'Thou shalt not commit adultery,' 'Thou shalt not commit fraud'–nowhere do we find it thus clearly declared: 'Thou shalt not go to the circus,' 'Thou shalt not go to the theater,' 'Thou shalt not watch a contest or show of gladiators.' ³ But we do find that to this special case there can be applied that first verse of David, where he says: 'Happy is the man who has not gone to the gathering of the ungodly, nor stood in the ways of sinners, nor sat in the chair of pestilence.' ⁴ For, even though David seems to have praised that well-known just man, because he took no part in the gathering and meeting of the Jews deliberating on the killing of the Lord, divine Scripture admits always a broader interpretation wherever a passage, after its actual sense has been exhausted, serves to strengthen discipline. So, in this case, too, the verse of David is not inapplicable to the prohibition of spectacles. ⁵ For, if then he called a mere handful of Jews 'a gathering of the ungodly,' how much more such a vast crowd of heathen people? Are the heathens less ungodly, less sinners, less the enemies of Christ that the Jews were then? ⁶ Moreover, the other details also fit in well. For at the spectacles there is both sitting 'in the chair' (in cathedra) and standing 'in the way' (in via). For 'ways' (viae) they term both the gangways that run round the girding walls and the aisles that slope down the incline and divide the seats of the populace; in like manner is the very place for chairs in the curving gallery called 'chair' (cathedra). ⁷ And so, to take the converse of the verse of David, 'he is unhappy who has gone to any gathering whatsoever of the ungodly, stood in any way at all of sinners, and sat in any chair of pestilence.' Let us take, then, the general application, even when, besides the general, a special interpretation is conceded. For some things that are said with special intent have also a general meaning. ⁸ When God reminds the Israelites of discipline and upbraids them, His words apply undoubtedly to all men; and when He threatens destruction to Egypt and Ethiopia, He certainly cautions every sinful nation against judgment to come. Thus, if we reason from a special case to the general type that every sinful nation is an Egypt and Ethiopia, in the same manner we reason from the general class to a special case that every spectacle is a gathering of the ungodly.

4

¹ Lest anyone think that I am avoiding the point in question, I shall now appeal to the prime and principal authority of our 'seal' itself. When we step into the water and profess the Christian faith in the terms prescribed by its law, we bear public witness that we have renounced the Devil and his pomp and his angels. ² What, however, shall we call the chief and foremost manifestation by which the Devil and his pomp and his angels are recognized, if not idolatry? From this source, in a few words–because I will not dwell any longer on this subject–comes every unclean and evil spirit. ³ So, if it shall be proved true that the entire apparatus of the spectacles originates from idolatry, we will have reached a decision in advance that our profession of faith in baptism refers also to the spectacles, since they belong to the Devil and his pomp and his angels because of the idolatry involved. ⁴ We shall, therefore, set forth the origins of the various spectacles, explaining in what nurseries they grew up; next in order, the titles of some of them, that is, the names by which they are called; then their equipment and the superstitions observed in them; thereafter the places and the presiding spirits to whom they are dedicated; and finally the arts employed in them and the authors to whom they are ascribed. If, among these, we find anything that is not related to an idol, we shall declare it to be free from the stain of idolatry and, as a result, to have no connection with our renunciation.

5

¹ Concerning the origins of the spectacles, which are somewhat obscure and, therefore, unknown among most of our people, we had to make a rather thorough investigation, our authority being none other than the works of pagan literature. ² There are many authors who have published treatises on the subject. They give the following report on the origin of the games. The Lydians migrated from Asia and settled in Etruria, according to the account of Timaeus, under the leadership of Tyrrhenus, who, in the struggle for the kingship, had succumbed to his brother. In Etruria, then, they also introduced, along with their other superstitious customs, the spectacles in the name of religion. From that place, in turn, the Romans invited the performers, borrowing also the name, so that the 'performers' (ludii) were so called from the 'Lydians' (Lydii). ³ And though Varro derives "ludii" from "ludus," that is, from "lusus" ('the play'), as they used to call also the Luperci "ludii," because, as "ludendo" ('in play') indicates, they ran to and fro, this play of the youths belongs in his view to festal days, temples, and religious ceremonies. ⁴ But it is, after all, not the name that matters; the real issue is idolatry. For, since the games also went under the general name of Liberalia, they clearly proclaimed the honor of Father Liber. They were first held in honor of Liber by the country folk because of the blessing which they say he bestowed upon them by making known to them the delicious taste of wine. ⁵ Then came the games called Consualia, which originally were celebrated in honor of Neptune, because he is also called Consus. After that, Romulus consecrated the Ecurria, derived from "equi" (horses), to Mars, though they claim the Consualia as well for Romulus on the ground that he consecrated them to Consus, the god, as they will have it, of counsel, to wit, of that very counsel by which he arrived at the scheme of carrying off the Sabine girls to be wives for his soldiers. ⁶ A noble counsel, indeed, even now considered just and lawful among the Romans themselves, not to say in the eyes of a god! For, also, this tends to stain their origin, lest you think something good that, had its origin in evil, in shamelessness, violence and hatred, in a founder who was a fratricide and the son of Mars. ⁷ Even now, at the first goal posts in the Circus, there is an underground altar dedicated to that Consus with an inscription that reads as follows: CONSUS MIGHTY IN COUNSEL, MARS IN WAR, THE LARES AT THE CROSSROAD. Sacrifice in offered on this altar on the seventh day of July by the priests of the state, and on the twenty-first of August by the Flamen of Quirinus and the Vestal Virgins. ⁸ On a later date, the same Romulus instituted games in honor of Jupiter Feretrius at the Tarpeian Rock, which, according to the tradition handed down by Piso, were called Tarpeian and Capitoline Games. After him, Numa Pompilius initiated games in honor of Mars and Robigo–for they invented also a goddess of "robigo" (mildew). Later still came Tullus Hostilius, then Ancus Martius and, in their order, the other founders of games. As to the idols in whose honor they instituted these games, information is found in Tranquillus Suetonius or in his sources. But this will suffice to prove the guilty origin of the games in idolatry.

6

¹ The testimony of antiquity is confirmed by that of the succeeding generations. For the titles by which the games still go today betray the nature of their origin. In these titles there is clearly expressed for what idol and for what superstition of one kind or other they were designed. For instance, the games of the Great Mother and Apollo, and also those of Ceres, Neptune, Jupiter Latiaris, and Flora are general festivals; the remaining trace their superstitious origin back to birthdays and commemorative celebrations of the emperors, to happy political events, and municipal feasts. ² Among them are also the funeral games, established by bequests to render honor to the memory of private persons. This, too, is in accordance with ancient custom. For from the very beginning two kinds of games were distinguished: sacred and funereal; that is, games in honor of pagan deities and those in honor of dead persons. ³ But in the question of

idolatry, it makes no difference to us under what name and title they are exhibited, as long as the matter concerns the same spirits that we renounce. Whether they exhibit these games in honor of their dead or in honor of their gods, they render the very same honor to their dead as to their gods. On either side you have one and the same situation: it is one and the same idolatry on their part, and one and the same renunciation of idolatry on our part.

7

[1] Both kinds of games, then, have a common origin; common, too, are their names, inasmuch as the reasons for their being held are the same. Therefore, also, their equipment must be the same because of the common guilt of idolatry which founded them. [2] Somewhat greater pomp, however, is displayed in the spectacles in the circus to which the term is properly applied. The "pompa"'procession'–which comes first, proves in itself to whom it belongs, with the long line of idols, the unbroken train of images, the cars and chariots and conveyances for carrying them, the portable thrones and garlands and the attributes of the gods. [3] Moreover, how many sacred rites are observed, how many sacrifices offered at the beginning, in the course, and at the end of the procession, how many religious corporations, furthermore, how many priesthoods, how many bodies of magistrates are called upon to march in it–each is known to the inhabitants of that city where all the demons have gathered and taken up their abode. [4] And if in the provinces less care is given to management of the games because of less ample funds, all the spectacles in the circus everywhere must be considered as belonging to the model from which they are copied, and are contaminated by the source from which they are drawn. For also, the small brook from its spring, and the tiny shoot from its stem, contain in them the nature of their origin. [5] Let splendor and frugality look to it where they come from. The pomp of the circus, whatever its nature, offends God. Even if there be carried but a few idols in procession, it takes only one to have idolatry; even if there be driven but one chariot, it is Jupiter's car; every kind of idolatry, even one meanly or moderately equipped, is still rich and splendid because of its sinful origin.

8

[1] In accordance with my plan, I shall deal next with the places. The circus is primarily consecrated to the Sun. His temple stands in the middle of it, and his image shines forth from the pediment of the temple. For they did not think it proper to worship beneath a roof a god whom they see above them in the open. [2] Those who maintain that the first circus show was exhibited by Circe in honor of the Sun, her father, as they will have it, conclude also that the name is derived from her. Plainly, the sorceress undoubtedly transacted the business in behalf of those whose priestess she was, namely, the demons and evil spirits. How many evidences of idol worship do you recognize accordingly in the decoration of the place? [3] Every ornament of the circus is a temple by itself. The eggs are regarded as sacred to Castor and Pollux by people who do not feel ashamed to believe the story of their origin from the egg made fertile by the swan, Jupiter. The dolphins spout water in honor of Neptune; the columns bear aloft images of Seia, so called from "sementatio" ('sowing'); of Messia, so called as deity of "messis" ('reaping'); and of Tutulina, so called as 'tutelary spirit' of the crops. [4] In front of these are seen three altars for the triple gods: the Great, the Potent, the Prevailing. They think these deities are Samothracean. The huge obelisk, as Hermateles maintains, has been set up in honor of the Sun. Its inscription which, like its origin, is Egyptian, contains a superstition. The gathering of the demons would be dull without their Great Mother, so she presides there over the ditch. [5] Consus, as we have mentioned, keeps in hiding underground at the Murcian Goals. The latter are also the work of an idol. For Murcia, as they will have it, is a goddess of love to whom they have dedicated a temple in that part (of the valley). [6] Take note, O Christian, how many unclean deities have taken possession of the circus. You have nothing to do with a place which so many diabolic spirits have made their own. Speaking of places, this is the appropriate occasion for throwing more light on the subject in order to anticipate a question that some may raise. [7] What will happen, you say, if I enter the circus at some other time? Shall I be then, too, in danger of contamination? There is no law laid down with regard to places as such. For not only these places where people gather for the spectacles but also the temples may be entered by the servant of God without peril to his rule of life, provided that he do so for an urgent and honest reason which has no connection with the business and function proper of the place. [8] Moreover, there is no place–whether streets or marketplace or baths or taverns or even our own homes–that is completely free of idols: Satan and his angels have filled the whole world. [9] Yet, it is not by our being in the world that we fall away from God, but by taking part in some sins of the world. Therefore, if I enter the temple of Jupiter on the Capitol or that of Serapis as a sacrificer or worshiper, I shall fall away from God, just as I do if I enter the circus theater as a spectator. It is not the places in themselves the defile us, but the things done in them, by which the places themselves, as we have contended, are defiled; it is by defiled that we are defiled. [10] It is for this reason that we remind you who those to whom places of this kind are dedicated to prove what takes place in them is the work of those to whom very places are sacred.

9

[1] Next let us consider the arts displayed in the circus games. In times past, equestrian skill was simply a matter riding on horseback, and certainly no guilt was involved the ordinary use of the horse. But when this skill was pressed into the service of the games, it was changed from a gift God into an instrument of the demons. [2] Accordingly, t kind of exhibition is regarded as sacred to Castor and Pollux to whom horses were allotted by Mercury, as Stesichorus tells us. Also, Neptune is an equestrian deity, since the Greeks call him "Hippios" ('Lord of Steeds'). [3] Moreover, concerning the chariot, the four-horse team was consecrated to the Sun; the two-horse team, to the Moon. But we also read: "Erichthonius first dared to yoke four steeds to the car And to ride upon its wheels with victorious swiftness." This Erichthonius, a son of Minerva and Vulcan, fruit of lust, in truth, that fell to earth, is a demon-monster, or, rather, the Devil himself, not a mere snake. [4] If, however, the Argive Trochilus is the inventor of the chariot, he dedicated this work of his in the first place to Juno. And if, at Rome, Romulus was the first to display a four-horse chariot, he, too, in my view, has been enrolled among the idols himself, provided that he is identical with Quirinus. [5] The chariots having been produced by such inventors, it was only fitting that they clad their drivers in the colors of idolatry. For at first there were only two colors: white and red. White was sacred to Winter because of the whiteness of its snow; red, to Summer because of the redness of its sun. But afterwards, when both love of pleasure and superstition had grown apace, some dedicated the red to Mars, others the white to the Zephyrs, the green to Mother Earth or Spring, the blue to Sky and Sea or Autumn. [6] Since, however, every kind of idolatry is condemned by God, this condemnation certainly applies also to that kind which is impiously offered to the elements of nature.

10

[2] Let us pass on to the exhibitions on the stage. We have already shown that they have a common origin with those in the circus, that they bear identical titles, inasmuch as they were called "ludi" ('games') and were exhibited together with equestrian displays. [3] The pageantry is likewise the same, inasmuch as a procession is held to the theater from the temples and altars, with that whole wretched business of incense and blood, to the tune of flutes and trumpets, under the direction of the two most polluted masters of ceremonies at funerals and sacrifices: the undertaker and soothsayer. [4] And so, as we passed from the origins of the games to the spectacles in the circus, now we will turn to the performances on the stage. Because of the evil character of the place, the theater is, strictly speaking, a shrine of Venus. It was in that capacity, after all, that this type of structure gained influence in the world. [5] For many a time the censors would tear down theaters at the very moment they began to rise. In their solicitude for public morals, they foresaw, no doubt, the great danger arising from the theater's lasciviousness. In this occurrence already, then, the heathens have their own opinion coinciding with ours as evidence, and we have the foreboding situation of a merely human code of morality giving additional strength to our way of life. [6] So, when Pompey the Great, a man who was surpassed only by his theater in greatness, had erected that citadel of all vile practices, he was afraid that some day the censors would condemn his memory. He therefore built on top of it a shrine of Venus, and when he summoned the people by edict to its dedication, he termed it not a theater, but a temple of Venus, 'under which,' he said, 'we have put tiers of seats for viewing the shows.' [7] In this way he misrepresented the character of a building, condemned and worthy of condemnation, with a temple's name, and employed superstition to make sport of morality. Venus and Liber (Bacchus), however, are close companions. The two demons of lust and drunkenness have banded together in sworn confederacy. [8] Therefore, the temple of Venus is also the house of Liber. For they appropriately gave the name of Liberalia also to other stage performances which, besides being dedicated to Liber (and called Dionysia among the Greeks), were also instituted by him. [9] And, quite obviously, the arts of the stage are under the patronage of Liber and Venus. Those features which are peculiar to, and characteristic of, the stage, that wantonness in gesture and posture, they dedicate to Venus and Liber, deities both dissolute: the former by sex perversion, the latter by effeminate dress. [10] And all else that is performed with voice and melodies, instruments and script, belongs to the Apollos and the Muses, the Minervas and Mercuries. You will hate, O Christian, the things whose authors you cannot help but hate. [11] At this point we intend to

make a few remarks concerning the arts and things whose authors we utterly detest in their very names. We know that the names of dead men are nothing, even as their images are nothing. But we are not unaware of the identity of those who are at work behind those displayed names and images, who exult in the homage paid to them and pretend to be divine, namely, the evil spirits, the demons. [12] We see then, also, that the arts are consecrated to the honor of those who appropriate the names of the inventors of those arts, and that they are not free from the taint of idolatry when their inventors for that very reason are considered gods. [13] Even more, as far as the arts are concerned, we ought to have gone further back and take exception to all further arguments, on the ground that the demons, from the very beginning looking out for themselves contrived, along with the other foul practices of idolatry, also those of the shows in order to turn man from the Lord and bind him to their glorification, and gave inspiration to men of genius in these particular arts. [14] For no one else but the demons would have contrived what was going to redound to their advantage, nor would they have produced the arts at that time through the agency of anyone except those very men in whose names and images and fables they accomplished the fraud of consecration which would work out to their advantage. To follow our plan, let us now begin the treatment of the contests (agones).

11

[1] Their origin is akin to that of the games. As a result, they, too, are instituted either as sacred or as funereal, and are performed in honor either of the gods of the Gentiles or of the dead. Accordingly, you have such titles as the Olympian contests in honor of Jupiter (these are called the Capitoline at Rome), the Nemean in honor of Hercules, the Isthmian in honor of Neptune; the rest are various contests to honor the dead. [2] What wonder is it, then, if the whole paraphernalia of these contests are tainted with idolatry–with unholy crowns, priestly superintendents, assistants from the sacred colleges, and last, but not least, with the blood of bulls? [3] To add a supplementary remark concerning the place: as you may expect from a place where the arts of the Muses, of Minerva, of Apollo, and even of Mars meet in common, with contest and sound of trumpet they endeavor to equal the circus in the stadium, which is no doubt a temple, too–I mean of the very idol whose festival is celebrated there. The gymnastic arts also had their origin in the teaching of the Castors and Herculeses and Mercuries.

12

[1] It still remains to examine the most prominent an most popular spectacle of all. It is called "munus" ('a obligatory service') from being an "officium" ('a duty'). For "munus" and "officium" are synonyms. The ancients thought they were performing a duty to the dead by this sort of spectacle e after they had tempered its character by a more refined form of cruelty. [2] For in time long past, in accordance with the belief that the souls of the-dead are propitiated by human blood, they used to purchase captives or slaves of inferior ability and to sacrifice them at funerals. [3] Afterwards, they preferred to disguise this ungodly usage by making it a pleasure. So, after the persons thus procured had been trained–for the sole purpose of learning how to be killed!– in the use of such arms as they then had and as best as they could wield, they then exposed them to death at the tombs on the day appointed for sacrifices in honor of the dead. Thus they found consolation for death in murder. [4] Such is the origin of the gladiatorial contest. But gradually their refinement progressed in the same proportion as their cruelty. For the pleasure of these beasts in human shape was not satisfied unless human bodies were torn to pieces also by wild beasts. What was then a sacrifice offered for the appeasement of the dead was no doubt considered a rite in honor of the dead. This sort of thing is, therefore, idolatry, because idolatry, too, is a kind of rite in honor of the dead: the one and the other is a service rendered to dead persons. [5] It is, furthermore, in the images of the dead that the demons have their abode. To come to the consideration of the titles also: though this type of exhibition has been changed from being an act in honor of the dead to being one in honor of the living–I mean those entering upon quaestorships, magistracies, flaminates, and priesthoods– still, since the guilt of idolatry cleaves the dignity of the title, whatever is carried out in the name this dignity shares necessarily in the taint of its origin. In the same way we must interpret the paraphernal which are considered as belonging to the ceremonies of the very offices. For the purple robes, the fasces, the fillets, and crowns–finally, also, the announcements made in meeting and on posters, and the pottage dinners given on the eve of exhibitions–do not lack the pomp of the Devil and the invocation of demons. [6] In conclusion, what shall I say about that horrible place which not even perjurers can bear? For the amphitheater is consecrated to names more numerous and more dreadful than the Capitol, temple of all demons as it is. There, as many unclean spirits have their abode as the place can seat men. And to say a final word about the arts concerned, we know that Mars and Diana are the patrons of both types of games.

13

[1] I have, I think, adequately carried out my plan by showing in how many and in what ways the spectacles involve idolatry. I discussed their origins, their names, their equipment, their locations, and their arts–all that we may be certain that the spectacles in no way become us who twice renounce idols. [2] 'Not that an idol is anything,' as the Apostle says, 'but because what they do, they do in honor of demons' who take up their abode there at the consecration of idols, whether of the dead, or, as they think, of gods. [3] It is for this reason, therefore, since both kinds of idols belong to one and the same category (the dead and the gods being the same thing) that we refrain from both types of idolatry. [4] Temples and tombs, we detest both equally; we know neither kind of altar, we adore neither kind of image, we offer no sacrifice, we celebrate no funeral rites. Nor do we eat of what is sacrificed, or offered at funeral rites, because 'we cannot share the Lord's supper and the supper of demons.' [5] If we keep, then, our palate and stomach free from defilement, how much more should we guard our nobler organs, our ears and eyes, from pleasures connected with sacrifices to idols and sacrificers to the dead–pleasures which do not pass through the bowels, but are digested in the very spirit and so with whose purity God is more concerned than with that of the bowels.

14

[1] Having established the charge of idolatry, which itself should be reason enough for our giving up the spectacles, let us now treat the matter fully from another point of view, chiefly for the benefit of those who delude themselves with the thought that such abstention is not expressly enjoined. [2] The latter excuse sounds as if judgment enough were not pronounced on spectacles, when the lusts of the world are condemned. For, just as there is a lust for money, a lust for high station in life, for gluttony, for sensual gratification, for fame, so there is a lust for pleasure. The spectacles, however are a sort of pleasure. [3] In my opinion, under the general heading of lust, there are also included pleasures; similarly, under the general idea of pleasures, spectacles are treated as a special class.

15

[1] Dealing with the matter of the places, we have already mentioned above that they do not contaminate us of themselves, but on account of what is done in them, that is, once these places have imbibed contamination by such actions, they spit it out again to the same degree on others. So much, then, as we have said, for the main charge: idolatry. Now let us also point out that the other characteristics of the things which are going on at the spectacles are all opposed to God. [2] God has given us the command both to deal with the Holy Spirit in tranquillity, gentleness, quiet, and peace, inasmuch as, in accordance with the goodness of His nature, He is tender and sensitive, and also not to vex Him by frenzy, bitterness of feeling, anger, and grief. [3] How, then, can the Holy Spirit have anything to do with spectacles? There is no spectacle without violent agitation of the soul. For, where you have pleasure, there also is desire which gives pleasure its savor; where you have desire, there is rivalry which gives desire its savor. [4] And where, in turn, you have rivalry, there also are frenzy and bitterness of feeling and anger and grief and the other effects that spring from them, and, moreover, are incompatible with our moral discipline. [5] For, even if a man enjoys spectacles modestly and soberly, as befits his rank, age, and natural disposition, he cannot go to them without his mind being roused and his soul being stirred by some unspoken agitation. [6] No one ever approaches a pleasure such as this without passion; no one experiences this passion without its damaging effects. These very effects are incitements to passion. On the other hand, if the passion ceases, there is no pleasure, and he who goes where he gains nothing is convicted of foolishness. [7] But I think that foolishness also is foreign to us. Is it, further, not true that a man really condemns himself when he has taken his place among those whose company he does not want and whom, at any rate, he confesses to detest? [8] It is not enough to refrain from such acts, unless we also shun those who commit them. 'If thou didst see a thief,' says holy Scripture, 'thou didst run with him.' Would that we did not live in the world with them! Still, we are separated from them in the things of the world. For the world is God's, but the things of the world are the Devil's.

16

[1] Since, then, frenzy is forbidden us, we are debarred from every type of spectacle, including the circus, where frenzy rules supreme. Look at the populace, frenzied even as it comes to the show, already in violent commotion, blind, wildly excited over its wagers. [2] The praetor is too slow for them; all the time their eyes are rolling as though in rhythm with the lots he shakes up in his urn. Then they await the signal with bated breath; one outcry voices the common madness. Recognize the madness from their

foolish behavior. 'He has thrown it!' they shout; everyone tells everybody else what all of them have seen just that moment. This I take as a proof of their blindness: they do not see what has been thrown–a signal cloth, they think–but it is the symbol of the Devil hurled headlong from on high. ³ Accordingly, from such beginnings the affair progresses to outbursts of fury and passion and discord and to everything forbidden to the priests of peace. Next come curses, insults without any justified reason for the hatred, and rounds of applause without the reward of affection. What are the partakers in all this –no longer their own masters–likely to achieve for themselves? At best, the loss of their self-control. They are saddened by another's bad luck; they rejoice in another's success. What they hope for and what they dread has nothing to do with themselves, and so their affection is to no purpose and their hatred is unjust. ⁴ Or are we, perhaps, permitted love without cause any more than to hate without cause? God who bids us to love our enemies certainly forbids us to hate even with cause; God who commands us to bless those who curse us does not permit us to curse even with cause. ⁵ But what is more merciless than the circus, where they do not even spare their rulers or their fellow citizens? If any of these frenzies of the circus become the faithful elsewhere, then it will be lawful also in the circus; but, if nowhere, then neither in the circus.

17

¹ In like manner we are commanded to steer clear of every kind of impurity. By this command, therefore, we are precluded also from the theater, which is impurity's own peculiar home, where nothing wins approval but what elsewhere finds approval. ² And so, the theater's greatest charm is above all produced by its filth–filth which the actor of the Atellan farces conveys by gestures; filth which the mimic actor even exhibits by womanish apparel, banishing all reverence for sex and sense of shame so that they blush more readily at home than on the stage; filth, finally, which the pantomime experiences in his own body from boyhood in order to become an artist. ³ Even the very prostitutes, the victims of public lust, are brought upon the stage, creatures feeling yet more wretched in the presence of women, the only members in the community who were unaware of their existence; now they are exhibited in public before the eyes of persons of every age and rank; their address, their price, their record are publicly announced, even to those who do not need the information, and (to say nothing of the rest) things which ought to remain hidden in the darkness of their dens so as not to contaminate the daylight. ⁴ Let the senate blush, let all the orders blush, let even those very women who have committed murder on their own shame blush once a year when, by their own gestures, they betray their fear of the light of the day and the gaze of the people. ⁵ Now, if we must detest every kind of impurity, why should we be allowed to hear what we are not allowed to speak, when we know that vile jocularity and every idle word are judged by God? Why, in like manner, should we be permitted to see that which is sinful to do? Why should things which, spoken by the mouth, defile a man not be regarded as defiling a man when allowed access by the ears and eyes, since the ears and eyes are the servants of the spirit, and he whose servants are filthy cannot claim to be clean himself? ⁶ You have, therefore, the theater prohibited in the prohibition of uncleanness. Again, if we reject the learning of the world's literature as convicted of foolishness before God, we have a sufficiently clear rule also concerning those types of spectacles which, in profane literature, are classified as belonging to the comic or tragic stage. ⁷ Now, if tragedies and comedies are bloody and wanton, impious and prodigal inventors of outrage and lust, the recounting of what is atrocious or base is no better; neither is what is objectionable in deed acceptable in word.

18

¹ Now, if you maintain that the stadium is mentioned in the Scriptures, I will admit at once that you have a point. But as for what is done in the stadium, you cannot deny that it is unfit for you to see–punches and kicks and blows and all the reckless use of the fist and every disfiguration of the human face, that is, of God's image. ² Never can you approve the foolish racing and throwing feats and the more foolish jumping contests ; never can you be pleased with either harmful or foolish exhibitions of strength nor with the cultivation of an unnatural body, outdoing the craftsmanship of God; you will hate men bred to amuse the idleness of Greece. ³ Also, the art of wrestling belongs to the Devil's trade: it was the Devil who first crushed men. The very movements of the wrestler have a snakelike quality: the grip that takes hold of the opponent, the twist that binds him, the sleekness with which he slips away from him. Crowns are of no use to you; why do you seek pleasure from crowns?

19

¹ Are we now to wait for a scriptural repudiation of the amphitheater, also? If we can claim that cruelty, impiety, and brutality are permitted us, let us by all means go to the amphi-theater. If we are what people say we are, let us take delight in human blood. ² It is a good thing when the guilty are punished. Who will deny this but the guilty? Yet it is not becoming for the guiltless to take pleasure in the punishment of another; rather, it befits the guiltless to grieve that a man like himself, has become so guilty that he is treated with such cruelty. ³ And who is my voucher that it is the guilty always who are condemned to the beasts, or whatever punishment, and that it is never inflicted on innocence, too, through the vindictiveness of the judge or the weakness of the defense or the intensity of the torture? How much better it is, then, not to know when the wicked are punished, lest I come to know also when the good are destroyed, provided, of course, that there is savor of good in them. ⁴ Certain it is that innocent men are sold as gladiators to serve as victims of public pleasure. Even in the case of those who are condemned to the games, what a preposterous idea is it that, in atonement for a smaller offense, they should be driven to the extreme of murder! ⁵ This reply I have addressed to Gentiles. Heaven forbid that a Christian should need any further instruction about the detestableness of this kind of spectacle. No one, however, is able to describe all the details at full length except one who is still in the habit of going to the spectacles. I myself prefer to leave the picture incomplete rather than to recall it.

20

¹ How foolish, then–rather, how desperate–is the reasoning of those who, obviously as a subterfuge to avoid the loss of pleasure, plead as their excuse that no regulation concerning such an abstinence is laid down in Scripture, precise terms or in a definite passage, forbidding the servant of God to enter gatherings of this kind. ² Only recently heard a novel defense offered by one of these devotees of games. 'The sun,' he said, 'nay, even God Himself, looks from heaven and is not defiled.' Why, the sun also sends rays into the sewer and is not soiled! ³ Would that God looked on at no sins of men that we might all escape judgment! But He looks on at robberies, He looks on at falsehood and adulteries and frauds and acts of idolatry and at the very spectacles. And it is for that reason that we will not look at them, lest we be seen by Him who looks on at everything. ⁴ My man, you are putting the defendant on the same footing as the judge: the defendant who is a defendant because he is seen, and the judge who, because he sees, is judge. ⁵ Do we, perhaps, indulge in frenzy also outside the confines of the circus, outside the gates of the theater give free play to lewdness, outside the stadium to haughty deportment, outside the amphitheater to cruelty, just because God has eyes also outside the covered seats and the tiers and the stage? We are wrong: nowhere and never is there any exemption from what God condemns; nowhere and never is there any permission for what is forbidden always and everywhere. ⁶ It is the freedom from the change of opinion and from the mutability of judgment that constitutes the fullness of truth and–what is due to truth–perfect morality, unvarying reverence, and faithful obedience. What is intrinsically good or evil cannot be anything else.

21

¹ All things, we maintain, are firmly defined by the truth of God. The heathens who do not possess the fullness of truth, since their teacher of truth is not God, form their judgment of good and evil in accordance with their own opinion and inclination, making what is good in one place evil in another, and what is evil in one place good in another. ² Thus it happens that the same man who in public will scarcely raise the tunic to ease nature will put it off in the circus in such a way as to expose himself completely to the gaze of all; and the man who protects the ears of his maiden daughter from every foul word will take her himself to the theater to hear such words and see the gestures which accompany them. ³ The same man who tries to break up or denounces a quarrel in the streets which has come to fisticuffs will in the stadium applaud fights far more dangerous; and the same man who shudders at the sight of the body of a man who died in accordance with nature's law common to all will in the amphitheater look down with tolerant eyes upon bodies mangled, rent asunder, and smeared with their own blood. ⁴ What is more, the same man who allegedly comes to the spectacle to show his approval of the punishment for murder will have a reluctant gladiator driven on with lashes and with rods to commit murder; and the same man who wants every more notorious murderer to be cast before the lion will have the staff and cap of liberty granted as a reward to a savage gladiator, while he will demand that the other man who has been slain be dragged back to feast his eyes upon him, taking delight in scrutinizing close at hand the man he wished killed at a distance–and, if that was not his wish, so much more heartless he!

22

¹ What wonder! Such are the inconsistencies of men who confuse and confound the nature of good and evil through their fickleness of feeling and instability in judgment. ² Take the treatment the very providers and managers of the spectacles accord to those idolized charioteers, actors,

athletes, and gladiators, to whom men surrender their souls and women even their bodies, on whose account they commit the sins they censure: for the very same skill for which they glorify them, they debase and degrade them; worse, they publicly condemn them to dishonor and deprivation of civil rights, excluding them from the council chamber, the orator's platform, the senatorial and equestrian orders, from all other offices and certain distinctions. [3] What perversity! They love whom they penalize; they bring into disrepute whom they applaud; they extol the art and brand the artist with disgrace. [4] What sort of judgment is this–that a man should be vilified for the things that win him a reputation? Yes, what an admission that these things are evil, when their authors, at the very peak of their popularity, are marked with disgrace!

23

[1] Since, then, man reflecting on these matters, even over against the protest and appeal of pleasure, comes to the conclusion that these people should be deprived of the benefits of posts of honor and exiled to some island of infamy, how much more will divine justice inflict punishment on those who follow such professions? [2] Or will God take pleasure in the charioteer, the disturber of so many souls, the minister to many outbursts of frenzy, flaunting his rostral crown as a priest wears his wreath, dressed up in gay colors like a pimp, attired by the Devil as a ludicrous counterpart of Elias to be swept away in his chariot? [3] Will God be pleased with the man who alters his features with a razor, belying his own countenance and, not content with making it resemble that of Saturn or Isis or Liber, on top of that submits it to the indignity of being slapped, as if in mockery of the Lord's commandment? [4] The Devil, to be sure, also teaches that one should meekly offer his cheek to be struck. In the same way, he also makes the tragic actors taller by means of their high shoes, because 'no one can add a single cubit to his stature.' He wishes to make Christ a liar. [5] Again, I ask whether this whole business of masks is pleasing to God, who forbids the likeness of anything to be made–how much more of His own image? The Author of truth does not love anything deceitful; all that is counterfeit is a kind of adultery in His eyes. [6] Accordingly, He will not approve the man who feigns voice, sex, or age, or who pretends love, anger, groans, or tears, for He condemns all hypocrisy. Moreover, since in His law He brands the man as accursed who dresses in woman's clothes, what will be His judgment upon the pantomime who is trained to play the woman? [7] No doubt, also, the artist in punching will go unpunished. For those scars and wales, marks left by boxing gloves and blows, and those growths upon his ears he got from God when his body was being fashioned; God gave him eyes to have them blinded in fighting! [8] I say nothing of the man who pushes another to the lion lest he seem less a murderer than the fellow who afterwards cuts the same victim's throat.

24

[1] In how many ways are we expected to prove that none of the things connected with the spectacles is pleasing to God? Or, because it is not pleasing to God, befits His servant? [2] If we have shown that all these things have been instituted for the Devil's sake, and furnished from the Devil's stores (for everything which is not God's or which displeases God is the Devil's), then this represents the pomp of the Devil which we renounce in the 'seal' of faith. [3] No share, however, ought we to have, whether in deed or word, whether by beholding or watching, in what we renounce. Moreover, if we ourselves renounce and rescind the 'seal' by making void our testimony to it, does it remain, then, for us to seek an answer from the heathen? Yes, let them tell us whether it be permitted for Christians to attend a spectacle. Why, for them this is the principal sign of a man's conversion to the Christian faith, that he renounces the spectacles. [4] A man, therefore, who removes the mark by which he is recognized, openly denies his faith. What hope is there left for such a man? No one deserts to the camp of the enemy without first throwing away weapons, deserting his standards, renouncing his oath of allegiance to his leader, and without pledging himself to die with the enemy.

25

[1] Will the man, seated where there is nothing of God, at that moment think of God? He will have peace in his soul, I suppose, as he cheers for the charioteer; he will learn purity as he gazes with fascination at the mimic actors. [2] No, indeed, in every kind of spectacle he will meet with no greater temptation than that over careful attire of women and men. That sharing of feelings and that agreement or disagreement over favorites fan the sparks of lust from their fellowship. [3] Finally, no one going to a spectacle has any other thought but to see and be seen. But, while the tragic actor is ranting, our good friend will probably recall the outcries of some prophet! Amid the strains of the effeminate flute-player, he will no doubt meditate on a psalm! And while the athletes are engaged in combat, he is sure to say that a blow must not be struck in return for a blow! [4] He will, therefore, also be in a position to let himself be stirred by pity, with his eyes fixed on the bears as they bite, and the net-fighters as they roll up their nets. May God avert from His own such a passion for murderous delight! [5] What sort of behavior is it to go from the assembly of God to the assembly of the Devil, from sky to sty, as the saying goes? Those hands which you have lifted up to God, to tire them out afterwards applauding an actor? To cheer a gladiator with the same lips with which you have said 'Amen' over the Most Holy? To call out 'for ever and ever' to anyone else but to God and Christ?

26

[1] Why, then, should such people not also be susceptible to demoniac possession? For we have the case of that woman–the Lord is witness–who went to the theater and returned home having a demon. [2] So, when in the course of exorcism the unclean spirit was hard pressed with the accusation that he had dared to seize a woman who believed, he answered boldly: 'I was fully justified in doing so, for I found her in my own domain.' [3] It is well known, too, that to another woman, during the night following the very day on which she had listened to a tragic actor, a shroud was shown in a dream, and a rebuke called out to her, mentioning the tragic actor by name; nor was that woman still alive after five days. [4] Indeed, how many other proofs can be drawn from those who, by consorting with the Devil at the spectacles, have fallen away from the Lord. For 'no man can serve two masters. ' 'What fellowship has light with darkness?' What has life to do with death?

27

[1] We ought to hate those gatherings and meetings of the heathen, seeing that there the name of God is blasphemed, there the cry to set the lions upon us is raised every day, there persecutions have their source, thence temptations are let loose. [2] What will you do when you are caught in that surging tide of wicked applause? Not that you are likely to suffer anything there at the hands of men (no one recognizes you as a Christian), but consider how you would fare in heaven. [3] Do you doubt that at the very moment when the Devil is raging in his assembly, all the angels look forth from heaven and note down every individual who has uttered blasphemy, who has listened to it, who has lent his tongue, who has lent his ears to the service of the Devil against God? [4] Will you, therefore, not shun the seats of Christ's enemies, that 'chair of pestilences', and the very air that hangs over it and is polluted with sinful cries? I grant you that you have there some things that are sweet, pleasant, harmless, and even honorable. No one flavors poison with gall and hellebore; it is into spicy, well-flavored, and mostly sweet dishes that he instills that noxious stuff. So, too, the Devil pours into the deadly draught he prepares the most agreeable and most welcome gifts of God. [5] Everything, then, you find there, whether manly or honorable or sonorous or melodious or tender, take it for drippings of honey from a poisoned cake, and do not consider your appetite for the pleasure worth the danger you run from its sweetness.

28

[1] Let the Devil's own guests stuff themselves with sweets of that sort: the places, the times, and the host who invites are theirs. Our banquet, or marriage feast, has not yet come. We cannot recline with them at table, as they cannot with us. Things in this matter run their course in succession. Now they rejoice, and we are afflicted. [2] 'The world,' holy Scripture says, 'will rejoice, you will be sad.' Let us mourn therefore while the heathen rejoice, that, when they have begun to mourn, we may rejoice: lest sharing their joy now, then we may be sharing their mourning too. [3] You are too dainty, O Christian, if you desire pleasure also in this world; nay, more, you are a fool altogether if you deem this pleasure. The philosophers at least have given the name 'pleasure' to quiet and tranquillity; in it they rejoice, they find their diversion in it, they even glory in it. But you–why, I find you sighing for goal posts, the stage, dust, the arena. [4] I wish you would say plainly: 'We cannot live without pleasure!' Whereas we ought to die with pleasure. For what other prayer have we but that of the Apostle–'to leave the world and find our place with the Lord'? Our pleasure is where our prayer is.

29

[1] And finally, if you think that you are to pass this span of life in delights, why are you so ungrateful as not to be satisfied with so many and so exquisite pleasures given you by God, and not to recognize them? For what is more delightful than reconciliation with God, our Father and Lord, than the revelation of truth, the recognition of errors, and pardon for such grievous sins of the past? [2] What greater pleasure is there than distaste of pleasure itself, than contempt of all the world can give, than true liberty, than a pure conscience, than a contented life, than freedom from fear of death? [3] To trample under foot the gods of the heathen, to drive out demons, to effect cures, to seek revelations, to live unto God –these are the pleasures, these are the spectacles of the Christians, holy, everlasting, and free of

charge. In these find your circus games: behold the course of the world, count the generations slipping by, bear in mind the goal of the final consummation, defend the bonds of unity among the local churches, awake at the signal of God, arise at the angel trumpet, glory in the palms of martyrdom. [4] If the literary accomplishments of the stage delight you, we have sufficient literature of our own, enough verses and maxims, also enough songs and melodies; and ours are not fables, but truths, not artful devices, but plain realities. [5] Do you want contests in boxing and wrestling? Here they are –contests of no slight account, and plenty of them. Behold impurity overthrown by chastity, faithlessness slain by faith, cruelty crushed by mercy, impudence put in the shade by modesty. Such are the contests among us, and in these we win our crowns. Do you have desire for blood, too? You have the blood of Christ.

30

[1] Moreover, what a spectacle is already at hand–the second coming of the Lord, now no object of doubt, now exalted, now triumphant! What exultation will that be of the angels, what glory of the saints as they rise again! What a kingdom, the kingdom of the just thereafter! What a city, the new Jerusalem! [2] But there are yet other spectacles to come–that day of the Last Judgment with its everlasting issues, unlooked for by the heathen, the object of their derision, when the hoary age of the world and all its generations will be consumed in one file. [3] What a panorama of spectacle on that day! Which sight shall excite my wonder? Which, my laughter? Where shall I rejoice, where exult–as I see so many and so mighty kings, whose ascent to heaven used to be made known by public announcement, now along with Jupiter himself, along with the very witnesses of their ascent, groaning in the depths of darkness? Governors of provinces, too, who persecuted the name of the Lord, melting in flames fiercer than those they themselves kindled in their rage against the Christians braving them with contempt? [4] Whom else shall I behold? Those wise philosophers blushing before their followers as they burn together, the followers whom they taught that the world is no concern of God's whom they assured that either they had no souls at all or that what souls they had would never return to their former bodies? The poets also, trembling, not before the judgment seat of Rhadamanthus or of Minos, but of Christ whom they did not expect to meet. [5] Then will the tragic actors be worth hearing, more vocal in their own catastrophe; then the comic actors will be worth watching, more lither of limb in the fire; then the charioteer will be worth seeing, red all over on his fiery wheel; then the athletes will be worth observing, not in their gymnasiums, but thrown about by fire–unless I might not wish to look at them even then but would prefer to turn an insatiable gaze on those who vented their rage on the Lord. [6] 'This is He,' I will say, 'the son of the carpenter and the harlot, the sabbath-breaker, the Samaritan who had a devil. This is He whom you purchased from Judas, this is He who was struck with reed and fist, defiled with spittle, given gall and vinegar to drink. This is He whom the disciples secretly stole away to spread the story of His resurrection, or whom the gardener removed lest his lettuces be trampled by the throng of curious idlers.' [7] What praetor or consul or quaestor or priest with all his munificence will ever bestow on you the favor of beholding and exulting in such sights? Yet, such scenes as these are in a measure already ours by faith in the vision of the spirit. But what are those things which 'eye has not seen nor ear heard and which have not entered into the heart of man'? Things of greater delight, I believe, than circus, both kinds of theater, and any stadium.

Tertullian On Prayer

1

[1] Jesus Christ our Lord the Spirit of God and the Word of God and the Reason of God–the Word (which expresses) the Reason, and the Reason (which possesses) the Word, and the Spirit of both–has prescribed for His new disciples of the New Testament a new form of prayer. For in this matter, also, it was fitting that new wine be stored in new wine skins and that a new patch be sewed upon a new garment. Whatever had prevailed in days gone by was either abolished, like circumcision, or completed, like the rest of the Law, or fulfilled, like the prophecies, or brought to its perfection, like faith itself. [2] Everything has been changed from carnal to spiritual by the new grace of God which, with the coming of the Gospel, has wiped out the old completely; and in this grace it has been proved there is the Spirit of God and the Word of God and the Reason of God, Jesus Christ our Lord; as the Spirit wherein He prevailed, the Word whereby He taught, and the Reason or which He came. Consequently, the prayer formulated by Christ consists of three elements: the spirit whereby it can have such power, the word by which it is expressed, and the reason why it produces reconciliation. [3] John, too, had taught his disciples to pray, but everything that John did was a preparation for Christ, until He would increase–even as John himself announced that He (Christ) must increase, but he himself must decrease–and the entire work of the servant would pass over, along with the spirit itself, to the Master. Hence it is that the words in which John taught men to offer their prayer are not extant, for the earthly have given place to the heavenly. 'He who is from the earth,' He says, 'of the earth speaks, and he who comes from heaven bears witness to that which he has seen.' And what that is of Christ the Lord is not of heaven, as is also this instruction concerning prayer? [4] Let us then, my blessed ones, consider His heavenly wisdom, in the first place with regard to the admonition to pray in secret. By this, He demanded of man the faith to believe that he is seen and heard by Almighty God even when he is within the house and out of sight; and He desired a modest reserve in the manifestation of his faith so that he would offer his homage to God alone who he believed was listening and observing everywhere. [5] The next recommendation in the following precept would, then, pertain to faith and the proper display of faith; we should not think that the Lord is to be approached with a barrage of words since we are certain that of His own accord He has regard for His creatures. [6] Yet, that concise phrase which forms the third point of His teaching rests for support upon a profound and effective figure of speech: the thought compressed within such few words carries a flood of meaning to the mind. For not only does it embrace the proper duties of prayer, namely, worship of God and man's act of supplication, but practically every word of the Lord, the whole content of His teaching, so that, really, in (the Lord's) Prayer, there is contained an abridgment of the entire Gospel.

2

[1] It begins with a proof of (our belief in) God and a meritorious act of faith when we say, 'Father, who art in heaven.' For we adore God and prove our faith, of which this form of address is the result. It is written: 'To them that believe in God He gave the power to be called the sons of God.' [2] Our Lord very frequently spoke to us of God as a Father; in fact, He even taught us to call none on earth 'father,' but only the one we have in heaven. Therefore, when we pray like this we are observing this precept, too. [3] Happy they who know the Father! This is the reproach made against Israel, when the Spirit calls heaven and earth to witness saying: 'I have begotten sons and they have not known me.' [4] Moreover, when we say 'Father,' we also add a title to God's name. This form of address is one of filial love and at the same time one of power. [4] In the Father, the Son is also addressed. For Christ said, 'I and the Father are one.' [5] Nor is Mother Church passed over without mention, for in the Son and the Father the Mother is recognized, since upon her the terms 'Father' and 'Son' depend for their meaning. With this one form, then, or word, we honor God with His own, we heed His precept, and we reproach those who are unmindful of the Father.

3

[1] The title 'God the Father' had not been revealed to anyone. Even Moses who had inquired about God's name had heard a different one. It has been revealed to us in His Son. For, before the Son (came) the name of the Father did not exist. 'I have come,' said Christ, 'in the name of my Father.' And again: 'Father, glorify thy name.' And, more explicitly: 'I have manifested thy name to men.' [2] We ask that this name be hallowed; not that it would be the proper thing for men to wish God well as if He were (just) another man and we could express some wish in his regard; or as if it would hurt Him if we did not express the wish. Certainly it is right that God should be blessed in all places and at all times because it is every man's duty to be ever mindful of His benefits, but this wish takes the form of a benediction. [3]

Moreover, when is the name of God not holy and blessed in itself, when of itself it makes others holy? To Him the attending hosts of angels cease not to say: 'Holy, holy, holy!' Therefore, we, too–the future comrades of the angels, if we earn this reward–become familiar even while here on this earth with that heavenly cry of praise to God and the duty of our future glory. [4] So much for the glory we give to God. Over and above that, there is reference to our own petition when we say 'Hallowed be thy name.' We are asking that it be sanctified in us who are in Him, as well as in all other men for whom the grace of God is still waiting. In this, too, we obey the precept by praying for all men, even our enemies. And thus, by an ellipsis, we say, not: 'May Thy name be hallowed among us,' but, we say: 'Among all men.'

4

[1] Next, we add this phrase: 'Thy will be done in heaven and on earth.' Not that anyone could prevent the fulfillment of God's will and we should pray that His will be successfully accomplished, but we pray that in everything His will may be done. For, by a figure of speech, under the symbol of flesh and spirit we represent heaven and earth. [2] But, even if this is to be understood literally, the sense of the petition is the same, namely, that the will of God be done in us on earth, in order that it may be done (by us) also in heaven. Now, what does God will but that we walk according to His teaching? We ask, therefore, that He grant us the substance and riches of His will, for our salvation both in heaven and on earth, since the sum total of His will is the salvation of those whom He has adopted as His children. [3] This is the will of God which our Lord accomplished by His teaching, His works, and His sufferings. For, if He Himself said that He did not His own will, but the will of His Father, without a doubt what He did was the will of His Father, to which we are now summoned as to a model, that we, too, may teach and work and suffer even unto death. That we may accomplish this there is need of God's will. [4] Likewise, when we say: 'Thy will be done,' we thereby wish well to ourselves because there is no evil in God's will, even if some adversity be inflicted upon one according to his deserts. [5] Now, by this phrase we forearm ourselves for patient endurance since our Lord, too, willed to point out in His own flesh under the intensity of His Passion the weakness of the flesh. 'Father,' He said, 'remove this cup from Me,' and then, after reflection, He added: 'Yet not my will but thine be done.' He Himself was the will and power of the Father, yet He surrendered Himself to the will of His Father to indicate the patient endurance which is rightly due.

5

[1] The phrase, 'Thy kingdom come,' also refers to the same end as 'Thy will be done,' namely, (May Thy kingdom come) in ourselves. For, when does God not reign, 'in whose hand is the heart of every king'? But, whatever we wish for ourselves, we direct our hope toward Him, and we attribute to Him what we expect from Him. Well, then, if the realization of our Lord's kingdom has reference to the will of God and to our uncertain condition, how is it that some ask for an extension of time, as it were, for this world, since the kingdom of God–for the coming of which we pray–tends toward the consummation of the world? Our hope is that we may sooner reign, and not be slaves any longer. [2] Even if it were not prescribed to ask in prayer for the coming of His kingdom, we would, of our own accord, have expressed this desire in our eagerness to embrace the object of our hope. [3] With indignation the souls of the martyrs beneath the altar cry aloud to the Lord: 'How long, O Lord, dost thou refrain from avenging our blood on those who dwell on the earth?' For, at least from the end of the world vengeance for them is ordained. [4] Indeed, as quickly as possible, O Lord, may Thy kingdom come! This is the prayer of Christians; this shall bring shame to the heathens; this shall bring joy to the angels; it is for the coming of this kingdom that we are harassed now, or rather, it is for this coming that we pray.

6

[1] With what exquisite choice has divine Wisdom arranged the order of this prayer that, after the matters which pertain to heaven–that is, after the name of God, the will of God, and the kingdom of God–it should make a place for a petition for our earthly needs, too! For our Lord has taught us: 'Seek first the kingdom, and then these things shall be given you besides.' [2] However, we should rather understand 'Give us this day our daily bread' in a spiritual sense. For Christ is 'our bread,' because Christ is Life and the Life is Bread. 'I am,' said He, 'the bread of life.' And shortly before: 'The bread is the word of the living God who hath come down from heaven.' Then, because His Body is considered to be in the bread: 'This is my body.' Therefore, when we ask for our daily bread, we are asking to live forever in Christ and to be inseparably united with His Body. [3] But, since there is admitted also an interpretation of this phrase according to the flesh, it cannot be devoid of religious sense and spiritual instruction. Christ commands that we ask for bread, which, for the faithful, is the only thing necessary, for the pagans seek all other things. Thus, too, He impresses His teaching by examples and He instructs by parables, saying, for example: 'Does a father take bread from his children and cast it to the dogs?' And again: 'If his son asks him for a loaf, will he hand him a stone?' He indicates what children expect from their father. That caller, too, who knocked upon the door in the night was asking for bread. [4] Moreover, He has rightly added: 'Give us this day' in view of what He had previously said: 'Do not be anxious about tomorrow, what you shall eat.' To this idea He also referred in the parable of that man who, when his crops were plentiful, laid plans for an addition to his barns and a long-range program of security–though he was destined to die that very night.

7

[1] Having considered God's generosity, we pray next for His indulgence. For, of what benefit is food if, in reality, we are bent on it like a bull on his victim? Our Lord knew that He alone was without sin. Therefore, He taught us to say in prayer: 'Forgive us our trespasses.' A prayer for pardon is an acknowledgment of sin, since one who asks for pardon confesses his guilt. Thus, too, repentance is shown to be acceptable to God, because God wills this rather than the death of the sinner. [2] Now, in Scripture, 'debt' is used figuratively to mean sin, because of this analogy: When a man owes something to a judge and payment is exacted from him, he does not escape the just demand unless excused from the payment of the debt, just as the master forgave the debt to that servant. Now, this is the point of the whole parable: Just as the servant was freed by his lord, but failed in turn to be merciful to his debtor and therefore, when brought before his lord, was handed over to the torturer until he paid the last penny, that is, the least and last of his faults, (Christ) intended by this parable to get us, also, to forgive our debtors. [3] This is expressed elsewhere under this aspect of prayer; 'Forgive,' He said, 'and you shall be forgiven.' And when Peter asked if one should forgive his brother seven times, our Lord said, 'Rather, seventy times seven times,' that He might improve upon the Law, for in Genesis vengeance was demanded of Cain seven times, of Lamech seventy times seven.

8

[1] To complete the prayer which was so well arranged, Christ added that we should pray not only that our sins be forgiven, but that they be shunned completely: 'Lead us not into temptation,' that is, do not allow us to be led by the Tempter. [2] God forbid that our Lord should seem to be the tempter, as if He were not aware of one's faith or were eager to upset it! [3] That weakness and spitefulness belongs to the Devil. For, even in the case of Abraham, God had ordered the sacrifice of his son not to tempt his faith, but to prove it, that in him He-might set forth an example for His precept whereby He was later to teach that no one should hold his loved ones dearer than God. [4] Christ Himself was tempted by the Devil and pointed out the subtle director of the temptation. This passage He confirms (by His words to His Apostles) later when He says: 'Pray that you may not enter into temptation.' They were so tempted to desert their Lord because they had indulged in sleep instead of prayer. [5] Therefore, the phrase which balances and interprets 'Lead us not into temptation' is 'But deliver us from evil.'

9

[1] How many utterances of the Prophets, Evangelists, and Apostles; how many of our Lord's sermons, parables, examples, and precepts are touched in the brief compass of a few little words! How many duties are fulfilled! [2] The honor due to God in the word 'Father'; a testimony of faith in the very title used; the offering of obedience in the mention of God's will; the remembrance of hope in the mention of His kingdom; a petition for life in the mention of bread; the confession of sins in asking for pardon; solicitude regarding temptation in the request for protection. [3] Yet, why be surprised? God alone could teach us how He would have us pray. The homage of prayer, then, as arranged by Him and animated by His Spirit at the very moment it went forth from His divine lips, because of the prerogative granted to Him, ascends to heaven, recommending to the Father what the Son has taught.

10

[1] Since, however, our Lord, who saw the needs of men, after giving them the method of prayer, said: 'Ask and you shall receive,' and since every man has petitions to make according to his own circumstances, everyone first sends ahead the prescribed and customary prayer which will, so to speak, lay the ground work for his additional desires. He then has the right to heap upon this (substructure) petitions, over and above–ever keeping in mind, however, the prescribed conditions, that we may be no farther from the ears of God than from His teachings.

11

¹ The remembrance of these teachings paves the way for our prayers to reach heaven, and the first of these is not to approach the altar of God without settling any controversy or quarrel we may have contracted with our brethren. For, how can one approach the peace of God without peace, or the forgiveness of sin when he nurses a grudge? How will he please his Father if he be angry with his brother, when all anger has been forbidden us from the beginning? ² For Joseph, sending his brothers home to bring their father, said: 'Do not quarrel on the way!' He was, in fact, admonishing us–for elsewhere our manner of life is called our 'way'–that on the way of prayer that has been set up we must not approach the Father if we are angry. ³ Furthermore, our Lord, clearly enlarging upon the Law, adds anger with one's brother to the sin of murder. He does not permit even an evil word to be expressed; even if one must experience anger, it should not outlast the setting of the sun, as the Apostle reminds us. How foolhardy it is, moreover, either to pass a day without prayer, while you fail to give satisfaction to your brother, or to pray to no avail since your anger persists!

12

¹ Since the attention of our prayer is bestowed by and directed to the same Spirit, it should be free not only from anger, but from any and every disturbance of the mind. For the Holy Spirit does not acknowledge an impure spirit, neither is a sad spirit recognized by the Spirit of Joy, nor a spirit that is bound by one that is free. No one extends a welcoming hand to an opponent; no one admits another unless he is a kindred spirit.

13

¹ Furthermore, what is the sense of approaching prayer with hands that have been cleansed but with a spirit that is stained? Why, even the hands themselves need a spiritual cleansing that they may be raised to heaven cleansed of falsehood, murder, cruelty, poisoning, idolatry, and all other stains which, conceived in the spirit, are accomplished by the operation of the hands. This is the real cleansing, not the kind which many, in superstitious anxiety, attend to, taking water at every prayer, even when they come after a complete bath! ² When I pondered this in detail and sought an explanation, I found it told of Pilate that he washed his hands in the act of surrendering Christ. We adore Christ, we do not surrender Him. Surely, we ought rather to follow a course of conduct different from that of the traitor and for that very reason not wash our hands; except to wash them because of some stain resulting from our dealings with men, for our conscience's sake; but the hands are sufficiently clean which we have washed once and for all, together with the whole body, in Christ.

14

¹ Though Israel may wash all its members every day, it is never clean. Its hands, at least, are always stained, forever red with the blood of the Prophets and of our Lord Himself. Conscious, therefore, of this hereditary stain of their fathers, they do not dare to raise their hands to the Lord, lest some Isaias cry out, lest Christ abominate them. In our case, not only do we raise them, we even spread them out, and, imitating the Passion of our Lord, we confess Christ as we pray.

15

¹ Now, since we have mentioned one detail of religious observance that is foolish, we shall not be loathe to censure the others, too, in which vanity deserves to be reproved, inasmuch as they are without the authority of any precept, either on the part of our Lord or any of the Apostles. Practices such as this are to be considered superstition rather than devout homage; affected and forced and indicative of scrupulosity rather than of a rational service; at any rate, constrained to match those of the pagans. ² Take, for example, the practice some have of laying aside their cloaks when they pray. This is the way pagans approach their idols. Now certainly, if this were necessary, the Apostles would have included it in their instructions about the dress for prayer; unless there are some who think that it was during his prayer that Paul left his cloak with Carpus! I suppose that the God who heeded the prayer of the three holy youths in the furnace of the Babylonian king when they prayed in their wide oriental trousers and turbans would not listen to those who wear their cloaks during prayer!

16

¹ Similarly, regarding the custom some have of sitting down when their prayer is ended: I see no reason for it except that they are acting like children. What do I mean? If that Hermas, whose writings generally bear the title 'The Shepherd,' had not sat upon his bed when his prayer was finished, but had done something else, would we adopt this practice, too? Certainly not! ² For the phrase, 'When I had offered my prayer and had seated myself on the bed,' was set down simply and solely in the course of the narrative, not as a point of discipline. ³ Otherwise, we would not be obliged to offer prayers anywhere except where there was a bed! ⁴ On the other hand, it would be violating his directions to sit upon a chair or bench! ⁵ Furthermore, since this is what the pagans do–sit down before the images of the gods which they adore–it is on this score that what is done before idols deserves to be reproved in us. ⁶ For this reason it is set down as a charge of irreverence, and would be so understood, even by those pagans, if they had any understanding. For, if it is disrespectful to sit down in the presence and sight of one whom you hold in very high esteem and honor, how much more is it the height of disrespect to do so in the presence of the living God with the angel of prayer standing beside Him? Unless we are offering a reproach to God because our prayer has wearied us!

17

¹ On the other hand, when we offer our prayer with modesty and humility, we commend our petitions to God all the more, even though our hands have not been raised very high in the air, but only slightly and to a proper position, and even though our gaze has not been lifted up in presumption. ² For, even the publican who, not only in his words but in his countenance as well, was humble and prayed with downcast eyes went away justified rather than the haughty Pharisee. ³ The tone of voice, too, should be lowered; otherwise, what lungs we will need, if being heard depended upon the noise we make! But God is not one who heeds the voice; rather, it is the heart which He hears and beholds. ⁴ 'Even the speechless I hear, and the silent petition I answer.' So runs an oracle of the Pythian demon. Do the ears of God await a sound? If they did, how could Jonas' prayer from the depths of the whale's belly have made its way to heaven, up through the organs of such a great beast from the very bottom of the sea, up through such a vast amount of water? ⁵ As for those who pray in such a loud voice, what else will they attain but the annoyance of their neighbors? Let us say, rather, when they thus publicize their petitions, what else are they doing but praying in public?

18

¹ There is another custom which has now become established: when those who are fasting have finished their prayer with their brethren, they withhold the kiss of peace; yet this is the seal of prayer. ² But, when is the kiss of peace to be given to our brethren if not when our prayer ascends to heaven, made more worthy of praise because of our charity? So that they themselves may share in our charity, who have contributed to it by passing on their peace to their brother. ³ What prayer is complete without the bond of a holy kiss? ⁴ With whom does the kiss of peace interfere in his service of the Lord? ⁵ What kind of sacrifice is it from which one departs without giving the kiss of peace? ⁶ Whatever the reason may be, it will not outweigh the observance of the precept whereby we are bidden to conceal our fasting. For, when we refrain from the kiss, it is recognized that we are fasting. But, even if there is some reason for it, still, that you may not be guilty of transgressing this precept, you may, if you wish, dispense with the kiss of peace at home, since there you are among those from whom it is not entirely possible to conceal your fasting. But, wherever else you can conceal your acts of mortification, you ought to remember this precept; in this way you will satisfactorily comply with religious discipline in public, and with ordinary usage at home. ⁷ Thus, too, on Good Friday, when the fasting is a general and, as it were, a public religious obligation, we rightly omit the kiss of peace, having no anxiety about concealing that which we are doing along with everyone else.

19

¹ Similarly, with regard to the station days, many do not think that there should be any attendance at the prayers of sacrifice, because the station should be ended when the Lord's Body is received. ² Has the Eucharist, then, dispensed with a duty vowed to God, or does it place upon us a greater obligation to God? ³ Will not your station be more solemn if you stand at the altar of God? ⁴ When the Body of our Lord is received and reserved, both are preserved: the participation in the sacrifice and the fulfillment of a duty. ⁵ Since 'station' has taken its name from military procedure (for we are God's militia), certainly no joy nor sadness which befalls the camp releases the soldiers on guard duty. For, in joy one will perform his duty more readily, and, in sadness, more conscientiously.

20

¹ As regards dress–I refer only to that of women–the difference of custom since the time of the holy Apostle has caused me, though a man of no rank (in the Church), to deal with this matter, which is a daring thing to do; except that it is not so daring if we deal with it as did the Apostle. ² As for the modesty of their attire and adornment, the admonition of Peter, too, is clearly expressed. Using the same words as Paul, because inspired by the same Spirit, he imposes restraint regarding ostentation in their dress, the proud display of gold, and the overcareful, meretricious arrangement of their hair.

21

¹ A point which must be treated, since in general, throughout the Church, it is regarded as a matter of dispute, is the question of whether or not virgins should be veiled. ² Those who grant to virgins the right of having their heads uncovered seem to support their position by the fact that the Apostle designated specifically, not that virgins, but that women, are to be veiled; that is, he referred not to the sex, using the generic term 'females,' but to one group within the sex, saying 'women.' ³ For, if he had specified the (entire) sex by the term 'females' he would have laid down an absolute law relating to every woman; but since he designates one group within the sex, he sets it apart by his silence regarding another group. ⁴ For, they say, he could have included them in the general term 'females.'

22

¹ Those who take this stand ought to give some thought to the basic meaning of this word. What does 'woman' mean right from the first pages of holy Scripture? They will discover that it is the term used to designate the sex, not a group within the sex; for God called Eve, although she had not yet known man, both woman and female: female, as an over-all term for the sex; woman, with special reference to a stage of life within the sex. Thus, since Eve, who up to that time was still unmarried, was designated by the term 'woman,' this term came to be commonly applied to a virgin, also. No wonder, then, if the Apostle, actuated by the same Spirit which has inspired all the sacred Scriptures as well as that Book of Genesis, used this same word, 'woman,' which, because of its application to the unmarried Eve, means also a virgin. ² Everything else, then, is in agreement. For, by the very fact that he has not named virgins, just as is the case in another passage, where he is teaching about marriage, he makes it clear that he is speaking about all women and the entire sex and that there is no distinction between a woman and a virgin since he does not mention the latter at all. For, since he did not forget to make a distinction in another passage where the difference demands it (he distinguishes both classes by designating each with its proper term), in a passage where he does not distinguish, since he does not name each, he does not intend any distinction. ³ But what of the fact that in the Greek, in which the Apostle wrote his epistles, the ordinary usage is to speak of 'women' rather than 'females,' that is, γυναῖκα (*gunaikas*) rather than θηλείας (*theleias*)? Well, if this word is the one commonly used to designate the sex, then the Apostle, in saying γυναῖκα, referred to the (entire) sex (by using) a word which, in translation, means 'females.' But in the (entire) sex the virgin, too, is included. ⁴ The form of expression is unmistakable: 'Every woman,' he says, 'praying or prophesying with her head uncovered disgraces her head.' What is the meaning of the expression 'every woman' except women of every age, every rank, and every circumstance? In saying 'every,' he excepts no member of the female sex, even as he does not command that men should have their heads covered. For then he would say 'every man.' Therefore, as in the reference to the male sex, under the term 'man' he forbids that even unmarried men should have their heads covered, similarly, in reference to the female sex, under the term 'woman' he commands that even a virgin should have her head covered. Without discrimination, in the case of both sexes, the younger should follow the rule for the elder; or else unmarried men should have their heads covered, too, if unmarried women should not have their heads covered; for the former are not specifically named in the regulation; let the (married) man be different from the unmarried if the woman is different from the virgin. ⁵ Of course, it is on account of the angels, he says, that the woman's head is to be covered, because the angels revolted from God on account of the daughters of men. Who, then, would contend that it is only women, that is, married women no longer virgins, that are a source of temptation? ⁶ Unless, of course, unmarried women may not present an attractive appearance and find their lovers? Rather, let us see whether it was virgins alone whom they desired when Scripture speaks of the 'daughters of men'; for it could have used the terms 'men's wives' or 'women' indifferently. ⁷ But, since it says: 'And they took to themselves wives,' it does so because they took as their wives those without husbands. Scripture would have used a different expression for those who had husbands. Now, they could be without husbands either because they were widows or virgins. So, in naming the sex in general by the term 'daughters,' he embraced species in genus. ⁸ Likewise, when he says that nature itself teaches that women should cover their heads because it has bestowed hair on woman both as a covering and an adornment, has not this same covering and this same adornment for the head been bestowed upon virgins as well? If it is a disgrace for a woman to have her hair shorn, it is for a virgin then, also. Since, then, one and the same condition is attributed to each in regard to the head, then one and the same regulation regarding the head is imposed upon them–even upon those virgins whom their tender age protects. For, right from the start she is included in the term 'woman.' Finally, Israel has the same regulation. But even if it did not, our law, amplified and supplemented, would demand an addition, imposing a veil upon virgins, also. Granted that at the moment that period of life which is unaware of its own sex should be excused. (Granted that it should retain the privilege of its innocence; for both Eve and Adam, when realization came to them, immediately covered what they had come to know.) At any rate, in the case of those who have left childhood, their age ought to confer much both by way of nature and of discipline. For women are revealed by their members and their duties. No one is a virgin from the time she is of marriageable age, since the age now in her has become the bride of its own partner, that is, time. ⁹ 'But (suppose that) someone has consecrated herself to God.' Nevertheless, from this time on, she rearranges her hair and changes her whole appearance to that of a woman. Therefore, let her be earnest about the whole business and present the complete appearance of a virgin; what she conceals for God's sake let her keep completely out of sight. It is to our interest to entrust to the knowledge of God alone what is done for the sake of God, lest we bargain with men for what we hope to receive from God. Why do you expose before the eyes of God what you cover in the presence of men? Will you be more modest in the public street than in church? If it is a gift from God and 'thou hast received it, why dost thou boast,' says the Apostle, 'as if thou hadst not received it?' Why do you condemn other women by this exhibition of yourself? Or are you inviting others to good by your vanity? Yet you are in danger of losing it yourself if you boast of it, and you force others to the same dangers. That is easily destroyed which is assumed with an inclination to vanity. Virgin, cover your head if you are a virgin, for you ought to blush for shame! If you are a virgin, avoid the gaze of many eyes. Let no one look in admiration upon your face. Let no one realize your deceit. It is praiseworthy for you to create the false impression that you are married by covering your head. Rather, it will not be a false impression you are creating; for you are the bride of Christ. To Him you have surrendered your body; act according to the instructions of your Spouse. If He bids other men's brides to cover their heads, how much more His own! ¹⁰ 'But (suppose that) someone thinks the arrangement of his predecessor should not be changed.' Many apply their own ideas and persistence in the same to the custom established by another. Granted that virgins should not be forced to cover their heads; at any rate, those who are willing to do so should not be prevented. If some cannot deny that they are virgins, they should be content, for the sake of preserving their conscience before God, to risk their reputation. However, in regard to those who are betrothed, I can declare and avow this with more than my usual firmness: their heads should be covered from the day when they first trembled at the kiss and handclasp of their future husband. For, in these symbols they have pledged every bit of themselves–their life throughout its full development, their flesh throughout their lifetime, their spirit through their understanding (of the contract), their modesty through the exchange of a kiss, their hope through their expectation, and their mind through their willingness. For us, Rebecca stands as sufficient example; when her future husband had been pointed out to her, she covered her head with her veil merely because she knew she was to marry him.

23

¹ With regard to kneeling, too, prayer allows a difference in custom because of certain ones–a very few–who stay off their knees on the Sabbath, an opposing point of view which is just now strongly defending itself in the churches. ² The Lord will give His grace so that either they will yield, or else maintain their own opinion without giving scandal to others. As for ourselves, according to our tradition, only on the day (which commemorates) our Lord's Resurrection should we refrain from this custom; and not only from this, but from every sign that bespeaks solicitude and every ceremony arising therefrom. This includes deferring business, lest we give any opportunity to the Devil. The same holds for the season of Pentecost, which is marked by the same joyous celebration. ³ But who would hesitate every day to prostrate himself before God for at least the first prayer with which we approach the light of day? ⁴ Moreover, during the periods of fasting and on the station days no prayer should be said except on the knees and with every other sign of a humble spirit. For we are not merely praying, but beseeching and offering satisfaction to God our Lord.

24

¹ Regarding the time for prayer there has been no regulation at all, except that we are to pray at all times and everywhere. But how can we pray everywhere when we are forbidden to pray in public? 'In every place,' He said, which circumstance or even necessity provides. For it is not considered that when the Apostles, within the hearing of their guards, prayed in prison and sang to God they were acting contrary to the precept any more was Paul when, aboard ship, in the sight of all, he gave thanks to God.

25

[1] With regard to the time, the outward observance of certain hours will not be without profit. I refer to those hours of community prayer which mark the main divisions of the day, namely, Terce, Sext, and None. These, it can be found, are mentioned in holy Scripture as being more deserving of note. [2] It was at the third hour–Terce–when the disciples were assembled, that the Holy Spirit was infused into them for the first time. [3] It was at the sixth hour–Sext– on the day when he had the vision of all creatures in the sheet that Peter had climbed to a higher spot in order to pray. [4] Similarly, it was at the ninth hour–None–that he went into the Temple with John where he restored the paralytic to health. [5] Although these incidents simply happen without any precept of observing (these hours), it would be good to establish some precedent which would make the admonition to pray a binding force to wrest us violently at times, as by a law, from our business to such an obligation so that we may offer adoration no less than three times a day at least, being debtors to the three divine Persons, Father, Son and Holy Spirit. And this, too, we read was observed by Daniel according to the rites of Israel. Of course, we are excepting the appropriate prayers which are due without any admonition at the approach of dawn and evening. It is befitting for the faithful not to take food and not to bathe before saying a prayer. For the refreshment and food of the spirit are to be put before (the needs) of the flesh, because the things of heaven are to be put before those of the earth.

26

[1] When a brother has entered your home, do not let him go away without a prayer. ('You have seen,' He said, 'a brother; you have seen your Lord'). Particularly should this be observed in the case of a stranger, lest he should happen to be an angel. [2] But, even after one has been welcomed by his brethren, you should not attend to earthly refreshment before the heavenly. For immediately will your faith be revealed. Or how can you say, according to the precept, 'Peace to this house,' unless you exchange the kiss of peace with those who are in the house?

27

[1] Those who are more exact about prayer are in the habit of adding to their prayers an 'Alleluia' and psalms of such a character that those who are present may respond with the final phrases. Assuredly, the practice is excellent in every respect which by its high praise and reverence of God is competent to offer Him, as a rich victim, a prayer that has been filled out in every detail.

28

[1] Now, this is the spiritual victim which has set aside the earlier sacrifice. 'To what purpose do you offer me the multitude of your victims,' saith the Lord? 'I am full, I desire not holocausts of rams, and fat of fatlings, and blood of calves and goats. For who required these things at your hands?' [2] The Gospel teaches what God demands. 'The hour is coming,' He says, 'when the true worshipers will worship the Father in spirit and in truth. For God is spirit,' and therefore He requires that His worshipers be of the same nature. [3] We are the true worshipers and true priests who, offering our prayer in the spirit, offer sacrifice in the spirit–that is, prayer–as a victim that is appropriate and acceptable to God; this is what He has demanded and what He has foreordained for Himself. [4] This prayer, consecrated to Him with our whole heart, nurtured by faith, prepared with truth–a prayer that is without blemish because of our innocence, clean because of our chastity–a prayer that has received the victor's crown because of our love for one another–this prayer we should bring to the altar of God with a display of good works amid the singing of psalms and hymns and it will obtain for us from God all that we ask.

29

[1] For what will God refuse to the prayer that comes to Him from the spirit and in truth, since this is the prayer He has exacted? What proofs of its efficacy do we read of an hear of and believe! To be sure, the prayer of old would save one from fires and wild beasts and starvation; yet, had not received its form from Christ. But how much more wrought by Christian prayer! It does not cause an angel (dew to appear in the midst of fire, nor does it stop the mouth of lions nor take the breakfast of country folk to the hungry it does not destroy all sense of pain by the grace that is conferred; but by patient endurance it teaches those who suffer, those who are sensitive, and those who have sorrow; by virtue it increases grace that our faith may know what comes from the Lord and understand what it suffers for the name of God. [2] Then, too, in the past, prayer would impose stripes, set loose the armies of the enemy, and prevent the beneficent effects of rain. But now, the prayer of justice averts the wrath of God, is on the alert for enemies, and intercedes for persecutors. What wonder if it could wrest water from the heavens, when it could even ask for fire and obtain it! Prayer alone overcomes God; but Christ has willed that it work no evil, upon it He has conferred all power for good. Therefore, it has no power except to recall the souls of the dead from the very path of death, to make the weak recover, to heal the sick, to exorcise demons, to open prison doors, to loosen the chains of the innocent. It likewise remits sins, repels temptations, stamps out persecution, consoles the fainthearted, delights the courageous, brings travelers safely home, calms the waves, stuns robbers, feeds the poor, directs the rich, raises up the fallen, sustains the falling, and supports those who are on their feet. [3] Prayer is the wall of faith, our shield and weapons against the foe who studies us from all sides. Hence, let us never set forth unarmed. Let us be mindful of our guard-duty by day and our vigil by night. Beneath the arms of prayer let us guard the standard of our general, and let us pray as we await the bugle call of the angel. [4] All the angels pray, too; every creature prays; the beasts, domestic and wild, bend their knees, and as they go forth from their stables and caves they look up to heaven with no idle gaze. Even the birds, upon rising in the morning, mount into the sky and stretch out their wings as a cross in place of hands and say something which might seem to be a prayer. What need, then, is there of further discussion of the duty of prayer? Even our Lord Himself prayed, to whom be honor and power forever and ever.

Tertullian On Patience

1

[1] Confess to the Lord my God that I certainly have courage, not to say presumption, to have dared to write on patience, a virtue which I am utterly unfit to practice, being, as I am, a man of no account. For, those who undertake to set forth and recommend any virtue should first give some evidence of practicing this virtue, and they should give proper direction to their constant admonition by the example of their own conduct, lest they be put to the blush at the discrepancy between their words and deeds. [2] And would that the blushing brought an improvement, that the shame (we feel) at not doing what we have suggested to others would teach us to do it! But, of course, it is with certain virtues as with certain vices: their greatness is so overwhelming that only the grace of divine inspiration can help us to attain and practice them. For, that which is in the highest sense good belongs in the highest degree to God, and no one dispenses it save He who possesses it, to each one as He sees fit. [3] It will be, then, a comfort to discuss that which it is not granted us to enjoy, somewhat in the manner of the sick, who, when deprived of health, cannot refrain from proclaiming its blessings. Thus, in my pitiable state, ever suffering from the fever of impatience, I must sigh after the health of patience which I do not possess, and I must beg and beseech it, remembering and reflecting, as I consider my weakness, that one does not easily attain the good health of faith and the soundness of the discipline of the Lord unless patience lends assistance thereto. [4] Patience has been given such pre-eminence in matters pertaining to God that no one can fulfill any precept or perform any work pleasing to the Lord without patience. [5] Even those who do not possess it pay recognition to its excellence by giving it the honorable title of 'the highest virtue.' In fact, the philosophers, who are regarded as creatures possessing some degree of wisdom, attribute such value to it that, while there are disagreements among them because of the various inclinations of the schools and their opposing tenets, they are, nevertheless, of one mind with regard to patience alone, and in this alone of their interests they enter into agreement. With regard to this they are in accord: for this they band together, with one mind they apply themselves to it in their efforts to attain virtue; every display of wisdom they usher in with a show of patience. [6] A great compliment it is to this virtue to be the moving force behind even the vain pursuits of the world to their praise and renown! Or is it rather an insult that divine things are involved in the doings of the world? [7] Let them see to it who will one day be ashamed of their wisdom when it is destroyed and brought to disgrace along with this world!

2

[1] There has been given to us as a model in the practice of patience no (merely) human product fashioned of the dullness of Cynic indifference, but the divine ordinance of a life-giving and heavenly way of life which points out as an exemplar of patience God Himself. Long has He been scattering the brilliance of this light (of the sun) upon the just and unjust alike and has allowed the deserving as well as the undeserving to enjoy the benefits of the seasons, the services of the elements, and the gifts of all creation. [2] He endures ungrateful peoples who worship the trifles fashioned by their skill and the works of their hands, who persecute His name and His children, and who, in their lewdness, their greed, their godlessness and depravity, grow worse from day to day; by His patience He hopes to draw them to Himself. There are many, you see, who do not believe in the Lord because for so long a time they have no experience of His wrath (directed) against the world.

3

[1] This is, indeed, a picture of the divine patience which exists, so to speak, far away from us, the patience, we might say, which prevails on high. But what about that patience which exists openly among men on earth, which is, as it were, within our reach? [2] God allows Himself to become incarnate: in His mother's womb He awaits (the time of birth) and after His birth suffers Himself to grow into manhood, and, when an adult, shows no eagerness to become known, but bears reproaches and is baptized by His own servant and by His words alone repels the attacks of the Tempter. [3] When He, (begotten) of the Lord, becomes a master teaching man how to avoid death, He teaches him for his own good how to offer reparation to outraged patience. [4] He did not wrangle or cry aloud; neither did anyone hear His voice in the streets; a bruised reed He did not break, a smoking wick He did not quench. (Now, the Prophet–or, rather, the testimony of God Himself, placing His own spirit in His Son with all patience–has not lied!) [5] He did not force one who was unwilling to stay close to Him; He scorned no one's table or dwelling; in fact, He ministered personally to His disciples by washing their feet. [6] He did not despise sinners or publicans, He showed no anger even toward that city which refused to receive Him, even when the disciples wished fire from heaven to fall upon such a shameful town; He healed the ungrateful, yielded to His persecutors. [7] More than this, He even kept in His company the one who would betray Him and did not firmly denounce him. Why, even when He is betrayed, when He is led like a beast to the slaughter–for thus (is it written): 'He does not open His mouth any more than does a lamb in the power of its shearer'–He who could have had if He wished, at a single word, legions of angels from heaven to assist Him did not approve of an avenging sword on the part of even one of His disciples. It was the forbearance of the Lord that was wounded in (the person of) Malchus. And so, He actually cursed for all time the works of the sword and by healing him whom He had not Himself struck, He made satisfaction by forbearance, which is the mother of mercy. [8] I say nothing about His crucifixion; it was for this that He had come. Still, did there have to be such insults attending the death He must undergo? No; but as He went forward to His death, He willed to have His fill of joy in suffering: He is spat upon, beaten, mocked, disgracefully clothed, and even more disgracefully crowned. [9] Marvel at the constancy of His meekness: He who had proposed to escape notice in the guise of man has in no degree imitated man's impatience. For this reason particularly, you Pharisees, you should have recognized the Lord! Patience such as this no mere man had ever practiced! [10] Such were the manifestations (of His patience), the very magnitude of which is the reason why pagan nations reject the faith; for us they are its rational foundation. For those to whom there has been granted the gift of faith they suffice to make it very clear, not only by the words our Lord used in His precepts, but also by the sufferings which He endured, that patience is the very nature of God, the effect and manifestation of a certain connatural property (of His being).

4

[1] Now, if we see that all servants of righteous character and good disposition live according to the mind of their lord–obedience, as you know, is a facility in rendering service, but the principle of obedience is compliant submission–how much more does it behoove us to be found modeled upon our Lord! Servants indeed we are of the living God whose sway over His (creatures) consists not in manacles or the granting of the slave's cap, but in allotting everlasting punishment or salvation. [2] To escape His severity or to invite His liberality one needs diligence in obeying which is proportionate to the threats uttered by His severity or the promises made by His liberality. [3] Yet, we ourselves exact obedience not only from men who are bound to us by the bonds of slavery or who, because of some other legal bond, are under obligation to us, but also from our flocks and even from the wild animals. We understand that they have been provided and granted by the Lord for our purposes. [4] I ask you: in the practice of obedience, shall those creatures which God has made subject to us surpass us? In a word, creatures which obey (their masters) acknowledge (their condition as creatures): do we hesitate to heed Him to whom alone we are subject, namely, the Lord? Why, how unjust it would be, and in addition how ungrateful, for you not to make a return of what you have obtained from others through the kindness of a third party, to him through whom you obtained it! [5] But, no more about the manifestation of the obedience which we owe to the Lord our God. For, in the act of recognition of God one understands sufficiently what is incumbent upon him. However, lest we seem to have inserted something irrelevant to this discussion of obedience, (let me remark that) obedience itself also stems from patience: never does one who is impatient obey nor does a patient man ever refuse obedience. [6] Who, then, could deal adequately with the value of that patience which the Lord our God, the model and patron of all that is good, has displayed in Himself? Who would doubt that those who belong to God have an obligation to strive with their whole soul for every good, since it has reference to God? By these considerations our recommendation and exhortation on the subject of patience is briefly established in a summary, as it were, of the prescribed rule.

5

[1] Now, to thrash out a question about essential points of faith is not wearisome, since it is not without profit. Verboseness, though a fault at times, is no fault when it tends to edification. [2] Therefore, if some good is being discussed, the matter demands that we examine also the evil which is its opposite. You will throw a better light upon what one should strive for if you discuss in connection with it what should be avoided. [3] Let us, then, with regard to impatience, consider whether, as patience (exists) in God, its opposite was born and discovered in our adversary. From this it will appear how impatience, more than anything else, is opposed to faith. [4] For, that which is conceived by God's rival is certainly not a friend to the things of God. There is the same hostility in the things as there is in their authors. Furthermore, since God is infinitely good, and the Devil, on the other hand, is superlatively evil, by their very difference they bear witness that neither

one effects anything for the other; it can no more seem to us that some good is produced from evil than some evil from good. ⁵ Now, I find the origin of impatience in the Devil himself. Even when the Lord God subjected to His own image, that is, to man, all the works He had made, the Devil bore it with impatience. ⁶ For, he would not have grieved, had he endured it, nor would he have envied man, had he not grieved; he deceived man because he envied him; he envied him because he grieved; he grieved because he certainly had not borne it with patience. ⁷ What the angel of perdition was first–I mean, whether he was first evil or impatient–I do not bother to inquire; it is clear that, whether impatience had its beginning in evil or evil in impatience, they entered into combination and grew as one in the bosom of one father. ⁸ For, as soon as he perceived that it was through his impatience that he had committed the first sin, having learned from his own experience what would assist in wrong-doing, he availed himself of this same impatience to lead men into sin. ⁹ Without delay, and would say not without forethought, he contrived a meeting with the woman, and simply and solely through their conversation she was touched by his breath, already infected with impatience. But never would she have sinned at all had she preserved her patience according to the divine command! ¹⁰ And what of the fact that she could not endure having met (the Devil) alone but, being unable to remain silent about it in the presence of Adam–he was not yet her husband, nor as yet under any obligation to lend her his ear–she makes him the carrier of that which she had imbibed from the Evil One? ¹¹ Thus, a second member, too, of the human race falls through the impatience of the first; and his fall, too, results from his own impatience committed in two ways: with regard to the forewarning of God, and with regard to the deceit of the Devil; for he was unable to observe the former or to oppose the latter. ¹² Condemnation began with him in whom sin originated; God's anger began with him by whom man was induced to offend Him. God's patience began with him who had aroused His indignation; for at that time He was content with simply cursing him and He refrained from inflicting punishment upon the Devil. ¹³ What sin previous to this sin of impatience can be imputed to man? He was innocent and a close friend of God and a tenant dwelling in paradise. But, when once he yielded to impatience, he ceased to relish God and could no longer endure the things of heaven. ¹⁴ From that time on, as a man delivered up to the earth and cast away from the eyes of God, he began to serve as an easy instrument for impatience to use for everything that would offend God. ¹⁵ For, immediately, that impatience which was conceived by the seed of the Devil with the fecundity of evil gave birth to a child of wrath and instructed its offspring in its own arts. Since it had plunged Adam and Eve into death, it taught their son, also, to commit the first murder. Vain were it for me to ascribe this sin to impatience, had Cain, the first homicide and the first fratricide, accepted it with equanimity and without impatience when his offerings were refused by the Lord; if he had not been angry with his brother; if, in fine, he had killed no one. ¹⁶ Therefore, since he could not commit murder unless he were angry, and could not be angry unless he were impatient, it proves that what he did in anger is to be referred to that which prompted the anger. ¹⁷ Such was the cradle of impatience which was then, so to speak, in its infancy. But to what proportions it soon grew! And no wonder: if it was the prime source of sin, it follows that, being the prime source, it was therefore also the sole fashioner of all sin, pouring forth from its own abundant resources the varied channels of crimes. ¹⁸ Homicide has already been mentioned. It sprang originally from anger, and whatever causes it finds for itself afterwards, it ascribes them to impatience at its origin. For, whether one commits this crime through enmity or for some gain, the original cause is that one is overwhelmed by hatred or greed. ¹⁹ Whatever is the motivating force, a crime could not be perpetrated unless one lacks patience. Who has ever attempted adultery save one who was unable to withstand his lustful desires? Even the fact that (disgrace) is forced upon (some) women for a price, that sale of one's honor is certainly set in order by an inability to set at naught despicable gain. ²⁰ Impatience is, as it were, the original sin in the eyes of the Lord. For, to put it in a nutshell, every sin is to be traced back to impatience. Evil cannot endure good. No unchaste person but is intolerant of chastity; no scoundrel but is irked by righteousness; no negligent person but resents his obligations; no agitator but is impatient of peace. Although anyone may become evil, not everyone can persevere in good. ²¹ Why, then, should not this hydra-like generator of sins offend the Lord, who condemns all wickedness? Is it not clear that Israel itself, through its impatience, was ever sinning against God? ²² Forgetting the heavenly arm whereby it had been rescued from the afflictions of the Egyptians, it demanded of Aaron gods to be its leaders, while it poured its contributions into an idol of its own gold. For, it had borne without patience the delay necessitated by Moses' meeting with the Lord. ²³ After the rain of manna as food, after the water that followed and flowed from the rock, they gave up hope in the Lord, unable to endure a three-days' thirst. For this, too, they were charged with impatience by the Lord. ²⁴ But, not to range over individual instances: never would they have been destroyed had they not fallen into sin by impatience. Why did they lay hands on the Prophets, except that they could not bear to listen to them? And more than that: they laid hands upon the Lord Himself, being unable to endure even the sight of Him. But had they acquired patience, they would now be free.

6

¹ Such is the patience which is both subsequent to and antecedent to faith. Accordingly, Abraham believed in God and it was credited to him by God as justice. Now, he proved his faith by patience, when he was commanded to offer in sacrifice his son–I do not say for a trial, but rather for a typical attestation, of his faith. ² But God knew the man whom He had reputed for his justice. This severe command, which the Lord did not intend should be carried out, Abraham heard with patience and, had God so willed, he would have fulfilled it. Rightly, then, is he blessed because he was faithful; and rightly was he faithful because he was patient. ³ Thus faith was illuminated by patience, since it was sown among the heathens by the seed of Abraham which is Christ and added grace to the Law, and it has made patience its helpmate in amplifying and fulfilling the Law, because in times past this was the only thing lacking to the teaching of justice. ⁴ Heretofore, men demanded an eye for an eye and a tooth for a tooth and they returned evil for evil. As yet, patience was not found upon the earth, for as yet, you see, there was not faith. Meanwhile, impatience was enjoying the opportunities occasioned by the Law. It was easy when the Lord and Teacher of patience was not on hand. ⁵ But after He came and united the grace of faith with patience, no longer was one permitted to do injury with so much as a word, or even say 'Thou fool!' without being in danger of the judgment. Wrath was forbidden, passions were kept in check, unruly hands were restrained, the poison of the tongue was removed. ⁶ The Law acquired more than it lost when Christ said: 'Love your enemies and bless those who curse you and pray for those who persecute you, so that you may be children of your Father in heaven.' Just see what a Father patience acquires for us!

7

¹ The entire practice of patience is compressed within this fundamental precept whereby not even a lawful injury is permitted. But now, as we run through the causes of impatience, all the other precepts, too, will correspond in their own context. ² Is the mind disturbed by the loss of property? In practically every passage of the holy Scriptures one is admonished to despise the world, and no greater exhortation is there to an indifference toward money than that our Lord Himself is without it. ³ He always justifies the poor and condemns the rich. Thus He has set disdain for wealth ahead of the endurance of losses, pointing out through His rejection of riches that one should make no account of the loss of them. ⁴ Hence, we need not seek wealth, since our Lord did not seek it; and we ought to bear the deprivation of even the theft of it without regret. The Spirit of the Lord, through the Apostle, has called the desire of money the root of all evils. We may infer that this consists not only in the desire for that which belongs to another; even that which seems to be our own belongs to another; for nothing is our own, since all things belong to God to whom we, too, belong. ⁵ Therefore, if we feel impatient when we suffer some loss, we will be found to possess a desire for money, since we grieve over the loss of that which is not our own. We are seeking what belongs to another when we are unwilling to bear the loss of that which belongs to another. The man who is upset and unable to bear his loss sins, you might say, against God Himself by preferring the things of earth to those of heaven. For, the soul which he has received from the Lord is upset by the attractiveness of worldly goods. ⁶ Let us, then, with glad hearts, relinquish earthly goods that we may preserve those of heaven! Let the whole world fall in ruins provided I gain the patience to endure it! In all probability, a man who has not resolved to bear with fortitude a slight loss occasioned by theft or violence or even by his own stupidity will not readily or willingly touch what he owns for the sake of charity. ⁷ For, what man who refuses to undergo any operation at all at the hands of another puts a knife to his own body? Patience to endure, shown on occasions of loss, is a training in giving and sharing. He who does not fear loss is not reluctant to give. ⁸ Otherwise, how would one who has two tunics give one of them to him who is destitute, unless the same is one who can offer his cloak as well to the one going off with his tunic? How will we make friends for ourselves with mammon if we love him only to the extent that we do not share in his loss? We shall be damned together with the damned. ⁹ What do we find here where we have (only something) to lose? It is for pagans to be unable to sustain all loss; they would set worldly goods before their life perhaps. ¹⁰ And they do this when, in their eager desire for wealth, they engage in lucrative but dangerous commerce on the sea; when, for money's sake, they unhesitatingly engage in transactions also in the forum, even though there be reason to fear loss; they

do it, in fine, when they hire themselves out for the games and military service or when, in desolate regions, they commit robbery regardless of the wild beasts. ¹¹ On the other hand, in view of the difference between them and ourselves, it befits us to give up not our life for money but money for our life, either by voluntary charity or by the patient endurance of loss.

8

¹ Our very life and our very body we have exposed in this world as a target for all manner of injury and we endure this injury with patience; shall we, then, be vexed by the deprivation of lesser things? Far be such shame from the servant of Christ, that his patience, trained by greater trials, should fail in trifling ones! ² If one tries to provoke you to a fight, there is at hand the admonition of the Lord: 'If someone strike thee,' He says, ' on the right cheek, turn to him the other also.' Let wrong-doing grow weary from your patience; whoever be struck, the one who strikes, weighed down by pain and shame, will suffer more severely from the Lord; by your meekness you will strike a more severe blow to the wrong-doer; for he will suffer at the hands of Him by whose grace you practice meekness. If a spiteful tongue bursts out in cursing or wrangling, recall the saying: 'When men reproach you, rejoice.' The Lord Himself was accursed before the Law, yet He alone is blessed. Let us, then, His servants, follow our Lord and patiently submit to maledictions that we may be blessed! ³ If, with slight forbearance, I hear some bitter or evil remark directed against me, I may return it, and then I shall inevitably be bitter myself. Either that, or I shall be tormented by unexpressed resentment. ⁴ If, then, I retaliate when cursed, how shall I be found to have followed the teaching of our Lord? For it has been handed down that a man is not defiled by unclean dishes, but by the words which proceed from his mouth; and, what is more, that it remains for us to render an account for every vain and idle word. ⁵ It follows, then, that our Lord forbids us to do certain acts, but at the same time admonishes us to endure with meekness the same treatment at the hands of another. ⁶ (We shall speak) now of the joy which comes from patience. For every injury, whether occasioned by the tongue or the hand, coming in contact with patience, will meet the same end as a weapon which is flung and dashed upon a hard, unyielding rock. An ineffectual and fruitless action will lose its force immediately and will sometimes vent its passion and strike with the force of a boomerang upon him who sent it forth. ⁷ This is true, of course, since one insults you with the intention of causing you pain, because the one who inflicts the injury reaps his reward in the pain of the one injured. Consequently, if you cheat him of his reward by not showing any pain, he will himself inevitably feel pain because he has lost his reward. ⁸ Then you will go off, not only uninjured (which of itself should suffice for you) but over and above that you will have the pleasure of seeing your enemy frustrated while you yourself are preserved from pain. Herein lies the advantage of patience and the joy which derives from it

9

¹ Not even that form of impatience which results from the loss of our dear ones is excused, although in this case a sort of rightful claim to grieve justifies it. Observance of the precept of the Apostle must be put first: 'Grieve not,' he says,' over one who has fallen asleep even as the gentiles who have no hope.' ² And rightly so. For, if we believe in the resurrection of Christ, we believe in our own, also, since it was for us that He died and rose again. Therefore, since there is sure ground for faith in the resurrection of the dead, there is no grief associated with death, and no inability to bear grief. ³ Why should you grieve if you believe that (the loved one) has not perished utterly? Why should you show impatience that one has been taken away for the time being if you believe he will return? That which you think of as death is merely the beginning of a journey. He who has gone ahead is not to be mourned, though certainly he will be missed. But this lonesomeness must be alleviated by patience. Why should you be inconsolable over the departure of one whom you are soon to follow? ⁴ Moreover, impatience in such things is a sad indication of our own hope and gives the lie to our faith. Likewise, we injure Christ when we fail to accept with resignation (the death of) those whom He has called, as though they were to be pitied. ⁵ 'I desire,' says the Apostle, 'to be welcomed home now and to be with the Lord.' How much better a prayer he holds forth! As for the Christians' prayer, then, if we bear it with impatience and grief that others have attained their goal, we ourselves do not want to attain our goal!

10

¹ There is another, and very strong, motive which gives rise to impatience, namely, the desire for revenge, which busies itself in the interest of either reputation or wrong-doing. Now, reputation is everywhere empty, and evil never fails to be hateful to the Lord, especially in this situation when, occasioned by wrong-doing on the part of another, it takes the upper hand in executing vengeance and, in paying back the evil, does twice as much as was done in the first place. ² Revenge mistakenly appears to be a soothing of one's pain, but in the light of truth it is seen to be only evil contending with evil. What difference is there between the one who provokes and the one provoked except that the one is caught doing wrong sooner than the other? Nevertheless, before the Lord each is guilty of having injured a fellow man and the Lord forbids and condemns every act of wrong-doing. ³ There is no hierarchical arrangement in wrong-doing, nor does position make any distinction in that which similarity makes one. Therefore, the precept is unequivocally laid down: evil is not to be rendered for evil. Like deed merits like treatment. ⁴ But how shall we observe this precept if, in loathing (evil), we have no loathing for revenge? What tribute of honor shall we offer to the Lord our God if we assume to ourselves the right to inflict punishment? ⁵ We who are matter subject to decay, vessels of clay, are grievously offended when our servants take it upon themselves to seek revenge from their fellow slaves; as for those who show us patience, we not only praise them as slaves who are conscious of their lowly position, men attentive to the respect they owe their lord, but we recompense them even more than they had themselves anticipated. Is there any risk for us in such a course when we have a Lord so just in His judgments, so powerful in His deeds? ⁶ Why, then, do we believe Him a judge, but not also an avenger? Of this He assures us when He says: 'Revenge is mine and I will repay them,' that is: 'Have patience with Me and I will reward your patience.' ⁷ When He says: 'Do not judge, that you may not be judged,' is He not demanding patience? What man will refrain from judging another except one who will forego (the right) of self-defense? What man judges with the intention of forgiving? And if he does forgive, he has but shied away from the impatience of a man who judges and has usurped the honor of the true Judge, that is, God! ⁸ What misfortunes has such impatience, as a rule, brought upon itself! How often has it regretted its self-defense! How often has its obstinacy become worse than the occasions which provoked it! Now, nothing undertaken through impatience can be transacted without violence, and everything done with violence has either met with no success or has collapsed or has plunged to its own destruction. ⁹ If you are too mild in your self-defense, you will be acting like a madman; if your defense is excessive, you will be depressed. Why should I be concerned about revenge when I cannot regulate its extent because of my inability to endure pain? Whereas, if I yield and suffer the injury, I shall have no pain; and if I have no pain, I shall have no desire for revenge.

11

¹ Now that we have, to the best of our ability, set forth these principal provocations to impatience in the order of their intensity, with which of the rest that (we encounter) at home and in public life should we concern ourselves? Widespread and extensive are the workings of the Evil One who extends innumerable incentives to impatience which, at times, are slight, at times very great. ² The slight ones you should ignore for their insignificance; to the great you should yield in view of their invincible power. When the injury is not very important, there is no need for impatience, but when the injury is more serious, then there is greater need for a remedy against the injury, namely, patience. ³ Let us strive, then, to bear the injuries that are inflicted by the Evil One, that the struggle to maintain our self-control may put to shame the enemy's efforts. If, however, through imprudence or even of our own free will we draw down upon ourselves some misfortune, we should submit with equal patience to that which we impute to ourselves. ⁴ But if we believe some blow of misfortune is struck by God, to whom would it be better that we manifest patience than to our Lord? In fact, more than this, it befits us to rejoice at being deemed worthy of divine chastisement: 'As for me,' He says, 'those whom I love I chastise.' Blessed is that servant upon whose amendment the Lord insists, at whom He deigns to be angry, whom He does not deceive by omitting His admonition! ⁵ From every angle, then, we are obliged to practice patience, because we meet up with our own mistakes or the wiles of the Evil One or the warnings of the Lord alike. Great is the recompense for practicing it, namely, happiness. ⁶ Whom has the Lord declared happy? Those who are patient; for He said: 'Blessed are the poor in spirit, for theirs is the kingdom of heaven.' Assuredly, no one but the humble man is poor in spirit. And who is humble but the man who is patient? No one can take a position of subjection without patience, the prime factor in subjection. ⁷ 'Blessed,' He says, 'are those who weep and mourn.' Who can endure such things without patience? To such, then, is consolation and joy promised. ⁸ 'Blessed are the meek.' Certainly, in this word one cannot by any means include the impatient. Likewise, when He applies this same title of happiness to the peace-makers and calls them the children of God, I ask you: Do the impatient share in this peace? Only a fool would think so! ⁹ And when He says: 'Rejoice and exult when men reproach you and persecute you because your reward is great in heaven,' certainly this promise of great joy is not

made to the impatient, for no one will rejoice in adversity unless he has first come to despise it; no one will despise it unless he possesses patience.

12

¹ As for what pertains to the practice of this peace so pleasing to God (I ask you): What man, completely given over to impatience, will forgive his brother, I will not say seven times and seventy times seven times, but even once? ² What man, taking his case with his adversary to a judge, will settle his trouble to the accommodation of the other party, unless he first puts an end to his wrath, his resentment, his harshness and bitterness, that is, his impatient disposition? ³ How will you forgive and experience forgiveness if you cling to your injury through a total lack of patience? No one whose mind is violently disturbed against his brother will complete his offering at the altar unless first he has been reconciled to his brother through patience. ⁴ If the sun goes down upon our anger, we are in danger. We may not live a single day without patience. Yet, since patience governs every aspect of a salutary way of life, what wonder that it also paves the way for repentance which, as a rule, comes to the assistance of those who have fallen? ⁵ What benefits it produces in both parties when, in spite of their forbearance from their marriage rights–provided it be only for that reason which makes it lawful for a man or woman to persist in their separation–it waits for, hopes for, wins by its prayers repentance for those who will eventually be saved. It purifies the one without causing the other to become an adulterer! ⁶ So, too, in those examples in our Lord's parables there is a breath of patience: it is the patience of the shepherd that seeks and finds the straying sheep (for impatience would readily take no account of a single sheep, whereas patience undertakes the wearisome search) and he carries it on his shoulders, a patient bearer of a forsaken sinner. ⁷ In the case of the prodigal son, too, it is the patience of his father that welcomes him and clothes him and feeds him and finds an excuse for him in the face of the impatience of his angry brother. The one who had perished is rescued, therefore, because he embraced repentance; repentance is not wasted because it meets up with patience! ⁸ Consider now charity, the great bond of faith, the treasure of the Christian religion, which the Apostle extols with all the power of the Holy Spirit: how is it learned except by the exercise of patience? ⁹ 'Charity,' he says, 'is magnanimous.' It derives this from patience. 'It is kind.' Patience works no evil. 'It does not envy.' Envy is certainly a characteristic of impatience. 'It is not pretentious.' It has derived its contentment from patience. 'It is not puffed up, is not ambitious,' for that does not befit patience. 'It is not self-seeking.' It suffers (the loss of) its own goods provided that it be to another's advantage. 'It is not provoked.' What, then, would it have left to impatience? Therefore, he says, 'charity bears with all things, endures all things.' Of course it does, because it is itself patient. ¹⁰ He is correct, then, in stating that it will never fall away. Everything else will pass away and come to an end. Tongues, knowledge, prophecies are made void, but there persist faith, hope, and charity: faith, which the patience of Christ has instilled; hope, to which the patience of man looks forward; charity, which patience accompanies, according to the teaching of God.

13

¹ Thus far (we have been speaking), however, of a patience which constitutes simply and uniformly and solely an operation of the soul, whereas in various ways we should strive for this same patience also in the body in order to attain the good pleasure of the Lord, inasmuch as it was practiced by the Lord Himself as a virtue also of the body; for the soul, as the directing agent, readily shares the inspirations of the Spirit with that wherein it dwells. ² What, then, is the operation of patience in the body? Primarily, mortification of the flesh as a sacrifice acceptable to the Lord. This is an offering of (one's) humility, since it offers to the Lord a sacrifice of mourning dress along with meager rations, contenting itself with plain food and a drink of clear water, joining fast with fast and persevering in sackcloth and ashes. ³ This patience on the part of the body contributes to the value of our petitions and strengthens our prayers for deliverance. It opens the ears of Christ our Lord, dispels His severity, elicits His mercy. ⁴ Thus, after offending the Lord, the King of Babylon lived for seven years in squalor and filth, an exile from human society. By this offering of the patient endurance of bodily (discomfort) not only did he regain his kingdom, but–and this is even more desirable in a man–he made satisfaction to God. ⁵ Now, if we go on to consider the higher and more blessed degrees of bodily patience, (we see that) it turns continence, too, into an opportunity for sanctity: this it is which preserves the widow (in her state), places its seal upon the virgin, and raises to the kingdom of heaven one who of his own free will embraces a life of celibacy. ⁶ That which derives from the power of the soul finds its fulfillment in the flesh. In persecutions the endurance of the flesh engages in battle. If flight besets one, the flesh surmounts the hardships of flight. If imprisonment precludes flight, it is the flesh which submits to the chains, the block of wood, and the bare ground. It is the flesh which endures both the scanty light (of the dungeon) and the deprivation of worldly comforts. ⁷ But, when one is led forth to the ordeal that will prove his happiness, to the opportunity to renew one's baptism, to the very ascent to the throne of divinity, there is nothing (which avails) more in that situation than endurance on the part of the body. If the spirit is willing but the flesh–without patience–weak, where is there salvation for the spirit as well as for the flesh itself? ⁸ On the other hand, when the Lord speaks thus of the flesh and declares it weak, He points out what is needed for strengthening it, namely, patience in the face of everything that is ready to overthrow our faith and impose a penalty for it, that one may bear with constancy stripes, and fire, the cross, wild beasts, or the sword as the Prophets and Apostles bore them and won the victory.

14

¹ In virtue of his power of endurance, Isaias, though cut in pieces, does not refrain from speaking of the Lord. Stephen, as he is stoned, prays for pardon for his enemies. ² Happy, too, was that man who displayed every manner of patience against every vicious attack of the Devil! His flocks were driven away, his wealth in cattle destroyed by lightning, his children killed at a single stroke when his house collapsed, his own body, finally, was tortured by painful sores –yet, by none of these was he lured from his patience and the trust he owed the Lord. Though the Devil struck him with all his strength, he struck in vain! ³ Far from being turned away by so many misfortunes from the reverence which he owed to God, he set for us an example and proof of how we must practice patience in the spirit as well as in the flesh, in soul as well as in body, that we may not succumb under the loss of worldly goods, the death of our dear ones, or any bodily afflictions. ⁴ What a trophy over the Devil God erected in the case of that man! What a banner of His glory He raised above His enemy when that man let fall from his lips no other word than 'Thanks be to God!' as each bitter message reached him; when he severely rebuked his wife who, weary by now of misfortunes, was urging him to improper remedies. ⁵ How God laughed, and how the Evil One was split asunder, when Job, with perfect calm, would wipe away the discharge oozing from his ulcer and, with a jesting remark, would call back to the cavity and sustenance of his open flesh the tiny creatures that were trying to make their way out! ⁶ Thus did that hero who brought about a victory for his God beat back all the darts of temptation and with the breastplate and shield of patience soon after recover from God complete health of body and the possession of twice as much as he had lost. ⁷ Had he wanted his sons to be restored, too, he would once again have heard himself called 'father.' But he preferred that they be restored to him on the last day; placing all his trust in the Lord, he deferred that great joy; for the prevent, he was willing to endure the loss of his children that he might not live without something to suffer!

15

¹ God is fully capable of being the trustee of our patience: if you place in His hands an injustice you have suffered, He will see that justice is done; if a loss, He will see that you receive compensation; if a pain, He acts as healer; if death, He restores life. How much is granted to patience that it should have God for a debtor! ² And not without reason. For it pays attention to all His prescriptions, it becomes surety for all His commands: it strengthens faith, governs peace, sustains love, instructs humility, awaits repentance, places its seal upon the discipline of penance, controls the flesh, preserves the spirit, puts restraint upon the tongue, holds back the (violent) hand, treads under foot temptations, pushes scandal aside, consummates martyrdom. ³ In poverty it supplies consolation; upon wealth it imposes moderation; the sick it does not destroy, nor does it, for the man in health, prolong his life; for the man of faith it is a source of delight. It attracts the heathen, recommends the slave to his master, the master to God. It adorns a woman, perfects a man. It is loved in a child, praised in a youth, esteemed in the aged. In both man and woman, at every age of life, it is exceedingly attractive. ³ Now, then! If you will, let us try to grasp the features and appearance of patience. Its countenance is peaceful and untroubled. Its brow is clear, unruffled by any lines of melancholy or anger. The eyebrows are relaxed, giving an impression of joyousness. The eyes are lowered, in an attitude rather of humility than moroseness. ⁴ The mouth is closed in becoming silence. Its complexion is that of the serene and blameless. It shakes its head frequently in the direction of the Devil, and its laughter conveys a threat to him. The upper part of its garment is white and close-fitting so that it is not blown about or disturbed (by the wind). ⁵ It sits on the throne of its spirit which is extremely mild and gentle and is not whipped into a knot by the whirlwind, is not made livid by a cloud, but is a breeze of soft light, clear and simple, such as Elias saw the third time. For where God is, there, too, is the child of His nurturing, namely, patience. ⁶ When the Spirit of God descends, patience is His inseparable companion.

If we fail to welcome it along with the Spirit, will the latter remain within us at all times? As a matter of fact, I rather think the Spirit would not remain at all. Without its companion and assistant it would feel very uncomfortable anywhere and at any time. It could not endure, all by itself, the blows which its enemy inflicts, if stripped of the means which helps it to endure.

16

[1] This is the theory, this the practice, this the operation of the patience which is divine and true, namely, Christian; a patience not like the patience practiced by the peoples of the earth, which is false and disgraceful. [2] For, that the Devil might rival the Lord in this respect, also, and be really on an equal footing with Him as it were (except that good and evil are extremes of equal magnitude) the Devil also taught his own a special brand of patience. [3] It is a patience, I say, which renders subject to the power of their wives husbands who are purchased by a dowry or who negotiate with panderers; a patience in virtue of which (a wife) bears, with feigned affection, all the irritation resulting from a forced association so that, as a childless widow, she may lay hands upon her husband's estate; a patience which sentences gormandizers to sacrifice their freedom and become disgraceful slaves to their gluttony. [4] Such are the goals of patience as the heathens know it and by such despicable efforts they appropriate the name of so noble a virtue; they live in patient endurance of their rivals, the wealthy, and their hosts; it is only God alone whom they cannot endure. But let their patience and the patience of their chief take care: there is fire beneath the earth awaiting this kind of patience. [5] Let us, then, love the patience that is of God, the patience of Christ; let us return to Him that which He expended for us; let us who believe in the resurrection of the flesh and of the spirit offer Him both the patience of the spirit and the patience of the flesh.

Tertullian On Martyrs
1

[1] Blessed martyrs elect, along with the nourishment for the body which our Lady Mother the Church from her breast, as well as individual brethren from their private resources, furnish you in prison, accept also from me some offering that will contribute to the sustenance of the spirit. For it is not good that the flesh be feasted while the spirit goes hungry. Indeed, if care is bestowed on that which is weak, there is all the more reason not to neglect that which is still weaker. [2] Not that I am specially entitled to exhort you. Yet, even the most accomplished gladiators are spurred on not only by their trainers and managers but also from afar by people inexperienced in this art and by all who choose, without the slightest need for it, with the result that hints issuing from the crowd have often proved profitable for them. [3] In the first place, then, O blessed, 'do not grieve the Holy Spirit who has entered prison with you. For, if He had not accompanied you there in your present trial, you would not be there today. See to it, therefore, that He remain with you there and so lead you out of that place to the Lord. [4] Indeed, the prison is the Devil's house too, where he keeps his household. But you have come to the prison for the very purpose of trampling upon him right in his own house. For you have engaged him in battle already outside the prison and trampled him underfoot. [5] Let him, therefore, not say: 'Now that they are in my domain, I will tempt them with base hatreds, with defections or dissensions among themselves.' Let him flee from your presence, and let him, coiled and numb, like a snake that is driven out by charms or smoke, hide away in the depths of his den. Do not allow him the good fortune in his own kingdom of setting you against one another, but let him find you fortified by the arms of peace among yourselves, because peace among yourselves means war with him. [6] Some, not able to find this peace in the Church, are accustomed to seek it from the martyrs in prison. For this reason, too, then, you ought to possess, cherish and preserve it among yourselves that you may perhaps be able to bestow it upon others also.

2

[1] Other attachments, equally burdensome to the spirit, may have accompanied you to the prison gate; so far your relatives, too, may have escorted you. From that very moment on you have been separated from the very world. How much more, then, from its spirit and its ways and doings? Nor let this separation from the world trouble you. For, if we reflect that it is the very world that is more truly a prison, we shall realize that you have left a prison rather than entered one. [2] The world holds the greater darkness, blinding men's hearts. The world puts on the heavier chains, fettering the very souls of men. The world breathes forth the fouler impurities–human lusts. Finally, the world contains the larger number of criminals, namely, the entire human race. In fact, it awaits sentence not from the proconsul but from God. [3] Wherefore, O blessed consider yourselves as having been transferred from prison to what we may call a place of safety. Darkness is there, but you are light; fetters are there, but you are free before God. It breathes forth a foul smell, but you are an odor of sweetness. There the judge is expected at every moment, but you are going to pass sentence upon the judges themselves. [4] There sadness may come upon the man who sighs for the pleasures of the world The Christian, however even when he is outside the prison, has renounced the world and, when in prison, even prison itself. It does not matter what part of the world you are in, you who are apart from the world. [5] And if you have missed some of the enjoyments of life, remember that it is the way of business to suffer one losses in order to make larger profits. I say nothing yet about the reward to which God invites the martyrs. Meanwhile, let us compare the life in the world with that in prison to see if the spirit does not gain more in prison than the flesh loses there. [6] In fact, owing to the solicitude of the Church and the charity of the brethren, the flesh does not miss there what it ought to have, while, in addition, the spirit obtains what is always beneficial to the faith: you do not look at strange gods; you do not chance upon their images; you do not, even by mere physical contact, participate in heathen holidays; you are not plagued by the foul fumes of the sacrificial banquets, not tormented by the noise of the spectacles, nor by the atrocity or frenzy or shamelessness of those taking part in the celebrations; your eyes do not fall on houses of lewdness; you are free from inducements to sin, from temptations, from unholy reminiscences, free, indeed, even from persecution. [7] The prison now offers to the Christian what the desert once gave to the Prophets. Our Lord Himself quite often spent time in solitude to pray there more freely, to be there away from the world. In fact, it was in a secluded place that He manifested His glory to His disciples. Let us drop the name 'prison' and call it a place of seclusion. [8] Though the body is confined, though the flesh is detained, there is nothing that is not open to the spirit. In spirit wander about, in spirit take a walk, setting before yourselves not shady promenades and long porticoes but that path which leads to God. As often as you walk

that path, you will not be in prison. [9] The leg does not feel the fetter when the spirit is in heaven. The spirit carries about the whole man and brings him wherever he wishes. And where your heart is, there will your treasure be also. There, then, let our heart be where we would have our treasure.

3

[1] Granted now, O blessed, that even to Christians the prison is unpleasant–yet, we were called to the service in the army of the living God in the very moment when we gave response to the words of the sacramental oath. No soldier goes out to war encumbered with luxuries, nor does he march to the line of battle from the sleeping chamber, but from light and cramped tents where every kind of austerity, discomfort, and inconvenience is experienced. [2] Even in time of peace soldiers are toughened to warfare by toils and hardships: by marching in arms, by practicing swift maneuvers in the field, by digging a trench, by joining closely together to form a tortoise-shield. Everything is set in sweating toil, lest bodies and minds be frightened at having to pass from shade to sunshine, from sunshine to icy cold, from the tunic to the breastplate, from hushed silence to the warcry, from rest to the din of battle. [3] In like manner, O blessed, consider whatever is hard in your present situation as an exercise of your powers of mind and body. You are about to enter a noble contest in which the living God acts the part of superintendent and the Holy Spirit is your trainer, a contest whose crown is eternity, whose prize is angelic nature, citizenship in heaven and glory for ever and ever. [4] And so your Master, Jesus Christ, who has anointed you with His Spirit and has brought you to this training ground, has resolved, before the day of the contest, to take you from a softer way of life to a harsher treatment that your strength may be increased. For athletes, too, are set apart for more rigid training that they may apply themselves to the building up of their physical strength. They are kept from lavish living, from more tempting dishes, from more pleasurable drinks. They are urged on, they are subjected to torturing toils, they are worn out: the more strenuously they have exerted themselves, the greater is their hope of victory. [5] And they do this, says the Apostle, to win a perishable crown. We who are about to win an eternal one recognize in the prison our training ground, that we may be led forth to the actual contest before the seat of the presiding judge well practiced in all hardships, because strength is built up by austerity, but destroyed by softness.

4

[1] We know from our Lord's teaching that, while the spirit is willing, the flesh is weak. Let us, however, not derive delusive gratification from the Lord's acknowledgment of the weakness of the flesh. For it was on purpose that He first declared the spirit willing: He wanted to show which of the two ought to be subject to the other, that is to say, that the flesh should be submissive to the spirit, the weaker to the stronger, so that the former may draw strength from the latter. [2] Let the spirit converse with the flesh on their common salvation, no longer thinking about the hardships of prison but, rather, about the struggle of the actual contest. The flesh will perhaps fear the heavy sword and the lofty cross and the wild beasts mad with rage and the most terrible punishment of all–death by fire–and, finally, all the executioner's cunning during the torture. [3] But let the spirit present to both itself and the flesh the other side of the picture: granted, these sufferings are grievous, yet many have borne them patiently nay, have even sought them on their own accord for the sake of fame and glory; and this is true not only of men but also of women so that you, too, O blessed women may be worthy of your sex. [4] It would lead me too far were I to enumerate each one of those who, led by the impulse of their own mind put an end to their lives by the sword. Among women there is the well-known instance of Lucretia. A victim of violence, she stabbed herself in the presence of her kinsfolk to gain glory for her chastity. Mucius burnt his right hand on the altar that his fair fame might include this deed. [5] Nor did the philosophers act less courageously: Heraclitus, for instance, who put an end to his life by smearing himself with cow dung ; Empedocles, too, who leaped down into the fires of Mt. Etna; and Peregrinus who not long ago threw himself upon a funeral pile. Why, even women have despised the flames: Dido did so in order not to be forced to marry after the departure of the man she had loved most dearly; the wife of Hasdrubal, too, with Carthage in flames, cast herself along with her children into the fire that was destroying her native city, that she might not see her husband a suppliant at Scipio's feet. [6] Regulus, a Roman general, was taken prisoner by the Carthaginians, but refused to be the only Roman exchanged for a large number of Carthaginian captives. He preferred to be returned to the enemy, and, crammed into a kind of chest, suffered as many crucifixions as nails were driven in from the outside in all directions to pierce him. A woman voluntarily sought out wild beasts, namely, vipers, serpents more horrible than either bull or bear, which Cleopatra let loose upon herself as not to fall into the hands of the enemy. [7] You may object: 'But the fear of death is not so great as the fear of torture.' Did the Athenian courtesan yield on that account to the executioner? For, being privy to a conspiracy, she was subjected to torture by the tyrant. But she did not betray her fellow conspirators, and at last bit off her own tongue and spat it into the tyrant's face to let him know that torments, however prolonged, could achieve nothing against her. [8] Everybody knows that to this day the most important festival of the Lacedaemonians is the "diamastigosis," that is, The Whipping. In this sacred rite all the noble youth are scourged with whips before the altar, while their parents and kinsfolk stand by and exhort them to perseverance. For they regard it as a mark of greater distinction and glory if the soul rather than the body has submitted to the stripes. [9] Therefore, if earthly glory accruing from strength of body and soul is valued so highly that one despises sword, fire, piercing with nails, wild beasts and tortures for the reward of human praise, then I may say the sufferings you endure are but trifling in comparison with the heavenly glory and divine reward. If the bead made of glass is rated so highly, how much must the true pearl be worth? Who, therefore, does not most gladly spend as much for the true as others spend for the false?

5

[1] I omit here an account of the motive of glory. For inordinate ambition among men as well as a certain morbidity of mind have already set at naught all the cruel and torturing contests mentioned above. How many of the leisure class are urged by an excessive love of arms to become gladiators? Surely it is from vanity that they descend to the wild beasts in the very arena, and think themselves more handsome because of the bites and scars. Some have even hired themselves out to tests by fire, with the result that they ran a certain distance in a burning tunic. Others have pranced up and down amid the bullwhips of the animal-baiters, unflinchingly exposing their shoulders. [2] All this, O blessed, the Lord tolerates in the world for good reason, that is, for the sake of encouraging us in the present moment and of confounding us on that final day, if we have recoiled from suffering for the truth unto salvation what others have pursued out of vanity unto perdition.

6

[1] Let us, however, no longer talk about those examples of perseverance proceeding from inordinate ambition. Let us, rather, turn to a simple contemplation of man's ordinary lot so that, if we ever have to undergo such trials with fortitude, we may also learn from those misfortunes which sometimes even befall unwilling victims. For how often have people been burned to death in conflagrations! How often have wild beasts devoured men either in the forests or in the heart of cities after escaping from their cages! How many have been slain by the sword of robbers! How many have even suffered the death of the cross at the hands of enemies, after having been tortured first and, indeed, treated with every kind of insult! [2] Furthermore, many a man is able to suffer in the cause of a mere human being what he hesitates to suffer in the cause of God. To this fact, indeed, our present days may bear witness. How many prominent persons have met with death in the cause of a man, though such a fate seemed most unlikely in view of their birth and their rank, their physical condition and their age! Death came to them either from him, if they had opposed him, or from his enemies, if they had sided with him.

Made in the USA
Las Vegas, NV
07 September 2024

f1aee9d6-e282-46eb-8dca-6edb85e42dbaR01